HOR

IN TRAININ

133rd YEAR OF PUBLICATION

RACING POST

INDEX TO GENERAL CONTENTS

Editor	**Graham Dench** E-mail: hitraceform@weatherbys.co.uk
Production Editor	**Joe Ball** Weatherbys, Sanders Road, Wellingborough, NN8 4BX.
Orders	Racing Post Books, Sanders Road, Wellingborough, Northants NN8 4BX. Tel: 01933 304858 www.racingpost.com/shop E-mail: Shop@racingpost.com
Advertisements	kay.brown@archantdialogue.co.uk and gary.millone@archantdialogue.co.uk
ISBN	978-1-83950-095-4

Printed and bound by Page Bros. Ltd, Norwich, NR6 6SA

INDEX TO ADVERTISERS

2023

RACING FIXTURES AND SALE DATES

(SUBJECT TO ALTERATION)

Flat fixtures are in **Black Type**; Jump in Light Type; Irish in *Italic*;
asterisk (★) indicates an evening or Twilight meeting;
† indicates an All Weather meeting. Sale dates are at foot of fixtures

MARCH

Sun	Mon	Tue	Wed	Thu	Fri	Sat
			1 **Kempton Park†★** **Lingfield Park†** Musselburgh Wincanton	**2** **Chelmsford City†★** *Clonmel* Ludlow **Newcastle†** Taunton	**3** Doncaster *Dundalk†★* **Lingfield Park†** Newbury **Newcastle†★**	**4** Doncaster Kelso **Lingfield Park†** *Navan* Newbury **Wolverhampton†★**
5 Ffos Las Huntingdon *Leopardstown* *Wexford*	**6** *Leopardstown* Southwell Wetherby **Wolverhampton†★**	**7** Newcastle Sandown Park **Southwell†★**	**8** Catterick Bridge Fontwell Park **Kempton Park†★** **Lingfield Park†**	**9** Carlisle **Newcastle†★** **Southwell†** *Thurles* Wincanton	**10** Ayr *Dundalk†★* Exeter **Kempton Park†★** Leicester	**11** Ayr **Chelmsford City†★** *Gowran Park* Hereford *Navan* Sandown Park **Wolverhampton†**
12 *Limerick* Market Rasen *Naas* Warwick	**13** Plumpton Stratford-On-Avon Taunton **Wolverhampton†★**	**14** Cheltenham **Newcastle†★** Sedgefield **Southwell†★**	**15** Cheltenham Huntingdon **Kempton Park†★** **Newcastle†★**	**16** **Chelmsford City†★** Cheltenham *Dundalk†★* Hexham **Southwell†★**	**17** Cheltenham Doncaster *Down Royal* Fakenham **Newcastle†★** **Wolverhampton†★**	**18** Fontwell Park Kempton Park Newcastle *Thurles* Uttoxeter **Wolverhampton†★**
19 Carlisle Chepstow	**20** Southwell Taunton	**21** *Clonmel* Market Rasen Plumpton Wetherby Goffs Sale	**22** Ffos Las Haydock Park Warwick	**23** Chepstow *Cork* Ludlow Sedgefield	**24** *Dundalk†★* Hereford Musselburgh Newbury **Newcastle†★**	**25** Bangor-On-Dee *Curragh* Kelso **Lingfield Park†** Newbury **Wolverhampton†★**
26 Carlisle Exeter *Limerick* *Naas*	**27** **Lingfield Park†** Wincanton **Wolverhampton†★**	**28** Hexham Huntingdon **Wolverhampton†★**	**29** **Kempton Park†★** **Lingfield Park†** Market Rasen *Navan* Newcastle	**30** *Limerick* *Naas* Newcastle Taunton Warwick **Wolverhampton†★**	**31** *Dundalk†★* **Lingfield Park†** **Newcastle†★** **Southwell†** Wetherby *Wexford ★*	

APRIL

Sun	Mon	Tue	Wed	Thu	Fri	Sat
30 **Musselburgh** *Sligo* **Wetherby**						**1** *Bellewstown* **Chelmsford City†★** **Doncaster** **Kempton Park†** Stratford-On-Avon Uttoxeter
2 Ascot **Doncaster** *Downpatrick* *Leopardstown*	**3** **Lingfield Park†** Ludlow **Newcastle†★**	**4** Fontwell Park **Southwell†★** **Thirsk**	**5** **Kempton Park†★** *Leopardstown* **Nottingham** Wincanton **Wolverhampton†**	**6** **Chelmsford City†** *Clonmel ★* Hereford **Southwell†★** Wetherby	**7** **Bath** **Lingfield Park†** **Newcastle†**	**8** Carlisle *Cork* *Fairyhouse* Haydock Park **Kempton Park†** **Musselburgh** Newton Abbot **Wolverhampton†★**
9 *Cork* *Fairyhouse* Ffos Las Market Rasen Plumpton **Southwell†**	**10** Chepstow *Cork* *Fairyhouse* Fakenham Huntingdon Plumpton **Redcar** **Wolverhampton†**	**11** *Dundalk†★* Exeter **Pontefract** **Wolverhampton†★**	**12** **Catterick Bridge** *Gowran Park* **Kempton Park†★** **Nottingham** Southwell	**13** Aintree **Chelmsford City†★** **Newcastle†** Taunton Goffs Sale	**14** Aintree *Ballinrobe ★* *Dundalk†★* **Leicester** Sedgefield **Southwell†★**	**15** Aintree Chepstow Newcastle **Wolverhampton†★** **Yarmouth†**
16 *Curragh* Huntingdon *Tramore* Wincanton	**17** Kelso **Kempton Park†★** **Redcar** *Tramore ★* **Windsor**	**18** **Lingfield Park†** **Newmarket** Newton Abbot **Southwell†★** *Tipperary*	**19** **Beverley** Cheltenham *Gowran Park* **Kempton Park†★** **Newmarket**	**20** **Chelmsford City†★** Cheltenham *Kilbeggan ★* **Newmarket** **Ripon** *Tipperary ★*	**21** Ayr **Bath★** *Cork* Exeter★ Fontwell Park *Kilbeggan ★* **Newbury**	**22** Ayr Bangor-On-Dee **Brighton★** *Limerick* *Navan* **Newbury** **Nottingham★** **Thirsk** Goffs Sale
23 Plumpton Stratford-On-Avon Goffs Sale	**24** Hexham Kempton Park★ *Naas ★* **Pontefract** **Windsor** Goffs Sale	**25** **Epsom Downs** Ffos Las *Punchestown ★* **Wolverhampton†★** **Yarmouth**	**26** **Catterick Bridge** **Lingfield Park†★** Ludlow Perth *Punchestown ★*	**27** **Beverley** **Chelmsford City†★** Perth *Punchestown ★* Taunton★ Warwick Goffs Sale	**28** Chepstow★ **Doncaster†** Perth *Punchestown ★* **Sandown Park** Southwell★ Keeneland Sale	**29** **Doncaster★** **Haydock Park** **Leicester** *Punchestown* **Ripon** Sandown Park **Wolverhampton†★**

MAY

Sun	Mon	Tue	Wed	Thu	Fri	Sat
	1 **Bath** **Beverley** *Curragh* *Down Royal* Kempton Park Warwick **Windsor**	**2** *Ballinrobe* ★ **Brighton** **Newcastle†★** **Nottingham** **Wolverhampton†★** **Yarmouth** Tattersalls Sale	**3** **Ascot** **Brighton★** *Gowran Park* **Kempton Park†★** **Pontefract** **Wolverhampton†** Tattersalls Sale	**4** **Ayr** **Chelmsford City†★** **Lingfield Park†★** **Redcar** **Salisbury** *Tipperary* ★ Tattersalls Sale	**5** Cheltenham★ *Cork* ★ *Downpatrick* ★ **Goodwood** **Musselburgh** **Newcastle†★** **Newmarket**	**6** *Cork* **Doncaster★** **Goodwood** Hexham★ *Naas* **Newmarket** **Thirsk** Uttoxeter
7 **Hamilton Park** *Leopardstown* **Newmarket** **Salisbury**	**8** **Ayr** **Newcastle†★** *Roscommon* ★ **Southwell†** **Windsor★** Worcester	**9** Fakenham Ffos Las **Lingfield Park†** Ludlow★ **Newcastle†★**	**10** **Chester** Fontwell Park★ *Gowran Park* Kelso **Kempton Park†★** Newton Abbot	**11** **Chelmsford City†★** **Chester** *Clonmel* ★ Huntingdon **Southwell†** **Thirsk★**	**12** **Ascot** **Chester** *Kilbeggan* ★ Market Rasen **Nottingham★** **Ripon★** **Wolverhampton†★**	**13** **Ascot** FALSEHaydock Park Hexham **Leicester★** **Lingfield Park** *Navan* **Nottingham** Warwick★
14 **Hamilton Park** *Killarney* Ludlow Plumpton	**15** **Catterick Bridge** *Killarney* ★ **Musselburgh** Southwell★ **Windsor★** **Wolverhampton†**	**16** **Beverley** **Chepstow** *Killarney* ★ Newcastle **Sandown Park★** *Sligo* ★ **Wetherby★** Tattersalls Sale	**17** **Bath★** *Cork* ★ Newton Abbot Perth★ Worcester **York**	**18** Fontwell Park★ **Newmarket★** Perth **Salisbury** *Tipperary* ★ **York**	**19** Aintree★ *Downpatrick* ★ **Hamilton Park★** *Leopardstown* ★ **Newbury** **Newmarket** **York** BBAG Sale	**20** Bangor-On-Dee **Doncaster★** **Newbury** **Newmarket** **Thirsk** Uttoxeter★ *Wexford* Arqana Sale
21 *Naas* **Ripon** Stratford-On-Avon	**22** **Carlisle** Ffos Las Market Rasen★ **Redcar** *Roscommon* ★ **Windsor★** Goffs Sale	**23** **Ayr★** **Brighton** *Gowran Park* Hexham★ Huntingdon **Wolverhampton†** Goffs Sale	**24** **Ayr** **Kempton Park†★** Southwell★ Warwick **Yarmouth** Goffs Sale	**25** **Catterick Bridge** **Chelmsford City†★** **Haydock Park** *Limerick* ★ **Sandown Park★** **Wolverhampton†** Goffs Sale Tattersalls Sale	**26** **Bath** *Curragh* ★ **Goodwood** **Haydock Park** *Limerick* ★ **Pontefract★** Worcester★ Tattersalls Sale	**27** Cartmel **Chester** *Curragh* Ffos Las★ **Goodwood** **Haydock Park** **Salisbury★** **York**
28 *Curragh* Fontwell Park Kelso Uttoxeter	**29** *Ballinrobe* ★ Cartmel Huntingdon **Leicester** **Redcar** **Windsor**	**30** *Ballinrobe* ★ **Brighton** **Leicester** **Lingfield Park★** **Nottingham★** **Redcar** *Tipperary* ★	**31** **Beverley** Cartmel★ **Hamilton Park** Newton Abbot Warwick★ *Wexford* ★			

JUNE

Sun	Mon	Tue	Wed	Thu	Fri	Sat
				1 **Carlisle★** *Fairyhouse* ★ **Lingfield Park** Market Rasen★ **Ripon** **Yarmouth**	**2** **Carlisle** **Catterick Bridge★** **Chepstow** **Doncaster★** *Down Royal* **Epsom Downs** Stratford-On-Avon★ *Tramore* ★	**3** **Doncaster** **Epsom Downs** Hexham **Lingfield Park★** *Listowel* **Musselburgh** Stratford-On-Avon★ *Tramore* ★ Worcester
4 Fakenham *Kilbeggan* *Listowel* **Nottingham**	**5** **Ayr** *Gowran Park* *Listowel* **Thirsk** **Windsor★** **Wolverhampton†★**	**6** **Leicester** **Lingfield Park†★** Southwell **Wetherby★**	**7** *Curragh* ★ **Kempton Park†★** **Newbury** Newton Abbot **Nottingham** **Ripon★**	**8** **Chelmsford City†★** Ffos Las **Hamilton Park** *Leopardstown* ★ Uttoxeter **Yarmouth★**	**9** **Bath★** **Brighton** *Clonmel* ★ *Fairyhouse* ★ **Goodwood★** **Haydock Park★** Market Rasen **Thirsk**	**10** Bangor-On-Dee **Beverley** **Catterick Bridge** **Chepstow★** **Haydock Park** **Lingfield Park★** *Punchestown*
11 **Beverley** **Goodwood** *Navan* Perth *Punchestown*	**12** **Lingfield Park** **Pontefract★** *Roscommon* ★ Southwell **Windsor★**	**13** **Ayr★** **Brighton** **Salisbury** *Sligo* ★ **Southwell†** **Wetherby★** Goffs Sale	**14** **Hamilton Park★** **Haydock Park** **Kempton Park†★** *Limerick* ★ Newton Abbot **Yarmouth** Goffs Sale	**15** **Haydock Park★** *Leopardstown* ★ **Newbury** **Nottingham** Worcester★ **Yarmouth** Goffs Sale	**16** Aintree★ **Chepstow** *Cork* ★ *Fairyhouse* ★ Fontwell Park★ **Goodwood★** **Sandown Park** **York**	**17** **Bath** **Chester** *Downpatrick* Hexham **Leicester★** **Sandown Park** Uttoxeter★ **York**
18 **Doncaster** *Downpatrick* *Gowran Park* **Salisbury**	**19** **Carlisle** *Kilbeggan* ★ **Lingfield Park†** **Nottingham★** **Windsor★** **Wolverhampton†** Goffs Sale	**20** **Ascot** **Beverley★** **Brighton★** Stratford-On-Avon **Thirsk** *Wexford*	**21** **Ascot** **Hamilton Park** **Newcastle†★** **Ripon★** *Wexford* ★ Worcester	**22** **Ascot** **Chelmsford City†** *Leopardstown* ★ **Lingfield Park†★** **Ripon** Uttoxeter★	**23** **Ascot** *Down Royal* **Goodwood★** *Limerick* ★ Market Rasen **Musselburgh★** **Newmarket★** **Redcar**	**24** **Ascot** **Ayr** *Down Royal* **Haydock Park★** **Lingfield Park★** **Newmarket** Perth **Redcar**
25 **Ffos Las** Hexham **Pontefract**	**26** *Ballinrobe* ★ **Chepstow** Southwell **Windsor★** **Wolverhampton†★**	**27** **Beverley** **Brighton** **Newbury★** Newton Abbot★	**28** **Bath★** **Carlisle** **Kempton Park†★** *Naas* ★ **Salisbury** Worcester Tattersalls Sale	**29** **Hamilton Park★** **Leicester★** **Newcastle†** **Newmarket** **Nottingham** Tattersalls Sale	**30** Cartmel **Chester★** *Curragh* ★ **Doncaster** **Newcastle†★** **Newmarket★** **Yarmouth**	

JULY

Sun	Mon	Tue	Wed	Thu	Fri	Sat
30 **Pontefract** Uttoxeter	**31** **Ayr** **Ffos Las★** *Galway* ★ **Lingfield Park★** Newton Abbot					**1** **Chester** *Curragh* **Doncaster★** **Lingfield Park★** **Newcastle†** **Newmarket** **Windsor**
2 Cartmel *Curragh* Uttoxeter **Windsor**	**3** **Musselburgh★** **Pontefract** Southwell **Windsor★**	**4** **Brighton** **Ffos Las★** **Hamilton Park** *Roscommon* ★ Stratford-On-Avon★ *Tipperary* Arqana Sale	**5** **Bath★** **Epsom Downs★** **Musselburgh** **Thirsk** *Tipperary* ★ Worcester Arqana Sale	**6** *Bellewstown* ★ **Haydock Park** **Kempton Park†★** **Newbury★** Perth *Tipperary* ★ **Yarmouth** Arqana Sale	**7** *Bellewstown* ★ **Beverley★** **Doncaster** **Haydock Park★** Newton Abbot **Sandown Park** *Wexford* ★	**8** *Bellewstown* ★ **Beverley** **Carlisle★** **Haydock Park** **Leicester** *Naas* **Nottingham★** **Sandown Park**
9 **Ayr** **Chelmsford City†** Market Rasen *Sligo*	**10** **Ayr** **Chepstow★** **Ripon★** *Roscommon* ★ Worcester	**11** **Brighton★** **Pontefract** *Tramore* ★ Uttoxeter★ **Wolverhampton†**	**12** **Bath★** **Catterick Bridge** *Dundalk†* *Fairyhouse* ★ **Kempton Park†★** **Lingfield Park** **Yarmouth** Tattersalls Sale	**13** **Carlisle** **Doncaster** *Downpatrick* **Epsom Downs★** *Leopardstown* ★ **Newbury★** **Newmarket** Tattersalls Sale	**14** **Ascot** **Chepstow★** **Chester★** *Cork* ★ *Kilbeggan* ★ **Newmarket** **York** Tattersalls Sale	**15** **Ascot** **Chester** **Hamilton Park★** *Navan* **Newmarket** **Salisbury★** **York**
16 Perth Stratford-On-Avon	**17** **Ayr** *Killarney* ★ Newton Abbot **Windsor★** **Wolverhampton†★**	**18** **Beverley** *Killarney* ★ **Lingfield Park** **Nottingham★** Southwell★	**19** **Bath** **Catterick Bridge** *Killarney* ★ Uttoxeter **Wolverhampton†★** **Yarmouth★**	**20** **Chepstow** **Epsom Downs★** **Hamilton Park** *Killarney* ★ **Leicester** *Leopardstown* ★ Worcester★	**21** **Hamilton Park★** **Haydock Park** *Kilbeggan* ★ *Killarney* **Newbury** **Newmarket★** **Nottingham** **Pontefract★**	**22** Cartmel *Curragh* **Doncaster★** **Haydock Park★** Market Rasen **Newbury** **Newmarket** **Ripon**
23 *Curragh* Newton Abbot **Redcar** Stratford-On-Avon	**24** **Ayr** *Ballinrobe* ★ **Beverley★** Cartmel **Windsor★**	**25** *Ballinrobe* ★ **Chelmsford City†★** **Musselburgh** Southwell **Wolverhampton†★** Tattersalls Sale	**26** **Bath** **Catterick Bridge** **Leicester★** *Limerick* ★ **Lingfield Park** *Naas* ★ **Sandown Park★** Tattersalls Sale	**27** **Doncaster** *Leopardstown* ★ *Limerick* ★ **Newbury★** **Sandown Park** Worcester **Yarmouth★** Tattersalls Sale	**28** **Ascot** **Chepstow★** *Cork* ★ *Down Royal* **Newmarket★** **Thirsk** Uttoxeter **York★**	**29** **Ascot** *Gowran Park* **Newcastle†** **Newmarket** **Salisbury★** **Windsor★** **York**

AUGUST

Sun	Mon	Tue	Wed	Thu	Fri	Sat
		1 Beverley Galway ★ Goodwood Perth★ Worcester★ Yarmouth Goffs Sale	**2** Galway ★ Goodwood Leicester★ Perth Redcar Sandown Park★ Goffs Sale	**3** Epsom Downs★ Galway Goodwood Newcastle†★ Nottingham Stratford-On-Avon	**4** Bangor-On-Dee Bath★ Galway ★ Goodwood Musselburgh★ Newmarket★ Wolverhampton†	**5** Doncaster Galway Goodwood Hamilton Park★ Lingfield Park★ Newmarket Thirsk
6 Chester Galway Haydock Park Market Rasen	**7** Ayr Carlisle★ Cork Naas Ripon Windsor★	**8** Catterick Bridge Chelmsford City†★ Ffos Las Ripon★ Roscommon ★	**9** Bath Brighton Kempton Park†★ Pontefract Sligo ★ Yarmouth★	**10** Brighton Chepstow★ Nottingham Salisbury★ Sandown Park★ Sligo ★ Yarmouth	**11** Brighton Haydock Park★ Musselburgh Newmarket★ Thirsk Tipperary ★ Wexford ★	**12** Ascot Ayr★ Curragh Haydock Park Kilbeggan ★ Lingfield Park★ Newmarket Redcar
13 Downpatrick Leicester Windsor	**14** Ballinrobe ★ Hamilton Park★ Kempton Park† Windsor★ Wolverhampton†	**15** Chelmsford City†★ Dundalk† Lingfield Park Newcastle†★ Nottingham	**16** Beverley Ffos Las★ Gowran Park Kempton Park†★ Salisbury Yarmouth	**17** Ayr★ Beverley Leopardstown ★ Salisbury Tramore ★ Windsor★ Wolverhampton†	**18** Cork ★ Epsom Downs Newbury Newmarket★ Thirsk★ Tramore ★ Wolverhampton† Arqana Sale	**19** Bath★ Curragh Doncaster Market Rasen★ Newbury Newmarket Perth Ripon Tramore (E) Arqana Sale
20 Curragh Pontefract Sandown Park Southwell† Tramore Arqana Sale	**21** Bangor-On-Dee★ Brighton Catterick Bridge Lingfield Park★	**22** Newton Abbot Roscommon ★ Worcester★	**23** Bath Carlisle Kempton Park†★ Leicester★ Sligo ★ York	**24** Chelmsford City†★ Chepstow Fontwell Park★ Killarney ★ Leopardstown ★ Stratford-On-Avon York	**25** Ffos Las Goodwood★ Hamilton Park★ Kilbeggan ★ Killarney ★ Newmarket York	**26** Cartmel Curragh ★ Goodwood Killarney Newmarket Redcar★ Windsor★ York
27 Beverley Goodwood Naas Yarmouth	**28** Ballinrobe ★ Cartmel Chepstow Downpatrick Epsom Downs Ripon Southwell†	**29** Bellewstown ★ Musselburgh★ Newbury Ripon Worcester★ Goffs Sale	**30** Bellewstown ★ Catterick Bridge Kempton Park†★ Lingfield Park Musselburgh Sedgefield★ Goffs Sale	**31** Bath Carlisle Chelmsford City† Navan Newcastle†★ Stratford-On-Avon★		

SEPTEMBER

Sun	Mon	Tue	Wed	Thu	Fri	Sat
					1 **Carlisle** *Down Royal* **Ffos Las★** Fontwell Park **Salisbury★** **Thirsk** *Wexford ★* **Wolverhampton†★** Tattersalls Sale BBAG Sale	**2** **Beverley** **Chelmsford City†★** **Chester** *Navan* Newton Abbot **Sandown Park** **Wolverhampton†★**
3 **Brighton** *Tipperary* Worcester	**4** **Brighton** **Chepstow** *Roscommon ★* **Windsor★** Tattersalls Sale	**5** Bangor-On-Dee **Goodwood** **Hamilton Park★** **Ripon★** Tattersalls Sale	**6** **Bath** *Cork ★* *Gowran Park* Hexham★ **Kempton Park†★** **Lingfield Park** **Southwell†** Goffs Sale	**7** **Carlisle★** *Clonmel ★* **Haydock Park** **Salisbury** Sedgefield **Wolverhampton†★** Goffs Sale	**8** **Ascot** *Down Royal* **Haydock Park** **Kempton Park†★** *Kilbeggan ★* **Newcastle†**	**9** **Ascot** **Haydock Park** **Kempton Park†** *Leopardstown* Stratford-On-Avon **Thirsk** **Wolverhampton†★** Goffs Sale
10 *Curragh* Fontwell Park **York**	**11** **Brighton** *Galway ★* **Newcastle†★** Newton Abbot Perth Keeneland Sale	**12** **Catterick Bridge** *Galway ★* Kelso★ *Laytown ★* **Leicester** Worcester Keeneland Sale	**13** **Bath** **Carlisle** **Kempton Park†★** *Punchestown* **Southwell†★** Uttoxeter Keeneland Sale	**14** **Chelmsford City†★** **Doncaster** **Epsom Downs** **Ffos Las** *Naas* Keeneland Sale	**15** *Ballinrobe ★* **Chester** **Doncaster** *Downpatrick* **Salisbury★** **Sandown Park** Keeneland Sale	**16** **Bath** **Chester** **Doncaster** *Gowran Park* **Lingfield Park** **Musselburgh★** *Navan* Keeneland Sale
17 **Doncaster** *Listowel* **Musselburgh** Keeneland Sale	**18** **Brighton** *Fairyhouse ★* **Kempton Park†★** *Listowel* **Thirsk** Worcester Keeneland Sale	**19** *Listowel* **Newcastle†★** **Redcar** Uttoxeter **Yarmouth** Keeneland Sale Tattersalls Sale	**20** **Beverley** Kelso★ *Listowel* **Sandown Park** **Yarmouth** Keeneland Sale Tattersalls Sale	**21** **Ayr** **Chelmsford City†★** *Listowel* **Pontefract** **Yarmouth** Keeneland Sale Tattersalls Sale	**22** **Ayr** *Dundalk†★* **Kempton Park†★** *Listowel* **Newbury** Newton Abbot Keeneland Sale	**23** **Ayr** **Catterick Bridge** *Curragh* *Listowel* **Newbury** **Newmarket** **Wolverhampton†★** **York** Keeneland Sale
24 *Curragh* **Hamilton Park** Plumpton	**25** *Down Royal* **Hamilton Park** **Leicester** *Roscommon* Warwick **Wolverhampton†★**	**26** **Beverley** *Cork* **Lingfield Park†** **Newcastle†★** **Nottingham** Goffs Sale	**27** *Bellewstown* **Goodwood** **Kempton Park†★** Perth **Redcar** *Sligo* Goffs Sale	**28** *Bellewstown* *Clonmel* **Newmarket** Perth **Pontefract** **Southwell†★** Arqana Sale Goffs Sale	**29** *Dundalk†★* *Gowran Park* **Haydock Park** **Newcastle†★** **Newmarket** Worcester Goffs Sale	**30** **Chelmsford City†★** **Chester** *Gowran Park* **Haydock Park** *Killarney* Market Rasen **Newmarket** **Ripon** Arqana Sale

OCTOBER

Sun	Mon	Tue	Wed	Thu	Fri	Sat
1 **Epsom Downs** **Ffos Las** *Killarney* *Tipperary*	**2** **Bath** *Fairyhouse* **Hamilton Park** **Newcastle†★** Newton Abbot	**3** **Ayr** *Galway* Sedgefield Southwell **Wolverhampton†★** Tattersalls Sale	**4** Bangor-On-Dee **Catterick Bridge** **Kempton Park†★** *Navan* **Nottingham** Tattersalls Sale	**5** **Chelmsford City†★** **Lingfield Park†** **Salisbury** *Thurles* Warwick Tattersalls Sale	**6** **Ascot** *Downpatrick* *Dundalk†★* Fontwell Park Hexham **Newcastle†★**	**7** **Ascot** *Curragh* *Fairyhouse* Fontwell Park **Newmarket** **Redcar** **Wolverhampton†★**
8 Kelso Uttoxeter	**9** **Pontefract** Stratford-On-Avon **Windsor** **Wolverhampton†★** Tattersalls Sale	**10** **Brighton** Huntingdon **Leicester** *Punchestown* **Southwell†★** Tattersalls Sale	**11** **Kempton Park†★** Ludlow **Nottingham** *Punchestown* Sedgefield Tattersalls Sale	**12** **Ayr** **Chelmsford City†★** *Curragh* Exeter *Tramore* Worcester Tattersalls Sale	**13** Chepstow *Dundalk†★* **Newcastle†★** **Newmarket** **York** Tattersalls Sale BBAG Sales	**14** **Chelmsford City†★** Chepstow **Chester** Hexham *Naas* **Newmarket** **York** Tattersalls Sale Tattersalls Sale BBAG Sales
15 *Cork* Ffos Las **Goodwood** *Naas*	**16** **Kempton Park†★** **Musselburgh** **Windsor** **Yarmouth** Arqana Sale	**17** *Gowran Park* Hereford Huntingdon **Leicester** **Newcastle†★** Arqana Sale	**18** **Bath** **Kempton Park†★** *Navan* **Nottingham** Wetherby Arqana Sale Goffs Sale	**19** **Brighton** Carlisle **Chelmsford City†★** *Thurles* Wincanton Arqana Sale Goffs Sale	**20** *Dundalk†★* Fakenham **Haydock Park** **Newcastle†★** **Redcar** Uttoxeter Arqana Sale	**21** **Ascot** **Catterick Bridge** *Leopardstown* *Limerick* Market Rasen Newton Abbot Stratford-On-Avon **Wolverhampton†★**
22 Kempton Park *Leopardstown* *Limerick* Sedgefield	**23** Plumpton **Pontefract** **Southwell†★** **Windsor** Tattersalls Sale	**24** Exeter Hereford **Wolverhampton†★** **Yarmouth** Tattersalls Sale	**25** *Curragh* Fontwell Park **Kempton Park†★** **Newmarket** Worcester Tattersalls Sale	**26** Carlisle *Clonmel* Ludlow **Southwell†** **Wolverhampton†★** Tattersalls Sale	**27** Cheltenham **Doncaster** *Dundalk†★* **Newbury** *Sligo* **Wolverhampton†★** Tattersalls Sale	**28** **Chelmsford City†★** Cheltenham **Doncaster** *Galway* Kelso **Newbury**
29 Aintree *Galway* *Wexford* Wincanton	**30** *Galway* Huntingdon **Leicester** **Redcar** **Southwell†★** *Wexford* Goffs Sale	**31** Bangor-On-Dee **Catterick Bridge** Chepstow **Newcastle†★** Goffs Sale				

NOVEMBER

Sun	Mon	Tue	Wed	Thu	Fri	Sat
			1 *Dundalk†* Fakenham **Kempton Park†★** Lingfield Park **Nottingham** Goffs Sale	**2** **Chelmsford City†★** **Lingfield Park†** Stratford-On-Avon *Thurles* Worcester Goffs Sale	**3** *Down Royal* *Dundalk†★* **Newcastle†★** **Newmarket** Uttoxeter Wetherby	**4** Ascot Ayr *Down Royal* **Newmarket** **Southwell†★** Wetherby
5 Carlisle *Cork* *Curragh* Huntingdon	**6** Hereford **Kempton Park†** Plumpton **Wolverhampton†★**	**7** *Fairyhouse* **Newcastle†★** **Redcar** **Southwell†** Warwick Keeneland Sale	**8** Chepstow *Dundalk†* **Kempton Park†★** Musselburgh Warwick Keeneland Sale	**9** **Chelmsford City†★** *Clonmel* Ludlow Newbury Sedgefield Keeneland Sale	**10** *Dundalk†★* Exeter Fontwell Park Hexham **Newcastle†★** Keeneland Sale Tattersalls Sale	**11** Aintree **Chelmsford City†★** **Doncaster** *Gowran Park* Kelso Wincanton Keeneland Sale Tattersalls Sale
12 Ffos Las *Naas* Sandown Park Keeneland Sale Tattersalls Sale	**13** Carlisle Kempton Park **Wolverhampton†★** Keeneland Sale Tattersalls Sale	**14** *Fairyhouse* Huntingdon Lingfield Park **Newcastle†** **Wolverhampton†★** Keeneland Sale Tattersalls Sale	**15** Ayr Bangor-On-Dee *Dundalk†* **Kempton Park†** **Southwell†★** Keeneland Sale Tattersalls Sale	**16** **Chelmsford City†★** Market Rasen *Punchestown* Sedgefield Taunton Keeneland Sale Tattersalls Sale	**17** Cheltenham *Dundalk†★* **Newcastle†** Southwell **Wolverhampton†★** Keeneland Sale Tattersalls Sale	**18** Cheltenham **Lingfield Park†** *Navan* Uttoxeter Wetherby **Wolverhampton†★** Arqana Sale Tattersalls Sale
19 Cheltenham Fontwell Park *Navan* Goffs Sale	**20** Exeter **Kempton Park†★** Leicester Plumpton Arqana Sale Goffs Sale	**21** **Chelmsford City†★** Fakenham Hereford *Limerick* Lingfield Park Arqana Sale Goffs Sale	**22** *Dundalk†* Ffos Las Hexham **Southwell†★** Warwick Arqana Sale Goffs Sale	**23** Market Rasen Newcastle *Thurles* Wincanton **Wolverhampton†★** Goffs Sale	**24** Ascot Catterick Bridge Chepstow *Dundalk†★* **Southwell†★** Goffs Sale	**25** Ascot Haydock Park Huntingdon **Lingfield Park†** *Punchestown* **Wolverhampton†★** Goffs Sale
26 *Cork* Exeter *Punchestown* Uttoxeter Goffs Sale	**27** Kempton Park Ludlow Tattersalls Sale	**28** Sedgefield Southwell *Tramore*	**29** *Dundalk†* Hereford Kelso Wetherby Tattersalls Sale	**30** Lingfield Park Musselburgh Taunton *Thurles* Tattersalls Sale		

DECEMBER

Sun	Mon	Tue	Wed	Thu	Fri	Sat
31 **Lingfield Park†** *Punchestown* Uttoxeter Warwick					**1** Doncaster *Dundalk†★* Musselburgh Newbury Tattersalls Sale	**2** Bangor-On-Dee Doncaster *Fairyhouse* Newbury Newcastle Tattersalls Sale
3 Carlisle *Fairyhouse* Leicester	**4** Ayr Plumpton **Wolverhampton†★** Tattersalls Sale	**5** **Lingfield Park†** Southwell **Wolverhampton†★** Tattersalls Sale	**6** *Dundalk†* Haydock Park **Kempton Park†★** **Lingfield Park†** Ludlow Tattersalls Sale	**7** **Chelmsford City†★** *Clonmel* Leicester Market Rasen Wincanton Tattersalls Sale	**8** *Dundalk†★* Exeter **Newcastle†★** Sandown Park Sedgefield Arqana Sale	**9** Aintree Chepstow *Navan* **Newcastle†★** Sandown Park Wetherby **Wolverhampton†★** Arqana Sale Goffs Sale
10 *Cork* Huntingdon Kelso Arqana Sale	**11** Ayr **Chelmsford City†★** Lingfield Park Arqana Sale Goffs Sale	**12** Fontwell Park *Punchestown* **Southwell†★** Uttoxeter Goffs Sale	**13** *Dundalk†* Hexham **Kempton Park†★** Leicester **Lingfield Park†** Goffs Sale	**14** **Chelmsford City†★** *Naas* Newcastle Taunton Warwick Goffs Sale	**15** Bangor-On-Dee Cheltenham Doncaster *Dundalk†★* **Southwell†★**	**16** Cheltenham Doncaster *Fairyhouse* Hereford **Newcastle†** **Wolverhampton†★**
17 Carlisle *Navan* Southwell *Thurles*	**18** Musselburgh Plumpton **Wolverhampton†★**	**19** Catterick Bridge Fakenham Wincanton **Wolverhampton†★**	**20** *Dundalk†★* **Kempton Park†★** **Lingfield Park†** Ludlow Newbury	**21** **Chelmsford City†★** Exeter Ffos Las **Southwell†**	**22** Ascot *Dundalk†★* **Southwell†** Uttoxeter **Wolverhampton†★**	**23** Ascot Haydock Park **Lingfield Park†** Newcastle
24	**25**	**26** Aintree *Down Royal* Fontwell Park Kempton Park *Leopardstown* *Limerick* Market Rasen Sedgefield Wetherby Wincanton **Wolverhampton†**	**27** Chepstow Kempton Park *Leopardstown* *Limerick* Wetherby **Wolverhampton†★**	**28** Catterick Bridge Leicester *Leopardstown* *Limerick* **Newcastle†★**	**29** Doncaster Kelso *Leopardstown* *Limerick* **Southwell†★**	**30** Haydock Park Newbury Taunton **Wolverhampton†★**

DATES OF PRINCIPAL RACES

(SUBJECT TO ALTERATION)

JANUARY

The Dornan Engineering Relkeel Hurdle Race (Grade 2)	Cheltenham	Sun 01
The Paddy Power Novices' Chase (Dipper) (Grade 2)	Cheltenham	Sun 01
The Paddy Power New Year's Day Handicap Chase (Premier Handicap)	Cheltenham	Sun 01
The Ballymore Novices' Hurdle (Listed)	Cheltenham	Sun 01
The Pony Club "Junior" National Hunt Flat Race (Listed)	Cheltenham	Sun 01
The John Fowler Memorial Mares Chase (Grade 3)	Fairyhouse	Sun 01
The Metal Man Chase (Grade 3)	Tramore	Sun 01
The Unibet Tolworth Novices' Hurdle (Grade 1)	Sandown Park	Sat 07
The Unibet 3 Uniboosts A Day Mares' Hurdle (Listed)	Sandown Park	Sat 07
The Slaney Novice Hurdle (Grade 1)	Naas	Sun 08
The Pertemps Network Mares' Chase (Listed)	Leicester	Wed 11
The Coral Lanzarote Handicap Hurdle (Listed)	Kempton Park	Sat 14
The Coral Silviniaco Conti Chase (Grade 2)	Kempton Park	Sat 14
The Ballymore Leamington Novices' Hurdle (Grade 2)	Warwick	Sat 14
The Wigley Group Hampton Novices' Chase (Grade 2)	Warwick	Sat 14
The Agetur UK Ltd Classic Handicap Chase (Premier Handicap)	Warwick	Sat 14
The Dan Moore Mem Handicap Chase (Grade A)	Fairyhouse	Sat 14
The Moscow Flyer Novice Hurdle (Grade 2)	Punchestown	Sun 15
The Killiney Novice Chase (Grade 3)	Punchestown	Sun 15
The Alan Swinbank Mares' Standard Open National Hunt Flat Race (Listed)	Market Rasen	Fri 20
The SBK Clarence House Chase (Grade 1)	Ascot	Sat 21
The SBK Mares' Hurdle (Warfield) (Grade 2)	Ascot	Sat 21
The New One Unibet Hurdle (Champion Hurdle Trial Race) (Grade 2)	Haydock Park	Sat 21
The Patrick Coyne Memorial Altcar Novices' Chase (Grade 2)	Haydock Park	Sat 21
The Sky Bet Supreme Trial Rossington Main Novices' Hurdle (Grade 2)	Haydock Park	Sat 21
The Peter Marsh Handicap Chase (Grade 2)	Haydock Park	Sat 21
The Navan Handicap Hurdle (Grade B)	Navan	Sat 21
The Coolmore EBF Mares Novice Chase (Grade 2)	Thurles	Sun 22
The Kinloch Brae Chase (Grade 2)	Thurles	Sun 22
The Galmoy Hurdle (Grade 2)	Gowran Park	Thu 26
The Goffs Thyestes Handicap Chase (Grade A)	Gowran Park	Thu 26
The Sky Bet Fillies' Juvenile Hurdle (Listed)	Doncaster	Fri 27
The Pertemps Lady Protectress Mares' Chase (Listed)	Huntingdon	Fri 27
The Paddy Power Cotswold Chase (Grade 2)	Cheltenham	Sat 28
The JCB Triumph Trial Juvenile Hurdle (Finesse) (Grade 2)	Cheltenham	Sat 28
The Welsh Marches Stallions At Chapel Stud Cleeve Hurdle (Grade 2)	Cheltenham	Sat 28
The Ballymore Novices' Hurdle (Classic) (Grade 2)	Cheltenham	Sat 28
The Cheltenham Countdown Podcast Handicap Chase (Premier Handicap)	Cheltenham	Sat 28
The attheraces.com Lightning Novices' Chase (Grade 2)	Doncaster	Sat 28
The Albert Bartlett River Don Novices' Hurdle (Grade 2)	Doncaster	Sat 28
The Sky Bet Yorkshire Rose Mares' Hurdle (Grade 2)	Doncaster	Sat 28
The Sky Bet Handicap Chase (Listed)	Doncaster	Sat 28
The Solerina Mares Novice Hurdle (Grade 3)	Fairyhouse	Sat 28
The Limestone Lad Hurdle (Grade 3)	Naas	Sun 29
The Woodlands Novice Chase (Grade 3)	Naas	Sun 2

FEBRUARY

The Betway Kachy Stakes (Listed)	Lingfield Park	Sat 04
The Betway Tandridge Stakes (Listed)	Lingfield Park	Sat 04
The Virgin Bet Scilly Isles Novices' Chase (Grade 1)	Sandown Park	Sat 04
The Virgin Bet Heroes Handicap Hurdle (Premier Handicap)	Sandown Park	Sat 04
The Virgin Bet Contenders Hurdle (Listed)	Sandown Park	Sat 04
The William Hill Towton Novices' Chase (Grade 2)	Wetherby	Sat 04
The Paddy Power Irish Gold Cup (Grade 1)	Leopardstown	Sat 04
The Nathaniel Lacy Golden Cygnet Novice Hurdle (Grade 1)	Leopardstown	Sat 04
The Arkle Novice Chase (Grade 1)	Leopardstown	Sat 04
The Spring 4yo Hurdle (Grade 1)	Leopardstown	Sat 04
The Goffs (C & G) INH Flat Race (Grade 2)	Leopardstown	Sat 04
The Sandyford Handicap Chase (Grade B)	Leopardstown	Sat 04
The Glencullen Handicap Hurdle (Grade B)	Leopardstown	Sat 04
The Bet365 Scottish Triumph Hurdle (Listed)	Musselburgh	Sun 05
The Chanelle Pharma Irish Champion Hurdle (Grade 1)	Leopardstown	Sun 05
The Ladbrokes Dublin Chase (Grade 1)	Leopardstown	Sun 05
The Brave Inca Novice Hurdle (Grade 1)	Leopardstown	Sun 05
The Scalp Novice Chase (Grade 1)	Leopardstown	Sun 05
The Coolmore Stud NH Sires Deep Run Mares INH Flat Race (Grade 2)	Leopardstown	Sun 05
The Leopardstown Chase (Grade A)	Leopardstown	Sun 05

The Liffey Handicap Hurdle (Grade B)	Leopardstown	Sun 05
The Paddy Mullins EBF Mares Handicap Hurdle (Grade B)	Leopardstown	Sun 05
The Urban Logistics Reit Sidney Banks Memorial Novices' Hurdle (Listed)	Huntingdon	Thu 09
The Betfair Denman Chase (Grade 2)	Newbury	Sat 11
The Betfair Exchange Game Spirit Chase (Grade 2)	Newbury	Sat 11
The Betfair Hurdle (Handicap) (Grade 3)	Newbury	Sat 11
The Best Odds On The Betfair Exchange Standard Open National Hunt Flat Race (Listed)	Newbury	Sat 11
The Virgin Bet Kingmaker Novices' Chase (Grade 2)	Warwick	Sat 11
The Virgin Bet Warwick Mares' Hurdle (Listed)	Warwick	Sat 11
The Opera Hat Mares Chase (Listed)	Naas	Sat 11
The Virgin Bet Mares' Chase (Listed)	Exeter	Sun 12
The Virgin Bet Novices' Hurdle (Listed)	Exeter	Sun 12
The Boyne Hurdle (Grade 2)	Navan	Sun 12
The Ten Up Novice Chase (Grade 2)	Navan	Sun 12
The Apple's Jade Mares Novice Hurdle (Listed)	Navan	Sun 12
The Jane Seymour Mares' Novices' Hurdle (Grade 2)	Sandown Park	Thu 16
The Powerstown Novice Hurdle (Grade 3)	Clonmel	Thu 16
The Betfair Ascot Chase (Grade 1)	Ascot	Sat 18
The Bateaux London Reynoldstown Novices' Chase (Grade 2)	Ascot	Sat 18
The Greatbritishstallionshowcase.co.uk Swinley Chase (Listed)	Ascot	Sat 18
The William Hill Rendlesham Hurdle (Grade 2)	Haydock Park	Sat 18
The Albert Bartlett Prestige Novices' Hurdle (Grade 2)	Haydock Park	Sat 18
The William Hill Grand National Trial Handicap Chase (Premier Handicap)	Haydock Park	Sat 18
The Wincanton Matchbook Betting Exchange Kingwell Hurdle (Grade 2)	Wincanton	Sat 18
The Red Mills Chase (Grade 2)	Gowran Park	Sat 18
The Red Mills Trial Hurdle (Grade 3)	Gowran Park	Sat 18
The EBF Novice Hurdle (Listed)	Punchestown	Sun 19
The Grand National Trial Handicap Chase (Grade B)	Punchestown	Sun 19
The Quevega Mares Hurdle (Grade 3)	Punchestown	Wed 22
The Michael Purcell Novice Hurdle (Grade 3)	Thurles	Thu 23
The Coral Pendil Novices' Chase (Grade 2)	Kempton Park	Sat 25
The Coral Adonis Juvenile Hurdle (Grade 2)	Kempton Park	Sat 25
The Sky Bet Dovecote Novices' Hurdle (Grade 2)	Kempton Park	Sat 25
The Coral Trophy Handicap Chase (Premier Handicap)	Kempton Park	Sat 25
The Betway Winter Derby Stakes (Group 3)	Lingfield Park	Sat 25
The Betway Hever Sprint Stakes (Listed)	Lingfield Park	Sat 25
The Bobbyjo Chase (Grade 3)	Fairyhouse	Sat 25
The Winning Fair Juvenile Hurdle (Grade 3)	Fairyhouse	Sat 25
The Royalequestrian Bedding And Manor Elite Horsebox National Spirit Hurdle (Grade 2)	Fontwell Park	Sun 26
The Paddy Power Johnstown Novice Hurdle (Grade 2)	Naas	Sun 26
The Paddy Power Newlands Chase (Grade 3)	Naas	Sun 26
The Nas na Riogh Novice Handicap Chase (Grade B)	Naas	Sun 26

MARCH

The Patton Stakes (Listed)	Dundalk	Fri 03
The Virgin Bet Mares' Novices' Hurdle (Listed)	Doncaster	Sat 04
The Bet365 Premier Novices' Hurdle (Grade 2)	Kelso	Sat 04
The Bet365 Premier Chase (Listed)	Kelso	Sat 04
The Coral Spring Cup Stakes (Listed)	Lingfield Park	Sat 04
The Betvictor Greatwood Gold Cup Handicap Chase (Premier Handicap)	Newbury	Sat 04
The Flyingbolt Novice Chase (Grade 3)	Navan	Sat 04
The TRI Equestrian Carrickmines Handicap Chase (Grade B)	Leopardstown	Sun 05
The Paddy Power Imperial Cup Handicap Hurdle (Premier Handicap)	Sandown Park	Sat 11
The European Breeders' Fund Paddy Power 'National Hunt' Novices' Handicap Hurdle Final (Grade 3)	Sandown Park	Sat 11
The Paddy Power Novices' Handicap Chase (Listed)	Sandown Park	Sat 11
The British Stallion Studs EBF Mares' Standard Open National Hunt Flat Race (Listed)	Sandown Park	Sat 11
The Lady Wulfruna Stakes (Listed)	Wolverhampton	Sat 11
The Shamrock Handicap Chase (Grade B)	Gowran Park	Sat 11
The An Uaimh Chase (Grade 2)	Navan	Sat 11
The EBF Novice Final Handicap Chase (Grade B)	Navan	Sat 11
The Shannon Spray EBF Mares Novice Hurdle (Grade 3)	Limerick	Sun 12
The Directors Plate Novice Chase (Grade 3)	Naas	Sun 12
The Kingsfurze Novice Hurdle (Grade 3)	Naas	Sun 12
The Leinster National (Grade A)	Naas	Sun 12
The Unibet Champion Hurdle Challenge Trophy (Grade 1)	Cheltenham	Tue 14
The Close Brothers Mares' Hurdle (David Nicholson) (Grade 1)	Cheltenham	Tue 14
The Sky Bet Supreme Novices' Hurdle (Grade 1)	Cheltenham	Tue 14
The Sporting Life Arkle Challenge Trophy Novices' Chase (Grade 1)	Cheltenham	Tue 14
The Ukraine Appeal National Hunt Challenge Cup Amateur Jockeys' Novices' Chase (Grade 2)	Cheltenham	Tue 14
The Ultima Handicap Chase (Premier Handicap)	Cheltenham	Tue 14
The Boodles Juvenile Handicap Hurdle (Fred Winter) (Grade 3)	Cheltenham	Tue 14
The Betway Queen Mother Champion Chase (Grade 1)	Cheltenham	Wed 15
The Brown Advisory Novices' Chase (Broadway) (Grade 1)	Cheltenham	Wed 15
The Ballymore Novices' Hurdle (Baring Bingham) (Grade 1)	Cheltenham	Wed 15

The Weatherbys Champion Bumper (Grade 1)	Cheltenham	Wed 15
The Johnny Henderson Grand Annual Challenge Cup Handicap Chase (Premier Handicap)	Cheltenham	Wed 15
The Coral Cup Handicap Hurdle (Premier Handicap)	Cheltenham	Wed 15
The Ryanair Chase (Festival Trophy) (Grade 1)	Cheltenham	Thu 16
The Paddy Power Stayers' Hurdle (Grade 1)	Cheltenham	Thu 16
The Turners Novices' Chase (Golden Miller) (Grade 1)	Cheltenham	Thu 16
The Ryanair Mares' Novices' Hurdle (Dawn Run) (Grade 2)	Cheltenham	Thu 16
The Craft Irish Whiskey Co. Plate Handicap Chase (Premier Handicap)	Cheltenham	Thu 16
The Pertemps Network Final Handicap Hurdle (Premier Handicap)	Cheltenham	Thu 16
The Cheltenham Gold Cup Chase (Grade 1)	Cheltenham	Fri 17
The Albert Bartlett Novices' Hurdle (Spa) (Grade 1)	Cheltenham	Fri 17
The JCB Triumph Hurdle (Grade 1)	Cheltenham	Fri 17
The Mrs Paddy Power Mares' Chase (Liberthine) (Grade 2)	Cheltenham	Fri 17
The McCoy Contractors County Handicap Hurdle (Premier Handicap)	Cheltenham	Fri 17
The Boulton Group Midlands Grand National (Listed)	Uttoxeter	Sat 18
The Native Upmanship Novice Chase (Grade 3)	Thurles	Sat 18
The EBF Park Express (Group 3)	Curragh	Sat 25
The Irish Lincolnshire	Curragh	Sat 25
The Hugh McMahon Mem Novice Chase (Grade 3)	Limerick	Sun 26
The Kevin McManus Bumper (Listed)	Limerick	Sun 26
The Devoy Stakes (Listed)	Naas	Sun 26

APRIL

The SBK Cammidge Trophy Stakes (Listed)	Doncaster	Sat 01
The SBK Doncaster Mile Stakes (Listed)	Doncaster	Sat 01
The SBK Lincoln (Heritage Handicap)	Doncaster	Sat 01
The Unibet Magnolia Stakes (Listed)	Kempton Park	Sat 01
The Ballysax Stakes (Group 3)	Leopardstown	Sun 02
The Leopardstown 1000 Guineas Trial (Group 3)	Leopardstown	Sun 02
The Leopardstown 2000 Guineas Trial (Listed)	Leopardstown	Sun 02
The Heritage Stakes (Listed)	Leopardstown	Wed 05
The Ire-Incentive, It Pays To Buy Irish Chelmer Fillies' Stakes (Listed)	Chelmsford City	Thu 06
The Racing TV Snowdrop Fillies' Stakes (Listed)	Kempton Park	Sat 08
The Cork Sprint (Listed)	Cork	Sat 08
The Noblesse Stakes (Listed)	Cork	Sat 08
The Glasscarn Handicap Hurdle (Grade A)	Fairyhouse	Sat 08
The INHSO Final Novice Handicap Hurdle (Grade B)	Fairyhouse	Sat 08
The Total Enjoyment Mares Bumper (Listed)	Fairyhouse	Sat 08
The Maid Of Money Mares Chase (Listed)	Fairyhouse	Sat 08
The Imperial Call Chase (Grade 3)	Cork	Sun 09
The Easter Handicap Hurdle (Grade B)	Cork	Sun 09
The EBF Mares Novice Hurdle Final (Grade 1)	Fairyhouse	Sun 09
The Gold Cup Novice Chase (Grade 1)	Fairyhouse	Sun 09
The Easter Festival Novice Hurdle (Grade 2)	Fairyhouse	Sun 09
The Hardy Eustace Novice Hurdle (Grade 2)	Fairyhouse	Sun 09
The Greenogue Novice Handicap Chase (Grade B)	Fairyhouse	Sun 09
The Boylesports Irish Grand National (Grade A)	Fairyhouse	Mon 10
The Ballybin Hurdle (Grade 2)	Fairyhouse	Mon 10
The Percy Maynard 4yo Hurdle (Grade 2)	Fairyhouse	Mon 10
The Fairyhouse Chase (Grade 2)	Fairyhouse	Mon 10
The Barry Hills Further Flight Stakes (Listed)	Nottingham	Wed 12
The Betway Bowl Chase (Grade 1)	Aintree	Thu 13
The Aintree Hurdle (Grade 1)	Aintree	Thu 13
The SSS Super Alloys Manifesto Novices' Chase (Grade 1)	Aintree	Thu 13
The Jewson Anniversary 4-Y-O Juvenile Hurdle (Grade 1)	Aintree	Thu 13
The Goffs Uk Nickel Coin Mares' Standard Open National Hunt Flat Race (Grade 2)	Aintree	Thu 13
The Close Brothers Red Rum Handicap Chase (Premier Handicap)	Aintree	Thu 13
The Coral Burradon Stakes (Listed)	Newcastle	Thu 13
The Marsh Chase (Melling) (Grade 1)	Aintree	Fri 14
The Cavani Menswear Sefton Novices' Hurdle (Grade 1)	Aintree	Fri 14
The Betway Top Novices' Hurdle (Grade 1)	Aintree	Fri 14
The Betway Mildmay Novices' Chase (Grade 1)	Aintree	Fri 14
The Randox Topham Handicap Chase (Premier Handicap)	Aintree	Fri 14
The Aintree Handicap Hurdle (Premier Handicap)	Aintree	Fri 14
The JRL Group Liverpool Hurdle (Grade 1)	Aintree	Sat 15
The Betway Mersey Novices' Hurdle (Grade 1)	Aintree	Sat 15
The Poundland Maghull Novices' Chase (Grade 1)	Aintree	Sat 15
The Weatherbys nhstallions.co.uk Standard Open National Hunt Flat Race (Grade 2)	Aintree	Sat 15
The EFT Construction Handicap Hurdle (Premier Handicap)	Aintree	Sat 15
The Betway Handicap Chase (Premier Handicap)	Aintree	Sat 15
The Randox Grand National Handicap Chase (Premier Handicap)	Aintree	Sat 15
The Alleged Stakes (Group 3)	Curragh	Sun 16
The Gladness Stakes (Group 3)	Curragh	Sun 16
The Lanwades Stud Nell Gwyn Stakes (Group 3)	Newmarket	Tue 18

The Bet365 Earl Of Sefton Stakes (Group 3)	Newmarket	Tue 18
The Matt Hampson Foundation Silver Trophy Handicap Chase (Grade 2)	Cheltenham	Wed 19
The Bet365 Craven Stakes (Group 3)	Newmarket	Wed 19
The Connaught Access Flooring Abernant Stakes (Group 3)	Newmarket	Wed 19
The Junior Jumpers Membership Fillies' Juvenile Handicap Hurdle (Premier Handicap)	Cheltenham	Thu 20
The Catesby Estates Plc Mares' Handicap Hurdle (Listed)	Cheltenham	Thu 20
The British EBF Mares' Novices' Handicap Chase Final (Listed)	Cheltenham	Thu 20
The bearrene.com Mares' Novices' Hurdle (Listed)	Cheltenham	Thu 20
The Bet365 Feilden Stakes (Listed)	Newmarket	Thu 20
The Hillhouse Quarry Handicap Chase (Listed)	Ayr	Fri 21
The Whitsbury Manor Stud / British EBF Lansdown Stakes (Listed)	Bath	Fri 21
The Watership Down Stud Too Darn Hot Greenham Stakes (Group 3)	Newbury	Fri 21
The Dubai Duty Free Stakes (Fred Darling) (Group 3)	Newbury	Fri 21
The Dubai Duty Free Finest Surprise Stakes (John Porter) (Group 3)	Newbury	Fri 21
The Coral Scottish Champion Hurdle (Grade 2)	Ayr	Sat 22
The Jordan Electrics Ltd Future Champion Novices' Chase (Grade 2)	Ayr	Sat 22
The Coral Scottish Grand National Handicap Chase (Premier Handicap)	Ayr	Sat 22
The Scotty Brand Handicap Chase (Listed)	Ayr	Sat 22
The Vintage Crop Stakes (Group 3)	Navan	Sat 22
The Committed Stakes (Listed)	Navan	Sat 22
The Salsabil Stakes(Listed)	Navan	Sat 22
The Woodlands Sprint (Listed)	Naas	Mon 24
The Cazoo Blue Riband Trial (Listed)	Epsom Downs	Tue 25
The Champion Chase (Grade 1)	Punchestown	Tue 25
The Champion Novice Hurdle (Grade 1)	Punchestown	Tue 25
The Ellier Novice Chase (Grade 1)	Punchestown	Tue 25
The British EBF William Hill Gold Castle 'National Hunt' Novices' Hurdle (Listed)	Perth	Wed 26
The William Hill Fair Maid Of Perth Mares' Chase (Listed)	Perth	Wed 26
The Punchestown Gold Cup (Grade 1)	Punchestown	Wed 26
The Irish Daily Mirror War of Attrition Novice Hurdle (Grade 1)	Punchestown	Wed 26
The Champion Bumper (Grade 1)	Punchestown	Wed 26
The Guinness Handicap Chase (Grade A)	Punchestown	Wed 26
The Ladbrokes World Series Hurdle (Grade 1)	Punchestown	Thu 27
The Ryanair Novice Chase (Grade 1)	Punchestown	Thu 27
The Shawiya Mares Novice Hurdle (Listed)	Punchestown	Thu 27
The Ballymore Eustace Handicap Hurdle (Grade B)	Punchestown	Thu 27
The Black Hills Handicap Steeplechase (Grade B)	Punchestown	Thu 27
The Bet365 Mile (Group 2)	Sandown Park	Fri 28
The Bet365 Gordon Richards Stakes (Group 3)	Sandown Park	Fri 28
The Bet365 Classic Trial (Group 3)	Sandown Park	Fri 28
The Punchestown Champion Hurdle (Grade 1)	Punchestown	Fri 28
The Tickell Champion Novice Hurdle (Grade 1)	Punchestown	Fri 28
The Glencarraig Lady Mares Handicap Chase (Grade 2)	Punchestown	Fri 28
The Punchestown Novice Handicap Chase (Grade A)	Punchestown	Fri 28
The Bet365 Celebration Chase (Grade 1)	Sandown Park	Sat 29
The Bet365 Oaksey Chase (Grade 2)	Sandown Park	Sat 29
The Bet365 Select Hurdle (Grade 2)	Sandown Park	Sat 29
The Bet365 Gold Cup Handicap Chase (Premier Handicap)	Sandown Park	Sat 29
The Aes Champion 4yo Hurdle (Grade 1)	Punchestown	Sat 29
The EBF Mares Champion Hurdle (Grade 1)	Punchestown	Sat 29
The Ballymore Handicap Hurdle (Grade B)	Punchestown	Sat 29

MAY

The Mooresbridge Stakes (Group 2)	Curragh	Mon 01
The Athasi Stakes (Group 3)	Curragh	Mon 01
The Tetrarch Stakes (Listed)	Curragh	Mon 01
The First Flier Stakes (Listed)	Curragh	Mon 01
The British EBF Supporting Racing To School Nottinghamshire Oaks Stakes (Listed)	Nottingham	Tue 02
The Longines Sagaro Stakes (Group 3)	Ascot	Wed 03
The Merriebelle Stables Commonwealth Cup Trial Stakes (Pavilion) (Group 3)	Ascot	Wed 03
The Paradise Stakes (Listed)	Ascot	Wed 03
The Vintage Tipple Stakes (Listed)	Gowran Park	Wed 03
The Victor McCalmont Stakes (Listed)	Gowran Park	Wed 03
The British Stallion Studs EBF Daisy Warwick Fillies' Stakes (Listed)	Goodwood	Fri 05
The Betfair Exchange Jockey Club Stakes (Group 2)	Newmarket	Fri 05
The Betfair King Charles II Stakes (Listed)	Newmarket	Fri 05
The Best Odds On The Betfair Exchange Newmarket Stakes (Listed)	Newmarket	Fri 05
The Polonia Stakes (Listed)	Cork	Fri 05
The William Hill Conqueror Fillies' Stakes (Listed)	Goodwood	Sat 06
The QIPCO 2000 Guineas Stakes (Group 1)	Newmarket	Sat 06
The Betfair Palace House Stakes (Group 3)	Newmarket	Sat 06
The Read Ryan Moore On Betting.Betfair British EBF Kilvington Stakes (Listed)	Newmarket	Sat 06
The Blue Wind Stakes (Group 3)	Naas	Sat 06

The QIPCO 1000 Guineas Stakes (Group 1) ... Newmarket ... Sun 07
The Betfair Exchange Dahlia Stakes (Group 2) ... Newmarket ... Sun 07
The Betfair Pretty Polly Stakes (Listed) ... Newmarket ... Sun 07
The Amethyst Stakes (Group 3) ... Leopardstown ... Sun 07
The Cornelscourt Stakes (Group 3) ... Leopardstown ... Sun 07
The Derby Trial Stakes (Group 3) ... Leopardstown ... Sun 07
The Boodles Chester Vase Stakes (Group 3) ... Chester ... Wed 10
The Weatherbys Bloodstock Pro Cheshire Oaks (Listed) ... Chester ... Wed 10
The tote.co.uk Proud To Support Chester Racecourse Ormonde Stakes (Group 3) ... Chester ... Thu 11
The Homeserve Dee Stakes (Listed) ... Chester ... Thu 11
The Irish Thoroughbred Marketing Ire-Incentive Scheme Huxley Stakes (Group 2) ... Chester ... Fri 12
The Chester Cup (Heritage Handicap) ... Chester ... Fri 12
The Victoria Cup (Heritage Handicap) ... Ascot ... Sat 13
The Pertemps Network Swinton Handicap Hurdle (Premier Handicap) ... Haydock Park ... Sat 13
The Pertemps Network Spring Trophy Stakes (Listed) ... Haydock Park ... Sat 13
The SBK Chartwell Fillies' Stakes (Group 3) ... Lingfield Park ... Sat 13
The SBK Derby Trial Stakes (Listed) ... Lingfield Park ... Sat 13
The SBK Oaks Trial Fillies' Stakes (Listed) ... Lingfield Park ... Sat 13
The Yeats Stakes (Listed) ... Navan ... Sat 13
The Tourist Attraction Mares Hurdle (Listed) ... Killarney ... Sun 14
The Killarney Handicap Hurdle (Grade B) ... Killarney ... Sun 14
The An Riocht Chase (Grade 3) ... Killarney ... Mon 15
The Coral Brigadier Gerard Stakes (Group 3) ... Sandown Park ... Tue 16
The Coral Henry II Stakes (Group 3) ... Sandown Park ... Tue 16
The Coral National Stakes (Listed) ... Sandown Park ... Tue 16
The 1895 Duke Of York Clipper Logistics Stakes (Group 2) ... York ... Wed 17
The Tattersalls Musidora Stakes (Group 3) ... York ... Wed 17
The Al Basti Equiworld Dubai Dante Stakes (Group 2) ... York ... Thu 18
The Al Basti Equiworld Dubai Middleton Fillies' Stakes (Group 2) ... York ... Thu 18
The British Stallion Studs EBF Westow Stakes (Listed) ... York ... Thu 18
The Paddy Power Yorkshire Cup Stakes (Group 2) ... York ... Fri 19
The Knights The New Name For Langleys British EBF Marygate Fillies' Stakes (Listed) ... York ... Fri 19
The Oaks Farm Stables Fillies' Stakes (Michael Seely Memorial) (Listed) ... York ... Fri 19
The Savel Beg Stakes (Listed) ... Leopardstown ... Fri 19
The Al Shaqab Lockinge Stakes (Group 1) ... Newbury ... Sat 20
The Al Rayyan Stakes (Aston Park) (Group 3) ... Newbury ... Sat 20
The Betvictor Carnarvon Stakes (Listed) ... Newbury ... Sat 20
The Haras De Bouquetot Fillies' Trial Stakes (Listed) ... Newbury ... Sat 20
The Coolmore Stud Juvenile Fillies Stakes (Group 3) ... Naas ... Sun 21
The Lacken Stakes (Group 3) ... Naas ... Sun 21
The Whitehead Memorial Stakes (Listed) ... Naas ... Sun 21
The Sole Power Stakes (Listed) ... Naas ... Sun 21
The Tennent's Lager British Stallion Studs EBF Rothesay Stakes (Listed) ... Ayr ... Wed 24
The Coral Heron Stakes (Listed) ... Sandown Park ... Thu 25
The British Stallion Studs EBF Cocked Hat Stakes (Listed) ... Goodwood ... Fri 26
The William Hill Height Of Fashion Stakes (Listed) ... Goodwood ... Fri 26
The EBF British Stallion Studs Cecil Frail (Listed) ... Haydock Park ... Fri 26
The William Hill Tapster Stakes (Listed) ... Goodwood ... Sat 27
The William Hill Festival Stakes (Listed) ... Goodwood ... Sat 27
The Betfred Pinnacle Stakes (Group 3) ... Haydock Park ... Sat 27
The Betfred John Of Gaunt Stakes (Group 3) ... Haydock Park ... Sat 27
The Betfred Nifty Fifty Achilles Stakes (Listed) ... Haydock Park ... Sat 27
The William Hill Bronte Cup Fillies' Stakes (Group 3) ... York ... Sat 27
The Tattersalls Irish 2000 Guineas (Group 1) ... Curragh ... Sat 27
The Weatherbys Greenlands Stakes (Group 2) ... Curragh ... Sat 27
The Marble Hill Stakes (Group 3) ... Curragh ... Sat 27
The Lanwades Stud Stakes (Group 3) ... Curragh ... Sat 27
The Tattersalls Irish 1000 Guineas (Group 1) ... Curragh ... Sun 28
The Tattersalls Gold Cup (Group 1) ... Curragh ... Sun 28
The Gallinule Stakes (Group 3) ... Curragh ... Sun 28
The Orby Stakes (Listed) ... Curragh ... Sun 28
The Mayo Grand National (Grade B) ... Ballinrobe ... Tue 30

JUNE

The Cazoo Oaks (Group 1) ... Epsom Downs ... Fri 02
The Dahlbury Coronation Cup (Group 1) ... Epsom Downs ... Fri 02
The Poundland Surrey Stakes (Listed) ... Epsom Downs ... Fri 02
The Cazoo Derby (Group 1) ... Epsom Downs ... Sat 03
The Princess Elizabeth Stakes (Sponsored By Cazoo) (Group 3) ... Epsom Downs ... Sat 03
The Cazoo Diomed Stakes (Group 3) ... Epsom Downs ... Sat 03
The Dash (Heritage Handicap) ... Epsom Downs ... Sat 03
The Queen Of Scots Fillies' Stakes (Listed) ... Musselburgh ... Sat 03
The Glencairn Stakes (Listed) ... Leopardstown ... Thu 08
The Nijinsky Stakes (Listed) ... Leopardstown ... Thu 08

The Cazoo Temple Stakes (Group 2)	Haydock Park	Sat 10
The Cazoo Sandy Lane Stakes (Group 2)	Haydock Park	Sat 10
The Greatwood British EBF Stakes (Abingdon) (Listed)	Newbury	Thu 15
The Ballycorus Stakes (Group 3)	Leopardstown	Thu 15
The Seat Unique Ganton Stakes (Listed)	York	Fri 16
The Munster Oaks (Group 3)	Cork	Fri 16
The Midsummer Sprint (Listed)	Cork	Fri 16
The Coral Scurry Stakes (Listed)	Sandown Park	Sat 17
The Sky Bet Race To The Ebor Grand Cup Stakes (Listed)	York	Sat 17
The British Stallion Studs EBF Cathedral Stakes (Listed)	Salisbury	Sun 18
The St James's Palace Stakes (Group 1)	Ascot	Tue 20
The Queen Anne Stakes (Group 1)	Ascot	Tue 20
The King's Stand Stakes (Group 1)	Ascot	Tue 20
The Coventry Stakes (Group 2)	Ascot	Tue 20
The Wolferton Stakes (Listed)	Ascot	Tue 20
The Ascot Stakes (Heritage Handicap)	Ascot	Tue 20
The Prince Of Wales's Stakes (Group 1)	Ascot	Wed 21
The Queen Mary Stakes (Group 2)	Ascot	Wed 21
The Duke Of Cambridge Stakes (Group 2)	Ascot	Wed 21
The Queen's Vase (Group 2)	Ascot	Wed 21
The Windsor Castle Stakes (Listed)	Ascot	Wed 21
The Royal Hunt Cup (Heritage Handicap)	Ascot	Wed 21
The Gold Cup (Group 1)	Ascot	Thu 22
The Norfolk Stakes (Group 2)	Ascot	Thu 22
The Ribblesdale Stakes (Group 2)	Ascot	Thu 22
The Hampton Court Stakes (Group 3)	Ascot	Thu 22
The Britannia Stakes (Heritage Handicap)	Ascot	Thu 22
The King George V Stakes (Heritage Handicap)	Ascot	Thu 22
The Albany Stakes (Group 3)	Ascot	Fri 23
The King Edward Vii Stakes (Group 2)	Ascot	Fri 23
The Commonwealth Cup (Group 1)	Ascot	Fri 23
The Coronation Stakes (Group 1)	Ascot	Fri 23
The Martin Molony Stakes (Listed)	Limerick	Fri 23
The Platinum Jubilee Stakes (Group 1)	Ascot	Sat 24
The Hardwicke Stakes (Group 2)	Ascot	Sat 24
The Jersey Stakes (Group 3)	Ascot	Sat 24
The Chesham Stakes (Listed)	Ascot	Sat 24
The Wokingham Stakes (Heritage Handicap)	Ascot	Sat 24
The Russell 'Rusty Boy' Smith Irish Stallion Farms EBF Land O'Burns Fillies' Stakes (Listed)	Ayr	Sat 24
The Sky Bet Sunday Series Pontefract Castle Fillies' Stakes (Listed)	Pontefract	Sun 25
The British Stallion Studs EBF Eternal Stakes (Listed)	Carlisle	Wed 28
The Naas Oaks Trial (Listed)	Naas	Wed 28
The Jenningsbet Hoppings Fillies' Stakes (Group 3)	Newcastle	Fri 30

JULY

The Pertemps Network Chipchase Stakes (Group 3)	Newcastle	Sat 01
The Northumberland Plate (Heritage Handicap)	Newcastle	Sat 01
The House Of Cavani Menswear Criterion Stakes (Group 3)	Newmarket	Sat 01
The House Of Cavani Menswear Fred Archer Stakes (Listed)	Newmarket	Sat 01
The Maureen Brittain Memorial Empress Fillies' Stakes (Listed)	Newmarket	Sat 01
The Dubai Duty Free Irish Derby (Group 1)	Curragh	Sat 01
The Gain Railway Stakes (Group 2)	Curragh	Sat 01
The Dubai Duty Free Belgrave Stakes (Listed)	Curragh	Sat 01
The Dubai Duty Free Celebration Stakes (Listed)	Curragh	Sat 01
The Bet365 Summer Cup (Open Handicap Chase) (Listed)	Uttoxeter	Sun 02
The Pretty Polly Stakes (Group 1)	Curragh	Sun 02
The Comer International Curragh Cup (Group 2)	Curragh	Sun 02
The Balanchine Stakes (Group 2)	Curragh	Sun 02
The International Stakes (Group 3)	Curragh	Sun 02
The Lenebane Stakes (Listed)	Roscommon	Tue 04
The Tipperary Stakes (Listed)	Tipperary	Wed 05
The Grimes Hurdle (Grade 3)	Tipperary	Thu 06
The Davies Insurance Services Gala Stakes (Listed)	Sandown Park	Fri 07
The Coral Marathon (Esher) (Listed)	Sandown Park	Fri 07
The Coral Dragon Stakes (Listed)	Sandown Park	Fri 07
The Bet365 Lancashire Oaks (Group 2)	Haydock Park	Sat 08
The bet365 Old Newton Cup (Heritage Handicap)	Haydock Park	Sat 08
The Coral-Eclipse (Group 1)	Sandown Park	Sat 08
The Coral Charge (Sprint) (Group 3)	Sandown Park	Sat 08
The Coral Distaff (Listed)	Sandown Park	Sat 08
The Louis Roederer Queen Charlotte Fillies' Stakes (Listed)	Chelmsford City	Sun 09
The Weatherbys Bloodstock Pro Pipalong Stakes (Listed)	Pontefract	Tue 11
The Brownstown Stakes (Group 3)	Fairyhouse	Wed 12

The Princess Of Wales's Close Brothers Stakes (Group 2)	Newmarket	Thu 13
The Edmondson Hall Solicitors Sir Henry Cecil Stakes (Listed)	Newmarket	Thu 13
The Bahrain Trophy Stakes (Group 3)	Newmarket	Thu 13
The Close Brothers July Stakes (Group 2)	Newmarket	Thu 13
The Stanerra Stakes (Group 3)	Leopardstown	Thu 13
The Tattersalls Falmouth Stakes (Group 1)	Newmarket	Fri 14
The Duchess Of Cambridge Stakes (Group 2)	Newmarket	Fri 14
The William Hill Summer Stakes (Group 3)	York	Fri 14
The Midlands Grand National (Grade B)	Kilbeggan	Fri 14
The Fred Cowley MBE Memorial Summer Mile Stakes (Group 2)	Ascot	Sat 15
The Raymond & Kathleen Corbett Memorial City Plate Stakes (Listed)	Chester	Sat 15
The Darley July Cup Stakes (Group 1)	Newmarket	Sat 15
The Bet365 Superlative Stakes (Group 2)	Newmarket	Sat 15
The bet365 Bunbury Cup (Heritage Handicap)	Newmarket	Sat 15
The John Smith's Silver Cup Stakes (Group 3)	York	Sat 15
The John Smith's City Walls Stakes (Listed)	York	Sat 15
The John Smith's Cup (Heritage Handicap)	York	Sat 15
The Cairn Rouge Stakes (Listed)	Killarney	Wed 19
The Green Room Meld Stakes (Group 3)	Leopardstown	Thu 20
The British Stallions Studs EBF Glasgow Stakes (Listed)	Hamilton Park	Fri 21
The Irish Thoroughbred Marketing (IRE) Incentive Scheme Rose Bowl Stakes (Listed)	Newbury	Fri 21
The Bourn Vincent Memorial Handicap Chase (Grade B)	Killarney	Fri 21
The Unibet Summer Plate Handicap Chase (Premier Handicap)	Market Rasen	Sat 22
The Bet365 Hackwood Stakes (Group 3)	Newbury	Sat 22
The Bet365 Stakes (Steventon) (Listed)	Newbury	Sat 22
The Ric And Mary Hambro Aphrodite Fillies' Stakes (Listed)	Newmarket	Sat 22
The Juddmonte Irish Oaks (Group 1)	Curragh	Sat 22
The Jebel Ali Anglesey Stakes (Group 3)	Curragh	Sat 22
The Minstrel Stakes (Group 3)	Curragh	Sat 22
The Kilboy Estate Stakes (Group 2)	Curragh	Sun 23
The Sapphire Stakes (Group 2)	Curragh	Sun 23
The Sweet Mimosa Stakes (Listed)	Naas	Wed 26
The Marwell Stakes (Listed)	Naas	Wed 26
The European Bloodstock News EBF Star Stakes (Listed)	Sandown Park	Thu 27
The Silver Flash Stakes (Group 3)	Leopardstown	Thu 27
The Tyros Stakes (Group 3)	Leopardstown	Thu 27
The British Stallion Studs EBF Lyric Fillies' Stakes (Listed)	York	Fri 28
The Her Majesty's Plate (Listed)	Down Royal	Fri 28
The King George VI And Queen Elizabeth QIPCO Stakes (Group 1)	Ascot	Sat 29
The Longines Valiant Stakes (Group 3)	Ascot	Sat 29
The Princess Margaret Keeneland Stakes (Group 3)	Ascot	Sat 29
The Flexjet Pat Eddery Stakes (Winkfield) (Listed)	Ascot	Sat 29
The International Stakes (Heritage Handicap)	Ascot	Sat 29
The Sky Bet York Stakes (Group 2)	York	Sat 29
The Sky Bet Go-Racing-In-Yorkshire Summer Festival Pomfret Stakes (Listed)	Pontefract	Sun 30

AUGUST

The Al Shaqab Goodwood Cup Stakes (Group 1)	Goodwood	Tue 0
The World Pool Lennox Stakes (Group 2)	Goodwood	Tue 0
The Japan Racing Association Vintage Stakes (Group 2)	Goodwood	Tue 0
The Castlegar Novice Hurdle (Listed)	Galway	Tue 0
The Qatar Sussex Stakes (Group 1)	Goodwood	Wed 0
The Whispering Angel Oak Tree Stakes (Group 3)	Goodwood	Wed 0
The Markel Molecomb Stakes (Group 3)	Goodwood	Wed 0
The Tote Galway Plate (Handicap Chase) (Grade A)	Galway	Wed 0
The Qatar Nassau Stakes (Group 1)	Goodwood	Thu 0
The Richmond Stakes (Group 2)	Goodwood	Thu 0
The John Pearce Racing Gordon Stakes (Group 3)	Goodwood	Thu 0
The Ballybrit Novice Chase (Grade 3)	Galway	Thu 0
The Corrib EBF Fillies (Listed)	Galway	Thu 0
The Guinness Galway Hurdle (Handicap) (Grade A)	Galway	Thu 0
The King George Qatar Stakes (Group 2)	Goodwood	Fri 0
The L'Ormarins Queen's Plate Glorious Stakes (Group 3)	Goodwood	Fri 0
The Bonhams Thoroughbred Stakes (Group 3)	Goodwood	Fri 0
The Qatar Lillie Langtry Stakes (Group 2)	Goodwood	Sat 0
The Stewards' Cup (Heritage Handicap)	Goodwood	Sat 0
The British Stallion Studs EBF Chalice Stakes (Listed)	Newmarket	Sat 0
The Mervue Handicap Hurdle (Grade B)	Galway	Sat 0
The Freddie Wilson Queensferry Stakes (Listed)	Chester	Sun 0
The Irish EBF Ballyhane Stud Median Sires Stakes	Naas	Mon 0
The El Gran Senor Stakes (Listed)	Tipperary	Fri 1
The Betfred Rose Of Lancaster Stakes (Group 3)	Haydock Park	Sat 1
The British Stallion Studs EBF Dick Hern Stakes (Listed)	Haydock Park	Sat 1

The Jewson Sweet Solera Stakes (Group 3)	Newmarket	Sat 12
The Keeneland Phoenix Stakes (Group 1)	Curragh	Sat 12
The Phoenix Sprint Stakes (Group 3)	Curragh	Sat 12
The British Stallion Studs EBF Upavon Fillies' Stakes (Listed)	Salisbury	Wed 16
The Hurry Harriet Stakes (Listed)	Gowran Park	Wed 16
The Tattersalls Sovereign Stakes (Group 3)	Salisbury	Thu 17
The Ballyroan Stakes (Group 3)	Leopardstown	Thu 17
The Desmond Stakes (Group 3)	Leopardstown	Thu 17
The Betvictor St Hugh's Stakes (Listed)	Newbury	Fri 18
The Platinum Stakes (Listed)	Cork	Fri 18
The Give Thanks Stakes	Cork	Fri 18
The Betvictor Hungerford Stakes (Group 2)	Newbury	Sat 19
The Betvictor Geoffrey Freer Stakes (Group 3)	Newbury	Sat 19
The Debutante Stakes (Group 2)	Curragh	Sat 19
The Futurity Stakes (Group 2)	Curragh	Sat 19
The EBF Stallions Highfield Farm Flying Fillies' Stakes (Listed)	Pontefract	Sun 20
The Ballycullen Stakes (Group 3)	Curragh	Sun 20
The Royal Whip Stakes (Group 3)	Curragh	Sun 20
The Curragh Stakes (Listed)	Curragh	Sun 20
The Juddmonte International Stakes (Group 1)	York	Wed 23
The Sky Bet Great Voltigeur Stakes (Group 2)	York	Wed 23
The Tattersalls Acomb Stakes (Group 3)	York	Wed 23
The Darley Yorkshire Oaks (Group 1)	York	Thu 24
The Sky Bet Lowther Stakes (Group 2)	York	Thu 24
The British EBF & Sir Henry Cecil Galtres Stakes (Listed)	York	Thu 24
The Ruby Stakes (Listed)	Killarney	Thu 24
The Vinnie Roe Stakes (Listed)	Leopardstown	Thu 24
The Coolmore Wootton Bassett Nunthorpe Stakes (Group 1)	York	Fri 25
The Weatherbys Hamilton Lonsdale Cup Stakes (Group 2)	York	Fri 25
The Al Basti Equiworld Dubai Gimcrack Stakes (Group 2)	York	Fri 25
The Mount Brandon Handicap Hurdle (Grade B)	Killarney	Fri 25
The William Hill Celebration Mile Stakes (Group 2)	Goodwood	Sat 26
The William Hill Prestige Fillies' Stakes (Group 3)	Goodwood	Sat 26
The Jenningsbet Hopeful Stakes (Listed)	Newmarket	Sat 26
The Sytner Sunningdale & Maidenhead BMW Winter Hill Stakes (Group 3)	Windsor	Sat 26
The Royal Windsor August Stakes (Listed)	Windsor	Sat 26
The Sky Bet City Of York Stakes (Group 2)	York	Sat 26
The Sky Bet And Symphony Group Strensall Stakes (Group 3)	York	Sat 26
The Julia Graves Roses Stakes (Listed)	York	Sat 26
The Sky Bet Ebor (Heritage Handicap)	York	Sat 26
The Sky Bet Melrose Stakes (Heritage Handicap)	York	Sat 26
The Flame Of Tara Stakes (Group 3)	Curragh	Sat 26
The Round Tower Stakes (Group 3)	Curragh	Sat 26
The Snow Fairy Stakes (Group 3)	Curragh	Sat 26
The Lough Leane Handicap Chase (Grade B)	Killarney	Sat 26
The Ballyogan Stakes (Group 3)	Naas	Sun 27
The British Stallion Studs EBF Ripon Champion Two Yrs Old Trophy Stakes (Listed)	Ripon	Mon 28

SEPTEMBER

The Longines Irish Champions Weekend EBF Stonehenge Stakes (Listed)	Salisbury	Fri 01
The William Hill Beverley Bullet Sprint Stakes (Listed)	Beverley	Sat 02
The Chester Stakes (Listed)	Chester	Sat 02
The Fasig-Tipton Night Of The Stars Solario Stakes (Group 3)	Sandown Park	Sat 02
The JRL Group Atalanta Stakes (Group 3)	Sandown Park	Sat 02
The Fairy Bridge Stakes (Group 3)	Tipperary	Sun 03
The Abergwaun Stakes (Listed)	Tipperary	Sun 03
The Ire-Incentive, It Pays To Buy Irish Dick Poole Fillies' Stakes (Group 3)	Salisbury	Thu 07
The Betfair Sprint Cup Stakes (Group 1)	Haydock Park	Sat 09
The Best Odds On The Betfair Exchange Superior Mile Stakes (Group 3)	Haydock Park	Sat 09
The Betfair Daily Tips On Betting.Betfair Ascendant Stakes (Listed)	Haydock Park	Sat 09
The Unibet September Stakes (Group 3)	Kempton Park	Sat 09
The Unibet 3 Uniboosts A Day Sirenia Stakes (Group 3)	Kempton Park	Sat 09
The Irish Champion Stakes (Group 1)	Leopardstown	Sat 09
The Coolmore Matron Stakes (Group 1)	Leopardstown	Sat 09
The Clipper Logistics Solonoway Stakes (Group 2)	Leopardstown	Sat 09
The KPMG Golden Fleece Stakes (Group 2)	Leopardstown	Sat 09
The Kilternan Stakes (Group 3)	Leopardstown	Sat 09
The Ingabelle Stakes (Listed)	Leopardstown	Sat 09
The Elevator Company Garrowby Stakes (Listed)	York	Sun 10
The Comer Group International St Leger Stakes (Group 1)	Curragh	Sun 10
The Derrinstown Stud Flying Five Stakes (Group 1)	Curragh	Sun 10
The Goffs Vincent O'Brien National Stakes (Group 1)	Curragh	Sun 10
The Moyglare Stud Stakes (Group 1)	Curragh	Sun 10
The Moyglare Stud Blandford Stakes (Group 2)	Curragh	Sun 10

Race	Course	Date
The Oyster Stakes (Listed)	Galway	Tue 12
The Coral Park Hill Fillies' Stakes (Group 2)	Doncaster	Thu 14
The Cazoo May Hill Stakes (Group 2)	Doncaster	Thu 14
The Coral Doncaster Cup Stakes (Group 2)	Doncaster	Fri 15
The Wainwright Flying Childers Stakes (Group 2)	Doncaster	Fri 15
The Cazoo Flying Scotsman Stakes (Listed)	Doncaster	Fri 15
The tote.co.uk Betting Tournaments Stand Cup Stakes (Listed)	Chester	Sat 16
The Cazoo St Leger Stakes (Group 1)	Doncaster	Sat 16
The Coral Champagne Stakes (Group 2)	Doncaster	Sat 16
The Cazoo Park Stakes (Group 2)	Doncaster	Sat 16
The Cordell Lavarack Stakes (Group 3)	Gowran Park	Sat 16
The Japan Racing Association Sceptre Fillies' Stakes (Group 3)	Doncaster	Sun 17
The Cazoo Scarbrough Stakes (Listed)	Doncaster	Sun 17
The Blenheim Stakes (Listed)	Fairyhouse	Mon 18
The Latrigue 4yo Handicap Hurdle (Grade B)	Listowel	Mon 18
The Listowel Stakes (Listed)	Listowel	Tue 19
The Chasemore Farm Fortune Stakes (Listed)	Sandown Park	Wed 20
The EBF Stallions John Musker Fillies' Stakes (Listed)	Yarmouth	Wed 20
The Guinness Kerry National (Handicap Chase) (Grade A)	Listowel	Wed 20
The British EBF Stallions Harry Rosebery Stakes (Listed)	Ayr	Fri 22
The Arran Scottish Sprint EBF Fillies' Stakes (Listed)	Ayr	Fri 22
The Dubai Duty Free Cup Stakes (Listed)	Newbury	Fri 22
The Ladbrokes Handicap Hurdle (Grade B)	Listowel	Fri 22
The Virgin Bet Firth Of Clyde Fillies' Stakes (Group 3)	Ayr	Sat 23
The Virgin Bet Doonside Cup Stakes (Listed)	Ayr	Sat 23
The Ayr Gold Cup (Heritage Handicap)	Ayr	Sat 23
The Dubai Duty Free Mill Reef Stakes (Group 2)	Newbury	Sat 23
The Dubai International Airport World Trophy Stakes (Group 3)	Newbury	Sat 23
The Beresford Stakes (Group 2)	Curragh	Sun 24
The Weld Park Stakes (Group 3)	Curragh	Sun 24
The Loughbrown Stakes (Group 3)	Curragh	Sun 24
The Renaissance Stakes (Group 3)	Curragh	Sun 24
The Kilbegnet NoviceChase (Grade 3)	Roscommon	Mon 25
The Navigation Stakes (Listed)	Cork	Tue 26
The Bahrain Turf Club Foundation Stakes (Listed)	Goodwood	Wed 27
The Tattersalls Stakes (Somerville Tattersall) (Group 3)	Newmarket	Thu 28
The Jockey Club Rose Bowl Stakes (Listed)	Newmarket	Thu 28
The Al Basti Equiworld, Dubai Rockfel Stakes (Group 2)	Newmarket	Fri 29
The Al Basti Equiworld, Dubai Joel Stakes (Group 2)	Newmarket	Fri 29
The Princess Royal Al Basti Equiworld, Dubai Stakes (Group 3)	Newmarket	Fri 29
The Al Basti Equiworld, Dubai British EBF Rosemary Stakes (Listed)	Newmarket	Fri 29
The Al Basti Equiworld, Dubai Godolphin Stakes (Listed)	Newmarket	Fri 29
The Diamond Stakes (Group 3)	Dundalk	Fri 29
The Mucklemeg Mares Bumper (Listed)	Gowran Park	Fri 29
The Pat Walsh Memorial Mares Hurdle (Listed)	Gowran Park	Fri 29
The Juddmonte Cheveley Park Stakes (Group 1)	Newmarket	Sat 30
The Juddmonte Middle Park Stakes (Group 1)	Newmarket	Sat 30
The Juddmonte Royal Lodge Stakes (Group 2)	Newmarket	Sat 30
The bet365 Cambridgeshire (Heritage Handicap)	Newmarket	Sat 3
The Gowran Champion Chase (Grade 2)	Gowran Park	Sat 3

OCTOBER

Race	Course	Date
The Tipperary Hurdle (Grade 2)	Tipperary	Sun 0
The Joe Mac Novice Hurdle (Grade 3)	Tipperary	Sun 0
The Like A Butterfly Novice Chase (Grade 3)	Tipperary	Sun 0
The Concorde Stakes (Group 3)	Tipperary	Sun 0
The Peroni Nastro Azzurro Noel Murless Stakes (Listed)	Ascot	Fri 0
The Star Appeal Stakes (Listed)	Dundalk	Fri 0
The Legacy Stakes (Listed)	Dundalk	Fri 0
The Peroni Nastro Azzurro Cumberland Lodge Stakes (Group 3)	Ascot	Sat 0
The John Guest Racing Bengough Stakes (Group 3)	Ascot	Sat 0
The Oakman Inns Rous Stakes (Listed)	Ascot	Sat 0
The Peroni Nastro Azzurro British EBF Stakes (October) (Listed)	Ascot	Sat 0
The Royal Bahrain Sun Chariot Stakes (Group 1)	Newmarket	Sat 0
The Racing TV EBF Stallions Guisborough Stakes (Listed)	Redcar	Sat 0
The William Hill Two Year Old Trophy (Listed)	Redcar	Sat 0
The Lanwades and Staffordstown Studs Silken Glider Stakes (Listed)	Curragh	Sat 0
The Waterford Testimonial Stakes (Listed)	Curragh	Sat 0
The Buck House Novice Chase (Grade 3) Carvills Hill Chase (Grade 3)	Punchestown	Wed 1
The Buck House Novice Chase (Grade 3)	Punchestown	Wed 1
The Unibet Persian War Novices' Hurdle (Grade 2)	Chepstow	Fri 1
The Bet365 Fillies' Mile (Group 1)	Newmarket	Fri 1
The Thoroughbred Industry Employee Awards Challenge Stakes (Group 2)	Newmarket	Fri 1
The Newmarket Academy Godolphin Beacon Project Cornwallis Stakes (Group 3)	Newmarket	Fri 1

Race	Course	Date
The Newmarket Pony Academy Pride Stakes (Group 3)	Newmarket	Fri 13
The Godolphin Lifetime Care Oh So Sharp Stakes (Group 3)	Newmarket	Fri 13
The bet365 Old Rowley Cup (Heritage Handicap)	Newmarket	Fri 13
The Dunraven Windows Novices' Chase (Listed)	Chepstow	Sat 14
The Darley Dewhurst Stakes (Group 1)	Newmarket	Sat 14
The Godolphin Flying Start Zetland Stakes (Group 3)	Newmarket	Sat 14
The Emirates Autumn Stakes (Group 3)	Newmarket	Sat 14
The Masar Darley Stakes (Group 3)	Newmarket	Sat 14
The Blue Point British EBF Boadicea Stakes (Listed)	Newmarket	Sat 14
The Cesarewitch (Heritage Handicap)	Newmarket	Sat 14
The Coral Rockingham Stakes (Class 1)(Listed)	York	Sat 14
The Coral Sprint Tophy (Heritage Handicap)	York	Sat 14
The Finale Stakes (Listed)	Naas	Sat 14
The Kinsale Handicap Chase (Grade B)	Cork	Sun 15
The Bluebell Stakes (Listed)	Naas	Sun 15
The Garnet Stakes (Listed)	Naas	Sun 15
The British Stallion Studs EBF Beckford Stakes (Listed)	Bath	Wed 18
The Mercury Stakes (Group 3)	Dundalk	Fri 20
The QIPCO Champion Stakes (Group 1)	Ascot	Sat 21
The Queen Elizabeth II Stakes (Group 1)	Ascot	Sat 21
The QIPCO British Champions Fillies & Mares Stakes (Group 1)	Ascot	Sat 21
The QIPCO British Champions Sprint Stakes (Group 1)	Ascot	Sat 21
The QIPCO British Champions Long Distance Cup (Group 2)	Ascot	Sat 21
The Eyrefield Stakes (Group 3)	Leopardstown	Sat 21
The Knockaire Stakes (Listed)	Leopardstown	Sat 21
The Bet@Racingtv.com Hurdle (Listed)	Kempton Park	Sun 22
The Racing TV Novices' Hurdle (Listed)	Kempton Park	Sun 22
The Killavullan Stakes (Group 3)	Leopardstown	Sun 22
The Trigo Stakes (Listed)	Leopardstown	Sun 22
The Greenmount Park Novice Hurdle (Listed)	Limerick	Sun 22
The Cailain Alainn Mares Hurdle (Listed)	Limerick	Sun 22
The Ladbrokes Munster National Handicap Chase (Grade A)	Limerick	Sun 22
The British Stallion Studs EBF Silver Tankard Stakes (Listed)	Pontefract	Mon 23
he Vertem Futurity Trophy Stakes (Group 1)	Doncaster	Sat 28
he Virgin Bet Doncaster Stakes (Listed)	Doncaster	Sat 28
he Virgin Bet Horris Hill Stakes (Group 3)	Newbury	Sat 28
he Virgin Bet St Simon Stakes (Group 3)	Newbury	Sat 28
he Galloping To Give Stakes (Radley) (Listed)	Newbury	Sat 28
he Jewson Monet's Garden Old Roan Limited Handicap Chase (Grade 2)	Aintree	Sun 29
he Bettyville Steeplechase (Listed)	Wexford	Sun 29

NOVEMBER

Race	Course	Date
he Ben Marshall Stakes (Listed)	Nottingham	Wed 01
he Coral EBF Fleur De Lys Fillies' Stakes (Listed)	Lingfield Park	Thu 02
he Coral EBF River Eden Fillies' Stakes (Listed)	Lingfield Park	Thu 02
he Irish Stallion Farms EBF 'Bosra Sham' Fillies' Stakes (Listed)	Newmarket	Fri 03
he Weatherbys nhstallions.co.uk Wensleydale Juvenile Hurdle (Listed)	Wetherby	Fri 03
he Each Way Extra At Bet365 Handicap Chase (Premier Handicap)	Wetherby	Fri 03
he WKD Hurdle (Grade 2)	Down Royal	Fri 03
he Hamptons EBF Mares Novice Hurdle (Grade 3)	Down Royal	Fri 03
he Cooley Stakes (Listed)	Dundalk	Fri 03
he Bateaux London Gold Cup Handicap Chase (Premier Handicap)	Ascot	Sat 04
he Byrne Group Handicap Chase (Premier Handicap)	Ascot	Sat 04
he British Stallion Studs EBF Montrose Fillies' Stakes (Listed)	Newmarket	Sat 04
he James Seymour Stakes (Listed)	Newmarket	Sat 04
he Bet365 Charlie Hall Chase (Grade 2)	Wetherby	Sat 04
he Bet365 Hurdle (West Yorkshire Hurdle) (Grade 2)	Wetherby	Sat 04
he Bet365 Mares' Hurdle (Listed)	Wetherby	Sat 04
he Colin Parker Memorial Intermediate Chase (Listed)	Carlisle	Sun 05
he Paddy Power EBF Novice Chase (Grade 3)	Cork	Sun 05
he Paddy Power EBF Novice Hurdle (Listed)	Cork	Sun 05
he Paddy Power Cork Grand National Handicap Chase (Grade B))	Cork	Sun 05
he NFRC Floodlit Stakes (Listed)	Kempton Park	Mon 06
he Clonmel Oil Chase (Grade 2)	Clonmel	Thu 09
he EBF TA Morris Mem Mares Chase (Listed)	Clonmel	Thu 09
he Betway Haldon Gold Cup (Grade 2)	Exeter	Fri 10
he British EBF Gillies Fillies' Stakes (Listed)	Doncaster	Sat 11
he Virgin Bet Wentworth Stakes (Listed)	Doncaster	Sat 11
he Unibet Elite Hurdle (Grade 2)	Wincanton	Sat 11
he Boodles 'Rising Stars' Novices' Chase (Grade 2)	Wincanton	Sat 11
he 61st Badger Beer Handicap Chase (Premier Handicap)	Wincanton	Sat 11
he Future Stars Intermediate Chase (Listed)	Sandown Park	Sun 12
ne Poplar Square Chase (Grade 3)	Naas	Sun 12
ne Fishery Lane 4yo Hurdle (Grade 3)	Naas	Sun 12

The Brown Lad Handicap Hurdle Grade B .... Naas .... Sun 12
The Potter Group Mares' Novices' Chase (Listed) .... Bangor-On-Dee .... Wed 15
The Bud Booth Mares' Chase (Listed) .... Market Rasen .... Thu 16
The Ballymore Novices' Hurdle (Hyde) (Grade 2) .... Cheltenham .... Fri 17
The JCB Triumph Trial Juvenile Hurdle (Prestbury) (Grade 2) .... Cheltenham .... Sat 18
The From The Horse's Mouth Podcast Novices' Chase (November) (Grade 2) .... Cheltenham .... Sat 18
The Mares' Open National Hunt Flat Race (Class 1)(Listed) .... Cheltenham .... Sat 18
The Paddy Power Gold Cup Handicap Chase (Premier Handicap) .... Cheltenham .... Sat 18
The Betway Golden Rose Stakes (Listed) .... Lingfield Park .... Sat 18
The Betway Churchill Stakes (Listed) .... Lingfield Park .... Sat 18
The Fortria Chase (Grade 2) .... Navan .... Sat 18
The Lismullen Hurdle (Grade 2) .... Navan .... Sat 18
The For Auction Novice Hurdle (Grade 3) .... Navan .... Sat 18
The Cheltenham Chase (Grade 2) .... Cheltenham .... Sun 19
The Sky Bet Supreme Trial Novices' Hurdle (Sharp) (Grade 2) .... Cheltenham .... Sun 19
The High Sheriff Of Gloucestershire Open National Hunt Flat Race) (Listed) .... Cheltenham .... Sun 19
The Unibet Greatwood Handicap Hurdle (Premier Handicap) .... Cheltenham .... Sun 19
The Jewson Click And Collect Handicap Chase (Premier Handicap) .... Cheltenham .... Sun 19
The Monksfield Novice Hurdle (Grade 3) .... Navan .... Sun 19
The Aries Girl Mares Bumper (Listed) .... Navan .... Sun 19
The Ladbrokes Troytown Handicap Chase (Grade B) .... Navan .... Sun 19
The Thurles Chase (Listed) .... Thurles .... Thu 23
The Chanelle Pharma 1965 Chase (Grade 2) .... Ascot .... Sat 25
The Coral Hurdle (Ascot) (Grade 2) .... Ascot .... Sat 25
The Betfair Chase (Lancashire) (Grade 1) .... Haydock Park .... Sat 25
The Betfair Weighed In Podcast Newton Novices' Hurdle (Listed) .... Haydock Park .... Sat 25
The Betfair Exchange Stayers' Handicap Hurdle (Premier Handicap) .... Haydock Park .... Sat 25
The John Durkan Memorial Chase (Grade 1) .... Punchestown .... Sat 25
The Craddockstown Novice Chase (Grade 2) .... Punchestown .... Sat 25
The Voler La Vedette Mares Novice Hurdle (Listed) .... Punchestown .... Sat 25
The Morgiana Hurdle (Grade 1) .... Punchestown .... Sun 26
The Florida Pearl Novice Chase (Grade 2) .... Punchestown .... Sun 26
The Grabel Mares Hurdle (Listed) .... Punchestown .... Sun 26
The Racing TV Mares' Hurdle (Listed) .... Kempton Park .... Mon 27

DECEMBER

The Ladbrokes Long Distance Hurdle (Grade 2) .... Newbury .... Fri 01
The Coral Novices' Chase (Berkshire) (Grade 2) .... Newbury .... Fri 01
The Ladbrokes John Francome Novices' Chase (Grade 2) .... Newbury .... Sat 02
The Ladbrokes Mares' Novices' Hurdle (Listed) .... Newbury .... Sat 02
The Coral Gold Cup Handicap Chase (Premier Handicap) .... Newbury .... Sat 02
The Coral Intermediate Handicap Hurdle (Gerry Feilden) (Premier Handicap) .... Newbury .... Sat 02
The Betfair Fighting Fifth Hurdle (Grade 1) .... Newcastle .... Sat 02
The Betfair Exchange Rehearsal Handicap Chase (Premier Handicap) .... Newcastle .... Sat 02
The Ballyhack Handicap Chase (Grade B) .... Punchestown .... Sat 02
The Houghton Mares' Chase (Listed) .... Carlisle .... Sun 03
The Bar One Drinmore Novice Chase (Grade 1) .... Fairyhouse .... Sun 03
The Bar One Hattons Grace Hurdle (Grade 1) .... Fairyhouse .... Sun 03
The Bar One Royal Bond Novice Hurdle (Grade 1) .... Fairyhouse .... Sun 03
The Winter Festival Juvenile Hurdle (Grade 3) .... Fairyhouse .... Sun 03
The New Stand Handicap Hurdle Grade A .... Fairyhouse .... Sun 03
The Porterstown Handicap Chase Grade B .... Fairyhouse .... Sun 03
The British Stallion Studs EBF Hyde Stakes (Listed) .... Kempton Park .... Wed 06
The Unibet Wild Flower Stakes (Listed) .... Kempton Park .... Wed 06
The Ballymore Winter Novices' Hurdle (Grade 2) .... Sandown Park .... Fri 08
The Many Clouds Chase (Grade 2) .... Aintree .... Sat 09
The racingtv.com Fillies' Juvenile Hurdle (Listed) .... Aintree .... Sat 09
The Becher Handicap Chase (Premier Handicap) .... Aintree .... Sat 09
The Betfair Tingle Creek Chase (Grade 1) .... Sandown Park .... Sat 09
The Close Brothers Henry VIII Novices' Chase (Grade 1) .... Sandown Park .... Sat 09
The Fitzdares Peterborough Chase (Grade 2) .... Huntingdon .... Sun 10
The Fitzdares Adores Henrietta Knight Mares' Open National Hunt Flat Race (Listed) .... Huntingdon .... Sun 10
The Kerry Group Hilly Way Chase (Grade 2) .... Cork .... Sun 10
The Lombardstown EBF Mares Novice Chase (Grade 2) .... Cork .... Sun 10
The Kerry Group Cork Stayers Novice Hurdle (Grade 3) .... Cork .... Sun 10
The Lady Godiva Mares' Novices' Chase (Listed) .... Warwick .... Thu 14
The Betfair Handicap Chase (Premier Handicap) .... Cheltenham .... Fri 15
The Unibet International Hurdle (Grade 2) .... Cheltenham .... Sat 16
The Albert Bartlett Novices' Hurdle (Bristol) (Grade 2) .... Cheltenham .... Sat 16
The Racing Post Gold Cup Handicap Chase (Premier Handicap) .... Cheltenham .... Sat 16
The Bet365 December Novices' Chase (Grade 2) .... Doncaster .... Sat 16
The Bet365 Summit Juvenile Hurdle (Listed) .... Doncaster .... Sat 16
The Future Champions Bumper (Listed) .... Navan .... Sun 17
The Tara Handicap Hurdle (Grade B) .... Navan .... Sun 17

The Boreen Belle EBF Mares Novice Hurdle (Listed)	Thurles	Sun 17
The Make Your Best Bet At Betvictor Mares' Chase (Listed)	Newbury	Wed 20
The Howden Noel Novices' Chase (Grade 2)	Ascot	Fri 22
The Howden Kennel Gate Novices' Hurdle (Grade 2)	Ascot	Fri 22
The Lexicon Recruitment Championship Open National Hunt Flat Race (Listed)	Ascot	Fri 22
The Howden Long Walk Hurdle (Grade 1)	Ascot	Sat 23
The Betfair Exchange Trophy (Premier Handicap)	Ascot	Sat 23
The Howden Silver Cup Handicap Chase (Premier Handicap)	Ascot	Sat 23
The Mares' Novices' Hurdle (Abram) (Listed)	Haydock Park	Sat 23
The Betway Quebec Stakes (Listed)	Lingfield Park	Sat 23
The Ladbrokes King George VI Chase (Grade 1)	Kempton Park	Tue 26
The Ladbrokes Christmas Hurdle (Grade 1)	Kempton Park	Tue 26
The Ladbrokes Kauto Star Novices' Chase (Grade 1)	Kempton Park	Tue 26
The William Hill Rowland Meyrick Handicap Chase (Premier Handicap)	Wetherby	Tue 26
The Racing Post Novice Chase (Grade 1)	Leopardstown	Tue 26
The Knight Frank Juvenile Hurdle (Grade 2)	Leopardstown	Tue 26
The Greenmount Park Novice Chase (Grade 1)	Limerick	Tue 26
The Coral Finale Juvenile Hurdle (Grade 2)	Chepstow	Wed 27
The Coral Welsh Grand National Handicap Chase (Premier Handicap)	Chepstow	Wed 27
The Ladbrokes Desert Orchid Chase (Grade 2)	Kempton Park	Wed 27
The Ladbrokes Wayward Lad Novices' Chase (Grade 2)	Kempton Park	Wed 27
The Paddy Power Dial A Bet Chase (Grade 1)	Leopardstown	Wed 27
The Paddy Power Future Champions Novice Hurdle (Grade 1)	Leopardstown	Wed 27
The Paddy Power Handicap Chase Grade B	Leopardstown	Wed 27
The Dorans Pride Novice Hurdle (Grade 2)	Limerick	Wed 27
The Savills Christmas Chase (Grade 1)	Leopardstown	Thu 28
The Christmas Hurdle (Grade 1)	Leopardstown	Thu 28
The Dawn Run EBF Mares Novice Chase (Grade 2)	Limerick	Thu 28
The Tim Duggan Mem Handicap Chase (Grade B)	Limerick	Thu 28
The Yorkshire Silver Vase Mares' Chase (Listed)	Doncaster	Fri 29
The Fort Leney Novice Chase (Grade 1)	Leopardstown	Fri 29
The Matheson December Hurdle (Grade 1)	Leopardstown	Fri 29
The EBF Mares Hurdle (Grade 3)	Leopardstown	Fri 29
The Sporting Limerick 4yo Hurdle (Grade 2)	Limerick	Fri 29
The Mansionbet Challow Novices' Hurdle (Grade 1)	Newbury	Sat 30
The Byerley Stud Mares' Novices' Hurdle (Listed)	Taunton	Sat 30

The list of Principal Races has been supplied by the BHA and Horse Racing Ireland and is provisional.
In all cases, the dates, venues, and names of sponsors are correct at time of going to press, but also subject to possible alteration.

Front cover -	First lot canter up the hill on a cold bright morning at Seven Barrows Lambourn. (Photo by Edward Whitaker)

INDEX TO TRAINERS

†denotes Permit to train under N.H. Rules only

Name	Team No.
BURKE, MR KEIRAN	067
†BURNS, MR HUGH	068
BURROWS, MR OWEN	069
BUTLER, MR JOHN	070
BUTLER, MR PADDY	071

C

Name	Team No.
CAMACHO, MISS JULIE	072
CAMPION, MR MARK	073
CANDLISH, MS JENNIE	074
CANDY, MR HENRY	075
CANN, MR GRANT	076
CANTILLON, MR DON	077
CARR, MRS RUTH	078
CARROLL, MR DECLAN	079
CARROLL, MR TONY	080
CARSON, MR TONY	081
CARTER, MR LEE	082
CASE, MR BEN	083
CHAMINGS, MR PATRICK	084
CHANNON, MR JACK	085
CHAPMAN, MR MICHAEL	086
†CHAPMAN, MR RYAN	087
CHAPPET, MR FABRICE	088
CHAPPLE-HYAM, MRS JANE	089
CHAPPLE-HYAM, MR PETER	090
CHARALAMBOUS, MR PETER AND JAMES CLUTTERBUCK,	091
CHARLTON, MR HARRY AND MR ROGER	092
CLARKE, MR BEN	093
CLEMENT, MR NICOLAS	094
CLOVER, MR TOM	095
COAKLEY, MR DENIS	096
COLE, MS DEBORAH	097
COLE, MR PAUL & OLIVER	098
COLLIER, MR TJADE	099
COLLINS, MR PAUL	100
COLTHERD, MR STUART	101
CORBETT, MRS SUSAN	102
†CORNWALL, MR JOHN	103
COULSON, MR JAKE	104
COWARD, MISS JACQUELINE	105
COWELL, MR ROBERT	106
COX, MR CLIVE	107
COYLE, MR TONY	108
CRAGGS, MR RAY	109
CRATE, MR PETER	110
CRAWLEY, MR MATTHEW	111
CRISFORD, MR SIMON AND ED	112
CROOK, MR ANDREW	113
CUNHA, MR DYLAN LIONEL	114
CURRAN, MR SEAN	115
CURTIS, MISS REBECCA	116
CUTHBERT, MISS HELEN	117

D

Name	Team No.
DACE, MR LUKE	118
DALGLEISH, MR KEITH	119
DALY, MR HENRY	120
DANDO, MR PHILLIP	121
DARTNALL, MR VICTOR	122
DAVIDSON, MR TRISTAN	123
DAVIES, MR JOHN	124
DAVIES, MISS SARAH-JAYNE	125
DAVIS, MISS JO	126
†DAVIS, MISS KATHARINE	127
†DAY, MR ANTHONY	128
DE BEST-TURNER, MR WILLIAM	129
DE GILES, MR ED	130
DEACON, MR GEOFFREY	131
DERHAM, MR HARRY WILLIAM	132
DICKIN, MISS HARRIET	133
†DIXON, MR JOHN	134
DIXON, MR SCOTT	135
DOBBIN, MRS ROSE	136
†DODGSON, MR ASHLEY	137
DODS, MR MICHAEL	138
DOW, MR SIMON	139
DOWN, MR CHRIS	140
DRINKWATER, MR SAMUEL	141
DU PLESSIS, MISS JACKIE	142
DUFFIELD, MRS ANN	143
DUNCAN, MR IAN	144
†DUNGER, MR NIGEL	145
DUNLOP, MR ED	146

Name	Team No.
†HAMILTON, MR ANDREW	224
†HAMILTON, MRS ANN	225
HAMMOND, MR MICKY	226
HANMER, MR GARY	227
HANNON, MR RICHARD	228
HARKER, MR GEOFFREY	229
†HARPER, MR RICHARD	230
HARRINGTON, MRS JESSICA	231
HARRIS, MISS CLAIRE LOUISE	232
HARRIS, MISS GRACE	233
HARRIS, MR MILTON	234
HARRIS, MR RONALD	235
HARRIS, MR SHAUN	236
HARRISON, MR GARY	237
HARRISON, MISS LISA	238
HASLAM, MR BEN	239
HAWKE, MR NIGEL	240
†HAWKER, MR MICHAEL	241
HAWKER, MR RICHARD	242
HAYNES, MISS ALICE ELIZABETH	243
†HAYNES, MR JONATHAN	244
HAYWOOD, MISS GAIL	245
†HAZARD, MRS KATE LOUISE	246
HENDERSON, MR NICKY	247
HENDERSON, MR PAUL	248
HERRINGTON, MR MICHAEL	249
HILL, MRS LAWNEY	250
HILLS, MR CHARLES	251
†HITCH, MRS CLAIRE WENDY	252
HOAD, MR MARK	253
HOBBS, MR PHILIP	254
HOBSON, MISS CLARE	255
HOBSON, MR RICHARD	256
HODGSON, MR SIMON	257
†HOGARTH, MR HENRY	258
†HOLDSWORTH, MR ANTHONY	259
HOLLAND, MR DARRYLL PAUL	260
HOLLINSHEAD, MISS SARAH	261
HOLLINSHEAD, MRS STEPH	262
HONEYBALL, MR ANTHONY	263
HONOUR, MR CHRISTOPHER	264
HORSFALL, MISS LAURA	265

Name	Team No.
HORTON, MR JAMES	266
†HOSIE, MR SYD	267
†HOWELL, MS GEORGIE	268
HUGHES, MRS DEBBIE	269
HUGHES, MR RICHARD	270
HUMPHREY, MRS SARAH	271
HUNT, MR MITCHELL ANTHONY	272
†HUNTER, MR KEVIN	273
I	
INGRAM, MR ROGER	274
IRVINE, MR ANDY	275
IVORY, MR DEAN	276
J	
JACKSON, MISS TINA	277
†JAMES, MISS HANNAH	278
JARDINE, MR IAIN	279
JARVIS, MR WILLIAM	280
JEFFERSON, MISS RUTH	281
JEFFREYS, MR D J	282
JENKINS, MR J. R.	283
JOHNSON, MR BRETT	284
JOHNSON HOUGHTON, MISS EVE	285
JOHNSTON, MR CHARLIE	286
JONES, MR ALAN	287
JONES, MR JACK	288
K	
KEADY, MR M AND, MR M MURPHY	289
KEATLEY, MR ADRIAN PAUL	290
†KEHOE, MRS FIONA	291
KEIGHLEY, MR MARTIN	292
KELLETT, MR CHRISTOPHER	293
KELLEWAY, MISS GAY	294
KENT, MR NICK	295
KENT, MR T J	296
†KERR, MR LEONARD	297
KING, MR ALAN	298
KING, MR NEIL	299
KIRBY, MR PHILIP	300
KIRK, MR SYLVESTER	301
KITTOW, MR STUART	302
KNIGHT, MR WILLIAM	303
KOBEISSI, MR HILAL	304

Name	Team No.
KUBLER, MR DANIEL AND CLAIRE	305

L

Name	Team No.
LACEY, MR TOM	306
†LANDY, MR JUSTIN	307
LAVELLE, MISS EMMA	308
LAWES, MR TOBY	309
†LECKENBY, MISS KATE	310
LEE, MISS KERRY	311
LEECH, MRS SOPHIE	312
LEESON, MISS TRACEY	313
LEWIS, MRS SHEILA	314
LIDSTER, MR CRAIG	315
LLEWELLYN, MR BERNARD	316
LLEWELLYN, MR ROBERT	317
LONG, MR JOHN	318
LONGSDON, MR CHARLIE	319
LOUGHNANE, MR DAVID	320
LOUGHNANE, MR MARK	321
†LUKE, MR ROBERT	322
LUND, MR BENJAMIN VINCENT	323
LYCETT, MR SHAUN	324

M

Name	Team No.
MACEY, MISS JESSICA	325
MACKIE, MR JOHN	326
MADGWICK, MR MICHAEL	327
MAIN, MRS HEATHER	328
MAKIN, MR PHILLIP	329
MARGARSON, MR GEORGE	330
MARTIN, MR ANDREW J.	331
MARTIN, MISS NICKY	332
MASON, MR CHRISTOPHER	333
MCBRIDE, MR PHILIP	334
MCCAIN, MR DONALD	335
MCENTEE, MR PHIL	336
MCGRATH, MR MURTY	337
MCGREGOR, MRS JEAN	338
†MCKIE, MISS JESSICA	339
†MCMAHON, MISS HANNAH MICHELLE	340
MCSHARRY, MISS FIONN	341
MEADE, MR FREDDIE AND MARTYN	342
MEADE, MR NOEL	343
MECHIE, MR NEIL	344
MEEHAN, MR BRIAN	345
MENUISIER, MR DAVID	346
MENZIES, MISS REBECCA	347
MIDGLEY, MR PAUL	348
MILLMAN, MR ROD	349
MITCHELL, MR RICHARD	350
MITFORD-SLADE, MR RICHARD	351
MOFFATT, MR JAMES	352
MOHAMMED, MR ISMAIL	353
MONGAN, MRS LAURA	354
MOORE, MR GARY	355
MOORE, MR J.S.	356
MORGAN, MISS LAURA	357
MORRIS, MR MOUSE	358
MORRIS, MR PATRICK	359
MORRISON, MR HUGHIE	360
MUIR, MR WILLIAM AND CHRIS GRASSICK,	361
MULHALL, MR CLIVE	362
MULHOLLAND, MR NEIL	363
MULLANEY, MR LAWRENCE	364
MULLINEAUX, MR MICHAEL	365
MULLINS, MR SEAMUS	366
MULLINS, MR WILLIAM P	367
MURPHY, MISS AMY	368
MURPHY, MR OLLY	369
MURPHY, MR PAT	370
MURTAGH, MR BARRY	371

N

Name	Team No.
†NEEDHAM, MRS FIONA	372
NELMES, MRS HELEN	373
NEVILLE, MR PATRICK	374
NEWCOMBE, MR TONY	375
NEWLAND, DR RICHARD	376
NEWTON-SMITH, MISS ANNA	377
NICHOLLS, MR ADRIAN	378
NICHOLLS, MR PAUL	379
NICOL, MR ADAM	380
NIVEN, MR PETER	381
NORTON, MR JOHN	382

O

Name	Team No.
O'BRIEN, MR A. P.	383

Name	Team No.
O'BRIEN, MR DONNACHA	384
O'BRIEN, MR FERGAL	385
O'KEEFFE, MR JEDD	386
O'MEARA, MR DAVID	387
†O'NEILL, MRS DANIELLE	388
O'NEILL, MR JOHN	389
O'NEILL, MR JONJO	390
O'ROURKE, MR BRIAN	391
O'SHEA, MR JOHN	392
OLDROYD, MR GEOFFREY	393
OLIVER, MR HENRY	394
OSBORNE, MR JAMIE	395
OWEN, MISS EMMA	396
OWEN, MR JAMES	397
OWENS, MR PATRICK	398
P	
PALMER, MR HUGO	399
PARR, MR JOSEPH	400
PATTINSON, MR MARK	401
PAULING, MR BEN	402
PEARCE, MR SIMON	403
PEARS, MR OLLIE	404
PERRATT, MISS LINDA	405
PERRETT, MRS AMANDA	406
PHELAN, MR PAT	407
PHILIPPART DE FOY, MR KEVIN	408
PHILLIPS, MR RICHARD	409
PIPE, MR DAVID EDWARD	410
POGSON, MR CHARLES AND ADAM	411
PONTING, MR JOE	412
PORTMAN, MR JONATHAN	413
POTTER, MR RYAN	414
POULTON, MRS CAMILLA	415
PRESCOTT BT, SIR MARK	416
PRICE, MISS KATY	417
PRICE, MR RICHARD	418
PRITCHARD, MR PETER	419
Q	
QUINLAN, MRS ELIZABETH	420
QUINN, MR DENIS	421
QUINN, MR JOHN	422

Name	Team No.
R	
RALPH, MR ALASTAIR	423
REED, MR TIM	424
REES, MR DAVID	425
†REES, MRS HELEN	426
RICHARDS, MRS LYDIA	427
RICHARDS, MR NICKY	428
RICHES, MR JOHN DAVID	429
RIMELL, MR MARK	430
ROBERTS, MR DAVE	431
ROBERTS, MR MIKE	432
ROBINSON, MISS SARAH	433
ROBSON, MR PAUL D	434
ROBSON, MISS PAULINE	435
†ROSS, MR RUSSELL	436
ROTHWELL, MR BRIAN	437
ROWE, MR RICHARD	438
ROWLEY, MRS MELANIE	439
RUSSELL, MS LUCINDA	440
RYAN, MR JOHN	441
RYAN, MR KEVIN	442
S	
SADIK, MR AYTACH	443
SAUNDERS, MR MALCOLM	444
SAYER, MRS DIANNE	445
SCARGILL, DR JON	446
SCOTT, MR GEORGE	447
SCOTT, MR JEREMY	448
SCOTT, MISS KATIE	449
SCUDAMORE, MR MICHAEL	450
SHAW, MR DEREK	451
SHAW, MRS FIONA	452
SHEPPARD, MR MATT	453
SHERWOOD, MR OLIVER	454
SIGNY, MR OLIVER	455
SIMCOCK, MR DAVID	456
SKELTON, MR DAN	457
SLY, MRS PAM	458
SMART, MR BRYAN	459
SMITH, MR JULIAN	460
SMITH, MR MARTIN	461
†SMITH, MISS PAULA	462

Name	Team No.
SMITH, MR R. MIKE	463
SMITH, MRS SUE	464
SMITH, MISS SUZY	465
SNOWDEN, MR JAMIE	466
SOWERSBY, MR MIKE	467
SPEARING, MR JOHN	468
SPENCER, MR RICHARD	469
SPENCER, MR SEB	470
SPILLER, MR HENRY	471
STACK, MR FOZZY	472
STEELE, MR DANIEL	473
STEPHEN, MRS JACKIE	474
STEPHENS, MR ROBERT	475
STIMPSON, MR JOHN	476
STONE, MR WILLIAM	477
STOREY, MR WILF	478
STOUTE, SIR MICHAEL	479
STRONGE, MRS ALI	480
STUBBS, MRS LINDA	481
SUMMERS, MR ROB	482
SYMONDS, MR TOM	483
T	
TATE, MR JAMES	484
TATE, MR TOM	485
†TAYLOR, MRS PHILLIPPA	486
TEAGUE, MR COLIN	487
TEAL, MR ROGER	488
THOMAS, MR SAM	489
†THOMASON-MURPHY, MRS JOANNE	490
THOMPSON, MR DAVID	491
THOMPSON, MR RONALD	492
†THOMPSON, MR VICTOR	493
THOMSON, MR SANDY	494
TICKLE, MR JOE	495
TINKLER, MR NIGEL	496
TIZZARD, MR JOE	497
TODD, SIR MARK	498
TODHUNTER, MR MARTIN	499
TREGONING, MR MARCUS	500
TUER, MR GRANT	501
TURNER, MR BILL	502
TUTTY, MISS GEMMA	503
TWISTON-DAVIES, MR NIGEL	504
U	
USHER, MR MARK	505
V	
VARIAN, MR ROGER	506
VAUGHAN, MR TIM	507
W	
WADHAM, MRS LUCY	509
WAGGOTT, MISS TRACY	510
WAINWRIGHT, MR JOHN	511
†WALEY-COHEN, MR ROBERT	512
WALFORD, MR MARK	513
WALFORD, MR ROBERT	514
WALKER, MR ED	515
WALL, MR TREVOR	516
WALLIS, MR CHARLIE	517
WALTON, MRS JANE	518
†WALTON, MR JIMMY	519
WARD, MR TOM	520
WATSON, MR ARCHIE	521
WATSON, MR FRED	522
WAUGH, MR SIMON	523
WEATHERER, MR MARK	524
WEBBER, MR PAUL	525
WEST, MR ADAM	526
WEST, MISS SHEENA	527
WEST, MR SIMON	528
WESTON, MR DAVID	529
WESTON, MR TOM	530
WHILLANS, MR DONALD	531
WHILLANS, MR EWAN ALISTAIR	532
WHITAKER, MR SIMON	533
WHITTINGTON, MR HARRY	534
WIGHAM, MR MICHAEL	535
WILLIAMS, MR CHRISTIAN	536
WILLIAMS, MR EVAN	537
WILLIAMS, MR IAN	538
WILLIAMS, MRS JANE	539
WILLIAMS, MR NOEL	540
WILLIAMS, MR OLLY	541
WILLIAMS, MR STUART	542
WILLIAMS, MISS VENETIA	543

Name	Team No.
WILLIAMSON, **MRS LISA**	544
WILSON, **MR ANDREW**	545
WINGROVE, **MR KEN**	546
WINKS, **MR PETER**	547
WINTLE, **MR ADRIAN**	548
WOODMAN, **MISS REBECCA**	549
WOODMAN, **MR STEVE**	550
WOODS, **MRS CYNTHIA**	551
WOODS, **MR SEAN**	552
WOOLLACOTT, **MRS KAYLEY**	553
Y	
†YORK, **MR PHILLIP**	554
YOUNG, **MRS LAURA**	555
YOUNG, **MR MAXWELL**	556
†YOUNG, **MR WILLIAM**	557

SOME TRAINERS' STRINGS ARE TAKEN FROM THE BHA RACING ADMINISTRATION WEBSITE AND INCLUDE HORSES LISTED ON THERE AS IN 'PRE-TRAINING', 'AT GRASS' OR 'RESTING'

---

1 MR N. W. ALEXANDER, Kinneston

Postal: **Kinneston, Leslie, Glenrothes, Fife, KY6 3JJ**
Contacts: **PHONE 01592 840774 MOBILE 07831 488210**
EMAIL nicholasalexander@kinneston.com WEBSITE www.kinneston.com

1 **ARNICA,** 10, b g Champs Elysees—Cordoba **Team Kinneston Club**
2 **ARTIC MANN,** 9, b g Sulamani (IRE)—Line Artic (FR) **Alexander, Baxter & Jardine-Paterson**
3 **ARTIC ROW,** 6, b g Yeats (IRE)—Line Artic (FR) **Exors of the Late Mr T. J. Hemmings**
4 **ATLANTIC DANCER (IRE),** 10, b m Waky Nao—Sarika (IRE) **Mr C. Lynn**
5 **BEAT THE RETREAT (IRE),** 4, b g Getaway (GER)—Lindy Lou **N Hodge & I Hodge**
6 **BLAZING PORT (IRE),** 8, b g Yeats (IRE)—Despute (IRE) **Turcan, Borwick, Dunning & McGarrity**
7 **BLUEBELL GLEN,** 5, b m Blue Bresil (FR)—Little Glenshee (IRE) **Sandy's Angels**
8 **BROADWAY JOE (IRE),** 9, b g Milan—Greenhall Rambler (IRE) **Clan Gathering**
9 **CANCAN (FR),** 7, b m Al Namix (FR)—Kestrel Mail (FR) **The Dregs Of Humanity**
10 **CARRIGEEN KALI (IRE),** 5, b m Soldier of Fortune (IRE)—Carrigeen Kalmia (IRE) **Clan Gathering**
11 **CHANTING HILL (IRE),** 9, b m Milan—Kitty Dillon (IRE) **Quandt & Cochrane**
12 **CHARM OFFENSIVE (FR),** 9, b m Le Triton (USA)—Go Lison (FR) **The Nags to Riches Partnership**
13 **CREAM OF THE WEST (IRE),** 7, b g Westerner—Clare Hogan (IRE) **Quandt & Cochrane**
14 5, B m Walk In The Park (IRE)—Decision Made (IRE)
15 **DONNY BOY (IRE),** 7, b g Westerner—Lady Roania (IRE) **Mrs L. Maclennan**
16 **DUBAI DAYS (IRE),** 9, b g Dubai Destination (USA)—Comeragh Girl (IRE) **Alexander, McGarrity, Morris & Parker**
17 **DUYFKEN,** 4, b g Le Havre (IRE)—Australienne (IRE) **Douglas Miller, Coltman, Dunning, Turcan**
18 **ELOI DU PUY (FR),** 5, b g Jeu St Eloi (FR)—Martalina (FR) **Coltman Cundall Matterson & Stephenson**
19 **ELVIS MAIL (FR),** 9, gr g Great Pretender (IRE)—Queenly Mail (FR) **The Ladies Who**
20 **FORTESCUE WOOD (IRE),** 8, b g Westerner—Primrose Time **Bowen & Nicol**
21 **GAILLIMH A STOR (IRE),** 7, b g Presenting—Gaillimh A Chroi (IRE) **Turcan Dunning Black & Elles**
22 **GINGER MAIL (FR),** 7, gr g Sinndar (IRE)—Queenly Mail (FR) **David & J Miller**
23 **GIPSY LEE ROSE (FR),** 9, gr m Walk In The Park (IRE)—Vanoo d'Orthe (FR) **Mrs S. M. Irwin**
24 **HALF TRACK (IRE),** 7, b g Fame And Glory—Presenting Brook (IRE) **Drew & Ailsa Russell**
25 **HIERACHY (FR),** 5, b m On Est Bien (IRE)—Kestrel Mail (FR) **Finhathan Ltd**
26 **HIGH ROLLER (FR),** 6, gr g Al Namix (FR)—Mandchou (FR) **Turcan Dunning Borwick & Wemyss**
27 **HOMBRE DE GUERRA (IRE),** 5, b g Soldier of Fortune (IRE)—Lindy Lou **Mrs I Hodge & Hugh Hodge Ltd**
28 **JIRKO (FR),** 4, bl g Balko (FR)—Belle du Luy (FR) **Mr N. W. Alexander**
29 **LACILA BLUE (FR),** 5, b m Muhaymin (USA)—Hispanola (FR) **Coltman, Douglas Miller, Matterson**
30 **LUCKY SOLDIER (IRE),** 5, br g Soldier of Fortune (IRE)—Kilbarry Flame (IRE) **Dudgeon, Loudon, Monroe & Morris**
31 **MASTER BRICKLAYER (IRE),** 5, b g Sholokhov (IRE)—Present Eile (IRE) **Exors of the Late Mr T. J. Hemmings**
32 **MELCHOIR (FR),** 6, b m Montmartre (FR)—Arvicaya **The Roasters**
33 **MRS FOX (FR),** 4, ch f No Risk At All (FR)—Bletchley (FR) **Finhathan Ltd**
34 **NED TANNER (IRE),** 7, b g Milan—Rose Tanner (IRE) **Hands and Heels**
35 **NICEANDEASY (IRE),** 10, b g Kalanisi (IRE)—High Priestess (IRE) **Katie & Brian Castle**
36 **NOT IN KANSAS,** 6, b m Gentlewave (IRE)—Spinning Away **Alexander, Baxter & Jardine-Paterson**
37 **NOT THE CHABLIS (IRE),** 9, b g Scorpion (IRE)—De Street (IRE) **Dunning, Stewart**
38 **ONE WAY OR ANOTHER (FR),** 4, b f Gris de Gris (IRE)—Ryde (FR) **Finhathan Ltd**
39 **QUEEN BELLATRIX,** 5, b m Clovis du Berlais (FR)—Swift Getaway (IRE) **The Dregs Of Humanity**
40 **SANOSUKE (IRE),** 5, b g Galileo (IRE)—Fix (NZ) **H Turcan S Dunning E Skinner & F Skinner**
41 **SCALLOWAY BAY (IRE),** 7, br g And Beyond (IRE)—Gretton **J Matterson & J Douglas Miller**
42 **SEPTEMBER DAISY,** 8, b m September Storm (GER)—Alleged To Rhyme (IRE) **& Racing**
43 **STAINSBY GIRL,** 9, ch m Shirocco (GER)—Charmaine Wood **Alexander Family**
44 **TANGIERS (FR),** 5, b m Masked Marvel—Jacira (FR) **Bowen & Nicol**
45 **THEME TUNE (IRE),** 8, b g Fame And Glory—Supreme Melody (IRE) **Katie & Brian Castle**
46 **TRAVAIL D'ORFEVRE (FR),** 7, gr g Martaline—Lady Needles (IRE) **Bowen & Nicol**
47 **ULTRA VIOLET (GER),** 5, b g Sea The Moon (GER)—United Germany (GER) **Quandt, Cochrane, Lysaght**
48 **UP HELLY AA KING,** 12, ch g And Beyond (IRE)—Gretton **Jean Matterson & J Douglas Miller**
49 **UPANDATIT (IRE),** 8, b g Winged Love (IRE)—Betty Beck (IRE) **Miss J. G. K. Matterson**
50 **WAKOOL (FR),** 7, gr g Motivator—Symba's Dream (USA) **Turcan, Borwick, Dunning & Elles**
51 **WARRIORS STORY,** 7, b g Midnight Legend—Samandara (FR) **The Warriors**

MR N.W. ALEXANDER - continued

52 **WAVELENGTH (FR),** 8, b g Gentlewave (IRE)—Mrs Percival **Mrs J. M. Walker**
53 **WHATHAVEYOU (IRE),** 4, b g Soldier of Fortune (IRE)—Tip Tap Toe (IRE) **Katie & Brian Castle**

THREE-YEAR-OLDS

54 **MONEGA PASS,** gr f Blue Bresil (FR)—Little Glenshee (IRE) **Alexander Family**

Assistant Trainer: Catriona Bissett.

Amateur Jockey: Mr Kit Alexander.

2

MISS LOUISE ALLAN, Newmarket

Postal: **2 London Road, Newmarket, Suffolk, CB8 0TW**
Contacts: **MOBILE 07703 355878**
EMAIL louiseallan1@hotmail.co.uk

1 4, B g Telescope (IRE)—A Fistful of Euros **Miss V. L. Allan**
2 **ARIS DE CRAT,** 5, b g Swiss Spirit—Titled Lady **Miss V. L. Allan**
3 **BOND SPIRIT,** 4, ch g Monsieur Bond (IRE)—Spirit Na Heireann (IRE) **The Early Birds**
4 **EASTER SUNDAE,** 4, ch g Polish Power (GER)—My Stroppy Poppy **Orchard Racing Club**
5 4, Ch c Malinas (GER)—Honour And Obey (IRE) **Mr P. W. Clifton**
6 **INDURO DE FONTAINE (FR),** 6, b g Manduro (GER)—Indian View (GER) **Clifton, Banks, Bona, Kelleway & Ashbrook**
7 **MENEJEWELS (IRE),** 6, br m Yeats (IRE)—Menepresents (IRE) **Miss C. Spurrier**
8 **REALMS OF FIRE,** 10, ch g Malinas (GER)—Realms of Gold (USA) **J. W. Whyte**

3

MR CONRAD ALLEN, Newmarket

Trainer did not wish details of their string to appear

4

MR SAM ALLWOOD, Whitchurch

Postal: **Church Farm, Church Lane, Ash Magna, Whitchurch, Shropshire, SY13 4EA**
Contacts: **PHONE 07738 413579**
EMAIL office@samallwood.co.uk

1 **ALRIGHT CHIEF (IRE),** 11, b br g Daylami (IRE)—Lee Valley Native (IRE) **Beverley & Steve Evason**
2 **AQUILA SKY (IRE),** 8, b g Arcadio (GER)—Starventure (IRE) **The Lygon Lot**
3 **BALLYNAVEEN BOY (IRE),** 4, gr g El Kabeir (USA)—Ballet Move **S. J. Allwood**
4 **BEMPTON CLIFFS (IRE),** 8, gr g Canford Cliffs (IRE)—Grand Lili **Mr M Dunlevy & Mrs H McGuinness**
5 **BITASWEETSYMPHONY (IRE),** 8, b g Mahler—Libertango (IRE) **Bostock Dunlevy McGuinness Bradshaw**
6 **CONINGBEG (IRE),** 8, b m Flemensfirth (USA)—Blue Gale (IRE) **Church Farm Racing Club**
7 **DOOBY,** 5, b m Pearl Secret—Moonshine Ridge (IRE) **Mr D. J. Todd**
8 **HAPPY NEWS,** 10, gr m Fair Mix (IRE)—Welcome News **Mrs C. L. Shaw**
9 **HOWYOUPLAYTHEGAME (FR),** 7, b g Montmartre (FR)—Maille Asie (FR) **R. B. Francis**
10 **JOBSONFIRE,** 11, b g Sulamani (IRE)—Seviot **Paul Clifton & Sarah Thomas**
11 **KALABANA (IRE),** 5, b g Kalanisi (IRE)—Life Is A Gift (IRE) **Maximum Racing & Sam Allwood**
12 **KING OF THE HILL (IRE),** 5, b g Kingston Hill—Gaye West (IRE) **Mrs B. A. Bostock**
13 **KINGS JUSTICE,** 5, b g Pether's Moon (IRE)—Queen's Law **Beverley & Friends**

MR SAM ALLWOOD - continued

14 **LEPASHE (IRE),** 6, bl g Ocovango—River Mill (IRE) **Mr G. J. Ashton**
15 **MONEY FOR JAM (IRE),** 6, b g Westerner—She's All Talk (IRE) **Ashton & Gittins**
16 **OUT ON THE TEAR (IRE),** 9, b g Arcadio (GER)—Madame Coco (IRE) **Sam Allwood Racing Club**
17 **R BERNARD,** 7, b g Norse Dancer (IRE)—Channel Treat **Mr R. J. W. Broadley**
18 **STRAIGHTUPSNICKET (IRE),** 5, b g Westerner—Gerry's Girl (IRE) **David Harris Racing Ltd.**
19 **THE GRAFTER (IRE),** 4, b g Workforce—Shokalocka Baby (IRE) **Richard & Steve Evason**
20 **TWOTWOTHREE (IRE),** 10, b g Shantou (USA)—Sibury (IRE)
21 **YAMBOCHARLIE,** 6, ch g Gentlewave (IRE)—Materiality **S. J. Allwood**

---

5 MR CHARLIE APPLEBY, Newmarket

Postal: **Godolphin Management Co Ltd, Moulton Paddocks, Newmarket, Suffolk, CB8 7PJ**
WEBSITE www.godolphin.com

1 **ADAYAR (IRE),** 5, b h Frankel—Anna Salai (USA)
2 **AL NAFIR (IRE),** 4, ch g Dubawi (IRE)—Nightime (IRE)
3 **AL SUHAIL,** 6, b g Dubawi (IRE)—Shirocco Star
4 **BANDINELLI,** 5, ch g Dubawi (IRE)—Indian Petal
5 **BAY OF HONOUR (IRE),** 4, b g Shamardal (USA)—Kazimiera
6 **BLUE TRAIL (IRE),** 4, b g Teofilo (IRE)—Pietrafiore (IRE)
7 **CREATIVE FORCE (IRE),** 5, ch g Dubawi (IRE)—Choose Me (IRE)
8 **DHAHABI (IRE),** 5, b g Frankel—Fleche d'Or
9 **ETERNAL PEARL,** 4, b f Frankel—Pearly Steph (FR)
10 **FALLING SHADOW (IRE),** 4, b g Invincible Spirit (IRE)—Belonging
11 **FIRST RULER,** 4, b g Dubawi (IRE)—Zhukova (IRE)
12 **GLOBAL STORM (IRE),** 6, ch g Night of Thunder (IRE)—Travel (USA)
13 **GOLDSPUR (IRE),** 4, b g Dubawi (IRE)—Pomology (USA)
14 **HAFIT (IRE),** 4, b g Dubawi (IRE)—Cushion
15 **HURRICANE LANE (IRE),** 5, ch h Frankel—Gale Force
16 **KEMARI,** 5, b g Dubawi (IRE)—Koora
17 **KING OF CONQUEST,** 4, b g Lope de Vega (IRE)—Moi Meme
18 **LAZULI (IRE),** 6, b g Dubawi (IRE)—Floristry
19 **LIFE OF DREAMS,** 4, b f Dubawi (IRE)—Endless Time (IRE)
20 **LIGHT OF PEACE (IRE),** 4, b f Dubawi (IRE)—Majestic Queen (IRE)
21 **MAN OF PROMISE (USA),** 6, b g Into Mischief (USA)—Involved (USA)
22 **MASTER OF THE SEAS (IRE),** 5, b g Dubawi (IRE)—Firth of Lorne (IRE)
23 **MODERN GAMES (IRE),** 4, ch c Dubawi (IRE)—Modern Ideals
24 **MODERN NEWS,** 5, ch g Shamardal (USA)—Modern Ideals
25 **NATIONS PRIDE (IRE),** 4, b c Teofilo (IRE)—Important Time (IRE)
26 **NATIVE TRAIL,** 4, b c Oasis Dream—Needleleaf
27 **NEW KINGDOM,** 4, ch g Dubawi (IRE)—Provenance
28 **NEW LONDON (IRE),** 4, b c Dubawi (IRE)—Bright Beacon
29 **NOBLE DYNASTY,** 5, b g Dubawi (IRE)—Alina (IRE)
30 **NOBLE ORDER (IRE),** 4, b g Dubawi (IRE)—Zibelina (IRE)
31 **NOBLE TRUTH (FR),** 4, b g Kingman—Speralita (FR)
32 **OTTOMAN FLEET,** 4, b g Sea The Stars (IRE)—Innevera (FR)
33 **REBEL'S ROMANCE (IRE),** 5, b br g Dubawi (IRE)—Minidress
34 **ROYAL SYMBOL (IRE),** 4, b g Sea The Stars (IRE)—Measured Tempo
35 **RULING DYNASTY,** 4, ch g Night of Thunder (IRE)—Indian Petal
36 **SECRET STATE (IRE),** 4, ch g Dubawi (IRE)—Jacqueline Quest (IRE)
37 **SENSE OF WISDOM,** 4, b g Shamardal (USA)—Tajriba (IRE)
38 **SILENT FILM,** 5, ch g New Approach (IRE)—Dibajj (FR)
39 **SILENT SPEECH,** 4, ch g Dubawi (IRE)—Epitome (IRE)
40 **SISKANY,** 5, b g Dubawi (IRE)—Halay
41 **SOVEREIGN PRINCE,** 4, b g Dubawi (IRE)—Gamilati
42 **TRANQUIL LADY (IRE),** 4, ch f Australia—Repose (USA)

MR CHARLIE APPLEBY - continued

43 **TRANQUIL NIGHT,** 4, b g Invincible Spirit (IRE)—Serene Beauty (USA)
44 **VALIANT PRINCE (IRE),** 5, b g Dubawi (IRE)—Chachamaidee (IRE)
45 **WARREN POINT,** 4, b g Dubawi (IRE)—Gaterie (USA)
46 **WILD BEAUTY,** 4, b f Frankel—Tulips (IRE)
47 **WILD CRUSADE,** 4, b g Dubawi (IRE)—Rumh (GER)
48 **WITH THE MOONLIGHT (IRE),** 4, b f Frankel—Sand Vixen
49 **YIBIR,** 5, ch g Dubawi (IRE)—Rumh (GER)

THREE-YEAR-OLDS

50 **ACT OF NATURE (IRE),** ch c Shamardal (USA)—Lava Flow (IRE)
51 **ANCIENT ROME (IRE),** b c Teofilo (IRE)—Waitress (USA)
52 **ANCIENT RULES (IRE),** ch c Lope de Vega (IRE)—Carriwitchet (IRE)
53 **BEAUTIFUL SUMMER,** b gr f Dark Angel (IRE)—Miss Lucifer (FR)
54 **BOLD ACT (IRE),** b c New Approach (IRE)—Dancing Sands (IRE)
55 B g Teofilo (IRE)—Calare (IRE)
56 **CANNON ROCK,** b g Fastnet Rock (AUS)—Fintry (IRE)
57 **CASTLE PEAK (USA),** b g Uncle Mo (USA)—Premura (USA)
58 **CASTLE WAY,** ch c Almanzor (FR)—Beach Frolic
59 **CHANGING COLOURS,** b g Dubawi (IRE)—Blossomtime
60 **CITY OF KINGS,** b c Kingman—Horseplay
61 **COURAGEOUS KNIGHT,** b g Dubawi (IRE)—Spring Mist
62 **DANCING GODDESS (IRE),** b f Dubawi (IRE)—Winter Lightning (IRE)
63 **DESERT ORDER (IRE),** b c Dubawi (IRE)—Duchess of Berry
64 **DREAM OF LOVE (IRE),** b f Shamardal (USA)—Secret Gesture
65 **ELEGANT CHARM (IRE),** b f Exceed And Excel (AUS)—Silk Words
66 **ENGLISH ROSE (IRE),** ch f Frankel—Sobetsu
67 **ETERNAL HOPE (IRE),** ch f Teofilo (IRE)—Voice of Truth (IRE)
68 **FAIRY CROSS (IRE),** b f Dubawi (IRE)—Devonshire (IRE)
69 **FIRST SIGHT,** ch c Dubawi (IRE)—Phiz (GER)
70 **FLYING HONOURS,** b c Sea The Stars (IRE)—Powder Snow (USA)
71 **GLORY LILY,** b f Shamardal (USA)—Autumn Lily (USA)
72 **GOLDEN SMILE,** b f Sea The Stars (IRE)—Sahraah (USA)
73 **HIDDEN STORY,** b g Dubawi (IRE)—Bound (IRE)
74 **HIGH HONOUR,** b g Frankel—As Good As Gold (IRE)
75 **HIGHBANK (IRE),** b g Kingman—Bristol Bay (IRE)
76 **IMPERIAL EMPEROR (IRE),** b c Dubawi (IRE)—Zhukova (IRE)
77 **ISLE OF JURA,** b g New Approach (IRE)—Falls of Lora (IRE)
78 **JOYFUL ACT,** b f Frankel—Blue Bunting (USA)
79 B f New Approach (IRE)—Khawlah (IRE)
80 **LAST TRADITION,** b g Dubawi (IRE)—Speirbhean (IRE)
81 **LENORMAND,** b c Dubawi (IRE)—Baisse
82 **LOCAL DYNASTY (IRE),** b c Dubawi (IRE)—Really Special
83 **MAJESTIC PRIDE,** b c Shamardal (USA)—Gonbarda (GER)
84 **MARRAKUSHI,** ch g Dubawi (IRE)—Extra Mile
85 **MEASURED TIME,** b c Frankel—Minidress
86 **MILITARY ORDER (IRE),** b c Frankel—Anna Salai (USA)
87 **MISCHIEF MAGIC (IRE),** b c Exceed And Excel (AUS)—Veil of Silence (IRE)
88 **MODERN DANCER,** b c Kingman—Epitome (IRE)
89 **MOUNTAIN SONG (IRE),** b f Sea The Stars (IRE)—Yodelling (USA)
90 **MYSTERIOUS NIGHT (IRE),** b c Dark Angel (IRE)—Mistrusting (IRE)
91 **NAHORI,** b f Night of Thunder (IRE)—Avongrove
92 **NATURE WATCH (USA),** ch c Curlin (USA)—Saucy Dame (USA)
93 **NAVAL POWER,** b c Teofilo (IRE)—Emirates Rewards
94 **NOBLE STYLE,** b c Kingman—Eartha Kitt
95 **ONE NATION,** ch g Dubawi (IRE)—Lacey's Lane
96 **PHERENIKOS (IRE),** b g Shamardal (USA)—First Victory (IRE)
97 **PRINCEVILLE,** b g Exceed And Excel (AUS)—Lacily (USA)
98 **QUEEN OF FAIRIES,** ch f Cracksman—Bean Feasa
99 **RAINBOW SKY,** ch f Sea The Stars (IRE)—Best Terms

MR CHARLIE APPLEBY - continued

100 RAINFALL OF COLOUR (IRE), b f Frankel—Mujarah (IRE)
101 REFLECTIVE STAR, b f Dubawi (IRE)—Switching (USA)
102 REGAL HONOUR (IRE), b c Dubawi (IRE)—Serena's Storm (IRE)
103 SACRED FLOWER, ch f Dubawi (IRE)—Indian Petal
104 SAHARA MIST, b f Deep Impact (JPN)—Hibaayeb
105 SAPPHIRE SEAS, b f Frankel—Pure Diamond
106 SHINING JEWEL, b f Siyouni (FR)—Gaterie (USA)
107 SILVER KNOTT, b c Lope de Vega (IRE)—God Given
108 SILVER LADY, b f Sea The Stars (IRE)—Lumiere
109 SITHCHEAN (IRE), b f Dark Angel (IRE)—Firth of Lorne (IRE)
110 SPRING DAWN (IRE), b f Kodiac—Policoro (IRE)
111 SPRING PROMISE (IRE), ch f Lope de Vega (IRE)—Come Alive
112 STAR GUEST, b f Dubawi (IRE)—Usherette (IRE)
113 STRIKING STAR, ch g Dubawi (IRE)—Lucida (IRE)
114 SUNSET POINT, b f Dubawi (IRE)—Hidden Gold (IRE)
115 TABARETTA (FR), ch g Dubawi (IRE)—Davantage (FR)
116 TAGABAWA, ch c New Approach (IRE)—Tasaday (USA)
117 THEATRE HONOURS, b c Kingman—Sperry (IRE)
118 THROUGH THE AGES, b g Golden Horn—Rumh (GER)
119 TRANQUIL ROSE (FR), b f Kingman—Needleleaf
120 TREASURE COVE, b g New Approach (IRE)—Serene Beauty (USA)
121 VEIL OF SHADOWS, b f Frankel—Violante (USA)
122 VIA CORONE (IRE), b f Invincible Spirit (IRE)—Pietrafiore (IRE)
123 VICTORY DANCE (IRE), br c Dubawi (IRE)—Dane Street (USA)
124 WHISPERING DREAM (IRE), b f Invincible Spirit (IRE)—Grecian Light (IRE)
125 WHISPERING WORDS (IRE), b f Dubawi (IRE)—Hadith (IRE)
126 WILD NATURE (IRE), ch c Galileo (IRE)—Dancing Rain (IRE)

TWO-YEAR-OLDS

127 Ch c 31/01 No Nay Never (USA)—Adventure Seeker (FR) (Bering) (500000)
128 B c 15/03 Dubawi (IRE)—Aim of Artemis (IRE) (Leroidesanimaux (BRZ))
129 B c 21/03 Dubawi (IRE)—Alina (IRE) (Galileo (IRE)) (750000)
130 B f 25/02 Bated Breath—Always A Dream (Oasis Dream) (600000)
131 B f 22/01 Dubawi (IRE)—Anamba (Shamardal (USA))
132 Ch f 04/04 New Approach (IRE)—Anna Sophia (IRE) (Sea The Stars (IRE))
133 B f 21/02 Shamardal (USA)—Antiquities (Kaldounevees (FR))
134 B f 16/03 Too Darn Hot—Astonishing (IRE) (Galileo (IRE))
135 Ch c 21/03 Dubawi (IRE)—Beyond Reason (IRE) (Australia)
136 B f 30/03 Dubawi (IRE)—Birch Grove (IRE) (Galileo (IRE)) (460184)
137 B c 12/03 Frankel—Bold Lass (IRE) (Sea The Stars (IRE)) (2000000)
138 B c 05/03 Too Darn Hot—Bright Beacon (Manduro (GER))
139 B c 27/01 Dubawi (IRE)—Broderie Anglaise (IRE) (Galileo (IRE)) (525000)
140 B c 16/02 Frankel—Cash In The Hand (USA) (Exchange Rate (USA)) (400000)
141 B f 08/02 Lope de Vega (IRE)—Chablis (IRE) (Galileo (IRE)) (425000)
142 B f 23/03 Exceed And Excel (AUS)—Chapelli (Poet's Voice)
143 B f 10/02 Shamardal (USA)—Come Alive (Dansili)
144 B c 15/03 Dubawi (IRE)—Dabyah (IRE) (Sepoy (AUS)) (650000)
145 B f 01/03 Shamardal (USA)—Dancing Rain (IRE) (Danehill Dancer (IRE))
146 B f 07/03 Blue Point (IRE)—Dancing Sands (IRE) (Dubawi (IRE))
147 B c 31/03 Blue Point (IRE)—Davantage (FR) (Galileo (IRE)) (160064)
148 B c 11/04 Too Darn Hot—Dazzling (IRE) (Galileo (IRE))
149 B c 02/02 Frankel—Desirous (Kingman) (400000)
150 B c 13/04 No Nay Never (USA)—Detailed (IRE) (Motivator) (550000)
151 B c 10/04 Blue Point (IRE)—Devonshire (IRE) (Fast Company (IRE))
152 Ch c 24/02 Dubawi (IRE)—Disavow (Shamardal (USA))
153 Ch f 21/03 Dubawi (IRE)—Divine Image (USA) (Scat Daddy (USA))
154 B c 05/03 Dubawi (IRE)—Dubai Beauty (IRE) (Frankel)
155 B c 12/02 Dubawi (IRE)—Dubai Rose (Dubai Destination (USA)) (480192)
156 Ch c 04/03 Teofilo (IRE)—Empress Consort (Dubawi (IRE)) (260000)

MR CHARLIE APPLEBY - continued

157 Ch f 24/03 New Approach (IRE)—Endless Charm (Dubawi (IRE))
158 B c 09/02 Too Darn Hot—Endless Time (IRE) (Sea The Stars (IRE))
159 B f 26/02 Shamardal (USA)—Espadrille (Dubawi (IRE))
160 B c 09/03 Frankel—Evita Peron (Pivotal) (750000)
161 B f 12/02 Too Darn Hot—Falls of Lora (IRE) (Street Cry (IRE))
162 B f 21/02 Kingman—Fintry (IRE) (Shamardal (USA))
163 B f 01/04 Kingman—Flowrider (USA) (Street Cry (IRE))
164 B f 20/02 Oasis Dream—Fond Words (IRE) (Shamardal (USA))
165 Ch f 10/03 Dubawi (IRE)—Gaterie (USA) (Dubai Destination (USA))
166 B c 19/04 Dubawi (IRE)—God Given (Nathaniel (IRE)) (1500000)
167 B c 28/02 Lope de Vega (IRE)—Golden Lilas (IRE) (Galileo (IRE)) (460184)
168 B c 12/04 Dubawi (IRE)—Golden Valentine (FR) (Dalakhani (IRE)) (1600640)
169 Ch c 27/03 Masar (IRE)—Great Hope (IRE) (Halling (USA)) (350000)
170 B f 04/02 Camelot—Grecian Light (IRE) (Shamardal (USA))
171 Ch f 11/04 Sea The Stars (IRE)—Hand Puppet (IRE) (Manduro (GER))
172 B c 31/03 Teofilo (IRE)—Heartily (IRE) (Dubawi (IRE))
173 B f 18/02 Sea The Stars (IRE)—Hibaayeb (Singspiel (IRE))
174 Br c 14/04 Dubawi (IRE)—Horseplay (Cape Cross (IRE)) (800000)
175 B c 03/03 Dubawi (IRE)—How (IRE) (Galileo (IRE)) (1600000)
176 Br c 18/04 Dubawi (IRE)—I'm Wonderful (USA) (Giant's Causeway (USA)) (625000)
177 B f 12/02 Dark Angel (IRE)—Important Time (IRE) (Oasis Dream)
178 B f 12/02 Dubawi (IRE)—Inner Secret (USA) (Singspiel (IRE))
179 B f 20/02 Dubawi (IRE)—Jazzi Top (Danehill Dancer (IRE)) (1300000)
180 B f 05/02 Sea The Stars (IRE)—Jollify (IRE) (Manduro (GER))
181 B f 05/02 Masar (IRE)—Kazziana (Shamardal (USA))
182 B f 14/03 Teofilo (IRE)—Kenspeckle (Dubawi (IRE))
183 B c 01/03 Too Darn Hot—Khawlah (IRE) (Cape Cross (IRE))
184 B c 15/03 Sea The Stars (IRE)—Kissable (IRE) (Danehill Dancer (IRE)) (150000)
185 B c 26/01 Siyouni (FR)—Klassique (Galileo (IRE)) (525000)
186 B f 08/02 Iffraaj—La Pelosa (IRE) (Dandy Man (IRE))
187 B c 09/03 Shamardal (USA)—La Rosetta (New Approach (IRE))
188 B c 30/01 Shamardal (USA)—Lady Frankel (Frankel) (1280512)
189 Ch f 30/04 Lope de Vega (IRE)—Lava Flow (IRE) (Dalakhani (IRE))
190 Ch c 20/01 Sea The Stars (IRE)—Lillian Russell (IRE) (Dubawi (IRE))
191 B f 09/03 Dubawi (IRE)—Lumiere (Shamardal (USA))
192 B c 18/02 Teofilo (IRE)—Lunar Maria (Dubawi (IRE))
193 B c 03/02 Dubawi (IRE)—Madonna Dell'orto (Montjeu (IRE))
194 Ch c 17/02 Australia—Magic Image (Dubawi (IRE))
195 B f 25/02 Frankel—Magical Touch (Dubawi (IRE))
196 B f 12/04 Frankel—Mairwen (Dubawi (IRE))
197 B f 28/02 Dubawi (IRE)—Maria Danilova (IRE) (Galileo (IRE))
198 B f 25/02 Dubawi (IRE)—Mary Somerville (Galileo (IRE))
199 B f 11/03 Shamardal (USA)—Measured Tempo (Sadler's Wells (USA))
200 B c 10/05 No Nay Never (USA)—Miss Nouriya (Galileo (IRE)) (200000)
201 B f 05/03 Kodiac—Mistrusting (IRE) (Shamardal (USA))
202 Ro f 11/04 Mastercraftsman (IRE)—Modern Ideals (New Approach (IRE))
203 B c 14/02 New Approach (IRE)—Morgan Le Faye (Shamardal (USA))
204 B f 09/04 Too Darn Hot—Najoum (USA) (Giant's Causeway (USA))
205 B c 30/04 Dubawi (IRE)—Opera Comique (FR) (Singspiel (IRE))
206 B c 02/04 Teofilo (IRE)—Patroness (Dubawi (IRE))
207 B c 08/05 Dubawi (IRE)—Peace In Motion (USA) (Hat Trick (JPN)) (550000)
208 Ch c 07/03 Dubawi (IRE)—Pepita (IRE) (Sir Prancealot (IRE)) (400000)
209 B c 02/03 Dubawi (IRE)—Persuasive (IRE) (Dark Angel (IRE)) (1000000)
210 B f 11/02 Dubawi (IRE)—Petticoat (Cape Cross (IRE))
211 Ch f 03/03 Night of Thunder (IRE)—Placidia (IRE) (Sea The Stars (IRE))
212 Gr c 18/01 Dark Angel (IRE)—Poetic Charm (Dubawi (IRE))
213 Ch f 10/02 Siyouni (FR)—Powder Snow (USA) (Dubawi (IRE))
214 B c 22/02 Dubawi (IRE)—Promising Run (USA) (Hard Spun (USA))
215 B c 06/03 Kingman—Pure Diamond (Street Cry (IRE))
216 Ch f 15/05 Sea The Stars (IRE)—Really Special (Shamardal (USA))

MR CHARLIE APPLEBY - continued

217 Ch f 20/02 Dubawi (IRE)—Richmond Avenue (IRE) (Invincible Spirit (IRE))
218 Ch f 11/02 Shamardal (USA)—Right Direction (IRE) (Cape Cross (IRE))
219 B c 02/05 Dubawi (IRE)—Ring The Bell (IRE) (Galileo (IRE)) (1500000)
220 B f 06/02 Dubawi (IRE)—River Melody (IRE) (Dansili)
221 B f 30/03 Frankel—Rosa Imperial (IRE) (Pivotal)
222 B c 03/02 Sea The Stars (IRE)—Sahrawi (GER) (Pivotal) (550000)
223 B f 12/03 Blue Point (IRE)—Sand Vixen (Dubawi (IRE))
224 B c 23/04 Dubawi (IRE)—Secret Gesture (Galileo (IRE))
225 B f 27/01 Kodiac—Shobobb (Shamardal (USA)) (475000)
226 B c 05/05 Dubawi (IRE)—Show Day (IRE) (Shamardal (USA))
227 B c 26/03 Blue Point (IRE)—Siamsaiocht (IRE) (Teofilo (IRE)) (200000)
228 B c 14/03 Frankel—So Mi Dar (Dubawi (IRE)) (2800000)
229 B c 20/02 Frankel—Soliloquy (Dubawi (IRE))
230 Br c 25/03 Sea The Stars (IRE)—Soltada (IRE) (Dawn Approach (IRE)) (270000)
231 B c 23/02 Too Darn Hot—Sperry (IRE) (Shamardal (USA))
232 B c 04/02 Dubawi (IRE)—Spinning Cloud (USA) (Street Cry (IRE))
233 B c 27/03 Sea The Stars (IRE)—Sunny Again (Shirocco (GER)) (550000)
234 Ch f 23/03 Night of Thunder (IRE)—Sweety Dream (FR) (Dream Ahead (USA)) (550000)
235 Ch c 10/03 Dubawi (IRE)—Swift Rose (IRE) (Invincible Spirit (IRE))
236 Ch c 01/03 Dubawi (IRE)—Tajriba (IRE) (Teofilo (IRE))
237 B f 19/03 Dubawi (IRE)—Tearless (Street Cry (IRE))
238 B f 31/03 Dark Angel (IRE)—Threading (IRE) (Exceed And Excel (AUS))
239 B c 28/02 Frankel—Tulips (IRE) (Pivotal)
240 B c 20/04 Frankel—Umniyah (IRE) (Shamardal (USA)) (150000)
241 B c 12/02 Dubawi (IRE)—Urban Fox (Foxwedge (AUS)) (1100000)
242 B c 18/02 Dubawi (IRE)—Valentine's Day (IRE) (Galileo (IRE))
243 B f 03/04 Exceed And Excel (AUS)—Veil of Silence (IRE) (Elusive Quality (USA))
244 B c 02/03 Dubawi (IRE)—Via Condotti (IRE) (Galileo (IRE)) (800000)
245 B c 27/01 Too Darn Hot—Volume (Mount Nelson)
246 B c 18/03 Sea The Stars (IRE)—Warless (IRE) (War Command (USA)) (240096)
247 B f 19/02 Night of Thunder (IRE)—Warning Fire (Shamardal (USA))
248 Ch f 14/03 Galileo (IRE)—Wild Illusion (Dubawi (IRE))
249 B c 12/02 Exceed And Excel (AUS)—Windsor County (USA) (Elusive Quality (USA))
250 B f 04/04 Galileo (IRE)—Winter Lightning (IRE) (Shamardal (USA))
251 B c 03/03 Frankel—Without You Babe (USA) (Lemon Drop Kid (USA)) (1300000)
252 B c 10/02 Shamardal (USA)—Zhukova (IRE) (Fastnet Rock (AUS))
253 B c 04/05 Blue Point (IRE)—Zibelina (IRE) (Dansili)
254 Ch f 22/04 Frankel—Zindaya (USA) (More Than Ready (USA)) (450000)

Assistant Trainer: Alex Merriam, Marie Murphy. **Racing Secretary:** Hannah Pollard.

Flat Jockey: William Buick, James Doyle.

---

6 MR MICHAEL APPLEBY, Oakham

Postal: **The Homestead, Langham, Oakham, Leicestershire, LE15 7EJ**
Contacts: **PHONE 01572 722772 MOBILE 07884 366421**
EMAIL mickappleby@icloud.com WEBSITE www.mickappleby.com

1 **ALEXANDER JAMES (IRE),** 7, b g Camelot—Plying (USA) **Magna Carter Bloodstock**
2 **ALL ABOARD (IRE),** 4, b g Anjaal—Dialing Tone (USA) **The Horse Watchers 1**
3 **ALSAAQY (IRE),** 4, gr c Sea The Stars (IRE)—Natagora (FR) **The Double Deckers**
4 **ANNAF (IRE),** 4, br c Muhaarar—Shimah (USA) **Fosnic Racing**
5 **APHELIOS,** 4, b g Kodiac—Homily **The Horse Watchers**
6 **AR EZRA,** 4, b c Ardad (IRE)—Lulu The Zulu (IRE) **The Ab Kettlebys**
7 **ARAB CINDER (IRE),** 4, b f Zoffany (IRE)—Athreyaa **Mr R. Oliver**
8 **AYR HARBOUR,** 6, b g Harbour Watch (IRE)—Sorella Bella (IRE) **Magna Carter Bloodstock**

MR MICHAEL APPLEBY - continued

9 **BALDOMERO (IRE),** 5, b g Shalaa (IRE)—Besotted (IRE) **The Horse Watchers 6**
10 **BANCNUANAHEIREANN (IRE),** 16, b g Chevalier (IRE)—Alamanta (IRE)
11 **BIG NARSTIE (FR),** 5, b br g Cable Bay (IRE)—Granadilla **Mr Z. Ison**
12 **BLIND BEGGAR (IRE),** 5, b g Equiano (FR)—Beylerbey (USA) **B & M Pallets Ltd**
13 **BOARHUNT,** 4, b g Equiano (FR)—Guishan **B. D. Cantle**
14 **BOND BOY,** 4, b g Equiano (FR)—Poppy Bond **Mr M. E. White**
15 **BORA BORA,** 5, b g Kingman—Beach Bunny (IRE) **The Southwell Snipers**
16 **BURABACK (IRE),** 4, b g Buratino (IRE)—Gailes First (IRE) **Andrew & Raymond Wright**
17 **CAZEVA PRINCESS,** 6, b m Equiano (FR)—Enford Princess **Mr C. A. Blyth**
18 **CHANNEL PACKET,** 9, b h Champs Elysees—Etarre (IRE) **Howdale Bloodstock**
19 **CHORUS SONG,** 4, b f Havana Gold (IRE)—Angelic Note (IRE) **Magna Carter Bloodstock**
20 **COME ON GIRL,** 6, gr m Outstrip—Floating **Mrs D. Hopkins**
21 **CRIMSON KING (IRE),** 7, b g Kingman—Toi Et Moi (IRE) **T. R. Pryke**
22 **DE VEGA'S WARRIOR (IRE),** 4, b g Lope de Vega (IRE)—Oh Sedulous (IRE) **J & A Young (Leicester) Ltd**
23 **DEW YOU BELIEVE (IRE),** 5, b g Make Believe—Dew (IRE) **Mr D. B. Gillett**
24 **DREAMS DELIVERED (IRE),** 5, b g Morpheus—Quick Sketch (IRE) **Dr M. Makratzakis**
25 **EAGLE EYED FREDDIE,** 5, b g Gleneagles (IRE)—Spice Trail **Mr E. Foster**
26 **EAGLE PATH (IRE),** 4, gr f Gleneagles (IRE)—Shirin of Persia (IRE) **Future Champions Racing Syndicate**
27 **EL ROYALE,** 4, gr g Hellvelyn—Sofia Royale **Mr Wayne Brackstone, Mr Steve Whitear**
28 **EPONINA (IRE),** 9, b m Zoffany (IRE)—Dame Rochelle (IRE) **Mrs E. Cash**
29 **EXPERT OPINION,** 5, b g Worthadd (IRE)—Calypso Choir **Aj Racing**
30 **FANTASY NAVIGATOR,** 4, b g Heeraat (IRE)—Mocca (IRE) **The Fantasy Fellowship**
31 **FAST STYLE (IRE),** 4, b g Camacho—That's My Style **Honestly Racing**
32 **FINERY,** 6, b m Al Kazeem—Elysian **Mr M. O. Ward**
33 **GLASSTREES,** 4, gr f Heeraat (IRE)—Goadby **Cleartherm Glass Sealed Units Ltd**
34 **GOLDEN SANDS (IRE),** 4, ch g Footstepsinthesand—Varna **HJW Partnership**
35 **HA'AN,** 5, b h Black Sam Bellamy (IRE)—Luna de Ventura **Howdale Bloodstock**
36 **HEZAHUNK (IRE),** 4, b g Fast Company (IRE)—Temecula (IRE) **ValueRacingClub.co.uk**
37 **IN THE BREEZE (IRE),** 5, b g Harzand (IRE)—Its In The Air (IRE) **J & A Young (Leicester) Ltd**
38 **INTERVENTION,** 6, b g Swiss Spirit—Lady Lube Rye (IRE) **The Horse Watchers 8**
39 **IVY AVENUE (IRE),** 6, ch m Ivawood (IRE)—Dance Avenue (IRE) **Diamond Racing Ltd**
40 **JENNYS JACK DANIEL,** 4, b c Jack Hobbs—Vodka Island (IRE) **Mr D. G. Skelton**
41 **JIMMYJEROO,** 5, b g Telescope (IRE)—Danarama **J & A Young (Leicester) Ltd**
42 **JUAN LES PINS,** 6, b g Invincible Spirit (IRE)—Miss Cap Ferrat **Mr M. J. Taylor**
43 **JUPITER EXPRESS (IRE),** 4, b g Kodiac—Spinola (FR) **The Horse Watchers**
44 **KARDINYA (IRE),** 4, b g Mehmas (IRE)—Sapphire Diva (IRE) **B & M Pallets Ltd**
45 **KATTANI (IRE),** 7, b g Tamayuz—Katiola (IRE) **Kaizen Racing**
46 **KING OF BAVARIA (IRE),** 4, bl g No Nay Never (USA)—Enharmonic (USA) **Craig & Laura Buckingham**
47 **KING OF STARS (IRE),** 6, gr g Starspangledbanner (AUS)—Glowing Star (IRE) **Mr William Esdaile**
48 **KOTYONOK,** 4, b g Bobby's Kitten (USA)—Nezhenka **ValueRacingClub.co.uk**
49 **LARADO (FR),** 5, b g Shalaa (IRE)—Suertez (USA) **Mrs E. Cash**
50 **LION'S DREAM (FR),** 4, b g Dabirsim (FR)—Full Rose **The Horse Watchers**
51 **MAWKEB (USA),** 5, b g Kitten's Joy (USA)—Illegal Search (USA) **Mrs D. Hopkins**
52 **MAXZENO,** 4, b g Bated Breath—Demora **Pete & Gillian Wragg & Angie Balderstone**
53 **MEGA MARVEL,** 4, b g Equiano (FR)—Megaleka **North Cheshire Trading & Storage Ltd**
54 **MEHMO (IRE),** 5, ch g Mehmas (IRE)—Baltic Belle (IRE) **Mr T. O. Bownes**
55 **MINESBIGGERTHANURS,** 4, b g Brazen Beau (AUS)—Laguna Belle **B & M Pallets Ltd**
56 **MOBASHR (USA),** 5, b g Mshawish (USA)—Refreshing **The Horse Watchers 4**
57 **MOHAREB,** 7, b g Delegator—Irrational **Mr I. Lawrence**
58 **MOP'S A LEGEND,** 6, b g Schiaparelli (GER)—Midnight Fun **Mick Appleby Racing**
59 **MOPS GEM,** 5, b m Equiano (FR)—Mops Angel **Mick Appleby Racing**
60 **MOSTALLIM,** 6, b g Bated Breath—Lifting Me Higher (IRE) **The Hobbits**
61 **MOTAWAAFEQ (FR),** 7, b g Wootton Bassett—Crossed Fingers (IRE) **Middleham Park Racing XX**
62 **NASIM,** 4, ch g Galileo Gold—Ashwaq **The Horse Watchers 2**
63 **PLASTIC PADDY,** 5, b g Buratino (IRE)—Bereka **Mr M. J. Goggin**
64 **POLITICS (IRE),** 5, b g Muhaarar—Wrong Answer **The Horse Watchers 1**
65 **POWER OF STATES (IRE),** 7, b g Lope de Vega (IRE)—Allegation (FR) **Middleham Park Racing CXXI**
66 **QUEEN OF BURGUNDY,** 7, b m Lethal Force (IRE)—Empress Adelaide **Mrs D. Hopkins**
67 **RAASEL,** 6, ch g Showcasing—Dubai Affair **The Horse Watchers**
68 **RICHARD R H B (IRE),** 6, b g Fulbright—Royal Interlude (IRE) **Peter R Ball & Gentech Products Ltd**

MR MICHAEL APPLEBY - continued

69 **SAMPERS SEVEN (IRE),** 6, b m Anjaal—Sampers (IRE) **ValueRacingClub.co.uk**
70 **SECRET ARMY,** 4, ch g Territories (IRE)—Secret Insider (USA) **M. Appleby**
71 **SHADOWFAX,** 4, gr g Galileo (IRE)—Golden Valentine (FR) **The Fellowship Of The Ring**
72 **SICARIO (IRE),** 8, b g Thewayyouare (USA)—Blessed Beauty (IRE) **Mr J. J. Gerrard**
73 **SIR GREGORY (FR),** 5, ch g Equiano (FR)—Tegara **B & M Pallets Ltd**
74 **SKEETER PARK (IRE),** 6, b g Yeats (IRE)—Biondo (IRE) **M. Appleby**
75 **SMILING SUNFLOWER (IRE),** 4, b f Fulbright—Hankering (IRE) **Mr M. J. Goggin**
76 **SNOW BERRY (IRE),** 5, b m Dragon Pulse (IRE)—Primal Snow (USA) **J & A Young (Leicester) Ltd**
77 **SPRING ROMANCE (IRE),** 8, gr g Zebedee—Love And Devotion **M. Appleby**
78 **STARSONG (IRE),** 4, b f Starspangledbanner (AUS)—Meetyouatthemoon (IRE) **Mick Appleby Racing**
79 **STONE OF DESTINY,** 8, b g Acclamation—Irishstone (IRE) **Mr M. J. Taylor**
80 **THRAVE,** 8, b g Sir Percy—Feis Ceoil (IRE) **MIDEST 1**
81 **TWISTALINE,** 4, b f Showcasing—Tongue Twista **ValueRacingClub.co.uk**
82 **UNITED FRONT (USA),** 6, b g War Front (USA)—Shell House (IRE) **Mr N. Brereton**
83 **WAR IN HEAVEN (IRE),** 4, b g Exceed And Excel (AUS)—Burma Sun (IRE) **Mr M. J. Taylor**
84 **WIN WIN POWER (IRE),** 6, b g Exceed And Excel (AUS)—Spesialta **Honestly Racing**
85 **WOODERS DREAM,** 4, ch f Equiano (FR)—Psychic's Dream **M. Appleby**
86 **ZEALOT,** 5, b g Pivotal—Devotion (IRE) **The Horse Watchers 1**
87 **ZUUL,** 5, ch h Black Sam Bellamy (IRE)—Sharp Dresser (USA) **Howdale Bloodstock**

THREE-YEAR-OLDS

88 **ARTISTIC DREAMER,** b f Caravaggio (USA)—So You Dream (IRE) **Magna Carter Bloodstock**
89 **BARLOW BARLOW,** b f Havana Gold (IRE)—Porcini **Honestly Racing**
90 **FAVORITE BOY,** b g Mukhadram—Favorite Girl (GER) **T. R. Pryke**
91 **FURNICOE (IRE),** b f Dandy Man (IRE)—Right Rave (IRE) **SBK Racing Ltd**
92 **MICHAELA'S BOY (IRE),** ch c Ribchester (IRE)—Joyce Compton (IRE) **Newtownstewart Construction UK Ltd**
93 **ROSSMORE NATION (IRE),** b c Sioux Nation (USA)—Alutiq (IRE) **M. Appleby**
94 **SECRETARY,** b f Zoustar (AUS)—Zakhrafa (IRE) **Mrs D. Curran**
95 **SHOT OF LOVE,** b c Invincible Spirit (IRE)—Dufay (IRE) **B & M Pallets Ltd**
96 **TWILIGHT JAZZ,** b f Twilight Son—Jasmine Royale **Mr L. J. M. J. Vaessen**
97 **TYKE (IRE),** b g Bobby's Kitten (USA)—Lady Clair (IRE) **White Rose Racing**

TWO-YEAR-OLDS

98 **GO WILD,** b f 03/04 Zoffany (IRE)—Hells Babe (Hellvelyn) (3200) **M. Appleby**
99 B c 09/02 Time Test—Paris Winds (IRE) (Galileo (IRE)) (10000) **Magna Carter Bloodstock**

Assistant Trainer: Jonathan Clayton.

Flat Jockey: Alistair Rawlinson, Jason Watson. **Apprentice Jockey:** Theodore Ladd, Frederick Larson.

---

7 MR BILLY APRAHAMIAN, Towcester

Postal: **The Gallops, Banbury Lane, Adstone, Northamptonshire, NN12 8DT**
Contacts: **PHONE 07739 819804**
EMAIL billyaprahamian@hotmail.com

1 **CONCEAL (IRE),** 8, ch g Stowaway—Babyshan (IRE) **The JGF Racing Club**
2 **DAZZLING DOVE,** 8, b m Winged Love (IRE)—Dans Desert **Old Bloxhamist Racing**
3 **GOOD LORD (GER),** 4, b g Lord of England (GER)—Good Harmony **Pury Racing**
4 **GRAIN TRADE,** 4, b g Telescope (IRE)—Halo Flora **Mr B. Aprahamian**
5 **HEROSS DU SEUIL (FR),** 6, b g Rail Link—Tulipe du Seuil (FR) **Kevin Boothby & John Lynk**
6 **KALKAS (FR),** 7, b g Kapgarde (FR)—Fortunateencounter (FR) **Old Bloxhamist Racing**
7 **KING OTIS (IRE),** 7, b g Ocovango—Fame Forever (IRE) **Mr B. Aprahamian**
8 **MAYHEBLUCKY (IRE),** 6, b g Libertarian—Golden Ard (IRE) **The Fairfax and Favor Racing Club**
9 **MRS KINSELLA (IRE),** 7, b m Beat Hollow—Islandbane (IRE) **Kevin Boothby & John Lynk**
10 **MUTUAL RESPECT (IRE),** 7, b g Valirann (FR)—By Heavens (IRE) **Hip Flask Racing (MR)**

MR BILLY APRAHAMIAN - continued

11 **SURREY FORTUNE (IRE),** 4, b g Soldier of Fortune (IRE)—Brog Beanri (IRE) **Surrey Racing (SFo)**
12 **TEETON SPIRIT,** 4, b f Telescope (IRE)—Teeton Priceless **Ms K. M. Payne**
13 **TEETON SUNRISE,** 7, ch m Black Sam Bellamy (IRE)—Sunley Shines **Ms K. M. Payne**

8

MR RICHARD ARMSON, Melbourne

Postal: **Scotlands Farm, Burney Lane, Staunton-Harold, Melbourne, Derbyshire, DE73 8BH**

1 **ALBURN,** 13, b g Alflora (IRE)—Burn Brook **R. J. Armson**
2 **KILCARAGH BOY (IRE),** 14, b g King's Theatre (IRE)—Histologie (FR) **R. J. Armson**
3 **MACKIE DEE (IRE),** 11, b g Westerner—Whatdoyouthinkmac (IRE) **R. J. Armson**
4 **THE FULL PASTY (IRE),** 6, b g Sans Frontieres (IRE)—Shannon Pearl (IRE) **R. J. Armson**

9

MR PETER ATKINSON, Northallerton

Postal: **Yafforth Hill Farm, Yafforth, Northallerton, North Yorkshire, DL7 0LT**
Contacts: **PHONE 01609 772598 MOBILE 07751 131215**

1 **BLACK MINSTER,** 8, bl g Trans Island—Mini Minster **Mr P. G. Atkinson**
2 **CENTIMENTALJOURNEY,** 6, b m Telescope (IRE)—Elusive Swallow **Mrs L. Atkinson**
3 **FINGAL'S HILL (IRE),** 7, b g Shirocco (GER)—Fingal's Sister (IRE) **Mr P. G. Atkinson**
4 **PRIDE PARK (IRE),** 7, b g Yeats (IRE)—Ballyallia Pride (IRE) **Mr P. G. Atkinson**
5 **RIBEYE,** 8, b g Lucarno (USA)—Elusive Swallow **Mrs L. Atkinson**
6 **YOURNOTLISTENING,** 7, ch m Trans Island—Mini Minster **Mr P. G. Atkinson**

10

MR MICHAEL ATTWATER, Epsom

Postal: **Tattenham Corner Stables, Tattenham Corner Road, Epsom Downs, Surrey, KT18 5PP**
Contacts: **PHONE 01737 360066 MOBILE 07725 423633**
EMAIL Attwaterracing@hotmail.co.uk WEBSITE www.attwaterracing.com

1 **ACADIAN CITY,** 4, ch f Cityscape—Cajun Moon **Canisbay Bloodstock**
2 **AJRAD,** 5, ch g New Approach (IRE)—Princess Cammie (IRE) **Canisbay Bloodstock**
3 **AMERIGHI (IRE),** 4, b g Caravaggio (USA)—Small Sacrifice (IRE) **Dare To Dream & the Attwater Partnership**
4 **BATTLE POINT (IRE),** 4, b g Dandy Man (IRE)—Paddy Again (IRE) **Canisbay Bloodstock**
5 **BEAR TO DREAM (IRE),** 4, b f Kodi Bear (IRE)—Wind In Her Sails (IRE) **Dare To Dream Racing**
6 **BEAUEN ARROWS,** 4, b g Brazen Beau (AUS)—Kindia (IRE) **Canisbay Bloodstock**
7 **CABEZA DE LLAVE,** 4, ch g Pearl Secret—Speed Princess (IRE) **Dare To Dream Racing**
8 **CAPPANANTY CON,** 9, gr g Zebedee—Fairmont (IRE) **Dare To Dream Racing**
9 **COME ON JOHN (IRE),** 4, b g Kodiac—Miss Glitters (IRE) **The Attwater Partnership**
10 **COMPERE,** 4, b g Gleneagles (IRE)—Emergent **Dare To Dream Racing**
11 **CONCIERGE (IRE),** 7, br g Society Rock (IRE)—Warm Welcome **Dare To Dream Racing**
12 **EMULATION,** 4, b f Ulysses (IRE)—My Hope (USA) **Dare To Dream Racing**
13 **EZZRAH,** 7, b g Garswood—Tessie **Dare To Dream Racing**
14 **FAR TOO BEAUTIFUL,** 5, b m Farhh—Four Miracles **BG Racing Partnership**
15 **FUJAIRA KING (USA),** 7, b g Kitten's Joy (USA)—Cat On a Tin Roof (USA) **Dare To Dream Racing**
16 **I'M MABLE,** 5, b m Cable Bay (IRE)—Triskel **Mr B. Neaves**
17 **KINGSTON KURRAJONG,** 10, b g Authorized (IRE)—Kingston Acacia **Canisbay Bloodstock**

MR MICHAEL ATTWATER - continued

18 **LAWN RANGER,** 8, b g Cityscape—Baylini **Canisbay Bloodstock**
19 **LONG TIME COMIN,** 4, ch f Postponed (IRE)—Bowstar **Canisbay Bloodstock**
20 **LOTHIAN,** 5, b g Coach House (IRE)—Gracilia (FR) **Haxted Racing**
21 **MARY OF MODENA,** 4, b f Bated Breath—Miss Chicane **Haxted Racing**
22 **MISS SHIRLEY (IRE),** 4, b f Dandy Man (IRE)—Shirley (IRE) **Mr B. Neaves**
23 **MOFRIDGE,** 4, ch g Iffraaj—Danega **Dare To Dream Racing**
24 **MR MONEYPENNY,** 5, b g Monsieur Bond (IRE)—Normandy Maid **Haxted Racing**
25 **MY KIND OF LADY,** 5, b m Proconsul—Lady Suesanne (IRE) **The Attwater Partnership**
26 **NORDIC GLORY (IRE),** 4, ch g Cotai Glory—Norwegian Highness (FR) **Dare To Dream Racing**
27 **PHYSICS (IRE),** 7, b g Acclamation—Precipitous (IRE) **Dare To Dream Racing**
28 **REAL ESTATE (IRE),** 8, b g Dansili—Maskunah (IRE) **Mr A. C. D. Main**
29 **RHUBARB BIKINI (IRE),** 6, b g Zoffany (IRE)—Pearlitas Passion (IRE) **Dare To Dream Racing**
30 **SAVOY BROWN,** 7, b g Epaulette (AUS)—Kindia (IRE) **Canisbay Bloodstock**
31 **STEPMOTHER (IRE),** 4, b f Dark Angel (IRE)—Divorces (AUS) **The Attwater Partnership**
32 **STREET PARADE,** 7, b g Swiss Spirit—Jollification (IRE) **Dare To Dream Racing**
33 **TADREEB (IRE),** 5, b g Oasis Dream—Wake Up Call **Canisbay Bloodstock**
34 **THISMYDREAM (IRE),** 4, b g Camacho—Ponty Royale (IRE) **Dare To Dream Racing**
35 **UBAHHA,** 5, ch g Dubawi (IRE)—Taqaareed (IRE) **Mr M. F. Cruse**
36 **VANDAD (IRE),** 6, b g Dandy Man (IRE)—Ruby Girl (IRE) **Haxted Racing**

THREE-YEAR-OLDS

37 **BREAK THE SPELL (IRE),** b f Zoffany (IRE)—Altogether (IRE) **The Attwater Partnership**
38 **CAMOUR (IRE),** b f Camacho—Tussie Mussie **Dare To Dream Racing & Peter & Dee Airey**
39 **DEE'S DREAM (IRE),** b f James Garfield (IRE)—Aquarius Star (IRE) **Dare To Dream Racing**
40 **SAJWAAN (IRE),** b c Kodiac—Aberlady (USA) **BG Racing Partnership**
41 **SMASHER (IRE),** b g Dandy Man (IRE)—Mercifilly (FR) **Dare To Dream Racing**

TWO-YEAR-OLDS

42 B c 09/03 Charming Thought—Kindia (IRE) (Cape Cross (IRE)) **Canisbay Bloodstock**
43 B f 14/02 Harry Angel (IRE)—Plover (Oasis Dream) **Canisbay Bloodstock**
44 **RUDIES IN COURT,** b g 20/04 Massaat (IRE)—Emperatriz (Holy Roman Emperor (IRE)) (7000) **The Attwater Partnership**
45 **SKA,** b c 28/04 Advertise—Diamond Blaise (Iffraaj) (32000) **The Attwater Partnership**

Assistant Trainer: S. Sawyer.

11 MR JEAN-RENE AUVRAY, Calne

Postal: **West Nolands Farm, Nolands Road, Yatesbury, Calne, Wiltshire, SN11 8YD**
Contacts: **MOBILE 07798 645796**
EMAIL jr.auvray@outlook.com WEBSITE www.jrauvrayracing.co.uk

1 **BEAT THE BREEZE,** 6, gr g Outstrip—Tranquil Flight **Sara Spratt, Nigel Kelly & Alison Auvray**
2 **MY FRIEND WOODY,** 4, br g Garswood—Wotnot (IRE) **The Yatesbury Racing Syndicate**
3 **STREETS OF FIRE (IRE),** 9, br m Milan—Flaming Brandy (IRE) **Lady E. Mays-Smith**
4 **TABLES TURNED,** 4, ch g Ulysses (IRE)—Mesa Fresca (USA) **Nigel Kelly & Jr Auvray Racing**
5 **TRIGGER HAPPY (IRE),** 6, b g Gutaifan (IRE)—Boom And Bloom (IRE) **Nigel Kelly & Jr Auvray Racing**
6 **UMMSUQUAIM (USA),** 4, br f More Than Ready (USA)—Jiwen (CAN) **Nigel Kelly & Jr Auvray Racing**

TWO-YEAR-OLDS

7 B c 11/03 Time Test—Havana Jane (Havana Gold (IRE)) (4000) **Mrs S. Spratt**

12 MR KIM BAILEY, Cheltenham

Postal: **Thorndale Farm, Withington Road, Andoversford, Cheltenham, Gloucestershire, GL54 4LL**
Contacts: **PHONE 01242 890241 MOBILE 07831 416859 FAX 01242 890193**
EMAIL info@kimbaileyracing.com WEBSITE www.kimbaileyracing.com

1 **AJERO (IRE),** 8, b g Red Jazz (USA)—Eoz (IRE) **Julie & David R Martin & Dan Hall**
2 **ARCTIC SAINT (IRE),** 5, gr g Saint des Saints (FR)—Nomad Attitude (FR) **Lady M. B. Dulverton**
3 **BARE ASSETS (IRE),** 6, b br m Konig Turf (GER)—Lady Hawk (GER) **Mrs A. Game**
4 **BEHIND THE VEIL,** 5, b m Kayf Tara—Amazing d'Azy (IRE) **Mr & Mrs K. R. Ellis**
5 **BOBHOPEORNOHOPE (IRE),** 8, b g Westerner—Bandelaro (IRE) **Mr J. F. Perriss**
6 **BRENDAS ASKING (IRE),** 5, b m Ask—Lost It (IRE) **Dr David Carey (Not The Turf Club)**
7 **BROOMFIELD PRESENT (IRE),** 7, b g Presenting—Diklers Oscar (IRE) **Turf 2022 & Mr K C Bailey**
8 **CHIANTI CLASSICO (IRE),** 6, b g Shantou (USA)—Ballinderry Lady (IRE) **Brooke Pilkington**
9 **DESIGN ICON,** 7, ch g Schiaparelli (GER)—Bisaat (USA) **It's Only Money**
10 **DESTROYTHEEVIDENCE,** 5, b g Kayf Tara—Mathine (FR) **Mr P. J. Andrews**
11 **DOES HE KNOW,** 8, b g Alkaased (USA)—Diavoleria **Yes He Does Syndicate**
12 **DUKE OF EARL (FR),** 7, br g Noroit (GER)—Visiorienne (FR) **Mr P. J. Andrews**
13 **EL PRESENTE,** 10, b g Presenting—Raitera (FR) **Davies Pilkington Yarborough Brooke**
14 **EL RIO (IRE),** 6, b g Elusive Pimpernel (USA)—Princess Jaffa (IRE) **Rio Grandees**
15 **EQUUS DREAMER (IRE),** 8, ch g Getaway (GER)—
Thornleigh Blossom (IRE) **Mr M Laws & Mr & Mrs P Woodhall**
16 **ESPOIR DE ROMAY (FR),** 9, b g Kap Rock (FR)—Miss du Seuil (FR) **The Midgelets**
17 **FAERIE CUTLASS,** 5, b m Black Sam Bellamy (IRE)—Faerie Reel (FR) **Mrs E. A. Kellar**
18 **FAIR FRONTIERES (IRE),** 8, ch g Sans Frontieres (IRE)—Cappawhite Lass (IRE) **The Front Ears**
19 **FIRST FLOW (IRE),** 11, b g Primary (USA)—Clonroche Wells (IRE) **A. N. Solomons**
20 **FLIRTATIOUS GIRL (IRE),** 7, b m Flemensfirth (USA)—
Another Gaye (IRE) **Mrs I. C. Sellars & Major & Mrs P. Arkwright**
21 **GALANTE DE ROMAY (FR),** 7, gr m Lord du Sud (FR)—Miss du Seuil (FR) **The Galante Gallopers**
22 **GALAXY MOON (FR),** 5, b g Spanish Moon (USA)—Porquerollaise (FR) **Wendy Prince Racing**
23 **GENERAL HUBBLE (IRE),** 5, b g Telescope (IRE)—Jennifer Eccles **Youneverknow**
24 **GERARD MENTOR (FR),** 7, b g Policy Maker (IRE)—Trephine du Sulon (FR) **Garrett, Meacham & Woodhall**
25 **GETAWEAPON (IRE),** 8, b m Getaway (GER)—Milan Serenade (IRE) **Mr J. F. Perriss**
26 **GRAND ESCAPARDE (IRE),** 5, b g Getaway (GER)—Liane de Pougy (FR) **The Xtra Specials**
27 **GRAVE LA KLASS (FR),** 7, gr ro g Saddler Maker (IRE)—Marbela (FR) **Mr & Mrs Mark Laws**
28 **HALLIGATOR (FR),** 6, b g Saddler Maker (IRE)—Quick des Sacart (FR) **Imperial Racing Partnership 2016**
29 **HAPPYGOLUCKY (IRE),** 9, br g Jeremy (USA)—Mydadsabishop (IRE) **Lady M. B. Dulverton**
30 **HEROS DE ROMAY (FR),** 6, b g My Risk (FR)—Miss du Seuil (FR) **This Horse Is For Sale Partnership**
31 **HURLERONTHEDITCH (IRE),** 7, ch g Shirocco (GER)—Maid of Malabar (IRE) **Mrs P. A. Perriss**
32 **I SPY A DIVA,** 6, b m Telescope (IRE)—Molly's A Diva **Mr J. F. Perriss**
33 **IDAMIX (FR),** 5, b g Al Namix (FR)—Lonita d'Airy (FR) **Lady M. B. Dulverton**
34 **IMPERIAL ADMIRAL (IRE),** 5, b g Mount Nelson—Boherna Lady (IRE) **Imperial Racing Partnership 2016**
35 **IMPERIAL HURRICANE,** 6, b g Black Sam Bellamy (IRE)—Silverlined **Imperial Racing & Mr John Blackburn**
36 **INFLAGRANTE (IRE),** 7, ch g Getaway (GER)—Maggie Connolly (IRE) **Mrs V. W. H. Johnson**
37 **ISLE OF GOLD (IRE),** 5, b g Milan—Head For Heights (IRE) **The Going For Gold Syndicate**
38 **KILLIGARTH,** 5, b g Telescope (IRE)—A Shade of Bay **The Real Partnership**
39 **KYNTARA,** 7, b g Kayf Tara—Speed Bonnie Boat **Lady M. B. Dulverton**
40 **LADY OF THE NIGHT,** 10, b m Midnight Legend—Even Flo **Mr J. F. Perriss**
41 **LET'S GO AMIGO (IRE),** 5, b g Getaway (GER)—You Should Know Me (IRE) **Going Places**
42 **MAGICAL ESCAPE (IRE),** 5, b g Getaway (GER)—Chestnut (IRE) **Surprise Syndicate**
43 **MIKHAILOVICH (IRE),** 6, b g Sholokhov (IRE)—Putland's Bridge (IRE) **The Thrill Seekers**
44 5, B g Scorpion (IRE)—Molly's A Diva **Mr J. F. Perriss**
45 **MOONLIGHTER,** 10, b g Midnight Legend—Countess Camilla **Huw & Richard Davies & Friends**
46 **MR GREY SKY (IRE),** 9, gr g Fame And Glory—Lakil Princess (IRE) **Mr P. J. Andrews**
47 **PARC D'AMOUR (IRE),** 6, b g Walk In The Park (IRE)—Mal d'Amour (IRE) **The Strollers**
48 **PARTY FUZZ,** 8, b g Great Pretender (IRE)—Very Special One (IRE) **Mr P. J. Andrews**
49 **PAY THE PILOT,** 6, b g Telescope (IRE)—Becky B **Julie & David R Martin & Dan Hall**
50 **PERCY VEERING,** 6, ch g Sir Percy—Saltpetre (IRE) **The Percy Vera's**
51 **PHANTOM GETAWAY (IRE),** 6, ch g Getaway (GER)—Belle Provence (FR) **The P G Tipsters**
52 **PICKS LAD,** 7, b g Westlake—Pic of The Paddock **S W Racing**
53 **SAINT BIBIANA (IRE),** 6, b m Sholokhov (IRE)—En Vedette (FR) **Ms M. L. Peterson**
54 **SALT ROCK,** 5, br g Soldier of Fortune (IRE)—Saltbarrow **Julie & David R Martin & Dan Hall**

MR KIM BAILEY - continued

55 **SAMATIAN (IRE),** 6, bl g Sageburg (IRE)—Bodhran Davis (FR) **Mr N. Carter**
56 **SANDMARTIN,** 5, b g Martaline—Parthenia (IRE) **Lady M. B. Dulverton**
57 **SAYADAM (FR),** 6, b g Saint des Saints (FR)—Catmoves (FR) **Lady M. B. Dulverton**
58 **SHANTOU EXPRESS (IRE),** 8, ch g Shantou (USA)—Spanker **The Second Chancers**
59 **SPRUCEFRONTIERS (IRE),** 6, ch g Sans Frontieres (IRE)—Wayward Winnie (IRE) **The All Spruced Up Syndicate**
60 **STARVOSKI (IRE),** 8, b m Aizavoski (IRE)—Telstar (IRE) **The Grapevine Syndicate**
61 **TALK OF THE MOON,** 6, b m Pether's Moon (IRE)—Tara The Gossip (IRE) **E Hawkings A Lofts B Harding M Harris**
62 **THE BULL MCCABE (IRE),** 9, b g Yeats (IRE)—Twilight View (IRE) **Park View**
63 **THE EDGAR WALLACE (IRE),** 8, b g Flemensfirth (USA)—Annalecky (IRE) **Mr P. J. Andrews**
64 **THE KEMBLE BREWERY,** 4, b g Blue Bresil (FR)—Legendara **Breakfast at 10 Syndicate**
65 **THRUTHELOOKINGLASS,** 6, b g Kayf Tara—Amazing d'Azy (IRE) **Mr & Mrs K. R. Ellis**
66 **TOP TARGET (IRE),** 5, b g Westerner—New Targets (IRE) **Mr J. F. Perriss**
67 **TREGELE (IRE),** 5, b g Mahler—Emily Gray (IRE) **Julie & David R Martin & Dan Hall**
68 **TRELAWNE,** 7, b g Geordieland (FR)—Black Collar **The Real Partnership**
69 **TWO FOR GOLD (IRE),** 10, b g Gold Well—Two of Each (IRE) **May We Never Be Found Out Partnership 2**
70 **UNDERCOVER LOVER (IRE),** 5, b g Cloudings (IRE)—
Another Gaye (IRE) **Mrs I. C. Sellars & Major & Mrs P. Arkwright**
71 **VOYBURG (IRE),** 7, br g Sageburg (IRE)—Slevoy Ahoy (IRE) **The Ten Sages**

Assistant Trainer: Matthew Nicholls.

NH Jockey: David Bass, Ciaran Gethings. **Conditional Jockey:** Kai Lenihan. **Amateur Jockey:** Lauren Keen-Hawkins.

13

MR LIAM BAILEY, Middleham

Postal: **2 Little Spigot, Coverham, Middleham, Leyburn, North Yorkshire, DL8 4TL**
Contacts: **PHONE 07807 519220**
EMAIL liambailey_foulricefarm@hotmail.com

1 **BUTTERFLY ISLAND (IRE),** 4, b f Acclamation—Cumbfree (IRE)
2 **CEASE AND DESIST (IRE),** 5, b g No Nay Never (USA)—Mackenzie's Friend **Oakfield Racing**
3 **CITY CENTRAL (IRE),** 5, b m Camacho—Boucheron **Mrs C M Clarke, Foulrice Park Racing Ltd**
4 **CLANSMAN,** 5, b g Nathaniel (IRE)—Pearl Dance (USA) **Mrs C M Clarke, Foulrice Park Racing Ltd**
5 **DOOMSDAY,** 4, b g Lethal Force (IRE)—Ayasha
6 **ESSENCIAL (IRE),** 4, b g Awtaad (IRE)—Passionable **Foulrice Park Racing Limited**
7 **FANZONE (IRE),** 6, b g Gutaifan (IRE)—Dame Alicia (IRE) **Foulrice Park Racing Limited**
8 **GORDONSTOUN (IRE),** 5, b g Gleneagles (IRE)—Elusive Girl (IRE) **Mrs C M Clarke, Foulrice Park Racing Ltd**
9 **HOW BIZARRE,** 8, ch g Society Rock (IRE)—Amanda Carter **Foulrice Park Racing Limited**
10 **KIRK HOUSE,** 4, b g Dragon Dancer—Lil Sophella (IRE) **Mrs S. Porteous**
11 **QUANAH (IRE),** 7, ch g Dandy Man (IRE)—Boucheron **Mrs A. M. Stirling**
12 **STRONSAY (IRE),** 7, b g Gale Force Ten—Perfect Blossom **Mrs C M Clarke, Foulrice Park Racing Ltd**
13 **STROXX (IRE),** 6, b g Camacho—Labisa (IRE) **Stroxx Partnership**
14 **THE VIK (IRE),** 4, b g Fast Company (IRE)—Flood Plain
15 **YAKHABAR,** 4, b g Ulysses (IRE)—End of An Era (IRE) **Foulrice Park Racing Limited**

THREE-YEAR-OLDS

16 **CROWN BRIDGES (IRE),** b g Kuroshio (AUS)—Shnnaas
17 **KEEPONBELIEVING (IRE),** gr f Make Believe—Slope **Foulrice Park Racing Limited**
18 **NAUGHTY TED,** ch c Mondialiste (IRE)—Just The Tonic **Wyndrinkers Racing**

TWO-YEAR-OLDS

19 B f 07/02 Time Test—Aerodrome (Nathaniel (IRE)) (8003)
20 B f 28/04 Free Eagle (IRE)—Media Room (USA) (Street Cry (IRE)) (4802)

14 MR GEORGE BAKER, Chiddingfold

Postal: **Robins Farm, Fisher Lane, Chiddingfold, Godalming, Surrey, GU8 4TB**
Contacts: **PHONE 01428 682059 MOBILE 07889 514881**
EMAIL gbakerracing@gmail.com WEBSITE www.georgebakerracing.com

1 **ATLANTIS BLUE,** 4, b c Cityscape—Deep Blue Sea
2 **AWESOME DANCER (IRE),** 4, ch g Highland Reel (IRE)—Adutchgirl (GER) **Carbine of London Racing (2)**
3 **BONDI SPICE (IRE),** 4, ch g Australia—La Spezia (IRE) **One Day Rodney Partnership, Mr M. J. Tracey, Mr M. A. C. Rudd**
4 **BONNET,** 5, ch m Helmet (AUS)—Tanda Tula (IRE) **Seaton Partnership**
5 **CEMHAAN,** 6, b g Muhaarar—Shalwa **PJL Racing**
6 **CONFILS (FR),** 7, b m Olympic Glory (IRE)—Mambo Mistress (USA) **Confidence Partnership**
7 **DESTINY QUEEN (FR),** 4, b f Al Wukair (IRE)—Trissa (FR) **The Wise Old Al Partnership**
8 **DEVORGILLA,** 5, ch m Mukhadram—Sweetheart Abbey **Miss S. Bannatyne**
9 **ETON BLUE (IRE),** 5, b g Starspangledbanner (AUS)—Naturotopia (FR) **The Eton Ramblers**
10 **FAT GLADIATOR (IRE),** 4, b g Cotai Glory—New Magic (IRE) **The Fat Gladiators**
11 **GET IT,** 5, b g Twilight Son—Pine Ridge **MyRacehorse & Partners, Mr G. Baker, Myracehorse Ltd, George Baker Racing International, MyRacehorse VI**
12 **GRAIGNES (FR),** 7, b g Zoffany (IRE)—Grey Anatomy **Delancey Real Estate Asset Management Limited**
13 **HECTOR (IRE),** 4, b g Bated Breath—Typhoon Della (FR) **Sir John Ritblat & Suki Ritblat, Creditincome Investments (No 3) Limited, Oakburr Limited**
14 **HELLO SUNSHINE,** 7, ch m Kapgarde—Louisvy
15 **HIERONYMUS,** 7, b g Dutch Art—Sleek **Mrs Pao, Mr Stafford & Mr Tucker, S. P. Tucker, Mr N. J. Stafford, Mrs A. Pao**
16 **HIGHWAY ONE (USA),** 9, b m Quality Road (USA)—Kinda Wonderful (USA) **George Baker Racing Bahrain Syndicate**
17 **IKKARI (IRE),** 4, b f Mehmas (IRE)—Ease The Jets **Mr Rupert Williams & Friends**
18 **JOHN BALLIOL,** 4, b g Sixties Icon—Sweetheart Abbey **Miss S. Bannatyne**
19 **JON SNOW (FR),** 8, br g Le Havre (IRE)—Saroushka (FR) **Mr G. Baker, Mr P. Bowden, PJL Racing, Pjl Racing & Paul Bowden**
20 **LA MAQUINA,** 8, b g Dutch Art—Miss Meltemi (IRE) **George Baker and Partners - Super Six**
21 **LOCKDOWN,** 5, b g Charm Spirit (IRE)—Bounty Box **Mrs Benjamin Newton & Friends**
22 **LUCANDER (IRE),** 6, b g Footstepsinthesand—Lady Sefton **Nigel Jones & Paul Bowden, Mr P. Bowden, Dr N. Jones**
23 **MAMILLIUS,** 10, b g Exceed And Excel (AUS)—Laika Lane (USA) **The Mamillius Partnership**
24 **MARSH BENHAM (IRE),** 4, ch g Galileo Gold—Zelie Martin (IRE) **The Red House Racing Club**
25 **MOTAZZEN (IRE),** 5, b g Dubawi (IRE)—Yaazy (IRE) **Paul Hudson Partnership**
26 **PINWHEEL (IRE),** 5, b g Exceed And Excel (AUS)—Quilting (USA) **The Quixotic Partnership**
27 **RAWYAAN,** 4, gr g Markaz (IRE)—Rathaath (IRE) **Highclere Thoroughbred Racing & Mr C Norman**
28 **RECHERCHER,** 4, b f Nathaniel (IRE)—Regardez **Mr B. R. Lindley**
29 **RILEY'S AYADA,** 4, b f Churchill (IRE)—Tobacco Bay (IRE)
30 **RILEY'S POSITANO (IRE),** 4, br g Bated Breath—Metal Precious (FR)
31 **ROCHEBRUNE,** 4, b f Postponed (IRE)—Singuliere (IRE) **Adams, Baker, Buckland & Green**
32 **SENSE OF SECURITY,** 4, b f Havana Gold (IRE)—Lilly Junior **Fellowship Racing**
33 **SHE'S A LADY,** 5, b m Telescope (IRE)—Acapella Star (IRE) **Fame n Fortune Syndicate**
34 **SHOWLAN SPIRIT,** 4, ch f Showcasing—Seolan (IRE) **Sir John Ritblat & Suki Ritblat, Creditincome Investments (No 3) Limited, Oakburr Limited**
35 **SPIRIT WARNING,** 7, b g Charm Spirit (IRE)—Averami **Kidd, Russell & Baker**
36 **STUDY THE STARS,** 5, b g Due Diligence (USA)—Celestial Bay **Homebred Racing**
37 **TAMPERE (IRE),** 6, b m Sea The Moon (GER)—Brigitta (IRE) **The Tampere Partnership**
38 **THE LAMPLIGHTER (FR),** 8, b g Elusive City (USA)—Plume Rouge **Mr G. Baker, Turf Club 2022 & Co 2, Mr A. N. Cheyne, Turf Club 2022, Col A. J. E. Malcolm, The Lamplighter Syndicate**
39 **WARHOL (IRE),** 4, b g Belardo (IRE)—Darsan (IRE) **C & F McKay, Mr C. S. Norman, Mr F. McKay**
40 **WATCHYA,** 4, gr g Dark Angel (IRE)—Barroche (IRE) **MyRacehorse & Partners, Mr G. Baker, Myracehorse Ltd, George Baker Racing International, MyRacehorse VI**

THREE-YEAR-OLDS

41 **ALBERTO (IRE),** b g Kodiac—Viadeigiardini **Mr G. Darling**
42 **ARGENTALI,** gr f Cracksman—Runner Runner (IRE) **S. P. Tucker, Mr N. J. Stafford, Mrs A. Pao, Tucker, Stafford, Pao & McCormack, E. McCormack**

MR GEORGE BAKER - continued

43 **BEAULD AS BRASS,** b g Brazen Beau (AUS)—Camelopardalis **Greens Racing**
44 **BILLAKI MOU (FR),** b g Belgian Bill—Billie Jean **PJL Racing**
45 **CARBINE STAR,** b f Starspangledbanner (AUS)—Pure Elegance (IRE) **Carbine of London Racing**
46 **EIGHT FIFTEEN (IRE),** b f New Approach (IRE)—Expecting To Fly (USA) **Rupert Williams & Partners**
47 **ELECTRIC AVENUE,** b f Outstrip—School Fees **Mr G. Baker**
48 Ch f Rajasinghe (IRE)—Jimmy's Girl (IRE) **Mr G. Baker**
49 **KITARO KICH (IRE),** br c Karakontie (JPN)—The Tulip (IRE) **J MacHale, S. Tucker & S. Jewell**
50 **LA MUJER (IRE),** b f Saxon Warrior (JPN)—Cocoa Beach (IRE) **The La Mujer Syndicate**
51 **QUIETNESS,** b f Bated Breath—Quiet Queen **Alvediston Stud & Miss Saba Bannatyne, Mr A. D. Wardall, Miss S. Bannatyne**

TWO-YEAR-OLDS

52 **PERLA MARINA (IRE),** b f 30/03 Zoffany (IRE)—Evangelical (Dutch Art) (25000) **Mr G. Baker**
53 B c 07/05 Bunglеinthejungle—Promiscuous (Kingman)
54 B c 21/03 Dark Angel (IRE)—Sudu Queen (GER) (Invincible Spirit (IRE)) (65626) **George Baker Racing International**
55 B g 14/02 Land Force (IRE)—Tanda Tula (IRE) (Alhaarth (IRE)) **Seaton Partnership**

Assistant Trainer: Barney Baker, Patrick Murphy, Valerie Murphy.

Flat Jockey: Pat Cosgrave, Trevor Whelan. **NH Jockey:** Marc Goldstein.

---

15 MR ANDREW BALDING, Kingsclere

Postal: **Park House Stables, Kingsclere, Newbury, Berkshire, RG20 5PY**
Contacts: **PHONE 01635 298210**
EMAIL admin@kingsclere.com WEBSITE www.kingsclere.com

1 **AEGIS POWER,** 4, b g Nathaniel (IRE)—Robema **King Power Racing Co Ltd**
2 **AL MARMAR (IRE),** 4, br g Kodiac—Fraulein **Al Shaqab Racing UK Limited**
3 **AUSTRALIAN ANGEL,** 4, ch f Australia—Angel Terrace (USA) **G. Strawbridge**
4 **AZTEC EMPIRE (IRE),** 4, b c Sea The Stars (IRE)—Azanara (IRE) **Sheikh I. S. Al Khalifa**
5 **BERKSHIRE BREEZE (IRE),** 4, gr c Mastercraftsman (IRE)—Bright And Shining (IRE) **Berkshire Parts & Panels Ltd No1 Fanclub**
6 **BERKSHIRE ROCCO (FR),** 6, ch g Sir Percy—Sunny Again **Berkshire Parts & Panels Ltd No1 Fanclub**
7 **BERKSHIRE SHADOW,** 4, gr g Dark Angel (IRE)—Angel Vision (IRE) **Berkshire Parts & Panels Ltd No1 Fanclub**
8 **BIZARRE LAW,** 4, b g Lawman (FR)—Bizzarria **Apollo Racing & Opulence T/breds**
9 **CITY STREAK,** 4, ch g Cityscape—Daffydowndilly **Lord J. Blyth**
10 **COLTRANE (IRE),** 6, b g Mastercraftsman (IRE)—Promise Me (IRE) **Mick and Janice Mariscotti**
11 **EYDON (IRE),** 4, b c Olden Times—Moon Mountain **Prince A. A. Faisal**
12 **FIVETHOUSANDTOONE (IRE),** 5, b g Frankel—Promised Money (IRE) **King Power Racing Co Ltd**
13 **FOX TAL,** 7, b g Sea The Stars (IRE)—Maskunah (IRE) **King Power Racing Co Ltd**
14 **FOXES TALES (IRE),** 5, b g Zoffany (IRE)—Starfish (IRE) **King Power Racing Co Ltd**
15 **GROUNDBREAKER (GER),** 4, b g Oasis Dream—Guajara (GER) **Sheikh Mohammed Obaid Al Maktoum**
16 **IMPERIAL FIGHTER (IRE),** 4, b g The Gurkha (IRE)—Endure (IRE) **Mr M. A. R. Blencowe**
17 **JUAN BERMUDEZ,** 4, ch g Nathaniel (IRE)—Long Face (USA) **The Bermuda Salman Morris Partnership**
18 **KING'S LYNN,** 6, b g Cable Bay (IRE)—Kinematic **The King**
19 **LADY LABELLE (IRE),** 4, ch f The Gurkha (IRE)—Duchess of Marmite (IRE) **Team Valor LLC**
20 **MASEKELA (IRE),** 4, b g El Kabeir (USA)—Lady's Purse **Mick and Janice Mariscotti**
21 **NATE THE GREAT,** 7, b g Nathaniel (IRE)—Theladyinquestion **Mildmay Racing & D. H. Caslon**
22 **NEANDRA (GER),** 4, gr f Jukebox Jury (IRE)—Noble Rose (GER) **DJT Racing & Partner**
23 **NOBEL (IRE),** 4, ch c Lope de Vega (IRE)—Starlet (IRE) **Qatar Racing Limited**
24 **NOTRE BELLE BETE,** 5, gr g Zoffany (IRE)—Angelic Guest (IRE) **King Power Racing Co Ltd**
25 **NYMPHADORA,** 4, b f No Nay Never (USA)—Bewitchment **St Albans Bloodstock Limited**
26 **ORZO,** 4, b f Aclaim (IRE)—Chibola (ARG) **Mrs A. Wigan**
27 **RANCH HAND,** 7, b g Dunaden (FR)—Victoria Montoya **Kingsclere Racing Club**

MR ANDREW BALDING - continued

28 **RING FENCED,** 4, b f Haafhd—Victoria Pollard **Kingsclere Racing Club**
29 **ROSCIOLI,** 5, b g Territories (IRE)—Never Lose **Mr Philip Fox & Partner**
30 **SANDRINE,** 4, b f Bobby's Kitten (USA)—Seychelloise **Miss K. Rausing**
31 **SCAMPI,** 5, b g Nayef (USA)—Preveza (FR) **RaceShare - Scampi**
32 **SPIRIT MIXER,** 5, ch g Frankel—Arabian Queen (IRE) **J. C. Smith**
33 **TEUMESSIAS FOX (IRE),** 4, ch g Lope de Vega (IRE)—Princess Serena (USA) **King Power Racing Co Ltd**
34 **TYPEWRITER (IRE),** 4, b f Gleneagles (IRE)—On Location (USA) **Mrs F. H. Hay**
35 **WHIMSY,** 4, ch f Charming Thought—Cape Victoria **Kingsclere Racing Club**

THREE-YEAR-OLDS

36 **ALSAKIB,** gr c Kingman—America Nova (FR) **Al Wasmiyah Stud**
37 **ANOTHER RUN (IRE),** b c Zoffany (IRE)—Mais Si **Another Bottle Racing 2**
38 **ARABIAN STORM,** b c Kingman—Arabian Queen (IRE) **J. C. Smith**
39 **BARRIER (FR),** ch f Australia—Pure Fantasy **The King**
40 **BATISTET,** b g Bated Breath—Bermondsey Girl **Miss S. Phipps Hornby**
41 **BELL SONG (FR),** b f Saxon Warrior (JPN)—Summer Chorus **Sheikh J. D. Al Maktoum**
42 **BERKSHIRE BRAVE (IRE),** b c Churchill (IRE)—Mitzi Winks (USA) **Berkshire Parts & Panels Ltd No1 Fanclub**
43 **BERKSHIRE CRUZ (IRE),** b c Exceed And Excel (AUS)—
Special Dancer **Berkshire Parts & Panels Ltd No1 Fanclub**
44 **BERKSHIRE PHANTOM (IRE),** gr g Expert Eye—Silver Step (FR) **Berkshire Parts & Panels Ltd No1 Fanclub**
45 **BERKSHIRE SUNDANCE (IRE),** ch c Decorated Knight—
Hugs 'n Kisses (IRE) **Berkshire Parts & Panels Ltd No1 Fanclub**
46 **BRITANNICA,** ch f Lope de Vega (IRE)—Guerriere (IRE) **Louisa Stone & St Albans Bloodstock**
47 **BRORA BREEZE,** b f Shirocco (GER)—Highland Pass **Kingsclere Racing Club**
48 **CELLO,** b c Intello (GER)—Make Music **Kingsclere Racing Club**
49 **CELTIC CHAMPION,** gr c Adaay (IRE)—Arcamist **Opulence Thoroughbreds**
50 **CHALDEAN,** ch c Frankel—Suelita **Juddmonte Farms Ltd**
51 **CHARITABLE,** b f Iffraaj—Send Up (IRE) **Highclere - Ernest Hemingway**
52 **CHASSERAL,** b f Exceed And Excel (AUS)—Swiss Range **Juddmonte Farms Ltd**
53 **CLOCHETTE (IRE),** b f No Nay Never (USA)—Handbell (IRE) **Sheikh Mohammed Obaid Al Maktoum**
54 **COPY ARTIST,** b f No Nay Never (USA)—Sleep Walk **Juddmonte Farms Ltd**
55 **DEEP IN MY HEART (IRE),** b f Saxon Warrior (JPN)—Remember You (IRE) **Healthy Wood Co., Ltd.**
56 **DELLA,** b f Brazen Beau (AUS)—Tricksy Spirit **Mr F. A. M. R. Alrafi**
57 **DESERT COP,** b g Oasis Dream—Speed Cop **J. C. Smith**
58 **ELEANOR CROSS,** b f Pivotal—Field of Miracles (IRE) **Cheveley Park Stud Limited**
59 **ELWASME,** b c Cracksman—Bahia Breeze **Mr S. Suhail**
60 **ENBORNE,** b f Tamayuz—Highest **Denford Stud Limited**
61 **ESTATE,** b g Showcasing—Cashla Bay **Highclere T'Bred Racing - James Chadwick**
62 **FAIR WIND,** gr g Tasleet—Gone Sailing **Kennet Valley Thoroughbreds**
63 **FAIRBANKS,** b c Nathaniel (IRE)—Fantasia **G. Strawbridge**
64 **FLEET ADMIRAL,** br c No Nay Never (USA)—Fleeting Fancy (IRE) **Sheikh Mohammed Obaid Al Maktoum**
65 **FLOATING SPIRIT,** b f Charm Spirit (IRE)—Zero Gravity **Juddmonte Farms Ltd**
66 **FRANKNESS,** ch f Frankel—Cosmopolitan Queen **J. C. Smith**
67 **FREQUENT FLYER (IRE),** b c Acclamation—Fashion Theory **Mr M. A. R. Blencowe**
68 **GALACTIC JACK (IRE),** b c Galileo (IRE)—Jack Naylor **J. C. Smith**
69 **GARRICK STREET (IRE),** b g Zoffany (IRE)—Danidh Dubai (IRE) **Thurloe Thoroughbreds LIII**
70 **GENTLE,** b f No Nay Never (USA)—Light The Stars (IRE) **Qatar Racing Limited**
71 **GLENFINNAN (IRE),** b c Harry Angel (IRE)—Fatanah (IRE) **Mick and Janice Mariscotti**
72 **GOLDSBOROUGH,** ch c Pearl Secret—Emily Carr (IRE) **Ms S. M. Pritchard-Jones**
73 **GREEN MACHINE (IRE),** b c Free Eagle (IRE)—Constant Comment (IRE) **A. Al Shaikh**
74 **GRENHAM BAY (IRE),** gr g Dark Angel (IRE)—Dawn of Empire (USA) **Martin & Valerie Slade & Partner**
75 **HAVANAZAM,** b c Havana Gold (IRE)—Mirzam (IRE) **Dahlbury Racing**
76 **HEDDEWIGII,** b f Sea The Moon (GER)—Night Carnation **G. Strawbridge**
77 **HOLGUIN,** gr c Havana Grey—Roxie Lot **J. Palmer-Brown & Partner 2**
78 **HOPEFUL,** b f Make Believe—Moon Mountain **Prince A. A. Faisal**
79 **IT'S MARVELLOUS,** ch f Intello (GER)—One So Marvellous **Helena Springfield Ltd**
80 **KADOVAR (IRE),** b c Dark Angel (IRE)—Bulrushes **Al Wasmiyah Stud**
81 **LAHAB,** b c U S Navy Flag (USA)—Cristielle **Mr I. Alsagar**
82 **LEADMAN,** b c Kingman—Big Break **Juddmonte Farms Ltd**

MR ANDREW BALDING - continued

83 **LEGACY POWER,** b c Time Test—Aurelia **King Power Racing Co Ltd**
84 **LIEBER POWER,** b c Cracksman—Astrelle (IRE) **King Power Racing Co Ltd**
85 **LOPE DE LIGHT,** ch c Lope de Vega (IRE)—Freedom's Light **G. Strawbridge**
86 **LORD OF EXCESS,** ch g Zoffany (IRE)—Frabjous **Mr M. A. R. Blencowe**
87 **MARZOCCO (IRE),** gr c Roaring Lion (USA)—Sand Shoe **Mick and Janice Mariscotti**
88 **MATCHING SOX (IRE),** b g Camacho—Follow My Lead **The Pink Hat Racing Partnership**
89 **MCLEAN HOUSE (FR),** ch c Dream Ahead (USA)—Private Cashier **Mr R. J. C. Wilmot-Smith**
90 **MLLE CHANEL,** b f Bobby's Kitten (USA)—Miss Cap Ferrat **Miss K. Rausing**
91 **MY LION,** b f Roaring Lion (USA)—Diamonds Pour Moi **Qatar Racing Limited**
92 **NDAAWI,** b c Cracksman—Mount Elbrus **S. Ali**
93 **NEW BUSINESS,** ch c Sea The Stars (IRE)—Instance **Mr S. Suhail**
94 **NIGHT AT SEA,** br f Sea The Stars (IRE)—Wordless (IRE) **Denford Stud Limited**
95 **OPERA FOREVER,** b f No Nay Never (USA)—Opera Gal (IRE) **J. C. Smith**
96 **ORANGE MARTINI,** ch f Roaring Lion (USA)—Strawberry Martini **Mrs J Redvers, S Lock & I A Balding**
97 **PASSING TIME,** b c Time Test—Flashing Colour (GER) **Pimlico Racing - Time Test**
98 **PAVISE,** ch g Camacho—Sacred Shield **Juddmonte Farms Ltd**
99 **PLATINUM JUBILEE (IRE),** b f Oasis Dream—Marisol (IRE) **The Royal Ascot Racing Club**
100 **POSTERGAL,** b f Postponed (IRE)—Astragal **Lord J. Blyth**
101 **PROSECCO,** ch f Gleneagles (IRE)—Elbereth **Westerberg, Magnier, Tabor & Smith**
102 B c Sea The Moon (GER)—Queen's Dream (GER) **Sir A. Ferguson**
103 **QUICK RESPONSE (IRE),** b f Time Test—Bari (IRE) **Sheikh J. D. Al Maktoum**
104 **RELENTLESS VOYAGER,** ch c Ulysses (IRE)—Nashama (IRE) **Relentless Dreamers Racing & Partner**
105 **REMINDER,** b f Dubawi (IRE)—Memory (IRE) **The King**
106 **RIBAL,** gr c Roaring Lion (USA)—Manasarova (USA) **Mr I. Alsagar**
107 **RISING BAY (IRE),** b f Kingman—Rosaline (IRE) **Sheikh Mohammed Obaid Al Maktoum**
108 **ROYAL JET,** ch c Exceed And Excel (AUS)—Goleta (IRE) **Mr M. A. R. Blencowe, A. F. O'Callaghan**
109 **ROYAL WOOTTON,** b f Wootton Bassett—Rimth **Denford Stud Limited**
110 **SAINT GEORGE,** gr c Roaring Lion (USA)—Lady Dragon (IRE) **Qatar Racing Limited**
111 B f Nathaniel (IRE)—Same Jurisdiction (SAF) **Cayton Park Stud Limited**
112 **SCEPTIC (IRE),** b g No Nay Never (USA)—Aljaazya (USA) **Mrs F. H. Hay**
113 **SCINTILLANTE,** gr c Roaring Lion (USA)—Freesia (IRE) **Mr Philip Fox & Partner**
114 **SEA OF ROSES,** b f Sea The Moon (GER)—Plume Rose **Weldspec Glasgow Limited**
115 **SILVRETTA,** b f Invincible Spirit (IRE)—Icespire **Juddmonte Farms Ltd**
116 **SISYPHUS STRENGTH,** b f Sea The Stars (IRE)—Childa (IRE) **Victorious Racing**
117 **SOVEREIGN SPIRIT,** b g Le Havre (IRE)—Shutka (FR) **Mr M. A. R. Blencowe**
118 **STARLIGHTER,** b f Sea The Stars (IRE)—Crafty (AUS) **Qatar Racing Limited**
119 **STORM VALLEY,** b f Lightning Spear—Hidden Valley **Kingsclere Racing Club**
120 **STORMBUSTER,** b c Dubawi (IRE)—Barshiba (IRE) **J. C. Smith**
121 **STRIKE ALLIANCE (IRE),** gr c El Kabeir (USA)—Delma (IRE) **Mr M. A. R. Blencowe**
122 **SUDDEN AMBUSH,** b c Cracksman—Al Mahmeyah **Mr H. R. Bin Ghedayer**
123 **SWORDOFHONOR (IRE),** b c Siyouni (FR)—Cercle de La Vie (IRE) **Victorious Racing**
124 **SYDNEY MEWS (IRE),** ch f New Bay—La Superba (IRE) **Chelsea Thoroughbreds - SM**
125 **THE FOXES (IRE),** b c Churchill (IRE)—Tanaghum **King Power Racing Co Ltd**
126 **THE GOAT,** ch c Cracksman—My Hope (USA) **The True Acre Partnership 1**
127 **THERAPIST,** b f Le Havre (IRE)—Homeopathic **Cheveley Park Stud Limited**
128 **TOPKAPI,** b g Bobby's Kitten (USA)—Cape Spirit (IRE) **Kingsclere Racing Club**
129 **TORRE DEL ORO (IRE),** b c Almanzor (FR)—Roystonia (IRE) **Mick and Janice Mariscotti**
130 **TOTNES (IRE),** b f Kingman—Havant **Mr & Mrs James Wigan**
131 **TWIN EARTH (IRE),** b c Teofilo (IRE)—Sularina (IRE) **Sheikh Mohammed Obaid Al Maktoum**
132 **URBAN OUTLOOK,** b g Cityscape—Casual Glance **Kingsclere Racing Club**
133 **VERMILION (IRE),** b f Kodiac—Western Sky **Highclere - Sir Alexander Fleming**
134 **VETIVER,** ch f Twilight Son—Poana (FR) **Cheveley Park Stud Limited**
135 **WINNARETTA (IRE),** gr f No Nay Never (USA)—Freezy (IRE) **Mr J Gladstone & Partner**
136 **WINTER MOON (IRE),** gr f Roaring Lion (USA)—Piscean Dream (IRE) **Mrs B Keller, Cambridge Stud & D Redvers**
137 **ZU RUN,** b c Zoustar (AUS)—Bewitchment **Mr D. P. Howden**

MR ANDREW BALDING - continued

TWO-YEAR-OLDS

138 B c 05/05 Make Believe—Adelasia (IRE) (Iffraaj) (65000) **Mr M. A. R. Blencowe**
139 Ch c 15/01 Galileo (IRE)—After (IRE) (Danehill Dancer (IRE)) (135000) **Mrs F. H. Hay**
140 Ch c 03/03 Night of Thunder (IRE)—Al Andalyya (USA) (Kingmambo (USA)) (170000) **Mr Zhang Yuesheng**
141 AL SHABAB (FR), b c 04/02 Saxon Warrior (JPN)—Pink Paint (FR) (Redoute's Choice (AUS)) (28011) **A. Al Shaikh**
142 B c 13/03 Study of Man (IRE)—Alma Mater (Sadler's Wells (USA)) (140000) **Mr H. Dalmook Al Maktoum**
143 B c 20/02 Night of Thunder (IRE)—Ancestral (Bated Breath) (270000) **Clipper Group Holdings Ltd**
144 ANCIENT MYTH (IRE), b c 13/04 Camelot—
Queen Rabab (IRE) (Fastnet Rock (AUS)) (425000) **Sheikh Mohammed Obaid Al Maktoum**
145 ARABIC LEGEND, b c 09/03 Dubawi (IRE)—
Sheikha Reika (FR) (Shamardal (USA)) **Sheikh Mohammed Obaid Al Maktoum**
146 ARAGON CASTLE, ch c 08/03 Territories (IRE)—
Wearing Wings (Sea The Stars (IRE)) (120000) **Mick and Janice Mariscotti**
147 ARCTIC THUNDER (IRE), b c 17/02 Night of Thunder (IRE)—
Al Kirana (IRE) (Exceed And Excel (AUS)) (110000) **Opulence Thoroughbreds**
148 BLUEBELL GROVE, b f 13/04 Blue Point (IRE)—
Moojha (USA) (Forest Wildcat (USA)) (190000) **Sheikh I. S. Al Khalifa**
149 Ch c 31/03 Le Havre (IRE)—Borja (IRE) (Lope de Vega (IRE)) (45000) **Mr S. Suhail**
150 BYE BYE SALAM, ch c 11/03 Frankel—September Stars (IRE) (Sea The Stars (IRE)) (450000) **Mr S. Suhail**
151 CATCH THE LIGHT, ch f 27/02 Siyouni (FR)—
Bay Light (IRE) (Lope de Vega (IRE)) (500000) **Cheveley Park Stud Limited**
152 B c 01/03 Sea The Stars (IRE)—Cava (IRE) (Acclamation) (300000) **Sheikh Mohammed Obaid Al Maktoum**
153 CHELSEA HARBOUR (IRE), b c 14/04 American Pharoah (USA)—
Miss Mahalia (USA) (Uncle Mo (USA)) (90000) **Chelsea Thoroughbreds - SM**
154 B c 14/03 Too Darn Hot—Compostela (Sea The Stars (IRE)) (170000) **Mr S. Suhail**
155 B f 17/04 Iffraaj—Coyote (Indian Ridge) **Wardley Bloodstock**
156 CUBAN MELODY, b f 07/02 Havana Grey—
Jacquotte Delahaye (Kyllachy) (155000) **Highclere Thoroughbred Racing - Van Gogh**
157 CUBAN TIGER, b c 14/02 Havana Grey—
Shirley's Kitten (USA) (Kitten's Joy (USA)) (160064) **Sheikh Mohammed Obaid Al Maktoum**
158 DAWN SUCCESS, b c 17/02 Exceed And Excel (AUS)—
Granola (Makfi) (55000) **Sheikh Mohammed Obaid Al Maktoum**
159 B c 18/02 Mehmas (IRE)—Dutch Monarch (Dutch Art) (150000) **Ecurie Ama Zingteam**
160 B f 16/02 Oasis Dream—Dutch Treat (Dutch Art) (33333) **Mildmay Racing**
161 B c 21/04 Too Darn Hot—Golden Reign (IRE) (Champs Elysees) **Clipper Group Holdings Ltd**
162 B f 20/04 Saxon Warrior (JPN)—Good Hope (Cape Cross (IRE)) **The King**
163 HAYA, b f 29/03 Ulysses (IRE)—Arabian Beauty (IRE) (Shamardal (USA)) (4309) **Cheveley Park Stud Limited**
164 HEET, b c 21/03 Dabirsim (FR)—Rimth (Oasis Dream) **Denford Stud Limited**
165 B c 19/02 Masar (IRE)—Highland Pass (Passing Glance) **Kingsclere Racing Club**
166 B c 01/05 Land Force (IRE)—Humdrum (Dr Fong (USA)) **The King**
167 B c 23/01 Camelot—Ighraa (IRE) (Tamayuz) (110000) **Mr J. B. A. Al Attiyah**
168 INFINITY BLUE, b c 23/04 Blue Point (IRE)—
Our Joy (IRE) (Kodiac) (250000) **Sheikh Mohammed Obaid Al Maktoum**
169 B c 10/05 Highland Reel (IRE)—Inhibition (Nayef (USA)) **Kingsclere Racing Club**
170 JUANTORENA (IRE), b c 01/03 Havana Gold (IRE)—
Freiheit (IRE) (Acclamation) (100000) **Jeremy & Germaine Hitchins**
171 LADY BIRDIE, b f 03/02 Gleneagles (IRE)—Lady Mascara (Cacique (IRE)) (30000) **DJT Racing & Partner**
172 B f 15/03 Masar (IRE)—Lady Brora (Dashing Blade) **Kingsclere Racing Club**
173 B c 26/03 Saxon Warrior (JPN)—Lady Rasha (Dansili) **Mr I. Alsagar**
174 B c 16/02 Too Darn Hot—Lixirova (FR) (Slickly (FR)) (85000)
175 B br c 08/05 No Nay Never (USA)—Llew Law (Verglas (IRE)) **Ecurie Ama Zingteam**
176 B f 10/02 Zoustar (AUS)—Mabs Cross (Dutch Art) **Qatar Racing Limited**
177 MACH TEN, b c 14/03 Ten Sovereigns (IRE)—
Western Sky (Barathea (IRE)) (150000) **Sheikh Mohammed Obaid Al Maktoum**
178 MAGIC FORCE (IRE), b c 27/03 Soldier's Call—Magic Mirror (Dutch Art) (20952) **J. Palmer-Brown & Partner 2**
179 B f 14/02 Zoffany (IRE)—Make Fast (Makfi) **The King**
180 B f 01/05 Charm Spirit (IRE)—Make Music (Acclamation) **Kingsclere Racing Club**
181 B c 09/04 Ulysses (IRE)—Marenko (Exceed And Excel (AUS)) (40000) **The Yippees & Partner**
182 B f 13/02 Areion (GER)—Maria (GER) (Sea The Moon (GER)) (46419)

MR ANDREW BALDING - continued

183 **MIMASUSA (IRE),** gr f 13/04 Australia—Watsdaplan (IRE) (Verglas (IRE)) (32013) **Nick Bradley Racing**
184 **MISS INFORMATION (IRE),** b f 19/03 Blue Point (IRE)—
Newsletter (IRE) (Sir Percy) (90000) **Norman Court Stud & Partner**
185 Ch c 20/02 Cracksman—Nabaraat (USA) (War Front (USA)) (64026) **Mr M. A. R. Blencowe**
186 B f 08/04 Churchill (IRE)—Najma (Cape Cross (IRE)) (184074) **F. Carmichael**
187 B c 21/04 Sea The Stars (IRE)—Natural Beauty (Oasis Dream) (375000) **King Power Racing Co Ltd**
188 B f 09/04 Churchill (IRE)—Nayarra (IRE) (Cape Cross (IRE)) (160064) **Victorious Racing**
189 **NOBLE GALAHAD (IRE),** ch c 13/02 Decorated Knight—
Noble Fantasy (GER) (Big Shuffle (USA)) (40016) **Knight Fantasy Syndicate**
190 B c 01/04 Dandy Man (IRE)—Perfect Beauty (Mount Nelson) (120000) **Al Shaqab Racing UK Limited**
191 B c 04/02 Cracksman—Perfect Delight (Dubai Destination (USA)) (130000) **King Power Racing Co Ltd**
192 **PIANOFORTE,** b c 02/02 Land Force (IRE)—
Musical Art (IRE) (Dutch Art) (96038) **Highclere Thoroughbred Racing - Cezanne**
193 Ch c 27/03 Frankel—Proserpine (USA) (Hat Trick (JPN)) (100000) **Mr H. Dalmook Al Maktoum**
194 B c 27/04 U S Navy Flag (USA)—Puzzled (IRE) (Peintre Celebre (USA)) (70000) **First Bloodstock**
195 **RELENTLESS WARRIOR (IRE),** ch c 04/02 Soldier's Call—
Iuturna (USA) (Intidab (USA)) (28571) **Relentless Dreamers Racing & Partner**
196 **SAYEDATY SADATY (IRE),** b c 03/05 Anodin (IRE)—Bell Su River (Galileo (IRE)) (24010) **A. Al Shaikh**
197 Ch c 15/02 Masar (IRE)—
Shalanaya (IRE) (Lomitas) (160000) **Qatar Racing Limited, China Horse Club International Ltd**
198 B c 06/04 Saxon Warrior (JPN)—Short Call (IRE) (Kodiac) (125000) **Mrs F. H. Hay**
199 B c 07/03 James Garfield (IRE)—Smart Mover (IRE) (Fast Company (IRE)) (16000) **Mr M. A. R. Blencowe**
200 B f 12/03 Inns of Court (IRE)—Soft Power (IRE) (Balmont (USA)) (175000) **Mr M. A. R. Blencowe**
201 **SPANISH PHOENIX (IRE),** b c 02/02 Phoenix of Spain (IRE)—
Freedom March (Oasis Dream) (44018) **Mr J. Maldonado**
202 B c 17/04 Fastnet Rock (AUS)—Stars At Night (IRE) (Galileo (IRE)) (95000) **King Power Racing Co Ltd**
203 **SUGAR ROAD,** ch c 31/03 Masar (IRE)—
Muscovado (USA) (Mr Greeley (USA)) (160000) **Jeremy & Germaine Hitchins**
204 **SUNDANCER GIRL,** b f 16/01 Dabirsim (FR)—Quemada (IRE) (Teofilo (IRE)) (20808)
205 **TAKE CARE,** b g 22/03 Due Diligence (USA)—Ortiz (Havana Gold (IRE)) **Mr T Briam, Mr P Jacobs**
206 B c 03/04 Zoustar (AUS)—Talampaya (USA) (Elusive Quality (USA)) (200000) **Mr S. Suhail**
207 B c 03/03 Magna Grecia (IRE)—Temerity (IRE) (Zoffany (IRE)) (60024) **Mr M. A. R. Blencowe**
208 B c 02/04 Lope de Vega (IRE)—Tesoro (IRE) (Galileo (IRE)) (525000) **Prince A. A. Faisal**
209 B c 08/02 Fast Company (IRE)—The Singing Hills (Nathaniel (IRE)) (46419) **Kennet Valley Thoroughbreds**
210 B c 10/03 Invincible Spirit (IRE)—Tiana (Diktat) (350000) **King Power Racing Co Ltd**
211 B f 23/02 Blue Point (IRE)—Tisa River (IRE) (Equiano (FR)) **Mr I. Alsagar**
212 B c 16/02 Kingman—Tisbutadream (IRE) (Dream Ahead (USA)) **King Power Racing Co Ltd**
213 **TOPANGA,** b f 29/01 Siyouni (FR)—
Time Tunnel (Invincible Spirit (IRE)) (230000) **St Albans Bloodstock Limited, Fittocks Stud**
214 **TURING,** ch c 02/02 New Approach (IRE)—
Rainbow's Arch (IRE) (Dubawi (IRE)) (80000) **Mick and Janice Mariscotti**
215 B c 02/03 Too Darn Hot—Turret Rocks (IRE) (Fastnet Rock (AUS)) (600000) **Qatar Racing Limited**
216 **URESHII,** b c 28/03 Too Darn Hot—Margaret's Mission (IRE) (Shamardal (USA)) (62000) **Opulence Thoroughbreds**
217 B c 26/02 Kodiac—Vibe Queen (IRE) (Invincible Spirit (IRE)) (160000) **Al Shaqab Racing UK Limited**
218 **WILD WAVES (IRE),** ch c 05/02 Crystal Ocean—Guenea (Sinndar (IRE)) (135000) **Jeremy & Germaine Hitchins**

Assistant Trainer: Paul Morkan.

Flat Jockey: Rob Hornby, Oisin Murphy, David Probert. **Apprentice Jockey:** William Carver, Harry Davies, Callum Hutchinson.

---

16 MR RICHARD J. BANDEY, Kingsclere

Postal: **Plantation House, Wolverton, Tadley, Hampshire, RG26 5RP**
Contacts: **MOBILE 07887 535615**

1 **ALL THE FAME (IRE),** 8, b g Fame And Glory—Abhainn Ri (IRE) **Miss A. M. Reed**
2 **ARTHURIAN FABLE (IRE),** 6, ch g Sea The Stars (IRE)—Abstain **Mrs M. P. O'Rourke**

MR RICHARD J. BANDEY - continued

3 **BRULURE NOIRE (IRE),** 6, b g Califet (FR)—Julia Glynn (IRE) **Miss A. M. Reed**
4 **COMME SEA COMME CA,** 5, b g Gentlewave (IRE)—Et Voila **Mr C. J. Boreham**
5 **CORRAN CROSS (IRE),** 8, b g Doyen (IRE)—Steel Lady (IRE) **Miss A. M. Reed**
6 **DELTA RUN (IRE),** 6, b g Ocovango—Curragheen (IRE) **Wendy & Malcolm Hezel**
7 **DIESEL D'ALLIER (FR),** 10, gr g Kap Rock (FR)—Iena d'Allier (FR) **The French Link**
8 **DIVINE INSPIRATION (IRE),** 6, b g Malinas (GER)—Byerley Beauty (IRE) **Syders & Burkes**
9 **ECLAIR MAG (FR),** 9, b g Network (GER)—Katerinette (FR) **R. M. Kirkland**
10 **ECUME ATLANTIQUE (FR),** 9, b g Satri (IRE)—Force Atlantique (FR) **R. M. Kirkland**
11 **ERNIE BILKO (IRE),** 6, ch g Shirocco (GER)—Molly's Case (IRE) **You'll Never Get Rich Racing Club**
12 **FLINTARA,** 8, b m Kayf Tara—Flinders **Leith Hill Chasers**
13 **FRONTIER GENERAL (IRE),** 6, b g Mahler—Lady Zephyr (IRE) **Mr M. J. P. Wheeler**
14 **GIVE ME A MOMENT (IRE),** 8, b g Mountain High (IRE)—Maryann (IRE) **The Plantation Racing Club**
15 **GODREVY POINT (FR),** 7, b g Coastal Path—Quetzalya (FR) **Syders & Burkes**
16 **HORS GUARD (FR),** 6, br g Kitkou (FR)—Soulte (FR) **Mr C. J. Boreham**
17 **HOWAYA NOW (IRE),** 5, b g Califet (FR)—Howaya Pet (IRE) **Mr S. R. Cross**
18 **ICAQUE DE L'ISLE (FR),** 5, b g Free Port Lux—Quetsche de L'Isle (FR) **Harper Girls**
19 **JACKALANI,** 4, bl c Jack Hobbs—Taniokey (IRE) **Mr M. A. Burton**
20 **LA BREILLE (FR),** 4, ch f Spanish Moon (USA)—Duchesse Pierji (FR) **The Golden Decade Syndicate**
21 **MASTER DANCER (FR),** 6, b g Masterstroke (USA)—Perle d'Ainay (FR) **The Dancer Quartet**
22 **MISTER MALARKY,** 10, ch g Malinas (GER)—Priscilla **Wendy & Malcolm Hezel**
23 **OAKLEY (IRE),** 10, b g Oscar (IRE)—Tirolean Dance (IRE) **Mr T. D. J. Syder**
24 **PASS ME BY,** 7, ch g Shirocco (GER)—Materiality **Wendy & Malcolm Hezel**
25 **SAINT PALAIS (FR),** 6, b g Saint des Saints (FR)—Ladies Choice (FR) **Syders & Burkes**
26 **SHIPTON MOYNE,** 4, b f Coach House (IRE)—Blissamore **Miss R. Jones**
27 **SOUTHERN SAM,** 9, b g Black Sam Bellamy (IRE)—Pougatcheva (FR) **Mr T. D. J. Syder**
28 **SPANISH DANCER (FR),** 4, ch g Spanish Moon (USA)—Aurore Celtique (FR) **The Make It So Partnership**
29 **THE CATHAL DON (IRE),** 7, b br g Westerner—Flying Answer (IRE) **The Rumble Racing Club**
30 **THEATRE MAN (IRE),** 7, b g Ocovango—Theatre Bird (IRE) **Burkes & Syders**
31 **WEWILLGOWITHPLANB (IRE),** 6, b g Fame And Glory—Our Polly (IRE) **The Test Valley Partnership**

---

17 MISS CHELSEA BANHAM, Newmarket

Postal: **Mulligans Cottage, Cowlinge, Newmarket, Suffolk, CB8 9HP**
Contacts: **PHONE 07387 169781**

1 **ADMIRABLE LAD,** 5, ch g Bated Breath—Admirable Spirit **Mulligans Racing club**
2 **AT YOUR SERVICE,** 9, b g Frankel—Crystal Gaze (IRE) **Chelsea Banham Pre Training ltd**
3 **AXEL JACKLIN,** 7, b g Iffraaj—Reroute (IRE) **Mr A. Searle**
4 **BANKRUPT (IRE),** 4, b g Adaay (IRE)—Scintillating (IRE) **Mulligans Racing club**
5 **CAFE ESPRESSO,** 7, b m Sir Percy—Forest Express (AUS) **Chelsea Banham Pre Training ltd**
6 **CHOCCO STAR (IRE),** 7, b m Lawman (FR)—Sharplaw Star **Mulligans Racing club**
7 **HANDEL (USA),** 5, b g Pioneerof The Nile (USA)—Party Starter (USA) **Chelsea Banham Pre Training ltd**
8 **HEAVENS LIGHT (IRE),** 4, gr g Dark Angel (IRE)—Kurland (IRE) **Chelsea Banham Pre Training ltd**
9 **INDEPENDENCE DAY (IRE),** 10, b g Dansili—Damson (IRE) **Chelsea Banham Pre Training ltd**
10 **LADY OF YORK,** 9, b m Sir Percy—Parsonagehotelyork (IRE) **Chelsea Banham Pre Training ltd**
11 **MARIONETTE (IRE),** 6, b m Dark Angel (IRE)—Hand Puppet (IRE) **Mr M. Bartram**
12 **MUNIFICENT,** 5, b g Pearl Secret—Hulcote Rose (IRE) **Mulligans Racing club**
13 **OXYGEN THIEF (IRE),** 4, gr g Prince of Lir (IRE)—Spavento (IRE) **Mulligans Racing club**
14 **RUSHMORE,** 5, b g Lope de Vega (IRE)—Qushchi **Chelsea Banham Pre Training ltd**
15 **SECRET STRIPPER,** 4, ch f Outstrip—Secret Advice **Chelsea Banham Pre Training ltd**
16 **WATERMELON SUGAR (IRE),** 4, gr g Gutaifan (IRE)—Looks Great **Mulligans Racing club**

THREE-YEAR-OLDS

17 **TWILIGHT FUN,** b g Twilight Son—Sweet Applause (IRE) **Mr M. Bartram**

---

18 MRS STELLA BARCLAY, Garstang

Postal: **Lancashire Racing Stables, The Paddocks, Strickens Lane, Barnacre, Garstang, Lancashire, PR3 1UD**
Contacts: **PHONE 01995 605790 MOBILE 07802 764094**
EMAIL paul@lancashireracingstables.co.uk

1 **AN ANGEL'S DREAM (FR),** 4, ch f Dream Ahead (USA)—Sandy's Charm (FR) **Mr A. Bamford**
2 **BALQAA,** 5, b m Cable Bay (IRE)—Angels Wings (IRE) **Kettledrum Racing**
3 **BASHOLO (IRE),** 4, b f Caravaggio (USA)—Golden Shine **Tony Culhane Racing**
4 **BAZALGETTE (IRE),** 4, gr g Clodovil (IRE)—Irene Adler (IRE) **Ann Kershaw, Bernie Keegan & the Mwp**
5 **BUACHAILL (IRE),** 4, b g Gregorian (IRE)—Anazah (USA) **The Haydock Badgeholders**
6 **BUYING MONEY (IRE),** 5, b m Yeats (IRE)—She's Our Banker (IRE) **Keith Dodd & Network Racing**
7 **CAPTAIN CORCORAN (IRE),** 6, b g Anjaal—Hms Pinafore (IRE) **Matt Watkinson Racing II**
8 **CHEESE THE ONE,** 4, gr f Outstrip—Arabian Music (IRE) **Mr P. Sedgwick**
9 **CLATTERBRIDGE (IRE),** 6, ch g Valirann (FR)—Marinnette (IRE) **Hedgehoppers**
10 **CLOCH NUA,** 4, b g Exceed And Excel (AUS)—Lady Alienor (IRE) **Tony & Bev Culhane**
11 **COLEY'S KOKO (IRE),** 5, b m Kodiac—Acclimatisation (IRE) **Stella Barclay Racing Club**
12 **DANZART (IRE),** 5, b g Dandy Man (IRE)—Surava **Carl Pye & Gary Prescott**
13 **DEOLALI,** 9, b g Sleeping Indian—Dulally **Matt Watkinson Racing Club**
14 **DEPART A MINUIT,** 4, b g Twilight Son—Grand Depart **Stella Barclay Racing Club**
15 **ENSEL DU PERCHE (FR),** 9, b g Anabaa Blue—Onvavoir (FR) **Matt Watkinson Racing I**
16 **GHOSTLY,** 5, gr g Outstrip—Alpha Spirit **Stella Barclay Racing Club**
17 **GLORIOUS RIO (IRE),** 6, b g Gutaifan (IRE)—Renaissance Rio (IRE) **Matt Watkinson Racing Club**
18 **HARROGATE (IRE),** 8, br g Society Rock (IRE)—Invincible Me (IRE) **Matt Watkinson Racing Club**
19 **LANCASHIRE LIFE,** 5, b m Coach House (IRE)—Betty's Pride **Betty's Brigade**
20 **LAOCH GACH LA,** 4, gr g Lethal Force (IRE)—Poetic Dancer **Mr R. P. Quinn**
21 **MIGHTY POWER (IRE),** 5, gr g Markaz (IRE)—Tooley Woods (IRE) **Tony & Bev Culhane**
22 **MIVVI,** 4, b f Sixties Icon—Dozen (FR) **The Style Council**
23 **PAPA COCKTAIL (IRE),** 4, b g Churchill (IRE)—Anklet (IRE) **Tony & Bev Culhane**
24 **PENUMBRA,** 4, b f Sixties Icon—Shadows Ofthenight (IRE) **Andy Clarke & the Four Aces**
25 **SELECTO,** 6, b g Paco Boy (IRE)—Telescopic **The Haydock Badgeholders**
26 **SHARRABANG,** 7, b g Coach House (IRE)—Dulally **Matt Watkinson Racing Club**
27 **SIR BENEDICT (IRE),** 5, ch g Dandy Man (IRE)—Kingdomforthebride (IRE) **Village Racing**
28 **SPIRIT OF BOWLAND,** 4, b g Coach House (IRE)—Ella Rosie **Bowland Racing**
29 **STARJIK,** 6, b g Exceed And Excel (AUS)—Ice Palace **Mr P. Sedgwick**
30 **STORM TIGER,** 7, b g Shirocco (GER)—Lucys Pet **G Seward & Stella Barclay**
31 **THE NU FORM WAY (FR),** 5, b g Le Havre (IRE)—Jamboree (IRE) **& Carswell**
32 **VET BILL,** 5, b g And Beyond (IRE)—Nevsky Bridge **The Bounty Hunters**
33 **WILDMOUNTAINTHYME,** 7, b m Doncaster Rover (USA)—Awaywithefairies **Mr P. J. Metcalfe**

THREE-YEAR-OLDS

34 B f Coach House (IRE)—Ella Rosie **Mrs S. E. Barclay**
35 B g Coach House (IRE)—Melanna (IRE) **Bowland Racing**
36 B g Monsieur Bond (IRE)—Stolen Glance **R. S. Cockerill (Farms) Ltd**

---

19 MRS TRACEY BARFOOT-SAUNT, Wotton-under-Edge

Postal: **Cosy Farm, Huntingford, Charfield, Wotton-under-Edge, Gloucestershire, GL12 8EY**
Contacts: **PHONE 01453 520312 MOBILE 07976 360626 FAX 01453 520312**

1 **EARTH SPIRIT,** 10, b g Black Sam Bellamy (IRE)—Samandara (FR) **Mrs T. M. Barfoot-Saunt**
2 **JOHNTHEPOSTMAN (IRE),** 5, ch g Sans Frontieres (IRE)—Moon Over Moscow (IRE) **Mrs T. M. Barfoot-Saunt**
3 **MACS LEGEND (IRE),** 15, b g Blueprint (IRE)—Rosealdi (IRE) **BS Racing**
4 **MRS JONES,** 7, b m Multiplex—Gertrude Webb **BS Racing**
5 **NUMERO UNO,** 7, b g Dubawi (IRE)—Casual Look (USA) **A Good Days Racing**

20 MR MAURICE BARNES, Brampton

Postal: **Tarnside, Farlam, Brampton, Cumbria, CA8 1LA**
Contacts: **PHONE 016977 46675 MOBILE 07760 433191**
EMAIL anne.barnes1@btinternet.com

1 **ACOUSTIC (IRE),** 4, b g Kodiac—Operissimo **Mr M. A. Barnes**
2 **BALKALIN (FR),** 11, ch g Balko (FR)—Rose Caline (FR) **Mr M. A. Barnes**
3 **BREAKING RECORDS (IRE),** 8, b g Kodiac—Querulous (USA) **Mr M. A. Barnes**
4 **DAPPER GENT,** 6, b g Dapper—Overpriced **Mr M. A. Barnes**
5 **DEERFOOT,** 7, ch g Archipenko (USA)—Danceatdusk **Mr M. A. Barnes**
6 **DOLLY DANCER (IRE),** 9, b m Yeats (IRE)—Scrapper Jack (IRE) **Mr E. Cassie**
7 **FLLANA BAY,** 6, b m Lucarno (USA)—Flaybay **Miss A. P. Lee**
8 **GET 'EM IN (IRE),** 7, b g Getaway (GER)—Swap Shop (IRE) **Miss H. M. Crichton**
9 **HALFWAY HOUSE LAD,** 4, b g Recharge (IRE)—Pezula **Halfway House Syndicate**
10 **ILE DE MEMOIRES,** 7, ch m Trans Island—Treasured Memories **Miss H. M. Crichton**
11 **IZZY BELL,** 5, gr m Eagle Top—Urbane Bell **Mr W. K. Waters**
12 **JAD MAHAL (FR),** 4, b g Dabirsim (FR)—Cheveley (IRE) **Mr G. Lochner**
13 **LAST MISSION (FR),** 5, br g Invincible Spirit (IRE)—Magic Mission **Miss A. P. Lee**
14 **MASTERMINDING (IRE),** 4, ch g Mastercraftsman (IRE)—Enjoy Life (IRE) **Mr M. A. Barnes**
15 **MRINDEPENDANT,** 6, b g Recharge (IRE)—Lady Jinks **Miss A. P. Lee**
16 **OISHIN,** 11, b g Paco Boy (IRE)—Roshina (IRE) **Mr M. A. Barnes**
17 **ON YER SCHNAPPS,** 6, b m Schiaparelli (GER)—On Yer Own **Mr M. A. Barnes**
18 **PLACEDELA CONCORDE,** 10, b g Champs Elysees—Kasakiya (IRE) **Mr M. A. Barnes**
19 **SAINT ARVANS (FR),** 9, b g Motivator—Castellina (USA) **D & A Lee**
20 **SKIDDAW TARA,** 9, b g Kayf Tara—Bob Back's Lady (IRE) **Exors of the Late J. R. Wills**
21 **SWASHBUCKLER,** 4, b g Sea The Stars (IRE)—Majestic Jasmine (IRE) **Mr M. A. Barnes**
22 **VICTORY ECHO (IRE),** 10, b g Cloudings (IRE)—Serendipity (IRE) **Mr M. A. Barnes**

---

21 MR BRIAN BARR, Sherborne

Postal: **Tall Trees Stud, Longburton, Sherborne, Dorset, DT9 5PH**
Contacts: **PHONE 01963 210173 MOBILE 07826 867881**
EMAIL brianbarrracing@hotmail.com WEBSITE www.brianbarrracing.co.uk TWITTER @ brianbarrracing

1 **BEGIN THE LUCK (IRE),** 7, b g Le Fou (IRE)—Bobsyourdad (IRE) **K9 King & Partner**
2 **BENANDGONE,** 6, b g Hallowed Crown (AUS)—Peaceful Soul (USA) **Mr G. Hitchins**
3 4, B g Telescope (IRE)—Blackwater Bay (IRE) **Mr Michael Davies**
4 **BY JOVE,** 6, b g Nathaniel (IRE)—Calima Breeze **Miss D. Hitchins**
5 **COCONUT TWIST (IRE),** 5, ch g Shantou (USA)—Presenting Chaos (IRE) **Troika Racing**
6 **INDEPENDENCE (USA),** 7, br g More Than Ready (USA)—Frivolous Alex (USA) **Chris Clark & Daisy Hitchins**
7 **LYNWOOD GOLD (IRE),** 8, gr ro g Mastercraftsman (IRE)—Witch of Fife (USA) **Miss D. Hitchins**
8 **MADAME BIJOUX,** 5, b m Geordieland (FR)—Madam Be **Mrs Caroline Louise Balmer & Partner**
9 **MANOR PARK,** 8, b g Medicean—Jadeel **Chris Clark & Daisy Hitchins**
10 **PAK ARMY (IRE),** 8, ch g Arcano (IRE)—Charity Box **Troika Racing**
11 5, Ch m Schiaparelli (GER)—Shehadtorun **Mr Mike Harris**
12 4, B f Court Cave (IRE)—Supreme Touch (IRE) **Mr S. Hosie**
13 **TORONTO (IRE),** 6, b g Galileo (IRE)—Mrs Marsh **Troika Racing**
14 **YONCONOR (FR),** 6, b g Diamond Boy (FR)—Sainterose (FR) **Mr Michael Phillips & Partner**

MR BRIAN BARR - continued

THREE-YEAR-OLDS

15 B f Califet (FR)—Coppenagh Beat (IRE) **The B's Knees Racing**
16 **LA TRAVIATA (IRE),** b f Kingman—Carpe Vita (IRE) **Mr Luc Boermans**
17 **POR TI VOLARE,** b f Ardad (IRE)—Fairmont (IRE) **Mr Michael Phillips & Partner**
18 **ZA DRUZBA,** ch f Havana Gold (IRE)—Sciarra **Mr S. Hosie**

Assistant Trainer: Daisy Hitchins.

22 MR RON BARR, Middlesbrough

Postal: **Carr House Farm, Seamer, Stokesley, Middlesbrough, Cleveland, TS9 5LL**
Contacts: **PHONE 01642 710687 MOBILE 07711 895309**
EMAIL christinebarr1@aol.com

1 **COLLETTE (IRE),** 6, ch m New Approach (IRE)—Shallow Lake (USA) **Mrs C. Barr**
2 5, B g Eagle Top—Karate Queen **Mrs C. Barr**
3 **MIGHTASWELLSMILE,** 9, b m Elnadim (USA)—Intishaar (IRE) **R. E. Barr**
4 5, Ch g Eagle Top—Pay Time **Mrs V. G. Davies**
5 **SKEDADDLED (IRE),** 5, b m Fast Company (IRE)—Knock Twice (USA) **D Thomson & C Barr**

THREE-YEAR-OLDS

6 **MEGATRON,** b g Zoustar (AUS)—Rohlindi **Mrs C. Barr**

Assistant Trainer: C. Barr. **Head Girl:** V. Barr.

23 MR DAVID AND NICOLA BARRON, Thirsk

Postal: **Maunby House, Maunby, Thirsk, Yorkshire, YO7 4HD**
Contacts: **PHONE 01845 587435**
EMAIL david.barron@maunbyhouse.com

1 **ABOVE THE REST (IRE),** 12, b g Excellent Art—Aspasias Tizzy (USA) **L. G. O'Kane**
2 **AHAMOMENT (IRE),** 4, b g Alhebayeb (IRE)—Taispeantas (IRE) **D. P. Van Der Hoeven & D. G. Pryde**
3 **ANOTHER BATT (IRE),** 8, ch g Windsor Knot (IRE)—Mrs Batt (IRE) **L. G. O'Kane**
4 **ATIYAH,** 5, br m Swiss Spirit—Jofranka **Mrs Anne Atkinson & Partner**
5 **BARYSHNIKOV,** 7, ch g Mastercraftsman (IRE)—Tara Moon **Mr John Knotts & Partner**
6 **BERT KIBBLER,** 5, b g Fountain of Youth (IRE)—Annie Beach (IRE) **Mrs D. Dalby & Harrowgate Bloodstock Ltd**
7 **COAXING,** 4, b f Outstrip—Blandish (USA) **Harrowgate Bloodstock Ltd**
8 **CONTACT (IRE),** 5, gr h Gutaifan (IRE)—La Tulipe (FR) **Mr H. D. Atkinson**
9 **ESTICKY END (IRE),** 5, b g Estidhkaar (IRE)—Hay Now (IRE) **Dr N. J. Barron**
10 **GENTLE ELLEN (IRE),** 4, b f Bungle Inthejungle—Art of Gold **D Ellis & Partner**
11 **HOMER STOKES,** 5, b g Stimulation (IRE)—Thicket **Harrowgate Bloodstock Ltd**
12 **HUDDLE UP (IRE),** 5, ch g Anjaal—Red Red Rose **Harrowgate Bloodstock Ltd & Associate**
13 **LILIKOI (IRE),** 5, b m Alhebayeb (IRE)—Passion Fruit **Mr James A Cringan & Partner**
14 **MERESIDE ANGEL (IRE),** 4, gr g Gutaifan (IRE)—Mary Thomas (IRE) **Mereside Racing Limited & Partner**
15 **MODULAR MAGIC,** 6, b g Swiss Spirit—Lucy Parsons (IRE) **Mr P McKenna, Mr L O'Kane & Partner**
16 **MOSSBAWN,** 6, b g Brazen Beau (AUS)—Maziona **Mr Laurence O'Kane/Harrowgatebloodstock Ltd**
17 **ON A SESSION (USA),** 7, b g Noble Mission—Destiny Calls (USA) **Penton Hill Racing Limited & Mr L O'Kane**
18 **PERSUASION (IRE),** 6, b g Acclamation—Effervesce (IRE) **L. G. O'Kane**
19 **POET'S LADY,** 6, gr m Farhh—La Gessa **L. G. O'Kane**
20 **POLAM LANE,** 5, b g Swiss Spirit—La Zamora **Mr David A Jones & Partner**

MR DAVID AND NICOLA BARRON - continued

21 **STREETSCAPE,** 4, ch g Cityscape—Maziona **Dr N. J. Barron**
22 **TEESCOMPONENTSTWO,** 4, b f Scorpion (IRE)—Hula Ballew **Tees Components Ltd**
23 **VENTUROUS (IRE),** 10, ch g Raven's Pass (USA)—Bold Desire **Mr Laurence O'Kane/Harrowgatebloodstock Ltd**
24 **VIVA VOCE (IRE),** 6, b g Intense Focus (USA)—Moonbi Haven (IRE) **Dr N. J. Barron**
25 **WILLARD CREEK,** 5, b g Havana Gold (IRE)—Zaaneh (IRE) **Mrs S. C. Barron**
26 **ZARZYNI (IRE),** 6, b g Siyouni (FR)—Zunera (IRE) **Mr Laurence O'Kane/Harrowgatebloodstock Ltd**

THREE-YEAR-OLDS

27 **BROWNLEE (IRE),** ch g Bungle Inthejungle—Flashy Queen (IRE) **Peter & Liz Jones**
28 **BURNING THE BAILS,** b g Time Test—Flame Out **Shropshire Wolves**
29 **DALEY T (IRE),** ch g Dragon Pulse (IRE)—Elizabeth Swann **Peter & Liz Jones**
30 **ERAZMUS,** b g Massaat (IRE)—Rosecomb (IRE) **Mrs S. C. Barron**
31 **GOLD GUY (IRE),** ch g Gustav Klimt (IRE)—Lella Beya **Peter & Liz Jones**
32 **HOPE TO DANCE,** b f Equiano (FR)—High On Light **D. G. Pryde**
33 **JER BATT (IRE),** ch g Dragon Pulse (IRE)—Nora Batt (IRE) **L. G. O'Kane**
34 **MERESIDE DIVA (IRE),** ch f Ivawood (IRE)—Mujaesce (ITY) **Mereside Racing Limited & Partner**
35 **PARISH COUNCILLOR (IRE),** b g Ruler of The World (IRE)—Sweet Surprise (IRE) **Dr N. J. Barron**
36 Ch c Dawn Approach (IRE)—Taispeantas (IRE) **D. G. Pryde**
37 **THE FOLLOWER (IRE),** gr g Galileo Gold—Morethanafeeling (IRE) **Mr Laurence O'Kane/Harrowgatebloodstock Ltd**

TWO-YEAR-OLDS

38 B c 01/04 Cable Bay (IRE)—Angel Carlotta (IRE) (Camelot)
39 B c 07/02 Palace Malice (USA)—Artilena (CAN) (Artie Schiller (USA)) **Peter & Liz Jones**
40 Ch c 07/04 Mor Spirit (USA)—Chambray (USA) (Alphabet Soup (USA)) **Peter & Liz Jones**
41 **DEGALE,** b c 31/03 Due Diligence (USA)—Nuptials (USA) (Broken Vow (USA)) (25610) **Peter & Liz Jones**
42 **FARAH M (USA),** b c 03/02 Free Drop Billy (USA)—Stormin' Taffy (USA) (Seeking The Dia (USA)) **Peter & Liz Jones**
43 B f 02/04 Swiss Spirit—Jofranka (Paris House)
44 Ch c 02/02 Buratino (IRE)—Ma Bella Paola (FR) (Naaqoos) (12005) **Mereside Racing Limited & Partner**
45 B f 16/03 Mondialiste (IRE)—Pantera Negra (IRE) (Champs Elysees) **D. G. Pryde**
46 **PILGRIM,** gr c 27/02 Havana Grey—Hot Secret (Sakhee's Secret) (61905) **Mr H. D. Atkinson**
47 B c 09/04 Invincible Army (IRE)—
Ragtime Dancer (Medicean) (38415) **Mr Laurence O'Kane/Harrowgatebloodstock Ltd**
48 B c 03/03 Territories (IRE)—Scattered Petals (IRE) (Dark Angel (IRE)) (27000) **Peter & Liz Jones**
49 B c 27/04 Land Force (IRE)—Secret Charge (Recharge (IRE)) (12005)
50 Gr c 24/02 Havana Grey—Sufficient (Showcasing) (57000) **Peter & Liz Jones**
51 **SWIFT SALIAN (IRE),** b c 20/03 Holy Roman Emperor (IRE)—
Dynalosca (USA) (Dynaformer (USA)) (23810) **Mr D. B. Ellis**
52 B f 18/03 Swiss Spirit—Vigorito (Arcano (IRE))
53 **WIGGINS B (USA),** b c 11/02 West Coast (USA)—Star Affair (USA) (Tiznow (USA)) **Peter & Liz Jones**

---

24 MR RALPH BECKETT, Kimpton

Postal: **Kimpton Down Stables, Kimpton, Andover, Hampshire, SP11 8QQ**
Contacts: **PHONE 01264 772278**
EMAIL trainer@rbeckett.com

1 **ANGEL BLEU (FR),** 4, b c Dark Angel (IRE)—Cercle de La Vie (IRE) **Mr M. Chan**
2 **BIGGLES,** 6, b g Zoffany (IRE)—At A Clip **Lady N. F. Cobham**
3 **CRESTA DE VEGA (IRE),** 4, b g Lope de Vega (IRE)—Bibury **Mr M. Chan**
4 **HASKOY,** 4, b f Golden Horn—Natavia **Juddmonte Farms Ltd**
5 **JIMI HENDRIX (IRE),** 4, ch g New Bay—Planchart (USA) **Chelsea Thoroughbreds - Purple Haze**
6 **KINROSS,** 6, b g Kingman—Ceilidh House **Mr M. Chan**
7 **LONE EAGLE (IRE),** 5, b h Galileo (IRE)—Modernstone **Mr Marc Chan & Ballylinch Stud**
8 **LORD PROTECTOR (GER),** 5, b br g Pastorius (GER)—Lady Jacamira (GER) **Quantum Leap Racing X & Partner**
9 **MAX VEGA (IRE),** 6, ch g Lope de Vega (IRE)—Paraphernalia (IRE) **The Pickford Hill Partnership**

MR RALPH BECKETT - continued

10 **PROSPEROUS VOYAGE (IRE),** 4, b f Zoffany (IRE)—Seatone (USA) **Andrew Rosen and Marc Chan**
11 **RICH RHYTHM,** 4, b g Profitable (IRE)—Gift of Music (IRE) **Clarendon Partnership**
12 **RIVER OF STARS (IRE),** 4, b f Sea The Stars (IRE)—Amazone (GER) **Woodford Thoroughbreds LLC**
13 **SAM COOKE (IRE),** 7, b g Pour Moi (IRE)—Saturday Girl **Chelsea Thoroughbreds - Wonderful World**
14 **STAR FORTRESS (IRE),** 4, gr f Sea The Stars (IRE)—Lady Aquitaine (USA) **J. Gunther & T. Gunther**
15 **STAR OF ORION (IRE),** 5, b g Footstepsinthesand—Harpist (IRE) **Miss T. A. Ashbee**
16 **STATE OCCASION,** 5, b m Iffraaj—Forest Crown **The Eclipse Partnership**
17 **TAMARAMA,** 4, b f Muhaarar—Kalsa (IRE) **Mr A. Rosen**
18 **THANKS MONICA (IRE),** 4, b f Teofilo (IRE)—Wedding Wish (IRE) **Mr M. Chan**
19 **TIEMPO STAR,** 4, b g Time Test—Tanaasub (IRE) **Michael and Roya Rembaum**
20 **WESTOVER,** 4, b c Frankel—Mirabilis (USA) **Juddmonte Farms Ltd**

THREE-YEAR-OLDS

21 **ALBA LONGA,** b f Muhaarar—Alla Speranza **Miss K. Rausing**
22 **ALBANY,** ch f Lope de Vega (IRE)—Alyssa **Miss K. Rausing**
23 **ALSHADHIAN (IRE),** b g Awtaad (IRE)—Alshadhia (IRE) **Mr G. C. Myddelton**
24 **ARTISTIC STAR (IRE),** b c Galileo (IRE)—Nechita (AUS) **J. C. Smith**
25 **BALANCE PLAY (IRE),** ch g Lope de Vega (IRE)—Bezique **Valmont**
26 **BALTIC VOYAGE,** b g Frankel—Baltic Duchess (IRE) **Mr M. Chan**
27 **BATEMANS BAY (FR),** b c New Bay—Inconceivable (IRE) **Mr B. Flannery**
28 **BLUESTOCKING,** b f Camelot—Emulous **Juddmonte Farms Ltd**
29 **CAMPAIGN TRAIL (IRE),** b g Mastercraftsman (IRE)—Greta (FR) **The Lucra Partnership III**
30 **CAPTAIN WIERZBA,** ch c Night of Thunder (IRE)—Return Ace **Valmont**
31 **CHERRY,** b f Dubawi (IRE)—Mori **Juddmonte Farms Ltd**
32 **CIRCUIT BREAKER,** b g Nathaniel (IRE)—Australian Queen **J. C. Smith**
33 **CLAN CHIEFTAIN,** b c Gleneagles (IRE)—Pink Symphony **Mrs F. H. Hay**
34 **COME TOGETHER (IRE),** b g Gleneagles (IRE)—Zut Alors (IRE) **Ellipsis II - Come Together**
35 **DANDY ALYS (IRE),** b f Dandy Man (IRE)—
Alyssum (IRE) **Magnier, Wachman, Mr C. P. E. Brooks, Mrs L. M. Shanahan**
36 **DAVIDEO,** b c Galileo (IRE)—Here To Eternity (USA) **Valmont**
37 **DIAMOND VEGA,** ch f Lope de Vega (IRE)—Megan Lily (IRE) **Regents Consulting**
38 **ESMERAY (IRE),** b f Sea The Moon (GER)—Exploitation (IRE) **Mrs Lynn Turner & Mr Guy Brook**
39 **FALCON,** b c Exceed And Excel (AUS)—Festivale (IRE) **Sheikh A. B. I. Al Khalifa**
40 **FEUD,** b g Dubawi (IRE)—Agnes Stewart (IRE) **Clipper Group Holdings Ltd**
41 **FUNNY STORY,** gr f Havana Grey—Funny Enough **Whitsbury Manor Stud & Mrs M. E. Slade**
42 **GALILAEUS,** b g Galileo (IRE)—Madame Chiang **Mrs F. H. Hay**
43 **GLENCALVIE (IRE),** b f Gleneagles (IRE)—Considered Opinion **The Eclipse Partnership**
44 **GREY'S MONUMENT,** b c Territories (IRE)—Matron of Honour (IRE) **Miss T. A. Ashbee**
45 **IF NOT NOW,** gr c Iffraaj—Amona (IRE) **Quantum Leap Racing I & Partner**
46 **JALAPA,** b f Expert Eye—Mirabilis (USA) **Juddmonte Farms Ltd**
47 **JULIET SIERRA,** b f Bated Breath—Kilo Alpha **Juddmonte Farms Ltd**
48 **LA ISLA MUJERES (FR),** b f Lope de Vega (IRE)—Honor Bound **Valmont**
49 **LADY BOBA,** b f Lope de Vega (IRE)—Moi Meme **Andrew Rosen & Barry K Schwartz**
50 **LATIN VERSE,** b g Postponed (IRE)—Parnell's Dream **Mr & Mrs David Aykroyd**
51 **LEADENHALL,** b g Kingman—Promising Lead **Juddmonte Farms Ltd**
52 **LEZOO,** b f Zoustar (AUS)—Roger Sez (IRE) **Marc Chan & Andrew Rosen**
53 **LOCK THE VAULT (FR),** b g Cracksman—Starring Guest (IRE) **The Lucra Partnership III**
54 **LOSE YOURSELF (IRE),** b f Lope de Vega (IRE)—Stellar Path (FR) **Valmont**
55 **LUCKIN BREW (IRE),** b f Lope de Vega (IRE)—Witches Brew (IRE) **Mr M.Chan & Mr M.Tabor**
56 **LUCKY FIFTEEN (FR),** ch g Lope de Vega (IRE)—Bess of Hardwick **Valmont**
57 **MEXICALI ROSE,** ch f Zoffany (IRE)—Apache Storm **Philip Newton & Elizabeth Railton**
58 **MILDYJAMA (IRE),** b f Zoffany (IRE)—Moment Juste **Mr P Stokes & Mr S Krase**
59 **MISTRESSOFILLUSION (IRE),** gr f Mastercraftsman (IRE)—Il Palazzo (USA) **Andrew Rosen & Barry K Schwartz**
60 **MR BUSTER (IRE),** br c Sea The Stars (IRE)—Olympienne (IRE) **Valmont**
61 **NIGIRI (IRE),** ch f Lope de Vega (IRE)—Disclose **Valmont**
62 **NOTHING TO SEA (GER),** b g Sea The Moon (GER)—Nada (GER) **The Lucra Partnership III**
63 **OVERACTIVE,** b g Awtaad (IRE)—Hyperactive **The Lucra Partnership III**
64 **PAISANO (IRE),** b g Dubawi (IRE)—Posset **J. Gunther & T. Gunther**
65 **PALM LILY (IRE),** b f Expert Eye—Lady Livius (IRE) **Juddmonte Farms Ltd**

MR RALPH BECKETT - continued

66 **PRETTY FANCY,** b f Iffraaj—Very Dashing **Helena Springfield Ltd**
67 **PROMOTER,** ch c Showcasing—Hereawi **J. H. Richmond-Watson**
68 **PUFFABLE,** b f Kodiac—Puff (IRE) **Mr & Mrs David Aykroyd**
69 **QUANTUM IMPACT (IRE),** b c Invincible Spirit (IRE)—Marie Celeste (IRE) **Mr M. Chan**
70 **QUANTUM LIGHT (IRE),** b f Kodiac—Emeriya (USA) **Mr M. Chan**
71 B f Galileo (IRE)—Quiet Oasis (IRE) **M. Tabor**
72 **REMARQUEE,** b f Kingman—Regardez **J. H. Richmond-Watson**
73 B g Lope de Vega (IRE)—Rococo **Valmont**
74 **ROOST,** b c Sea The Moon (GER)—Redstart **Mr A. D. G. Oldrey & Mr G. C. Hartigan**
75 **SALT BAY (GER),** ch c Farhh—Saltita (IRE) **Valmont**
76 **SEA SPARKLE,** ch f Sea The Stars (IRE)—Forte **Mr J L Rowsell & Mr M H Dixon**
77 **SEAHOUSES,** b g Sea The Moon (GER)—Ceilidh House **J. H. Richmond-Watson**
78 **SOLUTION,** b g New Approach (IRE)—Luisa Calderon **The Lucra Partnership III**
79 **TIME'S EYE,** b f Expert Eye—Time Honoured **R. Barnett**
80 **TRUST THE STARS (IRE),** b f Sea The Stars (IRE)—Son Macia (GER) **Valmont**
81 **UNDERSTATED,** b f Nathaniel (IRE)—Catalyst (IRE) **Peter Jensen & Partners**
82 **VERBIER (IRE),** b f Frankel—Permission Slip (IRE) **Mrs D. A. Tabor**
83 B f Frankel—Wildwood Flower (USA) **Mr J. D. Gunther**
84 **WIND IN YOUR SAILS (IRE),** b f Sea The Stars (IRE)—Buying Trouble (USA) **Valmont**

TWO-YEAR-OLDS

85 B c 13/04 Territories (IRE)—Alle Stelle (Sea The Stars (IRE)) (33333) **The Obank Partnership**
86 **ALLONSY,** b f 05/04 Study of Man (IRE)—Alyssa (Sir Percy) **Miss K. Rausing**
87 **BASIC INSTINCT (IRE),** b f 22/04 Mehmas (IRE)—Ahaaly (Exceed And Excel (AUS)) (145000) **Valmont**
88 Ch c 09/03 Lope de Vega (IRE)—Bearlita (GER) (Lomitas) (128051) **Mrs F. H. Hay**
89 **BERNESE,** b f 19/02 Expert Eye—Swiss Range (Zamindar (USA)) **Juddmonte Farms Ltd**
90 B c 20/04 Zoustar (AUS)—Beyond Desire (Invincible Spirit (IRE)) (55000) **Mrs F. H. Hay**
91 B c 21/01 Kingman—Beyond The Sea (USA) (Sea The Stars (IRE)) (200000) **J. Gunther & T. Gunther**
92 B f 06/02 Bated Breath—Blinking (Marju (IRE)) (36000) **First Bloodstock**
93 **BLUE AKOYA,** b f 12/03 Sea The Moon (GER)—Blue Oyster (Medicean) (70000) **Mrs E. C. Roberts**
94 B c 06/03 Lope de Vega (IRE)—Colonia (FR) (Champs Elysees) (128051) **Mr M. Chan**
95 **CONSUELO,** b f 02/03 Study of Man (IRE)—Cubanita (Selkirk (USA)) **Miss K. Rausing**
96 B c 29/03 Cracksman—Cosmopolitan Queen (Dubawi (IRE)) **J. C. Smith**
97 B f 01/05 Le Havre (IRE)—Darting (Shamardal (USA)) (350000) **M. Tabor**
98 B c 01/04 Exceed And Excel (AUS)—Di Fede (IRE) (Shamardal (USA)) **Mr Robert Ng**
99 **DIVINE BREATH,** ch f 23/04 Harry Angel (IRE)—Puff (IRE) (Camacho) **Mr & Mrs David Aykroyd**
100 **DUNSTAN,** b c 13/05 Saxon Warrior (JPN)—
My Fairy (IRE) (Sea The Stars (IRE)) (32000) **Mrs Philip Snow & Partners I**
101 **DYNAMITE DORA (GER),** b f 10/02 Zoffany (IRE)—Diamond Dove (GER) (Dr Fong (USA)) (104042) **Mr M. Chan**
102 **ECHO LIMA,** b f 05/03 Kingman—Kilo Alpha (King's Best (USA)) **Juddmonte Farms Ltd**
103 **EMBODY (IRE),** b f 25/02 Acclamation—Exemplify (Dansili) **Juddmonte Farms Ltd**
104 B f 10/04 Kingman—Enticement (Montjeu (IRE)) **HM The King and HM The Queen Consort**
105 B c 10/05 Awtaad (IRE)—Ezima (IRE) (Sadler's Wells (USA)) (54422) **The Lucra Partnership IV**
106 **FAIR POINT,** b f 02/03 Farhh—Fair Daughter (Nathaniel (IRE)) **The Eclipse Partnership**
107 **FARIZIO,** b c 14/02 Dubawi (IRE)—Mori (Frankel) **Juddmonte Farms Ltd**
108 **FEIGNING MADNESS,** ch c 02/03 Ulysses (IRE)—Dance The Dream (Sir Percy) (170000) **Valmont**
109 Ch f 08/04 Masar (IRE)—First City (Diktat) (100000) **First Bloodstock**
110 **FOREST FAIRY (IRE),** ch f 22/02 Waldgeist—Bahama Girl (IRE) (Lope de Vega (IRE)) (62425) **Mr G. C. Myddelton**
111 **FOREVER BLUE,** b f 09/04 Blue Point (IRE)—
Toujours L'Amour (Authorized (IRE)) (80000) **The Sunshine Partnership & Partner**
112 **FRANKELIAN,** b f 02/04 Frankel—Australian Queen (Fastnet Rock (AUS)) **J. C. Smith**
113 **FRIGHTENING,** b f 23/02 Night of Thunder (IRE)—Twist 'n' Shake (Kingman) (260000) **Valmont**
114 **GAMES PEOPLE PLAY (IRE),** b f 11/05 Sea The Stars (IRE)—
Pretty Diamond (IRE) (Hurricane Run (IRE)) (170000) **Valmont**
115 **GOLDEN MYRRH (IRE),** b f 01/04 Frankel—Shepherdia (IRE) (Pivotal) (200000) **Mr & Mrs David Aykroyd**
116 **GREEN KEEPER,** ch c 17/02 Gleneagles (IRE)—Glance (Dansili) **J. H. Richmond-Watson**
117 B f 30/01 Showcasing—Hello Glory (Zamindar (USA)) (52381) **Whitsbury Manor Stud & Mrs M. E. Slade**
118 **HUTCHENCE,** ch c 09/05 Frankel—Baisse (High Chaparral (IRE)) (310000) **Valmont**
119 **INDELIBLE (IRE),** b f 14/02 Shamardal (USA)—Midday (Oasis Dream) **Juddmonte Farms Ltd**

MR RALPH BECKETT - continued

120 Br f 14/02 Le Havre (IRE)—Innevera (FR) (Motivator) (350000) **Mr D. P. Howden**
121 B f 14/02 Masar (IRE)—Kallisha (Whipper (USA)) **D & J Newell**
122 Br f 14/03 Cable Bay (IRE)—Kinematic (Kyllachy) **HM The King and HM The Queen Consort**
123 B f 10/04 Lope de Vega (IRE)—La Patria (Dubawi (IRE)) (85000) **Newsells, Redvers, Beckett**
124 LOVED BY YOU, b f 14/05 Too Darn Hot—Wiener Valkyrie (Shamardal (USA)) **The Eclipse Partnership**
125 MACDUFF, b c 08/03 Sea The Stars—Present Tense (Bated Breath) **Juddmonte Farms Ltd**
126 MAYO NEIGHS (IRE), b c 14/02 Dandy Man (IRE)—Tropical Mist (IRE) (Marju (IRE)) (95000) **Mr P. Mellett**
127 MERIBELLA, b f 19/01 Sea The Stars (IRE)—Incharge (Kingman) **Mr & Mrs David Aykroyd**
128 B f 17/02 Land Force (IRE)—Miss President (Oasis Dream) (50000) **King Power Racing Co Ltd**
129 Ch c 05/03 Ulysses (IRE)—Mystic Storm (Pivotal) (52000) **The Lucra Partnership IV**
130 NEW CHELSEA (GER), b c 21/02 New Bay—
Nightlight Angel (USA) (Manduro (GER)) (96038) **Chelsea Thoroughbreds & Ballylinch Stud**
131 OXFORD COMMA (IRE), ch f 12/04 Nathaniel (IRE)—Abilene (Samum (GER)) (80000) **Valmont & Ballylinch Stud**
132 B c 06/03 Land Force (IRE)—Pack Together (Paco Boy (IRE)) **HM The King and HM The Queen Consort**
133 PICK YOUR BATTLES, b c 08/02 Ulysses (IRE)—Traditionelle (Indesatchel (IRE)) (75000) **Valmont**
134 B f 27/02 Invincible Spirit (IRE)—Playful Sound (Street Cry (IRE)) (320000) **M. Tabor**
135 QIRAT, ch c 22/02 Showcasing—Emulous (Dansili) **Juddmonte Farms Ltd**
136 B c 19/01 Wootton Bassett—Quara (IRE) (Pivotal) (180000) **Clipper Group Holdings Ltd**
137 RAGING AL (IRE), b c 07/03 Sea The Moon (GER)—Mountain Bell (Mount Nelson) (100000) **Valmont**
138 B f 27/04 Invincible Spirit—Rekindle (Frankel) **Mr Brandon Barker, Mr Ryan Kent**
139 REVEAL, b c 18/01 Oasis Dream—Regardez (Champs Elysees) **J. H. Richmond-Watson**
140 B c 17/02 Golden Horn—Rue Renan (IRE) (Lope de Vega (IRE)) (76030) **Amo Racing**
141 B f 05/03 More Than Ready (USA)—Rumble Doll (USA) (Street Boss (USA)) **Mr M. Chan**
142 SEEK AND DESTROY (IRE), b f 12/04 Sea The Stars (IRE)—
Swizzle Stick (IRE) (Sadler's Wells (USA)) (260000) **Valmont**
143 B f 12/04 Advertise—Self Centred (Medicean) (120000) **Mr A. Rosen**
144 SENOR BUSTER (IRE), b c 04/06 Night of Thunder (IRE)—
Olympienne (IRE) (Sadler's Wells (USA)) (110000) **Valmont**
145 B c 12/02 Churchill (IRE)—Serenity Dove (Harbour Watch (IRE)) (100000) **Quantum Leap Racing & Partner I**
146 Ch f 06/04 Mastercraftsman (IRE)—Shimmering Light (Dubawi (IRE)) **HM The King and HM The Queen Consort**
147 SO LOGICAL, b f 02/03 Footstepsinthesand—
Dainty's Daughter (Cape Cross (IRE)) (40000) **Tactful Finance & Partners**
148 B f 07/03 Soldier's Call—Spanish Fly (IRE) (Iffraaj) (96038) **Mr M. Chan**
149 B c 07/03 Advertise—Squash (Pastoral Pursuits) (500000) **Mr Robert Ng**
150 ST LUKES CHELSEA, b c 05/03 Territories (IRE)—Desert Liaison (Dansili) (78000) **Chelsea Thoroughbreds Ltd**
151 STOP THE CAVALRY, b f 03/03 Lope de Vega (IRE)—Cartiem (FR) (Cape Cross (IRE)) (200000) **Valmont**
152 STORMIN AWAY, b c 15/03 Vadamos (FR)—Reyamour (Azamour (IRE)) **M.Rembaum, M.Tuckey & S.Kemble**
153 B c 20/02 Time Test—Tebee's Oasis (Oasis Dream) (50000) **The Lucra Partnership IV**
154 Ch c 21/03 Sea The Moon (GER)—Truly Honoured (Frankel) (120048) **King Power Racing Co Ltd**
155 TUMBLEWEED, b f 25/04 Time Test—Prairie Flower (IRE) (Zieten (USA)) **J. H. Richmond-Watson**
156 VALVANO (IRE), ch c 14/05 Night of Thunder (IRE)—Vuela (Duke of Marmalade (IRE)) (220000) **Valmont**
157 WHERE I WANNA BE, b f 02/05 Camelot—Travel (Street Cry) **Mr P Stokes & Mr S Krase**
158 WITHOUT ME (IRE), ch f 17/05 Frankel—Dulcian (IRE) (Shamardal (USA)) (130000) **Valmont**
159 Gr f 25/03 Dandy Man (IRE)—Wrong Answer (Verglas (IRE)) (170000) **Mr M. Chan**
160 YOU GOT TO ME, b f 26/02 Nathaniel (IRE)—Brushing (Medicean) (200000) **Valmont**
161 B f 10/02 Sea The Stars (IRE)—
Zvarkhova (FR) (Makfi) (368147) **Mr M. Chan, Mr A. Rosen, Gainsway Ventures SC, LNJ Foxwoods SC**

Assistant Trainer: Gary Plasted.

Flat Jockey: Hector Crouch, Rob Hornby, Rossa Ryan. **Apprentice Jockey:** Laura Pearson.

25 MISS JESSICA BEDI, Yarm

Postal: **Hill House Farm, Kirklevington, Yarm, Cleveland, TS15 9PY**
Contacts: **PHONE 01642 780202**

1 **BUCK DANCING (IRE),** 14, b g King's Theatre (IRE)—Polly Anthus **Mrs S. M. Barker**
2 **CALYPSO STORM (IRE),** 12, b g Trans Island—Valin Thyne (IRE) **Mrs S. M. Barker**
3 **OLIVER'S ISLAND (IRE),** 11, b g Milan—Leading Rank (IRE) **Hill House Racing Club**
4 **PATEEN (IRE),** 11, b br g Vinnie Roe (IRE)—Richards Claire (IRE) **Hill House Racing Club**
5 **PERCY'S WORD,** 9, b g Sir Percy—Laverre (IRE)
6 **POPATANGO (IRE),** 6, b m Getaway (GER)—Popalong (IRE)
7 **SINGIRISHMANSING (IRE),** 10, ch g Beat Hollow—Mrs Dempsey (IRE) **Hill House Racing Club**
8 **THUNDEROSA (IRE),** 11, b g Westerner—Montanara (IRE) **Mrs S. M. Barker**
9 **TUFF MCCOOL (IRE),** 9, gr g Arcadio (GER)—Mrs Wallensky (IRE) **Hill House Racing Club**

---

26 MR MICHAEL BELL, Newmarket

Postal: **Fitzroy House, Newmarket, Suffolk, CB8 0JT**
Contacts: **PHONE 01638 666567 MOBILE 07802 264514**
EMAIL office@fitzroyhouse.co.uk WEBSITE www.michaelbellracing.co.uk

1 **ADJUVANT (IRE),** 4, b g New Bay—Levanto (IRE) **Mr A. Bound**
2 **ARTISTIC CHOICE (IRE),** 4, gr g Caravaggio (USA)—Chicago Girl (IRE) **Mr S. Mizon**
3 **AT LIBERTY (IRE),** 4, b g Muhaarar—Federation **Mr David Fish & Partner**
4 **BALTIMORE BOY (IRE),** 4, b g Starspangledbanner (AUS)—Biaraafa (IRE) **M.B. & I Hawtin Family & Corbani**
5 **CARUSO,** 4, ch g Lope de Vega (IRE)—Carpe Vita (IRE) **M. L. W. Bell Racing Ltd**
6 **HAARAR,** 4, b g Muhaarar—Interchange (IRE) **D.W. & L.Y. Payne and G. & T. Blackiston**
7 **HEATHERDOWN HERO,** 4, b g Sea The Moon (GER)—Mariee **The Heatherdonians 1**
8 **JOHN O'GROATS (FR),** 4, b g Dabirsim (FR)—Ecume du Jour (FR) **Mr C. Hazzard**
9 **KING FRANCIS (IRE),** 5, b g Le Havre (IRE)—Princess Nada **Mr Peter Trainor & Partner 1**
10 **MISS HARMONY,** 4, ch f Tamayuz—Muaamara **Mr C Philipps Mr T Redman & Mr T Trotter**
11 **ONE MORNING (IRE),** 4, b f Gleneagles (IRE)—All's Forgotten (USA) **Lady Bamford**
12 **STONE CIRCLE (IRE),** 6, ch g No Nay Never (USA)—Candlehill Girl (IRE) **The Fitzrovians 3**
13 **STYLISH ICON (IRE),** 4, b f Starspangledbanner (AUS)—Refreshed (IRE) **Middleham Park Racing Xv & Partner**
14 **THE GREEN AMIGO,** 4, b g Frankel—Majmu (AUS) **Trev Group**
15 **TRUE COURAGE,** 5, br g Le Havre (IRE)—Pearly Steph (FR) **Mr S. Mizon**

THREE-YEAR-OLDS

16 **ALL THAT GLITTERS,** gr g Churchill (IRE)—Luire (IRE) **Mascalls Stud**
17 **ANNIE MAHER,** b f Zoustar (AUS)—Cordial **The Gredley Family**
18 **ATLANTIC DREAM (IRE),** b c Starspangledbanner (AUS)—Tafawoq **T C & Alex Ferguson**
19 **BANDERAS (IRE),** ch c Lope de Vega (IRE)—Glamorous Approach (IRE) **Oti Racing, Ballylinch Stud & Partner**
20 **BLETCHLEY STORM,** ch f Night of Thunder (IRE)—Mystery Code **The Fitzrovians 3**
21 **BLUEFLAGFLYINGHIGH (IRE),** ch g Starspangledbanner (AUS)—Addictedtoprogress (IRE) **Middleham Park Racing LII**
22 **BRAVE NATION (IRE),** b c Sioux Nation (USA)—Suite (IRE) **C. B. Goodyear**
23 **BURDETT ROAD,** b c Muhaarar—Diamond Bangle (IRE) **The Gredley Family**
24 **CLIMATE PRECEDENT,** ch c Ulysses (IRE)—Ozone Kindly **The Gredley Family**
25 **CONCEITO,** b f Dandy Man (IRE)—Ojai (IRE) **Wood Hall Stud Limited**
26 **CREME CHANTILLY (IRE),** b f New Bay—Creme Anglaise **Mrs G. Rowland Clark & Mr J. O'Connor**
27 **DOVES OF PEACE (IRE),** b g Camacho—Petits Potins (IRE) **Mr J Lonsdale & Partner**
28 **DUKE OF OXFORD,** b g Kingman—Miss Marjurie (IRE) **Mr A Cope, Mr B Roberts & Mr J Biggane**
29 **HEAVENLY WISH (IRE),** ch f Pivotal—Gertrude Gray (IRE) **Lady Bamford**
30 **IBRAHIMOVIC (IRE),** gr c Le Havre (IRE)—Isanous (FR) **Mr P. Trainor**
31 **INVESTED (IRE),** ch f Smooth Daddy (USA)—Galeaza **Mr A. York**
32 **LADY D'ASCOYNE,** ch f Showcasing—Victory Garden **H & Dm Swinburn**
33 **LEAP TO GLORY (IRE),** b g Toronado (IRE)—Highborne (FR) **Stuart & Lee Baker**
34 **LIBERALIST,** b f Pivotal—Carenot (IRE) **Maclennan, Sangster, Magnier & Shanahan**
35 **LOCH CARRON (IRE),** gr f Gregorian (IRE)—Farran (IRE) **In-n-out Partnership**

MR MICHAEL BELL - continued

36 **MAYLANDSEA,** br gr f Havana Grey—Different **Middleham Park Racing Lxxi & Partners**
37 **METAHORSE,** gr ro g Havana Grey—Highly Spiced **Amo Racing Limited**
38 **MILE END,** b f Expert Eye—Roulette **The Gredley Family**
39 **MINDSET,** ch g New Approach (IRE)—Tight Lines **Mr E. J. Ware**
40 **NO SAINT,** b g Koropick (IRE)—Lady Kyllar **The Fitzrovians 3**
41 **NOODLE MISSION (USA),** b g Noble Mission—Driver's Girl (USA) **Mr Ed Babington & Partner**
42 **ODIN OWNS YOU ALL (IRE),** b c No Nay Never (USA)—Kitty Love (USA) **H.E. R. Munfaredi**
43 **ORO ORO (IRE),** b c New Bay—Millport **Mr P. Trainor**
44 **SAIL ON SILVERBIRD (USA),** gr ro f Twirling Candy (USA)—
Cheval Blanche (USA) **Hon Mrs J. M. The Corbett & Mr Chris Wright**
45 **SELENACHORUS,** b f Sea The Moon (GER)—Wood Chorus **Mrs P. B. E. P. Farr**
46 **SERAPHIA (IRE),** b f Dark Angel (IRE)—Lolwah **Lily & Andy Harter**
47 **SINDRI,** b f New Approach (IRE)—Marie Baa (FR) **Jastar Capital Limited**
48 **URBAN DECAY,** b f Frankel—Main Desire (IRE) **Clipper Group Holdings Ltd**
49 **WILDE AND DANDY,** b g Dandy Man (IRE)—Image **Mr D. Fravigar, Mr S. Jones & Partner**
50 **WILLOW TREE,** b f Harry Angel (IRE)—Bark (IRE) **The Gredley Family**

TWO-YEAR-OLDS

51 **A MAJOR PAYNE,** b c 01/04 Harry Angel (IRE)—Thankful (Diesis) (92000) **A Major Payne Syndicate**
52 B c 20/03 Noble Mission—Almashooqa (USA) (Dubawi (IRE)) (30000)
53 Br f 13/02 Wootton Bassett—Apres Midi (IRE) (Galileo (IRE)) (57000)
54 Ch f 26/02 Bated Breath—Ascended (IRE) (Dark Angel (IRE)) **Mrs Michelle Morris & K. Breen**
55 **BEVERAGINO (IRE),** br f 11/05 Soldier's Call—
Warm Welcome (Motivator) (58000) **Opulence Thoroughbreds & Partner**
56 **CLOUD FREE (IRE),** ch c 12/03 Sea The Stars (IRE)—
Fresnay (Rainbow Quest (USA)) (55000) **Mr David Fish & Partner**
57 B f 12/03 Oasis Dream—Coquet (Sir Percy) (50000) **Mr Jim Biggane & Partner**
58 Gr f 01/04 Phoenix of Spain (IRE)—Dreamaway (IRE) (Oasis Dream) (32013) **C. & D. Kilburn**
59 B c 05/04 Make Believe—Drifting Mist (Muhtathir) (35000) **Wayne & Sarah Dale & Ian Foster**
60 B c 21/03 Wootton Bassett—Elas Ruby (Raven's Pass (USA)) (55000)
61 **FOREST SPIRIT (IRE),** b gr f 02/05 Waldgeist—
Helisa (FR) (Elusive City (USA)) (55000) **Mrs G. Rowland Clark & Mr J. O'Connor**
62 **GALACTIC CHARM,** b c 10/02 Sea The Moon (GER)—
Gold Charm (GER) (Key of Luck (USA)) (48019) **Middleham Park Racing XV & Partner**
63 **HEATER (IRE),** br c 09/05 No Nay Never (USA)—Weekend Fling (USA) (Forest Wildcat (USA)) (145000) **Valmont**
64 B f 04/05 Showcasing—La Petite Reine (Galileo (IRE)) **Lady Bamford**
65 B c 01/05 Footstepsinthesand—Made By Hand (IRE) (Mastercraftsman (IRE)) **Lady Bamford**
66 **MART,** b gr c 04/02 Dark Angel (IRE)—Adorn (Kyllachy) (130000) **Valmont**
67 **MEDICIAN STAR (IRE),** b c 12/01 Galileo Gold—Excelled (IRE) (Exceed And Excel (AUS)) (28000) **Mr A. Bound**
68 B f 20/03 Awtaad (IRE)—Min Banat Alreeh (IRE) (Oasis Dream) (52381) **Mrs I Corbani & Partner**
69 B f 04/04 Masar (IRE)—Roman Holiday (IRE) (Holy Roman Emperor (IRE)) (27000) **Mr M. L. W. Bell**
70 **SCOTTISH BREEZE (IRE),** b c 29/03 Gleneagles (IRE)—
Tanyeli (IRE) (Mastercraftsman (IRE)) (44018) **Mr David Fish, Mrs E O'Leary & Partner**
71 B c 17/01 Territories (IRE)—Shiba (FR) (Rail Link) (75000) **Mr A. Bound**
72 **SHOW ME A HERO (IRE),** b c 30/03 Churchill (IRE)—
Vrai (IRE) (Dark Angel (IRE)) (50000) **Mr M. Buckley, Mrs E O'Leary & Partner**
73 **TRAMELL,** b f 25/04 Havana Gold (IRE)—Lavetta (Peintre Celebre (USA)) (26000) **Valmont**
74 B f 27/02 Iffraaj—Voge (IRE) (Clodovil (IRE)) (15000) **Wood Hall Stud Limited**

Assistant Trainer: Nick Bell.

Flat Jockey: Dylan Hogan. **Apprentice Jockey:** Joe Bradnam, Jay Mackay.

27 MR JAMES BENNETT, Wantage

Postal: **2 Filley Alley, Letcombe Bassett, Wantage, Oxfordshire, OX12 9LT**
Contacts: **PHONE 01235 762163 MOBILE 07771 523076**
EMAIL jbennett345@btinternet.com

1 **GONZAGA,** 8, b g Oasis Dream—Symposia **Miss J. C. Blackwell**
2 **PARISIAN PRINCESSE,** 7, ch m Schiaparelli (GER)—Princesse Katie (IRE) **Miss J. C. Blackwell**
3 **THE LAST MELON,** 11, ch g Sir Percy—Step Fast (USA) **Miss J. C. Blackwell**

Assistant Trainer: Jackie Blackwell.

NH Jockey: David Bass. **Conditional Jockey:** Harriet Tucker.

---

28 MR JOHN BERRY, Newmarket

Postal: **Beverley House Stables, Exeter Road, Newmarket, Suffolk, CB8 8LR**
Contacts: **PHONE 01638 660663**
EMAIL johnwathenberry@yahoo.co.uk WEBSITE www.johnberryracing.com

1 **BERYL BURTON,** 5, b m Sixties Icon—Miss Moses (USA) **Beryl's Bunch**
2 **CLOUDY ROSE,** 5, ch m Proconsul—Zarosa (IRE) **Runfortheroses**
3 **DAS KAPITAL,** 8, b g Cityscape—Narla **J. C. De P. Berry**
4 **DEREHAM,** 7, b g Sir Percy—Desiree (IRE) **Mrs E. L. Berry**
5 **DUCHESS (FR),** 4, b f The Grey Gatsby (IRE)—Queen To Be (IRE)
6 **ELJAYTEE (IRE),** 5, br g Rock of Gibraltar (IRE)—Yukon Girl (IRE) **Mr D. Tunmore**
7 **HIDDEN PEARL,** 7, ch m Dunaden (FR)—Volkovkha **The Sisters of Mercy & John Berry**
8 **LITTLE PETER,** 5, b g Mukhadram—Sweet Child O'Mine **Mr J. A. Byrne**
9 **MERRIJIG,** 5, b g Schiaparelli (GER)—Near Wild Heaven **The Beverley House Stables Partnership**
10 **MRS MAISEL,** 4, b f Dunaden (FR)—Minnie's Mystery (FR) **McCarthy & Berry**
11 **SUROOJ,** 6, br m Mukhadram—Eldalil **J. C. De P. Berry**
12 **TARBAT NESS,** 4, br gr g Reliable Man—Ethics Girl (IRE) **The 1997 Partnership & Rhd**
13 **TRUMPER,** 4, b g Jack Hobbs—Indira **J. C. De P. Berry**
14 **TURN OF PHRASE,** 6, ch m Kitten's Joy (USA)—Gotcha Good (USA) **The Sisters of Mercy & John Berry**

THREE-YEAR-OLDS

15 **FLYING STAR (IRE),** gr f Camacho—Guiletta (IRE)

TWO-YEAR-OLDS

16 **MORAL DILEMMA,** b f 14/02 Bobby's Kitten (USA)—Ethics Girl (IRE) (Hernando (FR))

Flat Jockey: Nicola Currie, John Egan, Josephine Gordon, Faye McManoman. **NH Jockey:** Will Kennedy, Jack Quinlan. **Amateur Jockey:** Mr R. Birkett, Mr F. Yarham.

---

29 MR JIM AND SUZI BEST, Lewes

Postal: **Grandstand Stables, The Old Racecourse, Lewes, Sussex, BN7 1UR**
Contacts: **PHONE 07804 487296**

1 **EARLY MORNING DEW (FR),** 7, ch g Muhtathir—Rosee Matinale (FR) **Mr Guy Dunphy & Mr Leon Best**
2 **EVENTFUL,** 6, b m Oasis Dream—Spectacle **Guy Dunphy, Chris Dillon, Mr C Seeney**
3 **FORLANO (FR),** 6, b g Papal Bull—Floriana (GER) **South Downs Super 6 & If Only Partnershp**
4 **GLOBAL WONDER (IRE),** 8, b g Kodiac—Traveller's Tales **The Global Wonder Partnership**
5 **GOOD OLD SUSSEX (IRE),** 5, gr m Sageburg (IRE)—Secret Leave **5 Jolly Boys Tc Matthews Mr T Helliwell**
6 **GOOD TIME AHEAD (IRE),** 9, b g Iffraaj—Good Time Sue (IRE) **G Dunphy, C Seeney, S Cooper-reade, Best**

MR JIM AND SUZI BEST - continued

7 **GRANDEE (IRE),** 9, b g Lope de Vega (IRE)—Caravan of Dreams (IRE) **Mr A Coupland, Mr C Dillon & Leon Best**
8 **GRANGECLARE NORTH (IRE),** 6, ch m Presenting—Hayabusa **If Only Partnership**
9 **GUINESSED (IRE),** 6, b m Sageburg (IRE)—Swap Shop (IRE) **Grandstand Stables Partnership**
10 **LADY SALVADOR (IRE),** 7, b m El Salvador (IRE)—Flora May **Mr J. R. D. Burnside**
11 **LEWESIAN LASS (IRE),** 6, b m Yeats (IRE)—O Mio My (IRE) **Lewes Dream Syndicate**
12 **NAUTICAL HAVEN,** 9, b g Harbour Watch (IRE)—Mania (IRE) **Mr Chris Dillon & Mr D G Edmonston**
13 **SOLID AS A ROCK (IRE),** 6, br m Malinas (GER)—Neat 'n Nimble **Mildean Racing & Cheam Marketing**
14 **THE TRAMPOLINIST (IRE),** 8, b m Flemensfirth (USA)—D'Gigi **If Only Partnership**
15 **WANG DANG DOODLE,** 8, b g Trans Island—Queen of The Blues (IRE) **If Only Partnership**
16 **WELLS GLORY (IRE),** 7, b g Fame And Glory—Annas Theatre **Milldean Racing Syndicate**

---

30 MR JOHN BEST AND KAREN JEWELL, Sittingbourne

Postal: **Eyehorn Farm, Munsgore Lane, Borden, Sittingbourne, Kent, ME9 8JU**
Contacts: **PHONE 07889 362154**
EMAIL office@bestjewellracing.com

1 **BELLA COLOROSSA,** 5, b m Toronado (IRE)—Shesells Seashells **Smarden Thoroughbreds**
2 **BERRAHRI (IRE),** 12, b g Bahri (USA)—Band of Colour (IRE) **Mr J. R. Best**
3 **BOLBERRY DOWN (IRE),** 7, ch g Frozen Power (IRE)—Miss Barbados (IRE) **Mr David Yeadon & Mrs Linda Jewell**
4 **CHEEKY CHESTER,** 4, ch g Life Force (IRE)—Indispensabelle **Mr R. Churcher**
5 **DANCE IN THE PARK,** 5, b m Walk In The Park (IRE)—Serpentine River (IRE) **Mr H J Jarvis & Mrs P Jarvis**
6 **DANCEN QUEEN (IRE),** 5, ch m Dansant—Virginia Woolf **Mrs L. C. Jewell**
7 **DANSIER (IRE),** 5, b g Dansant—Goodthyne Miss (IRE) **Mr H J Jarvis & Mrs P Jarvis**
8 **DELVEY (IRE),** 4, b f Iffraaj—Fashion Darling (IRE) **Curtis Bloodstock**
9 **DIVINATION (IRE),** 4, gr g Alhebayeb (IRE)—Maria Milena **Mrs L. C. Jewell**
10 **ELMEJOR (IRE),** 7, b g Xtension (IRE)—Lyca Ballerina **& Racing**
11 **ELZAARO (IRE),** 5, b g Elzaam (AUS)—Uncharted Waters (IRE) **Mr H J Jarvis & Mrs P Jarvis**
12 **GALWAY MAHLER (IRE),** 6, ch g Mahler—Kitty The Hare (IRE) **Peter & Linda Jewell**
13 **LADY BEACONSFIELD (IRE),** 4, b f Lawman (FR)—Belanoiva (IRE) **Mr S. D. Malcolm**
14 **MILLIES MITE (IRE),** 7, ch m Zoffany (IRE)—Charmingly (USA) **CS Partnership**
15 **PABLO PRINCE,** 5, b gr g Outstrip—French Accent **Littleoak Racing**
16 **PLEASURE GARDEN (USA),** 6, b g Union Rags (USA)—Garden of Eden (USA) **Mr H J Jarvis & Mrs P Jarvis**
17 **RED FLYER (IRE),** 5, ch g Free Eagle (IRE)—Hip **From Little Acorns Partnership**
18 **SANTIBURI SPIRIT,** 5, gr ro m Outstrip—Santiburi Spring **Hill Paine & Partners**
19 5, B g Kayf Tara—She's Humble (IRE) **Mr H J Jarvis & Mrs P Jarvis**
20 **SMARDEN FLYER (IRE),** 4, gr g Markaz (IRE)—Seminole Sun (IRE) **Mr K. De la Plain**
21 **TORBELLINO,** 7, b m Maxios—Tiny Smile (IRE) **Mr & Mrs N. F. Maltby**
22 **UALLRIGHTHARRY (IRE),** 11, b g Craigsteel—Enchanted Valley (IRE) **Mrs S. M. Stanier**

THREE-YEAR-OLDS

23 **MANILA MIST,** b f U S Navy Flag (USA)—Counterpoise **Mr H J Jarvis & Mrs P Jarvis**
24 **MARION OF ELMSTONE,** b f Golden Horn—Ever Love (BRZ) **Keaveney & Butcher**
25 B g Outstrip—Princess Spirit **Mr N. Dyshaev**
26 **TAKE MY BREATH (IRE),** b f Kuroshio (AUS)—Aberavon **Mr B. P. Keogh**

31 MR EDWARD BETHELL, Middleham

Postal: **Thorngill House, Middleham, Leyburn, Yorkshire, DL8 4TJ**
Contacts: **PHONE 07767 622921**
EMAIL edward@bethellracing.co.uk

1 **BIG CHEESE (FR),** 4, b g New Approach (IRE)—Kunegunda **The Earl Of Halifax**
2 **CHILLINGHAM (IRE),** 4, b g Ulysses (IRE)—Last Jewel (IRE) **Mr J Carrick & Mr S Taylor**
3 **EMILY POST,** 4, b f Charming Thought—Mary Read **Hot to Trot Racing 2**
4 **NIGWA,** 4, b f Sea The Stars (IRE)—Daban (IRE) **Abdullah Saeed Al Naboodah**
5 **POINT LYNAS (IRE),** 4, b g Iffraaj—Initially **Julie & David R Martin & Dan Hall**
6 **QUANTUM LEAP,** 4, ch g New Approach (IRE)—Disavow **Mr Richard Christison**
7 **REEL ROSIE (IRE),** 4, b f Highland Reel (IRE)—Lady Canford (IRE) **The Reel Wheelers and Dealers**
8 **REGIONAL,** 5, b g Territories (IRE)—Favulusa **Future Champions Racing Regional**
9 **SANDBECK,** 4, b f Ardad (IRE)—Astley Park **Mr David W. Armstrong**
10 **SKYE BREEZE (IRE),** 4, ch g Pride of Dubai (AUS)—Zelloof (IRE) **Mr M. Dawson**
11 **STELLAR QUEEN,** 4, b f Muhaarar—Bella Lulu **D & R Vickers Racing**

THREE-YEAR-OLDS

12 **BELLINGHAM,** ch c Dutch Art—Miss Meggy **Mr David W. Armstrong**
13 **CAPE POINT,** b f Muhaarar—Key Point (IRE) **Mr A. C. Cook**
14 **CHAOTIC,** gr g Bungle Inthejungle—Silver Games (IRE) **The Hon Mrs J. M. Corbett & Mr C. Wright**
15 **CHARLI SANDS (IRE),** b f Footstepsinthesand—Lady Canford (IRE) **Charli and the Dealmakers**
16 **CIG (IRE),** b g Fascinating Rock (IRE)—Eoz (IRE) **Julie & David R Martin & Dan Hall**
17 **CORNISH RIVIERA,** b f Zoustar (AUS)—Bournemouth Belle **Mr Jeremy Gompertz & Mr Patrick Milmo**
18 **COVERDALE (IRE),** b g Expert Eye—Brynica (FR) **Clarendon Thoroughbred Racing**
19 **DREAM FINAL,** b g Mukhadram—Fen Ali **Mr M. M. Foulger**
20 **ELIM (IRE),** b f Make Believe—Majestic Dancer (IRE) **Julie & David R Martin & Dan Hall**
21 **INDIANA BE,** b g Sioux Nation (USA)—Because (IRE) **Mr J Carrick & Mr S Taylor**
22 **INITIO,** b g Highland Reel (IRE)—Khobaraa **Mr M. Rozenbroek**
23 **JAMES MCHENRY,** gr c Starspangledbanner (AUS)—Savvy (IRE) **Mr Peter Jeffers**
24 **KARDIA,** b f Kingman—Elpida (USA) **St Albans Bloodstock Limited**
25 **LADY ROAMER,** b f Oasis Dream—Royal Eloquence (IRE) **C. Lewis (UK) Ltd**
26 **LERWICK,** b g Awtaad (IRE)—Mystique **The Marquess of Zetland**
27 **LOWTON,** b c Pivotal—Heskin (IRE) **Mr David W. Armstrong**
28 **MASTER CHARTWELL (IRE),** b c Churchill (IRE)—Springlike (IRE) **Mr P. B. Moorhead**
29 **MINT EDITION,** b g Showcasing—Starflower **Titanium Racing Club**
30 **MOUNTAIN WARRIOR,** b g Brazen Beau (AUS)—Plucky **Paul Morrison & James Lambert**
31 **NUKETOWN (IRE),** b c Oasis Dream—Comeback Queen **Kingwood Stud Management Co Ltd**
32 **OPEN CHOICE (USA),** ch c Classic Empire (USA)—Miss Mockingbird (USA) **Mr Peter Jeffers**
33 **OVIEDO (IRE),** b c Lope de Vega (IRE)—Gallitea (IRE) **Ms Fiona Carmichael & Ballylinch Stud**
34 **PENDLEBURY LANE,** b f Pivotal—Hilldale **Mr David W. Armstrong**
35 **POWERFUL RESPONSE (IRE),** b c Starspangledbanner (AUS)—Aja (IRE)
36 **QUANDARY,** ch f Intello (GER)—Augusta Ada **Sigsworth Partners**
37 **ROCK OF ENGLAND (IRE),** ch g Unfortunately (IRE)—Miss Fay (IRE) **Ricky Martin Philips & Jim Morris**
38 **SWANLAND (IRE),** b g Profitable (IRE)—Water Hole (IRE) **Mr G. N. van Cutsem**
39 **TIAMAT (IRE),** b f Aclaim (IRE)—Tenerife Song **Kingwood Stud Management Co Ltd**
40 **YORKSHIRE (IRE),** b c Harry Angel (IRE)—Totsiyah (IRE) **Clarendon Thoroughbred Racing**

TWO-YEAR-OLDS

41 **ANGEL OF ENGLAND,** b c 29/01 Harry Angel (IRE)—
Poana (FR) (New Approach (IRE)) (22857) **Ricky Martin Philips & Jim Morris**
42 **BERRYGATE (IRE),** gr ro f 22/04 Gregorian (IRE)—
Jungle Secret (IRE) (Bungle Inthejungle) (23000) **Clarendon Thoroughbred Racing**
43 B f 22/03 Profitable (IRE)—Coolminx (IRE) (One Cool Cat (USA)) **Mr David Howden & Mr David Redvers**
44 Br f 03/02 Caravaggio (USA)—Cosmogyral (IRE) (Camelot) **Kingwood Stud Management Co Ltd**
45 B c 31/03 Twilight Son—Dance Diva (Mayson) (85000) **Titanium Racing Club**
46 B g 30/04 Territories (IRE)—Dharwa (Equiano (FR)) (7000) **Mr M. Rozenbroek**
47 **GRESSINGTON (IRE),** ch c 11/03 Outstrip—Silver Games (IRE) (Verglas (IRE)) **Mr C Wright & Mr D Kilburn**
48 B f 22/04 Ten Sovereigns (IRE)—
Habbat Reeh (IRE) (Mastercraftsman (IRE)) (52000) **Clarendon Thoroughbred Racing**

MR EDWARD BETHELL - continued

49 **HAVANA ROSE (IRE),** gr f 24/01 Havana Gold (IRE)—
Rue Bonaparte (IRE) (Dark Angel (IRE)) (19208) **Richard Christison / Nicola Alton**
50 **MARIANGLAS (IRE),** b f 20/01 Almanzor (FR)—
Firelight (FR) (Oasis Dream) (75000) **Julie & David R Martin & Dan Hall**
51 Ch c 27/02 Dutch Art—Melrose Way (Mayson) **Mr David W. Armstrong**
52 B f 09/02 Mayson—Ocean Boulevard (Danehill Dancer (IRE)) **Mr David W. Armstrong**
53 **OLD COCK (IRE),** b c 14/04 Calyx—Love Potion (IRE) (Galileo (IRE)) (32000) **Mr & Mrs David Aykroyd**
54 B c 05/03 Soldier's Call—Parle Moi (USA) (Giant's Causeway (USA)) (20000) **Clarendon Thoroughbred Racing**
55 B c 12/03 Recoletos (FR)—Patuano (IRE) (Choisir (AUS)) (28000) **The Yorbus Syndicate**
56 **RICH GLORY (IRE),** b c 04/02 Cotai Glory—Zalpa (USA) (More Than Ready (USA)) (45000) **D & R Vickers Racing**
57 B c 11/03 Advertise—Twist Moor Lane (Mayson) **Mr David W. Armstrong**
58 B f 06/04 Too Darn Hot—Victorian Beauty (USA) (Rahy (USA)) (42000) **Mrs Charles Cyzer**
59 **VITRINA,** ch f 15/03 Showcasing—Elpida (USA) (Giant's Causeway (USA)) **St Albans Bloodstock Limited**
60 B f 11/03 Highland Reel (IRE)—Xaloc (IRE) (Shirocco (GER)) **Mr M. Rozenbroek**

---

32 MISS HARRIET BETHELL, Arnold

Postal: **Arnold Manor, Black Tup Lane, Arnold, Hull, Yorkshire, HU11 5JA**
EMAIL harrietbethell@hotmail.co.uk

1 **BEARWITH,** 5, gr g Brazen Beau (AUS)—Baylini **The Rise One Partnership**
2 **CHINESE WHISPERER (FR),** 6, b g Poet's Voice—Shanghai Noon (FR) **W. A. Bethell**
3 **DHARAN (FR),** 10, b g Slickly Royal (FR)—Kelle Home (FR) **W. A. Bethell**
4 **HOOFLEPUFF (IRE),** 7, b g Gale Force Ten—Hflah (IRE) **Mr K. Brown**
5 **ISLE OF WOLVES,** 7, b g Nathaniel (IRE)—L'Ile Aux Loups (IRE) **W. A. Bethell**
6 **LOPES DANCER (IRE),** 11, b g Lope de Vega (IRE)—Ballet Dancer (IRE) **W. A. Bethell**
7 **MIAMI PRESENT (IRE),** 13, b br g Presenting—Miami Nights (GER) **W. A. Bethell**
8 **NEWBERRY NEW (IRE),** 11, b g Kodiac—Sunblush (UAE) **W. A. Bethell**
9 **ON THE RIVER,** 4, b g Heeraat (IRE)—Lady Lekki (IRE) **W. A. Bethell**
10 **STEEL HELMET (IRE),** 9, ch g Helmet (AUS)—Marine City (JPN) **W. A. Bethell**
11 **YANIFER,** 5, b g Dandy Man (IRE)—Fondie (IRE) **T & W Bethell**

THREE-YEAR-OLDS

12 **ORIGINAL THINKER,** b f Oasis Dream—Royal Rascal **N. H. T. Wrigley**

Trainer did not supply details of their two-year-olds.

Flat Jockey: Josephine Gordon, Cam Hardie, Jo Mason. **NH Jockey:** Harry Bannister.

---

33 MR ROBERT BEVIS, Duckington

Postal: **The White House, Old Coach Road, Duckington, Cheshire, SY14 8LH**
EMAIL robertjbevis66@aol.com

1 **DANILO D'AIRY (FR),** 10, ch g Anzillero (GER)—Monita d'Airy (FR) **R. J. Bevis**
2 **DIAMAND DE VINDECY (FR),** 4, b g Diamond Green (FR)—Miss Chic'vindecy (FR) **E. Williams & J. Brooke**
3 **IMPERIAL CLOUD (IRE),** 6, b g Saddler Maker (IRE)—Ringaround **Imperial Racing Partnership 2016**
4 **LARKIN (IRE),** 4, gr g Dark Angel (IRE)—Plagiarism (USA) **R. J. Bevis**
5 **MASKED ARTIST,** 6, b m Masked Marvel—Definite Artist (IRE) **Port Antonio Syndicate**
6 **QUITE THE GETAWAY,** 5, gr m Getaway (GER)—Buddy Love **R. Bevis**
7 **TURNING GOLD,** 9, ch g Pivotal—Illusion **R. J. Bevis**
8 **UNBLINKING,** 10, b g Cacique (IRE)—Deliberate **R. Bevis**

---

34 MR GEORGE BEWLEY, Appleby-In-Westmorland

Postal: **Jerusalem Farm, Colby, Appleby-In-Westmorland, Cumbria, CA16 6BB**
Contacts: **PHONE 017683 53003 MOBILE 07704 924783**
EMAIL bewleyracing@outlook.com WEBSITE www.georgebewleyracing.co.uk

1 **ALCANTANGO (IRE),** 6, ch g Getaway (GER)—Rathleek **Mr A. Udale**
2 **AZOF DES MOTTES (FR),** 6, b g Sinndar (IRE)—Wavy (FR) **Montgomerie, Mandle, Annett & Davidson**
3 **BREAKING THE ICE (IRE),** 8, b g Frozen Power (IRE)—Specific (IRE) **Montgomerie & Bewley**
4 **BROOMFIELDS KAN (IRE),** 8, gr g Arakan (USA)—Roses And Wine (IRE) **Southdean Racing Club**
5 **CLONDAW FIXER (IRE),** 11, b g Court Cave (IRE)—The Millers Tale (IRE) **Mrs C. J. Todd**
6 **FAMOUS RESPONSE (IRE),** 9, b g Fame And Glory—Any Response (IRE) **Mr R Fisher & Bewley**
7 **FOLLOW YOUR ARROW (FR),** 7, b br g Crillon (FR)—Rakane Rouge (FR) **Annett, Richardson, Eales & Todd**
8 **FOXWOOD (IRE),** 5, b g Milan—She Took A Tree (FR) **J. Wade**
9 **GLENAVADDRA (IRE),** 7, br g Jet Away—Kerryhead Sunshine (IRE) **Holland & Bewley**
10 **HOGANVILLE (IRE),** 6, b g Frozen Fire (GER)—Wings To Soar (USA) **Annett, Gibson & Holland**
11 **HUNGRY TIGER (IRE),** 9, b g Morozov (USA)—Ballinamona Wish (IRE) **Mrs C. Holland**
12 **LIGHTS ARE GREEN (IRE),** 6, b g Califet (FR)—Katjakem (IRE) **Miss V. F. Bewley**
13 **LOVELY MOON (IRE),** 8, b g Le Fou (IRE)—Half The Battle (IRE) **Annett, Mandle & Davidson**
14 **MAH MATE BOB (IRE),** 11, b g Mahler—Bobset Leader (IRE) **J. Wade**
15 **MALIN DAZE (IRE),** 5, b g Milan—Daisy's Sister **J. Wade**
16 **PADDY THE HORSE (IRE),** 8, b g Imperial Monarch (IRE)—Dendelady (IRE) **Mr A. Udale**
17 **ROBERT D'ORES (FR),** 6, gr g Great Pretender (IRE)—Sister du Berlais (FR) **Mr A. Udale**
18 **ROCCO MOLLY,** 6, b m Shirocco (GER)—Langley House (IRE) **Mr E. G. Tunstall**
19 **STAR VANTAGE (IRE),** 6, b g Ocovango—Laura's Star (IRE) **J. Wade**
20 **STRIKE OF LIGHTING (IRE),** 7, ch g Jet Away—Will She Smile (IRE) **Montgomerie, Atkinson & Graham**
21 **WAR AT SEA (IRE),** 9, gr g Mastercraftsman (IRE)—Swirling (IRE) **Mrs Lesley Bewley & Mr John Gibson**
22 **WELL EDUCATED (IRE),** 7, ch g Getaway (GER)—Collegeofknowledge **Annett & Mandle**

NH Jockey: Jonathon Bewley.

---

35 MR SAEED BIN SUROOR, Newmarket

Postal: **Godolphin Office, Snailwell Road, Newmarket, Suffolk, CB8 7YE**
Contacts: **PHONE 01638 569956**
WEBSITE www.godolphin.com

1 **ARABIAN WARRIOR,** 6, b g Dubawi (IRE)—Siyaadah **Godolphin Management Company Ltd**
2 **BEAUTIFUL SECRET,** 4, b f Invincible Spirit (IRE)—Beautiful Forest **Godolphin Management Company Ltd**
3 **BIG MEETING (IRE),** 6, b br g Shamardal (USA)—Beta **Godolphin Management Company Ltd**
4 **BIG TEAM (USA),** 6, b br g Speightstown (USA)—Kotuku **Godolphin Management Company Ltd**
5 **BRIGHT START (USA),** 6, b br g Medaglia d'Oro (USA)—Blue Petrel (USA) **Godolphin Management Company Ltd**
6 **BRILLIANT LIGHT,** 6, b g Sea The Stars (IRE)—Flame of Gibraltar (IRE) **Godolphin Management Company Ltd**
7 **CITY WALK (IRE),** 6, b g Brazen Beau (AUS)—My Lucky Liz (IRE) **Godolphin Management Company Ltd**
8 **COLOUR IMAGE (IRE),** 6, b g Kodiac—Chroussa (IRE) **Godolphin Management Company Ltd**
9 **DESERT FIRE (IRE),** 8, b g Cape Cross (IRE)—Crystal House (CHI) **Godolphin Management Company Ltd**
10 **DUBAI FUTURE,** 7, b g Dubawi (IRE)—Anjaz (USA) **Godolphin Management Company Ltd**
11 **DUBAI LEGACY (USA),** 7, b g Discreet Cat (USA)—Afsana (USA) **Godolphin Management Company Ltd**
12 **DUBAI MIRAGE (IRE),** 6, ch g Dubawi (IRE)—Callpatria **Godolphin Management Company Ltd**
13 **DUBAI SOUQ (IRE),** 6, b g Dubawi (IRE)—Balsamine (USA) **Godolphin Management Company Ltd**
14 **DUBAI WELCOME,** 6, gr ro g Dubawi (IRE)—Emily Bronte **Godolphin Management Company Ltd**
15 **ELECTRICAL STORM,** 6, b g Dubawi (IRE)—Mujarah (IRE) **Godolphin Management Company Ltd**
16 **FIRST VIEW (IRE),** 6, b g Exceed And Excel (AUS)—Love Charm **Godolphin Management Company Ltd**
17 **FUTURE KING (IRE),** 6, b g Dark Angel (IRE)—Relation Alexander (IRE) **Godolphin Management Company Ltd**
18 **GHALY,** 7, ch g Dubawi (IRE)—Hanky Panky (IRE) **Godolphin Management Company Ltd**
19 **GLOBAL HEAT (IRE),** 7, b g Toronado (IRE)—Raskutani **Godolphin Management Company Ltd**
20 **GLOBAL WALK (IRE),** 6, b g Society Rock (IRE)—Shehila (IRE) **Godolphin Management Company Ltd**
21 **GREAT HUNTER (IRE),** 5, gr g Dark Angel (IRE)—Floristry **Godolphin Management Company Ltd**

MR SAEED BIN SUROOR - continued

22 **GREAT NEWS,** 5, gr g Shamardal (USA)—Nahoodh (IRE) **Godolphin Management Company Ltd**
23 **HOME CITY (IRE),** 4, b g Profitable (IRE)—Nafura **Godolphin Management Company Ltd**
24 **ISLAND FALCON (IRE),** 4, b br c Iffraaj—Adoringly (IRE) **Godolphin Management Company Ltd**
25 **LAND OF LEGENDS (IRE),** 7, b br g Iffraaj—Homily **Godolphin Management Company Ltd**
26 **LASER SHOW (IRE),** 6, ch g New Approach (IRE)—Entertains (AUS) **Godolphin Management Company Ltd**
27 **LIGHT AND DARK,** 7, b g Shamardal (USA)—Colour (AUS) **Godolphin Management Company Ltd**
28 **LIVE YOUR DREAM (IRE),** 6, b g Iffraaj—Dream Book **Godolphin Management Company Ltd**
29 **LONG TRADITION (IRE),** 6, b g Shamardal (USA)—Irish History (IRE) **Godolphin Management Company Ltd**
30 **MAJOR PARTNERSHIP (IRE),** 8, gr g Iffraaj—Roystonea **Godolphin Management Company Ltd**
31 **MARCHING ARMY,** 5, ch g Iffraaj—Show Day (IRE) **Godolphin Management Company Ltd**
32 **MILITARY MARCH,** 6, b g New Approach (IRE)—Punctilious **Godolphin Management Company Ltd**
33 **MO'ASSESS (IRE),** 5, ch g Pivotal—Hush Money (CHI) **Godolphin Management Company Ltd**
34 **MOVING LIGHT (IRE),** 6, ch g Night of Thunder (IRE)—
North East Bay (USA) **Godolphin Management Company Ltd**
35 **MUTAFAWWIG,** 7, b g Oasis Dream—Reunite (IRE) **Godolphin Management Company Ltd**
36 **NADER,** 4, b g Iffraaj—Manaboo (USA) **Godolphin Management Company Ltd**
37 **NIGHT HUNTER (USA),** 6, gr g Tapit (USA)—Wickedly Wise (USA) **Godolphin Management Company Ltd**
38 **NIGHT OF LUXURY,** 4, b g Postponed (IRE)—Moonlife (IRE) **Godolphin Management Company Ltd**
39 **OPEN MIND,** 4, br g Cable Bay (IRE)—Bonhomie **Godolphin Management Company Ltd**
40 **PASSION AND GLORY (IRE),** 7, b g Cape Cross (IRE)—
Potent Embrace (USA) **Godolphin Management Company Ltd**
41 **PIECE OF HISTORY (IRE),** 8, b g Iffraaj—Moonlife (IRE) **Godolphin Management Company Ltd**
42 **RAYAT (IRE),** 4, b g Starspangledbanner (AUS)—Violet's Gift (IRE) **Godolphin Management Company Ltd**
43 **REAL WORLD (IRE),** 6, b g Dark Angel (IRE)—Nafura **Godolphin Management Company Ltd**
44 **RETURN TO DUBAI (IRE),** 4, ch g Ribchester (IRE)—Farthing (IRE) **Godolphin Management Company Ltd**
45 **SECRET MOMENT (IRE),** 6, b g Exceed And Excel (AUS)—Devotee (USA) **Godolphin Management Company Ltd**
46 **SHINING BLUE (IRE),** 5, b g Exceed And Excel (AUS)—Braided (USA) **Godolphin Management Company Ltd**
47 **SHINING EXAMPLE (IRE),** 6, b g Shamardal (USA)—Kailani **Godolphin Management Company Ltd**
48 **SOFT WHISPER (IRE),** 5, b m Dubawi (IRE)—Placidia (IRE) **Godolphin Management Company Ltd**
49 **STORM FRONT,** 5, ch g Helmet (AUS)—Vituisa **Godolphin Management Company Ltd**
50 **UNTOLD STORY,** 6, ch g Teofilo (IRE)—Tanzania (USA) **Godolphin Management Company Ltd**
51 **WHITE MOONLIGHT (USA),** 6, b m Medaglia d'Oro (USA)—
Fitful Skies (IRE) **Godolphin Management Company Ltd**
52 **WHITE WOLF (IRE),** 4, b g Invincible Spirit (IRE)—Long Lashes (USA) **Godolphin Management Company Ltd**
53 **WILD HURRICANE (IRE),** 5, b g Dubawi (IRE)—Wavering (IRE) **Godolphin Management Company Ltd**
54 **WILD LION (IRE),** 5, ch g The Last Lion (IRE)—Snow Powder (IRE) **Godolphin Management Company Ltd**
55 **WILD PLACE (IRE),** 4, b f Mehmas (IRE)—Turuqaat **Godolphin Management Company Ltd**
56 **WILD TIGER,** 4, b g Frankel—Antara (GER) **Godolphin Management Company Ltd**

THREE-YEAR-OLDS

57 **AIN DUBAI (IRE),** b c Iffraaj—La Rosetta **Godolphin Management Company Ltd**
58 **AL KHAZNEH (IRE),** b g Exceed And Excel (AUS)—Heartily (IRE) **Godolphin Management Company Ltd**
59 **AL WASL DREAM (IRE),** b g Invincible Spirit (IRE)—Aurora Leigh **Godolphin Management Company Ltd**
60 B f Dark Angel (IRE)—Albasharah (USA) **Godolphin Management Company Ltd**
61 **BANDDAR (IRE),** gr g Dark Angel (IRE)—Good Place (USA) **Godolphin Management Company Ltd**
62 B f Dark Angel (IRE)—Betimes **Godolphin Management Company Ltd**
63 **BLACK DIAMOND (IRE),** b f Dark Angel (IRE)—Long Lashes (USA) **Godolphin Management Company Ltd**
64 B f Exceed And Excel (AUS)—Days of Old **Godolphin Management Company Ltd**
65 **DEEP THOUGHTS,** b f Lope de Vega (IRE)—Bint Almatar (USA) **Godolphin Management Company Ltd**
66 **DUBAI VIEW,** b c Caravaggio (USA)—Tandragee (USA) **Godolphin Management Company Ltd**
67 B f Teofilo (IRE)—Dutota Desejada (BRZ) **Godolphin Management Company Ltd**
68 **EGYPTIAN KING (IRE),** b c Fast Company (IRE)—Belle Boyd **Godolphin Management Company Ltd**
69 **ENDLESS WHISPER,** b f Teofilo (IRE)—All Clear **Godolphin Management Company Ltd**
70 **FIRST MAGIC (IRE),** ro f Mastercraftsman (IRE)—Hawsa (USA) **Godolphin Management Company Ltd**
71 Gr f Dubawi (IRE)—Heart's Content (IRE) **Godolphin Management Company Ltd**
72 **ICE CLIMBER,** b gr c Dark Angel (IRE)—Dark Orchid (USA) **Godolphin Management Company Ltd**
73 B c Nathaniel (IRE)—Lura (USA) **Godolphin Management Company Ltd**
74 **MAWJ (IRE),** b f Exceed And Excel (AUS)—Modern Ideals **Godolphin Management Company Ltd**
75 B c Ribchester (IRE)—Michita (USA) **Godolphin Management Company Ltd**

MR SAEED BIN SUROOR - continued

76 MOUNTAIN LAKE, b f Postponed (IRE)—Moonsail **Godolphin Management Company Ltd**
77 NEW TERRITORY, ch c Postponed (IRE)—Perfect Light (IRE) **Godolphin Management Company Ltd**
78 OPEN ROAD (IRE), b c Teofilo (IRE)—West Wind **Godolphin Management Company Ltd**
79 OPEN STORY (IRE), b f Invincible Spirit (IRE)—Aiming For Rio (FR) **Godolphin Management Company Ltd**
80 B c Dubawi (IRE)—Pleascach (IRE) **Godolphin Management Company Ltd**
81 B f Iffraaj—Ragsah (IRE) **Godolphin Management Company Ltd**
82 Ch f Harry Angel (IRE)—Saoirse Abu (USA) **Godolphin Management Company Ltd**
83 STAND STRONG, ch c Cracksman—Summer Flower (IRE) **Godolphin Management Company Ltd**
84 SUMMER SOLSTICE (IRE), b f Exceed And Excel (AUS)—Bitter Lake (USA) **Godolphin Management Company Ltd**
85 TOMOUH DUBAI (IRE), b f Iffraaj—Flora Sandes (USA) **Godolphin Management Company Ltd**

TWO-YEAR-OLDS

86 Ch c 04/03 Iffraaj—Bint Almatar (USA) (Kingmambo (USA)) **Godolphin Management Company Ltd**
87 B c 03/03 Shamardal (USA)—Carriwitchet (IRE) (Dubawi (IRE)) **Godolphin Management Company Ltd**
88 B c 23/02 Profitable (IRE)—Delphinidae (IRE) (Sepoy (AUS)) **Godolphin Management Company Ltd**
89 B f 17/02 Farhh—Ethereal Sky (IRE) (Invincible Spirit (IRE)) **Godolphin Management Company Ltd**
90 Gr f 22/03 Blue Point (IRE)—Fire Blaze (IRE) (Dubawi (IRE)) **Godolphin Management Company Ltd**
91 Gr c 26/04 Invincible Spirit (IRE)—Isabella Linton (IRE) (New Approach (IRE)) **Godolphin Management Company Ltd**
92 B f 14/02 Exceed And Excel (AUS)—Juneau (IRE) (Dubawi (IRE)) **Godolphin Management Company Ltd**
93 B c 05/05 Exceed And Excel (AUS)—Karenine (High Chaparral (IRE)) **Godolphin Management Company Ltd**
94 B f 21/02 Blue Point (IRE)—Luceita (IRE) (Dawn Approach (IRE)) **Godolphin Management Company Ltd**
95 B f 13/03 Invincible Spirit (IRE)—Lura (USA) (Street Cry (IRE)) **Godolphin Management Company Ltd**
96 B c 28/04 Night of Thunder (IRE)—Manaboo (USA) (Hard Spun (USA)) **Godolphin Management Company Ltd**
97 B f 11/04 Iffraaj—Panegyric (Monsun (GER)) **Godolphin Management Company Ltd**
98 B c 28/02 Night of Thunder (IRE)—Peace Trail (Kyllachy) **Godolphin Management Company Ltd**
99 B c 04/02 Masar (IRE)—Punctilious (Danehill (USA)) **Godolphin Management Company Ltd**
100 B f 20/03 Kingman—Qualify (IRE) (Fastnet Rock (AUS)) **Godolphin Management Company Ltd**
101 B c 22/02 Kodiac—Saoirse Abu (USA) (Mr Greeley (USA)) **Godolphin Management Company Ltd**
102 B f 07/02 Night of Thunder (IRE)—Seneca Falls (Invincible Spirit (IRE)) **Godolphin Management Company Ltd**
103 B c 04/02 Belardo (IRE)—Silk Words (Dubawi (IRE)) **Godolphin Management Company Ltd**
104 B c 19/02 Profitable (IRE)—Snowstar (IRE) (Raven's Pass (USA)) **Godolphin Management Company Ltd**
105 B c 06/02 Dark Angel (IRE)—Wanderwell (New Approach (IRE)) **Godolphin Management Company Ltd**

Assistant Trainer: Anthony Paul Howarth.

36

MRS EMMA-JANE BISHOP, Cheltenham

Postal: **Brockhill, Naunton, Cheltenham, Gloucestershire, GL54 3BA**
Contacts: **MOBILE 07887 845970 FAX 01451 850199**
EMAIL emmabishopracing@hotmail.com WEBSITE www.emmabishopracing.com

1 ANOTHER GLANCE, 7, br m Passing Glance—Roberta Back (IRE) **Emma Bishop Racing Club**
2 BOURDING PASS, 4, b g Passing Glance—Bourdello
3 FORCE DE FRAP (FR), 8, b g Desir d'Un Soir (FR)—Flaurella (FR) **Mrs E. J. Bishop**
4 HAAFBACK, 5, b g Haafhd—Roberta Back (IRE) **Mrs J. Arnold**
5 HAAFBOURD, 5, b g Haafhd—Bourdello **Mrs J. Arnold**
6 MASTER MALCOLM, 6, ch g Mastercraftsman (IRE)—Desert Sage **Mrs C. Richmond-Watson**
7 MAX DYNAMO, 13, b g Midnight Legend—Vivante (IRE) **Mrs M. J. Wilson**
8 RUBY'S PEARL, 6, b m Passing Glance—Ruby Valentine (FR) **Mrs M. J. Wilson**
9 STAAR (IRE), 9, b g Sea The Stars (IRE)—Bitooh **Mrs J. Arnold**
10 THEOULE (FR), 7, b br g Le Havre (IRE)—Santa Louisia **Emma Bishop Racing Club**

---

37 MISS CATRIONA BISSETT, Leslie

Postal: **East Bowhouse Farm, Leslie, Glenrothes, Fife, KY6 3JH**
Contacts: **PHONE 07581 367154**
EMAIL catchbissett@live.co.uk

1 **BRAVE BAIRN (FR),** 7, b m Brave Mansonnien (FR)—Miss Laveron (FR) **Bissett Racing**
2 **BRAY DALE,** 6, b g Scorpion (IRE)—Cherry West (IRE) **Bissett Racing**
3 **HELL ON EARTH (IRE),** 9, gr g Germany (USA)—Ceol Tire (IRE) **Bissett Racing**
4 **LEWA HOUSE,** 7, b g Yeats (IRE)—Primrose Time **Bissett Racing**
5 **RYEDALE RACER,** 12, b g Indian Danehill (IRE)—Jontys' lass **Bissett Racing**

38 MISS LINDA BLACKFORD, Tiverton

Postal: **Shortlane Stables, Rackenford, Tiverton, Devon, EX16 8EH**
Contacts: **PHONE 01884 881589 MOBILE 07887 947832**
EMAIL overthelast@outlook.com WEBSITE www.overthelast.com

1 **BAILY GORSE (IRE),** 9, b g Milan—Lillies Bordello (IRE) **Mrs V. W. Jones & Mr B. P. Jones**
2 **LURE DES PRES (IRE),** 11, b g Robin des Pres (FR)—Pinkeen Lady (IRE) **Mr M. J. Vanstone**
3 **POET'S REFLECTION (IRE),** 8, b m Dylan Thomas (IRE)—Lola's Reflection **Mrs S. H. Livesey-Van Dorst**
4 **PRINCE RHINEGOLD (IRE),** 5, b g Getaway (GER)—Water Rock **Mrs D Robinson Mrs&Mrs Livesey-Van Dorst**
5 **RANGATIRA JACK,** 5, ch g Mount Nelson—Woodland Walk **Mrs D Robinson Mrs & Mrs Livesey-Van Dorst**

Assistant Trainer: M. J. Vanstone.

NH Jockey: James Best, Micheal Nolan, Nick Scholfield. **Conditional Jockey:** Sean Houlihan.

39 MR MICHAEL BLAKE, Trowbridge

Postal: **Staverton Farm, Trowbridge, Wiltshire, BA14 6PE**
Contacts: **PHONE 01225 782327 MOBILE 07971 675180**
EMAIL mblakestavertonfarm@btinternet.com WEBSITE www.michaelblakeracing.co.uk

1 **ATHEBY,** 4, b g Gutaifan (IRE)—Meet Marhaba (IRE) **Racing For A Cause**
2 **BOUNTY PURSUIT,** 11, b g Pastoral Pursuits—Poyle Dee Dee **Racing For A Cause**
3 **CLEARANCE,** 9, b g Authorized (IRE)—Four Miracles **Racing For A Cause**
4 **EAGLE COURT (IRE),** 6, b g Free Eagle (IRE)—Classic Remark (IRE) **Mr A. D. Potts**
5 **LOVE DREAMS (IRE),** 9, b g Dream Ahead (USA)—Kimola (IRE) **Mr A. D. Potts**
6 **MR ZEE (IRE),** 6, b g Zebedee—Monsusu (IRE) **Staverton Owners Group**
7 **PADLEYOUROWNCANOE,** 9, b g Nayef (USA)—Pooka's Daughter (IRE) **K.A.C. Bloodstock Limited**
8 **ROCKTREERUNNER,** 6, ch m Saddler's Rock (IRE)—Gaelic Gold (IRE) **K.A.C. Bloodstock Limited**
9 **UNDER THE TWILIGHT,** 5, b m Twilight Son—Rococoa (IRE) **Mr R. Gould**
10 **WE'RE REUNITED (IRE),** 6, b g Kodiac—Caelis **Staverton Owners Group**
11 **WOTASTUNNER,** 6, b g Passing Glance—Posh Emily **R. J. House**

Assistant Trainer: Sharon Blake.

40 MISS GILLIAN BOANAS, Saltburn

Postal: **Groundhill Farm, Lingdale, Saltburn-By-The-Sea, Cleveland, TS12 3HD**
Contacts: **MOBILE 07976 280154**
EMAIL gillianboanas@aol.com

1 **ARMY'S DREAM (IRE),** 6, b g Dylan Thomas (IRE)—Cappa Or (IRE) **WASPS Syndicate**
2 **BABY JANE (IRE),** 8, b m Oscar (IRE)—Young Lady (IRE) **Miss G. L. Boanas**
3 **BALCOMIE BREEZE (FR),** 5, b g Joshua Tree (IRE)—The Lady Maggi (FR) **Mr A. N. Seymour**
4 **BESTIARIUS (IRE),** 11, b g Vinnie Roe (IRE)—Chione (IRE) **Gillian Boanas & Douglas Renton**
5 **BRIDGET BREEZE (FR),** 6, gr m Montmartre (FR)—The Lady Maggi (FR) **Gary Wood & Neil Hixon**
6 **BROCTUNE AZURE,** 5, b m Cannock Chase (USA)—Fairlie **Mrs M. B. Thwaites**
7 **BROCTUNE RED,** 8, ch g Haafhd—Fairlie **Mrs M. B. Thwaites**
8 **CRIXUS'S ESCAPE (IRE),** 10, ch g Beneficial—Tierneys Choice (IRE) **Rug, Grub & Pub Partnership**
9 **FLEXI FURLOUGH (IRE),** 7, gr m Milan—Young Lady (IRE) **Douglas & David Barclay**
10 **GREAT COLACI,** 10, b g Sulamani (IRE)—Fairlie **Rug, Grub & Pub Partnership**
11 **HIGH SHERIFF (IRE),** 9, b g Fame And Glory—Morning Legend (IRE) **Mrs K. Elliott**
12 **JACK OF ALL SHAPES (IRE),** 7, b g Arcadio (GER)—Arequipa (IRE) **Rug, Grub & Pub Partnership**
13 **JUST CALL ME AL (IRE),** 10, br g Presenting—Tonaphuca Girl (IRE) **M.B.Thwaites G Halder**
14 4, B f Milan—Kitty Power (IRE) **Miss G. L. Boanas**
15 5, B m Kayf Tara—La Calinda **Tees Components Ltd**
16 **LOCH LINNHE,** 11, b g Tobougg (IRE)—Quistaquay **Miss G. L. Boanas**
17 **LUNAR GLOW,** 5, b m Pether's Moon (IRE)—Just For Pleasure (IRE) **R & & Harwood**
18 **MAD ARTYMAISE (IRE),** 4, ch f Dandy Man (IRE)—El Mirage (IRE) **Smith, White G Wood**
19 **MOROCCAN MOON,** 4, b f Pether's Moon (IRE)—Atomic Tangerine **Supreme Partners & Rosie Robson-tinsley**
20 4, B f Westerner—New Targets (IRE) **Mr John Coates Mr Richard Smith**
21 5, Ch g Black Sam Bellamy (IRE)—Northern Native (IRE) **Tees Components Ltd**
22 **ON WE GO (IRE),** 10, b m Robin des Pres (FR)—Clan Music (IRE) **Mrs K. Elliott**
23 **POUND OFF YOU,** 7, ch m Haafhd—Let It Be **Miss G. L. Boanas**
24 **SULTANS PRIDE,** 11, b g Sulamani (IRE)—Pennys Pride (IRE) **Reveley Racing 1**
25 **TEESCOMPONENTS LAD,** 10, b g Midnight Legend—Northern Native (IRE) **Gillian Boanas Racing**
26 **TEESCOMPONENTSFLY,** 6, ch g Shirocco (GER)—Hula Ballew **Tees Components Ltd**
27 **TEESCOMPONENTSTRIG,** 8, ch g Black Sam Bellamy (IRE)—La Calinda **Tees Components Ltd**
28 **TRY TEESCOMPONENTS,** 6, br g Shirocco (GER)—Northern Native (IRE) **Tees Components Ltd**
29 4, B f Milan—Young Lady (IRE)

41 MRS MYRIAM BOLLACK-BADEL, Chantilly-Lamorlaye

Postal: **20 Rue Blanche, 60260 Chantilly-Lamorlaye, France**
Contacts: **HOME +33 3 44 21 33 67 MOBILE +33 6 10 80 93 47 FAX +33 3 44 21 33 67**
EMAIL myriam.bollack@gmail.com

1 **ACREGATE,** 4, b f Ribchester (IRE)—Green Speed (FR) **Philippe Stein**
2 **BLACKBIRDFLY (ITY),** 6, b h Frozen Power (IRE)—Hunting Queen (ITY) **Oscar Ortmans**
3 **COGOLIN (FR),** 5, ch h Goken (FR)—Albicocca (FR) **Mr Patrick Fellous**
4 **DAIQUIRI DREAM,** 4, b f Dubawi (IRE)—Cocktail Queen (IRE) **Mr J. C. Smith**
5 **GREEN SPIRIT (FR),** 6, b h Charm Spirit (IRE)—Green Speed (FR) **Mr Djamel Bentenah**
6 **LUNE DE RIO (FR),** 4, ch f Rio de La Plata (USA)—Rocheville (FR) **Mr Henri d'Aillieres**
7 **OPERA GIFT,** 6, b g Nathaniel (IRE)—Opera Glass **Mr J. C. Smith**
8 **PENTAOUR (FR),** 4, ch c Toronado (IRE)—Perpetual Glory **Ecurie Noel Forgeard**
9 **WELCOME SIGHT,** 4, br f Aclaim (IRE)—Loch Mirage **Mme M. Bollack-Badel**
10 **ZINNIA (FR),** 4, ch c Waldpark (GER)—Zython (FR) **Mme M. Bollack-Badel**
11 **ZYGFRYD (FR),** 5, ch h Literato (FR)—Zython (FR) **Zygfryd Partnership**

THREE-YEAR-OLDS

12 **BRUTALIST (IRE),** b f Free Eagle (IRE)—Fiuntach (IRE) **Mme M. Bollack-Badel**

MRS MYRIAM BOLLACK-BADEL - continued

13 **COCKTAIL PRINCE,** b c Exceed And Excel (AUS)—Cocktail Queen (IRE) **Mr J. C. Smith**
14 **MOON DASH,** ch c Sea The Moon (GER)—Dawn Dash **Mr J. C. Smith**
15 **PASIPHAE (FR),** b f Al Wukair (IRE)—Perpetual Glory **Ecurie Noel Forgeard**
16 **SMART STYLE (IRE),** b f Raven's Pass (USA)—Some Style (IRE) **Mr J. C. Smith**
17 **SPELLBINDER,** b f Camelot—Angel Wing **Mr J. C. Smith**

TWO-YEAR-OLDS

18 **ASHKENAZIM (FR),** ch g 04/04 Ultra (IRE)—Ardeatina (Harbour Watch (IRE)) **Mme M. Bollack-Badel**
19 **MYSTERY TRAIN (FR),** ch c 13/03 Intello (GER)—My Girl (FR) (Kendargent (FR)) **Oscar Ortmans**
20 **PAINTELLO (FR),** ch g 14/04 Intello (GER)—Perpetual Glory (Dansili) **Ecurie Noel Forgeard**
21 **SALAMALEK (FR),** b c 01/01 Tunis (POL)—Salinas Grande (FR) (Muhtathir) **Ecurie Noel Forgeard**
22 **SARIMARES (FR),** b f 18/03 Recoletos (FR)—Sinnderelle (FR) (Sinndar (IRE)) **Ecurie Noel Forgeard**

Assistant Trainer: Alain Badel. **Travelling Head:** Philippe Celier, **Racing Secretary:** Marie Helene Coulomb.

Flat Jockey: Stephane Pasquier.

---

42 MR MARCO BOTTI, Newmarket

Postal: **Prestige Place, Snailwell Road, Newmarket, Suffolk, CB8 7DP**
Contacts: **PHONE 01638 662416 MOBILE 07775 803007 FAX 01638 662417**
EMAIL office@marcobotti.co.uk WEBSITE www.marcobotti.co.uk

1 **ALMODOVAR DEL RIO (IRE),** 4, b g Dabirsim (FR)—Everglow (FR) **Mrs L. Botti**
2 **ARDAKAN,** 4, gr c Reliable Man—Alaskakonigin (GER) **Bennett Racing**
3 **FELIX,** 7, ch g Lope de Vega (IRE)—Luminance (IRE) **Gary Allsopp & Partner**
4 **GIAVELLOTTO (IRE),** 4, ch c Mastercraftsman (IRE)—Gerika (FR) **Scuderia La Tesa Limited**
5 **LAHEG (FR),** 4, b g Dabirsim (FR)—Sierra Leona (FR) **Mr R. El Youssef**
6 **LUCKY SAN JORE,** 4, gr g Lope de Vega (IRE)—Claba di San Jore (IRE) **Mr P. Hunt**
7 **RAINBOW FIRE (IRE),** 5, b g Kodiac—Heroine Chic (IRE) **Middleham Park Racing Iv & Les Boyer**
8 **SEE YOU BOY,** 4, b g Siyouni (FR)—Alamarie (FR) **R Bruni & Les Boyer Partnership**
9 **SILVER GUNN (IRE),** 5, gr g Lope de Vega (IRE)—Claba di San Jore (IRE) **Mr P. Hunt**
10 **SILVER SAMURAI,** 6, gr g Cable Bay (IRE)—High Tan **What A Time To Be Alive 1**
11 **VALENTINKA,** 5, ch m Helmet (AUS)—Pantile **Mrs L. Botti**
12 **WARD CASTLE (IRE),** 4, b g Flintshire—Endless Light **Milan Racing Club 1**

THREE-YEAR-OLDS

13 **ADVANCED NOTICE (IRE),** ch g New Approach (IRE)—Brazilian Bride (IRE) **Keep Kicking Racing & Partner**
14 **BARREL AGED,** b g Golden Horn—Brandybend (IRE) **A J Suited Partnership**
15 **BLENHEIM PRINCE,** b c Churchill (IRE)—Snow Dust **Keep Kicking Racing & Partner**
16 **BRIDGE WATER (FR),** b f Starspangledbanner (AUS)—Valkyries (FR) **Scuderia Sagam Srls & Partner**
17 **CARBIS BAY,** b c Siyouni (FR)—Lady Darshaan (IRE) **Newsells Park Stud & Partner**
18 **CAVERN CLUB (IRE),** ch g Ribchester (IRE)—Merseybeat **Mr C. J. Murfitt & Partner**
19 **COCO JAMBOO (IRE),** b f Massaat (IRE)—Beta Tauri (USA) **Scuderia Sagam Srls & Partner**
20 **COME MUSICA (ITY),** b g Muhaarar—Winter Serenade (ITY) **Scuderia La Tesa Limited**
21 **DAYSOFOURLIVES (IRE),** b g Churchill (IRE)—Komedy (IRE) **Mr R. El Youssef**
22 **DENSETSU (IRE),** b f Gleneagles (IRE)—Zenara (IRE) **Ahmad Bintouq & Partner**
23 **EDEN STORM (IRE),** b g Starspangledbanner (AUS)—Fou Rire (IRE) **Mr I. Bin Haider**
24 **FLYING CIRCUS,** b f Cracksman—At A Clip **Lady Cobham & Partner**
25 **GOLD AS GLASS (IRE),** ch f Australia—Crisolles (FR) **Ontoawinner & Les Boyer Partnership**
26 **HOBSON POINT,** b c Oasis Dream—Catalina Bay (IRE) **Mr Manfredini & Partner**
27 **INSPIRED KNOWHOW,** b c Exceed And Excel (AUS)—Simmy's Temple **Middleham Park Racing & Partner**
28 **INSPIRITED,** b c Lightning Spear—Moonlight Rhapsody (IRE) **Keep Kicking Racing & Partner**
29 **KASHMEER (IRE),** b f Holy Roman Emperor (IRE)—Hanzada (USA) **Mr A. Anne**
30 **KING OF ITHACA,** b g Ulysses (IRE)—Rhagori **Heart of the South Racing 129 & Partner**
31 **LEGEND OF LEROS (IRE),** b c Kuroshio (AUS)—Elusive Legend (USA) **Mr P. Hunt**

MR MARCO BOTTI - continued

32 **MAXIMILIAN CAESAR (IRE),** b g Holy Roman Emperor (IRE)—Primrose Gate (IRE) **Keep Kicking Racing & Partner**
33 **MORE THAN A GREY,** gr g Havana Grey—Eleusis **Middleham Park Racing LXXIV & Partner 2**
34 **MORNING COLOURS,** b f Oasis Dream—Za Za Zoom (IRE) **Scuderia Archi Romani**
35 **MOTASALEETA,** ch f Tasleet—Buttercross **Ahmad Bintouq & Partner**
36 **OUT OF SHADOWS,** b g Outstrip—Capla Ishtar (IRE) **Mr Manfredini & Milan Racing Club**
37 **RAVEN'S UP (IRE),** b f Raven's Pass (USA)—Up Tempo **Blueberry R. & Boyer Boyer**
38 **RESONANCE (IRE),** b f Dark Angel (IRE)—Maqaasid **Mr R. El Youssef**
39 **RUBINA ROSE,** b f Nathaniel (IRE)—Elas Ruby **Newsells Park Stud Limited**
40 **SEXY REXY (IRE),** ch f Saxon Warrior (JPN)—Kittens **Scuderia Archi Romani & Partner**
41 **STORYINTHESAND (IRE),** b f Footstepsinthesand—Storyline (IRE) **Scuderia La Tesa Limited**
42 **STRATEGIA (ITY),** b g Shalaa (IRE)—Tribulina **Scuderia La Tesa Limited**
43 **THAWG,** b f Golden Horn—Vandergirl (IRE) **Mr A. Bintouq**
44 **VICTORS DREAM,** b g Oasis Dream—Victors Lady (IRE) **Mr P. Hunt**

TWO-YEAR-OLDS

45 **ACROSS EARTH (IRE),** b c 18/04 Golden Horn—
War No More (USA) (War Front (USA)) (22000) **Scuderia Sagam Srls**
46 B f 13/03 Holy Roman Emperor (IRE)—Adutchgirl (GER) (Dutch Art) (39000) **Scuderia Sagam Srls**
47 B c 04/03 Australia—Allure (IRE) (Oasis Dream) (28011) **Les Boyer Partnership**
48 B c 02/05 Coach House (IRE)—Amber Lane (Compton Place) (4000) **Scuderia Blueberry & Partner**
49 Br c 05/04 Profitable (IRE)—Artistic Legacy (IRE) (Teofilo (IRE)) (25000) **Mr C. J. Murfitt & Partner**
50 **BEAUTY GENERATION (IRE),** b c 09/04 Ulysses (IRE)—Banana Split (Kyllachy) (18000) **Mr F. Sorge**
51 Ch c 04/02 Phoenix of Spain (IRE)—Breda Castle (Dutch Art) (35000) **Mrs L. Botti**
52 B c 08/04 Invincible Army (IRE)—Bright Approach (IRE) (New Approach (IRE)) (22000) **A To Alive & Boyer Boyer**
53 **CHEEKY BLIMEY (IRE),** b c 08/02 Ribchester (IRE)—Demesne (Dansili) (24000) **Scuderia Sagam Srls**
54 B f 14/02 Bated Breath—Dancer Cross (Cape Cross (IRE)) (28000) **Hold Your Horses Racing & Partner**
55 B f 28/01 Expert Eye—Dancing Warrior (War Command (USA)) (30000) **Ahmad Bintouq & Partner**
56 Ch c 10/05 Le Havre (IRE)—Endless Light (Pivotal) (45000)
57 B c 19/01 Kuroshio (AUS)—Firey Flower (IRE) (Lemon Drop Kid (USA)) (5602)
58 B c 01/02 Tamayuz—Fou Rire (IRE) (Iffraaj) (6403)
59 B c 24/02 Saxon Warrior (JPN)—Foxy Loxy (IRE) (Rock of Gibraltar (IRE)) (22409)
60 **HAVANA FORCE (ITY),** gr f 09/03 Havana Grey—
Lan Force (ITY) (Blu Air Force (IRE)) (25610) **Mr R Bruni & Partner**
61 Gr f 28/01 Eqtidaar (IRE)—High Tan (High Chaparral (IRE)) (33333) **Ahmad Bintouq & Les Boyer**
62 **KEEP MY SECRET,** b f 28/01 Cable Bay (IRE)—Lost Control (IRE) (Helmet (AUS)) **Scuderia La Tesa Limited**
63 B f 21/03 Aclaim (IRE)—Lady Crossmar (IRE) (Duke of Marmalade (IRE)) (13000) **Ahmad Bintouq & Partner**
64 B f 12/02 Shalaa (IRE)—Lady of The Lake (FR) (Camelot) (14406) **Keep Kicking Racing & Partner**
65 Gr c 26/02 Exceed And Excel (AUS)—Lady Rosamunde (Maria's Mon (USA)) (130000) **E. I. Mack**
66 B f 25/03 Saxon Warrior (JPN)—Lysanda (GER) (Lando (GER)) (16006)
67 Ch c 15/04 Saxon Warrior (JPN)—Moonlit View (IRE) (Exceed And Excel (AUS)) (17607) **Kicking & Boyer**
68 Ch f 03/02 Calyx—Plane Tree Fairy (IRE) (Oasis Dream) (30476) **Ahmad Bintouq & Partner**
69 B f 19/02 Iffraaj—Ronja (USA) (El Corredor (USA)) (80000) **Mr A. Bintouq**
70 **ROSY KISS,** br f 29/04 Calyx—Bristol Fashion (Dansili) (28000) **Archi & Boyer**
71 B f 13/04 Advertise—Saniyaat (Galileo (IRE)) **Mr F. A. A. Nass**
72 B f 18/02 Oasis Dream—Savida (IRE) (King's Best (USA)) (28011)
73 **SEE ALL MATCH (IRE),** b c 20/04 Acclamation—Peppard (Dansili) (29612) **Scuderia Sagam Srls**
74 **SHIELD WALL (IRE),** b c 08/04 Inns of Court (IRE)—
Viking Fair (Zamindar (USA)) (19048) **Sheikh K. A. I. S. Al Khalifa**
75 B c 21/03 Wootton Bassett—Shoot (FR) (Lawman (FR)) (30000) **Mr A. Bintouq**
76 B c 23/04 Land Force (IRE)—Slieve Mish (IRE) (Cape Cross (IRE)) (32000) **Ontoawinner & Les Boyer Partnership**
77 **SNEAKY GIRL,** b f 15/04 Holy Roman Emperor (IRE)—Maglietta Fina (IRE) (Verglas (IRE)) **Scuderia Archi Romani**
78 **SOMMELIER,** b c 11/03 Due Diligence (USA)—
Champagne Queen (Showcasing) (9000) **Mr Jonny Allison & Partner**
79 B f 06/04 Make Believe—Star Story (Sea The Stars (IRE)) (7000)
80 B c 17/03 Massaat (IRE)—Villabella (FR) (Hernando (FR)) (3000) **Scuderia Blueberry & Partner**
81 B c 19/01 Advertise—Volcanique (IRE) (Galileo (IRE)) **Fittocks, Bengough, Booth & Partner**

Assistant Trainer: Alberto Baragiola, Lucie Botti. **Pupil Assistant:** Conor Norris.

MR MARCO BOTTI - continued

Apprentice Jockey: Morgan Cole, Bradley Furniss.

---

43 MR GEORGE BOUGHEY, Newmarket

Postal: **Saffron House Stables, Hamilton Road, Newmarket, Suffolk, CB8 0NY**
Contacts: **WORK 01638 590643**
EMAIL george@georgeboughey.com

1 **AIR TO AIR,** 5, ch g Toronado (IRE)—Blossom Mills
2 **AL AMEEN (IRE),** 4, br g Aclaim (IRE)—Kendal Mint
3 **ALL THE KING'S MEN (FR),** 5, b g Kingman—Gooseley Chope (FR)
4 **ARION,** 4, b f Dubawi (IRE)—Filia Regina
5 **BARADAR (IRE),** 5, b br g Muhaarar—Go Lovely Rose (IRE)
6 **BRASIL POWER (FR),** 4, b g Dark Angel (IRE)—Venturous Spirit (FR)
7 **CACHET (IRE),** 4, b br f Aclaim (IRE)—Poyle Sophie
8 **CADILLAC (IRE),** 5, b g Lope de Vega (IRE)—Seas of Wells (IRE)
9 **CLEMENT DANES,** 4, b f Ribchester (IRE)—Blossom Mills
10 **DIAMOND RANGER (IRE),** 4, b g Kodiac—Eavesdrop (IRE)
11 **EHTEYAT (GER),** 4, b g Toronado (IRE)—Ella Ransom (GER)
12 **FORCA BRASIL (IRE),** 4, ch g Cotai Glory—Naias (IRE)
13 **HIT MAC (IRE),** 4, b g Exceed And Excel (AUS)—Hoodna (IRE)
14 **KOY KOY,** 4, b g Acclamation—Lynique (IRE)
15 **MINISTER FOR MAGIC (IRE),** 5, b m Make Believe—Rose of Africa (IRE)
16 **MISSED THE CUT (USA),** 4, b c Quality Road (USA)—Beauly
17 **MR ALAN,** 4, ch g Ulysses (IRE)—Interlace
18 **NAVELLO,** 4, b g Ivawood (IRE)—Caprella
19 **PARIS LIGHTS (IRE),** 4, b g Siyouni (FR)—Cabaret (IRE)
20 **PHANTASY MAC (IRE),** 4, b f Bobby's Kitten (USA)—Phantasmagoric (IRE)
21 **POCKET THE PROFIT,** 4, b g Mayson—Musical Beat (IRE)
22 **QUEEN OF IPANEMA (IRE),** 4, ch f Teofilo (IRE)—Aiming For Rio (FR)
23 **RIVER PRIDE,** 4, b f Oasis Dream—Highest
24 **SIMPLY SONDHEIM (IRE),** 4, b g Pivotal—Finishingthehat
25 **SPANGLED MAC (IRE),** 4, b g Starspangledbanner (AUS)—Intermittent
26 **STOWELL,** 5, b g Zoffany (IRE)—Marywell
27 **SUN KING (IRE),** 4, b g Galileo (IRE)—Song of My Heart (IRE)
28 **THUNDERSHOWER (IRE),** 4, ch f Iffraaj—Rainswept
29 **TOLLARD ROYAL (IRE),** 4, b g Ribchester (IRE)—Dew Line (IRE)
30 **TOTALLY CHARMING,** 5, b g Charming Thought—Totally Millie
31 **VIA SISTINA (IRE),** 5, b m Fastnet Rock (AUS)—Nigh (IRE)

THREE-YEAR-OLDS

32 **ABBADIA (IRE),** b f Mastercraftsman (IRE)—Orcia (IRE)
33 **ABSOLUTE QUEEN (IRE),** b f Zoffany (IRE)—Beat The Stars (IRE)
34 **AL DASIM (IRE),** ch c Harry Angel (IRE)—Dance Hall Girl (IRE)
35 **ANGEL DE LUZ (IRE),** b f Camacho—Angel Grace (IRE)
36 **APEX (IRE),** b g Kessaar (IRE)—Bisous Y Besos (IRE)
37 **BEAU ROC,** b f Brazen Beau (AUS)—Kicker Rock
38 **BEAUTIFULASALWAYS,** b f Kingman—Bastet (IRE)
39 **BELIEVING (IRE),** b f Mehmas (IRE)—Misfortunate (IRE)
40 **CALIFORNIA GEM,** b f Cable Bay (IRE)—Angels Wings (IRE)
41 **CALLUNA (USA),** b f More Than Ready (USA)—Halljoy (IRE)
42 **CANTORA,** b br f Time Test—Umthoulah (IRE)
43 **CHILLI PEPPER (IRE),** b f Sea The Stars (IRE)—Wo de Xin
44 **CLASS MEMBER,** b f Charm Spirit (IRE)—Mabinia (IRE)
45 **CONCORDE,** ch g Sixties Icon—Silca Chiave
46 **CONQUISTADOR,** b g U S Navy Flag (USA)—El Diamante (FR)

MR GEORGE BOUGHEY - continued

47 **CRAZY ABOUT HER (IRE),** b f Vadamos (FR)—Gravina
48 **CROW'S NEST (IRE),** b g U S Navy Flag (USA)—Argentina (IRE)
49 **CROWN LAND,** b f Territories (IRE)—La Roumegue (USA)
50 **DABBOUS (IRE),** b c Kodiac—Serafina's Flight
51 **DALLAS COWGIRL (FR),** ch f Kheleyf (USA)—Laureva Chope (FR)
52 **DANGER ALERT,** b g Ardad (IRE)—Sandy Times (IRE)
53 **DAWN MISSION,** ch c No Nay Never (USA)—Predawn (IRE)
54 **DOUGIE (IRE),** b g Tasleet—All On Red (IRE)
55 **EVENSTAR,** b f Havana Grey—Star Squared
56 **FORCEFUL SPEED (IRE),** ch c New Bay—Praden (USA)
57 **GALLIMIMUS,** b c Charm Spirit (IRE)—Amarullah (FR)
58 **HELLO MENAHI (IRE),** b g Kuroshio (AUS)—Breathless Kiss (USA)
59 **HOWYOULIKEMENOW (IRE),** b f Bated Breath—My Wish (IRE)
60 **JUST LOOKING,** b f Kingman—Ruby Rocket (IRE)
61 **KING LEAR (IRE),** b c Galileo (IRE)—Amazing Maria (IRE)
62 **KING'S GEM (IRE),** b g Kingman—Earring (USA)
63 **KINTA (IRE),** b f Sioux Nation (USA)—Qamarain (USA)
64 **LADY RASCAL,** br f Nathaniel (IRE)—Theladyinquestion
65 **LUMACHO (IRE),** b f Camacho—Southern Belle (IRE)
66 **MAID IN KENTUCKY (USA),** b f American Pharoah (USA)—Tiburtina (IRE)
67 **MALRESCIA (IRE),** b f Acclamation—Tecla (IRE)
68 **MARMARA STAR,** b f Golden Horn—Lunearia (IRE)
69 **MORBOKA,** ch f Iffraaj—Lady of Persia (JPN)
70 **MRS U S A (IRE),** ch f Starspangledbanner (AUS)—Intermittent
71 **MYSTERY PLAY,** b f Golden Horn—Monday Show (USA)
72 **NAASER (IRE),** b g New Bay—L'Ambre Gris (IRE)
73 **NAXOS,** ch g Saxon Warrior (JPN)—Ecureuil (IRE)
74 **NEVER LEFT,** b g Ribchester (IRE)—Norway Cross
75 Gr f Caravaggio (USA)—New Terms
76 **NINE SIX FIVE (IRE),** ch g Mehmas (IRE)—Interweave
77 **PASTICHE,** ch f Zoustar (AUS)—Crying Lightening (IRE)
78 **PAULTONS SQUARE (IRE),** b c Churchill (IRE)—Star Now
79 **PEACE OF MINE (IRE),** b f Fast Company (IRE)—Aurora Butterfly (IRE)
80 **PERDIKA,** b f Unfortunately (IRE)—Golden Dirham
81 **POCKET THE PACKET (IRE),** ch g Mayson—Oakley Star
82 **PRETTY FLAG (IRE),** b f U S Navy Flag (USA)—Pyrean (IRE)
83 **PROVERB (IRE),** b c Harry Angel (IRE)—Posh Perfect
84 **PURENESS,** b f Iffraaj—Ego
85 **QUEEN OF SPARTA (USA),** b f Lope de Vega (IRE)—Glittering Tax (USA)
86 **RAPALLO (IRE),** ch f Sea The Stars (IRE)—Parade Militaire (IRE)
87 **RAZONI (IRE),** b c Lope de Vega (IRE)—Malaspina (IRE)
88 **SERIOUS LOOK (IRE),** gr g Dark Angel (IRE)—Fregate First
89 **SPORTING HERO,** b c Bobby's Kitten (USA)—Clouds Rest
90 **STORYMAKER,** b f Ulysses (IRE)—Panova
91 **TEMPERED SOUL,** b c Massaat (IRE)—Kalia Asha (IRE)
92 **TEPHI (IRE),** b f Invincible Spirit (IRE)—Ghurra (USA)
93 **THUNDER MOOR (IRE),** ch g Dandy Man (IRE)—Play Mate
94 **TIGULLIO,** b f Kingman—Crystal Capella
95 **TIME IN MOTION,** b f Time Test—Bridge Poseidon (IRE)
96 **TRILBY,** b g Twilight Son—Fascinator
97 **WILD SIDE (IRE),** b f Kodiac—Inverse (IRE)
98 **ZEBRA STAR (IRE),** gr f Gregorian (IRE)—Queen Zain (IRE)

TWO-YEAR-OLDS

99 Ch f 27/04 Lope de Vega (IRE)—Adool (IRE) (Teofilo (IRE))
100 **ANGEL MAC (IRE),** ch f 30/03 Zoffany (IRE)—Sweet Sienna (Harbour Watch (IRE)) (45000)
101 B c 24/04 Harry Angel (IRE)—Balance (Pivotal) (9524)
102 B f 02/04 Blue Point (IRE)—Beautiful Filly (Oasis Dream)
103 **BULLDOG DRUMMOND,** b c 31/03 Aclaim (IRE)—Eternal Sun (Mayson) (14286)

MR GEORGE BOUGHEY - continued

104 B c 14/03 Kingman—Butterscotch (IRE) (Galileo (IRE)) (80000)
105 B c 28/04 Harry Angel (IRE)—Caldy Dancer (IRE) (Soviet Star (USA)) (18000)
106 B f 20/02 Too Darn Hot—Cape Bunting (IRE) (Cape Cross (IRE)) (50000)
107 **DARK BEFORE DAWN (IRE),** b c 04/03 Dark Angel (IRE)—Mystic Dawn (IRE) (Oasis Dream)
108 B f 09/04 Dandy Man (IRE)—Disko (IRE) (Kodiac) (65000)
109 B f 08/04 Mayson—Dream Dancing (IRE) (Dream Ahead (USA)) (4762)
110 B f 27/02 Invincible Army (IRE)—Edge of The World (IRE) (Fastnet Rock (AUS)) (83810)
111 B f 12/04 Blue Point (IRE)—Erysimum (IRE) (Arcano (IRE)) (80000)
112 Ch f 21/02 Night of Thunder (IRE)—Eva's Request (IRE) (Soviet Star (USA))
113 B c 25/02 Due Diligence (USA)—Ever Amber (IRE) (Ivawood (IRE)) (16000)
114 B f 10/02 Mehmas (IRE)—Excellent View (Shamardal (USA))
115 B c 15/05 Calyx—Finishingthehat (Sixties Icon)
116 Ch f 18/02 Masar (IRE)—Fligaz (FR) (Panis (USA)) (15000)
117 B c 20/02 Cracksman—Forbidden Love (Dubawi (IRE))
118 Ch f 30/01 Masar (IRE)—Francisca (USA) (Mizzen Mast (USA)) (15000)
119 Ch f 04/04 Territories (IRE)—Glee Club (Kyllachy) (62000)
120 B c 18/03 Siyouni (FR)—Glories (USA) (Galileo (IRE))
121 **GREEN SIGMA,** ch f 27/03 Havana Gold (IRE)—Honky Tonk Sally (Dansili) (32000)
122 B c 19/03 Blue Point (IRE)—Guerriere (IRE) (Invincible Spirit (IRE)) (100000)
123 B f 07/03 Advertise—Handana (IRE) (Desert Style (IRE))
124 B f 23/04 Camelot—Happy Face (IRE) (Kingman) (100000)
125 B f 14/03 Kingman—Hawaafez (Nayef (USA))
126 **HEARTWARMER,** b f 25/03 Holy Roman Emperor (IRE)—Heatwave (Leroidesanimaux (BRZ))
127 B f 17/04 Too Darn Hot—Honorina (Sea The Stars (IRE))
128 B f 14/04 Sioux Nation (USA)—Intermittent (Cacique (IRE)) (75000)
129 Ch f 22/03 Saxon Warrior (JPN)—Its All For Luck (IRE) (Fast Company (IRE))
130 B f 05/02 Sea The Moon (GER)—L'Age d'Or (Iffraaj) (115000)
131 Gr ro c 05/04 El Kabeir (USA)—Lady Heart (Kyllachy) (14406)
132 Ch f 12/02 Masar (IRE)—Lovely Surprise (IRE) (Shamardal (USA))
133 B c 10/02 Bobby's Kitten (USA)—Luisa Calderon (Nayef (USA)) (9604)
134 B c 29/01 Showcasing—New Day Dawn (IRE) (Dawn Approach (IRE)) (140000)
135 **NOVATION,** b br c 10/03 Havana Grey—Caprella (Kheleyf (USA)) (47619)
136 **ORGANIC (IRE),** b f 14/02 Land Force (IRE)—Duchy (Kyllachy) (38415)
137 B c 29/04 U S Navy Flag (USA)—Peinture Rare (IRE) (Sadler's Wells (USA)) (40000)
138 B c 11/02 Almanzor (FR)—Playing Trix (War Front (USA))
139 B f 18/02 Magna Grecia (IRE)—Pontenuovo (FR) (Green Tune (USA)) (95000)
140 B gr f 28/03 U S Navy Flag (USA)—Posh Perfect (Showcasing) (17607)
141 B f 22/02 Kingman—Predawn (IRE) (Fastnet Rock (AUS)) (150000)
142 Ch c 18/03 Cracksman—Qatari Perfection (Dubawi (IRE)) (148059)
143 **QUANTUM FORCE,** b c 20/03 Land Force (IRE)—High Luminosity (USA) (Elusive Quality (USA)) (61905)
144 Ch f 13/04 Galileo Gold—Queen's Code (IRE) (Shamardal (USA))
145 Ch c 31/01 Zoustar (AUS)—Really Lovely (IRE) (Galileo (IRE)) (75000)
146 **REINE DES COEURS (IRE),** b f 03/03 Calyx—Haddajah (IRE) (Sea The Stars (IRE)) (64026)
147 Ch c 16/03 Dutch Art—Rosebride (Mayson) (62000)
148 B c 15/03 Calyx—Second Glance (IRE) (Galileo (IRE)) (40000)
149 B f 21/04 Havana Grey—Secret Romance (Sakhee's Secret) (115000)
150 B f 25/03 Invincible Spirit (IRE)—She's Mine (IRE) (Sea The Stars (IRE)) (220000)
151 B f 21/01 Territories (IRE)—Snowdon (Iffraaj) (47000)
152 **SOPRANO (IRE),** ch f 23/02 Starspangledbanner (AUS)—Lealas Daughter (IRE) (Excelebration (IRE)) (100000)
153 Ch f 30/04 Mehmas (IRE)—Speed Freak (Fastnet Rock (AUS)) (220000)
154 Gr c 05/05 Havana Grey—Strictly Silca (Danehill Dancer (IRE)) (33613)
155 **SUPERFLUIDITY (USA),** b c 22/03 Quality Road (USA)—Faufiler (IRE) (Galileo (IRE))
156 B c 30/01 Exceed And Excel (AUS)—Symposia (Galileo (IRE)) (28011)
157 **TUNEFUL (IRE),** b f 30/01 Blue Point (IRE)—Pretty Face (Rainbow Quest (USA)) (52000)
158 B f 11/03 Galileo Gold—Turuqaat (Fantastic Light (USA)) (27000)
159 **TWILIGHT VISION (IRE),** b f 02/02 Sea The Stars (IRE)—Flying Fairies (IRE) (Holy Roman Emperor (IRE)) (360000)
160 B c 29/03 Due Diligence (USA)—Two In The Pink (IRE) (Clodovil (IRE)) (25000)
161 Ch c 01/04 Australia—Vasilia (Dansili)
162 B f 17/03 Night of Thunder (IRE)—Violet's Gift (IRE) (Cadeaux Genereux) (265000)
163 B f 03/04 Churchill (IRE)—Where's Sue (IRE) (Dark Angel (IRE)) (400000)

MR GEORGE BOUGHEY - continued

164 WIDE MARGIN (IRE), b c 15/03 Too Darn Hot—Layaleena (IRE) (Sea The Stars (IRE)) (75000)
165 B c 14/02 Golden Horn—Ya Hala (IRE) (Shamardal (USA))

Owners: Al Asayl Bloodstock Ltd, Mr J. B. A. Al Attiyah, Sheikh I. S. Al Khalifa, Sheikh A. H. F. M. A. Al Sabah, A. Al Shaikh, Al Wasmiyah Stud, S. Ali, Mr M. N. M. A. Almutairi, Mr A. Alotaibi, Mrs A. Althani, Amo Racing Limited, Amo Racing Ltd & Jean-etienne Dubois, Mr V. I. Araci, Mr E. P. Babington, Edward Babington & Phil Cunningham, Babington, Lanes End, St Elias & Hudson, Miss A. C. Bamford, Lady Bamford, Lady C. Bamford & Miss A. Bamford, Mr S. R. Bin Ghadayer, Mr G. R. D. Boughey, Mr J. Boughey, Mr N. Bradley, Mrs F. J. Carmichael, Mr C. L. Chen, Clearwater Stud, Clipper Group Holdings Ltd, Lady N. F. Cobham, Mr P. M. Cunningham, Mr J. E. Dubois, Ever Equine, Flaxman Stables Ireland Ltd, Mr H. R. Bin Ghedayer, Mrs M. Gill, Mrs E. J. Gregson-Williams, Mr R. W. Gregson-Williams, HIghclere Thoroughbred Racing - Goya, HIghclere Thoroughbred Racing - Matisse, Highclere - Jean-Paul Sartre, Highclere T'Bred Racing - John Steinbeck, Highclere T'bred Racing - Jane Addams, Highclere T'bred Racing - Wild Flower, Highclere Thoroughbred Racing - Angel, Highclere Thoroughbred Racing - Da Vinci, Highclere Thoroughbred Racing Angel 1, Highclere Thoroughbred Racing Ltd, Highclere Thoroughbred Racing Matisse 1, Mrs R. G. Hillen, Mr C. R. Hirst, Miss S. Holden, Mr R. S. Hoskins, Hot To Trot Racing 2, Hot To Trot Racing 2 & Partner, J. Harron Racing P'ship, JJ Henry Ltd, Jamie Perkins & Partner, Ms L. Judah, Mrs A. G. Kavanagh, Lanes End Bloodstock, Hudson & St Elias, Mrs J. C. Lascelles, L. Lillingston, Angela & M Lund, Ms M. B. Lund, Mr K. MacLennan, Mr J. P. Magnier, Mr M. V. Magnier, Mathis Stables LLC, Mathis Stables, Rosier & Rosier, Mrs A. M. McAlpine, Mr A. N. R. McAlpine, Middleham Park Racing CXXVII, Mr S. Mistry, Mrs R G Hillen & Partner, S. E. Munir, Mr Simon Munir & Mr Isaac Souede, Mr F. A. A. Nass, Mrs S. E. Nicholls, Nick Bradley Racing 27, Nick Bradley Racing 27 & Partner, Nick Bradley Racing 44, Northam Racing, O.T.I. Racing, Opulence Thoroughbreds, A. Ownership Change Pending, Paul Watson & Partner, Mr R. Peel, Mr J. H. Perkins, Qatar Racing Limited, Mr M. Rashid, Dr A. Ridha, Mrs S. Rogers, Mr C. F. J. Rosier, Mrs J. E. Rosier, Mr Charlie Rosier & Mrs Julia Rosier, Mrs S. M. Roy, Mr & Mrs R. Scott, Seventh Lap Racing, Shadwell Estate Company Ltd, Mrs L. M. Shanahan, Mrs M. Slack, Mr I. Souede, Sporting Hero Partnership, Babington, Peter & Stanley, P. H.C. Stanley, Teme Valley, The Blossom Mills Partnership, The Inver Park Partnership, Mr E. D. Tynan, Tynan, Maclennan, Magnier & Shanahan, Sir P. J. Vela, Veracity Racing, Victorious Racing Limited, Victorious Racing Limited & Fawzi Nass, Wardley Bloodstock, Mr E. J. Ware, Mr C. J. Waters, Mr P. Watson, Woodhurst, Nelson, Chrysanthou & Castle.

Racing Secretary: Mrs Nicky Pellatt.

MR CLIVE BOULTBEE-BROOKS, Woolhope

Postal: **C Boultbee-Brooks, 32-35 Broad Street, Hereford, Herefordshire, HR4 9AR**
Contacts: **PHONE 01432 347935**
EMAIL helen@bbre.co.uk

1 ALLAVINA (IRE), 8, b m Getaway (GER)—One Cool Kate (IRE) **C&C Boultbee Brooks**
2 BERTIE B, 5, b g Kayf Tara—Toubeera **C&C Boultbee Brooks**
3 BLACK OF THE GLADE (FR), 6, b g Tirwanako (FR)—Vega of The Clade (FR) **C&C Boultbee Brooks**
4 4, B f Flemensfirth (USA)—Daydream Beach (IRE) **C&C Boultbee Brooks**
5 FELICIE DU MAQUIS (FR), 8, b m Saddler Maker (IRE)—Qualine du Maquis (FR) **C&C Boultbee Brooks**
6 GENTLEMAN (GER), 5, ch g Sea The Moon (GER)—Gillenia (GER) **C&C Boultbee Brooks**
7 GEORDIE B, 10, gr g Geordieland (FR)—Sari Rose (FR) **C&C Boultbee Brooks**
8 5, Ch g Doyen (IRE)—Highly Presentable (IRE) **C&C Boultbee Brooks**
9 IPSOS DES BORDES (FR), 5, b g Cokoriko (FR)—Ahkel Vie (FR) **C&C Boultbee Brooks**
10 LARRIKIN (IRE), 5, ch g Golden Lariat (USA)—Social Society (IRE) **C&C Boultbee Brooks**
11 4, B f Flemensfirth (USA)—Petrovic (IRE) **C&C Boultbee Brooks**
12 RACING SNAKE, 8, b g Mount Nelson—Queen Soraya **C&C Boultbee Brooks**
13 SHADY B, 5, br g Saint des Saints (FR)—La Bombonera (FR) **C&C Boultbee Brooks**
14 SHANAKAL (GER), 5, ch g Kallisto (GER)—Shana Doyenne (GER) **Mr C. Boultbee-Brooks**
15 SHESASUPERSTAR (IRE), 6, b m Ocovango—Jills Oscar (IRE) **C&C Boultbee Brooks**
16 SWEET HONEY B (IRE), 5, b m Getaway (GER)—Kilbarry Classic (IRE) **C&C Boultbee Brooks**
17 4, B c Milan—Swincombe Flame **C&C Boultbee Brooks**
18 4, B c Kayf Tara—Toubeera **C&C Boultbee Brooks**
19 TRIO FOR RIO (IRE), 10, b br g Getaway (GER)—Rio Trio (IRE) **C&C Boultbee Brooks**

45 MR DARAGH BOURKE, Lockerbie

Postal: **Cherrybank, Waterbeck, Lockerbie, Dumfries and Galloway, DG11 3EY**
Contacts: **MOBILE 07495 948493**

1 4, Ch f Mahler—Ballybrowney Hall (IRE) **S Townshend & S Lowther**
2 **CORAL BLUE (IRE),** 8, b g Big Bad Bob (IRE)—Eva's Time (IRE) **Mr D. McCready**
3 **GAINSBOURG,** 5, b g Sixties Icon—Aromatherapy **Lowther, McCready, Scarlett**
4 **GAME BEAAA (IRE),** 6, br m Libertarian—Balla Brack (IRE) **Cherrybank Crusaders**
5 **MASTER OF THE MALT,** 7, b g Yeats (IRE)—Mrs Malt (IRE) **Mr S. Lowther**
6 **MORE TO FOLLOW (IRE),** 6, b g Soldier of Fortune (IRE)—Fast Finisher (IRE) **Lowther, McCready, Scarlett**
7 **NON MOLLARE (IRE),** 6, b m Cappella Sansevero—Confirm (IRE) **Mr D. F. Bourke**
8 **OLD JEWRY (IRE),** 9, b g Le Fou (IRE)—Clerken Bridge (IRE) **Mr D. McCready**
9 **PADDY THE PANDA (IRE),** 8, b g Flemensfirth (USA)—Pandorama Lady (IRE) **Mr S. Lowther**
10 **ROOKIE TRAINER (IRE),** 9, b g Gold Well—Crazy Falcon (IRE) **S Townshend & S Lowther**
11 **WEE BAZ (IRE),** 5, b g Getaway (GER)—Flame Supreme (IRE) **Mrs J. Lowther**
12 **YOUNG MOLONEY (IRE),** 6, b m Mustameet (USA)—Run Fly Run (IRE) **Lowther,Carruthers**

THREE-YEAR-OLDS

13 **VAMPIRE SLAYER (IRE),** b g Camacho—Bionic Buffy (IRE) **Mr D. F. Bourke**

46 MR DANIEL JOHN BOURNE, Varteg

Postal: **Tyddau Farm, Penylan Fields, Varteg, Pontypool, Gwent, NP4 7SA**
Contacts: **PHONE 01495 772444**
EMAIL bournegroundworks@gmail.com

1 **GERTCHA (IRE),** 6, b g Slade Power (IRE)—Elouges (IRE) **Mr D. J. Bourne**
2 **HARDE FASHION,** 7, b g Schiaparelli (GER)—La Harde (FR) **Mr D. J. Bourne**
3 **INCA ROSE,** 8, ch g Malinas (GER)—Cinderella Rose **Mr D. J. Bourne**
4 **LUCKY DRAW,** 6, b m Roderic O'Connor (IRE)—Lucky Breeze (IRE) **Mr D. J. Bourne**
5 **MONTAQEM (FR),** 6, b g Muhaarar—African Skies **Mr D. J. Bourne**
6 **PASCHALS DREAM (IRE),** 11, b g Primary (USA)—State Ur Case (IRE) **James Bourne Daniel Bourne**
7 **TOURNE BRIDE (FR),** 6, gr g Al Namix (FR)—Ambroise (FR) **Mr D. J. Bourne**

47 MR PETER BOWEN, Haverfordwest

Postal: **Yet-Y-Rhug, Letterston, Haverfordwest, Pembrokeshire, SA62 5TB**
Contacts: **PHONE 01348 840486 MOBILE 07811 111234 FAX 01348 840486**
EMAIL info@peterbowenracing.co.uk WEBSITE www.peterbowenracing.co.uk

1 **ALFA DAWN (IRE),** 7, b m No Nay Never (USA)—Aitch (IRE) **Mr H. Jones & Mrs E. Evans**
2 **BLUE BRASILIAN,** 5, b m Blue Bresil (FR)—Alfies Gift **Mrs G. A. Davies**
3 **BRYN BLACK SAM,** 5, gr g Black Sam Bellamy (IRE)—Fair Ask **Exors of the Late F. Lloyd**
4 **BRYN TELESCOPE,** 5, b g Telescope (IRE)—Grape Tree Flame **Exors of the Late F. Lloyd**
5 **BUCKS DREAM (IRE),** 7, ch g Salutino (GER)—The Devils Sister (IRE) **Mr H. Jones & Mrs E. Evans**
6 **COAL FIRE (IRE),** 7, b g Frozen Fire (GER)—Heartansoul (IRE) **M. G. Jones**
7 **COURTLAND (IRE),** 8, b g Court Cave (IRE)—Media View (IRE) **Miss Jayne Brace & Mr Gwyn Brace**
8 **DALKINGSTOWN,** 9, ch g Malinas (GER)—True Rose (IRE) **R. R. Owen**
9 **DICEY RIELLY (IRE),** 6, b m Getaway (GER)—Saintly Lady (IRE) **Mr D. Devereux**
10 **DREAMS OF DIAMONDS (IRE),** 6, ch g Malinas (GER)—Double Dream (IRE) **Mrs N. Unsworth**

MR PETER BOWEN - continued

11 **DREAMS OF FORTUNE (IRE),** 5, b g Soldier of Fortune (IRE)—Brooklyn View (IRE) **The Brace & Bowen Racing Group**
12 **DYSANIA (IRE),** 8, b g Califet (FR)—She's Supersonic (IRE) **Ms G. E. Morgan**
13 **EASY BUCKS,** 8, b g Getaway (GER)—Tushana (IRE) **Mr M. B. Bowen**
14 **EQUUS DANCER (IRE),** 9, b g Jeremy (USA)—Celtic Cailin (IRE) **R. R. Owen**
15 **FAIRLAWN FLYER,** 7, b g Dr Massini (IRE)—She's Our Native (IRE) **Mr R. Williams**
16 **FLYING FORTUNE (IRE),** 4, br f Soldier of Fortune (IRE)—Turbo Linn **Fortune N'Fame Fillies**
17 **FRANCKY DU BERLAIS (FR),** 10, b g Saint des Saints (FR)—Legende du Luy (FR) **R. R. Owen**
18 **GET A HIGH (IRE),** 8, b m Getaway (GER)—Top Nurse (IRE) **Mrs K. Bowen**
19 **GETASTAR (IRE),** 7, ch g Getaway (GER)—Metro Star (IRE) **Amanda & Patrick Bancroft**
20 **JACKTOT,** 6, b m Gentlewave (IRE)—Tot of The Knar **Steve & Jackie Fleetham**
21 **KARAVOMYLOS (IRE),** 4, b g Milan—Jet Empress (IRE) **Vernon & Anna Phillips & Bowen Group**
22 **LERMOOS LEGEND,** 8, b g Midnight Legend—Absalom's Girl **Mr J. A. Martin**
23 **LETTERSTON LADY,** 5, ch m Getaway (GER)—Whenskiesareblue (IRE) **Williams, Brace A Davies**
24 **MAC TOTTIE,** 10, b g Midnight Legend—Tot of The Knar **Steve & Jackie Fleetham**
25 **MO TOTTIE,** 9, b m Midnight Legend—Tot of The Knar **Steve & Jackie Fleetham**
26 **NIKHI,** 4, ch f Nathaniel (IRE)—Elysian Fields (GR) **Mr L. Mulryan**
27 **OUR FLYING ANGEL (IRE),** 5, b m Soldier of Fortune (IRE)—L'Etoile du Nord (IRE) **Our Flying Angel Partnership**
28 **PILGRIMS KING (IRE),** 7, b g Sholokhov (IRE)—So You Said (IRE) **Mr W. E. V. Harries**
29 **RESERVE TANK (IRE),** 9, b g Jeremy (USA)—Lady Bellamy (IRE) **R. R. Owen**
30 **ROOSTER COGBURN (IRE),** 10, b g Westerner—Hollygrove (IRE) **G. J. Morris**
31 **RUNASIMI RIVER,** 10, ch m Generous (IRE)—Zaffaranni (IRE) **Peter Bowen Racing Club & Mickey Bowen**
32 **SHANTOU CHAMPAGNE (IRE),** 6, b m Shantou (USA)—Couture Daisy (IRE) **Mrs J. Iddon**
33 **SOURIYAN (FR),** 12, b g Alhaarth (IRE)—Serasana **G. J. Morris**
34 **STATUARIO,** 8, b g Helmet (AUS)—Cat Hunter **Mrs N. Unsworth**
35 **UNIVERSAL BROOK,** 7, b m Universal (IRE)—Alfies Gift **Mrs G. A. Davies**

Assistant Trainer: Karen Bowen, Michael Bowen.

NH Jockey: James Bowen, Sean Bowen.

---

48 MISS SARAH BOWEN, Bromsgrove

Postal: **New House, Forest Farm, Forest Lane, Hanbury, Bromsgrove, Worcestershire, B60 4HP**
Contacts: **PHONE 07718 069485**
EMAIL sarah.bowen25@hotmail.com

1 **AL KHERB,** 8, b g Al Kazeem—Perfect Spirit (IRE) **Mrs S. A. Bowen**
2 **MISTER ALLEGRO,** 5, b g Bernardini (USA)—Joyful Hope **Mrs S. A. Bowen**

---

49 MR ROY BOWRING, Edwinstowe

Postal: **Fir Tree Farm, Edwinstowe, Mansfield, Nottinghamshire, NG21 9JG**
Contacts: **PHONE 01623 822451 MOBILE 07973 712942**
EMAIL srbowring@outlook.com

1 **BACK FROM DUBAI (IRE),** 6, b g Exceed And Excel (AUS)—Emirates Rewards **Mr K. Nicholls**
2 **CLIFFCAKE (IRE),** 5, b h Canford Cliffs (IRE)—Cake (IRE) **S. R. Bowring**
3 **DYLAN'S LAD (IRE),** 6, b g G Force (IRE)—Chizzler (IRE) **S. R. Bowring**
4 **HEERBEGOOD,** 4, b br f Heeraat (IRE)—Exceedingly Good (IRE) **S. R. Bowring**

MR ROY BOWRING - continued

5 **HIYA MAITE,** 5, b g Heeraat (IRE)—Misu's Maite **S. R. Bowring**
6 **JEANS MAITE,** 7, b m Burwaaz—Misu's Maite **S. R. Bowring**
7 **LIV LUCKY (IRE),** 4, b f Profitable (IRE)—Living Art (USA) **Mr L. P. Keane**
8 **MISS ANACO,** 4, b f Adaay (IRE)—Sonko (IRE) **Mr L. P. Keane**
9 **NINE ELMS (USA),** 8, ch g Street Cry (IRE)—Nawaiet (USA) **Mr K. Nicholls**
10 **SHE'S THE DANGER (IRE),** 4, b f Pride of Dubai (AUS)—Moment In The Sun **Mr L. P. Keane**
11 **TOPTIME,** 5, b g Gregorian (IRE)—Dominance **S. R. Bowring**
12 **TRULIE GOOD,** 5, b m Heeraat (IRE)—Exceedingly Good (IRE) **S. R. Bowring**

---

50 MR JIM BOYLE, Epsom

Postal: **South Hatch Stables, Burgh Heath Road, Epsom, Surrey, KT17 4LX**
Contacts: **WORK 07719 554147 MOBILE 07719 554147**
WORK EMAIL info@jamesboyle.co.uk HOME EMAIL Jimboyle17@hotmail.com
EMAIL pippaboyle@hotmail.com WEBSITE www.jamesboyle.co.uk

1 **ANGELS ROC,** 6, b g Roderic O'Connor (IRE)—Divine Pamina (IRE) **Lady R. M. Prosser**
2 **BAD COMPANY,** 6, b g Fast Company (IRE)—Clearing **The Clean Sweep Partnership**
3 **BEAT THE HEAT,** 6, b g Hot Streak (IRE)—Touriga **Inside Track Racing Club**
4 **BONUS,** 6, b g Roderic O'Connor (IRE)—Spring Clean (FR) **The Clean Sweep Partnership**
5 **CLASSIC ANTHEM (IRE),** 5, b g Affinisea (IRE)—Clohass Lane **Taylor & O'Dwyer**
6 **DOWNSMAN (IRE),** 5, b g Fast Company (IRE)—Hawk Dance (IRE) **The Paddock Space Partnership 2**
7 **HAVEAGOBEAU,** 4, b g Brazen Beau (AUS)—Jethou Island **Mr G. G. Stevens**
8 **HODLER (GER),** 4, b g Sea The Moon (GER)—Herzprinzessin (GER) **Taylor & O'Dwyer**
9 **MARLAY PARK,** 5, b br g Cable Bay (IRE)—Lovers' Vows **Inside Track Racing Club**
10 **MELERI,** 4, b f Nathaniel (IRE)—Divine Pamina (IRE) **Lady R. M. Prosser**
11 **NONSUCH LAD (IRE),** 4, ch g Tamayuz—Solandia (IRE) **South Hatch Partners**
12 **OTAGO,** 6, b g Cable Bay (IRE)—Spinning Top **Mr P and Mrs L Rowe and Mr John Turner**
13 **SECRET STRENGTH (IRE),** 4, b g Mehmas (IRE)—Midnight Destiny (IRE) **The BeeGeeZ**
14 **SPARKED,** 4, b f Night of Thunder (IRE)—Clearing **The Clean Sweep Partnership**
15 **TWINING (IRE),** 4, ch f Fast Company (IRE)—Interlacing **Inside Track Racing Club**
16 **WETAKECAREOFOUROWN (IRE),** 6, b g Mahler—Cooksgrove Lady (IRE) **Taylor & O'Dwyer**

THREE-YEAR-OLDS

17 **BUY THE DIP,** b g New Bay—Crossover **Taylor & O'Dwyer**
18 **CHINTHURST,** ch g Nathaniel (IRE)—Sonnetation (IRE) **The Paddock Space Partnership**
19 **DELIGHTFULLY YOURS (IRE),** b f Zoffany (IRE)—Sherbert **Maid In Heaven Partnership**
20 **IREZUMI,** b g Hawkbill (USA)—Inke (IRE) **Harrier Racing 2**

---

51 MR DAVID BRACE OBE, Bridgend

Postal: **Llanmihangel Farm, Pyle, Bridgend, Mid Glamorgan, CF33 6RL**
Contacts: **HOME 01656 742313 MOBILE 07900 495510**

1 **CARRIGLUX (IRE),** 7, b g Jet Away—Two of Each (IRE) **Mr D. Brace**
2 **CLASSIC CONCORDE (IRE),** 10, b g Shantou (USA)—Morning Calm **Mr D. Brace**
3 **COLORADO DOC,** 12, b g Dr Massini (IRE)—First Royal (GER) **Mr D. Brace**
4 **DARIYA (USA),** 8, b m Include (USA)—Dubai (IRE) **Mr D. Brace**
5 **DON'T LAUGH AT ME,** 8, b g Schiaparelli (GER)—Nurse Brace **Mr D. Brace**
6 **GATS AND CO,** 8, b g Dr Massini (IRE)—Vineuil (FR) **Mr D. Brace**

MR DAVID BRACE OBE - continued

7 **LESSANKAN (GER),** 8, b g Samum (GER)—Larena (GER) **Mr D. Brace**
8 **LILY MAY BLU,** 5, b m Blue Bresil (FR)—Lady Veronica **Mr D. Brace**
9 **LOOKSNOWTLIKEBRIAN (IRE),** 12, b g Brian Boru—Sheebadiva (IRE) **Mr D. Brace**
10 **MANGROVE RIVER (IRE),** 6, ch g Getaway (GER)—Tastytimes (IRE) **Mr D. Brace**
11 **PENNYFORAPOUND (IRE),** 9, b g Winged Love (IRE)—Recession Lass (IRE) **Mr D. Brace**
12 **PINK EYED PEDRO,** 12, b g Dr Massini (IRE)—Poacher's Paddy (IRE) **Mr D. Brace**
13 **QUILAURA (FR),** 6, b m Lauro (GER)—Qualite Controlee (FR) **Mr D. Brace**
14 **ROBIN DES PEOPLE (IRE),** 13, br g Robin des Pres (FR)—Zelea (IRE) **Mr D. Brace**
15 **ROKOCOKO BLUE (IRE),** 5, b m Shirocco (GER)—Freefairngenuine (IRE) **Mr D. Brace**
16 **SEPARATE WAYS (IRE),** 7, b g Darsi (FR)—Emily Vard (IRE) **Mr D. Brace**

NH Jockey: Connor Brace.

---

52 MR MARK BRADSTOCK, Wantage

Postal: **Old Manor Stables, Foresters Lane, Letcombe Bassett, Wantage, Oxfordshire, OX12 9NB**
Contacts: **WORK 01235 760780 HOME 01235 760780 PHONE 01235 760754 MOBILE 07887 686697**
EMAIL mark.bradstock@btconnect.com WEBSITE www.markbradstockracing.co.uk

1 **BATSMAN,** 4, b g Jack Hobbs—Maid of Oaksey **The Buster Syndicate**
2 **CRAWFORD,** 7, b g Kayf Tara—Maid of Oaksey **The Billy Partnership**
3 **DIAMOND TIKI (FR),** 5, ch g Diamond Boy (FR)—Belle Tiki (FR) **M. F. Bradstock**
4 **EGLANTIER (FR),** 9, b g Bonbon Rose (FR)—Kyalami (FR) **M. F. Bradstock**
5 **HELIX,** 6, ch g Helmet (AUS)—Child Bride (USA) **The Leiter Partnership**
6 **HERMIN D'OUDAIRIES (FR),** 6, b g Masterstroke (USA)—Ukalee (FR) **Mr G. Faber**
7 **JAKAMANI,** 9, b g Sulamani (IRE)—Kentford Grebe **Miss C Fordham & Mr C Vernon**
8 **MR VANGO (IRE),** 7, b g Ocovango—African Miss (IRE) **Cracker and Smodge Partnership**
9 **STEP BACK (IRE),** 13, ch g Indian River (FR)—Stepitoutmary (IRE) **Mr J. B. G. Macleod**

Assistant Trainer: Sara Bradstock. **Head Girl:** Lily Bradstock. **Racing Secretary:** Samantha Partridge.

NH Jockey: Nico De Boinville.

---

53 MR BARRY BRENNAN, Lambourn

Postal: **2 Rockfel Road, Lambourn, Hungerford, Berkshire, RG17 8NG**
Contacts: **MOBILE 07907 529780**
EMAIL barrybrennan2@hotmail.co.uk WEBSITE www.barrybrennanracing.co.uk

1 **BIRKIE GIRL,** 4, b f Buratino (IRE)—Noble Nova **M. J. Hills**
2 **CREM FRESH,** 9, b m Malinas (GER)—Clotted Cream (USA) **D. R. T. Gibbons**
3 **KANUKANKAN (IRE),** 8, ch g Arakan (USA)—Blow A Gasket (IRE) **F. J. Brennan**
4 **KERRKENNY GOLD (IRE),** 9, ch g Sans Frontieres (IRE)—Cailins Honour (IRE) **F. J. Brennan**
5 **SEA OF CHARM (FR),** 5, b m Charm Spirit (IRE)—Sea Meets Sky (FR) **Mrs C. A. M. Dunlop**
6 **STARSKY (IRE),** 9, b g Shantou (USA)—Lunar Star (IRE) **F. J. Brennan**
7 **VAXHOLM (IRE),** 4, b g Estidhkaar (IRE)—Lovely Dancer (IRE) **F. J. Brennan**

---

54 MR JOHN BRIDGER, Liphook

Postal: **Upper Hatch Farm, Liphook, Hampshire, GU30 7EL**
Contacts: **PHONE 01428 722528 MOBILE 07785 716614**
EMAIL jbridger@sky.com

1 **BE PREPARED,** 6, b g Due Diligence (USA)—Chicklade **Mr P. Cook**
2 **BEAU JARDINE (IRE),** 5, b g Make Believe—
Akira (IRE) **Happy Families, Mrs R. Cook, Mrs M. D. White, Mr J. J. Bridger, Mrs A. R. Bridger**
3 **DEBBIE'S CHOICE (IRE),** 4, b f Ardad (IRE)—Alnawiyah **The Deers Hut, Northcott & Steel**
4 5, B m Kier Park (IRE)—Devils In My Head **Mr J. J. Bridger**
5 **ESSME,** 5, b m Twilight Son—Desert Kiss **Mrs D. J. Ellison**
6 **FIRENZE ROSA (IRE),** 8, b m Zebedee—Our Nana Rose (IRE) **Mr & Mrs K. Finch, Mrs D. Finch, K. Finch**
7 **OLIVIA MARY (IRE),** 5, gr m Dark Angel (IRE)—Lapis Blue (IRE) **Miss V. J. Baalham**
8 **PEARLY GIRL,** 5, b m Telescope (IRE)—Posh Pearl **T. M. Jones, Mr M J Evans & Mr T M Jones, Mr M. J. Evans**
9 **RAPHEL JAKE,** 5, b g Charm Spirit (IRE)—Portrait **Mr J. J. Bridger**

THREE-YEAR-OLDS

10 B f New Approach (IRE)—Faeroes (IRE) **T. M. Jones**
11 **LAHINA BAY (IRE),** b f Cracksman—Serendipitously (IRE) **Mr & Mrs K. Finch, Mrs D. Finch, K. Finch**
12 **PENNY BE,** b f Havana Grey—Chicklade **Mr P. Cook**
13 B f Swiss Spirit—Raspberry Ripple **Double-R-Racing**
14 **RHYTHM DANCER,** b f Expert Eye—Haydn's Lass **Mr & Mrs K. Finch, Mrs D. Finch, K. Finch**

TWO-YEAR-OLDS

15 **DREAM OF KEDA,** b f 30/04 Aclaim (IRE)—
Glen Molly (IRE) (Danetime (IRE)) (9000) **Mr & Mrs K. Finch, Mrs D. Finch, K. Finch**
16 **KISS AND RUN,** b f 17/03 Twilight Son—Desert Kiss (Cape Cross (IRE)) (7000) **Mr J. E. Burrows**
17 Br g 24/04 Coach House (IRE)—La Fortunata (Lucky Story (USA)) (5000)
18 **LAND OF MAGIC,** b f 07/05 Land Force (IRE)—
Kelowna (IRE) (Pivotal) (6000) **Mr & Mrs K. Finch, Mrs D. Finch, K. Finch**
19 B c 27/03 Swiss Spirit—Parisean Artiste (IRE) (Zoffany (IRE)) (952)

Assistant Trainer: Rachel Cook.

---

55 MR DAVID BRIDGWATER, Stow-on-the-Wold

Postal: **Wyck Hill Farm, Wyck Hill, Stow-on-the-Wold, Cheltenham, Gloucestershire, GL54 1HT**
Contacts: **PHONE 01451 830349 MOBILE 07831 635817 FAX 01451 830349**
EMAIL sales@bridgwaterracing.co.uk WEBSITE www.bridgwaterracing.co.uk

1 **BARNAVIDDAUN (IRE),** 10, b g Scorpion (IRE)—Lucy Murphy (IRE) **Graham Clarkson & Andrew Smelt**
2 **CARPE DIEM (FR),** 5, b g Walzertakt (GER)—Chance Bleue (FR) **Terry & Sarah Amos**
3 **DAME DU SOIR (FR),** 10, br m Axxos (GER)—Kassing (FR) **Graham Clarkson & Andrew Smelt**
4 **DOM OF MARY (FR),** 7, b g Saddler Maker (IRE)—Antinea Marie (FR) **P. J. Cave**
5 **DUTCH ADMIRAL (IRE),** 6, ch g Dutch Art—Apasionata Sonata (USA) **P. J. Cave**
6 **ESTACAS (GER),** 6, b g Galileo (IRE)—Earthly Paradise (GER) **Constructive Equine**
7 **EXTRAORDINARY MAN (FR),** 7, b g No Risk At All (FR)—Argovie (FR) **Mr S. Hunt**
8 **FREDDIE'S SONG (FR),** 5, bl g Great Pretender (IRE)—Athinea (FR) **Mr S. Hunt**
9 **FREDDY BOY,** 7, b g Midnight Legend—Aster (IRE) **P. J. Cave**
10 **GAIA VALLIS (FR),** 7, b m Saint des Saints (FR)—Toccata Vallis (FR) **David Bridgwater Racing**
11 **IT'S FOR YOU MUM (FR),** 5, gr m Lord du Sud (FR)—Odile (FR) **Mr S. Hunt**
12 **ONE MAN PARTY (FR),** 6, b g Authorized (IRE)—Ahdaaf (USA) **Mr S. Hunt**
13 **PAWPAW,** 6, b g Showcasing—Papaya (IRE) **Mr T. Gaden**
14 **PIRATE SAM,** 8, b g Black Sam Bellamy (IRE)—Teenero **J.A & R.J Chenery & Partners**

MR DAVID BRIDGWATER - continued

15 **TELLAIRSUE (GER),** 5, ch g Zoffany (IRE)—Tiangua **Mr R. Wilson**
16 **URANUS DES BORDES (FR),** 7, b g Kapgarde (FR)—Queen des Bordes (FR) **Mr S. Hunt**

Assistant Trainer: Mrs Lucy K. Bridgwater.

56

MR ROBYN BRISLAND, Stockbridge

Postal: **Stud House, Danebury, Stockbridge, Hampshire, SO20 6JX**
Contacts: **MOBILE 07771 656081**
EMAIL robbris@me.com

1 **A LADY FOREVER,** 4, b f Adaay (IRE)—Lady Filly **Mrs M. S. Teversham**
2 **ANDRE AMAR (IRE),** 7, b g Dandy Man (IRE)—Heaven's Vault (IRE) **Mr M. Seedel**
3 **APACHE JEWEL (IRE),** 5, b m Teofilo (IRE)—Floating Along (IRE) **Ferrybank Properties Limited**
4 **APACHE PORTIA,** 4, b f Twilight Son—Nizhoni (USA) **Ferrybank Properties Limited**
5 **BIG IMPACT,** 6, b g Lethal Force (IRE)—Valandraud (IRE) **Mr D. R. J. Freeman**
6 **BLACK BOX,** 6, b m Iffraaj—Perfect Story (IRE) **Cross Channel Racing Club**
7 **BLUE COLLAR LAD,** 4, b g Ardad (IRE)—Wonderful Life (IRE) **Cross Channel Racing & Partner**
8 **BLUE COLLAR LASS,** 4, b f Due Diligence (USA)—Night Premiere (IRE) **Cross Channel Racing Club**
9 **BOMBASTIC (IRE),** 8, ch g Raven's Pass (USA)—Star of The West **Cross Channel Racing Club**
10 **BONNYRIGG (IRE),** 5, b g Zoffany (IRE)—Impressionist Art (USA)
11 **CALONNE (IRE),** 7, gr g Alhebayeb (IRE)—Lady Pastrana (IRE) **Cross Channel Racing Club**
12 **CARPE FORTUNA (IRE),** 4, b g Camacho—Phoenix Clubs (IRE) **Mrs J. Brisland**
13 **CLARITY SPIRIT,** 4, b f Time Test—Matron of Honour (IRE) **Cross Channel Racing & Partner**
14 **COLONIAL LOVE,** 5, b m Australia—Fondly (IRE) **Ferrybank Properties Limited**
15 **COMPASS POINT,** 8, b g Helmet (AUS)—Takarna (IRE) **Cross Channel Racing & Partner**
16 **COOL VIXEN (IRE),** 6, b m Dandy Man (IRE)—Cool Tarifa (IRE) **Mrs J. Brisland**
17 **COOLAGH MAGIC,** 7, b g Sepoy (AUS)—Miliika **Mrs J. Brisland**
18 **CUBAN STRIKE,** 4, b g Havana Gold (IRE)—Adalene **A. N. Page**
19 **DELAGATE THE LADY,** 7, b m Delegator—Lady Phill **Mrs M. S. Teversham**
20 4, B g Kodi Bear (IRE)—Dubai Flower
21 **ELLIE PIPER,** 5, b m Acclamation—Corncockle **Luther Lives On**
22 **EVASIVE POWER (USA),** 7, b g Elusive Quality (USA)—Casting Director (USA)
23 4, B g Al Kazeem—Folly Bridge **Mrs J. A. Cornwell**
24 **HARBOUR STORM,** 8, br g Sayif (IRE)—Minette **Mr C. J. Harding**
25 **IMPERIAL MAJESTY (IRE),** 4, b f Ribchester (IRE)—Dreaming of Rubies **Mrs J. Brisland**
26 **LOVERS' LANE (IRE),** 4, b f Sea The Stars (IRE)—Fondly (IRE) **Ferrybank Properties Limited**
27 **MONSIEUR PATAT,** 6, b g Coach House (IRE)—Miss Trish (IRE) **Wackey Racers Harefield**
28 **NAVAL COMMANDER,** 6, b br g French Navy—Quail Landing **Mrs Jackie Cornwell & Mrs Jo Brisland**
29 **NICK VEDDER,** 9, b g Rip Van Winkle (IRE)—Devotion (IRE) **Wackey Racers Harefield**
30 **PORTERINTHEJUNGLE (IRE),** 7, ch m Bungle Inthejungle—Porto Calero **Cross Channel Racing & Partner**
31 **POWER OVER ME (IRE),** 6, b g Ivawood (IRE)—Bridge Note (USA) **Cross Channel Racing & Partner**
32 **REGATTA QUEEN,** 4, b f Aclaim (IRE)—Sea Regatta (IRE) **Mrs J. A. Cornwell**
33 **REVOLUTIONARY MAN (IRE),** 8, b g Exceed And Excel (AUS)—Bint Almukhtar (IRE) **Mr M. Seedel**
34 **SERGEANT TIBBS,** 5, b g Bobby's Kitten (USA)—Beautiful View **Nick Andersen & Partner**
35 **SHOOT TO KILL (IRE),** 6, b g Dandy Man (IRE)—Nancy Astor **Mrs A. L. Heayns**
36 **SHOWDIEMLAD (IRE),** 4, b g Showcasing—Carpe Diem Lady (IRE) **Sheepwash Syndicate**
37 **SWATCH (IRE),** 4, b g Time Test—Gliding (IRE) **Mrs J. Brisland**
38 **THE CRUISING LORD,** 7, b g Coach House (IRE)—Lady Filly **Mrs M. S. Teversham**
39 **THEREHEGOES,** 4, b g Charming Thought—Chatalong (IRE) **Mrs A. L. Heayns**
40 **ZANDORA (IRE),** 4, b f Ulysses (IRE)—Mayberain (IRE) **Cross Channel Racing & Partner**

THREE-YEAR-OLDS

41 **ANGE DE L'AMOUR,** b f Harry Angel (IRE)—Ocelot **Mrs A. L. Heayns**

MR ROBYN BRISLAND - continued

42 **ANGEL TIME (IRE),** b f Penny's Picnic (IRE)—Tarawa (FR) **Mrs J. Brisland**
43 **BALA HATUN,** b f Iffraaj—Lyricist **Houghton Bloodstock**
44 **CAPTAIN CISCO (IRE),** b g Ivawood (IRE)—Another World (GER) **Cross Channel Racing & Partner**
45 **CLIMATE QUEEN,** b f Mukhadram—Dawaa
46 **DADAVIC (IRE),** b g Ivawood (IRE)—Amelino (IRE)
47 B c Raven's Pass (USA)—Daliana
48 Ch f Mayson—Dea Caelestis (FR)
49 **DORAS TAMAR (IRE),** b f Holy Roman Emperor (IRE)—Amber Morning
50 **GREENBRIDGE BOY,** b g Equiano (FR)—Rocco Rumbled **Cross Channel Racing Club**
51 Ch c Harbour Law—Harbour Star
52 B f Territories (IRE)—Haven's Wave (IRE)
53 **KINGSBURY (IRE),** b g Bungle Inthejungle—Without Doubt (IRE) **Cross Channel Racing & Partner**
54 B g Bobby's Kitten (USA)—Lassies Envoi **Houghton Bloodstock**
55 **LUNARIO (IRE),** gr c Gregorian (IRE)—Levade **Mrs J. Brisland**
56 B g Muhaarar—Making Eyes (IRE)
57 **RANGER THUNDERBOLT (IRE),** b g Dragon Pulse (IRE)—Mary Ann Bugg (IRE) **Mrs J. Brisland**
58 **RIXO LAD (IRE),** b g Kuroshio (AUS)—Alba Verde
59 B g Mayson—Royal Grace
60 **SANGUIS DIAMOND (IRE),** b f Camacho—Quickstyx
61 B c Harbour Law—Sea Whisper **Mrs J. A. Cornwell**
62 **SECRET NOTE (IRE),** b c Kessaar (IRE)—Love Note (USA) **Mrs J. Brisland**
63 B c Territories (IRE)—Sensible **Houghton Bloodstock**
64 Ch g Galileo Gold—Silca Boo
65 B f Harbour Law—Six Diamonds
66 **STOCKS PARK,** b f Mayson—Lever Park (IRE) **Mrs J. Brisland**
67 Ch f Harbour Law—Straviethirteen
68 B c Harbour Law—Sugar Beach (FR)
69 Ch c Harbour Law—Tohfa (IRE) **Mrs J. A. Cornwell**
70 **ZALICIA FIRE (IRE),** b f Cable Bay (IRE)—Tamara Moon (IRE) **Cross Channel Racing & Partner**

TWO-YEAR-OLDS

71 B f 24/04 Eqtidaar (IRE)—Be Amazing (IRE) (Refuse To Bend (IRE)) (5000)
72 B f 16/04 Land Force (IRE)—Commence (Oasis Dream) (3333)
73 B c 20/03 Outstrip—Diktalina (Diktat) (7000)
74 B f 27/02 Bungle Inthejungle—Excellent World (IRE) (Excellent Art) (4286)
75 B c 19/02 Pearl Secret—Rock Cake (IRE) (Fastnet Rock (AUS)) (5714)
76 B c 08/04 Washington DC (IRE)—Seaperle (Firebreak) (952)

Flat Jockey: Martin Harley, Luke Morris.

---

57 MR ANTONY BRITTAIN, Warthill

Postal: **Northgate Lodge, Warthill, York, YO19 5XR**
Contacts: **PHONE 01759 371472 FAX 01759 372915**
EMAIL email@antonybrittain.co.uk WEBSITE www.antonybrittain.co.uk

1 **ABNAA,** 6, b g Dark Angel (IRE)—Along Came Casey (IRE) **John & Tony Jarvis & Partner**
2 **ANOTHER ANGEL (IRE),** 9, b g Dark Angel (IRE)—Kermana (IRE) **Mr Antony Brittain**
3 **ASADJUMEIRAH,** 5, b g Adaay (IRE)—Place In My Heart **Made Profiles Ltd & Partner**
4 **BELLAGIO MAN (IRE),** 5, b g Dandy Man (IRE)—Rouge Noir **Paul Musson & Antony Brittain**
5 **CAVALRYMAN,** 4, b g Muhaarar—Noozhah **Mr Antony Brittain**
6 **DALGLISH (IRE),** 4, b g Aclaim (IRE)—Lamps of Heaven (IRE) **Mrs C. Brittain**
7 **DREAM SHOW,** 4, b g Tamayuz—Got To Dream
8 **EL JAD (IRE),** 5, ch g Shamardal (USA)—Doors To Manual (USA) **Mrs C. Brittain**
9 **ELDEYAAR (IRE),** 4, br g Slade Power (IRE)—Wardat Dubai **Made Profiles Ltd & Partner**
10 **FAI FAI,** 4, b g Acclamation—Sabratah

MR ANTONY BRITTAIN - continued

11 **GALTON,** 4, b g Kingman—Ultrasonic (USA) **Tykes & Terriers Racing Club & Partner**
12 **GUN SALUTE (IRE),** 4, b g Bated Breath—Guana (IRE) **Mrs C. Brittain**
13 **INEXPLICABLE (IRE),** 6, gr g Dark Angel (IRE)—Bikini Babe (IRE) **R Wherritt & Partner**
14 **INTERNATIONAL LAW,** 9, gr g Exceed And Excel (AUS)—Cruel Sea (USA) **John & Tony Jarvis & Partner**
15 **MONDAMMEJ,** 6, b g Lope de Vega (IRE)—Lamps of Heaven (IRE) **Mrs C. Brittain**
16 **MURBIH (IRE),** 4, b g Kodiac—Leyburn **Paul Musson & Antony Brittain**
17 **MUTABAAHY (IRE),** 8, b g Oasis Dream—Habaayib **Mr Antony Brittain**
18 **SPARTAN FIGHTER,** 6, b g Dutch Art—Survived **John & Tony Jarvis & Partner**
19 **TATHMEEN (IRE),** 8, b g Exceed And Excel (AUS)—Deyaar (USA) **Mr Antony Brittain**
20 **YAAHOBBY (IRE),** 4, b g Kodiac—Nations Alexander (IRE) **Styler, Chambers A Brittain**

THREE-YEAR-OLDS

21 B f Pastoral Pursuits—Ananda Kanda (USA)
22 **KEEP IT HUSH,** b f Charm Spirit (IRE)—Kept Under Wraps (IRE) **Mrs C. Brittain**
23 **TURBO TIGER (IRE),** b g Markaz (IRE)—Wardat Dubai **Made Profiles Ltd & Partner**

TWO-YEAR-OLDS

24 B c 11/03 Dutch Art—Prominence (Pivotal) (15000)

Flat Jockey: Cam Hardie.

58

MR DANIEL BROOKE, Middleham

Postal: **Brough Farm, Middleham, LEYBURN, North Yorkshire, DL8 4SG**
Contacts: **PHONE 01969 625259**
EMAIL danny.brooke@yahoo.com

1 **CARAMELLO (IRE),** 4, ch f Ultra (IRE)—Putaringonit (IRE) **Mr D. Thomas**
2 **DERWENT DEALER (IRE),** 7, gr g Cloudings (IRE)—Feenakilmeedy (IRE) **D & SJ Barker**
3 **DREAM DEAL,** 4, b g Due Diligence (USA)—Triveni (FR) **D & SJ Barker**
4 **FEARLESS (IRE),** 8, b g Arakan (USA)—La Spezia (IRE) **The Fearless Partnership**
5 **FLAVIUS TITUS,** 8, ch g Lethal Force (IRE)—Furbelow **Mr Foster & Partner**
6 **FRISCO QUEEN (IRE),** 7, b m Kalanisi (IRE)—Brownlow Castle (IRE) **Mr J. Flaherty**
7 **GET PHAR (IRE),** 7, b g Getaway (GER)—Lasado (IRE) **The Rolypoly Partnership**
8 **GRIFTER,** 4, b g Dandy Man (IRE)—Fleabiscuit (IRE) **Mr S. A. Sowray**
9 **HUMPS AND BUMPS (IRE),** 10, b m Court Cave (IRE)—
Cat Burglar (IRE) **Mary Sadler, Mervyn Buckley & the Bfrp**
10 **MELVICH BAY,** 6, b m Telescope (IRE)—Douryna **Mr Allan A Grant & Mrs Julia Brooke**
11 **REDESDALE REBEL,** 7, ch g Mayson—Jubilee **Mrs J. A. Brooke**
12 **ROCCO STORM (IRE),** 8, b g Shirocco (GER)—Line White (FR) **The Rolypoly Partnership**
13 **SILKSTONE (IRE),** 7, b g Alhebayeb (IRE)—Fine Silk (USA) **The Dalby Family**
14 **SONNING (IRE),** 5, gr g The Gurkha (IRE)—Moon Empress (FR) **The Sonning Syndicate**

THREE-YEAR-OLDS

15 **ACT OF WILL,** b g Mondialiste (IRE)—Silver Act (IRE) **Geoff & Sandra Turnbull & Mrs J A Brooke**
16 B f Mondialiste (IRE)—Red Hibiscus **Miss S. J. Turner**

TWO-YEAR-OLDS

17 B g 19/01 Phoenix of Spain (IRE)—Josette (IRE) (Danehill (USA)) (11204) **Mrs J. A. Brooke**
18 B f 21/01 Mondialiste (IRE)—Winter Bloom (USA) (Aptitude (USA)) **Geoff & Sandra Turnbull & Alice Brooke**

---

59 MR BENJAMIN BROOKHOUSE, Newmarket

Postal: **St Marys Square, Newmarket , Suffolk, CB8 0HZ**
Contacts: **PHONE 07488 710423**
EMAIL ben@brookhouseracing.co.uk

1 **ASLUKGOES,** 5, b g Yorgunnabelucky (USA)—She's The Lady **R. S. Brookhouse**
2 **ATHGARVAN (IRE),** 6, b g Soldier of Fortune (IRE)—Foildearg (IRE) **R. S. Brookhouse**
3 **BIG BRESIL,** 8, b g Blue Bresil (FR)—Cutielilou (FR) **R. S. Brookhouse**
4 **BLUE HOP (IRE),** 6, b g Soldier of Fortune (IRE)—Afaraka (IRE) **R. S. Brookhouse**
5 **BOBBY THE GREAT,** 6, b g Frankel—Riberac **R. S. Brookhouse**
6 **CARDANO (USA),** 7, b g Oasis Dream—Astorgs Galaxy **R. S. Brookhouse**
7 **CHAMPAGNE CITY,** 10, ch g Tobougg (IRE)—City of Angels **R. S. Brookhouse**
8 **DARK MYSTERY (IRE),** 4, b g Dark Angel (IRE)—Jakonda (USA) **R. S. Brookhouse**
9 **ESPOIR DE TEILLEE (FR),** 11, b g Martaline—Belle de Lyphard (FR) **R. S. Brookhouse**
10 **LUCKY'S DREAM,** 8, ch g Yorgunnabelucky (USA)—Dream Esteem **R. S. Brookhouse**
11 **MISS CHANTELLE,** 6, b m Yorgunnabelucky (USA)—Miss Estela (IRE) **R. S. Brookhouse**
12 **MY CHIQUITA,** 4, b f Postponed (IRE)—Warling (IRE) **R. S. Brookhouse**
13 **RAYA TIME (FR),** 10, gr g Al Namix (FR)—Ruthenoise (FR) **R. S. Brookhouse**
14 **RESET BUTTON,** 5, b g Yorgunnabelucky (USA)—Reset City **R. S. Brookhouse**
15 **SARSONS RISK (IRE),** 4, gr g Caravaggio (USA)—Pink Damsel (IRE) **R. S. Brookhouse**
16 **TELLITASITIS,** 4, b f Telescope (IRE)—Alasi **R. S. Brookhouse**
17 **WEST WARHORSE (IRE),** 5, b g Westerner—An Banog (IRE) **R. S. Brookhouse**
18 **YORADREAMER,** 4, ch g Yorgunnabelucky (USA)—Dream Esteem **R. S. Brookhouse**

TWO-YEAR-OLDS

19 B c 29/04 Phoenix of Spain (IRE)—Chicita Banana (Danehill Dancer (IRE)) (100000) **R. S. Brookhouse**
20 B c 18/04 Invincible Army (IRE)—Cracking Lass (IRE) (Whipper (USA)) (25000) **R. S. Brookhouse**
21 B c 26/03 Footstepsinthesand—Dubai (IRE) (Galileo (IRE)) (90000) **R. S. Brookhouse**
22 B c 13/02 Profitable (IRE)—Ibergman (IRE) (Big Bad Bob (IRE)) (36190) **R. S. Brookhouse**
23 B c 27/04 Ten Sovereigns (IRE)—Pink Damsel (IRE) (Galileo (IRE)) (90000) **R. S. Brookhouse**
24 Br c 17/04 Golden Horn—Terentia (Diktat) (4000) **R. S. Brookhouse**
25 B c 16/02 Postponed (IRE)—Warling (IRE) (Montjeu (IRE)) (33000) **R. S. Brookhouse**
26 B c 08/04 Golden Horn—Whirly Bird (Nashwan (USA)) (75000) **R. S. Brookhouse**
27 B c 24/03 Too Darn Hot—Whispering Bell (IRE) (Galileo (IRE)) (142857) **R. S. Brookhouse**

---

60 MR ROY BROTHERTON, Pershore

Postal: **Mill End Racing Stables, Netherton Road, Elmley Castle, Pershore, Worcestershire, WR10 3JF**
Contacts: **PHONE 01386 710772 MOBILE 07973 877280**

1 **AUNTIE JUNE,** 7, ch m Piccolo—Basle **Mr M. A. Geobey**
2 **CNOC SION (IRE),** 13, b g Gold Well—Bondi Babe (IRE) **Exors of the Late C. A. Newman**
3 **DEISE VU (IRE),** 15, b g Brian Boru—Deise Dreamer (IRE) **Elmley Queen**
4 **DUN BAY CREEK,** 12, b g Dubai Destination (USA)—Over It **Elmley Queen 2**
5 **EVA'S DIVA (IRE),** 9, b m Getaway (GER)—Shouette (IRE) **Miss S. C. Longford**
6 **FILBERT STREET,** 8, ch g Poet's Voice—Tinnarinka **R. Brotherton**
7 5, B m Norse Dancer (IRE)—Prairie Light **Elmley Queen 2**
8 **WHERE'S THE DOG,** 5, ch m Mortga (FR)—So Belle **Miss S. C. Longford**

Assistant Trainer: Justin Brotherton.

NH Jockey: Jamie Moore.

---

61 MR ALAN BROWN, Malton

Postal: **Lilac Farm, Yedingham, Malton, North Yorkshire, YO17 8SS**
Contacts: **PHONE 07970 672845 MOBILE 07970 672845**
EMAIL ad.brown@hotmail.co.uk WEBSITE www.alanbrownracing.co.uk

1 **ATRAFAN (IRE),** 9, b g Atraf—Up Front (IRE) **Mr F. E. Reay**
2 **BESSAH,** 8, b m Dick Turpin (IRE)—Trompette (USA) **David Furman & John Sugarman**
3 **BLACKCURRENT,** 7, b g Kuroshio (AUS)—Mamounia (IRE) **A. D. Brown, S. E. Pedersen**
4 **BLACKJACK,** 6, b g Sleeping Indian—Medam **The Hon Mrs E. S. Cunliffe-Lister**
5 **BOBBA TEE,** 11, b g Rail Link—Trompette (USA) **Mr D. E. Furman, Mr J. B. Sugarman**
6 **BOBBING ALONG,** 4, b g Albaasil (IRE)—Medam **The Hon Mrs E. S. Cunliffe-Lister**
7 **CROWNTHORPE,** 8, b g Monsieur Bond (IRE)—Normandy Maid **A. D. Brown**
8 **EMBLA,** 5, b m Albaasil (IRE)—Medam **The Hon Mrs E. S. Cunliffe-Lister**
9 **ICE SHADOW (IRE),** 4, b g Buratino (IRE)—Chicane **A. D. Brown**
10 **JEMS BOND,** 6, ch g Monsieur Bond (IRE)—Saphire **A. D. Brown, Mr F. E. Reay**
11 **LADY CELIA,** 6, b m Mayson—Fairy Shoes **A. D. Brown**
12 **MILKY TEAL,** 5, gr m Milk It Mick—Tealstoken Girl **Mr C. I. Ratcliffe**
13 **THORDIAC,** 4, b f Night of Thunder (IRE)—Nefetari **Mr F. E. Reay**
14 **URBAN ROAD,** 4, ch g Monsieur Bond (IRE)—Normandy Maid **A. D. Brown**

THREE-YEAR-OLDS

15 **CLEMENTYNE,** b f Peace Envoy (FR)—Miss Mohawk (IRE) **Mrs M. A. Doherty**
16 **CYBELE,** ch f Pastoral Pursuits—Medam **The Hon Mrs E. S. Cunliffe-Lister**
17 **LITTLE RED DANCER,** b f Pastoral Pursuits—Meandmyshadow **Mr A. Brown & Mr I. Stewart**
18 **MINCHINHAMPTON,** ch f Mayson—Normandy Maid **The Odd Partnership**
19 **RODBOROUGH,** b f Mayson—Fairy Shoes **The Odd Partnership**

TWO-YEAR-OLDS

20 B f 14/04 Massaat (IRE)—Meandmyshadow (Tobougg (IRE))
21 B f 09/03 Sogann (FR)—Rubis (Monsieur Bond (IRE)) (1429)

---

62 MR ANDI BROWN, Newmarket

Postal: **Southfields Stables, Hamilton Road, Newmarket, Suffolk, CB8 7JQ**
Contacts: **PHONE 01638 669652 MOBILE 07980 393263 FAX 01638 669652**
EMAIL southfieldsstables@btinternet.com WEBSITE www.southfieldsstables.co.uk

1 **KIRTLING,** 12, gr g Araafa (IRE)—Cape Maya **Faith Hope and Charity**
2 **MAKTER,** 6, b g Sepoy (AUS)—Perfect Silence **Miss L. J. Knocker**
3 **MR FUSTIC (IRE),** 5, b g Epaulette (AUS)—Marion Antoinette (IRE) **Dave Tonge, Steph Collins. Phil Mills**

THREE-YEAR-OLDS

4 **RAY THE HAY,** b c Dream Eater (IRE)—Noora Dream

Assistant Trainer: Miss Linsey Knocker.

---

63 MR GARY BROWN, Compton

Postal: **East Yard, Hamilton Stables, Hockham Road, Compton, Berkshire, RG20 6QJ**
Contacts: **PHONE 07545 915253**
EMAIL gbrownracing@hotmail.co.uk

1 **ALIOSKI,** 6, b g Kodiac—Luluti (IRE) **G. Cheshire**
2 **CARDS ARE DEALT (IRE),** 7, ch g Mastercraftsman (IRE)—High Praise (USA) **Mr K. W. Sneath**

MR GARY BROWN - continued

3 **EATON LADY (IRE),** 7, b m Presenting—Beluckyagain (IRE) **Brighton Girls**
4 **GRAFFITI,** 4, b g Sixties Icon—Outside Art **Enigma**
5 **HANNAH'S RETURN,** 4, b f Holy Roman Emperor (IRE)—Hannahs Turn **Mr K. W. Sneath**
6 **HE IS A CRACKER (IRE),** 7, b g Califet (FR)—She Is A Cracker (FR) **Enigma**
7 5, B g Soldier of Fortune (IRE)—Regal Maya
8 **REINE FEE (IRE),** 10, b m Kalanisi (IRE)—Cave Woman (IRE) **Enigma**
9 **SHALOTT (IRE),** 6, b g Camelot—Nasanice (IRE) **B & N Byrne**
10 **YOUCONDUIT (IRE),** 5, b g Conduit (IRE)—Hathamore **The Milk Sheiks**

---

64 MISS HARRIET BROWN, Sturminster Newton

Postal: **Blenheim Cottage,Quar Close, Mappowder, Sturminster Newton, Dorset, DT10 2EN**
Contacts: **MOBILE 07798 613111**
EMAIL harriet_brown1@hotmail.co.uk

1 **COSMORE,** 5, b m Davidoff (GER)—Cantzagua (FR) **Glanvilles Stud Partners**
2 **DANNYSTORY (IRE),** 6, b g Arcadio (GER)—Detente **Harriet Brown Racing Club**
3 **DESIGNER JET (IRE),** 7, gr g Jet Away—Casa Queen (IRE) **Miss H. Brown**
4 **JOYFUL KIT (IRE),** 7, b m Getaway (GER)—Kitara (GER) **Harriet Brown Racing Club**
5 **MR ONE MORE (IRE),** 11, b g Asian Heights—Norah's Quay (IRE)
6 **NOMOREDANCING,** 7, b m Norse Dancer (IRE)—Morebutwhen **R. J. King**
7 7, Br g Geordieland (FR)—On Oath (IRE)
8 5, B g Saddler's Rock (IRE)—On Oath (IRE)
9 **VALIRANN GOLD (IRE),** 6, b g Valirann (FR)—Gola Star (IRE) **Andrew & Mark Bentley**

THREE-YEAR-OLDS

10 B f Great Pretender (IRE)—Cosmic Diamond **Miss H. Brown**

---

65 MR TOBY BULGIN, Thetford

Postal: **High Fen, Thornham Road, Methwold, Thetford, Norfolk, IP26 4PJ**
EMAIL toby@beatbushfarm.co.uk

1 5, Ch g Norse Dancer (IRE)—Amber Cloud **Mrs N. H. Bulgin**
2 **ARTHUR'S SEAT (IRE),** 6, b g Champs Elysees—Sojitzen (FR) **Arthur's Seat Partnership**
3 **DARLING ALKO (FR),** 10, b g Al Namix (FR)—Padalko Tatou (FR) **Mrs N. H. Bulgin**
4 8, B m Librettist (USA)—Jessie May (IRE) **Mrs N. H. Bulgin**
5 **LUCKOFTHEDRAW (FR),** 10, gr g Martaline—La Perspective (FR) **Mrs M.E.Latham Mr John R Latham**
6 4, B f Telescope (IRE)—Materiality **Mrs N. H. Bulgin**
7 5, B m Clovis du Berlais (FR)—Mere Detail (IRE) **Mrs N. H. Bulgin**
8 4, B g Youmzain (IRE)—Our Lucky Venture (IRE) **Mrs N. H. Bulgin**
9 **RAPAPORT,** 11, b m Dr Massini (IRE)—Seemarye **Mrs N. H. Bulgin**
10 **SOLAR SOVEREIGN (IRE),** 8, b g Multiplex—Royal Roxy (IRE) **Mrs N. H. Bulgin**
11 **TRICOMI,** 8, b br m Getaway (GER)—Annaghbrack (IRE) **Mrs N. H. Bulgin**

THREE-YEAR-OLDS

12 B f Kayf Tara—Mere Detail (IRE) **Mrs N. H. Bulgin**

66 MR KARL BURKE, Leyburn

Postal: **Spigot Lodge, Middleham, Leyburn, North Yorkshire, DL8 4TL**
Contacts: **PHONE 01969 625088 MOBILE 07778 458777 FAX 01969 625099**
EMAIL karl@karlburke.co.uk WEBSITE www.karlburke.co.uk

1 **AL QAREEM (IRE),** 4, b g Awtaad (IRE)—Moqla **Nick Bradley Racing 33 + Burke**
2 **BARON RUN,** 13, ch g Bertolini (USA)—Bhima **Mr Eric Burke & Partner**
3 **BEGGARMANS ROAD (IRE),** 4, b g Elzaam (AUS)—Kiralik **West Shaw Farm & Burke**
4 **BENEFICIARY,** 4, b g Profitable (IRE)—La Roumegue (USA) **Almohamediya Racing & Mrs E Burke**
5 **EILEAN DUBH (IRE),** 5, b h Vadamos (FR)—Kenwana (FR) **Pau - Perth Partnership**
6 **EL CABALLO,** 4, b c Havana Gold (IRE)—Showstoppa **Grange Park Racing XVIII & Ofo Partners**
7 **EXALTED ANGEL (FR),** 7, b g Dark Angel (IRE)—Hurryupharriet (IRE) **Pau-Perth Partnership & Mrs E Burke**
8 **FAST RESPONSE (IRE),** 4, b f Fast Company (IRE)—Deemah (IRE) **Nick Bradley Racing 39**
9 **FEMME PATRONNE (IRE),** 4, gr f El Kabeir (USA)—Little Audio (IRE) **More Turf Racing & Mrs E Burke**
10 **FORGETMENOTBLUE (IRE),** 4, ch f Pivotal—Love In The Sun (IRE) **Mr Z. Yuesheng**
11 **FRONTLINE PHANTOM (IRE),** 16, b g Noverre (USA)—Daisy Hill **Mr Eric Burke & Partner**
12 **GIFTED GOLD (IRE),** 4, ch f Galileo Gold—Flare of Firelight (USA) **Mr Carl Waters & Mrs E Burke**
13 **HONEY SWEET (IRE),** 4, b f Adaay (IRE)—Sweet Sienna **Nick Bradley Racing 14 & Mrs E Burke**
14 **JUBILEE GIRL,** 4, b f Nathaniel (IRE)—Chincoteague (IRE) **Mr W. R. Kinsey**
15 **KABOO (USA),** 4, b br c More Than Ready (USA)—Follow Moon (USA) **Nick Bradley Racing 49 & Mrs E Burke**
16 **KORKER (IRE),** 4, b g Dandy Man (IRE)—Adaptation **Claret & Racing**
17 **LAST CRUSADER (IRE),** 4, b g Oasis Dream—Spanish Fly (IRE) **Clipper Group Holdings Ltd**
18 **LETHAL LEVI,** 4, b g Lethal Force (IRE)—Dartrix **Made in Thailand**
19 **LIAMARTY DREAMS,** 4, b g Oasis Dream—Heavenly Verse **Mr Liam Kelly & Mrs E Burke**
20 **LORD OF THE LODGE (IRE),** 6, b h Dandy Man (IRE)—Archetypal (IRE) **Mrs E. M. Burke**
21 **PARALLEL WORLD (IRE),** 7, b g Morpheus—Miss Glitters (IRE) **Mrs E. M. Burke**
22 **POPTRONIC,** 4, b f Nathaniel (IRE)—Alpine Dream (IRE) **David & Yvonne Blunt**
23 **QUICK CHANGE,** 4, b f New Approach (IRE)—Ensemble (FR) **The All About York Partnership**
24 **RIVELLINO,** 13, b g Invincible Spirit (IRE)—Brazilian Bride (IRE) **Mrs E. M. Burke**
25 **RUN TEDDY RUN (FR),** 4, b g Mayson—Idealist **C & E Burke**
26 **SHALLOW HAL,** 7, b g Mayson—Bazelle **Ontoawinner 14 & Mrs E Burke**
27 **SHE'S NO ANGEL (IRE),** 5, ch m Libertarian—Angel Voices (IRE) **Mrs E. M. Burke**
28 **SILKY WILKIE (IRE),** 4, b g Mehmas (IRE)—Vasoni (IRE) **Middleham Park Racing LXXXI & E Burke**
29 **SIR ROBIN (IRE),** 4, gr g El Kabeir (USA)—Lightwood Lady (IRE) **Mrs Barbara Facchino**
30 **SPYCATCHER (IRE),** 5, b h Vadamos (FR)—Damask (IRE) **Highclere T'BredRacing-Adriana Zaefferer**
31 **TOTHENINES (IRE),** 4, gr g Dandy Man (IRE)—Ultimate Best **Middleham Park Racing CI & Mrs E Burke**
32 **TRUE JEM (FR),** 4, b f Dabirsim (FR)—Vally Jem (FR) **Nick Bradley Racing 47**
33 **WHITE LAVENDER (IRE),** 5, b m Heeraat (IRE)—Goodnight And Joy (IRE) **Mrs B. M. Keller**

THREE-YEAR-OLDS

34 **AL NAJADA (IRE),** b c Exceed And Excel (AUS)—Stay Silent (IRE) **Promenade Bloodstock Limited**
35 **ALEXA'S PRINCESS (IRE),** ch f Dandy Man (IRE)—Born To Spend (IRE) **Nick Bradley Racing 9 & Mrs E Burke**
36 **ALICE MC CLORY (IRE),** b f Galileo Gold—Danza Nera (IRE) **Clipper Group Holdings Ltd**
37 **BACK SEE DAA,** b f Lope de Vega (IRE)—Zoella (USA) **Mr C. R. Hirst**
38 **BRIGHT DIAMOND (IRE),** b f El Kabeir (USA)—Starlite Sienna (IRE) **Sheikh R. D. Al Maktoum**
39 B f Night of Thunder (IRE)—Burlesque Star (IRE) **Mrs S. Kelly**
40 **CAMILA VARGAS (IRE),** b f Dandy Man (IRE)—Tilly Trotter (IRE) **Ontoawinner 14 & Mrs E Burke**
41 **CARIAD ANGEL (IRE),** b f Dark Angel (IRE)—Plagiarism (USA) **Nick Bradley Racing 30 & Partner 1**
42 **CINQUE VERDE,** b f Sioux Nation (USA)—Gregoria (IRE) **Mr B & Miss C Green**
43 **COLD CASE,** b c Showcasing—Killermont Street (IRE) **Sheikh Mohammed Obaid Al Maktoum**
44 **COLNAGO (IRE),** b c Sioux Nation (USA)—Dorothy Parker (IRE) **Mr S. B. M. Al Qassimi**
45 **DEE SEE ARE,** b f Massaat (IRE)—Delizia (IRE) **Mr C. R. Hirst**
46 **DESIGN,** b g Expert Eye—Betty Loch **Highclere T'Bred Racing -Mother Teresa**
47 **DRAMATISED (IRE),** b br f Showcasing—Katie's Diamond (FR) **Clipper Group Holdings Ltd**
48 **DUBAI CRYSTAL (IRE),** b f Fastnet Rock (AUS)—Lady Of Dubai **Sheikh Mohammed Obaid Al Maktoum**
49 **EDMUND IRONSIDE,** b g Saxon Warrior (JPN)—Garden Row (IRE) **Claret & Racing**
50 **ELECTRIC EYES (IRE),** b f Siyouni (FR)—Love Is Blindness (IRE) **Clipper Group Holdings Ltd**
51 **ESPIONNE,** b f Dubawi (IRE)—Lunar Vega (IRE) **Sheikh Mohammed Obaid Al Maktoum**

MR KARL BURKE - continued

52 **ETERNAL CLASS,** b f Night of Thunder (IRE)—Gadwa **Clipper Group Holdings Ltd**
53 **EXQUISITELY,** b f Zoustar (AUS)—Ainippe (IRE) **Harron & Pegum**
54 **FLIGHT PLAN,** b c Night of Thunder (IRE)—Romp **Clipper Group Holdings Ltd**
55 **GEORGIAVA,** gr f Havana Grey—Shohrah (IRE) **G & E Burke**
56 **GOLDCASING (IRE),** b f Showcasing—Fort Del Oro (IRE) **Ballylinch Stud**
57 **GREYCIOUS ANNA,** gr f Havana Grey—Annawi **Pau - Perth Partnership**
58 **HOLLOWAY BOY,** ch c Ulysses (IRE)—Sultry **Nick White & Mrs E Burke**
59 **INDESTRUCTIBLE (IRE),** b c Kodiac—Shareva (IRE) **Amo Racing Limited**
60 **JAHIDIN (FR),** b g Kheleyf (USA)—Loda (FR) **Pau - Perth Partnership**
61 **JIM'S CRACKER,** b gr g Havana Grey—Ruby Slippers **Ontoawinner, S Evans & E Burke**
62 **LADY HAMANA (AUS),** b f I Am Invincible (AUS)—Lake Hamana **Mr Z. Yuesheng**
63 **LADY MANYARA (IRE),** ch f Ribchester (IRE)—Tides **Mrs E. M. Burke**
64 **LAST STAND (IRE),** b g Gustav Klimt (IRE)—Queen Elsa (IRE) **Ontoawinner 14 & Mrs E Burke**
65 **LATEST EDITION (IRE),** b f Ribchester (IRE)—Catchline (USA) **Hambleton Racing Ltd XXXV & E Burke**
66 **LIBERTY LANE (IRE),** b c Teofilo (IRE)—Cape Liberty (IRE) **Sheikh Mohammed Obaid Al Maktoum**
67 **LOOKING FOR LYNDA (IRE),** ch g Unfortunately (IRE)—Designated **D & E Burke**
68 **MARSHMAN,** b c Harry Angel (IRE)—White Rosa (IRE) **Nick Bradley Racing 2 & Mrs E Burke**
69 **MISS JUNGLE CAT,** b f Jungle Cat (IRE)—Honky Tonk Sally **The Jungle Partnership**
70 **MONTY MAN (IRE),** b g Kessaar (IRE)—Red Ivy (IRE) **Mr & Mrs Paul & Clare Rooney**
71 **NAOMI'S CHARM (IRE),** b f Charm Spirit (IRE)—Quilita (GER) **Nick Bradley Racing 51 & Mrs E Burke**
72 **NOVAKAI,** b f Lope de Vega (IRE)—Elasia **Sheikh Mohammed Obaid Al Maktoum**
73 **O' DELLS STAR (FR),** b f Whitecliffsofdover (USA)—Ajab Bere (FR) **Nick Bradley Racing 2 & Mrs E Burke**
74 **OVERRULE (IRE),** b c New Bay—Goldamour (IRE) **Clipper Group Holdings Ltd**
75 **PILLOW TALK (IRE),** b f Kodiac—Flawless Jewel (FR) **Clipper Group Holdings Ltd**
76 **QAMRAH (IRE),** b f Decorated Knight—Sounds of April (IRE) **Mr A. Mohamdi**
77 B f Roaring Lion (USA)—Rive Gauche **Mrs E. M. Burke**
78 **ROYAL RHYME (IRE),** b c Lope de Vega (IRE)—Dubai Queen (USA) **Sheikh Mohammed Obaid Al Maktoum**
79 **SECRET ANGEL (IRE),** b f Dark Angel (IRE)—Meydan Princess (IRE) **Nick Bradley Racing 40, Burke & Partner**
80 **SHINE HONEY SHINE,** b f Havana Grey—Military Madame (IRE) **Gove & Shaw 02 & Whitsbury Manor Stud**
81 **SWEET FORTUNE (FR),** b f Unfortunately (IRE)—Sugar Hiccup (IRE) **Wolf Pack 6 & Partners**
82 **SWINGALONG (IRE),** ch f Showcasing—Pilates (IRE) **Sheikh J. D. Al Maktoum**
83 **TAH LUV (FR),** b f Shalaa (IRE)—Crystal War (IRE) **Mr R. Kent**
84 **TILT AT WINDMILLS (IRE),** ch f Dandy Man (IRE)—Satin Ribbon **Middleham Park Racing CXIX**
85 **TONDEUSE (FR),** bl f Dabirsim (FR)—Fresh Laurels (IRE) **Nick Bradley Racing 45**
86 **WINTER MELODY,** gr f Havana Grey—Rebecca de Winter **Clipper Group Holdings Ltd**
87 **YAHSAT (IRE),** b f Dandy Man (IRE)—Barqeyya (IRE) **Mr S. B. M. Al Qassimi**

TWO-YEAR-OLDS

88 Gr f 31/03 Too Darn Hot—Agnes Stewart (IRE) (Lawman (FR)) **Clipper Group Holdings Ltd**
89 B c 16/03 Mehmas (IRE)—Ajla (IRE) (Exceed And Excel (AUS)) (180000) **Mr Z. Yuesheng**
90 B f 08/05 Dark Angel (IRE)—Alexandrite (Oasis Dream) (40000)
91 Gr c 15/02 Soldier's Call—Alicia Darcy (IRE) (Sir Prancealot (IRE)) (33613) **Bronte Collection 1**
92 B f 25/02 Showcasing—All Out (Acclamation) **R. Barnett**
93 B c 10/02 Territories (IRE)—Anew (Oasis Dream) **Mr A. Mohamdi**
94 **BAZBALL (IRE),** b f 10/03 Estidhkaar (IRE)—
Sofi's Spirit (IRE) (Captain Marvelous (IRE)) (8003) **Nick Bradley Racing 5 & E Burke**
95 B f 20/02 Profitable (IRE)—Big Sky (Fastnet Rock (AUS)) (20000) **Fitzwilliams, Railton**
96 Br c 19/02 Dark Angel (IRE)—Blackgold Fairy (USA) (More Than Ready (USA)) **Mr Z. Yuesheng**
97 B c 31/03 Wootton Bassett—Blossom Mills (Bahamian Bounty) (280000) **John & Jessica Dance**
98 Br c 01/02 Bated Breath—Caped Lady (IRE) (Cape Cross (IRE)) (80032) **Clipper Group Holdings Ltd**
99 B f 25/03 Kodiac—Cartesienne (IRE) (Pivotal) (32013) **Mr R. Kent**
100 **CHURROS,** b c 26/01 Calyx—Winter Light (Bated Breath) (17143) **Mrs M. Bryce**
101 Gr c 23/03 Dark Angel (IRE)—
Cool Kitten (IRE) (One Cool Cat (USA)) (105000) **Sheikh Mohammed Obaid Al Maktoum**
102 **CUBAN SLIDE,** gr c 04/03 Havana Grey—Piper Bomb (IRE) (Dandy Man (IRE)) (57000) **Justwow Ltd & Mrs E Burke**
103 **DANDIVA,** ch f 16/04 Dandy Man (IRE)—Castleton Girl (IRE) (Hallowed Crown (AUS)) **Made in Thailand**
104 B f 28/02 Zoustar (AUS)—Dice Game (Shamardal (USA)) (325000) **Sheikh Mohammed Obaid Al Maktoum**
105 B c 29/01 Havana Grey—Dotted Swiss (IRE) (Swiss Spirit) (325000) **Sheikh Mohammed Obaid Al Maktoum**
106 B f 27/03 Dandy Man (IRE)—Dream Sleep (Rip Van Winkle (IRE)) (35214) **G & E Burke**

MR KARL BURKE - continued

107 B c 07/03 Calyx—Dubai Affair (Dubawi (IRE)) (72000) **Timmins, Rhodes & Burke**
108 B f 20/02 Soldier's Call—Dushlan (IRE) (New Approach (IRE)) (32013) **Mohammad & Burke**
109 B f 05/05 Dabirsim (FR)—Elnadwa (USA) (Daaher (CAN)) (6403) **Nick Bradley Racing 5 & E Burke**
110 Gr c 08/02 Cracksman—Fearlessly (IRE) (Dalakhani (IRE)) **S. Ali**
111 B f 26/03 Soldier's Call—Festoso (IRE) (Diesis) **Clipper Group Holdings Ltd**
112 FLIGHT RADAR (IRE), b c 10/04 James Garfield (IRE)—
Academicienne (CAN) (Royal Academy (USA)) (22857) **Titanium Racing Club**
113 B f 07/04 Siyouni (FR)—Foreign Legionary (IRE) (Galileo (IRE)) (200000) **Sheikh Mohammed Obaid Al Maktoum**
114 B c 10/04 Soldier's Call—Forever More (IRE) (Galileo (IRE)) (27211) **Ahmad Bintouq & E Burke**
115 B f 02/02 Magna Grecia (IRE)—Four's Company (IRE) (Fast Company (IRE)) (38095) **John & Jessica Dance**
116 B f 21/01 Showcasing—Funny Enough (Dansili) (110000) **John & Jessica Dance**
117 B f 17/02 Too Darn Hot—Galicuix (Galileo (IRE)) (240000) **Mr H. Dalmook Al Maktoum**
118 B c 12/02 Showcasing—Give And Take (Cityscape) (300000) **Sheikh Mohammed Obaid Al Maktoum**
119 HAIL CEASAR, b c 29/04 Holy Roman Emperor (IRE)—Hail Shower (IRE) (Red Clubs (IRE)) **Hunscote Stud Limited**
120 HARVANNA, b f 05/03 Havana Grey—Weisse Socken (IRE) (Acclamation) (46419) **Clarets & E Burke**
121 B c 28/02 Invincible Spirit (IRE)—Hikmaa (IRE) (Roderic O'Connor (IRE)) **Mr H. Dalmook Al Maktoum**
122 INSTANT RECALL, b c 27/04 Showcasing—
Delizia (IRE) (Dark Angel (IRE)) (50000) **Ken Lawrence, Justwow Ltd & Burke**
123 Br c 27/03 Kodiac—Kendal Mint (Kyllachy) (144058) **Clipper Group Holdings Ltd**
124 Br c 09/04 No Nay Never (USA)—Lady Corsica (IRE) (Galileo (IRE)) (155000) **Mr Z. Yuesheng**
125 Ch f 23/04 Showcasing—Lady Estella (IRE) (Equiano (FR)) (115000) **Sheikh J. D. Al Maktoum**
126 B f 20/04 Dark Angel (IRE)—Lidanski (IRE) (Soviet Star (USA)) (190000) **Mr Z. Yuesheng**
127 Ch f 24/01 Le Havre (IRE)—Like (IRE) (Frankel) (50000) **Mr Z. Yuesheng**
128 B c 29/03 Invincible Army (IRE)—Little Audio (IRE) (Shamardal (USA)) (52021) **Titanium Racing Club**
129 LIVINNXTDORTOALICE (IRE), b f 16/01 Dark Angel (IRE)—
Wings of The Rock (IRE) (Rock of Gibraltar (IRE)) (35214) **Nick Bradley Racing 40, Burke & Partner**
130 LOCHABER, b c 01/02 Havana Grey—
Yolo Star (IRE) (Society Rock (IRE)) (37000) **Pau-Perth Partnership & Mrs E Burke**
131 LONGHAIRED GENERAL (IRE), b c 04/02 Kessaar (IRE)—
Miss Glitters (IRE) (Chevalier (IRE)) (8003) **Gove & Shaw Racing**
132 B f 16/03 Inns of Court (IRE)—Luna Rosa (IRE) (Marju (IRE)) **R & K Mrs R Heaton & West Shaw Farm**
133 MAKING DREAMS (IRE), b f 28/04 Make Believe—
Sweet Dream (Oasis Dream) (33000) **Nick Bradley Racing 5 & E Burke**
134 MANNERISM (IRE), b c 13/02 Caravaggio (USA)—
Bright And Sunny (IRE) (Galileo (IRE)) (90000) **Highclere Thoroughbred Racing-Rembrandt**
135 B c 30/03 Ardad (IRE)—Mara Grey (IRE) (Azamour (IRE)) (130000) **Sheikh J. D. Al Maktoum**
136 B c 28/02 Oasis Dream—Marie of Lyon (Royal Applause) **Clipper Group Holdings Ltd**
137 B c 20/04 Dandy Man (IRE)—More Respect (IRE) (Spectrum (IRE)) (156062) **Mr Z. Yuesheng**
138 B c 20/01 Blue Point (IRE)—
Music Chart (USA) (Exchange Rate (USA)) (76190) **Victorious Racing Limited & Fawzi Nass**
139 B f 29/03 Showcasing—Must Be Me (Trade Fair) (57143) **Victorious Racing Limited & Fawzi Nass**
140 B f 08/04 Bungle Inthejungle—Naadrah (Muhtathir) (12805) **Hambleton Racing Ltd XXXV & E Burke**
141 NU DISCO (IRE), b c 24/04 Siyouni (FR)—Sequined (USA) (Street Cry (IRE)) (160064) **John & Jessica Dance**
142 B c 01/02 Showcasing—Parliament House (IRE) (Slade Power (IRE)) (115000) **Mr H. Dalmook Al Maktoum**
143 PETRA CELERA (IRE), b f 05/03 Inns of Court (IRE)—
Frabrika (IRE) (Intense Focus (USA)) (15000) **Nick Bradley Racing 5 & E Burke**
144 B f 31/03 Saxon Warrior (JPN)—Pyrean (IRE) (Teofilo (IRE)) (350000) **Mrs Barbara Facchino**
145 B c 30/03 Soldier's Call—Queen Elsa (IRE) (Frozen Power (IRE)) (33613) **Nick Bradley Racing 5 & E Burke**
146 Ch c 09/04 Mehmas (IRE)—Queensgate (Compton Place) (210000) **Clipper Group Holdings Ltd**
147 B c 06/03 Soldier's Call—Safeenah (Oasis Dream) **Clipper Group Holdings Ltd**
148 B c 12/03 Kodiac—Scarlet Pimpernel (Sir Percy) (88000) **Timmins, Rhodes, Burke & Partner**
149 Bl f 05/03 Dabirsim (FR)—Snowbright (Pivotal) (20808) **Nick Bradley Racing 5 & E Burke**
150 B c 02/02 Advertise—Velvet Revolver (IRE) (Mujahid (USA)) (71429) **Bronte Collection 1**
151 B c 02/04 Unfortunately (IRE)—
Vulnicura (IRE) (Frozen Power (IRE)) (40000) **Middleham Park Racing LXIII & E Burke**
152 WASHEEK (IRE), b c 23/04 Saxon Warrior (JPN)—Desert Version (Green Desert (USA)) (64026) **Mr M. S. Al Shahi**
153 B f 10/02 Saxon Warrior (JPN)—Water Hole (IRE) (Oasis Dream) (46419) **Bronte Collection 1**
154 WEDYAN, b f 13/03 Advertise—Button Moon (IRE) (Compton Place) (62000) **Mr M. S. Al Shahi**
155 B f 23/02 Night of Thunder (IRE)—Zoella (USA) (Invincible Spirit (IRE)) (100000) **Mr Z. Yuesheng**

MR KARL BURKE - continued

Assistant Trainer: Mrs Elaine Burke, Kelly Burke, Lucy Burke, Joe O'Gorman, **Pupil Assistant:** Ian Hickey.

Flat Jockey: Ben Curtis, Clifford Lee. **Apprentice Jockey:** Rhona Pindar, Harrison Shaw.

---

67 MR KEIRAN BURKE, Dorchester

Postal: **Whitcombe Monymusk Racing Stables, Whitcombe, Dorchester, Dorset, DT2 8NY**
Contacts: **MOBILE 07855 860993**
WORK EMAIL info@kieranburkeracing.co.uk

1 **BROADSHARE,** 4, gr g Kodiac—Bruxcalina (FR) **Mrs M. A. Crook**
2 **CALL ME TLALOK,** 8, ch g Tiger Groom—Laureldean Belle (IRE) **Mrs V. Perrott**
3 **CAPTAIN PROBUS,** 6, gr g Geordieland (FR)—Drop The Hammer **Mr E. G. M. Beard**
4 **CHARLIE MY BOY (IRE),** 6, gr g Leading Light (IRE)—Theionlady (IRE) **Mr A. J. Taylor**
5 **CHEDINGTON'S GUEST,** 4, b g Jack Hobbs—Doubly Guest **Dr G. W. Guy**
6 **DANZINI (IRE),** 7, br m Ocovango—Grainne Delight (IRE) **Whitcombe Racing Club**
7 **ENVOYE SPECIAL (FR),** 9, b g Coastal Path—Santa Bamba (FR) **Mrs P. Bunter**
8 4, B f Ocovango—Gayeroyale (IRE) **K. G. Kerley**
9 **GENERAL PROBUS,** 9, b br g Geordieland (FR)—Drop The Hammer **E G M Beard & R A Scott**
10 **GOLDEN POET (IRE),** 11, b g Urban Poet (USA)—Little Linnet **Mr K. M. F. Burke**
11 **HOTEL DU NORD (FR),** 10, b g Voix du Nord (FR)—Iu Mi Nao (IRE) **Mr C. J. Sprake**
12 **LADY WILBERRY,** 6, br m Montmartre (FR)—Lady Willa (IRE) **Balham Hill Racing**
13 **LAST ROYAL,** 8, b g Sulamani (IRE)—First Royal (GER) **Dr G. W. Guy**
14 **LETSBE AVENUE (IRE),** 8, b g Lawman (FR)—Aguilas Perla (IRE) **Mr C. J. Sprake**
15 **LOVE ACTUALLY (IRE),** 7, br m Shirocco (GER)—Elsie (IRE) **Mrs M. A. Crook**
16 **MAROOCHI,** 6, b m Presenting—Makadamia **Whitcombe Racing Club**
17 **MAROONED,** 4, b f Black Sam Bellamy (IRE)—Solitairy Girl **Dr G. W. Guy**
18 **MOURNE SUPREME (IRE),** 6, b g Doyen (IRE)—Dar Dar Supreme **Goodfellers Racing**
19 **NATHAN WALKER,** 5, b m Blue Bresil (FR)—West River (USA) **This Time Next Year Maybe**
20 **POTTERS VENTURE (IRE),** 9, b g Arcadio (GER)—Starventure (IRE) **Whitcombe Racing Club**
21 **PUTDECASHONTHEDASH (IRE),** 10, b g Doyen (IRE)—Be My Adelina (IRE) **Goodfellers Racing**
22 **SAM'S AMOUR,** 6, b m Black Sam Bellamy (IRE)—Aphrodisias (FR) **Dr G. W. Guy**
23 **SCRUMPY BOY,** 11, b g Apple Tree (FR)—Presuming **SMLC Racing**
24 **SOUL ICON,** 6, b g Sixties Icon—Solitairy Girl **This Time Next Year Maybe**
25 **STILETTO,** 5, b g Frankel—High Heeled (IRE) **Mrs M. A. Crook**
26 **THE HEIGHT OF FAME,** 6, b m Fame And Glory—Good Thinking **Barrow Hill**
27 4, Gr g Geordieland (FR)—Viking Treasure
28 **VITALLINE,** 5, b g Due Diligence (USA)—Vitta's Touch (USA) **Mrs M. A. Crook**
29 **WHITCOMBE ROCKSTAR,** 4, b g Footstepsinthesand—Roshina (IRE) **Mrs M. A. Crook**
30 **WHYNOTNOWROY (IRE),** 5, ch g Notnowcato—Midnight Lira **B. A. Derrick**

---

68 MR HUGH BURNS, Alnwick

Postal: **Rose Cottage, Hedgeley Hall, Powburn, Alnwick, Northumberland, NE66 4HZ**
Contacts: **PHONE 01665 578647 MOBILE 07503 539571**
EMAIL hughburns123@hotmail.co.uk

1 **COUNTRY DELIGHTS (IRE),** 10, b m Mahler—Nadwell (IRE) **Mr H. Burns**
2 **HENRY BROWN (IRE),** 8, b g Mahler—Blackeyedsue (IRE) **Mr H. Burns**
3 **LE FOU'S KEEP (IRE),** 8, b m Le Fou (IRE)—Slaney Conflict (IRE) **Mr H. Burns**
4 **LONGSTONE COWBOY (IRE),** 7, bl g Yeats (IRE)—The Munyabure **Mr H. Burns**
5 **MR JESSE JAMES (IRE),** 7, b g Kalanisi (IRE)—Balinacary **Mr H. Burns**

MR HUGH BURNS - continued

6 **WITH A START (IRE),** 8, b g Sea The Stars (IRE)—Sudden Blaze (IRE) **Mr H. Burns**

---

69 MR OWEN BURROWS, Lambourn

Postal: **Farncombe Down Stables, Baydon Road, Lambourn Woodlands, Hungerford, Berkshire, RG17 7AQ**
Contacts: **PHONE 01488 71631**
WORK EMAIL robyn@owenburrowsracing.com

1 **AL NAMIR (IRE),** 6, b g Shamardal (USA)—Rayaheen **Shadwell Estate Company Ltd**
2 **ALFLAILA,** 4, b c Dark Angel (IRE)—Adhwaa **Shadwell Estate Company Ltd**
3 **ANMAAT (IRE),** 5, b g Awtaad (IRE)—African Moonlight (UAE) **Shadwell Estate Company Ltd**
4 **HUKUM (IRE),** 6, b h Sea The Stars (IRE)—Aghareed (USA) **Shadwell Estate Company Ltd**
5 **MURAAD (IRE),** 7, gr g Dark Angel (IRE)—Hidden Girl (IRE) **Shadwell Estate Company Ltd**
6 **TARRABB (IRE),** 4, b f Exceed And Excel (AUS)—Bahjtee **Sheikh Ahmed Al Maktoum**

THREE-YEAR-OLDS

7 B c Kodiac—Deleyla **Sheikh Ahmed Al Maktoum**
8 Ch f Australia—Diamond Tango (FR) **Mr O. S. Harris**
9 **EDDIE TEMPLE (IRE),** b c Sioux Nation (USA)—Xema **Mr O. S. Harris**
10 **ELRAAED,** ch c Dubawi (IRE)—Into The Mystic (IRE) **Sheikh Ahmed Al Maktoum**
11 **EMBRACE (IRE),** b f Lope de Vega (IRE)—Whazzis **Mr A. A. Alkhallafi**
12 **FAIR WIND,** gr g Tasleet—Gone Sailing **Kennet Valley Thoroughbreds V**
13 **HAILEY YA MAL (IRE),** gr c Dark Angel (IRE)—Miranda Frost (IRE) **A. Al Shaikh**
14 **HALLA DUBAI (IRE),** b c Expert Eye—Soft Ice (IRE) **A. Al Shaikh**
15 **LAJOOJE,** b c Showcasing—Evita Peron **Sheikh Ahmed Al Maktoum**
16 **MANTOOG,** b f Kingman—Mudawanah **Shadwell Estate Company Ltd**
17 B f Dandy Man (IRE)—Ocean Myth **Sheikh Ahmed Al Maktoum**
18 B c Exceed And Excel (AUS)—Raaqyah (USA) **Sheikh Ahmed Al Maktoum**
19 **ROWAYEH (IRE),** b f Dubawi (IRE)—Alaflaak (USA) **Shadwell Estate Company Ltd**
20 **SHAFFOF (IRE),** ch f Siyouni (FR)—Wohileh **Sheikh Ahmed Al Maktoum**
21 B c Expert Eye—Shamandar (FR) **Mr O. S. Harris**
22 **SO FARHH SO GOOD (IRE),** b f Farhh—Collate **Mr R. E. Tillett**
23 **TAMALUK (IRE),** b f Dubawi (IRE)—Mutebah (IRE) **Shadwell Estate Company Ltd**
24 **TARJEEH (IRE),** b c Churchill (IRE)—Myturn (IRE) **Sheikh Ahmed Al Maktoum**
25 **WELLEEF (IRE),** b c Lope de Vega (IRE)—Romaana **Sheikh Ahmed Al Maktoum**
26 **YOUTH'S VOICE,** b c Nathaniel (IRE)—Indian Love Bird **A. Al Shaikh**

TWO-YEAR-OLDS

27 B f 24/01 Ribchester (IRE)—Al Raahba (IRE) (Frankel) **Shadwell Estate Company Ltd**
28 B c 03/03 Too Darn Hot—Alyamaama (USA) (Kitten's Joy (USA)) **Shadwell Estate Company Ltd**
29 B c 05/05 Churchill (IRE)—Apticanti (USA) (Aptitude (USA)) (200000) **Brook Farm Bloodstock**
30 B c 25/02 Zoustar (AUS)—Arabda (Elnadim (USA)) (70000) **Sheikh Ahmed Al Maktoum**
31 B c 10/04 Frankel—Baiddaa (IRE) (Dubawi (IRE)) **Sheikh Ahmed Al Maktoum**
32 **BUR DUBAI,** ch c 06/05 Night of Thunder (IRE)—Ana Shababiya (IRE) (Teofilo (IRE)) **A. Al Shaikh**
33 B c 25/04 Calyx—Decima (IRE) (Dream Ahead (USA)) **Empire State Racing Partnership**
34 Ch f 05/04 Dubawi (IRE)—Into The Mystic (IRE) (Galileo (IRE)) **Sheikh Ahmed Al Maktoum**
35 B c 17/02 Frankel—Jahafil (Kingman) **Shadwell Estate Company Ltd**
36 Ch c 16/04 Al Kazeem—Kentucky Belle (IRE) (Heliostatic (IRE)) (28571) **In the Mix Racing**
37 B c 16/04 Postponed (IRE)—Meet Marhaba (IRE) (Marju (IRE))
38 B f 04/04 Night of Thunder (IRE)—Monteja (Shamardal (USA)) **Sheikh Ahmed Al Maktoum**
39 Ch f 13/04 Frankel—Mubhirah (Raven's Pass (USA)) **Shadwell Estate Company Ltd**
40 **NAJM ALDAR (GER),** b c 04/03 Territories (IRE)—Navarra Sun (IRE) (Lope de Vega (IRE)) (22409) **A. Al Shaikh**
41 B f 19/02 Frankel—Ojooba (Dubawi (IRE)) **Shadwell Estate Company Ltd**
42 B c 23/02 Wootton Bassett—Olma (SAF) (Dynasty (SAF)) (64026) **Mr O. S. Harris**

MR OWEN BURROWS - continued

43 B c 27/04 Exceed And Excel (AUS)—Raaqyah (USA) (Elusive Quality (USA)) **Sheikh Ahmed Al Maktoum**
44 B f 15/03 Blue Point (IRE)—Rihaam (IRE) (Dansili) **Shadwell Estate Company Ltd**
45 **SEE THE GREEN,** b c 07/02 Postponed (IRE)—Clarentine (Dalakhani (IRE)) **A. Al Shaikh**
46 B c 24/04 Zoffany (IRE)—Solar Echo (IRE) (Galileo (IRE)) (110000) **Sheikh Ahmed Al Maktoum**
47 B f 24/05 Kingman—Talaayeb (Dansili) **Shadwell Estate Company Ltd**
48 B f 28/01 Awtaad (IRE)—Tatweej (Invincible Spirit (IRE)) **Shadwell Estate Company Ltd**

Assistant Trainer: Robert McDowall.

MR JOHN BUTLER, Newmarket

Postal: **The Cottage, Charnwood Stables, Hamilton Road, Newmarket, Suffolk, CB8 7JQ**
Contacts: **MOBILE 07764 999743**
EMAIL johnbutler1@btinternet.com

1 **AEROPLANE MODE,** 4, b g Gleneagles (IRE)—So In Love **Mr J. Butler**
2 **ANALYTICS (IRE),** 5, b m Zoffany (IRE)—Logique (FR) **Mr J. Butler**
3 **ANNULMENT (IRE),** 4, b c Fascinating Rock (IRE)—Imdancinwithurwife (IRE)
4 **ARABESCATO,** 6, gr g Outstrip—Cat Hunter **D. Cohen**
5 **ATTENTIVE,** 4, b f Oasis Dream—Visoliya (FR) **R Favarulo & Mr & Mrs R W Reed**
6 **AVARICE (IRE),** 6, b g Zoffany (IRE)—Spirit Watch (IRE) **Power Geneva Ltd**
7 **BEEBEE,** 4, b f Outstrip—Shadow of The Sun **Mr M. Ricketts**
8 **BRAINS (IRE),** 7, b g Dandy Man (IRE)—Pure Jazz (IRE) **Power Geneva Ltd**
9 **BRAZEN GIRL,** 4, b f Brazen Beau (AUS)—Easter Diva (IRE) **K. J. Quinn**
10 **BREACH,** 4, b f Intello (GER)—Flood Warning **Mr J. Butler**
11 **CONTROL,** 4, b f Havana Gold (IRE)—Love And Cherish (IRE) **Mr J. Butler**
12 **DARK ICON,** 6, br m Sixties Icon—Dark Raider (IRE) **Recycled Products Limited**
13 **DARWELL LION (IRE),** 5, b g The Last Lion (IRE)—Darwell (IRE) **Mr P. Holden**
14 **DESIGNER,** 4, ch f Pearl Secret—Curly Come Home **Mr A. L. Al Zeer**
15 **GLOBAL WARNING,** 7, b g Poet's Voice—Persario **Mr J. Butler**
16 **GOLD COAST (IRE),** 6, ch g Galileo (IRE)—Come To Heel (IRE) **Power Geneva Ltd**
17 **GOOD HUMOR,** 6, b g Distorted Humor (USA)—Time On **Mr G. Simons**
18 **HAVEONEYERSELF (IRE),** 8, b g Requinto (IRE)—Charismas Birthday (IRE) **Mr J. Butler**
19 **HONKY TONK TOWN (USA),** 4, b f Speightstown (USA)—Principle Equation (IRE) **Mrs A. J. Nicol**
20 **INAAM (IRE),** 10, b g Camacho—Duckmore Bay (IRE) **Power Geneva Ltd**
21 **IT'S A LOVE THING,** 5, b g Intrinsic—Lady Kyllar **Mr D. Pittack**
22 **JACK SPAROWE (IRE),** 4, b g Zoffany (IRE)—Red Stars (IRE) **Mr J. Butler**
23 **KAARANAH (IRE),** 5, b g Estidhkaar (IRE)—Chevanah (IRE) **Univit Ltd**
24 **KADIMA IMPERIAL,** 4, gr f Outstrip—Tibibit **D. Cohen**
25 **KNIGHT OF KINGS,** 5, b g New Approach (IRE)—Night Lily (IRE) **Mr K. Snell**
26 **LAFAN (IRE),** 5, b g Dandy Man (IRE)—Light Glass (IRE) **Mr J. Butler**
27 **LYNNS BOY,** 5, ch g Coach House (IRE)—La Fortunata **Mr M. Ricketts**
28 **MARTINEO,** 8, b g Declaration of War (USA)—Woodland Scene (IRE) **Power Geneva Ltd**
29 **MEASURED MOMENTS,** 4, b f Time Test—Hope And Fortune (IRE) **K. J. Quinn**
30 **MEGANSEIGHTHTEEN,** 4, b f Ardad (IRE)—Mea Parvitas (IRE) **Mr S. L. Clarke**
31 **MET OFFICE (IRE),** 6, b g Dansili—Paratonnerre **Mr G. Dolan**
32 **MIDNIGHT GLOW (IRE),** 4, b f Fascinating Rock (IRE)—Campfire Glow (IRE) **Newtown Anner Stud Farm Ltd**
33 **NO DIGGITY (IRE),** 7, b g Sir Prancealot (IRE)—Monarchy (IRE) **Mr R. Favarulo**
34 **PINK JAZZ (IRE),** 6, b g Red Jazz (USA)—Marvelofthelodge (IRE) **Power Geneva Ltd**
35 6, B m First Samurai (USA)—Principle Equation (IRE) **Mrs A. J. Nicol**
36 **QUTEY ZEE (IRE),** 6, b m Ivawood (IRE)—Cute Cait **Mr J. Butler**
37 **RARE FIND,** 4, b gr f Geordieland (FR)—Lady Blade (IRE) **E. A. Condon**
38 **RHYTHM N ROCK (IRE),** 5, b g Fascinating Rock (IRE)—Rythmic **Newtown Anner Stud Farm Ltd**
39 **SEAS OF ELZAAM (IRE),** 6, b g Elzaam (AUS)—Ocean Sands (IRE) **Power Geneva Ltd**
40 **SIR DANCEALOT (IRE),** 9, b g Sir Prancealot (IRE)—
Majesty's Dancer (IRE) **C Benham/ D Whitford/ L Quinn/ K Quinn**

MR JOHN BUTLER - continued

41 **SOAR ABOVE,** 8, gr ro g Lethal Force (IRE)—Soar **Miss M. Bishop-Peck**
42 **SOLANNA,** 4, ch g Helmet (AUS)—Night Lily (IRE) **Mr K. Snell**
43 **SOPHAR SOGOOD (IRE),** 6, b g French Navy—Cloud Break **Mr R. Ford**
44 **SPLIT ELEVENS,** 5, b g Ajaya—Woodland Scene (IRE) **Mr D. James**
45 **STRATEGIC FORTUNE (IRE),** 6, b g Power—Jenniings (IRE) **B. N. Fulton**
46 **SWEET BERTIE (IRE),** 5, ch g Dandy Man (IRE)—Tartiflette **Power Brothers**
47 **TOTAL LOCKDOWN,** 4, b g Finjaan—Diamondsaretrumps (IRE) **Mr R. Favarulo**
48 **ULTRAMARINE (IRE),** 4, b g Zoffany (IRE)—Onyali (IRE) **Mr J. Butler**
49 **UZINCSO,** 7, b g Mayson—Capacious **Recycled Products Limited**
50 **WELOOF (FR),** 9, b g Redoute's Choice (AUS)—Peinted Song (USA) **Power Geneva Ltd**
51 **WILKIE,** 5, ch g New Approach (IRE)—Victorian Beauty (USA) **Mr G. Dolan**

THREE-YEAR-OLDS

52 **ADORATION,** b g Tamayuz—Adore **C Benham/ D Whitford/ L Quinn/ K Quinn**
53 **AZEEZAN (FR),** b c Dabirsim (FR)—Louve des Neiges (IRE) **Mr A. Bahbahani**
54 **CAPTAIN WENTWORTH,** gr c Dark Angel (IRE)—Jumira Princess (IRE) **Mr J. Butler**
55 **DALOOLAH (IRE),** ch f Galileo Gold—Blue Enzian (USA) **Mr A. Bahbahani**
56 **EMPEROR ZEN (IRE),** b g Holy Roman Emperor (IRE)—Lady Zen (IRE) **Mr J. Butler**
57 **KUWAIT CITY (IRE),** b g Pearl Secret—Ahaaly **Mr A. L. Al Zeer**
58 **ORIGINALLY (IRE),** ch c Anjaal—Callanish **Mr A. L. Al Zeer**
59 **STRUCK GOLD (IRE),** b g No Nay Never (USA)—Yesterday (IRE) **Northumbria Leisure Ltd**

TWO-YEAR-OLDS

60 B c 24/04 Make Believe—Am I (USA) (Thunder Gulch (USA)) (35000) **Mr A. Bahbahani**
61 B c 08/02 Advertise—Glade (Bertolini (USA)) (30000) **Mr N. Buresli**
62 B f 22/03 Land Force (IRE)—Marysienka (Primo Dominie) (27000) **Mr N. Buresli**
63 Ch c 19/02 Pearl Secret—Midnight (IRE) (Galileo (IRE)) (19000) **Mr J. Butler**
64 B f 19/04 Zoffany (IRE)—Teeky (Daylami (IRE)) (23000) **Mr J. Butler**

---

71 MR PADDY BUTLER, Lewes

Postal: **Homewood Gate Racing Stables, Novington Lane, East Chiltington, Lewes, East Sussex, BN7 3AU**
Contacts: **PHONE 01273 890124 MOBILE 07973 873846**
EMAIL homewoodgate@aol.com

1 **ALBERT VAN ORNUM (FR),** 6, b g Authorized (IRE)—Diena (FR) **Homewoodgate Racing Club**
2 **EL HAGEB ROSE (FR),** 9, b g Coastal Path—Ile Rose (FR) **Homewoodgate Racing Club**
3 **ENGAGING SAM,** 6, ch g Casamento (IRE)—Engaging **Mrs E. Lucey-Butler**
4 **FITZY,** 7, b g Epaulette (AUS)—Zagarock **Miss M. P. Bryant**
5 **KLIP KLOPP,** 4, ch g Night of Thunder (IRE)—Wakeup Little Suzy (IRE) **C. W. Wilson**
6 **MARTIN SPIRIT (IRE),** 6, gr g Dark Angel (IRE)—Tribune Libre (IRE) **Mrs E. Lucey-Butler**
7 **MILTON,** 11, br g Nomadic Way (USA)—Jesmund **Mrs C. A. Webber**
8 **PENNY STREET,** 4, b f Mullionmileanhour (IRE)—Quality Street **Mrs E. Lucey-Butler**
9 **POPPYEQUIANO,** 4, b f Equiano (FR)—Zubaidah **Mr R Pattenden & Partner**

Assistant Trainer: Mrs E Lucey-Butler.

Amateur Jockey: Miss M. Bryant, Miss J. Oliver.

72 MISS JULIE CAMACHO, Malton

Postal: **Star Cottage, Welham Road, Norton, Malton, North Yorkshire, YO17 9QE**
Contacts: **PHONE 01653 696205 MOBILE 07950 356440, 07779 318135 FAX 01653 696205**
EMAIL julie@jacracing.co.uk WEBSITE www.juliecamacho.com

1 **AINSDALE,** 6, b h Mayson—Bruni Heinke (IRE) **Mr D. W. Armstrong**
2 **ARMY OF INDIA (IRE),** 5, gr g Sepoy (AUS)—Sudfah (USA) **Ian Clements & Julie Camacho**
3 **BABA REZA,** 5, ch g Garswood—Friendship Is Love **Judy & Richard Peck**
4 **BALLYCONNEELY BAY (IRE),** 5, b g Fast Company (IRE)—Kathy Sun (IRE) **Mr M. B. Hughes**
5 **BERAZ,** 5, b g ZOFFANY—BESHARA
6 **BURTONWOOD,** 11, b g Acclamation—Green Poppy **Judy & Richard Peck & Partner**
7 **CAPTAIN CORELLI (IRE),** 6, ch g Anjaal—Disprove (IRE) **Judy & Richard Peck**
8 **DAN DE MAN CAN,** 4, b g Dandy Man (IRE)—Last of The Dixies **S & J Camacho**
9 **DINGLE (IRE),** 5, b g Footstepsinthesand—Beal Ban (IRE) **Mr M. B. Hughes**
10 **EASTER ISLAND,** 4, b g Teofilo (IRE)—Pacific Pride (USA) **Mr & Mrs G. Turnbull**
11 **ENRAGED,** 4, b f Adaay (IRE)—Little Lady Katie (IRE) **A Barnes & Julie Camacho**
12 **FLASH THE DASH (IRE),** 4, b g Estidhkaar (IRE)—Anamarka **Miss J. A. Camacho**
13 **INSPIRATIONELLIE (IRE),** 4, ch f Dandy Man (IRE)—Bahamian Wishes (IRE) **Judy & Richard Peck**
14 **JUDICIAL (IRE),** 11, b g Iffraaj—Marlinka **Elite Racing Club**
15 **LESS IS MORE,** 4, b f Tamayuz—Vassaria (IRE) **Miss J. A. Camacho**
16 **LOOK OUT LOUIS,** 7, b g Harbour Watch (IRE)—Perfect Act **V.Watt,G Howard & J Jenkinson**
17 **MAKANAH,** 8, b g Mayson—Diane's Choice **Axom LXXI**
18 **MAKEEN,** 6, b g Dubawi (IRE)—Estidraaj (USA) **Verity, Pritchard & Simpson**
19 **MAPLE JACK,** 5, ch g Mayson—Porcelain (IRE) **Owners Group 075**
20 **MISTER FALSETTO,** 4, b g Twilight Son—Bint Arcano (FR) **Edwards, Rush & Camacho**
21 **NEVERBATSANEYELID,** 4, b f Due Diligence (USA)—Lady Lube Rye (IRE) **D. & S. L. Tanker Transport Limited**
22 **NICKLEBY (IRE),** 4, b g Kodi Bear (IRE)—Laheen (IRE) **Owners Group 088**
23 **NORTHBOUND (IRE),** 5, b g Fast Company (IRE)—Natalisa (IRE) **Edwards Harland & Hitchman**
24 **PROCLAIMER,** 6, b g Free Eagle (IRE)—Pious **Owners Group 033**
25 **QAASID (IRE),** 5, b g Awtaad (IRE)—Nisriyna (IRE) **Mr M. B. Hughes**
26 **RAATEA,** 6, b g Invincible Spirit (IRE)—Darajaat (USA) **Mr M. B. Hughes**
27 **READY TO SHINE (IRE),** 4, b f Camelot—Matorio (FR) **G. B. Turnbull Ltd**
28 **RED HOW,** 4, ch f Equiano (FR)—Diane's Choice **Miss J. A. Camacho**
29 **RIVERSWAY,** 4, b f Mayson—Capesthorne (IRE) **Mr D. W. Armstrong**
30 **ROSHAMBO,** 4, b f Due Diligence (USA)—Horsforth **Morecool Racing**
31 **RUGGLES,** 4, b f Exceed And Excel (AUS)—Madame Defarge (IRE) **Mr N. Edwards**
32 **SACRED JEWEL,** 4, ch f Dubawi (IRE)—Priceless **Mr M. B. Hughes**
33 **SECRET EQUITY,** 6, ch m Equiano (FR)—Secret Charge **B A McGarrigle & Julie Camacho**
34 **SHAKE A LEG (IRE),** 6, b g Excelebration (IRE)—Sos Brillante (CHI) **Hey Ho**
35 **SIGNIFICANTLY,** 5, b g Garswood—Rosebride **Mr N. O'Keeffe**
36 **SYMBOL OF LIGHT,** 4, br g Shamardal (USA)—Pure Diamond **Mr M. B. Hughes**
37 **SYMBOLIZE (IRE),** 6, ch g Starspangledbanner (AUS)—French Flirt **Mr N. O'Keeffe**
38 **TACTICAL,** 5, b g Toronado (IRE)—Make Fast **Mr N. O'Keeffe**
39 **TITIAN (IRE),** 5, b g Iffraaj—Lucelle (IRE) **W. F. Frewen**

THREE-YEAR-OLDS

40 **BANQUO (IRE),** b g Bungle Inthejungle—Balqaa (USA) **Mr M. B. Hughes**
41 **BOWLEAZE,** b f Dandy Man (IRE)—Bahamian Wishes (IRE) **Judy & Richard Peck**
42 **BUSAN,** b g Mondialiste (IRE)—Craic Agus Spraoi (IRE) **Mr & Mrs G. Turnbull**
43 **CALDER VALLEY (IRE),** b c Camacho—Sparkling (IRE) **Owners Group 103**
44 **CLIMATE CHANGE,** b g Mondialiste (IRE)—Reluctant Heroine (USA) **Mr & Mrs G. Turnbull**
45 **COCO STARLIGHT,** b f Gregorian (IRE)—Passionate Love (IRE) **Let's Get Racing Ltd**
46 **DERWENT BOY,** b g Harry Angel (IRE)—Bint Arcano (FR) **G. B. Turnbull Ltd**
47 **EQUITY'S DARLING,** b f Equiano (FR)—Magic Approach **Miss J. A. Camacho**
48 **EUPHROSYNE,** ch f Havana Gold (IRE)—Muqantara (USA) **Mrs V. Machen**
49 **GEORGE LODGE (IRE),** gr f Dark Angel (IRE)—Edge of The World (IRE) **George Lodge & Sons Ltd**
50 **HOUGOUMONT,** ch g Rajasinghe (IRE)—New Road Side **Morecool Racing & Andy Barnes**
51 **MARINE LAKE,** b f Oasis Dream—Bruni Heinke (IRE) **Mr D. W. Armstrong**
52 **OSCAR'S SISTER (IRE),** ch f Dandy Man (IRE)—Wishing Chair (USA) **Judy & Richard Peck**
53 **PROFANITIES,** b g Mondialiste (IRE)—Lady Percy (IRE) **Miss J. A. Camacho**
54 **SHAQUILLE,** b c Charm Spirit (IRE)—Magic (IRE) **Hughes, Rawlings, O'Shaughnessy**

MISS JULIE CAMACHO - continued

55 **STRIP OUT,** gr f Outstrip—Horsforth **Morecool Racing**
56 **WASDALE,** b f Twilight Son—L'Eglise **G. B. Turnbull Ltd**
57 **WINTER CROWN,** b g Invincible Spirit (IRE)—Berengaria (IRE) **Mr M. B. Hughes**
58 **ZAPPHIRE (IRE),** b f Zoffany (IRE)—Madison **Elite Racing Club**

TWO-YEAR-OLDS

59 **BRIGHT AS BUTTONS,** b f 13/04 Havana Gold (IRE)—
Bahamian Wishes (IRE) (Bahamian Bounty) (4500) **Judy & Richard Peck**
60 B f 24/03 Mayson—Delft Blue (Lethal Force (IRE)) (1500) **Miss J. A. Camacho**
61 **GRAND LADY,** ch f 14/04 Lightning Spear—Money Note (Librettist (USA)) (1000) **Rjh Ltd & Facts & Figures**
62 **GREGORIANNA (IRE),** b f 07/04 Gregorian (IRE)—Rahanna (GER) (Azamour (IRE)) (15000) **Quadrille Partnership**
63 **INTERTWINED (IRE),** b f 13/03 Cable Bay (IRE)—Tinted (IRE) (Galileo (IRE)) **Mr M. B. Hughes**
64 **LORTON VALE,** ch f 28/01 Twilight Son—Red Guana (IRE) (Famous Name) **G. B. Turnbull Ltd**
65 **TRIGGERMAN,** b c 30/04 Ribchester (IRE)—How Sweet It Is (IRE) (Kodiac) (9000) **Bland, Hall & Camacho**
66 **WINGED MESSENGER,** b c 30/04 Postponed (IRE)—Equimou (Equiano (FR)) (1600) **Bland, Hall & Camacho**

Assistant Trainer: Steve Brown.

Flat Jockey: Graham Lee, Paul Mulrennan, Callum Rodriguez.

---

73 MR MARK CAMPION, Malton

Postal: **Whitewell House Stables, Whitewall, Malton, North Yorkshire, YO17 9EH**
Contacts: **PHONE 01653 692729 MOBILE 07973 178311 FAX 01653 600066**
EMAIL info@markcampion-racing.com WEBSITE www.markcampion-racing.com

1 **BALLYWOOD (FR),** 9, b g Ballingarry (IRE)—Miss Hollywood (FR) **Whitewall Racing**
2 **BURGUNDY MAN (FR),** 6, b g Manduro (GER)—Kapirovska (FR) **Whitewall Racing**
3 **CIVIL ENSIGN (FR),** 9, b g Rob Roy (USA)—Petillante Royale (FR) **Whitewall Racing**
4 **DINONS (FR),** 10, b g Balko (FR)—Beni Abbes (FR) **Whitewall Racing**
5 **ISLE OF OIR (IRE),** 9, b g Gold Well—Patsy Cline (IRE) **Mark Campion Racing Club**
6 **LAAFY (USA),** 7, b g Noble Mission—Miner's Secret (USA) **Whitewall Racing**
7 **LAXEY (IRE),** 9, b g Yeats (IRE)—Nerissa (IRE) **Whitewall Racing**
8 **LORD WARBURTON (IRE),** 6, ch g Zoffany (IRE)—Portrait of A Lady (IRE) **Whitewall Racing**
9 **MELDRUM WAY (IRE),** 10, b g Getaway (GER)—Meldrum Hall (IRE) **Mark Campion Racing Club**
10 **MOUNTAIN RAPID (IRE),** 11, ch m Getaway (GER)—Founding Daughter (IRE) **Whitewall Racing**
11 **SE YOU,** 8, b g Sepoy (AUS)—Lady Hestia (USA) **Mark Campion Racing Club**
12 **TROIS BON AMIS (IRE),** 9, gr g Lilbourne Lad (IRE)—Vanozza (FR) **Whitewall Racing**

Assistant Trainer: Mrs F. Campion.

---

74 MS JENNIE CANDLISH, Leek

Postal: **Basford Grange Farm, Basford, Leek, Staffordshire, ST13 7ET**
Contacts: **PHONE 07976 825134, 07889 413639 FAX 01538 360324**
EMAIL jenniecandlish@yahoo.co.uk WEBSITE www.jenniecandlishracing.co.uk

1 **ABSOLUTE RULER (USA),** 4, b g War Front (USA)—Together Forever (IRE) **Mr B. W. Verinder**
2 **BASFORD (IRE),** 6, b g Soldier of Fortune (IRE)—Be My Present **Brian Verinder & Alan Baxter**
3 **BERTIE'S WISH (IRE),** 5, b g Fast Company (IRE)—Dance Bid **Mr A. J. Baxter**
4 **BRIDGE ROAD (IRE),** 7, b g Sholokhov (IRE)—Lucy's Legend (IRE) **Alan Baxter & Brian Hall**

MS JENNIE CANDLISH - continued

5 **CATCHMEIFYOUCAN (IRE),** 9, b m Touch of Land (FR)—Irish Honey (IRE) **A Baxter, C Burke & N Sobreperez**
6 **CHEDDLETON,** 8, br g Shirocco (GER)—Over Sixty **Mr P. & Mrs G. A. Clarke**
7 **COSHESTON,** 10, ch g Black Sam Bellamy (IRE)—Rare Ruby (IRE) **Mrs J. M. Ratcliff**
8 **CRACK DU NINIAN (FR),** 8, b g Le Houssais (FR)—Syphaline (FR) **Mr P. & Mrs G. A. Clarke**
9 **FOLLOW YOUR FIRE (IRE),** 8, b g Le Fou (IRE)—Jollie Bollie (IRE) **Jennie Candlish & Jillian McKeown**
10 **FOR JIM (IRE),** 11, gr g Milan—Dromhale Lady (IRE) **Ms J. Candlish**
11 **FORTIFIED BAY (IRE),** 11, b g Makfi—Divergence (USA) **Mr A. J. Baxter**
12 **FORTUITOUS FIND,** 6, b g Shirocco (GER)—Ruby Royale **J. L. Marriott**
13 **GOLAN CLOUD (IRE),** 10, b g Golan (IRE)—Mite Be Cloudy (IRE) **Ms J. Candlish**
14 **HACHERT,** 6, b g Lope de Vega (IRE)—Sense of Joy **Paul Wright-bevans & Mark Harrison**
15 **HAPPY HOLLOW,** 11, b g Beat Hollow—Dombeya (IRE) **Ms J. Candlish**
16 **IT'S GOOD TO LAUGH (IRE),** 6, b g Tamayuz—London Plane (IRE) **Brian Verinder & Alan Baxter**
17 **LAWRENNY,** 4, b g Black Sam Bellamy (IRE)—Rare Ruby (IRE) **Mrs J. M. Ratcliff**
18 **LEAVE ME ALONE (IRE),** 4, gr f Caravaggio (USA)—French Friend (IRE) **Mr & Mrs Paul & Clare Rooney**
19 **LECHRO (IRE),** 4, ch f Highland Reel (IRE)—Sirici (IRE) **The West Awake Partnership**
20 **LOUGH CARRA (IRE),** 6, b g Policy Maker (IRE)—Utrillo's Art (IRE) **Everything Is Aok**
21 **MARTHA YEATS (IRE),** 8, b m Yeats (IRE)—Stratosphere **Mrs F. M. Draper**
22 **MATCHLESS (IRE),** 5, b g Galileo (IRE)—Bye Bye Birdie (IRE) **J. L. Marriott**
23 **MCGOWAN'S PASS,** 12, b g Central Park (IRE)—Function Dreamer **Mrs A. E. Lee**
24 **MISS SOLITAIRE (IRE),** 5, b m Valirann (FR)—Estuary Princess (IRE) **The Brothers Grimm**
25 **NERO ROCK (IRE),** 8, b g Shirocco (GER)—Gilt Benefit (IRE) **J. L. Marriott**
26 **OCTOPUS (IRE),** 4, gr g Kendargent (FR)—Mountain Melody (GER) **Brian Verinder & Alan Baxter**
27 **OSCARS LEADER (IRE),** 10, b g Oscar (IRE)—Lead'er Inn (IRE) **J. L. Marriott**
28 **OUT FOR THE COUNT (IRE),** 5, b g Barely A Moment (AUS)—Annabaskey (IRE) **4 Left Footers & A Blewnose**
29 **ROCKET ROBBO,** 6, b g Multiplex—Sphere (IRE) **Mr S. Smithurst**
30 **SCUDAMORE (FR),** 6, ch g Dawn Approach (IRE)—Emirates Comfort (IRE) **The Sunset Crew**
31 4, Br g Court Cave (IRE)—Stormy Spirit (IRE) **Mr A. J. Baxter**
32 **TELHIMLISTEN (IRE),** 7, b g Fame And Glory—Hiwaitilitellu (IRE) **Mr A. Okeeffe**
33 **TOMMYDAN (IRE),** 8, b g Recital (FR)—Sovienne (IRE) **The Mere Partnership**
34 **YEALAND (IRE),** 4, b g Shirocco (GER)—Jane Hall (IRE) **Mr P. & Mrs G. A. Clarke**
35 **ZUCKERBERG (GER),** 7, b g Kamsin (GER)—Zazera (FR) **J. L. Marriott**

Assistant Trainer: Alan O'Keeffe.

Flat Jockey: Joe Fanning. **NH Jockey:** Sean Quinlan.

75

MR HENRY CANDY, Wantage

Postal: **Kingstone Warren, Wantage, Oxfordshire, OX12 9QF**
Contacts: **PHONE 01367 820276 MOBILE 07836 211264**
EMAIL henrycandy@btconnect.com

1 **AUTUMNAL DANCER (IRE),** 4, gr f El Kabeir (USA)—Autumn Tide (IRE) **Autumn Decs**
2 **CLOUD CUCKOO,** 4, b g Mayson—Crimson Cloud **Henry D. N. B. Candy**
3 **FOUR FEET (IRE),** 7, b g Harbour Watch (IRE)—Royal Connection **Henry D. N. B. Candy**
4 **HEARTBREAK LASS,** 4, b f Cotai Glory—Motion Lass **Mr A. J. Davis**
5 **NEPHALIST (IRE),** 4, b f Elzaam (AUS)—Cant Hurry Love **Mr A. J. Davis**
6 **NIARBYL BAY,** 4, b g Nayef (USA)—Danae **Girsonfield Ltd**
7 **PENGUIN ISLAND,** 4, b f The Gurkha (IRE)—In Secret **The Earl Cadogan**
8 **RING OF LIGHT,** 5, gr g Mayson—Silver Halo **T A Frost & Simon Broke & Partners**
9 **RUN TO FREEDOM,** 5, b h Muhaarar—Twilight Mistress **G. A. Wilson**
10 **SAINTE COLETTE,** 4, gr f Mastercraftsman (IRE)—La Chapelle (IRE) **T A Frost, Candy, Clayton & Lamb**
11 **SAN FRANCISCO BAY (IRE),** 4, b g Muhaarar—Stor Mo Chroi (IRE) **Henry D. N. B. Candy**
12 **SOVEREIGN SLIPPER,** 5, b g Charm Spirit (IRE)—Last Slipper **Mr D B Clark & Mr H Candy**
13 **TWILIGHT CALLS,** 5, b g Twilight Son—Zawiyah **Cheveley Park Stud Limited**

MR HENRY CANDY - continued

THREE-YEAR-OLDS

14 **ARAMINTA (IRE),** ch f Gleneagles (IRE)—Mince **St Albans Bloodstock, Acloque & Frost**
15 **BE FRANK,** b g Cable Bay (IRE)—Bonnie Arlene (IRE) **NinePM Limited**
16 **BUGANVILLEA (IRE),** b f Holy Roman Emperor (IRE)—Borghesa (GER) **Hot To Trot**
17 **CAPE VINCENT,** b g Kuroshio (AUS)—Cape Violet (IRE) **Henry D. N. B. Candy**
18 **CLUEDO (IRE),** b f Kodiac—Symbol of Peace (IRE) **Six Too Many**
19 **FEATH (IRE),** b f Aclaim (IRE)—Dream On Me (GER) **Mr A. J. Davis**
20 **FITZROY RIVER,** b f Oasis Dream—In Secret **The Earl Cadogan**
21 **GOSMORE,** b f Oasis Dream—Gosbeck **Major M. G. Wyatt**
22 **HIGH SPIRITED (IRE),** b f Belardo (IRE)—Spirited Charm **T. A. F. Frost**
23 **JIMMY LIFESTYLE,** b g Havana Gold (IRE)—Elite **Six Too Many**
24 **SIMPLE MAN (IRE),** b c Invincible Spirit (IRE)—Lethal Quality (USA) **Andrew Davis & Ryan Kent**
25 **SINFUL,** b f Aclaim (IRE)—Quiet Protest (USA) **NinePM Limited**
26 **TIGER BAY,** b f Harry Angel (IRE)—Totally Lost (IRE) **Mrs Lidsey & H Candy**
27 **WALL GAME,** b g Shalaa (IRE)—Wall of Light **David Coombs & Henry Candy**

TWO-YEAR-OLDS

28 **BESET,** b f 30/04 Expert Eye—Beshayer (FR) (Galileo (IRE)) **Major M. G. Wyatt**
29 **DOUBLE RED,** gr c 25/03 Belardo (IRE)—Red Boots (IRE) (Verglas (IRE)) (14000) **T. A. F. Frost**
30 **HIGHLAND SLIPPER,** b c 29/03 Highland Reel (IRE)—Intricate (Showcasing) (10000) **Mr D B Clark & Mr H Candy**
31 **PORT HEDLAND,** b c 23/03 Cable Bay (IRE)—In Secret (Dalakhani (IRE)) **The Earl Cadogan**
32 **PRESTON RIVER,** ch f 02/03 Masar (IRE)—Free Offer (Generous (IRE)) **The Earl Cadogan**
33 **RICARDO PHILLIPS,** b g 02/05 Aclaim (IRE)—Arlene Phillips (Groom Dancer (USA)) (5000) **Henry D. N. B. Candy**
34 **SNOOZY BEAR (IRE),** b g 23/04 Belardo (IRE)—
Sleeping Princess (IRE) (Dalakhani (IRE)) (12000) **Henry D. N. B. Candy**
35 **TWILIGHT TRUTH,** b f 21/02 Twilight Son—Verity (Redoute's Choice (AUS)) **Cheveley Park Stud Limited**
36 **ZAMBEZI DIAMOND,** b f 30/03 Muhaarar—Zamzama (IRE) (Shamardal (USA)) (16000) **Henry D. N. B. Candy**

Assistant Trainer: Amy Scott.

---

76 MR GRANT CANN, Lower Hamswell

Postal: **Park Field, Hall Lane, Lower Hamswell, Bath, Gloucestershire, BA1 9DE**
Contacts: **PHONE 01225 891674 MOBILE 07968 271118**

1 **CADEAU DU BRESIL (FR),** 11, b g Blue Bresil (FR)—Melanie du Chenet (FR) **J. G. Cann**
2 **MR PALM (IRE),** 8, ch g Mountain High (IRE)—Miss Palm (IRE) **J. G. Cann**
3 **QUEEN OF THE COURT (IRE),** 10, b m Court Cave (IRE)—Waydale Hill **J. G. Cann**

---

77 MR DON CANTILLON, Newmarket

Postal: **63 Exeter Road, Newmarket, Suffolk, CB8 8LP**
Contacts: **PHONE 01638 668507 MOBILE 07709 377601**

1 **ADMIRING GLANCE (IRE),** 6, b m Shantou (USA)—As I Am (IRE) **D. E. Cantillon**
2 **BOLD VISION (IRE),** 7, b g Shirocco (GER)—As I Am (IRE) **D. E. Cantillon**
3 4, Br f Walk In The Park (IRE)—Milanteea (IRE) **D. E. Cantillon**
4 **NAVARRA PRINCESS (IRE),** 8, b m Intense Focus (USA)—Navarra Queen **D. E. Cantillon**

THREE-YEAR-OLDS

5 **STEP AHEAD (IRE),** b c Walk In The Park (IRE)—As I Am (IRE)

---

78 MRS RUTH CARR, Stillington

Postal: **Mowbray House Farm, Easingwold Road, Stillington, York, North Yorkshire, YO61 1LT**
Contacts: **WORK 01347 823776 MOBILE 07721 926772**
EMAIL ruth@ruthcarrracing.co.uk, chrissie@ruthcarrracing.co.uk
WEBSITE www.ruthcarrracing.co.uk

1 **ALHABOR,** 4, b g Intello (GER)—Eternally **Mrs R. A. Carr, Clear Cut Racing**
2 **ATHMAD (IRE),** 7, b g Olympic Glory (IRE)—Black Mascara (IRE) **R J H Limited & Ruth Carr**
3 **BADRI,** 6, b g Dark Angel (IRE)—Penny Drops **Rjh Ltd & Mr D Padgett**
4 **BOBBY JOE LEG,** 9, ch g Pastoral Pursuits—China Cherub **Mrs A. Clark**
5 **CAESAR NERO,** 4, b g Territories (IRE)—Publilia **Mr D. E. Balfe**
6 **COPPER AND FIVE,** 7, ch g Paco Boy (IRE)—Peachez **Mrs R. A. Carr, Mrs S. J. Doyle**
7 **DARKER,** 4, b g Twilight Son—Spinatrix **Mr J. A. Knox and Mrs M. A. Knox**
8 **EMBOUR (IRE),** 8, b g Acclamation—Carpet Lady (IRE) **Formulated Polymer Products Ltd**
9 **FINAL FRONTIER (IRE),** 10, b g Dream Ahead (USA)—Polly Perkins (IRE) **V. Khosla**
10 **FORESEEABLE FUTURE (FR),** 8, b g Harbour Watch (IRE)—Russian Spirit **RHD & Ruth Carr**
11 **FREEDOM FLYER (IRE),** 6, b g Invincible Spirit (IRE)—Liberating **Mrs R. A. Carr**
12 **HARD SOLUTION,** 7, ch g Showcasing—Copy-Cat **Mrs R. A. Carr**
13 **HOSTELRY,** 6, ch m Coach House (IRE)—Queens Jubilee **Dennis Clayton & Ruth Carr**
14 **JOJO RABBIT,** 5, b g Due Diligence (USA)—Berkshire Honey **Grange Park Racing XIII & Ruth Carr**
15 **LITTLE EARL (IRE),** 4, b g Havana Gold (IRE)—Majestic Alexander (IRE) **Rjh Ltd & Facts & Figures**
16 **MAGICAL EFFECT (IRE),** 11, ch g New Approach (IRE)—Purple Glow (IRE) **Miss Vanessa Church**
17 **MAKALU (IRE),** 4, b g Mehmas (IRE)—Jolly Juicester (IRE) **Bruce Jamieson & Ruth Carr**
18 **MILBANKE,** 4, b g Intello (GER)—Augusta Ada **Mr D. Padgett**
19 **MONAADHIL (IRE),** 9, b g Dark Angel (IRE)—Urban Daydream (IRE) **Mrs R. A. Carr**
20 **MUTANAASEQ (IRE),** 8, ch g Red Jazz (USA)—Indaba (IRE) **Grange Park Racing VIII & Mrs R Carr**
21 **NEWYORKSTATEOFMIND,** 6, b g Brazen Beau (AUS)—Albany Rose (IRE) **Mrs R. A. Carr**
22 **NEXT SECOND,** 4, b f Hot Streak (IRE)—Millisecond **J Greaves, R Willcock & Ruth Carr**
23 **REIGNING PROFIT (IRE),** 4, ch g Profitable (IRE)—Reign (IRE) **The Chancers**
24 **REPUTATION (IRE),** 10, b g Royal Applause—Semaphore **Mrs Karen John**
25 **RHYTHM (IRE),** 5, b m Acclamation—Strasbourg Place **Mr D. Padgett**
26 **SEVEN FOR A POUND (USA),** 7, b g Scat Daddy (USA)—Gimlet Witha Twist (USA) **Mr E. D. Broadwith**
27 **SIRAJU,** 4, b g Showcasing—Bereka **Mr S. R. Jackson**
28 **SPANISH ANGEL (IRE),** 6, br g Gutaifan (IRE)—
City Dazzler (IRE) **Mrs R. A. Carr, Mrs M. Chapman, Mr G. A. Shields**
29 **STREAK LIGHTNING (IRE),** 6, ch g Night of Thunder (IRE)—Emreliya (IRE) **Grange Park Racing Club & Ruth Carr**
30 **SWISS ACE,** 5, b g Kingman—Swiss Lake (USA) **The Bottom Liners & Mrs R. Carr**
31 **TOUCHWOOD (IRE),** 5, b g Invincible Spirit (IRE)—Aaraamm (USA) **Mr D. E. Balfe**
32 **TWELFTH KNIGHT (IRE),** 4, b g Haatef (USA)—Balm **Mrs N. C. Padgett**
33 **VAN ZANT,** 4, b g Lethal Force (IRE)—Emmuska **Mrs R. A. Carr**

THREE-YEAR-OLDS

34 **CAVALIER APPROACH (IRE),** ch g Profitable (IRE)—Beauty Pageant (IRE) **G. Murray**
35 Ch g Pastoral Pursuits—China Cherub **Mrs A. Clark**
36 **DRESDEN GREEN,** b g Brazen Beau (AUS)—Necklace (AUS) **Mrs R. A. Carr, J. Berry, Mrs S. Hibbert**
37 **ROCKIN ROSA,** ch f Bated Breath—Rosalie Bonheur **The Beer Stalkers & Ruth Carr**
38 **SHOTLEY ROYALE,** b g Hot Streak (IRE)—Royal Pardon **Mr J. A. Swinburne & Mrs Ruth A. Carr**

TWO-YEAR-OLDS

39 B f 02/05 Sogann (FR)—China Cherub (Inchinor) **Mrs A. Clark**

Racing Secretary: Mrs Chrissie Skyes, **Yard Sponsor:** Darren Walker www.xreconstructiontraining.co.uk.

Flat Jockey: James Sullivan.

79 MR DECLAN CARROLL, Malton

Postal: **Santry Stables, Langton Road, Norton, Malton, North Yorkshire, YO17 9PZ**
Contacts: **MOBILE 07801 553779**
EMAIL declancarrollracing@gmail.com

1 **ASMUND (IRE),** 6, b g Zebedee—Suffer Her (IRE) **Mrs S. A. Bryan**
2 **EMIYN (FR),** 6, b g Invincible Spirit (IRE)—Edelmira (IRE) **Fab Five**
3 **IRELAND'S EYE (IRE),** 5, b g Canford Cliffs (IRE)—Sofi's Spirit (IRE) **Mrs S. A. Bryan**
4 **ISLE OF DREAMS,** 5, gr m Gutaifan (IRE)—Munaa's Dream **J. A. Duffy**
5 **JACK DANIEL (IRE),** 5, b h Equiano (FR)—Mirdhak **Danny Fantom Racing Ltd**
6 **KING OF TONGA (IRE),** 7, gr g Dark Angel (IRE)—Bronze Queen (IRE) **Mrs S. A. Bryan**
7 **LAAKHOF (IRE),** 4, b g Profitable (IRE)—Ihtifal **Rakjam Ltd**
8 **LADY PASCHA,** 4, b f Garswood—Sirenuse (IRE) **Terry Johnston & Andy Turton**
9 **NATCHEZ TRACE,** 6, b g Invincible Spirit (IRE)—Passage of Time **Second Chancers**
10 **SHEIKH MAZ MAHOOD (IRE),** 4, br g Fast Company (IRE)—All In Green (IRE) **Four Juniperus**
11 **SIMULATION THEORY (IRE),** 5, ch g Starspangledbanner (AUS)—Barawin (IRE) **Mrs S. A. Bryan**
12 **STAR OF ARIA,** 4, b g Starspangledbanner (AUS)—Partitia **Starlight N.E. Ltd**
13 **TRUE MASON,** 7, b g Mayson—Marysienka **Mr J. T. Hanbury**
14 **VICTORY FLAGSHIP,** 4, b g Garswood—Mis Chicaf (IRE) **Highgreen Partnership**
15 **YELLOW BEAR,** 4, ch g Poet's Voice—Roman Holiday (IRE) **Ray Flegg & John Bousfield**

THREE-YEAR-OLDS

16 **AREWENEARLYHOME (IRE),** b g Cotai Glory—Annella (IRE) **Mr J. N. Blackburn**
17 **CARVETII (IRE),** ch g Dandy Man (IRE)—Sundown Sally (IRE) **Santry Racing**
18 **CHANGEOFMIND (IRE),** ch c Sioux Nation (USA)—Dusty **Mr B. Cooney**
19 **CLERYS CLOCK (IRE),** b g Estidhkaar (IRE)—Dancing Soprano (IRE) **Dreams**
20 B g Dandy Man (IRE)—Elzana (IRE) **Mr J. T. Hanbury**
21 **FORTUNATE STAR (IRE),** ch g Unfortunately (IRE)—Effusive **Mr Ray Flegg & Mr John Bousfield.**
22 **GIMCRACK WARRIOR,** b g Muhaarar—Da'quonde (IRE) **Mr J. T. Hanbury**
23 **GLOBAL CRISIS (FR),** b g Shalaa (IRE)—Antalia (FR) **Sapphire Print Solutions Ltd**
24 **IRISH DANCER (IRE),** ch g Galileo Gold—Catamaran (IRE) **Mr J. T. Hanbury**
25 **RWENEARLYTHEREDAD,** b g Havana Grey—King's Guest (IRE) **Mr J. N. Blackburn**
26 **SEANTRABH (IRE),** b g Tasleet—Hot Stone (IRE) **Mr Brian Chambers**
27 **TEN BOB NOTE,** b g Muhaarar—Ha'penny Beacon **Mr C H Stephenson & Mr T A Stephenson**
28 **TERESA GRACE (IRE),** ch f Camacho—Lady Heart **Mr J. T. Hanbury**
29 **THE CAMACHO KID (IRE),** b g Camacho—Latina Reach (IRE) **Santry Racing**

TWO-YEAR-OLDS

30 **DAMISA (IRE),** b c 22/02 Magna Grecia (IRE)—Escape Proof (Cityscape) (16006) **Rakjam Ltd**
31 Ch c 18/04 Buratino (IRE)—Dixiedoodledandy (IRE) (Desert Style (IRE)) (7203)
32 B c 18/03 Churchill (IRE)—Dusty (Paco Boy (IRE)) **Mr J. T. Hanbury**
33 B gr c 07/05 Due Diligence (USA)—Kalia Asha (IRE) (Dark Angel (IRE)) (9524)
34 **MISS PHOENIX,** ch f 28/03 Phoenix of Spain (IRE)—Cherika (IRE) (Cape Cross (IRE)) **Olympus Racing**
35 B f 23/01 Starspangledbanner (AUS)—Patience Alexander (IRE) (Kodiac) (78000) **Danny Fantom Racing Ltd**
36 **WHOGOESTHERE,** b c 17/03 Soldier's Call—Backstreet Girl (IRE) (Shamardal (USA)) (24010) **Santry Racing II**
37 **WILLOLARUPI,** b c 11/04 Camacho—Moving Waves (IRE) (Intense Focus (USA)) (16807) **Dp Fabricators Ltd**
38 **WOODLEIGH,** b c 10/01 Inns of Court (IRE)—Naqrah (IRE) (Haatef (USA)) (75000) **Mr L. Ryan**

Assistant Trainer: Kym Dee.

Flat Jockey: Harrison Shaw. **Apprentice Jockey:** Zak Wheatley.

80

MR TONY CARROLL, Cropthorne

Postal: **Mill House Racing, Cropthorne, Pershore, Worcs**
Contacts: **PHONE 01386 861020 MOBILE 07770 472431 FAX 01386 861628**
EMAIL a.w.carroll@btconnect.com WEBSITE www.awcarroll.co.uk

1 **ABSTRACT (IRE),** 5, ch g Sea The Stars (IRE)—Sense of Purpose (IRE) **KHDRP**
2 **AFTERNOON TEA (IRE),** 5, b g Epaulette (AUS)—Dunbrody (FR) **Rideo Partnership**
3 **ALFRED COVE,** 4, b g Ardad (IRE)—Cards **SF Racing Club**
4 **ASTROPHYSICS,** 11, ch g Paco Boy (IRE)—Jodrell Bank (IRE) **Lynn Siddall Memorial Syndicate**
5 4, B g Mahsoob—Audley **KHDRP**
6 **AUTUMN ANGEL (IRE),** 4, b f Dark Angel (IRE)—Elshabakiya (IRE) **Cropthorne Syndicate**
7 **BE FAIR,** 7, b g Kyllachy—Going For Gold **Surefire Racing & Partner**
8 **BE MY SEA (IRE),** 12, b g Sea The Stars (IRE)—Bitooh **Mr Layton T. Cheshire L. T. Cheshire**
9 **BEARING BOB,** 4, ch g Bobby's Kitten (USA)—Danlia (IRE) **KJB Racing**
10 **BEAU GESTE (IRE),** 7, b g Lilbourne Lad (IRE)—Valbonne (IRE) **Mr A. W. Carroll**
11 **BEZZAS LAD (IRE),** 6, b g Society Rock (IRE)—Red Rosanna **KHDRP**
12 **BLACK BUBLE (FR),** 10, b g Valanour (IRE)—Miss Bubble Rose (FR) **Northway Lodge Racing**
13 **BOOM THE GROOM (IRE),** 12, b g Kodiac—Ecco Mi (IRE) **Mr B. J. Millen**
14 **CAFE SYDNEY (IRE),** 7, ch m Foxwedge (AUS)—Carafe **Contubernium Racing**
15 **CALIN'S LAD,** 8, ch g Equiano (FR)—Lalina (GER) **Lycett Racing Ltd**
16 **CAPTAIN PUGWASH (IRE),** 9, b g Sir Prancealot (IRE)—Liscoa (IRE) **A.W.Carroll & Partner**
17 **CAZCADE,** 4, b f Slade Power (IRE)—New Falcon (IRE) **Mr C. J. Dingwall**
18 **CHERISH (FR),** 6, b m Hunter's Light (IRE)—Agent Kensington **Wedgewood Estates**
19 **CHRISTINES ANGEL (IRE),** 6, gr m Gutaifan (IRE)—Salmon Rose (IRE) **Mr A. W. Carroll**
20 **COME TO PASS (IRE),** 4, ch g Mastercraftsman (IRE)—Chittenden (USA) **Northway Lodge Racing**
21 **DARKE HORSE,** 4, br g Outstrip—Atyaab **Wedgewood Estates**
22 **DE VEGAS KID (IRE),** 9, ch g Lope de Vega (IRE)—Fravolina (USA) **The Rebelle Boys**
23 **DELLA MARE,** 7, b m Delegator—Golbelini **The Fine Gild Racing Partnership**
24 **DEQUINTO (IRE),** 4, b g Requinto (IRE)—Moss Nation **Mr A. W. Carroll**
25 **DESTINADO,** 5, b g Lope de Vega (IRE)—Contribution **Green lighting Ltd**
26 **DOC SPORTELLO (IRE),** 11, b g Majestic Missile (IRE)—Queen of Silk (IRE) **International Racing Club & Partner**
27 **EASTERN STAR (IRE),** 7, b m Dylan Thomas (IRE)—Sweet Surprise (IRE) **The Fruit Flow Partners**
28 **EL HIBRI (IRE),** 4, b g Havana Gold (IRE)—Shawka **Mr M. I. Greaves**
29 **ENOUGH ALREADY,** 7, b g Coach House (IRE)—Funny Enough **Miss V. J. Baalham**
30 **EQUION,** 5, b g Mayson—Eleodora **Royale Racing Syndicate**
31 **FIELDSMAN (USA),** 11, b g Hard Spun (USA)—R Charlie's Angel (USA) **SF Racing Club**
32 **FLY THE NEST (IRE),** 7, b g Kodiac—Queen Wasp (IRE) **Mr B. J. Millen**
33 **FORBEARING (IRE),** 5, b g Kodi Bear (IRE)—Mercifilly (FR) **Keith Cosby & Partner**
34 **GLENCOE BOY (IRE),** 6, b g Gleneagles (IRE)—Eastern Appeal (IRE) **Mrs A. Cowley**
35 **GLOBAL STYLE (IRE),** 8, b g Nathaniel (IRE)—Danaskaya (IRE) **Curry House Corner & Partner**
36 **GOLD STANDARD (IRE),** 7, ch g Casamento (IRE)—Goldplated (IRE) **Mr J. M. Wall**
37 **HARBOUR PROJECT,** 6, b g Harbour Watch (IRE)—Quelle Affaire **Mr A. W. Carroll**
38 **HAZIYM (IRE),** 4, ch c Lope de Vega (IRE)—Hazmiyra (IRE) **Mr B. J. Millen**
39 **HE'S OUR STAR (IRE),** 8, b g Lord Shanakill (USA)—Afilla **Mrs S. R. Keable**
40 **HEADSHOT,** 5, b g Awtaad (IRE)—Kesara **Lycett Racing Ltd**
41 **HOOVES LIKE JAGGER (IRE),** 5, b g Sir Prancealot (IRE)—Roseisarose (IRE) **Mr A. Mills**
42 **HOT DIGGITY DOG (IRE),** 4, b g Dandy Man (IRE)—Unusually Hot (IRE) **KHDRP**
43 **HOT HOT HOT,** 6, ch m Hot Streak (IRE)—Just Emma **Mrs Susan Keable & Partner**
44 **HOW HARD CAN IT BE,** 5, gr m Style Vendome (FR)—Louya (IRE) **T & B Partnership**
45 **HUNTSMAN'S MOON (FR),** 4, b g Hunter's Light (IRE)—Song of India **Wedgewood Estates**
46 **ICONIC KNIGHT (IRE),** 8, b g Sir Prancealot (IRE)—Teutonic (IRE) **Mill House Racing Syndicate**
47 **ILHABELA FACT,** 9, b gr h High Chaparral (IRE)—Ilhabela (IRE) **Cooke & Millen**
48 **KELLS (IRE),** 6, b g Galileo (IRE)—Christmas Kid (USA) **Lycett Racing Ltd**
49 **KENSINGTON AGENT (FR),** 4, b f Elusive City (USA)—Agent Kensington **Wedgewood Estates**
50 **KONDRATIEV WAVE (IRE),** 6, ch g Dragon Pulse (IRE)—Right Reason (IRE) **Mr B. J. Millen**
51 **LATENT HEAT (IRE),** 7, b g Papal Bull—Taziria (SWI) **Mr J. M. Wall**
52 **LEQUINTO (IRE),** 6, b g Requinto (IRE)—Moss Nation **Mrs Y. T. Wallace**
53 **LOCAL BAY,** 5, br h Cable Bay (IRE)—Local Fancy **Mr N. Sfrantzis**
54 **LONG CALL,** 10, b g Authorized (IRE)—Gacequita (URU) **Northway Lodge Racing**
55 **MADRINHO (IRE),** 10, ch g Frozen Power (IRE)—Perfectly Clear (USA) **Mr A. Mills**
56 **MAISON BEAU,** 4, b f Coach House (IRE)—Beau Mistral (IRE) **Mr A. Mills**

MR TONY CARROLL - continued

57 **MANY WORDS (IRE),** 5, b g Kodi Bear (IRE)—Few Words **Northway Lodge Racing**
58 **MAYBE TONIGHT,** 4, b g Muhaarar—Night Affair **Lady Whent**
59 **MOON OVER THE SEA,** 4, b g Sea The Moon (GER)—Veiled Beauty (USA) **D. J. Oseman**
60 **MR PC (IRE),** 5, b g Acclamation—Beramana (FR) **Six Pack**
61 **MUMAYAZ (IRE),** 4, b g Tamayuz—Rashaaqa **Mr N. Sfrantzis**
62 **MY GENGHIS,** 4, b g Mukhadram—Assertive Agent **Wedgewood Estates**
63 **MY SAND BOY,** 4, b g Proconsul—Queen of Heaven (USA) **Wedgewood Estates**
64 **NELSON RIVER,** 8, b g Mount Nelson—I Say (IRE) **CCCP Syndicate**
65 **NEPTUNE LEGEND (IRE),** 4, b g Invincible Spirit (IRE)—Kate The Great **Mr N. Sfrantzis**
66 **NIGHT BEAR,** 6, ch g Dragon Pulse (IRE)—Contenance (IRE) **Mr R. Bellamy**
67 **NIGHT TRAVELLER,** 4, ch f Night of Thunder (IRE)—Travelling **Longview Stud & Bloodstock Ltd**
68 **OEIL DE TIGRE (FR),** 12, b g Footstepsinthesand—Suerte **Mr A. W. Carroll**
69 **OKAIDI (USA),** 6, ch g Anodin (IRE)—Oceanique (USA) **Mr A. W. Carroll**
70 **OUR MAN IN HAVANA,** 8, b g Havana Gold (IRE)—Auntie Kathryn (IRE) **D. J. Oseman**
71 **PERFECT FOCUS (IRE),** 6, b g Acclamation—Tonle Sap (IRE) **Miss V. J. Baalham**
72 **POETIC FORCE (IRE),** 9, ch g Lope de Vega (IRE)—Obligada (IRE) **International Racing Club & Partner**
73 **POP DANCER (IRE),** 6, b g Kodiac—Pop Art (IRE) **Mr B. J. Millen**
74 **PROUD WARRIOR (IRE),** 4, b g The Gurkha (IRE)—Rockshine **Mr D. Boocock**
75 **QUEEN SARABI (IRE),** 5, b m The Last Lion (IRE)—Tango Tonic (IRE) **L Judd, T Stamp, J Hardcastle, R Miles**
76 **RECON MISSION (IRE),** 7, b g Kodiac—Ermine Ruby **Mr B. J. Millen**
77 **RED ALERT,** 9, b g Sleeping Indian—Red Sovereign **Mill House Racing Syndicate**
78 **REPARTEE (IRE),** 6, br g Invincible Spirit (IRE)—Pleasantry **Miss V. J. Baalham**
79 **RIVER WHARFE,** 5, ch g Showcasing—Wahylah (IRE) **Mr B. J. Millen**
80 **SABAARELLI,** 6, ch m Schiaparelli (GER)—Princess Sabaah (IRE) **Mr D. Boocock**
81 **SAPPHIRE'S MOON,** 4, b f Ardad (IRE)—Shifting Moon **Curry House Corner**
82 **SECOND COLLECTION,** 7, b m Delegator—Quelle Affaire **Mr Ian Furlong & Partner**
83 **SEND IN THE CLOUDS,** 6, b g Delegator—Saharan Song (IRE) **Mrs Y. T. Wallace**
84 **SENSE OF WORTH (IRE),** 7, b g Street Sense (USA)—Desert Song (USA) **Miss V. J. Baalham**
85 **SILVER BYRNE,** 5, gr g Hot Streak (IRE)—Cool Angel (IRE) **Mr A. W. Carroll**
86 **SIR TITAN,** 9, b g Aqlaam—Femme de Fer **Wedgewood Estates**
87 **SOCIAL CITY,** 7, b g Cityscape—Society Rose **H. M. W. Clifford**
88 **SOCIAL CONTACT,** 4, ch f Night of Thunder (IRE)—Operettist **Longview Stud & Bloodstock Ltd**
89 **SOMEDAYONEDAYNEVER (IRE),** 4, b f Moohaajim (IRE)—Fravolina (USA) **Mr A. W. Carroll**
90 **STORM ASSET,** 4, b g Postponed (IRE)—Clear Water (IRE) **KHDRP**
91 **TEAH,** 4, b f Bobby's Kitten (USA)—Zeteah **Wedgewood Estates**
92 **THREE DONS (IRE),** 4, b g Fast Company (IRE)—Avizare (IRE) **KHDRP**
93 **TOPLIGHT,** 5, b g Bated Breath—Operettist **Longview Stud & Bloodstock Ltd**
94 **TRUSTY RUSTY,** 6, ch m Roderic O'Connor (IRE)—Madame Rouge **H. M. W. Clifford**
95 **UNDER CURFEW,** 7, ch g Stimulation (IRE)—Thicket **Mr M. J. Wellbelove**
96 **VOLTAIC,** 7, ch g Power—Seramindar **SF Racing Club**
97 **WINNETKA (IRE),** 6, ch g Camacho—Little Audio (IRE) **International Racing Club &molony Racing**
98 **YOU ARE EVERYTHING (FR),** 4, b br f Belardo (IRE)—Sensa (FR) **Wedgewood Estates**
99 **YOU ARE MY WORLD (FR),** 4, ch f French Fifteen (FR)—Etrangere (USA) **Wedgewood Estates**
100 **ZOFFANY PORTRAIT (IRE),** 4, ch g Zoffany (IRE)—Bunood (IRE) **Mr M S Cooke & Partner**

THREE-YEAR-OLDS

101 **ABILLITY,** ch c Ulysses (IRE)—Adaptability **Longview Stud & Bloodstock Ltd**
102 **AGENT MAYFAIR,** b g Tasleet—Wedgewood Estates **Wedgewood Estates**
103 **ESKIMO FLO,** ch f Garswood—Baby Dreamer (IRE)
104 **GALLANT LION,** ro g Roaring Lion (USA)—Lysanda (GER) **Green lighting Ltd**
105 **INTERCEPTEUR,** b c Intello (GER)—Midst **Longview Stud & Bloodstock Ltd**
106 **KAY CERAAR (IRE),** b c Kessaar (IRE)—Love To Dream (IRE) **Carroll, Williams & Wykes**
107 **LADY OF NEPAL,** ch f The Gurkha (IRE)—Atlantic Isle (GER) **P M Claydon & D Boocock**
108 B f Adaay (IRE)—Madame Rouge **H. M. W. Clifford**
109 **OK PAL,** b g Stimulation (IRE)—Despacito **S. &. A. Giannini**
110 **ONESHOT,** b c Cracksman—Doddinel **Longview Stud & Bloodstock Ltd**
111 **OVERLAND,** b g Territories (IRE)—Authoritarian **Longview Stud & Bloodstock Ltd**
112 **ROYAL AGENT,** b f Outstrip—Royal Circles **Wedgewood Estates**
113 **SMART CHARGER (IRE),** b c Saxon Warrior (JPN)—Stormy Blessing (USA) **Green lighting Ltd**

MR TONY CARROLL - continued

114 SMART SHOT, gr g Outstrip—Sinaadi (IRE) **Longview Stud & Bloodstock Ltd**
115 TEA SEA (FR), b g Hunter's Light (IRE)—Sensa (FR) **Wedgewood Estates**
116 THINK CHAMPAGNE (IRE), b g Gleneagles (IRE)—Rockshine **Mr D. Boocock**
117 TIME PATROL, b g Time Test—Travelling **Longview Stud & Bloodstock Ltd**
118 WEDGEWOOD, b f Outstrip—Gorgeous (FR) **Wedgewood Estates**

81

MR TONY CARSON, Newmarket

Postal: **Barn 2 Red House Stables , Hamilton Road, Newmarket, Suffolk, CB8 0TE**
Contacts: **MOBILE 07837 601867**
WORK EMAIL tcarsonracing@gmail.com INSTAGRAM tcarsonracing

1 COURTNEY SILVER (IRE), 5, b m Court Cave (IRE)—Jennifers Diary (IRE) **Mr C. Butler**
2 DENABLE, 7, b g Champs Elysees—Surprise (IRE) **Mr C. Butler**
3 HENRY THE FIFTH (IRE), 5, ch g Dawn Approach (IRE)—Vincennes **Lady E. L. Oshea**
4 HEY BAILS, 4, b g Muhaarar—White Dress (IRE) **Mr M. R. Francis**
5 MUTALAAQY (IRE), 5, br g Dark Angel (IRE)—Misdaqeya **Well Connected Electrics UK Ltd**
6 NITRO NEMO, 4, b g Marcel (IRE)—Believe In Dreams
7 PLANTATREE, 4, b f Helmet (AUS)—Chatline (IRE) **Michelle B Fernandes & Partners T Carson**

THREE-YEAR-OLDS

8 DARLO PRIDE, bl ro g Outstrip—Doric Lady **Mr C. T. Dennett**
9 DEED POLE, b g Poet's Word (IRE)—Bright Girl (IRE) **Mr C. T. Dennett**
10 DEEP SPIRIT, b f Charm Spirit (IRE)—Deep Blue Sea **Lady E. L. Oshea**
11 DUVEEN, b f Poet's Word (IRE)—Cool Catena **Mr C. T. Dennett**

TWO-YEAR-OLDS

12 B c 12/03 Postponed (IRE)—Velvet Charm (Excelebration (IRE)) (3000) **Mr C. Butler**

Flat Jockey: William Carson. **NH Jockey:** Mr Graham Carson. **Amateur Jockey:** Kerryanne Alexander.

82

MR LEE CARTER, Epsom

Postal: **The Old Yard, Clear Height Stables, Epsom, Surrey, KT18 5LB**
Contacts: **PHONE 01372 740878 MOBILE 07539 354819 FAX 01372 740898**
EMAIL leecarterracing@aol.co.uk WEBSITE www.leecarterracing.com

1 AL TARMAAH (IRE), 6, b g Muhaarar—How's She Cuttin' (IRE) **Mr J. J. Smith**
2 BIG WING (IRE), 6, b g Free Eagle (IRE)—Orafinitis (IRE) **Mr J. J. Smith**
3 COME ON TIER (FR), 8, b g Kendargent (FR)—Milwaukee (FR) **Mr J. J. Smith**
4 CREATIONIST (USA), 7, b g Noble Mission—Bargain Blitz (USA) **Mr J. J. Smith**
5 DUTUGAMUNU (IRE), 6, ch g Ivawood (IRE)—Bunditten (IRE) **Clear Racing**
6 DYNAKITE, 5, b g Adaay (IRE)—Ahwahnee **Mr J. J. Smith**
7 LA RAV (IRE), 9, b g Footstepsinthesand—Swift Acclaim (IRE) **Mr J. J. Smith**
8 MISS ELSA, 7, b m Frozen Power (IRE)—Support Fund (IRE) **Mr J. J. Smith**
9 PLYMOUTH ROCK (IRE), 6, b g Starspangledbanner (AUS)—Welcome Spring (IRE) **Ewell Never Know**

MR LEE CARTER - continued

10 **SIR SEDRIC (FR),** 5, b g Dragon Pulse (IRE)—Rajastani (IRE) **Tattenham Corner Racing IV**
11 **VILLEURBANNE,** 5, b g Iffraaj—Ninas Rainbow **Mr J. J. Smith**

THREE-YEAR-OLDS

12 **HOODOO,** b f Dark Angel (IRE)—Hoodna (IRE) **Mrs K. T. Carter**

---

83 MR BEN CASE, Banbury

Postal: **Wardington Gate Farm, Edgcote, Banbury, Oxfordshire, OX17 1AG**
Contacts: **PHONE 01295 750959 MOBILE 07808 061223**
EMAIL info@bencaseracing.com WEBSITE www.bencaseracing.com TWITTER @bencaseracing
INSTAGRAM bencaseracing

1 **ANNIE DAY (IRE),** 8, br m Arcadio (GER)—Aunt Annie (IRE) **BDRSyndicates**
2 **BASHERS REFLECTION,** 6, ch g Mount Nelson—Dungarvan Lass (IRE) **Mrs S. R. Bailey**
3 **BELLES BENEFIT (IRE),** 7, b m Leading Light (IRE)—Snowbelle (IRE) **Mr A. H. Harvey**
4 **BOLEYN BOY (IRE),** 5, b g Elusive Pimpernel (USA)—Fuchsia Delight (IRE) **Mr D P Walsh & Mr A Barry**
5 **CELESTIAL PARK (IRE),** 5, b m Walk In The Park (IRE)—Corona Moon (IRE) **Foran & Harrison**
6 **COBBLERS DREAM (IRE),** 7, br g Yeats (IRE)—Miss Parkington (IRE) **Lady Jane Grosvenor**
7 **CONCEROE (IRE),** 7, br g Yeats (IRE)—Made In Kk (IRE) **Fakenham Race Club**
8 **DASH OF BLUE,** 8, b g Great Pretender (IRE)—Madame Bleue **Bluebuyu**
9 **DORADO DOLLAR (IRE),** 9, ch g Golden Lariat (USA)—Stability Treaty (IRE) **Miss P. Murray**
10 **FELTON BELLEVUE (FR),** 8, b g Kap Rock (FR)—Sister du Berlais (FR) **Mrs H Munn, Mr R E Good, Mr B Case**
11 **FERN HILL (IRE),** 8, b g Dylan Thomas (IRE)—Water Rock **Cross Foran Harrison**
12 **GAZETTE BOURGEOISE (FR),** 7, b m Spanish Moon (USA)—Jasmine (FR) **Mr A. H. Harvey**
13 **J'HABITE EN FRANCE (FR),** 4, b g Gris de Gris (IRE)—Saintete (FR)
14 **JACK DOYEN (IRE),** 7, b g Doyen (IRE)—Reynella Cross (IRE) **Wardington Hopefuls**
15 **MIDNIGHTREFLECTION,** 8, b m Midnight Legend—Hymn To Love (FR) **Case Racing Partnership & Anita J Lush**
16 **MIGHTY DUCHESS (IRE),** 5, b m Vendangeur (IRE)—The Mighty Matron (IRE)
17 **MISS CONNAISSEUR,** 5, ch m Monsieur Bond (IRE)—China Cherub **Mr J. W. Stevenson**
18 **NICKELFORCE (IRE),** 4, b g Workforce—Nickel (IRE) **Lovell, Massey, Meads, Smith, Walsh**
19 **NORVICS REFLECTION (IRE),** 8, b g Mahler—Finallyfree (IRE) **Mrs S. R. Bailey**
20 5, B g Poet's Voice—Parlez Vous **Mrs S. R. Bailey**
21 **REBEL ROYAL (IRE),** 10, b g Getaway (GER)—Molly Duffy (IRE) **Case Racing Partnership**
22 **RED ROMEO,** 8, ch g Midnight Legend—Easter Comet **MirEmMark**
23 **REGALLY BLONDE,** 4, ch f Mukhadram—Jolie Blonde **Case Racing Partnership & Anita J Lush**
24 4, B f Black Sam Bellamy (IRE)—Sarahs Quay (IRE) **Fakenham Race Club**
25 **SEEK HIM THERE (IRE),** 4, b g Elusive Pimpernel (USA)—Isnt Dat Right (IRE) **Lovell Okninski Walsh**
26 **SHANTY ALLEY,** 9, b g Shantou (USA)—Alexander Road (IRE) **Jerry Wright Adam Lucock Patricia Murray**
27 **STARGAZER BELLE,** 5, b m Telescope (IRE)—Theatre Belle **Pat Murray Martin Redman Maurice Thomas**
28 **STORMWALKER (IRE),** 4, b g Walk In The Park (IRE)—Tempest Belle (IRE) **Lady Jane Grosvenor**
29 **THE GOLDEN REBEL (IRE),** 9, b g Gold Well—Good Thought (IRE) **The Golden Rebels**
30 **TROUVILLE LADY,** 6, b m Boris de Deauville (IRE)—Artofmen (FR) **Foran Lovell Moore**
31 **UNIKA ETOILE,** 5, b m Telescope (IRE)—Unika La Reconce (FR) **Martin Redman & Maurice Thomas**
32 **WINDSURFER,** 4, b g Getaway (GER)—Baby Shine (IRE) **Lady Jane Grosvenor**

NH Jockey: Harry Bannister, Jack Quinlan. **Amateur Jockey:** Charlie Case.

---

84 MR PATRICK CHAMINGS, Tadley

Postal: **Inhurst Farm Stables, Baughurst, Tadley, Hampshire, RG26 5JS**
Contacts: **PHONE 0118 981 4494 MOBILE 07831 360970 FAX 0118 982 0454**
EMAIL chamingsracing@talk21.com

1 **AMATHUS (IRE),** 6, b g Anjaal—Effige (IRE) **Mr D. F. Henery**

MR PATRICK CHAMINGS - continued

2 **BHUBEZI,** 5, ch g Starspangledbanner (AUS)—Lulani (IRE) **The Foxford House Partnership**
3 **COCO BEAR (IRE),** 5, br g Kodi Bear (IRE)—House of Roses **Trish & Colin Fletcher-Hall & Partner**
4 **DARVEL (IRE),** 5, b g Dark Angel (IRE)—Anthem Alexander (IRE) **Howard and Shirley Symonds**
5 **DOURADO (IRE),** 9, b h Dark Angel (IRE)—Skehana (IRE) **Mrs B. C. Wickens**
6 **EMINENT HIPSTER (IRE),** 5, b g Make Believe—Organza **Mr D. F. Henery**
7 **GLOBAL ACCLAMATION,** 7, b g Acclamation—High Luminosity (USA) **Inhurst Players**
8 **GUILTY PARTY (IRE),** 6, b m Lawman (FR)—Coolree Marj (IRE) **Mrs R. Lyon & Mr P. R. Chamings**
9 **LAST IN LINE,** 6, ch g Saddler's Rock (IRE)—Methodical **Abrahams,Reed,Truan & Spershott**
10 **LOOKSEE,** 5, b g Passing Glance—Orphina (IRE) **Mr J. A. Mould**
11 **MAGICAL DRAGON (IRE),** 6, b g Dragon Pulse (IRE)—Place That Face **Howard and Shirley Symonds**
12 **MOTATAABEQ (IRE),** 5, b g Kodiac—Jabhaat (USA) **The Foxford House Partnership**
13 **MY LADY CLAIRE,** 7, ch m Cityscape—Lady Sylvia **The Foxford House Partnership**
14 **RAQRAAQ (USA),** 5, b g War Front (USA)—Firdaws (USA) **The Foxford House Partnership**
15 **SHIP TO SHORE,** 5, b g Famous Name—Sea Regatta (IRE) **Mr D. F. Henery**
16 **SPANISH STAR (IRE),** 8, b g Requinto (IRE)—Rancho Star (IRE) **Shirley Symonds & Fred Camis**
17 **TAWTHEEF (IRE),** 6, b g Muhaarar—Miss Beatrix (IRE) **Trolley Action**

THREE-YEAR-OLDS

18 **ARTAVIAN,** b g Tasleet—Miss Villefranche **G E Bassett & P R Chamings**
19 **BRAGALOT,** b c Brazen Beau (AUS)—Arculinge **The Berks & Hants Racing Partnership**
20 **LETHAL SECRET,** b g Lethal Force (IRE)—Secret Night **Hants & Herts**
21 **MISS REQUINTO (IRE),** b f Requinto (IRE)—Rancho Star (IRE) **Shirley Symonds & Fred Camis**
22 **SPANISH STORM (IRE),** b g Requinto (IRE)—Mezogiorno (IRE) **F. D. Camis**

Assistant Trainer: Phillippa Chamings.

---

85 MR JACK CHANNON, West Ilsley

Postal: **West Ilsley Stables, West Ilsley, Newbury, Berkshire, RG20 7AE**
Contacts: **WORK 01635 281166**
EMAIL laura@jackchannonracing.co.uk, jackchannonracing@gmail.com

1 **BAROQUE STAR (IRE),** 4, ch f Lope de Vega (IRE)—Gallic Star (IRE) **Mrs T. Burns**
2 **CERTAIN LAD,** 7, b g Clodovil (IRE)—Chelsey Jayne (IRE) **Mr C. R. Hirst**
3 **CHAIRMANOFTHEBOARD (IRE),** 7, b g Slade Power (IRE)—Bound Copy (USA) **David Kilburn & Chris Wright**
4 **EASTER ICON,** 4, ch g Sixties Icon—Vive Ma Fille (GER) **Mr J. M. Mitchell**
5 **HIROMICHI (FR),** 5, gr g Dabirsim (FR)—Pachelbelle (FR) **Jon & Julia Aisbitt**
6 **INDIAN CREAK (IRE),** 6, b g Camacho—Ushindi (IRE) **Norman Court Stud & Susan Bunney**
7 **INGRA TOR (IRE),** 4, b g Churchill (IRE)—Kassia (IRE) **Jon & Julia Aisbitt**
8 **JOHAN,** 6, b g Zoffany (IRE)—Sandreamer (IRE) **Jon & Julia Aisbitt**
9 **MAJESTIC (IRE),** 5, b g Conduit (IRE)—Grevillea (IRE) **Mr N. J. Hitchins**
10 **SINGLE (IRE),** 6, ch m Nathaniel (IRE)—Solita (USA)
11 **TRAIS FLUORS,** 9, b br g Dansili—Trois Lunes (FR) **M. R. Channon**
12 **URBAN VIOLET,** 5, b m Cityscape—Just Violet **Eternal Folly Partnership**
13 **WHISTLEDOWN,** 4, gr f Gregorian (IRE)—El Che **Norman Court Stud & Susan Bunney**
14 **WONDERFUL WORLD,** 4, b g Bungle Inthejungle—La Gifted **M. R. Channon**

THREE-YEAR-OLDS

15 **BETWEENTHESTICKS,** b g Captain Gerrard (IRE)—Jollyhockeysticks **The Wilsley Partnership**
16 **CAERNARFON,** b f Cityscape—Royal Ffanci **Hunscote Stud, P Humphreys & J Sweeney**
17 **CALSHOT SPIT (IRE),** b g New Bay—Nour'spirit (IRE) **M. R. Channon**
18 **CHOURMO,** b g Postponed (IRE)—Indicia **Mr J. M. Mitchell**
19 **DESPERATE HERO,** gr ro g Captain Gerrard (IRE)—El Che **Norman Court Stud & Partner**
20 B f Gregorian (IRE)—Fanditha (IRE) **Mrs T. Burns**

MR JACK CHANNON - continued

21 **FERROUS (IRE),** gr c Dark Angel (IRE)—Grizzel (IRE) **Recycled Products Limited & Partner**
22 **FLAME QUEEN,** b f Oasis Dream—Opal Tiara (IRE) **The Filly Folly & Sweet Partnership**
23 **FLASH BARDOT,** b f Sixties Icon—Bridie Ffrench **Six or Sticks (Sixties)**
24 **GATHER YE ROSEBUDS,** ch f Zoffany (IRE)—Chelsey Jayne (IRE) **Mrs P Shanahan & Mrs M V Magnier**
25 **KALAMA SUNRISE,** b f Coulsty (IRE)—Evanesce **Dave & Gill Hedley**
26 **KANAWHA,** b f Kodiac—Kassia (IRE) **Box 41**
27 **KITBAG,** b g Territories (IRE)—Weigelia **M. R. Channon**
28 **LEXINGTON HERO,** b g Massaat (IRE)—Lexington Rose **R. Kent**
29 **MACARI,** b g Sixties Icon—Potternello (IRE) **M. R. Channon**
30 **METAL MERCHANT (IRE),** b c Make Believe—Whipped (IRE) **Recycled Products Limited & Partner**
31 **MILTEYE,** b c Cable Bay (IRE)—Fondie (IRE) **Mr D. Hunt**
32 **MISS ATTITUDE,** b f Cityscape—Rebecca Romero **Norman Court Stud**
33 **MMA RAMOTSWE (IRE),** b f Bungle Inthejungle—Dierama (IRE) **Mrs T. Burns**
34 **MOUSH,** b c Charm Spirit (IRE)—Fiumicino **Mr. P Trant & Partner**
35 **NIGHT STALKER,** ch g Sixties Icon—Shadows Ofthenight **M. R. Channon**
36 **OBAMA ARMY,** b g Washington DC (IRE)—Intrusion **Six or Sticks (Washington DC)**
37 **PHOENIX GLOW (IRE),** b f Bungle Inthejungle—Jillnextdoor (IRE) **Jolly Folly Syndicate I**
38 **RATHGAR,** ch c Ulysses (IRE)—Why We Dream (IRE) **Jon & Julia Aisbitt**
39 **RETETI,** b g Sixties Icon—Siri **Dave & Gill Hedley**
40 B f Wootton Bassett—Sea Claria (FR) **Mr C. R. Hirst**
41 **SERA DAWN,** b f Bated Breath—Amahoro **Dave & Gill Hedley**
42 **SIXTIES CHIC,** b f Sixties Icon—Chicago Star **Box 41**
43 **SPITFIRE BRIDGE,** b g Sixties Icon—Outside Art **M. R. Channon**
44 **THEM THAT CAN,** b f Kingman—Impressionist (IRE) **Mr C. R. Hirst**
45 **TIRIAC,** b c Sixties Icon—Rough Courte (IRE) **Mr J Widdows & Partner**
46 **TOMAHAWK KING (IRE),** b c Camacho—Amaany **The Wilsley Partnership**
47 **WOODSTOCK,** b c Sixties Icon—Isabella Bird **Jon & Julia Aisbitt**

TWO-YEAR-OLDS

48 B c 24/03 Inns of Court (IRE)—Abiquiu (IRE) (Roderic O'Connor (IRE)) (25000) **SYPS**
49 Ch c 23/02 Kessaar (IRE)—Balaawy (Bated Breath) **Mr. T. Radford & Partner**
50 **BRINDLEY (IRE),** b c 30/04 Calyx—
Shanghai Rose (Mastercraftsman (IRE)) (75000) **Rory O'Rourke, MPS Racing & Partners**
51 Ch c 27/04 Phoenix of Spain (IRE)—Brioniya (Pivotal) (10500) **M. R. Channon**
52 **CLARA BARTON,** b f 10/04 Mukhadram—Isabella Bird (Invincible Spirit (IRE)) **Jon & Julia Aisbitt**
53 **CONTINUANCE,** b c 17/02 Postponed (IRE)—Caravela (IRE) (Henrythenavigator (USA)) **Jon & Julia Aisbitt**
54 **DANCING THE DREAM,** b f 05/03 Bated Breath—Hazy Dancer (Oasis Dream) (6000) **Mr W H Carson**
55 B f 14/02 Zoustar (AUS)—Effie B (Sixties Icon) **Bastian Family**
56 B c 02/05 Sixties Icon—Estrellada (Oasis Dream) **Mr. R. Windridge**
57 B c 14/02 Ulysses (IRE)—Fervid (Dutch Art) (32000) **John & Zoe Webster**
58 **GALYX (IRE),** b c 17/04 Calyx—Gallic Star (IRE) (Galileo (IRE)) **Jon & Julia Aisbitt**
59 B f 11/04 Profitable (IRE)—Jillnextdoor (IRE) (Henrythenavigator (USA)) **Ballylinch Stud**
60 B c 29/03 Soldier's Call—La Perla (SPA) (Sinndar (IRE)) (20808) **SYPS & Partner**
61 **METALLO (IRE),** b c 09/02 Caravaggio (USA)—
Sweet Dreams Baby (IRE) (Montjeu (IRE)) (52021) **Recycled Products Limited & Partner**
62 B c 31/03 Postponed (IRE)—Mistaken Love (USA) (Bernardini (USA)) (18000) **Box 41**
63 B c 26/04 Bungle Inthejungle—Myladyjane (IRE) (Mastercraftsman (IRE)) **John & Zoe Webster**
64 B f 05/04 Harry Angel (IRE)—Never Lose (Diktat) **Mr. Jaber Abdullah**
65 B f 11/04 Invincible Army (IRE)—Promised Money (IRE) (Dark Angel (IRE)) (40000) **M. R. Channon**
66 B c 12/04 Sixties Icon—Rebecca Romero (Exceed And Excel (AUS)) **M. R. Channon**
67 B g 16/03 Gregorian (IRE)—Rinaria (IRE) (Tamayuz) (17000) **M. R. Channon**
68 **SAIGON DREAM,** b c 09/03 Oasis Dream—
Gracious Diana (Foxwedge (AUS)) (42000) **Mr. C. Hirst & Mr. B. Malcolm**
69 B c 17/03 Time Test—Salve Etoiles (IRE) (Sea The Stars (IRE)) (5000) **Hunscote Stud Limited**
70 B f 09/04 Dark Angel (IRE)—Sheba Five (USA) (Five Star Day (USA)) **Mr. Jaber Abdullah**
71 B c 27/03 Bungle Inthejungle—Society Guest (IRE) (Society Rock (IRE)) **John Guest Racing Ltd**
72 B c 22/04 Advertise—South Bay (Exceed And Excel (AUS)) (80000) **M. R. Channon**
73 B f 10/03 Advertise—Swing Out Sister (IRE) (Kodiac) (200000) **Mr C. R. Hirst**
74 B c 15/03 Ten Sovereigns (IRE)—Swinging Jean (Sixties Icon) **M. R. Channon**

MR JACK CHANNON - continued

75 B f 16/02 Havana Gold (IRE)—Tasman Sea (Champs Elysees) (43000) **Mr. B. Walters**
76 Ch f 12/04 Bated Breath—The Thrill Is Gone (Bahamian Bounty) **Christopher Wright & George Brooksbank**

Assistant Trainer: Allana Mason, **Pupil Assistant:** Suzannah Stevens, **Racing Secretary:** Laura Allan.

86

MR MICHAEL CHAPMAN, Market Rasen

Postal: **Woodlands Racing Stables, Woodlands Lane, Willingham Road, Market Rasen, Lincolnshire, LN8 3RE**
Contacts: **PHONE 01673 843663 MOBILE 07971 940087**
EMAIL woodlands.stables@btconnect.com WEBSITE www.woodlandsracingstables.co.uk

1 **FAST DEAL,** 6, ch g Fast Company (IRE)—Maven **Mrs M. M. Chapman**
2 **L'ES FREMANTLE (FR),** 12, b g Orpen (USA)—Grand Design **Mrs M. M. Chapman**
3 **LUDUAMF (IRE),** 9, ch g Tamayuz—Aphorism **Mrs M. M. Chapman**
4 **SMART CONNECTION (IRE),** 6, b g Dutch Art—Endless Love (IRE) **Mrs M. M. Chapman**
5 **STRAITOUTTACOMPTON,** 7, b g Compton Place—Red Mischief (IRE) **Mrs M. M. Chapman**

Assistant Trainer: Mrs M. Chapman.

MR RYAN CHAPMAN, St Mawgan

Postal: **Trevenna Forge, St Mawgan, Newquay, Cornwall, Tr8 4ez**

1 **ALBERTS BAY (IRE),** 6, b g Leading Light (IRE)—My Viking Bay (IRE) **Mr R. G. Chapman**
2 **BALLY DUN (IRE),** 8, b g Arcadio (GER)—Queen's Forest (IRE) **Mr R. G. Chapman**
3 **BLUE RIBBON,** 8, b g Sayif (IRE)—Mar Blue (FR) **Mr R. G. Chapman**
4 **FORRARD AWAY (IRE),** 8, b br g Califet (FR)—Hunting Spirit (IRE) **Mr R. G. Chapman**
5 **LEADING KNIGHT (IRE),** 7, b g Leading Light (IRE)—Miss McGoldrick (IRE) **Mr R. G. Chapman**
6 4, Ch g Linda's Lad—Onwegoagain (IRE) **Mr R. G. Chapman**
7 **RISKY WHISKEY (IRE),** 6, b g Watar (IRE)—Sapphire Rouge (IRE) **Mr R. G. Chapman**

THREE-YEAR-OLDS

8 Ch f Linda's Lad—Doctor Thea
9 B f Linda's Lad—Onwegoagain (IRE)

88

MR FABRICE CHAPPET, Chantilly

Postal: **29 Avenue de Joinville, Chantilly, 60500, France**
Contacts: **PHONE +33 3 44 21 03 00**
EMAIL chappet.office@chappetracing.fr WEBSITE www.chappetracing.com

1 **AFGHANY (FR),** 5, b h The Gurkha—Texaloula **F. Chappet**
2 **ALBA POWER (IRE),** 8, b g Fast Company (IRE)—Shehila (IRE) **F. J. Carmichael**
3 **EARLY LIGHT (FR),** 5, b h Wootton Bassett—Accalmie **F. Chappet**
4 **FOREST OF WISDOM,** 5, b h Ifraaj—Wiesenlerche **R. Shaykhutdinov**
5 **FREJA (FR),** 4, b f Toronado (IRE)—No Wind No Rain **A. Gilibert**
6 **GREGARINA (FR),** 4, ch f De Treville—Gagarina (IRE) **R. Shaykhutdinov**
7 **MACHETE (FR),** 4, b c Myboycharlie (IRE)—Maid To Believe **R. Shaykhutdinov**

MR FABRICE CHAPPET - continued

8 **NEPALAIS,** 5, b h The Gurkha—Daltiana (FR) **A. Gilibert**
9 **ONESTO (IRE),** 4, ch c Frankel—Onshore **G. Augustin-Normand**
10 **PLESENT JANE,** 4, b f Pivotal—Jane The Star **R. Shaykhutdinov**
11 **PRINCE LANCELOT,** 5, b h Sir Prancealot (IRE)—Rainbow Vale (FR) **A. Gilibert**
12 **PRIVATE LOUNGE,** 4, ch f Toronado (IRE)—Polarized **Haras de Saint Julien**
13 **ROYAUMONT (FR),** 6, b g Dabirsim (FR)—Rosie Thomas (IRE) **A. Gilibert**
14 **SICILIA (FR),** 4, b f Shalaa—Nigwah **F. Chappet**
15 **TOPGEAR (FR),** 4, b c Wootton Bassett—Miss Lech (USA) **H. Saito**

THREE-YEAR-OLDS

16 **AL MUNDHER (FR),** b c Toronado (IRE)—Vicieuse (FR) **K. M. Al Attiyah**
17 **ALMOND CHOUQUETTE (FR),** b f Almanzor (FR)—Minted (USA) **T Lines**
18 **ALVA (FR),** ch f Sea The Moon (GER)—America's Best (USA) **A. Gilibert**
19 **AMANDA'S CHOICE,** b f Brazen Beau (AUS)—Super Midge **A. Gilibert**
20 **AUSTRAL (FR),** b c Zelzal (FR)—Saga Boreale (USA) **Al Shaqab Racing**
21 **BASSAC (FR),** b f Gleneagles (IRE)—Segonzac (IRE) **H. de Pracomtal**
22 **BE THE KING (FR),** b c Kingman—Kosmische (IRE) **R. Shaykhutdinov**
23 **BLESS (FR),** ch c Toronado (IRE)—Mlayhah (FR) **R. Simmons**
24 **CROWN PRINCESSE (FR),** ch f Zarak (FR)—Lovemedo (FR) **Haras de Saint Julien**
25 **DAINTY BIT (FR),** b c De Treville—Dance In The Moon **R. Shaykhutdinov**
26 **DEEP WISH,** b c De Treville—Wiesenlerche (IRE) **R. Shaykhutdinov**
27 **DRIVABLE (FR),** b g De Treville—Barbara
28 **EMPATHIC (FR),** ch c Showcasing—Empreinte (USA) **R. Shaykhutdinov**
29 **FORTUNE (FR),** ch c De Treville—February Sun **R. Shaykhutdinov**
30 **GAIN IT,** b f De Treville—Gagarina (IRE) **R. Shaykhutdinov**
31 **GALLANT DEED (FR),** b c Frankel—Global Magic (GER) **R. Shaykhutdinov**
32 **GOOD GUESS,** b c Kodiac—Zykina **H. Saito**
33 **HIALEAH (FR),** b f Wootton Bassett—Gratefully (IRE) **Ecurie F. Defosse**
34 **I'M A BELIEVER (FR),** b c Seabhac (USA)—Winds Up (USA) **A. Gilibert**
35 **KING OF RECORDS (FR),** b c Sea The Stars (IRE)—Super Woman (FR) **Ecurie J-L. Bouchard**
36 **KITTY (FR),** b f De Treville—Kate's Winnie **R. Shaykhutdinov**
37 **KLEORA,** b f Le Havre (IRE)—Kleo (GR) **Tolmi Racing**
38 **LADY GLENHAM (IRE),** b f Zoffany (IRE)—Lady Babooshka **C. Bernick**
39 **LEMON ZEST (FR),** b c Almanzor—Lemon Twist **Ecurie Jeffroy**
40 **LEWIS CHOP (FR),** b c Kheleyf (USA)—Laia Chope (FR) **A Chopard**
41 **LIGHTNING BOLT (FR),** b c Sea The Moon—Wonderous Light **R. Shaykhutdinov**
42 **MEMORY ROAD,** b c Sea The Moon (GER)—Pure Song **H. Saito**
43 **MERCI ELIE (FR),** b c Ectot—Elegante (FR) **L. Mineo**
44 **METEOR SHOWER,** b br f Sea The Stars (IRE)—Megera (FR) **R. Shaykhutdinov**
45 **MILLE DREAMS,** ch f Dream Ahead—La Milletiere **A. Gilibert**
46 **PAZ,** b f Siyouni (FR)—Pinkster **Haras d'Etreham**
47 **PROTECTOR (FR),** b c Toronado (IRE)—Siyana (FR) **M. Rizieri**
48 **SAUCY JADE (IRE),** gr f De Treville—Jane The Star **R. Shaykhutdinov**
49 **SAY AGAIN (FR),** b f Zarak (FR)—Babylove (FR) **Haras de Saint Julien**
50 **SIVKA BURKA (FR),** ch f Siyouni (FR)—Dynadin **R. Shaykhutdinov**
51 **SOCIETY MAN (FR),** b c Cracksman—Society Lady **Haras de Saint Julien**
52 **SUNLIKE (FR),** b f De Treville—Sunny Frankel **R. Shaykhutdinov**
53 **THANKYOU (FR),** ch f Postponed (IRE)—Trully Belle (IRE) **A. Tamagni**
54 **THE LAST WALTZ (FR),** b f Golden Horn—Lavande Violet (GER) **C.N. Wright**
55 **TIMETOSHINE (FR),** bl f The Grey Gatsby (IRE)—This Time (FR) **A. Tamagni**
56 **VALENTINO FACE (FR),** ch c Almanzor (FR)—Asumi (IRE) **A. Gilibert**
57 **WATCHOUT (FR),** b f Golden Horn—Watchful (IRE) **Haras de Saint Julien**
58 **ZALAMO (FR),** b c Seahenge (USA)—Zylpha (IRE) **S. Vidal**
59 **ZINDERELLA (FR),** b f Almanzor (FR)—Zain Al Boldan **F. J. Carmichael**

Trainer did not supply details of their two-year-olds.

89 MRS JANE CHAPPLE-HYAM, Newmarket

Postal: **Abington Place Racing Stables, 44 Bury Road, Newmarket, Suffolk, CB8 7BT**
Contacts: **MOBILE 07899 000555**
EMAIL janechapplehyam@hotmail.co.uk, janechapplehyamracing@outlook.com

1 **AMBASSADORIAL (USA),** 9, b g Elusive Quality (USA)—Tactfully (IRE) **Jane Chapple-Hyam**
2 **APLOMB (IRE),** 7, b g Lope de Vega (IRE)—Mickleberry (IRE) **Mrs F. J. Carmichael**
3 **ARIKA (USA),** 4, b g Speightstown (USA)—Josette (IRE) **Kenjiro Private Office Limited**
4 **CLAYMORE (FR),** 4, b c New Bay—Brit Wit **Mrs M Slack**
5 **FIDUCIARY,** 6, b m Bated Breath—Ombre **China Horse Club International Limited**
6 **FIRST OFFICER (IRE),** 4, b c Galileo (IRE)—Weekend Strike (USA) **Mr Bryan Hirst & Jane Chapple-Hyam**
7 **HEAT OF THE MOMENT,** 4, ch f Bobby's Kitten (USA)—Heat of The Night **Miss K Rausing**
8 **IDEE FIXEE,** 4, ch c Dubawi (IRE)—Our Obsession (IRE) **A. E. Oppenheimer**
9 **INTELLOGENT (IRE),** 8, ch g Intello (GER)—Nuit Polaire (IRE) **Mrs F. J. Carmichael**
10 **INTERNATIONALANGEL (IRE),** 6, gr m Dark Angel (IRE)—Wrong Answer **Mr L. Holder**
11 **MEISHAR (ARG),** 7, b g Exchange Rate (USA)—My Palestina (ARG) **Mr L. Holder**
12 **NIZAAKA (FR),** 5, b m New Bay—Dusky Queen (IRE) **Jastar Capital Ltd & WH Bloodstock**
13 **OUR BOY SAM,** 4, ch g Mazameer (IRE)—Bobby Vee **Mr R. Beadle & Mrs S. Beadle**
14 **PARTHENOPAEUS,** 4, b g Pivotal—Atalante **Mrs D. M. Swinburn**
15 **POPPY BOUCHET,** 4, b f Havana Gold (IRE)—Audacia (IRE) **Mrs F. J. Carmichael**
16 **PRENUP (IRE),** 4, b f Profitable (IRE)—Intimacy (IRE) **Jastar Ltd, Murt Khan & Harry Wigan**
17 **QUEEN OF THE SKIES,** 4, ch f Lope de Vega (IRE)—Westwiththenight (IRE) **A. E. Oppenheimer**
18 **SUZI'S CONNOISSEUR,** 12, b g Art Connoisseur (IRE)—Suzi Spends (IRE) **Jane Chapple-Hyam**

THREE-YEAR-OLDS

19 **BLANCHLAND (IRE),** b c Farhh—Examinee (GER) **Mr P. W. Harris**
20 **CLIMATE FRIENDLY,** ch f Frankel—Unex Mona Lisa **The Gredley Family**
21 **CROWN BOARD (IRE),** b g Lope de Vega (IRE)—Against Rules (FR) **Mr P. W. Harris**
22 **DECIPHER (IRE),** b f Noble Mission—Multilingual **Mrs P Shanahan, B V Sangster, S Sangster**
23 **EYETRAP,** b c Ulysses (IRE)—Miss Dashwood **Mr P. W. Harris**
24 **GEMSTAR,** b f Zoustar (AUS)—Permission **Mrs F. J. Carmichael**
25 **GOLDEN DELITE,** b c Golden Horn—Inchina **A. E. Oppenheimer**
26 **HOLLINGBERY (IRE),** b g Lope de Vega (IRE)—Playfull Spirit **Mr P. W. Harris**
27 **I AM LEGEND (SWE),** b f Barocci (JPN)—Rock The Legend (IRE) **Abigail Harrison & Jane Chapple-Hyam**
28 **MARMARA SEA,** b f Golden Horn—Handana (IRE) **Mrs M Slack**
29 **MAURICES MEN,** b c Adaay (IRE)—Bobby Vee **Mr R. Beadle & Mrs S. Beadle**
30 **MIDNIGHTDANDY (IRE),** gr g Dandy Man (IRE)—Sweet Alabama **Mr L. Holder**
31 **MILL STREAM (IRE),** b c Gleneagles (IRE)—Swirral Edge **Mr P. W. Harris**
32 **ORANGE N BLUE (IRE),** ch c Saxon Warrior (JPN)—Fashion Darling (IRE) **Mr G. W. Y. Li**
33 **RISOTTO (IRE),** gr f Roaring Lion (USA)—Caster Sugar (USA) **Mrs A. Wigan**
34 **ROCHA DO LEAO (IRE),** b f Footstepsinthesand—Shaleela (IRE) **Peate, Martin, Harrison, Chapple-Hyam**
35 **SOLRAY,** b c New Bay—Lait Au Chocolat (USA) **Mr Ahmad Alotaibi & Jane Chapple-Hyam**
36 **STAVVY (IRE),** gr c Roaring Lion (USA)—Every Time **Harlequin Direct Ltd**
37 **THINK CLIMATE,** b c Exceed And Excel (AUS)—Whazzat **The Gredley Family**
38 **WANTOPLANTATREE,** b f Iffraaj—Madame Defarge (IRE) **The Gredley Family**

TWO-YEAR-OLDS

39 B br c 14/03 Sea The Stars (IRE)—Amorella (IRE) (Nathaniel (IRE)) (650000) **Mr P. W. Harris**
40 B f 21/02 Churchill (IRE)—
Aquamarine (JPN) (Deep Impact (JPN)) (240096) **China Horse Club International Limited**
41 Ch c 31/01 Kitten's Joy (USA)—Auntinet (Invincible Spirit (IRE)) (85000) **Mr P. W. Harris**
42 B c 12/02 Sea The Stars (IRE)—Awesometank (Intense Focus (USA)) (335000) **Mr P. W. Harris**
43 **CAPTAIN BRADY (IRE),** b c 08/04 Calyx—Alexis Carrington (IRE) (Mastercraftsman (IRE)) (35000) **Mr G. W. Y. Li**
44 B c 28/04 Dark Angel (IRE)—Crisolles (FR) (Le Havre (IRE)) (75000) **China Horse Club International Limited**
45 **ELDERFLOWER (IRE),** b f 03/03 Ten Sovereigns (IRE)—
Almoner (Oasis Dream) (50000) **Mrs M Slack & Mrs T Brudenell**
46 Ch c 09/03 New Bay—Falling Petals (IRE) (Raven's Pass (USA)) (360144) **Mrs F. J. Carmichael**
47 **FLAG OF ST GEORGE (IRE),** b c 13/04 U S Navy Flag (USA)—
Tamazug (Machiavellian (USA)) (32000) **Mr L. Holder**
48 Ch c 03/05 Churchill (IRE)—Flawless Jewel (FR) (Kheleyf (USA)) (150000) **Mr P. W. Harris**

MRS JANE CHAPPLE-HYAM - continued

49 B c 20/03 Night of Thunder (IRE)—Looks A Million (Kyllachy) (190000) **Mr P. W. Harris**
50 Ro gr c 27/01 Lope de Vega (IRE)—Maid Up (Mastercraftsman (IRE)) (230000) **Mr P. W. Harris**
51 B f 11/02 Lope de Vega (IRE)—Moteo (IRE) (Teofilo (IRE)) (320000) **Mr P. W. Harris**
52 Ch f 25/02 Ulysses (IRE)—Never Enough (GER) (Monsun (GER)) **5 Wise Monkeys Club**
53 **SAPIENCE,** b f 01/03 Study of Man (IRE)—Sagesse (Smart Strike (CAN)) **Miss K Rausing**
54 **SONS AND LOVERS,** b c 08/04 Study of Man (IRE)—
So In Love (Smart Strike (CAN)) (32013) **Mr & Mrs H Morriss & Miss K Rausing**
55 **UNION JACKIE (IRE),** b f 03/04 U S Navy Flag (USA)—Shaleela (IRE) (Galileo (IRE)) (26667) **Mr L. Holder**
56 B f 24/04 Siyouni (FR)—Villa d'Amore (IRE) (Mastercraftsman (IRE)) (500000) **Mr P. W. Harris**
57 B c 19/02 Sea The Stars (IRE)—Waitingfortheday (IRE) (Elzaam (AUS)) (350000) **Mr P. W. Harris**

Assistant Trainer: Abi Harrison.

Flat Jockey: Dayverson De Barros, Marco Ghiani, Robert Tart. **Apprentice Jockey:** Tommie Jakes.

---

90 MR PETER CHAPPLE-HYAM, Newmarket

Postal: **St Gatien Stables, All Saints Road, Newmarket, Suffolk, CB8 8HJ**

1 **DEJA (FR),** 8, b g Youmzain (IRE)—Atarfe (IRE) **Miss S. E. Wall**
2 **FRANCO GRASSO,** 5, b g Frankel—Oakley Girl **Miss S. E. Wall**
3 **MARTINENGO (IRE),** 8, b g Elusive Pimpernel (USA)—Albiatra (USA) **Miss S. E. Wall**
4 **SAYF AL DAWLA,** 5, b g Frankel—Attraction **Fairlawns Racing Ltd**
5 **UNION SPIRIT,** 6, b br g Outstrip—Nouvelle Lune **Miss Sally Wall & Star Pointe Ltd**

THREE-YEAR-OLDS

6 **ALBERT CEE (FR),** b br g Aclaim (IRE)—Alzahra **Franconson Partners**
7 **ARIKARA,** ch f Showcasing—Glade **Fairlawns Racing Ltd**
8 **CHESTER TONIK (FR),** ch c Starspangledbanner (AUS)—Costa Rica (IRE) **Franconson Partners**
9 **CRYSTALLIUM,** b f Expert Eye—Crysdal **E & Hancock**
10 **DEFENCE OF FORT (IRE),** ch c Starspangledbanner (AUS)—Signs And Signals (IRE)
11 B f Kingman—Frenzified
12 **MARLEYS MIRACLE,** ch c Exceed And Excel (AUS)—Split Trois (FR) **Miss S. E. Wall**
13 **SCORCH,** b g Aclaim (IRE)—I Feel It Coming (USA) **Fairlawns Racing Ltd**

TWO-YEAR-OLDS

14 Br c 18/03 Ten Sovereigns (IRE)—Al Jawza (Nathaniel (IRE)) (19000) **Mr P. W. Chapple-Hyam**
15 Bl c 24/03 Twilight Son—Peters Spirit (IRE) (Invincible Spirit (IRE)) (14000) **Miss S. E. Wall**
16 B c 27/03 Profitable (IRE)—Skip To My Lou (Foxwedge (AUS)) (27000) **Miss S. E. Wall**

---

91 MR PETER CHARALAMBOUS AND JAMES CLUTTERBUCK, Newmarket

Postal: **31 Chapel Street, Exning, Newmarket, Suffolk, CB8 7HA**
Contacts: **PHONE 07921 858421**
EMAIL pondhouseracing@gmail.com

1 **ALPHA KING,** 5, b g Kingman—Kilo Alpha **Mr C. Pigram**
2 **APOLLO ONE,** 5, ch g Equiano (FR)—Boonga Roogeta **pcracing.co.uk**
3 **ARLO'S SUNSHINE,** 6, b g Cable Bay (IRE)—Touching (IRE) **Mr F. Sonny**
4 **COUL UNIVERSE (IRE),** 4, b g Coulsty (IRE)—Universal Circus **Mr C. Pigram**
5 **DRILL TO DREAM,** 4, b f Australia—Mascarene (USA) **Mr D. Hazelwood**
6 **INTREPIDLY (USA),** 9, b g Medaglia d'Oro (USA)—Trepidation (USA) **C Pigram & T Hind**

MR PETER CHARALAMBOUS AND JAMES CLUTTERBUCK - continued

7 **MAKARIOS,** 5, b g Toronado (IRE)—Ela Gorrie Mou **pcracing.co.uk**
8 **MAN ON A MISSION,** 4, b g Swiss Spirit—Loveatfirstsight **Miss K. L. Squance**
9 **MOONLIGHT TIARA,** 4, ch f Helmet (AUS)—Amarylis (IRE) **Mrs M. Bacon**
10 **POINT OF FACT,** 4, b g Almanzor (FR)—Rip Roaring **Mr C. Pigram**
11 **ROARING RIVER,** 4, b g Muhaarar—River Belle **Mr C. Pigram**
12 **SHES MY GIRL,** 4, b f Helmet (AUS)—Theydon Girls **pcracing.co.uk**

THREE-YEAR-OLDS

13 **CRIKEY JUICEY,** b f Tasleet—Chevise (IRE) **Bywater Thoroughbreds**
14 **KALOI,** b c Mayson—Kalon Brama (IRE) **pcracing.co.uk**
15 B f Dark Angel (IRE)—Lightning Mark (IRE) **Bywater Thoroughbreds**
16 **MARTINI LODGE,** b f Muhaarar—Poppet's Passion **Bywater Thoroughbreds**
17 **SPACE TROOPER,** gr ro c Lethal Force (IRE)—Boonga Roogeta **pcracing.co.uk**
18 B f Charming Thought—Theydon Girls **pcracing.co.uk**

TWO-YEAR-OLDS

19 B c 07/05 Land Force (IRE)—Midnight M (Green Desert (USA)) (7619) **Bywater Thoroughbreds**
20 B f 16/04 Caravaggio (USA)—Midnight Oasis (Oasis Dream) (12005) **Bywater Thoroughbreds**
21 B f 09/02 Kodiac—Munaajaat (IRE) (Tamayuz) (21429) **Bywater Thoroughbreds**
22 B f 20/03 Advertise—Ocelot (Poet's Voice) (21000) **Bywater Thoroughbreds**
23 B f 11/02 Camacho—Pianola (USA) (Arch (USA)) (2857)
24 B c 29/01 Tasleet—Princess Keira (IRE) (Acclamation) (3500)
25 Gr f 09/04 Havana Grey—Tout Va Bien (IRE) (Verglas (IRE))
26 B c 08/02 Iffraaj—Toy Theatre (Lonhro (AUS)) **Mr L. J. M. J. Vaessen**

---

92 MR ROGER AND HARRY CHARLTON, Beckhampton

Postal: **Beckhampton House, Beckhampton, Marlborough, Wiltshire, SN8 1QR**
Contacts: **PHONE 01672 539533**
EMAIL office@beckhamptonstables.com

1 **ALBION PRINCESS,** 4, b f Kingman—Langlauf (USA) **Mr A. G. Bloom**
2 **ASHKY (IRE),** 4, gr f Caravaggio (USA)—Pannonia (USA) **M. Alharbi**
3 **BLUE MIST,** 8, ch g Makfi—Namaskar **Beckhampton Stables Ltd**
4 **DISCRETION,** 4, b f Dubawi (IRE)—Momentary
5 **IMPERIUM (IRE),** 7, ch g Frankel—Ramruma (USA) **Weston Brook Farm & Bromfield**
6 **NOISY NIGHT,** 4, b g Night of Thunder (IRE)—Ya Hajar **Mr S. J. A. Alharbi**
7 **OKEECHOBEE,** 4, b c Time Test—Scuffle **Juddmonte Farms Ltd**
8 **SINJAARI (IRE),** 7, b g Camelot—Heavenly Song (IRE) **M. Alharbi**
9 **SLEEPING LION (USA),** 8, ch g Teofilo (IRE)—Flame of Hestia (IRE) **Merry Fox Stud Limited**
10 **TIME LOCK,** 4, b f Frankel—Time Chaser **Juddmonte Farms Ltd**
11 **VALSAD (IRE),** 4, b g Intello (GER)—Vuela **Mr S. A. Stuckey**
12 **VEGA SICILIA,** 4, ch g Lope de Vega (IRE)—Stone Roses (FR) **John Basquill & Dan Gilbert**
13 **WITHHOLD,** 10, b g Champs Elysees—Coming Back **Mr A. G. Bloom**
14 **ZAIN NIGHTS,** 4, b g Decorated Knight—Missy O' Gwaun (IRE) **Mr A. Al Banwan**

THREE-YEAR-OLDS

15 **ABBRISHAM,** b f Havana Gold (IRE)—Donatia **Dr J. Ahmadzadeh**
16 **ACOTANGO (IRE),** b g Kodiac—Chupalla **Dean, Gerber, Inglett and Partners**
17 **ALGERNON,** b c Showcasing—Caponata (USA) **Juddmonte Farms Ltd**
18 **ALICE KNYVET,** b f Acclamation—Battlement **Juddmonte Farms Ltd**
19 **BALTIC,** b c Frankel—Baltic Best (IRE) **David Chaplin and Fittocks Stud**
20 **BATAL DUBAI (IRE),** b c Profitable (IRE)—Sweet Sienna **J. Alharbi**
21 **BILLABONG,** b g Oasis Dream—Carding (USA) **P Inglett, S de Zoete, N Jones and Partner**

MR ROGER AND HARRY CHARLTON - continued

22 **BIRDLAND LULLABY,** b f Kingman—Be My Gal **D. J. Deer**
23 **CARAXES,** b g Al Kazeem—Serenada (FR) **D. J. Deer**
24 Ch c Shamardal (USA)—Choumicha **M. Alharbi**
25 **ELEGANCIA,** b f Lope de Vega (IRE)—So Sleek **St Albans Bloodstock Limited**
26 B f Zoustar (AUS)—Exceptionelle **D. J. Deer**
27 **FINEST LEADER (IRE),** b g Churchill (IRE)—Damselfly (IRE) **Inglett, Bengough Lady Tidbury**
28 **FROM BEYOND,** b f Zoustar (AUS)—Via Lazio **T & P Inglett**
29 **GREEK ORDER,** b c Kingman—Trojan Queen (USA) **Juddmonte Farms Ltd**
30 B f Saxon Warrior (JPN)—Happy Holly (IRE)
31 B g Starspangledbanner (AUS)—Heavenly Song (IRE) **M. Alharbi**
32 **HYDRATION,** b g Oasis Dream—Encore Moi **Brook Farm Bloodstock**
33 **I'M TOO TIRED (IRE),** b g Ribchester (IRE)—Ard Na Sidhe (IRE) **Mr & Mrs Paul & Clare Rooney**
34 **IT'S ALL ABOUT YOU (IRE),** b c Highland Reel (IRE)—Three Moons (IRE) **Mr & Mrs Paul & Clare Rooney**
35 **KARAKOY,** b g Golden Horn—Souville **Paul Inglett & Partner**
36 **LILLISTAR,** gr f Zoustar (AUS)—Langlauf (USA) **Mr A. G. Bloom**
37 **LOVE IS A ROSE,** ch f Churchill (IRE)—Parsnip (IRE) **Philip Newton & Elizabeth Railton**
38 **MAGICAL MERLIN (IRE),** gr g Kodiac—Aphrodite's Angel (IRE) **Paul Inglett & Beckhampton Racing**
39 **MAN OF EDEN,** b g Zoffany (IRE)—Longing To Dance **D. J. Deer**
40 **MERLIN THE WIZARD,** b g Camelot—Sweet Gentle Kiss (IRE) **Mr I. Alsagar**
41 **MONOGLOW (IRE),** b g Kodiac—Savida (IRE) **M. Alharbi**
42 **MOTHER MARGARET (IRE),** b f Kingman—September Stars (IRE) **Andrew Rosen & Edward W Easton**
43 **PRIMEVAL,** b f Lope de Vega (IRE)—Passage of Time **Juddmonte Farms Ltd**
44 **QUIET SEA,** b f Sea The Moon (GER)—Kind of Hush (IRE) **Elite Racing Club**
45 **ROARIN' SUCCESS,** ch f Roaring Lion (USA)—Random Success (IRE) **Mr P. Inglett**
46 **SHAHEEN SAQAAR (IRE),** b g Fastnet Rock (AUS)—Signora Queen (FR) **J. Alharbi**
47 **SO MANY QUESTIONS,** b c Showcasing—Fig Roll **Mr D. Channon**
48 **SPEED TO RUN (IRE),** b f Holy Roman Emperor (IRE)—Rainbow Royal (IRE) **J. Alharbi**
49 **STAGE SHOW,** b g Showcasing—Floria Tosca (IRE) **Brook Farm Bloodstock**
50 Ch g Bated Breath—Telescopic **Hugo Hunt Racing**
51 **ZAMAN JEMIL (IRE),** b c Invincible Spirit (IRE)—Zippy Rock (IRE) **J. Alharbi**
52 **ZOUZANNA,** b f Zoustar (AUS)—Gee Kel (IRE) **Brooke-Rankin, Frost, Hues, Inglett**

TWO-YEAR-OLDS

53 Ch c 05/02 New Bay—All I Need (IRE) (Peintre Celebre (USA)) (70000)
54 Br f 27/04 Too Darn Hot—Amona (IRE) (Aussie Rules (USA)) (62000) **Dean, Frost, Hues and Inglett**
55 Ch c 03/03 Churchill (IRE)—Barter (Daylami (IRE)) (145000) **M. Alharbi**
56 **COMPLETELY RANDOM,** b gr c 02/04 Havana Grey—Random Success (IRE) (Shamardal (USA))
57 B c 05/02 Sea The Stars (IRE)—Complexion (Hurricane Run (IRE)) (120000) **Brightwalton Bloodstock**
58 **DIFFERENT DRUM,** b c 05/02 Sea The Moon (GER)—Hi Calypso (IRE) (In The Wings) **P. Newton**
59 **FLAG OF LOVE (IRE),** gr f 16/04 Starspangledbanner (AUS)—Aphrodite's Angel (IRE) (Dark Angel (IRE)) (140000)
60 **GREY MOON,** gr c 15/02 Sea The Moon (GER)—
Contrive (IRE) (Mastercraftsman (IRE)) (90000) **Dean, de Zoete, Inglett, Jones and Rees**
61 B c 21/03 Gleneagles (IRE)—Heavenly Song (IRE) (Oratorio (IRE)) **M. Alharbi**
62 B c 15/03 Havana Gold (IRE)—Here's Two (Hellvelyn) **K.A.C. Bloodstock Limited**
63 B c 29/04 Ten Sovereigns (IRE)—Lady Fashion (Oasis Dream) (75000) **M. Alharbi**
64 Ch c 05/03 Saxon Warrior (JPN)—Pure Symmetry (USA) (Storm Cat (USA)) (125000) **M. Alharbi**
65 Ch c 13/02 Sea The Moon (GER)—Puzzling (Peintre Celebre (USA)) (40000) **Paul Inglett & Partners**
66 Ch c 07/02 Zoustar (AUS)—Quiet (Observatory (USA))
67 B f 06/03 Camelot—Shaden (IRE) (Kodiac) **Mr I. Alsagar**
68 B c 15/02 Blue Point (IRE)—Sooraah (Dubawi (IRE)) **M. Alharbi**
69 B f 28/01 Decorated Knight—Sweet Gentle Kiss (IRE) (Henrythenavigator (USA)) **Mr I. Alsagar**
70 **TO VRIKA,** b f 20/02 Too Darn Hot—Choumicha (Paco Boy (IRE)) **M. Alharbi**
71 B c 02/05 Galileo (IRE)—Vanzara (FR) (Redoute's Choice (AUS)) (200000) **Brook Farm Bloodstock**

93 MR BEN CLARKE, Chard

Postal: **Puthill Barn, Cricket St Thomas, Chard, Somerset, TA20 4EJ**
EMAIL benclarkeracing@gmail.com

1 **ARCTIC BLUE,** 5, b m Blue Bresil (FR)—Arctic Magic (IRE) **Midd Shire Racing**
2 **BLUE MOON SERENADE,** 4, b f Pether's Moon (IRE)—Asola Blue (FR) **Ann & Tony Gale**
3 **BOBALOT,** 6, gr g Camelot—Riva Snows (IRE) **Fusion Racing Club**
4 **CAST'S TASHA (IRE),** 6, b m Westerner—Samsha (IRE) **Sue & Clive Cole & Ann & Tony Gale**
5 **DR KANANGA,** 9, b g Dapper—Crepe de Chine (FR) **Tootell, Tomkies & Tory**
6 **ENDLESS ESCAPE (IRE),** 7, b m Getaway (GER)—Endless Wave **Butler, Langford, Tootell & The Hecks**
7 **INEBRANLABLE (FR),** 5, b g Spanish Moon (USA)—Vega de Beaumont (FR) **Mr A. Paterson**
8 **JELLICLE JEWEL (IRE),** 7, b m Shirocco (GER)—Strike's Oscar (IRE) **Lloyd Hill & Monica Tory**
9 **JUST A DIME (IRE),** 7, b g Doyen (IRE)—Somebody's Darling (IRE) **Mr A. Paterson**
10 **LETTIE LUTZ (IRE),** 7, b m Mahler—Grange Oscar (IRE) **Mr A. Paterson**
11 **LITTLE JESSTURE (IRE),** 7, b m Dylan Thomas (IRE)—The Legislator (IRE) **Bob Butler, Monica Tory & Lloyd Hill**
12 **MERRY DREAMER (IRE),** 7, b g Doyen (IRE)—Merry Heart (IRE) **Ben Clarke Racing I**
13 **OOH BETTY (IRE),** 5, b m Westerner—On The Prairie (IRE) **Butler, Langford, Paterson & Tory**
14 **PIXIE LOC,** 8, gr m Lucarno (USA)—Ixora (IRE) **Mr R. Butler**
15 **THE GALLOPING BEAR,** 10, b g Shantou (USA)—Cheshire Kat **Mr A. Paterson**
16 **WITHOUT A DOUBT,** 8, b g Black Sam Bellamy (IRE)—Solid Land (FR) **Mrs A. E. Baker**

94 MR NICOLAS CLEMENT, Chantilly

Postal: **37, Avenue de Joinville, 60500 Chantilly, France**
Contacts: **PHONE +33 3 44 57 59 60 MOBILE +33 6 07 23 46 40**
EMAIL office@nicolasclement.com WEBSITE www.nicolasclement.com

1 **AMIRAVATI,** 4, ch f Siyouni (FR)—Abhisheka (IRE)
2 **ANAMANDA (FR),** 4, gr f Reliable Man—Anyana
3 **BLLUSHING,** 5, ch h Sepoy (AUS)—Convention
4 **CAP SAN ROMAN (FR),** 4, b f Muhaarar—Cap Verite (IRE)
5 **FENELON (FR),** 5, b h Fastnet Rock (AUS)—Aigue Marine
6 **GALIFA (IRE),** 5, b m Frankel—Viva Rafaela (BRZ)
7 **NOW WE KNOW (FR),** 6, gr h Kendargent (FR)—Now Forever (GER)
8 **RADIANT SKY (FR),** 4, ch f Almanzor (FR)—Glowing Cloud
9 **ROSETTA STONE (FR),** 4, ch c Rock of Gibraltar (IRE)—Forewarned (IRE)
10 **SUNRAY (IRE),** 4, ch f Dawn Approach (IRE)—Snake Dancer (IRE)
11 **THEORETICAL (FR),** 4, ch f Tamayuz—Game Theory (IRE)
12 **WILDWOOD (FR),** 5, b br m Maxios—Walayta (GER)

THREE-YEAR-OLDS

13 **AMINATU,** b f Frankel—Just Sensual (SAF)
14 **BELAFONTE,** b g Le Havre (IRE)—Eiriamach Na Casca
15 **CONSORT ROYAL,** b f Mendelssohn (USA)—Royal Story (USA)
16 **COUP DE SOLEIL (FR),** b f Showcasing—Evaporation
17 **GALISIA (FR),** ch f Galiway—Temsia (FR)
18 **GOLDEN JUANITA (FR),** b f Cloth of Stars (IRE)—Vejer (IRE)
19 **GOLDEN LAND,** b c Territories (IRE)—Harvestide (IRE)
20 **JUANA INES (IRE),** b f Lope de Vega (IRE)—Wild Irish Rose (IRE)
21 **KOREA (GER),** ch f Amaron—Konigsbraut (GER)
22 **LUNALA (FR),** b f Penny's Picnic (IRE)—Noella (FR)
23 **MARFISA (IRE),** b f Lope de Vega (IRE)—Special Gal (FR)
24 **MINUIT A PARIS,** b f War Front (USA)—Exotic Notion
25 **MONAPIA (FR),** b g Harry Angel (IRE)—Heeyaam
26 **MOON RAY (FR),** ch f Saxon Warrior (JPN)—Demeanour (USA)
27 **NARIMAN POINT (IRE),** ch f Dubawi (IRE)—Traffic Jam (IRE)
28 **NEAR AMORE (GER),** b f Amaron—Near Galante (GER)

MR NICOLAS CLEMENT - continued

29 **RAGNAROK (FR),** br c Churchill (IRE)—Anna Simona
30 **SEA TOWER (FR),** b f Sea The Stars (IRE)—La Tour Rouge
31 **SUNSHINEFLED (FR),** b f Seabhac—Winshine
32 **SUNY YINA (FR),** b f Motivator—Theoricienne (FR)
33 **THANKSGIVING (IRE),** b f Justify (USA)—C'Est Ca (IRE)
34 **TOURGEVILLE,** ch f Le Havre (IRE)—The Madding Crowd
35 **TROPEIRA (FR),** b f Cloth Of Stars—Tropa De Elite
36 **VEGA STAR,** b c Lope de Vega (IRE)—With Your Spirit (FR)

TWO-YEAR-OLDS

37 Ch c 18/01 Ruler Of The World (IRE)—Ababeel (FR) (Dansili)
38 **BALTIC EMPRESS (IRE),** b f 17/01 Kingman—Baltic Duchess (IRE) (Lope de Vega (IRE)) (280112)
39 **BLACK GEM (IRE),** br c 08/05 Waldgeist—Black Ruby (IRE) (Dansili) (56022)
40 **BLUE THUNDER (IRE),** b f 30/03 Blue Point (IRE)—Pussycat Lips (IRE) (Holy Roman Emperor (IRE)) (104042)
41 **CATY FISH (FR),** b f 27/02 Churchill (IRE)—Sharavana (Fastnet Rock (AUS)) (64026)
42 **ERAINES (FR),** ch f 12/05 Le Havre (IRE)—Eiria (King's Best (USA))
43 **JOYFUL CROWN (IRE),** b f 10/02 Churchill (IRE)—Livvys Dream (IRE) (Declaration of War (USA)) (52021)
44 **L'IMPRESSIONNISTE (FR),** b c 12/04 Waldgeist—Djumama (IRE) (Aussie Rules (USA)) (96038)
45 **LA TOUR DU BOIS (FR),** b f 26/03 Wootton Bassett—La Tour Rouge (Monsun (GER))
46 B c 15/04 Shalaa (IRE)—Lady Glitters (FR) (Homme De Loi (IRE))
47 B f 24/01 Iffraaj—Ming Zhi Cosmos (Duke of Marmalade (IRE))
48 **MODERN ERA (IRE),** ch f 08/04 Starspangledbanner (AUS)—Kendar Rouge (FR) (Kendargent (FR)) (100040)
49 **O'NICE GIRL (FR),** ch f 20/04 Australia—O'Keefe (FR) (Peintre Celebre (USA)) (36014)
50 **PRIVATE DELIGHT (FR),** ch c 18/03 Iffraaj—Private Eye (FR) (American Post) (38415)
51 **REUILLY (IRE),** b f 22/01 Le Havre (IRE)—Rue de Russie (IRE) (Champs Elysees)
52 **ROYAL ROSI (GER),** b br f 20/02 Holy Roman Emperor (IRE)—Rosinante (IRE) (Maxios) (24010)
53 B f 23/01 Churchill (IRE)—Sibyla (Invincible Spirit (IRE)) (49620)
54 **SIYOUNI FLASH (FR),** b f 21/02 Siyouni (FR)—Aigue Marine (Galileo (IRE)) (480192)
55 **SURVIE (IRE),** b f 19/03 Churchill (IRE)—Sotteville (FR) (Le Havre (IRE))
56 **TONIGHT (IRE),** ch f 08/02 Waldgeist—Leenavesta (USA) (Arch (USA)) (60000)
57 B f 06/03 Camelot—Universal Beauty (Universal (IRE)) (72029)
58 **VERA (FR),** b f 15/04 Almanzor (FR)—Anna Simona (GER) (Slip Anchor) (84034)
59 B f 15/02 Lope de Vega (IRE)—Xaarienne (Xaar) (256102)
60 **ZOE,** b f 16/02 Ten Sovereigns (IRE)—Sariette (Oasis Dream)

Flat Jockey: Sebastien Maillot, Stephane Pasquier, Thomas Truillier.

---

95 MR TOM CLOVER, Newmarket

Postal: **Kremlin House Stables, Fordham Road, Newmarket, Suffolk, CB8 7AQ**
Contacts: **PHONE 07795 834960, 01638 660055**
EMAIL thomaspwclover@gmail.com WEBSITE www.tomcloverracing.com

1 **AL BAREZ,** 4, b c Dark Angel (IRE)—Jet Setting (IRE) **Mr R. El Youssef**
2 **ALJARI,** 7, b g Quality Road (USA)—Rhagori **Mr R. El Youssef**
3 **BALGAIR,** 9, ch g Foxwedge (AUS)—Glencal **Newmarket Racing Club HQi**
4 **BASS PLAYER (IRE),** 4, b g Iffraaj—Rhythm And Rhyme (IRE) **The Rogues Gallery & Partners**
5 **CELSIUS (IRE),** 7, ch g Dragon Pulse (IRE)—Grecian Artisan (IRE) **J. Collins, C. Fahy & S. Piper**
6 **DARING GUEST (IRE),** 9, b g Fast Company (IRE)—Balm **Mrs G. A. S. Jarvis**
7 **FARHH POINT,** 4, b g Farhh—Altyn Alqa **K. A. Dasmal**
8 **GRAND LIBYA,** 4, b c Churchill (IRE)—Sprinkling (USA) **Mr E. Elhrari**
9 **ROGUE FORCE (IRE),** 5, b g Iffraaj—Lonely Rock **The Rogues Gallery**
10 **ROGUE MILLENNIUM (IRE),** 4, b f Dubawi (IRE)—Hawaafez **The Rogues Gallery**
11 **ROGUE ROCKET (FR),** 4, ch g Recorder—Eva Kant **The Rogues Gallery**
12 **THEBEAUTIFULGAME,** 4, b f Slade Power (IRE)—Imasumaq (IRE) **The Tripletto Partnership & Partner**

MR TOM CLOVER - continued

THREE-YEAR-OLDS

13 **AL KARRAR (IRE),** b c Dark Angel (IRE)—Moghamarah **Mr R. El Youssef**
14 **BEAU VINTAGE,** b g Brazen Beau (AUS)—Madame Lafite **G Habershon-butcher & D Pitchford**
15 **FISHING RIGHTS,** ch g Le Havre (IRE)—Puzzler (IRE) **The Greenacre Partnership**
16 **JUMBEAU,** b f Brazen Beau (AUS)—Jumeirah Street (USA) **LPOG21 & Partners**
17 **KANGAROO (IRE),** b g Kuroshio (AUS)—Conquete (FR) **Marek Gumienny & Adam Signy**
18 **PRISHA,** b f Ribchester (IRE)—Snow Powder (IRE) **David Ben & Thomas Lockwood**
19 **RAJINDRI (IRE),** b f Profitable (IRE)—Ugneya (IRE) **Jastar Capital Limited**
20 **ROGUE DE VEGA,** b g Lope de Vega (IRE)—Lamps of Heaven (IRE) **The Rogues Gallery**
21 **ROGUE FOX (IRE),** b c Kodiac—Cionn Tsaile (IRE) **The Rogues Gallery**
22 **ROGUE LIGHTNING (IRE),** b c Kodiac—Field of Stars **The Rogues Gallery**
23 **ROGUE LION,** gr c Roaring Lion (USA)—Welsh Angel **The Rogues Gallery**
24 **ROGUE SEA,** b c Sea The Stars (IRE)—Tarfasha (IRE) **The Rogues Gallery**
25 **ROGUE SPIRIT,** b g Dark Angel (IRE)—Quite Sharp **The Rogues Gallery**
26 **ROGUE THUNDER,** ch g Night of Thunder (IRE)—Represent (IRE) **The Rogues Gallery**
27 **ROGUE WARRIOR (IRE),** b f Saxon Warrior (JPN)—Speciality (FR) **The Rogues Gallery**

TWO-YEAR-OLDS

28 Ch f 03/03 Sea The Stars (IRE)—Anasheed (Frankel) (40000) **Sheikh A. H. F. M. A. Al Sabah**
29 B c 16/04 Time Test—Characterized (Oasis Dream) (32000) **Carroll House Racing**
30 B c 20/02 Invincible Spirit (IRE)—Effervesce (IRE) (Galileo (IRE)) (150000) **M Bringloe & Hrd McCalmont**
31 B f 18/04 Too Darn Hot—Instance (Invincible Spirit (IRE))
32 B f 26/02 Dark Angel (IRE)—Lightning Mark (IRE) (Invincible Spirit (IRE)) (37000) **Sheikh A. H. F. M. A. Al Sabah**
33 B c 22/01 Magna Grecia (IRE)—Lina de Vega (IRE) (Lope de Vega (IRE)) (33613) **Carroll House Racing**
34 **LITTLE SISKIN,** b f 02/04 Aclaim (IRE)—Emily Goldfinch (Prime Defender)
35 **MAY,** b f 12/05 Le Brivido (FR)—Hoku (IRE) (Holy Roman Emperor (IRE)) (20952) **Mr J. Targett**
36 B c 20/02 Le Havre (IRE)—Mirrorblack (IRE) (Clodovil (IRE)) (28011) **Carroll House Racing**
37 Br f 09/04 Ten Sovereigns (IRE)—
My Propeller (IRE) (Holy Roman Emperor (IRE)) (10000) **David Ben & Thomas Lockwood**
38 B c 13/01 Showcasing—Mystical Moon (IRE) (Excelebration (IRE)) (34000) **Sheikh A. H. F. M. A. Al Sabah**
39 B c 16/04 Elzaam (AUS)—Oatmeal (Dalakhani (IRE)) (40000) **Carroll House Racing**
40 **PRINCESS JASTAR (IRE),** gr f 20/04 Dark Angel (IRE)—
Sliabh Luachra (IRE) (High Chaparral (IRE)) (45000) **Jastar Capital Limited**
41 **ROGUE DREAM (IRE),** b f 18/04 Dark Angel (IRE)—Seafront (Foxwedge (AUS)) (35000) **The Rogues Gallery**
42 **ROGUE FIGHTER (IRE),** b c 07/03 Dark Angel (IRE)—
Redmaven (IRE) (Teofilo (IRE)) (38095) **The Rogues Gallery & Partner**
43 **ROGUE ROSIE,** b f 02/03 Magna Grecia (IRE)—Loveheart (Dubawi (IRE)) (16000) **The Rogues Gallery**
44 **SKIPPER,** b c 14/02 Calyx—Skipinnish (Exceed And Excel (AUS)) **J. H. Richmond-Watson**
45 **THE IRISH ROGUE,** b c 24/03 Blue Point (IRE)—On Her Way (Medicean) (45000) **The Rogues Gallery**
46 B c 20/03 Ribchester (IRE)—Up In Time (Noverre (USA)) (55000) **Mr A. C. Waney**

---

96 MR DENIS COAKLEY, West Ilsley

Postal: **Keeper's Stables, West Ilsley, Newbury, Berkshire, RG20 7AH**
Contacts: **PHONE 01635 281622 MOBILE 07768 658056**
EMAIL racing@deniscoakley.com WEBSITE www.deniscoakley.com

1 **BOBBY KENNEDY,** 5, b g Bobby's Kitten (USA)—All Annalena (IRE) **Ms I. Coakley**
2 **HOORNBLOWER,** 4, ch c Ulysses (IRE)—Tulip Dress **Chris van Hoorn Racing**
3 **ISKAHEEN (IRE),** 4, b g Profitable (IRE)—Scarlet Rosefinch **Mrs U. M. Loughrey**
4 **LISDARRAGH (USA),** 5, b g Hit It A Bomb (USA)—Thewholeshebang (USA) **Mrs U. M. Loughrey**
5 **MY AMBITION (IRE),** 4, ch g Galileo Gold—Rise Up Lotus (IRE) **Mrs B. Coakley**
6 **PARTY ISLAND (IRE),** 6, ch g Tagula (IRE)—Pretty Demanding (IRE) **Mr T. A. Killoran**
7 **RUSKIN RED (IRE),** 6, ch g Mastercraftsman (IRE)—Firey Red (IRE) **Mrs B. Coakley**
8 **UNA NOTTE,** 4, b f Time Test—Goodnightsuzy (IRE) **West Ilsley Racing**

MR DENIS COAKLEY - continued

9 **WATERLOO SUNSET,** 5, b g Adaay (IRE)—Atwix **Mr T. A. Killoran**
10 **WONDER STARELZAAM (IRE),** 5, b g Elzaam (AUS)—Ava Star (IRE) **J. C. Kerr**

THREE-YEAR-OLDS

11 **GENTLE WHINNY (IRE),** b f Churchill (IRE)—Short Call (IRE) **Chris van Hoorn Racing**
12 **GOLDEN PHASE,** ch f Gustav Klimt (IRE)—Amour Fou (IRE) **West Ilsley - Platinum**
13 **LOOE P LOOE (IRE),** b f Acclamation—Subtle Affair (IRE) **M. Fahy**
14 **MILVUS (IRE),** b g Dark Angel (IRE)—Redmaven (IRE) **Sparkling Partners**

TWO-YEAR-OLDS

15 **MISTER SKETCH,** b c 03/02 Territories (IRE)—Drawing (Dark Angel (IRE))
16 B f 31/01 Ribchester (IRE)—Nawkhatha (USA) (Tapit (USA)) (15000) **Mr N. Y. O. Askar**
17 Ch c 23/05 Showcasing—Peace And Love (IRE) (Fantastic Light (USA)) (37000) **Mr N. Y. O. Askar**
18 **PHOENIX MOON (IRE),** gr f 23/03 Phoenix of Spain (IRE)—
Meetyouatthemoon (IRE) (Excelebration (IRE)) (15000) **Keeper's 12**
19 **SWEET SISTER,** b f 24/01 Iffraaj—Paulinie (Royal Applause) (40000) **Chris van Hoorn Racing**

---

97 MS DEBORAH COLE, Solihull

Postal: **1577 Warwick Road, Knowle, Solihull, West Midlands, B93 9LF**
EMAIL dbrh.cole@gmail.com

1 **CABAYO LADY,** 6, b m Midnight Legend—Santera (IRE) **Knowle Racing Stables Limited**
2 **FERYL BERYL,** 4, b f Scorpion (IRE)—Our Jess (IRE) **Knowle Racing Stables Limited**
3 **HAURAKI GULF,** 8, b g Kayf Tara—Leading On **Knowle Racing Stables Limited**
4 **IMAC WOOD (FR),** 5, b g Karaktar (IRE)—Carrieriste (FR) **Knowle Racing Stables Limited**
5 **LAURA BULLION (IRE),** 7, b m Canford Cliffs (IRE)—Vivachi (IRE) **Knowle Racing Stables Limited**
6 **LEYLAK (IRE),** 6, b g Born To Sea (IRE)—Lidaya (USA) **Knowle Racing Stables Limited**
7 4, B g Retirement Plan—Pleasetellmeittrue (IRE) **Knowle Racing Stables Limited**
8 **POLYPUTTHEKETTLEON,** 9, b m Arvico (FR)—Sainte Kadette (FR) **Knowle Racing Stables Limited**
9 **SIR JACK WEST (IRE),** 7, b g Westerner—Star Sprinkled Sky (IRE) **Knowle Racing Stables Limited**
10 **TRICKALIGHT (IRE),** 7, b m Leading Light (IRE)—Horner Mill (IRE) **Knowle Racing Stables Limited**

---

98 MR PAUL & OLIVER COLE, Whatcombe

Postal: **Whatcombe Racing Stables, Whatcombe, Wantage, Oxfordshire, OX12 9NW**
Contacts: **PHONE 01488 638433**
EMAIL admin@paulcole.co.uk

1 **DEACS DELIGHT,** 4, ch g Tamayuz—Keene Dancer **R Deacon And P F I Cole**
2 **ERNIE'S VALENTINE,** 4, gr g Havana Gold (IRE)—Eastern Destiny **Williams, Campbell, Sennett & Cole**
3 **FIRTH OF CLYDE (IRE),** 4, b g Gleneagles (IRE)—Chrysanthemum (IRE) **Mrs F. H. Hay**
4 **GEELONG (FR),** 4, b g Australia—Tioga Pass **The Fairy Story Partnership**
5 **IVATHEENGINE (IRE),** 6, br g Ivawood (IRE)—Sharp Applause (IRE) **Mr F. P. Stella**
6 **JACK DARCY (IRE),** 4, b g Gleneagles (IRE)—Pretty Face **Crypto Racing Club & M Burns**
7 **LEAP ABROAD (IRE),** 4, b g Gregorian (IRE)—Norfolk Broads (IRE) **Middleham Park Racing CIV, Cole & Deacon**
8 **MANY A STAR (IRE),** 6, ch g Starspangledbanner (AUS)—Many Hearts (USA) **Mrs L. P. Hobby**
9 **MEDIEVAL (IRE),** 9, b g Kodiac—Quickstyx **P. F. I. Cole Ltd**
10 **SPLENDENT (IRE),** 4, b c Fast Company (IRE)—Sweet Lilly **Mrs F. H. Hay**
11 **TOOPHAN (IRE),** 4, ch c New Approach (IRE)—Maoineach (USA) **Amo Racing Limited**
12 **WILD MOUNTAIN (IRE),** 4, b c Aclaim (IRE)—Rochitta (USA) **Mrs F. H. Hay**

MR PAUL & OLIVER COLE - continued

13 **ZHANG FEI (FR),** 5, b g Camelot—Mambomiss (FR) **P. F. I. Cole Ltd**

THREE-YEAR-OLDS

14 **DESERT FIGHTER (IRE),** b c Acclamation—Mesaria (IRE) **Rosier, Ryan-Beswick, Russell, SWD & Cole**
15 **GOLDKIT (FR),** b f Olympic Glory (IRE)—Kits (FR) **Mr F. P. Stella**
16 **HURTLE (IRE),** gr c Mastercraftsman (IRE)—Ghurfah **P. F. I. Cole Ltd**
17 **MAJESTIC NEWLAW,** b c New Bay—Cornlaw **Opulence Thoroughbreds**
18 **METARACE (IRE),** ch g Tasleet—Power To Exceed (IRE) **Crypto Racing Club**
19 **PHYSIQUE (IRE),** b g Kingman—Shapes (IRE) **Mrs F. H. Hay**
20 **ROYAL SCOTSMAN (IRE),** b c Gleneagles (IRE)—Enrol **Mrs F. H. Hay**
21 **SHE'S HOT,** ch f Sioux Nation (USA)—Timely Words **Mrs Fitri Hay & Charlie Methven**
22 **SUMO SAM,** b gr f Nathaniel (IRE)—Seaduced **Ben & Sir Martyn Arbib**
23 **TANGO MAN,** b c Kingman—Raskutani **Amo Racing Limited**
24 **THUNDER BALL,** ch g Night of Thunder (IRE)—Seradim **The Fairy Story Partnership**
25 **TWINKLE STAR,** b f Oasis Dream—Cloud's End **Amo Racing Limited**
26 **WYOMING,** b f Motivator—Tioga Pass **The Fairy Story Partnership**
27 **YACOWLEF (IRE),** ch c Kessaar (IRE)—Turkana Girl **Valmont & Opulence Thoroughbreds**

TWO-YEAR-OLDS

28 Ch c 11/02 Exceed And Excel (AUS)—Alchemilla (Dubai Destination (USA)) (125000) **Mrs F. H. Hay**
29 **BATEMAN (IRE),** b c 29/04 Ten Sovereigns (IRE)—Fiuise (IRE) (Montjeu (IRE)) (110000) **Valmont**
30 B c 06/03 Gleneagles (IRE)—Belladonna (Medicean) (35000)
31 B c 05/03 Nathaniel (IRE)—Born Cross (IRE) (Dubawi (IRE)) (27211)
32 B f 25/03 Gleneagles (IRE)—Cradle of Life (IRE) (Notnowcato) (25000) **P. F. I. Cole Ltd**
33 B c 11/02 Gleneagles (IRE)—Ivirka (FR) (Mastercraftsman (IRE)) (136054) **Mrs F. H. Hay**
34 **LET'S GET EM,** b c 17/04 Wootton Bassett—Loaves And Fishes (Oasis Dream) (130000) **Valmont**
35 **LET'S PARTY,** b f 24/04 Oasis Dream—Dheyaa (IRE) (Dream Ahead (USA)) (21000)
36 Ch f 06/03 Territories (IRE)—Melody of Love (Haafhd) (19000)
37 B f 29/04 Churchill (IRE)—Pink Symphony (Montjeu (IRE)) **Mrs F. H. Hay**
38 B c 26/02 Exceed And Excel (AUS)—
Scarlet And Gold (IRE) (Peintre Celebre (USA)) (80952) **Middleham Park Racing LXXXV**
39 Ch c 20/04 Sixties Icon—Shadows Ofthenight (IRE) (Fastnet Rock (AUS)) (35000) **P. F. I. Cole Ltd**
40 Ch f 27/03 Harry Angel (IRE)—Tahiti (Royal Applause) (32000) **P. F. I. Cole Ltd**
41 B f 17/04 Gleneagles (IRE)—Taste The Salt (IRE) (Born To Sea (IRE)) (140056) **Mrs F. H. Hay**

99

MR TJADE COLLIER, Wilsden

Postal: **Salter Royd House, Shay Lane, Wilsden, Bradford, West Yorkshire, BD15 0DJ**
Contacts: **PHONE 01535 271445**
EMAIL tjade331@icloud.com

1 **BLUE HAWAII (IRE),** 8, b m Jeremy (USA)—Luanna (IRE) **R. Banks & J. Sheard**
2 **CHEMICAL WARFARE (IRE),** 6, b g Fame And Glory—Blazing Sky (IRE) **SendEmOn**
3 4, B f Sageburg (IRE)—Cognitive (IRE) **Mr J. N. Sheard**
4 **DOORS BREAKER (FR),** 6, b g American Post—Polyandry (IRE) **SendEmOn**
5 4, B g Hillstar—Endless Ambition (IRE) **Mr J. N. Sheard**
6 4, B g Soldier of Fortune (IRE)—Jessies Delight
7 **LADRONNE (FR),** 9, b g Linda's Lad—Worldeta (FR) **T C Racing Syndicate**
8 4, B f Jukebox Jury (IRE)—Legende Volante (FR)
9 **PUB CRAWL (IRE),** 4, b g Noble Mission—Water Hole (IRE) **SendEmOn**
10 4, Gr f Soldier of Fortune (IRE)—Quality Street (GER)
11 **SNEAKY PETE,** 6, b g Black Sam Bellamy (IRE)—Damascena (GER) **T C Racing Syndicate**
12 **TACITUS (IRE),** 5, ch g Zoffany (IRE)—Kiss My Tiara (IRE) **T C Racing Syndicate**
13 **TOMMY'S FORTUNE (IRE),** 5, br g Soldier of Fortune (IRE)—Jessies Delight **T C Racing Syndicate**

MR TJADE COLLIER - continued

THREE-YEAR-OLDS

14 B f Frontiersman—Blackjax **Mr S. Smith**
15 **THE SPINMEISTER,** ch g Bated Breath—Spin Doctor **Elaine Banks & Sam Lambert**

---

100 MR PAUL COLLINS, Saltburn-By-The-Sea

Postal: **Groundhill Farm, Lingdale, Saltburn-By-The-Sea, Cleveland, TS12 2WP**
Contacts: **MOBILE 07779 794684**

1 **LADY HOBBS,** 4, b f Jack Hobbs—Definite Artist (IRE) **Mrs P. A. Cowey**
2 **SONGBIRD'S TALE,** 8, b m Sulamani (IRE)—She Likes To Boogy (IRE) **Mrs P. A. Cowey**

---

101 MR STUART COLTHERD, Selkirk

Postal: **Clarilawmuir Farm, Selkirk, Selkirkshire, TD7 4QA**
Contacts: **PHONE 01750 21251 MOBILE 07801 398199 FAX 01750 21251**
EMAIL wscoltherd@gmail.com

1 **ARCANDY (IRE),** 7, b m Arcadio (GER)—Turf (FR) **Gillie,Scott,Swinton**
2 **ARCHI'S AFFAIRE,** 9, ch g Archipenko (USA)—Affaire d'Amour **Coltherd Racing Club**
3 **ARD CHROS (IRE),** 11, b g Publisher (USA)—Threecrossmammies (IRE) **Coltherd McDougal**
4 **AUGHARUE (IRE),** 6, b g Rule of Law (USA)—Abbans Aunt (IRE) **Perryman Coltherd**
5 **BUDARRI,** 10, b g Supreme Sound—Amtaar **Cruikshank Coltherd**
6 **CHANCEANOTHERFIVE (IRE),** 11, b g Dubai Destination (USA)—Ryhall (IRE) **Mr Richard & Mrs Lisa McCulloch**
7 **COOPER'S CROSS (IRE),** 8, b g Getaway (GER)—Rocella (GER) **Mr J. Fyffe**
8 **DEEP CHARM,** 9, b g Kayf Tara—Reel Charmer **Mr Richard & Mrs Lisa McCulloch**
9 **DEQUALL,** 7, ch g Zoffany (IRE)—Bark (IRE) **W. S. Coltherd**
10 **FARON (IRE),** 5, b g Fascinating Rock (IRE)—Ataahua (GER) **W. S. Coltherd**
11 **GANDHI MAKER (FR),** 7, b g Policy Maker (IRE)—Thellya d'Arc (FR) **Mr A. McCormack**
12 **GRAND VOYAGE (FR),** 7, b g Network (GER)—Qape Noir (FR) **Shire Dreamers**
13 **GRAYSTOWN (IRE),** 11, b g Well Chosen—Temple Girl (IRE) **W. S. Coltherd**
14 **GREY MOSS,** 7, gr m Proclamation (IRE)—Mae Moss **W. S. Coltherd**
15 **HIDDEN COMMANDER (IRE),** 8, b g Shirocco (GER)—Gift of Freedom (IRE) **Coltherd McDougal**
16 **JACK YEATS (IRE),** 7, b g Galileo (IRE)—Fire Lily (IRE) **Coltherd Racing Club**
17 **JIMMY RABBITTE (IRE),** 10, b g Dubai Destination (USA)—Time To Act **W. S. Coltherd**
18 **MAID O'MALLEY,** 10, b m Black Sam Bellamy (IRE)—Jolie (IRE) **Debbie Crawford & Stuart Coltherd**
19 **MCGARRY (IRE),** 9, b g Mahler—Little Pearl (IRE) **The Vacuum Pouch Company Limited**
20 **MIDNIGHT SHUFFLE,** 8, br m Midnight Legend—Lifestyle **Mr A. McCormack**
21 **MISS MISTRAL (IRE),** 7, gr m War Command (USA)—Drifting Mist **Coltherd Racing Club**
22 **MOONACURA (IRE),** 6, b g Fame And Glory—Monks Charm (IRE) **Flannigan Newitt French Valender Herriot**
23 **NOTNOWBOB (IRE),** 6, b g Notnowcato—Meldrum Hall (IRE) **W. S. Coltherd**
24 **OSCAR WILDE (IRE),** 9, b g Oscar (IRE)—Deep Supreme (IRE) **W. S. Coltherd**
25 **POOKIE PEKAN (IRE),** 10, b g Putra Pekan—Shii-Take's Girl **Mr J. Muir**
26 **RING PRETENDER (FR),** 7, b m Great Pretender (IRE)—Ring Blood (FR) **The Vacuum Pouch Company Limited**
27 **SAN MIGUEL (IRE),** 7, b g El Salvador (IRE)—Majestic Benbulben (IRE) **Mr A. McCormack**
28 **SILKEN MOONLIGHT,** 9, b m Aqlaam—Silk (IRE) **Coltherd Racing Club**
29 **SILVER VISION,** 4, gr f Muhaarar—Surrealism **Whyte & Binnie**
30 **SLEEPING TOM,** 6, b g Sleeping Indian—Freedom Song **W. S. Coltherd**
31 **TO THE LIMIT (IRE),** 8, gr g Carlotamix (FR)—Miss Kilkeel (IRE) **Border Eagles**
32 **WARENDORF (FR),** 10, b g Speedmaster (GER)—Hyllisia (FR)
33 **WHEELBAHRI,** 9, b g Bahri (USA)—Midlem Melody **Coltherd Racing Club**

MRS SUSAN CORBETT - continued

34 **ZOPITO (FR),** 5, ch g No Risk At All (FR)—Klyne (FR) **W. S. Coltherd**

Conditional Jockey: Sam Coltherd.

---

102 MRS SUSAN CORBETT, Otterburn

Postal: **Girsonfield, Otterburn, Newcastle upon Tyne, Tyne and Wear, NE19 1NT**
Contacts: **PHONE 01830 520771 MOBILE 07713 651215 FAX 01830 520771**
EMAIL girsonfield@outlook.com WEBSITE www.girsonfield.co.uk

1 **ASK MY HEATHER (IRE),** 5, ch g Ask—Tilly Ann (IRE) **Mr R. Payne**
2 **ATOMIC ANGEL,** 8, gr m Geordieland (FR)—Sovereignoftheseas **Castle View Racing**
3 **AVOID DE MASTER (IRE),** 9, b g Getaway (GER)—Tanit **Castle View Racing, Girsonfield Racing Club**
4 **BEAUMESNIL (FR),** 6, ch g Konig Turf (GER)—Eau Tenebreuse (FR) **Mrs S. Corbett**
5 **BLAME ROSE (IRE),** 6, b m Sholokhov (IRE)—Christmas Cracker (IRE) **The Nelson Racing Partnership**
6 **CLEAR ANGEL,** 5, b g Dark Angel (IRE)—Calypso Beat (USA) **Castle View Racing**
7 **DEVOUR (IRE),** 10, b g Milan—Marble Desire (IRE) **Girsonfield Racing Club**
8 **EN MEME TEMPS (FR),** 9, b g Saddler Maker (IRE)—Lady Reine (FR) **Mr I. Turnbull**
9 **GOWANBUSTER,** 8, b g Bahri (USA)—Aahgowangowan (IRE) **Gowan Racing**
10 **IMPERIAL SACHIN'S (IRE),** 7, gr g Fame And Glory—
Queen of Tribes (IRE) **Castle View Racing, Susan Corbett Racing**
11 **JESSICA RABBIT,** 9, b m Mawatheeq (USA)—Intersky High (USA) **Lady Samantha Toomes & Mrs Susan Corbett**
12 **KINGSTON ROCK (IRE),** 5, gr gr g Kingston Hill—Rock High Lady (IRE) **Mr J L & Mrs H R Gledson**
13 **KONIK KING (IRE),** 7, b g Jet Away—Cuddle Ina Drizzle (IRE) **The Race4fun Syndicate**
14 **LES'S LEGACY,** 6, b g Kutub (IRE)—Morning With Ivan (IRE) **Mrs S. Corbett, Tweed Valley Racing Club**
15 **MAISIE TOO,** 6, b m Millenary—Listen Tarablue **Mr J L & Mrs H R Gledson**
16 **MEKBAT (FR),** 4, b g Zelzal (FR)—Al Markhiya (IRE) **The Northern Racing Club**
17 **NULLI SECUNDUS (IRE),** 6, b m Califet (FR)—Strike An Ark (IRE) **The Cheltenham Trail Racing Club**
18 **ORLAS' ABBEY,** 8, b m Multiplex—Evelith Abbey (IRE) **The Northern Racing Club**
19 **POSH ET NOIR,** 4, b g Black Sam Bellamy (IRE)—Fairly Posh **Mr J L & Mrs H R Gledson**
20 **SAMWISE (IRE),** 5, ch g Mizzou (IRE)—Lake Cresent (IRE) **Lady Samantha Toomes & Mrs Susan Corbett**
21 **THIS IS BOB (IRE),** 5, b g Imperial Monarch (IRE)—Annie Grit (IRE) **W F Corbett & Race4fun**
22 **VELASCO (IRE),** 7, b g Sholokhov (IRE)—Bilboa (FR) **Rutherford, Barker, Toomes & Corbett**
23 **WOR VERGE,** 10, b g Virtual—Hanover Gate **The Goodfellow Partnership**
24 **WOTYOUDUNNOW BUDDY (IRE),** 5, b g Laverock (IRE)—Bob Girl (IRE) **Mr G. Satchwell**

THREE-YEAR-OLDS

25 **NAUGHTY GEORGE,** ch g Top Trip—Bassinet (USA) **Naughty But Nice And Ours For Life**

TWO-YEAR-OLDS

26 Ch c 19/03 Dandy Man (IRE)—Feint (Teofilo (IRE)) (5500) **Castle View Racing**
27 Ch c 20/02 Decorated Knight—Spring Eternal (Oasis Dream) (5000) **Castle View Racing**

Assistant Trainer: Mr James Corbett, **Travelling Head:** Emma Tully, **Yard Sponsor:** Finnies Heavy Haulage.

Conditional Jockey: Dillan Hurst.

---

103 MR JOHN CORNWALL, Melton Mowbray

Postal: **April Cottage, Pasture Lane, Hose, Melton Mowbray, Leicestershire, LE14 4LB**
Contacts: **PHONE 01664 444453 MOBILE 07939 557091 FAX 01664 444754**
EMAIL johncornwall7@gmail.com

1 **LESKINFERE (IRE),** 10, b g Darsi (FR)—Taipans Girl (IRE) **Mr J. R. Cornwall**
2 **TORRENT DES MOTTES (FR),** 12, gr g Montmartre (FR)—Wavy (FR) **Mr J. R. Cornwall**

104 MR JAKE COULSON, Heaton

Postal: **Bent End Farm, Bearda Hill Racing, Heaton, Macclesfield, Cheshire, SK11 0SJ**
Contacts: **MOBILE 07460 471492**
EMAIL beardahillracing@gmail.com

1 **BARNAY,** 8, b g Nayef (USA)—Barnezet (GR) **D. Ashbrook**
2 **CLICK AND COLLECT,** 11, b g Humbel (USA)—Galena (GER) **D. Ashbrook**
3 **FARM THE ROCK (IRE),** 12, b g Yeats (IRE)—Shades of Lavender (IRE) **Mr N. Carter**
4 **FOREVER A DOVE (IRE),** 5, b m Westerner—Drumderry (IRE) **Mr K. Dove**
5 **GETALADY (IRE),** 7, b m Getaway (GER)—Knocksouna Lady (IRE) **D Barrow-Yates, S Walsh & S Hargreaves**
6 **GIBBERWELL (IRE),** 7, b g Getaway (GER)—Unique Snoopy (IRE) **All Or Nothing Racing Club**
7 4, Ch f Notnowcato—Had To Be Done (IRE) **Mr N. Carter**
8 **HEY BOB (IRE),** 11, br g Big Bad Bob (IRE)—Bounty Star (IRE) **Proper mon Racing**
9 **IMPERIAL LORD (IRE),** 7, b g Imperial Monarch (IRE)—Grannys Kitchen (IRE) **Mr N. Carter**
10 **IN ARREARS (IRE),** 11, b m Beneficial—Gullet Dawn (IRE) **Mr J. T. Coulson**
11 **KINGSON (IRE),** 7, b g Kingman—Gaditana **Mr N. Carter**
12 **KINGSTON KING (IRE),** 9, b g Morozov (USA)—Gra Mo Chroi **Mr N. Carter**
13 **PALLASKENRY (IRE),** 11, b g Olden Times—My Lehcareve (IRE) **Mr J. T. Coulson**
14 **ROB ROYAL (FR),** 11, gr g Rob Roy (USA)—Royale Trophy (FR) **Mr N. Carter**
15 4, B f Mahler—Seventh Surprise (IRE) **Mr N. Carter**
16 **SHE'S OUT OF REACH,** 5, ch m Phoenix Reach (IRE)—Beat Seven **All the Kings Men**
17 4, B f Ocovango—Tara The Tiger **Mr N. Carter**
18 4, Ch f Shantou (USA)—What Lies Ahead (IRE) **All Or Nothing Racing Club**

THREE-YEAR-OLDS

19 **ELLA'S ANGEL,** bl gr f Lethal Force (IRE)—Princess of Rock **Mr R. Spruce**
20 **NATIVE NELLIE,** gr f Geordieland (FR)—Not Now Nellie **Mr B. H. Banks**

Assistant Trainer: Sarah Carter.

105 MISS JACQUELINE COWARD, Dalby

Postal: **Low Moor Farm, Dalby, Yorkshire, YO60 6PF**
Contacts: **PHONE 01653 628995**

1 **MUMCAT,** 4, b f Bobby's Kitten (USA)—Tell Mum **Mrs S. E. Mason**
2 **VALLEY OF FLOWERS (IRE),** 5, b m Slade Power (IRE)—Miss Cape (IRE) **Mrs C. A. Coward**
3 **WEDDING STRESS,** 5, b m Casamento (IRE)—Chip N Pin **S Hollings & Mrs Susan E Mason**

106 MR ROBERT COWELL, Newmarket

Postal: **Bottisham Heath Stud, Six Mile Bottom, Newmarket, Suffolk, CB8 0TT**
Contacts: **PHONE 01638 570330 MOBILE 07785 512463**
EMAIL robert@robertcowellracing.co.uk WEBSITE www.robertcowellracing.co.uk

1 **ANGLE LAND,** 4, b f Mayson—Jumeirah Star (USA) **K Dasmal, A Rix, R Penney**
2 **ARECIBO (FR),** 8, b g Invincible Spirit (IRE)—Oceanique (USA) **Mr R. J. Moore**
3 **CLARENDON HOUSE,** 5, b h Mehmas (IRE)—Walaaa (IRE) **Middleham Park Racing VIII**
4 **FAUSTUS,** 5, b g Mayson—Israfel **Mrs S. F. Hadida**
5 **GOLDEN AGE (FR),** 6, b g Golden Horn—Farnesina (FR) **Mr C Humphris & Partner**
6 **GRANDFATHER TOM,** 8, b g Kheleyf (USA)—Kassuta **Bottisham Heath Stud**
7 **HAN SOLO BERGER (IRE),** 8, b g Lord Shanakill (USA)—Dreamaway (IRE) **Mrs B. J. Berresford**
8 **ISLE OF LISMORE (IRE),** 5, b g Zebedee—Spring Bouquet (IRE) **Mr P. S. Ryan**
9 **JACK'S POINT,** 7, b g Slade Power (IRE)—Electra Star **Mr P. A. Downing**
10 **LIPSINK (IRE),** 6, b g Kodiac—Iron Lips **Mr J. Sargeant**

MR ROBERT COWELL - continued

11 **PRIVILEGE (FR),** 5, b m Elusive City (USA)—Helen Fourment **Mr C Humphris & Partner**
12 **THAKRAH,** 4, b f Dubawi (IRE)—Thafeera (USA) **Mrs M Ferguson & Partner**
13 **TOMSHALFBROTHER,** 7, b g Sir Percy—Kassuta **Bottisham Heath Stud**

THREE-YEAR-OLDS

14 **AGOSTINO,** b g Harry Angel (IRE)—Firenze **Mr P. S. Ryan**
15 **ASIAN QUEEN,** b br f Twilight Son—Alsium (IRE) **Mr R. J. Moore**
16 **BLUFF,** b c The Gurkha (IRE)—Blodwyn **Bottisham Heath Stud**
17 **CROWN DREAMS,** b g Oasis Dream—Looks All Right (IRE) **Mrs F. H. Hay**
18 **CUBAN GREY,** gr c Havana Grey—Tout Va Bien (IRE) **Mr R. J. Moore**
19 **DEIRA STAR,** b f Intrinsic—Jumeirah Star (USA) **Mr Khalifa Dasmal & Bottisham Heath Stud**
20 **KANDY KING,** ch c Rajasinghe (IRE)—Most Tempting **Bottisham Heath Stud**
21 **MAKE CLEAR,** b f Tasleet—Falsify **Bottisham Heath Stud**
22 **MISS MARIANNE,** b f Showcasing—Little Voice (USA) **Mr & Mrs T O'Donohoe**
23 **MOONLIGHT DREAMER,** b c Oasis Dream—Peace Dreamer (IRE) **Mrs S. F. Hadida**
24 **POETIC JACK,** b c Peace Envoy (FR)—Suzi Spends (IRE) **Mr R. T. Speakman**
25 **POWEREDBYLOVE,** b f Cracksman—Sitar **Mr R. J. Moore**
26 **REWILDING,** ch c Night of Thunder (IRE)—Kassuta **Mr J. Sargeant**
27 **SHAKA,** b c Mayson—Sciacca (IRE) **Bottisham Heath Stud**
28 **ZENO (FR),** b c Iffraaj—Farnesina (FR) **C & D Howard**

TWO-YEAR-OLDS

29 B f 27/02 Havana Grey—Blynx (Equiano (FR)) (15000) **Manor Farm Stud & Partner**
30 **FIDELIUS,** b c 07/05 Harry Angel (IRE)—Peace Dreamer (IRE) (Sir Prancealot (IRE)) **Mrs S. F. Hadida**
31 Ch f 05/04 Intrinsic—Jumeirah Star (USA) (Street Boss (USA)) **Mr Khalifa Dasmal & Bottisham Heath Stud**
32 Ch f 07/02 Coach House (IRE)—Mia Tia (Equiano (FR)) **The Cool Silk Partnership**
33 B c 23/03 Aclaim (IRE)—Most Tempting (Showcasing) **Bottisham Heath Stud**
34 B c 17/02 Night of Thunder (IRE)—Royal Eloquence (IRE) (Duke of Marmalade (IRE)) (100000) **Mrs F. H. Hay**
35 **TOMSHALFSISTER,** b f 27/03 Charm Spirit (IRE)—Kassuta (Kyllachy) **Mr J. Sargeant**

Head Lad: Mark Gadsby, Gavin Hernon, **Racing Secretary:** Holly Roeder, **Secretary:** Katy Warren.

107

MR CLIVE COX, Hungerford

Postal: **Beechdown Farm, Sheepdrove Road, Lambourn, Hungerford, Berkshire, RG17 7UN**
Contacts: **WORK 01488 73072 MOBILE 07740 630521**
EMAIL clive@clivecox.com WEBSITE www.clivecox.com

1 **ARATUS (IRE),** 5, b g Free Eagle (IRE)—Shauna's Princess (IRE) **A. Butler**
2 **DILIGENT HARRY,** 5, b g Due Diligence (USA)—Harryana To **The Dilinquents**
3 **FERNANDO RAH,** 5, b g Lethal Force (IRE)—Lacing **Mr P. N. Ridgers**
4 **GET AHEAD,** 4, ch f Showcasing—Suelita **Hot To Trot Racing V**
5 **HARRY THREE,** 4, b g Adaay (IRE)—Harryana To **Clive Cox Racing Ltd**
6 **JUST AMBER,** 5, ch m Lethal Force (IRE)—Milly's Gift **Ken Lock Racing**
7 **KINGDOM COME (IRE),** 4, b g Kingman—Monami (GER) **China Horse Club International Limited**
8 **LETHAL NYMPH,** 4, b g Lethal Force (IRE)—Little Nymph **Mr T. H. S. Fox**
9 **MAMBO BEAT (IRE),** 4, ch g Red Jazz (USA)—Bulrushes **Middleham Park Racing CXIV**
10 **MAPPATASSIE (IRE),** 4, ch f Australia—Montezuma (GER) **S R Hope & S W Barrow**
11 **MOHI,** 4, b g Acclamation—Minalisa **AlMohamediya Racing**
12 **OASIS GIFT,** 4, b g Oasis Dream—Siren's Gift **J. C. Smith**
13 **POSITIVE,** 6, b g Dutch Art—Osipova **Mr Alan Spence**
14 **PROP FORWARD,** 5, b g Iffraaj—My Propeller (IRE) **J. C. Smith**
15 **RIVER NYMPH,** 6, b g Cable Bay (IRE)—Little Nymph **Mr T. H. S. Fox**
16 **SPIRIT OF THE BAY (IRE),** 5, b m Cable Bay (IRE)—Decorative (IRE) **The Baywatchers**
17 **TIS MARVELLOUS,** 9, b g Harbour Watch (IRE)—Mythicism **Miss J. Deadman & Mr S. Barrow**
18 **TRANS MONTANA,** 4, b f Mondialiste (IRE)—Tarqua (IRE) **Earl of Carnarvon**

MR CLIVE COX - continued

19 **TREGONY,** 5, ch m New Bay—Timarwa (IRE) **S R Hope & S W Barrow**

THREE-YEAR-OLDS

20 **ANCESTRAL LAND,** b br c Sioux Nation (USA)—Swing Out Sister (IRE) **Sheikh I. S. Al Khalifa**
21 **BONNY ANGEL,** b f Harry Angel (IRE)—Timeless Gift (IRE) **Mr P. N. Ridgers**
22 **CHESTER JESTER,** b c Ribchester (IRE)—Straight Away **J. C. Smith**
23 **CLASSIC SPEED (IRE),** b c Kodiac—Alluring Park (IRE) **Mrs Patricia J. Burns**
24 **CONSERVATIONIST,** b f Muhaarar—Zuhoor Baynoona (IRE) **Cheveley Park Stud Limited**
25 **CRIMSON ANGEL,** b f Harry Angel (IRE)—Fanrouge (IRE) **Oak Lodge Racing**
26 **DUE DATE,** b c Due Diligence (USA)—Harryana To **N. Bizakov**
27 **EMINENCY (IRE),** gr c Havana Grey—Kendamara (FR) **Mr J. Goddard**
28 **EXORBITANT,** b c Exceed And Excel (AUS)—Quinta Verde (IRE) **Woodhurst, Nelson, Chrysanthou & Castle**
29 **FOOLS AND HORSES,** b f Twilight Son—Zawiyah **Mr & Mrs Paul & Clare Rooney**
30 **GWENDOLINA,** b f Decorated Knight—Divine Touch **Earl of Carnarvon**
31 **HAVANA BLUE,** gr c Havana Grey—Exrating **Teme Valley**
32 **HEARTBREAKING (IRE),** b f Ribchester (IRE)—Puff Pastry **Mr J. Goddard**
33 **HEROISM (IRE),** b c Invincible Spirit (IRE)—Liberating **Mr J. Goddard**
34 **ICE COOL HARRY,** b g Harry Angel (IRE)—Snow Squaw **J. C. Smith**
35 **JOHN CHARD VC,** b g Ardad (IRE)—Wild Mimosa (IRE) **Woodhurst Construction Ltd**
36 **JUST BRING IT (IRE),** ch g Harry Angel (IRE)—Just Joan (IRE) **Atlantic Equine**
37 **KAIDU (IRE),** b g Profitable (IRE)—Sahaayef (IRE) **Al Mohamediya Racing**
38 **KARSAVINA,** b f Ulysses (IRE)—Osipova **Cheveley Park Stud Limited**
39 **KATEY KONTENT,** ch f Havana Grey—Showstoppa **S R Hope & S W Barrow**
40 **KERDOS (IRE),** b c Profitable (IRE)—The Mums **John Connolly & A D Spence**
41 **KRACKING,** gr g Muhaarar—Vallado (IRE) **Mr A. L. Cohen**
42 **LIKELY TYPE,** b g Shalaa (IRE)—Rowan Brae **Miss J. Deadman & Mr S. Barrow**
43 **MA FAMILLE (IRE),** ch f Starspangledbanner (AUS)—Our Joy (IRE) **Oak Lodge Racing**
44 **MONTY BAY,** b c Night of Thunder (IRE)—Fleabiscuit (IRE) **Mr & Mrs Paul & Clare Rooney**
45 **MOVIE STAR LOOKS,** br f Cracksman—Garanciere (FR) **S R Hope & S W Barrow**
46 **MY TURN NOW (IRE),** b f Belardo (IRE)—Rio's Pearl **Mr & Mrs Paul & Clare Rooney**
47 **OLYMPIC QUEST,** ch f Australia—Olympic Runner **J. C. Smith**
48 **PAPAL MUSIC (IRE),** gr g Gregorian (IRE)—Kabaya (FR) **Kennet Valley Thoroughbreds XIII**
49 **PIERCE (IRE),** b g Profitable (IRE)—Snooze (IRE) **Mr S. B. M. Al Qassimi**
50 **QUEEN OF THRONES (IRE),** b f Profitable (IRE)—Throne **The Profiteers**
51 **RAPID TEST,** b f Time Test—Cascades (IRE) **J. C. Smith**
52 **REDCLIFF GLEN (GER),** b g Gleneagles (IRE)—Relevant (IRE) **Clive Cox Racing Ltd**
53 **REDEMPTION TIME,** b g Harry Angel (IRE)—Red Box **Atlantic Equine**
54 **SCHOLARSHIP (IRE),** b g Profitable (IRE)—Thakerah (IRE) **Sheikh I. S. Al Khalifa**
55 **SERGEANT PEP (IRE),** b g Kodiac—Light Glass (IRE) **Middleham Park Racing LXIX**
56 **SHOWGIRL,** ch f Showcasing—Salonmare (GER) **Windmill Racing - Showgirl**
57 **STARLIGHT NATION (IRE),** b g Sioux Nation (USA)—Starlight Princess (IRE) **Mrs C. J. Black**
58 **TASWARA,** b f Tasleet—Timarwa (IRE) **S R Hope & S W Barrow**
59 **TICKET TO ALASKA (IRE),** b g Kodiac—Jira **Browns & Hornbys**
60 **VERDANSK,** b c No Nay Never (USA)—Boater (IRE) **Barker Creighton Davis Kent Partnership**
61 **VULTAR (IRE),** gr c Free Eagle (IRE)—Evening Frost (IRE) **A. Butler**

TWO-YEAR-OLDS

62 **ACER,** ch f 22/02 Harry Angel (IRE)—Heliograph (Ishiguru (USA)) (6667) **Mr P. N. Ridgers**
63 Ch c 24/03 Sioux Nation (USA)—Annie Fior (IRE) (Finsceal Fior (IRE)) (76190) **Al Mohamediya Racing**
64 **ASSEMA,** b f 09/01 Dark Angel (IRE)—Awesome (Bahamian Bounty) (70000) **N. Bizakov**
65 Gr c 05/03 Dark Angel (IRE)—Beldale Memory (IRE) (Camacho) (180000) **AlMohamediya Racing**
66 **BELLA TASLINA,** ch f 22/04 Tasleet—Bella Catalina (Acclamation) (28011) **The Top Barn Syndicate**
67 B c 05/04 Magna Grecia (IRE)—Chibola (ARG) (Roy (USA)) (150000) **Mr D. A. Creighton**
68 B c 16/02 Invincible Spirit (IRE)—Crafty Madam (IRE) (Mastercraftsman (IRE)) **Mr Con Harrington**
69 B f 11/02 Ten Sovereigns (IRE)—Crisaff's Queen (Zoffany (IRE)) (30000) **Clive Cox Racing Ltd**
70 **DASHING HARRY,** b c 22/02 Harry Angel (IRE)—
Meghan Sparkle (IRE) (Showcasing) (24762) **The Beechdown Sparklers**
71 **DRAGON LEADER,** ch c 07/02 El Kabeir (USA)—
Sweet Dragon Fly (Oasis Dream) (42857) **Kennet Valley Thoroughbreds III**

MR CLIVE COX - continued

72 **DREAM SEEKER,** b f 19/03 Oasis Dream—Snoqualmie Star (Galileo (IRE)) **J. C. Smith**
73 **ENGINEER,** b c 09/04 Showcasing—Corazon Canarias (FR) (Caradak (IRE)) (60000) **Sheikh I. S. Al Khalifa**
74 **GHOSTWRITER,** b c 16/03 Invincible Spirit (IRE)—Moorside (Champs Elysees) **J. C. Smith**
75 **GLITTERELLA,** ch f 20/01 Starspangledbanner (AUS)—Amore Bello (IRE) (Bated Breath) **J. C. Smith**
76 B c 16/03 Invincible Army (IRE)—Heavens Peak (Pivotal) (44018) **Mr & Mrs Paul & Clare Rooney**
77 Gr c 15/03 Dark Angel (IRE)—Holy Cat (IRE) (Kitten's Joy (USA)) (28571) **Woodhurst Ltd & Withernsea**
78 **INKARA (IRE),** b f 06/04 Profitable (IRE)—Cafetiere (Iffraaj) (65000) **N. Bizakov**
79 **INSIGNIA,** b c 10/02 Land Force (IRE)—Kasumi (Inchinor) (80952) **Mr J. Goddard**
80 B f 12/03 Kodiac—Jadanna (IRE) (Mujadil (USA)) (24762) **Mr Noel O'Callaghan**
81 B f 29/04 Profitable (IRE)—Lydia Becker (Sleeping Indian) (50000) **S R Hope & S W Barrow**
82 Ch c 23/04 Havana Gold (IRE)—Meaning of Time (Captain Gerrard (IRE)) (76030) **Mr & Mrs Paul & Clare Rooney**
83 B c 02/04 Kodiac—Milana (FR) (Mark of Esteem (IRE)) (85000) **Mrs Marie McCartan**
84 **MISS SHOW OFF,** gr f 26/01 Showcasing—
Greach (IRE) (Gregorian (IRE)) (65000) **Norman Court Stud & Susan Bunney**
85 **MISS STORMY NIGHT,** b f 10/02 Night of Thunder (IRE)—
Jumeirah Palm Star (Invincible Spirit (IRE)) (80000) **Norman Court Stud & Susan Bunney**
86 **NEMOV,** b c 09/03 Blue Point (IRE)—Barynya (Pivotal) (80000) **Cheveley Park Stud Limited**
87 B c 25/04 Twilight Son—Normandy Maid (American Post) (21000) **Mr & Mrs Paul & Clare Rooney**
88 B c 18/02 Mehmas (IRE)—On The Same Page (IRE) (Born To Sea (IRE)) (40016) **Miss J. Deadman & Mr S. Barrow**
89 B br f 10/03 No Nay Never (USA)—Priceless (Exceed And Excel (AUS)) (200000) **Mr Alan Spence**
90 Br f 04/04 Blue Point (IRE)—Ridge Ranger (IRE) (Bushranger (IRE)) **Mr Con Harrington**
91 B c 09/03 Oasis Dream—Sharqeyih (Shamardal (USA)) (75000) **AlMohamediya Racing**
92 **SMOULDERING,** b f 14/02 Profitable (IRE)—Street Fire (IRE) (Street Cry (IRE)) (30000) **A.D. & A.J. Pearson**
93 **SPIRIT OF THE ROSE,** b f 22/04 Showcasing—Osipova (Makfi) **Cheveley Park Stud Limited**
94 **STUDY UP,** b c 28/03 Due Diligence (USA)—Cross My Heart (Sakhee's Secret) (70000) **Atlantic Equine**
95 **SUCCESSION (IRE),** b c 03/02 Showcasing—Lady Aria (Kodiac) (61905) **Mr J. Goddard**
96 **SYMBOLOGY,** gr f 15/02 Havana Grey—Showstoppa (Showcasing) (219048) **Sheikh I. S. Al Khalifa**
97 B c 08/02 U S Navy Flag (USA)—Tedsmore Dame (Indesatchel (IRE)) (44762) **Mr J. Goddard**
98 Gr c 10/04 Havana Grey—Twilight Thyme (Bahamian Bounty) (80952) **AlMohamediya Racing**
99 **UNBREAK MY HEART,** ch f 26/02 Showcasing—Place In My Heart (Compton Place) **C. J. Harper**
100 Gr c 14/02 Phoenix of Spain (IRE)—Ventura Mist (Pastoral Pursuits) (50000) **Clive Cox Racing Ltd**
101 B c 23/01 James Garfield (IRE)—
Wind In Her Sails (IRE) (Lilbourne Lad (IRE)) (29612) **Miss J. Deadman & Mr S. Barrow**

Flat Jockey: John Fahy, Adam Kirby.

---

108 MR TONY COYLE, Norton

Postal: **Long Row Stables, Beverley Road, Norton, Malton, North Yorkshire, YO17 9PJ**
Contacts: **MOBILE 07976 621425**
EMAIL tonycoyleracing@hotmail.co.uk

1 **BROKEN SPEAR,** 7, b g Pastoral Pursuits—My Pretty Girl **Morecool Racing**
2 **EY UP IT'S MAGGIE,** 5, b m Equiano (FR)—Velvet Jaguar **Mrs M. Lingwood**
3 **EY UP ITS THE BOSS,** 4, br g Pastoral Pursuits—Velvet Jaguar **M. & S. Bland**
4 **FLEET OF FOOT,** 4, ch g French Navy—Full Bloom **Heather Raw & Partner**
5 **FLEETING BLUE (FR),** 5, ch m French Navy—My Pretty Girl **David Bishop & Tony Coyle**
6 **GOLDEN PROSPERITY (IRE),** 4, ch g Galileo Gold—April (IRE) **Stella Riley & Tony Coyle**
7 5, B g Eagle Top—Little Missmoffatt
8 **LOU MEL,** 4, b f Intrinsic—Till Carr Duchess **C. R. Green**
9 **SELBY'S PRIDE,** 4, gr f Lethal Force (IRE)—Vibrant **Mrs A. M. Johnson**
10 **WOTS THE WIFI CODE,** 6, b g Fast Company (IRE)—Velvet Jaguar **Mrs M. Lingwood**

THREE-YEAR-OLDS

11 **SELBY'S JOY,** b f Massaat (IRE)—Vibrant **Mrs A. M. Johnson**
12 **URBAN DANDY (IRE),** ch g Dandy Man (IRE)—Pretty Pebble (IRE) **Mr D. F. L. Bishop**

MR TONY COYLE - continued

TWO-YEAR-OLDS

13 B gr c 12/01 Havana Grey—Sciacca (IRE) (Royal Applause) (7619)

Flat Jockey: Barry McHugh.

---

109 MR RAY CRAGGS, Sedgefield

Postal: **East Close Farm, Sedgefield, Stockton-On-Tees, Cleveland, TS21 3HW**
Contacts: **PHONE 01740 620239 FAX 01740 623476**

1 **AMELIA R (IRE),** 7, b m Zoffany (IRE)—Xaloc (IRE) **R. Craggs**
2 **AMOURI GLEAM,** 8, b m Arabian Gleam—Tour d'Amour (IRE) **R. Craggs**
3 **AMOURIE,** 7, ch m Haafhd—Tour d'Amour (IRE) **R. Craggs**
4 **CASTLEBERG ROCK,** 4, b g Fastnet Rock (AUS)—Banzari **R. Craggs**
5 **KHABIB (IRE),** 5, b br g Mehmas (IRE)—Lady Mega (IRE) **R. Craggs**
6 **RON O,** 5, ch g Toronado (IRE)—Xaloc (IRE) **R. Craggs**
7 **SPYCRACKER,** 6, b g Monsieur Bond (IRE)—Tour d'Amour (IRE) **R. Craggs**
8 **WELL I NEVER,** 11, b g Josr Algarhoud (IRE)—Tour d'Amour (IRE) **R. Craggs**

Assistant Trainer: Miss J N Craggs.

---

110 MR PETER CRATE, Reigate

Postal: **June Farm, Trumpets Hill Road, Reigate, Surrey, RH2 8QY**
Contacts: **MOBILE 07775 821560**
EMAIL peterdcrate@jandjfranks.com

1 **HARB,** 4, b g Muhaarar—Maid For Winning (USA) **Gallagher Bloodstock Limited**

TWO-YEAR-OLDS

2 B f 21/02 Advertise—Blue Aegean (Invincible Spirit (IRE)) **P. D. Crate**

Flat Jockey: Shane Kelly. **Amateur Jockey:** Mr George Crate.

---

111 MR MATTHEW CRAWLEY, Newmarket

Postal: **73 Manderston Road, Newmarket, Suffolk, CB8 0NL**
Contacts: **PHONE 07719 616402**
EMAIL matcrawley73@hotmail.co.uk

1 **ALICE KITTY (IRE),** 5, ch m Bobby's Kitten (USA)—Classic Legend **Mr F. Michael**
2 **BODROY (IRE),** 5, b h Coulsty (IRE)—Youcouldntmakeitup (IRE) **Newhorse**
3 **CENDRILLON,** 5, ch m Bobby's Kitten (USA)—Midnight Ransom **Ms S. J. Humber**
4 **DREAM GAME,** 6, bl m Brazen Beau (AUS)—Dreamily (IRE) **Ms S. J. Humber**
5 **DUBH ROSE,** 5, b g Black Sam Bellamy (IRE)—Iconic Rose **The Stablemates**
6 **MYWON (IRE),** 4, br c Gutaifan (IRE)—Spirit of Alsace (IRE) **Newhorse**
7 **POTTERS BISHOP,** 5, b g Cardinal—Craughwell Suas (IRE) **Mrs J. May**
8 **STRANGER THINGS,** 5, ch m Mukhadram—Fairy Steps **Ms S. J. Humber**
9 **TARTARUS,** 4, b g Ruler of The World (IRE)—Respectfilly **Mr F. Michael**
10 **THREE DRAGONS,** 6, ch g Sakhee (USA)—Three Heart's **Ms S. J. Humber**
11 **WAR BONNET,** 4, b g Helmet (AUS)—House Maiden (IRE) **Ms S. J. Humber**

MR MATTHEW CRAWLEY - continued

THREE-YEAR-OLDS

12 Ch c Hawkbill (USA)—Three Heart's **Ms S. J. Humber**

TWO-YEAR-OLDS

13 B c 15/01 Eqtidaar (IRE)—Respectable (Champs Elysees) (2500)

---

112 MR SIMON AND ED CRISFORD, Newmarket

Postal: **Gainsborough Thoroughbreds Limited, Gainsborough Stables, Hamilton Road, Newmarket, Suffolk, CB8 0TE**
Contacts: **PHONE 01638 662661**
EMAIL info@gainsboroughoffice.com WEBSITE www.gainsboroughthoroughbreds.com
TWITTER @gainsboroughhq INSTAGRAM @gainsboroughhq

1 **AL AGAILA (IRE),** 4, b f Lope de Vega (IRE)—L'Amour de Ma Vie (USA)
2 **ALGIERS (IRE),** 6, ch g Shamardal (USA)—Antara (GER)
3 **ANOTHER ROMANCE (IRE),** 4, ch f Night of Thunder (IRE)—Late Romance (USA)
4 **AWAAL (IRE),** 4, b g Lope de Vega (IRE)—Anna's Rock (IRE)
5 **BASE NOTE,** 4, b g Shamardal (USA)—Fragrancy (IRE)
6 **COURT OF SESSION,** 4, br g Iffraaj—Sibilance
7 **CROUPIER (IRE),** 4, b g Invincible Spirit (IRE)—Aaraamm (USA)
8 **DUKEMAN (IRE),** 4, b g Kingman—She's Mine (IRE)
9 **JADOOMI (FR),** 5, b g Holy Roman Emperor (IRE)—South Sister
10 **KINGORI (USA),** 4, b g Animal Kingdom (USA)—Hawana (USA)
11 **LISEO (IRE),** 4, b g Lope de Vega (IRE)—Special Gal (FR)
12 **MISTY DANCER,** 4, gr ro f Dubawi (IRE)—Summer Fete (IRE)
13 **POKER FACE (IRE),** 4, b g Fastnet Rock (AUS)—Stars At Night (IRE)
14 **POSITIVE IMPACT (IRE),** 4, ch g Shamardal (USA)—Masarah (IRE)
15 **SEA THE CASPER (IRE),** 4, ch g Sea The Stars (IRE)—October Queen (IRE)
16 **SUNGLASSES,** 4, b f Iffraaj—Elle Shade
17 **WEST WIND BLOWS (IRE),** 4, b c Teofilo (IRE)—West Wind

THREE-YEAR-OLDS

18 **AL ALAALI (FR),** b c Showcasing—Fresh Air (IRE)
19 **ANIMATE (IRE),** b g Shamardal (USA)—Dark Liberty (IRE)
20 **APPROACH THE SUN,** b f New Approach (IRE)—Cairncross (IRE)
21 **BAAHILL,** b g Kingman—Pirouette
22 **BOLSTER,** b c Invincible Spirit (IRE)—Quilting (USA)
23 **BYSTANDER (IRE),** b c Dark Angel (IRE)—Witnessed
24 **CHESSPIECE,** b c Nathaniel (IRE)—Royal Solitaire (IRE)
25 **CHOISYA,** ch f Night of Thunder (IRE)—Fragrancy (IRE)
26 B f Exceed And Excel (AUS)—Cool Thunder (IRE)
27 **COSMIC VIEW,** ch g New Approach (IRE)—First Priority
28 **CREDIT NOTE,** b f Sea The Moon (GER)—Deborah
29 **DESERT GUEST,** b g Teofilo (IRE)—Special Guest
30 **DRESS OF DUBAI,** b f Cracksman—Dresden Doll (USA)
31 **ELMONIR (IRE),** ch g New Approach (IRE)—Jadeyra
32 **EMACULATE SOLDIER (GER),** b c Sea The Moon (GER)—Enjoy The Life
33 **FAHARI (IRE),** b f Shamardal (USA)—Tutu Nguru (USA)
34 **FLOWER OF DUBAI,** ch f New Approach (IRE)—Time To Blossom

MR SIMON AND ED CRISFORD - continued

35 **INTRICACY,** b c Dubawi (IRE)—Golden Valentine (FR)
36 **INVERLOCHY (FR),** b f Oasis Dream—Innevera (FR)
37 **KNIGHT (IRE),** b c Mehmas (IRE)—Fidaaha (IRE)
38 **LASER GUIDED (IRE),** b c Kingman—Cercle d'Or (IRE)
39 **MONTE LINAS (IRE),** b g Territories (IRE)—Miss Carbonia (IRE)
40 **MUKEEDD,** b c Exceed And Excel (AUS)—Bahjtee
41 **MYSTERIOUS MAESTRO (IRE),** b g Mastercraftsman (IRE)—Elusive Girl (IRE)
42 **OH SO GRAND,** b f Postponed (IRE)—Lady Zonda
43 **PENZANCE,** br gr c Wootton Bassett—Iromea (IRE)
44 **QUDDWAH,** b c Kingman—Sajjhaa
45 **RAQEEBB (FR),** gr c Wootton Bassett—Tubereuse (IRE)
46 **ROTATIONAL,** b br f Kingman—Pivotique
47 **SAAMYAA,** ch f Sea The Stars (IRE)—Nezwaah
48 **SOARING EAGLE (IRE),** b f Gleneagles (IRE)—Heartlines (USA)
49 **SPARTAN ARROW (IRE),** b c Sioux Nation (USA)—Thames Pageant
50 **STORM AND CONQUEST,** b g New Approach (IRE)—Lady Marian (GER)
51 **STORY OF PEACE,** ch g Pivotal—Greatest Virtue
52 **TAJAWAL (IRE),** b c Frankel—Feedyah (USA)
53 **TARRAFF (IRE),** b f Lope de Vega (IRE)—Majeyda (USA)
54 **THE BUNT,** b g Cracksman—Buntingford (IRE)
55 **TRIBUTE (IRE),** b g Acclamation—Party Whip (IRE)
56 **TWIRLING (IRE),** b f Churchill (IRE)—Turning Top (IRE)
57 **WIGMORE STREET (USA),** b c American Pharoah (USA)—Marylebone (USA)

TWO-YEAR-OLDS

58 B f 21/04 Blue Point (IRE)—Affina (IRE) (Kodiac)
59 B c 27/03 Showcasing—All of Me (Teofilo (IRE)) (75000)
60 **ARTISTIC MISSION,** b c 06/02 Showcasing—Lilian Baylis (IRE) (Shamardal (USA))
61 Ch c 28/04 New Approach (IRE)—Balsamine (USA) (Street Cry (IRE))
62 Ch c 20/02 Night of Thunder (IRE)—Beautiful Ending (Exceed And Excel (AUS))
63 Ch c 27/02 Night of Thunder (IRE)—Beautiful Memory (IRE) (Invincible Spirit (IRE))
64 **CAVALRY CALL (IRE),** b c 28/01 Invincible Army (IRE)—Michael's Song (IRE) (Refuse To Bend (IRE)) (77000)
65 **CRIMSON ROAD (IRE),** b c 23/01 Masar (IRE)—Redhawk (IRE) (Mastercraftsman (IRE)) (55000)
66 B c 27/03 Showcasing—Deciding Vote (Pivotal) (85000)
67 B c 02/02 Lope de Vega (IRE)—Deep Inside (FR) (Redoute's Choice (AUS))
68 B c 01/05 Golden Horn—Dresden Doll (USA) (Elusive Quality (USA))
69 Ch c 21/01 Masar (IRE)—Dubai One (IRE) (Exceed And Excel (AUS))
70 Ch c 09/03 Havana Grey—Dundunah (USA) (Sidney's Candy (USA)) (220000)
71 Ch f 05/02 Iffraaj—El Gumryah (IRE) (No Nay Never (USA))
72 B f 29/01 Sea The Stars (IRE)—Eleanor Powell (IRE) (Exceed And Excel (AUS)) (105000)
73 B c 13/03 Mehmas (IRE)—Fanciful Miss (New Approach (IRE)) (140000)
74 B f 12/04 Night of Thunder (IRE)—Feedyah (USA) (Street Cry (IRE))
75 B f 21/02 Farhh—Finespun (IRE) (Sea The Stars (IRE))
76 B f 14/02 No Nay Never (USA)—Follow A Star (IRE) (Galileo (IRE)) (625000)
77 B f 23/02 Zarak (FR)—Fuse (FR) (Teofilo (IRE)) (144058)
78 **IMPERIAL SOVEREIGN (IRE),** b c 23/03 Frankel—Imperial Charm (Dubawi (IRE))
79 B c 01/04 Kodiac—Koubalibre (IRE) (Galileo (IRE)) (88035)
80 B c 06/01 Wootton Bassett—Lincoln Tale (IRE) (Intello (GER)) (180000)
81 B f 07/03 Iffraaj—Lucie Manette (Shamardal (USA))
82 B f 21/02 Blue Point (IRE)—Mannaal (IRE) (Dubawi (IRE))
83 B c 08/04 Blue Point (IRE)—Masarah (IRE) (Cape Cross (IRE))
84 B f 19/02 Siyouni (FR)—Mawahib (IRE) (New Approach (IRE))
85 B c 13/03 Showcasing—Megan Lily (IRE) (Dragon Pulse (IRE)) (260000)
86 B c 25/02 Invincible Spirit (IRE)—Menuetto (Dubawi (IRE))
87 B f 10/04 Too Darn Hot—Minwah (IRE) (Oasis Dream) (230000)
88 B c 06/05 Caravaggio (USA)—Miss Carbonia (IRE) (Lilbourne Lad (IRE))
89 B c 11/02 Almanzor (FR)—Mission Impassible (IRE) (Galileo (IRE)) (88035)
90 B f 04/02 Farhh—Natural Scenery (Dubawi (IRE))
91 B c 22/02 Frankel—Nezwaah (Dubawi (IRE))

MR SIMON AND ED CRISFORD - continued

92 Ch c 01/03 More Than Ready (USA)—Noblesse Oblige (ITY) (Myboycharlie (IRE)) (48019)
93 Ch f 18/01 Bated Breath—Orchid Star (Dubawi (IRE))
94 Ch f 23/04 Nathaniel (IRE)—Pelerin (IRE) (Shamardal (USA)) (50000)
95 B c 09/03 Sea The Stars (IRE)—Pink Rose (Shirocco (GER))
96 Ch c 15/02 Masar (IRE)—Porcelain Girl (IRE) (Exceed And Excel (AUS))
97 B f 24/01 Frankel—Red Dune (IRE) (Red Ransom (USA))
98 B c 14/02 Street Sense (USA)—Rose Sapphire (USA) (Congrats (USA))
99 B c 11/05 Wootton Bassett—Seaella (IRE) (Canford Cliffs (IRE)) (112045)
100 **SERENITY DREAM (IRE),** ch c 04/05 Night of Thunder (IRE)—Playfull Spirit (Invincible Spirit (IRE)) (200000)
101 B c 15/03 Magna Grecia (IRE)—Silver Meadow (IRE) (Teofilo (IRE))
102 **SOUTH SHORE,** b c 28/02 Blue Point (IRE)—Angel's Glory (Invincible Spirit (IRE))
103 B f 15/04 Sea The Stars (IRE)—Tea Dancing (Dubawi (IRE))
104 Ch c 20/02 Night of Thunder (IRE)—Terzetto (IRE) (Iffraaj)
105 Ch c 13/02 Nathaniel (IRE)—Toride (FR) (Fuisse (FR)) (208083)
106 Ch f 12/03 Dubawi (IRE)—Unforgetable Filly (Sepoy (AUS))
107 Ch c 12/03 Night of Thunder (IRE)—Whimbrel (IRE) (Dark Angel (IRE))
108 Ch c 10/03 Lope de Vega (IRE)—Wishfully (IRE) (Invincible Spirit (IRE))
109 B c 26/02 Frankel—With Your Spirit (FR) (Invincible Spirit (IRE)) (208083)

Owners: Shaikh D. Al Khalifa, H.H. Sheikh Nasser Al Khalifa, Sheikh J. D. Al Maktoum, Sheikh Mohammed Obaid Al Maktoum, Sheikh R. D. Al Maktoum, Mr A. Al Mansoori, Mr A. S. Al Naboodah, M. Al Nabouda, S. Ali, Mr E. P. Babington, Mr A. J. Byrne, Mr H. Dalmook Al Maktoum, Mr P. E. Done, Mr J. E. Dubois, Edward Ware Et Al, Gail Brown Racing (XVI), Gainsborough Thoroughbreds Ltd, Mr M. F. Geoghegan, Godolphin Management Company Ltd, Highclere T'Bred Racing - Dalai Lama, Mr A. P. P. Hoyeau, J-e Dubois, B Kwok, E Babington Et Al, KHK Racing Ltd, Mr C. W. B. Kwok, Sheikh Ahmed Al Maktoum, Marwan Al Maktoum, Mr A. Menahi, Newsells Park Stud Limited, Rabbah Racing, Dr A. Ridha, A. Saeed, Serpentine Bloodstock Ltd, Shaikh Duaij al Khalifa & Khk Racing Ltd, Mrs D. A. Tabor, M. Tabor, The Royal Ascot Racing Club, Victorious Racing Limited, Mr E. J. Ware.

---

113 MR ANDREW CROOK, Middleham

Postal: **Ashgill Stables (Yard 2), Tupgill Park, Coverham, Middleham, North Yorkshire, DL8 4TJ**
Contacts: **PHONE 01969 640303 MOBILE 07764 158899**
EMAIL andycrookracing@gmail.com WEBSITE www.andrewcrookracing.co.uk

1 **BOLT FROM THE BLUE (USA),** 4, b g Air Force Blue (USA)—Collect the Fee (USA) **Miss A. Porritt**
2 **BUBBLES'N'TROUBLES,** 6, b m Flemensfirth (USA)—Jontys'lass **Mr D. Carter**
3 **DAKOTA MOIRETTE (FR),** 10, b g Voix du Nord (FR)—Rahana Moirette (FR) **The Golden Dream**
4 **DANKING,** 6, b g Dansili—Time Saved **Mrs H. Sinclair**
5 **DON PORT LUX (FR),** 4, b g Free Port Lux—Marie d'Altissima (FR) **R. P. E. Berry**
6 **EARLY BOY (FR),** 12, b g Early March—Eclat de Rose (FR) **R. P. E. Berry**
7 **HAUT BERRY (FR),** 6, bl g My Risk (FR)—Bonjour Madame (FR) **R. P. E. Berry**
8 4, B f Jack Hobbs—Jontys'lass
9 **KNACKER TRAPPER (IRE),** 5, b g Court Cave (IRE)—Present Line (IRE) **Mr D. Carter**
10 **LADY BABS,** 9, br m Malinas (GER)—Jontys'lass **Ashgill Stud**
11 4, B f Sandmason—Manorwalk (IRE) **Miss A. M. Crook**
12 **OUR CILLA,** 9, gr m Sixties Icon—Kinetix **The 100 Club**
13 **SIR DOTTI (IRE),** 6, b g Dandy Man (IRE)—Midas Haze **The 100 Club**
14 **THIRD AVENUE (IRE),** 6, ch g Born To Sea (IRE)—Third Dimension (FR) **Whod Have Thought**
15 **VESHENSKAYA (IRE),** 8, b m Sholokhov (IRE)—Manorville (IRE) **Signify Partnership**
16 **ZARA'S UNIVERSE,** 7, b m Universal (IRE)—Jontys'lass **Ashgill Stud 2**

TWO-YEAR-OLDS

17 **LITTLE VENICE,** ch f 27/03 Cityscape—La Havrese (FR) (Le Havre (IRE))

Assistant Trainer: Amy Crook.

MR ANDREW CROOK - continued

NH Jockey: John Kington.

---

114 MR DYLAN CUNHA, Newmarket

Postal: **168 Windsor Road, Newmarket, Suffolk, CB8 0QA**
Contacts: **PHONE 07548 918385**
EMAIL dylancunha737@gmail.com

1 **ALPINE SPRINGS (IRE),** 5, gr m Anjaal—Conciliatory **Mr A. Dal Pos**
2 **FARO DE SAN JUAN (IRE),** 4, b g Almanzor (FR)—Fixette (IRE) **Quest Thoroughbreds**
3 **MOLIWOOD,** 5, b g Fastnet Rock (AUS)—Shalwa **Sarkar**
4 **MR FAYEZ (IRE),** 5, b g Ajaya—Yellow Elder (FR) **Mr D. L. Cunha**

THREE-YEAR-OLDS

5 **CONFEDERATION,** gr g Brazen Beau (AUS)—My Angel **Catch Us If You Can Racing**
6 **EXPRESSIONLESS,** b g Intello (GER)—Putois Peace **Mr D. L. Cunha**
7 B f Aclaim (IRE)—Haiti Dancer **Quest Thoroughbreds**
8 **IF YOU ASK ME TO,** b f Muhaarar—Endless
9 **SILVER SWORD,** gr g Charm Spirit (IRE)—Aurora Gray **Mrs K. Dixon**

TWO-YEAR-OLDS

10 **BATTLEOFBALTIMORE,** b c 19/02 Starspangledbanner (AUS)—Sparkle (Oasis Dream) (3000) **Catch Us If You Can Racing**
11 B c 18/03 Eqtidaar (IRE)—Clinet (IRE) (Docksider (USA)) (5000) **Quest Thoroughbreds**
12 B c 30/04 Saxon Warrior (JPN)—Dawn of Empire (USA) (Empire Maker (USA)) (28000) **Quest Thoroughbreds**
13 **EMPRESS LULU,** b f 01/03 Muhaarar—Celestial Empire (USA) (Empire Maker (USA)) **Catch Us If You Can Racing**
14 B c 20/04 Time Test—Haiti Dancer (Josr Algarhoud (IRE)) (6000) **Quest Thoroughbreds**
15 **HELLO MISS LADY (IRE),** ch f 16/03 Gleneagles (IRE)—Luminous (Champs Elysees) (6500) **d'Arblay Partnership**
16 B c 23/04 Oasis Dream—Putois Peace (Pivotal) **Mr D. L. Cunha**
17 B f 10/02 Magna Grecia (IRE)—What A Picture (FR) (Peintre Celebre (USA)) **Quest Thoroughbreds**

---

115 MR SEAN CURRAN, Swindon

Postal: **Twelve Oaks, Lechlade Road, Highworth, Swindon, Wiltshire, SN6 7QR**
Contacts: **MOBILE 07774 146169**

1 **A MHACIN,** 4, ch c Night of Thunder (IRE)—Astromagick **Miss N. Rymsza**
2 **ACES FULL (FR),** 8, b g Blek (FR)—Albalonga (FR) **Mr J. M. S. Curran**
3 **ALMUFEED (IRE),** 6, b g Mukhadram—Anqooda (USA) **Power Geneva Ltd**
4 **BUSINESS (FR),** 6, b g Siyouni (FR)—Mambo Mistress (USA) **Power Brothers**
5 **C'EST QUELQU'UN (FR),** 6, br g Buck's Boum (FR)—Sangrilla (FR) **Mr R. Cooper**
6 **COCHISE,** 7, b g Intello (GER)—Ship's Biscuit **Mr G. Box**
7 **COURTSIDE (FR),** 8, ch g Siyouni (FR)—Memoire (FR) **Power Geneva Ltd**
8 **DOMAINE DE L'ISLE (FR),** 10, b g Network (GER)—Gratiene de L'Isle (FR) **Mr L M Power & Mr Ian Hutchins**
9 **GIVE A LITTLE BACK (FR),** 4, b g Zelzal (FR)—Boyarynya (USA) **RacehorseClub.com**
10 **GRAND KNIGHT (FR),** 7, b g Slickly (FR)—La Grande Dame (FR) **Mr N. Byrne**
11 **GROOM DE COTTE (FR),** 7, b g Tiger Groom—Traviata Valtat (FR) **Mr W. J. M. Byrne**
12 **LEMON ICE (IRE),** 4, ch f Mastercraftsman (IRE)—Sense of Purpose (IRE) **Mr J. M. S. Curran**
13 **LETMELIVEMYLIFE,** 5, b g Oasis Dream—Itiqad **G. Wilson**
14 **MUTARA,** 4, b g Muhaarar—Primo Lady **Promanco Ltd**
15 **NAWAR,** 8, b g Henrythenavigator (USA)—Nouriya **Quartet Racing**

MR SEAN CURRAN - continued

16 **RUBY RED EMPRESS (IRE),** 6, b m Holy Roman Emperor (IRE)—Rougette **Power Geneva Ltd**
17 **THE THUNDERER (IRE),** 5, b g Gleneagles (IRE)—Purple Sage (IRE) **Mr N. Sangster**

---

116 MISS REBECCA CURTIS, Newport

Postal: **Fforest Farm, Newport, Pembrokeshire, SA42 0UG**
Contacts: **PHONE 01348 811489 MOBILE 07970 710690**
EMAIL rebcurtis@hotmail.com

1 **BEATTHEBULLET (IRE),** 9, br g Flemensfirth (USA)—Top Quality **Conyers, O'Reilly, Roddis, Zeffman**
2 **BOSTON JOE (IRE),** 7, b g Sageburg (IRE)—Supreme Millie (IRE) **Miss R. Curtis**
3 **CUMHACHT (IRE),** 5, b g Camacho—Soliza (IRE) **R & J Farnham,P Burns,S Gammond,F Street**
4 **FFOREST DANCER (IRE),** 5, b g Dahjee (USA)—Haven't A Notion **Mr G. S. Gammond**
5 **GENIETOILE (FR),** 5, b g Spider Flight (FR)—Olafane (FR) **ConyersJ&WO'ReillypPalmerProwtingRoddis**
6 **HAITI COULEURS (FR),** 6, b g Dragon Dancer—Inchala (FR) **The Brizzle Boys**
7 **HIS OSCAR (IRE),** 8, b g Oscar (IRE)—St Helans Bay (IRE) **Got There In the End Partnership**
8 **HOUSE OF STORIES (IRE),** 7, b br g Presenting—Liss Aris (IRE) **Conyers, O'Reilly, Clerkson, Zeffman**
9 **IDEFIX DE CIERGUES (FR),** 5, b br g Buck's Boum (FR)—
Caline de Ferbet (FR) **Hydes,Waters,Frobisher,Prowting&Palmer**
10 **INDIGO BOY (FR),** 5, b g Diamond Boy (FR)—Perle Irlandaise (FR) **Miss R. Curtis**
11 **KING CODI (IRE),** 6, b g Califet (FR)—Quintara (IRE) **Fforest Star Racing Ltd**
12 **LUBEAT FORAS (IRE),** 8, ch g Aizavoski (IRE)—Roomier (IRE) **Relentless Dreamers Racing**
13 **MAC'S LEGACY (IRE),** 6, b g Fame And Glory—Eurowinner (IRE) **Claire Lockett & Rebecca Curtis**
14 **MINELLA BOBO (IRE),** 10, gr g Oscar (IRE)—Line Kendie (FR) **Moran, Outhart, McDermott, Hyde & Hill**
15 **MONBARI (FR),** 5, b g Zanzibari (USA)—Mondovi (FR) **Miss R. Curtis**
16 **MR KATANGA (IRE),** 9, b g Flemensfirth (USA)—Pomme Tiepy (FR) **All About the Birch**
17 **NELSONS STAR (IRE),** 5, b g Mount Nelson—Real Revival (IRE) **Mr S Hubble, Mr M Doocey & Mr P Mayling**
18 **PATS FANCY (IRE),** 8, b g Oscar (IRE)—Pat's Darling (IRE) **Hydes,McDermott,Spencer,Frobisher & Lee**
19 **ROUGE DE L'QUEST (IRE),** 7, b g Fame And Glory—What A Bleu (IRE) **Mark Sherwood & Francis Reid**
20 **RUTHLESS ARTICLE (IRE),** 10, b g Definite Article—Lady Kamando **J Rymer R Farnham C Rymer J Farnham**
21 **SCRATCH CARD (IRE),** 4, ch g Galileo Gold—Fondled **Mrs E. A. M. Balding**
22 5, B g Sageburg (IRE)—The Right Thing (IRE) **Miss R. Curtis**
23 **WAYFINDER (IRE),** 9, br g Shantou (USA)—Sibury (IRE) **The Wayfinders**
24 **ZOFFALAY (IRE),** 5, b g Zoffany (IRE)—Layalee (IRE) **Miss R. Curtis**

Assistant Trainer: Paul Sheldrake.

---

117 MISS HELEN CUTHBERT, Brampton

Postal: **Woodlands, Cowranbridge, How Mill, Brampton, Cumbria, CA8 9LH**
Contacts: **PHONE 01228 560822 MOBILE 07879 634494**
EMAIL cuthbertracing@gmail.com

1 **JOSHUA R (IRE),** 6, b g Canford Cliffs (IRE)—Khobaraa **Miss H. E. Cuthbert**
2 **MR COCO BEAN (USA),** 9, b g Gio Ponti (USA)—Ing Ing (FR) **Miss H. E. Cuthbert**

---

118 MR LUKE DACE, Billingshurst

Postal: **Copped Hall Farm and Stud, Okehurst House, Okehurst Lane, Billingshurst, West Sussex, RH14 9HR**
Contacts: **MOBILE 07949 401085 FAX 01403 612176**
EMAIL lukedace@yahoo.co.uk WEBSITE www.lukedace.co.uk

1 **BROUGHTONS COMPASS,** 6, b g Henrythenavigator (USA)—Sayrianna **Mr B Pay**
2 **EXECUTIVE,** 5, b m Swiss Spirit—Stylistik **L. A. Dace**
3 **GAZZAH (FR),** 4, b g Olympic Glory (IRE)—Ysandre **Mr Richard L Page & Mr Luke Dace**
4 **KHURUMBI (IRE),** 4, b f The Gurkha (IRE)—Sharaarah (IRE) **L. A. Dace**
5 **KING CABO (USA),** 4, b br g Carpe Diem (USA)—Cabo Queen (CAN) **Prof D. J. Lawrence-Watt**
6 **SAPPERDEAN,** 4, gr ro g Adaay (IRE)—Beleave **The Hamptons Racing Partnership**
7 **YOUTHFUL KING,** 4, b g Fountain of Youth (IRE)—Lady Moscou (IRE) **Mr Richard L Page & Mr Luke Dace**

THREE-YEAR-OLDS

8 **GREY ROSETTA,** gr f Adaay (IRE)—Beleave **Mr R. L. Page**
9 **RED ROSETTA,** ch f Hawkbill (USA)—Stylistik **Mr R. L. Page**

Assistant Trainer: Mrs L Dace.

---

119 MR KEITH DALGLEISH, Carluke

Postal: **Belstane Racing Stables, Carluke, Lanarkshire, ML8 5HN**
Contacts: **PHONE 01555 773335**
EMAIL dalgleish.racing@outlook.com

1 **ABERAMA GOLD,** 6, b g Heeraat (IRE)—Nigella
2 **AIN'T NO SUNSHINE (IRE),** 7, b g Shantou (USA)—
Screaming Witness (IRE) **Middleham Park Racing XX & Partner**
3 **ALPINE SIERRA (IRE),** 5, br g Distorted Humor (USA)—Unaccompanied (IRE) **Mr J S Morrison**
4 **ALRIGHT SUNSHINE (IRE),** 8, b g Casamento (IRE)—Miss Gibraltar **Richard & Katherine Gilbert**
5 **BAEZ,** 4, b f Sixties Icon—Sinndarina (FR) **Mr J S Morrison**
6 **BELLE OF ANNANDALE (IRE),** 4, ch f Australia—Fountain of Honour (IRE) **Richard & Katherine Gilbert**
7 **BELTANE (IRE),** 4, ch g Fast Company (IRE)—Northern Affair (IRE) **Middleham Park Racing LXIV & Partner**
8 **BREGUET BOY (IRE),** 6, br g Requinto (IRE)—Holly Hawk (IRE) **Haxted Racing**
9 **CELESTIAL STAR (IRE),** 4, ch f Ribchester (IRE)—Praskovia (IRE) **Weldspec Glasgow Limited**
10 **CHICHESTER,** 6, b g Dansili—Havant **Sir Ian & Ms Catriona Good**
11 **CHOOKIE DUNEDIN,** 8, b g Epaulette (AUS)—Lady of Windsor (IRE) **Raeburn Brick Limited**
12 **DIOCLETIAN (IRE),** 8, b g Camelot—Saturday Girl **Mr J. K. McGarrity**
13 **EDWARD CORNELIUS (IRE),** 4, b c Bungle Inthejungle—Calorie **John Kelly & John McNeill**
14 **EL PICADOR (IRE),** 7, b g Dansili—West of Venus (USA) **Sir Ian & Ms Catriona Good**
15 **EVALUATION,** 5, b g Dubawi (IRE)—Estimate (IRE) **Sir Ian & Ms Catriona Good**
16 **FIRST ACCOUNT,** 9, b br g Malinas (GER)—Kind Nell **The County Set (Two)**
17 **FROM THE CLOUDS (FR),** 6, b g No Risk At All (FR)—Saffarona
18 **GARDE DES CHAMPS (IRE),** 7, b g Robin des Champs (FR)—La Reine de Riogh (IRE) **I. T. Buchanan**
19 **GIOIA CIECA (USA),** 5, b g Kitten's Joy (USA)—Dynacielo (USA) **Weldspec Glasgow Limited**
20 **GOMETRA GINTY (IRE),** 7, b m Morpheus—Silver Cache (USA) **Ken McGarrity & Partner**
21 **GOOD SHOW,** 4, b g Nathaniel (IRE)—Maleficent Queen **Weldspec Glasgow Limited**
22 **HAIZOOM,** 5, ch m Sea The Stars (IRE)—Sortita (GER) **Mr J S Morrison**
23 **HEIGHTS OF ABRAHAM (IRE),** 5, b g Starspangledbanner (AUS)—High Vintage (IRE) **Two Goldfish & A Balloon**
24 **HIGHWAY COMPANION (IRE),** 9, b g Milan—Niffyrann (FR) **Weldspec Glasgow Limited**
25 **HOWZER BLACK (IRE),** 7, br g Requinto (IRE)—Mattinata **Middleham Park Racing LXXVI**
26 **LADY LADE,** 4, b f Havana Gold (IRE)—Accolade **Partick Partnership**
27 **MI CAPRICHO (IRE),** 8, b g Elzaam (AUS)—Mavemacullen (IRE) **Mr C. Jones**
28 **MISTY AYR (IRE),** 4, b f Kodi Bear (IRE)—Rasana **Middleham Park Racing III & Partner**
29 **MORNING SUN (IRE),** 4, b g Muhaarar—Jadanna (IRE) **Richard & Katherine Gilbert**
30 **NOTIMEFORANOTHER (IRE),** 4, b g Time Test—Lyric Art (USA) **The Gilbert's & Mr Campbell**
31 **PAGE THREE (USA),** 4, b f Dialed In (USA)—Pin Up (IRE) **Weldspec Glasgow Limited**
32 **PERSUER,** 7, ch m Intello (GER)—Chase The Lady (USA) **Richard & Katherine Gilbert**

MR KEITH DALGLEISH - continued

33 **PRETTY BOUQUET (IRE),** 4, b f Champs Elysees—Catwalk Queen (IRE) **Mr & Mrs Paul & Clare Rooney**
34 **RAYMOND (IRE),** 8, b g Tobougg (IRE)—Crack The Kicker (IRE) **Richard & Katherine Gilbert**
35 **RELENTLESS SUN,** 5, b g Twilight Son—Riccoche (IRE) **Richard & Katherine Gilbert**
36 **SCARRIFF (IRE),** 5, ch m Dandy Man (IRE)—Maria Milena **Richard & Katherine Gilbert**
37 **SCOTTISH DANCER (IRE),** 4, b g Highland Reel (IRE)—Destalink **Richard & Katherine Gilbert**
38 **SEXTANT,** 8, b g Sea The Stars (IRE)—Hypoteneuse (IRE) **Richard & Katherine Gilbert**
39 **SOLDIER'S MINUTE,** 8, b g Raven's Pass (USA)—Hadba (IRE) **Weldspec Glasgow Limited**
40 **SUMMA PETO (USA),** 5, gr ro g Dialed In (USA)—Unbridled Gem (USA) **Weldspec Glasgow Limited**
41 **SURPRISE PICTURE (IRE),** 5, b g Kodiac—Lovely Surprise (IRE) **Mr E. M. Sutherland**
42 **TAXMEIFYOUCAN (IRE),** 9, b g Beat Hollow—Accounting **Sir Ian & Ms Catriona Good**
43 **THE THIN BLUE LINE (IRE),** 5, b br g Mehmas (IRE)—Rahlah **Middleham Park Racing LI & Partner**
44 **THERMOSCOPE (IRE),** 5, b g Galileo (IRE)—Viz (IRE) **Richard & Katherine Gilbert**
45 **TRICKY BUSINESS,** 4, ch g Hot Streak (IRE)—Juncea **Richard & Katherine Gilbert**
46 **VENTURA FLAME (IRE),** 6, b m Dandy Man (IRE)—
Kramer Drive (IRE) **Middleham Park Racing LXXXIII & Partner**
47 **VOLATILE ANALYST (USA),** 6, b g Distorted Humor (USA)—
Gentle Caroline (USA) **Richard Gilbert & Keith Dalgleish**
48 **WHAT'S THE STORY,** 9, b g Harbour Watch (IRE)—Spring Fashion (IRE) **Weldspec Glasgow Limited**

THREE-YEAR-OLDS

49 **AMOR VICTORIOUS (IRE),** b f Caravaggio (USA)—Honourably (IRE) **Weldspec Glasgow Limited**
50 **ANGEL FROM ABOVE (IRE),** b f Galileo Gold—Cartoon **The Brady Girls**
51 **DEBYDINKS (IRE),** ch g Dandy Man (IRE)—Absolute Music (USA) **Middleham Park Racing CVIII & Partner**
52 **IATO'S ANGEL (IRE),** ch f Footstepsinthesand—Ziggy's Secret **Middleham Park Racing XXXII & Partner**
53 **LOVELY LADY,** ch f Mastercraftsman (IRE)—Kylia (USA) **Mr F. Brady**
54 **PRINCE OF PILLO (IRE),** ch c Prince of Lir (IRE)—Lucky Omen (IRE) **Middleham Park Racing V & Partner**
55 **QUEENIE ROONEY,** b f Havana Gold (IRE)—Bounty Box **Mr & Mrs Paul & Clare Rooney**
56 **RORY THE CAT (IRE),** ch g Starspangledbanner (AUS)—Obligada (IRE) **Middleham Park Racing CIX & Partner**
57 B g Free Eagle (IRE)—Scatina (IRE) **Richard & Katherine Gilbert**
58 B f Saxon Warrior (JPN)—Wishing Star (IRE) **Richard & Katherine Gilbert**

TWO-YEAR-OLDS

59 B f 22/01 Havana Grey—Blue Lyric (Refuse To Bend (IRE)) (65000)
60 B c 19/03 Invincible Army (IRE)—Capomento (IRE) (Casamento (IRE)) (95000)
61 B f 13/02 Dark Angel (IRE)—Nigella (Band On The Run) (76030) **Weldspec Glasgow Limited**

Assistant Trainer: Kevin Dalgleish, **Racing Secretary:** Leanne Gordon.

---

120 MR HENRY DALY, Ludlow

Trainer did not wish details of their string to appear

---

121 MR PHILLIP DANDO, Peterston-Super-Ely

Postal: **Springfield Court, Peterston-Super-Ely, Cardiff, South Glamorgan, CF5 6LG**
Contacts: **PHONE 01446 760012 MOBILE 07872 965395**

1 **BEAU HAZE,** 10, b g Black Sam Bellamy (IRE)—Bella Haze **P. C. Dando**
2 **CHANTILLY HAZE,** 8, b m Black Sam Bellamy (IRE)—Bella Haze **P. C. Dando**
3 **SAM HAZE,** 9, b g Black Sam Bellamy (IRE)—Bella Haze **P. C. Dando**

MR PHILLIP DANDO - continued

4 **TARA HAZE,** 7, b m Kayf Tara—Bella Haze **P. C. Dando**

Assistant Trainer: Mrs Rebecca Davies.

---

122 MR VICTOR DARTNALL, Barnstaple

Postal: **Higher Shutscombe Farm, Charles, Brayford, Barnstaple, Devon, EX32 7PU**
Contacts: **PHONE 01598 710280 MOBILE 07974 374272 FAX 01598 710708**
EMAIL victordartnall@gmail.com WEBSITE www.victordartnallracing.com

1 **ARTHALOT (IRE),** 6, b g Camelot—Annina (IRE) **Thethrillofitall**
2 **ATJIMA (IRE),** 8, b m Mahler—Qui Plus Est (FR) **Mr N. Viney**
3 **AURIGNY MILL (FR),** 6, b g Diamond Boy (FR)—Fresh Princess (FR) **Mrs E. S. Weld**
4 **BACK YOURSELF (IRE),** 6, gr g Maxios—Katch Me Katie **Mr G. Bamby**
5 **BILINGUAL,** 6, b m Le Havre (IRE)—Downhill Dancer (IRE) **Miss K. M. George**
6 **EXMOOR EXPRESS (IRE),** 7, b g Sans Frontieres (IRE)—Blue Article (IRE) **The First Shutscombe Syndicate**
7 **GYPSY HILL,** 6, b m Blue Bresil (FR)—Minnie Hill (IRE) **Mrs L. M. Northover**
8 **HALDON HILL (IRE),** 10, b g Mahler—Qui Plus Est (FR) **Mr J. P. McManus**
9 **I MATTER (IRE),** 4, b br f Slade Power (IRE)—Piccola Sissi (IRE) **Hughes, McDaid K. George**
10 **ISLADAAY (IRE),** 4, b f Adaay (IRE)—Sun Angel (IRE) **Ashton & Dartnall**
11 **LHEBAYEB (GER),** 5, b m Alhebayeb (IRE)—Lady Gabrielle (IRE) **Boddy, George, Kilby, Oram & Partner**
12 **MINNIE ESCAPE,** 11, b m Getaway (GER)—Minnie Hill (IRE) **The Second Brayford Partnership**
13 **NATIVE MOON (IRE),** 5, ch g Sea Moon—Toye Native (IRE)
14 **POCKET TOO,** 5, b g Cannock Chase (USA)—Dance A Daydream **Ashton & Dartnall**
15 **PRIDE OF PARIS (IRE),** 5, b g Champs Elysees—Bincas Beauty (IRE) **Dallyn, De Wilde, Haggett, Metters, Yeo**
16 **RIVER BRAY (IRE),** 10, ch g Arakan (USA)—Cill Fhearga (IRE) **The River Bray Syndicate**
17 **RUN TO MILAN (IRE),** 11, b g Milan—Run Supreme (IRE) **Barber, Birchenhough, De Wilde**
18 **SALTA RESTA,** 4, bl f Brazen Beau (AUS)—Be Joyful (IRE) **Mrs J. Scrivens**

Assistant Trainer: G. A. Dartnall.

---

123 MR TRISTAN DAVIDSON, Carlisle

Postal: **Bellmount, Laversdale, Irthington, Carlisle, Cumbria, CA6 4PS**
Contacts: **MOBILE 07789 684290**

1 **ASKGARMOR (IRE),** 11, b g Ask—Karmafair (IRE) **Mr E. G. Tunstall**
2 4, B c Pether's Moon (IRE)—Bannow Storm (IRE)
3 **COCONUT BAY,** 4, b f Bated Breath—Tropicana Bay **Border Raiders**
4 **GREENGAGE (IRE),** 8, b m Choisir (AUS)—Empowermentofwomen (IRE) **Poker & Davidson**
5 **IRIS DANCER,** 5, b m Kodiac—Rainbow's Arch (IRE) **Auld Pals**
6 **IRISH SOVEREIGN (IRE),** 8, b g Getaway (GER)—Magdoodle (IRE) **Mr P. Drinkwater**
7 **NORSE REIVER,** 4, b f Norse Dancer (IRE)—Rev Up Ruby **R Robson-Tinsley & P & B Harwood**
8 **OUR ABSENT FRIENDS (IRE),** 5, ch g Camacho—Practicallyperfect (IRE) **Mr R. W. Hislop**
9 **RUBENESQUE (IRE),** 11, b m Getaway (GER)—Shouette (IRE) **Toby Noble & Andy Bell**
10 **SHANTOU MOON (IRE),** 6, b g Shantou (USA)—Emma Ami (IRE) **Mr P. Drinkwater**
11 **THORSDA,** 6, ch m Norse Dancer (IRE)—Wheyaye **Mrs V. S. Jackson**
12 **TOMORROW'S ANGEL,** 8, ch m Teofilo (IRE)—Funday **Gary Etheridge Tristan Davidson**
13 **UP THE TEMPO,** 5, ch g Belardo (IRE)—Paulinie **Mrs Hugh Fraser**
14 **YEEEAAH (IRE),** 4, gr g El Kabeir (USA)—Red Savina **J. T. Davidson**

THREE-YEAR-OLDS

15 **MAI ALWARD,** gr f Havana Grey—Livella Fella (IRE)

MR TRISTAN DAVIDSON - continued

Racing Secretary: Mrs Sharon McManus.

---

124 MR JOHN DAVIES, Darlington

Postal: **Denton Grange, Piercebridge, Darlington, County Durham, DL2 3TZ**
Contacts: **PHONE 01325 374366 MOBILE 07746 292782**
EMAIL johndavieshorses@live.co.uk WEBSITE www.johndaviesracing.com

1 **CORNELL,** 5, b g Cannock Chase (USA)—Tsarina Louise **The Red and White Stripes**
2 **HIGHJACKED,** 7, b g Dick Turpin (IRE)—Vera Richardson (IRE) **J. J. Davies**
3 **IDEAL DREAM,** 5, b m Cannock Chase (USA)—Croftamie **Ideal Breeding Ltd**
4 **SOUND OF JURA,** 5, br m Cannock Chase (USA)—Floradorado **J. J. Davies**

THREE-YEAR-OLDS

5 B f Havana Gold (IRE)—Code Cracker
6 **GARIFULLINA,** b f Mondialiste (IRE)—Croftamie **J. J. Davies**

---

125 MISS SARAH-JAYNE DAVIES, Leominster

Postal: **The Upper Withers, Hundred Lane, Kimbolton, Leominster, Herefordshire, HR6 0HZ**
Contacts: **PHONE 01584 711138 MOBILE 07779 797079**
EMAIL sarah@sjdracing.co.uk WEBSITE www.sjdracing.co.uk

1 **AUTUMN BLAZE,** 5, ch m Black Sam Bellamy (IRE)—Blurred Lines (IRE) **Mrs F. G. Alderson**
2 **BELLSHILL BEAUTY (IRE),** 4, ch f Decorated Knight—Ellbeedee (IRE) **Mr R. D. Bradford**
3 **BETTWYN,** 5, b m Black Sam Bellamy (IRE)—Kansas City (FR) **Michael & Lesley Wilkes**
4 **BLAZER'S MILL (IRE),** 9, b g Westerner—Creation (IRE) **Miss S. J. Davies**
5 **DAWN WONDER (IRE),** 6, b m Conduit (IRE)—Presentingatdawn (IRE) **Mr A. J. Gough**
6 **EQUUS MILLAR (IRE),** 10, b g Masterofthehorse (IRE)—Lets Get Busy (IRE) **Mrs J. N. Mansfield**
7 **EST ILLIC (IRE),** 9, b br g Court Cave (IRE)—Ten Friends (IRE) **Mr A. J. Gough**
8 **FAIR TO DREAM,** 10, b g Fair Mix (IRE)—Sahara's Dream **Miss S. J. Davies**
9 **FINAWN BAWN (IRE),** 10, b g Robin des Champs (FR)—Kayanti (IRE) **Miss S. J. Davies**
10 **FITZROY (IRE),** 9, b g Fame And Glory—Forces of Destiny (IRE) **Michael & Lesley Wilkes**
11 **FORT NELSON,** 6, b g Mount Nelson—Iron Butterfly **Moorland Racing & Mark Hammond**
12 **GAMBIE TIEP (FR),** 7, b g Zambezi Sun—Uitiepy (FR) **K. E. Stait**
13 **GREAT RIDLEY,** 5, b g Garswood—Blue Maisey **Mr A. J. Gough**
14 **HIGGS (IRE),** 10, b g Scorpion (IRE)—Captain Supreme (IRE) **Mr A. J. Gough**
15 **INVINCIBLE WISH (IRE),** 11, b g Vale of York (IRE)—Moonlight Wish (IRE) **Michael & Lesley Wilkes**
16 **JASEY (IRE),** 4, b g Holy Roman Emperor (IRE)—Euroceleb (IRE) **Withers Winners**
17 **JIMMY JIMMY (IRE),** 8, b h Robin des Champs (FR)—Asturienne **Miss S. J. Davies**
18 **LUIS VAN ZANDT (IRE),** 9, b g Scorpion (IRE)—Banrion Na Boinne **Moorland Racing**
19 **MIGHT DO EMERY,** 5, b m Pether's Moon (IRE)—Materiality **Moorland Racing**
20 **NINE NINE NINE,** 6, ch g Soldier of Fortune (IRE)—Reves d'Amour (IRE) **Moorland Racing & P R Whilock**
21 **NO QUARTER ASKED (IRE),** 8, b g Jeremy (USA)—Louis's Teffia (IRE) **Mr A. J. Gough**
22 **POWER GENERATION (IRE),** 4, b g Profitable (IRE)—Dame Alicia (IRE) **Mr R. D. Bradford**
23 **ROYAL ACT,** 11, br g Royal Anthem (USA)—Native's Return (IRE) **Moorland Racing**
24 **TIKA MOON (IRE),** 6, b g Casamento (IRE)—Trikala (IRE) **Miss S. J. Davies**
25 **VOLATORE,** 7, b g Lucarno (USA)—Rocking Robin **Quadriga Racing**
26 **WHYZZAT,** 5, b g Dark Angel (IRE)—Whazzis **Moorland Racing**

MISS SARAH-JAYNE DAVIES - continued

Head Man: Ryan Bradford.

NH Jockey: William Kennedy.

---

126 MISS JO DAVIS, Highworth

Postal: **Eastrop, Highworth, Wiltshire, SN6 7PP**
Contacts: **PHONE 01793 762232 MOBILE 07879 811535 FAX 01793 762232**
EMAIL jo@jodavisracing.com WEBSITE www.jodavisracing.com

1 **DEMOCRITUS,** 5, gr g Universal (IRE)—Nant Y Mynydd **Tony Worth & Vic Bedley**
2 **DREAMINGOFASONG,** 7, b m Epaulette (AUS)—No Frills (IRE) **Mrs P. M. Brown**
3 **FIAMETTE (IRE),** 5, ch m Free Eagle (IRE)—High Reserve **Mr C. Butler**
4 **GREAT COMMISSION,** 5, b g Nathaniel (IRE)—Duchess of Gazeley (IRE) **The Unstoppables**
5 **IT'S FOR ALAN,** 10, b g Multiplex—Miss Keck **Miss J. S. Davis**
6 **JOLIE BAIE (FR),** 4, b f Gris de Gris (IRE)—Belle Sauvage (FR) **Jo Davis & Chris Butler**
7 **MORVAL (FR),** 5, b br g Morandi (FR)—Valley Girl (FR) **Jo Davis & Chris Butler**
8 **PIANISSIMO,** 7, b g Teofilo (IRE)—Perfect Note **The Unstoppables**
9 **UNSTOPPABLE (FR),** 5, b g Morandi (FR)—Perdicilla (FR) **The Unstoppables**

THREE-YEAR-OLDS

10 **CEEJAYBE,** ch g Free Eagle (IRE)—Marmande (IRE) **Mr C. Butler**

Assistant Trainer: Kendall Dickinson.

---

127 MISS KATHARINE DAVIS, Reading

Postal: **Brewery Fields Farm, Southend, Reading, Berkshire, RG7 6JP**
EMAIL katharinedavisracing@gmail.com

1 **CHANTECLER,** 12, b g Authorized (IRE)—Snow Goose **Mr D. White**
2 **GRAPEVINE (IRE),** 10, b g Lilbourne Lad (IRE)—High Vintage (IRE)
3 **PRINCE DES MALVAUX (FR),** 7, b g Martaline—Fanny Princess (FR) **Mr D. White**
4 **TELLEROFTALES (IRE),** 8, b g Yeats (IRE)—Sweetbitter (FR) **Mr D. White**
5 **WHISKEY TIMES (IRE),** 10, br m Olden Times—Tomcoole Oscar (IRE) **Mr D. White**

---

128 MR ANTHONY DAY, Hinckley

Postal: **Wolvey Fields Farm, Coalpit Lane, Wolvey, Hinckley, Leicestershire, LE10 3HD**

1 **FAMOUS OISIN (IRE),** 7, br g Famous Name—Peig Alainn (IRE) **Mrs K. D. Day**
2 **GETTYSBURGH (IRE),** 8, b m Presenting—Rhapsody In Blue (GER) **Mrs K. D. Day**
3 **NOBLE RECALL,** 4, b g Telescope (IRE)—Fluffy Clouds **Mrs K. D. Day**
4 **STRIPE OF HONOUR (IRE),** 10, b g Court Cave (IRE)—Miss Top (IRE) **Mrs K. D. Day**

129 MR WILLIAM DE BEST-TURNER, Lambourn

Postal: **Delamere Stables, Baydon Road, Lambourn, Berkshire, RG17 8NT**
Contacts: **HOME 01249 813850 PHONE 01249 811944 MOBILE 07977 910779**
EMAIL debestracing@hotmail.co.uk

1 **CALGARY TIGER,** 8, b g Tiger Groom—Sachiko **W. de Best-Turner**
2 **MOLLY'S ANGEL,** 6, ch m Arvico (FR)—Sterling Moll **Debestracing**
3 **NELSON'S HILL,** 13, b g Mount Nelson—Regal Step **Debestracing**
4 **TIGER PRINT,** 8, b m Tiger Groom—Maylan (IRE) **Debestracing**

Assistant Trainer: Mrs I. de Best.

130 MR ED DE GILES, Ledbury

Postal: **Lilly Hall Farm, Little Marcle, Ledbury, Herefordshire, HR8 2LD**
Contacts: **PHONE 01531 637369 MOBILE 07811 388345**
EMAIL ed@eddegilesracing.com WEBSITE www.eddegilesracing.com

1 **AE FOND KISS,** 4, b f Time Test—Aurora Gray **Simon Treacher, Robert Colvin & Partner**
2 **ALPINE STROLL,** 5, b g Nathaniel (IRE)—Kammaan **The LAM Partnership**
3 **CHIFA (IRE),** 6, gr g Gutaifan (IRE)—Inca Trail (USA) **Mr J. P. Carrington**
4 **FITZROVIA,** 8, br g Poet's Voice—Pompey Girl **Clarissa Casdgali & Partners**
5 **GOODISON GIRL,** 4, b f Helmet (AUS)—Cloudchaser (IRE) **The Tully Family**
6 **KALAMITY KITTY,** 5, b m Cityscape—Lucky Breeze (IRE) **Fair Wind Partnership & Partner**
7 **MACON BELLE,** 4, b f Due Diligence (USA)—Disco Ball **Woodham Walter Partnership**
8 **PRIVATE BRYAN,** 4, b g Helmet (AUS)—Lucky Breeze (IRE) **Life of Bryan Partnership**
9 **RUNNER BEAN,** 4, b f Heeraat (IRE)—Miss Meticulous **The LAM Partnership**
10 **TREACHEROUS,** 9, b g Paco Boy (IRE)—Black Baroness **Woodham Walter Partnership**
11 **TROJAN TRUTH,** 4, b g Ulysses (IRE)—Verity **Woodham Walter Partnership**
12 **URBAN FOREST,** 5, ch g Cityscape—Tijuca (IRE) **Friends In Low Places**

THREE-YEAR-OLDS

13 **ALPHA FEMALE,** b f Sea The Moon (GER)—Kammaan **The LAM Partnership**
14 **RACING DEMON,** b g Muhaarar—Whatdoiwantthatfor (IRE) **John Manser & Simon Treacher**
15 **TWO PLUS TWO (IRE),** ch g Free Eagle (IRE)—Pivotal's Princess (IRE) **The LAM Partnership**

TWO-YEAR-OLDS

16 Gr g 28/04 El Kabeir (USA)—Cloudchaser (IRE) (Red Ransom (USA))
17 B c 13/02 El Kabeir (USA)—Lucky Breeze (IRE) (Key of Luck (USA))

131 MR GEOFFREY DEACON, Compton

Postal: **Hamilton Stables, Hockham Road, Compton, Newbury, Berkshire, RG20 6QJ**
Contacts: **MOBILE 07967 626757**
EMAIL geoffdeacon5@gmail.com WEBSITE www.geoffreydeacontraining.com

1 **CAPTAIN RYAN,** 12, b g Captain Gerrard (IRE)—Ryan's Quest (IRE) **Geoffrey Deacon Racing Crew**
2 **CHARLIE MAGRI,** 7, b g Midnight Legend—Psychosis **Reed Truan & Spershott**
3 **DARK CROCODILE (IRE),** 8, b g Dark Angel (IRE)—Heaven's Vault (IRE) **Mr M. D. Drake**
4 **DOLLY DRAKE,** 5, b m Havana Gold (IRE)—Farletti **Mr M. D. Drake**
5 6, Gr m Heeraat (IRE)—Elderberry **Geoffrey Deacon Racing Crew**
6 **ENCHANTEE (IRE),** 6, b m Gale Force Ten—Love Valentine (IRE) **Geoffrey Deacon Racing Crew**
7 **HONOURS,** 5, b m Exceed And Excel (AUS)—Roses For The Lady (IRE) **Allinc Property Services**

MR GEOFFREY DEACON - continued

8 **JUST ALBERT,** 6, gr ro g Toronado (IRE)—Deire Na Sli (IRE) **Mr and Mrs Duckett**
9 7, B m Born To Sea (IRE)—Khajool (IRE) **Geoffrey Deacon Racing Crew**
10 **LA ROCA DEL FUEGO (IRE),** 7, br g Rock of Gibraltar (IRE)—Reign (IRE) **Mr M. D. Drake**
11 **MEMBERRY,** 4, gr g Heeraat (IRE)—Glastonberry **Let Me Tell You**
12 **NIGHT N GALE (IRE),** 7, b m Gale Force Ten—Hadya (IRE) **Geoffrey Deacon Racing Crew**
13 **WUDASHUDACUDA,** 5, b h Awtaad (IRE)—Chicita Banana **Geoffrey Deacon Racing Crew**
14 **YOULLOVEMEWHENIWIN (IRE),** 5, b g Cable Bay (IRE)—Ventura Falcon (IRE) **Allinc Property Services**

THREE-YEAR-OLDS

15 **CAPTAIN RED BLAZER,** b c Captain Gerrard (IRE)—Aunt Minnie **Hearty Racing**

Assistant Trainer: Sally Duckett.

---

132 MR HARRY DERHAM, Boxford

Postal: **Upper Farm House, High Street, Boxford, RG20 8BR**
Contacts: **PHONE 07808 331034**
EMAIL Office@harryderhamracing.com

1 **ANY BISCUITS (IRE),** 6, b g Westerner—Topathistle (IRE) **The Oh Crumbs Syndicate**
2 **BELLA CIVENA (IRE),** 4, ch f Mount Nelson—Civena (IRE) **Mr G. Snell**
3 **BEYOND REDEMPTION (IRE),** 9, b g Court Cave (IRE)—Hopeful Gleam (IRE) **Beyond Redemption Syndicate**
4 4, B g Flemensfirth (USA)—Black Rock Lady (IRE) **Mr H. Redknapp**
5 **DARGIANNINI (IRE),** 8, b g Fame And Glory—You Take Care (IRE) **Mr A. D. Mitchell**
6 **FIDELIO VALLIS (FR),** 8, b g Saint des Saints (FR)—Quora Vallis (FR) **Mr J. D. L. Gregory**
7 **FOUROFAKIND (IRE),** 4, b br g Make Believe—In The House (IRE) **Cleeks Racing Syndicate**
8 **GAME WINNER (FR),** 7, br g Diamond Boy (FR)—Quelle Eria (FR) **JDL Racing Club**
9 **HARD FROST (FR),** 6, b g Silver Frost (IRE)—Lottie Belle (FR) **The Tail Waggers Syndicate**
10 **HELENN CLERMONT (FR),** 6, b br m Cokoriko (FR)—Coco de Clermont (FR) **Lady F. Sutton**
11 **IL VA DE SOI (FR),** 5, gr g Gris de Gris (IRE)—Vara des Champs (FR) **The Lubricators**
12 **IRISH FORTUNE (IRE),** 4, b g Soldier of Fortune (IRE)—The Blarney Rose (IRE) **The Dominae**
13 **MONTYS MEDOC (IRE),** 7, b g Westerner—Kilbarry Medoc (IRE) **Insurance Friends**
14 **NORDIC TIGER (FR),** 4, b g Choeur du Nord (FR)—Tigresse Rose (FR) **Harry Derham Racing Club**
15 **PRINCE NINO (FR),** 6, ch g It's Gino (GER)—Down On My Knees (FR) **Midwicket Cowboys**
16 **PUFFIN BAY,** 6, b m Blue Bresil (FR)—Miss Rocco **Mr C. T. Pelham**
17 **SALVATORE (GER),** 4, ch g Helmet (AUS)—Salve Sardegna (IRE) **Mr Browns Boys**
18 **SEELOTMOREBUSINESS (IRE),** 8, b g Sholokhov (IRE)—Land of Pride (IRE) **Mrs J. Derham**
19 **SHARED,** 4, b g Almanzor (FR)—Between Us **Mr C. A. Donlon**
20 **THUNDER N LIGHTNIN (IRE),** 5, b g Alkaadhem—Dranamol (IRE) **Lady Sutton & Caroline Sutton**
21 **VISION OF HOPE,** 4, b f Mastercraftsman (IRE)—Utopian Dream **Mr G. R. D. Boughey**

---

133 MISS HARRIET DICKIN, Bourton-on-the-Water

Postal: **Bourton Hill Farm, Bourton Hill, Bourton-on-the-Water, Cheltenham, Gloucestershire, GL54 2LF**
Contacts: **PHONE 07515 280799**
EMAIL harrietdd1@gmail.com

1 **BALLINSLEA BRIDGE (IRE),** 11, b g Pierre—Feelin' Looser (IRE) **Robin Dickin Racing Club**
2 **CHAIRMAN FITZ (IRE),** 5, b g Califet (FR)—Dawson's Corner (IRE) **Matt Fitzgerald, Alan Waller Dave Gillet**
3 **CHEER'S DELBOY (IRE),** 10, ch g Golan (IRE)—Lindy Lou **Just 4 Fun**
4 **EL DIABLO (IRE),** 7, gr g Cloudings (IRE)—Mayfly **The Cocoa Nuts & The Tricksters**

MISS HARRIET DICKIN - continued

5 **GALACTIC POWER (IRE),** 13, ch g Gamut (IRE)—Celtic Peace (IRE) **Robin Dickin Racing Club**
6 **GETAWAY GWEN (IRE),** 7, b m Getaway (GER)—Native Caroline (IRE) **N. J. Allen**
7 **HOOKY STREET (IRE),** 7, ch g Shirocco (GER)—Academy Miss (IRE) **The Goodies & Tricksters & Mr D Gillett**
8 **KINGOFTHESWINGERZ (IRE),** 4, b g Diamond Boy (FR)—Miss Baloo (IRE) **Albermarle Racing**
9 **MOON OVER GERMANY (IRE),** 12, ch g Germany (USA)—Elea Moon (IRE) **The Moggy Syndicate**
10 **MR PALMTREE (IRE),** 10, gr g Robin des Pres (FR)—Mattys Joy (IRE) **The Cocoa Nuts & The Tricksters**
11 **PESCATORIUS (IRE),** 4, ch g Getaway (GER)—Lisdaleen (IRE) **Mrs R. Campbell Hill**
12 **PHOEBUS LESCRIBAA (FR),** 11, b g Policy Maker (IRE)—Mia Lescribaa (FR) **Medbourne Racing**
13 **ROBINS FIELD (IRE),** 8, b g Robin des Champs (FR)—Sweet Poli (IRE) **Robin Dickin Racing Club**
14 **SOFIA'S ROCK (FR),** 9, b g Rock of Gibraltar (IRE)—Princess Sofia (UAE) **Matt FitzGerald and The Songsters**
15 **THIEVING GAP (IRE),** 5, b g Califet (FR)—Innisrush Eden (IRE) **The Buddies**
16 **VICTORY CLUB (IRE),** 6, b br g Soldier of Fortune (IRE)—La Shalak (IRE) **Miss H. Dickin**
17 **WALKINTHECOTSWOLDS (IRE),** 4, b f Walk In The Park (IRE)—
Blueberry Bramble (IRE) **Raqui Ch/Sarah Waller/Petew/Daveh/Amyc**
18 **WILLIAMDECONQUEROR,** 7, b g Native Ruler—Dancing Daffodil **Mrs M A Cooper & Mrs C M Dickin**

---

134 MR JOHN DIXON, Carlisle

Postal: **Moorend, Thursby, Carlisle, Cumbria, CA5 6QP**
Contacts: **PHONE 01228 711019**

1 **CAPTAIN ZEBO (IRE),** 11, b g Brian Boru—Waydale Hill **Mrs S. F. Dixon**
2 **CROFTON LANE,** 17, b g And Beyond (IRE)—Joyful Imp
3 **JOYFUL BE,** 18, ch m And Beyond (IRE)—Joyful Imp
4 **PALM BEACH (IRE),** 6, b g Galileo (IRE)—Alta Anna (FR) **Mrs S. F. Dixon**
5 **PISTOL (IRE),** 14, b g High Chaparral (IRE)—Alinea (USA) **Mrs S. F. Dixon**
6 **PRESENCE FELT (IRE),** 15, br g Heron Island (IRE)—Faeroe Isle (IRE) **Mrs S. F. Dixon**
7 **ROAD TO ROSLEY,** 6, b g Millenary—Ballela Road (IRE) **Mrs S. F. Dixon**

Amateur Jockey: Mr J. J. Dixon.

---

135 MR SCOTT DIXON, Retford

Postal: **Haygarth House Stud, Haygarth House, Babworth, Retford, Nottinghamshire, DN22 8ES**
Contacts: **PHONE 01777 869079, 01777 701818, 01777 869300 MOBILE 07976 267019**
EMAIL scottdixon1987@hotmail.com, mrsyvettedixon@gmail.com WEBSITE www.scottdixonracing.com

1 **A PINT OF BEAR (IRE),** 5, gr g Kodi Bear (IRE)—Heart of An Angel **The Bear Partnership**
2 **AHLAWI,** 5, ch g Shamardal (USA)—Lovely Pass (IRE) **Chappell Dixon Tylicki**
3 5, B m Kodi Bear (IRE)—Al Jamal
4 **AL TILAL (IRE),** 4, ch f Anjaal—Anythingknappen (IRE) **Wolverhampton Racing Club**
5 4, B c Aeroplane—Always Roses
6 **AMBER DEW,** 4, b f Showcasing—Roxy Star (IRE) **Chappell & Dixon**
7 **BANANA,** 4, b f Aclaim (IRE)—Bazzana **Dixon , Mahony L Bond**
8 6, Gr h Aeroplane—Bella Sofia
9 **BROOMY LAW,** 5, b g Gleneagles (IRE)—Hooray **Wolverhampton Racing Club**
10 5, B m Pride of Dubai (AUS)—Camille's Secret (FR) **The Scott Dixon Racing Partnership**
11 **CANDY WARHOL (USA),** 4, b g Twirling Candy (USA)—Costume **The Bear Partnership**
12 **CAPTAIN'S BAR,** 4, b g Showcasing—Roxie Lot **Brennan , Dixon , Wright**
13 **CAPTAINHUGHJAMPTON,** 4, ch g Mondialiste (IRE)—Sibaya **Ian Buckley & Ben Buckley**
14 **CATESBY,** 6, b g Slade Power (IRE)—Bonfire Heart **The Scott Dixon Racing Partnership**
15 **COAST,** 4, b f Aclaim (IRE)—Rio's Cliffs **Southwell Racing Club**
16 **COBH KID,** 6, b g Kyllachy—Never A Quarrel (IRE) **Paul J Dixon Mr J Wylam & Mrs C J Wylam**
17 **CONSERVATIVE (IRE),** 4, b g Churchill (IRE)—Fairy Dancer (IRE) **Coral Racing Club**
18 **COUNTRY CHARM,** 5, b m Charming Thought—Alushta **Southwell Racing Club**
19 **CRACKLING (IRE),** 7, b g Vale of York (IRE)—Almatlaie (USA) **The Scott Dixon Racing Partnership**

MR SCOTT DIXON - continued

20 **DARK SHOT,** 10, b g Acclamation—Dark Missile **Chappell Rose & Radford**
21 **EBURY,** 7, ch g Iffraaj—Alabelle **P. J. Dixon**
22 **FEEL THE THUNDER,** 7, b g Milk It Mick—Totally Trusted **Ne-chance & Dixon**
23 **FINE WINE (FR),** 6, b g Dream Ahead (USA)—Mulled Wine (FR) **Dixon Brennan Mahony & Partners**
24 **GENTLY SPOKEN (IRE),** 6, b gr m Gutaifan (IRE)—Always Gentle (IRE) **The Scott Dixon Racing Partnership**
25 **GHARBEYIH,** 4, b f Oasis Dream—Sharqeyih **Mr S. E. Chappell**
26 **GIOGIOBBO,** 10, b h Bahamian Bounty—Legnani **ARC Racing Syndicate**
27 **GOSSIP,** 6, b m Exceed And Excel (AUS)—Al Sharood **ARC Racing Club**
28 **GYPSY WHISPER,** 6, b m Helmet (AUS)—Secret Insider (USA) **Mr P. Wright-Bevans**
29 **HARBOUR VISION,** 8, gr g Harbour Watch (IRE)—Holy Nola (USA) **Southwell Racing Club**
30 **HARMONIOUS,** 6, b br g New Approach (IRE)—Clear Voice (USA) **The Scott Dixon Racing Partnership**
31 **HEADLAND,** 7, b g Harbour Watch (IRE)—Bazzana **ARC Racing Club**
32 **KING OF YORK (IRE),** 4, b g Kingman—Archangel Gabriel (USA) **Baker , Dixon , Chappell & Cope**
33 **KISSES OF FIRE (IRE),** 4, b f Mehmas (IRE)—Pearly Brooks **Wolverhampton Racing Club**
34 **KITTEN'S DREAM,** 6, b g Kitten's Joy (USA)—Strathnaver **Mr McSharry & Southwell Racing Club**
35 **KODI GOLD (IRE),** 5, b g Kodi Bear (IRE)—Labisa (IRE) **Southwell Racing Club**
36 5, B m Fountain of Youth (IRE)—Kyllarney
37 5, Ch h Monsieur Bond (IRE)—La Capriosa **Paul J Dixon Mr J Wylam & Mrs C J Wylam**
38 **LIGHT UP OUR STARS (IRE),** 7, b g Rip Van Winkle (IRE)—
Shine Like A Star **Paul J Dixon Mr J Wylam & Mrs C J Wylam**
39 **MARNIE JAMES,** 8, b g Camacho—Privy Garden (IRE) **Redknapp Dixon Chappell Baker**
40 **MAY THE SIXTH,** 6, b m Mayson—Six Wives **Sexy Six Partnership**
41 **MOTAGALLY,** 7, b g Swiss Spirit—Gilt Linked **Baker , Dixon , Chappell & Cope**
42 **MUDLAHHIM (IRE),** 7, b g Tamayuz—So Sweet (IRE) **Southwell Racing Club**
43 **MYKONOS ST JOHN,** 6, b g Swiss Spirit—Royal Pardon **L Bond, R Matheson & Partner**
44 **ONE NIGHT STAND,** 6, b g Swiss Spirit—Tipsy Girl **Chappell & Dixon**
45 **PENWAY (IRE),** 4, b f Twilight Son—She's A Worldie (IRE) **Mr S. E. Chappell**
46 **PERSEVERANTS (FR),** 5, b g Zoffany (IRE)—Perle Rare (USA) **Ryan , Chappell & Dixon**
47 **POET,** 4, b g Kodiac—Swiss Diva **Wolverhampton Racing Club**
48 **POP FAVORITE,** 5, br g Fastnet Rock (AUS)—Soundstrings **Wolverhampton Racing Club**
49 **REBEL REDEMPTION,** 6, gr g Lethal Force (IRE)—Tempting **Southwell Racing Club**
50 **ROSEHILL (IRE),** 4, ch g Australia—Elbereth **The Scott Dixon Racing Partnership**
51 **SAMARA STAR,** 5, b m Adaay (IRE)—Starlight Walk **Southwell Racing Club**
52 **SEA FERN,** 5, b m Acclamation—Scots Fern **Southwell Racing Club**
53 **SEVEN BROTHERS (IRE),** 5, b g Slade Power (IRE)—Ihtifal **Mr L. Ryan**
54 **SHACKABOOAH,** 6, b g Swiss Spirit—Ginger Cookie **The Scott Dixon Racing Partnership**
55 **SHAW PARK (IRE),** 4, b g Aclaim (IRE)—Waterways (IRE) **Wright Bevans & Dixon**
56 4, B f Aclaim (IRE)—Simballina (IRE)
57 **SIX O' HEARTS,** 4, b g Finjaan—Six Wives **Sexy Six Partnership**
58 **SOCIOLOGIST (FR),** 8, ch g Society Rock (IRE)—Fabiola (GER) **Rob Massheder, A J Turton & Partners**
59 **SYCAMORE (IRE),** 6, b g Kingman—Scarborough Fair **P Dixon & A Turton**
60 **TANGLEWOOD TALES,** 5, ch g Nathaniel (IRE)—Camdora (IRE) **The Farnworth Secret Circle**
61 **TERUNTUM STAR (FR),** 11, ch g Dutch Art—Seralia **Mrs E. Jepson**
62 **THEOTHERSIDE (IRE),** 6, br m Dandy Man (IRE)—New Magic (IRE) **Homecroft Wealth Racing & Partners**
63 **TOM TULLIVER,** 6, b g Hot Streak (IRE)—Belle Isle **Wolverhampton Racing Club**
64 **VALENTINE BLUES (IRE),** 6, gr m Clodovil (IRE)—Grecian Artisan (IRE) **Wolverhampton Racing Club**
65 **VALORANT,** 5, b m Showcasing—Comeback Queen **Turton Rhodes Bond Massheder**
66 **VISIBILITY (IRE),** 6, b g Raven's Pass (USA)—Cry Pearl (USA) **Paul J Dixon Mr J Wylam & Mrs C J Wylam**
67 **ZARGUN (GER),** 8, b g Rock of Gibraltar (IRE)—Zenaat **Sexy Six Partnership**

THREE-YEAR-OLDS

68 **CREATE (IRE),** b f Harry Angel (IRE)—Patent Joy (IRE) **The Scott Dixon Racing Partnership**
69 B f Master Carpenter (IRE)—Grass Green
70 **LIL WADE (IRE),** b g Dandy Man (IRE)—Wu Zetian **Bond Dixon Matheson**
71 B g Twilight Son—Never A Quarrel (IRE)
72 **PEDRAR (FR),** b f Pedro The Great (USA)—Just Another Day (FR) **Baker , Cloran , Chappell & Dixon**
73 **ROSE KING (IRE),** b c Tasleet—Chrissycross (IRE) **Mr S. E. Chappell**
74 **VERYGOOD VERYNICE (IRE),** b c Mehmas (IRE)—Taraba (IRE)

136 MRS ROSE DOBBIN, Alnwick

Postal: **South Hazelrigg Farm, Chatton, Alnwick, Northumberland, NE66 5RZ**
Contacts: **PHONE 01668 215151, 01668 215395 MOBILE 07969 993563 FAX 01668 215114**
EMAIL hazelriggracing1@btconnect.com WEBSITE www.rosedobbinracing.co.uk

1 **AAZZA (IRE),** 7, b m Beat Hollow—Kalygarde (FR) **Helen Ray & Isabel Tebay**
2 **CAILIN DEARG (IRE),** 8, ch m Getaway (GER)—Lepidina (IRE) **Jacobs,Tebay & Dobbin**
3 **CAPTAIN QUINT (IRE),** 7, b g Flemensfirth (USA)—Vics Miller (IRE) **Mr & Mrs Duncan Davidson**
4 **CHOSEN FLAME (IRE),** 11, b g Well Chosen—Flaming Misty (IRE) **Mrs R. Dobbin**
5 **CLIFFS OF DOONEEN (IRE),** 8, b g Galileo (IRE)—Devoted To You (IRE) **Mrs Dobbin & The Dimhorns**
6 **COSMIC OUTLAW (IRE),** 7, b g Arctic Cosmos (USA)—Golden Moro (IRE) **The Friday Lions 2**
7 **DO NOT DISTURB (IRE),** 10, b g Mahler—Galbertstown Run (IRE) **Mr & Mrs Duncan Davidson**
8 **ELMLEY LOVETT (IRE),** 6, b m Elusive Pimpernel (USA)—Blue Bell Walk (IRE)
9 **ESPOIR MORIVIERE (FR),** 9, ch g Saddex—Sagesse Moriviere (FR) **Dickson, Dobbin & Ray**
10 **FETE CHAMPETRE (IRE),** 8, b g Robin des Champs (FR)—John's Eliza (IRE) **Mr & Mrs Duncan Davidson**
11 **FIRTH OF FORTH (IRE),** 7, b g Flemensfirth (USA)—Gypsy Mo Chara (IRE) **Mark & Caroline Hunter**
12 **FOREVA ALFIE (IRE),** 5, b g Arcadio (GER)—Chitty Bang Bang (IRE) **Mr R. Roberts**
13 **GENTLEMAN DE MAI (FR),** 7, b g Saddler Maker (IRE)—Ula de Mai (FR) **Mr & Mrs Duncan Davidson**
14 **GET WITH IT (IRE),** 8, b g Getaway (GER)—Listening (IRE) **Mr & Mrs Duncan Davidson**
15 **HERE COMES THE MAN (IRE),** 8, b g Flemensfirth (USA)—Nifty Nuala (IRE) **Mrs R. Dobbin**
16 **HITMAN FRED (IRE),** 10, b g Getaway (GER)—Garravagh Lass (IRE) **The Friday Lions 2**
17 **IWA (FR),** 5, b br g Free Port Lux—Anavera (GER) **M. S. Hunter**
18 **JACK DEVINE (IRE),** 11, b g Kalanisi (IRE)—Sybil Says (IRE) **Roger Brown & Lizzy Annett**
19 **LE CHEVAL NOIR (IRE),** 9, b g Le Fou (IRE)—Bonny Lass **The Gathering**
20 **LIMERICK LEADER (FR),** 6, b g Joshua Tree (IRE)—Out Law d'Oc (FR) **Mr & Mrs Duncan Davidson**
21 **MISTER FREDDIE,** 7, b g Black Sam Bellamy (IRE)—Amaretto Rose **Ian Macconnachie & Barry Smith**
22 **MONFASS (IRE),** 12, b g Trans Island—Ajo Green (IRE) **Mrs Dobbin & The Dimhorns**
23 **OKAVANGO DELTA (IRE),** 7, b g Ocovango—Court My Eye **One For the Road Flower**
24 **PATS DREAM (IRE),** 6, b g Getaway (GER)—Ice Princess (IRE) **J. M. & Mrs M. R. Edwardson**
25 **RAE DES CHAMPS (IRE),** 6, ch m Robin des Champs (FR)—Dani Salamanca (IRE) **Mr & Mrs Duncan Davidson**
26 **RATH AN IUIR (IRE),** 10, b g Flemensfirth (USA)—Amathea (FR) **Mr & Mrs Duncan Davidson**
27 **ROCKONSOPH (IRE),** 6, ch m Notnowcato—Fromthecloudsabove (IRE) **Mr & Mrs Duncan Davidson**
28 **SEVEN EYE BRIDGE (IRE),** 8, b g Sans Frontieres (IRE)—Woodland Path (IRE) **Mr J. A. F. Filmer-Wilson**
29 **SHANBALLY ROSE (IRE),** 9, b m Court Cave (IRE)—Amy's Song (IRE) **Mrs C Hunter & Mr & Mrs M Edwardson**
30 **SHE'S A STEAL (IRE),** 6, b m Flemensfirth (USA)—Thanks Awfully (IRE) **Mr & Mrs J. Morrison-Bell**
31 **SLANELOUGH (IRE),** 11, b g Westerner—Tango Lady (IRE) **Miss J. Matterson & Mrs D. Davidson**
32 **THE PLAYER QUEEN (IRE),** 7, b m Yeats (IRE)—Seductive Dance **Mr & Mrs Duncan Davidson**
33 **WHELANS BRIDGE (IRE),** 7, b g Finsceal Fior (IRE)—Saintly Wish (USA) **Ian Macconnachie & Rose Dobbin**
34 **WILD POLLY (IRE),** 9, ch m Mahler—Dalzenia (FR) **Ms Borders Racing Club & Ronnie Jacobs**
35 **WORCESTER PEARMAIN,** 13, b m Beat All (USA)—Granoski Gala **Mr & Mrs Duncan Davidson**

Assistant Trainer: Tony Dobbin.

NH Jockey: Craig Nichol.

---

137 MR ASHLEY DODGSON, Thirsk

Postal: **Southerby House, Catton, Thirsk, North Yorkshire, YO7 4SQ**

1 **MR DEALER (IRE),** 11, b g Mr Dinos (IRE)—Vera Glynn (IRE) **Mrs F. M. G. Dodgson**

138 MR MICHAEL DODS, Darlington

Postal: **Denton Hall Farm, Piercebridge, Darlington, County Durham, DL2 3TY**
Contacts: **HOME 01325 374270 MOBILE 07860 411590, 07773 290830, 07590 048619 FAX 01325 374020**
EMAIL dods@michaeldodsracing.co.uk WEBSITE www.michaeldodsracing.co.uk

1 **ABRUZZO MIA,** 6, b g Bated Breath—Serenata Mia **Mrs H. I. S. Calzini**
2 **ALETHIOMETER (FR),** 4, b f Aclaim (IRE)—Live Love Laugh (FR) **Mrs C. Mr D Stone & Mrs C Dods**
3 **ARCH MOON,** 6, b g Sea The Moon (GER)—Archduchess **Mr Allan Mcluckie & Mr M. J. K. Dods**
4 **ATOMISE,** 4, b f Ardad (IRE)—Eolith **Dods Racing Club**
5 **AZURE BLUE (IRE),** 4, gr f El Kabeir (USA)—Sea of Dreams (IRE) **Mr P Appleton & Mrs Anne Elliott**
6 **BERRY EDGE (IRE),** 5, b g Mukhadram—Amaany **Elliott Brothers And Peacock**
7 **BILLY NO MATES (IRE),** 7, b g Clodovil (IRE)—Sabaidee (IRE) **Mr J Sagar & Mr M Dods**
8 **BOLD TERRITORIES (IRE),** 5, ch g Territories (IRE)—Amberley Heights (IRE) **Tg Racing**
9 **BRUNCH,** 6, b g Harbour Watch (IRE)—Granola **Mrs F. Denniff**
10 **CHALLET (IRE),** 6, b g Clodovil (IRE)—Eileenlilian **Dunham Trading Ltd**
11 **COMMANCHE FALLS,** 6, br g Lethal Force (IRE)—Joyeaux **Mr Doug Graham, Davison & Drysdale**
12 **DAKOTA GOLD,** 9, b g Equiano (FR)—Joyeaux **Doug Graham, Ian Davison, Alan Drysdale 1**
13 **DEPUTY (IRE),** 5, b br g Lawman (FR)—Finagle (IRE) **Mr V Spinks & Partner**
14 **DIAMOND HAZE (IRE),** 5, b g Coulsty (IRE)—Cannot Give (USA) **Denton Hall Racing Ltd**
15 **DIAMONDONTHEHILL,** 5, b g Al Kazeem—It's My Time **Sekura Group & John Burns**
16 **EMERALDS PRIDE,** 4, br f Pride of Dubai (AUS)—Emeralds Spirit (IRE) **T. A. Scothern**
17 **EXCEEDINGLY SONIC,** 4, ch f Exceed And Excel (AUS)—Modify **Mrs F. Denniff**
18 **FIFTY SENT,** 4, br g Dabirsim (FR)—Sentaril **Mrs C. E. Dods**
19 **FIRST GREYED (IRE),** 5, gr g Gutaifan (IRE)—Hidden Girl (IRE) **The Gorijeb Partnership**
20 **GALE FORCE MAYA,** 7, ch m Gale Force Ten—Parabola **Mr F. Lowe**
21 **HAVAGOMECCA,** 5, ch m Havana Gold (IRE)—Bikini **Mr David T J Metcalfe & Mr M J K Dods**
22 **IRISH FLAME,** 4, b g Dark Angel (IRE)—Dream of Tara (IRE) **Teresa Blackett & M Dods**
23 **LANGHOLM (IRE),** 7, b g Dark Angel (IRE)—Pindrop **Dods Racing Club**
24 **LORD ABAMA (IRE),** 4, ch g Profitable (IRE)—Dancing Years (IRE) **K Pratt, P Blackett, M Dods**
25 **MARCELLO SI,** 5, b g Marcel (IRE)—Serenata Mia **Mrs H. I. S. Calzini**
26 **MOTAWAAZY,** 7, b g Kingman—Shimah (USA) **Miss V. Greetham**
27 **NELSON GAY (IRE),** 5, b g Mehmas (IRE)—Rublevka Star (USA) **R Gander & Partner**
28 **NORTHERN EXPRESS (IRE),** 5, ch g Zoffany (IRE)—Hint of A Tint (IRE) **Sekura Trade Frames Ltd**
29 **PURPLE ICE (IRE),** 4, gr g El Kabeir (USA)—Maybe Now Baby (IRE) **High Hopes Partnership & Partner**
30 **QUEEN'S SARGENT (FR),** 8, gr g Kendargent (FR)—Queen's Conquer **Mr D. Stone**
31 **SEZAAM (IRE),** 4, gr g Elzaam (AUS)—Sesmen **Dunham Trading & Carole Dods**
32 **SHOW COMPASSION,** 4, ch f Showcasing—Khaseeb **Mr D. Stone**
33 **SIR TITUS (IRE),** 5, ch g Dandy Man (IRE)—Moss Top (IRE) **Mr Michael Moses & Mr Terry Moses**
34 **STALLONE (IRE),** 7, b g Dandy Man (IRE)—Titian Queen **Dods Racing Club**
35 **TINTO,** 7, b g Compton Place—Amirah (IRE) **F. Watson**
36 **VACCINE (IRE),** 4, b g Vadamos (FR)—Strike A Light **Rjh Ltd & D Stone**
37 **WOR WILLIE,** 5, b g Mukhadram—Caterina de Medici (FR) **D. Neale**
38 **WOVEN,** 7, ch g Dutch Art—Regal Silk **Mr John Sagar & Dunham Trading Ltd**

THREE-YEAR-OLDS

39 **ALCAZARA (IRE),** gr f Gregorian (IRE)—Eileenlilian **Mrs T. Burns**
40 **ARKENSTAAR,** b g Kessaar (IRE)—Never Lose **Mr P Appleton & Mrs Anne Elliott**
41 **AZAIM,** b g Aclaim (IRE)—Azhar **Trevor Scothern & Dave Stone**
42 **BOY DOUGLAS (IRE),** b g New Bay—Lola Ridge (IRE) **F & M Dods**
43 **BROCKLESBY (IRE),** ch g Tagula (IRE)—Beat of My Heart (IRE) **Mr S. Phelan**
44 **CAPOFAN (IRE),** b f Gutaifan (IRE)—Capomento (IRE) **Denton Hall Racing Ltd**
45 **CHEYENNE NATION (IRE),** b g Bungle Inthejungle—Fol O'Yasmine **Mr D. R. Graham**
46 **DESTINED,** b f Havana Grey—Cross My Heart **Ontoawinner,Whitsbury Manor & Partner**
47 **DISTRICT COUNTY,** b g Washington DC (IRE)—Bold Bidder **Bearstone Stud Limited**
48 **HALE END (IRE),** b g Mehmas (IRE)—Would It Matter (IRE) **Game on Racing**
49 B f Harry Angel (IRE)—Hill Welcome **Mrs F. Denniff**
50 **HILLS OF GOLD,** ch g Pivotal—Posterity (IRE) **Sekura Trade Frames Ltd**
51 **JACK OF CLUBS,** b g Equiano (FR)—Lavetta **Mr J Sagar & Mr M Dods**
52 **MASTERPAINTER (IRE),** b g Caravaggio (USA)—Hand On Heart (IRE) **Mr F. Lowe**
53 **NAVY WREN (IRE),** b f U S Navy Flag (USA)—Front House (IRE) **Mr W. R. Arblaster**

MR MICHAEL DODS - continued

54 **PHOENIX FIRE (IRE),** b g Fast Company (IRE)—Lydia Becker **Mrs C. E. Dods**
55 **POL ROGER (IRE),** b g Churchill (IRE)—Passegiata **Mr J Sagar & Mr S Lowthian**
56 **PRAIRIE FALCON,** b c Belardo (IRE)—New Falcon (IRE) **Bearstone Stud Limited**
57 **ROARING RALPH,** b g Roaring Lion (USA)—Seychelloise **Mr F. Lowe**
58 **ROCKONMECCA (IRE),** b f El Kabeir (USA)—Wings of The Rock (IRE) **D. T. J. Metcalfe**
59 **SEA IN THE DARK (IRE),** b f Sea The Moon (GER)—Realt Eile (IRE) **The Gorijeb Partnership**
60 **SPARKLING RED (IRE),** b f Bungle Inthejungle—Hint of Red (IRE) **R Saunders,G Thompson,I Davison**
61 **STATU OF LIBERTY,** b f Washington DC (IRE)—Mania (IRE) **Bearstone Stud Limited**
62 **TATTERSTALL (IRE),** b g Bungle Inthejungle—Nafa (IRE) **Mrs C. Mr D Stone & Mrs C Dods**
63 **THE KING'S MEN,** b g Unfortunately (IRE)—Natty Bumppo (IRE) **Mr W. A. Tinkler**
64 **TREMENDOUS TIMES,** b g Time Test—Summers Lease **D. Neale**
65 **VORTIGAN,** ch g Ulysses (IRE)—Aristocratic **Mr D. A. Bardsley**
66 **ZUFFOLO (IRE),** b g Bungle Inthejungle—Red Red Rose **Thompson,Saunders,Drysdale,Davison**

TWO-YEAR-OLDS

67 **A GIRL NAMED IVY (IRE),** gr f 02/02 Dark Angel (IRE)—May Girl (Mayson) (75000) **Mr F. Lowe**
68 Ch c 02/02 Soldier's Call—Bahaarah (IRE) (Iffraaj) (19208) **M. J. K. Dods**
69 Bl gr f 06/04 Dark Angel (IRE)—Bunraku (Cacique (IRE)) **Dods Racing Club**
70 **CARVALHAL (IRE),** b c 07/03 Profitable (IRE)—Peig (IRE) (Refuse To Bend (IRE)) (41617) **J & Dods**
71 **CLOSE CONNECTION (IRE),** b c 19/03 Cracksman—
Too Familiar (IRE) (Clodovil (IRE)) (41617) **Davison Geoff & Dods Dods**
72 **CUBAN STORM,** gr c 16/02 Havana Grey—Sunny York (IRE) (Vale of York (IRE)) (55000) **Sekura Trade Frames Ltd**
73 Ch f 29/03 Showcasing—Different (Bahamian Bounty) (45000) **Mrs F. Denniff**
74 Ch f 09/03 Cracksman—Dragon Beat (IRE) (Dragon Pulse (IRE)) (31000) **NSL Investments Limited**
75 B c 11/02 Twilight Son—First Eclipse (IRE) (Fayruz) (75000) **Doug Graham & Damian Flynn**
76 Ch f 18/03 Starspangledbanner (AUS)—
Holley Shiftwell (Bahamian Bounty) (40000) **Mr P Appleton & Mrs Anne Elliott**
77 **INSPIRING SPEECHES (IRE),** ch c 07/03 Churchill (IRE)—
Vallambrosa (IRE) (Holy Roman Emperor (IRE)) (37615) **D & M Dods**
78 B g 19/02 Churchill (IRE)—Intense Romance (IRE) (Intense Focus (USA)) (48000) **Stone, Neale J Sagar**
79 B g 07/03 Prince of Lir (IRE)—Kerineya (IRE) (Elusive City (USA)) (18407) **Denton Hall Racing Ltd**
80 **MECCA'S DUCHESS (IRE),** gr f 08/02 Dark Angel (IRE)—
Faithful Duchess (IRE) (Bachelor Duke (USA)) (38415) **Mr David T J Metcalfe & Mr M J K Dods**
81 Ch c 23/01 Territories (IRE)—Passionada (Avonbridge)
82 B f 22/04 Golden Horn—Pure Shores (Dubawi (IRE)) (37000) **Mr F. Lowe**
83 **TAYGAR (IRE),** b f 26/02 Churchill (IRE)—Leoube (IRE) (Kodiac) (24010) **Tg Racing**
84 B c 02/03 Kodi Bear (IRE)—Top Row (Observatory (USA)) (40000) **Mr Michael Moses & Mr Terry Moses**
85 B g 05/04 Belardo (IRE)—Victorious Secret (IRE) (Holy Roman Emperor (IRE)) (22857) **Mrs C. E. Dods**

Assistant Trainer: Carole Dods, Miss Chloe Dods. **Head Lad:** Steve Alderson.

Flat Jockey: Connor Beasley, Paul Mulrennan. **Apprentice Jockey:** Rhys Elliott. **Amateur Jockey:** Miss Sophie Dods.

---

139 MR SIMON DOW, Epsom

Postal: **Clear Height Stable, Derby Stables Road, Epsom, Surrey, KT18 5LB**
Contacts: **PHONE 01372 721490 MOBILE 07860 800109**
EMAIL simon@simondow.co.uk WEBSITE www.simondow.co.uk TWITTER @SimonDowRacing

1 **ARCTICIAN (IRE),** 5, gr g Dark Angel (IRE)—Atlantic Drift **R. A. Murray-Obodynski**
2 **ARENAS DEL TIEMPO,** 5, b br m Footstepsinthesand—Vezere (USA) **Mr R. J. Moss**
3 **CAFE MILANO,** 6, b g Al Kazeem—Selka (FR) **S. L. Dow**
4 **HEADLEY GEORGE (IRE),** 6, b g Due Diligence (USA)—Silent Secret (IRE) **Mr M. J. Convey**
5 **HECTOR LOZA,** 6, b g Kodiac—Queen Sarra **Mr R. J. Moss**
6 **HUL AH BAH LOO (IRE),** 4, b g Raven's Pass (USA)—Susiescot (IRE) **Mr M. McAllister**
7 **JEREMIAH JOHNSON (IRE),** 5, b g Camacho—Lady Lassie (IRE) **S. L. Dow**

MR SIMON DOW - continued

8 **MOOSMEE (IRE),** 6, br g Society Rock (IRE)—Tara Too (IRE) **Miss S. D. Groves**
9 **NEFARIOUS (IRE),** 7, ro g Zebedee—Tellelle (IRE) **R Moss, H Redknapp**
10 **PABLO DEL PUEBLO (IRE),** 5, b g Kodiac—Solar Event **Mr R. J. Moss**
11 **RECUERDAME (USA),** 7, b g The Factor (USA)—B R's Girl (USA) **Mr R. J. Moss**
12 **ROMAN TEMPEST (FR),** 4, b c Tiberius Caesar (FR)—Seasonal Cross **Malcolm & Alicia Aldis**
13 **ROUNDABOUT SILVER,** 4, gr g Silver Pond (FR)—Mumtaza **Roundabout Magic Racing**
14 **WAKE UP HARRY,** 5, b g Le Havre (IRE)—Regatta (FR) **Mr H. Redknapp**
15 **WOE BETIDE,** 4, b g Siyouni (FR)—Kenzadargent (FR) **Chasemore Farm LLP**

THREE-YEAR-OLDS

16 **DESFONDADO (IRE),** b c Australia—Baroness (IRE) **Mr R. J. Moss**
17 **ECTOCROSS (FR),** b c Ectot—Seasonal Cross **Malcolm & Alicia Aldis**
18 **EL PEQUENO PULPO,** ch g Proconsul—Vezere (USA) **Mr R. J. Moss**
19 **MUY MUY GUAPO,** b c Ardad (IRE)—Belvoir Diva **Mr R. J. Moss**
20 **RICARDO OFWORTHING (IRE),** b c Dandy Man (IRE)—Shamardyh (IRE) **Miss S. D. Groves**

TWO-YEAR-OLDS

21 **REY DE LA BATALLA,** b c 05/02 Le Brivido (FR)—Chica de La Noche (Teofilo (IRE)) **Mr R. J. Moss**
22 **TEJESUENO,** b f 28/04 Coach House (IRE)—Pacificadora (USA) (Declaration of War (USA)) **Mr R. J. Moss**
23 **TRONIDO,** b f 17/03 Aclaim (IRE)—Vezere (USA) (Point Given (USA)) **Mr R. J. Moss**

140

MR CHRIS DOWN, Cullompton

Postal: **Upton, Cullompton, Devon, EX15 1RA**
Contacts: **PHONE 01884 32212 MOBILE 07828 021232 FAX 01884 32212**
EMAIL cjdownracing@gmail.com

1 **ALKHATTAAF,** 5, b g Mukhadram—Rewaaya (IRE) **Knights of Ni**
2 **ARCTIC FOOTPRINT,** 9, br m Blueprint (IRE)—Arctic Flow **Mrs H. R. Dunn**
3 **BALLYGOE (IRE),** 7, ch g Shantou (USA)—Paradise Lily (IRE) **Paul & Valerie Holland**
4 **BATTLE MARCH (USA),** 6, b g War Front (USA)—Lahinch Classics (IRE) **Chris Down Racing**
5 **BRYHER,** 6, b g Dream Eater (IRE)—Angel Sprints **Miss V. M. Halloran**
6 **FAT SAM,** 9, b h Denham Red (FR)—Emergence (FR)
7 **HECTOR'S HOPE,** 5, b g Bollin Eric—Friends Hope **Mrs S. M. Trump**
8 **JOHNNY B (IRE),** 9, b g Famous Name—Zoudie **Mrs P. Roffe-Silvester**
9 **LIGHT IN THE SKY (FR),** 7, b g Anodin (IRE)—Arsila (IRE) **Kittymore Racing & R.A Davies**
10 **MISS MARETTE,** 7, b m Passing Glance—La Marette **Culm Valley Racing**
11 **MR SOCIABLE,** 8, b g Geordieland (FR)—Secret Queen **Kittymore Racing**
12 **OPENING BID,** 8, b g Native Ruler—Clifton Encore (USA) **Mr T Hamlin & Mr J M Dare**
13 **RADDON TOP (IRE),** 10, ch g Getaway (GER)—Knockbrack Vic (IRE) **Mrs S. M. Trump**
14 **REGAL 'N BOLD,** 6, bl m Royal Anthem (USA)—Secret Queen **Kittymore Racing**
15 5, Ch m Linda's Lad—Russie With Love **C. J. Down**
16 **RUSSIES DREAM,** 7, b g Dream Eater (IRE)—Russie With Love **Howzat Partnership**
17 **SECRET POTION (GER),** 7, b g Dabirsim (FR)—Sola Gratia (IRE) **Paul Carter And Chris Down**
18 **SILVER CHORD,** 5, gr m Linda's Lad—Lily Potts **C. J. Down**
19 **TRIBESMANS GLORY (IRE),** 9, b g Jeremy (USA)—Benecash (IRE) **Mr N. Tucker**
20 **WHAT A PLEASURE,** 7, gr m Al Namix (FR)—Emergence (FR) **Mr D. Lockwood**

THREE-YEAR-OLDS

21 **CINQ DOUZAINE,** b f Sixties Icon—Dozen (FR) **C. J. Down**
22 **WHAT AN ICON,** b f Sixties Icon—Inffiraaj (IRE) **Mr N. Tucker**

NH Jockey: James Davies, Paige Fuller, David Noonan. **Conditional Jockey:** Jo Anderson, Harriet Tucker.

141 MR SAMUEL DRINKWATER, Strensham

Postal: **The Granary, Twyning Road, Strensham, Worcester, Worcestershire, WR8 9LH**
Contacts: **MOBILE 07747 444633**
EMAIL samdrinkwater@gmail.com

1 **BALLYBREEZE,** 7, b g Schiaparelli (GER)—Cottstown Gold (IRE) **Mr K. J. Price**
2 **BEST PAL (IRE),** 6, b g Soldier of Fortune (IRE)—Shapley Shadow (IRE) **All Bar None Racing**
3 **BLUE RIDGE HILL,** 6, b g Blue Bresil (FR)—Asola Blue (FR) **Mrs J. C. Venvell**
4 **CAPTAIN JACK,** 10, b g Mount Nelson—Court Princess **Mr & Mrs D. C. Holder**
5 **CUP OF COFFEE (FR),** 9, b m Dragon Dancer—Danser Sur La Lune (FR) **Mr D. A. Hunt**
6 **FLIGHT COMMAND (IRE),** 6, br g War Command (USA)—Regency Girl (IRE) **Prestbury Thoroughbreds**
7 **FONTANA ELLISSI (FR),** 7, b g Sinndar (IRE)—Leni Riefenstahl (IRE) **Anthony & Family**
8 **GALLIC GEORDIE,** 10, b g Geordieland (FR)—Je Ne Sais Plus (FR) **Glastonbury & On the Gallops 1**
9 **GENERAL CONSENSUS,** 11, br g Black Sam Bellamy (IRE)—Charlottes Webb (IRE) **Mrs K. Drinkwater**
10 **GENTLE FIRE,** 7, b m Phoenix Reach (IRE)—Pugnacious Lady **Court Reclamation & Salvage Ltd**
11 **HELLO BOB,** 8, ch m Cityscape—Maid of Perth **Mrs J. Drinkwater**
12 **HOWLING MILAN (IRE),** 9, b g Milan—Fantasia Filly (FR) **P. Drinkwater**
13 **JEN'S GEORGIE,** 8, gr m Geordieland (FR)—Je Ne Sais Plus (FR) **Glastonburys & On the Gallops 2**
14 **KAPAMAZOV,** 6, b g Kapgarde (FR)—Miss Poli **Court Reclamation & Salvage Ltd**
15 **LETHAL INDUSTRY (IRE),** 5, b g Champs Elysees—Na Habair Tada (IRE) **P. Drinkwater**
16 **MAX'S CHAMP (FR),** 7, ch g Champs Elysees—On The Line (FR) **Drinkwater Family & Cheltenham Boys**
17 **MY MONTY,** 6, b g Mount Nelson—Court Princess **Mr & Mrs D. C. Holder**
18 **NO REMATCH (IRE),** 9, b g Westerner—Loadsofability (IRE) **All Bar None Racing & Paul Drinkwater**
19 **NO TACKLE,** 6, ch g Gentlewave (IRE)—Wychwoods Legend **Glastonburys & On The Gallops**
20 **POWDER TRICK (IRE),** 6, b g Notnowcato—Castle Supreme (IRE) **Mr G. T. W. Miller**
21 **RATH GAUL HILL (IRE),** 5, b g Doyen (IRE)—Toler Street (IRE) **Mr K. J. Price**
22 **RUSSIAN SERVICE,** 11, b g Robin des Champs (FR)—Just Kate **Stephen Mattick & Mr D.P. Drinkwater**
23 **SAWPIT SAMANTHA,** 5, b m Champs Elysees—Sawpit Supreme **Mr D. A. Hunt**
24 **SAWPIT SIENNA,** 8, b m Dylan Thomas (IRE)—Sawpit Supreme **Mr D. A. Hunt**
25 **SIZING MAURITIUS (IRE),** 6, b g Martaline—Beau Bridget (IRE) **Anthony & Family**
26 **SPIKE JONES,** 6, b g Walk In The Park (IRE)—Mathine (FR) **Drinkwater Family & Cheltenham Boys**
27 **STRENSHAM COURT,** 8, b g Great Pretender (IRE)—Diktalina **P. Drinkwater**
28 **THE BRIMMING WATER (IRE),** 8, b g Yeats (IRE)—Dollar's Worth (IRE) **Mrs K. Drinkwater**
29 **TOP DECISION (IRE),** 10, ch g Beneficial—Great Decision (IRE) **Prestbury Thoroughbreds**

---

142 MISS JACKIE DU PLESSIS, Saltash

Postal: **Burell Farm, Longlands, Saltash, Cornwall, PL12 4QH**
Contacts: **PHONE 01752 842362 MOBILE 07970 871505**
EMAIL ziggerson@aol.com

1 **BOTUS FLEMING,** 8, ch g Tiger Groom—Chelsea Express **Miss J. M. du Plessis**
2 **DEADWOOD DIVA,** 6, ch m Recharge (IRE)—Theatre Diva (IRE) **Miss J. M. du Plessis**
3 **FORGET YOU NOT (FR),** 8, ch g Smadoun (FR)—Baby Sitter (FR) **Mr R. C. Dodson**
4 **HALOA MAIL (FR),** 6, gr m Zanzibari (USA)—Queenly Mail (FR) **Miss J. M. du Plessis**
5 **KINGSMILL GIN,** 10, b m Fair Mix (IRE)—Kingsmill Lake **Miss J. M. du Plessis**
6 **LITTLE PEACHEY (IRE),** 7, b m September Storm (GER)—Mrs Peachey (IRE) **Miss J. M. du Plessis**
7 **MABEL KINGSMILL,** 8, b m Lucarno (USA)—Kingsmill Lake **Miss J. M. du Plessis**
8 **MARTHA BURELL,** 8, ch m Lucarno (USA)—Theatre Diva (IRE) **Miss J. M. du Plessis**
9 **ST ERNEY,** 12, ch g Kadastrof (FR)—Ticket To The Moon **Miss J. M. du Plessis**
10 **THEATRE MIX,** 10, gr m Fair Mix (IRE)—Theatre Diva (IRE) **Miss J. M. du Plessis**
11 **VALENTINO,** 8, b g Sulamani (IRE)—Romance Dance **Jackie Du Plessis & Sarah Pridham**

---

143 MRS ANN DUFFIELD, Leyburn

Postal: **Sun Hill Racing Ltd, Sun Hill Farm, Constable Burton, Leyburn, North Yorkshire, DL8 5RL**
Contacts: **PHONE 01677 450303 MOBILE 07802 496332 FAX 01677 450993**
EMAIL ann@annduffield.co.uk WEBSITE www.annduffield.co.uk

1 **ARNOLD,** 9, b g Equiano (FR)—Azurinta (IRE) **Patterson, Jolley**
2 **BILLYB (FR),** 4, b g Raven's Pass (USA)—Aztec Queen **D. K. Barker**
3 **CLOTHERHOLME (IRE),** 6, b g Sir Prancealot (IRE)—Giorgi (IRE) **Mr T. S. Ingham & Mrs Liz Ingham**
4 **EEH BAH GUM (IRE),** 8, b g Dandy Man (IRE)—Moonline Dancer (FR) **Mr N. A. Rhodes**
5 **JARVIS (IRE),** 4, ch g Profitable (IRE)—Sorry Woman (FR) **Ingham Racing Syndicate**
6 **LADY NECTAR (IRE),** 6, b m Zebedee—Mitchelton (FR) **Mr T. S. Ingham & Mrs Liz Ingham**
7 **MASTER RICHARD,** 4, b g Aclaim (IRE)—Movementneverlies **Mr T. S. Ingham & Mrs Liz Ingham**
8 **MISS SNUGGLES (IRE),** 4, ch f Dragon Pulse (IRE)—Miss Frime (IRE) **The Jolley Partnership**
9 **MR TREVOR (IRE),** 5, b g Kodi Bear (IRE)—Muscadelle **Mr T. S. Ingham & Mrs Liz Ingham**
10 **QUERCUS (IRE),** 6, b g Nayef (USA)—Dufoof (IRE) **Mrs C. A. Gledhill**
11 **RUNNINWILD,** 5, b g Fountain of Youth (IRE)—Dont Tell Nan **Mr Ian Farrington & Partner**
12 **SYDNEY BAY,** 4, b g Australia—Sudu Queen (GER) **Mr J. A. Kay**

THREE-YEAR-OLDS

13 **AZUCENA (IRE),** b f Exceed And Excel (AUS)—Mandinga (BRZ) **Mr Jimmy Kay & Partner**
14 **ELIZABETH'S JOY,** b f Washington DC (IRE)—Ice Mayden **Mrs E Ingham & Partner**
15 **HOW EXCITING (IRE),** b f Invincible Spirit (IRE)—Iron Lady (IRE) **Middleham Park Racing XXXIII & Partner**
16 **LONDON LEGEND (IRE),** b g Zoustar (AUS)—London Welsh **Mark & Nichola Jolley, Kay, Goodair**
17 **MADDISONELLE,** b f Territories (IRE)—Royal Silk **Mr Gary Wood & Partner**
18 **MISS REBECCA,** b f Washington DC (IRE)—Punchie **Mr T Ingham & Partner**
19 **SIR ARTHUR'S BOY,** b g Night of Thunder (IRE)—Shallika (IRE) **Mark Jolley, Nigel Leech & Partner**
20 **ZERBINETTA (IRE),** b f Kodiac—Escapism (IRE) **J Kay, P Dyson, N Leech & Partner**

---

144 MR IAN DUNCAN, Coylton

Postal: **Sandhill Farm, Coylton, Ayr, Ayrshire, KA6 6HE**
Contacts: **MOBILE 07731 473668**
EMAIL idracing@outlook.com

1 **ADVERAM,** 4, b g Walk In The Park (IRE)—Lochnell (IRE) **The Macdonald Family**
2 **BANNSIDE (IRE),** 7, b g Robin des Champs (FR)—Milogan (IRE) **Mr S. Sinclair**
3 **BOLT MAN,** 5, b g Millenary—Miss Chatterbox **Mrs Camille Macdonald**
4 **BONNIE DAY (IRE),** 5, ch m Ask—Red Card (IRE) **Mrs J. A. Duncan**
5 **CAVE HILL,** 4, ch g Universal (IRE)—Belfast Central (IRE) **Stephen Sinclair & Ian Duncan**
6 **CELESTIAL FASHION,** 5, b m Telescope (IRE)—French Fashion (IRE) **Stephen Sinclair & Ian Duncan**
7 **FAME VALLEY (IRE),** 8, b g Fame And Glory—Miss Island (IRE) **Mr S. Sinclair**
8 4, B g Telescope (IRE)—Golden Sparkle (IRE) **Stephen Sinclair & Ian Duncan**
9 **GUINNESS VILLAGE (IRE),** 7, bl g Sholokhov (IRE)—Lowroad Cross (IRE) **Mr C. Davidson**
10 **HIGHLAND FASHION,** 4, b g Champs Elysees—French Fashion (IRE) **Stephen Sinclair & Ian Duncan**
11 **JESSIEMAC (IRE),** 9, br m Sholokhov (IRE)—All Our Blessings (IRE) **The Macdonald Family**
12 **KING OF FASHION (IRE),** 13, ch g Desert King (IRE)—French Fashion (IRE) **I. A. Duncan**
13 **MANFROMINVERLOCHY (IRE),** 5, b g Workforce—Subbys Daughter (IRE) **Mr R. Lilley**
14 **MAURA JEANNE,** 6, ch m Sulamani (IRE)—Watch Closely Now (IRE) **Land of Burns Racing Club**
15 **STRONG ECONOMY (IRE),** 11, ch g Sandmason—Odd Decision (IRE) **The Macdonald Family**
16 **TEDDY MAC,** 4, ch g Black Sam Bellamy (IRE)—Spring Over (IRE) **The Macdonald Family**
17 **TOOMBRIDGE,** 7, b g Kayf Tara—Supreme Present **Mr S. Sinclair**
18 4, B f Champs Elysees—Watch Closely Now (IRE) **Stephen Sinclair & Ian Duncan**

---

145 MR NIGEL DUNGER, Pulborough

Postal: **17 Allfrey Plat, Pulborough, West Sussex, RH20 2BU**
Contacts: **PHONE 07494 344167 MOBILE 07790 631962**
EMAIL debdunger05@gmail.com

1 **HIER ENCORE (FR),** 11, ch g Kentucky Dynamite (USA)—Hierarchie (FR) **N. A. Dunger**
2 **PRIDE OF PEMBERLEY (IRE),** 11, ch g Flemensfirth (USA)—On Galley Head (IRE) **N. A. Dunger**

Assistant Trainer: Mrs D Dunger.

146 MR ED DUNLOP, Newmarket

Postal: **La Grange Stables, Fordham Road, Newmarket, Suffolk, CB8 7AA**
Contacts: **WORK 01638 661998 PHONE 07885 151567 MOBILE 07785 328537**
EMAIL edunlop@eddunlopracing.co.uk WEBSITE www.edunlop.com

1 **ARTHUR'S REALM (IRE),** 5, b g Camelot—Morning Line (FR)
2 **CITIZEN GENERAL (IRE),** 4, b g Camelot—Capriole
3 **FEARLESS BAY (IRE),** 4, b g Siyouni (FR)—Monroe Bay (IRE)
4 **GATWICK KITTEN (USA),** 6, b g Kitten's Joy (USA)—Maibaby (IRE)
5 **GIRL INTHE PICTURE (IRE),** 4, b f Lawman (FR)—Hidden Girl (IRE)
6 **HAUNTED DREAM (IRE),** 4, gr g Oasis Dream—Red Halo (IRE)
7 **HEATHEN,** 4, b g Lope de Vega (IRE)—Great Heavens
8 **JOHN LEEPER (IRE),** 5, b g Frankel—Snow Fairy (IRE)
9 **LENNY'S SPIRIT (FR),** 5, b br g Intello (GER)—Moonee Valley (FR)
10 **MY SILENT SONG,** 4, b f Postponed (IRE)—Sky Crystal (GER)
11 **NIKKI'S GIRL (IRE),** 4, b f Mehmas (IRE)—Dame Judi (IRE)
12 **PURPLE REIGN (IRE),** 4, b g Camelot—Button Up (IRE)
13 **RICHARD P SMITH (IRE),** 4, b g Belardo (IRE)—Illico
14 **ROCKABILL ANGEL,** 4, b f Fastnet Rock (AUS)—Anzhelika (IRE)
15 **SARKHA (IRE),** 4, b g The Gurkha (IRE)—Saga Celebre (FR)
16 **SEAL OF SOLOMON (IRE),** 4, br g Make Believe—Sapphire Waters (IRE)
17 **SOCIETY LION,** 6, b g Invincible Spirit (IRE)—Pavlosk (USA)
18 **STERLING KNIGHT,** 4, b g Camelot—Sterling Sound (USA)
19 **TURNER GIRL (IRE),** 4, b f Mastercraftsman (IRE)—Music In My Heart
20 **WESTERN STARS (FR),** 4, b g Almanzor (FR)—Waikika (FR)

THREE-YEAR-OLDS

21 **ATWATER NINE (IRE),** b f Camelot—Carol (IRE)
22 **CENTERSTAGE (IRE),** b g Showcasing—Landmark (USA)
23 **CHORUS LINE,** b f Territories (IRE)—Angelic Note (IRE)
24 **CLOUD QUEEN,** b f Garswood—Royal Seal
25 **CRACKERZ (IRE),** b f Cracksman—Sea Horn (FR)
26 **CUE'S BEAU,** b f Brazen Beau (AUS)—Cue's Folly
27 **DALRYMPLE,** ch f Cracksman—Dalvina
28 **DAMASCUS STEEL (IRE),** gr g Mastercraftsman (IRE)—Shanjia (GER)
29 **DAME SARRA,** ch f Decorated Knight—Queen Sarra
30 **DARK NOTIONS (IRE),** b g Caravaggio (USA)—Allegrezza
31 **DEBBY'S DELIGHT,** b f Ulysses (IRE)—Miss Pinkerton
32 **DOG FOX,** ch g Cityscape—Dragonera
33 **EMILY'S ECLIPSE,** b f Sea The Moon (GER)—Lonely Rock
34 **GILDED MOON,** b f Sea The Moon (GER)—Gulden Gorl (GER)
35 **GREEK GIANT (IRE),** b g Teofilo (IRE)—Balakera (IRE)
36 **HARRIET'S ANGEL,** b f Harry Angel (IRE)—Via Lattea (IRE)
37 **INTOXICATA (FR),** b f U S Navy Flag (USA)—Epsom Icon
38 **LA CHICANIERE,** b f Le Havre (IRE)—Capricious Cantor (IRE)
39 **LAURA'S BREEZE (IRE),** b br f Ribchester (IRE)—Etesian Flow

MR ED DUNLOP - continued

40 **LETABA,** b g Muhaarar—Shingwedzi (SAF)
41 **LUCIDITY (IRE),** b f Zoffany (IRE)—Roystonea
42 **NARASHA (IRE),** gr f Zoustar (AUS)—Cheetah
43 **NO SURRENDER (IRE),** b g Gleneagles (IRE)—Queen Myrine (IRE)
44 **ORCHESTRA (FR),** b g Golden Horn—Optica (FR)
45 **PEROVSKIA,** ch f Mukhadram—Oulianovsk (IRE)
46 **PHILOS (IRE),** ch g Teofilo (IRE)—Ilulisset (FR)
47 **PUZZLETOWN,** ch g Iffraaj—Ravensburg
48 **RAVEN'S APPLAUSE (IRE),** b g Acclamation—Cravin Raven (USA)
49 **RED TREASURE (IRE),** b f Muhaarar—Red Fantasy (IRE)
50 **ROYAL DREAM,** b g Muhaarar—Royale Danehill (IRE)
51 **SIERRA VISTA (IRE),** b g Almanzor (FR)—Just Gorgeous (IRE)
52 **STAR MAP,** b f Starspangledbanner (AUS)—Map of Heaven
53 **STREETSTORM,** b f Night of Thunder (IRE)—Upper Street (IRE)
54 **TRIP TO ROME (IRE),** b g Holy Roman Emperor (IRE)—Marthamydear (USA)

TWO-YEAR-OLDS

55 B f 22/04 Muhaarar—Abhasana (IRE) (Hawk Wing (USA)) (62000)
56 **ADAAY TO WIN,** b f 09/02 Adaay (IRE)—Salvo (Acclamation) (6000)
57 B f 13/03 Outstrip—Belle Dormant (IRE) (Rip Van Winkle (IRE)) (20000)
58 B f 16/04 Lope de Vega (IRE)—Capricious Cantor (IRE) (Cape Cross (IRE))
59 B c 17/03 Soldier's Call—Classy Lassy (IRE) (Tagula (IRE)) (9204)
60 **DON SIMON (IRE),** br c 21/05 Sea The Stars (IRE)—Snow Fairy (IRE) (Intikhab (USA))
61 **HAVANA SKY,** br c 29/03 Havana Gold (IRE)—Midnight Sky (Desert Prince (IRE)) (16000)
62 **KATIE G,** b f 23/04 Zoustar (AUS)—Kiyoshi (Dubawi (IRE)) (8000)
63 **LADY AVA (IRE),** b f 24/04 New Bay—Ladysiy (FR) (Siyouni (FR)) (17607)
64 Ch f 28/02 Masar (IRE)—Lady Liberty (IRE) (Shirocco (GER)) (13000)
65 Br f 18/04 Le Havre (IRE)—Loch Ma Naire (IRE) (Galileo (IRE))
66 B f 10/02 Expert Eye—Manana Chica (IRE) (Kodiac) (7000)
67 **MANOS ARRIBA (IRE),** b c 16/02 Tamayuz—Mo Chara (USA) (Street Cry (IRE)) (16000)
68 B f 24/04 Zoustar (AUS)—Map of Heaven (Pivotal)
69 B c 05/04 Land Force (IRE)—Olvia (IRE) (Giant's Causeway (USA)) (35000)
70 **PALAZZO PERSICO (IRE),** b c 03/03 Profitable (IRE)—Little Italy (USA) (Proud Citizen (USA)) (15000)
71 B c 16/01 Magna Grecia (IRE)—Purple Glow (IRE) (Orientate (USA)) (4000)
72 B c 21/03 Acclamation—Silken Soul (Dansili) (35000)
73 B f 12/04 Muhaarar—Sterling Sound (USA) (Street Cry (IRE)) (30000)
74 B f 14/04 Harry Angel (IRE)—Timeless Gift (IRE) (Camacho) (7619)
75 **TRIP TO VENICE (IRE),** br c 01/02 Bated Breath—La Grande Zoa (IRE) (Fantastic Light (USA)) (42000)

Assistant Trainer: Jack Morland. **Head Lad:** Joey Brown.

MRS ALEXANDRA DUNN, Wellington

Postal: **The Gallops, West Buckland, Wellington, Somerset, TA21 9LE**
Contacts: **MOBILE 07738 512924**
WEBSITE www.alexandradunnracing.com

1 **ANNIE NAIL (IRE),** 6, ch m Doyen (IRE)—Castletown Girl **Racehorse Ownership Club**
2 **ARGUS (IRE),** 11, b g Rip Van Winkle (IRE)—Steel Princess (IRE) **Helium Racing LTD**
3 **ATHOLL STREET (IRE),** 8, b g Jeremy (USA)—Allthewhile (IRE) **West Buckland Bloodstock Ltd**
4 **BEAT THE STORM (IRE),** 5, b g Dragon Pulse (IRE)—Before The Storm **Gangbusters**
5 **BLACKHILLSOFDAKOTA (IRE),** 8, b g Galileo (IRE)—Aymara **The Profile Partnership 2**
6 **BLITZ SPIRIT (IRE),** 5, b m Free Eagle (IRE)—All Clear **Racehorse Ownership Club**
7 **BOOLAMORE GLORY (IRE),** 6, b g Ocovango—Go Sandy Go (IRE) **Racehorse Ownership Club**
8 **CAILIN SAOIRSE,** 4, b f Bated Breath—Belle Travers **Gangbusters**
9 **COLDSTREAM (IRE),** 5, b g Australia—Balandra **Racehorse Ownership Club**

MRS ALEXANDRA DUNN - continued

10 **CONFIRMATION BIAS (IRE),** 8, b g Presenting—Bonnie Parker (IRE) **Wbb & Gold & Green**
11 **DARK MOON (FR),** 5, b m Spanish Moon (USA)—Vida Sure Bailly (FR) **Team Dunn**
12 **DOUBLE OR QUITS,** 6, b m Kayf Tara—Double Mead **Mrs K. R. Smith-Maxwell**
13 **ECCO,** 8, b g Maxios—Enjoy The Life **Miss R. J. Smith-Maxwell**
14 **ESTATE ITALIANA (USA),** 6, b br g Elusive Quality (USA)—Unaccompanied (IRE) **Team Dunn**
15 **ETOILE BRILLANTE (IRE),** 5, ch m Sholokhov (IRE)—Dam Royale (FR) **Racehorse Ownership Club**
16 **FREESTYLE (FR),** 5, b br m Magadino (FR)—Fristar (FR)
17 **GETOVERTHATHILL (IRE),** 6, b g Getaway (GER)—Vale of Avocia (IRE) **Racehorse Ownership Club**
18 **HO QUE OUI (FR),** 6, ch m Network (GER)—Highest Card (FR) **West Buckland Bloodstock Ltd**
19 4, B g Passing Glance—Holy Veil
20 **INSTANT GAMBLER (IRE),** 7, b g Getaway (GER)—Ostarakov (GER) **Lycett & Wbb**
21 **IRENE'S PEARL (IRE),** 4, b f Doyen (IRE)—Castletown Girl **Racehorse Ownership Club**
22 **KAPITALISTE (FR),** 7, b g Intello (GER)—Kapitale (GER) **The Profile Partnership 2**
23 **KAYF BAHA,** 7, b g Kayf Tara—Ishka Baha (IRE) **West Buckland Bloodstock Ltd**
24 **KEPALA,** 6, gr m Mastercraftsman (IRE)—Kebaya **Racehorse Ownership Club**
25 **KING OF WAR,** 4, b g Churchill (IRE)—Materialistic **Racehorse Ownership Club**
26 **KYBER CRYSTAL (IRE),** 4, gr f El Kabeir (USA)—Lapis Blue (IRE) **Racehorse Ownership Club**
27 **MINELLA VOUCHER,** 12, b g King's Theatre (IRE)—All Rise (GER) **Taunton Town Peacocks**
28 **MYFANWY'S JEWEL,** 8, b m Arvico (FR)—Lady Myfanwy **Mrs A. Dunn**
29 **NAEVA (FR),** 4, b f Pastorius (GER)—Todaraba (FR) **The Profile Partnership 2**
30 **NEAR DARK (IRE),** 7, b m Westerner—Mollyash (IRE) **Racehorse Ownership Club**
31 **ONE FOR BILLY,** 11, b g Midnight Legend—Saxona (IRE) **Mrs K. R. Smith-Maxwell**
32 **ROCK OF STAR (FR),** 6, b g Nom de d'La (FR)—Rolie de Vindecy (FR) **Racehorse Ownership Club**
33 **SAILED AWAY (GER),** 5, b g Sea The Moon (GER)—Sail (IRE) **The Danum Partnership**
34 **SAM'S THE MAN,** 6, b h Black Sam Bellamy (IRE)—Blurred Lines (IRE) **Berbillion & West Buckland Bloodstock**
35 **SARCEAUX (FR),** 6, gr m Rajsaman (FR)—Sainte Adresse **Racehorse Ownership Club**
36 **SAUSALITO SUNRISE (IRE),** 15, b g Gold Well—Villaflor (IRE) **Mrs K. R. Smith-Maxwell**
37 **SIGNAL TWENTY NINE,** 6, gr g Gregorian (IRE)—Beacon Lady **West Buckland Bloodstock Ltd**
38 **SNIPER POINT (FR),** 4, b f Pastorius (GER)—Ejina (FR) **Ms L. L. Clune**
39 **THAHAB IFRAJ (IRE),** 10, ch g Frozen Power (IRE)—Penny Rouge (IRE) **The Dunnitalls & Partner**
40 **THE RAIN KING (IRE),** 6, b g No Nay Never (USA)—Brigids Cross (IRE) **Racehorse Ownership Club**
41 **THIBOUVILLE (FR),** 5, b m Rajsaman (FR)—Tarnag (FR) **Helium Racing LTD**
42 **TOAD OF TOAD HALL,** 7, b g Universal (IRE)—Double Mead **Team Dunn**

TWO-YEAR-OLDS

43 B f 28/04 Sixties Icon—Holy Veil (Kayf Tara) **Mrs A. Dunn**

---

148 MRS CHRISTINE DUNNETT, Norwich

Postal: **College Farm, Hingham, Norwich, Norfolk, NR9 4PP**
Contacts: **PHONE 01953 851364 MOBILE 07775 793523**
EMAIL christine@christinedunnett.com WEBSITE www.christinedunnett.com

1 **BAD ATTITUDE,** 6, b g Canford Cliffs (IRE)—Cry Freedom (IRE) **Mr Nigel Hardy**
2 **BELOVED OF ALL (IRE),** 4, ch g Starspangledbanner (AUS)—Midnight Oasis **Christine Dunnett Racing (Arryzona)**
3 **BRAZEN ARROW,** 5, br g Brazen Beau (AUS)—Patience **Pete West & Christine Dunnett**
4 **ENCHANTED NIGHT,** 5, ch m Night of Thunder (IRE)—Khaseeb **Howard Lupton & Christine Dunnett**
5 **FAST FLO,** 4, b f Garswood—College Doll **Mrs C. A. Dunnett**
6 **FLOWER OF THUNDER (IRE),** 6, b m Night of Thunder (IRE)—Flower Fairy (USA) **Sparkes, Machin, Amey & Dunnett**
7 **GRAFFA,** 5, b g Bobby's Kitten (USA)—Marigay's Magic **Sparkes & Dunnett**
8 **JUST PERCY (IRE),** 4, b g Sir Percy—Sandtail (IRE) **Alan & Barbara Brown**
9 **KRAKA (IRE),** 8, b g Dark Angel (IRE)—Manuelita Rose (ITY) **Team Kraka**
10 **LATE BLOOM,** 4, b f Charm Spirit (IRE)—Lovely Memory (IRE) **Sparkes, Machin, Amey & Dunnett**
11 4, B g Outstrip—Patience **Pete West & Christine Dunnett**
12 **SHYJACK,** 8, ch g Archipenko (USA)—Coconut Shy **Christine Dunnett Racing (Arryzona)**

MRS CHRISTINE DUNNETT - continued

13 **SWOOPER,** 5, b g Brazen Beau (AUS)—Most Tempting **Mrs C. A. Dunnett**
14 **WATCH YOUR TOES,** 5, b g Lethal Force (IRE)—Barathea Dancer (IRE) **Mr P. D. West**

THREE-YEAR-OLDS

15 B f Mayson—Barathea Dancer (IRE) **Mr P. D. West**
16 **IDIOPATHIC,** b f Charm Spirit (IRE)—Zhanna (IRE) **Mr A. Machin & Mrs C. Dunnett**
17 **MISS MAISIEPAIGE,** b f Charming Thought—Born To Fly (IRE) **Miss M. Greenbank-Solomon**
18 **PRIMROSE MAID,** b f Harry Angel (IRE)—Cat O' Nine Tails **Howard Lupton & Christine Dunnett**

TWO-YEAR-OLDS

19 B f 09/05 Territories (IRE)—Entitlement (Authorized (IRE)) (1000) **Mr A. S. Machin**
20 B f 03/02 Intello (GER)—Regal Banner (Lope de Vega (IRE)) (15000) **Alan & Barbara Brown**

---

149 MR SEAMUS DURACK, Upper Lambourn

Postal: **The Croft Stables, Upper Lambourn, Hungerford, Berkshire, RG17 8QH**
Contacts: **PHONE 01488 491480 MOBILE 07770 537971**
EMAIL sd.111@btinternet.com WEBSITE www.seamusdurack.com

1 **DARKEST DREAM,** 7, b m Albaasil (IRE)—Rare Ruby (IRE) **Mr R. S. Fiddes**
2 6, B m Albaasil (IRE)—Duchess of Ripon (IRE) **Mr R. S. Fiddes**
3 6, B m Albaasil (IRE)—Grand Slam Maria (FR) **Mr R. S. Fiddes**
4 **HERESY,** 7, b m Albaasil (IRE)—Straversjoy **Mr R. S. Fiddes**
5 5, B g Albaasil (IRE)—Kayo Koko (IRE) **Mr R. S. Fiddes**
6 4, B c Albaasil (IRE)—Koala Bear **Mr R. S. Fiddes**
7 5, B h Albaasil (IRE)—L'Artiste (IRE) **Mr R. S. Fiddes**
8 6, B m Albaasil (IRE)—Majestic Treasure (IRE)
9 **PHOENIX AQUILUS (IRE),** 6, b g Slade Power (IRE)—Permsiri (IRE) **Phoenix Aquilus Partnership**
10 **PROPHECY,** 7, b g Albaasil (IRE)—Littlemoor Lass **Stamford Bridge Racing**
11 **REFLECT,** 6, b m Albaasil (IRE)—True Rose (IRE) **Mr R. S. Fiddes**
12 **SHALFA (IRE),** 4, ch f Ribchester (IRE)—Mikandy (IRE) **Aura (Gas) Holdings Ltd**
13 **SIR THOMAS GRESHAM (IRE),** 8, b h Dutch Art—Loquacity **Mrs P. Walshe**
14 4, B c Albaasil (IRE)—Sweet Charlie **Mr R. S. Fiddes**
15 **THUNDER LILY (IRE),** 5, b m Night of Thunder (IRE)—Permsiri (IRE) **Mr Stephen Tucker and Mr S Durack**
16 **TWILIGHT HEIR,** 5, b g Twilight Son—Xtrasensory **Mr R. S. Fiddes**
17 **VOLENTI (IRE),** 4, b g Estidhkaar (IRE)—Izba (IRE) **Mr R. S. Fiddes**

THREE-YEAR-OLDS

18 **GASMAN (IRE),** b c Cracksman—Anne of Kiev (IRE) **Aura (Gas) Holdings Ltd**
19 B f Albaasil (IRE)—Grand Slam Maria (FR) **Mr R. S. Fiddes**
20 B f Albaasil (IRE)—Kayo Koko (IRE) **Mr R. S. Fiddes**
21 **WADI BANI,** b c Oasis Dream—Semaral (IRE) **Stephen Tucker & Chris Howell**
22 B g Massaat (IRE)—Word Perfect

Assistant Trainer: Sam Beddoes.

MR CHRIS DWYER, Newmarket

Postal: **Paddocks View, Brickfield Stud, Exning Road, Newmarket, Suffolk, CB8 7JH**
EMAIL getadwyer@aol.com

1 **EPIC EXPRESS,** 5, ch g Twilight Son—Keep The Secret **Mr M. M. Foulger**
2 **ESPIRITU MORENO,** 4, b g Equiano (FR)—Annie Salts **Mrs S. Dwyer**
3 4, B g Garswood—Great White Hope (IRE) **Strawberry Fields Stud**

MR CHRIS DWYER - continued

4 **MIDRARR (IRE),** 6, b m Dubawi (IRE)—Oojooba **Strawberry Fields Stud**
5 **SIR OLIVER (IRE),** 6, b g Dark Angel (IRE)—Folga **Flying High Syndicate (Sir Oliver)**

THREE-YEAR-OLDS

6 B f Al Kazeem—Desert Berry **Strawberry Fields Stud**
7 **HAULFRONHOBBS,** b f Bobby's Kitten (USA)—Junket **Strawberry Fields Stud**
8 **SPECIALIST VIEW,** b f Expert Eye—Sugar Mill **Strawberry Fields Stud & Mrs S Dwyer**
9 **TWAYBLADE,** ch g Mayson—Arcanista (IRE) **Mr & Mrs J. & P. Harris**

TWO-YEAR-OLDS

10 B f 12/03 Study of Man (IRE)—Ichigo (Myboycharlie (IRE)) (22000) **Strawberry Fields Stud**
11 B f 19/04 Bobby's Kitten (USA)—Quick Thought (IRE) (Sir Percy) **Strawberry Fields Stud**
12 B c 01/04 Expert Eye—Rose Berry (Archipenko (USA)) (25000) **Strawberry Fields Stud**

---

151 MISS CLAIRE DYSON, Evesham

Postal: **Froglands Stud Farm, Froglands Lane, Cleeve Prior, Evesham, Worcestershire, WR11 8LB**
Contacts: **PHONE 01789 774000, 07803 720183 FAX 01789 774000**
EMAIL cdyson@live.co.uk WEBSITE www.clairedysonracing.co.uk

1 **BLUE HEAVEN,** 6, b m Blue Bresil (FR)—Spring Flight **DYDB Marketing Limited**
2 **CLASSIC TUNE,** 13, b g Scorpion (IRE)—Classic Fantasy **D. J. Dyson**
3 **DARQUESSE (IRE),** 5, b m Affinisea (IRE)—Judys Gift (IRE) **DYDB Marketing Limited**
4 **FOREVER DES LONG (FR),** 8, b g Blue Bresil (FR)—Fetuque Du Moulin (FR) **DYDB Marketing Limited**
5 **HARBIE,** 7, b g Harbour Watch (IRE)—Pigeon Pie **D. J. Dyson**
6 **HY BRASIL (IRE),** 6, b g Fastnet Rock (AUS)—Kahyasi Moll (IRE) **DYDB Marketing Limited**
7 **JUST ORLANDO,** 6, b g Universal (IRE)—Adiynara (IRE) **FSF Racing**
8 **KEEPER,** 5, b g Frankel—Portodora (USA) **DYDB Marketing Limited**
9 **LINGER (IRE),** 10, b g Cape Cross (IRE)—Await So **DYDB Marketing & C Dyson**
10 **MIDNIGHT OWLE,** 13, ch g Midnight Legend—Owlesbury Dream (IRE) **FSF Racing**
11 **PASSAM,** 11, b g Black Sam Bellamy (IRE)—One Wild Night **FSF Racing**
12 **SIR VALENTINE (GER),** 10, b g Cacique (IRE)—Singuna (GER) **DYDB Marketing Limited**
13 **TARBUCK,** 5, b h Telescope (IRE)—Tarbay **FSF Racing**

NH Jockey: David Noonan. **Conditional Jockey:** Charlie Hammond.

---

152 MR SIMON EARLE, Sutton Veny

Postal: **The Lower Barn, The Beeches Farm, Deverill Road, Sutton Veny, Wiltshire, BA12 7BY**
Contacts: **PHONE 01985 840450 MOBILE 07850 350116 FAX 01985 840450**
EMAIL simonearleracing@btinternet.com WEBSITE www.simonearleracing.co.uk

1 **BELLA MADONNA,** 5, b m Eastern Anthem (IRE)—Goochypoochyprader **The Ivy**
2 **CRIMSON SAND (IRE),** 5, b g Footstepsinthesand—Crimson Sunrise (IRE) **Mr R. H. J. Martin**
3 **GOLDEN DOVE,** 5, b m Golden Horn—Laughing Dove (IRE) **Mrs M. Williams**
4 **GOLDEN MILLIE,** 5, b m Walk In The Park (IRE)—Mille Et Une (FR) **Mrs M. Williams**
5 **JOUR D'ORAGE (FR),** 4, b g Great Pretender (IRE)—Ne M'Oubliez Pas (FR) **Mr K. M. Harris**
6 **KILKEASKIN MOLLY (IRE),** 9, b br m Mountain High (IRE)—Nicola's Girl (IRE) **Mr C Church, S Earle**
7 **MALAGO ROSE (IRE),** 5, b m Malinas (GER)—Avichi (IRE) **Mr K. M. Harris**
8 **MERAKI MIST (FR),** 5, gr g Tin Horse (IRE)—Merka (FR) **Mr R. H. J. Martin**
9 **NIVELLE'S MAGIC,** 4, b f Hellvelyn—Nihal (IRE) **Mr I. P. Patten**
10 **NOWYOUVEBINANDUNIT,** 6, b m Roderic O'Connor (IRE)—Oceana Blue **Mr W. Simmons**
11 **RARE CLOUDS,** 9, b g Cloudings (IRE)—Rare Vintage (IRE) **Mr R. H. J. Martin**
12 **ROBBER'S BRIDGE (IRE),** 5, b g Frammassone (IRE)—Mille Et Une Nuits (FR) **Mr R. H. J. Martin**

Racing Secretary: Mrs Katie Earle.

153 MR MICHAEL AND DAVID EASTERBY, Sheriff Hutton

Postal: **New House Farm, Stittenham Farms, Sheriff Hutton, York, Yorkshire, YO60 6TN**
EMAIL office@stittenham.com

1 **ALBERT'S BACK,** 9, b g Champs Elysees—Neath **Golden Ratio & J Blackburn**
2 **ASHKHABAD (IRE),** 5, b m Harzand (IRE)—Athenaire (IRE) **Gay & Peter Hartley Racing**
3 **BEAUTY CHOICE,** 6, b g Bated Breath—Modesty's Way (USA) **Silkstone United Racing**
4 **CALCUTTA DREAM (IRE),** 5, b g Iffraaj—Short Affair **Stittenham Racing**
5 **CARLTON AND CO,** 4, b f Havana Gold (IRE)—Rocking The Boat (IRE) **Mr S. A. Hollings, Mr M. Peacock**
6 **CAROLUS MAGNUS (IRE),** 5, b g Holy Roman Emperor (IRE)—Izola **Mr Jack Turton**
7 **CASILLI,** 6, b m Cacique (IRE)—Lilli Marlane **Tinning, Wallis & Hollings**
8 4, Gr g El Kabeir (USA)—Cesca (IRE) **Imperial Racing Partnership 2016**
9 **CHICAGO GAL,** 4, ch f Cityscape—Crooked Wood (USA) **The Chicago Gal Partnership**
10 **CONTRAST (IRE),** 9, ch g Dutch Art—Israar **The Laura Mason Syndicate**
11 **COPPER MOUNTAIN,** 4, b f Sir Percy—Aetna **The Laura Mason Syndicate**
12 **DESERT EMPEROR,** 6, b g Camelot—Praia (GER) **Mr L. J. Westwood, Mr Stephen Rainford**
13 **DREAMS AND VISIONS (IRE),** 7, b g Archipenko (USA)—Kibini **Imperial Racing & Partner**
14 **EAGLE CREEK (IRE),** 9, b g Raven's Pass (USA)—Blue Angel (IRE) **The Mick & David Easterby Racing Group**
15 **ELIGIBLE (IRE),** 7, b g Dark Angel (IRE)—Secrets Away (IRE) **Mr L. J. Westwood**
16 **ELYSIAN FLAME,** 7, ch g Champs Elysees—Combustible (IRE) **Mr J Blackburn & Imperial Racing P'ship**
17 **FALCON KING,** 4, b g Pivotal—Queen's Castle **Mr J Blackburn & Imperial Racing P'ship**
18 **FIERY DAWN (IRE),** 4, b g Lawman (FR)—Maidin Maith (IRE) **Imperial Racing & Mr J Blackburn**
19 **GRANTLEY HALL,** 4, b f Ardad (IRE)—Combustible (IRE) **Imperial Racing P'Ship & Mr J Blackburn**
20 **HAZY GLEN (FR),** 4, gr g Lawman (FR)—Skyline Dancer **Imperial Racing & Partner**
21 **HOOTS TOOTS,** 4, gr ro g Outstrip—Bow Bridge **Laura Mason Syndicate Racing**
22 **JAZZ SAMBA (IRE),** 4, gr f El Kabeir (USA)—
Sensational Samba (IRE) **Mr S. A. Hollings, Southbank Racing, Mrs A. Butler**
23 **KING OF EUROPE (IRE),** 4, b g Ardad (IRE)—High Cross (IRE) **The Lee Westwood Partnership**
24 **LAERTES (USA),** 4, ch g Kantharos (USA)—Raging Atlantic (USA) **Mr B. Padgett**
25 **LATE ARRIVAL (IRE),** 6, b g Night of Thunder (IRE)—Powdermill **Mr S. A. Windle, Mr G. Routledge**
26 **LE BEAU GARCON,** 4, b g Brazen Beau (AUS)—Bacall **Bernard Hoggarth Racing**
27 **LUKE,** 6, b g Lucarno (USA)—More Ballet Money **Falcon's Line Ltd**
28 **MARWARI (IRE),** 7, b g Exceed And Excel (AUS)—Miss Polaris **A & J Fordham & M Hickling**
29 **MENELAUS (IRE),** 4, br g Galileo Gold—Empress Rock (IRE) **Southbank Racing, Mr B. Padgett**
30 **MIN TILL,** 4, b f Al Kazeem—Avessia **Mrs C E Mason & Amity Finance**
31 **MISTER CAMACHO (IRE),** 4, b g Camacho—Drifting Mist **The Lee Westwood Partnership**
32 **NEVERWRONGFORLONG,** 5, ch m Eagle Top—Poetic Verse **Mr J. N. Blackburn**
33 **PIRANHEER,** 4, b g Heeraat (IRE)—Piranha (IRE) **Mr M. Hancock**
34 **POINT LOUISE,** 5, b m Free Eagle (IRE)—Cape Mystery **M. W. Easterby**
35 **REACH (IRE),** 5, b m Sea The Stars (IRE)—Ameliorate (IRE) **Amity Finance Racing**
36 **REFUGE,** 6, b g Harbour Watch (IRE)—Beldale Memory (IRE) **Laura Mason Syndicate & Julia Lukas**
37 **RING OF GOLD,** 6, b g Havana Gold (IRE)—Pitter Patter **Laura Mason Syndicate Racing**
38 **RUN RESDEV RUN,** 5, b g Cityscape—Heart Locket **Mr L. J. Westwood, Resdev Ltd**
39 **SAM'S CALL,** 6, b g Finjaan—Winner's Call **Westy Partnership**
40 **SHIMMERING SANDS,** 4, b g Teofilo (IRE)—Milady **Imperial Racing & Mr J Blackburn**
41 **SO GRATEFUL,** 5, b g Swiss Spirit—Bow Bridge **The Mick & David Easterby Racing Group**
42 **THE GREY LASS,** 4, ro f Outstrip—Be Lucky **The Lee Westwood Partnership**
43 **TWO BROTHERS,** 5, b g Sir Percy—Blandish (USA) **Thompson Brothers**
44 **UNPLUGGED (IRE),** 7, b g Alhebayeb (IRE)—Crown Light **Pellon Racing**
45 **WESTERN BEAT (IRE),** 5, ch m Mehmas (IRE)—Western Sky **Mark Hickling Racing**
46 **WHERE'S HECTOR,** 6, b g Schiaparelli (GER)—Diavoleria **Mr J Goodrick Racing**
47 **WHERE'S JEFF,** 8, b g Haafhd—Piece of Magic **Mr A. G. Pollock**
48 **YORKSHIRE LADY,** 5, gr m Mukhadram—Brave Mave **Munroe, McHale K Wreglesworth**

THREE-YEAR-OLDS

49 **ANIERES GIRL,** b f Aclaim (IRE)—On A Whim **Mr B. Padgett**
50 B g Sir Percy—Apalis (FR) **Mr J. N. Blackburn**
51 **BAY OF HOPE (IRE),** b g Cable Bay (IRE)—Selka (FR) **Mick & David Easterby 100 Racing**
52 **CANTALUPO BELLA,** b f Massaat (IRE)—Otrooha (IRE) **The Cantalupo Bella Partnership**
53 **CAPLA QUEST (IRE),** b f New Approach (IRE)—Some Site (IRE) **Capla Developments Racing**

MR MICHAEL AND DAVID EASTERBY - continued

54 Ch f Cityscape—Englishwoman **Mr Richard Chadwick**
55 Ch f Ulysses (IRE)—Ferrier **Mr Anthony Guerriero**
56 B g El Kabeir (USA)—Hazardous **Mr B Padgett Racing**
57 **HICKO'S GIRL (IRE),** b f Camacho—Mistress Makfi (IRE) **Mr K. M. Hickling**
58 **KING OF THE JUNGLE (IRE),** b g Bungle Inthejungle—Bonne **Mick & David Easterby 100 Racing**
59 **LA JOLIE FILLE (IRE),** ch f Decorated Knight—Fligaz (FR) **Bernard Hoggarth Racing**
60 **LADY BEECHFIELD,** b f Harry Angel (IRE)—Blue Maiden **Beechfield Racing**
61 **LADY DOUGLAS,** b f Massaat (IRE)—Angel Grigio **Mr D. A. Shaw, Mr A. Gove**
62 **MASTER SHERIDAN,** b g Farhh—Miss Sheridan (IRE) **Mr J Blackburn Racing**
63 **MINNEAPOLIS SOUND (IRE),** gr g Gregorian (IRE)—Generous Heart **Saltire Paper**
64 **MISS BRAZEN,** b f Brazen Beau (AUS)—
Quelle Affaire **Mrs J. A. Tinning, W. H. Tinning, Mrs C. M. Wallis, Mr D. O. Chapman**
65 **MY HONEY B,** b f Zoffany (IRE)—Midnight Dance (IRE) **Fraine, Fraine, Windle, Porter**
66 **ON SABBATICAL (IRE),** b g Awtaad (IRE)—Butoolat **D. Scott, A & J Fordham & M Hickling**
67 **PLEASURE VAMPIRE,** b f Massaat (IRE)—
Lady Suesanne (IRE) **Mr S. A. Windle, Mr A. M. Fraine, Mr M. J. Fraine, Mr G. Routledge**
68 **ROLL IT IN GLITTER (IRE),** b g Gustav Klimt (IRE)—Glitter Baby (IRE) **Middleham Park & South Bank Racing**
69 **SECRET JOY (IRE),** b c Camacho—Cape Joy (IRE) **Graham Simpson Racing**
70 **SLINGSBYTOO (IRE),** b g Bungle Inthejungle—Al Sultana **Bernard Hoggarth Racing**
71 **TENNESSEE BLAZE,** ch g Highland Reel (IRE)—Don't Forget Faith (USA) **Mr K. M. Hickling**
72 **Y B SOBER,** b f Outstrip—Brave Mave **MAYO 4 SAM, Mr R. Wreglesworth**
73 **YORKSTONE,** b g Mayson—La Gessa **The Mick & David Easterby Racing Group**

TWO-YEAR-OLDS

74 B g 07/03 Golden Horn—America Mon Amie (USA) (All American (AUS)) **Mr A. G. Pollock**
75 B c 29/03 Coach House (IRE)—Bengers Lass (USA) (Orientate (USA)) **Mr A. G. Pollock**
76 B c 05/04 Awtaad (IRE)—Brazilian Bride (IRE) (Pivotal) (45000) **Mr M. McHale**
77 **CATTON LADY,** b f 31/03 Time Test—
Soodad (King's Best (USA)) (10000) **Mrs J. A. Tinning, W. H. Tinning, Mrs C. M. Wallis**
78 B g 20/03 Postponed (IRE)—Darkandstormy (Hurricane Run (IRE)) **Mr J. N. Blackburn, Mr H A Cram, Mr S Winter**
79 Ch g 09/05 Zoffany (IRE)—Desert Sage (Selkirk (USA)) (9000) **Mr S. A. Windle**
80 B g 14/01 Due Diligence (USA)—Doobahdeedoo (USA) (Animal Kingdom (USA)) **Resdev & Partner**
81 B f 05/04 Land Force (IRE)—Dozy (IRE) (Exceed And Excel (AUS)) (26000) **Bernard Hoggarth Racing**
82 B g 07/04 Postponed (IRE)—Favorite Girl (GER) (Shirocco (GER)) (21000) **Mr J. N. Blackburn**
83 Gr g 26/02 Phoenix of Spain (IRE)—
Fleur de Sel (Linamix (FR)) (45000) **Capla Developments Racing, Mr B. Padgett**
84 B g 17/01 Adaay (IRE)—Ile Deserte (Green Desert (USA)) **Mick & David Easterby 100 Racing**
85 Ch c 18/01 Soldier's Call—In The Lurch (Mount Nelson) (61905) **Mr B. Padgett**
86 B g 26/01 Washington DC (IRE)—Jive (Major Cadeaux) (2857) **Mr D. O. Chapman**
87 B f 21/04 Postponed (IRE)—Miss Sheridan (IRE) (Lilbourne Lad (IRE)) **Mr J. N. Blackburn**
88 B g 11/02 Washington DC (IRE)—Penny Garcia (Indesatchel (IRE)) **Mr G. Routledge**
89 B c 04/04 Expert Eye—Pretty Paper (IRE) (Medaglia d'Oro (USA)) (22000) **Mr Jack Turton**
90 B g 05/02 Ribchester (IRE)—Roses For Grace (FR) (Redoute's Choice (AUS)) (20000) **Mr J. N. Blackburn**
91 B g 22/04 Lightning Spear—Sabrewing (IRE) (Fast Company (IRE)) (11500) **Mr J. N. Blackburn**
92 B f 01/02 Eqtidaar (IRE)—Santafiora (Poet's Voice) (12500) **Mick & David Easterby 100 Racing**
93 **SPIRIT OF ACKLAM,** b c 19/02 Cracksman—Zacchera (Zamindar (USA)) (27000) **Amity Finance Racing**
94 B g 07/03 Havana Gold (IRE)—Stereo Love (FR) (Champs Elysees) (21000) **Mr A. Morse**
95 B c 04/04 Zoustar (AUS)—Swiss Dream (Oasis Dream) (32000) **Mr M. McHale**
96 **ZOUS JUICE (IRE),** b g 23/03 Zoustar (AUS)—Elusive Horizon (USA) (Elusive Quality (USA)) **Mr H. Jones**

154

MR TIM EASTERBY, Malton

Postal: **Habton Grange, Great Habton, Malton, North Yorkshire, YO17 6TY**
Contacts: **PHONE 01653 668566 FAX 01653 668621**
EMAIL easterby@habtonfarms.co.uk WEBSITE www.timeasterby.co.uk

1 **ALBEGONE,** 5, b g Alhebayeb (IRE)—Pacngo **Mr D B & Mrs C Lamplough & Partner**
2 **ALBEGREY,** 4, b gr g Alhebayeb (IRE)—Maybeagrey **Reality Partnerships XIII**

MR TIM EASTERBY - continued

3 **ART POWER (IRE),** 6, gr g Dark Angel (IRE)—Evening Time (IRE) **King Power Racing Co Ltd**
4 **ATOMIC LADY (FR),** 4, b f Kodiac—Fusion (IRE) **Reality Partnerships II**
5 **BARLEY (IRE),** 4, b g Mehmas (IRE)—Cornakill (USA) **Reality Partnerships**
6 **BARNEY'S BAY,** 5, b g Cable Bay (IRE)—Fisadara **Mr J. R. Saville**
7 **BAY BREEZE,** 4, b g Buratino (IRE)—Midnight Mojito **Mr D. A. West & Partner**
8 **BEAT THE EDGE (IRE),** 6, b g Beat Hollow—Darsi O'Grady (IRE) **smartwater utilities**
9 **BENNY BALOO,** 6, ch g Schiaparelli (GER)—Tarabaloo **R. W. Metcalfe**
10 **BETTY BALOO,** 7, b m Schiaparelli (GER)—Tarabaloo **R. W. Metcalfe**
11 **BOARDMAN,** 7, b g Kingman—Nimble Thimble (USA) **Mr Ball, Mr Hodkinson, Mr Malley & Ptr**
12 **BOLLIN MARGARET,** 6, b m Fountain of Youth (IRE)—Bollin Greta **Mr D B & Mrs C Lamplough & Partner**
13 **BOLLIN NEIL,** 7, ch g Haafhd—Bollin Nellie **Habton Racing club**
14 **BUNGLEY (IRE),** 4, b f Bungle Inthejungle—Milly's Secret (IRE) **Mr Craig Wilson & Partner**
15 **CANARIA PRINCE,** 5, bl g Alhebayeb (IRE)—Gran Canaria Queen **The Senators**
16 **CARRIGILLIHY,** 5, gr g New Bay—Spectacle **The Harmonious Lot & Partner**
17 **CASSY O (IRE),** 6, b g Camacho—Hawaajib (FR) **R. Taylor & Mr P. Hebdon**
18 **CHIEF CRAFTSMAN,** 9, gr ro g Mastercraftsman (IRE)—Eurolink Raindance (IRE) **Habton Racing**
19 **CILLUIRID (IRE),** 9, b g Arcadio (GER)—Garw Valley **Reality Partnerships IV**
20 **CLAIM THE STARS (IRE),** 4, b g Starspangledbanner (AUS)—Ponty Acclaim (IRE) **Reality Partnerships XV**
21 **COPPER KNIGHT (IRE),** 9, b g Sir Prancealot (IRE)—Mystic Dream **Middleham Park, Ventura Racing 6 & Partner**
22 **COUNT D'ORSAY (IRE),** 7, b g Dandy Man (IRE)—Deira (USA) **Mr Ambrose Turnbull & John Cruces**
23 **COURT AT SLIP (IRE),** 6, b g Court Cave (IRE)—Lady Fame (IRE) **Mrs Anne Dawson & Partner**
24 **CRUYFF TURN,** 6, ch g Dutch Art—Provenance **Aberdeen Park & Partner**
25 **DANDY BAY (IRE),** 4, b f Dandy Man (IRE)—Harmony Bay (IRE) **Hart Inn Racing & Partner**
26 **DANZAN (IRE),** 8, b g Lawman (FR)—Charanga **Reality Partnerships XVII**
27 **DARK JEDI (IRE),** 7, b g Kodiac—Whitefall (USA) **Mr Evan M Sutherland & Partner**
28 **DEVILWALA (IRE),** 5, b g Kodiac—Najraan **Mr M. J. Macleod**
29 **EAST STREET REVUE,** 10, ch g Pastoral Pursuits—Revue Princess (IRE) **Mr S. A. Heley & Partner**
30 **EDITH GARRUD,** 4, b f Kingman—Regina Cordium (IRE) **Habton Racing**
31 **ERNEST RUTHERFORD,** 4, b g Ardad (IRE)—Rutherford (IRE) **Mr T Scothern, Mr D Stone & Partner**
32 **FOUNTAIN CROSS,** 5, b g Muhaarar—Infamous Angel **Ryedale Partners No 8**
33 **FYLINGDALE (IRE),** 4, b f National Defense—Pulp Idol (USA) **Mr Martin Adams, Mr Neil Arton & Partner**
34 **GARDEN OASIS,** 8, b g Excelebration (IRE)—Queen Arabella **Mr T. A. Scothern & Partner**
35 **GIBSIDE,** 4, b g Time Test—Ardbrae Tara (IRE) **Elsa Crankshaw, Gordon Allan & Partner**
36 **GIVE IT SOME TEDDY,** 9, b g Bahamian Bounty—Croeso Cariad **Mr L. Bond**
37 **GOLDEN APOLLO,** 9, ch g Pivotal—Elan **Mr David Scott & Partner**
38 **GOLDEN MELODY (IRE),** 5, ch m Belardo (IRE)—Chanter **Mr M. J. Macleod**
39 **GRACELANDS GIRL,** 4, b f Iffraaj—Stella Point (IRE) **The Wolf Pack 2 & Partner**
40 **HELLENISTA,** 5, b m Nathaniel (IRE)—Maven
41 **HIGHWAYGREY,** 7, b g Dick Turpin (IRE)—Maybeagrey **Reality Partnerships VII**
42 **HILDENLEY,** 6, ch g Teofilo (IRE)—Alpine Storm (IRE) **Elsa Crankshaw, Gordon Allan & Partner**
43 **HOW MUCH (IRE),** 5, ch g Ask—Womanofthemountain (IRE) **Mrs Anne Dawson & Partner**
44 **HYPERFOCUS (IRE),** 9, b br g Intense Focus (USA)—Jouel (FR) **Ryedale Partners No 14**
45 **IMPELLER,** 5, b g Pivotal—Musical Beat (IRE) **D Scott & Co (Pattern Makers) Ltd & Ptr**
46 **IS SO CUTE DIMARIA (FR),** 5, gr g Fly With Me (FR)—Kley du Paradis (FR) **Reality Partnerships XII**
47 **JEWEL MAKER (IRE),** 8, b g Invincible Spirit (IRE)—Sapphire (IRE) **Reality Partnerships I**
48 **JUST HISS,** 10, b g Lawman (FR)—Feather Boa (IRE) **The Sandmoor Partnership**
49 **KODIELLEN (IRE),** 6, b m Kodiac—Newellen (IRE) **Habton Racing**
50 **LAMPANG (IRE),** 6, b g Dandy Man (IRE)—Black Mascara (IRE) **King Power Racing Co Ltd**
51 **LICIT (IRE),** 6, b m Poet's Voice—Deserted **Mr I. P. Crane**
52 **LIKE A LION (IRE),** 4, b g Kodiac—Termagant (IRE) **Reality Partnerships III**
53 **LITTLE TED,** 6, ch g Cityscape—Speedy Utmost Meg **Mr M. J. Macleod**
54 **MAC AILEY,** 7, ch g Firebreak—Rosabee (IRE) **Dubelem (Racing) Limited & Partner**
55 **MAHANAKHON,** 4, b g Siyouni (FR)—Belle Josephine **King Power Racing Co Ltd**
56 **MANIGORDO (USA),** 6, b br g Kitten's Joy (USA)—Cutting Edge (USA) **Mr M. J. Macleod**
57 **MANILA SCOUSE,** 4, b g Aclaim (IRE)—Forever Excel (IRE) **Mr Ambrose Turnbull & John Cruces**
58 **MARBUZET,** 4, b g Farhh—Estournel
59 **MATTELLA,** 4, bl f Mattmu—Gran Canaria Queen **Habton Racing**
60 **MATTICE,** 4, b g Mattmu—Ice Mayden **Mr B Valentine & Partner**
61 **MICKY MICHAELIS,** 4, b g Fountain of Youth (IRE)—Katie Boo (IRE) **Mr J. F. Bowers**
62 **MOROZOV COCKTAIL (IRE),** 7, b g Morozov (USA)—Gold Platinum (IRE) **Mr & Mrs N Wrigley & Partner**

MR TIM EASTERBY - continued

63 **MOTARAJEL,** 6, b g Camacho—Vereri Senes **Reality Partnerships XVIII**
64 **MR CURIOSITY,** 6, b g Frankel—Our Obsession (IRE) **The Wolf Pack 2 & Partner**
65 **MUSIC SOCIETY (IRE),** 8, gr g Society Rock (IRE)—Absolutely Cool (IRE) **R. Taylor & Mr P. Hebdon**
66 **NEARLY WED (IRE),** 6, b g Ocovango—Bernie'stheboss (IRE) **Mr J Cruces & Partner**
67 **OBEE JO (IRE),** 7, b g Kodiac—Maleha (IRE) **Mrs Joanne Boxcer & Partner**
68 **OBJECT,** 4, b g Aclaim (IRE)—Quiet Protest (USA) **Mr John Matthews & Partner**
69 **PANAMA CITY,** 4, b g Iffraaj—Guavia (GER) **Ryedale Partners No 11**
70 **PARYS MOUNTAIN (IRE),** 9, gr g Dark Angel (IRE)—Muzdaan (IRE) **Reality Partnerships XII**
71 **PERFECT SWISS,** 7, b g Swiss Spirit—Perfect Practice **Mr Craig Wilson & Partner**
72 **POET'S DAWN,** 8, ch g Poet's Voice—Dudley Queen (IRE) **Mr Timothy O'Gram & Partner**
73 **PREMIER POWER,** 6, ch g Siyouni (FR)—Pelerin (IRE) **King Power Racing Co Ltd**
74 **QUEST FOR FUN,** 5, ch g Lope de Vega (IRE)—Craic Agus Spraoi (IRE) **Habton Racing**
75 **RED ASTAIRE,** 4, ch g Intello (GER)—Barynya **The Wolf Pack 2 & Partner**
76 **RELKADAM (FR),** 9, ch g Muhtathir—Gloirez (FR) **Ryedale Partners No 12**
77 **REVOQUABLE,** 4, b g Pastoral Pursuits—Breakable **Ryedale Partners No 9**
78 **RING OF BEARA (FR),** 4, b g Wootton Bassett—Harem Mistress (IRE) **Matt Fitzgerald, The Songsters & PARTNER**
79 **ROACH POWER (IRE),** 4, gr g Ribchester (IRE)—Evening Time (IRE) **King Power Racing Co Ltd**
80 **RUE GALILEE (IRE),** 5, ch g Champs Elysees—Granny Weatherwax (IRE) **Habton Racing club**
81 **SAMEEM (IRE),** 7, b g New Approach (IRE)—Ahla Wasahl **Habton Racing**
82 **SAULIRE STAR (IRE),** 5, b m Awtaad (IRE)—Gallic Star (IRE) **Habton Racing club**
83 **SHERIFF GARRETT (IRE),** 9, b g Lawman (FR)—Few Are Chosen (IRE) **Ontoawinner 10 & Partner 4**
84 **SHOWALONG,** 5, ch g Showcasing—Muaamara **Racing Knights & Ptnr**
85 **SNASH (IRE),** 5, b g Markaz (IRE)—Wardat Dubai **Mr J Musgrave & Partner**
86 **STRONGBOWE (FR),** 7, b g Siyouni (FR)—Landing Site (FR) **Ryedale Partners No 6**
87 **TELEGRAM BOB,** 5, b g Telescope (IRE)—Linagram **Reality Partnerships IX**
88 **THE DUNKIRK LADS,** 4, b g Pivotal—Spatial **Mr David Scott & Partner**
89 **UGO GREGORY,** 7, gr g Gregorian (IRE)—Raajis (IRE) **Mr F. Gillespie**
90 **WADE'S MAGIC,** 6, gr g Lethal Force (IRE)—Miliika **Reality Partnerships XVI**
91 **WAKEY WAKEY (IRE),** 4, b g Estidhkaar (IRE)—Sleeping Princess (IRE) **Hp Racing Wakey Wakey & Partner**
92 **WAR DEFENDER,** 6, b g War Command (USA)—Never Lose **Ryedale Partners No.15**
93 **WELLS FARHH GO (IRE),** 8, b h Farhh—Mowazana (IRE) **Mr S A Heley & Partner**
94 **WHISKY WOLF,** 4, ch g Territories (IRE)—Cartimandua **Mr Lee Bond & Partner**
95 **ZIMMERMAN,** 4, ch g Poet's Voice—Cresta Gold **Linkenholt Racing & Partner**

THREE-YEAR-OLDS

96 **AMAZING ARTHUR,** b g Showcasing—Majestic Song **Mr Evan M Sutherland & Partner**
97 **AMERICAN OAK (IRE),** b g Golden Horn—Lady Grace (IRE) **Middleham Park, Ventura Racing 6 & Partner**
98 **BEAUTRON,** br f Brazen Beau (AUS)—Alpine Dream (IRE) **David & Yvonne Blunt**
99 **BOWLAND PRINCE (IRE),** b g Ribchester (IRE)—Lady Catherine **Ryedale Partners No 3**
100 **BRAVEHEART BOY (IRE),** b g Harry Angel (IRE)—Bureau (IRE) **Reality Partnerships XI**
101 **BROTHER SEBASTIAN (IRE),** br g Kodiac—Tooraweenah **Mr F. Gillespie**
102 **BURGLAR'S DREAM (IRE),** ch g Cracksman—Jameela's Dream **Mr Ambrose Turnbull & Partner**
103 **CAWTHORNES GEM,** b g Pivotal—Honour **E. A. Brook**
104 Ch g Havana Grey—Choisette **Habton Racing**
105 **COMMON ACCLAIM (IRE),** b g Acclamation—Casual Remark (IRE) **Mr & Mrs J. D. Cotton**
106 **COURTNBOWLED (IRE),** ch g Dragon Pulse (IRE)—Dunleer (IRE) **Habton Racing**
107 **CWENHILD,** b f Saxon Warrior (JPN)—Dawreya (IRE) **Mr Ambrose Turnbull & Partner**
108 **DIRECT HIT (IRE),** br g Lightning Spear—The Silver Kebaya (FR) **E. A. Brook**
109 **EMERALD DUCHESS,** b f Massaat (IRE)—Caledonia Duchess **The 1891 Group & Partners**
110 B f Expert Eye—Esteemable **Habton Racing**
111 **EYEOFTHEBEHOLDER,** b g Expert Eye—Oh Dream **Mr John Hanbury & Ptr**
112 Bl f Pastoral Pursuits—Gran Canaria Queen **Habton Racing**
113 **HAPPIER (IRE),** b f Profitable (IRE)—Joy For Life **Habton Racing**
114 **HAPPY DANCER (IRE),** b g Highland Reel (IRE)—Cawett (IRE) **VeniVidiVici**
115 **HARDY ANGEL,** b g Harry Angel (IRE)—Cadeaux Power **Mr R Hardgrave & Partner**
116 **HE'S AN ANGEL,** ch c Harry Angel (IRE)—Secret Keeper **Mr J Musgrave & Partner**
117 **HEADABOVETHEREST (IRE),** ch g Churchill (IRE)—Evangelical **E. A. Brook**
118 **HOOF IT HOOF IT (IRE),** b f Prince of Lir (IRE)—So Devoted (IRE) **Habton Racing**
119 **HOWYADOIN (IRE),** b g Dragon Pulse (IRE)—Sensational Samba (IRE) **Mr B Valentine & Partner**

MR TIM EASTERBY - continued

120 IMPULSIVE REACTION (IRE), b g Fast Company (IRE)—Key Moment (IRE) **Mr T. A. Scothern & Partner**
121 JAZZAGAL (IRE), b f James Garfield (IRE)—Can Dance **Matt Fitzgerald, The Songsters & Ptr**
122 KNIGHTS ARTIST (IRE), b g Caravaggio (USA)—Cape Elizabeth (IRE) **Racing Knights & Ptnr**
123 KNIGHTS SPEAR, b g Lightning Spear—Riccoche (IRE) **Racing Knights & Ptnr**
124 LOLA'S MOMENT, b f Ardad (IRE)—Cards **Mews Mules Racing 1**
125 MALIBU MOONLIGHT, b f Pastoral Pursuits—Midnight Malibu (IRE) **Mr D. A. West & Partner**
126 MANILA STYLE, b g Aclaim (IRE)—Elvira Delight (IRE) **Habton Racing**
127 MISS HAVRE, br f Le Havre (IRE)—Fair Hill **Mr & Mrs J. D. Cotton**
128 MISTER SOX, ch g Pivotal—Crowning Glory (FR) **Huggymac Racing & Ptnr**
129 MISTY BLUES (IRE), b f Expert Eye—Ventura Mist **The Wolf Pack 2 & Partner**
130 MONTELUSA, b c Washington DC (IRE)—Rose Eclair **Mr J. F. Bowers**
131 MOON FRIEND (IRE), ch g Camacho—Acushladear (IRE) **Kate Barrett & Partner**
132 MOUNT KING (IRE), ch g National Defense—Christmas Joy (IRE) **Ryedale Partners No1**
133 MY DUTY (IRE), b c Muhaarar—New Plays (IRE) **King Power Racing Co Ltd**
134 NIGHTOUT, gr gr g Outstrip—Midnight Mojito **Mr D. A. West & Partner**
135 NORTHCLIFF (IRE), ch g Dandy Man (IRE)—Colgin **Bulmer, Hebdon R Taylor**
136 OPTICIAN, b g Expert Eye—Starlit Sands **Mrs J Pallister & Partner**
137 PETE THE BRIEF (IRE), b g Bungle Inthejungle—Sunblush (UAE) **Mr John Hanbury & Partner**
138 PLATINUM GIRL, b f Ardad (IRE)—Maybeagrey **Reality Partnerships VIII**
139 PREMIER OPTION (IRE), b g Profitable (IRE)—Piccola Sissi (IRE) **Mrs J Pallister & Partner**
140 RIBBLE ROUSER (IRE), ch c Ribchester (IRE)—Liel **Aberdeen Park & Partner**
141 RIBKANA (IRE), b f Ribchester (IRE)—Simkana (IRE)
142 SALEET, br f Tasleet—Sally (FR) **Mr B Valentine & Partner**
143 SEAGRAVE FOX (IRE), ch c Bungle Inthejungle—Pearl Power **King Power Racing Co Ltd**
144 SLING YER HOOK, b g Shalaa (IRE)—Isole Canarie (IRE) **Nick Rhodes & Partner**
145 SPIRIT OF APPLAUSE, b g Charm Spirit (IRE)—Accolade **Mr S A Heley & Partner**
146 STORM FOX (IRE), ch f Bungle Inthejungle—Guana (IRE) **King Power Racing Co Ltd**
147 STREETWISE GIRL, b f Aclaim (IRE)—Street Chic (USA) **Habton Racing club**
148 SUNNY ORANGE (IRE), b g Expert Eye—Orangey Red (IRE) **Habton Racing**
149 B f Camacho—Tartiflette **Habton Racing**
150 TASEVER, b c Tasleet—Forever Excel (IRE) **Mr Ambrose Turnbull & John Cruces**
151 THE GO TO (IRE), b f Ribchester (IRE)—Laura's Oasis **Jonathan Shack, Gawain Barnard & Partner**
152 UNKNOWN ANGEL, b f Harry Angel (IRE)—First Destinity (FR) **KJM Racing**
153 UPNGO, b f Mayson—Pacngo **Habton Racing**
154 VALSTAR (IRE), b f Zoustar (AUS)—Valonia **Elsa Crankshaw, Gordon Allan & Partner**
155 VINCE LE PRINCE, b g Iffraaj—Crecy **Reality Partnerships V**
156 WHISKY MCGONAGALL (IRE), b g Camacho—Laila Honiwillow **Reality Partnerships VI**
157 B g Gregorian (IRE)—Yearbook **Habton Racing club**

TWO-YEAR-OLDS

158 ACT OF VIOLENCE, gr c 12/04 Outstrip—Bacall (Paco Boy (IRE)) (15238) **Peter R. Ball, Gentech Ltd & Partners**
159 B c 22/04 Lope de Vega (IRE)—Belle Josephine (Dubawi (IRE)) **King Power Racing Co Ltd**
160 B c 22/03 Unfortunately (IRE)—Celestial Dream (IRE) (Oasis Dream) (4802) **Habton Racing**
161 DANDY FITZ (IRE), b c 11/04 Dandy Man (IRE)—New Magic (IRE) (Statue of Liberty (USA)) (20808) **A. R. Turnbull**
162 B c 27/01 Camacho—Disco Doris (Poet's Voice) (28000) **E. A. Brook**
163 B c 25/04 Invincible Army (IRE)—Fancy Feathers (IRE) (Redback) (140000) **King Power Racing Co Ltd**
164 FAST LOVE, b f 22/03 Time Test—Peak Spirit (IRE) (Invincible Spirit (IRE)) **Mr A. Al Alawi**
165 B f 19/02 Harry Angel (IRE)—Fleur de Lis (Nayef (USA)) (22000) **Mr J Musgrave & Partner**
166 B c 14/02 Bated Breath—Flycatcher (IRE) (Medicean) (23000) **Mr J Musgrave & Partner**
167 FORT YATES (IRE), ch c 26/04 Sioux Nation (USA)—
My Sweet Georgia (IRE) (Royal Applause) (17607) **Ryedale Partners No. 10**
168 GEORGIE WOOSTER (IRE), b c 14/03 Inns of Court (IRE)—Classic Legend (Galileo (IRE)) (22000) **Mules Racing 1**
169 B f 22/02 Bungle Inthejungle—Gizi Gazelle (IRE) (Fast Company (IRE)) (6500) **Mr Lee Bond & Partner**
170 Br f 25/03 Tasleet—Gold At Midnight (Havana Gold (IRE)) (26667) **Reality Partnerships XIV**
171 B c 05/04 Ardad (IRE)—Gran Canaria Queen (Compton Place) (34286) **Bulmer, Hebdon R Taylor**
172 B c 05/04 Kodiac—Grecian Artisan (IRE) (Mastercraftsman (IRE)) (36000) **Mr G Horsford & Partner**
173 Gr c 09/02 Ulysses (IRE)—Hula Girl (Oasis Dream) (10000) **Habton Racing**
174 B f 29/04 Time Test—Imperialistic (IRE) (Imperial Ballet (IRE)) (18000) **Mr G Horsford & Partner**
175 B c 22/04 Footstepsinthesand—Intrigue (Fastnet Rock (AUS)) (12000) **Habton Racing**

MR TIM EASTERBY - continued

176 B c 16/03 Cracksman—Isa (Approve (IRE)) (20000) **Bulmer, Hebdon, R Taylor**
177 Br c 07/02 Le Havre (IRE)—Kalaatah (USA) (Dynaformer (USA)) (42000) **Habton Racing**
178 B c 03/02 Equiano (FR)—Keriyka (IRE) (Indian Ridge) (13000) **Habton Racing**
179 B f 07/02 Soldier's Call—Megec Blis (IRE) (Soviet Star (USA)) (30000) **Habton Racing**
180 B c 17/02 Land Force (IRE)—Merry Diva (Bahamian Bounty) (9000) **Habton Racing**
181 B c 31/03 Dandy Man (IRE)—Obligada (IRE) (Beat Hollow) (10404) **Habton Racing**
182 B c 12/02 Massaat (IRE)—Ocicat (USA) (Storm Cat (USA)) (15000) **Habton Racing**
183 B f 04/04 Cable Bay (IRE)—Olive Mary (Authorized (IRE)) (24762) **The Wolf Pack 2 & Partner**
184 B c 15/03 Phoenix of Spain (IRE)—Pebbles Place (Oasis Dream) (24762) **Mr J. R. Saville**
185 Ch c 23/05 Ulysses (IRE)—Pivotting (Pivotal) (28000) **Mr M. J. Macleod**
186 B c 19/01 Invincible Army (IRE)—Red Romance (Dutch Art) (21905) **Reality Partnerships X**
187 Gr f 31/03 El Kabeir (USA)—Red Tulip (Kheleyf (USA)) (5000) **Mrs Doreen Swinburn & Partner**
188 **RIVERBOAT,** b c 25/04 Washington DC (IRE)—Katie Boo (IRE) (Namid) (7000) **Bearstone Stud Limited**
189 B c 06/03 Profitable (IRE)—Roxelana (IRE) (Oasis Dream) (26667) **Habton Racing**
190 B g 27/02 Due Diligence (USA)—Silvery Blue (Paco Boy (IRE)) (7000) **Habton Racing**
191 B f 25/05 Cable Bay (IRE)—Street Chic (USA) (Street Cry (IRE)) (1500) **Habton Racing**
192 B g 15/05 Aclaim (IRE)—Sunflower (Dutch Art) (4000) **Habton Racing**
193 B c 02/05 Ribchester (IRE)—Sweet Serendipity (Stimulation (IRE)) (19048) **Mr Neil Arton & Partner**
194 B c 21/03 Kodiac—Tooraweenah (Notnowcato) (22409) **Habton Racing**
195 Ch c 22/03 Soldier's Call—Union City Blues (IRE) (Encosta de Lago (AUS)) (19048) **Kate Barrett & Partner**
196 B f 14/03 Dandy Man (IRE)—Wind Storm (Holy Roman Emperor (IRE)) (12005) **Habton Racing**

---

155 MR BRIAN ECKLEY, Brecon

Postal: **Closcedi Farm, Llanspyddid, Brecon, Powys, LD3 8NS**
Contacts: **PHONE 01874 622422 MOBILE 07891 445409**
EMAIL brian.eckley@live.co.uk

1 4, B f Dartmouth—Any Pearl **B. J. Eckley**
2 4, B g Telescope (IRE)—Jaunty Spirit **B. J. Eckley**
3 **JAUNTY VIKING,** 8, b g Norse Dancer (IRE)—Jaunty Spirit **B. J. Eckley**
4 4, B g Dartmouth—Jaunty Walk **B. J. Eckley**
5 4, B f Dartmouth—Sunsational Girl **B. J. Eckley**
6 **TIMEFORADANCE,** 8, b g Norse Dancer (IRE)—Timeforagin **B. J. Eckley**
7 **TIMEFORARUM,** 5, b g Proconsul—Timeforagin **B. J. Eckley**
8 **YORGUNNABEALADY,** 5, b m Yorgunnabelucky (USA)—Sunsational Girl **B. J. Eckley**

---

156 MR ROBERT EDDERY, Newmarket

Postal: **Robert Eddery Racing Limited, Heyward Place Stables, Hamilton Road, Newmarket, Suffolk, CB8 7JQ**
Contacts: **PHONE 01638 428001 MOBILE 07938 898455**
EMAIL info@roberteddery racing.com WEBSITE www.robertedderyracing.com

1 **FELLOWSHIP (IRE),** 4, b g Fulbright—Street Kitty (IRE) **Graham & Lynn Knight**
2 **HOTSPUR HARRY (IRE),** 6, b g Zoffany (IRE)—Dark Crusader (IRE) **R. J. Creese**
3 **NEW SHEPARD (IRE),** 4, b g No Nay Never (USA)—Caelis **Julia Rayment & Brett Lawrence**
4 **SILVER DOLLAR (IRE),** 5, gr g Markaz (IRE)—Bunditten (IRE) **Mr B. Lawrence**
5 **SPRING BLOOM,** 6, ch g Power—Almond Branches **Mrs P. Aitken**

MR ROBERT EDDERY - continued

THREE-YEAR-OLDS

6 **CROCODILE ROLL,** gr c Lethal Force (IRE)—Make It Snappy **Mr C. R. Eddery**
7 **DRUM BRAE BOY,** ch g Bobby's Kitten (USA)—Wilbury Twist **Mrs P. Aitken, Mr P. H. Matthews**
8 **O'MHAIRE,** b f Scorpion (IRE)—Kompete **World Racing Network**
9 **PRIMA VALENTINA (IRE),** ch f Dandy Man (IRE)—Rosy Morning (IRE) **Mr B. Lawrence**
10 **RHEA OF THE YEAR,** b f Postponed (IRE)—Equimou **E. S. Phillips**

Flat Jockey: Andrea Atzeni. **Amateur Jockey:** Mr George Eddery.

157 MR STUART EDMUNDS, Newport Pagnell

Postal: **6 Fences Farm, Tyringham, Newport Pagnell, Buckinghamshire, MK16 9EN**
Contacts: **PHONE 01908 611369, 01908 611406 MOBILE 07778 782591 FAX 01908 611255 EMAIL Trishandstu@aol.com**

1 **ADDOSH,** 5, b m The Gurkha (IRE)—Wild Storm **Stuart Edmunds Racing Club**
2 **ALLO ALLO,** 7, b g Milan—Ravello Bay **Fakenham Race Club**
3 **ARISTOBULUS,** 4, b g Adaay (IRE)—Salome (FR) **Mr J. Gill**
4 **ARIZONA CARDINAL,** 7, b g Kayf Tara—Mathine (FR) **Oakman Racing Club**
5 **BIRDHOUSE,** 4, ch f New Approach (IRE)—Avongrove **The Danum Partnership**
6 **BLUE DAUPHIN,** 5, b g Blue Bresil (FR)—Ready To Crown (USA) **Braybrooke Lodge Partnership**
7 **BLUEGRASS (IRE),** 4, b g Galileo (IRE)—Quiet Reflection **Mrs D. E. Gardiner**
8 **BUBBLE DUBI (FR),** 6, b g Waldpark (GER)—Miss Bubble Rose (FR) **The Garratt Family**
9 **CHAOS CONTROL (IRE),** 4, b g Mastercraftsman (IRE)—Va Pensiero (IRE) **Oakman Racing Club**
10 **DOIREANN (IRE),** 6, b m Shirocco (GER)—Sew N Sew (IRE) **Stuart Edmunds Racing Club**
11 **EAGLE OF THE GLEN,** 4, gr g Gleneagles (IRE)—Mussoorie (FR) **Mr D. Mitson**
12 **ERIGMOOR,** 5, ch g Schiaparelli (GER)—Milliegait **M. Kehoe**
13 **GENTLEMAN AT ARMS (IRE),** 6, gr g Reliable Man—Sworn Sold (GER) **Mrs D. E. Gardiner**
14 **GLOBE PLAYER,** 4, b g Nathaniel (IRE)—La Dorotea (IRE) **M. Kehoe**
15 **GRAND LORD (FR),** 7, gr g Lord du Sud (FR)—Toscane des Fleurs (FR) **The Garratt Family**
16 **GUNNERY OFFICER (IRE),** 7, br g Califet (FR)—Blackthorne Winter (IRE) **Gunnery Officer Syndicate**
17 **HILLFINCH,** 6, ch m Hillstar—Grassfinch **BDRSyndicates**
18 **HOMETOWN BOY (IRE),** 8, ch g Curtain Time (IRE)—Mercy Mission **The Garratt Family**
19 **INNISFREE LASS (IRE),** 5, b m Yeats (IRE)—Topless (IRE) **The Danum Partnership**
20 **KOSASIEMPRE (FR),** 5, b m Masked Marvel—Cosavita (FR) **M. Kehoe**
21 **KRYPTON GOLD (IRE),** 5, b g Holy Roman Emperor (IRE)—Red Planet **The Danum Partnership**
22 **LARUSSO (IRE),** 6, ch g Doyen (IRE)—Muckle Flugga (IRE) **The Larusso Partnership**
23 **LORD SPARKY,** 9, ch g Sulamani (IRE)—Braybrooke Lady (IRE) **The On The Bridle Partnership**
24 **MANDOCELLO (FR),** 7, b g Motivator—Serenada (FR) **Mrs R. L. Banks**
25 **MARSH WREN,** 7, b m Schiaparelli (GER)—Carolina Wren **Far Bihoue Partnership**
26 **MEXICO (GER),** 7, b g Sea The Moon (GER)—Mexicali (IRE) **The High Kites**
27 **MISS MCGUGEN (IRE),** 8, b m Arakan (USA)—Sixties Girl (IRE) **BDRSyndicates**
28 **MY GIRL LOLLIPOP (IRE),** 7, b m Mahler—Pop Princess **Mrs N. C. Kappler**
29 **ONE EYE ON VEGAS,** 6, b g Blue Bresil (FR)—Savingforvegas (IRE) **Mr B. H. Turner**
30 **OVERSTATE,** 4, b g Oasis Dream—Zaminast **Mr J. Gill**
31 **PETITE SOURIS (FR),** 4, ch f Masked Marvel—Albufera (FR) **GMG**
32 **PRIDE OF HAWRIDGE (IRE),** 5, b g Vadamos (FR)—Face The Storm (IRE) **E. J. S. Gadsden**
33 **READY TO PLEASE,** 7, b m Kayf Tara—Ready To Crown (USA) **Braybrooke Lodge Partnership**
34 **RED ROYALIST,** 9, b g Royal Applause—Scarlet Royal **Mrs R. L. Banks**
35 **RENDITION (IRE),** 4, ch f Ulysses (IRE)—Penny Lane Forever **Stuart Edmunds Racing Club**
36 **ROYAL THUNDER,** 4, b g Night of Thunder (IRE)—Spinning Melody (USA) **Oakman Racing Club**
37 **SEDGE WREN,** 5, b m Blue Bresil (FR)—Carolina Wren **Ben Turner Racing Partnership**
38 **SHIYRVANN (FR),** 5, b g Kingman—Shemima **BDRSyndicates**
39 **SWAFFHAM BULBECK (IRE),** 9, b g Jeremy (USA)—Ballygologue (IRE) **D Bassom & P Cardosi**
40 **TREEFINCH,** 5, b m Telescope (IRE)—Grassfinch **The Long Hop Syndicate**
41 **YOUNG OFFENDER (IRE),** 8, b g Rule of Law (USA)—Cayetina **Mr D. Mitson**

Assistant Trainer: Miss Harriet Edmunds.

158 MR GORDON EDWARDS, Minehead

Trainer did not wish details of their string to appear

159 MR SIMON EDWARDS, Shrewsbury

Postal: **Blakeley Grange, Blakeley, Stanton Upon Hine Heath, Shrewsbury, Shropshire, SY4 4ND**
Contacts: **PHONE 01939 251387**

1 **BURY WALLS,** 6, b g Black Sam Bellamy (IRE)—Shuile Role **Mr S. Edwards**
2 **CHEROKEES PRAYER (IRE),** 6, b br g Hillstar—Old Madam (IRE) **Mr S. Edwards**
3 **NAME AND SHAME (IRE),** 10, b g Stowaway—Grannys Kitchen (IRE) **Mr S. Edwards**
4 **SWALLOWS RETURN (IRE),** 7, gr g Grey Swallow (IRE)—Sparkling Gem (IRE) **Mr S. Edwards**
5 **THISTLE DO (IRE),** 7, b g Dylan Thomas (IRE)—Nora's Flame (IRE) **Mr S. Edwards**

160 MISS CLARE ELLAM, Market Drayton

Postal: **Lostford Manor Stables, Mickley, Tern Hill, Market Drayton, Shropshire, TF9 3QW**
Contacts: **MOBILE 07974 075042**
EMAIL clareellam@btinternet.com WEBSITE www.clareellamracing.com

1 **AFRAID TO FEEL (IRE),** 4, b g Outstrip—La Dama Boba (IRE) **Mr R. P. Clarke**
2 **ARCHIE STEVENS,** 13, b g Pastoral Pursuits—Miss Wells (IRE) **Miss Clare L. Ellam**
3 **EIGHTYTWO TEAM (IRE),** 7, b m Mahler—Lady Hillingdon **Miss Clare L. Ellam**
4 **MY BOY GRIZZLE (IRE),** 8, b g Fame And Glory—Luminous Lizzie **Miss Clare L. Ellam**

Assistant Trainer: Amy Myatt.

161 MR BRIAN ELLISON, Malton

Postal: **Spring Cottage Stables, Langton Road, Norton, Malton, North Yorkshire, YO17 9PY**
Contacts: **PHONE 01653 690004 MOBILE 07785 747426 FAX 01653 690008**
EMAIL office@brianellisonracing.co.uk WEBSITE www.brianellisonracing.co.uk

1 **BARON DE MIDLETON (IRE),** 10, b g Brian Boru—Present Climate (IRE) **Brian Ellison Racing Club**
2 **BRIAN'S JET (IRE),** 5, gr g Jet Away—Carryonblue (IRE) **Mr J McAvoy, Mr C Lowther & Partners**
3 **CIANCIANA,** 4, ch f Cityscape—Golden Valley **Brian Ellison Racing Club, A Morton**
4 **CORMIER (IRE),** 7, b g Born To Sea (IRE)—Scotch Bonnet (IRE) **Dan Gilbert & Andrew Bruce**
5 **EXPLORERS WAY (IRE),** 4, ch g Australia—Into The Lane (IRE) **Mr P. Boyle**
6 **FREDDY ROBINSON,** 4, b g Adaay (IRE)—Bling Bling (IRE) **Brian Ellison Racing Club**
7 4, B g Nathaniel (IRE)—Full Day **Mr Dan Gilbert**
8 **IDOAPOLOGISE,** 6, b g Havana Gold (IRE)—Shiba (FR) **Dan Gilbert & Andrew Bruce**
9 **KEARNEY HILL (IRE),** 8, b g Dylan Thomas (IRE)—Sunny Glen (IRE) **Julie & Phil Martin**
10 **KILTORCAN BOY (IRE),** 8, b g Stowaway—Hathamore **Chris Lowther, Ian Smith & Partner**
11 **KING VIKTOR,** 5, ch g Cityscape—Ananda Kanda (USA) **Mrs Claire Ellison**
12 **KISS MY FACE,** 6, b g Nathaniel (IRE)—Bridle Belle **Dan Gilbert & Andrew Bruce**
13 **LANGTON WOLD (IRE),** 4, b g Cotai Glory—Ceylon Round (FR) **Mr B Dunn & Partner**
14 **LUCKY ROBIN (IRE),** 11, ch g Mister Fotis (USA)—Bewilderment (IRE) **Brian Ellison Racing Club**
15 **MINHAAJ (IRE),** 6, b m Invincible Spirit (IRE)—Sharqeyih **Mrs Claire Ellison & Partner**

MR BRIAN ELLISON - continued

16 **MONTEPLEX,** 6, b m Multiplex—Montelfolene (IRE) **Mickley Stud & Derrick Mossop**
17 **ONESMOOTHOPERATOR (USA),** 5, br g Dialed In (USA)—Sueno d'Oro (USA) **Mr P. Boyle**
18 **OSCAR DOODLE,** 4, gr g Outstrip—Dusty Blue **Miss V. Watt**
19 **PALLAS DANCER,** 6, b g War Command (USA)—Dance Card **Spring Cottage Syndicate 3**
20 **PUNXSUTAWNEY PHIL (IRE),** 6, b g Shirocco (GER)—Chilly Filly (IRE) **Mr Dan Gilbert**
21 **RALEAGH FLORA,** 8, b g Red Rocks (IRE)—Sommerflora (GER) **Mrs Claire Ellison**
22 **RAMIRO (IRE),** 7, ch g Born To Sea (IRE)—Whispering Lady (IRE) **Brian's Mates 2**
23 **RECLAIM VICTORY (IRE),** 6, b m Helmet (AUS)—Doctor's Note **Quickly Group Holdings Ltd & Partner**
24 **SALSADA (IRE),** 6, ch m Mukhadram—Mokaraba **Geoff & Sandra Turnbull & Partner**
25 **SAM'S ADVENTURE,** 11, b g Black Sam Bellamy (IRE)—My Adventure (IRE) **Julie & Phil Martin**
26 **SNOOKERED (IRE),** 9, b g Born To Sea (IRE)—Secret Quest **Brian Ellison Racing Club**
27 **SON OF THE SOMME (IRE),** 8, b g Yeats (IRE)—Present Venture (IRE) **Mr Daniel Blake**
28 **TASHKHAN (IRE),** 5, b g Born To Sea (IRE)—Tarziyna (IRE) **Mr P. Boyle**
29 **TEDTWO,** 4, b g Black Sam Bellamy (IRE)—Showtime Annie **Mr M. M. Allen**
30 **THE DANCING POET,** 7, ch g Poet's Voice—Caldy Dancer (IRE) **Spring Cottage Syndicate**
31 **THE KING OF MAY (FR),** 9, b g High Rock (IRE)—Waltzing (IRE) **Phil & Julie Martin**
32 **TIGER JET (IRE),** 7, ch g Jet Away—Just A Moment (IRE) **Mr S Gale & Partner**
33 **TUPELO MISSISSIPPI (IRE),** 8, b h Yeats (IRE)—Misleain (IRE) **Phil & Julie Martin & Graeme Preston**
34 **VICTORIANO (IRE),** 7, b g Teofilo (IRE)—Victorian Beauty (USA) **Mr Leigh Taylor**
35 **WHISKEY AND WATER,** 7, b g Harbour Watch (IRE)—Bahamamia **Dan Gilbert & Andrew Bruce**
36 **WINDSOR AVENUE (IRE),** 11, b g Winged Love (IRE)—Zaffarella (IRE) **Phil & Julie Martin**

THREE-YEAR-OLDS

37 **BREATH CATCHER,** ch f Bated Breath—Bronte Sister (IRE) **Mr Keith Brown**
38 **CHATTEL VILLAGE (IRE),** b br g Mondialiste (IRE)—Dame Hester (IRE) **Geoff & Sandra Turnbull & Partner**
39 **CHILLHI (IRE),** b g Churchill (IRE)—Hi Katriona (IRE) **Mr P. Boyle**
40 **DELAYED ACTION (IRE),** b f Postponed (IRE)—Al Rowaiyah **Mr Keith Brown**
41 **EAGLE PRINCE (IRE),** ch g Free Eagle (IRE)—Shauna's Princess (IRE) **Mr Keith Brown**
42 **GEORDIE MACKEM,** b g Jack Hobbs—The Pirate's Queen (IRE) **The Cat & the Mag Partnership**
43 **GRANDAD,** b g War Command (USA)—Livia Drusilla (IRE) **Mrs Claire Ellison**
44 **GREEK SIREN,** ch f Ulysses (IRE)—Topatoo **Mr Keith Brown**
45 **IMAGINEER (IRE),** b g Make Believe—Abilene **The Artis Partnership**
46 **MY ROXANNE (IRE),** b f James Garfield (IRE)—Magic Motif (USA) **Mr P. Boyle**
47 **MYSTICAL DREAMS (IRE),** b f Exceed And Excel (AUS)—Mystic Dream **Spring Cottage Syndicate 3**
48 **NORTHERN SPIRIT,** b g Adaay (IRE)—Amelia Grace (IRE) **Northern Water Services & Brian Ellison**
49 **SILVERLODE (IRE),** gr g Gutaifan (IRE)—Freedom Pass (USA) **The Artis Partnership**
50 **SUNFYRE,** ch g Twilight Son—Lunar Corona **The Artis Partnership**
51 **UTILIS (IRE),** b g Profitable (IRE)—Mysterious Burg (FR) **Linsey & Ian Pallas**

TWO-YEAR-OLDS

52 Ch f 01/04 Masar (IRE)—Cool Catena (One Cool Cat (USA))
53 Ch f 24/01 Mondialiste (IRE)—Countess Wells (IRE) (So You Think (NZ)) **Mr Keith Brown**
54 B c 02/02 Churchill (IRE)—Deep Influence (Kingman) (56022)
55 Ch f 08/02 Ulysses (IRE)—Full Day (Champs Elysees) **Mr Dan Gilbert**
56 **GRID IRON MAIDEN,** b f 12/04 Sogann (FR)—Next Stop (Rail Link)
57 **HABITUAL,** b g 26/02 Al Kazeem—Habita (IRE) (Montjeu (IRE)) (40000) **Artis 2**
58 B c 26/03 Mondialiste (IRE)—Kaiulani (IRE) (Danehill Dancer (IRE)) **Geoff & Sandra Turnbull**
59 B g 23/03 Pastoral Pursuits—Mad Jazz (Sir Percy) **Mr Keith Brown**
60 **MINERS GAMBLE (IRE),** b c 10/04 Tamayuz—Adeste (Dansili) (24010)
61 **TERRORISE,** b g 12/04 Territories (IRE)—Timely Words (Galileo (IRE)) (20000) **Mr A Barnes & Mr M Hulin**
62 **THEA BELL,** br gr f 29/03 Outstrip—Little Legs (Captain Gerrard (IRE)) **Mrs Claire Ellison**
63 **TRYFAN,** b c 21/04 Nathaniel (IRE)—Rhagori (Exceed And Excel (AUS)) (60024) **Artis 2**
64 B f 08/02 Sogann (FR)—Velvet Jaguar (Hurricane Run (IRE))

Assistant Trainer: Jessica Robinson.

Flat Jockey: Cam Hardie, Ben Robinson. **NH Jockey:** Henry Brooke, Sam Coltherd, Brian Hughes, Sean Quinlan. **Apprentice Jockey:** Harry Russell.

162 MISS SARA ENDER, Malton

Postal: **Swallows Barn, East Heslerton, Malton, North Yorkshire, YO17 8RN**
Contacts: **MOBILE 07983 462314**
EMAIL seequineservices@hotmail.com WEBSITE www.enderracing.co.uk

1 **ACCOMPANIED (USA),** 7, b g Distorted Humor (USA)—Unaccompanied (IRE) **Mr N. P. Ender**
2 **CALCULUS (IRE),** 6, b g Frankel—Vital Statistics **Yorkshire Horseracing**
3 **COLD HENRY,** 4, b g Sixties Icon—Flashyfrances **Mr L. Murray**
4 **DEMI SANG (FR),** 10, b g Gris de Gris (IRE)—Morvandelle (FR) **Mr N. P. Ender**
5 **DURLINGTON (FR),** 10, ch g Montmartre (FR)—Dalyonne (FR)
6 **EVISCERATING (IRE),** 11, gr g Court Cave (IRE)—Titanic Quarter (IRE)
7 **GOLD ARCH,** 7, b g Archipenko (USA)—Goldrenched (IRE) **Mr L. Murray**
8 **GOOD BYE (GER),** 8, ch g Tertullian (USA)—Guantana (GER) **Mr L. Murray**
9 **HIGH YIELD,** 6, b g Yeats (IRE)—Midsummer Magic **Rm&t Holdings Limited & Neville Ender**
10 **INDIAN SUNBIRD (IRE),** 6, b g Hillstar—Mausin (IRE) **Mr N. P. Ender**
11 **KING ATHELSTAN (IRE),** 8, b g Mayson—Ashtaroute (USA) **Mr N. P. Ender**
12 **MORO ROCK (IRE),** 6, b g Morozov (USA)—Ms Jilly Maaye (IRE) **Mr L. Murray**
13 **MR ZIPPI,** 4, b g Intello (GER)—Izzi Top **Mr N. P. Ender**
14 **NORTHANDSOUTH (IRE),** 13, ch g Spadoun (FR)—Ennel Lady (IRE)
15 **ROGAN'S FANCY (IRE),** 7, b g Frozen Power (IRE)—Kanuri (IRE) **Yorkshire Horseracing**
16 **WHEREWOULDUGETIT (IRE),** 9, b g Morozov (USA)—Matinee Show (IRE) **Mr N. P. Ender**

Assistant Trainer: Mr Neville Ender.

---

163 MRS SAM ENGLAND, Guiseley

Postal: **Brentwood, Manor Farm, Guiseley, Leeds, West Yorkshire, LS20 8EW**
Contacts: **MOBILE 07921 003155**

1 **BRIDES BAY (IRE),** 4, b f Cable Bay (IRE)—State Anthem **Marching On Together racing**
2 **CRAFTY LADY,** 4, gr f Mastercraftsman (IRE)—Kindu **Ursa Major -England**
3 **CROAGH PATRICK (IRE),** 8, b g Mountain High (IRE)—Benedicta Rose (IRE) **R. J. Hewitt**
4 **ELLEON (FR),** 8, b g Martaline—Ailette **Worcester Racing Club**
5 **EMILY WADE (IRE),** 6, ch m Lucky Speed (IRE)—Bealath Champ (IRE) **Mr S. Smith**
6 **FENLAND TIGER,** 7, ch g Schiaparelli (GER)—La Calinda **Mr J C England and Valerie Beattie**
7 **KINONDO KWETU,** 7, b g Casamento (IRE)—Asinara (GER) **Gunalt Partnership**
8 **MANWELL (IRE),** 13, b g Gold Well—Roborette (FR) **Sam England Racing Club**
9 **NO CRUISE YET,** 8, b g Passing Glance—Claradotnet **Rgm Partnership**
10 **QUIET FLOW,** 8, b g Sholokhov (IRE)—Sardagna (FR) **Pink & Purple Partnership**
11 **RIGGSBY (IRE),** 5, b g Acclamation—Silk Affair (IRE) **The Hands & Heels Partnership**
12 **SIR APOLLO (IRE),** 8, b g Westerner—Fieldtown (IRE) **Mrs S. Fawcett, Mrs J. Holgate**
13 **SPOT ON SOPH (IRE),** 7, b m Walk In The Park (IRE)—Gwenadu (FR) **Mrs S. A. England, Mr M. V. Atkinson**
14 **TOM CREEN (IRE),** 8, b g Yeats (IRE)—Casiana (GER) **J. W. Hardy**
15 **UMNEYAAT (IRE),** 5, br m Dansili—Tarayef (IRE) **The Marina Partnership**
16 **VINDOBALA (IRE),** 5, b m Pride of Dubai (AUS)—Sphere of Grace (FR) **The Marina Partnership**
17 **WHATABOUTYEH (IRE),** 6, b g Notnowcato—Correctandpresent (IRE) **R & G Malanga**

---

164 MR HARRY EUSTACE, Newmarket

Postal: **Park Lodge Stables, Newmarket, Suffolk, CB8 8AX**
Contacts: **WORK 01638 664277 MOBILE 07733 413771**
WORK EMAIL harry@harryeustaceracing.com, office@harryeustaceracing.com WEBSITE www.harryeustaceracing.com

1 **ALAROOS (IRE),** 4, b f Golden Horn—Aaraas **Shadwell Estate Company Ltd**
2 **ALDBOURNE (IRE),** 4, b g Awtaad (IRE)—Always Gentle (IRE) **Mr D. H. Batten**
3 **ALNWICK CASTLE,** 4, b f Sir Percy—Iron Butterfly **H. D. Nass**
4 **AMOR VINCIT OMNIA (IRE),** 4, b g Caravaggio (USA)—Dress Rehearsal (IRE) **The MacDougall Two**
5 **ANCIENT TIMES,** 5, b g Exceed And Excel (AUS)—Oriental Step (IRE) **The MacDougall Two**
6 **AT A PINCH,** 5, b m Lope de Vega (IRE)—Inchina **Andrew McGladdery & Park Lodge Stables**
7 **BELHAVEN (IRE),** 4, ch f Belardo (IRE)—Park Haven (IRE) **A. M. Mitchell**
8 **CHASING APHRODITE,** 4, b c Profitable (IRE)—Tutti Frutti **Gullwing Enterprises W.L.L.**
9 **CLARITUDO,** 4, b g Nathaniel (IRE)—Clarentine **Jackson XV**
10 **DIVINE COMEDY (IRE),** 5, b m Le Havre (IRE)—Epic Emirates **The Equema Partnership**
11 **FREE STEP (IRE),** 4, b f Muhaarar—Oriental Step (IRE) **Hughes & Scott**
12 **MAKINMEDOIT (IRE),** 4, b f Golden Horn—Tranquil Star (IRE) **Mr. R. M. Levitt & Mr A. Bromley**
13 **MUSTAZEED (IRE),** 5, br g Territories (IRE)—Mejala (IRE) **Newmarket Racing Club HQiii**
14 **OH SO AUDACIOUS,** 4, b f Mukhadram—Oh So Saucy **Eight Of Diamonds**
15 **TURNTABLE,** 7, b g Pivotal—Masarah (IRE) **Induna Racing**
16 **ZIGGY,** 5, b g Sixties Icon—Brushing **Sarabex & Aragon Racing**

THREE-YEAR-OLDS

17 **BETWEEN THE COVERS (IRE),** ch f Belardo (IRE)—Novel Fun (IRE) **Chief Singer Racing II**
18 **BILL SILVERS,** br gr c Farhh—Faughill (IRE) **Clipper Group Holdings Ltd**
19 **CITE D'OR (FR),** b f Galiway—Tin Rebel (FR) **Nick Bradley Racing 18**
20 **COUPLET,** b f Zoustar (AUS)—Arabda **Andrew Rosen and Marc Chan**
21 **DOCKLANDS,** b c Massaat (IRE)—Icky Woo **O.T.I. Racing**
22 **DREAMING SPIRES,** b f Cityscape—Liberisque **Chief Singer Racing III**
23 **ELUSIVE ANGEL (IRE),** b f Harry Angel (IRE)—Areyaam (USA) **Mrs I. Corbani**
24 **GOLD ROBBER,** b g Cracksman—Prize Diva **J. C. Smith**
25 **MAN OF A'AN (IRE),** b g Highland Reel (IRE)—Three Decades (IRE) **Aragon Racing 2**
26 **MOONFLEET MOMENT (IRE),** b g Sioux Nation (USA)—Moment In The Sun **The MacDougall Two**
27 **MUSICAL TRIBUTE,** b f Acclamation—Gift of Music (IRE) **J. C. Smith**
28 **MY FINEST HOUR (IRE),** b c Churchill (IRE)—Partita **Fortuna Racing**
29 **MYSTICAL APPLAUSE,** b g Aclaim (IRE)—Siren's Gift **J. C. Smith**
30 **PLUS POINT,** ch f Mastercraftsman (IRE)—Beshayer (FR) **Major M. G. Wyatt**
31 **REALISED,** b f Wootton Bassett—Wake Up Call **Park Lodge Racing**
32 **STARLIGHT MAGIC,** b f Ribchester (IRE)—Celestial Secret **J. C. Smith**
33 **VALTELLINA (IRE),** b f Caravaggio (USA)—El Cuerpo E L'Alma (USA) **Hughes & Scott**

TWO-YEAR-OLDS

34 B f 09/04 Blue Point (IRE)—Alnajmah (Dansili) **Shadwell Estate Company Ltd**
35 B br f 08/03 Dubawi (IRE)—Aneen (IRE) (Lawman (FR)) **Shadwell Estate Company Ltd**
36 B f 22/02 Calyx—Bellajeu (Montjeu (IRE)) (17607) **Nick Bradley Racing 48 and Partner**
37 **BOADICIA (IRE),** b f 27/03 Holy Roman Emperor (IRE)—Ketifa (IRE) (Iffraaj) **Gullwing Enterprises W.L.L.**
38 **BOSS DOG,** b c 22/01 Zoustar (AUS)—Lady McKell (IRE) (Raven's Pass (USA)) **Mr David Howden & Mr David Redvers**
39 B c 19/03 Starspangledbanner (AUS)—Callistan (IRE) (Galileo (IRE)) (68027) **Titanium Racing Club**
40 B c 23/02 Kingman—Ettisaal (Dubawi (IRE)) **Shadwell Estate Company Ltd**
41 B c 24/02 Zoustar (AUS)—Evil Spell (Dutch Art) (85000) **Hedge Woodside & Redvers**
42 **FLAG CARRIER,** b c 19/01 Starspangledbanner (AUS)—Evies Wish (IRE) (Holy Roman Emperor (IRE)) **J. C. Smith**
43 **HAPPY PLACE,** b f 15/03 Crystal Ocean—Happy Land (IRE) (Refuse To Bend (IRE)) (22000) **D Arnold & Thunder From Down Under**
44 **JAZZY ANGEL,** b f 30/03 Harry Angel (IRE)—Jasmiralda (FR) (Desert Style (IRE)) **Mrs I. Corbani**
45 Ch c 10/04 Churchill (IRE)—Kimblewick (IRE) (Iffraaj) (70000) **One More For the Road II**
46 **MISS GALIWAY (FR),** b f 15/05 Galiway—Free Flying (FR) (Authorized (IRE)) (21609) **Nick Bradley Racing 48 and Partner**
47 **MOON ANGEL,** b f 13/02 Time Test—Lost The Moon (Authorized (IRE)) **Mrs Sharon Goddard**

MR HARRY EUSTACE - continued

48 **NOTHING TO FEAR (IRE),** b f 03/02 Churchill (IRE)—
Withorwithoutyou (IRE) (Danehill (USA)) (37615) **Next Wave Racing**
49 B c 06/03 Muhaarar—Nurse Nightingale (Nathaniel (IRE)) (57623) **O.T.I. Racing**
50 **PAYMENT IN KIND,** b c 13/03 Profitable (IRE)—
Caring Touch (USA) (Elusive Quality (USA)) (21609) **Mr D Bevan & Mrs D Bevan**
51 **PHOENIX DUCHESS (IRE),** gr f 22/04 Phoenix of Spain (IRE)—
Kassandra (IRE) (Dandy Man (IRE)) (42000) **Johnstone Partnership**
52 **SATIRE,** b f 02/03 Time Test—Sated (Manduro (GER)) **Major M. G. Wyatt**
53 B g 03/02 Exceed And Excel (AUS)—Shaaqaaf (IRE) (Sepoy (AUS)) (58000) **Park Lodge Stables Ltd**
54 **SHIMMERING MOON (IRE),** b f 13/02 Kuroshio (AUS)—
Subtle Shimmer (Danehill Dancer (IRE)) (45714) **Titanium Racing Club**
55 **STRAIGHT A,** b c 08/04 Aclaim (IRE)—Straight Away (Dubawi (IRE)) **J. C. Smith**
56 Ch f 01/03 Masar (IRE)—Strawberry Martini (Mount Nelson) (110000) **Shadwell Estate Company Ltd**
57 **SYLVAN SPIRIT,** ch f 12/03 Waldgeist—Feline Groovy (USA) (Kitten's Joy (USA)) (20808) **J Wall, T Bater, D Redvers, Woodside BS**
58 B f 27/03 Time Test—Topaling (Halling (USA)) **Mr M Bowring & Mr R Smith**

Racing Secretary: Kelly Guillambert.

Apprentice Jockey: Kaiya Fraser.

---

165 MR DAVID EVANS, Abergavenny

Postal: **Ty Derlwyn Farm, Pandy, Abergavenny, Monmouthshire, NP7 8DR**
Contacts: **PHONE 07834 834775, 01873 890837 MOBILE 07860 668499 FAX 01873 890837**
EMAIL pdevansracing@btinternet.com WEBSITE www.pdevansracing.co.uk

1 **CUBAN BREEZE,** 5, b m Bated Breath—Madam Mojito (USA) **Dalwhinnie Bloodstock Ltd & Richard Kent**
2 **DORA PENNY,** 4, b f Mayson—Aubrietia **Shropshire Wolves**
3 **GALILEO GLASS (IRE),** 4, b g Galileo Gold—Tahoo (IRE) **Mr P. J. Glass**
4 **HASEEF (IRE),** 5, gr g Dark Angel (IRE)—Silver Shoon (IRE) **Brian & Irene Folkes**
5 **JACKS PROFIT (IRE),** 4, b c Profitable (IRE)—Violet Flame (IRE) **D. E. Edwards**
6 **KODIAC SIGN (IRE),** 4, b c Kodiac—Querulous (USA) **T. H. Gallienne**
7 **LEVEL UP (IRE),** 4, b g Hot Streak (IRE)—Kamarinskaya (USA) **Dave & Emma Evans**
8 **LIHOU,** 7, ch g Mayson—Kodiac Island **T. H. Gallienne**
9 **MABRE (IRE),** 6, gr g Make Believe—Slope **Mr K. McCabe**
10 **MIDGETONAMISSION (IRE),** 4, b f Holy Roman Emperor (IRE)—Kramer Drive (IRE) **Mrs I. M. Folkes**
11 **OCEAN OF STARS (IRE),** 4, b g Sea The Stars (IRE)—Legitimus (IRE) **Walters Plant Hire Ltd**
12 **OOH IS IT,** 5, ch g Es Que Love (IRE)—Candleberry **P. D. Evans**
13 **PORTELET BAY,** 5, b g Mayson—Fenella Rose **T. H. Gallienne**
14 **ROHAAN (IRE),** 5, b g Mayson—Vive Les Rouges **Mr Kieran McCabe & Partner**
15 **SO SMART (IRE),** 4, b g Dandy Man (IRE)—Model Looks (IRE) **John Abbey & Mike Nolan**
16 **SUN POWER (FR),** 6, b g Night of Thunder (IRE)—Sparkling Smile (IRE) **Mr P. J. Glass**
17 **WIND YOUR NECK IN (IRE),** 4, ch g Decorated Knight—Samite (USA) **Mr & Mrs Paul & Clare Rooney**
18 **WINKLEVI (FR),** 8, br g Maxios—Wild Star (IRE) **T. H. Gallienne**

THREE-YEAR-OLDS

19 **ALL IN THE HIPS (IRE),** b f Ivawood (IRE)—Raseel **Spiers & Hartwell Ltd & Mrs E. Evans**
20 **BILLY'S JOY,** b f Brazen Beau (AUS)—Aubrietia **Shropshire Wolves**
21 **BRIDLE BEAUTY,** ch f Casamento (IRE)—Primobella **Dalwhinnie Bloodstock Ltd & Richard Kent**
22 **DEMOCRACY DILEMMA (IRE),** b g Cotai Glory—Majestic Alexander (IRE) **Mr K. McCabe**
23 **DOCTOR MOZART (IRE),** b g Dandy Man (IRE)—Counter Ridge (SAF) **Dave & Emma Evans**
24 **EROSION RISK (IRE),** b g Dandy Man (IRE)—Kadesh (IRE) **Rocbrook Racing Club**
25 **EVOLICATT,** b f Massaat (IRE)—Erica Bing **Mr S. W. Banks**
26 **GIRLSWANNAHAVEFUN,** b f Massaat (IRE)—Only For Fun (IRE) **Mr E. R. Griffiths**
27 **LET'S HAVE A FLYER (IRE),** b f Camacho—Wavebreak **John Abbey, Mike Nolan & Jimmy Fairhurst**

MR DAVID EVANS - continued

28 **MAN MADE OF SMOKE,** gr g Havana Gold (IRE)—Ya Halla (IRE) **Mrs I M Folkes & Richard Kent**
29 **ON THE PULSE (IRE),** b f Dragon Pulse (IRE)—Amthal (IRE)
30 **PRINCESS ANGELA,** b f Massaat (IRE)—Adele Blanc Sec (FR) **G & A Racing**
31 **RADIO GOO GOO,** b gr f Havana Grey—Radio Gaga **Brian Mould, Richard Kent & Partner**
32 **SHE'S A MIRAGE,** b f Kodiac—Aqlaam Vision **T. H. Gallienne**
33 **YANKEE SPIRIT,** b g Washington DC (IRE)—Phantom Spirit **Mrs I. M. Folkes**
34 **ZEPHINA,** b f Zoustar (AUS)—Soho Susie (IRE) **Banks, Windsor R Kent**

TWO-YEAR-OLDS

35 B c 17/04 Mayson—Aubrietia (Dutch Art) **Shropshire Wolves**
36 B f 28/03 Dandy Man (IRE)—Chasing The Rain (Toronado (IRE)) (36014) **P. D. Evans**
37 B c 15/04 Due Diligence (USA)—Curious Fox (Bertolini (USA)) (14286) **Mr & Mrs Paul & Clare Rooney**
38 B c 14/01 Inns of Court (IRE)—Elysium Dream (Champs Elysees) (29612) **P. D. Evans**
39 B f 27/04 Havana Grey—Fire Line (Firebreak)
40 B c 05/01 Inns of Court (IRE)—Forgiving Flower (New Approach (IRE)) (18095) **P. D. Evans**
41 B f 07/04 Massaat (IRE)—Madam Mojito (USA) (Smart Strike (CAN)) **Dalwhinnie Bloodstock, R Kent & Partner**
42 B g 11/03 Massaat (IRE)—Otrooha (IRE) (Oasis Dream) (21000) **Mrs I. M. Folkes**
43 B f 16/02 Sea The Moon (GER)—Piccola Collina (IRE) (Dubawi (IRE)) (36014) **Mr & Mrs Paul & Clare Rooney**
44 **RAMBEAU,** b c 26/04 Washington DC (IRE)—Newton Bomb (IRE) (Fast Company (IRE)) **Mr E. A. R. Morgans**
45 **RED CHATAN,** ch c 12/04 Sioux Nation (USA)—Miss Chamanda (IRE) (Choisir (AUS)) **Mr E. A. R. Morgans**
46 B c 15/01 Markaz (IRE)—Reeh (IRE) (Invincible Spirit (IRE)) (6403) **P. D. Evans**
47 **SARAJEVO BOY (IRE),** ch c 15/02 Dragon Pulse (IRE)—
Sarajevo Rose (IRE) (Dylan Thomas (IRE)) (37615) **Stuart Banks & Partner**
48 B g 05/03 Proconsul—Song To The Moon (IRE) (Oratorio (IRE)) **R. Kent**
49 **STORM ALICE,** b f 12/02 Advertise—Graceful (IRE) (Zoffany (IRE)) (24000) **R. Kent**
50 B f 30/03 Too Darn Hot—Talema (FR) (Sunday Break (JPN)) (19048) **T. H. Gallienne**
51 Ch c 22/04 Exceed And Excel (AUS)—Wavebreak (Tiger Hill (IRE)) (60024) **Mr K. McCabe**

Assistant Trainer: Emma Evans.

---

166 MR JAMES EVANS, Worcester

Postal: **14-16 Kinnersley Severn Stoke, Worcester, Worcestershire**
Contacts: **MOBILE 07813 166430**
EMAIL herbie_evans@hotmail.com WEBSITE www.hjamesevans.co.uk

1 **A MIDNIGHT KISS,** 8, b m Midnight Legend—Wise Little Girl **Mr R. R. Evans**
2 **AMIDNIGHTSTAR,** 6, b m Midnight Legend—Wise Little Girl **Richard Evans Bloodstock**
3 **BUNGLE BAY (IRE),** 4, b g Bungle Inthejungle—Jenny's Dancer **Mrs J. Evans**
4 **CROESO CYMRAEG,** 9, b g Dick Turpin (IRE)—Croeso Cusan **Richard Evans Bloodstock**
5 **DREAM COMPOSER (FR),** 5, b g Dream Ahead (USA)—High Spice (USA) **Peter Clarke Racing Partners**
6 **JUSTCALLMEPETE,** 4, b g Bated Breath—Firenze **Peter Clarke Racing Partners**
7 **KENTUCKY KINGDOM (IRE),** 7, b g Camacho—Venetian Rhapsody (IRE) **Mr B. W. Preece**
8 **LOCKANDLOAD,** 7, b h Midnight Legend—Coldabri (IRE) **Richard Evans Bloodstock**
9 **LORD GETAWAY (IRE),** 11, b g Getaway (GER)—Terre d'Orient (FR) **Mrs J. Evans**
10 **MASQOOL (IRE),** 5, br g Invincible Spirit (IRE)—Eshaadeh (USA) **Peter Clarke Racing Partners**
11 **MOSSING,** 11, b m Passing Glance—Missy Moscow (IRE) **Mrs J. Evans**
12 **RISK AND ROLL (FR),** 9, b g No Risk At All (FR)—Rolie de Vindecy (FR) **Mr B. W. Preece**
13 **ROBERT WALPOLE,** 6, b g Golden Horn—Whazzat **Peter Clarke Racing Partners**

THREE-YEAR-OLDS

14 **AMERICAN ROSE,** b f Washington DC (IRE)—Mortitia **Mr B. W. Preece**

MRS NIKKI EVANS - continued

15 **LADY GAZELLE,** b c Decorated Knight—Lady Rasha **Mr B. W. Preece**
16 **LANDLORDTOTHESTARS (IRE),** b g City of Light (USA)—Dream (USA) **Mr B. W. Preece**
17 B f Cityscape—Malindi Bay (FR) **Mr B. W. Preece**
18 **MINTANA,** gr f Havana Grey—Catmint **Mr B. W. Preece**
19 **THE FLYING FALCO,** b g Falco (USA)—Whocalledmespeedy (IRE) **Mr B. W. Preece**

TWO-YEAR-OLDS

20 B c 17/03 Dark Angel (IRE)—Elusive Beauty (IRE) (Elusive Pimpernel (USA)) (27000) **Mr B. W. Preece**

Assistant Trainer: Mrs Jane Evans.

---

167 MRS NIKKI EVANS, Abergavenny

Postal: **Penbiddle Farm, Penbidwal, Pandy, Abergavenny, Gwent, NP7 8EA**
Contacts: **MOBILE 07977 753437**
EMAIL penbiddleracing@gmail.com WEBSITE NikkiEvansracing.com FACEBOOK NikkiEvansRacing
TWITTER @PenbiddleRacing WHATSAPP 07977753437

1 **AHEAD OF SCHEDULE (IRE),** 8, ch g Shirocco (GER)—Colleen Bawn (FR) **Mr R. Singh**
2 **CONNA SUE (IRE),** 7, b m Imperial Monarch (IRE)—Runaround Sue (IRE) **Hanford's Chemist Ltd**
3 **DANCING DANI (IRE),** 8, ch m Stowaway—Nodelay (IRE) **Hanford's Chemist Ltd & Partner**
4 **EMERALD LADY (IRE),** 4, ch f Garswood—Bahia Emerald (IRE) **Mr A. T. L. Clayton**
5 4, Ch f Black Sam Bellamy (IRE)—Faithful May (IRE) **Hanford's Chemist Ltd**
6 **FULL AUTHORITY (IRE),** 6, gr g Kingman—Ashley Hall (USA) **Tip of the Sword Racing**
7 **HACKBERRY,** 6, b g Nathaniel (IRE)—Dumfriesshire **Mrs N. S. Evans**
8 **HOWDY PARTNER (IRE),** 7, b g Califet (FR)—Areyououtofurmind (IRE) **Mr J. Berry**
9 **MINELLA MAGICAL (IRE),** 5, b g Champs Elysees—Histoire de Moeurs (FR) **Evans & Donlin**
10 **MONTY'S MISSION (IRE),** 9, b m Arctic Cosmos (USA)—Montys Miss (IRE) **Hanford's Chemist Ltd**
11 **MORE THAN LIKELY,** 7, b m Coach House (IRE)—Moss Likely (IRE) **Mr A. T. L. Clayton**
12 **OCEAN'S OF MONEY (IRE),** 7, b m Califet (FR)—Black Money **Mike Sheridan & Partner**
13 **ORANGE GINA,** 7, ch m Schiaparelli (GER)—Bobs Present **Martin Donlin & Lynne Bodman**
14 **REIGN SUEPREME (IRE),** 8, b g Imperial Monarch (IRE)—Runaround Sue (IRE) **Hanford's Chemist Ltd**
15 **SPIRITUS MUNDI (IRE),** 8, b g Yeats (IRE)—Maiden City (IRE) **Mr P. T. Evans & Partner**
16 **TWP STORI,** 5, ch g Proconsul—Gulf Punch **Mrs T. P. James**
17 **WELSH WARRIOR,** 7, b g Harbour Watch (IRE)—Crimson Queen **Mr A. T. L. Clayton**

THREE-YEAR-OLDS

18 **WOOD FARM WAG,** b f Muhaarar—Encore Encore (FR) **Mr J. Berry**

Assistant Trainer: Mr P. T. Evans.

---

168 MR JAMES EWART, Langholm

Postal: **James Ewart Racing Limited, Craig Farm, Westerkirk, Langholm, Dumfriesshire, DG13 0NZ**
Contacts: **PHONE 013873 70707 MOBILE 07786 995073**
EMAIL office@jeracing.co.uk WEBSITE www.jamesewartracing.com

1 **ALLTHEROADRUNNING,** 5, b m Telescope (IRE)—Becky B **The Southrigg Partnership & James Ewart**
2 **BEAT BOX (FR),** 7, b g Cokoriko (FR)—Niemen (FR) **Exors of the Late J. D. Gordon**
3 **BENACK (IRE),** 7, b g Shirocco (GER)—Maggies Oscar (IRE) **Team Benack**
4 **BRAYHILL (IRE),** 8, b g Sholokhov (IRE)—Definite Love (IRE) **Mr A Phillips, Dr C Kesson & Mr N Ewart**
5 **CLONDAW FAME (IRE),** 6, b g Fame And Glory—Aguida (FR) **N. M. L. Ewart**
6 **COMMUNITY REBEL (IRE),** 7, b g Asian Heights—Cnocbui Cailin (IRE) **The Craig Farm Syndicate**
7 **DON'T TELL ALLEN (IRE),** 8, b g Presenting—Liss Alainn (IRE) **Mr R. Cooper**
8 **EMPIRE DE MAULDE (FR),** 9, b g Spanish Moon (USA)—Ondine de Brejoux (FR) **Mr S Murrills & Mr J Ewart**
9 **ERIMITIS,** 5, b m Black Sam Bellamy (IRE)—Think Green
10 **ESCAPEANDEVADE (IRE),** 7, b g Westerner—Sandrinechoix (FR) **The Escapees**

MR JAMES EWART - continued

11 **FARNON (IRE),** 6, b g Arctic Cosmos (USA)—Arts And Music (IRE) **Mr J. Ewart**
12 **FOSTERED PHIL (IRE),** 9, b g Arcadio (GER)—Knock Na Shee (IRE) **N. M. L. Ewart**
13 **HAPY LA VIE (FR),** 6, b g Brave Mansonnien (FR)—Byzantion (FR) **Mr J. Ewart**
14 **HASHTAG LORD (FR),** 6, ch g Coastal Path—Serie Limitee (FR) **Mrs Hugh Fraser**
15 **HEROIQUE DE MAULDE (FR),** 6, ch g Jeu St Eloi (FR)—Ondine de Brejoux (FR) **Mr S Murrills & Mr J Ewart**
16 **HOLD ONTO THE LINE (IRE),** 6, br g Westerner—Dedoctorsdaughter (IRE) **Carruthers, Drew, Kesson & Phillips**
17 **JIMS APPLE (IRE),** 7, br m Sageburg (IRE)—Good Thyne Lucy (IRE) **The Craig Farm Syndicate**
18 **JUGE ET PARTI (FR),** 10, gr g Martaline—Nakota Rag (FR) **The Jp's**
19 **LAKE TAKAPUNA (IRE),** 12, b g Shantou (USA)—Close To Shore (IRE) **Carruthers,Graham,Hughes,Kesson**
20 **LEITRIM CHIEF (IRE),** 7, ch g Leading Light (IRE)—Leitrim Bridge (IRE) **Mrs J. E. Dodd**
21 **LEMOINE,** 4, b g Black Sam Bellamy (IRE)—Think Green **Mr J. Ewart**
22 **LORD ROCO,** 7, b g Rocamadour—Dolly Penrose **N. M. L. Ewart**
23 **NIKGARDE (FR),** 8, b g Kapgarde (FR)—Nikoline (FR) **Mrs J. E. Dodd**
24 **SCARLET N' BLACK,** 5, b g Black Sam Bellamy (IRE)—Overlady
25 **THE BLAME GAME (IRE),** 9, b g Getaway (GER)—Tribal Princess (IRE) **Exors of the Late J. D. Gordon**
26 **THISTLE ASK (IRE),** 6, b g Ask—Thistle Lane (IRE) **The Steel Bonnets**

Assistant Trainer: Briony Ewart.

NH Jockey: Rachael McDonald.

---

169 MR LES EYRE, Beverley

Postal: **Ivy House Stables, Main Street, Catwick, Beverley, North Humberside, HU17 5PJ**
Contacts: **MOBILE 07864 677444**
EMAIL leseyreracing@hotmail.co.uk

1 **ARKID,** 4, b g Ardad (IRE)—Lady Vermeer **Mr G. Parkinson & Mr J. L. Eyre**
2 **BEARCARDI (IRE),** 4, b g Kodi Bear (IRE)—Mojita (IRE) **RP Racing Ltd**
3 **BEDFORD FLYER (IRE),** 5, b g Clodovil (IRE)—Nafa (IRE) **RP Racing Ltd**
4 **FAME AND ACCLAIM (IRE),** 6, b g Acclamation—Applause (IRE) **RP Racing Ltd**
5 **HILARY'S BOY,** 4, b g Lethal Force (IRE)—Mitigate **RP Racing Ltd**
6 **JUST FRANK,** 5, b g Epaulette (AUS)—Mabinia (IRE) **Billy Parker & Steven Parker**
7 **LE BAYOU (FR),** 6, b g Dabirsim (FR)—Kastiya (FR) **Dr V. Webb**

THREE-YEAR-OLDS

8 **DANDILLY (IRE),** b g Dandy Man (IRE)—Lily's Rainbow (IRE) **RP Racing Ltd**

Assistant Trainer: Tracy Johnson.

---

170 MR RICHARD FAHEY, Malton

Trainer did not wish details of their string to appear

---

171 MR CHRIS FAIRHURST, Middleham

Postal: **Glasgow House, Middleham, Leyburn, North Yorkshire, DL8 4QG**
Contacts: **PHONE 01969 622039 MOBILE 07889 410840**
EMAIL cfairhurst@tiscali.co.uk

1 **BENADALID,** 8, b g Assertive—Gambatte **Mrs S. France**
2 **HEZMIE (IRE),** 4, b f Divine Prophet (AUS)—Zoumie (IRE) **Mr A. Davies**
3 **KAYLYN,** 5, b m Charm Spirit (IRE)—Dark Quest **Mr A. Davies**
4 **MADAM ARKATI,** 4, br f Pastoral Pursuits—Accamelia **Mrs C. Arnold**
5 **MASHAM MOOR,** 6, b g Music Master—Jane's Payoff (IRE) **Mrs C. Arnold**
6 **THE ARMED MAN,** 10, b g Misu Bond (IRE)—Accamelia **Mrs C. Arnold**
7 **TOP ATTRACTION,** 6, b g Fountain of Youth (IRE)—Symphonic Dancer (USA) **The PQD Partnership**
8 **VALLAMOREY,** 5, gr m Outstrip—Zagaleta **Mrs A. M. Leggett**
9 **VELMA,** 6, b m Fast Company (IRE)—Valoria **Mr A. Davies**

THREE-YEAR-OLDS

10 **GREY FORCE ONE,** gr g Lethal Force (IRE)—Flamenco **Hugh T. Redhead**
11 **VIXEY,** b f Cable Bay (IRE)—Valoria **Mr A. Davies**

---

172 MR JAMES FANSHAWE, Newmarket

Postal: **Pegasus Stables, Snailwell Road, Newmarket, Suffolk, CB8 7DJ**
Contacts: **PHONE 01638 664525 FAX 01638 664523**
EMAIL james@jamesfanshawe.com WEBSITE www.jamesfanshawe.com

1 **CHIPS AND RICE,** 4, b f Golden Horn—Semaral (IRE) **Mr D. M. Thurlby**
2 **COMPLIANT,** 4, b f Pivotal—Royal Seal **Cheveley Park Stud Limited**
3 **ENDUED (IRE),** 4, b g Footstepsinthesand—Amethystos (IRE) **Mr B. C. M. Wong**
4 **FRESH,** 6, b g Bated Breath—Kendal Mint **Clipper Group Holdings Ltd**
5 **HICKORY (IRE),** 5, b g Free Eagle (IRE)—Badr Al Badoor (IRE) **Fred Archer Racing - Galliard**
6 **LAILAH,** 4, b f Australia—Wedding Speech (IRE) **Mr G. Marney**
7 **LIBERTUS,** 4, b g Equiano (FR)—Italian Connection **Fred Archer Racing - Peeping Tom**
8 **NOVEL LEGEND (IRE),** 4, b g Nathaniel (IRE)—Majestic Dubawi **Mr K. K. B. Ho**
9 **ROYAL SCANDAL,** 4, ch f Dubawi (IRE)—Seal of Approval **T. R. G. Vestey**
10 **SECOND SLIP (IRE),** 6, b g Lope de Vega (IRE)—Arkadina (IRE) **Merry Fox Stud Limited**
11 **SPIT SPOT,** 4, ch f Sir Percy—Taweyla (IRE) **Mr D. M. Thurlby**
12 **TUXEDO JUNCTION,** 4, b g Iffraaj—Dash To The Front **Castle Down Racing**
13 **WANDERING ROCKS,** 4, ch g Ulysses (IRE)—West of The Moon **Cheveley Park Stud Limited**
14 **WANNABE BRAVE (IRE),** 4, b g Fastnet Rock (AUS)—Wannabe Special **Mrs G. J. Davey**
15 **WILLEM TWEE,** 4, b g Ribchester (IRE)—Paulinie **Chris van Hoorn Racing**

THREE-YEAR-OLDS

16 **ALPINE GIRL (IRE),** b f Acclamation—Almond Brook **Owners Group 097**
17 **AMERICAN BELLE (IRE),** b f Starspangledbanner (AUS)—Syndicate **Fred Archer Racing - Little Sister**
18 **ANNIE LAW,** b f Havana Grey—Song Lark **Law Fertilisers Ltd**
19 **BERNADINE (IRE),** b f Kodi Bear (IRE)—Alosha (IRE) **Mr A. R. Boyd-Rochfort**
20 **BRIGITTE,** b f Sixties Icon—Esteemed Lady (IRE) **Mrs Doreen M Swinburn & Partner**
21 **CRACKSKING,** ch c Frankel—Calyxa **Mrs J. Ostermann**
22 **DENIS ANTHONY (IRE),** b g Australia—Dolce Strega (IRE) **Sir William & Mr David Russell**
23 **ELLADONNA (GER),** b f Belardo (IRE)—Elle Gala (IRE) **The Macaroni Beach Society**
24 **EMMA EMILLEEN,** b f Lope de Vega (IRE)—Millistar **Helena Springfield Ltd**
25 **ENSUED (USA),** b c Lemon Drop Kid (USA)—Alluvial Gold (IRE) **Mr B. C. M. Wong**
26 **FAST AFFAIR,** b f Cracksman—Felicity (GER) **Mrs J. Ostermann**
27 **FIRST OF MAY,** b f Mayson—Roubles (USA) **Elite Racing Club**

MR JAMES FANSHAWE - continued

28 **INTERGALACTICAT,** b c Bobby's Kitten (USA)—Interstella **Fred Archer Racing - Thunder**
29 **LADY WORMSLEY (IRE),** ch f Twilight Son—Dutch Princess **Sir William Russell B McManus Mrs S Roy**
30 **LION KINGDOM,** gr c Roaring Lion (USA)—Granny Franny (USA) **Qatar Racing Limited**
31 **MASO BASTIE,** b g Churchill (IRE)—Opportuna **Mrs A. M. Swinburn**
32 **MASTER DANDY (IRE),** ch g Dandy Man (IRE)—Honeymead (IRE) **Fred Archer Racing - Grandmaster**
33 **MINEKO (FR),** b f Wootton Bassett—Harem Lady (FR) **Mrs A. M. Swinburn**
34 **MISS MAI TAI,** b f Prince of Lir (IRE)—Mia Tia **The Cool Silk Partnership**
35 **MOOGIE,** gr f Mastercraftsman (IRE)—Starlet (IRE) **The Earl Of Halifax**
36 B f Muhaarar—Peacehaven (IRE) **Manor Farm Stud & Mr J. E. Rose**
37 **PRAISING,** b f Acclamation—Spirit Raiser (IRE) **Lord Vestey**
38 **ROCK GODDESS,** b br f Teofilo (IRE)—Bentayga Girl **The Cool Silk Partnership**
39 **SEA OF TRANQUILITY,** b g Sea The Moon (GER)—She's Gorgeous (IRE) **Johnstone Partnership**
40 **SONG OF SUCCESS,** b f Havana Gold (IRE)—Rio's Cliffs **Mr J. E. Rose**
41 **STARBASE,** b g Sea The Stars (IRE)—Silk Sari **Fittocks, Bengough, Booth, Silver, Steed**
42 **THROUBI (IRE),** b f Teofilo (IRE)—Dubai Fashion (IRE) **Mrs A. M. Swinburn**
43 **THUNDER PRINCESS (IRE),** ch f Night of Thunder (IRE)—Peak Princess (IRE) **Mr S. D. Bradley**
44 **YEOMAN,** b g Tamayuz—Harmonica **Owners Group 108**

TWO-YEAR-OLDS

45 **ALL GREEK TO ME,** ch c 25/03 Ulysses (IRE)—Angeleno (IRE) (Belong To Me (USA)) (55000) **JUSTWOW Ltd**
46 **ASIMOV,** b c 03/04 Pivotal—Interstella (Sea The Stars (IRE)) **Castle Down Racing**
47 **CAMBRIA LEGEND (IRE),** b c 21/02 Camelot—
Enchanted Empress (IRE) (Holy Roman Emperor (IRE)) (100000) **Mr K. K. B. Ho**
48 **CHARMAINE,** b f 01/04 Camelot—Zest (IRE) (Duke of Marmalade (IRE)) **Elite Racing Club**
49 Ch g 12/02 Territories (IRE)—Chetwynd Abbey (Nathaniel (IRE)) (20000)
50 B f 06/05 Cracksman—Constant Dream (Kheleyf (USA)) (125000) **Mrs A. M. Swinburn**
51 **EMERALD CITY,** b c 22/01 Dream Ahead (USA)—Taweyla (IRE) (Teofilo (IRE)) **Mr D. M. Thurlby**
52 **GLASTONBURY,** b c 04/02 Showcasing—
Mecca's Gift (IRE) (Dark Angel (IRE)) (50000) **Fred Archer Racing - Ormonde II**
53 **HAVRAISE (FR),** b f 10/05 Le Havre (IRE)—
Restiadargent (FR) (Kendargent (FR)) (108043) **Cornthrop Bloodstock Limited**
54 **HEATHCLIFF,** b c 14/02 Iffraaj—Isola Verde (Oasis Dream) **Jan & Peter Hopper & Michelle Morris**
55 **KIND OF BLUE,** b c 25/02 Blue Point (IRE)—Blues Sister (Compton Place) **Michelle Morris & Jan & Peter Hopper**
56 B c 11/02 Churchill (IRE)—Miss Frangipane (IRE) (Acclamation) (210000) **Mr B. C. M. Wong**
57 B f 10/02 Zoustar (AUS)—Moonlight Sonata (Galileo (IRE)) **Mrs M. Slack**
58 B f 31/03 Siyouni (FR)—Moonlit Garden (IRE) (Exceed And Excel (AUS)) (160000) **Mrs A. M. Swinburn**
59 **PIQUE',** ch f 15/03 Nathaniel (IRE)—Pongee (Barathea (IRE)) **Fittocks Stud**
60 **RAINPROOF,** ch f 22/03 Ulysses (IRE)—Flood Warning (Pivotal) **Cheveley Park Stud Limited**
61 B f 24/02 Nathaniel (IRE)—Royal Empress (IRE) (Holy Roman Emperor (IRE)) (120000) **Mrs A. M. Swinburn**
62 **SALAMANCA CITY (IRE),** b f 17/03 Phoenix of Spain (IRE)—
Sharqawiyah (Dubawi (IRE)) (100000) **Mrs J. Ostermann**
63 **SURVEYOR,** b f 16/03 Pivotal—Spatial (New Approach (IRE)) **Cheveley Park Stud Limited**
64 **SWEET MILLEFEUILLE,** b f 21/04 Territories (IRE)—Millistar (Galileo (IRE)) **Helena Springfield Ltd**
65 **WONDER,** ch c 18/03 Masar (IRE)—High Drama (IRE) (High Chaparral (IRE)) **Senel Nafi & Gary Marney**

Assistant Trainer: Tom Fanshawe.

173

MISS JULIA FEILDEN, Newmarket

Postal: **Harraton Stud, Laceys Lane, Exning, Newmarket, Suffolk, CB8 7HW**
Contacts: **MOBILE 07974 817694**
EMAIL juliafeilden@gmail.com WEBSITE www.juliafeildenracing.com

1 **ALIBABA,** 6, b g Lawman (FR)—Fantasy In Blue **Ahamed Farook & Julia Feilden**
2 **ARPINA (IRE),** 4, ch f Starspangledbanner (AUS)—Lara Amelia (IRE) **Steve Clarke & Partner**
3 **ENGRAVE,** 7, gr m Dark Angel (IRE)—Hot Wired **Newmarket Equine Tours Racing Club**

MISS JULIA FEILDEN - continued

4 **FEN TIGER (IRE),** 5, b g Vadamos (FR)—Three Knots (IRE) **Mrs C. T. Bushnell**
5 **HEER'S SADIE,** 5, b m Heeraat (IRE)—Sadiigah **Mr J. W. Ford**
6 **MRS MEADER,** 7, b m Cityscape—Bavarica **Nj Bloodstock**
7 **QUEEN'S COMPANY,** 4, b f Siyouni (FR)—Queen's Charter **Good Company Partnership**
8 **ROSE FANDANGO,** 5, ch m Exceed And Excel (AUS)—Mumtaza **Mr U. Hormann**
9 **SCOTCH MIST,** 4, gr f Time Test—Positive Spin **Carol Bushnell & Partners**
10 **SMOKEY MALONE,** 5, gr g Outstrip—Trixie Malone **The Sultans of Speed**
11 **SPANISH MANE (IRE),** 8, b m Havana Gold (IRE)—Kiva **Stowstowquickquickstow Partnership**
12 **THE MOUSE KING (IRE),** 4, gr g El Kabeir (USA)—Empress Anna (IRE) **Mrs C. T. Bushnell**

THREE-YEAR-OLDS

13 **CLENCHED,** ch f Cityscape—Grasped **Adrian Sparks & Partner**
14 **CORPORATE RAIDER (IRE),** b g Profitable (IRE)—Zenella **Newmarket Equine Tours Racing Club**
15 **HURRICANE KIKO (IRE),** gr g Kuroshio (AUS)—Madame Thunder (IRE) **Carol Bushnell & Partners**
16 **LADY CLEMMIE,** b f Churchill (IRE)—Joquina (IRE) **Chris Cleevely & Partners**
17 **MACHO SUN (IRE),** b g Camacho—Morning Jewel (IRE) **In It To Win Partnership**
18 **SAVANNAH SONG,** gr f Roaring Lion (USA)—Dynaglow (USA) **Carol Bushnell & Partners**
19 **STINTINO SUNSET,** b f Twilight Son—Sunset Kitty (USA) **Steve Clarke & Partners 3**
20 **THREE BEAUZ,** br f Brazen Beau (AUS)—Three Gracez **Mr U. Hormann**
21 **TRINIDAD CALYPSO,** gr f Roaring Lion (USA)—My Only One **Mrs C. T. Bushnell**
22 **ZANAGOR,** b f Zarak (FR)—Jasmiralda (FR) **Mrs I. Corbani**
23 **ZANY IDEA (IRE),** b f Zoffany (IRE)—Novel Concept (IRE) **Newmarket Equine Tours Racing Club**

TWO-YEAR-OLDS

24 **LEON TROTSKY,** b g 19/02 Michigan (USA)—Moana (Kheleyf (USA)) **Edwards & Spells**
25 **RUSHEEN BOY,** b c 20/04 Coach House (IRE)—Displaying Amber (Showcasing) (4000) **Munster Heroes**
26 **SILVER SHAMROCK (IRE),** gr f 08/03 El Kabeir (USA)—
La Grande Elisa (IRE) (Ad Valorem (USA)) (11204) **Carol Bushnell & Partners**

Assistant Trainer: Ross Birkett.

Flat Jockey: Dylan Hogan. **Apprentice Jockey:** Mr Sam Feilden. **Amateur Jockey:** Mr R. Birkett.

---

174 MR ROGER FELL, Nawton

Postal: **Arthington Barn House, Highfield Lane, Nawton, York, North Yorkshire, YO62 7TU**
Contacts: **PHONE 01439 770184**
EMAIL rogerfellracing@gmail.com WEBSITE www.rogerfell.co.uk

1 **BRAWBY (IRE),** 4, b g Vadamos (FR)—Last Hooray **Fell & Collier**
2 **COCKALORUM (IRE),** 8, b g Cape Cross (IRE)—Opinionated (IRE) **K Hardy & R Fell**
3 **COLTOR (IRE),** 6, b g Free Eagle (IRE)—Reclamation (IRE) **Nick Bradley Racing 3 & Partner**
4 **DANDY SPIRIT (IRE),** 6, b g Dandy Man (IRE)—Spirit of Grace **Gove & Shaw Racing 03 & Partner**
5 **DANDYS GOLD (IRE),** 9, b m Dandy Man (IRE)—Proud Penny (IRE) **Fell & Windress**
6 **DAPPER MAN (IRE),** 9, b g Dandy Man (IRE)—Gist (IRE) **Colne Valley Racing & Partner**
7 **DIGITAL (IRE),** 5, b g Kodi Bear (IRE)—Notte Illuminata (IRE) **Fine Claret Racing & Partner**
8 **ELDRICKJONES (IRE),** 4, b g Cotai Glory—Dream Impossible (IRE) **Mr R. G. Fell**
9 **END ZONE,** 6, b g Dark Angel (IRE)—Brown Eyed Honey **Middleham Park Racing XIX & Partner 1**
10 **GIFT OF RAAJ (IRE),** 8, b g Iffraaj—Gift of Spring (USA) **Fishlake Commercial Motors Ltd**
11 **GINATO (IRE),** 5, b g Footstepsinthesand—Jacquelin Jag (IRE) **Mr R. G. Fell**
12 **GLOBAL SPIRIT,** 8, b g Invincible Spirit (IRE)—Centime **Swales & Fell**
13 **HARSWELL DUKE (IRE),** 5, b g Garswood—Grafitti **Harswell Thoroughbred Racing**
14 **IRON SHERIFF (IRE),** 5, b g Lawman (FR)—Rebelline (IRE) **Mr R. G. Fell**
15 **JEAN BAPTISTE (IRE),** 6, b g Invincible Spirit (IRE)—Pioneer Bride (USA) **Woodhurst Construction Ltd**
16 **KAPONO,** 7, b g Kuroshio (AUS)—Fair Maiden (JPN) **Mr S. M. Al Sabah**
17 **LA TRINIDAD,** 6, b g Bated Breath—High Drama (IRE) **Mrs D. W. Davenport**

MR ROGER FELL - continued

18 **LARGE ACTION,** 7, b g Iffraaj—Titian's Pride (USA) **Nick Bradley Racing 46**
19 **LOTUS ROSE,** 4, b f Showcasing—Ealaan (USA) **The Roses Partnership & R G Fell**
20 **MARIE'S DIAMOND (IRE),** 7, b br h Footstepsinthesand—Sindiyma (IRE) **The Wolf Pack & Partner**
21 **METHINKS (IRE),** 4, b g Showcasing—Landale **Mr S. M. Al Sabah**
22 **MUNTADAB (IRE),** 11, b g Invincible Spirit (IRE)—Chibola (ARG) **Swales & Fell**
23 **OSO RAPIDO (IRE),** 6, b g Kodiac—Burke's Rock **Woodhurst Construction & G Chrysanthou**
24 **PRIMO,** 4, b g Acclamation—Border Bloom **Mr S. M. Al Sabah**
25 **SHE'S GOT BOTTLE,** 4, b f Lethal Force (IRE)—Lady Tabitha (IRE) **Gordon Bulloch & S Hardcastle D Szepler**
26 **THE FLYING GINGER (IRE),** 5, ch m Showcasing—Law of The Range **Mr S. M. Al Sabah**
27 **TOSHIZOU (IRE),** 5, b h Galileo (IRE)—Remember You (IRE) **Nick Bradley Racing 3 & Partner**
28 **USTATH,** 7, ch g Exceed And Excel (AUS)—Adorn **MPR LXXXII & Peter Hewitson & Partner**
29 **WHERE'S DIANA (IRE),** 4, gr f Markaz (IRE)—Maid In Heaven (IRE) **Mr R. G. Fell**

THREE-YEAR-OLDS

30 **CHAMPAGNY (FR),** b f Shalaa (IRE)—Trainnah **Nick Bradley Racing 3 & Partner**
31 **CONGRESS,** b c Washington DC (IRE)—La Cabana **R Hadley & R Fell**
32 **EDWINA SHEERAN (IRE),** ch f Decorated Knight—Rooney O'Mara **Mr S. M. Al Sabah**
33 **HARSWELL ROSE,** b f Adaay (IRE)—Ealaan (USA) **Harswell Tb Racing & Roses Partnership**
34 **HENZAR (IRE),** b br c Gutaifan (IRE)—Amallna **Nick Bradley Racing 3 & Partner**
35 **KINDNESS MATTERS (IRE),** b f Union Rags (USA)—Sea of Laughter (USA) **Mr S. M. Al Sabah**
36 **LADYWANTAWAY (IRE),** b f Awtaad (IRE)—Lady Vyrnwy (IRE) **Nick Bradley Racing 3 & Partner**
37 **MAGGIE'S TERN (IRE),** b f Bungle Inthejungle—Khayrat (IRE) **Nick Bradley Racing 3 & Partner**
38 **MARIE'S JEWEL (IRE),** b g Kodiac—Silque **R Hadley & R Fell**
39 **MR SQUIRES (IRE),** ch c Zoffany (IRE)—Of Course Darling **Gove & Shaw Racing 03 & Partner**
40 **RIEVAULX RAVER (IRE),** b g Elzaam (AUS)—Juste Pour Moi (IRE) **Grange Park Racing, Collier & Fell**
41 **SHANDY STAR (IRE),** b f Cotai Glory—Nouvelle Nova (IRE) **Nick Bradley Racing 3 & Partner**
42 **SHINE'S AMBITION (IRE),** b c Kessaar (IRE)—January Morn (USA) **Gove & Shaw Racing 03 & Partner**
43 **TERRITORIAL WATERS (IRE),** b f National Defense—Poker Hospital **Nick Bradley Racing 3 & Partner**
44 **TRABAJO DETECHO,** b g Bated Breath—Grand Depart **Nick Bradley Racing 3 & Partner**

TWO-YEAR-OLDS

45 B f 15/02 Time Test—Kelamita (IRE) (Pivotal) (10000)
46 **LOUELLA (IRE),** b f 03/05 Invincible Army (IRE)—All On Red (IRE) (Red Clubs (IRE)) (15000) **Mr D. A. Swales**
47 Ch f 21/05 Dandy Man (IRE)—Prem Ramya (GER) (Big Shuffle (USA)) (15206) **Nick Bradley Racing 3 & Partner**
48 **YEULAN (IRE),** b f 14/05 Advertise—Wahylah (IRE) (Shamardal (USA)) (20000) **Grange Park Racing XX & Partner**

Assistant Trainer: Sean Murray.

---

175 MR CHARLIE FELLOWES, Newmarket

Postal: **Bedford House Stables, 7 Bury Road, Newmarket, Suffolk, CB8 7BX**
Contacts: **PHONE 01638 666948 MOBILE 07968 499596**
EMAIL charlie@charliefellowesracing.co.uk WEBSITE www.charliefellowesracing.co.uk

1 **AL RUFAA (FR),** 6, b g Kingman—Clarmina (IRE) **Mr P. E. Wildes**
2 **ATRIUM,** 4, b g Holy Roman Emperor (IRE)—Hail Shower (IRE) **Highclere Thoroughbred Racing - Pergola**
3 **CUMULONIMBUS (IRE),** 4, ch g Night of Thunder (IRE)—Queen's Novel **Mr D. R. J. King, Mr P. J. Hickman**
4 **FRESH HOPE,** 4, b f New Approach (IRE)—Wiener Valkyrie **The Eclipse Partnership**
5 **GORAK (FR),** 4, b g Goken (FR)—Ponte Bawi (IRE) **First Tuesday Syndicate**
6 **GRAND ALLIANCE (IRE),** 4, b g Churchill (IRE)—Endless Love (IRE) **Mrs S. M. Roy**
7 **HELLO ZABEEL (IRE),** 5, b g Frankel—Lady of The Desert (USA) **Mr P. E. Wildes**
8 **MEDRARA,** 4, b g Lope de Vega (IRE)—Moderah **Sohi, C Fellowes**
9 **PIRATE KING,** 8, br g Farhh—Generous Diana **Daniel MacAuliffe & Anoj Don**
10 **POWER OF DARKNESS,** 8, b g Power—Summers Lease **Mr C. H. Fellowes**

MR CHARLIE FELLOWS - continued

11 **PURPLE RIBBON,** 5, b m Gleneagles (IRE)—Crimson Ribbon (USA) **A. E. Oppenheimer**
12 **SATURN FIVE (IRE),** 4, b g Ulysses (IRE)—Dawning (USA) **Mr P. E. Wildes**
13 **SURREY KNIGHT (FR),** 4, b g Le Havre (IRE)—Millionaia (IRE) **Surrey Racing (SK)**
14 **TEQUILAMOCKINGBIRD,** 4, ch f New Approach (IRE)—Tequila Sunrise **Mr C. N. Wright**
15 **TROIS VALLEES,** 4, b f New Bay—Bellwether **A. M. Mitchell**
16 **VADREAM,** 5, b m Brazen Beau (AUS)—Her Honour (IRE) **Mr D. R. J. King**
17 **VANITY AFFAIR (IRE),** 6, b g Mayson—Height of Vanity (IRE) **Dun Lee & Charlie Fellowes**
18 **VIA SERENDIPITY,** 9, b g Invincible Spirit (IRE)—Mambo Light (USA) **D. S. Lovatt**
19 **WYNTER WILDES,** 4, b f Tamayuz—Khazeena **Mr P. E. Wildes**
20 **YOUNG ENDLESS,** 4, b g Champs Elysees—Eternity Ring **The Endless Acres Five**

THREE-YEAR-OLDS

21 **ART DE VIVRE,** b f Golden Horn—Sinnamary (IRE) **A. E. Oppenheimer**
22 **AUSSIE MYSTIC,** b g Australia—Hyper Dream (IRE) **Dahab Racing**
23 **BECCARA ROSE (IRE),** ch f Sea The Stars (IRE)—Nectar de Rose (FR) **Mr D. R. J. King, Mr P. J. Hickman**
24 **CHURCHILL ROSE (IRE),** b f Churchill (IRE)—Market Day **Newmarket Racing Club HQiv**
25 **CLOUDBREAKER,** br f Sea The Stars (IRE)—Deveron (USA) **Mr D. R. J. King**
26 **CRACKED UP,** b f Cracksman—Golden Laughter (USA) **A. E. Oppenheimer**
27 **EL JASOR (IRE),** br c Le Havre (IRE)—Manaha (FR) **Sheikh Ahmed Al Maktoum**
28 **FITZ PERFECTLY (FR),** b f No Nay Never (USA)—Kalimenta (USA) **Fitzdares & Friends**
29 **HALLROSE,** ch f Tasleet—Leap of Joy (IRE) **Craft Thoroughbreds & Charlie Fellowes**
30 **HOLY FIRE,** b f Unfortunately (IRE)—Abonos (IRE) **Offthebridle Podcast**
31 **ITALIAN MAGIC (IRE),** b g Mukhadram—Carsulae (IRE) **Moore, Clark, Loftus, Jubb & Fellowes**
32 **LADY PRIMROSE (IRE),** b f Dandy Man (IRE)—Kayak **Mathis Stables & Mr John O'Connor**
33 **MARBAAN,** b c Oasis Dream—Zahoo (IRE) **Sheikh Ahmed Al Maktoum**
34 **QUIZLET,** b g Time Test—Speed Date **Mathis Stables LLC, Joe Soiza & Charlie Fellowes**
35 **REFLEX (IRE),** gr g El Kabeir (USA)—Knapton Hill **Highclere - Ernest Rutherford**
36 **ROYAL RAZZMATAZZ (IRE),** ch c Tasleet—Royal Visit (IRE) **Mr A. C. Waney**
37 **SCYLLA,** ch f Ulysses (IRE)—Cosseted **Lady De Ramsey**
38 **SHAHBAZ (IRE),** b g Free Eagle (IRE)—Middle Persia **The Wolfpack & Partners Five**
39 **SMOKY MOUNTAIN (IRE),** b g Frankel—The Wagon Wheel (IRE) **Lady C. Bamford & Miss A. Bamford**
40 **SURREY NOIR (FR),** b c Dream Ahead (USA)—Model Black (IRE) **Surrey Racing SN**
41 **TANGLED IN TIME,** b f Dandy Man (IRE)—Tangled Thread
42 **TAWALLA (IRE),** b c Invincible Spirit (IRE)—Afdhaad **Sheikh Ahmed Al Maktoum**
43 **VICTORY HOUSE (IRE),** b g Dubawi (IRE)—Yaazy (IRE)
44 **WALDERSTERN,** b g Sea The Stars (IRE)—Waldnah **Mr D. R. J. King, Mr P. J. Hickman**

TWO-YEAR-OLDS

45 B c 01/01 Havana Grey—Berkshire Honey (Sakhee's Secret) **Mr P. E. Wildes**
46 **BESPOKE,** b f 12/03 Ardad (IRE)—Kiringa (Kyllachy) (26000) **Highclere Thoroughbred Racing**
47 B f 15/01 Zoustar (AUS)—Carolinae (Makfi) (140000) **Mathis, D Redvers, A&E Frost & Fellowes**
48 B c 01/01 Zoustar (AUS)—Crimson Rosette (IRE) (Teofilo (IRE)) **St Albans Bloodstock Ltd**
49 B c 10/05 Too Darn Hot—Deveron (USA) (Cozzene (USA)) (75000) **S. Ali**
50 B f 01/01 Gleneagles (IRE)—Endless Love (IRE) (Dubai Destination (USA)) **Mrs S. M. Roy**
51 B c 10/02 Make Believe—Fleur de Cactus (IRE) (Montjeu (IRE)) (136054) **Sheikh Ahmed Al Maktoum**
52 Br c 14/02 Bated Breath—If So (Iffraaj) (48000) **Bedford House Racing I**
53 Ch f 19/02 Showcasing—Mimram (Kheleyf (USA)) (35000) **Bedford House Racing II**
54 B c 14/04 Kodi Bear (IRE)—Moulane Lady (IRE) (Lilbourne Lad (IRE)) (32000) **Mr J. B. A. Al Attiyah**
55 Br c 03/03 Ten Sovereigns (IRE)—My Dorris (IRE) (Uncle Mo (USA)) (40016) **Sheikh Ahmed Al Maktoum**
56 B c 19/03 Crystal Ocean—Nateeja (IRE) (Shamardal (USA)) (115000) **Mr D. R. J. King**
57 Gr f 01/01 Muhaarar—Night Thrills (Dark Angel) **Mr C Wright & Mr A Macdonald**
58 B f 17/02 Bated Breath—Ocean Paradise (New Approach (IRE)) (42000) **The Paradise Partnership**
59 Ch c 11/02 Masar (IRE)—Pas de Soucis (IRE) (Footstepsinthesand) (84034) **Sheikh Ahmed Al Maktoum**
60 B c 25/04 Kodiac—Postulant (Kyllachy) (70000) **Dahab Racing**
61 B c 01/01 Exceeed and Excel (AUS)—Romaana (Iffraaj) **Sheikh Ahmed Al Maktoum**
62 B f 25/02 Cable Bay—Run Of The Day (Three Valleys (USA)) **Mr D. R. J. King**
63 B c 30/01 Cracksman—Singing Sky (Oasis Dream) (105000) **Mr D. R. J. King, Mr P. J. Hickman**
64 B c 01/01 Lope De Vega (IRE)—The Waggon Wheel (IRE) (Acclamation (IRE)) **Lady C. Bamford & Miss A. Bamford**
65 **THUNDERETTE (IRE),** b f 15/02 Night of Thunder (IRE)—Whazzis (Desert Prince (IRE)) (50000) **Dahab Racing**

MR CHARLIE FELLOWES - continued

66 Ch f 01/01 Night Of Thunder (IRE)—Vine Street (IRE) (Singspiel (IRE)) **Sheikh Ahmed Al Maktoum**
67 B c 29/03 Australia—Wazin (Dutch Art) (65000) **Mr P. J. Hickman**
68 B f 24/01 Kingman—Winning Ways (AUS) (Declaration of War (USA)) (300000) **Mr D. R. J. King, Mr P. J. Hickman**

Apprentice Jockey: Mikkel Mortensen.

---

176 MR JAMES FERGUSON, Newmarket

Postal: **Kremlin Cottage Stables, Snailwell Road, Newmarket, Suffolk, CB8 7DP**
Contacts: **WORK 01638 599581**
WORK EMAIL james@jamesfergusonracing.com

1 **BAGUE D'OR (IRE),** 5, ch g Belardo (IRE)—Ravensburg **Mr S. Fustok**
2 **COTOPAXI MOON,** 4, b g Farhh—Patroness **Dr C. Osborne, Dr A. Osborne**
3 **CURRENCY EXCHANGE (IRE),** 5, ch g Night of Thunder (IRE)—Mon Bijou (IRE) **Mr J. J. Ferguson**
4 **DEAUVILLE LEGEND (IRE),** 4, b g Sea The Stars (IRE)—Soho Rose (IRE) **Mr K. K. B. Ho**
5 **DIDEROT,** 5, br g Bated Breath—Modern Look **Owners Group 091**
6 **FIRST FOLIO,** 5, gr g Dark Angel (IRE)—Lilian Baylis (IRE) **Owners Group 083**
7 **KINGMANIA (IRE),** 5, b m Kingman—Greek Goddess (IRE) **Mr S. Fustok**
8 **MORE DIAMONDS (IRE),** 4, b f Zoffany (IRE)—Pellinore (USA) **Ahmed Jaber**
9 **PULCHERIA (IRE),** 4, b f Shamardal (USA)—Placidia (IRE) **Natalma**
10 **SAN ISIDRO (IRE),** 5, ch g Power—Olanthia (IRE) **Owners Group 102**
11 **SAVROLA (IRE),** 4, b g Churchill (IRE)—Toujours L'Amour **Mr S. Fustok**
12 **SHAMEKH,** 4, ch g New Bay—Ever Love (BRZ) **J Taylor, A Taylor, C Osborne & Partner**
13 **SUNSTRIKE (IRE),** 4, b f Dark Angel (IRE)—Extricate (IRE) **Natalma**

THREE-YEAR-OLDS

14 **ALPHA ZULU,** b c Zoustar (AUS)—La Rioja **Qatar Racing Limited**
15 **BEAUTIFUL SUNRISE (IRE),** b g Exceed And Excel (AUS)—Spanish Fly (IRE) **Mr S. Siddiqui**
16 **BEELZEBUB (IRE),** b g Dark Angel (IRE)—Hay Chewed (IRE) **Nas Syndicate Ii & Partners**
17 **CALYPSO (IRE),** b g Tamayuz—Alors Quoi (IRE) **Nas Syndicate, M Buckley & Mrs A M Hayes**
18 **CANBERRA LEGEND (IRE),** ch c Australia—Rocana **Mr K. K. B. Ho**
19 **CHEALAMY,** gr f Siyouni (FR)—Carnachy (IRE) **St Albans Bloodstock Limited**
20 **CROWNING,** b f Oasis Dream—Learned Friend (GER)
21 **ENGELBERT,** b g Havana Grey—Dare To Dream **Owners Group 105**
22 **FLAXEN FIELDS (IRE),** b f Galileo Gold—Victoria Montoya **G Bishop & A Kirkland**
23 **GLORIOUS LION,** b c Roaring Lion (USA)—Glories (USA) **Qatar Racing Limited**
24 **GOOD KARMA,** gr g Dark Angel (IRE)—Prontamente **Michael Buckley & China Horse Club**
25 **HOVER ON THE WIND (IRE),** b c No Nay Never (USA)—Casila (IRE) **Mrs N. S. L. Thorne**
26 **LADY CHAPEL (IRE),** b f Dandy Man (IRE)—Sistine **Elite Racing Club**
27 **LADY CLAYPOOLE (IRE),** b f Starspangledbanner (AUS)—Short Affair **Mr W. K. Wycoff**
28 **LAND LEGEND (FR),** ch c Galileo (IRE)—Landikusic (IRE) **Mr K. K. B. Ho**
29 **LIKE A TIGER,** ch c Farhh—Last Tango Inparis **Nas Syndicate Ii, Castledown & L Lynam**
30 **LOUAIZEH (IRE),** b f Ribchester (IRE)—Toujours L'Amour **Mr S. Fustok**
31 **MAPOGO,** gr c Roaring Lion (USA)—Mutatis Mutandis (IRE) **Qatar Racing Limited**
32 **MENALIPPE (IRE),** b f Bungle Inthejungle—Scarlet Wings **Hasmonean Racing & Mr A Chapman**
33 **OUTWARD BOUND,** gr f Outstrip—Shamara (IRE) **Lady Juliet Tadgell**
34 **RAGOSINA,** b f Teofilo (IRE)—Hadeeqa (IRE) **O.T.I. Racing**
35 **ROARING LEGEND (FR),** gr ro c Roaring Lion (USA)—Amarysia (FR) **Mr K. K. B. Ho**
36 **STAR ROCKETTE (IRE),** b f Fastnet Rock (AUS)—Stars At Night (IRE) **NAS Syndicate II**
37 **STORMY DENISE,** ch f Intello (GER)—Gracious Diana **Canary Thoroughbreds**
38 **VELVET THUNDER,** b f Zoustar (AUS)—Stella Blue (FR)
39 **VILLAGE LEGEND (IRE),** b c Australia—Imalwayshotforyou (USA) **Mr K. K. B. Ho**
40 **WONDER LEGEND (IRE),** b c Sea The Stars (IRE)—Sea of Wonders (IRE) **Mr K. K. B. Ho**
41 **ZOOLOGY,** b c Zoustar (AUS)—Peach Melba **Qatar Racing Limited**

MR JAMES FERGUSON - continued

TWO-YEAR-OLDS

42 **BORN THIS WAY (IRE),** b c 10/02 Lope de Vega (IRE)—
Wizz Kid (IRE) (Whipper (USA)) (128051) **Michael Buckley & Ballylinch Stud**
43 B f 13/01 Zoustar (AUS)—Coral Sea (Excelebration (IRE)) (120000)
44 B gr f 15/01 Time Test—Dabble (IRE) (Mastercraftsman (IRE)) (10000) **Mr G. S. Bishop**
45 **DARING LEGEND,** b c 28/02 Dark Angel (IRE)—Swiss Air (Oasis Dream) (150000) **Mr K. K. B. Ho**
46 B f 11/02 Waldgeist—Donau (IRE) (High Chaparral (IRE)) (16807)
47 **DRAMA,** b c 08/03 Havana Grey—
Reedanjas (IRE) (Sir Prancealot (IRE)) (27000) **Highclere Thoroughbred Racing Ltd**
48 B c 04/05 Dark Angel (IRE)—Fanciful Dancer (Groom Dancer (USA)) (45000) **Mrs S. M. Roy**
49 B c 22/02 Australia—Gatamalata (IRE) (Spartacus (IRE)) (25000) **Mr K. K. B. Ho**
50 **GULF LEGEND (FR),** b c 27/04 Dubawi (IRE)—Knyazhna (IRE) (Montjeu (IRE)) (240096)
51 Ch c 01/02 Lope de Vega (IRE)—Hertford Dancer (Foxwedge (AUS)) (140000)
52 **KILDARE LEGEND (IRE),** ch c 27/03 Sea The Stars (IRE)—
Miss Aiglonne (Dawn Approach (IRE)) (200080) **Mr K. K. B. Ho**
53 **LA SONNAMBULA,** ch f 21/04 Masar (IRE)—Drift And Dream (Exceed And Excel (AUS)) (16000) **Lady Juliet Tadgell**
54 B c 27/02 Farhh—Maria Letizia (Galileo (IRE)) (85000)
55 **MARIAMNE,** gr f 11/03 Dandy Man (IRE)—Ilsereno (Lethal Force (IRE)) (18000) **Hasmonean Racing & Partner**
56 B c 24/04 Sea The Stars (IRE)—Miss Katie Mae (IRE) (Dark Angel (IRE)) (200000)
57 B c 19/01 Sea The Stars (IRE)—Miss Marjurie (IRE) (Marju (IRE)) (264106) **Mr K. K. B. Ho**
58 B f 06/03 Zoustar (AUS)—Moons of Jupiter (USA) (War Front (USA)) (100000)
59 B c 30/04 Sea The Stars (IRE)—Qareenah (USA) (Arch (USA)) (60024)
60 B f 05/03 Zoustar (AUS)—Samasana (IRE) (Redback) (85000)
61 B c 09/03 Nathaniel (IRE)—Secret Soul (Street Cry (IRE)) (80000)
62 **SIR GALAHAD (IRE),** b c 05/03 Churchill (IRE)—
Katiyra (IRE) (Peintre Celebre (USA)) (56022) **T A Rahman, S Siddiqui, R Gray & Partner**
63 B c 08/05 Study of Man (IRE)—Starlit Sands (Oasis Dream) (148059)
64 **STARSHINE LEGEND (IRE),** b c 08/04 Sea The Stars (IRE)—Blissful Beat (Beat Hollow) (152061) **Mr K. K. B. Ho**
65 B c 24/04 Kodiac—Tarasila (IRE) (Shamardal (USA)) (78000)
66 B c 27/03 Teofilo (IRE)—Tayara (Lawman (FR)) (33613)
67 B c 07/04 Farhh—Theladyinquestion (Dubawi (IRE)) (160000)

Assistant Trainer: Tory Hayter, **Head Girl:** Aideen Marshall, **Travelling Head:** Alyson West.

MR DOMINIC FFRENCH DAVIS, Lambourn

Postal: **College House, 3 Oxford Street, Lambourn, Hungerford, Berkshire, RG17 8XP**
Contacts: **HOME 01488 72342 PHONE 01488 73675 MOBILE 07831 118764 FAX 01488 73675**
EMAIL ffrenchdavis@btinternet.com WEBSITE www.ffrenchdavis.com

1 **BOY GEORGE,** 6, b g Equiano (FR)—If I Were A Boy (IRE) **Mr R. F. Haynes**
2 **CALL MY BLUFF (IRE),** 6, b g Make Believe—Ocean Bluff (IRE) **The Ffrench Connection**
3 **CAPONE (GER),** 8, br g Nathaniel (IRE)—Codera (GER) **D. J. S. Ffrench Davis**
4 **CUCHAVIVA,** 7, ch m Lucarno (USA)—A Fistful of Euros **Mr M. Salaman**
5 **EGYPSYAN CRACKAJAK,** 6, b g Kutub (IRE)—Three Scoops **G. King Haulage Ltd**
6 **EGYPSYAN CRACKELLI,** 4, b g Sixties Icon—Three Scoops **G. King Haulage Ltd**
7 **ELSIEANNE,** 5, b m Haafhd—If I Were A Boy (IRE) **Mr R. F. Haynes**
8 **HOT LEGS LIL (IRE),** 4, ch f Hot Streak (IRE)—Flashy Queen (IRE) **Penny/Adrian Burton, Bob/Angela Lampard**
9 **IVILNOBLE (IRE),** 10, b g Alfred Nobel (IRE)—Almutamore (IRE) **D. J. S. Ffrench Davis**
10 **JAMES PARK WOODS (IRE),** 7, b g Australia—Happy Holly (IRE) **Philip Banfield & Dominic Ffrench Davis**
11 **PULL THE LEVER (IRE),** 4, b g Tagula (IRE)—Hi Milady (IRE) **Drop the Flag**
12 **ROCK AND BEL (FR),** 10, b g Laverock (IRE)—Belmiesque (FR) **D. J. S. Ffrench Davis**
13 **SASHENKA (GER),** 7, b m Maxios—Sarabia (GER) **N. Pickett**
14 **SOUS SURVEILLANCE,** 4, b g Passing Glance—Liddle Dwiggs **Mr M. Butler**

MR DOMINIC FFRENCH DAVIS - continued

THREE-YEAR-OLDS

15 **CHERRYHAWK,** ch f Hawkbill (USA)—Cherry Orchard (IRE) **Stapleford Racing Ltd**
16 **DAZZLING GEM (IRE),** b f Dandy Man (IRE)—Looks Great **Amo Racing Limited**
17 **DESTINY'S SPIRIT,** ch f Lightning Spear—Ellen Gates **J & G Ash**
18 **HOUSE OF DRAGONS,** b c Washington DC (IRE)—Hakuraa (IRE) **Mrs W. Edwards**
19 **ITHACA'S ARROW,** ch c Ulysses (IRE)—Eyeshine **The Agincourt Partnership**
20 **J J STINGLETON,** ch g Washington DC (IRE)—Bee Ina Bonnet **Ffrench Polish**
21 **JACKIE DIAMOND,** b f Territories (IRE)—The Dukkerer (IRE) **Mrs T. Cass**
22 **SURELY NOT (IRE),** b g National Defense—Thanks (IRE) **The Agincourt Partnership & Other**

TWO-YEAR-OLDS

23 Ch f 06/04 Ulysses (IRE)—Cherry Orchard (IRE) (King's Best (USA)) (10000) **Stapleford Racing Ltd**
24 B f 16/02 Soldier's Call—Jelly Monger (IRE) (Strategic Prince) (14406)
25 Ch c 15/03 Mayson—Poetic Smile (IRE) (Exceed And Excel (AUS)) (2000) **Ffrench Nickers**

Assistant Trainer: Ben Ffrench Davis.

---

178 MR GUISEPPE FIERRO, Hednesford

Postal: **Brook House, Rawnsley Road, Hednesford, Cannock, Staffordshire, WS12 1RB**
Contacts: **PHONE 01543 879611 MOBILE 07976 321468**

1 **JUST LIKE BETH,** 15, b m Proclamation (IRE)—Just Beth **G. Fierro**
2 **LAFILIA (GER),** 8, b m Teofilo (IRE)—Labrice **G. Fierro**
3 **LITTLE DOTTY,** 14, br m Erhaab (USA)—Marsh Marigold **G. Fierro**
4 **RAMBLING RIVER,** 12, b g Revoque (IRE)—Just Beth **G. Fierro**
5 **SUNDANCE BOY,** 14, gr g Proclamation (IRE)—Just Beth **G. Fierro**
6 **TOMMY TUCKER,** 6, b g Multiplex—Eternal Legacy (IRE) **G. Fierro**
7 6, Gr g Geordieland (FR)—Woodland Retreat **G. Fierro**

Assistant Trainer: M Fierro.

---

179 MR JOHN FLINT, Bridgend

Postal: **Woodland Lodge, Waunbant Road, Kenfig Hill, Bridgend, Mid Glamorgan, CF33 6FF**
Contacts: **MOBILE 07581 428173 FAX 01656 744347**
EMAIL johnflint900@gmail.com WEBSITE www.johnflintracing.com

1 **ALASKAN JEWEL (IRE),** 4, b f Kodiac—Dutch Destiny **J. L. Flint**
2 **ALYARA,** 5, b m Cable Bay (IRE)—Norway Cross **Mr D. A. Poole**
3 **AMATEUR (IRE),** 10, ch g Giant's Causeway (USA)—Adja (IRE) **Burnham Plastering & Drylining Ltd**
4 **BLAZE A TRAIL (IRE),** 9, b g Morozov (USA)—Bright Blaze (IRE) **Belly's Heroes**
5 **CARP KID (IRE),** 8, b g Lope de Vega (IRE)—Homegrown (IRE) **JACK Racing**
6 **FLOWER OF GOWER,** 5, b m Telescope (IRE)—Regal Fairy (IRE) **Mr D. Thomas**
7 **GLINT OF AN EYE (IRE),** 6, b m Australia—Call This Cat (IRE) **J. L. Flint**
8 **JADE COUNTRY,** 4, b g Territories (IRE)—Oasis Jade
9 **LILANDRA (FR),** 6, b m Equiano (FR)—Indigo River (IRE) **Katchar Racing**
10 **LOVE AND BE LOVED,** 9, b m Lawman (FR)—Rightside **J. L. Flint**
11 **LYNDON B (IRE),** 7, b g Charm Spirit (IRE)—Kelsey Rose **PDuffyD.SemmensVWilliamsRHarperMLoveday**
12 **MARTY BYRDE,** 6, b g Blue Bresil (FR)—Dancing Emily (IRE) **Burnham Plastering & Drylining Ltd**
13 **OUTER SPACE,** 12, b g Acclamation—Venoge (IRE) **Mr D. A. Poole**
14 **RIVAL,** 5, b g Iffraaj—Pamona (IRE) **P.Duffy, D.Semmens, V.Williams, R.Harper, M.Loveday**
15 **STIGWOOD (IRE),** 5, b g Kodiac—Time Honoured **J. L. Flint**
16 **THE WIRE FLYER,** 8, b g Champs Elysees—Good Morning Star (IRE) **Aled Evans & Tommy Williams**
17 **TIME INTERVAL,** 5, b g Adaay (IRE)—Kuriosa (IRE) **J. L. Flint**

MR JOHN FLINT - continued

18 **TOO SHY SHY (IRE),** 6, gr m Kodiac—Satwa Ruby (FR) **J. L. Flint**
19 **VAPE,** 6, gr g Dark Angel (IRE)—Puff (IRE) **J. L. Flint**
20 **WITH PLEASURE,** 10, b g Poet's Voice—With Fascination (USA) **The Highlife Racing Club**

Assistant Trainer: Mrs Martine Louise Flint, Rhys Flint.

---

180 MR TONY FORBES, Uttoxeter

Postal: **Hill House Farm, Poppits Lane, Stramshall, Uttoxeter, Staffordshire, ST14 5EX**
Contacts: **PHONE 01889 562722 MOBILE 07967 246571**
EMAIL tony@thimble.net

1 **CHEF DE TROUPE (FR),** 10, b g Air Chief Marshal (IRE)—Tazminya **Mr A. L. Forbes**
2 **FLEURSALS,** 7, b m Poet's Voice—Entitlement **Mr A. L. Forbes**
3 **SWEET DIME,** 7, b br m Toronado (IRE)—Rainbow's Edge **Mr A. L. Forbes**

Assistant Trainer: Mr Tim Eley.

---

181 MRS RICHENDA FORD, Blandford Forum

Postal: **Garlands Farm, The Common, Okeford Fitzpaine, Blandford Forum, Dorset, DT11 0RT**
Contacts: **MOBILE 07800 634846**
WORK EMAIL Richendafordracing@gmail.com WEBSITE www.richendafordracing.co.uk FACEBOOK RichendaFordRacing INSTAGRAM RichendaFordRacing

1 **CALL ME FREDDIE,** 8, ch g Black Sam Bellamy (IRE)—Still Runs Deep **Richenda Ford Racing Club**
2 **CAMPESE,** 4, b g Australia—Dubka
3 **DONT BE ROBIN (IRE),** 11, b g Robin des Pres (FR)—Rainbow Times (IRE) **Mr & Mrs K. B. Snook**
4 **FLAMENCO DE KERSER (FR),** 8, b g Vendangeur (IRE)—
Nouba de Kerser (FR) **Sturminster Newton Building Supplies Ltd**
5 **GOOD SOUL,** 5, gr m Mukhadram—Royal Dalakhani (IRE)
6 **HENZO DES BOULLATS (FR),** 6, b g Saddler Maker (IRE)—Becky des Boulats (FR) **Mr & Mrs K. B. Snook**
7 **MASTER MIKEY DEE (IRE),** 8, b g Fame And Glory—Miss Lauren Dee (IRE) **Mr & Mrs K. B. Snook**
8 **NOAH'S LIGHT (IRE),** 6, b g Leading Light (IRE)—Scrapper Jack (IRE) **Mr & Mrs K. B. Snook**
9 **O'FAOLAINS LAD (IRE),** 9, b g Oscar (IRE)—O'Faolains Fancy (IRE) **Lloyd Builders Investments Ltd**
10 **SIR JACKSCHIAPAREL (IRE),** 7, b g Schiaparelli (GER)—Royal Moll (IRE) **Mr & Mrs K. B. Snook**
11 6, B m Pether's Moon (IRE)—Sovereignsflagship (IRE) **Mr & Mrs K. B. Snook**
12 **TOPOFTHETRIFLE (IRE),** 4, b f Galileo Gold—Pretty Pebble (IRE) **Mrs S. M. Maine**

---

182 MISS SANDY FORSTER, Kelso

Postal: **Halterburn Head, Yetholm, Kelso, Roxburghshire, TD5 8PP**
Contacts: **PHONE 01573 420615 MOBILE 07976 587315, 07880 727877 FAX 01573 420615**
EMAIL clivestorey@btinternet.com

1 **ASHJAN,** 10, b g Medicean—Violet (IRE) **Dave Skeldon & Sandy Forster**
2 **CHUMLEE (IRE),** 8, b g Recital (FR)—Oceanna Mist (IRE) **The Border Racers**
3 **DIVAS DOYEN (IRE),** 6, b m Doyen (IRE)—Sleeping Diva (FR) **The Unlikely Tenors**

MISS SANDY FORSTER - continued

4 **DR SHIROCCO (IRE),** 8, ch g Shirocco (GER)—Uncommited (IRE) **I I F T F**
5 **DUTY CALLS (IRE),** 10, b g Arcadio (GER)—Inniskeen (IRE) **Dont Mind If We Do**
6 **FORTCANYON (IRE),** 7, b g Yeats (IRE)—Thegoodwans Sister (IRE) **C. Storey**
7 **GYPSEY'S SECRET (IRE),** 8, b m Dylan Thomas (IRE)—Lady Howe **Mr M. H. Walton**
8 **LASTIN' MEMORIES,** 11, b g Overbury (IRE)—Dusky Dante (IRE) **Dave Skeldon & Sandy Forster**
9 **LISSEN TO THE LADY (IRE),** 9, b m Fame And Glory—Liss Rua (IRE) **Mr M. H. Walton**
10 **MORNINGSIDE,** 10, b g Kayf Tara—Bouncing Bean **I I F T F**
11 **PIPERS CROSS (IRE),** 6, b m Soldier of Fortune (IRE)—Oatfield Lady (IRE) **Mr M. H. Walton**
12 **STOWAWAY JOHN (IRE),** 9, b g Stowaway—Figlette **Dave Skeldon & Clive Storey**
13 **ZIHUATANEJO (IRE),** 9, b g Flemensfirth (USA)—Cara Mara (IRE) **The Border Racers**

Assistant Trainer: C. Storey.

Amateur Jockey: Miss J. Walton.

---

183 MISS JO FOSTER, Ilkley

Postal: **The Old Mistal, Brookleigh Farm, Burley Road, Menston, Ilkley, West Yorkshire, LS29 6NS**
Contacts: **PHONE 07980 301808 MOBILE 07980 301808**
EMAIL info@jofosterracing.co.uk WEBSITE www.jofosterracing.co.uk

1 **BALLYNAGRAN (IRE),** 8, br g Imperial Monarch (IRE)—Fancyfacia (IRE) **The Yorkshire Racing Partnership**
2 **BIG BEE HIVE (IRE),** 6, b g Imperial Monarch (IRE)—Matinee Time (IRE) **R. J. Hewitt**
3 **CHASE THE WIND (IRE),** 14, ch g Spadoun (FR)—Asfreeasthewind (IRE) **Mr J. Nixon**
4 **DA VINCI HAND (IRE),** 8, b g Champs Elysees—Thousandkissesdeep (IRE) **Mr J. Nixon**
5 **DILLARCHIE,** 6, b m Sulamani (IRE)—Cute N You Know It **J Saxby, M Simmons Partnership**
6 **ESKENDASH (USA),** 10, ch g Eskendereya (USA)—Daffaash (USA) **Sticky Wicket Racing Partners**
7 **GLASCAR MORE (IRE),** 7, br g Es Que Love (IRE)—Ruby Ridge (IRE) **Mr E. C. Wilkin**
8 **ROCCOWITHLOVE,** 9, b g Shirocco (GER)—Love Train (IRE) **The Golden Syndicate**
9 **SIGURD (GER),** 11, ch g Sholokhov (IRE)—Sky News (GER) **Mrs E. A. Verity**

Assistant Trainer: P. Foster.

NH Jockey: Craig Nichol.

---

184 MR JIMMY FOX, Marlborough

Postal: **Highlands Farm Stables, Herridge, Collingbourne Ducis, Marlborough, Wiltshire, SN8 3EG**
Contacts: **PHONE 01264 850218, 07931 724358 MOBILE 07702 880010**
EMAIL jcfoxtrainer@aol.com

1 **ALBUS ANNE,** 4, b f Mayson—Asmahan **Miss F. L. Thomas**
2 **GRACIOUS GEORGE (IRE),** 13, b g Oratorio (IRE)—Little Miss Gracie **Highlands Farm Racing Partnership**
3 **LADY HOLLY,** 5, b m Sepoy (AUS)—Night Affair **SP9 Racing Club**
4 **MARCHETTI (IRE),** 6, b m Camelot—Though (IRE) **Mr Y. T. Mehmet**
5 **PURPLE POPPY,** 5, b m Swiss Spirit—Stunning In Purple (IRE) **The Brazen Racing Club**
6 **TRIDEVI,** 5, b m Sepoy (AUS)—Female Spring **SP9 Racing Club**

THREE-YEAR-OLDS

7 **ON THE OTHER HAND (IRE),** b f Ribchester (IRE)—Shaarfa (USA) **Mr T. J. Ashe**

Assistant Trainer: Sarah-Jane Fox.

---

185 MISS SUZZANNE FRANCE, Norton on Derwent

Postal: **Cheesecake Hill House, Highfield, Beverley Road, Norton on Derwent, North Yorkshire, YO17 9PJ**
Contacts: **PHONE 07904 117531 MOBILE 07904 117531 FAX 01653 691947**
EMAIL suzzanne@newstartracing.co.uk WEBSITE www.suzzannefranceracing.com, www.newstartracing.co.uk

1 **ARCHIVE (FR),** 13, b g Sulamani (IRE)—Royale Dorothy (FR) **Newstartracing.com Club**
2 **BIG MUDDY,** 6, b g Monsieur Bond (IRE)—Nine Red **Newstartracing.com Club**
3 **BILLY DYLAN (IRE),** 8, b g Excelebration (IRE)—It's True (IRE) **Newstartracing.com Club**
4 **CAPTAIN ST LUCIFER,** 6, b g Casamento (IRE)—Delaware Dancer (IRE) **Newstart Partnership.Com**
5 **KITTYBREWSTER,** 4, br f Brazen Beau (AUS)—Ivory Silk **Newstartracing.com Club**
6 **PHOTOGRAPH (IRE),** 6, b g Kodiac—Supreme Occasion (IRE) **Mr M. Steel**

Assistant Trainer: Mr Aaron James.

---

186 MR ALEX FRENCH, Averham Park

Postal: **Averham Park Farm, Averham Park, Averham, Newark, Nottinghamshire, NG23 5RU**
Contacts: **PHONE 07776 306588**
EMAIL alex@alexfrenchracing.com

1 **CHARMING BERRY (IRE),** 5, gr g Charm Spirit (IRE)—Frosty Berry **Ms J. A. French**
2 **CLASSICAL MUSIC (IRE),** 4, b g Muhaarar—Mu'ajiza **Ms J. A. French**
3 4, Ch f Sixties Icon—Excellent World (IRE)
4 **FLYING INSTRUCTOR (IRE),** 5, b g Nayef (USA)—Devonelli (IRE)
5 **GRANGECLARE VIEW (IRE),** 5, b g Ajaya—Eucharist (IRE) **Newgen Racing Group**
6 **KARATAYKA (IRE),** 5, b m Dariyan (FR)—Karamaya (IRE) **Ms J. A. French**
7 **LAWMANS BLIS (IRE),** 5, b g Lawman (FR)—Megec Blis (IRE) **Mr J. R. Dwyer**
8 **OUT OF SIGHT (IRE),** 5, b g Outstrip—Bountiful Girl **Ms J. A. French**
9 **SPELLS AT DAWN (IRE),** 4, b g Dawn Approach (IRE)—Spellcraft
10 **TEA GARDEN,** 5, ch m Helmet (AUS)—Tea Gown (IRE) **Alex French Racing Club**
11 **WAR OF WORDS (IRE),** 4, b g War Command (USA)—Zainda (IRE) **Ms J. A. French**

THREE-YEAR-OLDS

12 **REJOYCEFILLY,** b f Ulysses (IRE)—Cheerfilly (IRE) **Ms J. A. French**

TWO-YEAR-OLDS

13 **KING BERRY (IRE),** gr c 08/04 Kingston Hill—Frosty Berry (Proclamation (IRE))
14 Ch c 28/04 Tagula (IRE)—Musicology (USA) (Singspiel (IRE)) (12005)
15 B c 10/04 Muhaarar—Spellcraft (Dubawi (IRE))

---

187 MR JAMES FROST, Buckfastleigh

Postal: **Hawson Stables, Buckfastleigh, Devon, TQ11 0HP**
Contacts: **HOME 01364 642332 PHONE 01364 642267 MOBILE 07860 220229 FAX 01364 643182**
EMAIL info@frostracingclub.co.uk

1 **ASIAN SPICE,** 5, b m Scorpion (IRE)—Kim Tian Road (IRE)
2 **CAITLIN'S COURT (IRE),** 6, b m Court Cave (IRE)—Secret Can't Say (IRE) **G. D. Thompson**
3 **DEMOTHI (IRE),** 8, b g Le Fou (IRE)—Tuscarora (IRE) **Mr P. Tosh & Partner**
4 **FINDUSATGORCOMBE,** 11, b g Tobougg (IRE)—Seemma **Mr P. R. Meaden**
5 **FOILLMORE (IRE),** 8, gr g Carlotamix (FR)—Beale Native (IRE) **Frost Racing Club**
6 **GRACEFULL DANCER,** 5, ch g Alqaahir (USA)—Miss Grace **J. D. Frost**
7 **KING OF THE WOODS,** 5, b g Swiss Spirit—Love Is More **J. D. Frost**

8 **LITTLE MISS ALICE,** 7, b m Alqaahir (USA)—Miss Grace **J. D. Frost**
9 **PRESGRAVE (IRE),** 6, b g Camelot—Alamouna (IRE) **Frost Racing Club**
10 **RITE BITE,** 4, b c Scorpion (IRE)—Rite Breeze **Mrs R. Welch**
11 **SAINTEMILION (FR),** 10, b g Diamond Green (FR)—Matakana (FR) **J. D. Frost**
12 **SANS OF GOLD (IRE),** 5, ch g Sans Frontieres (IRE)—Shannon Pearl (IRE) **4Racing Owners Club**
13 **TREACYS JIM (IRE),** 9, b g Milan—Bridge Hotel Lilly (IRE) **Frost Racing Club**
14 **WRAP YOUR WINGS (IRE),** 8, gr m Cloudings (IRE)—Help Yourself (IRE) **4Racing Owners Club**
15 **ZUFAL,** 6, b g Worthadd (IRE)—Easy To Sing **J. D. Frost**

Assistant Trainer: G. Frost.

NH Jockey: Bryony Frost.

---

188 MR KEVIN FROST, Newark

Postal: **Hill Top Equestrian Centre, Danethorpe Lane, Danethorpe Hill, Newark, Nottinghamshire, NG24 2PD**
Contacts: **PHONE 07748 873092 MOBILE 07919 370081**
EMAIL info@kevinfrostracing.co.uk WEBSITE www.kevinfrostracing.co.uk

1 **AL BAAHY,** 4, b g Kingman—Secret Keeper **Curzon House Partnership**
2 **AMAYSMONT,** 6, b g Mayson—Montjen (IRE) **Miss L. Frost**
3 **APPROACH THE CITY (IRE),** 7, b g New Approach (IRE)—First City **The Kevin Frost Racing Club**
4 **ARABIAN KING,** 7, ch g New Approach (IRE)—Barshiba (IRE) **The Kevin Frost Racing Club**
5 **ATACAMA DESERT (IRE),** 5, ch g Galileo (IRE)—Ikat (IRE) **Rocky Canzone Partnership**
6 **BILLIEBROOKEDIT (IRE),** 8, ch g Dragon Pulse (IRE)—Klang (IRE) **Mr K. Frost**
7 **BOASTED,** 4, b f Showcasing—Tinted (IRE) **M & S Voikhanskaya**
8 **BRISTOL HILL (IRE),** 5, b g New Bay—Bristol Bay (IRE) **The Kevin Frost Racing Club**
9 **CHAMPAGNE TOWN,** 6, b g Kayf Tara—Kind Heart **Kevin Frost Racing Club & David Orr**
10 **CLONDAW SECRET (IRE),** 8, b g Court Cave (IRE)—Secret Can't Say (IRE) **Miss L. Frost**
11 **DAARIS (IRE),** 4, ch g Dawn Approach (IRE)—Reyaadah **Mr S. W. Turner**
12 **DOCUMENTING,** 10, b g Zamindar (USA)—Namaskar **Racing, Orr, Priest**
13 **ELSHAAMEQ,** 4, b g Awtaad (IRE)—Elraazy **Rocky Canzone Partnership**
14 **FIFTYSHADESOFRED (FR),** 5, b g Siyouni (FR)—Candinie (USA) **Mr D Orr & Mr M Humphreys**
15 **FRANCIS XAVIER (IRE),** 9, b g High Chaparral (IRE)—Missionary Hymn (USA) **Curzon House Partnership**
16 **HELVETIAN,** 8, b g Swiss Spirit—Lucky Dip **Ms T. Keane**
17 **INFINITI (IRE),** 10, b m Arcano (IRE)—Seraphina (IRE) **Total Asbestos Solutions Ltd & A Frost**
18 **KATH'S TOYBOY,** 5, gr g Gregorian (IRE)—It's Dubai Dolly **Mr K. Frost**
19 **LONGCLAW (USA),** 6, b g Kitten's Joy (USA)—Secret Union (USA) **The Kevin Frost Racing Club**
20 **MASTER OF COMBAT (IRE),** 5, b g Invincible Spirit (IRE)—Sharja Queen **Law Abiding Citizens**
21 **PAPA DON'T PREACH (IRE),** 4, b g Kodiac—Paella (IRE) **Kevin Frost Racing Club & David Orr**
22 **POSTER CHILD (IRE),** 6, b m Fracas (IRE)—Rachida (IRE) **Robin Hood Racing 2022**
23 **SIAM FOX (IRE),** 5, b g Prince of Lir (IRE)—Folegandros Island (FR) **Orbital Racing & Miss L Frost**
24 **SNAG IT (IRE),** 6, gr g Dream Ahead (USA)—Killura (USA) **The Kevin Frost Racing Club**
25 **SPOOF,** 8, b g Poet's Voice—Filona (IRE) **Mr K. Frost**
26 **STAN (FR),** 4, b g Highland Reel (IRE)—Scottish Stage (IRE) **D & A Frost**
27 **THE BREADMAN (IRE),** 6, b g Conduit (IRE)—Kathy Jet (USA)
28 **VIENNA GIRL,** 5, b m Golden Horn—Bint Doyen **Turner & Frost**

THREE-YEAR-OLDS

29 **DE LA HOYA (IRE),** b g Tasleet—Ardwinna (IRE) **Robin Hood Racing XXII**
30 **HARRY'S HALO (IRE),** ch g Harry Angel (IRE)—Postale **Kevin Frost Racing Club & David Orr**
31 **MR GLOVERMAN,** ch g Lethal Force (IRE)—Xylophone **Glover Priest Solicitors Ltd & Partner**
32 B g Invincible Spirit (IRE)—Oakley Girl
33 **SIR JOHN MONASH,** b g Sea The Stars (IRE)—Crystal Path (IRE) **The Kevin Frost Racing Club**

Assistant Trainer: Lauren Frost.

189 MR HARRY FRY, Dorchester

Postal: **Corscombe, Dorchester, Dorset, DT2 0PD**
Contacts: **WORK 01935 350330 PHONE 01935 350330**
EMAIL info@harryfryracing.com WEBSITE www.harryfryracing.com

1 **ACHNAMARA,** 4, b g Kodiac—Albamara **Noel Fehily Racing Syndicate - Achnamara**
2 **ALTOBELLI (IRE),** 5, b g Maxios—Atiana **Charlie Walker and Jonny Craib**
3 **APPLESHAW,** 4, b gr f Kayf Tara—Shades of Grey **Dr John Merrington**
4 **ARMATHIA,** 4, b f Cityscape—Slide Show **Somerset Racing**
5 **ASK ME EARLY (IRE),** 9, gr g Ask—Cotton Ali (IRE) **The Dare Family**
6 **BEAT THE BAT (IRE),** 5, b g Walk In The Park (IRE)—Dani Salamanca (IRE) **Twelfth Man Partnership 6**
7 **BERMEO (IRE),** 12, b g Definite Article—Miss Blueyes (IRE) **Manhole Covers Ltd**
8 **BOOTHILL (IRE),** 8, b br g Presenting—Oyster Pipit (IRE) **Brian & Sandy Lambert**
9 **BURROWS TREAT (FR),** 7, b m Muhtathir—La Vie de Boitron (FR) **Mr M. Stenning**
10 **CARRIGMOORNA ROWAN (IRE),** 6, b g Sea Moon—Carrigmoorna Fame (IRE) **Noel Fehily Racing Syndicate Carrigmoorn**
11 4, B f Jet Away—Classic Girl (IRE) **David's Partnership**
12 **COASTAL ROCK (FR),** 4, ch g Coastal Path—Adamantina (FR) **John McGeady Ltd**
13 **COLDEN'S DREAM (IRE),** 6, b g Ocovango—Now Were Broke (IRE) **Mr I F Gosden & Mr Dj Coles**
14 **CREDROJAVA (IRE),** 6, b m Presenting—Knock View Vic (IRE) **H&C Barrett S&A McDonald, Dolan-Abrahams**
15 **DANTON (IRE),** 6, b g Soldier of Fortune (IRE)—Fair Present (IRE) **Manhole Covers Ltd**
16 **DEEPER BLUE (FR),** 7, ch g Muhtathir—Divine Cayras (FR) **Charlie Walker**
17 **DUBROVNIK HARRY (IRE),** 7, b g Yeats (IRE)—Kashmir Lady (FR) **Manhole Covers Ltd**
18 **FAIRY GEM (IRE),** 7, b m Shantou (USA)—Mystic Masie (IRE) **Chasing Gold Limited**
19 **FOREVER BLESSED (IRE),** 5, b g Zoffany (IRE)—Yet Again **Thornton, Gibbs, Davies & Andrews**
20 **FORTUNES MELODY,** 6, b m Yorgunnabelucky (USA)—Fulgora **Mr Simon Munir & Mr Isaac Souede**
21 **GET BACK GET BACK (IRE),** 8, b g Lord Shanakill (USA)—Bawaakeer (USA) **GDM Partnership**
22 **GIDLEIGH PARK,** 5, b g Walk In The Park (IRE)—Lindeman (IRE) **The Eyre Family**
23 **GIN COCO (FR),** 7, b g Cokoriko (FR)—Qlementine (FR) **David's Partnership**
24 **GOODTIMECREW (IRE),** 5, b m Walk In The Park (IRE)—Glacial Drift **Jago & Allhusen**
25 **GOUDHURST STAR (IRE),** 7, b g Yeats (IRE)—Baliya (IRE) **Nigel & Barbara Collison**
26 **GREAT NAME THAT (IRE),** 6, b g Flemensfirth (USA)—Tokenella (IRE) **GDM Partnership**
27 **HAY THERE MONA (IRE),** 6, b m Mustameet (USA)—Turf (FR) **Ms M. E. Hannaford**
28 **HIGH FIBRE (IRE),** 4, b g Vadamos (FR)—Multi Grain **Gary Stevens & Manhole Covers Limited**
29 **HOT ROD LINCOLN (IRE),** 7, b g Westerner—Flaming Annie (IRE) **Gale Force Wins**
30 **HOW WILL I KNOW (IRE),** 6, b g Ocovango—Balleen Rose (IRE) **Wait & See Partnership**
31 **HOW'S THE CRICKET (IRE),** 8, b g Doyen (IRE)—Hayley Cometh (IRE) **Manhole Covers Ltd**
32 **HUBBLE TRUBBLE,** 5, b m Telescope (IRE)—Juno Mint **Sandie & David Newton**
33 **HYMAC (IRE),** 7, b g Ask—Katie Cranny (IRE) **Denny, Stuart-Jervis & Walsh**
34 **IN EXCELSIS DEO (FR),** 5, b g Saddex—Gratia Plena (FR) **Mr J. P. McManus**
35 **JUST A HEARTBEAT,** 4, b f Scorpion (IRE)—Kentford Grebe **Mr E Knowlton**
36 **KAP OUEST (FR),** 4, b g Kapgarde (FR)—Jahra (FR) **Mr J. P. McManus**
37 **LADY ADARE (IRE),** 7, b m Sholokhov (IRE)—En Vedette (FR) **Dare & Dolan-Abrahams Families**
38 **LAST OF A LEGEND,** 6, b m Midnight Legend—Blue Buttons (IRE) **Hot To Trot Jumping**
39 **LIGHTLY SQUEEZE,** 9, b g Poet's Voice—Zuleika Dobson **J Davies & Govier & Brown**
40 **LOVE ENVOI (IRE),** 7, b m Westerner—Love Divided (IRE) **Noel Fehily Racing Syndicates Love Envoi**
41 **LYDFORD LAD (IRE),** 8, b g Yeats (IRE)—Shannon Rose (IRE) **Mr David Martin & Mr Paul Barber**
42 **MA BELLE NOIRE,** 6, br m Soldier of Fortune (IRE)—Loxhill Lady **The Zoomers**
43 **METIER (IRE),** 7, b g Mastercraftsman (IRE)—We'll Go Walking (IRE) **G. C. Stevens**
44 **MIGHT I (IRE),** 7, b g Fame And Glory—Our Honey (IRE) **Brian & Sandy Lambert**
45 **MISS GOLDFIRE (IRE),** 4, b f Yeats (IRE)—Miss McGoldrick (IRE) **Mrs C. Fry**
46 **MONJULES (FR),** 5, b g Rajsaman (FR)—Equilibriste (IRE) **David's Partnership**
47 **OLD TOWN GARDE (IRE),** 7, b g Robin des Champs (FR)—Old Town Queen (IRE) **GDM Partnership**
48 **OUR NEL (IRE),** 5, ch m Mount Nelson—Hopeful Gleam (IRE) **A. R. Bromley**
49 **PHOENIX WAY (IRE),** 10, b g Stowaway—Arcuate **Mr J. P. McManus**
50 **QUEEN ANNIE (IRE),** 5, b m Westerner—Ben's Turn (IRE) **John McGeady Ltd**
51 **REE OKKA,** 7, b g Getaway (GER)—Presenteea (IRE) **The Jago Family Partnership**
52 **REVELS HILL (IRE),** 8, b g Mahler—Chlolo Supreme (IRE) **Noel Fehily Racing Syndicates-Revels Hil**
53 4, Ch g Getaway (GER)—Rock's Field (IRE) **L & K Haring, H Doubtfire**
54 **SAN GIOVANNI (IRE),** 7, b g Milan—Down By The Sea (IRE) **GDM Partnership**
55 **SIR IVAN,** 13, b g Midnight Legend—Tisho **The Eyre Family**

MR HARRY FRY - continued

56 **WALK ON HIGH,** 6, b g Walk In The Park (IRE)—Highland Retreat **The Highland Walkers**
57 **WHISKY EXPRESS,** 7, ch m Imperial Monarch (IRE)—Loxhill Lady **Lorna Squire, R Metherell, D German**
58 **WHITEHOTCHILLIFILI (IRE),** 9, b m Milan—Mhuire Na Gale (IRE) **Chasing Gold Limited**
59 **WINTERWATCH (GER),** 5, b g Lord of England (GER)—Wildlife Lodge (GER) **Dolan-Abrahams, Jago & Allhusen.**

THREE-YEAR-OLDS

60 **VALADON (IRE),** b g Vadamos (FR)—Art Festival **Bond, Thornton & Manhole Covers Ltd**

Assistant Trainer: Ciara Fry, Hugo Hunt.

NH Jockey: Sean Bowen, Jonathan Burke. **Conditional Jockey:** Ben Bromley, Lorcan Murtagh.

Amateur Jockey: Miss A. B. O'Connor.

---

190 MS CAROLINE FRYER, Wymondham

Postal: **Browick Hall Cottage, Browick Road, Wymondham, Norfolk, NR18 9RB**
Contacts: **PHONE 07768 056076 MOBILE 07768 056076**
EMAIL caroline@carolinefryerracing.co.uk, c.fryer528@btinternet.com WEBSITE www.carolinefryerracing.co.uk

1 **CANYON CITY,** 10, b g Authorized (IRE)—Colorado Dawn **A Whyte & D Nott**
2 **CLOUDY WEDNESDAY (IRE),** 7, b g Cloudings (IRE)—Hansel Monday (IRE) **Miss C. Fryer**
3 **GOODNIGHT CHARLIE,** 13, gr m Midnight Legend—Over To Charlie **Miss C. Fryer**
4 **MANOFTHEMOMENT (IRE),** 9, b g Jeremy (USA)—Endless Ambition (IRE) **Miss C. Fryer**
5 **RATOUTE YUTTY,** 10, b m Midnight Legend—Easibrook Jane **C J Underwood & Caroline Fryer**

---

191 MRS CHARLOTTE FULLER, Penwood

Postal: **Penwood Grange, Penwood, Newbury, Berkshire, RG20 9EW**
Contacts: **PHONE 01635 250658 MOBILE 07775 713107**
EMAIL charlotte.fuller@me.com

1 **MAXIMA,** 4, b f Telescope (IRE)—Tamara King (IRE) **Mrs C. Fuller**
2 **OUR THREE SONS (IRE),** 12, b g Shantou (USA)—Ballyquinn (IRE) **Mr & Mrs R. H. F. Fuller**
3 **SKANDIBURG (FR),** 9, b g Sageburg (IRE)—Skandia (FR) **R. H. F. Fuller**

---

192 MR IVAN FURTADO, Newark

Postal: **The Old Stables, Averham Park Farm, Averham, Newark, Nottinghamshire, NG23 5RU**
Contacts: **MOBILE 07783 520746**
EMAIL ivan.furtado@hotmail.co.uk

1 **BOASTY (IRE),** 6, b g Sir Prancealot (IRE)—Caffe Latte (IRE) **Daniel MacAuliffe & Anoj Don**
2 **CHANTREYS,** 6, gr ro m Mayson—Raajis (IRE) **The Giggle Factor Partnership**
3 **CHIPIRON (FR),** 7, ch g Rio de La Plata (USA)—Chicago May (FR) **Mr D. Croot**

MR IVAN FURTADO - continued

4 **CRAZY SPIN,** 7, b m Epaulette (AUS)—George's Gift **The Giggle Factor Partnership**
5 **DARK ENCHANTMENT (IRE),** 4, br f Vadamos (FR)—Listen Alexander (IRE) **The Giggle Factor Partnership**
6 **DARK KRIS (IRE),** 6, b g Dark Angel (IRE)—My Spirit (IRE) **B & Factor**
7 **DOWN TO THE KID (IRE),** 4, ch g Pride of Dubai (AUS)—Classic Lass **GB Civil, Sennett & Furtado**
8 **FAIRY FOOTPRINTS,** 4, b f Free Eagle (IRE)—Maggie Lou (IRE) **The Giggle Factor Partnership**
9 **FLOATS ON AIR,** 4, b g Heeraat (IRE)—Almaviva (IRE) **Amazing Racing**
10 **FUNKY TOWN PINKIE,** 4, b f Sun Central (IRE)—Maggie Pink **Mr A. W. Bult**
11 **GIORGIO VASARI (IRE),** 5, b g Air Force Blue (USA)—Dream The Blues (IRE) **The Giggle Factor Partnership**
12 **GREY BELLE (FR),** 4, gr f Johnny Barnes (IRE)—Coldgirl (FR) **Daniel MacAuliffe & Anoj Don**
13 **HEALING POWER,** 7, b g Kodiac—Loch Ma Naire (IRE) **Mr D. Croot**
14 **HECTOR'S HERE,** 7, b g Cityscape—L'Addition **The Giggle Factor Partnership**
15 **I'M GRATEFUL,** 5, b g Assertive—Tanning **Mr E. P. Spain**
16 **KENYX (FR),** 6, b g Kendargent (FR)—Onyx (FR) **Mr G. White**
17 **KODIACLAIM,** 4, b f Aclaim (IRE)—Gumhrear (IRE) **Mr P. L. Coe**
18 **LAST DATE,** 6, br g Music Master—Tanning **Mr E. P. Spain**
19 **LEDNIKOV,** 5, b g Footstepsinthesand—Ledena **Mr P. Tait**
20 **LEGAL REFORM (IRE),** 6, b g Lawman (FR)—Amhrasach (IRE) **GB Civil Engineering (Leicester) LTD**
21 **LINCOLN GAMBLE,** 6, gr g Zebedee—Lincolnrose (IRE) **G.P.S. Heart of Racing (Bloodstock) Ltd**
22 **LIZZIE JEAN,** 4, b f Nathaniel (IRE)—Mensoora (SAF) **GB Civil Engineering & The Gigle Factor**
23 **MADAME MARMALADE,** 4, b f Fountain of Youth (IRE)—Cuppatee (IRE) **The Giggle Factor Partnership**
24 **MAGICAL MAX,** 6, gr g Coach House (IRE)—Vellena **The Follow the Majer Partnership**
25 **MAY REMAIN,** 8, b g Mayson—Ultimate Best **The Giggle Factor Partnership**
26 **MOAI (FR),** 5, b g Showcasing—Psychometry (FR) **I. Furtado**
27 **NAT LOVE (IRE),** 6, b g Gregorian (IRE)—Chaguaramas (IRE) **Mr H Travis, Mr B Stephens & Partner**
28 **OKEANOS (FR),** 4, b g War Front (USA)—Oceanique (USA) **B Stephens & Giggle Factor**
29 **PROBE,** 5, b g Kingman—Tested **J. L. Marriott**
30 **RECORWOMAN (FR),** 4, b f Recorder—Pearlred (FR) **Mr D. Croot**
31 **ROCKET ACTION,** 7, gr g Toronado (IRE)—Winning Express (IRE) **Mr D. Croot**
32 **RUBY ARABELLA,** 4, b f Peace Envoy (FR)—Anagallis (IRE) **Mr K. Lane**
33 **SEESAWING,** 6, br g Music Master—Stunning In Purple (IRE) **Mr J. C. Levey**
34 **SOLAR QUEEN,** 5, b m Maxios—Solola (GER) **Mr W. P. Flynn**
35 **STARTER FOR TEN,** 6, b g Bated Breath—Scariff Hornet (IRE) **21st Century Racing & The Giggle Factor**
36 **THE NAIL GUNNER (IRE),** 5, b g Tough As Nails (IRE)—Remediate (USA) **Mr W. P. Flynn**
37 **TICKETS,** 4, b g Aclaim (IRE)—Czarna Roza **J. C. Fretwell**
38 **TIN PAN ALLEY,** 15, b g Singspiel (IRE)—Tazmeen
39 **TIPPERARY MOON (IRE),** 6, b g Sea Moon—Rathaal (IRE) **Mr W. P. Flynn**
40 **WALLAROO (IRE),** 5, b g Australia—Dancequest (IRE) **Mr C. Hodgson**

THREE-YEAR-OLDS

41 **ALCHIMIA (IRE),** b f Fast Company (IRE)—Pearlitas Passion (IRE)
42 **ANOTHER BEAUTIFUL,** b f National Defense—Voleuse de Coeurs (IRE) **A Night In Newmarket**
43 **BIRD OF PLAY (IRE),** b g Free Eagle (IRE)—Spiaggia (IRE) **Mr J. Phelan**
44 **BRABUSACH (FR),** ch g Profitable (IRE)—Tantivy (USA) **Daniel MacAuliffe & Anoj Don**
45 **BRIGHT BOOTS,** b c Time Test—Hannah Frank (IRE) **Norcroft Park Stud**
46 **CRAZY CRACKERS (IRE),** b g Cracksman—Roanne (USA)
47 **CROSSTITCH,** ch g Recorder—Craftiness **J. L. Marriott**
48 **EXTERNAL CAPITAL (FR),** b g Dabirsim (FR)—Campina **Alchemy Bloodstock & Partner**
49 **FRANKIE'S WISH (IRE),** b c Cracksman—Rajar **A Night In Newmarket**
50 **FREYA'S TEARS (IRE),** ch f Gustav Klimt (IRE)—Trust Your Opinion (IRE) **Mr S. Radymski**
51 Ch f Sun Central (IRE)—Maggie Pink **Mr A. W. Bult**
52 Gr g Zoffany (IRE)—Modern Love (IRE) **The Giggle Factor Partnership**
53 **MOLLY MISCHIEF,** b f Muhaarar—Adjudicate **J. L. Marriott**
54 **RAVANELLI (IRE),** gr g Dark Angel (IRE)—Sacred Aspect (IRE) **A Night In Newmarket**
55 **SHAMALAMA (IRE),** b g Kodiac—Rayda (IRE) **J. L. Marriott**
56 **WAMALAMA (IRE),** b g Kodiac—Stage Name **J. L. Marriott**

TWO-YEAR-OLDS

57 B f 03/05 Magna Grecia (IRE)—Adja (IRE) (Rock of Gibraltar (IRE)) (5602) **6 Bit Racing**
58 Ch f 20/02 Harry Angel (IRE)—Dancing Elegance (Nathaniel (IRE)) (4000) **The Giggle Factor Partnership**

MR IVAN FURTADO - continued

59 Ch f 03/03 Decorated Knight—Duna (GER) (Lomitas) (3000)
60 Ch g 05/04 Galileo Gold—Esterlina (IRE) (Highest Honor (FR)) (3000) **J. L. Marriott**
61 B f 01/02 Kuroshio (AUS)—Gold Bracelet (IRE) (Montjeu (IRE)) (2001)
62 **KESTEVEN RDA (IRE),** b f 03/04 Inns of Court (IRE)—
Shrewd Approach (IRE) (Dawn Approach (IRE)) (1200) **The Mystery Men**
63 B f 03/04 Inns of Court (IRE)—Kodiac Express (IRE) (Kodiac) (4002)
64 Ch f 08/04 Mayson—Lincolnrose (IRE) (Verglas (IRE)) **G.P.S. Heart of Racing (Bloodstock) Ltd**
65 B g 18/03 Eqtidaar (IRE)—Love In The Park (Pivotal) (6500) **GB Civil Engineering (Leicester) LTD**
66 **NASSAU BAY,** b f 23/02 Washington DC (IRE)—Oneroa (IRE) (Dandy Man (IRE)) **The Entainers**
67 Ch g 20/03 Footstepsinthesand—Pass The Moon (IRE) (Raven's Pass (USA)) (5500) **The Giggle Factor Partnership**
68 **QUEEN MAGGIE,** b f 30/03 Magna Grecia (IRE)—Sweet Coconut (Bahamian Bounty) (8000) **We Do Racing**
69 B f 15/02 Soldier's Call—Rising Wind (IRE) (Shirocco (GER)) (6403)
70 Ch f 04/03 Cracksman—Silken Express (IRE) (Speightstown (USA)) (3000)
71 B f 26/04 Invincible Army (IRE)—Streetlady (USA) (Street Boss (USA)) (5000)

---

193 MR JOHN GALLAGHER, Moreton-In-Marsh

Postal: **Grove Farm, Chastleton, Moreton-In-Marsh, Gloucestershire, GL56 0SZ**
Contacts: **PHONE 01608 674492 MOBILE 07780 972663**
EMAIL john@gallagherracing.com WEBSITE www.gallagherracing.com

1 **BATCHELOR BOY (IRE),** 6, ch g Footstepsinthesand—Kathoe (IRE) **C. R. Marks (Banbury)**
2 **BEAUPARC SEVEN,** 5, b g Cannock Chase (USA)—Molly Cat **John Gallagher**
3 **BIBURYINMAY,** 4, b f Mayson—Bibury Lass **Mr C. Rogers**
4 **BUDDY'S BEAUTY,** 4, b f Equiano (FR)—Hollybell **Mr T. J. F. Smith**
5 **GLOBAL ESTEEM (IRE),** 6, b g Kodiac—Baltic Belle (IRE) **Caveat Emptor Partnership**
6 **GREEN POWER,** 8, b g Kheleyf (USA)—Hakuraa (IRE) **John Gallagher**
7 **INTERCESSOR,** 6, b g Due Diligence (USA)—Miss Meticulous **The LAM Partnership**
8 **JUNOESQUE,** 9, b m Virtual—Snake Skin **Andrew Bell & Michael Wright**
9 **KATIE K,** 4, b f Garswood—Princess Luna (GER) **Andrew Bell & Michael Wright**
10 **LOS CAMACHOS (IRE),** 8, b g Camacho—Illuminise (IRE) **Mr A. Bell**
11 **PADDY K,** 4, b g Ardad (IRE)—Bella Catalina **Andrew Bell & Michael Wright**
12 **PUSEY STREET,** 5, ch m Equiano (FR)—Pusey Street Lady **C R Marks (banbury) & J Gallagher**
13 **RIVAS ROB ROY,** 8, ch g Archipenko (USA)—Rivas Rhapsody (IRE) **Mr T. J. F. Smith**
14 **SECRET HANDSHEIKH,** 5, b g Mayson—Descriptive (IRE) **The Old Deer Racing Partnership**
15 **SILVER DIVA,** 5, gr m Hellvelyn—Heartsong (IRE) **J & L Wetherald - M & M Glover**
16 **STUNGBYTHEMASTER,** 4, ch g Jack Hobbs—Scorpion Princess (IRE) **Mr J. N. Greenley**

THREE-YEAR-OLDS

17 **GET BUSY,** ch g Unfortunately (IRE)—Heartsong (IRE) **J & L Wetherald - M & M Glover**
18 **HAVANA PUSEY,** b f Havana Grey—Pusey Street Lady **C. R. Marks (Banbury)**

TWO-YEAR-OLDS

19 B c 08/03 Le Brivido (FR)—Miss Meticulous (Bahamian Bounty) **The LAM Partnership**
20 B f 04/02 Cityscape—Ortenzia (IRE) (Lawman (FR)) **Mr J. N. Greenley**
21 B c 12/03 Frontiersman—Scorpion Princess (IRE) (Scorpion (IRE)) **Mr J. N. Greenley**

194 MR THOMAS GALLAGHER, Borehamwood

Postal: **5 Old Priory Park, Old London Road, St. Albans, Hertfordshire, AL1 1QF**

1 5, B g Harzand (IRE)—Deep Winter **Mr J. Reddington**
2 **EIRE STREET (IRE),** 6, b g Flemensfirth (USA)—Miss Xian (IRE) **Mr J. Reddington**
3 **GRASS'S JET (IRE),** 6, br g Jet Away—Emily's Belle (IRE) **Mr J. Reddington**
4 **ICARE COLOMBE (FR),** 5, b g Cokoriko (FR)—Valse de Touzaine (FR) **Mr J. Reddington**
5 **JACK HYDE (IRE),** 5, b g Soldier of Fortune (IRE)—Ballinahow Tara (IRE) **Mr J. Reddington**
6 4, B g Marcel (IRE)—Jersey Cream (IRE) **John Reddington Ltd**
7 **JUPETTES (FR),** 4, bl gr f Magneticjim (IRE)—Quelle Robe (FR) **Mr J. Reddington**
8 **KAYF HOPE (IRE),** 6, b m Kayf Tara—No Time For Tears (IRE) **Mr J. Reddington**
9 **LOVE AT SEA (IRE),** 5, b m Affinisea (IRE)—Luna Lovegood (IRE) **Mr J. Reddington**
10 **MR HARP (IRE),** 10, b g Court Cave (IRE)—Chapel Wood Lady (IRE) **Conor O'Dea Racing Club**
11 **PLAISIR DES FLOS (FR),** 4, ch g Joshua Tree (IRE)—Flot des Flos (FR) **Mr J. Reddington**
12 **QUIAN (GER),** 7, gr h Mastercraftsman (IRE)—Quiana (GER) **Mr J. Reddington**
13 **SARATOGA LASS (IRE),** 7, ch m Valirann (FR)—Grangeclare Star (IRE) **Mr J. Reddington**
14 **SHIROCCOSMAGICGEM (IRE),** 5, b m Shirocco (GER)—Black Magic Baby (IRE) **Mr J. Reddington**
15 **STATION HILL (IRE),** 5, b g Raven's Pass (USA)—Freya Tricks **Mr J. Reddington**
16 **TAMBUKAN (FR),** 4, b c Manduro (GER)—Taraf (USA) **Mr J. Reddington**
17 **TYNWALD,** 5, b g Toronado (IRE)—Queen's Prize **Mr J. Reddington**

195 MRS ILKA GANSERA-LEVEQUE, Newmarket

Postal: **Saint Wendreds, Hamilton Road, Newmarket, Suffolk, CB8 7JQ**
Contacts: **PHONE 01638 454973 MOBILE 07855 532072**
EMAIL office@gansera-leveque.com WEBSITE www.gansera-leveque.com

1 **JUST ONCE,** 7, b m Holy Roman Emperor (IRE)—Nur Jahan (IRE) **Vantage Point Racing Club**
2 **KINGWELL,** 4, b g Kingman—Frenzified **Vantage Point Racing Club**
3 **MISS BELLA BRAND,** 5, b m Poet's Voice—Miss Toldyaso (IRE) **M. Hebbard, L. Blackmore & Partners**
4 **RABAT (IRE),** 5, b m Mehmas (IRE)—Refuse To Give Up (IRE)
5 **RETROUVAILLES,** 5, b br m Iffraaj—Badweia (USA) **Vantage Point Racing Club**
6 **SCOT'S GRACE (IRE),** 4, b f Mehmas (IRE)—Ms O'Malley (IRE) **Mr B. Havern**

THREE-YEAR-OLDS

7 **DARING GREATLY,** ch f Decorated Knight—Epiphany **Team Turf Racing Club**
8 **MAID FOR HARRY,** b f Harry Angel (IRE)—Maid For Winning (USA) **Mr M. Percival**
9 **ONCE ADAAY,** b c Adaay (IRE)—Sonko (IRE) **Saint Wendred's Racing**
10 **WHITE MIST,** b gr f Dark Angel (IRE)—Wild Bud (USA) **JARAZ Enterprises GmbH & Co KG**

TWO-YEAR-OLDS

11 **THANKYOU BARONESS,** b br f 02/03 Sea The Moon (GER)—
Tosca (GER) (Amadeus Wolf) (5000) **Mrs I. Gansera-Leveque**
12 **UNIVERSAL SALLY,** b f 19/03 Havana Grey—Daring Day (Acclamation) (25610) **Mr B. Havern**
13 Ch f 14/03 Birchwood (IRE)—Upendi (FR) (Siyouni (FR)) **Carte Blanche Racing**

Assistant Trainer: Stephane Leveque.

196 MRS SUSAN GARDNER, Longdown

Postal: **Woodhayes Farm, Longdown, Exeter**
Contacts: **PHONE 01392 811213 MOBILE 07936 380492**
EMAIL woodhayesstudfarm@btinternet.com WEBSITE www.suegardnerracing.co.uk

1 **ALRAMZ,** 7, b g Intello (GER)—Rewaaya (IRE) **Miss Jane Edgar & Mr D. V. Gardner**
2 **ASTRONOMIC VIEW,** 6, ch g Schiaparelli (GER)—Winter Scene (IRE) **Mr D. V. Gardner**
3 **BLUFFMEIFYOUCAN,** 6, br g Yorgunnabelucky (USA)—Cita Verda (FR) **A & D Gardner**
4 **COEUR BLIMEY (IRE),** 12, b br g Winged Love (IRE)—Eastender **Keith Harris & Tom Gardner**
5 **EMMPRESSIVE LADY (IRE),** 8, b m Jeremy (USA)—Court Lexi (IRE) **Clear Racing**
6 **IVESCENEASPIDER,** 5, b g Scorpion (IRE)—Winter Scene (IRE) **Mr D. V. Gardner**
7 **KING ORRY (IRE),** 8, b g Oscar (IRE)—Deer Island Peg (IRE) **Gardner Wheeler**
8 **LIGHTONTHEWING (IRE),** 8, b g Winged Love (IRE)—Neat 'n Nimble **Woodhayes Racing Club**
9 **MIDSUMMER LASS,** 5, ch m Linda's Lad—Midsummer Legend **Mr N. A. Eggleton**
10 **MR CRAFTSMAN,** 6, ch g Trans Island—La Hoofon **Mrs L. Osborne**
11 **PRELINSIA (IRE),** 5, b m Presenting—Our Pride **V & P Sampson**
12 **RAPID RIVER (IRE),** 5, b g Ol' Man River (IRE)—More Equity **Mr D. V. Gardner**
13 **SNUG AS A BUG (IRE),** 8, b m Shirocco (GER)—More Equity **Mrs L. Osborne**
14 **STARWALKER,** 6, b g Telescope (IRE)—Holly Walk **Mr J. Cole**
15 **SWEET SAFFRON,** 6, br m Telescope (IRE)—Miss Saffron **P. A. Tylor**
16 **TALKTOMENOW,** 9, b g Shirocco (GER)—Sweet Stormy (IRE) **Clear Racing & Partner**
17 **TESTFLIGHT,** 6, b g Kayf Tara—Molly Flight (FR) **Mrs B. Russell & Mr D. V. Gardner**
18 **ZILLION (IRE),** 9, b g Zebedee—Redelusion (IRE) **Miss Jane Edgar & Mr D. V. Gardner**

Assistant Trainer: D. V. Gardner.

NH Jockey: Lucy Gardner, Micheal Nolan.

197 MRS ROSEMARY GASSON, Banbury

Postal: **Alkerton Grounds, Balscote, Banbury, Oxfordshire, OX15 6JS**
Contacts: **PHONE 01295 730248 MOBILE 07769 798430**
EMAIL arb@agf.myzen.co.uk

1 **BIGNORM (IRE),** 11, b g Mahler—Merry Heart (IRE) **Mrs R. Gasson**
2 **DEADLY MISSILE (IRE),** 6, br g Presenting—Daisy's Sister **Mrs R. Gasson**
3 **EVEN BREAK (IRE),** 5, b g Alkaadhem—Lady Marnay (IRE) **Mrs R. Gasson**
4 **MASKIA (FR),** 6, b g Masked Marvel—Rasia (FR) **Mrs R. Gasson**
5 **MEETMELATER (IRE),** 6, b g Mustameet (USA)—Emilies Pearl (IRE) **Mrs R. Gasson**

NH Jockey: Ben Poste.

198 MR MICHAEL GATES, Stratford-Upon-Avon

Postal: **Comfort Park Stud & Racing Stables, Campden Road, Clifford Chambers, Stratford-Upon-Avon, Warwickshire, CV37 8LW**
Contacts: **PHONE 07581 246070**
EMAIL comfortparkstud@hotmail.co.uk

1 **DAYBREAK BOY (IRE),** 10, b br g Kingsalsa (USA)—Aloisi **Mr M. Gates**
2 **DRUMNAGREAGH (IRE),** 10, b m September Storm (GER)—Saffron Pride (IRE) **Mr M. Gates**
3 **FLOATING ROCK (GER),** 8, b g It's Gino (GER)—Fly Osoria (GER) **Mr M. Gates**
4 **HITTHEKETTLE (IRE),** 7, b g Ocovango—Ballyquin Queen (IRE) **Mr M. Gates**
5 **HURRICANE ALEX,** 6, b g Canford Cliffs (IRE)—Azharia

199 MR PAUL GEORGE, Crediton

Postal: **Higher Eastington, Lapford, Crediton, Devon, EX17 6NE**
Contacts: **MOBILE 07733 171112**
EMAIL paul.george1@icloud.com WEBSITE www.paulgeorgeracing.co.uk

1 **RATHAGAN,** 6, b g Kyllachy—Ardessie **P. J. H. George**
2 **SYMPATHISE (IRE),** 5, b m Kodi Bear (IRE)—Starfly (IRE) **P. J. H. George**

THREE-YEAR-OLDS

3 **BACK IN TENNESSEE (IRE),** b g Air Force Blue (USA)—Purr And Prowl (USA) **P. J. H. George**

Assistant Trainer: Cassie Haughton.

Apprentice Jockey: Rhiain Ingram.

200 MR TOM GEORGE, Slad

Postal: **Down Farm, Slad, Stroud, Gloucestershire, GL6 7QE**
Contacts: **PHONE 01452 814267 MOBILE 07850 793483**
EMAIL tom@trgeorge.com WEBSITE www.tomgeorgeracing.co.uk

1 **BANNISTER (FR),** 6, gr g Olympic Glory (IRE)—Amou Daria (FR) **Crossed Fingers Partnership**
2 **BOAGRIUS (IRE),** 11, ch g Beneficial—Greenhall Rambler (IRE) **The MerseyClyde Partnership**
3 **BUN DORAN (IRE),** 12, b g Shantou (USA)—Village Queen (IRE) **Crossed Fingers Partnership**
4 **CALL ME RAFA (IRE),** 6, b g Mahler—Annie Grit (IRE) **Mr C. B. Compton**
5 **CASA TALL (FR),** 9, b g No Risk At All (FR)—Gribouille Parcs (FR) **Nelson, O'Donohoe, Mcdermott**
6 **CHAMPAGNE MYSTERY (IRE),** 9, b g Shantou (USA)—Spanker **The Franglais Partnership**
7 **CHARLES RITZ,** 7, b g Milan—Miss Ballantyne **Mr & Mrs R. G. Kelvin-Hughes**
8 **CLEAR ON TOP (IRE),** 7, b g Robin des Champs (FR)—Homelander (IRE) **Nelson, Bovington, Taylor, Delarocha**
9 **CLONDAW CASTLE (IRE),** 11, b g Oscar (IRE)—Lohort Castle (IRE) **J French, D McDermott, S Nelson, T Syder**
10 **COME ON GRUFF (IRE),** 7, b g Mahler—Annie Grit (IRE) **Mr N T Griffith & H M Haddock**
11 **COOL VIEW,** 5, b g Telescope (IRE)—Arctic Lady (IRE) **Mr S. W. Clarke**
12 **COTTUN (FR),** 7, b g Le Havre (IRE)—Montebella (FR) **Sharon Nelson & Katya Taylor Delarocha**
13 **COUPDEBOL (FR),** 8, gr g Rajsaman (FR)—Chance Bleue (FR) **Terry Warner & Tim Syder**
14 **CREALION (FR),** 7, b g Creachadoir (IRE)—Lady La Lionne (FR) **S Nelson, T Keelan, H Polito, C Compton**
15 **DOCTOR DOTTY,** 8, b m Dr Massini (IRE)—Anadama (IRE) **Mr P. Isaac**
16 **DOM BOSCO,** 6, b g Blue Bresil (FR)—Definitely Better (IRE) **Miss J. A. Hoskins**
17 **DUNSTALL RAMBLER (IRE),** 5, b g Walk In The Park (IRE)—Toungara (FR) **Mr S. W. Clarke**
18 **FARO DE KERSER (FR),** 8, b g Ungaro (GER)—Nuit de Kerser (FR) **The Twenty One Partnership**
19 **FORGOT TO ASK (IRE),** 11, b g Ask—Lady Transcend (IRE) **Miss J. A. Hoskins**
20 **G A HENTY,** 6, b g Milan—Lindeman (IRE) **Mr & Mrs R. G. Kelvin-Hughes**
21 **GO ON BRYCEY LAD (FR),** 7, b g Saddler Maker (IRE)—Lonita d'Airy (FR) **The MerseyClyde Partnership**
22 **GREAT D'ANGE (FR),** 7, b g Great Pretender (IRE)—Vickx (FR) **Mr T. D. J. Syder**
23 **HOODLUM (IRE),** 5, b g Aizavoski (IRE)—Lough Ennell (IRE) **Sharon Nelson & Vicki Robinson**
24 **HOOLIGAN (IRE),** 8, b g Aizavoski (IRE)—Victory Run (IRE) **O'Donohoe, Cavanagh, Robinson, Nelson**
25 **IL EST FRANCAIS (FR),** 5, b g Karaktar (IRE)—Millesimee (FR) **R Kelvin-Hughes & Haras De Saint-Voir**
26 **ILTONE (FR),** 5, b br g Cokoriko (FR)—Maciga (FR) **The Franglais Partnership**
27 **INEDIT STAR (FR),** 5, gr g Lord du Sud (FR)—Tulipe Star (FR) **Crossed Fingers Partnership**
28 **INFLEXIBLE (FR),** 5, b g Tirwanako (FR)—Clemence (FR) **H Stephen Smith & The Gabbertas Family**
29 **JACHAR (FR),** 4, b g Cokoriko (FR)—Creatina (FR) **Mr & Mrs R. G. Kelvin-Hughes**
30 **JAR DU DESERT (FR),** 4, b g Kapgarde (FR)—Dora du Desert (FR) **Crossed Fingers Partnership**
31 **JAVA POINT (IRE),** 8, b g Stowaway—Classic Sun (GER) **Fanning, Griffith, Haddock**
32 **JOBESGREEN GIRL,** 6, b m Passing Glance—Overnight Fame (IRE) **Mr R. T. Cornock**
33 **JOBESGREEN LAD,** 8, b g Passing Glance—Overnight Fame (IRE) **Mr R. T. Cornock**
34 **KAKAMORA,** 8, b g Great Pretender (IRE)—Roche d'Or **Mr T. D. J. Syder**

MR TOM GEORGE - continued

35 **LYDIA VIOLET (IRE),** 8, br m Kalanisi (IRE)—Anne Hathaway (IRE) **Chasing Gold Limited**
36 **MENGLI KHAN (IRE),** 10, b g Lope de Vega (IRE)—Danielli (IRE) **The Franglais Partnership**
37 **OAK CREEK (IRE),** 6, b g Fame And Glory—Flirthing Around (IRE) **N. R. A. Sutton**
38 **OSCAR ROBERTSON (IRE),** 9, b g Oscar (IRE)—Beaus Polly (IRE) **Crossed Fingers Partnership**
39 **RASCAL,** 5, b g Blue Bresil (FR)—Fairy Theatre (IRE) **Sharon Nelson & Vicki Robinson**
40 **SMUGGLER'S BLUES (IRE),** 11, b g Yeats (IRE)—Rosy de Cyborg (FR) **D Rea & K Bebbington**
41 **SOMERWAY (IRE),** 5, b m Getaway (GER)—Way Back When **Somerset Racing**
42 **STORMIN CROSSGALES (IRE),** 6, b g Sageburg (IRE)—Nodelay (IRE) **Noel Fehily Racing Syndicates-Stormin Cr**
43 **SWEET THREAT (FR),** 5, b g Triple Threat (FR)—Sweet Chestnut (FR) **Mr M. Stenning**
44 **THE LIKELY LAD (FR),** 4, b g Great Pretender (IRE)—Turgotine (FR) **Mr & Mrs R. G. Kelvin-Hughes**
45 **TIBIA (FR),** 4, b br g Manduro (GER)—Triceps (IRE) **Mr T. George**
46 **WHAT A STEAL (IRE),** 6, b g Flemensfirth (USA)—Misty Heather (IRE) **O'Donohoe, Delchar, Jack, Nelson**
47 **ZOEMAN (FR),** 4, b g Great Pretender (IRE)—Voulay (FR) **Silkword Racing Partnership**

THREE-YEAR-OLDS

48 **KASHMIR DE CORTON (FR),** b g Karaktar (IRE)—Comete de Corton (FR) **Mr T. D. J. Syder**
49 **KELANNEE (FR),** b f Nom de d'La (FR)—Quoi d'Autre (FR) **Mr T. George**

Assistant Trainer: Darren O'Dwyer, **Travelling Head:** Sarah Peacock, **Racing Secretary:** Lizzie Simpson-Pattison, **Secretary:** Lauren Thompson.

NH Jockey: Jonathan Burke, Ciaran Gethings.

201 MR ALEXANDER GIBBONS, Wroughton

Postal: **4 Easton Farm Cottages, Bishop's Cannings, Devizes, Wiltshire, SN10 2LR**
Contacts: **PHONE 07920 280539**
EMAIL alexander1.racing@gmail.com

1 **BAY SAM BELLA,** 8, b m Black Sam Bellamy (IRE)—With Grace **Mr A. Gibbons**

---

202 MR NICK GIFFORD, Findon

Postal: **The Downs, Stable Lane, Findon, West Sussex, BN14 0RT**
Contacts: **PHONE 01903 872226 MOBILE 07940 518077**
WORK EMAIL giffordracing@outlook.com WEBSITE www.nickgiffordracing.co.uk

1 **AMI BONDHU (FR),** 4, b g Choeur du Nord (FR)—Rogation (FR) **Mrs R. E. Gifford**
2 **BELARGUS (FR),** 8, b g Authorized (IRE)—Belga Wood (USA) **Mr J. P. McManus**
3 **CHURCHILLS BOY (IRE),** 6, b g Malinas (GER)—Lindas Last (IRE) **H & L Meagher**
4 **COBBS CORNER (IRE),** 7, b g Ocovango—A Long Way **Mr M. P. Jones**
5 **DELTA ROSE (IRE),** 9, br m Robin des Champs (FR)—Cruising Katie (IRE) **J. R. Hulme**
6 **DRISHOGUE (IRE),** 4, ch f Mount Nelson—African Keys (IRE) **Nick Gifford Racing Club**
7 **ELIZA DOLITTLE (IRE),** 5, b m Califet (FR)—Cove (IRE) **Mr M. K. O'Shea**
8 **FAIRWAY FREDDY (IRE),** 10, b g Elusive Pimpernel (USA)—Silent Supreme (IRE) **New Gold Dream**
9 **FIRST OFFENCE (IRE),** 6, gr h Ask—Umadachar (FR) **Mrs T. J. Stone-Brown**
10 **FOLLOW INTELLO (IRE),** 8, b g Intello (GER)—Sauvage (FR) **Findon Flyers**
11 **GRAND SABRE,** 4, b g Dartmouth—Unika La Reconce (FR) **Mr G. F. Brooks**
12 **JASPER BOY (FR),** 4, b g Kapgarde (FR)—Soleiade (FR) **Nick Gifford Racing Club**
13 **KILFORDS QUEEN (IRE),** 6, b m Dylan Thomas (IRE)—Lunar Gift (IRE) **Nick Gifford Racing Club**
14 **KINGS KRACKERTARA,** 8, b m Kayf Tara—Firecracker Lady (IRE) **J.C.Harrison Lee & T.Howard Partnership**
15 **KINGS KUROSHIO,** 7, b m Kuroshio (AUS)—Firecracker Lady (IRE) **J.C.Harrison Lee & T.Howard Partnership**
16 5, B m Pour Moi (IRE)—Lady Bernie (IRE) **Mr T Allan and Mrs H Allan**

MR NICK GIFFORD - continued

17 **LEDDERS (IRE),** 5, ch g Jet Away—Miss Penny Pincher (IRE) **Ledwardian Legacy Partnership**
18 **LEGENDARY GRACE,** 6, b m Multiplex—Fairyinthewind (IRE) **Mr R. J. Delnevo**
19 6, B m Finsceal Fior (IRE)—Lounaos (FR) **Mrs R. E. Gifford**
20 **MARINE JAG (FR),** 6, b m Saint des Saints (FR)—Soif d'Aimer (FR) **Paul & Louise Bowtell**
21 **MISS GET THE VEUVE,** 5, b m Getaway (GER)—Miss Milborne **Miss S. Searle**
22 **MISSFIT (IRE),** 6, gr m Kalanisi (IRE)—Miss Miracle **Heart Racing**
23 **MY BAD LUCY,** 7, b g Kayf Tara—Luci di Mezzanotte **Mr M. K. O'Shea**
24 **NORTHERN POET (IRE),** 8, b g Yeats (IRE)—Crowning Virtue (IRE) **The Hope Springs Syndicate**
25 **ONESTEPTWOSTEPS (IRE),** 6, b br g Getaway (GER)—Total Gossip (IRE) **Paul & Louise Bowtell**
26 **PADDY'S POEM,** 12, b g Proclamation (IRE)—Ashleys Petale (IRE) **Mrs T. J. Stone-Brown**
27 **PIP AWAY (IRE),** 6, b m Getaway (GER)—Justamemory (IRE) **The Lavender Chickens**
28 4, B g Elusive Pimpernel (USA)—Point The Toes (IRE)
29 **RIVER TYNE,** 8, b m Geordieland (FR)—Not Now Nellie **Mr T Allan and Mrs H Allan**
30 **RUM COVE,** 5, ch g Black Sam Bellamy (IRE)—First Wonder (FR) **Hope Springs Too**
31 **SALLYANN (IRE),** 6, ch m Soldier of Fortune (IRE)—Golden Bay **Mrs S. A. Addington-Smith**
32 **THE MIGHTY DON (IRE),** 11, ch g Shantou (USA)—Flying Answer (IRE) **Golden Rose Partnership**
33 **WHISPERING GOLD,** 5, ch m Proconsul—Fairyinthewind (IRE) **The Rose Tinted Partnership**
34 **YESNOSORRY (IRE),** 6, ch m Sans Frontieres (IRE)—Graces Island (IRE) **The Willow & Bridle Partnership**
35 **ZUBA,** 7, b g Dubawi (IRE)—Purr Along **The South Downs Partnership**

NH Jockey: James Davies, Tabitha Worsley.

---

203 MR MARK GILLARD, Dorset

Postal: **Hawkes Field Farm, Hilton, Blandford Forum, Dorset, DT11 0DN**
Contacts: **PHONE 01258 881111 MOBILE 07970 700605**
EMAIL office@markgillardracing.com WEBSITE www.markgillardracing.com

1 **BLUEBLOOD (IRE),** 7, b br g Dawn Approach (IRE)—Ghany (IRE) **Mr I. T. Booth**
2 **CAPTAIN CUCKOO,** 11, ch g Black Sam Bellamy (IRE)—Shiny Thing (USA) **Mrs P. M. R. Gillard**
3 **CLINTON LANE,** 5, ch g Linda's Lad—Midnight Seranade (IRE) **T. J. C. Seegar**
4 **ELLENCARNE (IRE),** 4, b f Churchill (IRE)—Regalline (IRE) **M. C. Denning**
5 **GENI DE LA COUR (FR),** 7, b g Maresca Sorrento (FR)—Reveuse de La Cour (FR) **Mrs P. M. R. Gillard**
6 **GIRANDOLE (FR),** 5, b g No Nay Never (USA)—Laber Ildut (IRE) **Mr S. J. Garnett**
7 **HAZMAT (IRE),** 5, br m Harzand (IRE)—Suite (IRE) **Mr R. M. Rivers**
8 **JOHN BETJEMAN,** 7, b g Poet's Voice—A Great Beauty **Robin Gillard & Rory Gillard**
9 **NO NO TONIC,** 9, b m Sulamani (IRE)—Karinga Madame **N. J. McMullan**
10 **OLLY'S FOLLY,** 9, b g Poet's Voice—Pearl Diva (IRE) **Red Star Racing**

Assistant Trainer: Mrs Pippa Gillard, **Yard Sponsor:** Ascot Park Polo Club.

Conditional Jockey: Fergus Gillard, Theo Gillard.

---

204 MR JIM GOLDIE, Glasgow

Postal: **Libo Hill Farm, Uplawmoor, Glasgow, Lanarkshire, G78 4BA**
Contacts: **PHONE 01505 850212 MOBILE 07778 241522**
WEBSITE www.jimgoldieracing.com

1 **A LA FRANCAISE,** 4, ch f Postponed (IRE)—Alamode **Summerstorm Bloodstock Ltd**
2 **ABDUCTION (FR),** 5, b g Acclamation—Perfect Day (IRE) **Dab Hand Racing**
3 **AIGHEAR,** 5, b m Farhh—Kabjoy (IRE) **The Fair Lasses**
4 **AYR POET,** 8, b g Poet's Voice—Jabbara (IRE) **The Reluctant Suitor's**

MR JIM GOLDIE - continued

5 **BANNER ROAD (IRE),** 4, b f Make Believe—Trempjane **Mr J. M. Long**
6 **BE PROUD (IRE),** 7, b g Roderic O'Connor (IRE)—Agnista (IRE) **Whitestonecliffe Racing Partnership**
7 **BOBBY SHAFTOE,** 5, ch g Mazameer (IRE)—Sister Red (IRE) **Mr James Callow & Mr J. S. Goldie**
8 **BONITO CAVALO,** 4, b g Orientor—Eternal Instinct **Whitestonecliffe Racing Partnership**
9 **BRAES OF DOUNE,** 5, b g Orientor—Gargoyle Girl **Johnnie Delta Racing**
10 **CALL ME GINGER,** 7, ch g Orientor—Primo Heights **Johnnie Delta Racing**
11 **CLASSY AL,** 5, b g Fountain of Youth (IRE)—Classy Anne **Barraston Racing & Mr J S Goldie**
12 **COSA SARA (IRE),** 5, b m Gleneagles (IRE)—Antique Platinum (IRE) **Summerstorm Bloodstock Ltd**
13 **EUCHEN GLEN,** 10, b g Authorized (IRE)—Jabbara (IRE) **W. M. Johnstone**
14 **FAYLAQ,** 7, b g Dubawi (IRE)—Danedream (GER) **B Jordan, Brian Jordan, S Jordan & N McConnell**
15 **FOOLS RUSH IN (IRE),** 5, b g Mehmas (IRE)—Faddwa (IRE) **Dab Hand Racing**
16 **GENEVIEVE,** 4, b f Orientor—Eternalist **Johnnie Delta Racing**
17 **GEREMIA (IRE),** 5, b g Fastnet Rock (AUS)—Gerika (FR) **Mr James Fyffe & Mr Scott Fyffe**
18 **GLEN LOMOND,** 5, ch g Orientor—Glenlini **Johnnie Delta Racing**
19 4, B g Orientor—Glenlini **Johnnie Delta Racing**
20 **GLOBAL HUMOR (USA),** 8, b g Distorted Humor (USA)—In Bloom (USA) **Mr P. Stewart**
21 **GRACES QUEST,** 5, b m Telescope (IRE)—Ballinargh Girl (IRE) **Summerstorm Bloodstock Ltd**
22 **GRAND CANAL (IRE),** 6, b g Australia—Loreto (IRE) **Summerstorm Bloodstock Ltd**
23 **JORDAN ELECTRICS,** 7, b g Dandy Man (IRE)—Ruby Slippers **B Jordan, Brian Jordan, S Jordan & N McConnell**
24 **KRAKEN POWER (IRE),** 5, b g The Last Lion (IRE)—Throne **Mr P. Stewart**
25 **LOCHNAVER,** 5, b m Frankel—Strathnaver **Summerstorm Bloodstock Ltd**
26 **NICHOLAS T,** 11, b g Rail Link—Thorntoun Piccolo **Mr James Callow & Mr J. S. Goldie**
27 **ORIENTAL LILLY,** 9, ch m Orientor—Eternal Instinct **Johnnie Delta Racing**
28 **PAMMI,** 8, b m Poet's Voice—Bright Girl (IRE) **Ayrshire Racing & Partner**
29 **PRIMO'S COMET,** 8, b g Orientor—Primo Heights **Johnnie Delta Racing**
30 **ROCK MELODY (IRE),** 4, b f Fascinating Rock (IRE)—Legal Lyric (IRE) **Summerstorm Bloodstock Ltd**
31 **RORY,** 5, ch g Orientor—Eternal Instinct **Mr H. Connor**
32 **SHINE ON BRENDAN (IRE),** 6, b g Society Rock (IRE)—Something Magic **Let's Be Lucky Racing 29**
33 **SIR CHAUVELIN,** 11, b g Authorized (IRE)—Jabbara (IRE) **Mr J. Fyffe & Mr J. S. Goldie**
34 **SOUND OF IONA,** 7, ch m Orientor—Eternal Instinct **Mr & Mrs G Grant & the Reluctant Suitors**
35 **SPANISH HUSTLE,** 5, b g Pearl Secret—Dos Lunas (IRE) **Let's Be Lucky Racing 31**
36 **ST ANDREW'S CASTLE,** 4, b g Iffraaj—Age of Chivalry (IRE) **Johnnie Delta Racing**
37 **TAFSIR (USA),** 4, b f Tamarkuz (USA)—Jannattan (USA) **Summerstorm Bloodstock Ltd**
38 **TOMMY G,** 10, ch g Makfi—Primo Heights **Johnnie Delta Racing**
39 **TWO AULD PALS (IRE),** 5, b g The Carbon Unit (USA)—Lady Jock (IRE) **Mr J. M. Long**
40 **WATER OF LEITH (IRE),** 5, b g Kodiac—Zakhrafa (IRE) **Mr J. S. Goldie**

THREE-YEAR-OLDS

41 **ANA EMARAATY (IRE),** b g Awtaad (IRE)—Sundus (USA) **Mr J. S. Goldie**
42 **B ASSOCIATES (IRE),** b g War Command (USA)—Spirit of The Sea (IRE) **Mr S. Fyffe**
43 B g Washington DC (IRE)—Classy Anne **Barraston Racing & Mr J S Goldie**
44 **EPONA PAS (IRE),** b g Gustav Klimt (IRE)—Dream Scenario **ASAP Racing**
45 B f Orientor—Eternal Instinct **Mr James Callow & Mr J. S. Goldie**
46 **HUMBLE SPARK (IRE),** b g Acclamation—Maiden Approach **Mr F. Brady**
47 **KELPIE GREY,** gr g Havana Grey—Malelane (IRE) **Mr E. G. Murray**

TWO-YEAR-OLDS

48 B f 03/05 Muhaarar—Firenze (Efisio) (12000) **Summerstorm Bloodstock Ltd**
49 B c 03/02 Cotai Glory—Saikung (IRE) (Acclamation) (8095) **The Vital Sparks & David D Smith**
50 Ch f 23/03 Portamento (IRE)—Trasparencia (ARG) (Dynamix (USA)) (1905) **The Vital Sparks & David D Smith**

Assistant Trainer: George Goldie, James Goldie.

205 MR CHRIS GORDON, Winchester

Postal: **Morestead Farm Stables, Morestead, Winchester, Hampshire, SO21 1JD**
Contacts: **MOBILE 07713 082392**
EMAIL chrisgordon68@hotmail.co.uk WEBSITE www.chrisgordonracing.com

1 **ALTO ALTO (FR),** 6, ch g Falco (USA)—Beautyful (IRE) **Mrs C. New**
2 **ANNUAL INVICTUS (IRE),** 8, b g Mahler—Shantou Rose (IRE) **Mr T. M. Smith**
3 **AUCUNRISQUE (FR),** 7, b g No Risk At All (FR)—Saintheze (FR) **Goodwin Racing Ltd**
4 **BADDESLEY (IRE),** 8, b g Presenting—Fox Theatre (IRE) **Mr Richard & Mrs Carol Cheshire**
5 **BENTLEY'S RETURN (IRE),** 5, b g Mahler—Deianira (IRE) **Mr J. P. Pfitzner**
6 **BETGOODWIN (FR),** 4, ch g Castle du Berlais (FR)—Fol' Allegria (USA) **Goodwin Racing Ltd**
7 **BLADE RUNNER (FR),** 7, b g Great Pretender (IRE)—Cutting Edge (FR) **Holman,Widdows,Banks,Lloyd**
8 **BLAME THE GAME (IRE),** 8, b g Darsi (FR)—Lucy Walters (IRE) **Redz Together**
9 **CARD DEALER (IRE),** 6, ch g Aizavoski (IRE)—Oscar Invitation (IRE) **Mr D. S. Dennis**
10 **CHESH (IRE),** 4, br g Getaway (GER)—Through The Lens (IRE) **Mr Richard & Mrs Carol Cheshire**
11 **COOLVALLA (IRE),** 7, b g Westerner—Valleyboggan (IRE) **L. Gilbert**
12 **DIAMOND EGG (FR),** 5, b g Diamond Boy (FR)—Chamoss World (FR) **Henrietta Knight Racing Syndicate**
13 **DJIN CONTI (FR),** 10, b g Lucarno (USA)—Regina Conti (FR) **S C Robinson & Mrs C Gilsenan**
14 **DUKE OF BADDESLEY (IRE),** 4, br g Kalanisi (IRE)—Anotherlady (IRE) **Mr Richard & Mrs Carol Cheshire**
15 **FOREST JUMP (IRE),** 6, b g Mahler—Deianira (IRE) **Mrs N. Morris**
16 **GERICO VILLE (FR),** 7, b g Protektor (GER)—Jadoudy Ville (FR) **Cox, Russell, Lloyd, Finnegan & Scanlon**
17 **GOODWIN (IRE),** 5, b g Champs Elysees—Mount Corkish Girl (IRE) **Goodwin Racing Ltd**
18 **GOODWIN RACING (IRE),** 6, b g Califet (FR)—Ballinahow Tara (IRE) **Goodwin Racing Ltd**
19 **HAPPY BOY (FR),** 6, gr g Rail Link—Vrai Bonheur (FR) **Brenda Ansell & Jane Goddard**
20 **HEYDOUR (IRE),** 10, br g Presenting—Our Lucky Venture (IRE) **L. Gilbert**
21 **HIGHWAY ONE O FIVE (IRE),** 4, b br g Sageburg (IRE)—Shuil A Hocht (IRE) **A. C. Ward-Thomas**
22 **HIGHWAY ONE O FOUR (IRE),** 5, b g Sageburg (IRE)—Good Time In Milan (IRE) **A. C. Ward-Thomas**
23 **HIGHWAY ONE O TWO (IRE),** 8, b br g Shirocco (GER)—Supreme Dreamer (IRE) **A. C. Ward-Thomas**
24 **HIWAY ONE O THREE (IRE),** 6, b g Sageburg (IRE)—Good Time In Milan (IRE) **Ward-Thomas & Dennis**
25 **I'D LIKE TO KNOW (IRE),** 6, b g Mahler—The Boys Dont Know (IRE) **The Jolly Farmers**
26 **INVICTUS DE BRION (FR),** 5, b g Vespone (IRE)—Assemblee A Brion (FR) **Goodwin Racing Ltd**
27 **IPSO FALCO (FR),** 5, b g Falco (USA)—Roselaine (FR) **Party People**
28 **JEFE TRIUNFO (FR),** 4, gr g Cima de Triomphe (IRE)—Assemblee A Brion (FR) **Mrs J. L. Gordon**
29 **KAYF LEGEND,** 5, b g Kayf Tara—Camina **The Morestead Remount Syndicate**
30 **KING WILLIAM RUFUS (FR),** 6, b g Diamond Boy (FR)—Clochette de Sou (FR) **Mrs B. M. Ansell**
31 **LAKE ROAD (IRE),** 5, b m Shantou (USA)—Caheronaun (IRE) **Mr Richard & Mrs Carol Cheshire**
32 **LEAVE OF ABSENCE (FR),** 6, ch g Masked Marvel—To Much Fun **Mr Richard & Mrs Carol Cheshire**
33 **LORD BADDESLEY (IRE),** 8, b br g Doyen (IRE)—Tropical Ocean (IRE) **Mr Richard & Mrs Carol Cheshire**
34 **MISTER UPTON,** 4, b g Norse Dancer (IRE)—Whispering Grace **Mrs L. Finnegan**
35 **MOUNT BONETE,** 5, ch g Proconsul—Cita Verda (FR) **A. C. Ward-Thomas**
36 **MY TICKETYBOO (IRE),** 5, b g Shirocco (GER)—Subtle Hint (IRE) **L. Gilbert**
37 **ONE FOR THE WALL (IRE),** 7, br g Yeats (IRE)—Abinitio Lady (IRE) **The Select Syndicate**
38 **ONLY MONEY (IRE),** 9, ch g Getaway (GER)—Kings Diva (IRE) **Mr D. S. Dennis**
39 **PASVOLSKY (IRE),** 8, ch g Aizavoski (IRE)—Snowlaw (IRE) **The Augean Stables Syndicate**
40 **PRESENTING A QUEEN,** 6, br m Presenting—Queens Regatta (IRE) **Mr Richard & Mrs Carol Cheshire**
41 **PRESS YOUR LUCK (IRE),** 8, b g Doyen (IRE)—Merry Gladness (IRE) **Cox, Lloyd & Finden**
42 **PROPER TWELVE (IRE),** 5, br g Presenting—Ruby Reel (IRE) **Mr Richard & Mrs Carol Cheshire**
43 **PSYCHE,** 6, b g Lope de Vega (IRE)—Ode To Psyche (IRE) **L. Gilbert**
44 **RAMORE WILL (IRE),** 12, gr g Tikkanen (USA)—Gill Hall Lady **E. J. Farrant**
45 **RED WINDSOR (IRE),** 6, b g Elusive Pimpernel (USA)—Pros 'n' Cons (IRE) **Party People 2**
46 **SALADINS SON (IRE),** 5, b g Tobougg (IRE)—Denny de Lap (IRE) **Mrs C. L. Cheshire**
47 **SAMI BEAR,** 7, b g Sulamani (IRE)—Dalriath **Team ABC**
48 **SANDY BROOK (IRE),** 8, ch g Sandmason—Lovely Lolly (IRE) **Goodwin Racing Ltd**
49 **SEA INVASION (IRE),** 5, ch g Sea Moon—Aloha Iwanaga (GER) **Mr Richard & Mrs Carol Cheshire**
50 **SHUT THE BOX (IRE),** 9, ch g Doyen (IRE)—Bond Holder (IRE) **The Shut The Box Syndicate**
51 **STANLEY PINCOMBE (IRE),** 6, b g Multiplex—Allez Zane **Ms E. J. Southall**
52 **STORM DENNIS (IRE),** 7, b g Libertarian—Lady Eile (IRE) **Mr D. S. Dennis**
53 **TEA AND CHATS (IRE),** 6, b g Westerner—Dartmeet (IRE) **L. Gilbert**
54 **THE RAVEN'S RETURN,** 10, b g Scorpion (IRE)—Mimis Bonnet (FR) **Mrs J. L. Gordon**
55 **THE TIN MINER (IRE),** 12, br g Presenting—Sidalcea (IRE) **Mrs B. M. Ansell**

MR CHRIS GORDON - continued

56 **TOP MAN (IRE),** 9, b g Milan—Get In There (IRE) **Broadsword Group Ltd**
57 **UNANSWERED PRAYERS (IRE),** 7, b g Ocovango—Fitanga Speed (IRE) **The Pres Partnership**
58 **WHO IS THAT (IRE),** 7, ch g Shirocco (GER)—Nodelay (IRE) **Mr D. S. Dennis**

Assistant Trainer: Jenny Gordon.

NH Jockey: Tom Cannon. **Amateur Jockey:** Mr Freddie Gordon, Miss Molly Landau.

---

206 MR JOHN AND THADY GOSDEN, Newmarket

Postal: **Clarehaven , Bury Road, Newmarket, Suffolk, CB8 7BY**

1 **AUDIENCE,** 4, b g Iffraaj—Ladyship
2 **BELT BUCKLE,** 4, br f Golden Horn—Bible Belt (IRE)
3 **COURAGE MON AMI,** 4, b g Frankel—Crimson Ribbon (USA)
4 **DHABAB (IRE),** 4, ch g No Nay Never (USA)—Habbat Reeh (IRE)
5 **EMILY UPJOHN,** 4, b f Sea The Stars (IRE)—Hidden Brief
6 **FILISTINE (IRE),** 4, b c Almanzor (FR)—Desire To Win (IRE)
7 **FOREST OF DEAN,** 7, b g Iffraaj—Forest Crown
8 **FRANCESCO CLEMENTE (IRE),** 4, b c Dubawi (IRE)—Justlookdontouch (IRE)
9 **FRANTASTIC,** 4, b c Frankel—Rhadegunda
10 **FREE WIND (IRE),** 5, b m Galileo (IRE)—Alive Alive Oh
11 **GRANDE DAME,** 4, b f Lope de Vega (IRE)—Minwah (IRE)
12 **HARROVIAN,** 7, b g Leroidesanimaux (BRZ)—Alma Mater
13 **HONITON (IRE),** 4, gr g Dark Angel (IRE)—Lacily (USA)
14 **INSPIRAL,** 4, b f Frankel—Starscope
15 **ISRAR,** 4, b c Muhaarar—Taghrooda
16 **KENSINGTON (IRE),** 4, b f Frankel—Canonbury (IRE)
17 **LAUREL,** 4, b f Kingman—Promising Lead
18 **LORD NORTH (IRE),** 7, b g Dubawi (IRE)—Najoum (USA)
19 **MIGHTY ULYSSES,** 4, b c Ulysses (IRE)—Token of Love
20 **MIMIKYU,** 4, b f Dubawi (IRE)—Montare (IRE)
21 **MORNING POEM,** 4, b f Kingman—Mill Springs
22 **MOSTAHDAF (IRE),** 5, br h Frankel—Handassa
23 **MR INSPIRATION (IRE),** 4, b c Dubawi (IRE)—Fireglow
24 **NASHWA,** 4, b f Frankel—Princess Loulou (IRE)
25 **ONE EVENING,** 4, ch f Galileo (IRE)—Seta
26 **PEACE MAN,** 4, b c Kingman—Peacehaven (IRE)
27 **PENNYMOOR,** 5, b m Frankel—Penelopa
28 **REACH FOR THE MOON,** 4, b g Sea The Stars (IRE)—Golden Stream (IRE)
29 **SAGA,** 4, gr ro g Invincible Spirit (IRE)—Emily Bronte
30 **SECURITY CODE,** 4, b c Territories (IRE)—Moment of Time
31 **SHAARA,** 4, b f Shamardal (USA)—Yasmeen
32 **SWEET WILLIAM (IRE),** 4, b g Sea The Stars (IRE)—Gale Force
33 **TRAWLERMAN (IRE),** 5, b g Golden Horn—Tidespring (IRE)
34 **UNFORGOTTEN (IRE),** 5, gr ro g Exceed And Excel (AUS)—Souviens Toi
35 **VAGUELY REGAL (IRE),** 4, b f Galileo (IRE)—Danilovna (IRE)

THREE-YEAR-OLDS

36 **A DUBLIN LAD,** b c Ulysses (IRE)—Sacre Caroline (USA)
37 **A GIFT OF LOVE,** b f Frankel—Our Obsession (IRE)
38 **AL ASIFAH,** b f Frankel—Aneen (IRE)
39 **ALRASHAKA (IRE),** b f Frankel—Rumoush (USA)
40 **ALZAHIR (FR),** ch g Sea The Stars (IRE)—Cup Cake (IRE)
41 **AMPHITRITE,** b f Sea The Stars (IRE)—Belle d'Or (USA)
42 **ANANDA,** b f Frankel—Sotka
43 **ANDARAX (IRE),** ch g New Bay—Young Special (IRE)
44 **APOLO,** gr c Kingman—Sky Lantern (IRE)
45 **ARREST (IRE),** b c Frankel—Nisriyna (IRE)

MR JOHN AND THADY GOSDEN - continued

46 **ASTRODOME,** b c Sea The Stars (IRE)—So Mi Dar
47 **ATARAMA,** b f Sea The Stars (IRE)—Fly
48 **ATLANTIC BELLE,** b f Nathaniel (IRE)—Atlantic Drift
49 **AUGUST (IRE),** b c Almanzor (FR)—Nicky's Brown Miss (USA)
50 **BATTISTA (IRE),** ch c New Bay—Vuela
51 **BRESSON,** b c Dubawi (IRE)—Shutter Speed
52 **BRIDESTONES (IRE),** b f Teofilo (IRE)—White Moonstone (USA)
53 **BRIGHTLY (FR),** b f Sea The Stars (IRE)—Aurora Gold
54 **BRISBANE ROAD,** ch f Australia—Gale Force
55 **BURGLAR,** ch c Cracksman—Hidden Hope
56 **CALLIGRAPHY,** b c Night of Thunder (IRE)—Letterfromamerica (USA)
57 **CARLTON,** br c Frankel—Chantra (GER)
58 **CEANNA,** b f Showcasing—Penelopa
59 **CHALICE (IRE),** b f Sea The Stars (IRE)—Fleche d'Or
60 **CLOUD ANGEL,** ch f Frankel—Angel Terrace (USA)
61 **COPPICE,** b f Kingman—Helleborine
62 **COVEY,** b c Frankel—Quail
63 **CRUELLA DE VILL (IRE),** b f Dubawi (IRE)—Hoity Toity
64 **CRYPTO FORCE,** b c Time Test—Luna Mare (IRE)
65 **DARK KESTREL (IRE),** b g Dark Angel (IRE)—Goodnight And Joy (IRE)
66 **DOLCE COURAGE,** b c Siyouni (FR)—Valiant Girl
67 **EASTERN EMPRESS,** b f Dubawi (IRE)—Intrigued
68 **ELHAYBA,** ch f Justify (USA)—Woodland Scene (IRE)
69 **EPICTETUS (IRE),** b c Kingman—Thistle Bird
70 **FREE LOVIN',** b f Roaring Lion (USA)—Hippy Hippy Shake
71 **FREEDOM DAY (IRE),** b g No Nay Never (USA)—Pioneer Spirit
72 **FULLY WET,** b f Kodiac—Rainfall Radar (USA)
73 **GHARA,** b f Frankel—Ballet De La Reine (USA)
74 **GINZA,** b f Wootton Bassett—Shada (IRE)
75 **GLOWING SKY (IRE),** b f Sea The Stars (IRE)—Bella Qatara (IRE)
76 **GOVERNOR OF INDIA,** b c Dubawi (IRE)—Star of Seville
77 **GREGORY,** b c Golden Horn—Gretchen
78 **GUARD,** b c Kingman—California (IRE)
79 **HOWEITAT (IRE),** b c Dubawi (IRE)—Justlookdontouch (IRE)
80 **HUMANITY (IRE),** b c Roaring Lion (USA)—Cheriearch (USA)
81 **INNER SPACE,** ch f Siyouni (FR)—Journey
82 **INQUIRING MINDS,** b c Kingman—Precious Ramotswe
83 **INTINSO,** gr c Siyouni (FR)—Rose of Miracles
84 **JEFF KOONS (IRE),** b br c Frankel—Quidura
85 **JUMEIRA VISION (IRE),** b c Iffraaj—Manaboo (USA)
86 **KEITH DOUGLAS,** b c Dubawi (IRE)—The Black Princess (FR)
87 **LEADING LION (IRE),** b c Roaring Lion (USA)—Giofra
88 **LIFTOFF (FR),** ch f New Bay—Borgia's Best (IRE)
89 **LION TAMER,** ch c Roaring Lion (USA)—Exceedingly Rare (IRE)
90 **LION'S PRIDE,** b gr c Roaring Lion (USA)—Crimson Ribbon (USA)
91 **LMAY (IRE),** b f Frankel—Alienate
92 **LOTUSLAND (IRE),** b f Dark Angel (IRE)—Pleasemetoo (IRE)
93 **LOVING FEELING,** b c Sea The Stars (IRE)—Loving Things
94 **LUDMILLA,** b f Kingman—Rostova (USA)
95 **MAASAI MARA,** b g Roaring Lion (USA)—Wekeela (FR)
96 **MAGICAL STORY,** b f Nathaniel (IRE)—Magical Romance (IRE)
97 **MAHBOOB (IRE),** b c Sea The Stars (IRE)—Albaraah (IRE)
98 **MAREMMA,** b f Oasis Dream—Deciding Vote
99 **MARKSMAN QUEEN,** b f Dubawi (IRE)—Sharp Susan (USA)
100 **MASTERKEY,** b c Cracksman—Exceed Sensazione
101 **MEDICI CHAPEL,** ch f Iffraaj—Nannina
102 **MIDDLE EARTH,** b c Roaring Lion (USA)—Roheryn (IRE)
103 **MIDSUMMER DANCE (USA),** b f Mendelssohn (USA)—Dance With Another (IRE)
104 **MISCHIEVOUS MADAME (USA),** ch f Kitten's Joy (USA)—Auntinet
105 **MOSTABSHIR,** gr c Dark Angel (IRE)—Handassa

MR JOHN AND THADY GOSDEN - continued

106 **MUSING,** ch f Sea The Moon (GER)—Priola (GER)
107 **NAAEY,** b f Lope de Vega (IRE)—Materialistic
108 **NEVER ENDING (IRE),** b f No Nay Never (USA)—Lady Ederle (USA)
109 **OBELIX,** b c Sea The Stars (IRE)—La Mortola
110 **POLAR PRINCESS,** ch f Ulysses (IRE)—Ice Palace
111 **PORT JACKSON,** br gr g Australia—Miss Kenton (IRE)
112 **POSTMAN'S PARK,** gr ro c Mastercraftsman (IRE)—Dawn Delivers
113 **PRIDE AND GLORY (USA),** b br c Kitten's Joy (USA)—Forever Beautiful (USA)
114 **PROVIDENCIALES (IRE),** ch f Australia—Falling Petals (IRE)
115 **QUANTUM CAT (USA),** ch c Kitten's Joy (USA)—Blue Grass Music (USA)
116 **QUEEN FLEUR (IRE),** b f Kingman—Fleur Forsyte
117 **QUEEN FOR YOU (IRE),** b f Kingman—Fallen For You
118 **QUEEN OF THE PRIDE,** b f Roaring Lion (USA)—Simple Verse (IRE)
119 **QUEEN REGENT,** b f Roaring Lion (USA)—Common Knowledge
120 **RAJASTHAN,** ch c Dubawi (IRE)—Beautiful Morning
121 **REBECCA WEST,** b f Iffraaj—Scala Regia (FR)
122 **RIBLA (IRE),** b f Make Believe—Simple Magic (IRE)
123 **ROADWAY (USA),** b f Quality Road (USA)—Love Me Only (IRE)
124 **RUNNING LION,** gr f Roaring Lion (USA)—Bella Nouf
125 **SATIRICAL,** b f Kingman—Believable
126 **SAVANNA KING,** gr c Roaring Lion (USA)—An Ghalanta (IRE)
127 **SERENGETI SUNSET,** b c Roaring Lion (USA)—Really Lovely (IRE)
128 **SHADOW OF WAR,** b gr c Roaring Lion (USA)—Reckoning (IRE)
129 **SHIVA SHAKTI (IRE),** ch f Siyouni (FR)—Sacred Path
130 **SLIPOFTHEPEN,** ch c Night of Thunder (IRE)—Free Verse
131 **SOUL SISTER (IRE),** b f Frankel—Dream Peace (IRE)
132 **SPRING FEVER,** b f Dubawi (IRE)—Primevere (IRE)
133 **STAR OF CASSANDRA (IRE),** b f Sea The Stars (IRE)—Aegean Girl (IRE)
134 **SUNBELT (IRE),** ch f Zoffany (IRE)—Curtsy (IRE)
135 **SWEET MEMORIES (IRE),** b f Sea The Stars (IRE)—Time Control
136 **TARJAMAH,** br f Dubawi (IRE)—Tarayef (IRE)
137 **TEOWINGS (IRE),** b f Teofilo (IRE)—Celeste de La Mer (IRE)
138 **THEORYOFEVERYTHING,** gr c Frankel—Persuasive (IRE)
139 **TONY MONTANA,** b c Kingman—Mischief Making (USA)
140 **TORCHLIGHT,** b f Invincible Spirit (IRE)—Fireglow
141 **TORITO,** b c Kingman—Montare (IRE)
142 **VAGUELY ROYAL (IRE),** br c Galileo (IRE)—Danilovna (IRE)
143 **VELVET CRUSH (IRE),** b f Invincible Spirit (IRE)—Ship of Dreams (IRE)
144 **VENUS ROSEWATER (IRE),** ch f Frankel—Bold Lass (IRE)
145 **WEST BENGAL,** b c Oasis Dream—Seta
146 **WILTSHIRE WONDER,** b c Wootton Bassett—Chanterelle (FR)
147 **ZIRYAB,** b c Kingman—Reem (AUS)

Trainer did not supply details of their two-year-olds.

Flat Jockey: L. Dettori, Robert Havlin, Kieran O'Neill, Collen Storey. **Apprentice Jockey:** Benoit De La Sayette.

---

207 MRS HARRIET GRAHAM AND GARY RUTHERFORD, Jedburgh

Postal: **Strip End, Jedburgh, Roxburghshire, TD8 6NE**
Contacts: **PHONE 07780 009101**

1 **AYE RIGHT (IRE),** 10, b g Yeats (IRE)—Gaybric (IRE) **Mr & Mrs G & E Adam**
2 **BETTER BE DEFINITE,** 5, b g Clovis du Berlais (FR)—Definitely Better (IRE) **P & F Racing**
3 **BIG ARTHUR,** 6, b g Passing Glance—Xpectations (IRE) **The Potassium Partnership 2**
4 **BRANDY MCQUEEN (IRE),** 6, b g Yeats (IRE)—Down Ace (IRE) **Townshend, Irving & Graham**
5 **DANCEWITHTHEWIND (IRE),** 8, br g Jeremy (USA)—Sithgaoithe (IRE) **Mr & Mrs G & E Adam**

MRS HARRIET GRAHAM AND GARY RUTHERFORD - continued

6 **DON BROCCO,** 7, gr g Shirocco (GER)—Brantingham Breeze **Rutherford Racing**
7 **FLY AWAY BLUES,** 5, b m And Beyond (IRE)—Maggie Blue (IRE) **H G Racing**
8 **HEER HE GOES,** 6, b g Heeraat (IRE)—Abbeyleix Lady (IRE) **Mr & Mrs G & E Adam**
9 **MADAME BLUEBELLE,** 4, b f Blue Bresil (FR)—Definitely Better (IRE) **P & F Racing**
10 **MIDNIGHT FIDDLER,** 7, ch g Midnight Legend—Overlady **Mr W. F. Jeffrey**
11 **MILLARVILLE (IRE),** 10, b m Court Cave (IRE)—Portavoe (IRE) **Mr & Mrs G & E Adam**
12 5, B m Yorgunnabelucky (USA)—More Play **Mrs H. O. Graham**
13 **OVERCOURT,** 9, b g Court Cave (IRE)—Overlady **Mr W. F. Jeffrey**
14 **PUDDLEDUB I FROGET,** 7, b g Bollin Eric—Pollywog **H G Racing**
15 **SHOUGHALL'S BOY (IRE),** 7, b g Watar (IRE)—Lady Shackleton (IRE) **Mr R. Chapman**

THREE-YEAR-OLDS

16 **BLUE INDIGO,** b g Blue Bresil (FR)—Maggie Blue (IRE) **H G Racing**
17 Ch c Jack Hobbs—Primrose Time **Mrs F. M. Whitaker**
18 **WOR LAD,** b c Harbour Law—Wor Lass

TWO-YEAR-OLDS

19 B g 08/03 Slade Power (IRE)—Genuinely Crowded (IRE) (Zoffany (IRE)) **Mrs L. B. Normile**
20 Ch g 08/05 Postponed (IRE)—Kabjoy (IRE) (Intikhab (USA)) **Mrs L. B. Normile**
21 B g 06/05 Belardo (IRE)—Sarista (IRE) (Kodiac) **Mrs L. B. Normile**
22 B c 02/06 Manduro (GER)—Sense of Urgency (IRE) (Captain Rio) **Mrs L. B. Normile**
23 B br f 15/03 Berkshire (IRE)—Timoca (IRE) (Marju (IRE)) **Adams, Laws & Graham**
24 B f 15/03 Order of St George (IRE)—Xpectations (IRE) (Milan) **The Potassium Partnership 2**

---

208 MR CHRIS GRANT, Billingham

Postal: **Low Burntoft Farm, Wolviston, Billingham, Cleveland, TS22 5PD**
Contacts: **PHONE 01740 644054 MOBILE 07860 577998**
EMAIL chrisgrantracing@gmail.com WEBSITE www.chrisgrantracing.co.uk

1 **AATEKEMHOR,** 5, b m Black Sam Bellamy (IRE)—Cinnomhor **Miss A. P. Lee**
2 **BALLINTOGHER BOY (IRE),** 9, b g Flemensfirth (USA)—Room Seven (IRE) **Chris Grant Racing Club**
3 **BEBSIDE BANTER (IRE),** 6, b g Westerner—Hard Fought (IRE) **D&D Armstrong Limited**
4 **BEECHMOUNT (IRE),** 6, b g Masterofthehorse (IRE)—What's For Tea **G. F. White**
5 **BLACKSAMMHOR,** 4, b g Black Sam Bellamy (IRE)—Cinnomhor **Miss A. P. Lee**
6 **CHAMPAGNE BREEZE,** 4, b f Cannock Chase (USA)—Miss Chatterbox **Chasing the Dream**
7 **CHASE A FORTUNE,** 5, b g Cannock Chase (USA)—Lucematic **Chasing the Dream**
8 **DARJINK,** 4, b g Dartmouth—Lady Jinks **Miss A. P. Lee**
9 **FEARLESS ACTION (IRE),** 7, b g Yeats (IRE)—Hello Kitty (IRE) **G. F. White**
10 **FIADH (IRE),** 7, b m Fame And Glory—Lady Charisma **G. F. White**
11 **FOSTER'S FORTUNE,** 4, b g Cannock Chase (USA)—Mrs Eff **Chasing the Dream**
12 **FRANKS FANCY (IRE),** 8, b g Stowaway—Palesa Accord (IRE) **G. F. White**
13 **GLORY HIGHTS,** 7, b g Fame And Glory—Lady Hight (FR) **John Wade & Chris Grant**
14 4, B g Milan—Helen Wood
15 **JACQANINA,** 8, b m Fame And Glory—Ninna Nanna (FR) **Mr J. Kenny**
16 **NATIONAL CHARTER (IRE),** 4, b f Lawman (FR)—Debuetantin **Mrs H. N. Eubank**
17 **RATHGEARAN (IRE),** 7, b g Califet (FR)—Strong Lady (IRE) **Mrs H. N. Eubank**
18 **RED OCHRE,** 10, b g Virtual—Red Hibiscus **Mrs M Nicholas & Chris Grant**
19 **RED REMINDER,** 9, b m Mount Nelson—Red Hibiscus **Mrs H. N. Eubank**
20 **RULEOUT (IRE),** 7, b g Rule of Law (USA)—Galingale (IRE) **Miss A. P. Lee**
21 **SAMBEL BAY,** 5, b g Black Sam Bellamy (IRE)—Flaybay **Miss A. P. Lee**
22 **SHADOWS IN THE SKY (IRE),** 7, br g Arcadio (GER)—Ballinacraig (IRE) **D & D Armstrong Ltd & Mr L Westwood**
23 **SIX ONE NINE (IRE),** 8, b g Cloudings (IRE)—Indian Athlete (IRE) **D&D Armstrong Limited**
24 **STRONG TEAM (IRE),** 10, b g Exceed And Excel (AUS)—Star Blossom (USA) **Chris Grant Racing Club**
25 **THEATRE LEGEND,** 10, b g Midnight Legend—Theatre Belle **C. Grant**

MR CHRIS GRANT - continued

26 **TOP CLOUD,** 6, gr g Cloudings (IRE)—Too Generous **Exors of the Late Mr T. J. Hemmings**

Assistant Trainer: Mrs S. Grant.

NH Jockey: Callum Bewley, Brian Hughes.

---

209 MR MICHAEL GRASSICK, Curragh

Postal: **Fenpark House, Pollardstown, Curragh, Co. Kildare, Ireland**
Contacts: **MOBILE +353 86 364 8829**
EMAIL michaelgrassick1@gmail.com WEBSITE www.michaelcgrassick.com

1 **ALQABEELA (IRE),** 5, b m Awtaad (IRE)—Intimacy (IRE) **Mr M C Grassick**
2 **AMANIRENAS (IRE),** 4, b f War Command (USA)—Via Aurelia (IRE) **Ms Renata Coleman**
3 **BLUE PEAK,** 4, b f Fascinating Rock (IRE)—Mood Indigo (IRE) **Mr William Keeling**
4 **BOMBAY GLORY (IRE),** 6, b m Fame And Glory—Backinthere (IRE) **Mr Aidan Gleeson**
5 **BROWN EAGLE (IRE),** 4, b g Gleneagles (IRE)—Blueberry Gal (IRE) **Mr J. Keeling**
6 **ELANORA (IRE),** 5, br m No Nay Never (USA)—Vestavia (IRE) **Mr J. Keeling**
7 **LOINGSEOIR (IRE),** 7, b g Henrythenavigator (USA)—Only Exception (IRE) **Mrs M. J. Grassick**
8 **MOLLYS GLORY (IRE),** 8, b m Fame And Glory—Pellerossa (IRE) **Mr Aidan Gleeson**
9 4, B f Elusive Pimpernel (USA)—Pine Valley (IRE) **Mr Conor O'Daly**
10 **STELLIUM (IRE),** 5, b g Elzaam (AUS)—Gleaming Silver (IRE) **Mr J. Keeling**
11 **VERHOYEN,** 8, b g Piccolo—Memory Lane **Mr P. Cullen**

THREE-YEAR-OLDS

12 **BEAUMADIER (IRE),** b c Kuroshio (AUS)—Bird of Light (IRE) **Mr P. Cullen**
13 B c Highland Reel (IRE)—Desert Lily (IRE) **Ms Renata Coleman**
14 **IRRESISTIBLE YOU (IRE),** b f Decorated Knight—Miss Estrada (IRE) **Ms Renata Coleman**
15 **L'IMMORTALE,** b c Gregorian (IRE)—Maqueda (USA) **Ms Ciara Doyle**
16 **LILAC LADY,** b f Churchill (IRE)—Flowers Will Bloom (IRE) **Mr J. Keeling**
17 **MIMOSA PARK (IRE),** b f Dragon Pulse (IRE)—Vestavia (IRE) **Mr M C Grassick**
18 **MINGLE (IRE),** b f Fast Company (IRE)—Await So **Mr T. J. Pabst, Mrs S Grassick**
19 Gr c Beat Hollow—Perruche Grise (FR) **Mr Aidan Gleeson**
20 **SPIRIT OF EAGLES,** b f Gleneagles—Tranquil Spirit **Ms Renata Coleman**
21 **TASMANIAN GIRL,** b f Australia—Blueberry Gal (IRE) **Mr J. Keeling**

TWO-YEAR-OLDS

22 B c 05/03 Saxon Warrior (JPN)—Boundless Joy (AUS) (Montjeu (IRE)) (27211) **Ms Renata Coleman**
23 B f 09/05 Churchill (IRE)—Desert Lily (IRE) (Redoute's Choice (AUS)) (9604) **Ms Renata Coleman**
24 B g 10/04 Highland Reel (IRE)—Only Exception (IRE) (Jeremy (USA)) **Ms R Walshe**
25 B c 12/04 Poet's Word (IRE)—Pine Valley (IRE) (Entrepreneur) **Ms R Walshe**
26 **SOMPTUEUSE (IRE),** b f 10/03 Footstepsinthesand—Sommore (IRE) (Anjaal) (6403) **Ms Cathy Grassick**

Flat Jockey: W J Lee.

---

210 MR CARROLL GRAY, Bridgwater

Postal: **The Little Glen, Peartwater Road, Spaxton, Bridgwater, Somerset, TA5 1DG**
Contacts: **MOBILE 07989 768163**

1 **BELLAMY'S GREY,** 11, gr g Black Sam Bellamy (IRE)—Lambrini Queen **Riverdance Consortium 2**

MR CARROLL GRAY

2 **FRAME RATE,** 8, b g Arcano (IRE)—Miss Quality (USA) **Mrs M. E. Gittings-Watts**
3 **FREDDIE FLEETFOOT,** 5, b g Blue Bresil (FR)—Eardisland **Unity Farm Holiday Centre Ltd**
4 **LADY IRONSIDE (IRE),** 6, gr m Lawman (FR)—Expedience (USA) **Mr S. A. Reeves**

Assistant Trainer: Mrs C. M. L. Gray.

NH Jockey: Micheal Nolan.

---

211 MR WARREN GREATREX, Upper Lambourn

Postal: **Rhonehurst, Upper Lambourn, Hungerford, Berkshire, RG17 8QN**
Contacts: **PHONE 01488 670279 MOBILE 07920 039114**
EMAIL info@wgreatrexracing.com WEBSITE www.wgreatrexracing.com

1 **ABUFFALOSOLDIER (IRE),** 6, br g Mahler—Adderstonlee (IRE) **Mahler & The Wailers**
2 **ALLANAH'S BOY (IRE),** 6, b g Westerner—Countess Eileen (IRE) **Fitorfat Racing**
3 **ANOTHER EMOTION (FR),** 11, gr g Turgeon (USA)—Line Perle (FR) **Fitorfat Racing**
4 **ART OF ILLUSION (IRE),** 6, b g Malinas (GER)—Zara (IRE) **Mr A. Pegley**
5 **BEL MARE,** 5, b m Pether's Moon (IRE)—Uppermost **Mr A. Pegley**
6 **BIG JIM BEAM (IRE),** 7, b g Westerner—Brighid (IRE) **Mrs J & Miss C Shipp & W Greatrex**
7 **BILL BAXTER (IRE),** 7, gr g Milan—Blossom Rose (IRE) **Glassex Holdings Ltd**
8 **BOLD SOLDIER,** 8, b g Kayf Tara—Major Hoolihan **Alan & Andrew Turner**
9 **BOLSOVER BILL (IRE),** 6, b g Getaway (GER)—Peripheral Vision (IRE) **Jim and Claire Limited**
10 **CHATSHOW TV (IRE),** 5, b g Soldier of Fortune (IRE)—Back On Stage (IRE) **Jim and Claire Limited**
11 **CRIMSON RUBY,** 5, b m Soldier of Fortune (IRE)—Ruby Royale **Velocity Racing**
12 **DREADPOETSSOCIETY (IRE),** 5, b g Mahler—Deadly Pursuit (IRE) **Mr A. Pegley**
13 **GALLOPADE,** 7, b g Schiaparelli (GER)—Shikra **Mr N. J. Hussey**
14 4, Br g Soldier of Fortune (IRE)—Grangeclare Rosa (IRE)
15 **HELLO MARIE (FR),** 6, b m Network (GER)—Vive Marie (FR) **Glassex Holdings Ltd**
16 **HENERYETTA BAY (IRE),** 7, b m Jet Away—Elisabetta (IRE) **The Irc & Molony Racing Ltd**
17 **HENSCHKE (IRE),** 9, b g Mahler—Reserve The Right (IRE) **Mrs T. J. Stone-Brown**
18 **HERAKLES WESTWOOD (FR),** 6, b g Saddler Maker (IRE)—Une Histoire (FR) **The Albatross Club**
19 **HERMES LE GRIS (FR),** 6, gr g Gris de Gris (IRE)—Lola Lolita (FR) **David Turner & Ellie Lines**
20 **HIDALGO DES BORDES (FR),** 6, b g Coastal Path—Ahkel Vie (FR)
21 **HIGH STAKES (IRE),** 9, b g Scorpion (IRE)—High Performer (IRE) **Jim and Claire Limited**
22 **ICI LA REINE (IRE),** 5, b m Presenting—Reine Angevine (FR) **Mrs Julien Turner & Mr Andrew Merriam**
23 **JAMES JET (IRE),** 6, b g Yeats (IRE)—Givehertime (IRE) **Miss C. S. D. Shipp**
24 **JARAMILLO,** 5, b g Oasis Dream—Guajara (GER) **Owners Group 098**
25 **JET OF DREAMS (IRE),** 5, b g Jet Away—Lady J D (IRE) **Glassex Holdings Ltd**
26 **JUST A MEMORY (FR),** 4, b f Muhtathir—L'Aulniere (FR) **Jim and Claire Limited**
27 4, B f Blue Bresil (FR)—Karamel
28 **LARGY FORCE (IRE),** 5, br m Workforce—Aunt Rosalie (IRE) **Jim and Claire Limited**
29 **LINE OF DESCENT (IRE),** 5, b g Nathaniel (IRE)—Joys of Spring (IRE) **Jim and Claire Limited**
30 4, Br f Soldier of Fortune (IRE)—Magic Money **Dejeuner de Dames**
31 **MILITAIRE,** 6, b g Soldier of Fortune (IRE)—La Dame Brune (FR) **Jim and Claire Limited**
32 **PILOT SHOW (IRE),** 6, b g Yeats (IRE)—Castle Jane (IRE) **Eynon, Bryce & Rowley**
33 **SAGEBURG COUNTY (IRE),** 6, b g Sageburg (IRE)—Sounds Charming (IRE) **Alan & Andrew Turner**
34 **SHILLANAVOGY (IRE),** 5, b g Soldier of Fortune (IRE)—Lady Azamour (IRE)
35 **STAR FLYER (IRE),** 6, ch g Jet Away—Gaye Mercy **Jim and Claire Limited**
36 **STORM RYDER (IRE),** 5, b g Valirann (FR)—Daraheen Diamond (IRE) **Albatross Hinds Westwood**
37 **THEYSEEKHIMTHERE (IRE),** 5, b g Elusive Pimpernel (USA)—Wild Spell (IRE) **BadJams 5 Syndicate**
38 **TIPPERARY STAR,** 5, b m Getaway (GER)—Presenteea (IRE) **Glassex Holdings Ltd**
39 **TITANIUM BULLET (IRE),** 5, gr ro g Shirocco (GER)—Marta Mes (FR) **Unique Financial Racing Partnership**
40 **VALSHEDA,** 8, b g Milan—Candy Creek (IRE) **Mrs Jill Eynon & Mr Robin Eynon**
41 **VIA GALACTICA,** 5, b g Telescope (IRE)—La Grande Villez (FR) **Mr W. J. Greatrex**

Assistant Trainer: Oliver Kozak, **Head Girl:** Fred Gandolfo, **Head Lad:** Ian Yeates.

Flat Jockey: Thomas Greatrex. **NH Jockey:** Harry Bannister, James Bowen, Brendan Powell. **Conditional Jockey:** Dylan Kitts.

212 MR JOSH GUERRIERO AND OLIVER GREENALL, Malpas

Postal: **Stockton Hall Farm, Oldcastle, Malpas, Cheshire, SY14 7AE**
Contacts: **PHONE 01948 861157**
EMAIL ocg@stocktonhall.co.uk

1 **ADJOURNMENT (IRE),** 7, b g Court Cave (IRE)—Cherry Eile (IRE) **Stockton Hall Farm Racing**
2 **ANDONNO,** 5, b g Dansili—Lavender And Lace **The Andonno Syndicate**
3 **ANTI BRIDGIE (IRE),** 6, b m Doyen (IRE)—Tobrigids (IRE) **Foxtrot Anti Bridgie & Dreamweavers**
4 **APOLOGISE (IRE),** 4, b g Fascinating Rock (IRE)—Spirited Acclaim (IRE) **Malcolm Jones & John Norbury**
5 **BOUNDSY BOY,** 5, b g Awtaad (IRE)—Wadaat **The Oldcastle Racing Syndicate**
6 **BRAVETHEWAVES,** 6, b g Gentlewave (IRE)—Miss Lucky Penny **The Brave Bunch**
7 **CAWTHORNE,** 9, b g Sulamani (IRE)—Kings Maiden (IRE) **Back to the Track Syndicate**
8 **CAWTHORNE CRACKER (IRE),** 4, b g Frammassone (IRE)—Ball Park (IRE) **E. A. Brook**
9 **CHRIS COOL,** 7, b g Sulamani (IRE)—Cool Friend (IRE) **Evason, Harney & Greenall**
10 **CINCO SALTOS (IRE),** 4, ch f Ruler of The World (IRE)—Queen of Malta (IRE) **The Cinco Saltos Syndicate**
11 **CLONDAW PRETENDER,** 8, br g Great Pretender (IRE)—Shropshire Girl **Peavoy Emdells Daresbury Adams Lewis**
12 **CONCETTO (FR),** 6, b g Kapgarde (FR)—Lulu Rouge (FR) **5 O'clock Somewhere Syndicate**
13 **DANDYS DERRIERE,** 5, b g Dandy Man (IRE)—Overheard (IRE)
14 **DIEU VIVANT (FR),** 10, b g Network (GER)—Panique Pas (FR) **Mr P. J. Chesters**
15 **DOOYORK (IRE),** 7, b m Shantou (USA)—Hannah Rose (IRE) **Manchester Tennis & Racquet Club Racing**
16 **DRAGONFRUIT,** 8, ch g Black Sam Bellamy (IRE)—Fruity Farm **Mrs B. A. Bostock**
17 **DUKE OF DECEPTION (IRE),** 6, b g September Storm (GER)—Mrs Peachey (IRE) **Salmon Racing**
18 **DUN DANCING,** 4, b g Dunaden (FR)—Onetwobeat **Mr A. Park**
19 **ECOSSAIS (FR),** 9, b g Saddler Maker (IRE)—Sacade (FR) **Oliver Greenall Racing Club**
20 **EL BORRACHO (IRE),** 8, br g Society Rock (IRE)—Flame of Hibernia (IRE) **El Borracho Syndicate**
21 **EVANDER (IRE),** 8, br g Arcadio (GER)—Blazing Belle (IRE)
22 **FARO (FR),** 8, b g Cokoriko (FR)—Teskaline (FR) **The Oldcastle Racing Syndicate**
23 **FEUILLE DE LUNE (FR),** 8, b m Saddler Maker (IRE)—Arcafet (FR) **The Feuille De Lune Syndicate**
24 **FIRST MAN (IRE),** 8, b g Lilbourne Lad (IRE)—Dos Lunas (IRE) **The Haydock Park Racing Syndicate**
25 **FURIUS DE CIERGUES (FR),** 8, gr g Lord du Sud (FR)—Java de Ciergues (FR) **Mr O. C. Greenall**
26 **GABORIOT (FR),** 7, ch g Muhtathir—Uddy (FR) **The Jockey Club Haydock Park Racing Club Ltd**
27 **GAMESTERS GIRL,** 5, b m Telescope (IRE)—Gamesters Lady **Gamesters Partnership**
28 **GAMESTERS GUY,** 4, ch g Black Sam Bellamy (IRE)—Gamesters Lady **Gamesters Partnership**
29 **GARETH CAEL (FR),** 7, gr g Montmartre (FR)—Dallia (FR) **The Good Friends Syndicate**
30 **GENTLE VICTOR,** 5, b g Gentlewave (IRE)—Onetwobeat **The Gentle Victor Racing Syndicate**
31 **GESSKILLE (FR),** 7, b g Network (GER)—Nashkille (FR) **The Nevers Racing Partnership I**
32 **GO ON CHEZ,** 7, b g Malinas (GER)—Who's Afraid **Mr K. I. Roberts**
33 **GOLD DESERT,** 6, ch g Mastercraftsman (IRE)—Tendency (IRE) **Harbour Rose Partnership**
34 **GOLDEN GLANCE,** 4, b f Golden Horn—Zeeba (IRE) **Bcc Racing Partnership**
35 **GOOD WORK (FR),** 7, gr g Network (GER)—Teskaline (FR) **The Cool Runnings Syndicate II**
36 **GOUET DES BRUYERES (FR),** 7, b g Policy Maker (IRE)—
Innsbruck (FR) **Daresbury,Buckley,R Mills,D Mills,Walsh**
37 **HASHEHADHISOATSYET (IRE),** 5, gr g Carlotamix (FR)—Gortbofearna (IRE) **E. A. Brook**
38 **HERBIERS (FR),** 6, b g Waldpark (GER)—Qualanke (FR) **Nevers & Stockton Hall Farm Racing**
39 **HERITIER (FR),** 6, b g Fuisse (FR)—Toscane (FR) **Gardiner & the Cool Runnings Team**
40 **HOLLOW RON (IRE),** 5, b g Beat Hollow—Kiltiernan Road **Mr P. G. Scott**
41 **HOMME PUBLIC (FR),** 6, b g Cokoriko (FR)—Uddy (FR) **The Nevers Racing Partnership Ii**
42 **HORACIO APPLE'S (FR),** 6, ch g Saddex—Apple's Noa (FR) **Highclere Tb Racing - Apple & Dudgeon**
43 **HORSESOMEHARRY,** 5, b g Pether's Moon (IRE)—Miss Lucky Penny
44 **IBIZA ROCKS,** 5, gr g Dark Angel (IRE)—The Thrill Is Gone **Mrs R. L. Dawson**
45 **ICE COAST (FR),** 5, b g Coastal Path—Chez Lulu (FR) **The Nevers Racing Partnership III**
46 **IMPORT EXPORT (FR),** 5, b g Free Port Lux—Tes Belle (FR) **The Oldcastle Racing Syndicate**
47 **IROKO (FR),** 5, b g Cokoriko (FR)—Boscraie (FR) **Mr J. P. McManus**
48 **JAGWAR (FR),** 4, b g Karaktar (IRE)—Quizas Jolie (FR)
49 **LATE ROMANTIC (IRE),** 13, b g Mahler—Mere Gaye (IRE) **Spitalized Racing**
50 **LUCKY LOVER BOY (IRE),** 8, b g Teofilo (IRE)—Mayonga (IRE) **The Lucky Lovers Partnership**
51 **LUNE DE LA MER (IRE),** 6, b g Sea Moon—Printing Polly (IRE) **5 O'clock Somewhere Syndicate**
52 **MAKING HEADWAY (IRE),** 5, b g Malinas (GER)—Times Like These (IRE) **M. B. Jones**
53 **MCPHERSON,** 5, b br g Golden Horn—Moonlight Sonata **The McPherson Partnership**
54 **MIDNIGHT MOSS,** 11, ch g Midnight Legend—Brackenmoss (IRE) **Midnight Moss Partnership**
55 **MONTE IGUELDO (FR),** 6, b g Cokoriko (FR)—Petite Nany (FR) **Mr S. Beetham**

MR JOSH GUERRIERO AND OLIVER GREENALL - continued

56 **MRS TABITHA,** 4, b f Jack Hobbs—Hunca Munca (IRE) **The Preston Lodge Syndicate**
57 **MY POEM,** 6, ch m Poet's Voice—Watchoverme **Back to the Track Syndicate**
58 **NO BUT I WILL,** 6, b g Telescope (IRE)—Little Carmela **Mr K. I. Roberts**
59 **OCEANS RED,** 7, ch g Yorgunnabelucky (USA)—Djess **Spitalized Racing**
60 **PADDY'S FANCY,** 4, gr f New Bay—Likelihood (USA) **Zoe Hassall & George Hassall**
61 **PHIL DE PAIL (FR),** 6, gr g Silver Frost (IRE)—Dame de Pail (FR) **Stockton Hall Farm Racing**
62 **POST CHAISE (IRE),** 6, gr g Shirocco (GER)—Trazona Kit (IRE) **Mr G. Cardwell**
63 **POT OF PAINT,** 6, b g New Approach (IRE)—Regency (JPN) **Mr O. C. Greenall**
64 **REBEL MC,** 6, b g Black Sam Bellamy (IRE)—Ifni du Luc (FR) **Mr M. A. Cottam**
65 **ROCAMBOLAS (FR),** 6, b g Muhtathir—Trudente (FR) **Mr M. Astbury**
66 **ROYAL PLEASURE (IRE),** 5, b g Kingman—Merry Jaunt (USA)
67 **SHE'S ALL IN GOLD (IRE),** 6, b m Golden Horn—Simonetta (IRE) **The Gold Diggers**
68 **SNOWY EVENING (IRE),** 6, b g Snow Sky—Sherwolf (IRE) **The Stockton Hopefuls**
69 **SPECIAL DRAGON,** 4, b f Kayf Tara—Dragonera **The Preston Lodge Syndicate**
70 **STAR ZINC (IRE),** 4, b g Kodiac—Night Queen (IRE)
71 **SWIFT TUTTLE (IRE),** 4, ch g Fast Company (IRE)—Lumiere Astrale (FR) **Salmon Racing**
72 **TELEFENNEY,** 4, b f Telescope (IRE)—Fenney Spring **Oliver Greenall Racing Club**
73 **THE QUESTIONER (IRE),** 7, ch g Ask—Cush Bach (IRE) **Salmon Racing**
74 **TRE A PENI,** 6, b m Pether's Moon (IRE)—Cerise Bleue (FR) **The Malpas Syndicate**
75 **WELL DONE DANI,** 6, b m Multiplex—Do It On Dani **The Perthy Partnership**
76 4, Br f Getaway (GER)—West Bridge (IRE) **Spitalized Racing**
77 **WHITE RHINO (IRE),** 7, b g Doyen (IRE)—Aventia (IRE) **The Rhino Syndicate**
78 **WHODINI (IRE),** 6, ch g Conduit (IRE)—Mosey On Molly (IRE) **Malcolm Jones & John Norbury**
79 **WINDTOTHELIGHTNING (IRE),** 5, b m Sans Frontieres (IRE)—Derrylea Girl (IRE) **Mr G. C. Myddelton**

THREE-YEAR-OLDS

80 **ANGEL'S VOICE (IRE),** b g Ribchester (IRE)—Evies Wish (IRE) **Mr D. J. Astbury**
81 **CHAMBER CHOIR,** br f Ardad (IRE)—Polymnia **Mr O. C. Greenall**
82 Ch g Free Eagle (IRE)—Only Together (IRE)
83 **RED FORT (FR),** b c Zoustar (AUS)—Fortitude (IRE) **Dawson, Martin and Nolan**

---

213 MR TOM GRETTON, Inkberrow

Postal: **C/o Gretton & Co Ltd, Middle Bouts Farm, Bouts Lane, Inkberrow, Worcester**
Contacts: **PHONE 01386 792240 MOBILE 07866 116928 FAX 01386 792472**
EMAIL tomgretton@hotmail.co.uk WEBSITE www.tomgrettonracing.com

1 **ARINI,** 6, b m Blue Bresil (FR)—Polly Potter **James and Jean Potter Ltd**
2 **AURELIA FADILLA,** 6, b m Milan—Faustina Pius (IRE) **Miss J. Green**
3 **COMMITTEE OF ONE,** 8, b m Universal (IRE)—Inkberrow Rose (IRE) **Lewis Family & Tom Gretton Racing Club**
4 **EL CAPOTE,** 5, b m Blue Bresil (FR)—Camelia des Bordes (FR) **Mrs J. Green**
5 **FROMPOSTTOPILLAR,** 5, b g Clovis du Berlais (FR)—Altesse de Sou (FR) **Mr B. P. Keogh**
6 **GETBAZOUTOFHERE,** 7, ch m Gentlewave (IRE)—Present Your Case (IRE) **Mr I. M. Lewis**
7 **HARKANGEL,** 5, b m Black Sam Bellamy (IRE)—Supreme Gem (IRE) **F J Allen & Partners**
8 **JOHNNY MAC (IRE),** 8, b g Imperial Monarch (IRE)—Killowen Pam (IRE) **Mr M. Slingsby**
9 **JUKEBOX D'EDDY (FR),** 4, b g Fly With Me (FR)—Ultime Creek (FR) **Mrs D. E. Lewis**
10 **JUMBO VESTE VERTE (FR),** 4, b g Indomito (GER)—Ocara d'Airy (FR) **The Green Jackets**
11 **KAUTO RIKO (FR),** 12, b g Ballingarry (IRE)—Kauto Relstar (FR) **Mr & Mrs J.Dale & Partners**
12 **LICKPENNY LARRY,** 12, gr g Sagamix (FR)—Myriah (IRE) **Alan Clarke & Tom Gretton Racing Club**
13 **LINCOLN LYN,** 7, b m Universal (IRE)—Altesse de Sou (FR) **Team Burton, Ray & Warburton**
14 **MOON EAGLE (IRE),** 6, b m Free Eagle (IRE)—Behrama (IRE) **G1 Racing Club Ltd**
15 **ONE LAST GLANCE,** 6, b g Passing Glance—Lillie Lou **Fred Camis, Ray Fielder & Mel Clarke**
16 **PASSING SECRETS,** 7, bl g Passing Glance—Tabora **Rees, Gretton & McKay**
17 **SADLER'S BAY,** 6, b g Black Sam Bellamy (IRE)—Cormorant Cove **Mr T. Wheeler**
18 **THE OLD BULL,** 4, b g Blue Bresil (FR)—Auld Fyffee (IRE) **Not The Peloton Partnership**
19 **URBLEREAGH (FR),** 6, ch g High Rock (IRE)—Kelly des Cotieres (FR) **D. R. & E. E. Brown**

MR TOM GRETTON - continued

20 **WILDKATZE (GER),** 7, b m Kamsin (GER)—Zaynaat **Mr J. P. Edwards**

Assistant Trainer: Laura Gretton.

---

214 MR DAVID C. GRIFFITHS, Bawtry

Postal: **Martin Hall farm, Martin Common, Bawtry, Doncaster, South Yorkshire, DN10 6DA**
Contacts: **PHONE 01302 714247 MOBILE 07816 924621**
EMAIL davidgriffiths250@hotmail.com WEBSITE www.davidgriffithsracing.co.uk

1 **CANZONE,** 6, ch g Siyouni (FR)—Stirring Ballad **Martin Hall Farm Racing**
2 **COOL SPIRIT,** 8, b g Swiss Spirit—Marmot Bay (IRE) **Martin Hall Farm Racing**
3 **ENDOFASTORM (IRE),** 4, b f Galileo Gold—Red Fuschia **Ontoawinner 2 & Partners**
4 **FIREWATER,** 7, ch g Monsieur Bond (IRE)—Spirit Na Heireann (IRE) **Ladies & The Tramps**
5 **LUCKY BEGGAR (IRE),** 13, gr g Verglas (IRE)—Lucky Clio (IRE) **Griffiths And John Fox**
6 **ORNATE,** 10, b g Bahamian Bounty—Adorn **Kings Road Racing Partnership**

THREE-YEAR-OLDS

7 **BEECHWOOD ISABELLE,** ch f Territories (IRE)—Respectable **Ontoawinner 2 & Partners**
8 B f Heeraat (IRE)—Lookalike **Mrs S. Noble**

Assistant Trainer: Mrs S. E. Griffiths.

Flat Jockey: David Allan, Phil Dennis.

---

215 MRS DIANA GRISSELL, Robertsbridge

Postal: **Brightling Park, Robertsbridge, East Sussex, TN32 5HH**
Contacts: **PHONE 01424 838241 MOBILE 07950 312610**
EMAIL digrissell@aol.com WEBSITE www.brightlingpark.com

1 **BORDER LORD,** 5, ch g Lucarno (USA)—Kadenis **Mr M. Park**
2 **DUNATARA,** 7, b m Dunaden (FR)—Miltara (IRE) **B Cockerell & Mrs D Grissell**
3 **JAPPELOUP (IRE),** 14, b br g Presenting—Crackin' Liss (IRE) **Mrs C. A. Bailey**
4 5, B g Ask—Nothin To Say (IRE)
5 **SQUIRE HOCKEY,** 10, b g Green Horizon—Luisa Miller (IRE) **Mr M. Park**

Assistant Trainer: Paul Hacking, **Head Girl:** Donna French.

Amateur Jockey: Mr James Rawdon-Mogg.

---

216 MR JOHN GROUCOTT, Much Wenlock

Postal: **Dairy Cottage, Bourton, Much Wenlock, Shropshire, TF13 6QD**
Contacts: **PHONE 01746 785603**

1 **BROCKARNO,** 5, ch g Lucarno (USA)—Brockwell Abbey **Mrs B. Clarke**
2 **COLUMN OF FIRE (IRE),** 9, b g Robin des Champs (FR)—Ghillie's Bay (IRE) **Miss L. Richardson**
3 **DOM PERRY,** 7, b g Doyen (IRE)—Aphrodisias (FR) **Rushmoor Stud**
4 **EL SCORPIO (IRE),** 11, b g Scorpion (IRE)—El Monica (IRE) **Mr D. W. Jagger**
5 **HAND AND DIAMOND,** 8, b m Westerner—Heels Overhead **Miss J. Balmer**
6 **MAISIEBELLA,** 10, b m Black Sam Bellamy (IRE)—Lucylou (IRE) **Mrs B. Clarke**

MR JOHN GROUCOTT - continued

7 **ON THE PLATFORM (IRE),** 7, b g Valirann (FR)—Coca's Lady (IRE) **Mrs B. Clarke**
8 6, B m Rule of Law (USA)—One Move (IRE)
9 **PEARLYMOON,** 5, b g Telescope (IRE)—Any Pearl **Mrs B. Clarke**
10 **RED BUCCANEER,** 8, ch g Black Sam Bellamy (IRE)—Florarossa **Mrs B. Clarke**
11 **RICHARDSON,** 8, ch g Kirkwall—Makeover **Mrs B. Clarke**
12 **SAMMIX,** 6, gr g Black Sam Bellamy (IRE)—Morville **Mrs B. Clarke**
13 **TREVELLAS,** 7, b g Yorgunnabelucky (USA)—Susie Bury
14 **UNAI (IRE),** 8, b g Court Cave (IRE)—The Millers Tale (IRE) **Mrs B. Clarke**

---

217 MR RAE GUEST, Newmarket

Postal: **Chestnut Tree Stables, Hamilton Road, Newmarket, Suffolk, CB8 0NY**
Contacts: **WORK 01638 661508 MOBILE 07711 301095**
EMAIL raeguest@raeguest.com WEBSITE www.raeguest.com

1 **ARAMIS GREY (IRE),** 6, gr m Gutaifan (IRE)—Sveva (IRE) **The Musketeers**
2 **CRY HAVOC (IRE),** 6, b m War Command (USA)—Na Zdorovie **The Musketeers**
3 **DAYTONA BEACH (IRE),** 4, b f Dubawi (IRE)—Dalkova **Mr R. Guest**
4 **EKLIL,** 4, b g Invincible Spirit (IRE)—Raaqy (IRE) **Mr D. J. Willis**
5 **JEWEL IN MY CROWN,** 5, gr m Mukhadram—Rosa Grace **Mr E. P. Duggan**
6 **LAND OF WINTER (FR),** 7, b g Camelot—Gaselee (USA) **Paul Smith & Rae Guest**
7 **ONE COLOUR (IRE),** 4, ch f Teofilo (IRE)—Bluefire **Mr R. Guest**

THREE-YEAR-OLDS

8 **AFLOAT,** b f Sea The Moon (GER)—Planete Bleue (IRE) **Mr J. M. Mitchell**
9 **DIVINA GRACE (IRE),** b f Golden Horn—Beautiful Forest **Top Hat and Tails**
10 **EMPIRE OF THE SUN,** b g Dariyan (FR)—Boleyna (USA) **Mr P. J. Smith**
11 **FRUITFUL,** ch f Profitable (IRE)—Showbird **The Unusual Suspects Syndicate**
12 **GRAND DUCHESS OLGA,** b f Sir Percy—Archduchess **Miss K. Rausing**
13 **LADY JANE GREY,** gr f Havana Grey—Inagh River **The Unusual Suspects Syndicate**
14 **PASSION TANGO (USA),** b f California Chrome (USA)—Berryessa (IRE) **Mr P. L. Martin**
15 **SHOW OF HANDS,** b f Showcasing—Yali (IRE) **Mr C. S. Joseph**
16 **WAR CHANT (IRE),** b g War Command (USA)—Fanci That (IRE) **Miss V. Markowiak**

TWO-YEAR-OLDS

17 **HITS THE FRONT,** b c 06/04 Tasleet—Mawqed (IRE) (Invincible Spirit (IRE)) **The Storm Again Syndicate**
18 **KIMCHI,** b f 09/03 Postponed (IRE)—Indicia (Bated Breath) **Mr J. M. Mitchell**
19 **LIA ROSE,** gr f 03/03 Ulysses (IRE)—Rosa Grace (Lomitas) **Mr E. P. Duggan**
20 **LOST IN CUBA,** b f 20/03 Havana Grey—Soul Searching (Iffraaj) **The Raffles Syndicate**
21 **MALIBU RISING,** b f 30/04 Expert Eye—La Chapelle (IRE) (Holy Roman Emperor (IRE)) (35000) **Mr D. J. Willis**
22 **MASAR WAY,** ch f 23/02 Masar (IRE)—Ape Attack (Nayef (USA)) (11000) **The Raffles Syndicate**
23 **MEMORANDA,** ch f 29/04 Bobby's Kitten (USA)—Memory Lane (With Approval (CAN)) **Miss K. Rausing**
24 **NATURALIA,** b f 12/03 Sea The Moon (GER)—Na Balada (BRZ) (Forestry (USA)) **Miss K. Rausing**
25 **NOBLE MISS,** b f 01/04 Noble Mission—Volver (IRE) (Danehill Dancer (IRE)) (9000) **Lady Cecil & Family**
26 **NOUVEAUX,** b f 22/03 Tasleet—Alwafaa (IRE) (Invincible Spirit (IRE)) (7000) **Lady Cecil & Family**
27 **RAFFLES ANGEL,** br f 24/03 Harry Angel (IRE)—L'Eglise (Le Havre (IRE)) (21000) **The Raffles Syndicate**
28 B f 07/02 Due Diligence (USA)—Really Chic (USA) (Street Cry (IRE)) **Mr K. Walton**
29 B f 23/02 Camelot—Trail of Tears (IRE) (Exceed And Excel (AUS)) (16000)
30 B f 01/03 Camelot—Whirlygig (Mukhadram) (15000) **The Rainy Day Partnership**

218 MS POLLY GUNDRY, Ottery St Mary

Postal: **Holcombe Brook, Holcombe Lane, Ottery St Mary, Devon, EX11 1PH**
Contacts: **PHONE 01404 811181 MOBILE 07932 780621**
EMAIL pollygundrytraining@live.co.uk WEBSITE www.pollygundrytraining.co.uk

1 **CAN YOU SEE HER,** 6, gr m Telescope (IRE)—Sylvan Wings **Mrs A. E. R. Goodwin**
2 **DAWSON CITY,** 14, b g Midnight Legend—Running For Annie **Mrs P. Walker**
3 **DON'T RIGHTLY KNOW,** 8, ch m Malinas (GER)—Thebelloftheball **Mr J. P. Selby**
4 **DREAM BET,** 5, gr m Dream Eater (IRE)—Tanner Bet **Michael & Will Potter**
5 **ECHO OF PROMISE,** 5, ch m Shantou (USA)—Topette (FR) **Mrs P. Walker**
6 **FANFAN LA COLMINE (FR),** 8, b g No Risk At All (FR)—Union Leto (FR) **Mr P. R. Carter**
7 **GIO'S GIRL,** 10, ch m Schiaparelli (GER)—Programme Girl (IRE) **Pearn, Shires & Walker**
8 **HERESMAX (IRE),** 5, b g Gutaifan (IRE)—Euroceleb (IRE) **Mr M. J. P. Wheeler**
9 4, B g Yeats (IRE)—Lindeman (IRE) **Mr & Mrs R. G. Kelvin-Hughes**
10 4, B f Flemensfirth (USA)—My Petra **Mr & Mrs R. G. Kelvin-Hughes**
11 **PALLADIUM,** 7, ch g Champs Elysees—Galicuix **Mr & Mrs R. G. Kelvin-Hughes**
12 **WIND TOR,** 11, b m Midnight Legend—Flowing On **The Group of Otters**
13 **WOMBA,** 4, b f Walk In The Park (IRE)—Chomba Womba (IRE) **Mr & Mrs R. G. Kelvin-Hughes**

Assistant Trainer: Edward Walker.

NH Jockey: James Best, Nick Schofield. **Amateur Jockey:** Mr Josh Newman.

---

219 MR WILLIAM HAGGAS, Newmarket

Postal: **Somerville Lodge, Fordham Road, Newmarket, Suffolk, CB8 7AA**
Contacts: **PHONE 01638 667013 MOBILE 07860 282281 FAX 01638 660534**
EMAIL william@somerville-lodge.co.uk WEBSITE www.somerville-lodge.co.uk

1 **AL AASY (IRE),** 6, b g Sea The Stars (IRE)—Kitcara **Shadwell Estate Company Ltd**
2 **AL MUBHIR,** 4, ch c Frankel—Muffri'Ha (IRE) **Sheikh Juma Dalmook Al Maktoum**
3 **ALDAARY,** 5, ch g Territories (IRE)—Broughtons Revival **Shadwell Estate Company Ltd**
4 **AMANZOE (IRE),** 4, b f Fastnet Rock (AUS)—Starship (IRE) **The Starship Partnership II**
5 **ARAMAIC (IRE),** 5, b br g Le Havre (IRE)—Middle Persia **Sheikh Isa Salman Al Khalifa**
6 **BREWING,** 4, b g Showcasing—Cloud Line **Lael Stable**
7 **CANDLEFORD (IRE),** 5, b g Kingman—Dorcas Lane **Barnane Stud Ltd**
8 **DUBAI HONOUR (IRE),** 5, b g Pride of Dubai (AUS)—Mondelice **M. Obaida**
9 **EDUCATOR,** 4, br g Deep Impact (JPN)—Diploma **HM The King & HM The Queen Consort**
10 **ESTIDAMA,** 4, b f Farhh—Kitty For Me **Sheikh Rashid Dalmook Al Maktoum**
11 **GAASSEE (IRE),** 5, b g Sea The Stars (IRE)—Oojooba **Sheikh Ahmed Al Maktoum**
12 **GOLDEN LYRA (IRE),** 4, ch f Lope de Vega (IRE)—Sea The Sun (GER) **Sunderland Holding Inc.**
13 **HAMISH,** 7, b g Motivator—Tweed **Mr J. B. Haggas**
14 **HEBRIDES (IRE),** 4, ch g Mehmas (IRE)—Woodland Maiden (IRE) **Highclere Thoroughbred Racing - Oak Tree**
15 **KHANJAR (IRE),** 4, b g Kodiac—Naafer **Shadwell Estate Company Ltd**
16 **LA YAKEL,** 4, b g Time Test—Tebee's Oasis **Sheikh Ahmed Al Maktoum**
17 **LATTAM (IRE),** 4, ch g Lope de Vega (IRE)—Alaata (USA) **Wrigleys & Wyatts**
18 **LYSANDER,** 4, br g New Approach (IRE)—Darting **Highclere Thoroughbred Racing - Beehives**
19 **MALJOOM (IRE),** 4, b c Caravaggio (USA)—Nictate (IRE) **Sheikh Ahmed Al Maktoum**
20 **MILLEBOSC (FR),** 5, b g Le Havre (IRE)—Mixed Intention (IRE) **Mr G. L. R. Augustin-Normand**
21 **MUJTABA,** 5, b g Dubawi (IRE)—Majmu (AUS) **Shadwell Estate Company Ltd**
22 **MY ASTRA (IRE),** 5, b m Lope de Vega (IRE)—My Titania (IRE) **Sunderland Holding Inc.**
23 **MY PROSPERO (IRE),** 4, b c Iffraaj—My Titania (IRE) **Sunderland Holding Inc.**
24 **NATHANAEL GREENE,** 4, b g Nathaniel (IRE)—My Special J's (USA) **Sheikh Isa Salman Al Khalifa**
25 **PERFECT ALIBI,** 4, b f Le Havre (IRE)—Daphne **HM The King & HM The Queen Consort**
26 **PERFECT NEWS,** 4, b f Frankel—Besharah (IRE) **Sheikh Rashid Dalmook Al Maktoum**
27 **PERSIST,** 4, b f Frankel—Persuasive (IRE) **Cheveley Park Stud**
28 **PINK CRYSTAL (IRE),** 4, ch f Shamardal (USA)—Cristal Fizz (IRE) **Sheikh Juma Dalmook Al Maktoum**
29 **POST IMPRESSIONIST (IRE),** 4, b g Teofilo (IRE)—Island Remede **Mr R. Green**

MR WILLIAM HAGGAS - continued

30 **PRIDE OF PRIORY,** 5, b g Pivotal—Millennium Star (IRE) **Mr T. J. W. Bridge**
31 **PURPLEPAY (FR),** 4, b f Zarak (FR)—Piedra (IRE) **Lael Stable**
32 **QUEEN AMINATU,** 4, br f Muhaarar—Zeb Un Nisa **Mr A. E. Oppenheimer**
33 **RAZEYNA (IRE),** 4, b f Kodiac—Deleyla **Sheikh Ahmed Al Maktoum**
34 **ROBERTO ESCOBARR (IRE),** 6, b g Galileo (IRE)—Bewitched (IRE) **Mr H. A. Lootah**
35 **SACRED,** 5, b m Exceed And Excel (AUS)—Sacre Caroline (USA) **Cheveley Park Stud**
36 **SEA FLAWLESS (IRE),** 4, br f Sea The Stars (IRE)—Kitcara **The Zennor Partnership**
37 **SEA SILK ROAD (IRE),** 4, b f Sea The Stars (IRE)—Oriental Magic (GER) **Sunderland Holding Inc.**
38 **SENSE OF DUTY,** 4, b br f Showcasing—Margaret's Mission (IRE) **St Albans Bloodstock Limited**
39 **SPIRIT OF NGURU (IRE),** 4, b g Invincible Spirit (IRE)—Tutu Nguru (USA) **Sheikh Juma Dalmook Al Maktoum**
40 **TAMILLA,** 4, b f Nathaniel (IRE)—Miss Pinkerton **Abdulla Belhab**
41 **TASMAN BAY (FR),** 5, b g Le Havre (IRE)—Purely Priceless (IRE) **Sir P. J. Vela**
42 **TIBER FLOW (IRE),** 4, br gr g Caravaggio (USA)—Malabar **Jon & Julia Aisbitt**
43 **WILKINS,** 4, b g Lope de Vega (IRE)—Tiptree (IRE) **Mrs M. L. Morris**

THREE-YEAR-OLDS

44 **ALHAMBRA PALACE,** b g Le Havre (IRE)—Lady Francesca **Sheikh Isa Salman Al Khalifa**
45 **ALPHA CAPTURE (IRE),** b g Cotai Glory—York Express **Mr Simon Munir & Mr Isaac Souede**
46 **AMLETO (IRE),** br c Sea The Stars (IRE)—Holy Moon (IRE) **Sunderland Holding Inc.**
47 **ANNADER (IRE),** b c Australia—Cumbfree (IRE) **HRH Prince Faisal Bin Khaled**
48 **BLEAK (IRE),** ch c Highland Reel (IRE)—On A Cloud (USA) **J. Wigan**
49 **BLUE MISSILE,** b f Galileo (IRE)—Nathra (IRE) **HM The King & HM The Queen Consort**
50 **BLUEBOTTLE BLUE,** ch f Zoffany (IRE)—Ebbesbourne (IRE) **Mr T. J. W. Bridge**
51 **BUGLE BEADS,** b f Pivotal—Glitter Girl **Cheveley Park Stud**
52 **BURNISH,** b g Kingman—In The Light **J. Wigan**
53 **CAPTURE THE HEART (IRE),** b f Sea The Stars (IRE)—Amazone (GER) **Mr N. Jonsson**
54 **CHARMING STAR (IRE),** b c Sea The Stars (IRE)—Baino Hope (FR) **Ecurie Ama.Zingteam**
55 **COCO ROYALE,** b f Frankel—Coconut Creme **Mr T Johnson & Newsells Park Stud Ltd**
56 **CRACK OF LIGHT,** b f Kingman—Dawn Horizons **Mr A. E. Oppenheimer**
57 **DELTA LEGEND (IRE),** b c Camelot—Delta Dreamer **Mr K. K. B. Ho**
58 **DESERT HERO,** ch c Sea The Stars (IRE)—Desert Breeze **HM The King & HM The Queen Consort**
59 **DOOM,** b f Dubawi (IRE)—Dank **J. Wigan**
60 **ELNAJMM,** b c Sea The Stars (IRE)—Muneyra **Sheikh Ahmed Al Maktoum**
61 **EXPOSED,** b f Mukhadram—Undress (IRE) **Mr J. B. Haggas**
62 **FAKHAMA (IRE),** gr f Kingman—Majmu (AUS) **Shadwell Estate Company Ltd**
63 **FIVE TOWNS,** b f Lord Kanaloa (JPN)—Guilty Twelve (USA) **Merry Fox Stud**
64 **FLINDRIKIN (IRE),** ch f Frankel—Cold As Ice (SAF) **Barnane Stud Ltd**
65 **FLORIDA (IRE),** b c No Nay Never (USA)—Balankiya (IRE) **Michael Buckley**
66 **GARDEN ROUTE (IRE),** b c Galileo (IRE)—Cloth of Cloud (SAF) **Magnier/Shanahan/Nagle/Kantor**
67 **GIRL RACER (IRE),** ch f No Nay Never (USA)—In The Fast Lane (SAF) **Barnane Stud Ltd**
68 **GODWINSON,** b c Saxon Warrior (JPN)—Malabar **Jon & Julia Aisbitt**
69 **GOOD GRACIOUS,** b f Kingman—Give And Take **Nicholas Jones**
70 **HEAVENS TO BETSY,** b f Kingman—Wonderstruck (IRE) **Lael Stable**
71 **IN THE GIVING (IRE),** ch f Night of Thunder (IRE)—Elope (GER) **Mr R. Green**
72 **KARAT KARAT (IRE),** b br f Australia—Kitcara **Sunderland Holding Inc.**
73 **KATHAB (IRE),** br g Kingman—Deep Inside (FR) **Shadwell Estate Company Ltd**
74 **KINGFISHER KING,** ch c Farhh—Queen Consort (USA) **Mr T. J. W. Bridge**
75 **KLONDIKE,** b c Galileo (IRE)—Koora **Jonsson/Magnier/Tabor/Fittocks Stud**
76 **LAAFI (FR),** b c Cloth of Stars (IRE)—Mediteranea (FR) **Sheikh Hamed Dalmook Al Maktoum**
77 **LOHENGRIN,** ch c Ulysses (IRE)—Diyavana (FR) **Cheveley Park Stud**
78 **LORD BERTIE (FR),** b g Wootton Bassett—Bhageerathi (IRE) **Mrs F. J. Carmichael**
79 **LORDSHIP (GER),** ch g Lord of England (GER)—La Caldera **Ian & Christine Beard & Family**
80 **MARINE DRIVE (IRE),** b c Australia—Valais Girl **Sunderland Holding Inc.**
81 **MARKET VALUE (IRE),** b f Siyouni (FR)—Estimate (IRE) **HM The King & HM The Queen Consort**
82 **MEDIEVAL GOLD,** bl c Camelot—Mill Springs **Teme Valley & Mrs R. Philipps**
83 **MISTRESS LIGHT,** ch f Mastercraftsman (IRE)—Legerete (USA) **Merry Fox Stud & Newsells Park Stud**
84 **MOLAQAB,** b c Zoustar (AUS)—Saniyaat **Sheikh Ahmed Al Maktoum**
85 **MYSTIC PEARL (FR),** b f Invincible Spirit (IRE)—Ertiyad **Sheikh Juma Dalmook Al Maktoum**
86 **NAQEEB (IRE),** b c Nathaniel (IRE)—Aghareed (USA) **Shadwell Estate Company Ltd**

MR WILLIAM HAGGAS - continued

87 **NINE TENTHS (IRE),** b f Kodiac—Covetous **St Albans Bloodstock Limited**
88 **ONE LAST TIME (IRE),** b f Fastnet Rock (AUS)—Starship (IRE) **The Starship Partnership II**
89 **OPERA LEGEND,** b g Night of Thunder (IRE)—Operettist **Mr K. K. B. Ho**
90 **ORCHID BLOOM,** gr f Farhh—Fire Orchid **Sheikh Rashid Dalmook Al Maktoum**
91 **OUTFOXED (IRE),** ch g Dubawi (IRE)—Urban Fox **Barnane Stud Ltd**
92 **PINAFORE (IRE),** br f Dark Angel (IRE)—Naafer **Mr & Mrs R. Scott**
93 **PROSPER LEGEND (IRE),** gr c Australia—Prosper **Mr K. K. B. Ho**
94 **QUEEN EMMA,** ch f Saxon Warrior (JPN)—Amelia May **Mr A E Oppenheimer & Miss A Morris**
95 **QUEEN FOREVER (IRE),** b f Kingman—Signe (IRE) **Mrs F. J. Carmichael**
96 **RAMENSKY,** b g Cracksman—Agathe Sainte **Highclere - Martin Luther King**
97 **ROMILDA (FR),** b f Kingman—Alta Lilea (IRE) **Mr Frederick & Ms Jenny Bianco**
98 **ROYAL CHARTER,** b f Expert Eye—Queen's Charter **Apple Tree Stud**
99 **ROYAL DESIGN,** b f Iffraaj—Miskin Diamond (IRE) **Sheikh Juma Dalmook Al Maktoum**
100 **ROYAL MILA,** b f Nathaniel (IRE)—Russian Finale **Sunderland Holding Inc.**
101 **RUBELLITE (IRE),** b f Iffraaj—Posh Claret **Sheikh Hamed Dalmook Al Maktoum**
102 **SAFETY CATCH,** b f Cracksman—Tempest Fugit (IRE) **Mr A. E. Oppenheimer**
103 **SANCTION,** b f Camelot—Margaret's Mission (IRE) **St Albans Bloodstock Limited**
104 **SEA CLARET (IRE),** ch f Sea The Stars (IRE)—Creggs Pipes (IRE) **Sunderland Holding Inc.**
105 **SEA EAGLE,** br g Time Test—Vassaria (IRE) **Highclere Thoroughbred Racing - Time**
106 **SEENDID (IRE),** b c Dubawi (IRE)—Ferdoos **Sheikh Ahmed Al Maktoum**
107 **SILVER LEGEND (IRE),** gr c Dark Angel (IRE)—Propel (IRE) **Mr K. K. B. Ho**
108 **STAR AHOY,** b c Sea The Stars (IRE)—Infallible **Cheveley Park Stud**
109 **SYLLABUS (IRE),** b c Sea The Stars (IRE)—Nancy O (IRE) **Clipper Logistics**
110 **TAFREEJ (IRE),** b g Shamardal (USA)—Taqaareed (IRE) **Shadwell Estate Company Ltd**
111 **TO CATCH A THIEF,** b c Cracksman—Westwiththenight (IRE) **Mr A. E. Oppenheimer**
112 **TRUTHFUL (IRE),** b f Sea The Stars (IRE)—My Timing **Highclere T'Bred Racing - Nelson Mandela**
113 **TURQUOISE DIAMOND,** b f Dubawi (IRE)—Besharah (IRE) **Sheikh Rashid Dalmook Al Maktoum**
114 **UNEQUAL LOVE,** ch f Dutch Art—Heavenly Dawn **Cheveley Park Stud**
115 **VIVA BOLIVIA,** b f Galileo (IRE)—Aljazzi **Mrs M.Smith Bernal & Newsells Park Stud**
116 **ZARAZA (GER),** b g Sea The Stars (IRE)—Zarzali (AUS) **Sheikh Juma Dalmook Al Maktoum**

TWO-YEAR-OLDS

117 Ch c 20/05 Night of Thunder (IRE)—Aghareed (USA) (Kingmambo (USA)) **Shadwell Estate Company Ltd**
118 **ALTMORE,** b c 19/02 Showcasing—Keegsquaw (IRE) (Street Cry (IRE)) (288115) **Mrs F. J. Carmichael**
119 B f 12/03 Sea The Stars (IRE)—Amazone (GER) (Adlerflug (GER)) (350000) **Sheikh Isa Salman Al Khalifa**
120 B f 11/03 Kingman—Apphia (IRE) (High Chaparral (IRE)) **Barnane Stud Ltd**
121 **APPROVAL,** ch c 21/01 Le Havre (IRE)—Alnoras (Kingman) (160000) **Highclere Thoroughbred Racing - Dali**
122 B f 09/02 Sea The Stars (IRE)—Asheerah (Shamardal (USA)) **Shadwell Estate Company Ltd**
123 B c 16/01 Dark Angel (IRE)—Azwah (Invincible Spirit (IRE)) (148059) **Sheikh Ahmed Al Maktoum**
124 B c 14/02 Dubawi (IRE)—Beshaayir (Iffraaj) **Sheikh Rashid Dalmook Al Maktoum**
125 B c 03/02 Lope de Vega (IRE)—Burning Rules (IRE) (Aussie Rules (USA)) (150000) **First Bloodstock**
126 **BURSINEL (IRE),** b c 05/05 Fastnet Rock (AUS)—Starship (IRE) (Galileo (IRE)) **The Starship Partnership II**
127 B f 01/03 Dubawi (IRE)—Bustaan (USA) (Distorted Humor (USA)) **Sheikh Ahmed Al Maktoum**
128 **CASTLE COVE (IRE),** b c 05/02 Camelot—Lavender Lane (Shamardal) **Jon & Julia Aisbitt**
129 **CHORUS,** b f 03/05 Kingman—Koora (Pivotal) **Fittocks Stud**
130 **CHRISTIAN BRUCE,** b br f 03/04 Le Havre (IRE)—Bess of Hardwick (Dansili) **The Duke of Devonshire**
131 Ch f 17/04 Lope de Vega (IRE)—
Coconut Creme (Cape Cross (IRE)) (120000) **Mr. Jonathan Barnett/Newsells Park Stud**
132 **COGNISANCE,** b f 06/02 Sea The Stars (IRE)—Careful Thought (Brazen Beau (AUS)) **St Albans Bloodstock Limited**
133 **COLLEGE CHOIR,** b f 11/03 Nathaniel (IRE)—Rock Choir (Pivotal) **Cheveley Park Stud**
134 **COOL LEGEND,** gr c 05/02 Sea The Stars (IRE)—Childa (IRE) (Duke of Marmalade (IRE)) (328131) **Mr K. K. B. Ho**
135 B c 01/04 Kingman—Dardiza (IRE) (Street Cry (IRE)) (640256) **Victorious Racing Ltd**
136 B c 29/03 Sea The Stars (IRE)—Dramatic Queen (USA) (Kitten's Joy (USA)) **Sheikh Juma Dalmook Al Maktoum**
137 **ECONOMICS,** ch c 01/03 Night of Thunder (IRE)—
La Pomme d'Amour (Peintre Celebre (USA)) (160000) **Sheikh Isa Salman Al Khalifa**
138 B c 16/02 Le Havre (IRE)—End Over End (Intello (GER)) (58000) **Mr. Jonathan Barnett**
139 B f 19/02 Storm The Stars (USA)—Ertiyad (Dark Angel (IRE)) **Sheikh Juma Dalmook Al Maktoum**
140 **ETMAARI,** ch f 30/03 Dubawi (IRE)—Rizeena (IRE) (Iffraaj) **Sheikh Rashid Dalmook Al Maktoum**

MR WILLIAM HAGGAS - continued

141 B f 26/03 Sea The Stars (IRE)—
Faraday Light (IRE) (Rainbow Quest (USA)) (800000) **Victorious Racing Ltd & Fawzi Nass**
142 B f 17/03 Exceed And Excel (AUS)—Fashion Queen (Aqlaam) **Clipper Logistics**
143 B f 14/05 Night of Thunder (IRE)—Ferdoos (Dansili) **Sheikh Ahmed Al Maktoum**
144 B c 08/02 Fastnet Rock (AUS)—Fiery Sunset (Galileo (IRE)) **HM The King & HM The Queen Consort**
145 B f 21/04 Lope de Vega (IRE)—Fine Time (Dansili) (160000) **Sheikh Juma Dalmook Al Maktoum**
146 GERMANIC (IRE), ch c 19/03 Saxon Warrior (JPN)—
Alice Liddel (IRE) (Dark Angel (IRE)) (320000) **Sheikh Isa Salman Al Khalifa**
147 B c 25/01 Zoustar (AUS)—Golden Stunner (IRE) (Dream Ahead (USA)) (140000) **Sheikh Ahmed Al Maktoum**
148 Ch c 24/03 Night of Thunder (IRE)—
Gravity Flow (IRE) (Exceed And Excel (AUS)) **Sheikh Juma Dalmook Al Maktoum**
149 GREATEST HEAVENS, b f 02/02 Kingman—Great Heavens (Galileo (IRE)) **Nat Rothschild/Eduoard De Rothschild**
150 B f 12/04 Blue Point (IRE)—Greatest Virtue (Poet's Voice) **A. Saeed**
151 ICECAP, ch f 31/01 Ulysses (IRE)—Ice Gala (Invincible Spirit (IRE)) **Cheveley Park Stud**
152 B c 19/05 Zarak—Imperialistic Deva (Haafhd) **Sheikh Hamed Dalmook Al Maktoum**
153 INDISPENSABLE, b f 27/01 Ten Sovereigns (IRE)—Invaluable (Invincible Spirit (IRE)) **Cheveley Park Stud**
154 Gr c 20/03 Caravaggio (USA)—Isabella (IRE) (Galileo (IRE)) (58000) **Saeed Suhail**
155 KEEN INTEREST, b c 23/04 Kodiac—Sea of Dreams (IRE) (Oasis Dream) (130000) **Wrigleys & Wyatts**
156 KILT (IRE), b c 16/04 Kingman—Dank (Dansili) (220000) **J. Wigan**
157 B f 23/02 Sea The Stars (IRE)—Koala (FR) (Kodiac) (304122) **Sunderland Holding Inc.**
158 Ch c 08/04 No Nay Never (USA)—Lady Aquitaine (USA) (El Prado (IRE)) (130000) **First Bloodstock**
159 B f 28/01 Siyouni (FR)—Lah Ti Dar (Dubawi (IRE)) (880000) **Shadwell Estate Company Ltd**
160 Ch c 12/02 Zoffany (IRE)—Lambari (FR) (Medicean) (65000) **Saeed Suhail**
161 B f 23/01 Golden Horn—Livia's Dream (IRE) (Teofilo (IRE)) (290000) **First Bloodstock**
162 LOOSE CANNON, b c 12/04 Territories (IRE)—Varega (FR) (Danehill Dancer (IRE)) (68027) **Loose Cannons**
163 B c 21/03 Dubawi (IRE)—Luminate (IRE) (Lawman (FR)) **Merry Fox Stud & Newsells Park Stud**
164 B f 22/01 Dubawi (IRE)—Magnetic Charm (Exceed And Excel (AUS)) **HM The King & HM The Queen Consort**
165 B c 10/02 Kingman—Maqsad (FR) (Siyouni (FR)) **Shadwell Estate Company Ltd**
166 MARAMA, b f 16/03 Sea The Moon—Belle Above All (New Approach) **Tim & Debbie James**
167 MEGASTAR, ch c 08/04 Siyouni (FR)—Starscope (Selkirk (USA)) (350000) **Cheveley Park Stud**
168 MOLTEN SEA, b f 17/03 Too Darn Hot—Mill Springs (Shirocco (GER)) **Mrs R. Philipps**
169 B f 08/02 Shamardal (USA)—Muffri'Ha (IRE) (Iffraaj) **Sheikh Juma Dalmook Al Maktoum**
170 B c 28/04 Night of Thunder (IRE)—Mythie (FR) (Octagonal (NZ)) (176070) **Mrs F. J. Carmichael**
171 NIGHT OF THE STAR (IRE), b f 13/03 Sea The Stars (IRE)—
Angel of The Gwaun (IRE) (Sadler's Wells (USA)) **Neil Jones**
172 PERSIAN BLUE (USA), b f 17/03 Blue Point (IRE)—
Pichola Dance (IRE) (Distorted Humor (USA)) (80000) **Merry Fox Stud**
173 POINTOFBLUE, b f 06/03 Blue Point (IRE)—Karisma (IRE) (Lawman (FR)) (30000) **Yvonne Jacques**
174 Ch f 28/01 Sea The Moon (GER)—
Praise Dancing (IRE) (Blame (USA)) (280112) **Victorious Racing Ltd & Fawzi Nass**
175 Gr c 06/04 Tasleet—Rawaaf (IRE) (Dark Angel (IRE)) (88035) **Sheikh Ahmed Al Maktoum**
176 RELIEF RALLY (IRE), b f 19/04 Kodiac—Kathoe (IRE) (Fayruz) (58000) **Mr Simon Munir & Mr Isaac Souede**
177 RETRACEMENT (IRE), ch c 28/04 Australia—
Piccadilly Filly (IRE) (Exceed And Excel (AUS)) (120000) **Mr Simon Munir & Mr Isaac Souede**
178 RHETORICAL, b c 05/04 Wootton Bassett—Motivation (FR) (Muhtathir) (200000) **Highclere Thoroughbred Racing**
179 B f 09/03 Dandy Man (IRE)—Rouge Noir (Showcasing) (30476) **Mrs Michael Buckley**
180 RUSSIAN CRESCENDO, b f 12/03 Cracksman—Russian Finale (Dansili) **Cheveley Park Stud**
181 B f 20/01 Too Darn Hot—Secret Sense (USA) (Shamardal (USA)) (320000) **Shadwell Estate Company Ltd**
182 B c 11/01 Dubawi (IRE)—Shama (IRE) (Danehill Dancer (IRE)) **HM The King & HM The Queen Consort**
183 SKIPPING, b f 21/02 Ulysses (IRE)—On Her Toes (IRE) (Kodiac) **Cheveley Park Stud**
184 SPACE LEGEND (IRE), b c 23/03 Sea The Stars (IRE)—
Newton's Angel (IRE) (Dark Angel (IRE)) (150000) **Mr K. K. B. Ho**
185 Ch f 29/03 Havana Gold (IRE)—Star Girl (Dutch Art) (38000) **Ian & Christine Beard & Family**
186 B c 13/04 Zoustar (AUS)—Starboard Watch (Harbour Watch (IRE)) (38000) **Mr N. Jonsson**
187 B c 29/04 Churchill (IRE)—Steel Princess (IRE) (Danehill (USA)) **Ecurie Ama.Zingteam**
188 SUMMIT (IRE), b f 09/05 Kodiac—Shareva (IRE) (Rip Van Winkle (IRE)) (320000) **Cheveley Park Stud**
189 SUNFALL, b gr f 24/02 Twilight Son—Volition (IRE) (Dark Angel (IRE)) **Cheveley Park Stud**
190 B f 05/04 Kingman—Sweet Idea (AUS) (Snitzel (AUS)) **HM The King & HM The Queen Consort**
191 B c 26/03 Exceed And Excel (AUS)—Tazffin (IRE) (Iffraaj) **Sheikh Ahmed Al Maktoum**
192 TREASURE TIME, b c 18/02 Time Test—Penny Drops (Invincible Spirit (IRE)) (80000) **RaceShare - Treasure Time**

MR WILLIAM HAGGAS - continued

193 **TRIUMPH OF PEACE,** br f 12/03 No Nay Never (USA)—Tapisserie (Le Havre (IRE)) **Sheikh Isa Salman Al Khalifa**
194 B c 28/01 Soldier's Call—Under The Covers (Stimulation (IRE)) (57000) **Bronte Collection**
195 **VICTORIA LEGEND,** b c 07/05 Australia—
Rivers of Babylon (IRE) (Holy Roman Emperor (IRE)) (48019) **Mr K. K. B. Ho**
196 **VIRIDIAN (IRE),** b c 03/03 Acclamation—
Blue Willow (Exceed And Excel (AUS)) (80000) **The Royal Ascot Racing Club**
197 **WONDERFUL FEELING,** b f 02/02 Sea The Moon (GER)—Wonderful Filly (GER) (Lomitas) **Heike & Nico Bishoff**
198 **YOSEMITE GOLD,** b c 08/03 Golden Horn—
Tuolumne Meadows (High Chaparral (IRE)) (75000) **Souede/Munir/Levitt/Bromley**

Assistant Trainer: Josh Hamer, Andy McIntyre, Isabella Paul.

Flat Jockey: Tom Marquand, Cieren Fallon. **Apprentice Jockey:** Adam Farragher.

---

220 MR ALEX HALES, Edgecote

Postal: **Trafford Bridge Stables, Edgecote, Banbury, Oxfordshire, OX17 1AG**
Contacts: **PHONE 01295 660131 MOBILE 07771 511652 FAX 01295 660128**
EMAIL alex@alexhalesracing.co.uk WEBSITE www.alexhalesracing.co.uk

1 **ABINGTON PARK,** 8, br g Passing Glance—Epicurean **Red Cap Racing**
2 **BEDFORD HOUSE,** 4, b g Dabirsim (FR)—Akhmatova
3 **BOLDMERE,** 10, b g Multiplex—Pugnacious Lady **W. J. Odell**
4 **CASI CRUDO,** 4, b g Authorized (IRE)—Adalawa (IRE) **Acott, Cross, Cross, Johnston**
5 **CHOSEN SHANT (IRE),** 7, b br m Shantou (USA)—Ratheniska (IRE) **Golden Equinox Racing**
6 **CRIQUETTE (FR),** 6, b m Crillon (FR)—Lost Maiby (FR) **Mr S. N. Brackenbury**
7 **EASTER MIRACLE,** 5, b m Clovis du Berlais (FR)—It Doesn't Matter **The The Easter Miracle Racing Syndicate**
8 **EZ TIGER (IRE),** 6, b g Sholokhov (IRE)—Miss Opera **Mr N Rodway & Partner**
9 **FAGAN,** 13, gr g Fair Mix (IRE)—Northwood May **Stowe 100 Club**
10 **FAMILY TIME,** 5, b g Excelebration (IRE)—Porcini **Mr S. N. Brackenbury**
11 **FEEL LIKE DE BAUNE (FR),** 7, b g Feel Like Dancing—Sofia de Baune (FR) **Mr S. N. Brackenbury**
12 **FOR PLEASURE (IRE),** 8, ch g Excelebration (IRE)—Darsan (IRE) **Premier Plastering (UK) Limited**
13 **FOX'S SOCKS (FR),** 8, br g Crillon (FR)—Queva de Sarti (FR) **The Lost My Socks Racing Syndicate**
14 **GARDENER (FR),** 7, b g Dragon Dancer—Alliance Doree (FR) **Premier Plastering (UK) Limited**
15 **GONE IN SIXTY,** 6, b g Sixties Icon—Gib (IRE) **Golden Equinox Racing**
16 **GRASSE D'OLIVERIE (FR),** 6, b m Balko (FR)—My Belle du Rheu (FR) **Mrs J. M. Mayo**
17 **HAPPY AND FINE (FR),** 6, b g Balko (FR)—Richona (FR) **Mr T Acott, Mr L Cross, Mr S Cross**
18 **HARA KIRI (FR),** 6, b g Diamond Boy (FR)—Beauty du Bidou (FR) **Premier Plastering (UK) Limited**
19 **HARRY GULLIVER,** 5, b g Linda's Lad—Drombeg West
20 **HAS TROKE (FR),** 6, b g Masterstroke (USA)—Shifa (FR) **The Arty Syndicate**
21 **HICONIC,** 6, b m Sixties Icon—Hi Note **Golden Equinox Racing & Partner**
22 **HOUSTON BERE (FR),** 6, b g Hurricane Cat (USA)—Kunoichi (USA) **The Bere Necessities**
23 **I AM DE CHAILLAC (FR),** 5, b g Jeu St Eloi (FR)—Vivaldi du Pecos (FR) **Mr Michael & Mrs Norma Tuckey**
24 **ILARY DE L'ECU (FR),** 5, b m Great Pretender (IRE)—Alary de L'Ecu (FR) **Mrs John Thorneloe**
25 **INCLEMENT WEATHER,** 5, b m Bated Breath—Rapid Recruit (IRE) **Golden Equinox Racing**
26 **KAITUNA RIVER (IRE),** 6, b g Ask—Kaituna (IRE) **Money Down The River**
27 **KANKIN,** 7, ch g Archipenko (USA)—Touriga **Mr A. L. Cohen**
28 **LA GOMERA,** 5, b m Kayf Tara—Fernello **Miss S. M. L. Parden**
29 **MARIA MAGDALENA (IRE),** 7, b m Battle of Marengo (IRE)—Few Words **The Problem Solvers**
30 **MIDNIGHTINBRESIL,** 6, b m Blue Bresil (FR)—Farewellatmidnight **Mrs J. Way**
31 **MILLERS BANK,** 9, b g Passing Glance—It Doesn't Matter **Millers Bank Partnership**
32 **NEXTDOORTOALICE (IRE),** 7, b m Mahler—Lady Zephyr (IRE) **The Syndicate Next Door**
33 **NO RISK WITH LOU (FR),** 6, b g No Risk At All (FR)—Miss Meteore (FR) **The Risk and Reward Racing Syndicate**
34 **OL'RIVER SHINE (IRE),** 5, b m Ol' Man River (IRE)—Tosca Shine (IRE) **Old Stoics Racing Club 2**
35 **OMAR MARETTI (IRE),** 9, b g Fame And Glory—Parsons Hall (IRE) **J. T. B. Hunt**
36 **OUR BILL'S AUNT (IRE),** 7, b m Blueprint (IRE)—Carrigmoorna Oak (IRE) **The 25 Club**
37 **POLLYPOCKETT (IRE),** 6, b m Presenting—Mtpockets (IRE) **Edging Ahead**
38 **QUEENS HIGHWAY (IRE),** 7, br m Presenting—Augusta Bay **Golden Equinox Racing**

MR ALEX HALES - continued

39 **RIGHTOFWAY,** 4, b f Clovis du Berlais (FR)—Mawaweel (IRE) **Mrs J. Way**
40 **ROUGH NIGHT (IRE),** 10, b g Doyen (IRE)—Sunny Bob (IRE) **Miss P. M. Morris**
41 **SAY NOTHING,** 7, b m Nathaniel (IRE)—I Say (IRE) **The The Silent Partners**
42 **SEA PRINCE,** 7, b g Born To Sea (IRE)—Briery (IRE) **The Sea Prince Racing Partnership**
43 **SOLO SAXOPHONE (IRE),** 9, b g Frankel—Society Hostess (USA) **Golden Equinox Racing**
44 **THE LION DANCER (IRE),** 11, b g Let The Lion Roar—Shesadoll (IRE) **The 25 Club**
45 **YELLOWSTONE PARK (IRE),** 7, b g Arctic Cosmos (USA)—Cool Island (IRE) **Premier Plastering (UK) Limited**

---

221 MR MICHAEL HALFORD AND TRACEY COLLINS, Kildare

Postal: **Conyngham Lodge, The Curragh, Co. Kildare, R56 AF30, Ireland**
Contacts: **WORK +353 87 819 4680 MOBILE +353 87 257 9204**
WORK EMAIL info@michaelhalford.com WEBSITE www.michaelhalford.com

1 **ARCANEARS (IRE),** 8, b g Arcano (IRE)—Ondeafears (IRE) **Mrs Caroline Roper**
2 **CEALLACH (IRE),** 4, ch c Lope de Vega (IRE)—Alvee (IRE) **Mr P Rooney**
3 **CHALLY CHUTE (IRE),** 5, ch g Fast Company (IRE)—Edith Somerville (IRE) **Ms. Julie White**
4 **COSMIC VEGA (IRE),** 5, b g Lope de Vega (IRE)—Pivotal Era **Long Inch Ltd**
5 **ELZAAMSAN (IRE),** 5, b h Elzaam (AUS)—Lady Conway (USA) **Mr P Rooney**
6 **GOLDEN DAYS (IRE),** 6, b m Canford Cliffs (IRE)—Lisa Gherardini (IRE) **Front Row Partnership**
7 **GOLDEN TWILIGHT (IRE),** 6, b g Dawn Approach (IRE)—Great Hope (IRE) **Mr F W Lynch**
8 **INCHTURK (IRE),** 4, bl c Le Havre (IRE)—Pirita (IRE) **Mr N Hartery & Mr J McGee**
9 **KAMPALA BEACH (IRE),** 4, b c Belardo (IRE)—Translator (IRE) **Mr M Phelan**
10 **MASTER MATT (IRE),** 7, b g Slade Power—Ahaaly
11 **REGINALDS TOWER (IRE),** 6, b g Canford Cliffs (IRE)—La Femme (IRE) **Mr N Hartery**
12 **RICCARDI MEDIDI (IRE),** 4, ch c No Nay Never (USA)—Duchessofflorence **Mr M Enright**
13 **SAMEASITEVERWAS (IRE),** 6, br g Sageburg (IRE)—Print It On Lips (IRE) **Mrs L Halford**
14 **SLIEVE BEARNAGH (IRE),** 6, b h Zoffany (IRE)—Angels Story (IRE) **Mr P Rooney**
15 **VADIANA (IRE),** 4, br f Vadamos (FR)—Vassiana (FR) **Celbridge Estates Ltd**
16 **ZILEO,** 5, b g Galileo (IRE)—Lady Zuzu (USA) **Mr P Rooney**

THREE-YEAR-OLDS

17 **AMEERAT JUMAIRA,** ch f Australia—Nourah (IRE) **Mr Isa Bin Haider**
18 **BARNEY'S JOY,** gr c Gutaifan (IRE)—Jeremy's Girl (IRE) **Cornate Ltd**
19 **CHERRY PINK,** b f Elzaam (AUS)—Esmaggie
20 **DIYABA,** ch f Australia—Diylawa (IRE) **H. H. The Aga Khan**
21 **DOCTOR GRACE,** b f Buratino (IRE)—Firecrown (IRE) **Dundalk Racing Club**
22 **DROMANTINE (IRE),** ch f Lope De Vega—Via Ballycroy
23 **IMADPOUR (IRE),** gr c Le Havre (IRE)—Imrana **H. H. The Aga Khan**
24 **KADEEN (IRE),** b c New Approach (IRE)—Kadra (IRE) **H. H. The Aga Khan**
25 **KALIKAPOUR (IRE),** b c Lope De Vega—Kalaxana
26 **LIMESTONE RED,** ch c Cotai Glory—Kocna (IRE) **Castle Beech Partnership**
27 **NOT FORGOTTEN (IRE),** gr g National Defense—
Discreet Spy (USA) **Lillian A Stanley & M T Cunningham & Justin Comer**
28 **NYOTA,** b f Elzaam (AUS)—Playamongthestars (AUS) **Mr. O.B.P. Carroll, Mr. Dermot Kelly and Mr. Tony Vaughan**
29 **OSTRAKA (IRE),** bl f Profitable—Ostatnia
30 **PITTSFORD (IRE),** ch g Ulysses (IRE)—Influence (FR)
31 B f Gregorian (IRE)—Ranallagh Rocket (IRE)
32 **RAUZAN (IRE),** b c Australia—Rayisa (IRE) **H. H. The Aga Khan**

MR MICHAEL HALFORD AND TRACEY COLLINS - continued

33 **RAVSHAN (IRE),** b c Harzand—Rayna
34 **RYHTHM AND TYNE,** b c Elzaam (AUS)—Lady Tyne **Castle Beech Partnership**
35 **SHANADAR (IRE),** b c Siyouni—Alwaysandforever
36 **SLIEVE BINNIAN (IRE),** gr c Awtaad (IRE)—Qertaas (IRE) **Mr P Rooney**
37 **SON OF SAMPERS (IRE),** b g Starspangledbanner—Sampers

TWO-YEAR-OLDS

38 B f 21/04 Invincible Spirit (IRE)—Alwaysandforever (IRE) (Teofilo (IRE)) (180000)
39 B f 27/03 Free Eagle (IRE)—Discreet Spy (USA) (Discreet Cat (USA)) (2801)
40 Ch f 13/02 Waldgeist—Exotic Isle (Exceed And Excel (AUS)) (17607)
41 B c 07/03 Holy Roman Emperor—Marie Josephe (Cape Cross)
42 Bl c 10/04 Rock of Gibraltar (IRE)—Nalout (USA) (Afleet Alex (USA))
43 B f 20/03 Ten Sovereigns (IRE)—Paimpolaise (IRE) (Priolo (USA))
44 B c 04/04 Churchill—Roseraie (Marju)
45 B c 07/02 Harzand—Sharliyna (Pivotal)
46 **SWANZY (IRE),** b f 12/03 Elzaam (AUS)—Angelou (Poet's Voice) (4002)
47 B c 04/02 Mastercraftsman—Timiniya (Footstepsinthesand)
48 B c 19/03 Churchill—Vadaiyma (Galileo (IRE))

Assistant Trainer: Stephen Craine, **Head Man:** Nikica Jenjic.

Flat Jockey: Ross Coakley, Niall McCullagh, Ronan Whelan. **Amateur Jockey:** Mr Evan Halford, Mr Joshua Halford.

---

222 MRS DEBRA HAMER, Carmarthen

Postal: **Bryngors Uchaf, Nantycaws, Carmarthen, Dyfed, SA32 8EY**
Contacts: **HOME 01267 234585 MOBILE 07980 665274**
EMAIL hamerracing@hotmail.co.uk

1 **BERG NELLIE (IRE),** 4, b f Mount Nelson—Grangeclare Lark (IRE) **Mr D. R. Jones**
2 **CRESSWELL QUEEN,** 8, b m Brian Boru—Cresswell Willow (IRE) **Mr P. J. Woolley**
3 **DEAL EM HIGH,** 6, ch g Mountain High (IRE)—Dirty Deal **Mr I. R. Goatson**
4 **DEAL EM LUCKY,** 7, b m Yorgunnabelucky (USA)—Dirty Deal
5 **LAYERTHORPE (IRE),** 11, b bl g Vale of York (IRE)—Strobinia (IRE) **Mr C. A. Hanbury**
6 **LOOKS LIKE POWER (IRE),** 13, ch g Spadoun (FR)—Martovic (IRE) **Mr C. A. Hanbury**
7 **MEECHLANDS MAGIC,** 7, b br g Multiplex—Do It On Dani **Mrs J. M. Edmonds**
8 **RUBY'S COMET,** 5, b g Telescope (IRE)—Cresswell Ruby (IRE) **Eddie & John**
9 **RUBYS REWARD,** 7, b m Dr Massini (IRE)—Cresswell Ruby (IRE) **Eddie & John**
10 **SADDLERS QUEST,** 9, b m Dr Massini (IRE)—Lady Maranzi **Mrs D. A. Hamer**
11 **SHEE'S A STELLA,** 5, ch m Mountain High (IRE)—Another Stella **Mr R. W. J. Willcox**

Assistant Trainer: Mr M. P. Hamer.

---

223 MRS ALISON HAMILTON, Denholm

Postal: **Dykes Farm House, Denholm, Hawick, Roxburghshire, TD9 8TB**
Contacts: **PHONE 01450 870323 MOBILE 07885 477349**
EMAIL Alisonhamilton53@yahoo.com

1 **BALRANALD (FR),** 7, b gr g Mastercraftsman (IRE)—Shining Glory (GER) **J. P. G. Hamilton**
2 **CHARLIE'S ROCKSTAR (IRE),** 6, b g Shirocco (GER)—John's Eliza (IRE) **J. P. G. Hamilton**
3 **CHOIX DES ARMES (FR),** 11, b g Saint des Saints (FR)—Kicka **J. P. G. Hamilton**
4 **DRAKEHOLES,** 4, b g Gutaifan (IRE)—Elfine (IRE) **J. P. G. Hamilton**

MRS ALISON HAMILTON - continued

5 **GUN MERCHANT,** 10, b g Kayf Tara—Pearly Legend **Mr & Mrs D S Byers & Jpg Hamilton**
6 **MOUNT MELLERAY (IRE),** 8, ch g Flemensfirth (USA)—Prowler (IRE) **J. P. G. Hamilton**
7 **SHAUGHNESSY,** 10, b g Shantou (USA)—Sudden Beat **J. P. G. Hamilton**
8 **SKYHILL (IRE),** 10, b g Gold Well—Classic Mari (IRE) **Mr & Mrs D S Byers & Jpg Hamilton**
9 **STAND STAUNCH (IRE),** 5, b g Camelot—Takawiri (IRE) **J. P. G. Hamilton**
10 **TOWERBURN (IRE),** 14, b g Cloudings (IRE)—Lady Newmill (IRE) **J. P. G. Hamilton**
11 **TURBO COMMAND (IRE),** 6, gr g War Command (USA)—The Tempest **J. P. G. Hamilton**

Assistant Trainer: Mr G. Hamilton.

---

224 MR ANDREW HAMILTON, Carluke

Postal: **Nellfield House, Braidwood, Carluke, Lanarkshire, ML8 4PP**
Contacts: **PHONE 01555 771502**

1 **ALL ABOUT JOE (IRE),** 8, b g Oscar (IRE)—Sunny Native (IRE) **Mr A. B. Hamilton**
2 **EL JEFE (IRE),** 6, b g Born To Sea (IRE)—Ros Mountain (IRE) **Mr A. B. Hamilton**
3 **FLASH MORIVIERE (FR),** 8, b g Maresca Sorrento (FR)—Fleur de Princesse (FR) **Mr A. B. Hamilton**
4 **GALLANT FLAME (IRE),** 7, b g Doyen (IRE)—Angels Flame (IRE) **Mr A. B. Hamilton**
5 **IF NOT FOR DYLAN (IRE),** 8, b g Doyen (IRE)—Exit Stage Left (IRE) **Mr A. B. Hamilton**
6 **NO HIDING PLACE (IRE),** 10, b g Stowaway—Subtle Gem (IRE) **Mr A. B. Hamilton**
7 **STRAIGHT SWAP (IRE),** 8, b br g Yeats (IRE)—Alittlebitofheaven **Mr A. B. Hamilton**
8 **TOUCAN SAM,** 5, b g Frankel—Ridafa (IRE) **Mr A. B. Hamilton**

---

225 MRS ANN HAMILTON, Newcastle Upon Tyne

Postal: **Claywalls Farm, Capheaton, Newcastle Upon Tyne, Tyne and Wear, NE19 2BP**
Contacts: **PHONE 01830 530219 MOBILE 07704 670704**
EMAIL annhamilton1952@hotmail.com

1 **BAVINGTON BOB (IRE),** 8, br g Court Cave (IRE)—Chocolate Silk (IRE) **Mr I. Hamilton**
2 **DARE TO SHOUT,** 6, gr g Martaline—Dare To Doubt **Mr I. Hamilton**
3 **FIVE DOLLAR FINE (IRE),** 8, b g Shantou (USA)—Danecole (IRE) **Mr I. Hamilton**
4 **HELLO JUDGE,** 7, b g Martaline—Oeuvre Vive (FR) **Mr I. Hamilton**
5 **NUTS WELL,** 12, b g Dylan Thomas (IRE)—Renada **Mr I. Hamilton**
6 **PAY THE PIPER (IRE),** 8, b g Court Cave (IRE)—Regal Holly **Mr I. Hamilton**
7 4, B g Blue Bresil (FR)—Renada **Mr I. Hamilton**
8 **TOMMY'S OSCAR (IRE),** 8, b g Oscar (IRE)—Glibin (IRE) **Mr I. Hamilton**

Assistant Trainer: Ian Hamilton.

---

226 MR MICKY HAMMOND, Middleham

Postal: **Oakwood Stables, East Witton Road, Middleham, Leyburn, North Yorkshire, DL8 4PT**
Contacts: **PHONE 01969 625223 MOBILE 07808 572777**
EMAIL micky@mickyhammondracing.co.uk WEBSITE www.mickyhammondracing.co.uk

1 **ADMIRAL HORATIO (IRE),** 5, b g Mount Nelson—Kerry's Girl (IRE) **Mrs B. M. Lofthouse**
2 **AIR OF APPROVAL (IRE),** 5, gr m Mastercraftsman (IRE)—Rhiannon (IRE) **Mrs A. King**

MR MICKY HAMMOND - continued

3 **ALONG LONG STORY (IRE),** 7, b g Morozov (USA)—Bluebell Wedding **The Chronicles**
4 **AMBER RUN (IRE),** 8, b g Arcadio (GER)—Dorcet'slast Stand (IRE) **M.H.O.G.**
5 **APPLAUS (GER),** 11, b g Tiger Hill (IRE)—All About Love (GER) **Mrs G. Hogg**
6 **BALKOTIC (FR),** 7, b g Balko (FR)—Aurore Celtique (FR) **Raypasha**
7 **BANDIT D'AINAY (FR),** 12, b g Crossharbour—Ne M'Oubliez Pas (FR) **The Golden Cuckoo**
8 **BANNOCKBURN (FR),** 4, b f Ballingarry (IRE)—Nile Divine (FR) **Mr J. Connor**
9 **BELLE NA BANN (IRE),** 7, b m Califet (FR)—Cut 'n' Run (IRE) **Ms D Morley, Mr S Dobson & Partner**
10 **BONNE VITESSE (IRE),** 5, b m Fast Company (IRE)—Mirabile Dictu (IRE) **The Golden Cuckoo**
11 **BRICKADANK (IRE),** 7, b g Cape Cross (IRE)—Tralanza (IRE) **A & S Associates**
12 **BULLDOZE (IRE),** 8, gr g Notnowcato—Cap The Rose (IRE) **R M & T Holdings Limited & Partners**
13 **BURNAGE BOY (IRE),** 7, b g Footstepsinthesand—Speedi Mouse **JFW Properties Limited**
14 **BUTO,** 6, ch g Nathaniel (IRE)—Mea Parvitas (IRE) **Oakwood Racing**
15 **CARNIVAL ZAIN,** 6, b g Youmzain (IRE)—Lady Fashion **Newroc & Partner**
16 **CEDAR RAPIDS (IRE),** 5, ch g Australia—Song of My Heart (IRE) **Ian Barran & Oakwood**
17 **CONTRE ORDRE (FR),** 5, b g Martinborough (JPN)—Turga de La Tour (FR) **Mr G. Newton**
18 **CORNERSTONE LAD,** 9, b g Delegator—Chapel Corner (IRE) **Mrs B. M. Lofthouse**
19 **COUNTESS OLIVIA (IRE),** 6, ch m Ruler of The World (IRE)—Twelfth Night (IRE) **John & Kate Sidebottom**
20 **DESARAY GIRL (FR),** 8, gr m Montmartre (FR)—Feria To Bitch (FR) **Resdev Ltd**
21 **DIS DONC (FR),** 10, b g Kingsalsa (USA)—Skarina (FR) **The Monday Club**
22 **DRAGONS WILL RISE (IRE),** 7, b g Dragon Pulse (IRE)—Jaldini (IRE) **The Golden Cuckoo**
23 4, B f Mahler—Ebony Empress (IRE) **Sharp Hill Thoroughbreds**
24 **ERAGONE (FR),** 9, gr g Martaline—Sharonne (FR) **Mr S. Sutton**
25 **FAINCHE (IRE),** 6, b m Fame And Glory—Voodoo Magic (GER)
26 **FAMILLE VERTE (IRE),** 4, b f No Nay Never (USA)—Falling Rain (IRE) **Raymond Tooth & Oakwood Racing**
27 **FIFTYSHADESARESDEV (FR),** 4, gr g Johnny Barnes (IRE)—Tina Nova (FR) **Resdev Ltd**
28 **FOSTER'SISLAND,** 8, b g Trans Island—Mrs Eff **The Oakwood Nobels**
29 **FRANKELIO (FR),** 8, b g Frankel—Restiadargent (FR) **Forty Forty Twenty**
30 **GARDE LE SOLEIL (FR),** 6, b g Kapgarde (FR)—Toi Et Le Soleil (FR)
31 **GERYVILLE (FR),** 7, b g Rail Link—Rosaville (FR) **Mr R. M. Howard**
32 **GETAWAY JEWEL (IRE),** 9, b g Getaway (GER)—Fada's Jewel (IRE) **Mr P. Ellerby**
33 **GRAND DU NORD (FR),** 7, b g Montmartre (FR)—Vanille d'Ainay (FR) **Middleham Park & the Cheltenham Trail 7**
34 **GRANGE RANGER (IRE),** 11, b g Kalanisi (IRE)—Grangeclare Flight (IRE) **Oakwood Rainbow**
35 **GREAT BALLINBORIS (FR),** 7, b g Ballingarry (IRE)—Rotswana (FR) **Mr J. W. Burnett**
36 **GREAT RAFFLES (FR),** 7, b g Kapgarde (FR)—Une Artiste (FR) **The Golden Cuckoo**
37 **HIDEO (FR),** 6, b g Cokoriko (FR)—Saora (FR) **Two Nicks & A Mick**
38 **HIGH NOON (IRE),** 11, b g Westerner—Seymourswift **Mr Nick Pietrzyk & Partner**
39 **HOWZAT HIRIS (FR),** 6, gr m Al Namix (FR)—Une Dame d'Or (FR) **Sticky Wicket Racing**
40 **I'M DOUGAL ROCKS (FR),** 6, ch g Kap Rock (FR)—Anicka d'Or (FR) **Middleham Park Racing XXIII**
41 **ILAYA (FR),** 9, gr m Kapgarde (FR)—Tour Magic (FR) **The Golden Cuckoo**
42 **IRV (IRE),** 7, ch g Zoffany (IRE)—Marion Antoinette (IRE) **Anthony Bithall & Partner**
43 **JAKES WISH,** 4, b g Kayf Tara—Camillas Wish (IRE)
44 **JUS DE FRUIT (FR),** 4, b g Gris de Gris (IRE)—Soft Drink (FR) **Mrs N. J. McGrath**
45 **KILDRUM (IRE),** 10, b g Milan—Close Flame (IRE) **Mr T. M. Clarke**
46 **KING OF UNICORNS,** 6, b g Night of Thunder (IRE)—Aviacion (BRZ) **J. Buzzeo**
47 **KNOCKNAMONA (IRE),** 12, b g Trans Island—Faraday Lady (IRE) **The Rat Pack Racing Club**
48 **LARRY LOOBY (IRE),** 10, b g Golden Lariat (USA)—
Panglao Island (IRE) **Mr & Mrs D Lees Mr J Kaye & Mr D Pollitt**
49 **LE GRAND VERT (FR),** 7, b g Great Pretender (IRE)—Eliga (FR) **Mr Richard Howard & Mr Ben Howard**
50 **LINCOLN BURROWS (IRE),** 6, b g Dylan Thomas (IRE)—Avida Star (IRE) **K Jardine R Griffiths**
51 **MAC SUIBHNE (IRE),** 8, b g Virtual—Hepahepa Naeney (IRE) **Mr P. Ellerby**
52 **MASTER GUSTAV,** 7, b g Mahler—Annaghbrack (IRE) **Mrs B. M. Lofthouse**
53 **MILLTOWN LILY (IRE),** 5, b m Sir Prancealot (IRE)—Danetime Lily (IRE) **Maybe The Last Time**
54 **MISTER BELLS (IRE),** 9, b g Power—Keyaza (IRE) **Mr & Mrs P. Chapman**
55 **MONAGHAN BOY (IRE),** 6, b g Court Cave (IRE)—Ferrestown Lady (IRE) **The Golden Cuckoo**
56 **MORE JOY (FR),** 5, b m Morandi (FR)—La Joie (FR) **Mr S. Sutton**
57 **MYBOYMAX (FR),** 5, b g Myboycharlie (IRE)—Plebeya (IRE) **Mr A. Bithell**
58 **NOT WHAT IT SEEMS (IRE),** 7, b g Robin des Pres (FR)—Kyle Ruby (IRE) **Piecederesistance**
59 **ODD VENTURE (IRE),** 6, b g Epaulette (AUS)—Homegrown (IRE)
60 **ONENIGHTINTOWN (IRE),** 9, b g Robin des Pres (FR)—Snug Bunch (IRE) **The Rat Pack Racing Club**
61 **PENPAL (FR),** 8, ch g Muhtathir—Penkinella (FR) **The Golden Cuckoo**

MR MICKY HAMMOND - continued

62 **PERFECT MAN (IRE),** 12, b g Morozov (USA)—Garrisker (IRE) **The Rat Pack Racing Club**
63 **PIECEDERESISTANCE (IRE),** 5, b g Gleneagles (IRE)—Positive Step (IRE) **& Sugden**
64 **POLISUD (FR),** 7, gr g Lord du Sud (FR)—Polimere (FR) **The Cheltenham Trail**
65 **QUOTELINE DIRECT,** 10, ch g Sir Percy—Queen's Pudding (IRE) **JFW Properties Limited**
66 **RORY AND ME (FR),** 8, b g Shamardal (USA)—Rosawa (FR) **Mr Richard Howard & Mr Ben Howard**
67 **ROXYFET (FR),** 13, b g Califet (FR)—Roxalamour (FR) **Mr Samuel Sutton & Partners**
68 **ROYLE STEEL (FR),** 5, gr g Spanish Moon (USA)—Suffisante (FR) **Mr A. E. Tasker**
69 **SCHIEHALLION MUNRO,** 10, ch g Schiaparelli (GER)—Mrs Fawlty **Tennant, Lynch,Sharpe and Boston**
70 **SHADOW ROYAL,** 4, br f Alhebayeb (IRE)—Show Willing (IRE) **Sharp Hill Thoroughbreds**
71 **SHAWS BRIDGE (IRE),** 10, b g Kalanisi (IRE)—Zaffarella (IRE) **Newroc & Co**
72 **SHIGHNESS,** 6, b m Passing Glance—Sharwakom (IRE) **Keep The Faith Partnership**
73 **SPARKLE IN HIS EYE,** 7, ch g Sea The Stars (IRE)—Nyarhini **Mr S. Sutton**
74 **SPLIT THE BILL (IRE),** 5, b g Champs Elysees—Spin The Wheel (IRE) **Mr J. N. Swinbank**
75 **STORM SPIRIT,** 4, b f Passing Glance—Concentrate **Keep The Faith Partnership**
76 **THE RESDEV WAY,** 10, b g Multiplex—Lady Duxyana **Resdev Ltd**
77 **THE RUTLAND REBEL (IRE),** 7, b g Delegator—Do Disturb (IRE) **Ryder And Alex Sugden**
78 **THE VERY THING (IRE),** 9, b g Getaway (GER)—Katie Quinn (IRE) **Mr D. Walpole**
79 **TOUCH OF A DRAGON,** 4, b f Dragon Dancer—Touch of Ivory (IRE) **The Oakwood Nobels**
80 **TRAC (FR),** 6, b g Kingsalsa (USA)—Belobaka (FR) **Randall Orchard & Partners**
81 **TREVELYN'S CORN (IRE),** 10, b g Oscar (IRE)—Present Venture (IRE) **Mr & Mrs D Lees Mr J Kaye & Mr D Pollitt**
82 **VISITE OFFICIELLE (FR),** 5, gr m Martinborough (JPN)—Visite Royale (FR) **Resdev, Mr J Kaye & Mr D Lees**
83 **WESTERN MELODY (IRE),** 6, b m Sir Prancealot (IRE)—Western Tune (IRE) **The Rat Pack Racing Club**
84 **WESTY FOX (IRE),** 9, b g Westerner—Brogarais (IRE) **Rust, Stevenson & the Smiths**
85 **WHO'S THE GUV'NOR (IRE),** 9, b g Gold Well—Clamit Brook (IRE) **Mr & Mrs I P Earnshaw**
86 **WISTERIAROSE,** 7, b m Leading Light (IRE)—Mille Et Une (FR) **Mrs J. E. Newett**
87 **WOTYA MACALLIT,** 4, b g Orientor—Full of Love (IRE) **Mr K. S. Ward**

THREE-YEAR-OLDS

88 **ANJO BONITA,** b f Harry Angel (IRE)—Cape Mystery **Keep The Faith Partnership**
89 **EXPERT LADY,** b f Expert Eye—Iridescence **Sharp Hill Thoroughbreds**
90 **FINAL CHANT (IRE),** ch g Gleneagles (IRE)—Teide Lady **The Munro's**
91 **MAGNOLIA HAWKS (IRE),** br f Footstepsinthesand—Kofariti (IRE) **Peter Davies & Sons Limited**
92 **WITCHFORD,** b f Expert Eye—Interchange (IRE) **Keep The Faith Partnership**

Assistant Trainer: Mrs G. Hogg.

NH Jockey: Alain Cawley, Joe Colliver. **Conditional Jockey:** Billy Garritty, Aidan Macdonald, Emma Smith-Chaston. **Apprentice Jockey:** Aiden Brookes. **Amateur Jockey:** Miss R. Smith, James Waggott.

---

227 MR GARY HANMER, Tattenhall

Postal: **Church Farm, Harthill Lane, Harthill, Tattenhall, Chester, Cheshire, CH3 9LQ**
Contacts: **MOBILE 07737 181165**

1 **BELLELOISE,** 5, b m Blue Bresil (FR)—Sabreflight **Mr D. Coates**
2 **BRIGHT SUNBIRD (IRE),** 8, b m Milan—Mrs Marples (IRE) **Hammond, Racing J Menzies**
3 **COSTLY DIAMOND (IRE),** 9, ch m Mahler—Sweet Ouzel (IRE) **TGK Construction Co. Ltd**
4 **DARANOVA (IRE),** 9, b g Arctic Cosmos (USA)—Dara Supreme (IRE) **Mr C. F. Moore**
5 **DAWN RAIDER (IRE),** 11, b g Mahler—Woodview Dawn (IRE) **Mr T. G. Kelly**
6 **DEE EIRE,** 6, bl m Gentlewave (IRE)—Kahipiroska (FR) **The Deeside Partnership**
7 **DEE STAR (IRE),** 10, b g Shantou (USA)—Alicias Lady (IRE) **The Deeside Partnership**
8 **ERIC CARMEN (IRE),** 7, b g Fame And Glory—Cooper's Joy (IRE) **The Ed-chester Partnership**
9 **FANDABIDOZI (IRE),** 5, ch g Mastercraftsman (IRE)—Cranky Spanky (IRE) **Mr G. Evans**
10 **FLAMING AMBITION (IRE),** 6, b g Fame And Glory—Gran Chis (IRE) **S Beetham & Dpl Fab Ltd**
11 **FLOUEUR (FR),** 8, b g Legolas (JPN)—Saraska d'Airy (FR) **Hammond, Racing J Menzies**
12 **FUSIONFORCE (IRE),** 16, b g Overbury (IRE)—Seviot **Mr S. P. Edkins**

MR GARY HANMER - continued

13 **GRANGE ROAD (IRE),** 8, b g Oscar (IRE)—Niamh's Away (IRE) **Deva Racing (GR)**
14 **HADDOCK DE GRISSAY (FR),** 6, b g Maresca Sorrento (FR)—Kubana (FR)
15 **HIGH COUNSEL (IRE),** 14, br g Presenting—The Bench (IRE) **Herongate Racers**
16 **HILLVIEW (IRE),** 7, b g Fruits of Love (USA)—Da Das Delight (IRE) **Mr D. O. Pickering**
17 **IBERIA (IRE),** 6, b g Galileo (IRE)—Beauty Bright (IRE) **Mr H. Bourchier**
18 **ISTHEBAROPEN,** 10, b m Grape Tree Road—Seviot **P Morris R Watt & P Emmett**
19 **KNOCKNAGOSHEL (IRE),** 10, b g Kalanisi (IRE)—Granny Clark (IRE) **Knock Knock Syndicate**
20 **LEDHAM (IRE),** 8, b g Shamardal (USA)—Pioneer Bride (USA) **Mr G. Evans**
21 **LILOO D'ORES (FR),** 6, b m Great Pretender (IRE)—Diagora (FR) **Le Soleil Racing**
22 **LOCH GARMAN ARIS (IRE),** 13, b g Jammaal—See Em Aime (IRE) **The Brookes Family**
23 **LOCKDOWN LASS,** 5, b m Albaasil (IRE)—Littlemoor Lass **Lockdown Racing**
24 **LOU TREK (FR),** 9, b g Linda's Lad—Nara Eria (FR) **Mr T. G. Kelly**
25 **MAGHEROARTY STAR (IRE),** 7, b m Watar (IRE)—Cailin Aoibhinn (IRE) **Mr D. O. Pickering**
26 **MALINA OCARINA,** 8, b m Malinas (GER)—Ocarina Davis (FR) **M.H. Racing Malina**
27 **MUSE OF FIRE (IRE),** 9, b g Getaway (GER)—Maria Sophia (IRE) **C. J. Tipton**
28 **O'GRADY'S BOY (IRE),** 12, b g Kalanisi (IRE)—Jemima Jay (IRE) **The Deeside Partnership**
29 **OSCAR NOMINATION (IRE),** 11, b g Getaway (GER)—Nightofthe Oscars (IRE) **The Deeside Partnership**
30 **RAZZO ITALIANO (IRE),** 6, br g Frammassone (IRE)—Funny Fish (FR) **Mrs J. A. Ashley**
31 **SIR TIVO (FR),** 9, b g Deportivo—Miss Possibility (USA) **Mrs J. A. Ashley**
32 **STEEL WAVE (IRE),** 13, br g Craigsteel—Musical Waves (IRE)
33 **STONIFIC (IRE),** 10, b g Sea The Stars (IRE)—Sapphire Pendant (IRE) **Mr S. W. Jones**
34 **STONY MAN (IRE),** 7, b g Getaway (GER)—Answer My Question (IRE) **Lockdown Racing**
35 **SUPERIOR GLANCE,** 8, br m Passing Glance—Qualitee **The Ed-chester Partnership**
36 **TIO MIO (IRE),** 5, b g Teofilo (IRE)—Celeste de La Mer (IRE) **Ovia Racing Group**
37 **WBEE (IRE),** 8, b g Yeats (IRE)—Consultation (IRE) **Mrs M. D. Ritson**
38 **WHAT A TIME (IRE),** 7, b g Fame And Glory—Baden's Firth (IRE) **Steve Mace, Paul Whilock & Mark Hammond**

---

228 MR RICHARD HANNON, Marlborough

Postal: **Herridge Racing Stables, Herridge, Collingbourne Ducis, Wiltshire, SN8 3EG**
Contacts: **WORK 01264 850254 PHONE 01264 850820**
EMAIL kevin@richardhannonracing.co.uk WEBSITE www.richardhannonracing.co.uk

1 **ALWAYS FEARLESS (IRE),** 6, ch g Camacho—Zenella
2 **ARISTIA (IRE),** 5, b m Starspangledbanner (AUS)—Aloisi
3 **BOSH (IRE),** 4, b g Profitable (IRE)—Tropical Mist (IRE)
4 **CHINDIT (IRE),** 5, b h Wootton Bassett—Always A Dream
5 **CIAO ADIOS (IRE),** 4, b f The Gurkha (IRE)—Couragetocontinue (IRE)
6 **DAWN OF LIBERATION (IRE),** 4, b c Churchill (IRE)—Danetime Out (IRE)
7 **DILLYDINGDILLYDONG,** 5, b g Territories (IRE)—Cephalonie (USA)
8 **EHRAZ,** 4, ch g Showcasing—Exrating
9 **ELLADE,** 4, b f Showcasing—Entree
10 **GISBURN (IRE),** 4, ch c Ribchester (IRE)—Disclose
11 **GOD OF THUNDER (IRE),** 4, b g Tagula (IRE)—Tawjeeh
12 **HAPPY ROMANCE (IRE),** 5, b m Dandy Man (IRE)—Rugged Up (IRE)
13 **HEREDIA,** 4, br gr f Dark Angel (IRE)—Nakuti (IRE)
14 **LEXINGTON KNIGHT (IRE),** 5, ch g Night of Thunder (IRE)—Petit Adagio (IRE)
15 **LUSAIL (IRE),** 4, b c Mehmas (IRE)—Diaminda (IRE)
16 **MOJO STAR (IRE),** 5, b h Sea The Stars (IRE)—Galley
17 **MR TYRRELL (IRE),** 9, b g Helmet (AUS)—Rocking
18 **MUGADER,** 4, ch c Olympic Glory (IRE)—Al Anqa
19 **MUMS TIPPLE (IRE),** 6, ch g Footstepsinthesand—Colomone Cross (IRE)
20 **NIGHT ARC,** 4, b c Twilight Son—Gymnaste (IRE)
21 **OH HERBERTS REIGN (IRE),** 4, b g Acclamation—Western Safari (IRE)
22 **OWER STARLIGHT,** 5, b h Cityscape—Rebel Magic
23 **RATTLING,** 4, b f Acclamation—Westadora (IRE)

MR RICHARD HANNON - continued

24 **ROUSAY (IRE),** 4, gr ro f Muhaarar—Ronaldsay
25 **SALCOMBE STORM,** 4, b g Night of Thunder (IRE)—Surprise (IRE)
26 **SIR RUMI (IRE),** 5, ch g Gleneagles (IRE)—Reine des Plages (IRE)
27 **TACARIB BAY,** 4, b c Night of Thunder (IRE)—Bassmah
28 **TAHITIAN PRINCE (FR),** 6, b g Siyouni (FR)—Tehamana (IRE)
29 **THUNDER MAX,** 4, ch g Night of Thunder (IRE)—Tuolumne Meadows
30 **WINDSEEKER,** 4, b g Aclaim (IRE)—Itsinthestars
31 **WITCH HUNTER (FR),** 4, b g Siyouni (FR)—Sorciere (IRE)

THREE-YEAR-OLDS

32 **AJJAJ (FR),** b c Dark Angel (IRE)—Ajayeb (IRE)
33 **AL HARGAH (IRE),** b f Muhaarar—Platinum Pearl
34 **AMARETTI VIRGINIA (IRE),** b f Mehmas (IRE)—Soft Power (IRE)
35 **AUSSI MANDATE,** b f Zoustar (AUS)—Full Mandate (IRE)
36 **BALLYMORE VISION,** b g Night of Thunder (IRE)—Labise (IRE)
37 **CAPTAIN CUDDLES (IRE),** b c Kodiac—Golden Shine
38 **CLASSIC,** b c Dubawi (IRE)—Date With Destiny (IRE)
39 **CONGRESBURY,** b c Unfortunately (IRE)—Eleventh Hour (IRE)
40 **DAAHES (IRE),** b c Oasis Dream—Alghabrah (IRE)
41 **DARK THIRTY (IRE),** b c Starspangledbanner (AUS)—Beach Wedding (IRE)
42 **FAKHRA (IRE),** br f Zoustar (AUS)—Felissa (GER)
43 **FERENSBY,** b f Zoustar (AUS)—Festoso (IRE)
44 **FORCA TIMAO (IRE),** b c Kessaar (IRE)—Belle Diva (IRE)
45 **FOX ISLAND,** b f Territories (IRE)—Round The Cape
46 **GALEXIA,** b f Galileo (IRE)—Illuminate (IRE)
47 **GHASSAN (IRE),** b c Footstepsinthesand—Fine Judgment
48 **GLORY SKY (IRE),** ch f Cotai Glory—Artax Hope (IRE)
49 **GOLD AURA,** b f Golden Horn—Lady Heidi
50 **GRAHAM,** b g Time Test—Gravitation
51 **GREAT BEDWYN,** b c Showcasing—Mistress Quickly (IRE)
52 **GREATEST TIME (IRE),** b c No Nay Never (USA)—Teofilo's Princess (IRE)
53 **HAWAJES (IRE),** b c Mehmas (IRE)—Strange Magic (IRE)
54 **HECTIC,** b g Massaat (IRE)—Ceedwell
55 **IMMORTAL BEAUTY (IRE),** b f Cotai Glory—Invincible Me (IRE)
56 **ISLAND LUCK,** b c Havana Gold (IRE)—Golden Spell
57 **KING SHARJA,** b c Kingman—Sharja Queen
58 **KING'S CODE,** b c Saxon Warrior (JPN)—Polygon (USA)
59 **KING'S CONQUEST (IRE),** b c Kingman—Nashmiah (IRE)
60 **LADY AMANDA (IRE),** b f Camacho—Lido Lady (IRE)
61 **LAND OF SUMMER (IRE),** br gr f Clodovil (IRE)—Deora De
62 **LE MANS (IRE),** b f Kodiac—Diaminda (IRE)
63 **LULWORTH COVE (IRE),** b f New Bay—Areeda (IRE)
64 **MAGICAL SUNSET (IRE),** b f Kodiac—Fikrah
65 **MAJOR MAJOR (IRE),** b c Iffraaj—Spinaminnie (IRE)
66 **MAMAN JOON (IRE),** ch f Sea The Stars (IRE)—Dorcas Lane
67 **MAMMAS GIRL,** ch f Havana Grey—Mamma Morton (IRE)
68 **MANUELITO,** b c Cracksman—Navajo Charm
69 **MEHME (IRE),** b f Acclamation—Lucina
70 **MINDTHEGAP (IRE),** b c Kodiac—Pashmina (IRE)
71 **MINNETONKA (IRE),** b f Kingman—Perfect Angel (IRE)
72 **MOCHI (IRE),** gr f Acclamation—Free To Roam (IRE)
73 **MORCAR,** b c Saxon Warrior (JPN)—Loved So Much
74 **ONE NIGHT THUNDER,** ch c Night of Thunder (IRE)—Elis Eliz (IRE)
75 **ONSLOW GARDENS (IRE),** br g Footstepsinthesand—Just Darcy
76 **OPTIVA STAR (IRE),** b c U S Navy Flag (USA)—Leaf (IRE)
77 **ORIENTAL DANCER,** ch f Dubawi (IRE)—Geisha Girl (IRE)
78 **OUTRACE (IRE),** ch c Camacho—Trace of Scent (IRE)
79 **PALAMON (IRE),** ch c Decorated Knight—Seschat (IRE)
80 **PEACEFUL STORY (IRE),** b f Churchill (IRE)—Divisimo

MR RICHARD HANNON - continued

81 **PINK LILY,** ch f Sixties Icon—Mellow
82 **PLAYACTOR,** b c Make Believe—Say To Me (FR)
83 **POWERDRESS (IRE),** b f Dandy Man (IRE)—Nuclear Option (IRE)
84 **PRETTY PEG (IRE),** b f Awtaad (IRE)—Letizia (IRE)
85 **PRIDE OF SPAIN (IRE),** ch c Lope de Vega (IRE)—Pride (FR)
86 **PRINCE MAXI (IRE),** ch c Sea The Stars (IRE)—Soltada (IRE)
87 **PURPLE LOVE (FR),** b f Wootton Bassett—Ajou (FR)
88 **REVISIT,** b f Invincible Spirit (IRE)—You're Back (USA)
89 **RICH,** ch f Cracksman—Mademoiselle Marie (FR)
90 **ROMAN SPRING (IRE),** br c Caravaggio (USA)—Aurora Spring (IRE)
91 **ROYAL DRESS (IRE),** b f Night of Thunder (IRE)—Wadaa (USA)
92 **SALOMON PICO (FR),** b c Almanzor (FR)—Alta Stima (IRE)
93 **SAM'S HOPE,** b f Awtaad (IRE)—Delightful Belle (USA)
94 **SEDUCTIVE POWER (IRE),** b c Kodi Bear (IRE)—Final Treat (IRE)
95 **SHOULDVEBEENARING,** gr c Havana Grey—Lady Estella (IRE)
96 **SIGNCASTLE CITY (IRE),** gr c Dark Angel (IRE)—Uae Queen
97 **SKALLYWAG BAY,** gr f Havana Grey—Bassmah
98 **STAMFORD BLUE (IRE),** b c Fast Company (IRE)—Chelsea Corsage (IRE)
99 **STARNBERG (IRE),** b g Clodovil (IRE)—Taaluf (IRE)
100 **SUPREME KING (IRE),** b c Kingman—Alsindi (IRE)
101 **SWIFT ASSET (IRE),** b c Profitable (IRE)—Flick Show (IRE)
102 **TALIS EVOLVERE (IRE),** b c Awtaad (IRE)—My Henrietta (USA)
103 **TALISMAN,** b c Cracksman—Tamaanee (AUS)
104 **TAMANGO SANDS (IRE),** b g Footstepsinthesand—Couragetocontinue (IRE)
105 **THE BIG BOARD (IRE),** b f Profitable (IRE)—Singapore Lilly (IRE)
106 **THE PARENT,** b c Frankel—Sophie P
107 **THREEBARS (IRE),** ch f Cotai Glory—Lady Mega (IRE)
108 **TRILLIUM,** b f No Nay Never (USA)—Marsh Hawk
109 **TUJJAAR,** b c Frankel—Tajaanus (IRE)
110 **VASILISSA,** b f Kingman—Nakuti (IRE)
111 **VIRTUAL DREAM (IRE),** b f Camelot—Quixotic
112 **WALLOP (IRE),** b c Harry Angel (IRE)—Samaah (IRE)
113 **YELLOW LION,** b c Bobby's Kitten (USA)—Fair Value (IRE)
114 **YELLOW STAR (FR),** b c Sea The Moon (GER)—Aliyfa (IRE)
115 **YESISAIDYES (IRE),** b c Ulysses (IRE)—Endless Love (IRE)
116 **ZABBIE,** b f Poet's Word (IRE)—Barnezet (GR)

TWO-YEAR-OLDS

117 B c 08/02 Kodi Bear (IRE)—Agent Allison (Dutch Art)
118 B c 08/03 Soldier's Call—Ahazeej (IRE) (Dubawi (IRE)) (57143)
119 B f 02/03 Inns of Court (IRE)—Airbrush (IRE) (Camacho) (72000)
120 **AL DURRA,** b f 08/02 Sea The Moon (GER)—Temida (IRE) (Oratorio (IRE)) (100000)
121 B f 02/02 Kodiac—Anything Goes (IRE) (Nayef (USA)) (70000)
122 **ARAMRAM (IRE),** b c 30/03 Blue Point (IRE)—Queen's Pearl (IRE) (Exceed And Excel (AUS))
123 **ARDARA ROSE (IRE),** b f 15/03 Churchill (IRE)—Zenara (IRE) (Sea The Stars (IRE)) (24010)
124 B f 11/04 Blue Point (IRE)—Belle Dauphine (Dalakhani (IRE)) (65000)
125 **BLUE COLLAR (IRE),** b c 08/03 Starspangledbanner (AUS)—Navigate By Stars (IRE) (Sea The Stars (IRE)) (135000)
126 B f 04/02 No Nay Never (USA)—Bolshina (Galileo (IRE))
127 **BOYFRIEND,** b c 21/02 Twilight Son—Tallow (IRE) (Kodiac)
128 B c 07/04 No Nay Never (USA)—Bright Eyed (IRE) (Galileo (IRE))
129 **BRIGHT FIRE (IRE),** b c 28/04 Kessaar (IRE)—Shushu Sugartown (IRE) (Invincible Spirit (IRE)) (40016)
130 Gr c 12/04 Saxon Warrior (JPN)—Cay Dancer (Danehill Dancer (IRE))
131 **CHEQUERS COURT,** b c 28/02 Belardo (IRE)—Fanfair (Royal Applause)
132 B c 02/05 No Nay Never (USA)—Chrissycross (IRE) (Cape Cross (IRE)) (115000)
133 **CHRISTIAN DAVID (IRE),** b c 11/02 Profitable (IRE)—Liberty Sky (IRE) (Rip Van Winkle (IRE)) (49524)
134 **CLAXTON BAY,** b c 10/02 Due Diligence (USA)—Bassmah (Harbour Watch (IRE))
135 B c 10/04 Dandy Man (IRE)—Colgin (Canford Cliffs (IRE)) (72000)
136 **COMMANDER CROUCH (IRE),** b c 20/04 Mehmas (IRE)—Seven Magicians (USA) (Silver Hawk (USA)) (45000)
137 **COUSIN MARY,** b f 24/04 Advertise—Raggety Ann (IRE) (Galileo (IRE)) (75000)

MR RICHARD HANNON - continued

138 DARK VIPER, b gr c 18/03 Dark Angel (IRE)—Grande Bleue (IRE) (Oasis Dream) (76190)
139 B f 23/03 Cotai Glory—Diaminda (IRE) (Diamond Green (FR)) (240000)
140 DIMSONS (IRE), ch c 02/03 Footstepsinthesand—Herridge (IRE) (Bahamian Bounty) (47619)
141 B f 17/03 Profitable (IRE)—Dream Craft (IRE) (Mastercraftsman (IRE)) (19048)
142 B c 24/03 Crystal Ocean—Dream of The Hill (IRE) (Tiger Hill (IRE)) (50000)
143 DUBAWI DREAM, b f 21/02 Dubawi (IRE)—Elasia (Nathaniel (IRE))
144 B c 19/04 Dandy Man (IRE)—Duchess of Foxland (IRE) (Medecis) (47619)
145 B f 04/03 Kodiac—Elmaliya (IRE) (Sepoy (AUS)) (40952)
146 FINALLY (IRE), gr f 22/04 Clodovil (IRE)—Scarlet Wings (Sir Percy) (37000)
147 B f 01/04 Dandy Man (IRE)—Floating Along (IRE) (Oasis Dream) (42857)
148 GAIDEN (IRE), b f 11/02 Mehmas (IRE)—Silque (Aqlaam) (61905)
149 B c 31/03 Twilight Son—Glitter Girl (Invincible Spirit (IRE)) (110000)
150 B c 02/03 Phoenix of Spain (IRE)—Hard Walnut (IRE) (Cape Cross (IRE)) (27000)
151 HATADORA (IRE), b f 09/02 Invincible Army (IRE)—Senadora (GER) (Tertullian (USA)) (60000)
152 HEARTFULLOFSTARS (IRE), b f 24/03 Starspangledbanner (AUS)—Kendamara (FR) (Kendargent (FR)) (100040)
153 HOUSTONN, b c 27/01 Expert Eye—Moment In Time (IRE) (Tiger Hill (IRE)) (90000)
154 JOLLY SAILOR, b c 08/02 Adaay (IRE)—Rahaaba (IRE) (Dubawi (IRE)) (16000)
155 B c 28/02 Profitable (IRE)—Kasankaya (IRE) (Raven's Pass (USA)) (64762)
156 B f 06/03 Acclamation—Kiss of Spring (IRE) (Dansili) (58000)
157 B c 29/04 Waldgeist—Lady Livius (IRE) (Titus Livius (FR)) (55000)
158 B c 11/03 Time Test—Leonica (Lion Cavern (USA)) (35000)
159 LIV MY LIFE (IRE), b f 02/02 Awtaad (IRE)—My Wish (IRE) (Galileo (IRE)) (48019)
160 LOCAL HERO (IRE), ch c 12/04 Phoenix of Spain (IRE)—Pearl Diva (IRE) (Acclamation) (37000)
161 LOVE BILLY BOY (IRE), b c 20/02 Invincible Army (IRE)—Katrine (IRE) (Kodiac) (85714)
162 LYRAISA, b f 23/04 Masar (IRE)—Sagres (Henrythenavigator (USA)) (95000)
163 B c 31/03 Advertise—Mama Rocco (Shirocco (GER)) (20000)
164 B c 11/04 Kodi Bear (IRE)—Manaahil (Dubawi (IRE)) (42000)
165 B f 21/02 Sioux Nation (USA)—Midnight Martini (Night Shift (USA)) (40000)
166 B c 23/03 Due Diligence (USA)—Miskin Diamond (IRE) (Diamond Green (FR)) (20952)
167 MISS IDUNN (IRE), b f 31/03 Acclamation—Winter Snow (IRE) (Raven's Pass (USA))
168 MORE LIGHT, b f 18/03 Dream Ahead (USA)—Illuminate (IRE) (Zoffany (IRE))
169 NEW KINGS ROAD (IRE), b c 05/03 Sioux Nation (USA)—Thistlestar (USA) (Lion Heart (USA)) (57623)
170 B c 16/03 Ten Sovereigns (IRE)—Nigh (IRE) (Galileo (IRE)) (72029)
171 NOTTA NOTHER, gr c 12/02 Havana Grey—Tulip Dress (Dutch Art) (56022)
172 ODIN LEGACY (IRE), b c 31/03 Kodiac—Fikrah (Medicean) (460184)
173 B c 08/03 Mehmas (IRE)—Opinionated Lady (IRE) (Society Rock (IRE)) (100000)
174 B c 10/02 Awtaad (IRE)—Oriental Step (IRE) (Tamayuz) (69628)
175 B f 11/02 Blue Point (IRE)—Pacific Angel (IRE) (Dalakhani (IRE)) (80000)
176 PANNONICA (IRE), b f 11/03 Acclamation—Spring Leaf (FR) (Footstepsinthesand) (52381)
177 B c 31/03 Galileo (IRE)—Perfect Angel (IRE) (Dark Angel (IRE))
178 PERSICA (IRE), ch c 12/02 New Bay—Rubira (AUS) (Lope de Vega (IRE)) (190476)
179 PILOTO PARDO (IRE), b c 11/02 Bated Breath—Ivory Charm (Charm Spirit (IRE)) (55238)
180 PINK FIZZ, ch f 06/03 Masar (IRE)—Lipstick Rose (IRE) (Dream Ahead (USA)) (32000)
181 B c 09/04 Due Diligence (USA)—Primrose Place (Compton Place) (20000)
182 B f 27/01 Justify (USA)—Pushkinskaya (IRE) (Galileo (IRE))
183 QANDIL (IRE), ch f 17/04 Churchill (IRE)—Sweet Firebird (IRE) (Sadler's Wells (USA)) (32000)
184 B c 24/02 Kingman—Rayaheen (Nayef (USA))
185 B c 14/03 Blue Point (IRE)—Roman Venture (IRE) (Holy Roman Emperor (IRE)) (130000)
186 ROSALLION (IRE), b c 14/04 Blue Point (IRE)—Rosaline (IRE) (New Approach (IRE))
187 B c 11/03 Blue Point (IRE)—Sar Oiche (IRE) (Teofilo (IRE)) (160000)
188 SEDGEMOOR (IRE), b c 04/02 Churchill (IRE)—Kemble (IRE) (Kodiac) (40016)
189 B c 20/04 Cable Bay (IRE)—Sefaat (Haatef (USA))
190 SHEILA'S PARADISE, gr c 16/02 Havana Grey—Sheila's Rock (IRE) (Fastnet Rock (AUS)) (80952)
191 B c 26/02 Inns of Court (IRE)—Shoshoni Wind (Sleeping Indian) (80000)
192 SHOW BIZ KID (IRE), b c 09/04 Acclamation—Fashion Theory (Dubawi (IRE)) (55000)
193 SIGHTER, b f 24/03 Expert Eye—Tanouma (USA) (Mr Greeley (USA)) (64026)
194 Ch c 20/02 American Pharoah (USA)—Sizzling (IRE) (Galileo (IRE))
195 B f 03/03 Siyouni (FR)—So Hi Society (IRE) (Society Rock (IRE)) (150000)
196 B c 18/02 Blue Point (IRE)—Solar Event (Galileo (IRE)) (130000)
197 SON, b c 19/01 Too Darn Hot—Mia Diletta (Selkirk (USA))

MR RICHARD HANNON - continued

198 SPECIALISATION, b c 15/03 Dubawi (IRE)—Jumira Princess (IRE) (Redoute's Choice (AUS))
199 Gr c 03/03 Dark Angel (IRE)—Star Approval (IRE) (Hawk Wing (USA)) (190476)
200 STAR STYLE, b f 13/03 Zoustar (AUS)—Sweet Cecily (IRE) (Kodiac)
201 B c 04/03 Dandy Man (IRE)—Tauriel (IRE) (Sea The Stars (IRE)) (40016)
202 TIMEBAR, b c 04/03 Time Test—Barnezet (GR) (Invincible Spirit (IRE))
203 VENI VIDI VINCI (IRE), b f 16/04 Invincible Army (IRE)—Lisa Gherardini (IRE) (Barathea (IRE)) (42857)
204 Ch c 24/04 Footstepsinthesand—Venus de Medici (IRE) (Duke of Marmalade (IRE)) (40016)
205 B c 25/02 Inns of Court (IRE)—Vexatious (IRE) (Shamardal (USA)) (92000)
206 VOYAGE, b c 15/03 Golden Horn—Too In Love (IRE) (Galileo (IRE))
207 B f 08/02 Adaay (IRE)—Walaaa (IRE) (Exceed And Excel (AUS)) (40000)
208 WESTERN (IRE), b c 15/02 Magna Grecia (IRE)—Murhibaany (USA) (Elusive Quality (USA)) (80032)
209 Ch f 12/03 New Bay—Whispered Dreams (USA) (Mr Greeley (USA)) (44818)

Head Girl: Emma Christian, **Head Man:** Tony Gorman, **Racing Secretary:** Kevin Mason.

Flat Jockey: Pat Dobbs, Sean Levey, Rossa Ryan. **Apprentice Jockey:** Tyrese Cameron, Joe Leavy, Alec Voikhansky.

229

MR GEOFFREY HARKER, Thirsk

Postal: **Stockhill Green, York Rd, Thirkelby, Thirsk, North Yorkshire, YO7 3AS**
Contacts: **PHONE 01845 501117 MOBILE 07803 116412, 07930 125544**
EMAIL gandjhome@aol.com WEBSITE www.geoffharkerracing.com

1 **ELDELBAR (SPA),** 9, ch g Footstepsinthesand—Malinche **Mr G. A. Harker**
2 **HAIL SEZER,** 6, b g Intrinsic—Nice One **Mr G. A. Harker**
3 **MUDAMER (IRE),** 4, gr g Dark Angel (IRE)—Mesadah (IRE) **P. I. Harker**
4 **ROCKET ROD (IRE),** 6, b g Australia—Tessa Reef (IRE) **Mr G. A. Harker**
5 **RUM RUNNER,** 8, b g Havana Gold (IRE)—Thermopylae **Mr G. A. Harker**
6 **SCOTTISH SUMMIT (IRE),** 10, b g Shamardal (USA)—Scottish Stage (IRE) **T Banerjee,N Mather & G Harker**
7 **WENTWORTH FALLS,** 11, gr g Dansili—Strawberry Morn (CAN) **The Fall Guys Club**

Assistant Trainer: Jenny Harker.

NH Jockey: W. T. Kennedy.

230

MR RICHARD HARPER, Kings Sutton

Postal: **Home Farm, Kings Sutton, Banbury, Oxfordshire, OX17 3RS**
Contacts: **PHONE 01295 810997 MOBILE 07970 223481**
EMAIL richard@harpersfarm.co.uk

1 **STORM RISING (IRE),** 10, b g Canford Cliffs (IRE)—Before The Storm **R. C. Harper**
2 **THOMAS BLOSSOM (IRE),** 13, b g Dylan Thomas (IRE)—Woman Secret (IRE) **R. C. Harper**
3 **WEE WILLIE NAIL (IRE),** 5, b g Yeats (IRE)—Siba de La Pampa (FR) **& Harper**

Assistant Trainer: C. Harper.

---

231 MRS JESSICA HARRINGTON, Kildare

Postal: **Commonstown Stud, Moone, Co. Kildare, Ireland**
Contacts: **PHONE +353 59 862 4153 MOBILE +353 87 256 6129**
EMAIL jessica@jessicaharringtonracing.com WEBSITE www.jessicaharringtonracing.com

1 **ARUNTOTHEQUEEN (IRE),** 4, b br f Milan—Burn And Turn (IRE)
2 **ASHDALE BOB (IRE),** 8, b g Shantou (USA)—Ceol Rua (IRE)
3 **ASHDALE FLYER (IRE),** 4, b f Walk In The Park (IRE)—Miss Brandywell (IRE)
4 **AUTUMN EVENING,** 6, ch g Tamayuz—Martagon Lily
5 **BABY CHOU (IRE),** 5, b m Sholokhov (IRE)—Angel Lopez (IRE)
6 **BOOLA BOOLA (IRE),** 6, b g Invincible Spirit (IRE)—We Can Say It Now (AUS)
7 **CHANGING THE RULES (IRE),** 6, b g Walk In The Park (IRE)—Blooming Quick (IRE)
8 **HURRICANE IVOR (IRE),** 6, b g Ivawood (IRE)—Quickstep Queen
9 **IRISH LULLABY,** 4, gr f Nathaniel (IRE)—Victoria Regina (IRE)
10 **IT'S SNOWING (IRE),** 4, b ro f Kodiac—Snow Pixie (USA)
11 **JEKIKI (IRE),** 5, b m Soldier of Fortune (IRE)—Jeree (IRE)
12 **JETARA (IRE),** 5, b m Walk In The Park (IRE)—Jelan (IRE)
13 **JUNGLE COVE (IRE),** 6, gr g Mastercraftsman (IRE)—Purple Glow (IRE)
14 **JUNGLE JUNCTION (IRE),** 8, br g Elusive Pimpernel (USA)—Consignia (IRE)
15 **LIFETIME AMBITION,** 8, b g Kapgarde—Jeanquiri
16 **MAC'S XPRESS (IRE),** 5, ch g Mount Nelson—Snob's Supreme (IRE)
17 **MANHATTAN LADY (IRE),** 5, b br m Robin des Champs (FR)—Manhattan Babe (IRE)
18 **MARIE PHILIPPE (IRE),** 5, b m Flemensfirth (USA)—Fleur d'Ainay (FR)
19 **MAUD GONNE SPIRIT (IRE),** 6, ch m Intello—Bari
20 **MELLOW MAGIC,** 5, b m Nathaniel (IRE)—Lady Brora
21 **MIGHTY MO MISSOURI (IRE),** 4, b g Zoffany (IRE)—What Say You (IRE)
22 **NICKY'S CHAMP (IRE),** 4, b g Champs Elysees—Zaafran
23 **NJORD (IRE),** 7, b g Roderic O'Connor—Rosalind Franklin
24 **PORT STANLEY (IRE),** 9, b g Papal Bull—Prairie Moonlight (GER)
25 **PRINCESS RAJJ,** 4, b f Rajj (IRE)—Princess Aloof (IRE)
26 **QUEEN OF SEDUCTION (IRE),** 4, b f Mastercraftsman (IRE)—Supreme Seductress (IRE)
27 **SCARLET GRACE (IRE),** 4, b f Elusive Pimpernel (USA)—Alabama Rose (IRE)
28 **SHONA MEA (IRE),** 6, b m Dragon Pulse (IRE)—Weekend Getaway (IRE)
29 **SIERRA NEVADA (USA),** 4, b f American Pharoah (USA)—Visions of Clarity (IRE)
30 **STRIKING (FR),** 5, b g Equiano (FR)—Distinctive Look (IRE)
31 **SUMMER GALE (IRE),** 5, b g Camelot—Luas Line (IRE)
32 **TAIPAN (FR),** 5, b h Frankel—Kenzadargent (FR)
33 **THE VERY MAN (IRE),** 9, b g Jeremy (USA)—Mill Meadow (IRE)
34 **TREVAUNANCE (IRE),** 4, b f Muhaarar—Liber Nauticus (IRE)
35 **VALKYRIE GRAY (IRE),** 4, gr f Caravaggio (USA)—Flaming Sea (IRE)
36 **VILLANOVA QUEEN (IRE),** 4, ch f Mastercraftsman (IRE)—Quads (IRE)
37 **YASHIN (IRE),** 4, b c Churchill (IRE)—Mirdhak

THREE-YEAR-OLDS

38 **ALALCANCE,** gr f Mastercraftsman (IRE)—Albamara
39 **ANGELIC APPEAL (IRE),** b f Siyouni (FR)—Gabrielle (FR)
40 **AUTOLINE (IRE),** b c Exceed And Excel (AUS)—Mzyoon (IRE)
41 **BEAUTY'S STAR (IRE),** b f Starspangledbanner (AUS)—Belle de Neige (IRE)
42 **BEYOND THE STEPS (IRE),** b c Footstepsinthesand—Queen of Carthage (USA)
43 **BLANC DE NOIR (IRE),** b c Showcasing—Blanc de Chine (IRE)
44 **BOLD DISCOVERY (USA),** b c Bolt D'oro (USA)—Caribbean Babe (USA)
45 **CHILLAXING (IRE),** ch c Galileo (IRE)—Danetime Out (IRE)
46 **COSMIC LADY (IRE),** gr f Mastercraftsman (IRE)—Lady of The Lamp (IRE)
47 **CURVATURE (IRE),** ch f Lope de Vega (IRE)—Gravitee (FR)
48 **DANVERS GOLD (IRE),** gr f Galileo (IRE)—Mrs Danvers
49 **DUBAWI DELIGHT,** b g Dubawi (IRE)—Attraction
50 **DUBAWI SPECTRE,** b g Dubawi (IRE)—Spectre (FR)
51 **ENDLESS SUNSHINE (IRE),** b f Churchill (IRE)—Crazy Volume (IRE)
52 **ETERNAL SILENCE (USA),** b f War Front (USA)—Princess Highway (USA)
53 **FEATHERTOP,** b f Australia—Mt of Beatitudes (IRE)
54 **FIRST GENTLEMAN (IRE),** b c Camacho—Floriade (IRE)

MRS JESSICA HARRINGTON - continued

55 FONISKA (IRE), b f Galileo (IRE)—Bocca Baciata (IRE)
56 GALILEO'S COMPASS (IRE), b c Galileo (IRE)—Lady Lara (IRE)
57 HARDPOINT (IRE), b c Camelot—Los Ojitos (USA)
58 KINGS TIME (IRE), ch c Exceed And Excel (AUS)—Mrs King (IRE)
59 KISS ME DIXIE (IRE), b f Galileo (IRE)—Dixieland Kiss (USA)
60 LADY PRO, ch f Gleneagles (IRE)—Lamyaa
61 LAN CINNTE (IRE), b f Saxon Warrior (JPN)—Yellowhammer
62 LOVE MOCHA, br f Awtaad (IRE)—Nabaraat (USA)
63 MISS YVONNE (IRE), ch f Churchill (IRE)—Bright Snow (USA)
64 NATIONAL EMBLEM (IRE), b c National Defense—Clenaghcastle Lady (IRE)
65 NELDA (IRE), b f Dark Angel (IRE)—Choose Me (IRE)
66 NEOWISE (USA), b f Recoletos (FR)—Ode To Psyche (IRE)
67 NET A PORTER QUEEN (IRE), br f Sioux Nation (USA)—La Fee Verte (IRE)
68 NEW PHENOMENON (IRE), b f Churchill (IRE)—Queenscliff (IRE)
69 NIGHT BLUE (IRE), b f Sioux Nation (USA)—Takaliyda (IRE)
70 NORTH DORSET, b g Oasis Dream—Sandstone
71 OCEAN QUEST (IRE), ch f Sioux Nation (USA)—Gold Zain
72 ONE BOSS, b f Saxon Warrior (JPN)—Encore L'Amour
73 PANIC ALARM (IRE), br g Kuroshio (AUS)—Thraya Queen
74 PARIS REVIEW (IRE), b f Zoffany (IRE)—Allez Y (IRE)
75 PIGEON HOUSE (IRE), ch g Saxon Warrior (JPN)—Zaitana (IRE)
76 PIVOTAL REVIVE, ro gr c Pivotal—Tigrilla (IRE)
77 PIVOTAL TRIGGER, ch c Pivotal—Allegretto (IRE)
78 POLAR BEAR (IRE), b g Kodi Bear (IRE)—Blue Marmalade (IRE)
79 PORTREATH (IRE), b g Kodiac—Liber Nauticus (IRE)
80 QUAR SHAMAR (GER), ch c Shamardal (USA)—Quariana (GER)
81 ROCHESTER MIKE (IRE), b c Wootton Bassett—Siderante (FR)
82 ROMAN HANDS (IRE), b c Holy Roman Emperor (IRE)—Rhigolter Rose (IRE)
83 SATIN, ch f Australia—Countryside
84 SATURN (IRE), gr c Galileo (IRE)—Alpha Centauri (IRE)
85 SCARLETT O'HARA (FR), b f Frankel—Dream of Tara (IRE)
86 SEA SPRAY, b c Zoustar (AUS)—Wingingit (IRE)
87 SIMPSON'S PARADOX (IRE), b c Mastercraftsman (IRE)—Alpha Lupi (IRE)
88 SMALL OASIS, b f Sioux Nation (USA)—Collegiate (IRE)
89 SNOWCAPPED (IRE), b br f Churchill (IRE)—Snow Pixie (USA)
90 SNOWHAVEN (IRE), b f Le Havre (IRE)—Sandsnow (IRE)
91 SOUNDS OF HEAVEN, b f Kingman—Ring The Bell (IRE)
92 SPIRIT GENIE (IRE), b c Invincible Spirit (IRE)—Prima Luce (IRE)
93 SPIRIT OF PARADISE (IRE), b f Invincible Spirit (IRE)—The Sky Is Blazing (IRE)
94 SPREWELL (IRE), b c Churchill (IRE)—Lahaleeb (IRE)
95 STARIAM (IRE), ch f Sea The Stars (IRE)—I Am (IRE)
96 STARRY HEAVENS (IRE), gr f Mastercraftsman (IRE)—Etoile Filante
97 SUNDAY EVENING (IRE), b f Fastnet Rock (AUS)—Evening Rain (USA)
98 THE FIRST AND LAST (IRE), b c No Nay Never (USA)—Princess Sinead (IRE)
99 TIMELESS PIECE (IRE), b f Saxon Warrior (JPN)—Cosmodrome (USA)
100 VILLAGE VOICE, b f Zarak (FR)—Sensible Way (USA)
101 B f Intilaaq (USA)—Waseefa
102 YOUCRACKMEUP, b f Cracksman—Epic Emirates
103 YUZU, b f Daiwa Major (JPN)—Diaphora (GER)

TWO-YEAR-OLDS

104 B c 13/03 Time Test—Amami (IRE) (Peintre Celebre (USA)) (52000)
105 ANNUPURI, b f 10/03 Too Darn Hot—Mirror City (Street Cry (IRE)) (120000)
106 BETULA, ch f 01/03 Lope de Vega (IRE)—Galileo Gal (IRE) (Galileo (IRE))
107 CAMELOT ALEXANDER (IRE), b f 04/03 Camelot—Remember Alexander (Teofilo (IRE)) (100000)
108 B f 30/04 Fastnet Rock (AUS)—Celestial Beast (USA) (Kitten's Joy (USA)) (100000)
109 B c 30/03 Kodi Bear (IRE)—Dat Il Do (Bahamian Bounty) (60000)
110 Ch f 14/03 Pearl Secret—Dreamily (IRE) (New Approach (IRE))
111 EARTH (IRE), gr f 09/03 Galileo (IRE)—Alpha Centauri (IRE) (Mastercraftsman (IRE))

MRS JESSICA HARRINGTON - continued

112 EL REGALO (IRE), b c 12/04 Australia—Minnie Haha (FR) (Style Vendome (FR)) (17607)
113 EXCILLA (IRE), b f 28/04 Exceed And Excel (AUS)—Almira Wells (IRE) (High Chaparral (IRE))
114 B f 30/04 Dark Angel (IRE)—Fashionable (Nashwan (USA)) (60024)
115 Ch f 26/03 New Bay—Findhorn Magic (Kyllachy) (40016)
116 B c 25/03 Siyouni (FR)—Flora Danica (IRE) (Galileo (IRE)) (188075)
117 Ch f 07/03 Starspangledbanner (AUS)—Green Castle (IRE) (Indian Ridge)
118 HIGHLAND BLING (IRE), b c 09/03 Highland Reel (IRE)—Padma (Three Valleys (USA)) (17607)
119 B f 14/02 Teofilo (IRE)—Hymn of The Dawn (USA) (Phone Trick (USA)) (196078)
120 B f 10/04 Frankel—Improve (IRE) (Iffraaj) (232093)
121 B f 04/05 No Nay Never (USA)—Inca Wood (UAE) (Timber Country (USA)) (120048)
122 B f 25/02 Holy Roman Emperor (IRE)—Jeanne Girl (IRE) (Rip Van Winkle (IRE)) (32013)
123 B c 11/02 Study of Man (IRE)—Kinaesthesia (Sea The Stars (IRE)) (52021)
124 Br c 03/05 Holy Roman Emperor (IRE)—La Folie (IRE) (Footstepsinthesand) (38415)
125 B f 29/05 Galileo (IRE)—Laugh Out Loud (Clodovil (IRE)) (675000)
126 B c 30/03 Due Diligence (USA)—Livella Fella (IRE) (Strategic Prince) (36815)
127 B c 30/04 Kodiac—Lumi (IRE) (Canford Cliffs (IRE)) (40000)
128 MATTER OF FACT (IRE), b f 26/03 No Nay Never (USA)—Malicieuse (IRE) (Galileo (IRE))
129 B f 17/02 Ten Sovereigns (IRE)—Mississippilanding (IRE) (Galileo (IRE)) (76030)
130 MO GHILLE MAR (IRE), b f 22/02 Zoffany (IRE)—First Love (IRE) (Galileo (IRE)) (30412)
131 B c 03/04 Advertise—Moment of Time (Rainbow Quest (USA)) (78000)
132 B f 04/02 Australia—Moonrise Landing (IRE) (Dalakhani (IRE))
133 B f 21/03 National Defense—Myth Creation (USA) (More Than Ready (USA)) (37000)
134 NORWALK HAVOC, ch c 04/02 Showcasing—Light of Joy (USA) (Kitten's Joy (USA))
135 OLD SEA (IRE), b c 05/05 Blue Point (IRE)—Liber Nauticus (IRE) (Azamour (IRE))
136 B f 05/04 Mehmas (IRE)—One For June (IRE) (Arcano (IRE)) (26411)
137 B c 09/04 Magna Grecia (IRE)—Prosper (Exceed And Excel (AUS)) (32013)
138 Gr f 14/03 Phoenix of Spain (IRE)—Queen of Carthage (USA) (Cape Cross (IRE))
139 B f 01/05 Night of Thunder (IRE)—Rapacity Alexander (IRE) (Dandy Man (IRE)) (420168)
140 REHEARSAL (IRE), b f 29/04 Calyx—Melodrama (IRE) (Oratorio (IRE))
141 RIVIERA QUEEN (IRE), gr f 04/03 Camelot—Pakora (FR) (Gentlewave (IRE)) (112045)
142 B c 14/02 Profitable (IRE)—Rosy Morning (IRE) (Exceed And Excel (AUS)) (24810)
143 B f 21/04 Time Test—Salome (FR) (Fuisse (FR)) (40016)
144 SEA THE BOSS, ch f 21/01 Sea The Moon (GER)—Shaella (IRE) (Casamento (IRE)) (28011)
145 SEPTEMBER LEAVES (IRE), b f 05/05 Night of Thunder (IRE)—Antique Platinum (IRE) (Holy Roman Emperor (IRE))
146 SERIALISE (IRE), ch f 28/02 Footstepsinthesand—Dramatise (IRE) (Intikhab (USA))
147 B c 23/04 Lope de Vega (IRE)—She's Complete (IRE) (Oratorio (IRE))
148 B f 05/03 Gleneagles (IRE)—Shenanigans (IRE) (Arcano (IRE)) (112045)
149 B c 19/05 Galileo (IRE)—Snow Queen (IRE) (Danehill Dancer (IRE)) (144058)
150 SOLAR DRIVE (IRE), gr c 14/04 Mastercraftsman (IRE)—Trimurti (USA) (Harlan's Holiday (USA))
151 Ch c 28/04 Showcasing—Solfilia (Teofilo (IRE)) (160064)
152 B f 22/03 Kingman—Starfish (IRE) (Galileo (IRE))
153 STARRY DEW, gr f 20/02 Caravaggio (USA)—Etoile Filante (So You Think (NZ))
154 B f 05/04 War Front (USA)—Tocco d'Amore (IRE) (Raven's Pass (USA))
155 B f 11/02 Too Darn Hot—Transhumance (IRE) (Galileo (IRE)) (80032)
156 B f 12/04 Frankel—Vagabonde (IRE) (Acclamation) (200080)
157 B c 10/03 Al Rifai (IRE)—Venturous Spirit (IRE) (Invincible Spirit (IRE))
158 Br gr f 23/02 Caravaggio (USA)—Vivere (IRE) (Montjeu (IRE)) (21609)
159 B c 17/03 Al Rifai (IRE)—Wasmiya (Frankel)
160 B f 24/04 Sioux Nation (USA)—Way of Light (IRE) (Dylan Thomas (IRE)) (34414)

Assistant Trainer: Miss Kate Harrington, Eamonn Leigh.

232 MISS CLAIRE LOUISE HARRIS, Umberleigh

Postal: **Langridge Farm, Atherington , Barnstaple , Devon, EX37 9HP**
Contacts: **PHONE 07458 381716**
EMAIL clharris1986@hotmail.co.uk

1 **BREFFNIBOY (FR),** 9, b g Sageburg (IRE)—Dawn Cat (USA) **F. A. Clegg**
2 **CHRISTOPHER CLIVE,** 5, b g Mountain High (IRE)—Badb Catha (IRE) **Mr G. F. Mugleston**
3 **COLONEL LESLEY (IRE),** 7, gr g Lilbourne Lad (IRE)—Tagula Mon (IRE) **F. A. Clegg**
4 **FLUTISTE (FR),** 8, b g Secret Singer (FR)—Nanny (FR) **Mr M. G. Tucker**
5 **GETALEAD (IRE),** 7, b g Getaway (GER)—Site-Leader (IRE) **Pickard Racing Club**
6 **INCHAGOILL LADY (IRE),** 7, ch m Mahler—Kitty The Hare (IRE) **Pickard Racing**
7 **STOPHERANDGO (IRE),** 6, b m Aizavoski (IRE)—
Bonjour Bella (IRE) **Langridgefarm Racing Gin Light Syndicate**

---

233 MISS GRACE HARRIS, Shirenewton

Postal: **White House, Shirenewton, Chepstow, Gwent, NP16 6AQ**
Contacts: **MOBILE 07912 359425**
EMAIL graceharris90@gmail.com WEBSITE www.graceharrisracing.com

1 **DIAMOND RIVER (IRE),** 8, ch g Imperial Monarch (IRE)—River Clyde (IRE) **Jonathan Thomas & Partner**
2 **DRUMLEES PET (IRE),** 8, gr m Golden Lariat (USA)—Geraldine's Pet (IRE) **Brendon Sabin & Partner**
3 **HALF NELSON,** 8, ch g Mount Nelson—Maria Antonia (IRE) **Jonathan Thomas & Partner**
4 **HALIFAX (FR),** 6, b g Saddler Maker (IRE)—Oudette (FR) **Mrs E. Banks**
5 **INION TIOGAIR (IRE),** 6, br m Westerner—Tiger Bay Lady (IRE) **Foxhills Racing Limited**
6 **JUSTSHORTOFABUBBLE,** 6, b g Midnight Legend—Auld Fyffee (IRE) **Michelle Harris & Deberah Lawton**
7 **KARAKORAM,** 8, b g Excelebration (IRE)—Portrait **Grace Harris Racing**
8 **LADYPACKSAPUNCH,** 4, b f Time Test—Punchy Lady **Mr J. Thomas**
9 **LORD BILL (IRE),** 6, ch g Touch of Land (FR)—Hayward's Heath **Andrew & James Colthart**
10 **MOSCOW SPY (IRE),** 6, gr g Jet Away—Regents Ballerina (IRE) **Mrs E. Banks**
11 **MUSAYTIR (IRE),** 5, gr g Showcasing—Top of The Art (IRE) **Paul & Ann de Weck**
12 **MY GIRL KATIE (IRE),** 6, b m Ocovango—Kings Sister (IRE) **Foxhills Racing Limited**
13 **PASSING KATE,** 6, b m Passing Glance—Another Kate (IRE) **D. M. Richards**
14 **SHEEKA SUPREME (IRE),** 5, b m Flemensfirth (USA)—Thanks Awfully (IRE) **Foxhills Racing Limited**
15 **SOLDIER'S SON,** 7, b g Epaulette (AUS)—Elsie's Orphan **Grace Harris Racing**
16 **SYMBOL OF HOPE,** 5, b g Dandy Man (IRE)—Catalina Bay (IRE) **2 Counties Racing**
17 **THE BIG REVEAL (IRE),** 5, ch g Soldier of Fortune (IRE)—Fuel Queen (IRE) **Foxhills Racing Limited**
18 **THE COLA KID,** 6, gr g Lethal Force (IRE)—George's Gift **Mrs S. M. Maine**
19 **THEWAYTOTHESTARS,** 4, b f Due Diligence (USA)—Last Supper **Mr Ronald Davies & Mrs Candida Davies**
20 **WISE GLORY (IRE),** 6, b g Muhaarar—Bint Almukhtar (IRE) **Foxhills Racing Limited**

THREE-YEAR-OLDS

21 B g Heeraat (IRE)—Tahiti One **Mrs V. C. Gilbert**

TWO-YEAR-OLDS

22 B f 30/01 Belardo (IRE)—Spangle (Galileo (IRE)) **John Heaney & Simon Heaney**

Assistant Trainer: Michelle Harris, **Head Girl:** Christina Berry.

---

234 MR MILTON HARRIS, Warminster

Postal: **The Beeches, Deverill Road, Sutton Veny, Warminster, Wiltshire, BA12 7BY**
Contacts: **MOBILE 07879 634308**

1 **ALIOMAANA,** 5, ch m Raven's Pass (USA)—Taqdees (IRE) **Aliomaana Partnership**
2 **ANTUNES,** 9, b g Nathaniel (IRE)—Aigrette Garzette (IRE) **Mr M. Harris**
3 **APPRECIATE (IRE),** 5, ch g Australia—Became (USA) **Appreciate Partnership**
4 **ARCHER (GER),** 4, b g Nutan (IRE)—Amora (IRE) **Mr M. Harris**
5 **BALGOWAN (IRE),** 4, ch g Australia—Star Search **Mr J. F. Pearl**
6 **BARI BREEZE (IRE),** 8, b g Shirocco (GER)—Byerley Sophie (IRE) **Mr M. Harris**
7 **BRADFORD LADY,** 4, ch f Sir Percy—Malice **S & M Mr S Harvey & Mr M Griffiths**
8 **CABRAKAN (IRE),** 4, b g Divine Prophet (AUS)—Ready's Legend (USA) **Honestly Racing**
9 **CARLOW FARMER (IRE),** 10, b g Stowaway—Supreme Fivestar (IRE) **The Carlow Farmer Partnership**
10 **CHASE PARK (IRE),** 5, b m Walk In The Park (IRE)—Scarlet Feather (IRE) **Mrs Anthea Williams & Partner**
11 **CHESKY'S IN MILAN (IRE),** 4, b f Milan—Well Tuned (IRE) **Mr L. B. Carenza**
12 4, B g Forever Now—Choral Singer **Mark & Maria Adams**
13 **CIRRUS,** 5, ch m Starspangledbanner (AUS)—Callendula **Mr M. Harris**
14 **COIN BASKET (IRE),** 6, b m Flemensfirth (USA)—Garraidubh (IRE) **Eventmasters Racing**
15 **COPSHILL LAD (IRE),** 5, gr g Kingston Hill—Una Sorpresa (GER) **Middleham Park Racing XLVII**
16 **DANNY WHIZZBANG (IRE),** 10, b g Getaway (GER)—Lakil Princess (IRE) **Danny Whizzbang Partnership**
17 **DEFINITE,** 4, b g Kingman—Zulema **Mr M. Harris**
18 **DIAMOND DESTROYER (IRE),** 4, ch g El Kabeir (USA)—Diamond Duchess (IRE) **The Sophisticates**
19 **EARTH CRY (IRE),** 5, b g Pride of Dubai (AUS)—Freefourracing (USA) **Mr A. Badri**
20 **EDINBURGH ROCK (IRE),** 4, b g Highland Reel (IRE)—Sixpenny Sweets (IRE) **The Box 8 Partnership**
21 **EL MUCHACHO (IRE),** 6, gr g Walk In The Park (IRE)—La Segnora (FR) **Four Candles Partnership**
22 **ESCOBEDO,** 5, b g Nathaniel (IRE)—Notary **The Sophisticates**
23 **FAKIR (FR),** 8, b g Day Flight—Lazary (FR) **In For A Penny Partnership**
24 **FIRE LAKE (IRE),** 6, ch m Mustajeeb—Saiddaa (USA) **Mr A. Badri**
25 **GALAH,** 5, b m Australia—Lunar Spirit **Mr A. Badri**
26 **GASPALINE,** 6, b m Martaline—Gaspaisielle
27 **GAVROCHE D'ALLIER (FR),** 7, b g Apsis—Crouesty (FR) **Honestly Racing**
28 **GENTLE SLOPES,** 6, b g Gentlewave (IRE)—Dalriath **Mr A. Badri**
29 **GENUFLEX,** 5, b g Holy Roman Emperor (IRE)—Gravitation **Mr M. Harris**
30 **GLOBAL AGREEMENT,** 6, ch g Mayson—Amicable Terms **Global Partnership**
31 **HASTY PARISIAN (IRE),** 5, ch g Champs Elysees—Va'vite (IRE) **The Hasty Parisian Partnership**
32 **HAVAILA (IRE),** 4, ch g Le Havre (IRE)—Waila **Havaila Partnership**
33 5, B m Ol' Man River (IRE)—Hazy Outlook (IRE)
34 **HIGHLAND FROLIC (FR),** 4, b g Highland Reel (IRE)—Beach Frolic **Mark & Maria Adams**
35 **HUNTSMANS JOG (IRE),** 9, b g Milan—Faucon **The Box 8 Partnership**
36 **HURRICANE VICHI (IRE),** 6, b g Flemensfirth (USA)—Avichi (IRE) **Trailer Resources Ltd**
37 **IF KARL'S BERG DID,** 8, b g Fame And Glory—Mayberry **Air-water Treatments Ltd**
38 **ILANZ (FR),** 5, b g Rail Link—Vadrouille (FR) **Mrs A. M. Williams**
39 **JACAMAR (GER),** 8, b g Maxios—Juvena (GER) **Mark & Maria Adams**
40 **JORDAN (GER),** 4, ch g Guiliani (IRE)—Juvena (GER) **Mark & Maria Adams**
41 **KNIGHT SALUTE,** 5, b g Sir Percy—Shadow Dancing **Four Candles Partnership**
42 **KNOWWHENTOHOLDEM (IRE),** 8, b br g Flemensfirth (USA)—Definite Design (IRE) **Sutton Veny Racing Syndicate**
43 **LARIO (GER),** 4, b g Nutan (IRE)—Larmina (FR) **Honestly Racing**
44 **LEGIONAR (GER),** 5, ch g Protectionist (GER)—Lomitas Dream **Four Candles Partnership**
45 **LEN BRENNAN (IRE),** 10, b g Westerner—Letthedancebegin (IRE) **The Oxymorons**
46 **MARINE (IRE),** 5, b g Sea The Stars (IRE)—Ignis Away (FR) **Four Candles**
47 **MASTEROFTHEHEIGHTS (IRE),** 7, b g Masterofthehorse (IRE)—Martha's Way **Mr J R B Williams & Partner**
48 **MITIGATION,** 4, b g Nathaniel (IRE)—Maskunah (IRE) **Mr M. Woods**
49 **MORDRED (IRE),** 7, b g Camelot—Endure (IRE) **Middleham Park Racing Xcv & M Harris**
50 **MR YEATS (IRE),** 6, b g Yeats (IRE)—Va'vite (IRE) **Emdells Limited**
51 **MUCUNA (GER),** 4, b f Guiliani (IRE)—Monaway (IRE) **Mr D. K. Tye**
52 **MULLENBEG (IRE),** 6, b m Walk In The Park (IRE)—Oscars Joy (IRE) **Mullenbeg Partnership**
53 **MULLINAREE (IRE),** 7, b g Kayf Tara—Rydalis (FR) **Mr K. Sohi**
54 **NADIM (IRE),** 4, b g Highland Reel (IRE)—Nymphea (IRE) **D Tye & M Harris**
55 **OMEGA (GER),** 5, b g Adlerflug (GER)—Ormita (GER) **Mr M. Harris**
56 **PANDA SEVEN (FR),** 6, b g Wootton Bassett—Hermanville (IRE) **Mr M. Harris**

MR MILTON HARRIS - continued

57 **PHILLIPSTOWN ELLEN (IRE),** 6, b m Xtension (IRE)—Royal Bean (USA) **Mr C. J. Harding**
58 **POLYPHONIC (IRE),** 4, b g Sea The Stars (IRE)—Aim To Please (FR) **Honestly Racing**
59 **POSTMARK,** 4, b g Postponed (IRE)—Dream Wild **Mr H Redknapp, Mr A Badri & Mr K Monk**
60 **PRESENTING YEATS (IRE),** 7, b g Yeats (IRE)—Va'vite (IRE) **Mrs D. Dewbery**
61 **PYRAMID PLACE (IRE),** 6, b g Authorized (IRE)—Attima **PP & R Syndicate**
62 4, Gr f Universal (IRE)—Qeethaara (USA)
63 **RAASED (IRE),** 6, b g Teofilo (IRE)—Yanabeeaa (USA) **PP & R Syndicate**
64 **ROGUE MISSION (IRE),** 4, gr g El Kabeir (USA)—Ascot Lady (IRE) **Mr M. Harris**
65 **ROSY REDRUM (IRE),** 5, ch m Pride of Dubai (AUS)—Diamond Duchess (IRE) **Mark & Maria Adams**
66 **ROYAL SAM,** 6, b g Black Sam Bellamy (IRE)—Royal Nashkova **Racecourse & Clifford**
67 **SASSY MISS MARGOT,** 5, b m Schiaparelli (GER)—Sherwood Rose (IRE) **Mr N. Plumb**
68 **SCRIPTWRITER (IRE),** 4, b g Churchill (IRE)—Pivotalia (IRE) **Mark & Maria Adams**
69 **SEIGNEUR DES AS (FR),** 5, b g It's Gino (GER)—Dallidas (FR) **Mr A. Badri**
70 **SERGEANT (FR),** 6, b g Nutan (IRE)—Stella Marina (IRE) **Mr D. K. Tye**
71 **SILVER SHADE (FR),** 5, gr g Kendargent (FR)—Lady's Secret (IRE) **Mr C. J. Baldwin**
72 **SISTERANDBROTHER,** 5, ch g Sixties Icon—Picalily **Mr W. A. Harrison-Allan**
73 **SONGO (IRE),** 7, b g Most Improved (IRE)—Sacre Fleur (IRE) **The Songo Partnership**
74 **SOUTH OMO ZONE (IRE),** 5, b g Court Cave (IRE)—Starry Lady (IRE)
75 **SPY LADY (IRE),** 7, b m Shirocco (GER)—Present Attraction (IRE) **Future Champions Racing Syndicate**
76 **STEPNEY CAUSEWAY,** 6, b g New Approach (IRE)—Wake Up Call **Middleham Park Racing XCV**
77 **STIMULATING SONG,** 8, ch g Stimulation (IRE)—Choral Singer **Mark & Maria Adams**
78 **SUFI,** 9, ch g Pivotal—Basanti (USA) **WLT Racing Syndicate**
79 **TWINJETS (IRE),** 6, b g Jet Away—Shenamar (IRE) **Mr C. W. Rodgers**
80 **UGGY UGGY UGGY,** 5, ch g Saddler's Rock (IRE)—Aragons Gambler **Mr P. J. Bradley**
81 **VENTURA TORMENTA (IRE),** 5, b h Acclamation—Midnight Oasis **Middleham Park Racing IV**
82 **WATCHING OVER YOU,** 4, ch g Nathaniel (IRE)—Sonnetation (IRE) **Watching Over You Partnership**
83 **WHENITRAINSITPOURS (IRE),** 5, ch g Leading Light (IRE)—Zaharath Al Bustan **The Rebels**

THREE-YEAR-OLDS

84 **COCHIN,** b f Churchill (IRE)—Slatey Hen (IRE) **Mr M. Harris**
85 **GIDDYUPADINGDONG (IRE),** ch g El Kabeir (USA)—Wind Inher Sleeves (USA) **Mr G. Wells**
86 B f Sixties Icon—Shemriyna (IRE)
87 **STAFF SERGEANT LEN (GER),** b g Nutan (IRE)—Stella Marina (IRE) **Mr D. K. Tye**

---

235 MR RONALD HARRIS, Chepstow

Postal: **Ridge House Stables, Earlswood, Chepstow, Monmouthshire, NP16 6AN**
Contacts: **PHONE 01291 641689 MOBILE 07831 770899 FAX 01291 641258**
EMAIL ridgehousestables.ltd@btinternet.com WEBSITE www.ronharrisracing.co.uk

1 **EAGLE ONE,** 5, b g Gleneagles (IRE)—Gloryette **Ridge House Stables Ltd**
2 **EYE OF THE WATER (IRE),** 7, b g Lilbourne Lad (IRE)—Desert Location **Mr M. E. Wright**
3 **FAIR AND SQUARE,** 4, b g Kodiac—Slatey Hen (IRE) **Mr Malcolm Wright & Ridgehouse Stables Ltd**
4 **GLAMOROUS EXPRESS (IRE),** 4, b g Gutaifan (IRE)—Glamorous Air (IRE) **M Doocey, S Doocey & P J Doocey**
5 **GLAMOROUS FORCE,** 6, b g Lethal Force (IRE)—Glamorous Spirit (IRE) **Ridge House Stables Ltd**
6 **LUSCIFER,** 6, b g Heeraat (IRE)—Nut (IRE) **Mr S. Doocey**
7 **SARAH'S VERSE,** 6, b m Poet's Voice—Sancai (USA) **Mr N. Sfrantzis**
8 **SECRET POTION,** 9, b g Stimulation (IRE)—Fiancee (IRE) **Ridge House Stables Ltd**
9 **THE DALEY EXPRESS (IRE),** 9, b g Elzaam (AUS)—Seraphina (IRE) **The W.H.O. Society**
10 **THEGREYVTRAIN,** 7, gr m Coach House (IRE)—Debutante Blues (USA) **Ridge House Stables Ltd**

THREE-YEAR-OLDS

11 **GLAMOROUS STAR (IRE),** b f Gutaifan (IRE)—Glamorous Air (IRE) **M Doocey, S Doocey & P J Doocey**

MR RONALD HARRIS - continued

TWO-YEAR-OLDS

12 B f 31/03 Inns of Court (IRE)—Lady Heartbeat (Avonbridge) (3601) **H. M. W. Clifford**

Flat Jockey: Luke Morris.

---

236 MR SHAUN HARRIS, Worksop

Postal: **Pinewood Stables, Carburton, Worksop, Nottinghamshire, S80 3BT**
Contacts: **PHONE 01909 470936 MOBILE 07761 395596**
EMAIL shaunharrisracing@yahoo.com

1 **AL SUIL EILE (FR),** 7, gr g Alhebayeb (IRE)—Visual Element (USA) **J. Morris**
2 **ALI STAR BERT,** 7, b g Phoenix Reach (IRE)—Clumber Pursuits **S. A. Harris**
3 **GAAZOOO (IRE),** 4, ch g Cotai Glory—Gaazaal **J. Morris**
4 **TOMMYTWOHOOTS,** 5, b g Bated Breath—Lady Lube Rye (IRE) **J. Morris**
5 **UNCLE HENRY (IRE),** 9, b g Henrythenavigator (USA)—Shebelia (GER) **Mrs G. H. Harris**

THREE-YEAR-OLDS

6 **DARAMOUNT SUNLIGHT,** ch f Sun Central (IRE)—Delphyne **Mrs G. H. Harris**

Assistant Trainer: Mrs G. H. Harris.

---

237 MR GARY HARRISON, Lanark

Postal: **Highacre, New Trows Road, Lesmahagow, Lanark, Lanarkshire, ML11 0JS**
Contacts: **PHONE 07717 757162**
EMAIL garyharrison1968@gmail.com

1 **DAIJOOR,** 7, br g Cape Cross (IRE)—Angel Oak **Miss S. K. Harrison**
2 **FOX HILL,** 7, b m Foxwedge (AUS)—Siryena **Miss S. K. Harrison**
3 **NIGHT MOON,** 7, b g Dubawi (IRE)—Scatina (IRE) **Miss S. K. Harrison**
4 **VENUSTA (IRE),** 7, b m Medicean—Grevillea (IRE) **Miss S. K. Harrison**

---

238 MISS LISA HARRISON, Wigton

Postal: **Cobble Hall, Aldoth, Nr Silloth, Cumbria, CA7 4NE**
Contacts: **PHONE 016973 61753 MOBILE 07725 535554 FAX 016973 42250**
EMAIL lisa@daharrison.co.uk

1 **A PLACE APART (IRE),** 9, b g Power—Simadartha (USA) **Abbadis Racing & D A Harrison Racing**
2 **DALILEO (IRE),** 8, b g Galileo (IRE)—Snow Queen (IRE) **D A Harrison Racing**
3 **GREEN ZONE (IRE),** 12, b g Bushranger (IRE)—Incense **T Hunter & D A Harrison Racing**
4 **HATTAAB,** 10, b g Intikhab (USA)—Sundus (USA) **T Hunter & D A Harrison Racing**
5 **INSTINGTIVE (IRE),** 12, b g Scorpion (IRE)—Fully Focused (IRE) **D A Harrison & Abbadis Racing & Thompson**
6 **LIZZY'S GIRL,** 8, b m Multiplex—Might Do
7 **MALANGEN (IRE),** 8, b g Born To Sea (IRE)—Lady's Locket (IRE) **T Hunter & D A Harrison Racing**
8 **MILEVA ROLLER,** 11, b m Multiplex—Alikat (IRE) **D A Harrison Racing**
9 **MUWALLA,** 16, b g Bahri (USA)—Easy Sunshine (IRE) **Bell Bridge Racing**

MISS LISA HARRISON - continued

10 **SOLWAY HONEY,** 8, b m Multiplex—Solway Brook (IRE) **D A Harrison Racing**
11 **SOLWAY MOLLY,** 8, b m Trans Island—Solway Sunset **D A Harrison Racing**
12 **SOLWAY PRIMROSE,** 9, b m Overbury (IRE)—Solway Rose **D A Harrison Racing**
13 **SOLWAY STAREE,** 5, b m Yorgunnabelucky (USA)—Kashstaree **D A Harrison Racing**
14 **WASDELL DUNDALK (FR),** 8, ch g Spirit One (FR)—Linda Queen (FR) **D A Harrison Racing**
15 **WILLY NILLY (IRE),** 6, b g Morpheus—Subtle Shimmer **Abbadis Racing & D A Harrison Racing**

---

239 MR BEN HASLAM, Middleham

Postal: **Castle Hill Stables, Castle Hill, Middleham, Leyburn, North Yorkshire, DL8 4QW**
Contacts: **PHONE 01969 624351 MOBILE 07764 411660**
EMAIL office@benhaslamracing.com WEBSITE www.benhaslamracing.com

1 **AGONYCLITE,** 4, b g Dabirsim (FR)—Hoku (IRE) **Daniel Shapiro & David Clifford**
2 **ALFA MIX,** 8, b g Fair Mix (IRE)—Alora Money **Mr J. P. McManus**
3 **ARAMAX (GER),** 7, b g Maxios—Aramina (GER) **Mr J. P. McManus**
4 **ARTHUR'S QUAY (IRE),** 9, b g Beat Hollow—Bannow Girl (IRE) **Mr J. P. McManus**
5 **BAND OF OUTLAWS (IRE),** 8, b g Fast Company (IRE)—Band of Colour (IRE) **Mr J. P. McManus**
6 **CALEVADE (IRE),** 7, gr g Gregorian (IRE)—
Avoidance (USA) **Mr D. Shapiro, Mr P. G. Wood, Mr K. Nicol, Mrs A. M. C. Haslam, Mrs J. M. Feeney**
7 **CASH AGAIN (FR),** 11, br g Great Pretender (IRE)—Jeu de Lune (FR) **Mrs C Barclay & Mr P Adams**
8 **CELESTIAL HORIZON (IRE),** 5, b g Fastnet Rock (AUS)—Cocoon (IRE) **Mr J. P. McManus**
9 **CODE PURPLE,** 4, b g Ribchester (IRE)—Sugar Free (GER) **Daniel Shapiro & David Clifford**
10 **DIDTHEYLEAVEUOUTTO (IRE),** 10, ch g Presenting—Pretty Puttens (IRE) **Mr J. P. McManus**
11 **DO I DREAM (IRE),** 4, b f Mondialiste (IRE)—Novita (FR) **Chris Cleevely & Racing Knights**
12 **DR SANDERSON (IRE),** 9, b g Jeremy (USA)—Guydus (IRE) **Mr J. P. McManus**
13 **FORTAMOUR (IRE),** 7, b g Es Que Love (IRE)—Kathy Sun (IRE) **Chris Cleevely & Racing Knights**
14 **GUIRI (GER),** 8, ch g Motivator—Guardia (GER) **Mr J. P. McManus**
15 **HORN CAPE (FR),** 6, gr g Fame And Glory—Capstone (FR) **Mr J. P. McManus**
16 **JERRYSBACK (IRE),** 11, b g Jeremy (USA)—Get A Few Bob Back (IRE) **Mr J. P. McManus**
17 **LIGHTENING COMPANY (IRE),** 5, b g Fast Company (IRE)—
Shama's Song (IRE) **Mrs C. Barclay, Middleham Park Racing CXV, Mr D. P. Widdup**
18 **LORD CAPRIO (IRE),** 8, b g Lord Shanakill (USA)—Azzurra du Caprio (IRE) **Blue Lion Racing IX**
19 **MACHO PRIDE (IRE),** 5, b g Camacho—Proud Maria (IRE) **The Auckland Lodge Partnership**
20 **MARSHALLED (IRE),** 9, b g Flemensfirth (USA)—Serious Fun (IRE) **Mr J. P. McManus**
21 **MILLIONAIRE WALTZ,** 6, b g Heeraat (IRE)—Radio Gaga **Mr S. J. Robinson**
22 **ORIGINTRAIL (IRE),** 4, b f Profitable (IRE)—Miss Azeza **Daniel Shapiro & David Clifford**
23 **OUR LAURA B (IRE),** 5, b m Sans Frontieres (IRE)—Dear Bach (IRE) **Racing Knights**
24 **PINKIE BROWN (FR),** 11, gr g Gentlewave (IRE)—Natt Musik (FR) **Mr S. J. Robinson**
25 **PROTEK DES FLOS (FR),** 11, b g Protektor (GER)—Flore de Chantenay (FR) **Mr J. P. McManus**
26 **ROXBORO ROAD (IRE),** 10, b g Oscar (IRE)—Pretty Neat (IRE) **Mr J. P. McManus**
27 **SANDRET (IRE),** 7, b g Zebedee—Sava Sunset (IRE) **Mr B. M. R. Haslam**
28 **SASSOON,** 7, ch g Poet's Voice—Seradim **Mr S. J. Robinson**
29 **THATBEATSBANAGHER (IRE),** 9, b g Flemensfirth (USA)—Katie's Jem (IRE) **Mr J. P. McManus**
30 **WE STILL BELIEVE (IRE),** 5, b br g Lawman (FR)—
Curious Lashes (IRE) **Sam Farthing, Linda McGarry & Ken Nicol**

THREE-YEAR-OLDS

31 **CARMENTIS (IRE),** b f Kodiac—Capriole **Daniel Shapiro & David Clifford**
32 **PURPLE MARTINI,** b f Mayson—Lady Lekki (IRE) **Mr D. Shapiro, Mr D. Clifford, Blue Lion Racing IX**
33 **TANTALUS (IRE),** b g Kodiac—Chatham Islands (USA) **Daniel Shapiro & David Clifford**
34 **VIOLETA (IRE),** b f Kodiac—Welsh Anthem **Daniel Shapiro & David Clifford**
35 **WEN MOON (IRE),** b g Mehmas (IRE)—Luminous Gold **Daniel Shapiro & David Clifford**
36 **WILLIAM DEWHIRST (IRE),** b g Sioux Nation (USA)—
Two Pass (IRE) **Mr C. R. Cleevely, Mr D. P. Widdup, Mr R. Tocher, Mr K. Nicol**

MR BEN HASLAM - continued

TWO-YEAR-OLDS

37 **ON THE BUBBLE,** b f 29/05 Land Force (IRE)—O Fourlunda (Halling (USA)) (3810) **The Multifruit Syndicate**

---

240 MR NIGEL HAWKE, Tiverton

Postal: **Thorne Farm, Stoodleigh, Tiverton, Devon, EX16 9QG**
Contacts: **PHONE 01884 881666 MOBILE 07769 295839**
EMAIL nigel@thornefarmracingltd.co.uk WEBSITE www.nigelhawkethornefarmracing.co.uk

1 **A NEW SIEGE (IRE),** 8, ch m New Approach (IRE)—Arminta (USA) **Atlantic Friends Racing**
2 **ATLANTIC BREEZE (IRE),** 4, ch g No Nay Never (USA)—Flashy Wings **Mr Richard Weeks & Partner**
3 **BALLYMAGROARTY BOY (IRE),** 10, b g Milan—Glazed Storm (IRE) **Nigel Hawke Racing Club & Partners**
4 **BEAUTIFUL SURPRISE,** 4, ch f Ribchester (IRE)—Lovely Surprise (IRE) **Mr Samuel Quigley Thornefarmracing Ltd**
5 **BERT WILSON (IRE),** 6, b g Canford Cliffs (IRE)—Inishkea (USA) **Kapinhand**
6 **BIRDIE PUTT (IRE),** 4, b f Gleneagles (IRE)—Inch Perfect (USA) **Sam Quigley & Neil Tucker**
7 **BRING THE ACTION (IRE),** 7, b g Jet Away—Lady Firefly (IRE) **Exors of the Late C. Holmes-Elliott**
8 **CALL ME SAINTE (FR),** 6, b m Saint des Saints (FR)—Call Me Blue (FR) **Simms, Capps**
9 **CAPTAIN BILL (IRE),** 4, br c Sageburg (IRE)—Pomme **Hawke, Simms, Phillips**
10 **DAWN TROUPER (IRE),** 8, b g Dawn Approach (IRE)—Dance Troupe **Mr R. Lane**
11 **DONNACHA (IRE),** 5, br g Jet Away—Archdale Ambush (IRE) **Mrs M. J. Martin**
12 **ELMAFTUN (IRE),** 4, gr g Dark Angel (IRE)—Tamadhor (IRE) **The Cheltenham Trail Racing Club**
13 **EUROWORK (FR),** 9, bl g Network (GER)—Nandina (FR) **R. J. & Mrs J. A. Peake**
14 **GALORE DESASSENCES (FR),** 7, b g Rail Link—Villezbelle (FR) **Mr M. J. Phillips**
15 **GEORDIE WASHINGTON (IRE),** 7, b br g Sageburg (IRE)—Rathturtin Brief (IRE) **Mr N. J. Hawke**
16 **GETUPTHEYARD (IRE),** 4, b g Getaway (GER)—Harbour Mistress (IRE) **Mr N. J. Hawke**
17 **HOBSONS BAY (IRE),** 5, b g Camelot—Emirates Joy (USA) **Mr S. Jefford**
18 **I HAVE A VOICE (IRE),** 4, b g Vocalised (USA)—Fionnuar (IRE) **Molly & Paul Willis**
19 **INFERNO SACREE (FR),** 5, b g Saint des Saints (FR)—Altesse Sacree (FR) **Mr R. Lane**
20 **INSTANT DE BONHEUR (FR),** 5, b m Karaktar (IRE)—Par Bonheur (FR) **Mr Mike Izaby White & Partner**
21 **INTRIGUING LADY (IRE),** 4, b f Fascinating Rock (IRE)—Anam Allta (IRE) **Mrs D. E. Smith**
22 **JUST ANOTHER ONE (IRE),** 4, b g Vocalised (USA)—Teacht An Earraig (USA) **Atlantic Friends Racing**
23 **KENDELU (IRE),** 8, b g Yeats (IRE)—Supreme Baloo (IRE) **K & D Neilson & Nigel Hawke Racing Club**
24 **LA REFERI (IRE),** 4, ch f Pride of Dubai (AUS)—Referio (IRE) **Atlantic Friends Racing**
25 **MILTON BOY (FR),** 4, b g Doctor Dino (FR)—Valgenceuse (IRE) **Mr N. J. Hawke**
26 **MY GRANNY LILY,** 5, b m Pether's Moon (IRE)—Pont Royal (FR) **Sam Quigley & Denise Smith**
27 4, B f Dunaden (FR)—Ocarina Davis (FR)
28 **ONNAROLL (FR),** 5, b g Kapgarde (FR)—Sainte Borgue (FR) **Mrs K. Hawke & Mr W. Simms**
29 **PEARL ROYALE (IRE),** 11, b m Robin des Champs (FR)—Dartmeet (IRE) **Mr M. J. Phillips**
30 **PLAY BY THE RULES (IRE),** 4, b g Vocalised (USA)—Teodolite (IRE) **& Willis**
31 **POMME,** 12, b m Observatory (USA)—Mirthful (USA)
32 **PROFESSOR CALCULUS,** 5, b g Twilight Son—Roslea Lady (IRE) **Nigel Hawke Racing Club & Associate**
33 **RANCO (IRE),** 6, b g Makfi—Guerande (IRE) **R. J. Weeks**
34 **RUN AT DAWN (IRE),** 4, ch g Dawn Approach (IRE)—Ringside Humour (IRE) **& Willis**
35 **SINDABELLA (FR),** 7, b m Sinndar (IRE)—Figarella Gaugain (FR) **Surefire Racing 1**
36 **SOME DETAIL (IRE),** 9, b g Getaway (GER)—You Should Know Me (IRE) **& Willis**
37 **SYNCHRONICITY (FR),** 4, ch g Spanish Moon (USA)—Hotel California (FR)
38 **THE IMPOSTER (FR),** 6, b g Authorized (IRE)—Miss Dixie **Mark Philips & J H Gumbley**
39 **TIME TO BURN (IRE),** 5, b m Bobby's Kitten (USA)—Wholesome (USA) **R. J. Weeks**
40 **TIMELESS CLASSIC,** 4, b gr f Outstrip—Timeless **The Time Enough Stud Partnership**
41 **WATCHOUTITSCOOKIE (IRE),** 5, ch g Doyen (IRE)—Medimli (IRE) **Mr R. Lane**
42 **YAAZAAIN,** 7, b g Iffraaj—Tamazirte (IRE) **Mead Vale, Sam Quigley & Gerry Flanagan**

THREE-YEAR-OLDS

43 **BRIEF ENCOUNTER (FR),** b f Buck's Boum (FR)—Carmona (FR) **Thorne Farm Racing Limited**

MR NIGEL HAWKE - continued

44 **GEALACH IARIANN,** gr g Outstrip—Peace March **Thorne Farm Racing Limited**
45 B g Frontiersman—Ocarina Davis (FR)
46 B c Frontiersman—Sedgemoor Classact (IRE)
47 **SQUARE DU ROULE (FR),** b c It's Gino (GER)—Semur (FR) **Thorne Farm Racing Limited**

Assistant Trainer: Edward Buckley, Katherine Hawke.

---

241 MR MICHAEL HAWKER, Chippenham

Postal: **Battens Farm, Allington, Chippenham, Wiltshire, SN14 6LT**

1 **FAMA ET GLORIA (IRE),** 7, b g Fame And Glory—Clonogan (IRE) **Mr M. R. E. Hawker**
2 **MORTENS LEAM,** 11, b g Sulamani (IRE)—Bonnet's Pieces **Mr M. R. E. Hawker**
3 **MR JORROCKS,** 8, b g Scorpion (IRE)—Sheknowsyouknow **Mr M. R. E. Hawker**
4 **SPOTTY DOG,** 8, ch g Sixties Icon—Where's My Slave (IRE) **Mr M. R. E. Hawker**

---

242 MR RICHARD HAWKER, Frome

Postal: **Rode Farm, Rode, Bath, Somerset, BA11 6QQ**
Contacts: **PHONE 01373 831479**

1 **FARCEUR DE MAULNE (FR),** 8, b g Doctor Dino (FR)—Alize de La Prise (FR) **Landowners, Penwill, Skuse**
2 **FIVE GOLD BARS (IRE),** 10, b g Gold Well—Native Euro (IRE) **R. G. B. Hawker**
3 **HAVANA RIVER (IRE),** 10, b m Mahler—Dancingonthemoon (IRE) **R. J. Francome**
4 **JACK SNIPE,** 14, b g Kirkwall—Sea Snipe
5 **KILBRICKEN STORM (IRE),** 12, b g Oscar (IRE)—Kilbricken Leader (IRE) **R. G. B. Hawker**
6 **THIRSTY FARMER,** 9, b g Sulamani (IRE)—Sweet Shooter **Rolling Aces**

---

243 MISS ALICE ELIZABETH HAYNES, Newmarket

Postal: **11 Park Cottages, Park Lane, Newmarket, Suffolk, CB8 8BB**
Contacts: **PHONE 07585 558717**
EMAIL alice@alicehaynesracing.co.uk

1 **CAVALLUCCIO (IRE),** 4, br g Caravaggio (USA)—Gale Song
2 **GOLDSMITH (IRE),** 4, b g Shalaa (IRE)—Ingot of Gold **Scuderia Di Vincitori**
3 **GREAT MAX (IRE),** 4, b g Wootton Bassett—Teeslemee (FR) **Amo Racing Limited**
4 **JOSIES KID (IRE),** 4, b g Ardad (IRE)—Low Cut Affair (IRE)
5 **LIVE IN THE MOMENT (IRE),** 6, ch g Zebedee—Approaching Autumn **Steve & Jolene de'Lemos**
6 **MAYSONG,** 6, ch g Mayson—Aldeburgh Music (IRE) **Beaverbrook**
7 **MR PROFESSOR (IRE),** 4, b g Profitable (IRE)—Law of The Range **Amo Racing Limited**
8 **PARISIAC (IRE),** 4, b g Kodiac—Colgin
9 **RAMDON ROCKS,** 4, b g Iffraaj—Panova **Racing Unity & Partner**
10 **REGAL RAMBLER (IRE),** 4, b g Dark Angel (IRE)—Rural Celebration **P Murphy & Partner**
11 **STRONG POWER (IRE),** 6, b g Kodiac—Soft Power (IRE)

MISS ALICE ELIZABETH HAYNES - continued

THREE-YEAR-OLDS

12 **AJYAD (IRE),** b f Australia—Lady Design (IRE) **Mr M. S. Al Shahi**
13 **ALEXI BOY,** b c Oasis Dream—Abbakova (IRE) **Amo Racing Limited**
14 **DANCE HAVANA,** b f Havana Gold (IRE)—First Secretary **Independent Women**
15 **DISTINGUISHED LADY (FR),** b f Zoustar (AUS)—Saccharose **Amo Racing Limited**
16 **DON'T WHAT ME BOY (IRE),** ch g Dandy Man (IRE)—Summer Blues (USA) **Mrs V. De Sousa**
17 **FIX YOU,** ch f Night of Thunder (IRE)—Ifubelieveindreams (IRE) **Amo Racing Limited**
18 **GEMINI STAR (IRE),** b f Starspangledbanner (AUS)—Star Fire **Mr G. P. Budd**
19 **GIRL MAGIC,** b f Havana Grey—Blithe Spirit **Amo Racing Limited**
20 **IBIZA LOVE (IRE),** b f U S Navy Flag (USA)—Ibiza Dream **Roudee Racing**
21 **INNY LAD (IRE),** b c Cappella Sansevero—Laguna Salada (IRE) **Mr J. Acheson**
22 **ITHRA,** b f Ardad (IRE)—Insaaf **Mr S. B. M. Al Qassimi**
23 **LADY BULLET (IRE),** b f James Garfield (IRE)—Lil's Joy (IRE) **The Three Bullets**
24 **LADY CAMACHO (IRE),** b f Camacho—Guthanna Gaoithe **Roudee Racing**
25 **MAHBOOBAH (IRE),** b f Sea The Moon (GER)—Goldschatzchen (GER) **Sheikh A. H. F. M. A. Al Sabah**
26 **MASTER OF CHANT,** gr g Gregorian (IRE)—Arctic Moon (USA) **Mrs S. Dunn**
27 **MILLUNA,** b f Dandy Man (IRE)—Maid A Million **Mrs E. F. Harte**
28 **MINE THAT SHIP (IRE),** b f Kodiac—Royal Sister Two (IRE) **Dr V. Chhabria**
29 **MISHRAQ (IRE),** b c Cracksman—Fashion Parade **Sheikh A. H. F. M. A. Al Sabah**
30 **MOTHER INDIA (IRE),** ch f Profitable (IRE)—Fuaigh Mor (IRE) **Dr V. Chhabria**
31 **NEW HOPE BULLET (IRE),** b f New Bay—Morning Frost (IRE) **The Bruiser Boyz**
32 **PLAYUPSKYBLUES (IRE),** gr g Kodiac—Angelic Guest (IRE) **Mr G. Allsopp**
33 **RAINCLOUD,** ch f Ulysses (IRE)—Flood Warning
34 **RAMZ (IRE),** ch g Havana Gold (IRE)—Storybook (UAE) **Mrs S. Dunn**
35 **REMARKABLE FORCE (IRE),** b g Acclamation—Vastitas (IRE) **Amo Racing Limited**
36 **SHE'S CENTIMENTAL (USA),** b f Goldencents (USA)—Shesabitdistorted (USA) **Roudee Racing**
37 **SONGWRITER (IRE),** b c Kodi Bear (IRE)—Irish Cliff (IRE) **Amo Racing Limited**

TWO-YEAR-OLDS

38 **ALBERT LASKER (IRE),** b c 03/02 Advertise—Samuna (FR) (Samum (GER)) (28011) **NG Racing**
39 **BUMBLEBEE BULLET (IRE),** b f 20/03 Invincible Army (IRE)—Amurra (Oasis Dream) (12805)
40 B c 26/03 Kodiac—Chicadoro (Paco Boy (IRE)) (35238) **Sheikh A. H. F. M. A. Al Sabah**
41 **ELEGANT ELLOISE (IRE),** b f 12/04 U S Navy Flag (USA)—Karasiyra (IRE) (Alhaarth (IRE)) (11204) **Mrs H. Dacosta**
42 **ELYSIAN WOLF,** b c 26/03 Bungle Inthejungle—T Shirt Sun Tan (Sayif (IRE)) (26667) **Mrs Fiona Shaw**
43 **JAUNTY DANCER,** ch f 22/02 Decorated Knight—Dutch Monument (Dutch Art) (8000)
44 B f 22/01 Land Force (IRE)—Josefa Goya (Sakhee's Secret) (15000)
45 **MY LADY SAMANTHA,** b f 15/04 Ten Sovereigns (IRE)—Vitello (Raven's Pass (USA)) (35000) **Miss S. Elliott**
46 **NIGHTS OF HAVANA,** ch f 30/03 Havana Gold (IRE)—Gertrude Versed (Manduro (GER)) (6000) **Miss S. Elliott**
47 B c 26/04 Time Test—Raymi Coya (CAN) (Van Nistelrooy (USA)) (46419) **Titanium Racing Club**
48 B c 24/02 Inns of Court (IRE)—Silk Fan (IRE) (Unfuwain (USA)) (88035) **Titanium Racing Club**
49 B f 20/02 No Nay Never (USA)—Sophie P (Bushranger (IRE)) (85000)
50 B f 07/03 Twilight Son—Sweet And Dandy (IRE) (Dandy Man (IRE)) (18000)
51 **TOO MUCH TREVOR,** br c 02/03 Magna Grecia (IRE)—
Walk On Bye (IRE) (Danehill Dancer (IRE)) (18000) **New Star Partnership**

Racing Secretary: Miss Holly Hall, **Business & Racing Manager:** Charlie Sutton.

Flat Jockey: Kieran O'Neill. **Apprentice Jockey:** Mark Crehan, Shariq Mohd.

---

244 MR JONATHAN HAYNES, Brampton

Postal: **Cleugh Head, Low Row, Brampton, Cumbria, CA8 2JB**
Contacts: **PHONE 016977 46253 MOBILE 07771 511471**

1 **BERTIELICIOUS,** 15, b g And Beyond (IRE)—Pennepoint **J. C. Haynes**
2 **COMEONRITA,** 5, ch m Black Sam Bellamy (IRE)—Pennepoint **J. C. Haynes**

MR JONATHAN HAYNES - continued

3 **DOROTHY'S FLAME,** 11, ch m Black Sam Bellamy (IRE)—Flame of Zara **J. C. Haynes**
4 **HIDDEN CARGO (IRE),** 11, b g Stowaway—All Heart **J. C. Haynes**
5 **JACK GRASS,** 4, b g Jack Hobbs—Mrs Grass
6 **MR JV,** 7, ch g And Beyond (IRE)—Flame of Zara **J. C. Haynes**

---

245 MISS GAIL HAYWOOD, Moretonhampstead

Postal: **Stacombe Farm, Doccombe, Moretonhampstead, Newton Abbot, Devon, TQ13 8SS**
Contacts: **PHONE 01647 440826**
EMAIL gail@gghracing.com WEBSITE www.gghracing.com

1 **BALKEO (FR),** 6, b g Galiway—Hukba (IRE) **The Nascent Partnership**
2 **GRAND MOGUL (IRE),** 9, b g Presenting—Oligarch Society (IRE) **The Nascent Partnership**
3 **POL MA CREE,** 8, b g Arvico (FR)—Mere Salome (IRE) **Phillip & Mary Creese & Nicky Dunford**
4 **REAL REWARDS (IRE),** 6, b g Sageburg (IRE)—Serpentine Mine (IRE) **Phillip & Mary Creese**
5 5, B g Arvico (FR)—Torridge Lily **Miss G. G. Haywood**
6 **VINNIE THE HODDIE (IRE),** 9, b g Vinnie Roe (IRE)—Blackwater Babe (IRE) **The Nascent Partnership**
7 **ZULU,** 9, b g Cockney Rebel (IRE)—Pantita **Haywood's Heroes**

NH Jockey: David Noonan, Ben Poste. **Conditional Jockey:** Rex Dingle.

---

246 MRS KATE LOUISE HAZARD, Saltby

Postal: **7 Main Street, Saltby, Melton Mowbray, Leicestershire, LE14 4QN**
Contacts: **PHONE 07881 422137**
EMAIL katewoo1989@icloud.com

1 **BOOLEY BEACH (IRE),** 7, b m Valirann (FR)—Booley Bay (IRE) **Mrs J. Hanson**
2 **DEJA ROUGE (FR),** 6, ch g No Risk At All (FR)—Roselia Rouge (FR) **Mrs J. Hanson**
3 **THE WILD WESTERNER (IRE),** 8, b g Westerner—Nosey Oscar (IRE) **Mrs J. Hanson**

---

247 MR NICKY HENDERSON, Lambourn

Postal: **Seven Barrows, Lambourn, Hungerford, Berkshire, RG17 8UH**
Contacts: **PHONE 01488 72259 MOBILE 07774 608168**
EMAIL office@njhenderson.com

1 **AHORSEWITHNONAME,** 8, b m Cacique (IRE)—Sea of Galilee **Mr D. J. Burke & Mr P Alderson**
2 **AMRONS SAGE (IRE),** 6, b g Sageburg (IRE)—Vincenta (IRE) **G. B. Barlow**
3 **ARCLIGHT,** 4, b f Champs Elysees—Florentia **Fortnum Racing**
4 **ASTON MARTINI,** 4, b f Getaway (GER)—Gabriella Rose
5 **ATTACCA (IRE),** 5, b g Mahler—Listening (IRE) **Mrs P. J. Pugh**
6 **BALCO COASTAL (FR),** 7, b g Coastal Path—Fliugika (FR) **Mr M. R. Blandford**
7 **BALLYHIGH (IRE),** 6, b g Canford Cliffs (IRE)—Storm Run (IRE) **Unique Financial Racing Partnership**

MR NICKY HENDERSON - continued

8 **BENEFACT (IRE),** 5, gr g Sholokhov (IRE)—Sagarich (FR) **Mr J. Palmer-Brown**
9 **BETWEEN WATERS (IRE),** 5, b m Walk In The Park (IRE)—Clear Riposte (IRE) **Mrs D. A. Tabor**
10 **BLAIRGOWRIE (IRE),** 7, b g Yeats (IRE)—Gaye Preskina (IRE) **Highclere T'Bred Racing - Blairgowrie**
11 **BLUE STELLO (FR),** 7, b g Spider Flight (FR)—Benina (FR) **Owners Group 081**
12 **BOLD ENDEAVOUR,** 7, b g Fame And Glory—Araucaria (IRE) **Countrywide Park Homes Ltd**
13 **BOLD REACTION (FR),** 6, ch g Waldpark (GER)—Queen Dream (FR) **Tracey Bell & Caroline Lyons**
14 **BOMBAY SAPPHIRE (IRE),** 6, br m Shirocco (GER)—The Keane Edge (IRE) **Mrs C. Kendrick**
15 **BOOM BOOM (IRE),** 5, b g Califet (FR)—She Is A Cracker (FR) **Unique Financial Racing Partnership**
16 **BOTHWELL BRIDGE (IRE),** 8, b g Stowaway—Raise The Issue (IRE) **Victoria Dunn & Nicholas Mustoe**
17 **BRAVE JEN,** 5, b m Kayf Tara—Fenney Spring **Unique Financial Racing Partnership**
18 **BUZZ (FR),** 9, gr g Motivator—Tiysha (IRE) **Thurloe for Royal Marsden Cancer Charity**
19 **BY THE GRACE,** 4, b f Blue Bresil (FR)—Handmaid **Middleham Park Racing CXXII**
20 **CALL ME LORD (FR),** 10, b br g Slickly (FR)—Sosa (GER) **Mr Simon Munir & Mr Isaac Souede**
21 **CALL THE DANCE,** 5, b m Kayf Tara—Hora **James and Jean Potter Ltd**
22 **CAPTAIN MORGS (IRE),** 7, b g Milan—Gold Donn (IRE) **The Albatross Club**
23 **CARIBEAN BOY (FR),** 9, gr g Myboycharlie (IRE)—Caribena (FR) **Mr Simon Munir & Mr Isaac Souede**
24 **CHAMP (IRE),** 11, b g King's Theatre (IRE)—China Sky (IRE) **Mr J. P. McManus**
25 **CHANTRY HOUSE (IRE),** 9, br g Yeats (IRE)—The Last Bank (IRE) **Mr J. P. McManus**
26 **CHIVES,** 9, b g Sulamani (IRE)—Ceilidh Royal **Mrs R. H. Brown**
27 **CHOCCABLOC,** 5, b g Blue Bresil (FR)—Chocca Wocca **J & J Potter Ltd & Kelvin-hughes**
28 **CITY CHIEF (IRE),** 6, b g Soldier of Fortune (IRE)—Galant Ferns (IRE) **Mrs M. Donnelly**
29 **CONSTITUTION HILL,** 6, b g Blue Bresil (FR)—Queen of The Stage (IRE) **M. A. C. Buckley**
30 **CORNAMONA (IRE),** 5, ch m Doyen (IRE)—Belle Bora (IRE) **Countrywide Park Homes Ltd**
31 4, B g Jukebox Jury (IRE)—Dalamine (FR) **Middleham Park Racing XCIV**
32 **DODDIETHEGREAT (IRE),** 7, b g Fame And Glory—Asturienne **Mr K. Alexander**
33 **DUSART (IRE),** 8, b g Flemensfirth (USA)—Dusty Too **R. A. Bartlett**
34 **EAST INDIA EXPRESS,** 4, b g Milan—Roztoc (IRE) **Eic Racing & Table Five**
35 **EASY RIDER,** 5, b g Sixties Icon—Rose Row **Mrs S. M. Roy**
36 **EL KALDOUN (FR),** 9, b g Special Kaldoun (IRE)—Kermesse d'Estruval (FR) **Middleham Park Racing CIV**
37 **EMIR SACREE (FR),** 9, b g Network (GER)—Altesse Sacree (FR) **G. L. Porter**
38 **EPATANTE (FR),** 9, b m No Risk At All (FR)—Kadjara (FR) **Mr J. P. McManus**
39 **FABLE (FR),** 8, b m Coastal Path—Toscane des Fleurs (FR) **Owners Group 078**
40 **FANTASTIC LADY (FR),** 8, b m Network (GER)—Latitude (FR) **E. R. Hanbury**
41 **FAROUK DE CHENEAU (FR),** 8, b g Day Flight—Kardamone (FR) **Owners Group 049**
42 **FIRST STREET,** 6, b g Golden Horn—Ladys First **Lady C. Bamford & Miss A. Bamford**
43 **FRESH AS A DAISY,** 4, b f Kapgarde (FR)—Whoops A Daisy **Just Four Men**
44 **FULL OF LIGHT (IRE),** 7, gr g Leading Light (IRE)—Scartara (FR) **Deva Racing (FOL)**
45 **FUSIL RAFFLES (FR),** 8, b g Saint des Saints (FR)—Tali des Obeaux (FR) **Mr Simon Munir & Mr Isaac Souede**
46 **GENTLEMAN'S RELISH (IRE),** 4, br g Doyen (IRE)—Temple Juno (IRE) **Lindsey Nash & The Famous Five**
47 **GIPSY DE CHOISEL (FR),** 7, b br g Great Pretender (IRE)—
Beautiful Choisel (FR) **Mr Simon Munir & Mr Isaac Souede**
48 **GLYNN (IRE),** 9, b g Winged Love (IRE)—Barnish River (IRE) **Owners Group 039**
49 **GO CHIQUE (FR),** 7, b m Crillon (FR)—Similaresisoldofa (FR) **Middleham Park Racing CX**
50 **HANDS OFF (IRE),** 5, ch g Getaway (GER)—Gaye Lady (IRE) **Bartlett & Speelman**
51 **HOOPER,** 7, b g Rip Van Winkle (IRE)—Earth Amber **Mr Michael Clent**
52 **HYLAND (FR),** 6, gr g Turgeon (USA)—Medine (FR) **The Ten From Seven**
53 **IBERICO LORD (FR),** 5, b g Cokoriko (FR)—Valcelita (FR) **Mr J. P. McManus**
54 **IDEAL DES BORDES (FR),** 5, b g Coastal Path—
Carmen des Bordes (FR) **Mrs B. A. Hanbury, Mrs A. P. Mackenzie Smith**
55 **ILE DE JERSEY (FR),** 5, b m Night Wish (GER)—Zenita des Brosses (FR) **Owners Group 094**
56 **IMMORTAL (FR),** 5, gr g Montmartre (FR)—Cagnes Sur Mer (FR) **West Coast Haulage Limited**
57 **IMPOSE TOI (FR),** 5, b g It's Gino (GER)—Saraska d'Airy (FR) **Mr J. P. McManus**
58 **IMPULSIVE ONE (USA),** 5, b g Union Rags (USA)—Hokey Okey (USA) **Mr Simon Munir & Mr Isaac Souede**
59 **IOLAOS DU MOU (FR),** 5, b g Coastal Path—Thelemise du Mou (FR) **Loose Ends, Hosking & Knox**
60 **ISSUING AUTHORITY (IRE),** 6, ch g Flemensfirth (USA)—Mini's Last (IRE) **Owners Group 101**
61 **JAITROPLACLASSE (FR),** 4, b g Secret Singer (FR)—Bibracje (FR) **Mr M. A. R. Blencowe**
62 **JEMURA (IRE),** 5, b g Mahler—Joe's Dream Catch (IRE) **Mick Fitzgerald Racing Syndicate 1**
63 **JEN'S BOY,** 9, b g Malinas (GER)—Friendly Craic (IRE) **Middleham Park Racing CV**
64 **JET POWERED (IRE),** 6, b g Jet Away—Cloghoge Lady (IRE) **Mrs M. Donnelly**
65 **JINA (FR),** 4, b f Wings of Eagles (FR)—Valoise (FR) **FB Racing Club**

MR NICKY HENDERSON - continued

66 **JOHNNY BLUE (IRE),** 4, br g Soldier of Fortune (IRE)—Accordian Lady (IRE) **Mr J. Neocleous**
67 **JONBON (FR),** 7, b g Walk In The Park (IRE)—Star Face (FR) **Mr J. P. McManus**
68 **JOYEUSE (FR),** 4, b f No Risk At All (FR)—Virfolette (FR) **Mr J. P. McManus**
69 **JUNGLE WOOD (FR),** 4, b g Cokoriko (FR)—A Dormir Debout (FR) **Mr Stewart Andrew**
70 **KINCARDINE,** 6, b g Kayf Tara—Side Step **The King**
71 **KING ALEXANDER (IRE),** 5, b g Mount Nelson—Pale Face (IRE) **Mr J. Neocleous**
72 **KING EAGLE (IRE),** 4, ch g Frankel—The Lark **Lady Bamford**
73 **KING OTTOKAR (FR),** 7, b g Motivator—Treasure (FR) **Mrs S. M. Roy**
74 **KINTAIL,** 4, b g Blue Bresil (FR)—Speed Bonnie Boat **Lady M. B. Dulverton**
75 4, B br g Sholokhov (IRE)—Kris Kindle (IRE) **Middleham Park Racing LXXV**
76 **KUTAIBA,** 4, b f Golden Horn—Maktaba **Dash Grange Stud**
77 **LADY D'ARBANVILLE,** 5, bl m Authorized (IRE)—Miracle Maid **Syders & Burkes**
78 **LELANTOS (IRE),** 7, br g Presenting—Western Focus (IRE) **Middleham Park Racing XCI**
79 **LIGHTFOOT LADY (IRE),** 6, b m Leading Light (IRE)—Springinherstep (IRE) **The Knot Again Partnership**
80 **LOVE BITE (IRE),** 5, b m Milan—Knotted Midge (IRE) **Hot To Trot Jumping**
81 **LUCCIA,** 5, ch m The Gurkha (IRE)—Earth Amber **Pump & Plant Services Ltd**
82 **LUCKY PLACE (FR),** 4, b g Pastorius (GER)—Luckystar du Frene (FR) **Mrs G Van Geest & Mr M George**
83 5, B m Blue Bresil (FR)—Madam Fontaine (FR)
84 **MANALA (FR),** 4, b f Walzertakt (GER)—Aratiyna (FR) **Mr N. C. Wilson, Mrs R. K. Wilson**
85 **MARIE'S ROCK (IRE),** 8, b br m Milan—By The Hour (IRE) **Middleham Park Racing XLII**
86 **MARMALAID,** 6, gr m Martaline—Miracle Maid **Burkes & Syders**
87 **MEADOWSUITE (IRE),** 5, b m Spanish Moon (USA)—La Premiere Dame (FR) **Lady Tennant**
88 **MILITARY MISTRESS (IRE),** 4, b f Soldier of Fortune (IRE)—Flirthing Around (IRE)
89 **MILL GREEN,** 11, b g Black Sam Bellamy (IRE)—Ceilidh Royal **Mrs R. H. Brown**
90 **MISTER COFFEY (FR),** 8, b g Authorized (IRE)—Mamitador **Lady C. Bamford & Miss A. Bamford**
91 **MISTER FISHER (IRE),** 9, b g Jeremy (USA)—That's Amazing (IRE) **James and Jean Potter Ltd**
92 **MISTER PARK (IRE),** 6, b g Walk In The Park (IRE)—Anniesthyne (IRE) **Unique Financial Racing Partnership**
93 **MONTECAM (IRE),** 4, b g Camelot—Monte Solaro (IRE) **Mr K. Doyle**
94 **MOON LADY,** 5, b m Pether's Moon (IRE)—Lady Beaufort **James and Jean Potter Ltd**
95 **MORNING LINE (IRE),** 5, b g Shantou (USA)—Blodge (IRE) **Mr J. P. McManus**
96 **MOUNT ETNA (IRE),** 5, b g Milan—Flowers On Sunday (IRE) **Mrs C. Kendrick**
97 **NEXT DESTINATION (IRE),** 11, b g Dubai Destination (USA)—Liss Alainn (IRE) **M. C. Denmark**
98 **NO ORDINARY JOE (IRE),** 7, b g Getaway (GER)—Shadow Dearg (IRE) **Mr J. P. McManus**
99 **OLD TIME CHASER (IRE),** 5, b g Affinisea (IRE)—Simply Erin (IRE) **McNeill Family & Stone Family**
100 **ON MY COMMAND (IRE),** 7, b m War Command (USA)—Highindi **Mr J. Neocleous**
101 **ON THE BLIND SIDE (IRE),** 11, b g Stowaway—Such A Set Up (IRE) **Mr Alan Spence**
102 **OVERPRICED MIXER,** 6, b g Harbour Watch (IRE)—Chincoteague (IRE) **Owners Group 051**
103 **PARK HILL DANCER (FR),** 6, b g Waldpark (GER)—Sweni Hill (IRE) **Middleham Park Racing XXXVIII & Partner**
104 **PAROS (FR),** 6, ch g Masterstroke (USA)—Soft Blue (FR) **Middleham Park Racing CXXV**
105 **PAWAPURI,** 4, b br f Golden Horn—Palitana (USA) **Sullivan Bloodstock Ltd**
106 **PEACE OF ROME (GER),** 5, gr g Jukebox Jury (IRE)—Peace Flower (IRE) **Mr Alan Spence**
107 **PENTLAND HILLS (IRE),** 8, b g Motivator—Elle Galante (GER) **Owners Group 031**
108 **PERSIAN TIME,** 5, b g Califet (FR)—Persian Forest **McNeill Family & Stone Family**
109 **PRIVATE RYAN (IRE),** 6, ch g Presenting—Sea Jewel (IRE) **The Blue Bar Partnership**
110 **PROPELLED,** 6, b g Kapgarde (FR)—Polly Peachum (IRE) **Middleham Park Racing LXI & Peter Lamb**
111 **QUEENS ROCK (IRE),** 6, b m Shirocco (GER)—Lohort Castle (IRE) **Noel Fehily Racing Syndicate-Queens Rock**
112 **QUICK DRAW (IRE),** 7, b g Getaway (GER)—Sept Verites (FR) **Miss A. C. Bamford**
113 **RATHMACKNEE (IRE),** 7, b g Jet Away—Let's Park (IRE) **Million in Mind Partnership**
114 **ROCCSTAR BAY,** 5, b m Telescope (IRE)—Miss Rocco **E. R. Hanbury**
115 **ROYAL MAX (FR),** 5, b g Maxios—Rahada (GER) **Lady M. B. Dulverton**
116 **RUSSIAN RULER (IRE),** 6, b br g Sholokhov (IRE)—Hot Choice **Unique Financial Racing Partnership**
117 5, B m Blue Bresil (FR)—Safari Run (IRE) **Walters Plant Hire Ltd**
118 **SCANDISK PARK (IRE),** 5, b g Walk In The Park (IRE)—Scandisk (IRE) **Mr P. Holden**
119 **SCARPERED (IRE),** 6, b g Getaway (GER)—Finola's Gift (IRE) **Seven Barrows Limited**
120 **SCARPIA (IRE),** 9, ch g Sans Frontieres (IRE)—Bunglasha Lady (IRE) **Mrs T. J. Stone-Brown**
121 **SHANAGH BOB (IRE),** 5, b g Mahler—Exit Bob (IRE) **Mrs M. Donnelly**
122 **SHISHKIN (IRE),** 9, b g Sholokhov (IRE)—Labarynth (IRE) **Mrs M. Donnelly**
123 **SOUTHOFTHEBORDER (IRE),** 5, b g Leading Light (IRE)—Dante's Queen (IRE) **West Coast Haulage Limited**
124 **SPRING NOTE (IRE),** 5, ch m Mahler—Spring Baloo (IRE) **Canter Banter Racing**
125 4, B g Battle of Marengo (IRE)—St Helans Bay (IRE)

MR NICKY HENDERSON - continued

126 **STEAL A MARCH,** 8, b g Mount Nelson—Side Step **The King**
127 **STRUTTER,** 4, b g Racinger (FR)—Minute Blonde (FR) **Mr J. Neocleous**
128 **SURREY QUEST (IRE),** 6, b g Milan—Roztoc (IRE) **Surrey Racing (SQ)**
129 **SWAPPED (FR),** 6, b g Sinndar (IRE)—La Bezizais (FR) **Mr A. Speelman & Mr M. Speelman**
130 **TED DA TITAN,** 7, b g Kayf Tara—Aeronautica (IRE) **Mrs C. Kendrick**
131 **THE BOMBER LISTON (IRE),** 7, b g Yeats (IRE)—True Britannia **Mr J. P. McManus**
132 **THE CARPENTER (IRE),** 7, gr g Shantaram—Just Another Penny (IRE) **Owners Group 086**
133 **THE HAPPY CHAPATI (IRE),** 4, b g Champs Elysees—Thuringe (FR) **C. N. Barnes**
134 **THEATRE GLORY (IRE),** 6, b m Fame And Glory—Native Beauty (IRE) **Canter Banter Racing 2**
135 **TIME FLIES BY (IRE),** 8, ch g Getaway (GER)—What A Mewsment (IRE) **Mr J. P. McManus**
136 **TOUCHY FEELY,** 6, b m Kayf Tara—Liberthine (FR) **Robert Waley-Cohen & Turf Club 2022**
137 **TRADECRAFT (IRE),** 4, b g Blue Bresil (FR)—Rowlestone Lass **M. A. C. Buckley**
138 **TREYARNON BAY (IRE),** 5, b m Mastercraftsman (IRE)—
Dynalosca (USA) **Highclere Thoroughbred Racing -Treyarnon**
139 **TWEED SKIRT,** 6, b m Martaline—Theatre Girl **Just Four Men With Rose Tinted Glasses**
140 **UNDER CONTROL (FR),** 4, b f Doctor Dino (FR)—Delinda (FR) **Mr J. P. McManus**
141 **WALKING ON AIR (IRE),** 6, b g Walk In The Park (IRE)—Refinement (IRE) **Mrs D. A. Tabor**
142 **WESTWOOD RYDER (IRE),** 6, b g Flemensfirth (USA)—Beeverstown Girl (IRE) **The Albatross Club**
143 **WILL CARVER (IRE),** 8, b g Califet (FR)—Rock Angel (IRE) **Owners Group 064**
144 4, B g Milan—Windsor Higgins (IRE)
145 **WISEGUY (IRE),** 7, b g Fame And Glory—Sunset Queen (IRE) **Mrs John Magnier & Mrs Paul Shanahan**

NH Jockey: James Bowen, Nico De Boinville, Daryl Jacob. **Conditional Jockey:** Sean O'Briain.

---

248 MR PAUL HENDERSON, Whitsbury

Postal: **1 Manor Farm Cottage, Whitsbury, Fordingbridge, Hampshire, SP6 3QP**
Contacts: **PHONE 01725 518113 MOBILE 07958 482213 FAX 01725 518113**
EMAIL phendersonracing@gmail.com

1 **ALLARDYCE,** 11, b g Black Sam Bellamy (IRE)—Woore Lass (IRE) **Table 8 & Mr J Duffy**
2 **BALLYEGAN HERO (IRE),** 12, b g Oscar (IRE)—Kelly Gales (IRE) **Table 8 & Mr J Duffy**
3 **DOUBTCHA MOSSY BOY (IRE),** 7, b g Curtain Time (IRE)—Fernhill Queen (IRE) **The Rockbourne Partnership**
4 **DOYEN QUEEN (IRE),** 9, b m Doyen (IRE)—Panoora Queen (IRE) **NHRE Racing Club**
5 **ENTRE DEUX (FR),** 9, b g Khalkevi (IRE)—Evitta (FR) **Mr S. Tulk**
6 **HOLKHAM HALL (IRE),** 7, b g Kalanisi (IRE)—Royal Bride **The Ray Of Hope Partnership**
7 **KAY'S LIGHT (IRE),** 6, b m Leading Light (IRE)—Chlolo Supreme (IRE) **NHRE Racing Club**
8 **KYLENOE DANCER,** 5, ch m Norse Dancer (IRE)—Kylenoe Fairy (IRE) **Mr E. J. Hawkings**
9 **LUNCHABLE BOB,** 8, b g Big Bad Bob (IRE)—Kekova **Mr J. Pyatt**
10 **MEGALODON (IRE),** 10, b g Getaway (GER)—Fitzgrey (IRE) **Hawkings Finch Harding Stubbs Willis**
11 **MISTER MOSE (IRE),** 8, b g Jeremy (USA)—Gypsy Lou (IRE) **Mr J. H. W. Finch**
12 **NO DRAMA (IRE),** 8, ch g Mahler—Calimesa (IRE) **The Sundowners**
13 **OUR CHAMP (IRE),** 5, b g Champs Elysees—Affascinare (IRE) **Pearson,Jenner,Hawkings,Dunford&Harding**
14 **ROCK ON BARNEY (IRE),** 12, b g Fracas (IRE)—Monthly Sessions (IRE) **Mr R. G. Henderson**
15 **SAN PEDRO (IRE),** 6, b g Gleneagles (IRE)—Elle Woods (IRE) **The Rockbourne Partnership**
16 **SHAW'S CROSS (IRE),** 11, b g Mr Dinos (IRE)—Capparoe Cross (IRE) **Mareildar Racing Part 1**
17 **SMALL BAD BOB (IRE),** 8, b g Big Bad Bob (IRE)—Baileys Gleam **John H W Finch & Rockbourne Partnership**
18 **STORM HILL (IRE),** 8, gr g Mahler—Midnight Pleasure (IRE) **Hawkings Harding Lofts Pearson Willis**
19 **TZUNAMI,** 7, ch g Gentlewave (IRE)—Kylenoe Fairy (IRE) **Mr E. J. Hawkings**

249 MR MICHAEL HERRINGTON, Thirsk

Postal: **Garbutt Farm, Cold Kirby, Thirsk, North Yorkshire, YO7 2HJ**
Contacts: **MOBILE 07855 396858**
EMAIL info@michaelherringtonracing.co.uk WEBSITE www.michaelherringtonracing.co.uk

1 **ANIF (IRE),** 9, b g Cape Cross (IRE)—Cadenza (FR) **Stuart Herrington & Peter Forster**
2 **ARAIFJAN,** 6, ch g Kyllachy—Light Hearted **Mrs H. J. Lloyd-Herrington**
3 **BAY OF NAPLES (IRE),** 7, b g Exceed And Excel (AUS)—Copperbeech (IRE) **Mrs S. E. Lloyd**
4 **BEYOND INFINITY,** 6, ch g Bated Breath—Lady Gloria **Team Given 5**
5 **CONNIE R (IRE),** 4, b f Gutaifan (IRE)—Amurra **Mr P. S. Riley**
6 **DUBAI JEANIUS (IRE),** 5, b g Pride of Dubai (AUS)—Tempura (GER) **Mrs H. J. Lloyd-Herrington**
7 **GLORIOUS CHARMER,** 7, b g Charm Spirit (IRE)—Fantacise **Mrs H. J. Lloyd-Herrington**
8 **GOOD EARTH (IRE),** 6, b g Acclamation—Madhatten (IRE) **Mrs H. J. Lloyd-Herrington**
9 **KODEBREAKER (IRE),** 4, b g Kodi Bear (IRE)—Coachhouse Lady (USA) **Michael Herrington Racing Club**
10 **LOVE DESTINY,** 6, b g Lethal Force (IRE)—Danehill Destiny **S Herrington, P Forster & Team Given 5**
11 **MAHARASHTRA,** 7, ch g Schiaparelli (GER)—Khandala (IRE) **Nicholas Baines, Team Given 5 & Partner**
12 **RATAFIA,** 5, b g Iffraaj—Aetna **Ingram Racing**
13 **RATHBONE,** 7, b g Foxwedge (AUS)—Frequent **Mrs H. J. Lloyd-Herrington**
14 **THAAYER,** 8, b g Helmet (AUS)—Sakhya (IRE) **Mrs H. S Herrington, P Forster & Partner**
15 **THE GAME OF LIFE,** 8, b g Oasis Dream—Velvet Star (IRE) **Mrs H. J. Lloyd-Herrington**
16 **TIGER SPIRIT (IRE),** 6, b m Charm Spirit (IRE)—Tiger Lilly (IRE) **K & L Fitzsimons**
17 **YOSHIMI (IRE),** 6, gr g Dream Ahead (USA)—Dawn Dew (GER) **Mrs S. E. Lloyd**

THREE-YEAR-OLDS

18 **I AM SIMBA,** b c Roaring Lion (USA)—Sea Chorus **Mr M. Sharpe**
19 **MUSICAL YOUTH,** b g Fountain of Youth (IRE)—Tawaasul **David Frame & Mrs H Lloyd-herrington**
20 **ROXY'S CHARM,** b f Charm Spirit (IRE)—Roxy Star (IRE) **Mr M. Sharpe**

Assistant Trainer: Helen Lloyd-Herrington.

---

250 MRS LAWNEY HILL, Aston Rowant

Trainer did not wish details of their string to appear

---

251 MR CHARLES HILLS, Lambourn

Postal: **Wetherdown House, Lambourn, Hungerford, Berkshire, RG17 8UB**
Contacts: **PHONE 01488 71548**
EMAIL info@charleshills.co.uk WEBSITE www.charleshills.co.uk

1 **CARAUSIUS,** 6, b g Cacique (IRE)—Domitia **Mrs Fiona Williams**
2 **EQUALITY,** 5, b g Equiano (FR)—Penny Drops **Kennet Valley Thoroughbreds II**
3 **EQUILATERAL,** 8, b g Equiano (FR)—Tarentaise **Mrs Fitri Hay**
4 **GARRUS (IRE),** 7, gr g Acclamation—Queen of Power (IRE) **Mrs Susan Roy**
5 **HERSILIA,** 4, b f Adaay (IRE)—Vespasia **Mrs Fiona Williams**
6 **IBN ALDAR,** 4, br g Twilight Son—Bint Aldar **Mr Ziad A. Galadari**
7 **KHAADEM (IRE),** 7, br g Dark Angel (IRE)—White Daffodil (IRE) **Mrs Fitri Hay**
8 **KING'S KNIGHT (IRE),** 6, b g Dark Angel (IRE)—Oatcake **Mr Ziad A. Galadari**
9 **MAGHLAAK,** 4, b c Muhaarar—Ghanaati (USA) **Shadwell Estate Company Ltd**
10 **MAY SONIC,** 7, b g Mayson—Aromatherapy **Hills Angels**
11 **MUTASAABEQ,** 5, br h Invincible Spirit (IRE)—Ghanaati (USA) **Shadwell Estate Company Ltd**

MR CHARLES HILLS - continued

12 **ORAZIO (IRE),** 4, gr c Caravaggio (USA)—Lady Fashion **Mrs Susan Roy**
13 **POGO (IRE),** 7, b h Zebedee—Cute **Gary & Linnet Woodward**
14 **SARATOGA GOLD,** 5, ch g Mayson—Lady Sylvia **David J Keast & Faringdon Place 1**
15 **SHALFA (IRE),** 4, ch f Ribchester (IRE)—Kikandy (IRE) **Aura (Gas) Holdings Ltd**
16 **SHOBIZ,** 5, b g Showcasing—Royal Confidence **Mr D. M. James**
17 **SONNY LISTON (IRE),** 4, b g Lawman (FR)—Stars In Your Eyes **Chelsea Thoroughbreds - The Big Bear**
18 **TANMAWWY (IRE),** 5, b g Invincible Spirit (IRE)—Rufoof **Mr H. Frost**
19 **VAYNOR (IRE),** 4, ro g Mastercraftsman (IRE)—Sanaya (IRE) **Mrs Fitri Hay**
20 **VINDOLANDA,** 7, ch m Nathaniel (IRE)—Cartimandua **Mrs Fiona Williams**
21 **WANEES,** 4, b g Le Havre (IRE)—Waldnah **Shadwell Estate Company Ltd**

THREE-YEAR-OLDS

22 **AGRICOLA,** gr c Tasleet—Servilia **Mrs Fiona Williams**
23 **AL MUQDAD,** ch c Zoustar (AUS)—Miss Work of Art **Mr Ziad A. Galadari**
24 **ALASKAN (IRE),** b g Kodiac—Fixed Gaze (USA) **Kennet Valley Thoroughbreds XV**
25 B f Acclamation—Beatify (IRE) **AlMohamediya Racing**
26 **BLOODHOUND (IRE),** gr c Wootton Bassett—Amaranthe (FR) **Mrs Fitri Hay**
27 **BODORGAN (IRE),** gr c El Kabeir (USA)—Silver Rose (IRE) **Julie Martin & David R. Martin & Partner**
28 **CICERO'S GIFT,** b c Muhaarar—Terentia **Rosehill Racing**
29 **DIVINE LIBRA (IRE),** gr c Dark Angel (IRE)—Rakiza (IRE) **Alara Investments Limited**
30 **EAGLE EYED TOM,** b g Gleneagles (IRE)—Fauran (IRE) **Mr Tony Cocum**
31 B c Bated Breath—Enfijaar (IRE) **Mr Jerry Hinds & Mr Ashley Head**
32 **EXERTIVE (IRE),** b f Expert Eye—Garraun (IRE) **Mr John C Grant & Mr B W Hills**
33 **GALERON (IRE),** b c Camacho—Society Gal (IRE) **Teme Valley & Aura (gas) Holdings Ltd**
34 **GASMAN (IRE),** b c Cracksman—Anne Of Kiev (IRE) **Aura (Gas) Holdings Ltd**
35 **GERALT OF RIVIA (IRE),** ch c El Kabeir (USA)—Wojha (IRE) **Alara Investments Limited & Partner**
36 **GHOST LIGHTS (IRE),** b c Gustav Klimt (IRE)—Cuilaphuca (IRE) **The Albert Alickadoos & Partner**
37 **HARRY MAGNUS (IRE),** b c Harry Angel (IRE)—Music And Dance **One More Moment of Madness**
38 **HAVANA HEAT,** b c Havana Grey—Light of Love **The Hot Shots Syndicate & Phoebe Hobby**
39 **LABIQA (IRE),** b f Muhaarar—Inez **Mr Ziad A. Galadari**
40 **LADY ALARA (IRE),** b f Invincible Spirit (IRE)—Red Halo (IRE) **Alara Investments Limited**
41 **LADY OF ANJOU (IRE),** b f Awtaad (IRE)—Angevine **Rosehill Racing**
42 **LAKOTA LASS (IRE),** b f Sioux Nation (USA)—Iffraaj Pink (IRE) **Mrs Fitri Hay**
43 **LORD UHTRED (IRE),** b c Siyouni (FR)—Faay (IRE) **KHK Racing Ltd**
44 **LOSE YOUR WAD (IRE),** b c Muhaarar—Mission Secrete (IRE) **Jerry Hinds & Philip Herbert**
45 **LUDDEN LASS (IRE),** b f Dandy Man (IRE)—Xinji (IRE) **Mr John C. Grant**
46 **MIDNIGHTATTHEOASIS,** b c Oasis Dream—Love On The Rocks (IRE) **Mr Christopher Wright & Mr W H Carson**
47 **MINKA (IRE),** b f Kodiac—Queen's Code (IRE) **Mr Steven Rocco**
48 **MISS LIGHTFANDANGO,** gr f Dark Angel (IRE)—Elegante Bere (FR) **The Hon Mrs J. M. Corbett & Mr C. Wright**
49 **MOJITO BOY,** b c Havana Grey—Fashion Trade **Jerry Hinds & Philip Herbert**
50 **MOUNTAIN FLOWER (IRE),** b f Iffraaj—Moonlife (IRE) **Mrs Susan Roy**
51 **MUTAANY,** b c Invincible Spirit (IRE)—Madany (IRE) **Shadwell Estate Company Ltd**
52 **PADDY'S DAY (IRE),** b c Starspangledbanner (AUS)—
Elusive Gold (IRE) **McGoff, Ferguson, Mason, Nicholls, Hills**
53 **PEARLING TRAIL,** ch c Zoustar (AUS)—Shumoos (USA) **Mrs Victoria Machen**
54 **PENDING APPEAL,** b f Lawman (FR)—Influent (IRE) **Rosehill Racing**
55 **POPPAEA,** b f Oasis Dream—Cartimandua **Mrs Fiona Williams**
56 **RABAAH (IRE),** b c Dubawi (IRE)—Rufoof **Shadwell Estate Company Ltd**
57 **RACINGBREAKS RYDER (IRE),** b c Fast Company (IRE)—Nisma (IRE) **Racing Breaks & Friends**
58 **SARATOGA SPIRIT,** ch f Tasleet—Lady Sylvia **David J Keast & Mrs Wendy Soliman**
59 **SAXON KING,** b c Zoustar (AUS)—Brevity (USA) **JJ Culhane & Cliveden Stud**
60 **SHOGUN'S KATANA,** br c Territories (IRE)—Rock Ace (IRE) **Mr Ziad A. Galadari**
61 **SO CHIC (IRE),** b f Exceed And Excel (AUS)—Kaks Roosid (FR) **JJ Culhane,C Rosier & G & L Woodward**
62 **SPECIAL EVENT (IRE),** gr f Caravaggio (USA)—Anyone Special (IRE) **Mrs E O'Leary & Mr B W Hills**
63 **STAR CONTENDER,** b f Muhaarar—Perfect Star **Mildmay Racing & Aura (gas) Holdings Ltd**
64 **SUGAR HILL (IRE),** b g Invincible Spirit (IRE)—Coconut Kreek **Lady Bamford**
65 **SYDNEYARMS CHELSEA (IRE),** b f Sioux Nation (USA)—Wedding Dress **Cornthrop Bs & Sydney Arms Chelsea**
66 **TAJDIF (IRE),** b c Invincible Spirit (IRE)—Safeenah **Shadwell Estate Company Ltd**
67 **TENNESSEE DREAM,** b f Oasis Dream—Belle Meade (IRE) **Mildmay Racing & Aura (gas) Holdings Ltd**

MR CHARLES HILLS - continued

68 THE TOFF (IRE), b g Dandy Man (IRE)—Parakopi (IRE) **Rosehill Racing**
69 THEMAINPROTAGONIST (IRE), gr g Dark Angel (IRE)—White Daffodil (IRE) **Mrs Annette O'Callaghan**
70 TIMELY ESCAPE, b c Cityscape—In Your Time **Rosehill Racing**

TWO-YEAR-OLDS

71 B c 08/04 Sioux Nation (USA)—Armageddon (War Command (USA)) (48000)
72 ASINARA, b f 24/05 Harry Angel (IRE)—Kalsa (IRE) (Whipper (USA))
73 AUTUMN DREAM (IRE), b f 09/02 Sioux Nation (USA)—Ydillique (IRE) (Sadler's Wells (USA)) (150000)
74 B f 27/03 Teofilo (IRE)—Baqqa (IRE) (Shamardal (USA)) (38000)
75 B c 11/03 Land Force (IRE)—Basque Beauty (Nayef)
76 B c 15/02 Lope de Vega (IRE)—Bella Estrella (IRE) (High Chaparral (IRE)) (200000)
77 Ch f 25/02 Showcasing—Biri's Angel (IRE) (Sir Prancealot (IRE)) (200000)
78 CADOGAN GARDENS (IRE), b f 01/05 No Nay Never (USA)—Gale Song (Invincible Spirit (IRE))
79 B f 24/04 Acclamation—Caribbean Ace (IRE) (Red Clubs (IRE)) (32013)
80 B c 04/04 Dark Angel (IRE)—Clem Fandango (FR) (Elzaam (AUS)) (80032)
81 CONDE (IRE), ch c 05/02 Phoenix of Spain (IRE)—Grandee Daisy (Sepoy (AUS)) (36190)
82 B c 26/01 Churchill (IRE)—Damaniyat Girl (USA) (Elusive Quality (USA)) (105000)
83 DOOLEY (IRE), b c 06/03 Magna Grecia (IRE)—Greatest Place (IRE) (Shamardal (USA)) (76190)
84 B f 09/05 Kingman—Efaadah (IRE) (Dansili)
85 B c 26/02 Blue Point (IRE)—Familliarity (Nayef (USA))
86 B f 31/03 Dark Angel (IRE)—Faradays Law (IRE) (Lawman (FR))
87 B f 26/01 Havana Gold (IRE)—Funday (Daylami (IRE))
88 B c 31/03 Oasis Dream—Granny Bea (IRE) (Galileo (IRE)) (68027)
89 B f 12/02 Teofilo (IRE)—Hope Lake (IRE) (Shamardal (USA)) (110000)
90 HOPE RISING (IRE), b f 14/02 Phoenix of Spain (IRE)—Jellicle Ball (IRE) (Invincible Spirit (IRE))
91 B c 13/04 Magna Grecia (IRE)—Iffraaj Pink (IRE) (Iffraaj)
92 B f 01/03 Galiway—Kendam (FR) (Kendargent (FR)) (160000)
93 B c 06/04 Advertise—Kerry's Dream (Tobougg (IRE)) (100000)
94 B c 02/04 Sioux Nation (USA)—Knock Stars (IRE) (Soviet Star (USA)) (120048)
95 B f 10/01 Churchill (IRE)—Land Girl (USA) (War Front (USA)) (59048)
96 Gr c 15/04 Dark Angel (IRE)—Last Bid (Vital Equine)
97 B c 14/03 Too Darn Hot—Liberating (Iffraaj) (80032)
98 Ch f 29/01 Havana Grey—Little Clarinet (IRE) (Requinto (IRE)) (64762)
99 B c 13/01 Camacho—Mandoria (GER) (Adlerflug (GER)) (38095)
100 B c 05/03 Twilight Son—Maybride (Mayson) (57623)
101 B c 26/03 Acclamation—Mickleberry (IRE) (Desert Style (IRE)) (42000)
102 B c 28/03 Too Darn Hot—Mudawanah (Dansili) (80000)
103 B c 21/03 Night of Thunder (IRE)—Muteela (Dansili)
104 B f 08/02 Galileo (IRE)—Naples Bay (USA) (Giant's Causeway (USA)) (230000)
105 B c 12/02 Zoffany (IRE)—Pioneer Spirit (Galileo (IRE))
106 B c 13/04 Magna Grecia (IRE)—Prima Luce (IRE) (Galileo (IRE)) (112045)
107 B f 07/05 Sea The Stars (IRE)—Rakiza (IRE) (Elnadim (USA))
108 RUKAANA, b gr c 23/03 Dark Angel (IRE)—Shurooq (Dubawi (IRE)) (60000)
109 SARATOGA STAR, b f 04/03 Al Kazeem—Lady Sylvia (Haafhd)
110 B f 09/03 Sea The Stars (IRE)—Sea of Wonders (IRE) (Fastnet Rock (AUS)) (80000)
111 B f 17/03 Land Force (IRE)—Seeing Red (IRE) (Sea The Stars (IRE)) (120000)
112 Gr c 02/04 Caravaggio (USA)—Spirit of India (Galileo (IRE))
113 B c 03/04 Kodiac—Stage Name (Famous Name) (85000)
114 B f 09/04 Highland Reel (IRE)—Suvenna (IRE) (Arcano (IRE)) (48019)
115 THE ICE PHOENIX (IRE), ro c 19/04 Phoenix of Spain (IRE)—Bratislava (Dr Fong (USA)) (52021)
116 TREFOR (IRE), b c 17/02 Invincible Army (IRE)—Silk Bow (Elusive City (USA)) (100000)
117 Br c 31/01 Advertise—Valletta Gold (IRE) (Gutaifan (IRE)) (100000)
118 B c 24/02 Ulysses (IRE)—Vaulted (Kyllachy) (40000)
119 B c 27/03 Sea The Stars (IRE)—Yaazy (IRE) (Teofilo (IRE))

Assistant Trainer: Nicola Dowell, Jamie Insole.

Apprentice Jockey: Owen Lewis.

252 MRS CLAIRE WENDY HITCH, Watchet

Postal: **Higher Sminhays Farm, Brendon Hill, WATCHET, Somerset, TA23 0LG**
EMAIL barnlane@btinternet.com

1 **BALLYATTY,** 8, b g Kayf Tara—Charmaine Wood **Mrs C. W. Hitch**
2 **BARBARIAN,** 7, b g Black Sam Bellamy (IRE)—Mizzurka **Mrs C. W. Hitch**
3 **BOTHIE LADY (IRE),** 6, b m Kalanisi (IRE)—Lackagh Lass (IRE) **Mrs C. W. Hitch**
4 4, B g Mahler—Cairnsforth (IRE) **Mrs C. W. Hitch**
5 **EVERY BREAKIN WAVE (IRE),** 13, b g Double Eclipse (IRE)—Striking Gold (USA) **Mrs C. W. Hitch**
6 **GEOFFS LAD (IRE),** 4, b g Kalanisi (IRE)—Doneraile Parke (IRE) **Mrs C. W. Hitch**
7 **HOLERDAY RIDGE (IRE),** 8, b g Mahler—Deep Lilly **Mrs C. W. Hitch**
8 **WINTER GETAWAY (IRE),** 10, b m Getaway (GER)—Galzig (IRE) **Mr R. M. E. Wright**

253 MR MARK HOAD, Lewes

Postal: **Windmill Lodge Stables, Spital Road, Lewes, East Sussex, BN7 1LS**
Contacts: **PHONE 01273 480691, 01273 477124 MOBILE 07742 446168 FAX 01273 477124**
EMAIL markhoad@aol.com

1 **CRAZY MAISIE (IRE),** 4, b f Belardo (IRE)—Circleofinfluence (USA) **Mr A. Bangs**
2 **HEY HO LET'S GO,** 7, b g Dream Ahead (USA)—Lookslikeanangel **Mrs K. B. Tester**
3 **HISTORY WRITER (IRE),** 8, b g Canford Cliffs (IRE)—Abhasana (IRE) **Mrs K. B. Tester**
4 **LORD CLENAGHCASTLE (IRE),** 9, b g Big Bad Bob (IRE)—Clenaghcastle Lady (IRE) **Mr M. R. Baldry**

254 MR PHILIP HOBBS, Minehead

Postal: **Sandhill, Bilbrook, Minehead, Somerset, TA24 6HA**
Contacts: **PHONE 01984 640366 MOBILE 07860 729795 FAX 01984 641124**
EMAIL pjhobbs@pjhobbs.com WEBSITE www.pjhobbs.com

1 **ABIGAEL,** 6, b m Cameron Highland (IRE)—Mere Blanche (IRE) **Team CH Racing**
2 **ADVANTURA (IRE),** 6, b g Watar (IRE)—Keys Hope (IRE) **A. P. Staple**
3 **ALBERIC (FR),** 6, b g Poliglote—Khayance (FR) **Corrina Ltd**
4 **ARC RYDER,** 5, b g Kayf Tara—Ryde Back **Mrs J. A. S. Luff**
5 **BALLYDISCO (IRE),** 6, b g Presenting—Alphadite (IRE) **N. R. A. Sutton**
6 **BLUE ANCHOR,** 5, b m Blue Bresil (FR)—Kayf Willow **The Philip Hobbs Racing Partnership**
7 **CAMPROND (FR),** 7, b g Lope de Vega (IRE)—Bernieres (IRE) **Mr J. P. McManus**
8 **CELEBRE D'ALLEN (FR),** 11, ch g Network (GER)—Revoltee (FR) **A. Stennett**
9 4, B g Mount Nelson—Coca's Well (IRE) **The Englands and Heywoods**
10 **CONTRAMAR,** 5, b g Blue Bresil (FR)—Sting In The Gale **Louisville Syndicate**
11 **COOLNAUGH HAZE (IRE),** 5, b g Lawman (FR)—Midas Haze **Highclere Thoroughbred Racing - Cool**
12 **DAN'S CHOSEN (IRE),** 8, b g Well Chosen—Miss Audacious (IRE) **The Philip Hobbs Racing Partnership II**
13 **DARK DUOMO (IRE),** 5, b g Milan—Aroka (FR) **Louisville Syndicate**
14 **DEISE ABA (IRE),** 10, b g Mahler—Kit Massini (IRE) **Exors of the Late Mr T. J. Hemmings**
15 **DOLLY DELIGHTFUL,** 5, b m Soldier of Fortune (IRE)—Dolores Delightful (FR) **My Racing Manager Friends**
16 **DOLPHIN SQUARE (IRE),** 9, b g Shantou (USA)—Carrig Eden Lass (IRE) **D. Maxwell**
17 **EARTH COMPANY (IRE),** 7, b br g Arcadio (GER)—Lady Rhinestone (IRE) **R. M. Penny**
18 **ECU DE LA NOVERIE (FR),** 9, b g Linda's Lad—Quat'sous d'Or (FR) **D. Maxwell**
19 **ENERGY ONE,** 5, b m Kayf Tara—One For Joules (IRE) **Mr D. M. Mathias**
20 **ENERGY TWO,** 4, b f Kayf Tara—One For Joules (IRE) **Mr D. M. Mathias**

MR PHILIP HOBBS - continued

21 **FANCY YOUR CHANCES (IRE),** 6, br m Presenting—May's June (IRE) **Mr J. P. McManus**
22 **FAR SIGHT,** 6, b g Telescope (IRE)—Miss Chinchilla **Dr V. M. G. Ferguson**
23 **FOR LANGY (FR),** 8, b g Day Flight—Jubilee II (FR) **D. Maxwell**
24 **GEORGI GIRL (IRE),** 4, ch f Getaway (GER)—Gales Hill (IRE) **Michael Rembaum & Michael Tuckey**
25 **GETUPEARLY,** 6, ch g Getaway (GER)—Come The Dawn **The Philip Hobbs Racing Partnership**
26 **GINGERBRED,** 5, ch g Universal (IRE)—Portrait Royale (IRE) **Unity Farm Holiday Centre Ltd**
27 **GOLDEN SOVEREIGN (IRE),** 9, b g Gold Well—Fugal Maid (IRE) **Mr L. Quinn**
28 **GOSHHOWPOSH (IRE),** 6, b g Malinas (GER)—Keelans Choice (IRE) **Mrs P. M. Bosley**
29 **HEAD AND HEART,** 6, b m Mount Nelson—Don't Stop Me Now (FR) **Mr L. Quinn**
30 **HIGH GAME ROYAL (FR),** 6, b g Martaline—Jouable (FR) **Mrs L. R. Lovell**
31 **HOLD UP LA COLMINE (FR),** 6, b g Choeur du Nord (FR)—Taiwan Leto (FR) **Mr Tim Syder & Martin St Quinton**
32 **IAMASTAR (FR),** 5, b g Balko (FR)—Victoria's Star (FR) **D. Maxwell**
33 **IBERIO (GER),** 6, b g Kamsin (GER)—Imogen (GER) **Brocade Racing**
34 **ISLAND RUN,** 6, b g Blue Bresil (FR)—Penneyrose Bay **Sir Christopher & Lady Wates**
35 **JATILUWIH (FR),** 9, ch g Linda's Lad—Jaune de Beaufai (FR) **D. Maxwell**
36 **JET MARSHALL (IRE),** 6, br g Jet Away—Little Hand (IRE) **N. R. A. Sutton**
37 **KAYF DANCER,** 5, b g Kayf Tara—Winning Counsel (IRE) **Mrs K. V. Vann**
38 4, B g Jack Hobbs—Kayf Willow **P. J. Hobbs**
39 **KEABLE (IRE),** 6, b g Fame And Glory—Sarahs Quay (IRE) **R. A. Bartlett**
40 **KEEP ROLLING (IRE),** 10, ch g Mahler—Kayles Castle (IRE) **Mick Fitzgerald Racing Club**
41 **KEEP WONDERING (IRE),** 9, b g Scorpion (IRE)—Supreme Touch (IRE) **Andy Bell & Fergus Lyons**
42 **LANGLEY HUNDRED (IRE),** 6, b g Sholokhov (IRE)—Theregoesthetruth (IRE) **The Englands and Heywoods**
43 **LILLYWAVE,** 7, ch m Gentlewave (IRE)—Our Ethel **Royale Racing Syndicate**
44 **LONGSHANKS (IRE),** 9, b g Scorpion (IRE)—Cash A Lawn (IRE) **Unity Farm Holiday Centre Ltd**
45 4, Gr g Kingston Hill—Lucky Pigeon (IRE) **P. J. Hobbs**
46 **MAD MIKE (IRE),** 5, b g Soldier of Fortune (IRE)—Manorville (IRE) **The Macaroni Beach Society**
47 **MADAKET,** 5, b g Kayf Tara—She Ranks Me (IRE) **Louisville Syndicate**
48 **MASTERS LEGACY (IRE),** 8, br g Getaway (GER)—Gently Go (IRE) **Mrs P. M. Bosley**
49 **MIDNIGHT MIDGE,** 9, b g Midnight Legend—Posh Emily **A Midgley, R J Hodges**
50 **MISTRAL LADY,** 5, b m Shirocco (GER)—Peggies Run **Sir Christopher & Lady Wates**
51 **MOMBASA (FR),** 4, gr g Martaline—Molly Has (FR) **D. Maxwell**
52 **MONVIEL (IRE),** 6, gr g Montmartre (FR)—Mont Doree (FR) **Dr V. M. G. Ferguson**
53 **MUSICAL SLAVE (IRE),** 10, b g Getaway (GER)—Inghwung **Mr J. P. McManus**
54 **NOT A LIGHT (IRE),** 6, b g Leading Light (IRE)—Famous Lady (IRE) **Mr Tim Syder & Martin St Quinton**
55 **QUALITY,** 4, gr f Mastercraftsman (IRE)—Sahalin **Mr D. M. Mathias**
56 **ROLLING DYLAN (IRE),** 12, ch g Indian River (FR)—Easter Saturday (IRE) **Mrs S. Hobbs**
57 **SANDY BOY (IRE),** 9, b g Tajraasi (USA)—Annienoora (IRE) **Mrs B. A. Hitchcock**
58 **SASSIFIED (IRE),** 5, ch g Excelebration (IRE)—Satwa Pearl **Mr J. P. McManus**
59 **SKIDDAW (IRE),** 5, b g Mount Nelson—Bonnie Theatre (IRE) **Exors of the Late Mr T. J. Hemmings**
60 4, B g Lauro (GER)—Skyra (IRE) **P. J. Hobbs**
61 **SMARTY WILD,** 9, b g Fair Mix (IRE)—Blaeberry **Mr Michael & Mrs Norma Tuckey**
62 **SOLAR SYSTEM (FR),** 4, b g Pastorius (GER)—Solar Wind (FR) **Mr J. P. McManus**
63 **SPORTING JOHN (IRE),** 8, b br g Getaway (GER)—Wild Spell (IRE) **Mr J. P. McManus**
64 **STELLAR MAGIC (IRE),** 8, b g Arctic Cosmos (USA)—Inter Alia (IRE) **A. Stennett**
65 **THYME HILL,** 9, b g Kayf Tara—Rosita Bay **The Englands and Heywoods**
66 **UMNDENI (FR),** 9, b br g Balko (FR)—Marie Royale (FR) **S. &. A. Giannini**
67 **WEST PARK BOY,** 5, b g Cannock Chase (USA)—Desirable Rhythm (IRE) **Two Hendred Partnership**
68 **WILDFIRE WARRIOR (IRE),** 8, b g Flemensfirth (USA)—Lady of Fortune (IRE) **Mrs J. J. Peppiatt**
69 **ZANZA (IRE),** 9, b g Arcadio (GER)—What A Bleu (IRE) **Louisville Syndicate Elite**

Assistant Trainer: Mr Ben Robarts, Mr Johnson White.

NH Jockey: Mr Sean Houlihan, Mr Ben Jones, Mr Micheal Nolan, Mr Tom O'Brien. **Conditional Jockey:** Miss Elizabeth Gale, Mr Jack Martin. **Amateur Jockey:** Miss Ella Herbison, Mr David Maxwell, Mr Callum Pritchard.

255 MISS CLARE HOBSON, Royston

Postal: **Upper Coombe Farm, Coombe Road, Kelshall, Royston, Hertfordshire, SG8 9SA**
Contacts: **MOBILE 07966 734889**
EMAIL clarehobsonracing@gmail.com

1 **BA NA HILLS (IRE),** 4, b g Fastnet Rock (AUS)—Sheba Five (USA) **Mr G. Molen**
2 **BROUGHTONS MISSION,** 5, b g Coach House (IRE)—Broughtons Flight (IRE) **Ivan Titmuss & Penelope Anderson**
3 **DESERT GLORY (IRE),** 4, b g Churchill (IRE)—Polygon (USA) **Mr I. G. Titmuss**
4 **DOYEN STREET (IRE),** 5, b g Doyen (IRE)—De Street (IRE) **Clare Hobson & P Sherriff**
5 **EMBOLDEN (IRE),** 6, b g Kodiac—Sassy Gal (IRE) **Molen, Ball, Judd, Dunne & White**
6 **KING CNUT (FR),** 9, ch g Kentucky Dynamite (USA)—Makadane **Mr H. R. Hobson**
7 6, B m Ask—Maberry (IRE)
8 **MUVVERS MONEY,** 5, b g Universal (IRE)—Jump To The Beat **Mr H. R. Hobson**
9 **NOBOOKWORK (IRE),** 7, ch g Shantaram—Glenbrook Memories (IRE) **Mr H. R. Hobson**
10 **PERCY'S PRINCE,** 7, b g Sir Percy—Attainable **Sarah Westerhuis & Rosemary Hobson**
11 **UNCLE O,** 9, gr g Fair Mix (IRE)—Clever Liz **Mr H. R. Hobson**
12 **VINNIE'S GETAWAY (IRE),** 9, b g Getaway (GER)—Trixskin (IRE) **The Fox and Duck syndicate**
13 **WARNER'S CROSS (IRE),** 6, b g Leading Light (IRE)—Cellar Door (IRE) **Mr J. Griffin**
14 **WOODFORD BRIDGE,** 7, b m Champs Elysees—A Lulu Ofa Menifee (USA) **Mr G. Molen**

THREE-YEAR-OLDS

15 B g Tagula (IRE)—Alphaba (IRE) **Miss Clare R. W. Hobson**

---

256 MR RICHARD HOBSON, Little Rissington

Postal: **Bobble Barn Farm, Little Rissington, Cheltenham, Gloucestershire, GL54 2NE**
Contacts: **PHONE 01451 820535 MOBILE 07939 155843**
EMAIL hobson.r1@sky.com WEBSITE www.richardhobsonracing.co.uk

1 **DISCKO DES PLAGES (FR),** 10, b g Balko (FR)—Lady des Plages (FR) **Gordon Farr & Gerry M Ward**
2 **ECHO WATT (FR),** 9, gr g Fragrant Mix (IRE)—Roxane du Bois (FR) **The Boom Syndicate**
3 **EUREU DU BOULAY (FR),** 9, b g Della Francesca (USA)—Idole du Boulay (FR) **J. & R. Hobson**
4 **FAMILY BUSINESS (FR),** 6, b g Kitkou (FR)—Santa Senam (FR) **The Boom Syndicate**
5 **FANZIO (FR),** 8, b g Day Flight—Tu L'As Eu (FR) **Mr R. H. Hobson**
6 **FUGITIF (FR),** 8, b g Ballingarry (IRE)—Turiane (FR) **Carl & E. Hussain**
7 **HI RIKO (FR),** 6, b g Cokoriko (FR)—Vanille d'Ex (FR) **Mr D. W. Brookes**
8 **ILLICO DE MOUTIERS (FR),** 5, b g Ballingarry (IRE)—Moriany (FR) **Mr M. S. Scott**
9 **INGENNIO (FR),** 5, b g Lauro (GER)—Casbah Rose (FR) **Ms S. A. Fox**
10 5, B g Sageburg (IRE)—La Feuillarde (FR) **Mr R. H. Hobson**
11 **LORD DU MESNIL (FR),** 10, b g Saint des Saints (FR)—Ladies Choice (FR) **Mr Paul Porter & Mike & Mandy Smith**
12 **OUR FOLLET,** 4, b g Kapgarde (FR)—Folie Lointaine (FR) **Rubicon Racing 1**
13 **RIDERS ONTHE STORM (IRE),** 10, br g Scorpion (IRE)—Endless Moments (IRE) **Carl Hinchy & Mark Scott**
14 **SAINT XAVIER (FR),** 11, b g Saint des Saints (FR)—Princesse Lucie (FR) **Mr R. H. Hobson**
15 **SOME SCOPE,** 5, b g Telescope (IRE)—Rosygo (IRE) **Rubicon Racing**
16 **VALADOM (FR),** 14, gr g Dadarissime (FR)—Laurana (FR) **Mr R. H. Hobson**

THREE-YEAR-OLDS

17 **KALIZE (FR),** gr f Nom de d'La (FR)—Alize du Berlais (FR) **Mrs G. S. Langford**

Assistant Trainer: Shirley Jane Becker, **Head Lad:** Dawson Lees.

257 MR SIMON HODGSON, Andover

Postal: **12 Hei-Lin Way, Ludgershall, Andover, Hampshire, SP11 9QH**
Contacts: **PHONE 07786 730853**
EMAIL hodgsters@hotmail.co.uk

1 **BONNIE BLANDFORD,** 4, b f Hot Streak (IRE)—Rose Ransom (IRE) **Bonnie Blandford Quartet**
2 **C'EST NO MOUR (GER),** 10, b g Champs Elysees—C'Est L'Amour (GER) **Mr P. R. Hedger & P C F Racing Ltd**
3 **CHARLIE ARTHUR (IRE),** 7, b g Slade Power (IRE)—Musical Bar (IRE) **The 19th Hole Syndicate**
4 **DELAGATE THIS LORD,** 9, b g Delegator—Lady Filly **Mrs M. S. Teversham**
5 **ITS UR ROUNDMYLORD,** 5, ch g Havana Gold (IRE)—La Palma **Miss L. J. Knocker**
6 **KILLARNEY MOUNTAIN,** 5, b h Cable Bay (IRE)—Afro **P C F Racing Ltd**
7 **MR MAC,** 9, b g Makfi—Veronica Franco **P C F Racing Ltd**
8 **PAY FOR ADAAY,** 4, b g Adaay (IRE)—Gracilia (FR) **P C F Racing Ltd**
9 **ROYAL DEBUT (IRE),** 4, b g Showcasing—Mathool (IRE) **Results Racing**
10 **STAR FOR A DAY (IRE),** 4, ch f Postponed (IRE)—Starscape (IRE) **P C F Racing Ltd**
11 **THANK THE LORD,** 4, ch g Coach House (IRE)—Lady Phill **Mrs M. S. Teversham**
12 **TRALEE HILLS,** 9, gr ro g Mount Nelson—Distant Waters **P C F Racing Ltd**
13 **TWILIGHT MADNESS,** 5, ch h Twilight Son—Rhal (IRE) **Mr P. R. Hedger & P C F Racing Ltd**

THREE-YEAR-OLDS

14 **BRAZEN INSANITY,** b f Brazen Beau (AUS)—Armageddon **Mr L. A. Hill**
15 **DAVE,** ch g Bated Breath—Milly's Gift **Results Racing**
16 **SPICE RACK,** b g Acclamation—Spice Trail **Mrs M. Gill**
17 **STAR ADORNED (IRE),** b f Starspangledbanner (AUS)—Celestial Love (IRE) **P C F Racing Ltd**

---

258 MR HENRY HOGARTH, Stillington

Postal: **New Grange Farm, Stillington, York**
Contacts: **PHONE 01347 811168 MOBILE 07788 777044 FAX 01347 811168**
EMAIL harryhogarth@ymail.com

1 **ARCHIE BROWN (IRE),** 9, b g Aizavoski (IRE)—Pure Beautiful (IRE) **Hogarth Racing**
2 **BARRANCO (IRE),** 6, b g Shirocco (GER)—Be My Presenting (IRE) **Hogarth Racing**
3 **GEMINI FIRE (IRE),** 6, ch g Mahler—Verde Goodwood **Hogarth Racing**
4 **GOLDRAPPER (IRE),** 10, b g Gold Well—Mrs Bukay (IRE) **Hogarth Racing**
5 **LANDACRE BRIDGE,** 7, b g Kayf Tara—Wee Dinns (IRE) **Hogarth Racing**
6 **LARGY TRAIN,** 6, b g Yorgunnabelucky (USA)—Snow Train **Hogarth Racing**
7 **MANCE RAYDER (IRE),** 10, b g Flemensfirth (USA)—J'Y Viens (FR) **Hogarth Racing**
8 **STONEY STREET,** 7, b g Gentlewave (IRE)—Flemengo (IRE) **Hogarth Racing**
9 **THE BLACK SQUIRREL (IRE),** 10, br g Craigsteel—Terra Lucida (IRE) **Hogarth Racing**

NH Jockey: Jamie Hamilton. **Conditional Jockey:** Billy Garritty.

---

259 MR ANTHONY HOLDSWORTH, Ivybridge

Postal: **Quarry Farm, Modbury, Ivybridge, Devon, PL21 0SF**
EMAIL sam.holdsworth@sky.com

1 **AIRTON,** 10, b g Champs Elysees—Fly In Style **A. S. T. Holdsworth**
2 **ALWAYS TEA TIME,** 7, b m Indian Haven—Magical Wonderland **A. S. T. Holdsworth**
3 **MISSYLADIE (FR),** 9, b m Born King (JPN)—Ladie de Briandais (FR) **A. S. T. Holdsworth**
4 **THE DEVON DUMPLING,** 10, b m Fair Mix (IRE)—Star of Magic **A. S. T. Holdsworth**

260 MR DARRYLL PAUL HOLLAND, Newmarket

Postal: **The Cottage,Harraton Court Stables, Chapel Street, Exning, Newmarket, Suffolk, CB8 7HA**
Contacts: **PHONE 07901 550909**
EMAIL info@harratoncourtstables.com

1 **ASTRO JAKK (IRE),** 7, b g Zoffany (IRE)—By The Edge (IRE) **Harraton Court Stables Ltd**
2 **BERNARD SPIERPOINT,** 6, b g Harbour Watch (IRE)—Para Siempre **Mr R. A. Popely**
3 **BLUEBELLS BOY,** 4, b g Outstrip—Pompeia **Mr R. A. Popely**
4 **DYNAMIC TALENT,** 4, b g Aclaim (IRE)—Burnt Fingers (IRE) **Harraton Court Stables Ltd**
5 **LILKIAN,** 6, ch g Sepoy (AUS)—Janie Runaway (IRE) **Harraton Court Stables Ltd**
6 **SUANNI,** 4, gr g Lethal Force (IRE)—Glee Club **Harraton Court Stables Ltd**
7 **THEY DON'T KNOW (IRE),** 4, b g Vocalised (USA)—Fields of May (IRE) **Harraton Court Stables Ltd**

THREE-YEAR-OLDS

8 **CITY OF ALIAA,** b f Cityscape—Meet Me Halfway **Mr M. N. Mudhoo**
9 **DUTCH KINGDOM (IRE),** b c Iffraaj—Kiyra Wells (IRE) **Harraton Court Stables Ltd**
10 **GRACE ANGEL,** b f Harry Angel (IRE)—Sparkle **Mr R. Nugent**
11 **PEARL EYE,** b c Expert Eye—Treat Gently **Mr R. Nugent**
12 **SILKS GRAPHITE,** gr g Brazen Beau (AUS)—Zia (GER) **Silkman Pascoe & Harraton Court Stables**

TWO-YEAR-OLDS

13 **EQUIART,** b c 16/02 Equiano (FR)—
Silca Mistress (Dutch Art) (14000) **C. Fahy, M. Fairhurst, T. Breden & HCS**

261 MISS SARAH HOLLINSHEAD, Upper Longdon

Postal: **Lodge Farm, Upper Longdon, Rugeley, Staffordshire, WS15 1QF**
Contacts: **PHONE 01543 490298**

1 **BONDI MAN,** 4, ch g Australia—Honorine (IRE) **Dallas Racing & Partner**
2 **BUT YOU SAID (IRE),** 6, b m No Nay Never (USA)—San Macchia **The Giddy Gang**
3 **CASTLEREA TESS,** 10, ch m Pastoral Pursuits—Zartwyda (IRE) **Mr John Graham & Sarah Hollinshead**
4 **DIAMOND JILL (IRE),** 6, b m Footstepsinthesand—Sindiyma (IRE) **Mr J. Gould**
5 **DIAMOND JOEL,** 11, b g Youmzain (IRE)—Miss Lacroix **Mrs N. S. Harris**
6 **DREAMS OF GOLD,** 8, b g Goldmark (USA)—Song of Kenda **L & A Holland**
7 **FLORA PAGET,** 7, b m Kayf Tara—Lysways **Miss S. A. Hollinshead**
8 **GEALACH GHORM (IRE),** 9, b g Finsceal Fior (IRE)—Saintly Wish (USA) **Miss S. A. Hollinshead**
9 **GMS PRINCE,** 8, b g Kayf Tara—Zartwyda (IRE) **Graham Brothers Racing Partnership**
10 **JENNY REN,** 8, b m Multiplex—Cherished Love (IRE) **Mr J. Gould**
11 **LOOK FOR A DAY,** 4, b f Adaay (IRE)—Look Here's Dee **S. L. Edwards**
12 **LOOKFORARAINBOW,** 10, b g Rainbow High—Look Here's May **The Giddy Gang**
13 **MAJESTIC CHARM,** 4, b f Charming Thought—Last Dance **Mr K. Khan**
14 **OUT OF IDEAS (FR),** 9, b g Sinndar (IRE)—Out of Honour (IRE) **C. D. James**
15 **PHIL THE THRILL (FR),** 7, gr g Dabirsim (FR)—Parirou (GER) **Miss B. Connop**
16 **QUIET THUNDER (IRE),** 5, b m Night of Thunder (IRE)—Elevator Action (IRE) **& Gould**
17 **RHODIA (IRE),** 7, ch g Fast Company (IRE)—Annie Greene (IRE) **L & A Holland**
18 **SINNDARELLA (IRE),** 7, b m Fast Company (IRE)—Alafzara (IRE) **R & M Moseley, Slater, Gould & Laughland**
19 **SNOOZE LANE (IRE),** 4, b g Free Eagle (IRE)—Sindiyma (IRE) **A & J Graham & S Hollinshead**
20 **SPARKINTHEDARK,** 5, b m Telescope (IRE)—Cherished Love (IRE) **Mr J. Gould**
21 **UNCLE BERNIE (IRE),** 13, gr g Aussie Rules (USA)—Alwiyda (USA) **Miss S. A. Hollinshead**

THREE-YEAR-OLDS

22 **BALMY BREESE,** b g Mayson—Florett (IRE) **Mr D. A. Breese**
23 Ch g Saddler's Rock (IRE)—Lady Blade (IRE) **Mr D. A. Breese**
24 **PRETTY DARN QUICK,** b g Heeraat (IRE)—Zartwyda (IRE) **Graham Brothers Racing Partnership**
25 B c Brazen Beau (AUS)—Tibibit

262 MRS STEPH HOLLINSHEAD, Rugeley, Staffordshire

Postal: **Catmint Lodge, Bardy Lane, Upper Longdon, Rugeley, Staffordshire, WS15 4LJ**
Contacts: **HOME 01543 327609 PHONE 07554 008405 MOBILE 07791 385335**
EMAIL steph_hollinshead@hotmail.co.uk WEBSITE www.stephhollinsheadracing.com

1 **AL SIMMO,** 6, b m Al Kazeem—Magic Destiny **R. Bailey**
2 **ALBESEEINGYER,** 4, b f Al Kazeem—Magic Destiny **R. Bailey**
3 **ALCHEMYSTIQUE (IRE),** 6, b m Authorized (IRE)—Nice To Know (FR) **Lysways Racing**
4 **ALSEEYERTHERE,** 5, b m Al Kazeem—Magic Destiny **R. Bailey**
5 **LADY MANDER,** 5, b m Albaasil (IRE)—Goldeva **Hollinshead & Pyle**
6 **LOCALLINK (IRE),** 9, b g Sandmason—Suny House **The Captain On the Bridge Partnership**
7 **MALHAM TARN COVE,** 4, gr ro g Heeraat (IRE)—Spirit of Rosanna **Mr J. Holcombe**
8 **MARCIE (IRE),** 5, b m Marcel (IRE)—Ayun (USA) **Mr N. A. Hayward**
9 **MISS MOCKTAIL (IRE),** 8, b m Getaway (GER)—Identity Parade (IRE) **Lysways Racing**
10 **ORO COSMICO,** 4, ch g Universal (IRE)—Corsa All Oro (USA) **P. S. Burke**
11 **PEPSI CAT (IRE),** 4, b f Tamayuz—Music Pearl (IRE) **Mrs D. A. Hodson**
12 **ROYAL MUSKETEER,** 5, b g Acclamation—Queen's Pearl (IRE) **S & S Racing**
13 **THE GOLDEN CUE,** 8, ch g Zebedee—Khafayif (USA) **The Golden Cue Partnership**
14 **TILIA CORDATA (IRE),** 5, b m Zoffany (IRE)—Limetree Lady **Mr N. A. Hayward**
15 **UNCLE JUMBO,** 5, gr g Territories (IRE)—Gone Sailing **S & S Racing**
16 **VIEWFINDER (IRE),** 4, ch g El Kabeir (USA)—Encore View

THREE-YEAR-OLDS

17 **BEANIE BLUE,** b f Aclaim (IRE)—Sovereign's Honour (USA) **Beanie Blue Syndicate**
18 **CUTTLESTONE BRIDGE,** b g Camacho—Compton Bird **Cuttlestone Racing**
19 **INDRAPURA STAR,** ro c Dark Angel (IRE)—Eyes On Asha (IRE) **Miss H. L. Thacker**
20 B f Massaat (IRE)—Magic Music (IRE) **R. Bailey**
21 **REGENCY BOY,** b c Sea The Moon (GER)—Lady Freyja **S & S Racing**
22 **SIR SIDNEY SMITH,** br g Bated Breath—Belledesert **Mrs D. A. Hodson**
23 B gr c Lethal Force (IRE)—Spirit of Rosanna **Mr J. Holcombe**

TWO-YEAR-OLDS

24 B f 06/02 Time Test—Affaire de Coeur (Dalakhani (IRE)) (11000)
25 B f 28/01 Havana Gold (IRE)—Broughtons Berry (IRE) (Bushranger (IRE)) (9524)
26 B f 12/05 Harry Angel (IRE)—Quelle Affaire (Bahamian Bounty) (9000) **Beaudesert Racing 1**

Assistant Trainer: Adam Hawkins.

---

263 MR ANTHONY HONEYBALL, Beaminster

Postal: **Potwell Farm, Mosterton, Beaminster, Dorset, DT8 3HG**
Contacts: **MOBILE 07815 898569**
WORK EMAIL office@ajhoneyballracing.co.uk WEBSITE www.ajhoneyballracing.co.uk

1 **ACEY MILAN (IRE),** 9, b g Milan—Strong Wishes (IRE) **Mr A. Honeyball**
2 **AMALFI BAY,** 5, b g Lope de Vega (IRE)—Affinity **Elite Racing Club**
3 **ASK LILEEN (IRE),** 6, br m Soldier of Fortune (IRE)—Trendy Native **Potwell Racing Syndicate I**
4 **BING BELLE,** 4, b f Royal Anthem (USA)—Roxy Belle **Mr J. Barber**
5 **BLACKJACK MAGIC,** 8, b g Black Sam Bellamy (IRE)—
One Wild Night **T Hayward, O'Gorman, Walker & Patersons**
6 **BOHEMIAN LAD (IRE),** 5, b g Mahler—Rehill Lass (IRE) **Decimus Racing IX**
7 **BORDERLANDS (IRE),** 4, br g Getaway (GER)—Knocknabrogue (IRE) **The Mighty Six**
8 **BREAKING COVER (IRE),** 5, b g Getaway (GER)—
Peace And The City (FR) **Cartwright, Langford, Redknapp, Saunders**
9 **CAPE VIDAL,** 6, b g Kayf Tara—Midnight Minx **Potwell Racing Syndicate III**
10 **CAPTAIN CLAUDE (IRE),** 6, b g Soldier of Fortune (IRE)—Princess Supreme (IRE) **Decimus Racing V**
11 **COCO BRAVE (IRE),** 4, b f Court Cave (IRE)—Coming Home (FR) **The Coconuts**

MR ANTHONY HONEYBALL - continued

12 **CONCLUDING ACT,** 4, b g Black Sam Bellamy (IRE)—Gan On **Mr A. Honeyball**
13 **COQUELICOT (FR),** 7, b br m Soldier of Fortune (IRE)—Moscow Nights (FR) **Geegeez.co.uk PA**
14 **CREDO (IRE),** 8, b m Fame And Glory—Tasmani (FR) **Potwell Racing Syndicate II**
15 **CREST OF GLORY,** 4, b g Black Sam Bellamy (IRE)—Dolly Penrose **Mr A. Honeyball**
16 **DARTMOOR PIRATE,** 4, b g Black Sam Bellamy (IRE)—Behra (IRE) **geegeez.co.uk XXII**
17 **DEAR RALPHY (IRE),** 7, b g Westerner—Letterwoman (IRE) **Mr J. M. Pike**
18 **DOCTOR FOLEY (IRE),** 6, b g Malinas (GER)—Quarryanna (IRE) **Mr E. J. Dolan-Abrahams, Mr O. P. Farrer, Mr M. Newton**
19 **DOYANNIE (IRE),** 9, ch m Doyen (IRE)—Annie May (IRE) **Mr J. J. Barber, Mr J. M. French**
20 **DOYEN FOR MONEY (IRE),** 5, b br g Doyen (IRE)—Mrs Jay Dee (IRE) **Mr H. Kingston**
21 **DREAMING BLUE,** 6, b g Showcasing—Got To Dream **R. W. Devlin**
22 **FANFARON DINO (FR),** 8, gr g Doctor Dino (FR)—Kadjara (FR) **Mr J. P. McManus**
23 **FERRET JEETER,** 6, ch g Recharge (IRE)—Halo Flora **R. J. Matthews**
24 **FILM D'ACTION (FR),** 4, b g Saddex—Action des Flos (FR) **Mr J. P. McManus**
25 **FIRESTREAM,** 6, b g Yeats (IRE)—Swincombe Flame **Buckingham, Chapman, Langford & Ritzema**
26 **FORTUITOUS FAVOUR (IRE),** 5, b m Soldier of Fortune (IRE)—Northwood Milan (IRE) **Decimus Racing XI**
27 **FORTUNA LIGNA (IRE),** 6, br m Soldier of Fortune (IRE)—Quiet Thought (IRE) **Owners for Owners Fortuna Ligna**
28 **FORWARD PLAN (IRE),** 7, br g Valirann (FR)—Culmore Native (IRE) **The Steeple Chasers**
29 **FOUNTAINS CHIEF,** 7, b g Native Ruler—Tigeralley **The Fountains Partnership**
30 **GABRIEL'S GETAWAY (IRE),** 6, b g Getaway (GER)—Chosen Destiny (IRE) **Buckingham, Chapman, Kingston &Langford**
31 **GETMETOTHEMOON,** 4, b f Pether's Moon (IRE)—Gertie Getaway (IRE) **Unity Farm Holiday Centre Ltd**
32 **GOOD LOOK CHARM (FR),** 7, b m Cokoriko (FR)—Une d'Ex (FR) **The Isle of Blue and White**
33 **GUSTAVIAN (IRE),** 8, b g Mahler—Grange Oscar (IRE) **Decimus Racing I**
34 **HATOS (FR),** 6, b g Diamond Boy (FR)—Santalisa (FR) **Hats off to Hatos**
35 **I GIORNI (IRE),** 6, b m Arcadio (GER)—Shechangedhermind (IRE) **The Soldiers of Fortune**
36 **JAIL NO BAIL (IRE),** 6, b g Mahler—Kittys Oscar (IRE) **Bryan Drew & Friends, Chapman & Kingston**
37 **JEPECK (IRE),** 14, b g Westerner—Jenny's Jewel (IRE) **Mr J. M. Pike**
38 **JITTERBUG GEORDIE,** 5, gr g Geordieland (FR)—Dancingtilmidnight **Mrs S. J. Maltby**
39 **JUGGERNAUT (FR),** 4, b g Spanish Moon (USA)—Sacoleva (FR) **Martyn Chapman & Ms Gill Langford**
40 **JUKEBOX JAZZ (IRE),** 4, gr f Jukebox Jury (IRE)—Sweetheart **Mr R. W. Huggins**
41 **KEEPITFROMBECKY (IRE),** 5, b g Diamond Boy (FR)—Tobetall **Barber, French, Rees & Baird**
42 **KILBEG KING (IRE),** 8, b g Doyen (IRE)—Prayuwin Drummer (IRE) **M.R.Chapman, E.Jones & H.Kingston**
43 **KONIGIN ISABELLA (GER),** 5, b m Isfahan (GER)—Konigin Cala (GER) **geegeez.co.uk KI**
44 **LE COEUR NET (FR),** 11, ch g Network (GER)—Silverwood (FR) **Wessex Racing Club**
45 **LILITH (IRE),** 8, b m Stowaway—Flirthing Around (IRE) **Decimus Racing VI**
46 **MARCO ISLAND (IRE),** 6, b g Mahler—Florida Belle (IRE) **Buckingham, Chapman, Langford & Ritzema**
47 **MATTHIAS,** 4, b g Black Sam Bellamy (IRE)—Rouquine Sauvage **Step By Step**
48 **MELK ABBEY (IRE),** 7, b m Sholokhov (IRE)—Carrig'n May (IRE) **Noel Fehily Racing Syndicates Melk Abby**
49 **MIDNIGHT CALLISTO,** 8, br m Midnight Legend—Carrigeen Queen (IRE) **Mrs G. S. Langford**
50 **MOLLIE BROWN,** 5, b m Black Sam Bellamy (IRE)—Midnight Crackle **Mr T. C. Frost**
51 **NORTON HILL (IRE),** 7, b g Fame And Glory—Charming Leader (IRE) **Mr & Mrs J. J. Barber & Mr A. Norman**
52 **ONEUPMANSHIP (IRE),** 8, ch g Mahler—Letthisbetheone (IRE) **Charlie Walker & Phil Fry**
53 **PURE THEATRE (IRE),** 5, b m Court Cave (IRE)—Faucon **Potwell Racing Syndicate IV**
54 **QUEENS FORTUNE (IRE),** 5, b m Soldier of Fortune (IRE)—Down By The Sea (IRE) **Noel Fehily Racing Syndicates Queens For**
55 **REGAL ENCORE (IRE),** 15, b g King's Theatre (IRE)—Go On Eileen (IRE) **Mr J. P. McManus**
56 **SAILING GRACE,** 4, b f Dartmouth—War Creation (IRE) **Wessex Racing Club**
57 **SAM BROWN,** 11, b g Black Sam Bellamy (IRE)—Cream Cracker **Mr T. C. Frost**
58 **SMART CASUAL,** 5, b g Black Sam Bellamy (IRE)—Rouquine Sauvage **Mr J. P. McManus**
59 **SOLSTICE SAINT (IRE),** 4, b g Court Cave (IRE)—South West Nine (IRE) **Mr G. E. Pike**
60 **SOMESPRING SPECIAL (IRE),** 5, b m Westerner—Natural Spring **Yeo Racing Partnership**
61 **TALKINGTOTHEMOON,** 5, b g Pether's Moon (IRE)—Blue Buttons (IRE) **The Lunatic Partnership**
62 **UCANAVER,** 7, bl m Maxios—Purely By Chance **Ifuwonner Partnership**
63 **WINDANCE (IRE),** 8, b g Shirocco (GER)—Maca Rince (IRE) **Decimus Racing III**
64 **WORLD OF DREAMS (IRE),** 7, b g Kayf Tara—Rose of The World (IRE) **R. Huggins, Bisogno P Williams**

Assistant Trainer: Rachael Honeyball.

NH Jockey: Aidan Coleman, Rex Dingle. **Conditional Jockey:** Ben Godfrey. **Amateur Jockey:** Chad Bament.

264 MR CHRISTOPHER HONOUR, Ashburton

Postal: **Higher Whiddon Farm, Ashburton Down, Newton Abbot, Devon, TQ13 7EY**
Contacts: **HOME 01364 652500 MOBILE 07771 861219**
EMAIL tojohonour@aol.com

1 DOLLY BIRD, 5, b m Shantou (USA)—Sparron Hawk (FR) **The Dolly Bird Syndicate**
2 DROPITLIKEITSHOT, 4, b f Pour Moi (IRE)—Darn Hot **Mr C. E. Honour**
3 GAELIC DREAMER, 6, gr g Dream Eater (IRE)—Gaelic Lime **Mrs J. Elliott**
4 GAELIC STORM, 4, b g Linda's Lad—Gaelic Lime **Mrs J. Elliott**
5 GAELIC THUNDER, 8, b g Arvico (FR)—Gaelic Lime **Mrs J. Elliott**
6 GRUMPY CHARLEY, 8, gr g Shirocco (GER)—Whisky Rose (IRE) **G. D. Thompson**
7 GRUMPY FREYA, 8, ch m Malinas (GER)—Thedeboftheyear **G. D. Thompson**
8 GRUMPY ROSIE, 4, b f Pour Moi (IRE)—Thedeboftheyear **G. D. Thompson**
9 MAYHEM MYA, 6, b m Authorized (IRE)—Thedeboftheyear **G. D. Thompson**
10 PORTENTOSO (GER), 8, b g Santiago (GER)—Piccola (GER) **Never forgotten**
11 SHORTCROSS STORM (IRE), 8, b g September Storm (GER)—Lady Leila (IRE) **Cotswold Stone Supplies Ltd**
12 TILE TAPPER, 9, b g Malinas (GER)—Darn Hot **Cotswold Stone Supplies Ltd**
13 TIME TO BITE (IRE), 8, b g Scorpion (IRE)—Time To Act **Mr C. E. Honour**
14 TROED Y MELIN (IRE), 11, b g Craigsteel—Kissangel (IRE) **No Illusions Partnership**
15 WITH POISE, 5, b m Telescope (IRE)—With Grace **No Illusions Partnership**

THREE-YEAR-OLDS

16 GAELIC ICEOLATION, ch g Linda's Lad—Gaelic Ice **Miss E. M. Pearse**

TWO-YEAR-OLDS

17 B f 24/04 Dartmouth—Darn Hot (Sir Harry Lewis (USA)) **Mr C. E. Honour**
18 B c 18/02 Telescope (IRE)—Lady of Lamanver (Lucarno (USA)) **Never forgotten**

Assistant Trainer: Rebekah Honour.

---

265 MISS LAURA HORSFALL, Towcester

Postal: **Mobile Home ,Glebe Barn Stables, Blakesley Road, Maidford, Towcester, Northamptonshire, NN12 8HN**
EMAIL horsfalllaura@hotmail.co.uk

1 BEAMING, 9, b m Shamardal (USA)—Connecting **Mr R G Robinson & Mr R D Robinson**
2 CHOSEN DAY (IRE), 6, ch g Well Chosen—Terrible Day (IRE) **Miss L. Horsfall**
3 CITY ROLLER (IRE), 5, b g Scorpion (IRE)—Pearl's A Singer (IRE) **The City Rollers**
4 CREADAN GRAE (IRE), 11, gr g Scorpion (IRE)—Tenerife Pearl (IRE) **Miss L. Horsfall**
5 GOTTHEREINTHEEND (IRE), 4, b f Soldier of Fortune (IRE)—
Highland Flower (IRE) **M Redman M Thomas L Horsfall**
6 JACK THE SAVAGE, 6, b g Passing Glance—Catching Zeds **M White J Frampton L Horsfall**
7 LASTORDERSPLEASE (IRE), 6, b m Arctic Cosmos (USA)—The Bar Maid **The Laura Horsfall Racing Club**
8 LONG SYMPHONY (IRE), 6, b g Mahler—Ashlings Princess (IRE) **The Laura Horsfall Racing Club**
9 MONYMUSK LAD (IRE), 7, b g Califet (FR)—Tasanak (IRE) **The Laura Horsfall Racing Club**
10 MUCH TOO DEAR (IRE), 5, ch g Getaway (GER)—
Redunderthebed (IRE) **Mr M Redman F Jarvey M Thomas N Allen**
11 4, Gr f Carlotamix (FR)—One Cool Kate (IRE)

THREE-YEAR-OLDS

12 B c Harbour Law—Beaming
13 B f Wings of Eagles (FR)—Mytara

266 MR JAMES HORTON, Leyburn

Postal: **Garden View, Brecongill, Coverham, Leyburn, Yorkshire, DL8 4TJ**
EMAIL james@jameshortonracing.co.uk

1 **ASJAD,** 5, b g Iffraaj—Riskit Fora Biskit (IRE) **John & Jessica Dance**
2 **ENCOURAGEABLE (IRE),** 4, b c Profitable (IRE)—Dutch Courage **John & Jessica Dance**
3 **PHANTOM FLIGHT,** 4, b c Siyouni (FR)—Qushchi **John & Jessica Dance**
4 **RHYTHM MASTER (IRE),** 5, b g Dark Angel (IRE)—Pastoral Girl **John & Jessica Dance**
5 **SAM MAXIMUS,** 4, b c Showcasing—Daring Day **John & Jessica Dance**

THREE-YEAR-OLDS

6 **COSMIC SOUL (IRE),** br c Sea The Stars (IRE)—My Spirit (IRE) **John & Jessica Dance**
7 **CROSSFADER (IRE),** b c Invincible Spirit (IRE)—Jolyne
8 **DRAFTED (IRE),** b g Showcasing—Flower Fashion (FR)
9 **FIFTH HARMONIC (FR),** b br f Dubawi (IRE)—Peace In Motion (USA) **John & Jessica Dance**
10 **FOREVER PROUD,** b f Sioux Nation (USA)—Marsh Pride **John & Jessica Dance**
11 **GOTTA SHOW ME (IRE),** b f Showcasing—Chibola (ARG) **John & Jessica Dance**
12 **GROOVE NATION,** b g Siyouni (FR)—Fusion (IRE)
13 **HARLEM NIGHTS (IRE),** b g Dark Angel (IRE)—Elusive Beauty (IRE) **John & Jessica Dance**
14 **MAMBO SUNSET (IRE),** ch f Sea The Stars (IRE)—Mambo Light (USA) **John & Jessica Dance**
15 **MARTINI NIGHTS,** b f No Nay Never (USA)—Broderie Anglaise (IRE) **John & Jessica Dance**
16 **NEW TYCOON (IRE),** b g Cotai Glory—Diamond Finesse (IRE) **John & Jessica Dance**
17 **NIGHTS OVER EGYPT (IRE),** b c Oasis Dream—Beychella (USA) **John & Jessica Dance**
18 **ORBITAL CHIME,** b c Gleneagles (IRE)—Simmie (IRE) **John & Jessica Dance**
19 **PURE ANGEL,** b f Ardad (IRE)—Be My Angel **John & Jessica Dance**
20 **QUITE SPICY (IRE),** b f Sea The Stars (IRE)—Sindjara (USA) **John & Jessica Dance**
21 **RETRACTION (IRE),** b c Dark Angel (IRE)—Relation Alexander (IRE) **John & Jessica Dance**
22 **SENSE OF MOTION,** b f No Nay Never (USA)—Aim To Please (FR) **John & Jessica Dance**
23 **SOL CAYO (IRE),** b c Havana Gold (IRE)—Epatha (IRE) **John & Jessica Dance**
24 **SOUND PRESSURE (IRE),** b c Kodiac—Milana (FR) **John & Jessica Dance**
25 **TOO MUCH,** br f Showcasing—Girls Talk (IRE) **John & Jessica Dance**
26 **WATCHING OUT,** b f Bated Breath—Susan Stroman **John & Jessica Dance**
27 **WHAT A STRIKE (IRE),** b c Churchill (IRE)—Rose Blossom **John & Jessica Dance**

TWO-YEAR-OLDS

28 B f 22/02 Saxon Warrior (JPN)—Campion (Exceed And Excel (AUS)) (41617)
29 **CHILLI ZING (IRE),** b c 13/04 Magna Grecia (IRE)—Maria Lee (IRE) (Rock of Gibraltar (IRE)) (300000)
30 **CHUCHUWA (IRE),** ch f 14/02 Bated Breath—Bounce (Bahamian Bounty) (114286) **John & Jessica Dance**
31 B f 04/04 Invincible Army (IRE)—Dabtiyra (IRE) (Dr Devious (IRE)) (36190) **John & Jessica Dance**
32 **DISCO SPIRIT (IRE),** b c 04/03 Acclamation—Party For Ever (IRE) (Iffraaj) (150000)
33 **FLEETING MOMENT (IRE),** b f 11/02 Le Havre (IRE)—
Elle Maxima (GER) (Maxios) (190000) **John & Jessica Dance**
34 **JUNGLE DEMON (IRE),** b c 29/04 Galileo (IRE)—Terror (IRE) (Kodiac) (192077)
35 **LOVE FANTASY,** b f 17/02 Bated Breath—Adore (Oasis Dream) (230000) **John & Jessica Dance**
36 **LUNAR SHINE (IRE),** b f 24/03 Kodiac—African Moonlight (UAE) (Halling (USA)) (300000) **John & Jessica Dance**
37 B f 21/03 Cable Bay (IRE)—Marsh Pride (Stimulation (IRE))
38 **NEVERSTOPDREAMING (IRE),** gr gr f 28/02 No Nay Never (USA)—
Snowflakes (IRE) (Galileo (IRE)) (176070) **John & Jessica Dance**
39 B f 24/02 No Nay Never (USA)—Park Bloom (IRE) (Galileo (IRE)) (375000) **John & Jessica Dance**
40 **SPACE NINJA (IRE),** b c 24/04 Kodiac—Night Queen (IRE) (Rip Van Winkle (IRE)) (152381)
41 **TECHNICAL FAULT (IRE),** ch c 09/04 No Nay Never (USA)—Shahralasal (IRE) (Oasis Dream) (184074)
42 **TOUCH THE MOON (IRE),** b c 08/02 Sea The Stars (IRE)—Holda (IRE) (Docksider (USA)) (340136)
43 **TRIBAL RHYTHM,** ch c 01/04 Ulysses (IRE)—Russian Punch (Archipenko (USA)) (142857)
44 **TWISTING PHYSICS,** b c 25/02 Dubawi (IRE)—Frangipanni (IRE) (Dansili) (1000000)

267 MR SYD HOSIE, Sherborne

Postal: **Sandhills Farm, Holwell, Sherborne, Dorset, DT9 5LE**
Contacts: **PHONE 01963 23200**

1 **ACROSS THE LINE (IRE),** 8, b g Fame And Glory—La Protagonista (IRE) **Mr S. Hosie**
2 **AFTA PARTY (IRE),** 5, gr g Mastercraftsman (IRE)—Wood Fairy **Mr S. Hosie**
3 **BBOLD (IRE),** 9, b g Aizavoski (IRE)—Molly Be **Mr S. Hosie**
4 **COUP DE PINCEAU (FR),** 11, b g Buck's Boum (FR)—Castagnette III (FR) **Mr S. Hosie**
5 **ERITAGE (FR),** 9, b g Martaline—Sauves La Reine (FR) **Mr S. Hosie**
6 **EYE KNEE,** 5, b g Territories (IRE)—Western Pearl **Mr S. Hosie**
7 **GREAT SCHEMA,** 5, ch g Free Eagle (IRE)—Presbyterian Nun (IRE) **Mr S. Hosie**
8 **HARLEM SOUL,** 5, ch g Frankel—Giants Play (USA) **Mr S. Hosie**
9 **KALYPTRA (FR),** 7, b g Fair Mix (IRE)—Lovely Origny (FR) **Sherborne Utilities & Mr Robert Frosell**
10 **KATOPOP (IRE),** 5, b g Yeats (IRE)—Ashbury (IRE) **Mr S. Hosie**
11 **LIEUTENANT ROCCO (IRE),** 8, ch g Shirocco (GER)—Five Star Present (IRE) **Mr S. Hosie**
12 **MILANFORD (IRE),** 9, b g Milan—Tabachines (FR) **Mr S. Hosie**
13 **MORE BEER (IRE),** 8, b br g Westerner—Whites Cross (IRE) **Mr S. Hosie**
14 **MOYTIER (FR),** 6, ch g Falco (USA)—C'Est Trop Injuste (FR) **Mr S. Hosie**
15 **PLENTY OF TIME (IRE),** 7, b m Robin des Champs (FR)—Give It Time **Sherborne Utilities & Mr Robert Frosell**
16 **PROMISEDUAMIRACLE,** 4, b f Telescope (IRE)—Deploy Or Die (IRE) **Mr S. Hosie**
17 **PROMISING MILAN (IRE),** 8, b g Milan—French Promise (IRE) **Mr S. Hosie**
18 **ROCK MY WAY (IRE),** 5, b g Getaway (GER)—Far Rock (IRE) **Mr S. Hosie**
19 **SATANIC MOON,** 4, b g Sea The Moon (GER)—Diablerette **Mr S. Hosie**
20 **SUPREME COMMANDER (IRE),** 6, b g Fame And Glory—Unique Snoopy (IRE) **Mr S. Hosie**
21 **TARA LINE (IRE),** 6, b m Kayf Tara—First Line (GER) **Mr S. Hosie**
22 **WAY OUT (IRE),** 6, b g Getaway (GER)—Send To War **Mr S. Hosie**

268 MS GEORGIE HOWELL, Tenbury Wells

Postal: **Woodstock Bower Farm, Broadheath, Tenbury Wells, Worcestershire, WR15 8QN**
Contacts: **PHONE 07968 864433**
EMAIL georgie@drill-service.co.uk

1 **BLACK LIGHTNING (IRE),** 10, br g Whitmore's Conn (USA)—Annie May (IRE) **Ms G. P. C. Howell**
2 **CATCH THE CRUMPET,** 5, b h Lucarno (USA)—Shropshirelass **Ms G. P. C. Howell**
3 **CHAIN SMOKER,** 10, ch g Shantou (USA)—Handmemy Moneydown (IRE) **Ms G. P. C. Howell**
4 **MAWLOOD (IRE),** 7, b g Dawn Approach (IRE)—Kalaatah (USA) **Ms G. P. C. Howell**
5 **ORNUA (IRE),** 12, ch g Mahler—Merry Heart (IRE) **Ms G. P. C. Howell**
6 **POLLARDS FEN (IRE),** 8, ch g Sans Frontieres (IRE)—Shy Sheila (IRE) **Ms G. P. C. Howell**
7 **PUPPET WARRIOR,** 11, ch g Black Sam Bellamy (IRE)—Rakajack **Ms G. P. C. Howell**
8 4, Ch f Schiaparelli (GER)—Shropshirelass
9 **SUB LIEUTENANT (IRE),** 14, b g Brian Boru—Satellite Dancer (IRE) **Ms G. P. C. Howell**
10 **TIS BUT A SCRATCH,** 7, br g Passing Glance—Shropshirelass **Ms G. P. C. Howell**
11 4, B f Passing Glance—Young Cheddar (IRE)
12 **YOURHOLIDAYISOVER (IRE),** 16, ch g Sulamani (IRE)—Whitehaven **Ms G. P. C. Howell**

269 MRS DEBBIE HUGHES, Porth

Postal: **Tyr Heol Farm, Pantybrad, Tonyrefail, Rhondda, Mid Glamorgan, CF39 8HX**
EMAIL dimots@btinternet.com

1 **CHIM CHIMNEY,** 5, b g Cockney Rebel (IRE)—Wonderful Life (IRE) **Mrs D. J. Hughes**
2 **DANCING LILLY,** 8, ch m Sir Percy—Bhima **Mrs D. J. Hughes**

MRS DEBBIE HUGHES - continued

3 4, B c Mayson—Elysee (IRE) **Mrs D. J. Hughes**
4 **HOLLOW STEEL (IRE),** 4, b f Cotai Glory—Sunny Hollow **Mrs D. J. Hughes**
5 5, Ch m Indian Haven—Jinks And Co **Mrs D. J. Hughes**
6 **LESS OF THAT (IRE),** 9, b m Canford Cliffs (IRE)—Night Glimmer (IRE) **Mrs D. J. Hughes**
7 **LOVELY ACCLAMATION (IRE),** 9, b m Acclamation—Titova **Mrs D. J. Hughes**
8 **MAJOR ASSAULT,** 10, b g Kyllachy—Night Premiere (IRE) **Mrs D. J. Hughes**
9 **NATTY DRESSER (IRE),** 8, b g Dandy Man (IRE)—Parlour **Mrs D. J. Hughes**
10 **PICC AN ANGEL,** 7, b m Piccolo—Bhima **Mrs D. J. Hughes**
11 **PRINCESS OLIVE,** 4, b f Mayson—Royal Assent **Mrs D. J. Hughes**
12 **STOP N START,** 11, ch m Piccolo—Dim Ots **Mrs D. J. Hughes**
13 **TIME HAS WINGS (IRE),** 5, b m Moohaajim (IRE)—Rozene (IRE) **Mrs D. J. Hughes**
14 **WIRRAWAY (USA),** 7, ch g Australia—Fly Past **Mrs D. J. Hughes**

---

270 MR RICHARD HUGHES, Upper Lambourn

Postal: **Weathercock House, Upper Lambourn, Hungerford, Berkshire, RG17 8QT**
Contacts: **PHONE 01488 71198 MOBILE 07768 894828**
EMAIL office@richardhughesracing.co.uk WEBSITE www.richardhughesracing.co.uk

1 **AUSSIE BANKER,** 4, b g Muhaarar—Aristotelicienne (IRE) **Mr P. Cook**
2 **BASCULE (FR),** 5, ch g Kendargent (FR)—New River (IRE) **The New River Partnership**
3 **BETHERSDEN BOY (IRE),** 4, b g Excelebration (IRE)—Doctor's Note **RJ Rexton & CD Dickens**
4 **BRENTFORD HOPE,** 6, b g Camelot—Miss Raven (IRE) **Bernardine & Sean Mulryan**
5 **BRIGANTES WARRIOR,** 4, b g Ribchester (IRE)—Saphira's Fire (IRE) **M. J. Caddy**
6 **BRUNEL CHARM,** 6, b g Charm Spirit (IRE)—Manyara **R & S Needham**
7 **BYRON HILL (IRE),** 6, b g Kingston Hill—Gwen Lady Byron (IRE) **Mr D. A. Thorpe**
8 **CALLING THE WIND (IRE),** 7, b g Authorized (IRE)—Al Jasrah (IRE) **Mrs J. A. Wakefield**
9 **FAST DANSEUSE (IRE),** 4, b f Fast Company (IRE)—Zalanga (IRE) **Alan & Christine Bright**
10 **GOLD MEDAL,** 4, b g Olympic Glory (IRE)—Velvet Revolver (IRE) **Chris Kelly Developments Ltd**
11 **KIMNGRACE (IRE),** 4, b f Profitable (IRE)—Estonia **Mr A. Whelan**
12 **MYRIAD (IRE),** 4, ch g Cotai Glory—Superabundance (IRE) **Mr John Henwood & Partner**
13 **PRINCE IMPERIAL (USA),** 6, b g Frankel—Proportional **Highclere T'Bred Racing-Prince Imperial**
14 **SANDY PARADISE (IRE),** 4, ch g Footstepsinthesand—Duljanah (IRE) **Mr D. A. Thorpe**
15 **SEA APPEAL (IRE),** 5, b g Fastnet Rock (AUS)—Sea Paint (IRE) **Mr J. Reddington**
16 **TESSY LAD (IRE),** 4, b g Australia—Maracuja **M&O Construction & Civil Engineering Ltd**
17 **VILLALOBOS (IRE),** 4, b g Footstepsinthesand—Swift Acclaim (IRE) **L Turland and A Smith**
18 **WHOLEOFTHEMOON (IRE),** 4, b g Zoffany (IRE)—Shared Experience **The Golfers & Partner**
19 **WINFORGLORY (IRE),** 4, ch g Cotai Glory—Sideliner (IRE) **DWPJ**
20 **ZERO CARBON (FR),** 4, b g Acclamation—Clotilde **Cognition Land & Water & M Clarke**

THREE-YEAR-OLDS

21 **CANDLE OF HOPE,** br f Cable Bay (IRE)—Good Hope **The King**
22 **CINNODIN,** b g Anodin (IRE)—Cinnilla **Ellipsis II-Cinnodin**
23 **CONNEMARA COAST,** b g Sea The Moon (GER)—Force One **Bernardine & Sean Mulryan**
24 **EDGE OF EMBER,** br gr g Cracksman—White Wedding (IRE) **Graham Doyle & Hazel Lawrence**
25 **EMPEROR'S CLOTHES (IRE),** b g Holy Roman Emperor (IRE)—Camisole (IRE) **Mr D. A. Thorpe**
26 **FADI (FR),** gr c Mehmas (IRE)—Perspective (IRE) **Mr Eamon Kelly & Partner**
27 **FICTIONAL (IRE),** b g Make Believe—Hidden Girl (IRE) **The Dakota Partnership**
28 **KIMNKATE (IRE),** b f Havana Gold (IRE)—Chicas Amigas (IRE) **Mr P. Cook**
29 **KNEBWORTH,** b g Awtaad (IRE)—Stereophonic (IRE) **Blake, Coombs, Dellar, Giles & Merritt**
30 **LADY BRYANSTON (IRE),** ch f Ulysses (IRE)—Piano **The Heffer Syndicate**
31 **MISSING YOU,** b c Zoffany (IRE)—Capella's Song (IRE) **R & K Lawrence**
32 **NAILS MURPHY (IRE),** b c Sioux Nation (USA)—Supernovae (IRE) **Mansergh Wallace & Murphy**

MR RICHARD HUGHES - continued

33 **NOAH DAVID,** ch c Night of Thunder (IRE)—Mia San Triple **Sir David Seale**
34 **NOGO'S DREAM,** b g Oasis Dream—Morning Chimes (IRE) **RJ Rexton & CD Dickens**
35 **ONE MORE OLLY,** b f Camacho—Electrify (IRE) **Amo Racing Limited**
36 **REAL GAIN (IRE),** b c Profitable (IRE)—Real Me **Clarke, Jeffries, Lawrence & Cox**
37 **SATURNALIA (GER),** b g Holy Roman Emperor (IRE)—Soprana (GER) **Ms H. N. Pinniger**
38 **SCHUMANN (IRE),** b g Dandy Man (IRE)—Bibliotheca (JPN) **Highclere T'Bred Racing - Louise Gluck**
39 **SHARP POWER (IRE),** b g Churchill (IRE)—Polly Perkins (IRE) **Doyle, Ivory F Young**
40 **SPARKLING BEAUTY (FR),** b f Oasis Dream—Soniechka **Amo Racing Limited**
41 **THE THAMES BOATMAN,** b g Havana Grey—Gilt Linked **Nigel Scandrett & Shane Buy**
42 **VALUE ADDED,** b f Iffraaj—Star Value (IRE) **The King**
43 **WE COULD BE HEROES (IRE),** ch g Ribchester (IRE)—Mirabile Dictu (IRE) **Bernardine & Sean Mulryan**

TWO-YEAR-OLDS

44 **ALIKA BREEZE (GER),** ch f 18/01 Cracksman—Adalea (Dalakhani (IRE)) (50000) **Neal & Sheralee Grayston**
45 **ARCTURIAN (IRE),** ch c 28/01 Cotai Glory—
Star of Malta (Kyllachy) (38095) **Mr John Henwood & Miss Sally M Howes**
46 B f 29/01 Ardad (IRE)—Athbah (Shamardal (USA)) (76190) **J. Alharbi**
47 **CAT AND THE FIDDLE (IRE),** ch c 21/04 Ribchester (IRE)—
Tributary (New Approach (IRE)) (35000) **R Gander, S Threadwell & Partner**
48 B f 22/02 Cable Bay (IRE)—Fascinator (Helmet (AUS)) (32381) **Mr R. P. Gallagher**
49 Ch f 31/03 Zoustar (AUS)—Fast Lily (IRE) (Fastnet Rock (AUS)) (160000) **J. Alharbi**
50 B f 16/02 Kodi Bear (IRE)—Final Treat (IRE) (Acclamation) (80000)
51 Ch c 10/04 Ribchester (IRE)—Gamrah (IRE) (Exceed And Excel (AUS)) (80000) **Martin & James Jeffries**
52 B f 20/04 Ten Sovereigns (IRE)—Grand Zafeen (Zafeen (FR)) (104762) **J. Alharbi**
53 **HAVANAGREATTIME (IRE),** b c 18/02 Havana Grey—Dame Shirley (Haafhd) (84034) **Merritt, Lawrence P Cook**
54 B f 29/03 No Nay Never (USA)—Hidden Charms (IRE) (Canford Cliffs (IRE)) (40000) **Weathercock Ladies & Partner**
55 B c 16/03 Starspangledbanner (AUS)—
In The Fast Lane (SAF) (Jet Master (SAF)) (105000) **Bernadine Mulryan & Partner**
56 B c 22/02 Make Believe—Marasil (IRE) (Azamour (IRE)) (38415) **M&O Construction & Civil Engineering Ltd**
57 **MY MARGIE (IRE),** b f 09/04 Dandy Man (IRE)—Agapantha (USA) (Dynaformer (USA)) (47619) **R. A. Gander**
58 Ch c 03/03 Sea The Moon (GER)—Nimiety (Stormy Atlantic (USA)) (120000) **Qatar Racing & Mr A Regan**
59 B c 17/03 Cracksman—Pavillon (Showcasing) (85714) **Mr A. Al Mansoori**
60 Gr f 25/02 Havana Grey—Perfect Cover (IRE) (Royal Applause) (45714) **J. Alharbi**
61 B c 18/04 Postponed (IRE)—Queen's Dream (GER) (Oasis Dream) **Sir A. Ferguson**
62 B c 02/05 Awtaad (IRE)—Quiritis (Galileo (IRE)) (72029) **Mr A. Al Mansoori**
63 B c 04/05 Zoustar (AUS)—Roedean (IRE) (Oratorio (IRE)) (40000) **Beccle, Clay, Fleming & Partner**
64 B f 07/04 Magna Grecia (IRE)—Showtank (Showcasing) **M. J. Caddy**
65 **STATES,** b c 20/03 Territories (IRE)—
Stereophonic (IRE) (Acclamation) (40000) **Blake, Henwood, Lawrence and Merritt**
66 B f 10/04 Dandy Man (IRE)—Summarise (GER) (Shamardal (USA)) (38095) **J. Alharbi**
67 **SUPER SCHWARTZ (IRE),** b c 02/04 Kodiac—Sagittarian Wind (Iffraaj) (30476) **Mr A. G. Smith**
68 B c 25/04 Time Test—Sweet As Honey (Duke of Marmalade (IRE)) (50000)
69 B c 26/03 Frankel—Tai Hang Dragon (IRE) (Tamayuz) (190476) **J. Alharbi**
70 B f 30/03 Oasis Dream—Tappity Tap (Leroidesanimaux (BRZ)) (28571) **J. Alharbi**
71 B c 08/04 Due Diligence (USA)—Trumpet Lily (Acclamation) (38095) **Mr Richard Hughes**
72 B c 21/02 Advertise—Welsh Cake (Fantastic Light (USA)) (18000) **M. J. Caddy**
73 B gr f 25/02 Havana Gold (IRE)—Wings Ablaze (IRE) (Dark Angel (IRE)) (36190) **J. Alharbi**
74 B c 25/02 Cracksman—Wonderworld (GER) (Sea The Moon (GER)) (160000) **Mr A. Al Mansoori**
75 **ZOLA POWER,** ch c 14/04 Ulysses (IRE)—
Suerte Loca (IRE) (Peintre Celebre (USA)) (32000) **Thames Boys & Chris Budgett**

Apprentice Jockey: Tyler Heard, Finley Marsh, George Rooke.

271 MRS SARAH HUMPHREY, West Wratting

Postal: **Yen Hall Farm, West Wratting, Cambridge, Cambridgeshire, CB21 5LP**
Contacts: **PHONE 01223 291445 MOBILE 07798 702484**
EMAIL sarah@yenhallfarm.com WEBSITE www.sarahhumphrey.co.uk

1 **AJAY'S WAYS (IRE),** 9, br g Stowaway—Beechfield Queen (IRE) **Mrs S. J. Humphrey**
2 5, B m Clovis du Berlais (FR)—Call At Midnight **Mrs S. J. Humphrey**
3 **FULGURANT (FR),** 6, gr g Loup Breton (IRE)—Tour Magic (FR) **Humphreys and Brown Racing**
4 **GLIMPSE OF GOLD,** 12, b g Passing Glance—Tizzy Blue (IRE) **Yen Hall Farm Racing**
5 **GLOIRE D'ATHON (FR),** 7, b g Doctor Dino (FR)—Aster d'Athon (FR) **Mrs J. Pitman**
6 **ITS GONNAHAPPEN (IRE),** 7, b g Flemensfirth (USA)—Royal Choice (IRE) **Liz Reid & Partners**
7 **JACKS TOUCH (IRE),** 8, b m Jeremy (USA)—Jennys Gem (IRE) **The Jack's Touch Partnership**
8 **LE TUEUR (IRE),** 8, ch g Flemensfirth (USA)—Golden Odyssey (IRE) **Yen Hall Farm Racing**
9 **LILY'S RUBY,** 4, ch f Nayef (USA)—Silver Lily (IRE) **Silver Lily Bloodstock**
10 **NICKLE BACK (IRE),** 7, b g Mustameet (USA)—Mill House Girl (IRE) **The Friday Lunch Club**
11 **RAILWAY MUICE (IRE),** 10, b g Yeats (IRE)—Ar Muin Na Muice (IRE) **Mrs S. J. Humphrey**
12 **REDBRIDGE ROSIE (IRE),** 6, b m Soldier of Fortune (IRE)—Miss Island (IRE) **The Good Old Days Racing Partnership**
13 **STOP THIS TRAIN (IRE),** 6, b m Ask—Helens Decree (IRE) **The Buffers**
14 **TEMPLIER (IRE),** 10, b g Mastercraftsman (IRE)—Tigertail (FR) **Yen Hall Farm Racing**
15 5, B m Sans Frontieres (IRE)—Triumph Davis (IRE) **Mrs H Alcoe, Mr C Burgass**

Assistant Trainer: Mr A. R. Humphrey.

NH Jockey: Aidan Coleman, Nick Scholfield, Tom Scudamore. **Conditional Jockey:** Alexander Thorne, Jay Tidball.

Amateur Jockey: George O'Shea, Oliver Watson.

---

272 MR MITCHELL ANTHONY HUNT, Bridgwater

Postal: **Barford Stables, Spaxton, Bridgwater, Somerset, TA5 1AF**
Contacts: **PHONE 07540 732460**
EMAIL mitchell.hunt@rocketmail.com

1 **ARMY OF ONE (GER),** 6, b m Kingston Hill—Auctorita (GER) **Mr L. Robins**
2 **BARFORD DIVA,** 6, b m Kingston Hill—Jaja de Jau **Mr M. A. Hunt**
3 **BARFORD GROOVER,** 4, b f Pether's Moon (IRE)—Briska des Bordes (FR) **Mr S. Rushworth**
4 **BETTY FLETCHER,** 4, b f Heeraat (IRE)—Jilmah (IRE) **Mr N. Zayani**
5 **BLACKHORSE LADY (IRE),** 6, b m Fame And Glory—Discover Wexford (IRE) **Mr S. Rushworth**
6 **CHANKAYA,** 6, ch g Dubawi (IRE)—Splashdown **Mitchell Hunt Racing Club**
7 **GINDERELLA (IRE),** 6, b m Ocovango—Derella (IRE) **Familia Venari Syndicate**
8 **GYLLEN (USA),** 8, b g Medaglia d'Oro (USA)—Miss Halory (USA) **Stables Business Park Ltd**
9 **IRISH ED,** 5, b g Norse Dancer (IRE)—Dancing Hill **Things Can Only Get Better Syndicate**
10 **ISHANI,** 4, b f Ardad (IRE)—Ishiamber **Mrs P. A. Scott-Dunn**
11 4, Ch g Royal Anthem (USA)—Jaja de Jau **Mr M. A. Hunt**
12 **JUST GO FOR IT,** 10, b m Passing Glance—Just Jasmine **Mr S. G. Atkinson**
13 **LETS GO DUTCHESS,** 13, b m Helissio (FR)—Lets Go Dutch **K. Bishop**
14 **MARDOOF (IRE),** 5, b g Awtaad (IRE)—Yanabeeaa (USA) **Barford Premier**
15 **MINI YEATS (IRE),** 6, br gr g Yeats (IRE)—Rocapella **Mitchell Hunt Racing Club**
16 **OPTICALITY,** 5, b m Coach House (IRE)—Panoptic **Mr P. Simmons**
17 **PYRRHOS,** 5, ch g Twilight Son—Ishiamber **Mrs P. A. Scott-Dunn**
18 **RAYS RABBLE,** 6, b br m Blue Bresil (FR)—Queens Grove **Slabs & Lucan**
19 **TANGO FOR SALLY,** 6, b m Arvico (FR)—Teachmetotango **Monday Boys Partnership**

THREE-YEAR-OLDS

20 **PIVOTAL SKY,** b g Falco (USA)—Koben Sky **Mr S. Rushworth**

MR MITCHELL ANTHONY HUNT - continued

TWO-YEAR-OLDS

21 Ch f 01/04 Equiano (FR)—Blue Silk (Compton Place) (1000) **Mr M. A. Hunt**
22 **CITY WATERS,** b f 14/05 Washington DC (IRE)—Distant Waters (Lomitas) (1000) **Mr P. Simmons**

---

273 MR KEVIN HUNTER, Natland

Postal: **Larkrigg, Natland, Cumbria, LA9 7QS**
Contacts: **PHONE 015395 60245**

1 **BAPTISM OF FIRE (IRE),** 8, b g Jeremy (USA)—Julia Glynn (IRE) **J. K. Hunter**
2 **KINGOFTHECOTSWOLDS (IRE),** 9, b g Arcadio (GER)—Damoiselle **J. K. Hunter**
3 **THAT'S MY DUBAI (IRE),** 10, b m Dubai Destination (USA)—Musical Accord (IRE) **J. K. Hunter**

---

274 MR ROGER INGRAM, Epsom

Postal: **Wendover Stables, Burgh Heath Road, Epsom, Surrey, KT17 4LX**
Contacts: **PHONE 01372 749157, 01372 748505 MOBILE 07773 665980, 07715 993911**
FAX 01372 748505
EMAIL roger.ingram.racing@virgin.net WEBSITE www.rogeringramhorseracing.com

1 **DOUBLE LEGEND (IRE),** 8, b g Finsceal Fior (IRE)—Damask Rose (IRE) **Mr M. F. Cruse**
2 **MY BEAUTY (IRE),** 4, ch f Prince of Lir (IRE)—Zanida (IRE) **Mr J. O'Connor**
3 **NO SUCH LUCK (IRE),** 6, b g Tamayuz—Laftah (IRE) **Mr M. F. Cruse**
4 **ONE STEP BEYOND (IRE),** 6, b g Exceed And Excel (AUS)—Yours Truly (IRE) **Fire Plus Security**
5 **WHAT A MAN,** 4, b g Hellvelyn—Silver Marizah (IRE) **Mr J. Rogan**

Assistant Trainer: Sharon Ingram.

Apprentice Jockey: Rhiain Ingram.

275 MR ANDY IRVINE, East Grinstead

Postal: **Shovelstrode Racing Stables, Homestall Road, Ashurst Wood, East Grinstead, West Sussex, RH19 3PN**
Contacts: **PHONE 07970 839357**
EMAIL andy01031976@yahoo.co.uk

1 **BACKINFORGLORY (IRE),** 7, b m Fame And Glory—Backinthere (IRE) **The Lump Oclock the Secret Circle**
2 6, B m Fame And Glory—Barloge Creek (IRE) **Dan Shaw Simon Clare Andy Irvine**
3 **BEAUFORT WEST (IRE),** 9, b g Getaway (GER)—Blessingindisguise (IRE) **Mr D. Shaw**
4 **BIRDMAN BOB (IRE),** 6, ch g Flemensfirth (USA)—Brijomi Queen (IRE) **Taylor & O'Dwyer**
5 **BROWN BULLET (IRE),** 8, b m Arcadio (GER)—Barrack Buster **Dan Shaw Simon Clare Andy Irvine**
6 **CLONDAW ROBIN (IRE),** 10, ch g Robin des Champs (FR)—Old Town Queen (IRE) **The Plum Merchants**
7 **DEN THE DIVA,** 4, b f Black Sam Bellamy (IRE)—Bisou **Eventmasters Racing**
8 **ESCAPEFROMALCATRAZ (FR),** 6, b g Youmzain (IRE)—Waajida **Taylor & O'Dwyer**
9 **FLEMEN'S TIPPLE (IRE),** 6, b g Flemensfirth (USA)—Marie des Anges (FR) **Jokulhlaup Syndicate**
10 **GODOT (IRE),** 6, ch g Getaway (GER)—La Cerisaie **Taylor & O'Dwyer**
11 **GOLD CLERMONT (FR),** 7, b m Balko (FR)—Une Dame d'Or (FR) **Doyoufollow Partnership**
12 **HARRY HAZARD,** 9, b g Schiaparelli (GER)—Eveon (IRE) **Mr A. Lewers**

MR ANDY IRVINE - continued

13 **HESBEHINDYOU (IRE),** 7, b g Curtain Time (IRE)—Veronica's Gift (IRE) **The Plum Merchants**
14 **HONEST OSCAR (IRE),** 8, b m Oscar (IRE)—Honest Chance (FR) **Adrian Lewers the Lump Oclock Syndicate**
15 **LUCKY MAC,** 7, b g Yorgunnabelucky (USA)—C J Mackintosh **The Secret Circle Racing Club**
16 **MONTY'S AWARD (IRE),** 11, b g Oscar (IRE)—Montys Miss (IRE) **Jokulhlaup Syndicate**
17 **MR JACK (IRE),** 11, ch g Papal Bull—Miss Barbados (IRE) **Mr R. Dean**
18 **OSCAR ASCHE (IRE),** 9, b g Oscar (IRE)—Boro Supreme (IRE) **Dare To Dream Racing**
19 **PRIVATEARING,** 7, b g Black Sam Bellamy (IRE)—Diamond Dee **Jokulhlaup Syndicate**
20 **SILENT PARTNER,** 6, b g Fast Company (IRE)—Peace Lily **The Secret Circle Racing Club**
21 **THE REAL JET (IRE),** 7, ch m Jet Away—Stonehouse (IRE) **Bowtell, Shinton, Clare V Lewis**
22 **VINTAGE ICON,** 4, b g Sixties Icon—Amazing d'Azy (IRE) **Five Star Racing Group**

THREE-YEAR-OLDS

23 **YOUM DEJRAAN (IRE),** b g Muhaarar—Blue Ruby (IRE) **The Secret Circle Racing Club**

---

276 MR DEAN IVORY, Radlett

Postal: **Harper Lodge Farm, Harper Lane, Radlett, Hertfordshire, WD7 7HU**
Contacts: **PHONE 01923 855337 MOBILE 07785 118658 FAX 01923 852470**
EMAIL deanivoryracing@gmail.com WEBSITE www.deanivoryracing.co.uk

1 **ADACE,** 5, b m Adaay (IRE)—Marjong **Mr J. L. Marsden**
2 **BROXI (IRE),** 5, b br g Kodi Bear (IRE)—Own Gift **Heather Yarrow & Lesley Ivory**
3 **DORS TOYBOY (IRE),** 6, gr g Dark Angel (IRE)—Rathaath (IRE) **Mrs D. A. Carter**
4 **FIGHTING TEMERAIRE (IRE),** 10, b g Invincible Spirit (IRE)—Hot Ticket (IRE) **Michael & Heather Yarrow**
5 **HOT CHESNUT,** 5, ch m Camacho—Hot Ticket (IRE) **Heather & Michael Yarrow**
6 **LAURENTIA (IRE),** 7, b m Iffraaj—Brynica (FR) **B.Edwards & M.Hayes**
7 **LOST IN TIME,** 6, b g Dubawi (IRE)—Reunite (IRE) **K. T. Ivory**
8 **LUNA LIGHT (IRE),** 4, b f Highland Reel (IRE)—Moonwise (IRE) **Radlett Racing**
9 **MOONLIT CLOUD,** 5, b m Sea The Moon (GER)—Apple Blossom (IRE) **Dr A. J. F. Gillespie**
10 **PLEDGE OF HONOUR,** 7, b g Shamardal (USA)—Lura (USA) **Mr D. K. Ivory**
11 **THE SPOTLIGHT KID,** 4, b g Mayson—Marjong **Mr J. L. Marsden**
12 **THOMAS EQUINAS,** 4, ch g Mayson—Hot Ticket (IRE) **Michael & Heather Yarrow**
13 **YIMOU (IRE),** 8, b g Kodiac—Heroine Chic (IRE) **K. T. Ivory**

THREE-YEAR-OLDS

14 **ACHILLEA,** b f Frankel—Bruxcalina (FR) **Michael & Heather Yarrow**
15 **CRACKING FILLY,** ch f Cracksman—Hot Ticket (IRE) **Heather & Michael Yarrow**
16 **FOUGERE,** ch f Bated Breath—Nigh (IRE) **Heather & Michael Yarrow**
17 B f Acclamation—Gamba (IRE) **Mr D. K. Ivory**
18 **HAVECHATMA,** b f Havana Grey—Marjong **Mr J. L. Marsden**
19 **MOLLY VALENTINE (IRE),** b f Tamayuz—Molly Dolly (IRE) **Heather & Michael Yarrow**
20 **MY MATE MIKE (IRE),** b g Camacho—Forgotten Wish (IRE) **Mr D. K. Ivory**
21 **OPPORTUNITY KNOCKS (IRE),** b g Kodiac—Wild Impala (FR) **Michael & Heather Yarrow**
22 **SELINA'S STAR,** ch f Havana Grey—Elysee (IRE) **Radlett Racing**
23 **STARLIGHT WONDER (IRE),** b f Kodiac—Sanna Bay (IRE) **Michael & Heather Yarrow**

TWO-YEAR-OLDS

24 **DORS DELIGHT,** b f 10/02 Havana Grey—Dor's Law (Lawman (FR)) **Mrs D. A. Carter**
25 B f 16/01 Too Darn Hot—Eirene (Declaration of War (USA)) **Michael & Heather Yarrow**
26 Ch c 10/04 Ulysses (IRE)—Hot Ticket (IRE) (Selkirk (USA)) **Michael & Heather Yarrow**

Assistant Trainer: Chris Scally.

277 MISS TINA JACKSON, Loftus

Postal: **Tick Hill Farm, Liverton, Loftus, Saltburn, Cleveland, TS13 4TG**
Contacts: **PHONE 01287 644952 MOBILE 07774 106906**

1 **BLACK OPIUM,** 9, b m Black Sam Bellamy (IRE)—Fragrant Rose **Mr H. L. Thompson**
2 **ENAMAY,** 5, b m Lethal Force (IRE)—Postulant **Mr H. L. Thompson**
3 **IVORS INVOLVEMENT (IRE),** 11, b g Amadeus Wolf—Summer Spice (IRE) **Mr H. L. Thompson**
4 **JAMIH,** 8, ch g Intello (GER)—Hannda (IRE) **Mr H. L. Thompson**
5 **JAMIL (IRE),** 8, b g Dansili—Havant **Mr H. L. Thompson**
6 **KINDER KID (IRE),** 5, b g Milan—Another Nudge (IRE) **Mr H. L. Thompson**
7 **MISTER SMARTY,** 6, ch g Black Sam Bellamy (IRE)—Miss Sunflower **Mr H. L. Thompson**
8 **PARK STREET,** 4, b g New Approach (IRE)—City Chic (USA) **Mr H. L. Thompson**
9 **POINT OF WOODS,** 10, b g Showcasing—Romantic Myth **Mr H. L. Thompson**
10 **THOMAS CRANMER (USA),** 9, b g Hard Spun (USA)—House of Grace (USA) **Mr H. L. Thompson**

THREE-YEAR-OLDS

11 **MISSMIMI,** b f Equiano (FR)—Bendis (GER) **Mr H. L. Thompson**

---

278 MISS HANNAH JAMES, Malvern

Postal: **The Merries Farm, Rye Street, Birtsmorton, Malvern, Worcestershire, WR13 6AS**

1 **BATCH ME,** 7, b m Native Ruler—Bach Me (IRE) **Miss H. L. James**
2 **EMMAS DILEMMA (IRE),** 11, b m Gold Well—Emmas Island (IRE) **Miss H. L. James**
3 **JUNIOR MASSINI,** 8, b g Dr Massini (IRE)—Bach Me (IRE) **Miss H. L. James**
4 **MEGASCOPE,** 6, b g Telescope (IRE)—Megan Mint **Miss H. L. James**
5 **SPROGZILLA,** 14, gr m Fair Mix (IRE)—Gentle Approach **Miss H. L. James**

---

279 MR IAIN JARDINE, Carrutherstown

Postal: **Hetlandhill Farm, Carrutherstown, Dumfries, Dumfriesshire, DG1 4JX**
Contacts: **PHONE 01387 840347 MOBILE 07738 351232**
WORK EMAIL office@iainjardineracing.com WEBSITE www.iainjardineracing.com

1 **ABOLISH,** 7, b g Sepoy (AUS)—Striking Choice (USA) **Lycett Racing Ltd**
2 **ACONCAGUA MOUNTAIN (IRE),** 5, b g Requinto (IRE)—My Rules (IRE) **The Duchess of Sutherland**
3 **AFTER JOHN,** 7, b g Dutch Art—Rosacara **Lady Jouse Partnership**
4 **ANIMORE,** 10, b m Sulamani (IRE)—More Likely **Mrs A. F. Tullie**
5 **BASHFUL,** 5, b g Manduro (GER)—Inhibition **Lycett Racing Ltd**
6 **BULLS AYE (IRE),** 5, ch g Intello (GER)—Wo de Xin **Mr G. R. McGladery**
7 **CALL ME HARRY (IRE),** 6, b g Make Believe—Lake Moon **D & D Armstrong Ltd & Mr L Westwood**
8 **CAN'T STOP NOW (IRE),** 6, ch g Starspangledbanner (AUS)—Sorry Woman (FR) **Let's Be Lucky Racing 30**
9 **CARNIVAL TIMES,** 4, b f Time Test—Gypsy Carnival **The Duchess of Sutherland**
10 **COOL MIX,** 11, gr g Fair Mix (IRE)—Lucylou (IRE)
11 **CRYSTAL GUARD (IRE),** 5, b g Lope de Vega (IRE)—Crystal Melody **Let's Be Lucky Racing 33**
12 **DUNNET HEAD (IRE),** 5, b g Sholokhov (IRE)—Champagne Ruby (IRE) **R. A. Green**
13 **EXCELCIUS (USA),** 7, b g Exceed And Excel (AUS)—Crying Shame (USA) **Mr G. R. McGladery**
14 **EXIT TO WHERE (FR),** 9, b r Kapgarde (FR)—Rapsodie Sea (FR) **R. A. Green**
15 **FLORAL SPLENDOUR,** 4, br f Farhh—Red Tulip **Colin Dorman & Tommy Dorman**
16 **GISELLES IZZY (IRE),** 4, b f Camacho—Miss Cape (IRE) **Sons of Stirling Ltd**

MR IAIN JARDINE - continued

17 **GIVE GRACE (IRE),** 4, b f Harzand (IRE)—Bobbi Grace (IRE) **Mr I. Jardine**
18 **GLEN ALI (IRE),** 8, b m Califet (FR)—Glen Eile (IRE) **Mr I. Jardine**
19 **GOLD DES BOIS (FR),** 9, ch g Full of Gold (FR)—Equatoriale (FR) **R. A. Green**
20 **HALF SHOT (IRE),** 9, b g Yeats (IRE)—Dochas Supreme (IRE) **The Farming Army**
21 **HAVANA PARTY,** 5, ch g Havana Gold (IRE)—Ferayha (IRE) **Let's Be Lucky Racing 27**
22 **HAVEYOUMISSEDME,** 5, b g Helmet (AUS)—Haydn's Lass **Lycett Racing Ltd & Mr I Jardine**
23 4, Gr f Mastercraftsman (IRE)—In The Soup (USA)
24 **INNSE GALL,** 5, b g Toronado (IRE)—Reaf **C. H. McGhie**
25 **JKR COBBLER (IRE),** 4, b g Awtaad (IRE)—Lady Vyrnwy (IRE) **Mr A. Rankin**
26 **JUMP THE GUN (IRE),** 6, b g Make Believe—Sound of Guns **Let's Be Lucky Racing 26**
27 **KATS BOB,** 5, ch g Bobby's Kitten (USA)—Dreaming of Stella (IRE) **Colin Dorman & Tommy Dorman**
28 **LASTOFTHECOSMICS,** 8, b g Shirocco (GER)—Cosmic Case **The Cosmic Cases**
29 **LOOM LARGE (IRE),** 4, b g Acclamation—Pyrenean Queen (IRE) **Bruce & Susan Jones**
30 **MANU ET CORDE (IRE),** 4, b g Teofilo (IRE)—Tiffilia (IRE) **Mr J. Fyffe**
31 **MASTER OLIVER (IRE),** 4, ch g Mastercraftsman (IRE)—Steal The Show (NZ) **Mr I. Jardine**
32 **MERRICOURT (IRE),** 7, gr g Mizzen Mast (USA)—Elite **Mr A. McLuckie**
33 **MINELLA YOUNGY (IRE),** 5, b br g Beat Hollow—Cheryls Island (IRE) **Mr B. P. Keogh**
34 **MINTNTHAT,** 4, b g Lawman (FR)—Dream Dancing (IRE) **Iain Jardine Racing Club**
35 **MONROE GOLD,** 4, ch f Highland Reel (IRE)—Marilyn (GER) **Kildonan Gold Racing**
36 **NEVER DARK,** 6, b g No Nay Never (USA)—Dark Missile **Alison Walker Sarah Cousins**
37 **NOVAK,** 4, gr g Mastercraftsman (IRE)—Parknasilla (IRE) **Mrs F. E. Mitchell**
38 **OOT MA WAY (FR),** 5, b m Power—Olvia (IRE) **Iain Jardine Racing Club**
39 **PARAMARIBO (IRE),** 5, b g Sea The Moon (GER)—Homepage **C. H. McGhie**
40 **PERFECT POLI,** 5, b m Dunaden (FR)—Miss Poli **Mr I. Kurdi**
41 **PERIBONKA RIVER (FR),** 4, b f Kapgarde (FR)—Savage River (FR) **Mr I. Kurdi**
42 **PRONTOANITA (FR),** 4, gr f Reliable Man—Floriana (GER) **R. A. Green**
43 **RAVENSCRAIG CASTLE,** 5, gr g Nathaniel (IRE)—In The Soup (USA) **Castle Racing Scotland**
44 **REVE DE NIAMH,** 6, b m Telescope (IRE)—En Reve **The Twelve Munkys**
45 **ROSE BANDIT (IRE),** 6, b m Requinto (IRE)—Poppy's Rose **The Strattonites**
46 **SHIR I DONT KNOW (IRE),** 6, b g Shirocco (GER)—Liss Na Siog (IRE) **Mr I. Jardine**
47 **SHOWMEDEMONEY (IRE),** 4, b g Divine Prophet (AUS)—Escapism (IRE) **Cool Jazz**
48 **SLUGGER,** 4, b g Ocovango—Dolly Boru **Fight Club**
49 **SMART LASS (IRE),** 8, b m Casamento (IRE)—Smart Ass (IRE) **Mr G. R. McGladery**
50 **SOLEIL DE CANNES (FR),** 4, ch g Quick Martin (FR)—Act of Honor (FR) **D & D Armstrong Ltd & Mr L Westwood**
51 **SOMETHING GOLDEN (IRE),** 7, ch g Dylan Thomas (IRE)—Shuil Le Vic (IRE) **Mrs C. Brown**
52 **SWALLOWS SONG,** 5, b g Kayf Tara—One Gulp **Ms E. Fallon**
53 **THE GAY BLADE,** 4, b g Mazameer (IRE)—Big Mystery (IRE) **Musselburgh Lunch Club**
54 **THE GLOAMING (IRE),** 5, gr m Gutaifan (IRE)—On High **The Strattonites**
55 **VAMOS CHICA (IRE),** 4, b f Vadamos (FR)—Krynica (USA) **Let's Be Lucky Racing 32**
56 **VOIX DU REVE (FR),** 11, br g Voix du Nord (FR)—Pommbelle (FR) **D & D Armstrong Ltd & Mr L Westwood**
57 **WEE FAT MAC,** 4, b g Swiss Spirit—Flylowflylong (IRE) **The Strattonites**
58 **ZEGOS SURPRISE (IRE),** 5, b m Zebedee—Emma's Surprise **Mr I. Jardine**
59 **ZUMAATY (IRE),** 5, b g Tamayuz—Blackangelheart (IRE) **Let's Be Lucky Racing 34**

THREE-YEAR-OLDS

60 **DADDY SCAT (FR),** b g Seahenge (USA)—Etoile de Kerfelec (FR) **D&D Armstrong Limited**
61 **HELLO HAVANA (IRE),** b f Galileo Gold—Hello Brigette (IRE) **The Duchess of Sutherland**
62 **HOUR BY HOUR,** b g Time Test—Steppe By Steppe **The Duchess of Sutherland**
63 **LORD SAM'S CASTLE (IRE),** b g Zoffany (IRE)—Pellinore (USA) **Racing & I Jardine**
64 **LUNACY,** b g New Bay—Lunar Spirit
65 B f Smooth Daddy (USA)—Mornington Belle (IRE)
66 **PADDY THE SQUIRE,** b c Golden Horn—Provenance **Mr I. C. Jones**
67 B g Sixties Icon—Push Me (IRE)
68 **SAVE THE WORLD,** b g James Garfield (IRE)—Just Be Friendly **Lycett Racing Ltd**
69 **SCAT MAGGIE (IRE),** ch f Smooth Daddy (USA)—Go Maggie Go (IRE) **Miss V. E. Renwick**
70 **SPREZZATURA (IRE),** b g Muhaarar—Parle Moi (USA) **The Strattonites**
71 **SUTUE ALSHAMS (IRE),** b g Golden Horn—Gile Na Greine (IRE) **Mr I. C. Jones**
72 **WURKIN NINETOFIVE (IRE),** ch f Fast Company (IRE)—Folk Singer **Mr I. Jardine**

MR IAIN JARDINE - continued

TWO-YEAR-OLDS

73 B c 28/02 Muhaarar—Etaab (USA) (Street Cry (IRE))
74 B c 10/03 Saxon Warrior (JPN)—Hope So (IRE) (Bated Breath) (45000)
75 **MOONSTONE BOY (IRE),** b c 15/03 Calyx—Star Fire (Dark Angel (IRE)) **The Duchess of Sutherland**
76 B c 12/03 Calyx—Please Sing (Royal Applause) (85000)
77 **PUMPKIN PIE,** b c 20/04 Equiano (FR)—Groomsport (IRE) (Footstepsinthesand) **Mr G. R. McGladery**
78 B c 24/04 Expert Eye—Time On (Sadler's Wells (USA)) (32000) **The Cricketers**
79 **TIMESWITCH,** b c 12/03 Time Test—Miss Bates (Holy Roman Emperor (IRE)) **The Duchess of Sutherland**
80 **TOMMY'S PROMISE,** b c 02/05 Saxon Warrior (JPN)—Sister Red (IRE) (Diamond Green (FR)) **Mr G. R. McGladery**

Racing Secretary: Valerie Renwick.

Flat Jockey: Andrew Mullen. **NH Jockey:** Conor O'Farrell. **Apprentice Jockey:** Poppy Wilson. **Amateur Jockey:** Ailsa McClung.

---

280 MR WILLIAM JARVIS, Newmarket

Postal: **Phantom House Stables, Fordham Road, Newmarket, Suffolk, CB8 7AA**
Contacts: **HOME 01638 662677 PHONE 01638 669873 MOBILE 07836 261884 FAX 01638 667328**
EMAIL mail@williamjarvis.com WEBSITE www.williamjarvis.com

1 **BULLEIT,** 4, ch g Helmet (AUS)—Flora Medici **The Raceology Partnership**
2 **CRYSTAL DELIGHT,** 4, ch c New Approach (IRE)—Crystal Capella **Little Staughton Farms Ltd**
3 **CRYSTAL FLOW,** 5, b m Camelot—Living Well **M. G. H. Heald**
4 **DR BRERETON (IRE),** 4, ch f Dawn Approach (IRE)—Back In The Frame **The Raceology Partnership**
5 **DUKE OF VERONA (IRE),** 5, gr g Belardo (IRE)—Somewhere (IRE) **R. C. C. Villers**
6 **KENILWORTH KING (USA),** 4, b g Kitten's Joy (USA)—Uniformly Yours (CAN) **Little Staughton Farms Ltd**
7 **LIVALOT (IRE),** 4, b f Camelot—Lucht Na Gaeilge (IRE) **Ms E. L. Banks**
8 **ROSE CAMIRA,** 4, b f Camelot—Silent Act (USA) **Ms R. Grubmuller**

THREE-YEAR-OLDS

9 **ALI JEWELS (IRE),** b f Aclaim (IRE)—Passionable **Mr T. C. O'Brien**
10 **CERVETTO (IRE),** ch c Zoffany (IRE)—Ribble (FR) **Mr W. Jarvis**
11 **COLOANE (IRE),** b f Cotai Glory—Stylish One (IRE) **Dr J. Walker**
12 **EXQUISITE BEAUTY,** b f Bobby's Kitten (USA)—Salome (FR) **Paul Malone & Damien Tiernan**
13 **HAKUNA BABE,** b f Roaring Lion (USA)—Purr Along **Ms E. L. Banks**
14 **JURYMAN,** b g Recorder—Kinematic **Mr D. H. Batten**
15 **LARKHILL (IRE),** b g Nathaniel (IRE)—Lanita (GER) **The Phantom House Partnership**
16 **LAWMAKER,** gr c Mastercraftsman (IRE)—Zacchera **The Raceology Partnership & WJ**
17 **MISS GALLAGHER,** b f Dark Angel (IRE)—Mrs Gallagher **Ms E. L. Banks**
18 **MYSTERY PLAY,** b f Golden Horn—Monday Show (USA)
19 **OUT RULE (IRE),** br g Karakontie (JPN)—Leaf Blower (USA) **The Raceology Partnership**
20 **PEMBROKESHIRE,** b g Iffraaj—Gwerrann **P. C. J. Dalby & R. D. Schuster**
21 **SEVEN PILLARS,** b f Oasis Dream—Anzac (IRE) **Seven Pillars Partnership**
22 **TWO FOOLS COLLIDE,** b f Mukhadram—Hathrah (IRE) **Mrs P Shanahan & Mrs M V Magnier**

TWO-YEAR-OLDS

23 **CUBAN SECRET (IRE),** gr f 04/03 Havana Grey—
Milly's Secret (IRE) (Sakhee's Secret) (50000) **The Raceology Partnership & WJ**
24 **JUNGLE CRUISE (IRE),** b c 24/03 Bungle Inthejungle—
Chantilly Cream (IRE) (Acclamation) (9000) **The Raceology Partnership**
25 B f 12/04 Postponed (IRE)—Pearl Earing (IRE) (Excellent Art) **The Raceology Partnership**
26 B c 28/04 Dark Angel (IRE)—Relevant (IRE) (So You Think (NZ)) (30000) **P. C. J. Dalby & R. D. Schuster**
27 Gr c 21/02 Phoenix of Spain (IRE)—Think Fashion (IRE) (So You Think (NZ)) (85000) **Ms E. L. Banks**
28 **TIME TESTED,** b c 30/04 Time Test—Luzia (Cape Cross (IRE)) **The Raceology Partnership**

Assistant Trainer: James Toller.

281 MISS RUTH JEFFERSON, Malton

Postal: **Newstead Stables, Beverley Road, Norton, Malton, North Yorkshire, YO17 9PJ**
Contacts: **PHONE 01653 697225 MOBILE 07976 568152**
WEBSITE www.ruthjefferson.co.uk

1 **AUTUMN RETURN (IRE),** 6, b m Fame And Glory—Fedaia (IRE) **Drew & Ailsa Russell**
2 **BALLYWHATSIT (IRE),** 5, b g Kalanisi (IRE)—Silver Charmer **Drew & Ailsa Russell**
3 **EDMOND DANTES (FR),** 7, b g Walk In The Park (IRE)—Divine Surprise (IRE) **Drew & Ailsa Russell**
4 **FETCH IT YOURSELF,** 5, b m Mount Nelson—Retrieve The Stick **Newstead Racing Partnership**
5 **FLINT HILL,** 7, ch g Excelebration (IRE)—Modify **Whitelock, Clemitson R Jefferson**
6 **HASHTAG BOUM (FR),** 6, b br m Al Namix (FR)—Engagee (FR) **They Are Never At Home Partnership**
7 **INCA PRINCE (IRE),** 5, b g Fast Company (IRE)—Angel Stevens (IRE) **Whitelock, Clemitson R Jefferson**
8 **LUNAR CHIEF,** 5, b g Pether's Moon (IRE)—Oleohneh (IRE) **Miss N. R. Jefferson**
9 **MAURITIAN BOLT (IRE),** 8, ch g Le Fou (IRE)—Fleeting Arrow (IRE) **Ruth Jefferson Racing Club**
10 **MOURNE LASS (IRE),** 7, b m Kalanisi (IRE)—Drapers Hill (IRE) **Miss N. R. Jefferson**
11 **ROEBUCK BAY,** 4, ch f Beat Hollow—Down Ace (IRE) **Miss N. R. Jefferson**
12 **SAGONIGE,** 4, b f Blue Bresil (FR)—Oleohneh (IRE) **Miss N. R. Jefferson**
13 **SILVER COIN (IRE),** 6, b gr m Fairly Ransom (USA)—Hayestown Lady (IRE) **Best Foot Forward & Partner**
14 **SIR JIM (IRE),** 8, gr g Shirocco (GER)—Stick Together **Derek Gennard & Gillian Gennard**
15 **SOUNDS RUSSIAN (IRE),** 8, b g Sholokhov (IRE)—Reevolesa (IRE) **Claxby & Co**
16 **SWEDISH ICON,** 5, b g Norse Dancer (IRE)—Our Ethel **Ruth Jefferson Racing Club**
17 **SWITCH PARTNER (IRE),** 6, b m Presenting—Almada (FR) **The Switched On Club**

THREE-YEAR-OLDS

18 B g Norse Dancer (IRE)—Ethelwyn
19 B g Yeats (IRE)—Oleohneh (IRE)
20 B f Passing Glance—Our Ethel **Miss N. R. Jefferson**

282 MR D J JEFFREYS, Evesham

Postal: **Ballards Farm, Hinton-on-the-Green, Evesham, Worcestershire, WR11 2QU**
Contacts: **PHONE 07917 714687**
EMAIL djjeffreys15@hotmail.co.uk

1 **AL MUFFRIH (IRE),** 8, b g Sea The Stars (IRE)—Scarlet And Gold (IRE) **Mr M. E. Smith**
2 **ARCTIC LODGE (IRE),** 7, b g Arctic Cosmos (USA)—Lodge Princess (IRE) **Ballards Racing**
3 **AUGHNACURRA KING (IRE),** 10, ch g Tajraasi (USA)—Cracking Kate (IRE) **Mark E Smith & Jaykayjay Pals Ak**
4 **AYR OF ELEGANCE,** 11, b m Motivator—Gaelic Swan (IRE) **DJ Jeffreys Racing Club**
5 **BALLELA SUNRISE (IRE),** 6, b m Morozov (USA)—Tricky Present (IRE) **Mr D. Jeffreys**
6 **BALLYCROSS,** 12, b g King's Theatre (IRE)—Ninna Nanna (FR) **Mr Oscar Singh & Miss Priya Purewal**
7 **BALLYVAUGHAN BAY (IRE),** 6, b g Fame And Glory—Roughan Daisy (IRE)
8 **BEN BRODY (IRE),** 13, b g Beneficial—Thethirstyscholars (IRE) **Mark E Smith & the Bb Pony Gang 5**
9 **BEST MATE DAVE,** 6, b g Passing Glance—Dillay Brook (IRE) **Dave's Best Mates**
10 **BIG CITY LIFE,** 5, ch g Dawn Approach (IRE)—Puppet Queen (USA) **Mr D. Jeffreys**
11 **BOOMTIME BANKER (IRE),** 9, b m Kalanisi (IRE)—Tiger Tiffney (IRE) **Ms K. J. Sweeting**
12 **CARDBOARD GANGSTER,** 8, gr g Norse Dancer (IRE)—Hiho Silver Lining **Mr M. E. Smith**
13 **CHAMPAGNE GIFT (IRE),** 7, ch g Presenting—Princess Dante (IRE) **Mr M. E. Smith**
14 **COILROCK (IRE),** 6, b g Sageburg (IRE)—Merry Moet (IRE) **Mr D. Jeffreys**
15 **DR LOCKDOWN (IRE),** 6, ch g Shirocco (GER)—Our Soiree (IRE) **Mr D. Jeffreys**
16 **EMOTIONAL MEMORIES (IRE),** 6, b g Arctic Cosmos (USA)—Emotional Melody (IRE) **Mark E Smith & Caren Walsh**
17 **ENEMENEMYNEMO (IRE),** 8, b g Lakeshore Road (USA)—Portobello Sunrise (IRE) **Mr M. E. Smith**
18 **FLIGHTY BRIDE,** 8, b m Bahri (USA)—Flighty Mist **J. R. Jeffreys**
19 **GEROLAMO CARDANO,** 7, b g Motivator—Dark Quest **Mr M. E. Smith**
20 **GETAMAN (IRE),** 10, b g Getaway (GER)—Zingarella's Joy (IRE) **DJ Jeffreys Racing Club**

MR D J JEFFREYS - continued

21 **GHYLL MANOR (IRE),** 4, b g Gleneagles (IRE)—Jubilant Lady (USA) **Mrs C. Kendrick**
22 **GOGUENARD (FR),** 7, b g Buck's Boum (FR)—Ouchka (FR) **Les Petits Coquins**
23 **HARRY D'ALENE (FR),** 6, ch g Coastal Path—Agatha d'Alene (FR) **Ballards Racing**
24 **KAYLEN'S MISCHIEF,** 10, ch g Doyen (IRE)—Pusey Street Girl **Mr M. E. Smith**
25 **KILDIMO (IRE),** 8, b br g Stowaway—Beananti (IRE) **Mr M. E. Smith**
26 **LAND OF MY DELIGHT (IRE),** 7, b g Shantou (USA)—Gurteen Flyer (IRE) **Turf Club 2022**
27 **LE BALCON (IRE),** 8, b g Robin des Champs (FR)—Annilogs Symphony (IRE) **Ballards Racing**
28 **LIVELY CITIZEN (IRE),** 8, b g Frammassone (IRE)—Acinorev (IRE) **Mark E Smith,Brake Horse Power Syndicate**
29 **MUSTANG ALPHA (IRE),** 8, b g Stowaway—Tupia (FR) **Mrs C. Kendrick**
30 **ORDER OF ST JOHN,** 6, b g Coach House (IRE)—Gospel Music **Rupert Frost & Ed Shaw**
31 **PETRASTAR,** 8, b g Passing Glance—Petrarchick (USA) **Mr M. E. Smith**
32 **PRINCESS PRIYA (IRE),** 6, b m Flemensfirth (USA)—Rosa Rugosa (IRE) **Mr Oscar Singh & Miss Priya Purewal**
33 **RAKHINE STATE (IRE),** 10, b g Arakan (USA)—Oiselina (FR) **Mr Stuart Stanley & Mr Adam Lucock**
34 **RATFACEMCDOUGALL (IRE),** 10, b g Robin des Champs (FR)—Milano Bay (IRE) **Mrs C. Kendrick**
35 **REAMS OF LOVE,** 5, b g Frankel—Night of Light (IRE) **Mr G. Houghton**
36 **SIMPLY TRUE (IRE),** 6, ch g Camacho—Faussement Simple (IRE) **Mr M. E. Smith**
37 4, B g Doyen (IRE)—Structura (USA)
38 **TEN TEN TWENTY (IRE),** 5, b g Vadamos (FR)—Echo River (USA) **Cheltenham Amigos**
39 **TEVIOT PRINCE (IRE),** 13, ch g Strategic Prince—Nashville Skyline **Mr D. Jeffreys**
40 **THE GOLD BUG (IRE),** 8, b g Shantou (USA)—Eva La Diva (IRE) **Mrs M. Fleming**

---

283 MR J. R. JENKINS, Royston

Postal: **Kings Ride, Therfield Heath, Royston, Hertfordshire, SG8 9NN**
Contacts: **PHONE 01763 241141, 01763 246611 MOBILE 07802 750855 FAX 01763 248223**
EMAIL john@johnjenkinsracing.co.uk WEBSITE www.johnjenkinsracing.co.uk

1 **ACE TIME,** 9, b g Sinndar (IRE)—Desert Run (IRE) **B. S. P. Dowling**
2 **AMAL (IRE),** 5, b m No Nay Never (USA)—Lundy Island **Mrs W. A. Jenkins**
3 **ARTEMISIA GENTILE (IRE),** 4, gr f Caravaggio (USA)—Horse Sense (IRE) **Mr T. C. Lines**
4 **BANG ON THE BELL,** 4, b g Heeraat (IRE)—Bella Beguine **Mr M. Turner**
5 **BASHARAT,** 5, br g Bated Breath—Nos Da **Ms A. Juskaite**
6 **BUNGLEDUPINBLUE (IRE),** 5, b m Bungle Inthejungle—Generous Heart **Mr Q. Khan**
7 **CARMELA SOPRANO,** 5, gr m Hellvelyn—Caramelita **Golden Equinox Racing**
8 **CHLOELLIE,** 8, b m Delegator—Caramelita **All Weather Racing Club**
9 **CHRYSSIPHUS LIMES (FR),** 4, b g Australia—Sheistheboss (FR) **Mr T. C. Lines**
10 **COCOA CABANA,** 6, b m Cappella Sansevero—Mediterranean Sea (IRE) **Mrs W. A. Jenkins**
11 **COMPANY MINX (IRE),** 6, gr m Fast Company (IRE)—Ice Haven (IRE) **Double-R-Racing**
12 **ELF RISING,** 4, ch g Hot Streak (IRE)—Rise **Elf Rising Partnership**
13 **ESTABLISHED (IRE),** 4, br g Estidhkaar (IRE)—Azzoom (IRE) **Mr R. M. Grover**
14 **GOOD TO GO,** 4, b g Heeraat (IRE)—Ellcon (IRE) **Mr M. Turner**
15 **HOLD THE PRESS (IRE),** 4, b g Profitable (IRE)—Hairicin (IRE) **Mrs W. A. Jenkins**
16 **ILONA TAMARA (FR),** 4, b f Pedro The Great (USA)—La Houssay (FR) **Mr T. C. Lines**
17 **MAYKIR,** 7, b g Mayson—Kiruna **Mr R. Stevens**
18 **MISS G GEE,** 6, b m Fast Company (IRE)—Teyateyaneng (IRE) **Mr Mark Goldstein & Mrs Wendy Jenkins**
19 **PARTY PLANNER,** 6, gr m Mastercraftsman (IRE)—Sweet Sixteen (IRE) **Mrs W. A. Jenkins**
20 **SHERELLA,** 7, b m Delegator—Mediterranean Sea (IRE) **Mrs W. A. Jenkins**
21 **SIR RODNEYREDBLOOD,** 6, ch g Roderic O'Connor (IRE)—Red Blooded Woman (USA) **Mrs C. Goddard**
22 **SUNSET IN PARIS (IRE),** 5, b g Camelot—Trail of Tears (IRE) **B. S. P. Dowling**
23 **TEASYWEASY,** 4, gr g Outstrip—Dangerous Moonlite (IRE) **Zeal Racing Limited**
24 **TELL ELL,** 5, b m Proconsul—Ellcon (IRE) **Mr M. Turner**
25 **TILSWORTH JADE,** 4, b f Ardad (IRE)—Ashwell Rose **Michael Ng**
26 **TILSWORTH ONY TA,** 4, b g Ardad (IRE)—Pallas **Michael Ng**

THREE-YEAR-OLDS

27 **CARRANITA,** b f Heeraat (IRE)—Ellcon (IRE) **Mr M. Turner**

MR J. R. JENKINS - continued

28 Ch g Outstrip—Cavallo da Corsa **Michael Ng**
29 B g Telescope (IRE)—Lady Bonanova (IRE) **Michael Ng**
30 NO NEWS (IRE), b c Prince of Lir (IRE)—Lost Highway (IRE) **Mrs I. C. Hampson**

TWO-YEAR-OLDS

31 BOLEYN FOREVER, br c 28/03 Outstrip—
Pretty Bubbles (Sleeping Indian) **Mr Mark Goldstein & Mrs Wendy Jenkins**
32 B f 16/04 Massaat (IRE)—Dancing Plates (Royal Applause) **Mrs W. A. Jenkins**
33 KOHANA GIRL (IRE), b f 18/01 Sioux Nation (USA)—Dandilion (IRE) (Dandy Man (IRE)) **Golden Equinox Racing**
34 MR PHILLIPS, b c 19/05 Yorgunnabelucky (USA)—Caramelita (Deportivo) **Golden Equinox Racing**

---

284 MR BRETT JOHNSON, Epsom

Postal: **The Durdans Stables, Chalk Lane, Epsom, Surrey, KT18 7AX**
Contacts: **MOBILE 07768 697141**
EMAIL thedurdansstables@googlemail.com WEBSITE www.brjohnsonracing.co.uk

1 ALSAMYAH, 4, ch f Farhh—Chasing Rubies (IRE) **Kestonracingclub**
2 ANISOPTERA (IRE), 6, ch m Casamento (IRE)—Dragonera **Tann & Mr N Jarvis**
3 BEAUTIFUL CROWN, 5, b g Helmet (AUS)—Bright Halo (IRE) **Mr C. Westley**
4 CABLE MOUNTAIN, 4, b g Cable Bay (IRE)—Esteemed Lady (IRE) **The Fat Jockey Partnership**
5 DAMASCUS FINISH (IRE), 4, gr g Markaz (IRE)—Impressive Victory (USA) **Tann & Mr N Jarvis**
6 DEMBE, 5, b g Garswood—Disco Ball **Kestonracingclub**
7 DULCET SPIRIT, 4, b f Invincible Spirit (IRE)—Dulcet (IRE) **Kestonracingclub**
8 FOZZIE BEAR (IRE), 4, b g Kodiac—Dabtiyra (IRE) **J. Daniels**
9 JOANIE'S GIRL, 4, b f Pearl Secret—Jackline **Only Fools Have Horses**
10 KATELLI (IRE), 6, br g Dragon Pulse (IRE)—Kateeva (IRE) **Roofnet Limited**
11 KINDERFRAU, 5, b m Sea The Stars (IRE)—Prussian **Mr R. E. Pain**
12 LETHAL ANGEL, 8, gr m Lethal Force (IRE)—Heliograph **Billy and The Boys**
13 LUCKY MASCOT (IRE), 4, b f Exceed And Excel (AUS)—Light Spirit **Mr R. E. Pain**
14 MOEL ARTHUR (USA), 5, b g Flintshire—Quest To Peak (USA) **Kestonracingclub**
15 NOBBY BRUSSELS (IRE), 4, b g Milan—Blazes Peg (IRE)
16 STARRY EYES (USA), 7, ch m Animal Kingdom (USA)—Starship Elusive (USA) **J. Daniels**
17 STOPNSEARCH, 6, b g War Command (USA)—Secret Suspect **Mr R. E. Pain**
18 VIOLET'S LADS (IRE), 9, b m Myboycharlie (IRE)—Cape Violet (IRE) **The Savy Group**

THREE-YEAR-OLDS

19 LUCY LIGHTFOOT (IRE), b f Fast Company (IRE)—Redoutable (IRE) **Mrs L. E. Peck**
20 ROCKING ENDS, gr g Havana Grey—Copper Penny **Mr C. Westley**
21 SAND TIMER, b f Time Test—Dusty Answer **Mr C. Westley**

Assistant Trainer: Vanessa Johnson.

---

285 MISS EVE JOHNSON HOUGHTON, Blewbury

Postal: **Woodway, Blewbury, Didcot, Oxfordshire, OX11 9EZ**
Contacts: **PHONE 01235 850480 MOBILE 07721 622700 FAX 01235 851045**
EMAIL Eve@JohnsonHoughton.com WEBSITE www.JohnsonHoughton.com

1 ACCIDENTAL AGENT, 9, b g Delegator—Roodle **Mrs F. M. Johnson Houghton**
2 BASCINET, 4, ch g Helmet (AUS)—Finale **Eden Racing Club**
3 CABINET OF CLOWNS (IRE), 4, gr ro g Tamayuz—
Silver Games (IRE) **Hon Mrs J. M. The Corbett & Mr Chris Wright**

MISS EVE JOHNSON HOUGHTON - continued

4 **FLYING SECRET,** 4, b g Showcasing—Secret Sense (USA) **Jacobsconstructionholdings& Mr E Kelly**
5 **GRANARY QUEEN (IRE),** 5, ch m Dragon Pulse (IRE)—Multi Grain **Ian Gray & John Whitworth**
6 **GREG THE GREAT,** 4, gr g Gregorian (IRE)—Fantasy Queen **The Spencer Ward Harris Partnership**
7 **JUMBY (IRE),** 5, b h New Bay—Sound of Guns **Anthony Pye-Jeary & David Ian**
8 **KING OF THE DANCE (IRE),** 4, b g Havana Gold (IRE)—Figurante (IRE) **HP Racing King Of The Dance**
9 **LOCKSMITH (IRE),** 4, gr g Mastercraftsman (IRE)—Notion of Beauty (USA) **Eden Racing**
10 **MICHAELS CHOICE,** 7, b g War Command (USA)—Todber **The Music Makers 2**
11 **NOBLE MASQUERADE,** 6, b g Sir Percy—Moi Aussi (USA) **HP Racing Noble Masquerade**
12 **ROBJON,** 4, b g Mukhadram—Barnezet (GR) **Robin Blunt & Jonathan Palmer-Brown**
13 **ROOFUL,** 5, b m Charming Thought—Roodle **Mrs F. M. Johnson Houghton**
14 **SHEER ROCKS,** 4, ch g Iffraaj—Paradise Cove **Anthony Pye-Jeary & David Ian**
15 **SUZY'S SHOES,** 4, ch f Nathaniel (IRE)—Wittgenstein (IRE) **Mr M. Middleton-Heath**
16 **TARATARI,** 4, gr g Caravaggio (USA)—Premiere Danseuse **Mr G. J. Owen**
17 **THE PRINCES POET,** 5, b g Brazen Beau (AUS)—Poesy **HP Racing The Princes Poet**

THREE-YEAR-OLDS

18 **ANOTHER THOUGHT,** bl ro f Charming Thought—Reprieval (FR) **The Ascot Colts & Fillies Club**
19 **ARUMADAAY,** b f Adaay (IRE)—Rum Swizzle **The Nigel Bennett Partnership**
20 **BARLEYBROWN,** b g Zoustar (AUS)—Shozita **Mr S. Barley**
21 **BAULAC,** b g Fulbright—Nuptials (USA) **Boanas & Raw**
22 **BIG R (IRE),** b g Cotai Glory—Turuqaat **The Nigel Bennett Partnership**
23 **BISHOP'S CROWN,** b g Havana Gold (IRE)—Jalela **J D Partnership & Gary Black**
24 **BLUELIGHT BAY (IRE),** b c Exceed And Excel (AUS)—Siren's Cove **Jacobsconstructionholdings and J.E. Harley**
25 **BOY BROWNING,** b c Brazen Beau (AUS)—Rahaaba (IRE) **HP Racing Boy Browning**
26 **BUCCABAY (IRE),** b g Saxon Warrior (JPN)—Fifth Commandment (IRE) **The Buckingham Partnership**
27 **BUSSENTO,** b c Oasis Dream—Super Saturday (IRE) **Mick and Janice Mariscotti**
28 **GOLSPIE (IRE),** b c Ribchester (IRE)—Surrey Storm **Mick and Janice Mariscotti**
29 **GREASED LIGHTNING,** ch g Lightning Spear—How High The Sky (IRE) **Mrs S Keable & Partner**
30 **JACKALOPE,** b g Sea The Moon (GER)—Nezhenka **T. C. Stewart**
31 **KANOHI BREEZE,** b f Expert Eye—Sommesnil (IRE) **The Kimber Family & Bob Bell**
32 **KINGS PAGEANT,** b g Massaat (IRE)—Queens Revenge **HP Racing Kings Pageant**
33 **LADY OF ARABIA,** b f Poet's Word (IRE)—Arabian Music (IRE) **KJB Racing**
34 **LAST CHANCE SALOON (IRE),** b f Mukhadram—Comfort In Sound (USA) **Mr C. N. Wright**
35 **LUNAR LANDSCAPE,** b g Sea The Moon (GER)—Kensington Gardens **Primera Partnership**
36 **LUNARSCAPE,** gr f Cityscape—Moon Song **Hunscote Stud Limited**
37 **OUT OF DREAMADREAMFORME (USA),** gr f Dark Angel (IRE)—Dreamadreamforme (USA) **Mr Tom Freeman**
38 **RAGE OF BAMBY (IRE),** b f Saxon Warrior (JPN)—Rabiosa Fiore **Hot To Trot Racing 2 & Mrs A G Kavanagh**
39 **SAILING ON,** ch c New Approach (IRE)—Prowess (IRE) **M H Dixon & J L Rowsell**
40 **SIR CILIA,** b c Lope de Vega (IRE)—Lunesque (IRE) **Anthony Pye-Jeary & David Ian**
41 **STREETS OF GOLD (IRE),** b c Havana Gold (IRE)—Truly Honoured **J Allison & G C Stevens**
42 **SUNDOWNER,** b f Twilight Son—Light Hearted **The Ascot Revellers**
43 **TIMEWAITSFORNOBODY (IRE),** b f Camacho—Time Over **Mr R. Allcock**
44 **TROON (IRE),** b c Gleneagles (IRE)—Sacred Harp **Primera Partnership**

TWO-YEAR-OLDS

45 **BATED BREEZE (IRE),** b c 02/04 Bated Breath—
Olga da Polga (IRE) (Casamento (IRE)) (28011) **Neal & Sheralee Grayston**
46 **BIG BROWN BEAR (IRE),** b c 18/03 Kodiac—
Smokey Quartz (IRE) (Dark Angel (IRE)) (24010) **J Allison & G C Stevens**
47 Gr c 09/05 Advertise—Cherubic (Dark Angel (IRE)) (26000) **Austin, June & Jonny Allison**
48 **COMPTON BAY,** ch c 13/04 New Bay—On A Cloud (USA) (Silver Hawk (USA)) (18000) **Mr T. Smith**
49 **DARYSINA GOLD,** b f 16/02 Golden Horn—
Darysina (USA) (Smart Strike (CAN)) (17000) **Ever Equine & J Whitworth**
50 **DAYMER BAY (IRE),** b c 13/03 Expert Eye—
Reset In Blue (IRE) (Fastnet Rock (AUS)) (15000) **Mr M. Middleton-Heath**
51 **DRAMATIC EFFECT,** ch f 11/02 Bated Breath—Daryana (Dutch Art) **The Daryana Partnership**

MISS EVE JOHNSON HOUGHTON - continued

52 **DUE TO HENRY,** b c 09/05 Due Diligence (USA)—
Rivas Rhapsody (IRE) (Hawk Wing (USA)) (15000) **HP Racing Due To Henry**
53 **ETHANDUN (IRE),** b c 23/04 Saxon Warrior (JPN)—
Tears In My Eyes (IRE) (Lilbourne Lad (IRE)) (19208) **Munir, Souede A Bromley**
54 B c 05/05 Gregorian (IRE)—Fanditha (IRE) (Danehill Dancer (IRE)) (14000) **Miss E. A. Johnson Houghton**
55 **FRANCESCO BARACCA,** br c 07/03 Golden Horn—
Bella Ferrari (Bated Breath) (23000) **The Saddleworth Players & Partners**
56 **GOD BLESS AMERICA,** b g 14/02 Due Diligence (USA)—
Compton Poppy (Compton Place) **Paul & Sharon Downing**
57 **GOLD MINX,** b f 10/05 Havana Gold (IRE)—
Coquette Noire (IRE) (Holy Roman Emperor (IRE)) (43000) **HP Racing Gold Minx**
58 **GREAT ACCLAIM,** b c 26/02 Aclaim (IRE)—Freedom Spirit (Muhaarar) (35000) **Mr G. J. Owen**
59 **HIGH POINT (IRE),** b c 11/04 New Bay—Pacharana (Oasis Dream) (34000) **Anthony Pye-Jeary & David Ian**
60 **IVYBANKS,** b f 24/01 Due Diligence (USA)—Tabassor (IRE) (Raven's Pass (USA)) **Paul & Sharon Downing**
61 **JUNIPER BERRIES,** b f 18/02 Expert Eye—Tricksy Spirit (Lethal Force (IRE)) (28000) **Norman Court Stud**
62 B c 23/02 Dandy Man (IRE)—Lady Lockwood (Harbour Watch (IRE)) (16006) **The Woodway 20**
63 B g 03/04 Elzaam (AUS)—Lady Rosebud (IRE) (Sir Prancealot (IRE)) (13605) **The Woodway 20**
64 B c 14/03 Time Test—Limelite (IRE) (Dark Angel (IRE)) (40000) **Viscount Astor**
65 **LUCKY GOLD,** b f 17/04 Havana Gold (IRE)—See Emily Play (IRE) (Galileo (IRE)) (37000) **Norman Court Stud**
66 **MAKES SENSE (IRE),** b c 25/03 Calyx—Logique (FR) (Whipper (USA)) (15000) **McNamee Hewitt Rice Harding**
67 **MERCIAN WARRIOR (IRE),** b c 12/03 Saxon Warrior (JPN)—
Loquacity (Diktat) (41617) **The Buckingham Partnership Ii**
68 B c 03/02 Soldier's Call—Peticoatgovernement (IRE) (Holy Roman Emperor (IRE)) **Bronte Collection 1**
69 B c 06/05 Cable Bay (IRE)—Quiet Protest (USA) (Kingmambo (USA)) (40000) **Mr T. Smith & Partner**
70 B f 06/03 Churchill (IRE)—Rabiosa Fiore (Sakhee's Secret) **Hot To Trot Racing 2 & Mrs A G Kavanagh**
71 **REVENUE (IRE),** ch c 26/03 Profitable (IRE)—Exceed My Budget (Exceed And Excel (AUS)) (17607) **Eden Racing IV**
72 B f 16/04 Eqtidaar (IRE)—Shurfah (IRE) (Sea The Stars (IRE)) (42000) **Bronte Collection 1**
73 Gr f 23/01 Waldgeist—Skrei (IRE) (Approve (IRE)) (19208) **Ms E. L. Banks**
74 **SPARKLIGHT,** b f 04/04 Cable Bay (IRE)—Lava Light (Sixties Icon) (10000) **Brightwalton Bloodstock Limited**
75 B f 09/04 Iffraaj—Sparring Queen (USA) (War Front (USA)) (15000) **KJB Racing**
76 **THUNDERING BREEZE (IRE),** b gr f 08/03 Dark Angel (IRE)—
Tamarisk (GER) (Selkirk (USA)) (80000) **Neal & Sheralee Grayston**
77 **TRESCA,** b f 06/04 Iffraaj—Lulani (IRE) (Royal Applause) **Mr & Mrs James Blyth Currie**
78 B g 23/04 New Bay—Utopian Dream (High Chaparral (IRE)) **Mick and Janice Mariscotti**
79 **VIDI VICI,** b c 15/03 Invincible Army (IRE)—Chiffonade (IRE) (Galileo (IRE)) (10000) **The Woodway 20**

Assistant Trainer: James Unett.

Apprentice Jockey: Mia Nicholls.

---

286 MR CHARLIE JOHNSTON, Middleham

Postal: **Kingsley Park Farm, Park Lane, Middleham, Leyburn, Yorkshire, DL8 4QZ**
Contacts: **WORK 01969 622237**
WORK EMAIL racing@johnston.racing WEBSITE johnston.racing TWITTER @johnston_racing

1 **APPROACHABILITY,** 4, ch g New Approach (IRE)—Posterity (IRE)
2 **ASDAA (IRE),** 7, b g Dutch Art—Danseuse de Reve (IRE)
3 **AUSTRIAN THEORY (IRE),** 4, b g Awtaad (IRE)—Cedar Sea (IRE)
4 **BOBBY'S BLESSING,** 4, b c Bobby's Kitten (USA)—Affirmatively
5 **BOY ABOUT TOWN,** 4, b g Frankel—Miss Marjurie (IRE)
6 **CAPITAL THEORY,** 4, b g Muhaarar—Montalcino (IRE)
7 **DUBAI LEADER,** 4, b g Golden Horn—Zaeema
8 **DUTCH DECOY,** 6, ch g Dutch Art—The Terrier
9 **EVIDENT (USA),** 4, ch c Not This Time (USA)—Ready At Nine (USA)
10 **FAIRMAC,** 5, gr g Lethal Force (IRE)—Kenyan Cat
11 **GOBI SUNSET,** 6, b g Oasis Dream—Dark Promise

MR CHARLIE JOHNSTON - continued

12 **JILLY COOPER (IRE),** 4, b f Lope de Vega (IRE)—Jillnextdoor (IRE)
13 **KNIGHTSWOOD (IRE),** 4, ch g Decorated Knight—Neuquen (IRE)
14 **LA PULGA (IRE),** 4, b g Kodiac—Nijah (IRE)
15 **LIVING LEGEND (IRE),** 7, b g Camelot—Jazz Girl (IRE)
16 **LOVE DE VEGA (IRE),** 4, ch c Lope de Vega (IRE)—Ribble (FR)
17 **MADAME AMBASSADOR,** 4, ch f Churchill (IRE)—Lady Jane Digby
18 **MILITARY TWO STEP (FR),** 5, gr m Jukebox Jury (IRE)—Step This Way (USA)
19 **OUTBREAK,** 4, b g Dark Angel (IRE)—Purr Along
20 **PILLAR OF HOPE,** 5, b g Awtaad (IRE)—Great Hope (IRE)
21 **PONS AELIUS (IRE),** 4, b c Galileo (IRE)—Laugh Out Loud
22 **SPIRIT CATCHER (IRE),** 4, ch g New Bay—Lidanski (IRE)
23 **SUBJECTIVIST,** 6, b h Teofilo (IRE)—Reckoning (IRE)
24 **SUFFRAJET (IRE),** 4, b f Golden Horn—Liberating
25 **TEMPORIZE,** 4, b g Postponed (IRE)—Party Line
26 **THE GATEKEEPER (IRE),** 4, b g Excelebration (IRE)—Cherry Creek (IRE)
27 **THEMAXWECAN (IRE),** 7, b g Maxios—Psychometry (FR)
28 **TOUSSAROK,** 5, b g Iffraaj—Frangipanni (IRE)
29 **WADACRE GRACE,** 4, b f Brazen Beau (AUS)—Glenreef
30 **WHITEFEATHERSFALL (IRE),** 4, ch g Zoffany (IRE)—Naomh Geileis (USA)
31 **WORLD WITHOUT LOVE,** 4, ch f Ulysses (IRE)—Reckoning (IRE)
32 **YORKINDNESS,** 4, b f Nathaniel (IRE)—Yorkidding

THREE-YEAR-OLDS

33 **A LITTLE RESPECT (IRE),** ch f Sea The Stars (IRE)—Simannka (IRE)
34 **ABU ROYAL (IRE),** b c Dark Angel (IRE)—Spesialta
35 **ALPINA EXPRESS (IRE),** ch f Sea The Moon (GER)—Adalawa (IRE)
36 **ALTA COMEDIA,** b f Bobby's Kitten (USA)—Alta Moda
37 **ALUMNUS,** gr g Kendargent (FR)—Alma Mater
38 **ARTISAN DANCER (FR),** b g Mastercraftsman (IRE)—Russiana (IRE)
39 **ARTISAND (IRE),** gr g Mastercraftsman (IRE)—Desert Haze
40 **BAILEYS KHELSTAR (FR),** b g Cloth of Stars (IRE)—Khelwa (FR)
41 **BEAUTIFUL EYES,** ch f Bobby's Kitten (USA)—Forthefirstime
42 **BENACRE (IRE),** b c Australia—Sent From Heaven (IRE)
43 **BERWICK LAW (IRE),** ch f Zoffany (IRE)—Standing Rock (IRE)
44 **BLUE ANTARES (IRE),** ch c Frankel—Scarlett Rose
45 **BLUE UNIVERSE (IRE),** b c Iffraaj—Zara (BRZ)
46 **BOHEMIAN BREEZE (IRE),** gr c Galileo (IRE)—Wind Chimes
47 **BOOK OF TALES,** b g Ribchester (IRE)—Dream Book
48 **BULLDOG SPIRIT (IRE),** b g Churchill (IRE)—Banimpire (IRE)
49 **CAMUSDARACH (IRE),** ch g Footstepsinthesand—Antebellum (FR)
50 **CAPTAIN POTTER,** b c Almanzor (FR)—Astroglia (USA)
51 **CAROUSELLE (IRE),** gr f Dark Angel (IRE)—Spinola (FR)
52 **CENTRE COURT (FR),** b f Showcasing—Game Zone (IRE)
53 **COOL PARTY,** b c Postponed (IRE)—Party Line
54 **CRACKOVIA,** ch f Cracksman—Olvia (IRE)
55 **DANCE IN THE GRASS,** ch f Cracksman—Dance The Dream
56 **DARK MAJESTY,** b f Dark Angel (IRE)—Majestic Jasmine (IRE)
57 **DEAR MY FRIEND,** ch c Pivotal—Dusty Red
58 **DEMILION (IRE),** gr c Roaring Lion (USA)—Cascading
59 **DORNOCH CASTLE (IRE),** ch c Gleneagles (IRE)—Crown Light
60 **DOWNTOWN DUBAI (IRE),** b g Exceed And Excel (AUS)—Zabeel Park (USA)
61 **DREAMS ADOZEN (FR),** b f Kingman—Ferevia (IRE)
62 **DUBAI MILE (IRE),** ch c Roaring Lion (USA)—Beach Bunny (IRE)
63 **EDGE OF DARKNESS (IRE),** ch g Australia—Forces of Darkness (IRE)
64 **FERRARI QUEEN (IRE),** gr f Decorated Knight—Katch Me Katie
65 **FINN'S CHARM,** b c Kingman—Annabelle's Charm (IRE)
66 **FLIGHT OF ANGELS,** b f Golden Horn—Hoyam
67 **FOX FLAME,** b f Iffraaj—Street Fire (IRE)
68 **FRENCH INVASION (IRE),** b c Le Havre (IRE)—Jumooh

MR CHARLIE JOHNSTON - continued

69 **GAREEB (IRE),** br f Sioux Nation (USA)—Fancy (IRE)
70 **GET STUCK IN (IRE),** gr g Dark Angel (IRE)—Ultra Appeal (IRE)
71 **GONE (IRE),** b f Gustav Klimt (IRE)—Assault On Rome (IRE)
72 **GOOD MORALS,** ch f Farhh—Great Virtues (IRE)
73 **GRAIN OF HOPE,** b f Anodin (IRE)—Grain Only
74 **HADRIANUS (IRE),** b c Galileo (IRE)—Laugh Out Loud
75 **HEY LYLA,** b f Oasis Dream—Lomapamar
76 **HI CLARE (IRE),** b f Kodiac—Shemda (IRE)
77 **HOPE YOU CAN RUN (IRE),** ch c Lope de Vega (IRE)—Shelbysmile (USA)
78 **IN THESE SHOES (IRE),** ch f Starspangledbanner (AUS)—Majenta (IRE)
79 **JUNGLE FEVER (IRE),** b g Bungle Inthejungle—Titian Saga (IRE)
80 **KHAL (IRE),** b g Roaring Lion (USA)—Penny Pepper (IRE)
81 **KILLYBEGS WARRIOR (IRE),** b c Saxon Warrior (JPN)—Alltherightmoves (IRE)
82 **KING ME,** b g Kingman—Gemstone (IRE)
83 **KING OF THE PLAINS (IRE),** b c Roaring Lion (USA)—Golden Lilac (IRE)
84 **KINGSLEY PRIDE,** gr g Roaring Lion (USA)—Whirly Bird
85 **KITAI (IRE),** b br f No Nay Never (USA)—Belle Isle
86 **KNOCKBREX,** ch c Ulysses (IRE)—Prominence
87 **KRONA,** b f Sea The Moon (GER)—Kwanza
88 **LADY BRACKEN (IRE),** ch f New Bay—Footsteps Forever (IRE)
89 **LADY LAVINA,** b f The Last Lion (IRE)—Step This Way (USA)
90 **LAKOTA SIOUX (IRE),** b f Sioux Nation (USA)—Shemiyla (FR)
91 **LIMERICK BOUND,** ch c Sea The Stars (IRE)—Alamode
92 **LION OF WAR,** b c Roaring Lion (USA)—Momentus (IRE)
93 **LOCH CARRON (IRE),** gr f Gregorian (IRE)—Farran (IRE)
94 **LOYAL TOUCH (IRE),** b c No Nay Never (USA)—Devoted To You (IRE)
95 **LUDO'S LANDING (IRE),** b g Kodiac—Most Beautiful
96 **MADAM MACHO,** ch f Camacho—Madam President
97 B c Zoustar (AUS)—Madam Valentine
98 **MAJESTIC JAMEELA,** b f Postponed (IRE)—Aviacion (BRZ)
99 **MAN OF MONACO (IRE),** ch g Lightning Spear—Molly Mayhem (IRE)
100 **MICKEY MONGOOSE,** b g Lope de Vega (IRE)—Midnight Crossing (IRE)
101 **MIDNIGHT LION,** b c Nathaniel (IRE)—Coyote
102 **MISS DYNAMIC,** b f Cracksman—Dynaforce (USA)
103 **MONTEVIDEO (IRE),** b f Teofilo (IRE)—Cherry Creek (IRE)
104 **MOVIE NIGHT,** ch f Postponed (IRE)—Entertainment
105 **MUIR WOOD,** b c Teofilo (IRE)—St Francis Wood (USA)
106 **PATRIOT'S CHOICE (IRE),** b c Starspangledbanner (AUS)—Dingle View (IRE)
107 **PEACEFUL NIGHT,** ch f New Approach (IRE)—Concordia
108 **PERFECT PLAY,** b g Siyouni (FR)—Giants Play (USA)
109 **QUEEN OF DEAUVILLE (IRE),** gr f Showcasing—Syann (IRE)
110 **RAY OF COLOURS (IRE),** b g Ribchester (IRE)—Colour Play (USA)
111 **RED BIRD (IRE),** ch f Australia—Tissiak (IRE)
112 **ROSETTE,** ch f Bobby's Kitten (USA)—La Vie En Rose
113 **ROYAL OBSERVATORY,** ch c Siyouni (FR)—Vue Fantastique (FR)
114 **SAX APPEAL,** b c Saxon Warrior (JPN)—Isobel Archer
115 **SEA MASTER,** ch g Sea The Stars (IRE)—Altesse
116 **SIR JOCK BENNETT (IRE),** b g Almanzor (FR)—Biswa (USA)
117 **SIRONA (GER),** b f Soldier Hollow—Si Luna (GER)
118 **SMOOTH RYDER (IRE),** b g Smooth Daddy (USA)—Silesie (USA)
119 **STAR MOOD (IRE),** ch c Sea The Stars (IRE)—Model (FR)
120 **STRUTH (IRE),** ch c Australia—Portrait of A Lady (IRE)
121 **SWIFT LIONESS (IRE),** gr f Roaring Lion (USA)—Dame d'Honneur (IRE)
122 Ch f Saxon Warrior (JPN)—Take A Deep Breath
123 **TENERIFE SUNSHINE,** ch c Lope de Vega (IRE)—Yarrow (IRE)
124 **TIMEWAVE (FR),** gr g Sea The Stars (IRE)—Five Fifteen (FR)
125 **TROJAN LEGEND,** ch g Ulysses (IRE)—Intimation
126 **TROJAN SPIRIT,** ch c Ulysses (IRE)—Local Spirit (USA)
127 **TRUE STATESMAN (IRE),** b br g Churchill (IRE)—True Verdict (IRE)
128 **URBAN SPRAWL,** ch c Iffraaj—City Glam (ARG)

MR CHARLIE JOHNSTON - continued

129 VENETIAN (IRE), b g Awtaad (IRE)—Venetian Beauty (USA)
130 WADACRE GOMEZ, b c Brazen Beau (AUS)—Wadacre Gigi
131 WADACRE INCA, gr f Hawkbill (USA)—In The Soup (USA)

TWO-YEAR-OLDS

132 Ch c 08/02 Mastercraftsman (IRE)—Akvavera (Leroidesanimaux (BRZ)) (12805)
133 B f 23/02 Muhaarar—Alaata (USA) (Smart Strike (CAN)) (17000)
134 ALIGN THE STARS (IRE), br c 29/04 Sea The Stars (IRE)—Kitcara (Shamardal (USA)) (100000)
135 B c 27/02 Bobby's Kitten (USA)—Alumna (USA) (Mr Greeley (USA)) (21609)
136 ARCH LEGEND, b c 23/02 Camelot—Nakuti (IRE) (Mastercraftsman (IRE)) (82000)
137 AVIEMORE, b c 02/02 Kodiac—Raincall (Pivotal) (90000)
138 B f 02/02 Sea The Moon (GER)—Bayshore Freeway (IRE) (Declaration of War (USA))
139 B br f 18/02 Masar (IRE)—Be Fabulous (GER) (Samum (GER))
140 B c 12/04 Blue Point (IRE)—Bergamask (USA) (Kingmambo (USA))
141 B f 13/05 Ten Sovereigns (IRE)—Big Boned (USA) (Street Sense (USA)) (33613)
142 Ch f 19/04 Masar (IRE)—Blossomtime (Shamardal (USA))
143 B c 03/04 Wootton Bassett—Brasileira (Dubai Destination (USA)) (56022)
144 B c 04/05 New Approach (IRE)—Cairncross (IRE) (Cape Cross (IRE))
145 CAROLINA REAPER, b f 10/03 Too Darn Hot—Dark Promise (Shamardal (USA)) (46000)
146 Ch f 05/04 Lope de Vega (IRE)—Ceisteach (IRE) (New Approach (IRE)) (55000)
147 B f 25/04 Churchill (IRE)—Celeste de La Mer (IRE) (Zoffany (IRE)) (17607)
148 CHINA TRADE (IRE), ch f 16/05 Belardo (IRE)—Chinese White (IRE) (Dalakhani (IRE))
149 B c 04/05 Kodiac—Cloghran (FR) (Muhtathir) (16006)
150 COVEHITHE (IRE), b f 16/05 Magna Grecia (IRE)—Sent From Heaven (IRE) (Footstepsinthesand) (36014)
151 CURRAN (IRE), ch c 10/02 Gleneagles (IRE)—Tipitena (Camelot) (36014)
152 B f 06/03 Blue Point (IRE)—Daily Times (Gleneagles (IRE))
153 B f 19/02 Le Havre (IRE)—Dalkova (Galileo (IRE))
154 B c 17/03 Blue Point (IRE)—Dark Rose Angel (IRE) (Dark Angel (IRE))
155 B c 20/02 Ten Sovereigns (IRE)—De Veer Cliffs (IRE) (Canford Cliffs (IRE))
156 DEIRA MILE (IRE), b c 17/03 Camelot—Fastnet Mist (IRE) (Fastnet Rock (AUS)) (47000)
157 Ch f 17/02 Exceed And Excel (AUS)—Dubai Ice (USA) (More Than Ready (USA))
158 B f 24/02 Night of Thunder (IRE)—Dutota Desejada (BRZ) (First American (USA))
159 Ch f 02/04 Zoffany (IRE)—Flame of Hestia (IRE) (Giant's Causeway (USA)) (40000)
160 B c 01/05 Teofilo (IRE)—Fountain of Time (IRE) (Iffraaj)
161 FRANCOPHONE, b f 09/04 Study of Man (IRE)—Francophilia (Frankel)
162 FREDS MATE (IRE), b c 27/05 Gleneagles (IRE)—Flamingo Sea (USA) (Woodman (USA)) (25610)
163 Ch c 29/01 Starspangledbanner (AUS)—Frilly (Frankel)
164 B f 22/03 Showcasing—Fyxenna (Foxwedge (AUS)) (28000)
165 GONE ROGUE (IRE), b c 14/04 Gustav Klimt (IRE)—Assault On Rome (IRE) (Holy Roman Emperor (IRE))
166 Ch c 15/02 Ulysses (IRE)—Hector's Girl (Hector Protector (USA)) (52000)
167 B f 25/02 Camacho—Hidden Girl (IRE) (Tamayuz) (33613)
168 B c 21/02 Cracksman—Hoodna (IRE) (Invincible Spirit (IRE))
169 B c 14/02 Le Havre (IRE)—Hulcote (Frankel) (15000)
170 B f 21/04 Siyouni (FR)—Indiana Wells (FR) (Sadler's Wells (USA)) (62000)
171 INDIVIDUALISM, b c 11/04 Too Darn Hot—Reckoning (IRE) (Danehill Dancer (IRE)) (110000)
172 Ch f 27/04 Sea The Stars (IRE)—Jane's Memory (IRE) (Captain Rio) (54422)
173 KANDY HOUSE (IRE), b f 18/04 Invincible Spirit (IRE)—Gower Song (Singspiel (IRE)) (38415)
174 B f 08/01 Phoenix of Spain (IRE)—Kiltara (IRE) (Lawman (FR)) (15206)
175 B c 12/04 Mastercraftsman (IRE)—Lady Darshaan (IRE) (High Chaparral (IRE)) (32000)
176 B c 31/01 Caravaggio (USA)—Lamya (GER) (Choisir (AUS))
177 LINCOLN LEGACY (IRE), b f 23/03 Footstepsinthesand—Crystal Valkyrie (IRE) (Danehill (USA)) (28812)
178 B f 19/03 Invincible Army (IRE)—Love In The Desert (Lemon Drop Kid (USA)) (52021)
179 LOVE SAFARI (IRE), b c 15/03 Galileo (IRE)—Just Pretending (USA) (Giant's Causeway (USA)) (57000)
180 LOVE WARRIOR (IRE), b c 23/02 Saxon Warrior (JPN)—In The Mist (Pivotal) (80000)
181 Gr f 16/04 Magna Grecia (IRE)—Luire (IRE) (Dark Angel (IRE)) (18000)
182 Gr f 06/01 Churchill (IRE)—Lush Life (IRE) (Mastercraftsman (IRE)) (8000)
183 B c 08/02 Footstepsinthesand—Lynique (IRE) (Dylan Thomas (IRE)) (22409)
184 MADAME SANS GENE, b f 21/01 Study of Man (IRE)—Lady Jane Digby (Oasis Dream)
185 MADE IN CHINA (IRE), b c 28/03 Almanzor (FR)—Consumer Credit (USA) (More Than Ready (USA))

MR CHARLIE JOHNSTON - continued

186 B c 04/04 Zoffany (IRE)—Many Colours (Green Desert (USA)) (64026)
187 MARHABA MILLION (IRE), ch c 30/04 Galileo (IRE)—Kheleyf's Silver (IRE) (Kheleyf (USA)) (65626)
188 Ch f 14/05 No Nay Never (USA)—Matorio (FR) (Oratorio (IRE)) (70000)
189 Ch f 29/01 Territories (IRE)—Middle Club (Fantastic Light (USA)) (20000)
190 Gr ro f 07/05 Phoenix of Spain (IRE)—Middle Persia (Dalakhani (IRE)) (15206)
191 B c 08/01 Wootton Bassett—Mint Julep (FR) (Mastercraftsman (IRE)) (52021)
192 B c 26/03 Shalaa (IRE)—Misty Night (IRE) (Galileo (IRE)) (9604)
193 B c 17/03 Masar (IRE)—Mur Hiba (IRE) (Helmet (AUS)) (9000)
194 MY CLEMENTINE (IRE), ch f 13/05 Churchill (IRE)—Beauty Bright (IRE) (Danehill (USA)) (16807)
195 B f 04/03 Caravaggio (USA)—Nancy O (IRE) (Pivotal) (10000)
196 B c 09/03 Sogann (FR)—New Number (Muhaarar)
197 B c 10/03 Wootton Bassett—Normandie (GER) (Redoute's Choice (AUS)) (40000)
198 NORMANDY VISTA (IRE), ch c 05/04 Le Havre (IRE)—Vue Fantastique (FR) (Motivator) (38000)
199 Gr c 09/02 Frankel—Nyaleti (IRE) (Arch (USA))
200 PALADIN (IRE), ch c 15/03 Justify (USA)—Golconda (FR) (Planteur (IRE)) (56022)
201 B c 25/04 Profitable (IRE)—Pilates (IRE) (Shamardal (USA)) (48000)
202 B f 12/03 Too Darn Hot—Princesse Dansante (IRE) (King's Best (USA))
203 B c 19/04 Cracksman—Pulcinella (IRE) (Dubawi (IRE))
204 B c 15/01 Kodiac—Querulous (USA) (Raven's Pass (USA)) (52000)
205 QUINTUS MAXIMUS, ch c 16/02 Kitten's Joy (USA)—Indian Blessing (Sepoy (AUS)) (85000)
206 RAKKI, ch c 01/03 Sea The Stars (IRE)—Waldmark (GER) (Mark of Esteem (IRE)) (100000)
207 B c 27/04 Highland Reel (IRE)—Recambe (IRE) (Cape Cross (IRE)) (40000)
208 Ch f 25/04 New Approach (IRE)—Reyaadah (Tamayuz) (24010)
209 ROSENZOO (IRE), ch c 20/04 Zoffany (IRE)—Rosenreihe (IRE) (Catcher In The Rye (IRE)) (72000)
210 SACRED ANGEL (IRE), gr f 24/03 Dark Angel (IRE)—Sacred Aspect (IRE) (Haatef (USA)) (49524)
211 B c 01/02 Advertise—Sahara Sky (IRE) (Danehill (USA)) (62000)
212 SENNOCKIAN (IRE), ch c 10/05 No Nay Never (USA)—Lady Gorgeous (Compton Place) (96038)
213 B f 02/04 Masar (IRE)—Serene Beauty (USA) (Street Cry (IRE))
214 B c 08/02 Blue Point (IRE)—Servalan (IRE) (No Nay Never (USA)) (50420)
215 B f 14/04 Kingman—Seventh Heaven (IRE) (Galileo (IRE)) (70000)
216 Ch f 01/05 Kitten's Joy (USA)—Shadan (FR) (Orpen (USA)) (20008)
217 SIR GEOFF HURST (FR), b c 02/04 Sea The Stars (IRE)—Desert Haze (New Approach (IRE)) (78000)
218 SPOOK (IRE), b f 15/03 Holy Roman Emperor (IRE)—Swish (GER) (Monsun (GER)) (24010)
219 B f 08/02 Sea The Moon (GER)—Swift Action (IRE) (Invincible Spirit (IRE)) (28000)
220 B c 18/04 Showcasing—Tandragee (USA) (Bernardini (USA))
221 B c 19/04 Make Believe—Teo's Sister (IRE) (Galileo (IRE)) (10404)
222 THE AFRICAN QUEEN, ch f 03/02 The Last Lion (IRE)—Burgonet (Helmet (AUS))
223 THERE'S NO LIMIT (IRE), gr c 16/05 No Nay Never (USA)—Mixfeeling (IRE) (Red Ransom (USA)) (48000)
224 B c 09/06 Galileo (IRE)—Tiggy Wiggy (IRE) (Kodiac) (115000)
225 B c 27/03 Wootton Bassett—Victoria College (FR) (Rock of Gibraltar (IRE)) (60024)
226 B f 02/02 Magna Grecia (IRE)—Viola d'Amour (IRE) (Teofilo (IRE)) (38095)
227 VOYEUR, b c 23/02 Invincible Spirit (IRE)—Love Your Looks (Iffraaj) (40000)
228 Gr f 17/02 Dark Angel (IRE)—World's Fair (Showcasing)
229 Br c 20/04 Too Darn Hot—Woven Lace (Hard Spun (USA))
230 YIPPEE, b c 18/04 Zoustar (AUS)—Bewitchment (Pivotal) (24000)
231 B f 12/03 Kingman—You're Back (USA) (Street Cry (IRE)) (75000)

Assistant Trainer: Mr Jock Bennett, Mr Andrew Bottomley, Mrs Deirdre Johnston, Mr Mark Johnston, Ms Hayley Kelly.

Flat Jockey: Mr Andrew Breslin, Mr Joe Fanning, Mr Franny Norton.

Apprentice Jockey: Mr Oliver Stammers, Mr Archie Young.

287 MR ALAN JONES, Timberscombe

Postal: **East Harwood Farm, Timberscombe, Minehead, Somerset, TA24 7UE**
Contacts: **MOBILE 07901 505064 FAX 01643 831717**
EMAIL Rider45@me.com WEBSITE www.alanjonesracing.co.uk

1 4, B f Linda's Lad—A Nun With A Gun (IRE)
2 **COCARDIER (FR),** 6, b g My Risk (FR)—Tamaline (FR) **Mr A. E. Jones**
3 5, B g Clovis du Berlais (FR)—Dancing Emily (IRE)
4 **DUHALLOW LAD (IRE),** 11, b g Papal Bull—Macca Luna (IRE) **Mr A. E. Jones**
5 **I'M NOTAPARTYGIRL,** 10, b m Arvico (FR)—Lady Shirley Hunt **Mr A. E. Jones**
6 **JACK'S A LEGEND,** 8, b g Midnight Legend—Dancing Emily (IRE) **Burnham Plastering & Drylining Ltd**
7 **LADY AVERY (IRE),** 11, b m Westerner—Bobs Article (IRE) **Mr A. E. Jones**
8 **LADY EXCALIBUR (IRE),** 6, b m Camelot—Market Forces **Burnham Plastering & Drylining Ltd**
9 **PALAWAN DU MAZET (FR),** 4, b g Papal Bull—Princesse du Large (FR) **Mr A. E. Jones**
10 **THE PUNT,** 6, b g Bollin Eric—Rest And Be (IRE) **Mr A. E. Jones**
11 **THEHARDERYOUWORK (IRE),** 6, b m Fame And Glory—Toile d'Auteuil (FR) **Mr A. E. Jones**
12 **US AND THEM (IRE),** 10, b g Stowaway—Manorville (IRE) **Burnham Plastering & Drylining Ltd**
13 **VETONCALL (IRE),** 11, b g Well Chosen—Miss Audacious (IRE) **Mr A. E. Jones**

THREE-YEAR-OLDS

14 B f Camelot—Market Forces **Burnham Plastering & Drylining Ltd**
15 B f Linda's Lad—Rest And Be (IRE)

TWO-YEAR-OLDS

16 B g 17/05 Sans Frontieres (IRE)—Lady Avery (IRE) (Westerner)
17 Ch f 13/08 Sans Frontieres (IRE)—Rest And Be (IRE) (Vinnie Roe (IRE))

Assistant Trainer: Miss A. Bartelink.

288 MR JACK JONES, Newmarket

Postal: **Chestnut Tree Stables, Hamilton Road, Newmarket, Suffolk, CB8 0NY**
Contacts: **PHONE 07870 610067**
EMAIL jackj-95@hotmail.com, info@jackjonesracing.co.uk

1 **AREILLE (IRE),** 4, b f The Last Lion (IRE)—Likewise (IRE) **Private Equineity**
2 **CHAGALL (IRE),** 7, b g Slade Power (IRE)—Dangle (IRE) **Mr D. Jolland**
3 **JACK D'OR,** 7, b g Raven's Pass (USA)—Inchberry **Mr M. Robinson**
4 **NAVY DRUMS (USA),** 5, b br g Super Saver (USA)—Beat to Quarters (USA) **Mr D. Jolland**
5 **OUR SCHOLAR (IRE),** 4, b g Exceed And Excel (AUS)—Olympienne (IRE) **Mrs M. Middleton**
6 **SILVER SCREEN,** 4, b f Lope de Vega (IRE)—Silver Mirage **Lifecycle Bloodstock Ltd**
7 **SON OF RED (IRE),** 6, b g French Navy—Tarziyma (IRE) **Mr Nicholas John Jones**
8 **THE WAITING GAME,** 4, b f Due Diligence (USA)—Critical Speed (IRE)

THREE-YEAR-OLDS

9 **FIVE WINDS,** b f Adaay (IRE)—Critical Speed (IRE) **Mr H. Jenkins**

TWO-YEAR-OLDS

10 **FENGARI,** b f 21/02 Territories (IRE)—Moon Song (Lethal Force (IRE)) (4762) **Mr S. W. Goodwin**
11 B c 07/05 Showcasing—Frabjous (Pivotal) (38095) **Old Monmothians**
12 **GOODEVENINGMRBOND (IRE),** b c 05/02 Acclamation—Amaira (IRE) (Excelebration (IRE)) (45000)

Assistant Trainer: Polly Peate.

289 MR M KEADY AND MR M MURPHY, Westoning

Postal: **Mike Murphy and Michael Keady Racing, Manor Park Stud Farm, Park Road, Westoning, Bedfordshire, MK45 5LA**
Contacts: **MOBILE 07770 496103**
EMAIL mmurphy@globalnet.co.uk

1 **ANTIPHON (IRE),** 4, b g Kodiac—Freedom's Light **Mr J. Gill**
2 **BOLD AND LOYAL,** 4, b g Frankel—Birdwood **The Frankophiles**
3 **BREEZYANDBRIGHT (IRE),** 5, b g Epaulette (AUS)—Tranquil Sky **Moir & Murphy**
4 **COOPERATION (IRE),** 5, b g Mehmas (IRE)—Ripalong (IRE) **Mr R. J. Moore**
5 **ENLIGHTENMENT (IRE),** 4, ch f Mehmas (IRE)—So Easy (IRE) **The Adams, Laws & Murphy**
6 **HOPEFORTHEBEST,** 4, ch g Helmet (AUS)—Bestfootforward **Mr J. Gill**
7 **LA EQUINATA,** 4, b f Equiano (FR)—La Fortunata **Mr J. Patton**
8 **LADY ANNE BLUNT,** 4, b f Brazen Beau (AUS)—Ada Lovelace **Mr D. A. Clark**
9 **LE REVEUR (IRE),** 6, b g Dream Ahead (USA)—Don't Be **Sarabex**
10 **MULZIM,** 9, b g Exceed And Excel (AUS)—Samaah (IRE) **Victoria Taylor & Family**
11 **MUMMY'S BOY,** 5, br g Footstepsinthesand—Dance On The Hill (IRE) **Mr C. I. Johnston**
12 **PARK FARM PERCY,** 4, b g Sir Percy—Aloha **Mr A. R. Thompson**
13 **SHOW ME A SUNSET,** 7, b g Showcasing—Sunrise Star **Mr J. Gill**
14 **TEEKANA,** 4, b f Havana Gold (IRE)—Teeky **Mr J. Gill**
15 **TEMPLE BRUER,** 5, b g Showcasing—Kendal Mint **Mr R. J. Moore**
16 **THE CHARMER (IRE),** 4, ch g Dandy Man (IRE)—Charmgoer (USA) **Mr J. Gill**
17 **TINY TANTRUM (IRE),** 7, b g Fame And Glory—Sara's Smile **Mrs N. C. Kappler**
18 **VELVET VULCAN,** 4, b g Nathaniel (IRE)—Battery Power **Sarabex**

THREE-YEAR-OLDS

19 B f Massaat (IRE)—Aruan **B. D. Cantle**
20 **CATHAYA,** b f Ulysses (IRE)—Tallow (IRE) **Mr J. Gill**
21 **CHAMPAGNE SARAH (IRE),** ch f Sioux Nation (USA)—Alice Rose (IRE) **URSA Major Racing**
22 **ETERNAL FAME,** ch f Ulysses (IRE)—Forever In Love **Moir & Murphy**
23 **FAYASEL (IRE),** ch c Dandy Man (IRE)—Selva Real **Mr J. Gill**
24 **HEDENHAM,** b f Heeraat (IRE)—Denham **B. D. Cantle**
25 **JESSE LUC,** b c Brazen Beau (AUS)—Be Amazing (IRE) **P. Banfield**
26 **KODI DANCER (IRE),** b f Kodiac—Nijah (IRE) **P. Banfield**
27 Ch c Garswood—La Fortunata
28 **LIMELIGHT (GER),** b f Sea The Moon (GER)—Lutania (GER) **Mr J. Gill**
29 **MEHLODY MAKER (IRE),** ch f Mehmas (IRE)—Melodize **The Mehlody Makers**
30 **MINOLI,** b f Night of Thunder (IRE)—Anosti **Mr R. J. Moore**
31 **SHOW ME THE WIRE,** b c Showcasing—Maleficent Queen **Mr R. J. Moore**
32 **TIMELY ARTIST (IRE),** b gr c Caravaggio (USA)—Out of Time (IRE) **Apollo Horses I**
33 **VELVET VOGUE,** b f Intello (GER)—Battery Power **Sarabex**

TWO-YEAR-OLDS

34 B c 26/02 Profitable (IRE)—Anne of Kiev (IRE) (Oasis Dream) (27000)
35 B c 06/03 Territories (IRE)—Clubora (USA) (Medaglia d'Oro (USA)) (16000)
36 B f 01/03 Blue Point (IRE)—Ensemble (FR) (Iron Mask (USA)) (32000)
37 **PAGAN KING,** b c 12/02 Cockney Rebel (IRE)—Cushat Law (IRE) (Montjeu (IRE))
38 B f 10/03 Churchill (IRE)—Queen of Desire (IRE) (Dubawi (IRE)) (11000)
39 **VELVET VORTEX,** b c 17/04 Territories (IRE)—Battery Power (Royal Applause) **Sarabex**
40 **VITRUVIAN DAWN,** b f 29/03 Study of Man (IRE)—Dawn Horizons (New Approach (IRE)) (42000)
41 **WILLOW'S KISS,** b f 10/02 Twilight Son—Whispered Kiss (Medicean) (2000)

290 MR ADRIAN PAUL KEATLEY, Malton

Postal: **36 The Gallops, Norton, Malton, North Yorkshire, YO17 9JU**
Contacts: **PHONE +353 87 354 5349**

1 **ALL DOWN TO ROSIE (IRE),** 5, ch m Dandy Man (IRE)—Welsh Diva **Keatley Racing, Doherty & Manson**
2 **BELVEDERE BLAST (IRE),** 5, ch g Buratino (IRE)—Zelie Martin (IRE) **Swanland Partnership**
3 **CLEAR WHITE LIGHT,** 7, b g Dubawi (IRE)—Dalkova **The cosy at home family and friends**
4 **DRUMCONNOR LAD (IRE),** 13, b g Winged Love (IRE)—
Drumconnor Lady (IRE) **Mr David Keys & Mrs Breda Keatley**
5 **DUNGAR GLORY (IRE),** 4, ch f Cotai Glory—Independent Girl (IRE) **Ontoawinner & B Keatley**
6 **FOG ON THE TYNE (IRE),** 6, b m Malinas (GER)—Flaming Poncho (IRE) **The cosy at home family and friends**
7 **JEWEL OF KABEIR (IRE),** 4, b f El Kabeir (USA)—Apple Spirit (USA) **The cosy at home family and friends**
8 **KIHAVAH,** 6, ch g Harbour Watch (IRE)—Roheryn (IRE) **JAB**
9 **LEGENDARY DAY,** 5, b g Adaay (IRE)—Dubai Legend **Keatley Racing, Doherty & Manson**
10 **MARK'S CHOICE (IRE),** 7, b g Bungle Inthejungle—Ramamara (IRE) **Cragg Wood Racing**
11 **OCTOPHOBIA (IRE),** 4, b f Acclamation—Billie Eria (IRE) **Ontoawinner & B Keatley**
12 **PENELOPEBLUEYES (IRE),** 4, b f National Defense—City Vaults Girl (IRE) **The cosy at home family and friends**
13 **SATIN SNAKE,** 4, b g Aclaim (IRE)—Snake's Head **Keatley Racing, Doherty & Manson**
14 **SHALAA ASKER,** 5, b g Shalaa (IRE)—Miracle Seeker **Ontoawinner, Andy Finneran Racing**
15 **SUPER STARS (IRE),** 4, b g Sea The Stars (IRE)—Valais Girl **JAB**
16 **TWO SUMMERS (IRE),** 4, b f Acclamation—Phalaborwa **Keatley Racing Owners Group**
17 **WOBWOBWOB (IRE),** 5, b g Prince of Lir (IRE)—Ishimagic **Ontoawinner, Andy Finneran Racing**
18 **WOTEVER NEXT,** 4, b f Pastoral Pursuits—Next Stop **Mrs M. Lingwood**

THREE-YEAR-OLDS

19 **ANOTHER BAAR,** b g Mayson—Rapid Recruit (IRE) **Ontoawinner Andy Finneran Richard Porter**
20 **BEYOND BEAUTY (IRE),** ch f Bated Breath—Soothing Anthem (IRE) **Cragg Wood Racing**
21 **CARLOTTA (IRE),** b f Kuroshio (AUS)—Miss Millar (IRE) **Keatley Racing, Doherty & Manson**
22 **HONOUR YOUR DREAMS (FR),** b g Dream Ahead (USA)—Golconde (IRE) **Keatley Racing Owners Group**
23 **THE MALTON MAULER,** b g Massaat (IRE)—Available (IRE) **Keatley Racing Owners Group**
24 **VARDEN KITE (IRE),** ch f Bungle Inthejungle—Ramamara (IRE) **Cragg Wood Racing**
25 B f Ribchester (IRE)—Zelloof (IRE)

TWO-YEAR-OLDS

26 B c 10/04 Smooth Daddy (USA)—Bird of Light (IRE) (Elnadim (USA)) (20808)
27 B f 06/03 Kuroshio (AUS)—Clodovine (FR) (Kyllachy) (7203)
28 **HOWARD'S CHOICE,** b c 30/01 Ulysses (IRE)—Adornment (Kodiac) (20000) **Cragg Wood Racing**
29 B c 24/04 Elzaam (AUS)—Kateeva (IRE) (Statue of Liberty (USA)) (27211)
30 B f 12/03 Phoenix of Spain (IRE)—Rathbride Raven (Raven's Pass (USA)) (7203)

---

291 MRS FIONA KEHOE, Leighton Buzzard

Postal: **The Croft Farm, Wing Road, Stewkley, Leighton Buzzard, Bedfordshire, LU7 0JB**
Contacts: **PHONE 07795 096908**
EMAIL f.kehoe@btinternet.com

1 **COURT CIAN (IRE),** 5, b g Court Cave (IRE)—Sophie Rose (IRE) **M. Kehoe**
2 **HIDALGO CONTI (FR),** 6, b g Masked Marvel—Djna Conti (FR) **M. Kehoe**

292 MR MARTIN KEIGHLEY, Moreton-In-Marsh

Postal: **Condicote Stables, Luckley, Longborough, Moreton-In-Marsh, Gloucestershire, GL56 0RD**
Contacts: **MOBILE 07767 472547**
EMAIL keighleyracing@btinternet.com WEBSITE www.martinkeighley.com

1 **AMBASSADOR (IRE),** 6, b g Invincible Spirit (IRE)—Natural Bloom (IRE) **Martin Keighley Racing Club**
2 **ANOTHER DAY OUT (IRE),** 5, b m Ocovango—Earthshan (IRE)
3 **BACK ON THE LASH,** 9, b g Malinas (GER)—Giovanna **Redknapp, Salters**
4 **BALLYVANGO (IRE),** 4, b g Ocovango—Minoras Return (IRE) **Martin Keighley Racing Partnership 14**
5 **BELLA CIAO,** 6, b m Blue Bresil (FR)—Play With Fire **Lady F. Sutton**
6 **BEN BUIE (IRE),** 9, br g Presenting—Change of Plan (IRE) **Martin Keighley Racing Partnership 10**
7 **BLAZING COURT (IRE),** 5, b g Court Cave (IRE)—Bright Blaze (IRE) **Maughan, Parry, James & Thackray**
8 **BLUETHORN BOY,** 5, b g Blue Bresil (FR)—Thornton Alice **Serendipity Syndicate 2006**
9 **BORDERLINE (IRE),** 5, b g Sans Frontieres (IRE)—Seana Ghael (IRE) **Mr R. M. E. Wright**
10 **BREIZH ALKO (FR),** 12, ch g Balko (FR)—Quisiera (FR) **Mr D. Parry**
11 **BRIANNA ROSE (IRE),** 6, ch m Ocovango—Coco Milan (IRE) **Mr M. P. Baker**
12 **COME ON ME BABBY (IRE),** 7, b g Westerner—Hudson Hope (IRE) **Williams & Powell**
13 **DEBDEN BANK,** 9, b g Cacique (IRE)—Rose Row **Martin Keighley Racing Partnership 6**
14 **DREAMSUNDERMYFEET (IRE),** 8, br g Yeats (IRE)—Change of Plan (IRE) **Owners for Owners Dreamers**
15 **DUKE OF LUCKLEY (IRE),** 6, b g Mahler—Emily's Princess (IRE) **Owners for Owners Duke Of Luckley**
16 **ENFORCEMENT (IRE),** 8, b g Lawman (FR)—Elodie **Martin Keighley Racing Club**
17 **FINESCOPE,** 5, b m Telescope (IRE)—Fine Moment **G & W Worthington**
18 **FORECAST,** 11, ch g Observatory (USA)—New Orchid (USA) **Martin Keighley Racing Club**
19 **FOUND ON (IRE),** 8, b m Mahler—Court Gamble (IRE) **Mr O. F. Ryan**
20 **GENOVESE (IRE),** 5, b g Sans Frontieres (IRE)—Killoughey Babe (IRE) **Martin Keighley Racing Partnership 9**
21 **HERECOMESHOGAN (IRE),** 6, b g Sageburg (IRE)—Constant Approach (IRE) **The Cotswold Lockdowners**
22 **JUST A DEAL,** 8, b g Arvico (FR)—Monte Mayor Golf (IRE) **Lloyd, Bailey & Jessup**
23 **KALIBRATE (IRE),** 5, br g Califet (FR)—Clondalee (IRE) **MKRP8**
24 **KAZONTHERAZZ,** 7, b m Kayf Tara—Giovanna **The Meagher Family**
25 **LANTIC BAY,** 6, b g Dream Eater (IRE)—Twiga Woods
26 **LOST IN THE MIST (IRE),** 7, ch g Shirocco (GER)—Spirit Rock (IRE) **Martin Keighley Racing Club**
27 **MILADYGRACE,** 8, b m Universal (IRE)—Milan Athlete (IRE) **Mrs J. Kinsey**
28 **MISS ANTIPOVA,** 11, b m Pasternak—Herballistic **The Batsford Stud**
29 **MOZZARO (IRE),** 8, b g Morozov (USA)—Baraza (IRE) **Owners for Owners Mozzaro**
30 **MR MAFIA (IRE),** 14, b g Zerpour (IRE)—Wizzy (IRE) **Mr P. F. Boggis**
31 **MYFANWY'S MAGIC,** 6, b g Mr Medici (IRE)—Lady Myfanwy **360 Racing Club**
32 **PAY THE WOMAN (IRE),** 9, b m Doyen (IRE)—Mono Dame (IRE) **Foxtrot Racing Pay The Woman**
33 **PINNACLE PEAK,** 8, b g Passing Glance—Giovanna **M Boothright & R Lloyd**
34 **PRAIRIE DIAMOND (IRE),** 4, b g Diamond Boy (FR)—Siba de La Pampa (FR)
35 **REDBRIDGE RAMBLER (IRE),** 5, b g Mahler—Entertain Me **Mr D. A. Maughan**
36 **REVE,** 9, b g Nathaniel (IRE)—Rouge (FR) **Mr O. F. Ryan**
37 **ROBSAM (IRE),** 8, b g Mahler—Silver Set (IRE) **Mr M. Capp**
38 **ROLLING CLOUDS (IRE),** 7, b g Cloudings (IRE)—Woolett (FR) **Foxtrot Racing Minella Encore**
39 **SAMTARA,** 9, b g Kayf Tara—Aunt Harriet **Mr & Mrs R. Allsop**
40 **SHE HAS NOTIONS (IRE),** 6, b g Soldier of Fortune (IRE)—
Moscow Mo Chuisle (IRE) **Martin Keighley Racing Partnership 11**
41 **SHINJI (IRE),** 4, b g Kingston Hill—Albemarle **Mrs L. Jones**
42 **SPANISH PRESENT (IRE),** 7, b g Presenting—Sesenta (IRE) **Mr D. A. Maughan**
43 **SPICE BOY,** 4, b c Black Sam Bellamy (IRE)—Karmest **Martin Keighley Racing Partnership 13**
44 **TEN PAST MIDNIGHT,** 7, b g Midnight Legend—Thornton Alice **Serendipity Syndicate 2006**
45 **WIDE TO WEST (IRE),** 6, b g Soldier of Fortune (IRE)—Norah's Quay (IRE) **Williams & Powell**
46 **WINDY COVE,** 6, b m Lawman (FR)—Gale Green **A Morgan & Mrs N Clifford**
47 **WITNESS PROTECTION (IRE),** 10, b g Witness Box (USA)—Queen's Exit **Foxtrot Racing Witness Protection**
48 **ZESTFUL,** 4, b f Postponed (IRE)—Heart's Content (IRE) **Martin Keighley Racing Partnership 16**

THREE-YEAR-OLDS

49 **KAUTO CASTILLO (FR),** b c Castle du Berlais (FR)—Kauto Tireless (FR) **Martin Keighley Racing Partnership 12**
50 B c Idaho (IRE)—Seana Ghael (IRE)

MR MARTIN KEIGHLEY - continued

Assistant Trainer: Mr Matthew Carter, **Business & Racing Manager:** Mrs Belinda Keighley, **Yard Sponsor:** Mr Neil Lloyd FBC Manby Bowdler.

NH Jockey: Sean Bowen. **Conditional Jockey:** Mr Harry Atkins.

---

293 MR CHRISTOPHER KELLETT, Lathom

Postal: **6 Canal Cottages, Ring O Bells Lane, Lathom, Ormskirk, Lancashire, L40 5TF**
Contacts: **PHONE 01704 643775 MOBILE 07966 097989**
EMAIL CNKellett@outlook.com WEBSITE www.chriskellettracing.co.uk

1 **BEGOODTOYOURSELF (IRE),** 8, b g Getaway (GER)—Loreley (IRE) **Blythe Stables LLP**
2 **BERKSHIRE ROYAL,** 8, b g Sir Percy—Forest Express (AUS) **Andy Bell & Fergus Lyons**
3 **BLISTERING BARNEY (IRE),** 7, b g Sir Prancealot (IRE)—Eternal View (IRE) **Andy Bell & Fergus Lyons**
4 **DARBUCKS (IRE),** 4, ch g Profitable (IRE)—By Jupiter **Red & Blue Alliance**
5 **DECONSO,** 7, b g Dandy Man (IRE)—Tranquil Flight **Andy Bell & Fergus Lyons**
6 **DORETTE (FR),** 10, b m Kingsalsa (USA)—Ombrelle (FR) **Blythe Stables LLP**
7 **ONEFORTHEGUTTER,** 4, b g Muhaarar—Rainbow Springs **Tracey Bell & Caroline Lyons**
8 **REDROSEZORRO,** 9, b g Foxwedge (AUS)—Garter Star **Red Rose Partnership**
9 **SOLAR IMPULSE (FR),** 13, b g Westerner—Moon Glow (FR) **Andy Bell & Fergus Lyons**
10 **SOMTHINGPHENOMENAL,** 6, b g Phenomena—Quite Something **Mrs J. S. Roscoe-Casey**
11 **THE GRAND VISIR,** 9, b g Frankel—Piping (IRE) **Andy Bell & Fergus Lyons**
12 **WHITE UMBRELLA,** 4, b f Night of Thunder (IRE)—Sharaakah (IRE) **Whitehills Racing Syndicate 3**

THREE-YEAR-OLDS

13 **STRENGTH 'N HONOUR,** b g Showcasing—Wiener Valkyrie **Whitehills Racing Syndicate 2**
14 **TWOFORTHEGUTTER (IRE),** b c Expert Eye—Dorella (GER) **Tracey Bell & Caroline Lyons**

TWO-YEAR-OLDS

15 B g 25/01 Masar (IRE)—Bithynia (IRE) (Kodiac)

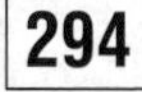

294 MISS GAY KELLEWAY, Newmarket

Postal: **Queen Alexandra Stables, 2 Chapel Street, Exning, Newmarket, Suffolk, CB8 7HA**
Contacts: **PHONE 01638 577778 MOBILE 07974 948768**
EMAIL gaykellewayracing@hotmail.co.uk WEBSITE www.gaykellewayracing.com

1 **ELOSO (IRE),** 5, b br g Kodi Bear (IRE)—Caelis **Strictly Fun Racing , Short & Robinson**
2 **HABANERO STAR,** 6, b m Mayson—Highly Spiced **Premier Thoroughbred Racing Ltd**
3 **MOVEONUP (IRE),** 7, gr g Zebedee—Emma Dora (IRE) **B. C. Oakley**
4 **MUKHA MAGIC,** 7, b g Mukhadram—Sweet Lemon (IRE) **Mr P. Bona, Moynihan,R & Robinson, Mr R. Mortlock**
5 **SHE'S OUT OF REACH,** 5, ch m Phoenix Reach (IRE)—Beat Seven **Mr P. Bona**
6 **SILVER BUBBLE,** 5, gr m Mayson—Skyrider (IRE) **W Robinson, G Kelleway & Partners**

THREE-YEAR-OLDS

7 **BISCOFF JOE,** ch g Cityscape—Royal Warranty **Mr M Pickett,Mr A Smith&miss G Kelleway**
8 **COMEDIAN LEADER,** b f Aclaim (IRE)—Last Frontier (FR) **Wolfpack X & Gay Kelleway**
9 **FOINIX,** b c Phoenix Reach (IRE)—Yeah Baby Yeah (IRE) **Winterbeck Manor Stud Ltd, Mr Adrian Johnson**
10 **HAALAND (IRE),** ch g Buratino (IRE)—Khajool (IRE) **Wrobinsonjmoynihanchilloutsyndgkelleway**
11 **MARGARET'S FUCHSIA,** ch f Dandy Man (IRE)—Quintessenz (GER) **Under The Hammer**
12 **MARKMILL,** b c Phoenix Reach (IRE)—Beat Seven **Mr P Bona & Mr M Watt**
13 **NATIVE MELODY (IRE),** b f Bungle Inthejungle—Native Picture (IRE) **Premier Thoroughbred Racing Ltd**

MISS GAY KELLEWAY - continued

14 **NEW YORK BAY,** b g New Bay—Seminova **Matthew.S, Paul.F, Arun.R, Keith.C & Gay.K**
15 **SILVER NIGHTFALL,** b f Adaay (IRE)—Godzilla's Girl **Under The Hammer**
16 **SILVER SEAHORSE,** gr f Muhaarar—Surrealism **Miss G. M. Kelleway**

TWO-YEAR-OLDS

17 B f 04/03 Le Brivido (FR)—Arbella (Primo Dominie) (12805) **Miss G. M. Kelleway, Mr T. V. Edwards**
18 **DUELY SPICED,** b f 23/04 Due Diligence (USA)—Highly Spiced (Cadeaux Genereux) (13333) **Miss G. M. Kelleway, Mr T. V. Edwards**
19 B c 05/02 Profitable (IRE)—So Funny (USA) (Distorted Humor (USA)) (32000) **Mr & Mrs H Parmar**
20 B f 04/04 Profitable (IRE)—Tiltili (IRE) (Spectrum (IRE)) (7000) **Hicky Parmar Racing**

Assistant Trainer: Sarah Kelleway, **Head Girl:** Liz Mullin.

---

295 MR NICK KENT, Brigg

Postal: **Newstead House, Newstead Priory, Cadney Road, Brigg, Lincolnshire, DN20 9HP**
Contacts: **PHONE 01652 650628 MOBILE 07710 644428**
EMAIL nick@nickkent.co.uk WEBSITE www.nickkent.co.uk

1 **BAGHDAD CENTRAL (IRE),** 7, br g Mores Wells—Katowice (IRE) **Half A Horse Partnership**
2 **BALLYCALLAN FAME (IRE),** 8, b m Fame And Glory—Sallie's Secret (IRE) **Wendy & Teresa Wesley & Mr Nick Kent**
3 **CATLIN,** 8, b m Bollin Eric—Linen Line **Cynthia Commons, Nick Kent**
4 **CROSSPARK,** 13, b g Midnight Legend—Blue Shannon (IRE) **Mrs W. M. Wesley**
5 **DEXPERADO (FR),** 4, b g Buck's Boum (FR)—Speedgirl (FR) **Crossed Fingers Partnership**
6 **DIAMOND KODA (IRE),** 4, b g Diamond Boy (FR)—Myakoda (FR) **Newstead Priory Racing Club**
7 **DOCTOR DEX (IRE),** 10, b g Oscar (IRE)—Larnalee (IRE) **Crossed Fingers Partnership**
8 **ERNE RIVER (IRE),** 8, b g Califet (FR)—Lusty Beg (IRE) **Crossed Fingers Partnership**
9 **FANFAN DU SEUIL (FR),** 8, b g Racinger (FR)—Nina du Seuil (FR) **Crossed Fingers Partnership**
10 **GAME OF WAR (IRE),** 11, b g Shantou (USA)—Carrig Eden Lass (IRE) **Mr M. Robinson**
11 **GEORDIE NIGHT,** 4, b gr g Geordieland (FR)—Night Symphonie **MMG Racing**
12 **GILBERTINA,** 6, b m Universal (IRE)—Saaboog **Mrs M. E. Kent**
13 **HARRY DU BERLAIS (IRE),** 6, b g Shirocco (GER)—Theatre Mole (IRE) **Crossed Fingers Partnership**
14 **KEEL OVER,** 12, b g Gamut (IRE)—Kayf Keel **Miss L. M. Haywood**
15 **MICK MAESTRO (FR),** 10, b br g Air Chief Marshal (IRE)—Mick Maya (FR) **Crossed Fingers Partnership**
16 5, B m Gentlewave (IRE)—Saaboog
17 **SAYAR (IRE),** 10, b g Azamour (IRE)—Seraya (FR) **Nick Kent Racing Club II**
18 **WHO'S IN THE BOX (IRE),** 9, b g Witness Box (USA)—See The Clouds **Mr Andy Parkin, Nick Kent**

Assistant Trainer: Mrs Jane Kent.

---

296 MR T J KENT, Newmarket

Postal: **Red House Stables, Hamilton Road, Newmarket, Suffolk, CB8 0NY**
Contacts: **WORK 07880 234291**
EMAIL terry@tjkentracing.co.uk

1 **ATASER,** 5, b g Sayif (IRE)—Psychic's Dream **Guaymas**
2 **DIFFIDENT SPIRIT,** 5, b g Sayif (IRE)—Abbotsfield (IRE) **Guaymas**
3 **GRAPHITE (FR),** 9, gr g Shamardal (USA)—Fairly Grey (FR) **T J Kent 1 (Graphite)**
4 **HEMMSA (IRE),** 5, b m Mehmas (IRE)—Hope And Faith (IRE) **Elpis Syndicate**

5 **INDIAN TERRITORIES,** 4, b g Territories (IRE)—Indian Story (IRE) **Mr & Mrs R. W. Reed**
6 **MOJITO MAGIC,** 4, b f Havana Gold (IRE)—Calm Attitude (IRE) **Gold Syndicate**
7 **MR MARVLOS (IRE),** 5, b g Vadamos (FR)—Petite Boulangere (IRE) **Insight Private Finance**
8 **NEMORUM,** 4, b g Stimulation (IRE)—Thicket **Kent Racing Club**
9 **OBSIDIAN KNIGHT (IRE),** 5, br g Awtaad (IRE)—Holda (IRE) **Insight Private Finance**
10 **ROBERT FROST (USA),** 6, ch g Munnings (USA)—Sorenstam (USA) **Mr T. Kent**
11 **SUPER DEN,** 6, b g Dutch Art—Loch Jipp (USA) **Guaymas**
12 **WARRIOR SQUARE,** 4, b g Adaay (IRE)—Ziefhd **Mr T. Kent**

THREE-YEAR-OLDS

13 **DREAM PIRATE,** b c Oasis Dream—Indian Story (IRE) **N Bromley, S Spampanato, R and E J Reed**
14 **KING OF FURY (IRE),** ch g Starspangledbanner (AUS)—Bequia (IRE) **Mrs Fiona Shaw**
15 **LITTLE ILFORD,** b f Buratino (IRE)—Ziefhd **Mr T. Kent**
16 B g Elzaam (AUS)—Sugarformyhoney (IRE)

TWO-YEAR-OLDS

17 B c 09/02 Cityscape—Lucky Charm (Charm Spirit (IRE)) (4500) **Mr T. Kent**
18 **ZENZIC,** b c 05/02 Territories (IRE)—Grande Rousse (FR) (Act One) (46000) **Insight Private Finance**

Assistant Trainer: Lewis Kent, Ryan Kent.

Apprentice Jockey: Levi Williams. **Amateur Jockey:** Lewis Kent.

297 MR LEONARD KERR, Irvine

Postal: **Annick Lodge, Irvine, Ayrshire, KA11 2AN**

1 **ALIEN ENCOUNTER,** 7, gr gr m Black Sam Bellamy (IRE)—Inthesettlement **Mr A Kerr Mr L Kerr**
2 **NEW ZEALANDER,** 6, b g Australia—Dalasyla (IRE) **Mr A Kerr Mr L Kerr**
3 **SWORD OF FATE (IRE),** 10, b g Beneficial—Beann Ard (IRE) **Mr A Kerr Mr L Kerr**
4 **WOTSMYNAME (IRE),** 6, ch g Famous Name—Nadeems Stella (IRE) **Mr A Kerr Mr L Kerr**

---

298 MR ALAN KING, Barbury Castle

Postal: **Barbury Castle Stables, Wroughton, Wiltshire, SN4 0QZ**
Contacts: **PHONE 01793 815009 MOBILE 07973 461233 FAX 01793 845080**
EMAIL alan@alanking.biz WEBSITE www.alankingracing.co.uk

1 **ADMIRALTY HOUSE,** 4, ch g Sea The Stars (IRE)—Akrivi (IRE) **Farrell, Hodgson A King**
2 **ALDSWORTH,** 5, b g Pether's Moon (IRE)—Handmaid **David J S Sewell & Burling Family**
3 **ALLEGRO FORTE,** 4, ch f Highland Reel (IRE)—Earth Amber **Pump & Plant Services Ltd**
4 **ANUBHUTI,** 6, br m Blue Bresil (FR)—Shatabdi (IRE) **Annabel Waley-Cohen & Family**
5 4, B f Blue Bresil (FR)—Arctic Actress **Alan King**
6 **BABY SAGE,** 5, b m Flemensfirth (USA)—Baby Shine (IRE) **Burkes & Syders**
7 **BENJAMIN BEAR (IRE),** 4, b g Kodiac—Mrs Robinson **Simon Ellen & Partners**
8 **BERINGER,** 8, b g Sea The Stars (IRE)—Edaraat (USA) **L Field, B Cognet, N Farrell, J Spack**
9 **BETTERFOREVERYONE,** 6, b g Cokoriko (FR)—Lady Emily **Mr J. R. D. Anton**
10 **BIG BOY BOBBY (IRE),** 5, b g Vadamos (FR)—Duchess of Foxland (IRE) **Incipe Partnership**
11 **BIT HARSH (IRE),** 4, b g Australia—Shortmile Lady (IRE) **Alan King & Anthony Bromley**
12 **BLAME IT ON SALLY (IRE),** 7, b g Canford Cliffs (IRE)—Sliding Scale **Owners Group 053**
13 4, B f Flemensfirth (USA)—Brijomi Queen (IRE) **Mr M. R. Haggas**
14 **BROOMHILL ROAD (IRE),** 4, b g Shirocco (GER)—Ussee (FR) **Mr J. A. Law**
15 **CAIRO KING (FR),** 4, b g Scalo—Ismailia (FR) **Mr N. Farrell**
16 **CALL OF THE WILD (IRE),** 6, b g Fame And Glory—Glory Days (GER) **Mr J. P. McManus**
17 **CHANDLERS BAY (IRE),** 4, b g Vadamos (FR)—Society Gal (IRE) **Mrs J. P. E. Cunningham**

MR ALAN KING - continued

18 **CRYSTAL MOON (IRE),** 6, ch g Shirocco (GER)—Liscannor (IRE) **Mrs J. A. Watts**
19 **DAL MALLART,** 4, b f Muhaarar—Dalvina **St Albans Bloodstock Limited**
20 **DANCING IN BRAZIL,** 4, b c Blue Bresil (FR)—Hora **James and Jean Potter Ltd**
21 **DENBURN (IRE),** 4, gr g Martaline—Shanon du Berlais (FR) **Mr J. A. Law**
22 **DEYRANN DE CARJAC (FR),** 10, b g Balko (FR)—Queyrann (FR) **Mr J. A. Law**
23 **DICKENS (IRE),** 5, b g Excelebration (IRE)—Open Book **McNeill Family & Niall Farrell**
24 **DIDONATO (IRE),** 8, b m Milan—Dream Lass (IRE) **Mr S. Smith**
25 **DINO VELVET (FR),** 10, b g Naaqoos—Matgil (FR) **Alan King**
26 **EDWARDSTONE,** 9, b g Kayf Tara—Nothingtoloose (IRE) **Robert Abrey & Ian Thurtle**
27 **EGBERT,** 6, b g Pether's Moon (IRE)—Karla June **James and Jean Potter Ltd**
28 **EMITOM (IRE),** 9, b g Gold Well—Avenging Angel (IRE) **The Spero Partnership Ltd**
29 **ERNEST GRAY (IRE),** 6, b g Walk In The Park (IRE)—Emily Gray (IRE) **Mr A. J. Peake**
30 **ES PERFECTO (IRE),** 8, ch g Shirocco (GER)—Shadow Dearg (IRE) **Mrs E. A. Prowting**
31 **EXIT POLL (IRE),** 9, b g Elusive Pimpernel (USA)—Carolobrian (IRE) **Mr G. C. Myddelton**
32 **FAST FORWARD (FR),** 4, b g Recorder—Forward Feline (IRE) **Kennet Valley Thoroughbreds IX**
33 **FAVOUR AND FORTUNE (IRE),** 5, br g Soldier of Fortune (IRE)—
Fleur Rose (IRE) **Exors of the Late Mr T. J. Hemmings**
34 **FIDUX (FR),** 10, b g Fine Grain (JPN)—Folle Tempete (FR) **AXOM LXVIII**
35 **FOREVER WILLIAM,** 5, ch g Sea The Moon (GER)—Archina (IRE) **The Barbury Lions 6**
36 **FORGET THE WAY,** 6, b g Getaway (GER)—Forget The Ref (IRE) **Robert Abrey, Ian Thurtle & David Gibbon**
37 **FORWARD FLIGHT (IRE),** 4, b g Declaration of War (USA)—On A Cloud (USA) **The Barbury Lions 7**
38 **FRATERNEL (FR),** 8, b g Kap Rock (FR)—Valence (FR) **Mr T. D. J. Syder**
39 **FUTURE INVESTMENT,** 7, b g Mount Nelson—Shenir **Mrs E. A. Prowting**
40 **GAVI DI GAVI (IRE),** 8, b g Camacho—Blossom Deary (IRE) **Alan King & Niall Farrell**
41 **GIRLS IN SKIRTS (IRE),** 4, b f Mahler—Lady On Track (IRE) **Mr C. B. J. Dingwall**
42 **GITCHE GUMEE,** 5, b g Clovis du Berlais (FR)—Fabrika **Mr J. P. McManus**
43 **GLIDE DOWN (USA),** 5, b g Point of Entry (USA)—On A Cloud (USA) **James Wigan & Alan King**
44 **GRANDEUR D'AME (FR),** 7, b g Desir d'Un Soir (FR)—Sourya d'Airy (FR) **Syders & Burkes**
45 **GREEN PLANET (IRE),** 6, b g Australia—Maleha (IRE) **The Unlikely Lads**
46 **GREYSTOKE,** 5, b g Sixties Icon—Siri **Robert & Lucy Dickinson**
47 **GROSVENOR COURT,** 7, b g Shirocco (GER)—Hurricane Milly (IRE) **Farrell, Gallagher, Gressier & Murray**
48 **HALL LANE (IRE),** 5, ch g Mount Nelson—Cashalass (IRE) **Jerry Wright & the Lee Family**
49 **HARBOUR LAKE (IRE),** 7, br g Shantou (USA)—Aibrean (IRE) **Exors of the Late Mr T. J. Hemmings**
50 **HASEEFAH,** 6, b m Teofilo (IRE)—Halaqa (IRE) **Michael Rembaum & Michael Tuckey**
51 **HEART OF A LION (IRE),** 8, b g Yeats (IRE)—Lady Secret (FR) **Mr J. P. McManus**
52 **HELNWEIN (IRE),** 5, b g Walk In The Park (IRE)—Synthe Davis (FR) **Noel Fehily Racing Syndicates Helnwein**
53 **HEY BROTHER (FR),** 6, b g Ballingarry (IRE)—Mick Maya (FR) **Alan King**
54 **I'M A LUMBERJACK,** 4, b g Jack Hobbs—Decision Made (IRE) **This Time Next Year Partnership**
55 **IRISH CHORUS,** 4, bl f Jack Hobbs—Mayfair Music (IRE) **Mrs E. C. Roberts**
56 **ISOLATE (FR),** 7, b g Maxios—Unaided **Noel Fehily Racing - Isolate**
57 **JAY BEE WHY (IRE),** 8, b g Yeats (IRE)—Lady Bernie (IRE) **David J S Sewell & Tim Leadbeater**
58 **KAY TARA TARA,** 5, b m Kayf Tara—Forever Present (IRE) **IBT Racing**
59 **KLITSCHKO,** 5, b g Blue Bresil (FR)—Arctic Actress **Mr J. P. McManus**
60 5, B g Kayf Tara—L'Unique (FR) **Mr D. J. Barry**
61 4, B g Milan—L'Unique (FR) **Mr D. J. Barry**
62 **LUNAR CONTACT (IRE),** 5, b g Sea Moon—Bobaway (IRE) **Million in Mind Partnership**
63 **LUNAR SHADOW,** 5, b m Sea The Moon (GER)—The Pirate's Queen (IRE) **Apple Tree Stud**
64 **MADIBA PASSION (FR),** 9, b g Al Namix (FR)—Birsheba (FR) **M Deeley, J Dale & A King**
65 **MAID ON THE MOON,** 6, b m Pether's Moon (IRE)—Handmaid **The Burling Family Ltd**
66 **MAJOR DUNDEE (IRE),** 8, b g Scorpion (IRE)—Be My Granny **Exors of the Late Mr T. J. Hemmings**
67 **MASACCIO (IRE),** 6, gr g Mastercraftsman (IRE)—Ange Bleu (USA) **McNeill Family & Niall Farrell**
68 **MAYFAIR GOLD (IRE),** 4, b f Havana Gold (IRE)—Cherrington (IRE) **Mr & Mrs R. G. Kelvin-Hughes**
69 **MAZZORBO,** 5, b g Cable Bay (IRE)—Pink Diamond **Dr A. J. F. Gillespie**
70 **MENAGGIO (IRE),** 4, b g Milan—Nova Stella (GER) **Mr D. J. S. Sewell**
71 **MESSIRE DES OBEAUX (FR),** 11, b g Saddler Maker (IRE)—
Madame Lys (FR) **Mr Simon Munir & Mr Isaac Souede**
72 **METHUSALAR (IRE),** 7, b g Sholokhov (IRE)—Pixie Dust (IRE) **Top Brass Partnership**
73 **MIDNIGHT GLANCE,** 8, b g Passing Glance—Magical Legend **R. H. Kerswell**
74 **MISTRAL MILLY (IRE),** 4, ch f Mount Nelson—Hurricane Milly (IRE) **John J. Murray & Niall Farrell**
75 **MOONAMACAROONA,** 7, b m Flemensfirth (USA)—Forever Present (IRE) **Netherfield House Stud**

MR ALAN KING - continued

76 **MOUNT OLYMPUS,** 5, b g Olympic Glory (IRE)—Ile Rouge **HP Racing Mount Olympus**
77 **MR RUMBALICIOUS (IRE),** 4, b g Kodiac—Intaglia **Let's Get Ready To Rumble Partnership**
78 **NELSON CRIQ (IRE),** 4, b g Mount Nelson—Real Revival (IRE) **Mr D. J. S. Sewell**
79 **NINA THE TERRIER (IRE),** 7, b m Milan—Shees A Dante (IRE) **Mr C. B. J. Dingwall**
80 **NORTH LODGE (IRE),** 6, b g Presenting—Saddleeruppat (IRE) **McNeill Family & Niall Farrell**
81 **NOTACHANCE (IRE),** 9, b g Mahler—Ballybrowney Hall (IRE) **David J S Sewell & Tim Leadbeater**
82 **NOTHINGTOCHANCE,** 6, b m Kayf Tara—Nothingtoloose (IRE) **Robert Abrey & Ian Thurtle**
83 **ON SE CALME (FR),** 5, ch m No Risk At All (FR)—Wedding Night (FR) **Mr G. C. Myddelton**
84 **ON TO VICTORY,** 9, b g Rock of Gibraltar (IRE)—Clouds of Magellan (USA) **HP Racing On To Victory**
85 **OPEN CHAMPION (IRE),** 4, b g Postponed (IRE)—Nargys (IRE) **Thurloe Royal Marsden Cancer Charity II**
86 **PANGLOSS,** 4, b g Havana Gold (IRE)—Fantastic Santanyi **R. Mathew**
87 **PARADIAS (GER),** 4, b g Kodiac—Paraisa **Dodds-Smith, Farrell, Hodgson & Coupland**
88 **PASS THE LOVE ON,** 6, b m Passing Glance—Call Me A Star **Pitchall Stud Partnership**
89 **PASSING REFLECTION,** 5, b m Passing Glance—Call Me A Star **Pitchall Stud Partnership**
90 **PASSIONATE PURSUIT (IRE),** 5, b m Champs Elysees—Passionate Lady (IRE) **Mr G. C. Myddelton**
91 **PICCADILLY LILLY,** 6, b m Authorized (IRE)—Hora **Trull House Stud & R. Waley-cohen**
92 5, B g Pether's Moon (IRE)—Polly Potter **James and Jean Potter Ltd**
93 **PUMPKIN'S PRIDE,** 7, b g Malinas (GER)—Peel Me A Grape **Mrs E. A. Prowting**
94 **QOYA,** 4, b f Almanzor (FR)—Plume Rose **Louisa Stone & St Albans Bloodstock**
95 **RAFIKI (FR),** 5, b g The Last Lion (IRE)—Adalawa (IRE) **Alan King & Niall Farrell**
96 **RAINBOW DREAMER,** 10, b g Aqlaam—Zamhrear **The Maple Street Partnership**
97 **RAYMOND TUSK (IRE),** 8, b h High Chaparral (IRE)—Dancing Shoes (IRE) **The Unlikely Lads**
98 **RESTITUTION (FR),** 5, b g Frankel—Restiana (FR) **Highclere T'Bred Racing - Restitution**
99 **ROCKWITHTHETIMES (IRE),** 6, br g Shirocco (GER)—Dare To Venture (IRE) **Alan King**
100 **ROSCOE TARA,** 8, b g Kayf Tara—Aunt Harriet **Mr & Mrs R. Allsop**
101 **ROYAL PRETENDER (FR),** 7, br g Great Pretender (IRE)—Robinia Directa (GER) **Mrs C. Skan**
102 4, B br g Bow Creek (IRE)—Saint Goustan (FR) **Alan King**
103 **SATURDAY SONG,** 7, b g Kayf Tara—Fernello **Gwen Meacham & Alan King**
104 **SAXONS LANE (IRE),** 4, b g Malinas (GER)—Local Lingo (IRE) **Alan King**
105 **SCEAU ROYAL (FR),** 11, b g Doctor Dino (FR)—Sandside (FR) **Mr Simon Munir & Mr Isaac Souede**
106 **SELWAN (IRE),** 4, b g Zelzal (FR)—Al Wathna **Andy Bell & Fergus Lyons**
107 **SENIOR CITIZEN,** 10, b g Tobougg (IRE)—Mothers Help **The McNeill Family**
108 5, B g Scorpion (IRE)—Shady Lane **Mrs S. C. Welch**
109 **SPARTAN ARMY (IRE),** 4, b g Highland Reel (IRE)—Trianon **McNeill Family & Patrick& Scott Bryceland**
110 **SWORD BEACH (IRE),** 6, ch g Ivawood (IRE)—Sleeping Princess (IRE) **Hp Racing Sword Beach & Ptnr**
111 **TECHNOLOGY (IRE),** 6, b g Yeats (IRE)—Little Fashionista (IRE) **McNeill Family & Stone Family**
112 **THE DOYEN CHIEF (IRE),** 6, b g Doyen (IRE)—Mandarli (IRE)
113 **THE OLYMPIAN (IRE),** 7, ch g Olympic Glory (IRE)—Basira (FR) **Mr J. P. McManus**
114 **THE UNIT (IRE),** 12, b g Gold Well—Sovana (FR) **International Plywood (Importers) Ltd**
115 **THEONLYWAYISWESSEX (FR),** 5, b br g Maxios—Terra Fina **Marsh, Kelly, Meacham, Davies & Mordaunt**
116 **THIS ONES FOR FRED (IRE),** 5, b br g Markaz (IRE)—Green Chorus (IRE) **Mr G. Coombs**
117 **THUNDER AHEAD,** 5, b g Dark Angel (IRE)—Champagne Time (IRE) **Maybe Only Fools Have Horses**
118 **TRITONIC,** 6, ch g Sea The Moon (GER)—Selenography **McNeill Family & Mr Ian Dale**
119 **TRUESHAN (FR),** 7, b g Planteur (IRE)—Shao Line (FR) **Singula Partnership**
120 **TUDDENHAM GREEN,** 4, b g Nathaniel (IRE)—Social Media **Simon Munir, Isaac Souede & Partners**
121 **TYING THE KNOT (USA),** 4, b g Noble Mission—Hope's Diamond (USA) **Mr A. J. Peake**
122 **UMAX (IRE),** 4, b g Kingman—Bella Nostalgia (IRE) **Amo Racing Limited & Arjun Waney**
123 **VAZIR (FR),** 5, b g Siyouni (FR)—Vazira (FR) **The Unlikely Lads**
124 **VICTORY (IRE),** 4, b g Churchill (IRE)—Mill Point **Barry, Trowbridge A King**
125 **VIVID PINK,** 4, b f Sea The Moon (GER)—Pink Diamond **Dr A. J. F. Gillespie**
126 **WURLITZER,** 5, b g Adaay (IRE)—Olympic Medal **Owners Group 067**
127 **WYNN HOUSE,** 8, ch m Presenting—Glorious Twelfth (IRE) **Mr J. R. D. Anton**

THREE-YEAR-OLDS

128 **DAWN VEGA,** b g Lope de Vega (IRE)—Ennaya (FR) **Regents Consulting**
129 **EZMERELLDA (IRE),** b f Intello (GER)—Elraazy **The Barbury Lions 7**
130 **HAUGHTY,** b f Adaay (IRE)—So Hoity Toity **R. Mathew**
131 **HOURLESS,** b g Time Test—Poly Pomona **Apple Tree Stud**
132 **INKAMAN,** gr c Cracksman—Lubinka (IRE) **Ian Gosden & Geoff Kennington**

MR ALAN KING - continued

133 **KERRY MOON,** b g Sea The Moon (GER)—Cosmea **Kingston Stud**
134 **LIONELLA,** gr f Roaring Lion (USA)—Ensaya (IRE) **W. R. Milner**
135 **LOUGHVILLE,** b f Mastercraftsman (IRE)—Distant (USA) **Glebe Farm Stud**
136 **NAP HAND (IRE),** b g Fast Company (IRE)—Dream Sleep **Elysees Partnership**
137 **OUTGUN,** gr g Outstrip—Triple Cee (IRE) **Kingston Stud**
138 **PALIO (IRE),** b g Vadamos (FR)—Figurante (IRE) **Alan King & Anthony Bromley**
139 **RAVIGILL (FR),** b f Showcasing—Loch Ma Naire (IRE) **St Albans Bloodstock Limited**
140 **ROYAL DEESIDE,** b g Churchill (IRE)—Ebb **Mr J. A. Law**
141 **SEA SQUARED,** b g Sea The Moon (GER)—Sea of Hope (IRE) **Singula Partnership 2**
142 **STAR TURN,** b g Zoustar (AUS)—Thousandkissesdeep (IRE) **Farrell, Marsh**
143 **TWO PAST EIGHT,** b g Sir Percy—Hazy Dancer **The Barbury Lions 7**
144 **WESTERTON (IRE),** b g Belardo (IRE)—Aubusson (IRE) **Mr J. A. Law**
145 **ZODIAC STAR (IRE),** b g Kodiac—An Cailin Orga (IRE) **The Barbury Boys**

Assistant Trainer: Dan Horsford, Robin Smith, **Yard Sponsor:** BETGOODWIN.

NH Jockey: Tom Bellamy, Tom Cannon, Gavin Sheehan. **Conditional Jockey:** Alexander Thorne. **Amateur Jockey:** Georgia King.

---

299 MR NEIL KING, Wroughton

Postal: **Upper Herdswick Farm, Burderop, Wroughton, Swindon, Wiltshire, SN4 0QH**
Contacts: **PHONE 01793 845011 MOBILE 07880 702325 FAX 01793 845011**
EMAIL neil@neil-king.co.uk WEBSITE www.neil-king.co.uk

1 **BALAGAN,** 8, b g Great Pretender (IRE)—Lovely Origny (FR) **Mr A. L. Cohen**
2 **CHARMIAN'S PLACE (IRE),** 5, b m Telescope (IRE)—Zahra's Place **Mrs H. M. Buckle**
3 **CHENG GONG,** 7, b g Archipenko (USA)—Kinetica **Three Kingdoms Racing**
4 **CLAY,** 5, b g Sixties Icon—Tamso (USA) **Davies,Govier,Govier,O'Callaghan&Brown**
5 **CLUAIN AODHA (IRE),** 6, b m Darsi (FR)—Wendy's Moan (IRE) **Mark Harrod, Bryan Agar & Nicky George**
6 **CUBAN COURT (IRE),** 5, b g Court Cave (IRE)—Havana Dancer (IRE) **Lingfield Park Owners Group19 & Partners**
7 **DON'T ASK FITZ (IRE),** 6, b g Ask—Decheekymonkey (IRE)
8 **GIVE ME A CUDDLE (IRE),** 7, b g Court Cave (IRE)—Social Society (IRE) **Mr A. L. Cohen**
9 **GO FOX,** 8, ch g Foxwedge (AUS)—Bling Bling (IRE) **The Ridgeway Racing For Fun Partnership**
10 **GRAND REVIVAL (USA),** 5, b g American Pharoah (USA)—
Rather Special (IRE) **The Ridgeway Racing For Fun Partnership**
11 5, B m Blue Bresil (FR)—Hope Royal
12 **I HOPE STAR (IRE),** 7, b g Casamento (IRE)—Bint Nayef (IRE) **Sal's Pals**
13 **IZAYTE (FR),** 5, b g Masked Marvel—Vakina (FR) **Simon & Patrick Evans**
14 **JUSTIFIED,** 6, br g Authorized (IRE)—Caribbean Dancer (USA) **Mr B Bell, Mr M Harrod & Mr G Sainsbury**
15 **KENYAN COWBOY (IRE),** 7, b g Sholokhov (IRE)—Joleen (IRE) **Mrs C. Kendrick**
16 **KEY INSTINCT,** 6, b m Intrinsic—Tellmethings **Mr M. H. Wood**
17 **LIFETIME LEGEND (IRE),** 5, b g Pride of Dubai (AUS)—Livia Galilei (IRE) **Ken Lawrence & Roy Mousley**
18 **LOOKAWAY (IRE),** 6, ch g Ask—Barrack's Choice (IRE) **Mr P. M. H. Beadles**
19 **LUWDVIG (FR),** 4, b g Creachadoir (IRE)—Grande Symphonie (FR)
20 **MALINA JAMILA,** 7, b m Malinas (GER)—Haveyoubeen (IRE) **Maundrell, Sawyer & Andrews**
21 **MARIDADI,** 7, b m Beat Hollow—Mighty Splash **Guy Sainsbury & Partners**
22 4, Ch f Jukebox Jury (IRE)—Mile From The Moon (IRE) **Mrs H. M. Buckle**
23 **MISTING,** 4, b f Scorpion (IRE)—Dream Performance (IRE) **A & D Smith**
24 **NEARLY PERFECT,** 9, b g Malinas (GER)—The Lyme Volunteer (IRE) **Mr P. M. H. Beadles**
25 **ONEMOREFORTHEROAD,** 8, b g Yorgunnabelucky (USA)—Vinomore **Rupert Dubai Racing**
26 **SANS CHOIX (IRE),** 5, ch m Sans Frontieres (IRE)—
Barrack's Choice (IRE) **Stephen Lower Insurance Services Limited**
27 **SPORTING ACE (IRE),** 7, b g Shantou (USA)—Knockbounce View (IRE) **Ken Lawrence & Roy Mousley**
28 **STATE OF BLISS (IRE),** 5, b g Gleneagles (IRE)—Crystal Valkyrie (IRE) **The Ridgeway Racing For Fun Partnership**
29 **THE BANDIT (IRE),** 8, br g Stowaway—Highly Presentable (IRE) **Mr P. M. H. Beadles**
30 **THE KNOT IS TIED (IRE),** 8, b g Casamento (IRE)—Really Polish (USA) **Ken Lawrence & Roy Mousley**
31 4, B g Scorpion (IRE)—Too Generous **Miss H. J. Williams**

MR NEIL KING - continued

Racing Secretary: Oriana-Jane Baines.

Flat Jockey: Ben Curtis, Luke Morris. **NH Jockey:** Bryony Frost.

---

300 MR PHILIP KIRBY, Richmond

Postal: **Green Oaks Farm, East Appleton, Richmond, North Yorkshire, DL10 7QE**
Contacts: **PHONE 01748 517337 MOBILE 07984 403558**
EMAIL pkirbyracing@gmail.com WEBSITE www.philipkirbyracing.co.uk

1 **ADELPHI SPRITE,** 7, b g Cityscape—Cailin Na Ri (IRE) **Barry and Virginia Brown**
2 **ALLIBABA,** 5, b g Alhebayeb (IRE)—Contenance (IRE) **Mr G. Nicholson**
3 **ALOISA,** 5, b m Kayf Tara—Alina Rheinberg (GER) **Epona Thoroughbreds Limited**
4 **ANNIE ROSE,** 5, b m Equiano (FR)—Tebee's Oasis **Alan Fairhurst & David Fairhurst**
5 **ASA (FR),** 4, gr f Balko (FR)—Reine de Glace (FR) **The Yorkshire Puddings**
6 **AUTONOMY,** 7, b g Dansili—Funsie (FR) **Hambleton Racing XXXIV & Partner**
7 **BAMBOO BAY (IRE),** 5, b g Camelot—Anna Karenina (USA) **Harbour Rose Partnership**
8 **BARLEY BREEZE,** 6, gr g Kapgarde (FR)—Attente de Sivola (FR) **Tor Side Racing**
9 **BARNEYS GIFT (FR),** 4, b g Johnny Barnes (IRE)—Diamond Surprise **Hold My Beer Syndicate Tom Hughes**
10 **BATEAU BAY (IRE),** 4, b f Nathaniel (IRE)—Assembly (USA) **First to Third Generation Partnership**
11 **BE THE DIFFERENCE (IRE),** 7, b g Califet (FR)—Rinroe Flyer (IRE) **Be The Difference Partnership**
12 **BILLIAN (IRE),** 5, b g Mehmas (IRE)—Truly Magnificent (USA) **The Philip Kirby Racing Club**
13 **BUSBY (IRE),** 8, b g Kodiac—Arabian Pearl (IRE) **The Busby Partnership**
14 **BUSHYPARK (IRE),** 9, b g Le Fou (IRE)—Aztec Pearl **The Green Oaks Partnership**
15 **CARACRISTI,** 4, b f Mondialiste (IRE)—Jen Jos Enigma (IRE) **Ace Bloodstock & P Kirby**
16 **CARLOS FELIX (IRE),** 6, ch g Lope de Vega (IRE)—Quad's Melody (IRE) **Mr & Mrs D. Yates**
17 **CASA LUNA (IRE),** 4, b f Starspangledbanner (AUS)—
Flowers of Spring (IRE) **James & Susan Cookson, Joss Coward**
18 **CLEAN GETAWAY (IRE),** 6, b g Getaway (GER)—Dee Two O Two (IRE) **Mr P. A. Kirby**
19 **COURT JUSTICE (IRE),** 6, b g Court Cave (IRE)—Killogan Lass (IRE) **Mr G. Nicholson**
20 **DEFINING BATTLE (IRE),** 7, gr g Lope de Vega (IRE)—Royal Fortune (IRE) **Mr & Mrs D. Yates**
21 **FARHAN (IRE),** 5, b h Zoffany (IRE)—Market Forces **James & Susan Cookson**
22 **FIRCOMBE HALL,** 5, ch g Charming Thought—Marmot Bay (IRE) **RedHotGardogs**
23 **GLAMOROUS ICON (IRE),** 5, ch m Presenting—Vic Chic (IRE) **The Glamorous Icon Partnership**
24 **GOLFE CLAIR (FR),** 7, b g Masked Marvel—Ocean Beach (FR) **Mr P. R. Rawcliffe**
25 **GOWANLAD,** 6, b g Mayson—Aahgowangowan (IRE) **Gowan Racing**
26 **GREEN OAKS TOP CAT,** 6, ch m Soldier of Fortune (IRE)—Molly Cat **The Philip Kirby Racing Club**
27 **HERITIER DE SIVOLA (FR),** 6, ch g Noroit (GER)—Quellevic (FR) **Mr G. Nicholson**
28 **HUBBEL BUBBEL,** 5, b g Telescope (IRE)—Cormorant Cove **Mr D. Carter**
29 **JASON THE MILITANT (IRE),** 9, b g Sans Frontieres (IRE)—Rock Angel (IRE) **Mr G. Nicholson**
30 **JOHN THE PIRATE,** 4, br g Mondialiste (IRE)—Musikhani **Ace Bloodstock & P Kirby**
31 4, B g Milan—Lady Chloe **FDC Holdings Ltd**
32 **LADY'S PRESENT (IRE),** 6, b m Presenting—Lady Chloe **The Team Kirby Partnership**
33 **LEOPOLDS ROCK (IRE),** 7, ch g Rock of Gibraltar (IRE)—Trianon **Tor Side Racing**
34 **LONE STAR,** 6, b m Kayf Tara—Supreme Gem (IRE) **John Cornforth & Peter Rawcliffe**
35 **LORD TORRANAGA (FR),** 8, b g Planteur (IRE)—Marie Cuddy (IRE) **Lord Torranaga Partnership**
36 **MAGICAL ARTHUR (IRE),** 5, b g Yeats (IRE)—Miss Cilla (IRE) **Harbour Rose Partnership**
37 **MARTALINDY,** 6, b m Martaline—Helen Wood **The Philip Kirby Racing Club**
38 **MICKS JET (IRE),** 5, ch m Jet Away—Miss Superior (IRE) **Mr J. A. Hall**
39 **MISSCARLETT (IRE),** 9, b m Red Rocks (IRE)—Coimbra (USA) **Mrs J. Porter**
40 **MY STRONG MAN (IRE),** 7, b g Authorized (IRE)—Lady Chloe **The Platinum Partnership**
41 **NOONIE,** 4, b f Almanzor (FR)—Gallice (IRE) **The Earl of R. L. Ronaldshay**
42 **PERIPETEIA,** 5, b m Sir Percy—Archduchess **RedHotGardogs**
43 **PORTO ERCOLE (IRE),** 4, gr f Caravaggio (USA)—Euphrasia (IRE) **Jowseybainbridgestephensonfraser**
44 **RAFFLES REBEL,** 5, ch g Al Kazeem—Go Between **Hope Eden Racing Limited**
45 **RAIFF (IRE),** 7, b g Shamardal (USA)—Estiqaama (USA) **Mr D. R. Platt**

MR PHILIP KIRBY - continued

46 **RAVENSCAR (IRE),** 7, b m Helmet (AUS)—Cry Pearl (USA) **Mr J. A. Hall**
47 **RED FORCE ONE,** 8, gr g Lethal Force (IRE)—Dusty Red **The Yorkshire Puddings**
48 **ROBERT JOHNSON,** 5, ch g Helmet (AUS)—Sensationally **Mr M. V. Coglan**
49 **SCALLOWAY CASTLE (IRE),** 5, b br g Ocovango—Ashlings Princess (IRE) **The Earl of R. L. Ronaldshay**
50 **SMART BOYO,** 5, b g War Command (USA)—Luluti (IRE) **Smartwater Utilities**
51 **SOARING STAR (IRE),** 6, b g Starspangledbanner (AUS)—Peig (IRE) **Hambleton Racing Ltd XXV**
52 **SPANISH BUTTONS (FR),** 4, b g Spanish Moon (USA)—Lady Westerner **The Spanish Buttons Partnership**
53 5, B g Sholokhov (IRE)—Sunlight (IRE) **Mr D. Carter**
54 **TELEMETRY,** 5, b g Telescope (IRE)—Emma Lee **Philip & Nicola Tyler**
55 4, B f Sholokhov (IRE)—The Sailors Bonnet (IRE) **The Good Looking Partnership**
56 **THE TABLET,** 7, b g Trans Island—Tushana (IRE) **Mr S. Silcock**
57 **TOMMASO (IRE),** 5, b g Bobby's Kitten (USA)—Aseela (IRE) **Mrs J. Porter**
58 **TOP VILLE BEN (IRE),** 11, b g Beneficial—Great Decision (IRE) **Harbour Rose Partnership**
59 **TWO THIRTY YEAT (IRE),** 8, b m Yeats (IRE)—Aneda Dubh (IRE) **Mr P. Bryan**
60 **WHITCLIFFE (IRE),** 4, gr g Kendargent (FR)—Lady Slippers (IRE) **L. M. Zetland**
61 **WHOSHOTTHESHERIFF (IRE),** 9, b g Dylan Thomas (IRE)—Dame Foraine (FR) **Hambleton Racing Ltd XXXIV**
62 **WILLING TO PLEASE,** 6, b m Iffraaj—Tebee's Oasis **Alan Fairhurst & David Fairhurst, R. G. Capstick**
63 **WYE AYE,** 8, b g Shirocco (GER)—A Media Luz (FR) **The Well Oiled Partnership**
64 **ZWICKY,** 6, b g Sixties Icon—Emma Lee **Philip & Nicola Tyler**

THREE-YEAR-OLDS

65 **DAZAMAY,** ch f Mayson—Dazakhee **Mr & Mrs D. Yates**
66 **HELIANTHUS,** b g Aclaim (IRE)—Sunflower **Coglan & Kilcran**
67 B g Yeats (IRE)—Lady Chloe **Mr P. A. Kirby**
68 **LILY IN THE JUNGLE (IRE),** ch f Bungle Inthejungle—Zuzinia (IRE) **The Well Oiled Partnership**
69 **MISAURA (IRE),** b f Free Eagle (IRE)—Etesian (IRE) **Mrs J. Porter**
70 Ch g Order of St George (IRE)—Miss Cilla (IRE) **Mr P. A. Kirby**
71 **NORTHERN CHANCER,** b g Brazen Beau (AUS)—Marmot Bay (IRE) **Ace Bloodstock Ltd**
72 **QUEENMAMBO,** ch f Sea The Moon (GER)—Best Side (IRE) **Fdc Holdings & Roofing Consultants Group**
73 B f Al Kazeem—Skid (IRE) **Ace Bloodstock Ltd**
74 **SMART BUCKS,** b g Buck's Boum (FR)—Lady Westerner **Mr P. A. Kirby**
75 Ch g Fast Company (IRE)—Village Fete **Fdc Holdings & Roofing Consultants Group**
76 **WOODCHIP,** ch g Getaway (GER)—Helen Wood **Mr P. A. Kirby**

Assistant Trainer: Simon Olley.

NH Jockey: Tommy Dowson, Joe Williamson. **Apprentice Jockey:** Madi Patzelt.

---

301 MR SYLVESTER KIRK, Upper Lambourn

Postal: **Cedar Lodge Stables, Upper Lambourn, Hungerford, Berkshire, RG17 8QT**
Contacts: **PHONE 01488 73215 MOBILE 07768 855261**
EMAIL info@sylvesterkirkracing.co.uk WEBSITE www.sylvesterkirkracing.co.uk

1 **EAUX DE VIE,** 5, b m Swiss Spirit—Delagoa Bay (IRE)
2 **EXIGENCY,** 4, b f Shalaa (IRE)—Emergency
3 **FURTHER MEASURE (USA),** 6, b g English Channel (USA)—Price Tag
4 **POUILLY FUISSE (IRE),** 4, b f Mastercraftsman (IRE)—Density
5 **SOUTHERLY STORM,** 4, b g Fastnet Rock (AUS)—Opera Gal (IRE)
6 **SUN TRACKER,** 4, b g Bated Breath—Solar Pursuit
7 **TROPICAL TALENT,** 4, b g Nathaniel (IRE)—Tropical Rock

THREE-YEAR-OLDS

8 **AFRICAN STAR (IRE),** b c Galileo (IRE)—Timbuktu (IRE)
9 **ALODIA,** ch f Saxon Warrior (JPN)—Atone
10 **BEND THE LIGHT,** b f Australia—Loch Mirage

MR SYLVESTER KIRK - continued

11 **BODEGA NIGHTS,** b br f Tasleet—Robbie Roo Roo
12 **CENTRE BACK,** b g Territories (IRE)—Finale
13 **CHINDWIN,** b c Saxon Warrior (JPN)—Cay Dancer
14 Gr g Acclamation—Chiringuita (USA)
15 **DALISO (IRE),** ch f Zoffany (IRE)—Wondrous Story (USA)
16 **FINN STAR (IRE),** b g National Defense—Attracted To You (IRE)
17 **MANY RIVERS (IRE),** b f Dandy Man (IRE)—Dubaya
18 **ME AND MRS JONES (IRE),** b f Acclamation—She Believes (IRE)
19 **MELLOW MOOD,** b f Bated Breath—Going For Gold
20 Ch f Air Force Blue (USA)—Peinture Rare (IRE)
21 **SEATTLE TIME,** b g Time Test—Snoqualmie Girl (IRE)
22 **THE PUG (IRE),** b g Churchill (IRE)—Alumni Award
23 **TONICITY,** b f Kodiac—City Girl (IRE)
24 **ZOUS BABY,** b g Zoustar (AUS)—Wishsong

TWO-YEAR-OLDS

25 B c 25/03 Dandy Man (IRE)—Autograph (Nathaniel (IRE)) (16006)
26 B g 10/03 Cappella Sansevero—Fol O'Yasmine (Dubawi (IRE)) (12005)
27 B f 08/04 Highland Reel (IRE)—Iconic Girl (Cape Cross (IRE))
28 B c 14/03 James Garfield (IRE)—Jane Rose (IRE) (Acclamation) (25000)
29 B c 07/03 Saxon Warrior (JPN)—Love And Laughter (IRE) (Theatrical)
30 **RITZY,** b f 24/04 Mendelssohn (USA)—Tiburtina (IRE) (Holy Roman Emperor (IRE)) (22000)
31 B f 10/03 Expert Eye—Tropical Treat (Bahamian Bounty)

Owners: Mr K. Balasuriya, Mr T. Crookenden, Deauville Daze Partnership, Family Amusements Ltd, Mrs J. A. Fowler, Homebred Racing, Miss Alison Jones, Miss F. Kirk, S. A. Kirk, Marchwood Aggregates, Marchwood Recycling Ltd, Mr N Simpson & Partners, Neil Simpson & Tom Crookenden, Paul Kilkenny and Son Limited, N. Pickett, Mrs L. M. Shanahan, Mr N. Simpson, J. C. Smith, Spear Family.

Assistant Trainer: Fanny Kirk.

MR STUART KITTOW, Cullompton

Postal: **Orchard House, Blackborough, Cullompton, Devon, EX15 2JD**
Contacts: **HOME 01823 680183 MOBILE 07714 218921**
EMAIL stuartkittowracing@hotmail.com WEBSITE www.stuartkittowracing.com

1 **BELLA'S PEARL,** 4, b f Pearl Secret—Plauseabella **Mrs G. R. Shire**
2 **BEYOND EQUAL,** 8, b g Kheleyf (USA)—Samasana (IRE) **Stuart Wood & Partner**
3 **CORNISH STORM,** 4, b g Coach House (IRE)—Dancing Storm **M. E. Harris**
4 **COUP DE FORCE,** 4, b f Lethal Force (IRE)—Dilgura **The Coup de Force Partnership**
5 **GHERKIN,** 6, b g Coach House (IRE)—Our Piccadilly (IRE) **Mrs G. R. Shire**
6 **MABEL JANE,** 6, b m Champs Elysees—Sabaweeya **Dr B. Blouin**
7 **MONTERIA (IRE),** 5, b g Mehmas (IRE)—Rip Van Music (IRE) **Elizabeth Gifford & Bernice Walter**
8 **NOTRE MAISON,** 4, b f Coach House (IRE)—Our Piccadilly (IRE) **Mrs G. R. Shire**
9 **ORIENTAL SPIRIT,** 5, b g Swiss Spirit—Yat Ding Yau (FR) **The Oriental Spirit Partnership**
10 **PERFECT MYTH,** 9, b m Midnight Legend—Perfect Silence **R. J. Vines**
11 **TIBBIE DUNBAR,** 7, b m Poet's Voice—Gold Approach **Mr J. R. Urquhart**

THREE-YEAR-OLDS

12 **BEAU GARS,** b g Brazen Beau (AUS)—Dilgura **The Coup de Force Partnership**
13 **CHALK MOUNTAIN,** gr gr g Outstrip—Perfect Muse **The Chalk Mountain Partnership**
14 B f Poet's Word (IRE)—Clanville Lass
15 **JIMMY MARK (IRE),** b g Intrinsic—Kodi da Capo (IRE) **Mr P. T. S. Lindsey**
16 **PAPABELLA,** b f Ardad (IRE)—Plauseabella **Mrs G. R. Shire**
17 **SONNET STAR,** gr f Poet's Word (IRE)—Reaching Ahead (USA) **Newton Barn Racing**

MR STUART KITTOW - continued

TWO-YEAR-OLDS

18 B f 15/03 Adaay (IRE)—Dancing Storm (Trans Island)
19 **MAISON DE BELLA,** b g 01/02 Coach House (IRE)—Plauseabella (Royal Applause) **Mrs G. R. Shire**
20 B g 24/03 Due Diligence (USA)—Shared Experience (Raven's Pass (USA)) **W. S. Kittow**
21 **SUNNY CORNER,** b c 25/04 Due Diligence (USA)—Nightingale Valley (Compton Place) **M. E. Harris**
22 **TIMETOBOUGGALOO,** b c 17/03 Time Test—Tobouggaloo (Tobougg (IRE)) **Dr G. S. Plastow**

Assistant Trainer: Mrs Judy Kittow.

Flat Jockey: Rob Hornby. **NH Jockey:** David Noonan.

303

MR WILLIAM KNIGHT, Newmarket

Postal: **Rathmoy Stables, Hamilton Road, Newmarket, Suffolk, CB8 0GU**
Contacts: **PHONE 01638 664063 MOBILE 07770 720828**
EMAIL william@wknightracing.co.uk WEBSITE www.wknightracing.co.uk FACEBOOK William-KnightRacing TWITTER @WKnightRacing INSTAGRAM williamknightracing1

1 **AUTHOR'S DREAM,** 10, gr g Authorized (IRE)—Spring Dream (IRE) **Mr & Mrs Conroy**
2 **BUNKER BAY (IRE),** 4, b g Australia—Alf Guineas (IRE) **Kennet Valley Thoroughbreds X**
3 **CHECKANDCHALLENGE,** 4, b br c Fast Company (IRE)—Likeable **Mr A. Hetherton**
4 **DUAL IDENTITY (IRE),** 5, b g Belardo (IRE)—Teide Lady **Kennet Valley Thoroughbreds IV**
5 **GAUNTLET (IRE),** 6, b g Galileo (IRE)—Danedrop (IRE) **J & P Seabrook & Tim Fisher**
6 **KING OF THE SOUTH (IRE),** 6, b g Kingman—South Atlantic (USA) **S. Ali**
7 **LORDSBRIDGE GIRL,** 4, b f Adaay (IRE)—Tempting **Mr R. Beadle & Mrs S. Beadle**
8 **MOKTASAAB,** 5, ch g Lope de Vega (IRE)—Dash To The Front **Mr H. Redknapp**
9 **REGAL ENVOY (IRE),** 4, b g Ardad (IRE)—Regina **Oakman Racing Club**
10 **SECRET TRYST,** 4, b f Brazen Beau (AUS)—Keep The Secret **Mr & Mrs N. Welby**
11 **SIR BUSKER (IRE),** 7, b g Sir Prancealot (IRE)—Street Kitty (IRE) **Kennet Valley Thoroughbreds Xi Racing**
12 **SPRING GLOW,** 6, gr m Mukhadram—Spring Dream
13 **SUNDAYINMAY (GER),** 5, b m Pastorius (GER)—Simply Noble (GER) **Mrs R. Baenziger-Gisi**

THREE-YEAR-OLDS

14 **AL TARFA,** b g Sea The Moon (GER)—Shegotloose (USA) **Promenade Bloodstock Limited**
15 **BEACH KITTY (IRE),** b f Gustav Klimt (IRE)—Street Kitty (IRE) **John & Peter Seabrook & Mrs Ann Foley**
16 **BEN DIKDUK (IRE),** ch g New Approach (IRE)—Halima Hatun (USA) **Mr A. Menahi**
17 **CHARTWELL HOUSE (IRE),** b g Churchill (IRE)—Ihtifal **Kennet Valley Thoroughbreds XIV**
18 **FIRST CUT,** b g Zoustar (AUS)—Brazilian Style **P. L. Winkworth**
19 **GOLDEN MOON,** b g Havana Gold (IRE)—Sorella Bella (IRE) **Park & Three**
20 **HOLKHAM BAY,** b g Aclaim (IRE)—Tumblewind **Norfolk Thoroughbreds**
21 **LORD LOUIS (IRE),** gr g Kodiac—Natheer (USA) **Mr J. I. Barnett**
22 **LORDSBRIDGE BLU,** b c Havana Grey—Tempting **Mr R. Beadle & Mrs S. Beadle**
23 **PARADISE ROW (IRE),** b f Zoffany (IRE)—Poplar Close (IRE) **J.I. Barnett & Rathmoy Racing**
24 **PRINCESS MILA (IRE),** br f Golden Horn—Qaafeya (IRE) **Mr J. I. Barnett**
25 **RED HAT EAGLE,** b g Gleneagles (IRE)—Sabaweeya **Pmg Partnership**
26 **STORY HORSE,** b g Bated Breath—Salutare (IRE) **Badger's Set III**
27 **SWIFT HAWK,** b g Hawkbill (USA)—Zacheta **S. Ali**
28 Ch f Intello (GER)—Westadora (IRE) **Mr & Mrs N. Welby**

TWO-YEAR-OLDS

29 **BEACH POINT (IRE),** br c 01/04 Blue Point (IRE)—Damselfly (IRE) (Power) (45000) **John & Peter Seabrook**
30 Ch c 13/02 Territories (IRE)—Brief Visit (Fastnet Rock (AUS)) (20008)
31 Br c 25/01 Highland Reel (IRE)—Four Eleven (CAN) (Arch (USA)) (52021) **Kennet Valley Thoroughbreds XII**
32 B f 06/03 Churchill (IRE)—Giennah (IRE) (Tamayuz) (14000) **Rathmoy Racing II**
33 Gr ro f 22/04 Frosted—Hawana
34 B f 10/02 Ten Sovereigns (IRE)—I Remember You (IRE) (Australia) **Mr & Mrs N. Welby**

MR WILLIAM KNIGHT - continued

35 B c 08/03 Lightning Spear—One Pixel (Primo Valentino (IRE)) (3000) **Badger's Set**
36 **ROYAL VELVET,** b f 26/03 Lightning Spear—Velvet Morn (IRE) (Epaulette (AUS)) **Mrs S. K. Hartley**
37 **STANDBACKANDLOOK,** b c 14/03 U S Navy Flag (USA)—
Chelsey Jayne (IRE) (Galileo (IRE)) (45000) **Mr A. Hetherton**
38 **SUGARLOAF LENNY (IRE),** b c 26/02 Land Force (IRE)—Ebb (Acclamation) (22409) **Caught Short Partnership**
39 **TIME SIGNATURE,** b c 25/01 Dark Angel (IRE)—Betty F (Frankel) (120000) **Wardley Bloodstock**

Assistant Trainer: Kayleigh Flower.

304 MR HILAL KOBEISSI, Newmarket

Postal: **8 Tom Jennings Close, Newmarket, Suffolk, CB8 0DU**
Contacts: **PHONE 07856 067990**
EMAIL hilalkob@live.com

TWO-YEAR-OLDS

1 B c 22/04 Ribchester (IRE)—Mad Existence (IRE) (Val Royal (FR)) (50000)
2 B c 30/04 Zoustar (AUS)—Purr Along (Mount Nelson) (36000)

---

305 MR DANIEL & CLAIRE KUBLER, Lambourn

Postal: **Sarsen Farm, Upper Lambourn, Hungerford, Berkshire, RG17 8RG**
Contacts: **PHONE 07984 287254**

1 **ABBEY HEIGHTS,** 5, b g Dark Angel (IRE)—Ducissa **Mr & Mrs G. Middlebrook**
2 **ANDALEEP (IRE),** 7, b g Siyouni (FR)—Oriental Magic (GER) **Mr J. T. Finch**
3 **ASTRO KING (IRE),** 6, b g Kingman—Astroglia (USA) **Kubler Racing Ltd**
4 **BOWLAND PARK,** 5, b g New Bay—Distinctive **Mr & Mrs G. Middlebrook**
5 **CLOSENESS,** 5, b m Iffraaj—Pack Together **Mr L. D. New**
6 **DON'T TELL CLAIRE,** 6, gr m Gutaifan (IRE)—Avenbury **Mr A. Stonehill**
7 **FISCAL POLICY (IRE),** 4, ch g Profitable (IRE)—Penny's Gift **Mr & Mrs G. Middlebrook**
8 **FLEETING LIGHT,** 4, b f Pearl Secret—Zophilly (IRE) **Mrs M. J. Hebbard**
9 **GLAM PUSS,** 5, b m Paco Boy (IRE)—La Donacella **Ms V. O'Sullivan**
10 **HELM ROCK,** 5, b g Pivotal—Nibbling (IRE) **Capture the Moment VII**
11 **LIL GUFF,** 4, b f Twilight Son—Lady McGuffy (IRE) **H. M. W. Clifford**
12 **OUTRAGE,** 11, ch g Exceed And Excel (AUS)—Ludynosa (USA) **Kubler Racing Ltd**
13 **PERCY'S LAD,** 5, ch g Sir Percy—Victory Garden **Mr A. Kerr**
14 **PRESENTLY,** 4, b f Time Test—Rosaceous **Mr & Mrs G. Middlebrook**
15 **SOUTHWOLD (IRE),** 4, b g Gleneagles (IRE)—Intrigue **Mr & Mrs G. Middlebrook**

THREE-YEAR-OLDS

16 **AIRA FORCE,** b f Oasis Dream—Dubai Affair **Mr & Mrs G. Middlebrook**
17 **BELATED,** b g Bobby's Kitten (USA)—Elation (IRE) **Mr & Mrs G. Middlebrook**
18 **CIARA PEARL,** b f Twilight Son—Upskittled **Mr A. Stonehill**
19 **CITY CYCLONE,** ch g Cityscape—Dubai Cyclone (USA) **Wayne Clifford & Ian Gosden**
20 **DALATARA,** b br f New Approach (IRE)—Dalasyla (IRE) **Maureen Coxon & Partners**
21 **DECEIVER,** b g Cracksman—Penny Drops **Oakmere Homes (North West) Ltd**
22 B g Invincible Spirit (IRE)—Distinctive **Mr & Mrs G. Middlebrook**
23 **DON'T TELL ROSIE,** gr f Telescope (IRE)—Crocus Rose **Wayne Clifford & Ian Gosden**

MR DANIEL & CLAIRE KUBLER - continued

24 **ELTERWATER,** b f Camelot—Acquainted **Mr & Mrs G. Middlebrook**
25 **EVENING STORY,** b f New Bay—Penny Rose **Mr & Mrs G. Middlebrook**
26 **FOREST DEMON (IRE),** b g Gustav Klimt (IRE)—Black Meyeden (FR) **Capture The Moment IX**
27 **JUBILEE PARTY,** ch g Ruler of The World (IRE)—Jubilant Lady (USA) **Mr & Mrs G. Middlebrook**
28 B c Poet's Word (IRE)—Kelamita (IRE) **Wayne Clifford & Ian Gosden**
29 B c Outstrip—La Donacella **Ms V. O'Sullivan**
30 **LOWICK (USA),** gr ro f The Factor (USA)—Chime Hope (USA) **Mr & Mrs G. Middlebrook**
31 **MOONDIAL,** b f Time Test—Quiet Elegance **Diskovery Partnership X**
32 **RAIMUNDA (USA),** b br f Blame (USA)—Volver (IRE) **Mr & Mrs G. Middlebrook**
33 **SILVER LEAF,** gr f Ribchester (IRE)—Albertine Rose **Mr & Mrs G. Middlebrook**
34 **SOLAR PORTRAIT (IRE),** b g Zoffany (IRE)—Future Energy **Innovate Racing**
35 **STATE OF HARMONY,** b f Territories (IRE)—Optimism **Mr & Mrs G. Middlebrook**

TWO-YEAR-OLDS

36 B gr c 05/03 Profitable (IRE)—Albertine Rose (Namid) (20952) **Mr & Mrs G. Middlebrook**
37 **AMONGST THE STARS,** b f 22/02 Sea The Moon (GER)—Choral Festival (Pivotal)
38 Ch f 05/03 Profitable (IRE)—Avenbury (Mount Nelson) (12405) **Mr A. Stonehill**
39 **CRIMSON SPIRIT,** b c 04/03 Harry Angel (IRE)—Fanrouge (IRE) (Red Clubs (IRE)) (25610) **Innovate Racing I**
40 B f 26/01 Zoustar (AUS)—Dream To Reality (Australia) **Mr & Mrs G. Middlebrook**
41 B f 24/04 Dark Angel (IRE)—Ducissa (Exceed And Excel (AUS)) **Mr & Mrs G. Middlebrook**
42 B c 20/04 Study of Man (IRE)—Elation (IRE) (Invincible Spirit (IRE)) **Mr & Mrs G. Middlebrook**
43 **ELLATRON (IRE),** b f 05/03 Caravaggio (USA)—
Dellaguista (IRE) (Sea The Stars (IRE)) (33333) **David & Yvonne Blunt**
44 **EXPERT ELSA,** b f 03/02 Expert Eye—Dubai Cyclone (USA) (Bernardini (USA)) (9000) **Alex & Julia Lukas**
45 **LA VERITE,** b f 15/03 Oasis Dream—Undeniable (Kyllachy) (3810)
46 B f 14/04 Saxon Warrior (JPN)—Mama Quilla (USA) (Smart Strike (CAN)) **Mr & Mrs G. Middlebrook**
47 B c 01/02 Inns of Court (IRE)—Pearly Brooks (Efisio) (20952) **Diskovery XI**
48 B f 04/05 Invincible Spirit (IRE)—Penny's Gift (Tobougg (IRE)) **Mr & Mrs G. Middlebrook**
49 B f 27/04 New Bay—Poetic Queen (IRE) (Dylan Thomas (IRE)) **Mr & Mrs G. Middlebrook**
50 B f 05/03 Land Force (IRE)—Rosaceous (Duke of Marmalade (IRE)) (25000) **Mr & Mrs G. Middlebrook**
51 Gr c 09/03 Blue Point (IRE)—Rose Diamond (IRE) (Daylami (IRE)) (70000) **Mr & Mrs G. Middlebrook**
52 Ch c 07/03 National Defense—Runway Giant (USA) (Giant's Causeway (USA)) (22409) **Capture The Moment XI**
53 B f 13/03 Due Diligence (USA)—Savannah's Show (Showcasing) (25000) **H. M. W. Clifford**
54 B c 24/03 Cable Bay (IRE)—Shamandar (FR) (Exceed And Excel (AUS)) (51429) **Capture The Moment X**
55 Ch c 21/03 Showcasing—Winifred Jo (Bahamian Bounty) (44000) **Mr & Mrs G. Middlebrook**

---

306 MR TOM LACEY, Woolhope

Postal: **Sapness Farm, Hereford, Herefordshire, County of, HR1 4RJ**
Contacts: **MOBILE 07768 398604**
EMAIL tom@cottagefield.co.uk WEBSITE www.cottagefield.co.uk

1 **ADRIMEL (FR),** 8, b br g Tirwanako (FR)—Irise De Gene (FR) **Lady C. Bamford & Miss A. Bamford**
2 **BANNOW BAY BOY (IRE),** 5, ch g Doyen (IRE)—Caedlih Davis (FR) **Mr D. Kellett**
3 **BEAN NORTY,** 7, gr m Malinas (GER)—Bouncing Bean **Ford Associated Racing Team**
4 4, Gr g Jukebox Jury (IRE)—Belle Fortune (IRE) **Mr Jerry Hinds & Mr Ashley Head**
5 **BIG BLUE MOON,** 6, b g Pether's Moon (IRE)—Don And Gerry (IRE) **Barrett, Meredith, Panniers, Wilde**
6 **BLOW YOUR WAD (IRE),** 5, b g Walk In The Park (IRE)—Molly's Mate (IRE) **Mr Jerry Hinds & Mr Ashley Head**
7 **BLUEBELLA,** 5, b m Blue Bresil (FR)—Henri Bella **Mrs T. P. James**
8 **CALL ME ARTHUR (IRE),** 4, ch g Soldier of Fortune (IRE)—Uliana (USA) **Mr C. B. Compton**
9 **CRUZ CONTROL (FR),** 6, b g Saint des Saints (FR)—En La Cruz (FR) **Mr F Green & Mr J Chinn**
10 **DANCING PAST,** 5, b m Passing Glance—Rebekah Rabbit (IRE) **Mr P. J. H. Wills**
11 **DIBBLE DECKER (IRE),** 7, b g Jet Away—Bella Minna (IRE) **ValueRacingClub.co.uk**
12 **DORKING BOY,** 9, ch g Schiaparelli (GER)—Megasue **Galloping On The South Downs Partnership**
13 **ELOGIO (IRE),** 4, b g Aclaim (IRE)—Scholarly **Roma Fittings Ltd t/a Plumbing World**
14 **FLASHY BOY (IRE),** 6, b g Sageburg (IRE)—Shining Lights (IRE) **N. R. A. Sutton**

MR TOM LACEY - continued

15 **GETAWAY TOM (IRE),** 5, b g Getaway (GER)—La Scala Diva (IRE) **Mr L. R. Attrill**
16 **GINNY'S DESTINY (IRE),** 7, b g Yeats (IRE)—Dantes Term (IRE) **Gordon & Su Hall**
17 **GLORY AND FORTUNE (IRE),** 8, b g Fame And Glory—Night Heron (IRE) **Mr J. Hinds**
18 **HIGHSTAKESPLAYER (IRE),** 7, b g Ocovango—Elivette (FR) **Mr Jerry Hinds & Mr Ashley Head**
19 **HOWLINGMADMURDOCK (IRE),** 6, b g Soldier of Fortune (IRE)—Bell Storm (IRE) **ValueRacingClub.co.uk**
20 **IKALIMIX (FR),** 5, b g Al Namix (FR)—Tersina (FR) **Mr L. R. Attrill**
21 **IMMORTAL FAME (IRE),** 7, b g Fame And Glory—Calverleigh Court (IRE) **Mr F. J. Allen**
22 **IMPERIAL ALEX (IRE),** 6, b g Imperial Monarch (IRE)—What Can I Say (IRE) **HFT Forklifts Limited**
23 **IVETWIGGEDIT,** 6, b m Schiaparelli (GER)—Southern Exit
24 4, B g Sholokhov (IRE)—Kaffie **Mr D. Kellett**
25 **KENNYS GIFT,** 4, b g Dartmouth—Come On Annie **Mrs E. V. A. Trotman**
26 **KIMBERLITE CANDY (IRE),** 11, b g Flemensfirth (USA)—Mandys Native (IRE) **Mr T. F. Lacey**
27 **LAMANVER STORM,** 8, b g Geordieland (FR)—Lamanver Homerun **Dr D. Christensen**
28 **LOSSIEMOUTH,** 8, b g Makfi—First Bloom (USA) **Lady N. F. Cobham**
29 **LUTTRELL LAD (IRE),** 7, b g Beat Hollow—Fairly Definite (IRE) **Owners for Owners Luttrell Lad**
30 **MACFIN (IRE),** 7, br g Dylan Thomas (IRE)—Justfour (IRE) **Mr T. F. Lacey**
31 **MAJOR FORTUNE (IRE),** 5, b g Soldier of Fortune (IRE)—
Numero Huit (IRE) **Noel Fehily Racing Syndicate-Major Fortu**
32 **MASKED MATGIL (FR),** 5, b m Masked Marvel—Matgil (FR) **Miss J. K. Allison**
33 **MONTREGARD (FR),** 4, ch c Joshua Tree (IRE)—Protektion (FR) **Mr J. P. McManus**
34 **NEVILLE'S CROSS (IRE),** 8, b g Stowaway—Dancing Bird (IRE) **Mr F Green & Mr J Chinn**
35 **NOCTE VOLATUS,** 8, b g Midnight Legend—Aeronautica (IRE) **Lady Cobham & Dauntsey Park**
36 **OPERATION MANNA,** 7, b g Champs Elysees—Vickers Vimy **Lady N. F. Cobham**
37 **POUNDING POET (IRE),** 7, b g Yeats (IRE)—Pestal And Mortar (IRE) **Mrs T. P. James**
38 **ROCK ON HARRY (IRE),** 7, b g Yeats (IRE)—Knockmehill Lady (IRE) **ValueRacingClub.co.uk**
39 **ROCKY HILL,** 6, gr g Kingston Hill—Blue Nymph **Mr F Green & Mr J Chinn**
40 **ROGER RAREBIT,** 6, b g Black Sam Bellamy (IRE)—Rebekah Rabbit (IRE) **Mr P. J. H. Wills**
41 **SCIPION (IRE),** 7, b g Shantou (USA)—Morning Calm **Mr Jerry Hinds & Mr Ashley Head**
42 **SEBASTOPOL (IRE),** 9, b g Fame And Glory—Knockcroghery (IRE) **& Boultbee Brooks**
43 **STEEL MY THUNDER (IRE),** 5, b g Zambezi Sun—Ask Carol (IRE) **ValueRacingClub.co.uk**
44 **SYR MAFFOS (IRE),** 5, b g Mount Nelson—Maple Mons (IRE) **Mrs T. P. James**
45 **TEA CLIPPER (IRE),** 8, b g Stowaway—A Plus Ma Puce (FR) **Mr Jerry Hinds & Mr Ashley Head**
46 **TEN LENGTHS TOM (IRE),** 4, ch g Mount Nelson—Tarentine (FR) **Mr Jerry Hinds & Mr Ashley Head**
47 **THE COX EXPRESS,** 4, b g Cityscape—Capestar (IRE) **D & J Newell**
48 **TOO MUCH HAMMER (IRE),** 4, b g Leading Light (IRE)—Joan's Girl (IRE) **Mr Jerry Hinds & Mr Ashley Head**
49 **TOP KAP (IRE),** 5, br g Kapgarde (FR)—Rose Indienne (FR) **Noel Fehily Racing Syndicate - Top Kap**
50 **TOWNHILL (IRE),** 5, ch g Presenting—Ladies Pride (IRE) **N. R. A. Sutton**
51 4, Ch f Proconsul—Where The Boys Are (IRE) **Mr P. A. Wilkins**
52 **YES NO MAYBE SO (IRE),** 9, br g Stowaway—Godlylady (IRE) **Mr T. F. Lacey**

Head Lad: Mr Eamonn O'Donnabhain.

NH Jockey: Tom Bellamy, Johnny Burke, Stan Sheppard. **Conditional Jockey:** Cameron Iles.

---

307 MR JUSTIN LANDY, Leyburn

Postal: **2 Beckwood, Spennithorne, Leyburn, North Yorkshire, DL8 5FB**
EMAIL jlandyracing@hotmail.com

1 **CORMACKSTOWN ROAD (IRE),** 8, b g Imperial Monarch (IRE)—Accordion To Pat (IRE) **Mrs P. Southerington**
2 **DO NO WRONG (IRE),** 7, br g Sageburg (IRE)—Uncommited (IRE) **Mrs P. Southerington**
3 **JIMVALE (IRE),** 6, b g Imperial Monarch (IRE)—Silver Serenade (IRE) **Mr J. P. G. Landy**
4 **LALOCHEZIA (IRE),** 8, ch g Shirocco (GER)—Flemens Pride **Mrs P. Southerington**
5 **LLEYTON (IRE),** 11, b br g Kalanisi (IRE)—Bonnie Parker (IRE) **Pauline & Camilla Southerington**
6 **MOONLIGHT BEAM (IRE),** 8, b g Kalanisi (IRE)—Assidua (IRE) **Mrs P. Southerington**
7 **RUMBLE B (IRE),** 9, b g Presenting—John's Eliza (IRE) **Miss C. Tinkler**

308 MISS EMMA LAVELLE, Marlborough

Postal: **Bonita Racing Stables, Ogbourne Maizey, Marlborough, Wiltshire, SN8 1RY**
Contacts: **PHONE 01672 511544 MOBILE 07774 993998 FAX 01672 511544**
EMAIL info@emmalavelle.com WEBSITE www.emmalavelle.com

1 **AHEAD OF THE FIELD (IRE),** 8, ch g Flemensfirth (USA)—Last of The Bunch **Andy & The Frisky Fillies**
2 **ARTEMISION,** 7, b g Gentlewave (IRE)—Miss Fahrenheit (IRE) **T K Racing Ltd**
3 **AUBA ME YANG (IRE),** 7, b g Fame And Glory—No Bodys Flame (IRE) **Mr N. Farrell**
4 **BERTIE BLUE,** 6, b g Blue Bresil (FR)—Madame Allsorts **Biltmore Syndicate**
5 **BETHPAGE (IRE),** 5, b m Getaway (GER)—Princess Knapping (IRE) **Bonita Racing Club**
6 **BIG FISH (IRE),** 5, b g Flemensfirth (USA)—Tweedledrum **N. Mustoe**
7 **CANTY BAY (IRE),** 6, b g Shantou (USA)—Afairs (IRE) **Mr G. P. MacIntosh**
8 **CAPTAIN BROOMFIELD (IRE),** 7, b g Arakan (USA)—Presenting d'Azy (IRE) **Mr A. Gemmell**
9 **CLASSIC KING (IRE),** 5, b g Champs Elysees—Hangar Six (IRE) **Mr & Mrs W & Dr T Davies & Mrs T Grundy**
10 **CONNOLLY (IRE),** 5, b g Califet (FR)—Bartlemy Bell (IRE) **Syders & Burkes**
11 **DAGUENEAU (IRE),** 8, b g Champs Elysees—Bright Enough **Mr A. Gemmell**
12 **DE RASHER COUNTER,** 11, b g Yeats (IRE)—Dedrunknmunky (IRE) **Makin' Bacon Partnership**
13 **DO YOU THINK,** 7, b m So You Think (NZ)—Leblon (IRE) **Bonita Racing Club**
14 **DOUGHMORE BAY (IRE),** 5, b g Milan—Ross Bay (IRE) **Mighty Acorn Stables**
15 **DREAM IN THE PARK (IRE),** 6, b g Walk In The Park (IRE)—Old Dreams (IRE) **P. G. Jacobs**
16 **EUREKA CREEK (IRE),** 7, b m Jet Away—Copper River (IRE) **Sailing to Byzantium**
17 **FLEMCARA (IRE),** 11, b g Flemensfirth (USA)—Cara Mara (IRE) **Andy & The Frisky Fillies**
18 **FLIGHT OF FREEDOM (IRE),** 5, b m Getaway (GER)—Dahara (FR) **The Cheltenham & South West Racing Club**
19 **FLYING NUN (IRE),** 8, b m Robin des Champs (FR)—Mystic Masie (IRE) **N. Mustoe & A. Gemmell**
20 **GALLOPING PRIDE (IRE),** 6, b g Yeats (IRE)—Rostellan (IRE) **The Diamonds**
21 4, B c Soldier of Fortune (IRE)—Gaye Memories **Mrs N. C. Turner**
22 **GENERAL MEDRANO (IRE),** 6, b g Ocovango—Talween **Elite Racing 003**
23 **GOLD LINK (FR),** 7, b g Rail Link—Une de Montot (FR) **Owners Group 057**
24 **GREY FOX (IRE),** 6, gr g Gutaifan (IRE)—Boucheron **Mrs Jennifer Simpson Racing**
25 **GROOVY BLUE,** 4, b g Blue Bresil (FR)—Miss Izzy (IRE) **Mr D. Donoghue**
26 **GUARD DUTY,** 6, b g Kapgarde (FR)—Ile de See (FR) **Owners Group 074**
27 **HANG IN THERE (IRE),** 9, b g Yeats (IRE)—Jaldemosa (FR) **Tim Syder & Andrew Gemmell**
28 **HARDY FELLA (IRE),** 6, b g Libertarian—Combustible Spirit (IRE) **Mighty Acorn Stables**
29 **HAWK'S WELL (IRE),** 9, b g Yeats (IRE)—Our Song **Mrs N. Turner & Mrs E. Fenton**
30 **HUNTING BROOK (IRE),** 6, b g Presenting—Fleur d'Ainay (FR) **Bryan & Philippa Burrough**
31 **IRISH PROPHECY (IRE),** 10, b g Azamour (IRE)—Prophets Honor (FR) **N. Mustoe**
32 **JEMIMA P (IRE),** 9, b m Jeremy (USA)—Peig Alainn (IRE) **The Three A's Syndicate**
33 **JESUILA DES MOTTES (FR),** 4, b f Voiladenuo (FR)—
Ouhetu des Mottes (FR) **KSB Bloodstock & Mrs Celia Djivanovic**
34 **JIGGAWAY,** 4, b f Telescope (IRE)—Jiggalong **Penn Wood Racing**
35 **KILLER CLOWN (IRE),** 9, b g Getaway (GER)—Our Soiree (IRE) **Burkes & Syders**
36 **KING'S THRESHOLD (IRE),** 6, b g Yeats (IRE)—Pearl Buttons **Sailing to Byzantium**
37 **LADY CARO (IRE),** 5, b m Soldier of Fortune (IRE)—
Springinherstep (IRE) **Alison & Tony Millett & Charles Dingwall**
38 **LIGHT N STRIKE (IRE),** 7, b g Leading Light (IRE)—One Rose **Salvo & Alex Giannini, N.Farrell**
39 **MANORBANK (IRE),** 8, b g Arcadio (GER)—Kind Word (IRE) **Owners Group 065**
40 **MASTER MILLINER (IRE),** 7, ch g Helmet (AUS)—Aqualina (IRE) **Mrs Jennifer Simpson Racing**
41 **MIKHAILA (IRE),** 5, b m Sholokhov (IRE)—Turica (IRE) **Alison & Tony Millett & Emma Fenton**
42 **MINELLA BUSTER (IRE),** 7, br g Beat Hollow—Itsallaracket (IRE) **The Pick 'N' Mix Partnership**
43 **MUMBO JUMBO (IRE),** 7, b g Califet (FR)—Touched By Angels (IRE) **N. Mustoe**
44 **MUSKOKA (IRE),** 5, b g Milan—Fine Fortune (IRE) **Mrs P. J. Travis**
45 **MY SILVER LINING (IRE),** 7, gr m Cloudings (IRE)—Welsh Connection (IRE) **Mrs C. J. Djivanovic**
46 **NOLLYADOR (FR),** 6, b g No Risk At All (FR)—Playa du Charmil (FR) **Highclere Thoroughbred Racing -Nollyador**
47 **ONEANDAHALFDEGREES (IRE),** 5, ch m Flemensfirth (USA)—Leading Lady **The High Altitude Partnership**
48 **PAISLEY PARK (IRE),** 11, b g Oscar (IRE)—Presenting Shares (IRE) **Mr A. Gemmell**
49 **PEMBERLEY (IRE),** 10, b g Darsi (FR)—Eyebright (IRE) **Laurie Kimber & Partners**
50 **POINT HIM OUT (USA),** 6, b g Point of Entry (USA)—Rahy's Colors (USA) **H.Pridham & D.Donoghue**
51 **PORTER IN THE PARK (IRE),** 6, b m Walk In The Park (IRE)—
Benefit of Porter (IRE) **Andrew Gemmell & Richard Lavelle**
52 **QUEEN ANTOINETTE,** 6, ch m Champs Elysees—Queen's Star **Mrs C. L. Bonner**
53 5, B m Mukhadram—Queen's Star **Mrs C. L. Bonner**

MISS EMMA LAVELLE - continued

54 **RAJARAN (FR),** 6, gr g Martaline—Ravna (FR) **The High Altitude Partnership**
55 **REBEL INTENTIONS (IRE),** 6, b g Aiken—Robin's Solo (IRE) **Hoe Racing**
56 **RED ROOKIE,** 8, ch g Black Sam Bellamy (IRE)—Auction Belle **The Hawk Inn Syndicate 3**
57 **ROCKET MAN (GER),** 4, b g Maxios—Royal Princess (GER) **N. Mustoe**
58 **ROCKY LAKE (IRE),** 7, b g Presenting—Cool Quest (IRE) **Exors of the Late Mr T. J. Hemmings**
59 **ROSALYS (IRE),** 4, b f Workforce—Saturday Girl **Mrs C. L. Bonner**
60 **RUNSWICK BAY,** 8, b g Arvico (FR)—Chantal **The Hon J. R. Drummond**
61 **SAM BARTON,** 8, b g Black Sam Bellamy (IRE)—Bartons Bride (IRE) **Exors of the Late Mr T. J. Hemmings**
62 **SHANG TANG (IRE),** 9, b g Shantou (USA)—Ballyguider Bridge (IRE) **T. Syder & N. Mustoe**
63 **SILVER THORN,** 4, gr g Martaline—Miracle Maid **Syders & Burkes**
64 **TABLE THIRTY FOUR,** 6, br g Blue Bresil (FR)—Whoops A Daisy **V.Burke, T.Syder & Mrs D.L.Whateley**
65 **TARAHUMARA,** 7, b g Kayf Tara—My World (FR) **N. Turner & C. Schicht**
66 **TEDWIN HILLS (IRE),** 6, b g Getaway (GER)—Ashwell Lady (IRE) **Mr S. W. Turner**
67 **THE STREET (IRE),** 7, b g Fame And Glory—Baileys Partytime **Exors of the Late Mr T. J. Hemmings**
68 **TIGHTENOURBELTS (IRE),** 6, b g Mahler—Miss McGoldrick (IRE) **Salvo Giannini & Andrew Gemmell**
69 **TWO TO TANGO,** 5, b g Kayf Tara—Folie Dancer **J.R. Lavelle & Paul G. Jacobs**
70 **VOICE OF CALM,** 7, b m Poet's Voice—Marliana (IRE) **Tim Syder & Hungerford Park Partnership**
71 **WHAT'S ONE MORE (IRE),** 4, ch f Mount Nelson—Madame Stella (FR) **Bonita Racing Club**
72 **WILD WILBUR (IRE),** 7, ch g Presenting—Kon Tiky (FR) **Mr & Mrs W & Dr T Davies & Mrs T Grundy**
73 **WOOLBERRY,** 4, ch f Jack Hobbs—Woolstone One **P. G. Jacobs**
74 **WOULDUBEWELL (IRE),** 9, b m Gold Well—Howrwedoin (IRE) **Owners Group 063**
75 **YOUNG BUTLER (IRE),** 7, b g Yeats (IRE)—Name For Fame (USA) **Burkes & Syders**
76 **ZARAFSHAN (IRE),** 7, b g Shamardal (USA)—Zarshana (IRE) **Mr R. J. Lavelle**

THREE-YEAR-OLDS

77 **GREY OWL,** gr c Australia—Dijlah **Mrs Jennifer Simpson Racing**
78 **HAWK JET,** b f Hawkbill (USA)—Taleteller (USA) **Mr S. P. Barry**

Assistant Trainer: Barry Fenton.

---

309 MR TOBY LAWES, Beare Green

Postal: **Henfold House Cottage, Henfold Lane, Beare Green, Dorking, Surrey, RH5 4RW**
EMAIL toby@tobylawesracing.com

1 **ALKOPOP (GER),** 9, gr g Jukebox Jury (IRE)—Alkeste (GER) **Mr Andrew & Sarah Wates**
2 **ARCADIAN ROSE,** 4, b f It's Gino (GER)—Protektrice (FR) **Mr T. Swerling**
3 4, B f Walk In The Park (IRE)—Betty Roe (IRE) **Mr A. J. McGladdery**
4 **BRIAR BANK,** 4, b g Garswood—Push Me (IRE) **Kent and Borders Syndicate**
5 **CHANCELLORSTOWN (IRE),** 5, b g Cloudings (IRE)—Joyride (GER) **Mr Andrew & Sarah Wates**
6 **DUHALLOW TOMMY (IRE),** 5, b g Dylan Thomas (IRE)—Grannie Liz (IRE) **Mr J. Terry**
7 **HAUL AWAY (IRE),** 10, b g Stowaway—Lisacul Queen (IRE) **R. M. Kirkland**
8 **KANNAPOLIS (IRE),** 8, b g Makfi—Alta Definizione (IRE) **Henfold Harriers**
9 **KAP AUTEUIL (FR),** 8, b g Kapgarde (FR)—Turboka (FR) **Mr Andrew & Sarah Wates**
10 **MISTER WHO (IRE),** 6, ch g Sholokhov (IRE)—Gortnagowna (IRE) **R. M. Kirkland**
11 **NASHVILLE NIPPER (IRE),** 9, b g Millenary—Benfrasea (IRE) **Beare With Us Wheeler, Hawkins & Copley**
12 **NICKOBOY (FR),** 8, b g Full of Gold (FR)—Dikanika (FR) **Mr Andrew & Sarah Wates**
13 **ONEWAYORTOTHER (FR),** 5, b g Great Pretender (IRE)—Betwixt (IRE) **Mr Andrew & Sarah Wates**
14 **REALTA ROYALE,** 5, b m Pether's Moon (IRE)—Sky Calling **Mr M. J. Allen**
15 **SILENT AUCTION,** 4, b f Blue Bresil (FR)—Odello **Eventmasters Racing**
16 **SUBLIME HEIGHTS (IRE),** 7, b g Arcadio (GER)—Corrag Lass (IRE) **Mr Andrew & Sarah Wates**
17 **SUPPORT ACT (IRE),** 5, b g Affinisea (IRE)—Carrigbuck (IRE) **The M Team**
18 **SURREY LORD (IRE),** 4, b g Getaway (GER)—Holly Royale (IRE) **Surrey Racing (SL)**
19 **THE BREW MASTER (IRE),** 6, b g Mahler—Raphuca (IRE) **R. M. Kirkland**
20 **TREVOR'S LAD (IRE),** 5, b g Milan—Jolie Landaise (FR) **Mr P. Mellett**
21 **ZACONY REBEL (IRE),** 8, b g Getaway (GER)—Bay Rebel (IRE) **Mr Andrew & Sarah Wates**

MR TOBY LAWES - continued

THREE-YEAR-OLDS

22 **ONE KNIGHT (IRE),** ch g Sir Percy—Woolstone One **P. G. Jacobs**

---

310 MISS KATE LECKENBY, Duns

Postal: **Lambden, Greenlaw, Duns, Berwickshire, TD10 6UN**
Contacts: **PHONE 01207 560491**
EMAIL farriersflight@gmail.com

1 **FEROCIOUS (IRE),** 9, b g Presenting—Accordingtoeileen (IRE) **Miss K. Leckenby**
2 **NIGHTS OF DOYEN (IRE),** 5, ch g Doyen (IRE)—Midnight Benefit (IRE) **Miss K. Leckenby**

---

311 MISS KERRY LEE, Byton, Powys

Postal: **Bell House, Byton, Presteigne, Powys, LD8 2HS**
Contacts: **MOBILE 07968 242663**
EMAIL kerry@kerrylee.co.uk WEBSITE www.kerrylee.co.uk

1 **ATLANTA BRAVE (IRE),** 5, b g Aizavoski (IRE)—Ominous Outcast (IRE) **W. Roseff**
2 **BALLYBEGG (IRE),** 8, b g Mahler—Rebel Flyer (IRE) **Glass Half Full**
3 **BLACK POPPY,** 7, b g Kayf Tara—Poppy Come Running (IRE) **West Coast Haulage Limited**
4 **DEMACHINE (IRE),** 9, b g Flemensfirth (USA)—Dancingonthemoon (IRE) **West Coast Haulage Limited**
5 **DESTINED TO SHINE (IRE),** 11, b g Dubai Destination (USA)—Good Shine (IRE) **Campbell-Mizen & Miss Kerry Lee**
6 **DO IT FOR THY SEN (IRE),** 9, ch g Mountain High (IRE)—Ashlings Princess (IRE) **R L Baker & R Lee**
7 **EATON COLLINA (IRE),** 8, b g Milan—Flowers On Sunday (IRE) **Mrs H. Watson**
8 **FAY CE QUE VOUDRAS (IRE),** 7, b m Getaway (GER)—Buck's Blue (FR) **W. Roseff**
9 **FINANCIER,** 10, ch g Dubawi (IRE)—Desired **W. Roseff**
10 **GREENROCK ABBEY (IRE),** 7, ch g El Salvador (IRE)—Aos Dana (IRE) **R L Baker & R Lee**
11 **HAVEN'T TIME (IRE),** 9, b g Curtain Time (IRE)—Good Thyne Lucy (IRE) **Miss S. L. McQueen**
12 **HELLFIRE PRINCESS,** 6, ch m Dunaden (FR)—Ryde Back **W. Roseff**
13 **HENRI LE BON (IRE),** 8, b g Sea The Stars (IRE)—Speed Song **W. Roseff**
14 **KESTREL VALLEY,** 9, b m Dr Massini (IRE)—Lady Karinga **Mrs J. M. Johnson**
15 **KINGS KEEPER (IRE),** 8, b g Getaway (GER)—Fingal's Sister (IRE) **Maurice Morgan Racing**
16 **KRAQUELINE (FR),** 6, gr m Martaline—Free Sky (FR) **West Coast Haulage Limited**
17 **MAGIC DANCER,** 11, b g Norse Dancer (IRE)—King's Siren (IRE) **The Magic Partnership**
18 **NEMEAN LION (GER),** 6, b g Golden Horn—Ninfea (GER) **W. Roseff**
19 **NEW FOUND FAME (IRE),** 7, b g Fame And Glory—Coco Opera (IRE) **West Coast Haulage Limited**
20 **NOT SURE (IRE),** 7, br g Presenting—Pink Mist (IRE) **W. Roseff**
21 **ORCHARD GROVE (IRE),** 7, b g Valirann (FR)—Little Vinnie (IRE) **Mr D. M. Morgan**
22 **PIMLICO POINT (IRE),** 6, ch g Flemensfirth (USA)—Royale Flag (FR) **W. Roseff**
23 **STORM CONTROL (IRE),** 10, b g September Storm (GER)—Double Dream (IRE) **W. Roseff**
24 **TOP GAMBLE (IRE),** 15, ch g Presenting—Zeferina (IRE) **Miss K. Lee**
25 **TOWN PARKS (IRE),** 12, b g Morozov (USA)—Outdoor Heather (IRE) **Mrs J. A. Beavan**

Assistant Trainer: Richard Lee.

NH Jockey: Richard Patrick.

312 MRS SOPHIE LEECH, Westbury-on-Severn

Postal: **T/A Leech Racing Limited, Tudor Racing Stables, Elton Road, Elton, Newnham, Gloucestershire, GL14 1JN**
Contacts: **PHONE 01452 760691 MOBILE 07775 874630**
EMAIL info@leechracing.co.uk WEBSITE www.leechracing.co.uk

1 **ADJALI (GER),** 8, b g Kamsin (GER)—Anabasis (GER) **The Has Been's**
2 **APPLESANDPIERRES (IRE),** 15, b g Pierre—Cluain Chaoin (IRE) **Exors of the Late C. J. Leech**
3 **CHESTNUT PETE,** 8, ch g Native Ruler—Rabbit **Mike Harris Racing Club**
4 **CLONDAW CIAN (IRE),** 13, br g Gold Well—Cocktail Bar (IRE) **G. D. Thompson**
5 **CRACKING SMART (FR),** 11, b g Great Pretender (IRE)—Maya du Frene (FR) **Mike Harris Racing Club & Partner**
6 **DEFILADE,** 7, b g Bated Breath—Zulema **Mike Harris Racing Club**
7 **DEMOISELLE KAP (FR),** 5, b m Kapgarde (FR)—Dabaratsa (FR) **J. L. Marriott**
8 **DESTRIER (FR),** 10, b g Voix du Nord (FR)—Razia (FR) **J. O'Brien**
9 **GARO DE JUILLEY (FR),** 11, b g Ungaro (GER)—Lucy de Juilley (FR) **G. D. Thompson**
10 6, Ch m Black Sam Bellamy (IRE)—Go For Coffee
11 **HYBRIS (FR),** 6, ch g Martaline—Oasice (FR) **Exors of the Late C. J. Leech**
12 **JOHN LOCKE,** 6, ch g Mastercraftsman (IRE)—Sacred Shield **Mr B. R. Halsall**
13 **LUCKY ONE (FR),** 8, br g Authorized (IRE)—Lady Anouchka (IRE) **Mr B. R. Halsall**
14 **MAILLOT BLANC,** 6, b g Sulamani (IRE)—Santoria (FR) **Happy Daze Racing Partnership**
15 **MAN OF PLENTY,** 14, ch g Manduro (GER)—Credit-A-Plenty **G. D. Thompson**
16 **MCGROARTY (IRE),** 12, b g Brian Boru—Uffizi (IRE) **The Has Been's**
17 **THE LONGEST DAY (IRE),** 7, b g Milan—Court Leader (IRE) **Exors of the Late C. J. Leech**
18 **THESE HAPPY DAZE,** 6, ch g Sholokhov (IRE)—Gaspaie (FR) **Happy Daze Racing Partnership**
19 **TRIBAL COMMANDER,** 7, gr g Intikhab (USA)—Jessica Ennis (USA) **Mike Harris Racing Club**
20 **VANITEUX (FR),** 14, br g Voix du Nord (FR)—Expoville (FR) **Mr C. R. Leech**

Assistant Trainer: Christian Leech.

---

313 MISS TRACEY LEESON, Maidford

Postal: **Glebe Stables, Blakesley Heath Farm, Maidford, Northants, NN12 8HN**
Contacts: **MOBILE 07761 537672**
EMAIL traceyl31@hotmail.co.uk WEBSITE www.traceyleesonracing.co.uk

1 **DELLBOY TROTTER (IRE),** 7, b g Dylan Thomas (IRE)—Super Daisy (IRE) **Mr P. A. Long**
2 **GODIVA'S BAY (IRE),** 9, b g Tobougg (IRE)—Ivy Lane (IRE) **Buzzing Again Partnership**
3 **HUNSBURY,** 5, b g Fast Company (IRE)—Nouvelle Lune **Mr P. A. Long**
4 **MASTER OF ALL (IRE),** 5, bl gr g Mastercraftsman (IRE)—That's My Style **The Blakesley Racing Club**
5 **MOROVAL (IRE),** 12, b g Morozov (USA)—Valerie Ellen (IRE) **The Blakesley Racing Club**
6 **NORTH SOUTH ROSIE (IRE),** 7, bl m Ocovango—South Street (IRE) **The Blakesley Racing Club**
7 **REMEMBER ALLY (FR),** 5, b g Sinndar (IRE)—Blue Lullaby (IRE) **Mr P. A. Long**
8 **SLEVE DONARD (IRE),** 9, b g Mountain High (IRE)—Ceart Go Leor (IRE) **The Blakesley Racing Club**
9 **TOP DRAWER (IRE),** 9, b g Doyen (IRE)—Merry Gladness (IRE) **The Peter Partnership**

---

314 MRS SHEILA LEWIS, Brecon

Postal: **Mill Service Station, Three Cocks, Brecon, Powys, LD3 0SL**
Contacts: **PHONE 01497 847081**
EMAIL sheilalewisracing1@gmail.com

1 **BEANNAIGH DO (IRE),** 6, b g Camelot—Thunder In Myheart (IRE) **Oaktree Racing Club**
2 **CHINOOK,** 5, b m Sea The Stars (IRE)—Papaya (IRE) **Oaktree Racing Club**
3 **COTTON END (IRE),** 9, gr m Scorpion (IRE)—Scartara (FR) **Mr G. Wilson**

MRS SHEILA LEWIS - continued

4 **FAMILY POT (FR),** 8, gr g Monitor Closely (IRE)—Nikitries (FR) **W. B. R. Davies**
5 **FASHION'S MODEL (IRE),** 7, gr m Flemensfirth (USA)—Fashion's Worth (IRE) **W. B. R. Davies**
6 **GRIS MAJEUR (FR),** 6, gr g Gris de Gris (IRE)—Partie Majeure (FR) **W. B. R. Davies**
7 **INGEBORG ZILLING (IRE),** 7, ch m Mahler—Lindy Lou **Mr R. M. O. Lloyd**
8 **IRON D'EX (FR),** 5, gr g Jeu St Eloi (FR)—Soiree d'Ex (FR) **Mr G. Wilson**
9 **MINNEIGH MOZZE (FR),** 7, gr m Phoenix Reach (IRE)—Mickie **Miss H. L. James**
10 **MISS PEARL (IRE),** 7, b m Mahler—Road To Pearls **Mr R. M. O. Lloyd**
11 **SINISTER MINISTER,** 8, gr g Malinas (GER)—Champagne Lil **Foxhunters In Mind**
12 **STRAW FAN JACK,** 8, gr g Geordieland (FR)—Callerlilly **Mr G. Wilson**
13 **TALKINGTHETALK (IRE),** 6, b m Aizavoski (IRE)—Talk of Rain (FR) **Mr G. Wilson**
14 **TOM O'ROUGHLEY (IRE),** 8, b g Yeats (IRE)—Thegoodwans Sister (IRE) **Oaktree Racing Club**
15 **VOLCANO (FR),** 9, gr g Martaline—Lyli Rose (FR) **W. B. R. Davies**

---

315 MR CRAIG LIDSTER, York

Postal: **Eboracum Racing Stables, Easingwold, Nr York, Yorkshire, YO61 3EN**
Contacts: **PHONE 07892 714425**

1 **BOBBY DALTON,** 4, b g Due Diligence (USA)—Nellie Ellis (IRE) **Lisa Thompson & Craig Lidster**
2 **CHESTER LE STREAK,** 4, ch g Hot Streak (IRE)—Serena's Pride **The Racing Emporium**
3 **DIVINE CONNECTION,** 6, b m Cable Bay (IRE)—Divine Power **Craig Lidster Racing Club**
4 **MASQUE OF ANARCHY (IRE),** 7, b g Sir Percy—Charming (IRE) **Mr C. Lidster**
5 **NOTEABLE (IRE),** 4, ch f Profitable (IRE)—Jenny Lind **Mrs W. Burdett**
6 **RESILIENCE,** 4, b g Aclaim (IRE)—Calypso Choir **Bradley & Wendy Burdett**
7 **STEP TO THE TOP (IRE),** 8, b m Doyen (IRE)—Step On My Soul (IRE) **Mr G. Wragg**
8 **THE MENSTONE GEM (IRE),** 4, ch g Galileo Gold—Masela (IRE) **JP Racing Club Limited**

THREE-YEAR-OLDS

9 **CAESARS PEARL (IRE),** b f Profitable (IRE)—Malilla (IRE) **Mrs W. Burdett**
10 **DICKIEBURD,** b g Cracksman—Lydia's Place **Bradley & Wendy Burdett**
11 **H KEY LAILS,** gr g Washington DC (IRE)—Natural Appeal (IRE) **White Rose Bloodstock**
12 **HAVANA BY THE SEA (IRE),** b f Havana Grey—Made of Talent **Wendy & Matthew Embleton**
13 **JUSTWATCHMESTRUGLE,** b g Bated Breath—Commence **Mrs W. Burdett**
14 **KANANGA,** b g Mondialiste (IRE)—Bondesire **Mr & Mrs G. Turnbull**
15 **KATAR (IRE),** b c Kessaar (IRE)—Applauding (IRE) **Syps & Mrs Wendy Burdett**
16 **LIOSA (IRE),** b c The Last Lion (IRE)—Sally Is The Boss (IRE) **Bradley & Wendy Burdett**
17 **SMILE AND PAY (IRE),** b g Kessaar (IRE)—Break Bread (IRE) **Craig Lidster Racing Club**
18 **TINTIN POTTER (IRE),** b c Kessaar (IRE)—Suffer Her (IRE) **Mrs W. Burdett**
19 **TOLLERTON FOREST,** b f Oasis Dream—Sommers Daughter (IRE) **Bradley & Wendy Burdett**
20 **WEEMISSGARYBLICK,** b f Pearl Secret—Indigo Beat **Craig Lidster Racing Club**
21 **WOWSHESOMTHINGELSE (IRE),** b f Exceed And Excel (AUS)—Delia Eria (IRE) **NE1 Racing Club**

TWO-YEAR-OLDS

22 **ALFA L'ANGEL,** b f 04/04 Tasleet—Ambriel (IRE) (Dark Angel (IRE)) (9000) **Wendy & A Jasper**
23 **CATENA (IRE),** b f 09/03 Cable Bay (IRE)—Koduro (IRE) (Kodiac) (46667) **Bradley & Wendy Burdett**
24 B br g 05/02 Unfortunately (IRE)—Clubbable (Mayson) (4002) **Mr M. J. Embleton**
25 Gr f 09/04 Outstrip—Cornlaw (Lawman (FR)) **Mr N. Bradley**
26 **EAST BANK,** b c 05/02 Aclaim (IRE)—Twist of Magic (IRE) (Arcano (IRE)) (20952) **Craig Lidster Racing Club**
27 B f 20/03 Land Force (IRE)—Ellen Gates (Mayson) (23000) **Mrs W. Burdett**
28 B f 04/04 Massaat (IRE)—High Speed (IRE) (Kodiac)
29 **HIGHLAND WELL,** b f 01/03 Highland Reel (IRE)—Bouvardia (Oasis Dream) (14000) **Bradley & Wendy Burdett**
30 B f 19/02 Inns of Court (IRE)—Masela (IRE) (Medicean) (23810) **Mrs W. Burdett**
31 B f 06/05 Ribchester (IRE)—Petite Georgia (IRE) (Camacho) (9204) **Bradley & Wendy Burdett**
32 B f 02/03 Massaat (IRE)—Piranha (IRE) (Exceed And Excel (AUS)) **Mrs W. Burdett**
33 B f 09/03 Havana Grey—Silhuette (IRE) (Canford Cliffs (IRE)) (19048) **Mrs W. Burdett**

MR CRAIG LIDSTER - continued

34 B c 27/03 Cotai Glory—Suaimhneach (IRE) (Vocalised (USA)) **White Rose Bloodstock**
35 Gr f 19/03 Havana Grey—Summerset (IRE) (Slade Power (IRE)) (20952) **Mrs W. Burdett**
36 Ch f 29/03 Profitable (IRE)—Surava (Big Bad Bob (IRE)) **Mrs W. Burdett**
37 **VITARLI (IRE),** b f 01/02 Adaay (IRE)—Inspirational (IRE) (Slade Power (IRE)) (14406) **Bradley & Wendy Burdett**
38 B f 18/02 Kessaar (IRE)—Would It Matter (IRE) (Morpheus) (11204) **Mrs W. Burdett**
39 B c 02/02 Due Diligence (USA)—Zelaniya (IRE) (Lawman (FR)) **Mrs W. Burdett**

---

316 MR BERNARD LLEWELLYN, Bargoed

Postal: **Ffynonau Duon Farm, Pentwyn, Fochriw, Bargoed, Mid Glamorgan, CF81 9NP**
Contacts: **PHONE 01685 841259 MOBILE 07960 151083, 07971 233473 FAX 01685 843838**
EMAIL bernard.llewellyn@btopenworld.com

1 **ADRIAN (GER),** 6, gr g Reliable Man—Anna Desta (GER) **B. J. Llewellyn**
2 **ASCOT DAY (FR),** 9, ch g Soave (GER)—Allez Hongkong (GER) **B. J. Llewellyn**
3 **CANAL ROCKS,** 7, gr g Aussie Rules (USA)—In Secret **Mr D Maddocks & Partner**
4 **CHANGE OF FORTUNE,** 4, ch g Cityscape—Secret Dream (IRE) **A. J. Williams**
5 **COGITAL,** 8, b g Invincible Spirit (IRE)—Galaxy Highflyer **Mr Alex James & Mr B. J. Llewellyn**
6 **GOOD IMPRESSION,** 8, b g Showcasing—Daintily Done **B. M. G. Group**
7 **INDIGO TIMES (IRE),** 6, gr g Alhebayeb (IRE)—Easy Times **Mr Gethyn Mills & Mr B. J. Llewellyn**
8 **KING CHARLES (USA),** 6, b g Lemon Drop Kid (USA)—La Reine Lionne (USA) **& Racing**
9 **MIND HUNTER,** 5, b g Gleneagles (IRE)—Gadwa **Mr Alex James & Mr B. J. Llewellyn**
10 **MONSIEUR LAMBRAYS,** 7, b g Champs Elysees—Windermere Island **Miss I. G. Tompsett**
11 **PORT OR STARBOARD (IRE),** 6, b g Epaulette (AUS)—Galley **Lland Af Cwrw**
12 **REMEDIUM,** 5, b g Adaay (IRE)—Lamentation **B. J. Llewellyn**
13 **SIR PLATO (IRE),** 9, b g Sir Prancealot (IRE)—Dessert Flower (IRE) **Mrs C. Llewellyn**
14 **TIGER VOICE (FR),** 8, b g Poet's Voice—Tarsia (GER) **The Bill & Ben Partnership**
15 **TRIPLE NICKLE (IRE),** 7, b m So You Think (NZ)—Secret Shine (IRE) **Mr Alex James & Mr B. J. Llewellyn**
16 **ZAMBEZI FIX (FR),** 8, gr g Zambezi Sun—Lady Fix (FR) **Mr Gethyn Mills & Mr B. J. Llewellyn**
17 **ZAMBEZI MAGIC,** 6, b g Zoffany (IRE)—Millestan (IRE) **Mr P G Amos & Partner**
18 **ZURAIG,** 5, gr g Teofilo (IRE)—Dakatari (FR) **B. J. Llewellyn**

Assistant Trainer: J L Llewellyn.

Flat Jockey: Daniel Muscutt, David Probert. **Conditional Jockey:** Jordan Williams, Robert Williams. **Amateur Jockey:** Miss Jessica Llewellyn.

---

317 MR ROBERT LLEWELLYN, Swindon

Postal: **1 Overtown, Wroughton, Swindon, Wiltshire, SN4 0SJ**
Contacts: **PHONE 01656 890621**
EMAIL robbie@rglracing.co.uk

1 **BENSINI,** 7, b g Dr Massini (IRE)—Grouch Onthe Couch (IRE) **Mr B Jones & Son**
2 4, Ch f Black Sam Bellamy (IRE)—Briery Vixen **Mr R. Llewellyn**
3 **CAP ST VINCENT (FR),** 10, b g Muhtathir—Criquetot (FR) **Mr B Jones & Son**
4 **DOCK ROAD (IRE),** 7, ch g Shirocco (GER)—Representing (IRE) **Rgl Racing & General Love Quote**
5 **EMRAAN (IRE),** 7, b g Invincible Spirit (IRE)—Wissal (USA) **Mr R. Llewellyn**
6 **FRANKIE ROY (IRE),** 6, b g Yeats (IRE)—Shipley **Mr B Jones & Son**
7 **HE'S MY SHADOW (IRE),** 6, gr g Fairly Ransom (USA)—Baylough Mist (IRE) **G. Mills**
8 **IBIZA ROCKS (FR),** 5, b m Rail Link—Banquise (FR) **Mr R. Llewellyn**
9 5, B h Pether's Moon (IRE)—It's A Discovery (IRE)
10 5, Bl m Eastern Anthem (IRE)—Je Ne Sais Plus (FR)
11 **LADY SAMSON (IRE),** 5, b m Court Cave (IRE)—Lady Kadina (IRE) **Mr R. Llewellyn**

MR ROBERT LLEWELLYN - continued

12 **LOUP DE MAULDE (FR),** 6, b g Loup Breton (IRE)—Onolita Saulaie (FR) **Martin Redman & Maurice Thomas**
13 **MIGHTY MISSISSIPPI,** 5, b m Ol' Man River (IRE)—Compton Chick (IRE) **General Love Quote**
14 **NO GETAWAY (IRE),** 10, ch g Getaway (GER)—Nonnetia (FR) **Mr R. Llewellyn**
15 **SHE'S MY SHADOW (IRE),** 5, gr m Jet Away—Lady Sagamix (FR) **G. Mills**
16 **SINNARAJA (FR),** 4, gr g Cima de Triomphe (IRE)—Kelly Day (FR) **Martin Redman & Maurice Thomas**
17 **TEL'ART (FR),** 9, gr g Montmartre (FR)—Textuelle (FR) **G. Mills**
18 **TODDAYS THE DAY,** 4, b g Adaay (IRE)—Abyssinia (FR) **Miss S. D. Redpath**
19 **TRUDIEMADLYDEEPLY,** 6, b m Aizavoski (IRE)—Compton Chick (IRE) **Coral Racing Club for Colleagues**
20 **TWASN'T THE PLAN (IRE),** 10, b g Presenting—Gentle Alice (IRE) **Mr B Jones & Son**

THREE-YEAR-OLDS

21 **U A E EMPIRE,** b c Cracksman—Kazeem **Mr R. Llewellyn**

TWO-YEAR-OLDS

22 **LYKKLERED,** b f 27/02 Yorgunnabelucky (USA)—Chebsey Jubilee (Multiplex)

---

318 MR JOHN LONG, Royston Hertfordshire

Postal: **Lower Yard, Kings Ride , Baldock Road , Royston, Hertfordshire, SG8 9NN**
Contacts: **MOBILE 07815 186085, 07958 296945**
EMAIL winalot@aol.com

1 **CATIVO RAGAZZO,** 8, b g Multiplex—Sea Isle **M. J. Gibbs**
2 **KINGMON'S BOY,** 8, b g Denounce—Ela d'Argent (IRE) **J. King**
3 **KNOCKOUT BLOW,** 8, b g Lethal Force (IRE)—Elidore **R Blyth & S Colville**
4 **LIBBRETTA,** 8, ch m Libranno—Dispol Katie **Mrs A. M. Sturges**
5 **MAGICINTHEMAKING (USA),** 9, br m Wildcat Heir (USA)—Love in Bloom (USA) **M. J. Gibbs**
6 **SOLDIER IN ACTION (FR),** 10, ch g Soldier of Fortune (IRE)—Ripley (GER) **M. J. Gibbs**

Assistant Trainer: Miss S Cassidy.

Flat Jockey: Hollie Doyle.

---

319 MR CHARLIE LONGSDON, Chipping Norton

Postal: **Hull Farm Stables, Stratford Road, Chipping Norton, Oxfordshire, OX7 5QF**
Contacts: **WORK 01608 645556 MOBILE 07775 993263**
EMAIL info@charlielongsdonracing.com WEBSITE www.charlielongsdonracing.com

1 **ALGHAZAAL,** 6, ch g Teofilo (IRE)—Tanfidh **Mr B. Bailey**
2 **ALIEN STORM (IRE),** 5, b g Getaway (GER)—Missusan (IRE) **Ian Brown & Philip Donnison**
3 **ALMAZHAR GARDE (FR),** 8, ch g Kapgarde (FR)—Loin de Moi (FR) **Arthur's Party**
4 **BUGISE SEAGULL (IRE),** 5, b g Mount Nelson—Golan Lady (IRE) **Mr G. Leon**
5 **CALIDAD (IRE),** 7, b g Califet (FR)—La Feuillarde (FR) **J Thwaite & C Longsdon**
6 **CAPTAINS ROAD (IRE),** 6, b g Doyen (IRE)—Temple Juno (IRE) **The Harlequins Racing**
7 **CASTLE ROBIN (IRE),** 8, ch g Robin des Champs (FR)—Coco Opera (IRE) **Bradley Partnership**
8 **CATUABA (IRE),** 5, ch g Jet Away—Catawollow **A.C. Bound & Mrs C. J. Djivanovic**
9 **EVERYONESGAME (IRE),** 6, ch g Jet Away—Rose Vic (IRE) **Mr M. Olden**
10 **FREETHINKER (IRE),** 7, b g Libertarian—Supreme Magical **The Free Thinkers**
11 **GAELIC PARK (IRE),** 7, br g Ocovango—The Last Bank (IRE) **The Gaelic Park Syndicate**

MR CHARLIE LONGSDON - continued

12 **GENTLEMAN JACQUES (IRE),** 4, b g Mount Nelson—Parkview Rose (IRE) **Mr M. Olden**
13 **GEORGE BANCROFT,** 5, ch g Australia—Extensive **Mr J. P. McManus**
14 **GLENCASSLEY (IRE),** 8, b g Yeats (IRE)—Reseda (GER) **Mr G. Leon**
15 **GLIMPSE OF GALA,** 7, b m Passing Glance—Apple Days **The Tweed Clad Fossils**
16 **GUETAPAN COLLONGES (FR),** 7, b g Saddler Maker (IRE)—Saturne Collonges (FR) **Mr J. P. McManus**
17 **HAAS BOY (FR),** 6, b g Diamond Boy (FR)—Naker Mome (FR) **Mr M. Olden**
18 **HARJO (IRE),** 6, b g Yeats (IRE)—Frankly Native (IRE) **Mr D. A. Halsall**
19 **HARRY THE NORSEMAN,** 7, ch g Norse Dancer (IRE)—Titled Lady **Mr J. Nettlefold**
20 **HECTOR JAVILEX (FR),** 6, b g Saddler Maker (IRE)—Peps Jarzeene (FR) **Mr D. M. Mason**
21 **IF I SAY (IRE),** 6, b m Free Eagle (IRE)—Wandering Star (IRE) **Stratford Racecourse 3**
22 **IMPERIAL JADE (IRE),** 4, b f Harzand (IRE)—Maggi Rocks (IRE) **Mr A. Fox-Pitt**
23 **INDELIBLE SPIN (IRE),** 6, b m Carlotamix (FR)—Spin The Wheel (IRE) **The Charlie Longsdon Racing Club**
24 **LARGY NIGHTS (IRE),** 9, b g Jeremy (USA)—Rowdy Nights (IRE) **Mrs J. A. Wakefield**
25 **LARGY VALLEY (IRE),** 5, b g Mount Nelson—Pine Valley (IRE) **Mr C. E. Longsdon**
26 **LYRICAL GENIUS (IRE),** 6, b g Milan—Rheinland (IRE) **Thackray, Ogilvy, King & Williams**
27 **MANINSANE (IRE),** 8, ch g Salutino (GER)—Don't Fall (IRE) **Barrels Of Courage**
28 **MISS APPLEJACK,** 4, ch f Jack Hobbs—Apple Days **The Applejacks**
29 **MOON KING (FR),** 7, br g Sea The Moon (GER)—Maraba (IRE) **Ever Optimistic**
30 **NO NO FIZZ (IRE),** 5, b m Getaway (GER)—Golden Firth (IRE) **Don Sebastiao Partnership**
31 **NO NO TANGO,** 6, ch g Sixties Icon—Until Forever (IRE) **Don Sebastiao Partnership**
32 **NO WORD (IRE),** 7, b m Shantaram—Pip 'n Pop (IRE) **Pay The Bill Syndicate**
33 **PARRAMOUNT,** 7, b g Mount Nelson—Queen Soraya **Mr A. Fox-Pitt**
34 **POTTERS LEGEND,** 13, b g Midnight Legend—Loose Morals (IRE) **Mrs J. May**
35 **QUEEN MANDANA,** 4, b f Black Sam Bellamy (IRE)—Queen Soraya **Mr A. Fox-Pitt**
36 **RARE EDITION (IRE),** 6, b g Califet (FR)—Quaspia (FR) **Pay The Bill Syndicate**
37 **REALISATION (FR),** 5, b m Masked Marvel—Four Green (FR) **Stratford Racecourse 3**
38 **SNOW LEOPARDESS,** 11, gr m Martaline—Queen Soraya **Mr A. Fox-Pitt**
39 **SOLDAT FORTE (IRE),** 6, b g Soldier of Fortune (IRE)—Rock Me Gently **Stratford Racecourse 2**
40 **STROLL ON BY (IRE),** 6, b g Walk In The Park (IRE)—Liss Croga (IRE) **Old Gold Racing 9**
41 **TEA FOR FREE (IRE),** 8, b g Court Cave (IRE)—Golan Gale (IRE) **Mrs S. M. Monkland**
42 **THE DARK EDGE (IRE),** 4, br g Sholokhov (IRE)—The Keane Edge (IRE) **The Dark Edge Partnership**
43 **THE MIGHTY ARC (IRE),** 8, b g Arcadio (GER)—Funcheon Lady (IRE) **Leon & Thornton Families**
44 **THE WISE TRAVELLER (IRE),** 7, b g Getaway (GER)—Butterfly Betty (IRE) **The Endeavour Racing Syndicate**
45 **THREE MACKS (IRE),** 4, ch f Pride of Dubai (AUS)—Anna David **Ms K. Neill & Mr W. Mackey**
46 **TOMMY CULLEN (IRE),** 5, ch g Hillstar—Minnie Maguire (IRE) **Mrs J. May**
47 **WELL DICK (IRE),** 6, b g Well Chosen—Midnight Benefit (IRE) **Mr M. Olden**
48 **WESTERN ZEPHYR (IRE),** 6, b g Westerner—Beneficial Breeze (IRE) **Swanee River Partnership**
49 **WHAT ABOUT TIME (IRE),** 9, br g Oscar (IRE)—Fennor Rose (IRE) **What About Time Syndicate**
50 **ZESTFUL HOPE (FR),** 6, b g Zanzibari (USA)—Chamdespoir (FR) **Ms G. E. Morgan**

NH Jockey: Paul O'Brien. **Conditional Jockey:** Cian Chester, Lilly Pinchin, Bradley Roberts.

---

320 MR DAVID LOUGHNANE, Tern Hill

Postal: **Helshaw Grange, Warrant Road, Tern Hill, Shropshire**
Contacts: **MOBILE 07527 173197**
EMAIL info@daveloughnaneracing.com WEBSITE www.daveloughnaneracing.com

1 **AMBER ISLAND (IRE),** 6, b m Exceed And Excel (AUS)—Raphinae **Mr D. J. Lowe**
2 **BABY STEPS,** 7, b g Paco Boy (IRE)—Stepping Out (IRE) **Mr D. J. Lowe**
3 **CHASE THE DOLLAR,** 5, b g Frankel—Cape Dollar (IRE) **Lydonford Ltd**
4 **CRAIC AT DAWN (IRE),** 4, ch g Dawn Approach (IRE)—Super Hoofer (IRE) **Miss S. L. Hoyland**
5 **DARK PINE (IRE),** 6, b g Dandy Man (IRE)—Suitably Discreet (USA) **Mr G. Dewhurst**
6 **DERRYMORE BOY (IRE),** 4, b g Dawn Approach (IRE)—Timeless Whisper (IRE) **Westshield Racing Club**
7 **DOLLY GRAY,** 4, b f Tamayuz—Exceedingly **Mr A. Gray**
8 **FFION,** 6, b m Sepoy (AUS)—Exceedingly **Mr A. Gray**

MR DAVID LOUGHNANE - continued

9 6, B g Telescope (IRE)—Goal Hanger
10 **INEVITABLE OUTCOME (IRE),** 6, b m Ivawood (IRE)—Foreplay (IRE) **Mr D. J. Lowe**
11 **KAPE MOSS,** 4, b f Equiano (FR)—Chrissycross (IRE) **Eclipse First Racing**
12 **KIM WEXLER (IRE),** 5, b m Mehmas (IRE)—Foreplay (IRE) **Mr D. J. Lowe**
13 **LUMBERJACK,** 4, gr g Mastercraftsman (IRE)—Wood Chorus **Mr T. R. Hartley**
14 **METABOLT,** 4, ch g Night of Thunder (IRE)—Something Exciting **Mr P. Brookes**
15 **MOJOMAKER (IRE),** 4, b g Mehmas (IRE)—Ajla (IRE) **Mr D. J. Lowe**
16 **OWENS LAD,** 5, b g Harbour Watch (IRE)—Dancing Primo **L. R. Owen**
17 **PLUMETTE,** 7, b m Compton Place—Belatorio (IRE) **Mr J. Rocke**
18 **QUICA,** 4, b f Heeraat (IRE)—Spate Rise **Mr P. Onslow**
19 **REAL QUIZ,** 4, b g Cityscape—Rattleyurjewellery **Mr P. Onslow**
20 **SHARRON MACREADY (IRE),** 4, b f Mehmas (IRE)—Foreplay (IRE) **Mr D. J. Lowe**
21 **SPACER (IRE),** 4, gr g Starspangledbanner (AUS)—First Party **Mr D. J. Lowe**
22 **TRIPLE M,** 4, gr f Mount Nelson—Nolas Lolly (IRE) **MMM**

THREE-YEAR-OLDS

23 **ABSOLUTELYFLAWLESS,** b f Ribchester (IRE)—Key Light (IRE) **Mr D. J. Lowe**
24 **BOXING ALEX,** b c Invincible Spirit (IRE)—Fresh Terms **Amo Racing Limited**
25 **CALL ME DIEGO (IRE),** br c Showcasing—Drumfad Bay (IRE) **Amo Racing Limited**
26 **CARMELA (IRE),** br f Tasleet—Jayla **The Many Saints**
27 **CHARLIE'S HUMOUR (IRE),** b f Camacho—Miracolia (IRE) **NSL Investments Limited**
28 **COMMANDER STRAKER (IRE),** b c Kodi Bear (IRE)—Slovak (IRE) **Mr D. J. Lowe**
29 **DANCE TIME,** b f Time Test—Dancing Primo **L. R. Owen**
30 **DEGUELLO (IRE),** b g Dark Angel (IRE)—Lady Springbank (IRE) **Mr T. R. Hartley**
31 **DOLORES ABERNATHY,** b f Footstepsinthesand—Kachess **Mr D. J. Lowe**
32 **FLAG FLYING,** b g Starspangledbanner (AUS)—Gavota **Mr D. J. Lowe**
33 **KING OF STEEL (USA),** gr c Wootton Bassett—Eldacar **Amo Racing Limited**
34 **MOLTISANTI (IRE),** b g Highland Reel (IRE)—Marah Dubai (FR) **The Many Saints**
35 **MY DELILAH (IRE),** b f Galileo Gold—Paella (IRE) **Mr D. J. Lowe**
36 **PORTRAITIST (IRE),** b f Awtaad (IRE)—Lyric Piece **Mr T. R. Hartley**
37 **PURPLE LADY (IRE),** b f Highland Reel (IRE)—Rock Kristal (IRE) **Amo Racing Limited**
38 **QUEEN OLLY (IRE),** b f No Nay Never (USA)—Surprisingly (IRE) **Amo Racing Limited**
39 **SAMBA LADY (IRE),** b f Kodi Bear (IRE)—Lynn's Memory **Amo Racing Limited**
40 **SANKS A MILLION (IRE),** b g Profitable (IRE)—Rasan **Mr R. A. Sankey**
41 **SPARKS FLY,** b f Muhaarar—Stepping Out (IRE) **Mr D. J. Lowe**
42 **STARMAS (IRE),** b f Mehmas (IRE)—Startori **Mr T. R. Hartley**
43 **TILLYBOB (IRE),** b f Kuroshio (AUS)—Midnight Destiny (IRE) **Mr A. Owen**
44 **WALBANK (IRE),** b c Kodiac—No Lippy (IRE) **Amo Racing Limited**

TWO-YEAR-OLDS

45 **ANGLESEY LAD (IRE),** b c 14/02 Kodi Bear (IRE)—Sign From Heaven (IRE) (Raven's Pass (USA)) (29612)
46 Gr c 28/03 Inns of Court (IRE)—Explosive Lady (IRE) (Alfred Nobel (IRE)) (50000) **Mr D. J. Lowe**
47 B f 16/03 Showcasing—Exrating (Exceed And Excel (AUS)) **Eclipse First Racing**
48 Br f 18/04 Soldier's Call—Harlem Dancer (Dr Devious (IRE)) (36014) **D Lowe, M Cantillon & Syndicates Racing**
49 B c 05/03 Cracksman—Hyper Dream (IRE) (Oasis Dream) (40000)
50 B f 04/03 Showcasing—Image (Sepoy (AUS)) (64762)
51 B f 29/04 Mehmas (IRE)—Kuaicoss (IRE) (Lujain (USA)) (37615)
52 **LUNA CATENA,** b f 17/02 Sea The Moon (GER)—Flying North (Raven's Pass (USA))
53 **QUESTIONABLE,** b f 10/02 Time Test—Rattleyurjewellery (Royal Applause) **Mr P. Onslow**
54 B f 20/04 Zoustar (AUS)—Sciarra (Monsieur Bond (IRE)) (32013)
55 Ch f 25/03 Smooth Daddy (USA)—Silesie (USA) (Magician (IRE)) (16006)
56 Ch f 23/03 New Bay—Tequila Sunrise (Dansili) (28011)

321 MR MARK LOUGHNANE, Kidderminster

Postal: **Rock Farm, Rock Cross, Rock, Kidderminster, Worcestershire, DY14 9SA**
Contacts: **MOBILE 07805 531021**

1 **ALGHEED (IRE),** 5, b m Dark Angel (IRE)—Rathaath (IRE) **S. & A. Mares**
2 **APACHE STAR (IRE),** 4, br g No Nay Never (USA)—Instinctively (IRE) **Xenon Workplace & Partner**
3 **ARCADIAN NIGHTS,** 5, b g Exceed And Excel (AUS)—Lady Lahar **Mr L. A. Bellman**
4 **BARBILL (IRE),** 7, b g Zebedee—Fiuise (IRE) **Mr K. Sohi**
5 **BOOKMARK,** 5, b m New Approach (IRE)—Free Verse **Live In Hope Partnership**
6 **BRASCA,** 7, ch g Nathaniel (IRE)—Regalline (IRE) **Over The Moon Racing**
7 **BROUGHTONS FLARE (IRE),** 7, ch g Rip Van Winkle (IRE)—Purple Glow (IRE) **Mrs C. M. Loughnane**
8 **CIOTOG (IRE),** 5, ch g Dandy Man (IRE)—Cristal Fashion (IRE) **Precision Facades Ltd**
9 **CITY ESCAPE (IRE),** 6, b m Cityscape—Lady Gabrielle (IRE) **Out Of Bounds Racing Club**
10 **COSMIC STAR,** 5, b gr m Charm Spirit (IRE)—Reaching Ahead (USA) **Mrs M. A. Cooke**
11 **CRAFTER (IRE),** 5, b g Muhaarar—Boston Rocker (IRE) **Mr L. A. Bellman**
12 **DAHEER (USA),** 6, ch g Speightstown (USA)—Elraazy (USA) **The Likely Lads**
13 **DELIGHTFILLY,** 4, b f Adaay (IRE)—Colourfilly **Mr L. A. Bellman**
14 **DELPHI DREAMER,** 4, b g Iffraaj—Dixie Dreamer **Promenade Bloodstock Limited**
15 **EL HOMBRE,** 9, ch g Camacho—Nigella **Over The Moon Racing**
16 **ERMIN STREET (IRE),** 4, ch g Belardo (IRE)—Ragtime Dancer **The Likely Lads**
17 **FIRST CHARGE (IRE),** 6, b g Dansili—Melodramatic (IRE) **Mr L. A. Bellman**
18 **FIRST COMPANY (IRE),** 5, b g Fast Company (IRE)—Pira Palace (IRE) **Northern Marking Ltd**
19 **FOLLOW YOUR HEART (IRE),** 5, b g Estidhkaar (IRE)—Al Gharrafa **S. & A. Mares**
20 **FRISTEL (IRE),** 4, b g Holy Roman Emperor (IRE)—Kyanight (IRE) **Mrs C. M. Loughnane**
21 **GLORY NIGHTS (IRE),** 4, b g Cotai Glory—Lady Lucia (IRE) **M J Refrigeration Transport Ltd**
22 **HAKU (IRE),** 4, b g Dragon Pulse (IRE)—Quiania (IRE) **Level Par Racing**
23 **IMPERIAL COMMAND (IRE),** 6, b g War Command (USA)—Acts Out Loud (USA) **M J Refrigeration Transport Ltd**
24 **JANAAT (IRE),** 4, ch f Ribchester (IRE)—Lexi's Love (USA) **S. & A. Mares**
25 **KEEP ME HAPPY,** 4, b f Stimulation (IRE)—Verus Delicia (IRE) **Mr R. M. Brilley**
26 **KING OF SPEED (IRE),** 4, b g Acclamation—Music And Dance **Ben Parish & Clare Loughnane**
27 **MOMAER (IRE),** 4, b f Belardo (IRE)—Khameela **D. S. Lovatt**
28 **PEARL REEF,** 4, b f Havana Gold (IRE)—Cockney Dancer **Mr K. Sohi**
29 **PERCY JONES,** 4, b g Sir Percy—Luisa Calderon **L Bellman & Racing Facades**
30 **PRECISION STORM,** 6, gr g Dragon Pulse (IRE)—Way To The Stars **Precision Facades Ltd**
31 **PYSANKA (FR),** 4, b g Holy Roman Emperor (IRE)—Ukraine (IRE) **Mr R. M. Brilley**
32 **SAN JUAN (IRE),** 6, b g Tagula (IRE)—Bigasiwannabe (IRE) **Mrs C. M. Loughnane**
33 **STARFIGHTER,** 7, b g Sea The Stars (IRE)—Starlit Sands **Mr L. A. Bellman**
34 **SWISS ROWE (IRE),** 5, b g Swiss Spirit—Hucking Hot **Level Par Racing**
35 **TRIGGERED (IRE),** 7, b g Dandy Man (IRE)—Triggers Broom (IRE) **L Bellman & S & A Mares**
36 **UNDER FOX (IRE),** 5, b g Dandy Man (IRE)—Lily's Rainbow (IRE) **S. & A. Mares**
37 **WELL PREPARED,** 6, b g Due Diligence (USA)—Amazed **Mr L. A. Bellman**
38 **WON LOVE (IRE),** 5, b g Frankel—Blhadawa (IRE) **Mr D. A. Olver**

THREE-YEAR-OLDS

39 **AL GHANIM,** ch g Iffraaj—Inala **Promenade Bloodstock Limited**
40 **ALL INCLUSIVE,** b g Tasleet—Stresa **& Mares S Turner**
41 **BLISSFILLY,** b f Dandy Man (IRE)—Colourfilly **Mr L. A. Bellman**
42 **ENTERPRISING LADY (IRE),** ch f Profitable (IRE)—Simonetta (IRE) **The Not for Profit Partnership**
43 **GRACIOUS GRACE (IRE),** b f Kodi Bear (IRE)—Lyca Ballerina **Middleham Park Racing LIII**
44 **LEONNA (IRE),** b f Expert Eye—Shy Audience (IRE) **Mr K. Sohi**
45 **LITTLE ROMAN (IRE),** b g Holy Roman Emperor (IRE)—Anna David **D Olver & the Likely Lads**
46 **MCCAULEY'S TAVERN (IRE),** b g Starspangledbanner (AUS)—Franzy (IRE) **D. Keoghan & James Stack**
47 B f Blue Bresil (FR)—Miss Sophierose (IRE)
48 **NINETYNINEPROBLEMS (IRE),** b f Sioux Nation (USA)—Worthington (IRE) **Mr K. Sohi**
49 B g Bated Breath—Primanora **D. S. Lovatt**
50 **SERENITY ROSE (IRE),** b f James Garfield (IRE)—Easton Arch (USA) **Mr C. Bacon**
51 Ch g Starspangledbanner (AUS)—Swept Away (IRE) **Level Par Racing**
52 **TOP OF THE CLASS,** ch f Zoustar (AUS)—The Gold Cheongsam (IRE) **Mr K. Sohi**
53 **WAKAI UMI (IRE),** b f Kuroshio (AUS)—Oceanella (IRE) **Orbital Racing, S&A Mares & S Turner**

MR MARK LOUGHNANE - continued

TWO-YEAR-OLDS

54 B c 30/04 Adaay (IRE)—Colourfilly (Compton Place) **Mr L. A. Bellman**
55 Ch f 04/03 Gustav Klimt (IRE)—Refuse Colette (IRE) (Refuse To Bend (IRE))
56 B c 10/02 Adaay (IRE)—Rose Ransom (IRE) (Oasis Dream) (6500) **D. S. Lovatt**

---

322 MR ROBERT LUKE, Haverfordwest

Postal: **Selvedge, CLARBESTON ROAD, Dyfed, SA63 4QR**
EMAIL robluke82@hotmail.com

1 **CIDER DRINKER,** 8, b m Apple Tree (FR)—Sniper Alley (IRE) **Mr R. E. Luke**
2 **GENERAL PICTON (IRE),** 11, b g Beneficial—Back To Cloghoge (IRE) **Mr R. E. Luke**
3 **GOOD GREEF,** 8, gr m Geordieland (FR)—Red Reef **Mr R. E. Luke**

---

323 MR BENJAMIN VINCENT LUND, Bridgwater

Postal: **Smocombe Racing Stables, Enmore, Bridgwater, Somerset, TA5 2DY**
EMAIL lundequine@gmail.com

1 **DARK HEATHER (IRE),** 6, b m Laverock (IRE)—Grainne Delight (IRE) **Ben Lund Racing Club**
2 **EXMOOR FOREST (IRE),** 6, b g Sageburg (IRE)—Horner Vale (IRE) **West Country Racing**
3 **GETMEGOLD (IRE),** 8, ch g Getaway (GER)—Sunset Gold (IRE) **Black Knight Racing Club**
4 **GLENGEEVER (IRE),** 7, gr g Scorpion (IRE)—Anns Island (IRE) **Black Knight Racing Club**
5 **GUN RUNNER CASH (IRE),** 6, b g Jet Away—Brownie Points (IRE) **Black Knight Racing Club**
6 **HURRICAN DREAM (IRE),** 6, b g Maxios—Welfare **Mr B. V. Lund**
7 **JACK THE FARMER,** 7, br g Kalanisi (IRE)—Deploys Dream (IRE) **West Country Racing**
8 **KIND WITNESS (IRE),** 10, b m Witness Box (USA)—Kind Oscar (IRE) **Ben Lund Racing Club**
9 **PONTRESINA (IRE),** 10, b g Milan—Gilt Benefit (IRE) **Ben Lund Racing Club**
10 **ROSSERK ABBEY (IRE),** 10, ch g Fruits of Love (USA)—Here Comes Alli (IRE) **Mr B. V. Lund**

THREE-YEAR-OLDS

11 **OLIVIA'S SECRET (IRE),** ch g Kessaar (IRE)—Maybe So **Mr B. V. Lund**

---

324 MR SHAUN LYCETT, Witney

Postal: **Fairspear Racing Stables, Fairspear Road, Leafield, Witney, Oxfordshire, OX29 9NT**
Contacts: **PHONE 01451 824143 MOBILE 07788 100894**
EMAIL trainer@bourtonhillracing.co.uk WEBSITE www.bourtonhillracing.co.uk

1 **BRANSON MISSOURI (IRE),** 7, b m Fame And Glory—Virtue **Bourton Racing**
2 **EXCELLENT PUCK (IRE),** 13, b g Excellent Art—Puck's Castle **S. Lycett**
3 **JENSON BENSON (IRE),** 5, b g Kodi Bear (IRE)—Star Fire **L & M Atkins**
4 **JOHNNY BOOM (IRE),** 5, ch g New Bay—Moody Blue (IRE) **Dan Gilbert & Andrew Bruce**

MR SHAUN LYCETT - continued

5 **LIVA (IRE),** 8, ch g Champs Elysees—Resistance Heroine **L & M Atkins**
6 **MARAYEL (IRE),** 4, b g Dandy Man (IRE)—Luvmedo (IRE) **Bourton Racing**
7 **MASHAAN,** 5, b g Kodiac—Vitello **Bourton Racing**
8 **PAINLESS POTTER (IRE),** 5, b g Camacho—Wider World (IRE) **Mr R. Gilbert**
9 **PARK PADDOCKS (IRE),** 9, b g Sea The Stars (IRE)—Dream of The Hill (IRE) **Mr D. R. Gilbert**
10 **RAINBOW MIRAGE,** 6, ch m Garswood—Oasis Mirage **Miss S. M. Howes**
11 **RICK BLAINE (IRE),** 6, b g Ruler of The World (IRE)—Saturday Girl **Mr D. R. Gilbert**
12 **SPEECH ROOM (IRE),** 6, b g Sea The Stars (IRE)—Dream of The Hill (IRE) **L & M Atkins**
13 **STATELY HOME (IRE),** 6, gr g Clodovil (IRE)—Lady Spangles (IRE) **Gilbert, Bruce, Wills**
14 **THE KING'S STEED,** 10, b g Equiano (FR)—King's Siren (IRE) **D Gilbert, J Lancaster, G Wills**
15 **TORCELLO (IRE),** 9, ch g Born To Sea (IRE)—Islandagore (IRE) **Mr D. R. Gilbert**
16 **WEEKLY GOSSIP (IRE),** 12, br g Kalanisi (IRE)—Mary's Little Vic (IRE) **L & M Atkins**

---

325 MISS JESSICA MACEY, Doncaster

Postal: **Mayflower Stables, Saracens Lane, Scrooby, DONCASTER, South Yorkshire, DN10 6AS**
Contacts: **PHONE 07588 374797**
EMAIL macey.jess@gmail.com

1 **BE BE EX (IRE),** 4, b g Harzand (IRE)—Juno Moneta (IRE) **Strawberry Fields Stud**
2 **BON SECRET,** 4, b f Territories (IRE)—Precious Secret (IRE) **Miss J. R. Macey**
3 **DARK SIDE PRINCE,** 6, b g Equiano (FR)—Dark Side Princess **Mr M. M. Foulger**
4 **DARK SIDE THUNDER,** 4, b g Night of Thunder (IRE)—Dark Side Princess **Mr M. M. Foulger**
5 **ELEVEN ELEVEN (FR),** 5, b g Olympic Glory (IRE)—Pretty Panther (FR) **Miss J. R. Macey**
6 **EYES (IRE),** 5, b m Dandy Man (IRE)—Ebony Street (USA) **Not Now Partnership**
7 **HARDY,** 5, bl g Heeraat (IRE)—Miss Lesley **Wentdale Limited**
8 **HE'S SO BRAZEN,** 4, b g Brazen Beau (AUS)—Sweet Lily Pea (USA) **Dawson, Elton, Harris W Hobson**
9 **JENEVER,** 4, b g Swiss Spirit—Dutch Mistress **Goldrush Racing**
10 **MERCURIUS POWER (IRE),** 5, b g Awtaad (IRE)—Dame Hester (IRE) **Miss J. R. Macey**
11 **PHOENIX STAR (IRE),** 7, b g Alhebayeb (IRE)—Volcanic Lady (IRE) **Flying High Syndicate**
12 **SHARK TWO ONE,** 5, b g Adaay (IRE)—Touching (IRE) **New Vision Bloodstock & Miss J R Macey**
13 **THAKI (IRE),** 6, b g Lope de Vega (IRE)—Mickleberry (IRE) **Dr J. Hon**
14 **TRINITY GIRL,** 6, b m Teofilo (IRE)—Micaela's Moon (USA) **G Mr Fowler, S Dwyer**
15 **WRATH OF HECTOR,** 6, b g Mayson—Dutch Mistress **Goldrush Racing & Miss J R Macey**

THREE-YEAR-OLDS

16 **NAUTICAL DREAM (IRE),** b c Dandy Man (IRE)—Dreaming of Gold (IRE) **Sheikh K Al Khalifa**
17 **THE MUFFIN MAN (IRE),** b g Make Believe—Speedi Mouse **Mrs S. Dwyer**
18 **THUNDER STAR,** b f Night of Thunder (IRE)—Dark Side Princess **Mr M. M. Foulger**

TWO-YEAR-OLDS

19 B c 28/02 Due Diligence (USA)—Bahamadam (Bahamian Bounty) (25000) **New Vision Bloodstock**
20 B c 12/02 Due Diligence (USA)—Mrs Ivy (Champs Elysees) (13333) **Wentdale Limited**
21 B f 12/03 Mayson—Spanish Gold (Vettori (IRE)) (16190) **Goldrush Racing & Miss J R Macey**
22 B c 21/04 Soldier's Call—Starbright (IRE) (Duke of Marmalade (IRE)) (12805)

326 MR JOHN MACKIE, Church Broughton

Postal: **The Bungalow, Barton Blount, Church Broughton, Derby**
Contacts: **PHONE 01283 585603, 01283 585604 MOBILE 07799 145283 FAX 01283 585603**
EMAIL jmackieracing@gmail.com

1 **AMAZING MOLLIE,** 4, b f Brazen Beau (AUS)—Avonrose **Moorland Racing**
2 **AVAILABLE ANGEL,** 5, b m Heeraat (IRE)—Available (IRE) **Derbyshire Racing II**
3 **BARTON KNOLL,** 11, b g Midnight Legend—Barton Flower **Mr S. W. Clarke**
4 **BOMB SQUAD (IRE),** 5, gr g Lethal Force (IRE)—Dutch Destiny **Derbyshire Racing III**
5 **CAVE BLEU,** 5, b g Arvico (FR)—Glan Lady (IRE) **Mrs C. L. Voce**
6 **COCONUT TUDOR (IRE),** 7, b g Mahler—Tudor Fashion (IRE) **Good Day Out Syndicate**
7 **CUSTARD THE DRAGON,** 10, b g Kyllachy—Autumn Pearl **Derbyshire Racing**
8 **DISTINCTION (IRE),** 5, b g Kodiac—Tajbell (IRE) **Mike And Wendy Yardley**
9 **ELHAFEI (USA),** 8, br g Speightstown (USA)—Albamara **Mrs E. M. Mackie**
10 **GLEBE ROAD (IRE),** 7, b g Fame And Glory—Poppy Baloo (IRE) **Mr S. N. Roberts**
11 **HURRICANE ALI (IRE),** 7, b g Alhebayeb (IRE)—Hurricane Irene (IRE) **Mr M. J. Fruhwald**
12 **JACKAMUNDO (FR),** 7, b g Fast Company (IRE)—Luxie (IRE) **Danny Fantom Racing Ltd**
13 **MINI RIVO (IRE),** 5, b m Nathaniel (IRE)—Toujours L'Amour **Phil Kelly & Peter Hiatt**
14 **NASHY (IRE),** 6, br g Camelot—Venus de Milo (IRE) **The Derbyshire Optimists**
15 **OFF TO ALABAMA,** 5, b g Telescope (IRE)—Off By Heart **Mrs E. M. Mackie**
16 **RAINBOW JET (IRE),** 6, b m Dream Ahead (USA)—Star Jet (IRE) **NSU Leisure & Mrs Carolyn Seymour**
17 **VIVENCY (USA),** 6, b m Noble Mission—Hint of Joy (USA) **Derbyshire Racing IV**
18 **YOUNG WINSTON,** 4, b g Churchill (IRE)—Come With Me **KHDRP**

THREE-YEAR-OLDS

19 **BLAKER (IRE),** gr f Mastercraftsman (IRE)—Petite Nymphe **Eventmasters Racing**
20 **BURROWS DREAM (FR),** b f Ultra (IRE)—See Your Dream
21 **DAZY MAZY,** br f Massaat (IRE)—Magical Daze **The Clarino Partnership**
22 B f Sioux Nation (USA)—Double High
23 B f Telescope (IRE)—Just Milly (IRE)

TWO-YEAR-OLDS

24 B c 05/04 Dartmouth—Fire Jet (IRE) (Ask)

---

327 MR MICHAEL MADGWICK, Denmead

Postal: **Forest Farm, Forest Road, Denmead, Waterlooville, Hampshire, PO7 6UA**
Contacts: **PHONE 023 9225 8313 MOBILE 07835 964969**

1 **BIG 'N BETTER,** 11, b g Revoque (IRE)—Donastrela (IRE) **W. M. Smith**
2 **BLUEBELL WAY,** 4, b f Sixties Icon—Whiteley (IRE) **Peter Taplin & Susan Bunney**
3 **FRAVANCO,** 4, ch g Proconsul—Meebo (IRE) **Whytehall Partnership**
4 **LARGO BAY (USA),** 5, ch g Flintshire—No Panic (USA) **Mr J. Lane**
5 **MISS MALOU,** 4, b f War Command (USA)—Nawaashi **Whytehall Partnership**
6 **STORMBOMBER (CAN),** 7, ch g Stormy Atlantic (USA)—Swanky Bubbles (CAN) **Mr T. Smith**
7 **TIME TO BREEZE,** 5, b m Mullionmileanhour (IRE)—Shantou Breeze (IRE) **M. J. Madgwick**
8 **VINLAND (IRE),** 5, b g Fastnet Rock (AUS)—Anadiyla (IRE) **W. M. Smith**
9 **WHAT'S MY LINE,** 6, b g Sixties Icon—Leading Star **M. J. Madgwick**
10 **WHERE'S TOM,** 8, b g Cape Cross (IRE)—Where's Susie **Recycled Products Limited**

THREE-YEAR-OLDS

11 **FULLFORWARD (IRE),** b g Tamayuz—Shakdara (USA) **Lane & Madgwick**
12 **PRIMROSE WAY,** b f Sixties Icon—Whiteley (IRE) **Norman Court Stud & Susan Bunney**

Assistant Trainer: David Madgwick.

Flat Jockey: Adam Kirby. **NH Jockey:** Marc Goldstein. **Amateur Jockey:** Mr Lance Madgwick.

328 MRS HEATHER MAIN, Wantage

Postal: **Kingston Common Farm, Kingston Lisle, Wantage, Oxfordshire, OX12 9QT**
Contacts: **WORK 01367 820124 MOBILE 07920 558860**
EMAIL heather.main@hotmail.com WEBSITE www.heathermainracing.com

1 **AGAPANTHER,** 4, b f Outstrip—Byroness **Share A Winner & Wetumpka Racing**
2 **CAPTAIN HADDOCK (IRE),** 6, b g Make Believe—Kayd Kodaun (IRE) **Mr C. M. T. Main**
3 **CELTIC EMPRESS,** 5, b m Golden Horn—Cartimandua **Llewelyn,Runeckles**
4 **DARK ISLAND,** 4, b g Night of Thunder (IRE)—Western Pearl **D. M. Kerr**
5 **ENGLISH SPIRIT,** 5, ch g Swiss Spirit—Cloud Illusions (USA) **Wetumpka Racing**
6 **ISLAND BANDIT (IRE),** 4, ch g Zarak (FR)—Lady of The Court (IRE) **D. M. Kerr**
7 **ISLAND BRAVE (IRE),** 9, b h Zebedee—Tip the Scale (USA) **D. M. Kerr**
8 5, B m Dunaden (FR)—Just Popsy **Wetumpka Racing**
9 **LA BELLE VIE,** 4, b f Iffraaj—Belle Dauphine **Andrew Knott & Wetumpka Racing**
10 **MARSHAL DAN (IRE),** 8, b g Lawman (FR)—Aunt Nicola **Coxwell Partnership**
11 **MISTER BLUEBIRD,** 5, gr g Outstrip—Childesplay **Dawn Aldham & Wetumpka Racing**
12 **MOSTAWAA,** 7, ch g Poet's Voice—Mumtaza **The Haroldians**
13 **MOSTLY SUNNY (IRE),** 4, ch g Zarak (FR)—Belle Above All **Till & Racing**
14 **NIGELLA SATIVA,** 7, gr m Gentlewave (IRE)—Just Popsy **Wetumpka Racing**
15 **NUMITOR,** 9, gr g Schiaparelli (GER)—Just Popsy **Mr Paul G. Jacobs & Wetumpka Racing**
16 **POLAR CLOUD,** 7, gr g Mount Nelson—Cloud Illusions (USA) **Wetumpka Racing**
17 **STONKING,** 4, b g Farhh—Vizinga (FR) **Mr Paul G. Jacobs & Wetumpka Racing**
18 **TINCHOO,** 5, b m Adaay (IRE)—Tinshu (IRE) **Llewelyn,Runeckles**
19 **UNSUNG HERO (IRE),** 4, b c Iffraaj—Red Avis **Mr Donald Kerr & Wetumpka Racing**
20 **WIZARDING,** 4, b g Showcasing—Dutch S **Mondial Racing & Robert Haim**

THREE-YEAR-OLDS

21 **BELIEVE YOU ME (IRE),** b f Make Believe—Beauthea (IRE) **Coxwell Partnership**
22 **FLYING SPIRIT,** b c Harry Angel (IRE)—Oilinda **D. M. Kerr**
23 **ICE CREAM CASTLES,** gr f Mukhadram—Cloud Illusions (USA) **Mr. Andrew Tuck & Wetumpka Racing**
24 **ISLAND KING (IRE),** b g Ribchester (IRE)—Diptych (USA) **D. M. Kerr**
25 **ISLAND NATIVE (IRE),** gr c Caravaggio (USA)—Way of Light (IRE) **D. M. Kerr**

TWO-YEAR-OLDS

26 Ch f 18/03 Nathaniel (IRE)—Arrowtown (Rail Link) (25000)
27 **ASH WEDNESDAY,** gr c 17/02 Outstrip—Medoras Childe (Nayef (USA)) **Mr & Mrs D. R. Guest**
28 B f 17/04 Aclaim (IRE)—Byroness (Byron) **Wetumpka Racing**
29 Ch c 21/01 Zoustar (AUS)—Courteous Crown (Helmet (AUS)) (27000) **Wetumpka Racing**
30 B c 02/03 Inns of Court (IRE)—Her Kindness (Night of Thunder (IRE)) (16000) **Wetumpka Racing**
31 B f 04/03 Advertise—Pale Pearl (IRE) (King's Best (USA)) (20008) **Hon Mrs J. M. The Corbett & Mr Chris Wright**
32 **SORONTAR,** ch c 12/03 Gleneagles (IRE)—
Miss Serenity (Dark Angel (IRE)) (11000) **Mr Paul G. Jacobs & Wetumpka Racing**
33 **WAHOO KING (IRE),** b c 02/02 Awtaad (IRE)—Vow (Motivator) (43000) **Coxwell Partnership**

---

329 MR PHILLIP MAKIN, Easingwold

Postal: **Well Close Farm, York Road, Easingwold, York, North Yorkshire, YO61 3EN**
Contacts: **PHONE 07968 045436**
EMAIL philmakin.21@hotmail.co.uk

1 **BIG DUTCHIE (IRE),** 5, b g Dutch Art—Exceedingly **Louise & Glen Mitton & Partners**
2 **BRAZEN AKOYA,** 4, b f Brazen Beau (AUS)—Broughtons Jewel (IRE) **White Rose Bloodstock**
3 **CAPTAIN VALLO (IRE),** 5, ch g Mehmas (IRE)—Top Dollar **J. Binks**
4 **IMPRESSOR (IRE),** 6, b g Footstepsinthesand—Little Empress (IRE) **Mr J Toes & Mr J O'Loan**
5 5, Ch g Eagle Top—Littlemiss **J. Binks**
6 **WOOGREY (IRE),** 4, gr f New Bay—Stella River (FR) **Mr J. A. Swinbank**

MR PHILLIP MAKIN - continued

THREE-YEAR-OLDS

7 B f Sioux Nation (USA)—Cabelo (IRE) **Maximum Racing & Partner Ii**
8 **CHICO DULCE,** b c Washington DC (IRE)—Deep Blue Diamond **Mr R. J. Moss**
9 **LADY LOVELESS,** b f Master Carpenter (IRE)—Lady Lonsdale (GER) **Peckham Bloodstock & Racing**
10 **LUPSET FLOSSY POP (IRE),** b f Kodiac—Lumi (IRE) **Mr P. S. Riley**
11 **NA SCOITEAR (IRE),** br g Footstepsinthesand—Nu Couche (FR) **Mr J Toes & Mr J O'Loan**
12 Gr g Gutaifan (IRE)—Ragtime Dancer **J. Binks**
13 **STELIOS (IRE),** b g Estidhkaar (IRE)—Xerxes (IRE) **P. J. Makin**

TWO-YEAR-OLDS

14 B f 15/04 Profitable (IRE)—Glen Ginnie (IRE) (Red Clubs (IRE)) (4002)
15 B c 07/03 Invincible Army (IRE)—Last Laugh (USA) (Smart Strike (CAN)) (7203)
16 B c 02/02 Massaat (IRE)—Miss Lesley (Needwood Blade) (16006)
17 B f 18/05 Massaat (IRE)—Rappel (Royal Applause) (7143)
18 B c 17/04 Rajasinghe (IRE)—Skeetah (Heeraat (IRE))
19 B f 23/04 Prince of Lir (IRE)—Turakina (IRE) (Teofilo (IRE)) (2001)
20 B c 03/05 Calyx—Zavaala (IRE) (Rock of Gibraltar (IRE)) (10000) **Mrs R. A. Gedge-Gibson**

---

330 MR GEORGE MARGARSON, Newmarket

Postal: **Graham Lodge, Birdcage Walk, Newmarket, Suffolk, CB8 0NE**
Contacts: **PHONE 01638 668043 MOBILE 07860 198303**
EMAIL george@georgemargarson.co.uk WEBSITE www.georgemargarson.co.uk

1 **BLAME CULTURE (USA),** 8, b g Blame (USA)—Pearl In The Sand (IRE) **The Bean Club**
2 **CARIBBEAN SPRING (IRE),** 10, b g Dark Angel (IRE)—Bogini (IRE) **The Bean Club**
3 **FARHH TO SHY,** 5, b m Farhh—Coconut Shy **Mr F. G. Butler**
4 **GOLDEN SPICE (USA),** 4, b f Golden Horn—Punita (USA) **Mr A. Al Mansoori**
5 **IDEAL GUEST (FR),** 4, b g Shalaa (IRE)—Rue Renan (IRE) **John Guest Racing Ltd**
6 **ISLAND OF SKYE,** 4, b g Ribchester (IRE)—Bonnie Brae **Davenport, Elsworth & Ten Green Bottles**
7 **MEDIA GUEST (FR),** 5, b br g Belardo (IRE)—Media Day (IRE) **John Guest Racing Ltd**
8 **PROTECTED GUEST,** 8, b g Helmet (AUS)—Reem Star **John Guest Racing Ltd**
9 **ROPEY GUEST,** 6, b g Cable Bay (IRE)—Hadeeya **John Guest Racing Ltd**
10 **SPIRITED GUEST,** 7, b g Swiss Spirit—Choisette **John Guest Racing Ltd**
11 **YOUNG BERTIE,** 4, b c Intrinsic—Young Jackie

THREE-YEAR-OLDS

12 **ABRAVAGGIO (IRE),** b c Caravaggio (USA)—Three Choirs (IRE) **Paul Kwok & Ms Angel Li**
13 **MYTHICAL GUEST (IRE),** b c Make Believe—Fonda (USA) **John Guest Racing Ltd**
14 **TWILIGHT GUEST,** b g Twilight Son—Astrosecret **John Guest Racing Ltd**
15 B f Intrinsic—Young Jackie
16 **ZINA COLADA,** b br f Brazen Beau (AUS)—Coconut Shy **Mr F. G. Butler**

TWO-YEAR-OLDS

17 **AUSSIE STAR,** b f 31/03 Zoustar (AUS)—Penelopa (Giant's Causeway (USA)) (30000) **Graham Lodge Partnership**
18 B c 09/02 Profitable (IRE)—Aussie View (IRE) (Australia) **Mr A. Al Mansoori**
19 B g 12/03 Cable Bay (IRE)—Hadeeya (Oratorio (IRE)) (25000) **John Guest Racing Ltd**
20 B f 11/04 Street Sense (USA)—Punita (USA) (Distorted Humor (USA)) **Mr A. Al Mansoori**
21 B f 01/03 Kessaar (IRE)—Rajmahal (UAE) (Indian Ridge) (155000) **Mr A. Al Mansoori**
22 **SHY NALA,** ch f 09/03 Postponed (IRE)—Coconut Shy (Bahamian Bounty) **Mr F. G. Butler**

Assistant Trainer: Katie Margarson.

Apprentice Jockey: Miss Abbie Pierce. **Amateur Jockey:** Miss Rosie Margarson.

331 MR ANDREW J. MARTIN, Chipping Norton

Postal: **Yew Tree Barn, Hook Norton Road, Swerford, Chipping Norton, Oxfordshire, OX7 4BF**
Contacts: **MOBILE 07815 698359**

1 **CASSOWARY (IRE),** 5, ch m Australia—Arose **Farrier Jump Jets**
2 **CHARLIE'S GLANCE,** 7, b g Passing Glance—Call Me A Legend **A. J. Martin**
3 **COME ON NIA,** 4, b f Telescope (IRE)—Call Me A Star **Mr A. V. John**
4 **FINEST VIEW,** 6, b m Passing Glance—Call Me A Legend **Pitchall Stud Partnership**
5 **GLANCE AT ME,** 5, b m Passing Glance—Marys Legend **Robert And Sandra Davenport**
6 **LION RING (IRE),** 5, b g The Last Lion (IRE)—Bling Ring (USA) **A. J. Martin**
7 **MIDNIGHT GINGER,** 7, ch m Midnight Legend—Calamintha **Mr A. V. John**
8 **MIDNIGHT POPSTAR,** 9, b m Midnight Legend—It's Missy Imp **Andy Martin Racing Club**
9 **MILITARIAN,** 13, b g Kayf Tara—Mille Et Une (FR) **Andy Martin Racing Club**
10 **RARE BEAR,** 5, b g Schiaparelli (GER)—Trifollet **A. J. Martin**
11 **SCHIAPARELLI TEDDY,** 7, ch g Schiaparelli (GER)—Trifollet **A. J. Martin**

---

332 MISS NICKY MARTIN, Minehead

Postal: **Great Bradley, Withypool, Minehead, Somerset, TA24 7RS**
Contacts: **PHONE 01643 831175 MOBILE 07980 269510**
EMAIL nickymartin3@hotmail.co.uk

1 **ALMOST GOTAWAY (IRE),** 6, b g Getaway (GER)—Isles of Icane (IRE) **Bradley Partnership**
2 **APPLES MOON (IRE),** 4, b f Diamond Boy (FR)—Trinity Rainbow (IRE) **Bradley Partnership**
3 **BEAR GHYLLS (IRE),** 8, br g Arcadio (GER)—Inch Princess (IRE) **Bradley Partnership**
4 **CRAIC MAGIC (IRE),** 8, b g Oscar (IRE)—Chantoue Royale (FR) **Bradley Partnership**
5 **DISH OF THE DAY (IRE),** 5, br g Famous Name—Inch Princess (IRE)
6 **FEVERTRE (IRE),** 8, ch g Sans Frontieres (IRE)—Avoca Star (IRE) **Bradley Partnership**
7 **HILL COUNTRY (FR),** 5, b g Masterstroke (USA)—Barbarasse (FR) **Bradley Partnership**
8 **INSPIRATRICE (IRE),** 4, gr f Galileo Gold—Telegraphy (USA) **Bradley Partnership**
9 **IPSOS PIERJI (FR),** 5, b g No Risk At All (FR)—Playa Pierji (FR) **Bradley Partnership**
10 **ITO DITTO (FR),** 5, b g Ito (GER)—Morning Moon **Bradley Partnership**
11 **JUST LOOSE CHANGE,** 6, gr g Yorgunnabelucky (USA)—Ovilia (IRE) **Bradley Partnership**
12 **LEADING CHOICE (IRE),** 6, b g Leading Light (IRE)—Rachel's Choice (IRE) **Bradley Partnership**
13 **LIGHT EM UP NIGEL (IRE),** 7, b g Leading Light (IRE)—Hushed Up (IRE) **Bradley Partnership**
14 **LUCKY SO AND SO (IRE),** 6, b g Lucky Speed (IRE)—Limerick Rose (IRE) **Bradley Partnership**
15 **MAGIC MARMALADE (IRE),** 20, ch g Mohaajir (USA)—Kylogue's Delight
16 **MOLE TRAP,** 12, b m Kayf Tara—Fairly High (IRE) **Bradley Partnership**
17 **MY LAST OSCAR (IRE),** 8, b g Oscar (IRE)—Power Again (GER) **Bradley Partnership**
18 **PENCIL (IRE),** 6, ch g Retirement Plan—Maggie From Dunlo (IRE) **Bradley Partnership**
19 **SPECIALAGENT MCGEE (IRE),** 5, b h Shirocco (GER)—Monks Charm (IRE) **Bradley Partnership**
20 **SYKES (IRE),** 14, b g Mountain High (IRE)—Our Trick (IRE) **Bradley Partnership**
21 **THE TWO AMIGOS,** 11, b g Midnight Legend—As Was **Bradley Partnership**
22 **VODKA ALL THE WAY (IRE),** 11, b g Oscar (IRE)—Fully Focused (IRE) **Bradley Partnership**
23 4, B g Getaway (GER)—Well Composed (IRE) **Bradley Partnership**

THREE-YEAR-OLDS

24 B f Youmzain (IRE)—Lornarette (IRE) **Bradley Partnership**

---

333 MR CHRISTOPHER MASON, Caerwent

Postal: **Whitehall Barn, Five Lanes, Caerwent, Newport, Monmouthshire, Np26 5pe**
Contacts: **HOME 01291 422172 PHONE 07767 808082 MOBILE 07970 202050**
WORK EMAIL cjmasonracing@yahoo.co.uk

1 **ATTY'S EDGE,** 7, b g Coach House (IRE)—Belle's Edge **International Plywood (Importers) Ltd**
2 **GILT EDGE,** 7, b m Havana Gold (IRE)—Bright Edge **Mr S Bishop & Mr C Mason**
3 **GLAMOROUS BREEZE,** 5, b m Cable Bay (IRE)—Go Glamorous (IRE) **Robert & Nina Bailey**
4 **HAGIA SOPHIA,** 5, b m Territories (IRE)—Aarti (IRE) **Mr K. B. Hodges**
5 **LIANGEL HOPE (IRE),** 4, b g The Last Lion (IRE)—Hope Against Hope (IRE) **B. G. Hicks**
6 **ON EDGE,** 5, b g Mayson—Edge of Light **Chris Mason Racing**

THREE-YEAR-OLDS

7 B f Cable Bay (IRE)—Edge of Light **Chris Mason Racing**
8 **JAX EDGE,** b f Cable Bay (IRE)—Bright Edge **International Plywood (Importers) Ltd**
9 B f Cable Bay (IRE)—Superior Edge **Chris Mason Racing**

TWO-YEAR-OLDS

10 **ALL WAYS GLAMOROUS,** b c 12/03 Cable Bay (IRE)—Go Glamorous (IRE) (Elnadim (USA)) **Robert & Nina Bailey**
11 B c 22/04 Due Diligence (USA)—Edged Out (Piccolo)
12 **GLAMOROUS JOY,** b gr f 06/05 Land Force (IRE)—Glamorous Rocket (IRE) (Dark Angel (IRE)) **Robert & Nina Bailey**
13 Gr ro c 08/04 Havana Grey—Sharpened Edge (Exceed And Excel (AUS))

Assistant Trainer: Miss Evie Young.

Apprentice Jockey: Miss Kerrie Raybould. **Amateur Jockey:** Miss Evie Young.

---

334 MR PHILIP MCBRIDE, Newmarket

Postal: **Exeter House Stables, 33 Exeter Road, Newmarket, Suffolk, CB8 8LP**
Contacts: **PHONE 01638 667841 MOBILE 07929 265711**

1 **CAMACHESS (IRE),** 7, b m Camacho—Heeby Jeeby **The Narc Partnership**
2 **HOPEMAN HARBOUR,** 4, b g Lethal Force (IRE)—Falling Angel **Mr C Massie & Mr Pj McBride**
3 **POKER MASTER (IRE),** 6, b g Sepoy (AUS)—Three Cards **Mr Ian Pattle & P J Mcbride**
4 **PRISCILLA'S WISH,** 5, b m Adaay (IRE)—Ghedi (IRE) **Mr C Massie & Mr Pj McBride**
5 **STO BENE,** 4, b g Brazen Beau (AUS)—Camelopardalis **P. J. McBride**

THREE-YEAR-OLDS

6 Ch g Profitable (IRE)—Autumn Tide (IRE) **The Narc Partnership**
7 **CARRY ON AITCH (IRE),** b f Fast Company (IRE)—Blue Willow **Mr Howard J. Cooke & Mr P. J. Mcbride**
8 **EQUIAMI,** b g Equiano (FR)—Handsome Molly **The Ten Fools & A Horse Partnership**
9 **RHYTHMIC ACCLAIM (IRE),** b f Acclamation—Lyric Harmony (IRE) **Pmracing (UK) Ltd**
10 B f Cracksman—Sayfoonisa (FR) **Mr S. Agodino**
11 **SPERIAMO,** gr f Outstrip—Suerte Loca (IRE) **Serafinoagodino, C.M.Budgett, P.J.Mcbride**
12 **ZOUKY,** b f Zoustar (AUS)—Kerry's Dream **Fravigar, Dixon R Mitchell**

TWO-YEAR-OLDS

13 B f 02/03 Cracksman—Ethaara (Green Desert (USA)) (12000) **P. J. McBride**

335 MR DONALD MCCAIN, Cholmondeley

Postal: **D McCain Racing Ltd, Bankhouse, Cholmondeley, Cheshire, SY14 8AL**
Contacts: **PHONE 01829 720351, 01829 720352 MOBILE 07903 066194**
EMAIL info@donaldmccain.co.uk WEBSITE www.donaldmccain.co.uk

1 **A DIFFERENT KIND (IRE),** 6, b g Doyen (IRE)—Ma Minx (IRE) **Mr D. Rowe**
2 **ARMATTIEKAN (IRE),** 9, b g Arakan (USA)—Serpentine Mine (IRE) **Clwydian International**
3 **BADLANDS BOY (IRE),** 4, b g Diamond Boy (FR)—Peace And The City (FR) **Mr J. M. Glews**
4 **BALLABAWN (IRE),** 5, b g Soldier of Fortune (IRE)—Coolfree (IRE) **David & Carol Shaw**
5 **BALLYBEG BOSS (IRE),** 5, b g Libertarian—Ballybeg Dusty (IRE) **Mr G. E. Fitzpatrick**
6 **BALLYGEARY (IRE),** 6, br g Flemensfirth (USA)—Sweet Poli (IRE) **Craig & Laura Buckingham**
7 **BAREBACK JACK (IRE),** 7, b g Getaway (GER)—Dubh Go Leir (IRE) **T. G. Leslie**
8 **BARNABAS COLLINS (IRE),** 8, b g Shantou (USA)—G Day Sile (IRE) **T. G. Leslie**
9 **BARRICHELLO,** 7, b g Gentlewave (IRE)—Tambourine Ridge (IRE) **Owners Group 066**
10 **BENTS HOLLOW (IRE),** 6, b br m Soldier of Fortune (IRE)—Blume (IRE) **Mr J. Fyffe**
11 **BIRD ON THE WIRE (FR),** 8, ch g Martaline—Titi Jolie (FR) **Donald McCain Racing Club**
12 **BLAKENEY POINT,** 10, b g Sir Percy—Cartoon **T W Johnson & G Maxwell**
13 **BLUE FIN (IRE),** 6, b g Shantou (USA)—Eluna **Spinners Winners**
14 **BLUEBERRY WINE (IRE),** 7, b g Dylan Thomas (IRE)—Buttonhole Rose (IRE) **Red Rum Racing 2**
15 **CAPE HELLES,** 4, b f Australia—Applause (IRE) **Mr T. G. Leslie & Mr David Redvers**
16 **CARTONNE (FR),** 6, b g Balko (FR)—Nuance Tartare (FR) **Dave & Matt Slater**
17 **CENOTICE,** 9, b g Phoenix Reach (IRE)—Kenny's Dream **Mr D. McMahon**
18 **CHALK THAT DOWN (IRE),** 5, b m Mount Nelson—Bob's Flame (IRE) **Exors of the Late Mr T. J. Hemmings**
19 **CHATSHOW HOST (IRE),** 6, b m Soldier of Fortune (IRE)—Back On Stage (IRE) **T W Johnson & G Maxwell**
20 **CHOIRMASTER,** 4, ch g Iffraaj—Lamentation **The Shinton Family**
21 **CHTI BALKO (FR),** 11, br g Balko (FR)—Ina Scoop (FR) **Dalwhinnie Bloodstock Limited**
22 **CHUVELO (IRE),** 8, b g Milan—Bargante (IRE) **T. G. Leslie**
23 **CLODY FLYER (IRE),** 6, b g Sholokhov (IRE)—Murphys Filly (IRE)
24 **COLLINGHAM (GER),** 5, b g Samum (GER)—Chandos Rose (IRE) **Mr J. Fyffe**
25 **CONQUREDALOFEUROPE (IRE),** 8, b g Presenting—Sleepless Eye **The Horse Watchers 9**
26 **COULD BE TROUBLE (IRE),** 8, b m Yeats (IRE)—She's No Trouble (IRE) **KC Sofas Ltd**
27 **CREATIVE CONTROL (IRE),** 7, b g Battle of Marengo (IRE)—Intricate Dance (USA) **Clwydian Connections**
28 **DEDANSER (IRE),** 7, b g Frammassone (IRE)—Courtown Bowe VII **Sarah & Wayne Dale**
29 **DINO BELLAGIO,** 4, b g Doyen (IRE)—Savingforvegas (IRE) **Nick Brown Racing**
30 **DREAMS OF HOME (IRE),** 7, b g Jet Away—Knocktartan (IRE) **Colin & Kay Taylor**
31 **EASTER JUNCTION (IRE),** 5, ch g Mount Nelson—Easter Day (IRE) **Noel Fehily Racing Syndicates- Easter Ju**
32 **ECLAIRANT LE MONDE,** 4, b f Champs Elysees—Clemency **David, Ben & Thomas Lockwood 1**
33 **ESME SHELBY (IRE),** 8, b m Arctic Cosmos (USA)—Kyle Again (IRE) **Red Rum Racing 1**
34 **FALANGHINA,** 6, gr m Ocovango—Whisky Rose (IRE) **Mrs C. A. Shaw**
35 **FFREE PEDRO (IRE),** 7, b g Yeats (IRE)—Ain't Misbehavin (IRE) **Ratkatcha Racing**
36 **FORCING BULL (FR),** 6, b g Papal Bull—Florice (GER) **The Turner Family**
37 **FORPADDYTHEPLUMBER (IRE),** 7, b g Ask—Doneraile Parke (IRE) **Mr G. E. Fitzpatrick**
38 **FRUIT N NUT (IRE),** 7, b g Carlotamix (FR)—Perilously (USA) **L. Buckley**
39 **GAELIK COAST (FR),** 9, br g Coastal Path—Gaelika (IRE) **T. G. Leslie**
40 **GALUNGGUNG (FR),** 7, gr g Khalkevi (IRE)—Unibelle (FR) **Nigel Dunnington & David Shaw**
41 **GAMETIME (IRE),** 6, b g Gatewood—Madame Von Meck (IRE) **Craig & Laura Buckingham**
42 **GENERAL OFFICER (IRE),** 6, br g Soldier of Fortune (IRE)—Oscar'swan (IRE) **Mr J. Fyffe**
43 **GENEVER DRAGON (IRE),** 6, b g Dragon Pulse (IRE)—Glen Ginnie (IRE) **Middleham Park Racing C**
44 **GEROMINO (FR),** 7, b g Masked Marvel—Romane Place (FR) **Mr G. E. Fitzpatrick**
45 **GLORY BRIDGE (IRE),** 7, b g Fame And Glory—Youngborogal (IRE) **Exors of the Late Mr T. J. Hemmings**
46 **GOLD EMERY (FR),** 7, gr g Doctor Dino (FR)—Queissa (FR) **Dalwhinnie Bloodstock Limited**
47 **GOOBINATOR (USA),** 7, ch g Noble Mission—Lilac Lilly (USA) **T. G. Leslie**
48 **GRAIN D'OUDAIRIES (FR),** 7, b g Kapgarde (FR)—Miss d'Estruval (FR) **Mr J. P. McManus**
49 **GREDIN (FR),** 7, ch g Masked Marvel—Valbrune (FR) **N.Y.P.D Racing**
50 **GREY SKIES (IRE),** 7, gr g Cloudings (IRE)—Garden Heaven (IRE) **Mr T. W. Fearn**
51 **GUILLAUME (IRE),** 6, b g Yeats (IRE)—Theleze (FR) **The Shinton Family 1**
52 **HAVEANOTHERGOFLO (IRE),** 6, b g Court Cave (IRE)—Gowiththeflo (IRE) **T. G. Leslie**
53 **HEARTBREAK KID (IRE),** 8, b g Getaway (GER)—Bella's Bury **T. G. Leslie**
54 **HENRY GRAY (IRE),** 7, gr g Doyen (IRE)—Gray's Anatomy (IRE) **L. Buckley**
55 **HEROS DE MOUTIERS (FR),** 6, b g Creachadoir (IRE)—Moriany (FR) **T W Johnson & G Maxwell**
56 **HIDALGO DE L'ISLE (FR),** 6, b g Coastal Path—Agence de L'Isle (FR) **T. G. Leslie**

MR DONALD MCCAIN - continued

57 **HOME SWEET HIGHWAY (IRE),** 6, b g Walk In The Park (IRE)—Dancing Bird (IRE) **Fine Claret Racing**
58 **I NEED YOU (FR),** 5, b m Great Pretender (IRE)—Similaresisoldofa (FR) **Middleham Park Racing C**
59 **ICE DE PAIL (FR),** 5, b m Cokoriko (FR)—Rosalie Malta (FR) **Ratkatcha Racing**
60 **ICEMAN DENNIS (FR),** 5, gr g Spanish Moon (USA)—Queissa (FR) **Mr J. M. Glews**
61 **INDEPENDENT JIMMY,** 4, b g Clovis du Berlais (FR)—Crystal Princess (IRE) **Mr I. Furlong**
62 **INKWELL,** 4, b f Intello (GER)—Three By Three (IRE) **P. Newton**
63 **INTO THE SUNSET (IRE),** 6, b g Ask—Try It Again (IRE) **Donald McCain Racing Club**
64 **IORANGI DE L'ISLE (FR),** 5, b g Lauro (GER)—Naiade de L'Isle (FR) **T. G. Leslie**
65 **JIPEKAA MACHIN (FR),** 4, b g Saonois (FR)—Salsavina (FR) **KC Sofas Ltd**
66 **JOMIG DES BOIS (FR),** 6, b g Great Pretender (IRE)—Norma Jean (IRE) **Greener Day Racing**
67 **JUNGLE JACK,** 7, ch g Doyen (IRE)—Skew **T. G. Leslie**
68 4, B f Cokoriko (FR)—Kayfleur
69 **KEROSINE LIGHT (IRE),** 6, b g Ask—Quadrennial (IRE) **Mark Kelly Racing Syndicate**
70 **KILBUNNY APLASIA (IRE),** 6, b m Flemensfirth (USA)—Gypsy Mo Chara (IRE) **Mr N. Hartley**
71 **KILLANE (IRE),** 8, b g Cloudings (IRE)—Kilkylane (IRE) **The Horses Mouth Racing Club**
72 **LADY TREMAINE (IRE),** 8, b m Kalanisi (IRE)—Lough Lein Leader (IRE) **Nigel Dunnington & David Shaw**
73 **LARGY REACH,** 7, b g Phoenix Reach (IRE)—Kallithea (IRE) **Red Rum Racing 3**
74 **LATINO FLING (IRE),** 8, b m Milan—Five of Spades (IRE) **Colin & Kay Taylor**
75 **LOST IN TRANSIT (IRE),** 6, gr g Libertarian—Rosafi (IRE) **David & Carol Shaw**
76 **LOVIN JUKEBOX (GER),** 5, b g Jukebox Jury (IRE)—Lovin Desert (GER) **Birkdale Bloodstock**
77 **LUCKIE MONEY (IRE),** 7, b m Most Improved (IRE)—Indian Bounty **Barry McGleenon & Thomas McAlister**
78 **MACKENBERG (GER),** 8, b g Jukebox Jury (IRE)—Mountain Melody (GER) **T. G. Leslie**
79 **MALPAS (IRE),** 8, b g Milan—Skipping Along (IRE) **Mr N. Hartley**
80 **MASKED CRUSADER (FR),** 7, gr g Masked Marvel—Textos (FR) **The Good Stock Syndicate**
81 **MASTER MALACHY (IRE),** 7, b g Mastercraftsman (IRE)—Stroke of Six (IRE) **T. G. Leslie**
82 **MAXIMILIAN (GER),** 7, ch g Adlerflug (GER)—Maxima (GER) **Owners Group 099**
83 **MERRY POPPINS (GER),** 6, gr m Authorized (IRE)—Manita (IRE) **Mrs C. O'Connor**
84 **MILANS EDGE (IRE),** 8, b m Milan—The Keane Edge (IRE) **James and Jean Potter Ltd**
85 **MINELLA DRAMA (IRE),** 8, b g Flemensfirth (USA)—Midsummer Drama (IRE) **Green Day Racing**
86 **MINELLA PLUS (IRE),** 6, b g Walk In The Park (IRE)—Violin Davis (FR) **Miss C. McCracken**
87 **MINELLA TRUMP (IRE),** 9, b g Shantou (USA)—One Theatre (IRE) **T. G. Leslie**
88 **MINELLADESTINATION (IRE),** 6, b m Flemensfirth (USA)—Tweedledrum **Penketh & Sankey Jech Racing Club**
89 **MISTER WHITAKER (IRE),** 11, b g Court Cave (IRE)—Benbradagh Vard (IRE) **T. G. Leslie**
90 **MOONLIT PARK (IRE),** 6, b m Walk In The Park (IRE)—Lakil Princess (IRE) **Mr T. G. Leslie & Partners**
91 **MY LITTLE TONI,** 5, br m Kayf Tara—Interim Lodge (IRE) **National Hunt Racing Club**
92 **NACHO (IRE),** 5, b g Camacho—Equinette (IRE) **Mrs Carol Shaw 1**
93 **NAVAJO PASS,** 7, b g Nathaniel (IRE)—Navajo Charm **T. G. Leslie**
94 **NAYATI (FR),** 9, b g Spirit One (FR)—Smadouce (FR) **CP Racing**
95 **NEFYN POINT,** 9, gr g Overbury (IRE)—So Cloudy **Dalwhinnie Bloodstock Limited**
96 **NELL'S BELLS (IRE),** 7, b m Milan—Miss Cilla (IRE) **Mrs S. C. Leslie**
97 **NEVER NO TROUBLE,** 4, b f Time Test—Kitba **D. R. McCain**
98 **NORA THE XPLORER,** 8, b m Norse Dancer (IRE)—Bijou Love (IRE) **Mr D. Sherlock**
99 **OLD FOLK TALE (IRE),** 6, b g Libertarian—Raheen Lady (IRE) **Mr T. W. Fearn**
100 **ON CLOUD NINE (IRE),** 5, b m Cloudings (IRE)—Role Model (FR) **Miss C. McCracken**
101 **ONTHEFRONTFOOT (IRE),** 9, b g Shantou (USA)—On The Backfoot (IRE) **Nigel Dunnington & David Shaw**
102 **PATIENT DREAM (FR),** 5, b g Al Kazeem—Parnell's Dream **More Turf Racing**
103 **PRESENT FAIR (IRE),** 6, b g Presenting—Premier Victory (IRE) **T. G. Leslie**
104 **PRESENTANDCOUNTING (IRE),** 9, b g Presenting—Count On Me (IRE) **The Turner Family**
105 **PUNTA PRIMA (IRE),** 6, br g Mahler—Ballinahow Ann (IRE) **Mrs J. L. Edwards**
106 **QUARESOME (IRE),** 5, b g Parish Hall (IRE)—Grinneas (IRE) **Owners Group 114**
107 **RED VISION (FR),** 8, b g Vision d'Etat (FR)—Petale Rouge (FR) **Miss C. Lees-Jones**
108 **REGGAE DE BAUNE (FR),** 5, ch g Spanish Moon (USA)—Sofia de Baune (FR)
109 **RICHMOND LAKE (IRE),** 7, b g Westerner—Chic Milan (IRE) **Exors of the Late Mr T. J. Hemmings**
110 **ROC OF DUNDEE (IRE),** 6, b m Shirocco (GER)—Miss Dundee (IRE) **Miss C. McCracken**
111 **ROYAL MOGUL (IRE),** 7, b g Doyen (IRE)—Tearaway Queen (IRE) **Craig & Laura Buckingham**
112 **SACRE PIERRE (FR),** 5, b g On Est Bien (IRE)—Goldance (FR) **Cheshire Bloodstock Racing 1**
113 **SEE THE SEA (IRE),** 9, b m Born To Sea (IRE)—Shahmina (IRE) **The Shinton Family 1**
114 **SILVER FLYER,** 7, b g Malinas (GER)—Silver Gypsy (IRE) **Nigel Dunnington & David Shaw**
115 **SINCE DAY ONE (IRE),** 7, b g Fame And Glory—Collou (IRE) **Mr C. B. Strang Steel**
116 **SISTER JULIENNE,** 5, b m Kayf Tara—Urticaire (FR) **R. K. Aston**

MR DONALD MCCAIN - continued

117 SLEEPING SATELLITE (IRE), 5, br g Mahler—Aneda Dubh (IRE) **The Good Stock Syndicate**
118 SOMEWHAT CLOUDY (IRE), 7, b m Presenting—Clara Mc Cloud (IRE) **Miss C. McCracken**
119 SOVEREIGN STAR (IRE), 5, b g Soldier of Fortune (IRE)—Sovereign Lass (IRE) **Old Gold Racing 16**
120 SPECTACULAR GENIUS (IRE), 6, ch g Doyen (IRE)—Present Line (IRE) **T. G. Leslie**
121 SPIRIT OF REGULUS (IRE), 5, gr g Walk In The Park (IRE)—La Segnora (FR) **Colin & Kay Taylor**
122 5, B m Doyen (IRE)—Stateable Case (IRE)
123 SULLIVAN'S BROW (IRE), 8, b g Flemensfirth (USA)—Beths Bell (IRE) **KC Sofas Ltd**
124 TARAGRACE (IRE), 7, b m Presenting—Seekayclaire (IRE) **Ceffyl cymraeg**
125 TEASING GEORGIA (IRE), 7, b m New Approach (IRE)—Hallowed Park (IRE) **Mr J. Turner**
126 THE CON MAN (IRE), 10, b g Oscar (IRE)—Phillis Hill **T. G. Leslie**
127 THEATRICAL LIGHT (IRE), 5, b m Leading Light (IRE)—Theatrical Cailin (IRE) **Sarah & Wayne Dale**
128 TIM PAT (IRE), 7, b g Mahler—April Thyne (IRE) **T. G. Leslie**
129 4, Br f Yorgunnabelucky (USA)—Tintera (IRE) **R. Kent**
130 TOUGHASOLDBOOTS (IRE), 5, b m Soldier of Fortune (IRE)—Khirahs Firth (IRE) **Donald McCain Racing Club**
131 TUNE THE CHELLO (IRE), 8, b m Ask—New Chello (IRE) **Mrs J. E. Graves**
132 UPAGAINSTIT (IRE), 6, b g Presenting—Sunami Storm (IRE) **Miss C. McCracken**
133 VE DAY (IRE), 4, b g Churchill (IRE)—Cochabamba (IRE) **Owners Group 111**
134 VINTAGE VALLEY (IRE), 4, gr g Mastercraftsman (IRE)—Lea Valley **Mr J. Fyffe**
135 VIRTUOSO, 4, b f Passing Glance—Make Music **Red Rum Racing**
136 WALL OF FAME (IRE), 8, b g Fame And Glory—Sanadja (IRE) **Mr A. Whelan**
137 WASPY (IRE), 5, b g Doyen (IRE)—Poly Kalo (IRE) **The Good Stock Syndicate**
138 WHITEHAVEN (FR), 6, bl g Le Havre (IRE)—Passion Blanche **Mr & Mrs G. Calder**
139 WINCHMORE HILL (IRE), 6, b g Walk In The Park (IRE)—Hats And Heels (IRE) **T. G. Leslie**
140 WORD HAS IT (IRE), 9, b g Jeremy (USA)—Rathfeigh (IRE) **T. G. Leslie**
141 YELLOW JACKET, 6, b g Blue Bresil (FR)—Cent Prime **Donald McCain Racing Club**
142 ZAFAR (GER), 8, b g Kamsin (GER)—Zambuka (FR) **Mrs S. K. McCain**
143 ZAMOND (FR), 7, b g Diamond Green (FR)—Cosavita (FR) **Hale Racing, the Lyle Family & Partner**

THREE-YEAR-OLDS

144 LECCE LADY, b f Golden Horn—Carlanda (FR) **Mrs S. C. Leslie**
145 B g Australia—Moondust (IRE) **T. G. Leslie**
146 WEIGH ANCHOR, ch f Nathaniel (IRE)—Miss Chaussini (IRE) **Mrs S. C. Leslie**

Assistant Trainer: Adrian Lane.

NH Jockey: Brian Hughes. **Conditional Jockey:** Theo Gillard, Peter Kavanagh, Abbie McCain. **Amateur Jockey:** Charlie Maggs, Will Maggs, Toby McCain-Mitchell.

---

336 MR PHIL MCENTEE, Newmarket

Postal: **Racefield Stables, Carriageway, Hamilton Road, Newmarket, Suffolk, CB8 7JQ**
Contacts: **PHONE 01638 662092 MOBILE 07802 663256**
WORK EMAIL mcenteephil@yahoo.com

1 ALAFDHAL (IRE), 5, ch g Lope de Vega (IRE)—Afdhaad **Miss M. Hancox**
2 AUTUMN FLIGHT (IRE), 7, b g Dandy Man (IRE)—Swallow Falls (IRE) **Miss R. B. McEntee**
3 BAKERSBOY, 5, b g Oasis Dream—Dubai Bounty **Carol & David Whymark**
4 BIG TIME MAYBE (IRE), 8, b g Dandy Man (IRE)—Divine Design (IRE) **Lamprell Roofing Ltd**
5 BILL PLUMB (IRE), 4, b g Footstepsinthesand—Provence **Miss M. Hancox**
6 BOBBY ON THE BEAT (IRE), 5, b g Bobby's Kitten (USA)—Late Night Movie (IRE) **Ruby Red Racing**
7 BRAVE DISPLAY (IRE), 9, b g Requinto (IRE)—Ashtown Girl (IRE) **Miss R. B. McEntee**
8 DIRTY BARRY (USA), 4, b g Blame (USA)—Cheer For Foxes (USA) **Miss M. Hancox**
9 EM JAY KAY, 4, b g Brazen Beau (AUS)—Skara Brae **T. D. Johnson**
10 FAITHLESS INSOMNIA, 4, b g Oasis Dream—Rive Gauche **D & C Watkins**
11 GO ON GAL (IRE), 10, b m Approve (IRE)—Jeritza **Mrs R. L. McEntee**
12 JACQUELINA (IRE), 4, b f Heeraat (IRE)—Springstride **T. D. Johnson**

MR PHIL MCENTEE - continued

13 **OSTILIO,** 8, ch g New Approach (IRE)—Reem Three **Miss M. Hancox**
14 **OUR LOUISE (IRE),** 4, b f Holy Roman Emperor (IRE)—A Place For Us (IRE) **Miss M. Hancox**
15 **PERSIAN WOLF (IRE),** 5, ch g Slade Power (IRE)—Riobamba (USA) **The Win Or Booze Racing Syndicate**
16 **PORFIN (IRE),** 5, b g Belardo (IRE)—Tropical Mist (IRE) **T. D. Johnson**
17 **RIVER CHORUS (IRE),** 5, b m Mehmas (IRE)—Scarlet Pimpernel **Carol & David Whymark**
18 **SEATTLE KING,** 4, b g Kingman—Snoqualmie Star **T. D. Johnson**
19 **SHORTS ON,** 4, b g Vadamos (FR)—Pearly Spirit (FR) **Ruby Red Racing II**
20 **SIMPLY GORGEOUS,** 4, b f Time Test—Leap of Joy (IRE) **E. A. Condon**
21 **SONNYSAURUS (IRE),** 4, b g Swiss Spirit—Hearsay **Miss R. B. McEntee**
22 **TIA DALMA (IRE),** 4, b f Prince of Lir (IRE)—Koh Tapu (IRE) **Ruby Red Racing III**
23 **TOM HAZELGROVE (IRE),** 4, gr g Alhebayeb (IRE)—With A Twist **Miss M. Hancox**

THREE-YEAR-OLDS

24 **GRAND CENTRAL,** b g Sioux Nation (USA)—Edessa (IRE) **Ruby Red Racing & Robin**
25 **LITTLE BETTY,** b f Bobby's Kitten (USA)—Twilight Sparkle (IRE) **Miss R. McEntee**
26 **RITAROCKS,** b f Heeraat (IRE)—Dutch Cat **Mrs R. L. Baker**

TWO-YEAR-OLDS

27 B f 23/03 Belardo (IRE)—Englishwoman (Acclamation) (4002) **Michelle Hancox & Robin McEntee**
28 **PADDY POWERFUL (IRE),** ch c 10/03 Free Eagle (IRE)—
Just Jealous (IRE) (Lope de Vega (IRE)) (1000) **Reynolds, Watkins R McEntee**

---

337 MR MURTY MCGRATH, Maidstone

Postal: **Galway Barn, Kiln Barn Road, East Malling, Kent, ME19 6BG**
Contacts: **PHONE 01732 840173 MOBILE 07818 098073**
EMAIL mjmcgrath@hotmail.com

1 **BALLYBAY (IRE),** 6, b g Walk In The Park (IRE)—Maple Lady (IRE) **Gallagher Bloodstock Limited**
2 **BALLYBAYMOONSHINER (FR),** 5, b g Dandy Man (IRE)—Haven's Wave (IRE) **Gallaghers**
3 **INIGO (FR),** 5, b g Authorized (IRE)—Cedilla (FR) **Gallagher Bloodstock Limited**
4 **REEL POWER,** 4, b g Highland Reel (IRE)—Ensaya (IRE) **Gallagher Bloodstock Limited**
5 **SEI BELLA,** 9, b m Crosspeace (IRE)—Dizzy Whizz **M. McGrath**

THREE-YEAR-OLDS

6 **LEITRIM ROCK (IRE),** b g Lope de Vega (IRE)—Dansky (IRE) **Gallagher Bloodstock & Ballylinch Stud**

Assistant Trainer: Heidi McGrath.

---

338 MRS JEAN MCGREGOR, Milnathort

Postal: **Wester Tillyrie Steading, Milnathort, Kinross, KY13 0RW**
Contacts: **PHONE 01577 861792 MOBILE 07764 464299**
EMAIL purebred68@hotmail.co.uk

1 **BURLINGTON BERT (FR),** 12, b g Califet (FR)—Melhi Sun (FR) **The Good To Soft Firm**
2 **DIAMOND ROAD (IRE),** 9, b g Tikkanen (USA)—Silver Tassie (FR) **Off and Running**
3 7, B m Bollin Eric—Ginger Brandy **Mrs D. Thomson**
4 **GO COMPLAIN,** 11, b m Mount Nelson—Trounce **Tillyrie Racing Club**
5 **IVYNATOR (IRE),** 5, b g Muhaarar—Venturous Spirit (FR) **The Good To Soft Firm**
6 **OSCAR BLUE (IRE),** 13, gr g Oscar (IRE)—Blossom Rose (IRE) **Tillyrie Racing Club**

MRS JEAN MCGREGOR - continued

NH Jockey: Henry Brooke, Sean Quinlan.

339

MISS JESSICA MCKIE, Wooler

Postal: **Lanton House, WOOLER, Northumberland, NE71 6TH**
Contacts: **PHONE 01668 216218**
EMAIL estateoffice@lantonestate.com

1 **TOKYO CALLING (IRE),** 6, b g Milan—Inch Native (IRE) **Miss J. Mckie**
2 **WATCH LAW (IRE),** 8, b g Court Cave (IRE)—Eyesabeatin (IRE) **Mrs V. J. McKie**

340

MISS HANNAH MICHELLE MCMAHON, Cousland

Postal: **Hansbury Stud, Quarrybank, Cousland,Dalkeith, Midlothian, EH22 2NT**
Contacts: **PHONE 07443 033976**
EMAIL jammyhanster@hotmail.co.uk

1 5, B m Dawn Approach (IRE)—Baila Me (GER) **Miss H. M. McMahon**
2 **BILBOA RIVER (IRE),** 7, b g Milan—Terracotta Queen (IRE) **Miss H. M. McMahon**
3 4, B g Proconsul—Chebsey Jubilee **Miss H. M. McMahon**
4 **CLONEYHURKE MAID (IRE),** 8, b m Tobougg (IRE)—Well Maid **Miss H. M. McMahon**
5 **GRAND MARIO (FR),** 6, ch g Nom de d'La (FR)—Nina La Belle (FR) **Miss H. M. McMahon**
6 **MISTAMEL (IRE),** 11, b g Rip Van Winkle (IRE)—Without Precedent (FR) **Miss H. M. McMahon**
7 **THE REAPING RACE (IRE),** 10, b g Flemensfirth (USA)—Native Design (IRE) **Miss H. M. McMahon**
8 **WONDEROFTHEWORLD (IRE),** 11, b g Beneficial—Our Lucky Supreme (IRE) **Miss H. M. McMahon**
9 **WORLDLY APPROACH (IRE),** 7, b m Dawn Approach (IRE)—Mundana (IRE) **Miss H. M. McMahon**

341

MISS FIONN MCSHARRY, Sheriff Hutton

Postal: **Dudley Barn, Sheriff Hutton, York, Yorkshire, YO60 6RU**
Contacts: **PHONE 07340 432785**
EMAIL mcsharry.fionn@gmail.com

1 **CEOLWULF,** 7, gr g Fame And Glory—Spieta (IRE) **Mr C. P. McSharry**
2 **TIGERPOMP,** 8, b m Fame And Glory—Saltbarrow **Mr C. P. McSharry**
3 **TIMETOTALK (IRE),** 7, b g Milan—Zalda **Mr C. P. McSharry**
4 **WELLFLEET WITCH,** 7, b m Black Sam Bellamy (IRE)—Indeed To Goodness (IRE) **Mr C. P. McSharry**

THREE-YEAR-OLDS

5 **ISADORA'S GIFT,** b f Tasleet—Dora's Sister (IRE) **Mr C. P. McSharry**

---

342 MR FREDDIE AND MARTYN MEADE, Manton Park

Postal: **Manton Park Racing, Marlborough, Wiltshire, SN8 4HB**
Contacts: **PHONE 01672 555000**
EMAIL racing@mantonpark.com

1 **CRESTA (FR),** 4, ch c New Bay—La Negra (IRE)
2 **EPIC POET (IRE),** 4, b c Lope de Vega (IRE)—Sagaciously (IRE)
3 **GLOUCESTERSHIRE (USA),** 5, b br g Flintshire—Ballade's Girl (USA)
4 **HOVER (IRE),** 6, ch g Free Eagle (IRE)—Badr Al Badoor (IRE)
5 **INFRASTRUCTURE,** 8, ch g Raven's Pass (USA)—Foundation Filly
6 **ZECHARIAH (IRE),** 4, b c Nathaniel (IRE)—Nancy O (IRE)

THREE-YEAR-OLDS

7 **ASHTANGA,** b f Nathaniel (IRE)—Yoga (IRE)
8 **CIARA STORM,** b f Nathaniel (IRE)—Francisca (USA)
9 **DAYZEE (IRE),** gr f Mastercraftsman (IRE)—Lizzy's Township (USA)
10 **ESCARPMENT (IRE),** b g Fastnet Rock (AUS)—Heroic Heart (FR)
11 **MODESTY (IRE),** b c Dubawi (IRE)—I Am Beautiful (IRE)
12 **SIERRA BLANCA (IRE),** b c No Nay Never (USA)—Alexandrova (IRE)
13 **VECCHIO (IRE),** b c Caravaggio (USA)—Private Paradise (IRE)
14 **WILTSHIRE,** b c Aclaim (IRE)—Simballina (IRE)
15 **YASMINA,** b f Iffraaj—Wilamina (IRE)

TWO-YEAR-OLDS

16 **AL BAHAR (QTR),** ch c 27/03 Saxon Warrior (JPN)—Favourable Terms (Selkirk (USA))
17 Ch c 12/01 Gleneagles (IRE)—Angel Love (GER) (Pivotal) (24810)
18 B f 01/03 Advertise—Aris (IRE) (Danroad (AUS))
19 B c 03/03 Advertise—Bazzana (Zebedee)
20 **BESTIE,** b c 12/04 Advertise—Simmy's Temple (Royal Applause) (51429)
21 B c 27/04 Advertise—Crown (IRE) (Royal Applause)
22 Ch c 24/02 Almanzor (FR)—Dieulefit (IRE) (Oasis Dream) (60024)
23 Ch c 29/03 Pastoral Pursuits—Engrossed (IRE) (Tamayuz)
24 B f 12/02 Eqtidaar (IRE)—Eolith (Pastoral Pursuits) (22000)
25 B f 26/01 Advertise—Flight To Fancy (Galileo (IRE)) (80032)
26 B c 20/03 Advertise—Grayling (Sea The Stars (IRE))
27 B f 03/02 Raven's Pass (USA)—Himalayan Queen (Poet's Voice) (19048)
28 Gr c 24/04 Golden Horn—Iromea (IRE) (Dansili)
29 B f 18/04 Advertise—Last Tango (FR) (Peintre Celebre (USA))
30 B f 31/03 Belardo (IRE)—Look of Love (IRE) (New Approach (IRE)) (12857)
31 B c 21/03 Too Darn Hot—Loveisallyouneed (IRE) (Sadler's Wells (USA)) (30000)
32 B f 26/04 Advertise—Lowanna (IRE) (Australia)
33 B f 27/04 Advertise—Marlyn (IRE) (Exceed And Excel (AUS))
34 B f 04/02 Awtaad (IRE)—Mesadah (IRE) (Raven's Pass (USA)) (38000)
35 B f 09/04 Advertise—Monogamy (Poet's Voice)
36 B br c 23/03 Kodi Bear (IRE)—Passionatta (IRE) (Intense Focus (USA)) (39048)
37 B c 02/03 Nathaniel (IRE)—Petits Fours (Lawman (FR)) (32000)
38 B c 15/03 Siyouni (FR)—Pilaster (Nathaniel (IRE)) (100000)
39 B c 14/05 Galileo (IRE)—Pink Dogwood (IRE) (Camelot) (130000)
40 B c 15/03 Advertise—Policy Term (IRE) (Authorized (IRE))
41 B f 19/03 Land Force (IRE)—Queen of Mean (Pivotal) (10000)
42 B c 29/04 Le Brivido (FR)—Rioticism (FR) (Rio de La Plata (USA)) (47619)
43 B c 13/02 Showcasing—Scintilating (Siyouni (FR)) (100000)
44 B c 07/02 New Bay—Smash (IRE) (Pivotal) (40016)
45 Ch c 17/02 Sea The Stars (IRE)—Swansdown (Dubawi (IRE)) (150000)
46 B f 12/03 Advertise—Wilamina (IRE) (Zoffany (IRE))

343 MR NOEL MEADE, Navan

Postal: **Tu Va Stables, Castletown KP, Navan, Co Meath, C15 F384, Ireland**
Contacts: **PHONE +353 46 905 4197 MOBILE +353 87 256 6039**
EMAIL tuvastables@gmail.com WEBSITE www.noelmeade.com

1 **AFTERCAER (IRE),** 4, b f Lauro—Onthebeach
2 **AZURE MAINE (IRE),** 6, br g Califet—Kizmehoney
3 **BARBARY MASTER,** 8, br g Presenting—Daisies Adventure
4 **BEACON EDGE (IRE),** 9, b g Doyen (IRE)—Laurel Gift (IRE)
5 **BLACK HAWK EAGLE (IRE),** 5, b g Awtaad—Nimboo
6 **BRIDGEHEAD (IRE),** 4, b g Belardo—Creese
7 **BUGS MORAN (IRE),** 6, b g Pour Moi—Vivachi
8 **CHESTNUTTER (IRE),** 4, ch f Anjaal—Sapporo
9 **CRASSUS (IRE),** 6, b h War Command—Buck Aspen
10 **DIOL KER (FR),** 9, b g Martaline—Stiren Bleue (FR)
11 **EUROBOT,** 9, ch g Malinas (GER)—L'Aventure (FR)
12 **EVERGLOW,** 8, b g Presenting—Cent Prime
13 **FARCEUR DU LARGE (FR),** 8, b g Turgeon (USA)—Antagua (FR)
14 **FERMOYLE,** 5, b g Fast Company—Mindy
15 **FLANKING MANEUVER (IRE),** 8, b g Beat Hollow—Corskeagh Shadow
16 **FOREIGN POLICY (IRE),** 4, gr g Outstrip—Seschat
17 **GANDERSTOWN (IRE),** 4, b g Vadamos—Celestial Fable
18 **GLOBAL BRIEF (IRE),** 5, b m Aizavoski—Grand Diem
19 **HARRY ALONZO (IRE),** 7, ch g Montmartre—Patrola
20 **HELVIC DREAM,** 6, b h Power—Rachevie (IRE)
21 **HIGHLAND CHARGE (IRE),** 8, b g Fame And Glory—Full Of Birds
22 **HYMIE WEISS,** 7, ch g Ocovango—Had To Be Done
23 **IDAS BOY (IRE),** 9, ch g Dubai Destination—Witness Express
24 **IN YOUR SHADOW (IRE),** 9, gr g Stowaway—Classic Lin (FR)
25 **JEFF KIDDER (IRE),** 6, b g Hallowed Crown (AUS)—Alpine
26 **JERANDME (IRE),** 9, b g Azamour—Estrelle
27 **JESSE EVANS (IRE),** 7, b g So You Think—American Princess
28 **JOE MASSERIA (IRE),** 4, b g Fast Company—Island Home
29 **JOSHUA WEBB,** 8, b g Flemensfirth (USA)—Lady of Appeal (IRE)
30 **KILLER MODE (IRE),** 8, b g Doyen—Cantou
31 5, B g Mount Nelson—Kizmehoney
32 **LADY OF INISHFREE (IRE),** 4, br f Farhh—Bittern
33 **LAYFAYETTE (IRE),** 6, b h French Navy—Scala Romana
34 **LIEUTENANT COMMAND (FR),** 9, gr g Kendargent (FR)—Maternelle (FR)
35 **LUKE SHORT,** 6, b g Sayif (IRE)—Acclamare (IRE)
36 **LUNAR POWER (IRE),** 5, ch g Power—Dusty Moon
37 **MAKINGACHAMP (IRE),** 5, b g Champs Elysees—Maka
38 **MIGHT AND MERCY,** 4, ch g Pearl Secret—Rocknahardplace
39 **MOUNT BROWN (IRE),** 6, b g Fulbright—Creese
40 **NUCKY JOHNSON (IRE),** 5, b g Vadamos—Sinful Pleasure
41 **PINKERTON,** 7, br g Ocovango—Mistress Pope
42 **POETS COTTAGE (IRE),** 4, b g Zoffany—Pearl Sea
43 5, B g Famous Name—Queen Commander
44 **RESILIENT FRONT (IRE),** 5, ch g Doyen—Magical Memoir
45 **ROAD TO RESPECT (IRE),** 12, ch g Gamut (IRE)—Lora Lady (IRE)
46 **ROSGALME (IRE),** 8, b g Mahler—Woodville Queen (IRE)
47 **ROYAL ROMEO (IRE),** 6, b g Mamool—Mariah Mooney
48 **SHEISBYBRID (IRE),** 5, gr m Mastercraftsman—Empowermentofwomen
49 **SIBERIAN PRINCE (IRE),** 7, ch g Shirocco—Sue N Win
50 **STEEL CABLE,** 8, b g Well Chosen—Apache Rose (IRE)
51 **THE MODEL KINGDOM (IRE),** 6, b m Aizavoski—Fickle Fortune
52 **THEDEVILSCOACHMAN (IRE),** 7, br g Elusive Pimpernel—Hagawi
53 **TOO BRIGHT (IRE),** 5, b g Fulbright—Galeaza
54 **ZOFFMAN (IRE),** 4, b g Zoffany—Empowermentofwomen

MR NOEL MEADE - continued

THREE-YEAR-OLDS

55 **BYZANTIUM BELLE,** b br f Churchill—Special Assignment
56 **DESERT HAVEN (IRE),** b c Oasis Dream—Fantacise
57 **DUTCH GOLD (IRE),** b c Galileo Gold—Dutch Monarch
58 **ENCOSTA,** b f Mukhadram—Maraaseem
59 B g Sea The Stars—Furia Cruzada
60 **GOLDEN TEMPLE,** b g Galileo Gold—Miss Sally
61 **GRANGE LADY (IRE),** b f Hawkbill—Aksaya
62 **HASTEN SLOWLY,** b f Kessaar—Hope Against Hope
63 **HEY WHATEVER,** gr f El Kabeir—Light Laughter
64 **HOKUSAI,** b g Raven's Pass—Maarit
65 **JALO,** b g Adaay—Firoza
66 **KATONAH (IRE),** gr f Dark Angel—Andorra
67 **KNOCKMORE PRINCE,** b g Dragon Pulse—Princesse Savoie
68 **LASTING PEACE (IRE),** ch g Helmet—Peace Of Glory
69 **MEGGY MOO,** b f Bungle Inthejungle—Zalanga
70 **MY BIRTHDAY GIRL,** ch f Churchill—Duljanah
71 **NOT JUST YET,** b g Nigh Of Thunder—Nefetari
72 **NOTTURNO (IRE),** b g Zoffany—Albarouche
73 **OPEN TO QUESTION,** ch g Noble Mission—Pick And Choose
74 **PEARL OF AUSTRALIA (IRE),** ch c Australia—Golden Pearl
75 **PULSE LIGHT,** ch g Dragon Pulse—Catch Light
76 **QUEENIE ST CLAIR,** b f Fast Company—Marmalade Cat
77 Ch g National Defense—Rarement
78 B g Berkshire—She's A Star
79 **SHE'S LOCAL (IRE),** br f Tasleet—Eshaadeh
80 **SPANISH SAINT (IRE),** b g Caravaggio—Shy Bride
81 **SPITFIRE FIGHTER,** b g Elusive Pimpernel—Summer Spice
82 **SUSIE WOSIE (IRE),** b f Zoffany—Pannonia
83 **TEA OLIVE (FR),** b f Mukhadram—Wahgah
84 **TENDER CAMILLA,** b f American Pharoah—Ana Luna
85 **UNION FLAG,** b g Starspangledbanner—Destalink
86 **VAN DEMON,** ch c Australia—Myrica
87 **WINSTON SPENCER,** b g Churchill—Glass Slipper
88 **ZERO FIGHTER,** b g Muhaarar—Kasayid

TWO-YEAR-OLDS

89 Bl g 08/04 Farhh—Adjudicate (Dansili)
90 Ch c 31/03 New Bay—Artesana (Mastercraftsman)
91 B c 05/05 Churchill—Athreyaa (Singspiel)
92 B c 11/05 Make Believe—Baby Love (It's Gino)
93 B c 16/02 US Navy Flag—Beramana (Nayef)
94 B f 21/03 Postponed—Double Diamond (Muhtathir)
95 B c 24/04 Kessaar—Drifting Spirit (Clodovil)
96 B c 07/05 Churchill—Glass Slipper (Danehill)
97 B c 25/03 Churchill—Little Kodi (Kodiac)
98 B g 06/02 Raven's Pass—Maarit (Harbour Watch)
99 B c 03/02 Inns Of Court—Malibu Beach (Mastercraftsman)
100 B f 02/05 Elzaam—Maqueda (Rock Hard Ten)
101 B g 11/03 Gregorian—Mindy (Zamindar)
102 Ch c 05/03 Belardo—Miss Dutee (Dubawi)
103 B c 25/01 James Garfield—Rebel Aclaim (Acclamation)
104 B c 15/04 Dragon Pulse—Rupa (Acclamation)
105 Gr f 08/04 Zoffany—Satwa Ruby (Verglas)
106 Gr c 24/03 Invincible Army—Silver Rainbow (Starspangledbanner)
107 B f 23/04 Zoffany—Simkana (Kalanisi)
108 B f 28/01 Churchill—Tammy Wynette (Tamayuz)
109 Ch f 04/03 Harzand—Wild Mix (Mastercraftsman)
110 B f 08/04 Showcasing—Wizara (Teofilo)

MR NOEL MEADE - continued

Assistant Trainer: Damien McGillick, **Head Man:** Paul Cullen, **Travelling Head:** Emma Connolly, **Racing Secretary:** Katie Daly.

NH Jockey: Bryan J Cooper. **Conditional Jockey:** Eoin Walsh. **Amateur Jockey:** Pat Taaffe.

---

344 MR NEIL MECHIE, Leyburn

Postal: **55 The Springs, Middleham, Leyburn, North Yorkshire, DL8 4RB**

1 **BILLY WEDGE,** 8, b g Arabian Gleam—Misu Billy **Kerr, Lawson**
2 **GOLD RING,** 6, b g Golden Horn—La Dorotea (IRE) **Kerr, Lawson**
3 **HAVANA CABANA,** 5, b m Havana Gold (IRE)—Word Perfect **The Kerr and Mechie Families**
4 **MEDICINE WHEEL,** 7, b g Multiplex—Blushing Heart **Mrs S. M. Pearson**
5 **MONTICELLO (IRE),** 9, b g Teofilo (IRE)—Towards (USA) **Mrs L. E. Mechie**

---

345 MR BRIAN MEEHAN, Manton

Trainer did not wish details of their string to appear

---

346 MR DAVID MENUISIER, Pulborough

Postal: **Shinco Racing Limited, Coombelands Racing Stables, Coombelands Lane, Pulborough, West Sussex, RH20 1BP**
Contacts: **MOBILE 07876 674095**
WORK EMAIL david@dmhorseracing.com WEBSITE www.dmhorseracing.com TWITTER @ DavidMenuisier

1 **ADELA OF CHAMPAGNE (FR),** 4, b f Kingman—Havre de Paix (FR) **Clive Washbourn & Peter Fagan**
2 **BELLOCCIO (FR),** 5, ro g Belardo (IRE)—Three Cards **All for One Racing**
3 **CAIUS CHORISTER (FR),** 4, b f Golden Horn—Corpus Chorister (FR) **Mr C. A. Washbourn**
4 **CANDY SHACK (FR),** 4, b f Almanzor (FR)—Dilbar (IRE) **Mr C. N. Wright**
5 **EGOISTE (USA),** 4, b g Flintshire—Denomination (USA) **Mr D. Menuisier**
6 **FLYIN' SOLO,** 6, br g Roderic O'Connor (IRE)—Fille Good **Mrs H. Ringrose & Mrs D. Thompson**
7 **GONNETOT (FR),** 4, b g Recorder—Gondole **Gerard Augustin-Normand & Partner**
8 **LA BELLE AURORE (FR),** 4, b f Motivator—Radiation (FR) **The Glow Worms**
9 **MIGRATION (IRE),** 7, b g Alhebayeb (IRE)—Caribbean Ace (IRE) **Gail Brown Racing (IX)**
10 **NUITS ST GEORGES (IRE),** 8, ch g Mount Nelson—Twelfth Night (IRE) **Boy George Partnership**
11 **SIR BOB PARKER (FR),** 4, b c Siyouni (FR)—Pacifique (IRE) **Michael & Brett Watkins**
12 **SPYFALL (FR),** 4, b f Iffraaj—Gallifrey **Chasemore Farm LLP**
13 **TOIMY SON (FR),** 4, b c Twilight Son—Miss Pimpernel (IRE) **Toimy Son Partnership**
14 **WINTER REPRISE (FR),** 6, b g Intello (GER)—Winter Fashion (FR) **Mr C. A. Washbourn**

THREE-YEAR-OLDS

15 **ANTICIPATING,** b f Bated Breath—Kekova **Mr T. G. Roddick**
16 **ASHMORE (IRE),** b c More Than Ready (USA)—Revolutionintheair (USA) **Gail Brown Racing/Shooting**
17 **BULLET (FR),** ch g Zoustar (AUS)—Pertinence (IRE) **Prime Equestrian Racing**
18 **BUXLOW BOY,** b c Cityscape—Buxlow Belle (FR) **Mrs A. K. Oldfield**
19 **CARAVANSERAI (IRE),** b f Camelot—High Fidelity (GER) **Quantum Leap Racing IV**
20 **ENTRANCEMENT (FR),** b f Expert Eye—Entree **Be Hopeful (2)**

MR DAVID MENUISIER - continued

21 **GEM,** b f Frankel—Keertana (USA) **Prime Equestrian Racing**
22 **GOODWOOD VISION,** b f Oasis Dream—Redskin Dancer (IRE) **Goodwood Racehorse Owners Group (28)**
23 **HEARTACHE TONIGHT (FR),** b f Recorder—Salvation **Chris Wright & Andy Macdonald**
24 **LA ESPANOLA (IRE),** b f Ribchester (IRE)—Corpus Chorister (FR) **Ignacio Bandres & Clive Washbourn**
25 **METAVERSE (IRE),** ch c Starspangledbanner (AUS)—Golden Song **Mr K. Sohi**
26 **MUDSKIPPER,** b c Le Havre (IRE)—Arendelle **Nicholas Mustoe & Chasemore**
27 **MYSTERIOUS LOVE (IRE),** b f Dark Angel (IRE)—Ma Cherie **Ms E. L. Banks**
28 **ON THE CARDS (FR),** b br c Attendu (FR)—Radiation (FR) **P & S Davis**
29 **PELISSANNE (FR),** b f Sioux Nation (USA)—Tahilla (IRE) **Michael Watt & Partner**
30 **PURE GOLD,** b f Golden Horn—Nathalie **Hurst-Brown, Ham, Needham**
31 **RULE OF THUMB (FR),** ch c Highland Reel (IRE)—Lockup (IRE) **Prime Equestrian Racing**
32 **SAKURA STAR,** b f Awtaad (IRE)—Shamakiya (IRE)
33 **SALAMANCAN (FR),** b g Recoletos (FR)—Vezina (FR) **Quantum Leap Racing VII**
34 **SEAGALA (FR),** b f Galiway—Kensea (FR) **Guy Pariente & Groupe KR**
35 **STAR SIGHT,** b f Expert Eye—Bizzarria **Tiger Racing**
36 **SURGE (FR),** b f Churchill (IRE)—Kapitale (GER) **Prime Equestrian Racing**
37 **WAXING GIBBOUS,** b f Sea The Moon (GER)—Mary Boleyn (IRE) **Chasemore Farm LLP**

TWO-YEAR-OLDS

38 Ch f 18/04 Ribchester (IRE)—Ashaaqah (IRE) (Dansili) (20808) **Mrs N. Hutchings**
39 B f 16/03 Masar (IRE)—Badweia (USA) (Kingmambo (USA)) (32000) **Five Arcs & A Covenant**
40 Gr f 05/03 Le Brivido (FR)—Buxlow Belle (FR) (Authorized (IRE)) **Mrs A. K. Oldfield**
41 B f 27/01 Camelot—Corinthian Girl (IRE) (Raven's Pass (USA)) (40000) **Austin, McCallum, Holtby & Clearwater**
42 B c 18/04 Ribchester (IRE)—Examinee (GER) (Monsun (GER)) (38000) **Quantum Leap Racing XIII**
43 **GOODWOOD ODYSSEY,** b c 20/02 Ulysses (IRE)—
Tropicana Bay (Oasis Dream) (50000) **Goodwood Racehorse Owners Group (29)**
44 **LAURA BAY (IRE),** b f 24/04 New Bay—Bridge of Peace (Anabaa (USA)) **Mr C. A. Washbourn**
45 **MASTER BUILDER,** b c 20/02 Mastercraftsman (IRE)—Laufeen (IRE) (Montjeu (IRE)) (19208) **Mr A. J. G. Walls**
46 **MYTHICAL LIGHT,** ch c 26/02 Waldgeist—Moonlight Danceuse (IRE) (Bering) (55000) **Gail Brown Racing (XV)**
47 **SISKARO (FR),** b c 05/02 Galiway—Siskadam (FR) (Kendargent (FR)) (48019) **Guy Pariente**
48 **SUNWAY (FR),** b c 23/03 Galiway—
Kensea (FR) (Kendargent (FR)) (240096) **Guy Pariente, Groupe KR & Thomas Lines**
49 B f 11/03 Le Havre (IRE)—
Super Eria (FR) (Hold That Tiger (USA)) (62000) **Chris Wright & Gerard St Augustin-Normand**
50 **THUNDER SPARKS (FR),** ch f 15/05 The Grey Gatsby (IRE)—
Soft Awakening (FR) (Rip Van Winkle (IRE)) (12005) **Shinco Racing Limited**
51 B f 29/03 Soldier Hollow—Tres Magnifique (FR) (Zoffany (IRE)) (16006) **Quantum Leap Racing VIII**
52 **TRIBAL CHIEF,** b c 31/03 Sioux Nation (USA)—Araca (FR) (Elusive Quality (USA)) (41617) **All For One Racing (II)**
53 **UNIVERSE (FR),** b c 05/04 Sea The Stars (IRE)—
Shamtee (IRE) (Shamardal (USA)) (272109) **Prime Equestrian Racing**
54 **WALDORA (FR),** ch f 13/03 Waldgeist—Imperatrice (IRE) (Kitten's Joy (USA)) (80032) **Guy Pariente & Partner**
55 **WAR CHIMES (FR),** b f 12/04 Summer Front (USA)—
Chipolata (FR) (Muhtathir) (49620) **Tars Farm Equestrian Stud**
56 **WAR DIRECTOR (IRE),** b c 28/02 Churchill (IRE)—Creative Director (USA) (War Front (USA)) (96038) **Tars Farm Equestrian Stud**
57 **XAARINE (FR),** b f 10/03 Goken (FR)—Xaarina (FR) (Aussie Rules (USA)) **Guy Pariente**
58 **XIOMARA (IRE),** b f 18/03 Lope de Vega (IRE)—Martlet (Dansili) (80032) **Tars Farm Equestrian Stud**

Assistant Trainer: Alex Badri, James Johnson, **Head Lad:** Dora Lenge, **Travelling Head:** Christophe Aebi, **Secretary:** Hayley Edgar, Katherine Hogan, Kim Johnstone.

347 MISS REBECCA MENZIES, Sedgefield

Postal: **Howe Hills Farm, Sedgefield, Stockton-On-Tees, Cleveland, TS21 2HG**
Contacts: **MOBILE 07843 169217**
WORK EMAIL Rebecca@rebeccamenziesracing.co.uk WEBSITE www.rebeccamenziesracing.com
TWITTER @Rebeccaemenzies

1 **ANGEL AMADEA,** 5, gr m Dark Angel (IRE)—Keene Dancer **Flash Figs Racing**
2 **AREYOUWITHUS (IRE),** 8, b g Watar (IRE)—Miss Sinnott (IRE) **J. Wade**
3 **ASKALLI (IRE),** 6, b g Ask—Gift Wrapped (IRE) **J. Wade**
4 4, B f Scorpion (IRE)—Astrodiamond
5 **ATTENTION ALL (IRE),** 5, b g Westerner—Moon Light Shadow **Emmerton, Johnson B Stevens**
6 **BALLYPOREEN (IRE),** 6, b g Fame And Glory—Littlemissthistle (IRE) **The Top Silk Syndicate**
7 **BATMAN FOR EVER (GER),** 6, gr g Jukebox Jury (IRE)—Bear Nora (GER) **Mr A. McCormack**
8 **BEWARE OF SAM,** 4, ch g Black Sam Bellamy (IRE)—Molly Pitcher (IRE) **J. Wade**
9 **BLOFELD (IRE),** 4, ch g Diamond Boy (FR)—Sorcillera **J. Wade**
10 **BOOMSLANG,** 6, b g Schiaparelli (GER)—Poisonous (FR) **Miss M. D. Myco**
11 **BOOT 'N' SHOE (IRE),** 5, b g Ask—Phecda (FR) **Mr D. Parry**
12 **BOWLAND BELLE,** 6, b m Black Sam Bellamy (IRE)—Samrana (FR) **Graham & Christine Seward**
13 **CABINET MAKER (IRE),** 4, gr g Mastercraftsman (IRE)—Elegant Peace (IRE) **Ursa Major Racing Club & Partner 1**
14 **CARLO STORM (IRE),** 7, gr g Carlotamix (FR)—Speedy River (IRE) **Mr I. C. Wilson**
15 **CHECK MY PULSE (IRE),** 7, b g Dragon Pulse (IRE)—Little Luxury (IRE) **Miss M. D. Myco**
16 **COCO LOCO (FR),** 4, ch g Ultra (IRE)—Kapirovska (FR) **Weight, Howe & Oliver**
17 **COURT CASE (IRE),** 5, b g Court Cave (IRE)—Dark Sari (IRE) **J. Wade**
18 **CURLEY FINGER (IRE),** 6, b g Getaway (GER)—Tooreen (IRE) **Club Racing Curley Partnership**
19 **DALYOTIN (FR),** 7, b g Poliglote—Dalyonne (FR) **Gay & Peter Hartley**
20 **DARK AGENT (IRE),** 5, gr g Dark Angel (IRE)—Lethal Lena (IRE) **Mr G. R. McGladery**
21 **DISCO ANNIE (IRE),** 5, b m Court Cave (IRE)—Betty Beck (IRE) **Graham & Christine Seward**
22 **DO YE WANNA (IRE),** 5, ch g Doyen (IRE)—Raphuca (IRE) **J. Wade**
23 **DOGGED,** 6, b g Due Diligence (USA)—Bling Bling (IRE) **Rebecca Menzies Racing Partnerships**
24 **EDGEWELL (IRE),** 5, b g Well Chosen—One Edge (IRE) **J. Wade**
25 5, Ch m Beat Hollow—Fairly Definite (IRE) **Mr I. Kurdi**
26 **FEVER ROQUE (FR),** 8, gr g Diamond Boy (FR)—Belle Saga (FR) **Graham & Christine Seward**
27 **FLURRY HEART,** 4, ch f Sea The Moon (GER)—Twilight Sparkle (IRE) **Mr G. R. McGladery**
28 **FONZERELLI (IRE),** 7, b m Schiaparelli (GER)—Cadoutene (FR) **Graham & Christine Seward**
29 **FRIENDLY FIRE (IRE),** 6, b m Walk In The Park (IRE)—Call Again (IRE) **Mrs J. Forster**
30 **FUTURE BENEFITS (IRE),** 6, b g Leading Light (IRE)—Benefit Miss (IRE) **J. Wade**
31 **GETAREASON (IRE),** 10, ch g Getaway (GER)—Simple Reason (IRE) **Titanium Racing Club**
32 4, Ch g Doyen (IRE)—Goaskhannah (IRE) **J. Wade**
33 **HAD TO BE HUGO (IRE),** 6, b g Ocovango—Had To Be Done (IRE) **ValueRacingClub.co.uk**
34 **HASTY BROOK (FR),** 6, b g Saddex—Brookdale (FR) **Who & Hasty Enterprise**
35 **HIGH MOON,** 8, b g Midnight Legend—Dizzy Frizzy **Miss M. D. Myco**
36 **HILLSIDE (IRE),** 5, b g Hillstar—Jennys Joy (IRE) **Miss M. D. Myco**
37 4, Br f Telescope (IRE)—I'm Delilah
38 **ICE DAY (FR),** 5, b m Walzertakt (GER)—Vanika Place (FR) **Mr I. Kurdi**
39 **ICE PYRAMID (IRE),** 8, ch g New Approach (IRE)—Coolnagree (IRE) **Bill Fraser & Adrian Pritchard**
40 **IVOIRE D'AVRIL (FR),** 5, ch m Magadino (FR)—Une Dame d'Avril (FR) **DFA Racing (Evie)**
41 **JERSEY STREAM (FR),** 4, b g Spanish Moon (USA)—Camiflora (FR) **Graham & Christine Seward**
42 **KING CARNEY,** 6, ch g Australia—Petit Trianon **The Risk Takers Partnership**
43 **KOPA KILANA (IRE),** 6, b g Milan—Kophinou (FR) **J. Wade**
44 **LADY MENDOZA (IRE),** 6, b m Court Cave (IRE)—Glen's Gift (IRE) **Coral Racing Club**
45 **LENEBANE (IRE),** 5, b m Vadamos (FR)—Callmeakhab (IRE) **Old Gold Racing 15**
46 **LIHYAN (IRE),** 5, b g Vendangeur (IRE)—Elle Est Milan (IRE) **Bill Fraser & Adrian Pritchard**
47 **LOVE YOUR WORK (IRE),** 7, ch g Helmet (AUS)—Little Italy (USA) **Greenwaste Solutions UK Ltd**
48 **MAJOR SNUGFIT,** 7, ch g Ruler of The World (IRE)—Bridle Belle **Breath Of Fresh Air Racing**
49 **MEWS HOUSE,** 6, ch g Coach House (IRE)—Beauty Pageant (IRE) **Flash Figs Racing**
50 **MISTER MOODLES,** 5, b g Phoenix Reach (IRE)—Sherry **Stonegrave Thoroughbreds**
51 4, B g Snow Sky—Moody Queen (IRE) **J. Wade**
52 4, B g Arctic Cosmos (USA)—Moscow Mistress (IRE) **Miss M. D. Myco**
53 **NORMAN KINDU,** 5, b g Lawman (FR)—Kindu **Diamond Racing Ltd**
54 **NORTONTHORPEBANKER,** 5, b br g Charming Thought—Scented Garden **E. A. Brook**
55 **ODD SOCKS HAVANA,** 5, b g Havana Gold (IRE)—Hamloola **Breath Of Fresh Air Racing**

MRS REBECCA MENZIES - continued

56 **OLIVER'S ARMY (FR),** 4, b g Pedro The Great (USA)—Douriya (USA) **Mr D. Stone**
57 **ONWARD ROUTE (IRE),** 9, b g Yeats (IRE)—Just Stunning (IRE) **J. Wade**
58 **PAINTERS PALETTE (IRE),** 4, ch g Lope de Vega (IRE)—Maimara (FR) **The Horse Watchers**
59 4, B g Black Sam Bellamy (IRE)—Pearl Buttons **Mr L. G. Aldsworth**
60 **PEPPERMILL (IRE),** 6, b m Getaway (GER)—Nouveau Moulin (IRE) **J. Wade**
61 **PIAFF BUBBLES (IRE),** 7, b br g Fame And Glory—Liss Na Tintri (IRE) **Titanium Racing Club**
62 **PINOT ROUGE (IRE),** 5, ch m Vendangeur (IRE)—Moanbaun Lady (IRE)
63 **POINT FRANKLIN (IRE),** 4, b g Camelot—Another Storm (USA) **The Connection**
64 **POSITIVE FORCE,** 4, gr g El Kabeir (USA)—Clann Force **Sapphire Print Solutions Ltd**
65 **PRINCE HECTOR (IRE),** 5, b g Camacho—Arabian Pearl (IRE) **Mr A. McCormack**
66 **QUICKASICAN (IRE),** 6, gr g Dylan Thomas (IRE)—Courting Shinney **Rebecca Menzies Racing Partnerships**
67 **RAECIUS FELIX (IRE),** 9, ch g Stowaway—Dances With Waves (IRE) **J. Wade**
68 **RAFFERTY'S RETURN,** 8, b g Schiaparelli (GER)—Duchess Theatre (IRE) **J. Wade**
69 **RAFFLES WONDER (FR),** 6, ch g Balko (FR)—Ruthenoise (FR) **Chris Roe & Andrew March**
70 **RAJMEISTER,** 5, b g Showcasing—Brilliant Sunshine **Flash Figs Racing**
71 **RESTANDBETHANKFUL,** 7, br g Califet (FR)—Persian Forest **Rebecca Menzies Racing Partnerships**
72 **RETURN TICKET (IRE),** 10, b g Getaway (GER)—Capelvenere (IRE) **J. Wade**
73 **RITSON (IRE),** 8, b g Jeremy (USA)—Ellen's Choice (IRE) **Mr P R Walker & Mr R Walker**
74 **ROAD WARRIOR,** 9, gr g Fair Mix (IRE)—Mimi Equal **Mr N. Taylor**
75 **ROUSE (IRE),** 4, ch g Australia—Snowfields (IRE) **Love To Race Partnership**
76 **RUSSIAN VIRTUE,** 6, b g Toronado (IRE)—Russian Rhapsody **Mr D. Thompson**
77 **SAO (FR),** 9, b br g Great Pretender (IRE)—Miss Country (FR) **Gary Eves & Partner**
78 **SCHALKE,** 8, b g Malinas (GER)—Prospero's Belle (IRE) **Sapphire Print Solutions Ltd**
79 **SNOWY BURROWS (FR),** 7, gr m Montmartre (FR)—Condoleezza (FR) **4Racing Owners Club**
80 4, Ch g Yorgunnabelucky (USA)—So Cannie **E. A. Brook**
81 **SOCKS OFF (IRE),** 6, br g Society Rock (IRE)—Deliziosa (IRE) **Cape Farming & Bloodstock Limited**
82 **SOLDIER AT ARMS (IRE),** 5, ch g Soldier of Fortune (IRE)—Hear The Thunder (IRE) **J. Wade**
83 **START IN FRONT (FR),** 4, ch g Hunter's Light (IRE)—Extra Terrestrial (FR) **Mr R. Oliver**
84 **STORM LORENZO (IRE),** 8, ch g Doyen (IRE)—Gallant Express (IRE) **Miss M. D. Myco**
85 4, B g Mahsoob—Sweet Belle **J. Wade**
86 **TAKE CENTRE STAGE (IRE),** 6, b g Fame And Glory—Glibin (IRE) **Mr C. M. Scholey**
87 **THE CHURCHILL LAD (IRE),** 4, b g Churchill (IRE)—Imalwayshotforyou (USA) **Flying High & Blacklock**
88 **THORNABY EXCEED,** 5, ch g Eagle Top—Ingleby Exceed (IRE) **Ingleby Bloodstock Limited**
89 **THREE PLATOON,** 5, b g Kingman—Brevity (USA) **Crowd Racing Partnership**
90 **TREATY BOY (IRE),** 6, ch g Well Chosen—Miss Taggle (IRE) **Rebecca Menzies Racing Partnerships**
91 **TWISTED DREAMS (USA),** 6, b br g Twirling Candy (USA)—Sweet Promises (USA) **Titanium Racing Club**
92 **TWOSHOTSOFTEQUILA (IRE),** 6, b g Snow Sky—Inouette (IRE) **Hetton Boys**
93 **UNBRIDLED POWER (IRE),** 5, b g Power—Via Aurelia (IRE) **Ursa Major Racing Club & Partner 1**
94 **YOU NAME HIM,** 7, b g Proclamation (IRE)—Scarlett O'Tara **Breath Of Fresh Air Racing**
95 **YOU SOME BOY (IRE),** 8, b g Dylan Thomas (IRE)—You Some Massini (IRE) **J. Wade**
96 **YOU SOME GIRL (IRE),** 6, b m Dylan Thomas (IRE)—Kallisti (IRE) **J. Wade**

THREE-YEAR-OLDS

97 **ACLAIM TO FAME (IRE),** b f Aclaim (IRE)—Lady Spangles (IRE) **Ursa Major Racing Club & Partner 1**
98 **BALALAIKA (IRE),** ch f No Nay Never (USA)—War And Peace **Lady A. F. Ogden**
99 B g Westerner—Be Mine Tonight (IRE) **J. Wade**
100 **GREENWICH,** bl g No Nay Never (USA)—Canonbury (IRE) **Lady A. F. Ogden**
101 **INDICATION ROCKET (IRE),** b g Dandy Man (IRE)—Rip Van Music (IRE) **Gold & Green Scott Shearsmith Crowd**
102 **IRONOPOLIS (IRE),** b g Gleneagles (IRE)—Silken Soul **Riverside Racing Syndicate**
103 B g Mount Nelson—La Reine de Riogh (IRE) **J. Wade**
104 Ch f No Risk At All (FR)—Mappa (FR)
105 **MASTERPIECE,** gr g Mastercraftsman (IRE)—Alegra **Lady A. F. Ogden**
106 **MONARCH BUTTERFLY,** gr f Mastercraftsman (IRE)—Madame Butterfly (IRE) **Lady A. F. Ogden**
107 **ONE OF OUR OWN,** b f Poet's Word (IRE)—Fangfoss Girls **Crowd Racing Partnership**
108 **PRESENTANDCORRECT (IRE),** b g Soldier of Fortune (IRE)—Coole Assembly (IRE) **J. Wade**
109 **STAR START (IRE),** b c U S Navy Flag (USA)—Button Up (IRE) **Mr S. F. S. A. Almutairi**
110 **STORMY PEARL,** b f Night of Thunder (IRE)—David's Duchess (IRE) **Mike and Eileen Newbould**
111 B g Snow Sky—Super Day (IRE) **J. Wade**
112 B g Malinas (GER)—Sweet Belle **J. Wade**

MRS REBECCA MENZIES - continued

113 TEXAS BOY (IRE), b c Fast Company (IRE)—Arizona Sun (IRE) **Ursa Major Racing Club & Partner 1**

TWO-YEAR-OLDS

114 B c 22/03 Kessaar (IRE)—Dutch Desire (Dutch Art) (10476) **Ursa Major Racing Club & Partner 1**
115 FIREBIRD, b f 21/03 Lope de Vega (IRE)—War And Peace (Frankel) **Lady A. F. Ogden**
116 Ch f 10/02 Silverwave (FR)—Kapirovska (FR) (Muhtathir) (6403) **Mr B. Stevens**
117 KATHMANDU (IRE), b f 20/02 Showcasing—Alegra (Galileo (IRE)) **Lady A. F. Ogden**
118 B f 03/03 Ectot—Mille Rubis (FR) (Great Pretender (IRE)) (9604)
119 NOTRE DAME, b f 07/05 Kingman—Madame Butterfly (IRE) (Rip Van Winkle (IRE)) **Lady A. F. Ogden**
120 SOLAR BENTLEY (IRE), gr c 17/03 Phoenix of Spain (IRE)—
Fresh Mint (IRE) (Sadler's Wells (USA)) (26000) **UK Farming Renewable Energy**

Secretary: Mrs Emma Ramsden, **Business & Racing Manager:** Philip Lawrenson, **Yard Sponsor:** Bluegrass Horse Feeds.

Flat Jockey: Cam Hardie, PJ McDonald. **NH Jockey:** Nathan Moscrop, Conor O'Farrell. **Amateur Jockey:** Miss Leah Cooper.

---

348 MR PAUL MIDGLEY, Westow

Postal: **The View, Sandfield Farm, Westow, York, North Yorkshire, YO60 7LS**
Contacts: **PHONE 07971 048550 MOBILE 07976 965220 FAX 01653 658790**
EMAIL ptmidgley@aol.com WEBSITE www.ptmidgley.com

1 A SHINING MOON (IRE), 5, ch g Sea The Moon (GER)—Aliana (GER) **R Wardlaw & Partners**
2 ATLANTIC HEART (IRE), 4, b f Twilight Son—Heaven's Sake **Sandfield Racing, Mr A. Turton**
3 BALLINTOY HARBOUR (IRE), 5, b m Vadamos (FR)—Fingal Nights (IRE) **Mr H. Thornton & Mr P. T. Midgley**
4 BEN MACDUI (IRE), 5, b g Kodiac—Candiland (IRE) **The Wolf Pack 7 & Partner**
5 BIRKENHEAD, 6, b g Captain Gerrard (IRE)—Vilnius **Chris Priestley & Ged Shields**
6 BURNING CASH (IRE), 5, b g Strath Burn—Passified Lady (USA) **C Priestley, M Hammond & D Flynn**
7 DIANA PRINCE, 7, b m Kayf Tara—Sweet Stormy (IRE) **Mr D. Padgett**
8 DR RIO (FR), 7, b g Rio de La Plata (USA)—Dr Wintringham (IRE) **Sandfield Racing**
9 ELEGANT ERIN (IRE), 6, b m Dandy Man (IRE)—Eriniya (IRE) **R J Bloodstock**
10 ELZAAL (IRE), 5, b g Elzaam (AUS)—Alice Liddel (IRE) **Mr P. T. Midgley**
11 ENDERMAN, 5, b g Bated Breath—Wish You Luck **Mr Colin Alton & Mr P. T. Midgley**
12 EXCUISITE, 5, gr m Gregorian (IRE)—Amour Fou (IRE) **Sandfield Racing**
13 GLORY FIGHTER, 7, b g Kyllachy—Isola Verde **Robert & Sheila Bradley**
14 GOLDEN RAINBOW, 4, b g Havana Gold (IRE)—Stereophonic (IRE) **Holmfirth Racing**
15 GOOD LUCK FOX (IRE), 7, b g Society Rock (IRE)—Violet Ballerina (IRE) **Mad 4 Fun & Paul Williamson**
16 GRANT WOOD (IRE), 4, gr g Caravaggio (USA)—Azagba (FR) **Mr L. Carlisle**
17 HEY MR, 5, b g Territories (IRE)—Filona (IRE) **Mr C. Priestley**
18 IMPERIAL KHAN (IRE), 4, b g Kodiac—Beatify (IRE) **Zacava Racing & Partner**
19 INDIAN SOUNDS (IRE), 7, b g Exceed And Excel (AUS)—Sarinda **Mr P. T. Midgley**
20 J R CAVAGIN (IRE), 5, b g Oasis Dream—International Love (IRE) **A Bell & M Hammond**
21 JAMES WATT (IRE), 7, b g Morpheus—Tomintoul Singer (IRE) **Mr M Hammond & Partner**
22 KEY LOOK (IRE), 6, ch m Dawn Approach (IRE)—Fashion Line (IRE) **Holmfirth Racing**
23 LADY ZIANA, 5, b m Dawn Approach (IRE)—Heartlines (USA) **Mount Pleasant Farm Syndicate**
24 LATIN FIVE (IRE), 6, b g Camacho—Penolva (IRE) **Sandfield**
25 LEODIS DREAM (IRE), 7, b g Dandy Man (IRE)—Paddy Again (IRE) **The Beer Stalkers & Partner**
26 MAJESKI MAN (IRE), 6, ch g Dandy Man (IRE)—Fly By Magic (IRE) **C Priestley & M Hammond**
27 MAKE A PROPHET (IRE), 4, b g Divine Prophet (AUS)—Miss Mirabeau **Northern Sealants Ltd & Mr R Wardlaw**
28 MID WINSTER, 7, b m Burwaaz—Cayman Fox **John Blackburn & Alan Bell**
29 MILITIA, 8, b g Equiano (FR)—Sweet As Honey **Mr A. Bell & Mr P. T. Midgley**
30 PROSPECT, 5, b g Shalaa (IRE)—Souville **Arms & Shields**
31 RUN THIS WAY, 5, b m Cannock Chase (USA)—Prime Run **Mr A. Bell & Mr P. T. Midgley**
32 SALUTI (IRE), 9, b g Acclamation—Greek Easter (IRE)

MR PAUL MIDGLEY - continued

33 **SHERDIL (IRE),** 4, b g Dandy Man (IRE)—Chicago Fall (IRE) **Stoneleigh Racing & Partner**
34 **SPRING IS SPRUNG (FR),** 4, b g Oasis Dream—Kinematic **Stoneleigh Racing LI & Partner**
35 **STRONG JOHNSON (IRE),** 7, b g Le Cadre Noir (IRE)—Isabella Rose (IRE) **Taylor's Bloodstock Ltd**
36 **TEXAS MAN (IRE),** 4, ch g Dandy Man (IRE)—Texas Queen **Syps & Mrs Wendy Burdett**
37 **THE BELL CONDUCTOR (IRE),** 6, b g Dandy Man (IRE)—Saffian **Mrs W. Burdett**
38 **THRILLA IN MANILA,** 7, b g Iffraaj—Tesary **Ian Massheder & Sandfield Racing**
39 **VADAMIAH (IRE),** 4, b f Vadamos (FR)—Ghanimah **The Blackburn Family**
40 **VAN GERWEN,** 10, ch g Bahamian Bounty—Disco Ball **Ryan Chapman & Partners**
41 **VENTURA EXPRESS,** 6, ch g Mayson—Mail Express (IRE) **Buist, Crowther & Shields**
42 **YAZAMAN (IRE),** 5, b g Kodiac—Online Alexander (IRE)

THREE-YEAR-OLDS

43 **COUNTESS KESS (IRE),** b f Kessaar (IRE)—Opinionated Lady (IRE) **D & D Poulter**
44 **DARK CRUSADE (IRE),** b g Camacho—Always Gentle (IRE) **J Blackburn, Imperial Racing & Sandfield**
45 **FAMILY TIES (IRE),** b f Expert Eye—Savannah's Dream **R J Bloodstock**
46 **FRANK THE SPARK,** ch g Orientor—Annie Gee **Mr F. Brady**
47 **GRANDAD BOB (IRE),** ch g Dandy Man (IRE)—Chantaleen (FR) **Mr K Everitt & Partner**
48 **LUKLA,** b g Aclaim (IRE)—Stately **Ryan Chapman & Partners**
49 **MATCH PLAY,** b g Dandy Man (IRE)—Corazon Canarias (FR) **Mr C. Priestley, Mr D. Flynn**
50 **MRS TRUMP (IRE),** b f James Garfield (IRE)—Musicora **Ryan Chapman & Partners**
51 **ONEFORSUE,** b f Bated Breath—Unveiling **Paul Buist & Mike Taylor**
52 **WRENEGADE LAD (IRE),** b g James Garfield (IRE)—Life Rely (USA) **Wrenegade Racing**
53 **YOUR SPIRIT (IRE),** b f Invincible Spirit (IRE)—Excel Yourself (IRE) **J Blackburn&Imperial Racing P'ship 2016**

TWO-YEAR-OLDS

54 Ch c 18/04 Exceed And Excel (AUS)—Shaya (IRE) (Invincible Spirit (IRE)) **SYPS (UK) Ltd**

Assistant Trainer: Mrs W. E. Midgley.

---

349 MR ROD MILLMAN, Cullompton

Postal: **The Paddocks, Dulford, Cullompton, Devon, EX15 2DX**
Contacts: **PHONE 01884 266620 MOBILE 07885 168447**
EMAIL rod.millman@ic24.net

1 **ABLE KANE,** 6, b g Due Diligence (USA)—Sugar Beet **Mr T. H. Chadney**
2 **AIRSHOW,** 8, ch g Showcasing—Belle des Airs (IRE) **Middleham Park Racing XXXIV**
3 **AMAZONIAN DREAM (IRE),** 4, b g Bungle Inthejungle—Grandmas Dream **Great Western Racing**
4 **BAMA LAMA,** 5, ch m Equiano (FR)—Kindia (IRE) **Canisbay Bloodstock**
5 **BILLY MILL,** 5, b g Adaay (IRE)—Phantom Spirit **Canisbay Bloodstock**
6 **CRAZY LUCK,** 5, b m Twilight Son—Suerte Loca (IRE) **Crown Connoisseurs**
7 **CRYSTAL CASQUE,** 8, ch m Helmet (AUS)—Crystal Moments **The Dirham Partnership**
8 **EDMOND,** 4, b f Nathaniel (IRE)—Seaham Hall **Mrs S. A. J. Kinsella**
9 **FAST STEPS (IRE),** 5, b g Footstepsinthesand—Inis Boffin **E. J. S. Gadsden**
10 **FOREVER DREAMING (IRE),** 4, ch f Dream Ahead (USA)—Melrose Abbey (IRE) **JPM Racing II**
11 **FOUR ADAAY,** 5, b m Adaay (IRE)—Sonko (IRE) **The Four Adaay Syndicate**
12 **MASTER GREY (IRE),** 8, gr g Mastercraftsman (IRE)—Market Day **The Links Partnership**
13 **RUMNOTRED,** 4, b g Coach House (IRE)—Artistic Muse (IRE) **Mr J. M. Hicks**
14 **SILENT FLAME,** 5, b m Al Kazeem—Burnt Fingers (IRE) **Miss G. J. Abbey**

THREE-YEAR-OLDS

15 **ATHENA BALLERINA,** b f Master Carpenter (IRE)—Tethys (IRE) **Kittymore Racing**
16 **CUBAN MISTRESS,** b f Havana Grey—Secret Romance **Middleham Park Racing LXXXVI BR Millman**
17 **DANTE'S POET,** b g Poet's Word (IRE)—Stockhill Diva **Mrs M Fairbairn, E Gadsden & P Dean**

MR ROD MILLMAN - continued

18 **DAVID'S DIVA,** b f Master Carpenter (IRE)—Imaginary Diva **The Links Partnership & B R Millman**
19 **DAVID'S GIFT,** ch f Master Carpenter (IRE)—Ladybird Blue **Kittymore Racing**
20 **GENEPI (IRE),** b f Galileo Gold—Last Hooray **Mr M. J. Watson**
21 **IGNAC LAMAR (IRE),** b g Dandy Man (IRE)—Bratislava **Crown Connoisseurs**
22 **JUST A SPARK,** b f Bungle Inthejungle—One Kiss **Next Ones A Grey Partnership**
23 **LITTLE HELEN,** b f Camacho—Dame Helen **B. R. Millman**
24 **MISS MOONSHINE,** gr f Outstrip—Cajun Moon **Canisbay Bloodstock**
25 **PRINCESS NAOMI,** ch f Master Carpenter (IRE)—Achianna (USA) **Mr C. Demetriou**
26 **SAFARI DREAM (IRE),** b g Bungle Inthejungle—Grandmas Dream **Great Western Racing Ii**
27 **STATE BORDER,** b f Territories (IRE)—Plover **Canisbay Bloodstock**
28 **WOOLHAMPTON (IRE),** b f Camacho—Mary Thomas (IRE) **Mr D. A. Klein**

TWO-YEAR-OLDS

29 B f 16/04 Adaay (IRE)—Achianna (USA) (Gemologist (USA)) **Mr C. Demetriou**
30 **ADAAY IN DEVON,** b f 06/04 Adaay (IRE)—
Favourite Girl (IRE) (Refuse To Bend (IRE)) **Horniwinks Racing Syndicate**
31 **BEENHAM,** b f 05/03 Havana Grey—Ares Choix (Choisir (AUS)) (30000) **Mr D. A. Klein**
32 Gr f 10/04 Outstrip—Cajun Moon (Showcasing) **Canisbay Bloodstock**
33 **CROOKED CROWN,** b f 11/03 Cable Bay (IRE)—Super Sleuth (IRE) (Selkirk (USA)) (11000) **Crown Connoisseurs**
34 B f 01/04 City Light (FR)—Jeune Et Jolie (IRE) (Verglas (IRE)) (48019) **Middleham Park Racing CXVI**
35 **JOHNNY JOHNSON,** b g 17/02 Due Diligence (USA)—
Military Madame (IRE) (Epaulette (AUS)) (14286) **Mr T. H. Chadney**
36 **LINE OF FIRE,** gr f 18/03 Havana Grey—Penny Royale (Monsieur Bond (IRE)) **Mainline Racing**
37 **MULLINS BEACH (IRE),** ch g 05/03 Unfortunately (IRE)—
Platinum Coast (USA) (Speightstown (USA)) (15000) **Anaco Racing Partnership**
38 **RUNAROUND SIOUX,** b f 16/03 Sioux Nation (USA)—Angel Mead (Archipenko (USA)) **Mr D. A. Klein**
39 **SHAWS PHOENIX (IRE),** gr f 01/02 Phoenix of Spain (IRE)—
Enliven (Dansili) (27000) **Central Facilities Services Ltd.**
40 **SILVER CHAPARRAL (IRE),** gr f 07/03 Bungle Inthejungle—
Syrian Pearl (Clodovil (IRE)) (17000) **Daddies Girl Partnership**
41 B f 02/04 Kodiac—Three Knots (IRE) (Chineur (FR)) **Three Knots Partnership**
42 **TWISTED TIARA (IRE),** b f 19/03 Ribchester (IRE)—
Aneedah (IRE) (Invincible Spirit (IRE)) (20000) **Crown Connoisseurs**

Assistant Trainer: Mr James Millman, Louise Millman, Pat Millman.

Flat Jockey: Ross Coakley, Oisin Murphy. **Apprentice Jockey:** Oliver Searle. **Amateur Jockey:** Mr Pat Millman.

---

350 MR RICHARD MITCHELL, Dorchester

Postal: **East Hill Stables, Piddletrenthide, Dorchester, Dorset, DT2 7QY**
Contacts: **PHONE 01300 348739 MOBILE 07775 843136**
EMAIL easthillstables@tiscali.co.uk

1 **BELLISSIMO MILAN (IRE),** 7, b m Milan—Opera Mask (IRE) **Mrs E. Mitchell**
2 **COTTON CLUB (IRE),** 12, b g Amadeus Wolf—Slow Jazz (USA) **Mr J. Boughey**
3 **POUR UNE RAISON (FR),** 8, b br g Kapgarde (FR)—Got Aba (FR) **Mrs S. H. May**

Assistant Trainer: Mrs E. Mitchell.

---

351 MR RICHARD MITFORD-SLADE, Norton Fitzwarren

Postal: **Pontispool Farm, Allerford, Norton Fitzwarren, Taunton, Somerset, TA4 1BG**
Contacts: **PHONE 01823 461196 MOBILE 07899 994420 FAX 01823 461508**
EMAIL rms@pontispool.com

1 **ALFIE SHARP,** 5, b g Scorpion (IRE)—Fluffy Clouds **Pontispool Racing Club**
2 **LAZY SUNDAY,** 9, b m Schiaparelli (GER)—Sari Rose (FR) **Pontispool Racing Club**
3 **MOJITO ROYALE (FR),** 7, ch g Champs Elysees—Sister Agnes (IRE) **Withyslade, Mr A. R. Newman**
4 **MORMON (IRE),** 10, b g Stowaway—A Plus Ma Puce (FR) **Pontispool Racing Club**
5 **SAMUEL JACKSON,** 11, b g Alflora (IRE)—Primitive Quest **R. C. Mitford-Slade, Mrs L. Fielding-Johnson**
6 **STAMP YOUR FEET (IRE),** 11, b g Galileo (IRE)—Nausicaa (USA) **Mr B. J. C. Wright**
7 **START POINT,** 7, b m Getaway (GER)—Allerford Annie (IRE) **Pontispool 1**

Assistant Trainer: Lucy Fielding-Johnson.

---

352 MR JAMES MOFFATT, Cartmel

Postal: **Pit Farm Racing Stables, Cartmel, Grange-Over-Sands, Cumbria, LA11 6PJ**
Contacts: **PHONE 015395 33808 MOBILE 07767 367282 FAX 015395 36236**
EMAIL jamesmoffatt@hotmail.co.uk WEBSITE www.jamesmoffatt.co.uk

1 **ALQAMAR,** 9, b g Dubawi (IRE)—Moonsail **Mrs E. Vyner-Brooks,Dave&Yvonne Simpson**
2 **BATTLE OF TORO (IRE),** 7, gr g New Approach (IRE)—Galician **Mr J. T. Hanbury**
3 **BELLS EXPRESS (IRE),** 6, ch g Sholokhov (IRE)—Bells Chance (IRE) **Mr J. T. Hanbury**
4 **BIG GANGSTA (IRE),** 7, b g Califet (FR)—Tempest Missile (IRE) **Mr J. T. Hanbury**
5 **BINGOO,** 7, b g Eastern Anthem (IRE)—It's A Discovery (IRE) **Kevin & Anne Glastonbury & Neil Bibby**
6 **BOY DE LA VIS (FR),** 5, b g Diamond Boy (FR)—Lorie de La Vis (FR) **Varlien Vyner Brooks / Sports Has Beens**
7 **BURBANK (IRE),** 11, b g Yeats (IRE)—Spring Swoon (FR) **D&y Simpson,D.Blyth,B.B Syndicate**
8 **CAPTAIN WESTIE (IRE),** 7, b g Westerner—Simons Niece (IRE) **Mr J. T. Hanbury**
9 **CITY VAULTS,** 4, gr g Dark Angel (IRE)—Priceless Jewel
10 **CUZCO DU MATHAN (FR),** 5, gr g Martaline—Thisbee du Mathan (FR) **Mr T. Gardner**
11 **GOLDEN TOWN (IRE),** 12, b g Invincible Spirit (IRE)—Princesse Dansante (IRE) **Gu on Big un**
12 **GRAND SOUFLE (FR),** 7, b g Network (GER)—Rafale d'Aron (FR) **Mr K. Bowron**
13 **JELSKI (GER),** 9, b g Kallisto (GER)—Just Zoud **The Running In Rail Partnership**
14 **JUDICIAL REVIEW (IRE),** 5, ch g Getaway (GER)—Chartani (IRE) **Racing in Furness**
15 **LADY BOWES,** 9, b m Malinas (GER)—Blazing Bay (IRE) **Bowes Lodge Stables**
16 **LUNAR DISCOVERY,** 6, b m Pether's Moon (IRE)—It's A Discovery (IRE) **Kevin & Anne Glastonbury**
17 **MOONLIGHT SPIRIT (IRE),** 7, b g Dubawi (IRE)—Moonsail **D&y Simpson,D Blyth,MLS Syndicate**
18 **NATIVE FIGHTER (IRE),** 9, b g Lawman (FR)—Night of Magic (IRE) **D&y Simpson & N.F Syndicate**
19 **OAKMONT (FR),** 10, ch g Turtle Bowl (IRE)—Onega Lake (IRE) **The Sheroot Partnership**
20 **ONE FINE MAN (IRE),** 8, br g Jeremy (USA)—American Jennie (IRE) **Mr J. T. Hanbury**
21 **OUR SAM,** 7, b g Black Sam Bellamy (IRE)—Arisea (IRE) **Geordie & Taffy**
22 **RAPID FLIGHT,** 7, b g Midnight Legend—Spring Flight **Mr D. Mills**
23 **VOCAL DUKE (IRE),** 7, b g Vocalised (USA)—Heir Today (IRE) **Jim Bracken, Keith Hadwin & DJM**
24 **YUKON (IRE),** 6, ro g Lope de Vega (IRE)—Alegra **The Vilprano Partnership**
25 **ZUMBI (GER),** 6, gr g Reliable Man—Zalexa (GER) **Dave & Yvonne Simpson**

Assistant Trainer: Nadine Moffatt.

NH Jockey: Henry Brooke, Brian Hughes. **Conditional Jockey:** Charlotte Jones.

353 MR ISMAIL MOHAMMED, Newmarket

Postal: **Grange House Stables, Hamilton Road, Newmarket, Suffolk, CB8 0TE**
Contacts: **PHONE 01638 669074 MOBILE 07747 191606, 07766 570271**
EMAIL justina.stone@dubairacingclub.com

1 **MAGICAL MILE (IRE),** 5, ch g Sepoy (AUS)—Magical Crown (USA) **Mr A. Al Mansoori**
2 **PROFIT GIVEN (IRE),** 4, ch f Profitable (IRE)—Kitty Softpaws (IRE) **Mr A. Al Mansoori**
3 **STARS ARE BORN (IRE),** 4, b f Sea The Stars (IRE)—Chachamaidee (IRE) **S. H. Altayer**
4 4, Gr f Caravaggio (USA)—Tassina (GER) **S. H. Altayer**
5 **TOTAL MASTER,** 4, ch c Mastercraftsman (IRE)—Totally Lost (IRE) **Mr A. Al Mansoori**
6 **WINNING EMPRESS,** 4, b f Bobby's Kitten (USA)—Flashing Colour (GER) **S. H. Altayer**

THREE-YEAR-OLDS

7 B f Harry Angel (IRE)—Always Thankful **S. H. Altayer**
8 B g Havana Grey—Chasing Rubies (IRE) **Mr I. Mohammed**
9 **DESERT ILLUSION (IRE),** b f Ribchester (IRE)—Natalisa (IRE) **Mr K. S. Sulaiman**
10 Ch c Mondialiste (IRE)—Dream Child (IRE) **S. Ali**
11 **GOING TO THE MOON (IRE),** b g Mastercraftsman (IRE)—Madeira Moon (IRE) **Mr A. Al Mansoori**
12 **HARD ACT TO FOLLOW (IRE),** ch f Exceed And Excel (AUS)—Claudette (USA) **S. H. Altayer**
13 **INVERINATE (IRE),** b c Kodiac—Say No Now (IRE) **Mr A. Al Mansoori**
14 **KITTEN GLOVES,** b f Bobby's Kitten (USA)—Skinny Love **Mr I. Mohammed**
15 B c Shamardal (USA)—Meeznah (USA) **Saif Ali & Saeed H. Altayer**
16 **MORALISA,** b f Jungle Cat (IRE)—Muhadathat **Mr A. Al Mansoori**
17 **NIBRAS RAINBOW (IRE),** b g U S Navy Flag (USA)—Show Rainbow **S. H. Altayer**
18 **ONCE MORE FOR LUCK (IRE),** b c Kodiac—Alkhawarah (USA) **Mr A. Al Mansoori**
19 Ch f Washington DC (IRE)—Symphonic Dancer (USA) **Mr A. Al Mansoori**
20 **TARBET,** b f Jungle Cat (IRE)—One Minute (IRE) **Mr A. Al Mansoori**

TWO-YEAR-OLDS

21 B c 20/04 New Bay—Alkhawarah (USA) (Intidab (USA)) (30476) **Mr I. Mohammed**
22 Ch f 04/03 Masar (IRE)—Bumptious (Acclamation) **Mr I. Mohammed**
23 Ch c 19/04 Waldgeist—Date With Destiny (IRE) (George Washington (IRE)) (65000) **Mr I. Mohammed**
24 B c 08/05 No Nay Never (USA)—Eloquent (IRE) (Galileo (IRE)) (120000) **Mr I. Mohammed**
25 B f 09/02 Havana Grey—Exceed Loose (Exceed And Excel (AUS)) (14000) **Mr A. Bintouq**
26 B f 22/03 Too Darn Hot—Just Wait (IRE) (Teofilo (IRE)) **Mr A. Al Mansoori**
27 B f 03/02 Shamardal (USA)—Kilmah (Sepoy (AUS)) **Mr A. Al Mansoori**
28 B f 04/04 Ten Sovereigns (IRE)—Lady Grace (IRE) (Orpen (USA)) (90000) **S. H. Altayer**
29 B f 02/06 Massaat (IRE)—Nantyglo (Mark of Esteem (IRE)) (20000) **Mr I. Mohammed**
30 B c 15/03 Universal (IRE)—One Minute (IRE) (Kodiac) **Mr A. Al Mansoori**
31 Ch f 24/03 No Nay Never (USA)—Poldhu (Cape Cross (IRE)) (150000) **S. H. Altayer**
32 B c 29/04 Churchill (IRE)—Shamwari Lodge (IRE) (Hawk Wing (USA)) (70000) **Mr I. Mohammed**
33 B c 16/04 Profitable (IRE)—Simple Thought (IRE) (Teofilo (IRE)) **Mr A. Al Mansoori**

Assistant Trainer: Mike Marshall.

---

354 MRS LAURA MONGAN, Epsom

Postal: **Condover Stables, Langley Vale Road, Epsom, Surrey, KT18 6AP**
Contacts: **PHONE 01372 271494 MOBILE 07788 122942 FAX 01372 271494**
EMAIL ljmongan@hotmail.co.uk WEBSITE www.lauramongan.co.uk

1 **ASCRAEUS,** 6, b m Poet's Voice—Sciacca (IRE) **Mrs P. J. Sheen**
2 **BLAIRLOGIE,** 6, b g Roderic O'Connor (IRE)—Desert Morning (IRE) **Mrs L. J. Mongan**
3 **BOWMAN (IRE),** 5, b g Lawman (FR)—Jo Bo Bo (IRE) **Mrs P. J. Sheen**
4 **CHARGO,** 4, b f Highland Reel (IRE)—Piano **Mrs P. J. Sheen**
5 **DAZZERLING (IRE),** 4, ch g Starspangledbanner (AUS)—Chances Are (IRE) **Mrs P. J. Sheen**
6 **KANUHURA,** 4, b f Kodiac—Gameday **Mrs L. J. Mongan**

MRS LAURA MONGAN - continued

7 **LAST ROAR (IRE),** 4, b g The Last Lion (IRE)—Western Tune (IRE) **Mrs P. J. Sheen**
8 **MADAM MAY,** 5, b m Telescope (IRE)—Madame de Guise (FR) **Mrs P. J. Sheen**
9 **MILLIONS MEMORIES,** 7, b g Zoffany (IRE)—Millestan (IRE) **Mrs P. J. Sheen**
10 **MOUNT MOGAN,** 6, b g Helmet (AUS)—Super Midge **Mrs P. J. Sheen**
11 **NEWS GIRL (IRE),** 4, b f New Bay—Lady Correspondent (USA) **Mrs P. J. Sheen**
12 **PATRIOCTIC (IRE),** 5, b g Vadamos (FR)—Height of Vanity (IRE) **Mrs P. J. Sheen**
13 **PLEDGE OF PEACE (IRE),** 6, b g New Approach (IRE)—Hoodna (IRE) **Mrs P. J. Sheen**
14 **SEA TIDE,** 9, b m Champs Elysees—Change Course **Mrs P. J. Sheen**

THREE-YEAR-OLDS

15 **CERTAIN STYLE,** b f Adaay (IRE)—Bling Bling (IRE) **Mrs P. J. Sheen**
16 **ESTEHWADH (IRE),** b g Profitable (IRE)—Packed House **Mrs P. J. Sheen**
17 **GINTINI (IRE),** b g Starspangledbanner (AUS)—Shama's Song (IRE) **Mrs P. J. Sheen**
18 **REGAL GLORY (IRE),** b f Cotai Glory—Regal Salute **Mrs P. J. Sheen**

Assistant Trainer: Ian Mongan.

NH Jockey: Tom Cannon.

---

355 MR GARY MOORE, Horsham

Postal: **Cisswood Racing Stables, Sandygate Lane, Lower Beeding, Horsham, West Sussex, RH13 6LR**
Contacts: **PHONE 01403 891912**
EMAIL info@garymooreracing.com

1 **ABINGWORTH,** 5, b g Kapgarde (FR)—Flute Bowl **Mr C. E. Stedman**
2 **AGE OF SAIL,** 4, b g Frankel—Concordia **Mr O. S. Harris**
3 **AGGAGIO (FR),** 5, b g Born To Sea (IRE)—Ravage **Aura (Gas) Holdings Ltd**
4 **ANGEL'S DREAM (FR),** 5, b g Martillo (GER)—My Angel (FR) **Five Star Racing Group**
5 **ANIFICAS BEAUTY (IRE),** 4, b f Exceed And Excel (AUS)—Khajool (IRE) **Mr K. Rummun**
6 **ASENSE,** 4, b f Equiano (FR)—Atwix **The Calculated Speculators**
7 **AUTHORISED SPEED (FR),** 6, b g Authorized (IRE)—Tangaspeed (FR) **Gallagher Bloodstock Limited**
8 **AVILES (FR),** 4, b g Saint des Saints (FR)—Ava (GER) **Mr P. Hunt**
9 **BIG BARD,** 5, b g Poet's Voice—Big Moza **Mr A Watson & Mr B Malyon**
10 **BIG JIMBO,** 6, ch g Helmet (AUS)—Big Moza **Mr A Watson & Mr B Malyon**
11 **BLACK GERRY (IRE),** 8, b g Westerner—Triptoshan (IRE) **Mrs M. Devine**
12 **BO ZENITH (FR),** 4, b g Zarak (FR)—Boreale du Berlais (FR) **Mr O. S. Harris**
13 **BOTOX HAS (FR),** 7, b g Dream Well (FR)—Bournie (FR) **John And Yvonne Stone**
14 **BRILLIANT BLUE (IRE),** 4, b g Ribchester (IRE)—Sea of Knowledge (IRE) **Mr T Jacobs & Mr J E Harley**
15 **CAPRICORN PRINCE,** 7, ch g Garswood—Sakhee's Pearl **Mrs A. P. Wilkinson**
16 **CASA LOUPI,** 6, ch g Casamento (IRE)—Kameruka **Mrs V. Pritchard-Gordon**
17 **CELESTIAL POINT (IRE),** 5, b m Pivotal—Hestia (FR) **Mr C. E. Stedman**
18 **CHAMPAGNE PIAFF (FR),** 5, b br g Le Havre (IRE)—Galaxe (FR) **Mr A. J. Head**
19 **CLOUD DANCER (IRE),** 4, gr g Jukebox Jury (IRE)—Donna Graciosa (GER) **The Keysoe Partnership**
20 **COPPERKNOB (IRE),** 4, ch c Churchill (IRE)—Mironica (IRE) **Mr S. Packham**
21 **DAPHNE MAY,** 5, b m Mayson—Cambridge Duchess **Naarn Breds**
22 **DECEIT,** 4, b f Karpino (GER)—Shiba (FR) **Lech Racing Ltd**
23 **DIRHAM EMIRATI (IRE),** 5, b g Vadamos (FR)—Allez Y (IRE) **Ashley, Carr, Duncan, Ives, Moorhead**
24 **DIYAKEN (FR),** 5, b g Goken (FR)—Dovima (IRE) **Mr O. S. Harris**
25 **DONALD LLEWELLYN,** 6, b g Pivotal—Rose Law **Mr C. E. Stedman**
26 **DORKING LAD,** 8, b g Sholokhov (IRE)—Brookville (IRE) **Galloping On The South Downs Partnership**
27 **EDITEUR DU GITE (FR),** 9, b g Saddex—Malaga de St Sulpice (FR) **The Preston Family, Friends & T Jacobs**
28 **EIRICK,** 5, gr g Geordieland (FR)—Viking Treasure **Miss L. J. Wallens**
29 **ERAGON DE CHANAY (FR),** 9, b g Racinger (FR)—Rose Celebre (FR) **Five Star Racing Group**
30 **EXECUTIVE POOL,** 4, b g Churchill (IRE)—She's So Flawless (IRE) **The Dubai Five**
31 **FASCINATING LIPS (IRE),** 6, b g Canford Cliffs (IRE)—Fantastic Lips (GER) **Mr H. Redknapp**

MR GARY MOORE - continued

32 **FIFTY BALL (FR),** 8, b g Cokoriko (FR)—Voix de Montot (FR) **Mr S. Packham**
33 **FLAMELCO (FR),** 5, b g Falco (USA)—Meldown (FR) **The Winning Hand**
34 4, B c Champs Elysees—Flute Bowl **Mr C. E. Stedman**
35 **FOXTROT SIZZLER (GER),** 5, b g Pride of Dubai (AUS)—Firedance (GER) **I. J. Heseltine**
36 **FULL BACK (FR),** 8, b g Sinndar (IRE)—Quatre Bleue (FR) **Mr A. J. Head**
37 **FUTURE PERFECT (IRE),** 5, b m Mount Nelson—Apple Trix (IRE) **Aura (Gas) Holdings Ltd**
38 4, B g Motivator—Galaxidi **Mr R. Gurney**
39 **GIVEGA (FR),** 7, b g Authorized (IRE)—Sivega (FR) **Mr A. J. Head**
40 **GOSHEN (FR),** 7, b g Authorized (IRE)—Hyde (FR) **Mr S. Packham**
41 **GUARDIA TOP (FR),** 7, b m Top Trip—Jour de Chance (FR) **Terence Wood, Samuel Jefford & Partners**
42 **HADDEX DES OBEAUX (FR),** 6, b g Saddex—Shifra (FR) **Mr O. S. Harris**
43 **HANSARD (IRE),** 5, b g The Gurkha (IRE)—Quiet Down (USA) **Noel Fehily Racing Syndicates Hansard**
44 **HAYEDO (GER),** 5, b g Sea The Moon (GER)—Hello Honey (GER) **Mr H. Redknapp**
45 **HE'S A LATCHICO (IRE),** 5, b g Fast Company (IRE)—Daliana **Danny & Gary Moore**
46 **HEAD OVER HINDS (IRE),** 5, b g Champs Elysees—Katie T (IRE) **Mr Jerry Hinds & Mr Ashley Head**
47 **HEAVEN SMART (FR),** 6, b g Saint des Saints (FR)—Barbarella Smart (FR) **The Seasiders**
48 **HECTOR JAGUEN (FR),** 6, b g Creachadoir (IRE)—Qu'en Dites Vous (FR) **Past The Post Racing**
49 **HENLEY PARK,** 6, ch g Paco Boy (IRE)—Sunny Afternoon **Mrs S. A. Windus**
50 **HERMINO AA (FR),** 6, b g Sinndar (IRE)—Acqua Luna (FR) **Galloping On The South Downs Partnership**
51 **HIGH UP IN THE AIR (FR),** 9, ch g Famous Name—You Got The Love **Mr P. T. Mott**
52 **HILL STATION (FR),** 4, b g Born To Sea (IRE)—Fulani's (IRE) **Mr M. L. Albon**
53 **HIT THE ROCKS (IRE),** 8, br g Fast Company (IRE)—Skerries (IRE) **P Moorhead, H Moorhead, J Collins 1**
54 **HUDSON DE GRUGY (FR),** 6, b g Falco (USA)—Queen de Grugy (FR) **Alan Jamieson Site Services Ltd**
55 **ICARE GRANDCHAMP (FR),** 5, b g Kapgarde (FR)—Qualia Grandchamp (FR) **Mr H. Redknapp**
56 **ICONIC MUDDLE,** 10, gr g Sixties Icon—Spatham Rose **Mrs C. S. Muddle**
57 **IMPHAL,** 9, b g Nathaniel (IRE)—Navajo Rainbow **A. Carr**
58 **IN THE AIR (FR),** 5, b g Coastal Path—Sably (FR) **Mr O. S. Harris**
59 **INNESTON (FR),** 5, b g Doctor Dino (FR)—Robbe (FR) **Mr O. S. Harris**
60 **INVINCIBLE NAO (FR),** 5, b g Gris de Gris (IRE)—Quetzalya (FR) **Paye, Darsey & Jamieson**
61 **ISAYALITTLEPRAYER,** 6, b m Nathaniel (IRE)—I Say (IRE) **Heart of the South Racing 117**
62 **ISKAR D'AIRY (FR),** 5, b g Sinndar (IRE)—Canzka d'Airy (FR) **Mr O. S. Harris**
63 **ISSAR D'AIRY (FR),** 5, b g Sinndar (IRE)—Bassika d'Airy (FR) **Mr O. S. Harris**
64 **JERRASH,** 6, b g Kayf Tara—Sudden Light (IRE) **Mr Jerry Hinds & Mr Ashley Head**
65 **JOLYJUMP (FR),** 4, b g Kapgarde (FR)—Pepite du Mathan (FR) **Mr Jerry Hinds & Mr Ashley Head**
66 **JUDOCA DE THAIX (FR),** 4, b g Castle du Berlais (FR)—Soca de Thaix (FR) **Mr Jerry Hinds & Mr Ashley Head**
67 **JUNKANOO,** 6, b g Epaulette (AUS)—Bahamian Music (IRE) **Jacobs Construction & Mr J Harley**
68 **JUPITER DU GITE (FR),** 4, b g Castle du Berlais (FR)—Malaga de St Sulpice (FR) **Alan Jamieson Site Services Ltd**
69 **KANSAS DU BERLAIS (FR),** 4, b g Martaline—Kadika (FR) **Mr O. S. Harris**
70 **KOTARI (FR),** 4, b g Nathaniel (IRE)—Kotama (FR) **Heart of the South Racing 134**
71 **KOTMASK (FR),** 5, ch g Masked Marvel—Kotkiline (FR) **Aura (Gas) Holdings Ltd**
72 **LAKE WASHINGTON (FR),** 10, ch g Muhtathir—La Curamalal (IRE) **Mr M. Gorman**
73 **LANGAFEL (IRE),** 5, b g Fast Company (IRE)—Miracle Steps (CAN) **Mrs Arnold & Partner**
74 **LARRY,** 10, b g Midnight Legend—Gaspaisie (FR) **Galloping On The South Downs Partnership**
75 **LE PATRON (FR),** 5, b g Balko (FR)—La Loute (FR) **Mrs E. H. Avery**
76 **LEGAL RIGHTS (GER),** 6, ch g Hunter's Light (IRE)—Lutindi (GER) **Heart of the South Racing 126**
77 **LOVE IS GOLDEN (IRE),** 5, b h Golden Horn—Holy Moon (IRE) **Aura (Gas) Holdings Ltd**
78 **MARK OF GOLD,** 6, b g Golden Horn—Polly's Mark (IRE) **Stevie Fisher & Friends**
79 **MARKS BEAR (IRE),** 5, b g Kodi Bear (IRE)—Elizabeth Swann **Mr P. C. R. Reed**
80 **MISTER TICKLE (IRE),** 9, b g Morozov (USA)—Tatiana (IRE) **Sunville Rail Limited**
81 **MOONIS (IRE),** 4, b g Muhaarar—Muhawalah (IRE) **Mr O. S. Harris**
82 **MOULINS CLERMONT (FR),** 5, b g Free Port Lux—Ania de Clermont (FR) **Alan Jamieson Site Services Ltd**
83 **MOVETHECHAINS (IRE),** 9, b g Robin des Champs (FR)—Clash Artist (IRE) **Mr O. S. Harris**
84 **NASSALAM (FR),** 6, ch g Dream Well (FR)—Ramina (GER) **John And Yvonne Stone**
85 **NATURALLY HIGH (FR),** 8, b g Camelot—Just Little (FR) **Hail Sargent Evans**
86 **NIGHT EAGLE (IRE),** 5, b g Free Eagle (IRE)—Life At Night (IRE) **Mr S. Chambers**
87 **NOT ANOTHER MUDDLE,** 12, b g Kayf Tara—Spatham Rose **Mrs C. S. Muddle**
88 **ODIN'S QUEST,** 5, b g Gentlewave (IRE)—Sablonne (USA) **Mr C. E. Stedman**
89 **OZZIE MAN (IRE),** 7, b g Ask—Parkdota (IRE) **Mr P. Hunt**
90 **PARIKARMA (IRE),** 6, b m Canford Cliffs (IRE)—Pushkar **G. L. Moore**
91 **PERMATA,** 5, b m Starspangledbanner (AUS)—Welsh Gem **Mr R. E. Tillett**

MR GARY MOORE - continued

92 **PERSEUS WAY (IRE),** 4, ch g Sea The Stars (IRE)—Bint Almatar (USA) **Mr O. S. Harris**
93 **PLATINUM PRINCE,** 6, gr g Harbour Watch (IRE)—Sakhee's Pearl **Mrs A. P. Wilkinson**
94 4, B g Authorized (IRE)—Polysheba (FR)
95 **PONCHO (FR),** 5, b g Motivator—Strelkita (FR) **Steven & Gary Moore**
96 **PRINCESS POPPY,** 5, b m Ocovango—Loxhill Lady **Mr R. R. Brinkley**
97 **PRIVATORY (FR),** 5, b g Motivator—Peinture Rose (USA) **Hale Sargent Evans Clifton**
98 **PURE BUBBLES (GER),** 5, b g Protectionist (GER)—Peace Society (USA) **Mr J. G. Jones**
99 **RECKON I'M HOT,** 4, b g Hot Streak (IRE)—Dark Reckoning **Heart of the South Racing 127**
100 **REINATOR (FR),** 7, b g Motivator—Vie de Reine (FR) **Mr C. E. Stedman**
101 **ROBS SECRET,** 4, b g Garswood—Snow Globe **Vicki & Sallyann Cross**
102 **ROCKEY ROAD,** 4, b c Saddler's Rock (IRE)—Maori Legend **Mr & Mrs R Sage**
103 **ROYAUME UNI (IRE),** 6, b br g Galileo (IRE)—Night Lagoon (GER) **Mrs E. H. Avery**
104 **SAGANO (IRE),** 6, b g Anodin (IRE)—Tristesse (USA) **Coldunell Limited**
105 **SALIGO BAY (IRE),** 5, b g New Bay—Glorification **Alan Jamieson Site Services Ltd**
106 **SAN PEDRO DE SENAM (FR),** 10, br g Saint des Saints (FR)—
Tetiaroa (FR) **Mrs Jane George & Mrs Helen Shelton**
107 **SAUSALITO,** 4, b g Frankel—One Last Dance (AUS) **The Southstand Syndicate**
108 **SEMSER,** 6, b g Siyouni (FR)—Serres (IRE) **Mr M. Warner**
109 **SILASTAR,** 6, b g Sea The Stars (IRE)—Silasol (IRE) **Silastar Racing Syndicate**
110 **SOBEGRAND,** 4, b c Decorated Knight—Nouriya **Mr R. R. Brinkley**
111 **SOPRAN THOR (FR),** 8, b g Authorized (IRE)—Sopran Slam (IRE) **Galloping On The South Downs Partnership**
112 **SOTO SIZZLER,** 8, b g Mastercraftsman (IRE)—Jalousie (IRE) **I. J. Heseltine**
113 **SPIRIT D'AUNOU (FR),** 4, b g Triple Threat (FR)—Miss Wind (FR) **Heart of the South Racing 130**
114 **STENATEE (FR),** 5, b g Manatee—Stenasia (FR) **Mr O. S. Harris**
115 **STORMINGIN (IRE),** 10, gr g Clodovil (IRE)—Magadar (USA) **Paul Reed & G L Moore**
116 4, B f Kayf Tara—Sudden Wish (IRE) **G. L. Moore**
117 **SYMPHORINE (FR),** 5, gr m Spanish Moon (USA)—Snow Berry (FR) **Mr Jerry Hinds & Mr Ashley Head**
118 **SYSTEMIC,** 6, b g Toronado (IRE)—Saskia's Dream **P Moorhead, H Moorhead & J Collins**
119 **TARA ITI,** 5, ch g Sixties Icon—Royal Warranty **Mark Albon & Gary Moore**
120 **TARA'S LIGHT,** 5, b m Kayf Tara—Sudden Light (IRE) **Heart of the South Racing 133 & Partner**
121 **TAZKA (FR),** 8, b m Network (GER)—Tazminya **B. Noakes & Baroness S. Noakes**
122 **TEDDY BLUE (GER),** 5, b g Sea The Moon (GER)—Tickle Me Blue (GER) **Hale Sargent Evans Clifton**
123 **TENFOLD (IRE),** 6, b g Born To Sea (IRE)—Dear Dream (IRE) **D Channon & G L Moore**
124 **THE WHIPMASTER (IRE),** 5, ch g Mastercraftsman (IRE)—Birdie Queen **The Golf Partnership**
125 **THINK TRIGGER (IRE),** 5, b g Epaulette (AUS)—Khibraat **J. & Davidson**
126 **TIME TO DAZZLE (IRE),** 5, b g Zambezi Sun—Born To Dazzle (IRE) **Mr David Leon & James Devine**
127 **TORONADO GREY,** 5, gr g Toronado (IRE)—Debutante Blues (USA) **Jacobs Construction (Holdings) Limited**
128 **TRANSATLANTIC (FR),** 6, b g Le Havre (IRE)—Aquamerica (USA) **Mr R. R. Brinkley**
129 **TWENTY TWENTY (IRE),** 8, b g Henrythenavigator (USA)—Distinctive Look (IRE) **Mark Albon & Gary Moore**
130 **VISION CLEAR (GER),** 8, b g Soldier Hollow—Vive Madame (GER) **A. Head**
131 **VOODOO RAY (IRE),** 4, ch g Ribchester (IRE)—Midget **Sunville Rail Limited**
132 **VORASHANN (FR),** 7, b g Sinndar (IRE)—Visorama (IRE) **T. Jacobs, J.E. Harley & Mr G.L. Moore**
133 **WALK IN THE WILD (FR),** 7, b g Walk In The Park (IRE)—Sublimissime (FR) **Heart of the South Racing 121**
134 **WARNING SIGN (FR),** 4, ch g Attendu (FR)—Modestie (FR) **Coldunell Limited**
135 **WARRANTY (FR),** 6, b g Authorized (IRE)—Ballymena Lassie **Ms A. R. Gross**
136 **YORKSEA (IRE),** 5, ch g Sea The Stars (IRE)—Queen's Jewel **Aura (Gas) Holdings Ltd**
137 **ZHIGULI (IRE),** 8, b g Flemensfirth (USA)—Grangeclare Flight (IRE) **Druzhba Racing Partnership**

THREE-YEAR-OLDS

138 **ALPHA CRUCIS (IRE),** b g Australia—Night Fairy (IRE) **Heart of the South Racing 131**
139 **ATWIXADAY,** b c Adaay (IRE)—Atwix **The Calculated Speculators**
140 **CLOUDY BREEZE (IRE),** b f Profitable (IRE)—Lily White Socks (IRE) **Neal And Sheralee Grayston**
141 **DICKO THE LEGEND (IRE),** b g Ardad (IRE)—Caledonia Princess **Mr O. S. Harris**
142 **EARTHY MANGOLD (IRE),** b f Bungle Inthejungle—Avizare (IRE) **Mr O. S. Harris**
143 **FIERCE (IRE),** b c Dandy Man (IRE)—Saffian **Danny & Gary Moore**
144 **LARRSEN,** b c Time Test—Zerka **Mrs Arnold & Partner**
145 **MAGIC MEMORIES (IRE),** b c Starspangledbanner (AUS)—Birdie Queen **The Golf Partnership**
146 **MILLER SPIRIT (IRE),** b c Australia—Esprit de Tauber (IRE) **Mr P. C. R. Reed**
147 **NOVUS (IRE),** b f Dandy Man (IRE)—Fleur de Nuit (IRE) **Mr O. Jackson**

MR GARY MOORE - continued

148 OJ LIFESTYLE (IRE), b c Gleneagles (IRE)—Vetlana (IRE) **Mr O. Jackson**
149 SPIRIT OF BREEZE (IRE), b g Invincible Spirit (IRE)—Gender Dance (USA) **Neal And Sheralee Grayston**
150 STAR OF SUSSEX (FR), b c Sea The Stars (IRE)—Natla (FR) **The The Tongdean Partnership**
151 TRUSSST IN ME (IRE), b f Fast Company (IRE)—La Tulipe (FR) **The Knights Of Pleasure**

TWO-YEAR-OLDS

152 AUTUMN'S BREEZE (IRE), b f 24/04 Le Brivido (FR)—
Whitefall (USA) (Street Cry (IRE)) (36014) **Neal And Sheralee Grayston**
153 RED CLOUD (IRE), b c 17/04 Sioux Nation (USA)—
Statenice (Montjeu (IRE)) (50000) **Mr J. Kimber & Aura (gas) Holdings Ltd**
154 THUNDERING BREEZE (IRE), b gr f 08/03 Dark Angel (IRE)—
Tamarisk (GER) (Selkirk (USA)) (80000) **Neal And Sheralee Grayston**
155 TIME TO ROLL, gr c 13/03 Time Test—Si Belle (IRE) (Dalakhani (IRE)) (25000) **The Fat Jockey Partnership**

Assistant Trainer: David Wilson, **Racing Secretary:** Maria Workman.

Flat Jockey: Rhys Clutterbuck, Hector Crouch, Ryan Moore, Tom Queally. **NH Jockey:** Jamie Moore. **Conditional Jockey:** Robert Hargreaves, Niall Houlihan, Caoilin Quinn. **Apprentice Jockey:** Anna Gibson. **Amateur Jockey:** Gina Gibson, Mr George Gorman, Miss Maddison Wright.

---

356 MR J. S. MOORE, Upper Lambourn

Postal: **Berkeley House Stables, Upper Lambourn, Hungerford, Berkshire, RG17 8QP**
Contacts: **PHONE 01488 73887 MOBILE 07860 811127, 07900 402856 FAX 01488 73997**
EMAIL jsmoore.racing@btopenworld.com WEBSITE www.stanmooreracing.co.uk

1 EASY EQUATION (FR), 5, b g Rajsaman (FR)—Simple Solution (USA) **Roy Humphrey & J S Moore**
2 FACT OR FABLE (IRE), 6, gr g Alhebayeb (IRE)—Unreal **Mrs Wendy Jarrett & J S Moore**
3 HAMMOCK, 4, b f Showcasing—Surcingle (USA) **Ms H. N. Pinniger**
4 HAVANA GOLDRUSH, 4, b g Havana Gold (IRE)—Riot of Colour **JS Moore & B Galloway**
5 HOT DAY, 5, b g Adaay (IRE)—Sunny York (IRE) **Gridline Racing & J S Moore**
6 RUITH LE TU, 4, b g Aclaim (IRE)—Let's Dance (IRE) **Mrs Wendy Jarrett & J S Moore**
7 THE WIZARD OF EYE (IRE), 4, ch c Galileo Gold—Prom Dress **O Humphrey A Favell R Humphrey J S Moore**
8 UTHER PENDRAGON (IRE), 8, b g Dragon Pulse (IRE)—Unreal **Mrs Wendy Jarrett & J S Moore**
9 WHOLELOTAFUN (IRE), 5, b h Sir Prancealot (IRE)—Gatamalata (IRE) **Mrs Wendy Jarrett & J S Moore**

THREE-YEAR-OLDS

10 ALAINN TU (IRE), b f Gregorian (IRE)—Debutante's Ball (IRE) **Mrs W Jarrett, Mrs T Burns, J S Moore**
11 DAFYRE, b f U S Navy Flag (USA)—Mille Tank **Lee Lun & S Moore**
12 KENTUCKY BOURBON (IRE), b g Mehmas (IRE)—Quiza **The 19th Hole Syndicate & J S Moore**
13 MIRABELLO BAY (IRE), ch g Belardo (IRE)—Stone Roses (IRE) **Ms Caroline Instone & J S Moore**
14 RAINTOWN (IRE), gr g Outstrip—Miss Fifty (IRE) **Mr Kieron Badger & J S Moore**
15 TIZ LIKELY (IRE), b f Elzaam (AUS)—Secret Liaison (IRE) **Ms H N Pinniger & Partner**

TWO-YEAR-OLDS

16 BIRKIE BOY (IRE), b g 07/04 Kuroshio (AUS)—Morazie (IRE) (Iffraaj) **Mr Ian Gray & Sara Moore**
17 B g 22/03 Bungle Inthejungle—Debutante's Ball (IRE) (Society Rock (IRE)) (2401) **The Moore The Merrier**
18 GO YOUR OWN WAY, gr ro c 07/04 Havana Grey—
Dubawi's Spirit (IRE) (Dubawi (IRE)) (7619) **Mr Kieron Badger & J S Moore**
19 Gr c 06/05 Phoenix of Spain (IRE)—Lismore (USA) (Tiznow (USA)) (10500) **J. S. Moore**
20 QUEUES LIKELY, b f 27/02 Massaat (IRE)—Bakoura (Green Desert (USA)) (14000) **Ms H N Pinniger & Partner**
21 SNOOKER MCCREW, ch g 29/03 Masar (IRE)—Stella Point (IRE) (Pivotal) (3000)
22 B g 24/02 Invincible Army (IRE)—Sojitzen (FR) (Great Journey (JPN)) (2401) **Eventmasters Racing & J S Moore**
23 B c 19/03 Soldier's Call—Tildiyna (IRE) (Sinndar (IRE))

MR J. S. MOORE - continued

24 **TOUCHING HANDS (IRE),** ch f 04/04 New Bay—
Rock Samphire (IRE) (Fastnet Rock (AUS)) (6002) **C Instone, K Badger & J S Moore**

Assistant Trainer: Mrs S. Moore, **Racing Secretary:** Miss Cathy Holding.

Apprentice Jockey: Miss Sophie Reed.

---

357 MISS LAURA MORGAN, Waltham On The Wolds

Postal: **Foxfield Stud, Goadby Road, Waltham On The Wolds, Melton Mowbray, Leicestershire, LE14 4AG**
Contacts: **PHONE 07543 836074 MOBILE 07817 616622**
EMAIL lauramorg@hotmail.co.uk

1 **AND THE NEW (IRE),** 12, b g Kalanisi (IRE)—Wheredidthemoneygo (IRE) **Mr Greenfingers Syndicate**
2 **ARTIC BREEZE (IRE),** 7, b g Arctic Cosmos (USA)—Barrell Rose (IRE) **JBFW Syndicate**
3 **BIG CHANGES,** 6, b g Kayf Tara—Harrys Whim **Mr A. Rogers**
4 **BLACKWELL BAY (IRE),** 6, ro g Carlotamix (FR)—Koochie Baby (IRE) **Ratkatcha Racing**
5 **CAPTAIN IVAN (IRE),** 9, ch g Stowaway—Western Starlight (IRE) **Racing On Together Club**
6 **CHAMP IS REAL,** 7, b g Kayf Tara—The Prime Viper (IRE) **Mr A. Rogers**
7 **CHARGING POINT,** 5, b g Sixties Icon—Lakaam **Scooby Doo Partnership**
8 **CLEAR THE RUNWAY (IRE),** 7, b g Jet Away—Minish Yeats (IRE) **Mr A. Rogers**
9 **CUDDLY DUDLEY (FR),** 6, b g Kapgarde (FR)—Cue To Cue **Mr & Mrs W. J. Williams**
10 **DALY TIGER (FR),** 10, b g Tiger Groom—Reine Tresor (FR) **Twist Your Arm Partnership**
11 **DIAKOSAINT (FR),** 8, b g Saint des Saints (FR)—Dianamisse (FR) **Worth the Ticket Partnership**
12 **DONDIAM (FR),** 6, b g Diamond Boy (FR)—Nouvelle Donne (FR) **National Hunt Racing Club**
13 **EMMA LAMB,** 9, b m Passing Glance—Lucinda Lamb **Capall Racing Club**
14 **FIRE AWAY (IRE),** 10, b g Getaway (GER)—Joan's Girl (IRE) **The Stagger Inn**
15 **FIRST ANGEL (FR),** 7, b g Anabaa Blue—Fontaine de Mars (FR) **Mr S. Sugden**
16 **FISHING FOR LIKES (IRE),** 7, b g Arcadio (GER)—Status Update (IRE) **Hanbury & Read**
17 **FRIARY ROCK (FR),** 8, b g Spanish Moon (USA)—Zenita des Brosses (FR) **The 1759 Syndicate**
18 **GLEN CANNEL (IRE),** 5, b g Flemensfirth (USA)—Shadow Eile (IRE) **Mr T. P. Radford**
19 **GLENTON,** 6, b g Casamento (IRE)—Sina (GER) **J Holt & G Archer**
20 **HASANKEY (IRE),** 7, gr g Mastercraftsman (IRE)—Haziyna (IRE) **The Hanky Panky Partnership**
21 **HERE WE HAVE IT (IRE),** 8, b g Mahler—Islands Sister (IRE) **The Stagger Inn**
22 **ILLUSION OF TIME (IRE),** 5, b g Sea The Stars (IRE)—Dolce Strega (IRE) **Mr Greenfingers Syndicate**
23 **J'AI FROID (IRE),** 10, b g Flemensfirth (USA)—Park Wave (IRE) **Mrs K. Bromley**
24 **LAKE SHORE DRIVE (IRE),** 11, b g Thewayyouare (USA)—Labrusca **Mr Greenfingers Syndicate**
25 **LOUGHDERG ROCCO (IRE),** 7, br g Shirocco (GER)—Banaltra (IRE) **Newark Castle Partnership**
26 **MY PORTIA,** 5, gr m Telescope (IRE)—Talk The Talk **Mrs J. E. Micklethwait**
27 **NOTLONGTILLMAY,** 7, b g Malinas (GER)—Tara Croft **Mr A. Rogers**
28 **PAT'S PICK (IRE),** 9, b g Shantou (USA)—Lady Lenson (IRE) **Barbara & Alex Faulconbridge**
29 **PERCUSSION,** 8, b g Malinas (GER)—Tambourine Ridge (IRE) **E. R. Hanbury**
30 **RADETZKY MARCH (IRE),** 8, b g Imperial Monarch (IRE)—Madgehil (IRE) **Mrs M. J. Pepperdine**
31 **RAFFERTY (IRE),** 9, b g Arcadio (GER)—Mighty Star (IRE) **Triumph In Mind**
32 **RELEASE THE KRAKEN (IRE),** 7, b g Shantou (USA)—Guydus (IRE) **Mrs H. Sugden**
33 **ROQUE IT (IRE),** 9, b g Presenting—Roque de Cyborg (IRE) **Gordon & Su Hall**
34 **SEHAYLI (IRE),** 10, b g Iffraaj—Quaich **Dream Team Partnership**
35 **SOCIALIST AGENDA,** 7, ch g Sir Percy—Mercy Pecksniff **Mr James Fyffe & Mr Scott Fyffe**
36 **SORCERESS MEDEA (IRE),** 6, b m Walk In The Park (IRE)—Nuit des Chartreux (FR) **Mr T. P. Radford**
37 **SUPREME YEATS (IRE),** 7, b g Yeats (IRE)—Supreme Bailerina (IRE) **The Old Stag Racing S.Y Partnership**
38 **TAQWAA (IRE),** 10, ch g Iffraaj—Hallowed Park (IRE) **Miss L. Morgan**
39 **TARDREE (IRE),** 9, ch g Mahler—Brownie Points (IRE) **Bennett & O'Brien**
40 **THE VOLLAN (IRE),** 9, b g Scorpion (IRE)—Print It On Lips (IRE) **Mrs E. Holmes**
41 **THEY CALL ME PETE,** 5, b g Shirocco (GER)—Pectora (IRE) **Miss C. L. Williamson**
42 **TOMMOUSE (IRE),** 7, b g Getaway (GER)—Run Supreme (IRE) **Gordon & Su Hall**
43 **WESTERN JILL (IRE),** 5, b m Westerner—Miss Pepperpot (IRE) **Mr A. Rogers**
44 **WESTERN SAFIRE (IRE),** 5, b m Westerner—Silver Sophfire **Miss C. L. Williamson**

MISS LAURA MORGAN - continued

45 **WHISTLEINTHEDARK (IRE),** 8, b g Fame And Glory—Last of Many (IRE) **Racing On Together Club**

Assistant Trainer: Patrick Cowley.

Amateur Jockey: Lewis Dobb.

---

358 MR MOUSE MORRIS, Fethard

Postal: **Everardsgrange, Fethard, Co. Tipperary, Ireland**
Contacts: **PHONE +353 52 613 1474 MOBILE +353 86 854 3010 FAX +353 52 613 1654**
EMAIL mouse@eircom.net

1 **BALLYSEEDY (IRE),** 5, b g Shirocco—Homelander **J. P. McManus**
2 **BLUEBELL DIVA,** 6, b m Walk In The Park (IRE)—In The Waves (IRE) **S. Casey**
3 **BOSSOFTHEBROWNIES (IRE),** 4, b g Ocovango—Gorgeousreach **Mrs A. Daly**
4 **CAESAR ROCK (IRE),** 7, b g Mahler—Supreme Von Pres (IRE) **M. O'Flynn, J. O'Flynn**
5 **CAMINO ROCK,** 6, b g Blue Bresil (FR)—Cresswell Ruby (IRE) **M. O'Flynn, J. O'Flynn**
6 **DIAMOND DUKE (IRE),** 4, b ch g Diamond Boy—Damefirth **Mr Kieran Evans**
7 **FOR FEAR OF FROST (IRE),** 5, b g Mahler—Pop Princess **Sean & Bernadine Mulryan**
8 **FOXY JACKS (IRE),** 9, b g Fame And Glory—Benefit Ball (IRE) **D. Desmond**
9 **FOXY ROCK (IRE),** 5, b g Mahler—Benefit Ball **M. O'Flynn, J. O'Flynn**
10 **FRANCISCIAN ROCK (IRE),** 6, b g Fame And Glory—Mrs Dempsey (IRE) **M. O'Flynn, J. O'Flynn**
11 **FRENCH DYNAMITE (FR),** 8, b g Kentucky Dynamite (USA)—Matnie (FR) **Robcour**
12 **GENTLEMANSGAME,** 7, b g Gentlewave (IRE)—Grainne Ni Maille **Robcour**
13 **GET MY DRIFT (FR),** 7, b g Spanish Moon (USA)—Voila (FR) **J. P. McManus**
14 **INDIANA JONES (IRE),** 7, b h Blue Bresil—Matnie **Robcour**
15 **LIMEKILN ROCK (IRE),** 6, b g Doyen (IRE)—Distelle (IRE) **M. O'Flynn, J. O'Flynn**
16 **MUSKERRY ROCK (IRE),** 4, b g Shirocco—One Treasure **M. O'Flynn, J. O'Flynn**
17 **SAMS PROFILE,** 9, b g Black Sam Bellamy (IRE)—Lucylou (IRE) **M. O'Flynn, J. O'Flynn**
18 4, B g Milan—Supreme Breda
19 **THE LAST THROW (IRE),** 7, b g Shirocco—Bridgequarter Girl
20 **WHATSAVAILABLE (IRE),** 6, b g Saddler Maker—Melancholy Hill **Mr R. A. Scott**
21 **WHATSITABOUT (FR),** 5, gr g Morandi (FR)—Top Crystal (IRE) **Mr R. A. Scott**
22 **WHATSNOTOKNOW (IRE),** 8, b g Mahler—Whos To Know (IRE) **Mr R. A. Scott**

---

359 MR PATRICK MORRIS, Prescot

Postal: **Avenue House, George Hale Avenue, Knowsley Park, Prescot, Merseyside, L34 4AJ**
Contacts: **MOBILE 07545 425235**
EMAIL Patrickmorris76@yahoo.com

1 **ALJARDAA (IRE),** 5, b m Muhaarar—Yasmeen **Dr S. Lane**
2 **BRIAN THE SNAIL (IRE),** 9, gr g Zebedee—Sweet Irish **Dr M. B. Q. S. Koukash**
3 **GABRIAL THE WIRE,** 7, b g Garswood—Nightunderthestars **Dr M. B. Q. S. Koukash**
4 **GLORY AND GOLD,** 4, b f Havana Gold (IRE)—Grace And Glory (IRE) **Mr A. Mather**
5 **HEART OF SOUL (IRE),** 8, b g Makfi—Hadrian's Waltz (IRE) **Dr M. B. Q. S. Koukash**
6 **HOCHFELD (IRE),** 9, b g Cape Cross (IRE)—What A Charm (IRE) **Mr T. Cross**
7 **HOT TEAM (IRE),** 7, b g Zoffany (IRE)—Ahd (USA) **Dr M. B. Q. S. Koukash**
8 **MANCINI,** 9, ch g Nathaniel (IRE)—Muscovado (USA) **Dr M. B. Q. S. Koukash**
9 **PALIFICO,** 5, ch m Siyouni (FR)—Montalcino (IRE) **TPT Syndicate**
10 **RESHOUN (FR),** 9, b g Shamardal (USA)—Radiyya (IRE) **Dr M. B. Q. S. Koukash**
11 **STREET LIFE,** 6, ch g Hot Streak (IRE)—Atheera (IRE) **Dr M. B. Q. S. Koukash**

360 MR HUGHIE MORRISON, East Ilsley

Postal: **Summerdown, East Ilsley, Newbury, Berkshire, RG20 7LB**
Contacts: **PHONE 01635 281678 MOBILE 07836 687799 FAX 01635 281746**
EMAIL jane@hughiemorrison.co.uk WEBSITE www.hughiemorrison.co.uk

1 **AFFAIR,** 9, b m Sakhee's Secret—Supatov (USA) **H. Morrison**
2 **AMERICAN GERRY (IRE),** 7, b g Americain (USA)—Hurricane Society (IRE) **Mrs M. R. Geake**
3 **BEGGARMAN,** 6, ch g Toronado (IRE)—Let's Dance (IRE) **Howses Stud**
4 **COUSIN KHEE,** 16, b g Sakhee (USA)—Cugina **Mrs M. D. W. Morrison**
5 **CURTIZ,** 6, b g Stimulation (IRE)—Supatov (USA) **Mrs J. Parkes**
6 **DOM PERRY,** 7, b g Doyen (IRE)—Aphrodisias (FR) **Rushmoor Stud**
7 **EX FLIRTATIOUS,** 6, b m Kayf Tara—Flirtatious **Mrs M. D. W. Morrison**
8 **FILANDERER,** 7, b g Kayf Tara—Flirtatious **Mrs M. D. W. Morrison**
9 **FINAL ENCORE,** 6, b g Dunaden (FR)—Act Three **Mrs A. J. Hamilton-Fairley**
10 6, B m Kayf Tara—Flirtatious **Mrs M. D. W. Morrison**
11 **GALLANT APPROACH,** 4, b g Garswood—Valencha **Pangfield Racing V**
12 **HARTFIELD (IRE),** 5, b m Robin des Champs (FR)—
Park Ella (IRE) **The Hill Stud, Mrs A. M. Garfield, L. A. Garfield**
13 **HAYMAKER,** 4, b g Muhaarar—Squash
H. Morrison, Collett, Morrison & Partners, The Hon Miss M. A. Morrison, Mr C. M. Budgett, Miss D. Collett
14 **LADY PERCIVAL,** 5, b m Sir Percy—Daffydowndilly **Lady Blyth**
15 **MAKSUD,** 4, b g Golden Horn—Althania (USA) **Thurloe Thoroughbreds LIV**
16 **MISS FAIRFAX (IRE),** 7, ch m Imperial Monarch (IRE)—
Stein Castle (IRE) **The Hill Stud, Mrs A. M. Garfield, L. A. Garfield**
17 **NOT SO SLEEPY,** 11, ch g Beat Hollow—Papillon de Bronze (IRE) **Lady Blyth**
18 **NOW THEN WENDY,** 6, bl m Mukhadram—Dusting (IRE) **Rushmoor Stud**
19 **ONE FOR BOBBY (IRE),** 4, b f Frankel—One Spirit (IRE) **Miss A H Marshall**
20 **PREMIERE LIGNE (FR),** 4, b g Lope de Vega (IRE)—Realism (USA) **Caveat Emptor Partnership**
21 **QUICKTHORN,** 6, b g Nathaniel (IRE)—Daffydowndilly **Lady Blyth**
22 **RAVENS ARK,** 6, ch g Raven's Pass (USA)—Wonderful Desert **Beachview Corporation Ltd**
23 **RODNEY (IRE),** 4, b g Golden Horn—Romina **Normandie Stud Ltd**
24 **SCANNING,** 7, b g Pastoral Pursuits—Yonder **Mrs M. D. W. Morrison**
25 **SCATTERING,** 4, b g Showcasing—Seed Corn **N. M. H. Jones**
26 **SECRET SQUIRREL,** 4, ch g Stimulation (IRE)—Trigger Point **Mrs M. D. W. Morrison**
27 **SELKIRK GRACE,** 4, ch f Cityscape—Jasmeno **MNC Racing**
28 **SHOCKWAVES,** 4, gr g Sea The Moon (GER)—Having A Blast (USA) **Mrs M. T. Bevan**
29 **STAY ALERT,** 4, b f Fastnet Rock (AUS)—Starfala **Ben & Sir Martyn Arbib, M. Arbib, Mr B. G. Arbib**
30 **STAY WELL,** 5, b g Iffraaj—Sweeping Up **Ben & Sir Martyn Arbib, M. Arbib, Mr B. G. Arbib**
31 **SUGAR CANDIE,** 4, b f Highland Reel (IRE)—Sweet Selection **Paul & Catriona Brocklehurst Bloodstock**
32 **TANGO TONIGHT,** 4, ch f Pivotal—Last Tango Inparis **Helena Springfield Ltd**
33 **THIRD WIND,** 9, b br g Shirocco (GER)—Act Three **Mrs A. J. Hamilton-Fairley**
34 **THUNDERCLAP (IRE),** 5, b g Night of Thunder (IRE)—
Former Drama (USA) **T. Pilkington & Mr R. A. Pilkington, Mr R. A. Pilkington, Sir Thomas Pilkington**
35 **URBAN ARTIST,** 8, ch m Cityscape—Cill Rialaig **Pangfield Racing V**
36 **VINO VICTRIX,** 5, b g Sir Percy—Valeria Victrix (IRE) **Mr S. B. S. Ronaldson**
37 **WAGGA WAGGA (IRE),** 4, ch g Australia—Quiz Mistress **The Fairy Story Partnership**
38 **WITH RESPECT (IRE),** 6, gr g Gutaifan (IRE)—More Respect (IRE) **Thurloe Thoroughbreds XLVIII**
39 **YODEL,** 6, b m Pastoral Pursuits—Yonder **Mrs M. D. W. Morrison**

THREE-YEAR-OLDS

40 **ASCARI,** b c Invincible Spirit (IRE)—
Monzza **M. Kerr-Dineen, Mr M. B. Hughes, Michael Kerr-Dineen & Martin Hughes**
41 **AZAHARA PALACE,** b f Adaay (IRE)—Josefa Goya **The TOD Partnership**
42 **CEILIDH,** ch c Highland Reel (IRE)—Rainbow's Arch (IRE) **Kerr-Dineen, Eason A Simpson, M. Kerr-Dineen,**
W. D. Eason, Alasdair Simpson Consulting Limited
43 **CEILIDH KING,** ch c Highland Reel (IRE)—Poet's Princess **Paul & Catriona Brocklehurst Bloodstock**
44 **CLEVER RELATION,** b c Intello (GER)—Sweet Selection **Bruton Street**
45 **EX SUPATOV,** b f Stimulation (IRE)—Supatov (USA) **H. Morrison**
46 **FAIR DINKUM (IRE),** b c Australia—Wannabe Posh (IRE) **Normandie Stud Ltd**
47 **HILL FILLY,** b f Kingston Hill—Respectfilly **The Fairy Story Partnership**
48 **ICY DIP,** b f Stimulation (IRE)—Inya Lake **H. Morrison, Mr Rod & Mrs Sherin Lloyd, Mrs S. A. Lloyd, R. E. Lloyd**

MR HUGHIE MORRISON - continued

49 **KATATELLA,** b f Intello (GER)—Katabatika **Lady Blyth**
50 **KYLE OF LOCHALSH,** b c Highland Reel (IRE)—Quiz Mistress **The Fairy Story Partnership**
51 **LOCH GLASS (IRE),** ch f Highland Reel (IRE)—Shimmering (IRE) **Selwood Bloodstock**
52 **LUNATICK,** b c Sea The Moon (GER)—
Alvarita **M. Kerr-Dineen, Martin Hughes & Michael Kerr-Dineen, Mr M. B. Hughes**
53 **MISTRAL STAR,** b f Frankel—Shirocco Star **Helena Springfield Ltd**
54 **MOTTISFONT (IRE),** b f Adaay (IRE)—Broadlands **H. Morrison, The End-R-Ways Partnership & Partners, Mr J. W. Parker, Mr A. R. Macdonald-Buchanan, The End-R-Ways Partnership**
55 **MR BOSON,** ch c Bobby's Kitten (USA)—Songerie **The Hon Miss M. A. Morrison, Miss D. Collett, Morrison, Pickford, Angliss, Collett, Malcolm, Mr S. D. Malcolm, A. C. Pickford, Mr R. A. Angliss**
56 **MR MISTOFFELEES (IRE),** b c Siyouni (FR)—Jellicle Ball (IRE) **One More Moment of Madness**
57 **ROMAN ART (IRE),** b g Ribchester (IRE)—Art Institute (USA) **Thurloe Thoroughbreds LII**
58 **ROYAL CAPE (IRE),** b c Gleneagles (IRE)—Kikonga **P. C. J. Dalby & R. D. Schuster**
59 **STAR ADAAY,** b f Adaay (IRE)—Noble Nova **Platinum Partners**
60 **SUN SPIRIT,** b g Pivotal—Sweeping Up **Ben & Sir Martyn Arbib, M. Arbib, Mr B. G. Arbib**
61 B f Stimulation (IRE)—Supatov (USA) **H. Morrison**
62 **SURREY BELLE,** b f Golden Horn—Al Reem **Surrey Racing (Be)**
63 **SURREY CHARM,** b f Havana Gold (IRE)—Stacey Sutton (FR) **Surrey Racing (SC)**
64 **SWITCHEL (IRE),** b f Golden Horn—Swizzle Stick (IRE) **Mr A. P. Rogers**
65 **TRANQUILLITY,** b f Massaat (IRE)—Tranquil Flight **Platinum Partners**
66 **TUKI TUKI,** b f Showcasing—Coquet **Mrs A Scott & Fonthill Farms, Lord Margadale, Mrs B. M. Scott**

TWO-YEAR-OLDS

67 **BELAMINDAR,** ch f 15/03 Belardo (IRE)—Seramindar (Zamindar (USA)) **The Fairy Story Partnership**
68 **BUDDING (IRE),** b f 21/04 Cracksman—Springlike (IRE) (Acclamation) (55000) **P. C. J. Dalby & R. D. Schuster**
69 B c 24/03 Ulysses (IRE)—Capriolla (In The Wings) (60000) **Collett, Lund, Morrison & Scott**
70 B c 27/04 Awtaad (IRE)—Celestial Girl (Dubai Destination (USA)) (20000)
71 **DASHINWHITESARGENT,** gr c 10/02 Highland Reel (IRE)—
Bella Regazza (Dutch Art) **Paul & Catriona Brocklehurst Bloodstock**
72 **EX BROADLANDS,** b f 25/04 Blue Point (IRE)—Broadlands (Kheleyf (USA)) **Mr A. R. Macdonald-Buchanan**
73 **EX LAST TANGO INPARIS,** b f 18/02 Nathaniel (IRE)—Last Tango Inparis (Aqlaam) **Helena Springfield Ltd**
74 **EX SHIROCCO STAR,** b f 12/02 Dubawi (IRE)—Shirocco Star (Shirocco (GER)) **Helena Springfield Ltd**
75 **HAPPY HADEDA (IRE),** b c 10/02 Invincible Spirit (IRE)—
Marsh Daisy (Pivotal) **Sir Thomas Pilkington & Mrs S Rogers**
76 B f 21/04 Acclamation—Marisol (IRE) (Teofilo (IRE)) (45000) **Thurloe Royal Marsden Cancer Charity II**
77 **MARMALADE LADY,** b f 12/04 Expert Eye—Got To Dream (Duke of Marmalade (IRE)) **Mr S. B. S. Ronaldson**
78 **NOWHERE,** ch f 05/05 Nathaniel (IRE)—Hereawi (Dubawi (IRE)) **Mr Julian Richmond-Watson**
79 **POST MISTRESS,** ch f 10/04 Postponed (IRE)—Quiz Mistress **The Fairy Story Partnership**
80 **RATTLER,** b c 25/04 Advertise—Ruby Rocket (IRE) (Indian Rocket) (55000) **M. Kerr-Dineen, Mr M. B. Hughes, Michael Kerr-Dineen & Martin Hughes**
81 B c 09/04 Fastnet Rock (AUS)—Seaduced (Lope de Vega (IRE)) **Ben & Sir Martyn Arbib, M. Arbib, Mr B. G. Arbib**
82 **SURREY FIRE,** ch c 08/03 Masar (IRE)—Sweet Selection (Stimulation (IRE)) (60000) **Surrey Racing (SF) & Mr Mark Symon**

Assistant Trainer: Mr Charles Harris.

Flat Jockey: Charlie Bennett. **Amateur Jockey:** Mr Robert Pooles.

---

361 MR WILLIAM MUIR AND CHRIS GRASSICK, Lambourn

Postal: **Linkslade, Wantage Road, Lambourn, Hungerford, Berkshire, RG17 8UG**
Contacts: **PHONE 01488 73748**
EMAIL william@williammuir.com

1 **COUNTRY PYLE,** 5, b m New Approach (IRE)—La Pyle (FR) **K & W Bloodstock Limited & Mr R W Devlin**
2 **GALIAC,** 4, b g Kodiac—Gallipot **Perspicacious Punters Racing Club**

MR WILLIAM MUIR AND CHRIS GRASSICK - continued

3 **HAMMY END (IRE),** 7, b g Mount Nelson—Northern Affair (IRE) **Mr J. M. O'Mulloy**
4 **IMAGINARY DRAGON (FR),** 5, b g Kapgarde (FR)—Call Me Dragon (FR) **Ms N J Grieve & Mr C A Turner**
5 **MAKING MUSIC (IRE),** 4, b f Mastercraftsman (IRE)—Rapacity Alexander (IRE) **Foursome Thoroughbreds**
6 **MAYTREE RESPITE (IRE),** 4, b g Mehmas (IRE)—Loveisreckless (IRE) **Mr J. M. O'Mulloy**
7 **MITROSONFIRE,** 5, gr g Lethal Force (IRE)—Blaugrana (IRE) **Mr J. M. O'Mulloy**
8 **PYLEDRIVER,** 6, b h Harbour Watch (IRE)—La Pyle (FR) **K & W Bloodstock Limited & Mr R W Devlin**
9 **RED VINEYARD (IRE),** 4, ch g Slade Power (IRE)—Artisia (IRE) **Foursome Thoroughbreds**
10 **SALT TREATY (IRE),** 4, ch g National Defense—Salty Sugar **Muir Racing Partnership - Flemington**
11 **SNAPCRACKLEPOP,** 4, b g Acclamation—Sweet Secret **Nigel Scandrett, Shane Buy & Partners**
12 **STOCKPYLE,** 4, b g Oasis Dream—La Pyle (FR) **K & W Bloodstock Limited & Mr R W Devlin**
13 **SWAYZE,** 4, b g Showcasing—Dream Dreamer **Baker, d'Arcy, Grassick**
14 **TOP SECRET,** 6, ch g Anjaal—Just Devine (IRE) **Carmel Stud**

THREE-YEAR-OLDS

15 **AVON LIGHT,** ch f Lightning Spear—Avon Lady **Helena Springfield Ltd**
16 **BEAUZEE,** gr g Brazen Beau (AUS)—Zeehan **d'Arcy & Baker Partnership**
17 **CARAMAY,** bl f Lethal Force (IRE)—Loveisreckless (IRE) **Mr J. M. O'Mulloy**
18 **EL HABANO,** b g Camacho—Sweet Secret **Muir Racing Partnership Newmarket**
19 **HERECOMESTHESTORM,** ch f Iffraaj—Yaa Mous **Folly Boys**
20 **HONEYMOONER (IRE),** gr f Mastercraftsman (IRE)—Meetyouatthemoon (IRE) **Mr C.L.A.Edginton & Mr K.Jeffery**
21 **MAGGIE'S WAY,** ch f Cityscape—Maggie Jonks **Dr J. A. E. Hobby**
22 **MOGOK VALLEY (IRE),** b c Zoffany (IRE)—Dreaming of Rubies **Muir Racing Partnership - Windsor**
23 **MRS TWIG (IRE),** gr f Mastercraftsman (IRE)—Desert Run (IRE) **Muir Racing Partnership - Ascot**
24 **MUSTAJAAB,** b br c Tasleet—Likeable **K. A. Dasmal**
25 **NEW DAYRELL,** b g New Approach (IRE)—Srda (USA) **Muir Racing Partnership - Saint Cloud**
26 **OVERNIGHT OATS,** b g Muhaarar—Integral **Wedgwell Partners**
27 **PRIORS DELL,** b g Charm Spirit (IRE)—Anya **Mrs L. M. Alexander**
28 **SHAGPYLE,** br f Frankel—La Pyle (FR) **K & W Bloodstock Limited & Mr R W Devlin**
29 **SO SLEEPY,** b f Oasis Dream—If So **Foursome Thoroughbreds**
30 **STARPROOF (IRE),** b f Camacho—Dufoof (IRE) **Muir Racing Partnership - Newbury**
31 **TENACIOUSLY,** ch c Showcasing—Tirania **Miss Y. M. G. Jacques**
32 **THE YODELLER,** b g Swiss Spirit—Bonne de Fleur **John H W Finch & Jo Stainer**
33 **UNLIMITED DATA,** b g Tasleet—Midnight Sky **Muir Racing Partnership - York**
34 **YOUNG CHAUCER (IRE),** b g Dandy Man (IRE)—Traveller's Tales **C. L. A. Edginton**

TWO-YEAR-OLDS

35 **DANGER ZONE,** ch c 31/01 Code Red—Ballymore Celebre (IRE) (Peintre Celebre (USA)) **Carmel Stud**
36 B g 20/04 Dandy Man (IRE)—Farthing (IRE) (Mujadil (USA)) (14406)
37 **I DARE YOU,** b f 26/03 Showcasing—Dare To Dream (Exceed And Excel (AUS)) (55000) **Carmel Stud Partnership**
38 **INNOCENT SPIRIT (IRE),** b f 29/03 Waldgeist—Seschat (IRE) (Sinndar (IRE)) (45000) **Clarke, Edginton, Niven**
39 Gr c 26/04 U S Navy Flag (USA)—Moon Empress (FR) (Rainbow Quest (USA)) (46419) **C. L. A. Edginton**
40 Br f 25/04 Cappella Sansevero—Rustam (Dansili) **Muir Racing Partnership - Spotted Dog**
41 **SURFER DUDE (IRE),** b c 23/03 Waldgeist—Tidewalker (IRE) (Lawman (FR)) (20000) **Foursome Thoroughbreds**
42 B c 22/02 Cable Bay (IRE)—Whims of Desire (Nathaniel (IRE)) (5000)

---

362 MR CLIVE MULHALL, Scarcroft

Postal: **Scarcroft Hall Farm, Thorner Lane, Scarcroft, Leeds, Yorkshire, LS14 3AQ**
Contacts: **HOME 0113 289 3095 MOBILE 07979 527675**
EMAIL clivemulhallracing@gmail.com, clive@scarcrofthallracing.co.uk

1 **ANEEDH,** 13, b g Lucky Story (USA)—Seed Al Maha (USA) **Mrs C. M. Mulhall**
2 **BIGBADBOY (IRE),** 10, b g Big Bad Bob (IRE)—Elegantly (IRE) **Ms Y Featherstone & Mrs M Mulhall**
3 **LORD SERENDIPITY (IRE),** 11, gr g Lord Shanakill (USA)—Elitista (FR) **Ms Y Featherstone & Mrs M Mulhall**
4 **SHE IS WHAT SHE IS,** 8, b m Desideratum—Alimure **Mrs C. M. Mulhall**

MR CLIVE MULHALL - continued

Assistant Trainer: Mrs Martina Mulhall.

Amateur Jockey: Miss Charlotte Mulhall.

363

MR NEIL MULHOLLAND, Limpley Stoke

Postal: **Conkwell Grange Stables, Conkwell, Limpley Stoke, Bath, Avon, BA2 7FD**
Contacts: **MOBILE 07739 258607**
EMAIL neil@neilmulhollandracing.com WEBSITE www.neilmulhollandracing.com

1 **ABBEYHILL (IRE),** 6, b g Shirocco (GER)—Tenable **Colony Stables , Bunch & Dicks**
2 **AGENT SAONOIS (FR),** 7, gr g Saonois (FR)—Agosta (FR) **The Affordable (3) Partnership**
3 **AMBUSH ANNIE (IRE),** 6, b br m Fame And Glory—Ambush Angel (IRE)
4 4, B g Black Sam Bellamy (IRE)—Angie Marinie **D. V. Stevens**
5 **ANNE BONNY,** 5, b m Black Sam Bellamy (IRE)—Presenting Taupo (IRE) **Heart Racing HR4**
6 **ANY NEWS (IRE),** 8, ch g Stowaway—Kisskiss Bang Bang (IRE) **Mrs J. N. Cartwright**
7 **BALINESKER BEACH (IRE),** 8, b g Fame And Glory—Minnie Ray (IRE) **Mrs P. J. Awdry**
8 5, B m Soldier of Fortune (IRE)—Ballycorrigan (IRE)
9 **BALLYMILAN,** 8, b m Milan—Ballyhoo (IRE) **Heart Racing HR2**
10 **BARNARDS GREEN (IRE),** 7, ch g Getaway (GER)—Strawberry Lane (IRE) **Mr M. C. Creed**
11 **BATWOMEN (IRE),** 5, b m Presenting—Avondhu Lady (IRE) **Miss J. A. Goddard**
12 **BLUE SUEDE SHOES (IRE),** 6, b m Walk In The Park (IRE)—Down By The Sea (IRE) **Heart Racing HR3**
13 **BRIEF TIMES (IRE),** 7, b g Doyen (IRE)—Dali's Theatre **Ms S. M. Exell**
14 **BROOMFIELDS CAVE (IRE),** 6, b g Court Cave (IRE)—Dreaming On (IRE) **Bristow Crofts & Flower**
15 **BUCEPHALUS (GER),** 6, b g Soldier Hollow—Batya (IRE) **C. E. Handford**
16 **CASTLE FROME (IRE),** 6, b m Walk In The Park (IRE)—Clear Riposte (IRE) **Mrs P. L. Bridel**
17 **CASTLE QUARTER (IRE),** 7, b g Zoffany (IRE)—Queen's Pudding (IRE) **Mr G. Teversham**
18 **CELTIC FORTUNE (IRE),** 6, b g Soldier of Fortune (IRE)—Rhinestone Cowgirl (IRE) **D. M. Bell**
19 **CHARIA,** 4, ch g Yorgunnabelucky (USA)—Midnight Sequel **Dajam Ltd**
20 **CHELSEA ANNIE (IRE),** 4, b f Mehmas (IRE)—Miss Sally (IRE) **Dajam Ltd**
21 **CHINWAG,** 8, b g Trans Island—Clohamon Gossip (IRE) **The Boot Inn Partnership**
22 **CHIRICO VALLIS (FR),** 11, b g Poliglote—Quora Vallis (FR) **Mr J. P. McManus**
23 **CLASSIC FLIGHT (IRE),** 5, br g Scalo—Classic Angel (GER) **James and Jean Potter Ltd**
24 **COME ON PADDY MAC (IRE),** 7, b g Libertarian—Mogs Delight (IRE) **C. E. Handford**
25 **CONCRETE KING (IRE),** 9, b g Morozov (USA)—Mags Millar (IRE) **Mr J. Hobbs**
26 **CONKWELL LEGEND,** 9, b g Midnight Legend—Gallimaufry **Mrs S. A. Keys**
27 **COUSU MAIN (FR),** 7, b g Buck's Boum (FR)—Just Pegasus (USA) **Lycett Racing Ltd**
28 **COWBOY (IRE),** 4, gr g Dark Angel (IRE)—Sea of Grace (IRE) **Neil Mulholland Racing Ltd**
29 **CREMANT (IRE),** 9, b g Getaway (GER)—Opera Season (IRE) **Mr P. M. Simmonds**
30 **CROSSING THE BAR (IRE),** 6, b g Poet's Voice—Ship's Biscuit **S. &. A. Giannini**
31 **DARKSIDEOFTARNSIDE (IRE),** 9, b g Intense Focus (USA)—Beautiful Dancer (IRE) **D. R. Fear**
32 **DEAD RIGHT,** 11, b g Alflora (IRE)—April Queen **Mr J. P. McManus**
33 **DJASEK (FR),** 7, b g Rip Van Winkle (IRE)—Darjana (IRE) **The Boot Inn Partnership**
34 **DYNAMIC KATE (IRE),** 7, br m Yeats (IRE)—Alverstone **BG Racing Partnership**
35 **EARTH KING (IRE),** 7, b g Shirocco (GER)—Beach Beauty (IRE) **R. M. Penny**
36 **EEL PIE ISLAND,** 5, b m Sixties Icon—Ificaniwill (IRE) **Mr P. Bowden**
37 **FEEL GOOD INC (IRE),** 5, b g Westerner—Brackforde (IRE) **Mrs L. Maclennan**
38 **FIRST QUEST (USA),** 9, b g First Defence (USA)—Dixie Quest (USA) **The Affordable Partnership**
39 **FRAU GEORGIA (IRE),** 9, b m Germany (USA)—Sumability (IRE) **Mr J. Henderson**
40 **FRED BEAR (IRE),** 5, b g Kodi Bear (IRE)—Subtle Affair (IRE) **Neil Mulholland Racing Ltd**
41 **FULL OF SURPRISES (FR),** 8, b m No Risk At All (FR)—Fontaine Riant (FR) **Mr J. P. McManus**
42 **GARINCHA (IRE),** 7, b g Ask—Mandy Winger **Mr R Flower & Dajam**
43 **GATA BAN (IRE),** 6, b m Getaway (GER)—Meryemnana (IRE) **The Boot Inn Partnership**
44 **GET WITH THE TIMES,** 5, b g Getaway (GER)—Pass The Time **Dajam Ltd**
45 **GIRLOFMYDREAMS,** 6, b br m Sir Percy—Fairy Slipper **Dajam Ltd**
46 **GLAJOU (FR),** 7, br g Network (GER)—Toscane (FR) **Mr J. Hobbs**

MR NEIL MULHOLLAND - continued

47 **GREAT OCEAN (FR),** 7, b g Great Pretender (IRE)—Diamond of Diana (FR) **S. &. A. Giannini**
48 **GREAT SNOW (FR),** 6, b m Great Pretender (IRE)—Snow Berry (FR) **Walters Plant Hire Ltd**
49 **HAPPY RETURNS,** 6, b m Recharge (IRE)—Bonne Anniversaire **Wincanton Race Club**
50 **HAWAII DU MESTIVEL (FR),** 6, ch g No Risk At All (FR)—Pensee du Mestivel (FR) **Mrs J. Gerard-Pearse**
51 **HIDDEN DEPTHS (IRE),** 8, b g Dark Angel (IRE)—Liber Nauticus (IRE) **Mr A. J. Russell**
52 **HOBB'S DELIGHT,** 7, b g Milan—Hobb's Dream (IRE) **Hobbs & Mulholland**
53 **HOBBS JOY,** 6, b g Norse Dancer (IRE)—Hobb's Dream (IRE) **Hobbs & Mulholland**
54 **HORIZON D'OR (FR),** 6, b g Nicaron (GER)—Unite Speciale (FR) **Neil Mulholland Racing Ltd**
55 **I'M ON MY WAY (IRE),** 6, b m Mahler—J'Arrive **D. M. Bell**
56 **ICONE D'AUBRELLE (FR),** 5, b g Cokoriko (FR)—Tiree A Part (FR) **Mr R. B. Waley-Cohen**
57 **IKE SPORT (FR),** 5, b g Spanish Moon (USA)—Safraniere (FR) **The Chosen Few**
58 **INOUI MACHIN (FR),** 5, b g Honolulu (IRE)—Firmini (FR) **Walters Plant Hire Ltd**
59 **INSPECTOR LYNLEY,** 6, b g Nathaniel (IRE)—Duchess of Seville **Mrs H. R. Cross**
60 **INVICTUS SMART (FR),** 5, b g Masterstroke (USA)—Barbarella Smart (FR) **Mr R. B. Waley-Cohen**
61 **ISLAND APPROACH (FR),** 5, b br g Scalo—Shabady (FR) **James and Jean Potter Ltd**
62 **JACOBS ACRE (IRE),** 5, b g Jet Away—Bethpage Black (IRE) **Ms S. M. Exell**
63 **JAMAICAINE (FR),** 4, gr f Martinborough (JPN)—Desideria (FR) **Mr J. P. McManus**
64 **JEAN PIERRE,** 5, b g Blue Bresil (FR)—Duchess of Seville **Mrs S. A. Keys**
65 **JOKER DE THAIX (FR),** 4, b g Karaktar (IRE)—Quete de Thaix (FR) **Mrs J. Gerard-Pearse**
66 **JONGLEUR D'ETOILES (FR),** 4, b g It's Gino (GER)—Salika (FR) **Mr J. P. McManus**
67 **LA PAGERIE (FR),** 6, b m Khalkevi (IRE)—Belle Yepa (FR) **Walters Plant Hire Ltd**
68 **LAHINCH WAVE (IRE),** 5, b m Affinisea (IRE)—Ballymartintheatre (IRE) **Lynne & Angus Maclennan**
69 **LORD ACCORD (IRE),** 8, b g Yeats (IRE)—Cush Jewel (IRE) **Lynne & Angus Maclennan**
70 **LORD CHIPS,** 5, b g Clovis du Berlais (FR)—Parstara
71 **LUMINARIES (IRE),** 6, b g Leading Light (IRE)—Pas de Chapeau (IRE) **Mr K. S. Ward**
72 **MAGNIFICENT BEN (IRE),** 8, b g Sans Frontieres (IRE)—Lakeshore Lodge (IRE) **Mr O. S. Harris**
73 **MALIBOO (IRE),** 10, b m Mahler—Aboo Lala (IRE) **Steve Bristow Hayley Williams**
74 **MALINAS ISLAND,** 8, ch g Malinas (GER)—Island of Memories (IRE) **P. C. Tory**
75 **MAN OF THE SEA (IRE),** 7, ch g Born To Sea (IRE)—Hurricane Lily (IRE) **Dajam Ltd**
76 **MASTERDREAM (FR),** 6, b g Sea The Stars (IRE)—Santa Christiana (FR) **Mr D. B. Harris**
77 **MICKYH (IRE),** 7, b g Sageburg (IRE)—Anna's Melody (IRE) **Mr M. J. Hemmings**
78 **MIDNIGHT GOLD (IRE),** 6, b m Fame And Glory—Midnight Fox (IRE) **Neil Mulholland Racing Club**
79 **MIDNIGHT SHIMMER,** 5, gr g Dream Eater (IRE)—Midnight Sequel **Dajam Ltd**
80 **MILANESE ROSE (IRE),** 7, gr m Milan—Ma Furie (FR) **Proudley & Whymark Partnership**
81 **MILKWOOD (IRE),** 9, b g Dylan Thomas (IRE)—Tropical Lake (IRE) **Ms J. Bridel**
82 **MINI MILDRED,** 4, b f Universal (IRE)—Pass The Time **Dajam Ltd**
83 5, B m Flemensfirth (USA)—Miss Mary Mac (IRE) **Mr T. Crowe**
84 **MISTER SWEETS (IRE),** 8, b g Scorpion (IRE)—Fast Finisher (IRE) **Equi ex Incertis Partners**
85 **MOLLIANA,** 8, b m Olden Times—The Screamer (IRE) **Dajam Ltd**
86 **MONGOL EMPEROR (IRE),** 8, b g Imperial Monarch (IRE)—Hurricane Bella (IRE) **Equi ex Incertis Partners**
87 **MOONSET (FR),** 5, b g Spanish Moon (USA)—Cerize (IRE) **Mr P. J. Proudley**
88 **MOTHILL (IRE),** 5, b g Golden Horn—Jilnaar (IRE) **Mr J. Gray**
89 **NO WORRIES,** 9, b g Passing Glance—Silver Sequel **Dajam Ltd**
90 **OF CORSE I CAN (FR),** 6, gr g Lord du Sud (FR)—Walk In Corsica (FR) **Mrs J. N. Cartwright**
91 **OF COURSE YOU CAN,** 5, b m Yeats (IRE)—Free Thinking **Hot To Trot Racing & Robert Waley-cohen**
92 **PELTWELL (IRE),** 10, b m Milan—Fast Finisher (IRE) **Mrs P. L. Bridel**
93 **PLANNED PARADISE (IRE),** 7, b g Westerner—Quel Bleu (IRE) **Mr O. S. Harris**
94 **PRINCESS T,** 8, gr m Aussie Rules (USA)—Fairy Slipper **Harte Investments Ltd & Dajam Ltd**
95 **QUEENS LEGACY,** 8, b m Passing Glance—April Queen **Mrs J. Fear**
96 **RAGAMUFFIN (IRE),** 8, b g Arcadio (GER)—Mill Race Annie (IRE) **Mrs J. N. Cartwright**
97 4, B f Shantaram—Realta Mo Croi (IRE)
98 **RENEGADE ARROW (FR),** 7, ch g Motivator—Cinders' Prize **Flower Abbott & Crofts**
99 **ROCK ON RITA (IRE),** 7, b m Shirocco (GER)—Gilt Free (IRE) **Mr J. P. McManus**
100 **SAINTE DOCTOR (FR),** 7, gr m Doctor Dino (FR)—Pakoonah **Mr J. P. McManus**
101 **SECRET SECRET (IRE),** 7, b g Born To Sea (IRE)—Maughami **Mrs K. Otoole**
102 **SHUIL CEOIL (IRE),** 5, ch g Mount Nelson—Shuil Bob (IRE) **Mr R. H. Flower**
103 **SIMPLY SIN (IRE),** 8, b g Footstepsinthesand—Miss Sally (IRE) **Neil Mulholland Racing Ltd**
104 **SUPER DUPER SAM,** 7, ch g Black Sam Bellamy (IRE)—With Grace **D. V. Stevens**
105 **TALLY'S SON,** 9, b g Assertive—Talamahana **Paul & Ann de Weck**
106 **TANGO BOY (IRE),** 10, ch g Flemensfirth (USA)—Hello Kitty (IRE) **Mr A. G. Bloom**

MR NEIL MULHOLLAND - continued

107 **THE BOLD THADY (IRE),** 6, b g Milan—Princesse Rooney (FR) **Strictly Come Racing**
108 **THE TURTLE SAID,** 6, b g Manduro (GER)—Goslar **Mrs P. M. Bunch**
109 **TRANSLINK,** 8, b g Rail Link—Ocean Transit (IRE) **Mr B. F. Mulholland**
110 **TROLLEY BOY,** 5, b g Casamento (IRE)—Where I Be **Equi ex Incertis Partners**
111 **TRUE ROMANCE (IRE),** 9, gr g Mastercraftsman (IRE)—Full of Love (IRE) **Mr K. S. Ward**
112 **TUSCAN ROSE (IRE),** 5, b m Milan—Ma Furie (FR) **Fighting Chance Syndicate**
113 **UNIVERSAL ISLAND,** 6, ch m Universal (IRE)—Island of Memories (IRE) **P. C. Tory**
114 **WATERGRANGE JACK (IRE),** 7, b g Sintarajan (IRE)—Prestissimo **Mrs J. N. Cartwright**
115 **WELL PAID SOLDIER (IRE),** 5, b m Soldier of Fortune (IRE)—High Dough (IRE) **Mrs P. L. Bridel**
116 **WILLMOUNT,** 5, b g Blue Bresil (FR)—Youngstar **Mr O. S. Harris**

THREE-YEAR-OLDS

117 B f Mount Nelson—Cool Quest (IRE)

Assistant Trainer: Andrew Doyle.

NH Jockey: James Best, Robbie Dunne, Sam Twiston-Davies. **Conditional Jockey:** Philip Donovan, Harry Reed.

---

364 MR LAWRENCE MULLANEY, Malton

Postal: **Raikes Farm, Great Habton, Malton, North Yorkshire, YO17 6RX**
Contacts: **PHONE 01653 668595 MOBILE 07899 902565**
EMAIL nicolamullaney@yahoo.co.uk

1 **FIRE EYES (FR),** 5, b m Toronado (IRE)—Aldayha (IRE) **Ian Buckley & Ben Buckley**
2 **GORGEOUS GENERAL,** 8, ch g Captain Gerrard (IRE)—Gorgeous Goblin (IRE) **Mr S. Humphries**
3 **MERRY SECRET (IRE),** 5, b g Elzaam (AUS)—Secret Liaison (IRE) **Mr S Rimmer & Partners**
4 **ROYAL PROSPECT (IRE),** 8, b g Thewayyouare (USA)—Jillian (USA) **Mr Shaun Humphries & Partner**
5 **SNAZZY JAZZY (IRE),** 8, b g Red Jazz (USA)—Bulrushes **Ian Buckley & Ben Buckley**

THREE-YEAR-OLDS

6 **ANNALEE LASS (IRE),** b f Gutaifan (IRE)—Think Snow (USA) **L. A. Mullaney**
7 B g Mondialiste (IRE)—File And Paint (IRE) **L. A. Mullaney**
8 **GUIDANCE,** b f Expert Eye—Villa Tora **David & Patrick Moorhead**
9 **INSTINCT,** b f Territories (IRE)—Oriental Romance (IRE) **David & Patrick Moorhead**
10 **SPURN POINT (IRE),** b f Dandy Man (IRE)—One For June (IRE) **Ontoawinner & Partner**

TWO-YEAR-OLDS

11 Br c 12/05 Pastoral Pursuits—Dark Intention (IRE) (High Chaparral (IRE))
12 B c 08/05 Berkshire (IRE)—Maggie Byrne (IRE) (Oscar (IRE))

---

365 MR MICHAEL MULLINEAUX, Tarporley

Postal: **Southley Farm, Alpraham, Tarporley, Cheshire, CW6 9JD**
Contacts: **PHONE 01829 261440 MOBILE 07753 650263 FAX 01829 261440**
EMAIL southlearacing@btinternet.com WEBSITE www.southleyfarm.co.uk

1 **BABYDUKE,** 6, b g Heeraat (IRE)—Baby Queen (IRE) **Mr J. P. Turner**
2 **BOB'S GIRL,** 8, b m Big Bad Bob (IRE)—Linda (FR) **S. A. Pritchard**
3 **DODGY BOB,** 10, b g Royal Applause—Rustam **Mr G. Cornes**
4 **INMEMORYOFMILLY (IRE),** 6, b m Fruits of Love (USA)—Lake Wakatipu **Mr G. Cornes**
5 **LUNAR JET,** 9, ch g Ask—Lightning Jet **County Charm Windows & Conservatories**
6 **OUR ROSIE (IRE),** 4, b f Rule of Law (USA)—County Gate (IRE) **Mr L. Tomlinson**
7 **PEACHEY CARNEHAN,** 9, ch g Foxwedge (AUS)—Zubova **Mr K. Jones**

MR MICHAEL MULLINEAUX - continued

8 **ROBEAM (IRE),** 7, b g Helmet (AUS)—Secret Flame **Mr K. Jones**
9 **SCREECHING DRAGON (IRE),** 6, b g Tagula (IRE)—
Array of Stars (IRE) **County Charm Windows & Conservatories**
10 **SHESADABBER,** 7, b m Heeraat (IRE)—Saorocain (IRE) **Mrs A. Turner**
11 **STOP THE WORLD (IRE),** 10, b g Oscar (IRE)—Coolsilver (IRE) **Mr J. P. Turner**
12 11, Ch m Sulamani (IRE)—Sunny Parkes **M. Mullineaux**

Assistant Trainer: Susan Mullineaux, Stuart Ross.

Amateur Jockey: Miss M. J. L. Mullineaux.

---

366 MR SEAMUS MULLINS, Amesbury

Postal: **Wilsford Stables, Wilsford-Cum-Lake, Amesbury, Salisbury, Wiltshire, SP4 7BL**
Contacts: **PHONE 01980 626344 MOBILE 07702 559634**
EMAIL info@seamusmullins.co.uk WEBSITE www.seamusmullins.co.uk

1 **ALL ABOUT ME,** 4, b f Pour Moi (IRE)—Zeldina **Simon & Christine Prout**
2 **BABY SHAM,** 5, b m Sir Percy—Zamzama (IRE) **Simon & Christine Prout**
3 **BAGAN,** 9, ch g Sulamani (IRE)—Aunt Rita (IRE) **J. W. Mullins**
4 **BAR THYME (IRE),** 5, b g Mahler—Jenny's Jewel (IRE) **Old Avenue Racing**
5 **BARROWMOUNT (IRE),** 7, b g Mountain High (IRE)—Nans Mare (IRE) **Mr G. Barnett**
6 **BASILETTE (IRE),** 4, b f Doyen (IRE)—Bahri Sugar (IRE) **J. W. Mullins**
7 **BERLAIS DU GEORGE,** 4, b g Clovis du Berlais (FR)—She's da One (IRE) **The St Georges Hill Racing Syndicate**
8 4, B g Red Jazz (USA)—Blase Chevalier (IRE) **Andrew Cocks & Tara Johnson**
9 **DAME PRESTIGE (FR),** 6, bl m Kapgarde (FR)—Prestige Girl (FR) **S Mullins Racing Club**
10 **ELPOLOGREG (FR),** 4, b g Creachadoir (IRE)—Zannkiya **J. W. Mullins**
11 **EN COEUR (FR),** 9, b g Kap Rock (FR)—Fairyleap (FR) **Woodford Valley Racing**
12 **HEDYCHIUM (IRE),** 5, b m Battle of Marengo (IRE)—Crystal Belle (IRE) **S Mullins Racing Club**
13 **HILLTOWN (IRE),** 5, b g Battle of Marengo (IRE)—California Rose **Hilltown Syndicate**
14 **I SEE YOU WELL (FR),** 10, b g Air Chief Marshal (IRE)—Bonne Mere (FR) **Philippa Downing, Clive Dunning & S Pitt**
15 **JACKELINE,** 4, ch f Jack Hobbs—Ballinlina **Mrs R. A. Jowett**
16 **KENTFORD MALLARD,** 10, b m Sulamani (IRE)—Kentford Grebe **D. I. Bare**
17 **KENTFORD SWANSONG,** 6, b m Sulamani (IRE)—Kentford Grebe **D. I. Bare**
18 4, Gr g Mount Nelson—Lady Friend **Mrs P. de W. Johnson**
19 **LAKESIDE LAD,** 8, b g Alkaased (USA)—Kimmeridge Bay **Simon & Christine Prout**
20 **LOUDSPEAKER,** 4, b g Recorder—Daring Aim **Simon & Christine Prout**
21 **MAIRIS ICON,** 4, b br f Sixties Icon—Alder Mairi (IRE) **F. G. Matthews**
22 **MARTINEAU (IRE),** 5, b g Mahler—Vicky Milan (IRE) **Andrew Cocks & Tara Johnson**
23 **MISS CURIOSITY (IRE),** 5, b m Life Force (IRE)—Lady Contessa (IRE) **Mr M. S. Rose**
24 **MISS FEDORA (IRE),** 4, b f Helmet (AUS)—Shahabad **Simon & Christine Prout**
25 **MORFEE (IRE),** 7, b g Dylan Thomas (IRE)—Ma Baker (IRE) **J. W. Mullins**
26 **MORODER (IRE),** 9, b g Morozov (USA)—Another Tonto (IRE) **Mrs A. Leftley**
27 **MOUNTAIN BAY (IRE),** 4, b g Dylan Thomas (IRE)—My Mountain (IRE) **New Venture Syndicate**
28 **MOUNTAIN GREY (IRE),** 5, gr ro g Mount Nelson—Lady Friend **Mrs P. de W. Johnson & Seamus Mullins**
29 **ROMANOR,** 9, b g Holy Roman Emperor (IRE)—Salinia (IRE) **Four Hens & A Cock**
30 **ROXHILL (IRE),** 4, b br g Ocovango—Thisthatandbaden (IRE) **J. W. Mullins**
31 **SHARP NOTE (IRE),** 6, b m Mahler—Last Campaign (IRE) **The 69 Racing Team**
32 **SHELDON (IRE),** 7, ch g Shantou (USA)—Feabhra (IRE) **Mrs D. H. Potter**
33 **SPARKLING AFFAIR (IRE),** 4, b g Profitable (IRE)—Exclusive Diamond **J. W. Mullins**
34 **STOWFORD (IRE),** 4, gr g Cloudings (IRE)—Tanya Thyne (IRE) **J. W. Mullins**
35 **THE BIG RED ONE,** 6, ch g Indian Haven—Brunette'sonly (IRE) **Mr J. R. Gerrelli**
36 **THE PINK'N,** 7, gr g Dunaden (FR)—Lady Friend **Mrs P. de W. Johnson**
37 **THINK FOR A MINIT,** 7, b g Sixties Icon—Time To Think **Mrs V. F. Hewett**
38 **TIME TO SMILE,** 5, b g Sixties Icon—Time To Think **Mrs V. F. Hewett**
39 **TIQUE,** 4, b br f Blue Bresil (FR)—Toberdowney (IRE) **Mrs H. M. Royle**
40 **TOMMIE BEAU (IRE),** 8, b g Brian Boru—Bajan Girl (FR) **Simon & Christine Prout**

MR SEAMUS MULLINS - continued

41 **VIN ROUGE (IRE),** 5, ch g Zoffany (IRE)—Adventure Seeker (FR) **Mrs D. H. Potter**
42 **WEST HILL MOTH (IRE),** 4, b g Masterofthehorse (IRE)—Epping **Mrs K. E. Kenyon**
43 **WEST HILL SHADOW (IRE),** 4, b br g Laverock (IRE)—Millys Girl (IRE) **Mrs K. E. Kenyon**
44 **WILDERNESS,** 8, b m Cityscape—Moonlight Applause **S Mullins Racing Club**

THREE-YEAR-OLDS

45 B g Casamento (IRE)—Lillian (IRE) **J. W. Mullins**
46 **SGIAN DUBH (FR),** b g Cloth of Stars (IRE)—Sans Peur (FR) **Mr C. Wilson**

Assistant Trainer: James Mullins, **Yard Sponsor:** Simon Prout/We Do Vans.

NH Jockey: James Best, Sean Houlihan, Micheal Nolan, Daniel Sansom.

---

367 MR WILLIAM P. MULLINS, Carlow

Postal: **Closutton, Bagenalstown, Co. Carlow, Ireland**
Contacts: **PHONE +353 59 972 1786 MOBILE +353 87 256 4940 FAX +353 59 972 2709**
EMAIL wpmullins@eircom.net WEBSITE www.wpmullins.com

1 **ABSURDE (FR),** 5, b g Fastnet Rock (AUS)—Incroyable (USA)
2 **ADAMANTLY CHOSEN (IRE),** 6, b g Well Chosen—Sher's Adamant (IRE)
3 **AIONE (FR),** 10, b g Coastal Path—La Horquela (IRE)
4 **ALLAHO (FR),** 9, b g No Risk At All (FR)—Idaho Falls (FR)
5 **ALLEGORIE DE VASSY (FR),** 6, b m No Risk At All (FR)—Autignac (FR)
6 **ANNAMIX (FR),** 10, gr g Martaline—Tashtiyana (IRE)
7 **APPRECIATE IT (IRE),** 9, b g Jeremy (USA)—Sainte Baronne (FR)
8 **ASTERION FORLONGE (FR),** 9, gr g Coastal Path—Belle du Brizais (FR)
9 **AUTHORIZED ART (FR),** 8, b g Authorized (IRE)—Rock Art (IRE)
10 **BACHASSON (FR),** 12, gr g Voix du Nord (FR)—Belledonne (FR)
11 **BERKSHIRE ROYAL,** 8, b g Sir Percy—Forest Express (AUS)
12 **BILLAWAY (IRE),** 11, b g Well Chosen—Taipans Girl (IRE)
13 **BLEU BERRY (FR),** 12, b g Special Kaldoun (IRE)—Somosierra (FR)
14 **BLUE LORD (FR),** 8, b g Blue Bresil (FR)—Lorette (FR)
15 **BLUE SARI (FR),** 8, b g Saddex—Blue Aster (FR)
16 **BRANDY LOVE (IRE),** 7, b m Jet Away—Bambootcha (IRE)
17 **BRING ON THE NIGHT,** 6, ch h Gleneagles (IRE)—Brasileira
18 **BRONN (IRE),** 6, b g Notnowcato—Cluain Easa (IRE)
19 **BURNING VICTORY (FR),** 7, b m Nathaniel (IRE)—M'Oubliez Pas (USA)
20 **BURROWS SAINT (FR),** 10, b g Saint des Saints (FR)—La Bombonera (FR)
21 **CAPODANNO (FR),** 7, ch g Manduro (GER)—Day Gets Up (FR)
22 **CAPTAIN CODY (IRE),** 5, b g Arctic Cosmos (USA)—Fromthecloudsabove (IRE)
23 **CAPTAIN KANGAROO (IRE),** 8, ch h Mastercraftsman (IRE)—We Can Say It Now (AUS)
24 **CAREFULLY SELECTED (IRE),** 11, b g Well Chosen—Knockamullen Girl (IRE)
25 **CASH BACK (FR),** 11, b g Linda's Lad—Holding (FR)
26 **CHACUN POUR SOI (FR),** 11, b g Policy Maker (IRE)—Kruscyna (FR)
27 **CHAMP KIELY (IRE),** 7, b g Ocovango—Cregg So (IRE)
28 **CHAPEAU DE SOLEIL (IRE),** 5, br g Soldier of Fortune (IRE)—On Line Tara (IRE)
29 **CHART TOPPER (FR),** 4, b g Walk In The Park (IRE)—Pink Hat (IRE)
30 **CHOSEN WITNESS (IRE),** 6, b g Well Chosen—Whatareyousaying (IRE)
31 **CIEL DE NEIGE (FR),** 8, b g Authorized (IRE)—In Caso di Neve (FR)
32 **CILAOS EMERY (FR),** 11, b g Califet (FR)—Queissa (FR)

MR WILLIAM P. MULLINS - continued

33 **CINSA (FR),** 4, b f Tirwanako (FR)—Passy Auteuil (IRE)
34 **CLASSIC GETAWAY (IRE),** 7, br g Getaway (GER)—Classic Magic (IRE)
35 **CUTA DES AS (FR),** 6, b m It's Gino (GER)—Negresse de Cuta (FR)
36 **DEPLOY THE GETAWAY (IRE),** 8, b g Getaway (GER)—Gaelic River (IRE)
37 **DID I ASK YOU THAT (IRE),** 5, b g Walk In The Park (IRE)—Ideal Song (IRE)
38 **DINOBLUE (FR),** 6, ch m Doctor Dino (FR)—Blue Aster (FR)
39 **DIVERGE,** 5, ch g Frankel—Sparkling Beam (IRE)
40 **DOLCITA (FR),** 8, b m Saint des Saints (FR)—Orcantara (FR)
41 **DR EGGMAN (FR),** 5, b g Saint des Saints (FR)—Jahra (FR)
42 **DYSART DASHER (IRE),** 6, b g Flemensfirth (USA)—Dysart Dancer (IRE)
43 **DYSART DYNAMO (IRE),** 7, b g Westerner—Dysart Dancer (IRE)
44 **EASY GAME (FR),** 9, b g Barastraight—Rule of The Game (FR)
45 **ECHOES IN RAIN (FR),** 7, b m Authorized (IRE)—Amarantine (FR)
46 **EGALITY MANS (FR),** 9, bl g Network (GER)—Quissisia Mans (FR)
47 **EL BARRA (FR),** 9, br g Racinger (FR)—Oasaka (FR)
48 **EL FABIOLO (FR),** 6, b g Spanish Moon (USA)—Sainte Mante (FR)
49 **ELIMAY (FR),** 9, gr m Montmartre (FR)—Hyde (FR)
50 **ELIXIR D'AINAY (FR),** 9, ch g Muhtathir—Perle du Bocage (FR)
51 **EN BETON (FR),** 9, br g Network (GER)—Nee A Saint Voir (FR)
52 **ENERGUMENE (FR),** 9, b g Denham Red (FR)—Olinight (FR)
53 **FACILE VEGA (IRE),** 6, b g Walk In The Park (IRE)—Quevega (FR)
54 **FACT TO FILE (FR),** 6, b g Poliglote—Mitemps (FR)
55 **FAN DE BLUES (FR),** 8, b g Poliglote—Tire En Touche (FR)
56 **FANCY GIRL (IRE),** 5, ch m Champs Elysees—Chase The Favorite (IRE)
57 **FAROUT (IRE),** 6, gr g Dark Angel (IRE)—Transhumance (IRE)
58 **FERNY HOLLOW (IRE),** 8, b br g Westerner—Mirazur (IRE)
59 **FIGHTER ALLEN (FR),** 8, b g Vision d'Etat (FR)—Reaction (FR)
60 **FINEST EVERMORE (IRE),** 7, b m Yeats (IRE)—St Helans Bay (IRE)
61 **FLAME BEARER (IRE),** 8, b g Fame And Glory—Banba (IRE)
62 **FOVEROS (FR),** 8, b g Authorized (IRE)—Fanurio's Angel (FR)
63 **FRANCO DE PORT (FR),** 8, b h Coastal Path—Ruth (FR)
64 **FUN FUN FUN (IRE),** 5, b m Martaline—Ocean Breeze (IRE)
65 **GAELIC WARRIOR (GER),** 5, b g Maxios—Game of Legs (FR)
66 **GAILLARD DU MESNIL (FR),** 7, gr g Saint des Saints (FR)—Athena du Mesnil (FR)
67 **GALA MARCEAU (FR),** 4, b f Galiway—Alma Marceau (FR)
68 **GALOPIN DES CHAMPS (FR),** 7, bl g Timos (GER)—Manon des Champs (FR)
69 **GARS EN NOIR (FR),** 7, b g Masked Marvel—Touche Noire (FR)
70 **GENTLEMAN DE MEE (FR),** 7, b g Saint des Saints (FR)—Koeur de Mee (FR)
71 **GLENGOULY (FR),** 7, b g Coastal Path—Roulmapoule (FR)
72 **GUST OF WIND (FR),** 4, br g Great Pretender (IRE)—Rafale Pearl (FR)
73 **HA D'OR (FR),** 6, b g Nidor (FR)—Rosewort (FR)
74 **HAUT EN COULEURS (FR),** 6, b g Saint des Saints (FR)—Sanouva (FR)
75 **HAUTURIERE (FR),** 6, ch m No Risk At All (FR)—Ocean Beach (FR)
76 **HEIA (FR),** 6, b m No Risk At All (FR)—Ulla de Montot (FR)
77 **HENN SEE (FR),** 6, br g Slickly Royal (FR)—Onvavoir (FR)
78 **HERCULE DU SEUIL (FR),** 6, br g Saddler Maker (IRE)—Cibelle du Seuil (FR)
79 **HI HO PHOENIX,** 7, gr g Phoenix Reach (IRE)—Silverlined
80 **HISTORIQUE RECONCE (FR),** 6, br m Lauro (GER)—Kruscyna (FR)
81 **HORANTZAU D'AIRY (FR),** 6, b g Legolas (JPN)—Panzara d'Airy (FR)
82 **HORS PISTE (FR),** 6, b m Kapgarde (FR)—Valgardena (FR)
83 **HUBRISKO (FR),** 6, b g Doctor Dino (FR)—Ubriska (FR)
84 **HUNTERS YARN (IRE),** 6, b g Fame And Glory—Full of Birds (FR)
85 **ICARE ALLEN (FR),** 5, b g Cokoriko (FR)—Coeur d'Allen (FR)
86 **IL ETAIT TEMPS (FR),** 5, ch g Jukebox Jury (IRE)—Une des Sources (FR)
87 **ILE ATLANTIQUE (FR),** 5, br g Coastal Path—Cote Atlantique (FR)
88 **IMPAIRE ET PASSE (FR),** 5, b g Diamond Boy (FR)—Brune Ecossaise (FR)
89 **IN EXCESS (FR),** 5, b g Walzertakt (GER)—Bouee En Mer (FR)
90 **INSTIT (FR),** 5, b m Saint des Saints (FR)—Bonne Maman (FR)
91 **IRIS EMERY (FR),** 5, b m Spanish Moon (USA)—Fleur d'Anjou (FR)
92 **IT'S FOR ME (FR),** 5, ch g Jeu St Eloi (FR)—Ugoline (FR)

MR WILLIAM P. MULLINS - continued

93 **JAMES DU BERLAIS (FR),** 7, ch g Muhtathir—King's Daughter (FR)
94 **JAMES GATE (IRE),** 6, b g Shantou (USA)—Annie May (IRE)
95 **JANIDIL (FR),** 9, b g Indian Daffodil (IRE)—Janidouce (FR)
96 **JUNTA MARVEL (FR),** 5, b m Masked Marvel—Junta des Champs (FR)
97 **KEMBOY (FR),** 11, b g Voix du Nord (FR)—Vitora (FR)
98 **KILCRUIT (IRE),** 8, b g Stowaway—Not Broke Yet (IRE)
99 **KING PEAK (IRE),** 4, ch g Mount Nelson—Sixhills (FR)
100 **KLARC KENT (FR),** 7, b g Spanish Moon (USA)—Kryptonie (FR)
101 **KLASSICAL DREAM (FR),** 9, b g Dream Well (FR)—Klassical Way (FR)
102 **LA PRIMA DONNA (FR),** 6, b m Saint des Saints (FR)—Princesse d'Anjou (FR)
103 **LARGY HILL (IRE),** 6, b g Flemensfirth (USA)—Rowansgift (IRE)
104 **LECKY WATSON (IRE),** 5, ch g Valirann (FR)—Anno Whyte (IRE)
105 **LOT OF JOY (IRE),** 5, b m Camelot—Miss Macnamara (IRE)
106 **M C MULDOON (IRE),** 8, gr g Mastercraftsman (IRE)—Alizaya (IRE)
107 **MADMANSGAME,** 6, bl g Blue Bresil (FR)—Grainne Ni Maille
108 **MAZE RUNNER (IRE),** 8, b g Authorized (IRE)—Alice Rose (IRE)
109 **MICRO MANAGE (IRE),** 7, ch h Rip Van Winkle (IRE)—Lillebonne (FR)
110 **MINELLA COCOONER (IRE),** 7, b g Flemensfirth (USA)—Askanna (IRE)
111 **MONKFISH (IRE),** 9, ch g Stowaway—Martovic (IRE)
112 **MT LEINSTER (IRE),** 9, ch g Beat Hollow—Sixhills (FR)
113 **NIGHT AND DAY,** 6, b m Sea The Moon (GER)—Distinctive Look (IRE)
114 **NIKINI (IRE),** 6, b m Sea Moon—Back Log (IRE)
115 **ONTHEROPES (IRE),** 9, b g Presenting—Dushion (IRE)
116 **PARMENION,** 5, b g Soldier Hollow—Pearls Or Passion (FR)
117 **PAUL MARVEL (FR),** 6, gr g Masked Marvel—Paulmie (FR)
118 **PINK IN THE PARK (IRE),** 6, b m Walk In The Park (IRE)—Pink Hat (IRE)
119 **PONT AVAL (FR),** 10, b m Soldier of Fortune (IRE)—Panzella (FR)
120 **POWER OF PAUSE (IRE),** 8, ch g Doyen (IRE)—Shady Pines (IRE)
121 **RAMILLIES (IRE),** 8, gr g Shantou (USA)—Mrs Wallensky (IRE)
122 **READIN TOMMY WRONG (IRE),** 5, b g Authorized (IRE)—Roque de Cyborg (IRE)
123 **RECITE A PRAYER (IRE),** 8, b g Recital (FR)—Old Madam (IRE)
124 **REDEMPTION DAY,** 6, b g Blue Bresil (FR)—Cutielilou (FR)
125 **ROYAL RENDEZVOUS (IRE),** 11, b g King's Theatre (IRE)—Novacella (FR)
126 **SAINT ROI (FR),** 8, b g Coastal Path—Sainte Vigne (FR)
127 **SAINT SAM (FR),** 6, b g Saint des Saints (FR)—Ladeka (FR)
128 **SALDIER (FR),** 9, b g Soldier Hollow—Salve Evita
129 **SAYLAVEE (IRE),** 6, b m Shantou (USA)—Mae's Choice (IRE)
130 **SHADOW RIDER (FR),** 9, ch g Martaline—Samansonnienne (FR)
131 **SHANBALLY KID (IRE),** 6, b g Presenting—Kalanisi's Lady (IRE)
132 **SHARJAH (FR),** 10, b g Doctor Dino (FR)—Saaryeh
133 **SHEWEARSITWELL (IRE),** 8, b m Shirocco (GER)—Ware It Vic (IRE)
134 **SIR ARGUS,** 6, b g Soldier of Fortune (IRE)—Oligarch Society (IRE)
135 **SIR GERHARD (IRE),** 8, b g Jeremy (USA)—Faanan Aldaar (IRE)
136 **SKY SPRINTER (IRE),** 6, b g Shantou (USA)—Levmoss Lady (IRE)
137 **SPANISH HARLEM (FR),** 5, ch g Spanish Moon (USA)—Souverainete (FR)
138 **STATE MAN (FR),** 6, ch g Doctor Dino (FR)—Arret Station (FR)
139 **STATTLER (IRE),** 8, br g Stowaway—Our Honey (IRE)
140 **STONES AND ROSES (IRE),** 9, b g Shantou (USA)—Compelled (IRE)
141 **STRATUM,** 10, b g Dansili—Lunar Phase (IRE)
142 **TAX FOR MAX (GER),** 6, b h Maxios—Tomato Finish (GER)
143 **TEKAO (FR),** 4, b g Doctor Dino (FR)—Texaloula (FR)
144 **THE NICE GUY (IRE),** 8, b g Fame And Glory—Kilbarry Beauty (IRE)
145 **TORNADO FLYER (IRE),** 10, b g Flemensfirth (USA)—Mucho Macabi (IRE)
146 **UNCLE PHIL (IRE),** 6, b g Walk In The Park (IRE)—Synthe Davis (FR)
147 **VAUBAN (FR),** 5, ch g Galiway—Waldfest
148 **VIVA DEVITO (IRE),** 6, br g Malinas (GER)—Red Cattiva
149 **WESTERN DIEGO (IRE),** 6, b g Westerner—Ask Me Sister (IRE)
150 **WESTPORT COVE (FR),** 5, b g Muhtathir—Reine Pieuse (FR)
151 **WHAT PATH (FR),** 6, b g Coastal Path—Quoi d'Autre (FR)
152 **WHATDEAWANT (IRE),** 7, b g Aizavoski (IRE)—Hidden Reserve (IRE)

MR WILLIAM P. MULLINS - continued

153 WHISKEY SOUR (IRE), 10, b h Jeremy (USA)—Swizzle Stick (IRE)
154 WILLIAMSTOWNDANCER (IRE), 5, b m Beat Hollow—Snag List (IRE)
155 WINTER FOG (IRE), 9, b g Papal Bull—Banphrionsa (IRE)
156 ZARAK THE BRAVE (FR), 4, b g Zarak (FR)—Tempo Royale (FR)

Owners: Barnane Stud, R. A. Bartlett, Anthony Bloom, Bruton Street IV Partnership, Cheveley Park Stud, George Creighton, Malcolm C. Denmark, Mrs J Donnelly, Mrs J. Donnelly, Dr S P Fitzgerald, N G King, Miss M A Masterson, Miss M. A. Masterson, Luke McMahon, Mrs M. McMahon, J. P McManus, John P McManus, Mrs J M Mullins, Mrs J. M. Mullins, Simon Munir & Isaac Souede, Edward O'Connell, P Reilly & C. Reilly, Mrs S Ricci, Mrs S. Ricci, Roaringwater Syndicate, Sullivan Bloodstock Limited, TFP Partnership, Mrs Audrey Turley, J Turner, J. Turner, Andrea Wylie, Closutton Racing Club, Mrs Joanne Coleman, C M Grech, Chris Jones, Kanga Racing & Brett Graham Syndicate, Kemboy/Brett Graham/Ken Sharp Syndicate, Merriebelle Irish Farm Limited, Sean & Bernadine Mulryan, Tim O'Driscoll, Nicholas Peacock, Mrs A.M & RJD Varmen, Edward J Ware, Watch This Space Syndicate.

---

368 MISS AMY MURPHY, Newmarket

Postal: **Southgate Stables, Hamilton Road, Newmarket, Suffolk, CB8 0NQ**
Contacts: **PHONE 01638 484907 MOBILE 07711 992500**
EMAIL info@amymurphyracing.com WEBSITE www.amymurphyracing.com

1 **ALBORKAN (FR),** 6, b g Joshua Tree (IRE)—Plaine Monceau (FR) **Jamie Hambro and Alan & Sally Coney**
2 **BAILEYS DERBYDAY,** 5, b g New Approach (IRE)—Posteritas (USA) **G R Bailey Ltd (Baileys Horse Feeds)**
3 4, B f Manduro (GER)—Carole's Destiny **Amy Murphy Racing Club**
4 **CAROLE'S PASS (FR),** 5, b m Authorized (IRE)—Carole's Spirit **Charles Auld & Partner**
5 **CHATEAU D'IF (FR),** 5, b g Intello (GER)—Moonlight Cass (IRE) **Amy Murphy Racing Club**
6 **DANCINGINTHEWOODS,** 6, b g Garswood—Pachanga **Solario Racing (Ashridge)**
7 **DANIEL DERONDA,** 6, b g Siyouni (FR)—Madonna Dell'orto **A White & Partner**
8 **DOUKAROV (FR),** 8, b g Le Havre (IRE)—Landskia (FR) **Mr A. J. White**
9 **ELEGANT ELLEN (FR),** 5, b m Shalaa (IRE)—Lily of The Lake (FR) **Just Back The Boreen**
10 **FILLYFUDGE,** 4, b f Charming Thought—Our Gal **Mrs F. A. Shaw**
11 **GEORGE MORLAND,** 5, b g Camacho—Baharah (USA) **Miss A. L. Murphy**
12 **GIVE ME A BOOM (IRE),** 5, b g Sageburg (IRE)—Knockara One (IRE) **Racing To Profit Syndicate**
13 4, Ch g Champs Elysees—Glorybe (GER) **The Rann Family**
14 **GOLDEN MAYFLOWER,** 4, b f Golden Horn—Pelerin (IRE) **Racing To Profit Syndicate & Partner**
15 **HAWTHORN COTTAGE (IRE),** 10, b m Gold Well—Miss Kilkeel (IRE) **Melbourne 10 Racing**
16 **KALAHARI KING,** 4, b g Califet (FR)—Kalane (IRE) **Mr P. Murphy**
17 **KALASHNIKOV (IRE),** 10, br g Kalanisi (IRE)—Fairy Lane (IRE) **Mr P. Murphy**
18 **KALEB (IRE),** 5, b g Sir Percy—Kalane (IRE) **Racing To Profit Syndicate & Partner**
19 **KALMOOR (IRE),** 6, b g Kalanisi (IRE)—Fairy On The Moor (IRE) **Mr P. Murphy**
20 **KIT GABRIEL (IRE),** 4, b g Kodiac—Maleha (IRE) **Mr C. Johnston**
21 **MAGICAL MORNING,** 6, b g Muhaarar—The Lark **Daniel MacAuliffe & Anoj Don**
22 **MERCIAN OMEN (IRE),** 5, b m Black Sam Bellamy (IRE)—Mariah Rollins (IRE) **Mr P. Murphy**
23 **MERCIAN PRINCE (IRE),** 12, b g Midnight Legend—Bongo Fury (FR) **Mr P. Murphy**
24 **OBTAIN,** 4, b f Oasis Dream—Facilitate **Just Back The Boreen**
25 **PRIDE OF AMERICA (FR),** 6, b g American Post—Atarfe (IRE) **Haven't A Pot, D. Macauliffe & Anoj Don**
26 **PROUD MARI,** 6, b m Shirocco (GER)—Mariah Rollins (IRE) **Racing To Profit Syndicate & Partner**
27 **RAQISA,** 5, b m Mukhadram—Hazy Dancer **A White & Partner**
28 **SHANDANCER (IRE),** 6, b g Morpheus—Mrs Popple **Racing To Profit Syndicate**
29 **SHARP DISTINCTION,** 4, ch g Tamayuz—Pin Cushion **Solario Racing (Berkhamsted)**
30 **SYMBOLIC SPIRIT (FR),** 6, b m Westerner—Carole's Spirit **Hot To Trot Jumping**
31 **TARBAAN (IRE),** 4, ch g Tamayuz—Rocana **Constellation Syndicate & Partner**
32 **THEGREATESTSHOWMAN,** 7, ch g Equiano (FR)—Conversational (IRE) **Amy Murphy Racing Club**
33 **TONYX,** 7, b m Nathaniel (IRE)—Kadoma **The Rann Family**

MISS AMY MURPHY - continued

THREE-YEAR-OLDS

34 **AL QADAM (FR),** b br g Al Wukair (IRE)—One River (FR) **Macauliffe, Don D de Souza**
35 **AUROPHOBIA (IRE),** b f Galileo Gold—Love Or Fear **Burns Farm Racing**
36 **AWTAAD PRINCE (IRE),** b c Awtaad (IRE)—Showcard **Eclipse Sports Racing Club & Partner**
37 **CALLEVERYONEUKNOW,** b f Cityscape—Shes Queen (IRE) **Empress Racing & Partner**
38 **CATWALK MODEL,** b f Charm Spirit (IRE)—Pizzarra **Mr M. P. Coleman**
39 **FLAME JET (IRE),** b g Saxon Warrior (JPN)—Star Jet (IRE) **Ladas**
40 **LOVE AFFAIRS,** b f Showcasing—Fond Words (IRE) **G R Bailey Ltd (Baileys Horse Feeds)**
41 **MEDINA GOLD (FR),** b f Seahenge (USA)—Eva Kant **Daniel MacAuliffe & Anoj Don**
42 **MISS CANTIK (FR),** b br f Recoletos (FR)—Atarfe (IRE) **Haven't A Pot, D. Macauliffe & Anoj Don**
43 **ROYAL BLISS (IRE),** b f Ribchester (IRE)—Chillala (IRE) **Daniel MacAuliffe & Anoj Don**
44 **TARITINO (IRE),** b g Buratino (IRE)—Archange (FR) **Solario Racing (Moulton)**
45 **TENRAI (FR),** b f U S Navy Flag (USA)—Hayaku (USA) **D Macauliffe & A Don, MP & RJ Coleman**
46 **VICTORY TIME,** b f Time Test—Be Free **Daniel MacAuliffe & Anoj Don**

TWO-YEAR-OLDS

47 B f 07/03 Land Force (IRE)—Aljumar (IRE) (Marju (IRE)) (25610) **Macauliffe, Don D de Souza**
48 B f 05/04 Equiano (FR)—Amber Road (IRE) (Anjaal) (4000) **Racing To Profit Syndicate & Partner**
49 B f 07/03 Raven's Pass (USA)—
Atlantic Queen (IRE) (Society Rock (IRE)) (20008) **Nick Radley Racing 50 & Partners**
50 B f 20/03 Highland Reel (IRE)—China Eyes (IRE) (Invincible Spirit (IRE)) (6403)
51 B f 10/03 Havana Grey—Cliffhanger (Canford Cliffs (IRE)) (40016)
52 B c 10/03 Unfortunately (IRE)—Concra Girl (IRE) (Footstepsinthesand) (19208) **Daniel MacAuliffe & Anoj Don**
53 Gr f 07/04 Mehmas (IRE)—Day Creek (Daylami (IRE)) (60024) **Daniel MacAuliffe & Anoj Don**
54 Ch f 28/01 Equiano (FR)—Freckles (Arakan (USA)) (28000) **Ontoawinner & Partner**
55 **GEOLOGIST,** ch f 13/03 Territories (IRE)—Parknasilla (IRE) (Dutch Art) (35000) **Eclipse Thoroughbred Partners**
56 B c 27/04 Blue Point (IRE)—Irish Abbey (IRE) (Invincible Spirit (IRE)) (49620) **Macauliffe, Don D de Souza**
57 B f 21/02 Churchill (IRE)—Island Drive (IRE) (Kodiac) **Bronte 1 Collection**
58 B c 19/02 Adaay (IRE)—Israfel (Dark Angel (IRE)) (26000) **Macauliffe, Don D de Souza**
59 B f 21/02 Inns Of Court—Jolie Et Belle (Oratorio) **G R Bailey Ltd (Baileys Horse Feeds)**
60 B c 07/03 Inns of Court (IRE)—La Roumegue (USA) (Henrythenavigator (USA)) (40000)
61 Ch f 17/02 Toranado—Lucky Lot (Exceed And Excel) **Nick Radley Racing 50 & Partners**
62 Br c 05/04 Al Wukair (IRE)—Maqam (IRE) (Dansili) (15000)
63 Gr f 08/04 El Kabeir (USA)—Maridiyna (IRE) (Sinndar (IRE)) (6403)
64 Gr f 03/03 Havana Grey—Minionette (IRE) (Manduro (GER)) (24010) **Macauliffe, Don D de Souza**
65 B f 08/04 Soldier's Call—Moonlight Bay (Pivotal) (40000) **Bronte 1 Collection**
66 **NEEDLEPOINT (IRE),** b f 14/04 Blue Point (IRE)—Zenella (Kyllachy) (49620) **Eclipse Thoroughbred Partners**
67 B f 02/03 Camacho—Nyanga (IRE) (Born To Sea (IRE)) (8804)
68 **PASSIONATELY (IRE),** b f 03/05 Night of Thunder (IRE)—
Lexi's Love (USA) (Big Top Cat (USA)) (55000) **Eclipse Thoroughbred Partners**
69 B f 05/04 Mayson—Shes Queen (IRE) (Baltic King) **Miss A. L. Murphy**
70 Ch c 25/04 Showcasing—Signs And Signals (IRE) (Kodiac) (46419) **Daniel MacAuliffe & Anoj Don**
71 B c 28/02 Magna Grecia (IRE)—Sirici (IRE) (Choisir (AUS)) (21609) **Daniel MacAuliffe & Anoj Don**
72 B br f 03/04 Zoustar (AUS)—Social Media (New Approach (IRE)) (7000) **Syndicates.Racing & Partner**
73 B f 07/02 Dandy Man (IRE)—Some Style (IRE) (Kodiac) (19048) **D. L. de Souza**
74 Ch f 11/03 Mehmas (IRE)—Tiz Only Me Daza (IRE) (Camacho) (20000)

---

369 MR OLLY MURPHY, Wilmcote

Postal: **Warren Chase Stables, Wilmcote, Stratford-Upon-Avon, Warwickshire, CV37 9XG**
Contacts: **PHONE 01789 613347**
EMAIL office@ollymurphyracing.com WEBSITE www.ollymurphyracing.com

1 **ACT OF AUTHORITY (FR),** 5, b g Authorized (IRE)—Leah Claire (IRE) **Mrs D. L. Whateley**
2 **AFRICAN DANCE (IRE),** 8, br g Shirocco (GER)—Dani California **Bective Stud**

MR OLLY MURPHY - continued

3 **AM I WRONG (IRE),** 6, gr g Soldier of Fortune (IRE)—Medimli (IRE) **Mr A. L. Cohen**
4 **AUDITORIA,** 6, b m Gleneagles (IRE)—Authora (IRE) **Nick Brown Racing**
5 **BARONY LEGENDS (IRE),** 7, b g Yeats (IRE)—Monty's Sister (IRE) **Bective Stud**
6 **BARRICANE,** 8, b g Kayf Tara—Alina Rheinberg (GER) **Mr O. J. Murphy**
7 **BELIEVE JACK (FR),** 6, b g Make Believe—Sandslide **Five Saints Racing**
8 **BENASSI (IRE),** 6, b g Westerner—Kylebeg Krystle (IRE) **The Mighty Men**
9 **BENIGN DICTATOR (IRE),** 6, b g Getaway (GER)—Canto Creek **The Wayward Pilgrims**
10 **BEST TRITION (IRE),** 8, b g Mustameet (USA)—Ad Astra (IRE) **Foxtrot Racing Syndicate 1**
11 **BOBBY SOCKS,** 6, b g Kayf Tara—Bobs Present **Stephen R Hodgkinson & Partner**
12 **BOOSTER BOB (IRE),** 5, b g Malinas (GER)—Ceka Dawn (IRE) **Mrs D. L. Whateley**
13 **BOREEN BOY (IRE),** 7, b g Valirann (FR)—Annas Back (IRE) **Owners Group 095**
14 **BORODALE (IRE),** 5, br g Flemensfirth (USA)—Portryan Native (IRE) **Mrs D. L. Whateley**
15 **BREWIN'UPASTORM (IRE),** 10, b g Milan—Daraheen Diamond (IRE) **Ms B. J. Abt**
16 **BUSHTUCKER PARK (IRE),** 5, b m Walk In The Park (IRE)—Kalico Kalista (IRE) **Cousins & Wells**
17 **BUTCH,** 6, b g Kayf Tara—Leading On **McNeill Family & Ralston Family**
18 **CALIPSO COLLONGES (FR),** 11, b g Crossharbour—Ivresse Collonges (FR) **The Black Horse Hotel Bridgnorth**
19 **CAPTAIN FANTASTIC (IRE),** 6, b g Soldier of Fortune (IRE)—Chapel Queen (IRE) **A. J. Wall**
20 **CELTIC TARA,** 9, b m Kayf Tara—Valdas Queen (GER) **A. P. Racing**
21 **CHAMPAGNESUPEROVER (IRE),** 8, b g Jeremy (USA)—
Meldrum Hall (IRE) **McNeill Family & Patrick & Scott Bryceland**
22 **CHASING FIRE,** 6, b g Maxios—Kahara **Mrs D. L. Whateley**
23 **CHORAL WORK,** 6, gr m Nathaniel (IRE)—Chapel Choir **Matt FitzGerald and The Songsters**
24 **CHOSEN PORT (IRE),** 7, b m Well Chosen—Despute (IRE) **Bective Stud**
25 **CLAY ROGERS (IRE),** 8, b g Imperial Monarch (IRE)—Fly Bid (IRE) **Future Champions Racing Syndicate**
26 **CLONAKILTY (IRE),** 6, b g Flemensfirth (USA)—Soeur Gael (IRE) **Burkes & Syders**
27 **COLEMANSTOWN LAD (IRE),** 7, b g Kalanisi (IRE)—Grangeclare Dancer (IRE) **D. Teevan**
28 **COLLOONEY (IRE),** 9, b g Yeats (IRE)—Amber Trix (IRE) **Mr J. P. McManus**
29 **CONTEMPLATEMYFAITH (IRE),** 7, b g Califet (FR)—Liss A Chroi (IRE) **Owners Group 087**
30 **COREY'S COURAGE,** 7, b m Dunaden (FR)—Valdas Queen (GER) **A. P. Racing**
31 **DAMARTA (FR),** 5, ch g Martaline—Viveda (FR) **A. Butler**
32 **DE CRAIC IS MIGHTY (IRE),** 5, br g Mount Nelson—Liz's d'Estruval (IRE) **Mrs D. L. Whateley**
33 **DEV OF TARA (IRE),** 7, br g Kayf Tara—Sinnaja **Touchwood Racing**
34 **DEXTERITY (IRE),** 6, ch g Shantou (USA)—Lurane (FR) **Mrs D. L. Whateley**
35 **DOCTOR KEN (FR),** 7, b g Doctor Dino (FR)—Kendoretta (FR) **Mrs D. L. Whateley**
36 **DOMINIC'S FAULT,** 6, b g Camelot—Midnight Angel (GER) **Mrs D. L. Whateley**
37 **DR SEB (FR),** 6, ch g Doctor Dino (FR)—Gareduhavre (FR) **Mrs D. L. Whateley**
38 **DR T J ECKLEBURG (IRE),** 5, b g Lawman (FR)—Imtidaad (USA) **Syders & Burkes**
39 **DROP HIM IN (IRE),** 7, br g Elusive Pimpernel (USA)—Dart Queen (GER) **Zavier Austin, Mrs Roz Wyles & Partner**
40 **EAVESDROPPING,** 7, b m Kayf Tara—Leading On **Deva Racing (ED) & M. Muldoon**
41 **ENDURING LOVE (IRE),** 11, br g Winged Love (IRE)—Strong Lady (IRE) **Olly Murphy Racing Club**
42 **FABRIQUE EN FRANCE (FR),** 8, b g Yeats (IRE)—Knar Mardy **Fitorfat Racing**
43 **FINGLE BRIDGE (IRE),** 5, br g Flemensfirth (USA)—Royale Video (FR) **McNeill Family & Stone Family**
44 **FIRST CLASS RETURN (IRE),** 10, b g Let The Lion Roar—Chitty Bang Bang (IRE) **Olly Murphy Racing Club**
45 **FISTON DE BECON (FR),** 8, b g Secret Singer (FR)—Sharonne (FR) **W Woodhouse & M James**
46 **FLETCH (FR),** 8, b g Kayf Tara—Oeuvre Vive (FR) **Jacques Law P'ship & Partner**
47 **FLEURMAN (IRE),** 5, gr g Mastercraftsman (IRE)—Fleur de Nuit (IRE) **Bective Stud**
48 **FLOATING LINE,** 5, b m Martaline—Stone Light (FR) **Burkes & Syders**
49 **FOLLOW THAT,** 9, b m Malinas (GER)—Leading On **Olly Murphy Racing Club**
50 **FORTUNATE SOLDIER (IRE),** 5, ch g Soldier of Fortune (IRE)—Ma Belle Amie **Mr J. Hales**
51 **FOXEY,** 8, b g Foxwedge (AUS)—Blue Lyric **Mr M. J. James**
52 **FOXINTHEBOX (IRE),** 7, b g Presenting—Forces of Destiny (IRE) **A. Butler**
53 **GAIUS,** 4, b g Havana Gold (IRE)—Gemina (IRE) **Mr T. C. McKeever**
54 **GETAWAY LILY BEAR (IRE),** 7, b m Getaway (GER)—Jemima Jones (IRE) **Owners Group 082**
55 **GO DANTE,** 7, b g Kayf Tara—Whoops A Daisy **Ms B. J. Abt**
56 **GRANDADS COTTAGE (IRE),** 8, ch g Shantou (USA)—Sarah's Cottage (IRE) **Mr J. Hales**
57 **GUNSIGHT RIDGE,** 8, b g Midnight Legend—Grandma Griffiths **Mrs D. L. Whateley**
58 **HALONDO (FR),** 6, b g Cokoriko (FR)—Rive Gauche (FR) **Mrs D. L. Whateley**
59 **HARDI DU MESNIL (FR),** 6, b g Masterstroke (USA)—Athena du Mesnil (FR) **Mr R. B. Waley-Cohen**
60 **HERE COMES MCCOY (IRE),** 8, br g Dylan Thomas (IRE)—Is It Here (IRE) **Mr C. J. Haughey**
61 **HERO (FR),** 6, b g Saddler Maker (IRE)—Burma (FR) **Mrs D. L. Whateley**

MR OLLY MURPHY - continued

62 **HOKELAMI (FR),** 6, b br g Coastal Path—Une Brik (FR) **A. Butler**
63 **HOURVARI (FR),** 6, b g My Risk (FR)—Ty Perrine (FR) **Mrs D. L. Whateley**
64 **HUNTERS CALL (IRE),** 13, b g Medaaly—Accordiontogelica (IRE) **Holloway,Clarke,Black**
65 **IDDERGEM (FR),** 7, b g Youmzain (IRE)—Hey Laura (FR) **& Racing**
66 **ILLICO DE NUIT (FR),** 5, ch g Gris de Gris (IRE)—Reine de Treve (FR)
67 **INDEEVAR BLEU (FR),** 5, b g Blue Bresil (FR)—Ardissone (FR) **Mrs D. L. Whateley**
68 **ITALIAN SPIRIT (IRE),** 7, b g Fame And Glory—Coco Milan (IRE) **Mr O. J. Murphy**
69 **ITCHY FEET (FR),** 9, b g Cima de Triomphe (IRE)—Maeva Candas (FR) **The Sherington Partnership**
70 **JACKPOT D'AINAY (FR),** 4, ch g No Risk At All (FR)—Vanille d'Ainay (FR) **H. A. Murphy**
71 **JAMES FORT (IRE),** 7, b g Fame And Glory—Well Clad (IRE) **Foxtrot Racing**
72 **JURI (GER),** 5, b g Sea The Moon (GER)—Josephine Blanche (GER)
73 **KENAHOPE (FR),** 5, b m Kendargent (FR)—Make Up (FR) **Mr P. D. Wells**
74 **LE BON VIVANT (FR),** 5, ch g Doctor Dino (FR)—School of Thought (FR) **Mr A. L. Cohen**
75 **LEARNTALOT (IRE),** 7, ch g Ask—Lady Alacoque (IRE) **Mr A. L. Cohen**
76 **LET'S HAVE ANOTHER (IRE),** 7, b g Fame And Glory—Rocella Lady (IRE) **Harry Redknapp & Aiden Murphy**
77 **LINELEE KING (FR),** 8, gr g Martaline—Queen Lee (FR) **Mrs D. L. Whateley**
78 **LITTLE MISS DANTE,** 5, b m Kayf Tara—Whoops A Daisy **Ms B. J. Abt**
79 **LIVERPOOL KNIGHT,** 5, b g Golden Horn—Nouriya **Mr P. Abrahams**
80 **LORD OF KERAK,** 8, b g Martaline—Mille Et Une (FR) **Mrs D. L. Whateley**
81 **LOVE MYSTERY,** 4, ch g Frankel—Mix And Mingle (IRE) **Premier Plastering (UK) Limited**
82 **LUPUS REGEM,** 7, b g Iffraaj—Miss Villefranche **Mrs D. L. Whateley**
83 **MACKELDUFF (FR),** 7, gr g Martaline—Evitta (FR) **Tommy Elphick & Mary Shalvey**
84 **MADE FOR YOU,** 8, b g Cape Cross (IRE)—Edallora (IRE) **H. A. Murphy**
85 **MEXICAN BOY (IRE),** 7, gr g Kayf Tara—J'Y Viens (FR) **The Four Timers**
86 **MINELLA DOUBLE (IRE),** 5, b g Shantou (USA)—Lady Dromlac (IRE) **Mrs D. L. Whateley**
87 **MOORE MARGAUX (IRE),** 8, b g Flemensfirth (USA)—Omas Glen (IRE) **Graeme Moore, Kate & Andrew Brooks**
88 **NEWTON (FR),** 5, b g No Risk At All (FR)—Price du Charmil (FR) **Mr T. D. J. Syder**
89 **NO RISK DES FLOS (FR),** 8, gr g No Risk At All (FR)—Marie Royale (FR) **Mrs D. L. Whateley**
90 **OAKLEY DANCER,** 6, b m Black Sam Bellamy (IRE)—Stravinsky Dance **Racing & Waley-cohen**
91 **OUT THE GLEN (IRE),** 10, b g Millenary—Dicera (IRE) **Sky's The Limit**
92 **PARLIAMENT HILL,** 5, ch g Sir Percy—Fauran (IRE) **Mrs D. L. Whateley**
93 **PLEASINGTON (IRE),** 5, br g Shantou (USA)—Bisoguet (IRE) **McNeill Family & Stone Family**
94 **PRESENT DE VANGO (IRE),** 5, br g Ocovango—Present Your Own (IRE) **FGD Limited**
95 **RACY LACEY (IRE),** 5, b m No Nay Never (USA)—Lace (IRE) **The UTV Syndicate**
96 **RAMBO T (IRE),** 6, b g Ocovango—Biddy's Boru (IRE) **MPB Contractors Limited**
97 **RANGING BEAR (IRE),** 5, b g Walk In The Park (IRE)—Eireann Rose (IRE) **Mr J. P. McManus**
98 **RESPLENDENT GREY (IRE),** 5, b gr g Walk In The Park (IRE)—Caltra Princess (IRE) **Mrs C. Skan**
99 **RIO SILVA,** 6, gr m Blue Bresil (FR)—A Cappella Lido (FR) **The Mighty Men**
100 **RIPPER ROO (FR),** 8, gr g Smadoun (FR)—Sninfia (IRE) **Deva Racing (RR), Shalvey & Partners**
101 **ROCK ON TOMMY,** 8, gr g Fair Mix (IRE)—Little Carmela **Premier Thoroughbred Racing Ltd**
102 **ROYAL BASSETT (FR),** 6, b g Wootton Bassett—Donna Roberta (GER) **The Bertie Allsorts**
103 **SALADAM (FR),** 6, b g Saint des Saints (FR)—Salsadame (FR) **A. Butler**
104 **SALLEY GARDENS (IRE),** 7, b g Yeats (IRE)—Glenlogan (IRE) **Oceana Racing & Partner**
105 **SAN FERMIN (IRE),** 7, b g Sans Frontieres (IRE)—Taipans Girl (IRE) **Mr A. E. Peterson**
106 **SAO CARLOS,** 5, b g Blue Bresil (FR)—Valleyofthedolls **H. A. Murphy**
107 4, B g Ultra (IRE)—Saroushka (FR) **H. A. Murphy**
108 **SECRET TRIX,** 6, b g Kayf Tara—Box of Trix (IRE) **D & C Racing**
109 **SHE'S A FINE WINE (IRE),** 5, b m Flemensfirth (USA)—Morning Run (IRE) **Mr P. Tumelty**
110 **SILENT APPROACH (IRE),** 5, b m Walk In The Park (IRE)—
Kilbarry Demon (IRE) **Mrs John Magnier & Mrs Paul Shanahan**
111 **SMACKWATER JACK (IRE),** 9, b g Flemensfirth (USA)—Malachy's Attic (IRE) **Par Four**
112 **SPACE VOYAGE,** 6, b m Kayf Tara—Maiden Voyage **Deva Racing SV**
113 **SPIRIT OF KINSALE,** 5, b g Blue Bresil (FR)—As Was **Mrs D. L. Whateley**
114 **SPORTY JIM (IRE),** 6, ch g Flemensfirth (USA)—Ma Belle Amie **Mr Terry Warner & the McNeill Family**
115 **STORM OF LIGHT (IRE),** 7, b g Fame And Glory—Blazing Moon (IRE) **Mrs D. L. Whateley**
116 **STRONG LEADER,** 6, b g Passing Glance—Strong Westerner (IRE) **Welfordgolf syndicate**
117 **SUNSET ON FIRE (IRE),** 5, b g Flemensfirth (USA)—Be My Sunset (IRE) **What the Elle**
118 **SURE TOUCH,** 7, b g Yeats (IRE)—Liberthine (FR) **Geegeez.Co.Uk Om & Partner**
119 **SWINGING LONDON (IRE),** 5, b g Dark Angel (IRE)—Malka (FR) **A. Butler**
120 **TAMAR BRIDGE (IRE),** 8, b g Jeremy (USA)—Mise En Place **McNeill Family & Stone Family**

MR OLLY MURPHY - continued

121 **THE SAME (FR),** 6, b g Network (GER)—Escort'beauty (FR) **Premier Plastering (UK) Limited**
122 **THE WOLF (FR),** 9, ch g Kapgarde (FR)—Ges (FR) **McNeill Family & Stone Family**
123 **THOMAS DARBY (IRE),** 10, b g Beneficial—Silaoce (FR) **Mrs D. L. Whateley**
124 **THREE FIGS (IRE),** 5, b g Affinisea (IRE)—Figlette **Mrs C. Skan**
125 **THUNDER ROCK (IRE),** 7, b g Shirocco (GER)—La Belle Sauvage **McNeill Family & Mr Ian Dale**
126 **TINNAHALLA (IRE),** 6, b g Starspangledbanner (AUS)—Bright Bank (IRE) **Future Champions Racing Syndicate**
127 **TINTAGEL QUEEN (IRE),** 5, b m Camelot—Condition **Nick Brown Racing**
128 5, B g Telescope (IRE)—Tintera (IRE) **Mr J. P. McManus**
129 **UKANTANGO (IRE),** 6, ch g Ocovango—Molly Be **Mr A. E. Peterson**
130 **VALUPO (IRE),** 7, b g Valirann (FR)—Sameaway (IRE) **Foxtrot NH Racing Partnership**
131 **VOKOLOHS (IRE),** 7, ch g Sholokhov (IRE)—Quarry Thyne (IRE) **Olly Murphy Racing Club**
132 **WASHINGTON,** 7, br g Westerner—Present Leader **Syders & Burkes**
133 **WEEBILL,** 11, b g Schiaparelli (GER)—Wee Dinns (IRE) **Olly Murphy Racing Club**
134 **WHAT WILL BE (IRE),** 7, b g Thewayyouare (USA)—Gali Gal (IRE) **The Dream Big Syndicate**

THREE-YEAR-OLDS

135 **NATIONAL HEALTH (FR),** b g Seabhac (USA)—Rainbow Rising (FR)

Assistant Trainer: Gerard Tumelty.

NH Jockey: Aidan Coleman, David England. **Conditional Jockey:** Fergus Gregory, Callum McKinnes, Lewis Stones. **Amateur Jockey:** Mr James King, Mr Luke Scott.

370 MR PAT MURPHY, Hungerford

Postal: **Glebe House, School Lane, East Garston, Hungerford, Berkshire, RG17 7HR**
Contacts: **PHONE 01488 648473**
EMAIL patgmurphy13@gmail.com

1 **AMALFI GEM (IRE),** 4, b f Cotai Glory—Diamond Circle **The Limoncello's**
2 **AMALFI SKYLINE,** 4, b g Telescope (IRE)—Maria Antonia (IRE) **Amalfi Bloodstock**
3 **CLONDAW BERTIE (IRE),** 8, b g Thewayyouare (USA)—Female (IRE) **Theoddsquad syndicate**
4 **GALTEE MOUNTAIN (IRE),** 8, br g Mountain High (IRE)—Kings Queen (IRE) **P. G. Murphy**
5 **JACK LESLIE,** 4, b g Twilight Son—Fenella Rose **P. G. Jacobs**
6 **MOORGATE (IRE),** 4, b g Mastercraftsman (IRE)—Private Paradise (IRE) **Mrs B. I. Chantler**
7 **NESSFIELD BLUE,** 9, b g Kayf Tara—Bella Medici **Murphy & Chantler**
8 **OHNODONTTAKEMEHOME (FR),** 6, gr g Cima de Triomphe (IRE)—Koyotte d'Agrostis (FR) **Graeme Moore, Kate & Andrew Brooks**

THREE-YEAR-OLDS

9 **AUTUMN LIGHTS,** b f Harry Angel (IRE)—Autumn Leaves **JQRacing Club**

371 MR BARRY MURTAGH, Carlisle

Postal: **Hurst Farm, Ivegill, Carlisle, Cumbria, CA4 0NL**
Contacts: **PHONE 017684 84649 MOBILE 07714 026741 FAX 017684 84744**
EMAIL suemurtagh7@gmail.com

1 **BOYNESIDE,** 4, b g Black Sam Bellamy (IRE)—Myrtle Drive (IRE) **Mrs S. A. Murtagh**
2 **BREEZE OF WIND (IRE),** 6, gr g Arctic Cosmos (USA)—Mite Be Cloudy (IRE) **Mrs S. A. Murtagh**
3 **DERRACRIN,** 6, ch g Mustajeeb—Transvaal Sky **Mr J. H. F. Proudfoot**
4 **ELUSIVE RED (IRE),** 9, b g Elusive Pimpernel (USA)—Spin In The Wind (IRE) **Hurst Farm Racing**
5 **GARSWOOD LADY,** 4, b f Garswood—Ailsa On My Mind (IRE) **Mrs A. Kenny**
6 **GEYSER,** 7, b g Gale Force Ten—Popocatepetl (FR) **Mrs A. Stamper**
7 **NAIROBI GIRL (IRE),** 7, b m Sans Frontieres (IRE)—Colligan Wood (IRE) **Mrs P. M. R. Groves**
8 **ROBIOLA (IRE),** 5, b g Harzand (IRE)—Weeping Wind **Hurst Farm Racing**

MR BARRY MURTAGH - continued

9 **SAIGON,** 5, b g Frankel—Silk Sari **Mr C. L. Metcalfe**
10 **SHE'S A GEM,** 6, b m Dapper—Tara Springs **Mrs A. Stamper**
11 **SORBONNE,** 7, ch g Cityscape—Sorcellerie **Mrs S. A. Murtagh**

TWO-YEAR-OLDS

12 B c 26/01 Intrinsic—Ailsa On My Mind (IRE) (Dark Angel (IRE)) **Mrs A. Kenny**

Assistant Trainer: S A Murtagh.

Conditional Jockey: Lorcan Murtagh. **Apprentice Jockey:** Connor Murtagh.

372 MRS FIONA NEEDHAM, Thirsk

Postal: **Moor View, Knayton, Thirsk, Yorkshire, YO7 4AZ**
Contacts: **PHONE 07831 688625**
EMAIL fiona@catterickbridge.co.uk

1 4, B f Telescope (IRE)—Cormorant Cove **R. Tate**
2 **MOONLIGHT FLIT (IRE),** 7, b g Getaway (GER)—Dreaming On (IRE) **R. Tate**
3 **RED DELTA,** 4, ch g Ocovango—Red Card (IRE) **R. Tate**
4 **SINE NOMINE,** 7, gr m Saint des Saints (FR)—Hymn To Love (FR) **R. Tate**

373 MRS HELEN NELMES, Dorchester

Postal: **Warmwell Stables, 2 Church Cottages, Warmwell, Dorchester, Dorset, DT2 8HQ**
Contacts: **PHONE 01305 852254 MOBILE 07977 510318**
EMAIL warmwellstud@tiscali.co.uk WEBSITE www.warmwellstables.co.uk

1 **ITSABOUTIME (IRE),** 13, gr g Whitmore's Conn (USA)—Blazing Love (IRE) **K. A. Nelmes**
2 **MENAPIAN (IRE),** 12, b br g Touch of Land (FR)—Mannequin (IRE) **T M W Partnership**
3 **MERCHANT IN MILAN (IRE),** 11, b g Milan—Azaban (IRE) **Mr L. J. Burden**
4 **UNIVERSAL SECRET (IRE),** 6, ch g Universal (IRE)—Quiet Beauty **Matt Hoskins & Julie Roche**
5 **WEARAPINKRIBBON (IRE),** 7, ch g Shantou (USA)—Pink Hat (IRE) **Warmwellcome Partnership**
6 **WELLWILLYA,** 5, gr b g Universal (IRE)—Mons Meg **Mr L. J. Burden**

Assistant Trainer: K Nelmes.

Conditional Jockey: Conor Ring.

374 MR PATRICK NEVILLE, Leyburn

Postal: **3 Castle Hill, Middleham, Leyburn, Yorkshire, DL8 4QR**
Contacts: **PHONE +353 87 255 3084**

1 **ARMOURED (IRE),** 4, b g Lope de Vega (IRE)—Rayisa (IRE) **Miss R. Dennis**
2 **BEAUTY TO BEHOLD (IRE),** 6, gr m Mahler—Castle Lake (IRE) **Mrs W. Duffus**
3 **BREAKDANCE KID,** 5, ch g Norse Dancer (IRE)—Pinamar **Mrs W. Duffus**
4 **FISTON DU MOU (FR),** 8, b g Cokoriko (FR)—Jane du Mou (FR) **Mrs W. Duffus**
5 **FUSAIN (FR),** 8, gr g Lord du Sud (FR)—Savigny (FR) **Mr E. McElligott**
6 **GANAPATHI (FR),** 7, b g Samum (GER)—Une Dame d'Avril (FR) **Mrs W. Duffus**
7 **GLENTRUAN (IRE),** 8, b g Getaway (GER)—Mac Idol (IRE) **Neville, Kehoe, Dennis & Scott**
8 **J C INTERNATIONAL,** 4, gr g Nayef (USA)—Pax Americana (FR) **Miss R. Dennis**
9 **KAVANAGHS CROSS (IRE),** 8, b g Califet (FR)—Mugs In Milan (IRE) **Mr D. I. Tomlinson**

MR PATRICK NEVILLE - continued

10 4, B f Snow Sky—Macville (IRE) **Mr P. Neville**
11 **MARTY MCFLY (IRE),** 5, b g Getaway (GER)—Barbalicious (IRE) **Mrs W. Duffus**
12 **MIRRIE DANCERS (IRE),** 5, b g Harzand (IRE)—Beatrice Aurore (IRE) **Miss R. Dennis**
13 **MORANDI SECOND (FR),** 4, b g Morandi (FR)—Hold The Thought **Cold Beer Sports Partnership**
14 **MYFAVOURITESISTER (IRE),** 4, b f Soldier of Fortune (IRE)—Credit Box (IRE) **Miss R. Dennis**
15 **N'GOLO (IRE),** 8, gr g Galileo (IRE)—Dame Again (AUS) **Mr E. McElligott**
16 **NEBUCHADNEZZAR (FR),** 8, b g Planteur (IRE)—Trexana **J Fyffe & S Townshend**
17 **NOT STAYING LONG (IRE),** 5, b br m Soldier of Fortune (IRE)—Princess Bella (IRE) **Mrs W. Duffus**
18 **OLYMPUS (IRE),** 5, b g Kingman—Carpe Vita (IRE) **Mr E. McElligott**
19 **RADDLE AND HUM (IRE),** 9, b m Milan—Gaybric (IRE) **Miss R. Dennis**
20 **RAINS OF CASTAMERE,** 6, ch g Harbour Watch (IRE)—Shrimpton **Mrs W. Duffus**
21 **RED AMAPOLA,** 5, gr m Marcel (IRE)—Si Belle (IRE) **Miss R. Dennis**
22 **ROYAL CREEK (IRE),** 5, b br m Getaway (GER)—Canto Creek **Rebecca Dennis and Wilma Duffus**
23 **THE BONGO KID (IRE),** 6, b g Soldier of Fortune (IRE)—Credit Box (IRE) **E McElligott & A Duffus**
24 **THE REAL WHACKER (IRE),** 7, b g Mahler—Credit Box (IRE) **Neville, Mann, Duffus & Dennis**
25 **THE WOUNDED KNEE,** 6, b g Yeats (IRE)—Gold Reef **R.Dennis, A.Tomlinson**
26 **THE WRITER,** 4, ch g Ulysses (IRE)—Arwaah (IRE) **Miss R. Dennis**

TWO-YEAR-OLDS

27 **VICTORIA CONCORDIA,** b f 07/02 Camelot—Arwaah (IRE) (Dalakhani (IRE)) (40000) **Miss R. Dennis**

---

375 MR TONY NEWCOMBE, Barnstaple

Postal: **Lower Delworthy, Yarnscombe, Barnstaple, Devon, EX31 3LT**
Contacts: **MOBILE 07785 297210**
EMAIL huntshawequineforest@talktalk.net

1 **BUG BOY (IRE),** 7, b g Big Bad Bob (IRE)—Velvetina (IRE) **Dr S. P. Hargreaves**
2 **IRON HEART,** 6, b g Muhaarar—Kiyoshi **Mr K. D. D. Morris**
3 **JOLI'S LEGACY (IRE),** 5, b m Elzaam (AUS)—Joli Elegant (IRE) **Joli Racing**
4 **JOYFUL SONG (IRE),** 6, b m Teofilo (IRE)—Good Friend (IRE) **Joli Racing**
5 **LIGHTNING ATTACK,** 7, b g Lethal Force (IRE)—Afrodita (IRE) **A. G. Newcombe**
6 **LIIMARI,** 10, b m Authorized (IRE)—Snow Polina (USA) **A. G. Newcombe**
7 **LIPPY LADY (IRE),** 7, b m Bungle Inthejungle—Sayrah **A. G. Newcombe**
8 **PRINCELY,** 8, b h Compton Place—Royal Award **A. G. Newcombe**
9 **SOVEREIGN STATE,** 8, b g Compton Place—One Night In May (IRE) **R. Eagle**
10 **STANCHESKI (IRE),** 5, b g Sans Frontieres (IRE)—Rose of Clare **Milsom Baker Racing**
11 **TARKA COUNTRY,** 4, gr c Outstrip—Turaathy (IRE) **Dr S. P. Hargreaves**

THREE-YEAR-OLDS

12 **KRYSTYNA,** ch f The Gurkha (IRE)—Skarbek **A. G. Newcombe**
13 **PERFECT LIBERTY,** b f Iffraaj—Perfect Spirit (IRE) **A. G. Newcombe**
14 **SCARLET,** ch f Sir Percy—Symbol **Mr K. D. D. Morris**

---

376 DR RICHARD NEWLAND, Droitwich

Postal: **Urloxhey Farm, Elmbridge lane, Droitwich, Worcestershire, WR9 0NQ**
Contacts: **MOBILE 07956 196535**
EMAIL office@richardnewlandracing.com

1 **AN MARCACH (IRE),** 9, b g Milan—Red Square Lady (IRE) **Dr R. D. P. Newland**
2 **ARLO (FR),** 7, b g Cokoriko (FR)—Nina La Belle (FR) **Mr M. Hough**
3 **ART OF DIPLOMACY,** 7, b g Archipenko (USA)—Rowlestone Express **Three Pears Racing**

DR RICHARD NEWLAND - continued

4 **ASTROMACHIA,** 8, b g Sea The Stars (IRE)—Fontley **Murcotts Ltd**
5 **BALI BODY (IRE),** 8, b g Doyen (IRE)—Burnt Oil Babe (IRE) **Foxtrot Racing Bali Body**
6 **BOLINTLEA (IRE),** 8, b m Le Fou (IRE)—Lady Boulea (IRE) **Foxtrot Racing Bolintlea**
7 **BROOKE BRESIL,** 5, b m Blue Bresil (FR)—Brookville (IRE) **Mrs L. J. Newland**
8 **CAPTAIN TOM CAT (IRE),** 8, b g Dylan Thomas (IRE)—Miss Molly Malone (IRE) **Deva Racing (CTC)**
9 **DIOMEDE DES MOTTES (FR),** 10, ch g Kapgarde (FR)—Nellyssa Bleu (FR) **Belbroughton Racing Club**
10 **DREAMWEAVER (IRE),** 7, b g Mastercraftsman (IRE)—Livia's Dream (IRE) **The Leicester Lads**
11 **DYNAMITE KENTUCKY (FR),** 8, ch g Kentucky Dynamite (USA)—
Madonna Incognito (USA) **Off The Clock Partners & Dr RDP Newland**
12 **ENDLESSPOSSIBILITY,** 5, b g Pour Moi (IRE)—Another Evening (IRE)
13 **ENQARDE (FR),** 9, b g Kapgarde (FR)—Usachaqa (FR) **Off The Clock Partners & Dr RDP Newland**
14 **FEIVEL (IRE),** 8, b br g Le Fou (IRE)—Much Appreciated (IRE) **The Boondogglers**
15 **FIFTY SHADES OVHAY (IRE),** 5, b g Westerner—Founding Daughter (IRE)
16 **FIRST SOLDIER (FR),** 7, ch g Soldier of Fortune (IRE)—First Choice (FR) **Mr C. E. Stedman**
17 **FULGURIX (FR),** 8, b g Maresca Sorrento (FR)—Union de Sevres (FR) **The The Tenovus Partnership**
18 **GALATA BRIDGE,** 6, b g Golden Horn—Infallible **Foxtrot Racing Galata Bridge**
19 **GAME SOCKS (IRE),** 7, ch g Leading Light (IRE)—Late Night Deed **Chris Stedman & Mark Albon**
20 **GETABUCK (IRE),** 10, ch g Getaway (GER)—Buck's Blue (FR) **Miss A. B. Hyde**
21 **GO ALL THE WAY,** 9, b g Fame And Glory—La Cerisaie **Celtic New Bees**
22 **GOLDEN COSMOS (IRE),** 7, b g Arctic Cosmos (USA)—Lilly Mais (IRE) **Ardroe Developments Ltd**
23 **HERON CREEK (IRE),** 6, b g Leading Light (IRE)—Campanella (GER) **M Albon & M P Tudor**
24 **HIGH TECH (FR),** 6, b g Intello (GER)—Highborne (FR) **Mr P. C. W. Green**
25 **HYPNOTIK (FR),** 6, b g Cokoriko (FR)—Advantime (FR) **Foxtrot Racing Galata Bridge**
26 **I'M SO BUSY,** 8, gr g Carlotamix (FR)—Ballcrina Girl (IRE) **Foxtrot Racing I'm So Busy**
27 **INDIGO LAKE,** 6, b g Frankel—Responsible **Foxtrot Racing Galata Bridge**
28 **JACKS ORCHARD (IRE),** 6, b br g Shantou (USA)—Royal Roxy (IRE) **Mr W. Jones**
29 **JESUITIQUE (FR),** 8, b g Saint des Saints (FR)—Jaune de Beaufai (FR) **The Three Amigos**
30 **JUBILEE GOLD (IRE),** 7, b g Libertarian—Simplyonelady (IRE) **Mr M. P. Tudor**
31 **KING ARISE (IRE),** 6, gr g Kingston Hill—Aries Ballerina (IRE) **Foxtrot Racing King Arise**
32 **LA RENOMMEE (FR),** 5, b m Doctor Dino (FR)—Grande Cavale (FR) **Mrs L. J. Newland**
33 **LAWTOP LEGEND (IRE),** 11, b g Milan—Nolagh Supreme (IRE) **JGS Partnership**
34 **LE PATRIOTE (FR),** 11, b g Poliglote—Sentosa (FR) **Canard Vert Racing Club**
35 **LET ME BE (IRE),** 7, b g Gale Force Ten—Peryzat (IRE) **Mr P. Drinkwater**
36 **LIGHTENING GESTURE,** 4, b g Estidhkaar (IRE)—Cornlaw **Mr R. M. Evans**
37 **MAHONS GLORY (IRE),** 7, b g Fame And Glory—Dark Sunshine (GER) **C Nightingale & Hold My Beer Partnership**
38 **MOTION IN LIMINE (IRE),** 8, b g Court Cave (IRE)—My Memory (IRE) **Mr J. H. Graham**
39 **MR HAILSTONE (IRE),** 7, b g Sageburg (IRE)—Gaye Steel (IRE) **Dr R. D. P. Newland**
40 **MR MULDOON (IRE),** 10, ch g Rajj (IRE)—Miss Muldoon (IRE) **Foxtrot Racing Mr Muldoon**
41 **ON THE WILD SIDE (IRE),** 10, b g Robin des Champs (FR)—Clear Riposte (IRE) **M Albon & M P Tudor**
42 **ORCHESTRAL RAIN (IRE),** 6, b g Born To Sea (IRE)—Musical Rain (IRE) **Mark Albon & Chris Stedman**
43 **PLANET LEGEND (IRE),** 4, ch g Galileo (IRE)—Zut Alors (IRE) **Mr M. Hough**
44 **PROGRESSIVE,** 6, b m Nathaniel (IRE)—Graduation **Mrs L. J. Newland**
45 **QUICK SHARPENER (IRE),** 6, b g Sageburg (IRE)—Flaming Flower (IRE) **Foxtrot Racing Quick Sharpener**
46 **RAJJAMATAZ (IRE),** 5, ch g Rajj (IRE)—Miss Muldoon (IRE) **Foxtrot Racing Rajjamataz**
47 **REBEL LEADER (IRE),** 9, b g Milan—Chicharito's Gem (IRE) **Celtic New Bees**
48 **REWIRED,** 5, ch g Power—Kekova **Opulence Thoroughbreds NH**
49 **ROSE SEA HAS (FR),** 8, gr g Kapgarde (FR)—Vaibuscar Has (FR) **The Berrow Hill Partnership**
50 **ROSTELLO (FR),** 8, ch g Fuisse (FR)—Rose d'Ete (FR) **Dr R. D. P. Newland**
51 **SAGE ADVICE (IRE),** 6, b g Make Believe—Purple Sage (IRE) **Dr R. D. P. Newland**
52 **SCARLET O'TARA,** 5, b m Kayf Tara—Run Ructions Run (IRE) **Laura Newland and Chris Stedman**
53 **SEAFORTH MANCY (IRE),** 7, b g Mustameet (USA)—Dark Victory (IRE) **Brackenrigg Partnership**
54 **SEINESATIONAL,** 8, b g Champs Elysees—Kibara **Mr C. E. Stedman**
55 **SHAR WHATS THERUSH (IRE),** 10, b g Doyen (IRE)—Turmoss (FR)
56 **SHETLAND BUS (GER),** 10, ch g Sholokhov (IRE)—Shali Tori (FR) **Mr D. Hague**
57 **SINGASONGSAM,** 6, b g Black Sam Bellamy (IRE)—Vin Rose **Mr P. Drinkwater**
58 **SIR CANFORD (IRE),** 7, b g Canford Cliffs (IRE)—Alexander Divine
59 **SOUTH TERRACE (IRE),** 8, b g Fame And Glory—Supreme Sales (IRE) **South Terrace Partnership**
60 **STELLAR SPRINTER,** 4, b f Kayf Tara—Run Ructions Run (IRE)
61 **SUPREMELY WEST (IRE),** 5, b g Westerner—Blue Supreme (IRE)
62 **SWEETTOWATCH (IRE),** 9, b m Fracas (IRE)—Molly's Mate (IRE) **Mr M. P. Tudor**

DR RICHARD NEWLAND - continued

63 **TANGO ECHO CHARLIE (IRE),** 9, b g Stowaway—Wrong In Okanagan (IRE) **Briton International & Partner**
64 **TASTE THE FEAR (IRE),** 8, b g Mores Wells—No Complaints But (IRE) **In It For Fun Partnership & Dr R Newland**
65 **TCHOUPINMINZAC (FR),** 6, b g Falco (USA)—Ninive (FR) **Marie's Dream Team**
66 **THE DREAM GOES ON,** 4, b f Kayf Tara—Adreamstillalive (IRE)
67 **THIRTYFOURSTITCHES (IRE),** 8, b g Fairly Ransom (USA)—Blue Berlais (IRE) **Doom Bar Beach Club**
68 **TIGER ORCHID (IRE),** 8, b g Mores Wells—Akarita (IRE) **Foxtrot Racing Tiger Orchid**
69 **TIP TOP TONTO (IRE),** 7, b g Milan—Sarahs Quay (IRE) **Foxtrot Racing Galata Bridge**
70 **WAKE UP EARLY (IRE),** 9, ch g Doyen (IRE)—Wake Me Gently (IRE) **Dr R. D. P. Newland**
71 **WHATSDASTORY (IRE),** 10, b m Beneficial—Supreme Contender (IRE) **Plan B**
72 **WHIZZ KID (GER),** 7, ch g Teofilo (IRE)—Wurfspiel (GER) **Foxtrot Racing Whizz Kid**
73 **YCCS PORTOCERVO (FR),** 8, gr g Martaline—Griva (FR) **Mrs P. J. Litton**

Secretary: Phoebe Peck.

NH Jockey: Charlie Hammond. **Conditional Jockey:** Cillin Leonard, Luke Scott.

---

377 MISS ANNA NEWTON-SMITH, Jevington

Postal: **Bull Pen Cottage, Jevington, Polegate, East Sussex, BN26 5QB**
Contacts: **PHONE 01323 488354 MOBILE 07970 914124**
EMAIL annanewtonsmith@gmail.com WEBSITE www.annanewtonsmith.co.uk

1 **DECORA (IRE),** 6, ch m Conduit (IRE)—Grevillea (IRE) **R Blyth & S Colville**
2 **FORGOT ONE (IRE),** 8, b g Le Fou (IRE)—Ready For Ballett (IRE)
3 **SHIROCCO'S DELIGHT (IRE),** 6, ch g Shirocco (GER)—Far Rock (IRE) **The Beano Partnership**
4 **UNCERTAIN TIMES (IRE),** 8, ch m Well Chosen—Moment of Destiny (IRE) **Mr K. E. Spencer**

Assistant Trainer: Nicola Worley.

NH Jockey: Paddy Brennan, Charlie Deutsch, Rex Dingle, David Noonan.

---

378 MR ADRIAN NICHOLLS, Sessay

Postal: **The Ranch, Sessay, Thirsk, North Yorkshire, YO7 3ND**
Contacts: **PHONE 01845 597428**

1 **ABATE,** 7, br g Bated Breath—Red Kyte **The Never Say No Racing Club**
2 **BURJ MALINKA (IRE),** 5, ch g Pride of Dubai (AUS)—Malinka (IRE) **Dubelem (Racing) Limited**
3 **HURT YOU NEVER (IRE),** 4, b f Dandy Man (IRE)—Kyllarney **Mr A. Nicholls**
4 **PEPPER STREAK (IRE),** 4, b f Hot Streak (IRE)—Rohesia **Roscourt**
5 **SAAHEQ,** 9, b g Invincible Spirit (IRE)—Brevity (USA) **Mr A. Nicholls**
6 **TEES SPIRIT,** 5, br g Swiss Spirit—Mistress Twister **Ingleby Bloodstock Ltd & The Ivy League**
7 **THORNABY PEARL,** 5, b g Pearl Secret—Juncea **Ingleby Bloodstock Limited**
8 **UNIVERSAL FOCUS (GER),** 10, b g Intense Focus (USA)—Unquenchable (USA) **Champagne and Dreams**

THREE-YEAR-OLDS

9 **CAN TO CAN (IRE),** b f Kodiac—Ridge Ranger (IRE) **Mr C. R. Hirst**
10 **CHEWSDAY (IRE),** b f Camacho—Aalia (IRE) **Champagne and Dreams**
11 **CRIME FICTION (IRE),** gr f El Kabeir (USA)—Fictitious **Mr A. N. Brooke Rankin**
12 **GETHIPTOTHETRIP,** br g Tasleet—Point Perfect **Mr D. Stone**
13 **KING'S CROWN (IRE),** b g Starspangledbanner (AUS)—Textured (IRE) **Mr D. Stone**
14 **SPIRIT IN MY SOUL (IRE),** b f Holy Roman Emperor (IRE)—Tasha's Dream (USA) **Mr D. Stone**
15 **SUPER SPY (IRE),** b g Gustav Klimt (IRE)—Ugo Fire (IRE) **The Never Say No Racing Club**

MR ADRIAN NICHOLLS - continued

16 **THORNABY BEAUTY,** b f Brazen Beau (AUS)—Ingleby Exceed (IRE) **Ingleby Bloodstock Limited**
17 **WHALLEY ROAD,** b g Dandy Man (IRE)—Ocean Boulevard **Mr D. W. Armstrong**

TWO-YEAR-OLDS

18 B f 12/02 Zoustar (AUS)—Dubara (Dubawi (IRE)) (9524) **Ingleby Bloodstock Limited**
19 B c 08/03 Due Diligence (USA)—Empress Livia (Paco Boy (IRE)) (21000) **Mr A. Nicholls**
20 B c 19/02 Massaat (IRE)—Heartstone (IRE) (Fastnet Rock (AUS)) (33333) **Ingleby Bloodstock Limited**
21 B f 23/02 Harry Angel (IRE)—Hilary J (Mount Nelson) (38095) **Ingleby Bloodstock Limited**
22 B c 13/01 Dream Ahead (USA)—Hulcote Rose (IRE) (Rock of Gibraltar (IRE)) (23810) **Ingleby Bloodstock Limited**
23 Gr f 03/01 Dark Angel (IRE)—Lady Kermit (IRE) (Starspangledbanner (AUS)) (61905) **Ingleby Bloodstock Limited**
24 B c 06/02 Invincible Spirit (IRE)—Late Rosebud (IRE) (Jeremy (USA)) (28571) **Ingleby Bloodstock Limited**
25 **MAMBHA (IRE),** b f 04/04 Elzaam (AUS)—Mistress of Rome (Holy Roman Emperor (IRE)) **Mr D. Stone**
26 **MARIE'S SECRET,** b f 19/02 Land Force (IRE)—Pure As Gold (Kingman) (23810) **Mr D. Stone**

---

379 MR PAUL NICHOLLS, Ditcheat

Postal: **Manor Farm Stables, Ditcheat, Shepton Mallet, Somerset, BA4 6RD**
Contacts: **PHONE 01749 860656 MOBILE 07977 270706**
EMAIL info@paulnichollsracing.com WEBSITE www.paulnichollsracing.com

1 **AFADIL (FR),** 4, b g Camelot—Afsheen (FR) **Mr P. J. Vogt**
2 **ALL DANCER (FR),** 6, ch g No Risk At All (FR)—Maia Dancer (FR) **D. Maxwell**
3 **AMENON (FR),** 8, b g Saint des Saints (FR)—La Couetrie (FR) **Mr & Mrs J. D. Cotton**
4 **ANNIE K (IRE),** 6, b m Valirann (FR)—Anno Whyte (IRE) **Mr P. J. Vogt**
5 **BANTEER (IRE),** 5, b g Westerner—Robyn's Rose (IRE) **Exors of the Late Mr T. J. Hemmings**
6 **BARBADOS BUCK'S (IRE),** 8, b g Getaway (GER)—Buck's Blue (FR) **The Stewart Family**
7 **BEAU BALKO (FR),** 5, b g Balko (FR)—Douce Ambiance (FR) **Highclere Thoroughbred Racing - Balko**
8 **BENY NAHAR ROAD (IRE),** 4, b g Nathaniel (IRE)—Wonder Why (GER) **Chris Giles & Brendan McManus**
9 **BLACKJACK KENTUCKY (IRE),** 10, b g Oscar (IRE)—My Name's Not Bin (IRE) **Owners Group 026**
10 4, B g Walk In The Park (IRE)—Blodge (IRE)
11 **BLUEKING D'OROUX (FR),** 4, b g Jeu St Eloi (FR)—Belle du Bresil (FR) **Mrs J. De La Hey**
12 **BRAVE KINGDOM (FR),** 7, b g Brave Mansonnien (FR)—
New Foundation (IRE) **Graeme Moore, Kate & Andrew Brooks**
13 **BRAVEMANSGAME (FR),** 8, b g Brave Mansonnien (FR)—Genifique (FR) **John Dance & Bryan Drew**
14 **BRITTAS BAY (FR),** 5, b m Coastal Path—Solivate (FR) **Mr C. A. Donlon**
15 **BROKEN HALO,** 8, b g Kayf Tara—Miss Invincible **Giraffa Racing - BH**
16 4, B g Sixties Icon—Bull And Bush (IRE) **Mr W. A. Harrison-Allan**
17 **BYORDEROFTHECOURT (IRE),** 5, b g Court Cave (IRE)—Lucky Hand (IRE) **Mrs J. Irish**
18 **CAP DU MATHAN (FR),** 8, b g Kapgarde (FR)—Nounjya du Mathan (FR) **The Stewart Family**
19 **CAPTAIN TEAGUE (IRE),** 5, ch g Doyen (IRE)—Dancingwithbubbles (IRE) **Mrs J. De La Hey**
20 **CASTLEWARD (IRE),** 6, b g Notnowcato—Maggie Byrne (IRE) **Middleham Park Racing**
21 **CAT TIGER (FR),** 9, b g Diamond Boy (FR)—Miss Canon (FR) **D. Maxwell**
22 **CENTARA (IRE),** 5, br g Sageburg (IRE)—Spartan Angel (IRE) **Mrs K. A. Stuart**
23 **CHEZ HANS (GER),** 7, b g Mamool (IRE)—Chandos Rose (IRE) **Owners Group 038**
24 **CLAN DES OBEAUX (FR),** 11, b g Kapgarde (FR)—
Nausicaa des Obeaux (FR) **Mr & Mrs P.K.Barber, G.Mason, Sir A Ferguson**
25 **COMPLETE UNKNOWN (IRE),** 7, b g Dylan Thomas (IRE)—Silver Stream (IRE) **Mr C. K. Ong & Mr I. Warwick**
26 **COUNTRY LADY,** 5, b m Kapgarde (FR)—Miss Country (FR) **The Brooks Family & P.J. Vogt**
27 4, B g Clovis du Berlais (FR)—Dalriath **Giraffa Racing**
28 **DANCINGONTHEEDGE (FR),** 6, b m Kapgarde (FR)—Solarize (FR) **Old Gold Racing 4**
29 **DANNY KIRWAN (IRE),** 10, b g Scorpion (IRE)—Sainte Baronne (FR) **Mrs J. De La Hey**
30 **DE WANTED WARRIOR (IRE),** 7, b g Ocovango—Brown Sheila (IRE) **Barber, Jackson & Eddy**
31 **DIEGO DU CHARMIL (FR),** 11, b g Ballingarry (IRE)—Daramour (FR) **Mrs J. De La Hey**
32 **DINO MAGIC (FR),** 4, b g Doctor Dino (FR)—La Bandera **Mr & Mrs J. D. Cotton**
33 **DIVILSKIN (IRE),** 5, b g Doyen (IRE)—Beauty Star (IRE) **Gordon & Su Hall**

MR PAUL NICHOLLS - continued

34 **DOLOS (FR),** 10, b g Kapgarde (FR)—Redowa (FR) **Mrs J. De La Hey**
35 **DON ALVARO,** 7, b g Muhtathir—New Destiny (FR) **Moger & Woodhouse**
36 **DON'T TELL SU (IRE),** 5, b g Soldier of Fortune (IRE)—Bell Walks Day (IRE) **Gordon & Su Hall**
37 **EMAILANDY (IRE),** 5, b g Mount Nelson—Eoz (IRE) **The Brooks & Stewart Families**
38 **ENRILO (FR),** 9, bl g Buck's Boum (FR)—Rock Treasure (FR) **Martin Broughton & Friends 4**
39 **ESPOIR DE GUYE (FR),** 9, b g Khalkevi (IRE)—Penelope de Guye (FR) **Mrs J. Hitchings**
40 **FAME AND FUN (IRE),** 6, b g Fame And Glory—Tabachines (FR) **Mrs J. Hitchings**
41 **FARNOGE,** 5, b g Camelot—Septembers Hawk (IRE) **Mr C. K. Ong & Mr I. Warwick**
42 **FIRE FLYER (IRE),** 5, b g Shantou (USA)—Eva La Diva (IRE) **Mr M. F. Geoghegan**
43 **FLASH COLLONGES (FR),** 8, b g Saddler Maker (IRE)—Prouesse Collonges (FR) **The Gi Gi Syndicate**
44 **FLEMENSTIDE (IRE),** 8, b g Flemensfirth (USA)—Keep Face (FR) **Mr P K Barber & Mr P J Vogt**
45 **FLIC OU VOYOU (FR),** 9, b g Kapgarde (FR)—Hillflower (FR) **Mr C. A. Donlon**
46 **FRIEND OR FOE (FR),** 8, b g Walk In The Park (IRE)—Mandchou (FR) **Gordon & Su Hall**
47 **FRODON (FR),** 11, b g Nickname (FR)—Miss Country (FR) **Mr P. J. Vogt**
48 **GELINO BELLO (FR),** 7, b g Saint des Saints (FR)—Parade (FR) **Mr & Mrs J. D. Cotton**
49 **GEORGE HENRY,** 4, b g Kayf Tara—Stravinsky Dance **Mr D. G Staddon & Mr Paul Nicholls**
50 **GO WEST (IRE),** 5, b g Westerner—Topathistle (IRE) **Owners Group 107**
51 **GOLDEN SON (FR),** 5, ch g Martaline—Thou In Gold (FR) **Mrs J. De La Hey**
52 **GRACE A VOUS ENKI (FR),** 7, b g Dream Well (FR)—Cadiane (FR) **Mrs J. Hitchings**
53 **GREANETEEN (FR),** 9, b g Great Pretender (IRE)—Manson Teene (FR) **Mr C. M. Giles**
54 **GRIVETANA (FR),** 5, ch m No Risk At All (FR)—Stourza (FR) **Syders & Burkes**
55 **HACKER DES PLACES (FR),** 6, gr g Great Pretender (IRE)—Plaisance (FR) **Owners Group 068**
56 **HALF DOZEN (IRE),** 6, b g Sageburg (IRE)—Sixofone (IRE) **John & Jessica Dance**
57 **HALO DES OBEAUX (FR),** 6, gr g Al Namix (FR)—Almeria des Obeaux (FR) **Mr P. J. Vogt**
58 **HELL RED (FR),** 6, gr g Martaline—Queen Margot (FR) **Sir Martin Broughton & Friends 6**
59 **HENRI THE SECOND (FR),** 6, b g Saddler Maker (IRE)—Rock Treasure (FR) **Martin Broughton & Friends 7**
60 **HERMES ALLEN (FR),** 6, b g Poliglote—
Une Destine (FR) **Sir A. Ferguson, G. A. Mason, Mr J. R. Hales, Mr J. Diver**
61 **HIKARI POMPADOUR AA (FR),** 4, b g Jeu St Eloi (FR)—Hestampe Japonaise (FR) **Mr J. P. McManus**
62 **HIM MALAYA (FR),** 4, b g Martaline—Clarte d'Or (FR) **Mrs J. De La Hey**
63 **HITMAN (FR),** 7, b g Falco (USA)—Tercah Girl (FR) **Mason, Hogarth, Ferguson & Done**
64 **HOLETOWN HERO (FR),** 6, br g Buck's Boum (FR)—Voix du Coeur (FR) **Mr M. F. Geoghegan**
65 **HUELGOAT (FR),** 6, b g Voiladenuo (FR)—Cavadee (FR) **Owners Group 080**
66 **HUFLOWER (FR),** 6, b g Saddex—Send Me Flower (FR) **Mr C. M. Giles, Mr D. Staddon**
67 **HUGOS NEW HORSE (FR),** 6, b g Coastal Path—Pour Le Meilleur (FR) **The Stewart Family**
68 **HURRICANE DANNY (FR),** 5, ch g No Risk At All (FR)—Tornade d'Ainay (FR) **Martin Broughton & Friends 2**
69 **IBIS DOCTOR (FR),** 5, ch g Doctor Dino (FR)—Bise de Mer (FR) **Mr J. P. McManus**
70 **ICEO (FR),** 5, b g Coastal Path—Rocroi (FR) **Mr C. M. Giles**
71 **IL RIDOTO (FR),** 6, b g Kapgarde (FR)—L'Exploratrice (FR) **Giles, Hogarth, Mason & McGoff**
72 **ILIADE ALLEN (FR),** 5, b m Rail Link—Atacames (FR) **Mr A. J. Peake**
73 **ILIKO D'OLIVATE (FR),** 5, b g Cokoriko (FR)—Dyna d'Olivate (FR) **Mr C. M. Giles**
74 **IMPACT DU BONHEUR (FR),** 5, b g Bathyrhon (GER)—Valownia (FR) **Highclere Thoroughbred Racing - Impact**
75 **IMPREVU DU LARGE (FR),** 5, b g Kapgarde (FR)—Emy Chope (FR) **D. G. Staddon**
76 **INCA DE LAFAYETTE (FR),** 5, gr g Gris de Gris (IRE)—Queen de Lafayette (FR) **Owners Group 100**
77 **INTHEWATERSIDE (FR),** 5, b g Jeu St Eloi (FR)—Vared (FR) **McNeill Family & G C Stevens**
78 **IOUPY COLLONGES (FR),** 5, b g Kitkou (FR)—Une Collonges (FR) **Million in Mind Partnership**
79 **IRANDANDO HAS (FR),** 4, b g No Risk At All (FR)—Irostare (FR) **Mr J. Hales, Miss L. J. Hales**
80 **IRISH HILL (GER),** 5, gr g Kingston Hill—Irresistable (GER) **Sir Martin Broughton & Friends 8**
81 **ISAAC DES OBEAUX (FR),** 5, b g Kapgarde (FR)—
Varda des Obeaux (FR) **G Mason, Sir A Ferguson, Mr & Mrs P K Barber**
82 **IVALDI (FR),** 5, b g Night Wish (GER)—Valence (FR) **Mrs J. De La Hey**
83 **JACKPOT D'ATHOU (FR),** 4, ch g Doctor Dino (FR)—Victoire d'Athom (FR)
84 **JACKPOT DES BORDES (FR),** 4, b g Vision d'Etat (FR)—
Carmen des Bordes (FR) **Sir Martin Broughton & Friends 9**
85 **JACOBIN (FR),** 4, gr g Magneticjim (IRE)—Boheme (FR) **Mr J. P. McManus**
86 **JALILA MORIVIERE (FR),** 4, b f Joshua Tree (IRE)—Princess Moriviere (FR) **Mr J. P. McManus**
87 **JENA D'OUDAIRIES (FR),** 4, b br f Buck's Boum (FR)—Une d'Oudairies (FR) **Giraffa Racing**
88 **JENNY WYSE (IRE),** 5, b m Flemensfirth (USA)—Morning Edition (IRE) **Mr C. M. Giles**
89 **JEREMY PASS (IRE),** 8, b g Jeremy (USA)—Toulon Pass (IRE) **John & Jessica Dance**
90 **JERIKO PLACE (FR),** 4, ch g Masked Marvel—Vanika Place (FR) **Miss Tanya Roach**

MR PAUL NICHOLLS - continued

91 4, B g Blue Bresil (FR)—Jessber's Dream (IRE)
92 **JET OF MAGIC (IRE),** 7, b g Jet Away—Ginandit (IRE) **Ratkatcha Racing**
93 **JUST LUCKY SIVOLA (FR),** 4, b g Noroit (GER)—Rue Pigalle (FR) **Lynne & Angus Maclennan**
94 **JUSTMYIMAGINATION,** 5, b m Sixties Icon—Kaylianni **Mr W. A. Harrison-Allan**
95 **KANDOO KID (FR),** 7, gr g Kapgarde (FR)—Scarlett du Mesnil (IRE) **Mr M. F. Geoghegan**
96 **KAP BOY (FR),** 4, b g Kapgarde (FR)—Bumble (FR) **Mrs D. L. Whateley**
97 **KICK UP A STORM (IRE),** 5, b g Shantou (USA)—Erins Stage (IRE) **Mrs C. H. Moger**
98 **KILLALOAN (IRE),** 5, b g Fastnet Rock (AUS)—Farranjordan **Owners Group 093**
99 **KNAPPERS HILL (IRE),** 7, b g Valirann (FR)—Brogella (IRE) **Mr P K Barber & Mr P J Vogt**
100 **KNOWSLEY ROAD (IRE),** 6, b g Flemensfirth (USA)—
Rowanville Lady (IRE) **Mr Charles Pelham & Mr Henry Pelham**
101 **KRUGER PARK (FR),** 5, ch g Kapgarde (FR)—Fleur De Sel De Re (FR) **The The BM Partnership**
102 **LALLYGAG (GER),** 6, b g It's Gino (GER)—Laviola (GER) **D. G. Staddon**
103 **LALOR (GER),** 11, b g It's Gino (GER)—Laviola (GER) **D. G. Staddon**
104 **LARCHMONT LASS (IRE),** 5, b m Walk In The Park (IRE)—Tocororo (IRE) **Mr M. F. Geoghegan**
105 **LE CHIFFRE D'OR (FR),** 7, gr g No Risk At All (FR)—Miss Vitoria (FR) **Gordon & Su Hall**
106 5, B g Mount Nelson—Letherbelucky (IRE) **McNeill Family & Mr G Mason**
107 **LIME AVENUE (IRE),** 6, b m Walk In The Park (IRE)—
Carrigeen Kohleria (IRE) **Highclere Thoroughbred Racing - WITP**
108 **MAGIC SAINT (FR),** 9, b g Saint des Saints (FR)—Magic Poline (FR) **Mr & Mrs J. D. Cotton**
109 **MAGISTRATO (FR),** 5, b g Kapgarde (FR)—Franche Alliance (FR) **Mrs J. De La Hey**
110 **MAKIN'YOURMINDUP,** 6, b g Kayf Tara—Subtilty **Owners Group 090**
111 4, B f Flemensfirth (USA)—Marie des Anges (FR)
112 **MARVELLOUS MICK,** 5, b g Blue Bresil (FR)—Mickie **Mr M. F. Geoghegan**
113 **MATTERHORN (FR),** 5, b g Martaline—Sacarine (FR) **Mrs J. De La Hey**
114 **MCFABULOUS (IRE),** 9, b g Milan—Rossavon (IRE) **Giraffa Racing**
115 **MEATLOAF (FR),** 4, ch g Doctor Dino (FR)—Jane (GER) **The Stewart Family, Sir A Ferguson & G Mason**
116 **MILAN BRIDGE (IRE),** 7, b g Milan—Ice Princess (IRE) **Exors of the Late Mr T. J. Hemmings**
117 **MONMIRAL (FR),** 6, bl g Saint des Saints (FR)—Achere (FR) **Sir A Ferguson G Mason J Hales & L Hales**
118 **MR GLASS (IRE),** 7, b g Sholokhov (IRE)—Maryota (FR) **John & Jessica Dance**
119 **MULLINS BAY,** 5, b g Kayf Tara—Gaye Sophie **The Stewart Family & Mr P. J. Vogt**
120 **OLD GOLD,** 5, b g Blue Bresil (FR)—She's da One (IRE) **Old Gold Racing 12**
121 **ONETHREEFIVENOTOUT (IRE),** 7, b g Milan—Back To Loughadera (IRE) **The Stewart Family**
122 **OSCARS MOONSHINE (IRE),** 8, b g Oscar (IRE)—Scrapper Jack (IRE) **Mrs E. Lane**
123 **OUTLAW PETER (IRE),** 7, b g Mustameet (USA)—My Katie (IRE) **The Stewart Family, Dench, Ferguson & Mason**
124 **PASO DOBLE (IRE),** 6, br g Dawn Approach (IRE)—Baila Me (GER) **Mr G. F. Brooks**
125 **PENTIRE HEAD (IRE),** 5, ch g Presenting—Kneeland Lass (IRE) **Mr Paul K. Barber & Mr Roger Eddy**
126 **PIC D'ORHY (FR),** 8, b g Turgeon (USA)—Rose Candy (FR) **Mrs J. De La Hey**
127 **PLEASANT MAN,** 5, b g Galileo (IRE)—Melito (AUS) **McNeill Family & Patrick & Scott Bryceland**
128 4, Br g Blue Bresil (FR)—Present Your Case (IRE) **Mr G. F. Brooks**
129 **QUEL DESTIN (FR),** 8, ch g Muhtathir—High Destiny (FR) **Martin Broughton & Friends**
130 **RARE MIDDLETON,** 4, b g Aclaim (IRE)—Blaise Chorus (IRE) **Bryan Drew & Diana L Whateley**
131 **RED RISK (FR),** 8, b g No Risk At All (FR)—Rolie de Vindecy (FR) **Middleham Park Racing XLIV & A&J Ryan**
132 **REGENT'S STROLL (IRE),** 4, b g Walk In The Park (IRE)—Pretty Puttens (IRE) **Mr C. M. Giles**
133 4, B g Getaway (GER)—Rose Indienne (FR) **Mr G. F. Brooks**
134 **RUBAUD (FR),** 5, b g Air Chief Marshal (IRE)—Fulgence (FR) **Chris Giles & Brendan McManus**
135 **RUE ST DENIS (IRE),** 5, b g Montmartre (FR)—Lady Denisa **Mr C. M. Giles**
136 **SABRINA (IRE),** 8, b m Yeats (IRE)—En Vedette (FR) **Owners Group 030**
137 **SAINT CALVADOS (FR),** 10, b g Saint des Saints (FR)—Lamorrese (FR) **D. Maxwell**
138 **SAMARRIVE (FR),** 6, b g Coastal Path—Sambirane (FR) **Mrs J. De La Hey**
139 **SANDALWOOD (FR),** 6, ch g Martaline—Balli Flight (FR) **Owners Group 072**
140 **SEASIDE LEGEND (IRE),** 5, b g Adlerflug (GER)—It Gorl (GER) **Jackson & Monk**
141 **SECRET INVESTOR,** 11, b g Kayf Tara—Silver Charmer **C. J. Hitchings**
142 **SECRET SHADOW (IRE),** 5, b m Camelot—Secret Pursuit (IRE) **Mrs R G Hillen**
143 **SEEYOUINMYDREAMS,** 5, b m Telescope (IRE)—Sierra (FR) **Mason, Hogarth, Ferguson, Done, McGoff**
144 **SHEARER (IRE),** 7, b g Flemensfirth (USA)—The Crown Jewel (IRE) **The McNeill Family**
145 **SILENT REVOLUTION (IRE),** 7, b g Sholokhov (IRE)—Watson River (IRE) **Mr C. A. Donlon**
146 **SIMPLY THE BETTS (IRE),** 10, b g Arcadio (GER)—Crimson Flower (IRE) **D. Maxwell**
147 **SIR PSYCHO (IRE),** 7, b g Zoffany (IRE)—Open Book **Martin Broughton & Friends 3**
148 **SISTER SAINT (FR),** 6, gr m Martaline—Minirose (FR) **Mrs J. De La Hey**

MR PAUL NICHOLLS - continued

149 **SKATMAN (IRE),** 8, br g Mustameet (USA)—Maid For Action (IRE) **Mr C. M. Giles**
150 **SOIR DE GALA (FR),** 4, b g Joshua Tree (IRE)—Solvalla (FR) **Mr J. P. McManus**
151 **SOLO (FR),** 7, b g Kapgarde (FR)—Flameche (FR) **Mrs J. De La Hey**
152 **SONIGINO (FR),** 6, b g It's Gino (GER)—Soniador (FR) **Sir A Ferguson G Mason J Hales & L Hales**
153 **SOUTHFIELD HARVEST,** 9, b g Kayf Tara—Chamoss Royale (FR) **Mrs Angela Yeoman & Mr Paul K. Barber**
154 **STAGE STAR (IRE),** 7, b g Fame And Glory—Sparky May **Owners Group 044**
155 **STATE OF POWER (IRE),** 6, b g Westerner—Strong Statement (IRE) **Gordon & Su Hall**
156 **STAY AWAY FAY (IRE),** 6, b g Shantou (USA)—Augusta Bay **Mr C. M. Giles**
157 **SUMMER BRISE,** 4, bl f Kapgarde (FR)—Brise Vendeenne (FR) **Burkes & Syders**
158 **SUPER SAINT (FR),** 4, b g Saint des Saints (FR)—La Champmesle (FR) **Mr & Mrs J. D. Cotton**
159 **SWITCH HITTER (IRE),** 8, b g Scorpion (IRE)—Country Time (IRE) **Hills of Ledbury Ltd**
160 **TAHMURAS (FR),** 6, b g Falco (USA)—Alinga's Lass (IRE) **Noel Fehily Racing Syndicates Tahmuras**
161 **TAKE YOUR TIME (IRE),** 8, b g Dubai Destination (USA)—Don't Be Bleu (IRE) **Owners Group 060**
162 **TANGO TARA,** 7, b g Kayf Tara—Bling Noir (FR) **Middleham Park Racing XXXIX & Peter Lamb**
163 **TARRAS WOOD (IRE),** 5, b g Kayf Tara—Wood Lily (IRE) **The Gi Gi Syndicate**
164 **THREEUNDERTHRUFIVE (IRE),** 8, b g Shantou (USA)—Didinas (FR) **The McNeill Family**
165 **THYME WHITE (FR),** 7, b g Anodin (IRE)—Jane (GER) **The Stewart Family & Michael Blencowe**
166 **TIME TO TINKER (IRE),** 8, br g Stowaway—Zuzka (IRE) **Mrs A. Tincknell**
167 **TIMEFORATUNE,** 7, b g Yorgunnabelucky (USA)—Timeforagin **Mr J. Hales**
168 **TINKLERS HILL (IRE),** 5, b g Milan—Beautiful War (IRE) **The Hon Mrs Townshend & Mr J.R.Townshend**
169 **TOOTHLESS (FR),** 5, b g Authorized (IRE)—Sandside (FR) **Mr C. A. Donlon**
170 **TOUQUET (FR),** 4, b g Kapgarde (FR)—Tahaza (FR) **Mr G. F. Brooks**
171 **TRUCKERS LODGE (IRE),** 11, b g Westerner—Galeacord (IRE) **Gordon & Su Hall**
172 **TWIN POWER (IRE),** 6, b g Milan—Knockfierna (IRE) **McNeill Family & M & A Wainwright**
173 **URBAN SOLDIER (IRE),** 6, br g Soldier of Fortune (IRE)—She's No Pet (IRE) **Middleham Park Racing CXI**
174 **WELCOM TO CARTRIES (FR),** 5, b g No Risk At All (FR)—Nasou (FR) **Mrs J. De La Hey**
175 **WRAPPEDUPINMAY (IRE),** 5, ch g Ocovango—Funny Times **Mrs J. De La Hey**
176 **YOUNG BUCK (IRE),** 9, b g Yeats (IRE)—Pepsi Starlet (IRE) **P. F. Nicholls, Mrs J. Irish**

THREE-YEAR-OLDS

177 **SORCELEUR (FR),** b g Saint des Saints (FR)—Biche d'Oo (FR)

Assistant Trainer: Charlie Davies, Conor Houlihan, Natalie Parker.

NH Jockey: Harry Cobden, Bryony Frost, Lorcan Williams. **Conditional Jockey:** Tom Buckley, Angus Cheleda, Freddie Gingell. **Amateur Jockey:** Mr Freddie Gordon, Mr David Maxwell, Miss Olive Nicholls, Miss Natalie Parker, Mr Charlie Sprake.

---

380 MR ADAM NICOL, Seahouses

Postal: **Springwood, South Lane, North Sunderland, SEAHOUSES, Northumberland, NE68 7UL**
Contacts: **PHONE 01665 720320**
EMAIL adamnicol89@hotmail.co.uk

1 **AGILULF,** 4, ch g Mondialiste (IRE)—Turin (IRE) **Mr & Mrs G. Turnbull**
2 **BARNEY STINSON (IRE),** 7, b g Fame And Glory—Which Thistle (IRE) **The Risk Takers Partnership**
3 **ECONOMIC EDITOR (IRE),** 7, b g Jet Away—How Provincial (IRE) **UP4B**
4 **FARNE ISLAND,** 6, gr m Trans Island—Tigerific (IRE) **Ian Nicol Racing**
5 **FOSHAN (IRE),** 4, b g The Last Lion (IRE)—China In My Hands **The MacDougall Two**
6 **QUERCUS ROBUR,** 4, br g Camelot—Wood Fairy **Mrs J. Sivills**
7 **SPIDER'S BITE (IRE),** 11, b g Scorpion (IRE)—Model Girl **James Wright & Tony Ogorman**
8 **TRAILBLAZER,** 4, b g Dark Angel (IRE)—Ballymore Celebre (IRE) **Ian Nicol Racing**
9 **VELKERA (IRE),** 9, br m Sholokhov (IRE)—April Gale (IRE) **The Seahouses Syndicate**
10 **WISE EAGLE (IRE),** 6, ch g Free Eagle (IRE)—Best Be Careful (IRE) **The Seahouses Syndicate**

381 MR PETER NIVEN, Malton

Postal: **Clovafield, Barton-Le-Street, Malton, North Yorkshire, YO17 6PN**
Contacts: **PHONE 01653 628176 MOBILE 07860 260999 FAX 01653 627295**
EMAIL pruniven@btinternet.com WEBSITE www.peterniven.co.uk

1 **CLOVA HOTEL,** 5, b g Sixties Icon—Simply Mystic **Mr P. D. Niven**
2 **HURSTWOOD,** 6, br gr g Dark Angel (IRE)—Haigh Hall **Hard Held Partnership & Angus Racing**
3 **MALYSTIC,** 9, b g Malinas (GER)—Mystic Glen **Clova Syndicate & Mrs J A Niven**
4 **MISTY MANI,** 8, b m Sulamani (IRE)—Mystic Glen **Mrs K Young & Mrs J A Niven**
5 4, Br f Malinas (GER)—Mystic Glen
6 **PROSPECT HOUSE (IRE),** 5, b g Retirement Plan—Niffyrann (FR) **Hard Held Partnership**
7 **STORM FORCE ONE,** 7, b m Schiaparelli (GER)—Force In The Wings (IRE) **Hedley, Little, Sharkey & Tomkins**
8 **SUGAR BABY,** 5, b g Monsieur Bond (IRE)—Sugar Town **Angus Racing Club & Mr P. D. Niven**

---

382 MR JOHN NORTON, Barnsley

Postal: **Globe Farm, High Hoyland, Barnsley, South Yorkshire, S75 4BE**
Contacts: **HOME 01226 387633 MOBILE 07970 212707**
HOME EMAIL johnrnorton@hotmail.com FACEBOOK JRNorton

1 **BLACK MARKET (IRE),** 9, b g Yeats (IRE)—Aneda Dubh (IRE) **Fellowship Of The Rose Partnership 2**
2 **DAKOTA BEAT (IRE),** 8, ch g Beat Hollow—Rushmore Rose (IRE) **Liz And Phil Woodcock-jones**
3 **MUFTAKKER,** 9, gr g Tamayuz—Qertaas (IRE) **Fellowship Of The Rose Partnership 2**
4 **NAASIK,** 10, b g Poet's Voice—Shemriyna (IRE) **Fellowship Of The Rose Partnership 2**
5 **OLD DURHAM TOWN,** 7, b g Fame And Glory—Oleohneh (IRE) **Jaffa Racing Syndicate**

TWO-YEAR-OLDS

6 B c 23/04 Land Force (IRE)—Miss Mediator (USA) (Consolidator (USA)) (2500) **J. R. Norton Ltd**
7 **MYSTIC MARIE,** b c 04/05 Outstrip—Marmande (IRE) (Duke of Marmalade (IRE)) (2000) **A. Tattersall**

---

383 MR A. P. O'BRIEN, Ballydoyle

Postal: **Ballydoyle Stables, Cashel, Co. Tipperary, Ireland**
Contacts: **PHONE +353 62 62615**
EMAIL Chris@ballydoyleracing.com

1 **BOLSHOI BALLET (IRE),** 5, b h Galileo (IRE)—Alta Anna (FR)
2 **BROOME (IRE),** 7, b h Australia—Sweepstake (IRE)
3 **CHANGINGOFTHEGUARD (IRE),** 4, b c Galileo (IRE)—Lady Lara (IRE)
4 **EMILY DICKINSON (IRE),** 4, b f Dubawi (IRE)—Chicquita (IRE)
5 **GULLIVER'S TRAVELS (IRE),** 4, b c Galileo (IRE)—Prudenzia (IRE)
6 **KYPRIOS (IRE),** 5, ch h Galileo (IRE)—Polished Gem (IRE)
7 **LUXEMBOURG (IRE),** 4, b c Camelot—Attire (IRE)
8 **MACQUARIE (IRE),** 7, ch h Australia—Beyond Brilliance (IRE)
9 **MARTINSTOWN (IRE),** 4, b c Galileo (IRE)—Alive Alive Oh
10 **ORDER OF AUSTRALIA (IRE),** 6, b h Australia—Senta's Dream
11 **POINT LONSDALE (IRE),** 4, b c Australia—Sweepstake (IRE)
12 **STONE AGE (IRE),** 4, b c Galileo (IRE)—Bonanza Creek (IRE)
13 **TENEBRISM (USA),** 4, b br f Caravaggio (USA)—Immortal Verse (IRE)
14 **THOUGHTS OF JUNE (IRE),** 4, gr f Galileo (IRE)—Discreet Marq (USA)

MR A.P. O'BRIEN - continued

THREE-YEAR-OLDS

15 **ADARE MANOR (IRE),** br c Camelot—Clear Skies
16 **ADELAIDE RIVER (IRE),** b c Australia—Could It Be Love (USA)
17 **AESOP'S FABLES (IRE),** b c No Nay Never (USA)—How's She Cuttin' (IRE)
18 **ALEXANDROUPOLIS (IRE),** b c Camelot—Jazz Cat (IRE)
19 **ALFRED MUNNINGS (IRE),** b c Dubawi (IRE)—Best In The World (IRE)
20 **ALL TIME GREAT (USA),** ch f Justify (USA)—Curvy
21 **AUGUSTE RODIN (IRE),** br c Deep Impact (JPN)—Rhododendron (IRE)
22 **BALLGOWN (IRE),** b f Galileo (IRE)—Legatissimo (IRE)
23 **BALLSBRIDGE (USA),** br c Lord Kanaloa (JPN)—Happily (IRE)
24 **BE HAPPY (IRE),** b f Camelot—Frequential
25 **BEGINNINGS (USA),** b f Lord Kanaloa (JPN)—Winter (IRE)
26 **BERTINELLI (USA),** ch c Justify (USA)—Together Forever (IRE)
27 **BOOGIE WOOGIE (IRE),** b f Dubawi (IRE)—Seventh Heaven (IRE)
28 **BROADHURST (IRE),** b c No Nay Never (USA)—Sweet Charity (FR)
29 **CAIRO (IRE),** b c Quality Road (USA)—Cuff (IRE)
30 **CANUTE (USA),** b c Quality Road (USA)—Alice Springs (IRE)
31 **CAPE BRIDGEWATER (IRE),** b c Australia—Itqaan (USA)
32 **CARRACCI (USA),** b c Quality Road (USA)—Butterflies (IRE)
33 **CITY OF CHICAGO (IRE),** bl c Justify (USA)—My Sister Sandy (USA)
34 **CLOCKWORK (IRE),** ch c Galileo (IRE)—Queen Boudica
35 **CONGO RIVER (USA),** b c Mendelssohn (USA)—Tessie Flip (USA)
36 **CONTINUOUS (JPN),** b c Heart's Cry (JPN)—Fluff (IRE)
37 **COVENT GARDEN (IRE),** b br c Galileo (IRE)—Inca Princess (IRE)
38 **DAME KIRI (USA),** ch f Justify (USA)—Hence (IRE)
39 **DELIGHTFUL (IRE),** b f Galileo (IRE)—Lillie Langtry (IRE)
40 **DENMARK,** b c Camelot—Board Meeting (IRE)
41 **DIAMONDSAREFOREVER (IRE),** b f Justify (USA)—Diamondsandrubies (IRE)
42 **DOWER HOUSE (IRE),** b f Galileo (IRE)—Meow (IRE)
43 **DRUMROLL (IRE),** br c Deep Impact (JPN)—Maybe (IRE)
44 **DUKE CADOR (IRE),** b c Camelot—Elbasana (IRE)
45 **ERATO (IRE),** ch f Galileo (IRE)—One Moment In Time (IRE)
46 **ESPIONAGE (IRE),** b c Galileo (IRE)—Even Song (IRE)
47 **FARNBOROUGH (IRE),** b c Galileo (IRE)—Sing Softly (USA)
48 **GOOLOOGONG (IRE),** ch c Australia—Muwakaba (USA)
49 **GREENLAND (IRE),** b c Saxon Warrior (JPN)—Aktoria (FR)
50 **GULF OF MEXICO (IRE),** b c Galileo (IRE)—Anthem Alexander (IRE)
51 **HANS ANDERSEN,** b c Frankel—Shadow Hunter (IRE)
52 **HIAWATHA (IRE),** b c Camelot—Attire (IRE)
53 **HIGH CHIEFTESS (IRE),** ch f Galileo (IRE)—Tiggy Wiggy (IRE)
54 **HIPPODROME (IRE),** br c Galileo (IRE)—Lightning Thunder
55 **HISPANIC (IRE),** br gr c No Nay Never (USA)—Fork Lightning (USA)
56 **HURST PARK (IRE),** b c Galileo (IRE)—Chanting (USA)
57 **JACKIE OH (IRE),** ch f Galileo (IRE)—Jacqueline Quest (IRE)
58 **KING LEODEGRANCE (IRE),** b c Camelot—Empowering (IRE)
59 **LAMBADA (IRE),** b f Dubawi (IRE)—Wading (IRE)
60 **LIBRARY (IRE),** b f Galileo (IRE)—Words (IRE)
61 **LITTLE BIG BEAR (IRE),** b c No Nay Never (USA)—Adventure Seeker (FR)
62 **LONDONER (IRE),** ch c Saxon Warrior (JPN)—Gilt Edge Girl
63 **MAYBE JUST MAYBE (JPN),** b f Lord Kanaloa (JPN)—Promise To Be True (IRE)
64 **MEDITATE (IRE),** gr ro f No Nay Never (USA)—Pembina (IRE)
65 **MILWAUKEE (USA),** ch c Justify (USA)—Moth (IRE)
66 **NEVER ENDING STORY (IRE),** b f Dubawi (IRE)—Athena (IRE)
67 **PEKING OPERA (IRE),** b c Galileo (IRE)—Bugle (USA)
68 **POP STAR (IRE),** b c Sioux Nation (USA)—Knock Stars (IRE)
69 **POWER AND GLORY (IRE),** b c Galileo (IRE)—Charlotte Bronte
70 **PRAGUE (IRE),** b c Galileo (IRE)—Princess Noor (IRE)
71 **PROMISES TO KEEP (IRE),** br f Galileo (IRE)—Mystical Lady (IRE)
72 **QUEENSTOWN (IRE),** b c Galileo (IRE)—Where (IRE)

MR A.P. O'BRIEN - continued

73 **RED CARPET (IRE),** b f Galileo (IRE)—Quiet Reflection
74 **RED RIDING HOOD (IRE),** ch f Justify (USA)—Ballydoyle (IRE)
75 **SALT LAKE CITY (IRE),** b c Galileo (IRE)—Heartache
76 **SAN ANTONIO (IRE),** b c Dubawi (IRE)—Rain Goddess (IRE)
77 **SAVETHELASTDANCE (IRE),** ch f Galileo (IRE)—Daddys Lil Darling (USA)
78 **SMART COOKIE (IRE),** ch f Dubawi (IRE)—Highest Ever (IRE)
79 **SNOWY (IRE),** b f Galileo (IRE)—Snow Queen (IRE)
80 **SQUARE MILE (IRE),** br c Galileo (IRE)—Penchant
81 **ST KITTS (IRE),** ch c No Nay Never (USA)—Bracelet (IRE)
82 **STARRY EYED (IRE),** b f Galileo (IRE)—Nickname (USA)
83 **STATUETTE (USA),** ch f Justify (USA)—Immortal Verse (IRE)
84 **SUBZERO (IRE),** b c Galileo (IRE)—Different League (FR)
85 **SWEETEST THING (IRE),** b f Galileo (IRE)—Mecca's Angel (IRE)
86 **TENDER KISS (IRE),** b f Galileo (IRE)—Marsha (IRE)
87 **THE ANTARCTIC (IRE),** gr c Dark Angel (IRE)—Anna Law (IRE)
88 **THE BLACK TIGER (USA),** b c Justify (USA)—Gagnoa (IRE)
89 **THE PRAIRIE (IRE),** b c Galileo (IRE)—Again (IRE)
90 **TIME TO BOOGIE (USA),** b f Quality Road (USA)—Magical Dream (IRE)
91 **TOWER OF LONDON (IRE),** b c Galileo (IRE)—Dialafara (FR)
92 **UNLESS (USA),** ch f Justify (USA)—Clemmie (IRE)
93 **VICTORIA ROAD (IRE),** b c Saxon Warrior (JPN)—Tickled Pink (IRE)
94 **WARM HEART (IRE),** b f Galileo (IRE)—Sea Siren (AUS)
95 **WATER NYMPH (IRE),** b f Saxon Warrior (JPN)—Chenchikova (IRE)
96 **WEDDING BOUQUET (IRE),** b f Galileo (IRE)—Hazariya (IRE)
97 **WORLD PEACE (IRE),** b f Frankel—How High The Moon (IRE)

TWO-YEAR-OLDS

98 B c 01/04 Galileo (IRE)—Abel Tasman (USA) (Quality Road (USA))
99 Ch f 15/02 Justify (USA)—Alice Springs (IRE) (Galileo (IRE))
100 B c 28/01 Galileo (IRE)—Alive Alive Oh (Duke of Marmalade (IRE)) (600000)
101 B c 15/02 Fastnet Rock (AUS)—All For Glory (USA) (Giant's Causeway (USA))
102 B c 13/04 Dubawi (IRE)—Amerique (IRE) (Galileo (IRE))
103 B c 02/05 Galileo (IRE)—Amicus (AUS) (Fastnet Rock (AUS))
104 B br f 05/05 American Pharoah (USA)—Antonia Autumn (USA) (Bernstein (USA)) (306878)
105 Ch c 07/03 Night of Thunder (IRE)—Asidious Alexander (IRE) (Windsor Knot (IRE)) (575000)
106 B c 02/02 Dubawi (IRE)—Athena (IRE) (Camelot)
107 B f 04/04 Camelot—Attire (IRE) (Danehill Dancer (IRE))
108 B c 25/04 Frankel—Auld Alliance (IRE) (Montjeu (IRE)) (800000)
109 **AUTUMN WINTER (IRE),** b c 22/03 Galileo (IRE)—Quidura (Dubawi (IRE))
110 B c 16/04 Galileo (IRE)—Awesome Maria (USA) (Maria's Mon (USA))
111 B f 11/03 Fastnet Rock (AUS)—Ballydoyle (IRE) (Galileo (IRE))
112 B c 24/01 No Nay Never (USA)—Beauly (Sea The Stars (IRE)) (650000)
113 B f 25/02 Ten Sovereigns (IRE)—Belong (IRE) (Fastnet Rock (AUS))
114 B c 24/03 Frankel—Blue Waltz (Pivotal) (1900000)
115 B c 04/01 Galileo (IRE)—Bridal Dance (IRE) (Danehill Dancer (IRE))
116 B f 24/03 No Nay Never (USA)—Canada Water (Dansili) (288115)
117 B f 06/05 Galileo (IRE)—Charlotte Bronte (Danehill Dancer (IRE))
118 B c 12/04 No Nay Never (USA)—Chenchikova (IRE) (Sadler's Wells (USA))
119 B f 30/01 Wootton Bassett—Chrysocolla (FR) (Sea The Stars (IRE)) (500000)
120 Ch f 13/03 Justify (USA)—Clemmie (IRE) (Galileo (IRE))
121 B c 06/03 Camelot—Clique (Bated Breath) (300000)
122 B c 23/01 Uncle Mo (USA)—Coin Broker (IRE) (Montjeu (IRE))
123 B c 20/02 No Nay Never (USA)—Compression (USA) (First Defence (USA))
124 B c 31/01 Dubawi (IRE)—Coolmore (IRE) (Galileo (IRE))
125 B br c 15/01 No Nay Never (USA)—Coral Shell (IRE) (High Chaparral (IRE))
126 B f 08/04 Kingman—Could It Be Love (USA) (War Front (USA))
127 B c 26/01 Justify (USA)—Credenza (IRE) (Galileo (IRE))
128 B c 17/04 No Nay Never (USA)—Cry Me A River (IRE) (Danehill Dancer (IRE))
129 B c 05/01 No Nay Never (USA)—Czabo (Sixties Icon) (325000)

MR A.P. O'BRIEN - continued

130 B c 08/02 Galileo (IRE)—Danedrop (IRE) (Danehill (USA))
131 B br c 12/04 No Nay Never (USA)—Data Dependent (USA) (More Than Ready (USA))
132 B c 07/05 Galileo (IRE)—Devoted To You (IRE) (Danehill Dancer (IRE))
133 B f 05/03 No Nay Never (USA)—Diamondsandrubies (IRE) (Fastnet Rock (AUS))
134 B c 31/05 Galileo (IRE)—Different League (FR) (Dabirsim (FR))
135 B br c 10/01 No Nay Never (USA)—Dream The Blues (IRE) (Oasis Dream)
136 B br f 14/01 Galileo (IRE)—Emerald Ring (IRE) (Johannesburg (USA))
137 Ch f 10/05 Australia—Fabulae (IRE) (Fastnet Rock (AUS))
138 B c 09/02 Ten Sovereigns (IRE)—Fancy Vivid (IRE) (Galileo (IRE)) (176070)
139 Br c 05/02 Ten Sovereigns (IRE)—Fashion Darling (IRE) (Sea The Stars (IRE)) (260000)
140 B c 01/04 Galileo (IRE)—Fire Lily (IRE) (Dansili)
141 B c 19/04 No Nay Never (USA)—Flower Fashion (FR) (Flower Alley (USA)) (230000)
142 B br c 22/02 Camelot—Frequential (Dansili)
143 B c 27/04 Sea The Stars (IRE)—Greenisland (IRE) (Fasliyev (USA)) (300000)
144 B c 03/03 No Nay Never (USA)—Hazakiyra (IRE) (Camelot)
145 B c 21/03 Galileo (IRE)—Hazariya (IRE) (Xaar)
146 B f 10/02 Justify (USA)—Heaven On Earth (IRE) (Galileo (IRE))
147 Ch c 23/02 Justify (USA)—Hence (IRE) (Galileo (IRE))
148 B c 13/02 No Nay Never (USA)—Hermosa (IRE) (Galileo (IRE))
149 B c 31/03 Galileo (IRE)—High Celebrity (FR) (Invincible Spirit (IRE)) (520208)
150 Br c 10/05 No Nay Never (USA)—Holy Alliance (IRE) (Holy Roman Emperor (IRE))
151 B c 29/01 Siyouni (FR)—Hostess (Iffraaj) (375000)
152 B f 04/02 Dubawi (IRE)—Hydrangea (IRE) (Galileo (IRE))
153 B c 26/01 Galileo (IRE)—I Can Fly (Fastnet Rock (AUS))
154 B br c 17/04 No Nay Never (USA)—I'll Have Another (IRE) (Dragon Pulse (IRE))
155 B c 24/02 Siyouni (FR)—Illaunmore (USA) (Shamardal (USA)) (200000)
156 B f 21/04 Galileo (IRE)—Inca Princess (IRE) (Holy Roman Emperor (IRE))
157 Br c 23/02 No Nay Never (USA)—Jigsaw (IRE) (Galileo (IRE))
158 B c 27/01 Galileo (IRE)—Just Wonderful (USA) (Dansili)
159 B c 05/05 Galileo (IRE)—Lady Eli (USA) (Divine Park (USA))
160 B c 26/05 Galileo (IRE)—Legatissimo (IRE) (Danehill Dancer (IRE))
161 B c 01/04 No Nay Never (USA)—Lesson In Life (Duke of Marmalade (IRE)) (272109)
162 B f 22/03 Justify (USA)—Liscanna (IRE) (Sadler's Wells (USA))
163 B c 14/02 Dubawi (IRE)—Marvellous (IRE) (Galileo (IRE))
164 B f 09/05 Galileo (IRE)—Mecca's Angel (IRE) (Dark Angel (IRE))
165 B c 22/03 Justify (USA)—Milam (USA) (Street Sense (USA)) (776014)
166 B c 28/01 Dubawi (IRE)—Minding (IRE) (Galileo (IRE))
167 Ch f 31/01 Galileo (IRE)—Missvinski (USA) (Stravinsky (USA))
168 B f 12/01 Justify (USA)—Misty For Me (IRE) (Galileo (IRE))
169 B f 19/02 No Nay Never (USA)—Muravka (IRE) (High Chaparral (IRE))
170 Ch c 15/04 Galileo (IRE)—Muwakaba (USA) (Elusive Quality (USA))
171 Br f 11/05 Galileo (IRE)—Mystical Lady (IRE) (Halling (USA))
172 B c 15/02 Galileo (IRE)—Palace (IRE) (Fastnet Rock (AUS))
173 Ch f 15/02 Justify (USA)—Peach Tree (IRE) (Galileo (IRE))
174 B c 22/02 Siyouni (FR)—Pelligrina (IRE) (Soldier Hollow) (300000)
175 Ch f 30/04 Gleneagles (IRE)—Plying (USA) (Hard Spun (USA)) (650000)
176 B c 25/04 Lord Kanaloa (JPN)—Promise To Be True (IRE) (Galileo (IRE))
177 B c 16/02 Galileo (IRE)—Quiet Reflection (Showcasing)
178 B c 15/02 No Nay Never (USA)—Rain Goddess (IRE) (Galileo (IRE))
179 B f 28/04 Galileo (IRE)—Red Evie (IRE) (Intikhab (USA))
180 B c 18/03 No Nay Never (USA)—Ruby Tuesday (IRE) (Galileo (IRE))
181 B f 09/03 Frankel—Shambolic (IRE) (Shamardal (USA)) (1500000)
182 B c 23/01 No Nay Never (USA)—Shermeen (IRE) (Desert Style (IRE))
183 Ch f 06/02 Galileo (IRE)—So Perfect (USA) (Scat Daddy (USA))
184 B f 08/04 Galileo (IRE)—Song of My Heart (IRE) (Footstepsinthesand) (360000)
185 B c 07/04 Wootton Bassett—Strawberry Lace (Sea The Stars (IRE)) (272109)
186 B c 29/04 Frankel—Sweepstake (IRE) (Acclamation) (2400000)
187 B c 05/05 Galileo (IRE)—Switch (USA) (Quiet American (USA))
188 B f 01/01 Ten Sovereigns (IRE)—Tara's Force (IRE) (Acclamation)
189 Ch f 22/02 Galileo (IRE)—Tepin (USA) (Bernstein (USA))

MR A. P. O'BRIEN - continued

190 B c 23/02 Camelot—The Fairy (IRE) (Invincible Spirit (IRE)) (450000)
191 B f 10/02 American Pharoah (USA)—The Tooth Fairy (IRE) (Galileo (IRE))
192 B c 07/03 Justify (USA)—Together Forever (IRE) (Galileo (IRE))
193 B c 15/02 Wootton Bassett—Transcendence (IRE) (Arcano (IRE)) (480000)
194 B c 25/02 Magna Grecia (IRE)—Twitch (IRE) (Azamour (IRE))
195 B c 03/02 Galileo (IRE)—Wadyhatta (Cape Cross (IRE))
196 B c 07/04 Justify (USA)—Wedding Vow (IRE) (Galileo (IRE))
197 Gr c 29/04 Justify (USA)—Winter (IRE) (Galileo (IRE))
198 B c 09/06 Galileo (IRE)—Words (IRE) (Dansili)
199 B c 09/05 Dubawi (IRE)—Zagitova (IRE) (Galileo (IRE))

---

384 MR DONNACHA O'BRIEN, Cashel

Postal: **Bawnmore Racing Stables, Ballyroe, Cashel, Tipperary, Ireland**
EMAIL Chris@ballydoyleracing.com

1 **EMPORIO (IRE),** 5, ch h Zoffany (IRE)—Eirnin (IRE)
2 **MOON DAISY (IRE),** 5, b m Australia—Holy Alliance (IRE)
3 **PIZ BADILE (IRE),** 4, b br c Ulysses (IRE)—That Which Is Not (USA)

THREE-YEAR-OLDS

4 **A MOMENT LIKE THIS (USA),** ch f Galileo (IRE)—Stellar Wind (USA)
5 **ALDER (IRE),** ch c Australia—Eccentricity (USA)
6 **AMUSEMENT (IRE),** ch f Galileo (IRE)—Rock Orchid (IRE)
7 **BADB (IRE),** b f Footstepsinthesand—Belong (IRE)
8 **BEWARE (IRE),** b f Dubawi (IRE)—Chicquita (IRE)
9 **BOLD AS LOVE (IRE),** b f Deep Impact (JPN)—Malicieuse (IRE)
10 **EARTH DANCE (IRE),** b g Australia—Jamrah (IRE)
11 **EL TESORO (IRE),** ch c Mehmas (IRE)—C'Est Ma Souer (IRE)
12 **GOLDEN GOOSE (IRE),** b g Showcasing—Horse Sense (IRE)
13 **LA DOLCE VITA (IRE),** gr f Caravaggio (USA)—Ask Me Nicely (IRE)
14 **LIVELONG (IRE),** b f No Nay Never (USA)—Cocoon (IRE)
15 **MOMENT OF CLARITY (IRE),** gr f Galileo (IRE)—Ysoldina (FR)
16 **NEWPORT,** b c Starspangledbanner (AUS)—Chamber Maid
17 **NOT EVEN CLOSE (IRE),** b f Zoustar (AUS)—Street Marie (USA)
18 **NUNCA (IRE),** b f No Nay Never (USA)—Inca Wood (UAE)
19 **PROUD AND REGAL (IRE),** ch c Galileo (IRE)—Simply Perfect
20 **REPORT (IRE),** ch f Australia—Madam Baroque
21 **SEGOMO (IRE),** b g Zoffany (IRE)—Inchikhan
22 **STREAM OF LIGHT (IRE),** b c No Nay Never (USA)—Seeking Solace
23 **TEUTATES (IRE),** b g Churchill (IRE)—War Goddess (IRE)
24 **TWINKLING (IRE),** b f Galileo (IRE)—Alluringly (USA)
25 **UNCANNY (IRE),** b f Churchill (IRE)—Eos (IRE)
26 **UNCHAINED MELODY (IRE),** b f Fastnet Rock (AUS)—Eloquent (IRE)
27 **WODAO (FR),** ch c Showcasing—Dadao
28 **YOSEMITE VALLEY,** b c Shamardal (USA)—That Which Is Not (USA)

TWO-YEAR-OLDS

29 B f 18/05 Galileo (IRE)—Again (IRE) (Danehill Dancer (IRE))
30 Br f 22/02 Le Havre (IRE)—Althea Rose (IRE) (Green Desert (USA)) (120000)
31 B c 02/02 Ten Sovereigns (IRE)—Anja (IRE) (Indian Ridge)
32 B c 07/05 Churchill (IRE)—Bint Al Reem (IRE) (Elusive Quality (USA)) (75000)
33 Ch c 07/02 Night of Thunder (IRE)—Braided (USA) (Elusive Quality (USA)) (40000)
34 B c 01/05 No Nay Never (USA)—Bright Sapphire (IRE) (Galileo (IRE)) (360000)
35 B f 30/05 Dubawi (IRE)—Chicquita (IRE) (Montjeu (IRE))

MR DONNACHA O'BRIEN - continued

36 Ch c 05/04 No Nay Never (USA)—Cocoon (IRE) (Galileo (IRE))
37 B f 30/05 Galileo (IRE)—Coral Beach (IRE) (Zoffany (IRE))
38 B br c 31/03 Showcasing—Dawning (USA) (War Chant (USA))
39 B f 25/02 Churchill (IRE)—Devious Diva (IRE) (Dr Devious (IRE)) (48019)
40 Ch f 17/05 Australia—Eccentricity (USA) (Kingmambo (USA))
41 B f 30/04 Zoffany (IRE)—Eirnin (IRE) (Galileo (IRE))
42 Ch f 03/05 Churchill (IRE)—Empowering (IRE) (Encosta de Lago (AUS))
43 B f 10/02 Ten Sovereigns (IRE)—Eria (IRE) (Zoffany (IRE)) (52381)
44 Ch c 03/04 Starspangledbanner (AUS)—Federation (Motivator) (140000)
45 B f 26/03 Lord Kanaloa (JPN)—Fluff (IRE) (Galileo (IRE))
46 Gr c 10/04 Ten Sovereigns (IRE)—Gossamer Seed (IRE) (Choisir (AUS))
47 Ch f 11/04 Galileo (IRE)—Gossamer Wings (USA) (Scat Daddy (USA))
48 Ch c 04/04 Profitable (IRE)—Grotta Del Fauno (IRE) (Galileo (IRE)) (78431)
49 B f 17/03 No Nay Never (USA)—Hand On Heart (IRE) (Mastercraftsman (IRE))
50 B f 03/02 Dubawi (IRE)—Happen (USA) (War Front (USA))
51 B f 07/05 Ten Sovereigns (IRE)—Hint of Pink (IRE) (Teofilo (IRE)) (84034)
52 B c 05/03 Zoffany (IRE)—In My Dreams (IRE) (Sadler's Wells (USA))
53 B f 19/04 Ten Sovereigns (IRE)—Irradiate (IRE) (Australia) (12805)
54 B c 13/04 Magna Grecia (IRE)—Lilting (IRE) (Montjeu (IRE)) (70000)
55 B c 14/03 Magna Grecia (IRE)—Loulwa (IRE) (Montjeu (IRE)) (95238)
56 B f 06/04 Ten Sovereigns (IRE)—Malayan Mist (IRE) (Dansili) (48000)
57 Ch f 18/03 Justify (USA)—Maryinsky (IRE) (Sadler's Wells (USA))
58 B c 04/02 Zoffany (IRE)—Noelani (GER) (Nayef (USA)) (32013)
59 B c 28/05 Galileo (IRE)—On A Pedestal (IRE) (Montjeu (IRE))
60 Ch f 07/02 Dutch Art—Scheme (Pivotal) (144058)
61 B c 30/05 Galileo (IRE)—Sea Siren (AUS) (Fastnet Rock (AUS))
62 B f 13/05 Galileo (IRE)—September (IRE) (Deep Impact (JPN))
63 B c 09/02 Gleneagles (IRE)—Shannow (IRE) (Pivotal) (140000)
64 B f 18/03 No Nay Never (USA)—Sheranda (IRE) (Siyouni (FR)) (150000)
65 Br f 02/03 Ten Sovereigns (IRE)—Sodashy (IRE) (Noverre (USA)) (188075)
66 **SOLDIER OF ROME,** b c 14/04 Cracksman—Tyrana (FR) (Motivator) (40952)
67 Ch f 31/01 Churchill (IRE)—Star Blossom (USA) (Good Reward (USA)) (12805)
68 B c 06/02 Galileo (IRE)—Strawberry Fledge (USA) (Kingmambo (USA))
69 B c 03/03 Saxon Warrior (JPN)—Sweetasever (IRE) (Power) (46419)
70 B c 06/02 Churchill (IRE)—Syrena (IRE) (Gale Force Ten) (11204)
71 B f 02/04 Kingman—That Which Is Not (USA) (Elusive Quality (USA))
72 B f 23/01 Caravaggio (USA)—Too Precious (IRE) (Holy Roman Emperor (IRE))
73 B c 17/04 Galileo (IRE)—Where (IRE) (Danehill Dancer (IRE)) (200080)

385

MR FERGAL O'BRIEN, Cheltenham

Postal: **Ravenswell Farm, Withington, Cheltenham, Gloucestershire, GL54 4DD**
Contacts: **MOBILE 07771 702829**
EMAIL admin@fergalobrienracing.com

1 **ACCIDENTAL LEGEND (IRE),** 6, b g Shirocco (GER)—Cloth Fair (IRE) **Mr N. Brereton**
2 **ACCIDENTAL REBEL,** 9, b g Kayf Tara—Special Choice (IRE) **KHDRP**
3 **AJP KINGDOM (IRE),** 6, b g Mahler—Mattys Joy (IRE) **The FOB Racing Partnership**
4 **ALAPHILIPPE (IRE),** 9, b g Morozov (USA)—Oscar Bird (IRE) **Mr N. Brereton**
5 **AMADORIO (FR),** 8, b g Authorized (IRE)—Carolles (FR) **R V Racing**
6 **AMARBELLE'S DREAM,** 4, b f Brazen Beau (AUS)—Amarullah (FR) **Mr W. Marzouk**
7 **AMI DESBOIS (FR),** 13, b g Dream Well (FR)—Baroya (FR) **Mr F. M. O'Brien**
8 **ARMCHAIR FARMER (IRE),** 7, b g Brian Boru—Cobajay Lady (IRE) **P J King & Son**
9 4, B f Blue Bresil (FR)—Arrucian **J. C. S. Wilson**
10 **ART APPROVAL (FR),** 7, b g Authorized (IRE)—Rock Art (IRE) **Mr R. J. G. Lowe**
11 **ASK A HONEY BEE (IRE),** 9, b g Ask—Pure Honey (IRE) **Lewis, Lawson and Hope**

MR FERGAL O'BRIEN - continued

12 **AUTONOMOUS CLOUD (IRE),** 7, b g Flemensfirth (USA)—
August Hill (IRE) **Mr Terry Warner & the McNeill Family**
13 **AVIEWTOSEA (IRE),** 8, b g Where Or When (IRE)—Final Run (IRE) **The O'Brien McPherson Syndicate 1**
14 **BABY BEN (IRE),** 7, b g Ask—Decheekymonkey (IRE) **BDRSyndicates**
15 **BALLYHOME (IRE),** 12, b g Westerner—Nostra (FR) **A & K Ecofilm Ltd**
16 **BARRAKHOV (IRE),** 7, b g Sholokhov (IRE)—Barrack Buster **Dl Adams, Ja Adams & G McPherson**
17 **BATHIVA (FR),** 9, b g Spanish Moon (USA)—Thithia (FR) **Mrs J. Rees**
18 **BHALOO (IRE),** 5, br g Sageburg (IRE)—Feldaline (IRE) **Miss J. E. McGivern**
19 **BILLAMS LEGACY,** 8, b m Black Sam Bellamy (IRE)—Liqueur Rose **The Cod and Chips Twice Racing Syndicate**
20 **BILLY BOI BLUE,** 6, b g Blue Bresil (FR)—Kentucky Sky **BDRSyndicates**
21 **BLACK KALANISI (IRE),** 10, b g Kalanisi (IRE)—Blackthorne Winter (IRE) **The Harefield Racing Club**
22 **BLUE BIKINI,** 7, b m Winged Love (IRE)—Bleu d'Avril (FR) **Nick Brown Racing**
23 **BLUE CLOVER,** 5, b m Clovis du Berlais (FR)—Asola Blue (FR) **F&M Bloodstock Limited**
24 **BLUE SANS (IRE),** 8, b m Sans Frontieres (IRE)—California Blue (FR) **The FOB Racing Partnership 12**
25 **BLUE THE MONEY,** 5, b m Blue Bresil (FR)—No More Money **M. D. C. Jenks**
26 4, B f Dartmouth—Bonnet's Pieces
27 **BONTTAY (IRE),** 6, b m Westerner—Ben's Turn (IRE) **Mr C. B Brookes & Fergal O'Brien**
28 **BRIEF AMBITION,** 9, b g Yeats (IRE)—Kentucky Sky **C Coley, D Porter, H Redknapp, P Smith**
29 **BYZANTINE EMPIRE,** 6, b g Golden Horn—Mainstay **Always Smiling**
30 4, B f Passing Glance—Call Me Emma (IRE) **Upthorpe Racing**
31 **CALL ME TARA,** 6, b m Kayf Tara—Call Me Emma (IRE) **Upthorpe Racing**
32 **CAPTAIN CATTISTOCK,** 10, b g Black Sam Bellamy (IRE)—Pearl Buttons **Mr N. Brereton**
33 **CARLO DU BERLAIS (IRE),** 6, b g Carlotamix (FR)—Dark Ebony (IRE) **Owners Group 089**
34 4, Br g Sholokhov (IRE)—Carrigeen Kalmia (IRE)
35 **CARRIGEEN KAMPALA (IRE),** 5, b m Mahler—Carrigeen Kariega (IRE) **National Hunt Racing Club**
36 **CASTEL GANDOLFO (IRE),** 6, gr g Dark Angel (IRE)—Capulet Monteque (IRE) **Mr N. Brereton**
37 **CAVALLINO (IRE),** 8, ch g Presenting—Roque de Cyborg (IRE) **M. C. Denmark**
38 **CELESTIAL GIFT (FR),** 5, ch g Spanish Moon (USA)—Rose Star (FR) **Dl Adams, Ja Adams & G McPherson**
39 **CHANCYCOURT (IRE),** 7, b g Court Cave (IRE)—She Saval (IRE) **O'Brien & Porter**
40 **CHARLES ST,** 4, b g Outstrip—Under The Rainbow **The Cheltenham & South West Racing Club**
41 **CLARAS SOLDIER (IRE),** 5, br g Soldier of Fortune (IRE)—Clara Bel La (IRE) **Mr L. B. Carenza**
42 **CORAL (FR),** 8, gr g Martaline—Clipsy (FR) **Against All Odds Racing**
43 **CRAMBO,** 6, b g Saddler Maker (IRE)—Cardline (FR) **Sullivan Bloodstock Ltd & Chris Giles**
44 **DANCILA (IRE),** 6, b g Teofilo (IRE)—Empress of Rome (IRE) **Dr Richard & Anne Rowland**
45 **DEAUVILLE DANCER (IRE),** 12, b g Tamayuz—Mathool (IRE) **Mr G.Brandrick & Partner**
46 **DEHRADUN,** 7, b g Australia—Ridafa (IRE) **Mrs L.Day, Mr H.Burdett & Mr G.McPherson**
47 **DIRK GENTLY (IRE),** 6, ch g Mahler—Jumpingjude (IRE) **Bdr Syndicates & Graeme McPherson**
48 **DIV INE TARA,** 8, b m Kayf Tara—Mid Div And Creep **Mrs K Exall & Mr G Molen**
49 **DONTYAWANTME (IRE),** 6, ch m Getaway (GER)—Glory Queen (IRE) **Cliff Stud Limited**
50 **DREAM CHASER (FR),** 5, b g Dream Ahead (USA)—Avodale (IRE) **The Dream Partnership**
51 **DREAMING DIAMOND (IRE),** 6, b m Shirocco (GER)—Run And Dream (IRE) **D. J. Shorey**
52 **DUBLIN FOUR (IRE),** 9, ch g Arakan (USA)—Eluna **Dl Adams, Ja Adams & G McPherson**
53 **DYSART ENOS (IRE),** 5, b m Malinas (GER)—Graces Benefit (IRE) **The Good Stock Syndicate**
54 **EAGLE'S REALM,** 5, b g Free Eagle (IRE)—Regal Realm **Mr G. P. McPherson**
55 **EBONY WARRIOR (IRE),** 5, br g Sholokhov (IRE)—Three Wood (IRE) **Dl Adams, Ja Adams & G McPherson**
56 **ELHAM VALLEY (FR),** 6, gr g Tin Horse (IRE)—Dame du Floc (IRE) **Caveat Emptor Partnership**
57 **ENDLESS SUPPLY (IRE),** 5, b m Westerner—Selective Hearing (IRE) **Endless Fun**
58 **EVENWOOD SONOFAGUN (IRE),** 5, b g The Gurkha (IRE)—Ravish **KHDRP**
59 **EYEOFTHESCORPION (IRE),** 9, b g Scorpion (IRE)—Shuil Sharp (IRE) **With Dl & Adams Adams**
60 **FEEL THE PINCH,** 9, b g Librettist (USA)—Liqueur Rose **Mr B Jones & Son**
61 **FESTIVE GLORY (IRE),** 7, b g Fame And Glory—Rose of Clare **Mrs J. Rees**
62 **FILS DE ROI (FR),** 4, b g Saint des Saints (FR)—Prodiga (FR) **The Yes No Wait Sorries**
63 5, B g Gamut (IRE)—Final Run (IRE)
64 **FLANN,** 8, b g Brian Boru—Lady Karinga **Flann's Fans**
65 **FORTHEGREATERGOOD (IRE),** 9, b m Yeats (IRE)—Feast Or Famine (IRE) **Mrs J. A. Watts**
66 **FORTUNE FOREVER (IRE),** 5, ch m Soldier of Fortune (IRE)—Forever Young (IRE) **The Ravenstone Partnership**
67 **FRUIT HILL (IRE),** 6, br g Kingston Hill—Bobs Star (IRE) **Mr G. P. McPherson**
68 **FUJI ROCKS (IRE),** 6, b g Jet Away—Star of The Season (IRE) **Guy Henriques & Michael Henriques**
69 **GENTLE LIFE,** 6, b m Gentlewave (IRE)—Luz de La Vida **The Yes No Wait Sorries**
70 5, B g Westerner—Get Me Home (IRE) **M. C. Denmark**

MR FERGAL O'BRIEN - continued

71 **GETTHEPOT (IRE),** 8, b g Getaway (GER)—Raheen Lady (IRE) **Shaw Racing & Graeme McPherson**
72 **GLORIOUS ZOFF (IRE),** 6, b g Zoffany (IRE)—Ardbrae Lady **Deva Racing GZ**
73 **GO GO CHICAGO (IRE),** 6, b g Shirocco (GER)—Chicago Vic (IRE) **The Good Racing Company Ltd**
74 **GO TO WAR (IRE),** 5, b g Soldier of Fortune (IRE)—Rate of Knots (IRE) **Mr G. Leon**
75 5, Br g Malinas (GER)—Golan Road (IRE)
76 **GOLDEN TAIPAN (IRE),** 9, b g Golden Lariat (USA)—Rose of Taipan (IRE) **Double Barrels Of Courage**
77 **GORTROE JOE (IRE),** 11, b g Beneficial—Rowlands Star (IRE) **J. T. Warner**
78 **GREAT HEART'JAC (FR),** 8, br g Blue Bresil (FR)—Aqua Fontana (FR) **Mr L. D. Craze**
79 **GREATEST STAR (FR),** 7, gr g Lord du Sud (FR)—Sacree Mome (FR) **Mrs J. A. Watts**
80 **GREYVAL (FR),** 4, gr f The Grey Gatsby (IRE)—Valley Girl (FR) **The Oakley Partnership**
81 **GUMBALL (FR),** 9, gr g No Risk At All (FR)—Good Time Girl (FR) **J. T. Warner**
82 **HARD AS NAILS,** 5, b m Black Sam Bellamy (IRE)—Cream Cracker **Ray Treacy & Shaun Staplehurst**
83 **HEART OVER HEAD (IRE),** 4, b g Soldier of Fortune (IRE)—Oscar Bird (IRE) **Mr N. Brereton**
84 **HEREWEGOHONEY (IRE),** 7, b m Sageburg (IRE)—
Knappogue Honey (IRE) **Middleham Park Racing & C and J Hobkirk**
85 **HIDDEN BEAUTY,** 6, b m Kapgarde (FR)—Ma Councha (FR) **Nick Brown Racing**
86 **HOLA HERMOSA (IRE),** 4, ch f Diamond Boy (FR)—Glorys Lass (IRE) **The FOB Racing Partnership 3**
87 **HORACES PEARL (FR),** 5, b g Authorized (IRE)—Yellow Queen (FR) **Matt & Sally Burford**
88 4, Br f Sageburg (IRE)—Horner Vale (IRE)
89 **HORSE POWER (FR),** 6, b g Coastal Path—Valle d'Ossau (FR) **Actionclad 2001 Ltd**
90 **HULLNBACK,** 6, b g Schiaparelli (GER)—Freydis (IRE) **We're Having A Mare (WHAM)**
91 **HURRICANE HARVEY,** 9, b g Doyen (IRE)—Camp Fire (IRE) **Dr Richard & Anne Rowland**
92 **IMPERIAL ALCAZAR (IRE),** 9, b g Vinnie Roe (IRE)—Maddy's Supreme (IRE) **Imperial Racing Partnership 2016**
93 **IMPERIAL LIGHTNING (IRE),** 6, ch g Shantou (USA)—Vindonissa (IRE) **Imperial Racing Partnership 2016**
94 **IMPERIAL STORM (IRE),** 7, ch g Shantou (USA)—Vindonissa (IRE) **Imperial Racing Partnership 2016**
95 **INCE (AUT),** 6, gr m Reliable Man—Intricate Talent (USA) **Mr P. Loftus**
96 **INTERNET BIDDY (IRE),** 5, b m Westerner—Benefit Days (IRE) **The B Lucky Partnership**
97 **INTREPIDE SUD (FR),** 5, b g Coastal Path—Altitude Sud (FR) **The Chicheley Partnership**
98 **ISABELLA BEE (IRE),** 6, b m Westerner—Myakoda (FR) **KHDRP**
99 **IT'S TUESDAY (FR),** 5, b g Ballingarry (IRE)—Santalisa (FR) **Craig & Laura Buckingham**
100 **JAKANA (IRE),** 4, ch f Soldier of Fortune (IRE)—Golden Firth (IRE) **C. B. Brookes**
101 **JE FEEL AU POTEAU (FR),** 4, ch g Feel Like Dancing—Six Pack (FR) **& Adams, Phillips G McPherson**
102 **JEREMY THE JINN (IRE),** 8, br g Jeremy (USA)—Phantom Waters **Mrs J. Rees**
103 **JOHN THE BAPTIST (IRE),** 4, b g Caravaggio (USA)—Scream Blue Murder (IRE) **Mr N. Brereton**
104 **JUST DEEGEETEEBEE,** 7, b g Malinas (GER)—Rising Bell **& A Fear**
105 **KALELULA,** 6, br m Kalanisi (IRE)—Akdara (IRE) **Craig & Laura Buckingham**
106 **KAMSINAS (FR),** 6, b g Kamsin (GER)—Louvadeus Has (FR) **Noel Fehily Racing Syndicates Kamsinas**
107 **KARL PHILIPPE (FR),** 8, ch g Kentucky Dynamite (USA)—
Kaer Gwell (FR) **C Coley, D Porter, H Redknapp, P Smith**
108 **KEEP ON DIGGING (IRE),** 6, br g Notnowcato—Strange Talk (IRE) **Celia & Michael Baker**
109 **KEPLERIAN,** 6, b g Telescope (IRE)—Countess Camilla **Huw & Richard Davies & Friends**
110 **KINGFAST (IRE),** 8, b g Fast Company (IRE)—Monarchy (IRE) **Mr G. Brandrick & Partner and Ed Davies**
111 **KINGSTON SUNFLOWER (FR),** 6, bl m Authorized (IRE)—Kingston Acacia **Mr R. J. G. Lowe**
112 5, Ch m Sixties Icon—Kristalette (IRE)
113 **LANDEN CALLING (IRE),** 7, gr g Watar (IRE)—Gill Hall Lady **The B Lucky Partnership**
114 **LASSUE,** 7, b m Geordieland (FR)—Annie Fleetwood **Mr W. Marzouk**
115 4, B g Jack Hobbs—Latitude (FR)
116 **LEADING THEATRE (IRE),** 7, b m Leading Light (IRE)—Theatre Days (IRE) **Mrs C. Kendrick**
117 **LEAVE HER TO ME,** 5, b m Kayf Tara—Marie Deja La (FR) **David Killahena & John Benfield**
118 **LILTING VERSE (IRE),** 6, b m Yeats (IRE)—Sorcillera **Baker, Burford, Haynes & Plumb**
119 **LONG STAY,** 8, b g Nathaniel (IRE)—Mainstay **Mr R. Treacy**
120 **LORD P,** 6, b g Brazen Beau (AUS)—Netta (IRE) **Mr M. R. Breeze**
121 **LUNAR SOVEREIGN (IRE),** 7, b g Dubawi (IRE)—Surprise Moment (IRE) **Craig & Laura Buckingham**
122 **LUTINEBELLA,** 7, b m Kayf Tara—West River (USA) **Blue StaRR Racing FOB**
123 **MAGISTRA EQUITUM (IRE),** 5, b m Masterofthehorse (IRE)—
Gorteen Robin (IRE) **Mr Oscar Singh & Miss Priya Purewal**
124 **MAHON POINT,** 8, b g Kayf Tara—Freydis (IRE) **The Gud Times Partnership**
125 **MAMOON STAR (IRE),** 5, b g Mamool (IRE)—Mariah Mooney (IRE) **The Sharnbrook Partnership**
126 **MANOTHEPEOPLE (IRE),** 8, b g Mahler—Midnight Insanity (IRE) **The FOB Racing Partnership 2**
127 **MARBLE SANDS (FR),** 7, gr g Martaline—Sans Rien (FR) **Dl Adams, Ja Adams & G McPherson**

MR FERGAL O'BRIEN - continued

128 **MARTALITE (FR),** 5, b g Martaline—Frivolite (FR) **Dl Adams, Ja Adams & G McPherson**
129 **MAYS HILL,** 5, b m Kayf Tara—May Hay **W. F. H. Carson**
130 **MERRY BERRY,** 7, b m Malinas (GER)—Mayberry **Keeping The Dream Alive**
131 **MISTRAL BLUE,** 5, b m Blue Bresil (FR)—Mistral Reine **Sara The Dennis Family & Dominic Reilly**
132 **MOON CHIME,** 5, b g Pether's Moon (IRE)—Bella (FR) **Dl Adams, Ja Adams & G McPherson**
133 **MOONSHINE SPIRIT,** 6, b g Telescope (IRE)—Liqueur Rose **The FOB Racing Partnership 5**
134 **MOOT COURT (IRE),** 8, b g Court Cave (IRE)—Leney Dancer (IRE) **Ravenswell Renegades**
135 **MORTLACH,** 8, b g Yeats (IRE)—Belle Brook (IRE) **Richard D A Hames & Doug Pocock**
136 **MULBERRY HILL (IRE),** 7, br m Califet (FR)—Massini Rose (IRE) **Dark Horse Racing Partnership Nine**
137 **MY BOY BEASTY,** 5, b g Passing Glance—Think of The Money **Three Saints One Sinner**
138 **NIGHT DUTY (IRE),** 7, br g Kalanisi (IRE)—Lerichi (IRE) **Dr Richard & Anne Rowland**
139 **NIGHT ON THE TOWN,** 7, b m Black Sam Bellamy (IRE)—One Wild Night **Mr F. M. O'Brien**
140 **NO NO MAESTRO (IRE),** 8, b g Mahler—Maisey Down **Don Sebastiao Partnership**
141 **NOTHIN TO ASK (IRE),** 8, b g Ask—Nothin To Say (IRE) **The FOB Racing Partnership 11**
142 **OLD BEGINNINGS (IRE),** 6, b g Presenting—Beluckyagain (IRE) **Old Beginnings Partnership**
143 **ONAGATHERINGSTORM (IRE),** 8, b g Imperial Monarch (IRE)—Springfield Mary (IRE) **Craig & Laura Buckingham**
144 **ONE HUNDRED NOTOUT (IRE),** 7, b m Getaway (GER)—Roxtown **Glos Gipsies CC**
145 **OSCAR THYNE (IRE),** 8, b g Oscar (IRE)—Coolsilver (IRE) **Mr P. Sheanon**
146 **OSLO,** 6, b g Gleneagles (IRE)—Intercontinental **Mr N. Brereton**
147 **PAINT THE DREAM,** 9, b g Brian Boru—Vineuil (FR) **Mr D. Brace**
148 **PALACE BOY (GER),** 6, b g Nathaniel (IRE)—Palace Princess (GER) **Mr R. J. G. Lowe**
149 **PEERLESS BEAUTY,** 7, b m Phoenix Reach (IRE)—Sudden Beat **Smell The Flowers**
150 **PEKING ROSE,** 8, br g Passing Glance—Miniature Rose **The Coln Valley Partnership**
151 **PHILLAPA SUE (IRE),** 8, b m Scorpion (IRE)—Shuil Sharp (IRE) **Adams, Graham & McPherson**
152 **POETIC MUSIC,** 5, ch m Poet's Voice—Mofeyda (IRE) **Mr I. El Magdoub**
153 **POLITACUS (IRE),** 5, b m Epaulette (AUS)—Santacus (IRE) **Mr J. C. Collett**
154 **POP THE CHAMPAGNE (FR),** 7, b m Spanish Moon (USA)—Six Pack (FR) **Mrs Jill Phillips & Graeme McPherson**
155 **POUGNE AMINTA (FR),** 6, br m Protektor (GER)—Amicus **A. Stennett**
156 **PRELUDE TO GLORY (IRE),** 7, b m Fame And Glory—Prelude **Dl Adams, Ja Adams & G McPherson**
157 **PRESENTING MARVIN (IRE),** 5, ch g Presenting—Gaye Future **Caveat Emptor Partnership**
158 **PULL AGAIN GREEN (IRE),** 7, b g Kalanisi (IRE)—Clogher Valley (IRE) **Roy & Sally Green Tony & Karen Exall**
159 **PUNCTUATION,** 6, b g Dansili—Key Point (IRE) **Mr G. Leon**
160 **RECORD ART (FR),** 4, ch g Recorder—Rock Art (IRE) **Mr R. J. G. Lowe**
161 **RED RIVER VALLEY (IRE),** 7, b g Imperial Monarch (IRE)—Sunset View (IRE) **R V Racing**
162 **ROCK DANSE (FR),** 6, b g Kap Rock (FR)—Magic Danse (FR) **Don't Tell The Missus Partnership**
163 **ROYAL PRACTITIONER,** 10, b m Dr Massini (IRE)—Valdas Queen (GER) **A. P. Racing**
164 **RYAN'S ROCKET (IRE),** 5, ch g Jet Away—Smiths Lady (IRE) **Noel Fehily Racing Syndicate - Ryan's**
165 **SAINT JAGUEN (FR),** 5, b g Saint des Saints (FR)—Soif d'Aimer (FR) **Imperial Racing Partnership**
166 **SAMMYLOU (IRE),** 10, b g Beneficial—Carrigeen Diamond (IRE) **Dl Adams, Ja Adams & G McPherson**
167 **SCARLETT CLIPPER (IRE),** 6, b m Milan—Crimson Flower (IRE) **Blue StaRR Racing FOB**
168 **SCHOOL DAYS OVER (IRE),** 6, br g Ocovango—Landenstown Rose (IRE) **Dark Horse Racing Ltd**
169 4, B f Pether's Moon (IRE)—Scotland Act (FR)
170 **SEAS THE DAY,** 5, b m Scorpion (IRE)—Liqueur Rose **Blue StaRR Racing FOB**
171 **SEISMIC WAVE,** 6, b g Gentlewave (IRE)—Sunnyland **Anne West and Pete James, Bill Foylan**
172 **SHALLOW RIVER (IRE),** 7, b br g Ocovango—Nicola's Girl (IRE) **Mick Fitzgerald Racing Club**
173 **SHE'S A NOVELTY (IRE),** 8, b m Approve (IRE)—Novel Fun (IRE) **Sally's Angels**
174 **SHELIKESTHELIGHTS (IRE),** 5, b m Kayf Tara—Unify **4 The Fun Partnership**
175 **SILVER HALLMARK,** 9, br gr g Shirocco (GER)—Gaye Sophie **Mr & Mrs William Rucker**
176 **SILVER RAJ,** 4, gr g Rajsaman (FR)—Monshak (IRE) **Lord C. D. Harrison**
177 **SILVER SHEEN,** 9, b g Sulamani (IRE)—Silver Gypsy (IRE) **The Turner Family**
178 5, Br g Kalanisi (IRE)—Simply Deep (IRE) **Mrs C. Kendrick**
179 **SIR JACK YEATS (IRE),** 12, b g Yeats (IRE)—Quadrennial (IRE) **Mr F. M. O'Brien**
180 **SISTER MICHAEL (IRE),** 7, b g Fame And Glory—Derriana (IRE) **The Odd Lot**
181 **SMOKING PIGEON,** 9, b g Midnight Legend—Velvet Dove **Kilkenny Racing Partnership**
182 **SPAGO (IRE),** 6, br g Sageburg (IRE)—Davids Delight (IRE) **M. C. Denmark**
183 **ST PATRICKS BRIDGE (IRE),** 6, b g Hillstar—Glazed Storm (IRE) **The FOB Racing Partnership 4**
184 **STAR LEGEND (IRE),** 4, b g Galileo (IRE)—Thai Haku (IRE) **Mr K. K. B. Ho**
185 **STONER'S CHOICE,** 8, br g Great Pretender (IRE)—High Benefit (IRE) **Mrs C. Kendrick**
186 **STOWAWAY JESS,** 6, b m Universal (IRE)—Kahlua Cove **The FOB Racing Partnership 6**
187 **STUDENT CHAP (IRE),** 7, br g Presenting—Prowler (IRE) **Shaw Racing & Graeme McPherson**

MR FERGAL O'BRIEN - continued

188 **SUNDAY SOLDIER (IRE),** 5, ch m Shantou (USA)—Fortunes Harvest (FR) **Sunday Digital Publishing limited**
189 **SUNSET MELODY (IRE),** 6, b m Westerner—Bobset Leader (IRE) **Nick Brown Racing**
190 **SURTITLE (IRE),** 7, b g Presenting—Annabaloo (IRE) **Burkes & Syders**
191 **SWORDSMAN (IRE),** 9, br g Doyen (IRE)—Battle Over (FR) **Miss J. E. McGivern**
192 **TED'S FRIEND (IRE),** 7, b g Dylan Thomas (IRE)—Water Rock **Mrs C. Kendrick**
193 **TEETOTALLER,** 5, b g Black Sam Bellamy (IRE)—One Wild Night **Mennell, Logan and Coneyworths**
194 **TEQANY (IRE),** 9, gr g Dark Angel (IRE)—Capulet Monteque (IRE) **Mrs J. A. Watts**
195 **TEQUILA BLAZE,** 9, b m Sakhee (USA)—Miss Sassi **The Tequila Tipplers**
196 **THATZA DAZZLER,** 5, b g Blue Bresil (FR)—Sainte Fortuna (FR) **Mr D. Brace**
197 **THE BOGMANS BALL,** 6, b g Kayf Tara—Gaspaisie (FR) **Mrs M. Devine**
198 **THE GALAHAD KID (IRE),** 7, ch g Quest For Peace (IRE)—Kyle Again (IRE) **KHDRP**
199 **THE TOOJUMPA,** 10, b m Midnight Legend—Sunnyland **The FOB Racing Partnership 9**
200 **THUNDERSOCKSSUNDAE (IRE),** 8, b g Yeats (IRE)—Roseabel (IRE) **4 Left Footers & A Blewnose**
201 **TIGGER (IRE),** 5, br g Doyen (IRE)—Battle Over (FR) **Miss J. E. McGivern**
202 **TINTINTIN (FR),** 4, gr g Tin Horse (IRE)—Vanoo d'Orthe (FR) **Caveat Emptor Partnership**
203 **TIP TOP CAT (IRE),** 8, b g Milan—Pilgara (IRE) **Miss J. E. McGivern**
204 **TRIPOLI FLYER (IRE),** 4, b g Getaway (GER)—Collen Beag (IRE) **Mr I. El Magdoub**
205 **ULTIMATE GETAWAY (IRE),** 9, b g Getaway (GER)—Ultimate Echo (IRE) **Foxtrot Racing: Ultimate Getaway**
206 **UNE DE LA SENIERE (FR),** 8, ch m Noroit (GER)—Smabelle (FR) **The General Asphalte Company Ltd**
207 **UNLEASH THE BEAST (IRE),** 4, b g Malinas (GER)—Cloth Fair (IRE) **Mr N. Brereton**
208 **VALENTIA,** 5, b m Kayf Tara—Molly Flight (FR) **Mr W. Marzouk**
209 **VALENTINO DANCER,** 8, ch g Mastercraftsman (IRE)—Bertie's Best **Richard Hames & Alex Govorusa**
210 **VOLKOVKA (FR),** 6, b m Camelot—Drole de Dame (IRE) **The Tyringham Partnership**
211 4, B g Getaway (GER)—Water Rock **Mr F. M. O'Brien**
212 **WE GOTTA GETAWAY (IRE),** 6, b g Getaway (GER)—Clooney Eile (IRE) **First with Mortgages DL Adams & JA Adams**
213 **WOLF PRINCE (IRE),** 7, b g Pour Moi (IRE)—Preach (IRE) **Mr P. Sheanon**
214 **YOULNEVERWALKALONE,** 5, b g Walk In The Park (IRE)—Easter Dancer **YoulNeverWalkAlone Racing Syndicate**
215 **YOUNG BUSTER (IRE),** 7, b g Yeats (IRE)—Shatani (IRE) **The Good Stock Syndicate**
216 **ZUCAYAN (FR),** 6, b g Lucayan (FR)—John Quatz (FR) **Mr I. Slatter**

TWO-YEAR-OLDS

217 B g 02/04 Blue Bresil (FR)—Savingforvegas (IRE) (Beneficial) **The Denton Partnership**

Assistant Trainer: Sally Randell.

NH Jockey: Connor Brace, Paddy Brennan, Max Kendrick, Kielan Woods. **Conditional Jockey:** Liam Harrison, Jack Hogan. **Amateur Jockey:** Mr Tom Broughton, Miss Fern O'Brien.

386

MR JEDD O'KEEFFE, Leyburn

Postal: **Highbeck Lodge, Brecongill, Coverham, Leyburn, North Yorkshire, DL8 4TJ**
Contacts: **PHONE 01969 640330 MOBILE 07710 476705**
EMAIL jedd@jeddokeefferacing.co.uk WEBSITE www.jeddokeefferacing.co.uk

1 **BEEP BEEP BURROW (IRE),** 6, ch g Malinas (GER)—Ballygambon Girl (IRE) **The Good Racing Company Ltd**
2 **BRASINGAMAN BELLA,** 4, b f Black Sam Bellamy (IRE)—Brasingaman Hifive **Mr R. J. Morgan**
3 **BURROW SEVEN,** 6, gr g Kayf Tara—Gaye Sophie **The Good Racing Company Ltd**
4 **DEVIL'S ANGEL,** 7, gr g Dark Angel (IRE)—Rocking The Boat (IRE) **Titanium Racing Club**
5 **DREAM TOGETHER (IRE),** 6, ch g Dream Ahead (USA)—Shamsalmaidan (IRE) **The Fatalists**
6 **FAIRFIELD FERRATA,** 7, b m Kayf Tara—Via Ferrata (FR) **Mrs J. A. Darling**
7 **FRANKIE LAMB,** 5, ch g Proconsul—Lucinda Lamb **Miss S.E. Hall & Mr C. Platts**
8 **FRINGILL DIKE (IRE),** 6, ch g Mahler—Credo Star (IRE) **Caron & Paul Chapman**
9 **GOLDEN VINTAGE,** 4, b f Golden Horn—Millevini (IRE) **Titanium Racing Club**
10 **GREEN PLANET (IRE),** 6, b g Australia—Maleha (IRE) **The Unlikely Lads**
11 **INSTANT ATTRACTION (IRE),** 12, b g Tagula (IRE)—Coup de Coeur (IRE) **J. E. D. O'Keeffe**
12 **LUNA AOIFE,** 5, b m Telescope (IRE)—Laetitia (IRE) **Mrs J. A. Darling**

MR JEDD O'KEEFFE - continued

13 **MACAVITY,** 5, b g Fountain of Youth (IRE)—Brom Felinity (AUS) **Sigsworth Partners**
14 **MIAH GRACE,** 8, b m Malinas (GER)—Silver Gypsy (IRE) **Caron & Paul Chapman**
15 **MISS LAMB,** 7, b m Passing Glance—Lucinda Lamb **Miss S. E. Hall**
16 **MONTY NEVETT (IRE),** 4, ch g Churchill (IRE)—Organza **Caron & Paul Chapman**
17 **MR BRAMLEY,** 5, ch g Schiaparelli (GER)—Apple Days **Mr H. M. Posner**
18 **MR SCRUMPY,** 9, b g Passing Glance—Apple Days **Mr H. M. Posner**
19 **PERCY WILLIS,** 5, b g Sir Percy—Peace Lily **The Unlikely Lads**
20 **PRINCE ACHILLE,** 4, b g Reliable Man—Halle Bop **J. E. D. O'Keeffe**
21 **RARE GROOVE (IRE),** 8, ch g Lope de Vega (IRE)—Ascot Lady (IRE) **John & Jessica Dance**
22 **RATTLE OWL,** 7, b g Kayf Tara—Rattlin **Racing4Business Ltd**
23 **SAISONS D'OR (IRE),** 8, ro g Havana Gold (IRE)—Deux Saisons **The Fatalists**
24 **UBETYA (IRE),** 8, b g Le Fou (IRE)—Valentina Gaye (IRE) **Mr A. J. Peake**
25 **VINTAGE FIZZ,** 6, ch g Sulamani (IRE)—Milan Athlete (IRE) **Claret & T.S. Ingham**

THREE-YEAR-OLDS

26 **CHUCK TAYLOR (IRE),** b g Exceed And Excel (AUS)—Pabouche (IRE) **Mr S. Molaris**
27 B f Brazen Beau (AUS)—Emerald Cliffs (IRE) **Mr Gary White, West Shaw Farm**
28 **FUTURE TIMES (FR),** b g Olympic Glory (IRE)—Para El Futuro (FR) **Highbeck Racing 2**
29 **MASS CONSUMPTION (IRE),** gr g Cotai Glory—Day Creek **John & Jessica Dance**
30 **NOBLE MAJESTY,** b g Holy Roman Emperor (IRE)—Last Lahar **Highbeck Racing 3**
31 **NOBODY TOLD ME,** b g Intello (GER)—Dubka **Ellipsis II**
32 **OUR DELIA,** b f Acclamation—Fanta Dielo (USA) **Caron & Paul Chapman**
33 **OUT OF MISCHIEF,** b f Invincible Spirit (IRE)—More Mischief **Caron & Paul Chapman**
34 **SILK BIRD,** b f Free Eagle (IRE)—Organza **Caron & Paul Chapman**

TWO-YEAR-OLDS

35 **BROMPTON CROSS (IRE),** b c 26/02 Farhh—Eneryda (FR) (Sinndar (IRE)) (70000) **Quantum**
36 B c 21/01 Expert Eye—Cozi Bay (Kingman) (50000) **John & Jessica Dance**
37 B f 03/02 Tamayuz—Lady Eclair (IRE) (Danehill Dancer (IRE)) (19000) **Highbeck Racing**
38 **MONSIEUR MELEE,** b c 09/03 Intello (GER)—Penny Rose (Danehill Dancer (IRE)) (37000) **Quantum**
39 B f 31/03 Golden Horn—More Mischief (Azamour (IRE)) **Caron & Paul Chapman**
40 B f 26/03 Iffraaj—Nutkin (Act One) (33000) **John & Jessica Dance**
41 B f 15/04 Oasis Dream—Organza (Pour Moi (IRE)) **Caron & Paul Chapman**
42 **SOMETHING,** br c 08/02 Golden Horn—Calipatria (Shamardal (USA)) (57000) **Quantum**
43 **STIPULATION (IRE),** b c 01/03 New Bay—Danamight (IRE) (Danetime (IRE)) (124050) **John & Jessica Dance**

Assistant Trainer: Miss Leanne Kershaw, **Pupil Assistant:** Miss Jessica Townend.

Amateur Jockey: Miss Jessica Barraclough, Mr Jonathan O'Keeffe.

---

387 MR DAVID O'MEARA, Upper Helmsley

Postal: **Willow Farm, Upper Helmsley, York, Yorkshire, YO41 1JX**
Contacts: **PHONE 01759 372427 MOBILE 07747 825418**
EMAIL enquiries@davidomeara.co.uk WEBSITE www.davidomeara.co.uk

1 **ALLIGATOR ALLEY,** 6, b g Kingman—Overturned **Akela Thoroughbreds Limited**
2 **ANIMATO,** 4, ch g Ulysses (IRE)—Blithe **Mr D. B. O'Meara**
3 **ASCOT ADVENTURE,** 5, ch g Mayson—Kasumi **Woodhurst Ltd & Withernsea**
4 **AULD TOON LOON (IRE),** 4, b g Belardo (IRE)—Snowtime (IRE) **Empire State Racing Partnership**
5 **AUTUMN FESTIVAL,** 4, b g Poet's Voice—Kammaan **The LAM Partnership**
6 **AZANO,** 7, b g Oasis Dream—Azanara (IRE) **M.J & L.A Taylor & Partner**
7 **BARENBOIM,** 5, b g Golden Horn—Labise (IRE) **Richard D.A. Hames & Mark Russell**
8 **BEAUZON,** 4, b g Brazen Beau (AUS)—Pepper Lane **Mr K. Nicholson**
9 **BIN HAYYAN (IRE),** 4, gr g Dark Angel (IRE)—Anahita (FR) **Mr S. R. Bin Ghadayer**
10 **BLUE FOR YOU (IRE),** 5, ch g New Approach (IRE)—Love In The Sun (IRE) **Alderson Burke Francis**

MR DAVID O'MEARA - continued

11 **BOPEDRO (FR),** 7, b g Pedro The Great (USA)—Breizh Touch (FR) **Mr L. Bond**
12 **CHARGING THUNDER,** 5, b g War Command (USA)—Storming Sioux **Mr & Mrs G. Turnbull**
13 **COLD STARE (IRE),** 8, b g Intense Focus (USA)—Ziria (IRE) **Middleham Park Racing XC, P & J Hewitson**
14 **COSMOS RAJ,** 5, b g Iffraaj—Cosmos Pink **Mr Stuart Graham & Partner 2**
15 **CULCOR,** 4, b g Invincible Spirit (IRE)—Hot Snap **Mr F. Gillespie**
16 **DANCE TO EXCEL,** 4, ch c Exceed And Excel (AUS)—Dear Dancer (IRE) **Mr M. Rashid**
17 **DARKNESS (FR),** 5, b g Siyouni (FR)—Kerila (FR) **Akela Thoroughbreds Limited**
18 **EEETEE (IRE),** 5, b g Fast Company (IRE)—Chiquita Picosa (USA) **Gallop Racing**
19 **ELISHEVA (IRE),** 5, ch m Camacho—Smoken Rosa (USA) **Mr D. B. O'Meara**
20 **ESCOBAR (IRE),** 9, b g Famous Name—Saying Grace (IRE) **Withernsea Thoroughbred Limited**
21 **GET SHIRTY (IRE),** 7, b g Teofilo (IRE)—Soccer Mom (GER) **Akela Thoroughbreds Limited**
22 **GLORY AND HONOUR (IRE),** 7, b g Elusive Pimpernel (USA)—On Khee **The Horse Watchers**
23 **GULLIVER,** 9, b g Sayif (IRE)—Sweet Coincidence **Withernsea Thoroughbred Limited**
24 **HEADINGLEY (IRE),** 5, b g Dawn Approach (IRE)—Gold Bubbles (USA) **Gallop Racing**
25 **HORTZADAR,** 8, b g Sepoy (AUS)—Clouds of Magellan (USA) **Akela Thoroughbreds Limited**
26 **ICONICDAAY,** 4, b f Adaay (IRE)—Bond Bombshell **Trendy Ladies**
27 **IMPROVISED (IRE),** 5, ch m Raven's Pass (USA)—Kirouna (FR) **Clipper Group Holdings Ltd**
28 **INFINITIVE,** 4, b f Ulysses (IRE)—Integral **Cheveley Park Stud Limited**
29 **KALAHARI PRINCE (IRE),** 4, ch g New Approach (IRE)—Desert Blossom (IRE) **Mr F. Gillespie**
30 **KALGANOV (FR),** 4, b g Gutaifan (IRE)—Nidina (IRE) **Mr F. Gillespie**
31 **LACONIC,** 4, b g Oasis Dream—Brevity (USA) **Middleham Park Racing CII & Partner 3**
32 **LOVE INTEREST,** 4, b f Time Test—Wild Mimosa (IRE) **Clipper Group Holdings Ltd**
33 **MAY BLOSSOM,** 4, b f Mayson—Almond Branches **Hambleton Racing Ltd 2c & Partner**
34 **MR BEAUFORT,** 4, b g Cable Bay (IRE)—Tan Tan **The Mr Beaufort Syndicate**
35 **MUSCIKA,** 9, b g Kyllachy—Miss Villefranche **Gallop Racing I**
36 **NOMADIC EMPIRE (IRE),** 5, b g Kodiac—Beatify (IRE) **AlMohamediya Racing**
37 **ORBAAN,** 8, b g Invincible Spirit (IRE)—Contradict **Mr C. G. J. Chua**
38 **PEARLE D'OR (IRE),** 4, ch g Starspangledbanner (AUS)—Thoughtless Moment (IRE) **Mr C. G. J. Chua**
39 **PISANELLO (IRE),** 6, b g Raven's Pass (USA)—Painting (IRE) **Trendy Ladies**
40 **REEL PROSPECT (IRE),** 4, b g Highland Reel (IRE)—Candy Ride (IRE) **Hambleton Racing Ltd XXXIX & Partner**
41 **RHOSCOLYN,** 5, b g Territories (IRE)—Zeyran (IRE) **The Horse Watchers**
42 **RIOT (IRE),** 6, b g Kingman—Alexander Queen (IRE) **Rasio Cymru 1 & Windmill House Tb Ltd**
43 **ROYAL PARADE (IRE),** 4, b g Kodiac—Supreme Occasion (IRE) **Hambleton Racing Ltd XXXIX**
44 **SCOTCH MISTRESS,** 4, br f Twilight Son—La Rosiere (USA) **Empire State Racing Partnership**
45 **SEA GREY,** 4, gr g Ulysses (IRE)—Sensory (IRE) **Mrs A. Althani**
46 **SHELIR (IRE),** 7, gr g Dark Angel (IRE)—Shelina (IRE) **Akela Thoroughbreds Limited**
47 **SKY DEFENDER,** 7, b g Farhh—Al Mahmeyah **Mr H. R. Bin Ghedayer**
48 **SOUL SEEKER (IRE),** 6, b g Oasis Dream—Mad About You (IRE)
49 **STAR SHIELD,** 8, ch g Helmet (AUS)—Perfect Star **Middleham Park Racing & Mr P&G Upton**
50 **STARSHIBA,** 6, b g Acclamation—Dashiba **The Horse Watchers 7**
51 **SUDONA,** 8, b m Zoffany (IRE)—Vickers Vimy **D. Hulse S. Saunders & Lady Cobham**
52 **SUMMERGHAND (IRE),** 9, b g Lope de Vega (IRE)—Kate The Great **Mr H. R. Bin Ghedayer**
53 **TARTAN SKIRT (IRE),** 4, ch f Mehmas (IRE)—Scottish Exile (IRE) **Akela Thoroughbreds & Partners**
54 **TENDENTIOUS,** 5, b g Intello (GER)—Capacious **Quantum Leap Racing XIII & Partner**
55 **TRUEMAN,** 4, b g Wootton Bassett—Dazzling Rose **Clipper Group Holdings Ltd**
56 **TUSCAN (IRE),** 4, b g Churchill (IRE)—Orcia (IRE) **Mr F. Gillespie**
57 **VAL BASSETT (FR),** 5, b g Wootton Bassett—Val d'Hiver (FR) **Diamond Racing & Hurn Racing Club**
58 **WESTERNESSE (IRE),** 4, b g Camelot—Truthwillsetufree (IRE) **The Horse Watchers 7**
59 **YOUNG FIRE (FR),** 8, b g Fuisse (FR)—Young Majesty (USA) **Mr E. M. Sutherland**
60 **ZOZIMUS (IRE),** 5, b g Footstepsinthesand—Comment **The Horse Watchers 3**

THREE-YEAR-OLDS

61 B f Harry Angel (IRE)—Absolutely Right (IRE) **Mr H. R. Bin Ghedayer**
62 **ADVANTAGE (IRE),** ch g Profitable (IRE)—Dutch Rose (IRE) **Mr L. A. Bellman**
63 **AIHAWAWI (IRE),** b c Ribchester (IRE)—Hoyamy **Mr S. R. Bin Ghadayer**
64 **CHURCHELLA (IRE),** b f Churchill (IRE)—Elizabelle (IRE) **Hambleton Racing Ltd - 2C & P Gallagher**
65 **CONCERT BOY (IRE),** b g Kodiac—Perfect Fun **Windmill House Thoroughbred Limited 1**
66 **CONRI,** b g U S Navy Flag (USA)—Fresh Strike (IRE) **Akela Thoroughbreds Limited**
67 **CUAN,** b f Zoustar (AUS)—Moons of Jupiter (USA) **Akela Thoroughbreds Limited**

MR DAVID O'MEARA - continued

68 **DANCE ANGEL (IRE),** b f Harry Angel (IRE)—Dear Dancer (IRE) **Mr M. Rashid**
69 **DORA MILAJE (IRE),** b f Mondialiste (IRE)—Barefoot Contessa (FR) **Mr & Mrs G. Turnbull**
70 **FEEL THE NEED,** b g Ribchester (IRE)—Patterned **Hambleton Racing Ltd XXII & Partner 2**
71 **FINAL CREDIT (IRE),** b g New Bay—D'Oro Princess (USA) **Clipper Group Holdings Ltd**
72 **FULL OF SECRETS (IRE),** b g War Command (USA)—Shearling **One For The Road**
73 **HOLLY BLACKMORE (IRE),** b f Kessaar (IRE)—Divine Design (IRE) **XLCR Vehicle Management Ltd**
74 B f Time Test—Imperialistic (IRE) **Hot To Trot Racing 1**
75 **IRON LION,** gr c Roaring Lion (USA)—Stream Song **Mr & Mrs G. Turnbull**
76 **JUST JANET,** b f Zoustar (AUS)—Coral Sea **Mr T. J. Perkins**
77 **KENTUCKY BLUEGRASS,** b g Requinto (IRE)—Snowtime (IRE) **Empire State Racing Partnership**
78 B g Bated Breath—Lady Guinevere
79 **LAKOTA LADY (IRE),** ch f Sioux Nation (USA)—Queen Grace (IRE) **Hambleton Racing Ltd XXXIX**
80 **LEITZEL,** ch f Teofilo (IRE)—Trapeze **Mrs S. Holtby**
81 **OWNERS DREAM,** b c Time Test—Four Miracles **Mrs A. Althani**
82 **PALACE GARDENS (IRE),** gr f Gutaifan (IRE)—Dancewithastranger (IRE) **Mr D. K. Kelly**
83 **PURNIKA,** b f Mondialiste (IRE)—Nepali Princess (IRE) **Mr & Mrs G. Turnbull**
84 **QUEEN OF CORDOBA,** b f Almanzor (FR)—Arabian Beauty (IRE) **Cheveley Park Stud Limited**
85 **SENSEOFENTITLEMENT (IRE),** gr g El Kabeir (USA)—Amurra **J Bromfield & R Treacy**
86 B f Zoffany (IRE)—Solfege **Mr S. Morris**
87 **SOUTH DAKOTA SIOUX (IRE),** b g Sioux Nation (USA)—Dutch Lilly **Mr S. Morris**
88 **STAR OF LADY M,** gr f Havana Grey—Abraj Dubai (USA) **Mr M. A. Madden**
89 **THE ANGELUS BELLE (IRE),** b f Dandy Man (IRE)—Annamanamoux (USA) **S Morris & Partner**
90 **VALE DOLOBO DANCER (IRE),** ch g Mastercraftsman (IRE)—Tolzey (USA) **Ray Treacy & Richard Hames**
91 **YURINOV,** b g Mondialiste (IRE)—Bogside Theatre (IRE) **Mr & Mrs G. Turnbull**
92 **ZAKRAM (IRE),** gr g Markaz (IRE)—Mattinata **Mr P. Renoso**
93 **ZEBADAAY,** b g Adaay (IRE)—Springing Baroness **The Horse Watchers 5**

TWO-YEAR-OLDS

94 B g 18/03 Study of Man (IRE)—Albizzia (Archipenko (USA)) (12805)
95 **BAREFOOT WARRIOR (IRE),** b c 29/01 Saxon Warrior (JPN)—
Barefoot Contessa (FR) (Dansili) **Mr & Mrs G. Turnbull**
96 B c 02/03 Dandy Man (IRE)—Beatify (IRE) (Big Bad Bob (IRE)) **AlMohamediya Racing**
97 **BIG TED (IRE),** b c 18/04 Kodi Bear (IRE)—Bahati (IRE) (Intikhab (USA)) (37000) **Gallop Racing**
98 **BLAISE PASCAL (IRE),** ch g 16/04 Mondialiste (IRE)—Dream Child (IRE) (Pivotal) **Mr & Mrs G. Turnbull**
99 B f 28/01 U S Navy Flag (USA)—By Jupiter (Sea The Stars (IRE)) (38095) **Akela Thoroughbreds Limited**
100 B c 18/02 Gleneagles (IRE)—Caridade (USA) (Medaglia d'Oro (USA)) (22000)
101 Ch f 16/04 Night of Thunder (IRE)—Dawn Delight (Dawn Approach (IRE)) (40000) **Mr H. R. Bin Ghedayer**
102 B f 08/04 Profitable (IRE)—Dear Dancer (IRE) (Teofilo (IRE)) (2000) **Mr M. Rashid**
103 B c 27/01 Magna Grecia (IRE)—Dikta Del Mar (SPA) (Diktat) (64026) **AlMohamediya Racing**
104 **EDIE C (IRE),** b f 29/04 Mehmas (IRE)—Claramara (IRE) (Epaulette (AUS)) (65000) **Mr T. J. Perkins**
105 Ch f 02/01 Soldier's Call—Fairy Falcon (Sepoy (AUS)) **Clipper Group Holdings Ltd**
106 B c 03/04 Blue Point (IRE)—Hoyamy (Dark Angel (IRE)) (35000) **Mr S. R. Bin Ghadayer**
107 B f 13/02 U S Navy Flag (USA)—Hummingbird (IRE) (Fast Company (IRE)) (20952)
108 B f 19/04 Zoffany (IRE)—Inala (Cape Cross (IRE)) (38095) **Mr D. K. Kelly**
109 B c 19/03 New Bay—Kathy Sun (IRE) (Intikhab (USA)) (60024) **Mr N. J. Cable**
110 B c 25/04 Mondialiste (IRE)—Kocollada (IRE) (Kodiac) **Mr & Mrs G. Turnbull**
111 **LAD NEXT DOOR (IRE),** ch c 01/04 Soldier's Call—Calorie (Sea The Stars (IRE)) (25000) **Eagle Racing**
112 B f 28/02 Inns of Court (IRE)—Lady Lucia (IRE) (Royal Applause) (108043) **Akela Thoroughbreds Limited**
113 Ch c 14/04 Footstepsinthesand—
Lady Sandy (IRE) (Dandy Man (IRE)) (30000) **Jcg Chua & Akela Thoroughbreds Limited**
114 **LAVA STREAM (IRE),** gr f 05/03 Too Darn Hot—Stream Song (Mastercraftsman (IRE)) **Mr & Mrs G. Turnbull**
115 Ch f 05/04 Dandy Man (IRE)—Love Match (Danehill Dancer (IRE)) (12000) **Bronte Collection 1**
116 B f 02/03 Time Test—Lunar Phase (IRE) (Galileo (IRE)) (12000)
117 B f 23/02 Due Diligence (USA)—
Mary Stewart (IRE) (Dawn Approach (IRE)) (2857) **Withernsea Thoroughbred Limited**
118 B c 20/03 Bungle Inthejungle—Mochachino (IRE) (Fast Company (IRE)) (13605) **Mr Richard Mustill 1**
119 B f 28/04 Kodiac—Moon Club (IRE) (Red Clubs (IRE)) (28812) **Mr D. K. Kelly**
120 B f 15/04 James Garfield (IRE)—Musical Bar (IRE) (Barathea (IRE)) (13605)
121 B c 17/03 James Garfield (IRE)—Park Glen (IRE) (Tagula (IRE)) (55000) **Bronte Collection 1**

MR DAVID O'MEARA - continued

122 B f 26/04 Night of Thunder (IRE)—Penny Pepper (IRE) (Fast Company (IRE)) (150000) **Akela Thoroughbreds Limited**
123 B c 12/04 Zoustar (AUS)—Pepper Lane (Exceed And Excel (AUS)) (42857) **Mr K. Nicholson**
124 B f 06/03 Showcasing—Predicted (Dansili) (28000)
125 B c 11/04 Pastoral Pursuits—Roys Dream (Monsieur Bond (IRE))
126 **SAYALITTLEPRAYER,** b f 27/01 Time Test—Tight Lines (Fastnet Rock (AUS)) **Alderson Burke Francis**
127 Ch c 26/02 Waldgeist—So Unique (FR) (Siyouni (FR)) (48019)
128 B f 03/03 Waldgeist—Sound of Guns (Acclamation) (65000) **Akela Thoroughbreds Limited**
129 **SPRING FESTIVAL,** b c 18/04 Territories (IRE)—Kammaan (Diktat) **The LAM Partnership**
130 B c 20/02 Time Test—Station House (IRE) (Galileo (IRE)) (10000) **Mr R. Treacy**
131 **STEPS IN TIME (IRE),** b g 11/03 Shalaa (IRE)—Flash Dance (IRE) (Zamindar (USA)) **Mr & Mrs G. Turnbull**
132 Ch f 14/02 Masar (IRE)—Summer Thunder (USA) (Street Cry (IRE)) (1905) **Mr C. J. Miller**
133 B g 27/04 Pastoral Pursuits—Venus Rising (Observatory (USA))
134 Br c 04/03 Twilight Son—Zawiyah (Invincible Spirit (IRE)) (49524) **Hambleton Racing XXII & Jinky Farms**

Assistant Trainer: Jason Kelly.

Flat Jockey: Daniel Tudhope, Jason Watson. **Apprentice Jockey:** Mark Winn.

---

388 MRS DANIELLE O'NEILL, North Fawley

Postal: **The Old Granary, North Fawley, Wantage, Oxfordshire, OX12 9NJ**
Contacts: **PHONE 01488 639350 MOBILE 07931 193790**
EMAIL danni@fawleyhousestud.com

1 **BARDD (IRE),** 11, b g Dylan Thomas (IRE)—Zarawa (IRE) **Fawley House Stud**
2 **COMMANDER MILLER,** 9, b g Shirocco (GER)—Milliegait **Fawley House Stud**
3 **COMMODORE MILLER,** 6, b g Blue Bresil (FR)—Milliegait **Fawley House Stud**
4 **DEER HUNTER (IRE),** 7, b g Fame And Glory—Subtle Gem (IRE) **Fawley House Stud**
5 **GOAHEADWITHTHEPLAN (IRE),** 8, b g Stowaway—Backandillo (IRE) **Fawley House Stud**
6 **ROPEMAN,** 5, b g Telescope (IRE)—Ley Lady Grey **Fawley House Stud**
7 **VERSATILITY,** 9, b g Yeats (IRE)—Stravinsky Dance **Fawley House Stud**

Assistant Trainer: Stephen O'Neill.

---

389 MR JOHN O'NEILL, Bicester

Postal: **Hall Farm, Stratton Audley, Nr Bicester, Oxfordshire, OX27 9BT**
Contacts: **PHONE 01869 277202 MOBILE 07785 394128**
EMAIL jgoneill4@gmail.com

1 **CAPPARATTIN,** 8, b g Universal (IRE)—Little Miss Prim **J. G. O'Neill**
2 **ONURBIKE,** 15, b g Exit To Nowhere (USA)—Lay It Off (IRE) **J. G. O'Neill**
3 **SLEPTWITHMEBOOTSON,** 8, b m Universal (IRE)—Temple Heather **Ms L. M. Keane**
4 **SONGDANCE,** 6, b m Norse Dancer (IRE)—Overlay **Ms L. M. Keane**
5 **W S GILBERT,** 9, b g Librettist (USA)—Little Miss Prim **Ms L. M. Keane**

---

390 MR JONJO O'NEILL, Cheltenham

Postal: **Jackdaws Castle, Temple Guiting, Cheltenham, Gloucestershire, GL54 5XU**
Contacts: **PHONE 01386 584209**
EMAIL racingoffice@jonjooneillracing.com WEBSITE www.jonjooneillracing.com

1 **ALL THE GLORY,** 6, b m Fame And Glory—Glorybe (GER) **TopSpeed Thoroughbreds**
2 **ALSO KNOWN AS (IRE),** 5, b g Presenting—Jay Lo (IRE) **Mrs Fitri Hay**
3 **AN TAILLIUR (FR),** 7, gr g Authorized (IRE)—Dirama (FR) **Mr Pat Hickey**
4 **ANN D'ARABIE (FR),** 4, b f Montmartre (FR)—Mer d'Arabie (FR) **Anne, Harriet & Lucinda Bond**
5 **ANYHARMINASKING (IRE),** 6, b g Getaway (GER)—Collen Beag (IRE) **Mrs Gay Smith**
6 **ANYTRIXWILLDO (IRE),** 5, b g Flemensfirth (USA)—Blossom Trix (IRE) **Trixothetrade Partnership**
7 **ARE U WISE TO THAT (IRE),** 6, b g Walk In The Park (IRE)—Pretty Puttens (IRE) **Mr Michael Geoghegan**
8 **ARRIVEDERCI (FR),** 8, gr g Martaline—Etoile d'Ainay (FR) **Martin Broughton & Friends 1**
9 **BARE MEADOWS (IRE),** 6, b g Fame And Glory—Diamond Smiles **David's Partnership**
10 **BEACHCOMBER (FR),** 5, b g Bathyrhon (GER)—Alpes du Sud (FR) **The Hon Mrs E. J. Wills**
11 4, B f Walk In The Park (IRE)—Bella Venezia (IRE) **Mrs Fitri Hay**
12 **BERTIE'S BANDANA (IRE),** 6, b g Notnowcato—Alright Kitty (IRE) **DYDB Marketing Limited**
13 **BETHKA (IRE),** 5, gr m Walk In The Park (IRE)—Lakil Princess (IRE) **Mr Steve Killalea**
14 **BETTY'S BANJO (IRE),** 6, b m Fame And Glory—Betty's The Best (IRE) **Mrs Fitri Hay**
15 **BIG AMBITIONS (IRE),** 5, b g Shantou (USA)—Midnight Gift (IRE) **Exors of the Late Mr Trevor Hemmings**
16 **BIOWAVEGO (IRE),** 6, b g Presenting—Clara Bel La (IRE) **P14 Medical Ltd & Dydb Marketing Ltd.**
17 4, B g Westerner—Blazing Sonnet (IRE) **Eric Brook**
18 **BLUE SHARK (IRE),** 6, b g Shirocco (GER)—Meara Trasna (IRE) **The Ocean Partnership**
19 **BOB BOB RICARD (IRE),** 5, b g Bathyrhon (GER)—Russian Memories (FR) **Mr Paul Downing**
20 **BROOK BAY (IRE),** 5, b g Affinisea (IRE)—Orchid Bay **Martin Tedham & Wasdell Properties Ltd.**
21 **BROUGHSHANE (IRE),** 5, b g Mahler—Shuil Milan (IRE) **Mrs Gay Smith**
22 **CAME FROM NOTHING (IRE),** 5, b g Beat Hollow—By The Hour (IRE) **Mr Danny Walker**
23 **CAWTHORNE BANKER (IRE),** 5, b g Flemensfirth (USA)—Shees A Dante (IRE) **Eric Brook**
24 **CEDAR ROW (IRE),** 6, b g Westerner—Because of You (IRE) **Exors of the Late Mr Trevor Hemmings**
25 **CLOTH CAP (IRE),** 11, b g Beneficial—Cloth Fair (IRE) **Exors of the Late Mr Trevor Hemmings**
26 **COBOLOBO (FR),** 11, br g Maresca Sorrento (FR)—Nanou des Brosses (FR) **Anne, Harriet & Lucinda Bond**
27 **COEUR SEREIN (IRE),** 9, b g Fame And Glory—Balvenie (IRE) **Mr Andy Ralph**
28 **COLLECTORS ITEM (IRE),** 6, b g Flemensfirth (USA)—Leading Lady **Jackdaws Antiques**
29 **COPPER COVE (IRE),** 6, b g Jet Away—Cherry Island (IRE) **The Hon Mrs E. J. Wills**
30 **CREBILLY (IRE),** 6, b g Soldier of Fortune (IRE)—Blueberry Bramble (IRE) **Mr J. P. McManus**
31 **DANA'S GEM (IRE),** 5, b m Milan—At Present (IRE) **Mr Graham Freeman**
32 **DOLLAR BAE (IRE),** 6, b m Sageburg (IRE)—Molly Round (IRE) **The Perfect Partnership**
33 **DON MARIONE (IRE),** 4, b g My Dream Boat (IRE)—Russian Memories (FR) **Mrs Mary Walsh**
34 **DR HEGARTY (IRE),** 6, b g Califet (FR)—Millrock Lady (IRE) **P14 Medical Ltd & Dydb Marketing Ltd.**
35 **EASYSLAND (FR),** 9, b br g Gentlewave (IRE)—Island du Frene (FR) **Mr J. P. McManus**
36 **FAME AND CONCRETE (IRE),** 7, b g Fame And Glory—Masiana (IRE) **Mr Pat Hickey**
37 **FILE ILLICO (FR),** 8, b g Cokoriko (FR)—Noryane (FR) **The Hon Mrs E. J. Wills**
38 **FLIGHT DECK (IRE),** 9, b g Getaway (GER)—Rate of Knots (IRE) **Mr J. P. McManus**
39 **FRONT VIEW (FR),** 8, gr g Konig Turf (GER)—Tumavue (FR) **Mr J. P. McManus**
40 **GWENNIE MAY BOY (IRE),** 5, b g Mahler—Samsha (IRE) **Ms Gwendoline Clarke**
41 **HALF THE FREEDOM,** 7, ch g Haafhd—Freedom Song **The Free At Last Partnership**
42 **HASTHING (FR),** 6, b g Konig Turf (GER)—Trendy (FR) **Mr J. P. McManus**
43 **HEAD LAW (FR),** 6, b g Network (GER)—Law (FR) **Mr J. P. McManus**
44 **HEY DAY BABY (IRE),** 5, b m Soldier of Fortune (IRE)—Midnight Choir (IRE) **Coral Champions Club**
45 **HIGHLAND GETAWAY (IRE),** 5, b g Getaway (GER)—Hollygrove Rumba (IRE) **The Hon Mrs E. J. Wills**
46 **HIGHLANDS LEGACY,** 4, b g Kayf Tara—Highland Retreat **The Hon Mrs E. J. Wills**
47 **HUNGRY HILL (IRE),** 6, b g Fame And Glory—Echo Queen (IRE) **Martin Tedham & Wasdell Properties Ltd.**
48 **ILESTDANCINGSPIRIT (FR),** 5, ch g Coastal Path—Une d'Ex (FR) **The Magic Circle Partnership**
49 **IMPATIENT (FR),** 5, gr g Montmartre (FR)—Vista Palma (FR) **R. A. Bartlett**
50 **IMPERIAL BEDE (FR),** 5, b g Robin du Nord (FR)—Amusez Moi (FR) **Mr J. P. McManus**
51 **INCH HOUSE (IRE),** 6, b g Ocovango—Ask Hazel (IRE) **Mr Michael Geoghegan**
52 **INCHESTER D'AMSYL (FR),** 5, b g No Risk At All (FR)—Virgine Place (FR) **Mr Alan Nolan**
53 **IRON BRIDGE (IRE),** 7, b g Milan—Chit Chat **Exors of the Late Mr Trevor Hemmings**
54 **ISOCRATE (FR),** 5, b g Petillo (FR)—Popins (FR) **Mr Toby Cole**
55 **ITSO FURY (IRE),** 6, b g Fame And Glory—Qui Plus Est (FR) **Mrs Gay Smith**
56 **JAXONNE (FR),** 4, b g Free Port Lux—Noisete (FR) **Eric Brook**

MR JONJO O'NEILL - continued

57 **JOHNNYWHO (IRE),** 6, br g Califet (FR)—Howaya Pet (IRE) **Mr J. P. McManus**
58 **JUDICIAL LAW (IRE),** 6, b g Fame And Glory—Miss Overdrive **Mrs Gay Smith**
59 **KENTANDDOVER,** 6, b g Sir Percy—Kristalette (IRE) **Graeme Moore, Kate & Andrew Brooks**
60 **KIOTO SUN (GER),** 5, b g Pastorius (GER)—Kurfurstin (GER) **The Hon Mrs E. J. Wills**
61 **LAND GENIE,** 5, b g Flemensfirth (USA)—Queen of The Stage (IRE) **Mr Terry McKeever**
62 **LETMETELLUSOMETHIN,** 5, b g Shirocco (GER)—Early Dawne **Letmetellusomethin Partnership**
63 **LIMETREE BOY (IRE),** 7, b g Shirocco (GER)—Bells Glory (IRE) **Mr Mike Gaskell**
64 4, Br g Soldier of Fortune (IRE)—Littlegrace Lady (IRE) **Eric Brook**
65 **MACMOLLY,** 4, b f Black Sam Bellamy (IRE)—Flutter Bye (IRE) **Mrs Siobhan McAuley**
66 **MAGIC SEVEN (IRE),** 5, b g Doyen (IRE)—Magic Maze (IRE) **Mr Christopher Johnston**
67 **MAMMIES BOY (IRE),** 5, b g Getaway (GER)—Tonaphuca Girl (IRE) **What's The Craic Syndicate**
68 **MANINTHESHADOWS (IRE),** 8, ch g Well Chosen—
Grannys Kitchen (IRE) **Martin Tedham & Wasdell Properties Ltd.**
69 **MARDY MONO (IRE),** 5, b m Walk In The Park (IRE)—Koko Rose (IRE) **Anne, Harriet & Lucinda Bond**
70 **MAYPOLE CLASS (IRE),** 9, b g Gold Well—
Maypole Queen (IRE) **Delancey Real Estate Asset Management Limited**
71 **MELLIFICENT (IRE),** 6, b m Fame And Glory—Mise En Place **Mr Semore Kurdi**
72 **MERSEY STREET (IRE),** 5, b g Califet (FR)—Seeking Susan (IRE) **The Iveragh Syndicate**
73 **MERVEILLO,** 5, b g Archipenko (USA)—Merville (FR) **Mr J. P. McManus**
74 4, B g Court Cave (IRE)—Miss Parkington (IRE)
75 **MONBEG GENIUS (IRE),** 7, b g Shantou (USA)—Ella Watson (IRE) **Barrowman Racing Limited**
76 **MONTMARTIN (FR),** 5, gr g Montmartre (FR)—Asiana (FR) **Mr Pat Hickey**
77 **MORNING SPIRIT (IRE),** 8, b g Milan—Morning Legend (IRE) **Mr Pat Hickey**
78 **MR BIGGS,** 6, b g Telescope (IRE)—Linagram **P14 Medical Ltd T/A Platform 14**
79 **NEW BEGINNINGS,** 6, b g Flemensfirth (USA)—W Six Times **Martin Tedham & Wasdell Properties Ltd.**
80 **NITWIT (IRE),** 5, b g Shirocco (GER)—Lady Elite (IRE) **Mr Danny Walker**
81 **ON THE BANDWAGON (IRE),** 8, b g Oscar (IRE)—Deep Supreme (IRE) **Mr Alan Nolan**
82 **ONLY BY NIGHT (IRE),** 5, b m Affinisea (IRE)—Leyhill (IRE) **Mr Colin Russell**
83 **ORRISDALE (IRE),** 9, b g Oscar (IRE)—Back To Loughadera (IRE) **Miss Katharine Holland**
84 **OUR FRIEND MO (IRE),** 5, b m Mahler—Avoca Star (IRE) **Anne, Harriet & Lucinda Bond**
85 **PENS MAN (IRE),** 8, ch g Sholokhov (IRE)—Dudeen (IRE) **Girls on Lockdown**
86 **PERFECT SCORE (IRE),** 4, b f Mahler—Clarification (IRE) **The Rumble Racing Club**
87 **PETIT TONNERRE (FR),** 5, b g Waldpark (GER)—Perpette (FR) **Mr J. P. McManus**
88 **PIPER TOM (IRE),** 5, b g Presenting—Fly Town (IRE) **Noel Fehily Racing Syndicate - Piper Tom**
89 **PLAYTOGETAWAY (IRE),** 5, ch g Getaway (GER)—Play Trix (IRE) **Betfred**
90 **POWERFUL HERO (AUS),** 6, br g Better Than Ready (AUS)—Glennie West (AUS) **Creative Earth Productions**
91 **PRESENT CHIEF (IRE),** 9, b g Presenting—Daizinni **Mrs K Squire, Chapman, Goodman**
92 **PRIDE ROCK (IRE),** 5, b g Westerner—Byerley Beauty (IRE) **Delancey & Mr Michael O'Flynn**
93 **PRINCE ESCALUS (IRE),** 8, b g Jeremy (USA)—So You Said (IRE) **The As You Like It Syndicate**
94 **PURE BLUE (IRE),** 4, b g Blue Bresil (FR)—Katalina **Martin Broughton & Friends 5**
95 **PYFFO (IRE),** 5, b g Shantou (USA)—Maryota (FR) **Mr Andy Ralph**
96 **RED DIRT ROAD (IRE),** 6, b g Fame And Glory—Miss Otis Regrets (IRE) **Mr Danny Walker**
97 **REGAL BLUE (IRE),** 6, b g French Navy—Deceptive **Martin Tedham & Wasdell Properties Ltd.**
98 **ROCCO ROYALE (IRE),** 5, b g Shirocco (GER)—Gayeroyale (IRE) **The Royales**
99 **ROCK OF THE NATION (IRE),** 5, b g Soldier of Fortune (IRE)—
You Take Care (IRE) **Mr Michael O'Flynn & Delancey**
100 **RULER LEGEND (IRE),** 4, b g Camelot—Avenue Dargent (FR) **Mrs Jonjo O'Neill**
101 **SACRE COEUR (FR),** 7, gr m Montmartre (FR)—Singaporette (FR) **David's Partnership**
102 **SAINT DAVY (FR),** 6, b g Balko (FR)—Saintejoie (FR) **Mrs Gay Smith**
103 **SERMANDO (FR),** 9, ch g Fuisse (FR)—Josephjuliusjodie (IRE) **Creative Earth Productions**
104 **SOARING GLORY (IRE),** 8, b g Fame And Glory—Hapeney (IRE) **Mr Pat Hickey**
105 **SOLDIEROFTHESTORM (IRE),** 5, ch g Soldier of Fortune (IRE)—Fiddlededee (IRE) **Mr Tom Bond**
106 **SPITALFIELD (IRE),** 5, b g Mahler—Hollygrove Bonnie (IRE) **Mrs Mairead Liston**
107 **SPRINGWELL BAY,** 6, b g Kayf Tara—Winning Counsel (IRE) **Mrs Gay Smith**
108 **STAY IF U WANT TO (IRE),** 4, ch g Soldier of Fortune (IRE)—Fiddlededee (IRE) **Mrs Peter Bond**
109 **SYD DEE YEATS (IRE),** 4, b f Yeats (IRE)—Croise Naofa (IRE) **Mrs Siobhan McAuley**
110 **TAP N GO LEO (IRE),** 4, b g Malinas (GER)—Avealittlepatience (IRE) **The Three Cabelleros**
111 **THE GOONER (IRE),** 5, b g Flemensfirth (USA)—Rose of Milana (IRE) **Gay & Paul Smith**
112 **TIME FOR A PINT (IRE),** 6, b g Ask—Eatons Way (IRE) **& Wordsworth**
113 **TIME TO GET UP (IRE),** 10, ch g Presenting—Gales Return (IRE) **Mr J. P. McManus**

MR JONJO O'NEILL - continued

114 **TOUTE CHIC (IRE),** 4, b f Violence (USA)—Creative Director (USA) **Mrs Carolyn Kendrick**
115 **TRACK AND TRACE (IRE),** 6, b g Mahler—Princess Bella (IRE) **Bruton Street**
116 **TRAPISTA (FR),** 6, b m Golden Horn—Quezon Sun (GER) **Mr J. P. McManus**
117 **UNSINKABLE MOLLY B,** 5, br m Blue Bresil (FR)—Perfect Promise (IRE) **Mr Danny Walker**
118 **UPTOWN LADY (IRE),** 8, b m Milan—Lady Zephyr (IRE) **Russell McAllister**
119 **VALENTINE GETAWAY (IRE),** 5, b m Getaway (GER)—Awesome Miracle (IRE) **The Valentine Partnership**
120 **WALK IN MY SHOES (IRE),** 7, b m Milan—Bonnies Island (IRE) **Creative Earth Productions**
121 **WALK OF NO SHAME (IRE),** 6, b m Walk In The Park (IRE)—
Ultimate Echo (IRE) **Mr P. G. Taiano, Mrs Sharon Wilks**
122 **WELLINGTON ARCH,** 4, b g Blue Bresil (FR)—Moyliscar **Mr Mike Gaskell**
123 **WIDEEYEDANDLEGLESS (IRE),** 6, b g El Salvador (IRE)—Ardcolm Collen (IRE) **London Design Group Limited**
124 **WILFUL (IRE),** 4, br g Westerner—Shuil Milan (IRE) **Mrs Fitri Hay**
125 **YES DAY (IRE),** 5, b g Court Cave (IRE)—Jiggle Joules (IRE) **Mr Ian Bullions**
126 **YES INDEED (FR),** 6, b g Martaline—She Hates Me (IRE) **Mr Michael O'Flynn & Delancey**
127 **YULONG MAGICREEF (IRE),** 6, b g Fastnet Rock (AUS)—Lindikhaya (IRE) **The Magic Circle Partnership**
128 **ZABEEL CHAMPION,** 6, b g Poet's Voice—Stars In Your Eyes **Martin Tedham & Wasdell Properties Ltd.**
129 **ZONDA (FR),** 5, gr g Martaline—Tornada (FR) **Martin Broughton Racing Partners 2**

THREE-YEAR-OLDS

130 **GLIMPSE OF GLORY,** b c Passing Glance—Dauphine Ereine (FR) **Martin, Jocelyn & Steve Broughton**

TWO-YEAR-OLDS

131 B c 31/03 Order of St George (IRE)—Fiddlededee (IRE) (Beneficial) **Mrs Peter Bond**

NH Jockey: Kevin Brogan, Richie McLernon, Jonjo O'Neill Jr, Nick Scholfield. **Conditional Jockey:** Jamie Brace, Ben Macey. **Amateur Jockey:** AJ O'Neill, Jack Wilmot.

---

391 MR BRIAN O'ROURKE, Upper Lambourn

Postal: **Maple Tree House, Newbury Road, Great Shefford, Hungerford, Berkshire, RG17 7DT**
Contacts: **PHONE 01488 670290**
EMAIL brian@brianorourkebloodstock.com

1 **BANSHEE (IRE),** 4, b f Iffraaj—Reflective (USA) **B. E. Nielsen**
2 **MAGNIFICENCE (FR),** 5, b m Kingman—Alamarie (FR) **Brian O'Rourke Bloodstock Ltd**
3 **SPINSTER (IRE),** 4, b f Sea The Stars (IRE)—Melodramatic (IRE) **B. E. Nielsen**

THREE-YEAR-OLDS

4 **KOKOMO,** b f Kodiac—Betty The Thief (IRE) **Mr D. Ward**

---

392 MR JOHN O'SHEA, Newnham-on-Severn

Postal: **The Stables, Bell House, Lumbars Lane, Newnham, Gloucestershire, GL14 1LH**
Contacts: **WORK 07891 496837 PHONE 01452 760835 MOBILE 07891 496837**
WEBSITE www.johnoshearacing.co.uk

1 **AWORKINGMAN,** 5, b g Kalanisi (IRE)—Try The Bell (IRE) **The Cross Racing Club**
2 **BANTRY,** 4, b g Lope de Vega (IRE)—Elysian
3 **DUNDORY (IRE),** 7, b g Holy Roman Emperor (IRE)—Lady Bones (IRE) **The Cross Racing Club**
4 **FIDDLERS GREEN (IRE),** 4, b g Awtaad (IRE)—Luanas Pearl (IRE)

MR JOHN O'SHEA - continued

5 **FIGHT FOR IT (IRE),** 5, b g Camelot—Dorothy B (IRE) **K. W. Bell**
6 **FLIP MODE,** 6, b g Lethal Force (IRE)—Canukeepasecret **Mr S. P. Price**
7 **FORTUNE TRAVELLER,** 6, b m Soldier of Fortune (IRE)—When In Roam (IRE) **Mr J. R. Salter**
8 **GET THE VALUE (IRE),** 5, b g Getaway (GER)—Valsugana (IRE) **The Cross Racing Club**
9 **GLEN ESK,** 6, b g Kyllachy—Ski Slope **K. W. Bell**
10 **HAPPY COMPANY (IRE),** 9, ch g Fast Company (IRE)—Miss Mauna Kea (IRE) **Mr R. Cooper**
11 **HARVIE WALLBANGER (IRE),** 7, b g Mahler—Initforthecrack (IRE) **K. W. Bell**
12 **JUST THE MAN (FR),** 7, gr g Rajsaman (FR)—Yachtclubgenoa (IRE) **K. W. Bell**
13 **KASWARAH (IRE),** 5, b m Mehmas (IRE)—Beautiful Dancer (IRE) **The Cross Racing Club**
14 **LETTER OF THE LAW (IRE),** 4, b g Lawman (FR)—Lady Ravenna (IRE) **Mr N. G. H. Ayliffe**
15 **MACS DILEMMA (IRE),** 5, b g Coulsty (IRE)—Ohsosecret **Miss H. O. G. Jones**
16 **MY OPINION (IRE),** 4, b g Pride of Dubai (AUS)—Trust Your Opinion (IRE) **K. W. Bell**
17 **OUTBACK FRONTIERS (IRE),** 7, ch g Sans Frontieres (IRE)—Bord de Loire (FR) **Mr S. P. Price**
18 **PUNCHBOWL FLYER (IRE),** 6, b g Dream Ahead (USA)—All On Red (IRE) **The Cross Racing Club**
19 **ROMANOVICH (IRE),** 4, gr g Dark Angel (IRE)—My Favourite Thing **The Cross Racing Club**
20 **SCARLET RUBY,** 6, b m Al Kazeem—Monisha (FR) **The Cross Racing Club**
21 **SOME NIGHTMARE (IRE),** 6, b g Dream Ahead (USA)—Isolde's Return **The Cross Racing Club**
22 **SONIC GOLD,** 7, b g Schiaparelli (GER)—Sonic Weld **K. W. Bell**
23 **THE LION STRIKES (IRE),** 4, b g The Last Lion (IRE)—Seasons **The Cross Racing Club**
24 **THREEWAYS BRUCE,** 4, b g Heeraat (IRE)—Under My Spell **Mr J. R. Salter**

THREE-YEAR-OLDS

25 **CHARMING OSCAR,** b g Charm Spirit (IRE)—Shiba (FR) **Mr Oscar Singh & Miss Priya Purewal**
26 **DANCING GYPSY,** ch g Intello (GER)—Paquerettza (FR) **Mr A. Kanji**
27 **MARISITTA,** b f Intello (GER)—Nessita **Mr A. Kanji**
28 **STELLA HOGAN (IRE),** ch f Gustav Klimt (IRE)—Fenagh (IRE) **The Cross Racing Club**

Flat Jockey: Gina Mangan, Luke Morris.

---

393 MR GEOFFREY OLDROYD, Pocklington

Postal: **Yapham Grange, Pocklington, York, Yorkshire, YO42 1PB**
Contacts: **PHONE 01653 668279**
EMAIL oldroydgeoff@gmail.com

1 **DOCTOR KHAN JUNIOR,** 4, b g Muhaarar—Ladies Are Forever **Bond Thoroughbred Limited**
2 **RISE HALL,** 8, b g Frankel—Forever Bond **Bond Thoroughbred Limited**
3 **SKY HIGH GIRL,** 4, b f Muhaarar—Forever's Girl **Bond Thoroughbred Limited**

THREE-YEAR-OLDS

4 **MARGOT ROBBIE,** b f Muhaarar—Ladies Are Forever **Bond Thoroughbred Limited**
5 **VERY CLASSY,** b f Muhaarar—Classic Code (IRE) **Bond Thoroughbred Limited**

TWO-YEAR-OLDS

6 B f 10/03 Calyx—Axxeleration (Monsieur Bond (IRE)) **Bond Thoroughbred Limited**
7 Br g 11/04 Calyx—Bond Artist (IRE) (Excellent Art) (2857) **Bond Thoroughbred Limited**
8 Ch f 18/04 Calyx—Forever's Girl (Monsieur Bond (IRE)) (15238) **Bond Thoroughbred Limited**
9 B c 02/03 Blue Point (IRE)—Ladies Are Forever (Monsieur Bond (IRE)) **Bond Thoroughbred Limited**
10 Ch f 28/01 Showcasing—Thatsallimsaying (IRE) (Dandy Man (IRE)) **Bond Thoroughbred Limited**

---

394 MR HENRY OLIVER, Worcester

Postal: **Kinnersley Racing Stables , Kinnersley , Severn Stoke, Worcester, Worcs, WR8 9JR**
Contacts: **PHONE 01299 890143 MOBILE 07701 068759**
EMAIL henryoliverracing@hotmail.co.uk WEBSITE www.henryoliverracing.co.uk

1 **ADAMHILL (IRE),** 8, b g Oscar (IRE)—Benefit of Porter (IRE) **Mr F. K. Baxter**
2 **BOYS OF WEXFORD,** 6, b g Millenary—Floradorado **R. G. Whitehead**
3 **CAN'T BEAT HISTORY (IRE),** 7, ch g Beat Hollow—Histologie (FR) **Mr F. K. Baxter**
4 **CAPTAIN ATTRIDGE (IRE),** 5, b g Raven's Pass (USA)—High Queen (IRE) **Ms S. A. Howell**
5 **COASTGUARD STATION (IRE),** 7, ch g Dylan Thomas (IRE)—Shuruwaat (IRE) **Catchtwentytwo,Andyfreight Holdingsltd**
6 **FORTUNE COOKIE (IRE),** 6, b m Soldier of Fortune (IRE)—Tukawhile (IRE) **Enduring Love Syndicate**
7 **GENEROUS DAY (IRE),** 11, b g Daylami (IRE)—Our Pride **R. G. Whitehead**
8 **GENTLE FRANK,** 7, ch g Gentlewave (IRE)—Himitas (FR) **Ms S. A. Howell**
9 **JESSIE LIGHTFOOT (IRE),** 9, b m Yeats (IRE)—Needle Doll (IRE) **Mr P. Price**
10 **KEY FACTOR (IRE),** 5, b g Ol' Man River (IRE)—Grannys House (IRE) **R. G. Whitehead**
11 **PATIENT OWNER (IRE),** 8, b g Getaway (GER)—La Femme Blanche (IRE) **Catchtwentytwo,Andyfreight Holdingsltd**
12 **SKINFLINT (IRE),** 11, b g Scorpion (IRE)—Gales Hill (IRE) **Mrs S. A. Gent**
13 **STRIKING OUT,** 9, b g Malinas (GER)—Cresswell Ruby (IRE) **Bill Hawkins & Catch Twenty Two**
14 **THE BIG BITE (IRE),** 10, b g Scorpion (IRE)—Thanks Noel (IRE) **Mr N T Griffith & H M Haddock**

NH Jockey: James Davies.

---

395 MR JAMIE OSBORNE, Upper Lambourn

Postal: **The Old Malthouse, Upper Lambourn, Hungerford, Berkshire, RG17 8RG**
Contacts: **PHONE 01488 73139 MOBILE 07860 533422**
EMAIL info@jamieosborne.com WEBSITE www.jamieosborne.com

1 **AIKHAL (IRE),** 4, b c Galileo (IRE)—Diamond Fields (IRE) **Ms Mary Slack**
2 **APPARATE,** 7, b g Dubawi (IRE)—Appearance **Mr C. Ryan**
3 **BOAFO BOY,** 4, b g Lope de Vega (IRE)—Royal Empress (IRE) **Mr A. M. A. S. Al-Hajri**
4 **CASHEW (IRE),** 4, b f Bated Breath—Taste The Salt (IRE) **Miss L. G. Robinson**
5 **CLADDAGHDUFF (IRE),** 5, b g Estidhkaar (IRE)—Attracted To You (IRE) **David N. Reynolds & Chris Watkins**
6 **CLIFFS OF CAPRI,** 9, b g Canford Cliffs (IRE)—Shannon Spree **Melbourne 10 Racing**
7 **CREMA INGLESA (IRE),** 5, b m Lope de Vega (IRE)—Creme Anglaise **Hunscote Stud Limited**
8 **DUTY OF CARE,** 5, b g Kingman—Exemplify **Gallagher Bloodstock Limited**
9 **ETON COLLEGE (IRE),** 6, b g Invincible Spirit (IRE)—Windsor County (USA) **Mr J. A. Osborne**
10 **GAME NATION (IRE),** 4, b g Le Havre (IRE)—Mt of Beatitudes (IRE) **Jacobs Construction Ltd&city Gaming Ltd**
11 **HASHTAGMETOO (USA),** 6, b m Declaration of War (USA)—Caribbean Princess (USA) **The Other Club**
12 **HIERARCHY (IRE),** 4, ch g Mehmas (IRE)—Cheworee **Dominic Griffiths & David Kavanagh**
13 **HUSCARI (IRE),** 4, gr f Caravaggio (USA)—Greatest Place (IRE) **Mrs H Allanson & Partners**
14 **INIGO JONES,** 5, b g New Approach (IRE)—Spacious **Gary Allsopp Partnership**
15 **ISLE OF SARK (USA),** 5, b g Kitten's Joy (USA)—Endless Fancy (USA) **Gary Allsopp Partnership**
16 **JERSEY GIFT (IRE),** 5, b g Nathaniel (IRE)—Pharadelle (IRE) **Mr Mr A. Taylor & Partner**
17 **LUNAR SPACE (IRE),** 5, ch g Dawn Approach (IRE)—Luminaria (IRE) **The Judges & Partner**
18 **MILLTOWN STAR,** 6, b g Roderic O'Connor (IRE)—Hail Shower (IRE) **Gary Allsopp & Partner**
19 **MISS SLIGO (IRE),** 6, b m New Approach (IRE)—Illandrane (IRE) **The Q Party**
20 **MR ALCHEMY,** 6, gr g Leroidesanimaux (BRZ)—Albaraka **The Q Party**
21 **NEW YORK CITY (IRE),** 4, b c Invincible Spirit (IRE)—Rajeem **Mr G Bryce & Partner**
22 **OUZO,** 7, b g Charm Spirit (IRE)—Miss Meltemi (IRE) **The Other Club**
23 **RAISING SAND,** 11, b g Oasis Dream—Balalaika **Nick Bradley Racing 22 & Partner**
24 **STEVENSON,** 4, b g Havana Gold (IRE)—In Your Time **V7 Recruitment Ltd**

MR JAMIE OSBORNE - continued

THREE-YEAR-OLDS

25 **ALL DUNN,** b g Oasis Dream—Bimbo **Alasdair Simpson,Victoria Dunn & Partner**
26 **ARDAD'S GREAT,** b f Ardad (IRE)—Belle Dormant (IRE) **Barratt Racing**
27 **BALBOA,** b g Mondialiste (IRE)—Reachforthestars (IRE) **Mr F. A. A. Nass**
28 **BEN LOMOND (IRE),** b g Gleneagles (IRE)—Coquette Rouge (IRE) **Mr J Palmer-Brown**
29 **CLARKO'S BACK,** b g Harry Angel (IRE)—Dubai Bounty **Seymour Bloodstock Pty Ltd**
30 **CONSTITUTION,** b g Churchill (IRE)—Pack Together **Nick Bradley Racing 26**
31 **EXECUTIVE DECISION (IRE),** b f Ardad (IRE)—Belle Travers **Barratt Racing**
32 **GREAVSIE (IRE),** ch c Equiano (FR)—Path of Peace **Homecroft Wealth Racing VIII**
33 **HAZEL BEAR,** ch f Zoustar (AUS)—Meeting Waters **Mr J. A. Osborne**
34 **JOPHIEL,** b f Harry Angel (IRE)—Atlaal **Griffiths de Kock Racing Syndicate**
35 **KARADOW (IRE),** ch c Starspangledbanner (AUS)—Vera Lilley (IRE) **Miss L. G. Robinson**
36 **KEHLANI (IRE),** b f Muhaarar—Pyrenean Queen (IRE) **Ms L G Robinson & Partner**
37 **KYNSA (IRE),** b f Make Believe—Fact Or Folklore (IRE) **Miss L. G. Robinson**
38 **LADY BIANCA,** b f Sir Percy—Six Cents (IRE) **Hunscote Stud Limited**
39 **NUTHATCH,** b f Expert Eye—Tanouma (USA) **Mr J. A. Osborne**
40 **ORMOLULU (IRE),** b f Havana Gold (IRE)—Camdora (IRE) **The Hon A. A. Blyth**
41 B c Galileo Gold—Red Blanche (IRE)
42 **STYLE OF LIFE (IRE),** b f New Bay—Caterina di Cesi **Clipper Group Holdings Ltd**
43 **VALKYRIAN (IRE),** b f Kodiac—Darrinah (IRE) **Holmes Family**

TWO-YEAR-OLDS

44 B f 26/04 Eqtidaar (IRE)—Alice Girl (IRE) (Oratorio (IRE)) (14000) **The 10 Club**
45 B f 20/03 Showcasing—Casting Spells (Lope de Vega (IRE)) (24010) **The 10 Club**
46 B c 08/04 Ribchester (IRE)—Crecy (Refuse To Bend (IRE)) (9000)
47 B f 16/02 Sea The Stars (IRE)—Fabulist (Dubawi (IRE)) (100000) **Holmes Family**
48 Gr f 13/03 Dark Angel (IRE)—Fashion Family (FR) (Frankel) (58000) **Holmes Family**
49 B f 27/02 Iffraaj—Galmarley (Sir Percy) (170000) **Holmes Family**
50 B c 04/04 Due Diligence (USA)—Gilt Linked (Compton Place) (11000) **The 10 Club**
51 B f 17/04 Havana Gold (IRE)—Granny Franny (USA) (Grand Slam (USA)) (55000) **EIC Racing Ltd Redvers & Winkworth**
52 B f 18/01 Showcasing—I'm Donna (IRE) (Frankel) (45000) **Holmes Family**
53 B f 24/03 Dandy Man (IRE)—Illegally Blonde (IRE) (Lawman (FR)) **Barratt Racing**
54 B f 17/04 Elzaam (AUS)—Marigold (FR) (Marju (IRE)) (8003) **The 10 Club**
55 B f 02/05 Ardad (IRE)—News Desk (Cape Cross (IRE)) (27211) **The 10 Club**
56 B c 05/01 Soldier's Call—Pursuit of Magic (IRE) (Kingman) (37000) **The 10 Club**
57 Br c 07/03 Dandy Man (IRE)—Queen Andorra (IRE) (Finsceal Fior (IRE)) (32000) **V7 Recruitment Ltd**
58 B c 25/04 The Last Lion (IRE)—Quiania (IRE) (Dansili) (22000) **The 10 Club**
59 B c 28/03 U S Navy Flag (USA)—Rohain (IRE) (Singspiel (IRE)) (8804) **The 10 Club**
60 **SIGNATURE BLUE (IRE),** b c 23/02 Gregorian (IRE)—La Femme (IRE) (Cape Cross (IRE)) (19208) **Mr & Mrs I. H. Bendelow**
61 B br c 04/04 Dandy Man (IRE)—Snow Scene (IRE) (Singspiel (IRE)) (25610) **The 10 Club**
62 B c 28/04 Inns of Court (IRE)—Suffer Her (IRE) (Whipper (USA)) **The 10 Club**

Assistant Trainer: Jimmy McCarthy.

Flat Jockey: Nicola Currie, Saffie Osborne.

---

396 MISS EMMA OWEN, Nether Winchendon

Postal: **Muskhill Farm, Nether Winchendon, Aylesbury, Buckinghamshire, HP18 0EB**
Contacts: **PHONE 01844 290282 MOBILE 07718 984799**
EMAIL emma.l.owen@hotmail.com

1 **ASHAREDMOMENT,** 8, b m Swiss Spirit—Shared Moment (IRE) **Miss E. L. Owen**
2 **DIVINE MESSENGER,** 9, b g Firebreak—Resentful Angel **Miss E. L. Owen**

MISS EMMA OWEN - continued

3 **MILLDEAN PANTHER,** 7, b g Mayson—Silver Halo **Miss E. L. Owen**
4 **MUSICAL COMEDY,** 12, b g Royal Applause—Spinning Top **Miss E. L. Owen**
5 **RED HANRAHAN (IRE),** 12, b g Yeats (IRE)—Monty's Sister (IRE) **Miss E. L. Owen**
6 **REIGNITE,** 8, b g Firebreak—Resentful Angel **Miss E. L. Owen**

---

397 MR JAMES OWEN, Newmarket

Postal: **Indian Lodge,Green Ridge Stables, Hamilton Road, Newmarket, Suffolk, CB8 7JQ**
Contacts: **PHONE 01638 676513**
EMAIL office@jamesowenracing.com

1 **ENTHUSED (IRE),** 6, b g Zoffany (IRE)—Question Times **Mr J. P. Owen**
2 **SMART DEAL,** 4, b g Kingman—Bargain Buy **James Owen Racing Club**
3 **THE BIG LENSE (IRE),** 10, b g Court Cave (IRE)—Megans Joy (IRE) **James Owen Racing Club**
4 **TWILIGHT GIRL (IRE),** 10, b m Craigsteel—Twilight Princess (IRE) **Mr J. P. Owen**

---

398 MR PATRICK OWENS, Newmarket

Postal: **Authorized Yard, St Gatien Stables, Vicarage Road, Newmarket, Suffolk, CB8 8HP**
Contacts: **PHONE 07796 036878**
EMAIL powens@patrickowens.co.uk

1 **ANGLO SAXSON (IRE),** 6, ch g Starspangledbanner (AUS)—Obligada (IRE) **Daniel MacAuliffe & Anoj Don**
2 **PERFECT THUNDER,** 4, b f Night of Thunder (IRE)—Perfect Delight **Daniel MacAuliffe & Anoj Don**
3 **TOOMEVARA (IRE),** 4, b g Bated Breath—Kerrys Requiem (IRE) **Mr Patrick Owens**

THREE-YEAR-OLDS

4 **ALMARIN (IRE),** b g Belardo (IRE)—Princess Severus (IRE) **Pinnacle Thoroughbreds 1**
5 **AWTAAR (IRE),** b f No Nay Never (USA)—Za'hara (IRE) **Mr M. S. Al Shahi**
6 **BALLYKESSANGEL (IRE),** b f Kessaar (IRE)—Sun Angel (IRE) **TP Racing Syndicate**
7 **GOODFELLA (IRE),** b g Footstepsinthesand—Musical Jewel (IRE) **Memento Vivere Racing**
8 **RAYENA (FR),** b f Harry Angel (IRE)—Rima (IRE) **S Fisher A Kirwan E Prosser & J Burke**

TWO-YEAR-OLDS

9 **AJWAAD (FR),** b c 31/03 Blue Point (IRE)—Madhulika (FR) (Marchand de Sable (USA)) (44018) **Mr M. S. Al Shahi**
10 **ODDYSSEY,** ch c 05/03 Ulysses (IRE)—Last Echo (IRE) (Whipper (USA)) (10500) **Pinnacle Thoroughbreds 3**
11 **TIORA,** b f 21/02 Time Test—Eleusis (Elnadim (USA)) (7203) **Pinnacle Thoroughbreds 2**

---

399 MR HUGO PALMER, Malpas

Postal: **Manor House Stables, Shay Lane, Malpas, Cheshire, SY14 8AD**
Contacts: **WORK 01948 820485 MOBILE 07824 887886**
EMAIL info@manorhousestables.com

1 **ARION,** 4, b f Dubawi (IRE)—Filia Regina **Lady Derby & Lady Ritblat**
2 **BATTERED,** 9, b g Foxwedge (AUS)—Swan Wings **Mr H. Palmer**
3 **BOX TO BOX (IRE),** 4, b g Kodiac—Alyaafel **The Running Order Partnership**

MR HUGO PALMER - continued

4 **BRAD THE BRIEF,** 6, b g Dutch Art—Kenzadargent (FR) **Chasemore Farm LLP**
5 **COMMONSENSICAL,** 5, b g Bated Breath—Critical Path (IRE) **More Turf Racing**
6 **DEDENNE,** 4, b f Kingman—Roedean (IRE) **Miss S. Y. D. Goh**
7 **FLAMING RIB (IRE),** 4, b c Ribchester (IRE)—Suddenly (GER) **Dale Dolan Dooley Owen**
8 **GIFTED RULER,** 6, b g Muhaarar—Dubai Bounty **Mr D. R. Passant**
9 **GLITTERING CHOICE,** 4, b f Havana Gold (IRE)—Adorable Choice (IRE) **Mr J. D. Brown**
10 **HE'S A GENTLEMAN (IRE),** 4, gr g Dark Angel (IRE)—Cut No Ice (IRE) **Owen Rothwell Studholme**
11 **HE'S A KEEPER (IRE),** 6, gr g Brazen Beau (AUS)—Silver Grey (IRE) **Mr N. Canning**
12 **HERETIC (IRE),** 4, ch g Galileo Gold—Al Jawza **Highclere Tbred Racing, C Fahy & Partner**
13 **HOW IMPRESSIVE (IRE),** 4, ch g Starspangledbanner (AUS)—Bright New Day (IRE) **Middleham Park Racing XCIX**
14 **NOLTON CROSS (IRE),** 4, b g Dark Angel (IRE)—Pandora's Box (IRE) **Middleham Park Racing XCII**
15 **RAJINSKY (IRE),** 7, b g Zoffany (IRE)—Pink Moon (IRE) **Jastar Capital Limited**
16 **ROMAN DRAGON,** 4, b g Heeraat (IRE)—Trixie Malone **Nick Hughes & Owen Promotions Ltd**
17 **ROUDEMENTAL (IRE),** 4, b g Footstepsinthesand—Nonetheless (IRE) **Roudee Racing**
18 **SOLENT GATEWAY (IRE),** 5, b g Awtaad (IRE)—Aoife Alainn (IRE) **Mr D. R. Passant & Hefin Williams**
19 **VICTORIA FALLS (IRE),** 4, b f Heeraat (IRE)—Lady Red Oak **Mr D. R. Passant**
20 **ZOFFEE,** 7, b g Zoffany (IRE)—Mount Crystal (IRE) **Mr A. E. Peterson**

THREE-YEAR-OLDS

21 **ACCLAIMER,** b c Acclamation—Lady Red Oak **Mr D. R. Passant**
22 **ACHERNAR (IRE),** ch c Galileo Gold—Operissimo **Mr L. L. Lee**
23 **AL MOTASIM,** b g Lope de Vega (IRE)—Maureen (IRE) **Al Shaqab Racing UK Limited**
24 Ch c Iffraaj—Anticipation (FR) **Batters & Owen**
25 **AUSDAISIA (IRE),** b g Australia—Young Daisy Miller (IRE) **Faulkner, Joynson, Morris & Simpson**
26 B g Free Eagle (IRE)—Candle Lit (IRE) **Military Syndicate & Mrs Clodagh McStay**
27 **CAPITANO,** br c Sea The Stars (IRE)—Chachamaidee (IRE) **Eddie & Fiona Carswell**
28 **CARVED IN STONE,** b g Mastercraftsman (IRE)—Bride Unbridled (IRE) **Al Asayl Bloodstock Ltd**
29 **CHELSEA GREEN (IRE),** b f U S Navy Flag (USA)—Agapantha (USA) **Chelsea Thoroughbreds - CG**
30 **CHRONOGRAPH,** ch c Recorder—Basque Beauty **Sheikh I. S. Al Khalifa**
31 **DARK STRIKE,** b c Lightning Spear—Dark Reckoning **The Roof Partnership**
32 **DEBATER,** br f No Nay Never (USA)—Now You're Talking (IRE) **Sheikh I. S. Al Khalifa**
33 **DHARIYE (FR),** b c Al Wukair (IRE)—Al Dweha (IRE) **Al Shaqab Racing UK Limited**
34 **DOUBLE OBAN,** b g Territories (IRE)—Zaaneh (IRE) **Mr R. Cotter**
35 **DRAGONBALL PRINCE (IRE),** b g Dragon Pulse (IRE)—Island Odyssey **& Maguire**
36 **ELOPED (FR),** b f Golden Horn—Mary's Choice (GER) **HackettJohnPaulRickMike**
37 **ERTEBAT,** b g Unfortunately (IRE)—The Chemist **Al Shaqab Racing UK Limited**
38 **FARNALEEN (IRE),** b f No Nay Never (USA)—Conniption (IRE) **Lady Mimi Manton & Partners**
39 **FLEUR DE MER (IRE),** gr f Dark Angel (IRE)—Hespera **Al Asayl Bloodstock Ltd**
40 **FOOLS GAMBIT (IRE),** b g Expert Eye—Gold Again (USA) **Check Mates Partnership**
41 **FRITILLARIA (IRE),** b f Galileo Gold—Pale Orchid (IRE) **Mr E. D. Tynan**
42 Ch g Footstepsinthesand—Gabardine **Al Shaqab Racing UK Limited**
43 **GOLDEN MOONSHAKE (IRE),** ch g Zoffany (IRE)—Shake The Moon (GER) **Mr A. E. Peterson**
44 B c Raven's Pass (USA)—Haughtily (IRE) **M & C Hirst**
45 **IMPERIAL ACE (IRE),** b c Lope de Vega (IRE)—Cottonmouth (IRE) **Michael Blencowe & J P M O'Connor**
46 **INVINCIBLE PASS (IRE),** br c Invincible Spirit (IRE)—Lovely Pass (IRE) **Dr A. Ridha**
47 **KRISTAL KLEAR (IRE),** b f Sioux Nation (USA)—Kristal Xenia (IRE) **Owen Grundy Carswell Studholme**
48 **MACHO MANIA (IRE),** b g Camacho—Dame Judi (IRE) **Deva Racing (CO)**
49 **MAID IN LONDON,** ch f Roaring Lion (USA)—Maid To Dream **Tony O'Connor & Reins Partners 2**
50 **MELWOOD BOY,** b g Massaat (IRE)—Kirrin Island (USA) **O'Halloran Owen Satchell**
51 **MONKMOOR PIP,** b g Fast Company (IRE)—Jal Mahal **Mr D. R. Passant**
52 **NAKANO (IRE),** b f Saxon Warrior (JPN)—Silky (IRE) **Lacy, Tynan**
53 **NAMMOS,** ch f Territories (IRE)—Doobahdeedoo (USA) **Babington, Gallagher, Al-Khail & Partners**
54 **NAVARRE EXPRESS,** gr f Roaring Lion (USA)—Great Court (IRE) **Hunscote Stud Ltd & Mrs Lynne Maclennan**
55 **O G BEACHWEAR,** b f Washington DC (IRE)—Show Willing (IRE) **Owen Promotions Limited**
56 **ORDER OF MALTA,** b c Lope de Vega (IRE)—Along Came Casey (IRE) **Batters Passant Owen**
57 **PEARLY STAR,** b f Zoustar (AUS)—Pearly Spirit (FR) **Michael Owen Racing Club**
58 **POWER OF GOLD,** b c Golden Horn—Power of Light (IRE) **Dr A. Ridha**
59 **PRINCE OF ZENDA,** b g Kingman—Priceless Jewel **Middleham Park Racing XXX**
60 **PRINCESS NIYLA,** b f Night of Thunder (IRE)—Coillte Cailin (IRE) **Sustainable Building Services UK Ltd**

MR HUGO PALMER - continued

61 **PROUD DRAGON (IRE),** ch g Dragon Pulse (IRE)—Proud Maria (IRE) **Blencowe Brothers**
62 **PUB CLUB,** b c Kodiac—Usra (IRE) **Ms Diamond & Owen Promotions Ltd**
63 B f Heeraat (IRE)—Raktina **Owen Promotions Limited**
64 **ROSE DONNELLY,** b f Massaat (IRE)—Trixie Malone **R Kent & Owen Promotions Ltd**
65 **RUNNING STAR,** ch c Zoustar (AUS)—Castle Hill Cassie (IRE) **Mr D. P. Howden**
66 **SAMAGON,** b g Lightning Spear—Velvet Revolver (IRE) **Mr A. S. Shawe**
67 **SARACEN HEAD,** b c Showcasing—Maelia (USA) **Done Ferguson Mason Owen**
68 **SELF ACLAIM (IRE),** b c Aclaim (IRE)—Selfara **The Roof Partnership**
69 **SIR RAJ (IRE),** b g Holy Roman Emperor (IRE)—Pink Moon (IRE) **Jastar Capital Limited**
70 **SOLUTRE (IRE),** ch c Havana Grey—Seven Magicians (USA) **Mr A. S. Shawe**
71 **SOUFFIONNE (IRE),** ch g No Nay Never (USA)—Coral Shell (IRE) **Mr A. S. Shawe**
72 **STENTON GLIDER (IRE),** b f Dandy Man (IRE)—Crystal Malt (IRE) **J & T Mairs**
73 **SUPASPECIALAWESOME (IRE),** ch g Cotai Glory—Special Chocolate (FR) **& Maguire**
74 **TEDDY'S DAWN (IRE),** b f Dawn Approach (IRE)—Suddenly (GER) **Dolan & Dooley**
75 **TERRY TWO JAGS,** b c Fountain of Youth (IRE)—Siren Song **Owen Promotions Limited**
76 **THE RENEGADE,** gr g Mastercraftsman (IRE)—Belle Above All **FOMO Syndicate**
77 **WICCAN,** b f Zoustar (AUS)—Evil Spell **Widden Stud & Partners**
78 **WOLF OF KINGSTREET (IRE),** b g Dandy Man (IRE)—Moonline Dancer (FR) **M3 Racing Limited**
79 **ZIVANIYA,** ch c Cityscape—Rosie Royce **Mr A. S. Shawe**

TWO-YEAR-OLDS

80 B f 17/02 Caravaggio (USA)—Darajaat (USA) (Elusive Quality (USA)) (47619) **Manor House Stables LLP**
81 B f 02/02 Time Test—Dream Melody (Selkirk (USA)) (14406)
82 B c 27/03 Exceed And Excel (AUS)—Facilitate (Bated Breath) **Mr L. L. Lee**
83 **HACKMAN (IRE),** ch c 15/03 Mehmas (IRE)—Ishimagic (Ishiguru (USA)) (123810) **The Gene Genies**
84 **HE'S GOT GAME (IRE),** b c 28/03 Oasis Dream—Thafeera (USA) (War Front (USA)) (49620) **Mr G. A. Hall**
85 B g 27/04 Buratino (IRE)—Kirrin Island (USA) (Arch (USA)) **Mr M. Satchell**
86 Gr f 19/04 Phoenix of Spain (IRE)—Kristal Xenia (IRE) (Xaar) (28812)
87 B c 26/01 Havana Grey—Madame Paco (Paco Boy (IRE)) (40016)
88 Ch f 18/03 No Nay Never (USA)—Magic America (USA) (High Yield (USA)) (112045)
89 B c 13/02 Kodiac—Martina Franca (Paco Boy (IRE)) (42857) **Manor House Stables LLP**
90 B c 03/03 Zoffany (IRE)—Miss Margarita (Scat Daddy (USA)) (16006) **More Turf Racing**
91 Ch c 13/04 Showcasing—Modify (New Approach (IRE)) (57143) **Manor House Stables LLP**
92 B c 18/02 Belardo (IRE)—Petits Potins (IRE) (Verglas (IRE)) (125000) **Mr L. L. Lee**
93 **PITNEY (IRE),** b c 23/04 Mehmas (IRE)—Mercifilly (FR) (Whipper (USA)) (48019) **The Gene Genies**
94 Gr c 11/04 Havana Grey—Serena Grae (Arakan (USA)) (19048) **Roudee Racing**
95 **SOLDIER'S GOLD (IRE),** b c 15/04 Soldier's Call—Copperbeech (IRE) (Red Ransom (USA)) **Nobody Ever Replies**
96 **SOUTH KENSINGTON (IRE),** b f 22/03 Blue Point (IRE)—Moonvoy (Cape Cross (IRE)) (85000)
97 B f 05/03 Too Darn Hot—Spirit Raiser (IRE) (Invincible Spirit (IRE)) **Lord W. G. Vestey**
98 Gr ro f 12/04 Havana Grey—Springing Baroness (Bertolini (USA)) (85000) **Middleham Park Racing XCII**
99 **THE BITTER MOOSE (IRE),** b c 08/04 Kodiac—Baroness (IRE) (Declaration of War (USA)) (140000) **AJT Group**
100 Br f 28/01 Sioux Nation (USA)—The Dylan Show (IRE) (Showcasing) (20952) **Manor House Stables LLP**
101 **TIERNEY (IRE),** b f 06/05 Mehmas (IRE)—Madam Macie (IRE) (Bertolini (USA)) (115000) **The Gene Genies**
102 **UNDER THE SUN,** b c 18/02 Golden Horn—Hasten (IRE) (Montjeu (IRE)) **Al Asayl Bloodstock Ltd**
103 B c 28/01 Kodiac—Usra (IRE) (Requinto (IRE))
104 B c 27/02 Havana Grey—Voicemail (Poet's Voice) (80000)
105 **WATCHA MATEY,** b c 16/03 Land Force (IRE)—
Kenzahope (FR) (Kendargent (FR)) (24010) **Austin, Moran, Rowlands, McCallum**

400 MR JOSEPH PARR, Newmarket

Postal: **5 Greenfields, Newmarket, Suffolk, CB8 8DR**
Contacts: **PHONE 07876 262169**
EMAIL josephparr@hotmail.com

1 **ARTHUR'S VICTORY (IRE),** 5, b m Buratino (IRE)—Impressive Victory (USA) **Mr M. Downey**
2 **BEDFORD BLAZE (IRE),** 5, b g Dandy Man (IRE)—Hawaajib (FR) **The Bears Syndicate**
3 **ENIGMATIC (IRE),** 9, b g Elnadim (USA)—Meanwhile (IRE) **Trevor & Ruth Milner**
4 **G'DAAY,** 5, b g Adaay (IRE)—Gilt Linked **Trevor & Ruth Milner**
5 4, B c Churchill (IRE)—Ghizlaan (USA) **Martley Hall Stud Ltd.**
6 **GIOVANNI BAGLIONE (IRE),** 4, gr g Caravaggio (USA)—Like A Star (IRE) **Trevor & Ruth Milner**
7 **HELLO ME (IRE),** 5, b m Mehmas (IRE)—Safe Place (USA) **Martley Hall Stud Ltd.**
8 **LETHAL TOUCH,** 4, gr f Lethal Force (IRE)—Loving Touch **Trevor & Ruth Milner**
9 **MC'TED,** 5, b g Garswood—Granny McPhee **Mr S. Bond**
10 **NAADYAA,** 4, b f Muhaarar—Nasmatt **The Skills People Group Ltd**
11 **NACHOS CHEESE (IRE),** 4, b f Australia—Artwork Genie (IRE) **Lash Come on Bear LLP**
12 **PRINCE OF BEL LIR (IRE),** 5, b g Prince of Lir (IRE)—Harvest Joy (IRE) **The Skills People Group Ltd**
13 **ROMAN DYNASTY (IRE),** 5, b g Mehmas (IRE)—Empress Ella (IRE) **Trevor & Ruth Milner**
14 **SUN FESTIVAL,** 5, b g Toronado (IRE)—Raymi Coya (CAN) **Mr S. Bond**
15 **THE GREEN MAN (IRE),** 4, b g Acclamation—Lydia Becker **Mr J. F. Stocker**

THREE-YEAR-OLDS

16 **A TOUCH OF SILVER,** ch f Ulysses (IRE)—Astromagick **Mr M. R. Gates**
17 **COVERT LEGEND,** b c Zoustar (AUS)—Miss You Too **Mr K. K. B. Ho**
18 B f Time Test—Diamond Run **Mrs S. J. Hearn**
19 **HIYA HIYA (IRE),** b g Exceed And Excel (AUS)—Somoushe (IRE) **Mr M. N. M. A. Almutairi**
20 **JUAN COOL DUDE (IRE),** b c Profitable (IRE)—Invernata (FR) **Trevor & Ruth Milner**
21 **KALAMUNDA,** b c Zoustar (AUS)—Karen's Caper (USA) **Trevor & Ruth Milner**
22 **KAMANIKA (IRE),** gr f Roaring Lion (USA)—Raddeh **Trevor & Ruth Milner**
23 **KILCUMMIN (IRE),** gr g Mastercraftsman (IRE)—Aspasi **The Kilcummin Partnership**
24 **LIBERTY MOUNTAIN,** b f Washington DC (IRE)—Cresta Gold **Mrs S. E. Tellwright**
25 **MC'S WAG,** b f Mayson—Granny McPhee **A J McNamee & L C McNamee**
26 **REVOLUCION,** ch g Havana Grey—Hope Island (IRE) **Team Lodge Racing**
27 **TOPO CHICO (IRE),** gr f Havana Grey—Conversational (IRE) **Mr D. Evans**

TWO-YEAR-OLDS

28 B f 23/02 Magna Grecia (IRE)—Cosmos Pink (Dansili) (42000)
29 Gr c 28/03 Mastercraftsman (IRE)—Elegant Peace (IRE) (Intense Focus (USA)) (20000)
30 B f 09/02 Advertise—Lady Alienor (IRE) (Elusive Quality (USA)) (3000) **Mrs S. J. Hearn**
31 Ch c 13/05 No Nay Never (USA)—Meeting (IRE) (Galileo (IRE)) (75000) **Trevor & Ruth Milner**

401 MR MARK PATTINSON, Epsom

Postal: **Flat 3, White House Stables, Tattenham Corner Road, Epsom, Surrey, KT18 5PP**
Contacts: **MOBILE 07961 835401**

1 **IMPERIAL CULT (IRE),** 4, ch g Sea The Moon (GER)—Proserpine (USA) **Miss N. J. Miliam**
2 **NUBOUGH (IRE),** 7, b g Kodiac—Qawaasem (IRE) **M I Pattinson Racing**
3 **PERFECT SYMPHONY (IRE),** 9, b g Dandy Man (IRE)—Fields of Joy (GER) **Mr M. Pattinson**
4 **RAINBOW SIGN,** 5, b g Adaay (IRE)—Pax Aeterna (USA) **Forever Amber**
5 **RAY'S THE ONE,** 6, b g Mount Nelson—Tenpence **M I Pattinson Racing**
6 **SIX O'CLOCK SWILL,** 5, ch g Bobby's Kitten (USA)—Golden Bottle (USA) **G. B. Partnership**

THREE-YEAR-OLDS

7 **KWIZ (IRE),** b g Prince of Lir (IRE)—Preferable (IRE) **Kathy & Margaret Elliott**

402 MR BEN PAULING, Naunton, Gloucestershire

Postal: **Ben Pauling Racing Ltd, Naunton Downs Estate, Naunton, Cheltenham, Gloucestershire, GL54 3AE**
Contacts: **WORK 01451 821252 MOBILE 07825 232888**
WORK EMAIL Hannah@benpaulingracing.com EMAIL ben@benpaulingracing.com WEBSITE www.benpaulingracing.com

1 **A DEFINITE GETAWAY (IRE),** 5, b g Getaway (GER)—Def It Vic (IRE) **Bruton Street UK - III**
2 **ACTIVE DUTY (FR),** 4, b g Almanzor (FR)—Minakshi (FR) **Mr T. P. Radford**
3 **AMARILLOBYMORNING (IRE),** 5, br g Soldier of Fortune (IRE)—Ultimate Echo (IRE)
4 **ANIGHTINLAMBOURN (IRE),** 9, b m Gold Well—Madgehil (IRE) **The Megsons**
5 **APPLE ROCK (IRE),** 9, b g Royal Anthem (USA)—Wayward Cove **Presumption in Favour Partnership**
6 **AWAYTHELAD (IRE),** 6, b g Getaway (GER)—Jennys Joy (IRE) **Geri and The Pacemakers**
7 **BAD (FR),** 4, gr g Morandi (FR)—Love Over Gold (FR) **Mr D. P. Howden**
8 **BANGERS AND CASH (IRE),** 7, b g Fame And Glory—Cash Customer (IRE) **OAP II**
9 **BETTY'S BELLE,** 6, b m Schiaparelli (GER)—Burgundy Betty (IRE) **Mrs B. M. Henley**
10 **BETTY'S TIARA,** 5, b m Kayf Tara—Burgundy Betty (IRE) **Mrs B. M. Henley**
11 **BINGO LITTLE (IRE),** 4, b g Elusive Pimpernel (USA)—Ile En Crise (IRE) **The Megsons**
12 **BOBBY BOW (IRE),** 9, b g Frammassone (IRE)—Bramble Cottage (IRE) **Mrs G. Morgan**
13 **BOWTOGREATNESS (IRE),** 7, br g Westerner—Miss Baden (IRE) **Harry Redknapp & Sophie Pauling**
14 **CHADLINGTON LAD (IRE),** 5, b g Estidhkaar (IRE)—Fuaigh Mor (IRE) **Mr R. J. Catling**
15 **CHESS PLAYER (IRE),** 8, ch g No Risk At All (FR)—Merci Jandrer (FR) **Mrs Rachel Brodie & Mr John Brodie**
16 **CLAPTON HILL,** 5, b g Dunaden (FR)—Rosita Bay **The Clapton Hill Partnership**
17 4, B g Alkaadhem—Clongeen Star (IRE) **Pimlico Racing - Fitzdares Cotswolds**
18 **COULDBEAWEAPON (IRE),** 6, ch g Mahler—Wild Fuchsia (IRE) **Easy Going Racing**
19 **DE BARLEY BASKET (IRE),** 10, b g Alkaadhem—Lady Willmurt (IRE) **Mrs S N J Embiricos & Ms A Embiricos**
20 **DEL LA MAR ROCKET (IRE),** 7, b g Fame And Glory—Pipe Lady (IRE) **Les de La Haye & Martin Mundy**
21 **DENSWORTH (IRE),** 6, b g Kayf Tara—Mariah's Way **OAP Syndicate**
22 4, B g Shirocco (GER)—Diamond Gesture (IRE)
23 **DUNSKAY (FR),** 4, gr g Night Wish (GER)—Ardissone (FR) **OAP Syndicate**
24 **ENCASHMENT,** 6, b m Casamento (IRE)—Burton Ash **Mrs S. Lee & Mr E. Lee**
25 **FAWSLEY SPIRIT (IRE),** 10, b g Stowaway—Apple Trix (IRE) **Mrs Rachel Brodie & Mr Clive Bush**
26 **FIERCELY PROUD (IRE),** 4, b g Iffraaj—Estiqaama (USA) **Mr T. P. Radford**
27 **FINE CASTING (IRE),** 7, b g Shantou (USA)—Fine Fortune (IRE) **Mrs S. P. Davis**
28 **FLASH IN THE PARK (IRE),** 5, b g Walk In The Park (IRE)—Mrs Masters (IRE) **The Megsons**
29 **GALAHAD THREEPWOOD,** 6, b g Nathaniel (IRE)—Tesary **The Megsons**
30 **GENTLEMAN VALLEY (FR),** 7, b g Kapgarde (FR)—Richona (FR) **The Megsons**
31 **GET PREPARED,** 8, b g Black Sam Bellamy (IRE)—Star Ar Aghaidh (IRE) **The Aldaniti Partnership**
32 **GETAWAY DRUMLEE (IRE),** 7, ch g Getaway (GER)—Miss Leele (IRE) **Mrs G. Collier**
33 **GIEVES (IRE),** 5, ch g Shirocco (GER)—Lady of Appeal (IRE) **Pump & Plant Services Ltd**
34 **GLOBAL CITIZEN (IRE),** 11, b g Alkaadhem—Lady Willmurt (IRE) **The Megsons**
35 **GLORIOUS OSCAR (IRE),** 6, b g Fame And Glory—Flowers On Sunday (IRE) **Mr & Mrs J Tuttiett**
36 **GOLDEN AMBITION (IRE),** 4, ch g Mount Nelson—Serpentine Mine (IRE) **The Shamrock and Rose Syndicate**
37 **GREATNESS AWAITS (IRE),** 4, b g Clodovil (IRE)—Top Act (FR) **Deva Racing GA**
38 **HARDY BOY (FR),** 6, gr g Diamond Boy (FR)—Alize du Berlais (FR) **Martin & Lynn Jones**
39 **HARPER'S BROOK (IRE),** 7, b g Ask—Un Jour D Ete (FR) **The Megsons**
40 **HENRY'S FRIEND (IRE),** 6, b g Shirocco (GER)—Easter Bonnie (IRE) **E Troup & Family**
41 **HERCULES MORSE,** 5, b g Blue Bresil (FR)—Ishka Baha (IRE) **The Megsons**
42 **HONOR GREY (IRE),** 8, b g Flemensfirth (USA)—Rose Island **Mr & Mrs J Tuttiett**
43 **I'M RAVENOUS (FR),** 5, b g Spanish Moon (USA)—Berry Emery (FR)
44 **JOE DADANCER (IRE),** 6, b g Califet (FR)—Sister Phoebe (IRE) **The Megsons**
45 **JUST CHASING MAY,** 4, b g Isfahan (GER)—Just For Show (IRE) **Mrs F. Hook**
46 **KERRYHILL (IRE),** 5, b g Soldier of Fortune (IRE)—Highland Flower (IRE)
47 **LADY ROBINN,** 6, br m Robin des Champs (FR)—Friendly Craic (IRE) **Nicholas Piper & Claire E. Piper**
48 **LE BREUIL (FR),** 11, ch g Anzillero (GER)—Slew Dancer **Mrs E. A. Palmer**
49 **LE GRAND LION (FR),** 7, gr g Turgeon (USA)—Grande Cavale (FR) **The Lion Tamers**
50 **LES'S DESTINY STAR (IRE),** 4, b g Blue Bresil (FR)—Spendajennie (IRE) **Mr L. De la Haye**
51 **LES'S JERSEY ROYAL (IRE),** 4, b g Soldier of Fortune (IRE)—Milano Glen (IRE) **Mr L. De la Haye**
52 **LOOKINGDANDY,** 5, b g Telescope (IRE)—Danisa **Mr N. Holder & Mr P. Glanville**
53 **MALINELLO,** 8, b g Malinas (GER)—Wyldello **Martin & Lynn Jones**
54 **MAN OF MY DREAMS (IRE),** 5, b g Champs Elysees—Storm Away (IRE) **Maranto Manor**
55 **MATTY TOO,** 4, b g Mattmu—Bustling Darcey **The Megsons**

MR BEN PAULING - continued

56 **MISTER WATSON,** 9, b g Mawatheeq (USA)—Island Odyssey **The Jp Girls**
57 **MOLE COURT (IRE),** 6, b g Court Cave (IRE)—Running Wild (IRE) **Mr O. Troup**
58 **MONTY BODKIN (IRE),** 4, b g Walk In The Park (IRE)—La Segnora (FR) **The Megsons**
59 **MRS GRIMLEY (IRE),** 5, b m Australia—Yakshini (IRE) **FB Racing Club**
60 **MUCHO MAS (IRE),** 7, b g Fame And Glory—Ceart Go Leor (IRE) **Mrs J. A. Wakefield**
61 **NESTOR PARK (FR),** 10, b g Walk In The Park (IRE)—Cila (FR) **Mrs S. P. Davis**
62 **NO QUESTIONS ASKED (IRE),** 5, ch g Ask—Fancy Fashion (IRE) **Newton LDP Ltd**
63 **NOELS DESTINY STAR,** 4, b f Blue Bresil (FR)—Who's Afraid **Mr L. De la Haye**
64 **NORLEY (IRE),** 8, b g Yeats (IRE)—No Moore Bills **Mrs G. Morgan**
65 **NORTHERN BOUND (IRE),** 9, b g Fruits of Love (USA)—Noble Choice **Mrs E. L. Kendall**
66 **NOT AT PRESENT (IRE),** 8, br g Presenting—Anna Magdalena (IRE) **Mrs Rachel Brodie & Mr John Brodie**
67 **ON SPRINGS (IRE),** 8, b g Mahler—Wild Fuchsia (IRE) **Sophie Pauling & Les de La Haye**
68 **ONE TOUCH (IRE),** 9, b g Court Cave (IRE)—Star Bui (IRE) **Martin & Lynn Jones**
69 4, B g Westerner—Onewayortheother (IRE)
70 **OPTIMISE PRIME (IRE),** 7, b g Shantou (USA)—Wilde Ruby (IRE) **Mrs Rachel Brodie & Mr John Brodie**
71 **PENCREEK (FR),** 10, ch g Konig Shuffle (GER)—Couture Fleurs (FR) **Mrs G. S. Worcester**
72 **PHIL THE SOCK (IRE),** 6, b g Fame And Glory—Quinnsboro Native (IRE) **The Stewkley Shindiggers Partnership**
73 **PIC ROC (IRE),** 5, ch g Mount Nelson—South Africa (FR) **Mrs E. L. Kendall**
74 **PLATENIUM (FR),** 4, b g Night Wish (GER)—Bella Lawena (IRE) **Mrs F. Hook**
75 **POMEROL GEORGE (IRE),** 7, b g Fame And Glory—My Native (IRE) **A Fine Claret**
76 **QUINTA DO MAR (IRE),** 8, b g Califet (FR)—Cara Mara (IRE) **The Bourtoneers**
77 4, B g Kayf Tara—Rattlin **The OA's**
78 **RAVEN'S TOWER (USA),** 13, b g Raven's Pass (USA)—Tizdubai (USA) **Mrs S. Pauling**
79 **ROCK ON COWBOY (IRE),** 6, b g Snow Sky—Rose of Dunamase (IRE) **The Megsons**
80 **SAMAZUL,** 5, b g Blue Bresil (FR)—Samandara (FR) **OAP III**
81 **SAMUEL SPADE (GER),** 4, b g Myboycharlie (IRE)—Summarily (IRE) **Mrs E. A. Palmer**
82 **SANDA RENA (IRE),** 5, b m Getaway (GER)—Conors Miracle (IRE) **The Megsons**
83 **SCOTCH ON DA ROCKS (IRE),** 6, b g Fame And Glory—Final Episode (IRE) **Dominic Griffiths & David Kavanagh**
84 **SERJEANT PAINTER,** 8, b g Royal Applause—Szabo's Art **Mrs S. Pauling**
85 **SEVERANCE,** 7, b g Nathaniel (IRE)—Decorative (IRE) **The Megsons**
86 **SFORZA CASTLE (IRE),** 5, b g Milan—Jet Empress (IRE) **Mrs S. Pauling**
87 **SHAKEM UP'ARRY (IRE),** 9, b g Flemensfirth (USA)—Nun Better (IRE) **Mr H. Redknapp**
88 **SILVER ATOM (IRE),** 5, gr g Vadamos (FR)—Dalaway (IRE) **Mrs E. A. Palmer**
89 **SLIPWAY (IRE),** 8, b g Stowaway—Little Sioux (IRE) **Mrs S. N. J. Embiricos**
90 **SOUND AND FURY (IRE),** 6, b g Milan—Tarantella Lady **Foxtrot Racing Fortyfive West**
91 **SPECIAL BUDDY (IRE),** 9, b g Robin des Pres (FR)—Annees d'Or (IRE) **Mrs S. Pauling**
92 **SPORTING MIKE (IRE),** 6, b g Walk In The Park (IRE)—Kates The Boss (IRE) **Mrs Rachel Brodie & Mr John Brodie**
93 **STORMINHOME (IRE),** 6, b g Frammassone (IRE)—Storminoora (IRE) **The Megsons**
94 4, B g Mahler—Suetsu (IRE) **The Cob Nuts**
95 **SULOCHANA (IRE),** 6, br m Lope de Vega (IRE)—Yakshini (IRE) **Mr P. Brocklehurst**
96 **THE EMINENT GOOSE,** 7, ch m Malinas (GER)—Hope Royal **The Ben Pauling Racing Club**
97 **THE GREY FALCO (FR),** 8, gr g Falco (USA)—Take A Chance (FR) **The Roaming Roosters**
98 **THE JUKEBOX MAN (IRE),** 5, b g Ask—My Twist (IRE) **Mr H. Redknapp**
99 **THE MACON LUGNATIC,** 9, b g Shirocco (GER)—Didbrook **Genesis Racing Partnership II**
100 **TWIG,** 8, b g Sulamani (IRE)—Southern Exit **Mrs G. Morgan**
101 **UNIT SIXTYFOUR (IRE),** 8, b g Sholokhov (IRE)—Dixie Chick (IRE) **Owners Group 062**
102 **WEE TONY (IRE),** 5, b g Califet (FR)—Afar Story (IRE) **Mr S Reddin & Partner**
103 **WHATSUPWITHYOU (IRE),** 9, b g Shantou (USA)—Whats Up Britta (IRE) **Co-Foundations Ltd**
104 **WICK GREEN,** 10, b g Sagamix (FR)—Jolly Dancer **Shy John Partnership**
105 **YOUR DARLING (IRE),** 8, b g Shirocco (GER)—Carries Darling **Lord W. G. Vestey**

THREE-YEAR-OLDS

106 **BINGLEY CROCKER (IRE),** b g Bungle Inthejungle—Ellbeedee (IRE) **The Megsons**
107 **BLUE BETTY,** b f Blue Bresil (FR)—Bit of A Geordie **The Megsons**
108 **KAYLAN (GER),** b br g Protectionist (GER)—Koffi Cherie (GER) **The Megsons**
109 **KINGLY FIGHTER (GER),** br g Lord of England (GER)—Konigin (GER) **Mrs Rachel Brodie & Mr John Brodie**
110 **POLLY POTT,** b f Muhaarar—Must Be Me **The Megsons**
111 **TALYSH,** b f Linda's Lad—Persian Forest **Mrs Rachel Brodie & Mr John Brodie**
112 **WONDERFUL DELIGHT (GER),** ch g Amaron—Wonderful Pearl (GER) **Mrs G. Morgan**

MR BEN PAULING - continued

113 **WRECKLESS ERIC,** ch g Masterstroke (USA)—Santa Diana (FR) **The Megsons**

TWO-YEAR-OLDS

114 **WIND RIVER (IRE),** ch c 18/04 Sioux Nation (USA)—Decorative (IRE) (Danehill Dancer (IRE)) (80032) **The Megsons**

Assistant Trainer: Thomas David, **Head Girl:** Gill Tate, **Secretary:** Hannah Vowles.

NH Jockey: Kielan Woods, Luca Morgan.

---

403 MR SIMON PEARCE, Newmarket

Postal: **1 Whitegates, Newmarket, Suffolk, CB8 8DS**
Contacts: **PHONE 01638 664669**
EMAIL spearceracing@hotmail.co.uk

1 **ABRAAJ (FR),** 5, b g Shalaa (IRE)—Wonderous Light (IRE) **Conde, Hanger, Jones, Noone & Noone**
2 **BARTHOLOMEW J (IRE),** 9, ch g Fast Company (IRE)—Mana (IRE) **Nigel Hanger, Eric Jones & Partners**
3 **BRAZEN IDOL,** 4, br g Brazen Beau (AUS)—Babylon Lane **The Infinite Folly Partnership**
4 **DESERT BOOTS,** 5, b g Belardo (IRE)—City Chic (USA) **Deerfield Syndicate**
5 **FLOY JOY (IRE),** 7, b g Arcadio (GER)—The Scorpion Queen (IRE) **Nigel Hanger & Eric Jones**
6 **FRISKY,** 4, ch f Bated Breath—Thrill **Deerfield Syndicate**
7 **FULL INTENTION,** 9, b g Showcasing—My Delirium **Killarney Glen & Lydia Pearce**
8 **HANOVERIAN KING (GER),** 5, b g Showcasing—Hasay **The Showstoppers**
9 **RACING COUNTRY (IRE),** 8, b g Dubawi (IRE)—Movin' Out (AUS) **Deerfield Syndicate**
10 **RED EVELYN,** 5, ch m Garswood—Skara Brae **Deerfield Syndicate**
11 **STORM CATCHER (IRE),** 5, b g Vadamos (FR)—Next Life **Nigel Hanger & Eric Jones**
12 **TARAVARA (IRE),** 5, b g The Gurkha (IRE)—Red Blossom **Killarney Glen**
13 **WRENS ROSE (FR),** 6, b m Zanzibari (USA)—Montoria (FR) **Deerfield Syndicate**

THREE-YEAR-OLDS

14 **GEORGIA MADELEINE (IRE),** ch f Pearl Secret—Rocknahardplace (IRE) **Howard Duff Racing**
15 **GRIGIO (IRE),** gr c El Kabeir (USA)—Prequel (IRE) **Killarney Glen**
16 **TRACKMAN,** b c Cracksman—Devotion (IRE) **Killarney Glen**

---

404 MR OLLIE PEARS, Malton

Postal: **The Old Farmhouse, Beverley Road, Norton, Malton, North Yorkshire, YO17 9PJ**
Contacts: **MOBILE 07760 197103**
EMAIL info@olliepearsracing.co.uk WEBSITE www.olliepearsracing.co.uk

1 **COLIGONE KATE,** 4, ch f Garswood—Dubai Walk (ITY) **H Bradshaws LTD Coligone**
2 **CROWN PRINCESS (IRE),** 5, b m Mehmas (IRE)—Al Hanyora **Ownaracehorse Ltd, M Reay & K West**
3 **GOLDEN GAL (IRE),** 4, br f Galileo Gold—Dubai Princess (IRE) **Ownaracehorse Ltd & Mr Ollie Pears**
4 **KRYSTAL MAZE (IRE),** 5, b m Kodiac—Escapism (IRE) **Sheila Elsey, Ollie Pears & Keith West**
5 **MY BROTHER JACK (IRE),** 4, b g Decorated Knight—Bella Bella (IRE) **Jo-co Partnership**
6 **OUTSMART (IRE),** 4, gr g Outstrip—Mi Rubina (IRE) **Jo-co Partnership**
7 **READY FREDDIE GO (IRE),** 5, b g Swiss Spirit—Barbieri (IRE) **Ownaracehorse Ltd, Keates & West**
8 **WRITTEN BROADCAST (IRE),** 6, gr g Gutaifan (IRE)—Teeline (IRE) **Harvey Bastiman & Ollie Pears**

THREE-YEAR-OLDS

9 **A DAY TO DREAM (IRE),** b g Adaay (IRE)—Tara Too (IRE) **Ownaracehorse Ltd, Pears & West**
10 **AFTERWARDS (IRE),** b g Time Test—Noahs Ark (IRE) **Kavanagh, Downey O Pears**

MR OLLIE PEARS - continued

11 **AURORA GLORY (IRE),** b f Cotai Glory—Al Hanyora **Pam Moll, Timothy O'Gram & Mike Reay**
12 **BREATHTAKER (IRE),** b g Buratino (IRE)—Impressive Victory (USA) **Michael Downey & Ollie Pears**
13 **GLORY CALL (IRE),** b g Cotai Glory—Miriam's Song **Crystal Clear Racing**
14 **HIDDEN CODE (IRE),** b g Kessaar (IRE)—Khibrah **Ownaracehorse Ltd, O Pears & A Caygill**
15 **LET'S GO HUGO (IRE),** ch g Unfortunately (IRE)—Barbieri (IRE) **Ownaracehorse & Dave Keates**
16 **LOVELIEST,** br f Unfortunately (IRE)—Harbour Siren **O. J. Pears**
17 **THE VAN MAN,** b g Brazen Beau (AUS)—Anushka Noo Noo **Mr A. Caygill**

TWO-YEAR-OLDS

18 B g 02/03 Twilight Son—Anushka Noo Noo (Makfi) **Mr A. Caygill**
19 **BOBINA (IRE),** b f 02/03 Bobby's Kitten (USA)—
Sosian (Showcasing) (1200) **Ownaracehorse Ltd & Mr Ollie Pears**
20 Br c 09/03 Time Test—Carnival Rose (Harbour Watch (IRE)) (55000) **Crystal Clear Racing**
21 B c 08/03 Kodiac—Ceist Eile (IRE) (Noverre (USA)) (44018) **Crystal Clear Racing**
22 **CELESTIAL FLIGHT,** b g 25/03 Harry Angel (IRE)—
Ebrah (Singspiel (IRE)) (2857) **Ownaracehorse Ltd & Mr Ollie Pears**
23 B g 19/04 Dandy Man (IRE)—Ceol Loch Aoidh (IRE) (Medecis) (17607) **Crystal Clear Racing**
24 B f 06/02 Land Force (IRE)—Cthulhu (USA) (Henrythenavigator (USA)) (1601) **O. J. Pears**
25 Br c 23/02 Kodiac—Dance Club (IRE) (Fasliyev (USA)) (40000) **Mr A. Caygill**
26 B c 05/03 Expert Eye—Electric Feel (Firebreak) (25610) **Crystal Clear Racing**
27 **KAARESS (IRE),** b f 02/04 Kessaar (IRE)—
Baltic Time (IRE) (Baltic King) (3201) **Ownaracehorse Ltd & Mr Ollie Pears**
28 **KELDEO,** gr f 05/03 Land Force (IRE)—
Kept Under Wraps (IRE) (Clodovil (IRE)) (7000) **Ownaracehorse Ltd & Mr Ollie Pears**
29 **LUCKY JUDE,** b g 06/03 Due Diligence (USA)—
Khaki (IRE) (Key of Luck (USA)) (1000) **Ownaracehorse Ltd & Mr Ollie Pears**
30 B c 21/04 Cotai Glory—Lucrezia (Nathaniel (IRE)) (20008) **Crystal Clear Racing**
31 B c 01/04 Inns of Court (IRE)—Moon Sister (IRE) (Cadeaux Genereux) (49524) **Crystal Clear Racing**
32 **RYOTO (IRE),** ch g 06/04 Dragon Pulse (IRE)—
Foot of Pride (IRE) (Footstepsinthesand) (2401) **Ownaracehorse Ltd & Mr Ollie Pears**
33 B c 16/04 Unfortunately (IRE)—Shahaama (Showcasing) (22409) **Crystal Clear Racing**
34 B f 09/04 Inns of Court (IRE)—Solace (USA) (Langfuhr (CAN)) (18000) **Crystal Clear Racing**
35 Gr f 16/02 Inns of Court (IRE)—Syamantaka (IRE) (Clodovil (IRE)) (10000) **Crystal Clear Racing**
36 B c 02/04 Time Test—Trust Fund Babe (IRE) (Captain Rio) (5000)
37 Br f 20/02 Kuroshio (AUS)—Village Gossip (IRE) (Pivotal) **O. J. Pears**
38 B c 10/04 Time Test—With Distinction (Zafonic (USA)) (35000) **O. J. Pears**

Assistant Trainer: Vicky Pears.

405

MISS LINDA PERRATT, East Kilbride

Postal: **North Allerton Farm, East Kilbride, Glasgow, Lanarkshire, G75 8RR**
Contacts: **PHONE 01355 303425 MOBILE 07931 306147**
EMAIL linda.perratt@btinternet.com

1 **BURTONLODGE BEAUTY (IRE),** 4, b f Bungle Inthejungle—Katevan (IRE) **M & L Perratt**
2 **CHINESE SPIRIT (IRE),** 9, gr g Clodovil (IRE)—In The Ribbons **Mr Sandy Jarvie & Miss L. Perratt**
3 **CLASS CLOWN (IRE),** 6, ch g Intense Focus (USA)—Joli Elegant (IRE) **Miss L. A. Perratt**
4 **HARD NUT (IRE),** 6, b g Gutaifan (IRE)—With A Twist **Mr W. F. Perratt**
5 **HENERY HAWK,** 4, b g Heeraat (IRE)—Rosecomb (IRE) **Jackton Racing Club**
6 **HOLLIS BROWN,** 4, b g Bobby's Kitten (USA)—Akranti **William Burns & Alan Berry**
7 **JUDGMENT CALL,** 5, br g Pivotal—Madonna Dell'orto **M. Sawers**
8 **KEEP COMING (IRE),** 7, b g Leading Light (IRE)—Pretty Present (IRE) **M & L Perratt**
9 **MARAAKIZ (IRE),** 5, b g Muhaarar—Entisaar (AUS) **Mr B. A. Jordan**

MISS LINDA PERRATT - continued

10 **MONHAMMER,** 5, b g Awtaad (IRE)—Soviet Terms **Jackton Racing Club**
11 **MRS DIBBLE (FR),** 5, b br m Dabirsim (FR)—Ossun (FR) **Mr A. Grant**
12 **NAZCA,** 4, b g Oasis Dream—Pure Line **Mr P. Corrigan**
13 **NODSASGOODASAWINK,** 5, ch m Sixties Icon—Winkaway **Miss L. A. Perratt**
14 **PASHA BAY,** 4, b g Cable Bay (IRE)—Cafe Express (IRE) **The Hon Miss H. Galbraith**
15 **POCKLEY,** 5, b g Shalaa (IRE)—Wanting (IRE) **J & R Winning**
16 **RETIREMENT BECKONS,** 8, b g Epaulette (AUS)—Mystical Ayr (IRE) **R. Winning & Partner**
17 **SIXCOR,** 5, b g Sixties Icon—Roccor **Linda Perratt Racing Club**
18 **STREAMLINE,** 6, b g Due Diligence (USA)—Ahwahnee **Mr R. Winning**
19 **THE CALTONIAN,** 4, b g Swiss Spirit—Azelle **M. Sawers**

THREE-YEAR-OLDS

20 **KEEP ME STABLE (IRE),** b f Galileo Gold—Sketching **Mr P. Corrigan**
21 **ONTHEBUNNY,** b f Bungle Inthejungle—Hi Note **Miss L. A. Perratt**

TWO-YEAR-OLDS

22 Gr f 17/03 Gregorian (IRE)—Avizare (IRE) (Lawman (FR)) (10000) **Miss L. A. Perratt**

Flat Jockey: Tom Eaves, P. J. McDonald. **Apprentice Jockey:** Leanne Ferguson.

---

406 MRS AMANDA PERRETT, Pulborough

Postal: **Coombelands Racing Stables, Pulborough, West Sussex, RH20 1BP**
Contacts: **PHONE 01798 873011 MOBILE 07803 088713**
EMAIL aperrett@coombelands-stables.com WEBSITE www.amandaperrett.com

1 **BALLET BLANC,** 4, ch f Highland Reel (IRE)—Bouvardia **Amanda Perrett & Partners**
2 **COUNT OTTO (IRE),** 8, b g Sir Prancealot (IRE)—Dessert Flower (IRE) **Count Otto Partnership**
3 **LATER DARLING,** 4, b g Postponed (IRE)—Saucy Minx (IRE) **F & P Conway**
4 **MISS DOWN UNDER (IRE),** 4, ch f Australia—Pocket of Stars (IRE) **Miss Down Under Partnership**
5 **NELLIE MOON,** 5, b br m Sea The Moon (GER)—Queen's Dream (IRE) **Nellie Moon Partnership**
6 **REBEL TERRITORY,** 5, b g Territories (IRE)—Saucy Minx (IRE) **F & P Conway**
7 **SAYIFYOUWILL,** 5, b m Sayif (IRE)—Amirah (IRE) **Richard Cheadle & Partners**
8 **STAR CALIBER,** 5, b g Golden Horn—Lombatina (FR) **Mrs S. M. Conway**
9 **ZIKANY,** 5, b g Zoffany (IRE)—Rosika **Mrs A. M. Lewis**

THREE-YEAR-OLDS

10 **AUTOLYCUS,** ch g Cracksman—Elysian Fields (GR) **Mr John P Connolly**
11 **DOVENA,** ch f Nathaniel (IRE)—Curtains **The Dovena Partnership**
12 **DREAM OF MISCHIEF,** b g Oasis Dream—Saucy Minx (IRE) **F & P Conway**
13 **FREETODREAM,** b g Muhaarar—Twilight Spirit **Freetodream Partnership**
14 **IMPERIOUSITY,** ch g Tasleet—Great Hope (IRE) **D & B James and Partners**

TWO-YEAR-OLDS

15 **GOLDEN ARC,** b f 22/02 Golden Horn—Longing To Dance (Danehill Dancer (IRE)) (30000) **D James & Partners**
16 **OUR ELYSIUM,** b c 14/03 Advertise—Jeu de Plume (IRE) (Montjeu (IRE)) (12000) **Mr I. Skinner**
17 **PLATINUM PERFECT,** b f 22/02 Postponed (IRE)—Point Perfect (Dansili) (6000) **The Another Point Partners**
18 **UNREAL CONNECTION,** b f 26/03 Calyx—Susan Stroman (Monsun (GER)) (22000) **Mr D. Woods**
19 **WILD TEMPO,** b c 05/04 Time Test—Wild Mimosa (IRE) (Dynaformer (USA)) (22000) **The Wild Tempo Partnership**

Assistant Trainer: Mark Perrett.

407 MR PAT PHELAN, Epsom

Postal: **Ermyn Lodge, Shepherds Walk, Epsom, Surrey, KT18 6DF**
Contacts: **PHONE 01372 229014 MOBILE 07917 762781 FAX 01372 229001**
EMAIL pat.phelan@ermynlodge.com WEBSITE www.ermynlodge.com

1 **ABIE MY BOY,** 4, ch g Equiano (FR)—Ellie In The Pink (IRE) **A. B. Pope**
2 **CELTIC NED (IRE),** 5, b g Well Chosen—Belsalsa (FR) **Celtic Contractors Limited**
3 **DEVIZES (IRE),** 7, b g Dubawi (IRE)—Dalasyla (IRE) **Celtic Contractors Limited**
4 **DOTTIES STAR,** 4, b g Sea The Moon (GER)—Young Dottie **Ermyn Lodge Stud Limited**
5 **EPSOM FAITHFULL,** 6, b m Coach House (IRE)—La Fortunata **Epsom Racegoers No.2**
6 **FIVEOCLOCKSOMEWHER,** 4, ch f Sir Percy—My Amalie (IRE) **P. P. Mclaughlin**
7 **HONORE,** 5, b g Telescope (IRE)—Saint Honore **Mr M. Houlihan**
8 **ICONIC MOVER,** 5, ch g Sixties Icon—Run For Ede's **Ermyn Lodge Stud Limited**
9 **NAASMA (IRE),** 4, b f Churchill (IRE)—Music Show (IRE) **Mr P. J. Wheatley**
10 **NO TURNING BACK,** 4, b f Equiano (FR)—Isabella Beeton **P. P. Mclaughlin**
11 **OPTIMISTIC BELIEF (IRE),** 5, b g Make Believe—Panglossian (IRE) **Mr J. F. Lang**
12 **QEYAADY,** 5, b g Muhaarar—Starflower **Mr P. J. Wheatley**
13 **REECELTIC,** 8, b g Champs Elysees—Sense of Pride **Celtic Contractors Limited**
14 **SHERPA TRAIL (USA),** 7, gr ro g Gio Ponti (USA)—Vapour Musing **Mr P. J. Wheatley**
15 **STAR OF EPSOM,** 5, b m Sir Percy—Isabella Beeton **Epsom Racegoers No.3**
16 **WEARDIDITALLGORONG,** 11, b m Fast Company (IRE)—Little Oz (IRE) **P. P. Mclaughlin**

THREE-YEAR-OLDS

17 **THE GAME IS UP,** b f Adaay (IRE)—Falcon In Flight **I. W. Harfitt**

Flat Jockey: J. F. Egan, Shane Kelly, Kieran O'Neill. **NH Jockey:** James Best. **Conditional Jockey:** Sean Houlihan. **Apprentice Jockey:** Paddy Bradley.

---

408 MR KEVIN PHILIPPART DE FOY, Newmarket

Postal: **Machell Place Stables, Old Station Road, Newmarket, Suffolk, CB8 8DW**
Contacts: **PHONE 07551 498273**
EMAIL office@kpfracing.com

1 **ALREHB (USA),** 6, gr g War Front (USA)—Tahrir (IRE)
2 **BAILEYSGUTFEELING (IRE),** 4, b g Gutaifan (IRE)—Baileys Pursuit
3 **CAIRN GORM,** 5, ch h Bated Breath—In Your Time
4 **CICELY (IRE),** 4, b f The Gurkha (IRE)—Wingspan (USA)
5 **CLIPSHAM GOLD (IRE),** 4, ch f Galileo Gold—Tilly Two (IRE)
6 **CORSINI (IRE),** 4, ch f Mastercraftsman (IRE)—Il Palazzo (USA)
7 **COVERT MISSION (FR),** 5, b g Lope de Vega (IRE)—Beach Belle
8 **D DAY ODETTE,** 4, br f Lawman (FR)—Morning Chimes (IRE)
9 **DESERT MIRACLE,** 4, ch g Postponed (IRE)—Mia San Triple
10 **DREAM BY DAY,** 4, b g Shalaa (IRE)—Illaunmore (USA)
11 **EDWARD JENNER (IRE),** 4, b g Vadamos (FR)—Zakyah
12 **EL HABEEB (IRE),** 4, b c Al Rifai (IRE)—Los Ojitos (USA)
13 **ENTHRALLMENT (IRE),** 4, b g Fastnet Rock (AUS)—Magen's Star (IRE)
14 **EVANIA,** 5, b m Golden Horn—Hanami
15 **LIGHTSHIP (IRE),** 4, b f Fascinating Rock (IRE)—Kayak
16 **MAX MAYHEM,** 5, b g New Bay—Maybe Grace (IRE)
17 **MILLION THANKS (IRE),** 4, ch g Churchill (IRE)—Queen's Rose
18 **MY BOY JACK,** 4, ch g No Nay Never (USA)—Great Court (IRE)
19 **RIKONA,** 4, b f Shalaa (IRE)—Paradise Sea (USA)
20 **SPINAROUND (IRE),** 4, b g Kodiac—Spinamiss (IRE)
21 **STREET KID (IRE),** 5, ch g Street Boss (USA)—Brushed Gold (USA)
22 **SURREY MIST (FR),** 4, gr g Kendargent (FR)—Kindly Dismiss (FR)
23 **TORIOUS,** 4, ch f Lethal Force (IRE)—Authora (IRE)

MR KEVIN PHILIPPART DE FOY - continued

24 **TUDOR (IRE),** 4, b g Zoffany (IRE)—Tiger Lilly (IRE)
25 **TWENTYSHARESOFGREY,** 5, gr m Markaz (IRE)—Carsulae (IRE)
26 **VAFORTINO (IRE),** 5, b g New Bay—Arbaah (USA)

THREE-YEAR-OLDS

27 **APOLLO'S ANGEL,** gr f Dark Angel (IRE)—Ebony Flyer (SAF)
28 **BEAR ON THE LOOSE (IRE),** b g Footstepsinthesand—Ihtiraam (IRE)
29 **BURNING SKIES,** b f Kingman—Flower of Life (IRE)
30 **BYEFORNOW,** b f Charm Spirit (IRE)—Zumran
31 **CLIPSHAM LA HABANA,** gr c Havana Grey—Vitta's Touch (USA)
32 **CONGRUENT (IRE),** b f Acclamation—Back In The Frame
33 **CORSICAN CAPER (IRE),** gr c Fast Company (IRE)—Kanshe (IRE)
34 **CRESTA CAT,** b c Bobby's Kitten (USA)—Alpensinfonie (IRE)
35 **D DAY ARVALENREEVA (IRE),** ch f Mastercraftsman (IRE)—Eccellente Idea (IRE)
36 **ERMESINDE (IRE),** b f Golden Horn—Eye Witness (GER)
37 **EURYTHMICAL (IRE),** b f Territories (IRE)—Sweet Dream
38 **EXPERT AGENT,** b g Expert Eye—Oeuvre d'Art (IRE)
39 **FARIBA (IRE),** b f Farhh—Last Pearl
40 **FRENCH MISTRESS,** b f Kingman—French Dressing
41 Ch f Sea The Stars (IRE)—Future Generation (IRE)
42 B f Golden Horn—Hanami
43 **IN THE TRENCHES,** b g Kodiac—Bristol Fashion
44 **KESSAAR POWER (IRE),** b c Kessaar (IRE)—Lady Willpower
45 **KLIMOVA,** ch f Intello (GER)—Queen of Ice
46 **MAGNUSSON,** b g Territories (IRE)—Broughtons Revival
47 **MALKA (IRE),** ch f Nathaniel (IRE)—Carisolo
48 **PRECIOUS LAGATHA,** ch f Pearl Secret—Yukon Girl (IRE)
49 **RENESMEE,** b f Iffraaj—Magique (IRE)
50 **SEA THE BUCKTHORN,** b g Sea The Moon (GER)—Pax Aeterna (USA)
51 **SENESI,** b f Kingman—Montalcino (IRE)
52 **SHAZAM (IRE),** b br f Almanzor (FR)—Shalanaya (IRE)
53 **SONEMOS (IRE),** b f Vadamos (FR)—Adroit (IRE)
54 **STAR PLAYER,** b g Zoffany (IRE)—Lunar Phase (IRE)
55 **TULEKYA,** b f Wootton Bassett—Kuna Yala (GER)
56 **UMBERTO,** b c Expert Eye—Maria Letizia
57 **ZAFAAN (IRE),** b g Zoffany (IRE)—Gush (USA)

TWO-YEAR-OLDS

58 B c 16/03 Golden Horn—Above The Clouds (FR) (High Chaparral (IRE)) (41617)
59 B f 17/04 Siyouni (FR)—Alandalos (Invincible Spirit (IRE))
60 Ch f 16/03 Lope de Vega (IRE)—Anipa (Sea The Stars (IRE)) (35000)
61 B f 12/03 Camacho—Blockade (IRE) (Kheleyf (USA)) (14406)
62 B br f 21/02 Cloth of Stars (IRE)—Desert Image (Beat Hollow) (26411)
63 **DIANARA (FR),** b f 17/04 Goken (FR)—Kindly Dismiss (FR) (Excellent Art) (72029)
64 **ELECTRIFIED,** b c 24/01 Expert Eye—Electrify (IRE) (Invincible Spirit (IRE)) (16006)
65 B c 25/02 Advertise—Fen Breeze (Bated Breath) (62000)
66 B c 12/03 Invincible Spirit (IRE)—Flash Flood (Shamardal (USA)) (32000)
67 B f 13/03 Noble Mission—Garmoosha (USA) (Kingmambo (USA))
68 **GLIMPSE THE MOON,** b gr f 19/02 Sea The Moon (GER)—Lady Bergamot (FR) (Mastercraftsman (IRE))
69 Ch f 24/02 Territories (IRE)—Graine de Maille (IRE) (Pivotal) (23000)
70 Ch f 02/02 Galileo Gold—Height of Vanity (IRE) (Erhaab (USA)) (13605)
71 B c 03/04 Prince of Lir (IRE)—Kaplinsky (IRE) (Fath (USA)) (45000)
72 **KESTEVEN RDA (IRE),** b f 03/04 Inns of Court (IRE)—Shrewd Approach (IRE) (Dawn Approach (IRE)) (1200)
73 Br f 11/03 Twilight Son—Litigious (Lawman (FR)) (65000)
74 **LOVES LOVING,** b f 29/03 Expert Eye—Fallen In Love (Galileo (IRE))
75 **LUAS (IRE),** gr c 16/05 Dark Angel (IRE)—Dansky (IRE) (Dansili) (52000)
76 B c 03/02 Le Havre (IRE)—Murviel (FR) (Siyouni (FR)) (32013)
77 Ch f 27/04 New Bay—Need You Now (IRE) (Kheleyf (USA)) (20008)
78 **QUICKLY (GER),** b c 17/03 Soldier Hollow—Queenie (GER) (Areion (GER)) (56022)

MR KEVIN PHILIPPART DE FOY - continued

79 **REFLEXION FAITE (FR),** b f 10/05 Intello (GER)—Lady Ascot (IRE) (Excellent Art) (8003)
80 B f 04/04 Dandy Man (IRE)—Royal Order (USA) (Medaglia d'Oro (USA)) (16000)
81 B f 09/02 Farhh—Shahnila (FR) (Elusive City (USA)) (24010)
82 B c 25/01 Due Diligence (USA)—Sri Kandi (Pivotal)
83 B f 19/03 Expert Eye—Sunchisetagioo (Exceed And Excel (AUS)) (38095)
84 **TARAMASALATA (IRE),** b f 17/02 Too Darn Hot—Sultanina (New Approach (IRE))
85 B f 24/01 Golden Horn—Tarap (IRE) (Myboycharlie (IRE))
86 Ch f 21/04 Dubawi (IRE)—Tarfasha (IRE) (Teofilo (IRE))
87 B c 11/02 Blue Point (IRE)—Tasleya (Frankel)
88 B c 04/03 Expert Eye—Tutti Frutti (Teofilo (IRE)) (38000)
89 Ch f 06/03 Masar (IRE)—Wall of Light (Zamindar (USA)) (26000)
90 Gr c 06/02 Zarak (FR)—Zegna (GER) (Shirocco (GER)) (60000)

---

409 MR RICHARD PHILLIPS, Moreton-in-Marsh

Postal: **Adlestrop Stables, Adlestrop, Moreton-in-Marsh, Gloucestershire, GL56 0YN**
Contacts: **WORK 01608 658710 MOBILE 07774 832715**
EMAIL info@richardphillipsracing.com WEBSITE www.richardphillipsracing.com

1 **ALRIGHT CHAP (IRE),** 6, b g Sageburg (IRE)—Brown Arrow (IRE) **The Aspirationals**
2 **BLUENOSE BELLE (USA),** 5, b m Noble Mission—Poster Girl (USA) **Mr G. Lansbury**
3 **CORRANY (IRE),** 9, br g Court Cave (IRE)—Time For An Audit **Dozen Dreamers**
4 6, Ch m Gentlewave (IRE)—Days Like These
5 **ELFRIDE,** 7, ch m Black Sam Bellamy (IRE)—Just Missie **Mr D. G. Redfern**
6 **FIGHTING POET (IRE),** 5, b g The Gurkha (IRE)—Inkling (USA) **Richard Phillips Racing Syndicate**
7 **FINE THEATRE (IRE),** 13, b g King's Theatre (IRE)—Finemar Lady (IRE) **Richard Phillips Racing Syndicate**
8 4, B g Sans Frontieres (IRE)—Gaelic River (IRE) **Hopeful Travellers**
9 **IRON HORSE,** 12, b g Kayf Tara—What A Vintage (IRE) **The Someday's Here Racing Partnership**
10 **LESSER (IRE),** 9, b g Stowaway—Aine Dubh (IRE) **The C Level Partnership**
11 **LIZZIE REY,** 6, b m Kingston Hill—Mayolynn (USA) **The Cavallo Syndicate**
12 4, B g Malinas (GER)—Lucy Rouge (IRE)
13 **MATTIE ROSS,** 7, b m Champs Elysees—Ommadawn (IRE) **The Zara Syndicate**
14 **METHODTOTHEMAGIC (IRE),** 8, b m Sans Frontieres (IRE)—
Cindy's Fancy (IRE) **Dalziel Family, T White, J Inverdale**
15 **NED CASH,** 5, b g Blue Bresil (FR)—Folie Lointaine (FR) **Mrs A. Barclay**
16 **ORGANDI (FR),** 11, br m Early March—Creme Pralinee (FR) **Beautiful People**
17 **PICANHA,** 9, br g Malinas (GER)—Royal Bride **Mrs E. A. Prowting**
18 **POP MISTRESS (IRE),** 7, ch m Sixties Icon—Mayolynn (USA) **Goodwood Owners Drinks Session**
19 **ROSSBEIGH STRAND (IRE),** 8, b g Mahler—Could Do **Nut Club Partnership**
20 4, Ch f Prince of Lir (IRE)—Shadow Mountain
21 **SHIBUYA SONG,** 4, ch f New Approach (IRE)—Silent Music (IRE) **The Firebirds**
22 4, Bl f Black Sam Bellamy (IRE)—Supreme Gem (IRE) **Dalziel Family, Rogers, Vowles**
23 **TOTTERDOWN,** 12, b g Pasternak—Yeldham Lady **The Adlestrop Club**

THREE-YEAR-OLDS

24 **URBAN CHAMPION,** ch g Cityscape—L'Addition **Hunscote Stud Limited**

Yard Sponsor: Tori Global.

---

410 MR DAVID EDWARD PIPE, Wellington

Postal: **Pond House, Nicholashayne, Wellington, Somerset, TA21 9QY**
Contacts: **PHONE 07774 622014**
EMAIL david@davidpipe.com

1 **ABAYA DU MATHAN (FR),** 11, b g Al Namix (FR)—Swahilie du Mathan (FR) **Mrs J. E. Wilson**
2 **ACTIVIST (FR),** 4, b g Iffraaj—Above The Clouds (FR) **Mrs L. Maclennan**
3 **AMERICAN SNIPER (IRE),** 5, b g Malinas (GER)—Mountain Leap (IRE) **Mrs A. Jeal**
4 **ANGLERS CRAG,** 8, bl g Multiplex—Overyou **D. Mossop**
5 **ASTIGAR (FR),** 7, gr g No Risk At All (FR)—Sissi de Teille (FR) **The Angove Family**
6 **BARRIER PEAKS (FR),** 7, b g Blue Bresil (FR)—La Balzane (FR) **David Pipe Racing Club**
7 **BASHFUL BOY (IRE),** 7, b g Magician (IRE)—Bacheliere (USA) **Milldean Racing Syndicate**
8 **BASHFUL KATE (IRE),** 6, b m El Salvador (IRE)—Hester Lady (IRE) **Milldean Racing Syndicate**
9 **BEHIND THE CURTAIN (IRE),** 9, br g Curtain Time (IRE)—Veronica's Gift (IRE) **David Pipe Racing Club**
10 **BEN LILLY (IRE),** 6, b g Gleneagles (IRE)—Aristocratic Lady (USA) **David Pipe Racing Club**
11 **BONHEUR DE BALLON (FR),** 4, b g Doctor Dino (FR)—Bonheur de Stara (FR) **Mr S. Sutton**
12 **BORNTOBEALEADER (IRE),** 4, ch g Churchill (IRE)—Shake The Moon (GER) **Mr A. J. Ryan**
13 **BRINKLEY (FR),** 8, gr g Martaline—Royale Majesty (FR) **Brocade Racing**
14 **BUMPY JOHNSON (IRE),** 7, ch g Imperial Monarch (IRE)—Country Flora **Brocade Racing**
15 **CADEAU D'OR (FR),** 6, ch g Le Havre (IRE)—Hill of Grace **The Golden Gift Partnership**
16 **CALL HER CLEVER (IRE),** 5, gr ro m Califet (FR)—Pure Genius (IRE) **ValueRacingClub.co.uk**
17 **CASTLE DARAGH (IRE),** 6, b g Watar (IRE)—Old Glenort Daragh (IRE)
18 **COLONY QUEEN,** 7, b m Gregorian (IRE)—Queen Margrethe **The Angove Family**
19 **D'JANGO (FR),** 10, br g Balko (FR)—Quizas Jolie (FR) **Mrs J. E. Wilson**
20 **DANCES ON THE SAND (IRE),** 7, gr g Kalanisi (IRE)—Pure Anticipation (IRE) **Rio Racing**
21 **DINDIN (FR),** 10, b g Balko (FR)—Taguy Star (FR) **David Pipe Racing Club**
22 **DUC DE BEAUCHENE (FR),** 10, b g Saddler Maker (IRE)—Quatia d'Angron (FR) **Mr J. P. McManus**
23 **EDEN DU HOUX (FR),** 9, b g Irish Wells (FR)—Maralypha (FR) **Prof C. Tisdall**
24 **FERDINAND STAR,** 6, b g Kalanisi (IRE)—Hells House **Mr P. W. Garnsworthy**
25 **FIRST LORD DE CUET (FR),** 9, gr g Lord du Sud (FR)—Alyce (FR) **Potter, Pipe and Pete**
26 **FREE CHAKARTE (FR),** 4, b f Highland Reel (IRE)—Piroska (IRE) **D. E. Pipe**
27 **GERICAULT ROQUE (FR),** 7, b g Montmartre (FR)—Nijinska Delaroque (FR) **Prof C. Tisdall & Mr B. Drew**
28 **GRANGECLARE GLORY (IRE),** 8, b g Fame And Glory—Annies Joy (IRE) **Prof C. Tisdall**
29 **GWENCILY BERBAS (FR),** 12, b g Nickname (FR)—Lesorial (FR) **Mr A. J. Ryan**
30 **HEURE DE GLOIRE (FR),** 6, b m Kapgarde (FR)—Lounoas (FR) **Mrs J P E Cunningham & Mr G M Cunningham**
31 **HORY (FR),** 6, br g Crossharbour—Tempete d'Ory (FR)
32 **ISRAEL CHAMP (IRE),** 8, b g Milan—La Dariska (FR) **John White & Anne Underhill**
33 **ITACARE (FR),** 6, gr g Silver Frost (IRE)—Steadfast (FR) **Somerset Racing**
34 **JAZZ WOMAN (FR),** 4, bl f Voiladenuo (FR)—Villzane (FR) **Middleham Park Racing LXX**
35 **JET SMART (IRE),** 5, ch g Jet Away—Cherry Island (IRE) **Clan McNeil**
36 **JILAIJONE (FR),** 4, b g Walzertakt (GER)—Alauda (FR) **Mr S. Sutton**
37 **KALMA,** 5, b m Mukhadram—Peters Spirit (IRE) **David Pipe Racing Club**
38 **KATPOLI (FR),** 8, b g Poliglote—Katkogarie (FR) **Mr S. Sutton**
39 **KEPAGGE (IRE),** 9, b g Getaway (GER)—Miracle Lady **Mrs S. J. Ling**
40 **KING TURGEON (FR),** 5, gr g Turgeon (USA)—King's Crystal **Mrs A. Jeal**
41 **KINGOFTHEWEST (IRE),** 7, b g Westerner—Other Salsa (FR) **Friends From the West**
42 **KOI DODVILLE (FR),** 5, b g French Fifteen (FR)—Konkan (IRE) **David Pipe Racing Club**
43 **KOLISI (IRE),** 5, b g Harzand (IRE)—Wild Step (GER) **W. F. Frewen**
44 **LADY RESET,** 7, ch m Yorgunnabelucky (USA)—Reset City **Mrs L. Webb**
45 **LAST QUARTER (IRE),** 6, b g Walk In The Park (IRE)—Lunar Path (IRE) **Brocade Racing**
46 **LITTLE RED LION (IRE),** 9, b g Sans Frontieres (IRE)—Rever Up (IRE) **Friends of Ebony Horse Club**
47 **LOCK OUT (IRE),** 6, b g Watar (IRE)—Swift And Late (IRE) **Chris & David Stam**
48 4, Ch f Mahler—Magie du Ma (FR) **Mr K. Alexander**
49 **MAIN FACT (USA),** 10, b g Blame (USA)—Reflections **Munrowd's Partnership**
50 **MAKE ME A BELIEVER (IRE),** 8, br g Presenting—Kiltiernan Robin (IRE) **Prof. C. Tisdall & Jane Gerard-Pearse**
51 **MAN AGAIN (FR),** 4, ch g Manduro (GER)—Now Again (GER) **W. F. Frewen**
52 **MAN AT WORK (IRE),** 5, b g Workforce—Shokalocka Baby (IRE) **Prof C. Tisdall & Mr B. Drew**
53 **MARTINHAL (IRE),** 8, b g Westerner—Gweedara (IRE) **Mrs L. Maclennan**
54 **MICRONORMOUS (IRE),** 5, b m Walk In The Park (IRE)—Foxy Lauren (IRE) **Micro Managers**
55 **MOODOFTHEMOMENT (IRE),** 6, ch g Shantou (USA)—Mood I'm In (GER) **Clan McNeil**
56 **MR TAMBOURINE MAN (IRE),** 6, b g Galileo (IRE)—Snow Queen (IRE) **Midd Shire Racing**

MR DAVID EDWARD PIPE - continued

57 **MYRISTICA (IRE),** 5, br m Harzand (IRE)—Black Mascara (IRE) **Prof C. Tisdall**
58 **NEON MOON (IRE),** 7, b g No Risk At All (FR)—Hidden Horizons (IRE) **Brocade Racing**
59 **NEW AGE DAWNING (IRE),** 9, ch g Stowaway—Captain Supreme (IRE) **Brocade Racing**
60 **NILA (IRE),** 4, b f Nutan (IRE)—Nicea (GER) **What a mare racing group**
61 **NOBEL JOSHUA (AUT),** 7, b br g Joshua Tree (IRE)—Namat (IRE) **Avalon Surfacing & Construction Co Ltd**
62 **OCEAN HEIGHTS,** 6, ch g Dubawi (IRE)—Ethereal Sky (IRE) **Mrs Lynne Webb & Partner**
63 **OCEANLINE (IRE),** 5, b g Adaay (IRE)—Ocean Bluff (IRE) **R M & Wright**
64 **ONLY FOOLS (IRE),** 4, b f Mondialiste (IRE)—Only Together (IRE) **David Pipe Racing Club**
65 **ONLY THE BOLD (IRE),** 8, b g Jeremy (USA)—Cloghoge Lady (IRE) **ValueRacingClub.co.uk**
66 **PACHACUTI (IRE),** 6, b g Walk In The Park (IRE)—Mrs Mac Veale (IRE) **The Arthur White Partnership**
67 **PANIC ATTACK (IRE),** 7, b m Canford Cliffs (IRE)—Toto Corde Meo (IRE) **Mr B. J. C. Drew**
68 **PARICOLOR (FR),** 7, b g Orpen (USA)—Kadiana (IRE) **Mrs J P E Cunningham & Mr G M Cunningham**
69 **PESO IN MY POCKET (IRE),** 5, b g Champs Elysees—Horner Hill (IRE) **Mrs L. Jones**
70 **PLATINUMCARD (IRE),** 8, b g Golden Lariat (USA)—Flemensfirth Lady (IRE) **Redeemers Syndicate**
71 **PORT O'CLOCK (IRE),** 8, ch g Sans Frontieres (IRE)—Rever Up (IRE) **David Pipe Racing Club**
72 **POSEIDON (IRE),** 9, ch g Born To Sea (IRE)—Maskaya (IRE) **David Pipe Racing Club**
73 **RAMSES DE TEILLEE (FR),** 11, gr g Martaline—Princesse d'Orton (FR) **John White & Anne Underhill**
74 **RED HAPPY (FR),** 6, ch g Red Dubawi (IRE)—Happynees (FR) **Mrs J. E. Wilson**
75 **REMASTERED,** 10, ch g Network (GER)—Cathodine Cayras (FR) **Brocade Racing**
76 **ROYAL DEFENDER (IRE),** 5, b g Soldier of Fortune (IRE)—Kings Sister (IRE) **Prof C. Tisdall & Mr B. Drew**
77 **ROYAL MER (FR),** 5, gr g Montmartre (FR)—Princesse Pauline (FR) **Mr S. Sutton**
78 **SETME STRAIGHTMATE,** 7, ch g Malinas (GER)—Karamel **Prof C Tisdall & The Angove Family**
79 **SHOT BOII (IRE),** 6, b g Malinas (GER)—Moncherie (IRE) **W. F. Frewen**
80 **SIDI ISMAEL (FR),** 9, b g Great Pretender (IRE)—Tetouane (FR) **The Show is Over Syndicate**
81 **SIZING POTTSIE (FR),** 9, b br g Kapgarde (FR)—Line Salsa (FR) **Tracey, Alexander, Apiafi, Kuyt, Harman**
82 **TANGO ARUMBA (IRE),** 6, b m Shantou (USA)—Thricha (IRE) **Mrs J. Gerard-Pearse**
83 **TEXARD (FR),** 8, b g Kapgarde (FR)—Textuelle (FR) **Mrs J. E. Wilson**
84 **THANKSFORTHEHELP (FR),** 6, gr g Martaline—Agathe du Berlais (FR) **Mr J. P. McManus**
85 **THOMAS MOR (IRE),** 6, ch g Dylan Thomas (IRE)—Lusty Beg (IRE) **Wayne Clifford & Ian Gosden**
86 **UMBRIGADO (IRE),** 9, br g Stowaway—Dame O'Neill (IRE) **John White & Anne Underhill**
87 **VIA DANTE (IRE),** 6, b g Milan—Jessies Delight **David Pipe Racing Club**
88 **WALK OF THE ROSES (IRE),** 4, b f Walk In The Park (IRE)—Koko Rose (IRE) **ValueRacingClub.co.uk**
89 **YA KNOW YASEFF (IRE),** 6, ch m Jet Away—Back To Cloghoge (IRE) **Mr A. J. Ryan**

---

411 MR CHARLES AND ADAM POGSON, Farnsfield

Postal: **Allamoor Farm, Mansfield Road, Farnsfield, Nottinghamshire, NG22 8HZ**
Contacts: **PHONE 07977 016155**
EMAIL adampogson@hotmail.co.uk

1 **GEORGE MALLORY,** 7, b g Kingman—Rose Et Noire (IRE) **C. T. Pogson**
2 **GOLDEN GETAWAY (IRE),** 6, ch m Getaway (GER)—Native Caroline (IRE) **Mrs S. Tucker**
3 **JUMPING JUPITER (IRE),** 5, br g Sageburg (IRE)—Mazaryne (FR) **Mr A. Tucker**
4 **MARAJMAN (FR),** 9, gr g Rajsaman (FR)—Mascarpone (FR) **Stephanie Kaye and M.T Hughes**
5 **MR COLDSTONE (IRE),** 7, b g Tamayuz—Dance Lively (USA) **Robert & Marie Smith & M T Hughes**
6 **OVERTOUGEORGE,** 9, b g Overbury (IRE)—Captivating Tyna (IRE) **C. T. Pogson**
7 **SECOND KINGDOM,** 5, b g Make Believe—Simple Magic (IRE) **Mr W. Berridge**
8 **THE SKIFFLE KING (IRE),** 7, b g Dylan Thomas (IRE)—Joe's Dream Catch (IRE) **M. Tucker**
9 **WARRIOR'S FATE (IRE),** 6, b g Soldier of Fortune (IRE)—In Fact (IRE) **Hughes, Pogson**

412 MR JOE PONTING, Wotton-Under-Edge

Postal: **Woodmans Farm, Hawkesbury Road, Hillesley, Wotton-Under-Edge, Gloucestershire, GL12 7RD**
Contacts: **PHONE 01454 294554**
EMAIL joeponting02@gmail.com

1 **AL GAIYA (FR),** 6, b m Olympic Glory (IRE)—Lathah (IRE) **Mr J. Ponting**
2 **ARCHIE MACDART,** 4, b g Dartmouth—Tara Mactwo **Mr M. T. Davies**
3 **DEFFERELLA,** 4, b f Postponed (IRE)—Cradle of Life (IRE) **Mr J. Ponting**
4 **GAVIN,** 5, b g Bated Breath—Under Milk Wood **P. J. Ponting**
5 **GRIMSBY TOWN (IRE),** 4, b g Garswood—Fantasy In Blue **P. J. Ponting**
6 **KRAKEN FILLY (IRE),** 5, b m Camacho—Tip It On The Top (IRE) **P. J. Ponting**
7 **LORD MARBURY (IRE),** 5, b g Galileo (IRE)—Convocate (USA) **P. J. Ponting**
8 **LOST HISTORY (IRE),** 10, b g Strategic Prince—Prelude **P. J. Ponting**
9 **MAX THE MISFIT,** 5, b g Mountain High (IRE)—Tara Mactwo **Mr M. T. Davies**
10 **MUG BOOKIES (IRE),** 5, b m Soldier of Fortune (IRE)—Last Century (IRE) **Back Pages**
11 **OCTAVIUS SABINI (IRE),** 6, b g Yeats (IRE)—Feathard Lady (IRE) **P. J. Ponting**
12 **SUSANBEQUICK (IRE),** 4, b f Dabirsim (FR)—Brynica (FR) **P. J. Ponting**
13 5, Ch g Schiaparelli (GER)—Sweet Like You **P. J. Ponting**
14 4, B f Schiaparelli (GER)—Sweet Like You
15 **THERE'S LOVELY,** 4, b f Jeu St Eloi (FR)—Monopolime (FR) **Mrs S. Ponting**
16 **YKIKAHOBBSIE,** 4, ch c Jack Hobbs—Ykikamoocow **Mr M. T. Davies**
17 **YOU GO GIRL,** 4, b f Twilight Son—Hard Walnut (IRE) **P. J. Ponting**

---

413 MR JONATHAN PORTMAN, Upper Lambourn

Postal: **Whitcoombe House Stables, Upper Lambourn, Hungerford, Berkshire, RG17 8RA**
Contacts: **PHONE 01488 73894 MOBILE 07798 824513**
EMAIL jonathan@jonathanportmanracing.com WEBSITE www.jonathanportmanracing.com

1 **BROAD APPEAL,** 9, ch g Medicean—Shy Appeal (IRE) **J. G. B. Portman**
2 **ELITE ETOILE,** 4, br g Vadamos (FR)—Way To The Stars **Portlee Bloodstock**
3 **HELLAVAPACE,** 5, br gr m Hellvelyn—Hasten (USA) **Fillies First**
4 **KNIGHT'S GAMBIT,** 4, b g Sir Percy—Play Street **J. G. B. Portman**
5 **MANYANA,** 4, b f Postponed (IRE)—Tenerife Song **Fillies First & Partners**
6 **MREMBO,** 4, b f Albaasil (IRE)—Shesha Bear **RWH Partnership**
7 **NEW HEIGHTS,** 5, b m Intello (GER)—How High The Sky (IRE) **Simon Skinner & Partner**
8 **ORIN SWIFT (IRE),** 9, b g Dragon Pulse (IRE)—Hollow Green (IRE) **Mr L. A. Bellman**
9 **ROMANTIC MEMORIES,** 4, b f Time Test—Midnight Fling **Mr S. Emmet & Miss R. Emmet**
10 **ROSE LIGHT,** 4, b f Nathaniel—Rosie Briar **Mrs Joy Hobby**
11 **RUSSIAN RUMOUR (IRE),** 6, b m Make Believe—Russian Rave **Fillies First**
12 **STRIKE,** 5, gr g Lethal Force (IRE)—Midnight Fling **Mr S. Emmet & Miss R. Emmet**
13 **SWEET REWARD (IRE),** 6, b g Acclamation—Dangle (IRE) **Old Stoic Racing Club & Partner**
14 **TOYBOX,** 7, ch m Paco Boy (IRE)—Play Street **J. G. B. Portman**
15 **TWO TEMPTING (IRE),** 4, ch g New Bay—Dangle (IRE) **Berkeley Racing**
16 **WAY OF LIFE,** 5, b g Havana Gold (IRE)—Upskittled **Berkeley Racing**

THREE-YEAR-OLDS

17 **ANNA AURELIA,** b f Wootton Bassett—Faustinatheyounger (IRE) **Adc Bloodstock & Partner**
18 **BEAR FORCE (IRE),** b g Kodi Bear (IRE)—Dew (IRE) **Berkeley Racing**
19 **BONNE SUZETTE (IRE),** b f Ulysses (IRE)—Retake **Mrs Suzanne Williams & Partner**
20 **CORINTHIAN KID (IRE),** b f Kodi Bear (IRE)—Columbia Kid (IRE) **Old Stoic Racing Club & Partner**
21 **DRAGON POWER (IRE),** ch g Dragon Pulse (IRE)—Monteamiata (IRE)
22 **ENOCHDHU (FR),** b g Muhaarar—Gloryette **Mrs J. M. M. Scott**
23 **ENOLA GREY (IRE),** gr f Havana Grey—Izola **Mrs M. Parker**
24 **GIDDY AUNT,** gr f Mayson—Jessie's Spirit (IRE) **Farraday Equine Partnership**

MR JONATHAN PORTMAN - continued

25 **HIGHLAND FLYER,** ch g Highland Reel (IRE)—Tobruk (IRE) **Mr L. A. Bellman**
26 **LYNWOOD LAD,** b g Mayson—Faithful Promise **Simpson, Tierney, Portman**
27 **MRS VAN HOPPER,** b f Adaay (IRE)—Beatrice Lacey **Turf Club 2022 & Partner 1**
28 **ONE MORE WAVE,** b g Bated Breath—Elbow Beach **Whitcoombe Park Racing**
29 **PUNTARELLE,** b f Footstepsinthesand—Maybelater **Hot To Trot Racing 2 & Anita Wigan**
30 **RIVER CHAT,** ch f Raven's Pass (USA)—Rivercat **Portlee Bloodstock**
31 **ROAR EMOTION (IRE),** b g The Last Lion (IRE)—Singuita (GER) **Whitcoombe Park Racing**
32 **RUMSTAR,** b c Havana Grey—Stellarta **Mr V. G. Ward**
33 **SHOWY,** b f Golden Horn—Steal The Show **Bloomsbury Stud**
34 **SISTER OF THOR (IRE),** b f Anodin (IRE)—Helisa (FR) **Mr A. N. Brooke Rankin**
35 **SNOW FORECAST,** b g Sea The Moon (GER)—Snow Ballerina **Mr A. N. Brooke Rankin**
36 **TWILIGHT DANCER,** b f Twilight Son—Accede **Mrs D. O. Joly**

TWO-YEAR-OLDS

37 B f 20/04 Lightning Spear—Air Stricker (FR) (Acclamation) **Whitcoombe Park Racing**
38 **AIRGUNNER,** b c 02/03 Pearl Secret—Air Biscuit (Galileo)
39 **BRINTON,** b f 27/03 Zoustar (AUS)—Bounty Box (Bahamian Bounty) (15238) **Mr M Sinclair & Partner**
40 B c 11/02 Bated Breath—Choco Box (Harbour Watch (IRE))
41 **CRY FICTION (IRE),** ch f 29/03 El Kabeir (USA)—Fictitious (Mayson) (5602) **Mr A. N. Brooke Rankin**
42 Ch c 30/04 New Bay—Dangle (IRE) (Desert Style (IRE)) (20808) **Berkeley Racing**
43 **EASEL,** br f 01/04 Tasleet—Szabo's Art (Excellent Art) (14000) **Berkeley Dollar Powell**
44 B f 24/03 Churchill (IRE)—Faustinatheyounger (IRE) (Antonius Pius (USA)) (8000) **Mrs Suzanne Williams & Partner**
45 **MAXIM DE WINTER (IRE),** gr c 03/05 Galileo (IRE)—
Mrs Danvers (Hellvelyn) (65000) **Ladyswood Stud, Mr A E Frost**
46 **OCEAN BLUE (IRE),** b f 09/02 Ten Sovereigns (IRE)—Chance of Bubbles (IRE) (Exceed And Excel (AUS)) (18000)
C.R. Lambourne, M. Forbes, D. Losse
47 B c 09/04 Havana Gold (IRE)—Riccoche (IRE) (Oasis Dream)
48 **ROSADILLY,** b f 27/01 Due Diligence (USA)—
Fenella Rose (Compton Place) (9000) **C.R. Lambourne, M. Forbes, D. Losse**
49 B c 21/03 Le Brivido (FR)—Samantha (Black Sam Bellamy (IRE)) **Mrs R Pease**
50 **SI SI LA BONNE (IRE),** b f 21/03 Kodi Bear (IRE)—
Nymfia (IRE) (Invincible Spirit (IRE)) (16807) **Mrs Suzanne Williams & Partner**
51 B f 21/03 Nathaniel (IRE)—Tallulah Rose (Exceed And Excel (AUS)) (10000) **Whitcoombe Park Racing**

Amateur Jockey: Mr J. Harding.

---

414 MR RYAN POTTER, Sellack

Postal: **The Coach House, Sellack, Ross-On-Wye, Herefordshire, HR9 6LS**
EMAIL rdpotter88@googlemail.com

1 **ANGUS DE BULL (IRE),** 7, b g Papal Bull—Diskretion (GER) **Mr S. A. B. Steel**
2 **BIG BAD BUZZ (IRE),** 7, b g Doyen (IRE)—Little Moscow (IRE) **Carl & Emma Pyne**
3 **BRUSHED UP,** 10, b m Doyen (IRE)—Definite Artist (IRE) **R. F. Bailey**
4 **D'EDGE OF GLORY (IRE),** 7, b m Fame And Glory—D'Gigi **Mr R. D. Potter**
5 **DAVITT ROAD GLORY (IRE),** 8, b m Fame And Glory—Ballydunne Present (IRE) **Didn't Cost A Lot Racing Club**
6 **DOGEM BY DESIGN (IRE),** 6, b br g Sageburg (IRE)—Janal (IRE) **Mr R. D. Potter**
7 **DON BERSY (FR),** 10, b g Califet (FR)—Tropulka God (FR) **Mr R. D. Potter**
8 **EATON MILLER (IRE),** 11, b g Milan—Four Fields (IRE) **Mr R. D. Potter**
9 **FAZAYTE (FR),** 8, b g Spider Flight (FR)—Vakina (FR) **Mr S. McCafferty**
10 **FIRST DU CHARMIL (FR),** 11, ch g Ballingarry (IRE)—Famous Member (FR) **Mr R. D. Potter**
11 **GOODWILLHUNTING (IRE),** 8, b g Carlotamix (FR)—One Edge (IRE) **Mr S. A. B. Steel**
12 **GUATEMALA LE DUN (FR),** 7, gr g Poliglote—Uranus Le Dun (FR) **Mrs L. P. Vaughan**
13 **HIGH GROUNDS (IRE),** 10, b g High Chaparral (IRE)—Civility Cat (USA) **Mr R. D. Potter**
14 **I DIDN'T COST ALOT,** 4, br f Ardad (IRE)—Cool Crescendo **Didn't Cost A Lot Racing Club**
15 **ITHAKA (IRE),** 7, b g Libranno—Taras Choice **Mr R. D. Potter**

MR RYAN POTTER - continued

16 **JANE DU BERLAIS,** 5, b m Clovis du Berlais (FR)—Bet Davis (IRE) **Ms J. Bennett**
17 **JETOILE (IRE),** 8, b g Jeremy (USA)—Accordingtoherself (IRE) **Ms J. Bennett**
18 **KNOCKANORE (IRE),** 6, b g Shantou (USA)—Ballyoscar (IRE) **Ms J. Bennett**
19 **LIGHT FLICKER (IRE),** 11, b g Royal Anthem (USA)—Five Cents More (IRE) **S & V Peets**
20 **LILY'S GEM (IRE),** 10, b m Scorpion (IRE)—Kegster (IRE) **Mr R. D. Potter**
21 **LITTLE WINDMILL (IRE),** 13, ch g Mahler—Ennismore Queen (IRE) **Mr R. D. Potter**
22 **LUCKY BOUNCE (IRE),** 6, b g Milan—Gracie B (IRE) **Mr R. D. Potter**
23 **MARIAS LAD (FR),** 7, b g Martaline—Marie Deja La (FR) **Ryan Potter Racing Club**
24 **MISTERTOMMYSHELBY (IRE),** 7, b g Alkaadhem—Coolkenna Contact (IRE) **Mr R. D. Potter**
25 **MON RAY (IRE),** 6, b m Montmartre (FR)—Seven Even (FR) **Carl & Emma Pyne**
26 **OUT BY SIX (FR),** 9, b g Scalo—Sixty Six (IRE) **Mr R. D. Potter**
27 **PAULS HILL (IRE),** 11, b g Marienbard (IRE)—Lunar Star (IRE) **Ryan Potter Racing Club**
28 **PICKAMIX,** 12, gr g Sagamix (FR)—Star of Wonder (FR) **Mr W. Fox**
29 **PITTSBURG (IRE),** 7, b g Sageburg (IRE)—Constant Approach (IRE) **Mr R. D. Potter**
30 **POST NO BILLS (IRE),** 8, b g Mahler—Shining Lights (IRE) **Pyne Swinburne Partnership**
31 **PRINCE OF BAD LINS (GER),** 5, ch g Nutan (IRE)—Pastellrosa (IRE) **Mr R. D. Potter**
32 **SHESUPINCOURT,** 6, b m Court Cave (IRE)—Supreme Cove **Ryan Potter Racing Club**
33 **SISSINGHURST (IRE),** 13, b g Kalanisi (IRE)—Sissinghurst Storm (IRE) **Mr R. D. Potter**
34 **SUEZOOKI,** 4, b f Cityscape—Floriane (IRE) **Mr R. D. Potter**
35 **UNWANTED ATTENTION (IRE),** 5, b g Pour Moi (IRE)—Balinacary **Carl & Emma Pyne**

---

415 MRS CAMILLA POULTON, Lewes

Postal: **White Cottage, Stud Farm, Telscombe Village, Lewes, BN7 3HZ**
Contacts: **PHONE 01273 300127**
EMAIL camilla.poulton67@outlook.com

1 **ACED IT (IRE),** 7, b g Lope de Vega (IRE)—Farranjordan **Crowd Racing Partnership**
2 **D'AMBONNAY (IRE),** 5, b g Hallowed Crown (AUS)—Encore du Cristal (USA) **P. S. Wardle**
3 **GOKOTTA (IRE),** 5, b m Pride of Dubai (AUS)—Sivensen (IRE) **Mrs L. G. Talbot**
4 **MAIRE'S DREAM (IRE),** 6, ch m Sholokhov (IRE)—Wild Fern (IRE) **Gold & Green Crowd & Camilla Poulton**
5 **MILITRY DECORATION (IRE),** 8, b g Epaulette (AUS)—Funcheon Vale (IRE) **Gold & Green Crowd & Camilla Poulton**
6 **PENNA ROSSA (IRE),** 4, b g Belardo (IRE)—Alpine **R Allen, Blythe Hill Racing2, the Crowd**
7 **PHOTO BOMB (IRE),** 4, b f Haatef (USA)—Formidable Guest **Mr L. Stevens**
8 **TOUCH OF THUNDER (IRE),** 5, b g Beat Hollow—Sweetheart **Blythe Hill Racing, L.Talbot & the Crowd**
9 **UNIVERSAL EFFECT,** 7, b m Universal (IRE)—Saaboog **Kestonracingclub**

THREE-YEAR-OLDS

10 **DREAM FRONTIER,** b g Massaat (IRE)—Miss Lesley **Mrs C. D. Poulton**

---

416 SIR MARK PRESCOTT BT, Newmarket

Postal: **Heath House, Moulton Road, Newmarket, Suffolk, CB8 8DU**
Contacts: **PHONE 01638 662117**
EMAIL sirmark@heathhousestables.com WEBSITE www.heathhousestables.com TWITTER @ HeathHouseNkt

1 **ARCADIAN FRIEND,** 4, b g Lope de Vega (IRE)—Best Friend (IRE) **John Pearce Racing Limited**
2 **AT THE DOUBLE (FR),** 4, b br g Almanzor (FR)—Express American (FR) **Charlie Walker - Osborne House II**
3 **EAGLE'S WAY,** 4, ch g Gleneagles (IRE)—Martlet **Tim Bunting - Osborne House II**

SIR MARK PRESCOTT BT - continued

4 **FLYAWAYDREAM,** 4, b g Farhh—Mockinbird (IRE) **Caroline Gregson & the GD Partnership**
5 **GENESIUS (IRE),** 6, ch g Teofilo (IRE)—Craic Agus Spraoi (IRE) **Owners Group 076**
6 **GLENISTER (IRE),** 4, b g Gleneagles (IRE)—Sistine **Elite Racing Club**
7 **GOLDEN SHOT,** 4, b g Golden Horn—Quenelle **W E Sturt - Osborne House**
8 **OMNISCIENT,** 4, b g Mukhadram—Miss Dashwood **Ne'er Do Wells VII**
9 **SEA KING,** 4, br g Sea The Stars (IRE)—Pamona (IRE) **Mr N. R. Boyden**
10 **WHATAWIT,** 5, b g Sakhee (USA)—Florie **Strawberry Fields Stud**
11 **WHISPERING SONG,** 4, b f Danon Ballade (JPN)—Jewelled **M & M Franklin**
12 **ZONISTY (IRE),** 5, b g Zoffany (IRE)—Promise Me (IRE) **Mr W. J. S. Prosser**

THREE-YEAR-OLDS

13 **ALEXANDRETTA,** b f Sea The Moon (GER)—Alinstante **Miss K. Rausing**
14 **BLINDEDBYTHELIGHTS (GER),** b g Protectionist (GER)—Batya (IRE) **Middleham Park Racing XXXV**
15 **BORN RULER,** b c Kingman—Filia Regina **Charlie Walker - Osborne House**
16 **BRAVE KNIGHT,** b c Sir Percy—Belladonna **Neil Greig - Osborne House**
17 **BRAVURA,** b g Saxon Warrior (JPN)—Approach **Denford Stud Limited**
18 **DARK GOLD,** br g Havana Gold (IRE)—Muscovado (USA) **Philip Bamford - Osborne House**
19 **DESERT FALCON (IRE),** b g Gleneagles (IRE)—Love Oasis **Allison, Gregson, Matterson & Satchell**
20 **IMPERIAL DREAM (IRE),** b g Holy Roman Emperor (IRE)—Iffa Red (IRE) **Gregson, Jenkins, Lee & Warman**
21 **MISS CYNTHIA,** b f Sea The Moon (GER)—Best Friend (IRE) **John Pearce Racing Limited**
22 **MOON FLIGHT (IRE),** b g Sea The Moon (GER)—Miss Margarita **Mr W. J. S. Prosser**
23 **NATACATA,** gr f Kitten's Joy (USA)—Na Balada (BRZ) **Miss K. Rausing**
24 **OTTOMAN PRINCE (IRE),** ch g Zoffany (IRE)—Byzantium **Baxter, Charnley, Jones & Prosser**
25 **PLEDGEOFALLEGIANCE (IRE),** b c Sea The Stars (IRE)—Vow **Victorious Racing Limited**
26 **ROBUSTO (IRE),** b g Churchill (IRE)—Blackgold Fairy (USA) **Heath House Optimists**
27 **SPRITZIN' (IRE),** b f Sea The Stars (IRE)—Affability (IRE) **Mt. Brilliant Farm & Ranch, LLC**
28 **SURE SPIRIT (IRE),** b f Invincible Spirit (IRE)—Don't Be **Hot To Trot Racing 1, Mr J. S. M. Fill**
29 **TIFFANY (IRE),** b f Farhh—Affinity **Elite Racing Club**
30 **TROOPER BISDEE (IRE),** ch g Australia—Merritt Island **Mr & Mrs John Kelsey-Fry**
31 **TRUE LEGEND (IRE),** b c Camelot—Scarlet And Gold (IRE) **Tim Bunting - Osborne House IV**

TWO-YEAR-OLDS

32 B f 14/04 Shalaa (IRE)—Al Wathna (Nayef (USA)) **HM The King and HM The Queen Consort**
33 **ALMUDENA,** b f 11/04 Study of Man (IRE)—Albamara (Galileo (IRE)) **Miss K. Rausing**
34 B c 02/02 Time Test—Alys Love (New Approach (IRE)) (37000) **Middleham Park Racing CIII**
35 Gr c 29/03 Frankel—America Nova (FR) (Verglas (IRE)) (300000) **Al Wasmiyah Stud**
36 **ANGEL PASS (IRE),** b f 16/04 Dark Angel (IRE)—Aintisari (IRE) (Helmet (AUS)) (104042) **Lady C. J. O'Reilly**
37 **APOSTLE,** ch f 14/02 Ulysses (IRE)—Heaven Sent (Pivotal) **Cheveley Park Stud Limited**
38 **AWAY DAY (IRE),** b c 25/03 Camelot—Daytona (GER) (Lando (GER)) (70000) **Graeme Moore - Osborne House**
39 **GODSEND,** ch c 26/01 Nathaniel (IRE)—
Floriss (Medicean) (180000) **BuntingOsb/Newsells/NewEnglandStanleyEst**
40 **HAUMEA (IRE),** br f 24/03 Invincible Spirit (IRE)—Finagle (IRE) (Azamour (IRE)) (55000) **Mr N. R. Boyden**
41 **HEAT OF PASSION,** b f 20/03 Dubawi (IRE)—
Here To Eternity (USA) (Stormy Atlantic (USA)) (280112) **Miss K. Rausing**
42 B g 22/02 Golden Horn—Inshiraah (FR) (Holy Roman Emperor (IRE)) **Mrs V. Machen**
43 **JUDGEMENTOFSOLOMON,** b c 09/02 Study of Man (IRE)—Diablerette (Green Desert (USA)) (35000)
Troubridge,Mailer,Gregson,Greenwood,Budd
44 **KINEMATICA,** ch f 19/03 Kendargent (FR)—Kinetica (Stormy Atlantic (USA)) **Miss K. Rausing**
45 **KNIGHT TEMPLAR,** b c 03/02 Haafhd—Jewelled (Fantastic Light (USA)) **M & M Franklin**
46 **LINGUA FRANCA,** b f 16/02 Study of Man (IRE)—Leaderene (Selkirk (USA)) **Miss K. Rausing**
47 **MISS GITANA (IRE),** b f 27/02 Nathaniel (IRE)—
Miss Celestial (IRE) (Exceed And Excel (AUS)) **John Pearce Racing Limited**
48 **NIGHT OF DECREE,** b f 02/03 Night of Thunder (IRE)—Intrigued (Darshaan) **Denford Stud Limited**
49 **OPAL ROSE,** b f 05/03 Workforce—Norfolk Sky (Haafhd) **Richborough Stud**
50 **ORBITAL,** b f 15/02 Pivotal—Lunar Corona (Dansili) **Cheveley Park Stud Limited**
51 **OVERTURE,** ch f 25/02 New Approach (IRE)—Tribute Act (Exceed And Excel (AUS)) **Elite Racing Club**
52 **PAGLIACCI (IRE),** ch c 06/03 Gleneagles (IRE)—California (IRE) (Azamour (IRE)) **Denford Stud Limited**
53 **RECALL,** b c 11/02 Golden Horn—
Always Remembered (IRE) (Galileo (IRE)) (160000) **Charlie Walker - Osborne House III**

SIR MARK PRESCOTT BT - continued

54 **RISHI,** b c 25/04 Massaat (IRE)—Sitting Pretty (IRE) (Compton Place) (28571) **Mr J. B. Haggas**
55 **ROUGE SELLIER,** ch f 19/02 Lope de Vega (IRE)—
Screen Star (IRE) (Tobougg (IRE)) (260000) **Memento Vivere Racing**
56 **SCARBOROUGHWARNING,** b f 08/05 Harry Angel (IRE)—
Scarborough (IRE) (Dandy Man (IRE)) **Taylor's Bloodstock Ltd**
57 B g 30/03 Too Darn Hot—Seta (Pivotal) **Lady Bamford**
58 B f 19/03 Almanzor (FR)—Star Value (IRE) (Danehill Dancer (IRE)) **HM The King and HM The Queen Consort**
59 **TAPIS ROUGE (IRE),** ch c 22/02 Le Havre (IRE)—
Starring Guest (IRE) (Teofilo (IRE)) (35000) **Cavendish, Gregson, Royle & Scouller**
60 **VALIDATED,** b c 07/03 Iffraaj—Believable (Acclamation) (25000) **Cheveley Park Stud Limited**
61 **WARMONGER (IRE),** b c 27/03 Camelot—
War Goddess (IRE) (Champs Elysees) (52000) **Tim Bunting - Osborne House III**

Assistant Trainer: William Butler, **Pupil Assistant:** Ben James.

Flat Jockey: Luke Morris.

---

417 MISS KATY PRICE, Llanigon

Postal: **Willow Croft, Llanigon, Hay-On-Wye, Herefordshire, HR3 5PN**
Contacts: **PHONE 07976 820819**
EMAIL katyprice2005@aol.com WEBSITE www.facebook.com/katypriceracing

1 **ALL GUNS BLAZING (IRE),** 4, b g Bullet Train—Gaye Future **Miss K. J. Price**
2 **EL ROJO GRANDE (IRE),** 6, ch g Ocovango—Matt Wood (IRE) **Mr N. Elliott**
3 **GALLOW FORD (IRE),** 8, b g Westerner—Magical Theatre (IRE) **Mr N. Elliott**
4 **KING OF BRAZIL,** 6, b g Blue Bresil (FR)—Blue Ride (IRE) **Nick Elliott & Heather Shane**
5 **LOST CONNECTIONS (IRE),** 7, b m Dylan Thomas (IRE)—Mini Shan (IRE) **Peter Hearn & David Lipsey**
6 **MIX MASTER,** 9, b g Fair Mix (IRE)—Foxchapel Queen (IRE) **Mr L. J. Williams**
7 **PEACENIK (IRE),** 4, b g Mount Nelson—Liss Agragh (IRE) **Mr N. Elliott**
8 **PREMIER D'TROICE (FR),** 9, b g Great Pretender (IRE)—Mick Bora (FR) **Nick Elliott & Heather Shane**
9 **ROCK THE HOUSE (IRE),** 8, b g Scorpion (IRE)—Holiday Time (IRE) **Mike Harris Racing Club**
10 **THE REBEL BREEN,** 4, b g Bated Breath—Style And Grace (IRE) **I. M. McGready**

---

418 MR RICHARD PRICE, Hereford

Postal: **Criftage Farm, Ullingswick, Hereford, Herefordshire, HR1 3JG**
Contacts: **PHONE 01432 820263 MOBILE 07929 200598**

1 **BAKEWELL,** 4, b f Alhebayeb (IRE)—Rock Cake (IRE) **J & V Morse**
2 **BEAR A HAND,** 6, b m Pether's Moon (IRE)—River Beauty **Mrs V. J. Morse**
3 **BESTGETGOING (IRE),** 5, b m Jet Away—Across The River (IRE) **Alastair & Pippa McLeish**
4 **HIGHLAND LASS (FR),** 4, ch f Highland Reel (IRE)—Palace Princess (FR) **Mr G E Amey & Mr D M Boddy**
5 **OCEAN REACH,** 7, b m Phoenix Reach (IRE)—Ocean Transit (IRE) **Mr G E Amey & Mr D M Boddy**
6 **OUT FOR JUSTICE (IRE),** 10, b g Beneficial—Dustys Delight (IRE) **Alastair & Pippa McLeish**
7 **PADDINGTON EXPRESS (IRE),** 5, b g Shirocco (GER)—True Dedication (IRE) **Alastair & Pippa McLeish**
8 **RHUBARB,** 6, b m Nayef (USA)—Cockney Fire **Ocean's Five**

THREE-YEAR-OLDS

9 B f Frontiersman—Ocean Transit (IRE)

Assistant Trainer: Jane Price.

419 MR PETER PRITCHARD, Shipston-on-Stour

Postal: **Upper Farm Lodge, Upper Farm, Whatcote, Shipston-On-Stour, Warwickshire, CV36 5EF**
Contacts: **MOBILE 07376 500499**
EMAIL pennypritch55@hotmail.co.uk

1 4, B c Passing Glance—Astral Affair (IRE)
2 6, B m Passing Glance—Astral Affair (IRE)
3 4, Br f Passing Glance—Earcomesannie (IRE)
4 **EARCOMESBOB,** 8, ch g Yorgunnabelucky (USA)—Earcomesannie (IRE) **R W Stowe & Marc Miller**
5 **EARCOMESSUE,** 6, b m Passing Glance—Earcomesannie (IRE) **Mr R. W. Stowe**
6 **FRANZ KLAMMER,** 11, b g Midnight Legend—Ski **Mr M. J. Miller**
7 5, B m Passing Glance—Tilinisi (IRE)

420 MRS ELIZABETH QUINLAN, Appleby-in-Westmorland

Postal: **Bolton Mill, Bolton, Appleby, Cumbria, CA16 6AL**
Contacts: **PHONE 017683 61363**
EMAIL lizb_345@hotmail.com

1 **ANGE ENDORMI (IRE),** 7, ch g Leading Light (IRE)—Maxford Lady (IRE) **Mrs E. Quinlan**
2 **BENITO (FR),** 6, b g Rail Link—Aspolina (IRE) **Mrs E. Quinlan**
3 **CITY DERBY (IRE),** 7, ch g Ask—Reine d'Or (IRE) **Fools Who Dream Partnership**
4 **COEUR AIMANT (FR),** 8, b g Maresca Sorrento (FR)—Babet (IRE) **Mrs B. Butterworth**
5 **COMEDAYGODAY (IRE),** 6, ch m Soldier of Fortune (IRE)—Whatagoa (IRE) **Mrs E J Quinlan & Partner**
6 **GETAWAY LUV (IRE),** 8, b g Getaway (GER)—Ut Love (FR) **Fools Who Dream Partnership**
7 **KITTY HALL (IRE),** 9, b m Fame And Glory—Set In Her Ways (IRE) **Mrs E. Quinlan**
8 **POWERS DILEMMA (IRE),** 6, br g Kalanisi (IRE)—Maggie Howard (IRE) **Fools Who Dream Partnership**
9 **SNOWED IN (IRE),** 14, gr g Dark Angel (IRE)—Spinning Gold **Mrs E. Quinlan**
10 **THATSY (FR),** 9, gr g Martaline—Rainallday (FR) **Mrs B Butterworth & Mrs Jackie Holliday**

421 MR DENIS QUINN, Newmarket

Postal: **Stockbridge Stables, 192 High Street, Newmarket, Suffolk, CB8 9AP**
Contacts: **MOBILE 07435 340008**

1 **ALDERSHOT,** 4, b f Cityscape—Elegant Annie **Mr D. P. Quinn**
2 **BO TAIFAN (IRE),** 6, gr g Gutaifan (IRE)—Scarlet Rosefinch **Mr A. F. Keane**
3 **CLOUGHROE (IRE),** 5, b g Sans Frontieres (IRE)—Capparoe Cross (IRE) **Mr D. P. Quinn**
4 4, B g Intrinsic—Cthulhu (USA)
5 **DANCING ZEBEDEE (IRE),** 6, gr g Zebedee—Yaqoot **Mr D. P. Quinn**
6 **DAYEM (IRE),** 4, b c Acclamation—Slovak (IRE)
7 **DE ROCKER,** 4, ch g Equiano (FR)—Kawaii **Four Winds Racing Partnership**
8 4, Ro f Coach House (IRE)—Fast Menantie (FR)
9 **GOSSAMER SILK,** 5, ch m Equiano (FR)—Gossamer Seed (IRE) **Mr A. F. Keane**
10 **HEY ELVIS,** 5, b g Excelebration (IRE)—Sky Boat (IRE) **Mrs J. J. Beasley**
11 **HYBA,** 6, b m Muhaarar—Jellwa (IRE) **Miss C. McKernan**

MR DENIS QUINN - continued

12 **ISLE OF HOPE,** 4, b g Due Diligence (USA)—Rip Van Suzy (IRE) **Mr D. P. Quinn**
13 **MAWINGO,** 4, b g Oasis Dream—Million Faces **C. J. Mills**
14 **PILLARS OF EARTH,** 6, b g Nathaniel (IRE)—Aliena (IRE) **Four Winds Racing Partnership**
15 **ROUGE ROMANCE (IRE),** 4, b f Profitable (IRE)—Red Ivy (IRE)
16 **SAMMY SUNSHINE (GER),** 5, ch m Sea The Moon (GER)—Summertime (GER) **Zeal Racing Limited**
17 4, B c Dragon Pulse (IRE)—Sense of A Woman (USA)
18 **STAR OF ST LOUIS (FR),** 6, b g Style Vendome (FR)—Momix **Zeal Racing Limited**
19 **SUNSET SALUTE,** 5, b g Twilight Son—Hill Welcome **Mrs J. E. Lambert**
20 **TO THE BAR (IRE),** 5, ch g Tamayuz—Coachhouse Lady (USA) **Mr D. P. Quinn**

THREE-YEAR-OLDS

21 **KINKY BOOTS,** b f Aclaim (IRE)—Woomera **Just Wing It**
22 B g Dragon Pulse (IRE)—Tilly Two (IRE) **Mrs J. J. Beasley**

---

422 MR JOHN QUINN, Malton

Trainer did not wish details of their string to appear

---

423 MR ALASTAIR RALPH, Bridgnorth

Postal: **Bynd Farm, Bynd Lane, Billingsley, Bridgnorth, Shropshire, WV16 6PQ**
Contacts: **WORK 01746 860807 PHONE 07912 184217**
WORK EMAIL info@alastairralphracing.co.uk WEBSITE www.alastairralphracing.co.uk

1 **BALLINOULART (IRE),** 5, b br g Court Cave (IRE)—Lace Parasol (IRE) **Taylormaid**
2 **BILLINGSLEY (IRE),** 11, b g Millenary—Retain That Magic (IRE) **Alastair Ralph Racing**
3 **BLACK SAM VICKI,** 5, b m Black Sam Bellamy (IRE)—Overthrow **Strutting Cockerels Syndicate**
4 4, B g Telescope (IRE)—Bollin Across **Mrs N. S. Harris**
5 **BUTLER'S BRIEF (IRE),** 8, b g Yeats (IRE)—She's On The Case (IRE) **You Can Be Sure**
6 **CHANCEUX (IRE),** 7, b g Mahler—Granny Mc Cann (IRE) **Rskm Bloodstock**
7 **CHEVINGTON,** 4, b g Jack Hobbs—Norma Hill **Mr G. Lloyd**
8 **CHURCHMAN,** 5, b g Dunaden (FR)—Pickersleigh (IRE) **Mr M. H. Jones**
9 **CLOVER PASS,** 6, b m Passing Glance—Allforclover (IRE) **Miss S. Troughton**
10 **ELMOUNT (IRE),** 7, b g Yeats (IRE)—Maltesse (IRE) **B. Hawkins**
11 **GLANCE FROM CLOVER,** 8, b g Passing Glance—Allforclover (IRE) **Miss S. Troughton**
12 **GOVERNOR GREEN (IRE),** 6, b g Aiken—Little Green (IRE) **The Fortune Hunters**
13 **GUERLAIN DE VAUX (FR),** 7, b g Tiger Groom—Que du Charmil (FR) **S W Racing**
14 **HEY MISTER DJ (IRE),** 5, gr g Jukebox Jury (IRE)—Margarita (GER) **Mr R. J. Simpson**
15 **HOLLY HARTINGO (IRE),** 7, b m Well Chosen—Hazel Toi (IRE) **The HHH Partnership**
16 **ICONIC ROCK (IRE),** 7, b m Yeats (IRE)—Forgotten Lady (IRE) **Fothergill & Ralph**
17 **IONTACH CHEVAL,** 7, b g Dunaden (FR)—Dancing Emily (IRE) **RSKM Bloodstock**
18 **KABRIT (IRE),** 8, ch g Mastercraftsman (IRE)—Twinkling Ice (USA) **Alastair Ralph Racing**
19 **KATESON,** 10, gr g Black Sam Bellamy (IRE)—Silver Kate (IRE) **D. M. Richards**
20 **KRACQUER,** 9, ch g Schiaparelli (GER)—Norma Hill **Mr G. Lloyd**
21 **LETS GO TO VEGAS (IRE),** 5, b m Getaway (GER)—Danielle's Journey **Let's Go To Vegas Partnership**
22 **MAGICAL MAGGIE,** 6, gr m Geordieland (FR)—Bollin Across **Mrs N. S. Harris**
23 **MAGNA BELLA,** 4, b f Due Diligence (USA)—Sugar Beet **Mr S. Price**
24 **MAGNA SAM,** 9, b g Black Sam Bellamy (IRE)—Angie Marinie **Mr S. Price**
25 **MANKHOOL (IRE),** 5, ch g New Approach (IRE)—Majestic Manner **B. Hawkins**
26 **METHOD MADNESS (IRE),** 8, b g Sans Frontieres (IRE)—Inishbeg House (IRE) **Fothergills Sparey and Lewis**
27 **MIX OF CLOVER,** 9, b g Fair Mix (IRE)—Allforclover (IRE) **Miss S. Troughton**
28 **OSELETA,** 5, b m Clovis du Berlais (FR)—Cedelor (FR) **The Oseleta Partnership**

MR ALASTAIR RALPH - continued

29 **OSPREY CALL (IRE),** 8, br g Winged Love (IRE)—Courting Whitney (IRE) **Gentech, Franklin, Archer & James**
30 **PAVLODAR (FR),** 4, ch g Recorder—Sampaquita (FR) **Pavlodar Partnership**
31 **POLLYONESOCK (IRE),** 5, b m Mount Nelson—Kenzie (IRE) **Mrs P. Simpson**
32 **PRINCE DE JUILLEY (FR),** 6, b g Honolulu (IRE)—Horemsaf (IRE) **The Big Dog Partnership**
33 **QUESHI BRIDGE (IRE),** 7, b m Shantou (USA)—Royal Robin (IRE) **Mr A. Ralph**
34 **RISK D'ARGENT (FR),** 7, gr g My Risk (FR)—Villebruyere (FR) **The Risk d'Argent Partnership**
35 **SADIE HILL (IRE),** 6, ch m Kingston Hill—Sadie Thompson (IRE) **Making Hay**
36 **SCHERBOBALOB,** 5, gr ro g Cityscape—Cloudy Spirit **Mrs N. S. Harris**
37 **SWEET MAGIC (IRE),** 5, b m Flemensfirth (USA)—Garraidubh (IRE) **Fwittery Racing**
38 **TAP TAP BOOM,** 9, ro g Foxwedge (AUS)—Exclusive Approval (USA) **Gentech,James,Franklin,Bickmore&ralph**
39 **THANKYOURLUCKYSTAR,** 7, b g Dunaden (FR)—Cloudy Spirit **Mrs N. S. Harris**
40 **TINTERN ABBEY (IRE),** 6, b m Mahler—Portobello Sunrise (IRE) **The Tintern Abbey Partnership**
41 **TWYFORD'S DIAMOND,** 4, b f Black Sam Bellamy (IRE)—Overthrow **Strutting Cockerels 2**
42 **WELL VICKY (IRE),** 6, b m Well Chosen—Vicante (IRE) **The Hawkins Partnership**
43 **WELSH CHARGER (IRE),** 5, b g Westerner—Answer Ur Phone (IRE) **Jones, Spiers & Hartwell**
44 **YOUR BAND,** 8, b g Helmet (AUS)—Kampai **Only Fools Own Horses**

Yard Sponsor: Planned Office Interiors Ltd.

NH Jockey: Jonathan Burke, Nick Schofield. **Conditional Jockey:** Jay Tidball.

---

424 MR TIM REED, Hexham

Postal: **Moss Kennels, Haydon Bridge, Hexham, Northumberland, NE47 6NL**
Contacts: **PHONE 01434 344016 MOBILE 07703 270408**
EMAIL timreedracing@gmail.com

1 **ANOTHER PARK (IRE),** 6, b m Walk In The Park (IRE)—Another Cliche (IRE) **Davies, Huddleston, Reed**
2 **BIG DIFFERENCE (IRE),** 10, b g Presenting—Roque de Cyborg (IRE) **Mr W. T. Reed**
3 **RUINOUS (IRE),** 8, b br g Aizavoski (IRE)—Will She Smile (IRE) **Mothers & Daughters**

THREE-YEAR-OLDS

4 Ch f Doyen (IRE)—Windsor Higgins (IRE) **Mr W. T. Reed**

Assistant Trainer: Mrs E. J. Reed.

Conditional Jockey: Harry Reed.

---

425 MR DAVID REES, Haverfordwest

Postal: **Knock Moor, Clarbeston Road, Haverfordwest, Pembrokeshire, SA63 4SL**
Contacts: **PHONE 01437 731308 MOBILE 07775 662463 FAX 01437 731308**
EMAIL accounts@davidreesfencing.co.uk

1 **DUNBAR (FR),** 10, gr g Lord du Sud (FR)—Jiletta (FR) **D & J Rees**
2 **ESPERTI (IRE),** 6, b g Presenting—Elsie (IRE) **D. A. Rees**
3 **JAUNTY BELLE,** 5, ch m Yorgunnabelucky (USA)—Jaunty Spirit **Three Men & The Filly**
4 **KARANNELLE (IRE),** 8, b m Nathaniel (IRE)—Dance Lively (USA) **D. A. Rees**
5 **MISTY MAI (IRE),** 13, b m Westerner—Arcanum (IRE) **D. A. Rees**
6 **ROBIN OF SHERWOOD (IRE),** 10, b br g Robin des Pres (FR)—Galleta **West Is Best**

---

426 MRS HELEN REES, Dorchester

Postal: **Distant Hills, Chalmington, Dorchester, Dorset, DT2 0HB**
Contacts: **PHONE 07715 558289**
EMAIL helen-rees@live.co.uk

1 **BEYOND SUPREMACY (IRE),** 11, b g Beneficial—Slaney Athlete (IRE) **Mrs H. E. Rees**
2 **MY ROCKSTAR (IRE),** 7, b g Valirann (FR)—All Notoriety (IRE) **Mrs H. E. Rees**

---

427 MRS LYDIA RICHARDS, Chichester

Postal: **Lynch Farm, Hares Lane, Funtington, Chichester, West Sussex, PO18 9LW**
Contacts: **PHONE 01243 574882 MOBILE 07803 199061**
EMAIL lydia.richards@sky.com

1 **CAPSTAN,** 4, b g Kingman—Arizona Jewel **Aura (Gas) Holdings Ltd**
2 **CERTAINLY RED,** 9, ch g Midnight Legend—Venetian Lass **The Venetian Lad Partnership**
3 **CITY TOUR,** 7, b g Dutch Art—Privacy Order **Mrs E. F. J. Seal**
4 **EYE CANDY (IRE),** 4, b f Jukebox Jury (IRE)—Chinara (IRE) **Mrs D. J. Fleming**
5 **FLORENCE STREET,** 5, b m Iffraaj—Queen's Dream (GER) **Mrs L. Richards**
6 **GOOD NEWS,** 11, b g Midnight Legend—Venetian Lass **The Good News Partnership**
7 5, B m Passing Glance—Leyla's Gift **Mrs L. Richards**
8 **MURHIB (IRE),** 11, b g Sea The Stars (IRE)—Mood Swings (IRE) **The Murhib Partnership**
9 **RUBY RICHARDS,** 7, gr ro m Alkaased (USA)—Venetian Lass **Mrs L. Richards**
10 **SMITH (IRE),** 7, ch g Dawn Approach (IRE)—Alazeya (IRE) **Bryan Mathieson & Lydia Richards**
11 **TARA,** 5, b m Toronado (IRE)—Demoiselle Bond **The Demoiselle Bond Partnership**

---

428 MR NICKY RICHARDS, Greystoke

Postal: **Rectory Farm, Greystoke, Penrith, Cumbria, CA11 0UJ**
Contacts: **HOME 017684 83160 PHONE 017684 83392 MOBILE 07771 906609**
EMAIL office@nickyrichardsracing.com WEBSITE www.nickyrichardsracing.com

1 **AUBIS WALK (FR),** 7, b m Walk In The Park (IRE)—Aubisquinette (FR) **Mr K. Alexander**
2 **BETTER GETALONG (IRE),** 12, b g Gold Well—Arequipa (IRE) **Tarzan Bloodstock**
3 **BIG BAD BEAR (IRE),** 9, br g Jeremy (USA)—Our Polly (IRE) **Tor Side Racing**
4 **CAIUS MARCIUS (IRE),** 12, b g King's Theatre (IRE)—
Ain't Misbehavin (IRE) **Mr C P Norbury & Tarzan Bloodstock**
5 **CASTLE RUSHEN (IRE),** 8, b g Fame And Glory—Rosie Suspect (IRE) **Exors of the Late Mr T. J. Hemmings**
6 **CLOVIS ISLAND,** 5, b g Clovis du Berlais (FR)—Egretta Island (IRE) **Charlie Doocey / Cathal Doocey**
7 **CNOC NA SI (IRE),** 6, ch m Flemensfirth (USA)—Fairy Hill (IRE) **The Spirit Partnership**
8 **CONISTON CLOUDS (IRE),** 7, gr g Cloudings (IRE)—Lincon Lady (IRE) **Accurite Racing**
9 **CONISTON GEORGE (IRE),** 5, ch g Flemensfirth (USA)—Dazza **Accurite Racing**
10 **COURT DREAMING (IRE),** 10, b g Court Cave (IRE)—Louis's Teffia (IRE) **Dark Horse Racing Ltd**
11 **EVERYDAY CHAMPAGNE (IRE),** 7, gr g Doyen (IRE)—Magie de Toulouse (FR) **Katie & Brian Castle**
12 **FAMOUS BRIDGE (IRE),** 7, b g Fame And Glory—Wahiba Hall (IRE) **Exors of the Late Mr T. J. Hemmings**
13 **FINDTHETIME (IRE),** 7, b g Shantou (USA)—Bisoguet (IRE) **Tor Side Racing**
14 **FINNTHEMAGICIAN (IRE),** 5, b g Shantou (USA)—Twentytwo's Taken (IRE) **Mr P. D. Bird**
15 **FLORIDA DREAMS (IRE),** 5, b g Doyen (IRE)—First Line (GER) **Mr J. Fyffe**
16 **FLY BY MILAN (IRE),** 8, b g Milan—So Proper (IRE) **Langdale Bloodstock**
17 **GEGE VILLE (FR),** 7, b g Protektor (GER)—Auvloo Ville (FR) **Mrs A. Starkie**
18 **GLINGER FLAME (IRE),** 11, gr g Daylami (IRE)—Titian Flame (IRE) **Mr James Westoll**
19 **GLITTERING LOVE (IRE),** 11, b g Winged Love (IRE)—Glittering Image (IRE) **The Fife Boys + 1**
20 **GONFALONIER (FR),** 7, ch g Spanish Moon (USA)—Tuffe (FR) **Mr P. Polly**

MR NICKY RICHARDS - continued

21 **HEADSCARF LIL (IRE),** 9, b m Getaway (GER)—Bleu Money (IRE) **Accurite Racing & Tarzan Bloodstock**
22 **HOUSTON TEXAS (IRE),** 9, b g Dylan Thomas (IRE)—Royal Robin (IRE) **Mr A. S. Crawford**
23 **JUNIOR COMANDEUR (FR),** 4, b g Cokoriko (FR)—Nobless d'Aron (FR) **Mr P. Polly**
24 **KAJAKI (IRE),** 10, gr g Mastercraftsman (IRE)—No Quest (IRE) **Multiple Sclerosis Borders Racing Club 1**
25 **LUCKIE SEVEN (IRE),** 5, b g Soldier of Fortune (IRE)—
Uimhir A Seacht (IRE) **Mrs I. C. Sellars & Major P. Arkwright**
26 **MAROWN (IRE),** 9, b g Milan—Rosie Suspect (IRE) **Exors of the Late Mr T. J. Hemmings**
27 **MAUGHOLD HEAD,** 6, b g Fame And Glory—Misty Lass (IRE) **Exors of the Late Mr T. J. Hemmings**
28 **MILLIE OF MAYO,** 8, b m Overbury (IRE)—Gertrude Webb **Mr A. C. R. Stubbs, R. Kent**
29 **MISS MILANO (IRE),** 8, b m Milan—Dewasentah (IRE) **Tor Side Racing**
30 **NAB WOOD (IRE),** 6, b g Court Cave (IRE)—Glenark (IRE) **Tarzan Bloodstock**
31 **NELLS SON,** 8, b g Trans Island—Miss Nellie (IRE) **Langdale Bloodstock**
32 **NO REGRETS (IRE),** 9, b g Presenting—E Mac (IRE) **Jim Ennis & Tony Killoran**
33 **ONE STEP UP (FR),** 5, b g Cockney Rebel (IRE)—Or des Joncs (FR) **Tor Side Racing**
34 **PADDOCK COTTAGE (IRE),** 7, b g Pour Moi (IRE)—Blend **D. Wesley-Yates**
35 **PARISENCORE (FR),** 7, b g Walk In The Park (IRE)—Folk Dancing (FR) **Mrs I. C. Sellars & Major P. Arkwright**
36 **PRESIDENT SCOTTIE (IRE),** 5, b g Milan—Kinard True (IRE) **Hargrove, Parker & Rafferty**
37 **RICKETY GATE,** 8, b g Trans Island—Hannah Jacques (IRE) **Tarzan Bloodstock**
38 **ROSE OF SIENA (IRE),** 6, b m Califet (FR)—The Tabster (IRE) **Mrs Pat Sloan**
39 **SAUCE OF LIFE (IRE),** 8, b g Califet (FR)—Salsaparilla (FR) **Mrs I. C. Sellars & Major P. Arkwright**
40 **SERIOUS EGO (GER),** 10, b g Sholokhov (IRE)—Sunshine Story (IRE) **Greystoke Owners**
41 **SHE'S A ROCCA (IRE),** 8, b m Shirocco (GER)—Hannigan's Lodger (IRE) **Mrs I. C. Sellars & Major P. Arkwright**
42 **SNOWY CLOUDS (IRE),** 7, gr g Cloudings (IRE)—
Wednesday Girl (IRE) **Highclere T/bred Racing - Snowy Clouds 1**
43 **SOFT RISK (FR),** 7, b g My Risk (FR)—Douce Ambiance (FR) **Mr James Westoll**
44 **SUMMERGROUNDS,** 7, b g Phoenix Reach (IRE)—Hannah Jacques (IRE) **Summergrounds Partnership**
45 **TFOU (FR),** 7, b g Authorized (IRE)—Fire Moon Julie (FR) **Tarzan Bloodstock**
46 **THE KALOOKI KID,** 5, gr g Gentlewave (IRE)—Wild Blueberry (IRE) **Eddie Melville & Kenny Haughey**
47 **UNCLE ALASTAIR,** 11, b g Midnight Legend—Cyd Charisse **Mr Eddie Melville & Partners**
48 **UNIVERSAL FOLLY,** 8, b g Universal (IRE)—Madam Jolie (IRE) **Tor Side Racing**
49 **YAKALEO (FR),** 4, b g Buck's Boum (FR)—Implora (FR) **Mr P. Polly**

Assistant Trainer: Harry Haynes, Joey Haynes, **Secretary:** Antonia Reid.

NH Jockey: Brian Hughes, Danny McMenamin, Sean Quinlan. **Conditional Jockey:** Conor Rabbitt. **Amateur Jockey:** Amy Corrado, Jack Power.

---

429 MR JOHN DAVID RICHES, Pilling

Postal: **Moss Side Farm, Off Lancaster Road, Scronkey, Pilling, Lancashire, PR3 6SR**
Contacts: **PHONE 01253 799190**
EMAIL jrracing@btinternet.com

1 **ANGEL EYES,** 8, b m Piccolo—Miacarla **J R Racing**
2 **ASTAPOR,** 5, b g Sixties Icon—Good Morning Lady **J R Racing**
3 **MR GAMBINO,** 6, b g Music Master—Snow Dancer (IRE) **J R Racing**
4 **RAIN CAP,** 6, b g Fountain of Youth (IRE)—Rough Courte (IRE) **J R Racing**
5 **STORM MASTER,** 6, b g Music Master—Miacarla **J R Racing**

THREE-YEAR-OLDS

6 **BLUE JAY WAY,** b g Sixties Icon—Dark Blue (IRE) **J R Racing**
7 **FUMBLEINTHEJUNGLE,** b g Bungle Inthejungle—Good Morning Lady **J R Racing**

---

430 MR MARK RIMELL, Witney

Postal: **Fairspear Equestrian Centre, Fairspear Road, Leafield, Witney, Oxfordshire, OX29 9NT**
Contacts: **PHONE 07778 648303 MOBILE 07778 648303, 07973 627054**
EMAIL rimell@rimellracing.com WEBSITE www.rimellracing.com

1 **ASSEMBLED,** 7, gr g Iffraaj—Bezique **Ms J. Williams**
2 **HALLWOOD (FR),** 6, gr g Martaline—Ball of Wood (FR) **Roel Hill Farm limited**
3 **I'M A STARMAN,** 10, ch g Schiaparelli (GER)—Strathtay **M. G. Rimell**
4 **IMPRINT (IRE),** 4, ch g Footstepsinthesand—Aine (IRE) **PremierRacing.club**
5 **THAPA VC (IRE),** 5, b g The Gurkha (IRE)—Merritt Island **The Circle of five**
6 **TIGER BEETLE,** 5, b g Camelot—Beach Frolic **M. G. Rimell**

THREE-YEAR-OLDS

7 **KHANGAI,** b g Twilight Son—Samasana (IRE) **M. G. Rimell**
8 **RED MAIDS,** b f Invincible Spirit (IRE)—Desert Blossom (IRE) **PremierRacing.club**
9 **TOUS LES GRIS,** gr ro f Lethal Force (IRE)—Tiger Milly
10 B c Adaay (IRE)—What Excitement

Assistant Trainer: Annie Rimell.

---

431 MR DAVE ROBERTS, Kenley

Postal: **Leasowes Farm, Kenley, Shrewsbury, Shropshire, SY5 6NY**
Contacts: **PHONE 07854 550606**

1 **BILLY BUTCHER (IRE),** 5, b g Mahler—Reillys Daughter **Mr D. Bradbury**
2 5, Ch g Cannock Chase (USA)—Cat Six (USA) **D. B. Roberts**
3 **G'DAY AUSSIE,** 10, b g Aussie Rules (USA)—Moi Aussi (USA) **Mr D. Bradbury**
4 **MAN OF THE NORTH,** 10, b g And Beyond (IRE)—Latin Beauty (IRE) **Last Day Racing Partnership**
5 **PARKED IN A PUDDLE,** 7, b m Norse Dancer (IRE)—Cat Six (USA) **D. B. Roberts**
6 **QUICK OF THE NIGHT,** 6, b m Gentlewave (IRE)—Message Personnel (FR) **Mr D. T. Carder**
7 **RACHEL LOUISE,** 8, b m Shirocco (GER)—Avoine (IRE) **Shropshire Racing**
8 **RACING SPIRIT,** 11, ch g Sir Percy—Suertuda **D. B. Roberts**
9 **SHROPSHIRE,** 6, b m Telescope (IRE)—With Grace **D. B. Roberts**
10 **STAMINA CHOPE (FR),** 7, ch m Muhaymin (USA)—My Virginia (FR) **Mr D. Bradbury**
11 **TAMPICO ROCCO (IRE),** 6, b br g Shirocco (GER)—Opera Gale (IRE) **Carder & Roberts**

---

432 MR MIKE ROBERTS, Hailsham

Postal: **Summertree Farm, Bodle Street Green, Hailsham, East Sussex, BN27 4QT**
Contacts: **PHONE 01435 830231 MOBILE 07774 208040**
EMAIL mike@summertree-racing.com

1 **ANDAPA (FR),** 9, br m Kapgarde (FR)—Daniety (FR) **M. J. Roberts**
2 **CAP D'ANTIBES (IRE),** 6, b g Society Rock (IRE)—Miss Verdoyante **M. J. Roberts**
3 **CLIFFS OF MALTA (IRE),** 5, b m Canford Cliffs (IRE)—Queen of Malta (IRE) **M. J. Roberts**
4 **CONCHITA (GER),** 8, b m Zoffany (IRE)—Cross Check (IRE) **M. J. Roberts**
5 **FORT DE L'OCEAN (FR),** 8, b g Racinger (FR)—Iconea (FR) **M. J. Roberts**
6 **GOT BRIGHT (FR),** 5, b g Intello (GER)—Rumored (USA) **M. J. Roberts**
7 **KIRUNA PEAK (IRE),** 9, ch m Arcano (IRE)—Kirunavaara (IRE) **M. J. Roberts**

MR MIKE ROBERTS - continued

8 **MISS TIKI,** 5, ch m Zoffany (IRE)—Teeky **M. J. Roberts**
9 **PERFECT MOMENT (IRE),** 10, b m Milan—Faucon **M. J. Roberts**
10 **PETIT BIJOU,** 6, b m Delegator—Native Ring (FR) **Mrs M. Martin**
11 **PUMP IT UP,** 5, ch m Charming Thought—Cherry Malotte **M. J. Roberts**

Assistant Trainer: Marie Martin.

---

433 MISS SARAH ROBINSON, Bridgwater

Postal: **Newnham Farm, Shurton, Stogursey, Bridgwater, Somerset, TA5 1QG**
Contacts: **PHONE 01278 732357 MOBILE 07866 435197, 07518 785291 FAX 01278 732357**
EMAIL info@sarahrobinsonracing.co.uk WEBSITE www.sarahrobinsonracing.co.uk

1 **BRUCIE BONUS,** 6, gr ro g Indian Haven—Magical Wonderland **Mr B. Robinson**
2 **DONT CALL ME DORIS,** 13, b m Franklins Gardens—Grove Dancer **Mr M. L. J. Fooks**
3 **FAMILY MAN (IRE),** 10, b g Gold Well—Greenacre Mandalay (IRE) **Mr A. Woodley-Milburn**
4 **GETAWAY TOTHE WOOD (IRE),** 8, b g Getaway (GER)—Salty Wind Lady (IRE) **Mr B. Robinson**
5 7, B m Franklins Gardens—Lofaire (IRE)
6 **MILLIE'S FLYING,** 10, b m Franklins Gardens—Grove Dancer **Mr M. L. J. Fooks**
7 **MY FOREVER FRIEND (IRE),** 15, b g Dr Massini (IRE)—Stormy Rose (IRE) **Mr B. Robinson**
8 **TIME IS TIME (IRE),** 14, ch g Golan (IRE)—Minnie Ray (IRE) **Mr A. Woodley-Milburn**

Assistant Trainer: Mr R. J. Bailey, Mr B. Robinson.

---

434 MR PAUL D ROBSON, Hawick

Postal: **1 Spittal On Rule, Hawick, Roxburghshire, TD9 8TA**
EMAIL spittalonrule@gmail.com

1 **ABOUTTIMEYOUTOLDME,** 9, ch g Mastercraftsman (IRE)—Mary Boleyn (IRE) **Miss D. Auld**
2 **BEN ASKER (IRE),** 5, b g Rock of Gibraltar (IRE)—Roskeen (IRE) **A. Robson**
3 **BREIZH RIVER (FR),** 5, b g Stormy River (FR)—Ilerda (GER) **Border Caravans Ltd**
4 **CANNOCK PARK,** 5, b g Cannock Chase (USA)—Van Mildert (IRE) **J. R. Bewley**
5 **GONNINO (IRE),** 4, ch g Doyen (IRE)—Scotch Beg (IRE)
6 **HAVEYOUGOTMYMONEY (IRE),** 5, b g Ol' Man River (IRE)—Killenagh Oscar (IRE) **Out of the Shed Racing**
7 **HIGHLANDER HILL (IRE),** 6, ch g Mahler—Cherish The Pear (IRE) **A. Robson**
8 **INTO THE FIRE (FR),** 5, ch g Intello (GER)—Roman Ridge (FR) **Mr & Mrs G & E Adam**
9 **JUST DON'T KNOW (IRE),** 10, b g Kalanisi (IRE)—Desperado Queen (IRE) **Border Caravans Ltd**
10 **KINERTON HILL (IRE),** 7, b g Kalanisi (IRE)—Gingerlina (IRE) **A & J Robson Limited**
11 5, B g Bollin Eric—Lethem Present (IRE) **Raceline Scotland Ltd**
12 **MAGIC MIKE (IRE),** 6, ch g Doyen (IRE)—Lady Gogo (IRE) **A. Robson**

435 MISS PAULINE ROBSON, Capheaton

Postal: **Kidlaw Farm, Capheaton, Newcastle Upon Tyne, NE19 2AW**
Contacts: **PHONE 01830 530241 MOBILE 07814 708725, 07721 887489**
EMAIL pauline@prracing.co.uk

1 **ANDRE LE NOTRE,** 6, br g Champs Elysees—Audaz **Mr E. A. Elliott**
2 **BALLIN BAY (IRE),** 5, b br g Milan—Ballinahow Ann (IRE) **J. Wade**
3 **BLUE PLAN (IRE),** 4, b g Retirement Plan—Blueberrythethird (IRE) **J. Wade**
4 **DOYEN DU BAR (IRE),** 7, b g Doyen (IRE)—Hollygrove Native (IRE) **Mr E. A. Elliott**
5 **GEORDIES DREAM,** 8, gr g Geordieland (FR)—Dream Leader (IRE) **J. Wade**
6 **HEEZTHEBOY (IRE),** 6, b g Dylan Thomas (IRE)—Lovely Native (IRE) **J. Wade**
7 **NORTHERN FALCON,** 8, b g Kayf Tara—Special Trinket (IRE) **Mr I. Kurdi**
8 **SHANTOU'S TEMPLE,** 6, b g Shantou (USA)—Temple Green **P Mayland & J Martin-Mayland**
9 **UPSILON BLEU (FR),** 15, b g Panoramic—Glycine Bleue (FR) **Mr & Mrs Raymond Anderson Green**

Assistant Trainer: David Parker.

NH Jockey: Brian Hughes, Craig Nichol.

436 MR RUSSELL ROSS, Consett

Postal: **Rock Cottage Farm, 79 Iveston Lane, Consett, County Durham, DH8 7TB**

1 **LISLORAN (IRE),** 7, b g Imperial Monarch (IRE)—Now Were Broke (IRE) **R. A. Ross**

437 MR BRIAN ROTHWELL, Oswaldkirk

Postal: **Old Post Office, Oswaldkirk, York, North Yorkshire, YO62 5XT**
Contacts: **PHONE 01439 788859 MOBILE 07969 968241**
EMAIL brian.rothwell1@googlemail.com

1 4, B f Time Test—Artistic Dawn (IRE) **B. S. Rothwell**
2 5, B g Ruler of The World (IRE)—Artistic Dawn (IRE) **Mr S. P. Hudson & Mr Brian Rothwell**
3 **BRIGHT DAWN (IRE),** 6, b g Helmet (AUS)—Skywards Miles (IRE) **B. S. Rothwell**
4 4, B g Viking Raider—Ceiriog Valley **The Jelly Boys**
5 **GURKHALI,** 4, gr g Gregorian (IRE)—Skywards Miles (IRE) **A & J Grimshaw**
6 **LADY'S SURPRISE,** 4, b f Cityscape—Kodiac Lady (IRE) **Mr S. P. Hudson & Mr Brian Rothwell**
7 **STONEGATE,** 4, b g Proconsul—Bonnie Burnett (IRE) **Mrs Greta Sparks & Mr Andrew Sparks**
8 **TURBULENT POWER,** 5, b m Power—Skywards Miles (IRE) **Mr S. P. Hudson & Mr Brian Rothwell**

THREE-YEAR-OLDS

9 **LADY'S CHARM,** br f Massaat (IRE)—Kodiac Lady (IRE) **B. S. Rothwell**
10 B f Heeraat (IRE)—Rambling Queen (IRE) **B. S. Rothwell**
11 B c Massaat (IRE)—Thornton Mary **Mr N. Al Habtoor**
12 B f Rajasinghe (IRE)—Yawail **Mr S. P. Hudson & Mr Brian Rothwell**

TWO-YEAR-OLDS

13 B f 04/05 Massaat (IRE)—Kodiac Lady (IRE) (Kodiac) **B. S. Rothwell**
14 B c 07/04 Aclaim (IRE)—Rambling Queen (IRE) (Mastercraftsman (IRE)) (952) **B. S. Rothwell**
15 B f 21/04 Rajasinghe (IRE)—Skywards Miles (IRE) (New Approach (IRE)) **B. S. Rothwell**

438 MR RICHARD ROWE, Pulborough

Postal: **Ashleigh House Stables, Sullington Lane, Storrington, Pulborough, West Sussex, RH20 4AE**
Contacts: **PHONE 01903 742871 MOBILE 07831 345636**
EMAIL richard@richardroweracing.com WEBSITE www.richardroweracing.co.uk/horses
FACEBOOK RichardRoweRacehorseTrainer TWITTER @rowe_racing

1 **AIKENBREAKINHEART (IRE),** 8, b g Aiken—Stelobel **Any Port In a Storm**
2 **BANNIXTOWN BOY (IRE),** 9, b g Oscar (IRE)—Lucky Loch (IRE) **Any Port In a Storm**
3 **CELMA DES BOIS (FR),** 11, b g Ballingarry (IRE)—Palafixe (FR) **Encore Partnership V**
4 **COLONEL KEATING (IRE),** 11, b g Yeats (IRE)—Jabroot (IRE) **Capt Adrian Pratt & Friends**
5 **CONSTANT FRIDAY (IRE),** 8, gr g Mahler—Mattys Joy (IRE) **Pink Birds**
6 **DANCE TO FAME (IRE),** 8, b g Fame And Glory—Cooline Jana (IRE) **The Winterlee Partnership**
7 **DANDYLYON (IRE),** 6, b m Gamut (IRE)—Agladora (FR) **Mr D. Scott**
8 **DELGANY MONARCH (IRE),** 8, ch g Imperial Monarch (IRE)—Naughty Marietta (IRE) **Encore Partnership V11**
9 **EL PACO,** 7, b g Paco Boy (IRE)—Miss Marauder **The Blazing Partnership**
10 **ENDERSEN (IRE),** 6, b g Ask—Molly Con (IRE) **The Forever Partnership Two**
11 5, B m Ask—Fair And Aisey (IRE) **R. Rowe**
12 **GREY D'ALCO (FR),** 6, gr g Gris de Gris (IRE)—Chutiquetta (FR) **Winterfields Farm Ltd & Mr David Scott**
13 **KICKS AND ALE (IRE),** 6, b g Pour Moi (IRE)—Spice Patrol (IRE) **The Encore Partnership VIII**
14 **KNOWLEDGEABLE KING,** 6, ch g Schiaparelli (GER)—Encyclopedia **Scott Parnell Limited**
15 **LEAD THE FIELD (IRE),** 7, b g Notnowcato—County Champions (IRE) **Pink Birds**
16 **MEETMEATTHEARCH (IRE),** 7, b g Jet Away—Golden Fantasy (IRE) **Mr D. Scott**
17 **MISTER MURCHAN (IRE),** 10, b g Westerner—So Supreme (IRE) **The Winterlee Partnership**
18 **REMEMBER FOREVER (IRE),** 13, b g Indian River (FR)—Running Wild (IRE) **R. Rowe**
19 **SET IN THE WEST (IRE),** 7, b m Westerner—Set In Her Ways (IRE) **Mr D. Scott**
20 **SOARLIKEANEAGLE (IRE),** 11, b g Scorpion (IRE)—Wayward Cove **B. H. Page**
21 **TOMMY DILLION (IRE),** 7, b g Dylan Thomas (IRE)—Coolaghmore Yeats (IRE) **Winterfields Farm Ltd**
22 **UP THE STRAIGHT (IRE),** 9, b g Arcadio (GER)—Kings Artist (IRE) **The Forever Partnership**
23 **VENDANT (IRE),** 5, b g Vendangeur (IRE)—Arrive In Style (IRE) **Winterfields Farm Ltd**

439 MRS MELANIE ROWLEY, Bridgnorth

Postal: **Poplar Cottage Farm, Morville, Bridgnorth, Shropshire, WV16 4RS**
Contacts: **PHONE 01746 714025**
EMAIL mel@mrpequestrian.co.uk

1 **ANOTHER BROWN BEAR (IRE),** 7, b g Shirocco (GER)—Full of Spirit (IRE) **G. B. Barlow**
2 **BLUE BEACH,** 6, b m Kayf Tara—Flutter Bye (IRE) **Poplar Cottage Racing Club**
3 **COCCO MADONNA (IRE),** 4, b f Malinas (GER)—Ostarakov (GER)
4 **COMMANDING VIEW (IRE),** 5, b g Mount Nelson—Clogher Valley (IRE) **P&T Andrews/M&S Carroll**
5 **FINALSHOT,** 10, b g Phoenix Reach (IRE)—Ryoshi **J. N. Dalton**
6 **GALASSIAN,** 6, ch g Schiaparelli (GER)—La Harde (FR) **Mr P. Rowley**
7 **HIGHLY RECOMMENDED,** 4, b g Highland Reel (IRE)—Celestial Harmony **Mr P. Rowley**
8 **HOUSTON CALLING,** 6, b m Masked Marvel—Houston du Berlais (FR) **James and Jean Potter Ltd**
9 **IDEALDES VILLERETS (FR),** 5, b g Maresca Sorrento (FR)—Qui L'Eut Cru (FR) **Mrs D. L. Whateley**
10 **KEY COMMANDER (IRE),** 8, b g Elusive Pimpernel (USA)—Ten Commandments (IRE) **Mr P. Freeman**
11 **LATITUDE (IRE),** 7, b g Shirocco (GER)—Gift of Freedom (IRE) **Mrs A. D. Williams**
12 **MALAITA,** 7, b m Malinas (GER)—Aimela (FR) **Fourgentsandalady**
13 **MARMALADE TIME,** 4, ch f Black Sam Bellamy (IRE)—Madame Bleue **Mr P. Rowley**
14 **MARTALMIX'JAC (FR),** 6, gr g Lord du Sud (FR)—Andria (FR) **High and Low**
15 **MASKED DANCE (FR),** 5, ch m Masked Marvel—Breakdance (FR) **Mr P. Rowley**
16 **MAXCEL,** 6, b g Excelebration (IRE)—Katess (IRE) **Mrs M. C. Sweeney**
17 **MY BOBBY DAZZLER,** 8, b g Malinas (GER)—Ease And Grace **Mr R. Barrett**
18 **MY BOBBY'S LASS,** 4, b f Pether's Moon (IRE)—Chocca Wocca **Mr R. Barrett**
19 **MY VIRTUE,** 5, b m Blue Bresil (FR)—No Virtue **S. M. Flook**

MRS MELANIE ROWLEY - continued

20 **PERRYVILLE (IRE),** 6, b g Mahler—How Is Things (IRE) **Mrs C. J. Bibbey**
21 **PRIME TIME LADY,** 6, br m Westerner—Lady Everywhere **Poplar Cottage Racing Club**
22 **RAFFLE TICKET,** 9, b g Fair Mix (IRE)—Halo Flora **Countess V. C. Cathcart**
23 **TIKITOV (IRE),** 7, b g Sholokhov (IRE)—Goodthyme Ticket (IRE) **Mr P. Rowley**
24 **TROOP SHIP,** 5, br g Soldier of Fortune (IRE)—Lady of The Clyde
25 **VAL DANCER (IRE),** 6, b g Valirann (FR)—Katies Dancer (IRE) **The Val Dancers**
26 **WHISPERONTHEWIND,** 5, gr m Shirocco (GER)—Brantingham Breeze **Swanbridge Bloodstock Limited**
27 **WISHING AND HOPING (IRE),** 13, b g Beneficial—Desperately Hoping (IRE) **Mrs P. Andrews**

---

440 MS LUCINDA RUSSELL, Kinross

Postal: **Arlary House Stables, Milnathort, Kinross, Tayside, KY13 9SJ**
Contacts: **PHONE 01577 865512 MOBILE 07970 645261 FAX 01577 861171**
EMAIL lucindarussellracing@outlook.com WEBSITE www.lucindarussell.com

1 **AHOY SENOR (IRE),** 8, b g Dylan Thomas (IRE)—Dara Supreme (IRE) **Mrs C Wymer & Mr PJS Russell**
2 4, Ch g Dylan Thomas (IRE)—Ajo Green (IRE)
3 **ANTEY (GER),** 10, b g Lord of England (GER)—Achinora **Gerry & Beaumont**
4 **AONE ALLY,** 5, b g Mayson—Infatuate **Mrs H. Kelly**
5 **APPLE AWAY (IRE),** 6, b m Arctic Cosmos (USA)—Dr A Day (IRE) **Old Gold Racing 14**
6 **AURORA THUNDER,** 9, b m Malinas (GER)—Ninna Nanna (FR) **Thunder Holdings Ltd**
7 **BALLYARE,** 6, b g Hot Streak (IRE)—Saddlers Bend (IRE) **The Bristol Boys**
8 **BIG RIVER (IRE),** 13, b g Milan—Call Kate (IRE) **Two Black Labs**
9 **BIX BEIDERBECKE (FR),** 5, b gr g Mawatheeq (USA)—Like It Is (FR) **Mrs S Russell & A M Russell**
10 **BLAZING SHIROCCO (IRE),** 5, b g Shirocco (GER)—Blazing Tempo (IRE) **Mr K. Alexander**
11 **BLOORIEDOTCOM (IRE),** 8, b g Holy Roman Emperor (IRE)—Peaceful Kingdom (USA) **Mutual Friends**
12 **BOIS GUILLBERT (FR),** 4, ch g Ivanhowe (GER)—Ready Kap (FR) **Mr R. B. H. Young**
13 **BOLLINGERANDKRUG (IRE),** 8, b g Getaway (GER)—Out Performer (IRE) **Two Black Labs**
14 **BRYDEN (IRE),** 6, b g Getaway (GER)—Lady Madison (FR) **R. A. Bartlett**
15 **BUDDHA SCHEME (IRE),** 9, b g Milan—Benefit Scheme (IRE) **Mr G. R. McGladery**
16 **CABOY (FR),** 11, b g Nidor (FR)—Cadouya Girl (FR) **Goodtimes**
17 **CALLE MALVA (IRE),** 8, b m Getaway (GER)—Waydale Hill **Mrs C Wymer & Mr Pjs Russell**
18 **CAMP BELAN (IRE),** 7, b g Milan—Glencree Spirit (IRE) **Mrs S Russell & A M Russell**
19 **CHAPEL GREEN (IRE),** 6, b g Dylan Thomas (IRE)—The Coolest Cat (IRE) **The Kestrel Partnership**
20 **CLOVIS BOY,** 4, b g Clovis du Berlais (FR)—Denisette (FR) **Mrs S Russell & A M Russell**
21 **CORACH RAMBLER (IRE),** 9, b g Jeremy (USA)—Heart N Hope (IRE) **The Ramblers**
22 **CORRIGEEN ROCK (IRE),** 6, b g Westerner—Set In Her Ways (IRE) **The Caledonian Racing Society**
23 **CUBAN CIGAR,** 5, b g Havana Gold (IRE)—Semayyel (IRE) **Mr Gerry McGladery & Mr PJS Russell**
24 **DE LEGISLATOR (IRE),** 6, b g Shirocco (GER)—Reynard's Glen (IRE) **Sword, Russell & Boys**
25 **DESTINY IS ALL (IRE),** 9, b g Prince Flori (GER)—Hearts Delight (IRE) **Mr J. R. Adam**
26 **DIAMOND STATE (FR),** 7, b g Vision d'Etat (FR)—Wonderful Diamond (GER) **Mr G. R. McGladery**
27 **DOMANDLOUIS (IRE),** 6, b g Getaway (GER)—Drive On Kate (IRE) **Two Black Labs**
28 **DON'T LOOK BACK,** 5, gr g Oasis Dream—Ronaldsay **Mrs H. Kelly**
29 **DOUGLAS TALKING (IRE),** 7, b g Dylan Thomas (IRE)—Look Who's Talking **The Bristol Boys & Peter J S Russell**
30 **ENGLES ROCK (IRE),** 7, b m Excelebration (IRE)—Lisa Gherardini (IRE) **Mrs H. Kelly**
31 **ESPRIT DU POTIER (FR),** 4, b gr g Montmartre (FR)—Absent Minded **The Four Lushes**
32 **FLYLIKEANEAGLE (IRE),** 6, b g Free Eagle (IRE)—Dulcian (IRE) **The Osprey Partnership**
33 **FOX'S FANCY (IRE),** 5, b m Kayf Tara—Nonnetia (FR) **The Nostalgics**
34 **FRENCH HIGHLANDS (IRE),** 4, b f Shirocco (GER)—Terre Haute (IRE) **A. Brooke Rankin & Russell**
35 4, B f Jack Hobbs—Gaye Flier (IRE) **Mr J. R. Adam**
36 **GIOVINCO (IRE),** 6, b g Walk In The Park (IRE)—Whyalla (IRE) **Ms L. V. Russell**
37 **GOLDEN POINT (FR),** 4, b f Bathyrhon (GER)—Diteou (FR) **Mr & Mrs J. Morrison-Bell**
38 **GREENHILL GARDENS,** 4, b g Westerner—The Toft **Mr P. J. S. Russell**
39 **HAUTE ESTIME (IRE),** 6, b m Walk In The Park (IRE)—Terre Haute (IRE) **Brahms & Liszt**
40 **HECTOR MASTER (FR),** 6, b g Masterstroke (USA)—Queen Maresca (FR) **Mrs S Russell & A M Russell**
41 **HELSGETAWAY (IRE),** 4, ch g Getaway (GER)—Heltornic (IRE) **The Red Shoes**

MS LUCINDA RUSSELL - continued

42 **IDEM (FR),** 5, b g Rail Link—Reflexion (FR) **The Boltons & Atholl Duncan**
43 **INIS OIRR (IRE),** 6, b g Ocovango—Peace Time Beauty (IRE) **Mr G. R. McGladery**
44 **ITS A MIDNIGHT,** 6, ch m Midnight Legend—Just For Pleasure (IRE) **The Midnight Chasers**
45 **IZZY'S CHAMPION (IRE),** 9, b g Gold Well—Native Crystal (IRE) **Mr & Mrs T. P. Winnell**
46 **JEM IN EM (IRE),** 5, b g Well Chosen—Apache Rose (IRE) **The Jemsters**
47 **JEUNE PRINCE (FR),** 4, gr g Al Namix (FR)—Une d'Ex (FR) **Misses P & F Simpson**
48 4, Br f Malinas (GER)—Jigs'n Reels (IRE)
49 **LIFE MADE SIMPLE,** 6, b g Sulamani (IRE)—Swift Getaway (IRE) **The Crick Girls**
50 **METHODTOTHEMADNESS (IRE),** 9, b m Gold Well—Odeeka (IRE) **Mrs S Russell & A M Russell**
51 **MIGHTY THUNDER,** 10, b g Malinas (GER)—Cool Island (IRE) **Thunder Holdings Ltd**
52 **MINT GOLD (IRE),** 9, b g Gold Well—Lady Flyer (IRE) **Mrs S Russell & A M Russell**
53 **MONOCHROMIX (FR),** 5, gr g Morandi (FR)—Lounamix (FR) **Mr Michael & Lady Jane Kaplan**
54 **MYRETOWN (IRE),** 6, b g Dylan Thomas (IRE)—Miss Platinum (IRE) **Mrs C Wymer & Mr Pjs Russell**
55 **NETYWELL (FR),** 6, b g Willywell (FR)—Netova (FR) **Set & Hunter**
56 **NORTHERN CARDINAL (FR),** 4, b br g Bathyrhon (GER)—Sagadoune (FR) **Ms L. V. Russell**
57 **OLD GREGORIAN,** 4, b g Jack Hobbs—Thankyou Very Much **R. F. Gibbons**
58 **ONE MILL HARBOUR (FR),** 6, gr g Diamond Boy (FR)—Kavusakan (FR) **Bernardine & Sean Mulryan**
59 **OPERATION OVERLORD (IRE),** 8, b g Jeremy (USA)—Alfreeze **Mr J. P. McManus**
60 **OUR MARTY (FR),** 5, b g Martinborough (JPN)—Dercia (FR) **Mrs S Russell & A M Russell**
61 **PASTURE BEACH (IRE),** 6, ch m Sholokhov (IRE)—Maryota (FR) **R. A. Green**
62 **PETITE RHAPSODY (IRE),** 8, b g Shirocco (GER)—Peggy Cullen (IRE) **Tay Valley Chasers Racing Club**
63 **PRINCE DUNDEE (IRE),** 10, b g Stowaway—Miss Dundee (IRE) **McNeill Racing & County Set Three**
64 **PRINCE OF PERTH (IRE),** 5, b g Malinas (GER)—Emma Ami (IRE) **County Set Four & L V Russell**
65 7, B g Dylan Thomas (IRE)—Princess Nina (IRE) **Ms L. V. Russell**
66 **QARBATSI (IRE),** 7, b g Barely A Moment (AUS)—Robin Victoria (IRE) **Mrs S Russell & A M Russell**
67 **RAPID RAIDER (IRE),** 9, ch g Golden Lariat (USA)—Golden Court (IRE) **Mrs S Russell & A M Russell**
68 **RATTLING ROAD (IRE),** 6, b g Arctic Cosmos (USA)—Rossa Parks (IRE) **Misses P & F Simpson**
69 **READYSTEADYBEAU (FR),** 7, ch g Kapgarde (FR)—La Ville Aux Dames (FR) **Joanne & Peter Russell**
70 **RED MISSILE (IRE),** 6, b g Battle of Marengo (IRE)—Plym **Mr Michael & Lady Jane Kaplan**
71 **RETURN FIRE (IRE),** 7, b g Leading Light (IRE)—There On Time (IRE) **Tay Valley Chasers Racing Club**
72 **ROWDY RUSTLER (IRE),** 8, b g Getaway (GER)—Posh Posy (IRE) **Mr J. R. Adam**
73 **SCOTTISH WIND (FR),** 5, b g Territories (IRE)—Isalou (FR) **Lamont Racing**
74 **SERIOUS OPERATOR (IRE),** 6, b g Malinas (GER)—Idrather Not Say (IRE) **The Operators**
75 4, Br f Malinas (GER)—Skellig Mist (FR) **Ms L. V. Russell**
76 **SNAKE ROLL (IRE),** 6, b g Jet Away—Cuddle Ina Drizzle (IRE) **The Ormello Way**
77 **SO THEY SAY,** 7, b m Malinas (GER)—Feisty Lass (IRE) **The Osprey Partnership**
78 **SPARK OF MADNESS (FR),** 7, b g Walk In The Park (IRE)—Prosopopee (FR) **Mrs S Russell & A M Russell**
79 **SPEAK OF THE DEVIL (IRE),** 10, ch g Mahler—A Fine Romance (IRE) **The County Set & Mr P Russell & Friends**
80 **STARLYTE (IRE),** 6, b m Sir Percy—Virevolle (FR) **Mr A. Grant**
81 **STEP ABOVE (IRE),** 6, b g Jet Away—Tansyaster (IRE) **One Step Beyond**
82 **STYLISH MOMENT (IRE),** 10, b g Milan—Up The Style (IRE) **The Crick Girls**
83 **TENBOBEACHWAY (IRE),** 5, br g Malinas (GER)—Gift Wrapped (IRE) **Mrs C Wymer & Mr Pjs Russell**
84 **THEREISNODOUBT (IRE),** 10, ch g Primary (USA)—Doubt (IRE) **Mrs H. Kelly**
85 **THISTLEBUFFS (IRE),** 6, b g Fame And Glory—Doransfirth (IRE) **Mrs Jo Tracey & Mr K Alexander**
86 **THUNDER IN MILAN (IRE),** 7, b g Milan—Baby Briggs (IRE) **Thunder Holdings Ltd**
87 **TOROSAY (IRE),** 5, b m Getaway (GER)—The Toft **Mr P. J. S. Russell**
88 **TRAPRAIN LAW (FR),** 5, gr g Martaline—Pina (FR) **R. A. Green**
89 **WELL ABOVE PAR (IRE),** 11, b g Gold Well—Glynn Glory (IRE) **The Eagle Partnership**
90 **WEST END LADY (IRE),** 8, b m Westerner—Nightofthe Oscars (IRE) **The Falcon Partnership**
91 **WITHOUT CONVICTION (IRE),** 8, b m Aizavoski (IRE)—With Conviction (IRE) **Kelso Lowflyers & Mr PJS Russell**
92 **YOUR OWN STORY (IRE),** 7, b g Shantaram—Forest Heiress (IRE) **Mrs J Kehoe, Wymer & Russell**
93 **YOUR PLACE (IRE),** 7, b m Scorpion (IRE)—Sheebadiva (IRE) **Dig In Racing**

THREE-YEAR-OLDS

94 **EASTVAN (IRE),** b g Make Believe—Empress Anna (IRE) **Mrs H. Kelly**
95 **I WISH YOU (FR),** ch g Night Wish (GER)—Native Story (FR) **Mr R. B. H. Young**
96 **LOUGH SWILLY LASS,** b f Adaay (IRE)—Plage Depampelonne **Mrs H. Kelly**
97 B f Milan—Miss Joeking (IRE) **Ms L. V. Russell**
98 **ROCHEVAL (FR),** b c Kapgarde (FR)—County Fun (FR) **Mrs S Russell & A M Russell**

MS LUCINDA RUSSELL - continued

TWO-YEAR-OLDS

99 Ch c 01/04 Recorder—Blanchefleur (IRE) (Camelot) (1601) **Lamont Racing**
100 B f 24/03 Sir Percy—Dona Viola (Cacique (IRE)) (6000) **Mrs H. Kelly**
101 MIX DE GRIS (FR), gr c 23/02 Master's Spirit (IRE)—Goldamix (IRE) (Linamix (FR)) (17607) **Lamont Racing**
102 B c 16/04 Adaay (IRE)—Nellie Ellis (IRE) (Compton Place) (3500) **Mrs H. Kelly**
103 B c 10/03 Make Believe—Ready When You Are (IRE) (Royal Applause) (3201) **Mrs H. Kelly**
104 SNOW DRAGON (IRE), gr c 22/04 Decorated Knight—Rose of Miracles (Dalakhani (IRE)) (11000) **Lamont Racing**

Assistant Trainer: Blair Campbell, Jaimie Duff, Steven Kelly, Peter Scudamore, Cameron Wadge. **Head Girl:** Vicky Haughton, Hannah Wilson. **Travelling Head:** Eleanor Warren.

NH Jockey: Derek Fox, Stephen Mulqueen. **Conditional Jockey:** Conner McCann, Patrick Wadge. **Amateur Jockey:** Mr Gregor Walkingshaw.

---

441 MR JOHN RYAN, Newmarket

Postal: **Cadland Stables, Moulton Road, Newmarket, Suffolk, CB8 8DU**
Contacts: **PHONE 01638 664172 MOBILE 07739 801235**
EMAIL john.ryan@jryanracing.com WEBSITE www.jryanracing.com TWITTER @JohnRyanRacing

1 **ANGER MANAGEMENT,** 4, b g Ribchester (IRE)—Despatch **BB Thoroughbreds**
2 **BATTLE OF MARATHON (USA),** 11, b g War Front (USA)—Sayedah (IRE) **Emma Ryan & Partner**
3 **CATCH MY BREATH,** 7, gr g Bated Breath—Likeable **The Out of Puff Partnership**
4 **FIRST EMPEROR,** 4, b c Galileo (IRE)—Sky Lantern (IRE) **BB Thoroughbreds**
5 **GAUTREY,** 4, ch c Farhh—Si Belle (IRE) **Mr F. P. Maghery**
6 **GODDESS OF FIRE,** 6, b m Toronado (IRE)—Burnt Fingers (IRE) **Mr M. M. Foulger**
7 **HIROSHIMA,** 7, b g Nathaniel (IRE)—Lisiere (IRE) **Russell, Thompson, DAS Racing, Ryan**
8 **JACK RYAN (IRE),** 6, b g Harbour Watch (IRE)—Anything (IRE) **Emma Ryan & Partner**
9 **MANACCAN,** 4, ch c Exceed And Excel (AUS)—Shyrl **Newsells Park Stud - Ossie Ardiles Synd.**
10 **PISTOLETTO (USA),** 6, b g War Front (USA)—Lerici (USA) **J A Thompson & S Russell**
11 **REEL OF FORTUNE (IRE),** 4, b f Highland Reel (IRE)—Romantic Stroll (IRE) **Das Racing & Mr J Ryan**
12 **SONAIRT (FR),** 4, ch g Territories (IRE)—Wall of Light **Mr A. Cryans**

THREE-YEAR-OLDS

13 **DAYTONA LADY (IRE),** b f Bungle Inthejungle—Roseau City **Mr A. Cryans**
14 **DO IT FOR LOVE,** b f Zoustar (AUS)—Magic Florence (IRE) **Mr F. P. Maghery**
15 B f Expert Eye—Dona Viola
16 **HARRY WITH STYLE,** ch g Dutch Art—Thrill **S & J Ryan**
17 **MY FIRST RODEO (IRE),** br g Kodiac—Rashaaqa **Mr A. Cryans**
18 **PRINCE NABEEL (IRE),** b g Smooth Daddy (USA)—Luminance (IRE) **Mr J. F. Stocker**
19 **STEVEN SEAGULL,** b g War Command (USA)—Mercy Me **The Leolli Partnership**
20 **THE X O (IRE),** b c Zoffany (IRE)—Pivotal Era **Mr G Smith- Bernal & Mr Anthony Verrier**
21 **WARMINSTER,** b c Ardad (IRE)—Lady Vermeer **Mr G. F. Smith-Bernal**

TWO-YEAR-OLDS

22 B c 17/02 Exceed And Excel (AUS)—Asoof (Dubawi (IRE)) (6000)
23 **ROMAN EMPEROR,** b c 09/03 Magna Grecia (IRE)—Alsaaden (Acclamation) **BB Thoroughbreds**
24 B f 28/02 Time Test—Twilight Sparkle (IRE) (Rock of Gibraltar (IRE)) **Mr G. R. McGladery**

Amateur Jockey: Miss Tia Phillips.

442 MR KEVIN RYAN, Hambleton

Postal: **Hambleton Lodge, Hambleton, Thirsk, North Yorkshire, YO7 2HA**
Contacts: **PHONE 01845 597010, 01845 597622 FAX 01845 597622**
EMAIL office@kevinryanracing.com WEBSITE www.kevinryanracing.com

1 **ALEEZDANCER (IRE),** 4, b g Fast Company (IRE)—Clifton Dancer **Jack Berry & John Matthews**
2 **BERGERAC (IRE),** 5, b g Kodi Bear (IRE)—Fancy Vivid (IRE) **Mrs Angie Bailey**
3 **BIELSA (IRE),** 8, b g Invincible Spirit (IRE)—Bourbon Ball (USA) **King Power Racing Co Ltd**
4 **CATCH CUNNINGHAM (IRE),** 4, b g Kodiac—Faithful Duchess (IRE) **Mr Steve Ryan**
5 **COTAI WEST (IRE),** 4, b f Cotai Glory—Capote West (USA) **Clara Stud & Partner**
6 **DARK MOON RISING (IRE),** 4, b g Night of Thunder (IRE)—Al Nassa (USA) **Mrs Angie Bailey**
7 **EMARAATY ANA,** 7, b g Shamardal (USA)—Spirit of Dubai (IRE) **Sheikh Mohammed Obaid Al Maktoum**
8 **FAST AND LOOSE,** 4, b g No Nay Never (USA)—Madam Valentine **Mr Steve Ryan**
9 **FORZA ORTA (IRE),** 5, b g Fastnet Rock (AUS)—Follow A Star (IRE) **Highbank Stud**
10 **GIS A SUB (IRE),** 4, b g Acclamation—Monclaire (GER) **Mr Steve Ryan**
11 **INVISIBLE FRIEND (IRE),** 4, b f Sea The Stars (IRE)—Stealth Missile (IRE) **Highbank Stud**
12 **JUSTANOTHERBOTTLE (IRE),** 9, ch g Intense Focus (USA)—Duchess K (IRE) **Mr Steve Ryan & Mr M J Tedham**
13 **LULLABY BAY,** 4, b f Profitable (IRE)—Dubai Affair **Bearstone Stud Limited**
14 **MAGICAL SPIRIT (IRE),** 7, ch g Zebedee—La Dame de Fer (IRE) **Hambleton Racing Ltd XXXII**
15 **MARHABA THE CHAMP,** 4, ch c Galileo (IRE)—Lady of The Desert (USA) **Mr Jaber Abdullah**
16 **MERSEYSIDE (IRE),** 4, b c Lope de Vega (IRE)—Megera (FR) **Sheikh Mohammed Obaid Al Maktoum**
17 **RAMBUSO CREEK (IRE),** 4, b g Tagula (IRE)—Fine Prospect (IRE) **Hambleton Racing Ltd XXV**
18 **SHALADAR (FR),** 4, b g Shalaa (IRE)—Ultradargent (FR) **Hambleton Racing Ltd XLVII**
19 **SOUND REASON,** 5, ch g Hot Streak (IRE)—Brown Eyed Honey **Hambleton Racing Ltd XXIX**
20 **SPIRITOFTHENORTH (FR),** 6, br g Bated Breath—Danlepordamsterdam (IRE) **Middleham Park Racing XLVI**
21 **THE COOKSTOWN CAFU,** 4, b g Invincible Spirit (IRE)—Miss Delila (USA) **Highbank Stud**
22 **THUNDER ROAR,** 4, ch c Night of Thunder (IRE)—Dominike (ITY) **Thunder Roar Partners**
23 **THUNDERING,** 4, b g Night of Thunder (IRE)—Cosmea **Mr Steve Ryan**
24 **TRIPLE TIME (IRE),** 4, b c Frankel—Reem Three **Sheikh Mohammed Obaid Al Maktoum**
25 **VENTURA RASCAL,** 6, b g Fountain of Youth (IRE)—Choisette **Middleham Park Racing CVII**

THREE-YEAR-OLDS

26 **BELSITO (GER),** b g Areion (GER)—Best Moving (GER) **Hambleton Racing Ltd XXXII**
27 **BINT AL DAAR,** br f Muhaarar—Sharqeyih **Mr Jaber Abdullah**
28 **CAMACHO STAR (IRE),** ch g Camacho—Desert Way (IRE) **Pallister Racing**
29 **CAPTAIN WINTERS,** b c Lope de Vega (IRE)—Reem Three **Sheikh Mohammed Obaid Al Maktoum**
30 **CATCH THE PADDY (IRE),** b c No Nay Never (USA)—Pandora's Box (IRE) **Mr Steve Ryan**
31 **CHUZZLEWIT,** b c Showcasing—Furbelow **Sheikh Mohammed Obaid Al Maktoum**
32 **DREAM FOR GOLD (IRE),** b c U S Navy Flag (USA)—Why Not Queen (IRE) **Mr Jaber Abdullah**
33 **DUBAI JEMILA,** ch f Dubawi (IRE)—Joyful Hope **Mr Jaber Abdullah**
34 **EAGLE DAY (IRE),** b c Kodiac—Ramone (IRE) **Sheikh Mohammed Obaid Al Maktoum**
35 **ELVENIA (IRE),** br f Dark Angel (IRE)—Pixeleen **Sheikh Mohammed Obaid Al Maktoum**
36 **FLOWER DESERT (FR),** b f Mehmas (IRE)—Mojave Desert (IRE) **Mr Jaber Abdullah**
37 **GLENLAUREL (IRE),** b f Lope de Vega (IRE)—Nada **Sheikh Mohammed Obaid Al Maktoum**
38 **HELLO QUEEN (IRE),** b f Acclamation—Elnadim Star (IRE) **Mr Jaber Abdullah**
39 **HI ROYAL (IRE),** b c Kodiac—Majestic Roi (USA) **Mr Jaber Abdullah**
40 **HOLLOWAY GIRL,** b f Night of Thunder (IRE)—Special Miss **Nick White & Partner**
41 **LEAP YEAR LAD (IRE),** gr ro g Havana Grey—Skeleton (IRE) **My Vein Clinic Syndicate 1**
42 **MAGICDOLLAR,** b g Washington DC (IRE)—She Mystifies **Y&R Engineering Ltd**
43 **MONTE FORTE,** b g Cotai Glory—Miss Poppy **J Blackburn & Partner 1**
44 **MUNTASIRA (IRE),** b f Night of Thunder (IRE)—Etive (USA) **Mr Jaber Abdullah**
45 **NAHWAND (IRE),** b c Dark Angel (IRE)—Bunditten (IRE) **Mr Jaber Abdullah**
46 **NO BARRIER,** b c Kingman—Swiss Affair **Mrs A Althani**
47 **NWAIRA (IRE),** b f No Nay Never (USA)—Zee Zee Gee **Mr Jaber Abdullah**
48 **POWDERING (IRE),** b f Ribchester (IRE)—Sufoof (IRE) **Hambleton Racing Ltd XXXVIII**
49 **PRIDE OF YORKSHIRE,** ch g Zoustar (AUS)—Worship (IRE) **Hambleton Racing Ltd Xxvii & Partner**
50 **PRINCESS SAVANNAH,** b f Ardad (IRE)—Juncea **Mr Roger Peel**
51 **PROFESSOR PESCA (IRE),** b g Kodiac—Marian Halcombe (USA) **J Blackburn & Partner 1**
52 **QUEEN ME (IRE),** ch f Dubawi (IRE)—Queen Kindly **Mr Jaber Abdullah**
53 **QUINTUS ARRIUS (IRE),** b c Mehmas (IRE)—Juxtaposed **Sheikh Mohammed Obaid Al Maktoum**
54 **REVISION,** b g Ardad (IRE)—Relaxez Vous (IRE) **Highclere T'bred Racing - Alice Munro 1**

MR KEVIN RYAN - continued

55 **SILENT WORDS,** ch f Zoustar (AUS)—Thatsallimsaying (IRE) **Clipper Logistics**
56 **STAR OF HAVANA,** b f Havana Gold (IRE)—Keladora (USA) **Hambleton Racing Ltd XVI**
57 **STAR SOUND,** b f Zoustar (AUS)—Sterling Sound (USA) **Hambleton Racing Ltd XXIX**
58 **STELLA BLUE (IRE),** b f Bungle Inthejungle—Cliodhna (IRE) **Mr Allan Kerr**
59 **UNREQUITED LOVE (IRE),** ch f No Nay Never (USA)—
Passion Overflow (USA) **Hambleton Racing Ltd XXXII & Partner 1**
60 **WASHINGTON HEIGHTS,** b g Washington DC (IRE)—Epping Rose (IRE) **Hambleton Racing Ltd XXVII**
61 **YOUM JAMEEL (IRE),** b g No Nay Never (USA)—Spasha **Mr Jaber Abdullah**

TWO-YEAR-OLDS

62 Br c 02/01 No Nay Never (USA)—Aurora Spring (IRE) (Power) (310000) **Mr T A Rahman**
63 **BARNABY (IRE),** b c 20/03 Soldier's Call—Aegean Sunset (IRE) (Shamardal (USA)) (47619) **Mrs Angie Bailey**
64 **BORDERLINE BOSS,** b c 21/05 Harry Angel (IRE)—Bourbon Ball (USA) (Peintre Celebre (USA)) **Highbank Stud**
65 Gr f 17/03 Mastercraftsman (IRE)—Bright Bank (IRE) (Sadler's Wells (USA)) (52021) **Mr Jaber Abdullah**
66 B f 03/03 Holy Roman Emperor (IRE)—Bright Birdie (IRE) (Sadler's Wells (USA)) (68027) **Mr Jaber Abdullah**
67 B f 17/02 Camacho—Carina (IRE) (Sea The Stars (IRE)) (20000) **Hambleton Racing Ltd XXXVIII**
68 **DEIMOS (IRE),** ch c 30/03 Night of Thunder (IRE)—
Step Sequence (Nayef (USA)) (180000) **Sheikh Mohammed Obaid Al Maktoum**
69 B c 03/04 Cotai Glory—Deliziosa (IRE) (Iffraaj) (66667) **Mr B T McDonald**
70 **ELINOR DASHWOOD (IRE),** b br f 21/01 Kodi Bear (IRE)—
Scarlet Plum (Pivotal) (210000) **Sheikh Mohammed Obaid Al Maktoum**
71 Ch f 08/02 Churchill (IRE)—Elnadim Star (IRE) (Elnadim (USA)) **Mr Jaber Abdullah**
72 B f 13/01 Cable Bay (IRE)—Eyes On Asha (IRE) (Redoute's Choice (AUS)) **Mr T A Rahman**
73 **INISHERIN,** b c 22/02 Shamardal (USA)—
Ajman Princess (IRE) (Teofilo (IRE)) **Sheikh Mohammed Obaid Al Maktoum**
74 B f 21/01 Magna Grecia (IRE)—Lady Cedar (IRE) (Exceed And Excel (AUS)) (36190)
75 B c 27/03 Bungle Inthejungle—Lady Spangles (IRE) (Starspangledbanner (AUS)) (40016)
76 B c 03/02 Mukhadram—Lady Tabitha (IRE) (Tamayuz) **Mr Gordon Bulloch**
77 B f 29/03 Dark Angel (IRE)—Layla Jamil (IRE) (Exceed And Excel (AUS)) (120048) **Mr Jaber Abdullah**
78 B c 13/03 Night of Thunder (IRE)—Merry Jaunt (USA) (Street Sense (USA)) (110000) **Mr T A Rahman**
79 **MISSTERIOUS,** b f 22/02 Dream Ahead (USA)—She Mystifies (Indesatchel (IRE)) **Bearstone Stud Limited**
80 Gr f 15/02 Dark Angel (IRE)—Moonlit Show (Showcasing) (36014) **Mr Jaber Abdullah**
81 **NOVARRO (IRE),** b c 13/02 Invincible Army (IRE)—
Meydan Princess (IRE) (Choisir (AUS)) (110000) **Sheikh Mohammed Obaid Al Maktoum**
82 B c 15/02 Invincible Spirit (IRE)—Paco's Angel (Paco Boy (IRE)) (50000) **Mr Steve Ryan**
83 B c 14/03 Bungle Inthejungle—Play Mate (Showcasing)
84 B f 31/03 Kingman—Reem Three (Mark of Esteem (IRE)) **Sheikh Mohammed Obaid Al Maktoum**
85 **RICHMOND COUNTY (IRE),** br c 08/05 No Nay Never (USA)—
Belle Isle (Pastoral Pursuits) (325000) **Sheikh Mohammed Obaid Al Maktoum**
86 **RIVERSOUL,** ch f 20/01 Washington DC (IRE)—River Song (USA) (Siphon (BRZ)) **Bearstone Stud Limited**
87 B f 28/02 Advertise—Rowan Brae (Haafhd) (25610) **Mr Jaber Abdullah**
88 Ch c 05/02 Night of Thunder (IRE)—Royal Rose (IRE) (Exceed And Excel (AUS)) **Mr Jaber Abdullah**
89 B c 25/01 Washington DC (IRE)—Saltwater (Fountain of Youth (IRE)) (24762) **Hambleton Racing Ltd XVI**
90 B c 11/02 Night of Thunder (IRE)—Samdaniya (Machiavellian (USA)) (100000) **Mr Steve Ryan**
91 Ch c 24/03 Bungle Inthejungle—Shawhill (Dr Fong (USA)) (45714) **Middleham Park Racing LXXIX**
92 **SISYPHEAN (IRE),** b c 23/04 Dubawi (IRE)—
Lunar Vega (IRE) (Lope de Vega (IRE)) **Sheikh Mohammed Obaid Al Maktoum**
93 B c 04/04 Kodiac—Spasha (Shamardal (USA)) **Mr Jaber Abdullah**
94 B g 13/03 Kodi Bear (IRE)—Speed Skater (Olympic Glory (IRE)) (27619) **Hambleton Racing Ltd XLVII**
95 B c 28/04 Kodi Bear (IRE)—Tamara Love (IRE) (Tamayuz) (115000)
96 **TRUE PROMISE,** ch g 28/01 Washington DC (IRE)—In Trutina (Firebreak) (20952) **John Matthews & Partner**
97 B f 03/02 Kodiac—Vallecupa (ITY) (Mujahid (USA)) (80032)
98 **VANTHEMAN (IRE),** b c 28/02 Invincible Army (IRE)—
Laila Honiwillow (Bahamian Bounty) (42857) **Tom Muir / Colin Paterson**
99 **VARDEN (IRE),** ch c 16/04 Bungle Inthejungle—
Yogi's Girl (IRE) (Harbour Watch (IRE)) (65000) **Sheikh Mohammed Obaid Al Maktoum**
100 **VENTURE CAPITAL,** b c 25/02 Washington DC (IRE)—Ventura Blues (IRE) (Bated Breath) **Ms Leslie Clune**
101 **VOLTERRA (IRE),** b c 08/03 Farhh—Lajatico (Equiano (FR)) (400000) **Sheikh Mohammed Obaid Al Maktoum**

MR KEVIN RYAN - continued

102 WAHKAN (IRE), ch c 05/02 Sioux Nation (USA)—
Refusetolisten (IRE) (Clodovil (IRE)) (250000) **Sheikh Mohammed Obaid Al Maktoum**

Assistant Trainer: Adam Ryan.

Flat Jockey: Tom Eaves, Shane Gray. **Apprentice Jockey:** Louise Akehurst, Curtis Wilson-Ruddock.

---

443 MR AYTACH SADIK, Kidderminster

Postal: **Wolverley Court Coach House, Wolverley, Kidderminster, Worcestershire, DY10 3RP**
Contacts: **PHONE 01562 852362 MOBILE 07803 040344**

1 **BAWAADER (IRE),** 8, gr g Dark Angel (IRE)—Aspen Falls (IRE) **A. M. Sadik**
2 **NYOUFSEA,** 8, gr g Fair Mix (IRE)—Just Smokie **A. M. Sadik**
3 **OLD PAGE (IRE),** 6, b g Snow Sky—Dual Rose (IRE) **A. M. Sadik**

---

444 MR MALCOLM SAUNDERS, Wells

Postal: **Blue Mountain Farm, Wells Hill Bottom, Haydon, Wells, Somerset, BA5 3EZ**
Contacts: **PHONE 01749 841011 MOBILE 07771 601035**
EMAIL malcolm@malcolmsaunders.co.uk WEBSITE www.malcolmsaunders.co.uk

1 **BARRYOKI,** 5, ch g Coach House (IRE)—Lady Bayside **M. S. Saunders**
2 **BLUEBELL TIME (IRE),** 7, b m Coach House (IRE)—Matterofact (IRE) **Mrs Ginny Nicholas & Mr M. S. Saunders**
3 **CORONATION COTTAGE,** 9, b m Pastoral Pursuits—Avrilo **Pat Hancock & Eric Jones**
4 **DESERT (IRE),** 4, b f Havana Gold (IRE)—Jewel In The Sand (IRE) **Paul Nicholas / M S Saunders**
5 **DIAMOND COTTAGE,** 6, ch m Cappella Sansevero—Avrilo **Pat Hancock & Eric Jones**
6 **JOY CHOI (IRE),** 5, b m Territories (IRE)—Vintage Molly **Paul Nicholas / M S Saunders**
7 **REDREDROBIN,** 6, b m Helmet (AUS)—Cape Rosie **M. S. Saunders**
8 **RUBY COTTAGE (IRE),** 5, b m Coach House (IRE)—Avrilo **Pat Hancock & Eric Jones**
9 **SOWS (IRE),** 4, b f Kodiac—Zvarkhova (FR) **M. S. Saunders**

THREE-YEAR-OLDS

10 B g Pearl Secret—Sarangoo **M. S. Saunders**

---

445 MRS DIANNE SAYER, Penrith

Postal: **Town End Farm, Hackthorpe, Penrith, Cumbria, CA10 2HX**
Contacts: **PHONE 01931 712245 MOBILE 07980 295316**

1 **APPLE MOON (FR),** 4, b g Spanish Moon (USA)—La Berciere (FR) **Mr G. N. Critchley**
2 **ARRANMORE,** 6, b g Oasis Dream—Ceisteach (IRE) **D & M Lynch**
3 **BALKING (FR),** 5, ch g Balko (FR)—Anaqueen (FR) **Mr G. N. Critchley**
4 **BERTIE'S BALLET,** 5, b g Albaasil (IRE)—More Ballet Money **Falcon's Line Ltd**
5 **CALLIOPE,** 10, b m Poet's Voice—Costa Brava (IRE) **Mr E. G. Tunstall**
6 **CHARLIE UBERALLES,** 7, ch g Geordieland (FR)—Sovereignoftheseas **Mr G. N. Critchley**
7 **DALLAS DES PICTONS (FR),** 10, b g Spanish Moon (USA)—Nadia des Pictons (FR) **Mrs M. R. Lewis**
8 **DETECTIVE,** 7, b g Kingman—Promising Lead **A. Slack**
9 **DIAMOND TRILOGY (IRE),** 4, br g Diamond Boy (FR)—For A While (IRE) **Mr G. N. Critchley**

MRS DIANNE SAYER - continued

10 **FRIGHTENED RABBIT (USA),** 11, b g Hard Spun (USA)—Champagne Ending (USA) **Mr R. A. Harrison**
11 **HEART ABOVE,** 5, b g Shirocco (GER)—Cool Baranca (GER) **Margaret Coppola & Dianne Sayer**
12 **IDILICO (FR),** 8, b g Lawman (FR)—Ydillique (IRE) **Mr Dennis J. Coppola & Mrs Dianne Sayer**
13 **IOLANI (GER),** 11, b g Sholokhov (IRE)—Imogen (GER) **SJD Racing & Dianne Sayer**
14 **JACKHAMMER (IRE),** 9, b g Thewayyouare (USA)—Ask Annie (IRE) **Margaret Coppola & Dianne Sayer**
15 **MILLIE THE MINX (IRE),** 9, b m Medicean—Popocatepetl (FR) **A. R. White**
16 **PROPAGATION (IRE),** 5, b g Acclamation—Thakerah (IRE) **A. R. White**
17 **RACQUET CLUB (IRE),** 4, b g Almanzor (FR)—Galipette
18 **REDARNA,** 9, ch g Aqlaam—Curtains **Graham Lund & Dianne Sayer**
19 **SAMS ROSEABELLE,** 7, b m Black Sam Bellamy (IRE)—Cashback Rose (IRE) **Mrs M. R. Lewis**
20 **SIMPLE STAR (IRE),** 5, b g Sea The Stars (IRE)—Simple Elegance (USA) **Mrs D. M. Monteith**
21 **THE NAVIGATOR,** 8, gr g Mastercraftsman (IRE)—Blessing (USA) **Mr G. H. Bell**

Assistant Trainer: Miss Joanna Sayer.

Amateur Jockey: Miss Liz Butterworth, Miss Emma Sayer.

---

446 DR JON SCARGILL, Newmarket

Postal: **Red House Stables, Hamilton Road, Newmarket, Suffolk, CB8 0TE**
Contacts: **PHONE 01638 667767 MOBILE 07785 350705**
EMAIL jdscargill@gmail.com WEBSITE www.jonscargill.co.uk

1 **PLACATED,** 5, b m Archipenko (USA)—Cosseted **Stuart Howard & GB Horseracing**
2 **VERTICAL,** 5, ch m Al Kazeem—Greenery (IRE) **Dr Edna Robson & Partner**

THREE-YEAR-OLDS

3 **ASTRONOMICA,** b f Belardo (IRE)—Itsinthestars **Stuart Howard & GB Horseracing**
4 **LA PODEROSA,** b gr f Havana Grey—Khaki (IRE) **Strawberry Fields Stud & Partner**
5 **PAY SCALE (IRE),** b f Profitable (IRE)—Harmonic Note **Silent Partners**
6 B g Mukhadram—Qualification (USA) **Mr P. J. Darlington**

---

447 MR GEORGE SCOTT, Newmarket

Postal: **Eve Lodge Stables, Hamilton Road, Newmarket, Suffolk, CB8 0NY**
Contacts: **WORK 07833 461294**
EMAIL george@georgescottracing.com WEBSITE www.georgescottracing.com

1 **CAPTAIN KANE,** 4, ch g Ulysses (IRE)—Foundation Filly **Bluestarr Racing & Partners**
2 **MELLYS FLYER,** 5, b g Dandy Man (IRE)—Azhar **Investasurge Consulting Ltd**
3 **PRYDWEN (IRE),** 5, b g Camelot—Honey Hunter (IRE) **Blue Starr Racing**
4 **STRAWBERRY JACK,** 7, b g Foxwedge (AUS)—Strawberry Leaf **Mr J. Stephenson**
5 **TIMESTAMP (IRE),** 4, b g No Nay Never (USA)—Sandglass **The Black Dragon**

THREE-YEAR-OLDS

6 **BUTTERFLY EFFECT (IRE),** gr f James Garfield (IRE)—Angel de La Gesse (FR) **The Grey Racehorse**
7 **CARIAD,** b f Cityscape—Edge of Love **Mr E. W. B. Williams**
8 **COCO JACK (IRE),** bl g Wings of Eagles (FR)—Bright Morning (USA) **Kelly & Stephenson**
9 **COPPER BAY (IRE),** ch f Starspangledbanner (AUS)—Abend (IRE) **Spangled Ballet**
10 **DEAR DAPHNE (IRE),** b f Tamayuz—Rebecca Rolfe **Breen, Williams, Lilley, Rosier & Underwood**
11 **EIGHT MILE (IRE),** b g Dandy Man (IRE)—Fashion Central **Mr E Williams & Partner**
12 **EMBROIDERED CLOTH,** ch g Buratino (IRE)—Ribbon Royale **Mr E Williams & Partner**

MR GEORGE SCOTT - continued

13 B g Sioux Nation (USA)—Enliven **The Pals**
14 **GOOSE ROCK (IRE),** b g Mehmas (IRE)—Drifting Spirit (IRE) **Breen, Stephenson & Birkett**
15 **KING KRAKEN,** b g Washington DC (IRE)—Minty Fox **Blue Starr Racing**
16 **MARGARET BEAUFORT,** b f Iffraaj—Janabiya **Mrs V. Machen**
17 **PERFECT GENTLEMAN (IRE),** b g Dawn Approach (IRE)—Silver Moon **Eve Lodge Racing**
18 **PROVOCATEUR (IRE),** gr f El Kabeir (USA)—Little Audio (IRE) **Ms E. L. Banks**
19 **ROCKET RODNEY,** b g Dandy Man (IRE)—Alushta **Victorious Racing Limited**
20 **SPARE RIB,** b g Ribchester (IRE)—Fortune Hunter (FR) **Bluestarr Racing & Mr E Williams**
21 **ZEPPLIN,** b g Adaay (IRE)—Tamaara (IRE) **Offthebridle Podcast**

TWO-YEAR-OLDS

22 B f 27/04 Awtaad (IRE)—Aghaany (Dubawi (IRE)) (38415) **One More for the Road**
23 B f 18/04 Massaat (IRE)—Caledonia Duchess (Dutch Art) (17143)
24 B g 26/02 Bungle Inthejungle—Cold Comfort (IRE) (Gutaifan (IRE)) (14000) **The Trading Partnership**
25 Br c 11/02 Twilight Son—Darwinia (GER) (Acatenango (GER)) (20952) **Victorious Racing Limited & Fawzi Nass**
26 B f 06/03 Havana Grey—Emerald Cliffs (IRE) (Canford Cliffs (IRE)) (19048) **Amo Racing Limited**
27 B g 22/01 Dandy Man (IRE)—
Feelinlikeasomeone (Requinto (IRE)) (26667) **Victorious Racing Limited & Fawzi Nass**
28 **FIBONACCI SEQUENCE (IRE),** b f 04/04 Gleneagles (IRE)—
Elltaaf (IRE) (Invincible Spirit (IRE)) (35000) **Mr K. J. Breen, Ms A. R. Wang**
29 **FIGHT BACK,** ch c 26/02 Ulysses (IRE)—Entity (Shamardal (USA)) (75000) **Valmont**
30 **FISTRAL BEACH (IRE),** b f 09/04 New Bay—
Lamsa (IRE) (Invincible Spirit (IRE)) (30000) **Williams, Townbraccan & Partner**
31 B f 23/03 New Bay—For Henry (IRE) (Galileo (IRE)) (50000) **Ms E. L. Banks**
32 B c 31/01 Kodiac—Get Up And Dance (Makfi) (55238) **Victorious Racing Limited & Fawzi Nass**
33 Gr c 24/04 Dandy Man (IRE)—Heavenly Angel (Dark Angel (IRE)) (75000) **Victorious Racing Limited & Fawzi Nass**
34 Br g 31/01 Outstrip—Hindsight (Sayif (IRE)) (15000) **Ms E Banks, Mr C Rosier & Mrs J Rosier**
35 Ch g 30/03 Dandy Man (IRE)—Kramer Drive (IRE) (Medicean) (8003) **The Trading Partnership**
36 B c 23/02 Footstepsinthesand—Kykuit (IRE) (Green Desert (USA)) (25000) **Sheikh K. B. H. Al Maktoum**
37 B c 11/04 Sioux Nation (USA)—Lanita (GER) (Anabaa (USA)) (25000) **The Trading Partnership**
38 B c 15/01 Caravaggio (USA)—Layalee (IRE) (Lawman (FR)) (50000) **Bluestarr Racing & Partner Ii**
39 B c 25/04 Bated Breath—Lovee Dovee (Galileo (IRE)) **Flaxman Stables Ireland Ltd**
40 **MARY BAGOT (IRE),** b f 01/05 Magna Grecia (IRE)—
Stupendous Miss (USA) (Dynaformer (USA)) (40016) **Mr E. W. B. Williams, Mr D. Underwood**
41 **MELANIES JOY,** b c 08/03 Time Test—
Heading North (Teofilo (IRE)) (57000) **Opulence Thoroughbreds & Partner Ii**
42 B c 11/01 Gleneagles (IRE)—Nazli (IRE) (Invincible Spirit (IRE)) (16006) **The Trading Partnership**
43 Ch c 22/02 Phoenix of Spain (IRE)—Oberyn (IRE) (Holy Roman Emperor (IRE)) (26411) **Mr M. J. Lilley**
44 B f 17/01 New Bay—Paza (USA) (Galileo (IRE)) **Mr M. Chan**
45 B c 06/02 Cracksman—Perfect Showdance (Showcasing) (23000) **The Trading Partnership**
46 **QUEENOFPUDDINGS (IRE),** b f 16/02 Cotai Glory—Pudding (IRE) (Bushranger (IRE)) **Mr C. Woodhouse**
47 B c 21/02 Bungle Inthejungle—
Seafaring (IRE) (Born To Sea (IRE)) (35000) **Ms E Banks, Mr C Rosier & Mrs J Rosier**
48 B g 09/03 Profitable (IRE)—Some Site (IRE) (Nayef (USA)) (30000) **The Trading Partnership**
49 B f 13/03 Cable Bay (IRE)—Srda (USA) (Kingmambo (USA)) (22000) **The Consortium**
50 B f 21/02 U S Navy Flag (USA)—
Style And Grace (IRE) (So You Think (NZ)) (17143) **Ms E Banks, Mr C Rosier & Mrs J Rosier**
51 B c 25/04 Muhaarar—Super Midge (Royal Applause) (25000) **The Trading Partnership**
52 B c 04/03 U S Navy Flag (USA)—Try Yes (Dutch Art) (20000) **Ms E Banks, Mr C Rosier & Mrs J Rosier**
53 B g 29/03 Kodi Bear (IRE)—Turn On The Tears (USA) (Cape Blanco (IRE)) (23810) **The Trading Partnership**
54 **VICE CAPTAIN,** b g 30/04 Land Force (IRE)—Foundation Filly (Lando (GER)) (3000) **Perth Racing**

448 MR JEREMY SCOTT, Dulverton

Postal: **Higher Holworthy Farm, Brompton Regis, Dulverton, Somerset, TA22 9NY**
Contacts: **WORK 01398 371414 MOBILE 07709 279483**
EMAIL holworthyfarm@yahoo.com WEBSITE Jeremyscottracing.net INSTAGRAM @jeremyscottracing

1 **ANNIE MAGIC (IRE),** 7, br m Westerner—Sound Case (IRE) **Pillhead House Partners**
2 **BAMPTON STAR,** 6, b g Kayf Tara—United (GER) **George & Glenda Giles**
3 **BONZA BOY,** 6, ch g Schiaparelli (GER)—Purple Patch **Mr G. T. Lever**
4 **CELTIC ART (FR),** 6, ch g Mastercraftsman (IRE)—Irish Song (FR) **Mr J. P. Carrington**
5 **CHAMPAGNE COURT (IRE),** 10, b g Court Cave (IRE)—Lady Taipan (IRE) **Coles, Smith, McManus & Broughton**
6 **DASHEL DRASHER,** 10, b g Passing Glance—So Long **Mrs B Tully & Mr R Lock**
7 **DIESEL LINE (IRE),** 5, br g Malinas (GER)—Ryans Robin (IRE) **Langley's**
8 **DRASH ON RUBY,** 7, b m Passing Glance—So Long **Mrs B Tully & Mr R Lock**
9 **EMBERSCOMBE (IRE),** 6, br m Califet (FR)—Market Niche (IRE) **The Exmoor Partners**
10 **EXMOOR LAD,** 5, b g Arvico (FR)—Tabello **Mike Wright & Mrs C Scott**
11 **GOLDEN ACE,** 5, b m Golden Horn—Deuce Again **Mr I. F. Gosden**
12 **GREGOR (FR),** 7, gr g Montmartre (FR)—Agathe du Berlais (FR) **Coles, Langley D Skelton**
13 4, Br f Schiaparelli (GER)—Kim Tian Road (IRE) **Mr J. R. M. Scott**
14 **KING'S CASTLE (IRE),** 6, b g Camelot—Kikonga **Mr D. E. Langley**
15 **KISSESFORKATIE (IRE),** 9, b m Jeremy (USA)—Now Were Broke (IRE) **Derek Coles & Ian Gosden**
16 **LA BRETESCHE (FR),** 4, ch f Barastraight—Sandslide **Mr J. H. Frost**
17 **LADY KK (IRE),** 8, br m Shirocco (GER)—Lissard Lady (IRE) **Friends From Insurance**
18 **LEISSIERES EXPRESS,** 6, b g Telescope (IRE)—Maria Antonia (IRE) **Mr M. James**
19 **LILY LUNA (IRE),** 5, gr m Soldier of Fortune (IRE)—Argento Luna **Derek Coles & Ian Gosden**
20 **LITTLE ELSE,** 7, b m Midnight Legend—Real Treasure **The Real Partnership**
21 4, Gr g Mount Nelson—Miss Blueyes (IRE) **Mrs H. L. Stoneman**
22 **MR SNOW WAY (IRE),** 6, b g Snow Sky—Suny House **G. P. and Miss S. J. Hayes**
23 **MY LADY PHOENIX,** 5, b m Telescope (IRE)—Solid Land (FR) **Mike & Maggie Horton**
24 **NATIVE ROBIN (IRE),** 13, br g Robin des Pres (FR)—Homebird (IRE) **Mr P. D. Moore**
25 4, B g Shirocco (GER)—Nowhere Fast (IRE) **Mr J. R. M. Scott**
26 **PETTICOAT LUCY (IRE),** 7, b m Fame And Glory—Matties Isle (IRE) **Mr I F Gosden & Mr DJ Coles**
27 **PHOENIX RISEN,** 6, ch g Conduit (IRE)—Tchatchacoya (FR) **Mike & Maggie Horton**
28 **PILSDON PEN,** 6, b g Helmet (AUS)—Bisou **Mr D. E. Langley**
29 **PRIDE OF NEPAL,** 5, b g The Gurkha (IRE)—Best Regards (IRE) **The Punchestown Syndicate**
30 5, Br m Scorpion (IRE)—Real Treasure **The Real Partnership**
31 4, B g Doyen (IRE)—Rock Garden (IRE) **Mr J. R. M. Scott**
32 **ROLLO'S KINGDOM,** 6, b g Yorgunnabelucky (USA)—Tashkiyla (FR) **Mrs W. Ward**
33 5, B g Kayf Tara—Shanxi Girl **Mrs C. C. Scott**
34 **SIZABLE SAM,** 8, ch g Black Sam Bellamy (IRE)—Halo Flora **The Hopefuls & Kelvin-Hughes**
35 **STARVIDOV (FR),** 5, gr g Davidoff (GER)—Starglas (FR) **Mrs S. Rising**
36 **STORMY FLIGHT (IRE),** 9, gr g Cloudings (IRE)—Help Yourself (IRE) **Mr Ian Murray & Mr Dave Smith**
37 **THE MULCAIR (IRE),** 9, b g Flemensfirth (USA)—Black Lassie (IRE) **The Reverse Forecast**
38 **THE PLIMSOLL LINE (IRE),** 7, b g Dylan Thomas (IRE)—Patsy Choice (IRE) **Dave Smith & Mike Wright**
39 **THE RUSSIAN DOYEN (IRE),** 10, b g Doyen (IRE)—Namloc (IRE) **Mr J. H. Frost**
40 **THE SAINTED CANARY (IRE),** 4, br g Malinas (GER)—Bonny Blackdoe (IRE) **James Barnard & Derek Coles**
41 **TIKKINTHEBOX (IRE),** 11, b g Tikkanen (USA)—Surfing France (FR) **On A Mission**
42 **WAVERING DOWN (IRE),** 8, b g Jeremy (USA)—Gortbofearna (IRE) **Mr J. H. Frost**

Assistant Trainer: Camilla Scott, Georgina Scott, **Head Girl:** Laura Scott. **Racing Secretary:** Joe Scott. **Yard Sponsor:** Chris Hendy Brendon Powerwashers.

NH Jockey: Rex Dingle, Lorcan Williams. **Conditional Jockey:** Jack Martin, David Pritchard.

449 MISS KATIE SCOTT, Galashiels

Postal: **Stables Cottage, Millhaugh, Lindean, Galashiels, Scottish Borders**
Contacts: **MOBILE 07826 344577**

1 **BOLD LIGHT (IRE),** 6, ch g Leading Light (IRE)—Turmoss (FR) **Mr J. Scott**
2 **CASTLEGRANGE (IRE),** 9, b g Arcadio (GER)—Tintown Lady (IRE) **James Scott, Warren Black, Katie Scott**
3 **CHRISTY'S STAR,** 4, b g Fulbright—Teide Mistress (USA) **Star Racing**
4 **COLINTON,** 5, b g Red Jazz (USA)—Magic Maisie **Star Racing**
5 **COOLDINE BOG (IRE),** 10, b g Court Cave (IRE)—Express Mail (IRE) **Miss K. Scott**
6 **ELLADORA,** 5, b m Equiano (FR)—Somersault **Stevens Taylor Clark Raeburn Scott**
7 **ENEMY COAST AHEAD,** 9, br g Malinas (GER)—Penang Princess **Mrs L. J. McLeod**
8 **FAR FROM A RUBY,** 6, b m Farhh—Pretty Miss **Ursa Major Racing & Partner**
9 **FLASH BULB (IRE),** 4, b f Camelot—Ethel **Headway & Scott**
10 **GETAWAY GERRY,** 9, b g Getaway (GER)—Loch Dhu (IRE) **Mark Hay, Andrew Machray, Murray Scott**
11 **GINGER POINTE (FR),** 6, b g Denon (USA)—Rainbow Pointe (ITY) **Mr M. A. Robertson**
12 **GUEST LIST (IRE),** 4, gr f Ardad (IRE)—Heavenly Angel **Mr S. Wallace**
13 **GWEEDORE,** 6, b g Epaulette (AUS)—Ares Choix **Lamont Racing**
14 **HALCYON DREAMS (IRE),** 8, b m Shantaram—Tobrigids (IRE) **Miss K. Scott**
15 **JACKMEISTER RUDI,** 4, b g Churchill (IRE)—Beyond Desire **Making Headway Racing**
16 **JUSTATHIMBLE (IRE),** 4, gr f Gutaifan (IRE)—Dazzling Valentine **Ursa Major Racing & Partner**
17 **KITTY PI,** 4, b f Danon Ballade (JPN)—Moonlight Babe (USA) **Mrs N. Naylor**
18 **MEET ME THERE (IRE),** 4, b f Churchill (IRE)—Shorana (IRE) **Mr A. R. Pollard**
19 **MY MACHO MAN (IRE),** 6, ch g Camacho—Mypreciousblue **Mr E. Cassie**
20 **NELLIE FRENCH (IRE),** 6, b m Dragon Pulse (IRE)—Texas Ruby (USA) **Mrs S. Scott**
21 **ROCKLEY POINT,** 10, b g Canford Cliffs (IRE)—Statua (IRE) **The Vintage Flyers**
22 **SAMURAI SNEDDZ,** 4, b g Highland Reel (IRE)—Self Centred **Paddock Panners & Katie Scott**
23 **SLAINTE MHATH,** 5, ch m Mayson—Ofelia (IRE) **Katie Scott Racing Syndicate**
24 **SPARTAKOS,** 5, b g Rajsaman (FR)—Medicean Bliss (IRE) **Making Headway Racing**

THREE-YEAR-OLDS

25 **ARTEMIS FLYER (IRE),** ch f Dandy Man (IRE)—Tipperary Boutique (IRE) **Making Headway Racing**
26 **KILLING EVE (IRE),** b f Dawn Approach (IRE)—Whisp (GER) **Lamont Racing**
27 **MAUREEN'S LASS (IRE),** b f Cotai Glory—Lovely Lou (IRE) **Making Headway Racing**

TWO-YEAR-OLDS

28 B f 06/04 Land Force (IRE)—Insaaf (Averti (IRE)) (16000) **Black, Clark, Scott and Scott**

---

450 MR MICHAEL SCUDAMORE, Bromsash

Postal: **Eccleswall Court, Bromsash, Nr. Ross-on-Wye, Herefordshire, HR9 7PP**
Contacts: **PHONE 01989 750844 MOBILE 07901 853520**
EMAIL michael.scu@btconnect.com WEBSITE www.michaelscudamoreracing.co.uk

1 **BAYA LESCRIBAA (FR),** 5, b m Spanish Moon (USA)—Anoaita Lescribaa (FR) **Mr A. J. Edwards**
2 **BLAZER TWO,** 5, b g Cable Bay (IRE)—Tamara Moon (IRE) **Mrs B. V. Evans**
3 **BLOW THE BUDGET,** 5, b m Kayf Tara—Roche d'Or **Mr P. E. Truscott**
4 **CALDWELL,** 6, b g Dansili—Milford Sound **Mr And Mrs N Dower**
5 **COMMANDER OF TEN (IRE),** 6, b g Doyen (IRE)—Some Sport (IRE) **Mrs L. Maclennan**
6 **COPPER COIN,** 10, ch g Sulamani (IRE)—Silken Pearls **Mr P. E. Truscott**
7 **COURT MASTER (IRE),** 10, b g Court Cave (IRE)—Lusos Wonder (IRE) **Mrs L. Maclennan**
8 **CZECH HER OUT (IRE),** 9, b m Fame And Glory—Molly Hussey (IRE) **Having A Mare & Michael Scudamore**
9 **DINSDALE,** 10, b g Cape Cross (IRE)—Emmy Award (IRE) **Gabby Gajova and Friends**
10 **DO YOUR JOB (IRE),** 9, b g Fame And Glory—Full of Birds (FR) **Mr M. P. Dunphy**

11 **FAITQUE DE L'ISLE (FR),** 8, ch g Secret Singer (FR)—
Naiade de L'Isle (FR) **dfa racing (Donaldson, Currie, Edwards)**
12 **FAR HORIZON (IRE),** 5, b g Free Eagle (IRE)—Sparkling View (IRE) **Mark & Michael Scudamore**
13 **FIX AT ALL (FR),** 7, b g No Risk At All (FR)—Lady Fix (FR) **Mrs L. Maclennan**
14 **FRIEZE FRAME,** 4, b f Cable Bay (IRE)—Clinet (IRE) **Frieze Racing & Steven Dobson**
15 **GRIS GRIS TOP (FR),** 7, gr g Gris de Gris (IRE)—Tiptop Hugaux (FR) **Mrs L. Maclennan**
16 **HEADS OR HARPS,** 6, b g Flemensfirth (USA)—Dametori (FR) **Mr M. R. Blandford**
17 **HERECOMESFREDDIE,** 5, b g Gregorian (IRE)—Forever Loved **Racehorse Friends Partnership**
18 **HEY FRANKIE (IRE),** 7, gr m Mahler—Flaming Poncho (IRE) **Mr M. P. Dunphy**
19 **I AM GONNA BE (IRE),** 6, b m Barely A Moment (AUS)—Janet Lindup **Mr M. P. Dunphy**
20 **IL GRUSCHEN (IRE),** 4, b g Free Eagle (IRE)—Topaz Clear (IRE) **Mr M. G. Savidge**
21 **KARLIE,** 8, b m Schiaparelli (GER)—Deianira (IRE) **Mr M. P. Dunphy**
22 **LEBOWSKI (IRE),** 8, b g Aizavoski (IRE)—Castle Supreme (IRE) **Mr M. P. Dunphy**
23 **LET IT SHINE,** 5, bl g Pether's Moon (IRE)—My Belle (FR) **Mark & Michael Scudamore**
24 **LET ME ENTERTAIN U,** 7, gr g Saint des Saints (FR)—My Belle (FR) **Mr M. P. Dunphy**
25 **MOFASA,** 7, b g Ocovango—Ninna Nanna (FR) **Mrs L. Maclennan**
26 **MOLLY SANDERSON (IRE),** 5, br m Affinisea (IRE)—Kayanti (IRE) **Mr O. S. Harris**
27 **NOPLACETOBE (IRE),** 6, b m Kalanisi (IRE)—Definite Asset (IRE) **Mr P. E. Truscott & Mr M. Scudamore**
28 **PEAKY BOY (IRE),** 5, b g Kayf Tara—Joanne One (IRE) **Mr O. S. Harris**
29 **PRINCESS OF MERCIA,** 6, b m Blue Bresil (FR)—Very Special One (IRE) **Mrs M. L. Scudamore**
30 **ROBBIE DAZZLER,** 6, ch g Leading Light (IRE)—Mrs Roberts **Having A Mare & Michael Scudamore**
31 **ROBIN DES THEATRE (IRE),** 8, b br m Robin des Champs (FR)—Shannon Theatre (IRE) **Mr M. P. Dunphy**
32 **ROLFE REMBRANDT,** 5, ch g Dutch Art—Rebecca Rolfe **Hunscote Stud Limited**
33 **ROSSEA (IRE),** 5, b m Affinisea (IRE)—Rossbridge Lass (IRE) **Mr M. P. Dunphy**
34 **SINURITA (IRE),** 7, b m Yeats (IRE)—Hard To Please (IRE) **Mrs L. Maclennan**
35 **SOUTHERN BABYLON (IRE),** 5, b m Workforce—Double Diamond (IRE) **Mrs L. Maclennan**
36 **THOR DE CERISY (FR),** 9, b g Enrique—Midalisy (FR) **Mrs L. Maclennan**
37 **THYME 'N' TYDE (IRE),** 5, b m Lucky Speed (IRE)—High Priestess (IRE) **Mr P. E. Truscott & Mr M. Scudamore**
38 **UPTON ROAD (IRE),** 9, b g Jeremy (USA)—Reynard's Glen (IRE) **Mr M. R. Blandford**
39 **VIVE DE CHARNIE (FR),** 6, b m Zambezi Sun—Hecate (IRE) **Mr A. J. Edwards**
40 **WHOZATGIRL (IRE),** 4, b f Estidhkaar (IRE)—Cantaloupe **Mr C. G. J. Chua**
41 **WOLF OF OXSHOTT,** 4, gr g Almanzor (FR)—Marie Rossa **Mr O. S. Harris**

THREE-YEAR-OLDS

42 **RAISE YOUR GLASS,** br f Jack Hobbs—Sparkling River (IRE) **Mr M. P. Dunphy**

Racing Secretary: Marilyn Scudamore.

NH Jockey: Richard Patrick, Ben Poste, Brendan Powell.

---

451 MR DEREK SHAW, Sproxton

Postal: **The Sidings, Saltby Road, Sproxton, Melton Mowbray, Leicestershire, LE14 4RA**
Contacts: **PHONE 01476 860578 MOBILE 07721 039645 FAX 01476 860578**
EMAIL mail@derekshawracing.com WEBSITE www.derekshawracing.com

1 **AMAZING AMAYA,** 8, b m New Approach (IRE)—Faslen (USA) **P. E. Barrett**
2 **ANOTHER BERTIE (IRE),** 4, b g Acclamation—Temerity (IRE) **Mr J. R. Saville**
3 **CEDAR CAGE,** 6, b g Golden Horn—Faslen (USA) **P. E. Barrett**
4 **DAAFY (USA),** 6, b g The Factor (USA)—Ishraak (USA) **Mr D. Shaw**
5 **DIAMOND MEMORIES,** 5, b m Due Diligence (USA)—Shaws Diamond (USA) **Mrs L. J. Shaw**
6 **DUBAI ELEGANCE,** 9, ch m Sepoy (AUS)—Some Sunny Day **Million Dreams Racing 1**
7 **GUSTAV GRAVES,** 5, b g Bobby's Kitten (USA)—Bondesire **Big Lachie Syndicate**
8 **HALA BE ZAIN (IRE),** 5, b m Zoffany (IRE)—We Are Ninety (IRE) **Mr D. Shaw**
9 **HEAVENS DEW,** 4, b f New Approach (IRE)—Tahlia Ree (IRE) **P. E. Barrett**
10 **JAZZ MUSIC,** 6, b m Muhaarar—Propel (IRE) **Mrs L. J. Shaw**

MR DEREK SHAW - continued

11 **JUMIRA BRIDGE,** 9, b g Invincible Spirit (IRE)—Zykina **Mr N. P. Franklin**
12 **LITTLEMISSATTITUDE,** 6, b m Due Diligence (USA)—Lady Elalmadol (IRE) **Million Dreams Racing 1**
13 **MADAME FENELLA,** 4, b f Due Diligence (USA)—Fenella Fudge **Shawthing Racing Partnership & L Shaw**
14 **MISS BELLADONNA,** 4, b f Brazen Beau (AUS)—Ming Meng (IRE) **P. E. Barrett**
15 **MR FUNKY MONKEY,** 4, b g Hellvelyn—Nabat Sultan **Mrs L. J. Shaw**
16 **MR GINJA NINJA,** 4, ch g Coach House (IRE)—Divasesque (IRE) **Mrs L. J. Shaw**
17 **PISELLI MOLLI (IRE),** 5, ch m Dragon Pulse (IRE)—Dancing Duchess (IRE) **P. E. Barrett**
18 **PRINCE ABU (IRE),** 6, gr g Dark Angel (IRE)—Saoirse Abu (USA) **Million Dreams Racing**
19 **SEABOROUGH (IRE),** 8, b g Born To Sea (IRE)—Nobilissima (IRE) **Mr J. Souster**
20 **SIX STRINGS,** 9, b g Requinto (IRE)—Island Music (IRE) **Million Dreams Racing**
21 **THE TRON,** 5, gr g Outstrip—Ming Meng (IRE) **P. E. Barrett**
22 **TIGER TOUCH (USA),** 6, b g American Pharoah (USA)—Osaila (IRE) **Mr J. Souster**
23 **TRUSTY SCOUT (IRE),** 5, ch g Gleneagles (IRE)—Dutch Lilly **Million Dreams Racing**
24 **ULYSSES (GER),** 9, b g Sinndar (IRE)—Ungarin (GER) **Million Dreams Racing**
25 **YOU'RE COOL,** 11, b g Exceed And Excel (AUS)—Ja One (IRE) **Mr D. Bichan**
26 **ZEYDAR (IRE),** 4, b g War Command (USA)—Zaralanta (IRE) **Mr G. Simons**

THREE-YEAR-OLDS

27 **CARNIVAL LAD (IRE),** b g Fastnet Rock (AUS)—Mardie Gras **Mr D. Shaw**
28 **GINNY JO,** b f Massaat (IRE)—Skylla **Facts & Figures**
29 **HEIDI OF ARENDELLE,** gr f Outstrip—Princess Heidi (IRE) **D & L Shaw**
30 **KODI HAWK,** b g Kodiac—Millevini (IRE) **Mr D. Shaw**
31 **L'SARAFINA,** b f Hellvelyn—Naralsaif (IRE) **Shawthing Racing Partnership (D Shaw)**
32 **MIKKA,** b g Expert Eye—Faslen (USA) **P. E. Barrett**

TWO-YEAR-OLDS

33 B f 08/04 Fastnet Rock (AUS)—Sarinda (Dubawi (IRE)) (13000) **P. E. Barrett**
34 B g 01/02 Time Test—Tahlia Ree (IRE) (Acclamation) (40000) **P. E. Barrett**

Yard Sponsor: N & L Franklin Ltd.

452 MRS FIONA SHAW, Dorchester

Postal: **Skippet Cottage, Bradford Peverell, Dorchester, Dorset, DT2 9SE**
Contacts: **PHONE 01305 889350 MOBILE 07970 370444**
EMAIL fiona.shaw05@gmail.com

1 **BENVILLE BRIDGE,** 6, b g Bollin Eric—Kiwi Katie **John & Heather Snook**
2 **BROADOAK,** 8, b g Kayf Tara—Bird Without Wings (IRE) **John & Heather Snook**
3 **ETINCELLE ARTISTE (FR),** 6, b g Great Pretender (IRE)—Forcat (FR) **Miss A. E. Fletcher**
4 **HYMN AND A PRAYER,** 10, br g Eastern Anthem (IRE)—Kryssa **Mrs F. M. Shaw**
5 **MAX WOLF,** 6, ch g Schiaparelli (GER)—Cerise Sauvage **P. B. Shaw**
6 5, B g Arvico (FR)—Petite Pois **P. B. Shaw**
7 **SHOW ON THE ROAD,** 12, b g Flemensfirth (USA)—Roses of Picardy (IRE) **Mrs F. M. Shaw**
8 **SURE LISTEN (FR),** 6, ch g Diamond Boy (FR)—Califea (FR) **Miss A. E. Fletcher**

453 MR MATT SHEPPARD, Ledbury

Postal: **Home Farm Cottage, Eastnor, Ledbury, Herefordshire, HR8 1RD**
Contacts: **MOBILE 07770 625061 FAX 01531 634846**
EMAIL matthew.sheppard@cmail.co.uk

1 **ALWAYS ABLE (IRE),** 8, b m Stowaway—Twotrailerparkgirl (IRE) **Veronica Silber & Marcus Jordan**
2 **BALIYAD (IRE),** 8, gr g Sea The Stars (IRE)—Baliyana (IRE) **The Evron Experience**
3 **COOL RAIN (IRE),** 7, b m Yeats (IRE)—Catleen (IRE) **Silber, Jordan & Lost In the Summer Wine**
4 **LITTLE PI (FR),** 5, b g Dunaden (FR)—Faustina Pius (IRE) **Lost In The Summer Wine**

MR MATT SHEPPARD - continued

5 **NOT AVAILABLE (IRE),** 8, b g Milan—Miss Arteea (IRE) **Mr A. J. Scrivin**
6 **ONE FER MAMMA (IRE),** 7, b g Dylan Thomas (IRE)—Miss Martel (IRE) **D. K. Yearsley**
7 **POTTLERATH (IRE),** 8, b g Yeats (IRE)—Truffle Fairy (IRE) **Lost In The Summer Wine**

NH Jockey: Stan Sheppard.

---

454 MR OLIVER SHERWOOD, Upper Lambourn

Postal: **Neardown Stables, Upper Lambourn, Hungerford, Berkshire, RG17 8QP**
Contacts: **PHONE 01488 71411 MOBILE 07979 591867 FAX 01488 72786**
EMAIL oliver.sherwood@virgin.net WEBSITE www.oliversherwood.co.uk

1 **A TIME TO SHINE (IRE),** 8, b br g Malinas (GER)—Royal Bride **Our Racing Club**
2 4, B g Court Cave (IRE)—Alexander Road (IRE) **Heart of the South Racing 132**
3 **BABY SPICE,** 5, b m Kendargent (FR)—Blast Furnace (IRE) **Apiafi, Frost & Black**
4 **BAL AMIE (FR),** 9, b g Ballingarry (IRE)—Amie Roli (FR) **Mr A. Taylor**
5 **BALLAQUANE (IRE),** 8, b g Scorpion (IRE)—Barreenagh Beag (IRE) **Mrs S. A. White**
6 **CAPTAIN LARA (IRE),** 5, b g Maxios—La Superba (IRE) **Mr Mark Dixon & Luke Lillingston**
7 **CILAOS GLACE (FR),** 10, br g Voix du Nord (FR)—Miss Glacee (FR) **Heart of the South Racing 118**
8 **COKYTHO (FR),** 5, b g Joshua Tree (IRE)—Domidale (FR) **The Neardowners**
9 **CRYPTO CURRENCY (IRE),** 6, b g Yeats (IRE)—Jeunopse (IRE) **Mr T. D. J. Syder**
10 **DJ PETE (IRE),** 5, gr g Malinas (GER)—Rosealainn (IRE) **Lady Thompson**
11 **EAST BRIDGE (IRE),** 7, b g Shirocco (GER)—Ballinahow Lady (IRE) **Exors of the Late Mr T. J. Hemmings**
12 **HAVANELLA (FR),** 6, b m Saddler Maker (IRE)—Kavalle (FR) **The 4 Musketeers**
13 **IMPERIAL HOPE (IRE),** 7, b g Imperial Monarch (IRE)—Ebony Hope (IRE) **Michael Fiddy & Richard Fleming**
14 **JERSEY GEM (IRE),** 4, b br f Mount Nelson—Rose Revived **Mr A. Taylor**
15 **JERSEY LADY (FR),** 7, ch m Martaline—La Bombonera (FR) **Mr A. Taylor**
16 **JERSEY WONDER (IRE),** 7, ch g Zoffany (IRE)—Magena (USA) **Mr A. Taylor**
17 **KANSAS CITY CHIEF (IRE),** 14, b g Westerner—Badawi Street **Jersey Racing Friends**
18 **LITTLE AWKWARD (FR),** 7, gr g Montmartre (FR)—Seven Even (FR) **Michael Fiddy & Richard Fleming**
19 **MACLAINE,** 6, ch g Masked Marvel—Aisance (FR) **Burkes & Syders**
20 **MAKETY,** 9, ch m Black Sam Bellamy (IRE)—Mi Money **Mrs S. A. White**
21 **MINELLA ROYALE,** 10, b g Shirocco (GER)—Lisa du Chenet (FR) **Minella Royale Partnership**
22 **MOUNT FERNS (IRE),** 5, b g Mount Nelson—Galant Ferns (IRE) **Exors of the Late Mr T. J. Hemmings**
23 **MYSTIC MAN (IRE),** 6, b g Sageburg (IRE)—Mystic Cherry (IRE) **The The Dragon Partnership**
24 **NAZWA (IRE),** 5, b g Sepoy (AUS)—Kahalah Fantasy **Quicksilver Racing Partnership**
25 **NEWTONIAN,** 6, b g Telescope (IRE)—Mi Money **Mr P. Mellett**
26 **NORN IRON (IRE),** 5, br g Soldier of Fortune (IRE)—Coco des Champs (IRE) **Dr P. Kelly**
27 **OCEAN DRIFTER (IRE),** 8, b g Aizavoski (IRE)—Driftaway (IRE) **Burkes & Syders**
28 **PEUR DE RIEN (FR),** 10, b g Kapgarde (FR)—Tango Princess (FR) **Peur de Rien Syndicate**
29 **POLICE ACADEMY (IRE),** 6, b m Arctic Cosmos (USA)—Academy Miss (IRE) **Million in Mind Partnership**
30 **PURE CARBON,** 4, bl g Diamond Boy (FR)—Rosie's Rein (IRE) **Mr J. Palmer-Brown**
31 **QUEENS GAMBLE (IRE),** 5, ch m Getaway (GER)—Gambling Girl (IRE) **A & E Galvin**
32 **RED BOND (IRE),** 7, b g Red Jazz (USA)—Faithfulbond (IRE) **Mr J Luck**
33 **REPUBLICAN,** 8, b g Kayf Tara—Noun de La Thinte (FR) **Mr E. J. Ware**
34 **RHEBUS ROAD (IRE),** 5, ch g Champs Elysees—Red Riddle (IRE) **Burkes & Syders**
35 **ROUGE ET BLANC (FR),** 18, ch g Mansonnien (FR)—Fidelety (FR) **Mr O. M. C. Sherwood**
36 **ROYAL LAKE (IRE),** 7, b g Fame And Glory—Gran Chis (IRE) **Exors of the Late Mr T. J. Hemmings**
37 4, B g Mount Nelson—Run Like The Wind (IRE) **Mr O. M. C. Sherwood**
38 **SCAMALLACH LIATH (IRE),** 6, gr g Shantou (USA)—Lady Cloudings (IRE) **Mr & Mrs Norman**
39 **SCRUM DIDDLY (IRE),** 5, b g Malinas (GER)—Diamond Gesture (IRE) **Winterfields Farm Ltd & M Burton**
40 **SEASTON SPIRIT,** 10, b g Kayf Tara—Aphrodisias (FR) **Mr M. Fiddy**
41 **SONIFICATION,** 5, b g Telescope (IRE)—Moonlight Music (IRE) **Quicksilver Racing Partnership**
42 4, B g Kingston Hill—Tara Tara (IRE) **Mr O. M. C. Sherwood**
43 **TIMES ARE BLUE (IRE),** 5, gr g Champs Elysees—Times Are Grey (IRE) **Mr R. E. Kingston**

MR OLIVER SHERWOOD - continued

44 **TREVADA,** 7, b g Kayf Tara—Kerada (FR) **Hot To Trot Jumping & Mrs R Chugg**
45 **VINTAGE RASCAL (FR),** 6, b g Nathaniel (IRE)—Irish Vintage (FR) **Mr O. M. C. Sherwood**

Assistant Trainer: Andy Llewellyn, **Head Lad:** Stefan Namesansky, **Secretary:** Emma Chugg.

---

455 MR OLIVER SIGNY, Lambourn

Postal: **The Croft Stables, Upper Lambourn, Hungerford, Berkshire, RG17 8QH**
EMAIL oliver@oliversignyracing.com

1 **AGENT EMPIRE (GER),** 5, gr g Sidestep (AUS)—Adalea **Dunkley, Gumienny, Mackenzie & Signy**
2 **BE THE BEST (USA),** 7, b g Declaration of War (USA)—Memories For Us (USA)
3 **CHEF BOGO (FR),** 6, b g Balko (FR)—Ascella (FR) **Dunkley, Gumienny, Mackenzie & Signy**
4 **COACHMAN (FR),** 7, b g Maresca Sorrento (FR)—La Pelodette (FR) **Mrs S. McLean**
5 **COME DANCING (IRE),** 6, b g Fame And Glory—Minnie Ray (IRE) **Come Dancing Partnership**
6 **DAVE AND BERNIE (IRE),** 8, b g Papal Bull—Iseult (IRE) **Oliver Signy Racing Club**
7 **DECORATED,** 5, ch g Nathaniel (IRE)—Trapeze **Oliver Signy Racing Club**
8 **ETAT MAJOR AULMES (FR),** 9, b g Della Francesca (USA)—River Gold Aulmes (FR) **Oliver Signy Racing Club**
9 **FRENCH PARADOXE (FR),** 8, b g Day Flight—Sculture (FR) **Mick Fitzgerald Racing Club**
10 **HEDERA PARK (IRE),** 5, b m Walk In The Park (IRE)—Ivy Queen (IRE) **Mr D. R. Jones**
11 **J'VENTILE (FR),** 4, b f Cokoriko (FR)—Valia du Reponet (FR) **Oliver Signy Racing Club**
12 **JIGGINSTOWN KING (IRE),** 6, b g Lucky Speed (IRE)—Miss Baden (IRE) **I Barratt, A Signy & B Spiers**
13 4, B g Lawman (FR)—Luminata (IRE) **Oliver Signy Racing Club**
14 **MAD ABOUT SALLY (IRE),** 8, b br m Califet (FR)—Lou's Coole Girl (IRE) **Oliver Signy Racing Club**
15 **MARSHELLA (IRE),** 4, b f Getaway (GER)—Assistance **Bart Ryan-beswick & Warwick Ryan-beswick**
16 **MARYAH ISLAND,** 4, b g Blue Bresil (FR)—Hidden Rebel **Feather & Hay Racing**
17 **NO WORD OF A LIE,** 7, b g Milan—Agnese **Dunkley, Gumienny, Mackenzie & Signy**
18 **PINK POWER,** 6, b m Kayf Tara—Presenting Taupo (IRE) **R Triple H**
19 **ROBIN DES FOX (IRE),** 7, b g Robin des Champs (FR)—Shesafoxylady (IRE) **I Barratt, A Signy & B Spiers**
20 **ROLLING RIVER (IRE),** 5, b g Ol' Man River (IRE)—Joan d'Arc (IRE) **Oliver Signy Racing Club**
21 **SAMBEZI (FR),** 7, b g Rajsaman (FR)—Tunis (FR) **Mrs S. McLean**
22 **SEA VILLAGE (IRE),** 5, b g Affinisea (IRE)—Etoile Margot (FR) **Mick Fitzgerald Racing Club**
23 **THE SCORPION KING,** 5, b g Scorpion (IRE)—Big Time Billy (IRE) **Mr & Mrs A. Signy**
24 5, B m Soldier of Fortune (IRE)—What A Lark (IRE) **Mr O. Signy**
25 4, B g Sageburg (IRE)—Willow Rose (IRE) **Oliver Signy Racing Club**

Racing Secretary: Mrs Katherine Signy.

---

456 MR DAVID SIMCOCK, Newmarket

Postal: **The Office, Trillium Place, Birdcage Walk, Newmarket, Suffolk, CB8 0NE**
Contacts: **PHONE 01638 662968 MOBILE 07808 954109, 07702 851561 FAX 01638 663888**
EMAIL david@davidsimcock.co.uk WEBSITE www.davidsimcock.co.uk

1 **AIMING HIGH,** 4, ch f Lope de Vega (IRE)—High Hopes
2 **BLESS HIM (IRE),** 9, b g Sea The Stars (IRE)—Happy Land (IRE)
3 **CASH (IRE),** 4, gr c Shamardal (USA)—Lady Rosamunde
4 **CHING SHIH (IRE),** 4, b f Lope de Vega (IRE)—Madame Chiang
5 **CHOLA EMPIRE,** 4, b g Territories (IRE)—Veena (FR)
6 **CUERNAVACA (FR),** 4, b f Lope de Vega (IRE)—Lady Darshaan (IRE)
7 **DALBY FOREST,** 4, ch g Equiano (FR)—Primrose Valley
8 **FORGE VALLEY LAD,** 6, b g Cityscape—Tamara
9 **FOX POWER (IRE),** 7, gr g Dark Angel (IRE)—Zenella
10 **FULFILLED,** 4, b g Ulysses (IRE)—Zoella (USA)
11 **GLEN COVE (IRE),** 4, b g Ardad (IRE)—North East Bay (USA)
12 **HEATH RISE,** 5, b g Gleneagles (IRE)—Cubanita

MR DAVID SIMCOCK - continued

13 **KINGSTON JOY (IRE),** 4, b f Kingston Hill—Archetypal (IRE)
14 **KIWANO (FR),** 4, b g Dabirsim (FR)—Araca (FR)
15 **LIGHT INFANTRY (FR),** 4, ch c Fast Company (IRE)—Lights On Me
16 **MASTERCLASS,** 4, gr g Lethal Force (IRE)—Kensington Gardens
17 **MELEK ALREEH (USA),** 4, b c Lemon Drop Kid (USA)—Bargain Blitz (USA)
18 **MOUNTAIN ROAD (FR),** 4, b g Churchill (IRE)—La Corniche (FR)
19 **ORIENTAL ART,** 5, b g Archipenko (USA)—Robe Chinoise
20 **REPERTOIRE,** 7, b g Bated Breath—Binche (USA)
21 **SCARBOROUGH CASTLE,** 6, b g Fastnet Rock (AUS)—Charlotte O Fraise (IRE)
22 **SMART CHAMPION,** 8, b g Teofilo (IRE)—Soryah (IRE)
23 **TIDES OF WAR (IRE),** 5, ch h Galileo (IRE)—Walklikeanegyptian (IRE)
24 **TIGER CRUSADE (FR),** 6, b g No Nay Never (USA)—Folle Allure (FR)
25 **TRADESMAN (IRE),** 4, b g Mastercraftsman (IRE)—Casila (IRE)
26 **TRAILA,** 5, ch g Australia—Waila
27 **VIVE LA REINE,** 4, b f Twilight Son—Aiming

THREE-YEAR-OLDS

28 **AIM STRAIGHT,** b g Australia—High Hopes
29 **ALEX THE GREAT (IRE),** gr g Camelot—Moonrise Landing (IRE)
30 **ARARAT (IRE),** b c Kodiac—Recife (GER)
31 **CHARLATAN (IRE),** ch c Mastercraftsman (IRE)—Lyin Eyes
32 **CHARLIE'S CHOICE,** b g Lightning Spear—Aliyana (IRE)
33 **CITY OF YORK,** b g Cityscape—Primrose Valley
34 **DAGMAR RUN (IRE),** b c Muhaarar—Zabeel Princess
35 **DMANI,** ch f Dubawi (IRE)—Dabyah (IRE)
36 **DOUBLE TOT (IRE),** b f Starspangledbanner (AUS)—Spirited Girl (IRE)
37 **EMPRESS WU,** b f Sea The Moon (GER)—Chinoiseries
38 **FOLK STAR,** ch f Le Havre (IRE)—Folk Opera (IRE)
39 **HARROGATE BETTY,** b f Cityscape—Miss Fridaythorpe
40 **HARRY BROWN,** b g Harry Angel (IRE)—Sarshampla (IRE)
41 **HIGHLAND SONG (IRE),** b c Kingman—Longing (IRE)
42 **HITCHED (IRE),** b g Cotai Glory—Newlywed (IRE)
43 B g Cloth of Stars (IRE)—Ihsas (USA)
44 **LADY MARIE (IRE),** b f Shamardal (USA)—Lady Rosamunde
45 **LIGHTNING SPARK,** ch f Lightning Spear—Starlit Sky
46 **LOUGH LEANE (IRE),** b g Cityscape—Kyllarney
47 **LUNAR BIRD (IRE),** b f Cracksman—Singyoursong (IRE)
48 **MASCAPONE,** b c Massaat (IRE)—Capelita
49 **MORDOR (FR),** b c Roaring Lion (USA)—Secrete (FR)
50 **MS GREER,** b f Bobby's Kitten (USA)—Ms Gillard
51 **OPTIK (IRE),** b g Expert Eye—Sliabh Luachra (IRE)
52 **PANNING FOR GOLD (IRE),** b g Galileo Gold—Sweet Temptation (IRE)
53 **PFINGSTBERG (GER),** ch c Protectionist (GER)—Peace of Paradise (GER)
54 Ch c No Nay Never (USA)—Pink Damsel (IRE)
55 **RESTRICT (USA),** ch c Collected (USA)—Short Squeeze (USA)
56 **SAGAMI BAY (IRE),** b c New Bay—Kymera (IRE)
57 **SECRET CONTACT (FR),** b f Dabirsim (FR)—Heliocentric (FR)
58 **SHERBET FOUNTAIN (USA),** b f Twirling Candy (USA)—Church Camp (USA)
59 **SNIPER'S EYE (FR),** b c Expert Eye—Popular
60 **SUPER MO (USA),** b c Uncle Mo (USA)—Sweet Connie (USA)
61 B f Iffraaj—Zubeida

TWO-YEAR-OLDS

62 **ALTANERA,** gr f 28/04 Oasis Dream—Albaraka (Selkirk (USA))
63 B f 09/03 Land Force (IRE)—Born To Day (IRE) (Born To Sea (IRE)) (80000)
64 **CLOUDSIDE ROCK,** b c 04/04 Rock of Gibraltar (IRE)—Go Georgie (Sagamix (FR))
65 B c 05/04 Camelot—Dillydallydo (IRE) (Holy Roman Emperor (IRE)) (24000)
66 B c 10/04 Lightning Spear—Elenora Delight (Dansili) (30000)
67 B c 27/02 Kodiac—Hairpin (USA) (Bernardini (USA)) (90000)

MR DAVID SIMCOCK - continued

68 B f 25/02 Oasis Dream—Happy Hiker (IRE) (Dalakhani (IRE))
69 **LUCY LOCKETT,** b f 19/02 Lightning Spear—Aliyana (IRE) (Iffraaj)
70 B c 28/03 Invincible Spirit (IRE)—Mardie Gras (Galileo (IRE))
71 B f 03/02 Lightning Spear—Marine Bleue (IRE) (Desert Prince (IRE))
72 B c 27/04 Saxon Warrior (JPN)—Mirage (IRE) (Oasis Dream)
73 B f 24/02 Advertise—Miss Latin (IRE) (Galileo (IRE))
74 B f 19/04 Cable Bay (IRE)—Montjeu's Lady (Motivator) (45000)
75 **NORTHSTEAD GARDENS,** ch f 03/03 Cityscape—Miss Fridaythorpe (Pastoral Pursuits)
76 B c 12/02 Magna Grecia (IRE)—Occupation (IRE) (Dragon Pulse (IRE)) (23000)
77 Ch f 28/03 Cracksman—Oud Metha (Manduro (GER))
78 Gr f 20/02 Night of Thunder (IRE)—Princess de Lune (IRE) (Shamardal (USA)) (280112)
79 B c 23/03 Masar (IRE)—Privacy Order (Azamour (IRE)) (30000)
80 B c 08/04 Noble Mission—Queen of Time (Harbour Watch (IRE)) (135000)
81 **RAJA RAJA,** b c 10/04 Nathaniel (IRE)—Veena (FR) (Elusive City (USA))
82 B c 31/03 Too Darn Hot—Realism (USA) (First Defence (USA)) (55000)
83 B f 22/04 Pivotal—Sarshampla (IRE) (Elzaam (AUS))
84 B c 21/02 Blue Point (IRE)—Sharaakah (IRE) (Roderic O'Connor (IRE))
85 **SHIN FALLS,** b f 14/04 Gleneagles (IRE)—Carnachy (IRE) (Mastercraftsman (IRE))
86 **SINOLOGY,** b f 19/04 Study of Man (IRE)—Madame Chiang (Archipenko (USA))
87 B c 11/03 Tasleet—Sparkling Eyes (Lujain (USA)) (26667)
88 **THORNTONLEDALE MAX,** b c 13/02 Cityscape—Primrose Valley (Pastoral Pursuits)
89 B c 10/04 Nathaniel (IRE)—Veena (FR) (Elusive City (USA))
90 Gr f 12/03 Nathaniel (IRE)—White Chocolate (IRE) (Mastercraftsman (IRE)) (36000)

Owners: A Jackson, K Stewart & Partners, Sheikh J. D. Al Maktoum, Mr A. Al Mansoori, Mr A. S. Al Naboodah, Mr S. B. M. Al Qassimi, Amo Racing Limited, Artemis Thoroughbred Racing, Australian Bloodstock, Mr A. S. Belhab, Brookfields Racing, Mr R. G. W. Brown, Chola Dynasty, Rumble Racing Club, J. M. Cook, Axel Cornez, K. A. Dasmal, Khalifa Dasmal & Bryan Payne, Mr R. El Youssef, Mrs F. H. Hay, Honorable Earle I Mack International, Mohammed Jaber, Mrs A. J. Jackson, Katherine Stewart & Alison Jackson, Khalifa Dasmal & Partners, Mr J. Lovett, E. I. Mack, Never Say Die Partnership, Neversaydie & Light Infantry Partnership, Mr E. M. O'Connor, Twenty Stars Partnership, Mr C. C. Payne, A. J. Perkins, A. M. Pickering, Qatar Racing Limited, Quantum Leap Racing II, Ms A. Quinn, Highclere Thoroughbred Racing, Mr R. Rauscher, Miss K. Rausing, Miss K. J. Reed, Mr J. Rodosthenous, Mrs J. Rodosthenous, Dr A. Sivananthan, Mrs K. Sivananthan, St Albans Bloodstock Limited, Mrs K. Stewart, Tick Tock Partnership, Tony Perkins & Partners, Mr E. J. Ware, Major M. G. Wyatt.

Assistant Trainer: Thomas Lyon-Smith.

Flat Jockey: Jamie Spencer. **Apprentice Jockey:** Olivia Haines.

---

457 MR DAN SKELTON, Alcester

Postal: **Lodge Hill, Shelfield Green, Shelfield, Alcester, Warwickshire, B49 6JR**
Contacts: **PHONE 01789 336339**
EMAIL office@danskeltonracing.com WEBSITE www.danskeltonracing.com FACEBOOK @ DanSkeltonHorseracing TWITTER @DSkeltonRacing INSTAGRAM @DSkeltonRacing

1 5, B g Doyen (IRE)—African Keys (IRE) **P. H. Betts**
2 **ALLIHIES (IRE),** 4, ch g Anjaal—Ahd (USA) **Share My Dream**
3 **ALLJANI (GER),** 4, br f Guiliani (IRE)—Aireen (GER) **Mr J. J. Reilly**
4 **ALLMANKIND,** 7, b g Sea The Moon (GER)—Wemyss Bay **The Gredley Family**
5 **ALNADAM (FR),** 10, b g Poliglote—Rosadame (FR) **Mr B. J. C. Drew**
6 **ALRIGHT DAI (IRE),** 5, ch g No Risk At All (FR)—The Cookie Jar (IRE) **Lycett Racing Ltd**
7 **AMOOLA GOLD (GER),** 10, b g Mamool (IRE)—Aughamore Beauty (IRE) **Mr & Mrs Gordon Pink**
8 4, B g Mahler—April Thyne (IRE) **Speelman Thoroughbreds Ltd**

MR DAN SKELTON - continued

9 **ARTEMIS KIMBO,** 6, b m Saint des Saints (FR)—Early Dawne **Stuart & Shelly Parkin**
10 **ASHTOWN LAD (IRE),** 9, b g Flemensfirth (USA)—Blossom Trix (IRE) **Mr & Mrs D. Yates**
11 **ASTA LA PASTA (IRE),** 5, b g Walk In The Park (IRE)—Asian Maze (IRE) **The Asta La Pasta Partnership**
12 **BAHIO BOUM (FR),** 4, gr g Buck's Boum (FR)—Bahia Do Brasil (FR) **Mr D. N. Skelton**
13 **BALLYGRIFINCOTTAGE (IRE),** 8, b g Stowaway—Long Long Time (IRE) **Friends From Insurance**
14 **BALLYWITE (IRE),** 4, b g Sholokhov (IRE)—Wite Lioness **R. M. Kirkland**
15 5, B m Presenting—Banjaxed Girl **Little Lodge Farm**
16 **BEAKSTOWN (IRE),** 10, b g Stowaway—Midnight Reel (IRE) **Mr B. J. C. Drew**
17 **BENNY'S OSCAR (IRE),** 8, b br g Oscar (IRE)—Benefit Ball (IRE) **Craig & Laura Buckingham**
18 **BENNYS KING (IRE),** 12, b g Beneficial—Hellofafaithful (IRE) **Mezzone Family**
19 **BERAZ (FR),** 5, b g Zoffany (IRE)—Beshara (FR) **Owners Group 096**
20 **BIZZY MOON,** 5, b m Telescope (IRE)—September Moon **Mrs E. M. Pugh**
21 **BLAKLION,** 14, b g Kayf Tara—Franciscaine (FR) **Mr & Mrs D. Yates**
22 **BLUE BUBBLES,** 6, b m Blue Bresil (FR)—Araucaria (IRE) **L & H Hales**
23 4, B g Flemensfirth (USA)—Blue Maxi (IRE)
24 **BOOK OF SECRETS (IRE),** 5, b g Free Eagle (IRE)—Alice Treasure (IRE) **Craig & Laura Buckingham**
25 **CALICO (GER),** 7, b g Soldier Hollow—Casanga (IRE) **Mr J. J. Reilly**
26 **CALLISTO'S KING (IRE),** 6, b g Imperial Monarch (IRE)—Exit Bob (IRE) **Noel Fehily Racing Syndicates - C King**
27 **CAMDONIAN (IRE),** 7, b g Shantou (USA)—Miss Garbo (IRE) **Masterson Holdings Limited**
28 **CATCH HIM DERRY (IRE),** 5, b g Milan—Pretty Present (IRE) **Jolly Boys Outing**
29 **CHANTILLY ROSE,** 6, gr m Turgeon (USA)—Nicknack (FR) **Mr I. Lawrence**
30 **CHER TARA (IRE),** 4, b f Kayf Tara—Rock Chick Supremo (IRE) **Judy Craymer & Nick Skelton**
31 **CHERIE D'AM (FR),** 5, b m Great Pretender (IRE)—Flemens Pride **Mr & Mrs D. Yates**
32 **CHILINLIKEAVILLAIN (IRE),** 6, b g Imperial Monarch (IRE)—Witneses Daughter (IRE) **Craig & Laura Buckingham**
33 **CLARAROSE (IRE),** 5, b m Yeats (IRE)—Garranlea Maree (IRE) **Mezzone Family**
34 **COOGAN'S BLUFF (IRE),** 5, b g Westerner—Louve Sereine (FR) **Mr Frank McAleavy & Mr Ian McAleavy**
35 **DEAFENING SILENCE (IRE),** 6, b g Alkaadhem—Taipers (IRE) **My Racing Manager Friends**
36 **DELGANY BOBBY BLUE,** 5, b g Blue Bresil (FR)—Pretty Neat (IRE) **Charles & Rachel Wilson**
37 **DELGANY DREAMER,** 5, gr m Blue Bresil (FR)—New Bridge (FR) **Charles & Rachel Wilson**
38 **DIAMOND TWIN (FR),** 5, b g Diamond Boy (FR)—Lady La Lionne (FR) **Winter Gold Racing 2**
39 **DIME STORE COWGIRL,** 6, ch m Gentlewave (IRE)—Bold Fire **Honestly Racing**
40 **DOCTOR PARNASSUS (IRE),** 5, b g Make Believe—We'll Go Walking (IRE) **Mr D. W. Fox**
41 **DOG OF WAR (FR),** 9, b g Soldier of Fortune (IRE)—Zainzana (FR) **Mr C. A. Donlon**
42 **DON HOLLOW (GER),** 6, b g Soldier Hollow—Donna Philippa (GER) **Honestly Racing**
43 **DON OCCHETTI (IRE),** 5, b g Presenting—Baileys Partytime
44 **DOYEN QUEST (IRE),** 5, ch g Doyen (IRE)—Queen of Questions (IRE) **N. W. Lake**
45 **DOYOUKNOWWHATIMEAN,** 6, b g Martaline—Knar Mardy **R. M. Kirkland**
46 **ECLAIR D'AINAY (FR),** 9, b br g Network (GER)—Etoile d'Ainay (FR) **Mr J. Hales**
47 **ELLE EST BEAU (IRE),** 5, b m Walk In The Park (IRE)—Autumn Clouds (IRE) **Mrs S. Lawrence**
48 5, B m Kayf Tara—Ellnando Queen **Mr J. J. Reilly**
49 **EMILY'S STAR,** 6, b m Kayf Tara—Lisa du Chenet (FR) **1863 Racing**
50 **ENTITY OF SUBSTANZ,** 4, gr g No Risk At All (FR)—Sardagna (FR) **Mr C. A. Donlon**
51 **ETALON (IRE),** 6, br g Sholokhov (IRE)—So You Said (IRE) **Mrs S. Lawrence**
52 **FAIVOIR (FR),** 8, b g Coastal Path—Qape Noir (FR) **Mrs S. Lawrence**
53 **FANCY STUFF (IRE),** 6, br m Presenting—Deep Supreme (IRE) **Thirsty Thursday Syndicate**
54 **FARMER'S GAMBLE,** 7, ch g Geordieland (FR)—Callerlilly **Farmer's Friends**
55 **FATHER OF JAZZ,** 6, b g Kingman—Bark (IRE) **The Gredley Family**
56 **FLEGMATIK (FR),** 8, ch g Fuisse (FR)—Crack d'Emble (FR) **N. W. Lake**
57 **FRERE D'ARMES (FR),** 6, b g Bathyrhon (GER)—Ville Sainte (FR) **Belbroughton Racing Club**
58 **GALIA DES LITEAUX (FR),** 7, b m Saddler Maker (IRE)—Serie Love (FR) **Mr M. Ariss**
59 **GET A TONIC (IRE),** 7, b m Getaway (GER)—Atomic Winner (IRE) **Cherry Knoll Farm, M&T Ward & D Skelton**
60 **GET SKY HIGH (IRE),** 8, ch m Getaway (GER)—Tell Me Emma (IRE) **Mr & Mrs Gordon Pink**
61 **GET UP MUSH (IRE),** 5, b g Getaway (GER)—Steel Lady (IRE) **Mr M. Ariss**
62 **GIULIETTA (IRE),** 6, br m Great Pretender (IRE)—Sardagna (FR) **Mrs S. J. Faulks**
63 **GLOBAL FAMENGLORY (IRE),** 7, b m Fame And Glory—Noble Pearl (GER) **Mrs S. Carsberg**
64 **GLORIOUS FUN (IRE),** 6, b g Fame And Glory—Itsalark (IRE) **R. M. Kirkland**
65 **GO STEADY,** 11, b g Indian Danehill (IRE)—Pyleigh Lady **Popham, Rogers**
66 **GOD'S OWN GETAWAY (IRE),** 5, b g Getaway (GER)—Yorkshire Girl (IRE) **SRW Partnership**
67 **GOONHILLY (IRE),** 5, ch g Mount Nelson—Holly Baloo (IRE) **Mike and Eileen Newbould**
68 **GREAT SAMOURAI (FR),** 6, b g Great Pretender (IRE)—Bahama Pearl (FR) **ST Racing - Great Samourai**

MR DAN SKELTON - continued

69 **GREY DAWNING (IRE),** 6, gr g Flemensfirth (USA)—Lady Wagtail (IRE) **R. M. Kirkland**
70 **GRILLON DE MONTY (FR),** 8, b g Crillon (FR)—Pat's Girl (FR) **Mr C. Ohrstrom**
71 **HARTUR D'OUDAIRIES (FR),** 6, b g Kapgarde (FR)—Brise d'Oudairies (FR) **Mr J. P. McManus**
72 **HATCHER (IRE),** 10, b g Doyen (IRE)—African Keys (IRE) **P. H. Betts**
73 **HAVOCK (IRE),** 5, b g Walk In The Park (IRE)—Pipe Lady (IRE) **Simon & Lisa Hobson**
74 **HEEZER GEEZER (FR),** 6, b g Cokoriko (FR)—Queen du Vallon (FR) **Mr S. M. Bough**
75 **HELLO POPS,** 6, b g Kayf Tara—Venceremos **Mr A. L. Cohen**
76 **HELTENHAM (FR),** 6, b g Masked Marvel—Souris Blanche (FR) **N. W. Lake**
77 4, B g Getaway (GER)—Hestina (FR)
78 **HIDDEN HEROICS (FR),** 6, b g Coastal Path—Quine de Sivola (FR) **Mr I. Lawrence**
79 **HITCHING JACKING (FR),** 6, b g Honolulu (IRE)—Omirande (FR) **Noel Fehily Racing Syndicate-Hitching Ja**
80 **HOE JOLY SMOKE,** 5, b g Black Sam Bellamy (IRE)—My Miss Lucy **Babbitt Racing**
81 **HOME FREE (IRE),** 5, b g Soldier of Fortune (IRE)—Shuriken (IRE) **Mrs S. Magnier**
82 **HOMETOWN HERO (IRE),** 8, b g Darsi (FR)—Kilcoltrim Society (IRE) **Estate Research Limited**
83 **HORIZON D'AINAY (FR),** 6, ch g Network (GER)—Sirene d'Ainay (FR) **Simon & Lisa Hobson**
84 **HOT FIZZY LIZZY (IRE),** 4, gr f Doyen (IRE)—Carrigeen Acebo (IRE) **Mr C. B. J. Dingwall**
85 **I LOOK HOW I LOOK (SPA),** 4, b f Dink (FR)—Manly Dream (FR) **Mr D. N. Skelton**
86 4, Br f Getaway (GER)—Illwalktheline (IRE) **Speelman Thoroughbreds Ltd**
87 **IN THIS WORLD (FR),** 5, b h Saint des Saints (FR)—Maia Royale (FR) **In This World Syndicate**
88 **IORENS (FR),** 5, ch m Coastal Path—Anglica (FR) **Mrs S. Lawrence**
89 **IRLANDAIS (FR),** 5, b g Buck's Boum (FR)—Saboum (FR) **Mr C. A. Donlon**
90 **ITTACK BLUE (FR),** 5, gr g Coastal Path—Beauty Blue (FR) **A G J & Diver**
91 **JACK BLACK (FR),** 4, b g Tirwanako (FR)—Loriane de Vonnas (FR)
92 **JAY JAY REILLY (IRE),** 7, b g Fame And Glory—Garden City (IRE) **Mr J. J. Reilly**
93 **JAZZ QUEEN,** 4, br f Jack Hobbs—Ellnando Queen **Mrs R. I. Vaughan**
94 **JEFFERY'S CROSS (IRE),** 7, b g Flemensfirth (USA)—Gleaming Spire **Mr P. Beck**
95 **JET PLANE (IRE),** 7, b g Jet Away—Court Gamble (IRE) **Norman Lake & Susan Carsberg**
96 **JUVENTUS DE BRION (FR),** 4, b g Creachadoir (IRE)—Reunion A Brion (FR) **Mr D. N. Skelton**
97 **KASH TARA,** 5, b g Kayf Tara—Rock Chick Supremo (IRE) **Judy Craymer & Nick Skelton**
98 **KATEIRA,** 6, b m Kayf Tara—Raitera (FR) **Little Lodge Farm & Dan Skelton**
99 **KATTEGAT,** 4, b f Black Sam Bellamy (IRE)—Chilla Cilla **Alne Park Stud**
100 **KAYF HERNANDO,** 7, b g Kayf Tara—Thrice Nice **Dick,Stevenson and Partners**
101 **KELSEY PARK (IRE),** 6, b g Walk In The Park (IRE)—Vast Consumption (IRE) **Mr T. Crowe**
102 **KINGSFORT HILL,** 8, b g Multiplex—Pugnacious Lady **Ms D. O Connor**
103 **KNICKERBOCKERGLORY (IRE),** 7, b g Fame And Glory—
The Brass Lady (IRE) **Chelsea Thoroughbreds - Knickerbocker**
104 **KNIGHT IN DUBAI (IRE),** 10, b g Dubai Destination (USA)—Bobbies Storm (IRE) **Mr & Mrs Ben Houghton**
105 **KRACKA NUT,** 6, b g Blue Bresil (FR)—More Like That (IRE) **Mike and Eileen Newbould**
106 **L'EAU DU SUD (FR),** 5, gr g Lord du Sud (FR)—Eaux Fortes (FR) **Sir A Ferguson G Mason J Hales & L Hales**
107 **LAC DE CONSTANCE (FR),** 7, gr g Martaline—Kendova (FR) **Mr A. L. Cohen**
108 **LANGER DAN (IRE),** 7, b g Ocovango—What A Fashion (IRE) **Mr C. A. Donlon**
109 **LATHAN (FR),** 4, ch g Doctor Dino (FR)—Venerie (FR) **Mike and Eileen Newbould**
110 **LE MILOS,** 8, b g Shirocco (GER)—Banjaxed Girl **The Jolly Good Partnership**
111 **LET IT RAIN,** 4, b f Kayf Tara—Tazzarine (FR) **Mr D. N. Skelton**
112 4, B f Getaway (GER)—Little Acorn **Andy & Sharon Measham**
113 **LOLLOBRIGIDA (IRE),** 5, b m It's Gino (GER)—Laviola (GER) **Mr Michael Fennessy & Alne Park Stud**
114 **LONE SOLDIER,** 5, b g Soldier of Fortune (IRE)—Alegralil **Mr Frank McAleavy & Mr Ian McAleavy**
115 **MAHLER MOON (IRE),** 5, b g Mahler—Celestial Spirit (IRE) **Mr & Mrs Gordon Pink**
116 **MARADA,** 8, ch m Martaline—Kerada (FR) **Little Lodge Farm & Dan Skelton**
117 **MARTHA BRAE,** 8, b m Shirocco (GER)—Harringay **Mrs R. I. Vaughan**
118 **MEDYAF,** 4, b g Sea The Moon (GER)—Questabella (GER) **Craig & Laura Buckingham**
119 **MESSAGE PERSONNEL (FR),** 5, b g Saint des Saints (FR)—Victoria Princess (FR) **Mr J. Hales**
120 **MIDNIGHT RIVER,** 8, ch g Midnight Legend—Well Connected **Mr Frank McAleavy & Mr Ian McAleavy**
121 **MILAGROSA (FR),** 5, b m Masked Marvel—Macara (GER) **Mrs S. J. Faulks**
122 **MISSED TEE (IRE),** 6, b m Fame And Glory—Paradise Lily (IRE) **Mr C. A. Donlon**
123 **MOLLY OLLYS WISHES,** 9, b m Black Sam Bellamy (IRE)—September Moon **Mr D. Pugh**
124 **MON KAPLAIS (FR),** 4, b g Kapgarde (FR)—Iris du Berlais (FR) **Mr & Mrs D. Yates**
125 4, B g Pillar Coral—Mont Doree (FR) **Dick and Mandy Higgins**
126 **MOST AGREEABLE,** 5, b m Kayf Tara—Susie Sheep **Little Lodge Farm & Dan Skelton**

MR DAN SKELTON - continued

127 **MOUNT TEMPEST (IRE),** 6, b g Walk In The Park (IRE)—
Tempest Missile (IRE) **Highclere T'Bred Racing - The Tempest**
128 **MR HOPE STREET (IRE),** 5, br g Jet Away—The Scorpion Queen (IRE) **Mr M. A. Williams**
129 **MYLESFROMWICKLOW (IRE),** 6, b g Ocovango—Hayes Princess (IRE) **Norman Lake & Susan Carsberg**
130 **NO I DIDN'T,** 5, b m Kayf Tara—Yes I Did (IRE) **Mike and Eileen Newbould**
131 **NOT THAT FUISSE (FR),** 10, b g Fuisse (FR)—Edelmira (FR) **Mr C. A. Donlon**
132 **NOTNOWLINDA (IRE),** 6, br m Notnowcato—Moll Bawn (IRE) **Mr M. Ariss**
133 **NUBE NEGRA (SPA),** 9, br g Dink (FR)—Manly Dream (FR) **Mr T. Spraggett**
134 **NURSE SUSAN (FR),** 6, ch m Doctor Dino (FR)—Hembra (FR) **Mr C. A. Donlon**
135 **OMAHA WISH (FR),** 5, b m Night Wish (GER)—Chattleya (FR) **Mr S. M. Bough**
136 **OUR JET (IRE),** 7, ch g Jet Away—She's Bitting (IRE) **Mr C. Ohrstrom**
137 **PEMBROKE,** 6, b g Blue Bresil (FR)—Moyliscar **Jon & Julia Aisbitt**
138 **PIKAR (FR),** 6, b g Masterstroke (USA)—Prairie Scilla (GER) **Yorton Racing**
139 **PLAYFUL SAINT (FR),** 8, b g Saint des Saints (FR)—Playact (IRE) **Mr & Mrs J. D. Cotton**
140 **PONY SOPRANO (IRE),** 4, b g Blue Bresil (FR)—Milanese Queen **Mr S. M. Bough**
141 **PRESENTING JEREMY (IRE),** 8, b g Jeremy (USA)—Present Company (IRE) **Dick,Stevenson and Partners**
142 **PRESENTING NELLY,** 6, b m Kayf Tara—Forever Present (IRE) **Stuart & Shelly Parkin**
143 **PROSCHEMA (IRE),** 8, ch g Declaration of War (USA)—Notable **Empire State Racing Partnership**
144 **PROTEKTORAT (FR),** 8, b g Saint des Saints (FR)—Protektion (FR) **Sir A Ferguson G Mason J Hales & L Hales**
145 **QUID PRO QUO (IRE),** 7, ch g Beat Hollow—Thieving Gypsy (IRE) **Mr J. P. McManus**
146 4, B g Pillar Coral—Quine de Sivola (FR)
147 4, B g Shantou (USA)—Ratheniska (IRE) **Mr C. A. Donlon**
148 **REAL STONE,** 8, b g Arvico (FR)—Stoney Path **Mrs S. C. Welch**
149 **REILLY (IRE),** 7, b g Milan—Flowers On Sunday (IRE) **Mr J. J. Reilly**
150 **RICHHILL (IRE),** 6, b g Presenting—Our Pride **Owners Group 109**
151 **RIDGEWAY (FR),** 6, gr g Outstrip—Bocca Bianca (GER) **Foxtrot Racing Ridgeway**
152 **RISKINTHEGROUND (IRE),** 6, b g Presenting—The Folkes Choice **3 Sons**
153 **ROBYNSON,** 5, b g Kayf Tara—Robyn de Galles (IRE) **Mrs C. M. Graves**
154 **ROCK HOUSE (IRE),** 5, b g Westerner—Rose of Dunamase (IRE) **Mr D. N. Skelton**
155 **ROCKETTE (IRE),** 5, gr m Fascinating Rock (IRE)—Zariziyna (IRE) **Mr O. Williams**
156 **ROCKY MAN (FR),** 5, b h Doctor Dino (FR)—Lady Speedy (IRE) **Mr C. A. Donlon**
157 **ROYALE DANCE (FR),** 6, b m Muhtathir—Sky Royale (FR) **Noel Fehily Racing Syndicate-Royale Danc**
158 **SAIL AWAY (FR),** 7, gr g Martaline—Baraka du Berlais (FR) **Mr & Mrs J. D. Cotton**
159 **SANTOS BLUE,** 6, b g Blue Bresil (FR)—Maybe Plenty **N. R. A. Sutton**
160 **SCOTS GOLD (IRE),** 5, gr g Dark Angel (IRE)—Duchess Andorra (IRE) **Empire State Racing Partnership**
161 **SEVEN NO TRUMPS (IRE),** 8, b g Milan—Ballyknock Present (IRE) **Mr Frank McAleavy & Mr Ian McAleavy**
162 **SHAN BLUE (IRE),** 9, b g Shantou (USA)—Lady Roberta (IRE) **Mr C. A. Donlon**
163 **SHE'S A SAINT (IRE),** 6, b m Saint des Saints (FR)—Charade (IRE) **Estate Research Limited**
164 **SHE'S SO LOVELY (IRE),** 7, b m Mahler—House-of-Hearts (IRE) **Winter Gold Racing 2**
165 **SHOLOKJACK (IRE),** 7, b g Sholokhov (IRE)—Another Pet (IRE) **Sullivan Bloodstock & Hughes Crowley**
166 4, B g Blue Bresil (FR)—Silver Spinner **Speelman Thoroughbreds Ltd**
167 **SKYCUTTER (FR),** 5, b g Scissor Kick (AUS)—Skysweeper (FR) **The French Connection**
168 **SMILING GETAWAY,** 6, ch m Getaway (GER)—One More Cookie (IRE) **James and Jean Potter Ltd**
169 **SMURFETTE,** 5, b m Blue Bresil (FR)—Veronaise (FR) **Colm Donlon & Alne Park Stud**
170 **SNIPE (IRE),** 6, b g Soldier of Fortune (IRE)—Pisces **Foxtrot Racing Snipe**
171 **SOLOMOON,** 4, br g Pether's Moon (IRE)—Solojorie (FR) **Yorton Racing**
172 **SPIRITOFTHEGAMES (IRE),** 11, b g Darsi (FR)—Lucy Walters (IRE) **N. W. Lake**
173 **STEAL MY SUNSHINE,** 6, b g Black Sam Bellamy (IRE)—Amber Cloud **Mark & Maria Adams**
174 **STELLAR ONE (IRE),** 5, b m Kayf Tara—Nova Stella (GER) **Mike and Eileen Newbould**
175 **SWEET OR DRY,** 4, ch f Jack Hobbs—Sherry **Mike and Eileen Newbould**
176 **TAKE NO CHANCES (IRE),** 5, b m Milan—Coscorrig (IRE) **Mr G. J. Wilson**
177 4, B g Ocovango—Talktothetail (IRE) **Mr N. Skelton**
178 **THE KING OF RYHOPE,** 7, ch g Malinas (GER)—Eleven Fifty Nine **Sullivan Bloodstock Ltd & Chris Giles**
179 **THE NEW LION,** 4, b g Kayf Tara—Raitera (FR) **Mr & Mrs D. Yates**
180 **THEFORMISMIGHTY,** 6, b g Black Sam Bellamy (IRE)—Mimi Equal **Mr G. J. Wilson**
181 **THIRD TIME LUCKI (IRE),** 8, br g Arcadio (GER)—Definite Valley (IRE) **Mike and Eileen Newbould**
182 **TOKAY DOKEY (IRE),** 9, b g Gold Well—Charming Present (IRE) **Mr C. A. Donlon**
183 **TOO FRIENDLY,** 5, b g Camelot—Chatline (IRE) **The Gredley Family**
184 **TRIP SWITCH (IRE),** 6, b br g Soldier of Fortune (IRE)—Sunset Gold (IRE) **Mr D. N. Skelton**
185 **TRUDIE GLEN (FR),** 5, b m Blue Bresil (FR)—Only For Love **Mr N. Skelton**

MR DAN SKELTON - continued

186 **TURNAWAY (IRE),** 6, ch g Getaway (GER)—Robins Turn (IRE) **Mr G. J. Wilson**
187 **UHTRED (IRE),** 8, b g Fame And Glory—Ingred Hans (IRE) **Craig & Laura Buckingham**
188 **UNEXPECTED PARTY (FR),** 8, gr g Martaline—Reform Act (USA) **O'Reilly Maclennan Tynan Carthy Shanahan**
189 4, B f Blue Bresil (FR)—Veronaise (FR) **Colm Donlon & Alne Park Stud**
190 **VICKI VALE (IRE),** 6, b m Westerner—Byerley Sophie (IRE) **Bullen-Smith & Faulks**
191 **VIGILANCE (IRE),** 6, b g Flemensfirth (USA)—Erins Stage (IRE) **Simon & Lisa Hobson**
192 **VIKING'S WAY (FR),** 7, gr g Martaline—Virgata (FR) **Craig & Laura Buckingham**
193 **VINNIE SPARKLES (IRE),** 5, b g Elzaam (AUS)—Four Kicks (IRE) **Mr D. N. Skelton**
194 **VIVA LAVILLA (IRE),** 7, br g Getaway (GER)—Viva Forever (FR) **Mr & Mrs D. Yates**
195 **VIVA VALENTINA (IRE),** 5, b br m Masked Marvel—Sainte Russy (FR) **Mr S. M. Bough**
196 **WALK IN CLOVER (IRE),** 6, b m Walk In The Park (IRE)—Bridgequarter Girl (IRE) **The Blind Squirrels**
197 **WEST BALBOA (IRE),** 7, b m Yeats (IRE)—Rostellan (IRE) **Bullen-Smith & Faulks**
198 **WEST CORK,** 9, b g Midnight Legend—Calamintha **Mike and Eileen Newbould**
199 **WEST TO THE BRIDGE (IRE),** 10, b g Flemensfirth (USA)—Godlylady (IRE) **Mr P. J. Tierney**
200 **WHENTHEPENNYDROPS,** 7, b m Kayf Tara—Subtilty **Noel Fehily Racing Syndicates - Whenthep**
201 **WILD ROMANCE (IRE),** 8, br m Kalanisi (IRE)—Aboo Lala (IRE) **& Skelton**
202 **WILDE ABOUT OSCAR (IRE),** 8, b g Oscar (IRE)—Baie Barbara (IRE) **Mike and Eileen Newbould**
203 **WILLIAM OF YORK,** 7, b g Kayf Tara—Shady Anne **Mike and Eileen Newbould**
204 **YEOMEN WARDER (IRE),** 6, gr g Shirocco (GER)—Quarry Endeavour (IRE) **Bedlam Bound Syndicate**
205 **YESANNA,** 4, b f Blue Bresil (FR)—Alegralil **Mr I. Lawrence**
206 **YGRITTE (IRE),** 4, gr f Pillar Coral—Zariziyna (IRE) **Mr J. Lane**
207 **YHPRUM'S LAW (IRE),** 4, gr g Kayf Tara—She Ranks Me (IRE) **Mrs S. Lawrence**
208 4, B g Jack Hobbs—Young Mags (IRE) **Masterson Holdings Limited**

THREE-YEAR-OLDS

209 Ch c Kingston Hill—Hestina (FR) **Mr D. N. Skelton**
210 **WHERE'S THE RISK (FR),** b c My Risk (FR)—Not Lost (FR)

Assistant Trainer: Tom Messenger,**Head Girl:** Amber Blythe, Gemma Double,**Head Lad:** James Heaney, Joe Knox, Fin Mulrine, Nick Pearce,**Travelling Head:** Andy Gardner, Hannah Haywood, Phil Haywood, **Racing Secretary:** Natalie Fisher, Ella Pearce, Tiggy Vale-Titterton.

NH Jockey: Bridget Andrews, Harry Skelton. **Conditional Jockey:** Mr Tristan Durrell. **Amateur Jockey:** Miss Heidi Palin.

458

MRS PAM SLY, Peterborough

Postal: **Singlecote, Thorney, Peterborough, Cambridgeshire, PE6 0PB**
Contacts: **PHONE 01733 270212 MOBILE 07850 511267**

1 **ACERTAIN CIRCUS,** 13, ch g Definite Article—Circus Rose **Mrs P. M. Sly**
2 **ANNIVERSARY BELLE (IRE),** 4, b f No Nay Never (USA)—Annamanamoux (USA) **D.L. Bayliss & G.A. Libson**
3 **ASTRAL BEAU,** 4, b f Brazen Beau (AUS)—Asteroidea **Family Sly**
4 **CHIC AVENUE,** 5, b m Champs Elysees—Chicklemix **Gary Smitheringale & Pam Sly**
5 **CUBANISTA,** 4, b g Havana Gold (IRE)—Multicultural (IRE) **D.L. Bayliss & G.A. Libson**
6 **DARK MIX,** 4, b g Black Sam Bellamy (IRE)—Chicklemix **Mrs P. M. Sly**
7 **DARTING ROSE,** 4, b f Dartmouth—Circus Rose **Mrs P. M. Sly**
8 **ELEANOR DUMONT,** 6, b m Westerner—Circus Rose **Mrs P. M. Sly**
9 **EVER READY,** 4, b f Recharge (IRE)—Wistow **Mrs P. M. Sly**
10 **FRANSHAM,** 9, b g Sulamani (IRE)—Circus Rose **G. Libson, D. Bayliss, T. Davies & P. Sly**
11 **GENTLE ROSE,** 7, b m Gentlewave (IRE)—Iconic Rose **The Stablemates**
12 **HAAFAPIECE,** 10, ch g Haafhd—Bonnet's Pieces **Mrs I. A. Coles**
13 **JOHN CLARE (IRE),** 7, b g Poet's Voice—Specialty (IRE) **Michael H. Sly & Mrs Pam Sly**
14 **LIAM'S LASS (IRE),** 7, b m Dandy Man (IRE)—Rupa (IRE) **Mrs P. M. Sly**
15 **MIXEDWAVE (IRE),** 6, b g Gentlewave (IRE)—Chicklemix **Mrs P. M. Sly**
16 **RUMOURSAREFLYING,** 5, b g Blue Bresil (FR)—Circus Rose **Mrs P. M. Sly**
17 **SLEEPING LATE,** 5, ch g Gentlewave (IRE)—Wistow **Mrs P. M. Sly**

MRS PAM SLY - continued

18 **SPECIAL MAYSON,** 5, b g Mayson—Specialty (IRE) **Michael H. Sly & Mrs Pam Sly**
19 **TAKEIT EASY,** 8, b g Malinas (GER)—Circus Rose **Pam's People**
20 **WILLIAM CODY,** 6, b g Westerner—Wistow **Mr M. R. Davis**
21 **XCITATIONS,** 8, b g Universal (IRE)—Bonnet's Pieces **G. Libson,D. Bayliss,T. Davies & P. Sly**

THREE-YEAR-OLDS

22 **ASTRAL SPIRIT,** b f Charm Spirit (IRE)—Asteroidea **Michael H. Sly & Mrs Pam Sly**
23 **TORFRIDA,** b f Aclaim (IRE)—Vernatti **Michael H. Sly & Mrs Pam Sly**
24 **WINTERCRACK,** b f Cracksman—Speciosa (IRE) **M. H. Sly, Dr T. Davies & Mrs P. Sly**

TWO-YEAR-OLDS

25 **FENLANDER,** b g 10/04 Territories (IRE)—Specialty (IRE) (Oasis Dream) **Michael H. Sly & Mrs Pam Sly**

NH Jockey: Kielan Woods. **Conditional Jockey:** Jack Andrews. **Amateur Jockey:** Miss Gina Andrews.

---

459 MR BRYAN SMART, Hambleton

Postal: **Hambleton House, Sutton Bank, Thirsk, North Yorkshire, YO7 2HA**
Contacts: **PHONE 01845 597481 MOBILE 07748 634797**
EMAIL office@bryansmart.plus.com WEBSITE www.bryansmart-racing.com FACEBOOK Bryan-Smart-Racing TWITTER @BryanSmartRacin INSTAGRAM bryan_smart_racing

1 **ANTAGONIZE,** 7, b g Epaulette (AUS)—Hakuraa (IRE) **Crossfields Racing**
2 **BLAZING SON,** 5, ch g Mayson—Emblaze **The Smart Emblaze Partnership**
3 **BOND CHAIRMAN,** 4, br g Kodiac—Wunders Dream (IRE) **Bond Thoroughbred Limited**
4 **EMPEROR CARADOC (FR),** 4, b g Siyouni (FR)—Tribune Libre (IRE) **Dan Maltby Bloodstock Ltd & Mr B. Smart**
5 **HIGH OPINION,** 4, b g Hellvelyn—Vanity (IRE) **The Smart Set**
6 **HIGHLAND QUEEN (IRE),** 4, b f Acclamation—Medicean Queen (IRE) **Moody, Thompson & Powell**
7 **PRINCESS KARINE,** 4, b f Aclaim (IRE)—Hakuraa (IRE) **Mr N. Derbyshire & Partner**
8 **PROJECT DANTE,** 4, ch g Showcasing—Thatsallimsaying (IRE) **Bond Thoroughbred Limited**
9 **REDZONE,** 6, b g Sepoy (AUS)—Mythicism **Crossfields Racing**
10 **ZOOM STAR,** 5, b m Mayson—Chinaconnection (IRE) **Woodcock Electrical Limited**

THREE-YEAR-OLDS

11 **CASTAN,** ch g Charming Thought—Astley Park **Ceffyl Racing**
12 **DATA LEAK (IRE),** br g Dandy Man (IRE)—Dora de Green (IRE) **Clipper Group Holdings Ltd**
13 **HERAKLES (IRE),** b c Dandy Man (IRE)—Air of Mystery **Mr F. A. A. Nass**
14 **JAMIE BOND,** b g Zoustar (AUS)—Always A Drama (IRE) **Bond Thoroughbred Limited**
15 **KASINO,** b f Equiano (FR)—Katabatik Katie **The Wheel Of Fortune Partnership**
16 **OPERATION GIMCRACK (IRE),** ch c Showcasing—Folk Melody (IRE) **Bond Thoroughbred Limited**
17 **PROJECT BLACK,** b c Showcasing—Dot Hill **Bond Thoroughbred Limited**
18 **REGINALD CHARLES,** b g Zoustar (AUS)—Melbourne Memories **Bond Thoroughbred Limited**
19 **SECRET GUEST,** gr g Havana Grey—Lady Macduff (IRE) **The Unscrupulous Judges**
20 **SENATE QUEEN,** ch f Washington DC (IRE)—Rhal (IRE) **Mr S. D. Bradley**

TWO-YEAR-OLDS

21 Gr c 09/02 Aclaim (IRE)—Analytical (Lethal Force (IRE)) (42857) **Mr F. A. A. Nass**
22 B f 13/02 Lope de Vega (IRE)—Anna Law (IRE) (Lawman (FR)) (1800000) **Bond Thoroughbred Limited**
23 B c 02/02 Kingman—Best Terms (Exceed And Excel (AUS)) (450000) **Bond Thoroughbred Limited**
24 B f 17/04 Gleneagles (IRE)—Excelette (IRE) (Exceed And Excel (AUS)) **Crossfields Racing**
25 Ch c 26/03 Washington DC (IRE)—Nizhoni (USA) (Mineshaft (USA)) **Crossfields Racing**
26 B f 21/02 Mehmas (IRE)—No Lippy (IRE) (Oasis Dream) (450000) **Bond Thoroughbred Limited**
27 **POLY JOKE,** ch f 25/04 Tasleet—Katabatik Katie (Sir Percy) **Mrs P. A. Clark**
28 Ch f 03/03 Sioux Nation (USA)—Rhal (IRE) (Rahy (USA)) **Crossfields Racing**
29 Br c 18/02 Blue Point (IRE)—She's A Worldie (IRE) (Kodiac) **Mr S. Chappell & Partner**
30 B f 06/03 Washington DC (IRE)—Spontaneity (IRE) (Holy Roman Emperor (IRE)) (4000) **Crossfields Racing**

MR BRYAN SMART - continued

Assistant Trainer: Beth Smart, **Head Man:** Ian Howell, **Business & Racing Manager:** Victoria Smart.

---

460 MR JULIAN SMITH, Tirley

Postal: **Tirley Court, Tirley, Gloucester, Gl19 4HA**
Contacts: **PHONE 01452 780461 MOBILE 07748 901175 FAX 01452 780461**
EMAIL Julian.smith461@gmail.com

1 **AFTER MIDNIGHT,** 6, b m Sulamani (IRE)—Midnight Ocean **Exors of the Late Mr D. E. S. Smith**
2 **CARO DES FLOS (FR),** 11, b g Tiger Groom—Royale Marie (FR) **Mrs J.A. Benson & Miss S.N. Benson**
3 **DIAMOND ROSE,** 11, b m Sagamix (FR)—Swiss Rose **Grand Jury Partnership**
4 **FINE BY HER,** 7, b m Shirocco (GER)—High Benefit (IRE) **Mrs J.A. Benson & Miss S.N. Benson**
5 **GONE TO TEXAS (IRE),** 7, b g Imperial Monarch (IRE)—Echo Falls (IRE) **Exors of the Late Mr D. E. S. Smith**
6 **SALLY'S GIRL,** 6, b m Black Sam Bellamy (IRE)—Shayana **Grand Jury Partnership**
7 **SONG OF EARTH (IRE),** 8, b g Mahler—Lady Lenson (IRE) **Mrs J.A. Benson & Miss S.N. Benson**
8 **STAY OUT OF COURT (IRE),** 12, b g Court Cave (IRE)—Lucky To Live (IRE) **Exors of the Late Mr D. E. S. Smith**

Assistant Trainer: Mrs Nicky Smith.

---

461 MR MARTIN SMITH, Newmarket

Postal: **Kremlin House Stables, Fordham Road, Newmarket, Suffolk, CB8 7AQ**
Contacts: **MOBILE 07712 493589**
WEBSITE www.martinsmithracing.com

1 **ACE ROTHSTEIN (USA),** 5, b g More Than Ready (USA)—A P Cindy (USA) **Mrs A. M. Stokes**
2 **ALEATORIC (IRE),** 7, b g Dylan Thomas (IRE)—Castalian Spring (IRE) **Mr M. P. B. Smith**
3 **ALL ABOUT ALICE (IRE),** 4, b f Excelebration (IRE)—Castalian Spring (IRE) **The Affluence Partnership**
4 4, Ch g Garswood—Donna Giovanna **Mr Robert P Clarke & Partners**
5 **FRIENDS DON'T ASK,** 8, b g Champs Elysees—Kintyre **Mr Robert P Clarke & Partners**
6 **GUITAR,** 4, b g Mayson—Clapperboard **Two By Two Racing**
7 **MORANI KALI,** 5, ch g Charming Thought—Crystal Moments **Angela & Smith Racing**
8 **RIFFA FORT,** 4, b c Helmet (AUS)—Beyond Fashion **M and E Racing**
9 **ROCK ON TEDDY,** 4, b g Scorpion (IRE)—Freedom Rock **Mrs D. Wilkinson**
10 **SHABS,** 4, b g Aclaim (IRE)—Inagh River **Mr S. Rankine**

THREE-YEAR-OLDS

11 **FOOTSTEPS ON MARS (IRE),** b f Footstepsinthesand—Castalian Spring (IRE) **Mr M. P. B. Smith**

TWO-YEAR-OLDS

12 **ALCHEMYSTERY,** gr f 24/03 Nathaniel (IRE)—Alsacienne (Dalakhani (IRE)) (8000) **Mrs A. M. Stokes**
13 B c 14/04 Le Brivido (FR)—Grand Myla (IRE) (Dark Angel (IRE)) (2000) **Mr Robert P Clarke & Partners**
14 B f 15/05 Equiano (FR)—Isis (USA) (Royal Academy (USA)) (2500) **Mr Robert P Clarke & Partners**
15 B f 22/02 Postponed (IRE)—Perfect Spirit (IRE) (Invincible Spirit (IRE)) (3500) **Mr Robert P Clarke & Partners**

Racing Secretary: Mrs Rachel Rennie.

462 MISS PAULA SMITH, Malton

Postal: **Woodyard Barn, Ruffin Lane, Eddlethorpe, Malton, North Yorkshire, YO17 9QU**
Contacts: **PHONE 07760 247207**
EMAIL Paulamsmith4@gmail.com

1 **ACROSS THE CHANNEL (FR),** 8, b g Dunkerque (FR)—Aulne River (FR) **Miss P. M. Smith**
2 **BLOOMING FORTUNE (IRE),** 6, br m Soldier of Fortune (IRE)—Ballyknock Present (IRE) **Miss P. M. Smith**
3 **HALLOWED GROUND (IRE),** 8, b g Mahler—Castlehaven (IRE) **Miss P. M. Smith**
4 **IHEARDUPAINTHOUSES (IRE),** 6, b g Born To Sea (IRE)—Miracle Steps (CAN) **Miss M. Chaston**
5 **MELROSE JACK,** 6, ch g Shirocco (GER)—Daisies Adventure (IRE) **Miss M. Chaston**
6 4, B br f Westerner—Queens Regatta (IRE)
7 **SHANNON HILL,** 9, b g Kayf Tara—Shannon Native (IRE) **Miss P. M. Smith**
8 **WELSH REIGN (IRE),** 8, b g Imperial Monarch (IRE)—Marians Gem (IRE) **Miss P. M. Smith**

---

463 MR R. MIKE SMITH, Galston

Postal: **West Loudoun Farm, Galston, Ayrshire, KA4 8PB**
Contacts: **PHONE 01563 822062 MOBILE 07711 692122**
EMAIL mike@mikesmithracing.co.uk WEBSITE www.mikesmithracing.co.uk

1 **BINTHEREDONETHAT (IRE),** 9, b g Yeats (IRE)—Would You Do That (IRE) **Mr R. M. Smith**
2 **BLACK FRIDAY,** 8, b g Equiano (FR)—The Clan Macdonald **Riverside Racing**
3 **BORN TO SPARKLE,** 5, ch m Schiaparelli (GER)—Primrose Time **Miss P A Carnaby & B Thomson**
4 **CAPTAIN NELSON (IRE),** 5, ch g Mount Nelson—Dromod Mour (IRE) **The Racing Suite**
5 **COULDNTGIVAMONKEYS (IRE),** 5, b g Valirann (FR)—Monets Dream (IRE) **Green Spittal & Smith**
6 **DANCE THIEF (IRE),** 5, b g Leading Light (IRE)—Don't Wait (IRE) **Mr R. M. Smith**
7 **DESERT STRANGER,** 5, b g Helmet (AUS)—Jillanar (IRE) **Spittal Family**
8 **DONSO STAR,** 5, ch m Sun Central (IRE)—Fame Is The Spur **Burns Partnership**
9 **DOT COTTON (IRE),** 6, b m Califet (FR)—Katariya (IRE) **Mr R. M. Smith**
10 **EARN YOUR STRIPES,** 5, b m Epaulette (AUS)—Midnight Bahia (IRE) **Burns Partnership**
11 **EUCHAN FALLS (IRE),** 6, ch g Poet's Voice—Miss Anneliese (IRE) **Blue Circle Racing**
12 **FATHERS ADVICE (IRE),** 6, b g Aiken—I'll Have It (IRE) **The Racing Suite**
13 **FLYING MOON (GER),** 7, b g Sea The Moon (GER)—Finity (USA) **West Loudoun Racing Club**
14 **FOURTH OF JULY (IRE),** 8, b g Salutino (GER)—Akasha (IRE) **Bruce, & Smith**
15 **GLASSES UP (USA),** 8, ch g English Channel (USA)—Hurricane Hallie (USA) **The Jolly Beggars**
16 **GO BOB GO (IRE),** 6, b g Big Bad Bob (IRE)—Fire Up **Riverside Racing**
17 **GOLDEN VALOUR,** 7, b g Kingman—Gracefield (USA) **Great Northern Partnership**
18 5, B m Elusive Pimpernel (USA)—Hot On Her Heels (IRE)
19 5, Ch m Vendangeur (IRE)—I'll Have It (IRE)
20 **JUST DOTTIE,** 5, b br m Al Kazeem—Blaise Chorus (IRE) **Mr J. G. Brown**
21 4, B g Ol' Man River (IRE)—Karinswift
22 **KONDO ISAMI (IRE),** 5, ch h Galileo (IRE)—Zouzou (AUS) **Mr J. Murphy**
23 **LAY DOWN THE LAW (IRE),** 5, ch g Rule of Law (USA)—Theatre Fool (IRE) **Green Spittal & Smith**
24 **MELANAMIX (IRE),** 8, gr m Carlotamix (FR)—Melanjo (IRE) **Six In the Mix**
25 4, B g Sans Frontieres (IRE)—New Sensation
26 4, B g Elusive Pimpernel (USA)—Ories Light (IRE)
27 **ROYAL COUNTESS,** 7, b m Coach House (IRE)—Dont Tell Nan **Mr S. W. Dick**
28 **ROYAL REGENT,** 11, b g Urgent Request (IRE)—Royal Citadel (IRE) **Mr S. W. Dick**
29 **SEA PRINCE (FR),** 6, br g Great Pretender (IRE)—Sea Pearl (FR) **K Jardine R Griffiths S Greig**
30 5, B g Vendangeur (IRE)—Shady Pines (IRE)
31 **SPANISH LARIAT (IRE),** 5, b g Golden Lariat (USA)—Miracle Millie (IRE) **Green Spittal & Smith**
32 4, B g Ol' Man River (IRE)—Star of The Season (IRE)
33 5, B g Ol' Man River (IRE)—Sumability (IRE)
34 **TANGLED (IRE),** 8, b g Society Rock (IRE)—Open Verse (USA) **Mr R. Gibson**
35 **THE ELECTRICIAN (IRE),** 7, ch g Leading Light (IRE)—Spring Flower (IRE) **Spittal & Smith**
36 **THE JAD FACTOR (IRE),** 7, b g Arcadio (GER)—Sumability (IRE) **Mr J. A. Dickson**
37 **TILSITT (FR),** 6, b g Charm Spirit (IRE)—Azores (IRE) **Mr A. Mills**

MR R. MIKE SMITH - continued

38 4, B f Valirann (FR)—Vinnie Knows (IRE)
39 **WELL PLANTED (FR),** 6, b g Planteur (IRE)—Next Dream (FR) **Drew & Ailsa Russell**
40 **WESTERN RUN (IRE),** 8, b g Westerner—Stitch Pockets (IRE) **Mr R. M. Smith**
41 **WIND OF HOPE (IRE),** 14, b g September Storm (GER)—Ciara's Run (IRE) **Mr R. M. Smith**
42 **WRECKED IT RALPH,** 5, b g Orientor—Rafta (IRE) **Toytown**

THREE-YEAR-OLDS

43 B g Orientor—Ss Vega
44 **TIANNA FALLS,** br f Equiano (FR)—Midnight Bahia (IRE) **Mr A. J. Bogle**

---

464 MRS SUE SMITH, Bingley

Postal: **Craiglands Farm, High Eldwick, Bingley, West Yorkshire, BD16 3BE**
WORK EMAIL office@craiglandsracing.co.uk WEBSITE www.suesmithracing.co.uk

1 **ABSOLUTELY DYLAN (IRE),** 10, b g Scorpion (IRE)—Cash Customer (IRE) **Mrs S. J. Smith**
2 **AIRE VALLEY LAD,** 9, b g Schiaparelli (GER)—Bonnie Rock (IRE) **Mrs S. J. Smith**
3 **ALGESIRAS,** 7, gr g Martaline—Message Personnel (FR) **Mrs S. J. Smith**
4 **ANNAHARVEY LAD (IRE),** 7, b g Famous Name—Annaharvey Pride (IRE) **Mrs S. J. Smith**
5 4, Br g Sageburg (IRE)—Arts Theater (IRE) **Mrs S. J. Smith**
6 **BEA MY SHADOW,** 4, b f Flemensfirth (USA)—Lolli (IRE) **Mrs A. Clarke**
7 **BURROWS CLOSE (FR),** 4, b g Dabirsim (FR)—See Your Dream **Mrs J. Morgan**
8 **BURROWS DIAMOND (FR),** 8, b m Diamond Boy (FR)—La Vie de Boitron (FR)
9 **BURROWS HALL (FR),** 6, b g Hunter's Light (IRE)—La Vie de Boitron (FR)
10 **BURROWS LIGHT (FR),** 5, ch g Hunter's Light (IRE)—Condoleezza (FR) **J & S Smith**
11 **CALL HIM NOW (IRE),** 5, b g Presenting—Shuil Away (IRE) **Mrs S. J. Smith**
12 **CERENDIPITY (IRE),** 6, b g Sageburg (IRE)—Check The Forecast (IRE) **Mrs A. Clarke**
13 4, B g Scorpion (IRE)—Cherry West (IRE) **Mrs A. Clarke**
14 **COPPER BEACH (IRE),** 6, ch g Getaway (GER)—Lady McBride (IRE) **Mrs S. J. Smith**
15 **CRACKING FIND (IRE),** 12, b g Robin des Pres (FR)—Crack The Kicker (IRE) **Mrs A. Ellis**
16 **DARSI'S DARLING (IRE),** 7, b m Darsi (FR)—The Farmers Sister (IRE) **Mrs S. J. Smith**
17 **EAST STREET (IRE),** 7, b g Mores Wells—Serpentine Mine (IRE) **Exors of the Late Mr T. J. Hemmings**
18 **EDDIE MUSH (IRE),** 5, br g Sageburg (IRE)—So Proper (IRE) **Beechfield**
19 **EDGAR ALLAN POE (IRE),** 9, b g Zoffany (IRE)—Swingsky (IRE) **I. B. Barker**
20 **FAT HARRY,** 6, b g Multiplex—Linen Line **Mrs S. J. Smith**
21 **FRIMEUR DE LANCRAY (FR),** 8, b g Saddler Maker (IRE)—Jecyfly (FR) **Mrs A. Ellis**
22 4, B g Cloudings (IRE)—Garnock (IRE) **Mrs S. J. Smith**
23 **HEATHER HONEY,** 4, ch f Getaway (GER)—Firth of Malt **Mrs S. J. Smith**
24 **HOPE HILL (IRE),** 5, b g Sageburg (IRE)—Lightning Breeze (IRE) **Mrs S. J. Smith**
25 **INFORMATEUR (FR),** 10, b g Maresca Sorrento (FR)—Isarella (GER) **Mrs J M Gray & Mr G R Orchard**
26 **IT'S MAISY (IRE),** 5, b m Sageburg (IRE)—Arts Theater (IRE) **Mrs S. J. Smith**
27 **JOKE DANCER,** 10, ch g Authorized (IRE)—Missy Dancer **D G Pryde & D Van Der Hoeven**
28 **JUST JESS (IRE),** 7, b m Yeats (IRE)—She's On The Case (IRE) **Widdop Wanderers**
29 **KAPHUMOR (FR),** 7, b g Kapgarde (FR)—Money Humor (IRE) **Mrs S. J. Smith**
30 **KAUTO D'AMOUR (FR),** 8, b g Anabaa Blue—Kauto Luisa (FR) **Mrs S. J. Smith**
31 **KONFUSION,** 5, ch g Schiaparelli (GER)—Tahira (GER) **Mrs S. J. Smith**
32 4, B g Cloudings (IRE)—Lake Cresent (IRE) **Mrs S. J. Smith**
33 **LANZEALOT,** 6, b g Camelot—Blue Zealot (IRE) **Mrs S. J. Smith**
34 **LOCAL DRAMA (IRE),** 5, b g Kayf Tara—Me Ould Buttie (IRE) **Mrs S. J. Smith**
35 **MARTY TIME (FR),** 7, gr g Martaline—Shahwarda (FR) **Mrs S. J. Smith**
36 **MIDNIGHT PHANTOM (FR),** 4, b g Vif Monsieur (GER)—Perceverense (FR) **Mrs A. Clarke**
37 **MR MAHLER (IRE),** 5, ch g Mahler—Catcheragain (IRE) **Mrs S. J. Smith**
38 **MYBURG (IRE),** 7, br g Sageburg (IRE)—Prairie Call (IRE) **Mrs S. J. Smith**
39 **NAVIGATE WEST (IRE),** 5, b g Westerner—Onewayortheother (IRE) **Exors of the Late Mr T. J. Hemmings**
40 **NORTH PARADE (IRE),** 8, br g Dylan Thomas (IRE)—Retain That Magic (IRE) **Mrs S. J. Smith**

MRS SUE SMITH - continued

41 **O'CONNELL (IRE),** 7, b g Westerner—Brixen (IRE) **R & T Ford**
42 **ONESOC (IRE),** 6, b g Valirann (FR)—Hollyvillaexpress (IRE) **Mrs A. Ellis**
43 **PADDY O'MAHLER (IRE),** 5, b g Mahler—Miss Massini (IRE) **McGoldrick Racing**
44 **PARELLIROC,** 7, b g Schiaparelli (GER)—Roc Mirage **Mrs S. J. Smith**
45 **PRAIRIE WOLF (IRE),** 6, br g Sageburg (IRE)—Applause For Amy (IRE) **Mr G. R. Orchard & Mrs J. M. Gray**
46 **RICH SPIRIT,** 5, b g Iktibas—Silly Gilly (IRE) **Mrs S. J. Smith**
47 **RIGHT SAID TED (IRE),** 6, b g Dylan Thomas (IRE)—Patsy Choice (IRE) **Mrs S. J. Smith**
48 **ROMEO BROWN,** 9, br g Yeats (IRE)—Santia **McGoldrick Racing**
49 **SILVA ECLIPSE,** 10, gr g Multiplex—Linen Line **The Acre Bottom Syndicate**
50 **SMALL PRESENT (IRE),** 8, b g Presenting—Serpentaria **Mrs A. Clarke**
51 **THE FOREMAN,** 5, b g Workforce—Princess Oriane (IRE) **Mrs S. J. Smith**
52 **THE PADDY PIE (IRE),** 10, b g Beneficial—Salsita (FR) **J. Wade**
53 **TREASURED COMPANY (IRE),** 7, b g Fast Company (IRE)—Lady's Locket (IRE) **Mrs S. J. Smith**
54 **TRESHNISH (FR),** 10, ch g Gold Away (IRE)—Didn't I Tell You (IRE) **D G Pryde & D Van Der Hoeven**
55 **VALENCE D'AUMONT (FR),** 9, b g Sinndar (IRE)—Ice Ti (ITY) **Mrs J. Morgan**
56 **WOLF RUN (IRE),** 8, b br g Presenting—Our Pride **Mr G. R. Orchard & Mrs J. M. Gray**

Assistant Trainer: Joel Parkinson, **Head Lad:** Reece Jarosiewicz, **Racing Secretary:** Rachel Swinden.

NH Jockey: Ross Chapman. **Conditional Jockey:** Thomas Willmott.

---

465 MISS SUZY SMITH, Angmering

Postal: **Lower Coombe Stables, Angmering Park, Angmering , Littlehampton , West Sussex, BN16 4EX**
Contacts: **WORK 01903 298968 MOBILE 07970 550828 FAX 01903 298967**
EMAIL suzy@suzysmithracing.co.uk WEBSITE www.suzysmithracing.co.uk FACEBOOK @ suzysmithracing

1 **ANIMAL (IRE),** 7, b g Arcadio (GER)—Fantine (IRE) **James Rimmer & Chris Ames**
2 **COUNTERACT,** 8, b g Dr Massini (IRE)—Aimigayle **Ms S. A. S. Palmer**
3 4, B f September Storm (GER)—Material World **Mr J. Sennett, Miss S. Smith, Mr Andrew Gifford**
4 **NOBLE ENCORE (IRE),** 5, b g Pour Moi (IRE)—She's Noble **Crawford-Smith Family**
5 **OSCARSMAN (IRE),** 9, b g Oscar (IRE)—Ashwell Lady (IRE) **J Logan J Rimmer & Everard Bloodstock**
6 **PILBARA,** 8, b g Tiger Groom—Golden Benefit (IRE) **J. A. A. S. Logan, Mr G. R. Jones, Mr J. Sennett**
7 **RECORD HIGH (IRE),** 6, b g Mahler—Leapy Lady (IRE) **Wallace Racing**
8 **SELSEY SIZZLER,** 6, b g Nathaniel (IRE)—Heho **I. J. Heseltine**
9 **SILVER HILL FLYER (IRE),** 4, b f Court Cave (IRE)—Jennifer Eccles **Kate Allisat & Chris Ames**
10 **SUPERSTYLIN (IRE),** 6, b g Califet (FR)—Bright Blaze (IRE) **Mrs V. Palmer**
11 **TAPLEY,** 6, gr g Geordieland (FR)—Cathodine Cayras (FR) **The Plumpton Party**

THREE-YEAR-OLDS

12 Ch f Jack Hobbs—Storm Patrol

TWO-YEAR-OLDS

13 B g 17/06 Poet's Word (IRE)—Aimigayle (Midnight Legend)
14 **JIMMY JAZZ,** b g 15/03 Jack Hobbs—Storm Patrol (Shirocco (GER)) **Mr J. Rimmer**
15 B g 29/03 Poet's Word (IRE)—Material World (Karinga Bay)

Assistant Trainer: Mr S E Gordon-Watson, **Racing Secretary:** Tina Ford.

Flat Jockey: Luke Morris, Jason Watson. **NH Jockey:** Charlie Hammond, Micheal Nolan.

466 MR JAMIE SNOWDEN, Lambourn

Postal: **Folly House, Upper Lambourn Road, Lambourn, Hungerford, Berkshire, RG17 8QG**
Contacts: **PHONE 01488 72800 MOBILE 07779 497563**
EMAIL info@jamiesnowdenracing.co.uk WEBSITE www.jamiesnowdenracing.co.uk
TWITTER @jamiesnowden INSTAGRAM jamie_snowden

1 **A PRO PO (IRE),** 5, b br g Milan—Bonny River (IRE) **Mr & Mrs R Cooper**
2 **ARBENNIG (IRE),** 7, b br g Yeats (IRE)—Ultra Light (FR) **AWR Consultancy, Stacey, Kirk & Fields**
3 **BEHOLDEN,** 7, b g Cacique (IRE)—Pure Joy **Foxtrot Racing Beholden**
4 **BILL JACK (IRE),** 5, b g Shantou (USA)—Couture Daisy (IRE) **Sheep As A Lamb Syndicate**
5 **BRAVEHEART (IRE),** 7, b g Westerner—Miss Knowall (IRE) **The Cherry Pickers**
6 **BUCKO'S BOY,** 8, b g Midnight Legend—Buxom (IRE) **A. J. & Mrs J. Ward**
7 **CINDYSOX,** 5, b m Kayf Tara—Golden Gael **Mr E. J. M. Spurrier**
8 **CLIMBING,** 5, b g Clovis du Berlais (FR)—Spring Flight **The Queen Consort & Chips Keswick**
9 **COASTAL SUN (FR),** 5, b m Coastal Path—Valle Fleurie (FR) **Prospect Racing**
10 **COLLEGE OAK,** 8, ch g Norse Dancer (IRE)—Katmai (IRE) **Mr A. C. T. Bath**
11 **COLONEL HARRY (IRE),** 6, ch g Shirocco (GER)—Stateable Case (IRE) **The GD Partnership**
12 **CORNICELLO (FR),** 5, b g Penny's Picnic (IRE)—Breezy Hawk (GER) **ValueRacingClub.co.uk**
13 **DATSALRIGHTGINO (GER),** 7, b g It's Gino (GER)—Delightful Sofie (GER) **The GD Partnership**
14 **DOC MCCOY (IRE),** 5, ch g Getaway (GER)—Salvatrice (IRE) **League Of Nations**
15 **DONNIE AZOFF (IRE),** 7, ch g Dylan Thomas (IRE)—Bonny River (IRE) **The Footie Partnership**
16 **DOUBLE CLICK (IRE),** 5, ch g Flemensfirth (USA)—Katmai (IRE) **Foxtrot Racing Double Click**
17 **DUSKY DAYS (IRE),** 6, ch g Flemensfirth (USA)—Day's Over **Mrs K. Gunn**
18 **EBONELLO (IRE),** 6, b m Presenting—Ravello Bay **Friends of Ebony Horse Club**
19 **ELLIES SISTER (IRE),** 6, b m Court Cave (IRE)—Dizzy's Whisper (IRE) **Sheep As A Lamb Syndicate**
20 **FORTUNATE FRED (FR),** 8, b g Cokoriko (FR)—Rosalie Malta (FR) **Foxtrot Racing Fortunate Fred**
21 **GA LAW (FR),** 7, b g Sinndar (IRE)—Law (FR) **The Footie Partnership**
22 **GIT MAKER (FR),** 7, b g Saddler Maker (IRE)—Bamos (FR) **Sheep As A Lamb Syndicate**
23 **GREAT D'TROICE (FR),** 5, b g Great Pretender (IRE)—Mick Bora (FR) **Buckett Flach Woodward Moran Sperling**
24 **GUINNESS AFFAIR (FR),** 7, b g Fuisse (FR)—Ashkiyra (FR) **ValueRacingClub.co.uk**
25 **HARDY DU SEUIL (FR),** 6, b g Coastal Path—Pervenche du Seuil (FR) **The Hardy Souls**
26 **JACK SPRAT (IRE),** 5, b g Walk In The Park (IRE)—Hell Cat Maggie (IRE) **Mr E. J. M. Spurrier**
27 **JANWORTH,** 6, b m Norse Dancer (IRE)—Buxom (IRE) **Mr & Mrs Ward Jamie Snowden Racing Club**
28 **KILTEALY BRIGGS (IRE),** 9, b g Fame And Glory—Baby Briggs (IRE) **The McNeill Family**
29 **LADY VALENTINE (IRE),** 4, b f No Nay Never (USA)—Mais Si **ValueRacingClub.co.uk**
30 **LEGENDS RYDE,** 8, ch m Midnight Legend—Ryde Back **AWTP Racing Partnership**
31 **MIDNIGHT CENTURION,** 7, b g Midnight Legend—Centoria (IRE) **The Wife Loves It Partnership**
32 **MILLDAM (FR),** 5, gr g Martaline—Santa Dame (FR) **Goulden, & Hopgood**
33 **MIMI ZURI,** 4, b br f Kayf Tara—Manaphy (FR) **Mr & Mrs R Wilkinson**
34 **MOTIVE,** 5, b m Kayf Tara—Midsummer Magic **The Queen Consort & Chips Keswick**
35 **NIGHT FEVER (GER),** 6, b m Dylan Thomas (IRE)—Night Heart (IRE) **Foxtrot Racing Night Fever**
36 **NO ANXIETY (IRE),** 7, ch g Presenting—Joanne One (IRE) **Mr J. E. Snowden**
37 **OBSESSEDWITHYOU (FR),** 4, b f Bathyrhon (GER)—Carmona (FR) **AWR Consultancy & the Picnic Partnership**
38 **PARK THIS ONE (IRE),** 6, b g Walk In The Park (IRE)—Soraya Pearl **Dellar Doel Syson Reid Williamson & One**
39 **PASSING WELL (FR),** 6, b g Coastal Path—Passing Lore (FR) **Gouldenhopgood Gilliesmethvensanderdson**
40 **PHAR FROM MILAN (IRE),** 5, b g Milan—Pharenna (IRE) **ValueRacingClub.co.uk**
41 **PHONE HOME,** 4, b f Telescope (IRE)—Ring Back (IRE) **The Turf Club, Mr Bryan Mayoh**
42 **PISGAH PIKE (IRE),** 8, br g Famous Name—Music On D Waters (IRE) **ValueRacingClub.co.uk**
43 4, B g Westerner—Poem (IRE) **Richard Wilmot-Smith**
44 **REGARDE (IRE),** 6, ch br g Kapgarde (FR)—Mazaryne (FR) **Mr F. McAleavy**
45 **REPRESENTING BOB (IRE),** 7, ch g Presenting—Some Bob Back (IRE) **Beccle, Sperling, Allen & Hague**
46 **ROGER POL (IRE),** 5, b g Shantou (USA)—Laren (GER) **Cobbold Allen Ogilvy Shaw Morley**
47 **SCHEMATIC,** 5, b g Schiaparelli (GER)—Wishing Wind **The Queen Consort & Chips Keswick**
48 **SEA THE CLOUDS (IRE),** 6, b g Born To Sea (IRE)—Leo's Spirit (IRE) **ValueRacingClub.co.uk**
49 **SHADY DAISY (IRE),** 5, b m Flemensfirth (USA)—Day's Over **Jamie Snowden Racing Club**
50 **SHAKERMAKER (IRE),** 6, gr g Mastercraftsman (IRE)—Fine Threads **Mr J. E. Snowden**
51 **SHOLOKHOV COCKTAIL,** 5, ch m Sholokhov (IRE)—Centoria (IRE) **The Wife Loves It Partnership**
52 **SOCIALISER (IRE),** 7, b g Milan—Simonsoeur (IRE) **Foxtrot Racing Socialiser**
53 **SOLDIER OF DESTINY (IRE),** 7, b g Presenting—Sagarich (FR) **Sir Chippendale Keswick**
54 **SPICE HEAVEN,** 5, b m Telescope (IRE)—La Doelenaise **Foxtrot Racing Spice Heaven**
55 **SPITFIRE GIRL (IRE),** 6, b m Walk In The Park (IRE)—Calomeria **A Walk In The Park Partnership**

MR JAMIE SNOWDEN - continued

56 **STAREVITCH (FR),** 7, b g Sinndar (IRE)—Folie Star Gate (FR) **Friends of Ebony Horse Club**
57 **SUPER SURVIVOR (IRE),** 7, b g Shantou (USA)—All The Best Mate (IRE) **Goulden, & Hopgood**
58 **TALLOW FOR COAL (IRE),** 7, b g Arctic Cosmos (USA)—South Queen Lady (IRE) **Apache Star Racing**
59 **TEECEETHREE,** 5, b m Native Ruler—Tea Caddy **The Galloping Grannies**
60 **THOMAS MACDONAGH,** 10, b g Black Sam Bellamy (IRE)—
Taqreem (IRE) **Sperling, Coomes, Davies, Hague, Collins**
61 **UP FOR PAROL (IRE),** 7, b g Flemensfirth (USA)—Clarification (IRE) **Duck Jordan Wright Dellar Doel Woodward**
62 **VALAMIX (IRE),** 6, b g Valirann (FR)—Julimark (IRE) **The Folly Partnership**
63 **VILLAINESS (IRE),** 5, b m Yeats (IRE)—En Vedette (FR) **Mrs J. A. Thomas**
64 **YOU WEAR IT WELL,** 6, b m Midnight Legend—Annie's Answer (IRE) **Sir Chippendale Keswick**

Head Girl: Kate Robinson.

NH Jockey: Jonathan Burke, Page Fuller, Gavin Sheehan.

---

467 MR MIKE SOWERSBY, York

Postal: **Southwold Farm, Goodmanham Wold, Market Weighton, York, East Yorkshire, YO43 3NA**
Contacts: **PHONE 01430 810534 MOBILE 07855 551056**

1 **CHOUNGAYA (FR),** 10, b g Walk In The Park (IRE)—Autorite (FR) **Mrs J Cooper & Mrs J Plummer**
2 5, B m Arcadio (GER)—Detente **M. E. Sowersby**
3 **FORCETA (IRE),** 5, b m Life Force (IRE)—Coleta (IRE) **M. E. Sowersby**
4 **GOOSEWOOD,** 6, b g Nathaniel (IRE)—Regina Cordium (IRE) **Mrs J. M. Plummer**
5 **ISLA DIAMONDS,** 8, ch m Trans Island—Queen of Diamonds (IRE) **Mr A. G. Waite**
6 **MAGNA MORALIA (IRE),** 6, gr g Gregorian (IRE)—Trentini (IRE) **Miss E. C. Forman**
7 **MATOURY,** 4, b g Kingman—Sinnamary (IRE) **Mrs J. M. Plummer**
8 **MISS BLENNERHASSET (IRE),** 4, b f Nathaniel (IRE)—Elizabelle (IRE) **Miss E. C. Forman**
9 **ONLY FOR PASCAL (IRE),** 7, b m Arcadio (GER)—Emmas' House (IRE) **Mounted Gamess Assoc Syndicate**
10 **SIGHT NOR SEEN (IRE),** 9, b g Morozov (USA)—Baby Cat (IRE) **The Southwold Set**
11 **UJUMPTHELASTUWIN,** 9, b g Multiplex—Rosa Canina **Mr A. G. Waite**
12 **VERY EXCELLENT (IRE),** 7, ch g Casamento (IRE)—Step With Style (USA) **Mr A. G. Waite**
13 **WILLA,** 6, b m Dutch Art—Holberg Suite **M. E. Sowersby**
14 **ZEN MASTER (IRE),** 11, b g Shantou (USA)—Back Log (IRE) **M. E. Sowersby**
15 **ZOFFALEE (FR),** 8, ch g Zoffany (IRE)—Senderlea (IRE) **Mounted Gamess Assoc Syndicate**

Assistant Trainer: Mary Sowersby.

Flat Jockey: Tom Eaves, James Sullivan. **NH Jockey:** Brian Hughes. **Amateur Jockey:** Mr Russell Lindsay.

---

468 MR JOHN SPEARING, Kinnersley

Postal: **Kinnersley Racing Limited, Kinnersley Racing Stables, Kinnersley, Severn Stoke, Worcestershire, WR8 9JR**
Contacts: **PHONE 01905 371054 MOBILE 07801 552922 FAX 01905 371054**
EMAIL jlspearing@aol.com

1 **A SURE WELCOME,** 9, b g Pastoral Pursuits—Croeso Bach **Kinnersley Partnership 3**
2 **CALISSON,** 5, b g Califet (FR)—Miss Conduct **Miss C. J. Ive**
3 **DANNY BLEU (IRE),** 5, gr g Clodovil (IRE)—Casual Remark (IRE) **Mr J. L. Spearing**
4 **HY EALES (IRE),** 6, b m Passing Glance—Miss Conduct **Graham Eales & Kate Ive**
5 **IT'S HOW WE ROLL (IRE),** 9, b g Fastnet Rock (AUS)—Clodora (FR) **Kinnersley Partnership**

MR JOHN SPEARING - continued

6 **KINZ (IRE),** 5, b m Footstepsinthesand—Talitha Kum (IRE) **Mr H. James**
7 **PILLAR OF STEEL,** 8, b m Shirocco (GER)—Miss Conduct **Miss C. J. Ive**
8 **SHUTTHEGATE (IRE),** 9, b g Milan—Miss Conduct **Kinnersley Partnership II**
9 **TOWER PRINCESS (IRE),** 5, ch m Prince of Lir (IRE)—Malory Towers **Miss C. J. Ive**

THREE-YEAR-OLDS

10 **MAYZ (IRE),** b f Mayson—Malikayah (IRE) **Mr H. James**
11 B g Elzaam (AUS)—Plym

Assistant Trainer: Miss C. Ive.

---

469 MR RICHARD SPENCER, Newmarket

Postal: **Sefton Lodge, 8 Bury Road, Newmarket, Suffolk, CB8 7BT**
Contacts: **PHONE 01638 675780 MOBILE 07720 064053**
WORK EMAIL richard.spencer@rebel-racing.co.uk

1 **BERNARDO O'REILLY,** 9, b g Intikhab (USA)—Baldovina **Rebel Racing (2)**
2 **CAN'TSMILEWITHOUTU (IRE),** 6, b g Shantou (USA)—Maggies Oscar (IRE) **Phil, Philip & Aidan Cunningham**
3 **CHAMPAGNE SUPANOVA (IRE),** 6, b g Camacho—Flawless Pink **Mr P. M. Cunningham**
4 **CIGARETTESNALCOHOL (IRE),** 7, ch g Ocovango—Moylisha Red (IRE) **Rebel Jumping II**
5 **DANDY MAESTRO,** 5, ch g Dandy Man (IRE)—Maids Causeway (IRE) **Mr J. Power**
6 **DANNI CALIFORNIA (IRE),** 5, gr m The Gurkha (IRE)—Satwa Ruby (FR) **Mr P. M. Cunningham**
7 **FUEGO,** 4, b g Cityscape—La Pantera **Mr A. Cunningham**
8 **KEYSER SOZE (IRE),** 9, ch g Arcano (IRE)—Causeway Queen (IRE) **Rebel Racing (2)**
9 **LUCKY MAN (IRE),** 4, b c Kodi Bear (IRE)—Vastitas (IRE) **Rebel Racing Premier IV**
10 **MR BIG STUFF,** 4, b g Iffraaj—Groovejet **Mr P. M. Cunningham**
11 **PEEJAYBEE (FR),** 7, ch g Ballingarry (IRE)—Playa du Charmil (FR) **Martin Gowing & Paul Booker**
12 **REVICH (IRE),** 7, b g Requinto (IRE)—Kathleen Rafferty (IRE) **Middleham Park Lxvii & Phil Cunningham**
13 **ROLL WITH IT (IRE),** 7, b g Sholokhov (IRE)—Que Pasa (IRE) **Rebel Jumping II**
14 **SPACE COWBOY (IRE),** 4, b c Kodi Bear (IRE)—Usem **Rebel Racing Premier IV**
15 **STAY CLASSY (IRE),** 7, ch m Camacho—Hollow Green (IRE) **Balasuriya,Cook, Cunningham, Gowing, Spencer**
16 **SUPERSTAR DJ,** 4, b g Time Test—Excello **Mr P. M. Cunningham**
17 **THE CITY'S PHANTOM,** 6, b g Free Eagle (IRE)—Meet Marhaba (IRE) **Mr P. M. Cunningham**
18 **THEFASTNTHECURIOUS,** 5, ch m Fast Company (IRE)—Dame Plume (IRE) **Mr P. M. Cunningham**
19 **TOO FUNKY,** 4, b f Mayson—Instructress **Mr P. M. Cunningham**
20 **TWISTEDFIRESTARTER (IRE),** 7, b g Sageburg (IRE)—Mercy Mission **Rebel Jumping II**
21 **TYSON FURY,** 6, ch g Iffraaj—Za Za Zoom (IRE) **Balasuriya, Cook, Cunningham, Gowing, Spencer**
22 **WONDERWALL (IRE),** 7, b g Yeats (IRE)—Rock Me Gently **Rebel Jumping II**

THREE-YEAR-OLDS

23 **ANOTHER DIMENSION,** b c Time Test—Heather Lark (IRE) **Mr P. M. Cunningham**
24 **BACK TOMORROW,** b f Rajasinghe (IRE)—Wonderful Life (IRE) **Mr P. M. Cunningham**
25 **BELO HORIZONTE,** ch g Rajasinghe (IRE)—Lucia de Medici **Mr P. M. Cunningham**
26 **BODYGROOVE,** b g Iffraaj—Groovejet **Mr P. M. Cunningham**
27 **EXPRESS YOURSELF,** b f Rajasinghe (IRE)—Dame Plume (IRE) **Mr P. M. Cunningham**
28 **GIANT,** b c Rajasinghe (IRE)—Rebel Surge (IRE) **Mr P. M. Cunningham**
29 **IVORY MADONNA (IRE),** gr f Dark Angel (IRE)—Clem Fandango (FR) **Mr P. M. Cunningham**
30 **JUICY,** b f Rajasinghe (IRE)—Twizzell **Mr P. M. Cunningham**
31 **LITTLE EDI,** b g Rajasinghe (IRE)—Oneroa (IRE) **Mr P. M. Cunningham**
32 **MAHARAJAS EXPRESS,** ch c Rajasinghe (IRE)—Instructress **Mr P. M. Cunningham**
33 **MISS SARAJEVO,** b f Rajasinghe (IRE)—Cherry Malotte **Mr P. M. Cunningham**
34 **NAOMI LAPAGLIA,** b f Awtaad (IRE)—Hawaafez **Edward Babington & Phil Cunningham**
35 **NUTBUSH CITY,** ch f Rajasinghe (IRE)—Bronte Flyer **Mr P. M. Cunningham**
36 **PHENOMENON,** b g Rajasinghe (IRE)—Encantar **Mr P. M. Cunningham**
37 **PJANOO,** b c Muhaarar—Cockney Dancer **Mr P. M. Cunningham**

MR RICHARD SPENCER - continued

38 **PRETTY YOUNG THING (IRE),** b f Rajasinghe (IRE)—Perfect Pose (IRE) **Mr P. M. Cunningham**
39 **SWEET HARMONY (IRE),** b f No Nay Never (USA)—Last Waltz (IRE) **Mr P. M. Cunningham**
40 **TALAMANCA,** ch g Rajasinghe (IRE)—Bakoura **Mr P. M. Cunningham**
41 **WAITING ALL NIGHT,** b g Rajasinghe (IRE)—Goodnightsuzy (IRE) **Mr P. M. Cunningham**

TWO-YEAR-OLDS

42 **AIDAN ANDABETTIN,** b c 20/02 Blue Point (IRE)—Nadia Glory (Oasis Dream) (61905) **Mr P. M. Cunningham**
43 **CON TE PARTIRO,** b c 10/03 Time Test—Groovejet (Cockney Rebel (IRE)) **Mr P. M. Cunningham**
44 **CROSS THE TRACKS,** b c 12/03 Rajasinghe (IRE)—Local Fancy (Bahamian Bounty) **Mr P. M. Cunningham**
45 **FOOL'S GOLD (IRE),** b c 14/03 Galileo Gold—Thrilled (IRE) (Kodiac) (161905) **Mr P. M. Cunningham**
46 **GIVE IT UP,** b c 26/04 Rajasinghe (IRE)—Dame Plume (IRE) (Amadeus Wolf) **Mr P. M. Cunningham**
47 **RUN BOY RUN,** b c 29/03 Rajasinghe (IRE)—Instructress (Diktat) **Mr P. M. Cunningham**
48 **SHALLOW,** ch f 03/03 Rajasinghe (IRE)—Velvet Band (Verglas (IRE)) (17000) **Mr P. M. Cunningham**
49 **TOXIC,** b f 16/04 Rajasinghe (IRE)—Encantar (Equiano (FR)) **Mr P. M. Cunningham**
50 **TWO TRIBES,** ch c 05/02 Rajasinghe (IRE)—Warsash (IRE) (War Command (USA)) **Mr P. M. Cunningham**

Assistant Trainer: Mr Joe Akehurst, **Pupil Assistant:** Mr Jack Jones, **Travelling Head:** Miss Tegan Kerr.

Apprentice Jockey: Mr Angus Villiers.

---

470 MR SEB SPENCER, Malton

Postal: **79 Harvest Drive, Malton, North Yorkshire, YO17 7BF**
Contacts: **MOBILE 07790 060050**
EMAIL sebspencerracing@gmail.com

1 **BEARAWAY (IRE),** 5, b g Kodiac—Fair Sailing (IRE) **The Bears Syndicate**
2 **DESERT DREAM,** 9, b g Oasis Dream—Rosika **The Racing Emporium**
3 **LITTLE MUDDY,** 7, b m Mr Medici (IRE)—Secret Oasis **Mac Racing**
4 **MUDDAGENT,** 4, b g Mahsoob—Nine Red **N. Bycroft**
5 **MUDDY LYNN,** 4, b f Intrinsic—She's So Pretty (IRE) **Mac Racing**
6 **NOOO MORE (IRE),** 4, b g Ribchester (IRE)—Lyric of Fife (IRE) **Mr K. G. E. Skow**
7 **SALVE JAPAN,** 4, b f Dabirsim (FR)—Salve Diana (GER)
8 **VICTORY MARCH (IRE),** 6, b g Zoffany (IRE)—Seatone (USA) **Magna Carter Bloodstock**

THREE-YEAR-OLDS

9 Ch c Koropick (IRE)—Misu Mac
10 B c Koropick (IRE)—She's So Pretty (IRE)

TWO-YEAR-OLDS

11 Ch f 27/04 Mayson—Bond's Girl (Monsieur Bond (IRE)) (10000) **Mr M. Marsh**
12 B c 21/02 Muhaarar—Dubai Media (CAN) (Songandaprayer (USA)) (5000) **Mr M. Marsh**
13 B c 23/02 Time Test—Jostle (USA) (Brocco (USA)) (11000) **Mr M. Marsh**
14 B c 31/01 Intrinsic—Misu Mac (Misu Bond (IRE))
15 B c 20/02 Harry Angel (IRE)—Vespasia (Medicean) (12000) **Mr M. Marsh**

471 MR HENRY SPILLER, Newmarket

Postal: **Henry Spiller Racing, Sackville House Stables, Sackville Street, Newmarket, Suffolk, CB8 8DX**
Contacts: **MOBILE 07786 263997**
WORK EMAIL henry@henryspiller.com EMAIL office@henryspiller.com WEBSITE www.henryspiller.com

1 **APFELSTRUDEL,** 4, b f Intello (GER)—Appointee (IRE) **Mr R. P. A. Spiller**
2 **BAKED ALASKA,** 4, b f Iffraaj—Figment
3 **BOOK OF VERSE (USA),** 5, ch g Curlin (USA)—Silvester Lady **Mr K. Clarke & Partner**
4 **BRAULIA,** 4, b f Swiss Spirit—Faeroes (IRE) **G. B. Partnership**
5 **CAMERATA (GER),** 5, b m Kingman—Calyxa **Dethrone Racing**
6 **CRACK REGIMENT (FR),** 6, b g Siyouni (FR)—Coiffure **Mr R. P. A. Spiller**
7 **DARK DESIGN (IRE),** 6, b g Gutaifan (IRE)—Divine Design (IRE) **Aj Racing**
8 **KODIAS SANGARIUS (IRE),** 4, b f Kodiac—Oui Say Oui (IRE) **Sarkar**
9 **LEGENDE D'ART (IRE),** 6, b g Kingman—Legende Bleue **Dethrone Racing**
10 **MASHAAER (IRE),** 4, b f Muhaarar—Fleeting Smile (USA) **Sarkar**
11 **MCQUEEN (IRE),** 4, ch g Zoffany (IRE)—Shahralasal (IRE) **Sarkar**
12 **MIDNIGHT LUCK,** 5, b gr m Gregorian (IRE)—Maybe Enough **Mr S. Davies**
13 **MOVING FOR GOLD (IRE),** 5, b g Acclamation—Church Melody **Henry Mak, Koon Sing Li & John Lee**
14 **SIRIUS WHITE (IRE),** 4, gr g Markaz (IRE)—Piacere (IRE) **Dark Horse Partnership**
15 **TAHASUN (IRE),** 4, b f Tamayuz—Urjuwaan **Sarkar**
16 **THE THIRD MAN,** 12, gr g Dalakhani (IRE)—Spinning Queen **Mrs D. Spiller**
17 **VICTORIA GROVE,** 4, b f Siyouni (FR)—Baltic Best (IRE) **Mr R. P. A. Spiller**
18 5, Ch g Night of Thunder (IRE)—Whitefall (USA)

THREE-YEAR-OLDS

19 **FULLY DEPLOYED,** b g Muhaarar—Thafeera (USA) **Sarkar**
20 **HIGH COURT JUDGE (USA),** ch g Kitten's Joy (USA)—Proctor's Ledge (USA) **Mr K. Clarke & Partner**
21 **MARINARA (IRE),** b f U S Navy Flag (USA)—Sapore di Roma (IRE) **d'Arblay Partnership**
22 **PROFITABLE DAWN (IRE),** b f Profitable (IRE)—Light At Dawn (IRE) **Sarkar**
23 **SENOR POCKETS,** b g Aclaim (IRE)—Ulfah Dream **Sarkar**

TWO-YEAR-OLDS

24 B f 28/04 Camacho—Beach Candy (IRE) (Footstepsinthesand) (30000) **Sarkar**

472 MR FOZZY STACK, Cashel

Postal: **Thomastown Castle Stud, Golden, Cashel, Co. Tipperary, Ireland**
Contacts: **PHONE +353 62 54129**
EMAIL contact@stackracing.ie WEBSITE www.stackracing.ie

1 **CASTLE STAR,** 4, b c Starspangledbanner (AUS)—Awohaam
2 **CHAZZESMEE (IRE),** 5, b h Excelebration—Elope
3 **FIZZICAL,** 4, ch f Starspangledbanner (AUS)—Medicean Star (IRE)
4 **MY EYES ADORE YOU,** 4, ch f Profitable—Crossanza

THREE-YEAR-OLDS

5 B f Camelot—American Spirit (IRE)
6 **ASPEN GROVE,** b f Justify (USA)—Data Dependent (USA)
7 **AUSSIE GIRL,** ch f Starspangledbanner (AUS)—Ravissante (IRE)
8 **BRIGHT LEGEND,** b c Zoustar (AUS)—Alexiade (IRE)
9 **DINGLE DANCER (IRE),** b c Awtaad—Babberina
10 Ch c No Nay Never (USA)—Dowager
11 **ELSA'S PRIDE (IRE),** gr f Roaring lion—Colonial Classic
12 B f Camelot—Fastnet Mist (IRE)
13 **GLAMS GAMS (IRE),** b f Zoffany—Hot legs

MR FOZZY STACK - continued

14 **HIGHLAND RAHY,** b c Hard Spun (USA)—Patti O'Rahy (USA)
15 Ch f Footstepsinthesand—Inis Boffin
16 **LIGHTNING LEGEND,** ch g Night of Thunder (IRE)—Precious Dream (USA)
17 **MANDO ECLIPSE,** b c Churchill—Gentle Breeze
18 **MARSH LOCK,** b f No Nay Never (USA)—Canada Water
19 **NATHALIA ECLIPSE (IRE),** ch f Churchill (IRE)—Emirate Jewel (USA)
20 **NEVER SHOUT NEVER,** b c No Nay Never (USA)—Catch The Eye (IRE)
21 **PARTING GLASS,** ch c Starspangledbanner (AUS)—Keep Dancing (IRE)
22 **PASSIONATE,** ch f Churchill (IRE)—Many Hearts (USA)
23 **RAINBOW REEL (IRE),** b f Highland Reel—Brunch Bellini
24 **RUN RAN RUN (IRE),** ch c No Nay Never (USA)—Scream Blue Murder (IRE)
25 **SEA LEGEND,** ch c Sea The Stars (IRE)—Dame du Roi (IRE)
26 **SECRET SAUCE,** ch c Starspangledbanner (AUS)—Pure Greed (IRE)
27 **TWO STARS (IRE),** b g Starspangledbanner (AUS)—Glowing Star
28 **YOU SEND ME,** ch f Starspangledbanner (AUS)—Coco Rouge (IRE)

TWO-YEAR-OLDS

29 Ch f 01/04 Starspangledbanner (AUS)—Bright Glow (Exceed and Excel)
30 B f 04/04 Waldgeist—Call Me Katie (Kodiac)
31 Br c 29/01 Caravaggio—Castle Cross (Cape Cross)
32 Br gr f 01/03 Starspangledbanner (AUS)—Face Off (CAN) (Mizzen Mast (USA)) (33333)
33 B f 13/05 Territories—Flashing Colour (Pivotal)
34 B f 14/02 Starspangledbanner (AUS)—Heavenly Snow (Australia)
35 B g 20/04 US Navy Flag—Lahabah (Invincible Spirit)
36 B c 14/03 Ten Sovereigns—Miss Understood (Excellent Art)
37 B f 20/02 Inns of Court—Overheard (Lope de Vega)
38 Ch c 03/04 Starspangledbanner (AUS)—Postale (Zamindar)
39 B c 06/02 Oasis Dream—Red Intrigue (Selkirk)
40 B f 10/02 Starspangledbanner (AUS)—Sandtail (Verglas)
41 B f 08/05 Galileo—Scream Blue Murder (Oratorio)
42 **SMASH FACTOR (IRE),** b c 29/03 Showcasing—Ultrasonic (USA) (Mizzen Mast (USA)) (64026)
43 B f 26/02 Churchill (IRE)—Solstice (Dubawi)

Owners: Mr Rick Barnes, Mr Michael Begley, Craig Bernick, Peter Chiu, Iman Hartono, Mr T. Hyde Jnr, Mr D. Keoghan, Mrs J. Magnier, Mr Casey McLiney, Mr P. Piller, Mrs Jane Rowlinson, J. A. Stack, Mr Michael Tabor, Francis Brooke, Mr John Byrne, Mrs Anne Gaffney partnership, Mr Bon Ho, Mrs MV Magnier, Toshihiro Matsimoto, Mrs Eimear Mulhearne, Brosnan Racing, Mrs P Shanahan, Cayton Park Stud, Ms Patricia Casement/D Harron partnership.

Flat Jockey: Mark Enright, Andrew Slattery.

473 MR DANIEL STEELE, Henfield

Postal: **Blacklands House, Wheatsheaf Road, Wineham, Henfield, West Sussex, BN5 9BE**
Contacts: **PHONE 07809 405036**
EMAIL danielsteele14@hotmail.co.uk

1 **CLONGOWES (IRE),** 9, b g New Approach (IRE)—Punctilious **Sam Tingey & Charlie Tingey**
2 **GOLD SOUK (IRE),** 6, b g Casamento (IRE)—Dubai Sunrise (USA) **Sam Tingey & Charlie Tingey**
3 4, B f Diamond Boy (FR)—Oscar Invitation (IRE) **Mr D. R. Steele**
4 **TASKHEER (IRE),** 5, b g Golden Horn—Shaarfa (USA) **Sam Tingey & Charlie Tingey**
5 **THE DEFIANT,** 7, b g Morpheus—Killer Class **Mrs L. Chester**

THREE-YEAR-OLDS

6 B f Media Hype—Dainty Diva (IRE) **Mr D. R. Steele**

TWO-YEAR-OLDS

7 B c 26/03 Postponed (IRE)—Flylowflylong (IRE) (Danetime (IRE)) (4000) **Mr D. R. Steele**
8 B f 23/02 Massaat (IRE)—Magical Daze (Showcasing) (2000) **Mr D. R. Steele**
9 B c 13/01 Equiano (FR)—Omaha Gold (IRE) (Kodiac) (2000) **Mr D. R. Steele**

474 MRS JACKIE STEPHEN, Melrose

Postal: **Firth Farm, Lilliesleaf, Melrose, Roxburghshire, TD6 9JW**
Contacts: **MOBILE 07980 785924, 07887 902733**
EMAIL jackiestephen123@hotmail.com WEBSITE www.jackiestephenracing.com

1 **ALONE NO MORE (IRE),** 11, b g Gold Well—Cherry In A Hurry (IRE) **Miss L. Brown**
2 **ANY JOB WILL DO (IRE),** 7, ch g Shirocco (GER)—Funcheon Lady (IRE) **Northern Lights Racing**
3 4, B g Sandmason—Blue Article (IRE) **Mrs J. S. Stephen**
4 4, B g Shirocco (GER)—Borboleta (IRE) **Mr P. G. Stephen**
5 **CLEAR ABILITY (IRE),** 7, ch m Imperial Monarch (IRE)—Celtic Peace (IRE) **Lessells & Ritchie**
6 **DUNNOTTAR CASTLE,** 7, b g Kalanisi (IRE)—Sister Shannon (IRE) **Horn & Stephen**
7 **GLEN CLOVIS,** 5, b m Clovis du Berlais (FR)—Present Leader **Horn & Stephen**
8 **JOANNA I'M FINE (IRE),** 6, ch m Famous Name—Toye Native (IRE) **Mr G. Truscott**
9 **KILFINAN BAY (IRE),** 8, b g Mahler—Midnight Special (IRE) **Jackie Stephen Racing Club**
10 **LOCK DOWN LUKE,** 7, b g Lucarno (USA)—La Grande Villez (FR) **P. & Mark Fleming**
11 **SPUTNIK (IRE),** 8, b g Recital (FR)—Itlallendintears (IRE) **Jackie Stephen Racing Club**
12 **THE GREAT GEORGIE,** 8, b g Multiplex—For More (FR) **Mr P. G. Stephen**
13 **THE REAL RASCAL (IRE),** 6, b g Sageburg (IRE)—Real Revival (IRE) **Mr P. G. Stephen**
14 **TOUGH OUT (IRE),** 6, br g Tough As Nails (IRE)—Doutzen (IRE) **High Country Racing**
15 **WOLFCATCHER (IRE),** 11, b g King's Best (USA)—Miss Particular (IRE) **Northern Lights Racing**

Assistant Trainer: Patrick Stephen.

---

475 MR ROBERT STEPHENS, Newport

Postal: **Penhow, Newport, NP26 3AD**
Contacts: **MOBILE 07717 477177**
EMAIL robertdavidstephens@btinternet.com WEBSITE www.robertstephensracing.com

1 **ALYA'S GOLD AWARD (IRE),** 4, b f Starspangledbanner (AUS)—Quinta Verde (IRE)
2 **ANCIENT CAPITAL,** 4, b g Frankel—Spirit of Xian (IRE)
3 **BECOMING (IRE),** 4, b f Gleneagles (IRE)—Crystal Morning (IRE)
4 **BRECCIA,** 5, b m Intello (GER)—Rock Choir
5 **BUMBLE BAY,** 13, b g Trade Fair—Amica
6 **CARIBOU,** 5, b g Adaay (IRE)—Blue Lyric
7 **ESPRESSO FREDDO (IRE),** 9, b g Fast Company (IRE)—Spring Bouquet (IRE)
8 **FOOTSY,** 4, ch g Siyouni (FR)—Barter
9 **KUMASI,** 6, ch g New Approach (IRE)—Ghanaian (FR)
10 **MELAKAZ (IRE),** 5, br g Markaz (IRE)—Melatonina (IRE)
11 **PARSONS STONE (IRE),** 6, ch g Leading Light (IRE)—Tetou (IRE)
12 **PORT NOIR,** 6, bl m Harbour Watch (IRE)—Cocabana
13 **SKY POWER (IRE),** 6, b g Fastnet Rock (AUS)—Dame Blanche (IRE)
14 **SON OF OZ,** 6, ch g Australia—Ambria (GER)
15 **TUDORS TREASURE,** 12, b g Dr Massini (IRE)—Rude Health
16 **WALEYFA,** 5, b m Awtaad (IRE)—Sweet Secret

THREE-YEAR-OLDS

17 **BERAGON,** b g Zoffany (IRE)—Got To Dream
18 B f Free Eagle (IRE)—Grain de Beaute (IRE)
19 **SAO TIMOTHY (IRE),** b g Fast Company (IRE)—Starbright (IRE)

TWO-YEAR-OLDS

20 B c 28/04 Free Eagle (IRE)—Party Angel (IRE) (Dark Angel (IRE)) (10804)

476 MR JOHN STIMPSON, Newcastle-under-Lyme

Postal: **Trainers Lodge, Park Road, Butterton, Newcastle-under-Lyme, Staffordshire, ST5 4DZ**
Contacts: **PHONE 01782 636020**
EMAIL john@redskyuk.com

1 **APACHE PRINCESS,** 4, b f Fountain of Youth (IRE)—Apache Glory (USA) **Mr J. Stimpson**
2 **HURRICANE DYLAN (IRE),** 12, b g Brian Boru—Definetly Sarah (IRE) **Mr J. Stimpson**
3 **MY BROTHER MIKE (IRE),** 9, b g Bated Breath—Coming Back **Mr J. Stimpson**
4 **PERUVIAN SUMMER (IRE),** 7, ch g Lope de Vega (IRE)—Need You Now (IRE) **Mr J. Stimpson**
5 **POPPOP (FR),** 7, b g Great Pretender (IRE)—Bloody Sunday (FR) **Mr J. Stimpson**
6 **ROMAN PRINCESS,** 4, b f Fountain of Youth (IRE)—Diletta Tommasa (IRE) **Mr J. Stimpson**
7 **THE GREY BANDIT,** 6, bl g Gregorian (IRE)—Reel Cool **Mr J. Stimpson**

THREE-YEAR-OLDS

8 B g Fountain of Youth (IRE)—Apache Glory (USA) **Mr J. Stimpson**
9 B f Fountain of Youth (IRE)—Diletta Tommasa (IRE) **Mr J. Stimpson**

---

477 MR WILLIAM STONE, West Wickham

Postal: **The Meadow, Streetly End, West Wickham, Cambridge, Cambridgeshire, CB21 4RP**
Contacts: **MOBILE 07788 971094**
EMAIL williamstone1@hotmail.co.uk

1 **DASHING DICK (IRE),** 5, b g Cable Bay (IRE)—Raggiante (IRE) **Ron Spore & Dr C Scott**
2 **DASHING PANTHER,** 4, b g Slade Power (IRE)—Irrational **Ron Spore & Dr C Scott**
3 **DASHING RAT,** 4, b g Adaay (IRE)—Hot Secret **R. C. Spore**
4 **DASHING ROGER,** 6, b g Fast Company (IRE)—Croeso Cusan **R. C. Spore**
5 **DASHING TO YOU,** 4, b g Olympic Glory (IRE)—Libre A Vous (FR) **Ron Spore & Dr C Scott**
6 **JEANETTE MAY,** 7, b m Dick Turpin (IRE)—Clock Opera (IRE) **Mr Shane Fairweather & Dr C Scott**
7 4, B g Showcasing—Khaki (IRE) **R. C. Spore**
8 **LALANIA,** 8, br m Kheleyf (USA)—George's Gift **Dr C. M. Scott**
9 **LITTLE BROWN TROUT,** 6, b g Casamento (IRE)—Clock Opera (IRE) **Dr C. M. Scott**
10 4, B c Gregorian (IRE)—Satin Waters **Ron Spore & P D West**

THREE-YEAR-OLDS

11 **AWESOME GEORGIE (IRE),** b f Awtaad (IRE)—Georgie Hyde **R. C. Spore**
12 B g Equiano (FR)—East Coast Lady (IRE) **Dr C. M. Scott**
13 **LITTLE TIGER,** b g Night of Thunder (IRE)—Tigerfish (IRE) **Dr C. M. Scott**
14 **ROMANTIC SUNLIGHT,** b f Tasleet—Percy's Romance **Dr C. M. Scott**
15 **SASSY REDHEAD,** ch f Harry Angel (IRE)—Passcode **R. C. Spore**
16 **SOOTHING BLAZE,** b c Oasis Dream—Afternoon (IRE) **Kalabak Ltd**
17 **ZARA'S RETURN,** br f Zarak (FR)—Quandreviendrastu (IRE) **R. C. Spore**

TWO-YEAR-OLDS

18 **BREATH OF WRETS,** ch c 02/02 Territories (IRE)—Give Me Breath (Bated Breath) **Mrs E. A. P. Haynes**
19 B c 02/03 Charm Spirit (IRE)—Diamond Lady (Multiplex) **Dr C. M. Scott**
20 B f 28/04 Equiano (FR)—East Coast Lady (IRE) (Kodiac) **Dr C. M. Scott**
21 B c 26/04 Cable Bay (IRE)—Pointer (Bated Breath) (6500) **Ron Spore & P D West**
22 B c 18/03 Time Test—Quandreviendrastu (IRE) (Dream Ahead (USA)) (4000) **R. C. Spore**
23 B c 16/04 Postponed (IRE)—Tigerfish (IRE) (Lilbourne Lad (IRE)) **Dr C. M. Scott**

478 MR WILF STOREY, Consett

Postal: **Grange Farm & Stud, Muggleswick, Consett, County Durham, DH8 9DW**
Contacts: **PHONE 01207 255259 MOBILE 07860 510441**
EMAIL wilf.storey@hotmail.com

1 **GOING UNDERGROUND,** 6, ch g Lope de Vega (IRE)—Jam Jar **H S Hutchinson and W Glass**
2 **LADY HAMILTON (IRE),** 4, b f Teofilo (IRE)—Heartily (IRE) **Exors of the Late J. A. Lister**
3 **PERFECT SOLDIER (IRE),** 9, b g Kodiac—Independent Girl (IRE) **Gremlin Racing**
4 **SHIFTER,** 4, b f Muhaarar—Holley Shiftwell **Mr W. L. Storey**
5 **TARNHELM,** 8, b m Helmet (AUS)—Anosti **wilfstoreyracingclub**
6 **THE WHITE VOLCANO (IRE),** 11, b g September Storm (GER)—Ravishing Rita (IRE) **Mr W. L. Storey**

Assistant Trainer: Miss S. M. Doolan, Miss S. Storey.

---

479 SIR MICHAEL STOUTE, Newmarket

Postal: **Freemason Lodge, Bury Road, Newmarket, Suffolk, CB8 7BY**
Contacts: **PHONE 01638 663801 FAX 01638 667276**

1 **AERION POWER (IRE),** 5, b h Kingman—Applauded (IRE)
2 **ASSESSMENT,** 4, b g Kingman—Clinical
3 **BALHAMBAR (FR),** 4, b g Almanzor (FR)—Moojeh (IRE)
4 **BAY BRIDGE,** 5, b h New Bay—Hayyona
5 **BELIEVE IN STARS (IRE),** 4, b g Make Believe—Cruck Realta
6 **CRYSTAL CAPRICE (IRE),** 4, b f Frankel—Crystal Zvezda
7 **CRYSTAL ESTRELLA,** 4, b f Iffraaj—Crystal Etoile
8 **DESERT CROWN,** 4, b c Nathaniel (IRE)—Desert Berry
9 **HASTY SAILOR (IRE),** 6, b g Fastnet Rock (AUS)—Galileano (IRE)
10 **HIGHEST GROUND (IRE),** 6, b g Frankel—Celestial Lagoon (JPN)
11 **LOVE YOU GRANDPA (IRE),** 4, b f Frankel—Baldovina
12 **MIGDAM (FR),** 4, b g Zelzal (FR)—Asyad (IRE)
13 **NEW DIMENSION,** 4, b g Ulysses (IRE)—Azhar
14 **OUIJA DREAM (IRE),** 4, ch g Australia—Dubian To (IRE)
15 **POTAPOVA,** 5, b m Invincible Spirit (IRE)—Safina
16 **REAL DREAM (IRE),** 4, b g Lope de Vega (IRE)—Laganore (IRE)
17 **RED RAMBLER,** 4, ch c Iffraaj—Blushing Rose
18 **REGAL REALITY,** 8, b g Intello (GER)—Regal Realm
19 **SEE (USA),** 4, br f War Front (USA)—Faufiler (IRE)
20 **SOLID STONE (IRE),** 7, br g Shamardal (USA)—Landmark (USA)
21 **WAHRAAN (FR),** 5, ch g Le Havre (IRE)—Al Jassasiyah (IRE)

THREE-YEAR-OLDS

22 **CIENFUEGOS (IRE),** ch f Ulysses (IRE)—Celestial Lagoon (JPN)
23 **CIRCLE OF FIRE,** br c Almanzor (FR)—Fiery Sunset
24 **CORYMBOSA,** b f Frankel—Diamond Fields (IRE)
25 **CRYSTAL MARINER (IRE),** ch c Sea The Stars (IRE)—Crystal Zvezda
26 **ELEUTHEROMANIA (FR),** b f Invincible Spirit (IRE)—Rajaratna (IRE)
27 **FALCON NINE,** ch g Ulysses (IRE)—Freedonia
28 **FLY ZONE,** b c Expert Eye—Lilyfire (USA)
29 **FOX JOURNEY,** gr c Roaring Lion (USA)—Follow A Star (IRE)
30 **GENTLE LIGHT,** ch f Frankel—Light Music
31 **HIGH FASHION (IRE),** b f Siyouni (FR)—Fashion Family (FR)
32 B f Lope de Vega (IRE)—Highlands Queen (FR)
33 **HOSANNA POWER (IRE),** ch c Frankel—Belle Josephine
34 **HUMANKIND (IRE),** b f Frankel—Ama (USA)
35 **INFINITE COSMOS (IRE),** ch f Sea The Stars (IRE)—Waila
36 **LET LIFE HAPPEN,** b f Siyouni (FR)—Transhumance (IRE)

SIR MICHAEL STOUTE - continued

37 **LIABLE,** b c Frankel—Responsible
38 **LONG AGO,** ch f Roaring Lion (USA)—Let It Be Me (USA)
39 **MARCHING BAND,** b c Ribchester (IRE)—Medley
40 **NADER KING (IRE),** b c Camelot—Coppertop (IRE)
41 **NOSTRUM,** b c Kingman—Mirror Lake
42 **OLIVER SHOW (IRE),** ch c No Nay Never (USA)—Ashley Hall (USA)
43 **PASSENGER (USA),** b c Ulysses (IRE)—Dilmun (USA)
44 **PERFUSE,** ch c Lope de Vega (IRE)—Suffused
45 **PREPENSE,** b f Kingman—Deliberate
46 **PUMALIN PARK (IRE),** b c Exceed And Excel (AUS)—Galileano (IRE)
47 **REGAL FANFARE,** b f Intello (GER)—Regal Realm
48 **RIGHTEOUS,** b f Kingman—Criteria (IRE)
49 **ROUEN,** ch f Intello (GER)—Troarn (FR)
50 **STORMY SEA,** b f Territories (IRE)—Hayyona
51 **WODHOOH (FR),** b f Le Havre (IRE)—Dhan (IRE)
52 **ZAAKARA,** b f Bobby's Kitten (USA)—Kesara
53 **ZARGA (FR),** gr f Camelot—Strawberrydaiquiri

Trainer did not supply details of their two-year-olds.

Owners: The King, Al Shaqab Racing UK Limited, Ballylinch Stud, Mr S. M. Bel Obaida, Cheveley Park Stud Limited, Mr P. E. Done, Exors of the late Sir E. D. Rothschild, Niarchos Family, Flaxman Stables Ireland Ltd, Mrs Denis Haynes, Juddmonte Farms Ltd, King Power Racing Co Ltd, Newsells Park Stud, Mr R. Ng, Qatar Racing Limited, Miss K. Rausing, Mr A. P. Rogers & Mrs S. Rogers - Airlie Stud, Mrs M. Slack, Mr S. Suhail, Team Valor Llc & Gary Barber, Lord W. G. Vestey, J. Wigan.

---

480 MRS ALI STRONGE, Eastbury

Postal: **Castle Piece Racing Stables, Eastbury, Hungerford, Berkshire, RG17 7JR**
Contacts: **PHONE 01488 72818 MOBILE 07779 285205 FAX 01488 670378**
EMAIL office@castlepiecestables.com WEBSITE www.castlepiecestables.com

1 **ARDMAYLE (IRE),** 11, ch g Whitmore's Conn (USA)—Welsh Connection (IRE) **The One and Only Partnership**
2 **ESTRELA STAR (IRE),** 7, ch g Casamento (IRE)—Reem Star **Mrs A. J. Stronge**
3 **JUST JOSH,** 4, b g Nathaniel (IRE)—Joshua's Princess **Spencer-Herbert,Herbert,Simmons&Kidger**
4 **LAKE SAND (IRE),** 6, b g Footstepsinthesand—Lake Louise (IRE) **Mr L. A. Bellman**
5 **MUSICAL MYSTERY,** 4, b g Showcasing—Puzzled Look **G Bishop & A Kirkland**
6 **OUR NOBLE LORD,** 4, ch g Sir Percy—Lady Stardust **Mrs B. V. Evans**
7 **PEERLESS PERCY (IRE),** 6, b g Sir Percy—Victoria Montoya **Friends Of Castle Piece**
8 **RENARDEAU,** 7, b g Foxwedge (AUS)—La Cucina (IRE) **Mr L. A. Bellman**
9 **SKY STORM,** 6, ch m Night of Thunder (IRE)—Dinvar Diva **Mrs A. J. Stronge**
10 **STORM MELODY,** 10, b g Royal Applause—Plume **Shaw Racing Partnership 2 & Ali Stronge**
11 **SUNSETS DREAMERS (IRE),** 4, b f Awtaad (IRE)—Oasis Sunset (IRE) **Shaw Racing Partnership 2 & Ali Stronge**
12 **VALEGRO (IRE),** 4, b g Highland Reel (IRE)—Promise Me (IRE) **Kings Of The Castle**
13 **YORKTOWN (IRE),** 6, b g Free Eagle (IRE)—Bryanstown (IRE) **C Spencer-Herbert, M Herbert & L Bellman**

THREE-YEAR-OLDS

14 **ANGEL OF ANTRIM (IRE),** b g Dark Angel (IRE)—Todegica **G Bishop & A Kirkland**
15 **FANTASTIC ARTIST (IRE),** b g Zoffany (IRE)—Fantastic Account **Friends Of Castle Piece**
16 B f Gregorian (IRE)—Greenery (IRE)
17 Ch g Mondialiste (IRE)—Just Jealous (IRE)
18 B g Churchill (IRE)—Rose of Africa (IRE) **Mr G. S. Bishop**

Assistant Trainer: Sam Stronge.

481 MRS LINDA STUBBS, Malton

Postal: **Beverley House Stables, Beverley Road, Malton, North Yorkshire, YO17 9PJ**
Contacts: **HOME 01653 698731 MOBILE 07801 167707**
EMAIL l.stubbs@btconnect.com

1 **CAREY STREET (IRE),** 7, b g Bungle Inthejungle—Undulant Way **Mr P. G. Shorrock, P.G.Shorrock & L.Stubbs, Mrs L. Stubbs**
2 **FINAL ACCOUNT,** 4, b g Adaay (IRE)—Vitta's Touch (USA) **Verona Racing**
3 **OLD NEWS,** 6, b g Dutch Art—Queen's Charter **Mr P. G. Shorrock**

---

482 MR ROB SUMMERS, Solihull

Postal: **Summerhill Cottage, Danzey Green, Tanworth-in-Arden, Solihull**
Contacts: **PHONE 01564 742667 MOBILE 07775 898327**

1 **ATLANTIC STORM (IRE),** 11, b g September Storm (GER)—Double Dream (IRE) **Mr A. R. Price**
2 **LONIMOSS BARELIERE (FR),** 7, b g Palamoss (IRE)—Lonia Blue (FR) **Mr C. Hayes**
3 **PECKINPAH (IRE),** 7, ch g Excelebration (IRE)—Melodrama (IRE) **Mr P. Waldron**
4 **RED ROLY,** 7, b g Native Ruler—Photogenique (FR) **Mrs G. M. Summers**
5 **SECRET MOSS,** 8, ch m Schiaparelli (GER)—Secret Whisper **Mrs G. M. Summers**
6 **TREMWEDGE,** 7, b g Foxwedge (AUS)—Tremelo Pointe (IRE) **Mr S. Wood**

Assistant Trainer: Mrs G. M. Summers.

---

483 MR TOM SYMONDS, Hentland

Postal: **Dason Court Cottage, Hentland, Ross-On-Wye, Herefordshire, HR9 6LW**
Contacts: **PHONE 01989 730869 MOBILE 07823 324649**
EMAIL dasoncourt@gmail.com WEBSITE www.thomassymonds.co.uk

1 **AH WHISHT (IRE),** 6, b m Getaway (GER)—Listening (IRE) **Dahlbury Racing**
2 **BOBO MAC (IRE),** 12, gr g Whitmore's Conn (USA)—Blazing Love (IRE) **C & M Baker, K Ibberson, H Pearman**
3 **CITIZEN JANE,** 4, b f Scorpion (IRE)—Janes Boutique (IRE) **Dahlbury Racing**
4 **COBRA COMMANDER (IRE),** 9, b g Beneficial—Run For Help (IRE) **Dean, Willetts & Vernon**
5 **DAMASK (FR),** 4, b f Walzertakt (GER)—Lyric Melody (FR) **Dahlbury Racing & Chapel Stud Ltd**
6 **FIRST VENTURE (IRE),** 5, b m Soldier of Fortune (IRE)—Be My Gesture (IRE) **Dahlbury Racing**
7 **GAYE LEGACY (IRE),** 5, b m Flemensfirth (USA)—Gaye Memories **Chase The Dream And Mrs R F Knipe**
8 **HIDOR DE BERSY (FR),** 6, ch g Nidor (FR)—Tropulka God (FR) **The Hon Lady Gibbings**
9 **HYSTERY BERE (FR),** 6, b g Pedro The Great (USA)—Mysteryonthebounty (USA) **The Hon Lady Gibbings**
10 **IRRESISTABLE (POL),** 5, ch m Silvaner (GER)—Irkucja (POL) **Dahlbury Racing**
11 **ISSAM (FR),** 5, b g Nicaron (GER)—Venus de Re (FR) **The Hon Lady Gibbings**
12 **KELLAHEN (GER),** 6, b g Wiesenpfad (FR)—Kurfurstin (GER) **Gun Dog Gin Limited**
13 **LADY BERLAIS,** 5, b m Clovis du Berlais (FR)—Lady of Llanarmon **The Nigel Jones & Roy Ovel Syndicate**
14 **LEGENDARY RHYTHM,** 7, b m Midnight Legend—Hot Rhythm **David Clark & Partner**
15 **LIBERTARIAN ROYALE (IRE),** 5, b m Libertarian—Sheestown (IRE) **The Nigel Jones & Roy Ovel Syndicate**
16 **LLANDINABO LAD,** 8, ch g Malinas (GER)—Hot Rhythm **Celia & Michael Baker**
17 **LOUD AS LIONS (IRE),** 10, b g Flemensfirth (USA)—Misspublican (IRE) **C & M Baker, K Ibberson, H Pearman**
18 **LUNA DORA,** 6, gr m Pether's Moon (IRE)—Ixora (IRE) **Chase the Dream - Luna Dora**
19 **MARTA DES MOTTES (FR),** 6, b m Montmartre (FR)—Oktavia des Mottes (FR) **Dahlbury Racing**
20 **MISTER BARCLAY,** 5, b g Nathaniel (IRE)—Singapore Harbour (IRE) **C & M Baker, K Ibberson, H Pearman**
21 **MOLLY HASTINGS,** 4, b f Clovis du Berlais (FR)—Catherines Well **Mr J. Palmer-Brown**
22 **MORIKO DE VASSY (FR),** 6, b g Cokoriko (FR)—Mona Vassy (FR) **Amis de Vassy**
23 **NAVAJO INDY,** 4, b g Nathaniel (IRE)—Navajo Charm **C & M Baker, K Ibberson, H Pearman**
24 **NIGHT JET,** 6, b g Telescope (IRE)—Midnight Belle **Mrs P. E. Holtorp**
25 **RHIAN DE SIVOLA,** 7, b m Kayf Tara—R de Rien Sivola (FR) **Mr S. Davies**
26 **ROYALE MARGAUX (FR),** 5, ch m Doctor Dino (FR)—Royale Cazoumaille (FR) **Dahlbury Racing**
27 **SANTA CLARITA (FR),** 5, gr m Walzertakt (GER)—New Delice (FR) **Dahlbury Racing**

MR TOM SYMONDS - continued

28 **STRIKE MIDNIGHT,** 5, b g Telescope (IRE)—Midnight Belle **Mrs P. E. Holtorp**
29 **THE WINSLOW BOY,** 4, b g Dartmouth—Mizzurka **Golden Cap**

THREE-YEAR-OLDS

30 **GOLD FOR ALEC (FR),** ch g Planteur (IRE)—Gold For Tina (FR) **Dahlbury Racing**
31 **QUINN'S REWARD (GER),** b g Maxios—Quirigua **The Hon Lady Gibbings**

---

484 MR JAMES TATE, Newmarket

Postal: **Jamesfield Place, Hamilton Road, Newmarket, Suffolk, CB8 7JQ**
Contacts: **PHONE 01638 669861 MOBILE 07703 601283**
EMAIL james@jamestateracing.com WEBSITE www.jamestateracing.com

1 **COOL LIGHTNING (IRE),** 4, b f Exceed And Excel (AUS)—Cool Thunder (IRE) **Sheikh J. D. Al Maktoum**
2 **DIVINE RAPTURE,** 4, gr f Dark Angel (IRE)—Titivation **S. Manana**
3 **HIGH VELOCITY (IRE),** 4, gr c Gutaifan (IRE)—Reflect Alexander (IRE) **S. Manana**
4 **MOUNT ATHOS,** 4, b c Dark Angel (IRE)—Ceaseless (IRE) **Sheikh R. D. Al Maktoum**
5 **ROYAL ACLAIM (IRE),** 4, b f Aclaim (IRE)—Knock Stars (IRE) **Sheikh J. D. Al Maktoum**
6 **SHADES OF SUMMER (IRE),** 4, b f Shamardal (USA)—Jira **S. Manana**
7 **WAIT TO EXCEL,** 4, b c Postponed (IRE)—Al Baidaa **S. Ali**

THREE-YEAR-OLDS

8 **ACLAIMED ART (IRE),** b br c Aclaim (IRE)—Aloisi **Sheikh J. D. Al Maktoum**
9 **ALWAYS TOMORROW (IRE),** b c Unfortunately (IRE)—Maybe Tomorrow **S. Manana**
10 Ch f Night of Thunder (IRE)—Ancestral **S. Manana**
11 **BEHIND THE SCENES (IRE),** ch f Saxon Warrior (JPN)—Doors To Manual (USA) **S. Manana**
12 Ch c Dawn Approach (IRE)—Dorraar (IRE) **Mr H. Dalmook Al Maktoum**
13 **DREAM CHOICE,** b f Dubawi (IRE)—Prefer (IRE) **S. Manana**
14 **DUBAI HARBOUR,** b c Invincible Spirit (IRE)—Asanta Sana (IRE) **S. Manana**
15 **ENDLESS POWER,** b c Fastnet Rock (AUS)—Heaven's Angel (IRE) **S. Manana**
16 **FLAME SPIRIT (IRE),** ch c Iffraaj—Spirit of Cuba (IRE) **S. Manana**
17 **FLYING FRONTIER,** b c Farhh—Alaia (IRE) **S. Manana**
18 B f Night of Thunder (IRE)—Hokkaido **S. Manana**
19 **ICONIC MOMENT (IRE),** b c Harry Angel (IRE)—Purplest **S. Ali**
20 **IMAGINARY WORLD (IRE),** ch c Shamardal (USA)—Galactic Heroine **S. Manana**
21 **LOVE ANGEL,** ch f Farhh—Heartsease **James Tate Racing Limited**
22 **MAJESTIC WARRIOR (IRE),** ch c Churchill (IRE)—Zam Zoom (IRE) **S. Manana**
23 **MIGHTY RIVER (IRE),** b c Siyouni (FR)—Coral Garden **S. Manana**
24 **NEW DEFINITION,** b c Invincible Spirit (IRE)—Second Generation **Sheikh R. D. Al Maktoum**
25 **OPENING SHOW,** br c Showcasing—Regal Hawk **S. Manana**
26 **POPULAR DREAM,** b c Oasis Dream—Populist (IRE) **S. Manana**
27 **REGAL EMPIRE (IRE),** ch c Farhh—Saltanat (IRE) **S. Manana**
28 Ch f Night of Thunder (IRE)—Rekindle **S. Manana**
29 B f Storm The Stars (USA)—Reroute (IRE) **Sheikh R. D. Al Maktoum**
30 **SEA LORD (FR),** b c Le Havre (IRE)—Gold Sands (IRE) **S. Manana**
31 Ch f Frankel—Shepherdia (IRE) **S. Manana**
32 **SOVEREIGN KING,** b c Shamardal (USA)—Lamar (IRE) **S. Ali**
33 **SPEED DIAL BAILEYS,** ch f Harry Angel (IRE)—Ring For Baileys **G R Bailey Ltd (Baileys Horse Feeds)**
34 **THINK FIRST (IRE),** b c Kessaar (IRE)—Willow Beck **S. Ali**
35 **TOUGH ENOUGH,** b c Showcasing—Puzzled Look **Sheikh J. D. Al Maktoum**
36 B f Storm The Stars (USA)—Umneyati **Sheikh R. D. Al Maktoum**
37 **UNITED APPROACH (IRE),** b c Fastnet Rock (AUS)—Bright Approach (IRE) **S. Manana**

TWO-YEAR-OLDS

38 B c 17/03 Blue Point (IRE)—Al Fareej (IRE) (Iffraaj) **S. Ali**

MR JAMES TATE - continued

39 Ch f 13/02 Bated Breath—Always Gold (New Approach (IRE)) (18000) **S. Manana**
40 B c 06/04 Bobby's Kitten (USA)—Belvoir Diva (Exceed And Excel (AUS)) (35000) **S. Manana**
41 B f 16/02 Storm The Stars (USA)—Blhadawa (IRE) (Iffraaj) **Sheikh J. D. Al Maktoum**
42 Ch c 24/03 Masar (IRE)—Carlanda (FR) (Lando (GER)) (8000) **Houghton Bloodstock**
43 Ch c 08/04 Masar (IRE)—Cartimandua (Medicean) (27000) **S. Manana**
44 B f 05/03 Invincible Army (IRE)—Coral Garden (Halling (USA)) (65000) **S. Manana**
45 B c 08/02 Land Force (IRE)—Delevigne (Redoute's Choice (AUS)) (55000) **S. Manana**
46 B f 22/02 New Approach (IRE)—Dubawi Meeznah (IRE) (Dubawi (IRE)) **S. Ali**
47 B f 21/03 Masar (IRE)—Dubka (Dubawi (IRE)) (45000) **S. Ali**
48 B c 27/04 Farhh—Dulcet (IRE) (Halling (USA)) **Mr H. Dalmook Al Maktoum**
49 Gr c 24/02 Oasis Dream—Eastern Destiny (Dubai Destination (USA)) (40000) **S. Manana**
50 B c 17/04 Caravaggio (USA)—El Manati (IRE) (Iffraaj) **Sheikh R. D. Al Maktoum**
51 B f 04/02 Inns of Court (IRE)—Emeriya (USA) (Giant's Causeway (USA)) (35000) **S. Manana**
52 B c 06/02 Expert Eye—Fair Dubawi (IRE) (Dubawi (IRE)) (55000) **S. Manana**
53 B f 01/03 Invincible Army (IRE)—Forever In Love (Dutch Art) **James Tate Racing Limited**
54 B f 07/04 Muhaarar—Furqaan (IRE) (Dark Angel (IRE)) **Mr A Dale**
55 Gr c 26/03 Havana Grey—Ghedi (IRE) (Aussie Rules (USA)) (55000) **S. Manana**
56 B c 29/01 Blue Point (IRE)—Havergate (Dansili) (57000) **S. Manana**
57 B c 23/02 Too Darn Hot—Heaven's Angel (IRE) (Henrythenavigator (USA)) (50000) **S. Manana**
58 B f 03/02 Dark Angel (IRE)—Hidden Steps (Footstepsinthesand) (38000) **Sheikh J. D. Al Maktoum**
59 B c 24/04 Invincible Army (IRE)—Hokkaido (Street Cry (IRE)) (2000) **S. Manana**
60 B c 17/04 Night of Thunder (IRE)—Impala (Oasis Dream) (180000) **S. Manana**
61 Ch c 22/03 Mehmas (IRE)—La Seine (USA) (Rahy (USA)) (25000) **Sheikh J. D. Al Maktoum**
62 B c 17/04 Dandy Man (IRE)—Lady Beware (IRE) (Dragon Pulse (IRE)) (35000) **S. Manana**
63 B f 02/05 Too Darn Hot—Lamar (IRE) (Cape Cross (IRE)) (100000) **S. Ali**
64 B c 30/03 Blue Point (IRE)—Madeline (IRE) (Kodiac) (45000) **S. Manana**
65 B c 07/04 Invincible Spirit (IRE)—Making Memories (IRE) (New Approach (IRE)) **Sheikh J. D. Al Maktoum**
66 B f 05/02 Invincible Army (IRE)—Manyatta (IRE) (Iffraaj) (42857) **S. Manana**
67 B c 10/01 Inns of Court (IRE)—Mild Illusion (IRE) (Requinto (IRE)) (27000) **S. Manana**
68 B c 30/03 Invincible Army (IRE)—Muluk (IRE) (Rainbow Quest (USA)) (40000) **S. Manana**
69 Ch f 24/02 Masar (IRE)—Murasaki (Dubawi (IRE)) (22000) **S. Manana**
70 Gr c 30/04 Dark Angel (IRE)—My Favourite Thing (Oasis Dream) (45000) **S. Manana**
71 Ch f 13/03 Ulysses (IRE)—Oasis Mirage (Oasis Dream) (20000) **S. Manana**
72 B c 23/02 Shamardal (USA)—October Queen (IRE) (Iffraaj) **Sheikh R. D. Al Maktoum**
73 B f 13/04 Territories (IRE)—Persepone (Dubawi (IRE)) (45000) **S. Manana**
74 B f 21/04 Invincible Army (IRE)—Purple Tiger (IRE) (Rainbow Quest (USA)) **S. Ali**
75 B f 03/03 Too Darn Hot—Queen of The Stars (Sea The Stars (IRE)) **S. Ali**
76 B c 03/02 Study of Man (IRE)—Quintada (Leroidesanimaux (BRZ)) (58000) **S. Manana**
77 B c 28/04 Farhh—Reroute (IRE) (Acclamation) **Sheikh R. D. Al Maktoum**
78 B br c 15/04 Blue Point (IRE)—Riskit Fora Biskit (IRE) (Kodiac) (71429) **S. Ali**
79 Ch c 30/01 Kitten's Joy (USA)—Sea of Snow (USA) (Distorted Humor (USA)) **Sheikh J. D. Al Maktoum**
80 B c 01/02 Kodiac—Smile Ahead (IRE) (Dream Ahead (USA)) (48000) **S. Manana**
81 **STANLEY SPENCER (IRE),** b c 30/03 Iffraaj—Marsh Hawk (Invincible Spirit (IRE)) (47619) **Mr A. G. D. Hogarth**
82 B c 21/04 Exceed And Excel (AUS)—Sunset Avenue (USA) (Street Cry (IRE)) **S. Ali**
83 **SURVIVALIST (IRE),** b c 16/04 Invincible Army (IRE)—
Peak Princess (IRE) (Foxwedge (AUS)) (37000) **Mr A. G. D. Hogarth**
84 Ch c 06/02 Saxon Warrior (JPN)—Swift Campaign (IRE) (Intikhab (USA)) **Sheikh J. D. Al Maktoum**
85 B f 15/01 Kodiac—Taliyna (IRE) (Dawn Approach (IRE)) (52381) **Sheikh J. D. Al Maktoum**
86 B f 16/04 Ardad (IRE)—Totally Lost (IRE) (Rip Van Winkle (IRE)) (58000) **S. Manana**
87 B f 10/04 Iffraaj—Utterly Charming (IRE) (Dandy Man (IRE)) (42000) **S. Manana**
88 B c 09/04 Kodiac—Veiled Intrigue (Pastoral Pursuits) (50000) **S. Manana**
89 B c 28/04 Invincible Army (IRE)—Wojha (IRE) (Pivotal) (85000) **S. Manana**
90 B f 12/04 Masar (IRE)—Zacheta (Polish Precedent (USA)) **S. Ali**

Assistant Trainer: Mrs Lucinda Tate.

485 MR TOM TATE, Tadcaster

Postal: **Castle Farm, Hazelwood, Tadcaster, North Yorkshire, LS24 9NJ**
Contacts: **PHONE 01937 836036 MOBILE 07970 122818**
EMAIL tomptate@zen.co.uk WEBSITE www.tomtate.co.uk

1 **BAYRAAT,** 7, b g Heeraat (IRE)—Baymist **T T Racing**
2 **BRUNELLO BREEZE,** 4, b g Bated Breath—Calima Breeze **T T Racing**
3 **EQUIANO SPRINGS,** 9, b g Equiano (FR)—Spring Clean (FR) **T T Racing**
4 **FREEWHEELIN,** 5, b g Poet's Voice—Certral **T T Racing**
5 **THUNDER GAP,** 6, b g Night of Thunder (IRE)—Regal Hawk **T T Racing**

THREE-YEAR-OLDS

6 **CANDY EYE,** b f Expert Eye—Sugar Free (IRE) **T T Racing**
7 **HAVE YOU A MINUTE,** b g Muhaarar—One Second **T T Racing**
8 **TIGER TRAP,** b g Massaat (IRE)—Blades Princess **T T Racing**

TWO-YEAR-OLDS

9 B c 29/03 Cable Bay (IRE)—Esteemable (Nayef (USA)) (12381)
10 B f 18/02 Tasleet—Mookhlesa (Marju (IRE)) (12381)

Assistant Trainer: Hazel Tate.

Flat Jockey: Billy Garrity, Tom Queally.

---

486 MRS PHILLIPPA TAYLOR, Fringford

Postal: **Waterloo Farm, Fringford, Bicester, Oxfordshire, OX27 8RH**
Contacts: **PHONE 01869 277241**
EMAIL phillippa.taylor@btconnect.com

1 **ELMDALE (FR),** 9, gr g Martaline—Victoire Jaguine (FR) **Mrs P. Taylor**
2 **GUTTURAL (IRE),** 9, b g Gold Well—Our Fair Lady (IRE) **Mrs P. Taylor**
3 **IDEE DE GARDE (FR),** 10, b g Kapgarde (FR)—Idee Recue (FR) **Mrs P. Taylor**
4 **MADRA MORJOHN,** 5, b g Black Sam Bellamy (IRE)—Overlay **Mrs P. Taylor**
5 **ULTRA VIERS (IRE),** 7, b g Fame And Glory—Endless Moments (IRE) **Mrs P. Taylor**

---

487 MR COLIN TEAGUE, Wingate

Postal: **Bridgefield Farm, Trimdon Lane, Station Town, Wingate, County Durham, TS28 5NE**
Contacts: **PHONE 01429 837087 MOBILE 07967 330929**
EMAIL colin.teague@btopenworld.com

1 **BRAZEN BELLE,** 5, b m Brazen Beau (AUS)—Pepper Lane **Collins Chauffeur Driven Executive Cars**
2 **COWBOY SOLDIER (IRE),** 8, b g Kodiac—Urgele (FR) **Collins Chauffeur Driven Executive Cars**
3 **INGLEBY COMMAND,** 6, b g War Command (USA)—Mistress Twister **Collins Chauffeur Driven Executive Cars**
4 **KOROPICK (IRE),** 9, b g Kodiac—Kathoe (IRE) **Mr A. Rice**
5 **LOLA REBEL (IRE),** 5, b m Dandy Man (IRE)—Copperbeech (IRE) **Collins Chauffeur Driven Executive Cars**
6 **TAAMER,** 6, ch m Tamayuz—Abhajat (IRE) **Mr A. Rice**

488 MR ROGER TEAL, Hungerford

Postal: **Windsor House Stables, Crowle Road, Lambourn, Hungerford, Berkshire, RG17 8NR**
Contacts: **PHONE 01488 491623 MOBILE 07710 325521**
EMAIL info@rogertealracing.com WEBSITE www.rogertealracing.co.uk

1 **ALCAZAN,** 5, b m Al Kazeem—Glorious Dreams (USA) **Mr J. O'Donnell**
2 **BEAR FORCE ONE,** 7, b g Swiss Spirit—Shesha Bear **Joe Bear Racing**
3 **BICKERSTAFFE,** 5, b h Mayson—Ocean Boulevard **Mr D. W. Armstrong**
4 **BLACKROD,** 5, b h Mayson—Hilldale **Mr D. W. Armstrong**
5 **BLAZEON FIVE,** 5, b m Indian Haven—Precision Five **Calne Engineering Ltd**
6 **CHIPSTEAD,** 5, b h Mayson—Charlotte Rosina **Homecroft, Crampsie & Sullivan**
7 **CINZENTO (IRE),** 7, gr g Lawman (FR)—Silver Samba **Mr R. A. Teal**
8 **CIVIL LAW (IRE),** 6, gr g Dark Angel (IRE)—Tribune (FR) **D Bassom & P Cardosi**
9 **DAKOTA POWER,** 4, b g Aclaim (IRE)—Vivid Blue **Dakota Racing**
10 **DANCING HARRY (IRE),** 6, b g Camelot—Poisson d'Or **Fishdance Ltd**
11 **DANCING REEL (IRE),** 4, b c Highland Reel (IRE)—Poisson d'Or **Fishdance Ltd**
12 **DICKTATE,** 4, b g Lawman (FR)—Gakku **Mr R. A. Teal**
13 **EVERBEST ST GEORGE,** 5, ch g Steele Tango (USA)—Villarrica Lady **Mr Steve Robinson & Miss Heather Best**
14 **GERT LUSH (IRE),** 6, b m Bated Breath—Agent Allison **Mrs Muriel Forward & Dr G C Forward**
15 **GUGUSS COLLONGES (FR),** 7, b g Secret Singer (FR)—
Une Collonges (FR) **Mr David Gilmour & Mr James Dellaway**
16 **GURKHA GIRL (IRE),** 5, b m The Gurkha (IRE)—Freddie's Girl (USA) **Mrs A. Cowley**
17 **KAMAXOS (FR),** 6, b g Maxios—Kamellata (FR) **Mr A. J. Edwards**
18 **KENZAI WARRIOR (USA),** 6, b br g Karakontie (JPN)—Lemon Sakhee (CAN) **Rae & Carol Borras**
19 **KNOWWHENTORUN,** 5, b g Mayson—Josefa Goya **Homecroft Wealth Racing**
20 **MARION'S BOY (IRE),** 6, ch g Mastercraftsman (IRE)—Freddie's Girl (USA) **Mrs A. Cowley**
21 **MASTER SULLY,** 5, ch g Coach House (IRE)—Dawn Catcher **Mayden Stud**
22 **MICKS DREAM,** 5, b g Adaay (IRE)—Malelane (IRE) **Bhatti Brothers**
23 **MUMINAMILLION (IRE),** 4, ch f Galileo Gold—Lady Dettoria (FR) **Rockingham Reins Limited**
24 **MY MATE TED (IRE),** 4, gr c Caravaggio (USA)—Pop Art (IRE) **Mr A. Whelan**
25 **NEVER IN FOURTH,** 4, ch g Coach House (IRE)—Bengers Lass (USA) **Mrs Muriel Forward & Dr G C Forward**
26 **OCEAN WIND,** 7, b h Teofilo (IRE)—Chan Tong (BRZ) **Rockingham Reins Limited**
27 **OUR BOY BUDDY,** 4, b g Coach House (IRE)—Rose Garnet (IRE) **J. A. Dewhurst**
28 **OXTED,** 7, b g Mayson—Charlotte Rosina **S Piper,T.Hirschfeld,D.Fish & J.Collins**
29 **PERFECT LESCRIBAA (FR),** 5, b m Rajsaman (FR)—Mia Lescribaa (FR) **DFA Racing & Value Rater Ltd**
30 **SILENCE IS GOLDEN,** 4, b f Golden Horn—Mia Diletta **A D Spence, A J Pearson & M B Spence**
31 **SILVERSCAPE,** 4, gr g Cityscape—Miss Minuty **Miss J. S. Dorey**
32 **SISTERS IN THE SKY,** 4, ch g Showcasing—Sunny York (IRE) **Mr David Gilmour & Mr James Dellaway**
33 **SPIRIT OF CAHALA,** 4, b g Swiss Spirit—Cahala Dancer (IRE) **Gunshot Paddocks Racing Club**
34 **SWISS PRIDE (IRE),** 7, b g Swiss Spirit—Encore Encore (FR) **Idle B's & Sue Teal**
35 **WHATS IN THE BAG (IRE),** 4, b g Dark Angel (IRE)—Kathoe (IRE) **Teme Valley**
36 **WHENTHEDEALINSDONE,** 5, b g Dark Angel (IRE)—Maureen (IRE) **Mr A. Whelan**

THREE-YEAR-OLDS

37 **ANGELIC DIVAS (IRE),** b f Ardad (IRE)—Low Cut Affair (IRE) **Mr David Gilmour & Mr James Dellaway**
38 **CARAGIO (IRE),** b g Caravaggio (USA)—Freddie's Girl (USA) **Mrs A. Cowley**
39 **DANCING MAGIC (IRE),** b c Camelot—Poisson d'Or **Fishdance Ltd**
40 **DAVE'LL DO,** b f Adaay (IRE)—Kristollini **Red Hot Partnership**
41 **DECISIVE CALL (IRE),** b c Footstepsinthesand—Tarfshi **Mr B. S. Chatwal**
42 **ELLEXIS (IRE),** b f Expert Eye—Three D Alexander (IRE) **Mr T. J. Smith**
43 **FRANKFREYA,** b c Cracksman—Posteritas (USA) **Mr M. J. Goggin**
44 **MIDSUMMER MUSIC (IRE),** b f Mendelssohn (USA)—Nabat Seif (USA) **Rae & Carol Borras**
45 **MISS DOLLY ROCKER,** b f Frontiersman—Miss Minuty **Miss J. S. Dorey**
46 **PHOTON (IRE),** b c Shalaa (IRE)—Alexander Queen (IRE) **Homecroft Wealth Racing**
47 **THATS DANDY HARRY (IRE),** b c Dandy Man (IRE)—
Fancy Feathers (IRE) **Mr David Gilmour & Mr James Dellaway**
48 **THE CRAFTYMASTER,** ch g Master Carpenter (IRE)—With Distinction **Mr S. Barton**

MR ROGER TEAL - continued

TWO-YEAR-OLDS

49 **BUILTINABILITY,** b f 02/04 Time Test—
Westwiththenight (IRE) (Cape Cross (IRE)) (18000) **Mr David Gilmour & Mr James Dellaway**
50 **CALVERT,** b c 21/03 Golden Horn—Criteria (IRE) (Galileo (IRE)) (22000) **Mrs H. I. Jinks**
51 **CHERRYBLOSSOM TIME (IRE),** b f 22/02 Kuroshio (AUS)—The Shrew (Dansili) (28000) **Norman Court Stud**
52 **HIYA HONEY (IRE),** b f 27/04 Dark Angel (IRE)—Pixeleen (Pastoral Pursuits) (105000) **Mr A. Whelan**
53 **MAMORA BAY,** b f 01/04 Time Test—
Keep The Moon (Rock of Gibraltar (IRE)) (22000) **The Antiguan Family Syndicate**
54 B f 23/05 Havana Grey—Oulianovsk (IRE) (Peintre Celebre (USA)) **The Hon R. T. A. Goff**
55 **ROSARIO (IRE),** ch c 20/04 Harry Angel (IRE)—City Glam (ARG) (Grand Reward (USA)) (20000) **Mrs S. M. Teal**
56 **SOLAR POWER,** b c 06/04 Exceed And Excel (AUS)—
Vereri Senes (Nayef (USA)) (50000) **Mr David Gilmour & Mr James Dellaway**
57 **ULTIMATE SHADOW (IRE),** br c 14/03 U S Navy Flag (USA)—
Cork Harbour (IRE) (Harbour Watch (IRE)) (32000) **Mr R. Hernandez**
58 **VORDERMAN,** b c 02/02 Study of Man (IRE)—Nadia Promise (Galileo (IRE)) (34000) **Homecroft Wealth Racing**

Assistant Trainer: Harry Teal.

---

489 MR SAM THOMAS, Cardiff

Postal: **Crossways, St Mellons Road, Lisvane, Cardiff, South Glamorgan, CF14 0SH**
Contacts: **PHONE 07929 101751**
EMAIL samthomasracing@outlook.com, emma@samthomasracing.com WEBSITE www.samthomasracing.com

1 **AL DANCER (FR),** 10, gr g Al Namix (FR)—Steel Dancer (FR) **Walters Plant Hire Ltd**
2 **ALFIE'S PRINCESS (IRE),** 6, b br m Shirocco (GER)—Dunahall Queen (IRE) **Walters Plant Hire & Potter Group**
3 **AMAZING TANGO (GER),** 6, b g Tai Chi (GER)—Amazing Model (GER) **Walters Plant Hire Ltd**
4 **ANGELS BREATH (IRE),** 9, gr g Shantou (USA)—Mystic Masie (IRE) **Walters Plant Hire & Ronnie Bartlett**
5 5, B m Norse Dancer (IRE)—Another Kate (IRE) **Mr S. J. Thomas**
6 **ARWENA,** 6, b m Telescope (IRE)—Precious Lady **Diamond Racing Ltd**
7 **BALLYBEEN (IRE),** 7, ch g Presenting—Dotchenka (FR) **Lightfoot, Mussell-Evans, Peart**
8 **BEFORE MIDNIGHT,** 10, ch g Midnight Legend—Lady Samantha **Walters Plant Hire & Potter Group**
9 **CANYOUSEEME,** 5, b m Universal (IRE)—Haidees Reflection **Mr S. J. Thomas**
10 **CELTIC DINO (FR),** 4, ch g Doctor Dino (FR)—Bal Celtique (FR) **Walters Plant Hire Ltd**
11 **DEERE MARK,** 6, b g Pether's Moon (IRE)—Henri Bella **Walters Plant Hire Ltd**
12 **DIAMOND MONARCH (IRE),** 6, b g Imperial Monarch (IRE)—Otorum (IRE) **Diamond Racing Ltd**
13 **ED KEEPER (FR),** 5, b g Hunter's Light (IRE)—Charbelle (FR) **Walters Plant Hire Ltd**
14 **GALILEO SILVER (IRE),** 8, gr g Galileo (IRE)—Famous (IRE) **Walters Plant Hire & Potter Group**
15 **GOOD RISK AT ALL (FR),** 7, ch g No Risk At All (FR)—Sissi Land (FR) **Walters Plant Hire Ltd**
16 **GREY DIAMOND (FR),** 9, b g Gris de Gris (IRE)—Diamond of Diana (FR) **Walters Plant Hire Ltd**
17 4, B f Passing Glance—Haidees Reflection **Mr S. J. Thomas**
18 **HURRICANE DEAL (FR),** 6, gr g Hurricane Cat (USA)—Diluvienne (FR) **Walters Plant Hire Ltd**
19 **INTEL DES BRUYERES (FR),** 5, b g Spanish Moon (USA)—Innsbruck (FR) **Walters Plant Hire Ltd**
20 **IWILLDOIT,** 10, b g Flying Legend (USA)—Lyricist's Dream **Diamond Racing Ltd**
21 **JAZZ KING (FR),** 7, gr g Kapgarde (FR)—Jaragua (FR) **Walters Plant Hire Ltd**
22 **JUBILEE EXPRESS (FR),** 6, b g No Risk At All (FR)—Bella Lawena (IRE) **Walters Plant Hire Ltd**
23 **JUST NO RISK (FR),** 7, ch g No Risk At All (FR)—Just Divine (FR) **Walters Plant,Spiers&Hartwell,Egan Waste**
24 **JUST OVER LAND (FR),** 4, ch g No Risk At All (FR)—Sissi Land (FR) **Walters Plant Hire & Spiers & Hartwell**
25 **KATATE DORI (FR),** 5, b g Bathyrhon (GER)—Vavea (FR) **Walters Plant Hire Ltd**
26 **LUMP SUM (FR),** 5, b g Authorized (IRE)—Fleur Enchantee (FR) **Walters Plant Hire Ltd**
27 **MARIO DE PAIL (FR),** 8, gr g Blue Bresil (FR)—Sauveterre (FR) **Walters Plant Hire & Potter Group**
28 **MASTER AUSTRALIA (IRE),** 4, b g Australia—Mohican Princess **Walters Plant Hire Ltd**
29 **MIND SUNDAY (FR),** 7, gr m Never On Sunday (FR)—Mind Master (USA) **Walters Plant Hire Ltd**
30 **MOT A MOT (FR),** 7, gr g Martaline—Gaily Zest (USA) **Walters Plant Hire & Potter Group**
31 4, B g Walk In The Park (IRE)—Norabelle (FR) **Walters Plant Hire Ltd**

MR SAM THOMAS - continued

32 **OUR POWER (IRE),** 8, b g Power—Scripture (IRE) **Walters Plant Hire & Potter Group**
33 **PADDYS MOTORBIKE (IRE),** 11, ch g Fast Company (IRE)—
Saffa Garden (IRE) **Walters Plant Hire Ltd Egan Waste Ltd**
34 **PALACIO (FR),** 5, b g Khalkevi (IRE)—Belle Yepa (FR) **Walters Plant Hire Ltd**
35 **POWERSTOWN PARK (IRE),** 10, b g Craigsteel—Smiths Lady (IRE) **The Ipsden Invincibles**
36 **PRESENT FOR ME,** 5, b g Pour Moi (IRE)—Gales Present (IRE) **James and Jean Potter Ltd**
37 **PRINCE DES FICHAUX (FR),** 6, b g No Risk At All (FR)—Princesse Kap (FR) **Walters Plant Hire Ltd**
38 **RANGE (IRE),** 6, b g Shantou (USA)—Grapevine Sally (IRE) **Walters Plant Hire & Potter Group**
39 **ROCKING MAN (FR),** 4, b c Manatee—Rockburn (FR) **Walters Plant Hire Ltd**
40 **ROYAL MAGIC (IRE),** 11, b g Whitmore's Conn (USA)—Room To Room Magic (IRE) **Sam Thomas Racing Club**
41 **SHOMEN UCHI (FR),** 6, b g Great Pretender (IRE)—Vavea (FR) **Walters Plant Hire Ltd**
42 **SKYTASTIC (FR),** 7, b g Way of Light (USA)—Verzasca (IRE) **Walters Plant Hire Ltd**
43 **SLIP ROAD (IRE),** 8, gr g Shantou (USA)—Agladora (FR) **Walters Plant Hire Ltd**
44 **SPONTHUS (FR),** 8, b g Alianthus (GER)—Pavane du Kalon (FR) **Walters Plant Hire Ltd**
45 **STEEL ALLY (FR),** 5, b g Doctor Dino (FR)—Poprock du Berlais (FR) **Walters Plant Hire Ltd**
46 **STOLEN SILVER (FR),** 8, gr g Lord du Sud (FR)—Change Partner (FR) **Walters Plant Hire & Potter Group**
47 **SWEDISHHORSEMAFIA (IRE),** 8, b g Shantou (USA)—Carrigmoorna Style (IRE) **Mr S. J. Thomas**
48 **THANK YOU BLUE,** 6, b g Blue Bresil (FR)—Tara Potter **Walters Plant Hire Ltd**
49 **TZARMIX (FR),** 5, ch g Gemix (FR)—Tzarine de La Mone (FR) **Walters Plant Hire Ltd**
50 **VINCENZO (FR),** 5, b g Doctor Dino (FR)—Sweet Nano (FR) **Walters Plant Hire Ltd**
51 **WE DONE IT (FR),** 5, gr g Montmartre (FR)—Glicine (GER) **Walters Plant Hire Ltd**
52 **WILLIAM HENRY (IRE),** 13, b g King's Theatre (IRE)—Cincuenta (IRE) **Walters Plant Hire Ltd**

THREE-YEAR-OLDS

53 **C'EST DIFFERENT (FR),** b g Manatee—Narvica Gravelle (FR) **Walters Plant Hire Ltd**
54 **DOCTOR BLUE (FR),** b g Doctor Dino (FR)—Version Originale (FR) **Walters Plant Hire Ltd**
55 **DOCTOR KILDARE (FR),** ch g Doctor Dino (FR)—Lofte Place (FR) **Walters Plant Hire Ltd**
56 **DOCTOR ON CALL (FR),** ch g Doctor Dino (FR)—Tornada (FR) **Walters Plant Hire Ltd**
57 **JUSTALARGEWHISKY (FR),** b g No Risk At All (FR)—Hojacaracois Has (FR) **Walters Plant Hire Ltd**
58 **KOP LAND (FR),** b g Bathyrhon (GER)—Sissi Land (FR) **Walters Plant Hire Ltd**
59 **SHANNON VICTOR (FR),** ch g Doctor Dino (FR)—Shannon Verse (FR) **Walters Plant Hire Ltd**
60 B f Ask—Stowaway Rose (IRE) **Mr S. J. Thomas**

NH Jockey: Charlie Deutsch, Sam Twiston-Davies

---

490 MRS JOANNE THOMASON-MURPHY, Chelmsford

Postal: **Oakview, Leighams Road, Bicknacre, Chelmsford, Essex, CM3 4HF**

1 **AFRICAN SUN (IRE),** 6, b g Teofilo (IRE)—Castle Cross (IRE) **Mrs J. Thomason-Murphy**
2 **BARBAROSA (IRE),** 7, br g Holy Roman Emperor (IRE)—Snow Scene (IRE) **Mrs J. Thomason-Murphy**
3 **BAY BELLE,** 7, b m Major Cadeaux—Belle Boleyn **Mrs J. Thomason-Murphy**
4 **CANDY LOU,** 9, b m Schiaparelli (GER)—Candello **Mrs J. Thomason-Murphy**
5 **DARCYS HILL (IRE),** 8, b m Milan—Royal Nora (IRE) **Mrs J. Thomason-Murphy**
6 **SOLID FUEL,** 5, b g Oasis Dream—Burlesque Star (IRE) **Mrs J. Thomason-Murphy**

---

491 MR DAVID THOMPSON, Darlington

Postal: **South View Racing, Ashley Cottage, South View, Bolam, Darlington, County Durham, DL2 2UP**
Contacts: **PHONE 01388 832658, 01388 835806 MOBILE 07795 161657 FAX 01325 835806**
EMAIL dwthompson61@hotmail.co.uk WEBSITE www.dwthompson.co.uk

1 **BIRDIE BOWERS (IRE),** 6, b g Bungle Inthejungle—Shamiya (IRE) **K. Kirkup**
2 **BLAME THE FARRIER (IRE),** 6, ch g Slade Power (IRE)—Silirisa (FR) **Mr A. J. Livingston**
3 **BUSHMILL BOY,** 9, b g Malinas (GER)—Miss Holly **Mr S. Murray**
4 **CALUM GILHOOLEY (IRE),** 9, br g Kalanisi (IRE)—Honeyed (IRE) **Mr F. B. Hawkins**
5 **COUP DE GOLD (IRE),** 7, br g Maxios—Astroglia (USA) **Mr & Mrs Kirkup & Mrs Anna Kenny**
6 **CUSACK,** 5, b g Heeraat (IRE)—Vera Richardson (IRE) **K. Kirkup**
7 **DANIELSFLYER (IRE),** 9, b g Dandy Man (IRE)—Warm Welcome **Elliott Brothers And Peacock**
8 **DIRCHILL (IRE),** 9, b g Power—Bawaakeer (USA) **Mr S. Murray**
9 **DRAGON ART,** 4, b g Dragon Dancer—Zahara Joy **A. B. Graham**
10 **JOHN KIRKUP,** 8, ch g Assertive—Bikini **Mrs Suzanne Kirkup & Mr Kevin Kirkup**
11 **KHILWAFY,** 7, b g Mukhadram—Almass (IRE) **Northumbria Leisure Ltd,Watson,Flemming**
12 **KHULU,** 7, ch g Burwaaz—Ingenti **D. A. J. Bartlett**
13 **LOSTNFOUND,** 10, b m Midnight Legend—La Cerisaie **Mr S. Murray**
14 **MACTAVISH,** 6, b g Yorgunnabelucky (USA)—On Holiday **Mr F. B. Hawkins**
15 **MARTIN'S BRIG (IRE),** 6, b g Equiano (FR)—Weeza (IRE) **J. A. Moore**
16 **MR STRUTTER (IRE),** 9, ch g Sir Prancealot (IRE)—Khajool (IRE) **Mrs A. Harrison**
17 **MR SUNDOWNER (USA),** 11, b br g Scat Daddy (USA)—Bold Answer (USA) **Mr R. Glendinning**
18 **OWZTHAT (FR),** 4, ch f Jack Hobbs—Vic's Last Stand (IRE) **Mr W. Fleming**
19 **TIDEWELL,** 4, ch g Sixties Icon—Lucy Parsons (IRE) **Mr D. Mawer**
20 4, Ch f Assertive—Vera Richardson (IRE) **K. Kirkup**
21 **VERTICE (IRE),** 6, ch m Toronado (IRE)—Asima (IRE) **Mick Martin Keith Boddy & Son**
22 **VISITANT,** 10, ch g Pivotal—Invitee **D. W. Thompson**
23 **WHERES THE CRUMPET,** 5, ch m Mukhadram—Jivry **Mr S. Murray**

THREE-YEAR-OLDS

24 B f Mondialiste (IRE)—Vera Richardson (IRE) **K. Kirkup**

Assistant Trainer: J. A. Moore.

Flat Jockey: Tony Hamilton.

---

492 MR RONALD THOMPSON, Doncaster

Postal: **No 2 Bungalow, Haggswood Racing Stable, Stainforth, Doncaster, South Yorkshire, DN7 5PS**
Contacts: **PHONE 01302 845904 MOBILE 07713 251141 FAX 01302 845904**
EMAIL ronracing@gmail.com

1 **BEAST OF BURDEN,** 4, b f Elzaam (AUS)—Katie Elder (FR) **Featherstone Racing**
2 **CHURCHILL BAY,** 5, b g The Last Lion (IRE)—Cape Cay **Featherstone Racing**
3 **CRYSTAL DAWN (IRE),** 7, b m Rip Van Winkle (IRE)—Awjila **Dallow Farm Stud**
4 **FURNITURE FACTORS (IRE),** 5, b g Pride of Dubai (AUS)—I Hearyou Knocking (IRE) **B. Bruce & R. Thompson**
5 **LADY VALLETTA (IRE),** 6, ch m Ivawood (IRE)—Cesca (IRE) **Ronald Thompson**

THREE-YEAR-OLDS

6 **MISS FURNY FACTOR (IRE),** b f Kodi Bear (IRE)—Irish Mint (IRE) **B. Bruce & R. Thompson**
7 **THE WHITE ELEPHANT,** b f Holy Roman Emperor (IRE)—Jellwa (IRE) **B. Bruce & R. Thompson**

TWO-YEAR-OLDS

8 **BROADWAY GIRL,** b f 16/02 Massaat (IRE)—Ligeia (Rail Link) (952) **Ronald Thompson**

493 MR VICTOR THOMPSON, Alnwick

Postal: **Link House Farm, Newton By The Sea, Embleton, Alnwick, Northumberland, NE66 3ED**
Contacts: **PHONE 01665 576272 MOBILE 07739 626248**

1 **DAVE THE RUSSIAN (IRE),** 5, b g Shantou (USA)—Smashing Leader (IRE) **V. Thompson**
2 **EX S'ELANCE (FR),** 9, b g Saddex—Pampa Brune (FR) **V. Thompson**
3 **GLORY,** 7, b g Olympic Glory (IRE)—Updated (FR) **V. Thompson**
4 **MUROOR,** 10, ch g Nayef (USA)—Raaya (USA) **V. Thompson**
5 **RAPID FRITZ (IRE),** 14, ch g Kutub (IRE)—Another Pet (IRE)
6 **SCORPO (IRE),** 12, b g Scorpion (IRE)—Maltesse (IRE) **V. Thompson**
7 **SWEET JUSTICE (IRE),** 6, b m Lawman (FR)—Muluk (IRE) **V. Thompson**
8 **UP WITH THE PLAY (IRE),** 6, b g Fracas (IRE)—Alertness (IRE) **V. Thompson**

Assistant Trainer: M Thompson.

---

494 MR SANDY THOMSON, Greenlaw

Postal: **Lambden, Greenlaw, Duns, Berwickshire, TD10 6UN**
Contacts: **PHONE 01361 810211 MOBILE 07876 142787**
EMAIL sandy@lambdenfarm.co.uk WEBSITE www.sandythomsonracing.co.uk

1 **BAK ROCKY (IRE),** 7, br g Shirocco (GER)—Leanne (IRE) **Mr A. M. Thomson**
2 **BASS ROCK (FR),** 7, b g Martaline—Horta (FR) **R. A. Green**
3 **BENSON,** 8, b g Beat Hollow—Karla June **J Fyffe & S Townshend**
4 **BLUE BALOO (IRE),** 5, b m Mahler—Dancing Baloo (IRE) **Trading Products Limited**
5 **BOWLER JACK (IRE),** 5, b g Mahler—Ballybrowney Hall (IRE) **J Fyffe & S Townshend**
6 **CARCACI CASTLE (IRE),** 7, b g Getaway (GER)—Hakuna (IRE) **Mr & Mrs M McPherson & Mrs Q Thomson**
7 **CEDAR HILL (IRE),** 9, br g Frammassone (IRE)—Dayamen **A & Tanclark**
8 **COOLBANE BOY (IRE),** 8, b g Mountain High (IRE)—Easter Saturday (IRE) **Michelle And Dan Macdonald**
9 **COOLKILL (IRE),** 9, b g Arcadio (GER)—Elisabetta (IRE) **Mr J. K. McGarrity**
10 **DANNO'S DOLLAR (IRE),** 4, ch g Golden Lariat (USA)—
Social Society (IRE) **Warren,Wright, Cockcroft,Jervis,Chapman**
11 **DELUXE RANGE (IRE),** 8, b g Westerner—Kildea Cailin (IRE) **Watson & Lawrence**
12 **DINGO DOLLAR (IRE),** 11, ch g Golden Lariat (USA)—
Social Society (IRE) **M Warren J Holmes R Kidner & J Wright**
13 **DONNA'S DELIGHT (IRE),** 12, b g Portrait Gallery (IRE)—Hot Lips (IRE) **D&D Armstrong Limited**
14 **DONNA'S DOUBLE,** 7, b g Fair Mix (IRE)—Elegant Accord (IRE) **D & D Armstrong Ltd & Mr L Westwood**
15 **DOYEN BREED (IRE),** 8, ch g Doyen (IRE)—Sweet Empire (IRE) **The Explorers**
16 **DUC DE GRISSAY (FR),** 10, b g Denham Red (FR)—Rhea de Grissay (FR) **Quona Thomson & Ken McGarrity**
17 **EMPIRE STEEL (IRE),** 9, gr g Aizavoski (IRE)—Talk of Rain (FR) **Mr A. J. Wight**
18 **FAITHFULFLYER (IRE),** 6, b g Sageburg (IRE)—Dakota Fire (IRE) **Midnight Racing Club**
19 **FLOWER OF SCOTLAND (FR),** 8, gr m Lord du Sud (FR)—Theme Song (FR) **R. A. Green**
20 **FOXHOLLOW (IRE),** 6, b g Westerner—Accordingtoherself (IRE) **Trading Products Limited**
21 **FRANZ JOSEF (IRE),** 7, b g Jet Away—Invisible Spirit (IRE) **Midnight Racing Club**
22 **GOODTIMES BADTIMES (IRE),** 8, b g Doyen (IRE)—One Love (IRE) **Chicken Hutch Racers**
23 **GORDON DAI DAI (FR),** 7, b br g Buck's Boum (FR)—Ubanika (FR) **Mr W. D. Macdonald**
24 **GOT TRUMPED,** 8, ch g Thewayyouare (USA)—Madam President **Midnight Racing Club**
25 **HATTONS GARDENS (IRE),** 7, b g Imperial Monarch (IRE)—Pretty Impressive (IRE) **The Daylight Robbers**
26 **HILL SIXTEEN,** 10, b g Court Cave (IRE)—Chasers Chic **J Fyffe & S Townshend**
27 **JIMMY'S JET,** 7, b g Jet Away—Southway Queen **Mr J. Fyffe**
28 **KILBRAINY (IRE),** 7, br g Beat Hollow—Portryan Native (IRE) **Mr W. D. Macdonald**
29 **LEADING FORCE (IRE),** 6, b g Leading Light (IRE)—
Good Looking Woman (IRE) **D & D Armstrong Ltd & Mr L Westwood**
30 **MARCH WIND (IRE),** 6, b m Doyen (IRE)—Gaye Preskina (IRE) **J Fyffe & S Townshend**
31 **MASSINI MAN,** 10, b g Dr Massini (IRE)—Alleged To Rhyme (IRE) **P And F Racing**
32 **MILVALE (IRE),** 9, b g Ask—House-of-Hearts (IRE) **Trading Products Limited**
33 **MISS ARABELLA,** 5, b m Nathaniel (IRE)—Helter Helter (USA) **Mrs Q. R. Thomson**

MR SANDY THOMSON - continued

34 **MOARINS MOARNIN (IRE),** 7, b g Getaway (GER)—Sharifa (GER) **Mr J. Fyffe**
35 **NINETOFIVE (IRE),** 6, b br g Malinas (GER)—Poulnasherry Dove (IRE) **The Williewin Partnership**
36 **PAVLIK (IRE),** 6, b g Morozov (USA)—Longwhitejemmy (IRE) **Mr And Mrs M McPherson And Mrs Q Thomson**
37 8, B m Getaway (GER)—Present Leader **Mrs Q. R. Thomson**
38 **ROB ROY MACGREGOR (IRE),** 5, b g Walk In The Park (IRE)—Miss Baloo (IRE) **Quona Thomson & Ken McGarrity**
39 **SALVINO (IRE),** 7, b g Leading Light (IRE)—Sagabolley (IRE) **Mr A. J. Wight**
40 **SEEMORELIGHTS (IRE),** 11, b g Echo of Light—Star Lodge **Watson & Lawrence**
41 **SIRWILLIAMWALLACE (IRE),** 10, b g Getaway (GER)—Mrs Milan (IRE) **Mr J. K. McGarrity**
42 **STONEY ROVER (IRE),** 10, b g Scorpion (IRE)—Consultation (IRE) **Mrs F. Telfer**
43 **STORM NELSON (IRE),** 10, b g Gold Well—Dabiyra (IRE) **Mr J. Fyffe**
44 **THE FERRY MASTER (IRE),** 10, b g Elusive Pimpernel (USA)—Dinghy (IRE) **The Potassium Partnership**
45 5, B g Mahler—The Malteasiereyes (IRE) **Marchcleuch Bloodstock**
46 **THEIRSHEGOES (IRE),** 6, b m Court Cave (IRE)—Betty Scott **Mr M. S. Scott**
47 5, B g Mustameet (USA)—Tub of Harte's (IRE) **Mr I. J. Herbert**
48 **WAR SOLDIER (IRE),** 6, b g Soldier of Fortune (IRE)—After Dark (IRE) **J Townson & P Thompson**
49 **WOLFBURG (IRE),** 4, b g Sageburg (IRE)—Presenting Melody (IRE) **Mrs A. R. B. Mania**

THREE-YEAR-OLDS

50 B f Schiaparelli (GER)—Red Con One (IRE) **Mrs A. R. B. Mania**

Assistant Trainer: Mrs A. M. Thomson.

---

495 MR JOE TICKLE, Tiverton

Postal: **Lower Ford, Warbrightsley Hill, Stoodleigh, Tiverton, Devon, EX16 9QQ**
EMAIL txi100@hotmail.com

1 **DAANY (IRE),** 6, b g Pivotal—Ejadah (IRE) **Miss D Kenealy & Duckhaven Stud**
2 **DANEHILL KODIAC (IRE),** 10, b g Kodiac—Meadow **J Davies & Govier & Brown**
3 **EPEIUS (IRE),** 10, b g Arakan (USA)—Gilda Lilly (USA) **Two Rivers Racing**
4 **GALACTIC GLOW (IRE),** 6, b g No Nay Never (USA)—Shine Like A Star **The Clueless Syndicate**
5 **HAZY DREAM,** 7, gr m Dream Eater (IRE)—Lily Potts **Duckhaven Stud**
6 **KINGCORMAC (IRE),** 7, b g Shirocco (GER)—On The Up (IRE) **Maddox Langdon Johns & Tickle**
7 **LOOK OUT TO SEA,** 6, b g Telescope (IRE)—Sainte Gig (FR) **P. G. Hepworth**
8 **MUJID (IRE),** 8, b g Frankel—Bethrah (IRE) **The Family Affair**
9 **ROSE ABOVE IT (IRE),** 7, b m Kalanisi (IRE)—West Hill Rose (IRE) **Mr K. Johns**
10 **SCHOOL FOR SCANDAL (FR),** 8, gr g Doctor Dino (FR)—School of Thought (FR) **Mr P. A. Mann**
11 **SWEARER (IRE),** 7, br g Kalanisi (IRE)—Dance Cover (IRE) **Mr K. Johns**
12 **VENDANGE (IRE),** 5, b g Le Havre (IRE)—Harvest Queen (IRE) **Two Rivers Racing**

THREE-YEAR-OLDS

13 **THE MENICE (IRE),** b c Tagula (IRE)—Classic Style (IRE) **Miss D. Kenealy**

---

496 MR NIGEL TINKLER, Malton

Postal: **Woodland Stables, Langton, Malton, North Yorkshire, YO17 9QR**
Contacts: **HOME 01653 658245 MOBILE 07836 384225 FAX 01653 658542**
WORK EMAIL nigel@nigeltinkler.com EMAIL sam@nigeltinkler.com

1 **ACKLAM EXPRESS (IRE),** 5, b g Mehmas (IRE)—York Express **MPS Racing & M B Spence**

MR NIGEL TINKLER - continued

2 **ANOTHER INVESTMENT (IRE),** 4, b g Awtaad (IRE)—Mitzi Winks (USA) **J Glover R O'Donnell J Short N Skinner**
3 **AS IF BY CHANCE,** 5, b g Fountain of Youth (IRE)—Citron **Ms Sara Hattersley & Miss Tracey Mann**
4 **ATHOLLBLAIR BOY (IRE),** 10, ch g Frozen Power (IRE)—Ellxell (IRE) **The Geezaaah Partnership**
5 **COTTAM LANE,** 5, b g Twilight Son—Alsium (IRE) **The Racing Emporium**
6 **DANDY DINMONT (IRE),** 4, b g Dandy Man (IRE)—Coconut Kisses **MPS Racing, The Olliers & S. Perkins**
7 **DOUGIES DREAM (IRE),** 4, b g Fast Company (IRE)—Sidney Girl **Martin Webb Racing**
8 **GLORY HALLELUJAH (IRE),** 4, ch g Cotai Glory—Island Vision (IRE) **Mr J Raybould & Mr S Perkins**
9 **GOLDEN DUKE (IRE),** 4, ch g Galileo Gold—Porta Portese **The Racing Emporium**
10 **HIGH SECURITY,** 5, b g Acclamation—Excelette (IRE) **Reliance Racing Partnership**
11 **ISLA KAI (IRE),** 5, b g Awtaad (IRE)—Sidney Girl **Martin Webb Racing**
12 **LUCKY LUCKY LUCKY (IRE),** 4, b g Footstepsinthesand—Lovers Peace (IRE) **G Maidment Racing**
13 **NOT ON YOUR NELLIE (IRE),** 6, b m Zebedee—Piccadilly Filly (IRE) **Exors of the Late J. D. Gordon**
14 **PRODIGIOUS BLUE (IRE),** 4, b g Bated Breath—Hellofahaste **Mr & Mrs I. H. Bendelow**
15 **ROUNDHAY PARK,** 8, ch g Mayson—Brave Mave **Exors of the Late J. D. Gordon**
16 **SELFISH BRIAN (IRE),** 4, b g Shalaa (IRE)—Mad Existence (IRE) **MPS Racing & Partners**
17 **STRANGERONTHESHORE,** 5, b m Cable Bay (IRE)—Stolen Glance **R S Cockerill (farms) & Crawford Society**
18 **TRUST BERTIE (IRE),** 4, b g Mehmas (IRE)—Crystal Theatre (IRE) **Mr J. R. Saville**
19 **VAUNTED,** 4, b f Ardad (IRE)—Vallila **P. Kelly**
20 **WHATWOULDYOUKNOW (IRE),** 8, b g Lope de Vega (IRE)—Holamo (IRE) **Dearing Plastics Ltd & Mark Ingram**
21 **WOODLANDS CHARM (IRE),** 4, b f Kodiac—
Causeway Charm (USA) **Woodlands Racing & Middleham Park Racing**

THREE-YEAR-OLDS

22 **ANNIE BE GOOD (IRE),** b f Blame (USA)—Goodthingstaketime (IRE) **David Balfe, The Olliers & Partner**
23 **BAROSSA (IRE),** b br f Awtaad (IRE)—Quenched **G Maidment Racing**
24 **BELLA KOPELLA (IRE),** b f Awtaad (IRE)—Ajla (IRE) **Martin Webb Racing**
25 **BIG BAD WOLF (IRE),** gr g Make Believe—Danamight (IRE) **Huff & Puff Partnership**
26 **BRYCE (IRE),** b g Galileo Gold—Petite Boulangere (IRE) **SYPS (UK) Ltd**
27 **CANDY CANE (IRE),** gr ro f Fast Company (IRE)—Saphira Silver (IRE) **The Racing Emporium**
28 **DUKE OF WYBOURNE (IRE),** b g Dandy Man (IRE)—Bahaarah (IRE) **The Dandymen**
29 **EXCEED (IRE),** b g Exceed And Excel (AUS)—Silver Grey (IRE) **Ontoawinner 1**
30 **GOBLET OF FIRE,** b g Saxon Warrior (JPN)—War No More (USA) **Miss A. Hodgson-Tuck**
31 **GOLDEN FIREFLY (IRE),** b g New Bay—Luciole **The Firefly Syndicate**
32 **HEART OF ACKLAM,** b g Zoffany (IRE)—Tingleo **Amity Finance Ltd**
33 **HEART OF SOFIA (IRE),** b f James Garfield (IRE)—Tut (IRE) **Sara Hattersley & Peter Blyth**
34 **KERPOW,** b g Showcasing—Impede **Mr Y. T. Szeto**
35 **LAKOTA BLUE,** br c Sioux Nation (USA)—Thiel **Mr & Mrs I. H. Bendelow**
36 **MAJIL (IRE),** b f Mehmas (IRE)—Damask (IRE) **Reliance Racing Partnership**
37 **OSKAR (IRE),** b g Awtaad (IRE)—Classic Legend **The Flying Raconteurs**
38 B g Awtaad (IRE)—Padma **J Derry J Glover R O'Donnell N Skinner**
39 **PARR FIRE (IRE),** b f James Garfield (IRE)—Vulnicura (IRE) **MPS Racing & Partners**
40 **SIDNEY'S SON (IRE),** b g Dandy Man (IRE)—Sidney Girl **Mps Racing, Stewart & Pals**
41 **SMALLEYTIME (IRE),** ch g Tamayuz—Into The Lane (IRE) **MPS Racing & Partners**
42 **SQUEALER (IRE),** b g Mehmas (IRE)—Sunny Hollow **Martin Webb & Syps (uk) Ltd**
43 **THANKUAPPRECIATE,** b g Fountain of Youth (IRE)—Illusions **Ms Sara Hattersley & Miss Tracey Mann**
44 **THEME PARK,** b c Lope de Vega (IRE)—Queen's Prize **Mr M. Webb**
45 **TREBLE GLORY (IRE),** b g Cotai Glory—Kodafine (IRE) **D Bloy, Harlequin Direct & Syps (uk)**
46 **UBETTABEQUICK (IRE),** br f Wootton Bassett—Broken Applause (IRE) **Martin Webb Racing**

TWO-YEAR-OLDS

47 B f 21/03 Zoffany (IRE)—Accipiter (Showcasing) (43810) **R.N.J. Partnership**
48 **ALL ABOUT NEVE (IRE),** gr f 31/01 Kuroshio (AUS)—Valen (IRE) (Acclamation) (24010) **Ms H. C. Gordon**
49 B f 23/02 Washington DC (IRE)—Citron (Reel Buddy (USA)) (7619)
50 B c 05/02 Oasis Dream—Clematis (USA) (First Defence (USA)) (50000)
51 Br g 04/02 Kuroshio (AUS)—Daffy Jane (Excelebration (IRE)) (24010)
52 B c 27/03 Showcasing—Danseuse d'Etoile (IRE) (Pivotal) (56022)
53 B c 11/04 Invincible Spirit (IRE)—Dolma (FR) (Marchand de Sable (USA)) (36014) **Caslin, Wilcock M Cantillon**
54 **DWINDLING FUNDS,** b c 20/04 Intrinsic—Kashtan (Sakhee's Secret) **D P Van Der Hoeven & D G Pryde**
55 B g 22/03 Cable Bay (IRE)—Essenza (IRE) (Alhebayeb (IRE)) (20000)

MR NIGEL TINKLER - continued

56 B f 29/01 Land Force (IRE)—Fille de Reve (Iffraaj) (28000)
57 B g 16/03 Mayson—Kilbaha Lady (IRE) (Elnadim (USA)) **Dapper Partnership**
58 B c 12/03 Mehmas (IRE)—Lost Comet (IRE) (Sea The Stars (IRE)) (34000) **Mr J. R. Saville**
59 **NOBILITY BLUE,** bl g 18/03 Calyx—Blanche Dubawi (IRE) (Dubawi (IRE)) (15000) **Mr & Mrs I. H. Bendelow**
60 B g 08/02 Advertise—Powerful Star (IRE) (Slade Power (IRE)) (45714) **Hart Inn Leisure**
61 **PROFIT STREET (IRE),** b g 31/03 Profitable (IRE)—
Street Marie (USA) (Street Cry (IRE)) (16000) **D Jenkins J Glover R O'Donnell J Short**
62 B f 27/02 Oasis Dream—Sassy Gal (IRE) (King's Best (USA)) (45714) **SYPS (UK) Ltd**
63 B c 05/05 Inns of Court (IRE)—Sidney Girl (Azamour (IRE)) (35000)
64 Bl ro f 06/04 Outstrip—Stolen Glance (Mujahid (USA)) (952)
65 B g 15/03 Blue Point (IRE)—Strathnaver (Oasis Dream) (32013) **Woodlands Racing 2**
66 B g 23/03 Soldier's Call—Suedehead (Cape Cross (IRE)) (38095)
67 B f 01/04 Muhaarar—Tingleo (Galileo (IRE)) **Ceramic Tile Merchants Ltd**
68 B f 25/04 Inns of Court (IRE)—York Express (Vale of York (IRE)) (64026)
69 **ZEITGEIST,** ch c 11/04 Showcasing—El Diamante (FR) (Royal Applause) (45000)

---

497 MR JOE TIZZARD, Sherborne

Postal: **Spurles Farm, Milborne Port, Sherborne, Dorset, DT9 5HE**
Contacts: **PHONE 01963 250425**
EMAIL joetizzard79@gmail.com

1 **AKI BOMAYE (IRE),** 8, gr g Stowaway—Line Grey (FR) **Mrs M. Middleton**
2 **ALLSFINEANDANDY (IRE),** 7, b g Dandy Man (IRE)—Swish Dancer (IRE) **Mr G. Kennington**
3 **AMARILLO SKY (IRE),** 7, b g Westerner—Bag of Tricks (IRE) **Mr J. P. Romans**
4 **AMBION HILL (IRE),** 8, b br g Getaway (GER)—Vertality (IRE) **Mr O. C. R. Wynne & Mrs S. J. Wynne**
5 **AMERICAN LAND (IRE),** 5, br g Malinas (GER)—Golan Annie (IRE) **Brocade Racing**
6 **ATAKAN (FR),** 7, b g Sinndar (IRE)—Accusation (IRE) **The Reserve Tankers**
7 **BALA BROOK,** 5, b g Getaway (GER)—The Wicked Kipper **C. L. Tizzard**
8 **BELGARUM (IRE),** 5, b g Shirocco (GER)—Cyrils Girl **Mrs G. C. Pritchard**
9 **BERTIE WOOSTER (IRE),** 5, b br g Beat Hollow—Fair Ina (IRE) **Mrs C. Knowles**
10 **BORN IN BORRIS (IRE),** 9, b m Arcadio (GER)—Honour Own (IRE) **Mr R. M. Harvey-Bailey**
11 **BOURBALI (FR),** 6, b g Sinndar (IRE)—Saintheze (FR) **Pope, Legg, Green T Swaffield**
12 **BUCKHORN GEORGE,** 8, gr g Geordieland (FR)—Waimea Bay **The Buckhorn Racing Team**
13 **BUCKHORN ROCCO,** 7, ch g Saddler's Rock (IRE)—Waimea Bay **The Buckhorn Racing Team**
14 **BUTTERFLYCOLLECTOR (IRE),** 5, ch m Flemensfirth (USA)—Jolivia (FR) **Susan & John Waterworth**
15 **BUTTERWICK BROOK (IRE),** 8, b g Getaway (GER)—Sheriussa (IRE) **The Butterwick Syndicate**
16 **C'EST BLEU,** 5, b m Blue Bresil (FR)—Super Cookie **The FTC Syndicate**
17 **CHAMPAGNE MESDAMES (FR),** 6, b g Diamond Boy (FR)—Olerone (FR) **The Wychwood Partnership**
18 **CHAMPS HILL,** 6, b g Champs Elysees—Grapes Hill **The Colin Tizzard Racing Club**
19 **COPPERHEAD,** 9, ch g Sulamani (IRE)—How's Business **Mrs G. C. Pritchard**
20 **COULD TALKABOUTIT (IRE),** 6, b g Kayf Tara—Glen Countess (IRE) **Mr J. P. Romans**
21 **DIAMOND RI (IRE),** 4, ch g Diamond Boy (FR)—Quaspia (FR) **The Wychwood Partnership**
22 **DYLAN'S DOUBLE (IRE),** 6, b g Getaway (GER)—Summer Again (IRE) **Brocade Racing**
23 **EARTH BUSINESS (IRE),** 7, b g Westerner—Shellys Creek (IRE) **Mrs C. E. Penny**
24 **ELDORADO ALLEN (FR),** 9, gr g Khalkevi (IRE)—Hesmeralda (FR) **J P Romans & Terry Warner**
25 **ELEGANT ESCAPE (IRE),** 11, b g Dubai Destination (USA)—Graineuaile (IRE) **Mr J. P. Romans**
26 **ELIXIR DE NUTZ (FR),** 9, gr g Al Namix (FR)—Nutz (FR) **J. T. Warner**
27 **FAUSTINOVICK,** 9, b g Black Sam Bellamy (IRE)—Cormorant Cove **The Faustinovick Syndicate**
28 **FIDDLERONTHEROOF (IRE),** 9, b g Stowaway—Inquisitive Look **Taylor, Burley & O'Dwyer**
29 **FURKASH (FR),** 8, b g Al Namix (FR)—Meralda (FR) **Swallowfield Racing**
30 **GUERNESEY (FR),** 7, gr g Martaline—Myrtille Jersey (FR) **J. T. Warner**
31 **GYENYAME,** 5, b g Nathaniel (IRE)—Lizzie Tudor **Anne Broom & Wendy Carter**
32 **HARTINGTON (IRE),** 4, gr g Jukebox Jury (IRE)—Duchess Dee (IRE) **The Wychwood Partnership**
33 **HONEY JACK,** 4, br g Jack Hobbs—Miss Serious (IRE) **Susan & John Waterworth**
34 **HOUR STAR,** 4, ch g Dunaden (FR)—Valdas Queen (GER) **Mrs K. Squire**

MR JOE TIZZARD - continued

35 **I SHUT THAT D'OR (FR),** 5, b g Barastraight—Anicka d'Or (FR) **J. K. Powell Racing**
36 **ILOVETHENIGHTLIFE,** 5, b m Walk In The Park (IRE)—
Belle De Londres (IRE) **Geoff Nicholas, Susan & John Waterworth**
37 **INVESTMENT MANAGER,** 7, b g Nathaniel (IRE)—Two Days In Paris (FR) **Brocade Racing**
38 **JPR ONE (IRE),** 6, b br g Court Cave (IRE)—Lady Knightess (IRE) **Mr J. P. Romans**
39 **KAUTO THE KING (FR),** 9, b g Ballingarry (IRE)—Kauto Luisa (FR) **Jenny Perry & Celia Goaman**
40 **KILLER KANE (IRE),** 8, b g Oscar (IRE)—Native Idea (IRE) **Mr J. P. Romans**
41 **KING OF LOMBARDY (IRE),** 5, b g Milan—Uranna (FR) **The Wychwood Partnership**
42 4, B g Norse Dancer (IRE)—Lady Beaufort
43 **LAMANVER BEL AMI,** 9, b g Black Sam Bellamy (IRE)—Lamanver Homerun **Dr D. Christensen**
44 **LANSPARK (IRE),** 8, b g Milan—Sparky May **Ruxley Holdings Ltd**
45 **LE LIGERIEN (FR),** 10, b g Turgeon (USA)—Etoile de Loir (FR) **D. R. Churches**
46 **MARLEY HEAD (IRE),** 4, ch g Pride of Dubai (AUS)—Boast **C. L. Tizzard**
47 **MISS CHAWNER,** 5, br m Blue Bresil (FR)—Ice Nelly (IRE) **Mr E. Jones**
48 **MOLINEAUX (IRE),** 12, b g King's Theatre (IRE)—Steel Grey Lady (IRE) **C. L. Tizzard**
49 **MOONLIGHT ARTIST,** 5, b g Pether's Moon (IRE)—Karla June **The Cheltenham & South West Racing Club**
50 **MY LADY GREY,** 9, gr m Presenting—Wassailing Queen **Mr J. Reed**
51 **NAME IN LIGHTS (IRE),** 7, b g Fame And Glory—Chevalier Jet (IRE) **Mrs M. Middleton**
52 **NELSONS ROCK,** 8, b g Mount Nelson—Neardown Beauty (IRE) **Middleham Park Racing LXXXVIII**
53 **NO HUBS NO HOOBS (IRE),** 7, b g Flemensfirth (USA)—Miss Brandywell (IRE) **Mrs R. James**
54 **NON STOP (FR),** 4, b g Starspangledbanner (AUS)—Saint Hilary **Gavigan Kennedy Sharp**
55 **OFF TO A FLYER (IRE),** 6, b g Shirocco (GER)—On The Up (IRE) **Mary-Ann & J Romans**
56 **OFTEN OVERLOOKED (IRE),** 7, b br g Elusive Pimpernel (USA)—Alpinia (IRE) **Coral Racing Club for Colleagues**
57 **OSCAR ELITE (IRE),** 8, b g Oscar (IRE)—Lady Elite (IRE) **Mrs M. Middleton**
58 **PEARL BEAUTY,** 4, gr f Pearl Secret—Wilspa's Magic (IRE) **The Gardens Entertainments Ltd**
59 **PEDLEY WOOD (IRE),** 6, b g Westerner—Rosin de Beau (IRE) **Messenger Family & John Reed**
60 **PER VINO VERITAS,** 8, b g Arvico (FR)—Countess Point **Mr D. S. Purdie**
61 **PREMIUMACCESS (IRE),** 8, b g Milan—De Loose Mongoose (IRE) **Mr J. Reed**
62 **RIVERS CORNER,** 5, b g Soldier of Fortune (IRE)—Whisky Rose (IRE) **Case, Hosie, Romans**
63 **ROBINSVILLE,** 6, b g Shirocco (GER)—This Town **John & Heather Snook**
64 **ROSE OF ARCADIA (IRE),** 8, b m Arcadio (GER)—Rosie Lea (IRE) **Mr G. Nicholas**
65 **RYDER'S ROCK,** 5, b m Fascinating Rock (IRE)—Featherweight (IRE) **C. L. Tizzard**
66 **SCARFACE (IRE),** 6, b g Milan—Consider Her Lucky (GER) **Mr K Leggett, Susan & John Waterworth**
67 **SEABORN (IRE),** 9, b g Born To Sea (IRE)—Next To The Top **Mr I. Beach**
68 **SEYMOUR PROMISE (IRE),** 7, b g Flemensfirth (USA)—Loadsapromise (IRE) **C. L. Tizzard**
69 **SHERBORNE (IRE),** 7, b g Getaway (GER)—Luck of The Deise (IRE) **Sharp, Nicholas & Kennington**
70 **SHIROCCO'S DREAM (IRE),** 8, b m Shirocco (GER)—Dream Function (IRE) **P & Geranio**
71 **SIXTY DOLLARS MORE (FR),** 7, b g Buck's Boum (FR)—Sacree City (FR) **C. L. Tizzard**
72 **SIZING CUSIMANO,** 10, b g Midnight Legend—Combe Florey **Peter Bennett & Colin Tizzard**
73 **SLATE HOUSE (IRE),** 11, b g Presenting—Bay Pearl (FR) **Eric Jones, Geoff Nicholas, John Romans**
74 **SO SAID I,** 7, gr m Malinas (GER)—Wassailing Queen **And So Say All Of Us Partnership**
75 **SPARKLING DUKE (IRE),** 4, b g Jukebox Jury (IRE)—Sparkling Sword **The Wychwood Partnership**
76 **SPICY NELSON (IRE),** 5, ch g Mount Nelson—Fairy Trader (IRE) **The Backburner syndicate**
77 **STAR OF AFFINITY (IRE),** 4, b g Affinisea (IRE)—Nansheen (IRE) **Kennington, Reed, Sharp & Goodsir**
78 **STAR OF VALOUR (IRE),** 8, b g Invincible Spirit (IRE)—Birthstone **Mr G. Kennington**
79 **STRIKING A POSE (IRE),** 7, b g Getaway (GER)—Clonsingle Native (IRE) **I & C Gosden, M Sharp & G Kennington**
80 **SWEET CARYLINE,** 5, b m Blue Bresil (FR)—Mollasses **Mr J. P. Romans**
81 **TALIMAR PEARL (FR),** 5, gr g Martaline—Be A Good One (GER) **D. R. Churches**
82 **TAMARIS (IRE),** 6, br g Dansili—Fleur de Cactus (IRE) **Team Tasker**
83 **TELLMESOMETHINGOOD (IRE),** 5, b g Walk In The Park (IRE)—Norabelle (FR) **The Reserve Tankers**
84 **THE BIG BREAKAWAY (IRE),** 8, ch g Getaway (GER)—
Princess Mairead (IRE) **Eric Jones, Geoff Nicholas, John Romans**
85 **THE CHANGING MAN (IRE),** 6, b g Walk In The Park (IRE)—Bitofapuzzle **Susan & John Waterworth**
86 **THE WHERRYMAN,** 5, b g Telescope (IRE)—La Perrotine (FR) **Susan & John Waterworth**
87 **THE WIDDOW MAKER,** 9, ch g Arvico (FR)—Countess Point **Mr D. S. Purdie**
88 **TRIPLE TRADE,** 7, b g Norse Dancer (IRE)—Doubly Guest **SJS Racing**
89 **U CANT BE SERIOUS (IRE),** 4, ch g Notnowcato—Whyyousoserious (IRE) **Mr D. S. Purdie**
90 **VENTARA,** 5, b g Kayf Tara—Venceremos **On the Case Syndicate**
91 **VISCOUNT VINYL (IRE),** 4, br gr g Jukebox Jury (IRE)—Vbadge Treat (FR) **The Wychwood Partnership**
92 **VISION DES FLOS (FR),** 10, b g Balko (FR)—Marie Royale (FR) **C. L. Tizzard**

MR JOE TIZZARD - continued

93 **WAR LORD (GER),** 8, gr g Jukebox Jury (IRE)—Westalin (GER) **The Wychwood Partnership**
94 4, B gr g Walk In The Park (IRE)—Wassailing Queen **Barrow Hill**
95 **WEST APPROACH,** 13, b g Westerner—Ardstown **C. L. Tizzard**
96 **WEST END BOY (IRE),** 5, b g Westerner—Eternally Grateful (IRE) **Coral Racing Club**
97 **WEST ORCHARD (IRE),** 6, b g Westerner—Shellys Creek (IRE) **Orchard Racing**
98 **WESTERN BARON (IRE),** 6, b g Westerner—Aylesbury Park (IRE) **The Alyasan Partnership**
99 **WESTERN GENERAL (IRE),** 5, ch g Valirann (FR)—Shocona (IRE) **Brocade Racing**
100 **WESTERN KNIGHT (IRE),** 4, b g Westerner—Milford Maggie (IRE) **The Wychwood Partnership**
101 **WHYDAH GALLY,** 7, b g Black Sam Bellamy (IRE)—Reverse Swing **Sam's Crew**

---

498 SIR MARK TODD, Swindon

Postal: **Badgerstown, Foxhill, Swindon, Wiltshire, SN4 0DR**
Contacts: **PHONE 01793 791228**
EMAIL mtoddracing@gmail.com

1 **CAPE CORNWALL ROSE (IRE),** 4, b f Awtaad (IRE)—Alice Rose (IRE) **Dr H. K. Tayton-Martin**
2 **DOUBLE TIME,** 5, b g Bated Breath—Darling Daisy **Mrs P. A. Scott-Dunn**
3 **WOW WILLIAM (FR),** 5, b g The Wow Signal (IRE)—Naive (IRE) **Wow William Partnership**

THREE-YEAR-OLDS

4 **DANEANN (IRE),** b f Zoffany (IRE)—Ketifa (IRE) **GullWing Enterprises W.L.L.**
5 **FILM STAR,** ch f Zoustar (AUS)—Station House (IRE)
6 **NATIVE BEACH (IRE),** b c Footstepsinthesand—
School Holidays (USA) **Badgerstown Red Syndicate/Sir Mark Todd**
7 **NOBLE SOVEREIGN,** b f Night of Thunder (IRE)—Daintily Done
8 **ROCKIT TOMMY,** ch g Tamayuz—Saving Grace **Peregrine Racing & Sir Mark & Lady Todd**
9 **ST JUST IN TIME,** b g Time Test—Porthledden Flight **Dr H. K. Tayton-Martin**
10 **UNO GRANDE,** b c Exceed And Excel (AUS)—Miss Chicane **Sir M. J. Todd**
11 B f Expert Eye—Upstanding **Sir M. J. Todd**

---

499 MR MARTIN TODHUNTER, Penrith

Postal: **The Park, Orton, Penrith, Cumbria, CA10 3SD**
Contacts: **PHONE 015396 24314 MOBILE 07976 440082 FAX 015396 24314**
WEBSITE www.martintodhunter.co.uk

1 **ARCTIC FOX,** 7, ch m Mastercraftsman (IRE)—Aurora Borealis (IRE) **Colin & Kay Taylor**
2 **ARRANGE (IRE),** 5, gr m Mastercraftsman (IRE)—Watsdaplan (IRE) **Mr & Mrs Ian Hall**
3 **ASKING FOR ANSWERS (IRE),** 10, ch g Ask—Equation (IRE) **Mrs Mrs Matthews & Mrs G Hazeldean**
4 **BOUNCING BOBBY (IRE),** 6, b g Raven's Pass (USA)—Silicon Star (FR) **J. W. Hazeldean**
5 **FIA FUINIDH (IRE),** 6, b g Flemensfirth (USA)—Western Garden (IRE) **The Surf & Turf Partnership**
6 **FIRST REVOLUTION (IRE),** 9, b g Jeremy (USA)—Shaigino (IRE) **Colin & Kay Taylor**
7 **JET LEGS (IRE),** 6, b g Jet Away—Supreme Magical **Mrs Suzy Brown & Mr Peter R Brown**
8 **JOIE DE VIVRE (IRE),** 8, gr m Mastercraftsman (IRE)—Fragonard **Exors of the Late J. D. Gordon**
9 **KICKSAFTERSIX (IRE),** 7, b g Scorpion (IRE)—Astalanda (FR) **Coniston Old Men Syndicate**
10 **KINGOFTHEGAME (IRE),** 5, b g Kingston Hill—Sand Lady **Murphy's Law Partnership**
11 **MOLINARI (IRE),** 6, gr g Mastercraftsman (IRE)—Moon Empress (FR) **Mr & Mrs Ian Hall**
12 **WELL CLICHE (IRE),** 8, b m Milan—Thyngreesa **Murphy's Law Partnership**

500 MR MARCUS TREGONING, Whitsbury

Postal: **Whitsbury Manor Racing Stables, Whitsbury, Fordingbridge, Hampshire, SP6 3QQ**
Contacts: **WORK 01725 518889 MOBILE 07767 888100**
EMAIL info@marcustregoningracing.co.uk

1 **AL AZHAR (IRE),** 4, b g Invincible Spirit (IRE)—Arabian Comet (IRE) **John Wallis, Stephen Wallis, Nona Baker**
2 **ATALANTA BREEZE,** 7, b m Champs Elysees—Craighall **Miss S. M. Sharp**
3 **LA FORZA,** 5, b g Shalaa (IRE)—Seven Magicians (USA) **Mr M. P. Tregoning**
4 **LADYBIRD (IRE),** 4, b f Australia—Bessichka **Mr M. P. Tregoning**
5 **LANDING STRIP,** 4, b f Outstrip—Quail Landing **Miss S Sharp & Mr M. P. N. Tregoning**
6 **MARGUB,** 8, ch g Bated Breath—Bahamian Babe **Mr M. P. Tregoning**
7 **MEADRAM,** 5, b g Mukhadram—Mea Parvitas (IRE)
8 **MISS BLUEBELLE (IRE),** 4, b f Awtaad (IRE)—Miss Bellbird (IRE) **Sir T Pilkington & The Rogers Family**
9 **NAWRAS,** 4, b g Sea The Stars (IRE)—Umniyah (IRE) **Shadwell Estate Company Ltd**
10 **STRATHSPEY STRETTO (IRE),** 8, ch m Kyllachy—
Rhythm And Rhyme (IRE) **Miss S Sharp & Mr M. P. N. Tregoning**
11 **WISPER (IRE),** 5, ch m Belardo (IRE)—Whisp (GER) **The Reignmakers**

THREE-YEAR-OLDS

12 **COMMISSION,** ch g Profitable (IRE)—Modify **Longstock Thoroughbreds**
13 Gr g Havana Grey—Darsan (IRE) **Shadwell Estate Company Ltd**
14 **DUMFRIES,** b c Cityscape—Milldale **Whitsbury II**
15 **FEYHA (IRE),** b f Sir Percy—Mariana (IRE) **Savernake Racing**
16 **MARIE LAVEAU,** b f Sir Percy—Mariee **Miss K. Rausing**
17 **MUKTAMIL (IRE),** b g Sea The Stars (IRE)—Intisaar (USA) **Shadwell Estate Company Ltd**
18 **SECRET SOLACE,** b f Gleneagles (IRE)—Secret Pursuit (IRE) **Mr G. C. B. Brook**
19 **SHAADEN (IRE),** b f Invincible Spirit (IRE)—Rihaam (IRE) **Shadwell Estate Company Ltd**
20 **SKYSAIL,** ch c Tasleet—Lady Marl **Whitsbury I**

TWO-YEAR-OLDS

21 B f 12/02 Sea The Stars (IRE)—Aaraas (Haafhd) **Shadwell Estate Company Ltd**
22 B c 21/04 Phoenix of Spain (IRE)—Billie Eria (IRE) (Tamayuz) (15000) **Whitsbury IV**
23 **DEIRA CLASSIC (FR),** b c 11/02 Dariyan (FR)—Zahrat Narjis (Exceed And Excel (AUS)) (7603) **Green Team Racing**
24 **DEMANDING LILLEY,** b f 04/05 Due Diligence (USA)—
On Demand (Teofilo (IRE)) **Ms Christine Thomas and Mr Jim Hoyland**
25 B f 17/04 Footstepsinthesand—Desert Run (IRE) (Desert Prince (IRE)) **Mr & Mrs A. E. Pakenham**
26 **ETIHAD RAIL (IRE),** b c 23/01 Fast Company (IRE)—Designation (IRE) (Acclamation) (2857) **A. Al Shaikh**
27 Ch f 03/05 Nathaniel (IRE)—Garanciere (FR) (Anabaa (USA)) (16000) **Whitsbury V**
28 B c 26/04 Lope de Vega (IRE)—Musaanada (Sea The Stars (IRE)) **Shadwell Estate Company Ltd**
29 **NEVER DREAM (IRE),** b c 29/03 Showcasing—Overtones (New Approach (IRE)) (28000) **Mrs C. J. Wates**
30 B c 09/03 Muhaarar—Scarlet Royal (Red Ransom (USA)) (18000) **Whitsbury III**
31 **SELECTIVITY,** ch f 09/03 Sea The Moon (GER)—Selenography (Selkirk (USA)) **Miss K. Rausing**
32 B c 02/05 Advertise—Slatey Hen (IRE) (Acclamation) (27000) **Mr M. P. Tregoning**
33 B f 25/02 Zoustar (AUS)—Spiced (Dansili)
34 B c 16/04 Bated Breath—Vote Often (Beat Hollow) (28000)

Assistant Trainer: Mrs Angela Kennedy.

Amateur Jockey: Miss Alice Tregoning.

---

501 MR GRANT TUER, Northallerton

Postal: **Home Farm, Great Smeaton, Northallerton, North Yorkshire, DL6 2EP**
Contacts: **PHONE 01609 881094 MOBILE 07879 698869 FAX 01609 881094**
EMAIL grant_tuer@btinternet.com

1 **ARABIC CULTURE (USA),** 9, b g Lonhro (AUS)—Kydd Gloves (USA) **Marjorie & Tuer**
2 **AWARD DANCER (IRE),** 5, b g Awtaad (IRE)—Music And Dance **Moment Of Madness**

MR GRANT TUER - continued

3 **BICEP (IRE),** 4, b g Mehmas (IRE)—Crafty Notion (IRE) **David & Tuer**
4 **CARIBBEAN SUNSET (IRE),** 5, b g Twilight Son—Guana (IRE) **Mr S. E. Chappell**
5 **CATHAYENSIS (IRE),** 5, b m Twilight Son—Chaenomeles (USA) **Allerton Racing & G Tuer**
6 **CUSTARD,** 7, ch g Monsieur Bond (IRE)—Ailsa Craig (IRE) **Mr G. F. Tuer**
7 **DIRTYOLDTOWN (IRE),** 4, b g No Nay Never (USA)—Tadris (USA) **Mr C. J. Miller**
8 **DREAMCASING,** 5, br g Showcasing—Nandiga (USA) **Marjorie & Tuer**
9 **ETIKAAL,** 9, ch g Sepoy (AUS)—Hezmah **Moment Of Madness**
10 **GHOST RIDER (IRE),** 5, b g Dark Angel (IRE)—Priceless Jewel **Mr G. F. Tuer**
11 **GOLD TERMS,** 5, b m Havana Gold (IRE)—Easy Terms **Mr G. F. Tuer**
12 **GUNNERSIDE (IRE),** 6, gr g Gutaifan (IRE)—Suite (IRE) **Mr G. F. Tuer**
13 **HART STOPPER,** 9, b g Compton Place—Angel Song **Mr G. F. Tuer**
14 **ILLUSIONIST (GER),** 6, b g Hot Streak (IRE)—Irishstone (IRE) **Miss M. A. Thompson**
15 **KAAFY (IRE),** 7, b g Alhebayeb (IRE)—Serene Dream **Marjorie & Tuer**
16 **KING TRITON (IRE),** 5, b g Invincible Spirit (IRE)—Nada **Mr E. J. Ware**
17 **LEZARDRIEUX,** 6, b g Due Diligence (USA)—M'Selle (IRE) **Allerton Racing & G Tuer**
18 **LION TOWER (IRE),** 6, b g Exceed And Excel (AUS)—Memorial (AUS) **Hornby Hornets**
19 **LITUUS (IRE),** 4, b g Holy Roman Emperor (IRE)—Rip Van Music (IRE) **Racing, Blackburn G. Tuer**
20 **MILWAUKEE BLIZZARD (IRE),** 5, b m French Navy—Glyndebourne (USA) **Mrs J. Keys**
21 **MOKAMAN,** 5, b g Dandy Man (IRE)—Percolator **Moment Of Madness**
22 **MYWAYISTHEONLYWAY (IRE),** 10, b g Tamayuz—Soul Custody (CAN) **Moment Of Madness**
23 **ONE HART (IRE),** 6, br g Gutaifan (IRE)—Crystal Morning (IRE) **Mr G. F. Tuer**
24 **PINK PARFAIT,** 4, b f Bated Breath—Rosehill Artist (IRE) **Mr G. F. Tuer**
25 **REAL TERMS,** 6, b m Champs Elysees—Easy Terms **Mr G. F. Tuer**
26 **RICH WATERS (IRE),** 5, b g Showcasing—Springlike (IRE) **Ebor Racing Club Ix & Grant Tuer**
27 **SHOWTIME MAHOMES,** 4, b g Dabirsim (FR)—Magic Florence (IRE) **The Muffed Punt Partnership**
28 **SKILLED WARRIOR (IRE),** 5, b g Holy Roman Emperor (IRE)—Sushi Tuna **David & Tuer**
29 **STALINGRAD,** 6, b g War Front (USA)—I Am Beautiful (IRE) **Marjorie & Tuer**
30 **SWINGING EDDIE,** 7, b g Swiss Spirit—Bling Bling (IRE) **NG Racing**
31 **TERMONATOR,** 7, ch g Monsieur Bond (IRE)—Easy Terms **Mr G. F. Tuer**
32 **THE TURPINATOR (IRE),** 6, b g Canford Cliffs (IRE)—Bessichka **Ursa Major Racing & G.Tuer**
33 **VINCE LOMBARDI,** 4, b g Sea The Moon (GER)—First Destinity (FR) **Dark Blue Bloodstock**
34 **WALKING ON CLOUDS (IRE),** 4, b g Gale Force Ten—Aglaia (IRE) **Moment Of Madness**
35 **WESTMORIAN,** 4, b g Holy Roman Emperor (IRE)—Inca Trail (USA) **Miss M. A. Thompson**
36 **WHITEANDBLUE,** 4, b f Fountain of Youth (IRE)—Whiteandgold **Akebar Park Leisure Ltd**
37 **ZAGHAL (IRE),** 5, b g Exceed And Excel (AUS)—Broadway Melody **Hornby Hornets**

THREE-YEAR-OLDS

38 **ACTON BELL,** ch g Dandy Man (IRE)—Divine Act (IRE) **Mr G. F. Tuer**
39 **ALL WHITE MATE (IRE),** b g Camacho—Global Alexander (IRE) **A. Ownership Change Pending**
40 **AMERRONE (IRE),** ch g Fast Company (IRE)—Avenbury **The Weighting Game**
41 **BAJAN BANDIT,** b g Oasis Dream—Dirayah (IRE) **A. R. Turnbull**
42 **BARROLO,** gr g Havana Grey—Belatorio (IRE) **The Weighting Game**
43 B g Gleneagles (IRE)—Celtic Cygnet (IRE) **The Weighting Game**
44 B g Mondialiste (IRE)—Easy Terms **Mr G. F. Tuer**
45 **ECCLES STREET (IRE),** b g Ulysses (IRE)—Wanna (IRE) **The Northern Partners**
46 B f Unfortunately (IRE)—End of An Era (IRE) **Mr G. F. Tuer**
47 **FORTUITOUS STAR (IRE),** b f Starspangledbanner (AUS)—Fortuities (IRE) **Ursa Major Racing & G.Tuer**
48 **GLENTEAGUE,** b f Gleneagles (IRE)—Chincoteague (IRE) **Beswick Brothers & Well Oiled Partners**
49 **GLORIOUS ANGEL (IRE),** b f Cotai Glory—Angel Meadow **Nick Bradley Racing 23**
50 Br f Unfortunately (IRE)—M'Selle (IRE) **Hornby Hornets**
51 **MADAM FLORENCE,** ch f Cityscape—La Havrese (FR) **Mr J. A. Kay**
52 **MERSEA (FR),** b f Born To Sea (IRE)—Bolga Bere (FR) **Nick Bradley Racing 11**
53 **MR JETMAN (IRE),** b g Territories (IRE)—Silent Secret (IRE) **The Northern Partners**
54 **OH SO CHARMING,** b g Charm Spirit (IRE)—Scattered Petals (IRE) **Mr J. A. Kay**
55 B g Mastercraftsman (IRE)—Ondeafears (IRE) **Mr G. F. Tuer**
56 Gr g Havana Grey—Rosehill Artist (IRE) **Mr G. F. Tuer**
57 **RUN CMC (IRE),** b g Gutaifan (IRE)—Sardenya (IRE) **The Muffed Punt Partnership**
58 B g Camacho—Rusookh **Mr G. F. Tuer**

MR GRANT TUER - continued

59 SMOOTH RED, ch g Jungle Cat (IRE)—Greek Tragedy **Mr N. Dalgarno**
60 SOPHIA'S STARLIGHT (FR), b f Hunter's Light (IRE)—Endeavor (FR) **Nick Bradley Racing 11**
61 WRECK IT RYLEY (IRE), gr g Gutaifan (IRE)—Bucks Frizz (IRE) **Ursa Major Racing & G.Tuer**

TWO-YEAR-OLDS

62 B f 05/02 Kodi Bear (IRE)—Alosha (IRE) (Alhebayeb (IRE)) (13000) **Nick Bradley Racing 19 & Partner**
63 B f 19/03 Muhaarar—Chandresh (Holy Roman Emperor (IRE)) (8500) **Nick Bradley Racing 19 & Partner**
64 Ch f 12/04 Mehmas (IRE)—Drop Dead Gorgeous (FR) (Sepoy (AUS)) (28571) **Nick Bradley Racing 19 & Partner**
65 B f 17/03 Camacho—Eriniya (IRE) (Acclamation) (27000) **Mr J. T. Finch**
66 HIGHLAND OLLY, b c 12/03 Cable Bay (IRE)—Roxy Star (IRE) (Fastnet Rock (AUS)) (20000) **M & Tuer**
67 B f 11/04 Expert Eye—Love And Cherish (IRE) (Excellent Art) (15714) **NG Racing**
68 Ch c 25/03 Free Eagle (IRE)—Princesa Del Sol (Kyllachy) (40016) **The Weighting Game**
69 B c 26/04 Land Force (IRE)—Say To Me (FR) (Redoute's Choice (AUS)) (60000) **The Weighting Game**
70 B f 17/04 Havana Gold (IRE)—Stella Blue (FR) (Anabaa (USA)) (41000) **Nick Bradley Racing 19 & Partner**
71 B c 28/02 Dawn Approach (IRE)—Strapless (IRE) (Whipper (USA)) (64026) **The Weighting Game**

---

502 MR BILL TURNER, Sherborne

Postal: **Sigwells Farm, Sigwells, Corton Denham, Sherborne, Dorset, DT9 4LN**
Contacts: **PHONE 01963 220523 MOBILE 07932 100173 FAX 01963 220046**
EMAIL billturnerracing@gmail.com

1 BORN AT MIDNIGHT, 8, b g Midnight Legend—Wavet **Mr B. J. Goldsmith**
2 BY PASS, 4, ch f Cityscape—Up And Running **Mrs P. A. Turner**
3 HILLBILLY, 5, b g Coach House (IRE)—Dusty Dazzler (IRE) **Mrs P. A. Turner**
4 LION'S VIGIL (USA), 6, ch g Kitten's Joy (USA)—Keeping Watch (IRE) **Mr & Mrs RJ Manning**
5 LITTLE BOY BLUE, 8, gr g Hellvelyn—Dusty Dazzler (IRE) **Mrs P. A. Turner**
6 MAJOR GATSBY (IRE), 4, gr g The Grey Gatsby (IRE)—Monteamiata (IRE) **Mr & Mrs RJ Manning**
7 MARETTIMO (IRE), 9, b g Harbour Watch (IRE)—Renowned (IRE) **Mrs P. A. Turner**
8 MILLY MOLLY MANDY, 4, gr f Hellvelyn—Charlevoix (IRE) **Mrs P. A. Turner**
9 SCRAPPY JACK (IRE), 5, b g Epaulette (AUS)—Jessie K **G A Haulage Ltd**
10 SIX FIVE SPECIAL, 5, gr g Hellvelyn—Hound Music **Mrs P. A. Turner**
11 WHO'S SORRY NOW, 5, b m Norse Dancer (IRE)—Pull The Wool (IRE) **Mrs P. A. Turner**

THREE-YEAR-OLDS

12 IT'S A MIRACLE, b g Mayson—Tuscan Light **E. A. Brook**
13 B g Pearl Secret—Mabrokah **R. J. Manning**
14 MOUNTAIN RUN, gr f Hellvelyn—Up And Running **The Hon Mrs R. Pease**
15 PEARLY GAITS, b f Pearl Secret—Spanish Gold **Chapel Stud Ltd**
16 UMMING N' AHING, ch g Lightning Spear—Life Is Golden (USA) **E. A. Brook**

TWO-YEAR-OLDS

17 B c 14/03 Coach House (IRE)—Lady Kyllar (Kyllachy) (5000) **Mrs P. A. Turner**
18 B c 01/05 Gregorian (IRE)—Limousine (Beat Hollow) (15000) **E. A. Brook**
19 B f 16/03 Cable Bay (IRE)—Poinsettia (IRE) (Galileo (IRE)) (24000) **Mr R. W. Clothier**

Assistant Trainer: Kathy While.

---

503 MISS GEMMA TUTTY, Yarm

Postal: **7 Belbrough Close, Hutton Rudby, Yarm, Yorkshire, TS15 0EH**
Contacts: **PHONE 01609 883624**
EMAIL gemma_tutty@hotmail.co.uk

1 **BUSHFIRE,** 4, ch g Australia—Aflame **Grange Park Racing VII**
2 **FREAK OUT (IRE),** 5, b g Kodiac—Herridge (IRE) **Grange Park Racing XIX**
3 **HER WAY,** 5, ch m Charming Thought—On Her Way **Thoroughbred Homes Ltd**
4 **HIGHLIGHTER (IRE),** 4, b g Australia—Cosmic Fire (FR) **Middleham Park Racing XXVII**
5 **LITTLE JO,** 9, b g Major Cadeaux—Discoed **Thoroughbred Homes Ltd**
6 **MISS BRITAIN (IRE),** 4, b f Dandy Man (IRE)—Britain's Pride **Miss G. Tutty**
7 **PATONTHEBACK (IRE),** 5, b g Kodi Bear (IRE)—Miss Brief (IRE) **Mr R & Mrs J E Huin**
8 **RISHES BAAR (IRE),** 4, gr f El Kabeir (USA)—Preobrajenska **Ontoawinner Andy Finneran Richard Porter**
9 **SHAHNAZ (IRE),** 4, b f Decorated Knight—Fol O'Yasmine **Maximum Racing & Thoroughbred Homes Ltd**
10 **STRAWMAN (IRE),** 6, b g Starspangledbanner (AUS)—Youve Got A Friend (IRE) **Mr K. Till**
11 **WHISPERING WINDS (IRE),** 4, ch f Buratino (IRE)—Guthanna Gaoithe **Thoroughbred Homes Ltd**

THREE-YEAR-OLDS

12 **DANCING CLOUD (IRE),** b c Mastercraftsman (IRE)—Dream Approach (IRE) **Miss G. Tutty**
13 **KING HARRY (IRE),** b c Harzand (IRE)—Vizean (IRE) **King Harry Partnership**
14 **LOOK BACK SMILING (IRE),** ch g Fast Company (IRE)—Portico **Nick Bradley Racing 21 & Partners**
15 **MAYJORITY,** b g Mayson—Concentrate **Keep The Faith Partnership**
16 **SHE'S A ROCKET,** b f Bungle Inthejungle—Ticktocks **Salthouse & Partners**
17 **VONDELPARK,** b c Mayson—Loving Touch **Keep The Faith Partnership**

TWO-YEAR-OLDS

18 **ALLROADSLEADTOROME,** b c 17/02 Golden Horn—New Desire (IRE) (Dansili) (37000) **Mostly Cloudy Syndicate**
19 B f 17/03 Invincible Army (IRE)—Dutch Heiress (Dutch Art) (16006) **Yorkshire Moors Racing**
20 B f 29/03 The Last Lion (IRE)—Lady Clair (IRE) (Canford Cliffs (IRE)) **White Rose Racing**
21 B c 23/01 Profitable (IRE)—Ohh Lala (IRE) (Clodovil (IRE)) (17143) **Mr D. J. Lowe**
22 B c 20/04 Inns of Court (IRE)—Startori (Vettori (IRE)) (19000) **Mr E. Eismark**

---

504 MR NIGEL TWISTON-DAVIES, Cheltenham

Postal: **T/a Grange Hill Farm Limited, Grange Hill Farm, Naunton, Cheltenham, Gloucestershire, GL54 3AY**
Contacts: **PHONE 01451 850278 MOBILE 07836 664440**
EMAIL nigel@nigeltwistondavies.co.uk WEBSITE www.nigeltwistondavies.co.uk

1 **AWESOME FOURSOME,** 6, b g Blue Bresil (FR)—Mini Muck **Noel Fehily Racing Syndicates-Awesome Fo**
2 **BAGHEERA GINGE,** 5, b g Clovis du Berlais (FR)—The Prime Viper (IRE) **Gingearmy Racing**
3 **BALLINTUBBER BOY (IRE),** 6, b g Robin des Champs (FR)—Manhattan Babe (IRE) **Mason and McGoff**
4 **BALLYANDY,** 12, b g Kayf Tara—Megalex **Options O Syndicate**
5 **BALLYCAMUS (IRE),** 6, b g Presenting—Dotchenka (FR) **Mrs C. S. C. Beresford-Wylie**
6 **BALLYELLIS (IRE),** 10, b g Shantou (USA)—Chalice Wells **Mr N. A. Twiston-Davies**
7 **BEAUPORT (IRE),** 7, b g Califet (FR)—Byerley Beauty (IRE) **Bryan & Philippa Burrough**
8 **BENNY SILVER (IRE),** 5, gr g Mastercraftsman (IRE)—Red Allie (IRE) **Twiston-Davies Equine**
9 **BLACKCAUSEWAY,** 7, b g Robin des Champs (FR)—Bellino Spirit (IRE) **Mr A. Gillman**
10 **BLENDED STEALTH,** 6, b g Walk In The Park (IRE)—Wyldello **Graham & Alison Jelley**
11 **BROADWAY BOY (IRE),** 5, b g Malinas (GER)—Broadway Theatre (IRE) **D. M. Proos**
12 **CAFE PUSHKIN (FR),** 7, b g Montmartre (FR)—Chausey (FR) **The Wasting Assets**
13 **CASA NO MENTO,** 5, b m Casamento (IRE)—Red Hibiscus **Ratkatcha Racing**
14 **CHANCE A TUNE (FR),** 8, b g My Risk (FR)—Lyric Melody (FR) **Mr N. A. Twiston-Davies**
15 **CHECKITOUT (IRE),** 9, b g Salutino (GER)—Akasha (IRE) **Mills & Mason Partnership**

MR NIGEL TWISTON-DAVIES - continued

16 **CORPORAL JACKJONES (IRE),** 4, b g Milan—Peinture Rose (IRE) **Mr N. A. Twiston-Davies**
17 **CUTHBERT DIBBLE (IRE),** 5, b g Kayf Tara—Molo **Graham & Alison Jelley**
18 **DANCE AT NIGHT,** 5, b g Dark Angel (IRE)—Strictly Dancing (IRE) **Mr J. Neild**
19 **DASHER (IRE),** 5, b g Soldier of Fortune (IRE)—High Dolly (IRE) **Mr N. A. Twiston-Davies**
20 **DEFENCE TREATY (IRE),** 7, b g Dandy Man (IRE)—Just Like Ivy (CAN) **Mr M. Barlow**
21 **EARLOFTHECOTSWOLDS (FR),** 9, bl g Axxos (GER)—Sissi Land (FR) **Twiston-Davies, Mason, Greer & Kiely**
22 **EQUINUS (IRE),** 5, b g Shantou (USA)—Merryisker (IRE) **Options O Syndicate**
23 **FANTASTIKAS (FR),** 8, b g Davidoff (GER)—Negresse de Cuta (FR) **Imperial Racing Partnership 2016**
24 **FANTOMAS (FR),** 7, b g Sinndar (IRE)—Trudente (FR) **Mr N. A. Twiston-Davies**
25 **FINEST HOUR (FR),** 5, gr g Coastal Path—Miss Vitoria (FR) **A. R. Bromley**
26 **FLINTSTONE (IRE),** 4, ch g Starspangledbanner (AUS)—Madame Cherie (USA) **J. K. Powell Racing**
27 **GOOD BOY BOBBY (IRE),** 10, b g Flemensfirth (USA)—Princess Gaia (IRE) **Mr Simon Munir & Mr Isaac Souede**
28 **GUARD YOUR DREAMS,** 7, b g Fame And Glory—Native Sunrise (IRE) **Graham & Alison Jelley**
29 **GUY (IRE),** 8, ch g Getaway (GER)—Sept Verites (FR) **The Hons W. G. & A. G. Vestey**
30 **HIGH TREASON,** 4, b g Kayf Tara—Amber Cloud **Bryan & Philippa Burrough**
31 **HIGHER GROUND,** 6, b g Black Sam Bellamy (IRE)—Reverse Swing **Twiston-Davies Equine**
32 4, B br g Soldier of Fortune (IRE)—Hollygrove Samba (IRE) **Graham & Alison Jelley**
33 **I LIKE TO MOVE IT,** 6, b g Trans Island—Nobratinetta (FR) **Anne-Marie & Jamie Shepperd**
34 **IDALKO BIHOUE (FR),** 5, br g Balko (FR)—Vann Bihouee (FR) **Anne-Marie & Jamie Shepperd**
35 **IMPERIAL B G (IRE),** 6, gr g Getaway (GER)—Milan Pride (IRE) **Imperial Racing Partnership**
36 **IMPERIAL SUN,** 5, b g Sea The Stars (IRE)—Abunai **Ratkatcha Racing**
37 **JASMIWA (FR),** 5, b m Authorized (IRE)—Maikawa (FR) **Anne-Marie & Jamie Shepperd**
38 **JOSH THE BOSS,** 4, b g Yorgunnabelucky (USA)—Bonsai (IRE) **Mr J. Neild**
39 **JUNIOR DES BORDES (FR),** 4, b g Free Port Lux—Baraka des Bordes (FR) **A. R. Bromley**
40 **KEEPYOURDREAMSBIG (FR),** 5, b g Vision d'Etat (FR)—Take This Waltz (FR) **Mr C. J. Haughey**
41 **KING OF QUINTA (FR),** 5, ch g Style Vendome (FR)—Dogaressa (IRE) **D. M. Proos**
42 **MANIMOLE,** 6, b m Sulamani (IRE)—Mabel Mole **The Jukes Family**
43 **MASTER CHEWY (IRE),** 6, b g Walk In The Park (IRE)—Shake The Tree (IRE) **Anne-Marie & Jamie Shepperd**
44 **MATATA (IRE),** 5, b g Vadamos (FR)—Wattrey **Mr Simon Munir & Mr Isaac Souede**
45 **MAVIS PIKE,** 4, b f Pether's Moon (IRE)—Definitley Lovely **Mr N. A. Twiston-Davies**
46 **MOVEIT LIKE MINNIE (IRE),** 6, b g Libertarian—Cassandrasway (IRE) **F. J. Mills**
47 **MR BARROWCLOUGH (IRE),** 4, b g Mount Nelson—Kizmehoney (IRE) **Mr Simon Munir & Mr Isaac Souede**
48 **MR MACKAY (IRE),** 4, ch g Mount Nelson—Soeur Gael (IRE) **Mr N. A. Twiston-Davies**
49 **NAVEGAON GATE,** 5, b g Frankel—Cascata (IRE) **Mr N. A. Twiston-Davies**
50 **NOBLE SAVAGE (IRE),** 8, b g Arcadio (GER)—Callerdiscallerdat (IRE) **Walker White Jenkins & Old**
51 **NORMAN FLETCHER,** 4, ch g No Risk At All (FR)—Hiho Silver Lining **Mr N. A. Twiston-Davies**
52 **ONE TRUE KING (IRE),** 8, ch g Getaway (GER)—Final Leave (IRE) **RacehorseClub.com**
53 **POPPA POUTINE (IRE),** 7, b g Sholokhov (IRE)—Sherchanceit (IRE) **Options O Syndicate**
54 **PUSH THE BUTTON (IRE),** 4, gr g Kingston Hill—Tara Rose **Jimmy & Susie Wenman**
55 **PYM (IRE),** 10, b g Stowaway—Liss Rua (IRE) **Ratkatcha Racing**
56 **ROCCO (IRE),** 10, b g Shantou (USA)—Navaro (IRE) **Mr & Mrs P Carter**
57 **SAFE DESTINATION,** 5, b g Pether's Moon (IRE)—Leighton Lass **Mr M. L. Berryman**
58 **SERGEANT WILSON (IRE),** 5, b g Soldier of Fortune (IRE)—In A Rush (IRE) **Mr Simon Munir & Mr Isaac Souede**
59 **SPIRITS BAY,** 5, b g Black Sam Bellamy (IRE)—Silver Coaster (IRE) **Mr & Mrs P Carter, J.A.B Old, M Sanders**
60 **SPRING MEADOW (IRE),** 6, b g Fame And Glory—Gales Present (IRE) **Walters Plant Hire & Potter Group**
61 **STREAM OF STARS,** 8, b g Sea The Stars (IRE)—Precious Gem (IRE) **Susie & Robert Frosell**
62 **STRONG BELLE,** 5, bl m Blue Bresil (FR)—Belle Berry (FR) **James and Jean Potter Ltd**
63 **SUPASUNRISE (IRE),** 7, b g Mores Wells—Sofia Aurora (USA) **Jump For Fun Racing**
64 **SUPER SIX,** 6, b gr g Montmartre (FR)—Hiho Silver Lining **Baker, Dodd & Lakin**
65 **TEDLEY,** 4, b g Sixties Icon—Six Cents (IRE) **Mr N. A. Twiston-Davies**
66 **TEMPLEHILLS (IRE),** 12, b br g Kalanisi (IRE)—Sissinghurst Storm (IRE) **Mr N. A. Twiston-Davies**
67 **THE KNIPHAND (FR),** 5, b g Choeur du Nord (FR)—La Chichina (FR) **Mr D. E. Owens**
68 **THE NEWEST ONE (IRE),** 8, b g Oscar (IRE)—Thuringe (FR) **S Such & CG Paletta**
69 **THELASTHIGHKING (IRE),** 7, ch g Roderic O'Connor (IRE)—End of The Affair (IRE) **Mr E. Whettam**
70 **TOP OF THE BILL (IRE),** 7, b g Fame And Glory—Glory Days (GER) **C. C. Walker**
71 **TOPOFTHECOTSWOLDS (IRE),** 9, b g Arcadio (GER)—Bambootcha (IRE) **Mr M. A. Reay**
72 **UNCLE ARTHUR,** 5, b g Blue Bresil (FR)—Mini Muck **Million in Mind Partnership**
73 **UNCLE BERT,** 6, b g Pether's Moon (IRE)—Azza (FR) **James and Jean Potter Ltd**
74 **UNDERSUPERVISION (IRE),** 7, ch g Doyen (IRE)—Dances With Waves (IRE) **Anne-Marie & Jamie Shepperd**
75 **VICTORIAS PEAK (IRE),** 8, b m Fame And Glory—Rosin de Beau (IRE) **Superior Enterprises LTD**

MR NIGEL TWISTON-DAVIES - continued

76 **WEVEALLBEENCAUGHT (IRE),** 6, b g Getaway (GER)—Curvacious (IRE) **& Wenman & James**
77 **WHOLESTONE (IRE),** 12, br g Craigsteel—Last Theatre (IRE) **Mr Simon Munir & Mr Isaac Souede**
78 **WONDER OF THE SEAS (IRE),** 5, b g Doyen (IRE)—Stay At Home Mum (IRE) **Gingearmy Racing**
79 **ZAMBELLA (FR),** 8, b m Zambezi Sun—Visby (FR) **Mr Simon Munir & Mr Isaac Souede**

Assistant Trainer: Carl LLewellyn, Jim Old.

NH Jockey: Tom Bellamy, Sam Twiston-Davies. **Conditional Jockey:** Finn Lambert, Jordan Nailor, Jack Savage.

Amateur Jockey: James Turner.

---

505 MR MARK USHER, Lambourn

Postal: **Rowdown House Stables, Upper Lambourn, Hungerford, Berkshire, RG17 8QP**
Contacts: **PHONE 01488 73630, 01488 72598 MOBILE 07831 873531**
EMAIL markusher.racing@btconnect.com WEBSITE www.markusherracing.co.uk

1 **ADAAYINOURLIFE,** 4, b g Adaay (IRE)—Sans Reward (IRE) **Andy & Lizzie Cova**
2 **ALCHEMIST'S DREAM,** 4, b f Lawman (FR)—Royal Alchemist **The Ridgeway Alchemist's**
3 **ARLECCHINO'S GIFT,** 4, b g Shalaa (IRE)—Represent (IRE) **Mr K. Senior**
4 **BIRD FOR LIFE,** 9, b m Delegator—Birdolini **The Mark Usher Racing Club**
5 **BORN TO PLEASE,** 9, b m Stimulation (IRE)—Heart Felt **The Mark Usher Racing Club**
6 **GUSTAV HOLST (IRE),** 5, b g Sea The Stars (IRE)—Scarlet And Gold (IRE) **Mr B. C. Rogan**
7 **HEERATHETRACK,** 4, gr g Heeraat (IRE)—Jessica Ennis (USA) **High Five Racing and Partners**
8 **LIBERTY BAY,** 5, b m Iffraaj—Light Fantastic **Ushers Court**
9 **MEISTERZINGER (IRE),** 5, br g Mastercraftsman (IRE)—Zingeeyah **The OAP Partnership (Mr J. Segust)**
10 **MOON KNIGHT,** 4, b g Garswood—Nightunderthestars **The Unraceables**
11 **ON THE RIGHT TRACK,** 6, gr g Mukhadram—Jessica Ennis (USA) **Mrs T. J. Channing-Williams**
12 **PERTHSHIRE (IRE),** 5, b g Gleneagles (IRE)—Destalink **Mr B. C. Rogan**
13 **Q TWENTY BOY (IRE),** 8, ch g Dandy Man (IRE)—Judies Child (IRE) **The Mark Usher Racing Club**
14 **RAVI ROAD (IRE),** 4, ch f Zoffany (IRE)—Crosstalk (IRE) **Ushers Court**
15 **SID'S ANNIE,** 4, b f Farhh—Blushing Beauty **Twenty Four Carrot Racing**
16 **THE BAY WARRIOR (IRE),** 5, b g The Gurkha (IRE)—Fraulein **Andy & Lizzie Cova**
17 **TIMEFORASPIN,** 9, b g Librettist (USA)—Timeforagin **The Unraceables**
18 **TIN FANDANGO,** 8, b g Steele Tango (USA)—Littlemoor Lass **Mr M. A. Humphreys**
19 **TWILIGHT REVENGE,** 4, ch g Twilight Son—Sweetest Revenge (IRE) **The Ridgeway Partnership**
20 **VIEWFROMTHESTARS (IRE),** 4, b g Starspangledbanner (AUS)—Condensed **Champagne And Shambles**
21 **WILLINGLY,** 6, ch m Hot Streak (IRE)—Paradise Place **Miss J. Hynes**

THREE-YEAR-OLDS

22 **ARLECCHINO'S STAR,** b f Zoustar (AUS)—Sandy Cay (USA) **Mr K. Senior**
23 **BOOM BOOM POW,** gr f Havana Grey—Sunburnt **Miss J. Hynes**
24 **CLOSE OF PLAY,** b f Assertive—Free To Love **Lady Whent**
25 **OUTREACH,** b gr g Outstrip—Willbeme **Mike Humphreys & Mark Usher**

TWO-YEAR-OLDS

26 Gr c 07/04 Outstrip—Abbotsfield (IRE) (Sakhee's Secret) (6000)
27 Ch f 27/03 Pearl Secret—Concentration (IRE) (Mind Games) (4500)
28 B c 24/03 U S Navy Flag (USA)—Danehurst (Danehill (USA)) (12000)
29 B f 07/03 French Navy—Dream Impossible (IRE) (Iffraaj) (11605)

506 MR ROGER VARIAN, Newmarket

Postal: **Carlburg Stables, 49 Bury Road, Newmarket, Suffolk, CB8 7BY**
Contacts: **PHONE 01638 661702 FAX 01638 667018**
EMAIL office@varianstable.com WEBSITE www.varianstable.com

1 **AIMERIC,** 4, b g Frankel—Aris (IRE) **Sheikh Mohammed Obaid Al Maktoum**
2 **AKHU NAJLA,** 4, b c Kingman—Galicuix **KHK Racing Ltd**
3 **AL HUSN (IRE),** 4, b f Dubawi (IRE)—Hadaatha (IRE) **Shadwell Estate Company Ltd**
4 **AMEYNAH (IRE),** 4, b f Exceed And Excel (AUS)—Tazffin (IRE) **Sheikh Ahmed Al Maktoum**
5 **CAPH STAR,** 4, b c Siyouni (FR)—Caskelena (IRE) **N. Bizakov**
6 **CHANTICO,** 4, b g Kingman—Deuce Again **KHK Racing Ltd**
7 **CROACHILL (IRE),** 4, b f Churchill (IRE)—Cronsa (GER) **Mr M. Saeed**
8 **DEFERRED,** 4, ch g Postponed (IRE)—Platinum Pearl **Z. A. Galadari**
9 **DINOO (IRE),** 5, b g Starspangledbanner (AUS)—Shirley Blade (IRE) **Mr D. Vakilgilani**
10 **DIVINE JEWEL,** 4, b f Frankel—Agnes Stewart (IRE) **Mr K. Maeda**
11 **DRAGON SYMBOL,** 5, gr h Cable Bay (IRE)—Arcamist **Mr Y. Kubota**
12 **EL DRAMA (IRE),** 5, ch h Lope de Vega (IRE)—Victoire Finale **Sheikh Mohammed Obaid Al Maktoum**
13 **ELDAR ELDAROV,** 4, b c Dubawi (IRE)—All At Sea **KHK Racing Ltd**
14 **EXTRICATION,** 4, ch g Iffraaj—Heavenly Scent **John Connolly & A D Spence**
15 **FANTASTIC FOX,** 5, ch g Frankel—Vasilia **King Power Racing Co Ltd**
16 **GASTRONOMY,** 4, ch g Ulysses (IRE)—Cantal **Cheveley Park Stud Limited**
17 **GLAM DE VEGA (IRE),** 4, ch c Lope de Vega (IRE)—
Glamorous Approach (IRE) **Sheikh Mohammed Obaid Al Maktoum**
18 **GREATGADIAN (GER),** 5, b g Siyouni (FR)—Goathemala (GER) **King Power Racing Co Ltd**
19 **INDEMNIFY,** 4, gr g Lope de Vega (IRE)—Karisma (IRE) **Miss Y. M. G. Jacques**
20 **JULIA AUGUSTA,** 4, b f Ulysses (IRE)—Empress Livia **Cheveley Park Stud Limited**
21 **KITSUNE POWER (IRE),** 4, b g Holy Roman Emperor (IRE)—Fire Heroine (USA) **King Power Racing Co Ltd**
22 **LEUVEN POWER (IRE),** 4, ch g Cotai Glory—Triggers Broom (IRE) **King Power Racing Co Ltd**
23 **LIR SPECIALE (IRE),** 4, b g Prince of Lir (IRE)—Ma Bella Paola (FR) **Opulence Thoroughbreds**
24 **MANAAFITH (USA),** 4, b f Exceed And Excel (AUS)—Almashooqa (USA) **Shadwell Estate Company Ltd**
25 **MITBAAHY (IRE),** 4, b c Profitable (IRE)—Wrood (USA) **Mr Hasan Mefareh Alajmi & Fawzi Nass**
26 **MODAARA,** 4, b f Dubawi (IRE)—Nahrain **Sheikh Ahmed Al Maktoum**
27 **MOSHAAWER,** 5, gr g Frankel—Hadaatha (IRE) **Shadwell Estate Company Ltd**
28 **MUKADDAMAH,** 4, b f New Approach (IRE)—Craighall **Shadwell Estate Company Ltd**
29 **NAGANO,** 5, b g Fastnet Rock (AUS)—Nazym (IRE) **N. Bizakov**
30 **PERIPATETIC,** 4, b f Ulysses (IRE)—Dublino (USA) **Cheveley Park Stud Limited**
31 **POSTILEO (IRE),** 6, b g Galileo (IRE)—Posterity (IRE) **Sheikh Mohammed Obaid Al Maktoum**
32 **PURE DIGNITY,** 4, ch f Dubawi (IRE)—Starlet's Sister (IRE) **Victorious Racing & KHK Racing**
33 **RIZG,** 4, b g No Nay Never (USA)—Azenzar **Mr I. Alsagar**
34 **ROYAL CHAMPION (IRE),** 5, b g Shamardal (USA)—Emirates Queen **Sheikh Mohammed Obaid Al Maktoum**
35 **SAINT LAWRENCE (IRE),** 5, b g Al Kazeem—Affluent **D. J. Deer**
36 **SHANDOZ,** 6, b g Golden Horn—Shabyt **N. Bizakov**
37 **SIR WINSTON (IRE),** 4, b g Churchill (IRE)—Boastful (IRE)
38 **SOLAR ORBITER (IRE),** 4, b c Showcasing—Heliosphere (USA) **Flaxman Stables Ireland Ltd**
39 **SONNERIE POWER (FR),** 4, ch g Almanzor (FR)—Nehalennia (USA) **King Power Racing Co Ltd**
40 **SOUND ANGELA,** 4, b f Muhaarar—Instance **Mr Y. Masuda**
41 **STRAWBERRI,** 5, ch m Gleneagles (IRE)—Altesse Imperiale (IRE) **D. J. Deer**
42 **SUBASTAR (IRE),** 4, b g Sea The Stars (IRE)—Suba (USA) **Sheikh Mohammed Obaid Al Maktoum**
43 **THREE PRIESTS (JPN),** 4, b f Deep Impact (JPN)—Guilty Twelve (USA) **Merry Fox Stud Limited**
44 **TINKER TOY,** 6, b g War Front (USA)—Cursory Glance (USA) **Merry Fox Stud Limited**
45 **TOSKANA BELLE (FR),** 4, ch f Shamalgan (FR)—Tristane (FR) **T. Yoshida**
46 **TYRRHENIAN SEA (IRE),** 5, gr g Dark Angel (IRE)—Nocturne (GER) **Flaxman Stables Ireland Ltd**
47 **VOODOO QUEEN,** 4, b f Frankel—Cursory Glance (USA) **Merry Fox Stud Limited**
48 **YAANAAS,** 4, ch g Ulysses (IRE)—Troarn (FR) **Shadwell Estate Company Ltd**
49 **ZAINALARAB,** 4, b g Wootton Bassett—Zimira (IRE) **Shadwell Estate Company Ltd**
50 **ZENGA,** 4, b f Lope de Vega (IRE)—Blending **Toudo LLC**

THREE-YEAR-OLDS

51 **AKKADIAN THUNDER,** ch c Night of Thunder (IRE)—Akhania **Opulence Thoroughbreds**
52 **AL MUZN (IRE),** b c Oasis Dream—Queen's Pearl (IRE) **Z. A. Galadari**
53 **ALIF POWER (IRE),** gr c El Kabeir (USA)—Extricate (IRE) **King Power Racing Co Ltd**

MR ROGER VARIAN - continued

54 **ALMATY STAR (IRE),** b c Kodiac—Sante (IRE) **N. Bizakov**
55 B f Kingman—Alwarga (USA) **Sheikh Ahmed Al Maktoum**
56 **AMAZING (IRE),** b f Siyouni (FR)—Missy O' Gwaun (IRE) **Mr I. Alsagar**
57 B c Gleneagles (IRE)—Anaamil (IRE) **Sheikh Ahmed Al Maktoum**
58 Ch c Frankel—Auld Alliance (IRE)
59 **AURORA CHARM,** ch f New Bay—Farewell To You **Sheikh Mohammed Obaid Al Maktoum**
60 **AZURE ANGEL,** ch f Harry Angel (IRE)—Silken Skies (IRE) **Opulence Thoroughbreds**
61 **BOTANICAL (IRE),** b g Lope de Vega (IRE)—Bloomfield (IRE) **Sheikh Mohammed Obaid Al Maktoum**
62 B f New Approach (IRE)—Bumptious **Mrs H. Varian**
63 **BUSH ROSE,** b f Australia—Tulipa Rosa (IRE) **Ed Babington, James Barnett & Partner**
64 **CELL SA BEELA,** br f Kingman—Sellsabeel (FR) **Sheikh M. B. K. Al Maktoum**
65 **CENTREFOLD,** b f Showcasing—Delevigne **Sheikh Mohammed Obaid Al Maktoum**
66 **CHARYN (IRE),** gr c Dark Angel (IRE)—Futoon (IRE) **N. Bizakov**
67 **CLASSIC TIMES,** b f Lope de Vega (IRE)—Sunday Times **Mr A. Belshaw**
68 **COBALT BLUE (IRE),** ch g Sioux Nation (USA)—Impressionist Art (USA) **C Fahy, R & S Marchant & Partner**
69 **CREME DE CACAO (IRE),** b f Iffraaj—Alwasmiya **Mr P R Jarvis & Partner**
70 B c Dubawi (IRE)—Crown Queen (USA) **Mr B. Leon**
71 **DECORATION (IRE),** b f Frankel—Weekend Strike (USA) **Magnier, Smith, Tabor & Westerberg**
72 **DEMI POINTE,** b f Pivotal—On Her Toes (IRE) **Cheveley Park Stud Limited**
73 **DRAGON ICON (IRE),** b c Lope de Vega (IRE)—Matauri Pearl (IRE) **Mr Y. Kubota**
74 **EMBESTO,** ch c Roaring Lion (USA)—Dibajj (FR) **Sheikh Ahmed Al Maktoum**
75 **ENFJAAR (IRE),** b c Lope de Vega (IRE)—Tesoro (IRE) **Shadwell Estate Company Ltd**
76 **EQUATORIAL (USA),** ch g Showcasing—Amuser (IRE) **Exors of the Late S. S. Niarchos**
77 **EXIMIOUS (IRE),** b f Exceed And Excel (AUS)—Estiqaama (USA) **Highclere T'Bred Racing - Marie Curie**
78 **EXOPLANET (FR),** b c Sea The Stars (IRE)—Gumriyah **Sheikh Mohammed Obaid Al Maktoum**
79 **EXTRA TIME,** b f Zoustar (AUS)—Time On **R. Barnett**
80 **FLEURIR,** ch f Justify (USA)—Butterscotch (IRE) **Mr K. Maeda**
81 **FOX MASTER,** b g Showcasing—Awesome **King Power Racing Co Ltd**
82 **FOX VISION,** b c New Approach (IRE)—Melinoe **King Power Racing Co Ltd**
83 **FRANBERRI,** b f Frankel—Altesse Imperiale (IRE) **D. J. Deer**
84 **GLISTENED,** ch f Iffraaj—Spangled **Cheveley Park Stud Limited**
85 **GREEN GO (IRE),** ch g Zoffany (IRE)—Queen of Stars (USA) **Newsells Park Stud - Ossie Ardiles Synd.**
86 **INDEMNITY (IRE),** b c Lope de Vega (IRE)—Oriental Magic (GER) **Highclere - George Bernard Shaw**
87 **INSPIRITUS (IRE),** b c Sea The Stars (IRE)—Pure Art **Varian Racing VII**
88 **IRREGULAR WARFARE (FR),** ch c Saxon Warrior (JPN)—Artistic Jewel (IRE) **Victorious Racing Limited**
89 **ISLAND STAR (IRE),** b c New Approach (IRE)—My Fairy (IRE) **The Matthew Family & Partner**
90 **JURI,** b f Invincible Spirit (IRE)—Nessina (USA) **K. M. Al-Mudhaf**
91 **KODIMAN (IRE),** b g Kodi Bear (IRE)—Manaahil **Varian Racing VIII**
92 **KOLSAI,** b c Oasis Dream—Fizzi Top **N. Bizakov**
93 **LIL' FRANK,** b g Frankel—Pepita (IRE) **Sheikh Mohammed Obaid Al Maktoum**
94 **LITTLE HUG,** b f Invincible Spirit (IRE)—Another Charm (IRE) **Glentree Pastoral Pty Ltd**
95 **LORD OF BISCAY (IRE),** b c Lope de Vega (IRE)—Alava (IRE) **Ballylinch Stud**
96 **LUNA EFFECT (IRE),** b g Sea The Stars (IRE)—Potent Embrace (USA) **King Power Racing Co Ltd**
97 **MARAKESH,** ch f Decorated Knight—Turama **Mr I. Alsagar**
98 **MATHEMATICIAN (IRE),** b g Starspangledbanner (AUS)—Stranagone (IRE) **Mr Alan Spence**
99 **MAWHOOBA,** ch f Sea The Stars (IRE)—Mur Hiba (IRE) **Sheikh M. B. K. Al Maktoum**
100 **MEGAN MOON (IRE),** ch f Starspangledbanner (AUS)—Apparel (IRE) **Opulence Thoroughbreds**
101 **MIGHTY NEBULA (IRE),** ch c Saxon Warrior (JPN)—Pure Symmetry (USA) **Mr F. A. Al Harthi**
102 **MIQDAAD (IRE),** br gr c Dark Angel (IRE)—Khatiba (IRE) **Sheikh Ahmed Al Maktoum**
103 **MUBHIJAH,** ch f Shamardal (USA)—Mubhirah **Shadwell Estate Company Ltd**
104 **NAZYMBEK (FR),** b c Kingman—Nazym (IRE) **N. Bizakov**
105 **NEW ENDEAVOUR (IRE),** b g New Bay—Moody Blue (IRE) **Teme Valley & Ballylinch Stud**
106 **OKAMI (IRE),** b g Showcasing—Brexitmeansbrexit **Mr A. Bintouq**
107 **PACO'S PRIDE,** gr f Roaring Lion (USA)—Paco's Angel **Biddestone Racing XIII**
108 **PILLARSOFCREATION,** b gr f Roaring Lion (USA)—Psychometry (FR) **Exors of the Late S. S. Niarchos**
109 **PIVOTAL DANCE,** ch f Pivotal—Strictly Lambada **Helena Springfield Ltd**
110 **PUSHY,** b f Dubawi (IRE)—Dash To The Front **Helena Springfield Ltd**
111 **RAZZAM (IRE),** br c Showcasing—Whispering Bell (IRE) **Mr Hasan Mefareh Alajmi & Fawzi Nass**
112 **RED DANIELLE,** b f Sea The Moon (GER)—Garabelle (IRE) **Mr M. J. Power**
113 **RESOLUTE MAN,** ch c Dubawi (IRE)—Lady Momoka (IRE) **Sheikh Mohammed Obaid Al Maktoum**

MR ROGER VARIAN - continued

114 REVENITE, b g Harry Angel (IRE)—Constant Dream **King Power Racing Co Ltd**
115 RUSSET GOLD, ch g Al Kazeem—Affluent **D. J. Deer**
116 SAKHEER (IRE), b c Zoffany (IRE)—Shortmile Lady (IRE) **KHK Racing Ltd**
117 SEALINE (IRE), ch c Australia—Zman Awal (IRE) **Mr M. B. H. K. Al Attiyah**
118 SHADOW DANCE, gr c Almanzor (FR)—Skyline Dancer **Newsells Park Stud Limited**
119 SHOOLAA, ch f Shamardal (USA)—Tranquil Star (IRE) **Sheikh Ahmed Al Maktoum**
120 STRONG IMPACT (IRE), b f Saxon Warrior (JPN)—Cascella (IRE) **Ed Babington, James Barnett & Partner**
121 SUB ROSA, b f Twilight Son—Between Us **Cheveley Park Stud Limited**
122 SWISS STAR, b f Dark Angel (IRE)—Swiss Dream **Lordship Stud**
123 TADSHIN, b c Muhaarar—Nahrain **Sheikh Ahmed Al Maktoum**
124 TAJALAT (IRE), ch f Showcasing—Ta Ammol **Sheikh Ahmed Al Maktoum**
125 TAJALLA (IRE), b c Kessaar (IRE)—Armum (IRE) **Sheikh Ahmed Al Maktoum**
126 TAWAFAG, gr ro c Starspangledbanner (AUS)—Bedouin Dancer (IRE) **Sheikh Ahmed Al Maktoum**
127 THE PLATINUM QUEEN (IRE), b f Cotai Glory—Thrilled (IRE) **Mr K. Yoshida**
128 TYNDRUM GOLD, b g Muhaarar—La Napoule **Opulence Thoroughbreds**
129 WARREN HILL (IRE), b f No Nay Never (USA)—Travel (USA) **Crager, Hassiakos, Moorhead, Collins & Partner**
130 WELLTIMED, b f Zoffany (IRE)—Well Yes (IRE) **Miss Y. M. G. Jacques**
131 WITCHING HOUR, b c Frankel—Cursory Glance (USA) **Merry Fox Stud Limited**
132 YA HAFHD (IRE), ch f Sea The Stars (IRE)—Daymooma **Shadwell Estate Company Ltd**
133 YOUNG AND FUN, b f Lope de Vega (IRE)—Crimson Rosette (IRE) **Mr M. Matsushima**
134 YOUNGEST, b f Dubawi (IRE)—Sheikha Reika (FR) **Sheikh Mohammed Obaid Al Maktoum**

TWO-YEAR-OLDS

135 AL HUJAIJA (IRE), b f 16/03 Kodiac—Majestic Jasmine (IRE) (New Approach (IRE)) (60000) **Z. A. Galadari**
136 AL KHAWSSAA (IRE), b f 28/03 Night of Thunder (IRE)—Platinum Pearl (Shamardal (USA)) **Z. A. Galadari**
137 Ch c 26/04 Sea The Stars (IRE)—
Along Came Casey (IRE) (Oratorio (IRE)) (700000) **Sheikh Mohammed Obaid Al Maktoum**
138 B c 19/01 Camelot—Alouja (IRE) (Raven's Pass (USA)) (190000) **HIghclere Thoroughbred Racing - Monet**
139 B f 24/03 Exceed And Excel (AUS)—Baheeja (Dubawi (IRE)) **Sheikh Ahmed Al Maktoum**
140 B br c 09/03 American Pharoah (USA)—Bint Huwaar (USA) (More Than Ready (USA)) **Victorious Racing Limited**
141 B c 22/01 Frankel—Come On Leicester (IRE) (Kodiac) **King Power Racing Co Ltd**
142 CONDOR PASA, ch c 26/02 Siyouni (FR)—Waldnah (New Approach (IRE)) (140000)
143 B c 01/05 Frankel—Crown Queen (USA) (Smart Strike (CAN)) **Mr B. Leon**
144 B c 13/03 Siyouni (FR)—Dame du Roi (IRE) (Dark Angel (IRE)) (250000) **Sheikh Mohammed Obaid Al Maktoum**
145 Br c 28/03 Calyx—Dazzling Rose (Raven's Pass (USA)) (170000)
146 B c 11/04 Kingman—Diamond Fields (IRE) (Fastnet Rock (AUS)) (375000) **N. Bizakov**
147 Br f 27/01 Sea The Stars (IRE)—
Diamonds Pour Moi (Pour Moi (IRE)) (304122) **Victorious Racing Limited & Fawzi Nass**
148 DILARA (IRE), ch f 21/03 Night of Thunder (IRE)—Divisimo (Dansili) (150000) **N. Bizakov**
149 B f 24/03 Invincible Spirit (IRE)—Dubai Queen (USA) (Kingmambo (USA)) **Sheikh Mohammed Obaid Al Maktoum**
150 B c 22/04 Sea The Stars (IRE)—Duchess of France (IRE) (Dylan Thomas (IRE)) (150000)
151 B f 31/01 Frankel—Estijaab (AUS) (Snitzel (AUS))
152 B c 05/04 Twilight Son—Faithful Promise (Acclamation) (47000) **Sheikh A. H. F. M. A. Al Sabah**
153 Br c 10/02 Showcasing—Falsafa (Dansili) (210000) **Sheikh Ahmed Al Maktoum**
154 B f 25/02 Churchill (IRE)—Fearn's Pippin (Dubawi (IRE)) (120000) **Mr W. Crager**
155 FLAVOUR MAKER (IRE), b c 10/02 Profitable (IRE)—
May Day Queen (IRE) (Danetime (IRE)) (65000) **Opulence Thoroughbreds**
156 FOREVER NOAH, b c 06/04 Dark Angel (IRE)—Poppet's Passion (Clodovil (IRE)) (76030) **Opulence Thoroughbreds**
157 B c 14/04 Cappella Sansevero—
Goodnight And Joy (IRE) (Rip Van Winkle (IRE)) (125000) **King Power Racing Co Ltd**
158 HALVA (IRE), b f 30/04 Kodiac—Home Cummins (IRE) (Rip Van Winkle (IRE)) (150000) **N. Bizakov**
159 Ch c 13/04 Mastercraftsman (IRE)—Hamasat (Pivotal)
160 B c 06/02 Twilight Son—Impressionable (Exceed And Excel (AUS)) (40000) **Sheikh A. H. F. M. A. Al Sabah**
161 B c 20/03 Kodiac—Irish Steps (USA) (Giant's Causeway (USA)) (150000) **Sheikh A. H. F. M. A. Al Sabah**
162 B c 07/04 Kessaar (IRE)—Khibrah (Dark Angel (IRE)) (45714) **Victorious Racing Limited & Fawzi Nass**
163 B c 12/02 Too Darn Hot—Lady Momoka (IRE) (Shamardal (USA)) **Sheikh Mohammed Obaid Al Maktoum**
164 Ch c 06/02 Churchill (IRE)—Lady's Purse (Doyen (IRE)) (160064) **King Power Racing Co Ltd**
165 LIGHTNING TOUCH, b f 05/03 Frankel—
Legerete (USA) (Rahy (USA)) (350000) **Newsells Park Stud & Merry Fox Stud**

MR ROGER VARIAN - continued

166 B c 14/04 Kingman—Majestic Silver (IRE) (Linamix (FR)) (256102) **Sheikh Mohammed Obaid Al Maktoum**
167 B f 31/01 Blue Point (IRE)—Maleficent Queen (Mount Nelson) (62000)
168 B c 18/04 U S Navy Flag (USA)—Many Hearts (USA) (Distorted Humor (USA)) (128051) **King Power Racing Co Ltd**
169 B c 01/03 Mehmas (IRE)—My Better Half (Rip Van Winkle (IRE)) (260000) **Sheikh Mohammed Obaid Al Maktoum**
170 B f 27/03 Kingman—Nahrain (Selkirk (USA)) **Sheikh Ahmed Al Maktoum**
171 B f 28/01 Phoenix of Spain (IRE)—Navette (IRE) (Invincible Spirit (IRE)) (40000)
172 B f 25/03 Iffraaj—Neesaan (New Approach (IRE)) **Sheikh Ahmed Al Maktoum**
173 B c 23/02 Sea The Stars (IRE)—Orange Sun (Duke of Marmalade (IRE)) (72029) **Mr M. Saeed**
174 B c 07/02 Night of Thunder (IRE)—Parton (Kitten's Joy (USA)) (95000) **Sheikh A. H. F. M. A. Al Sabah**
175 Ch c 01/03 Night of Thunder (IRE)—Partridge (IRE) (Zoffany (IRE)) (195000) **Clipper Group Holdings Ltd**
176 Gr c 21/04 Phoenix of Spain (IRE)—Pearly Empress (FR) (Holy Roman Emperor (IRE)) (70000) **VARIAN RACING IX**
177 B c 26/03 Gleneagles (IRE)—Polar Pearl (IRE) (Pivotal)
178 B c 21/03 Saxon Warrior (JPN)—Pour Deux (IRE) (Dansili) (300000) **Sheikh Mohammed Obaid Al Maktoum**
179 **QAZAQ (FR),** b c 24/02 Kingman—Qabala (USA) (Scat Daddy (USA)) (300000) **N. Bizakov**
180 B br c 11/03 Magna Grecia (IRE)—Rio Festival (USA) (First Defence (USA)) (124050) **Sheikh Ahmed Al Maktoum**
181 B c 29/03 Ulysses (IRE)—Sacre Caroline (USA) (Blame (USA)) (150000)
182 **SANAT (IRE),** b c 07/04 Invincible Spirit (IRE)—Sante (IRE) (Dream Ahead (USA)) (220000) **N. Bizakov**
183 Ch f 14/01 Siyouni (FR)—Sea of Grace (IRE) (Born To Sea (IRE)) (350000) **Sheikh Mohammed Obaid Al Maktoum**
184 B f 13/02 Too Darn Hot—Sellsabeel (FR) (Galileo (IRE)) **Sheikh M. B. K. Al Maktoum**
185 Gr c 04/02 Dark Angel (IRE)—
Shang Shang Shang (USA) (Shanghai Bobby (USA)) (120000) **Sheikh Ahmed Al Maktoum**
186 B c 04/02 Oasis Dream—Shimah (USA) (Storm Cat (USA)) **Shadwell Estate Company Ltd**
187 B c 18/04 Exceed And Excel (AUS)—Shortmile Lady (IRE) (Arcano (IRE)) (270000) **KHK Racing Ltd**
188 Ch c 14/01 No Nay Never (USA)—Simply A Star (IRE) (Giant's Causeway (USA))
189 **SO (USA),** b f 20/04 More Than Ready (USA)—Light Blow (USA) (Kingmambo (USA)) **Flaxman Stables Ireland Ltd**
190 B c 28/04 Rey De Oro (JPN)—Sound Paradise (JPN) (Workforce) **Mr Y. Masuda**
191 **SPETSES (USA),** br c 13/03 Get Stormy (USA)—Radiantly (Aussie Rules (USA)) **Flaxman Stables Ireland Ltd**
192 B f 05/02 Kingman—Sunday Times (Holy Roman Emperor (IRE)) **Mr A. Belshaw**
193 B f 14/02 Massaat (IRE)—Sweet Sixteen (IRE) (Sadler's Wells (USA)) **Mr F. A. Al Harthi**
194 B c 14/04 Too Darn Hot—Tantshi (IRE) (Invincible Spirit (IRE)) **Sheikh Ahmed Al Maktoum**
195 B f 04/02 U S Navy Flag (USA)—Tideflow (IRE) (Invincible Spirit (IRE))
196 **TRADITIONAL,** ch f 16/03 Ulysses (IRE)—Aristocratic (Exceed And Excel (AUS)) **Cheveley Park Stud Limited**
197 B c 14/03 Exceed And Excel (AUS)—Yourtimeisnow (Charm Spirit (IRE)) **Sheikh Mohammed Obaid Al Maktoum**
198 B c 11/04 No Nay Never (USA)—Zouzou (AUS) (Redoute's Choice (AUS))

Assistant Trainer: Jo Fowles, George Hills, Oli Rix, **Racing Secretary:** Jim Hiner.

507 MR TIM VAUGHAN, Cowbridge

Postal: **Pant Wilkin Stables, Aberthin, Cowbridge, CF71 7GX**
Contacts: **PHONE 01446 771626 MOBILE 07841 800081**
EMAIL tim@timvaughanracing.com WEBSITE www.timvaughanracing.com

1 **AIRTOTHETHRONE (IRE),** 7, b g Yeats (IRE)—Sorcillera **Mrs C. S. Wilson**
2 **ARTISTIC ENDEAVOUR,** 5, b g Kayf Tara—Dubh Eile (IRE) **Paul & Louise Bowtell**
3 **BELLS OF PETERBORO (IRE),** 8, gr g Carlotamix (FR)—Power of Future (GER) **Mr S. Grys & Mr M. O'Boyle**
4 **BELLS OF RUTLAND (IRE),** 6, gr g Kingston Hill—D'Gigi **Mr S. Grys & Mr M. O'Boyle**
5 **BELLS OF STAMFORD (IRE),** 6, b g Presenting—Passlands (IRE) **Mr S. Grys & Mr M. O'Boyle**
6 **BOBMAHLEY (IRE),** 8, b g Mahler—Supreme Von Pres (IRE) **Mr S. A. Clarke**
7 **BUMPY EVANS (IRE),** 5, ch g Ocovango—Gaye Native (IRE) **T. E. Vaughan**
8 **CLEMENCIA (IRE),** 7, b g Pour Moi (IRE)—Cleofila (IRE) **T. E. Vaughan**
9 **COLONIAL EMPIRE,** 6, b g Zoffany (IRE)—Susan Stroman **Mr S. Grys & Mr M. O'Boyle**
10 **COPPERFASTEN (IRE),** 6, b m Flemensfirth (USA)—Copper Dusht (IRE) **Paul & Louise Bowtell**
11 **DALAMOI (IRE),** 6, b g Pour Moi (IRE)—Dalamine (FR) **Mrs B. N. Ead**
12 **DESIGNER DESTINY (IRE),** 9, b m Jeremy (USA)—Gaye Steel (IRE) **T. E. Vaughan**
13 **EILE TARA,** 4, b f Kayf Tara—Dubh Eile (IRE) **Paul & Louise Bowtell**
14 **EVA'S OSKAR (IRE),** 9, gr g Shirocco (GER)—Sardagna (FR) **Mrs Sally & Richard Prince**
15 **GALOP DU BOSC (FR),** 7, ch g Vatori (FR)—Larisandre (FR) **The Optimistic Racing Group**
16 **GOLDEN IDENTITY,** 4, b g Kayf Tara—Hidden Identity (IRE) **Paul & Louise Bowtell**
17 **HIDDEN BELLE,** 5, b m Kayf Tara—Hidden Identity (IRE) **Paul & Louise Bowtell**

MR TIM VAUGHAN - continued

18 **INVINCIBLE DE MEE (FR),** 5, b g Authorized (IRE)—Koeur de Mee (FR) **Oceans Racing**
19 **ISLE OF ARON,** 7, gr g Kayf Tara—Maggie Aron **Oceans Racing**
20 **JEAN GENIE (FR),** 7, gr g Turgeon (USA)—Lady Koko **Oceans Racing**
21 **JUDEX LEFOU (IRE),** 8, b g Le Fou (IRE)—Knockalaghan Maid (IRE) **Mr S. A. Clarke**
22 **KALPAGA (FR),** 6, b m Kamsin (GER)—Via Carolina (FR) **ER Newnham & JD Shinton**
23 **KAP CHIDLEY (FR),** 5, b g Kapgarde (FR)—Savage River (FR) **Paul Bowtell & Jonathan Shinton**
24 **KEADEN HILL (IRE),** 6, b g Kingston Hill—Holy Vow (IRE) **Mrs C. S. Wilson**
25 **LOUKARAK (FR),** 4, b g Karaktar (IRE)—Louegarde (FR)
26 **LUCKELLO,** 7, b m Yorgunnabelucky (USA)—Timarello (IRE) **The Davies' Racing Team**
27 **MADERA MIST (IRE),** 9, ch m Stowaway—Odonimee (IRE) **Paul & Louise Bowtell**
28 **MARGARET'S LEGACY (FR),** 6, ch g Prince Gibraltar (FR)—Caphira **The Old Romantics**
29 **MOURZOUK (IRE),** 6, b g Declaration of War (USA)—Mouraniya (IRE) **Pimlico Racing - Mourzouk**
30 **MY DREAM,** 5, b m Proclamation (IRE)—Scarlett O'Tara **Mrs D. Thomas**
31 **MYUNCLECHARLIE (FR),** 5, b g Myboycharlie (IRE)—Medicis Lady (FR)
32 **NORDY LORDY (GER),** 6, b g Jukebox Jury (IRE)—Nur Bani (GER) **Bovian Racing**
33 **ORIENTAL CROSS (IRE),** 10, b m Cape Cross (IRE)—Orion Girl (GER) **Mr J Durston & Mr N Harris**
34 **OSCA LOCA (IRE),** 10, b m Oscar (IRE)—Lohort Castle (IRE) **Paul & Louise Bowtell**
35 **POINT OF PRINCIPLE (IRE),** 10, b g Rip Van Winkle (IRE)—L'Ancresse (IRE) **Oceans Racing**
36 **PRISON BREAK (IRE),** 5, b g Muhaarar—World Class **The Pant Wilkin Partnership**
37 4, B g Court Cave (IRE)—Rowdy Exit (IRE) **T. E. Vaughan**
38 **SHANTOU SUNSET,** 9, ch m Shantou (USA)—Kingara **Optimumracing.Co.Uk & Mr Andrew P. Bell**
39 **SILVER IN DISGUISE,** 9, gr g Sulamani (IRE)—Silver Spinner **Mr J Durston & Mr N Harris**
40 **STATE OF FAME (IRE),** 7, b g Fame And Glory—Nirphania (GER)
41 **STATE OF HONOR (IRE),** 6, b m Fame And Glory—Nirphania (GER) **Lycett Racing Ltd**
42 **TIGHT CALL (IRE),** 9, ch g Mahler—Victory Anthem (IRE) **ER Newnham & JD Shinton**
43 **TIPPINGITUPTONANCY (IRE),** 9, ch m Stowaway—Dyrick Daybreak (IRE) **Mr J. P. M. Bowtell**
44 **TRIXSTER (IRE),** 10, b g Beneficial—Our Trick (IRE) **The Pant Wilkin Partnership**
45 **TWILIGHT GLORY,** 7, b g Fame And Glory—Twilight Eclipse (IRE) **Tynewydd Investments Limited**
46 **WEAVER'S ANSWER,** 5, gr g Dunaden (FR)—Oskar's Eva (IRE) **Mrs Sally & Richard Prince**
47 **WONDERWEASLE,** 5, b m Clovis du Berlais (FR)—Silver Gypsy (IRE) **Paul & Louise Bowtell**

THREE-YEAR-OLDS

48 **FOREVER COPPER,** b g Kayf Tara—Dubh Eile (IRE) **Paul & Louise Bowtell**
49 **LIVY'S LAD,** b g Kayf Tara—Hidden Identity (IRE) **Paul & Louise Bowtell**
50 **RINGOCANRUN,** ch g Jack Hobbs—Oskar's Eva (IRE) **Mrs Sally & Richard Prince**

Flat Jockey: David Probert. **NH Jockey:** Alan Johns. **Conditional Jockey:** Charlie Price.

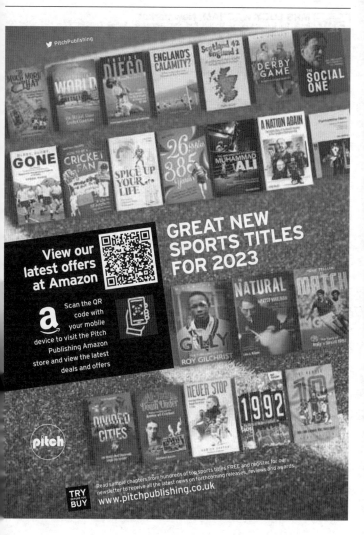

509 MRS LUCY WADHAM, Newmarket

Postal: **The Trainer's House, Moulton Paddocks, Newmarket, Suffolk, CB8 7PJ**
Contacts: **PHONE 01638 662411 MOBILE 07980 545776**
EMAIL lucy@wadhamracing.com WEBSITE www.lucywadhamracing.co.uk

1 **ADMIRAL BARRATRY (FR),** 10, b g Soldier of Fortune (IRE)—Haskilclara (FR) **Forster, Pepper & Summers**
2 **ANOTHER MYSTERY,** 6, b g Norse Dancer (IRE)—Misstree Pitcher **J & J McAndrew**
3 **ARQOOB (IRE),** 5, b g Estidhkaar (IRE)—Via Ballycroy (IRE) **Little Staughton Farms Ltd**
4 **BOMBAY SUNSET (IRE),** 5, ch g Shantaram—Naamah (IRE) **Mrs C. De Burgh Marsh**
5 **BOMBYX,** 8, ch g Sir Percy—Bombazine (IRE) **The FOPS**
6 **BRANDISOVA (IRE),** 7, b m Shirocco (GER)—Gentle Alice (IRE) **Ms E. L. Banks**
7 4, B f Westerner—Chase The Favorite (IRE) **Ms E. L. Banks**
8 **DANCE TO PARIS,** 8, b m Champs Elysees—Riabouchinska **The Calculated Speculators**
9 **DERSY SOCIAL,** 6, b m Pether's Moon (IRE)—Drop of Spirit (IRE) **Suiter Developments& Suiter Construction**
10 **DOUBLETHETROUBLE,** 5, ch g Pearl Secret—Kirunavaara (IRE) **R W Hayward & E R Wakelin**
11 **EAST END GIRL,** 6, b m Youmzain (IRE)—Bermondsey Girl **Mr & Mrs A E Pakenham & J J W Wadham**
12 **ECLAIR DE GUYE (FR),** 9, gr g Lord du Sud (FR)—
Jouvence de Guye (FR) **E R Wakelin, R W Hayward & J J W Wadham**
13 **FLAT WHITE (FR),** 6, ch m Olympic Glory (IRE)—Bolivia (GER) **Mr & Mrs A. E. Pakenham**
14 **FOR GINA,** 5, b m Kayf Tara—United (GER) **Louise Kemble & J J W Wadham**
15 **GAME ON FOR GLORY (IRE),** 7, b m Fame And Glory—Jeunopse (IRE) **Mr J. Summers**
16 **HURRICANE BAY,** 7, b g Malinas (GER)—Another Storm **The Hanseatic League**
17 **IZAR BALD (FR),** 5, b g Al Namix (FR)—Pruneyle Do (FR) **Suiter Developments & James Summers**
18 **JEUNE BELLE (IRE),** 5, b m Champs Elysees—Jeunopse (IRE) **Mr J. Summers**
19 **KADEX (FR),** 5, b g Saddex—Califete Royale (FR) **The The Sanguiners, Mrs G Redman & B Painter**
20 **MARTELLO SKY,** 7, gr m Martaline—Kentucky Sky **The Sky Partnership**
21 **MIDNIGHT MARY,** 7, b m Midnight Legend—Epee Celeste (FR) **Mr S A Richards & Louise Kemble**
22 **MISTRAL NELL,** 6, b m Mount Nelson—Mistral Reine **Sara The Dennis Family & Dominic Reilly**
23 4, B g Black Sam Bellamy (IRE)—Mistral Reine **Mistral Sam Partnership**
24 **PEARLY ISLAND,** 7, b g Trans Island—Shinrock Pearl (IRE) **Mr S. C. McIntyre**
25 4, B f Milan—Peggy Cullen (IRE) **Ms E. L. Banks**
26 **PRESENTING BELLE (IRE),** 6, b m Valirann (FR)—Lace Parasol (IRE) **J & J McAndrew**
27 **PRETENDING (IRE),** 4, gr f Make Believe—Gala **Mr J. Summers**
28 **REGARDING RUTH (IRE),** 9, b m Flemensfirth (USA)—
May's June (IRE) **Suiter Developments Ltd & JJW Wadham**
29 **REVASSER (IRE),** 6, b g Ask—Open Cry (IRE) **P. H. Betts**
30 **SAMOURAI ONE (FR),** 6, gr g Montmartre (FR)—Northern Ocean (FR) **Suiter Developments Limited**
31 **SCENE ONE (IRE),** 7, b g Curtain Time (IRE)—Isserkelly Lady (IRE) **The Scene One Partnership**
32 **SIENNA BREEZE (IRE),** 5, b m Camacho—Viking Rose (IRE) **Mr B. J. Painter**
33 **SORBET,** 8, b m Passing Glance—Fireburst **Mrs P. J. Toye**
34 **TARAS HALLS (IRE),** 5, b g Yeats (IRE)—Brixen (IRE) **R & T Ford**
35 **TELEPATHIQUE,** 5, b m Telescope (IRE)—Rhetorique (FR) **Mrs E. C. Gordon Lennox**
36 **TERRESITA (IRE),** 6, b m Westerner—Brixen (IRE) **R & T Ford**
37 **TRINCOMALEE,** 10, b g Malinas (GER)—Royal Tango **Hot to Trot Jumping&Mrs E Gordon Lennox**
38 **WILL STING (IRE),** 8, br g Scorpion (IRE)—Undecided Hall (IRE) **The Cyclones**

THREE-YEAR-OLDS

39 **HAVANA FLAME,** ch g Havana Gold (IRE)—Mischievous **Mr J. Summers**
40 **SUNRISE BOY (FR),** b c Belardo (IRE)—Sunrise Memory (FR) **Mr J. Summers**

TWO-YEAR-OLDS

41 B f 11/04 Getaway (GER)—Mistral Reine (King's Theatre (IRE)) **Dominic Reilly & Malcolm Kemp**

NH Jockey: Bryony Frost. **Conditional Jockey:** Corey McGivern.

510 MISS TRACY WAGGOTT, Spennymoor

Postal: **Awakening Stables, Merrington Road, Spennymoor, County Durham, DL16 7HD**
Contacts: **PHONE 01388 819012 MOBILE 07979 434498**
EMAIL tracywaggott@hotmail.com

1 **ARCHDUKE FERDINAND (IRE),** 4, b c Gutaifan (IRE)—Salariaq (USA) **Mr P. Slater**
2 **GHATHANFAR (IRE),** 7, br g Invincible Spirit (IRE)—Cuis Ghaire (IRE) **Mr W. J. Laws**
3 **HAJEY,** 6, ch g Raven's Pass (USA)—Almashooqa (USA) **Tracy Waggott & Sally Booth**
4 **HENLEY,** 11, b g Royal Applause—Making Waves (IRE) **Miss T. Waggott**
5 **INTRINSIC BOND,** 6, b g Intrinsic—Misu Billy **David & Daniel Lawson**
6 **MRS BAGERRAN (IRE),** 5, b m Kodiac—Habaayib **Mr S. W. Rain**
7 **PREMIERSHIP,** 4, b g Mahsoob—Misu Billy **David & Daniel Lawson**
8 **RAINBOW RAIN,** 4, b g Acclamation—Free Rein **Mr S. W. Rain**
9 **RED COMMAND (IRE),** 4, b g War Command (USA)—Wajaha (IRE) **Tracy Waggott & W J Laws**
10 **ROBIN GOODFELLOW (IRE),** 4, b g Dark Angel (IRE)—Bergamask (USA) **Mr W. G. Laws**
11 **WITHOUT DELAY (IRE),** 4, ch f Decorated Knight—Apace (IRE) **Mr W. J. Laws**

THREE-YEAR-OLDS

12 **MISS RAINDROP,** b f Iffraaj—Disdain (USA) **Mr S. W. Rain**

TWO-YEAR-OLDS

13 **LAUGHING LORD (IRE),** gr g 01/04 Waldgeist—
Catchphrase (IRE) (Dubawi (IRE)) (12805) **The Outrageous Partnership**
14 **MISS RAINBOW (IRE),** b f 26/02 Holy Roman Emperor (IRE)—
Allegrina (IRE) (Barathea (IRE)) (16006) **The Outrageous Partnership**

---

511 MR JOHN WAINWRIGHT, Malton

Postal: **Granary House, Beverley Road, Norton, Malton, North Yorkshire, YO17 9PJ**
Contacts: **PHONE 01653 692993 MOBILE 07798 778070**
EMAIL jswainwright@googlemail.com

1 **BIPLANE (USA),** 5, b m Noble Mission—Aviate **J. S. Wainwright & Peter Clarke**
2 **BOBBY SHAFT,** 7, b g Garswood—She Mystifies **Wayne Bavill & John Wainwright**
3 **DANDY'S ANGEL (IRE),** 6, b m Dandy Man (IRE)—Party Pipit (IRE) **Anthony Ross & David Lumley**
4 **DICK DATCHERY (IRE),** 6, b g Make Believe—Bayja (IRE) **Mr W Bavill & Mr D. Bavill**
5 **ELETTARIA (IRE),** 4, b f Mehmas (IRE)—Rayon Rouge (IRE) **John Wainwright Racing Club**
6 **KRAKEN FLORIDA (IRE),** 4, b g The Last Lion (IRE)—Duchess Dora (IRE) **Caballo Dos**
7 **LIVING'S BOY AN CO (FR),** 8, b g Diamond Boy (FR)—Living Start (FR) **I. J. Barran**
8 **MUATADEL,** 10, b g Exceed And Excel (AUS)—Rose Blossom **Caballo Racing**
9 **ONESTEPATATIME (IRE),** 8, b m Jeremy (USA)—Good Thyne Lucy (IRE) **Mr A. J. Ross**
10 **POWER POINT,** 6, br g Cable Bay (IRE)—Frabjous **Mr W Bavill & Mr D. Bavill**
11 **TANTASTIC,** 5, b g Mayson—Love Island **Fast Track Racing**
12 **WICKLOW FLYER (IRE),** 6, b m Ask—Good Bye Dolly (IRE) **I. J. Barran**

THREE-YEAR-OLDS

13 **MALINHEADSEAROVERS (IRE),** b g Zoffany (IRE)—Providencia **D. R. & E. E. Brown**

Assistant Trainer: Mrs Fiona Wainwright.

Flat Jockey: Tom Eaves.

---

512 MR ROBERT WALEY-COHEN, Banbury

Postal: **Upton Viva, Banbury, Oxfordshire, OX15 6HT**
Contacts: **PHONE 01295 670538**

1 **CHABICHOU DUPOITOU,** 7, gr m Martaline—Tidara Angel (IRE) **Mr R. B. Waley-Cohen**
2 **IGOR,** 10, b g Presenting—Stravinsky Dance **Mr R. B. Waley-Cohen**
3 **JETT (IRE),** 12, b g Flemensfirth (USA)—La Noire (IRE) **Mr R. B. Waley-Cohen**
4 **MAITREE EXPRESS,** 9, br g Malinas (GER)—Shatabdi (IRE) **Mr R. B. Waley-Cohen**
5 **WIND FROM THE WEST,** 6, b m Shirocco (GER)—Free Thinking **Mr R. B. Waley-Cohen**

513 MR MARK WALFORD, Sheriff Hutton

Postal: **Cornborough Manor, Cornborough Road, Sheriff Hutton, York, North Yorkshire, YO60 6QN**

1 **ALLBETSOFF (IRE),** 7, b g Carlotamix (FR)—Longer Lashes (IRE) **New Vision Bloodstock & G B Walford**
2 **AMBER GOLD,** 6, b m Iktibas—Nativus (IRE) **Mr G. Bonson**
3 **AOIFE'S JOY (IRE),** 6, b m Elzaam (AUS)—Spavento (IRE) **Mr K. Brown**
4 **ASHINGTON,** 8, b g Canford Cliffs (IRE)—Kadoma **URSA Major Racing**
5 **ASTROBRIO,** 4, ch f Garswood—Astrosecret **Mystic Meg Limited**
6 **ASTROMAN,** 6, b g Garswood—Mega (IRE) **Mystic Meg Limited**
7 **BAY DREAM BELIEVER (IRE),** 4, b f New Bay—Arabescatta **Ursa Major Racing & Partner**
8 **BIT OF A QUIRKE,** 10, ch g Monsieur Bond (IRE)—Silk (IRE) **Mr A. Quirke & Mrs G. B. Walford**
9 **BON RETOUR (IRE),** 8, b m Fame And Glory—Rosy de Cyborg (FR) **J. T. Ennis**
10 **BUSTER VALENTINE (IRE),** 10, b g Ask—Femme du Noir (IRE) **The Mount Fawcus Partnership**
11 **CALL ME JACK,** 4, b g Jack Hobbs—Gaspara (FR) **Mr J Scarrow & Partner**
12 **CARRAREA (IRE),** 6, ch g Notnowcato—Georgina Valleya (IRE) **Ursa Major Racing & Partner**
13 **CASH TO ASH (IRE),** 10, b g Westerner—Knocklayde Rose (IRE) **8 Amigos, Morrell, Evans, Cowan & Burns**
14 **CHOOSETHENEWS (IRE),** 6, b g Westerner—Leading Article (IRE) **The Mount Fawcus Partnership**
15 **CLASSIC LADY (IRE),** 8, ch m Flemensfirth (USA)—Another Gaye (IRE) **Allott & Wordingham**
16 **DROMOLOUGHT LAD (IRE),** 6, b g Brazen Beau (AUS)—She's A Pistol (IRE) **Ursa Major Racing & Partner**
17 **EL BELLO,** 4, gr g El Kabeir (USA)—Ya Halla (IRE) **Grey Horse Syndicates**
18 **EVENT OF SIVOLA (FR),** 9, ch g Noroit (GER)—Surprise de Sivola (FR) **Cw Racing Club & Ursa Major Racing**
19 **FENNA'S LOSS (IRE),** 6, br g Sageburg (IRE)—Caronova (IRE) **Major & S Morrell**
20 **FENNO'S SOLDIER (IRE),** 5, b g Soldier of Fortune (IRE)—Bachello (IRE) **Mrs G. B. Walford**
21 **FROG AND TOAD (IRE),** 5, b g Mehmas (IRE)—Fast Pick (IRE) **Mr A. L. Bosomworth**
22 5, B m Kayf Tara—Gaspara (FR) **Mrs G. B. Walford**
23 **GET GOING,** 6, b g Getaway (GER)—Bright Cloud (IRE) **Mrs M. Cooper**
24 **GHADBBAAN,** 7, ch g Intello (GER)—Rock Choir **Ursa Major Racing & Partner**
25 **GIOVANNI CHANGE (FR),** 8, gr g French Fifteen (FR)—Ask For Rain **Readers & Wiggy, the 8 Amigos & J Burns**
26 **GLOBAL VISION (IRE),** 5, gr g Markaz (IRE)—Vision of Peace (IRE) **Grey Horse Syndicates**
27 **HAVING A BARNEY (IRE),** 6, ch g Getaway (GER)—Batren's Garden (IRE) **Royal Blue Racing & Partner**
28 **INTO OVERDRIVE,** 8, b g Court Cave (IRE)—Lady Brig **Mrs W. Hamilton**
29 **IT JUST TAKES TIME (IRE),** 5, br g Power—War Bride (GER) **Go Alfresco Racing Partners**
30 4, Br g Kapgarde (FR)—Ixora (IRE)
31 **JANTE LAW,** 7, gr g Gentlewave (IRE)—Ixora (IRE) **Grey Horse Syndicates & Mr P Drury**
32 **JOHNSON'S BLUE (IRE),** 6, b g Westerner—Annimation (IRE) **Geoff Wilson & Cambridge Racing**
33 **JOSIEBOND,** 7, ch m Monsieur Bond (IRE)—Smiddy Hill **I. B. Barker**
34 **KATHLEEN,** 4, b f Jack Hobbs—Classic Palace (IRE) **Allott & Wordingham**
35 **KINGS CREEK (IRE),** 6, b g Elusive Quality (USA)—Nunavik (IRE) **New Vision Bloodstock**
36 **MAGIC WAVE,** 7, b g Gentlewave (IRE)—Annie's Gift (IRE) **The Magic Circle**
37 **MISSY AVA (IRE),** 5, b m Westerner—Sea Breeze Lady (IRE) **Cambridge Racing, Mr J Scarrow & Partner**
38 **MOLLYSLITTLEANGEL,** 4, b f Schiaparelli (GER)—All For Lily **Allott & Wordingham**
39 **MONTMARTRE ABBEY (FR),** 6, gr g Montmartre (FR)—La Pinede
40 **MOONLIGHT GLORY (IRE),** 8, b m Fame And Glory—Prairie Moonlight (GER) **Ursa Major Racing, Cw Racing & Partner**
41 **OASIS PRINCE,** 7, br g Oasis Dream—Demisemiquaver **Mr A. L. Bosomworth**
42 4, B f Cannock Chase (USA)—Peal of Bells

MR MARK WALFORD - continued

43 **PERCULATOR,** 6, b m Telescope (IRE)—Ancora (IRE) **SYPS (UK) Ltd & Mr M. Downing Hrl**
44 **PILEUP (IRE),** 6, b g Valirann (FR)—All Notoriety (IRE) **Grindal,Head & Scarrow**
45 **POETRIA,** 5, b m Poet's Voice—Jozafeen **Mrs C. Steel**
46 **POLLYJO,** 5, ch m Schiaparelli (GER)—Kaylan's Rose **Allott & Wordingham**
47 4, Ch g Black Sam Bellamy (IRE)—Presenteea (IRE) **Cowan & Drury**
48 **ROCKMANN (FR),** 8, b g Kap Rock (FR)—All Berry (FR) **Mr C. N. Herman**
49 **RUBY ISLAND,** 6, ch m Trans Island—Midnight Mayhem (IRE) **Buckingham & Ritzema**
50 4, B g Westerner—Sea Breeze Lady (IRE)
51 **TINEGGIORI (FR),** 4, gr g Bated Breath—Validora (FR) **8 Amigos, Readers & wiggy, Grey Horse Syn.**
52 **WANDERING WEST (IRE),** 5, b g Westerner—Banrion Na Boinne **Mrs M. Cooper**
53 **WILLASTON (IRE),** 7, b g Morozov (USA)—Bombalong (IRE) **New Vision Bloodstock**
54 **YORKSHIRE MAN SAM,** 5, b g Black Sam Bellamy (IRE)—Annie's Gift (IRE) **The Magic Circle**
55 5, B m Lucarno (USA)—Youamazeme
56 **ZUMURUD (IRE),** 8, gr g Zebedee—Thaisy (USA) **Ms M. Austerfield**

THREE-YEAR-OLDS

57 **ARTISTIC STEPS (IRE),** b f Footstepsinthesand—Artistica (IRE) **Mr K. Brown**
58 **EL MONTEJEAN,** b g Mondialiste (IRE)—Jeany (IRE) **SYPS (UK) Ltd**
59 **GIRL FROM ITALY (IRE),** b f Holy Roman Emperor (IRE)—Keilogue (IRE) **Mr K. Brown**
60 **HAVANAWING,** b f Havana Gold (IRE)—Sabrewing (IRE) **Ms M Austerfield, 8 Amigos, Mr J Burns**
61 **JILL'S JUNGLE,** b g Bungle Inthejungle—Diablo Dancer
62 **KITTEN'S BAY,** b g Kitten's Joy (USA)—Special Purpose (IRE) **Ms M Austerfield, 8 Amigos, Mr J Burns**
63 **SPIORADALTA,** b g Rajasinghe (IRE)—Broughtons Secret **Clayton Civils, S Morrell & Hathaway**
64 **WHATACRACKER,** ch g Cracksman—Isa **Mrs P A Johnson & Mr C H Stephenson**

TWO-YEAR-OLDS

65 Ch f 24/04 Masar (IRE)—Astromagick (Rainbow Quest (USA)) (10000)
66 **DOCTOR LIVINGSTONE (IRE),** b g 03/04 Bungle Inthejungle—Ask Not (Invincible Spirit (IRE)) (4200)
67 **ELECTRIC LIGHTNING,** gr g 14/04 Lightning Spear—Black Sails (Lope de Vega (IRE)) (10000) **Ms M. Austerfield**
68 **JAM LASS,** b f 30/03 U S Navy Flag (USA)—Counterpoise (Cape Cross (IRE)) (14000)
69 **MASTER ELI,** b c 07/04 Eqtidaar (IRE)—Tweety Pie (IRE) (Rock of Gibraltar (IRE))

MR ROBERT WALFORD, Blandford

Postal: **Heart of Oak Stables, Okeford Fitzpane, Blandford, Dorset, DT11 0LW**
Contacts: **MOBILE 07815 116209**
EMAIL robertwalford1@gmail.com

1 **AMELIA'S DANCE (IRE),** 8, ch m Flemensfirth (USA)—Madame McGoldrick (IRE) **Major-Gen R. Keightley**
2 **ART DECCO,** 7, br g Dapper—Lewesdon Duchess **Buckingham, Chapman, Langford & Ritzema**
3 **CAERULEUM,** 5, br g Millenary—Queen of The Blues (IRE) **Buckingham, Chapman, Langford & Ritzema**
4 **CHLOE'S COURT (IRE),** 10, br m Court Cave (IRE)—Howaya Pet (IRE) **Cole, Gale, Levy & Mortimer**
5 **EDE'IFFS ELTON,** 9, b g Geordieland (FR)—Ede'iff **Mr A. Lees**
6 **ELECTRIC ANNIE (IRE),** 8, b m Fame And Glory—Decent Dime (IRE) **Mr P. A. Hiscock**
7 **ELIOS D'OR (FR),** 9, b g Puit d'Or (IRE)—Naker Mome (FR) **Lewis Nettley Racing**
8 **FLAGRANT DELITIEP (FR),** 8, gr g Fragrant Mix (IRE)—Naltiepy (FR) **Mrs C. M. Hinks**
9 **FLASH GORCOMBE,** 6, b g Alqaahir (USA)—Seem of Gold **Mr P. R. Meaden**
10 **FOXBORO (GER),** 8, b g Maxios—Fair Breeze (GER) **Lewis Nettley Racing**
11 **GORCOMBE MOONSHINE,** 6, b g Alqaahir (USA)—Seemma **Mr P. R. Meaden**
12 **HIPOP DES ONGRAIS (FR),** 6, gr g Voiladenuo (FR)—Pretty des Ongrais (FR) **Baroness D. M. Harding**
13 **HITITI (FR),** 6, b g Great Pretender (IRE)—Val'melodie (FR) **Dr & Mrs John Millar**
14 **ILLICO DES PLACES (FR),** 5, b g Jeu St Eloi (FR)—Liliane Star (FR) **Acorn Builders Dorset LTD**
15 **JILL'S MEMORY,** 5, gr g Geordieland (FR)—Just Fee **Mr R. Walford**
16 **LEADING SWOOP (IRE),** 7, b g Leading Light (IRE)—One Swoop (IRE) **Gale Force One**
17 **LINDISFARNE,** 8, gr g Geordieland (FR)—Tin Symphony **B. J. M. Ryall**

MR ROBERT WALFORD - continued

18 **OUR MERLIN,** 11, b g Pasternak—Lorgnette **A. J. M. Trowbridge**
19 **SHUTUPSHIRLEY,** 6, b g Saddler's Rock (IRE)—Ede'iff **Chris Pugsley & Nigel Skinner**
20 **THE FLYING FIG,** 4, b g Scorpion (IRE)—Shoofly Milly (IRE) **Clive And Sue Cole**
21 **TIP TOP MOUNTAIN (IRE),** 8, b g Mountain High (IRE)—The Central Lady (IRE) **Mr R. J. Brown**
22 **WILLIAM PHILO,** 6, ch g Black Sam Bellamy (IRE)—Jambles **Tony & Susan Brimble**

NH Jockey: James Best.

---

515 MR ED WALKER, Upper Lambourn

Postal: **Kingsdown Stables, Upper Lambourn, Hungerford, Berkshire, RG17 8QX**
Contacts: **PHONE 01488 674148 MOBILE 07787 534145**
EMAIL libby@edwalkerracing.com WEBSITE www.edwalkerracing.com

1 **AMERICAN STAR (IRE),** 4, b g Starspangledbanner (AUS)—Signora Valentina (IRE) **Mr D. Ward**
2 **BLING ON THE MUSIC,** 4, ch g Sea The Stars (IRE)—Crysdal **Owners Group 115**
3 **CAME FROM THE DARK (IRE),** 7, gr g Dark Angel (IRE)—Silver Shoon (IRE) **Mr P. K. Siu**
4 **CANOODLED (IRE),** 5, b m Mehmas (IRE)—Fondled **Mr L. A. Bellman**
5 **FANTASY BELIEVER (IRE),** 6, b g Make Believe—Avizare (IRE) **Chris & David Stam**
6 **GREAT AMBASSADOR,** 6, ch g Exceed And Excel (AUS)—Snoqualmie Girl (IRE) **Ebury Racing 6**
7 **HAFEET ALAIN (IRE),** 7, b g Elzaam (AUS)—Batuta **Mr P. K. Siu**
8 **LIBRA TIGER,** 4, ch g Territories (IRE)—Show Aya (IRE) **S. Al Ansari**
9 **MAKAROVA,** 4, b f Acclamation—Vesnina **Brightwalton Bloodstock Limited**
10 **MOUNTAIN PEAK,** 8, b g Swiss Spirit—Nolas Lolly (IRE) **Ebury Racing**
11 **PEGGOTY,** 4, b f Hot Streak (IRE)—Semayyel (IRE)
12 **POPMASTER (IRE),** 5, gr g Gutaifan (IRE)—Best New Show (IRE) **Mr L. A. Bellman**
13 **RANDOM HARVEST (IRE),** 5, b m War Front (USA)—Seta **Lady Bamford**
14 **REINA DEL MAR (IRE),** 5, b m Awtaad (IRE)—Star Approval (IRE) **Mr D. Ward**
15 **RUM COCKTAIL,** 4, b f Muhaarar—Tropical Treat **Mr L. A. Bellman**
16 **STAR FROM AFARHH,** 4, b f Farhh—Tears of The Sun **Dr Bridget Drew & Partners**
17 **TIDAL STORM,** 4, b g Sea The Moon (GER)—Kinetica **Mrs G. Austen-Smith**
18 **V TWELVE (IRE),** 4, br g Slade Power (IRE)—Black Mascara (IRE) **Mr P. K. Siu**

THREE-YEAR-OLDS

19 **ANGEL OF PEACE (IRE),** b f Dark Angel (IRE)—Button Down **Thurloe Thoroughbreds LII**
20 **ARKENDALE,** br c Pivotal—Paris Rooftops (IRE) **Clipper Group Holdings Ltd**
21 **AUNT VIOLET (USA),** b f Noble Mission—Gianna Schicchi (USA) **MPVL Racing**
22 **AURORA DAWN (IRE),** b f Awtaad (IRE)—Bright New Day (IRE) **Dubai Thoroughbred Racing**
23 **BAUHINIA RHAPSODY,** b g Siyouni (FR)—Tai Hang Dragon (IRE) **Rockcliffe Stud**
24 **CRACK SHOT (IRE),** b c Kingman—Twitch (IRE) **Mrs F. H. Hay**
25 **CRAGGY RANGE (IRE),** b c Awtaad (IRE)—Arabian Pearl (IRE) **Mr B. R. Halsall**
26 **DARK TROOPER (IRE),** b g Dark Angel (IRE)—Warshah (IRE) **Mr C. U. F. Ma**
27 **DE BRUYNE,** b g Dutch Art—Danehill Revival **Mr D. Ward**
28 **DIFFERENT TONE,** b g Iffraaj—Justice Belle (IRE) **Mr R. Ng**
29 **DIVYA (IRE),** b f Galileo (IRE)—Nahema (IRE) **Lady Bamford**
30 **DREAMROCKER (IRE),** b f Fastnet Rock (AUS)—Livia's Dream (IRE) **Mr J. S. M. Fill**
31 **ENGLISH OAK,** b c Wootton Bassett—Forest Crown **Mr D. Ward**
32 **GLIMMER OF LIGHT,** b f Farhh—Gaze **Gaze Partnership**
33 **GOLDEN PASSPORT,** b c Acclamation—Fast Lily (IRE) **Mr P. K. Siu**
34 **HEDONISTA (IRE),** b f Ulysses (IRE)—Luminous **Opulence Thoroughbreds**
35 **INCA QUEEN (IRE),** b f Oasis Dream—Inca Trail (USA) **Mr M. J. Cottis**
36 **JUST A NOTION,** b f Le Havre (IRE)—Queen Cordelia (IRE) **East Wind Racing Ltd**
37 **KHINJANI,** b f Sir Percy—Kandahari **Miss K. Rausing**
38 **LODDON,** ch f Sea The Moon (GER)—Wylye **Wigan/Willis/Donald**
39 **MERRY MINISTER (IRE),** b g Churchill (IRE)—Merry Me (IRE) **Mrs F. H. Hay**
40 **MONOPOLISE,** bl g Showcasing—Simply Me **Mr L. A. Bellman**

MR ED WALKER - continued

41 **OBSERVED,** br f Sea The Stars (IRE)—Motivee (IRE) **The Ashes**
42 **PEONY,** b f Churchill (IRE)—Nancy Hart **Mr D. Ward**
43 **PERFECT PROPHET,** br f Nathaniel (IRE)—Perfect Lady **Mildmay Racing & Aura (gas) Holdings Ltd**
44 **PONDICHERRY (IRE),** b g No Nay Never (USA)—Sarita **Lady Bamford**
45 **PROSPERING (IRE),** b c Profitable (IRE)—Heavenly Angel **Greenwood, Dale, Silver, Homburg**
46 **PROTEST RALLY (IRE),** b c Dandy Man (IRE)—Odyssee (FR) **Clipper Group Holdings Ltd**
47 **QUEENS AWARD (IRE),** b f Mehmas (IRE)—Warda **Mr D. Ward**
48 **ROSE PRICK (IRE),** ch f No Nay Never (USA)—Ornelia Ruee (FR) **Mr D. Ward**
49 Ch c Night of Thunder (IRE)—Safe House (IRE) **Sheikh Ahmed Al Maktoum**
50 **SASSY BELLE (IRE),** b f Mehmas (IRE)—Peronism (USA) **Mr L. A. Bellman**
51 **SCENIC (FR),** b f Lope de Vega (IRE)—Ghalyah **Mr D. Ward**
52 **SEA OF THIEVES,** b f Cracksman—Grande Bleue (IRE) **Brightwalton Bloodstock Limited**
53 **SNUGGLE,** ch g Showcasing—Under The Covers **Kennet Valley Thoroughbreds VI**
54 **STAR OF COTAI (IRE),** ch f Cotai Glory—Triggers Broom (IRE) **Kangyu International Racing (HK) Limited**
55 **STAR SPRITE (IRE),** b f Sea The Stars (IRE)—The Fairy (IRE) **Mrs F. H. Hay**
56 **STRYDER (IRE),** b c Oasis Dream—Sorry Woman (FR) **Mrs S. Flatt**
57 **TERWADA (IRE),** b c Tamayuz—Bethrah (IRE) **Sheikh Ahmed Al Maktoum**
58 **THE KITE (IRE),** b g Kingman—Gull Wing (IRE) **Lady Bamford**
59 **WAIPIRO (IRE),** b c Australia—London Plane (IRE) **Mr P. K. Siu**
60 **WALK THE MOON,** b c Sea The Stars (IRE)—Ladys First **Lady Bamford**
61 **YOTARID (IRE),** br c Shamardal (USA)—Hadaatha (IRE) **Sheikh Ahmed Al Maktoum**
62 **ZOUKSTER,** b c Zoustar (AUS)—Dubai Media (CAN) **Mr C. E. Stedman**

TWO-YEAR-OLDS

63 **AKIMBO,** b f 13/04 Sir Percy—Akranti (Pivotal) **Miss K. Rausing**
64 B f 04/04 Invincible Army (IRE)—Alsalwa (IRE) (Nayef (USA)) (65000) **Mr L. A. Bellman**
65 **AMSTERDAM,** ch c 31/01 Dutch Art—
Wilde Ambition (IRE) (No Nay Never (USA)) (130000) **David Ward & Chasemore Farm**
66 B f 01/02 Aclaim (IRE)—Arendelle (Camelot) **Chasemore Farm LLP**
67 B f 15/04 Oasis Dream—Astronomy Domine (Galileo (IRE)) (80000) **Fountain Thoroughbreds**
68 B f 23/05 Showcasing—Bird Key (Cadeaux Genereux) **Mainline Racing**
69 B c 25/03 Night of Thunder (IRE)—Considered Opinion (Redoute's Choice (AUS)) **Car Colston Hall Stud**
70 **COPAIN (IRE),** b c 01/03 Postponed (IRE)—Best Friend (IRE) (Galileo (IRE)) **John Pearce Racing Limited**
71 **COTAI VISION (IRE),** ch f 29/04 Cotai Glory—
Island Vision (IRE) (Arcano (IRE)) **Kangyu International Racing (HK) Limited**
72 **DAZITOO (IRE),** ch f 13/02 Soldier's Call—Tartiflette (Dr Fong (USA)) **Mr A. R. F. Buxton**
73 **DEVOIRS CHOICE (IRE),** b c 20/01 Ten Sovereigns (IRE)—
Tracing (IRE) (Galileo (IRE)) (70000) **Opulence Thoroughbreds**
74 Ch f 15/02 Gleneagles (IRE)—Dowayla (IRE) (Sepoy (AUS)) **Sheikh Ahmed Al Maktoum**
75 B f 31/03 Cable Bay (IRE)—Elizabeth Bennet (IRE) (Acclamation) **Mr & Mrs T O'Donohoe**
76 B c 09/03 Havana Grey—Fair Maiden (JPN) (Carnegie (IRE)) (68000) **Mr L. A. Bellman**
77 **GELICEAUX,** b f 24/01 Cracksman—Wotnot (IRE) (Exceed And Excel (AUS)) (42000) **The Pipa Dobson Syndicate**
78 B f 24/04 Siyouni (FR)—Ghalyah (Frankel) (65000)
79 B c 03/03 Cotai Glory—Hellofahaste (Hellvelyn) **Kangyu International Racing (HK) Limited**
80 Ch c 30/03 Night of Thunder (IRE)—
Il Palazzo (USA) (Giant's Causeway (USA)) (185000) **Sheikh Ahmed Al Maktoum**
81 **INTO BATTLE (IRE),** ch c 15/03 Churchill (IRE)—
Madam Baroque (Royal Applause) (30412) **Philip Afia & Matthew Cottis**
82 **KEY TO COTAI (IRE),** ch f 11/05 Cotai Glory—Clef (Dutch Art) **Julia Scott & Fred Ma**
83 B f 24/04 Due Diligence (USA)—Lady Macduff (IRE) (Iffraaj) **Kingsdown Racing Club**
84 B f 08/03 Frankel—Ladys First (Dutch Art) **Lady Bamford**
85 B c 14/02 Acclamation—Miss Academe (IRE) (Born To Sea (IRE)) (110000) **Sheikh Ahmed Al Maktoum**
86 **MISS ALPILLES,** b f 04/02 Sea The Stars (IRE)—
Alma Linda (Invincible Spirit (IRE)) (200000) **John Pearce Racing Limited**
87 B f 01/04 Invincible Spirit (IRE)—Nahema (IRE) (Dubawi (IRE)) **Lady Bamford**
88 B f 11/04 Ulysses (IRE)—Perfect Lady (Excelebration (IRE)) (35000) **Mildmay Racing**
89 **PHOENIX PASSION (IRE),** b c 14/04 Too Darn Hot—
Souvenir Delondres (FR) (Siyouni (FR)) (125000) **Opulence Thoroughbreds**
90 B c 11/01 Camelot—Queen of India (IRE) (Fastnet Rock (AUS)) (128051) **Mrs F. H. Hay**

MR ED WALKER - continued

91 **QUICKFIRE,** b c 26/02 Land Force (IRE)—Byrony (IRE) (Byron) (47000) **Mr L. A. Bellman**
92 **RAVENSBOURNE,** b f 08/03 Dutch Art—Danehill Revival (Pivotal) (75000) **Matthew Cottis & Partner**
93 B c 01/04 Blue Point (IRE)—Rive Gauche (Fastnet Rock (AUS)) (43000)
94 **SAMBUCUS,** b f 12/02 Lope de Vega (IRE)—Black Cherry (Mount Nelson) **Rockcliffe Stud**
95 B c 06/04 Awtaad (IRE)—Scholarly (Authorized (IRE)) (41617) **Mr L. A. Bellman**
96 B f 25/04 Bated Breath—Simply Me (New Approach (IRE)) **Mr L. A. Bellman**
97 B c 11/03 Too Darn Hot—Starflower (Champs Elysees) (55000) **Mr C. E. Stedman**
98 Ch c 30/03 Masar (IRE)—Sweet Lady Rose (IRE) (Shamardal (USA)) (240000) **Mrs F. H. Hay**
99 B c 20/03 Lope de Vega (IRE)—Talmada (USA) (Cape Cross (IRE)) **Sheikh Ahmed Al Maktoum**
100 Ch f 02/03 Lope de Vega (IRE)—Vesnina (Sea The Stars (IRE)) **Brightwalton Bloodstock Limited**
101 Ch f 04/02 Siyouni (FR)—Vivianite (IRE) (Teofilo (IRE)) (280000) **Mr D. Ward**
102 B f 25/03 Too Darn Hot—Way To My Heart (IRE) (Galileo (IRE))
103 **WINKSTER,** b c 27/04 Night of Thunder (IRE)—
Polar Circle (USA) (Royal Academy (USA)) (115000) **Opulence Thoroughbreds**

Assistant Trainer: Jack Steels.

---

516 MR TREVOR WALL, Ludlow

Postal: **Gorsty Farm Flat, Whitcliffe, Ludlow, Shropshire, SY8 2HD**
Contacts: **PHONE 01588 660219 MOBILE 07972 732080**
EMAIL trevorwall56@outlook.com

1 4, B g Dunaden (FR)—Bringewood Belle
2 5, B g Telescope (IRE)—Fairy Alisha
3 5, B m Dunaden (FR)—Just For A Dream
4 4, B f Recharge (IRE)—Longville Anna
5 **LONGVILLE LILLY,** 8, b m Mawatheeq (USA)—Curtains **T. R. Wall**
6 **MAY MIST,** 11, b m Nayef (USA)—Midnight Mist (IRE) **A. H. Bennett**
7 **MY FOXY LADY,** 11, br m Sagamix (FR)—Marlbrook Fox **Miss J. C. L. Needham**
8 **PAT'S LIGHT,** 7, b m Black Sam Bellamy (IRE)—Kansas City (FR) **C. G. Johnson**
9 **RIGHT ROYALS DAY,** 14, b m Beneficial—Just For A Laugh **Miss J. C. L. Needham**

Assistant Trainer: Mrs J. A. Wall.

---

517 MR CHARLIE WALLIS, Ardleigh

Postal: **Benson Stud, Harts Lane, Ardleigh, Colchester, Essex, CO7 7QE**
Contacts: **PHONE 01206 230779 MOBILE 07725 059355**
EMAIL cwallis86@hotmail.com

1 **ARZAAK (IRE),** 9, br g Casamento (IRE)—Dixieland Kiss (USA) **Mr M. M. Foulger**
2 **HUDDLETON MAC (IRE),** 5, b g Awtaad (IRE)—Melodique (FR) **J & A Bangs**
3 **IESHA,** 5, b m Cable Bay (IRE)—Royal Silk **J. M. Bradley**
4 **INDIAN AFFAIR,** 13, br g Sleeping Indian—Rare Fling (USA) **Mrs H. Wallis**
5 **MUSTAFFIZ,** 4, b g Oasis Dream—Mulkeyya (IRE) **J. M. Bradley**
6 **PANDEMIC PRINCESS (IRE),** 4, b f Mehmas (IRE)—Pearl Bell (IRE)
7 **PROCLIVITY (IRE),** 4, b f Acclamation—Jameerah **Mr E. Hayward**
8 **REVERSION (IRE),** 4, b g Adaay (IRE)—Dutch Desire **P. E. Axon**

MR CHARLIE WALLIS - continued

THREE-YEAR-OLDS

9 **DANCHOVSKA,** b g Oasis Dream—Araminte **P. E. Axon**
10 **HUCKLEBERRY,** b g Unfortunately (IRE)—Enchanted Princess **P. E. Axon**
11 **JAMES BRADLEY,** b g Sea The Stars (IRE)—Nadia Glory **P. E. Axon**
12 **LENS LEGACY (IRE),** b g Muhaarar—Alexis Carrington (IRE) **Miss J. A. Challen**
13 B g Aclaim (IRE)—Saved My Bacon (IRE) **Mrs J. V. Hughes**
14 **SUMAC (IRE),** ch g Belardo (IRE)—Spring Eternal **Mr E. Hayward**

TWO-YEAR-OLDS

15 B c 20/03 Belardo (IRE)—Hakuraa (IRE) (Elnadim (USA)) (2000)
16 Ch g 24/03 Territories (IRE)—Holberg Suite (Azamour (IRE)) (3000)
17 B c 26/03 Eqtidaar (IRE)—Holder's Hill (IRE) (Danehill Dancer (IRE)) (3000) **Mrs H. Wallis**
18 **MARCUS,** b g 04/03 Twilight Son—Sadiigah (Medicean) (15714) **Mrs S. A. Shewring**
19 B f 15/04 Sixties Icon—Triple Dip (IRE) (Three Valleys (USA)) (2500) **Mrs H. Wallis**

Assistant Trainer: Hayley Wallis.

---

518 MRS JANE WALTON, Otterburn

Postal: **Dunns Houses Stables, Otterburn, Newcastle Upon Tyne, Northumberland, NE19 1LB**
Contacts: **PHONE 01830 520677 MOBILE 07808 592701 FAX 01830 520677**
EMAIL dunnshouses@hotmail.com WEBSITE www.janewaltonhorseracing.co.uk

1 **EVEQUE (FR),** 9, ch g Kotky Bleu (FR)—Gloria IV (FR) **Mrs J. M. Walton**
2 **GOODOLDBILL,** 7, b g Leading Light (IRE)—Golden Sunbird (IRE) **Jane Walton & David Woodman**
3 **NOBLE AFFAIR (IRE),** 7, b m Morozov (USA)—Tudor Glyn (IRE) **The Optimistic Syndicate**
4 **PARELLI POWER,** 7, ch m Schiaparelli (GER)—Shankhouse Wells (IRE) **Jane Walton & George Charlton Partner**
5 **REAL ARMANI,** 11, ch g Sulamani (IRE)—Reel Charmer **Jane Walton & George Charlton Partner**
6 **UPTOWN HARRY (IRE),** 9, b br g Morozov (USA)—Tudor Glyn (IRE) **Fresh Start Partnership**

Assistant Trainer: Mrs Patricia Robson.

NH Jockey: Ross Chapman

---

519 MR JIMMY WALTON, Morpeth

Postal: **Flotterton Hall, Thropton, Morpeth, Northumberland, NE65 7LF**
Contacts: **PHONE 01669 640253 MOBILE 07831 894120**

1 **BONNIE BANJO,** 5, b m Requinto (IRE)—Island Music (IRE) **J. B. Walton**
2 **CUDGEL,** 10, b g Sulamani (IRE)—Posh Stick **Messrs F. T. Walton**
3 **EAGLE WATCH,** 5, ch g Eagle Top—Watch The Wind **Messrs F. T. Walton**
4 **FEEL THE BREEZE,** 6, b m Kutub (IRE)—Watch The Wind **Messrs F. T. Walton**
5 **FRANKIES FIRE,** 10, b m Flying Legend (USA)—Watch The Wind **Messrs F. T. Walton**
6 **HIGH ON THE HILL,** 5, gr m Kingston Hill—Garden Feature **Messrs F. T. Walton**
7 **MATTHEW MAN,** 12, b g Bollin Eric—Garden Feature **Messrs F. T. Walton**
8 **ROLL OF THUNDER,** 14, b g Antonius Pius (USA)—Ischia **Messrs F. T. Walton**
9 **TWENTY'S PLENTY,** 5, b g Intrinsic—Strategic Island (IRE) **Messrs F. T. Walton**
10 **WEST LAWN,** 7, b m Westlake—Garden Feature **Messrs F. T. Walton**

---

520 MR TOM WARD, Upper Lambourn

Postal: **Whitehouse Stables, Upper Lambourn, Hungerford, Berkshire, RG17 8QP**
WORK EMAIL tom@tomwardracing.com

1 **BOBBY DASSLER (IRE),** 4, b g Awtaad (IRE)—Butoolat
2 **CAPOTE'S DREAM (IRE),** 6, br g Dream Ahead (USA)—Capote West (USA)
3 **DIAMOND BAY,** 5, ch g New Bay—Amarillo Starlight (IRE)
4 **FARASI LANE (IRE),** 5, b g Belardo (IRE)—No Such Zone
5 **LUISA CASATI (IRE),** 5, b m Vadamos (FR)—La Marchesa (IRE)
6 **TASHI (IRE),** 6, ch m Kingston Hill—Supercharged (IRE)
7 **TINTORETTO (IRE),** 8, b g Lilbourne Lad (IRE)—Fanacanta (IRE)
8 **ZHUI FENG (IRE),** 10, b g Invincible Spirit (IRE)—Es Que

THREE-YEAR-OLDS

9 **CABARET SHOW (IRE),** b f Showcasing—Iamfine (IRE)
10 **CHARMING LILY,** b f Charm Spirit (IRE)—Lilly Junior
11 **DOUBLE DOWN (IRE),** ch c Fast Company (IRE)—Dinaria (IRE)
12 B g Adaay (IRE)—Dry Your Eyes (ITY)
13 B f Showcasing—Ebrah
14 **FLYING PANTHER,** ch g Hawkbill (USA)—La Pantera
15 **FULL PRIME (IRE),** ch f Mehmas (IRE)—Mayorstone (IRE)
16 **GARRICK PAINTER (IRE),** b g Zoffany (IRE)—Suraat (IRE)
17 **INTRICATE PILLAR (IRE),** b f Awtaad (IRE)—Delicate
18 **LADY DREAMER (IRE),** b f Dandy Man (IRE)—Weekend Getaway (IRE)
19 **ROYAL ATHENA,** b f Golden Horn—Neartica (FR)
20 **SAVANNAH SMILES (IRE),** b f Unfortunately (IRE)—Silicon Star (FR)
21 **SEA OF ELEGANCE (IRE),** ch f Sea The Stars (IRE)—Shahah
22 **SHOT,** b f Acclamation—Gladiatrix
23 **SO GLORIOUS,** b f Bated Breath—Self Centred
24 **SWEET IDEA,** b f Charming Thought—Berkshire Honey
25 **URBAN JUNGLE (IRE),** ch f Bungle Inthejungle—City Dazzler (IRE)

TWO-YEAR-OLDS

26 **CRYSTAL FLYER,** b f 23/01 Magna Grecia (IRE)—Mount Crystal (IRE) (Montjeu (IRE)) (42000)
27 **ESCAPE THE GRAPE,** ch c 17/03 Cityscape—Sancerre (IRE) (Canford Cliffs (IRE)) (952)
28 B f 22/03 Awtaad (IRE)—Flanders (IRE) (Common Grounds)
29 B c 11/04 Harry Angel (IRE)—Miss Work of Art (Dutch Art)
30 B f 03/02 Exceed And Excel (AUS)—Night Charter (IRE) (Night of Thunder (IRE)) (75000)
31 B c 23/05 Cloth of Stars (IRE)—Passing Burg (FR) (Sageburg (IRE)) (44818)
32 B f 26/03 Golden Horn—Pleione (FR) (Sadler's Wells (USA))
33 B c 13/05 Portamento (IRE)—Rosealee (IRE) (Zebedee)
34 **SNOW EAGLE,** b c 13/01 Due Diligence (USA)—Acampe (Sky Mesa (USA))
35 B f 29/04 New Bay—Soft Lips (Rahy (USA)) (35214)
36 **THEWORLDSNOTENOUGH,** b f 12/02 Inns of Court (IRE)—Fondled (Selkirk (USA)) (33333)
37 B c 02/03 Night of Thunder (IRE)—Twilight Sky (Authorized (IRE)) (55000)
38 B f 16/02 U S Navy Flag (USA)—Uele River (Refuse To Bend (IRE)) (32000)
39 **WOODHAY WONDER,** b f 07/04 Tamayuz—Luang Prabang (IRE) (Invincible Spirit (IRE)) (26000)

Head Lad: James Hughes, Anthony James, **Travelling Head:** Matt Birch, Jemma Marshall,

Business & Racing Manager: Alex Lowe, **Yard Sponsor:** Smulders.

521 MR ARCHIE WATSON, Upper Lambourn

Postal: **Saxon Gate, Upper Lambourn, Hungerford, Berkshire, RG17 8QH**
Contacts: **PHONE 01488 491247**
EMAIL office@archiewatsonracing.com WEBSITE www.archiewatsonracing.com

1 **AADDEEY (IRE),** 6, b g New Approach (IRE)—Feedyah (USA)
2 **AL ZARAQAAN,** 6, br g Golden Horn—Asheerah
3 **ALAZWAR (IRE),** 5, b g Awtaad (IRE)—Venetian Beauty (USA)
4 **ALBASHEER (IRE),** 5, ch h Shamardal (USA)—Mutebah (IRE)
5 **AMOR DE MI VIDA (FR),** 5, b m Dabirsim (FR)—Troiecat (FR)
6 **BARGING THRU,** 4, b g Profitable (IRE)—Rhythm Excel
7 **BUGLE MAJOR (USA),** 8, gr g Mizzen Mast (USA)—Conference Call
8 **CHIEF'S WILL (IRE),** 4, ch g Slade Power (IRE)—Royal Debt
9 **CHOSEN HERO (IRE),** 5, ch m Flemensfirth (USA)—Chosen Destiny (IRE)
10 **CIRCUS MOON (IRE),** 5, b m Sholokhov (IRE)—Carrigeen Kohleria (IRE)
11 **CLIFFTOP HEAVEN,** 6, b g Canford Cliffs (IRE)—Heaven's Sake
12 **COLOURFUL DREAM,** 4, b f Dubawi (IRE)—Be My Gal
13 **CORINTHIA KNIGHT (IRE),** 8, ch g Society Rock (IRE)—Victoria Lodge (IRE)
14 **EXCEL POWER (IRE),** 5, b g Slade Power (IRE)—Rhythm Excel
15 **FLAG OF TRUTH (FR),** 4, b g Starspangledbanner (AUS)—Dalakania (IRE)
16 **GROVE ROAD (IRE),** 7, ch g Mahler—Dear Frankie (IRE)
17 **IMPERIAL SANDS (IRE),** 5, b g Footstepsinthesand—Hadrienne
18 **LAST HOORAH,** 4, ch g Bated Breath—Fibou (USA)
19 **LET HER LOOSE (IRE),** 6, ch m Mukhadram—Passionable
20 **LUNA MAGIC,** 9, br m Mayson—Dayia (IRE)
21 **MAFIA POWER,** 6, b g Gleneagles (IRE)—Rivara
22 **MENIN GATE (IRE),** 7, gr g Farhh—Telegraphy (USA)
23 **MIGHTY GURKHA (IRE),** 5, b g Sepoy (AUS)—Royal Debt
24 **MONSIEUR FANTAISIE (IRE),** 5, b g Make Believe—Rachel Tiffany (USA)
25 **MOUNTBATTEN (IRE),** 4, bl g Dabirsim (FR)—Sapore di Roma (IRE)
26 **NIFTY GETAWAY (IRE),** 7, b m Getaway (GER)—Buttonboard (IRE)
27 **NIKOVO,** 4, b g Kingman—Rostova (USA)
28 **NOBLE ANTHEM (IRE),** 4, b g Starspangledbanner (AUS)—Queen Margherita
29 **OTTO OYL,** 5, b g Mayson—Olive Mary
30 **OUTBOX,** 8, b g Frankel—Emirates Queen
31 **PINK CARNATION,** 4, b f Territories (IRE)—Dusty Red
32 **POLEMON,** 4, b g Frankel—Very Good News (USA)
33 **QUANTICO (IRE),** 4, b g Make Believe—Palladius
34 **SANITISER,** 4, b g The Gurkha (IRE)—Spicy Dal
35 **SHARVARA,** 4, b g Kingman—Tendency (IRE)
36 **SIR JOSEPH SWAN,** 5, b g Paco Boy (IRE)—Candle
37 **SPOT OF BOTHER (IRE),** 6, gr g Well Chosen—Mrs Jones (FR)
38 **STAG HORN,** 6, b g Golden Horn—Starfala
39 **TABDEED,** 8, ch g Havana Gold (IRE)—Puzzled (IRE)
40 **TEMPUS,** 7, b g Kingman—Passage of Time
41 **THRONE HALL,** 6, b g Kingman—Appearance
42 **TOUT EST PERMIS (FR),** 10, gr g Linda's Lad—Kadalbleue (FR)
43 **TYLOS (FR),** 4, b g Night of Thunder (IRE)—New Arrival (FR)
44 **UNILATERALISM (IRE),** 4, ch g Starspangledbanner (AUS)—Barnet
45 **VERONA STAR (IRE),** 4, b g Gutaifan (IRE)—Julieta (IRE)

THREE-YEAR-OLDS

46 **A TASTE OF HONEY,** b f Harry Angel (IRE)—Gimme Some Lovin (IRE)
47 **ABBEY'S DREAM,** b f Tasleet—Blue Oyster
48 **ANGEL OF THE ROCK (IRE),** b f Dark Angel (IRE)—Flame of Gibraltar (IRE)
49 **ATHENE'S KISS (IRE),** b f Gustav Klimt (IRE)—Low Cunning (IRE)
50 **BIRTHDAY ANGEL (IRE),** gr c Dark Angel (IRE)—Capulet Monteque (IRE)
51 **BISHOP'S GLORY (IRE),** ch g Cotai Glory—Bishop's Lake
52 **BRADSELL,** b c Tasleet—Russian Punch
53 **BRAVE EMPEROR (IRE),** b g Sioux Nation (USA)—Roman Gal (IRE)
54 B c Jungle Cat (IRE)—Caldy Dancer (IRE)

MR ARCHIE WATSON - continued

55 **CHRISZOFF (IRE),** b c Zoffany (IRE)—Countess Chrissy
56 **COLORS OF FREEDOM,** ch f Mayson—Scarborough (IRE)
57 **CONCON CANDY (IRE),** gr f Havana Grey—Child Bride (USA)
58 **CORAL REEF (IRE),** b f Invincible Spirit (IRE)—Mehronissa
59 **CORELLIAN STAR (IRE),** ch f Cotai Glory—Orelle
60 **CREATIVE STYLE (IRE),** b f Kodiac—New Style (USA)
61 **DESERT SWIRL (IRE),** b f Cracksman—Khaleesi Wind (IRE)
62 **DREAM MISSION,** b c Oasis Dream—Luna Mission (IRE)
63 **ELUSIVE EMPIRE (FR),** b c Territories (IRE)—Elusive Galaxy (IRE)
64 **ELUSIVE TIGER (IRE),** b c Jungle Cat (IRE)—Purple Tiger (IRE)
65 **FIFTY YEAR STORM (IRE),** b f Mehmas (IRE)—Fainleog (IRE)
66 **FLAMMABLE,** b f Almanzor (FR)—Danza Cavallo (FR)
67 **FLYING KISS (IRE),** b f Kessaar (IRE)—Ray of Sunshine
68 **GARNER,** b g Recorder—Dawn Glory
69 **GUSTAVAGO (IRE),** b g Gustav Klimt (IRE)—Harpist (IRE)
70 **GYPSY NATION (IRE),** br gr g Sioux Nation (USA)—Gypsy Style
71 **HE'S A MONSTER (IRE),** br c No Nay Never (USA)—Al Joza
72 **HEAVENLY BREATH,** gr f Dark Angel (IRE)—Astonishing (IRE)
73 **HILDEGARD (IRE),** b f Zoffany (IRE)—Gale Song
74 **IT'S SHOWTIME BABY,** b f Showcasing—Minoria
75 **JUNGLE CHARM,** ch f Jungle Cat (IRE)—Royal Debt
76 **KOHANA BREEZE (IRE),** b f Sioux Nation (USA)—Luxie (IRE)
77 **LAKOTA BRAVE,** b g Sioux Nation (USA)—Cartographer
78 **LOVE LIES (IRE),** b f Dandy Man (IRE)—Lahabah (IRE)
79 **MANITOU (IRE),** ch g Sioux Nation (USA)—Jowana (IRE)
80 Ch c New Approach (IRE)—Maoineach (USA)
81 **MOJEYRR (IRE),** b c Profitable (IRE)—For Joy
82 **NATZOR (FR),** b c Almanzor (FR)—Natty (IRE)
83 **ONIGHT,** b c Oasis Dream—Surcingle (USA)
84 **RADETSKY MARSCH (FR),** b c Seahenge (USA)—Baileys Applause
85 Ch c Night Of Thunder (IRE)—Rathaath (IRE)
86 **RHYTHM N HOOVES,** b g Pearl Secret—Street Jazz
87 **SEAHRENA (FR),** b f Seahenge (USA)—Rena Borghese (IRE)
88 **STAR (FR),** b g Cloth of Stars (IRE)—Municiadora (BRZ)
89 **STAR CHILD,** ch f Gleneagles (IRE)—Spicy Dal
90 **STOLEN ENCOUNTER,** br g Cracksman—Forbidden Love
91 **SUNDAZED (IRE),** ch f Australia—Sunbird
92 **UNITED FORCE (IRE),** b c Showcasing—Pure Innocence (IRE)
93 B br f Zoustar (AUS)—Utterly Charming (IRE)
94 **VICTORIA COUNTY (IRE),** ch g Starspangledbanner (AUS)—Victoria Bear (IRE)
95 **WAY TO AMARILLO (FR),** gr f Shalaa (IRE)—Peinted Song (USA)

Trainer did not supply details of their two-year-olds.

Assistant Trainer: Stephanie Joannides, Chris Martin, Rory O'Dowd.

Flat Jockey: Hollie Doyle. **Apprentice Jockey:** Taylor Fisher. **Amateur Jockey:** Miss Brodie Hampson.

522

MR FRED WATSON, Sedgefield

Postal: **Beacon Hill, Sedgefield, Stockton-On-Tees, Cleveland, TS21 3HN**
Contacts: **PHONE 01740 620582 MOBILE 07773 321472**
EMAIL fredwatson@talktalk.net

1 **DARK ECLIPSE (IRE),** 7, b g Slade Power (IRE)—Many Colours **F. Watson**
2 **GLEAMING ARCH,** 9, b g Arabian Gleam—Mrs Quince **F. Watson**
3 **JOYFUL STAR,** 13, b g Teofilo (IRE)—Extreme Beauty (USA) **F. Watson**

MR FRED WATSON - continued

4 **NEWSPEAK (IRE),** 11, b g New Approach (IRE)—Horatia (IRE) **F. Watson**
5 **ROYAL LEGEND,** 9, ch g New Approach (IRE)—Villarrica (USA) **F. Watson**
6 **STAR CITIZEN,** 11, b g New Approach (IRE)—Faslen (USA) **F. Watson**

---

523 MR SIMON WAUGH, Morpeth

Postal: **A G Waugh & Sons Limited, Molesden House, Molesden, Morpeth, Northumberland, NE61 3QF**
Contacts: **MOBILE 07860 561445**
EMAIL swaugh@dircon.co.uk

1 **COOLMOYNE,** 7, ch g Ocovango—High Life **Mrs S. A. York**
2 **DAN GUN (IRE),** 9, b g Intikhab (USA)—Lady Magdalena (IRE) **Northumberland Racing Club**
3 **DARK AND DANGEROUS (IRE),** 15, b g Cacique (IRE)—Gilah (IRE) **S. G. Waugh**
4 **HELLFIRE KODE,** 6, b g Helmet (AUS)—Secret Kode (IRE) **S. G. Waugh**
5 **LOUGHERMORE (IRE),** 9, b g Milan—Seductive Dance **Northumberland Racing Club**
6 **ROYAL FLUSH,** 12, b g Multiplex—Mystical Feelings (BEL) **S. G. Waugh**
7 **SEGEDUNUM,** 5, b g Cannock Chase (USA)—Arabian Sunset (IRE) **S. G. Waugh**
8 **THISTIMENEXTYEAR,** 9, gr g New Approach (IRE)—Scarlet Empire (IRE) **S. G. Waugh**

---

524 MR MARK WEATHERER, Leyburn

Postal: **The Flat, Bolton Hall Racing Stables, Wensley, Leyburn, North Yorkshire, DL8 4UF**
Contacts: **PHONE 01969 625735**
EMAIL markweatherer@btinternet.com

1 **AMANI,** 5, b m Adaay (IRE)—Miss Wells (IRE) **M. Weatherer**
2 **BARRISTER BLASTER,** 5, b g Toronado (IRE)—Dansante **Ownaracehorse And Tom Cusdenlaster**
3 **CASSIEL (IRE),** 4, gr g Dark Angel (IRE)—Masaya **B Lapham & Formidable Fillies**
4 **DEE DAY LANDING,** 6, b h Intrinsic—Heidenheim (IRE) **Mark Weatherer & Formidable Fellows**
5 **DIONYSIS (FR),** 10, ch g Lucarno (USA)—Oasice (FR) **Mr B. Lapham**
6 **FAIRY STREAM,** 4, b f Mayson—Fairy Shoes **Mr B. Lapham**
7 **FOR THREE (IRE),** 9, b g Pour Moi (IRE)—Asmaa (USA) **Ben Lapham & Formidable Fellows**
8 **GLAN Y GORS (IRE),** 11, b br g High Chaparral (IRE)—Trading Places **B Lapham & Formidable Fillies**
9 **HOLLIE POPS,** 5, b m Garswood—Chasin' Rainbows **Mr B. Lapham**
10 **LEANNES LADY (IRE),** 11, b m Ask—Wizzy (IRE) **Ben Lapham & Formidable Fellows**
11 **LITTLE GEM,** 5, b m Bobby's Kitten (USA)—Harlequin Twist **B & Fillies**
12 **PRETTY AS PINK,** 4, b f Intrinsic—Rubicon Bay (IRE) **M. Weatherer**
13 **SCATTER GILL,** 4, b f Mahsoob—Little Missmoffatt
14 **SPIRITTAPPERGOODE,** 5, b g Eagle Top—Dutch Girl **Mark Weatherer & Formidable Fellows**
15 **UNIQUE COMPANY (IRE),** 8, ch g Fast Company (IRE)—Unique Blanche **M. Weatherer**

THREE-YEAR-OLDS

16 Ch g Forever Now—Dudette
17 **FIRE HEART,** b f Pearl Secret—Winning Return (IRE) **Mr B. Lapham**

525 MR PAUL WEBBER, Banbury

Postal: **Cropredy Lawn, Cropredy, Banbury, Oxfordshire, OX17 1DR**
Contacts: **PHONE 01295 750226 MOBILE 07836 232465**
EMAIL paul@paulwebberracing.com WEBSITE www.paulwebberracing.com

1 **ALL A STRUGGLE,** 6, b g Kayf Tara—Hot Rhythm **Mr Martin Hughes**
2 6, Ch m Shirocco (GER)—Cabaret Girl **Ms Dillie Keane**
3 **CECI WELLS,** 6, b m Orientor—Theatrical Dancer **Exors of the Late Mr P. C. Smith**
4 **CHRONOS,** 6, b g Nayef (USA)—All Time **The Fitzdares Racing Syndicate**
5 **CLOUDY HILLS (IRE),** 7, b g Cloudings (IRE)—Phillis Hill **Miss Sheena Pilkington**
6 **CRYSTAL MER,** 4, b g Sea The Stars (IRE)—Yaazy (IRE) **Mr Martin Hughes**
7 **ELWING (IRE),** 4, b f Intello (GER)—Masandra (IRE) **Mr David Taylor**
8 **EURKASH (FR),** 9, b g Irish Wells (FR)—Meralda (FR) **Cropredy Lawn Racing**
9 **EYED,** 6, b g Kayf Tara—One Gulp **Mr Martin Hughes**
10 **GETAWAY WITH YOU,** 5, ch g Getaway (GER)—Dizzy Frizzy **The Starjac Partnership**
11 **GLENGOLLY,** 4, b g Black Sam Bellamy (IRE)—Tsarinova **Miss Sheena Pilkington**
12 **GO AS YOU PLEASE (IRE),** 10, b g Jeremy (USA)—Aweebounce (IRE) **Mr J. P. McManus**
13 **HAPPY INDEX,** 5, b m Blue Bresil (FR)—Alasi **Sir John Timpson**
14 **HE'S A KNOWALL (IRE),** 8, b br g Oscar (IRE)—Miss Knowall (IRE) **Old Gold Racing 5**
15 **HELPFUL,** 4, b g Oasis Dream—Magic (IRE) **Mr Martin Hughes**
16 **INDEFATIGABLE (IRE),** 10, b m Schiaparelli (GER)—Spin The Wheel (IRE) **Mr Philip Rocher**
17 **JAPON DE CARJAC (FR),** 4, b g Joshua Tree (IRE)—Queyrann (FR) **Mr Philip Rocher**
18 **KILFILUM WOODS (IRE),** 7, b g Beat Hollow—Cheryls Island (IRE) **Mr Martin Hughes**
19 **LUNAR OCEAN (IRE),** 4, br g Sea Moon—Lawfull (IRE) **Sox & Co**
20 **MASTER HOBBS,** 4, br g Jack Hobbs—Interim Lodge (IRE) **Mr Philip Rocher**
21 **MY GIFT TO YOU (IRE),** 5, b g Kingston Hill—Ariels Serenade (IRE) **Mrs Paul Shanahan**
22 **PEPITE DE AMOUR,** 5, b m Telescope (IRE)—Pepite de Soleil (FR) **Mrs T North**
23 **SPECIAL ACCEPTANCE,** 10, b g Malinas (GER)—Doubly Guest **The Syndicators 2**
24 **ZAIN FARHH,** 4, ch g Farhh—Local Spirit (USA) **Mr Martin Hughes**

THREE-YEAR-OLDS

25 **BONGO MAN,** b g Jack Hobbs—Miss Tongabezi **Cropredy Lawn Racing**
26 **EL RAYO,** b g Jack Hobbs—Viking Queen **The Jack, Queen, and King Syndicate**
27 Ch f Cityscape—September Blaze **Mr Paul Bowden**
28 Ch f Cityscape—Shuil Gealach (IRE) **Overbury Stud**

TWO-YEAR-OLDS

29 B c 14/04 Australia—Laka (IRE) (Oasis Dream) (27000) **Miss Sheena Pilkington**

---

526 MR ADAM WEST, Epsom

Postal: **Flat 2, Lorretta Lodge, Tilley Lane, Headley, Epsom, Surrey, KT18 6EP**
Contacts: **MOBILE 07939 030046**
EMAIL westtraining@outlook.com

1 **BAIKAL,** 4, b g No Nay Never (USA)—Foreign Assignment (IRE)
2 **BIG BEAR HUG,** 4, b f Belardo (IRE)—Silkenveil (IRE) **Ownaracehorse And R Kent**
3 **CAP'N (IRE),** 12, b g Gamut (IRE)—Dawn Princess (IRE) **Ishtar**
4 **CODSWALLOP,** 4, gr g Outstrip—Lady Benedicte (IRE) **Sills, Colegate, Amass & Ownaracehorse**
5 **COILLTE EILE (IRE),** 10, b m Stowaway—Aughwilliam Lady (IRE) **Mr P K & Mrs A J Adams**
6 **DARING DESTINY (IRE),** 4, b f Mehmas (IRE)—Flat White (IRE) **Mr S. K. McPhee**
7 **DEN GRIMME AELLING (IRE),** 4, b f Estidhkaar (IRE)—Veladiya (IRE)
8 **ELECKTRA,** 4, b f Telescope (IRE)—Haatefina **Mr T. Francis**
9 **GILBERT,** 4, b g Cityscape—Merry Diva **Ownaracehorse And Ross Deacon**
10 4, Ch g Sans Frontieres (IRE)—Hatton Park **Mr J. Webb**

MR ADAM WEST - continued

11 **KILGANER QUEEN (IRE),** 13, b m Trans Island—La Prima Diva (IRE) **Mr D. Amass**
12 **LADY PLUMTON,** 5, b m Mahler—Plumton Dawn (IRE) **Mrs A. Cantillon**
13 **LIVE IN THE DREAM (IRE),** 4, ch g Prince of Lir (IRE)—Approaching Autumn **Steve & Jolene de'Lemos**
14 **MALCOLM,** 4, b g Teofilo (IRE)—Interception (IRE) **SRDS Racing**
15 **MYTHICAL HERO (IRE),** 6, b g Soldier of Fortune (IRE)—Flamenco Lily (IRE) **Cusden & Parker**
16 **NIBLAWI (IRE),** 11, b g Vale of York (IRE)—Finnmark
17 **NOAHTHIRTYTWORED (IRE),** 7, b g Court Cave (IRE)—Royale Video (FR) **Mr D. Phelan**
18 **ONE FOR YOU (IRE),** 8, b g Yeats (IRE)—Tempest Belle (IRE) **Cusden & Parker**
19 **PRESUMING ED (IRE),** 8, br g Westerner—Maracana (IRE) **Seasons & Parker**
20 **QUEEN OF THE ROAD,** 6, b m Kingston Hill—Lily Rules (IRE) **Mr T. J. Cusden**
21 **ROLYPOLYMOLY,** 4, b g Heeraat (IRE)—Elzebieta (IRE) **S Brace, C Parker & All Seasons Racing**
22 **SATONO JAPAN (JPN),** 6, b g Deep Impact (JPN)—Dubawi Heights **Cusden & Parker**
23 **TELEFINA,** 5, b m Telescope (IRE)—Haatefina **Silver Lining Racing**
24 **THESPINNINGWHEEL (IRE),** 8, b g Arakan (USA)—Dancing Jest (IRE)
25 **THIBAULT,** 10, b g Kayf Tara—Seemarye **Farm fencing limited**
26 **ZYON,** 9, gr g Martaline—Temptation (FR) **Mr S. W. Lang**

THREE-YEAR-OLDS

27 **BILLIE LOU,** b f Intello (GER)—Silkenveil (IRE)
28 **DAISY ROOTS,** b f Footstepsinthesand—Cambridge Duchess **Ownaracehorse & Theakston Stud**
29 **HAWKES BAY,** b g Fountain of Youth (IRE)—Bay Tree (IRE) **Mr J. Stevens**
30 **LANGYTHELEGEND,** ch g Hawkbill (USA)—Hisaronu (IRE) **Mr S. W. Lang**
31 Ch f Night of Thunder (IRE)—Moonstone Rock
32 **MR POSTMAN,** ch g Bated Breath—Kitba **Mr T R Slater & Ownaracehorse**
33 B f Linda's Lad—Narla **Mr J. Webb**
34 **NORDIC STAR,** b g Kuroshio (AUS)—Dazzling View (USA) **David & Patrick Moorhead**
35 **VEGAS JACK,** ch g Bated Breath—Haigh Hall **T Cusden & Partner**
36 **VIOLETS STAR,** b f Ardad (IRE)—Poppy Seed **Mr C. Parker**
37 **VITANI,** gr f Roaring Lion (USA)—Kiyoshi **Stuart McPhee & Paul Webster**

TWO-YEAR-OLDS

38 B f 03/05 Massaat (IRE)—Aquasulis (IRE) (Titus Livius (FR))
39 B g 26/04 Harry Angel (IRE)—Aunt Minnie (Night Shift (USA)) (5000) **Farm Fencing Limited**
40 B f 18/04 Australia—D'Oro Princess (USA) (Medaglia d'Oro (USA)) (1500)
41 B f 31/03 Land Force (IRE)—Dame Helen (Royal Applause) (12000)
42 B c 16/01 Pearl Secret—Exceedingly (Exceed And Excel (AUS))
43 Br f 24/01 Belardo (IRE)—Kenyan Cat (One Cool Cat (USA)) **Mr T. J. Cusden**
44 B f 14/02 Churchill (IRE)—Mill Point (Champs Elysees) (10000) **Seasons & Brace**
45 B f 13/05 Nathaniel (IRE)—Porcini (Azamour (IRE)) (7000) **West Racing Partnership**
46 B f 18/02 Eqtidaar (IRE)—Poudretteite (Royal Applause) (5500) **Cusden & Parker**
47 B f 07/03 Bungle Inthejungle—Rose Crown (New Approach (IRE)) (4000)
48 **TANGLED UP IN BLUE (IRE),** ch f 15/04 Soldier's Call—Child Bride (USA) (Coronado's Quest (USA)) (17000)
49 B f 23/03 Showcasing—The Gold Cheongsam (IRE) (Red Clubs (IRE)) **Chasemore Farm LLP**

---

527 MISS SHEENA WEST, Lewes

Postal: **5 Balmer Farm Cottages, Brighton Road, Lewes, East Sussex, BN7 3JN**
Contacts: **MOBILE 07748 181804 FAX 01273 622189**
EMAIL sheenawest11@aol.com FACEBOOK @sheenawestracing

1 **A TICKATICKATIMING,** 5, b m Sixties Icon—Hi Note **Miss S. West**
2 **AIR HAIR LAIR (IRE),** 7, ch g Zebedee—Blond Beauty (USA) **I Poysden,R Heal,B Beesley,D Harper-Jones**
3 **ALEXANDRA ROMANOV (IRE),** 6, ch m Sixties Icon—Russian Empress (IRE) **Balmer Farm Racing**
4 **BARD OF BRITTANY,** 9, b g Sayif (IRE)—Lily Le Braz **Mr M. Moriarty**
5 **BAREST OF MARGINS (IRE),** 7, b g Shirocco (GER)—Holly Baloo (IRE) **Mr M. Moriarty**

MISS SHEENA WEST - continued

6 **BASS STRAIT,** 4, b f Cityscape—Rough Courte (IRE) **Miss S. West**
7 **CHERRY COLA,** 7, ch m Sixties Icon—Rose Cheval (USA) **The Affordable (4) Partnership**
8 **DANCE OF DRAGONS,** 4, b br f Gutaifan (IRE)—Sahafh (USA) **Miss S. West**
9 **GEARING'S POINT,** 5, b m Harbour Watch (IRE)—Amahoro **Mr S. K. Francis**
10 **JUSTANOTHER MUDDLE,** 14, gr g Kayf Tara—Spatham Rose **Saloop**
11 **KENNY GEORGE,** 8, b g Mawatheeq (USA)—One For Philip **Mr M. Moriarty**
12 **LAETOLI,** 5, b m Footstepsinthesand—Exentricity **Miss S. West**
13 **LIGHTNING GOLD,** 8, ch m Black Sam Bellamy (IRE)—Santera (IRE) **The Affordable (3) Partnership**
14 **MR FREEDOM,** 4, b g Sixties Icon—Waitingforachance **The Affordable (3) Partnership**
15 **SABYINYO,** 4, gr g Gregorian (IRE)—Amahoro **The Affordable (3) Partnership**
16 **SIXTIES SECRET,** 8, b m Sixties Icon—Jollyhockeysticks **Miss S. West**
17 **SLY MADAM,** 5, b m Sixties Icon—Tanojin (IRE) **Miss S. West**
18 **SUMATRAN TIGER (FR),** 6, b m Hurricane Cat (USA)—Malacca Straits **Miss S. West**
19 **ZOLTAN VARGA,** 9, b g Sayif (IRE)—Mar Blue (FR) **Dr M. Makratzakis**
20 **ZYRA'S LIONESS,** 5, b m Sixties Icon—Follow The Faith **Mr R. Vaughan**

Assistant Trainer: Megan Poulton.

NH Jockey: Marc Goldstein.

---

528 MR SIMON WEST, Middleham

Postal: **14A St Alkeldas Road, Middleham, Leyburn, North Yorkshire, DL8 4PW**
Contacts: **MOBILE 07855 924529**
EMAIL simonwest21@hotmail.co.uk WEBSITE www.mkmracing.co.uk

1 **BANDOL (IRE),** 15, b g Zagreb (USA)—Formal Affair **Mr P. Hothersall**
2 **BOBBIE THE DAZZLER (IRE),** 9, b m Lawman (FR)—Fashion Statement **Mr P. C. Bryan**
3 **CASAMARI ABBEY (IRE),** 9, br g Jeremy (USA)—Sprightly Gal (IRE) **Mr P. C. Bryan**
4 **CRANK EM UP (IRE),** 12, b g Royal Anthem (USA)—Carrawaystick (IRE) **Mr P. Hothersall**
5 **DORA DE JANEIRO (FR),** 10, b m Ballingarry (IRE)—Katana (GER) **Mr P. Hothersall**
6 **FABULEUX DU CLOS (FR),** 8, b g Blue Bresil (FR)—Osmazome (FR) **Mr P. Hothersall**
7 **FIGHTING CHANCE,** 4, ch g Pastoral Pursuits—Slim Chance (IRE) **Mrs B. Hothersall**
8 **GHOSTEEM FLECHOIS (FR),** 7, gr g Smadoun (FR)—Lesteem (FR) **Exors of the Late J. D. Gordon**
9 **HAPPY COUNTY (FR),** 6, b g High Rock (IRE)—Osmazome (FR) **Mr P. Hothersall**
10 **KODI KOH (IRE),** 8, b m Kodiac—Laywaan (USA) **Wild West Racing**
11 **LITTLE CHANCE,** 5, b m Milk It Mick—Slim Chance (IRE) **Mrs B. Hothersall**
12 **MIKE MCCANN (IRE),** 15, b g Helissio (FR)—Inzamaam (IRE) **Wild West Racing**
13 **QUERCUS SINUATA,** 5, ch m Garswood—Abonos (IRE) **Mr S. G. West**
14 **SHORT HEAD (GER),** 8, b m Fastnet Rock (AUS)—Slight Advantage (IRE) **Wild West Racing**
15 **SO YOU THOUGHT (USA),** 9, b g So You Think (NZ)—Lady of Akita (USA) **Exors of the Late J. D. Gordon**
16 **SUGARPIEHONEYBUNCH (IRE),** 5, b m Fast Company (IRE)—Jeewana **Mr P. C. Bryan**
17 **TOUCH KICK (IRE),** 12, b g Presenting—Bay Pearl (FR) **Hothersall & West**

---

529 MR DAVID WESTON, West Overton

Postal: **c/o Flintstone Stud, West Overton, Marlborough, Wiltshire, SN8 4ER**
Contacts: **MOBILE 07966 641001**
EMAIL flintstone007@icloud.com

1 **ADMIRAL'S SUNSET,** 10, b m Mount Nelson—Early Evening **Miss E. Tanner**
2 **LADY PACIFICO,** 5, b m Sir Percy—Silken Ocean **Miss E. Tanner**
3 **SIX AND OUT,** 5, ch g Sixties Icon—Extremely Rare (IRE) **Miss E. Tanner**

MR DAVID WESTON - continued

4 **SOLSTALLA,** 11, b m Halling (USA)—Solstice **Miss E. Tanner**

THREE-YEAR-OLDS

5 B f Gleneagles (IRE)—You Look So Good **Miss E. Tanner**

---

530 MR TOM WESTON, Hindlip

Postal: **Offerton Farm, Offerton Lane, Hindlip, Worcester, Worcestershire, WR3 8SX**
Contacts: **MOBILE 07752 313698**

1 **BLACK TONIC,** 5, b g Black Sam Bellamy (IRE)—Tullow Tonic (IRE) **Mr T. H. Weston**
2 **ELUSIVE ENEMY (IRE),** 4, bl g Elusive Pimpernel (USA)—Field Robin (IRE) **Mr T. H. Weston**
3 **STUMPS OR SLIPS (IRE),** 6, ch g Getaway (GER)—Queeny's Princess (IRE) **Big Winners Big Dinners**
4 **THE LATE LEGEND,** 10, ch g Midnight Legend—Vin Rose **Mr G. J. Fisher**

---

531 MR DONALD WHILLANS, Hawick

Postal: **Dodlands Steading, Hawick, Roxburghshire, TD9 8LG**
Contacts: **MOBILE 07565 609007**
EMAIL garrywhillans@gmail.com WEBSITE www.donaldwhillansracing.com

1 **BOLLIN MATILDA,** 5, b m Yorgunnabelucky (USA)—Bollin Julie **Mr C. S. Whillans**
2 **BONNY HOUXTY,** 10, b m Native Ruler—Izons Croft **Mr W. M. Aitchison**
3 5, B m Black Sam Bellamy (IRE)—Border Flora **Mr W. M. Aitchison**
4 **BOTH BARRELS,** 5, ch g Saddler's Rock (IRE)—Red Legend **Mrs A. Marshall**
5 **COWBOY COOPER (IRE),** 7, b g Frammassone (IRE)—Ball Park (IRE) **D. W. Whillans**
6 **EDEN MILL (IRE),** 6, ch g Leading Light (IRE)—Mistress Pope (IRE) **Td9 Racing**
7 4, B g Clovis du Berlais (FR)—Ellistrin Belle **Ellistrin Partnership**
8 **ELLISTRIN STAR,** 6, b m Passing Glance—Ellistrin Belle **Ellistrin Partnership**
9 **ENEMY AT THE GATE (IRE),** 7, b g Fame And Glory—Biondo (IRE) **D. W. Whillans**
10 **ETERNALLY YOURS,** 10, b m Sulamani (IRE)—Well Disguised (IRE) **D. W. Whillans**
11 **GIE IT LALDY,** 6, b gr g Multiplex—Celine Message **Simon & Angela Gillie**
12 **GOGO GLENDA,** 6, b m Schiaparelli (GER)—Glenda Lough (IRE) **D. W. Whillans**
13 **HOUXTY REIVER,** 6, b m Black Sam Bellamy (IRE)—Izons Croft **Reiver Racing Syndicate**
14 **KEYBOARD GANGSTER (IRE),** 12, b g Gamut (IRE)—Vic O'Tully (IRE)
15 4, Br g Malinas (GER)—Lis Goold (IRE)
16 4, B f Black Sam Bellamy (IRE)—Lonely Paradise
17 **MAID OF HOUXTY,** 8, b m Native Ruler—Izons Croft **Mr W. M. Aitchison**
18 **NIGHTS IN VENICE,** 7, ch g Midnight Legend—Well Disguised (IRE) **D. W. Whillans**
19 **PALLAS LORD (IRE),** 5, b g Dandy Man (IRE)—Nutshell **D. W. Whillans**
20 **PRINCESS APOLLO,** 9, b m Mullionmileanhour (IRE)—Speedy Senorita (IRE) **Mr S. B. Chamberlain**
21 **SEE MY BABY JIVE,** 7, ch m Coach House (IRE)—Lady Fiona **Mrs H. M. Whillans**
22 **SHOESHINE BOY (IRE),** 7, b br g Valirann (FR)—Godlylady (IRE) **Mousetrap Racing**
23 **SO MANY ROADS,** 6, b g Sulamani (IRE)—Spotthestripe **The The Wellfed Boys**
24 **UNDECIDED (IRE),** 7, b g Sageburg (IRE)—Your Place Or Mine (IRE) **The Buyers Club**

Assistant Trainer: Mr Callum Whillans.

532 MR EWAN ALISTAIR WHILLANS, Hawick

Postal: **Newmill On Slitrig, HAWICK, Roxburghshire, TD9 9UQ**
Contacts: **PHONE 01450 372350**
EMAIL ewanwhillans1@gmail.com

1 **AIKIDO (IRE),** 5, b g Dandy Man (IRE)—Quintessenz (GER) **Karen Spark & Christine Jordan**
2 **AMAZING ALBA,** 7, ch m Helmet (AUS)—Silcasue **John & Liz Elliot**
3 **ANCORA (GER),** 4, b f Amaron—Ajesha (GER) **Mr A. Turnbull**
4 4, B g Malinas (GER)—Beanri Mhaith (IRE) **Mrs K. Spark**
5 **BELLA BLUESKY,** 7, br m Dylan Thomas (IRE)—Lady Bluesky **Harrow Whillans**
6 **BILLY BATHGATE,** 7, ch g New Approach (IRE)—Bustling **Mrs E. B. Ferguson**
7 **BUFORD,** 5, b g Lawman (FR)—Sibaya **Mr G. Downie**
8 **CORRIEBEN REIVER,** 9, ch g Malinas (GER)—Wild Child Lucy **John & Liz Elliot**
9 **CRACKING DESTINY (IRE),** 10, b g Dubai Destination (USA)—Cracking Gale (IRE) **Mr A. G. Williams**
10 4, B g Sans Frontieres (IRE)—Cracking Gale (IRE) **Mr J D Wright & Mrs S Wright**
11 **DESERT QUEST (IRE),** 5, b g Footstepsinthesand—Waha (IRE) **Whillans, Orr, Spark, Wright**
12 **DEVIL LOCH,** 6, b g Dawn Approach (IRE)—Historian (IRE) **Mrs E. B. Ferguson**
13 **DIABLO LOCH,** 5, b g Golden Horn—Always Remembered (IRE) **Mrs E. B. Ferguson**
14 **DIAMANT SUR CANAPE (FR),** 5, b g Diamond Boy (FR)—Belledonne (FR) **Mr G. Downie**
15 **EBONY MAW,** 6, b g Iffraaj—Skirrid **Mr B. A. Jordan**
16 **EMPTY QUARTER,** 8, b g Pivotal—Desert Skies (IRE) **Mr R. Greggan**
17 **FOLKS LIKE US (IRE),** 8, b g Sans Frontieres (IRE)—Nia (IRE) **A. C. Whillans**
18 **GARLOGIE,** 4, gr g El Kabeir (USA)—Passing Stranger (IRE) **N J Dalgarno & W R Ellis**
19 **GRADY GASTON (IRE),** 5, b g Dawn Approach (IRE)—Hazium (IRE) **Clan Burns**
20 **GUIDING STAR,** 9, b m Iffraaj—Still I'm A Star (IRE) **A. C. Whillans**
21 **HOLD THE NOTE (IRE),** 9, b g Jeremy (USA)—Keys Hope (IRE) **BJordan,BrianJordan,SJordan&NMcconnell**
22 **HURAIZ (IRE),** 6, ch g Sepoy (AUS)—Samaah (IRE) **Big Teeree Racing & Partner**
23 **INGLEBY MACKENZIE,** 9, b g Sixties Icon—Natalie Jay **Ursa Major & Whillans**
24 **KAIZER,** 8, ch g Nathaniel (IRE)—Perse **Mrs E. B. Ferguson**
25 **KALAHARRY (IRE),** 11, b g Kalanisi (IRE)—Full Imperatrice (FR) **A. C. Whillans**
26 **KILCONQUHAR,** 6, b g Hallowed Crown (AUS)—Passing Stranger (IRE) **N J Dalgarno & W R Ellis**
27 **KINGSTON BRIDGE (IRE),** 5, b br g Kingston Hill—Lady Kate Ellen (IRE) **Mrs K. Spark**
28 **LEOSTAR,** 9, ch g Nathaniel (IRE)—Gaditana **Mrs E. B. Ferguson**
29 **LIZZIE LOCH,** 7, br m Maxios—Quenched **Mrs E. B. Ferguson**
30 **LOCKDOWN LEADER (IRE),** 7, b g Leading Light (IRE)—Holy Vow (IRE) **The Golf Inn Racers**
31 **LUSITANIEN (FR),** 7, b g Muhtathir—Easter Rose (FR) **Mr J D Wright & Mrs S Wright**
32 **MEDITUR (FR),** 6, gr g Turgeon (USA)—Medimix (FR) **E. A. Whillans**
33 **PITEMPTON POWER (IRE),** 8, b g Yeats (IRE)—Western Euro (IRE) **A. J. Brown**
34 **RAMON DI LORIA (IRE),** 5, ch g Dandy Man (IRE)—Pria Bona (IRE) **Clan Burns**
35 **RETICENT,** 4, b f Sixties Icon—Inhibition **Ursa Major & Whillans**
36 **SAFRAN (FR),** 6, b g Dabirsim (FR)—Sosquaw (FR) **A. C. Whillans**
37 **SCOTS POET,** 7, b g Yeats (IRE)—Blue Nymph **Distillery Racing Club**
38 **SYLTEZAR (IRE),** 6, b m Flemensfirth (USA)—August Hill (IRE) **John & Liz Elliot**
39 **TARQUIN STARDUST (FR),** 7, gr g Great Pretender (IRE)—Turgotine (FR) **Mr J D Wright & Mrs S Wright**
40 **TARTAN COOKIE (IRE),** 7, b g Leading Light (IRE)—Morning Breeze (IRE) **Mrs M. A. Scott**
41 **TOPKAPI STAR,** 6, b m Golden Horn—Burlesque Star (IRE) **McLafferty,Whillans &topkapi Partnership**
42 **TOUTATIS (USA),** 6, b g Karakontie (JPN)—Afleet Lass (USA) **Stuart Hogg Chris Spark**
43 **ZEALOUS (IRE),** 10, br g Intense Focus (USA)—Velvet Kiss (IRE) **Mrs M. A. Scott**
44 **ZEPHLYN (IRE),** 4, b g Iffraaj—Taqdees (IRE) **Mrs E. B. Ferguson**

533 MR SIMON WHITAKER, Scarcroft

Postal: **Hellwood Lane, Scarcroft, LEEDS, West Yorkshire, LS14 3BP**
Contacts: **MOBILE 07771 821955**
WORK EMAIL simonwhitakerracing@gmail.com WEBSITE simonwhitakerracing.co.uk

1 **BILLY ROBERTS (IRE),** 10, b g Multiplex—Mi Amor (IRE) **Country Lane Partnership**
2 **JILL ROSE,** 7, ch m Coach House (IRE)—Wotatomboy **J.W.'s Wotafun Club**
3 **LE FILS DE FORCE,** 5, b g Slade Power (IRE)—Hot Wired **Mr R. M. Whitaker**
4 **LIBERTY BREEZE,** 5, b m Equiano (FR)—Avon Breeze **Grange Park RacingXVII**
5 **LIL BIT OF MAGIC,** 4, ch f Spill The Beans (AUS)—Mey Blossom **Mr P. G. F. Ziegler**
6 **MISS WILLOWS,** 4, b f Outstrip—Wotatomboy **Escrick Environmental Services Ltd**
7 **MR HEINZ,** 4, b g Spill The Beans (AUS)—Velvet Band **Mrs J. Sivills**
8 **MYTHICAL (FR),** 6, b g Camelot—Inchmina **Mrs J. Sivills**
9 **NOAHS ABBEY,** 4, gr g Gregorian (IRE)—Bertha Burnett (IRE) **Mrs Greta Sparks & Mr Andrew Sparks**
10 **ROUND THE ISLAND,** 10, b g Royal Applause—Luanshya **Nice Day Out Partnership**
11 **SPEAR FIR,** 4, b f Spill The Beans (AUS)—Tumblewind **J & R Whitaker**
12 **STONEY LANE,** 8, b g Mayson—Spin A Wish
13 **THE GANGES (IRE),** 4, gr g Markaz (IRE)—Heavenly River (FR) **Mr A. Melville**
14 **TIBERIO FORCE,** 4, bl g Lethal Force (IRE)—Rio's Rosanna (IRE)
15 **VARIETY ISLAND,** 4, b g Spill The Beans (AUS)—Love Island **Grange Park Racing XVI & Partners**
16 **YASMIN FROM YORK,** 7, b m Sixties Icon—Bonnie Burnett (IRE) **Mrs Greta Sparks & Mr Andrew Sparks**

THREE-YEAR-OLDS

17 **BRAZEN RASCAL,** b g Brazen Beau (AUS)—Sweetnessandlight **Escrick Environmental Services Ltd**
18 **PENNY GHENT,** gr f Pastoral Pursuits—Velvet Band **Mr P. G. F. Ziegler**

TWO-YEAR-OLDS

19 **SALLY ANNE'S DREAM,** b ch f 02/04 Wusool—Mey Blossom
20 **UN-NAMED,** b f 18/02 Outstrip—Love Island **Mr R. M. Whitaker**

---

534 MR HARRY WHITTINGTON, Sparsholt

Postal: **Harry Whittington Racing Ltd, Hill Barn, Sparsholt, Wantage, Oxfordshire, OX12 9XB**
Contacts: **PHONE 01235 751869 MOBILE 07734 388357**
EMAIL info@harrywhittington.co.uk WEBSITE www.harrywhittington.co.uk

1 **BAHTIYAR (FR),** 5, b g Bathyrhon (GER)—Baladala Reconce (FR) **Menir La Voie**
2 **BREAKING WAVES (IRE),** 9, b g Yeats (IRE)—Acoola (IRE) **Colin Peake & Julie Slater**
3 **CHAMPETRE (IRE),** 5, b g Champs Elysees—Romantic Fashion (IRE) **The Hill Barn Syndicate**
4 **DOCPICKEDME (IRE),** 7, ch g Getaway (GER)—Hard Luck (IRE) **D Racing**
5 **EBONY SPIRIT (IRE),** 5, br g Frammassone (IRE)—Dayamen **Lead The Way Syndicate**
6 **FRANIGANE (FR),** 8, ch g Coastal Path—Nobless d'Aron (FR) **Edgedale & Robinson**
7 **GALUDON (FR),** 7, b g Saddler Maker (IRE)—Nobless d'Aron (FR) **The Queue Partnership**
8 **HARRY'S HOTTIE (IRE),** 6, b m Cloudings (IRE)—Really Royale (FR) **The Atkin Family**
9 **HE KNOWS BETTER (IRE),** 5, ch g Jet Away—She Knows Best (IRE) **Isobel & Julie Fowler**
10 **JUNIPER,** 9, b m Malinas (GER)—Prescelli (IRE) **Gin n It**
11 **KEEP RUNNING (FR),** 5, gr g Turgeon (USA)—Roxaline (FR) **Mrs J. A. Fowler**
12 **KITESURFER (FR),** 4, b g Karaktar (IRE)—Saintenitouche (FR) **The Atkin Family**
13 **OLD PAINLESS (IRE),** 7, b g Imperial Monarch (IRE)—Baby Goose (IRE) **The Racing Demon Partnership**
14 **POLDARK CROSS (IRE),** 8, b g Shantou (USA)—Diaconate (IRE) **The Racing Demons**
15 **ROGUE QUEEN (IRE),** 5, b m Malinas (GER)—Menepresents (IRE) **The Rogues Gallery**
16 **ROUGE VIF (FR),** 9, b g Sageburg (IRE)—Rouge Amour (FR) **Peake, Slater, Isy & Partners**
17 **THE BLUEBERRY ONE,** 4, b c Blue Bresil (FR)—The Strawberry One **Kykie Allsopp Cousins**
18 **VENGEANCE,** 5, b g Schiaparelli (GER)—Titch Strider (IRE) **Mr J. F. Panvert**
19 **YOUNG BULL (IRE),** 9, b g Dubai Destination (USA)—Jane Hall (IRE) **Nash & Webb**

Assistant Trainer: Joe Quintin.

NH Jockey: Harry Bannister.

535 MR MICHAEL WIGHAM, Newmarket

Postal: **Hamilton Stables, Hamilton Road, Newmarket, Suffolk, CB8 7JQ**
Contacts: **PHONE 01638 668806 MOBILE 07831 456426**
EMAIL michaelwigham@hotmail.co.uk WEBSITE www.michaelwighamracing.co.uk

1 **DEPUTISE,** 7, b g Kodiac—Dolly Colman (IRE)
2 **DION BAKER (IRE),** 4, b g Ribchester (IRE)—Tiga Tuan (FR)
3 **LONGLAI (FR),** 5, b g Shalaa (IRE)—Mojo Risin (IRE)
4 **RUMAILAH (USA),** 4, ch f Kitten's Joy (USA)—Sandiva (IRE)
5 **SEPTEMBER POWER (IRE),** 6, b m Mastercraftsman (IRE)—Lisanor

THREE-YEAR-OLDS

6 **MISS BILLIE,** b f Koropick (IRE)—Misu Billy
7 **MUCKY MULCONRY (IRE),** b g Profitable (IRE)—Exempt
8 **TOUGH GIRL,** b f Due Diligence (USA)—Todber

Assistant Trainer: Sharon Kenyon.

---

536 MR CHRISTIAN WILLIAMS, Bridgend

Postal: **Trainer did not wish details of their string to appear**

---

537 MR EVAN WILLIAMS, Llancarfan

Postal: **Fingerpost Farm, Llancarfan, Nr Barry, Vale of Glamorgan, CF62 3AE**
Contacts: **PHONE 01446 754069 MOBILE 07950 381227 FAX 01446 754069**
EMAIL cath@evanwilliamsracing.co.uk WEBSITE www.evanwilliamsracing.co.uk

1 **AERONISI (IRE),** 7, b g Kalanisi (IRE)—Carrigeen Lonicera (IRE) **Aircraft Tool Hire Ltd**
2 **ALMINAR (IRE),** 10, b g Arakan (USA)—Classic Magic (IRE) **Mr M. J. Phillips**
3 **ANNIE WICKS,** 6, b m Kayf Tara—Bathwick Annie **Wayne Clifford & Ian Gosden**
4 **ANNSAM,** 8, b g Black Sam Bellamy (IRE)—Bathwick Annie **H. M. W. Clifford**
5 **ARCADE ATTRACTION (IRE),** 9, b g Arcadio (GER)—Tobetall **Border Pointers & Feilim O'Muiri**
6 **ASTRA VIA,** 8, b m Multiplex—Wou Oodd **Mrs J. Davies**
7 **ATLANTIC FLEET (IRE),** 5, b g Beat Hollow—Rosa Fleet (IRE) **Mr & Mrs William Rucker**
8 **BALLINSKER (IRE),** 8, b g Court Cave (IRE)—Brownie Points (IRE) **Gg Thoroughbreds Xii & Partner**
9 **BALLYBREEN (IRE),** 10, b g Gold Well—Miss Colclough (IRE) **R. E. R. Williams**
10 **BEBRAVEFORGLORY (IRE),** 7, b g Fame And Glory—Brave Betsy (IRE) **Aircraft Tool Hire Ltd**
11 **BLACKO (FR),** 7, gr g Balko (FR)—Ascella (FR) **R J Gambarini Racing**
12 **BOLD PLAN (IRE),** 9, b g Jeremy (USA)—Kings Orchid (IRE) **Mr & Mrs William Rucker**
13 **CAN YOU CALL,** 8, b g Passing Glance—Call Me A Legend **Mr & Mrs William Rucker**
14 **CANFORD LIGHT (IRE),** 6, b g Canford Cliffs (IRE)—Way of Light (IRE) **Mrs Janet Davies**
15 **CASWELL BAY,** 8, b g Fame And Glory—Lauderdale (GER) **Mr David M. Williams**
16 **CHAMPAGNE RHYTHM (IRE),** 8, b g Oscar (IRE)—Before (IRE) **Mrs Janet Davies**
17 **COCONUT SPLASH (IRE),** 8, ch g Stowaway—Presenting Chaos (IRE) **Mr & Mrs William Rucker**
18 **COOLE CODY (IRE),** 12, b g Dubai Destination (USA)—Run For Cover (IRE) **H. M. W. Clifford**
19 **COURT ROYALE (IRE),** 10, b g Court Cave (IRE)—Windsor Dancer (IRE) **Mrs Janet Davies**
20 **CURRENT MOOD,** 8, ch m Sulamani (IRE)—Lambrini Queen **Mr W Corrigan Racing**
21 **DANS LE VENT (FR),** 10, b g Skins Game—Boreade (FR) **R J Gambarini Racing**
22 **DOYEN STAR (IRE),** 5, br g Doyen (IRE)—Leith Walk (IRE) **Mr & Mrs William Rucker**
23 **DUC DU RENE (IRE),** 5, b g Walk In The Park (IRE)—Lady Rene (IRE) **Mr & Mrs William Rucker**
24 **EMORELLE (IRE),** 6, ch m Shirocco (GER)—Flemerelle (IRE) **R.J.W Corrigan Racing**
25 **ESPRIT DU LARGE (FR),** 9, b g No Risk At All (FR)—Tuffslolyloly (FR) **Mr & Mrs William Rucker**
26 **GILWEN ROSIE,** 5, b m Telescope (IRE)—Gilwen Glory (IRE) **Keith & Sue Lowry**

MR EVAN WILLIAMS - continued

27 **GOLDEN WHISKY (IRE),** 10, ch g Flemensfirth (USA)—Derry Vale (IRE) **Mr & Mrs William Rucker**
28 **HAPPY DU MESNIL (FR),** 6, ch g Spanish Moon (USA)—Perle du Mesnil (FR)
29 **HARBOUR SHORE (IRE),** 5, br g Kalanisi (IRE)—Marina du Berlais (FR) **Mr & Mrs William Rucker**
30 **HENRY BOX BROWN (IRE),** 6, ch g Getaway (GER)—Lough Coyne (IRE) **Old Gold Racing 7**
31 **HOLDBACKTHERIVER (IRE),** 11, b g Presenting—Fairy Lane (IRE) **W J Evans Racing**
32 **HURRICANE HIGHWAY (IRE),** 5, br g Malinas (GER)—Florida Pet (IRE) **Mr & Mrs William Rucker**
33 **IDEALLKO (FR),** 5, b g Cokoriko (FR)—Umiska de Beaumont (FR) **R. E. R. Williams**
34 **IMPERIAL MEASURE (IRE),** 5, b g Imperial Monarch (IRE)—Boro Cruise (IRE) **Vale Racing 1**
35 4, B g Shirocco (GER)—Kayf Hampshire (IRE) **R. E. R. Williams**
36 **KYM EYRE (IRE),** 7, b m Mahler—Saddleoncemore (IRE) **R. E. R. Williams**
37 **L'ASTROBOY (GER),** 6, b g Kamsin (GER)—La Martina (GER) **Mr & Mrs William Rucker**
38 **LELANT (IRE),** 5, b g Soldier of Fortune (IRE)—Ab Initio (IRE) **R. E. R. Williams**
39 **LIBBERTY HUNTER,** 7, b g Yorgunnabelucky (USA)—Classy Crewella **Mr & Mrs William Rucker**
40 **LIPA K (IRE),** 5, b g Mamool (IRE)—Triennial (IRE)
41 **LOOP HEAD (IRE),** 5, b g Westerner—River Mill (IRE) **Mr & Mrs William Rucker**
42 **MAC BE LUCKY,** 6, b g Yorgunnabelucky (USA)—Macnance (IRE) **Keith & Sue Lowry**
43 **MACK THE MAN (IRE),** 9, b g Flemensfirth (USA)—Nifty Nuala (IRE) **Mr & Mrs William Rucker**
44 4, Ch g Jukebox Jury (IRE)—Mal d'Amour (IRE) **R. E. R. Williams**
45 **MODERN MONARCH (IRE),** 5, b g Imperial Monarch (IRE)—On Her Own (IRE) **R. E. R. Williams**
46 **MUMBLES (IRE),** 5, b g Mahler—She's Got Grit (IRE) **Mr D. M. Williams**
47 **OUT OF FOCUS (IRE),** 5, br g Montmartre (FR)—Nebuleuse (IRE) **R. E. R. Williams**
48 **OUT OF OFFICE (IRE),** 5, b g Shirocco (GER)—Shuil Dorcha (IRE) **Mr & Mrs William Rucker**
49 **OXWICH BAY (IRE),** 11, b g Westerner—Rose de Beaufai (FR) **T Hywel Jones Racing**
50 **PAGEANT MATERIAL (IRE),** 6, b m Soldier of Fortune (IRE)—House-of-Hearts (IRE) **W J Evans Racing**
51 **PALMAGREEN (FR),** 5, b m Kapgarde (FR)—Felindra (FR) **R. E. R. Williams**
52 **PETERBOROUGH (FR),** 10, b g Fuisse (FR)—Peony Girl (FR) **Norwester Racing Club & Partner**
53 **PRIME PRETENDER,** 8, b g Great Pretender (IRE)—The Prime Viper (IRE) **Mrs Janet Davies**
54 **PRIME VENTURE (IRE),** 12, br g Primary (USA)—Next Venture (IRE) **Mrs Janet Davies**
55 **PUDDLESINTHEPARK (IRE),** 5, b g Walk In The Park (IRE)—
Vast Consumption (IRE) **Opulence Thoroughbreds Nh & Partner**
56 **QUOI DE NEUF (FR),** 9, b g Anzillero (GER)—Qualite Controlee (FR) **Mr & Mrs William Rucker**
57 **RING THE MOON,** 10, b g Spanish Moon (USA)—Get The Ring (FR) **W. J. Evans**
58 **SABBATHICAL (FR),** 8, b g Sunday Break (JPN)—Ulcy Pressive (FR) **Maximum Racing & Partner**
59 **SECRET PLAN (IRE),** 5, b g Ocovango—Oscar's Reprieve (IRE) **Mr & Mrs William Rucker**
60 **SECRET REPRIEVE (IRE),** 9, b g Flemensfirth (USA)—Oscar's Reprieve (IRE) **Mr & Mrs William Rucker**
61 **SEREN Y TEIGR (IRE),** 4, ch g Dylan Thomas (IRE)—Belle of The Lodge (IRE) **Mr G. Hopkins**
62 **SIGN OF WAR (IRE),** 9, b g Oscar (IRE)—Irish Wedding (IRE) **R. E. R. Williams**
63 **SONNEMOSER (FR),** 6, b g Great Pretender (IRE)—Rainallday (FR) **Mr & Mrs William Rucker**
64 **TANRUDY (IRE),** 9, b g Presenting—Come In Moscow (IRE) **Mr M. J. Phillips**
65 **THE BOAT (IRE),** 7, gr g Dylan Thomas (IRE)—Whenever Wherever (IRE) **W J Evans Racing**
66 **THE LAST DAY (IRE),** 11, b g Oscar (IRE)—The Last Bank (IRE) **Mr & Mrs William Rucker**
67 **THREE CLIFFS BAY (GER),** 5, b g Jukebox Jury (IRE)—The Beauty (GER) **Mr D. M. Williams**
68 **TO BE SURE,** 8, b g Sulamani (IRE)—Egretta Island (IRE) **T Hywel Jones Racing**
69 **TOUR OVALIE (FR),** 4, b f Kamsin (GER)—Tour Ambition (FR) **R. E. R. Williams**
70 **TREASURE DILLON (IRE),** 9, b g Sans Frontieres (IRE)—Treasure Trix (IRE) **Mr R Abbott & Mr M Stavrou**
71 **VOODOO DOLL (IRE),** 10, b g Getaway (GER)—Voodoo Magic (GER) **R. E. R. Williams**
72 **WALKINTHEWOODS (IRE),** 6, b g Walk In The Park (IRE)—Mercy Mission **Vale Racing 1**
73 **WAVECREST (IRE),** 8, gr g Carlotamix (FR)—Go Girl (IRE) **Mr M. J. Phillips**
74 **WHITE TURF (FR),** 5, b g Spider Flight (FR)—Muisca du Turf (FR) **R. E. R. Williams**
75 **WINDS OF FIRE (USA),** 8, b g Kitten's Joy (USA)—Laureldean Gale (USA) **Mr T. L. Fell**
76 **ZERO TOLERANCE (GER),** 6, b g Lord of England (GER)—Zegna (GER) **Mr T. L. Fell**

Assistant Trainer: Catherine Williams, **Racing Secretary:** William Williams.

NH Jockey: Adam Wedge. **Conditional Jockey:** Conor Ring, Isabel Williams. **Amateur Jockey:** Lewis Gordon, Eleanor Williams.

538 MR IAN WILLIAMS, Alvechurch

Postal: **Dominion Racing Stables, Seafield Lane, Alvechurch, Birmingham, B48 7HL**
Contacts: **PHONE 01564 822392 MOBILE 07976 645384 FAX 01564 829475**
EMAIL info@ianwilliamsracing.com WEBSITE www.ianwilliamsracing.com

1 **AILES D'AMOUR (IRE),** 8, gr g Winged Love (IRE)—Ally Rose (IRE) **Mr A. Cocum**
2 **ALMOST GOLD (IRE),** 10, b g Gold Well—Shining Lights (IRE) **Mr S. Cox**
3 **ALWAJD (IRE),** 4, gr f Dark Angel (IRE)—Relation Alexander (IRE) **Smart Trax ltd**
4 **ANGELS LANDING (IRE),** 5, b m Fascinating Rock (IRE)—Kalinka Malinka (IRE) **The Piranha Partnership**
5 **AQWAAM,** 5, gr g Sea The Stars (IRE)—Aghaany **P. Kelly**
6 **ARTISTIC FIGHTER (IRE),** 5, b g The Gurkha (IRE)—Allegro Viva (USA) **Miss C. Douglas**
7 **BARNEY'S ANGEL,** 4, b g Ardad (IRE)—Highly Spiced **I. P. Williams**
8 **BLOW YOUR HORN (IRE),** 6, b g Golden Horn—She's Complete (IRE) **Ian Williams Racing Club**
9 **BUXTED REEL (IRE),** 4, b g Highland Reel (IRE)—Blue Lightning **Buxted Partnership**
10 **BUXTED TOO,** 5, ch g Iffraaj—Much Promise **Buxted Partnership**
11 **C'MON KENNY,** 7, gr g Dutch Art—Bite of The Cherry **Ne-Chance**
12 **CAP FRANCAIS,** 7, b g Frankel—Miss Cap Ferrat **Coomes Parmar Turner Dale**
13 **CAPTAIN TOMMY (IRE),** 9, b g Court Cave (IRE)—Freemantle Doctor (IRE) **Mr R. J. Gurr**
14 **CARAGHANN (FR),** 4, b g Almanzor (FR)—Candara (FR) **Ne-Chance**
15 **CATCH CATCHFIRE,** 4, b g Dartmouth—Becky B **Mr S. Cox**
16 **COOL STYLE,** 4, br g Dartmouth—Intersky High (USA) **Miss K. J. Keir**
17 **COUNSEL,** 5, ch g Frankel—Honorina **Mr S. Hashish**
18 **CRAZY MARY,** 6, br m Blue Bresil (FR)—Pistol At Dawn (IRE) **The Ferandlin Peaches**
19 **DESERT WILLIAM,** 4, b g Intello (GER)—Desert Kiss **Mr K. M. Harris**
20 **DEVASBOY,** 4, gr g Ectot—Belliflore (FR) **Deva Racing (DB)**
21 **DREAM HARDER (IRE),** 4, b g Muhaarar—Silent Thoughts (IRE) **Nationwide Racing**
22 **EAST ASIA (IRE),** 8, b g Iffraaj—Chan Tong (BRZ)
23 **ENEMY,** 6, b g Muhaarar—Prudenzia (IRE) **Tracey Bell & Caroline Lyons**
24 **ERNESTO (GER),** 8, ch g Reliable Man—Enrica **Midtech**
25 **FAMOUS LAST WORD (IRE),** 8, b br g Fame And Glory—Presenting Tara (IRE) **Mr T. J. & Mrs H. Parrott**
26 **FIFRELET (FR),** 8, br g Diamond Boy (FR)—Unique Star (FR) **ASD Contracts Ltd**
27 **GARITSA BAY (IRE),** 5, b g Walk In The Park (IRE)—Oscar Ladensa (IRE) **John Nicholls Racing**
28 **GENERATOR CITY (IRE),** 10, b g Primary (USA)—Sabbatical (IRE) **Dove Valley Holdings Ltd**
29 **GHASHAM (IRE),** 4, b c Churchill (IRE)—Shamarbelle (IRE) **Mr K. McKenna**
30 **GLEN AGAIN (IRE),** 5, b g Gleneagles (IRE)—Four Eleven (CAN) **R. C. Tooth**
31 **GREEN TEAM (FR),** 4, b c Wootton Bassett—On The Line (FR) **Fiji Racing Limited**
32 **HALIPHON,** 6, b g Showcasing—Harem Lady (FR) **Ne-Chance**
33 **HEAD ON (IRE),** 7, br g Robin des Champs (FR)—Miss Baloo (IRE) **Mr S. Cox**
34 **HYDROPLANE (IRE),** 7, b g Pour Moi (IRE)—Walk On Water **John Nicholls Racing**
35 **JAYTEE,** 8, ch g Schiaparelli (GER)—Archway Copse **J. Tredwell**
36 **JUSTUS (IRE),** 5, ch g Galileo (IRE)—Landikusic (IRE) **Coomes Parmar Turner Dale**
37 **KEMERTON (IRE),** 4, b g Kodi Bear (IRE)—Moynsha Lady (IRE) **Mr T. J. & Mrs H. Parrott**
38 **KIMBERLEY EVE,** 5, b m Black Sam Bellamy (IRE)—Ma Councha (FR) **Mr K. M. Harris**
39 **KIMIFIVE (IRE),** 8, ch g Born To Sea (IRE)—Appletreemagic (IRE) **Mr R. J. Gurr**
40 **KITAAB,** 4, b g Showcasing—Life of Pi **I. P. Williams**
41 **LAW SUPREME (FR),** 4, b c Lawman (FR)—Lope Supreme **Macable Partnership**
42 **LIBERATED LAD,** 5, b g Muhaarar—Puzzler (IRE) **Mr S. Coomes**
43 **LINDAKA (FR),** 6, b g Linda's Lad—Chamanka (FR) **A. Stennett**
44 **MALAKAHNA (FR),** 5, b m Manduro (GER)—Alakhana (FR) **Macable Partnership**
45 4, B f Yeats (IRE)—Maryann (IRE) **Eventmasters Racing**
46 **MINELLA CHOICE (IRE),** 7, b g Beat Hollow—Termsconditonsaply (IRE) **The DTTW Partnership**
47 **MOKAATIL,** 8, br g Lethal Force (IRE)—Moonlit Garden (IRE) **Midtech**
48 4, B g Highland Reel (IRE)—Moraine
49 **MOUNT SOUTH (IRE),** 6, b g Well Chosen—Hurry Up Helen (IRE) **Noel Fehily Racing Syndicate-Mount South**
50 **MR TRICK (IRE),** 5, b g Kodiac—Alkhawarah (USA) **Ian Williams Racing Club**
51 **MRS DOUBTFIRE,** 9, b m Jeremy (USA)—Monsignorita (IRE) **M. C. Denmark**
52 **NIGHT ON EARTH (IRE),** 5, b g Kodiac—Eternal View (IRE) **Mr S. Coomes**
53 **ONE MORE FLEURIE (IRE),** 9, b g Mustameet (USA)—Auburn Cherry (IRE) **Mr K. McKenna**
54 **PARTY BUSINESS (IRE),** 7, b g Shantou (USA)—Marias Dream (IRE) **Eventmasters Racing**
55 **PERTEMPS DIAMOND,** 4, gr g Dartmouth—Luna June (IRE) **Pertemps Ltd**
56 **RENOIR,** 4, b g Nathaniel (IRE)—Feis Ceoil (IRE) **Mr R. Allcock**

MR IAN WILLIAMS - continued

57 **RESTORER,** 11, gr g Mastercraftsman (IRE)—Moon Empress (FR) **I. P. Williams**
58 **ROCCOVANGO (IRE),** 7, br g Ocovango—Nouveau Moulin (IRE) **John Nicholls Racing**
59 **ROCK CHANT (USA),** 5, b g Flintshire—High Chant (USA) **I. P. Williams**
60 **RON BURGUNDY (IRE),** 6, ch g Presenting—Diklers Oscar (IRE) **The DTTW Partnership**
61 **SAINT RIQUIER (FR),** 5, gr g Le Havre (IRE)—Salamon **Mr D. W. Fox**
62 **SCREAMING LEEAGALE,** 4, b f Australia—Julia Dream **The Albatross Club**
63 **SIROBBIE (IRE),** 9, br g Arakan (USA)—Presentbreeze (IRE) **Mr R. J. Gurr**
64 **SOMETIMES ALWAYS (IRE),** 8, b g Presenting—Noras Fancy (IRE) **Mr S. Cox**
65 **SPEEDO BOY (FR),** 9, ch g Vision d'Etat (FR)—Shamardanse (IRE) **Mr P. R. Williams**
66 **SPIRIT OF LIGHT (IRE),** 6, gr g Dark Angel (IRE)—Inspiriter **Mr S. Hashish**
67 **STATE LEGEND (IRE),** 4, b g Churchill (IRE)—Zibeling (IRE) **Rubicon Racing**
68 **SWING TO THE STARS (IRE),** 4, b f Sea The Stars (IRE)—Simple Elegance (USA) **The Albatross Club**
69 **TEAM ENDEAVOUR,** 4, b g Bated Breath—Olympic Medal **Deva Racing (TE)**
70 **TESTING FAITH,** 4, b g Time Test—Midnight (IRE) **Midtech 3**
71 **THUNDER FLASH,** 6, b g Night of Thunder (IRE)—Sultanah Heyam **John Nicholls Racing**
72 **TIDE TIMES (IRE),** 9, gr g Vinnie Roe (IRE)—Lady Wagtail (IRE) **The DTTW Partnership**
73 **TIGERTEN,** 6, b g Born To Sea (IRE)—Morning Bride (IRE) **Mr R. J. Gurr**
74 **TYPICAL MAN,** 5, b g Territories (IRE)—Just Like A Woman **Mascalls Stud**
75 **TYPICAL WOMAN,** 4, ch f Nathaniel (IRE)—Just Like A Woman **Mascalls Stud**
76 **VISSANI (FR),** 5, gr g Dariyan (FR)—Visorama (IRE) **Ms S. A. Howell**
77 **WALK IN THE STORM (IRE),** 6, b m Walk In The Park (IRE)—Mucho Macabi (IRE) **TopSpeed Thoroughbreds**
78 **ZEALANDIA (FR),** 6, b g Sea The Moon (GER)—Belle Ambre **Mr P. E. Wildes**
79 **ZINC WHITE (IRE),** 5, gr g Vadamos (FR)—Chinese White (IRE) **Mr S. Beetham**

THREE-YEAR-OLDS

80 **C'MON ELLIE,** b f Massaat (IRE)—Zelaniya (IRE) **Ne-Chance**
81 **DAME LAURA KNIGHT,** b f Sir Percy—Feis Ceoil (IRE) **Mr R. Allcock**
82 **DANCING IN PARIS (FR),** b g Olympic Glory (IRE)—Ponte Sanangelo (FR) **J. Smith**
83 **FINN RUSSELL (IRE),** br g Caravaggio (USA)—Tawaareekh (USA) **M. H. Watt**
84 **GOLDEN MAVERICK (FR),** b g Zarak (FR)—Waritta **Midtech**
85 **GORDON GREY (IRE),** br gr c Australia—Lady Aquitaine (USA) **Michael & Brett Watkins**
86 **MARINAKIS (IRE),** b g Ulysses (IRE)—Giennah (IRE) **Ian Williams Racing Club**
87 **QUEENSLAND BOY (IRE),** b g Australia—Queen of France (USA) **Letsgiveitago**
88 **QUIET SMILE,** b f War Command (USA)—Glee Club **Miss K. J. Keir**
89 **SASSY BABE,** b f Zoffany (IRE)—Hells Babe **Mr T. Spraggett**
90 **SEA URCHIN (FR),** b g Seahenge (USA)—Lady of Light (IRE) **R. C. Tooth**

---

539 MRS JANE WILLIAMS, South Molton

Postal: **Culverhill Farm, George Nympton, South Molton, Devon, EX36 4JE**
Contacts: **HOME 01769 574174 MOBILE 07977 457350**

1 **AFTER THE FOX,** 8, b g Universal (IRE)—Foxglove **You Can Be Sure**
2 **AIMEE DE SIVOLA (FR),** 9, ch m Network (GER)—Neva de Sivola (FR) **Larkhills Racing Partnership IV**
3 **BALKO SAINT (FR),** 6, b g Balko (FR)—Sainte Cupid (FR) **Mrs J. R. Williams**
4 **DESPEREAUX (FR),** 4, b g Great Pretender (IRE)—Rouvraie (FR) **Chasing Gold Limited**
5 **FAST BUCK (FR),** 9, br g Kendargent (FR)—Juvenil Delinquent (USA) **KnightRiders III**
6 **FAVORI DE SIVOLA (FR),** 8, b g Noroit (GER)—Suave de Sivola (FR) **John White & Anne Underhill**
7 **FOLLY GATE (FR),** 8, b g Montmartre (FR)—Cate Bleue (FR) **Mrs J Williams & Mr R Stark**
8 **FOX PRO (FR),** 8, b g Coastal Path—Devise II (FR) **Mrs J. R. Williams**
9 **GALAHAD QUEST (FR),** 7, b g American Post—Atacames (FR) **Holt, Macnabb, Robinson & Jeffrey**
10 **GALICE MACALO (FR),** 7, b m Saddler Maker (IRE)—Victoire de Forme (FR) **Culverhill Racing Club II**

MRS JANE WILLIAMS - continued

11 **GLADIATEUR ALLEN (FR),** 7, b g Saint des Saints (FR)—Une Epoque (FR) **Mrs J. R. Williams**
12 **HELIOS ALLEN (FR),** 6, b g Coastal Path—Silane (FR) **French Gold Racing**
13 **HERMES BOY (FR),** 6, b g Diamond Boy (FR)—Roche Brune (FR) **The Culverhill Racing Club IV**
14 **HONNEUR D'AJONC (FR),** 6, b g Diamond Boy (FR)—Fleur d'Ajonc (FR) **Jonny Allison & Patrick Waldron**
15 **ILFONCE (FR),** 5, ch g Coastal Path—Une Brik (FR) **Len, Mason, Ray, Nicol, Cowell, Stevens& Booth**
16 **IN REM (FR),** 8, b g Kapgarde (FR)—Etoile des Iles (FR) **Chasing Gold Limited**
17 **INTERNE DE SIVOLA (FR),** 5, b g Noroit (GER)—Kerrana (FR) **Mr R. C. Watts**
18 **JAMINSKA (FR),** 4, b f Manatee—Pacifie du Charmil (FR) **Larkhills Racing Partnership III**
19 **JAVERT ALLEN (FR),** 4, ch g No Risk At All (FR)—Une Epoque (FR) **Holtmacnabbrobinsonmiltontuckerweedon**
20 **JUPITER ALLEN (FR),** 4, ch g Castle du Berlais (FR)—Bienvenue Allen (FR) **Mr R. C. Watts**
21 **KAP HORN (FR),** 4, b g Manatee—Palma du Charmil (FR) **Mrs J. R. Williams**
22 **KOOKY (FR),** 4, b g Kamsin (GER)—Kotkicha (FR) **Mrs J. R. Williams**
23 **LADY GWEN,** 5, b m Haafhd—Countess Camilla **Huw & Richard Davies N L Williams**
24 **LE CAMELEON,** 8, b br g Great Pretender (IRE)—Countess Camilla **The Pretenders & Partner**
25 **MOKA DE VASSY (FR),** 5, b g Karaktar (IRE)—Mona Vassy (FR) **Tom Chadney and Friends**
26 **MONSIEUR LECOQ (FR),** 9, b g Diamond Boy (FR)—Draga (FR) **Knightriders Racing**
27 **MOORLAND RAMBLER,** 5, b g Telescope (IRE)—Fragrant Rose **Mr R Stark & Mrs J Williams**
28 **PEPE LE MOKO (FR),** 5, b g Saint des Saints (FR)—Jolie Menthe (FR) **Mrs Len Jakeman & Mrs Jane Williams**
29 **ROMANCERO LE DUN (FR),** 4, b g Spanish Moon (USA)—Uranus Le Dun (FR) **Mrs J. R. Williams**
30 **SAINT CYR DE PAIL (FR),** 4, b g Kapgarde (FR)—Dame de Pail (FR) **The Culverhill Racing Club**
31 **SAINT SEGAL (FR),** 5, b g Saint des Saints (FR)—Bal Celtique (FR) **Culverhill Racing V**
32 **YGGDRASIL (FR),** 6, b g Kapgarde (FR)—Margerie (FR) **John White & Anne Underhill**

THREE-YEAR-OLDS

33 **AUTHOCELTIC (FR),** b c Authorized (IRE)—Bal Celtique (FR)
34 **CAPTAIN MARVELLOUS (FR),** ch g Masked Marvel—Praticks (IRE) **J Allison & Knightriders II**
35 **CASTELFORT (FR),** b g Castle du Berlais (FR)—Stellarmor (FR) **Mrs J. R. Williams**
36 **EXCELERO (FR),** b g Castle du Berlais (FR)—Si St Eloi (FR) **Holt, Macnabb, Robinson & Jeffrey**
37 **FIDUCIARY DUTY (FR),** b g Night Wish (GER)—Fadas (FR) **Holt, Robinson, Macnabb**
38 Ch g No Risk At All (FR)—Goddess Freja (FR) **Mr R. C. Watts**
39 **INSIDE MAN (FR),** b g Manatee—Rockburn (FR) **Mrs J. R. Williams**
40 **KEL DU LARGE (FR),** b g No Risk At All (FR)—Princesse Selenia (FR) **Tom Chadney and Friends**
41 **KNIGHT OF ALLEN (FR),** b g Masterstroke (USA)—Atacames (FR) **Holt, Macnabb, Robinson & Jeffrey**

TWO-YEAR-OLDS

42 B c 17/03 Beaumec de Houelle (FR)—Lady Butterfly (FR) (Lando (GER)) (23209)
43 **LANCELOT ALLEN (FR),** b c 02/04 Rail Link—
Triple Star (FR) (Dom Alco (FR)) **Holt, Robinson, Macnabb, Clark, Weedon**
44 **LYNYRD DU LARGE (FR),** b g 02/02 Nirvana Du Berlais (FR)—Kayagua (FR) (Kahyasi) **Mr J. Allison**
45 B c 14/04 Goliath Du Berlais (FR)—Toi Et Le Soleil (FR) (Poliglote) (30412)

---

540 MR NOEL WILLIAMS, Blewbury

Postal: **Churn Stables, Churn Estate, Blewbury, Didcot, Oxfordshire, OX11 9HG**
Contacts: **PHONE 01235 850806 MOBILE 07887 718678**
EMAIL info@noelwilliamsracing.co.uk WEBSITE www.noelwilliamsracing.co.uk FACEBOOK NoelWilliamsRacingSyndicates TWITTER @noelwilliams03 INSTAGRAM noelwilliamsracing

1 **ANOTHER CRICK,** 10, b g Arcadio (GER)—Suetsu (IRE) **Mr D. J. S. Sewell**
2 **BOHAMS ROAD (IRE),** 5, b g Vendangeur (IRE)—Contradeal (IRE) **Churn Bloodstock**
3 **BRIERY EXPRESS,** 10, b m Rail Link—Blackbriery Thyne (IRE) **Helen Plumbly & Kathryn Leadbeater**
4 **COTONEASTER,** 5, b m Telescope (IRE)—Easter Legend **Easter Racing Club**
5 **EASTER MOUSE,** 5, ch m Norse Dancer (IRE)—The Easter Rabbit **Easter Racing Club**
6 **FARNE (IRE),** 9, b m Stowaway—Bonnies Island (IRE) **Mr I. Kurdi**
7 **HARLEM CLERMONT (FR),** 6, b g Konig Turf (GER)—Flo de Clermont (FR) **Drover Bloodstock**

MR NOEL WILLIAMS - continued

8 **HASTON CLERMONT (FR),** 6, b g Coastal Path—Magie Brune (FR) **Burkes & Syders**
9 **JUST SOPHIE,** 5, b m Scorpion (IRE)—Theatre Goer **Noel Williams Racing Club**
10 **LUCKY ROSE (IRE),** 5, b m Soldier of Fortune (IRE)—Shantou Rose (IRE) **Allison, Allison, Williams**
11 **MAXIMUM EFFORT,** 4, br g Dartmouth—Theatre Goer **Waddington & Williams Thoroughbreds**
12 **MIGHTY MOTH (IRE),** 5, b m Champs Elysees—Ballinderry Moth (IRE) **Mr I. Kurdi**
13 **MOVIDDY (IRE),** 7, b m Urban Poet (USA)—Killiney Gold (IRE) **Noel Fehily Racing Syndicates - Moviddy**
14 **OUR PINK LADY (IRE),** 5, b br m Westerner—Littlegrace Lady (IRE) **Mr Neil Berry**
15 **SISTER AGATHA,** 4, b f Saint des Saints (FR)—Polygona (FR) **Syders & Burkes**
16 **SOUND OF MUSIC,** 8, ch m Universal (IRE)—Sounds Familiar (IRE) **Mr Nick Luck**
17 **SPEECH BUBBLE (IRE),** 8, b m Well Chosen—Teamplin (IRE) **Burkes & Syders**
18 **VINNIE DEV (IRE),** 9, b g Vinnie Roe (IRE)—Nifty Milan (IRE) **David J S Sewell & Tim Leadbeater**
19 **WONDER KING (FR),** 5, b g Creachadoir (IRE)—Walk Folie (FR) **Mr N. Williams**

THREE-YEAR-OLDS

20 B g Passing Glance—Theatre Goer **Waddington & Williams Thoroughbreds**

NH Jockey: James Davies, Tom O'Brien.

---

541 MR OLLY WILLIAMS, Market Rasen

Postal: **Stone Cottage, Nettleton Top, Market Rasen, Lincolnshire, LN7 6SY**
Contacts: **MOBILE 07793 111600**
EMAIL williams.olly@yahoo.co.uk WEBSITE www.ollywilliamsracing.co.uk

1 **CORIANO RIDGE,** 5, b g Al Kazeem—Melodica **Olly Williams, Rhys Williams, James Hanna**
2 **FOURSOME,** 4, ch f Highland Reel (IRE)—Putois Peace **D. L. Bayliss**
3 **FRENCH ROMANCE,** 4, b f Le Havre (IRE)—Soho Susie (IRE) **Mr I. Holt**
4 **GOING NATIVE,** 8, ch m Speightstown (USA)—Latin Love (IRE) **Mr O. R. Williams**
5 **LINCOLN RED,** 7, ch g Monsieur Bond (IRE)—Roxy Hart **Top of the Wolds Racing**
6 **LITTLE PUMPKIN,** 6, b m Mountain High (IRE)—Our Jess (IRE) **Mr Danny Ablott, Mr Olly Williams**
7 **LORRAINE'S GIRL,** 5, b m Scorpion (IRE)—Our Jess (IRE) **Mrs L. Truscott**
8 **RASPBERRY,** 7, b m Avonbridge—Spennymoor (IRE) **Olly Williams, Rhys Williams, James Hanna**

THREE-YEAR-OLDS

9 **OHNOJOE (IRE),** b g Footstepsinthesand—Tadkhirah **Mrs H. R. Townsend**

Assistant Trainer: Lynsey Williams.

---

542 MR STUART WILLIAMS, Newmarket

Postal: **Diomed Stables, Hamilton Road, Newmarket, Suffolk, CB8 0PD**
Contacts: **PHONE 01638 663984 MOBILE 07730 314102**
EMAIL stuart@stuartwilliamsracing.co.uk WEBSITE www.stuartwilliamsracing.co.uk
TWITTER @Williamsstuart INSTAGRAM stuartwilliams_racing

1 **ABOVE (FR),** 6, b g Anjaal—Broken Applause (IRE) **Mr N. R. Boyden, Mr C. Harrold**
2 **BEAR PROFIT (IRE),** 4, b c Profitable (IRE)—Orikawa (FR) **Spiers, Barratt & Signy**
3 **BLUE FLAME (IRE),** 6, gr g Dark Angel (IRE)—Bluefire **Diomed Racing**
4 **CIRCLE TIME (IRE),** 4, b g Oasis Dream—Maybe Grace (IRE) **Mr J. M. Norris**
5 **DUBAI STATION,** 6, b g Brazen Beau (AUS)—Princess Guest (IRE) **Regents Racing & Partners**
6 **DUSKY LORD,** 5, b g Twilight Son—Petit Trianon **Mrs M. J. Morley**

MR STUART WILLIAMS - continued

7 **ENZOS ANGEL,** 4, gr g Dark Angel (IRE)—Along Came Casey (IRE) **Opulence T/breds, Regents Racing Et Al**
8 **EXISTENT,** 5, b g Kingman—Entity **Mrs M. J. Morley**
9 **GOT NO DOLLARS (IRE),** 5, b g Showcasing—Canada Water **Mr W Enticknap & Mr B Ralph**
10 **LORD CHERRY (IRE),** 4, ch g Profitable (IRE)—Winning Sequence (FR) **Mr B Piper & Mr D Cobill**
11 **LORD RAPSCALLION (IRE),** 7, gr g Alhebayeb (IRE)—Simply Topping (IRE) **Tje Racing**
12 **MAY NIGHT,** 5, ch g Mayson—Dream Melody **Tje Racing**
13 **PAPA STOUR (USA),** 8, b g Scat Daddy (USA)—Illaunglass (IRE) **Mrs M. J. Morley**
14 **REVOLUTIONISE (IRE),** 7, gr g Lope de Vega (IRE)—Modeeroch (IRE) **Mrs M. J. Morley, Regents Racing**
15 **RHYTHMIC INTENT (IRE),** 7, ch g Lope de Vega (IRE)—Kerry Gal (IRE) **Proceed Nominees Pty Ltd**
16 **SHAMSHON (IRE),** 12, b g Invincible Spirit (IRE)—Greenisland (IRE) **Mr S. C. Williams**
17 **TOLSTOY (IRE),** 4, b g Kingman—War And Peace **Mr N. R. Boyden, Mr C. Harrold**
18 **TONE THE BARONE,** 7, ch g Lope de Vega (IRE)—A Huge Dream (IRE) **Mr B Piper & Partner**
19 **TOP EXHIBIT,** 4, b g Showcasing—Must Be Me **Mr David N Reynolds & Mr C D Watkins**
20 **WEYDAAD,** 4, b f Iffraaj—Lady of Persia (JPN) **Barker, Creighton, Davis, Kent & Partner**
21 **WYVERN,** 4, br g Bated Breath—Miramont **Mrs M. J. Morley**

THREE-YEAR-OLDS

22 **ANOTHER DREAM,** b f Oasis Dream—Orpha **Mr J W Parry and Mrs C Shekells**
23 **ARBAAWI (IRE),** b g Invincible Spirit (IRE)—Initially **Mr M. M. M. Owaimer**
24 **BAILAR CONTIGO (IRE),** b f Gleneagles (IRE)—Slieve Mish (IRE) **Mr P. Brosnan**
25 **DIOMED SPIRIT,** b g Charm Spirit (IRE)—Dainty Dandy (IRE) **Diomed Racing & Partner**
26 **DIONYSIAN,** ch c Exceed And Excel (AUS)—Magic Nymph (IRE) **Opulence Thoroughbreds**
27 **ENTERPRISER (IRE),** b g Fast Company (IRE)—Condensed **Opulence Thoroughbreds**
28 **EXPERT BEAR,** b f Expert Eye—Miss Marina Bay **Mr R. C. Watts**
29 **FLYING BARTY (IRE),** ch f Starspangledbanner (AUS)—Dice Game **Chasemore Farm & Seymour Bloodstock**
30 **FORNHAM ST MARTIN,** b c Zoustar (AUS)—Spiced **Mr N. R. Boyden, Mr C. Harrold**
31 **GOD OF FIRE (IRE),** b c Muhaarar—Loreto (IRE) **Opulence Thoroughbreds**
32 **HARRY THE HAGGLER (IRE),** ch g Gleneagles (IRE)—Tears In My Eyes (IRE) **Paul Stevens & Partner**
33 **HUBERTS DREAM (IRE),** gr c Oasis Dream—Raaqy (IRE) **Opulence Thoroughbreds**
34 **MISTER X (IRE),** b c Profitable (IRE)—Capote West (USA) **Mr S. C. Williams**
35 **MONT VALLON,** b g Invincible Spirit (IRE)—Murasaki **Mr N. R. Boyden**
36 **PREMIERE BEAUTY,** b f Churchill (IRE)—Rosie's Premiere (IRE) **Mr R. C. Watts**
37 **QUINAULT (GER),** b g Oasis Dream—Queimada (GER) **TJE Racing**
38 **RIVER LYNE,** b f Massaat (IRE)—Piranha (IRE) **Opulence Thoroughbreds**
39 B f Gleneagles (IRE)—Stellar Surprise **Mr J. W. Parry & Mr Robert Levitt**
40 **TALLULAH MYLA (IRE),** b f Oasis Dream—Sheikhakan (IRE) **Opulence Thoroughbreds**
41 **UNIVERSAL GRACE,** b f Brazen Beau (AUS)—Spritzig **D. P. Fremel**
42 **WEE GEORDIE,** b g Muhaarar—Perfect Blessings (IRE) **Opulence Thoroughbreds**
43 **WHERE'S FREDDY (IRE),** ch g Lope de Vega (IRE)—One Spirit (IRE) **Patrick B Doyle (Construction) Ltd**
44 **YOU SAW BRIGADOON (IRE),** b g Kingman—Stirring Ballad **Mr Glenn Thompson & Partner**

TWO-YEAR-OLDS

45 B f 11/04 Golden Horn—Amahoro (Sixties Icon) (6000) **J. W. Parry**
46 B f 20/03 Churchill (IRE)—Amthaal (Exceed And Excel (AUS)) (22409) **James Parry & Partners**
47 B f 29/04 Advertise—Baliyka (IRE) (Cape Cross (IRE)) (30000) **James Parry & Partners**
48 B f 25/04 Advertise—Indignant (Gold Away (IRE)) (17000) **Mr J. W. Parry & Mr Robert Levitt**
49 B c 20/02 Golden Horn—Kahlua Kiss (Mister Baileys) (26000) **Mr S. C. Williams**
50 **LAGUNA BOY (IRE),** ch c 05/02 Sioux Nation (USA)—Mary McPhee (Makfi) (68000) **Opulence Thoroughbreds**
51 B f 29/03 U S Navy Flag (USA)—Stor Mo Chroi (IRE) (Montjeu (IRE)) (130000) **Mr R. C. Watts**

Apprentice Jockey: Luke Catton.

543 MISS VENETIA WILLIAMS, Hereford

Postal: **Aramstone, Kings Caple, Hereford, Herefordshire, HR1 4TU**
Contacts: **PHONE 01432 840646 MOBILE 07770 627108**
EMAIL office@venetiawilliams.com WEBSITE www.venetiawilliams.com

1 **ACHILLE (FR),** 13, gr g Dom Alco (FR)—Hase (FR) **Mrs V. A. Bingham**
2 **ALCEDO (IRE),** 5, b g Vadamos (FR)—Deliziosa (IRE) **Mr P. Davies**
3 **BALLINGERS CORNER (IRE),** 8, br m Jeremy (USA)—Dances With Waves (IRE) **Mr M. G. Roberts**
4 **BELLATRIXSA (IRE),** 6, gr m Gregorian (IRE)—Aloisi **Mrs S. A. J. Kinsella**
5 **BELLE SAINT,** 6, b m Saint des Saints (FR)—Tazzarine (FR) **My Racing Manager Friends - Mako**
6 **BRAVE SEASCA (FR),** 8, bl g Brave Mansonnien (FR)—Miss Laveron (FR) **Brooks & Taylor Families**
7 **BRIANSTORM (IRE),** 11, b g Brian Boru—Coco Moon (IRE) **David & Carol Shaw**
8 **BURROWS PARK (FR),** 11, b g Astarabad (USA)—
La Vie de Boitron (FR) **Venetia Williams Racehorse Syndicate III**
9 **CHAMBARD (FR),** 11, b g Gris de Gris (IRE)—Regina Park (FR) **David & Carol Shaw**
10 **CHRISTOPHER WOOD (IRE),** 8, b g Fast Company (IRE)—Surf The Web (IRE) **Mrs S. A. J. Kinsella**
11 **CLOUDY GLEN (IRE),** 10, b g Cloudings (IRE)—Ribble (IRE) **Exors of the Late Mr T. J. Hemmings**
12 **COMMODORE (FR),** 11, gr g Fragrant Mix (IRE)—Morvandelle (FR) **Mrs C Watson & Mrs S Graham**
13 **COO STAR SIVOLA (FR),** 11, b g Assessor (IRE)—Santorine (FR) **Babbitt Racing**
14 **CRYPTO (IRE),** 9, b g Gold Well—Top Lot (IRE) **Mr P. Davies**
15 **CUBAN PETE (IRE),** 11, b g Flemensfirth (USA)—Gee Whizz (FR) **Mrs J. Jones**
16 **DENTLEY DE MEE (FR),** 10, b g Lauro (GER)—Natty Twigy (FR) **Babbitt Racing**
17 **DESQUE DE L'ISLE (FR),** 10, b g Special Kaldoun (IRE)—Naiade de L'Isle (FR) **The Hon Lady M. J. Heber-Percy**
18 **DIDERO VALLIS (FR),** 10, b g Poliglote—Oreade Vallis (FR) **Normans, Ramsay, Tufnell & Bishop**
19 **DJELO (FR),** 5, b g Montmartre (FR)—Djeville (FR) **Mr P. Davies**
20 **DON HERBAGER (FR),** 9, b g Saddler Maker (IRE)—Marie d'Altoria (FR) **Hereford Racing Club**
21 **EASY AS THAT (IRE),** 8, b g Sans Frontieres (IRE)—Bell Storm (IRE) **Brooks & Taylor Families**
22 **ECEPARTI (FR),** 9, b g Enrique—La Pommeraie (FR) **Mrs S. M. Champ**
23 **ENJOY YOUR LIFE (FR),** 6, b br g Bathyrhon (GER)—Madoudal (FR) **Mrs J. R. L. Young**
24 **ENZO D'AIRY (FR),** 9, b g Anzillero (GER)—Panzara d'Airy (FR) **Dr M. A. Hamlin**
25 **FANION D'ESTRUVAL (FR),** 8, b g Enrique—Urfe d'Estruval (FR) **Mr D. C. A. Wilson**
26 **FARINET (FR),** 8, gr g Lord du Sud (FR)—Mendy Tennise (FR) **Hammond, Coombs T Henriques**
27 **FAUTINETTE (FR),** 5, b m Bathyrhon (GER)—Fautina (FR) **DFA Racing (Anderson & Edwards)**
28 **FIRE DANCER (FR),** 7, b g Martaline—Steel Dancer (FR) **Mrs S. Ricci**
29 **FLOWING CADENZA,** 9, b m Yeats (IRE)—Over The Flow **Mrs H. R. Dunn**
30 **FONTAINE COLLONGES (FR),** 8, b m Saddler Maker (IRE)—Saturne Collonges (FR) **Mr P. Davies**
31 **FRENCHY DU LARGE (FR),** 8, gr g Al Namix (FR)—Quadence de Sivola (FR) **Mr A. O. Wiles**
32 **FRERO BANBOU (FR),** 8, b g Apsis—Lady Banbou (FR) **Mr P. Davies**
33 **FUJI FLIGHT (FR),** 8, b g Day Flight—Silverlea (FR) **George & Drury**
34 **FUNAMBULE SIVOLA (FR),** 8, b g Noroit (GER)—Little Memories (IRE) **My Racing Manager Friends**
35 **GALOP DE CHASSE (FR),** 7, b g Boris de Deauville (IRE)—Mousse des Bois (FR) **The Winter Partnership**
36 **GAMARET (FR),** 7, b g Coastal Path—Oppale (FR) **Kennet Valley Thoroughbreds VII**
37 **GEMIRANDE (FR),** 7, b g Al Namix (FR)—Queenjo (FR) **The Bellamy Partnership**
38 **GEORGES SAINT (FR),** 7, gr g Lord du Sud (FR)—Une Deux Trois (FR) **Mrs C. G. Watson**
39 **GREEN BOOK (FR),** 6, b g Authorized (IRE)—Mantissa **Price, Shaw, Boylan, Tagg**
40 **GRIZZLY JAMES (FR),** 7, b g Montmartre (FR)—Mariyara (FR) **Mr G. Hannon**
41 **HAUT FOLIN (FR),** 6, b g Coastal Path—Venise (FR) **The Autumn Partnership**
42 **HERMES DU GOUET (FR),** 6, b g Saddler Maker (IRE)—Dolly du Gouet (FR) **My Racing Manager Friends**
43 **HEROS (FR),** 6, b g Voiladenuo (FR)—La Colombe d'Or (FR) **Mr & Mrs Simon E Bown**
44 **HEVA ROSE (FR),** 6, gr m Saint des Saints (FR)—Wild Rose Bloom (FR) **The Hon Lady M. J. Heber-Percy**
45 **HILL OF TARA,** 6, b g Kayf Tara—Patsie Magern **B B Racing Club**
46 **HOLD THAT TAUGHT,** 8, b g Kayf Tara—Belle Magello (FR) **Mr P. Davies**
47 **HOUI CHERIE (FR),** 6, gr m Cima de Triomphe (IRE)—Joslaine (FR) **B B Racing Club**
48 **HUNTER LEGEND (FR),** 6, b g Buck's Boum (FR)—Sience Fiction (FR) **Gaskins Family**
49 **ICARAT (FR),** 5, b g Nicaron (GER)—Cemoua (FR) **The DTTW Partnership**
50 **IN D'OR (FR),** 5, b g Nidor (FR)—La Dauvilla (FR) **D. Maxwell**
51 **INTIMATE (FR),** 5, b g Montmartre (FR)—Quandaly (FR) **Mrs E. A. Ball**
52 **J'AIME EL MARS (FR),** 4, b g Elm Park—Perle de Sceaux (FR) **Ms L. A. Mars**
53 **JIKALA (FR),** 4, b f Berkshire (IRE)—Chakalaboumboum (FR) **Venetia Williams Racehorse Syndicate III**
54 **JOLLY NELLERIE (FR),** 4, ch g Nicaron (GER)—Jumper Nellerie (FR) **RaceShare - Jolly Nellerie**
55 **KALLOW POINT (IRE),** 6, br g Soldier of Fortune (IRE)—Centre Field (IRE) **Exors of the Late Mr T. J. Hemmings**

MISS VENETIA WILLIAMS - continued

56 **KAPGA DE LILY (FR),** 10, ch m Kapgarde (FR)—Louvisy (FR) **Lady Judith Price & Mrs Carol Shaw**
57 **L'HOMME PRESSE (FR),** 8, b g Diamond Boy (FR)—Romance Turgot (FR) **DFA Racing (Pink & Edwards)**
58 **LAGONDA,** 8, b m Great Pretender (IRE)—Lago d'Oro **Mrs S. M. Newell**
59 **LASKALIN (FR),** 8, b g Martaline—Laskadya (FR) **David & Carol Shaw**
60 **LILY GRACE,** 5, gr m Blue Bresil (FR)—Fine Lily **Mr & Mrs A. Powley**
61 **MARTATOR (FR),** 6, b g Martaline—Tornada (FR) **Mrs C. J. Norton**
62 **MOUNTAIN LEOPARD (IRE),** 8, b g Shantou (USA)—Laurel Gift (IRE) **The Shantou Partnership**
63 **NAMBITI (FR),** 5, b g Walk In The Park (IRE)—Cheyrac (FR) **Syders & Burkes**
64 **NATTY NIGHT,** 7, b g Nathaniel (IRE)—Danehill Dreamer (USA) **The GS & JS Partnership**
65 **OTTOLINE,** 7, b m Kayf Tara—Lily Grey (FR) **Ottoline Syndicate**
66 **OXYGEN (FR),** 5, gr g Martaline—Bella Lawena (IRE) **The DTTW Partnership**
67 **PASEO,** 7, b g Champs Elysees—Posteritas (USA) **My Racing Manager Friends**
68 **PENNY MALLOW (FR),** 9, b m Kapgarde (FR)—Louvisy (FR) **Miss V. M. Williams, Carol & David Shaw**
69 **PINK LEGEND,** 9, b m Midnight Legend—Red And White (IRE) **F. M. P. Mahon**
70 **PREVARICATE (IRE),** 7, b g Fame And Glory—Zita Hall (IRE) **East India Racing I**
71 **QUICK WAVE (FR),** 10, b m Gentlewave (IRE)—Magicaldoun (FR) **Mrs S. A. J. Kinsella**
72 **RAMO (FR),** 6, b g Kapgarde (FR)—Djeville (FR) **Mr L. DI Franco, Mr C. B. Compton**
73 **REALM OF GLORY (IRE),** 8, b g Fame And Glory—Ebony Queen **Venetia Williams Racehorse Syndicate V**
74 **ROBYNDZONE (IRE),** 9, b g Frammassone (IRE)—Rebecca Susan **East India Racing**
75 **ROCK OF FAME,** 6, b m Fastnet Rock (AUS)—Familliarity **Caroline Wilson & Lavinia Taylor**
76 **ROYALE PAGAILLE (FR),** 9, b g Blue Bresil (FR)—Royale Cazoumaille (FR) **Mrs S. Ricci**
77 **SHALAKAR (FR),** 10, b g Cape Cross (IRE)—Shalanaya (IRE) **Sheila Schwartz & Venetia Williams**
78 **SOLE SOLUTION (IRE),** 5, ch g Sans Frontieres (IRE)—Bell Storm (IRE) **Sir W. J. A. Timpson**
79 **STANLEY STANLEY,** 6, b m Camelot—Seaham Hall **Mrs S. A. J. Kinsella**
80 **SUPERVISOR (IRE),** 9, b g Flemensfirth (USA)—Coolamaine Star (IRE) **Sarah Williams & Charles Barlow**
81 **TANGANYIKA (FR),** 5, b g Martaline—Norita Has (FR) **Mrs C. S. Wilson**
82 **TOKYO LIVE (FR),** 6, gr g Ivory Land (FR)—Tracja (POL) **Old Gold Racing 10**
83 **VICTTORINO (FR),** 5, b br g It's Gino (GER)—Victtorie (FR) **Martians Racing**
84 **ZERTAKT (FR),** 5, b g Walzertakt (GER)—Qualivie (FR) **Michael Davies & Peter Davies**

NH Jockey: Charlie Deutsch. **Conditional Jockey:** Ned Fox, Shane Quinlan. **Amateur Jockey:** Miss Lucy Turner.

---

544 MRS LISA WILLIAMSON, Tarporley

Postal: **Kelsall Hill Equestrian Centre, Middlewich Road, Tarporley, Cheshire, CW6 0SR**
Contacts: **PHONE 07970 437679**
EMAIL info@lisawilliamson.co.uk WEBSITE www.lisawilliamson.co.uk

1 **AMICO AMORE,** 7, b g Universal (IRE)—Dusky Dancer **Mr P. R. D'Amato**
2 **AQUADABRA (IRE),** 8, b m Born To Sea (IRE)—Amazing Win (IRE) **Heath House Racing**
3 **BRANDY STATION (IRE),** 8, b g Fast Company (IRE)—Kardyls Hope (IRE) **A V Wilding (Chester) Ltd**
4 **CELERITY (IRE),** 9, ch m Casamento (IRE)—Shinko Dancer (IRE) **Heath House Racing**
5 **INDEPENDENT BEAUTY,** 5, b m Outstrip—Verus Decorus (IRE) **Mr I. Furlong**
6 **ISABELLA RUBY,** 8, b m Power—Scarlet Rocks (IRE) **Heath House Racing**
7 **LOCO LOBO,** 5, ch m Captain Gerrard (IRE)—Senora Lobo (IRE) **Miss H. J. Roberts**
8 **MRS TIFFEN,** 6, b m Finjaan—Fancy Rose (USA) **A V Wilding (Chester) Ltd**
9 **PACOPASH,** 5, b m Paco Boy (IRE)—Passionada **Mia Racing**
10 **PRINCE OF ROME (IRE),** 7, gr g Lethal Force (IRE)—Garraun (IRE) **G & A Racing**
11 **RED ALLURE,** 8, ch m Mayson—Lark In The Park (IRE) **Mia Racing**
12 **RED DEREK,** 7, b g Steele Tango (USA)—Maydream **JMH Racing Ltd**
13 **RED STRIPES (USA),** 11, b g Leroidesanimaux (BRZ)—Kaleidoscopic (USA) **E. H. Jones (Paints) Ltd**
14 **RED WALLS,** 5, b g Heeraat (IRE)—Gemini Glory (USA) **E. H. Jones (Paints) Ltd**
15 **SANTINHO (IRE),** 20, b g Double Eclipse (IRE)—Gina's Love
16 **SECRET ASSET (IRE),** 18, gr g Clodovil (IRE)—Skerray

MRS LISA WILLIAMSON - continued

THREE-YEAR-OLDS

17 **MAX STRIPES,** b g Heeraat (IRE)—Lily Jicaro (IRE) **Miss H. J. Roberts**
18 **PINK STRIPES,** gr f Heeraat (IRE)—Mariah's Melody (IRE) **E. H. Jones (Paints) Ltd**
19 **PINK WALLS,** b f Heeraat (IRE)—Gemini Glory (USA) **E. H. Jones (Paints) Ltd**
20 **SUGAR HILL BABE (IRE),** b f Bungle Inthejungle—Kardyls Hope (IRE) **JMH Racing Ltd**

---

545 MR ANDREW WILSON, Orton

Postal: **Silver Howe, Orton, Penrith, Cumbria, CA10 3RQ**
Contacts: **PHONE 015396 24071 MOBILE 07813 846768**
EMAIL andywilsonorton@gmail.com

1 **EBENDI (IRE),** 6, ch g Le Havre (IRE)—Ebalista (IRE) **Mr A. C. Wilson**
2 **KINGS ECLIPSE (IRE),** 13, b g Double Eclipse (IRE)—Good Times Ahead (IRE) **Mr A. C. Wilson**
3 **MOORE CLOUDS (IRE),** 8, gr m Cloudings (IRE)—Wednesday Girl (IRE) **Clouds of Orton**
4 **ZANAVI (IRE),** 6, gr g Champs Elysees—Zindana (IRE) **Mr A. C. Wilson**

---

546 MR KEN WINGROVE, Bridgnorth

Postal: **6 Netherton Farm Barns, Netherton Lane, Highley, Bridgnorth, Shropshire, WV16 6NJ**
Contacts: **HOME 01746 861534 MOBILE 07974 411267**
EMAIL kenwingrove@btinternet.com

1 **BOULIVAR (IRE),** 4, ch g Tagula (IRE)—Concra Girl (IRE) **Mr D. G. Wingrove**
2 **BRAMHAM (IRE),** 4, b g Ribchester (IRE)—Flute Enchante (FR) **Mr D. G. Wingrove**
3 **ELUSIVE ARTIST (IRE),** 5, ch g Zoffany (IRE)—Lady Pimpernel **Mr D. G. Wingrove**
4 **FRANKLIN SAINT (IRE),** 4, b g Caravaggio (USA)—I Am (IRE) **Mr J. M. Wingrove**
5 **HEY PRETTY (IRE),** 8, b g Society Rock (IRE)—Coffee Date (USA) **Mr D. G. Wingrove**
6 **JAFFATHEGAFFA,** 5, ch g Havana Gold (IRE)—Actionplatinum (IRE) **Mr J. M. Wingrove**
7 **PHILOSOPHY,** 4, b f Exceed And Excel (AUS)—Greatest Virtue **Mr J. M. Wingrove**
8 **URBAN HIGHWAY (IRE),** 7, b g Kodiac—Viking Fair **Mr J. M. Wingrove**

Assistant Trainer: Isobel Willer.

---

547 MR PETER WINKS, Barnsley

Postal: **Homefield, Rotherham Road, Little Houghton, Barnsley, South Yorkshire, S72 0HA**
Contacts: **MOBILE 07846 899993**
EMAIL pwracing@outlook.com

1 **BALLYFARSOON (IRE),** 12, ch g Medicean—Amzara (IRE) **Barnsley Burglars**
2 **BOB DELANEY,** 7, b g Haafhd—September Moon **Mr R. H. Lee**
3 **GROW NASA GROW (IRE),** 12, ch g Mahler—Dereenavurrig (IRE) **Mr P. Winks**
4 **HARTSIDE (GER),** 14, b g Montjeu (IRE)—Helvellyn (USA) **Peter Winks Racing Club**
5 **LOUGH SALT (IRE),** 12, b g Brian Boru—Castlehill Lady (IRE) **Mr J Toes & Mr J O'Loan**
6 **RHYME SCHEME (IRE),** 6, b m Poet's Voice—Tidal Moon **Simmons, Sambrook S. Woodcock**
7 **SCOTTSDALE,** 10, b g Cape Cross (IRE)—High Praise (USA) **P W O'Mara & P Winks**

MR PETER WINKS - continued

THREE-YEAR-OLDS

8 **DUNNINGTON LAD (IRE),** ch g Camacho—Streetlady (USA) **The Golden Partnership**

Assistant Trainer: Ryan Winks.

---

548 MR ADRIAN WINTLE, Westbury-On-Severn

Postal: **Yew Tree Stables, Rodley, Westbury-On-Severn, Gloucestershire, GL14 1QZ**
Contacts: **MOBILE 07767 351144**

1 **AMLOVI (IRE),** 10, b m Court Cave (IRE)—Portanob (IRE) **Mr S. R. Whistance**
2 **ANGEL ON HIGH (IRE),** 6, b g Dark Angel (IRE)—Angel of The Gwaun (IRE) **Mrs P. Goodwin**
3 **BLUE HERO (CAN),** 5, b g Air Force Blue (USA)—Pomarine (USA) **A. A. Wintle**
4 **CLASHANISKA (IRE),** 7, b g Dark Angel (IRE)—Spirit Watch (IRE) **Mrs Shelley Tucker Partnership**
5 **CREEK HARBOUR (IRE),** 8, b g Kodiac—Allegheny Creek (IRE) **Mrs H. Hawkins**
6 **GO BEYOND (IRE),** 4, b f No Nay Never (USA)—Pure Greed (IRE) **Oracle Horseracing**
7 **GRIGGY (IRE),** 7, b g Dandy Man (IRE)—Joint Destiny (IRE) **Mrs Shelley Tucker Partnership**
8 **HI TRIG,** 6, b g Stimulation (IRE)—Lily Le Braz **M. L. Brown**
9 **IGOTATEXT (IRE),** 5, b g Ajaya—Tifawt **Mrs P. Goodwin**
10 **JESSE'S LADY,** 8, b m Malinas (GER)—Lets Run **Mr D. A. Smerdon**
11 **KEEPER'S CHOICE (IRE),** 9, ch m Intikhab (USA)—Crossing **Wintle Racing Club**
12 **KENSTONE (FR),** 10, gr g Kendargent (FR)—Little Stone (FR) **Wintle Racing Club**
13 **KNOT ON TIME (IRE),** 8, ch g Windsor Knot (IRE)—There On Time (IRE) **Mr S. R. Whistance**
14 **LADY JANE P (IRE),** 7, b m Walk In The Park (IRE)—Rosee des Bieffes (FR) **The Shortlandoyle Syndicate**
15 **LITTLE BROWN MOUSE (IRE),** 6, b m Shantou (USA)—Maxwells Demon (IRE) **Ms L. Shahkarami**
16 **LUXY LOU (IRE),** 5, ch m The Last Lion (IRE)—Dutch Courage **A. A. Wintle**
17 **ORIENTAL BEAUTY,** 5, b m Oasis Dream—Mitre Peak **Wintle, & Crowd Maac**
18 **PESSOA,** 4, b g Ardad (IRE)—Firebelly **A. A. Wintle**
19 **RED BRAVO (IRE),** 7, b g Acclamation—Vision of Peace (IRE) **Mr D. A. Smerdon**
20 **RED RIPPLE,** 5, ch g Gentlewave (IRE)—Brackets (IRE) **Mrs P Corbett & Mrs A Thomas**
21 **RITA RANA (IRE),** 4, b f The Gurkha (IRE)—Tureyth (USA) **Mrs P. Goodwin**
22 **ROSE KAR (FR),** 7, b g Spider Flight (FR)—Rose Wells (FR) **Mr D. A. Smerdon**
23 **SATELLITE CALL (IRE),** 4, b g Kodiac—Ball Girl (IRE) **Dahlbury Racing**
24 **SAVALAS (IRE),** 8, gr g Zebedee—Tap The Dot (IRE) **A. A. Wintle**
25 **TAWAAFOQ,** 9, b g Showcasing—Gilt Linked **Mr S. R. Whistance**
26 **TEDDY THE KNIGHT,** 8, b g Kayf Tara—Michelle's Ella (IRE) **A. A. Wintle**
27 **WIFF WAFF,** 8, b g Poet's Voice—Eraadaat (IRE) **A. A. Wintle**

THREE-YEAR-OLDS

28 **CLANDESTINELY (IRE),** b f El Kabeir (USA)—Hidden Steps **Dahlbury Racing**
29 **ISABELLE (FR),** ch f Planteur (IRE)—Nizzy (FR) **Dahlbury Racing**
30 **LA MIA DUTCHESSA (IRE),** b f Kuroshio (AUS)—Dutch Heiress **A. A. Wintle**

---

549 MISS REBECCA WOODMAN, Chichester

Postal: **Souters Cottage, 21 East Lavant, Chichester, West Sussex, PO18 0AG**
Contacts: **PHONE 01243 527260 MOBILE 07821 603063**
EMAIL rebeccawoodman@msn.com

1 **CLOONEY,** 8, b g Dansili—Love Divine **Miss R. E. Woodman**

MISS REBECCA WOODMAN - continued

2 **ECHO BRAVA,** 13, gr g Proclamation (IRE)—Snake Skin **Miss R. E. Woodman**
3 **GIN AND TEA,** 4, b f Swiss Spirit—Deep Blue Diamond **Burtons Geegees & Budling Bloodstock**
4 **MILLDEAN FELIX (IRE),** 7, br g Red Jazz (USA)—Plausabelle **Miss R. E. Woodman**

THREE-YEAR-OLDS

5 **ALICEFROMUMBRIDGE,** ch f Master Carpenter (IRE)—Indian Flash **March Hare Stud Racing Club**

550 MR STEVE WOODMAN, Chichester

Postal: **Parkers Barn Stables, East Lavant, Chichester, West Sussex, PO18 0AU**
Contacts: **PHONE 01243 527136 MOBILE 07889 188519 FAX 01243 527136**
EMAIL stevewoodman83@msn.com

1 **HONEY P (IRE),** 12, b m Winged Love (IRE)—Luck's A Lady (IRE) **Mrs S. B. Woodman**
2 **MY BONNIE LASSIE,** 4, b f Highland Reel (IRE)—Bonnie Arlene (IRE) **Mrs S. B. Woodman**

THREE-YEAR-OLDS

3 **DON'T FIGHT IT (IRE),** b f Kessaar (IRE)—Malyana **Mrs S. B. Woodman**

---

551 MRS CYNTHIA WOODS, Crowborough

Postal: **Green Hedges Farm, Mark Cross, CROWBOROUGH, East Sussex, TN6 3PA**
Contacts: **PHONE 01892 750567**
EMAIL chaydon@hotmail.co.uk

1 **AULD SOD (IRE),** 10, b g Court Cave (IRE)—Didn't You Know (FR) **The Poucor Partnership**
2 **CHECKITSME,** 6, b m Telescope (IRE)—Sweet Charlie **Green Hedges Racing**
3 **GLORIOUS LADY (IRE),** 9, b m Fame And Glory—Lady Secret (FR) **Glorious Days Racing**
4 **HEART OF THE SUN,** 5, b m Fastnet Rock (AUS)—Heartless **Heartful Racing**
5 **POUCOR,** 8, b g Pour Moi (IRE)—Corinium (IRE) **The Poucor Partnership**

THREE-YEAR-OLDS

6 B g The Gurkha (IRE)—Tropical Rock **Mr G. Woods**

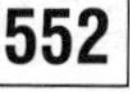

552 MR SEAN WOODS, Newmarket

Postal: **Shalfleet Stables, 17 Bury Road, Newmarket, Suffolk, CB8 7BX**
WORK EMAIL sean@seanwoods.co.uk EMAIL cheryl@seanwoods.co.uk

1 **APPIER (IRE),** 4, b g Holy Roman Emperor (IRE)—Dame Lucy (IRE) **Ignited**
2 **BLACK CAESAR (IRE),** 12, b g Bushranger (IRE)—Evictress (IRE) **The Long Furlong**
3 **BORGI (IRE),** 4, b g Anjaal—One Time (IRE) **S. P. C. Woods**
4 **FRANCESI (IRE),** 4, gr g Caravaggio (USA)—Show Me The Music **Mr N. O'Keeffe**
5 **GOLDEN KEEPER,** 4, b g Pivotal—Celeste **S. P. C. Woods**
6 **LITE AND AIRY,** 4, b g Twilight Son—Spin Doctor **Mr N. O'Keeffe**
7 **MENG TIAN,** 4, b g Territories (IRE)—Yearbook **S. P. C. Woods**
8 **MOGWAI,** 4, gr f Dark Angel (IRE)—Ferevia (IRE) **K. H. M. Doyle**

MR SEAN WOODS - continued

9 **ONE FOR THE FROG (IRE),** 4, b g Dabirsim (FR)—Delicate **Ignited**
10 **PRINCESS SHABNAM (IRE),** 4, b f Gregorian (IRE)—Green Vision (IRE) **A. Ali**
11 **SAVVY KNIGHT (IRE),** 4, b g Caravaggio (USA)—Seagull (IRE) **Mr J. C. H. Hui**
12 **SAVVY VICTORY (IRE),** 4, b c New Bay—Highlands Queen (FR) **Mr J. C. H. Hui**
13 **UDABERRI (IRE),** 4, gr g Mastercraftsman (IRE)—Eccellente Idea (IRE) **S. P. C. Woods**
14 **VITRALITE (IRE),** 7, br g Moohaajim (IRE)—Nellie Forbush **S. P. C. Woods**

THREE-YEAR-OLDS

15 **A POET'S SECRET,** b c Poet's Word (IRE)—Dreaming Beauty **Mr S. Suhail**
16 **AL ASMAKH,** b f Cracksman—Bella Varenna (IRE) **Promenade Bloodstock Limited**
17 **AYYAB,** b f Adaay (IRE)—Astrantia **Teme Valley**
18 **BAND OF STEEL,** b c Golden Horn—Shama's Crown (IRE) **Emirates Park PTY Ltd**
19 **BREAK POINT,** b c Iffraaj—Final Set (IRE) **Mr S. Suhail**
20 **CANADIANSMOKESHOW (IRE),** b f U S Navy Flag (USA)—Wrood (USA) **Mr N. O'Keeffe**
21 **DASHO LENNIE,** b c Territories (IRE)—Sami **Brook Stud**
22 **DOUBLE MARCH (IRE),** b f Kodiac—Flat White (IRE) **Victorious Racing Limited & Fawzi Nass**
23 **GULMARG (IRE),** b g Dandy Man (IRE)—Baileys Pursuit **Mr J William Rowley & Mr S P C Woods**
24 **HARD LINER (IRE),** ch f Profitable (IRE)—Cynthiana (FR) **Victorious Racing Limited**
25 **INANNA (IRE),** b f Acclamation—Kiss of Spring (IRE) **S. P. C. Woods**
26 **LADY NAGIN (IRE),** b f Kodiac—Top Dollar **Mr J William Rowley & Mr S P C Woods**
27 **LAOISMAN,** ch c Night of Thunder (IRE)—Harlequin Girl **Mr N. O'Keeffe**
28 **MASKED QUEEN,** b f Hawkbill (USA)—Cephalonie (USA) **Brook Stud**
29 **PAPA RICCO,** b g Almanzor (FR)—Borja (IRE) **S. P. C. Woods**
30 **POET'S PRIZE,** b f Poet's Word (IRE)—Cape Dollar (IRE) **Mr S. Suhail**
31 **SAVVY BRILLIANCE,** b c Cracksman—Pongee **Mr J. C. H. Hui**
32 **SEA ME DANCE,** b f Sea The Stars (IRE)—Whirly Dancer **Hot To Trot Racing 1**
33 **STRICTLY GOLD,** b g Havana Gold (IRE)—Strictly Silca **Mr N. O'Keeffe**
34 **TERRIMIA,** b f Territories (IRE)—Miaplacidus (IRE) **Mrs J. E. Wallsgrove**
35 **THIRD BATCH,** b f Expert Eye—Amanda Carter **A. Ali**
36 **VAUDEVILLIAN (IRE),** b c Dandy Man (IRE)—Vaudeville **The Storm Again Syndicate & Spc Woods**
37 **XAVIERA,** b f Twilight Son—High Class Girl **Altitude Racing & S.P.C Woods**

TWO-YEAR-OLDS

38 Br f 02/02 Bated Breath—Cirrus Minor (FR) (George Vancouver (USA)) (75000) **Victorious Racing Limited & Fawzi Nass**
39 B c 26/04 Iffraaj—Dirayah (IRE) (Dark Angel (IRE)) (55000) **Mr F. A. A. Nass**
40 Ch c 24/01 Starspangledbanner (AUS)—Emerald Approach (IRE) (New Approach (IRE)) (100000) **Mr N. A. D. Thomas**
41 B f 09/03 Aclaim (IRE)—Epping Rose (IRE) (Kodiac) (90000) **Mr N. O'Keeffe**
42 Ch f 27/04 Zoustar (AUS)—Lacarolina (FR) (Charge d'Affaires) (22000) **S. P. C. Woods**
43 B c 25/03 Tasleet—Poppy Pivot (IRE) (Pivotal) (38095) **A. Ali**
44 B c 26/03 Gleneagles (IRE)—Shahad (AUS) (Fastnet Rock (AUS)) **Emirates Park PTY Ltd**
45 B f 22/01 Cappella Sansevero—Shirin Jaan (Sepoy (AUS)) (7000) **Dr Jamal Ahmadzadeh & Mrs D Swinburn**
46 **ZARIELA,** b f 06/04 Eqtidaar (IRE)—Zia (GER) (Grand Lodge (USA)) (9000) **Mrs C. P. Campbell**

---

553 MRS KAYLEY WOOLLACOTT, South Molton

Postal: **Big Brook Park, Rose Ash, South Molton, Devon, EX36 4RQ**
Contacts: **PHONE 01769 550483**
EMAIL info@richardwoollacottracing.co.uk WEBSITE www.richardwoollacottracing.co.uk

1 **CASPERS COURT (IRE),** 9, gr g Court Cave (IRE)—Kindle Ball (FR) **Mr D Stevens & Mrs S Stevens**
2 **ENORMOUSE,** 10, b g Crosspeace (IRE)—Mousiemay **M. H. Dare**
3 **EROS (FR),** 9, b g Diamond Boy (FR)—Madame Lys (FR) **Mr D Stevens & Mrs S Stevens**
4 **ICE N SLICE (IRE),** 4, ch g New Approach (IRE)—La Superba (IRE) **Gin O'Clock Crew**

MRS KAYLEY WOOLLACOTT - continued

5 **MORNING GLORIA (IRE),** 7, b m Fame And Glory—Leading Article (IRE) **4Racing Owners Club**
6 **NICKELSONTHEDIME (IRE),** 9, b g Shantou (USA)—Penny Fiction (IRE) **T Hamlin, J E Gardener**
7 **SHANNON LODGE (IRE),** 9, b m Doyen (IRE)—Lady Cadia (FR)
8 **SHANNON ROCCO (IRE),** 8, b m Shirocco (GER)—Coco Moon (IRE) **Mr I. G. Thompson**
9 **STELLAR STREAM (IRE),** 6, b g Getaway (GER)—Gaelic River (IRE) **Mrs J. E. Slough**
10 **SURDOUE DE BALLON (FR),** 10, gr g Turgeon (USA)—Nile Breeze (FR) **4Racing Owners Club**
11 **THE KINGS WRIT (IRE),** 12, b g Brian Boru—Letterwoman (IRE) **Mr D Stevens & Mrs S Stevens**
12 **URABAMBA (IRE),** 8, b g Arctic Cosmos (USA)—Glaisdale **Kayley Woollacott Racing Club**

---

554 MR PHILLIP YORK, Effingham Common

Postal: **Mornshill Farm, Banks Lane, Effingham, Leatherhead, Surrey, KT24 5JB**
Contacts: **PHONE 01372 457102**

1 **BARB WIRE,** 9, b br m Amber Life—Eastern Point **Mrs K. H. York**
2 **DELIGHTFUL GUEST (IRE),** 10, b m Beneficial—Saddlers Green (IRE) **Mrs K. H. York**
3 **DINAH WASHINGTON (IRE),** 7, ch m Australia—Gainful (USA) **Mrs K. H. York**
4 **HAPPY LARRY (IRE),** 9, b g Stowaway—Lucky Start (IRE) **Mrs K. H. York**
5 **LEGAL OK (IRE),** 11, b g Echo of Light—Desert Trail (IRE) **P. York**
6 **MISS MASSEY (IRE),** 10, ch m Mahler—Finnow Turkle (IRE) **P. York**
7 **MOUNT CORBITT (IRE),** 8, b g Robin des Champs (FR)—Hanora O'Brien (IRE) **P. York**
8 **ROBIN DES MANA (IRE),** 12, br g Robin des Pres (FR)—Kokopelli Mana (IRE) **P. York**
9 **SPENDABLE,** 11, ch m Spendent—Eastern Point **Mrs K. H. York**
10 **TOUCH TIGHT (IRE),** 11, b g Touch of Land (FR)—Classic China **Mrs K. H. York**
11 **ZINAT (IRE),** 9, gr m Holy Roman Emperor (IRE)—Zariziyna (IRE) **Mrs K. H. York**

TWO-YEAR-OLDS

12 Ch f 29/06 Eastern Anthem (IRE)—Sammara (Black Sam Bellamy (IRE)) **P. York**

---

555 MRS LAURA YOUNG, Bridgwater

Postal: **Rooks Castle Stables, Broomfield, Bridgwater, Somerset, TA5 2EW**
Contacts: **PHONE 01278 664595 MOBILE 07766 514414 FAX 01278 661555**
EMAIL ljyracing@hotmail.com WEBSITE www.laurayoungracing.com

1 **AUENWIRBEL (GER),** 12, b g Sholokhov (IRE)—Auentime (GER) **Mrs L. J. Young**
2 **MEGAUDAIS SPEED (FR),** 11, b g Puit d'Or (IRE)—La Rouadiere (FR) **The Isle Of Frogs Partnership**
3 **ST ESTEPHE,** 7, br g Lethal Force (IRE)—Ha'penny Beacon **Mrs L. J. Young**
4 **THEDANCINGMAN,** 10, b g Jeremy (USA)—Broadway Dancer **Mrs L. J. Young**
5 **TOUT PARIS (FR),** 8, b g Kapgarde (FR)—Parice de La Borie (FR) **The Isle Of Frogs Partnership**

Assistant Trainer: James Young.

NH Jockey: Robert Dunne.

---

556 MR MAXWELL YOUNG, Droitwich

Postal: **Little Acton Farm, Sneads Green, Droitwich, Worcestershire, WR9 0PZ**
Contacts: **PHONE 01905 827795**
EMAIL max.young@hotmail.com

1 **ARTEMIS SKY,** 5, ch m Hunter's Light (IRE)—Starlit Sky **Max Young Racing Club**
2 **CHARLIE SIRINGO (IRE),** 8, ch g Getaway (GER)—Drumderry (IRE) **Mr R. M. Evans**
3 **CITYZEN SERG (IRE),** 6, b g Raven's Pass (USA)—Summer Dream (IRE) **Mrs D. Prosser**
4 **COUNTRY KITTEN (IRE),** 8, b m Recital (FR)—Kitty True (IRE) **Mr D. Jennings**
5 **DECORATION OF WAR (IRE),** 8, b g Declaration of War (USA)—Sea Paint (IRE) **Mrs D. Prosser**
6 **DOYENS DE ANTE (IRE),** 7, b g Doyen (IRE)—De Street (IRE) **Mrs D. Prosser**
7 **FERROBIN (IRE),** 9, br g Robin des Champs (FR)—Fedaia (IRE) **Mrs D. Prosser**
8 **FOU DILIGENCE (IRE),** 8, ch g Le Fou (IRE)—Peggy Maddock (IRE) **Lady Brooke**
9 **GOTADANCE (IRE),** 6, b m Mahler—Larnalee (IRE) **Mr M. J. Young**
10 **HAPPY SANCHEZ (IRE),** 5, b g Sholokhov (IRE)—Realta Mo Croi (IRE) **Lady Brooke**
11 **MAN OF RIDDLES (USA),** 5, b br g Temple City (USA)—Mien (USA) **Mr D. R. Broadhurst**
12 **PAUDIE (IRE),** 7, b g Fame And Glory—Honeyed (IRE) **Mr M. J. Young**
13 **QUECHUA,** 4, ch g Australia—Mama Quilla (USA) **Mr M. J. Young**
14 **SECOND CHAPTER (IRE),** 8, b g Arcadio (GER)—Tosca Shine (IRE) **Mr D. R. Broadhurst**
15 **SILVRETTA SCHWARZ (IRE),** 8, b m Silver Frost (IRE)—Perruche Grise (FR) **Max Young Racing Club**
16 **SNOWPIERCER (FR),** 9, b g Astarabad (USA)—My Darling Rose (FR) **Lady Brooke**
17 **STEVIE MCKEANE,** 6, b m Bated Breath—Eventfull Meet (IRE) **Mr M. J. Young**
18 **THE FECKENHAM FOX,** 9, ch m Malinas (GER)—Broughton Melody **Mr K. E. Hay**
19 **VOICE OF HOPE (IRE),** 6, br g Poet's Voice—Viennese Whirl **Mr D. R. Broadhurst**

---

557 MR WILLIAM YOUNG, Carluke

Postal: **Watchknowe Lodge, Crossford, Carluke, Lanarkshire, ML8 5QT**
Contacts: **PHONE 01555 860226, 01555 860856 MOBILE 07900 408210 FAX 01555 860137**
EMAIL watchknowe@talktalk.net

1 **ARDERA CROSS (IRE),** 12, ch g Shantou (USA)—Fair Maid Marion (IRE) **W. G. Young**
2 **COLONEL MANDERSON (FR),** 7, b g Kapgarde (FR)—Playact (IRE) **W. G. Young**
3 **DARKEST DAY (IRE),** 8, b g Aizavoski (IRE)—Dempseys Luck (IRE) **W. G. Young**
4 **GRIPPER,** 8, b g Thewayyouare (USA)—Hold On Tight (IRE) **W. G. Young**
5 **SO BE IT (IRE),** 7, b g Yeats (IRE)—Maple Valley Gale (IRE) **W. G. Young**
6 **SOME AMBITION (IRE),** 10, b g Westerner—Heath Heaven **W. G. Young**
7 **TUMBLING DICE,** 8, b g Lucarno (USA)—Arctic Ring **W. G. Young**

Assistant Trainer: William G Young Snr.

INDEX TO HORSES

The figure before the name of the horse refers to the number of the team in which it appears and
The figure after the horse supplies a ready reference to each animal. Horses are indexed strictly alphabetically, e.g. THE CON MAN appears in the T's, MR NICE GUY In the MR's, ST BASIL in the ST'S etc.
Unnamed animals are listed under their dam, along with their sex.

380 **AGILULF** 1
66 **AGNES STEWART** (IRE) F 88
239 **AGONYCLITE** 1
106 **AGOSTINO** 14
251 **AGRICOLA** 22
483 **AH WHISHT** (IRE) 1
23 **AHAMOMENT** (IRE) 2
228 **AHAZEEJ** (IRE) C 118
167 **AHEAD OF SCHEDULE** (IRE) 1
308 **AHEAD OF THE FIELD** (IRE) 1
135 **AHLAWI** 2
247 **AHORSEWITHNONAME** 1
440 **AHOY SENOR** (IRE) 1
469 **AIDAN ANDABETTIN** 42
204 **AIGHEAR** 3
387 **AIHAWAWI** (IRE) 63
438 **AIKENBREAKINHEART** (IRE) 1
395 **AIKHAL** (IRE) 1
532 **AIKIDO** (IRE) 1
538 **AILES D'AMOUR** (IRE) 1
371 **AILSA ON MY MIND** (IRE) C 12
5 **AIM OF ARTEMIS** (IRE) C 128
456 **AIM STRAIGHT** 28
539 **AIMEE DE SIVOLA** (FR) 2
506 **AIMERIC** 1
465 **AIMIGAYLE** G 13
456 **AIMING HIGH** 1
35 **AIN DUBAI** (IRE) 57
119 **AIN'T NO SUNSHINE** (IRE) 2
72 **AINSDALE** 1
367 **AIONE** (FR) 3
527 **AIR HAIR LAIR** (IRE) 2
226 **AIR OF APPROVAL** (IRE) 2
413 **AIR STRICKER** (FR) F 37
43 **AIR TO AIR** 1
305 **AIRA FORCE** 16
228 **AIRBRUSH** (IRE) F 119
464 **AIRE VALLEY LAD** 2
413 **AIRGUNNER** 38
349 **AIRSHOW** 2
259 **AIRTON** 1
507 **AIRTOTHETHRONE** (IRE) 1
271 **AJAY'S WAYS** (IRE) 1
12 **AJERO** (IRE) 1
228 **AJJAJ** (FR) 32
66 **AJLA** (IRE) C 89
440 **AJO GREEN** (IRE) G 2
385 **AJP KINGDOM** (IRE) 3
10 **AJRAD** 2
398 **AJWAAD** (FR) 9
243 **AJYAD** (IRE) 12
506 **AKHU NAJLA** 2
497 **AKI BOMAYE** (IRE) 1
515 **AKIMBO** 63
506 **AKKADIAN THUNDER** 51
286 **AKVAVERA** C 132
219 **AL AASY** (IRE) 1
112 **AL AGAILA** (IRE) 1
112 **AL ALAALI** (FR) 18
43 **AL AMEEN** (IRE) 2
15 **AL ANDALYYA** (USA) C 140
206 **AL ASIFAH** 38
552 **AL ASMAKH** 16
500 **AL AZHAR** (IRE) 1
188 **AL BAAHY** 1
342 **AL BAHAR** (QTR) 16
95 **AL BAREZ** 1
489 **AL DANCER** (FR) 1
43 **AL DASIM** (IRE) 34
228 **AL DURRA** 120
484 **AL FAREEJ** (IRE) C 38
412 **AL GAIYA** (FR) 1
321 **AL GHANIM** 39
228 **AL HARGAH** (IRE) 33
506 **AL HUJAIJA** (IRE) 135
506 **AL HUSN** (IRE) 3
135 **AL JAMAL** F 3
90 **AL JAWZA** C 14
95 **AL KARRAR** (IRE) 13
506 **AL KHAWSSAA** (IRE) 136
35 **AL KHAZNEH** (IRE) 58
48 **AL KHERB** 1
15 **AL MARMAR** (IRE) 2
399 **AL MOTASIM** 23
219 **AL MUBHIR** 2
282 **AL MUFFRIH** (IRE) 1
88 **AL MUNDHER** (FR) 16
251 **AL MUQDAD** 23
506 **AL MUZN** (IRE) 52
5 **AL NAFIR** (IRE) 2
66 **AL NAJADA** (IRE) 34
69 **AL NAMIR** (IRE) 1
368 **AL QADAM** (FR) 34
66 **AL QAREEM** (IRE) 1
69 **AL RAAHBA** (IRE) F 27
175 **AL RUFAA** (FR) 1
15 **AL SHABAB** (FR) 141
262 **AL SIMMO** 1
5 **AL SUHAIL** 3
236 **AL SUIL EILE** (FR) 1
303 **AL TARFA** 14
82 **AL TARMAAH** (IRE) 1
135 **AL TILAL** (IRE) 4
35 **AL WASL DREAM** (IRE) 59
416 **AL WATHNA** F 32
521 **AL ZARAQAAN** 2
286 **ALAATA** (USA) F 133
336 **ALAFDHAL** (IRE) 1
356 **ALAINN TU** (IRE) 10
231 **ALALCANCE** 38
408 **ALANDALOS** F 59
385 **ALAPHILIPPE** (IRE) 4
164 **ALAROOS** (IRE) 1
251 **ALASKAN** (IRE) 24
179 **ALASKAN JEWEL** (IRE) 1
521 **ALAZWAR** (IRE) 3
24 **ALBA LONGA** 21
88 **ALBA POWER** (IRE) 2
24 **ALBANY** 22
35 **ALBASHARAH** (USA) F 60
521 **ALBASHEER** (IRE) 4
154 **ALBEGONE** 1
154 **ALBEGREY** 2
254 **ALBERIC** (FR) 3
90 **ALBERT CEE** (FR) 6
243 **ALBERT LASKER** (IRE) 38
71 **ALBERT VAN ORNUM** (FR) 1
153 **ALBERT'S BACK** 1
305 **ALBERTINE ROSE** C 36
14 **ALBERTO** (IRE) 41
87 **ALBERTS BAY** (IRE) 1
262 **ALBESEEINGYER** 2
92 **ALBION PRINCESS** 1
387 **ALBIZZIA** G 94
368 **ALBORKAN** (FR) 1
8 **ALBURN** 1
184 **ALBUS ANNE** 1
34 **ALCANTANGO** (IRE) 1
488 **ALCAZAN** 1
138 **ALCAZARA** (IRE) 39
543 **ALCEDO** (IRE) 2
98 **ALCHEMILLA** C 28
505 **ALCHEMIST'S DREAM** 2
461 **ALCHEMYSTERY** 12
262 **ALCHEMYSTIQUE** (IRE) 3
192 **ALCHIMIA** (IRE) 41
219 **ALDAARY** 3
164 **ALDBOURNE** (IRE) 2
384 **ALDER** (IRE) 5
421 **ALDERSHOT** 1
298 **ALDSWORTH** 2
461 **ALEATORIC** (IRE) 2
442 **ALEEZDANCER** (IRE) 1
138 **ALETHIOMETER** (FR) 2
456 **ALEX THE GREAT** (IRE) 29
66 **ALEXA'S PRINCESS** (IRE) 35
6 **ALEXANDER JAMES** (IRE) 1
454 **ALEXANDER ROAD** (IRE) G 2
527 **ALEXANDRA ROMANOV** (IRE) 3
416 **ALEXANDRETTA** 13
66 **ALEXANDRITE** F 90
383 **ALEXANDROUPOLIS** (IRE) 18
243 **ALEXI BOY** 13
47 **ALFA DAWN** (IRE) 1
315 **ALFA L'ANGEL** 22
239 **ALFA MIX** 2
351 **ALFIE SHARP** 1
489 **ALFIE'S PRINCESS** (IRE) 2
69 **ALFLAILA** 2
80 **ALFRED COVE** 3
383 **ALFRED MUNNINGS** (IRE) 19
92 **ALGERNON** 17
464 **ALGESIRAS** 3
319 **ALGHAZAAL** 1
321 **ALGHEED** (IRE) 1
112 **ALGIERS** (IRE) 2
78 **ALHABOR** 1
219 **ALHAMBRA PALACE** 44
280 **ALI JEWELS** (IRE) 9
236 **ALI STAR BERT** 2
173 **ALIBABA** 1
395 **ALICE GIRL** (IRE) F 44
111 **ALICE KITTY** (IRE) 1
92 **ALICE KNYVET** 18
66 **ALICE MC CLORY** (IRE) 36
383 **ALICE SPRINGS** (IRE) F 99
549 **ALICEFROMUMBRIDGE** 5
66 **ALICIA DARCY** (IRE) C 91
297 **ALIEN ENCOUNTER** 1
319 **ALIEN STORM** (IRE) 2
506 **ALIF POWER** (IRE) 53
286 **ALIGN THE STARS** (IRE) 134
270 **ALIKA BREEZE** (GER) 44
5 **ALINA** (IRE) C 129
234 **ALIOMAANA** 1
63 **ALIOSKI** 1
383 **ALIVE ALIVE OH** C 100
359 **ALJARDAA** (IRE) 1
95 **ALJARI** 2
368 **ALJUMAR** (IRE) F 47
140 **ALKHATTAAF** 1

353 **ALKHAWARAH** (USA) C 21
309 **ALKOPOP** (GER) 1
525 **ALL A STRUGGLE** 1
6 **ALL ABOARD** (IRE) 2
461 **ALL ABOUT ALICE** (IRE) 3
224 **ALL ABOUT JOE** (IRE) 1
366 **ALL ABOUT ME** 1
496 **ALL ABOUT NEVE** (IRE) 48
379 **ALL DANCER** (FR) 2
290 **ALL DOWN TO ROSIE** (IRE) 1
395 **ALL DUNN** 25
383 **ALL FOR GLORY** (USA) C 101
172 **ALL GREEK TO ME** 45
417 **ALL GUNS BLAZING** (IRE) 1
92 **ALL I NEED** (IRE) C 53
165 **ALL IN THE HIPS** (IRE) 19
321 **ALL INCLUSIVE** 40
112 **ALL OF ME** C 59
66 **ALL OUT** F 92
26 **ALL THAT GLITTERS** 16
16 **ALL THE FAME** (IRE) 1
390 **ALL THE GLORY** 1
43 **ALL THE KING'S MEN** (FR) 3
383 **ALL TIME GREAT** (USA) 20
333 **ALL WAYS GLAMOROUS** 10
501 **ALL WHITE MATE** (IRE) 39
367 **ALLAHO** (FR) 4
211 **ALLANAH'S BOY** (IRE) 2
248 **ALLARDYCE** 1
44 **ALLAVINA** (IRE) 1
513 **ALLBETSOFF** (IRE) 1
24 **ALLE STELLE** C 85
367 **ALLEGORIE DE VASSY** (FR) 5
298 **ALLEGRO FORTE** 3
300 **ALLIBABA** 2
387 **ALLIGATOR ALLEY** 1
457 **ALLIHIES** (IRE) 2
457 **ALLJANI** (GER) 3
457 **ALLMANKIND** 4
157 **ALLO ALLO** 2
24 **ALLONSY** 86
503 **ALLROADSLEADTOROME** 18
497 **ALLSFINEANDANDY** (IRE) 2
168 **ALLTHEROADRUNNING** 1
42 **ALLURE** (IRE) C 47
15 **ALMA MATER** C 142
398 **ALMARIN** (IRE) 4
26 **ALMASHOOQA** (USA) C 52
506 **ALMATY STAR** (IRE) 54
319 **ALMAZHAR GARDE** (FR) 3
537 **ALMINAR** (IRE) 2
42 **ALMODOVAR DEL RIO** (IRE) 1
88 **ALMOND CHOUQUETTE** (FR) 17
538 **ALMOST GOLD** (IRE) 2
332 **ALMOST GOTAWAY** (IRE) 1
416 **ALMUDENA** 33
115 **ALMUFEED** (IRE) 3
457 **ALNADAM** (FR) 5
164 **ALNAJMAH** F 34
164 **ALNWICK CASTLE** 3
301 **ALODIA** 9
300 **ALOISA** 3
474 **ALONE NO MORE** (IRE) 1
506 **ALONG CAME CASEY** (IRE) C 137
226 **ALONG LONG STORY** (IRE) 3
501 **ALOSHA** (IRE) F 62
506 **ALOUJA** (IRE) C 138
219 **ALPHA CAPTURE** (IRE) 45
355 **ALPHA CRUCIS** (IRE) 138
130 **ALPHA FEMALE** 13
91 **ALPHA KING** 1
176 **ALPHA ZULU** 14
255 **ALPHABA** (IRE) G 15
286 **ALPINA EXPRESS** (IRE) 35
172 **ALPINE GIRL** (IRE) 16
119 **ALPINE SIERRA** (IRE) 3
114 **ALPINE SPRINGS** (IRE) 1
130 **ALPINE STROLL** 2
209 **ALQABEELA** (IRE) 1
352 **ALQAMAR** 1
196 **ALRAMZ** 1
206 **ALRASHAKA** (IRE) 39
408 **ALREHB** (USA) 1
409 **ALRIGHT CHAP** (IRE) 1
4 **ALRIGHT CHIEF** (IRE) 1
457 **ALRIGHT DAI** (IRE) 6
119 **ALRIGHT SUNSHINE** (IRE) 4
6 **ALSAAQY** (IRE) 3
15 **ALSAKIB** 36
515 **ALSALWA** (IRE) F 64
284 **ALSAMYAH** 1
262 **ALSEEYERTHERE** 4
24 **ALSHADHIAN** (IRE) 23
390 **ALSO KNOWN AS** (IRE) 2
286 **ALTA COMEDIA** 36
456 **ALTANERA** 62
384 **ALTHEA ROSE** (IRE) F 30
219 **ALTMORE** 118
205 **ALTO ALTO** (FR) 1
189 **ALTOBELLI** (IRE) 2
286 **ALUMNA** (USA) C 135
286 **ALUMNUS** 37
88 **ALVA** (FR) 18
538 **ALWAJD** (IRE) 3
506 **ALWARGA** (USA) F 55
5 **ALWAYS A DREAM** F 130
453 **ALWAYS ABLE** (IRE) 1
228 **ALWAYS FEARLESS** (IRE) 1
484 **ALWAYS GOLD** F 39
135 **ALWAYS ROSES** C 5
259 **ALWAYS TEA TIME** 2
353 **ALWAYS THANKFUL** F 7
484 **ALWAYS TOMORROW** (IRE) 9
221 **ALWAYSANDFOREVER** (IRE) F 38
475 **ALYA'S GOLD AWARD** (IRE) 1
69 **ALYAMAAMA** (USA) C 28
179 **ALYARA** 2
416 **ALYS LOVE** C 34
206 **ALZAHIR** (FR) 40
70 **AM I** (USA) C 60
369 **AM I WRONG** (IRE) 3
385 **AMADORIO** (FR) 5
542 **AMAHORO** F 45
283 **AMAL** (IRE) 2
263 **AMALFI BAY** 2
370 **AMALFI GEM** (IRE) 1
370 **AMALFI SKYLINE** 2
231 **AMAMI** (IRE) C 104
88 **AMANDA'S CHOICE** 19
524 **AMANI** 1
209 **AMANIRENAS** (IRE) 2
219 **AMANZOE** (IRE) 4
385 **AMARBELLE'S DREAM** 6
228 **AMARETTI VIRGINIA** (IRE) 34
497 **AMARILLO SKY** (IRE) 3
402 **AMARILLOBYMORNING** (IRE) 3
179 **AMATEUR** (IRE) 3
84 **AMATHUS** (IRE) 1
188 **AMAYSMONT** 2
506 **AMAZING** (IRE) 56
532 **AMAZING ALBA** 2
451 **AMAZING AMAYA** 1
154 **AMAZING ARTHUR** 96
326 **AMAZING MOLLIE** 1
489 **AMAZING TANGO** (GER) 3
219 **AMAZONE** (GER) F 119
349 **AMAZONIAN DREAM** (IRE) 3
292 **AMBASSADOR** (IRE) 1
89 **AMBASSADORIAL** (USA) 1
65 **AMBER CLOUD** G 1
135 **AMBER DEW** 6
513 **AMBER GOLD** 2
320 **AMBER ISLAND** (IRE) 1
42 **AMBER LANE** C 48
368 **AMBER ROAD** (IRE) F 48
226 **AMBER RUN** (IRE) 4
497 **AMBION HILL** (IRE) 4
363 **AMBUSH ANNIE** (IRE) 3
221 **AMEERAT JUMAIRA** 17
109 **AMELIA R** (IRE) 1
514 **AMELIA'S DANCE** (IRE) 1
379 **AMENON** (FR) 3
153 **AMERICA MON AMIE** (USA) G 74
416 **AMERICA NOVA** (FR) C 35
172 **AMERICAN BELLE** (IRE) 17
360 **AMERICAN GERRY** (IRE) 2
497 **AMERICAN LAND** (IRE) 5
154 **AMERICAN OAK** (IRE) 97
166 **AMERICAN ROSE** 14
410 **AMERICAN SNIPER** (IRE) 3
472 **AMERICAN SPIRIT** (IRE) F 5
515 **AMERICAN STAR** (IRE) 1
10 **AMERIGHI** (IRE) 3
383 **AMERIQUE** (IRE) C 102
501 **AMERRONE** (IRE) 40
506 **AMEYNAH** (IRE) 4
202 **AMI BONDHU** (FR) 1
385 **AMI DESBOIS** (FR) 7
544 **AMICO AMORE** 1
383 **AMICUS** (AUS) C 103
166 **AMIDNIGHTSTAR** 2
94 **AMINATU** 13
94 **AMIRAVATI** 1
219 **AMLETO** (IRE) 46
548 **AMLOVI** (IRE) 1
92 **AMONA** (IRE) F 54
305 **AMONGST THE STARS** 37
457 **AMOOLA GOLD** (GER) 7
521 **AMOR DE MI VIDA** (FR) 5
119 **AMOR VICTORIOUS** (IRE) 49
164 **AMOR VINCIT OMNIA** (IRE) 4
89 **AMORELLA** (IRE) C 39
109 **AMOURI GLEAM** 2
109 **AMOURIE** 3
206 **AMPHITRITE** 41
247 **AMRONS SAGE** (IRE) 2
515 **AMSTERDAM** 65
542 **AMTHAAL** F 46
384 **AMUSEMENT** (IRE) 6
18 **AN ANGEL'S DREAM** (FR) 1
376 **AN MARCACH** (IRE) 1

321 **ARCADIAN NIGHTS** 3
309 **ARCADIAN ROSE** 2
101 **ARCANDY** (IRE) 1
221 **ARCANEARS** (IRE) 1
286 **ARCH LEGEND** 136
138 **ARCH MOON** 3
510 **ARCHDUKE FERDINAND** (IRE) 1
234 **ARCHER** (GER) 4
101 **ARCHI'S AFFAIRE** 2
258 **ARCHIE BROWN** (IRE) 1
412 **ARCHIE MACDART** 2
160 **ARCHIE STEVENS** 2
185 **ARCHIVE** (FR) 1
247 **ARCLIGHT** 3
298 **ARCTIC ACTRESS** F 5
93 **ARCTIC BLUE** 1
140 **ARCTIC FOOTPRINT** 2
499 **ARCTIC FOX** 1
282 **ARCTIC LODGE** (IRE) 2
12 **ARCTIC SAINT** (IRE) 2
15 **ARCTIC THUNDER** (IRE) 147
139 **ARCTICIAN** (IRE) 1
270 **ARCTURIAN** (IRE) 45
101 **ARD CHROS** (IRE) 3
395 **ARDAD'S GREAT** 26
42 **ARDAKAN** 2
228 **ARDARA ROSE** (IRE) 123
557 **ARDERA CROSS** (IRE) 1
480 **ARDMAYLE** (IRE) 1
390 **ARE U WISE TO THAT** (IRE) 7
106 **ARECIBO** (FR) 2
288 **AREILLE** (IRE) 1
139 **ARENAS DEL TIEMPO** 2
515 **ARENDELLE** F 66
79 **AREWENEARLYHOME** (IRE) 16
347 **AREYOUWITHUS** (IRE) 2
14 **ARGENTALI** 42
147 **ARGUS** (IRE) 2
89 **ARIKA** (USA) 3
90 **ARIKARA** 7
213 **ARINI** 1
399 **ARION** 1
43 **ARION** 4
342 **ARIS** (IRE) F 18
2 **ARIS DE CRAT** 2
228 **ARISTIA** (IRE) 2
157 **ARISTOBULUS** 3
157 **ARIZONA CARDINAL** 4
515 **ARKENDALE** 20
138 **ARKENSTAAR** 40
169 **ARKID** 1
505 **ARLECCHINO'S GIFT** 3
505 **ARLECCHINO'S STAR** 22
376 **ARLO** (FR) 2
91 **ARLO'S SUNSHINE** 3
251 **ARMAGEDDON** C 71
189 **ARMATHIA** 4
335 **ARMATTIEKAN** (IRE) 2
385 **ARMCHAIR FARMER** (IRE) 8
374 **ARMOURED** (IRE) 1
72 **ARMY OF INDIA** (IRE) 2
272 **ARMY OF ONE** (GER) 1
40 **ARMY'S DREAM** (IRE) 1
1 **ARNICA** 1
143 **ARNOLD** 1
173 **ARPINA** (IRE) 2
509 **ARQOOB** (IRE) 3
499 **ARRANGE** (IRE) 2
445 **ARRANMORE** 2
206 **ARREST** (IRE) 45
390 **ARRIVEDERCI** (FR) 8
328 **ARROWTOWN** F 26
385 **ARRUCIAN** F 9
385 **ART APPROVAL** (FR) 10
175 **ART DE VIVRE** 21
514 **ART DECCO** 2
376 **ART OF DIPLOMACY** 3
211 **ART OF ILLUSION** (IRE) 4
154 **ART POWER** (IRE) 3
84 **ARTAVIAN** 18
449 **ARTEMIS FLYER** (IRE) 25
457 **ARTEMIS KIMBO** 9
556 **ARTEMIS SKY** 1
283 **ARTEMISIA GENTILE** (IRE) 3
308 **ARTEMISION** 2
343 **ARTESANA** C 90
122 **ARTHALOT** (IRE) 1
239 **ARTHUR'S QUAY** (IRE) 4
146 **ARTHUR'S REALM** (IRE) 1
65 **ARTHUR'S SEAT** (IRE) 2
400 **ARTHUR'S VICTORY** (IRE) 1
16 **ARTHURIAN FABLE** (IRE) 2
357 **ARTIC BREEZE** (IRE) 2
1 **ARTIC MANN** 2
1 **ARTIC ROW** 3
23 **ARTILENA** (CAN) C 39
286 **ARTISAN DANCER** (FR) 38
286 **ARTISAND** (IRE) 39
26 **ARTISTIC CHOICE** (IRE) 2
437 **ARTISTIC DAWN** (IRE) F 1
437 **ARTISTIC DAWN** (IRE) G 2
6 **ARTISTIC DREAMER** 88
507 **ARTISTIC ENDEAVOUR** 2
538 **ARTISTIC FIGHTER** (IRE) 6
42 **ARTISTIC LEGACY** (IRE) C 49
112 **ARTISTIC MISSION** 60
24 **ARTISTIC STAR** (IRE) 24
513 **ARTISTIC STEPS** (IRE) 57
464 **ARTS THEATER** (IRE) G 5
289 **ARUAN** F 19
285 **ARUMADAAY** 19
231 **ARUNTOTHEQUEEN** (IRE) 1
489 **ARWENA** 6
517 **ARZAAK** (IRE) 1
496 **AS IF BY CHANCE** 3
300 **ASA** (FR) 5
57 **ASADJUMEIRAH** 3
360 **ASCARI** 40
26 **ASCENDED** (IRE) F 54
387 **ASCOT ADVENTURE** 3
316 **ASCOT DAY** (FR) 2
354 **ASCRAEUS** 1
286 **ASDAA** (IRE) 2
355 **ASENSE** 6
328 **ASH WEDNESDAY** 27
346 **ASHAAQAH** (IRE) F 38
396 **ASHAREDMOMENT** 1
231 **ASHDALE BOB** (IRE) 2
231 **ASHDALE FLYER** (IRE) 3
219 **ASHEERAH** F 122
513 **ASHINGTON** 4
182 **ASHJAN** 1
41 **ASHKENAZIM** (FR) 18
153 **ASHKHABAD** (IRE) 2
92 **ASHKY** (IRE) 2
346 **ASHMORE** (IRE) 16
342 **ASHTANGA** 7
457 **ASHTOWN LAD** (IRE) 10
106 **ASIAN QUEEN** 15
187 **ASIAN SPICE** 1
383 **ASIDIOUS ALEXANDER** (IRE) C 105
172 **ASIMOV** 46
251 **ASINARA** 72
266 **ASJAD** 1
385 **ASK A HONEY BEE** (IRE) 11
263 **ASK LILEEN** (IRE) 3
189 **ASK ME EARLY** (IRE) 5
102 **ASK MY HEATHER** (IRE) 1
347 **ASKALLI** (IRE) 3
123 **ASKGARMOR** (IRE) 1
499 **ASKING FOR ANSWERS** (IRE) 3
59 **ASLUKGOES** 1
79 **ASMUND** (IRE) 1
441 **ASOOF** C 22
472 **ASPEN GROVE** 6
107 **ASSEMA** 64
430 **ASSEMBLED** 1
479 **ASSESSMENT** 2
457 **ASTA LA PASTA** (IRE) 11
429 **ASTAPOR** 2
367 **ASTERION FORLONGE** (FR) 8
410 **ASTIGAR** (FR) 5
247 **ASTON MARTINI** 4
5 **ASTONISHING** (IRE) F 134
537 **ASTRA VIA** 6
419 **ASTRAL AFFAIR** (IRE) C 1
419 **ASTRAL AFFAIR** (IRE) M 2
458 **ASTRAL BEAU** 3
458 **ASTRAL SPIRIT** 22
260 **ASTRO JAKK** (IRE) 1
305 **ASTRO KING** (IRE) 3
513 **ASTROBRIO** 5
347 **ASTRODIAMOND** F 4
206 **ASTRODOME** 46
376 **ASTROMACHIA** 4
513 **ASTROMAGICK** F 65
513 **ASTROMAN** 6
196 **ASTRONOMIC VIEW** 2
446 **ASTRONOMICA** 3
515 **ASTRONOMY DOMINE** F 67
80 **ASTROPHYSICS** 4
164 **AT A PINCH** 6
26 **AT LIBERTY** (IRE) 3
416 **AT THE DOUBLE** (FR) 2
17 **AT YOUR SERVICE** 2
188 **ATACAMA DESERT** (IRE) 5
497 **ATAKAN** (FR) 6
500 **ATALANTA BREEZE** 2
206 **ATARAMA** 47
296 **ATASER** 1
270 **ATHBAH** F 46
39 **ATHEBY** 1
383 **ATHENA** (IRE) C 106
349 **ATHENA BALLERINA** 15
521 **ATHENE'S KISS** (IRE) 49
59 **ATHGARVAN** (IRE) 2
78 **ATHMAD** (IRE) 2
147 **ATHOLL STREET** (IRE) 3
496 **ATHOLLBLAIR BOY** (IRE) 4
343 **ATHREYAA** C 91

23 **ATIYAH** 4
122 **ATJIMA** (IRE) 2
311 **ATLANTA BRAVE** (IRE) 1
206 **ATLANTIC BELLE** 48
240 **ATLANTIC BREEZE** (IRE) 2
1 **ATLANTIC DANCER** (IRE) 4
26 **ATLANTIC DREAM** (IRE) 18
537 **ATLANTIC FLEET** (IRE) 7
348 **ATLANTIC HEART** (IRE) 2
368 **ATLANTIC QUEEN** (IRE) F 49
482 **ATLANTIC STORM** (IRE) 1
14 **ATLANTIS BLUE** 1
102 **ATOMIC ANGEL** 2
154 **ATOMIC LADY** (FR) 4
138 **ATOMISE** 4
61 **ATRAFAN** (IRE) 1
175 **ATRIUM** 2
247 **ATTACCA** (IRE) 5
347 **ATTENTION ALL** (IRE) 5
70 **ATTENTIVE** 5
383 **ATTIRE** (IRE) F 107
333 **ATTY'S EDGE** 1
146 **ATWATER NINE** (IRE) 21
355 **ATWIXADAY** 139
308 **AUBA ME YANG** (IRE) 3
428 **AUBIS WALK** (FR) 1
165 **AUBRIETIA** C 35
205 **AUCUNRISQUE** (FR) 3
206 **AUDIENCE** 1
369 **AUDITORIA** 4
80 **AUDLEY** G 5
555 **AUENWIRBEL** (GER) 1
101 **AUGHARUE** (IRE) 4
282 **AUGHNACURRA KING** (IRE) 3
206 **AUGUST** (IRE) 49
383 **AUGUSTE RODIN** (IRE) 21
506 **AULD ALLIANCE** (IRE) C 58
383 **AULD ALLIANCE** (IRE) C 108
551 **AULD SOD** (IRE) 1
387 **AULD TOON LOON** (IRE) 4
526 **AUNT MINNIE** G 39
515 **AUNT VIOLET** (USA) 21
60 **AUNTIE JUNE** 1
89 **AUNTINET** C 41
213 **AURELIA FADILLA** 2
122 **AURIGNY MILL** (FR) 3
368 **AUROPHOBIA** (IRE) 35
506 **AURORA CHARM** 59
515 **AURORA DAWN** (IRE) 22
404 **AURORA GLORY** (IRE) 11
442 **AURORA SPRING** (IRE) C 62
440 **AURORA THUNDER** 6
399 **AUSDAISIA** (IRE) 25
228 **AUSSI MANDATE** 35
270 **AUSSIE BANKER** 1
472 **AUSSIE GIRL** 7
175 **AUSSIE MYSTIC** 22
330 **AUSSIE STAR** 17
330 **AUSSIE VIEW** (IRE) C 18
88 **AUSTRAL** (FR) 20
15 **AUSTRALIAN ANGEL** 3
286 **AUSTRIAN THEORY** (IRE) 3
539 **AUTHOCELTIC** (FR) 33
303 **AUTHOR'S DREAM** 1
355 **AUTHORISED SPEED** (FR) 7
367 **AUTHORIZED ART** (FR) 9
301 **AUTOGRAPH** C 25
231 **AUTOLINE** (IRE) 40
406 **AUTOLYCUS** 10
385 **AUTONOMOUS CLOUD** (IRE) 12
300 **AUTONOMY** 6
80 **AUTUMN ANGEL** (IRE) 6
125 **AUTUMN BLAZE** 1
251 **AUTUMN DREAM** (IRE) 73
231 **AUTUMN EVENING** 4
387 **AUTUMN FESTIVAL** 5
336 **AUTUMN FLIGHT** (IRE) 2
370 **AUTUMN LIGHTS** 9
281 **AUTUMN RETURN** (IRE) 1
334 **AUTUMN TIDE** (IRE) G 6
383 **AUTUMN WINTER** (IRE) 109
355 **AUTUMN'S BREEZE** (IRE) 152
75 **AUTUMNAL DANCER** (IRE) 1
326 **AVAILABLE ANGEL** 2
70 **AVARICE** (IRE) 6
305 **AVENBURY** F 38
286 **AVIEMORE** 137
385 **AVIEWTOSEA** (IRE) 13
355 **AVILES** (FR) 8
405 **AVIZARE** (IRE) F 22
102 **AVOID DE MASTER** (IRE) 3
361 **AVON LIGHT** 15
112 **AWAAL** (IRE) 4
501 **AWARD DANCER** (IRE) 2
416 **AWAY DAY** (IRE) 38
402 **AWAYTHELAD** (IRE) 6
14 **AWESOME DANCER** (IRE) 2
504 **AWESOME FOURSOME** 1
477 **AWESOME GEORGIE** (IRE) 11
383 **AWESOME MARIA** (USA) C 110
89 **AWESOMETANK** C 42
392 **AWORKINGMAN** 1
368 **AWTAAD PRINCE** (IRE) 36
398 **AWTAAR** (IRE) 5
17 **AXEL JACKLIN** 3
393 **AXXELERATION** F 6
207 **AYE RIGHT** (IRE) 1
6 **AYR HARBOUR** 8
282 **AYR OF ELEGANCE** 4
204 **AYR POET** 4
552 **AYYAB** 17
360 **AZAHARA PALACE** 41
138 **AZAIM** 41
387 **AZANO** 6
70 **AZEEZAN** (FR) 53
34 **AZOF DES MOTTES** (FR) 2
15 **AZTEC EMPIRE** (IRE) 4
143 **AZUCENA** (IRE) 13
506 **AZURE ANGEL** 60
138 **AZURE BLUE** (IRE) 5
343 **AZURE MAINE** (IRE) 2
219 **AZWAH** C 123
204 **B ASSOCIATES** (IRE) 42
255 **BA NA HILLS** (IRE) 1
112 **BAAHILL** 21
72 **BABA REZA** 3
385 **BABY BEN** (IRE) 14
231 **BABY CHOU** (IRE) 5
40 **BABY JANE** (IRE) 2
343 **BABY LOVE** C 92
298 **BABY SAGE** 6
366 **BABY SHAM** 2
454 **BABY SPICE** 3
320 **BABY STEPS** 2
365 **BABYDUKE** 1
367 **BACHASSON** (FR) 10
49 **BACK FROM DUBAI** (IRE) 1
199 **BACK IN TENNESSEE** (IRE) 3
292 **BACK ON THE LASH** 3
66 **BACK SEE DAA** 37
469 **BACK TOMORROW** 24
122 **BACK YOURSELF** (IRE) 4
275 **BACKINFORGLORY** (IRE) 1
402 **BAD** (FR) 7
148 **BAD ATTITUDE** 1
50 **BAD COMPANY** 2
384 **BADB** (IRE) 7
205 **BADDESLEY** (IRE) 4
335 **BADLANDS BOY** (IRE) 3
78 **BADRI** 3
346 **BADWEIA** (USA) F 39
119 **BAEZ** 5
366 **BAGAN** 3
295 **BAGHDAD CENTRAL** (IRE) 1
504 **BAGHEERA GINGE** 2
176 **BAGUE D'OR** (IRE) 1
138 **BAHAARAH** (IRE) C 68
325 **BAHAMADAM** C 19
506 **BAHEEJA** F 139
457 **BAHIO BOUM** (FR) 12
534 **BAHTIYAR** (FR) 1
69 **BAIDDAA** (IRE) C 31
526 **BAIKAL** 1
340 **BAILA ME** (GER) F 1
542 **BAILAR CONTIGO** (IRE) 24
368 **BAILEYS DERBYDAY** 2
286 **BAILEYS KHELSTAR** (FR) 40
408 **BAILEYSGUTFEELING** (IRE) 2
38 **BAILY GORSE** (IRE) 1
501 **BAJAN BANDIT** 41
494 **BAK ROCKY** (IRE) 1
471 **BAKED ALASKA** 2
336 **BAKERSBOY** 3
418 **BAKEWELL** 1
454 **BAL AMIE** (FR) 4
497 **BALA BROOK** 7
56 **BALA HATUN** 43
85 **BALAAWY** C 49
299 **BALAGAN** 1
347 **BALALAIKA** (IRE) 98
43 **BALANCE** C 101
24 **BALANCE PLAY** (IRE) 25
395 **BALBOA** 27
247 **BALCO COASTAL** (FR) 6
40 **BALCOMIE BREEZE** (FR) 3
6 **BALDOMERO** (IRE) 9
95 **BALGAIR** 3
234 **BALGOWAN** (IRE) 5
479 **BALHAMBAR** (FR) 3
376 **BALI BODY** (IRE) 5
363 **BALINESKER BEACH** (IRE) 7
453 **BALIYAD** (IRE) 2
542 **BALIYKA** (IRE) F 47
20 **BALKALIN** (FR) 2
245 **BALKEO** (FR) 1
445 **BALKING** (FR) 3
539 **BALKO SAINT** (FR) 3
226 **BALKOTIC** (FR) 6
335 **BALLABAWN** (IRE) 4
454 **BALLAQUANE** (IRE) 5
282 **BALLELA SUNRISE** (IRE) 5

406 **BALLET BLANC** 1
383 **BALLGOWN** (IRE) 22
435 **BALLIN BAY** (IRE) 2
543 **BALLINGERS CORNER** (IRE) 3
423 **BALLINOULART** (IRE) 1
537 **BALLINSKER** (IRE) 8
133 **BALLINSLEA BRIDGE** (IRE) 1
208 **BALLINTOGHER BOY** (IRE) 2
348 **BALLINTOY HARBOUR** (IRE) 3
504 **BALLINTUBBER BOY** (IRE) 3
383 **BALLSBRIDGE** (USA) 23
87 **BALLY DUN** (IRE) 2
504 **BALLYANDY** 4
440 **BALLYARE** 7
252 **BALLYATTY** 1
337 **BALLYBAY** (IRE) 1
337 **BALLYBAYMOONSHINER** (FR) 2
489 **BALLYBEEN** (IRE) 7
335 **BALLYBEG BOSS** (IRE) 5
311 **BALLYBEGG** (IRE) 2
537 **BALLYBREEN** (IRE) 9
141 **BALLYBREEZE** 1
45 **BALLYBROWNEY HALL** (IRE) F 1
295 **BALLYCALLAN FAME** (IRE) 2
504 **BALLYCAMUS** (IRE) 5
72 **BALLYCONNEELY BAY** (IRE) 4
363 **BALLYCORRIGAN** (IRE) F 8
282 **BALLYCROSS** 6
254 **BALLYDISCO** (IRE) 5
383 **BALLYDOYLE** (IRE) F 111
248 **BALLYEGAN HERO** (IRE) 2
504 **BALLYELLIS** (IRE) 6
547 **BALLYFARSOON** (IRE) 1
335 **BALLYGEARY** (IRE) 6
140 **BALLYGOE** (IRE) 3
457 **BALLYGRIFINCOTTAGE** (IRE) 13
247 **BALLYHIGH** (IRE) 7
385 **BALLYHOME** (IRE) 15
398 **BALLYKESSANGEL** (IRE) 6
240 **BALLYMAGROARTY BOY** (IRE) 3
363 **BALLYMILAN** 9
228 **BALLYMORE VISION** 36
183 **BALLYNAGRAN** (IRE) 1
4 **BALLYNAVEEN BOY** (IRE) 3
347 **BALLYPOREEN** (IRE) 6
358 **BALLYSEEDY** (IRE) 1
292 **BALLYVANGO** (IRE) 4
282 **BALLYVAUGHAN BAY** (IRE) 7
281 **BALLYWHATSIT** (IRE) 2
457 **BALLYWITE** (IRE) 14
73 **BALLYWOOD** (FR) 1
261 **BALMY BREESE** 22
18 **BALQAA** 2
223 **BALRANALD** (FR) 1
112 **BALSAMINE** (USA) C 61
92 **BALTIC** 19
94 **BALTIC EMPRESS** (IRE) 38
24 **BALTIC VOYAGE** 26
26 **BALTIMORE BOY** (IRE) 4
349 **BAMA LAMA** 4
300 **BAMBOO BAY** (IRE) 7
448 **BAMPTON STAR** 2
135 **BANANA** 7
6 **BANCNUANAHEIREANN** (IRE) 10
239 **BAND OF OUTLAWS** (IRE) 5
552 **BAND OF STEEL** 18
35 **BANDDAR** (IRE) 61
26 **BANDERAS** (IRE) 19
5 **BANDINELLI** 4
226 **BANDIT D'AINAY** (FR) 7
528 **BANDOL** (IRE) 1
283 **BANG ON THE BELL** 4
402 **BANGERS AND CASH** (IRE) 8
457 **BANJAXED GIRL** F 15
17 **BANKRUPT** (IRE) 4
204 **BANNER ROAD** (IRE) 5
200 **BANNISTER** (FR) 1
438 **BANNIXTOWN BOY** (IRE) 2
226 **BANNOCKBURN** (FR) 8
306 **BANNOW BAY BOY** (IRE) 2
123 **BANNOW STORM** (IRE) C 2
144 **BANNSIDE** (IRE) 2
72 **BANQUO** (IRE) 40
391 **BANSHEE** (IRE) 1
379 **BANTEER** (IRE) 5
392 **BANTRY** 2
273 **BAPTISM OF FIRE** (IRE) 1
251 **BAQQA** (IRE) F 74
366 **BAR THYME** (IRE) 4
43 **BARADAR** (IRE) 5
148 **BARATHEA DANCER** (IRE) F 15
554 **BARB WIRE** 1
379 **BARBADOS BUCK'S** (IRE) 6
252 **BARBARIAN** 2
490 **BARBAROSA** (IRE) 2
343 **BARBARY MASTER** 3
321 **BARBILL** (IRE) 4
527 **BARD OF BRITTANY** 4
388 **BARDD** (IRE) 1
12 **BARE ASSETS** (IRE) 3
390 **BARE MEADOWS** (IRE) 9
335 **BAREBACK JACK** (IRE) 7
387 **BAREFOOT WARRIOR** (IRE) 95
387 **BARENBOIM** 7
527 **BAREST OF MARGINS** (IRE) 5
272 **BARFORD DIVA** 2
272 **BARFORD GROOVER** 3
521 **BARGING THRU** 6
234 **BARI BREEZE** (IRE) 6
154 **BARLEY** (IRE) 5
300 **BARLEY BREEZE** 8
285 **BARLEYBROWN** 20
275 **BARLOGE CREEK** (IRE) M 2
6 **BARLOW BARLOW** 89
335 **BARNABAS COLLINS** (IRE) 8
442 **BARNABY** (IRE) 63
363 **BARNARDS GREEN** (IRE) 10
55 **BARNAVIDDAUN** (IRE) 1
104 **BARNAY** 1
380 **BARNEY STINSON** (IRE) 2
538 **BARNEY'S ANGEL** 7
154 **BARNEY'S BAY** 6
221 **BARNEY'S JOY** 18
300 **BARNEYS GIFT** (FR) 9
161 **BARON DE MIDLETON** (IRE) 1
66 **BARON RUN** 2
369 **BARONY LEGENDS** (IRE) 5
85 **BAROQUE STAR** (IRE) 1
496 **BAROSSA** (IRE) 23
385 **BARRAKHOV** (IRE) 16
258 **BARRANCO** (IRE) 2
42 **BARREL AGED** 14
369 **BARRICANE** 6
335 **BARRICHELLO** 9
15 **BARRIER** (FR) 39
410 **BARRIER PEAKS** (FR) 6
524 **BARRISTER BLASTER** 2
501 **BARROLO** 42
366 **BARROWMOUNT** (IRE) 5
444 **BARRYOKI** 1
92 **BARTER** C 55
403 **BARTHOLOMEW J** (IRE) 2
326 **BARTON KNOLL** 3
23 **BARYSHNIKOV** 5
285 **BASCINET** 2
270 **BASCULE** (FR) 2
112 **BASE NOTE** 5
74 **BASFORD** (IRE) 2
283 **BASHARAT** 5
83 **BASHERS REFLECTION** 2
279 **BASHFUL** 5
410 **BASHFUL BOY** (IRE) 7
410 **BASHFUL KATE** (IRE) 8
18 **BASHOLO** (IRE) 3
24 **BASIC INSTINCT** (IRE) 87
366 **BASILETTE** (IRE) 6
251 **BASQUE BEAUTY** C 75
95 **BASS PLAYER** (IRE) 4
494 **BASS ROCK** (FR) 2
527 **BASS STRAIT** 6
88 **BASSAC** (FR) 21
92 **BATAL DUBAI** (IRE) 20
278 **BATCH ME** 1
193 **BATCHELOR BOY** (IRE) 1
300 **BATEAU BAY** (IRE) 10
285 **BATED BREEZE** (IRE) 45
98 **BATEMAN** (IRE) 29
24 **BATEMANS BAY** (FR) 27
385 **BATHIVA** (FR) 17
15 **BATISTET** 40
347 **BATMAN FOR EVER** (GER) 7
52 **BATSMAN** 1
399 **BATTERED** 2
206 **BATTISTA** (IRE) 50
140 **BATTLE MARCH** (USA) 4
441 **BATTLE OF MARATHON** (USA) 2
352 **BATTLE OF TORO** (IRE) 2
10 **BATTLE POINT** (IRE) 4
114 **BATTLEOFBALTIMORE** 10
363 **BATWOMEN** (IRE) 11
515 **BAUHINIA RHAPSODY** 23
285 **BAULAC** 21
225 **BAVINGTON BOB** (IRE) 1
443 **BAWAADER** (IRE) 1
490 **BAY BELLE** 3
154 **BAY BREEZE** 7
479 **BAY BRIDGE** 4
513 **BAY DREAM BELIEVER** (IRE) 7
5 **BAY OF HONOUR** (IRE) 5
153 **BAY OF HOPE** (IRE) 51
249 **BAY OF NAPLES** (IRE) 3
201 **BAY SAM BELLA** 1
450 **BAYA LESCRIBAA** (FR) 1
485 **BAYRAAT** 1
286 **BAYSHORE FREEWAY** (IRE) F 138
18 **BAZALGETTE** (IRE) 4
66 **BAZBALL** (IRE) 94
342 **BAZZANA** C 19
267 **BBOLD** (IRE) 3
56 **BE AMAZING** (IRE) F 71
325 **BE BE EX** (IRE) 1

286 **BE FABULOUS** (GER) F 139
80 **BE FAIR** 7
75 **BE FRANK** 15
383 **BE HAPPY** (IRE) 24
347 **BE MINE TONIGHT** (IRE) G 99
80 **BE MY SEA** (IRE) 8
54 **BE PREPARED** 1
204 **BE PROUD** (IRE) 6
455 **BE THE BEST** (USA) 2
300 **BE THE DIFFERENCE** (IRE) 11
88 **BE THE KING** (FR) 22
464 **BEA MY SHADOW** 6
471 **BEACH CANDY** (IRE) F 24
303 **BEACH KITTY** (IRE) 15
303 **BEACH POINT** (IRE) 29
390 **BEACHCOMBER** (FR) 10
343 **BEACON EDGE** (IRE) 4
457 **BEAKSTOWN** (IRE) 16
265 **BEAMING** 1
265 **BEAMING** C 12
306 **BEAN NORTY** 3
262 **BEANIE BLUE** 17
314 **BEANNAIGH DO** (IRE) 1
532 **BEANRI MHAITH** (IRE) G 4
418 **BEAR A HAND** 2
413 **BEAR FORCE** (IRE) 18
488 **BEAR FORCE ONE** 2
332 **BEAR GHYLLS** (IRE) 3
408 **BEAR ON THE LOOSE** (IRE) 28
542 **BEAR PROFIT** (IRE) 2
10 **BEAR TO DREAM** (IRE) 5
470 **BEARAWAY** (IRE) 1
169 **BEARCARDI** (IRE) 2
80 **BEARING BOB** 9
24 **BEARLITA** (GER) C 88
32 **BEARWITH** 1
492 **BEAST OF BURDEN** 1
168 **BEAT BOX** (FR) 2
189 **BEAT THE BAT** (IRE) 6
11 **BEAT THE BREEZE** 1
154 **BEAT THE EDGE** (IRE) 8
50 **BEAT THE HEAT** 3
1 **BEAT THE RETREAT** (IRE) 5
147 **BEAT THE STORM** (IRE) 4
251 **BEATIFY** (IRE) F 25
387 **BEATIFY** (IRE) C 96
116 **BEATTHEBULLET** (IRE) 1
379 **BEAU BALKO** (FR) 7
302 **BEAU GARS** 12
80 **BEAU GESTE** (IRE) 10
121 **BEAU HAZE** 1
54 **BEAU JARDINE** (IRE) 2
43 **BEAU ROC** 37
95 **BEAU VINTAGE** 14
10 **BEAUEN ARROWS** 6
275 **BEAUFORT WEST** (IRE) 3
14 **BEAULD AS BRASS** 43
383 **BEAULY** C 112
209 **BEAUMADIER** (IRE) 12
102 **BEAUMESNIL** (FR) 4
193 **BEAUPARC SEVEN** 2
504 **BEAUPORT** (IRE) 7
284 **BEAUTIFUL CROWN** 3
112 **BEAUTIFUL ENDING** C 62
286 **BEAUTIFUL EYES** 41
43 **BEAUTIFUL FILLY** F 102
112 **BEAUTIFUL MEMORY** (IRE) C 63
35 **BEAUTIFUL SECRET** 2
5 **BEAUTIFUL SUMMER** 53
176 **BEAUTIFUL SUNRISE** (IRE) 15
240 **BEAUTIFUL SURPRISE** 4
43 **BEAUTIFULASALWAYS** 38
154 **BEAUTRON** 98
153 **BEAUTY CHOICE** 3
42 **BEAUTY GENERATION** (IRE) 50
374 **BEAUTY TO BEHOLD** (IRE) 2
231 **BEAUTY'S STAR** (IRE) 41
361 **BEAUZEE** 16
387 **BEAUZON** 8
537 **BEBRAVEFORGLORY** (IRE) 10
208 **BEBSIDE BANTER** (IRE) 3
175 **BECCARA ROSE** (IRE) 23
475 **BECOMING** (IRE) 3
400 **BEDFORD BLAZE** (IRE) 2
169 **BEDFORD FLYER** (IRE) 3
220 **BEDFORD HOUSE** 2
70 **BEEBEE** 7
208 **BEECHMOUNT** (IRE) 4
214 **BEECHWOOD ISABELLE** 7
176 **BEELZEBUB** (IRE) 16
349 **BEENHAM** 31
386 **BEEP BEEP BURROW** (IRE) 1
489 **BEFORE MIDNIGHT** 8
360 **BEGGARMAN** 3
66 **BEGGARMANS ROAD** (IRE) 3
21 **BEGIN THE LUCK** (IRE) 1
383 **BEGINNINGS** (USA) 25
293 **BEGOODTOYOURSELF** (IRE) 1
410 **BEHIND THE CURTAIN** (IRE) 9
484 **BEHIND THE SCENES** (IRE) 11
12 **BEHIND THE VEIL** 4
466 **BEHOLDEN** 3
211 **BEL MARE** 5
94 **BELAFONTE** 14
360 **BELAMINDAR** 67
202 **BELARGUS** (FR) 2
305 **BELATED** 17
107 **BELDALE MEMORY** (IRE) C 65
497 **BELGARUM** (IRE) 8
164 **BELHAVEN** (IRE) 7
479 **BELIEVE IN STARS** (IRE) 5
369 **BELIEVE JACK** (FR) 7
328 **BELIEVE YOU ME** (IRE) 21
43 **BELIEVING** (IRE) 39
15 **BELL SONG** (FR) 41
532 **BELLA BLUESKY** 5
292 **BELLA CIAO** 5
132 **BELLA CIVENA** (IRE) 2
30 **BELLA COLOROSSA** 1
251 **BELLA ESTRELLA** (IRE) C 76
496 **BELLA KOPELLA** (IRE) 24
152 **BELLA MADONNA** 1
135 **BELLA SOFIA** H 8
107 **BELLA TASLINA** 66
390 **BELLA VENEZIA** (IRE) F 11
302 **BELLA'S PEARL** 1
98 **BELLADONNA** C 30
57 **BELLAGIO MAN** (IRE) 4
164 **BELLAJEU** F 36
210 **BELLAMY'S GREY** 1
543 **BELLATRIXSA** (IRE) 4
228 **BELLE DAUPHINE** F 124
146 **BELLE DORMANT** (IRE) F 57
306 **BELLE FORTUNE** (IRE) G 4
154 **BELLE JOSEPHINE** C 159
226 **BELLE NA BANN** (IRE) 9
119 **BELLE OF ANNANDALE** (IRE) 6
543 **BELLE SAINT** 5
227 **BELLELOISE** 1
83 **BELLES BENEFIT** (IRE) 3
31 **BELLINGHAM** 12
350 **BELLISSIMO MILAN** (IRE) 1
346 **BELLOCCIO** (FR) 2
352 **BELLS EXPRESS** (IRE) 3
507 **BELLS OF PETERBORO** (IRE) 3
507 **BELLS OF RUTLAND** (IRE) 4
507 **BELLS OF STAMFORD** (IRE) 5
125 **BELLSHILL BEAUTY** (IRE) 2
469 **BELO HORIZONTE** 25
383 **BELONG** (IRE) F 113
148 **BELOVED OF ALL** (IRE) 2
442 **BELSITO** (GER) 26
206 **BELT BUCKLE** 2
119 **BELTANE** (IRE) 7
290 **BELVEDERE BLAST** (IRE) 2
484 **BELVOIR DIVA** C 40
4 **BEMPTON CLIFFS** (IRE) 4
434 **BEN ASKER** (IRE) 2
282 **BEN BRODY** (IRE) 8
292 **BEN BUIE** (IRE) 6
303 **BEN DIKDUK** (IRE) 16
410 **BEN LILLY** (IRE) 10
395 **BEN LOMOND** (IRE) 28
348 **BEN MACDUI** (IRE) 4
168 **BENACK** (IRE) 3
286 **BENACRE** (IRE) 42
171 **BENADALID** 1
21 **BENANDGONE** 2
369 **BENASSI** (IRE) 8
301 **BEND THE LIGHT** 10
247 **BENEFACT** (IRE) 8
66 **BENEFICIARY** 4
153 **BENGERS LASS** (USA) C 75
369 **BENIGN DICTATOR** (IRE) 9
420 **BENITO** (FR) 2
298 **BENJAMIN BEAR** (IRE) 7
154 **BENNY BALOO** 9
504 **BENNY SILVER** (IRE) 8
457 **BENNY'S OSCAR** (IRE) 17
457 **BENNYS KING** (IRE) 18
317 **BENSINI** 1
494 **BENSON** 3
205 **BENTLEY'S RETURN** (IRE) 5
335 **BENTS HOLLOW** (IRE) 10
452 **BENVILLE BRIDGE** 1
379 **BENY NAHAR ROAD** (IRE) 8
475 **BERAGON** 17
343 **BERAMANA** C 93
72 **BERAZ** 5
457 **BERAZ** (FR) 19
222 **BERG NELLIE** (IRE) 1
286 **BERGAMASK** (USA) C 140
442 **BERGERAC** (IRE) 2
298 **BERINGER** 8
15 **BERKSHIRE BRAVE** (IRE) 42
15 **BERKSHIRE BREEZE** (IRE) 5
15 **BERKSHIRE CRUZ** (IRE) 43
175 **BERKSHIRE HONEY** C 45
15 **BERKSHIRE PHANTOM** (IRE) 44
15 **BERKSHIRE ROCCO** (FR) 6
293 **BERKSHIRE ROYAL** 2

367 **BERKSHIRE ROYAL** 11
15 **BERKSHIRE SHADOW** 7
15 **BERKSHIRE SUNDANCE** (IRE) 45
366 **BERLAIS DU GEORGE** 7
189 **BERMEO** (IRE) 7
172 **BERNADINE** (IRE) 19
260 **BERNARD SPIERPOINT** 2
469 **BERNARDO O'REILLY** 1
24 **BERNESE** 89
30 **BERRAHRI** (IRE) 2
138 **BERRY EDGE** (IRE) 6
31 **BERRYGATE** (IRE) 42
23 **BERT KIBBLER** 6
240 **BERT WILSON** (IRE) 5
44 **BERTIE** B 2
308 **BERTIE BLUE** 4
497 **BERTIE WOOSTER** (IRE) 9
445 **BERTIE'S BALLET** 4
390 **BERTIE'S BANDANA** (IRE) 12
74 **BERTIE'S WISH** (IRE) 3
244 **BERTIELICIOUS** 1
383 **BERTINELLI** (USA) 26
286 **BERWICK LAW** (IRE) 43
28 **BERYL BURTON** 1
75 **BESET** 28
219 **BESHAAYIR** C 124
175 **BESPOKE** 46
61 **BESSAH** 2
282 **BEST MATE DAVE** 9
141 **BEST PAL** (IRE) 2
459 **BEST TERMS** C 23
369 **BEST TRITION** (IRE) 10
418 **BESTGETGOING** (IRE) 3
40 **BESTIARIUS** (IRE) 4
342 **BESTIE** 20
205 **BETGOODWIN** (FR) 6
270 **BETHERSDEN BOY** (IRE) 3
390 **BETHKA** (IRE) 13
308 **BETHPAGE** (IRE) 5
35 **BETIMES** F 62
207 **BETTER BE DEFINITE** 2
428 **BETTER GETALONG** (IRE) 2
298 **BETTERFOREVERYONE** 9
125 **BETTWYN** 3
154 **BETTY BALOO** 10
272 **BETTY FLETCHER** 4
309 **BETTY ROE** (IRE) F 3
390 **BETTY'S BANJO** (IRE) 14
402 **BETTY'S BELLE** 9
402 **BETTY'S TIARA** 10
231 **BETULA** 106
164 **BETWEEN THE COVERS** (IRE) 17
247 **BETWEEN WATERS** (IRE) 9
85 **BETWEENTHESTICKS** 15
26 **BEVERAGINO** (IRE) 55
384 **BEWARE** (IRE) 8
347 **BEWARE OF SAM** 8
290 **BEYOND BEAUTY** (IRE) 20
24 **BEYOND DESIRE** C 90
302 **BEYOND EQUAL** 2
249 **BEYOND INFINITY** 4
5 **BEYOND REASON** (IRE) C 135
132 **BEYOND REDEMPTION** (IRE) 3
426 **BEYOND SUPREMACY** (IRE) 1
24 **BEYOND THE SEA** (USA) C 91
231 **BEYOND THE STEPS** (IRE) 42
80 **BEZZAS LAD** (IRE) 11
385 **BHALOO** (IRE) 18
84 **BHUBEZI** 2
193 **BIBURYINMAY** 3
501 **BICEP** (IRE) 3
488 **BICKERSTAFFE** 3
442 **BIELSA** (IRE) 3
327 **BIG 'N BETTER** 1
390 **BIG AMBITIONS** (IRE) 15
207 **BIG ARTHUR** 3
428 **BIG BAD BEAR** (IRE) 3
414 **BIG BAD BUZZ** (IRE) 2
496 **BIG BAD WOLF** (IRE) 25
355 **BIG BARD** 9
526 **BIG BEAR HUG** 2
183 **BIG BEE HIVE** (IRE) 2
306 **BIG BLUE MOON** 5
286 **BIG BONED** (USA) F 141
298 **BIG BOY BOBBY** (IRE) 10
59 **BIG BRESIL** 3
285 **BIG BROWN BEAR** (IRE) 46
357 **BIG CHANGES** 3
31 **BIG CHEESE** (FR) 1
282 **BIG CITY LIFE** 10
424 **BIG DIFFERENCE** (IRE) 2
329 **BIG DUTCHIE** (IRE) 1
308 **BIG FISH** (IRE) 6
352 **BIG GANGSTA** (IRE) 4
56 **BIG IMPACT** 5
211 **BIG JIM BEAM** (IRE) 6
355 **BIG JIMBO** 10
35 **BIG MEETING** (IRE) 3
185 **BIG MUDDY** 2
6 **BIG NARSTIE** (FR) 11
285 **BIG R** (IRE) 22
440 **BIG RIVER** (IRE) 8
66 **BIG SKY** F 95
35 **BIG TEAM** (USA) 4
387 **BIG TED** (IRE) 97
336 **BIG TIME MAYBE** (IRE) 4
82 **BIG WING** (IRE) 2
362 **BIGBADBOY** (IRE) 2
24 **BIGGLES** 2
197 **BIGNORM** (IRE) 1
340 **BILBOA RIVER** (IRE) 2
122 **BILINGUAL** 5
211 **BILL BAXTER** (IRE) 7
466 **BILL JACK** (IRE) 4
336 **BILL PLUMB** (IRE) 5
164 **BILL SILVERS** 18
92 **BILLABONG** 21
14 **BILLAKI MOU** (FR) 44
385 **BILLAMS LEGACY** 19
367 **BILLAWAY** (IRE) 12
300 **BILLIAN** (IRE) 12
500 **BILLIE ERIA** (IRE) C 22
526 **BILLIE LOU** 27
188 **BILLIEBROOKEDIT** (IRE) 6
423 **BILLINGSLEY** (IRE) 2
532 **BILLY BATHGATE** 6
385 **BILLY BOI BLUE** 20
431 **BILLY BUTCHER** (IRE) 1
185 **BILLY DYLAN** (IRE) 3
349 **BILLY MILL** 5
138 **BILLY NO MATES** (IRE) 7
533 **BILLY ROBERTS** (IRE) 1
344 **BILLY WEDGE** 1
165 **BILLY'S JOY** 20
143 **BILLYB** (FR) 2
387 **BIN HAYYAN** (IRE) 9
263 **BING BELLE** 4
402 **BINGLEY CROCKER** (IRE) 106
402 **BINGO LITTLE** (IRE) 11
352 **BINGOO** 5
442 **BINT AL DAAR** 27
384 **BINT AL REEM** (IRE) C 32
35 **BINT ALMATAR** (USA) C 86
506 **BINT HUWAAR** (USA) C 140
463 **BINTHEREDONETHAT** (IRE) 1
390 **BIOWAVEGO** (IRE) 16
511 **BIPLANE** (USA) 1
5 **BIRCH GROVE** (IRE) F 136
505 **BIRD FOR LIFE** 4
515 **BIRD KEY** F 68
290 **BIRD OF LIGHT** (IRE) C 26
192 **BIRD OF PLAY** (IRE) 43
335 **BIRD ON THE WIRE** (FR) 11
157 **BIRDHOUSE** 5
491 **BIRDIE BOWERS** (IRE) 1
240 **BIRDIE PUTT** (IRE) 6
92 **BIRDLAND LULLABY** 22
275 **BIRDMAN BOB** (IRE) 4
251 **BIRI'S ANGEL** (IRE) F 77
348 **BIRKENHEAD** 5
356 **BIRKIE BOY** (IRE) 16
53 **BIRKIE GIRL** 1
521 **BIRTHDAY ANGEL** (IRE) 50
294 **BISCOFF JOE** 7
285 **BISHOP'S CROWN** 23
521 **BISHOP'S GLORY** (IRE) 51
298 **BIT HARSH** (IRE) 11
513 **BIT OF A QUIRKE** 8
4 **BITASWEETSYMPHONY** (IRE) 5
293 **BITHYNIA** (IRE) G 15
440 **BIX BEIDERBECKE** (FR) 9
15 **BIZARRE LAW** 8
457 **BIZZY MOON** 20
56 **BLACK BOX** 6
80 **BLACK BUBLE** (FR) 12
552 **BLACK CAESAR** (IRE) 2
35 **BLACK DIAMOND** (IRE) 63
463 **BLACK FRIDAY** 2
94 **BLACK GEM** (IRE) 39
355 **BLACK GERRY** (IRE) 11
343 **BLACK HAWK EAGLE** (IRE) 5
385 **BLACK KALANISI** (IRE) 21
268 **BLACK LIGHTNING** (IRE) 1
382 **BLACK MARKET** (IRE) 1
9 **BLACK MINSTER** 1
44 **BLACK OF THE GLADE** (FR) 3
277 **BLACK OPIUM** 1
311 **BLACK POPPY** 3
132 **BLACK ROCK LADY** (IRE) G 4
423 **BLACK SAM VICKI** 3
530 **BLACK TONIC** 1
41 **BLACKBIRDFLY** (ITY) 2
504 **BLACKCAUSEWAY** 9
61 **BLACKCURRENT** 3
66 **BLACKGOLD FAIRY** (USA) C 96
147 **BLACKHILLSOFDAKOTA** (IRE) 5
272 **BLACKHORSE LADY** (IRE) 5
61 **BLACKJACK** 4
379 **BLACKJACK KENTUCKY** (IRE) 9
263 **BLACKJACK MAGIC** 5
99 **BLACKJAX** F 14

537 **BLACKO** (FR) 11
488 **BLACKROD** 4
208 **BLACKSAMMHOR** 5
21 **BLACKWATER BAY** (IRE) G 3
357 **BLACKWELL BAY** (IRE) 4
205 **BLADE RUNNER** (FR) 7
247 **BLAIRGOWRIE** (IRE) 10
354 **BLAIRLOGIE** 2
387 **BLAISE PASCAL** (IRE) 98
335 **BLAKENEY POINT** 12
326 **BLAKER** (IRE) 19
457 **BLAKLION** 21
330 **BLAME CULTURE** (USA) 1
298 **BLAME IT ON SALLY** (IRE) 12
102 **BLAME ROSE** (IRE) 5
491 **BLAME THE FARRIER** (IRE) 2
205 **BLAME THE GAME** (IRE) 8
231 **BLANC DE NOIR** (IRE) 43
440 **BLANCHEFLEUR** (IRE) C 99
89 **BLANCHLAND** (IRE) 19
366 **BLASE CHEVALIER** (IRE) G 8
179 **BLAZE A TRAIL** (IRE) 4
488 **BLAZEON FIVE** 5
450 **BLAZER TWO** 2
125 **BLAZER'S MILL** (IRE) 4
292 **BLAZING COURT** (IRE) 7
1 **BLAZING PORT** (IRE) 6
440 **BLAZING SHIROCCO** (IRE) 10
459 **BLAZING SON** 2
390 **BLAZING SONNET** (IRE) G 17
219 **BLEAK** (IRE) 48
504 **BLENDED STEALTH** 10
42 **BLENHEIM PRINCE** 15
88 **BLESS** (FR) 23
456 **BLESS HIM** (IRE) 2
26 **BLETCHLEY STORM** 20
367 **BLEU BERRY** (FR) 13
484 **BLHADAWA** (IRE) F 41
6 **BLIND BEGGAR** (IRE) 12
416 **BLINDEDBYTHELIGHTS** (GER) 14
515 **BLING ON THE MUSIC** 2
24 **BLINKING** F 92
321 **BLISSFILLY** 41
293 **BLISTERING BARNEY** (IRE) 3
147 **BLITZ SPIRIT** (IRE) 6
94 **BLLUSHING** 3
408 **BLOCKADE** (IRE) F 61
379 **BLODGE** (IRE) G 10
347 **BLOFELD** (IRE) 9
251 **BLOODHOUND** (IRE) 26
462 **BLOOMING FORTUNE** (IRE) 2
440 **BLOORIEDOTCOM** (IRE) 11
66 **BLOSSOM MILLS** C 97
286 **BLOSSOMTIME** F 142
450 **BLOW THE BUDGET** 3
538 **BLOW YOUR HORN** (IRE) 8
306 **BLOW YOUR WAD** (IRE) 6
110 **BLUE AEGEAN** F 2
24 **BLUE AKOYA** 93
254 **BLUE ANCHOR** 6
286 **BLUE ANTARES** (IRE) 44
474 **BLUE ARTICLE** (IRE) G 3
494 **BLUE BALOO** (IRE) 4
439 **BLUE BEACH** 2
402 **BLUE BETTY** 107
385 **BLUE BIKINI** 22
47 **BLUE BRASILIAN** 2
457 **BLUE BUBBLES** 22
385 **BLUE CLOVER** 23
228 **BLUE COLLAR** (IRE) 125
56 **BLUE COLLAR LAD** 7
56 **BLUE COLLAR LASS** 8
157 **BLUE DAUPHIN** 6
335 **BLUE FIN** (IRE) 13
542 **BLUE FLAME** (IRE) 3
387 **BLUE FOR YOU** (IRE) 10
99 **BLUE HAWAII** (IRE) 1
151 **BLUE HEAVEN** 1
548 **BLUE HERO** (CAN) 3
59 **BLUE HOP** (IRE) 4
207 **BLUE INDIGO** 16
429 **BLUE JAY WAY** 6
367 **BLUE LORD** (FR) 14
119 **BLUE LYRIC** F 59
457 **BLUE MAXI** (IRE) G 23
219 **BLUE MISSILE** 49
92 **BLUE MIST** 3
93 **BLUE MOON SERENADE** 2
209 **BLUE PEAK** 3
435 **BLUE PLAN** (IRE) 3
87 **BLUE RIBBON** 3
141 **BLUE RIDGE HILL** 3
385 **BLUE SANS** (IRE) 24
367 **BLUE SARI** (FR) 15
390 **BLUE SHARK** (IRE) 18
272 **BLUE SILK** F 21
247 **BLUE STELLO** (FR) 11
363 **BLUE SUEDE SHOES** (IRE) 12
385 **BLUE THE MONEY** 25
94 **BLUE THUNDER** (IRE) 40
5 **BLUE TRAIL** (IRE) 6
286 **BLUE UNIVERSE** (IRE) 45
383 **BLUE WALTZ** C 114
358 **BLUEBELL DIVA** 2
1 **BLUEBELL GLEN** 7
15 **BLUEBELL GROVE** 148
444 **BLUEBELL TIME** (IRE) 2
327 **BLUEBELL WAY** 2
306 **BLUEBELLA** 7
260 **BLUEBELLS BOY** 3
335 **BLUEBERRY WINE** (IRE) 14
203 **BLUEBLOOD** (IRE) 1
219 **BLUEBOTTLE BLUE** 50
26 **BLUEFLAGFLYINGHIGH** (IRE) 21
157 **BLUEGRASS** (IRE) 7
379 **BLUEKING D'OROUX** (FR) 11
285 **BLUELIGHT BAY** (IRE) 24
409 **BLUENOSE BELLE** (USA) 2
24 **BLUESTOCKING** 28
292 **BLUETHORN BOY** 8
106 **BLUFF** 16
196 **BLUFFMEIFYOUCAN** 3
106 **BLYNX** F 29
421 **BO TAIFAN** (IRE) 2
355 **BO ZENITH** (FR) 12
164 **BOADICIA** (IRE) 37
395 **BOAFO BOY** 3
200 **BOAGRIUS** (IRE) 2
154 **BOARDMAN** 11
6 **BOARHUNT** 13
188 **BOASTED** 7
192 **BOASTY** (IRE) 1
390 **BOB BOB RICARD** (IRE) 19
547 **BOB DELANEY** 2
365 **BOB'S GIRL** 2
93 **BOBALOT** 3
61 **BOBBA TEE** 5
528 **BOBBIE THE DAZZLER** (IRE) 2
61 **BOBBING ALONG** 6
402 **BOBBY BOW** (IRE) 12
315 **BOBBY DALTON** 1
520 **BOBBY DASSLER** (IRE) 1
78 **BOBBY JOE LEG** 4
96 **BOBBY KENNEDY** 1
336 **BOBBY ON THE BEAT** (IRE) 6
511 **BOBBY SHAFT** 2
204 **BOBBY SHAFTOE** 7
369 **BOBBY SOCKS** 11
59 **BOBBY THE GREAT** 5
286 **BOBBY'S BLESSING** 4
12 **BOBHOPEORNOHOPE** (IRE) 5
404 **BOBINA** (IRE) 19
507 **BOBMAHLEY** (IRE) 6
483 **BOBO MAC** (IRE) 2
301 **BODEGA NIGHTS** 11
251 **BODORGAN** (IRE) 27
111 **BODROY** (IRE) 2
469 **BODYGROOVE** 26
540 **BOHAMS ROAD** (IRE) 2
286 **BOHEMIAN BREEZE** (IRE) 46
263 **BOHEMIAN LAD** (IRE) 6
440 **BOIS GUILLBERT** (FR) 12
30 **BOLBERRY DOWN** (IRE) 3
5 **BOLD ACT** (IRE) 54
289 **BOLD AND LOYAL** 2
384 **BOLD AS LOVE** (IRE) 9
231 **BOLD DISCOVERY** (USA) 44
247 **BOLD ENDEAVOUR** 12
5 **BOLD LASS** (IRE) C 137
449 **BOLD LIGHT** (IRE) 1
537 **BOLD PLAN** (IRE) 12
247 **BOLD REACTION** (FR) 13
211 **BOLD SOLDIER** 8
138 **BOLD TERRITORIES** (IRE) 8
77 **BOLD VISION** (IRE) 2
220 **BOLDMERE** 3
83 **BOLEYN BOY** (IRE) 4
283 **BOLEYN FOREVER** 31
376 **BOLINTLEA** (IRE) 6
423 **BOLLIN ACROSS** G 4
154 **BOLLIN MARGARET** 12
531 **BOLLIN MATILDA** 1
154 **BOLLIN NEIL** 13
440 **BOLLINGERANDKRUG** (IRE) 13
228 **BOLSHINA** F 126
383 **BOLSHOI BALLET** (IRE) 1
211 **BOLSOVER BILL** (IRE) 9
112 **BOLSTER** 22
113 **BOLT FROM THE BLUE** (USA) 1
144 **BOLT MAN** 3
326 **BOMB SQUAD** (IRE) 4
56 **BOMBASTIC** (IRE) 9
209 **BOMBAY GLORY** (IRE) 4
247 **BOMBAY SAPPHIRE** (IRE) 14
509 **BOMBAY SUNSET** (IRE) 4
509 **BOMBYX** 5
513 **BON RETOUR** (IRE) 9
325 **BON SECRET** 2
393 **BOND ARTIST** (IRE) G 7
6 **BOND BOY** 14
459 **BOND CHAIRMAN** 3

2 **BOND SPIRIT** 3
470 **BOND'S GIRL** F 11
261 **BONDI MAN** 1
14 **BONDI SPICE** (IRE) 3
525 **BONGO MAN** 25
410 **BONHEUR DE BALLON** (FR) 11
204 **BONITO CAVALO** 8
413 **BONNE SUZETTE** (IRE) 19
226 **BONNE VITESSE** (IRE) 10
14 **BONNET** 4
385 **BONNET'S PIECES** F 26
519 **BONNIE BANJO** 1
257 **BONNIE BLANDFORD** 1
144 **BONNIE DAY** (IRE) 4
107 **BONNY ANGEL** 21
531 **BONNY HOUXTY** 2
56 **BONNYRIGG** (IRE) 10
385 **BONTTAY** (IRE) 27
50 **BONUS** 4
448 **BONZA BOY** 3
383 **BOOGIE WOOGIE** (IRE) 27
457 **BOOK OF SECRETS** (IRE) 24
286 **BOOK OF TALES** 47
471 **BOOK OF VERSE** (USA) 3
321 **BOOKMARK** 5
231 **BOOLA BOOLA** (IRE) 6
147 **BOOLAMORE GLORY** (IRE) 7
246 **BOOLEY BEACH** (IRE) 1
247 **BOOM BOOM** (IRE) 15
505 **BOOM BOOM POW** 23
80 **BOOM THE GROOM** (IRE) 13
347 **BOOMSLANG** 10
282 **BOOMTIME BANKER** (IRE) 11
369 **BOOSTER BOB** (IRE) 12
347 **BOOT 'N' SHOE** (IRE) 11
189 **BOOTHILL** (IRE) 8
387 **BOPEDRO** (FR) 11
6 **BORA BORA** 15
474 **BORBOLETA** (IRE) G 4
531 **BORDER FLORA** F 3
215 **BORDER LORD** 1
263 **BORDERLANDS** (IRE) 7
292 **BORDERLINE** (IRE) 9
442 **BORDERLINE BOSS** 64
369 **BOREEN BOY** (IRE) 13
552 **BORGI** (IRE) 3
15 **BORJA** (IRE) C 149
502 **BORN AT MIDNIGHT** 1
98 **BORN CROSS** (IRE) C 31
497 **BORN IN BORRIS** (IRE) 10
416 **BORN RULER** 15
176 **BORN THIS WAY** (IRE) 42
456 **BORN TO DAY** (IRE) F 63
505 **BORN TO PLEASE** 5
463 **BORN TO SPARKLE** 3
410 **BORNTOBEALEADER** (IRE) 12
369 **BORODALE** (IRE) 14
228 **BOSH** (IRE) 3
164 **BOSS DOG** 38
358 **BOSSOFTHEBROWNIES** (IRE) 3
116 **BOSTON JOE** (IRE) 2
506 **BOTANICAL** (IRE) 61
531 **BOTH BARRELS** 4
252 **BOTHIE LADY** (IRE) 3
247 **BOTHWELL BRIDGE** (IRE) 16
355 **BOTOX HAS** (FR) 13
142 **BOTUS FLEMING** 1
546 **BOULIVAR** (IRE) 1
499 **BOUNCING BOBBY** (IRE) 4
209 **BOUNDLESS JOY** (AUS) C 22
212 **BOUNDSY BOY** 5
39 **BOUNTY PURSUIT** 2
497 **BOURBALI** (FR) 11
36 **BOURDING PASS** 2
347 **BOWLAND BELLE** 12
305 **BOWLAND PARK** 4
154 **BOWLAND PRINCE** (IRE) 99
72 **BOWLEAZE** 41
494 **BOWLER JACK** (IRE) 5
354 **BOWMAN** (IRE) 3
402 **BOWTOGREATNESS** (IRE) 13
399 **BOX TO BOX** (IRE) 3
320 **BOXING ALEX** 24
286 **BOY ABOUT TOWN** 5
285 **BOY BROWNING** 25
352 **BOY DE LA VIS** (FR) 6
138 **BOY DOUGLAS** (IRE) 42
177 **BOY GEORGE** 1
228 **BOYFRIEND** 127
371 **BOYNESIDE** 1
394 **BOYS OF WEXFORD** 2
192 **BRABUSACH** (FR) 44
399 **BRAD THE BRIEF** 4
234 **BRADFORD LADY** 7
521 **BRADSELL** 52
204 **BRAES OF DOUNE** 9
84 **BRAGALOT** 19
384 **BRAIDED** (USA) C 33
70 **BRAINS** (IRE) 8
546 **BRAMHAM** (IRE) 2
509 **BRANDISOVA** (IRE) 6
367 **BRANDY LOVE** (IRE) 16
207 **BRANDY MCQUEEN** (IRE) 4
544 **BRANDY STATION** (IRE) 3
324 **BRANSON MISSOURI** (IRE) 1
321 **BRASCA** 6
43 **BRASIL POWER** (FR) 6
286 **BRASILEIRA** C 143
386 **BRASINGAMAN BELLA** 2
471 **BRAULIA** 4
37 **BRAVE BAIRN** (FR) 1
336 **BRAVE DISPLAY** (IRE) 7
521 **BRAVE EMPEROR** (IRE) 53
247 **BRAVE JEN** 17
379 **BRAVE KINGDOM** (FR) 12
416 **BRAVE KNIGHT** 16
26 **BRAVE NATION** (IRE) 22
543 **BRAVE SEASCA** (FR) 6
466 **BRAVEHEART** (IRE) 5
154 **BRAVEHEART BOY** (IRE) 100
379 **BRAVEMANSGAME** (FR) 13
212 **BRAVETHEWAVES** 6
416 **BRAVURA** 17
174 **BRAWBY** (IRE) 1
37 **BRAY DALE** 2
168 **BRAYHILL** (IRE) 4
329 **BRAZEN AKOYA** 2
148 **BRAZEN ARROW** 3
487 **BRAZEN BELLE** 1
70 **BRAZEN GIRL** 9
403 **BRAZEN IDOL** 3
257 **BRAZEN INSANITY** 14
533 **BRAZEN RASCAL** 17
153 **BRAZILIAN BRIDE** (IRE) C 76
70 **BREACH** 10
552 **BREAK POINT** 19
10 **BREAK THE SPELL** (IRE) 37
374 **BREAKDANCE KID** 3
263 **BREAKING COVER** (IRE) 8
20 **BREAKING RECORDS** (IRE) 3
34 **BREAKING THE ICE** (IRE) 3
534 **BREAKING WAVES** (IRE) 2
161 **BREATH CATCHER** 37
477 **BREATH OF WRETS** 18
404 **BREATHTAKER** (IRE) 12
475 **BRECCIA** 4
42 **BREDA CASTLE** C 51
371 **BREEZE OF WIND** (IRE) 2
289 **BREEZYANDBRIGHT** (IRE) 3
232 **BREFFNIBOY** (FR) 1
119 **BREGUET BOY** (IRE) 8
292 **BREIZH ALKO** (FR) 10
434 **BREIZH RIVER** (FR) 3
12 **BRENDAS ASKING** (IRE) 6
270 **BRENTFORD HOPE** 4
206 **BRESSON** 51
369 **BREWIN'UPASTORM** (IRE) 15
219 **BREWING** 6
359 **BRIAN THE SNAIL** (IRE) 2
161 **BRIAN'S JET** (IRE) 2
292 **BRIANNA ROSE** (IRE) 11
543 **BRIANSTORM** (IRE) 7
309 **BRIAR BANK** 4
226 **BRICKADANK** (IRE) 11
383 **BRIDAL DANCE** (IRE) C 115
163 **BRIDES BAY** (IRE) 1
206 **BRIDESTONES** (IRE) 52
74 **BRIDGE ROAD** (IRE) 4
42 **BRIDGE WATER** (FR) 16
343 **BRIDGEHEAD** (IRE) 6
40 **BRIDGET BREEZE** (FR) 5
165 **BRIDLE BEAUTY** 21
385 **BRIEF AMBITION** 28
240 **BRIEF ENCOUNTER** (FR) 43
363 **BRIEF TIMES** (IRE) 13
303 **BRIEF VISIT** C 30
540 **BRIERY EXPRESS** 3
317 **BRIERY VIXEN** F 2
270 **BRIGANTES WARRIOR** 5
42 **BRIGHT APPROACH** (IRE) C 52
72 **BRIGHT AS BUTTONS** 59
442 **BRIGHT BANK** (IRE) F 65
5 **BRIGHT BEACON** C 138
442 **BRIGHT BIRDIE** (IRE) F 66
192 **BRIGHT BOOTS** 45
437 **BRIGHT DAWN** (IRE) 3
66 **BRIGHT DIAMOND** (IRE) 38
228 **BRIGHT EYED** (IRE) C 128
228 **BRIGHT FIRE** (IRE) 129
472 **BRIGHT GLOW** F 29
472 **BRIGHT LEGEND** 8
384 **BRIGHT SAPPHIRE** (IRE) C 34
35 **BRIGHT START** (USA) 5
227 **BRIGHT SUNBIRD** (IRE) 2
206 **BRIGHTLY** (FR) 53
172 **BRIGITTE** 20
298 **BRIJOMI QUEEN** (IRE) F 13
355 **BRILLIANT BLUE** (IRE) 14
35 **BRILLIANT LIGHT** 6
85 **BRINDLEY** (IRE) 50
367 **BRING ON THE NIGHT** 17

240 **BRING THE ACTION** (IRE) 7
516 **BRINGEWOOD BELLE** G 1
410 **BRINKLEY** (FR) 13
413 **BRINTON** 39
85 **BRIONIYA** C 51
206 **BRISBANE ROAD** 54
188 **BRISTOL HILL** (IRE) 8
15 **BRITANNICA** 46
379 **BRITTAS BAY** (FR) 14
413 **BROAD APPEAL** 1
383 **BROADHURST** (IRE) 28
452 **BROADOAK** 2
67 **BROADSHARE** 1
504 **BROADWAY BOY** (IRE) 11
492 **BROADWAY GIRL** 8
1 **BROADWAY JOE** (IRE) 8
216 **BROCKARNO** 1
138 **BROCKLESBY** (IRE) 43
40 **BROCTUNE AZURE** 6
40 **BROCTUNE RED** 7
5 **BRODERIE ANGLAISE** (IRE) C 139
379 **BROKEN HALO** 15
108 **BROKEN SPEAR** 1
386 **BROMPTON CROSS** (IRE) 35
367 **BRONN** (IRE) 18
390 **BROOK BAY** (IRE) 20
376 **BROOKE BRESIL** 7
383 **BROOME** (IRE) 2
12 **BROOMFIELD PRESENT** (IRE) 7
363 **BROOMFIELDS CAVE** (IRE) 14
34 **BROOMFIELDS KAN** (IRE) 4
298 **BROOMHILL ROAD** (IRE) 14
135 **BROOMY LAW** 9
15 **BRORA BREEZE** 47
154 **BROTHER SEBASTIAN** (IRE) 101
390 **BROUGHSHANE** (IRE) 21
262 **BROUGHTONS BERRY** (IRE) F 25
118 **BROUGHTONS COMPASS** 1
321 **BROUGHTONS FLARE** (IRE) 7
255 **BROUGHTONS MISSION** 2
275 **BROWN BULLET** (IRE) 5
209 **BROWN EAGLE** (IRE) 5
23 **BROWNLEE** (IRE) 27
276 **BROXI** (IRE) 2
433 **BRUCIE BONUS** 1
16 **BRULURE NOIRE** (IRE) 3
138 **BRUNCH** 9
270 **BRUNEL CHARM** 6
485 **BRUNELLO BREEZE** 2
414 **BRUSHED UP** 3
41 **BRUTALIST** (IRE) 12
496 **BRYCE** (IRE) 26
440 **BRYDEN** (IRE) 14
140 **BRYHER** 5
47 **BRYN BLACK SAM** 3
47 **BRYN TELESCOPE** 4
18 **BUACHAILL** (IRE) 5
157 **BUBBLE DUBI** (FR) 8
113 **BUBBLES'N'TROUBLES** 2
285 **BUCCABAY** (IRE) 26
363 **BUCEPHALUS** (GER) 15
25 **BUCK DANCING** (IRE) 1
497 **BUCKHORN GEORGE** 12
497 **BUCKHORN ROCCO** 13
466 **BUCKO'S BOY** 6
47 **BUCKS DREAM** (IRE) 5
101 **BUDARRI** 5
440 **BUDDHA SCHEME** (IRE) 15
360 **BUDDING** (IRE) 68
193 **BUDDY'S BEAUTY** 4
532 **BUFORD** 7
375 **BUG BOY** (IRE) 1
75 **BUGANVILLEA** (IRE) 16
319 **BUGISE SEAGULL** (IRE) 4
219 **BUGLE BEADS** 51
521 **BUGLE MAJOR** (USA) 7
343 **BUGS MORAN** (IRE) 7
488 **BUILTINABILITY** 49
379 **BULL AND BUSH** (IRE) G 16
43 **BULLDOG DRUMMOND** 103
286 **BULLDOG SPIRIT** (IRE) 48
226 **BULLDOZE** (IRE) 12
280 **BULLEIT** 1
346 **BULLET** (FR) 17
279 **BULLS AYE** (IRE) 6
475 **BUMBLE BAY** 5
243 **BUMBLEBEE BULLET** (IRE) 39
353 **BUMPTIOUS** F 22
506 **BUMPTIOUS** F 62
507 **BUMPY EVANS** (IRE) 7
410 **BUMPY JOHNSON** (IRE) 14
200 **BUN DORAN** (IRE) 3
166 **BUNGLE BAY** (IRE) 3
283 **BUNGLEDUPINBLUE** (IRE) 6
154 **BUNGLEY** (IRE) 14
303 **BUNKER BAY** (IRE) 2
138 **BUNRAKU** F 69
69 **BUR DUBAI** 32
6 **BURABACK** (IRE) 16
352 **BURBANK** (IRE) 7
26 **BURDETT ROAD** 23
206 **BURGLAR** 55
154 **BURGLAR'S DREAM** (IRE) 102
73 **BURGUNDY MAN** (FR) 2
378 **BURJ MALINKA** (IRE) 2
66 **BURLESQUE STAR** (IRE) F 39
338 **BURLINGTON BERT** (FR) 1
226 **BURNAGE BOY** (IRE) 13
348 **BURNING CASH** (IRE) 6
219 **BURNING RULES** (IRE) C 125
408 **BURNING SKIES** 29
23 **BURNING THE BAILS** 28
367 **BURNING VICTORY** (FR) 19
219 **BURNISH** 52
386 **BURROW SEVEN** 3
464 **BURROWS CLOSE** (FR) 7
464 **BURROWS DIAMOND** (FR) 8
326 **BURROWS DREAM** (FR) 20
464 **BURROWS HALL** (FR) 9
464 **BURROWS LIGHT** (FR) 10
543 **BURROWS PARK** (FR) 8
367 **BURROWS SAINT** (FR) 20
189 **BURROWS TREAT** (FR) 9
219 **BURSINEL** (IRE) 126
405 **BURTONLODGE BEAUTY** (IRE) 1
72 **BURTONWOOD** 6
159 **BURY WALLS** 1
72 **BUSAN** 42
300 **BUSBY** (IRE) 13
506 **BUSH ROSE** 63
503 **BUSHFIRE** 1
491 **BUSHMILL BOY** 3
369 **BUSHTUCKER PARK** (IRE) 16
300 **BUSHYPARK** (IRE) 14
115 **BUSINESS** (FR) 4
285 **BUSSENTO** 27
219 **BUSTAAN** (USA) F 127
513 **BUSTER VALENTINE** (IRE) 10
261 **BUT YOU SAID** (IRE) 2
369 **BUTCH** 17
423 **BUTLER'S BRIEF** (IRE) 5
226 **BUTO** 14
447 **BUTTERFLY EFFECT** (IRE) 6
13 **BUTTERFLY ISLAND** (IRE) 1
497 **BUTTERFLYCOLLECTOR** (IRE) 14
43 **BUTTERSCOTCH** (IRE) C 104
497 **BUTTERWICK BROOK** (IRE) 15
346 **BUXLOW BELLE** (FR) F 40
346 **BUXLOW BOY** 18
538 **BUXTED REEL** (IRE) 9
538 **BUXTED TOO** 10
50 **BUY THE DIP** 17
18 **BUYING MONEY** (IRE) 6
247 **BUZZ** (FR) 18
21 **BY JOVE** 4
387 **BY JUPITER** F 99
502 **BY PASS** 2
247 **BY THE GRACE** 19
15 **BYE BYE SALAM** 150
408 **BYEFORNOW** 30
379 **BYORDEROFTHECOURT** (IRE) 17
270 **BYRON HILL** (IRE) 7
328 **BYRONESS** F 28
112 **BYSTANDER** (IRE) 23
385 **BYZANTINE EMPIRE** 29
343 **BYZANTIUM BELLE** 55
497 **C'EST BLEU** 16
489 **C'EST DIFFERENT** (FR) 53
257 **C'EST NO MOUR** (GER) 2
115 **C'EST QUELQU'UN** (FR) 5
538 **C'MON ELLIE** 80
538 **C'MON KENNY** 11
525 **CABARET GIRL** M 2
520 **CABARET SHOW** (IRE) 9
97 **CABAYO LADY** 1
329 **CABELO** (IRE) F 7
10 **CABEZA DE LLAVE** 7
347 **CABINET MAKER** (IRE) 13
285 **CABINET OF CLOWNS** (IRE) 3
284 **CABLE MOUNTAIN** 4
440 **CABOY** (FR) 16
234 **CABRAKAN** (IRE) 8
43 **CACHET** (IRE) 7
410 **CADEAU D'OR** (FR) 15
76 **CADEAU DU BRESIL** (FR) 1
43 **CADILLAC** (IRE) 8
251 **CADOGAN GARDENS** (IRE) 78
85 **CAERNARFON** 16
514 **CAERULEUM** 3
78 **CAESAR NERO** 5
358 **CAESAR ROCK** (IRE) 4
315 **CAESARS PEARL** (IRE) 9
17 **CAFE ESPRESSO** 5
139 **CAFE MILANO** 3
504 **CAFE PUSHKIN** (FR) 12
80 **CAFE SYDNEY** (IRE) 14
136 **CAILIN DEARG** (IRE) 2
147 **CAILIN SAOIRSE** 8
408 **CAIRN GORM** 3
286 **CAIRNCROSS** (IRE) C 144
252 **CAIRNSFORTH** (IRE) G 4

383 **CAIRO** (IRE) 29
298 **CAIRO KING** (FR) 15
187 **CAITLIN'S COURT** (IRE) 2
346 **CAIUS CHORISTER** (FR) 3
428 **CAIUS MARCIUS** (IRE) 4
349 **CAJUN MOON** F 32
5 **CALARE** (IRE) G 55
162 **CALCULUS** (IRE) 2
153 **CALCUTTA DREAM** (IRE) 4
72 **CALDER VALLEY** (IRE) 43
450 **CALDWELL** 4
521 **CALDY DANCER** (IRE) C 54
43 **CALDY DANCER** (IRE) C 105
447 **CALEDONIA DUCHESS** F 23
239 **CALEVADE** (IRE) 6
129 **CALGARY TIGER** 1
457 **CALICO** (GER) 25
319 **CALIDAD** (IRE) 5
43 **CALIFORNIA GEM** 40
80 **CALIN'S LAD** 15
369 **CALIPSO COLLONGES** (FR) 18
468 **CALISSON** 2
271 **CALL AT MIDNIGHT** F 2
410 **CALL HER CLEVER** (IRE) 16
464 **CALL HIM NOW** (IRE) 11
306 **CALL ME ARTHUR** (IRE) 8
320 **CALL ME DIEGO** (IRE) 25
385 **CALL ME EMMA** (IRE) F 30
181 **CALL ME FREDDIE** 1
204 **CALL ME GINGER** 10
279 **CALL ME HARRY** (IRE) 7
513 **CALL ME JACK** 11
472 **CALL ME KATIE** F 30
247 **CALL ME LORD** (FR) 20
200 **CALL ME RAFA** (IRE) 4
240 **CALL ME SAINTE** (FR) 8
385 **CALL ME TARA** 31
67 **CALL ME TLALOK** 2
177 **CALL MY BLUFF** (IRE) 2
298 **CALL OF THE WILD** (IRE) 16
247 **CALL THE DANCE** 21
440 **CALLE MALVA** (IRE) 17
368 **CALLEVERYONEUKNOW** 37
206 **CALLIGRAPHY** 56
270 **CALLING THE WIND** (IRE) 8
445 **CALLIOPE** 5
164 **CALLISTAN** (IRE) C 39
457 **CALLISTO'S KING** (IRE) 26
43 **CALLUNA** (USA) 41
56 **CALONNE** (IRE) 11
85 **CALSHOT SPIT** (IRE) 17
491 **CALUM GILHOOLEY** (IRE) 4
488 **CALVERT** 50
176 **CALYPSO** (IRE) 17
25 **CALYPSO STORM** (IRE) 2
334 **CAMACHESS** (IRE) 1
442 **CAMACHO STAR** (IRE) 28
172 **CAMBRIA LEGEND** (IRE) 47
457 **CAMDONIAN** (IRE) 27
390 **CAME FROM NOTHING** (IRE) 22
515 **CAME FROM THE DARK** (IRE) 3
231 **CAMELOT ALEXANDER** (IRE) 107
471 **CAMERATA** (GER) 5
66 **CAMILA VARGAS** (IRE) 40
135 **CAMILLE'S SECRET** (FR) F 10
358 **CAMINO ROCK** 5
10 **CAMOUR** (IRE) 38
440 **CAMP BELAN** (IRE) 18
24 **CAMPAIGN TRAIL** (IRE) 29
181 **CAMPESE** 2
266 **CAMPION** F 28
254 **CAMPROND** (FR) 7
286 **CAMUSDARACH** (IRE) 49
378 **CAN TO CAN** (IRE) 9
537 **CAN YOU CALL** 13
218 **CAN YOU SEE HER** 1
394 **CAN'T BEAT HISTORY** (IRE) 3
279 **CAN'T STOP NOW** (IRE) 8
469 **CAN'TSMILEWITHOUTU** (IRE) 2
383 **CANADA WATER** F 116
552 **CANADIANSMOKESHOW** (IRE) 20
316 **CANAL ROCKS** 3
154 **CANARIA PRINCE** 15
176 **CANBERRA LEGEND** (IRE) 18
1 **CANCAN** (FR) 9
399 **CANDLE LIT** (IRE) G 26
270 **CANDLE OF HOPE** 21
219 **CANDLEFORD** (IRE) 7
496 **CANDY CANE** (IRE) 27
485 **CANDY EYE** 6
490 **CANDY LOU** 4
346 **CANDY SHACK** (FR) 4
135 **CANDY WARHOL** (USA) 11
537 **CANFORD LIGHT** (IRE) 14
434 **CANNOCK PARK** 4
5 **CANNON ROCK** 56
515 **CANOODLED** (IRE) 4
153 **CANTALUPO BELLA** 52
43 **CANTORA** 42
308 **CANTY BAY** (IRE) 7
383 **CANUTE** (USA) 30
190 **CANYON CITY** 1
489 **CANYOUSEEME** 9
214 **CANZONE** 1
432 **CAP D'ANTIBES** (IRE) 2
379 **CAP DU MATHAN** (FR) 18
538 **CAP FRANCAIS** 12
94 **CAP SAN ROMAN** (FR) 4
317 **CAP ST VINCENT** (FR) 3
526 **CAP'N** (IRE) 3
383 **CAPE BRIDGEWATER** (IRE) 31
43 **CAPE BUNTING** (IRE) F 106
498 **CAPE CORNWALL ROSE** (IRE) 1
335 **CAPE HELLES** 15
31 **CAPE POINT** 13
263 **CAPE VIDAL** 9
75 **CAPE VINCENT** 17
66 **CAPED LADY** (IRE) C 98
506 **CAPH STAR** 5
286 **CAPITAL THEORY** 6
399 **CAPITANO** 27
153 **CAPLA QUEST** (IRE) 53
367 **CAPODANNO** (FR) 21
138 **CAPOFAN** (IRE) 44
119 **CAPOMENTO** (IRE) C 60
177 **CAPONE** (GER) 3
520 **CAPOTE'S DREAM** (IRE) 2
10 **CAPPANANTY CON** 8
389 **CAPPARATTIN** 1
146 **CAPRICIOUS CANTOR** (IRE) F 58
355 **CAPRICORN PRINCE** 15
360 **CAPRIOLLA** C 69
427 **CAPSTAN** 1
394 **CAPTAIN ATTRIDGE** (IRE) 4
240 **CAPTAIN BILL** (IRE) 9
89 **CAPTAIN BRADY** (IRE) 43
308 **CAPTAIN BROOMFIELD** (IRE) 8
385 **CAPTAIN CATTISTOCK** 32
56 **CAPTAIN CISCO** (IRE) 44
263 **CAPTAIN CLAUDE** (IRE) 10
367 **CAPTAIN CODY** (IRE) 22
18 **CAPTAIN CORCORAN** (IRE) 7
72 **CAPTAIN CORELLI** (IRE) 7
203 **CAPTAIN CUCKOO** 2
228 **CAPTAIN CUDDLES** (IRE) 37
369 **CAPTAIN FANTASTIC** (IRE) 19
328 **CAPTAIN HADDOCK** (IRE) 2
357 **CAPTAIN IVAN** (IRE) 5
141 **CAPTAIN JACK** 4
447 **CAPTAIN KANE** 1
367 **CAPTAIN KANGAROO** (IRE) 23
454 **CAPTAIN LARA** (IRE) 6
539 **CAPTAIN MARVELLOUS** (FR) 34
247 **CAPTAIN MORGS** (IRE) 22
463 **CAPTAIN NELSON** (IRE) 4
286 **CAPTAIN POTTER** 50
67 **CAPTAIN PROBUS** 3
80 **CAPTAIN PUGWASH** (IRE) 16
136 **CAPTAIN QUINT** (IRE) 3
131 **CAPTAIN RED BLAZER** 15
131 **CAPTAIN RYAN** 1
185 **CAPTAIN ST LUCIFER** 4
379 **CAPTAIN TEAGUE** (IRE) 19
376 **CAPTAIN TOM CAT** (IRE) 8
538 **CAPTAIN TOMMY** (IRE) 13
329 **CAPTAIN VALLO** (IRE) 3
70 **CAPTAIN WENTWORTH** 54
352 **CAPTAIN WESTIE** (IRE) 8
24 **CAPTAIN WIERZBA** 30
442 **CAPTAIN WINTERS** 29
134 **CAPTAIN ZEBO** (IRE) 1
135 **CAPTAIN'S BAR** 12
135 **CAPTAINHUGHJAMPTON** 13
319 **CAPTAINS ROAD** (IRE) 6
219 **CAPTURE THE HEART** (IRE) 53
300 **CARACRISTI** 15
538 **CARAGHANN** (FR) 14
488 **CARAGIO** (IRE) 38
361 **CARAMAY** 17
58 **CARAMELLO** (IRE) 1
251 **CARAUSIUS** 1
346 **CARAVANSERAI** (IRE) 19
92 **CARAXES** 23
14 **CARBINE STAR** 45
42 **CARBIS BAY** 17
494 **CARCACI CASTLE** (IRE) 6
205 **CARD DEALER** (IRE) 9
59 **CARDANO** (USA) 6
282 **CARDBOARD GANGSTER** 12
63 **CARDS ARE DEALT** (IRE) 2
367 **CAREFULLY SELECTED** (IRE) 24
481 **CAREY STREET** (IRE) 1
447 **CARIAD** 7
66 **CARIAD ANGEL** (IRE) 41
251 **CARIBBEAN ACE** (IRE) F 79
330 **CARIBBEAN SPRING** (IRE) 2
501 **CARIBBEAN SUNSET** (IRE) 4
247 **CARIBEAN BOY** (FR) 23
475 **CARIBOU** 6
387 **CARIDADE** (USA) C 100
442 **CARINA** (IRE) F 67

484 **CARLANDA** (FR) C 42
385 **CARLO DU BERLAIS** (IRE) 33
347 **CARLO STORM** (IRE) 14
300 **CARLOS FELIX** (IRE) 16
290 **CARLOTTA** (IRE) 21
234 **CARLOW FARMER** (IRE) 9
206 **CARLTON** 57
153 **CARLTON AND CO** 5
320 **CARMELA** (IRE) 26
283 **CARMELA SOPRANO** 7
239 **CARMENTIS** (IRE) 31
451 **CARNIVAL LAD** (IRE) 27
404 **CARNIVAL ROSE** C 20
279 **CARNIVAL TIMES** 9
226 **CARNIVAL ZAIN** 15
460 **CARO DES FLOS** (FR) 2
368 **CAROLE'S DESTINY** F 3
368 **CAROLE'S PASS** (FR) 4
286 **CAROLINA REAPER** 145
175 **CAROLINAE** F 47
153 **CAROLUS MAGNUS** (IRE) 6
286 **CAROUSELLE** (IRE) 51
179 **CARP KID** (IRE) 5
55 **CARPE DIEM** (FR) 2
56 **CARPE FORTUNA** (IRE) 12
383 **CARRACCI** (USA) 32
283 **CARRANITA** 27
513 **CARRAREA** (IRE) 12
1 **CARRIGEEN KALI** (IRE) 10
385 **CARRIGEEN KALMIA** (IRE) G 34
385 **CARRIGEEN KAMPALA** (IRE) 35
154 **CARRIGILLIHY** 16
51 **CARRIGLUX** (IRE) 1
189 **CARRIGMOORNA ROWAN** (IRE) 10
35 **CARRIWITCHET** (IRE) C 87
334 **CARRY ON AITCH** (IRE) 7
66 **CARTESIENNE** (IRE) F 99
484 **CARTIMANDUA** C 43
335 **CARTONNE** (FR) 16
26 **CARUSO** 5
138 **CARVALHAL** (IRE) 70
399 **CARVED IN STONE** 28
79 **CARVETII** (IRE) 17
355 **CASA LOUPI** 16
300 **CASA LUNA** (IRE) 17
504 **CASA NO MENTO** 13
200 **CASA TALL** (FR) 5
528 **CASAMARI ABBEY** (IRE) 3
456 **CASH** (IRE) 3
239 **CASH AGAIN** (FR) 7
367 **CASH BACK** (FR) 25
5 **CASH IN THE HAND** (USA) C 140
513 **CASH TO ASH** (IRE) 13
395 **CASHEW** (IRE) 4
220 **CASI CRUDO** 4
153 **CASILLI** 7
553 **CASPERS COURT** (IRE) 1
524 **CASSIEL** (IRE) 3
331 **CASSOWARY** (IRE) 1
154 **CASSY O** (IRE) 17
93 **CAST'S TASHA** (IRE) 4
459 **CASTAN** 11
385 **CASTEL GANDOLFO** (IRE) 36
539 **CASTELFORT** (FR) 35
395 **CASTING SPELLS** F 45
219 **CASTLE COVE** (IRE) 128
472 **CASTLE CROSS** C 31
410 **CASTLE DARAGH** (IRE) 17
363 **CASTLE FROME** (IRE) 16
5 **CASTLE PEAK** (USA) 57
363 **CASTLE QUARTER** (IRE) 17
319 **CASTLE ROBIN** (IRE) 7
428 **CASTLE RUSHEN** (IRE) 5
472 **CASTLE STAR** 1
5 **CASTLE WAY** 58
109 **CASTLEBERG ROCK** 4
449 **CASTLEGRANGE** (IRE) 2
261 **CASTLEREA TESS** 3
379 **CASTLEWARD** (IRE) 20
537 **CASWELL BAY** 15
270 **CAT AND THE FIDDLE** (IRE) 47
431 **CAT SIX** (USA) G 2
379 **CAT TIGER** (FR) 21
538 **CATCH CATCHFIRE** 15
442 **CATCH CUNNINGHAM** (IRE) 4
457 **CATCH HIM DERRY** (IRE) 28
441 **CATCH MY BREATH** 3
268 **CATCH THE CRUMPET** 2
15 **CATCH THE LIGHT** 151
442 **CATCH THE PADDY** (IRE) 30
74 **CATCHMEIFYOUCAN** (IRE) 5
315 **CATENA** (IRE) 23
135 **CATESBY** 14
289 **CATHAYA** 20
501 **CATHAYENSIS** (IRE) 5
318 **CATIVO RAGAZZO** 1
295 **CATLIN** 3
153 **CATTON LADY** 77
319 **CATUABA** (IRE) 8
368 **CATWALK MODEL** 38
94 **CATY FISH** (FR) 41
15 **CAVA** (IRE) C 152
78 **CAVALIER APPROACH** (IRE) 34
385 **CAVALLINO** (IRE) 37
283 **CAVALLO DA CORSA** G 28
243 **CAVALLUCCIO** (IRE) 1
112 **CAVALRY CALL** (IRE) 64
57 **CAVALRYMAN** 5
326 **CAVE BLEU** 5
144 **CAVE HILL** 5
42 **CAVERN CLUB** (IRE) 18
212 **CAWTHORNE** 7
390 **CAWTHORNE BANKER** (IRE) 23
212 **CAWTHORNE CRACKER** (IRE) 8
154 **CAWTHORNES GEM** 103
228 **CAY DANCER** C 130
80 **CAZCADE** 17
6 **CAZEVA PRINCESS** 17
221 **CEALLACH** (IRE) 2
206 **CEANNA** 58
13 **CEASE AND DESIST** (IRE) 2
525 **CECI WELLS** 3
451 **CEDAR CAGE** 3
494 **CEDAR HILL** (IRE) 7
226 **CEDAR RAPIDS** (IRE) 16
390 **CEDAR ROW** (IRE) 24
126 **CEEJAYBE** 10
360 **CEILIDH** 42
360 **CEILIDH KING** 43
437 **CEIRIOG VALLEY** G 4
404 **CEIST EILE** (IRE) C 21
286 **CEISTEACH** (IRE) F 146
254 **CELEBRE D'ALLEN** (FR) 8
544 **CELERITY** (IRE) 4
286 **CELESTE DE LA MER** (IRE) F 147
231 **CELESTIAL BEAST** (USA) F 108
154 **CELESTIAL DREAM** (IRE) C 160
144 **CELESTIAL FASHION** 6
404 **CELESTIAL FLIGHT** 22
385 **CELESTIAL GIFT** (FR) 38
360 **CELESTIAL GIRL** C 70
239 **CELESTIAL HORIZON** (IRE) 8
83 **CELESTIAL PARK** (IRE) 5
355 **CELESTIAL POINT** (IRE) 17
119 **CELESTIAL STAR** (IRE) 9
506 **CELL SA BEELA** 64
15 **CELLO** 48
438 **CELMA DES BOIS** (FR) 3
95 **CELSIUS** (IRE) 5
448 **CELTIC ART** (FR) 4
15 **CELTIC CHAMPION** 49
501 **CELTIC CYGNET** (IRE) G 43
489 **CELTIC DINO** (FR) 10
328 **CELTIC EMPRESS** 3
363 **CELTIC FORTUNE** (IRE) 18
407 **CELTIC NED** (IRE) 2
369 **CELTIC TARA** 20
14 **CEMHAAN** 5
111 **CENDRILLON** 3
335 **CENOTICE** 17
379 **CENTARA** (IRE) 22
146 **CENTERSTAGE** (IRE) 22
9 **CENTIMENTALJOURNEY** 2
301 **CENTRE BACK** 12
286 **CENTRE COURT** (FR) 52
506 **CENTREFOLD** 65
404 **CEOL LOCH AOIDH** (IRE) G 23
341 **CEOLWULF** 1
464 **CERENDIPITY** (IRE) 12
85 **CERTAIN LAD** 2
354 **CERTAIN STYLE** 15
427 **CERTAINLY RED** 2
280 **CERVETTO** (IRE) 10
153 **CESCA** (IRE) G 8
512 **CHABICHOU DUPOITOU** 1
5 **CHABLIS** (IRE) F 141
367 **CHACUN POUR SOI** (FR) 26
402 **CHADLINGTON LAD** (IRE) 14
288 **CHAGALL** (IRE) 2
268 **CHAIN SMOKER** 3
133 **CHAIRMAN FITZ** (IRE) 2
85 **CHAIRMANOFTHEBOARD** (IRE) 3
15 **CHALDEAN** 50
206 **CHALICE** (IRE) 59
302 **CHALK MOUNTAIN** 13
335 **CHALK THAT DOWN** (IRE) 18
138 **CHALLET** (IRE) 10
221 **CHALLY CHUTE** (IRE) 3
543 **CHAMBARD** (FR) 9
212 **CHAMBER CHOIR** 81
23 **CHAMBRAY** (USA) C 40
247 **CHAMP** (IRE) 24
357 **CHAMP IS REAL** 6
367 **CHAMP KIELY** (IRE) 27
208 **CHAMPAGNE BREEZE** 6
59 **CHAMPAGNE CITY** 7
448 **CHAMPAGNE COURT** (IRE) 5
282 **CHAMPAGNE GIFT** (IRE) 13
497 **CHAMPAGNE MESDAMES** (FR) 17
200 **CHAMPAGNE MYSTERY** (IRE) 6
355 **CHAMPAGNE PIAFF** (FR) 18

283 **CHRYSSIPHUS LIMES** (FR) 9
335 **CHTI BALKO** (FR) 21
266 **CHUCHUWA** (IRE) 30
386 **CHUCK TAYLOR** (IRE) 26
182 **CHUMLEE** (IRE) 2
387 **CHURCHELLA** (IRE) 64
492 **CHURCHILL BAY** 2
175 **CHURCHILL ROSE** (IRE) 24
202 **CHURCHILLS BOY** (IRE) 3
423 **CHURCHMAN** 8
66 **CHURROS** 100
335 **CHUVELO** (IRE) 22
442 **CHUZZLEWIT** 31
161 **CIANCIANA** 3
228 **CIAO ADIOS** (IRE) 5
305 **CIARA PEARL** 18
342 **CIARA STORM** 8
408 **CICELY** (IRE) 4
251 **CICERO'S GIFT** 28
322 **CIDER DRINKER** 1
367 **CIEL DE NEIGE** (FR) 31
479 **CIENFUEGOS** (IRE) 22
31 **CIG** (IRE) 16
469 **CIGARETTESNALCOHOL** (IRE) 4
367 **CILAOS EMERY** (FR) 32
454 **CILAOS GLACE** (FR) 7
154 **CILLUIRID** (IRE) 19
212 **CINCO SALTOS** (IRE) 10
466 **CINDYSOX** 7
270 **CINNODIN** 22
140 **CINQ DOUZAINE** 21
66 **CINQUE VERDE** 42
367 **CINSA** (FR) 33
488 **CINZENTO** (IRE) 7
321 **CIOTOG** (IRE) 8
479 **CIRCLE OF FIRE** 23
542 **CIRCLE TIME** (IRE) 4
24 **CIRCUIT BREAKER** 32
521 **CIRCUS MOON** (IRE) 10
234 **CIRRUS** 13
552 **CIRRUS MINOR** (FR) F 38
164 **CITE D'OR** (FR) 19
146 **CITIZEN GENERAL** (IRE) 2
483 **CITIZEN JANE** 3
496 **CITRON** F 49
13 **CITY CENTRAL** (IRE) 3
247 **CITY CHIEF** (IRE) 28
305 **CITY CYCLONE** 19
420 **CITY DERBY** (IRE) 3
321 **CITY ESCAPE** (IRE) 9
260 **CITY OF ALIAA** 8
383 **CITY OF CHICAGO** (IRE) 33
5 **CITY OF KINGS** 60
456 **CITY OF YORK** 33
265 **CITY ROLLER** (IRE) 3
15 **CITY STREAK** 9
427 **CITY TOUR** 3
352 **CITY VAULTS** 9
35 **CITY WALK** (IRE) 7
272 **CITY WATERS** 22
556 **CITYZEN SERG** (IRE) 3
73 **CIVIL ENSIGN** (FR) 3
488 **CIVIL LAW** (IRE) 8
395 **CLADDAGHDUFF** (IRE) 5
154 **CLAIM THE STARS** (IRE) 20
24 **CLAN CHIEFTAIN** 33
379 **CLAN DES OBEAUX** (FR) 24
548 **CLANDESTINELY** (IRE) 28
13 **CLANSMAN** 4
302 **CLANVILLE LASS** F 14
402 **CLAPTON HILL** 16
85 **CLARA BARTON** 52
457 **CLARAROSE** (IRE) 33
385 **CLARAS SOLDIER** (IRE) 41
106 **CLARENDON HOUSE** 3
164 **CLARITUDO** 9
56 **CLARITY SPIRIT** 13
395 **CLARKO'S BACK** 29
548 **CLASHANISKA** (IRE) 4
405 **CLASS CLOWN** (IRE) 3
43 **CLASS MEMBER** 44
228 **CLASSIC** 38
50 **CLASSIC ANTHEM** (IRE) 5
51 **CLASSIC CONCORDE** (IRE) 2
363 **CLASSIC FLIGHT** (IRE) 23
367 **CLASSIC GETAWAY** (IRE) 34
189 **CLASSIC GIRL** (IRE) F 11
308 **CLASSIC KING** (IRE) 9
513 **CLASSIC LADY** (IRE) 15
107 **CLASSIC SPEED** (IRE) 23
506 **CLASSIC TIMES** 67
151 **CLASSIC TUNE** 2
186 **CLASSICAL MUSIC** (IRE) 2
204 **CLASSY AL** 11
204 **CLASSY ANNE** G 43
146 **CLASSY LASSY** (IRE) C 59
18 **CLATTERBRIDGE** (IRE) 9
228 **CLAXTON BAY** 134
299 **CLAY** 4
369 **CLAY ROGERS** (IRE) 25
89 **CLAYMORE** (FR) 4
300 **CLEAN GETAWAY** (IRE) 18
474 **CLEAR ABILITY** (IRE) 5
102 **CLEAR ANGEL** 6
200 **CLEAR ON TOP** (IRE) 8
357 **CLEAR THE RUNWAY** (IRE) 8
290 **CLEAR WHITE LIGHT** 3
39 **CLEARANCE** 3
251 **CLEM FANDANGO** (FR) C 80
496 **CLEMATIS** (USA) C 50
507 **CLEMENCIA** (IRE) 8
43 **CLEMENT DANES** 9
61 **CLEMENTYNE** 15
383 **CLEMMIE** (IRE) F 120
173 **CLENCHED** 13
79 **CLERYS CLOCK** (IRE) 19
360 **CLEVER RELATION** 44
104 **CLICK AND COLLECT** 2
49 **CLIFFCAKE** (IRE) 2
368 **CLIFFHANGER** F 51
395 **CLIFFS OF CAPRI** 6
136 **CLIFFS OF DOONEEN** (IRE) 5
432 **CLIFFS OF MALTA** (IRE) 3
521 **CLIFFTOP HEAVEN** 11
72 **CLIMATE CHANGE** 44
89 **CLIMATE FRIENDLY** 20
26 **CLIMATE PRECEDENT** 24
56 **CLIMATE QUEEN** 45
466 **CLIMBING** 8
114 **CLINET** (IRE) C 11
203 **CLINTON LANE** 3
408 **CLIPSHAM GOLD** (IRE) 5
408 **CLIPSHAM LA HABANA** 31
383 **CLIQUE** C 121
18 **CLOCH NUA** 10
15 **CLOCHETTE** (IRE) 53
383 **CLOCKWORK** (IRE) 34
290 **CLODOVINE** (FR) F 27
335 **CLODY FLYER** (IRE) 23
286 **CLOGHRAN** (FR) C 149
369 **CLONAKILTY** (IRE) 26
370 **CLONDAW BERTIE** (IRE) 3
200 **CLONDAW CASTLE** (IRE) 9
312 **CLONDAW CIAN** (IRE) 4
168 **CLONDAW FAME** (IRE) 5
34 **CLONDAW FIXER** (IRE) 5
212 **CLONDAW PRETENDER** 11
275 **CLONDAW ROBIN** (IRE) 6
188 **CLONDAW SECRET** (IRE) 10
340 **CLONEYHURKE MAID** (IRE) 4
402 **CLONGEEN STAR** (IRE) G 17
473 **CLONGOWES** (IRE) 1
549 **CLOONEY** 1
138 **CLOSE CONNECTION** (IRE) 71
505 **CLOSE OF PLAY** 24
305 **CLOSENESS** 5
390 **CLOTH CAP** (IRE) 25
143 **CLOTHERHOLME** (IRE) 3
206 **CLOUD ANGEL** 60
75 **CLOUD CUCKOO** 2
355 **CLOUD DANCER** (IRE) 19
26 **CLOUD FREE** (IRE) 56
146 **CLOUD QUEEN** 24
175 **CLOUDBREAKER** 25
130 **CLOUDCHASER** (IRE) G 16
456 **CLOUDSIDE ROCK** 64
355 **CLOUDY BREEZE** (IRE) 140
543 **CLOUDY GLEN** (IRE) 11
525 **CLOUDY HILLS** (IRE) 5
28 **CLOUDY ROSE** 2
190 **CLOUDY WEDNESDAY** (IRE) 2
421 **CLOUGHROE** (IRE) 3
381 **CLOVA HOTEL** 1
423 **CLOVER PASS** 9
440 **CLOVIS BOY** 20
428 **CLOVIS ISLAND** 6
299 **CLUAIN AODHA** (IRE) 5
315 **CLUBBABLE** G 24
289 **CLUBORA** (USA) C 35
75 **CLUEDO** (IRE) 18
428 **CNOC NA SI** (IRE) 7
60 **CNOC SION** (IRE) 2
455 **COACHMAN** (FR) 4
47 **COAL FIRE** (IRE) 6
135 **COAST** 15
189 **COASTAL ROCK** (FR) 12
466 **COASTAL SUN** (FR) 9
394 **COASTGUARD STATION** (IRE) 5
23 **COAXING** 7
506 **COBALT BLUE** (IRE) 68
83 **COBBLERS DREAM** (IRE) 6
202 **COBBS CORNER** (IRE) 4
135 **COBH KID** 16
390 **COBOLOBO** (FR) 26
483 **COBRA COMMANDER** (IRE) 4
254 **COCA'S WELL** (IRE) G 9
287 **COCARDIER** (FR) 2
439 **COCCO MADONNA** (IRE) 3
234 **COCHIN** 84
115 **COCHISE** 6
174 **COCKALORUM** (IRE) 2

41 **COCKTAIL PRINCE** 13
84 **COCO BEAR** (IRE) 3
263 **COCO BRAVE** (IRE) 11
447 **COCO JACK** (IRE) 8
42 **COCO JAMBOO** (IRE) 19
347 **COCO LOCO** (FR) 16
219 **COCO ROYALE** 55
72 **COCO STARLIGHT** 45
283 **COCOA CABANA** 10
123 **COCONUT BAY** 3
219 **COCONUT CREME** F 131
537 **COCONUT SPLASH** (IRE) 17
326 **COCONUT TUDOR** (IRE) 6
21 **COCONUT TWIST** (IRE) 5
384 **COCOON** (IRE) C 36
124 **CODE CRACKER** F 5
239 **CODE PURPLE** 9
526 **CODSWALLOP** 4
420 **COEUR AIMANT** (FR) 4
196 **COEUR BLIMEY** (IRE) 4
390 **COEUR SEREIN** (IRE) 27
316 **COGITAL** 5
219 **COGNISANCE** 132
99 **COGNITIVE** (IRE) F 3
41 **COGOLIN** (FR) 3
526 **COILLTE EILE** (IRE) 5
282 **COILROCK** (IRE) 14
234 **COIN BASKET** (IRE) 14
383 **COIN BROKER** (IRE) C 122
454 **COKYTHO** (FR) 8
66 **COLD CASE** 43
447 **COLD COMFORT** (IRE) G 24
162 **COLD HENRY** 3
387 **COLD STARE** (IRE) 13
189 **COLDEN'S DREAM** (IRE) 13
147 **COLDSTREAM** (IRE) 9
369 **COLEMANSTOWN LAD** (IRE) 27
18 **COLEY'S KOKO** (IRE) 11
228 **COLGIN** C 135
404 **COLIGONE KATE** 1
449 **COLINTON** 4
390 **COLLECTORS ITEM** (IRE) 28
219 **COLLEGE CHOIR** 133
466 **COLLEGE OAK** 10
22 **COLLETTE** (IRE) 1
335 **COLLINGHAM** (GER) 24
369 **COLLOONEY** (IRE) 28
66 **COLNAGO** (IRE) 44
280 **COLOANE** (IRE) 11
466 **COLONEL HARRY** (IRE) 11
438 **COLONEL KEATING** (IRE) 4
232 **COLONEL LESLEY** (IRE) 3
557 **COLONEL MANDERSON** (FR) 2
24 **COLONIA** (FR) C 94
507 **COLONIAL EMPIRE** 9
56 **COLONIAL LOVE** 14
410 **COLONY QUEEN** 18
51 **COLORADO DOC** 3
521 **COLORS OF FREEDOM** 56
35 **COLOUR IMAGE** (IRE) 8
321 **COLOURFILLY** C 54
521 **COLOURFUL DREAM** 12
174 **COLTOR** (IRE) 3
15 **COLTRANE** (IRE) 10
216 **COLUMN OF FIRE** (IRE) 2
5 **COME ALIVE** F 143
455 **COME DANCING** (IRE) 5
42 **COME MUSICA** (ITY) 20
6 **COME ON GIRL** 20
200 **COME ON GRUFF** (IRE) 10
10 **COME ON JOHN** (IRE) 9
506 **COME ON LEICESTER** (IRE) C 141
292 **COME ON ME BABBY** (IRE) 12
331 **COME ON NIA** 3
363 **COME ON PADDY MAC** (IRE) 24
82 **COME ON TIER** (FR) 3
80 **COME TO PASS** (IRE) 20
24 **COME TOGETHER** (IRE) 34
420 **COMEDAYGODAY** (IRE) 5
294 **COMEDIAN LEADER** 8
244 **COMEONRITA** 2
138 **COMMANCHE FALLS** 11
228 **COMMANDER CROUCH** (IRE) 136
388 **COMMANDER MILLER** 2
450 **COMMANDER OF TEN** (IRE) 5
320 **COMMANDER STRAKER** (IRE) 28
439 **COMMANDING VIEW** (IRE) 4
16 **COMME SEA COMME CA** 4
56 **COMMENCE** F 72
500 **COMMISSION** 12
213 **COMMITTEE OF ONE** 3
543 **COMMODORE** (FR) 12
388 **COMMODORE MILLER** 3
154 **COMMON ACCLAIM** (IRE) 105
399 **COMMONSENSICAL** 5
168 **COMMUNITY REBEL** (IRE) 6
283 **COMPANY MINX** (IRE) 11
56 **COMPASS POINT** 15
10 **COMPERE** 10
379 **COMPLETE UNKNOWN** (IRE) 25
92 **COMPLETELY RANDOM** 56
92 **COMPLEXION** C 57
172 **COMPLIANT** 2
15 **COMPOSTELA** C 154
383 **COMPRESSION** (USA) C 123
285 **COMPTON BAY** 48
469 **CON TE PARTIRO** 43
7 **CONCEAL** (IRE) 1
26 **CONCEITO** 25
505 **CONCENTRATION** (IRE) F 27
83 **CONCEROE** (IRE) 7
387 **CONCERT BOY** (IRE) 65
212 **CONCETTO** (FR) 12
432 **CONCHITA** (GER) 4
10 **CONCIERGE** (IRE) 11
263 **CONCLUDING ACT** 12
521 **CONCON CANDY** (IRE) 57
43 **CONCORDE** 45
368 **CONCRA GIRL** (IRE) C 52
363 **CONCRETE KING** (IRE) 25
251 **CONDE** (IRE) 81
506 **CONDOR PASA** 142
114 **CONFEDERATION** 5
14 **CONFILS** (FR) 6
147 **CONFIRMATION BIAS** (IRE) 10
383 **CONGO RIVER** (USA) 35
228 **CONGRESBURY** 39
174 **CONGRESS** 31
408 **CONGRUENT** (IRE) 32
4 **CONINGBEG** (IRE) 6
428 **CONISTON CLOUDS** (IRE) 8
428 **CONISTON GEORGE** (IRE) 9
363 **CONKWELL LEGEND** 26
167 **CONNA SUE** (IRE) 2
270 **CONNEMARA COAST** 23
249 **CONNIE R** (IRE) 5
308 **CONNOLLY** (IRE) 10
43 **CONQUISTADOR** 46
335 **CONQUREDALOFEUROPE** (IRE) 25
387 **CONRI** 66
107 **CONSERVATIONIST** 24
135 **CONSERVATIVE** (IRE) 17
515 **CONSIDERED OPINION** C 69
94 **CONSORT ROYAL** 15
172 **CONSTANT DREAM** F 50
438 **CONSTANT FRIDAY** (IRE) 5
395 **CONSTITUTION** 30
247 **CONSTITUTION HILL** 29
24 **CONSUELO** 95
23 **CONTACT** (IRE) 8
369 **CONTEMPLATEMYFAITH** (IRE) 29
85 **CONTINUANCE** 53
383 **CONTINUOUS** (JPN) 36
254 **CONTRAMAR** 10
153 **CONTRAST** (IRE) 10
226 **CONTRE ORDRE** (FR) 17
70 **CONTROL** 11
543 **COO STAR SIVOLA** (FR) 13
457 **COOGAN'S BLUFF** (IRE) 34
161 **COOL CATENA** F 52
66 **COOL KITTEN** (IRE) C 101
219 **COOL LEGEND** 134
484 **COOL LIGHTNING** (IRE) 1
279 **COOL MIX** 10
286 **COOL PARTY** 53
363 **COOL QUEST** (IRE) F 117
453 **COOL RAIN** (IRE) 3
214 **COOL SPIRIT** 2
538 **COOL STYLE** 16
112 **COOL THUNDER** (IRE) F 26
200 **COOL VIEW** 11
56 **COOL VIXEN** (IRE) 16
56 **COOLAGH MAGIC** 17
494 **COOLBANE BOY** (IRE) 8
449 **COOLDINE BOG** (IRE) 5
537 **COOLE CODY** (IRE) 18
494 **COOLKILL** (IRE) 9
31 **COOLMINX** (IRE) F 43
383 **COOLMORE** (IRE) C 124
523 **COOLMOYNE** 1
254 **COOLNAUGH HAZE** (IRE) 11
205 **COOLVALLA** (IRE) 11
101 **COOPER'S CROSS** (IRE) 7
289 **COOPERATION** (IRE) 4
515 **COPAIN** (IRE) 70
21 **COPPENAGH BEAT** (IRE) F 15
78 **COPPER AND FIVE** 6
447 **COPPER BAY** (IRE) 9
464 **COPPER BEACH** (IRE) 14
450 **COPPER COIN** 6
390 **COPPER COVE** (IRE) 29
154 **COPPER KNIGHT** (IRE) 21
153 **COPPER MOUNTAIN** 11
507 **COPPERFASTEN** (IRE) 10
497 **COPPERHEAD** 19
355 **COPPERKNOB** (IRE) 20
206 **COPPICE** 61
234 **COPSHILL LAD** (IRE) 15
15 **COPY ARTIST** 54
263 **COQUELICOT** (FR) 13
26 **COQUET** F 57

440 **CORACH RAMBLER** (IRE) 21
385 **CORAL** (FR) 42
384 **CORAL BEACH** (IRE) F 37
45 **CORAL BLUE** (IRE) 2
484 **CORAL GARDEN** F 44
521 **CORAL REEF** (IRE) 58
176 **CORAL SEA** F 43
383 **CORAL SHELL** (IRE) C 125
521 **CORELLIAN STAR** (IRE) 59
369 **COREY'S COURAGE** 30
541 **CORIANO RIDGE** 1
521 **CORINTHIA KNIGHT** (IRE) 13
346 **CORINTHIAN GIRL** (IRE) F 41
413 **CORINTHIAN KID** (IRE) 20
307 **CORMACKSTOWN ROAD** (IRE) 1
161 **CORMIER** (IRE) 4
372 **CORMORANT COVE** F 1
247 **CORNAMONA** (IRE) 30
124 **CORNELL** 1
226 **CORNERSTONE LAD** 18
466 **CORNICELLO** (FR) 12
31 **CORNISH RIVIERA** 17
302 **CORNISH STORM** 3
315 **CORNLAW** F 25
444 **CORONATION COTTAGE** 3
504 **CORPORAL JACKJONES** (IRE) 16
173 **CORPORATE RAIDER** (IRE) 14
16 **CORRAN CROSS** (IRE) 5
409 **CORRANY** (IRE) 3
532 **CORRIEBEN REIVER** 8
440 **CORRIGEEN ROCK** (IRE) 22
408 **CORSICAN CAPER** (IRE) 33
408 **CORSINI** (IRE) 6
479 **CORYMBOSA** 24
204 **COSA SARA** (IRE) 12
74 **COSHESTON** 7
64 **COSMIC DIAMOND** F 10
231 **COSMIC LADY** (IRE) 46
136 **COSMIC OUTLAW** (IRE) 6
266 **COSMIC SOUL** (IRE) 6
321 **COSMIC STAR** 10
221 **COSMIC VEGA** (IRE) 4
112 **COSMIC VIEW** 27
31 **COSMOGYRAL** (IRE) F 44
24 **COSMOPOLITAN QUEEN** C 96
64 **COSMORE** 1
400 **COSMOS PINK** F 28
387 **COSMOS RAJ** 14
227 **COSTLY DIAMOND** (IRE) 3
515 **COTAI VISION** (IRE) 71
442 **COTAI WEST** (IRE) 5
540 **COTONEASTER** 4
176 **COTOPAXI MOON** 2
496 **COTTAM LANE** 5
350 **COTTON CLUB** (IRE) 2
314 **COTTON END** (IRE) 3
200 **COTTUN** (FR) 12
91 **COUL UNIVERSE** (IRE) 4
335 **COULD BE TROUBLE** (IRE) 26
383 **COULD IT BE LOVE** (USA) F 126
497 **COULD TALKABOUTIT** (IRE) 20
402 **COULDBEAWEAPON** (IRE) 18
463 **COULDNTGIVAMONKEYS** (IRE) 5
538 **COUNSEL** 17
154 **COUNT D'ORSAY** (IRE) 22
406 **COUNT OTTO** (IRE) 2
465 **COUNTERACT** 2
348 **COUNTESS KESS** (IRE) 43
226 **COUNTESS OLIVIA** (IRE) 19
161 **COUNTESS WELLS** (IRE) F 53
135 **COUNTRY CHARM** 18
68 **COUNTRY DELIGHTS** (IRE) 1
556 **COUNTRY KITTEN** (IRE) 4
379 **COUNTRY LADY** 26
361 **COUNTRY PYLE** 1
302 **COUP DE FORCE** 4
491 **COUP DE GOLD** (IRE) 5
267 **COUP DE PINCEAU** (FR) 4
94 **COUP DE SOLEIL** (FR) 16
200 **COUPDEBOL** (FR) 13
164 **COUPLET** 20
206 **COURAGE MON AMI** 3
5 **COURAGEOUS KNIGHT** 61
154 **COURT AT SLIP** (IRE) 23
347 **COURT CASE** (IRE) 17
291 **COURT CIAN** (IRE) 1
428 **COURT DREAMING** (IRE) 10
300 **COURT JUSTICE** (IRE) 19
450 **COURT MASTER** (IRE) 7
112 **COURT OF SESSION** 6
537 **COURT ROYALE** (IRE) 19
328 **COURTEOUS CROWN** C 29
47 **COURTLAND** (IRE) 7
154 **COURTNBOWLED** (IRE) 106
81 **COURTNEY SILVER** (IRE) 1
115 **COURTSIDE** (FR) 7
360 **COUSIN KHEE** 4
228 **COUSIN MARY** 137
363 **COUSU MAIN** (FR) 27
286 **COVEHITHE** (IRE) 150
383 **COVENT GARDEN** (IRE) 37
31 **COVERDALE** (IRE) 18
400 **COVERT LEGEND** 17
408 **COVERT MISSION** (FR) 7
206 **COVEY** 62
363 **COWBOY** (IRE) 28
531 **COWBOY COOPER** (IRE) 5
487 **COWBOY SOLDIER** (IRE) 2
15 **COYOTE** F 155
386 **COZI BAY** C 36
74 **CRACK DU NINIAN** (FR) 8
219 **CRACK OF LIGHT** 56
471 **CRACK REGIMENT** (FR) 6
515 **CRACK SHOT** (IRE) 24
175 **CRACKED UP** 26
146 **CRACKERZ** (IRE) 25
532 **CRACKING DESTINY** (IRE) 9
276 **CRACKING FILLY** 15
464 **CRACKING FIND** (IRE) 15
532 **CRACKING GALE** (IRE) G 10
59 **CRACKING LASS** (IRE) C 20
312 **CRACKING SMART** (FR) 5
135 **CRACKLING** (IRE) 19
286 **CRACKOVIA** 54
172 **CRACKSKING** 21
98 **CRADLE OF LIFE** (IRE) F 32
321 **CRAFTER** (IRE) 11
163 **CRAFTY LADY** 2
107 **CRAFTY MADAM** (IRE) C 68
515 **CRAGGY RANGE** (IRE) 25
320 **CRAIC AT DAWN** (IRE) 4
332 **CRAIC MAGIC** (IRE) 4
385 **CRAMBO** 43
528 **CRANK EM UP** (IRE) 4
343 **CRASSUS** (IRE) 9
52 **CRAWFORD** 2
43 **CRAZY ABOUT HER** (IRE) 47
192 **CRAZY CRACKERS** (IRE) 46
349 **CRAZY LUCK** 6
253 **CRAZY MAISIE** (IRE) 1
538 **CRAZY MARY** 18
192 **CRAZY SPIN** 4
265 **CREADAN GRAE** (IRE) 4
200 **CREALION** (FR) 14
1 **CREAM OF THE WEST** (IRE) 13
135 **CREATE** (IRE) 68
82 **CREATIONIST** (USA) 4
335 **CREATIVE CONTROL** (IRE) 27
5 **CREATIVE FORCE** (IRE) 7
521 **CREATIVE STYLE** (IRE) 60
390 **CREBILLY** (IRE) 30
395 **CRECY** C 46
383 **CREDENZA** (IRE) C 127
112 **CREDIT NOTE** 28
263 **CREDO** (IRE) 14
189 **CREDROJAVA** (IRE) 14
548 **CREEK HARBOUR** (IRE) 5
53 **CREM FRESH** 2
395 **CREMA INGLESA** (IRE) 7
363 **CREMANT** (IRE) 29
26 **CREME CHANTILLY** (IRE) 26
506 **CREME DE CACAO** (IRE) 69
222 **CRESSWELL QUEEN** 2
263 **CREST OF GLORY** 15
342 **CRESTA** (FR) 1
408 **CRESTA CAT** 34
24 **CRESTA DE VEGA** (IRE) 3
91 **CRIKEY JUICEY** 13
378 **CRIME FICTION** (IRE) 11
107 **CRIMSON ANGEL** 25
6 **CRIMSON KING** (IRE) 21
112 **CRIMSON ROAD** (IRE) 65
175 **CRIMSON ROSETTE** (IRE) C 48
211 **CRIMSON RUBY** 11
152 **CRIMSON SAND** (IRE) 2
305 **CRIMSON SPIRIT** 39
220 **CRIQUETTE** (FR) 6
107 **CRISAFF'S QUEEN** F 69
89 **CRISOLLES** (FR) C 44
40 **CRIXUS'S ESCAPE** (IRE) 8
506 **CROACHILL** (IRE) 7
163 **CROAGH PATRICK** (IRE) 3
156 **CROCODILE ROLL** 6
166 **CROESO CYMRAEG** 4
134 **CROFTON LANE** 2
349 **CROOKED CROWN** 33
469 **CROSS THE TRACKS** 44
266 **CROSSFADER** (IRE) 7
363 **CROSSING THE BAR** (IRE) 30
295 **CROSSPARK** 4
192 **CROSSTITCH** 47
112 **CROUPIER** (IRE) 7
43 **CROW'S NEST** (IRE) 48
342 **CROWN** (IRE) C 21
89 **CROWN BOARD** (IRE) 21
13 **CROWN BRIDGES** (IRE) 16
106 **CROWN DREAMS** 17
43 **CROWN LAND** 49
404 **CROWN PRINCESS** (IRE) 2
88 **CROWN PRINCESSE** (FR) 24
506 **CROWN QUEEN** (USA) C 70

506 **CROWN QUEEN** (USA) C 143
176 **CROWNING** 20
61 **CROWNTHORPE** 7
206 **CRUELLA DE VILL** (IRE) 63
154 **CRUYFF TURN** 24
306 **CRUZ CONTROL** (FR) 9
413 **CRY FICTION** (IRE) 41
217 **CRY HAVOC** (IRE) 2
383 **CRY ME A RIVER** (IRE) C 128
543 **CRYPTO** (IRE) 14
454 **CRYPTO CURRENCY** (IRE) 9
206 **CRYPTO FORCE** 64
479 **CRYSTAL CAPRICE** (IRE) 6
349 **CRYSTAL CASQUE** 7
492 **CRYSTAL DAWN** (IRE) 3
280 **CRYSTAL DELIGHT** 2
479 **CRYSTAL ESTRELLA** 7
280 **CRYSTAL FLOW** 3
520 **CRYSTAL FLYER** 26
279 **CRYSTAL GUARD** (IRE) 11
479 **CRYSTAL MARINER** (IRE) 25
525 **CRYSTAL MER** 6
298 **CRYSTAL MOON** (IRE) 18
90 **CRYSTALLIUM** 9
421 **CTHULHU** (USA) G 4
404 **CTHULHU** (USA) F 24
387 **CUAN** 67
165 **CUBAN BREEZE** 1
440 **CUBAN CIGAR** 23
299 **CUBAN COURT** (IRE) 6
106 **CUBAN GREY** 18
15 **CUBAN MELODY** 156
349 **CUBAN MISTRESS** 16
543 **CUBAN PETE** (IRE) 15
280 **CUBAN SECRET** (IRE) 23
66 **CUBAN SLIDE** 102
138 **CUBAN STORM** 72
56 **CUBAN STRIKE** 18
15 **CUBAN TIGER** 157
458 **CUBANISTA** 5
177 **CUCHAVIVA** 4
357 **CUDDLY DUDLEY** (FR) 9
519 **CUDGEL** 2
146 **CUE'S BEAU** 26
456 **CUERNAVACA** (FR) 6
387 **CULCOR** 15
116 **CUMHACHT** (IRE) 3
175 **CUMULONIMBUS** (IRE) 3
141 **CUP OF COFFEE** (FR) 5
165 **CURIOUS FOX** C 37
347 **CURLEY FINGER** (IRE) 18
286 **CURRAN** (IRE) 151
176 **CURRENCY EXCHANGE** (IRE) 3
537 **CURRENT MOOD** 20
360 **CURTIZ** 5
231 **CURVATURE** (IRE) 47
491 **CUSACK** 6
501 **CUSTARD** 6
326 **CUSTARD THE DRAGON** 7
367 **CUTA DES AS** (FR) 35
504 **CUTHBERT DIBBLE** (IRE) 17
262 **CUTTLESTONE BRIDGE** 18
352 **CUZCO DU MATHAN** (FR) 10
154 **CWENHILD** 107
61 **CYBELE** 16
383 **CZABO** C 129
450 **CZECH HER OUT** (IRE) 8
408 **D DAY ARVALENREEVA** (IRE) 35
408 **D DAY ODETTE** 8
415 **D'AMBONNAY** (IRE) 2
414 **D'EDGE OF GLORY** (IRE) 4
410 **D'JANGO** (FR) 19
526 **D'ORO PRINCESS** (USA) F 40
183 **DA VINCI HAND** (IRE) 4
451 **DAAFY** (USA) 4
228 **DAAHES** (IRE) 40
495 **DAANY** (IRE) 1
188 **DAARIS** (IRE) 11
176 **DABBLE** (IRE) F 44
43 **DABBOUS** (IRE) 50
266 **DABTIYRA** (IRE) F 31
5 **DABYAH** (IRE) C 144
56 **DADAVIC** (IRE) 46
279 **DADDY SCAT** (FR) 60
496 **DAFFY JANE** G 51
356 **DAFYRE** 11
456 **DAGMAR RUN** (IRE) 34
308 **DAGUENEAU** (IRE) 11
321 **DAHEER** (USA) 12
237 **DAIJOOR** 1
286 **DAILY TIMES** F 152
88 **DAINTY BIT** (FR) 25
473 **DAINTY DIVA** (IRE) F 6
41 **DAIQUIRI DREAM** 4
526 **DAISY ROOTS** 28
382 **DAKOTA BEAT** (IRE) 2
138 **DAKOTA GOLD** 12
113 **DAKOTA MOIRETTE** (FR) 3
488 **DAKOTA POWER** 9
298 **DAL MALLART** 19
247 **DALAMINE** (FR) G 31
507 **DALAMOI** (IRE) 11
305 **DALATARA** 20
456 **DALBY FOREST** 7
23 **DALEY T** (IRE) 29
57 **DALGLISH** (IRE) 6
56 **DALIANA** C 47
238 **DALILEO** (IRE) 2
301 **DALISO** (IRE) 15
47 **DALKINGSTOWN** 8
286 **DALKOVA** F 153
43 **DALLAS COWGIRL** (FR) 51
445 **DALLAS DES PICTONS** (FR) 7
70 **DALOOLAH** (IRE) 55
379 **DALRIATH** G 27
146 **DALRYMPLE** 27
357 **DALY TIGER** (FR) 10
347 **DALYOTIN** (FR) 19
251 **DAMANIYAT GIRL** (USA) C 82
369 **DAMARTA** (FR) 31
284 **DAMASCUS FINISH** (IRE) 5
146 **DAMASCUS STEEL** (IRE) 28
483 **DAMASK** (FR) 5
506 **DAME DU ROI** (IRE) C 144
55 **DAME DU SOIR** (FR) 3
526 **DAME HELEN** F 41
383 **DAME KIRI** (USA) 38
538 **DAME LAURA KNIGHT** 81
366 **DAME PRESTIGE** (FR) 9
146 **DAME SARRA** 29
79 **DAMISA** (IRE) 30
72 **DAN DE MAN CAN** 8
523 **DAN GUN** (IRE) 2
254 **DAN'S CHOSEN** (IRE) 12
390 **DANA'S GEM** (IRE) 31
387 **DANCE ANGEL** (IRE) 68
504 **DANCE AT NIGHT** 18
404 **DANCE CLUB** (IRE) C 25
31 **DANCE DIVA** C 45
243 **DANCE HAVANA** 14
286 **DANCE IN THE GRASS** 55
30 **DANCE IN THE PARK** 5
527 **DANCE OF DRAGONS** 8
463 **DANCE THIEF** (IRE) 6
320 **DANCE TIME** 29
387 **DANCE TO EXCEL** 16
438 **DANCE TO FAME** (IRE) 6
509 **DANCE TO PARIS** 8
30 **DANCEN QUEEN** (IRE) 6
42 **DANCER CROSS** F 54
410 **DANCES ON THE SAND** (IRE) 20
207 **DANCEWITHTHEWIND** (IRE) 5
517 **DANCHOVSKA** 9
385 **DANCILA** (IRE) 44
503 **DANCING CLOUD** (IRE) 12
167 **DANCING DANI** (IRE) 3
192 **DANCING ELEGANCE** F 58
287 **DANCING EMILY** (IRE) G 3
5 **DANCING GODDESS** (IRE) 62
392 **DANCING GYPSY** 26
488 **DANCING HARRY** (IRE) 10
298 **DANCING IN BRAZIL** 20
538 **DANCING IN PARIS** (FR) 82
269 **DANCING LILLY** 2
488 **DANCING MAGIC** (IRE) 39
306 **DANCING PAST** 10
283 **DANCING PLATES** F 32
5 **DANCING RAIN** (IRE) F 145
488 **DANCING REEL** (IRE) 11
5 **DANCING SANDS** (IRE) F 146
302 **DANCING STORM** F 18
85 **DANCING THE DREAM** 54
42 **DANCING WARRIOR** F 55
421 **DANCING ZEBEDEE** (IRE) 5
368 **DANCINGINTHEWOODS** 6
379 **DANCINGONTHEEDGE** (FR) 28
169 **DANDILLY** (IRE) 8
66 **DANDIVA** 103
24 **DANDY ALYS** (IRE) 35
154 **DANDY BAY** (IRE) 25
496 **DANDY DINMONT** (IRE) 6
154 **DANDY FITZ** (IRE) 161
469 **DANDY MAESTRO** 5
174 **DANDY SPIRIT** (IRE) 4
511 **DANDY'S ANGEL** (IRE) 3
438 **DANDYLYON** (IRE) 7
212 **DANDYS DERRIERE** 13
174 **DANDYS GOLD** (IRE) 5
498 **DANEANN** (IRE) 4
383 **DANEDROP** (IRE) C 130
495 **DANEHILL KODIAC** (IRE) 2
505 **DANEHURST** C 28
43 **DANGER ALERT** 52
361 **DANGER ZONE** 35
413 **DANGLE** (IRE) C 42
368 **DANIEL DERONDA** 7
491 **DANIELSFLYER** (IRE) 7
33 **DANILO D'AIRY** (FR) 1
113 **DANKING** 4
469 **DANNI CALIFORNIA** (IRE) 6
494 **DANNO'S DOLLAR** (IRE) 10

468 **DANNY BLEU** (IRE) 3
379 **DANNY KIRWAN** (IRE) 29
234 **DANNY WHIZZBANG** (IRE) 16
64 **DANNYSTORY** (IRE) 2
537 **DANS LE VENT** (FR) 21
496 **DANSEUSE D'ETOILE** (IRE) C 52
30 **DANSIER** (IRE) 7
349 **DANTE'S POET** 17
189 **DANTON** (IRE) 15
231 **DANVERS GOLD** (IRE) 48
154 **DANZAN** (IRE) 26
18 **DANZART** (IRE) 12
67 **DANZINI** (IRE) 6
355 **DAPHNE MAY** 21
20 **DAPPER GENT** 4
174 **DAPPER MAN** (IRE) 6
399 **DARAJAAT** (USA) F 80
236 **DARAMOUNT SUNLIGHT** 6
227 **DARANOVA** (IRE) 4
293 **DARBUCKS** (IRE) 4
490 **DARCYS HILL** (IRE) 5
219 **DARDIZA** (IRE) C 135
225 **DARE TO SHOUT** 2
132 **DARGIANNINI** (IRE) 5
526 **DARING DESTINY** (IRE) 6
195 **DARING GREATLY** 7
95 **DARING GUEST** (IRE) 6
176 **DARING LEGEND** 45
51 **DARIYA** (USA) 4
208 **DARJINK** 8
347 **DARK AGENT** (IRE) 20
523 **DARK AND DANGEROUS** (IRE) 3
43 **DARK BEFORE DAWN** (IRE) 107
131 **DARK CROCODILE** (IRE) 3
348 **DARK CRUSADE** (IRE) 44
471 **DARK DESIGN** (IRE) 7
254 **DARK DUOMO** (IRE) 13
522 **DARK ECLIPSE** (IRE) 1
192 **DARK ENCHANTMENT** (IRE) 5
416 **DARK GOLD** 18
323 **DARK HEATHER** (IRE) 1
70 **DARK ICON** 12
364 **DARK INTENTION** (IRE) C 11
328 **DARK ISLAND** 4
154 **DARK JEDI** (IRE) 27
206 **DARK KESTREL** (IRE) 65
192 **DARK KRIS** (IRE) 6
286 **DARK MAJESTY** 56
458 **DARK MIX** 6
147 **DARK MOON** (FR) 11
442 **DARK MOON RISING** (IRE) 6
59 **DARK MYSTERY** (IRE) 8
146 **DARK NOTIONS** (IRE) 30
320 **DARK PINE** (IRE) 5
286 **DARK ROSE ANGEL** (IRE) C 154
135 **DARK SHOT** 20
325 **DARK SIDE PRINCE** 3
325 **DARK SIDE THUNDER** 4
399 **DARK STRIKE** 31
228 **DARK THIRTY** (IRE) 41
515 **DARK TROOPER** (IRE) 26
228 **DARK VIPER** 138
153 **DARKANDSTORMY** G 78
80 **DARKE HORSE** 21
78 **DARKER** 7
557 **DARKEST DAY** (IRE) 3
149 **DARKEST DREAM** 1
387 **DARKNESS** (FR) 17
363 **DARKSIDEOFTARNSIDE** (IRE) 31
65 **DARLING ALKO** (FR) 3
81 **DARLO PRIDE** 8
264 **DARN HOT** F 17
151 **DARQUESSE** (IRE) 3
500 **DARSAN** (IRE) G 13
464 **DARSI'S DARLING** (IRE) 16
24 **DARTING** F 97
458 **DARTING ROSE** 7
263 **DARTMOOR PIRATE** 16
84 **DARVEL** (IRE) 4
70 **DARWELL LION** (IRE) 13
447 **DARWINIA** (GER) C 25
285 **DARYSINA GOLD** 49
28 **DAS KAPITAL** 3
83 **DASH OF BLUE** 8
448 **DASHEL DRASHER** 6
504 **DASHER** (IRE) 19
477 **DASHING DICK** (IRE) 1
107 **DASHING HARRY** 70
477 **DASHING PANTHER** 2
477 **DASHING RAT** 3
477 **DASHING ROGER** 4
477 **DASHING TO YOU** 5
360 **DASHINWHITESARGENT** 71
552 **DASHO LENNIE** 21
231 **DAT IL DO** C 109
383 **DATA DEPENDENT** (USA) C 131
459 **DATA LEAK** (IRE) 12
353 **DATE WITH DESTINY** (IRE) C 23
466 **DATSALRIGHTGINO** (GER) 13
5 **DAVANTAGE** (FR) C 147
257 **DAVE** 15
455 **DAVE AND BERNIE** (IRE) 6
493 **DAVE THE RUSSIAN** (IRE) 1
488 **DAVE'LL DO** 40
349 **DAVID'S DIVA** 18
349 **DAVID'S GIFT** 19
24 **DAVIDEO** 36
414 **DAVITT ROAD GLORY** (IRE) 5
387 **DAWN DELIGHT** F 101
43 **DAWN MISSION** 53
114 **DAWN OF EMPIRE** (USA) C 12
228 **DAWN OF LIBERATION** (IRE) 6
227 **DAWN RAIDER** (IRE) 5
15 **DAWN SUCCESS** 158
240 **DAWN TROUPER** (IRE) 10
298 **DAWN VEGA** 128
125 **DAWN WONDER** (IRE) 5
384 **DAWNING** (USA) C 38
218 **DAWSON CITY** 2
368 **DAY CREEK** F 53
198 **DAYBREAK BOY** (IRE) 1
44 **DAYDREAM BEACH** (IRE) F 4
421 **DAYEM** (IRE) 6
285 **DAYMER BAY** (IRE) 50
409 **DAYS LIKE THESE** M 4
35 **DAYS OF OLD** F 64
42 **DAYSOFOURLIVES** (IRE) 21
217 **DAYTONA BEACH** (IRE) 3
441 **DAYTONA LADY** (IRE) 13
342 **DAYZEE** (IRE) 9
300 **DAZAMAY** 65
515 **DAZITOO** (IRE) 72
326 **DAZY MAZY** 21
354 **DAZZERLING** (IRE) 5
5 **DAZZLING** (IRE) C 148
7 **DAZZLING DOVE** 2
177 **DAZZLING GEM** (IRE) 16
506 **DAZZLING ROSE** C 145
402 **DE BARLEY BASKET** (IRE) 19
515 **DE BRUYNE** 27
369 **DE CRAIC IS MIGHTY** (IRE) 32
188 **DE LA HOYA** (IRE) 29
440 **DE LEGISLATOR** (IRE) 24
308 **DE RASHER COUNTER** 12
421 **DE ROCKER** 7
286 **DE VEER CLIFFS** (IRE) C 155
6 **DE VEGA'S WARRIOR** (IRE) 22
80 **DE VEGAS KID** (IRE) 22
379 **DE WANTED WARRIOR** (IRE) 30
56 **DEA CAELESTIS** (FR) F 48
98 **DEACS DELIGHT** 1
363 **DEAD RIGHT** 32
197 **DEADLY MISSILE** (IRE) 2
142 **DEADWOOD DIVA** 2
457 **DEAFENING SILENCE** (IRE) 35
222 **DEAL EM HIGH** 3
222 **DEAL EM LUCKY** 4
387 **DEAR DANCER** (IRE) F 102
447 **DEAR DAPHNE** (IRE) 10
286 **DEAR MY FRIEND** 57
263 **DEAR RALPHY** (IRE) 17
385 **DEAUVILLE DANCER** (IRE) 45
176 **DEAUVILLE LEGEND** (IRE) 4
399 **DEBATER** 32
54 **DEBBIE'S CHOICE** (IRE) 3
146 **DEBBY'S DELIGHT** 31
292 **DEBDEN BANK** 13
356 **DEBUTANTE'S BALL** (IRE) G 17
119 **DEBYDINKS** (IRE) 51
355 **DECEIT** 22
305 **DECEIVER** 21
112 **DECIDING VOTE** C 66
69 **DECIMA** (IRE) C 33
89 **DECIPHER** (IRE) 22
1 **DECISION MADE** (IRE) F 14
488 **DECISIVE CALL** (IRE) 41
293 **DECONSO** 5
377 **DECORA** (IRE) 1
455 **DECORATED** 7
506 **DECORATION** (IRE) 71
556 **DECORATION OF WAR** (IRE) 5
335 **DEDANSER** (IRE) 28
399 **DEDENNE** 6
524 **DEE DAY LANDING** 4
227 **DEE EIRE** 6
66 **DEE SEE ARE** 45
227 **DEE STAR** (IRE) 7
10 **DEE'S DREAM** (IRE) 39
81 **DEED POLE** 9
101 **DEEP CHARM** 8
15 **DEEP IN MY HEART** (IRE) 55
161 **DEEP INFLUENCE** C 54
112 **DEEP INSIDE** (FR) C 67
81 **DEEP SPIRIT** 10
35 **DEEP THOUGHTS** 65
194 **DEEP WINTER** G 1
88 **DEEP WISH** 26
189 **DEEPER BLUE** (FR) 16
388 **DEER HUNTER** (IRE) 4
489 **DEERE MARK** 11
20 **DEERFOOT** 5

90 **DEFENCE OF FORT** (IRE) 10
504 **DEFENCE TREATY** (IRE) 20
506 **DEFERRED** 8
412 **DEFFERELLA** 3
312 **DEFILADE** 6
300 **DEFINING BATTLE** (IRE) 20
234 **DEFINITE** 17
23 **DEGALE** 41
320 **DEGUELLO** (IRE) 30
385 **DEHRADUN** 46
442 **DEIMOS** (IRE) 68
500 **DEIRA CLASSIC** (FR) 23
286 **DEIRA MILE** (IRE) 156
106 **DEIRA STAR** 19
254 **DEISE ABA** (IRE) 14
60 **DEISE VU** (IRE) 3
90 **DEJA** (FR) 1
246 **DEJA ROUGE** (FR) 2
402 **DEL LA MAR ROCKET** (IRE) 20
56 **DELAGATE THE LADY** 19
257 **DELAGATE THIS LORD** 4
161 **DELAYED ACTION** (IRE) 40
484 **DELEVIGNE** C 45
69 **DELEYLA** C 7
72 **DELFT BLUE** F 60
457 **DELGANY BOBBY BLUE** 36
457 **DELGANY DREAMER** 37
438 **DELGANY MONARCH** (IRE) 8
321 **DELIGHTFILLY** 13
383 **DELIGHTFUL** (IRE) 39
554 **DELIGHTFUL GUEST** (IRE) 2
50 **DELIGHTFULLY YOURS** (IRE) 19
442 **DELIZIOSA** (IRE) C 69
15 **DELLA** 56
80 **DELLA MARE** 23
313 **DELLBOY TROTTER** (IRE) 1
321 **DELPHI DREAMER** 14
35 **DELPHINIDAE** (IRE) C 88
219 **DELTA LEGEND** (IRE) 57
202 **DELTA ROSE** (IRE) 5
16 **DELTA RUN** (IRE) 6
494 **DELUXE RANGE** (IRE) 11
30 **DELVEY** (IRE) 8
311 **DEMACHINE** (IRE) 4
500 **DEMANDING LILLEY** 24
284 **DEMBE** 6
506 **DEMI POINTE** 72
162 **DEMI SANG** (FR) 4
286 **DEMILION** (IRE) 58
165 **DEMOCRACY DILEMMA** (IRE) 22
126 **DEMOCRITUS** 1
312 **DEMOISELLE KAP** (FR) 7
187 **DEMOTHI** (IRE) 3
526 **DEN GRIMME AELLING** (IRE) 7
275 **DEN THE DIVA** 7
81 **DENABLE** 2
298 **DENBURN** (IRE) 21
172 **DENIS ANTHONY** (IRE) 22
383 **DENMARK** 40
42 **DENSETSU** (IRE) 22
402 **DENSWORTH** (IRE) 21
543 **DENTLEY DE MEE** (FR) 16
18 **DEOLALI** 13
18 **DEPART A MINUIT** 14
367 **DEPLOY THE GETAWAY** (IRE) 36
535 **DEPUTISE** 1
138 **DEPUTY** (IRE) 13
101 **DEQUALL** 9
80 **DEQUINTO** (IRE) 24
28 **DEREHAM** 4
371 **DERRACRIN** 3
320 **DERRYMORE BOY** (IRE) 6
509 **DERSY SOCIAL** 9
72 **DERWENT BOY** 46
58 **DERWENT DEALER** (IRE) 2
226 **DESARAY GIRL** (FR) 20
444 **DESERT** (IRE) 4
150 **DESERT BERRY** F 6
403 **DESERT BOOTS** 4
15 **DESERT COP** 57
479 **DESERT CROWN** 8
470 **DESERT DREAM** 2
153 **DESERT EMPEROR** 12
416 **DESERT FALCON** (IRE) 19
98 **DESERT FIGHTER** (IRE) 14
35 **DESERT FIRE** (IRE) 9
255 **DESERT GLORY** (IRE) 3
112 **DESERT GUEST** 29
343 **DESERT HAVEN** (IRE) 56
219 **DESERT HERO** 58
353 **DESERT ILLUSION** (IRE) 9
408 **DESERT IMAGE** F 62
209 **DESERT LILY** (IRE) C 13
209 **DESERT LILY** (IRE) F 23
408 **DESERT MIRACLE** 9
5 **DESERT ORDER** (IRE) 63
532 **DESERT QUEST** (IRE) 11
500 **DESERT RUN** (IRE) F 25
153 **DESERT SAGE** G 79
463 **DESERT STRANGER** 7
521 **DESERT SWIRL** (IRE) 61
538 **DESERT WILLIAM** 19
139 **DESFONDADO** (IRE) 16
66 **DESIGN** 46
12 **DESIGN ICON** 9
70 **DESIGNER** 14
507 **DESIGNER DESTINY** (IRE) 12
64 **DESIGNER JET** (IRE) 3
5 **DESIROUS** C 149
85 **DESPERATE HERO** 19
539 **DESPEREAUX** (FR) 4
543 **DESQUE DE L'ISLE** (FR) 17
80 **DESTINADO** 25
138 **DESTINED** 46
311 **DESTINED TO SHINE** (IRE) 5
440 **DESTINY IS ALL** (IRE) 25
14 **DESTINY QUEEN** (FR) 7
177 **DESTINY'S SPIRIT** 17
312 **DESTRIER** (FR) 8
12 **DESTROYTHEEVIDENCE** 10
5 **DETAILED** (IRE) C 150
445 **DETECTIVE** 8
467 **DETENTE** F 2
369 **DEV OF TARA** (IRE) 33
538 **DEVASBOY** 20
175 **DEVERON** (USA) C 49
532 **DEVIL LOCH** 12
386 **DEVIL'S ANGEL** 4
54 **DEVILS IN MY HEAD** F 4
154 **DEVILWALA** (IRE) 28
384 **DEVIOUS DIVA** (IRE) F 39
407 **DEVIZES** (IRE) 3
515 **DEVOIRS CHOICE** (IRE) 73
5 **DEVONSHIRE** (IRE) C 151
14 **DEVORGILLA** 8
383 **DEVOTED TO YOU** (IRE) C 132
102 **DEVOUR** (IRE) 7
6 **DEW YOU BELIEVE** (IRE) 23
295 **DEXPERADO** (FR) 5
369 **DEXTERITY** (IRE) 34
298 **DEYRANN DE CARJAC** (FR) 22
206 **DHABAB** (IRE) 4
5 **DHAHABI** (IRE) 8
32 **DHARAN** (FR) 3
399 **DHARIYE** (FR) 33
31 **DHARWA** G 46
24 **DI FEDE** (IRE) C 98
532 **DIABLO LOCH** 13
357 **DIAKOSAINT** (FR) 11
33 **DIAMAND DE VINDECY** (FR) 2
532 **DIAMANT SUR CANAPE** (FR) 14
228 **DIAMINDA** (IRE) F 139
520 **DIAMOND BAY** 3
444 **DIAMOND COTTAGE** 5
234 **DIAMOND DESTROYER** (IRE) 18
358 **DIAMOND DUKE** (IRE) 6
205 **DIAMOND EGG** (FR) 12
506 **DIAMOND FIELDS** (IRE) C 146
402 **DIAMOND GESTURE** (IRE) G 22
138 **DIAMOND HAZE** (IRE) 14
261 **DIAMOND JILL** (IRE) 4
261 **DIAMOND JOEL** 5
295 **DIAMOND KODA** (IRE) 6
477 **DIAMOND LADY** C 19
451 **DIAMOND MEMORIES** 5
489 **DIAMOND MONARCH** (IRE) 12
43 **DIAMOND RANGER** (IRE) 10
497 **DIAMOND RI** (IRE) 21
233 **DIAMOND RIVER** (IRE) 1
338 **DIAMOND ROAD** (IRE) 2
460 **DIAMOND ROSE** 3
400 **DIAMOND RUN** F 18
440 **DIAMOND STATE** (FR) 26
69 **DIAMOND TANGO** (FR) F 8
52 **DIAMOND TIKI** (FR) 3
445 **DIAMOND TRILOGY** (IRE) 9
457 **DIAMOND TWIN** (FR) 38
24 **DIAMOND VEGA** 37
138 **DIAMONDONTHEHILL** 15
506 **DIAMONDS POUR MOI** F 147
383 **DIAMONDSANDRUBIES** (IRE) F 133
383 **DIAMONDSAREFOREVER** (IRE) 41
348 **DIANA PRINCE** 7
408 **DIANARA** (FR) 63
306 **DIBBLE DECKER** (IRE) 11
66 **DICE GAME** F 104
47 **DICEY RIELLY** (IRE) 9
511 **DICK DATCHERY** (IRE) 4
298 **DICKENS** (IRE) 23
315 **DICKIEBURD** 10
355 **DICKO THE LEGEND** (IRE) 141
488 **DICKTATE** 12
367 **DID I ASK YOU THAT** (IRE) 37
543 **DIDERO VALLIS** (FR) 18
176 **DIDEROT** 5
298 **DIDONATO** (IRE) 24
239 **DIDTHEYLEAVEUOUTTO** (IRE) 10
379 **DIEGO DU CHARMIL** (FR) 31
16 **DIESEL D'ALLIER** (FR) 7
448 **DIESEL LINE** (IRE) 7
212 **DIEU VIVANT** (FR) 14

342 **DIEULEFIT** (IRE) C 22
138 **DIFFERENT** F 73
92 **DIFFERENT DRUM** 58
383 **DIFFERENT LEAGUE** (FR) C 134
515 **DIFFERENT TONE** 28
296 **DIFFIDENT SPIRIT** 2
174 **DIGITAL** (IRE) 7
387 **DIKTA DEL MAR** (SPA) C 103
56 **DIKTALINA** C 73
506 **DILARA** (IRE) 148
476 **DILETTA TOMMASA** (IRE) F 9
107 **DILIGENT HARRY** 2
183 **DILLARCHIE** 5
456 **DILLYDALLYDO** (IRE) C 65
228 **DILLYDINGDILLYDONG** 7
457 **DIME STORE COWGIRL** 39
228 **DIMSONS** (IRE) 140
554 **DINAH WASHINGTON** (IRE) 3
410 **DINDIN** (FR) 21
72 **DINGLE** (IRE) 9
472 **DINGLE DANCER** (IRE) 9
494 **DINGO DOLLAR** (IRE) 12
335 **DINO BELLAGIO** 29
379 **DINO MAGIC** (FR) 32
298 **DINO VELVET** (FR) 25
367 **DINOBLUE** (FR) 38
73 **DINONS** (FR) 4
506 **DINOO** (IRE) 9
450 **DINSDALE** 9
119 **DIOCLETIAN** (IRE) 12
343 **DIOL KER** (FR) 10
542 **DIOMED SPIRIT** 25
376 **DIOMEDE DES MOTTES** (FR) 9
535 **DION BAKER** (IRE) 2
542 **DIONYSIAN** 26
524 **DIONYSIS** (FR) 5
552 **DIRAYAH** (IRE) C 39
491 **DIRCHILL** (IRE) 8
154 **DIRECT HIT** (IRE) 108
355 **DIRHAM EMIRATI** (IRE) 23
385 **DIRK GENTLY** (IRE) 47
336 **DIRTY BARRY** (USA) 8
501 **DIRTYOLDTOWN** (IRE) 7
226 **DIS DONC** (FR) 21
5 **DISAVOW** C 152
256 **DISCKO DES PLAGES** (FR) 1
347 **DISCO ANNIE** (IRE) 21
154 **DISCO DORIS** C 162
266 **DISCO SPIRIT** (IRE) 32
221 **DISCREET SPY** (USA) F 39
92 **DISCRETION** 4
332 **DISH OF THE DAY** (IRE) 5
43 **DISKO** (IRE) F 108
326 **DISTINCTION** (IRE) 8
305 **DISTINCTIVE** G 22
243 **DISTINGUISHED LADY** (FR) 15
138 **DISTRICT COUNTY** 47
385 **DIV INE TARA** 48
182 **DIVAS DOYEN** (IRE) 3
367 **DIVERGE** 39
379 **DIVILSKIN** (IRE) 33
217 **DIVINA GRACE** (IRE) 9
30 **DIVINATION** (IRE) 9
24 **DIVINE BREATH** 99
164 **DIVINE COMEDY** (IRE) 10
315 **DIVINE CONNECTION** 3
5 **DIVINE IMAGE** (USA) F 153
16 **DIVINE INSPIRATION** (IRE) 8
506 **DIVINE JEWEL** 10
251 **DIVINE LIBRA** (IRE) 29
396 **DIVINE MESSENGER** 2
484 **DIVINE RAPTURE** 2
515 **DIVYA** (IRE) 29
79 **DIXIEDOODLEDANDY** (IRE) C 31
221 **DIYABA** 20
355 **DIYAKEN** (FR) 24
454 **DJ PETE** (IRE) 10
363 **DJASEK** (FR) 33
543 **DJELO** (FR) 19
205 **DJIN CONTI** (FR) 13
456 **DMANI** 35
239 **DO I DREAM** (IRE) 11
441 **DO IT FOR LOVE** 14
311 **DO IT FOR THY SEN** (IRE) 6
307 **DO NO WRONG** (IRE) 2
136 **DO NOT DISTURB** (IRE) 7
347 **DO YE WANNA** (IRE) 22
308 **DO YOU THINK** 13
450 **DO YOUR JOB** (IRE) 10
466 **DOC MCCOY** (IRE) 14
80 **DOC SPORTELLO** (IRE) 26
317 **DOCK ROAD** (IRE) 4
164 **DOCKLANDS** 21
534 **DOCPICKEDME** (IRE) 4
489 **DOCTOR BLUE** (FR) 54
295 **DOCTOR DEX** (IRE) 7
200 **DOCTOR DOTTY** 15
263 **DOCTOR FOLEY** (IRE) 18
221 **DOCTOR GRACE** 21
369 **DOCTOR KEN** (FR) 35
393 **DOCTOR KHAN JUNIOR** 1
489 **DOCTOR KILDARE** (FR) 55
513 **DOCTOR LIVINGSTONE** (IRE) 66
165 **DOCTOR MOZART** (IRE) 23
489 **DOCTOR ON CALL** (FR) 56
457 **DOCTOR PARNASSUS** (IRE) 40
87 **DOCTOR THEA** F 8
188 **DOCUMENTING** 12
247 **DODDIETHEGREAT** (IRE) 32
365 **DODGY BOB** 3
12 **DOES HE KNOW** 11
146 **DOG FOX** 32
457 **DOG OF WAR** (FR) 41
414 **DOGEM BY DESIGN** (IRE) 6
347 **DOGGED** 23
157 **DOIREANN** (IRE) 10
206 **DOLCE COURAGE** 66
367 **DOLCITA** (FR) 40
390 **DOLLAR BAE** (IRE) 32
264 **DOLLY BIRD** 1
20 **DOLLY DANCER** (IRE) 6
254 **DOLLY DELIGHTFUL** 15
131 **DOLLY DRAKE** 4
320 **DOLLY GRAY** 7
496 **DOLMA** (FR) C 53
320 **DOLORES ABERNATHY** 31
379 **DOLOS** (FR) 34
254 **DOLPHIN SQUARE** (IRE) 16
200 **DOM BOSCO** 16
55 **DOM OF MARY** (FR) 4
216 **DOM PERRY** 3
360 **DOM PERRY** 6
115 **DOMAINE DE L'ISLE** (FR) 8
440 **DOMANDLOUIS** (IRE) 27
369 **DOMINIC'S FAULT** 36
379 **DON ALVARO** 35
414 **DON BERSY** (FR) 7
207 **DON BROCCO** 6
543 **DON HERBAGER** (FR) 20
457 **DON HOLLOW** (GER) 42
390 **DON MARIONE** (IRE) 33
457 **DON OCCHETTI** (IRE) 43
113 **DON PORT LUX** (FR) 5
146 **DON SIMON** (IRE) 60
299 **DON'T ASK FITZ** (IRE) 7
550 **DON'T FIGHT IT** (IRE) 3
51 **DON'T LAUGH AT ME** 5
440 **DON'T LOOK BACK** 28
218 **DON'T RIGHTLY KNOW** 3
168 **DON'T TELL ALLEN** (IRE) 7
305 **DON'T TELL CLAIRE** 6
305 **DON'T TELL ROSIE** 23
379 **DON'T TELL SU** (IRE) 36
243 **DON'T WHAT ME BOY** (IRE) 16
441 **DONA VIOLA** F 15
440 **DONA VIOLA** F 100
355 **DONALD LLEWELLYN** 25
176 **DONAU** (IRE) F 46
357 **DONDIAM** (FR) 12
461 **DONNA GIOVANNA** G 4
494 **DONNA'S DELIGHT** (IRE) 13
494 **DONNA'S DOUBLE** 14
240 **DONNACHA** (IRE) 11
466 **DONNIE AZOFF** (IRE) 15
1 **DONNY BOY** (IRE) 15
463 **DONSO STAR** 8
181 **DONT BE ROBIN** (IRE) 3
433 **DONT CALL ME DORIS** 2
385 **DONTYAWANTME** (IRE) 49
153 **DOOBAHDEEDOO** (USA) G 80
4 **DOOBY** 7
251 **DOOLEY** (IRE) 83
219 **DOOM** 59
13 **DOOMSDAY** 5
99 **DOORS BREAKER** (FR) 4
212 **DOOYORK** (IRE) 15
528 **DORA DE JANEIRO** (FR) 5
387 **DORA MILAJE** (IRE) 69
165 **DORA PENNY** 2
83 **DORADO DOLLAR** (IRE) 9
56 **DORAS TAMAR** (IRE) 49
293 **DORETTE** (FR) 6
306 **DORKING BOY** 12
355 **DORKING LAD** 26
286 **DORNOCH CASTLE** (IRE) 59
244 **DOROTHY'S FLAME** 3
484 **DORRAAR** (IRE) C 12
276 **DORS DELIGHT** 24
276 **DORS TOYBOY** (IRE) 3
463 **DOT COTTON** (IRE) 9
66 **DOTTED SWISS** (IRE) C 105
407 **DOTTIES STAR** 4
466 **DOUBLE CLICK** (IRE) 16
343 **DOUBLE DIAMOND** F 94
520 **DOUBLE DOWN** (IRE) 11
326 **DOUBLE HIGH** F 22
274 **DOUBLE LEGEND** (IRE) 1
552 **DOUBLE MARCH** (IRE) 22
399 **DOUBLE OBAN** 34
147 **DOUBLE OR QUITS** 12
75 **DOUBLE RED** 29

498 **DOUBLE TIME** 2
456 **DOUBLE TOT** (IRE) 36
509 **DOUBLETHETROUBLE** 10
248 **DOUBTCHA MOSSY BOY** (IRE) 3
308 **DOUGHMORE BAY** (IRE) 14
43 **DOUGIE** (IRE) 54
496 **DOUGIES DREAM** (IRE) 7
440 **DOUGLAS TALKING** (IRE) 29
368 **DOUKAROV** (FR) 8
84 **DOURADO** (IRE) 5
406 **DOVENA** 11
26 **DOVES OF PEACE** (IRE) 27
472 **DOWAGER** C 10
515 **DOWAYLA** (IRE) F 74
383 **DOWER HOUSE** (IRE) 42
192 **DOWN TO THE KID** (IRE) 7
50 **DOWNSMAN** (IRE) 6
286 **DOWNTOWN DUBAI** (IRE) 60
263 **DOYANNIE** (IRE) 19
494 **DOYEN BREED** (IRE) 15
435 **DOYEN DU BAR** (IRE) 4
263 **DOYEN FOR MONEY** (IRE) 20
248 **DOYEN QUEEN** (IRE) 4
457 **DOYEN QUEST** (IRE) 44
537 **DOYEN STAR** (IRE) 22
255 **DOYEN STREET** (IRE) 4
556 **DOYENS DE ANTE** (IRE) 6
457 **DOYOUKNOWWHATIMEAN** 45
153 **DOZY** (IRE) F 81
280 **DR BRERETON** (IRE) 4
367 **DR EGGMAN** (FR) 41
390 **DR HEGARTY** (IRE) 34
93 **DR KANANGA** 5
282 **DR LOCKDOWN** (IRE) 15
348 **DR RIO** (FR) 8
239 **DR SANDERSON** (IRE) 12
369 **DR SEB** (FR) 37
182 **DR SHIROCCO** (IRE) 4
369 **DR T J ECKLEBURG** (IRE) 38
266 **DRAFTED** (IRE) 8
491 **DRAGON ART** 9
138 **DRAGON BEAT** (IRE) F 74
506 **DRAGON ICON** (IRE) 73
107 **DRAGON LEADER** 71
413 **DRAGON POWER** (IRE) 21
506 **DRAGON SYMBOL** 11
399 **DRAGONBALL PRINCE** (IRE) 35
212 **DRAGONFRUIT** 16
226 **DRAGONS WILL RISE** (IRE) 22
223 **DRAKEHOLES** 4
176 **DRAMA** 47
285 **DRAMATIC EFFECT** 51
219 **DRAMATIC QUEEN** (USA) C 136
66 **DRAMATISED** (IRE) 47
448 **DRASH ON RUBY** 8
211 **DREADPOETSSOCIETY** (IRE) 12
218 **DREAM BET** 4
408 **DREAM BY DAY** 10
385 **DREAM CHASER** (FR) 50
353 **DREAM CHILD** (IRE) C 10
484 **DREAM CHOICE** 13
166 **DREAM COMPOSER** (FR) 5
228 **DREAM CRAFT** (IRE) F 141
43 **DREAM DANCING** (IRE) F 109
58 **DREAM DEAL** 3
31 **DREAM FINAL** 19
442 **DREAM FOR GOLD** (IRE) 32
415 **DREAM FRONTIER** 10
111 **DREAM GAME** 4
538 **DREAM HARDER** (IRE) 21
505 **DREAM IMPOSSIBLE** (IRE) F 29
308 **DREAM IN THE PARK** (IRE) 15
399 **DREAM MELODY** F 81
521 **DREAM MISSION** 62
54 **DREAM OF KEDA** 15
5 **DREAM OF LOVE** (IRE) 64
406 **DREAM OF MISCHIEF** 12
228 **DREAM OF THE HILL** (IRE) C 142
296 **DREAM PIRATE** 13
107 **DREAM SEEKER** 72
57 **DREAM SHOW** 7
66 **DREAM SLEEP** F 106
383 **DREAM THE BLUES** (IRE) C 135
305 **DREAM TO REALITY** F 40
386 **DREAM TOGETHER** (IRE) 5
26 **DREAMAWAY** (IRE) F 58
501 **DREAMCASING** 8
231 **DREAMILY** (IRE) F 110
263 **DREAMING BLUE** 21
385 **DREAMING DIAMOND** (IRE) 51
164 **DREAMING SPIRES** 22
126 **DREAMINGOFASONG** 2
515 **DREAMROCKER** (IRE) 30
286 **DREAMS ADOZEN** (FR) 61
153 **DREAMS AND VISIONS** (IRE) 13
6 **DREAMS DELIVERED** (IRE) 24
47 **DREAMS OF DIAMONDS** (IRE) 10
47 **DREAMS OF FORTUNE** (IRE) 11
261 **DREAMS OF GOLD** 6
335 **DREAMS OF HOME** (IRE) 30
292 **DREAMSUNDERMYFEET** (IRE) 14
376 **DREAMWEAVER** (IRE) 10
112 **DRESDEN DOLL** (USA) C 68
78 **DRESDEN GREEN** 36
112 **DRESS OF DUBAI** 30
26 **DRIFTING MIST** C 59
343 **DRIFTING SPIRIT** C 95
91 **DRILL TO DREAM** 5
202 **DRISHOGUE** (IRE) 6
88 **DRIVABLE** (FR) 27
221 **DROMANTINE** (IRE) 22
513 **DROMOLOUGHT LAD** (IRE) 16
501 **DROP DEAD GORGEOUS** (FR) F 64
369 **DROP HIM IN** (IRE) 39
264 **DROPITLIKEITSHOT** 2
156 **DRUM BRAE BOY** 7
290 **DRUMCONNOR LAD** (IRE) 4
233 **DRUMLEES PET** (IRE) 2
198 **DRUMNAGREAGH** (IRE) 2
383 **DRUMROLL** (IRE) 43
520 **DRY YOUR EYES** (ITY) G 12
303 **DUAL IDENTITY** (IRE) 4
59 **DUBAI** (IRE) C 21
66 **DUBAI AFFAIR** C 107
5 **DUBAI BEAUTY** (IRE) C 154
66 **DUBAI CRYSTAL** (IRE) 48
1 **DUBAI DAYS** (IRE) 16
451 **DUBAI ELEGANCE** 6
56 **DUBAI FLOWER** G 20
35 **DUBAI FUTURE** 10
484 **DUBAI HARBOUR** 14
219 **DUBAI HONOUR** (IRE) 8
286 **DUBAI ICE** (USA) F 157
249 **DUBAI JEANIUS** (IRE) 6
442 **DUBAI JEMILA** 33
286 **DUBAI LEADER** 7
35 **DUBAI LEGACY** (USA) 11
470 **DUBAI MEDIA** (CAN) C 12
286 **DUBAI MILE** (IRE) 62
35 **DUBAI MIRAGE** (IRE) 12
112 **DUBAI ONE** (IRE) C 69
506 **DUBAI QUEEN** (USA) F 149
5 **DUBAI ROSE** C 155
35 **DUBAI SOUQ** (IRE) 13
542 **DUBAI STATION** 5
35 **DUBAI VIEW** 66
35 **DUBAI WELCOME** 14
378 **DUBARA** F 18
231 **DUBAWI DELIGHT** 49
228 **DUBAWI DREAM** 143
484 **DUBAWI MEEZNAH** (IRE) F 46
231 **DUBAWI SPECTRE** 50
111 **DUBH ROSE** 5
484 **DUBKA** F 47
385 **DUBLIN FOUR** (IRE) 52
189 **DUBROVNIK HARRY** (IRE) 17
410 **DUC DE BEAUCHENE** (FR) 22
494 **DUC DE GRISSAY** (FR) 16
537 **DUC DU RENE** (IRE) 23
28 **DUCHESS** (FR) 5
228 **DUCHESS OF FOXLAND** (IRE) C 144
506 **DUCHESS OF FRANCE** (IRE) C 150
149 **DUCHESS OF RIPON** (IRE) M 2
305 **DUCISSA** F 41
524 **DUDETTE** G 16
107 **DUE DATE** 26
285 **DUE TO HENRY** 52
294 **DUELY SPICED** 18
287 **DUHALLOW LAD** (IRE) 4
309 **DUHALLOW TOMMY** (IRE) 6
383 **DUKE CADOR** (IRE) 44
205 **DUKE OF BADDESLEY** (IRE) 14
212 **DUKE OF DECEPTION** (IRE) 17
12 **DUKE OF EARL** (FR) 12
292 **DUKE OF LUCKLEY** (IRE) 15
26 **DUKE OF OXFORD** 28
280 **DUKE OF VERONA** (IRE) 5
496 **DUKE OF WYBOURNE** (IRE) 28
112 **DUKEMAN** (IRE) 8
484 **DULCET** (IRE) C 48
284 **DULCET SPIRIT** 7
500 **DUMFRIES** 14
60 **DUN BAY CREEK** 4
212 **DUN DANCING** 18
192 **DUNA** (GER) F 59
215 **DUNATARA** 2
425 **DUNBAR** (FR) 1
392 **DUNDORY** (IRE) 3
112 **DUNDUNAH** (USA) C 70
290 **DUNGAR GLORY** (IRE) 5
279 **DUNNET HEAD** (IRE) 12
547 **DUNNINGTON LAD** (IRE) 8
474 **DUNNOTTAR CASTLE** 6
402 **DUNSKAY** (FR) 23
200 **DUNSTALL RAMBLER** (IRE) 17
24 **DUNSTAN** 100
162 **DURLINGTON** (FR) 5
247 **DUSART** (IRE) 33
66 **DUSHLAN** (IRE) F 108
466 **DUSKY DAYS** (IRE) 17
542 **DUSKY LORD** 6

79 **DUSTY** C 32
55 **DUTCH ADMIRAL** (IRE) 5
286 **DUTCH DECOY** 8
347 **DUTCH DESIRE** C 114
343 **DUTCH GOLD** (IRE) 57
503 **DUTCH HEIRESS** F 19
260 **DUTCH KINGDOM** (IRE) 9
15 **DUTCH MONARCH** C 159
15 **DUTCH TREAT** F 160
35 **DUTOTA DESEJADA** (BRZ) F 67
286 **DUTOTA DESEJADA** (BRZ) F 158
82 **DUTUGAMUNU** (IRE) 5
182 **DUTY CALLS** (IRE) 5
395 **DUTY OF CARE** 8
81 **DUVEEN** 11
1 **DUYFKEN** 17
496 **DWINDLING FUNDS** 54
497 **DYLAN'S DOUBLE** (IRE) 22
49 **DYLAN'S LAD** (IRE) 3
82 **DYNAKITE** 6
363 **DYNAMIC KATE** (IRE) 34
260 **DYNAMIC TALENT** 4
24 **DYNAMITE DORA** (GER) 101
376 **DYNAMITE KENTUCKY** (FR) 11
47 **DYSANIA** (IRE) 12
367 **DYSART DASHER** (IRE) 42
367 **DYSART DYNAMO** (IRE) 43
385 **DYSART ENOS** (IRE) 53
39 **EAGLE COURT** (IRE) 4
153 **EAGLE CREEK** (IRE) 14
442 **EAGLE DAY** (IRE) 34
6 **EAGLE EYED FREDDIE** 25
251 **EAGLE EYED TOM** 30
157 **EAGLE OF THE GLEN** 11
235 **EAGLE ONE** 1
6 **EAGLE PATH** (IRE) 26
161 **EAGLE PRINCE** (IRE) 41
519 **EAGLE WATCH** 3
385 **EAGLE'S REALM** 54
416 **EAGLE'S WAY** 3
419 **EARCOMESANNIE** (IRE) F 3
419 **EARCOMESBOB** 4
419 **EARCOMESSUE** 5
504 **EARLOFTHECOTSWOLDS** (FR) 21
113 **EARLY BOY** (FR) 6
88 **EARLY LIGHT** (FR) 3
29 **EARLY MORNING DEW** (FR) 1
463 **EARN YOUR STRIPES** 10
231 **EARTH** (IRE) 111
497 **EARTH BUSINESS** (IRE) 23
254 **EARTH COMPANY** (IRE) 17
234 **EARTH CRY** (IRE) 19
384 **EARTH DANCE** (IRE) 10
363 **EARTH KING** (IRE) 35
19 **EARTH SPIRIT** 1
355 **EARTHY MANGOLD** (IRE) 142
413 **EASEL** 43
538 **EAST ASIA** (IRE) 22
315 **EAST BANK** 26
454 **EAST BRIDGE** (IRE) 11
477 **EAST COAST LADY** (IRE) G 12
477 **EAST COAST LADY** (IRE) F 20
509 **EAST END GIRL** 11
247 **EAST INDIA EXPRESS** 34
464 **EAST STREET** (IRE) 17
154 **EAST STREET REVUE** 29
85 **EASTER ICON** 4
72 **EASTER ISLAND** 10
335 **EASTER JUNCTION** (IRE) 31
220 **EASTER MIRACLE** 7
540 **EASTER MOUSE** 5
2 **EASTER SUNDAE** 4
484 **EASTERN DESTINY** C 49
206 **EASTERN EMPRESS** 67
80 **EASTERN STAR** (IRE) 27
440 **EASTVAN** (IRE) 94
543 **EASY AS THAT** (IRE) 21
47 **EASY BUCKS** 13
356 **EASY EQUATION** (FR) 1
367 **EASY GAME** (FR) 44
247 **EASY RIDER** 35
501 **EASY TERMS** G 44
390 **EASYSLAND** (FR) 35
311 **EATON COLLINA** (IRE) 7
63 **EATON LADY** (IRE) 3
414 **EATON MILLER** (IRE) 8
301 **EAUX DE VIE** 1
369 **EAVESDROPPING** 40
545 **EBENDI** (IRE) 1
466 **EBONELLO** (IRE) 18
226 **EBONY EMPRESS** (IRE) F 23
532 **EBONY MAW** 15
534 **EBONY SPIRIT** (IRE) 5
385 **EBONY WARRIOR** (IRE) 55
520 **EBRAH** F 13
135 **EBURY** 21
384 **ECCENTRICITY** (USA) F 40
501 **ECCLES STREET** (IRE) 45
147 **ECCO** 13
543 **ECEPARTI** (FR) 22
549 **ECHO BRAVA** 2
24 **ECHO LIMA** 102
218 **ECHO OF PROMISE** 5
256 **ECHO WATT** (FR) 2
367 **ECHOES IN RAIN** (FR) 45
457 **ECLAIR D'AINAY** (FR) 46
509 **ECLAIR DE GUYE** (FR) 12
16 **ECLAIR MAG** (FR) 9
335 **ECLAIRANT LE MONDE** 32
380 **ECONOMIC EDITOR** (IRE) 3
219 **ECONOMICS** 137
212 **ECOSSAIS** (FR) 19
139 **ECTOCROSS** (FR) 17
254 **ECU DE LA NOVERIE** (FR) 18
16 **ECUME ATLANTIQUE** (FR) 10
489 **ED KEEPER** (FR) 13
464 **EDDIE MUSH** (IRE) 18
69 **EDDIE TEMPLE** (IRE) 9
514 **EDE'IFFS ELTON** 5
410 **EDEN DU HOUX** (FR) 23
531 **EDEN MILL** (IRE) 6
42 **EDEN STORM** (IRE) 23
464 **EDGAR ALLAN POE** (IRE) 19
286 **EDGE OF DARKNESS** (IRE) 63
270 **EDGE OF EMBER** 24
333 **EDGE OF LIGHT** F 7
43 **EDGE OF THE WORLD** (IRE) F 110
333 **EDGED OUT** C 11
347 **EDGEWELL** (IRE) 24
387 **EDIE C** (IRE) 104
234 **EDINBURGH ROCK** (IRE) 20
355 **EDITEUR DU GITE** (FR) 27
154 **EDITH GARRUD** 30
349 **EDMOND** 8
281 **EDMOND DANTES** (FR) 3
66 **EDMUND IRONSIDE** 49
219 **EDUCATOR** 9
119 **EDWARD CORNELIUS** (IRE) 13
408 **EDWARD JENNER** (IRE) 11
298 **EDWARDSTONE** 26
174 **EDWINA SHEERAN** (IRE) 32
387 **EEETEE** (IRE) 18
143 **EEH BAH GUM** (IRE) 4
363 **EEL PIE ISLAND** 36
251 **EFAADAH** (IRE) F 84
95 **EFFERVESCE** (IRE) C 30
85 **EFFIE B** F 55
367 **EGALITY MANS** (FR) 46
298 **EGBERT** 27
52 **EGLANTIER** (FR) 4
346 **EGOISTE** (USA) 5
177 **EGYPSYAN CRACKAJAK** 5
177 **EGYPSYAN CRACKELLI** 6
35 **EGYPTIAN KING** (IRE) 68
228 **EHRAZ** 8
43 **EHTEYAT** (GER) 11
14 **EIGHT FIFTEEN** (IRE) 46
447 **EIGHT MILE** (IRE) 11
160 **EIGHTYTWO TEAM** (IRE) 3
507 **EILE TARA** 13
66 **EILEAN DUBH** (IRE) 5
194 **EIRE STREET** (IRE) 2
276 **EIRENE** F 25
355 **EIRICK** 28
384 **EIRNIN** (IRE) F 41
217 **EKLIL** 4
367 **EL BARRA** (FR) 47
513 **EL BELLO** 17
212 **EL BORRACHO** (IRE) 20
66 **EL CABALLO** 6
213 **EL CAPOTE** 4
133 **EL DIABLO** (IRE) 4
506 **EL DRAMA** (IRE) 12
367 **EL FABIOLO** (FR) 48
112 **EL GUMRYAH** (IRE) F 71
361 **EL HABANO** 18
408 **EL HABEEB** (IRE) 12
71 **EL HAGEB ROSE** (FR) 2
80 **EL HIBRI** (IRE) 28
321 **EL HOMBRE** 15
57 **EL JAD** (IRE) 8
175 **EL JASOR** (IRE) 27
224 **EL JEFE** (IRE) 2
247 **EL KALDOUN** (FR) 36
484 **EL MANATI** (IRE) C 50
513 **EL MONTEJEAN** 58
234 **EL MUCHACHO** (IRE) 21
438 **EL PACO** 9
139 **EL PEQUENO PULPO** 18
119 **EL PICADOR** (IRE) 14
12 **EL PRESENTE** 13
525 **EL RAYO** 26
231 **EL REGALO** (IRE) 112
12 **EL RIO** (IRE) 14
417 **EL ROJO GRANDE** (IRE) 2
6 **EL ROYALE** 27
216 **EL SCORPIO** (IRE) 4
384 **EL TESORO** (IRE) 11
209 **ELANORA** (IRE) 6
26 **ELAS RUBY** C 60
305 **ELATION** (IRE) C 42

506 **ELDAR ELDAROV** 13
229 **ELDELBAR** (SPA) 1
131 **ELDERBERRY** M 5
89 **ELDERFLOWER** (IRE) 45
57 **ELDEYAAR** (IRE) 9
497 **ELDORADO ALLEN** (FR) 24
174 **ELDRICKJONES** (IRE) 8
15 **ELEANOR CROSS** 58
458 **ELEANOR DUMONT** 8
112 **ELEANOR POWELL** (IRE) F 72
526 **ELECKTRA** 8
514 **ELECTRIC ANNIE** (IRE) 6
14 **ELECTRIC AVENUE** 47
66 **ELECTRIC EYES** (IRE) 50
404 **ELECTRIC FEEL** C 26
513 **ELECTRIC LIGHTNING** 67
35 **ELECTRICAL STORM** 15
408 **ELECTRIFIED** 64
92 **ELEGANCIA** 25
5 **ELEGANT CHARM** (IRE) 65
368 **ELEGANT ELLEN** (FR) 9
243 **ELEGANT ELLOISE** (IRE) 41
348 **ELEGANT ERIN** (IRE) 9
497 **ELEGANT ESCAPE** (IRE) 25
400 **ELEGANT PEACE** (IRE) C 29
456 **ELENORA DELIGHT** C 66
511 **ELETTARIA** (IRE) 5
479 **ELEUTHEROMANIA** (FR) 26
325 **ELEVEN ELEVEN** (FR) 5
283 **ELF RISING** 12
409 **ELFRIDE** 5
326 **ELHAFEI** (USA) 9
385 **ELHAM VALLEY** (FR) 56
206 **ELHAYBA** 68
153 **ELIGIBLE** (IRE) 15
31 **ELIM** (IRE) 20
367 **ELIMAY** (FR) 49
442 **ELINOR DASHWOOD** (IRE) 70
514 **ELIOS D'OR** (FR) 7
387 **ELISHEVA** (IRE) 19
413 **ELITE ETOILE** 2
367 **ELIXIR D'AINAY** (FR) 50
497 **ELIXIR DE NUTZ** (FR) 26
202 **ELIZA DOLITTLE** (IRE) 7
515 **ELIZABETH BENNET** (IRE) F 75
143 **ELIZABETH'S JOY** 14
28 **ELJAYTEE** (IRE) 6
18 **ELLA ROSIE** F 34
104 **ELLA'S ANGEL** 19
228 **ELLADE** 9
172 **ELLADONNA** (GER) 23
449 **ELLADORA** 6
305 **ELLATRON** (IRE) 43
457 **ELLE EST BEAU** (IRE) 47
315 **ELLEN GATES** F 27
203 **ELLENCARNE** (IRE) 4
163 **ELLEON** (FR) 4
488 **ELLEXIS** (IRE) 42
56 **ELLIE PIPER** 21
466 **ELLIES SISTER** (IRE) 19
531 **ELLISTRIN BELLE** G 7
531 **ELLISTRIN STAR** 8
457 **ELLNANDO QUEEN** F 48
240 **ELMAFTUN** (IRE) 12
228 **ELMALIYA** (IRE) F 145
486 **ELMDALE** (FR) 1
30 **ELMEJOR** (IRE) 10
136 **ELMLEY LOVETT** (IRE) 8
112 **ELMONIR** (IRE) 31
423 **ELMOUNT** (IRE) 10
442 **ELNADIM STAR** (IRE) F 71
66 **ELNADWA** (USA) F 109
219 **ELNAJMM** 60
306 **ELOGIO** (IRE) 13
1 **ELOI DU PUY** (FR) 18
399 **ELOPED** (FR) 36
353 **ELOQUENT** (IRE) C 24
294 **ELOSO** (IRE) 1
366 **ELPOLOGREG** (FR) 10
69 **ELRAAED** 10
472 **ELSA'S PRIDE** (IRE) 11
188 **ELSHAAMEQ** 13
177 **ELSIEANNE** 7
305 **ELTERWATER** 24
164 **ELUSIVE ANGEL** (IRE) 23
546 **ELUSIVE ARTIST** (IRE) 3
166 **ELUSIVE BEAUTY** (IRE) C 20
521 **ELUSIVE EMPIRE** (FR) 63
530 **ELUSIVE ENEMY** (IRE) 2
371 **ELUSIVE RED** (IRE) 4
521 **ELUSIVE TIGER** (IRE) 64
442 **ELVENIA** (IRE) 35
1 **ELVIS MAIL** (FR) 19
15 **ELWASME** 59
525 **ELWING** (IRE) 7
269 **ELYSEE** (IRE) C 3
153 **ELYSIAN FLAME** 16
243 **ELYSIAN WOLF** 42
165 **ELYSIUM DREAM** C 38
348 **ELZAAL** (IRE) 10
221 **ELZAAMSAN** (IRE) 5
30 **ELZAARO** (IRE) 11
79 **ELZANA** (IRE) G 20
336 **EM JAY KAY** 9
112 **EMACULATE SOLDIER** (GER) 32
379 **EMAILANDY** (IRE) 37
442 **EMARAATY ANA** 7
448 **EMBERSCOMBE** (IRE) 9
506 **EMBESTO** 74
61 **EMBLA** 8
24 **EMBODY** (IRE) 103
255 **EMBOLDEN** (IRE) 5
78 **EMBOUR** (IRE) 8
69 **EMBRACE** (IRE) 11
447 **EMBROIDERED CLOTH** 12
552 **EMERALD APPROACH** (IRE) C 40
172 **EMERALD CITY** 51
447 **EMERALD CLIFFS** (IRE) F 26
386 **EMERALD CLIFFS** (IRE) F 27
154 **EMERALD DUCHESS** 109
167 **EMERALD LADY** (IRE) 4
383 **EMERALD RING** (IRE) F 136
138 **EMERALDS PRIDE** 16
484 **EMERIYA** (USA) F 51
383 **EMILY DICKINSON** (IRE) 4
31 **EMILY POST** 3
206 **EMILY UPJOHN** 5
163 **EMILY WADE** (IRE) 5
146 **EMILY'S ECLIPSE** 33
457 **EMILY'S STAR** 49
107 **EMINENCY** (IRE) 27
84 **EMINENT HIPSTER** (IRE) 6
247 **EMIR SACREE** (FR) 37
298 **EMITOM** (IRE) 28
79 **EMIYN** (FR) 2
172 **EMMA EMILLEEN** 24
357 **EMMA LAMB** 13
278 **EMMAS DILEMMA** (IRE) 2
196 **EMMPRESSIVE LADY** (IRE) 5
537 **EMORELLE** (IRE) 24
282 **EMOTIONAL MEMORIES** (IRE) 16
88 **EMPATHIC** (FR) 28
459 **EMPEROR CARADOC** (FR) 4
70 **EMPEROR ZEN** (IRE) 56
270 **EMPEROR'S CLOTHES** (IRE) 25
168 **EMPIRE DE MAULDE** (FR) 8
217 **EMPIRE OF THE SUN** 10
494 **EMPIRE STEEL** (IRE) 17
384 **EMPORIO** (IRE) 1
384 **EMPOWERING** (IRE) F 42
5 **EMPRESS CONSORT** C 156
378 **EMPRESS LIVIA** C 19
114 **EMPRESS LULU** 13
456 **EMPRESS WU** 37
532 **EMPTY QUARTER** 16
317 **EMRAAN** (IRE) 5
10 **EMULATION** 12
367 **EN BETON** (FR) 51
366 **EN COEUR** (FR) 11
102 **EN MEME TEMPS** (FR) 8
277 **ENAMAY** 2
15 **ENBORNE** 60
402 **ENCASHMENT** 24
148 **ENCHANTED NIGHT** 4
131 **ENCHANTEE** (IRE) 6
343 **ENCOSTA** 58
266 **ENCOURAGEABLE** (IRE) 2
501 **END OF AN ERA** (IRE) F 46
219 **END OVER END** C 138
174 **END ZONE** 9
348 **ENDERMAN** 11
438 **ENDERSEN** (IRE) 10
99 **ENDLESS AMBITION** (IRE) G 5
5 **ENDLESS CHARM** F 157
93 **ENDLESS ESCAPE** (IRE) 6
42 **ENDLESS LIGHT** C 56
175 **ENDLESS LOVE** (IRE) F 50
484 **ENDLESS POWER** 15
231 **ENDLESS SUNSHINE** (IRE) 51
385 **ENDLESS SUPPLY** (IRE) 57
5 **ENDLESS TIME** (IRE) C 158
35 **ENDLESS WHISPER** 69
376 **ENDLESSPOSSIBILITY** 12
214 **ENDOFASTORM** (IRE) 3
172 **ENDUED** (IRE) 3
369 **ENDURING LOVE** (IRE) 41
282 **ENEMENEMYNEMO** (IRE) 17
538 **ENEMY** 23
531 **ENEMY AT THE GATE** (IRE) 9
449 **ENEMY COAST AHEAD** 7
367 **ENERGUMENE** (FR) 52
254 **ENERGY ONE** 19
254 **ENERGY TWO** 20
251 **ENFIJAAR** (IRE) C 31
506 **ENFJAAR** (IRE) 75
292 **ENFORCEMENT** (IRE) 16
71 **ENGAGING SAM** 3
176 **ENGELBERT** 21
107 **ENGINEER** 73
440 **ENGLES ROCK** (IRE) 30
515 **ENGLISH OAK** 31

543 **FAUTINETTE** (FR) 27
539 **FAVORI DE SIVOLA** (FR) 6
6 **FAVORITE BOY** 90
153 **FAVORITE GIRL** (GER) G 82
298 **FAVOUR AND FORTUNE** (IRE) 33
402 **FAWSLEY SPIRIT** (IRE) 25
311 **FAY CE QUE VOUDRAS** (IRE) 8
289 **FAYASEL** (IRE) 23
204 **FAYLAQ** 14
414 **FAZAYTE** (FR) 9
58 **FEARLESS** (IRE) 4
208 **FEARLESS ACTION** (IRE) 9
146 **FEARLESS BAY** (IRE) 3
66 **FEARLESSLY** (IRE) C 110
506 **FEARN'S PIPPIN** F 154
75 **FEATH** (IRE) 19
231 **FEATHERTOP** 53
384 **FEDERATION** C 44
112 **FEEDYAH** (USA) F 74
363 **FEEL GOOD INC** (IRE) 37
220 **FEEL LIKE DE BAUNE** (FR) 11
519 **FEEL THE BREEZE** 4
387 **FEEL THE NEED** 70
385 **FEEL THE PINCH** 60
135 **FEEL THE THUNDER** 22
447 **FEELINLIKEASOMEONE** G 27
24 **FEIGNING MADNESS** 108
102 **FEINT** C 26
376 **FEIVEL** (IRE) 14
44 **FELICIE DU MAQUIS** (FR) 5
42 **FELIX** 3
156 **FELLOWSHIP** (IRE) 1
83 **FELTON BELLEVUE** (FR) 10
66 **FEMME PATRONNE** (IRE) 9
408 **FEN BREEZE** C 65
173 **FEN TIGER** (IRE) 4
94 **FENELON** (FR) 5
288 **FENGARI** 10
163 **FENLAND TIGER** 6
458 **FENLANDER** 25
513 **FENNA'S LOSS** (IRE) 19
513 **FENNO'S SOLDIER** (IRE) 20
410 **FERDINAND STAR** 24
219 **FERDOOS** F 143
228 **FERENSBY** 43
343 **FERMOYLE** 14
83 **FERN HILL** (IRE) 11
107 **FERNANDO RAH** 3
367 **FERNY HOLLOW** (IRE) 58
310 **FEROCIOUS** (IRE) 1
286 **FERRARI QUEEN** (IRE) 64
263 **FERRET JEETER** 23
153 **FERRIER** F 55
556 **FERROBIN** (IRE) 7
85 **FERROUS** (IRE) 21
85 **FERVID** C 57
97 **FERYL BERYL** 2
385 **FESTIVE GLORY** (IRE) 61
66 **FESTOSO** (IRE) F 111
281 **FETCH IT YOURSELF** 4
136 **FETE CHAMPETRE** (IRE) 10
24 **FEUD** 40
212 **FEUILLE DE LUNE** (FR) 23
347 **FEVER ROQUE** (FR) 26
332 **FEVERTRE** (IRE) 6
500 **FEYHA** (IRE) 15
320 **FFION** 8
116 **FFOREST DANCER** (IRE) 4
335 **FFREE PEDRO** (IRE) 35
499 **FIA FUINIDH** (IRE) 5
208 **FIADH** (IRE) 10
126 **FIAMETTE** (IRE) 3
447 **FIBONACCI SEQUENCE** (IRE) 28
270 **FICTIONAL** (IRE) 27
390 **FIDDLEDEDEE** (IRE) C 131
497 **FIDDLERONTHEROOF** (IRE) 28
392 **FIDDLERS GREEN** (IRE) 4
132 **FIDELIO VALLIS** (FR) 6
106 **FIDELIUS** 30
89 **FIDUCIARY** 5
539 **FIDUCIARY DUTY** (FR) 37
298 **FIDUX** (FR) 34
80 **FIELDSMAN** (USA) 31
355 **FIERCE** (IRE) 143
402 **FIERCELY PROUD** (IRE) 26
153 **FIERY DAWN** (IRE) 18
219 **FIERY SUNSET** C 144
538 **FIFRELET** (FR) 26
266 **FIFTH HARMONIC** (FR) 9
355 **FIFTY BALL** (FR) 32
138 **FIFTY SENT** 18
376 **FIFTY SHADES OVHAY** (IRE) 15
521 **FIFTY YEAR STORM** (IRE) 65
226 **FIFTYSHADESARESDEV** (FR) 27
188 **FIFTYSHADESOFRED** (FR) 14
447 **FIGHT BACK** 29
392 **FIGHT FOR IT** (IRE) 5
367 **FIGHTER ALLEN** (FR) 59
528 **FIGHTING CHANCE** 7
409 **FIGHTING POET** (IRE) 6
276 **FIGHTING TEMERAIRE** (IRE) 4
360 **FILANDERER** 8
60 **FILBERT STREET** 6
364 **FILE AND PAINT** (IRE) G 7
390 **FILE ILLICO** (FR) 37
206 **FILISTINE** (IRE) 6
496 **FILLE DE REVE** F 56
368 **FILLYFUDGE** 10
263 **FILM D'ACTION** (FR) 24
498 **FILM STAR** 5
385 **FILS DE ROI** (FR) 62
481 **FINAL ACCOUNT** 2
226 **FINAL CHANT** (IRE) 90
387 **FINAL CREDIT** (IRE) 71
360 **FINAL ENCORE** 9
78 **FINAL FRONTIER** (IRE) 9
385 **FINAL RUN** (IRE) G 63
270 **FINAL TREAT** (IRE) F 50
228 **FINALLY** (IRE) 146
439 **FINALSHOT** 5
311 **FINANCIER** 9
125 **FINAWN BAWN** (IRE) 9
231 **FINDHORN MAGIC** F 115
428 **FINDTHETIME** (IRE) 13
187 **FINDUSATGORCOMBE** 4
460 **FINE BY HER** 4
402 **FINE CASTING** (IRE) 27
409 **FINE THEATRE** (IRE) 7
219 **FINE TIME** F 145
135 **FINE WINE** (FR) 23
6 **FINERY** 32
292 **FINESCOPE** 17
112 **FINESPUN** (IRE) F 75
367 **FINEST EVERMORE** (IRE) 60
504 **FINEST HOUR** (FR) 25
92 **FINEST LEADER** (IRE) 27
331 **FINEST VIEW** 4
9 **FINGAL'S HILL** (IRE) 3
369 **FINGLE BRIDGE** (IRE) 43
43 **FINISHINGTHEHAT** C 115
538 **FINN RUSSELL** (IRE) 83
301 **FINN STAR** (IRE) 16
286 **FINN'S CHARM** 65
428 **FINNTHEMAGICIAN** (IRE) 14
5 **FINTRY** (IRE) F 162
300 **FIRCOMBE HALL** 22
357 **FIRE AWAY** (IRE) 14
35 **FIRE BLAZE** (IRE) F 90
543 **FIRE DANCER** (FR) 28
364 **FIRE EYES** (FR) 1
379 **FIRE FLYER** (IRE) 42
524 **FIRE HEART** 17
326 **FIRE JET** (IRE) C 24
234 **FIRE LAKE** (IRE) 24
383 **FIRE LILY** (IRE) C 140
165 **FIRE LINE** F 39
347 **FIREBIRD** 115
204 **FIRENZE** F 48
54 **FIRENZE ROSA** (IRE) 6
263 **FIRESTREAM** 25
214 **FIREWATER** 4
42 **FIREY FLOWER** (IRE) C 57
119 **FIRST ACCOUNT** 16
357 **FIRST ANGEL** (FR) 15
321 **FIRST CHARGE** (IRE) 17
24 **FIRST CITY** F 109
369 **FIRST CLASS RETURN** (IRE) 44
321 **FIRST COMPANY** (IRE) 18
303 **FIRST CUT** 18
414 **FIRST DU CHARMIL** (FR) 10
138 **FIRST ECLIPSE** (IRE) C 75
441 **FIRST EMPEROR** 4
12 **FIRST FLOW** (IRE) 19
176 **FIRST FOLIO** 6
231 **FIRST GENTLEMAN** (IRE) 54
138 **FIRST GREYED** (IRE) 19
410 **FIRST LORD DE CUET** (FR) 25
35 **FIRST MAGIC** (IRE) 70
212 **FIRST MAN** (IRE) 24
172 **FIRST OF MAY** 27
202 **FIRST OFFENCE** (IRE) 9
89 **FIRST OFFICER** (IRE) 6
363 **FIRST QUEST** (USA) 38
499 **FIRST REVOLUTION** (IRE) 6
5 **FIRST RULER** 11
5 **FIRST SIGHT** 69
376 **FIRST SOLDIER** (FR) 16
247 **FIRST STREET** 42
483 **FIRST VENTURE** (IRE) 6
35 **FIRST VIEW** (IRE) 16
98 **FIRTH OF CLYDE** (IRE) 3
136 **FIRTH OF FORTH** (IRE) 11
305 **FISCAL POLICY** (IRE) 7
357 **FISHING FOR LIKES** (IRE) 16
95 **FISHING RIGHTS** 15
369 **FISTON DE BECON** (FR) 45
374 **FISTON DU MOU** (FR) 4
447 **FISTRAL BEACH** (IRE) 30
175 **FITZ PERFECTLY** (FR) 28
130 **FITZROVIA** 4
125 **FITZROY** (IRE) 10

75 **FITZROY RIVER** 20
71 **FITZY** 4
225 **FIVE DOLLAR FINE** (IRE) 3
242 **FIVE GOLD BARS** (IRE) 2
219 **FIVE TOWNS** 63
288 **FIVE WINDS** 9
407 **FIVEOCLOCKSOMEWHER** 6
15 **FIVETHOUSANDTOONE** (IRE) 12
450 **FIX AT ALL** (FR) 13
243 **FIX YOU** 17
472 **FIZZICAL** 3
164 **FLAG CARRIER** 42
320 **FLAG FLYING** 32
92 **FLAG OF LOVE** (IRE) 59
89 **FLAG OF ST GEORGE** (IRE) 47
521 **FLAG OF TRUTH** (FR) 15
514 **FLAGRANT DELITIEP** (FR) 8
367 **FLAME BEARER** (IRE) 61
368 **FLAME JET** (IRE) 39
286 **FLAME OF HESTIA** (IRE) F 159
85 **FLAME QUEEN** 22
484 **FLAME SPIRIT** (IRE) 16
355 **FLAMELCO** (FR) 33
181 **FLAMENCO DE KERSER** (FR) 4
227 **FLAMING AMBITION** (IRE) 10
399 **FLAMING RIB** (IRE) 7
521 **FLAMMABLE** 66
520 **FLANDERS** (IRE) F 28
343 **FLANKING MANEUVER** (IRE) 15
385 **FLANN** 64
85 **FLASH BARDOT** 23
449 **FLASH BULB** (IRE) 9
379 **FLASH COLLONGES** (FR) 43
408 **FLASH FLOOD** C 66
514 **FLASH GORCOMBE** 9
402 **FLASH IN THE PARK** (IRE) 28
224 **FLASH MORIVIERE** (FR) 3
72 **FLASH THE DASH** (IRE) 12
472 **FLASHING COLOUR** F 33
306 **FLASHY BOY** (IRE) 14
509 **FLAT WHITE** (FR) 13
58 **FLAVIUS TITUS** 5
506 **FLAVOUR MAKER** (IRE) 155
89 **FLAWLESS JEWEL** (FR) C 48
176 **FLAXEN FIELDS** (IRE) 22
15 **FLEET ADMIRAL** 64
108 **FLEET OF FOOT** 4
108 **FLEETING BLUE** (FR) 5
305 **FLEETING LIGHT** 8
266 **FLEETING MOMENT** (IRE) 33
457 **FLEGMATIK** (FR) 56
308 **FLEMCARA** (IRE) 17
275 **FLEMEN'S TIPPLE** (IRE) 9
379 **FLEMENSTIDE** (IRE) 44
369 **FLETCH** (FR) 46
175 **FLEUR DE CACTUS** (IRE) C 51
154 **FLEUR DE LIS** F 165
399 **FLEUR DE MER** (IRE) 39
153 **FLEUR DE SEL** G 83
506 **FLEURIR** 80
369 **FLEURMAN** (IRE) 47
180 **FLEURSALS** 2
40 **FLEXI FURLOUGH** (IRE) 9
379 **FLIC OU VOYOU** (FR) 45
43 **FLIGAZ** (FR) F 116
141 **FLIGHT COMMAND** (IRE) 6
390 **FLIGHT DECK** (IRE) 38
286 **FLIGHT OF ANGELS** 66
308 **FLIGHT OF FREEDOM** (IRE) 18
66 **FLIGHT PLAN** 54
66 **FLIGHT RADAR** (IRE) 112
342 **FLIGHT TO FANCY** F 25
282 **FLIGHTY BRIDE** 18
219 **FLINDRIKIN** (IRE) 64
281 **FLINT HILL** 5
16 **FLINTARA** 12
504 **FLINTSTONE** (IRE) 26
392 **FLIP MODE** 6
360 **FLIRTATIOUS** M 10
12 **FLIRTATIOUS GIRL** (IRE) 20
20 **FLLANA BAY** 7
228 **FLOATING ALONG** (IRE) F 147
369 **FLOATING LINE** 48
198 **FLOATING ROCK** (GER) 3
15 **FLOATING SPIRIT** 65
192 **FLOATS ON AIR** 9
231 **FLORA DANICA** (IRE) C 116
261 **FLORA PAGET** 7
279 **FLORAL SPLENDOUR** 15
427 **FLORENCE STREET** 5
219 **FLORIDA** (IRE) 65
428 **FLORIDA DREAMS** (IRE) 15
227 **FLOUEUR** (FR) 11
442 **FLOWER DESERT** (FR) 36
383 **FLOWER FASHION** (FR) C 141
112 **FLOWER OF DUBAI** 34
179 **FLOWER OF GOWER** 6
494 **FLOWER OF SCOTLAND** (FR) 19
148 **FLOWER OF THUNDER** (IRE) 6
543 **FLOWING CADENZA** 29
5 **FLOWRIDER** (USA) F 163
403 **FLOY JOY** (IRE) 5
384 **FLUFF** (IRE) F 45
347 **FLURRY HEART** 27
355 **FLUTE BOWL** C 34
232 **FLUTISTE** (FR) 4
207 **FLY AWAY BLUES** 7
428 **FLY BY MILAN** (IRE) 16
80 **FLY THE NEST** (IRE) 32
479 **FLY ZONE** 28
416 **FLYAWAYDREAM** 4
154 **FLYCATCHER** (IRE) C 166
346 **FLYIN' SOLO** 6
542 **FLYING BARTY** (IRE) 29
42 **FLYING CIRCUS** 24
47 **FLYING FORTUNE** (IRE) 16
484 **FLYING FRONTIER** 17
5 **FLYING HONOURS** 70
186 **FLYING INSTRUCTOR** (IRE) 4
521 **FLYING KISS** (IRE) 67
463 **FLYING MOON** (GER) 13
308 **FLYING NUN** (IRE) 19
520 **FLYING PANTHER** 14
285 **FLYING SECRET** 4
328 **FLYING SPIRIT** 22
28 **FLYING STAR** (IRE) 15
440 **FLYLIKEANEAGLE** (IRE) 32
473 **FLYLOWFLYLONG** (IRE) C 7
290 **FOG ON THE TYNE** (IRE) 6
187 **FOILLMORE** (IRE) 5
294 **FOINIX** 9
301 **FOL O'YASMINE** G 26
456 **FOLK STAR** 38
532 **FOLKS LIKE US** (IRE) 17
112 **FOLLOW A STAR** (IRE) F 76
202 **FOLLOW INTELLO** (IRE) 10
369 **FOLLOW THAT** 49
34 **FOLLOW YOUR ARROW** (FR) 7
74 **FOLLOW YOUR FIRE** (IRE) 9
321 **FOLLOW YOUR HEART** (IRE) 19
56 **FOLLY BRIDGE** G 23
539 **FOLLY GATE** (FR) 7
5 **FOND WORDS** (IRE) F 164
231 **FONISKA** (IRE) 55
543 **FONTAINE COLLONGES** (FR) 30
141 **FONTANA ELLISSI** (FR) 7
347 **FONZERELLI** (IRE) 28
469 **FOOL'S GOLD** (IRE) 45
107 **FOOLS AND HORSES** 29
399 **FOOLS GAMBIT** (IRE) 40
204 **FOOLS RUSH IN** (IRE) 15
461 **FOOTSTEPS ON MARS** (IRE) 11
475 **FOOTSY** 8
358 **FOR FEAR OF FROST** (IRE) 7
509 **FOR GINA** 14
447 **FOR HENRY** (IRE) F 31
74 **FOR JIM** (IRE) 10
254 **FOR LANGY** (FR) 23
220 **FOR PLEASURE** (IRE) 12
524 **FOR THREE** (IRE) 7
80 **FORBEARING** (IRE) 33
43 **FORBIDDEN LOVE** C 117
43 **FORCA BRASIL** (IRE) 12
228 **FORCA TIMAO** (IRE) 44
36 **FORCE DE FRAP** (FR) 3
43 **FORCEFUL SPEED** (IRE) 56
467 **FORCETA** (IRE) 3
335 **FORCING BULL** (FR) 36
292 **FORECAST** 18
66 **FOREIGN LEGIONARY** (IRE) F 113
343 **FOREIGN POLICY** (IRE) 16
78 **FORESEEABLE FUTURE** (FR) 10
305 **FOREST DEMON** (IRE) 26
24 **FOREST FAIRY** (IRE) 110
205 **FOREST JUMP** (IRE) 15
206 **FOREST OF DEAN** 7
88 **FOREST OF WISDOM** 4
26 **FOREST SPIRIT** (IRE) 61
136 **FOREVA ALFIE** (IRE) 12
104 **FOREVER A DOVE** (IRE) 4
189 **FOREVER BLESSED** (IRE) 19
24 **FOREVER BLUE** 111
507 **FOREVER COPPER** 48
151 **FOREVER DES LONG** (FR) 4
349 **FOREVER DREAMING** (IRE) 10
484 **FOREVER IN LOVE** F 53
66 **FOREVER MORE** (IRE) C 114
506 **FOREVER NOAH** 156
266 **FOREVER PROUD** 10
298 **FOREVER WILLIAM** 35
393 **FOREVER'S GIRL** F 8
456 **FORGE VALLEY LAD** 8
298 **FORGET THE WAY** 36
142 **FORGET YOU NOT** (FR) 3
66 **FORGETMENOTBLUE** (IRE) 10
165 **FORGIVING FLOWER** C 40
377 **FORGOT ONE** (IRE) 2
200 **FORGOT TO ASK** (IRE) 19
29 **FORLANO** (FR) 3
542 **FORNHAM ST MARTIN** 30
335 **FORPADDYTHEPLUMBER** (IRE) 37

87 **FORRARD AWAY** (IRE) 4
432 **FORT DE L'OCEAN** (FR) 5
125 **FORT NELSON** 11
154 **FORT YATES** (IRE) 167
239 **FORTAMOUR** (IRE) 13
182 **FORTCANYON** (IRE) 6
1 **FORTESCUE WOOD** (IRE) 20
385 **FORTHEGREATERGOOD** (IRE) 65
74 **FORTIFIED BAY** (IRE) 11
263 **FORTUITOUS FAVOUR** (IRE) 26
74 **FORTUITOUS FIND** 12
501 **FORTUITOUS STAR** (IRE) 47
263 **FORTUNA LIGNA** (IRE) 27
466 **FORTUNATE FRED** (FR) 20
369 **FORTUNATE SOLDIER** (IRE) 50
79 **FORTUNATE STAR** (IRE) 21
88 **FORTUNE** (FR) 29
394 **FORTUNE COOKIE** (IRE) 6
385 **FORTUNE FOREVER** (IRE) 66
392 **FORTUNE TRAVELLER** 7
189 **FORTUNES MELODY** 20
298 **FORWARD FLIGHT** (IRE) 37
263 **FORWARD PLAN** (IRE) 28
442 **FORZA ORTA** (IRE) 9
380 **FOSHAN** (IRE) 5
208 **FOSTER'S FORTUNE** 11
226 **FOSTER'SISLAND** 28
168 **FOSTERED PHIL** (IRE) 12
556 **FOU DILIGENCE** (IRE) 8
42 **FOU RIRE** (IRE) C 58
276 **FOUGERE** 16
292 **FOUND ON** (IRE) 19
154 **FOUNTAIN CROSS** 32
286 **FOUNTAIN OF TIME** (IRE) C 160
263 **FOUNTAINS CHIEF** 29
349 **FOUR ADAAY** 11
303 **FOUR ELEVEN** (CAN) C 31
75 **FOUR FEET** (IRE) 3
66 **FOUR'S COMPANY** (IRE) F 115
132 **FOUROFAKIND** (IRE) 7
541 **FOURSOME** 2
463 **FOURTH OF JULY** (IRE) 14
367 **FOVEROS** (FR) 62
286 **FOX FLAME** 67
237 **FOX HILL** 2
228 **FOX ISLAND** 45
479 **FOX JOURNEY** 29
506 **FOX MASTER** 81
456 **FOX POWER** (IRE) 9
539 **FOX PRO** (FR) 8
15 **FOX TAL** 13
506 **FOX VISION** 82
440 **FOX'S FANCY** (IRE) 33
220 **FOX'S SOCKS** (FR) 13
514 **FOXBORO** (GER) 10
15 **FOXES TALES** (IRE) 14
369 **FOXEY** 51
494 **FOXHOLLOW** (IRE) 20
369 **FOXINTHEBOX** (IRE) 52
355 **FOXTROT SIZZLER** (GER) 35
34 **FOXWOOD** (IRE) 8
358 **FOXY JACKS** (IRE) 8
42 **FOXY LOXY** (IRE) C 59
358 **FOXY ROCK** (IRE) 9
284 **FOZZIE BEAR** (IRE) 8
288 **FRABJOUS** C 11
210 **FRAME RATE** 2
506 **FRANBERRI** 83
285 **FRANCESCO BARACCA** 55
206 **FRANCESCO CLEMENTE** (IRE) 8
552 **FRANCESI** (IRE) 4
188 **FRANCIS XAVIER** (IRE) 15
43 **FRANCISCA** (USA) F 118
358 **FRANCISCIAN ROCK** (IRE) 10
47 **FRANCKY DU BERLAIS** (FR) 17
367 **FRANCO DE PORT** (FR) 63
90 **FRANCO GRASSO** 2
286 **FRANCOPHONE** 161
534 **FRANIGANE** (FR) 6
348 **FRANK THE SPARK** 46
24 **FRANKELIAN** 112
226 **FRANKELIO** (FR) 29
488 **FRANKFREYA** 43
386 **FRANKIE LAMB** 7
317 **FRANKIE ROY** (IRE) 6
192 **FRANKIE'S WISH** (IRE) 49
519 **FRANKIES FIRE** 5
546 **FRANKLIN SAINT** (IRE) 4
15 **FRANKNESS** 66
208 **FRANKS FANCY** (IRE) 12
458 **FRANSHAM** 10
206 **FRANTASTIC** 9
494 **FRANZ JOSEF** (IRE) 21
419 **FRANZ KLAMMER** 6
298 **FRATERNEL** (FR) 38
363 **FRAU GEORGIA** (IRE) 39
327 **FRAVANCO** 3
503 **FREAK OUT** (IRE) 2
368 **FRECKLES** F 54
363 **FRED BEAR** (IRE) 40
210 **FREDDIE FLEETFOOT** 3
55 **FREDDIE'S SONG** (FR) 8
55 **FREDDY BOY** 9
161 **FREDDY ROBINSON** 6
286 **FREDS MATE** (IRE) 162
410 **FREE CHAKARTE** (FR) 26
206 **FREE LOVIN'** 70
164 **FREE STEP** (IRE) 11
206 **FREE WIND** (IRE) 10
206 **FREEDOM DAY** (IRE) 71
78 **FREEDOM FLYER** (IRE) 11
147 **FREESTYLE** (FR) 16
319 **FREETHINKER** (IRE) 10
406 **FREETODREAM** 13
485 **FREEWHEELIN** 4
88 **FREJA** (FR) 5
358 **FRENCH DYNAMITE** (FR) 11
440 **FRENCH HIGHLANDS** (IRE) 34
286 **FRENCH INVASION** (IRE) 68
408 **FRENCH MISTRESS** 40
455 **FRENCH PARADOXE** (FR) 9
541 **FRENCH ROMANCE** 3
543 **FRENCHY DU LARGE** (FR) 31
90 **FRENZIFIED** F 11
15 **FREQUENT FLYER** (IRE) 67
383 **FREQUENTIAL** C 142
457 **FRERE D'ARMES** (FR) 57
543 **FRERO BANBOU** (FR) 32
172 **FRESH** 4
247 **FRESH AS A DAISY** 43
175 **FRESH HOPE** 4
192 **FREYA'S TEARS** (IRE) 50
357 **FRIARY ROCK** (FR) 17
379 **FRIEND OR FOE** (FR) 46
347 **FRIENDLY FIRE** (IRE) 29
461 **FRIENDS DON'T ASK** 5
450 **FRIEZE FRAME** 14
445 **FRIGHTENED RABBIT** (USA) 10
24 **FRIGHTENING** 113
286 **FRILLY** C 163
464 **FRIMEUR DE LANCRAY** (FR) 21
386 **FRINGILL DIKE** (IRE) 8
58 **FRISCO QUEEN** (IRE) 6
403 **FRISKY** 6
321 **FRISTEL** (IRE) 20
399 **FRITILLARIA** (IRE) 41
379 **FRODON** (FR) 47
513 **FROG AND TOAD** (IRE) 21
92 **FROM BEYOND** 28
119 **FROM THE CLOUDS** (FR) 17
213 **FROMPOSTTOPILLAR** 5
390 **FRONT VIEW** (FR) 39
16 **FRONTIER GENERAL** (IRE) 13
66 **FRONTLINE PHANTOM** (IRE) 11
385 **FRUIT HILL** (IRE) 67
335 **FRUIT N NUT** (IRE) 38
217 **FRUITFUL** 11
469 **FUEGO** 7
256 **FUGITIF** (FR) 6
10 **FUJAIRA KING** (USA) 15
543 **FUJI FLIGHT** (FR) 33
385 **FUJI ROCKS** (IRE) 68
456 **FULFILLED** 10
271 **FULGURANT** (FR) 3
376 **FULGURIX** (FR) 17
167 **FULL AUTHORITY** (IRE) 6
355 **FULL BACK** (FR) 36
161 **FULL DAY** G 7
161 **FULL DAY** F 55
403 **FULL INTENTION** 7
247 **FULL OF LIGHT** (IRE) 44
387 **FULL OF SECRETS** (IRE) 72
363 **FULL OF SURPRISES** (FR) 41
520 **FULL PRIME** (IRE) 15
327 **FULLFORWARD** (IRE) 11
471 **FULLY DEPLOYED** 19
206 **FULLY WET** 72
429 **FUMBLEINTHEJUNGLE** 7
367 **FUN FUN FUN** (IRE) 64
543 **FUNAMBULE SIVOLA** (FR) 34
251 **FUNDAY** F 87
192 **FUNKY TOWN PINKIE** 10
66 **FUNNY ENOUGH** F 116
24 **FUNNY STORY** 41
343 **FURIA CRUZADA** G 59
212 **FURIUS DE CIERGUES** (FR) 25
497 **FURKASH** (FR) 29
6 **FURNICOE** (IRE) 91
492 **FURNITURE FACTORS** (IRE) 4
484 **FURQAAN** (IRE) F 54
301 **FURTHER MEASURE** (USA) 3
374 **FUSAIN** (FR) 5
112 **FUSE** (FR) F 77
247 **FUSIL RAFFLES** (FR) 45
227 **FUSIONFORCE** (IRE) 12
347 **FUTURE BENEFITS** (IRE) 30
408 **FUTURE GENERATION** (IRE) F 41
298 **FUTURE INVESTMENT** 39
35 **FUTURE KING** (IRE) 17
355 **FUTURE PERFECT** (IRE) 37
386 **FUTURE TIMES** (FR) 28

410 **GERICAULT ROQUE** (FR) 27
205 **GERICO VILLE** (FR) 16
219 **GERMANIC** (IRE) 146
282 **GEROLAMO CARDANO** 19
335 **GEROMINO** (FR) 44
488 **GERT LUSH** (IRE) 14
46 **GERTCHA** (IRE) 1
226 **GERYVILLE** (FR) 31
212 **GESSKILLE** (FR) 31
20 **GET 'EM IN** (IRE) 8
47 **GET A HIGH** (IRE) 18
457 **GET A TONIC** (IRE) 59
107 **GET AHEAD** 4
189 **GET BACK GET BACK** (IRE) 21
193 **GET BUSY** 17
513 **GET GOING** 23
14 **GET IT** 11
385 **GET ME HOME** (IRE) G 70
358 **GET MY DRIFT** (FR) 13
58 **GET PHAR** (IRE) 7
402 **GET PREPARED** 31
387 **GET SHIRTY** (IRE) 21
457 **GET SKY HIGH** (IRE) 60
286 **GET STUCK IN** (IRE) 70
392 **GET THE VALUE** (IRE) 8
447 **GET UP AND DANCE** C 32
457 **GET UP MUSH** (IRE) 61
136 **GET WITH IT** (IRE) 14
363 **GET WITH THE TIMES** 44
376 **GETABUCK** (IRE) 20
104 **GETALADY** (IRE) 5
232 **GETALEAD** (IRE) 5
282 **GETAMAN** (IRE) 20
347 **GETAREASON** (IRE) 31
47 **GETASTAR** (IRE) 19
402 **GETAWAY DRUMLEE** (IRE) 32
449 **GETAWAY GERRY** 10
133 **GETAWAY GWEN** (IRE) 6
226 **GETAWAY JEWEL** (IRE) 32
369 **GETAWAY LILY BEAR** (IRE) 54
420 **GETAWAY LUV** (IRE) 6
306 **GETAWAY TOM** (IRE) 15
433 **GETAWAY TOTHE WOOD** (IRE) 4
525 **GETAWAY WITH YOU** 10
12 **GETAWEAPON** (IRE) 25
213 **GETBAZOUTOFHERE** 6
378 **GETHIPTOTHETRIP** 12
323 **GETMEGOLD** (IRE) 3
263 **GETMETOTHEMOON** 31
147 **GETOVERTHATHILL** (IRE) 17
385 **GETTHEPOT** (IRE) 71
128 **GETTYSBURGH** (IRE) 2
254 **GETUPEARLY** 25
240 **GETUPTHEYARD** (IRE) 16
371 **GEYSER** 6
513 **GHADBBAAN** 24
35 **GHALY** 18
515 **GHALYAH** F 78
206 **GHARA** 73
135 **GHARBEYIH** 25
538 **GHASHAM** (IRE) 29
228 **GHASSAN** (IRE) 47
510 **GHATHANFAR** (IRE) 2
484 **GHEDI** (IRE) C 55
302 **GHERKIN** 5
400 **GHIZLAAN** (USA) C 5
251 **GHOST LIGHTS** (IRE) 36
501 **GHOST RIDER** (IRE) 10
528 **GHOSTEEM FLECHOIS** (FR) 8
18 **GHOSTLY** 16
107 **GHOSTWRITER** 74
282 **GHYLL MANOR** (IRE) 21
469 **GIANT** 28
42 **GIAVELLOTTO** (IRE) 4
104 **GIBBERWELL** (IRE) 6
154 **GIBSIDE** 35
413 **GIDDY AUNT** 24
234 **GIDDYUPADINGDONG** (IRE) 85
189 **GIDLEIGH PARK** 22
531 **GIE IT LALDY** 11
303 **GIENNAH** (IRE) F 32
402 **GIEVES** (IRE) 33
174 **GIFT OF RAAJ** (IRE) 10
66 **GIFTED GOLD** (IRE) 12
399 **GIFTED RULER** 8
526 **GILBERT** 9
295 **GILBERTINA** 12
146 **GILDED MOON** 34
333 **GILT EDGE** 2
395 **GILT LINKED** C 50
537 **GILWEN ROSIE** 26
79 **GIMCRACK WARRIOR** 22
549 **GIN AND TEA** 3
189 **GIN COCO** (FR) 23
174 **GINATO** (IRE) 11
272 **GINDERELLA** (IRE) 7
338 **GINGER BRANDY** M 3
1 **GINGER MAIL** (FR) 22
449 **GINGER POINTE** (FR) 11
254 **GINGERBRED** 26
451 **GINNY JO** 28
306 **GINNY'S DESTINY** (IRE) 16
354 **GINTINI** (IRE) 17
206 **GINZA** 74
218 **GIO'S GIRL** 7
135 **GIOGIOBBO** 26
119 **GIOIA CIECA** (USA) 19
192 **GIORGIO VASARI** (IRE) 11
400 **GIOVANNI BAGLIONE** (IRE) 6
513 **GIOVANNI CHANGE** (FR) 25
440 **GIOVINCO** (IRE) 36
247 **GIPSY DE CHOISEL** (FR) 47
1 **GIPSY LEE ROSE** (FR) 23
203 **GIRANDOLE** (FR) 6
513 **GIRL FROM ITALY** (IRE) 59
146 **GIRL INTHE PICTURE** (IRE) 5
243 **GIRL MAGIC** 19
219 **GIRL RACER** (IRE) 67
363 **GIRLOFMYDREAMS** 45
298 **GIRLS IN SKIRTS** (IRE) 41
165 **GIRLSWANNAHAVEFUN** 26
442 **GIS A SUB** (IRE) 10
228 **GISBURN** (IRE) 10
279 **GISELLES IZZY** (IRE) 16
466 **GIT MAKER** (FR) 22
298 **GITCHE GUMEE** 42
457 **GIULIETTA** (IRE) 62
115 **GIVE A LITTLE BACK** (FR) 9
66 **GIVE AND TAKE** C 118
279 **GIVE GRACE** (IRE) 17
154 **GIVE IT SOME TEDDY** 36
469 **GIVE IT UP** 46
368 **GIVE ME A BOOM** (IRE) 12
299 **GIVE ME A CUDDLE** (IRE) 8
16 **GIVE ME A MOMENT** (IRE) 14
355 **GIVEGA** (FR) 39
154 **GIZI GAZELLE** (IRE) F 169
70 **GLADE** C 61
539 **GLADIATEUR ALLEN** (FR) 11
363 **GLAJOU** (FR) 46
506 **GLAM DE VEGA** (IRE) 17
305 **GLAM PUSS** 9
333 **GLAMOROUS BREEZE** 3
235 **GLAMOROUS EXPRESS** (IRE) 4
235 **GLAMOROUS FORCE** 5
300 **GLAMOROUS ICON** (IRE) 23
333 **GLAMOROUS JOY** 12
235 **GLAMOROUS STAR** (IRE) 11
472 **GLAMS GAMS** (IRE) 13
524 **GLAN Y GORS** (IRE) 8
331 **GLANCE AT ME** 5
423 **GLANCE FROM CLOVER** 11
183 **GLASCAR MORE** (IRE) 7
343 **GLASS SLIPPER** C 96
463 **GLASSES UP** (USA) 15
6 **GLASSTREES** 33
172 **GLASTONBURY** 52
522 **GLEAMING ARCH** 2
326 **GLEBE ROAD** (IRE) 10
43 **GLEE CLUB** F 119
538 **GLEN AGAIN** (IRE) 30
279 **GLEN ALI** (IRE) 18
357 **GLEN CANNEL** (IRE) 18
474 **GLEN CLOVIS** 7
456 **GLEN COVE** (IRE) 11
392 **GLEN ESK** 9
329 **GLEN GINNIE** (IRE) F 14
204 **GLEN LOMOND** 18
34 **GLENAVADDRA** (IRE) 9
24 **GLENCALVIE** (IRE) 43
319 **GLENCASSLEY** (IRE) 14
80 **GLENCOE BOY** (IRE) 34
15 **GLENFINNAN** (IRE) 71
323 **GLENGEEVER** (IRE) 4
525 **GLENGOLLY** 11
367 **GLENGOULY** (FR) 71
416 **GLENISTER** (IRE) 6
442 **GLENLAUREL** (IRE) 37
204 **GLENLINI** G 19
501 **GLENTEAGUE** 48
357 **GLENTON** 19
374 **GLENTRUAN** (IRE) 7
298 **GLIDE DOWN** (USA) 43
515 **GLIMMER OF LIGHT** 32
319 **GLIMPSE OF GALA** 15
390 **GLIMPSE OF GLORY** 130
271 **GLIMPSE OF GOLD** 4
408 **GLIMPSE THE MOON** 68
428 **GLINGER FLAME** (IRE) 18
179 **GLINT OF AN EYE** (IRE) 7
506 **GLISTENED** 84
228 **GLITTER GIRL** C 149
107 **GLITTERELLA** 75
399 **GLITTERING CHOICE** 9
428 **GLITTERING LOVE** (IRE) 19
84 **GLOBAL ACCLAMATION** 7
234 **GLOBAL AGREEMENT** 30
343 **GLOBAL BRIEF** (IRE) 18
402 **GLOBAL CITIZEN** (IRE) 34
79 **GLOBAL CRISIS** (FR) 23
193 **GLOBAL ESTEEM** (IRE) 5

457 **GLOBAL FAMENGLORY** (IRE) 63
35 **GLOBAL HEAT** (IRE) 19
204 **GLOBAL HUMOR** (USA) 20
174 **GLOBAL SPIRIT** 12
5 **GLOBAL STORM** (IRE) 12
80 **GLOBAL STYLE** (IRE) 35
513 **GLOBAL VISION** (IRE) 26
35 **GLOBAL WALK** (IRE) 20
70 **GLOBAL WARNING** 15
29 **GLOBAL WONDER** (IRE) 4
157 **GLOBE PLAYER** 14
271 **GLOIRE D'ATHON** (FR) 5
43 **GLORIES** (USA) C 120
501 **GLORIOUS ANGEL** (IRE) 49
249 **GLORIOUS CHARMER** 7
457 **GLORIOUS FUN** (IRE) 64
551 **GLORIOUS LADY** (IRE) 3
176 **GLORIOUS LION** 23
402 **GLORIOUS OSCAR** (IRE) 35
18 **GLORIOUS RIO** (IRE) 17
385 **GLORIOUS ZOFF** (IRE) 72
493 **GLORY** 3
306 **GLORY AND FORTUNE** (IRE) 17
359 **GLORY AND GOLD** 4
387 **GLORY AND HONOUR** (IRE) 22
335 **GLORY BRIDGE** (IRE) 45
404 **GLORY CALL** (IRE) 13
348 **GLORY FIGHTER** 13
496 **GLORY HALLELUJAH** (IRE) 8
208 **GLORY HIGHTS** 13
5 **GLORY LILY** 71
321 **GLORY NIGHTS** (IRE) 21
228 **GLORY SKY** (IRE) 48
368 **GLORYBE** (GER) G 13
342 **GLOUCESTERSHIRE** (USA) 3
206 **GLOWING SKY** (IRE) 75
247 **GLYNN** (IRE) 48
261 **GMS PRINCE** 9
376 **GO ALL THE WAY** 21
525 **GO AS YOU PLEASE** (IRE) 12
548 **GO BEYOND** (IRE) 6
463 **GO BOB GO** (IRE) 16
247 **GO CHIQUE** (FR) 49
338 **GO COMPLAIN** 4
369 **GO DANTE** 55
312 **GO FOR COFFEE** M 10
299 **GO FOX** 9
385 **GO GO CHICAGO** (IRE) 73
200 **GO ON BRYCEY LAD** (FR) 21
212 **GO ON CHEZ** 32
336 **GO ON GAL** (IRE) 11
457 **GO STEADY** 65
385 **GO TO WAR** (IRE) 74
379 **GO WEST** (IRE) 50
6 **GO WILD** 98
356 **GO YOUR OWN WAY** 18
388 **GOAHEADWITHTHEPLAN** (IRE) 5
320 **GOAL HANGER** G 9
347 **GOASKHANNAH** (IRE) G 32
286 **GOBI SUNSET** 11
496 **GOBLET OF FIRE** 30
285 **GOD BLESS AMERICA** 56
5 **GOD GIVEN** C 166
542 **GOD OF FIRE** (IRE) 31
228 **GOD OF THUNDER** (IRE) 11
457 **GOD'S OWN GETAWAY** (IRE) 66
539 **GODDESS FREJA** (FR) G 38
441 **GODDESS OF FIRE** 6
313 **GODIVA'S BAY** (IRE) 2
275 **GODOT** (IRE) 10
16 **GODREVY POINT** (FR) 15
416 **GODSEND** 39
219 **GODWINSON** 68
531 **GOGO GLENDA** 12
282 **GOGUENARD** (FR) 22
541 **GOING NATIVE** 4
353 **GOING TO THE MOON** (IRE) 11
478 **GOING UNDERGROUND** 1
415 **GOKOTTA** (IRE) 3
74 **GOLAN CLOUD** (IRE) 13
385 **GOLAN ROAD** (IRE) G 75
162 **GOLD ARCH** 7
42 **GOLD AS GLASS** (IRE) 25
154 **GOLD AT MIDNIGHT** F 170
228 **GOLD AURA** 49
192 **GOLD BRACELET** (IRE) F 61
275 **GOLD CLERMONT** (FR) 11
70 **GOLD COAST** (IRE) 16
279 **GOLD DES BOIS** (FR) 19
212 **GOLD DESERT** 33
335 **GOLD EMERY** (FR) 46
483 **GOLD FOR ALEC** (FR) 30
23 **GOLD GUY** (IRE) 31
308 **GOLD LINK** (FR) 23
270 **GOLD MEDAL** 10
285 **GOLD MINX** 57
344 **GOLD RING** 2
164 **GOLD ROBBER** 24
473 **GOLD SOUK** (IRE) 2
80 **GOLD STANDARD** (IRE) 36
501 **GOLD TERMS** 11
66 **GOLDCASING** (IRE) 56
448 **GOLDEN ACE** 11
106 **GOLDEN AGE** (FR) 5
402 **GOLDEN AMBITION** (IRE) 36
154 **GOLDEN APOLLO** 37
406 **GOLDEN ARC** 15
376 **GOLDEN COSMOS** (IRE) 22
221 **GOLDEN DAYS** (IRE) 6
89 **GOLDEN DELITE** 25
152 **GOLDEN DOVE** 3
496 **GOLDEN DUKE** (IRE) 9
496 **GOLDEN FIREFLY** (IRE) 31
404 **GOLDEN GAL** (IRE) 3
411 **GOLDEN GETAWAY** (IRE) 2
212 **GOLDEN GLANCE** 34
384 **GOLDEN GOOSE** (IRE) 12
507 **GOLDEN IDENTITY** 16
94 **GOLDEN JUANITA** (FR) 18
552 **GOLDEN KEEPER** 5
94 **GOLDEN LAND** 19
5 **GOLDEN LILAS** (IRE) C 167
219 **GOLDEN LYRA** (IRE) 12
538 **GOLDEN MAVERICK** (FR) 84
368 **GOLDEN MAYFLOWER** 14
154 **GOLDEN MELODY** (IRE) 38
152 **GOLDEN MILLIE** 4
303 **GOLDEN MOON** 19
399 **GOLDEN MOONSHAKE** (IRE) 43
24 **GOLDEN MYRRH** (IRE) 115
515 **GOLDEN PASSPORT** 33
96 **GOLDEN PHASE** 12
67 **GOLDEN POET** (IRE) 10
440 **GOLDEN POINT** (FR) 37
108 **GOLDEN PROSPERITY** (IRE) 6
348 **GOLDEN RAINBOW** 14
15 **GOLDEN REIGN** (IRE) C 161
6 **GOLDEN SANDS** (IRE) 34
416 **GOLDEN SHOT** 7
5 **GOLDEN SMILE** 72
379 **GOLDEN SON** (FR) 51
254 **GOLDEN SOVEREIGN** (IRE) 27
144 **GOLDEN SPARKLE** (IRE) G 8
330 **GOLDEN SPICE** (USA) 4
219 **GOLDEN STUNNER** (IRE) C 147
385 **GOLDEN TAIPAN** (IRE) 76
343 **GOLDEN TEMPLE** 60
352 **GOLDEN TOWN** (IRE) 11
221 **GOLDEN TWILIGHT** (IRE) 7
5 **GOLDEN VALENTINE** (FR) C 168
463 **GOLDEN VALOUR** 17
386 **GOLDEN VINTAGE** 9
537 **GOLDEN WHISKY** (IRE) 27
98 **GOLDKIT** (FR) 15
258 **GOLDRAPPER** (IRE) 4
15 **GOLDSBOROUGH** 72
243 **GOLDSMITH** (IRE) 2
5 **GOLDSPUR** (IRE) 13
300 **GOLFE CLAIR** (FR) 24
285 **GOLSPIE** (IRE) 28
119 **GOMETRA GINTY** (IRE) 20
286 **GONE** (IRE) 71
220 **GONE IN SIXTY** 15
286 **GONE ROGUE** (IRE) 165
460 **GONE TO TEXAS** (IRE) 5
428 **GONFALONIER** (FR) 20
346 **GONNETOT** (FR) 7
434 **GONNINO** (IRE) 5
27 **GONZAGA** 1
335 **GOOBINATOR** (USA) 47
504 **GOOD BOY BOBBY** (IRE) 27
162 **GOOD BYE** (GER) 8
249 **GOOD EARTH** (IRE) 8
219 **GOOD GRACIOUS** 69
322 **GOOD GREEF** 3
88 **GOOD GUESS** 32
15 **GOOD HOPE** F 162
70 **GOOD HUMOR** 17
316 **GOOD IMPRESSION** 6
176 **GOOD KARMA** 24
263 **GOOD LOOK CHARM** (FR) 32
7 **GOOD LORD** (GER) 3
348 **GOOD LUCK FOX** (IRE) 15
286 **GOOD MORALS** 72
427 **GOOD NEWS** 6
29 **GOOD OLD SUSSEX** (IRE) 5
489 **GOOD RISK AT ALL** (FR) 15
119 **GOOD SHOW** 21
181 **GOOD SOUL** 5
29 **GOOD TIME AHEAD** (IRE) 6
283 **GOOD TO GO** 14
212 **GOOD WORK** (FR) 35
288 **GOODEVENINGMRBOND** (IRE) 12
398 **GOODFELLA** (IRE) 7
130 **GOODISON GIRL** 5
506 **GOODNIGHT AND JOY** (IRE) C 157
190 **GOODNIGHT CHARLIE** 3
518 **GOODOLDBILL** 2
189 **GOODTIMECREW** (IRE) 24
494 **GOODTIMES BADTIMES** (IRE) 22
414 **GOODWILLHUNTING** (IRE) 11

205 **GOODWIN** (IRE) 17
205 **GOODWIN RACING** (IRE) 18
346 **GOODWOOD ODYSSEY** 43
346 **GOODWOOD VISION** 22
383 **GOOLOOGONG** (IRE) 48
457 **GOONHILLY** (IRE) 67
447 **GOOSE ROCK** (IRE) 14
467 **GOOSEWOOD** 4
175 **GORAK** (FR) 5
514 **GORCOMBE MOONSHINE** 11
494 **GORDON DAI DAI** (FR) 23
538 **GORDON GREY** (IRE) 85
13 **GORDONSTOUN** (IRE) 8
364 **GORGEOUS GENERAL** 2
385 **GORTROE JOE** (IRE) 77
355 **GOSHEN** (FR) 40
254 **GOSHHOWPOSH** (IRE) 28
75 **GOSMORE** 21
384 **GOSSAMER SEED** (IRE) C 46
421 **GOSSAMER SILK** 9
384 **GOSSAMER WINGS** (USA) F 47
135 **GOSSIP** 27
432 **GOT BRIGHT** (FR) 6
542 **GOT NO DOLLARS** (IRE) 9
494 **GOT TRUMPED** 24
556 **GOTADANCE** (IRE) 9
266 **GOTTA SHOW ME** (IRE) 11
265 **GOTTHEREINTHEEND** (IRE) 5
189 **GOUDHURST STAR** (IRE) 25
212 **GOUET DES BRUYERES** (FR) 36
423 **GOVERNOR GREEN** (IRE) 12
206 **GOVERNOR OF INDIA** 76
102 **GOWANBUSTER** 9
300 **GOWANLAD** 25
379 **GRACE A VOUS ENKI** (FR) 52
260 **GRACE ANGEL** 10
187 **GRACEFULL DANCER** 6
154 **GRACELANDS GIRL** 39
204 **GRACES QUEST** 21
184 **GRACIOUS GEORGE** (IRE) 2
321 **GRACIOUS GRACE** (IRE) 43
532 **GRADY GASTON** (IRE) 19
148 **GRAFFA** 7
63 **GRAFFITI** 4
228 **GRAHAM** 50
14 **GRAIGNES** (FR) 12
335 **GRAIN D'OUDAIRIES** (FR) 48
475 **GRAIN DE BEAUTE** (IRE) F 18
286 **GRAIN OF HOPE** 73
7 **GRAIN TRADE** 4
408 **GRAINE DE MAILLE** (IRE) F 69
154 **GRAN CANARIA QUEEN** F 112
154 **GRAN CANARIA QUEEN** C 171
285 **GRANARY QUEEN** (IRE) 5
175 **GRAND ALLIANCE** (IRE) 6
204 **GRAND CANAL** (IRE) 22
336 **GRAND CENTRAL** 24
226 **GRAND DU NORD** (FR) 33
217 **GRAND DUCHESS OLGA** 12
12 **GRAND ESCAPARDE** (IRE) 26
115 **GRAND KNIGHT** (FR) 10
72 **GRAND LADY** 61
95 **GRAND LIBYA** 8
157 **GRAND LORD** (FR) 15
340 **GRAND MARIO** (FR) 5
245 **GRAND MOGUL** (IRE) 2
461 **GRAND MYLA** (IRE) C 13
299 **GRAND REVIVAL** (USA) 10
202 **GRAND SABRE** 11
149 **GRAND SLAM MARIA** (FR) M 3
149 **GRAND SLAM MARIA** (FR) F 19
352 **GRAND SOUFLE** (FR) 12
101 **GRAND VOYAGE** (FR) 12
270 **GRAND ZAFEEN** F 52
161 **GRANDAD** 43
348 **GRANDAD BOB** (IRE) 47
369 **GRANDADS COTTAGE** (IRE) 56
206 **GRANDE DAME** 11
29 **GRANDEE** (IRE) 7
298 **GRANDEUR D'AME** (FR) 44
106 **GRANDFATHER TOM** 6
343 **GRANGE LADY** (IRE) 61
226 **GRANGE RANGER** (IRE) 34
227 **GRANGE ROAD** (IRE) 13
410 **GRANGECLARE GLORY** (IRE) 28
29 **GRANGECLARE NORTH** (IRE) 8
211 **GRANGECLARE ROSA** (IRE) G 14
186 **GRANGECLARE VIEW** (IRE) 5
251 **GRANNY BEA** (IRE) C 88
395 **GRANNY FRANNY** (USA) F 51
348 **GRANT WOOD** (IRE) 16
153 **GRANTLEY HALL** 19
127 **GRAPEVINE** (IRE) 2
296 **GRAPHITE** (FR) 3
135 **GRASS GREEN** F 69
194 **GRASS'S JET** (IRE) 3
220 **GRASSE D'OLIVERIE** (FR) 16
12 **GRAVE LA KLASS** (FR) 27
219 **GRAVITY FLOW** (IRE) C 148
342 **GRAYLING** C 26
101 **GRAYSTOWN** (IRE) 13
379 **GREANETEEN** (FR) 53
285 **GREASED LIGHTNING** 29
285 **GREAT ACCLAIM** 58
515 **GREAT AMBASSADOR** 6
226 **GREAT BALLINBORIS** (FR) 35
228 **GREAT BEDWYN** 51
40 **GREAT COLACI** 10
126 **GREAT COMMISSION** 4
200 **GREAT D'ANGE** (FR) 22
466 **GREAT D'TROICE** (FR) 23
385 **GREAT HEART'JAC** (FR) 78
5 **GREAT HOPE** (IRE) C 169
35 **GREAT HUNTER** (IRE) 21
243 **GREAT MAX** (IRE) 3
189 **GREAT NAME THAT** (IRE) 26
35 **GREAT NEWS** 22
363 **GREAT OCEAN** (FR) 47
226 **GREAT RAFFLES** (FR) 36
125 **GREAT RIDLEY** 13
457 **GREAT SAMOURAI** (FR) 68
267 **GREAT SCHEMA** 7
363 **GREAT SNOW** (FR) 48
150 **GREAT WHITE HOPE** (IRE) G 3
219 **GREATEST HEAVENS** 149
385 **GREATEST STAR** (FR) 79
228 **GREATEST TIME** (IRE) 52
219 **GREATEST VIRTUE** F 150
506 **GREATGADIAN** (GER) 18
402 **GREATNESS AWAITS** (IRE) 37
395 **GREAVSIE** (IRE) 32
154 **GRECIAN ARTISAN** (IRE) C 172
5 **GRECIAN LIGHT** (IRE) F 170
335 **GREDIN** (FR) 49
146 **GREEK GIANT** (IRE) 35
92 **GREEK ORDER** 29
161 **GREEK SIREN** 44
543 **GREEN BOOK** (FR) 39
231 **GREEN CASTLE** (IRE) F 117
506 **GREEN GO** (IRE) 85
24 **GREEN KEEPER** 116
15 **GREEN MACHINE** (IRE) 73
300 **GREEN OAKS TOP CAT** 26
386 **GREEN PLANET** (IRE) 10
298 **GREEN PLANET** (IRE) 45
193 **GREEN POWER** 6
43 **GREEN SIGMA** 121
41 **GREEN SPIRIT** (FR) 5
538 **GREEN TEAM** (FR) 31
238 **GREEN ZONE** (IRE) 3
56 **GREENBRIDGE BOY** 50
480 **GREENERY** (IRE) F 16
123 **GREENGAGE** (IRE) 4
440 **GREENHILL GARDENS** 38
383 **GREENISLAND** (IRE) C 143
383 **GREENLAND** (IRE) 49
311 **GREENROCK ABBEY** (IRE) 10
347 **GREENWICH** 100
285 **GREG THE GREAT** 6
88 **GREGARINA** (FR) 6
448 **GREGOR** (FR) 12
72 **GREGORIANNA** (IRE) 62
206 **GREGORY** 77
15 **GRENHAM BAY** (IRE) 74
31 **GRESSINGTON** (IRE) 47
192 **GREY BELLE** (FR) 12
438 **GREY D'ALCO** (FR) 12
457 **GREY DAWNING** (IRE) 69
489 **GREY DIAMOND** (FR) 16
171 **GREY FORCE ONE** 10
308 **GREY FOX** (IRE) 24
92 **GREY MOON** 60
101 **GREY MOSS** 14
308 **GREY OWL** 77
118 **GREY ROSETTA** 8
335 **GREY SKIES** (IRE) 50
24 **GREY'S MONUMENT** 44
66 **GREYCIOUS ANNA** 57
298 **GREYSTOKE** 46
385 **GREYVAL** (FR) 80
161 **GRID IRON MAIDEN** 56
58 **GRIFTER** 8
548 **GRIGGY** (IRE) 7
403 **GRIGIO** (IRE) 15
457 **GRILLON DE MONTY** (FR) 70
412 **GRIMSBY TOWN** (IRE) 5
557 **GRIPPER** 4
450 **GRIS GRIS TOP** (FR) 15
314 **GRIS MAJEUR** (FR) 6
379 **GRIVETANA** (FR) 54
543 **GRIZZLY JAMES** (FR) 40
115 **GROOM DE COTTE** (FR) 11
266 **GROOVE NATION** 12
308 **GROOVY BLUE** 25
298 **GROSVENOR COURT** 47
384 **GROTTA DEL FAUNO** (IRE) C 48
15 **GROUNDBREAKER** (GER) 15
521 **GROVE ROAD** (IRE) 16
547 **GROW NASA GROW** (IRE) 3
264 **GRUMPY CHARLEY** 6
264 **GRUMPY FREYA** 7

264 **GRUMPY ROSIE** 8
206 **GUARD** 78
308 **GUARD DUTY** 26
504 **GUARD YOUR DREAMS** 28
355 **GUARDIA TOP** (FR) 41
414 **GUATEMALA LE DUN** (FR) 12
423 **GUERLAIN DE VAUX** (FR) 13
497 **GUERNESEY** (FR) 30
43 **GUERRIERE** (IRE) C 122
449 **GUEST LIST** (IRE) 12
319 **GUETAPAN COLLONGES** (FR) 16
488 **GUGUSS COLLONGES** (FR) 15
364 **GUIDANCE** 8
532 **GUIDING STAR** 20
335 **GUILLAUME** (IRE) 51
84 **GUILTY PARTY** (IRE) 8
29 **GUINESSED** (IRE) 9
466 **GUINNESS AFFAIR** (FR) 24
144 **GUINNESS VILLAGE** (IRE) 9
239 **GUIRI** (GER) 14
461 **GUITAR** 6
176 **GULF LEGEND** (FR) 50
383 **GULF OF MEXICO** (IRE) 50
387 **GULLIVER** 23
383 **GULLIVER'S TRAVELS** (IRE) 5
552 **GULMARG** (IRE) 23
385 **GUMBALL** (FR) 81
223 **GUN MERCHANT** 5
323 **GUN RUNNER CASH** (IRE) 5
57 **GUN SALUTE** (IRE) 12
501 **GUNNERSIDE** (IRE) 12
157 **GUNNERY OFFICER** (IRE) 16
369 **GUNSIGHT RIDGE** 57
488 **GURKHA GIRL** (IRE) 16
437 **GURKHALI** 5
367 **GUST OF WIND** (FR) 72
451 **GUSTAV GRAVES** 7
505 **GUSTAV HOLST** (IRE) 6
521 **GUSTAVAGO** (IRE) 69
263 **GUSTAVIAN** (IRE) 33
486 **GUTTURAL** (IRE) 2
504 **GUY** (IRE) 29
449 **GWEEDORE** 13
410 **GWENCILY BERBAS** (FR) 29
107 **GWENDOLINA** 30
390 **GWENNIE MAY BOY** (IRE) 40
497 **GYENYAME** 31
272 **GYLLEN** (USA) 8
182 **GYPSEY'S SECRET** (IRE) 7
122 **GYPSY HILL** 7
521 **GYPSY NATION** (IRE) 70
135 **GYPSY WHISPER** 28
315 **H KEY LAILS** 11
367 **HA D'OR** (FR) 73
6 **HA'AN** 35
458 **HAAFAPIECE** 12
36 **HAAFBACK** 4
36 **HAAFBOURD** 5
294 **HAALAND** (IRE) 10
26 **HAARAR** 6
319 **HAAS BOY** (FR) 17
294 **HABANERO STAR** 2
31 **HABBAT REEH** (IRE) F 48
161 **HABITUAL** 57
74 **HACHERT** 14
167 **HACKBERRY** 7
379 **HACKER DES PLACES** (FR) 55
399 **HACKMAN** (IRE) 83
104 **HAD TO BE DONE** (IRE) F 7
347 **HAD TO BE HUGO** (IRE) 33
355 **HADDEX DES OBEAUX** (FR) 42
227 **HADDOCK DE GRISSAY** (FR) 14
330 **HADEEYA** G 19
286 **HADRIANUS** (IRE) 74
515 **HAFEET ALAIN** (IRE) 7
5 **HAFIT** (IRE) 14
333 **HAGIA SOPHIA** 4
489 **HAIDEES REFLECTION** F 17
66 **HAIL CEASAR** 119
229 **HAIL SEZER** 2
69 **HAILEY YA MAL** (IRE) 13
456 **HAIRPIN** (USA) C 67
116 **HAITI COULEURS** (FR) 6
114 **HAITI DANCER** F 7
114 **HAITI DANCER** C 14
119 **HAIZOOM** 22
510 **HAJEY** 3
321 **HAKU** (IRE) 22
280 **HAKUNA BABE** 13
517 **HAKURAA** (IRE) C 15
451 **HALA BE ZAIN** (IRE) 8
449 **HALCYON DREAMS** (IRE) 14
122 **HALDON HILL** (IRE) 8
138 **HALE END** (IRE) 48
379 **HALF DOZEN** (IRE) 56
233 **HALF NELSON** 3
279 **HALF SHOT** (IRE) 20
390 **HALF THE FREEDOM** 41
1 **HALF TRACK** (IRE) 24
20 **HALFWAY HOUSE LAD** 9
233 **HALIFAX** (FR) 4
538 **HALIPHON** 32
298 **HALL LANE** (IRE) 48
69 **HALLA DUBAI** (IRE) 14
12 **HALLIGATOR** (FR) 28
462 **HALLOWED GROUND** (IRE) 3
175 **HALLROSE** 29
430 **HALLWOOD** (FR) 2
379 **HALO DES OBEAUX** (FR) 57
142 **HALOA MAIL** (FR) 4
369 **HALONDO** (FR) 58
506 **HALVA** (IRE) 158
506 **HAMASAT** C 159
219 **HAMISH** 13
356 **HAMMOCK** 3
361 **HAMMY END** (IRE) 3
106 **HAN SOLO BERGER** (IRE) 7
408 **HANAMI** F 42
216 **HAND AND DIAMOND** 5
384 **HAND ON HEART** (IRE) F 49
5 **HAND PUPPET** (IRE) F 171
43 **HANDANA** (IRE) F 123
17 **HANDEL** (USA) 7
247 **HANDS OFF** (IRE) 50
308 **HANG IN THERE** (IRE) 27
63 **HANNAH'S RETURN** 5
403 **HANOVERIAN KING** (GER) 8
383 **HANS ANDERSEN** 51
355 **HANSARD** (IRE) 43
384 **HAPPEN** (USA) F 50
154 **HAPPIER** (IRE) 113
220 **HAPPY AND FINE** (FR) 17
205 **HAPPY BOY** (FR) 19
392 **HAPPY COMPANY** (IRE) 10
528 **HAPPY COUNTY** (FR) 9
154 **HAPPY DANCER** (IRE) 114
537 **HAPPY DU MESNIL** (FR) 28
43 **HAPPY FACE** (IRE) F 124
360 **HAPPY HADEDA** (IRE) 75
456 **HAPPY HIKER** (IRE) F 68
74 **HAPPY HOLLOW** 15
92 **HAPPY HOLLY** (IRE) F 30
525 **HAPPY INDEX** 13
554 **HAPPY LARRY** (IRE) 4
4 **HAPPY NEWS** 8
164 **HAPPY PLACE** 43
363 **HAPPY RETURNS** 49
228 **HAPPY ROMANCE** (IRE) 12
556 **HAPPY SANCHEZ** (IRE) 10
12 **HAPPYGOLUCKY** (IRE) 29
168 **HAPY LA VIE** (FR) 13
220 **HARA KIRI** (FR) 18
110 **HARB** 1
151 **HARBIE** 5
298 **HARBOUR LAKE** (IRE) 49
80 **HARBOUR PROJECT** 37
537 **HARBOUR SHORE** (IRE) 29
56 **HARBOUR STAR** C 51
56 **HARBOUR STORM** 24
135 **HARBOUR VISION** 29
353 **HARD ACT TO FOLLOW** (IRE) 12
385 **HARD AS NAILS** 82
132 **HARD FROST** (FR) 9
552 **HARD LINER** (IRE) 24
405 **HARD NUT** (IRE) 4
78 **HARD SOLUTION** 12
228 **HARD WALNUT** (IRE) C 150
46 **HARDE FASHION** 2
369 **HARDI DU MESNIL** (FR) 59
231 **HARDPOINT** (IRE) 57
325 **HARDY** 7
154 **HARDY ANGEL** 115
402 **HARDY BOY** (FR) 38
466 **HARDY DU SEUIL** (FR) 25
308 **HARDY FELLA** (IRE) 28
319 **HARJO** (IRE) 18
213 **HARKANGEL** 7
540 **HARLEM CLERMONT** (FR) 7
320 **HARLEM DANCER** F 48
266 **HARLEM NIGHTS** (IRE) 13
267 **HARLEM SOUL** 8
135 **HARMONIOUS** 30
402 **HARPER'S BROOK** (IRE) 39
146 **HARRIET'S ANGEL** 36
18 **HARROGATE** (IRE) 18
456 **HARROGATE BETTY** 39
206 **HARROVIAN** 12
343 **HARRY ALONZO** (IRE) 19
456 **HARRY BROWN** 40
282 **HARRY D'ALENE** (FR) 23
295 **HARRY DU BERLAIS** (IRE) 13
220 **HARRY GULLIVER** 19
275 **HARRY HAZARD** 12
251 **HARRY MAGNUS** (IRE) 37
542 **HARRY THE HAGGLER** (IRE) 32
319 **HARRY THE NORSEMAN** 19
107 **HARRY THREE** 5
441 **HARRY WITH STYLE** 16
188 **HARRY'S HALO** (IRE) 30
534 **HARRY'S HOTTIE** (IRE) 8
174 **HARSWELL DUKE** (IRE) 13

174 **HARSWELL ROSE** 33
501 **HART STOPPER** 13
360 **HARTFIELD** (IRE) 12
497 **HARTINGTON** (IRE) 32
547 **HARTSIDE** (GER) 4
457 **HARTUR D'OUDAIRIES** (FR) 71
66 **HARVANNA** 120
392 **HARVIE WALLBANGER** (IRE) 11
220 **HAS TROKE** (FR) 20
357 **HASANKEY** (IRE) 20
165 **HASEEF** (IRE) 4
298 **HASEEFAH** 50
212 **HASHEHADHISOATSYET** (IRE) 37
281 **HASHTAG BOUM** (FR) 6
168 **HASHTAG LORD** (FR) 14
395 **HASHTAGMETOO** (USA) 11
24 **HASKOY** 4
343 **HASTEN SLOWLY** 62
390 **HASTHING** (FR) 42
540 **HASTON CLERMONT** (FR) 8
347 **HASTY BROOK** (FR) 34
234 **HASTY PARISIAN** (IRE) 31
479 **HASTY SAILOR** (IRE) 9
228 **HATADORA** (IRE) 151
457 **HATCHER** (IRE) 72
263 **HATOS** (FR) 34
238 **HATTAAB** 4
526 **HATTON PARK** G 10
494 **HATTONS GARDENS** (IRE) 25
399 **HAUGHTILY** (IRE) C 44
298 **HAUGHTY** 130
309 **HAUL AWAY** (IRE) 7
150 **HAULFRONHOBBS** 7
416 **HAUMEA** (IRE) 40
146 **HAUNTED DREAM** (IRE) 6
97 **HAURAKI GULF** 3
113 **HAUT BERRY** (FR) 7
367 **HAUT EN COULEURS** (FR) 74
543 **HAUT FOLIN** (FR) 41
440 **HAUTE ESTIME** (IRE) 39
367 **HAUTURIERE** (FR) 75
138 **HAVAGOMECCA** 21
234 **HAVAILA** (IRE) 32
107 **HAVANA BLUE** 31
315 **HAVANA BY THE SEA** (IRE) 12
344 **HAVANA CABANA** 3
509 **HAVANA FLAME** 39
42 **HAVANA FORCE** (ITY) 60
356 **HAVANA GOLDRUSH** 4
251 **HAVANA HEAT** 38
11 **HAVANA JANE** C 7
279 **HAVANA PARTY** 21
193 **HAVANA PUSEY** 18
242 **HAVANA RIVER** (IRE) 3
31 **HAVANA ROSE** (IRE) 49
146 **HAVANA SKY** 61
270 **HAVANAGREATTIME** (IRE) 53
513 **HAVANAWING** 60
15 **HAVANAZAM** 75
454 **HAVANELLA** (FR) 12
485 **HAVE YOU A MINUTE** 7
50 **HAVEAGOBEAU** 7
335 **HAVEANOTHERGOFLO** (IRE) 52
276 **HAVECHATMA** 18
56 **HAVEN'S WAVE** (IRE) F 52
311 **HAVEN'T TIME** (IRE) 11
70 **HAVEONEYERSELF** (IRE) 18
484 **HAVERGATE** C 56
434 **HAVEYOUGOTMYMONEY** (IRE) 6
279 **HAVEYOUMISSEDME** 22
513 **HAVING A BARNEY** (IRE) 27
457 **HAVOCK** (IRE) 73
172 **HAVRAISE** (FR) 53
43 **HAWAAFEZ** F 125
363 **HAWAII DU MESTIVEL** (FR) 50
228 **HAWAJES** (IRE) 53
303 **HAWANA** F 33
308 **HAWK JET** 78
308 **HAWK'S WELL** (IRE) 29
526 **HAWKES BAY** 29
368 **HAWTHORN COTTAGE** (IRE) 15
189 **HAY THERE MONA** (IRE) 27
15 **HAYA** 163
355 **HAYEDO** (GER) 44
360 **HAYMAKER** 13
383 **HAZAKIYRA** (IRE) C 144
153 **HAZARDOUS** G 56
383 **HAZARIYA** (IRE) C 145
395 **HAZEL BEAR** 33
80 **HAZIYM** (IRE) 38
203 **HAZMAT** (IRE) 7
495 **HAZY DREAM** 5
153 **HAZY GLEN** (FR) 20
234 **HAZY OUTLOOK** (IRE) F 33
63 **HE IS A CRACKER** (IRE) 6
534 **HE KNOWS BETTER** (IRE) 9
399 **HE'S A GENTLEMAN** (IRE) 10
399 **HE'S A KEEPER** (IRE) 11
525 **HE'S A KNOWALL** (IRE) 14
355 **HE'S A LATCHICO** (IRE) 45
521 **HE'S A MONSTER** (IRE) 71
154 **HE'S AN ANGEL** 116
399 **HE'S GOT GAME** (IRE) 84
317 **HE'S MY SHADOW** (IRE) 7
80 **HE'S OUR STAR** (IRE) 39
325 **HE'S SO BRAZEN** 8
254 **HEAD AND HEART** 29
390 **HEAD LAW** (FR) 43
538 **HEAD ON** (IRE) 33
355 **HEAD OVER HINDS** (IRE) 46
154 **HEADABOVETHEREST** (IRE) 117
387 **HEADINGLEY** (IRE) 24
135 **HEADLAND** 31
139 **HEADLEY GEORGE** (IRE) 4
450 **HEADS OR HARPS** 16
428 **HEADSCARF LIL** (IRE) 21
80 **HEADSHOT** 40
192 **HEALING POWER** 13
445 **HEART ABOVE** 11
298 **HEART OF A LION** (IRE) 51
496 **HEART OF ACKLAM** 32
496 **HEART OF SOFIA** (IRE) 33
359 **HEART OF SOUL** (IRE) 5
551 **HEART OF THE SUN** 4
385 **HEART OVER HEAD** (IRE) 83
35 **HEART'S CONTENT** (IRE) F 71
346 **HEARTACHE TONIGHT** (FR) 23
335 **HEARTBREAK KID** (IRE) 53
75 **HEARTBREAK LASS** 4
107 **HEARTBREAKING** (IRE) 32
228 **HEARTFULLOFSTARS** (IRE) 152
5 **HEARTILY** (IRE) C 172
378 **HEARTSTONE** (IRE) C 20
43 **HEARTWARMER** 126
416 **HEAT OF PASSION** 41
89 **HEAT OF THE MOMENT** 7
26 **HEATER** (IRE) 63
456 **HEATH RISE** 12
172 **HEATHCLIFF** 54
146 **HEATHEN** 7
464 **HEATHER HONEY** 23
26 **HEATHERDOWN HERO** 7
383 **HEAVEN ON EARTH** (IRE) F 146
355 **HEAVEN SMART** (FR) 47
484 **HEAVEN'S ANGEL** (IRE) C 57
447 **HEAVENLY ANGEL** C 33
521 **HEAVENLY BREATH** 72
472 **HEAVENLY SNOW** F 34
92 **HEAVENLY SONG** (IRE) G 31
92 **HEAVENLY SONG** (IRE) C 61
26 **HEAVENLY WISH** (IRE) 29
451 **HEAVENS DEW** 9
17 **HEAVENS LIGHT** (IRE) 8
107 **HEAVENS PEAK** C 76
219 **HEAVENS TO BETSY** 70
219 **HEBRIDES** (IRE) 14
228 **HECTIC** 54
14 **HECTOR** (IRE) 13
355 **HECTOR JAGUEN** (FR) 48
319 **HECTOR JAVILEX** (FR) 20
139 **HECTOR LOZA** 5
440 **HECTOR MASTER** (FR) 40
286 **HECTOR'S GIRL** C 166
192 **HECTOR'S HERE** 14
140 **HECTOR'S HOPE** 7
15 **HEDDEWIGII** 76
289 **HEDENHAM** 24
455 **HEDERA PARK** (IRE) 10
515 **HEDONISTA** (IRE) 34
366 **HEDYCHIUM** (IRE) 12
207 **HEER HE GOES** 8
173 **HEER'S SADIE** 5
505 **HEERATHETRACK** 7
49 **HEERBEGOOD** 4
15 **HEET** 164
457 **HEEZER GEEZER** (FR) 74
435 **HEEZTHEBOY** (IRE) 6
367 **HEIA** (FR) 76
451 **HEIDI OF ARENDELLE** 29
408 **HEIGHT OF VANITY** (IRE) F 70
119 **HEIGHTS OF ABRAHAM** (IRE) 23
208 **HELEN WOOD** G 14
132 **HELENN CLERMONT** (FR) 10
300 **HELIANTHUS** 66
539 **HELIOS ALLEN** (FR) 12
52 **HELIX** 5
37 **HELL ON EARTH** (IRE) 3
379 **HELL RED** (FR) 58
413 **HELLAVAPACE** 3
154 **HELLENISTA** 40
523 **HELLFIRE KODE** 4
311 **HELLFIRE PRINCESS** 12
141 **HELLO BOB** 11
24 **HELLO GLORY** F 117
279 **HELLO HAVANA** (IRE) 61
225 **HELLO JUDGE** 4
211 **HELLO MARIE** (FR) 15
400 **HELLO ME** (IRE) 7
43 **HELLO MENAHI** (IRE) 58
114 **HELLO MISS LADY** (IRE) 15
457 **HELLO POPS** 75

442 **HELLO QUEEN** (IRE) 38
14 **HELLO SUNSHINE** 14
175 **HELLO ZABEEL** (IRE) 7
515 **HELLOFAHASTE** C 79
305 **HELM ROCK** 10
298 **HELNWEIN** (IRE) 52
525 **HELPFUL** 15
440 **HELSGETAWAY** (IRE) 41
457 **HELTENHAM** (FR) 76
188 **HELVETIAN** 16
343 **HELVIC DREAM** 20
296 **HEMMSA** (IRE) 4
383 **HENCE** (IRE) C 147
405 **HENERY HAWK** 5
211 **HENERYETTA BAY** (IRE) 16
510 **HENLEY** 4
355 **HENLEY PARK** 49
367 **HENN SEE** (FR) 77
311 **HENRI LE BON** (IRE) 13
379 **HENRI THE SECOND** (FR) 59
537 **HENRY BOX BROWN** (IRE) 30
68 **HENRY BROWN** (IRE) 2
335 **HENRY GRAY** (IRE) 54
81 **HENRY THE FIFTH** (IRE) 3
402 **HENRY'S FRIEND** (IRE) 40
211 **HENSCHKE** (IRE) 17
174 **HENZAR** (IRE) 34
181 **HENZO DES BOULLATS** (FR) 6
328 **HER KINDNESS** C 30
503 **HER WAY** 3
459 **HERAKLES** (IRE) 13
211 **HERAKLES WESTWOOD** (FR) 18
212 **HERBIERS** (FR) 38
367 **HERCULE DU SEUIL** (FR) 78
402 **HERCULES MORSE** 41
369 **HERE COMES MCCOY** (IRE) 60
136 **HERE COMES THE MAN** (IRE) 15
357 **HERE WE HAVE IT** (IRE) 21
92 **HERE'S TWO** C 62
450 **HERECOMESFREDDIE** 17
292 **HERECOMESHOGAN** (IRE) 21
361 **HERECOMESTHESTORM** 19
228 **HEREDIA** 13
218 **HERESMAX** (IRE) 8
149 **HERESY** 4
399 **HERETIC** (IRE) 12
385 **HEREWEGOHONEY** (IRE) 84
212 **HERITIER** (FR) 39
300 **HERITIER DE SIVOLA** (FR) 27
379 **HERMES ALLEN** (FR) 60
539 **HERMES BOY** (FR) 13
543 **HERMES DU GOUET** (FR) 42
211 **HERMES LE GRIS** (FR) 19
52 **HERMIN D'OUDAIRIES** (FR) 6
355 **HERMINO AA** (FR) 50
383 **HERMOSA** (IRE) C 148
369 **HERO** (FR) 61
168 **HEROIQUE DE MAULDE** (FR) 15
107 **HEROISM** (IRE) 33
376 **HERON CREEK** (IRE) 23
543 **HEROS** (FR) 43
335 **HEROS DE MOUTIERS** (FR) 55
12 **HEROS DE ROMAY** (FR) 30
7 **HEROSS DU SEUIL** (FR) 5
251 **HERSILIA** 5
176 **HERTFORD DANCER** C 51
275 **HESBEHINDYOU** (IRE) 13
457 **HESTINA** (FR) G 77
457 **HESTINA** (FR) C 209
410 **HEURE DE GLOIRE** (FR) 30
543 **HEVA ROSE** (FR) 44
81 **HEY BAILS** 4
104 **HEY BOB** (IRE) 8
298 **HEY BROTHER** (FR) 53
390 **HEY DAY BABY** (IRE) 44
421 **HEY ELVIS** 10
450 **HEY FRANKIE** (IRE) 18
253 **HEY HO LET'S GO** 2
286 **HEY LYLA** 75
423 **HEY MISTER DJ** (IRE) 14
348 **HEY MR** 17
546 **HEY PRETTY** (IRE) 5
343 **HEY WHATEVER** 63
205 **HEYDOUR** (IRE) 20
6 **HEZAHUNK** (IRE) 36
171 **HEZMIE** (IRE) 2
286 **HI CLARE** (IRE) 76
367 **HI HO PHOENIX** 79
256 **HI RIKO** (FR) 7
442 **HI ROYAL** (IRE) 39
548 **HI TRIG** 8
88 **HIALEAH** (FR) 33
383 **HIAWATHA** (IRE) 52
5 **HIBAAYEB** F 173
153 **HICKO'S GIRL** (IRE) 57
172 **HICKORY** (IRE) 5
220 **HICONIC** 21
291 **HIDALGO CONTI** (FR) 2
335 **HIDALGO DE L'ISLE** (FR) 56
211 **HIDALGO DES BORDES** (FR) 20
385 **HIDDEN BEAUTY** 85
507 **HIDDEN BELLE** 17
244 **HIDDEN CARGO** (IRE) 4
270 **HIDDEN CHARMS** (IRE) F 54
404 **HIDDEN CODE** (IRE) 14
101 **HIDDEN COMMANDER** (IRE) 15
363 **HIDDEN DEPTHS** (IRE) 51
286 **HIDDEN GIRL** (IRE) F 167
457 **HIDDEN HEROICS** (FR) 78
28 **HIDDEN PEARL** 7
484 **HIDDEN STEPS** F 58
5 **HIDDEN STORY** 73
226 **HIDEO** (FR) 37
483 **HIDOR DE BERSY** (FR) 8
145 **HIER ENCORE** (FR) 1
1 **HIERACHY** (FR) 25
395 **HIERARCHY** (IRE) 12
14 **HIERONYMUS** 15
125 **HIGGS** (IRE) 14
383 **HIGH CELEBRITY** (FR) C 149
383 **HIGH CHIEFTESS** (IRE) 53
227 **HIGH COUNSEL** (IRE) 15
471 **HIGH COURT JUDGE** (USA) 20
479 **HIGH FASHION** (IRE) 31
189 **HIGH FIBRE** (IRE) 28
254 **HIGH GAME ROYAL** (FR) 30
414 **HIGH GROUNDS** (IRE) 13
5 **HIGH HONOUR** 74
347 **HIGH MOON** 35
226 **HIGH NOON** (IRE) 38
519 **HIGH ON THE HILL** 6
459 **HIGH OPINION** 5
285 **HIGH POINT** (IRE) 59
1 **HIGH ROLLER** (FR) 26
496 **HIGH SECURITY** 10
40 **HIGH SHERIFF** (IRE) 11
315 **HIGH SPEED** (IRE) F 28
75 **HIGH SPIRITED** (IRE) 22
211 **HIGH STAKES** (IRE) 21
42 **HIGH TAN** F 61
376 **HIGH TECH** (FR) 24
504 **HIGH TREASON** 30
355 **HIGH UP IN THE AIR** (FR) 51
484 **HIGH VELOCITY** (IRE) 3
162 **HIGH YIELD** 9
5 **HIGHBANK** (IRE) 75
504 **HIGHER GROUND** 31
479 **HIGHEST GROUND** (IRE) 10
124 **HIGHJACKED** 2
231 **HIGHLAND BLING** (IRE) 118
343 **HIGHLAND CHARGE** (IRE) 21
144 **HIGHLAND FASHION** 10
413 **HIGHLAND FLYER** 25
234 **HIGHLAND FROLIC** (FR) 34
390 **HIGHLAND GETAWAY** (IRE) 45
418 **HIGHLAND LASS** (FR) 4
501 **HIGHLAND OLLY** 66
15 **HIGHLAND PASS** C 165
459 **HIGHLAND QUEEN** (IRE) 6
472 **HIGHLAND RAHY** 14
75 **HIGHLAND SLIPPER** 30
456 **HIGHLAND SONG** (IRE) 41
315 **HIGHLAND WELL** 29
434 **HIGHLANDER HILL** (IRE) 7
390 **HIGHLANDS LEGACY** 46
479 **HIGHLANDS QUEEN** (FR) F 32
503 **HIGHLIGHTER** (IRE) 4
44 **HIGHLY PRESENTABLE** (IRE) G 8
439 **HIGHLY RECOMMENDED** 7
306 **HIGHSTAKESPLAYER** (IRE) 18
119 **HIGHWAY COMPANION** (IRE) 24
14 **HIGHWAY ONE** (USA) 16
205 **HIGHWAY ONE O FIVE** (IRE) 21
205 **HIGHWAY ONE O FOUR** (IRE) 22
205 **HIGHWAY ONE O TWO** (IRE) 23
154 **HIGHWAYGREY** 41
379 **HIKARI POMPADOUR AA** (FR) 61
66 **HIKMAA** (IRE) C 121
378 **HILARY J** F 21
169 **HILARY'S BOY** 5
521 **HILDEGARD** (IRE) 73
154 **HILDENLEY** 42
332 **HILL COUNTRY** (FR) 7
360 **HILL FILLY** 47
543 **HILL OF TARA** 45
494 **HILL SIXTEEN** 26
355 **HILL STATION** (FR) 52
138 **HILL WELCOME** F 49
502 **HILLBILLY** 3
157 **HILLFINCH** 17
138 **HILLS OF GOLD** 50
347 **HILLSIDE** (IRE) 36
366 **HILLTOWN** (IRE) 13
227 **HILLVIEW** (IRE) 16
379 **HIM MALAYA** (FR) 62
342 **HIMALAYAN QUEEN** F 27
447 **HINDSIGHT** G 34
384 **HINT OF PINK** (IRE) F 51
514 **HIPOP DES ONGRAIS** (FR) 12
383 **HIPPODROME** (IRE) 54
85 **HIROMICHI** (FR) 5

12 **HURLERONTHEDITCH** (IRE) 31
323 **HURRICAN DREAM** (IRE) 6
198 **HURRICANE ALEX** 5
326 **HURRICANE ALI** (IRE) 11
509 **HURRICANE BAY** 16
379 **HURRICANE DANNY** (FR) 68
489 **HURRICANE DEAL** (FR) 18
476 **HURRICANE DYLAN** (IRE) 2
385 **HURRICANE HARVEY** 91
537 **HURRICANE HIGHWAY** (IRE) 32
231 **HURRICANE IVOR** (IRE) 8
173 **HURRICANE KIKO** (IRE) 15
5 **HURRICANE LANE** (IRE) 15
234 **HURRICANE VICHI** (IRE) 36
383 **HURST PARK** (IRE) 56
381 **HURSTWOOD** 2
378 **HURT YOU NEVER** (IRE) 3
98 **HURTLE** (IRE) 16
395 **HUSCARI** (IRE) 13
24 **HUTCHENCE** 118
151 **HY BRASIL** (IRE) 6
468 **HY EALES** (IRE) 4
421 **HYBA** 11
312 **HYBRIS** (FR) 11
383 **HYDRANGEA** (IRE) F 152
92 **HYDRATION** 32
538 **HYDROPLANE** (IRE) 34
247 **HYLAND** (FR) 52
189 **HYMAC** (IRE) 33
343 **HYMIE WEISS** 22
452 **HYMN AND A PRAYER** 4
231 **HYMN OF THE DAWN** (USA) F 119
320 **HYPER DREAM** (IRE) C 49
154 **HYPERFOCUS** (IRE) 44
376 **HYPNOTIK** (FR) 25
483 **HYSTERY BERE** (FR) 9
220 **I AM DE CHAILLAC** (FR) 23
450 **I AM GONNA BE** (IRE) 19
89 **I AM LEGEND** (SWE) 27
249 **I AM SIMBA** 18
383 **I CAN FLY** C 153
361 **I DARE YOU** 37
414 **I DIDN'T COST ALOT** 14
263 **I GIORNI** (IRE) 35
240 **I HAVE A VOICE** (IRE) 18
299 **I HOPE STAR** (IRE) 12
504 **I LIKE TO MOVE IT** 33
457 **I LOOK HOW I LOOK** (SPA) 85
122 **I MATTER** (IRE) 9
335 **I NEED YOU** (FR) 58
303 **I REMEMBER YOU** (IRE) F 34
366 **I SEE YOU WELL** (FR) 14
497 **I SHUT THAT D'OR** (FR) 35
12 **I SPY A DIVA** 32
440 **I WISH YOU** (FR) 95
205 **I'D LIKE TO KNOW** (IRE) 25
383 **I'LL HAVE ANOTHER** (IRE) C 154
463 **I'LL HAVE IT** (IRE) F 19
88 **I'M A BELIEVER** (FR) 34
298 **I'M A LUMBERJACK** 54
430 **I'M A STARMAN** 3
347 **I'M DELILAH** F 37
395 **I'M DONNA** (IRE) F 52
226 **I'M DOUGAL ROCKS** (FR) 40
192 **I'M GRATEFUL** 15
10 **I'M MABLE** 16
287 **I'M NOTAPARTYGIRL** 5
363 **I'M ON MY WAY** (IRE) 55
402 **I'M RAVENOUS** (FR) 43
376 **I'M SO BUSY** 26
92 **I'M TOO TIRED** (IRE) 33
5 **I'M WONDERFUL** (USA) C 176
254 **IAMASTAR** (FR) 32
119 **IATO'S ANGEL** (IRE) 52
59 **IBERGMAN** (IRE) C 22
227 **IBERIA** (IRE) 17
247 **IBERICO LORD** (FR) 53
254 **IBERIO** (GER) 33
379 **IBIS DOCTOR** (FR) 69
243 **IBIZA LOVE** (IRE) 20
317 **IBIZA ROCKS** (FR) 8
212 **IBIZA ROCKS** 44
251 **IBN ALDAR** 6
26 **IBRAHIMOVIC** (IRE) 30
16 **ICAQUE DE L'ISLE** (FR) 18
543 **ICARAT** (FR) 49
367 **ICARE ALLEN** (FR) 85
194 **ICARE COLOMBE** (FR) 4
355 **ICARE GRANDCHAMP** (FR) 55
35 **ICE CLIMBER** 72
212 **ICE COAST** (FR) 45
107 **ICE COOL HARRY** 34
328 **ICE CREAM CASTLES** 23
347 **ICE DAY** (FR) 38
335 **ICE DE PAIL** (FR) 59
553 **ICE N SLICE** (IRE) 4
347 **ICE PYRAMID** (IRE) 39
61 **ICE SHADOW** (IRE) 9
219 **ICECAP** 151
335 **ICEMAN DENNIS** (FR) 60
379 **ICEO** (FR) 70
150 **ICHIGO** F 10
211 **ICI LA REINE** (IRE) 22
363 **ICONE D'AUBRELLE** (FR) 56
301 **ICONIC GIRL** F 27
80 **ICONIC KNIGHT** (IRE) 46
484 **ICONIC MOMENT** (IRE) 19
407 **ICONIC MOVER** 8
355 **ICONIC MUDDLE** 56
423 **ICONIC ROCK** (IRE) 16
387 **ICONICDAAY** 26
360 **ICY DIP** 48
504 **IDALKO BIHOUE** (FR) 34
12 **IDAMIX** (FR) 33
343 **IDAS BOY** (IRE) 23
369 **IDDERGEM** (FR) 65
247 **IDEAL DES BORDES** (FR) 54
124 **IDEAL DREAM** 3
330 **IDEAL GUEST** (FR) 5
439 **IDEALDES VILLERETS** (FR) 9
537 **IDEALLKO** (FR) 33
486 **IDEE DE GARDE** (FR) 3
89 **IDEE FIXEE** 8
116 **IDEFIX DE CIERGUES** (FR) 9
440 **IDEM** (FR) 42
445 **IDILICO** (FR) 12
148 **IDIOPATHIC** 16
161 **IDOAPOLOGISE** 8
517 **IESHA** 3
319 **IF I SAY** (IRE) 21
234 **IF KARL'S BERG DID** 37
224 **IF NOT FOR DYLAN** (IRE) 5
24 **IF NOT NOW** 45
175 **IF SO** C 52
114 **IF YOU ASK ME TO** 8
251 **IFFRAAJ PINK** (IRE) C 91
15 **IGHRAA** (IRE) C 167
349 **IGNAC LAMAR** (IRE) 21
512 **IGOR** 2
548 **IGOTATEXT** (IRE) 9
462 **IHEARDUPAINTHOUSES** (IRE) 4
456 **IHSAS** (USA) G 43
306 **IKALIMIX** (FR) 20
363 **IKE SPORT** (FR) 57
14 **IKKARI** (IRE) 17
200 **IL EST FRANCAIS** (FR) 25
367 **IL ETAIT TEMPS** (FR) 86
450 **IL GRUSCHEN** (IRE) 20
515 **IL PALAZZO** (USA) C 80
379 **IL RIDOTO** (FR) 71
132 **IL VA DE SOI** (FR) 11
234 **ILANZ** (FR) 38
220 **ILARY DE L'ECU** (FR) 24
226 **ILAYA** (FR) 41
367 **ILE ATLANTIQUE** (FR) 87
247 **ILE DE JERSEY** (FR) 55
20 **ILE DE MEMOIRES** 10
153 **ILE DESERTE** G 84
390 **ILESTDANCINGSPIRIT** (FR) 48
539 **ILFONCE** (FR) 15
80 **ILHABELA FACT** 47
379 **ILIADE ALLEN** (FR) 72
379 **ILIKO D'OLIVATE** (FR) 73
383 **ILLAUNMORE** (USA) C 155
395 **ILLEGALLY BLONDE** (IRE) F 53
256 **ILLICO DE MOUTIERS** (FR) 8
369 **ILLICO DE NUIT** (FR) 66
514 **ILLICO DES PLACES** (FR) 14
357 **ILLUSION OF TIME** (IRE) 22
501 **ILLUSIONIST** (GER) 14
457 **ILLWALKTHELINE** (IRE) F 86
283 **ILONA TAMARA** (FR) 16
497 **ILOVETHENIGHTLIFE** 36
200 **ILTONE** (FR) 26
97 **IMAC WOOD** (FR) 4
221 **IMADPOUR** (IRE) 23
320 **IMAGE** F 50
361 **IMAGINARY DRAGON** (FR) 4
484 **IMAGINARY WORLD** (IRE) 20
161 **IMAGINEER** (IRE) 45
247 **IMMORTAL** (FR) 56
228 **IMMORTAL BEAUTY** (IRE) 55
306 **IMMORTAL FAME** (IRE) 21
379 **IMPACT DU BONHEUR** (FR) 74
367 **IMPAIRE ET PASSE** (FR) 88
484 **IMPALA** C 60
390 **IMPATIENT** (FR) 49
154 **IMPELLER** 45
399 **IMPERIAL ACE** (IRE) 45
12 **IMPERIAL ADMIRAL** (IRE) 34
385 **IMPERIAL ALCAZAR** (IRE) 92
306 **IMPERIAL ALEX** (IRE) 22
504 **IMPERIAL B G** (IRE) 35
390 **IMPERIAL BEDE** (FR) 50
33 **IMPERIAL CLOUD** (IRE) 3
321 **IMPERIAL COMMAND** (IRE) 23
401 **IMPERIAL CULT** (IRE) 1
416 **IMPERIAL DREAM** (IRE) 20
5 **IMPERIAL EMPEROR** (IRE) 76
15 **IMPERIAL FIGHTER** (IRE) 16
454 **IMPERIAL HOPE** (IRE) 13

12 **IMPERIAL HURRICANE** 35
319 **IMPERIAL JADE** (IRE) 22
348 **IMPERIAL KHAN** (IRE) 18
385 **IMPERIAL LIGHTNING** (IRE) 93
104 **IMPERIAL LORD** (IRE) 9
56 **IMPERIAL MAJESTY** (IRE) 25
537 **IMPERIAL MEASURE** (IRE) 34
102 **IMPERIAL SACHIN'S** (IRE) 10
521 **IMPERIAL SANDS** (IRE) 17
112 **IMPERIAL SOVEREIGN** (IRE) 78
385 **IMPERIAL STORM** (IRE) 94
504 **IMPERIAL SUN** 36
387 **IMPERIALISTIC** (IRE) F 74
154 **IMPERIALISTIC** (IRE) F 174
219 **IMPERIALISTIC DEVA** C 152
406 **IMPERIOUSITY** 14
92 **IMPERIUM** (IRE) 5
355 **IMPHAL** 57
212 **IMPORT EXPORT** (FR) 46
5 **IMPORTANT TIME** (IRE) F 177
247 **IMPOSE TOI** (FR) 57
506 **IMPRESSIONABLE** C 160
329 **IMPRESSOR** (IRE) 4
379 **IMPREVU DU LARGE** (FR) 75
430 **IMPRINT** (IRE) 4
231 **IMPROVE** (IRE) F 120
387 **IMPROVISED** (IRE) 27
247 **IMPULSIVE ONE** (USA) 58
154 **IMPULSIVE REACTION** (IRE) 120
104 **IN ARREARS** (IRE) 10
543 **IN D'OR** (FR) 50
189 **IN EXCELSIS DEO** (FR) 34
367 **IN EXCESS** (FR) 89
384 **IN MY DREAMS** (IRE) C 52
539 **IN REM** (FR) 16
355 **IN THE AIR** (FR) 58
6 **IN THE BREEZE** (IRE) 37
270 **IN THE FAST LANE** (SAF) C 55
219 **IN THE GIVING** (IRE) 71
153 **IN THE LURCH** C 85
279 **IN THE SOUP** (USA) F 23
408 **IN THE TRENCHES** 43
286 **IN THESE SHOES** (IRE) 78
457 **IN THIS WORLD** (FR) 87
343 **IN YOUR SHADOW** (IRE) 24
70 **INAAM** (IRE) 20
387 **INALA** F 108
552 **INANNA** (IRE) 25
379 **INCA DE LAFAYETTE** (FR) 76
281 **INCA PRINCE** (IRE) 7
383 **INCA PRINCESS** (IRE) F 156
515 **INCA QUEEN** (IRE) 35
46 **INCA ROSE** 3
231 **INCA WOOD** (UAE) F 121
385 **INCE** (AUT) 95
390 **INCH HOUSE** (IRE) 51
232 **INCHAGOILL LADY** (IRE) 6
390 **INCHESTER D'AMSYL** (FR) 52
221 **INCHTURK** (IRE) 8
220 **INCLEMENT WEATHER** 25
369 **INDEEVAR BLEU** (FR) 67
525 **INDEFATIGABLE** (IRE) 16
24 **INDELIBLE** (IRE) 119
319 **INDELIBLE SPIN** (IRE) 23
506 **INDEMNIFY** 19
506 **INDEMNITY** (IRE) 86
21 **INDEPENDENCE** (USA) 6
17 **INDEPENDENCE DAY** (IRE) 9
544 **INDEPENDENT BEAUTY** 5
335 **INDEPENDENT JIMMY** 61
66 **INDESTRUCTIBLE** (IRE) 59
517 **INDIAN AFFAIR** 4
85 **INDIAN CREAK** (IRE) 6
348 **INDIAN SOUNDS** (IRE) 19
162 **INDIAN SUNBIRD** (IRE) 10
296 **INDIAN TERRITORIES** 5
31 **INDIANA BE** 21
358 **INDIANA JONES** (IRE) 14
286 **INDIANA WELLS** (FR) F 170
347 **INDICATION ROCKET** (IRE) 101
542 **INDIGNANT** F 48
116 **INDIGO BOY** (FR) 10
376 **INDIGO LAKE** 27
316 **INDIGO TIMES** (IRE) 7
219 **INDISPENSABLE** 153
286 **INDIVIDUALISM** 171
262 **INDRAPURA STAR** 19
2 **INDURO DE FONTAINE** (FR) 6
93 **INEBRANLABLE** (FR) 7
200 **INEDIT STAR** (FR) 27
320 **INEVITABLE OUTCOME** (IRE) 10
57 **INEXPLICABLE** (IRE) 13
240 **INFERNO SACREE** (FR) 19
479 **INFINITE COSMOS** (IRE) 35
188 **INFINITI** (IRE) 17
387 **INFINITIVE** 28
15 **INFINITY BLUE** 168
12 **INFLAGRANTE** (IRE) 36
200 **INFLEXIBLE** (FR) 28
464 **INFORMATEUR** (FR) 25
342 **INFRASTRUCTURE** 5
314 **INGEBORG ZILLING** (IRE) 7
256 **INGENNIO** (FR) 9
487 **INGLEBY COMMAND** 3
532 **INGLEBY MACKENZIE** 23
85 **INGRA TOR** (IRE) 7
15 **INHIBITION** C 169
337 **INIGO** (FR) 3
395 **INIGO JONES** 14
233 **INION TIOGAIR** (IRE) 5
472 **INIS BOFFIN** F 15
440 **INIS OIRR** (IRE) 43
442 **INISHERIN** 73
31 **INITIO** 22
298 **INKAMAN** 132
107 **INKARA** (IRE) 78
335 **INKWELL** 62
365 **INMEMORYOFMILLY** (IRE) 4
5 **INNER SECRET** (USA) F 178
206 **INNER SPACE** 81
355 **INNESTON** (FR) 59
24 **INNEVERA** (FR) F 120
157 **INNISFREE LASS** (IRE) 19
361 **INNOCENT SPIRIT** (IRE) 38
279 **INNSE GALL** 24
243 **INNY LAD** (IRE) 21
363 **INOUI MACHIN** (FR) 58
206 **INQUIRING MINDS** 82
449 **INSAAF** F 28
416 **INSHIRAAH** (FR) G 42
539 **INSIDE MAN** (FR) 39
107 **INSIGNIA** 79
363 **INSPECTOR LYNLEY** 59
206 **INSPIRAL** 14
72 **INSPIRATIONELLIE** (IRE) 13
332 **INSPIRATRICE** (IRE) 8
42 **INSPIRED KNOWHOW** 27
138 **INSPIRING SPEECHES** (IRE) 77
42 **INSPIRITED** 28
506 **INSPIRITUS** (IRE) 87
95 **INSTANCE** F 31
386 **INSTANT ATTRACTION** (IRE) 11
240 **INSTANT DE BONHEUR** (FR) 20
147 **INSTANT GAMBLER** (IRE) 20
66 **INSTANT RECALL** 122
364 **INSTINCT** 9
238 **INSTINGTIVE** (IRE) 5
367 **INSTIT** (FR) 90
489 **INTEL DES BRUYERES** (FR) 19
89 **INTELLOGENT** (IRE) 9
138 **INTENSE ROMANCE** (IRE) G 78
80 **INTERCEPTEUR** 105
193 **INTERCESSOR** 7
172 **INTERGALACTICAT** 28
43 **INTERMITTENT** F 128
57 **INTERNATIONAL LAW** 14
89 **INTERNATIONALANGEL** (IRE) 10
539 **INTERNE DE SIVOLA** (FR) 17
385 **INTERNET BIDDY** (IRE) 96
72 **INTERTWINED** (IRE) 63
6 **INTERVENTION** 38
379 **INTHEWATERSIDE** (FR) 77
543 **INTIMATE** (FR) 51
206 **INTINSO** 83
515 **INTO BATTLE** (IRE) 81
513 **INTO OVERDRIVE** 28
434 **INTO THE FIRE** (FR) 8
69 **INTO THE MYSTIC** (IRE) F 34
335 **INTO THE SUNSET** (IRE) 63
146 **INTOXICATA** (FR) 37
385 **INTREPIDE SUD** (FR) 97
91 **INTREPIDLY** (USA) 6
112 **INTRICACY** 35
520 **INTRICATE PILLAR** (IRE) 17
154 **INTRIGUE** C 175
240 **INTRIGUING LADY** (IRE) 21
510 **INTRINSIC BOND** 5
353 **INVERINATE** (IRE) 13
112 **INVERLOCHY** (FR) 36
26 **INVESTED** (IRE) 31
497 **INVESTMENT MANAGER** 37
205 **INVICTUS DE BRION** (FR) 26
363 **INVICTUS SMART** (FR) 60
507 **INVINCIBLE DE MEE** (FR) 18
355 **INVINCIBLE NAO** (FR) 60
399 **INVINCIBLE PASS** (IRE) 46
125 **INVINCIBLE WISH** (IRE) 15
442 **INVISIBLE FRIEND** (IRE) 11
445 **IOLANI** (GER) 13
247 **IOLAOS DU MOU** (FR) 59
423 **IONTACH CHEVAL** 17
335 **IORANGI DE L'ISLE** (FR) 64
457 **IORENS** (FR) 88
379 **IOUPY COLLONGES** (FR) 78
205 **IPSO FALCO** (FR) 27
44 **IPSOS DES BORDES** (FR) 9
332 **IPSOS PIERJI** (FR) 9
379 **IRANDANDO HAS** (FR) 79
79 **IRELAND'S EYE** (IRE) 3
147 **IRENE'S PEARL** (IRE) 21
50 **IREZUMI** 20

123 **IRIS DANCER** 5
367 **IRIS EMERY** (FR) 91
368 **IRISH ABBEY** (IRE) C 56
298 **IRISH CHORUS** 55
79 **IRISH DANCER** (IRE) 24
272 **IRISH ED** 9
138 **IRISH FLAME** 22
132 **IRISH FORTUNE** (IRE) 12
379 **IRISH HILL** (GER) 80
231 **IRISH LULLABY** 9
308 **IRISH PROPHECY** (IRE) 31
123 **IRISH SOVEREIGN** (IRE) 6
506 **IRISH STEPS** (USA) C 161
457 **IRLANDAIS** (FR) 89
212 **IROKO** (FR) 47
342 **IROMEA** (IRE) C 28
390 **IRON BRIDGE** (IRE) 53
314 **IRON D'EX** (FR) 8
375 **IRON HEART** 2
409 **IRON HORSE** 9
387 **IRON LION** 75
174 **IRON SHERIFF** (IRE) 14
347 **IRONOPOLIS** (IRE) 102
384 **IRRADIATE** (IRE) F 53
506 **IRREGULAR WARFARE** (FR) 88
483 **IRRESISTABLE** (POL) 10
209 **IRRESISTIBLE YOU** (IRE) 14
226 **IRV** (IRE) 42
154 **IS SO CUTE DIMARIA** (FR) 46
154 **ISA** C 176
379 **ISAAC DES OBEAUX** (FR) 81
219 **ISABELLA** (IRE) C 154
385 **ISABELLA BEE** (IRE) 98
35 **ISABELLA LINTON** (IRE) C 91
544 **ISABELLA RUBY** 6
548 **ISABELLE** (FR) 29
341 **ISADORA'S GIFT** 5
355 **ISAYALITTLEPRAYER** 61
272 **ISHANI** 10
461 **ISIS** (USA) F 14
96 **ISKAHEEN** (IRE) 3
355 **ISKAR D'AIRY** (FR) 62
467 **ISLA DIAMONDS** 5
496 **ISLA KAI** (IRE) 11
122 **ISLADAAY** (IRE) 10
363 **ISLAND APPROACH** (FR) 61
328 **ISLAND BANDIT** (IRE) 6
328 **ISLAND BRAVE** (IRE) 7
368 **ISLAND DRIVE** (IRE) F 57
35 **ISLAND FALCON** (IRE) 24
328 **ISLAND KING** (IRE) 24
228 **ISLAND LUCK** 56
328 **ISLAND NATIVE** (IRE) 25
330 **ISLAND OF SKYE** 6
254 **ISLAND RUN** 34
506 **ISLAND STAR** (IRE) 89
507 **ISLE OF ARON** 19
79 **ISLE OF DREAMS** 4
12 **ISLE OF GOLD** (IRE) 37
421 **ISLE OF HOPE** 12
5 **ISLE OF JURA** 77
106 **ISLE OF LISMORE** (IRE) 8
73 **ISLE OF OIR** (IRE) 5
395 **ISLE OF SARK** (USA) 15
32 **ISLE OF WOLVES** 5
390 **ISOCRATE** (FR) 54
298 **ISOLATE** (FR) 56
410 **ISRAEL CHAMP** (IRE) 32
368 **ISRAFEL** C 58
206 **ISRAR** 15
483 **ISSAM** (FR) 11
355 **ISSAR D'AIRY** (FR) 63
247 **ISSUING AUTHORITY** (IRE) 60
227 **ISTHEBAROPEN** 18
513 **IT JUST TAKES TIME** (IRE) 29
317 **IT'S A DISCOVERY** (IRE) C 9
70 **IT'S A LOVE THING** 21
502 **IT'S A MIRACLE** 12
92 **IT'S ALL ABOUT YOU** (IRE) 34
126 **IT'S FOR ALAN** 5
367 **IT'S FOR ME** (FR) 92
55 **IT'S FOR YOU MUM** (FR) 11
74 **IT'S GOOD TO LAUGH** (IRE) 16
468 **IT'S HOW WE ROLL** (IRE) 5
464 **IT'S MAISY** (IRE) 26
15 **IT'S MARVELLOUS** 79
521 **IT'S SHOWTIME BABY** 74
231 **IT'S SNOWING** (IRE) 10
385 **IT'S TUESDAY** (FR) 99
410 **ITACARE** (FR) 33
175 **ITALIAN MAGIC** (IRE) 31
369 **ITALIAN SPIRIT** (IRE) 68
369 **ITCHY FEET** (FR) 69
177 **ITHACA'S ARROW** 19
414 **ITHAKA** (IRE) 15
243 **ITHRA** 22
332 **ITO DITTO** (FR) 10
440 **ITS A MIDNIGHT** 44
43 **ITS ALL FOR LUCK** (IRE) F 129
271 **ITS GONNAHAPPEN** (IRE) 6
257 **ITS UR ROUNDMYLORD** 5
373 **ITSABOUTIME** (IRE) 1
390 **ITSO FURY** (IRE) 55
457 **ITTACK BLUE** (FR) 90
379 **IVALDI** (FR) 82
98 **IVATHEENGINE** (IRE) 5
196 **IVESCENEASPIDER** 6
306 **IVETWIGGEDIT** 23
177 **IVILNOBLE** (IRE) 9
98 **IVIRKA** (FR) C 33
347 **IVOIRE D'AVRIL** (FR) 40
277 **IVORS INVOLVEMENT** (IRE) 3
469 **IVORY MADONNA** (IRE) 29
6 **IVY AVENUE** (IRE) 39
285 **IVYBANKS** 60
338 **IVYNATOR** (IRE) 5
136 **IWA** (FR) 17
489 **IWILLDOIT** 20
513 **IXORA** (IRE) G 30
509 **IZAR BALD** (FR) 17
299 **IZAYTE** (FR) 13
20 **IZZY BELL** 11
440 **IZZY'S CHAMPION** (IRE) 45
374 **J C INTERNATIONAL** 8
177 **J J STINGLETON** 20
348 **J R CAVAGIN** (IRE) 20
357 **J'AI FROID** (IRE) 23
543 **J'AIME EL MARS** (FR) 52
83 **J'HABITE EN FRANCE** (FR) 13
455 **J'VENTILE** (FR) 11
234 **JACAMAR** (GER) 39
200 **JACHAR** (FR) 29
457 **JACK BLACK** (FR) 91
288 **JACK D'OR** 3
79 **JACK DANIEL** (IRE) 5
98 **JACK DARCY** (IRE) 6
136 **JACK DEVINE** (IRE) 18
83 **JACK DOYEN** (IRE) 14
244 **JACK GRASS** 5
194 **JACK HYDE** (IRE) 5
370 **JACK LESLIE** 5
40 **JACK OF ALL SHAPES** (IRE) 12
138 **JACK OF CLUBS** 51
441 **JACK RYAN** (IRE) 8
242 **JACK SNIPE** 4
70 **JACK SPAROWE** (IRE) 22
466 **JACK SPRAT** (IRE) 26
323 **JACK THE FARMER** 7
265 **JACK THE SAVAGE** 6
101 **JACK YEATS** (IRE) 16
287 **JACK'S A LEGEND** 6
106 **JACK'S POINT** 9
16 **JACKALANI** 19
285 **JACKALOPE** 30
326 **JACKAMUNDO** (FR) 12
366 **JACKELINE** 15
445 **JACKHAMMER** (IRE) 14
177 **JACKIE DIAMOND** 21
383 **JACKIE OH** (IRE) 57
449 **JACKMEISTER RUDI** 15
369 **JACKPOT D'AINAY** (FR) 70
379 **JACKPOT D'ATHOU** (FR) 83
379 **JACKPOT DES BORDES** (FR) 84
376 **JACKS ORCHARD** (IRE) 28
165 **JACKS PROFIT** (IRE) 5
271 **JACKS TOUCH** (IRE) 7
47 **JACKTOT** 20
379 **JACOBIN** (FR) 85
363 **JACOBS ACRE** (IRE) 62
208 **JACQANINA** 15
336 **JACQUELINA** (IRE) 12
20 **JAD MAHAL** (FR) 12
107 **JADANNA** (IRE) F 80
179 **JADE COUNTRY** 8
112 **JADOOMI** (FR) 9
546 **JAFFATHEGAFFA** 6
212 **JAGWAR** (FR) 48
69 **JAHAFIL** C 35
66 **JAHIDIN** (FR) 60
263 **JAIL NO BAIL** (IRE) 36
247 **JAITROPLACLASSE** (FR) 61
272 **JAJA DE JAU** G 11
52 **JAKAMANI** 7
385 **JAKANA** (IRE) 100
226 **JAKES WISH** 43
24 **JALAPA** 46
379 **JALILA MORIVIERE** (FR) 86
343 **JALO** 65
513 **JAM LASS** 68
363 **JAMAICAINE** (FR) 63
517 **JAMES BRADLEY** 11
367 **JAMES DU BERLAIS** (FR) 93
369 **JAMES FORT** (IRE) 71
367 **JAMES GATE** (IRE) 94
211 **JAMES JET** (IRE) 23
31 **JAMES MCHENRY** 23
177 **JAMES PARK WOODS** (IRE) 10
348 **JAMES WATT** (IRE) 21
459 **JAMIE BOND** 14
277 **JAMIH** 4
277 **JAMIL** (IRE) 5

497 **JPR ONE** (IRE) 38
15 **JUAN BERMUDEZ** 17
400 **JUAN COOL DUDE** (IRE) 20
6 **JUAN LES PINS** 42
94 **JUANA INES** (IRE) 20
15 **JUANTORENA** (IRE) 170
489 **JUBILEE EXPRESS** (FR) 22
66 **JUBILEE GIRL** 14
376 **JUBILEE GOLD** (IRE) 30
305 **JUBILEE PARTY** 27
507 **JUDEX LEFOU** (IRE) 21
416 **JUDGEMENTOFSOLOMON** 43
405 **JUDGMENT CALL** 7
72 **JUDICIAL** (IRE) 14
390 **JUDICIAL LAW** (IRE) 58
352 **JUDICIAL REVIEW** (IRE) 14
355 **JUDOCA DE THAIX** (FR) 66
168 **JUGE ET PARTI** (FR) 18
263 **JUGGERNAUT** (FR) 39
469 **JUICY** 30
213 **JUKEBOX D'EDDY** (FR) 9
263 **JUKEBOX JAZZ** (IRE) 40
506 **JULIA AUGUSTA** 20
24 **JULIET SIERRA** 47
95 **JUMBEAU** 16
213 **JUMBO VESTE VERTE** (FR) 10
285 **JUMBY** (IRE) 7
206 **JUMEIRA VISION** (IRE) 85
106 **JUMEIRAH STAR** (USA) F 31
451 **JUMIRA BRIDGE** 11
279 **JUMP THE GUN** (IRE) 26
411 **JUMPING JUPITER** (IRE) 3
35 **JUNEAU** (IRE) F 92
521 **JUNGLE CHARM** 75
231 **JUNGLE COVE** (IRE) 13
280 **JUNGLE CRUISE** (IRE) 24
266 **JUNGLE DEMON** (IRE) 34
286 **JUNGLE FEVER** (IRE) 79
335 **JUNGLE JACK** 67
231 **JUNGLE JUNCTION** (IRE) 14
247 **JUNGLE WOOD** (FR) 69
428 **JUNIOR COMANDEUR** (FR) 23
504 **JUNIOR DES BORDES** (FR) 39
278 **JUNIOR MASSINI** 3
534 **JUNIPER** 10
285 **JUNIPER BERRIES** 61
355 **JUNKANOO** 67
193 **JUNOESQUE** 8
367 **JUNTA MARVEL** (FR) 96
194 **JUPETTES** (FR) 7
539 **JUPITER ALLEN** (FR) 20
355 **JUPITER DU GITE** (FR) 68
6 **JUPITER EXPRESS** (IRE) 43
506 **JURI** 90
369 **JURI** (GER) 72
280 **JURYMAN** 14
226 **JUS DE FRUIT** (FR) 44
292 **JUST A DEAL** 22
93 **JUST A DIME** (IRE) 9
189 **JUST A HEARTBEAT** 35
211 **JUST A MEMORY** (FR) 26
515 **JUST A NOTION** 36
349 **JUST A SPARK** 22
131 **JUST ALBERT** 8
107 **JUST AMBER** 6
240 **JUST ANOTHER ONE** (IRE) 22
107 **JUST BRING IT** (IRE) 36
40 **JUST CALL ME AL** (IRE) 13
402 **JUST CHASING MAY** 45
385 **JUST DEEGEETEEBEE** 104
434 **JUST DON'T KNOW** (IRE) 9
463 **JUST DOTTIE** 20
516 **JUST FOR A DREAM** F 3
169 **JUST FRANK** 6
272 **JUST GO FOR IT** 12
154 **JUST HISS** 48
387 **JUST JANET** 76
480 **JUST JEALOUS** (IRE) G 17
464 **JUST JESS** (IRE) 28
480 **JUST JOSH** 3
178 **JUST LIKE BETH** 1
43 **JUST LOOKING** 60
332 **JUST LOOSE CHANGE** 11
379 **JUST LUCKY SIVOLA** (FR) 93
326 **JUST MILLY** (IRE) F 23
489 **JUST NO RISK** (FR) 23
195 **JUST ONCE** 1
151 **JUST ORLANDO** 7
489 **JUST OVER LAND** (FR) 24
148 **JUST PERCY** (IRE) 8
328 **JUST POPSY** F 8
540 **JUST SOPHIE** 9
392 **JUST THE MAN** (FR) 12
353 **JUST WAIT** (IRE) F 26
383 **JUST WONDERFUL** (USA) C 158
489 **JUSTALARGEWHISKY** (FR) 57
527 **JUSTANOTHER MUDDLE** 10
442 **JUSTANOTHERBOTTLE** (IRE) 12
449 **JUSTATHIMBLE** (IRE) 16
166 **JUSTCALLMEPETE** 6
299 **JUSTIFIED** 14
379 **JUSTMYIMAGINATION** 94
233 **JUSTSHORTOFABUBBLE** 6
538 **JUSTUS** (IRE) 36
315 **JUSTWATCHMESTRUGLE** 13
457 **JUVENTUS DE BRION** (FR) 96
501 **KAAFY** (IRE) 15
70 **KAARANAH** (IRE) 23
404 **KAARESS** (IRE) 27
207 **KABJOY** (IRE) G 20
66 **KABOO** (USA) 15
423 **KABRIT** (IRE) 18
221 **KADEEN** (IRE) 24
509 **KADEX** (FR) 19
70 **KADIMA IMPERIAL** 24
15 **KADOVAR** (IRE) 80
306 **KAFFIE** G 24
542 **KAHLUA KISS** C 49
107 **KAIDU** (IRE) 37
220 **KAITUNA RIVER** (IRE) 26
161 **KAIULANI** (IRE) C 58
532 **KAIZER** 24
428 **KAJAKI** (IRE) 24
200 **KAKAMORA** 34
154 **KALAATAH** (USA) C 177
4 **KALABANA** (IRE) 11
368 **KALAHARI KING** 16
387 **KALAHARI PRINCE** (IRE) 29
532 **KALAHARRY** (IRE) 25
85 **KALAMA SUNRISE** 25
130 **KALAMITY KITTY** 6
400 **KALAMUNDA** 21
368 **KALASHNIKOV** (IRE) 17
368 **KALEB** (IRE) 18
385 **KALELULA** 105
387 **KALGANOV** (FR) 30
79 **KALIA ASHA** (IRE) C 33
292 **KALIBRATE** (IRE) 23
221 **KALIKAPOUR** (IRE) 25
256 **KALIZE** (FR) 17
7 **KALKAS** (FR) 6
24 **KALLISHA** F 121
543 **KALLOW POINT** (IRE) 55
410 **KALMA** 37
368 **KALMOOR** (IRE) 19
91 **KALOI** 14
507 **KALPAGA** (FR) 22
267 **KALYPTRA** (FR) 9
400 **KAMANIKA** (IRE) 22
488 **KAMAXOS** (FR) 17
221 **KAMPALA BEACH** (IRE) 9
385 **KAMSINAS** (FR) 106
315 **KANANGA** 14
85 **KANAWHA** 26
379 **KANDOO KID** (FR) 95
286 **KANDY HOUSE** (IRE) 173
106 **KANDY KING** 20
95 **KANGAROO** (IRE) 17
220 **KANKIN** 27
309 **KANNAPOLIS** (IRE) 8
285 **KANOHI BREEZE** 31
454 **KANSAS CITY CHIEF** (IRE) 17
355 **KANSAS DU BERLAIS** (FR) 69
354 **KANUHURA** 6
53 **KANUKANKAN** (IRE) 3
309 **KAP AUTEUIL** (FR) 9
379 **KAP BOY** (FR) 96
507 **KAP CHIDLEY** (FR) 23
539 **KAP HORN** (FR) 21
189 **KAP OUEST** (FR) 36
141 **KAPAMAZOV** 14
320 **KAPE MOSS** 11
543 **KAPGA DE LILY** (FR) 56
464 **KAPHUMOR** (FR) 29
347 **KAPIROVSKA** (FR) F 116
147 **KAPITALISTE** (FR) 22
408 **KAPLINSKY** (IRE) C 71
174 **KAPONO** 16
395 **KARADOW** (IRE) 35
233 **KARAKORAM** 7
92 **KARAKOY** 35
211 **KARAMEL** F 27
425 **KARANNELLE** (IRE) 4
219 **KARAT KARAT** (IRE) 72
186 **KARATAYKA** (IRE) 6
22 **KARATE QUEEN** G 2
47 **KARAVOMYLOS** (IRE) 21
31 **KARDIA** 24
6 **KARDINYA** (IRE) 44
35 **KARENINE** C 93
463 **KARINSWIFT** G 21
385 **KARL PHILIPPE** (FR) 107
450 **KARLIE** 21
107 **KARSAVINA** 38
228 **KASANKAYA** (IRE) C 155
457 **KASH TARA** 97
42 **KASHMEER** (IRE) 29
200 **KASHMIR DE CORTON** (FR) 48
459 **KASINO** 15
392 **KASWARAH** (IRE) 13
315 **KATAR** (IRE) 15

489 **KATATE DORI** (FR) 25
360 **KATATELLA** 49
290 **KATEEVA** (IRE) C 29
457 **KATEIRA** 98
284 **KATELLI** (IRE) 10
423 **KATESON** 19
107 **KATEY KONTENT** 39
188 **KATH'S TOYBOY** 18
219 **KATHAB** (IRE) 73
513 **KATHLEEN** 34
347 **KATHMANDU** (IRE) 117
387 **KATHY SUN** (IRE) C 109
146 **KATIE** G 62
193 **KATIE** K 9
343 **KATONAH** (IRE) 66
267 **KATOPOP** (IRE) 10
410 **KATPOLI** (FR) 38
279 **KATS BOB** 27
6 **KATTANI** (IRE) 45
457 **KATTEGAT** 99
292 **KAUTO CASTILLO** (FR) 49
464 **KAUTO D'AMOUR** (FR) 30
213 **KAUTO RIKO** (FR) 11
497 **KAUTO THE KING** (FR) 39
374 **KAVANAGHS CROSS** (IRE) 9
80 **KAY CERAAR** (IRE) 106
298 **KAY TARA TARA** 58
248 **KAY'S LIGHT** (IRE) 7
147 **KAYF BAHA** 23
254 **KAYF DANCER** 37
537 **KAYF HAMPSHIRE** (IRE) G 35
457 **KAYF HERNANDO** 100
194 **KAYF HOPE** (IRE) 8
205 **KAYF LEGEND** 29
254 **KAYF WILLOW** G 38
335 **KAYFLEUR** F 68
402 **KAYLAN** (GER) 108
282 **KAYLEN'S MISCHIEF** 24
171 **KAYLYN** 3
149 **KAYO KOKO** (IRE) G 5
149 **KAYO KOKO** (IRE) F 20
292 **KAZONTHERAZZ** 24
5 **KAZZIANA** F 181
254 **KEABLE** (IRE) 39
507 **KEADEN HILL** (IRE) 24
161 **KEARNEY HILL** (IRE) 9
295 **KEEL OVER** 14
219 **KEEN INTEREST** 155
405 **KEEP COMING** (IRE) 8
57 **KEEP IT HUSH** 22
321 **KEEP ME HAPPY** 25
405 **KEEP ME STABLE** (IRE) 20
42 **KEEP MY SECRET** 62
385 **KEEP ON DIGGING** (IRE) 108
254 **KEEP ROLLING** (IRE) 40
534 **KEEP RUNNING** (FR) 11
254 **KEEP WONDERING** (IRE) 41
151 **KEEPER** 8
548 **KEEPER'S CHOICE** (IRE) 11
263 **KEEPITFROMBECKY** (IRE) 41
13 **KEEPONBELIEVING** (IRE) 17
504 **KEEPYOURDREAMSBIG** (FR) 40
395 **KEHLANI** (IRE) 36
206 **KEITH DOUGLAS** 86
539 **KEL DU LARGE** (FR) 40
305 **KELAMITA** (IRE) C 28
174 **KELAMITA** (IRE) F 45
200 **KELANNEE** (FR) 49
404 **KELDEO** 28
483 **KELLAHEN** (GER) 12
80 **KELLS** (IRE) 48
204 **KELPIE GREY** 47
457 **KELSEY PARK** (IRE) 101
5 **KEMARI** 16
367 **KEMBOY** (FR) 97
538 **KEMERTON** (IRE) 37
369 **KENAHOPE** (FR) 73
66 **KENDAL MINT** C 123
251 **KENDAM** (FR) F 92
240 **KENDELU** (IRE) 23
280 **KENILWORTH KING** (USA) 6
527 **KENNY GEORGE** 11
306 **KENNYS GIFT** 25
206 **KENSINGTON** (IRE) 16
80 **KENSINGTON AGENT** (FR) 49
5 **KENSPECKLE** F 182
548 **KENSTONE** (FR) 12
390 **KENTANDDOVER** 59
366 **KENTFORD MALLARD** 16
366 **KENTFORD SWANSONG** 17
69 **KENTUCKY BELLE** (IRE) C 36
387 **KENTUCKY BLUEGRASS** 77
356 **KENTUCKY BOURBON** (IRE) 12
166 **KENTUCKY KINGDOM** (IRE) 7
526 **KENYAN CAT** F 43
299 **KENYAN COWBOY** (IRE) 15
192 **KENYX** (FR) 16
488 **KENZAI WARRIOR** (USA) 18
410 **KEPAGGE** (IRE) 39
147 **KEPALA** 24
385 **KEPLERIAN** 109
107 **KERDOS** (IRE) 40
138 **KERINEYA** (IRE) G 79
154 **KERIYKA** (IRE) C 178
335 **KEROSINE LIGHT** (IRE) 69
496 **KERPOW** 34
53 **KERRKENNY GOLD** (IRE) 4
298 **KERRY MOON** 133
251 **KERRY'S DREAM** C 93
402 **KERRYHILL** (IRE) 46
408 **KESSAAR POWER** (IRE) 44
192 **KESTEVEN RDA** (IRE) 62
408 **KESTEVEN RDA** (IRE) 72
311 **KESTREL VALLEY** 14
439 **KEY COMMANDER** (IRE) 10
394 **KEY FACTOR** (IRE) 10
299 **KEY INSTINCT** 16
348 **KEY LOOK** (IRE) 22
515 **KEY TO COTAI** (IRE) 82
531 **KEYBOARD GANGSTER** (IRE) 14
469 **KEYSER SOZE** (IRE) 8
251 **KHAADEM** (IRE) 7
109 **KHABIB** (IRE) 5
131 **KHAJOOL** (IRE) M 9
477 **KHAKI** (IRE) G 7
286 **KHAL** (IRE) 80
430 **KHANGAI** 7
219 **KHANJAR** (IRE) 15
5 **KHAWLAH** (IRE) F 79
5 **KHAWLAH** (IRE) C 183
506 **KHIBRAH** C 162
491 **KHILWAFY** 11
515 **KHINJANI** 37
491 **KHULU** 12
118 **KHURUMBI** (IRE) 4
379 **KICK UP A STORM** (IRE) 97
438 **KICKS AND ALE** (IRE) 13
499 **KICKSAFTERSIX** (IRE) 9
290 **KIHAVAH** 8
496 **KILBAHA LADY** (IRE) G 57
263 **KILBEG KING** (IRE) 42
494 **KILBRAINY** (IRE) 28
242 **KILBRICKEN STORM** (IRE) 5
335 **KILBUNNY APLASIA** (IRE) 70
8 **KILCARAGH BOY** (IRE) 2
532 **KILCONQUHAR** 26
367 **KILCRUIT** (IRE) 98
400 **KILCUMMIN** (IRE) 23
176 **KILDARE LEGEND** (IRE) 52
282 **KILDIMO** (IRE) 25
226 **KILDRUM** (IRE) 45
525 **KILFILUM WOODS** (IRE) 18
474 **KILFINAN BAY** (IRE) 9
202 **KILFORDS QUEEN** (IRE) 13
526 **KILGANER QUEEN** (IRE) 11
152 **KILKEASKIN MOLLY** (IRE) 6
379 **KILLALOAN** (IRE) 98
335 **KILLANE** (IRE) 71
257 **KILLARNEY MOUNTAIN** 6
308 **KILLER CLOWN** (IRE) 35
497 **KILLER KANE** (IRE) 40
343 **KILLER MODE** (IRE) 30
12 **KILLIGARTH** 38
449 **KILLING EVE** (IRE) 26
286 **KILLYBEGS WARRIOR** (IRE) 81
353 **KILMAH** F 27
219 **KILT** (IRE) 156
286 **KILTARA** (IRE) F 174
466 **KILTEALY BRIGGS** (IRE) 28
161 **KILTORCAN BOY** (IRE) 10
448 **KIM TIAN ROAD** (IRE) F 13
320 **KIM WEXLER** (IRE) 12
538 **KIMBERLEY EVE** 38
306 **KIMBERLITE CANDY** (IRE) 26
164 **KIMBLEWICK** (IRE) C 45
217 **KIMCHI** 18
538 **KIMIFIVE** (IRE) 39
270 **KIMNGRACE** (IRE) 11
270 **KIMNKATE** (IRE) 28
231 **KINAESTHESIA** C 123
247 **KINCARDINE** 70
172 **KIND OF BLUE** 55
323 **KIND WITNESS** (IRE) 8
277 **KINDER KID** (IRE) 6
284 **KINDERFRAU** 11
10 **KINDIA** (IRE) C 42
174 **KINDNESS MATTERS** (IRE) 35
24 **KINEMATIC** F 122
416 **KINEMATICA** 44
434 **KINERTON HILL** (IRE) 10
247 **KING ALEXANDER** (IRE) 71
376 **KING ARISE** (IRE) 31
162 **KING ATHELSTAN** (IRE) 11
186 **KING BERRY** (IRE) 13
118 **KING CABO** (USA) 5
347 **KING CARNEY** 42
316 **KING CHARLES** (USA) 8
255 **KING CNUT** (FR) 6
116 **KING CODI** (IRE) 11
247 **KING EAGLE** (IRE) 72
26 **KING FRANCIS** (IRE) 9

503 **KING HARRY** (IRE) 13
447 **KING KRAKEN** 15
43 **KING LEAR** (IRE) 61
383 **KING LEODEGRANCE** (IRE) 58
286 **KING ME** 82
6 **KING OF BAVARIA** (IRE) 46
417 **KING OF BRAZIL** 4
5 **KING OF CONQUEST** 17
153 **KING OF EUROPE** (IRE) 23
144 **KING OF FASHION** (IRE) 12
296 **KING OF FURY** (IRE) 14
42 **KING OF ITHACA** 30
497 **KING OF LOMBARDY** (IRE) 41
504 **KING OF QUINTA** (FR) 41
88 **KING OF RECORDS** (FR) 35
321 **KING OF SPEED** (IRE) 26
6 **KING OF STARS** (IRE) 47
320 **KING OF STEEL** (USA) 33
285 **KING OF THE DANCE** (IRE) 8
4 **KING OF THE HILL** (IRE) 12
153 **KING OF THE JUNGLE** (IRE) 58
286 **KING OF THE PLAINS** (IRE) 83
303 **KING OF THE SOUTH** (IRE) 6
187 **KING OF THE WOODS** 7
79 **KING OF TONGA** (IRE) 6
226 **KING OF UNICORNS** 46
147 **KING OF WAR** 25
135 **KING OF YORK** (IRE) 32
196 **KING ORRY** (IRE) 7
7 **KING OTIS** (IRE) 7
247 **KING OTTOKAR** (FR) 73
367 **KING PEAK** (IRE) 99
228 **KING SHARJA** 57
501 **KING TRITON** (IRE) 16
410 **KING TURGEON** (FR) 40
161 **KING VIKTOR** 11
205 **KING WILLIAM RUFUS** (FR) 30
448 **KING'S CASTLE** (IRE) 14
228 **KING'S CODE** 58
228 **KING'S CONQUEST** (IRE) 59
378 **KING'S CROWN** (IRE) 13
43 **KING'S GEM** (IRE) 62
251 **KING'S KNIGHT** (IRE) 8
15 **KING'S LYNN** 18
308 **KING'S THRESHOLD** (IRE) 36
495 **KINGCORMAC** (IRE) 6
107 **KINGDOM COME** (IRE) 7
385 **KINGFAST** (IRE) 110
219 **KINGFISHER KING** 74
402 **KINGLY FIGHTER** (GER) 109
176 **KINGMANIA** (IRE) 7
318 **KINGMON'S BOY** 2
273 **KINGOFTHECOTSWOLDS** (IRE) 2
499 **KINGOFTHEGAME** (IRE) 10
133 **KINGOFTHESWINGERZ** (IRE) 8
410 **KINGOFTHEWEST** (IRE) 41
112 **KINGORI** (USA) 10
513 **KINGS CREEK** (IRE) 35
545 **KINGS ECLIPSE** (IRE) 2
4 **KINGS JUSTICE** 13
311 **KINGS KEEPER** (IRE) 15
202 **KINGS KRACKERTARA** 14
202 **KINGS KUROSHIO** 15
285 **KINGS PAGEANT** 32
231 **KINGS TIME** (IRE) 58
56 **KINGSBURY** (IRE) 53
457 **KINGSFORT HILL** 102
286 **KINGSLEY PRIDE** 84
142 **KINGSMILL GIN** 5
104 **KINGSON** (IRE) 11
532 **KINGSTON BRIDGE** (IRE) 27
456 **KINGSTON JOY** (IRE) 13
104 **KINGSTON KING** (IRE) 12
10 **KINGSTON KURRAJONG** 17
102 **KINGSTON ROCK** (IRE) 12
385 **KINGSTON SUNFLOWER** (FR) 111
195 **KINGWELL** 2
421 **KINKY BOOTS** 21
163 **KINONDO KWETU** 7
24 **KINROSS** 6
43 **KINTA** (IRE) 63
247 **KINTAIL** 74
468 **KINZ** (IRE) 6
390 **KIOTO SUN** (GER) 60
13 **KIRK HOUSE** 10
399 **KIRRIN ISLAND** (USA) G 85
62 **KIRTLING** 1
432 **KIRUNA PEAK** (IRE) 7
54 **KISS AND RUN** 16
231 **KISS ME DIXIE** (IRE) 59
161 **KISS MY FACE** 12
228 **KISS OF SPRING** (IRE) F 156
5 **KISSABLE** (IRE) C 184
135 **KISSES OF FIRE** (IRE) 33
448 **KISSESFORKATIE** (IRE) 15
368 **KIT GABRIEL** (IRE) 20
538 **KITAAB** 40
286 **KITAI** (IRE) 85
14 **KITARO KICH** (IRE) 49
85 **KITBAG** 27
534 **KITESURFER** (FR) 12
506 **KITSUNE POWER** (IRE) 21
353 **KITTEN GLOVES** 14
513 **KITTEN'S BAY** 62
135 **KITTEN'S DREAM** 34
88 **KITTY** (FR) 36
420 **KITTY HALL** (IRE) 7
449 **KITTY PI** 17
40 **KITTY POWER** (IRE) F 14
185 **KITTYBREWSTER** 5
456 **KIWANO** (FR) 14
343 **KIZMEHONEY** G 31
367 **KLARC KENT** (FR) 100
367 **KLASSICAL DREAM** (FR) 101
5 **KLASSIQUE** C 185
88 **KLEORA** 37
408 **KLIMOVA** 45
71 **KLIP KLOPP** 5
298 **KLITSCHKO** 59
219 **KLONDIKE** 75
113 **KNACKER TRAPPER** (IRE) 9
379 **KNAPPERS HILL** (IRE) 99
270 **KNEBWORTH** 29
457 **KNICKERBOCKERGLORY** (IRE) 103
112 **KNIGHT** (IRE) 37
457 **KNIGHT IN DUBAI** (IRE) 104
539 **KNIGHT OF ALLEN** (FR) 41
70 **KNIGHT OF KINGS** 25
234 **KNIGHT SALUTE** 41
416 **KNIGHT TEMPLAR** 45
413 **KNIGHT'S GAMBIT** 4
154 **KNIGHTS ARTIST** (IRE) 122
154 **KNIGHTS SPEAR** 123
286 **KNIGHTSWOOD** (IRE) 13
251 **KNOCK STARS** (IRE) C 94
414 **KNOCKANORE** (IRE) 18
286 **KNOCKBREX** 86
343 **KNOCKMORE PRINCE** 67
227 **KNOCKNAGOSHEL** (IRE) 19
226 **KNOCKNAMONA** (IRE) 47
318 **KNOCKOUT BLOW** 3
548 **KNOT ON TIME** (IRE) 13
438 **KNOWLEDGEABLE KING** 14
379 **KNOWSLEY ROAD** (IRE) 100
234 **KNOWWHENTOHOLDEM** (IRE) 42
488 **KNOWWHENTORUN** 19
219 **KOALA** (FR) F 157
149 **KOALA BEAR** C 6
387 **KOCOLLADA** (IRE) C 110
249 **KODEBREAKER** (IRE) 9
289 **KODI DANCER** (IRE) 26
135 **KODI GOLD** (IRE) 35
451 **KODI HAWK** 30
528 **KODI KOH** (IRE) 10
192 **KODIAC EXPRESS** (IRE) F 63
437 **KODIAC LADY** (IRE) F 13
165 **KODIAC SIGN** (IRE) 6
192 **KODIACLAIM** 17
471 **KODIAS SANGARIUS** (IRE) 8
154 **KODIELLEN** (IRE) 49
506 **KODIMAN** (IRE) 91
521 **KOHANA BREEZE** (IRE) 76
283 **KOHANA GIRL** (IRE) 33
410 **KOI DODVILLE** (FR) 42
391 **KOKOMO** 4
410 **KOLISI** (IRE) 43
506 **KOLSAI** 92
463 **KONDO ISAMI** (IRE) 22
80 **KONDRATIEV WAVE** (IRE) 50
464 **KONFUSION** 31
263 **KONIGIN ISABELLA** (GER) 43
102 **KONIK KING** (IRE) 13
539 **KOOKY** (FR) 22
489 **KOP LAND** (FR) 58
347 **KOPA KILANA** (IRE) 43
94 **KOREA** (GER) 21
66 **KORKER** (IRE) 16
487 **KOROPICK** (IRE) 4
157 **KOSASIEMPRE** (FR) 20
355 **KOTARI** (FR) 70
355 **KOTMASK** (FR) 71
6 **KOTYONOK** 48
112 **KOUBALIBRE** (IRE) C 79
43 **KOY KOY** 14
457 **KRACKA NUT** 105
107 **KRACKING** 41
423 **KRACQUER** 20
148 **KRAKA** (IRE) 9
412 **KRAKEN FILLY** (IRE) 6
511 **KRAKEN FLORIDA** (IRE) 6
204 **KRAKEN POWER** (IRE) 24
447 **KRAMER DRIVE** (IRE) G 35
311 **KRAQUELINE** (FR) 16
247 **KRIS KINDLE** (IRE) G 75
399 **KRISTAL KLEAR** (IRE) 47
399 **KRISTAL XENIA** (IRE) F 86
385 **KRISTALETTE** (IRE) F 112
286 **KRONA** 87
379 **KRUGER PARK** (FR) 101
157 **KRYPTON GOLD** (IRE) 21
404 **KRYSTAL MAZE** (IRE) 4

375 **KRYSTYNA** 12
320 **KUAICOSS** (IRE) F 51
475 **KUMASI** 9
247 **KUTAIBA** 76
70 **KUWAIT CITY** (IRE) 57
401 **KWIZ** (IRE) 7
147 **KYBER CRYSTAL** (IRE) 26
447 **KYKUIT** (IRE) C 36
360 **KYLE OF LOCHALSH** 50
248 **KYLENOE DANCER** 8
135 **KYLLARNEY** F 36
537 **KYM EYRE** (IRE) 36
395 **KYNSA** (IRE) 37
12 **KYNTARA** 39
383 **KYPRIOS** (IRE) 6
43 **L'AGE D'OR** F 130
149 **L'ARTISTE** (IRE) C 7
537 **L'ASTROBOY** (GER) 37
457 **L'EAU DU SUD** (FR) 106
86 **L'ES FREMANTLE** (FR) 2
543 **L'HOMME PRESSE** (FR) 57
209 **L'IMMORTALE** 15
94 **L'IMPRESSIONNISTE** (FR) 44
451 **L'SARAFINA** 31
298 **L'UNIQUE** (FR) G 60
298 **L'UNIQUE** (FR) G 61
346 **LA BELLE AURORE** (FR) 8
328 **LA BELLE VIE** 9
16 **LA BREILLE** (FR) 20
448 **LA BRETESCHE** (FR) 16
40 **LA CALINDA** F 15
135 **LA CAPRIOSA** C 37
146 **LA CHICANIERE** 38
384 **LA DOLCE VITA** (IRE) 13
305 **LA DONACELLA** C 29
289 **LA EQUINATA** 7
346 **LA ESPANOLA** (IRE) 24
256 **LA FEUILLARDE** (FR) G 10
231 **LA FOLIE** (IRE) C 124
54 **LA FORTUNATA** G 17
289 **LA FORTUNATA** C 27
500 **LA FORZA** 3
220 **LA GOMERA** 28
24 **LA ISLA MUJERES** (FR) 48
153 **LA JOLIE FILLE** (IRE) 59
14 **LA MAQUINA** 20
548 **LA MIA DUTCHESSA** (IRE) 30
14 **LA MUJER** (IRE) 50
363 **LA PAGERIE** (FR) 67
24 **LA PATRIA** F 123
5 **LA PELOSA** (IRE) F 186
85 **LA PERLA** (SPA) C 60
26 **LA PETITE REINE** F 64
446 **LA PODEROSA** 4
367 **LA PRIMA DONNA** (FR) 102
286 **LA PULGA** (IRE) 14
82 **LA RAV** (IRE) 7
240 **LA REFERI** (IRE) 24
347 **LA REINE DE RIOGH** (IRE) G 103
376 **LA RENOMMEE** (FR) 32
131 **LA ROCA DEL FUEGO** (IRE) 10
5 **LA ROSETTA** C 187
368 **LA ROUMEGUE** (USA) C 60
484 **LA SEINE** (USA) C 61
176 **LA SONNAMBULA** 53
94 **LA TOUR DU BOIS** (FR) 45
21 **LA TRAVIATA** (IRE) 16
174 **LA TRINIDAD** 17
305 **LA VERITE** 45
219 **LA YAKEL** 16
219 **LAAFI** (FR) 76
73 **LAAFY** (USA) 6
79 **LAAKHOF** (IRE) 7
251 **LABIQA** (IRE) 39
457 **LAC DE CONSTANCE** (FR) 107
552 **LACAROLINA** (FR) F 42
1 **LACILA BLUE** (FR) 29
387 **LACONIC** 31
387 **LAD NEXT DOOR** (IRE) 111
393 **LADIES ARE FOREVER** C 9
99 **LADRONNE** (FR) 7
189 **LADY ADARE** (IRE) 37
251 **LADY ALARA** (IRE) 40
400 **LADY ALIENOR** (IRE) F 30
228 **LADY AMANDA** (IRE) 60
289 **LADY ANNE BLUNT** 8
219 **LADY AQUITAINE** (USA) C 158
146 **LADY AVA** (IRE) 63
287 **LADY AVERY** (IRE) 7
287 **LADY AVERY** (IRE) G 16
113 **LADY BABS** 10
30 **LADY BEACONSFIELD** (IRE) 13
497 **LADY BEAUFORT** G 42
153 **LADY BEECHFIELD** 60
483 **LADY BERLAIS** 13
202 **LADY BERNIE** (IRE) F 16
484 **LADY BEWARE** (IRE) C 62
395 **LADY BIANCA** 38
15 **LADY BIRDIE** 171
261 **LADY BLADE** (IRE) G 23
24 **LADY BOBA** 49
283 **LADY BONANOVA** (IRE) G 29
352 **LADY BOWES** 15
286 **LADY BRACKEN** (IRE) 88
15 **LADY BRORA** F 172
270 **LADY BRYANSTON** (IRE) 30
243 **LADY BULLET** (IRE) 23
539 **LADY BUTTERFLY** (FR) C 42
243 **LADY CAMACHO** (IRE) 24
308 **LADY CARO** (IRE) 37
442 **LADY CEDAR** (IRE) F 74
61 **LADY CELIA** 11
176 **LADY CHAPEL** (IRE) 26
300 **LADY CHLOE** G 31
300 **LADY CHLOE** G 67
503 **LADY CLAIR** (IRE) F 20
176 **LADY CLAYPOOLE** (IRE) 27
173 **LADY CLEMMIE** 16
66 **LADY CORSICA** (IRE) C 124
42 **LADY CROSSMAR** (IRE) F 63
247 **LADY D'ARBANVILLE** 77
26 **LADY D'ASCOYNE** 32
286 **LADY DARSHAAN** (IRE) C 175
153 **LADY DOUGLAS** 61
520 **LADY DREAMER** (IRE) 18
386 **LADY ECLAIR** (IRE) F 37
383 **LADY ELI** (USA) C 159
66 **LADY ESTELLA** (IRE) F 125
287 **LADY EXCALIBUR** (IRE) 8
92 **LADY FASHION** C 63
5 **LADY FRANKEL** C 188
366 **LADY FRIEND** G 18
166 **LADY GAZELLE** 15
88 **LADY GLENHAM** (IRE) 38
94 **LADY GLITTERS** (FR) C 46
353 **LADY GRACE** (IRE) F 28
387 **LADY GUINEVERE** G 78
539 **LADY GWEN** 23
66 **LADY HAMANA** (AUS) 62
478 **LADY HAMILTON** (IRE) 2
43 **LADY HEART** C 131
235 **LADY HEARTBEAT** F 12
100 **LADY HOBBS** 1
184 **LADY HOLLY** 3
210 **LADY IRONSIDE** (IRE) 4
217 **LADY JANE GREY** 13
548 **LADY JANE P** (IRE) 14
378 **LADY KERMIT** (IRE) F 23
448 **LADY KK** (IRE) 17
502 **LADY KYLLAR** C 17
15 **LADY LABELLE** (IRE) 19
119 **LADY LADE** 26
286 **LADY LAVINA** 89
146 **LADY LIBERTY** (IRE) F 64
228 **LADY LIVIUS** (IRE) C 157
285 **LADY LOCKWOOD** C 62
329 **LADY LOVELESS** 9
387 **LADY LUCIA** (IRE) F 112
515 **LADY MACDUFF** (IRE) F 83
262 **LADY MANDER** 5
66 **LADY MANYARA** (IRE) 63
456 **LADY MARIE** (IRE) 44
347 **LADY MENDOZA** (IRE) 44
506 **LADY MOMOKA** (IRE) C 163
552 **LADY NAGIN** (IRE) 26
143 **LADY NECTAR** (IRE) 6
251 **LADY OF ANJOU** (IRE) 41
285 **LADY OF ARABIA** 33
343 **LADY OF INISHFREE** (IRE) 32
264 **LADY OF LAMANVER** C 18
80 **LADY OF NEPAL** 107
42 **LADY OF THE LAKE** (FR) F 64
12 **LADY OF THE NIGHT** 40
17 **LADY OF YORK** 10
529 **LADY PACIFICO** 2
79 **LADY PASCHA** 8
360 **LADY PERCIVAL** 14
526 **LADY PLUMTON** 12
175 **LADY PRIMROSE** (IRE) 32
231 **LADY PRO** 60
43 **LADY RASCAL** 64
15 **LADY RASHA** C 173
410 **LADY RESET** 44
31 **LADY ROAMER** 25
402 **LADY ROBINN** 47
42 **LADY ROSAMUNDE** C 65
285 **LADY ROSEBUD** (IRE) G 63
29 **LADY SALVADOR** (IRE) 10
317 **LADY SAMSON** (IRE) 11
387 **LADY SANDY** (IRE) C 113
442 **LADY SPANGLES** (IRE) C 75
442 **LADY TABITHA** (IRE) C 76
335 **LADY TREMAINE** (IRE) 72
466 **LADY VALENTINE** (IRE) 29
492 **LADY VALLETTA** (IRE) 5
67 **LADY WILBERRY** 12
172 **LADY WORMSLEY** (IRE) 29
348 **LADY ZIANA** 23
437 **LADY'S CHARM** 9
300 **LADY'S PRESENT** (IRE) 32
506 **LADY'S PURSE** C 164

437 **LADY'S SURPRISE** 6
500 **LADYBIRD** (IRE) 4
233 **LADYPACKSAPUNCH** 8
515 **LADYS FIRST** F 84
174 **LADYWANTAWAY** (IRE) 36
153 **LAERTES** (USA) 24
527 **LAETOLI** 12
70 **LAFAN** (IRE) 26
178 **LAFILIA** (GER) 2
543 **LAGONDA** 58
542 **LAGUNA BOY** (IRE) 50
219 **LAH TI DAR** F 159
15 **LAHAB** 81
472 **LAHABAH** G 35
42 **LAHEG** (FR) 5
54 **LAHINA BAY** (IRE) 11
363 **LAHINCH WAVE** (IRE) 68
172 **LAILAH** 6
69 **LAJOOJE** 15
525 **LAKA** (IRE) C 29
464 **LAKE CRESENT** (IRE) G 32
205 **LAKE ROAD** (IRE) 31
480 **LAKE SAND** (IRE) 4
357 **LAKE SHORE DRIVE** (IRE) 24
168 **LAKE TAKAPUNA** (IRE) 19
355 **LAKE WASHINGTON** (FR) 72
366 **LAKESIDE LAD** 19
496 **LAKOTA BLUE** 35
521 **LAKOTA BRAVE** 77
387 **LAKOTA LADY** (IRE) 79
251 **LAKOTA LASS** (IRE) 42
286 **LAKOTA SIOUX** (IRE) 90
477 **LALANIA** 8
379 **LALLYGAG** (GER) 102
307 **LALOCHEZIA** (IRE) 4
379 **LALOR** (GER) 103
497 **LAMANVER BEL AMI** 43
306 **LAMANVER STORM** 27
484 **LAMAR** (IRE) F 63
383 **LAMBADA** (IRE) 59
219 **LAMBARI** (FR) C 160
154 **LAMPANG** (IRE) 50
286 **LAMYA** (GER) C 176
231 **LAN CINNTE** (IRE) 61
18 **LANCASHIRE LIFE** 19
539 **LANCELOT ALLEN** (FR) 43
390 **LAND GENIE** 61
251 **LAND GIRL** (USA) F 95
176 **LAND LEGEND** (FR) 28
35 **LAND OF LEGENDS** (IRE) 25
54 **LAND OF MAGIC** 18
282 **LAND OF MY DELIGHT** (IRE) 26
228 **LAND OF SUMMER** (IRE) 61
217 **LAND OF WINTER** (FR) 6
258 **LANDACRE BRIDGE** 5
385 **LANDEN CALLING** (IRE) 113
500 **LANDING STRIP** 5
166 **LANDLORDTOTHESTARS** (IRE) 16
355 **LANGAFEL** (IRE) 73
457 **LANGER DAN** (IRE) 108
138 **LANGHOLM** (IRE) 23
254 **LANGLEY HUNDRED** (IRE) 42
161 **LANGTON WOLD** (IRE) 13
526 **LANGYTHELEGEND** 30
147 **LANITA** (GER) C 37
497 **LANSPARK** (IRE) 44
292 **LANTIC BAY** 25
464 **LANZEALOT** 33
18 **LAOCH GACH LA** 20
552 **LAOISMAN** 27
6 **LARADO** (FR) 49
379 **LARCHMONT LASS** (IRE) 104
174 **LARGE ACTION** 18
327 **LARGO BAY** (USA) 4
211 **LARGY FORCE** (IRE) 28
367 **LARGY HILL** (IRE) 103
319 **LARGY NIGHTS** (IRE) 24
335 **LARGY REACH** 73
258 **LARGY TRAIN** 6
319 **LARGY VALLEY** (IRE) 25
234 **LARIO** (GER) 43
280 **LARKHILL** (IRE) 15
33 **LARKIN** (IRE) 4
44 **LARRIKIN** (IRE) 10
355 **LARRSEN** 144
355 **LARRY** 74
226 **LARRY LOOBY** (IRE) 48
157 **LARUSSO** (IRE) 22
112 **LASER GUIDED** (IRE) 38
35 **LASER SHOW** (IRE) 26
543 **LASKALIN** (FR) 59
56 **LASSIES ENVOI** G 54
385 **LASSUE** 114
251 **LAST BID** C 96
285 **LAST CHANCE SALOON** (IRE) 34
66 **LAST CRUSADER** (IRE) 17
192 **LAST DATE** 18
521 **LAST HOORAH** 18
84 **LAST IN LINE** 9
329 **LAST LAUGH** (USA) C 15
20 **LAST MISSION** (FR) 13
189 **LAST OF A LEGEND** 38
410 **LAST QUARTER** (IRE) 45
354 **LAST ROAR** (IRE) 7
67 **LAST ROYAL** 13
66 **LAST STAND** (IRE) 64
342 **LAST TANGO** (FR) F 29
5 **LAST TRADITION** 80
182 **LASTIN' MEMORIES** 8
343 **LASTING PEACE** (IRE) 68
279 **LASTOFTHECOSMICS** 28
265 **LASTORDERSPLEASE** (IRE) 7
153 **LATE ARRIVAL** (IRE) 25
148 **LATE BLOOM** 10
212 **LATE ROMANTIC** (IRE) 49
378 **LATE ROSEBUD** (IRE) C 24
80 **LATENT HEAT** (IRE) 51
406 **LATER DARLING** 3
66 **LATEST EDITION** (IRE) 65
457 **LATHAN** (FR) 109
348 **LATIN FIVE** (IRE) 24
24 **LATIN VERSE** 50
335 **LATINO FLING** (IRE) 74
385 **LATITUDE** (FR) G 115
439 **LATITUDE** (IRE) 11
219 **LATTAM** (IRE) 17
231 **LAUGH OUT LOUD** F 125
510 **LAUGHING LORD** (IRE) 13
346 **LAURA BAY** (IRE) 44
97 **LAURA BULLION** (IRE) 5
146 **LAURA'S BREEZE** (IRE) 39
206 **LAUREL** 17
276 **LAURENTIA** (IRE) 6
5 **LAVA FLOW** (IRE) F 189
387 **LAVA STREAM** (IRE) 114
538 **LAW SUPREME** (FR) 41
280 **LAWMAKER** 16
186 **LAWMANS BLIS** (IRE) 7
10 **LAWN RANGER** 18
74 **LAWRENNY** 17
376 **LAWTOP LEGEND** (IRE) 33
73 **LAXEY** (IRE) 7
463 **LAY DOWN THE LAW** (IRE) 23
447 **LAYALEE** (IRE) C 38
222 **LAYERTHORPE** (IRE) 5
343 **LAYFAYETTE** (IRE) 33
442 **LAYLA JAMIL** (IRE) F 77
5 **LAZULI** (IRE) 18
351 **LAZY SUNDAY** 2
282 **LE BALCON** (IRE) 27
169 **LE BAYOU** (FR) 7
153 **LE BEAU GARCON** 26
369 **LE BON VIVANT** (FR) 74
402 **LE BREUIL** (FR) 48
539 **LE CAMELEON** 24
136 **LE CHEVAL NOIR** (IRE) 19
379 **LE CHIFFRE D'OR** (FR) 105
263 **LE COEUR NET** (FR) 44
533 **LE FILS DE FORCE** 3
68 **LE FOU'S KEEP** (IRE) 3
402 **LE GRAND LION** (FR) 49
226 **LE GRAND VERT** (FR) 49
497 **LE LIGERIEN** (FR) 45
228 **LE MANS** (IRE) 62
457 **LE MILOS** 110
376 **LE PATRIOTE** (FR) 34
355 **LE PATRON** (FR) 75
289 **LE REVEUR** (IRE) 9
271 **LE TUEUR** (IRE) 8
438 **LEAD THE FIELD** (IRE) 15
24 **LEADENHALL** 51
332 **LEADING CHOICE** (IRE) 12
494 **LEADING FORCE** (IRE) 29
87 **LEADING KNIGHT** (IRE) 5
206 **LEADING LION** (IRE) 87
514 **LEADING SWOOP** (IRE) 16
385 **LEADING THEATRE** (IRE) 116
15 **LEADMAN** 82
524 **LEANNES LADY** (IRE) 10
98 **LEAP ABROAD** (IRE) 7
26 **LEAP TO GLORY** (IRE) 33
442 **LEAP YEAR LAD** (IRE) 41
369 **LEARNTALOT** (IRE) 75
385 **LEAVE HER TO ME** 117
74 **LEAVE ME ALONE** (IRE) 18
205 **LEAVE OF ABSENCE** (FR) 32
450 **LEBOWSKI** (IRE) 22
335 **LECCE LADY** 144
74 **LECHRO** (IRE) 19
367 **LECKY WATSON** (IRE) 104
202 **LEDDERS** (IRE) 17
227 **LEDHAM** (IRE) 20
192 **LEDNIKOV** 19
15 **LEGACY POWER** 83
554 **LEGAL OK** (IRE) 5
192 **LEGAL REFORM** (IRE) 20
355 **LEGAL RIGHTS** (GER) 76
383 **LEGATISSIMO** (IRE) C 160
42 **LEGEND OF LEROS** (IRE) 31
290 **LEGENDARY DAY** 9
202 **LEGENDARY GRACE** 18

483 **LEGENDARY RHYTHM** 14
471 **LEGENDE D'ART** (IRE) 9
99 **LEGENDE VOLANTE** (FR) F 8
466 **LEGENDS RYDE** 30
234 **LEGIONAR** (GER) 44
448 **LEISSIERES EXPRESS** 18
168 **LEITRIM CHIEF** (IRE) 20
337 **LEITRIM ROCK** (IRE) 6
387 **LEITZEL** 80
537 **LELANT** (IRE) 38
247 **LELANTOS** (IRE) 78
168 **LEMOINE** 21
115 **LEMON ICE** (IRE) 12
88 **LEMON ZEST** (FR) 39
234 **LEN BRENNAN** (IRE) 45
347 **LENEBANE** (IRE) 45
146 **LENNY'S SPIRIT** (FR) 9
5 **LENORMAND** 81
517 **LENS LEGACY** (IRE) 12
348 **LEODIS DREAM** (IRE) 25
173 **LEON TROTSKY** 24
228 **LEONICA** C 158
321 **LEONNA** (IRE) 44
300 **LEOPOLDS ROCK** (IRE) 33
532 **LEOSTAR** 28
4 **LEPASHE** (IRE) 14
80 **LEQUINTO** (IRE) 52
47 **LERMOOS LEGEND** 22
31 **LERWICK** 26
402 **LES'S DESTINY STAR** (IRE) 50
402 **LES'S JERSEY ROYAL** (IRE) 51
102 **LES'S LEGACY** 14
103 **LESKINFERE** (IRE) 1
72 **LESS IS MORE** 15
269 **LESS OF THAT** (IRE) 6
51 **LESSANKAN** (GER) 7
409 **LESSER** (IRE) 10
383 **LESSON IN LIFE** C 161
521 **LET HER LOOSE** (IRE) 19
457 **LET IT RAIN** 111
450 **LET IT SHINE** 23
479 **LET LIFE HAPPEN** 36
376 **LET ME BE** (IRE) 35
450 **LET ME ENTERTAIN** U 24
98 **LET'S GET EM** 34
12 **LET'S GO AMIGO** (IRE) 41
404 **LET'S GO HUGO** (IRE) 15
165 **LET'S HAVE A FLYER** (IRE) 27
369 **LET'S HAVE ANOTHER** (IRE) 76
98 **LET'S PARTY** 35
146 **LETABA** 40
284 **LETHAL ANGEL** 12
141 **LETHAL INDUSTRY** (IRE) 15
66 **LETHAL LEVI** 18
107 **LETHAL NYMPH** 8
84 **LETHAL SECRET** 20
400 **LETHAL TOUCH** 8
434 **LETHEM PRESENT** (IRE) G 11
379 **LETHERBELUCKY** (IRE) G 106
115 **LETMELIVEMYLIFE** 13
390 **LETMETELLUSOMETHIN** 62
272 **LETS GO DUTCHESS** 13
423 **LETS GO TO VEGAS** (IRE) 21
67 **LETSBE AVENUE** (IRE) 14
392 **LETTER OF THE LAW** (IRE) 14
47 **LETTERSTON LADY** 23
93 **LETTIE LUTZ** (IRE) 10
506 **LEUVEN POWER** (IRE) 22
165 **LEVEL UP** (IRE) 7
37 **LEWA HOUSE** 4
29 **LEWESIAN LASS** (IRE) 11
88 **LEWIS CHOP** (FR) 40
85 **LEXINGTON HERO** 28
228 **LEXINGTON KNIGHT** (IRE) 14
427 **LEYLA'S GIFT** F 7
97 **LEYLAK** (IRE) 6
501 **LEZARDRIEUX** 17
24 **LEZOO** 52
122 **LHEBAYEB** (GER) 11
217 **LIA ROSE** 19
479 **LIABLE** 37
458 **LIAM'S LASS** (IRE) 14
66 **LIAMARTY DREAMS** 19
333 **LIANGEL HOPE** (IRE) 5
537 **LIBBERTY HUNTER** 39
318 **LIBBRETTA** 4
26 **LIBERALIST** 34
538 **LIBERATED LAD** 42
251 **LIBERATING** C 97
483 **LIBERTARIAN ROYALE** (IRE) 15
172 **LIBERTUS** 7
505 **LIBERTY BAY** 8
533 **LIBERTY BREEZE** 4
66 **LIBERTY LANE** (IRE) 66
400 **LIBERTY MOUNTAIN** 24
515 **LIBRA TIGER** 8
383 **LIBRARY** (IRE) 60
154 **LICIT** (IRE) 51
213 **LICKPENNY LARRY** 12
66 **LIDANSKI** (IRE) F 126
15 **LIEBER POWER** 84
343 **LIEUTENANT COMMAND** (FR) 34
267 **LIEUTENANT ROCCO** (IRE) 11
440 **LIFE MADE SIMPLE** 49
5 **LIFE OF DREAMS** 19
231 **LIFETIME AMBITION** 15
299 **LIFETIME LEGEND** (IRE) 17
206 **LIFTOFF** (FR) 88
35 **LIGHT AND DARK** 27
332 **LIGHT EM UP NIGEL** (IRE) 13
414 **LIGHT FLICKER** (IRE) 19
140 **LIGHT IN THE SKY** (FR) 9
456 **LIGHT INFANTRY** (FR) 15
308 **LIGHT N STRIKE** (IRE) 38
5 **LIGHT OF PEACE** (IRE) 20
135 **LIGHT UP OUR STARS** (IRE) 38
239 **LIGHTENING COMPANY** (IRE) 17
376 **LIGHTENING GESTURE** 36
247 **LIGHTFOOT LADY** (IRE) 79
189 **LIGHTLY SQUEEZE** 39
375 **LIGHTNING ATTACK** 5
88 **LIGHTNING BOLT** (FR) 41
527 **LIGHTNING GOLD** 13
472 **LIGHTNING LEGEND** 16
91 **LIGHTNING MARK** (IRE) F 15
95 **LIGHTNING MARK** (IRE) F 32
456 **LIGHTNING SPARK** 45
506 **LIGHTNING TOUCH** 165
196 **LIGHTONTHEWING** (IRE) 8
34 **LIGHTS ARE GREEN** (IRE) 12
408 **LIGHTSHIP** (IRE) 15
165 **LIHOU** 8
347 **LIHYAN** (IRE) 46
375 **LIIMARI** 6
66 **LIKE** (IRE) F 127
154 **LIKE A LION** (IRE) 52
176 **LIKE A TIGER** 29
107 **LIKELY TYPE** 42
533 **LIL BIT OF MAGIC** 5
305 **LIL GUFF** 11
135 **LIL WADE** (IRE) 70
506 **LIL' FRANK** 93
209 **LILAC LADY** 16
179 **LILANDRA** (FR) 9
23 **LILIKOI** (IRE) 13
263 **LILITH** (IRE) 45
260 **LILKIAN** 5
366 **LILLIAN** (IRE) G 45
5 **LILLIAN RUSSELL** (IRE) C 190
92 **LILLISTAR** 36
254 **LILLYWAVE** 43
227 **LILOO D'ORES** (FR) 21
384 **LILTING** (IRE) C 54
385 **LILTING VERSE** (IRE) 118
543 **LILY GRACE** 60
300 **LILY IN THE JUNGLE** (IRE) 68
448 **LILY LUNA** (IRE) 19
51 **LILY MAY BLU** 8
414 **LILY'S GEM** (IRE) 20
271 **LILY'S RUBY** 9
379 **LIME AVENUE** (IRE) 107
358 **LIMEKILN ROCK** (IRE) 15
289 **LIMELIGHT** (GER) 28
285 **LIMELITE** (IRE) C 64
286 **LIMERICK BOUND** 91
136 **LIMERICK LEADER** (FR) 20
221 **LIMESTONE RED** 26
390 **LIMETREE BOY** (IRE) 63
502 **LIMOUSINE** C 18
95 **LINA DE VEGA** (IRE) C 33
226 **LINCOLN BURROWS** (IRE) 50
192 **LINCOLN GAMBLE** 21
286 **LINCOLN LEGACY** (IRE) 177
213 **LINCOLN LYN** 13
541 **LINCOLN RED** 5
112 **LINCOLN TALE** (IRE) C 80
192 **LINCOLNROSE** (IRE) F 64
538 **LINDAKA** (FR) 43
218 **LINDEMAN** (IRE) G 9
514 **LINDISFARNE** 17
211 **LINE OF DESCENT** (IRE) 29
349 **LINE OF FIRE** 36
369 **LINELEE KING** (FR) 77
151 **LINGER** (IRE) 9
416 **LINGUA FRANCA** 46
172 **LION KINGDOM** 30
286 **LION OF WAR** 92
331 **LION RING** (IRE) 6
206 **LION TAMER** 89
501 **LION TOWER** (IRE) 18
6 **LION'S DREAM** (FR) 50
206 **LION'S PRIDE** 90
502 **LION'S VIGIL** (USA) 4
298 **LIONELLA** 134
315 **LIOSA** (IRE) 16
537 **LIPA K** (IRE) 40
375 **LIPPY LADY** (IRE) 7
106 **LIPSINK** (IRE) 10
506 **LIR SPECIALE** (IRE) 23
531 **LIS GOOLD** (IRE) G 15
383 **LISCANNA** (IRE) F 162

440 **LOUGH SWILLY LASS** 96
357 **LOUGHDERG ROCCO** (IRE) 25
523 **LOUGHERMORE** (IRE) 5
298 **LOUGHVILLE** 135
507 **LOUKARAK** (FR) 25
384 **LOULWA** (IRE) C 55
202 **LOUNAOS** (FR) M 19
317 **LOUP DE MAULDE** (FR) 12
67 **LOVE ACTUALLY** (IRE) 15
368 **LOVE AFFAIRS** 40
179 **LOVE AND BE LOVED** 10
501 **LOVE AND CHERISH** (IRE) F 67
301 **LOVE AND LAUGHTER** (IRE) C 29
484 **LOVE ANGEL** 21
194 **LOVE AT SEA** (IRE) 9
228 **LOVE BILLY BOY** (IRE) 161
247 **LOVE BITE** (IRE) 80
286 **LOVE DE VEGA** (IRE) 16
249 **LOVE DESTINY** 10
39 **LOVE DREAMS** (IRE) 5
189 **LOVE ENVOI** (IRE) 40
266 **LOVE FANTASY** 35
286 **LOVE IN THE DESERT** F 178
192 **LOVE IN THE PARK** G 65
387 **LOVE INTEREST** 32
92 **LOVE IS A ROSE** 37
355 **LOVE IS GOLDEN** (IRE) 77
521 **LOVE LIES** (IRE) 78
387 **LOVE MATCH** F 115
231 **LOVE MOCHA** 62
369 **LOVE MYSTERY** 81
286 **LOVE SAFARI** (IRE) 179
286 **LOVE WARRIOR** (IRE) 180
479 **LOVE YOU GRANDPA** (IRE) 11
347 **LOVE YOUR WORK** (IRE) 47
24 **LOVED BY YOU** 124
447 **LOVEE DOVEE** C 39
342 **LOVEISALLYOUNEED** (IRE) C 31
404 **LOVELIEST** 16
269 **LOVELY ACCLAMATION** (IRE) 7
119 **LOVELY LADY** 53
34 **LOVELY MOON** (IRE) 13
43 **LOVELY SURPRISE** (IRE) F 132
56 **LOVERS' LANE** (IRE) 26
408 **LOVES LOVING** 74
335 **LOVIN JUKEBOX** (GER) 76
206 **LOVING FEELING** 93
342 **LOWANNA** (IRE) F 32
305 **LOWICK** (USA) 30
31 **LOWTON** 27
286 **LOYAL TOUCH** (IRE) 94
408 **LUAS** (IRE) 75
116 **LUBEAT FORAS** (IRE) 12
14 **LUCANDER** (IRE) 22
247 **LUCCIA** 81
35 **LUCEITA** (IRE) F 94
146 **LUCIDITY** (IRE) 41
112 **LUCIE MANETTE** F 81
507 **LUCKELLO** 26
335 **LUCKIE MONEY** (IRE) 77
428 **LUCKIE SEVEN** (IRE) 25
24 **LUCKIN BREW** (IRE) 55
65 **LUCKOFTHEDRAW** (FR) 5
214 **LUCKY BEGGAR** (IRE) 5
414 **LUCKY BOUNCE** (IRE) 22
130 **LUCKY BREEZE** (IRE) C 17
296 **LUCKY CHARM** C 17
46 **LUCKY DRAW** 4
24 **LUCKY FIFTEEN** (FR) 56
285 **LUCKY GOLD** 65
404 **LUCKY JUDE** 29
368 **LUCKY LOT** F 61
212 **LUCKY LOVER BOY** (IRE) 50
496 **LUCKY LUCKY LUCKY** (IRE) 12
275 **LUCKY MAC** 15
469 **LUCKY MAN** (IRE) 9
284 **LUCKY MASCOT** (IRE) 13
312 **LUCKY ONE** (FR) 13
254 **LUCKY PIGEON** (IRE) G 45
247 **LUCKY PLACE** (FR) 82
161 **LUCKY ROBIN** (IRE) 14
540 **LUCKY ROSE** (IRE) 10
42 **LUCKY SAN JORE** 6
332 **LUCKY SO AND SO** (IRE) 14
1 **LUCKY SOLDIER** (IRE) 30
59 **LUCKY'S DREAM** 10
404 **LUCREZIA** C 30
284 **LUCY LIGHTFOOT** (IRE) 19
456 **LUCY LOCKETT** 69
409 **LUCY ROUGE** (IRE) G 12
251 **LUDDEN LASS** (IRE) 45
206 **LUDMILLA** 94
286 **LUDO'S LANDING** (IRE) 95
86 **LUDUAMF** (IRE) 3
286 **LUIRE** (IRE) F 181
125 **LUIS VAN ZANDT** (IRE) 18
43 **LUISA CALDERON** C 133
520 **LUISA CASATI** (IRE) 5
153 **LUKE** 27
343 **LUKE SHORT** 35
348 **LUKLA** 48
442 **LULLABY BAY** 13
228 **LULWORTH COVE** (IRE) 63
43 **LUMACHO** (IRE) 65
320 **LUMBERJACK** 13
231 **LUMI** (IRE) C 127
5 **LUMIERE** F 191
363 **LUMINARIES** (IRE) 71
455 **LUMINATA** (IRE) G 13
219 **LUMINATE** (IRE) C 163
489 **LUMP SUM** (FR) 26
386 **LUNA AOIFE** 12
320 **LUNA CATENA** 52
483 **LUNA DORA** 18
506 **LUNA EFFECT** (IRE) 96
276 **LUNA LIGHT** (IRE) 8
521 **LUNA MAGIC** 20
66 **LUNA ROSA** (IRE) F 132
279 **LUNACY** 64
94 **LUNALA** (FR) 22
456 **LUNAR BIRD** (IRE) 47
281 **LUNAR CHIEF** 8
298 **LUNAR CONTACT** (IRE) 62
352 **LUNAR DISCOVERY** 16
40 **LUNAR GLOW** 17
365 **LUNAR JET** 5
285 **LUNAR LANDSCAPE** 35
5 **LUNAR MARIA** C 192
525 **LUNAR OCEAN** (IRE) 19
387 **LUNAR PHASE** (IRE) F 116
343 **LUNAR POWER** (IRE) 36
298 **LUNAR SHADOW** 63
266 **LUNAR SHINE** (IRE) 36
385 **LUNAR SOVEREIGN** (IRE) 121
395 **LUNAR SPACE** (IRE) 17
56 **LUNARIO** (IRE) 55
285 **LUNARSCAPE** 36
360 **LUNATICK** 52
248 **LUNCHABLE BOB** 9
212 **LUNE DE LA MER** (IRE) 51
41 **LUNE DE RIO** (FR) 6
329 **LUPSET FLOSSY POP** (IRE) 10
369 **LUPUS REGEM** 82
35 **LURA** (USA) C 73
35 **LURA** (USA) F 95
38 **LURE DES PRES** (IRE) 2
228 **LUSAIL** (IRE) 15
235 **LUSCIFER** 6
286 **LUSH LIFE** (IRE) F 182
532 **LUSITANIEN** (FR) 31
385 **LUTINEBELLA** 122
306 **LUTTRELL LAD** (IRE) 29
299 **LUWDVIG** (FR) 19
383 **LUXEMBOURG** (IRE) 7
548 **LUXY LOU** (IRE) 16
189 **LYDFORD LAD** (IRE) 41
107 **LYDIA BECKER** F 81
200 **LYDIA VIOLET** (IRE) 35
317 **LYKKLERED** 22
179 **LYNDON B** (IRE) 11
286 **LYNIQUE** (IRE) C 183
70 **LYNNS BOY** 27
21 **LYNWOOD GOLD** (IRE) 7
413 **LYNWOOD LAD** 26
539 **LYNYRD DU LARGE** (FR) 44
228 **LYRAISA** 162
319 **LYRICAL GENIUS** (IRE) 26
42 **LYSANDA** (GER) F 66
219 **LYSANDER** 18
367 **M C MULDOON** (IRE) 106
501 **M'SELLE** (IRE) F 50
23 **MA BELLA PAOLA** (FR) C 44
189 **MA BELLE NOIRE** 42
107 **MA FAMILLE** (IRE) 43
343 **MAARIT** G 98
206 **MAASAI MARA** 95
302 **MABEL JANE** 6
142 **MABEL KINGSMILL** 7
255 **MABERRY** (IRE) M 7
165 **MABRE** (IRE) 9
502 **MABROKAH** G 13
15 **MABS CROSS** F 176
154 **MAC AILEY** 54
537 **MAC BE LUCKY** 42
226 **MAC SUIBHNE** (IRE) 51
47 **MAC TOTTIE** 24
116 **MAC'S LEGACY** (IRE) 13
231 **MAC'S XPRESS** (IRE) 16
85 **MACARI** 29
386 **MACAVITY** 13
24 **MACDUFF** 125
306 **MACFIN** (IRE) 30
15 **MACH TEN** 177
88 **MACHETE** (FR) 7
399 **MACHO MANIA** (IRE) 48
239 **MACHO PRIDE** (IRE) 19
173 **MACHO SUN** (IRE) 17
537 **MACK THE MAN** (IRE) 43
369 **MACKELDUFF** (FR) 83
335 **MACKENBERG** (GER) 78
8 **MACKIE DEE** (IRE) 3

454 **MACLAINE** 19
390 **MACMOLLY** 65
130 **MACON BELLE** 7
383 **MACQUARIE** (IRE) 8
392 **MACS DILEMMA** (IRE) 15
19 **MACS LEGEND** (IRE) 3
491 **MACTAVISH** 14
374 **MACVILLE** (IRE) F 10
455 **MAD ABOUT SALLY** (IRE) 14
40 **MAD ARTYMAISE** (IRE) 18
304 **MAD EXISTENCE** (IRE) C 1
161 **MAD JAZZ** G 59
254 **MAD MIKE** (IRE) 46
254 **MADAKET** 47
171 **MADAM ARKATI** 4
501 **MADAM FLORENCE** 51
247 **MADAM FONTAINE** (FR) F 83
286 **MADAM MACHO** 96
354 **MADAM MAY** 8
165 **MADAM MOJITO** (USA) F 41
286 **MADAM VALENTINE** C 97
286 **MADAME AMBASSADOR** 17
21 **MADAME BIJOUX** 8
207 **MADAME BLUEBELLE** 9
451 **MADAME FENELLA** 13
192 **MADAME MARMALADE** 23
399 **MADAME PACO** C 87
80 **MADAME ROUGE** F 108
286 **MADAME SANS GENE** 184
143 **MADDISONELLE** 17
26 **MADE BY HAND** (IRE) C 65
369 **MADE FOR YOU** 84
286 **MADE IN CHINA** (IRE) 185
484 **MADELINE** (IRE) C 64
507 **MADERA MIST** (IRE) 27
298 **MADIBA PASSION** (FR) 64
367 **MADMANSGAME** 107
5 **MADONNA DELL'ORTO** C 193
486 **MADRA MORJOHN** 4
80 **MADRINHO** (IRE) 55
521 **MAFIA POWER** 21
364 **MAGGIE BYRNE** (IRE) C 12
192 **MAGGIE PINK** F 51
174 **MAGGIE'S TERN** (IRE) 37
361 **MAGGIE'S WAY** 21
227 **MAGHEROARTY STAR** (IRE) 25
251 **MAGHLAAK** 9
399 **MAGIC AMERICA** (USA) F 88
311 **MAGIC DANCER** 17
15 **MAGIC FORCE** (IRE) 178
5 **MAGIC IMAGE** C 194
332 **MAGIC MARMALADE** (IRE) 15
355 **MAGIC MEMORIES** (IRE) 145
434 **MAGIC MIKE** (IRE) 12
211 **MAGIC MONEY** F 30
262 **MAGIC MUSIC** (IRE) F 20
379 **MAGIC SAINT** (FR) 108
390 **MAGIC SEVEN** (IRE) 66
513 **MAGIC WAVE** 36
300 **MAGICAL ARTHUR** (IRE) 36
473 **MAGICAL DAZE** F 8
84 **MAGICAL DRAGON** (IRE) 11
78 **MAGICAL EFFECT** (IRE) 16
12 **MAGICAL ESCAPE** (IRE) 42
423 **MAGICAL MAGGIE** 22
192 **MAGICAL MAX** 24
92 **MAGICAL MERLIN** (IRE) 38
353 **MAGICAL MILE** (IRE) 1
368 **MAGICAL MORNING** 21
442 **MAGICAL SPIRIT** (IRE) 14
206 **MAGICAL STORY** 96
228 **MAGICAL SUNSET** (IRE) 64
5 **MAGICAL TOUCH** F 195
442 **MAGICDOLLAR** 42
318 **MAGICINTHEMAKING** (USA) 5
410 **MAGIE DU MA** (FR) F 48
385 **MAGISTRA EQUITUM** (IRE) 123
379 **MAGISTRATO** (FR) 109
423 **MAGNA BELLA** 23
467 **MAGNA MORALIA** (IRE) 6
423 **MAGNA SAM** 24
219 **MAGNETIC CHARM** F 164
391 **MAGNIFICENCE** (FR) 2
363 **MAGNIFICENT BEN** (IRE) 72
226 **MAGNOLIA HAWKS** (IRE) 91
408 **MAGNUSSON** 46
34 **MAH MATE BOB** (IRE) 14
154 **MAHANAKHON** 55
469 **MAHARAJAS EXPRESS** 32
249 **MAHARASHTRA** 11
206 **MAHBOOB** (IRE) 97
243 **MAHBOOBAH** (IRE) 25
457 **MAHLER MOON** (IRE) 115
385 **MAHON POINT** 124
376 **MAHONS GLORY** (IRE) 37
123 **MAI ALWARD** 15
195 **MAID FOR HARRY** 8
43 **MAID IN KENTUCKY** (USA) 66
399 **MAID IN LONDON** 49
101 **MAID O'MALLEY** 18
531 **MAID OF HOUXTY** 17
298 **MAID ON THE MOON** 65
89 **MAID UP** C 50
312 **MAILLOT BLANC** 14
410 **MAIN FACT** (USA) 49
415 **MAIRE'S DREAM** (IRE) 4
366 **MAIRIS ICON** 21
5 **MAIRWEN** F 196
102 **MAISIE TOO** 15
216 **MAISIEBELLA** 6
80 **MAISON BEAU** 56
302 **MAISON DE BELLA** 19
512 **MAITREE EXPRESS** 4
348 **MAJESKI MAN** (IRE) 26
85 **MAJESTIC** (IRE) 9
261 **MAJESTIC CHARM** 13
286 **MAJESTIC JAMEELA** 98
98 **MAJESTIC NEWLAW** 17
5 **MAJESTIC PRIDE** 83
506 **MAJESTIC SILVER** (IRE) C 166
149 **MAJESTIC TREASURE** (IRE) M 8
484 **MAJESTIC WARRIOR** (IRE) 22
496 **MAJIL** (IRE) 36
269 **MAJOR ASSAULT** 8
298 **MAJOR DUNDEE** (IRE) 66
306 **MAJOR FORTUNE** (IRE) 31
502 **MAJOR GATSBY** (IRE) 6
228 **MAJOR MAJOR** (IRE) 65
35 **MAJOR PARTNERSHIP** (IRE) 30
347 **MAJOR SNUGFIT** 48
78 **MAKALU** (IRE) 17
72 **MAKANAH** 17
91 **MAKARIOS** 7
515 **MAKAROVA** 9
348 **MAKE A PROPHET** (IRE) 27
106 **MAKE CLEAR** 21
15 **MAKE FAST** F 179
410 **MAKE ME A BELIEVER** (IRE) 50
15 **MAKE MUSIC** F 180
72 **MAKEEN** 18
285 **MAKES SENSE** (IRE) 66
454 **MAKETY** 20
379 **MAKIN'YOURMINDUP** 110
66 **MAKING DREAMS** (IRE) 133
56 **MAKING EYES** (IRE) G 56
212 **MAKING HEADWAY** (IRE) 52
484 **MAKING MEMORIES** (IRE) C 65
361 **MAKING MUSIC** (IRE) 5
343 **MAKINGACHAMP** (IRE) 37
164 **MAKINMEDOIT** (IRE) 12
360 **MAKSUD** 15
62 **MAKTER** 2
537 **MAL D'AMOUR** (IRE) G 44
152 **MALAGO ROSE** (IRE) 7
439 **MALAITA** 12
538 **MALAKAHNA** (FR) 44
238 **MALANGEN** (IRE) 7
384 **MALAYAN MIST** (IRE) F 56
526 **MALCOLM** 14
506 **MALEFICENT QUEEN** F 167
262 **MALHAM TARN COVE** 7
363 **MALIBOO** (IRE) 73
343 **MALIBU BEACH** C 99
154 **MALIBU MOONLIGHT** 125
217 **MALIBU RISING** 21
34 **MALIN DAZE** (IRE) 15
299 **MALINA JAMILA** 20
227 **MALINA OCARINA** 26
363 **MALINAS ISLAND** 74
166 **MALINDI BAY** (FR) F 17
402 **MALINELLO** 53
511 **MALINHEADSEAROVERS** (IRE) 13
219 **MALJOOM** (IRE) 19
408 **MALKA** (IRE) 47
335 **MALPAS** (IRE) 79
43 **MALRESCIA** (IRE) 67
381 **MALYSTIC** 3
305 **MAMA QUILLA** (USA) F 46
228 **MAMA ROCCO** C 163
228 **MAMAN JOON** (IRE) 66
378 **MAMBHA** (IRE) 25
107 **MAMBO BEAT** (IRE) 9
266 **MAMBO SUNSET** (IRE) 14
14 **MAMILLIUS** 23
228 **MAMMAS GIRL** 67
390 **MAMMIES BOY** (IRE) 67
385 **MAMOON STAR** (IRE) 125
488 **MAMORA BAY** 53
410 **MAN AGAIN** (FR) 51
410 **MAN AT WORK** (IRE) 52
165 **MAN MADE OF SMOKE** 28
164 **MAN OF A'AN** (IRE) 25
92 **MAN OF EDEN** 39
286 **MAN OF MONACO** (IRE) 99
402 **MAN OF MY DREAMS** (IRE) 54
312 **MAN OF PLENTY** 15
5 **MAN OF PROMISE** (USA) 21
556 **MAN OF RIDDLES** (USA) 11
431 **MAN OF THE NORTH** 4
363 **MAN OF THE SEA** (IRE) 75
91 **MAN ON A MISSION** 8

506 **MANAAFITH** (USA) 24
228 **MANAAHIL** C 164
35 **MANABOO** (USA) C 96
441 **MANACCAN** 9
247 **MANALA** (FR) 84
146 **MANANA CHICA** (IRE) F 66
258 **MANCE RAYDER** (IRE) 7
359 **MANCINI** 8
472 **MANDO ECLIPSE** 17
157 **MANDOCELLO** (FR) 24
251 **MANDORIA** (GER) C 99
144 **MANFROMINVERLOCHY** (IRE) 13
51 **MANGROVE RIVER** (IRE) 10
231 **MANHATTAN LADY** (IRE) 17
154 **MANIGORDO** (USA) 56
30 **MANILA MIST** 23
154 **MANILA SCOUSE** 57
154 **MANILA STYLE** 126
504 **MANIMOLE** 42
319 **MANINSANE** (IRE) 27
390 **MANINTHESHADOWS** (IRE) 68
521 **MANITOU** (IRE) 79
423 **MANKHOOL** (IRE) 25
112 **MANNAAL** (IRE) F 82
66 **MANNERISM** (IRE) 134
190 **MANOFTHEMOMENT** (IRE) 4
21 **MANOR PARK** 9
308 **MANORBANK** (IRE) 39
113 **MANORWALK** (IRE) F 11
146 **MANOS ARRIBA** (IRE) 67
385 **MANOTHEPEOPLE** (IRE) 126
69 **MANTOOG** 16
279 **MANU ET CORDE** (IRE) 30
228 **MANUELITO** 68
163 **MANWELL** (IRE) 8
98 **MANY A STAR** (IRE) 8
286 **MANY COLOURS** C 186
506 **MANY HEARTS** (USA) C 168
301 **MANY RIVERS** (IRE) 17
80 **MANY WORDS** (IRE) 57
413 **MANYANA** 5
484 **MANYATTA** (IRE) F 66
521 **MAOINEACH** (USA) C 80
146 **MAP OF HEAVEN** F 68
72 **MAPLE JACK** 19
176 **MAPOGO** 31
347 **MAPPA** (FR) F 104
107 **MAPPATASSIE** (IRE) 10
368 **MAQAM** (IRE) C 62
219 **MAQSAD** (FR) C 165
343 **MAQUEDA** F 100
66 **MARA GREY** (IRE) C 135
405 **MARAAKIZ** (IRE) 9
457 **MARADA** 116
411 **MARAJMAN** (FR) 4
506 **MARAKESH** 97
219 **MARAMA** 166
270 **MARASIL** (IRE) C 56
324 **MARAYEL** (IRE) 6
175 **MARBAAN** 33
385 **MARBLE SANDS** (FR) 127
154 **MARBUZET** 58
138 **MARCELLO SI** 25
494 **MARCH WIND** (IRE) 30
184 **MARCHETTI** (IRE) 4
35 **MARCHING ARMY** 31
479 **MARCHING BAND** 39
262 **MARCIE** (IRE) 8
263 **MARCO ISLAND** (IRE) 46
517 **MARCUS** 18
456 **MARDIE GRAS** C 70
272 **MARDOOF** (IRE) 14
390 **MARDY MONO** (IRE) 69
206 **MAREMMA** 98
15 **MARENKO** C 181
502 **MARETTIMO** (IRE) 7
94 **MARFISA** (IRE) 23
447 **MARGARET BEAUFORT** 16
294 **MARGARET'S FUCHSIA** 11
507 **MARGARET'S LEGACY** (FR) 28
393 **MARGOT ROBBIE** 4
500 **MARGUB** 6
286 **MARHABA MILLION** (IRE) 187
442 **MARHABA THE CHAMP** 15
15 **MARIA** (GER) F 182
5 **MARIA DANILOVA** (IRE) F 197
176 **MARIA LETIZIA** C 54
220 **MARIA MAGDALENA** (IRE) 29
176 **MARIAMNE** 55
31 **MARIANGLAS** (IRE) 50
414 **MARIAS LAD** (FR) 23
299 **MARIDADI** 21
368 **MARIDIYNA** (IRE) F 63
379 **MARIE DES ANGES** (FR) F 111
221 **MARIE JOSEPHE** C 41
500 **MARIE LAVEAU** 16
66 **MARIE OF LYON** C 136
231 **MARIE PHILIPPE** (IRE) 18
174 **MARIE'S DIAMOND** (IRE) 20
174 **MARIE'S JEWEL** (IRE) 38
247 **MARIE'S ROCK** (IRE) 85
378 **MARIE'S SECRET** 26
395 **MARIGOLD** (FR) F 54
538 **MARINAKIS** (IRE) 86
471 **MARINARA** (IRE) 21
234 **MARINE** (IRE) 46
456 **MARINE BLEUE** (IRE) F 71
219 **MARINE DRIVE** (IRE) 80
202 **MARINE JAG** (FR) 20
72 **MARINE LAKE** 51
489 **MARIO DE PAIL** (FR) 27
30 **MARION OF ELMSTONE** 24
488 **MARION'S BOY** (IRE) 20
17 **MARIONETTE** (IRE) 11
392 **MARISITTA** 27
360 **MARISOL** (IRE) F 76
355 **MARK OF GOLD** 78
290 **MARK'S CHOICE** (IRE) 10
287 **MARKET FORCES** F 14
219 **MARKET VALUE** (IRE) 81
294 **MARKMILL** 12
355 **MARKS BEAR** (IRE) 79
206 **MARKSMAN QUEEN** 99
50 **MARLAY PARK** 9
497 **MARLEY HEAD** (IRE) 46
90 **MARLEYS MIRACLE** 12
342 **MARLYN** (IRE) F 33
360 **MARMALADE LADY** 77
439 **MARMALADE TIME** 13
247 **MARMALAID** 86
89 **MARMARA SEA** 28
43 **MARMARA STAR** 68
135 **MARNIE JAMES** 39
67 **MAROOCHI** 16
67 **MAROONED** 17
428 **MAROWN** (IRE) 26
5 **MARRAKUSHI** 84
14 **MARSH BENHAM** (IRE) 24
472 **MARSH LOCK** 18
266 **MARSH PRIDE** F 37
157 **MARSH WREN** 25
328 **MARSHAL DAN** (IRE) 10
239 **MARSHALLED** (IRE) 20
455 **MARSHELLA** (IRE) 15
66 **MARSHMAN** 68
26 **MART** 66
483 **MARTA DES MOTTES** (FR) 19
300 **MARTALINDY** 37
385 **MARTALITE** (FR) 128
439 **MARTALMIX'JAC** (FR) 14
543 **MARTATOR** (FR) 61
509 **MARTELLO SKY** 20
457 **MARTHA BRAE** 117
142 **MARTHA BURELL** 8
74 **MARTHA YEATS** (IRE) 21
71 **MARTIN SPIRIT** (IRE) 6
491 **MARTIN'S BRIG** (IRE) 15
399 **MARTINA FRANCA** C 89
366 **MARTINEAU** (IRE) 22
90 **MARTINENGO** (IRE) 3
70 **MARTINEO** 28
410 **MARTINHAL** (IRE) 53
91 **MARTINI LODGE** 16
266 **MARTINI NIGHTS** 15
383 **MARTINSTOWN** (IRE) 9
179 **MARTY BYRDE** 12
374 **MARTY MCFLY** (IRE) 11
464 **MARTY TIME** (FR) 35
383 **MARVELLOUS** (IRE) C 163
379 **MARVELLOUS MICK** 112
153 **MARWARI** (IRE) 28
447 **MARY BAGOT** (IRE) 40
10 **MARY OF MODENA** 21
5 **MARY SOMERVILLE** F 198
387 **MARY STEWART** (IRE) F 117
455 **MARYAH ISLAND** 16
538 **MARYANN** (IRE) F 45
384 **MARYINSKY** (IRE) F 57
70 **MARYSIENKA** F 62
15 **MARZOCCO** (IRE) 87
298 **MASACCIO** (IRE) 67
217 **MASAR WAY** 22
112 **MASARAH** (IRE) C 83
456 **MASCAPONE** 48
15 **MASEKELA** (IRE) 20
315 **MASELA** (IRE) F 30
471 **MASHAAER** (IRE) 10
324 **MASHAAN** 7
171 **MASHAM MOOR** 5
33 **MASKED ARTIST** 5
335 **MASKED CRUSADER** (FR) 80
439 **MASKED DANCE** (FR) 15
306 **MASKED MATGIL** (FR) 32
552 **MASKED QUEEN** 28
197 **MASKIA** (FR) 4
172 **MASO BASTIE** 31
166 **MASQOOL** (IRE) 10
315 **MASQUE OF ANARCHY** (IRE) 4
386 **MASS CONSUMPTION** (IRE) 29
494 **MASSINI MAN** 31
489 **MASTER AUSTRALIA** (IRE) 28

279 **MERRICOURT** (IRE) 32
28 **MERRIJIG** 9
385 **MERRY BERRY** 130
154 **MERRY DIVA** C 180
93 **MERRY DREAMER** (IRE) 12
442 **MERRY JAUNT** (USA) C 78
515 **MERRY MINISTER** (IRE) 39
335 **MERRY POPPINS** (GER) 83
364 **MERRY SECRET** (IRE) 3
501 **MERSEA** (FR) 52
390 **MERSEY STREET** (IRE) 72
442 **MERSEYSIDE** (IRE) 16
390 **MERVEILLO** 73
342 **MESADAH** (IRE) F 34
457 **MESSAGE PERSONNEL** (FR) 119
298 **MESSIRE DES OBEAUX** (FR) 71
70 **MET OFFICE** (IRE) 31
320 **METABOLT** 14
26 **METAHORSE** 37
85 **METAL MERCHANT** (IRE) 30
85 **METALLO** (IRE) 61
98 **METARACE** (IRE) 18
346 **METAVERSE** (IRE) 25
88 **METEOR SHOWER** 44
174 **METHINKS** (IRE) 21
423 **METHOD MADNESS** (IRE) 26
440 **METHODTOTHEMADNESS** (IRE) 50
409 **METHODTOTHEMAGIC** (IRE) 14
298 **METHUSALAR** (IRE) 72
189 **METIER** (IRE) 43
347 **MEWS HOUSE** 49
24 **MEXICALI ROSE** 57
369 **MEXICAN BOY** (IRE) 85
157 **MEXICO** (GER) 26
119 **MI CAPRICHO** (IRE) 27
106 **MIA TIA** F 32
386 **MIAH GRACE** 14
32 **MIAMI PRESENT** (IRE) 7
6 **MICHAELA'S BOY** (IRE) 92
285 **MICHAELS CHOICE** 10
35 **MICHITA** (USA) C 75
295 **MICK MAESTRO** (FR) 15
286 **MICKEY MONGOOSE** 100
251 **MICKLEBERRY** (IRE) C 101
488 **MICKS DREAM** 22
300 **MICKS JET** (IRE) 38
154 **MICKY MICHAELIS** 61
363 **MICKYH** (IRE) 77
367 **MICRO MANAGE** (IRE) 109
410 **MICRONORMOUS** (IRE) 54
348 **MID WINSTER** 28
286 **MIDDLE CLUB** F 189
206 **MIDDLE EARTH** 102
286 **MIDDLE PERSIA** F 190
165 **MIDGETONAMISSION** (IRE) 10
70 **MIDNIGHT** (IRE) C 63
263 **MIDNIGHT CALLISTO** 49
466 **MIDNIGHT CENTURION** 31
207 **MIDNIGHT FIDDLER** 10
331 **MIDNIGHT GINGER** 7
298 **MIDNIGHT GLANCE** 73
70 **MIDNIGHT GLOW** (IRE) 32
363 **MIDNIGHT GOLD** (IRE) 78
286 **MIDNIGHT LION** 101
471 **MIDNIGHT LUCK** 12
91 **MIDNIGHT M** C 19
228 **MIDNIGHT MARTINI** F 165
509 **MIDNIGHT MARY** 21
254 **MIDNIGHT MIDGE** 49
212 **MIDNIGHT MOSS** 54
91 **MIDNIGHT OASIS** F 20
151 **MIDNIGHT OWLE** 10
464 **MIDNIGHT PHANTOM** (FR) 36
331 **MIDNIGHT POPSTAR** 8
457 **MIDNIGHT RIVER** 120
363 **MIDNIGHT SHIMMER** 79
101 **MIDNIGHT SHUFFLE** 20
251 **MIDNIGHTATTHEOASIS** 46
89 **MIDNIGHTDANDY** (IRE) 30
220 **MIDNIGHTINBRESIL** 30
83 **MIDNIGHTREFLECTION** 15
150 **MIDRARR** (IRE) 4
206 **MIDSUMMER DANCE** (USA) 103
196 **MIDSUMMER LASS** 9
488 **MIDSUMMER MUSIC** (IRE) 44
479 **MIGDAM** (FR) 12
343 **MIGHT AND MERCY** 38
125 **MIGHT DO EMERY** 19
189 **MIGHT I** (IRE) 44
22 **MIGHTASWELLSMILE** 3
83 **MIGHTY DUCHESS** (IRE) 16
521 **MIGHTY GURKHA** (IRE) 23
317 **MIGHTY MISSISSIPPI** 13
231 **MIGHTY MO MISSOURI** (IRE) 21
540 **MIGHTY MOTH** (IRE) 12
506 **MIGHTY NEBULA** (IRE) 101
18 **MIGHTY POWER** (IRE) 21
484 **MIGHTY RIVER** (IRE) 23
440 **MIGHTY THUNDER** 51
206 **MIGHTY ULYSSES** 19
346 **MIGRATION** (IRE) 9
528 **MIKE MCCANN** (IRE) 12
308 **MIKHAILA** (IRE) 41
12 **MIKHAILOVICH** (IRE) 43
451 **MIKKA** 32
292 **MILADYGRACE** 27
457 **MILAGROSA** (FR) 121
383 **MILAM** (USA) C 165
379 **MILAN BRIDGE** (IRE) 116
107 **MILANA** (FR) C 83
363 **MILANESE ROSE** (IRE) 80
267 **MILANFORD** (IRE) 12
335 **MILANS EDGE** (IRE) 84
77 **MILANTEEA** (IRE) F 3
78 **MILBANKE** 18
484 **MILD ILLUSION** (IRE) C 67
24 **MILDYJAMA** (IRE) 58
26 **MILE END** 38
299 **MILE FROM THE MOON** (IRE) F 22
238 **MILEVA ROLLER** 8
211 **MILITAIRE** 31
331 **MILITARIAN** 9
35 **MILITARY MARCH** 32
247 **MILITARY MISTRESS** (IRE) 88
5 **MILITARY ORDER** (IRE) 86
286 **MILITARY TWO STEP** (FR) 18
348 **MILITIA** 29
415 **MILITRY DECORATION** (IRE) 5
363 **MILKWOOD** (IRE) 81
61 **MILKY TEAL** 12
247 **MILL GREEN** 89
526 **MILL POINT** F 44
89 **MILL STREAM** (IRE) 31
207 **MILLARVILLE** (IRE) 11
466 **MILLDAM** (FR) 32
549 **MILLDEAN FELIX** (IRE) 4
396 **MILLDEAN PANTHER** 3
88 **MILLE DREAMS** 45
347 **MILLE RUBIS** (FR) F 118
219 **MILLEBOSC** (FR) 20
355 **MILLER SPIRIT** (IRE) 146
220 **MILLERS BANK** 31
428 **MILLIE OF MAYO** 28
445 **MILLIE THE MINX** (IRE) 15
433 **MILLIE'S FLYING** 6
30 **MILLIES MITE** (IRE) 14
408 **MILLION THANKS** (IRE) 17
239 **MILLIONAIRE WALTZ** 21
354 **MILLIONS MEMORIES** 9
226 **MILLTOWN LILY** (IRE) 53
395 **MILLTOWN STAR** 18
243 **MILLUNA** 27
502 **MILLY MOLLY MANDY** 8
85 **MILTEYE** 31
71 **MILTON** 7
240 **MILTON BOY** (FR) 25
494 **MILVALE** (IRE) 32
96 **MILVUS** (IRE) 14
383 **MILWAUKEE** (USA) 65
501 **MILWAUKEE BLIZZARD** (IRE) 20
15 **MIMASUSA** (IRE) 183
466 **MIMI ZURI** 33
206 **MIMIKYU** 20
209 **MIMOSA PARK** (IRE) 17
175 **MIMRAM** F 53
26 **MIN BANAT ALREEH** (IRE) F 68
153 **MIN TILL** 30
61 **MINCHINHAMPTON** 18
316 **MIND HUNTER** 9
489 **MIND SUNDAY** (FR) 29
383 **MINDING** (IRE) C 166
26 **MINDSET** 39
228 **MINDTHEGAP** (IRE) 70
343 **MINDY** G 101
243 **MINE THAT SHIP** (IRE) 28
172 **MINEKO** (FR) 33
116 **MINELLA BOBO** (IRE) 14
308 **MINELLA BUSTER** (IRE) 42
538 **MINELLA CHOICE** (IRE) 46
367 **MINELLA COCOONER** (IRE) 110
369 **MINELLA DOUBLE** (IRE) 86
335 **MINELLA DRAMA** (IRE) 85
167 **MINELLA MAGICAL** (IRE) 9
335 **MINELLA PLUS** (IRE) 86
454 **MINELLA ROYALE** 21
335 **MINELLA TRUMP** (IRE) 87
147 **MINELLA VOUCHER** 27
279 **MINELLA YOUNGY** (IRE) 33
335 **MINELLADESTINATION** (IRE) 88
161 **MINERS GAMBLE** (IRE) 60
6 **MINESBIGGERTHANURS** 55
94 **MING ZHI COSMOS** F 47
209 **MINGLE** (IRE) 18
161 **MINHAAJ** (IRE) 15
363 **MINI MILDRED** 82
326 **MINI RIVO** (IRE) 13
272 **MINI YEATS** (IRE) 15
368 **MINIONETTE** (IRE) F 64
43 **MINISTER FOR MAGIC** (IRE) 15
251 **MINKA** (IRE) 47
153 **MINNEAPOLIS SOUND** (IRE) 63

314 **MINNEIGH MOZZE** (FR) 9
228 **MINNETONKA** (IRE) 71
122 **MINNIE ESCAPE** 12
289 **MINOLI** 30
31 **MINT EDITION** 29
440 **MINT GOLD** (IRE) 52
286 **MINT JULEP** (FR) C 191
166 **MINTANA** 18
279 **MINTNTHAT** 34
94 **MINUIT A PARIS** 24
112 **MINWAH** (IRE) F 87
506 **MIQDAAD** (IRE) 102
356 **MIRABELLO BAY** (IRE) 13
456 **MIRAGE** (IRE) C 72
374 **MIRRIE DANCERS** (IRE) 12
95 **MIRRORBLACK** (IRE) C 36
300 **MISAURA** (IRE) 69
5 **MISCHIEF MAGIC** (IRE) 87
206 **MISCHIEVOUS MADAME** (USA) 104
243 **MISHRAQ** (IRE) 29
228 **MISKIN DIAMOND** (IRE) C 166
515 **MISS ACADEME** (IRE) C 85
515 **MISS ALPILLES** 86
49 **MISS ANACO** 8
292 **MISS ANTIPOVA** 28
319 **MISS APPLEJACK** 28
494 **MISS ARABELLA** 33
85 **MISS ATTITUDE** 32
195 **MISS BELLA BRAND** 3
451 **MISS BELLADONNA** 14
535 **MISS BILLIE** 6
467 **MISS BLENNERHASSET** (IRE) 8
500 **MISS BLUEBELLE** (IRE) 8
448 **MISS BLUEYES** (IRE) G 21
153 **MISS BRAZEN** 64
503 **MISS BRITAIN** (IRE) 6
368 **MISS CANTIK** (FR) 42
112 **MISS CARBONIA** (IRE) C 88
59 **MISS CHANTELLE** 11
497 **MISS CHAWNER** 47
300 **MISS CILLA** (IRE) G 70
83 **MISS CONNAISSEUR** 17
366 **MISS CURIOSITY** (IRE) 23
416 **MISS CYNTHIA** 21
488 **MISS DOLLY ROCKER** 45
406 **MISS DOWN UNDER** (IRE) 4
343 **MISS DUTEE** C 102
286 **MISS DYNAMIC** 102
82 **MISS ELSA** 8
360 **MISS FAIRFAX** (IRE) 16
366 **MISS FEDORA** (IRE) 24
172 **MISS FRANGIPANE** (IRE) C 56
492 **MISS FURNY FACTOR** (IRE) 6
283 **MISS G GEE** 18
164 **MISS GALIWAY** (FR) 46
280 **MISS GALLAGHER** 17
202 **MISS GET THE VEUVE** 21
416 **MISS GITANA** (IRE) 47
189 **MISS GOLDFIRE** (IRE) 45
26 **MISS HARMONY** 10
154 **MISS HAVRE** 127
228 **MISS IDUNN** (IRE) 167
15 **MISS INFORMATION** (IRE) 184
440 **MISS JOEKING** (IRE) F 97
66 **MISS JUNGLE CAT** 69
176 **MISS KATIE MAE** (IRE) C 56
386 **MISS LAMB** 15
456 **MISS LATIN** (IRE) F 73
329 **MISS LESLEY** C 16
251 **MISS LIGHTFANDANGO** 48
172 **MISS MAI TAI** 34
148 **MISS MAISIEPAIGE** 17
327 **MISS MALOU** 5
140 **MISS MARETTE** 10
399 **MISS MARGARITA** C 90
106 **MISS MARIANNE** 22
176 **MISS MARJURIE** (IRE) C 57
363 **MISS MARY MAC** (IRE) F 83
554 **MISS MASSEY** (IRE) 6
157 **MISS MCGUGEN** (IRE) 27
382 **MISS MEDIATOR** (USA) C 6
193 **MISS METICULOUS** C 19
428 **MISS MILANO** (IRE) 29
101 **MISS MISTRAL** (IRE) 21
262 **MISS MOCKTAIL** (IRE) 9
349 **MISS MOONSHINE** 24
5 **MISS NOURIYA** C 200
390 **MISS PARKINGTON** (IRE) G 74
314 **MISS PEARL** (IRE) 10
79 **MISS PHOENIX** 34
24 **MISS PRESIDENT** F 128
510 **MISS RAINBOW** (IRE) 14
510 **MISS RAINDROP** 12
143 **MISS REBECCA** 18
84 **MISS REQUINTO** (IRE) 21
469 **MISS SARAJEVO** 33
153 **MISS SHERIDAN** (IRE) F 87
10 **MISS SHIRLEY** (IRE) 22
107 **MISS SHOW OFF** 84
395 **MISS SLIGO** (IRE) 19
143 **MISS SNUGGLES** (IRE) 8
74 **MISS SOLITAIRE** (IRE) 24
321 **MISS SOPHIEROSE** (IRE) F 47
107 **MISS STORMY NIGHT** 85
432 **MISS TIKI** 8
472 **MISS UNDERSTOOD** C 36
533 **MISS WILLOWS** 6
520 **MISS WORK OF ART** C 29
231 **MISS YVONNE** (IRE) 63
300 **MISSCARLETT** (IRE) 39
457 **MISSED TEE** (IRE) 122
43 **MISSED THE CUT** (USA) 16
202 **MISSFIT** (IRE) 22
270 **MISSING YOU** 31
112 **MISSION IMPASSIBLE** (IRE) C 89
231 **MISSISSIPPILANDING** (IRE) F 129
277 **MISSMIMI** 11
442 **MISSTERIOUS** 79
383 **MISSVINSKI** (USA) F 167
513 **MISSY AVA** (IRE) 37
259 **MISSYLADIE** (FR) 3
85 **MISTAKEN LOVE** (USA) C 62
340 **MISTAMEL** (IRE) 6
48 **MISTER ALLEGRO** 2
483 **MISTER BARCLAY** 20
226 **MISTER BELLS** (IRE) 54
328 **MISTER BLUEBIRD** 11
153 **MISTER CAMACHO** (IRE) 31
247 **MISTER COFFEY** (FR) 90
72 **MISTER FALSETTO** 20
247 **MISTER FISHER** (IRE) 91
136 **MISTER FREDDIE** 21
16 **MISTER MALARKY** 22
347 **MISTER MOODLES** 50
248 **MISTER MOSE** (IRE) 11
438 **MISTER MURCHAN** (IRE) 17
247 **MISTER PARK** (IRE) 92
96 **MISTER SKETCH** 15
277 **MISTER SMARTY** 7
154 **MISTER SOX** 128
363 **MISTER SWEETS** (IRE) 84
355 **MISTER TICKLE** (IRE) 80
205 **MISTER UPTON** 34
402 **MISTER WATSON** 56
335 **MISTER WHITAKER** (IRE) 89
309 **MISTER WHO** (IRE) 10
542 **MISTER X** (IRE) 34
414 **MISTERTOMMYSHELBY** (IRE) 24
299 **MISTING** 23
385 **MISTRAL BLUE** 131
254 **MISTRAL LADY** 50
298 **MISTRAL MILLY** (IRE) 74
509 **MISTRAL NELL** 22
509 **MISTRAL REINE** G 23
509 **MISTRAL REINE** F 41
360 **MISTRAL STAR** 53
219 **MISTRESS LIGHT** 83
24 **MISTRESSOFILLUSION** (IRE) 59
5 **MISTRUSTING** (IRE) F 201
119 **MISTY AYR** (IRE) 28
154 **MISTY BLUES** (IRE) 129
112 **MISTY DANCER** 12
383 **MISTY FOR ME** (IRE) F 168
425 **MISTY MAI** (IRE) 5
381 **MISTY MANI** 4
286 **MISTY NIGHT** (IRE) C 192
470 **MISU MAC** C 9
470 **MISU MAC** C 14
506 **MITBAAHY** (IRE) 25
234 **MITIGATION** 48
361 **MITROSONFIRE** 7
18 **MIVVI** 22
440 **MIX DE GRIS** (FR) 101
417 **MIX MASTER** 6
423 **MIX OF CLOVER** 27
458 **MIXEDWAVE** (IRE) 15
15 **MLLE CHANEL** 90
85 **MMA RAMOTSWE** (IRE) 33
231 **MO GHILLE MAR** (IRE) 130
47 **MO TOTTIE** 25
35 **MO'ASSESS** (IRE) 33
192 **MOAI** (FR) 26
494 **MOARINS MOARNIN** (IRE) 34
6 **MOBASHR** (USA) 56
387 **MOCHACHINO** (IRE) C 118
228 **MOCHI** (IRE) 72
506 **MODAARA** 26
5 **MODERN DANCER** 88
94 **MODERN ERA** (IRE) 48
5 **MODERN GAMES** (IRE) 23
5 **MODERN IDEALS** F 202
192 **MODERN LOVE** (IRE) G 52
537 **MODERN MONARCH** (IRE) 45
5 **MODERN NEWS** 24
342 **MODESTY** (IRE) 11
399 **MODIFY** C 91
23 **MODULAR MAGIC** 15
284 **MOEL ARTHUR** (USA) 14
450 **MOFASA** 25
10 **MOFRIDGE** 23
361 **MOGOK VALLEY** (IRE) 22

552 **MOGWAI** 8
6 **MOHAREB** 57
107 **MOHI** 11
521 **MOJEYRR** (IRE) 81
251 **MOJITO BOY** 49
296 **MOJITO MAGIC** 6
351 **MOJITO ROYALE** (FR) 3
228 **MOJO STAR** (IRE) 16
320 **MOJOMAKER** (IRE) 15
539 **MOKA DE VASSY** (FR) 25
538 **MOKAATIL** 47
501 **MOKAMAN** 21
303 **MOKTASAAB** 8
219 **MOLAQAB** 84
402 **MOLE COURT** (IRE) 57
332 **MOLE TRAP** 16
499 **MOLINARI** (IRE) 11
497 **MOLINEAUX** (IRE) 48
114 **MOLIWOOD** 3
363 **MOLLIANA** 85
263 **MOLLIE BROWN** 50
483 **MOLLY HASTINGS** 21
192 **MOLLY MISCHIEF** 53
457 **MOLLY OLLYS WISHES** 123
450 **MOLLY SANDERSON** (IRE) 26
276 **MOLLY VALENTINE** (IRE) 19
12 **MOLLY'S A DIVA** G 44
129 **MOLLY'S ANGEL** 2
209 **MOLLYS GLORY** (IRE) 8
513 **MOLLYSLITTLEANGEL** 38
219 **MOLTEN SEA** 168
320 **MOLTISANTI** (IRE) 34
321 **MOMAER** (IRE) 27
254 **MOMBASA** (FR) 51
384 **MOMENT OF CLARITY** (IRE) 15
231 **MOMENT OF TIME** C 131
457 **MON KAPLAIS** (FR) 124
414 **MON RAY** (IRE) 25
78 **MONAADHIL** (IRE) 19
226 **MONAGHAN BOY** (IRE) 55
94 **MONAPIA** (FR) 25
347 **MONARCH BUTTERFLY** 106
116 **MONBARI** (FR) 15
390 **MONBEG GENIUS** (IRE) 75
57 **MONDAMMEJ** 15
1 **MONEGA PASS** 54
4 **MONEY FOR JAM** (IRE) 15
136 **MONFASS** (IRE) 22
363 **MONGOL EMPEROR** (IRE) 86
405 **MONHAMMER** 10
189 **MONJULES** (FR) 46
367 **MONKFISH** (IRE) 111
399 **MONKMOOR PIP** 51
379 **MONMIRAL** (FR) 117
440 **MONOCHROMIX** (FR) 53
342 **MONOGAMY** F 35
92 **MONOGLOW** (IRE) 41
515 **MONOPOLISE** 40
279 **MONROE GOLD** 35
521 **MONSIEUR FANTAISIE** (IRE) 24
316 **MONSIEUR LAMBRAYS** 10
539 **MONSIEUR LECOQ** (FR) 26
386 **MONSIEUR MELEE** 38
56 **MONSIEUR PATAT** 27
457 **MONT DOREE** (FR) G 125
542 **MONT VALLON** 35
46 **MONTAQEM** (FR) 5
442 **MONTE FORTE** 43
212 **MONTE IGUELDO** (FR) 55
112 **MONTE LINAS** (IRE) 39
247 **MONTECAM** (IRE) 93
69 **MONTEJA** F 38
154 **MONTELUSA** 130
161 **MONTEPLEX** 16
302 **MONTERIA** (IRE) 7
286 **MONTEVIDEO** (IRE) 103
344 **MONTICELLO** (IRE) 5
456 **MONTJEU'S LADY** F 74
390 **MONTMARTIN** (FR) 76
513 **MONTMARTRE ABBEY** (FR) 39
306 **MONTREGARD** (FR) 33
107 **MONTY BAY** 44
402 **MONTY BODKIN** (IRE) 58
66 **MONTY MAN** (IRE) 70
386 **MONTY NEVETT** (IRE) 16
275 **MONTY'S AWARD** (IRE) 16
167 **MONTY'S MISSION** (IRE) 10
132 **MONTYS MEDOC** (IRE) 13
254 **MONVIEL** (IRE) 52
265 **MONYMUSK LAD** (IRE) 9
410 **MOODOFTHEMOMENT** (IRE) 55
347 **MOODY QUEEN** (IRE) G 51
172 **MOOGIE** 35
485 **MOOKHLESA** F 10
164 **MOON ANGEL** 47
385 **MOON CHIME** 132
387 **MOON CLUB** (IRE) F 119
384 **MOON DAISY** (IRE) 2
41 **MOON DASH** 14
213 **MOON EAGLE** (IRE) 14
361 **MOON EMPRESS** (FR) C 39
416 **MOON FLIGHT** (IRE) 22
154 **MOON FRIEND** (IRE) 131
319 **MOON KING** (FR) 29
505 **MOON KNIGHT** 10
247 **MOON LADY** 94
133 **MOON OVER GERMANY** (IRE) 9
80 **MOON OVER THE SEA** 59
94 **MOON RAY** (FR) 26
404 **MOON SISTER** (IRE) C 31
101 **MOONACURA** (IRE) 22
298 **MOONAMACAROONA** 75
305 **MOONDIAL** 31
335 **MOONDUST** (IRE) G 145
164 **MOONFLEET MOMENT** (IRE) 26
355 **MOONIS** (IRE) 81
497 **MOONLIGHT ARTIST** 49
368 **MOONLIGHT BAY** F 65
307 **MOONLIGHT BEAM** (IRE) 6
106 **MOONLIGHT DREAMER** 23
372 **MOONLIGHT FLIT** (IRE) 2
513 **MOONLIGHT GLORY** (IRE) 40
172 **MOONLIGHT SONATA** F 57
352 **MOONLIGHT SPIRIT** (IRE) 17
91 **MOONLIGHT TIARA** 9
12 **MOONLIGHTER** 45
276 **MOONLIT CLOUD** 9
172 **MOONLIT GARDEN** (IRE) F 58
335 **MOONLIT PARK** (IRE) 90
442 **MOONLIT SHOW** F 80
42 **MOONLIT VIEW** (IRE) C 67
231 **MOONRISE LANDING** (IRE) F 132
176 **MOONS OF JUPITER** (USA) F 58
363 **MOONSET** (FR) 87
385 **MOONSHINE SPIRIT** 133
279 **MOONSTONE BOY** (IRE) 75
526 **MOONSTONE ROCK** F 31
545 **MOORE CLOUDS** (IRE) 3
369 **MOORE MARGAUX** (IRE) 87
370 **MOORGATE** (IRE) 6
539 **MOORLAND RAMBLER** 27
139 **MOOSMEE** (IRE) 8
385 **MOOT COURT** (IRE) 134
6 **MOP'S A LEGEND** 58
6 **MOPS GEM** 59
538 **MORAINE** G 48
28 **MORAL DILEMMA** 16
353 **MORALISA** 16
374 **MORANDI SECOND** (FR) 13
461 **MORANI KALI** 7
43 **MORBOKA** 69
228 **MORCAR** 73
456 **MORDOR** (FR) 49
234 **MORDRED** (IRE) 49
267 **MORE BEER** (IRE) 13
176 **MORE DIAMONDS** (IRE) 8
226 **MORE JOY** (FR) 56
228 **MORE LIGHT** 168
386 **MORE MISCHIEF** F 39
207 **MORE PLAY** F 12
66 **MORE RESPECT** (IRE) C 137
42 **MORE THAN A GREY** 33
167 **MORE THAN LIKELY** 11
45 **MORE TO FOLLOW** (IRE) 6
366 **MORFEE** (IRE) 25
5 **MORGAN LE FAYE** C 203
483 **MORIKO DE VASSY** (FR) 22
351 **MORMON** (IRE) 4
42 **MORNING COLOURS** 34
553 **MORNING GLORIA** (IRE) 5
247 **MORNING LINE** (IRE) 95
206 **MORNING POEM** 21
390 **MORNING SPIRIT** (IRE) 77
119 **MORNING SUN** (IRE) 29
182 **MORNINGSIDE** 10
279 **MORNINGTON BELLE** (IRE) F 65
162 **MORO ROCK** (IRE) 12
40 **MOROCCAN MOON** 19
366 **MORODER** (IRE) 26
313 **MOROVAL** (IRE) 5
154 **MOROZOV COCKTAIL** (IRE) 62
241 **MORTENS LEAM** 2
385 **MORTLACH** 135
126 **MORVAL** (FR) 7
347 **MOSCOW MISTRESS** (IRE) G 52
233 **MOSCOW SPY** (IRE) 10
506 **MOSHAAWER** 27
23 **MOSSBAWN** 16
166 **MOSSING** 11
457 **MOST AGREEABLE** 126
106 **MOST TEMPTING** C 33
206 **MOSTABSHIR** 105
206 **MOSTAHDAF** (IRE) 22
6 **MOSTALLIM** 60
328 **MOSTAWAA** 12
328 **MOSTLY SUNNY** (IRE) 13
489 **MOT A MOT** (FR) 30
135 **MOTAGALLY** 41
154 **MOTARAJEL** 63
42 **MOTASALEETA** 35
84 **MOTATAABEQ** (IRE) 12

6 **MOTAWAAFEQ** (FR) 61
138 **MOTAWAAZY** 26
14 **MOTAZZEN** (IRE) 25
89 **MOTEO** (IRE) F 51
243 **MOTHER INDIA** (IRE) 30
92 **MOTHER MARGARET** (IRE) 42
363 **MOTHILL** (IRE) 88
376 **MOTION IN LIMINE** (IRE) 38
466 **MOTIVE** 34
360 **MOTTISFONT** (IRE) 54
175 **MOULANE LADY** (IRE) C 54
355 **MOULINS CLERMONT** (FR) 82
484 **MOUNT ATHOS** 4
205 **MOUNT BONETE** 35
343 **MOUNT BROWN** (IRE) 39
554 **MOUNT CORBITT** (IRE) 7
247 **MOUNT ETNA** (IRE) 96
454 **MOUNT FERNS** (IRE) 22
154 **MOUNT KING** (IRE) 132
223 **MOUNT MELLERAY** (IRE) 6
354 **MOUNT MOGAN** 10
298 **MOUNT OLYMPUS** 76
538 **MOUNT SOUTH** (IRE) 49
457 **MOUNT TEMPEST** (IRE) 127
366 **MOUNTAIN BAY** (IRE) 27
251 **MOUNTAIN FLOWER** (IRE) 50
366 **MOUNTAIN GREY** (IRE) 28
35 **MOUNTAIN LAKE** 76
543 **MOUNTAIN LEOPARD** (IRE) 62
515 **MOUNTAIN PEAK** 10
73 **MOUNTAIN RAPID** (IRE) 10
456 **MOUNTAIN ROAD** (FR) 18
502 **MOUNTAIN RUN** 14
5 **MOUNTAIN SONG** (IRE) 89
31 **MOUNTAIN WARRIOR** 30
521 **MOUNTBATTEN** (IRE) 25
281 **MOURNE LASS** (IRE) 10
67 **MOURNE SUPREME** (IRE) 18
507 **MOURZOUK** (IRE) 29
85 **MOUSH** 34
504 **MOVEIT LIKE MINNIE** (IRE) 46
294 **MOVEONUP** (IRE) 3
355 **MOVETHECHAINS** (IRE) 83
540 **MOVIDDY** (IRE) 13
286 **MOVIE NIGHT** 104
107 **MOVIE STAR LOOKS** 45
471 **MOVING FOR GOLD** (IRE) 13
35 **MOVING LIGHT** (IRE) 34
267 **MOYTIER** (FR) 14
292 **MOZZARO** (IRE) 29
43 **MR ALAN** 17
395 **MR ALCHEMY** 20
504 **MR BARROWCLOUGH** (IRE) 47
387 **MR BEAUFORT** 34
469 **MR BIG STUFF** 10
390 **MR BIGGS** 78
360 **MR BOSON** 55
386 **MR BRAMLEY** 17
24 **MR BUSTER** (IRE) 60
117 **MR COCO BEAN** (USA) 2
411 **MR COLDSTONE** (IRE) 5
196 **MR CRAFTSMAN** 10
154 **MR CURIOSITY** 64
137 **MR DEALER** (IRE) 1
114 **MR FAYEZ** (IRE) 4
527 **MR FREEDOM** 14
451 **MR FUNKY MONKEY** 15
62 **MR FUSTIC** (IRE) 3
429 **MR GAMBINO** 3
451 **MR GINJA NINJA** 16
379 **MR GLASS** (IRE) 118
188 **MR GLOVERMAN** 31
12 **MR GREY SKY** (IRE) 46
376 **MR HAILSTONE** (IRE) 39
194 **MR HARP** (IRE) 10
533 **MR HEINZ** 7
457 **MR HOPE STREET** (IRE) 128
206 **MR INSPIRATION** (IRE) 23
275 **MR JACK** (IRE) 17
68 **MR JESSE JAMES** (IRE) 5
501 **MR JETMAN** (IRE) 53
241 **MR JORROCKS** 3
244 **MR JV** 6
116 **MR KATANGA** (IRE) 16
257 **MR MAC** 7
504 **MR MACKAY** (IRE) 48
292 **MR MAFIA** (IRE) 30
464 **MR MAHLER** (IRE) 37
296 **MR MARVLOS** (IRE) 7
360 **MR MISTOFFELEES** (IRE) 56
10 **MR MONEYPENNY** 24
376 **MR MULDOON** (IRE) 40
64 **MR ONE MORE** (IRE) 5
76 **MR PALM** (IRE) 2
133 **MR PALMTREE** (IRE) 10
80 **MR PC** (IRE) 60
283 **MR PHILLIPS** 34
526 **MR POSTMAN** 32
243 **MR PROFESSOR** (IRE) 7
298 **MR RUMBALICIOUS** (IRE) 77
386 **MR SCRUMPY** 18
448 **MR SNOW WAY** (IRE) 22
140 **MR SOCIABLE** 11
174 **MR SQUIRES** (IRE) 39
491 **MR STRUTTER** (IRE) 16
491 **MR SUNDOWNER** (USA) 17
410 **MR TAMBOURINE MAN** (IRE) 56
143 **MR TREVOR** (IRE) 9
538 **MR TRICK** (IRE) 50
228 **MR TYRRELL** (IRE) 17
52 **MR VANGO** (IRE) 8
234 **MR YEATS** (IRE) 50
39 **MR ZEE** (IRE) 6
162 **MR ZIPPI** 13
413 **MREMBO** 6
20 **MRINDEPENDANT** 15
510 **MRS BAGERRAN** (IRE) 6
405 **MRS DIBBLE** (FR) 11
538 **MRS DOUBTFIRE** 51
1 **MRS FOX** (FR) 33
402 **MRS GRIMLEY** (IRE) 59
325 **MRS IVY** C 20
19 **MRS JONES** 4
7 **MRS KINSELLA** (IRE) 9
28 **MRS MAISEL** 10
173 **MRS MEADER** 6
212 **MRS TABITHA** 56
544 **MRS TIFFEN** 8
348 **MRS TRUMP** (IRE) 50
361 **MRS TWIG** (IRE) 23
43 **MRS U S A** (IRE) 70
413 **MRS VAN HOPPER** 27
456 **MS GREER** 50
367 **MT LEINSTER** (IRE) 112
511 **MUATADEL** 8
506 **MUBHIJAH** 103
69 **MUBHIRAH** F 39
265 **MUCH TOO DEAR** (IRE) 10
402 **MUCHO MAS** (IRE) 60
535 **MUCKY MULCONRY** (IRE) 7
234 **MUCUNA** (GER) 51
229 **MUDAMER** (IRE) 3
251 **MUDAWANAH** C 102
470 **MUDDAGENT** 4
470 **MUDDY LYNN** 5
135 **MUDLAHHIM** (IRE) 42
346 **MUDSKIPPER** 26
219 **MUFFRI'HA** (IRE) F 169
382 **MUFTAKKER** 3
412 **MUG BOOKIES** (IRE) 10
228 **MUGADER** 18
286 **MUIR WOOD** 105
495 **MUJID** (IRE) 8
219 **MUJTABA** 21
506 **MUKADDAMAH** 28
112 **MUKEEDD** 40
294 **MUKHA MAGIC** 4
500 **MUKTAMIL** (IRE) 17
385 **MULBERRY HILL** (IRE) 136
234 **MULLENBEG** (IRE) 52
234 **MULLINAREE** (IRE) 53
379 **MULLINS BAY** 119
349 **MULLINS BEACH** (IRE) 37
484 **MULUK** (IRE) C 68
289 **MULZIM** 10
80 **MUMAYAZ** (IRE) 61
537 **MUMBLES** (IRE) 46
308 **MUMBO JUMBO** (IRE) 43
105 **MUMCAT** 1
488 **MUMINAMILLION** (IRE) 23
289 **MUMMY'S BOY** 11
228 **MUMS TIPPLE** (IRE) 19
91 **MUNAAJAAT** (IRE) F 21
17 **MUNIFICENT** 12
174 **MUNTADAB** (IRE) 22
442 **MUNTASIRA** (IRE) 44
286 **MUR HIBA** (IRE) C 193
69 **MURAAD** (IRE) 5
484 **MURASAKI** F 69
383 **MURAVKA** (IRE) F 169
57 **MURBIH** (IRE) 16
427 **MURHIB** (IRE) 8
493 **MUROOR** 4
408 **MURVIEL** (FR) C 76
500 **MUSAANADA** C 28
233 **MUSAYTIR** (IRE) 11
387 **MUSCIKA** 35
227 **MUSE OF FIRE** (IRE) 27
66 **MUSIC CHART** (USA) C 138
154 **MUSIC SOCIETY** (IRE) 65
387 **MUSICAL BAR** (IRE) F 120
396 **MUSICAL COMEDY** 4
480 **MUSICAL MYSTERY** 5
254 **MUSICAL SLAVE** (IRE) 53
164 **MUSICAL TRIBUTE** 27
249 **MUSICAL YOUTH** 19
186 **MUSICOLOGY** (USA) C 14
206 **MUSING** 106
358 **MUSKERRY ROCK** (IRE) 16
308 **MUSKOKA** (IRE) 44
66 **MUST BE ME** F 139

517 **MUSTAFFIZ** 5
361 **MUSTAJAAB** 24
282 **MUSTANG ALPHA** (IRE) 29
164 **MUSTAZEED** (IRE) 13
251 **MUTAANY** 51
57 **MUTABAAHY** (IRE) 17
35 **MUTAFAWWIG** 35
81 **MUTALAAQY** (IRE) 5
78 **MUTANAASEQ** (IRE) 20
115 **MUTARA** 14
251 **MUTASAABEQ** 11
251 **MUTEELA** C 103
7 **MUTUAL RESPECT** (IRE) 10
255 **MUVVERS MONEY** 8
383 **MUWAKABA** (USA) C 170
238 **MUWALLA** 9
139 **MUY MUY GUAPO** 19
96 **MY AMBITION** (IRE) 5
219 **MY ASTRA** (IRE) 22
202 **MY BAD LUCY** 23
274 **MY BEAUTY** (IRE) 2
506 **MY BETTER HALF** C 169
343 **MY BIRTHDAY GIRL** 70
439 **MY BOBBY DAZZLER** 17
439 **MY BOBBY'S LASS** 18
550 **MY BONNIE LASSIE** 2
385 **MY BOY BEASTY** 137
160 **MY BOY GRIZZLE** (IRE) 4
408 **MY BOY JACK** 18
404 **MY BROTHER JACK** (IRE) 5
476 **MY BROTHER MIKE** (IRE) 3
59 **MY CHIQUITA** 12
286 **MY CLEMENTINE** (IRE) 194
320 **MY DELILAH** (IRE) 35
175 **MY DORRIS** (IRE) C 55
507 **MY DREAM** 30
154 **MY DUTY** (IRE) 133
472 **MY EYES ADORE YOU** 4
484 **MY FAVOURITE THING** C 70
164 **MY FINEST HOUR** (IRE) 28
441 **MY FIRST RODEO** (IRE) 17
433 **MY FOREVER FRIEND** (IRE) 7
516 **MY FOXY LADY** 7
11 **MY FRIEND WOODY** 2
80 **MY GENGHIS** 62
525 **MY GIFT TO YOU** (IRE) 21
233 **MY GIRL KATIE** (IRE) 12
157 **MY GIRL LOLLIPOP** (IRE) 28
240 **MY GRANNY LILY** 26
153 **MY HONEY** B 65
10 **MY KIND OF LADY** 25
84 **MY LADY CLAIRE** 13
497 **MY LADY GREY** 50
448 **MY LADY PHOENIX** 23
243 **MY LADY SAMANTHA** 45
332 **MY LAST OSCAR** (IRE) 17
15 **MY LION** 91
335 **MY LITTLE TONI** 91
449 **MY MACHO MAN** (IRE) 19
270 **MY MARGIE** (IRE) 57
276 **MY MATE MIKE** (IRE) 20
488 **MY MATE TED** (IRE) 24
141 **MY MONTY** 17
392 **MY OPINION** (IRE) 16
218 **MY PETRA** F 10
212 **MY POEM** 57
357 **MY PORTIA** 26
95 **MY PROPELLER** (IRE) F 37
219 **MY PROSPERO** (IRE) 23
426 **MY ROCKSTAR** (IRE) 2
161 **MY ROXANNE** (IRE) 46
80 **MY SAND BOY** 63
146 **MY SILENT SONG** 10
308 **MY SILVER LINING** (IRE) 45
300 **MY STRONG MAN** (IRE) 40
205 **MY TICKETYBOO** (IRE) 36
107 **MY TURN NOW** (IRE) 46
439 **MY VIRTUE** 19
226 **MYBOYMAX** (FR) 57
464 **MYBURG** (IRE) 38
147 **MYFANWY'S JEWEL** 28
292 **MYFANWY'S MAGIC** 31
374 **MYFAVOURITESISTER** (IRE) 14
135 **MYKONOS ST JOHN** 43
85 **MYLADYJANE** (IRE) C 63
457 **MYLESFROMWICKLOW** (IRE) 129
440 **MYRETOWN** (IRE) 54
270 **MYRIAD** (IRE) 12
410 **MYRISTICA** (IRE) 57
346 **MYSTERIOUS LOVE** (IRE) 27
112 **MYSTERIOUS MAESTRO** (IRE) 41
5 **MYSTERIOUS NIGHT** (IRE) 90
280 **MYSTERY PLAY** 18
43 **MYSTERY PLAY** 71
41 **MYSTERY TRAIN** (FR) 19
381 **MYSTIC GLEN** F 5
454 **MYSTIC MAN** (IRE) 23
382 **MYSTIC MARIE** 7
219 **MYSTIC PEARL** (FR) 85
24 **MYSTIC STORM** C 129
164 **MYSTICAL APPLAUSE** 29
161 **MYSTICAL DREAMS** (IRE) 47
383 **MYSTICAL LADY** (IRE) F 171
95 **MYSTICAL MOON** (IRE) C 38
265 **MYTARA** F 13
231 **MYTH CREATION** (USA) F 133
533 **MYTHICAL** (FR) 8
330 **MYTHICAL GUEST** (IRE) 13
526 **MYTHICAL HERO** (IRE) 15
346 **MYTHICAL LIGHT** 46
219 **MYTHIE** (FR) C 170
507 **MYUNCLECHARLIE** (FR) 31
501 **MYWAYISTHEONLYWAY** (IRE) 22
111 **MYWON** (IRE) 6
374 **N'GOLO** (IRE) 15
329 **NA SCOITEAR** (IRE) 11
66 **NAADRAH** F 140
400 **NAADYAA** 10
206 **NAAEY** 107
43 **NAASER** (IRE) 72
382 **NAASIK** 4
407 **NAASMA** (IRE) 9
428 **NAB WOOD** (IRE) 30
15 **NABARAAT** (USA) C 185
335 **NACHO** (IRE) 92
400 **NACHOS CHEESE** (IRE) 11
35 **NADER** 36
479 **NADER KING** (IRE) 40
234 **NADIM** (IRE) 54
147 **NAEVA** (FR) 29
506 **NAGANO** 29
515 **NAHEMA** (IRE) F 87
5 **NAHORI** 91
506 **NAHRAIN** F 170
442 **NAHWAND** (IRE) 45
270 **NAILS MURPHY** (IRE) 32
371 **NAIROBI GIRL** (IRE) 7
69 **NAJM ALDAR** (GER) 40
15 **NAJMA** F 186
5 **NAJOUM** (USA) F 204
399 **NAKANO** (IRE) 52
221 **NALOUT** (USA) C 42
543 **NAMBITI** (FR) 63
159 **NAME AND SHAME** (IRE) 3
497 **NAME IN LIGHTS** (IRE) 51
399 **NAMMOS** 53
286 **NANCY O** (IRE) F 195
353 **NANTYGLO** F 29
469 **NAOMI LAPAGLIA** 34
66 **NAOMI'S CHARM** (IRE) 71
298 **NAP HAND** (IRE) 136
251 **NAPLES BAY** (USA) F 104
219 **NAQEEB** (IRE) 86
146 **NARASHA** (IRE) 42
94 **NARIMAN POINT** (IRE) 27
526 **NARLA** F 33
309 **NASHVILLE NIPPER** (IRE) 11
206 **NASHWA** 24
326 **NASHY** (IRE) 14
6 **NASIM** 62
355 **NASSALAM** (FR) 84
192 **NASSAU BAY** 66
192 **NAT LOVE** (IRE) 27
416 **NATACATA** 23
79 **NATCHEZ TRACE** 9
15 **NATE THE GREAT** 21
175 **NATEEJA** (IRE) C 56
472 **NATHALIA ECLIPSE** (IRE) 19
67 **NATHAN WALKER** 19
219 **NATHANAEL GREENE** 24
208 **NATIONAL CHARTER** (IRE) 16
231 **NATIONAL EMBLEM** (IRE) 64
369 **NATIONAL HEALTH** (FR) 135
5 **NATIONS PRIDE** (IRE) 25
498 **NATIVE BEACH** (IRE) 6
352 **NATIVE FIGHTER** (IRE) 18
294 **NATIVE MELODY** (IRE) 13
122 **NATIVE MOON** (IRE) 13
104 **NATIVE NELLIE** 20
448 **NATIVE ROBIN** (IRE) 24
5 **NATIVE TRAIL** 26
269 **NATTY DRESSER** (IRE) 9
543 **NATTY NIGHT** 64
15 **NATURAL BEAUTY** C 187
112 **NATURAL SCENERY** F 90
217 **NATURALIA** 24
355 **NATURALLY HIGH** (FR) 85
5 **NATURE WATCH** (USA) 92
521 **NATZOR** (FR) 82
102 **NAUGHTY GEORGE** 25
13 **NAUGHTY TED** 18
325 **NAUTICAL DREAM** (IRE) 16
29 **NAUTICAL HAVEN** 12
483 **NAVAJO INDY** 23
335 **NAVAJO PASS** 93
56 **NAVAL COMMANDER** 28
5 **NAVAL POWER** 93
77 **NAVARRA PRINCESS** (IRE) 4
399 **NAVARRE EXPRESS** 54
504 **NAVEGAON GATE** 49
43 **NAVELLO** 18

326 **OFF TO ALABAMA** 15
497 **OFTEN OVERLOOKED** (IRE) 56
228 **OH HERBERTS REIGN** (IRE) 21
164 **OH SO AUDACIOUS** 14
501 **OH SO CHARMING** 54
112 **OH SO GRAND** 42
503 **OHH LALA** (IRE) C 21
370 **OHNODONTTAKEMEHOME** (FR) 8
541 **OHNOJOE** (IRE) 9
20 **OISHIN** 16
355 **OJ LIFESTYLE** (IRE) 148
69 **OJOOBA** F 41
80 **OK PAL** 109
80 **OKAIDI** (USA) 69
506 **OKAMI** (IRE) 106
136 **OKAVANGO DELTA** (IRE) 23
192 **OKEANOS** (FR) 28
92 **OKEECHOBEE** 7
220 **OL'RIVER SHINE** (IRE) 34
385 **OLD BEGINNINGS** (IRE) 142
31 **OLD COCK** (IRE) 53
382 **OLD DURHAM TOWN** 5
335 **OLD FOLK TALE** (IRE) 99
379 **OLD GOLD** 120
440 **OLD GREGORIAN** 57
45 **OLD JEWRY** (IRE) 8
481 **OLD NEWS** 3
443 **OLD PAGE** (IRE) 3
534 **OLD PAINLESS** (IRE) 13
231 **OLD SEA** (IRE) 135
247 **OLD TIME CHASER** (IRE) 99
189 **OLD TOWN GARDE** (IRE) 47
281 **OLEOHNEH** (IRE) G 19
154 **OLIVE MARY** F 183
479 **OLIVER SHOW** (IRE) 42
347 **OLIVER'S ARMY** (FR) 56
25 **OLIVER'S ISLAND** (IRE) 3
54 **OLIVIA MARY** (IRE) 7
323 **OLIVIA'S SECRET** (IRE) 11
203 **OLLY'S FOLLY** 10
69 **OLMA** (SAF) C 42
146 **OLVIA** (IRE) C 69
107 **OLYMPIC QUEST** 47
374 **OLYMPUS** (IRE) 18
473 **OMAHA GOLD** (IRE) C 9
457 **OMAHA WISH** (FR) 135
220 **OMAR MARETTI** (IRE) 35
234 **OMEGA** (GER) 55
416 **OMNISCIENT** 8
384 **ON A PEDESTAL** (IRE) C 59
23 **ON A SESSION** (USA) 17
335 **ON CLOUD NINE** (IRE) 100
333 **ON EDGE** 6
247 **ON MY COMMAND** (IRE) 100
64 **ON OATH** (IRE) G 7
64 **ON OATH** (IRE) G 8
153 **ON SABBATICAL** (IRE) 66
298 **ON SE CALME** (FR) 83
402 **ON SPRINGS** (IRE) 67
390 **ON THE BANDWAGON** (IRE) 81
247 **ON THE BLIND SIDE** (IRE) 101
239 **ON THE BUBBLE** 37
346 **ON THE CARDS** (FR) 28
184 **ON THE OTHER HAND** (IRE) 7
216 **ON THE PLATFORM** (IRE) 7
165 **ON THE PULSE** (IRE) 29
505 **ON THE RIGHT TRACK** 11
32 **ON THE RIVER** 9
107 **ON THE SAME PAGE** (IRE) C 88
376 **ON THE WILD SIDE** (IRE) 41
298 **ON TO VICTORY** 84
40 **ON WE GO** (IRE) 22
20 **ON YER SCHNAPPS** 17
385 **ONAGATHERINGSTORM** (IRE) 143
195 **ONCE ADAAY** 9
353 **ONCE MORE FOR LUCK** (IRE) 18
501 **ONDEAFEARS** (IRE) G 55
231 **ONE BOSS** 72
217 **ONE COLOUR** (IRE) 7
265 **ONE COOL KATE** (IRE) F 11
206 **ONE EVENING** 25
157 **ONE EYE ON VEGAS** 29
453 **ONE FER MAMMA** (IRE) 6
352 **ONE FINE MAN** (IRE) 20
147 **ONE FOR BILLY** 31
360 **ONE FOR BOBBY** (IRE) 19
231 **ONE FOR JUNE** (IRE) F 136
552 **ONE FOR THE FROG** (IRE) 9
205 **ONE FOR THE WALL** (IRE) 37
526 **ONE FOR YOU** (IRE) 18
501 **ONE HART** (IRE) 23
385 **ONE HUNDRED NOTOUT** (IRE) 144
309 **ONE KNIGHT** (IRE) 22
213 **ONE LAST GLANCE** 15
219 **ONE LAST TIME** (IRE) 88
55 **ONE MAN PARTY** (FR) 12
440 **ONE MILL HARBOUR** (FR) 58
353 **ONE MINUTE** (IRE) C 30
538 **ONE MORE FLEURIE** (IRE) 53
270 **ONE MORE OLLY** 35
413 **ONE MORE WAVE** 28
26 **ONE MORNING** (IRE) 11
216 **ONE MOVE** (IRE) M 8
5 **ONE NATION** 95
135 **ONE NIGHT STAND** 44
228 **ONE NIGHT THUNDER** 74
347 **ONE OF OUR OWN** 107
303 **ONE PIXEL** C 35
274 **ONE STEP BEYOND** (IRE) 4
428 **ONE STEP UP** (FR) 33
402 **ONE TOUCH** (IRE) 68
504 **ONE TRUE KING** (IRE) 52
1 **ONE WAY OR ANOTHER** (FR) 38
308 **ONEANDAHALFDEGREES** (IRE) 47
348 **ONEFORSUE** 51
293 **ONEFORTHEGUTTER** 7
299 **ONEMOREFORTHEROAD** 25
226 **ONENIGHTINTOWN** (IRE) 60
80 **ONESHOT** 110
161 **ONESMOOTHOPERATOR** (USA) 17
464 **ONESOC** (IRE) 42
511 **ONESTEPATATIME** (IRE) 9
202 **ONESTEPTWOSTEPS** (IRE) 25
88 **ONESTO** (IRE) 9
379 **ONETHREEFIVENOTOUT** (IRE) 121
263 **ONEUPMANSHIP** (IRE) 52
402 **ONEWAYORTHEOTHER** (IRE) G 69
309 **ONEWAYORTOTHER** (FR) 13
521 **ONIGHT** 83
390 **ONLY BY NIGHT** (IRE) 82
209 **ONLY EXCEPTION** (IRE) G 24
410 **ONLY FOOLS** (IRE) 64
467 **ONLY FOR PASCAL** (IRE) 9
205 **ONLY MONEY** (IRE) 38
410 **ONLY THE BOLD** (IRE) 65
212 **ONLY TOGETHER** (IRE) G 82
240 **ONNAROLL** (FR) 28
228 **ONSLOW GARDENS** (IRE) 75
405 **ONTHEBUNNY** 21
335 **ONTHEFRONTFOOT** (IRE) 101
367 **ONTHEROPES** (IRE) 115
389 **ONURBIKE** 2
347 **ONWARD ROUTE** (IRE) 57
87 **ONWEGOAGAIN** (IRE) G 6
87 **ONWEGOAGAIN** (IRE) F 9
93 **OOH BETTY** (IRE) 13
165 **OOH IS IT** 12
279 **OOT MA WAY** (FR) 38
416 **OPAL ROSE** 49
298 **OPEN CHAMPION** (IRE) 85
31 **OPEN CHOICE** (USA) 32
35 **OPEN MIND** 39
35 **OPEN ROAD** (IRE) 78
35 **OPEN STORY** (IRE) 79
343 **OPEN TO QUESTION** 73
140 **OPENING BID** 12
484 **OPENING SHOW** 25
5 **OPERA COMIQUE** (FR) C 205
15 **OPERA FOREVER** 95
41 **OPERA GIFT** 7
219 **OPERA LEGEND** 89
459 **OPERATION GIMCRACK** (IRE) 16
306 **OPERATION MANNA** 36
440 **OPERATION OVERLORD** (IRE) 59
228 **OPINIONATED LADY** (IRE) C 173
276 **OPPORTUNITY KNOCKS** (IRE) 21
272 **OPTICALITY** 16
154 **OPTICIAN** 136
456 **OPTIK** (IRE) 51
402 **OPTIMISE PRIME** (IRE) 70
407 **OPTIMISTIC BELIEF** (IRE) 11
228 **OPTIVA STAR** (IRE) 76
167 **ORANGE GINA** 13
15 **ORANGE MARTINI** 96
89 **ORANGE N BLUE** (IRE) 32
506 **ORANGE SUN** C 173
251 **ORAZIO** (IRE) 12
387 **ORBAAN** 37
416 **ORBITAL** 50
266 **ORBITAL CHIME** 18
311 **ORCHARD GROVE** (IRE) 21
146 **ORCHESTRA** (FR) 44
376 **ORCHESTRAL RAIN** (IRE) 42
219 **ORCHID BLOOM** 90
112 **ORCHID STAR** F 93
383 **ORDER OF AUSTRALIA** (IRE) 10
399 **ORDER OF MALTA** 56
282 **ORDER OF ST JOHN** 30
409 **ORGANDI** (FR) 16
43 **ORGANIC** (IRE) 136
386 **ORGANZA** F 41
456 **ORIENTAL ART** 19
548 **ORIENTAL BEAUTY** 17
507 **ORIENTAL CROSS** (IRE) 33
228 **ORIENTAL DANCER** 77
204 **ORIENTAL LILLY** 27
302 **ORIENTAL SPIRIT** 9
228 **ORIENTAL STEP** (IRE) C 174
463 **ORIES LIGHT** (IRE) G 26
32 **ORIGINAL THINKER** 12
70 **ORIGINALLY** (IRE) 58

266 **PARK BLOOM** (IRE) F 39
289 **PARK FARM PERCY** 12
387 **PARK GLEN** (IRE) C 121
247 **PARK HILL DANCER** (FR) 103
324 **PARK PADDOCKS** (IRE) 9
277 **PARK STREET** 8
466 **PARK THIS ONE** (IRE) 38
431 **PARKED IN A PUDDLE** 5
31 **PARLE MOI** (USA) C 54
83 **PARLEZ VOUS** G 20
369 **PARLIAMENT HILL** 92
66 **PARLIAMENT HOUSE** (IRE) C 142
367 **PARMENION** 116
247 **PAROS** (FR) 104
496 **PARR FIRE** (IRE) 39
319 **PARRAMOUNT** 33
475 **PARSONS STONE** (IRE) 11
89 **PARTHENOPAEUS** 14
472 **PARTING GLASS** 21
506 **PARTON** C 174
506 **PARTRIDGE** (IRE) C 175
475 **PARTY ANGEL** (IRE) C 20
538 **PARTY BUSINESS** (IRE) 54
12 **PARTY FUZZ** 48
96 **PARTY ISLAND** (IRE) 6
283 **PARTY PLANNER** 19
154 **PARYS MOUNTAIN** (IRE) 70
175 **PAS DE SOUCIS** (IRE) C 59
46 **PASCHALS DREAM** (IRE) 6
543 **PASEO** 67
405 **PASHA BAY** 14
41 **PASIPHAE** (FR) 15
379 **PASO DOBLE** (IRE) 124
16 **PASS ME BY** 24
298 **PASS THE LOVE ON** 88
192 **PASS THE MOON** (IRE) G 67
151 **PASSAM** 11
479 **PASSENGER** (USA) 43
520 **PASSING BURG** (FR) C 31
233 **PASSING KATE** 13
298 **PASSING REFLECTION** 89
213 **PASSING SECRETS** 16
15 **PASSING TIME** 97
466 **PASSING WELL** (FR) 39
35 **PASSION AND GLORY** (IRE) 40
217 **PASSION TANGO** (USA) 14
138 **PASSIONADA** C 81
472 **PASSIONATE** 22
298 **PASSIONATE PURSUIT** (IRE) 90
368 **PASSIONATELY** (IRE) 68
342 **PASSIONATTA** (IRE) C 36
43 **PASTICHE** 77
440 **PASTURE BEACH** (IRE) 61
205 **PASVOLSKY** (IRE) 39
516 **PAT'S LIGHT** 8
357 **PAT'S PICK** (IRE) 28
25 **PATEEN** (IRE) 4
148 **PATIENCE** G 11
79 **PATIENCE ALEXANDER** (IRE) F 35
335 **PATIENT DREAM** (FR) 102
394 **PATIENT OWNER** (IRE) 11
503 **PATONTHEBACK** (IRE) 7
354 **PATRIOCTIC** (IRE) 12
286 **PATRIOT'S CHOICE** (IRE) 106
5 **PATRONESS** C 206
136 **PATS DREAM** (IRE) 24
116 **PATS FANCY** (IRE) 18
31 **PATUANO** (IRE) C 55
556 **PAUDIE** (IRE) 12
367 **PAUL MARVEL** (FR) 117
414 **PAULS HILL** (IRE) 27
43 **PAULTONS SQUARE** (IRE) 78
270 **PAVILLON** C 59
15 **PAVISE** 98
494 **PAVLIK** (IRE) 36
423 **PAVLODAR** (FR) 30
247 **PAWAPURI** 105
55 **PAWPAW** 13
257 **PAY FOR ADAAY** 8
446 **PAY SCALE** (IRE) 5
12 **PAY THE PILOT** 49
225 **PAY THE PIPER** (IRE) 6
292 **PAY THE WOMAN** (IRE) 32
22 **PAY TIME** G 4
164 **PAYMENT IN KIND** 50
88 **PAZ** 46
447 **PAZA** (USA) F 44
96 **PEACE AND LOVE** (IRE) C 17
5 **PEACE IN MOTION** (USA) C 207
206 **PEACE MAN** 26
43 **PEACE OF MINE** (IRE) 79
247 **PEACE OF ROME** (GER) 106
35 **PEACE TRAIL** C 98
286 **PEACEFUL NIGHT** 107
228 **PEACEFUL STORY** (IRE) 80
172 **PEACEHAVEN** (IRE) F 36
417 **PEACENIK** (IRE) 7
383 **PEACH TREE** (IRE) F 173
365 **PEACHEY CARNEHAN** 7
450 **PEAKY BOY** (IRE) 28
513 **PEAL OF BELLS** F 42
497 **PEARL BEAUTY** 58
347 **PEARL BUTTONS** G 59
280 **PEARL EARING** (IRE) F 25
260 **PEARL EYE** 11
343 **PEARL OF AUSTRALIA** (IRE) 74
321 **PEARL REEF** 28
240 **PEARL ROYALE** (IRE) 29
387 **PEARLE D'OR** (IRE) 38
251 **PEARLING TRAIL** 53
305 **PEARLY BROOKS** C 47
506 **PEARLY EMPRESS** (FR) C 176
502 **PEARLY GAITS** 15
54 **PEARLY GIRL** 8
509 **PEARLY ISLAND** 24
399 **PEARLY STAR** 57
216 **PEARLYMOON** 9
154 **PEBBLES PLACE** C 184
482 **PECKINPAH** (IRE) 3
497 **PEDLEY WOOD** (IRE) 59
135 **PEDRAR** (FR) 72
469 **PEEJAYBEE** (FR) 11
385 **PEERLESS BEAUTY** 149
480 **PEERLESS PERCY** (IRE) 7
515 **PEGGOTY** 11
509 **PEGGY CULLEN** (IRE) F 25
301 **PEINTURE RARE** (IRE) F 20
43 **PEINTURE RARE** (IRE) C 137
383 **PEKING OPERA** (IRE) 67
385 **PEKING ROSE** 150
112 **PELERIN** (IRE) F 94
346 **PELISSANNE** (FR) 29
383 **PELLIGRINA** (IRE) C 174
363 **PELTWELL** (IRE) 92
308 **PEMBERLEY** (IRE) 49
457 **PEMBROKE** 137
280 **PEMBROKESHIRE** 20
332 **PENCIL** (IRE) 18
402 **PENCREEK** (FR) 71
251 **PENDING APPEAL** 54
31 **PENDLEBURY LANE** 34
290 **PENELOPEBLUEYES** (IRE) 12
75 **PENGUIN ISLAND** 7
415 **PENNA ROSSA** (IRE) 6
54 **PENNY BE** 12
153 **PENNY GARCIA** G 88
533 **PENNY GHENT** 18
543 **PENNY MALLOW** (FR) 68
387 **PENNY PEPPER** (IRE) F 122
71 **PENNY STREET** 8
305 **PENNY'S GIFT** F 48
51 **PENNYFORAPOUND** (IRE) 11
206 **PENNYMOOR** 27
226 **PENPAL** (FR) 61
390 **PENS MAN** (IRE) 85
41 **PENTAOUR** (FR) 8
379 **PENTIRE HEAD** (IRE) 125
247 **PENTLAND HILLS** (IRE) 107
18 **PENUMBRA** 24
135 **PENWAY** (IRE) 45
112 **PENZANCE** 43
515 **PEONY** 42
539 **PEPE LE MOKO** (FR) 28
5 **PEPITA** (IRE) C 208
525 **PEPITE DE AMOUR** 22
387 **PEPPER LANE** C 123
378 **PEPPER STREAK** (IRE) 4
347 **PEPPERMILL** (IRE) 60
262 **PEPSI CAT** (IRE) 11
497 **PER VINO VERITAS** 60
513 **PERCULATOR** 43
357 **PERCUSSION** 29
321 **PERCY JONES** 29
12 **PERCY VEERING** 50
386 **PERCY WILLIS** 19
305 **PERCY'S LAD** 13
255 **PERCY'S PRINCE** 10
25 **PERCY'S WORD** 5
43 **PERDIKA** 80
219 **PERFECT ALIBI** 25
228 **PERFECT ANGEL** (IRE) C 177
15 **PERFECT BEAUTY** C 190
270 **PERFECT COVER** (IRE) F 60
15 **PERFECT DELIGHT** C 191
80 **PERFECT FOCUS** (IRE) 71
447 **PERFECT GENTLEMAN** (IRE) 17
515 **PERFECT LADY** F 88
488 **PERFECT LESCRIBAA** (FR) 29
375 **PERFECT LIBERTY** 13
226 **PERFECT MAN** (IRE) 62
432 **PERFECT MOMENT** (IRE) 9
302 **PERFECT MYTH** 10
219 **PERFECT NEWS** 26
286 **PERFECT PLAY** 108
279 **PERFECT POLI** 40
515 **PERFECT PROPHET** 43
390 **PERFECT SCORE** (IRE) 86
447 **PERFECT SHOWDANCE** C 45
478 **PERFECT SOLDIER** (IRE) 3
461 **PERFECT SPIRIT** (IRE) F 15
154 **PERFECT SWISS** 71

401 **PERFECT SYMPHONY** (IRE) 3
398 **PERFECT THUNDER** 2
479 **PERFUSE** 44
279 **PERIBONKA RIVER** (FR) 41
506 **PERIPATETIC** 30
300 **PERIPETEIA** 42
14 **PERLA MARINA** (IRE) 52
355 **PERMATA** 91
146 **PEROVSKIA** 45
209 **PERRUCHE GRISE** (FR) C 19
439 **PERRYVILLE** (IRE) 20
484 **PERSEPONE** F 73
355 **PERSEUS WAY** (IRE) 92
135 **PERSEVERANTS** (FR) 46
219 **PERSIAN BLUE** (USA) 172
247 **PERSIAN TIME** 108
336 **PERSIAN WOLF** (IRE) 15
228 **PERSICA** (IRE) 178
219 **PERSIST** 27
23 **PERSUASION** (IRE) 18
5 **PERSUASIVE** (IRE) C 209
119 **PERSUER** 32
538 **PERTEMPS DIAMOND** 55
505 **PERTHSHIRE** (IRE) 12
476 **PERUVIAN SUMMER** (IRE) 4
133 **PESCATORIUS** (IRE) 11
410 **PESO IN MY POCKET** (IRE) 69
548 **PESSOA** 18
154 **PETE THE BRIEF** (IRE) 137
537 **PETERBOROUGH** (FR) 52
90 **PETERS SPIRIT** (IRE) C 15
285 **PETICOATGOVERNEMENT** (IRE) C 68
432 **PETIT BIJOU** 10
390 **PETIT TONNERRE** (FR) 87
315 **PETITE GEORGIA** (IRE) F 31
452 **PETITE POIS** G 6
440 **PETITE RHAPSODY** (IRE) 62
157 **PETITE SOURIS** (FR) 31
342 **PETITS FOURS** C 37
399 **PETITS POTINS** (IRE) C 92
66 **PETRA CELERA** (IRE) 143
282 **PETRASTAR** 31
44 **PETROVIC** (IRE) F 11
5 **PETTICOAT** F 210
448 **PETTICOAT LUCY** (IRE) 26
454 **PEUR DE RIEN** (FR) 28
456 **PFINGSTBERG** (GER) 53
43 **PHANTASY MAC** (IRE) 20
266 **PHANTOM FLIGHT** 3
12 **PHANTOM GETAWAY** (IRE) 51
466 **PHAR FROM MILAN** (IRE) 40
469 **PHENOMENON** 36
5 **PHERENIKOS** (IRE) 96
212 **PHIL DE PAIL** (FR) 61
402 **PHIL THE SOCK** (IRE) 72
261 **PHIL THE THRILL** (FR) 15
385 **PHILLAPA SUE** (IRE) 151
234 **PHILLIPSTOWN ELLEN** (IRE) 57
146 **PHILOS** (IRE) 46
546 **PHILOSOPHY** 7
133 **PHOEBUS LESCRIBAA** (FR) 12
149 **PHOENIX AQUILUS** (IRE) 9
164 **PHOENIX DUCHESS** (IRE) 51
138 **PHOENIX FIRE** (IRE) 54
85 **PHOENIX GLOW** (IRE) 37
96 **PHOENIX MOON** (IRE) 18
515 **PHOENIX PASSION** (IRE) 89
448 **PHOENIX RISEN** 27
325 **PHOENIX STAR** (IRE) 11
189 **PHOENIX WAY** (IRE) 49
466 **PHONE HOME** 41
415 **PHOTO BOMB** (IRE) 7
185 **PHOTOGRAPH** (IRE) 6
488 **PHOTON** (IRE) 46
10 **PHYSICS** (IRE) 27
98 **PHYSIQUE** (IRE) 19
347 **PIAFF BUBBLES** (IRE) 61
126 **PIANISSIMO** 8
15 **PIANOFORTE** 192
91 **PIANOLA** (USA) F 23
379 **PIC D'ORHY** (FR) 126
402 **PIC ROC** (IRE) 73
409 **PICANHA** 17
269 **PICC AN ANGEL** 10
298 **PICCADILLY LILLY** 91
165 **PICCOLA COLLINA** (IRE) F 43
24 **PICK YOUR BATTLES** 133
414 **PICKAMIX** 28
12 **PICKS LAD** 52
35 **PIECE OF HISTORY** (IRE) 41
226 **PIECEDERESISTANCE** (IRE) 63
107 **PIERCE** (IRE) 49
231 **PIGEON HOUSE** (IRE) 75
457 **PIKAR** (FR) 138
342 **PILASTER** C 38
286 **PILATES** (IRE) C 201
465 **PILBARA** 6
513 **PILEUP** (IRE) 44
23 **PILGRIM** 46
47 **PILGRIMS KING** (IRE) 28
286 **PILLAR OF HOPE** 20
468 **PILLAR OF STEEL** 7
421 **PILLARS OF EARTH** 14
506 **PILLARSOFCREATION** 108
66 **PILLOW TALK** (IRE) 75
211 **PILOT SHOW** (IRE) 32
228 **PILOTO PARDO** (IRE) 179
448 **PILSDON PEN** 28
311 **PIMLICO POINT** (IRE) 22
219 **PINAFORE** (IRE) 92
209 **PINE VALLEY** (IRE) F 9
209 **PINE VALLEY** (IRE) C 25
521 **PINK CARNATION** 31
219 **PINK CRYSTAL** (IRE) 28
59 **PINK DAMSEL** (IRE) C 23
456 **PINK DAMSEL** (IRE) C 54
342 **PINK DOGWOOD** (IRE) C 39
51 **PINK EYED PEDRO** 12
228 **PINK FIZZ** 180
367 **PINK IN THE PARK** (IRE) 118
70 **PINK JAZZ** (IRE) 34
543 **PINK LEGEND** 69
228 **PINK LILY** 81
501 **PINK PARFAIT** 24
455 **PINK POWER** 18
112 **PINK ROSE** C 95
544 **PINK STRIPES** 18
98 **PINK SYMPHONY** F 37
544 **PINK WALLS** 19
343 **PINKERTON** 41
239 **PINKIE BROWN** (FR) 24
292 **PINNACLE PEAK** 33
347 **PINOT ROUGE** (IRE) 62
14 **PINWHEEL** (IRE) 26
251 **PIONEER SPIRIT** C 105
202 **PIP AWAY** (IRE) 27
390 **PIPER TOM** (IRE) 88
182 **PIPERS CROSS** (IRE) 11
172 **PIQUE'** 59
315 **PIRANHA** (IRE) F 32
153 **PIRANHEER** 33
175 **PIRATE KING** 9
55 **PIRATE SAM** 14
387 **PISANELLO** (IRE) 39
451 **PISELLI MOLLI** (IRE) 17
466 **PISGAH PIKE** (IRE) 42
134 **PISTOL** (IRE) 5
441 **PISTOLETTO** (USA) 10
532 **PITEMPTON POWER** (IRE) 33
399 **PITNEY** (IRE) 93
414 **PITTSBURG** (IRE) 29
221 **PITTSFORD** (IRE) 30
506 **PIVOTAL DANCE** 109
231 **PIVOTAL REVIVE** 76
272 **PIVOTAL SKY** 20
231 **PIVOTAL TRIGGER** 77
154 **PIVOTTING** C 185
93 **PIXIE LOC** 14
384 **PIZ BADILE** (IRE) 3
469 **PJANOO** 37
446 **PLACATED** 1
20 **PLACEDELA CONCORDE** 18
5 **PLACIDIA** (IRE) F 211
194 **PLAISIR DES FLOS** (FR) 11
42 **PLANE TREE FAIRY** (IRE) F 68
376 **PLANET LEGEND** (IRE) 43
363 **PLANNED PARADISE** (IRE) 93
81 **PLANTATREE** 7
6 **PLASTIC PADDY** 63
402 **PLATENIUM** (FR) 74
154 **PLATINUM GIRL** 138
15 **PLATINUM JUBILEE** (IRE) 99
406 **PLATINUM PERFECT** 17
355 **PLATINUM PRINCE** 93
410 **PLATINUMCARD** (IRE) 70
240 **PLAY BY THE RULES** (IRE) 30
442 **PLAY MATE** C 83
228 **PLAYACTOR** 82
457 **PLAYFUL SAINT** (FR) 139
24 **PLAYFUL SOUND** F 134
43 **PLAYING TRIX** C 138
390 **PLAYTOGETAWAY** (IRE) 89
243 **PLAYUPSKYBLUES** (IRE) 32
379 **PLEASANT MAN** 127
35 **PLEASCACH** (IRE) C 80
279 **PLEASE SING** C 76
97 **PLEASETELLMEITTRUE** (IRE) G 7
369 **PLEASINGTON** (IRE) 93
30 **PLEASURE GARDEN** (USA) 16
153 **PLEASURE VAMPIRE** 67
276 **PLEDGE OF HONOUR** 10
354 **PLEDGE OF PEACE** (IRE) 13
416 **PLEDGEOFALLEGIANCE** (IRE) 25
520 **PLEIONE** (FR) F 32
267 **PLENTY OF TIME** (IRE) 15
88 **PLESENT JANE** 10
10 **PLOVER** F 43
320 **PLUMETTE** 17
164 **PLUS POINT** 30
383 **PLYING** (USA) F 175
468 **PLYM** G 11

347 **RAJMEISTER** 70
282 **RAKHINE STATE** (IRE) 33
251 **RAKIZA** (IRE) F 107
286 **RAKKI** 206
399 **RAKTINA** F 63
161 **RALEAGH FLORA** 21
165 **RAMBEAU** 44
437 **RAMBLING QUEEN** (IRE) F 10
437 **RAMBLING QUEEN** (IRE) C 14
178 **RAMBLING RIVER** 4
369 **RAMBO T** (IRE) 96
442 **RAMBUSO CREEK** (IRE) 17
243 **RAMDON ROCKS** 9
219 **RAMENSKY** 96
367 **RAMILLIES** (IRE) 121
161 **RAMIRO** (IRE) 22
543 **RAMO** (FR) 72
532 **RAMON DI LORIA** (IRE) 34
205 **RAMORE WILL** (IRE) 44
410 **RAMSES DE TEILLEE** (FR) 73
243 **RAMZ** (IRE) 34
221 **RANALLAGH ROCKET** (IRE) F 31
15 **RANCH HAND** 27
240 **RANCO** (IRE) 33
515 **RANDOM HARVEST** (IRE) 13
38 **RANGATIRA JACK** 5
489 **RANGE** (IRE) 38
56 **RANGER THUNDERBOLT** (IRE) 57
369 **RANGING BEAR** (IRE) 97
231 **RAPACITY ALEXANDER** (IRE) F 139
43 **RAPALLO** (IRE) 86
65 **RAPAPORT** 9
54 **RAPHEL JAKE** 9
352 **RAPID FLIGHT** 22
493 **RAPID FRITZ** (IRE) 5
440 **RAPID RAIDER** (IRE) 67
196 **RAPID RIVER** (IRE) 12
107 **RAPID TEST** 51
329 **RAPPEL** F 17
112 **RAQEEBB** (FR) 45
368 **RAQISA** 27
84 **RAQRAAQ** (USA) 14
331 **RARE BEAR** 10
152 **RARE CLOUDS** 11
319 **RARE EDITION** (IRE) 36
70 **RARE FIND** 37
386 **RARE GROOVE** (IRE) 21
379 **RARE MIDDLETON** 130
343 **RAREMENT** G 77
200 **RASCAL** 39
541 **RASPBERRY** 8
54 **RASPBERRY RIPPLE** F 13
249 **RATAFIA** 12
282 **RATFACEMCDOUGALL** (IRE) 34
136 **RATH AN IUIR** (IRE) 26
141 **RATH GAUL HILL** (IRE) 21
521 **RATHAATH** (IRE) C 85
199 **RATHAGAN** 1
249 **RATHBONE** 13
290 **RATHBRIDE RAVEN** F 30
457 **RATHENISKA** (IRE) G 147
85 **RATHGAR** 38
208 **RATHGEARAN** (IRE) 17
247 **RATHMACKNEE** (IRE) 113
190 **RATOUTE YUTTY** 5
386 **RATTLE OWL** 22
360 **RATTLER** 80
402 **RATTLIN** G 77
228 **RATTLING** 23
440 **RATTLING ROAD** (IRE) 68
221 **RAUZAN** (IRE) 32
192 **RAVANELLI** (IRE) 54
146 **RAVEN'S APPLAUSE** (IRE) 48
402 **RAVEN'S TOWER** (USA) 78
42 **RAVEN'S UP** (IRE) 37
360 **RAVENS ARK** 22
515 **RAVENSBOURNE** 92
300 **RAVENSCAR** (IRE) 46
279 **RAVENSCRAIG CASTLE** 43
505 **RAVI ROAD** (IRE) 14
298 **RAVIGILL** (FR) 139
221 **RAVSHAN** (IRE) 33
219 **RAWAAF** (IRE) C 175
14 **RAWYAAN** 27
286 **RAY OF COLOURS** (IRE) 110
62 **RAY THE HAY** 4
401 **RAY'S THE ONE** 5
59 **RAYA TIME** (FR) 13
228 **RAYAHEEN** C 184
35 **RAYAT** (IRE) 42
398 **RAYENA** (FR) 8
243 **RAYMI COYA** (CAN) C 47
119 **RAYMOND** (IRE) 34
298 **RAYMOND TUSK** (IRE) 97
272 **RAYS RABBLE** 18
219 **RAZEYNA** (IRE) 33
43 **RAZONI** (IRE) 87
506 **RAZZAM** (IRE) 111
227 **RAZZO ITALIANO** (IRE) 30
153 **REACH** (IRE) 35
206 **REACH FOR THE MOON** 28
367 **READIN TOMMY WRONG** (IRE) 122
404 **READY FREDDIE GO** (IRE) 7
157 **READY TO PLEASE** 33
72 **READY TO SHINE** (IRE) 27
440 **READY WHEN YOU ARE** (IRE) C 103
440 **READYSTEADYBEAU** (FR) 69
518 **REAL ARMANI** 5
479 **REAL DREAM** (IRE) 16
10 **REAL ESTATE** (IRE) 28
270 **REAL GAIN** (IRE) 36
320 **REAL QUIZ** 19
245 **REAL REWARDS** (IRE) 4
457 **REAL STONE** 148
501 **REAL TERMS** 25
448 **REAL TREASURE** F 30
35 **REAL WORLD** (IRE) 43
319 **REALISATION** (FR) 37
164 **REALISED** 31
456 **REALISM** (USA) C 82
217 **REALLY CHIC** (USA) F 28
43 **REALLY LOVELY** (IRE) C 145
5 **REALLY SPECIAL** F 216
543 **REALM OF GLORY** (IRE) 73
2 **REALMS OF FIRE** 8
363 **REALTA MO CROI** (IRE) F 97
309 **REALTA ROYALE** 14
282 **REAMS OF LOVE** 35
85 **REBECCA ROMERO** C 66
206 **REBECCA WEST** 121
343 **REBEL ACLAIM** C 103
308 **REBEL INTENTIONS** (IRE) 55
376 **REBEL LEADER** (IRE) 47
212 **REBEL MC** 64
135 **REBEL REDEMPTION** 49
83 **REBEL ROYAL** (IRE) 21
406 **REBEL TERRITORY** 6
5 **REBEL'S ROMANCE** (IRE) 33
416 **RECALL** 53
286 **RECAMBE** (IRE) C 207
14 **RECHERCHER** 28
367 **RECITE A PRAYER** (IRE) 123
355 **RECKON I'M HOT** 99
161 **RECLAIM VICTORY** (IRE) 23
80 **RECON MISSION** (IRE) 76
385 **RECORD ART** (FR) 160
465 **RECORD HIGH** (IRE) 7
192 **RECORWOMAN** (FR) 30
139 **RECUERDAME** (USA) 11
80 **RED ALERT** 77
544 **RED ALLURE** 11
374 **RED AMAPOLA** 21
154 **RED ASTAIRE** 75
286 **RED BIRD** (IRE) 111
395 **RED BLANCHE** (IRE) C 41
454 **RED BOND** (IRE) 32
548 **RED BRAVO** (IRE) 19
216 **RED BUCCANEER** 10
383 **RED CARPET** (IRE) 73
165 **RED CHATAN** 45
355 **RED CLOUD** (IRE) 153
510 **RED COMMAND** (IRE) 9
494 **RED CON ONE** (IRE) F 50
506 **RED DANIELLE** 112
372 **RED DELTA** 3
544 **RED DEREK** 12
390 **RED DIRT ROAD** (IRE) 96
112 **RED DUNE** (IRE) F 97
403 **RED EVELYN** 10
383 **RED EVIE** (IRE) F 179
30 **RED FLYER** (IRE) 17
300 **RED FORCE ONE** 47
212 **RED FORT** (FR) 83
396 **RED HANRAHAN** (IRE) 5
410 **RED HAPPY** (FR) 74
303 **RED HAT EAGLE** 25
58 **RED HIBISCUS** F 16
72 **RED HOW** 28
472 **RED INTRIGUE** C 39
430 **RED MAIDS** 8
440 **RED MISSILE** (IRE) 70
208 **RED OCHRE** 18
479 **RED RAMBLER** 17
208 **RED REMINDER** 19
383 **RED RIDING HOOD** (IRE) 74
548 **RED RIPPLE** 20
379 **RED RISK** (FR) 131
385 **RED RIVER VALLEY** (IRE) 161
482 **RED ROLY** 4
154 **RED ROMANCE** C 186
83 **RED ROMEO** 22
308 **RED ROOKIE** 56
118 **RED ROSETTA** 9
157 **RED ROYALIST** 34
544 **RED STRIPES** (USA) 13
146 **RED TREASURE** (IRE) 49
154 **RED TULIP** F 187
361 **RED VINEYARD** (IRE) 9
335 **RED VISION** (FR) 107
544 **RED WALLS** 14
205 **RED WINDSOR** (IRE) 45

445 **REDARNA** 18
292 **REDBRIDGE RAMBLER** (IRE) 35
271 **REDBRIDGE ROSIE** (IRE) 12
107 **REDCLIFF GLEN** (GER) 52
367 **REDEMPTION DAY** 124
107 **REDEMPTION TIME** 53
58 **REDESDALE REBEL** 11
444 **REDREDROBIN** 7
293 **REDROSEZORRO** 8
459 **REDZONE** 9
189 **REE OKKA** 51
407 **REECELTIC** 13
165 **REEH** (IRE) C 46
441 **REEL OF FORTUNE** (IRE) 11
337 **REEL POWER** 4
387 **REEL PROSPECT** (IRE) 40
31 **REEL ROSIE** (IRE) 7
442 **REEM THREE** F 84
149 **REFLECT** 11
5 **REFLECTIVE STAR** 101
175 **REFLEX** (IRE) 35
408 **REFLEXION FAITE** (FR) 79
153 **REFUGE** 36
321 **REFUSE COLETTE** (IRE) F 55
140 **REGAL 'N BOLD** 14
148 **REGAL BANNER** F 20
390 **REGAL BLUE** (IRE) 97
484 **REGAL EMPIRE** (IRE) 27
263 **REGAL ENCORE** (IRE) 55
303 **REGAL ENVOY** (IRE) 9
479 **REGAL FANFARE** 47
354 **REGAL GLORY** (IRE) 18
5 **REGAL HONOUR** (IRE) 102
63 **REGAL MAYA** G 7
243 **REGAL RAMBLER** (IRE) 10
479 **REGAL REALITY** 18
83 **REGALLY BLONDE** 23
466 **REGARDE** (IRE) 44
509 **REGARDING RUTH** (IRE) 28
56 **REGATTA QUEEN** 32
262 **REGENCY BOY** 21
379 **REGENT'S STROLL** (IRE) 132
335 **REGGAE DE BAUNE** (FR) 108
459 **REGINALD CHARLES** 18
221 **REGINALDS TOWER** (IRE) 11
31 **REGIONAL** 8
231 **REHEARSAL** (IRE) 140
167 **REIGN SUEPREME** (IRE) 14
78 **REIGNING PROFIT** (IRE) 23
396 **REIGNITE** 6
457 **REILLY** (IRE) 149
515 **REINA DEL MAR** (IRE) 14
355 **REINATOR** (FR) 100
43 **REINE DES COEURS** (IRE) 146
63 **REINE FEE** (IRE) 8
186 **REJOYCEFILLY** 12
24 **REKINDLE** F 138
484 **REKINDLE** F 28
357 **RELEASE THE KRAKEN** (IRE) 32
119 **RELENTLESS SUN** 35
15 **RELENTLESS VOYAGER** 104
15 **RELENTLESS WARRIOR** (IRE) 195
280 **RELEVANT** (IRE) C 26
219 **RELIEF RALLY** (IRE) 176
154 **RELKADAM** (FR) 76
243 **REMARKABLE FORCE** (IRE) 35
24 **REMARQUEE** 72
410 **REMASTERED** 75
316 **REMEDIUM** 12
313 **REMEMBER ALLY** (FR) 7
438 **REMEMBER FOREVER** (IRE) 18
15 **REMINDER** 105
225 **RENADA** G 7
480 **RENARDEAU** 8
157 **RENDITION** (IRE) 35
363 **RENEGADE ARROW** (FR) 98
408 **RENESMEE** 49
538 **RENOIR** 56
80 **REPARTEE** (IRE) 78
456 **REPERTOIRE** 20
384 **REPORT** (IRE) 20
466 **REPRESENTING BOB** (IRE) 45
454 **REPUBLICAN** 33
78 **REPUTATION** (IRE) 24
484 **REROUTE** (IRE) F 29
484 **REROUTE** (IRE) C 77
47 **RESERVE TANK** (IRE) 29
59 **RESET BUTTON** 14
359 **RESHOUN** (FR) 10
315 **RESILIENCE** 6
343 **RESILIENT FRONT** (IRE) 44
506 **RESOLUTE MAN** 113
42 **RESONANCE** (IRE) 38
111 **RESPECTABLE** C 13
369 **RESPLENDENT GREY** (IRE) 98
287 **REST AND BE** (IRE) F 15
287 **REST AND BE** (IRE) F 17
347 **RESTANDBETHANKFUL** 71
298 **RESTITUTION** (FR) 98
538 **RESTORER** 57
456 **RESTRICT** (USA) 55
85 **RETETI** 39
532 **RETICENT** 35
405 **RETIREMENT BECKONS** 16
219 **RETRACEMENT** (IRE) 177
266 **RETRACTION** (IRE) 21
195 **RETROUVAILLES** 5
440 **RETURN FIRE** (IRE) 71
347 **RETURN TICKET** (IRE) 72
35 **RETURN TO DUBAI** (IRE) 44
94 **REUILLY** (IRE) 51
509 **REVASSER** (IRE) 29
292 **REVE** 36
279 **REVE DE NIAMH** 44
24 **REVEAL** 139
189 **REVELS HILL** (IRE) 52
506 **REVENITE** 114
285 **REVENUE** (IRE) 71
517 **REVERSION** (IRE) 8
469 **REVICH** (IRE) 12
442 **REVISION** 54
228 **REVISIT** 88
400 **REVOLUCION** 26
56 **REVOLUTIONARY MAN** (IRE) 33
542 **REVOLUTIONISE** (IRE) 14
154 **REVOQUABLE** 77
106 **REWILDING** 26
376 **REWIRED** 48
139 **REY DE LA BATALLA** 21
286 **REYAADAH** F 208
459 **RHAL** (IRE) F 28
156 **RHEA OF THE YEAR** 10
454 **RHEBUS ROAD** (IRE) 34
219 **RHETORICAL** 178
483 **RHIAN DE SIVOLA** 25
261 **RHODIA** (IRE) 17
387 **RHOSCOLYN** 41
418 **RHUBARB** 8
10 **RHUBARB BIKINI** (IRE) 29
547 **RHYME SCHEME** (IRE) 6
78 **RHYTHM** (IRE) 25
54 **RHYTHM DANCER** 14
266 **RHYTHM MASTER** (IRE) 4
521 **RHYTHM N HOOVES** 86
70 **RHYTHM N ROCK** (IRE) 38
334 **RHYTHMIC ACCLAIM** (IRE) 9
542 **RHYTHMIC INTENT** (IRE) 15
15 **RIBAL** 106
154 **RIBBLE ROUSER** (IRE) 140
9 **RIBEYE** 5
154 **RIBKANA** (IRE) 141
206 **RIBLA** (IRE) 122
139 **RICARDO OFWORTHING** (IRE) 20
75 **RICARDO PHILLIPS** 33
221 **RICCARDI MEDIDI** (IRE) 12
413 **RICCOCHE** (IRE) C 47
228 **RICH** 89
31 **RICH GLORY** (IRE) 56
24 **RICH RHYTHM** 11
464 **RICH SPIRIT** 46
501 **RICH WATERS** (IRE) 26
146 **RICHARD P SMITH** (IRE) 13
6 **RICHARD R H B** (IRE) 68
216 **RICHARDSON** 11
457 **RICHHILL** (IRE) 150
5 **RICHMOND AVENUE** (IRE) F 217
442 **RICHMOND COUNTY** (IRE) 85
335 **RICHMOND LAKE** (IRE) 109
324 **RICK BLAINE** (IRE) 11
428 **RICKETY GATE** 37
256 **RIDERS ONTHE STORM** (IRE) 13
107 **RIDGE RANGER** (IRE) F 90
457 **RIDGEWAY** (FR) 151
174 **RIEVAULX RAVER** (IRE) 40
461 **RIFFA FORT** 8
163 **RIGGSBY** (IRE) 11
5 **RIGHT DIRECTION** (IRE) F 218
516 **RIGHT ROYALS DAY** 9
464 **RIGHT SAID TED** (IRE) 47
479 **RIGHTEOUS** 48
220 **RIGHTOFWAY** 39
69 **RIHAAM** (IRE) F 44
408 **RIKONA** 19
14 **RILEY'S AYADA** 29
14 **RILEY'S POSITANO** (IRE) 30
85 **RINARIA** (IRE) G 67
15 **RING FENCED** 28
154 **RING OF BEARA** (FR) 78
153 **RING OF GOLD** 37
75 **RING OF LIGHT** 8
101 **RING PRETENDER** (FR) 26
5 **RING THE BELL** (IRE) C 219
537 **RING THE MOON** 57
507 **RINGOCANRUN** 50
506 **RIO FESTIVAL** (USA) C 180
369 **RIO SILVA** 99
387 **RIOT** (IRE) 42
342 **RIOTICISM** (FR) C 42
369 **RIPPER ROO** (FR) 100
393 **RISE HALL** 2
503 **RISHES BAAR** (IRE) 8

495 **ROSE ABOVE IT** (IRE) 9
279 **ROSE BANDIT** (IRE) 45
150 **ROSE BERRY** C 12
280 **ROSE CAMIRA** 8
526 **ROSE CROWN** F 47
305 **ROSE DIAMOND** (IRE) C 51
399 **ROSE DONNELLY** 64
173 **ROSE FANDANGO** 8
379 **ROSE INDIENNE** (FR) G 133
548 **ROSE KAR** (FR) 22
135 **ROSE KING** (IRE) 73
413 **ROSE LIGHT** 10
480 **ROSE OF AFRICA** (IRE) G 18
497 **ROSE OF ARCADIA** (IRE) 64
428 **ROSE OF SIENA** (IRE) 38
515 **ROSE PRICK** (IRE) 48
321 **ROSE RANSOM** (IRE) C 56
112 **ROSE SAPPHIRE** (USA) C 98
376 **ROSE SEA HAS** (FR) 49
520 **ROSEALEE** (IRE) C 33
43 **ROSEBRIDE** C 147
135 **ROSEHILL** (IRE) 50
501 **ROSEHILL ARTIST** (IRE) G 56
286 **ROSENZOO** (IRE) 209
221 **ROSERAIE** C 44
153 **ROSES FOR GRACE** (FR) G 90
94 **ROSETTA STONE** (FR) 9
286 **ROSETTE** 112
343 **ROSGALME** (IRE) 46
72 **ROSHAMBO** 30
409 **ROSSBEIGH STRAND** (IRE) 19
450 **ROSSEA** (IRE) 33
323 **ROSSERK ABBEY** (IRE) 10
6 **ROSSMORE NATION** (IRE) 93
376 **ROSTELLO** (FR) 50
42 **ROSY KISS** 70
231 **ROSY MORNING** (IRE) C 142
234 **ROSY REDRUM** (IRE) 65
112 **ROTATIONAL** 46
399 **ROUDEMENTAL** (IRE) 17
479 **ROUEN** 49
116 **ROUGE DE L'QUEST** (IRE) 19
454 **ROUGE ET BLANC** (FR) 35
219 **ROUGE NOIR** F 179
421 **ROUGE ROMANCE** (IRE) 15
416 **ROUGE SELLIER** 55
534 **ROUGE VIF** (FR) 16
220 **ROUGH NIGHT** (IRE) 40
533 **ROUND THE ISLAND** 10
139 **ROUNDABOUT SILVER** 13
496 **ROUNDHAY PARK** 15
228 **ROUSAY** (IRE) 24
347 **ROUSE** (IRE) 75
442 **ROWAN BRAE** F 87
69 **ROWAYEH** (IRE) 19
507 **ROWDY EXIT** (IRE) G 37
440 **ROWDY RUSTLER** (IRE) 72
239 **ROXBORO ROAD** (IRE) 26
154 **ROXELANA** (IRE) C 189
366 **ROXHILL** (IRE) 30
249 **ROXY'S CHARM** 20
226 **ROXYFET** (FR) 67
484 **ROYAL ACLAIM** (IRE) 5
125 **ROYAL ACT** 23
80 **ROYAL AGENT** 112
520 **ROYAL ATHENA** 19
369 **ROYAL BASSETT** (FR) 102
368 **ROYAL BLISS** (IRE) 43
360 **ROYAL CAPE** (IRE) 58
506 **ROYAL CHAMPION** (IRE) 34
219 **ROYAL CHARTER** 98
463 **ROYAL COUNTESS** 27
374 **ROYAL CREEK** (IRE) 22
257 **ROYAL DEBUT** (IRE) 9
298 **ROYAL DEESIDE** 140
410 **ROYAL DEFENDER** (IRE) 76
219 **ROYAL DESIGN** 99
146 **ROYAL DREAM** 50
228 **ROYAL DRESS** (IRE) 91
106 **ROYAL ELOQUENCE** (IRE) C 34
172 **ROYAL EMPRESS** (IRE) F 61
523 **ROYAL FLUSH** 6
56 **ROYAL GRACE** G 59
15 **ROYAL JET** 108
454 **ROYAL LAKE** (IRE) 36
522 **ROYAL LEGEND** 5
489 **ROYAL MAGIC** (IRE) 40
247 **ROYAL MAX** (FR) 115
410 **ROYAL MER** (FR) 77
219 **ROYAL MILA** 100
335 **ROYAL MOGUL** (IRE) 111
262 **ROYAL MUSKETEER** 12
286 **ROYAL OBSERVATORY** 113
408 **ROYAL ORDER** (USA) F 80
387 **ROYAL PARADE** (IRE) 43
212 **ROYAL PLEASURE** (IRE) 66
385 **ROYAL PRACTITIONER** 163
298 **ROYAL PRETENDER** (FR) 101
364 **ROYAL PROSPECT** (IRE) 4
175 **ROYAL RAZZMATAZZ** (IRE) 36
463 **ROYAL REGENT** 28
367 **ROYAL RENDEZVOUS** (IRE) 125
66 **ROYAL RHYME** (IRE) 78
343 **ROYAL ROMEO** (IRE) 47
442 **ROYAL ROSE** (IRE) C 88
94 **ROYAL ROSI** (GER) 52
234 **ROYAL SAM** 66
172 **ROYAL SCANDAL** 9
98 **ROYAL SCOTSMAN** (IRE) 20
5 **ROYAL SYMBOL** (IRE) 34
157 **ROYAL THUNDER** 36
303 **ROYAL VELVET** 36
15 **ROYAL WOOTTON** 109
457 **ROYALE DANCE** (FR) 157
483 **ROYALE MARGAUX** (FR) 26
543 **ROYALE PAGAILLE** (FR) 76
355 **ROYAUME UNI** (IRE) 103
88 **ROYAUMONT** (FR) 13
226 **ROYLE STEEL** (FR) 68
387 **ROYS DREAM** C 125
379 **RUBAUD** (FR) 134
219 **RUBELLITE** (IRE) 101
123 **RUBENESQUE** (IRE) 9
42 **RUBINA ROSE** 39
61 **RUBIS** F 21
192 **RUBY ARABELLA** 32
444 **RUBY COTTAGE** (IRE) 8
513 **RUBY ISLAND** 49
115 **RUBY RED EMPRESS** (IRE) 16
427 **RUBY RICHARDS** 9
383 **RUBY TUESDAY** (IRE) C 180
222 **RUBY'S COMET** 8
36 **RUBY'S PEARL** 8
222 **RUBYS REWARD** 9
10 **RUDIES IN COURT** 44
154 **RUE GALILEE** (IRE) 80
24 **RUE RENAN** (IRE) C 140
379 **RUE ST DENIS** (IRE) 135
72 **RUGGLES** 31
424 **RUINOUS** (IRE) 3
356 **RUITH LE TU** 6
251 **RUKAANA** 108
346 **RULE OF THUMB** (FR) 31
208 **RULEOUT** (IRE) 20
390 **RULER LEGEND** (IRE) 100
5 **RULING DYNASTY** 35
515 **RUM COCKTAIL** 15
202 **RUM COVE** 30
229 **RUM RUNNER** 5
535 **RUMAILAH** (USA) 4
307 **RUMBLE B** (IRE) 7
24 **RUMBLE DOLL** (USA) F 141
349 **RUMNOTRED** 13
458 **RUMOURSAREFLYING** 16
413 **RUMSTAR** 32
240 **RUN AT DAWN** (IRE) 34
469 **RUN BOY RUN** 47
501 **RUN CMC** (IRE) 57
454 **RUN LIKE THE WIND** (IRE) G 37
175 **RUN OF THE DAY** F 62
472 **RUN RAN RUN** (IRE) 24
153 **RUN RESDEV RUN** 38
66 **RUN TEDDY RUN** (FR) 25
348 **RUN THIS WAY** 31
75 **RUN TO FREEDOM** 9
122 **RUN TO MILAN** (IRE) 17
349 **RUNAROUND SIOUX** 38
47 **RUNASIMI RIVER** 31
130 **RUNNER BEAN** 9
206 **RUNNING LION** 124
399 **RUNNING STAR** 65
143 **RUNNINWILD** 11
308 **RUNSWICK BAY** 60
305 **RUNWAY GIANT** (USA) C 52
343 **RUPA** C 104
173 **RUSHEEN BOY** 25
17 **RUSHMORE** 14
96 **RUSKIN RED** (IRE) 7
501 **RUSOOKH** G 58
506 **RUSSET GOLD** 115
219 **RUSSIAN CRESCENDO** 180
247 **RUSSIAN RULER** (IRE) 116
413 **RUSSIAN RUMOUR** (IRE) 11
141 **RUSSIAN SERVICE** 22
347 **RUSSIAN VIRTUE** 76
140 **RUSSIE WITH LOVE** F 15
140 **RUSSIES DREAM** 16
361 **RUSTAM** F 40
116 **RUTHLESS ARTICLE** (IRE) 20
79 **RWENEARLYTHEREDAD** 25
385 **RYAN'S ROCKET** (IRE) 164
497 **RYDER'S ROCK** 65
37 **RYEDALE RACER** 5
221 **RYHTHM AND TYNE** 34
404 **RYOTO** (IRE) 32
295 **SAABOOG** F 16
378 **SAAHEQ** 5
112 **SAAMYAA** 47
80 **SABAARELLI** 80
537 **SABBATHICAL** (FR) 58
153 **SABREWING** (IRE) G 91

379 **SABRINA** (IRE) 136
527 **SABYINYO** 15
506 **SACRE CAROLINE** (USA) C 181
390 **SACRE COEUR** (FR) 101
335 **SACRE PIERRE** (FR) 112
219 **SACRED** 35
286 **SACRED ANGEL** (IRE) 210
5 **SACRED FLOWER** 103
72 **SACRED JEWEL** 32
222 **SADDLERS QUEST** 10
423 **SADIE HILL** (IRE) 35
213 **SADLER'S BAY** 17
349 **SAFARI DREAM** (IRE) 26
247 **SAFARI RUN** (IRE) F 117
504 **SAFE DESTINATION** 57
515 **SAFE HOUSE** (IRE) C 49
66 **SAFEENAH** C 147
219 **SAFETY CATCH** 102
532 **SAFRAN** (FR) 36
206 **SAGA** 29
456 **SAGAMI BAY** (IRE) 56
355 **SAGANO** (IRE) 104
376 **SAGE ADVICE** (IRE) 51
211 **SAGEBURG COUNTY** (IRE) 33
281 **SAGONIGE** 12
5 **SAHARA MIST** 104
286 **SAHARA SKY** (IRE) C 211
5 **SAHRAWI** (GER) C 222
371 **SAIGON** 9
85 **SAIGON DREAM** 68
204 **SAIKUNG** (IRE) C 49
457 **SAIL AWAY** (FR) 158
26 **SAIL ON SILVERBIRD** (USA) 44
147 **SAILED AWAY** (GER) 33
263 **SAILING GRACE** 56
285 **SAILING ON** 39
20 **SAINT ARVANS** (FR) 19
12 **SAINT BIBIANA** (IRE) 53
379 **SAINT CALVADOS** (FR) 137
539 **SAINT CYR DE PAIL** (FR) 30
390 **SAINT DAVY** (FR) 102
15 **SAINT GEORGE** 110
298 **SAINT GOUSTAN** (FR) G 102
385 **SAINT JAGUEN** (FR) 165
506 **SAINT LAWRENCE** (IRE) 35
16 **SAINT PALAIS** (FR) 25
538 **SAINT RIQUIER** (FR) 61
367 **SAINT ROI** (FR) 126
367 **SAINT SAM** (FR) 127
539 **SAINT SEGAL** (FR) 31
256 **SAINT XAVIER** (FR) 14
75 **SAINTE COLETTE** 10
363 **SAINTE DOCTOR** (FR) 100
187 **SAINTEMILION** (FR) 11
386 **SAISONS D'OR** (IRE) 23
10 **SAJWAAN** (IRE) 40
506 **SAKHEER** (IRE) 116
346 **SAKURA STAR** 32
369 **SALADAM** (FR) 103
205 **SALADINS SON** (IRE) 46
41 **SALAMALEK** (FR) 21
172 **SALAMANCA CITY** (IRE) 62
346 **SALAMANCAN** (FR) 33
228 **SALCOMBE STORM** 25
367 **SALDIER** (FR) 128
154 **SALEET** 142
355 **SALIGO BAY** (IRE) 105
369 **SALLEY GARDENS** (IRE) 104
533 **SALLY ANNE'S DREAM** 19
460 **SALLY'S GIRL** 6
202 **SALLYANN** (IRE) 31
231 **SALOME** (FR) F 143
228 **SALOMON PICO** (FR) 92
161 **SALSADA** (IRE) 24
24 **SALT BAY** (GER) 75
383 **SALT LAKE CITY** (IRE) 75
12 **SALT ROCK** 54
361 **SALT TREATY** (IRE) 10
122 **SALTA RESTA** 18
442 **SALTWATER** C 89
348 **SALUTI** (IRE) 32
132 **SALVATORE** (GER) 17
85 **SALVE ETOILES** (IRE) C 69
470 **SALVE JAPAN** 7
494 **SALVINO** (IRE) 39
308 **SAM BARTON** 61
263 **SAM BROWN** 57
24 **SAM COOKE** (IRE) 13
121 **SAM HAZE** 3
266 **SAM MAXIMUS** 5
161 **SAM'S ADVENTURE** 25
67 **SAM'S AMOUR** 22
153 **SAM'S CALL** 39
228 **SAM'S HOPE** 93
147 **SAM'S THE MAN** 34
399 **SAMAGON** 66
413 **SAMANTHA** C 49
135 **SAMARA STAR** 51
379 **SAMARRIVE** (FR) 138
176 **SAMASANA** (IRE) F 60
12 **SAMATIAN** (IRE) 55
402 **SAMAZUL** 80
320 **SAMBA LADY** (IRE) 39
208 **SAMBEL BAY** 21
455 **SAMBEZI** (FR) 21
515 **SAMBUCUS** 94
442 **SAMDANIYA** C 90
15 **SAME JURISDICTION** (SAF) F 111
221 **SAMEASITEVERWAS** (IRE) 13
154 **SAMEEM** (IRE) 81
205 **SAMI BEAR** 47
554 **SAMMARA** F 12
216 **SAMMIX** 12
421 **SAMMY SUNSHINE** (GER) 16
385 **SAMMYLOU** (IRE) 166
509 **SAMOURAI ONE** (FR) 30
6 **SAMPERS SEVEN** (IRE) 69
358 **SAMS PROFILE** 17
445 **SAMS ROSEABELLE** 19
292 **SAMTARA** 39
351 **SAMUEL JACKSON** 5
402 **SAMUEL SPADE** (GER) 81
449 **SAMURAI SNEDDZ** 22
102 **SAMWISE** (IRE) 20
383 **SAN ANTONIO** (IRE) 76
369 **SAN FERMIN** (IRE) 105
75 **SAN FRANCISCO BAY** (IRE) 11
189 **SAN GIOVANNI** (IRE) 54
176 **SAN ISIDRO** (IRE) 10
321 **SAN JUAN** (IRE) 32
101 **SAN MIGUEL** (IRE) 27
248 **SAN PEDRO** (IRE) 15
355 **SAN PEDRO DE SENAM** (FR) 106
506 **SANAT** (IRE) 182
219 **SANCTION** 103
284 **SAND TIMER** 21
5 **SAND VIXEN** F 223
402 **SANDA RENA** (IRE) 82
379 **SANDALWOOD** (FR) 139
31 **SANDBECK** 9
12 **SANDMARTIN** 56
239 **SANDRET** (IRE) 27
15 **SANDRINE** 30
472 **SANDTAIL** F 40
254 **SANDY BOY** (IRE) 57
205 **SANDY BROOK** (IRE) 48
270 **SANDY PARADISE** (IRE) 14
56 **SANGUIS DIAMOND** (IRE) 60
521 **SANITISER** 34
42 **SANIYAAT** F 71
320 **SANKS A MILLION** (IRE) 40
1 **SANOSUKE** (IRE) 40
299 **SANS CHOIX** (IRE) 26
187 **SANS OF GOLD** (IRE) 12
483 **SANTA CLARITA** (FR) 27
153 **SANTAFIORA** F 92
30 **SANTIBURI SPIRIT** 18
544 **SANTINHO** (IRE) 15
457 **SANTOS BLUE** 159
347 **SAO** (FR) 77
369 **SAO CARLOS** 106
475 **SAO TIMOTHY** (IRE) 19
35 **SAOIRSE ABU** (USA) F 82
35 **SAOIRSE ABU** (USA) C 101
89 **SAPIENCE** 53
118 **SAPPERDEAN** 6
5 **SAPPHIRE SEAS** 105
80 **SAPPHIRE'S MOON** 81
228 **SAR OICHE** (IRE) C 187
399 **SARACEN HEAD** 67
235 **SARAH'S VERSE** 7
83 **SARAHS QUAY** (IRE) F 24
165 **SARAJEVO BOY** (IRE) 47
444 **SARANGOO** G 10
251 **SARATOGA GOLD** 14
194 **SARATOGA LASS** (IRE) 13
251 **SARATOGA SPIRIT** 58
251 **SARATOGA STAR** 109
147 **SARCEAUX** (FR) 35
41 **SARIMARES** (FR) 22
451 **SARINDA** F 33
207 **SARISTA** (IRE) G 21
146 **SARKHA** (IRE) 15
369 **SAROUSHKA** (FR) G 107
456 **SARSHAMPLA** (IRE) F 83
59 **SARSONS RISK** (IRE) 15
177 **SASHENKA** (GER) 13
254 **SASSIFIED** (IRE) 58
239 **SASSOON** 28
538 **SASSY BABE** 89
515 **SASSY BELLE** (IRE) 50
496 **SASSY GAL** (IRE) F 62
234 **SASSY MISS MARGOT** 67
477 **SASSY REDHEAD** 15
267 **SATANIC MOON** 19
548 **SATELLITE CALL** (IRE) 23
231 **SATIN** 83
290 **SATIN SNAKE** 13
477 **SATIN WATERS** C 10
164 **SATIRE** 52
206 **SATIRICAL** 125

521 **SHARVARA** 35
223 **SHAUGHNESSY** 7
135 **SHAW PARK** (IRE) 55
248 **SHAW'S CROSS** (IRE) 16
442 **SHAWHILL** C 91
226 **SHAWS BRIDGE** (IRE) 71
349 **SHAWS PHOENIX** (IRE) 39
348 **SHAYA** (IRE) C 54
408 **SHAZAM** (IRE) 52
292 **SHE HAS NOTIONS** (IRE) 40
362 **SHE IS WHAT SHE IS** 4
369 **SHE'S A FINE WINE** (IRE) 109
371 **SHE'S A GEM** 10
14 **SHE'S A LADY** 33
165 **SHE'S A MIRAGE** 32
385 **SHE'S A NOVELTY** (IRE) 173
428 **SHE'S A ROCCA** (IRE) 41
503 **SHE'S A ROCKET** 16
457 **SHE'S A SAINT** (IRE) 163
343 **SHE'S A STAR** G 78
136 **SHE'S A STEAL** (IRE) 30
459 **SHE'S A WORLDIE** (IRE) C 29
212 **SHE'S ALL IN GOLD** (IRE) 67
243 **SHE'S CENTIMENTAL** (USA) 36
231 **SHE'S COMPLETE** (IRE) C 147
174 **SHE'S GOT BOTTLE** 25
98 **SHE'S HOT** 21
30 **SHE'S HUMBLE** (IRE) G 19
343 **SHE'S LOCAL** (IRE) 79
43 **SHE'S MINE** (IRE) F 150
317 **SHE'S MY SHADOW** (IRE) 15
66 **SHE'S NO ANGEL** (IRE) 27
294 **SHE'S OUT OF REACH** 5
104 **SHE'S OUT OF REACH** 16
457 **SHE'S SO LOVELY** (IRE) 164
470 **SHE'S SO PRETTY** (IRE) C 10
49 **SHE'S THE DANGER** (IRE) 10
379 **SHEARER** (IRE) 144
85 **SHEBA FIVE** (USA) F 70
222 **SHEE'S A STELLA** 11
233 **SHEEKA SUPREME** (IRE) 14
285 **SHEER ROCKS** 14
21 **SHEHADTORUN** F 11
79 **SHEIKH MAZ MAHOOD** (IRE) 10
228 **SHEILA'S PARADISE** 190
343 **SHEISBYBRID** (IRE) 48
366 **SHELDON** (IRE) 32
385 **SHELIKESTHELIGHTS** (IRE) 174
387 **SHELIR** (IRE) 46
234 **SHEMRIYNA** (IRE) F 86
231 **SHENANIGANS** (IRE) F 148
484 **SHEPHERDIA** (IRE) F 31
384 **SHERANDA** (IRE) F 64
456 **SHERBET FOUNTAIN** (USA) 58
497 **SHERBORNE** (IRE) 69
348 **SHERDIL** (IRE) 33
283 **SHERELLA** 20
154 **SHERIFF GARRETT** (IRE) 83
383 **SHERMEEN** (IRE) C 182
407 **SHERPA TRAIL** (USA) 14
91 **SHES MY GIRL** 12
368 **SHES QUEEN** (IRE) F 69
365 **SHESADABBER** 10
44 **SHESASUPERSTAR** (IRE) 15
414 **SHESUPINCOURT** 32
376 **SHETLAND BUS** (GER) 56
367 **SHEWEARSITWELL** (IRE) 133
26 **SHIBA** (FR) C 71
409 **SHIBUYA SONG** 21
42 **SHIELD WALL** (IRE) 74
478 **SHIFTER** 4
226 **SHIGHNESS** 72
211 **SHILLANAVOGY** (IRE) 34
506 **SHIMAH** (USA) C 186
24 **SHIMMERING LIGHT** F 146
164 **SHIMMERING MOON** (IRE) 54
153 **SHIMMERING SANDS** 40
456 **SHIN FALLS** 85
66 **SHINE HONEY SHINE** 80
204 **SHINE ON BRENDAN** (IRE) 32
174 **SHINE'S AMBITION** (IRE) 42
35 **SHINING BLUE** (IRE) 46
35 **SHINING EXAMPLE** (IRE) 47
5 **SHINING JEWEL** 106
292 **SHINJI** (IRE) 41
84 **SHIP TO SHORE** 15
16 **SHIPTON MOYNE** 26
279 **SHIR I DONT KNOW** (IRE) 46
552 **SHIRIN JAAN** F 45
377 **SHIROCCO'S DELIGHT** (IRE) 3
497 **SHIROCCO'S DREAM** (IRE) 70
194 **SHIROCCOSMAGICGEM** (IRE) 14
247 **SHISHKIN** (IRE) 122
206 **SHIVA SHAKTI** (IRE) 129
157 **SHIYRVANN** (FR) 38
251 **SHOBIZ** 16
5 **SHOBOBB** F 225
360 **SHOCKWAVES** 28
531 **SHOESHINE BOY** (IRE) 22
251 **SHOGUN'S KATANA** 60
466 **SHOLOKHOV COCKTAIL** 51
457 **SHOLOKJACK** (IRE) 165
489 **SHOMEN UCHI** (FR) 41
231 **SHONA MEA** (IRE) 28
506 **SHOOLAA** 119
42 **SHOOT** (FR) C 75
56 **SHOOT TO KILL** (IRE) 35
15 **SHORT CALL** (IRE) C 198
528 **SHORT HEAD** (GER) 14
264 **SHORTCROSS STORM** (IRE) 11
506 **SHORTMILE LADY** (IRE) C 187
336 **SHORTS ON** 19
228 **SHOSHONI WIND** C 191
520 **SHOT** 22
410 **SHOT BOII** (IRE) 79
6 **SHOT OF LOVE** 95
78 **SHOTLEY ROYALE** 38
207 **SHOUGHALL'S BOY** (IRE) 15
228 **SHOULDVEBEENARING** 95
228 **SHOW BIZ KID** (IRE) 192
138 **SHOW COMPASSION** 32
5 **SHOW DAY** (IRE) C 226
26 **SHOW ME A HERO** (IRE) 72
289 **SHOW ME A SUNSET** 13
289 **SHOW ME THE WIRE** 31
217 **SHOW OF HANDS** 15
452 **SHOW ON THE ROAD** 7
154 **SHOWALONG** 84
56 **SHOWDIEMLAD** (IRE) 36
107 **SHOWGIRL** 56
14 **SHOWLAN SPIRIT** 34
279 **SHOWMEDEMONEY** (IRE) 47
270 **SHOWTANK** F 64
501 **SHOWTIME MAHOMES** 27
413 **SHOWY** 33
431 **SHROPSHIRE** 9
268 **SHROPSHIRELASS** F 8
363 **SHUIL CEOIL** (IRE) 102
525 **SHUIL GEALACH** (IRE) F 28
285 **SHURFAH** (IRE) F 72
205 **SHUT THE BOX** (IRE) 50
468 **SHUTTHEGATE** (IRE) 8
514 **SHUTUPSHIRLEY** 19
330 **SHY NALA** 22
148 **SHYJACK** 12
413 **SI SI LA BONNE** (IRE) 50
188 **SIAM FOX** (IRE) 23
5 **SIAMSAIOCHT** (IRE) C 227
343 **SIBERIAN PRINCE** (IRE) 49
94 **SIBYLA** F 53
6 **SICARIO** (IRE) 72
88 **SICILIA** (FR) 14
505 **SID'S ANNIE** 15
410 **SIDI ISMAEL** (FR) 80
496 **SIDNEY GIRL** C 63
496 **SIDNEY'S SON** (IRE) 40
509 **SIENNA BREEZE** (IRE) 32
342 **SIERRA BLANCA** (IRE) 12
231 **SIERRA NEVADA** (USA) 29
146 **SIERRA VISTA** (IRE) 51
467 **SIGHT NOR SEEN** (IRE) 10
228 **SIGHTER** 193
537 **SIGN OF WAR** (IRE) 62
147 **SIGNAL TWENTY NINE** 37
395 **SIGNATURE BLUE** (IRE) 60
228 **SIGNCASTLE CITY** (IRE) 96
72 **SIGNIFICANTLY** 35
368 **SIGNS AND SIGNALS** (IRE) C 70
183 **SIGURD** (GER) 9
355 **SILASTAR** 109
56 **SILCA BOO** G 64
488 **SILENCE IS GOLDEN** 30
369 **SILENT APPROACH** (IRE) 110
309 **SILENT AUCTION** 15
5 **SILENT FILM** 38
349 **SILENT FLAME** 14
275 **SILENT PARTNER** 20
379 **SILENT REVOLUTION** (IRE) 145
5 **SILENT SPEECH** 39
442 **SILENT WORDS** 55
320 **SILESIE** (USA) F 55
315 **SILHUETTE** (IRE) F 33
386 **SILK BIRD** 34
243 **SILK FAN** (IRE) C 48
35 **SILK WORDS** C 103
192 **SILKEN EXPRESS** (IRE) F 70
101 **SILKEN MOONLIGHT** 28
146 **SILKEN SOUL** C 72
260 **SILKS GRAPHITE** 12
58 **SILKSTONE** (IRE) 13
66 **SILKY WILKIE** (IRE) 28
464 **SILVA ECLIPSE** 49
402 **SILVER ATOM** (IRE) 88
294 **SILVER BUBBLE** 6
80 **SILVER BYRNE** 85
349 **SILVER CHAPARRAL** (IRE) 40
140 **SILVER CHORD** 18
281 **SILVER COIN** (IRE) 13
193 **SILVER DIVA** 15
156 **SILVER DOLLAR** (IRE) 4
335 **SILVER FLYER** 114

42 **SILVER GUNN** (IRE) 9
385 **SILVER HALLMARK** 175
465 **SILVER HILL FLYER** (IRE) 9
507 **SILVER IN DISGUISE** 39
5 **SILVER KNOTT** 107
5 **SILVER LADY** 108
305 **SILVER LEAF** 33
219 **SILVER LEGEND** (IRE) 107
112 **SILVER MEADOW** (IRE) C 101
294 **SILVER NIGHTFALL** 15
343 **SILVER RAINBOW** C 106
385 **SILVER RAJ** 176
42 **SILVER SAMURAI** 10
288 **SILVER SCREEN** 6
294 **SILVER SEAHORSE** 16
234 **SILVER SHADE** (FR) 71
173 **SILVER SHAMROCK** (IRE) 26
385 **SILVER SHEEN** 177
457 **SILVER SPINNER** G 166
114 **SILVER SWORD** 9
308 **SILVER THORN** 63
101 **SILVER VISION** 29
161 **SILVERLODE** (IRE) 49
488 **SILVERSCAPE** 31
154 **SILVERY BLUE** G 190
15 **SILVRETTA** 115
556 **SILVRETTA SCHWARZ** (IRE) 15
135 **SIMBALLINA** (IRE) F 56
343 **SIMKANA** F 107
75 **SIMPLE MAN** (IRE) 24
445 **SIMPLE STAR** (IRE) 20
353 **SIMPLE THOUGHT** (IRE) C 33
506 **SIMPLY A STAR** (IRE) C 188
385 **SIMPLY DEEP** (IRE) G 178
336 **SIMPLY GORGEOUS** 20
515 **SIMPLY ME** F 96
363 **SIMPLY SIN** (IRE) 103
43 **SIMPLY SONDHEIM** (IRE) 24
379 **SIMPLY THE BETTS** (IRE) 146
282 **SIMPLY TRUE** (IRE) 36
231 **SIMPSON'S PARADOX** (IRE) 87
79 **SIMULATION THEORY** (IRE) 11
335 **SINCE DAY ONE** (IRE) 115
240 **SINDABELLA** (FR) 35
26 **SINDRI** 47
372 **SINE NOMINE** 4
75 **SINFUL** 25
376 **SINGASONGSAM** 57
175 **SINGING SKY** C 63
25 **SINGIRISHMANSING** (IRE) 7
85 **SINGLE** (IRE) 10
314 **SINISTER MINISTER** 11
92 **SINJAARI** (IRE) 8
317 **SINNARAJA** (FR) 16
261 **SINNDARELLA** (IRE) 18
456 **SINOLOGY** 86
450 **SINURITA** (IRE) 34
163 **SIR APOLLO** (IRE) 12
367 **SIR ARGUS** 134
143 **SIR ARTHUR'S BOY** 19
18 **SIR BENEDICT** (IRE) 27
346 **SIR BOB PARKER** (FR) 11
303 **SIR BUSKER** (IRE) 11
376 **SIR CANFORD** (IRE) 58
204 **SIR CHAUVELIN** 33
285 **SIR CILIA** 40
70 **SIR DANCEALOT** (IRE) 40
113 **SIR DOTTI** (IRE) 13
176 **SIR GALAHAD** (IRE) 62
286 **SIR GEOFF HURST** (FR) 217
367 **SIR GERHARD** (IRE) 135
6 **SIR GREGORY** (FR) 73
189 **SIR IVAN** 55
97 **SIR JACK WEST** (IRE) 9
385 **SIR JACK YEATS** (IRE) 179
181 **SIR JACKSCHIAPAREL** (IRE) 10
281 **SIR JIM** (IRE) 14
286 **SIR JOCK BENNETT** (IRE) 116
188 **SIR JOHN MONASH** 33
521 **SIR JOSEPH SWAN** 36
150 **SIR OLIVER** (IRE) 5
316 **SIR PLATO** (IRE) 13
379 **SIR PSYCHO** (IRE) 147
399 **SIR RAJ** (IRE) 69
66 **SIR ROBIN** (IRE) 29
283 **SIR RODNEYREDBLOOD** 21
228 **SIR RUMI** (IRE) 26
82 **SIR SEDRIC** (FR) 10
262 **SIR SIDNEY SMITH** 22
149 **SIR THOMAS GRESHAM** (IRE) 13
80 **SIR TITAN** 86
138 **SIR TITUS** (IRE) 33
227 **SIR TIVO** (FR) 31
151 **SIR VALENTINE** (GER) 12
506 **SIR WINSTON** (IRE) 37
78 **SIRAJU** 27
368 **SIRICI** (IRE) C 71
471 **SIRIUS WHITE** (IRE) 14
538 **SIROBBIE** (IRE) 63
286 **SIRONA** (GER) 117
494 **SIRWILLIAMWALLACE** (IRE) 41
5 **SISKANY** 40
346 **SISKARO** (FR) 47
414 **SISSINGHURST** (IRE) 33
540 **SISTER AGATHA** 15
335 **SISTER JULIENNE** 116
385 **SISTER MICHAEL** (IRE) 180
413 **SISTER OF THOR** (IRE) 34
379 **SISTER SAINT** (FR) 148
234 **SISTERANDBROTHER** 72
488 **SISTERS IN THE SKY** 32
442 **SISYPHEAN** (IRE) 92
15 **SISYPHUS STRENGTH** 116
5 **SITHCHEAN** (IRE) 109
88 **SIVKA BURKA** (FR) 50
529 **SIX AND OUT** 3
56 **SIX DIAMONDS** F 65
502 **SIX FIVE SPECIAL** 10
135 **SIX O' HEARTS** 57
401 **SIX O'CLOCK SWILL** 6
208 **SIX ONE NINE** (IRE) 23
451 **SIX STRINGS** 20
405 **SIXCOR** 17
85 **SIXTIES CHIC** 42
527 **SIXTIES SECRET** 16
497 **SIXTY DOLLARS MORE** (FR) 71
94 **SIYOUNI FLASH** (FR) 54
448 **SIZABLE SAM** 34
497 **SIZING CUSIMANO** 72
141 **SIZING MAURITIUS** (IRE) 25
410 **SIZING POTTSIE** (FR) 81
228 **SIZZLING** (IRE) C 194
10 **SKA** 45
228 **SKALLYWAG BAY** 97
191 **SKANDIBURG** (FR) 3
379 **SKATMAN** (IRE) 149
22 **SKEDADDLED** (IRE) 5
329 **SKEETAH** C 18
6 **SKEETER PARK** (IRE) 74
440 **SKELLIG MIST** (FR) F 75
300 **SKID** (IRE) F 73
254 **SKIDDAW** (IRE) 59
20 **SKIDDAW TARA** 20
501 **SKILLED WARRIOR** (IRE) 28
394 **SKINFLINT** (IRE) 12
90 **SKIP TO MY LOU** C 16
95 **SKIPPER** 44
219 **SKIPPING** 183
285 **SKREI** (IRE) F 73
387 **SKY DEFENDER** 47
393 **SKY HIGH GIRL** 3
475 **SKY POWER** (IRE) 13
367 **SKY SPRINTER** (IRE) 136
480 **SKY STORM** 9
457 **SKYCUTTER** (FR) 167
31 **SKYE BREEZE** (IRE) 10
223 **SKYHILL** (IRE) 8
254 **SKYRA** (IRE) G 60
500 **SKYSAIL** 20
489 **SKYTASTIC** (FR) 42
437 **SKYWARDS MILES** (IRE) F 15
449 **SLAINTE MHATH** 23
136 **SLANELOUGH** (IRE) 31
497 **SLATE HOUSE** (IRE) 73
500 **SLATEY HEN** (IRE) C 32
458 **SLEEPING LATE** 17
92 **SLEEPING LION** (USA) 9
335 **SLEEPING SATELLITE** (IRE) 117
101 **SLEEPING TOM** 30
389 **SLEPTWITHMEBOOTSON** 3
313 **SLEVE DONARD** (IRE) 8
221 **SLIEVE BEARNAGH** (IRE) 14
221 **SLIEVE BINNIAN** (IRE) 36
42 **SLIEVE MISH** (IRE) C 76
154 **SLING YER HOOK** 144
153 **SLINGSBYTOO** (IRE) 70
489 **SLIP ROAD** (IRE) 43
206 **SLIPOFTHEPEN** 130
402 **SLIPWAY** (IRE) 89
279 **SLUGGER** 48
527 **SLY MADAM** 17
369 **SMACKWATER JACK** (IRE) 111
248 **SMALL BAD BOB** (IRE) 17
231 **SMALL OASIS** 88
464 **SMALL PRESENT** (IRE) 50
496 **SMALLEYTIME** (IRE) 41
30 **SMARDEN FLYER** (IRE) 20
300 **SMART BOYO** 50
300 **SMART BUCKS** 74
263 **SMART CASUAL** 58
456 **SMART CHAMPION** 22
80 **SMART CHARGER** (IRE) 113
86 **SMART CONNECTION** (IRE) 4
383 **SMART COOKIE** (IRE) 78
397 **SMART DEAL** 2
279 **SMART LASS** (IRE) 49
15 **SMART MOVER** (IRE) C 199
80 **SMART SHOT** 114
41 **SMART STYLE** (IRE) 16
254 **SMARTY WILD** 61
342 **SMASH** (IRE) C 44

472 **SMASH FACTOR** (IRE) 42
10 **SMASHER** (IRE) 41
484 **SMILE AHEAD** (IRE) C 80
315 **SMILE AND PAY** (IRE) 17
457 **SMILING GETAWAY** 168
6 **SMILING SUNFLOWER** (IRE) 75
427 **SMITH** (IRE) 10
173 **SMOKEY MALONE** 10
385 **SMOKING PIGEON** 181
175 **SMOKY MOUNTAIN** (IRE) 39
501 **SMOOTH RED** 59
286 **SMOOTH RYDER** (IRE) 118
107 **SMOULDERING** 92
200 **SMUGGLER'S BLUES** (IRE) 40
457 **SMURFETTE** 169
188 **SNAG IT** (IRE) 24
440 **SNAKE ROLL** (IRE) 76
361 **SNAPCRACKLEPOP** 11
154 **SNASH** (IRE) 85
364 **SNAZZY JAZZY** (IRE) 5
42 **SNEAKY GIRL** 77
99 **SNEAKY PETE** 11
457 **SNIPE** (IRE) 170
147 **SNIPER POINT** (FR) 38
456 **SNIPER'S EYE** (FR) 59
356 **SNOOKER MCCREW** 21
161 **SNOOKERED** (IRE) 26
261 **SNOOZE LANE** (IRE) 19
75 **SNOOZY BEAR** (IRE) 34
6 **SNOW BERRY** (IRE) 76
440 **SNOW DRAGON** (IRE) 104
520 **SNOW EAGLE** 34
413 **SNOW FORECAST** 35
319 **SNOW LEOPARDESS** 38
231 **SNOW QUEEN** (IRE) C 149
395 **SNOW SCENE** (IRE) C 61
66 **SNOWBRIGHT** F 149
231 **SNOWCAPPED** (IRE) 89
43 **SNOWDON** F 151
420 **SNOWED IN** (IRE) 9
231 **SNOWHAVEN** (IRE) 90
556 **SNOWPIERCER** (FR) 16
35 **SNOWSTAR** (IRE) C 104
383 **SNOWY** (IRE) 79
347 **SNOWY BURROWS** (FR) 79
428 **SNOWY CLOUDS** (IRE) 42
212 **SNOWY EVENING** (IRE) 68
196 **SNUG AS A BUG** (IRE) 13
515 **SNUGGLE** 53
506 **SO** (USA) 189
557 **SO BE IT** (IRE) 5
347 **SO CANNIE** G 80
251 **SO CHIC** (IRE) 61
69 **SO FARHH SO GOOD** (IRE) 22
294 **SO FUNNY** (USA) C 19
520 **SO GLORIOUS** 23
153 **SO GRATEFUL** 41
228 **SO HI SOCIETY** (IRE) F 195
24 **SO LOGICAL** 147
92 **SO MANY QUESTIONS** 47
531 **SO MANY ROADS** 23
5 **SO MI DAR** C 228
383 **SO PERFECT** (USA) F 183
497 **SO SAID** I 74
361 **SO SLEEPY** 29
165 **SO SMART** (IRE) 15
440 **SO THEY SAY** 77
387 **SO UNIQUE** (FR) C 127
528 **SO YOU THOUGHT** (USA) 15
70 **SOAR ABOVE** 41
112 **SOARING EAGLE** (IRE) 48
390 **SOARING GLORY** (IRE) 104
300 **SOARING STAR** (IRE) 51
438 **SOARLIKEANEAGLE** (IRE) 20
355 **SOBEGRAND** 110
80 **SOCIAL CITY** 87
80 **SOCIAL CONTACT** 88
368 **SOCIAL MEDIA** F 72
466 **SOCIALISER** (IRE) 52
357 **SOCIALIST AGENDA** 35
85 **SOCIETY GUEST** (IRE) C 71
146 **SOCIETY LION** 17
88 **SOCIETY MAN** (FR) 51
135 **SOCIOLOGIST** (FR) 58
347 **SOCKS OFF** (IRE) 81
384 **SODASHY** (IRE) F 65
133 **SOFIA'S ROCK** (FR) 14
520 **SOFT LIPS** F 35
15 **SOFT POWER** (IRE) F 200
428 **SOFT RISK** (FR) 43
35 **SOFT WHISPER** (IRE) 48
379 **SOIR DE GALA** (FR) 150
356 **SOJITZEN** (FR) G 22
266 **SOL CAYO** (IRE) 23
404 **SOLACE** (USA) F 34
70 **SOLANNA** 42
347 **SOLAR BENTLEY** (IRE) 120
231 **SOLAR DRIVE** (IRE) 150
69 **SOLAR ECHO** (IRE) C 46
228 **SOLAR EVENT** C 196
293 **SOLAR IMPULSE** (FR) 9
506 **SOLAR ORBITER** (IRE) 38
305 **SOLAR PORTRAIT** (IRE) 34
488 **SOLAR POWER** 56
192 **SOLAR QUEEN** 34
65 **SOLAR SOVEREIGN** (IRE) 10
254 **SOLAR SYSTEM** (FR) 62
319 **SOLDAT FORTE** (IRE) 39
347 **SOLDIER AT ARMS** (IRE) 82
318 **SOLDIER IN ACTION** (FR) 6
466 **SOLDIER OF DESTINY** (IRE) 53
384 **SOLDIER OF ROME** 66
399 **SOLDIER'S GOLD** (IRE) 95
119 **SOLDIER'S MINUTE** 39
233 **SOLDIER'S SON** 15
390 **SOLDIEROFTHESTORM** (IRE) 105
543 **SOLE SOLUTION** (IRE) 78
279 **SOLEIL DE CANNES** (FR) 50
399 **SOLENT GATEWAY** (IRE) 18
387 **SOLFEGE** F 86
231 **SOLFILIA** C 151
29 **SOLID AS A ROCK** (IRE) 13
490 **SOLID FUEL** 6
479 **SOLID STONE** (IRE) 20
5 **SOLILOQUY** C 229
379 **SOLO** (FR) 151
220 **SOLO SAXOPHONE** (IRE) 43
457 **SOLOMOON** 171
89 **SOLRAY** 35
529 **SOLSTALLA** 4
472 **SOLSTICE** F 43
263 **SOLSTICE SAINT** (IRE) 59
5 **SOLTADA** (IRE) C 230
24 **SOLUTION** 78
399 **SOLUTRE** (IRE) 70
238 **SOLWAY HONEY** 10
238 **SOLWAY MOLLY** 11
238 **SOLWAY PRIMROSE** 12
238 **SOLWAY STAREE** 13
557 **SOME AMBITION** (IRE) 6
240 **SOME DETAIL** (IRE) 36
392 **SOME NIGHTMARE** (IRE) 21
256 **SOME SCOPE** 15
447 **SOME SITE** (IRE) G 48
368 **SOME STYLE** (IRE) F 73
80 **SOMEDAYONEDAYNEVER** (IRE) 89
200 **SOMERWAY** (IRE) 41
263 **SOMESPRING SPECIAL** (IRE) 60
386 **SOMETHING** 42
279 **SOMETHING GOLDEN** (IRE) 51
538 **SOMETIMES ALWAYS** (IRE) 64
335 **SOMEWHAT CLOUDY** (IRE) 118
42 **SOMMELIER** 78
209 **SOMPTUEUSE** (IRE) 26
293 **SOMTHINGPHENOMENAL** 10
228 **SON** 197
475 **SON OF OZ** 14
288 **SON OF RED** (IRE) 7
221 **SON OF SAMPERS** (IRE) 37
161 **SON OF THE SOMME** (IRE) 27
441 **SONAIRT** (FR) 12
408 **SONEMOS** (IRE) 53
460 **SONG OF EARTH** (IRE) 7
383 **SONG OF MY HEART** (IRE) F 184
172 **SONG OF SUCCESS** 40
165 **SONG TO THE MOON** (IRE) G 48
100 **SONGBIRD'S TALE** 2
389 **SONGDANCE** 4
234 **SONGO** (IRE) 73
243 **SONGWRITER** (IRE) 37
392 **SONIC GOLD** 22
454 **SONIFICATION** 41
379 **SONIGINO** (FR) 152
537 **SONNEMOSER** (FR) 63
506 **SONNERIE POWER** (FR) 39
302 **SONNET STAR** 17
58 **SONNING** (IRE) 14
251 **SONNY LISTON** (IRE) 17
336 **SONNYSAURUS** (IRE) 21
89 **SONS AND LOVERS** 54
92 **SOORAAH** C 68
477 **SOOTHING BLAZE** 16
70 **SOPHAR SOGOOD** (IRE) 43
501 **SOPHIA'S STARLIGHT** (FR) 60
243 **SOPHIE P** F 49
355 **SOPRAN THOR** (FR) 111
43 **SOPRANO** (IRE) 152
509 **SORBET** 33
371 **SORBONNE** 11
379 **SORCELEUR** (FR) 177
357 **SORCERESS MEDEA** (IRE) 36
328 **SORONTAR** 32
355 **SOTO SIZZLER** 112
399 **SOUFFIONNE** (IRE) 71
67 **SOUL ICON** 24
387 **SOUL SEEKER** (IRE) 48
206 **SOUL SISTER** (IRE) 131
402 **SOUND AND FURY** (IRE) 90
506 **SOUND ANGELA** 40
387 **SOUND OF GUNS** F 128
204 **SOUND OF IONA** 34

124 **SOUND OF JURA** 4
540 **SOUND OF MUSIC** 16
506 **SOUND PARADISE** (JPN) C 190
266 **SOUND PRESSURE** (IRE) 24
442 **SOUND REASON** 19
231 **SOUNDS OF HEAVEN** 91
281 **SOUNDS RUSSIAN** (IRE) 15
47 **SOURIYAN** (FR) 33
177 **SOUS SURVEILLANCE** 14
85 **SOUTH BAY** C 72
387 **SOUTH DAKOTA SIOUX** (IRE) 87
399 **SOUTH KENSINGTON** (IRE) 96
234 **SOUTH OMO ZONE** (IRE) 74
112 **SOUTH SHORE** 102
376 **SOUTH TERRACE** (IRE) 59
301 **SOUTHERLY STORM** 5
450 **SOUTHERN BABYLON** (IRE) 35
16 **SOUTHERN SAM** 27
379 **SOUTHFIELD HARVEST** 153
247 **SOUTHOFTHEBORDER** (IRE) 123
305 **SOUTHWOLD** (IRE) 15
484 **SOVEREIGN KING** 32
5 **SOVEREIGN PRINCE** 41
75 **SOVEREIGN SLIPPER** 12
15 **SOVEREIGN SPIRIT** 117
335 **SOVEREIGN STAR** (IRE) 119
375 **SOVEREIGN STATE** 9
181 **SOVEREIGNSFLAGSHIP** (IRE) M 11
444 **SOWS** (IRE) 9
469 **SPACE COWBOY** (IRE) 14
219 **SPACE LEGEND** (IRE) 184
266 **SPACE NINJA** (IRE) 40
91 **SPACE TROOPER** 17
369 **SPACE VOYAGE** 112
320 **SPACER** (IRE) 21
385 **SPAGO** (IRE) 182
233 **SPANGLE** F 22
43 **SPANGLED MAC** (IRE) 25
78 **SPANISH ANGEL** (IRE) 28
300 **SPANISH BUTTONS** (FR) 52
16 **SPANISH DANCER** (FR) 28
24 **SPANISH FLY** (IRE) F 148
325 **SPANISH GOLD** F 21
367 **SPANISH HARLEM** (FR) 137
204 **SPANISH HUSTLE** 35
463 **SPANISH LARIAT** (IRE) 31
173 **SPANISH MANE** (IRE) 11
15 **SPANISH PHOENIX** (IRE) 201
292 **SPANISH PRESENT** (IRE) 42
343 **SPANISH SAINT** (IRE) 80
84 **SPANISH STAR** (IRE) 16
84 **SPANISH STORM** (IRE) 22
447 **SPARE RIB** 20
440 **SPARK OF MADNESS** (FR) 78
50 **SPARKED** 14
261 **SPARKINTHEDARK** 20
226 **SPARKLE IN HIS EYE** 73
285 **SPARKLIGHT** 74
366 **SPARKLING AFFAIR** (IRE) 33
270 **SPARKLING BEAUTY** (FR) 40
497 **SPARKLING DUKE** (IRE) 75
456 **SPARKLING EYES** C 87
138 **SPARKLING RED** (IRE) 60
320 **SPARKS FLY** 41
285 **SPARRING QUEEN** (USA) F 75
449 **SPARTAKOS** 24
298 **SPARTAN ARMY** (IRE) 109
112 **SPARTAN ARROW** (IRE) 49
57 **SPARTAN FIGHTER** 18
442 **SPASHA** C 93
440 **SPEAK OF THE DEVIL** (IRE) 79
533 **SPEAR FIR** 11
525 **SPECIAL ACCEPTANCE** 23
402 **SPECIAL BUDDY** (IRE) 91
212 **SPECIAL DRAGON** 69
251 **SPECIAL EVENT** (IRE) 62
458 **SPECIAL MAYSON** 18
332 **SPECIALAGENT MCGEE** (IRE) 19
228 **SPECIALISATION** 198
150 **SPECIALIST VIEW** 8
335 **SPECTACULAR GENIUS** (IRE) 120
540 **SPEECH BUBBLE** (IRE) 17
324 **SPEECH ROOM** (IRE) 12
484 **SPEED DIAL BAILEYS** 33
43 **SPEED FREAK** F 153
442 **SPEED SKATER** G 94
92 **SPEED TO RUN** (IRE) 48
538 **SPEEDO BOY** (FR) 65
41 **SPELLBINDER** 17
186 **SPELLCRAFT** C 15
186 **SPELLS AT DAWN** (IRE) 9
554 **SPENDABLE** 9
334 **SPERIAMO** 11
5 **SPERRY** (IRE) C 231
506 **SPETSES** (USA) 191
292 **SPICE BOY** 43
466 **SPICE HEAVEN** 54
257 **SPICE RACK** 16
500 **SPICED** F 33
497 **SPICY NELSON** (IRE) 76
380 **SPIDER'S BITE** (IRE) 7
141 **SPIKE JONES** 26
408 **SPINAROUND** (IRE) 20
5 **SPINNING CLOUD** (USA) C 232
391 **SPINSTER** (IRE) 3
513 **SPIORADALTA** 63
286 **SPIRIT CATCHER** (IRE) 22
355 **SPIRIT D'AUNOU** (FR) 113
231 **SPIRIT GENIE** (IRE) 92
378 **SPIRIT IN MY SOUL** (IRE) 14
15 **SPIRIT MIXER** 32
153 **SPIRIT OF ACKLAM** 93
154 **SPIRIT OF APPLAUSE** 145
18 **SPIRIT OF BOWLAND** 28
355 **SPIRIT OF BREEZE** (IRE) 149
488 **SPIRIT OF CAHALA** 33
209 **SPIRIT OF EAGLES** 20
251 **SPIRIT OF INDIA** C 112
369 **SPIRIT OF KINSALE** 113
538 **SPIRIT OF LIGHT** (IRE) 66
219 **SPIRIT OF NGURU** (IRE) 39
231 **SPIRIT OF PARADISE** (IRE) 93
335 **SPIRIT OF REGULUS** (IRE) 121
262 **SPIRIT OF ROSANNA** C 23
107 **SPIRIT OF THE BAY** (IRE) 16
107 **SPIRIT OF THE ROSE** 93
399 **SPIRIT RAISER** (IRE) F 97
14 **SPIRIT WARNING** 35
330 **SPIRITED GUEST** 10
457 **SPIRITOFTHEGAMES** (IRE) 172
442 **SPIRITOFTHENORTH** (FR) 20
504 **SPIRITS BAY** 59
524 **SPIRITTAPPERGOODE** 14
167 **SPIRITUS MUNDI** (IRE) 15
172 **SPIT SPOT** 11
390 **SPITALFIELD** (IRE) 106
85 **SPITFIRE BRIDGE** 43
343 **SPITFIRE FIGHTER** 81
466 **SPITFIRE GIRL** (IRE) 55
98 **SPLENDENT** (IRE) 10
70 **SPLIT ELEVENS** 44
226 **SPLIT THE BILL** (IRE) 74
459 **SPONTANEITY** (IRE) F 30
489 **SPONTHUS** (FR) 44
188 **SPOOF** 25
286 **SPOOK** (IRE) 218
299 **SPORTING ACE** (IRE) 27
43 **SPORTING HERO** 89
254 **SPORTING JOHN** (IRE) 63
402 **SPORTING MIKE** (IRE) 92
369 **SPORTY JIM** (IRE) 114
521 **SPOT OF BOTHER** (IRE) 37
163 **SPOT ON SOPH** (IRE) 13
241 **SPOTTY DOG** 4
231 **SPREWELL** (IRE) 94
279 **SPREZZATURA** (IRE) 70
156 **SPRING BLOOM** 5
5 **SPRING DAWN** (IRE) 110
102 **SPRING ETERNAL** C 27
387 **SPRING FESTIVAL** 129
206 **SPRING FEVER** 132
303 **SPRING GLOW** 12
348 **SPRING IS SPRUNG** (FR) 34
504 **SPRING MEADOW** (IRE) 60
247 **SPRING NOTE** (IRE) 124
5 **SPRING PROMISE** (IRE) 111
6 **SPRING ROMANCE** (IRE) 77
399 **SPRINGING BARONESS** F 98
390 **SPRINGWELL BAY** 107
416 **SPRITZIN'** (IRE) 27
278 **SPROGZILLA** 5
12 **SPRUCEFRONTIERS** (IRE) 59
364 **SPURN POINT** (IRE) 10
474 **SPUTNIK** (IRE) 11
234 **SPY LADY** (IRE) 75
66 **SPYCATCHER** (IRE) 30
109 **SPYCRACKER** 7
346 **SPYFALL** (FR) 12
240 **SQUARE DU ROULE** (FR) 47
383 **SQUARE MILE** (IRE) 80
24 **SQUASH** C 149
496 **SQUEALER** (IRE) 42
215 **SQUIRE HOCKEY** 5
447 **SRDA** (USA) F 49
408 **SRI KANDI** C 82
463 **SS VEGA** G 43
204 **ST ANDREW'S CASTLE** 36
142 **ST ERNEY** 9
555 **ST ESTEPHE** 3
247 **ST HELANS BAY** (IRE) G 125
498 **ST JUST IN TIME** 9
383 **ST KITTS** (IRE) 81
24 **ST LUKES CHELSEA** 150
385 **ST PATRICKS BRIDGE** (IRE) 183
36 **STAAR** (IRE) 9
234 **STAFF SERGEANT LEN** (GER) 87
521 **STAG HORN** 38
251 **STAGE NAME** C 113
92 **STAGE SHOW** 49
379 **STAGE STAR** (IRE) 154
1 **STAINSBY GIRL** 43

226 **STORM SPIRIT** 75
18 **STORM TIGER** 30
15 **STORM VALLEY** 119
327 **STORMBOMBER** (CAN) 6
15 **STORMBUSTER** 120
24 **STORMIN AWAY** 152
200 **STORMIN CROSSGALES** (IRE) 42
355 **STORMINGIN** (IRE) 115
402 **STORMINHOME** (IRE) 93
83 **STORMWALKER** (IRE) 28
176 **STORMY DENISE** 37
448 **STORMY FLIGHT** (IRE) 36
347 **STORMY PEARL** 110
479 **STORMY SEA** 50
74 **STORMY SPIRIT** (IRE) G 31
303 **STORY HORSE** 26
112 **STORY OF PEACE** 51
42 **STORYINTHESAND** (IRE) 41
43 **STORYMAKER** 90
385 **STOWAWAY JESS** 186
182 **STOWAWAY JOHN** (IRE) 12
489 **STOWAWAY ROSE** (IRE) F 60
43 **STOWELL** 26
366 **STOWFORD** (IRE) 34
164 **STRAIGHT** A 55
224 **STRAIGHT SWAP** (IRE) 7
4 **STRAIGHTUPSNICKET** (IRE) 18
86 **STRAITOUTTACOMPTON** 5
111 **STRANGER THINGS** 8
496 **STRANGERONTHESHORE** 17
501 **STRAPLESS** (IRE) C 71
42 **STRATEGIA** (ITY) 42
70 **STRATEGIC FORTUNE** (IRE) 45
496 **STRATHNAVER** G 65
500 **STRATHSPEY STRETTO** (IRE) 10
367 **STRATUM** 141
56 **STRAVIETHIRTEEN** F 67
314 **STRAW FAN JACK** 12
506 **STRAWBERRI** 41
384 **STRAWBERRY FLEDGE** (USA) C 68
447 **STRAWBERRY JACK** 4
383 **STRAWBERRY LACE** C 185
164 **STRAWBERRY MARTINI** F 56
503 **STRAWMAN** (IRE) 10
78 **STREAK LIGHTNING** (IRE) 29
384 **STREAM OF LIGHT** (IRE) 22
504 **STREAM OF STARS** 61
405 **STREAMLINE** 18
154 **STREET CHIC** (USA) F 191
408 **STREET KID** (IRE) 21
359 **STREET LIFE** 11
10 **STREET PARADE** 32
192 **STREETLADY** (USA) F 71
11 **STREETS OF FIRE** (IRE) 3
285 **STREETS OF GOLD** (IRE) 41
23 **STREETSCAPE** 21
146 **STREETSTORM** 53
154 **STREETWISE GIRL** 147
293 **STRENGTH 'N HONOUR** 13
141 **STRENSHAM COURT** 27
552 **STRICTLY GOLD** 33
43 **STRICTLY SILCA** C 154
413 **STRIKE** 12
15 **STRIKE ALLIANCE** (IRE) 121
483 **STRIKE MIDNIGHT** 28
34 **STRIKE OF LIGHTING** (IRE) 20
231 **STRIKING** (FR) 30
497 **STRIKING A POSE** (IRE) 79
394 **STRIKING OUT** 13
5 **STRIKING STAR** 113
72 **STRIP OUT** 55
128 **STRIPE OF HONOUR** (IRE) 4
319 **STROLL ON BY** (IRE) 40
504 **STRONG BELLE** 62
144 **STRONG ECONOMY** (IRE) 15
506 **STRONG IMPACT** (IRE) 120
348 **STRONG JOHNSON** (IRE) 35
369 **STRONG LEADER** 116
243 **STRONG POWER** (IRE) 11
208 **STRONG TEAM** (IRE) 24
154 **STRONGBOWE** (FR) 86
13 **STRONSAY** (IRE) 12
13 **STROXX** (IRE) 13
70 **STRUCK GOLD** (IRE) 59
282 **STRUCTURA** (USA) G 37
286 **STRUTH** (IRE) 120
247 **STRUTTER** 127
515 **STRYDER** (IRE) 56
385 **STUDENT CHAP** (IRE) 187
14 **STUDY THE STARS** 36
107 **STUDY UP** 94
530 **STUMPS OR SLIPS** (IRE) 3
193 **STUNGBYTHEMASTER** 16
447 **STYLE AND GRACE** (IRE) F 50
395 **STYLE OF LIFE** (IRE) 42
26 **STYLISH ICON** (IRE) 13
440 **STYLISH MOMENT** (IRE) 82
315 **SUAIMHNEACH** (IRE) C 34
260 **SUANNI** 6
268 **SUB LIEUTENANT** (IRE) 9
506 **SUB ROSA** 121
506 **SUBASTAR** (IRE) 42
286 **SUBJECTIVIST** 23
309 **SUBLIME HEIGHTS** (IRE) 16
383 **SUBZERO** (IRE) 84
107 **SUCCESSION** (IRE) 95
15 **SUDDEN AMBUSH** 122
355 **SUDDEN WISH** (IRE) F 116
387 **SUDONA** 51
14 **SUDU QUEEN** (GER) C 54
496 **SUEDEHEAD** G 66
402 **SUETSU** (IRE) G 94
414 **SUEZOOKI** 34
395 **SUFFER HER** (IRE) C 62
23 **SUFFICIENT** C 50
286 **SUFFRAJET** (IRE) 24
234 **SUFI** 78
381 **SUGAR BABY** 8
56 **SUGAR BEACH** (FR) C 68
360 **SUGAR CANDIE** 31
251 **SUGAR HILL** (IRE) 64
544 **SUGAR HILL BABE** (IRE) 20
15 **SUGAR ROAD** 203
296 **SUGARFORMYHONEY** (IRE) G 16
303 **SUGARLOAF LENNY** (IRE) 38
528 **SUGARPIEHONEYBUNCH** (IRE) 16
335 **SULLIVAN'S BROW** (IRE) 123
402 **SULOCHANA** (IRE) 95
40 **SULTANS PRIDE** 24
463 **SUMABILITY** (IRE) G 33
517 **SUMAC** (IRE) 14
527 **SUMATRAN TIGER** (FR) 18
119 **SUMMA PETO** (USA) 40
270 **SUMMARISE** (GER) F 66
379 **SUMMER BRISE** 157
231 **SUMMER GALE** (IRE) 31
35 **SUMMER SOLSTICE** (IRE) 84
387 **SUMMER THUNDER** (USA) F 132
387 **SUMMERGHAND** (IRE) 52
428 **SUMMERGROUNDS** 44
315 **SUMMERSET** (IRE) F 35
219 **SUMMIT** (IRE) 188
98 **SUMO SAM** 22
400 **SUN FESTIVAL** 14
43 **SUN KING** (IRE) 27
165 **SUN POWER** (FR) 16
360 **SUN SPIRIT** 60
301 **SUN TRACKER** 6
206 **SUNBELT** (IRE) 134
408 **SUNCHISETAGIOO** F 83
178 **SUNDANCE BOY** 5
15 **SUNDANCER GIRL** 204
231 **SUNDAY EVENING** (IRE) 97
385 **SUNDAY SOLDIER** (IRE) 188
506 **SUNDAY TIMES** F 192
303 **SUNDAYINMAY** (GER) 13
521 **SUNDAZED** (IRE) 91
285 **SUNDOWNER** 42
219 **SUNFALL** 189
154 **SUNFLOWER** G 192
161 **SUNFYRE** 50
112 **SUNGLASSES** 16
300 **SUNLIGHT** (IRE) G 53
88 **SUNLIKE** (FR) 52
5 **SUNNY AGAIN** C 233
302 **SUNNY CORNER** 21
154 **SUNNY ORANGE** (IRE) 148
365 **SUNNY PARKES** M 12
94 **SUNRAY** (IRE) 10
509 **SUNRISE BOY** (FR) 40
155 **SUNSATIONAL GIRL** F 5
484 **SUNSET AVENUE** (USA) C 82
283 **SUNSET IN PARIS** (IRE) 22
385 **SUNSET MELODY** (IRE) 189
369 **SUNSET ON FIRE** (IRE) 117
5 **SUNSET POINT** 114
421 **SUNSET SALUTE** 19
480 **SUNSETS DREAMERS** (IRE) 11
94 **SUNSHINEFLED** (FR) 31
176 **SUNSTRIKE** (IRE) 13
346 **SUNWAY** (FR) 48
94 **SUNY YINA** (FR) 32
399 **SUPASPECIALAWESOME** (IRE) 73
504 **SUPASUNRISE** (IRE) 63
360 **SUPATOV** (USA) F 61
347 **SUPER DAY** (IRE) G 111
296 **SUPER DEN** 11
363 **SUPER DUPER SAM** 104
346 **SUPER ERIA** (FR) F 49
447 **SUPER MIDGE** C 51
456 **SUPER MO** (USA) 60
379 **SUPER SAINT** (FR) 158
270 **SUPER SCHWARTZ** (IRE) 67
504 **SUPER SIX** 64
378 **SUPER SPY** (IRE) 15
290 **SUPER STARS** (IRE) 15
466 **SUPER SURVIVOR** (IRE) 57
43 **SUPERFLUIDITY** (USA) 155
333 **SUPERIOR EDGE** F 9
227 **SUPERIOR GLANCE** 35
469 **SUPERSTAR DJ** 16

465 **SUPERSTYLIN** (IRE) 10
543 **SUPERVISOR** (IRE) 80
309 **SUPPORT ACT** (IRE) 17
358 **SUPREME BREDA** G 18
267 **SUPREME COMMANDER** (IRE) 20
409 **SUPREME GEM** (IRE) F 22
228 **SUPREME KING** (IRE) 100
21 **SUPREME TOUCH** (IRE) F 12
357 **SUPREME YEATS** (IRE) 37
376 **SUPREMELY WEST** (IRE) 61
315 **SURAVA** F 36
553 **SURDOUE DE BALLON** (FR) 10
452 **SURE LISTEN** (FR) 8
416 **SURE SPIRIT** (IRE) 28
369 **SURE TOUCH** 118
177 **SURELY NOT** (IRE) 22
361 **SURFER DUDE** (IRE) 41
346 **SURGE** (FR) 36
28 **SUROOJ** 11
119 **SURPRISE PICTURE** (IRE) 41
360 **SURREY BELLE** 62
360 **SURREY CHARM** 63
360 **SURREY FIRE** 82
7 **SURREY FORTUNE** (IRE) 11
175 **SURREY KNIGHT** (FR) 13
309 **SURREY LORD** (IRE) 18
408 **SURREY MIST** (FR) 22
175 **SURREY NOIR** (FR) 40
247 **SURREY QUEST** (IRE) 128
385 **SURTITLE** (IRE) 190
172 **SURVEYOR** 63
94 **SURVIE** (IRE) 55
484 **SURVIVALIST** (IRE) 83
412 **SUSANBEQUICK** (IRE) 12
343 **SUSIE WOSIE** (IRE) 82
279 **SUTUE ALSHAMS** (IRE) 71
251 **SUVENNA** (IRE) F 114
89 **SUZI'S CONNOISSEUR** 18
285 **SUZY'S SHOES** 15
157 **SWAFFHAM BULBECK** (IRE) 39
159 **SWALLOWS RETURN** (IRE) 4
279 **SWALLOWS SONG** 52
31 **SWANLAND** (IRE) 38
342 **SWANSDOWN** C 45
221 **SWANZY** (IRE) 46
247 **SWAPPED** (FR) 129
20 **SWASHBUCKLER** 21
56 **SWATCH** (IRE) 37
361 **SWAYZE** 13
495 **SWEARER** (IRE) 11
281 **SWEDISH ICON** 16
489 **SWEDISHHORSEMAFIA** (IRE) 47
383 **SWEEPSTAKE** (IRE) C 186
243 **SWEET AND DANDY** (IRE) F 50
270 **SWEET AS HONEY** C 68
347 **SWEET BELLE** G 85
347 **SWEET BELLE** G 112
70 **SWEET BERTIE** (IRE) 46
497 **SWEET CARYLINE** 80
149 **SWEET CHARLIE** C 14
180 **SWEET DIME** 3
66 **SWEET FORTUNE** (FR) 81
92 **SWEET GENTLE KISS** (IRE) F 69
469 **SWEET HARMONY** (IRE) 39
44 **SWEET HONEY B** (IRE) 16
219 **SWEET IDEA** (AUS) F 190
520 **SWEET IDEA** 24
493 **SWEET JUSTICE** (IRE) 7
515 **SWEET LADY ROSE** (IRE) C 98
412 **SWEET LIKE YOU** G 13
412 **SWEET LIKE YOU** F 14
423 **SWEET MAGIC** (IRE) 37
206 **SWEET MEMORIES** (IRE) 135
172 **SWEET MILLEFEUILLE** 64
457 **SWEET OR DRY** 175
413 **SWEET REWARD** (IRE) 13
196 **SWEET SAFFRON** 15
154 **SWEET SERENDIPITY** C 193
96 **SWEET SISTER** 19
506 **SWEET SIXTEEN** (IRE) F 193
200 **SWEET THREAT** (FR) 43
206 **SWEET WILLIAM** (IRE) 32
384 **SWEETASEVER** (IRE) C 69
383 **SWEETEST THING** (IRE) 85
376 **SWEETTOWATCH** (IRE) 62
5 **SWEETY DREAM** (FR) F 234
321 **SWEPT AWAY** (IRE) G 51
286 **SWIFT ACTION** (IRE) F 219
228 **SWIFT ASSET** (IRE) 101
484 **SWIFT CAMPAIGN** (IRE) C 84
303 **SWIFT HAWK** 27
286 **SWIFT LIONESS** (IRE) 121
5 **SWIFT ROSE** (IRE) C 235
23 **SWIFT SALIAN** (IRE) 51
212 **SWIFT TUTTLE** (IRE) 71
44 **SWINCOMBE FLAME** C 17
85 **SWING OUT SISTER** (IRE) F 73
538 **SWING TO THE STARS** (IRE) 68
66 **SWINGALONG** (IRE) 82
501 **SWINGING EDDIE** 30
85 **SWINGING JEAN** C 74
369 **SWINGING LONDON** (IRE) 119
78 **SWISS ACE** 30
153 **SWISS DREAM** C 95
488 **SWISS PRIDE** (IRE) 34
321 **SWISS ROWE** (IRE) 34
506 **SWISS STAR** 122
383 **SWITCH** (USA) C 187
379 **SWITCH HITTER** (IRE) 159
281 **SWITCH PARTNER** (IRE) 17
360 **SWITCHEL** (IRE) 64
148 **SWOOPER** 13
298 **SWORD BEACH** (IRE) 110
297 **SWORD OF FATE** (IRE) 3
15 **SWORDOFHONOR** (IRE) 123
385 **SWORDSMAN** (IRE) 191
404 **SYAMANTAKA** (IRE) F 35
135 **SYCAMORE** (IRE) 59
390 **SYD DEE YEATS** (IRE) 109
143 **SYDNEY BAY** 12
15 **SYDNEY MEWS** (IRE) 124
251 **SYDNEYARMS CHELSEA** (IRE) 65
332 **SYKES** (IRE) 20
219 **SYLLABUS** (IRE) 109
532 **SYLTEZAR** (IRE) 38
164 **SYLVAN SPIRIT** 57
233 **SYMBOL OF HOPE** 16
72 **SYMBOL OF LIGHT** 36
368 **SYMBOLIC SPIRIT** (FR) 30
72 **SYMBOLIZE** (IRE) 37
107 **SYMBOLOGY** 96
199 **SYMPATHISE** (IRE) 2
353 **SYMPHONIC DANCER** (USA) F 19
355 **SYMPHORINE** (FR) 117
43 **SYMPOSIA** C 156
240 **SYNCHRONICITY** (FR) 37
306 **SYR MAFFOS** (IRE) 44
384 **SYRENA** (IRE) C 70
355 **SYSTEMIC** 118
487 **TAAMER** 6
5 **TABARETTA** (FR) 115
521 **TABDEED** 39
308 **TABLE THIRTY FOUR** 64
11 **TABLES TURNED** 4
228 **TACARIB BAY** 27
99 **TACITUS** (IRE) 12
72 **TACTICAL** 38
10 **TADREEB** (IRE) 33
506 **TADSHIN** 123
219 **TAFREEJ** (IRE) 110
204 **TAFSIR** (USA) 37
5 **TAGABAWA** 116
66 **TAH LUV** (FR) 83
471 **TAHASUN** (IRE) 15
98 **TAHITI** F 40
233 **TAHITI ONE** G 21
228 **TAHITIAN PRINCE** (FR) 28
451 **TAHLIA REE** (IRE) G 34
379 **TAHMURAS** (FR) 160
270 **TAI HANG DRAGON** (IRE) C 69
231 **TAIPAN** (FR) 32
23 **TAISPEANTAS** (IRE) C 36
506 **TAJALAT** (IRE) 124
506 **TAJALLA** (IRE) 125
112 **TAJAWAL** (IRE) 52
251 **TAJDIF** (IRE) 66
5 **TAJRIBA** (IRE) C 236
286 **TAKE A DEEP BREATH** F 122
15 **TAKE CARE** 205
347 **TAKE CENTRE STAGE** (IRE) 86
30 **TAKE MY BREATH** (IRE) 26
457 **TAKE NO CHANCES** (IRE) 176
379 **TAKE YOUR TIME** (IRE) 161
458 **TAKEIT EASY** 19
69 **TALAAYEB** F 47
469 **TALAMANCA** 40
15 **TALAMPAYA** (USA) C 206
165 **TALEMA** (FR) F 50
497 **TALIMAR PEARL** (FR) 81
228 **TALIS EVOLVERE** (IRE) 102
228 **TALISMAN** 103
484 **TALIYNA** (IRE) F 85
12 **TALK OF THE MOON** 61
314 **TALKINGTHETALK** (IRE) 13
263 **TALKINGTOTHEMOON** 61
196 **TALKTOMENOW** 16
457 **TALKTOTHETAIL** (IRE) G 177
466 **TALLOW FOR COAL** (IRE) 58
542 **TALLULAH MYLA** (IRE) 40
413 **TALLULAH ROSE** F 51
363 **TALLY'S SON** 105
515 **TALMADA** (USA) C 99
402 **TALYSH** 111
69 **TAMALUK** (IRE) 23
228 **TAMANGO SANDS** (IRE) 104
369 **TAMAR BRIDGE** (IRE) 120
442 **TAMARA LOVE** (IRE) C 95
24 **TAMARAMA** 17
497 **TAMARIS** (IRE) 82
194 **TAMBUKAN** (FR) 16
219 **TAMILLA** 40

410 **THANKSFORTHEHELP** (FR) 84
94 **THANKSGIVING** (IRE) 33
496 **THANKUAPPRECIATE** 43
88 **THANKYOU** (FR) 53
195 **THANKYOU BARONESS** 11
423 **THANKYOURLUCKYSTAR** 39
430 **THAPA VC** (IRE) 5
384 **THAT WHICH IS NOT** (USA) F 71
273 **THAT'S MY DUBAI** (IRE) 3
239 **THATBEATSBANAGHER** (IRE) 29
488 **THATS DANDY HARRY** (IRE) 47
393 **THATSALLIMSAYING** (IRE) F 10
420 **THATSY** (FR) 10
385 **THATZA DAZZLER** 196
42 **THAWG** 43
286 **THE AFRICAN QUEEN** 222
387 **THE ANGELUS BELLE** (IRE) 89
383 **THE ANTARCTIC** (IRE) 87
171 **THE ARMED MAN** 6
299 **THE BANDIT** (IRE) 29
505 **THE BAY WARRIOR** (IRE) 16
348 **THE BELL CONDUCTOR** (IRE) 37
394 **THE BIG BITE** (IRE) 14
228 **THE BIG BOARD** (IRE) 105
497 **THE BIG BREAKAWAY** (IRE) 84
397 **THE BIG LENSE** (IRE) 3
366 **THE BIG RED ONE** 35
233 **THE BIG REVEAL** (IRE) 17
399 **THE BITTER MOOSE** (IRE) 99
258 **THE BLACK SQUIRREL** (IRE) 9
383 **THE BLACK TIGER** (USA) 88
168 **THE BLAME GAME** (IRE) 25
534 **THE BLUEBERRY ONE** 17
537 **THE BOAT** (IRE) 65
385 **THE BOGMANS BALL** 197
363 **THE BOLD THADY** (IRE) 107
247 **THE BOMBER LISTON** (IRE) 131
374 **THE BONGO KID** (IRE) 23
188 **THE BREADMAN** (IRE) 27
309 **THE BREW MASTER** (IRE) 19
141 **THE BRIMMING WATER** (IRE) 28
12 **THE BULL MCCABE** (IRE) 62
112 **THE BUNT** 54
405 **THE CALTONIAN** 19
79 **THE CAMACHO KID** (IRE) 29
247 **THE CARPENTER** (IRE) 132
16 **THE CATHAL DON** (IRE) 29
497 **THE CHANGING MAN** (IRE) 85
289 **THE CHARMER** (IRE) 16
347 **THE CHURCHILL LAD** (IRE) 87
469 **THE CITY'S PHANTOM** 17
233 **THE COLA KID** 18
335 **THE CON MAN** (IRE) 126
442 **THE COOKSTOWN CAFU** 21
306 **THE COX EXPRESS** 47
488 **THE CRAFTYMASTER** 48
56 **THE CRUISING LORD** 38
235 **THE DALEY EXPRESS** (IRE) 9
161 **THE DANCING POET** 30
319 **THE DARK EDGE** (IRE) 42
473 **THE DEFIANT** 5
259 **THE DEVON DUMPLING** 4
298 **THE DOYEN CHIEF** (IRE) 112
376 **THE DREAM GOES ON** 66
154 **THE DUNKIRK LADS** 88
399 **THE DYLAN SHOW** (IRE) F 100
12 **THE EDGAR WALLACE** (IRE) 63
463 **THE ELECTRICIAN** (IRE) 35
402 **THE EMINENT GOOSE** 96
383 **THE FAIRY** (IRE) C 190
556 **THE FECKENHAM FOX** 18
494 **THE FERRY MASTER** (IRE) 44
231 **THE FIRST AND LAST** (IRE) 98
166 **THE FLYING FALCO** 19
514 **THE FLYING FIG** 20
174 **THE FLYING GINGER** (IRE) 26
23 **THE FOLLOWER** (IRE) 37
464 **THE FOREMAN** 51
15 **THE FOXES** (IRE) 125
8 **THE FULL PASTY** (IRE) 4
385 **THE GALAHAD KID** (IRE) 198
93 **THE GALLOPING BEAR** 15
407 **THE GAME IS UP** 17
249 **THE GAME OF LIFE** 15
533 **THE GANGES** (IRE) 13
286 **THE GATEKEEPER** (IRE) 26
279 **THE GAY BLADE** 53
279 **THE GLOAMING** (IRE) 54
154 **THE GO TO** (IRE) 151
15 **THE GOAT** 126
282 **THE GOLD BUG** (IRE) 40
526 **THE GOLD CHEONGSAM** (IRE) F 49
262 **THE GOLDEN CUE** 13
83 **THE GOLDEN REBEL** (IRE) 29
390 **THE GOONER** (IRE) 111
4 **THE GRAFTER** (IRE) 19
293 **THE GRAND VISIR** 11
474 **THE GREAT GEORGIE** 12
26 **THE GREEN AMIGO** 14
400 **THE GREEN MAN** (IRE) 15
476 **THE GREY BANDIT** 7
402 **THE GREY FALCO** (FR) 97
153 **THE GREY LASS** 42
247 **THE HAPPY CHAPATI** (IRE) 133
67 **THE HEIGHT OF FAME** 26
251 **THE ICE PHOENIX** (IRE) 115
240 **THE IMPOSTER** (FR) 38
95 **THE IRISH ROGUE** 45
463 **THE JAD FACTOR** (IRE) 36
402 **THE JUKEBOX MAN** (IRE) 98
428 **THE KALOOKI KID** 46
12 **THE KEMBLE BREWERY** 64
161 **THE KING OF MAY** (FR) 31
457 **THE KING OF RYHOPE** 178
138 **THE KING'S MEN** 63
324 **THE KING'S STEED** 14
553 **THE KINGS WRIT** (IRE) 11
515 **THE KITE** (IRE) 58
504 **THE KNIPHAND** (FR) 67
299 **THE KNOT IS TIED** (IRE) 30
14 **THE LAMPLIGHTER** (FR) 38
537 **THE LAST DAY** (IRE) 66
27 **THE LAST MELON** 3
358 **THE LAST THROW** (IRE) 19
88 **THE LAST WALTZ** (FR) 54
530 **THE LATE LEGEND** 4
200 **THE LIKELY LAD** (FR) 44
220 **THE LION DANCER** (IRE) 44
392 **THE LION STRIKES** (IRE) 23
312 **THE LONGEST DAY** (IRE) 17
402 **THE MACON LUGNATIC** 99
494 **THE MALTEASIEREYES** (IRE) G 45
290 **THE MALTON MAULER** 23
495 **THE MENICE** (IRE) 13
315 **THE MENSTONE GEM** (IRE) 8
319 **THE MIGHTY ARC** (IRE) 43
202 **THE MIGHTY DON** (IRE) 32
343 **THE MODEL KINGDOM** (IRE) 51
173 **THE MOUSE KING** (IRE) 12
325 **THE MUFFIN MAN** (IRE) 17
448 **THE MULCAIR** (IRE) 37
192 **THE NAIL GUNNER** (IRE) 36
445 **THE NAVIGATOR** 21
457 **THE NEW LION** 179
504 **THE NEWEST ONE** (IRE) 68
367 **THE NICE GUY** (IRE) 144
18 **THE NU FORM WAY** (FR) 31
213 **THE OLD BULL** 18
298 **THE OLYMPIAN** (IRE) 113
464 **THE PADDY PIE** (IRE) 52
228 **THE PARENT** 106
366 **THE PINK'N** 36
506 **THE PLATINUM QUEEN** (IRE) 127
136 **THE PLAYER QUEEN** (IRE) 32
448 **THE PLIMSOLL LINE** (IRE) 38
383 **THE PRAIRIE** (IRE) 89
285 **THE PRINCES POET** 17
301 **THE PUG** (IRE) 22
287 **THE PUNT** 10
212 **THE QUESTIONER** (IRE) 73
147 **THE RAIN KING** (IRE) 40
205 **THE RAVEN'S RETURN** 54
275 **THE REAL JET** (IRE) 21
474 **THE REAL RASCAL** (IRE) 13
374 **THE REAL WHACKER** (IRE) 24
340 **THE REAPING RACE** (IRE) 7
417 **THE REBEL BREEN** 10
399 **THE RENEGADE** 76
226 **THE RESDEV WAY** 76
116 **THE RIGHT THING** (IRE) G 22
448 **THE RUSSIAN DOYEN** (IRE) 39
226 **THE RUTLAND REBEL** (IRE) 77
300 **THE SAILORS BONNET** (IRE) F 55
448 **THE SAINTED CANARY** (IRE) 40
369 **THE SAME** (FR) 121
455 **THE SCORPION KING** 23
15 **THE SINGING HILLS** C 209
411 **THE SKIFFLE KING** (IRE) 8
99 **THE SPINMEISTER** 15
276 **THE SPOTLIGHT KID** 11
308 **THE STREET** (IRE) 67
300 **THE TABLET** 56
270 **THE THAMES BOATMAN** 41
119 **THE THIN BLUE LINE** (IRE) 43
471 **THE THIRD MAN** 16
85 **THE THRILL IS GONE** F 76
115 **THE THUNDERER** (IRE) 17
205 **THE TIN MINER** (IRE) 55
251 **THE TOFF** (IRE) 68
385 **THE TOOJUMPA** 199
383 **THE TOOTH FAIRY** (IRE) F 191
29 **THE TRAMPOLINIST** (IRE) 14
451 **THE TRON** 21
501 **THE TURPINATOR** (IRE) 32
363 **THE TURTLE SAID** 108
332 **THE TWO AMIGOS** 21
298 **THE UNIT** (IRE) 114
404 **THE VAN MAN** 17
231 **THE VERY MAN** (IRE) 33
226 **THE VERY THING** (IRE) 78
13 **THE VIK** (IRE) 14

357 **THE VOLLAN** (IRE) 40
175 **THE WAGGON WHEEL** (IRE) C 64
288 **THE WAITING GAME** 8
497 **THE WHERRYMAN** 86
355 **THE WHIPMASTER** (IRE) 124
492 **THE WHITE ELEPHANT** 7
478 **THE WHITE VOLCANO** (IRE) 6
497 **THE WIDDOW MAKER** 87
246 **THE WILD WESTERNER** (IRE) 3
483 **THE WINSLOW BOY** 29
179 **THE WIRE FLYER** 16
319 **THE WISE TRAVELLER** (IRE) 44
356 **THE WIZARD OF EYE** (IRE) 7
369 **THE WOLF** (FR) 122
374 **THE WOUNDED KNEE** 25
374 **THE WRITER** 26
441 **THE X O** (IRE) 20
361 **THE YODELLER** 32
161 **THEA BELL** 62
247 **THEATRE GLORY** (IRE) 134
540 **THEATRE GOER** G 20
5 **THEATRE HONOURS** 117
208 **THEATRE LEGEND** 25
16 **THEATRE MAN** (IRE) 30
142 **THEATRE MIX** 10
335 **THEATRICAL LIGHT** (IRE) 127
95 **THEBEAUTIFULGAME** 12
555 **THEDANCINGMAN** 4
343 **THEDEVILSCOACHMAN** (IRE) 52
469 **THEFASTNTHECURIOUS** 18
457 **THEFORMISMIGHTY** 180
368 **THEGREATESTSHOWMAN** 32
235 **THEGREYVTRAIN** 10
287 **THEHARDERYOUWORK** (IRE) 11
494 **THEIRSHEGOES** (IRE) 46
176 **THELADYINQUESTION** C 67
504 **THELASTHIGHKING** (IRE) 69
85 **THEM THAT CAN** 44
251 **THEMAINPROTAGONIST** (IRE) 69
286 **THEMAXWECAN** (IRE) 27
496 **THEME PARK** 44
1 **THEME TUNE** (IRE) 45
298 **THEONLYWAYISWESSEX** (FR) 115
94 **THEORETICAL** (FR) 11
206 **THEORYOFEVERYTHING** 138
135 **THEOTHERSIDE** (IRE) 62
36 **THEOULE** (FR) 10
15 **THERAPIST** 127
412 **THERE'S LOVELY** 15
286 **THERE'S NO LIMIT** (IRE) 223
56 **THEREHEGOES** 39
440 **THEREISNODOUBT** (IRE) 84
119 **THERMOSCOPE** (IRE) 44
312 **THESE HAPPY DAZE** 18
526 **THESPINNINGWHEEL** (IRE) 24
233 **THEWAYTOTHESTARS** 19
520 **THEWORLDSNOTENOUGH** 36
357 **THEY CALL ME PETE** 41
260 **THEY DON'T KNOW** (IRE) 7
91 **THEYDON GIRLS** F 18
211 **THEYSEEKHIMTHERE** (IRE) 37
526 **THIBAULT** 25
147 **THIBOUVILLE** (FR) 41
133 **THIEVING GAP** (IRE) 15
80 **THINK CHAMPAGNE** (IRE) 116
89 **THINK CLIMATE** 37
280 **THINK FASHION** (IRE) C 27
484 **THINK FIRST** (IRE) 34
366 **THINK FOR A MINIT** 37
355 **THINK TRIGGER** (IRE) 125
113 **THIRD AVENUE** (IRE) 14
552 **THIRD BATCH** 35
457 **THIRD TIME LUCKI** (IRE) 181
360 **THIRD WIND** 33
242 **THIRSTY FARMER** 6
376 **THIRTYFOURSTITCHES** (IRE) 67
102 **THIS IS BOB** (IRE) 21
298 **THIS ONES FOR FRED** (IRE) 116
10 **THISMYDREAM** (IRE) 34
523 **THISTIMENEXTYEAR** 8
168 **THISTLE ASK** (IRE) 26
159 **THISTLE DO** (IRE) 5
440 **THISTLEBUFFS** (IRE) 85
230 **THOMAS BLOSSOM** (IRE) 2
277 **THOMAS CRANMER** (USA) 10
369 **THOMAS DARBY** (IRE) 123
276 **THOMAS EQUINAS** 12
466 **THOMAS MACDONAGH** 60
410 **THOMAS MOR** (IRE) 85
450 **THOR DE CERISY** (FR) 36
61 **THORDIAC** 13
378 **THORNABY BEAUTY** 16
347 **THORNABY EXCEED** 88
378 **THORNABY PEARL** 7
437 **THORNTON MARY** C 11
456 **THORNTONLEDALE MAX** 88
123 **THORSDA** 11
383 **THOUGHTS OF JUNE** (IRE) 14
6 **THRAVE** 80
5 **THREADING** (IRE) F 238
173 **THREE BEAUZ** 20
537 **THREE CLIFFS BAY** (GER) 67
80 **THREE DONS** (IRE) 92
111 **THREE DRAGONS** 10
369 **THREE FIGS** (IRE) 124
111 **THREE HEART'S** C 12
349 **THREE KNOTS** (IRE) F 41
319 **THREE MACKS** (IRE) 45
347 **THREE PLATOON** 89
506 **THREE PRIESTS** (JPN) 43
228 **THREEBARS** (IRE) 107
379 **THREEUNDERTHRUFIVE** (IRE) 164
392 **THREEWAYS BRUCE** 24
348 **THRILLA IN MANILA** 38
521 **THRONE HALL** 41
172 **THROUBI** (IRE) 42
5 **THROUGH THE AGES** 118
12 **THRUTHELOOKINGLASS** 65
298 **THUNDER AHEAD** 117
98 **THUNDER BALL** 24
538 **THUNDER FLASH** 71
485 **THUNDER GAP** 5
440 **THUNDER IN MILAN** (IRE) 86
149 **THUNDER LILY** (IRE) 15
228 **THUNDER MAX** 29
43 **THUNDER MOOR** (IRE) 93
132 **THUNDER N LIGHTNIN** (IRE) 20
172 **THUNDER PRINCESS** (IRE) 43
442 **THUNDER ROAR** 22
369 **THUNDER ROCK** (IRE) 125
346 **THUNDER SPARKS** (FR) 50
325 **THUNDER STAR** 18
360 **THUNDERCLAP** (IRE) 34
175 **THUNDERETTE** (IRE) 65
442 **THUNDERING** 23
285 **THUNDERING BREEZE** (IRE) 76
355 **THUNDERING BREEZE** (IRE) 154
25 **THUNDEROSA** (IRE) 8
43 **THUNDERSHOWER** (IRE) 28
385 **THUNDERSOCKSSUNDAE** (IRE) 200
450 **THYME 'N' TYDE** (IRE) 37
254 **THYME HILL** 65
379 **THYME WHITE** (FR) 165
336 **TIA DALMA** (IRE) 22
31 **TIAMAT** (IRE) 39
15 **TIANA** C 210
463 **TIANNA FALLS** 44
302 **TIBBIE DUNBAR** 11
219 **TIBER FLOW** (IRE) 42
533 **TIBERIO FORCE** 14
200 **TIBIA** (FR) 45
261 **TIBIBIT** C 25
107 **TICKET TO ALASKA** (IRE) 59
192 **TICKETS** 37
515 **TIDAL STORM** 17
538 **TIDE TIMES** (IRE) 72
506 **TIDEFLOW** (IRE) F 195
456 **TIDES OF WAR** (IRE) 23
491 **TIDEWELL** 19
24 **TIEMPO STAR** 19
399 **TIERNEY** (IRE) 101
416 **TIFFANY** (IRE) 29
75 **TIGER BAY** 26
430 **TIGER BEETLE** 6
456 **TIGER CRUSADE** (FR) 24
161 **TIGER JET** (IRE) 32
376 **TIGER ORCHID** (IRE) 68
129 **TIGER PRINT** 4
249 **TIGER SPIRIT** (IRE) 16
451 **TIGER TOUCH** (USA) 22
485 **TIGER TRAP** 8
316 **TIGER VOICE** (FR) 14
477 **TIGERFISH** (IRE) C 23
341 **TIGERPOMP** 2
538 **TIGERTEN** 73
385 **TIGGER** (IRE) 201
286 **TIGGY WIGGY** (IRE) C 224
507 **TIGHT CALL** (IRE) 42
308 **TIGHTENOURBELTS** (IRE) 68
43 **TIGULLIO** 94
125 **TIKA MOON** (IRE) 24
439 **TIKITOV** (IRE) 23
448 **TIKKINTHEBOX** (IRE) 41
356 **TILDIYNA** (IRE) C 23
264 **TILE TAPPER** 12
262 **TILIA CORDATA** (IRE) 14
419 **TILINISI** (IRE) F 7
421 **TILLY TWO** (IRE) G 22
320 **TILLYBOB** (IRE) 43
463 **TILSITT** (FR) 37
283 **TILSWORTH JADE** 25
283 **TILSWORTH ONY TA** 26
66 **TILT AT WINDMILLS** (IRE) 84
294 **TILTILI** (IRE) F 20
335 **TIM PAT** (IRE) 128
247 **TIME FLIES BY** (IRE) 135
390 **TIME FOR A PINT** (IRE) 112
269 **TIME HAS WINGS** (IRE) 13
43 **TIME IN MOTION** 95
179 **TIME INTERVAL** 17
433 **TIME IS TIME** (IRE) 8

251 **VALLETTA GOLD** (IRE) C 117
105 **VALLEY OF FLOWERS** (IRE) 2
135 **VALORANT** 65
92 **VALSAD** (IRE) 11
211 **VALSHEDA** 40
154 **VALSTAR** (IRE) 154
164 **VALTELLINA** (IRE) 33
270 **VALUE ADDED** 42
369 **VALUPO** (IRE) 130
24 **VALVANO** (IRE) 156
279 **VAMOS CHICA** (IRE) 55
45 **VAMPIRE SLAYER** (IRE) 13
343 **VAN DEMON** 86
348 **VAN GERWEN** 40
78 **VAN ZANT** 33
10 **VANDAD** (IRE) 36
312 **VANITEUX** (FR) 20
175 **VANITY AFFAIR** (IRE) 17
442 **VANTHEMAN** (IRE) 98
92 **VANZARA** (FR) C 71
179 **VAPE** 19
442 **VARDEN** (IRE) 99
290 **VARDEN KITE** (IRE) 24
533 **VARIETY ISLAND** 15
43 **VASILIA** C 161
228 **VASILISSA** 110
367 **VAUBAN** (FR) 147
552 **VAUDEVILLIAN** (IRE) 36
251 **VAULTED** C 118
496 **VAUNTED** 19
53 **VAXHOLM** (IRE) 7
251 **VAYNOR** (IRE) 19
298 **VAZIR** (FR) 123
335 **VE DAY** (IRE) 133
342 **VECCHIO** (IRE) 13
456 **VEENA** (FR) C 89
92 **VEGA SICILIA** 12
94 **VEGA STAR** 36
526 **VEGAS JACK** 35
5 **VEIL OF SHADOWS** 121
5 **VEIL OF SILENCE** (IRE) F 243
484 **VEILED INTRIGUE** C 88
102 **VELASCO** (IRE) 22
380 **VELKERA** (IRE) 9
171 **VELMA** 9
81 **VELVET CHARM** C 12
206 **VELVET CRUSH** (IRE) 143
161 **VELVET JAGUAR** F 64
66 **VELVET REVOLVER** (IRE) C 150
176 **VELVET THUNDER** 38
289 **VELVET VOGUE** 33
289 **VELVET VORTEX** 39
289 **VELVET VULCAN** 18
495 **VENDANGE** (IRE) 12
438 **VENDANT** (IRE) 23
286 **VENETIAN** (IRE) 129
534 **VENGEANCE** 18
228 **VENI VIDI VINCI** (IRE) 203
497 **VENTARA** 90
348 **VENTURA EXPRESS** 41
119 **VENTURA FLAME** (IRE) 46
107 **VENTURA MIST** C 100
442 **VENTURA RASCAL** 25
234 **VENTURA TORMENTA** (IRE) 81
442 **VENTURE CAPITAL** 100
23 **VENTUROUS** (IRE) 23
231 **VENTUROUS SPIRIT** (IRE) C 157
228 **VENUS DE MEDICI** (IRE) C 204
387 **VENUS RISING** G 133
206 **VENUS ROSEWATER** (IRE) 144
237 **VENUSTA** (IRE) 4
94 **VERA** (FR) 58
491 **VERA RICHARDSON** (IRE) F 20
491 **VERA RICHARDSON** (IRE) F 24
24 **VERBIER** (IRE) 82
107 **VERDANSK** 60
209 **VERHOYEN** 11
15 **VERMILION** (IRE) 133
521 **VERONA STAR** (IRE) 45
457 **VERONAISE** (FR) F 189
388 **VERSATILITY** 7
446 **VERTICAL** 2
491 **VERTICE** (IRE) 21
393 **VERY CLASSY** 5
467 **VERY EXCELLENT** (IRE) 12
135 **VERYGOOD VERYNICE** (IRE) 74
113 **VESHENSKAYA** (IRE) 15
515 **VESNINA** F 100
470 **VESPASIA** C 15
18 **VET BILL** 32
15 **VETIVER** 134
287 **VETONCALL** (IRE) 13
228 **VEXATIOUS** (IRE) C 205
5 **VIA CONDOTTI** (IRE) C 244
5 **VIA CORONE** (IRE) 122
410 **VIA DANTE** (IRE) 87
211 **VIA GALACTICA** 41
175 **VIA SERENDIPITY** 18
43 **VIA SISTINA** (IRE) 31
15 **VIBE QUEEN** (IRE) C 217
447 **VICE CAPTAIN** 54
457 **VICKI VALE** (IRE) 190
286 **VICTORIA COLLEGE** (FR) C 225
374 **VICTORIA CONCORDIA** 27
521 **VICTORIA COUNTY** (IRE) 94
399 **VICTORIA FALLS** (IRE) 19
471 **VICTORIA GROVE** 17
219 **VICTORIA LEGEND** 195
383 **VICTORIA ROAD** (IRE) 93
31 **VICTORIAN BEAUTY** (USA) F 58
161 **VICTORIANO** (IRE) 34
504 **VICTORIAS PEAK** (IRE) 75
138 **VICTORIOUS SECRET** (IRE) G 85
42 **VICTORS DREAM** 44
298 **VICTORY** (IRE) 124
133 **VICTORY CLUB** (IRE) 16
5 **VICTORY DANCE** (IRE) 123
20 **VICTORY ECHO** (IRE) 22
79 **VICTORY FLAGSHIP** 14
175 **VICTORY HOUSE** (IRE) 43
470 **VICTORY MARCH** (IRE) 8
368 **VICTORY TIME** 46
543 **VICTTORINO** (FR) 83
285 **VIDI VICI** 79
188 **VIENNA GIRL** 28
262 **VIEWFINDER** (IRE) 16
505 **VIEWFROMTHESTARS** (IRE) 20
457 **VIGILANCE** (IRE) 191
23 **VIGORITO** F 52
67 **VIKING TREASURE** G 27
457 **VIKING'S WAY** (FR) 192
89 **VILLA D'AMORE** (IRE) F 56
42 **VILLABELLA** (FR) C 80
300 **VILLAGE FETE** G 75
404 **VILLAGE GOSSIP** (IRE) F 37
176 **VILLAGE LEGEND** (IRE) 39
231 **VILLAGE VOICE** 100
466 **VILLAINESS** (IRE) 63
270 **VILLALOBOS** (IRE) 17
231 **VILLANOVA QUEEN** (IRE) 36
82 **VILLEURBANNE** 11
366 **VIN ROUGE** (IRE) 41
154 **VINCE LE PRINCE** 155
501 **VINCE LOMBARDI** 33
489 **VINCENZO** (FR) 50
163 **VINDOBALA** (IRE) 16
251 **VINDOLANDA** 20
175 **VINE STREET** (IRE) F 66
327 **VINLAND** (IRE) 8
540 **VINNIE DEV** (IRE) 18
463 **VINNIE KNOWS** (IRE) F 38
457 **VINNIE SPARKLES** (IRE) 193
245 **VINNIE THE HODDIE** (IRE) 6
255 **VINNIE'S GETAWAY** (IRE) 12
360 **VINO VICTRIX** 36
386 **VINTAGE FIZZ** 25
275 **VINTAGE ICON** 22
454 **VINTAGE RASCAL** (FR) 45
335 **VINTAGE VALLEY** (IRE) 134
286 **VIOLA D'AMOUR** (IRE) F 226
43 **VIOLET'S GIFT** (IRE) F 162
284 **VIOLET'S LADS** (IRE) 18
239 **VIOLETA** (IRE) 34
526 **VIOLETS STAR** 36
219 **VIRIDIAN** (IRE) 196
228 **VIRTUAL DREAM** (IRE) 111
335 **VIRTUOSO** 135
497 **VISCOUNT VINYL** (IRE) 91
135 **VISIBILITY** (IRE) 66
355 **VISION CLEAR** (GER) 130
497 **VISION DES FLOS** (FR) 92
132 **VISION OF HOPE** 21
491 **VISITANT** 22
226 **VISITE OFFICIELLE** (FR) 82
538 **VISSANI** (FR) 76
67 **VITALLINE** 28
526 **VITANI** 37
315 **VITARLI** (IRE) 37
552 **VITRALITE** (IRE) 14
31 **VITRINA** 59
289 **VITRUVIAN DAWN** 40
219 **VIVA BOLIVIA** 115
367 **VIVA DEVITO** (IRE) 148
457 **VIVA LAVILLA** (IRE) 194
457 **VIVA VALENTINA** (IRE) 195
23 **VIVA VOCE** (IRE) 24
450 **VIVE DE CHARNIE** (FR) 39
456 **VIVE LA REINE** 27
326 **VIVENCY** (USA) 17
231 **VIVERE** (IRE) F 158
515 **VIVIANITE** (IRE) F 101
298 **VIVID PINK** 125
171 **VIXEY** 11
352 **VOCAL DUKE** (IRE) 23
332 **VODKA ALL THE WAY** (IRE) 22
26 **VOGE** (IRE) F 74
308 **VOICE OF CALM** 70
556 **VOICE OF HOPE** (IRE) 19
399 **VOICEMAIL** C 104
279 **VOIX DU REVE** (FR) 56
369 **VOKOLOHS** (IRE) 131

119 **VOLATILE ANALYST** (USA) 47
125 **VOLATORE** 25
42 **VOLCANIQUE** (IRE) C 81
314 **VOLCANO** (FR) 15
149 **VOLENTI** (IRE) 17
385 **VOLKOVKA** (FR) 210
80 **VOLTAIC** 96
442 **VOLTERRA** (IRE) 101
5 **VOLUME** C 245
503 **VONDELPARK** 17
537 **VOODOO DOLL** (IRE) 71
506 **VOODOO QUEEN** 47
355 **VOODOO RAY** (IRE) 131
355 **VORASHANN** (FR) 132
488 **VORDERMAN** 58
138 **VORTIGAN** 65
500 **VOTE OFTEN** C 34
228 **VOYAGE** 206
12 **VOYBURG** (IRE) 71
286 **VOYEUR** 227
66 **VULNICURA** (IRE) C 151
107 **VULTAR** (IRE) 61
389 **W S GILBERT** 5
286 **WADACRE GOMEZ** 130
286 **WADACRE GRACE** 29
286 **WADACRE INCA** 131
154 **WADE'S MAGIC** 90
149 **WADI BANI** 21
383 **WADYHATTA** C 195
360 **WAGGA WAGGA** (IRE) 37
442 **WAHKAN** (IRE) 102
328 **WAHOO KING** (IRE) 33
479 **WAHRAAN** (FR) 21
515 **WAIPIRO** (IRE) 59
484 **WAIT TO EXCEL** 7
469 **WAITING ALL NIGHT** 41
89 **WAITINGFORTHEDAY** (IRE) C 57
321 **WAKAI UMI** (IRE) 53
376 **WAKE UP EARLY** (IRE) 70
139 **WAKE UP HARRY** 14
154 **WAKEY WAKEY** (IRE) 91
1 **WAKOOL** (FR) 50
228 **WALAAA** (IRE) F 207
320 **WALBANK** (IRE) 44
175 **WALDERSTERN** 44
346 **WALDORA** (FR) 54
475 **WALEYFA** 16
457 **WALK IN CLOVER** (IRE) 196
390 **WALK IN MY SHOES** (IRE) 120
538 **WALK IN THE STORM** (IRE) 77
355 **WALK IN THE WILD** (FR) 133
390 **WALK OF NO SHAME** (IRE) 121
410 **WALK OF THE ROSES** (IRE) 88
189 **WALK ON HIGH** 56
515 **WALK THE MOON** 60
247 **WALKING ON AIR** (IRE) 141
501 **WALKING ON CLOUDS** (IRE) 34
133 **WALKINTHECOTSWOLDS** (IRE) 17
537 **WALKINTHEWOODS** (IRE) 72
75 **WALL GAME** 27
335 **WALL OF FAME** (IRE) 136
408 **WALL OF LIGHT** F 89
192 **WALLAROO** (IRE) 40
228 **WALLOP** (IRE) 112
192 **WAMALAMA** (IRE) 56
172 **WANDERING ROCKS** 13
513 **WANDERING WEST** (IRE) 52
35 **WANDERWELL** C 105
251 **WANEES** 21
29 **WANG DANG DOODLE** 15
172 **WANNABE BRAVE** (IRE) 14
89 **WANTOPLANTATREE** 38
34 **WAR AT SEA** (IRE) 21
111 **WAR BONNET** 11
217 **WAR CHANT** (IRE) 16
346 **WAR CHIMES** (FR) 55
154 **WAR DEFENDER** 92
346 **WAR DIRECTOR** (IRE) 56
6 **WAR IN HEAVEN** (IRE) 83
497 **WAR LORD** (GER) 93
186 **WAR OF WORDS** (IRE) 11
494 **WAR SOLDIER** (IRE) 48
42 **WARD CASTLE** (IRE) 12
101 **WARENDORF** (FR) 32
14 **WARHOL** (IRE) 39
5 **WARLESS** (IRE) C 246
59 **WARLING** (IRE) C 25
383 **WARM HEART** (IRE) 94
441 **WARMINSTER** 21
416 **WARMONGER** (IRE) 61
255 **WARNER'S CROSS** (IRE) 13
5 **WARNING FIRE** F 247
355 **WARNING SIGN** (FR) 134
355 **WARRANTY** (FR) 135
506 **WARREN HILL** (IRE) 129
5 **WARREN POINT** 45
296 **WARRIOR SQUARE** 12
411 **WARRIOR'S FATE** (IRE) 9
1 **WARRIORS STORY** 51
72 **WASDALE** 56
238 **WASDELL DUNDALK** (FR) 14
231 **WASEEFA** F 101
66 **WASHEEK** (IRE) 152
369 **WASHINGTON** 132
442 **WASHINGTON HEIGHTS** 60
231 **WASMIYA** C 159
335 **WASPY** (IRE) 137
497 **WASSAILING QUEEN** G 94
144 **WATCH CLOSELY NOW** (IRE) F 18
339 **WATCH LAW** (IRE) 2
148 **WATCH YOUR TOES** 14
399 **WATCHA MATEY** 105
266 **WATCHING OUT** 26
234 **WATCHING OVER YOU** 82
88 **WATCHOUT** (FR) 57
240 **WATCHOUTITSCOOKIE** (IRE) 41
14 **WATCHYA** 40
66 **WATER HOLE** (IRE) F 153
383 **WATER NYMPH** (IRE) 95
204 **WATER OF LEITH** (IRE) 40
385 **WATER ROCK** G 211
363 **WATERGRANGE JACK** (IRE) 114
96 **WATERLOO SUNSET** 9
17 **WATERMELON SUGAR** (IRE) 16
165 **WAVEBREAK** C 51
537 **WAVECREST** (IRE) 73
1 **WAVELENGTH** (FR) 52
448 **WAVERING DOWN** (IRE) 42
346 **WAXING GIBBOUS** 37
413 **WAY OF LIFE** 16
231 **WAY OF LIGHT** (IRE) F 160
267 **WAY OUT** (IRE) 22
521 **WAY TO AMARILLO** (FR) 95
515 **WAY TO MY HEART** (IRE) F 102
116 **WAYFINDER** (IRE) 23
175 **WAZIN** C 67
227 **WBEE** (IRE) 37
270 **WE COULD BE HEROES** (IRE) 43
489 **WE DONE IT** (FR) 51
385 **WE GOTTA GETAWAY** (IRE) 212
239 **WE STILL BELIEVE** (IRE) 30
39 **WE'RE REUNITED** (IRE) 10
373 **WEARAPINKRIBBON** (IRE) 5
407 **WEARDIDITALLGORONG** 16
507 **WEAVER'S ANSWER** 46
383 **WEDDING BOUQUET** (IRE) 96
105 **WEDDING STRESS** 3
383 **WEDDING VOW** (IRE) C 196
80 **WEDGEWOOD** 118
66 **WEDYAN** 154
45 **WEE BAZ** (IRE) 11
279 **WEE FAT MAC** 57
542 **WEE GEORDIE** 42
402 **WEE TONY** (IRE) 102
230 **WEE WILLIE NAIL** (IRE) 3
369 **WEEBILL** 133
324 **WEEKLY GOSSIP** (IRE) 16
315 **WEEMISSGARYBLICK** 20
335 **WEIGH ANCHOR** 146
379 **WELCOM TO CARTRIES** (FR) 174
41 **WELCOME SIGHT** 9
440 **WELL ABOVE PAR** (IRE) 89
499 **WELL CLICHE** (IRE) 12
332 **WELL COMPOSED** (IRE) G 23
319 **WELL DICK** (IRE) 47
212 **WELL DONE DANI** 75
34 **WELL EDUCATED** (IRE) 22
109 **WELL I NEVER** 8
363 **WELL PAID SOLDIER** (IRE) 115
463 **WELL PLANTED** (FR) 39
321 **WELL PREPARED** 37
423 **WELL VICKY** (IRE) 42
69 **WELLEEF** (IRE) 25
341 **WELLFLEET WITCH** 4
390 **WELLINGTON ARCH** 122
154 **WELLS FARHH GO** (IRE) 93
29 **WELLS GLORY** (IRE) 16
506 **WELLTIMED** 130
373 **WELLWILLYA** 6
70 **WELOOF** (FR) 50
270 **WELSH CAKE** C 72
423 **WELSH CHARGER** (IRE) 43
462 **WELSH REIGN** (IRE) 8
167 **WELSH WARRIOR** 17
239 **WEN MOON** (IRE) 35
229 **WENTWORTH FALLS** 7
497 **WEST APPROACH** 95
457 **WEST BALBOA** (IRE) 197
206 **WEST BENGAL** 145
212 **WEST BRIDGE** (IRE) F 76
457 **WEST CORK** 198
497 **WEST END BOY** (IRE) 96
440 **WEST END LADY** (IRE) 90
366 **WEST HILL MOTH** (IRE) 42
366 **WEST HILL SHADOW** (IRE) 43
519 **WEST LAWN** 10
497 **WEST ORCHARD** (IRE) 97
254 **WEST PARK BOY** 67
457 **WEST TO THE BRIDGE** (IRE) 199
59 **WEST WARHORSE** (IRE) 17
112 **WEST WIND BLOWS** (IRE) 17

24 **YOU GOT TO ME** 160
529 **YOU LOOK SO GOOD** F 5
347 **YOU NAME HIM** 94
542 **YOU SAW BRIGADOON** (IRE) 44
472 **YOU SEND ME** 28
347 **YOU SOME BOY** (IRE) 95
347 **YOU SOME GIRL** (IRE) 96
466 **YOU WEAR IT WELL** 64
286 **YOU'RE BACK** (USA) F 231
451 **YOU'RE COOL** 25
513 **YOUAMAZEME** F 55
63 **YOUCONDUIT** (IRE) 10
231 **YOUCRACKMEUP** 102
131 **YOULLOVEMEWHENIWIN** (IRE) 14
385 **YOULNEVERWALKALONE** 214
275 **YOUM DEJRAAN** (IRE) 23
442 **YOUM JAMEEL** (IRE) 61
506 **YOUNG AND FUN** 133
330 **YOUNG BERTIE** 11
379 **YOUNG BUCK** (IRE) 176
534 **YOUNG BULL** (IRE) 19
385 **YOUNG BUSTER** (IRE) 215
308 **YOUNG BUTLER** (IRE) 75
361 **YOUNG CHAUCER** (IRE) 34
268 **YOUNG CHEDDAR** (IRE) F 11
175 **YOUNG ENDLESS** 20
387 **YOUNG FIRE** (FR) 59
330 **YOUNG JACKIE** F 15
40 **YOUNG LADY** (IRE) F 29
457 **YOUNG MAGS** (IRE) G 208
45 **YOUNG MOLONEY** (IRE) 12
157 **YOUNG OFFENDER** (IRE) 41
326 **YOUNG WINSTON** 18
506 **YOUNGEST** 134
423 **YOUR BAND** 44
402 **YOUR DARLING** (IRE) 105
440 **YOUR OWN STORY** (IRE) 92
440 **YOUR PLACE** (IRE) 93
348 **YOUR SPIRIT** (IRE) 53
268 **YOURHOLIDAYISOVER** (IRE) 12
9 **YOURNOTLISTENING** 6
506 **YOURTIMEISNOW** C 197
69 **YOUTH'S VOICE** 26
118 **YOUTHFUL KING** 7
352 **YUKON** (IRE) 24
390 **YULONG MAGICREEF** (IRE) 127
387 **YURINOV** 91
231 **YUZU** 103
21 **ZA DRUZBA** 18
479 **ZAAKARA** 52
228 **ZABBIE** 116
390 **ZABEEL CHAMPION** 128
484 **ZACHETA** F 90
309 **ZACONY REBEL** (IRE) 21
408 **ZAFAAN** (IRE) 57
335 **ZAFAR** (GER) 142
501 **ZAGHAL** (IRE) 37
383 **ZAGITOVA** (IRE) C 199
525 **ZAIN FARHH** 24
92 **ZAIN NIGHTS** 14
506 **ZAINALARAB** 49
387 **ZAKRAM** (IRE) 92
88 **ZALAMO** (FR) 58
56 **ZALICIA FIRE** (IRE) 70
92 **ZAMAN JEMIL** (IRE) 51
504 **ZAMBELLA** (FR) 79
75 **ZAMBEZI DIAMOND** 36
316 **ZAMBEZI FIX** (FR) 16
316 **ZAMBEZI MAGIC** 17
335 **ZAMOND** (FR) 143
173 **ZANAGOR** 22
545 **ZANAVI** (IRE) 4
56 **ZANDORA** (IRE) 40
173 **ZANY IDEA** (IRE) 23
254 **ZANZA** (IRE) 69
72 **ZAPPHIRE** (IRE) 58
477 **ZARA'S RETURN** 17
113 **ZARA'S UNIVERSE** 16
308 **ZARAFSHAN** (IRE) 76
367 **ZARAK THE BRAVE** (FR) 156
219 **ZARAZA** (GER) 116
479 **ZARGA** (FR) 53
135 **ZARGUN** (GER) 67
552 **ZARIELA** 46
23 **ZARZYNI** (IRE) 26
329 **ZAVAALA** (IRE) C 20
387 **ZAWIYAH** C 134
538 **ZEALANDIA** (FR) 78
6 **ZEALOT** 86
532 **ZEALOUS** (IRE) 43
387 **ZEBADAAY** 93
43 **ZEBRA STAR** (IRE) 98
342 **ZECHARIAH** (IRE) 6
408 **ZEGNA** (GER) C 90
279 **ZEGOS SURPRISE** (IRE) 58
496 **ZEITGEIST** 69
315 **ZELANIYA** (IRE) C 39
290 **ZELLOOF** (IRE) F 25
467 **ZEN MASTER** (IRE) 14
506 **ZENGA** 50
106 **ZENO** (FR) 28
296 **ZENZIC** 18
165 **ZEPHINA** 34
532 **ZEPHLYN** (IRE) 44
447 **ZEPPLIN** 21
143 **ZERBINETTA** (IRE) 20
270 **ZERO CARBON** (FR) 20
343 **ZERO FIGHTER** 88
537 **ZERO TOLERANCE** (GER) 76
543 **ZERTAKT** (FR) 84
292 **ZESTFUL** 48
319 **ZESTFUL HOPE** (FR) 50
451 **ZEYDAR** (IRE) 26
98 **ZHANG FEI** (FR) 13
355 **ZHIGULI** (IRE) 137
520 **ZHUI FENG** (IRE) 8
5 **ZHUKOVA** (IRE) C 252
5 **ZIBELINA** (IRE) C 253
164 **ZIGGY** 16
182 **ZIHUATANEJO** (IRE) 13
406 **ZIKANY** 9
221 **ZILEO** 16
196 **ZILLION** (IRE) 18
154 **ZIMMERMAN** 95
330 **ZINA COLADA** 16
554 **ZINAT** (IRE) 11
538 **ZINC WHITE** (IRE) 79
5 **ZINDAYA** (USA) F 254
88 **ZINDERELLA** (FR) 59
41 **ZINNIA** (FR) 10
206 **ZIRYAB** 147
399 **ZIVANIYA** 79
298 **ZODIAC STAR** (IRE) 145
94 **ZOE** 60
66 **ZOELLA** (USA) F 155
200 **ZOEMAN** (FR) 47
116 **ZOFFALAY** (IRE) 24
467 **ZOFFALEE** (FR) 15
80 **ZOFFANY PORTRAIT** (IRE) 100
399 **ZOFFEE** 20
343 **ZOFFMAN** (IRE) 54
270 **ZOLA POWER** 75
527 **ZOLTAN VARGA** 19
390 **ZONDA** (FR) 129
416 **ZONISTY** (IRE) 12
176 **ZOOLOGY** 41
459 **ZOOM STAR** 10
101 **ZOPITO** (FR) 34
515 **ZOUKSTER** 62
334 **ZOUKY** 12
301 **ZOUS BABY** 24
153 **ZOUS JUICE** (IRE) 96
92 **ZOUZANNA** 52
506 **ZOUZOU** (AUS) C 198
387 **ZOZIMUS** (IRE) 60
15 **ZU RUN** 137
202 **ZUBA** 35
456 **ZUBEIDA** F 61
385 **ZUCAYAN** (FR) 216
74 **ZUCKERBERG** (GER) 35
187 **ZUFAL** 15
138 **ZUFFOLO** (IRE) 66
245 **ZULU** 7
279 **ZUMAATY** (IRE) 59
352 **ZUMBI** (GER) 25
513 **ZUMURUD** (IRE) 56
316 **ZURAIG** 18
6 **ZUUL** 87
24 **ZVARKHOVA** (FR) F 161
300 **ZWICKY** 64
41 **ZYGFRYD** (FR) 11
526 **ZYON** 26
527 **ZYRA'S LIONESS** 20

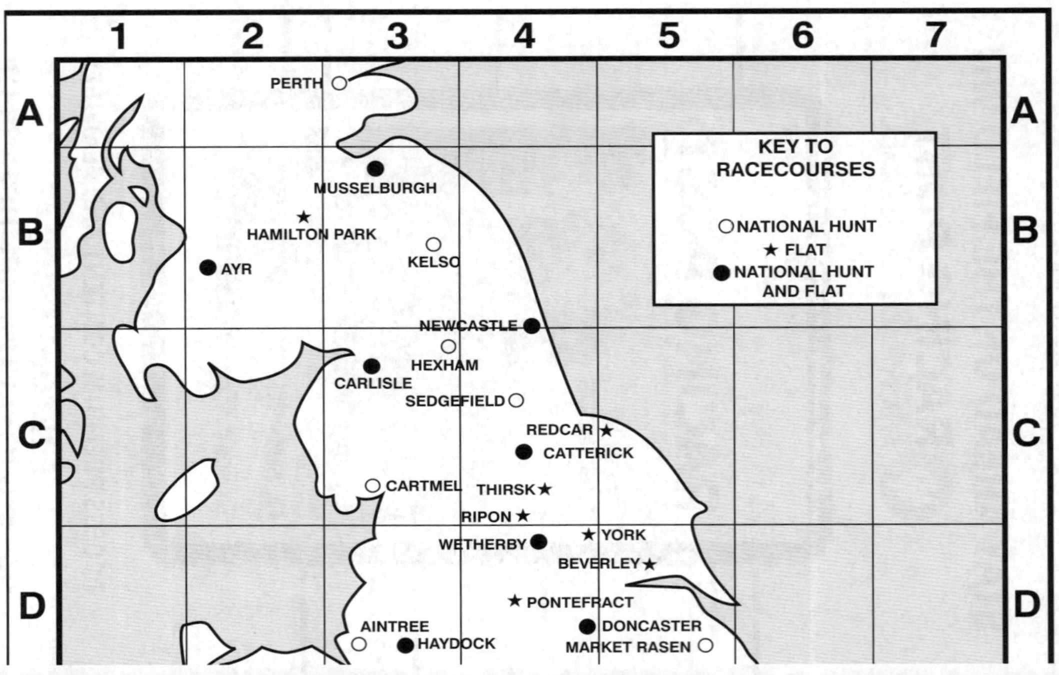
1
2
3
4
5
6
7
A
B
C
D
KEY TO RACECOURSES
NATIONAL HUNT
FLAT
NATIONAL HUNT AND FLAT
PERTH
MUSSELBURGH
HAMILTON PARK
AYR
KELSO
NEWCASTLE
HEXHAM
CARLISLE
SEDGEFIELD
REDCAR
CATTERICK
CARTMEL
THIRSK
RIPON
WETHERBY
YORK
BEVERLEY
PONTEFRACT
AINTREE
HAYDOCK
DONCASTER
MARKET RASEN

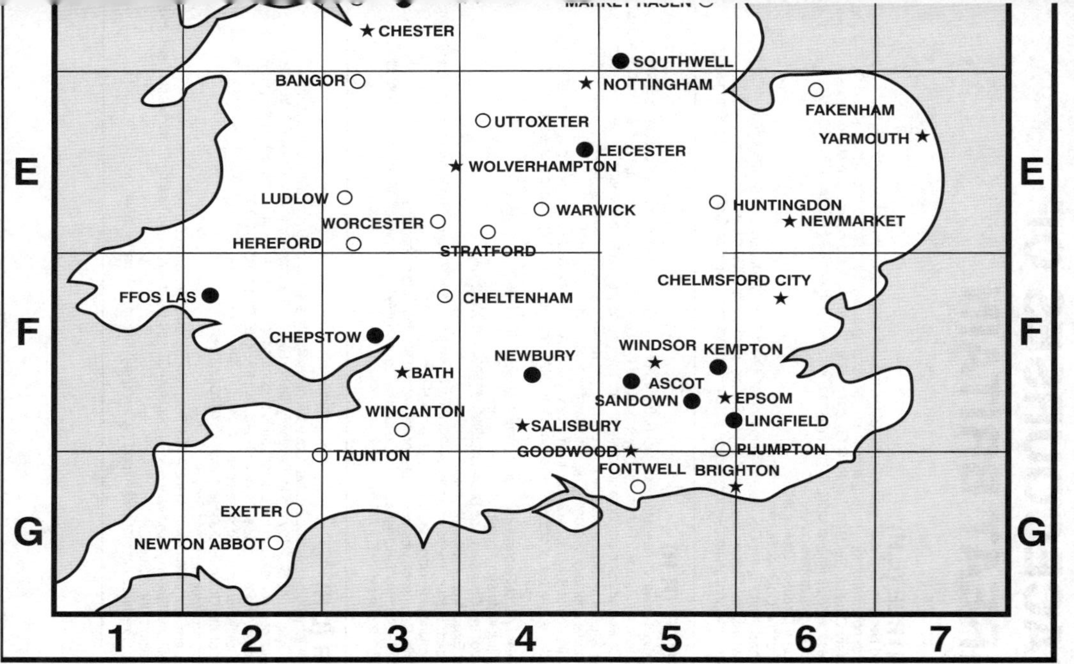
CHESTER
SOUTHWELL
BANGOR
NOTTINGHAM
FAKENHAM
UTTOXETER
YARMOUTH
LEICESTER
WOLVERHAMPTON
E
E
LUDLOW
WARWICK
HUNTINGDON
NEWMARKET
WORCESTER
HEREFORD
STRATFORD
CHELMSFORD CITY
FFOS LAS
CHELTENHAM
F
F
CHEPSTOW
WINDSOR
KEMPTON
NEWBURY
BATH
ASCOT
SANDOWN
EPSOM
WINCANTON
LINGFIELD
SALISBURY
TAUNTON
GOODWOOD
PLUMPTON
FONTWELL
BRIGHTON
EXETER
G
G
NEWTON ABBOT
1
2
3
4
5
6
7

RACECOURSES OF GREAT BRITAIN

AINTREE (L.H)

Grand National Course: Triangular, 2m2f (16 fences) 494y run-in with elbow. Perfectly flat. A severe test for both horse and rider, putting a premium on jumping ability, fitness and courage.
Mildmay Course: Rectangular, 1m4f (8) 260y run-in. A very fast, flat course with sharp bends.
Address: Aintree Racecourse, Ormskirk Road, Aintree, Liverpool, L9 5AS Tel: 0151 523 2600
Website: www.aintree.co.uk
Regional Director: Dickon White
Clerk of the Course: Sulekha Varma
By Road: North of the City, near the junction of the M57 and M58 with the A59 (Preston).
By Rail: Aintree Station is adjacent to the Stands, from Liverpool Central.
By Air: Liverpool (John Lennon) Airport is 10 miles. Helicopter landing facility by prior arrangement.

ASCOT (R.H)

Flat: Right-handed triangular track just under 1m6f in length. The Round course descends from the 1m4f start into Swinley Bottom, the lowest part of the track. It then turns right-handed and joins the Old Mile Course, which starts on a separate chute. The course then rises to the right-handed home turn over an underpass to join the straight mile course. The run-in is about 3f, rising slightly to the winning post. The whole course is of a galloping nature with easy turns.
N.H. Triangular, 1m6f (10), 240y run-in mostly uphill. A galloping course with an uphill finish, Ascot provides a real test of stamina. The fences are stiff and sound jumping is essential, especially for novices.
Address: Ascot Racecourse, Ascot, Berkshire SL5 7JX Tel: 08707 271234
Website: www.ascot.co.uk
Clerk of the Course: Chris Stickels 01344 878502 / 07970 621440
Chief Executive: Alastair Warwick
By Road: West of the town on the A329. Easy access from the M3 (Junction 3) and the M4 (Junction 6). Car parking adjoining the course and Ascot Heath.
By Rail: Regular service from Waterloo to Ascot (500y from the racecourse).
By Air: Helicopter landing facility at the course. London (Heathrow) Airport 15 miles, White Waltham Airfield 12 miles (01427) 718800.

AYR (L.H)

Flat: A left-handed, galloping, flat oval track of 1m4f with a 4f run-in. The straight 6f is essentially flat.
N.H. Oval, 1m4f (9), 210y run-in. Relatively flat and one of the fastest tracks in Great Britain. It is a well-drained course and the ground rarely becomes testing. The track suits the long-striding galloper.
Address: Ayr Racecourse, Whitletts Road, Ayr, KA8 0JE Tel: 01292 264179
Website: www.ayr-racecourse.co.uk
Clerk of the Course: Graeme Anderson 07768 651261
Managing Director: David Brown
By Road: East of the town on the A758. Free parking for buses and cars.
By Rail: Ayr Station (trains on the half hour from Glasgow Central). Journey time 55 minutes. Buses and taxis also to the course.
By Air: Prestwick International Airport (10 minutes), Glasgow Airport (1 hour).

BANGOR-ON-DEE (L.H)

N.H. Circular, 1m4f (9), 325y run-in. Apart from some 'ridge and furrow', this is a flat course notable for three sharp bends, especially the paddock turn. Suits handy, speedy sorts.
Address: Bangor-On-Dee Racecourse, Overton Road, Bangor-On-Dee, Wrexham, LL13 0DA Tel: 01978 782081
Website: www.bangorondeeraces.co.uk
Clerk of the Course: Andrew Tulloch
Chief Executive: Louise Stewart
General Manager: Patrick Chesters
By Road: 5 miles south-east of Wrexham, off the B5069.
By Rail: Wrexham Station (bus or taxi to the course).
By Air: Helicopters may land by prior arrangement with Clerk of the Course.

BATH (L.H)

Flat: Galloping, left-handed, level oval of 1m4f, with long, stiff run-in of about 4f which bends to the left. An extended chute provides for sprint races.
Address: The Racecourse, Lansdown, Bath, BA1 9BU Tel: 01225 424609
Website: www.bath-racecourse.co.uk
Clerk of the Course: Ben Hicks 07929 202277
Executive Director: Simon Tonge
By Road: 2 miles northwest of the City (M4 Junction 18) at Lansdown. Unlimited free car and coach parking immediately behind the stands. Special bus services operate from Bath to the racecourse.
By Rail: Bath Station (from Paddington).
By Air: Bristol or Colerne Airports. Helicopter landing facilities available by prior arrangement.

BEVERLEY (R.H)

Flat: A right-handed oval of 1m3f, generally galloping, with an uphill run-in of two and a half furlongs. The 5f course is very stiff.
Address: Beverley Race Co. Ltd., York Road, Beverley, Yorkshire HU17 9QZ Tel: 01482 867488 / 882645
Website: www.beverley-racecourse.co.uk
Chief Executive and Clerk of the Course: Sally Iggulden 07850 458605
By Road: 7 miles from the M62 (Junction 38) off the A1035. Free car parking opposite the course. Owners and trainers use a separate enclosure.
By Rail: Beverley Station (Hull-Scarborough line). Occasional bus service to the course (1 mile).

BRIGHTON (L.H)

Flat: Left-handed, 1m4f horseshoe with easy turns and a run-in of three and a half furlongs. Undulating and sharp, the track suits handy types.
Address: Brighton Racecourse, Brighton, East Sussex BN2 2XZ Tel: 01273 603580
Website: www.brighton-racecourse.co.uk
Clerk of the Course: Stephanie Wethered 07977 435569
Executive Director: Paul Ellison
By Road: East of the city on the A27 (Lewes Road). Car park adjoins the course.
By Rail: Brighton Station (from Victoria on the hour, London Bridge or Portsmouth). Special bus service to the course from the station (approx 2 miles).
By Air: Helicopters may land by prior arrangement.

CARLISLE (R.H)

Flat: Right-handed, 1m4f pear-shaped track. Galloping and undulating with easy turns and a stiff uphill run-in of three and a half furlongs. The 6f course begins on an extended chute.
N.H. Pear-shaped, 1m5f (9), 300y run-in uphill. Undulating and a stiff test of stamina, ideally suited to the long-striding thorough stayer.
Address: Carlisle Racecourse, Durdar Road, Carlisle CA2 4TS Tel: 01228 554700
Website: www.carlisle-races.co.uk
Regional Director: Dickon White
Joint Clerks of the Course: Sulekha Varma and Kirkland Tellwright
General Manager: Helen Willis
By Road: 2 miles south of the city (Durdar Road). Easy access from the M6 (Junction 42). The car park is free (adjacent to the course).
By Rail: Carlisle Station (2 miles from the course).
By Air: Helicopter landing facility by prior arrangement.

CARTMEL (L.H)

N.H. Oval, 1m1f (6), 800y run-in. Almost perfectly flat but very sharp, with the longest run-in in the country, approximately half a mile. The fences are stiff but fair.
Address: Cartmel Racecourse, Cartmel, nr Grange-Over-Sands, Cumbria LA11 6QF Tel: 01539 536340 Out of season: 01539 533335
Website: www.cartmel-racecourse.co.uk
General Manager: Geraldine McKay
Clerk of the Course: Anthea Leigh 07837 559861
By Road: 1 mile west of the town, 2 miles off the B5277 (Grange-Haverthwaite road). M6 (Junction 36).
By Rail: Cark-in-Cartmel Station (2 miles) (Carnforth-Barrow line). Raceday bus service.
By Air: Light aircraft facilities available at Cark Airport (4 miles from the course). Helicopter landing facility at the course, by prior arrangement only.

CATTERICK (L.H)

Flat: A sharp, left-handed, undulating oval of 1m180y with a downhill run-in of 3f.
N.H. Oval, 1m1f (9), 240y run-in. Undulating, sharp track that favours the handy, front-running sort, rather than the long-striding galloper.
Address: The Racecourse, Catterick Bridge, Richmond, North Yorkshire DL10 7PE Tel: 01748 811478
Website: www.catterickbridge.co.uk
Chief Executive: James Sanderson
General Commercial Manager: Emma Stevenson
By Road: The course is adjacent to the A1, 1 mile northwest of the town on the A6136. There is a free car park.
By Rail: Darlington Station (special buses to course - 14-mile journey).
By Air: Helicopters can land by prior arrangement. Fixed wing planes contact RAF Leeming Tel: 01677 423041

CHELMSFORD CITY (L.H)

Flat: A left-handed, floodlit Polytrack oval of 1m with sweeping bends and a 2f home straight. Races over 7f and 1m start from separate chutes.
Address: Chelmsford City Racecourse, Great Leighs, Essex, CM3 1QP Tel: 01245 362412
Website: www.chelmsfordcityracecourse.com
Clerk of the Course: Andy Waitt 07929 915731
By Road: At Great Leighs, five miles north of Chelmsford on the A31
By Rail: Chelmsford station (from Liverpool Street)
By Air: Stansted Airport (17 miles)

CHELTENHAM (L.H)

Old Course: Oval, 1m4f, (9) 350y run-in. A testing, undulating track with stiff fences. The ability to stay is essential.
New Course: Oval, 1m5f (10), 220y run-in. Undulating, stiff fences, testing course, uphill for the final half-mile.
Address: Cheltenham Racecourse, Prestbury Park, Cheltenham, Gloucestershire GL50 4SH Tel: 01242 513014
Website: www.cheltenham.co.uk
Regional Director: Ian Renton
Regional Head of Racing and Clerk of the Course: Jon Pullin 07966 154962
By Road: 1.5 miles north of the town on the A435. M5 (Junction 10 or 11).
By Rail: Cheltenham Spa Station. Buses and taxis to course.
By Air: Helicopter landing site to the northeast of the stands.

CHEPSTOW (L.H)

Flat: A left-handed, undulating oval of about 2m, with easy turns, and a straight run-in of 5f. There is a straight track of 1m14y.
N.H. Oval, 2m (11), 240y run-in. Many changing gradients, five fences in the home straight. Favours the long-striding front-runner, but stamina is important.
Address: Chepstow Racecourse, Chepstow, Monmouthshire NP16 6BE Tel: 01291 622260
Website: www.chepstow-racecourse.co.uk
Clerk of the Course: Libby O'Flaherty 07970 831987
Executive Director: Phil Bell
By Road: 1 mile north-west of the town on the A466. (1 mile from Junction 22 of the M4 (Severn Bridge) or M48 Junction 2. There is a free public car park opposite the entrance.
By Rail: Chepstow Station (from Paddington, change at Gloucester or Newport). The course is a mile from the station.
By Air: Helicopter landing facility in the centre of the course.

CHESTER (L.H)

Flat: A level, sharp, left-handed, circular course of 1m73y, with a short run-in of 230y.
Chester is a specialists' track which generally suits the sharp-actioned horse.
Address: The Racecourse, Chester CH1 2LY Tel: 01244 304600
Website: www.chester-races.co.uk
Clerk of the Course: Andrew Tulloch
Chief Executive: Louise Stewart
By Road: The course is near the centre of the city on the A548 (Queensferry Road). The Owners' and Trainers' car park is adjacent to the Leverhulme Stand. There is a public car park in the centre of the course.
By Rail: Chester Station (3/4 mile from the course). Services from Euston, Paddington and Northgate.
By Air: Hawarden Airport (2 miles). Helicopters are allowed to land on the racecourse by prior arrangement only.

DONCASTER (L.H)

Flat: A left-handed, flat, galloping course of 1m7f 110y, with a long run-in which extends to a straight mile.
N.H. Conical, 2m (11), 247y run-in. A very fair, flat track ideally suited to the long-striding galloper.
Address: Doncaster Racecourse, Leger Way, Doncaster, DN2 6BB Tel: 01302 304200
Website: www.doncaster-racecourse.co.uk
Clerk of the Course: Paul Barker 07966 472231
Executive Director: Rachel Harwood
General Manager: Nikki Griffiths
By Road: East of the town, off the A638 (M18 Junctions 3 and 4). Club members' car park reserved. Large public car park free and adjacent to the course.
By Rail: Doncaster Central Station (from King's Cross). Special bus service from the station (1 mile).
By Air: Helicopter landing facility by prior arrangement only. Doncaster Robin Hood Airport is 15 minutes from the racecourse.

EPSOM (L.H)

Flat: Left-handed and undulating with easy turns, and a run-in of just under 4f. The straight 5f course is also undulating and downhill all the way, making it the fastest 5f in the world.
Address: The Racecourse, Epsom Downs, Surrey KT18 5LQ Tel: 01372 726311
Website: www.epsomderby.co.uk
Regional Director: Amy Starkey
Clerk of the Course: Andrew Cooper Tel: 01372 726311 Mobile: 07774 230850
General Manager: James Crespi
By Road: Two miles south of the town on the B290 (M25 Junctions 8 and 9). For full car park particulars apply to: The Club Secretary, Epsom Grandstand, Epsom Downs, Surrey KT18 5LQ. Tel: 01372 726311.
By Rail: Epsom, Epsom Downs or Tattenham Corner Stations (trains from London Bridge, Waterloo, Victoria). Regular bus services run to the course from Epsom and Morden Underground Station.
By Air: London (Heathrow) and London (Gatwick) are both within 30 miles of the course. Heliport (Derby Meeting only) - apply to Hascombe Aviation. Tel: 01279 680291.

EXETER (R.H)

N.H. Oval, 2m (11), 300y run-in uphill. Undulating with a home straight of half a mile. A good test of stamina, suiting the handy, well-balanced sort.
Address: Exeter Racecourse, Kennford, Exeter, Devon EX6 7XS Tel: 01392 832599
Website: www.exeter-racecourse.co.uk
Regional Director: Ian Renton
Clerk of the Course: Daniel Cooper 07976 413045
General Manager: Jack Parkinson
By Road: The course is at Haldon, 5 miles south-west of Exeter on the A38 (Plymouth) road, 2 miles east of Chudleigh.
By Rail: Exeter (St Davids) Station. Free bus service to course.
By Air: Helicopters can land by prior arrangement.

FAKENHAM (L.H)

N.H. Square, 1m (6), 200y run-in. On the turn almost throughout and undulating, suiting the handy front-runner. The going rarely becomes heavy.
Address: The Racecourse, Fakenham, Norfolk NR21 7NY Tel: 01328 862388
Website: www.fakenhamracecourse.co.uk
Clerk of the Course and Chief Executive: David Hunter Tel: 01328 862388 Mobile: 07767 802206
By Road: A mile south of the town on the B1146 (East Dereham) road.
By Rail: Norwich Station (26 miles) (Liverpool Street line), King's Lynn (22 miles) (Liverpool Street/Kings Cross).
By Air: Helicopter landing facility in the centre of the course by prior arrangement only.

FFOS LAS (L.H)

Flat The track is a 60m wide, basically flat, 1m4f oval with sweeping bends. Races over 5f and 6f start on a chute.
N.H. A flat, 1m4f oval (9). The going is often testing which places the emphasis on stamina.
Address: Ffos Las Racecourse, Trimsaran, Carmarthenshire SA17 4DE Tel: 01554 811092
Website: www.ffoslasracecourse.com
General Manager: Kevin Hire
Clerk of the Course: Dai Jones 07970 828961
By Road: From the east take J48 from the M4 and join the A4138 to Llanelli, then follow the brown tourist signs to the racecourse. From the west take the A48 to Carmarthen then the A484 to Kidwelly before following the brown signs.
By Air: The course has the facilities to land helicopters on race days.

FONTWELL PARK (Fig. 8)

N.H. 2m (7), 230y run-in with left-hand bend close home. The figure-of-eight chase course suits handy types and is something of a specialists' track. The left-handed hurdle course is oval and one mile round. The bottom bend, which is shared, has been converted to Fibresand.
Address: Fontwell Park Racecourse, nr Arundel, West Sussex BN18 0SX Tel: 01243 543335
Website: www.fontwellpark.co.uk
Clerk of the Course: Philip Hide 07976 761945
Executive Director: Guy Pridie
By Road: South of village at the junction of the A29 (Bognor) and A27 (Brighton-Chichester) roads.
By Rail: Barnham Station (2 miles). Brighton-Portsmouth line (access via London Victoria).
By Air: Helicopter landing facility by prior arrangement with the Clerk of the Course.

GOODWOOD (R.H)

Flat: A sharp, undulating, essentially right-handed track with a long run-in. There is also a straight 6f course.
Address: Goodwood Racecourse Ltd., Goodwood, Chichester, West Sussex PO18 0PX Tel: 01243 755022
Website: www.goodwood.co.uk
Managing Director: Adam Waterworth
General Manager: Alex Eade
Clerk of the Course: Ed Arkell 07977 587713
By Road: 6 miles north of Chichester between the A286 and A285. There is a car park adjacent to the course. Ample free car and coach parking.
By Rail: Chichester Station (from Victoria or London Bridge). Regular bus service to the course (6 miles).
By Air: Helicopter landing facility by prior arrangement 01243 755030. Goodwood Airport 2 miles (taxi to the course).

HAMILTON PARK (R.H)

Flat: A sharp, undulating, right-handed course of 1m5f with a five and a half-furlong, uphill run-in. There is a straight track of 6f.
Address: Hamilton Park Racecourse, Bothwell Road, Hamilton, Lanarkshire ML3 0DW Tel: 01698 283806
Website: www.hamilton-park.co.uk
Clerk of the Course: Harriet Graham
Racecourse Managing Director : Ashley Moon
By Road: Off the A72 on the B7071 (Hamilton-Bothwell road). (M74 Junction 5). Free parking for cars and buses.
By Rail: Hamilton West Station (1 mile).
By Air: Glasgow Airport (20 miles).

HAYDOCK PARK (L.H)

Flat: A galloping, almost flat, oval track, 1m5f round, with a run-in of four and a half furlongs and a straight six-furlong course.
N.H. Oval, 1m5f (10), 440y run-in. A flat, galloping chase course using portable fences. The hurdles track, which is sharp, is inside the chase course and has some tight bends.
Address: Haydock Park Racecourse, Newton-le-Willows, Merseyside WA12 0HQ Tel: 01942 402609
Website: www.haydock-park.co.uk
Regional Director: Dickon White
General Manager: Molly Dingwall
Regional Head of Racing and Clerk of the Course: Kirkland Tellwright 01942 725963 or 07748 181595
By Road: The course is on the A49 near Junction 23 of the M6.
By Rail: Newton-le-Willows Station (Manchester-Liverpool line) is 2.5 miles from the course. Earlstown 3 miles from the course. Warrington Bank Quay and Wigan are on the London to Carlisle/Glasgow line.
By Air: Landing facilities in the centre of the course for helicopters and planes not exceeding 10,000lbs laden weight.

HEREFORD (R.H)

N.H. Square, 1m4f (9), 300y run-in. The turns, apart from the final one that is on falling ground, are easily negotiated, placing the emphasis on speed rather than stamina. A handy position round the home turn is vital, as winners rarely come from behind. The hurdle track is on the outside of the chase course.
Address: Hereford Racecourse, Roman Road, Holmer, Hereford, HR4 9QU Tel: (01432) 273560
Website: www.hereford-racecourse.co.uk
General Manager: Camilla Esling
Clerk of the Course: John Holliday
By Road: 1 mile north-west of the city centre off the A49 (Leominster) road.
By Rail: Hereford Station (1 mile from the course).

HEXHAM (L.H)

N.H. Oval, 1m4f (10), 220y run-in. An undulating course that becomes very testing when the ground is soft, it has easy fences and a stiff climb to the finishing straight, which is on a separate spur.
Address: Hexham Racecourse, The Riding, Hexham, Northumberland NE46 2JP Tel: 01434 606881
Racedays: 01434 603738
Website: www.hexham-racecourse.co.uk
Chief Executive: Robert Whitelock
Clerk of the Course: James Armstrong 01434 606881 or 07801 166820
By Road: 1.5 miles south-west of the town off the B6305.
By Rail: Hexham Station (Newcastle-Carlisle line). Free bus to the course.
By Air: Helicopter landing facility in centre of course (by special arrangement only).

HUNTINGDON (R.H)

N.H. Oval, 1m4f (9), 200y run-in. A perfectly flat, galloping track with a tricky open ditch in front of the stands. The two fences in the home straight can cause problems for novice chasers. Suits front-runners.
Address: The Racecourse, Brampton, Huntingdon, Cambridgeshire PE28 4NL Tel: 01480 453373
Website: www.huntingdon-racecourse.co.uk
Regional Director: Amy Starkey
Clerk of the Course: Roderick Duncan 07772 958685
General Manager: James Wilcox
By Road: The course is situated at Brampton, 2 miles west of Huntingdon on the A14. Easy access from the A1 (1/2 mile from the course).
By Rail: Huntingdon Station. Buses and taxis to course.
By Air: Helicopter landing facility by prior arrangement.

KELSO (L.H)

N.H. Oval, 1m1f (8), uphill run-in of just over a furlong. Rather undulating with two downhill fences opposite the stands, it suits the nippy, front-running sort, though the uphill finish helps the true stayer. The hurdle course is smaller and very sharp with a tight turn away from the stands.
Address: Kelso Racecourse, Kelso, Roxburghshire TD5 7SX Tel: 01668 280800
Website: www.kelso-races.co.uk
Clerk of the Course: Matthew Taylor 07521 517495
Managing Director: Jonathan Garratt
By Road: 1 mile north of the town, off the B6461.
By Rail: Berwick-upon-Tweed Station. 23-mile bus journey to Kelso.
By Air: Helicopters can land at course by arrangement, fixed wing aircraft at Winfield, regular aircraft at Edinburgh.

KEMPTON PARK (R.H)

Flat: A floodlit Polytrack circuit. A 1m2f outer track accommodates races over 6f, 7f, 1m, 1m3f, 1m4f and 2m. The 1m inner track caters for races over 5f and 1m2f.
N.H. Triangular, 1m5f (10), 175y run-in. A practically flat, sharp course where the long run between the last obstacle on the far side and the first in the home straight switches the emphasis from jumping to speed. The hurdles track is on the outside of the chase track. The course crosses the Polytrack at two points on each circuit.
Address: Kempton Park Racecourse, Sunbury-on-Thames, Middlesex TW16 5AQ Tel: 01932 782292
Website: www.kempton.co.uk
Regional Director: Amy Starkey
Clerk of the Course and Director of Racing: Brian Clifford 07880 784484
Assistant Clerk of the Course: Sarah Dunster
General Manager: Simon Durrant
By Road: On the A308 near Junction 1 of the M3.
By Rail: Kempton Park Station (from Waterloo).
By Air: London (Heathrow) Airport 6 miles.

LEICESTER (R.H)

Flat: A stiff, galloping, right-handed oval of 1m5f, with a 5f run-in. There is a straight course of seven furlongs.
N.H. Rectangular, 1m6f (10), 250y run-in uphill. An undulating course with an elbow 150y from the finish,it can demand a high degree of stamina, as the going can become extremely testing and the last three furlongs are uphill.
Address: Leicester Racecourse, Oadby, Leicester, LE2 4AL Tel: 01162 716515
Website: www.leicester-racecourse.co.uk
Clerk of the Course: Jimmy Stevenson 01162 712115 or 07774 497281
General Manager: Rob Bracken
By Road: The course is 2.5 miles south-east of the city on the A6 (M1, Junction 21). The car park is free.
By Rail: Leicester Station (from St Pancras) is 2.5 miles.
By Air: Helicopter landing facility in the centre of the course.

LINGFIELD PARK (L.H)

Flat, Turf: A sharp, undulating left-handed circuit, with a 7f 140y straight course.
Flat, Polytrack: The left-handed Polytrack is 1m2f round, with an extended chute to provide a 1m5f start. It is a sharp, level track with a short run-in.
N.H. Conical, 1m5f (10), 200y run-in. Severely undulating with a tight downhill turn into the straight, the chase course suits front-runners.
Address: Lingfield Park Racecourse, Lingfield, Surrey RH7 6PQ Tel: 01342 834800
Website: www.lingfield-racecourse.co.uk
Clerk of the Course: George Hill 07581 119984
Executive Director: Martin Wales
General Manager: Russell Bowes
By Road: South-east of the town off the A22; M25 (Junction 6). Ample free parking.
By Rail: Lingfield Station (regular services from London Bridge and Victoria). Half-mile walk to the course.
By Air: London (Gatwick) Airport 10 miles. Helicopter landing facility south of wind-sock.

LUDLOW (R.H)

N.H. Oval, 1m4f (9), 185y run-in. The chase course is flat and has quite sharp bends into and out of the home straight, although long-striding horses never seem to have any difficulties. The hurdle course is on the outside of the chase track and is not so sharp.
Address: Ludlow Race Club Ltd, The Racecourse, Bromfield, Ludlow, Shropshire SY8 2BT Tel: 01584 856221 (Racedays) or see below.
Website: www.ludlowracecourse.co.uk
General Manager and Clerk of the Course: Simon Sherwood 07836 215639
By Road: The course is situated at Bromfield, 2 miles north of Ludlow on the A49.
By Rail: Ludlow Station (Hereford-Shrewsbury line) 2 miles.
By Air: Helicopter landing facility in the centre of the course by arrangement with the Clerk of the Course

MARKET RASEN (R.H)

N.H. Oval, 1m2f (8), 250y run-in. A sharp, undulating course with a long run to the straight, it favours the handy, front-running type.
Address: Market Rasen Racecourse, Legsby Road, Market Rasen, Lincolnshire LN8 3EA Tel: 01673 843434
Website: www.marketrasenraces.co.uk
Regional Director: Amy Starkey
Clerk of the Course: Jack Pryor
General Manager: Nadia Powell
By Road: The town is just off the A46, and the racecourse is one mile east of the town on the A631. Free car parks.
By Rail: Market Rasen Station 1 mile (King's Cross - Cleethorpes line).
By Air: Helicopter landing facility by prior arrangement only.

MUSSELBURGH (R.H)

Flat: A sharp, level, right-handed oval of 1m2f, with a run-in of 4f. There is an additional 5f straight course.
N.H. Rectangular, 1m3f (8), 150y run-in (variable). A virtually flat track with sharp turns, suiting the handy, front-running sort. It drains well. There is a section of Polytrack going away from the stands.
Address: Musselburgh Racecourse, Linkfield Road, Musselburgh, East Lothian EH21 7RG
Tel: 01316 652859
Website: www.musselburgh-racecourse.co.uk
Clerk of the Course: Rory Innes 07922 410937
General Manager: Bill Farnsworth 07710 536134
By Road: The course is situated at Musselburgh, 5 miles east of Edinburgh on the A1. Car park, adjoining course, free for buses and cars.
By Rail: Waverley Station (Edinburgh). Local Rail service to Musselburgh.
By Air: Edinburgh (Turnhouse) Airport 30 minutes.

NEWBURY (L.H)

Flat: Left-handed, oval track of about 1m7f, with a slightly undulating straight mile. The round course is level and galloping with a four and a half-furlong straight. Races over the round mile start on the adjoining chute.
N.H. Oval, 1m6f (11), 255y run-in. Slightly undulating, wide and galloping in nature. The fences are stiff and sound jumping is essential. One of the fairest tracks in the country.
Address: Newbury Racecourse, Newbury, Berkshire RG14 7NZ Tel: 01635 40015
Website: www.newbury-racecourse.co.uk
Chief Executive: Julian Thick
Clerk of the Course: Keith Ottesen 07813 043453
By Road: East of the town off the A34 (M4, Junction 12 or 13). Car park, adjoining enclosures, free.
By Rail: Newbury Racecourse Station adjoins the course.
By Air: Light Aircraft landing strip East/West. 830 metres by 30 metres wide. Helicopter landing facilities.

NEWCASTLE (L.H)

Flat: A 1m6f Tapeta track outside the jumps course. The straight mile is floodlit.
N.H. Oval, 1m6f (11), 220y run-in. A gradually rising home straight of four furlongs makes this galloping track a true test of stamina, especially as the ground can become very heavy.
Address: High Gosforth Park, Newcastle-Upon-Tyne, NE3 5HP Tel: 01912 362020
Website: www.newcastle-racecourse.co.uk
Clerk of the Course: Eloise Quayle 07968 751087
Executive Director: Paul Elliott
By Road: 4 miles north of the city on the A6125 (near the A1). Car and coach park free.
By Rail: Newcastle Central Station (from King's Cross). A free bus service operates from South Gosforth and Regent Centre Metro Station.
By Air: Helicopter landing facility by prior arrangement. The Airport is 4 miles from the course.

NEWMARKET (R.H)

Rowley Mile Course: There is a straight ten-furlong course, which is wide and galloping. Races over 1m4f or more are right-handed. The Rowley Mile course has a long run-in and a stiff finish.
July Course: Races up to a mile are run on the Bunbury course, which is straight. Races over 1m2f or more are right-handed, with a 7f run-in. Like the Rowley Mile course, the July Course track is stiff.
Address: Newmarket Racecourse, Westfield House, The Links, Newmarket, Suffolk CB8 0TG Tel: 01638 663482 (Main Office) 01638 663762 (Rowley Mile) 01638 675416 (July) .
Website: www.newmarketracecourses.co.uk
Clerk of the Course and Racing Director: Michael Prosser 01638 675504 or 07802 844578
Regional Director: Amy Starkey
General Manager: Sophie Able
By Road: South-west of the town on the A1304 London Road (M11 Junction 9). Free car parking at the rear of the enclosure. Annual Badge Holders' car park free all days. Courtesy bus service from Newmarket Station, Bus Station and High Street, commencing 90 minutes prior to the first race.
By Rail: Infrequent rail service to Newmarket Station from Cambridge (Liverpool Street) or direct bus service from Cambridge (13-mile journey).
By Air: Landing facilities for light aircraft and helicopters on racedays at both racecourses. See Flight Guide. Cambridge Airport 11 miles.

NEWTON ABBOT (L.H)

N.H. Oval, 1m2f (7), 300y run-in. Flat with two tight bends. The nippy, agile sort is favoured. The run-in can be very short on the hurdle course.
Address: Newton Abbot Races Ltd., Kingsteignton Road, Newton Abbot, Devon TQ12 3AF Tel: 01626 353235
Website: www.newtonabbotracing.com
Clerk of the Course: Jason Loosemore 07766 228109
Managing Director: Pat Masterson Tel: 01626 353235 Mobile: 07917 830144
By Road: North of the town on the A380. Torquay 6 miles, Exeter 17 miles.
By Rail: Newton Abbot Station (from Paddington) 3/4 mile. Buses and taxis operate to and from the course.
By Air: Helicopter landing pad in the centre of the course.

NOTTINGHAM (L.H)

Flat: Left-handed, galloping, oval of about 1m4f, and a straight of four and a half furlongs. Flat with easy turns.
Address: Nottingham Racecourse, Colwick Park, Nottingham, NG2 4BE Tel: 0870 8507634
Website: www.nottinghamracecourse.co.uk
Regional Director: Amy Starkey
Clerk of the Course: Tom Ryall
By Road: 2 miles east of the city centre on the B686.
By Rail: Nottingham (Midland) Station. Regular bus service to course (2 miles).
By Air: Helicopter landing facility in the centre of the course.

PERTH (R.H)

N.H. Rectangular, 1m2f (8), 283y run-in. A flat, easy track with sweeping turns. Not a course for the long-striding galloper.
Address: Perth Racecourse, Scone Palace Park, Perth, PH2 6BB Tel: 01738 551597
Website: www.perth-races.co.uk
Clerk of the Course: Matthew Taylor
General Manager: Hazel Peplinski
By Road: 4 miles north of the town off the A93.
By Rail: Perth Station (from Dundee) 4 miles. There are buses to the course.
By Air: Scone Airport (3.75 miles). Edinburgh Airport 45 minutes.

PLUMPTON (L.H)

N.H. Oval, 1m1f (6), 200y run-in uphill. A tight, undulating circuit with an uphill finish, Plumpton favours the handy, fast jumper.
Address: Plumpton Racecourse, Plumpton, East Sussex BN7 3AL Tel: 01273 890383
Website: www.plumptonracecourse.co.uk
Clerk of the Course: Marcus Waters
By Road: 2 miles north of the village off the B2116.
By Rail: Plumpton Station (from Victoria) adjoins course.
By Air: Helicopter landing facility by prior arrangement with the Clerk of the Course.

PONTEFRACT (L.H)

Flat: Left-handed oval, undulating course of 2m133y, with a short run-in of 2f. It is a particularly stiff track with the last 3f uphill.
Address: Pontefract Park Race Co. Ltd., The Park, Pontefract, West Yorkshire Tel: 01977 781307
Website: www.pontefract-races.co.uk
Managing Director: Norman Gundill 01977 781307
Assistant Manager and Clerk of the Course: Richard Hamill
By Road: 1 mile north of the town on the A639. Junction 32 of M62. Free car park adjacent to the course.
By Rail: Pontefract Station (Tanshelf, every hour to Wakefield), 1 1/2 miles from the course. Regular bus service from Leeds.
By Air: Helicopters by arrangement only. (Nearest Airfields: Robin Hood (Doncaster), Sherburn-in-Elmet, Yeadon (Leeds Bradford).

REDCAR (L.H)

Flat: Left-handed, level, galloping, oval course of 1m6f with a straight run-in of 5f. There is also a straight mile.
Address: Redcar Racecourse, Redcar, Cleveland TS10 2BY Tel: 01642 484068
Website: www.redcarracing.com
Clerk of the Course: Jonjo Sanderson Tel: 01642 484068 Mobile: 07766 022893
General Manager: Amy Fair
By Road: In the town off the A1085. Free parking adjoining the course for buses and cars.
By Rail: Redcar Station (1/4 mile from the course).
By Air: Landing facilities at Turners Arms Farm (600yds runway) Yearby, Cleveland. Two miles south of the racecourse - transport available. Durham Tees Valley airport (18 miles west of Redcar).

RIPON (R.H)

Flat: A sharp, undulating, right-handed oval of 1m5f, with a 5f run-in. There is also a 6f straight course.
Address: Ripon Racecourse, Boroughbridge Road, Ripon, North Yorkshire HG4 1UG Tel: 01765 530530
Website: www.ripon-races.co.uk
Clerk of the Course and Managing Director: James Hutchinson 07860 679904
By Road: The course is situated 2 miles south-east of the city, on the B6265. There is ample free parking for cars and coaches.
By Rail: Harrogate Station (11 miles) or Thirsk (15 miles). Bus services to Ripon.
By Air: Helicopters only on the course. Otherwise Leeds/Bradford airport.

SALISBURY (R.H)

Flat: Right-handed and level, with a run-in of 4f. There is a straight mile track. The last half-mile is uphill, providing a stiff test of stamina.
Address: Salisbury Racecourse, Netherhampton, Salisbury, Wiltshire SP2 8PN Tel: 01722 326461
Website: www.salisburyracecourse.co.uk
Clerk of the Course and General Manager: Jeremy Martin 07880 744999
By Road: 3 miles south-west of the city on the A3094 at Netherhampton. Free car park adjoins the course.
By Rail: Salisbury Station is 3.5 miles (from London Waterloo). Bus service to the course.
By Air: Helicopter landing facility near the 1m2f start.

SANDOWN PARK (R.H)

Flat: An easy right-handed oval course of 1m5f with a stiff, straight uphill run-in of 4f. Separate straight 5f track is also uphill. Galloping.
N.H. Oval, 1m5f (11), 220y run-in uphill. Features seven fences on the back straight; the last three (the Railway Fences) are very close together and can often decide the outcome of races. The stiff climb to the finish puts the emphasis very much on stamina, but accurate-jumping, free-running sorts are also favoured. Hurdle races are run on the Flat course.
Address: Sandown Park Racecourse, Esher, Surrey KT10 9AJ Tel: 01372 464348
Website: www.sandown.co.uk
Regional Director: Amy Starkey
General Manager: Sarah Drabwell
Clerk of the Course: Andrew Cooper: 01372 461213 Mobile: 07774 230850
By Road: Four miles south-west of Kingston-on-Thames, on the A307 (M25 Junction 10).
By Rail: Esher Station (from Waterloo) adjoins the course.
By Air: London (Heathrow) Airport 12 miles.

SEDGEFIELD (L.H)

N.H. Oval, 1m2f (8), 200y run-in. Undulating with fairly tight turns, it doesn't suit big, long-striding horses.
Address: Sedgefield Racecourse, Sedgefield, Stockton-on-Tees, Cleveland TS21 2HW Tel: 01740 621925
Website: www.sedgefield-racecourse.co.uk
General Manager: Colin Smith
Clerk of the Course: Michael Naughton
By Road: 3/4 mile south-west of the town, near the junction of the A689 (Bishop Auckland) and the A177 (Durham) roads. The car park is free.
By Rail: Darlington Station (9 miles). Durham Station (12 miles).
By Air: Helicopter landing facility in car park area by prior arrangement only.

SOUTHWELL (L.H)

Flat, Tapeta: Left-handed oval, Tapeta course of 1m2f with a 3f run-in. There is a straight 5f. Tapeta replaced Fibresand in late 2021.
N.H. Oval, 1m 1f (7), 220y run-in. A tight, flat track with a short run-in, it suits front-runners.
Address: Southwell Racecourse, Rolleston, Newark, Nottinghamshire NG25 0TS Tel: 01636 814481
Website: www.southwell-racecourse.co.uk
Executive Director: Mark Clayton
Clerk of the Course: David Attwood 07860 274289
By Road: The course is situated at Rolleston, 3 miles south of Southwell, 5 miles from Newark.
By Rail: Rolleston Station (Nottingham-Newark line) adjoins the course.
By Air: Helicopters can land by prior arrangement.

STRATFORD-ON-AVON (L.H)

N.H. Triangular, 1m2f (8), 200y run-in. Virtually flat with two tight bends, and quite a short home straight. A sharp and turning course, it suits the well-balanced, handy sort.
Address: Stratford Racecourse, Luddington Road, Stratford-upon-Avon, Warwickshire CV37 9SE Tel: 01789 267949
Website: www.stratfordracecourse.net
Managing Director: Ilona Barnett
Clerk of the Course: Nessie Chanter
By Road: A mile from the town centre, off the A429 (Evesham road).
By Rail: Stratford-on-Avon Station (from Birmingham New Street or Leamington Spa) 1 mile.
By Air: Helicopter landing facility by prior arrangement.

TAUNTON (R.H)

N.H. Elongated oval, 1m2f (8), 150y run-in uphill. Sharp turns, especially after the winning post, with a steady climb from the home bend. Suits the handy sort.
Address: Taunton Racecourse, Orchard Portman, Taunton, Somerset TA3 7BL Tel: 01823 337172
Website: www.tauntonracecourse.co.uk
Clerk of the Course: Jason Loosemore 07766 228109
Chief Executive: Bob Young
By Road: Two miles south of the town on the B3170 (Honiton) road (M5 Junction 25).
By Rail: Taunton Station 2 miles. There are buses and taxis to course.
By Air: Helicopter landing facility by prior arrangement.

THIRSK (L.H)

Flat: Left-handed oval of 1m2f with sharp turns and an undulating run-in of 4f. There is a straight 6f track.
Address: The Racecourse, Station Road, Thirsk, North Yorkshire YO7 1QL Tel: 01845 522276
Website: www.thirskracecourse.net
Clerk of the Course and Managing Director: James Sanderson
By Road: West of the town on the A61. Free car park adjacent to the course for buses and cars.
By Rail: Thirsk Station (from King's Cross), 1/2 mile from the course.
By Air: Helicopters can land by prior arrangement. Tel: Racecourse 01845 522276. Fixed wing aircraft can land at RAF Leeming. Tel: 01677 423041. Light aircraft at Bagby. Tel: 01845 597385 or 01845 537555

UTTOXETER (L.H)

N.H. Oval, 1m2f (8), 170y run-in. A few undulations, easy bends and fences and a flat home straight of over half a mile. Suits front-runners, especially on the 2m hurdle course.
Address: The Racecourse, Wood Lane, Uttoxeter, Staffordshire ST14 8BD Tel: 01889 562561
Website: www.uttoxeter-racecourse.co.uk
Clerk of the Course: Richard Fothergill 07801 166820
General Manager: Brian Barrass
By Road: South-east of the town off the B5017 (Marchington Road).
By Rail: Uttoxeter Station (Crewe-Derby line) adjoins the course.
By Air: Helicopters can land by prior arrangement with the raceday office.

WARWICK (L.H)

N.H. Circular, 1m6f (10), 240y run-in. Undulating with tight bends, five quick fences in the back straight and a short home straight, Warwick favours handiness and speed rather than stamina.
Address: Warwick Racecourse, Hampton Street, Warwick, CV34 6HN Tel: 01926 491553
Website: www.warwickracecourse.co.uk
Regional Director: Ian Renton
Clerk of the Course: Tom Ryall
General Manager: Tommy Williams
By Road: West of the town on the B4095 adjacent to Junction 15 of the M40.
By Rail: Warwick or Warwick Parkway Stations.
By Air: Helicopters can land by prior arrangement with the Clerk of the Course.

WETHERBY (L.H)

Flat: First used in 2015, the Flat course is left-handed with a 1m4f circuit.
N.H. Oval, 1m4f (9), 200y run-in slightly uphill. A flat, very fair course which suits the long-striding galloper.
Address: The Racecourse, York Road, Wetherby, LS22 5EJ Tel: 01937 582035
Website: www.wetherbyracing.co.uk
Clerk of the Course and Chief Executive: Jonjo Sanderson 07831 437453
General Manager: Michelle Campbell
By Road: East of the town off the B1224 (York Road). Adjacent to the A1. Excellent bus and coach facilities. Car park free.
By Rail: Leeds Station 12 miles. Buses to Wetherby.
By Air: Helicopters can land by prior arrangement

WINCANTON (R.H)

N.H. Rectangular, 1m3f (9), 200y run-in. Good galloping course where the going rarely becomes heavy. The home straight is mainly downhill.
Address: Wincanton Racecourse, Wincanton, Somerset BA9 8BJ Tel: 01963 435840
Website: www.wincantonracecourse.co.uk
Regional Director: Ian Renton
Clerk of the Course: Daniel Cooper 07976 413045
General Manager: Jack Parkinson
By Road: 1 mile north of the town on the B3081.
By Rail: Gillingham Station (from Waterloo) or Castle Cary Station (from Paddington). Buses and taxis to the course.
By Air: Helicopter landing area is situated in the centre of the course.

WINDSOR (Fig. 8)

Flat: Figure of eight track of 1m4f 110y. The course is level and sharp with a long run-in. The 6f course is essentially straight.
Address: Royal Windsor Racecourse, Maidenhead Road, Windsor, Berkshire SL4 5JJ Tel: 01753 498400
Website: www.windsor-racecourse.co.uk
Clerk of the Course: Charlie Rees 07773 652379
Executive Director: Liam Johnson
By Road: North of the town on the A308 (M4 Junction 6).
By Rail: Windsor Central Station (from Paddington) or Windsor and Eton Riverside Station (from Waterloo).
By Air: London (Heathrow) Airport 15 minutes. Also White Waltham Airport (West London Aero Club) 15 minutes.
River Bus: Seven minutes from Barry Avenue promenade at Windsor.

WOLVERHAMPTON (L.H)

Flat: Left-handed, floodlit, oval Tapeta track of 1m, with a run-in of 380y. A level track with sharp bends.
Address: Wolverhampton Racecourse, Dunstall Park, Gorsebrook Road, Wolverhampton, WV6 0PE Tel: 01902 390000
Website: www.wolverhampton-racecourse.co.uk
Clerk of the Course: Fergus Cameron 07971 531162
General Manager: Dave Roberts
By Road: 1 mile north of the city centre on the A449 (M54 Junction 2 or M6 Junction 12). Car parking free.
By Rail: Wolverhampton Station (from Euston) 1 mile.
By Air: Halfpenny Green Airport 8 miles.

WORCESTER (L.H)

N.H. Elongated oval, 1m5f (9), 220y run-in. Flat with easy turns, it is a very fair, galloping track.
Address: Worcester Racecourse, Pitchcroft, Worcester, WR1 3EJ Tel: 01905 25364
Website: www.worcester-racecourse.co.uk
Clerk of the Course: Nessie Chanter 07812 202904
General Manager: Michael Thomas
By Road: West of the city centre off the A449 (Kidderminster road) (M5 Junction 8).
By Rail: Foregate Street Station, Worcester (from Paddington) 3/4 mile.
By Air: Helicopter landing facility in the centre of the course, by prior arrangement only.

YARMOUTH (L.H)

Flat: Left-handed, level circuit of 1m4f, with a run-in of 5f. The straight course is 1m long.
Address: The Racecourse, Jellicoe Road, Great Yarmouth, Norfolk NR30 4AU Tel: 01493 842527
Website: www.greatyarmouth-racecourse.co.uk
Clerk of the Course: Richard Aldous 07738 507643
Executive Director: Glenn Tubby
By Road: 1 mile east of town centre (well signposted from A47 and A12).
By Rail: Great Yarmouth Station (1 mile). Bus service to the course.
By Air: Helicopter landing available by prior arrangement with Racecourse Office

---

YORK (L.H)

Flat: Left-handed, level, galloping track, with a straight 6f. There is also an adjoining chute for races over 7f.
Address: The Racecourse, York, YO23 1EX Tel: 01904 683932
Website: www.yorkracecourse.co.uk
Clerk of the Course and Chief Executive: William Derby 07812 961176
Assistant Clerk of the Course: Anthea Leigh
By Road: 1 mile south-east of the city on the A1036.
By Rail: 1 1/2 miles York Station (from King's Cross). Special bus service from station to the course.
By Air: Light aircraft and helicopter landing facilities available at Rufforth aerodrome (5,000ft tarmac runway). Leeds Bradford airport (25 miles).

HE EUROPEAN LASSIFICATION OF WO-YEAR-OLDS

ting	Horse	Trainer
	Little Big Bear (IRE)	Aidan O'Brien
	Blackbeard (IRE)	Aidan O'Brien
	Chaldean (GB)	Andrew Balding
	Auguste Rodin (IRE)	Aidan O'Brien
	Royal Scotsman (IRE)	Paul & Oliver Cole
	Tahiyra (IRE)	Dermot Weld
	Noble Style (GB)	Charlie Appleby
	Commissioning (GB)	John & Thady Gosden
	Silver Knott (GB)	Charlie Appleby
	Victoria Road (IRE)	Aidan O'Brien
	Al Riffa (FR)	Joseph O'Brien
	Bradsell (GB)	Archie Watson
	Dubai Mile (IRE)	Charlie & Mark Johnston
	Lezoo (GB)	Ralph Beckett
	Meditate (IRE)	Aidan O'Brien
	Sakheer (IRE)	Roger Varian
	Arrest (IRE)	John & Thady Gosden
	Blue Rose Cen (IRE)	Christopher Head
	Marshman (GB)	Karl Burke
	Mischief Magic (IRE)	Charlie Appleby
	Nostrum (GB)	Sir Michael Stoute
	Novakai (GB)	Karl Burke
	Persian Force (IRE)	Richard Hannon
	Proud And Regal (IRE)	Donnacha O'Brien
	The Antarctic (IRE)	Aidan O'Brien
	Belbek (FR)	André Fabre
	Espionage (IRE)	Aidan O'Brien
	Epictetus (IRE)	John & Thady Gosden
	Gamestop (IRE)	Christophe Ferland
	The Foxes (IRE)	Andrew Balding
	The Platinum Queen (IRE)	Richard Fahey
	Trillium (GB)	Richard Hannon
	Aesop's Fables (IRE)	Aidan O'Brien
	Breizh Sky (FR)	A. & G. Botti
	Charyn (IRE)	Roger Varian
	Crypto Force (GB)	Michael O'Callaghan
	Flying Honours (GB)	Charlie Appleby
	Marbaan (GB)	Charlie Fellowes
	Mawj (IRE)	Saeed Bin Suroor
	Mysterious Night (IRE)	Charlie Appleby
	Naval Power (GB)	Charlie Appleby
	Quantanamera (GER)	Andreas Suborics
	Shartash (IRE)	Johnny Murtagh

LONGINES WORLD'S BEST RACEHORSE RANKINGS 2022

For **three-year-olds** rated 115 or greater by the IFHA World's Best Racehorse Rankings Conference.

Rating	Horse	Trained
140	**Flightline (USA)**	USA
135	**Baaeed (GB)**	GB
126	**Equinox (JPN)**	JPN
126	**Nature Strip (AUS)**	AUS
125	**Epicenter (USA)**	USA
125	**Life Is Good (USA)**	USA
125	**Vadeni (FR)**	FR
124	**Golden Sixty (AUS)**	HK
124	**Kyprios (IRE)**	IRE
124	**Olympiad (USA)**	USA
124	**Pyledriver (GB)**	GB
124	**Real World (IRE)**	GB
124	**Romantic Warrior (IRE)**	HK
124	**Titleholder (JPN)**	JPN
124	**Torquator Tasso (GER)**	GER
123	**Alpinista (GB)**	GB
123	**California Spangle (IRE)**	HK
123	**Desert Crown (GB)**	GB
123	**Luxembourg (IRE)**	IRE
123	**Taiba (USA)**	USA
123	**Vela Azul (JPN)**	JPN
122	**Bay Bridge (GB)**	GB
122	**Hukum (IRE)**	GB
122	**Onesto (IRE)**	FR
122	**Rebel's Romance (IRE)**	GB
122	**Serifos (JPN)**	JPN
122	**Speaker's Corner (USA)**	USA
122	**State of Rest (IRE)**	IRE
121	**Adayar (IRE)**	GB
121	**Al Hakeem (GB)**	FR
121	**Anamoe (AUS)**	AUS
121	**Coroebus (IRE)**	GB
121	**Country Grammer (USA)**	USA
121	**Golden Pal (USA)**	USA
121	**Hot Rod Charlie (USA)**	USA
121	**Jack Christopher (USA)**	USA
121	**Jackie's Warrior (USA)**	USA
121	**Minzaal (IRE)**	GB
121	**Modern Games (IRE)**	GB
121	**My Prospero (IRE)**	GB
121	**Shahryar (JPN)**	JPN
121	**Trueshan (FR)**	GB
121	**Wellington (AUS)**	HK
120	**Boldog Hos (JPN)**	JPN
120	**Do Deuce (JPN)**	JPN
120	**Dreamloper (IRE)**	GB
120	**El Bodegon (IRE)**	AUS
120	**Emblem Road (USA)**	KSA
120	**Giga Kick (AUS)**	AUS
120	**Gold Trip (FR)**	AUS
120	**Hishi Iguazu (JPN)**	JPN
120	**Home Affairs (AUS)**	AUS
120	**I'm Thunderstruck (NZ)**	AUS
120	**Inspiral (GB)**	GB
120	**Light Infantry (FR)**	GB
120	**Mishriff (IRE)**	GB
120	**Mo Donegal (USA)**	USA
120	**Panthalassa (JPN)**	JPN
120	**Private Eye (AUS)**	AUS
120	**Rich Strike (USA)**	USA
120	**Think It Over (AUS)**	AUS
120	**Tunnes (GER)**	GER
120	**Weltreisende (JPN)**	JPN
120	**Westover (GB)**	GB
120	**Zaaki (GB)**	AUS
119	**Alcohol Free (IRE)**	GB
119	**Alligator Blood (AUS)**	AUS
119	**Cody's Wish (USA)**	USA
119	**Cyberknife (USA)**	USA
119	**Danon Beluga (JPN)**	JPN
119	**Erevann (FR)**	FR
119	**Geoglyph (JPN)**	JPN
119	**Highfield Princess (FR)**	GB
119	**Homeless Songs (IRE)**	IRE
119	**Jet Dark (SAF)**	SAF
119	**Kinross (GB)**	GB
119	**Laurel River (USA)**	USA
119	**Laws of Indices (IRE)**	AUS
119	**Mandaloun (USA)**	USA
119	**Native Trail (GB)**	GB
119	**Yibir (GB)**	UAE
118	**A Case of You (IRE)**	IRE
118	**Alenquer (FR)**	GB
118	**Anmaat (IRE)**	GB
118	**Authority (JPN)**	JPN
118	**Bayside Boy (IRE)**	GB
118	**Broome (IRE)**	IRE
118	**Danon Scorpion (JPN)**	JPN
118	**Danon The Kid (JPN)**	JPN
118	**Early Voting (USA)**	USA
118	**Goodnight Olive (USA)**	USA
118	**Jack d'Or (JPN)**	JPN
118	**Jun Light Bolt (JPN)**	JPN
118	**Kommetdieding (SAF)**	SAF
118	**Letruska (USA)**	USA
118	**Lord North (IRE)**	GB
118	**Lost And Running (NZ)**	AUS
118	**Malathaat (USA)**	USA
118	**Malibu Spring (ARG)**	ARG
118	**Man of Promise (USA)**	UAE
118	**Mojo Star (IRE)**	GB
118	**Naval Crown (GB)**	GB
118	**Nest (USA)**	USA
118	**Order of Australia (IRE)**	IRE
118	**Pearls Galore (FR)**	IRE
118	**Salios (JPN)**	JPN
118	**Schnell Meister (GER)**	JPN
118	**Stone Age (IRE)**	IRE
118	**Stradivarius (IRE)**	GB
118	**T O Keynes (JPN)**	JPN
118	**Tuesday (IRE)**	IRE
118	**Waikuku (IRE)**	HK
117	**Art Collector (USA)**	USA
117	**Ask Victor More (JPN)**	JPN
117	**Cafe Pharoah (USA)**	JPN
117	**Casa Creed (USA)**	USA
117	**Cascadian (GB)**	AUS
117	**Chuwa Wizard (JPN)**	JPN
117	**Count Again (CAN)**	USA
117	**Creative Force (IRE)**	GB
117	**Dancing Prince (JPN)**	JPN
117	**Deep Bond (JPN)**	JPN
117	**Do It Again (SAF)**	SAF
117	**Eduardo (AUS)**	AUS
117	**Gufo (USA)**	USA
117	**Hamish (GB)**	GB
117	**Hezashocka (NZ)**	AUS
117	**High Definition (IRE)**	IRE
117	**In Italian (GB)**	USA
117	**Iresine (FR)**	FR
117	**Junko (GB)**	FR
117	**Luthier Blues (ARG)**	ARG
117	**Mazu (AUS)**	AUS
117	**Mendocino (GER)**	GER
117	**Midnight Bourbon (USA)**	USA

117 Mo'unga (NZ) AUS
117 Nations Pride (IRE) GB
117 O'Connor (CHI) CHI
117 Potager (JPN) JPN
117 Regal Glory (USA) USA
117 Russian Emperor (IRE) HK
117 Santin (USA) USA
117 Secret Oath (USA) USA
117 Simca Mille (IRE) FR
117 Soul Rush (JPN) JPN
117 Spendarella (USA) USA
117 Stay Foolish (JPN) JPN
117 Tuvalu (AUS) AUS
117 Vin de Garde (JPN) JPN
117 Zandon (USA) USA
116 Aldaary (GB) GB
116 Alflaila (GB) GB
116 Al Muthana (AUS) SAF
116 Annapolis (USA) USA
116 Arrivo (JPN) JPN
116 Artorius (AUS) AUS
116 Baratti (GB) FR
116 Blue Stripe (ARG) USA
116 Charge It (USA) USA
116 Charles Dickens (SAF) SAF
116 Clairiere (USA) USA
116 Coltrane (IRE) GB
116 Converge (AUS) AUS
116 Crown Pride (JPN) JPN
116 Deauville Legend (IRE) GB
116 Defunded (USA) USA
116 Durazzo (ARG) ARG
116 Echo Zulu (USA) USA
116 Efforia (JPN) JPN
116 Eldar Eldarov (GB) GB
116 Elite Power (USA) USA
116 El Musical (ARG) ARG
116 Emily Upjohn (GB) GB
116 Express Train (USA) USA
116 Forbidden Love (AUS) AUS
116 Grand Glory (GB) FR
116 Hitotsu (AUS) AUS
116 I Wish I Win (NZ) AUS
116 Jacquinot (AUS) AUS
116 Justin Cafe (JPN) JPN
116 Ka Ying Star (GB) (ex Urban Aspect) HK
116 Knicks Go (USA) USA
116 Linebacker (SAF) SAF
116 Mare Australis (IRE) FR
116 Mostahdaf (IRE) GB
116 Mr Brightside (NZ) AUS
116 Overpass (AUS) AUS
116 Pretty Tiger (IRE) FR
116 Quickthorn (GB) GB
116 Royal Ship (BRZ) USA
116 Saffron Beach (IRE) GB
116 Shirl's Speight (USA) CAN
116 Sir Busker (IRE) GB
116 Sky Field (AUS) HK
116 Sodashi (JPN) JPN
116 Tempus (GB) GB
116 Tofane (NZ) AUS
116 Tourbillon Diamond (AUS) (ex Eric The Eel) HK
116 Tribhuvan (FR) USA
116 Ushba Tesoro (JPN) JPN
115 Aegon (NZ) AUS
115 Air Lolonois (JPN) JPN
115 Alegron (AUS) AUS
115 Americanrevolution (USA) USA
115 American Theorem (USA) USA
115 Apache Chase (AUS) AUS
115 Baller (AUS) AUS
115 Bathrat Leon (JPN) JPN
115 Beauty Joy (AUS) (ex Talladega) HK
115 Bella Nipotina (AUS) AUS
115 Benaud (AUS) AUS
115 Botanik (IRE) FR
115 Bubble Gift (FR) FR
115 Cezanne (USA) USA
115 Daring Tact (JPN) JPN
115 Diatonic (JPN) JPN
115 Double Superlative (SAF) SAF
115 Duais (AUS) AUS
115 Dubai Honour (IRE) GB
115 Elite Street (AUS) AUS
115 Fearless (USA) USA
115 Free Wind (IRE) GB
115 Gendarme (USA) JPN
115 Geraldina (JPN) JPN
115 Glory Vase (JPN) JPN
115 Going Global (IRE) USA
115 Grocer Jack (GER) GB
115 Gunite (USA) USA
115 Happy Saver (USA) USA
115 Hoo Ya Mal (GB) GB
115 In Secret (AUS) AUS
115 In The Congo (AUS) AUS
115 Ivar (BRZ) USA
115 Jadoomi (FR) GB
115 Jorel (BRZ) BRZ
115 Justin Palace (JPN) JPN
115 Just On Time (ARG) ARG
115 Labrado (ARG) ARG
115 Lady Speightspeare (USA) CAN
115 La Petite Coco (IRE) IRE
115 Lieutenant Dan (USA) USA
115 Lombardo (AUS) AUS
115 Lucky Patch (NZ) (ex Paleontologist) HK
115 Lucky Sweynesse (NZ) HK
115 Maljoom (IRE) GB
115 Marabi (AUS) AUS
115 Masked Crusader (AUS) AUS
115 Matenro Orion (JPN) JPN
115 Meisho Hario (JPN) JPN
115 Mira Mission (USA) USA
115 MK's Pride (SAF) SAF
115 Montefilia (AUS) AUS
115 Nashwa (GB) GB
115 Natan (ARG) ARG
115 New London (IRE) GB
115 Nino Guapo (ARG) ARG
115 Nonconformist (AUS) AUS
115 Omega Perfume (JPN) JPN
115 Ottoman Fleet (GB) GB
115 Perfect Power (IRE) GB
115 Place du Carrousel (IRE) FR
115 Pogo (IRE) GB
115 Pomp And Power (SAF) SAF
115 Racatan (CHI) CHI
115 Safe Passage (SAF) SAF
115 Sammarco (IRE) GER
115 Scope (IRE) GB
115 Sealiway (FR) FR
115 Search Results (USA) USA
115 Shantisara (IRE) USA
115 Shedaresthedevil (USA) USA
115 Sight Success (AUS) HK
115 Skippylongstocking (USA) USA
115 Slow Down Andy (USA) USA
115 Snapdancer (AUS) AUS
115 Songline (JPN) JPN
115 Sonnyboyliston (IRE) IRE
115 Stars on Earth (JPN) JPN
115 Stilleto Boy (USA) USA
115 Stronger (AUS) HK
115 Super Corinto (ARG) PER
115 Super Wealthy (AUS) (ex Covert Operation) HK
115 The Punisher (ARG) ARG
115 There Goes Harvard (USA) USA
115 The Revenant (GB) FR
115 Top Ranked (IRE) (ex Top Rank) AUS
115 War Like Goddess (USA) USA
115 White Abarrio (USA) USA

OLDER HORSES 2022

For **four-year-olds and up** rated 115 or greater by the IFHA World's Best Racehorse Rankings Conference.

Rating		Age	Trained
129	**Knicks Go (USA)**	6	USA
127	**Mishriff (IRE)**	5	GB
126	**Contrail (JPN)**	5	JPN
125	**Golden Sixty (AUS)**	7	HK
125	**Palace Pier (GB)**	5	GB
125	**Torquator Tasso (GER)**	5	GER
124	**Nature Strip (AUS)**	8	AUS
123	**Glory Vase (JPN)**	7	JPN
123	**Verry Elleegant (NZ)**	7	AUS
123	**Subjectivist (GB)**	5	GB
122	**Incentivise (AUS)**	6	AUS
122	**Domestic Spending (GB)**	5	USA
122	**Mystic Guide (USA)**	5	USA
121	**Eduardo (AUS)**	9	AUS
121	**Zaaki (GB)**	7	AUS
121	**Masked Crusader (AUS)**	6	AUS
121	**Authority (JPN)**	5	JPN
121	**Charlatan (USA)**	5	USA
121	**Deep Bond (JPN)**	5	JPN
120	**Addeybb (IRE)**	8	GB
120	**Exultant (IRE) (ex Irishcorrespondent)**	8	HK
120	**Monomoy Girl (USA)**	7	USA
120	**Skalleti (FR)**	7	FR
120	**Chrono Genesis (JPN)**	6	JPN
120	**Gran Alegria (JPN)**	6	JPN
120	**Lord North (IRE)**	6	GB
120	**Tarnawa (IRE)**	6	IRE
120	**Trueshan (FR)**	6	GB
120	**Pyledriver (GB)**	5	GB
120	**T O Keynes (JPN)**	5	JPN
119	**Do It Again (SAF)**	8	SAF
119	**Rainbow Bridge (SAF)**	8	SAF
119	**Village King (ARG)**	8	ARG
119	**Mugatoo (IRE)**	7	AUS
119	**World Premiere (JPN)**	6	JPN
119	**Al Aasy (IRE)**	5	GB
119	**Aloha West (USA)**	5	USA
119	**Art Collector (USA)**	5	USA
119	**Colonel Liam (USA)**	5	USA
119	**Max Player (USA)**	5	USA
119	**Starman (GB)**	5	GB
118	**Southern Legend (AUS)**	10	HK
118	**Dream of Dreams (IRE)**	8	GB
118	**Stradivarius (IRE)**	8	GB
118	**Indy Champ (JPN)**	7	JPN
118	**Sanrei Pocket (JPN)**	7	JPN
118	**The Revenant (GB)**	7	FR
118	**Think It Over (AUS)**	7	AUS
118	**Waikuku (IRE)**	7	HK
118	**Broome (IRE)**	6	IRE
118	**Dalasan (AUS)**	6	AUS
118	**Danon Kingly (JPN)**	6	JPN
118	**Letruska (USA)**	6	USA
118	**Loves Only You (JPN)**	6	JPN
118	**More Than This (GB)**	6	HK
118	**Sir Dragonet (IRE)**	6	AUS
118	**Sir Ron Priestley (GB)**	6	GB
118	**Space Blues (IRE)**	6	GB
118	**Unicorn Lion (IRE)**	6	JPN
118	**Alpinista (GB)**	5	GB

Rating		Age	Trained
118	**Gamine (USA)**	5	USA
118	**Lei Papale (JPN)**	5	JPN
118	**Love (IRE)**	5	IRE
118	**Mare Australis (IRE)**	5	FR
118	**Maxfield (USA)**	5	USA
118	**Order of Australia (IRE)**	5	IRE
118	**Real World (IRE)**	5	GB
118	**Russian Camelot (IRE)**	5	AUS
117	**Furore (NZ)**	8	HK
117	**Hot King Prawn (AUS) (ex Join In)**	8	HK
117	**Angel of Truth (AUS)**	7	AUS
117	**Behemoth (AUS)**	7	AUS
117	**Cascadian (GB)**	7	AUS
117	**Fifty Stars (IRE)**	7	AUS
117	**Ka Ying Star (GB) (ex Urban Aspect)**	7	HK
117	**Kolding (NZ)**	7	AUS
117	**Lone Rock (USA)**	7	USA
117	**Marianafoot (FR)**	7	FR
117	**My Sister Nat (FR)**	7	USA
117	**Hishi Iguazu (JPN)**	6	JPN
117	**Lady Bowthorpe (GB)**	6	GB
117	**Mo Forza (USA)**	6	USA
117	**Probabeel (NZ)**	6	NZ
117	**Spanish Mission (USA)**	6	GB
117	**Tetaze (ARG)**	6	ARG
117	**Zenden (USA)**	6	USA
117	**Armory (IRE)**	5	IRE
117	**Gufo (USA)**	5	USA
117	**Jet Dark (SAF)**	5	SAF
117	**Kommetdieding (SAF)**	5	SAF
117	**Lope Y Fernandez (IRE)**	5	IRE
117	**Malmoos (SAF)**	5	SAF
117	**Mo'unga (NZ)**	5	AUS
117	**Salios (JPN)**	5	JPN
117	**Smooth Like Strait (USA)**	5	USA
117	**Swiss Skydiver (USA)**	5	USA
117	**Tripoli (USA)**	5	USA
117	**Victor Ludorum (GB)**	5	FR
117	**War Like Goddess (USA)**	5	USA
117	**Wonderful Tonight (FR)**	5	GB
116	**Dreamforce (AUS)**	10	AUS
116	**Lord Glitters (FR)**	9	GB
116	**Twilight Payment (IRE)**	9	IRE
116	**Avilius (GB)**	8	AUS
116	**Kiseki (JPN)**	8	JPN
116	**Melody Belle (NZ)**	8	NZ
116	**Aero Trem (BRZ)**	7	URU
116	**Arcadia Queen (AUS)**	7	AUS
116	**Avantage (AUS)**	7	NZ
116	**Chuwa Wizard (JPN)**	7	JPN
116	**Danon Smash (JPN)**	7	JPN
116	**George Washington (BRZ)**	7	BRZ
116	**Gytrash (AUS)**	7	AUS
116	**Mr Quickie (AUS)**	7	AUS
116	**Pimper's Paradise (BRZ)**	7	BRZ
116	**Savatoxl (AUS)**	7	AUS
116	**Strategos (ARG)**	7	ARG
116	**Tofane (NZ)**	7	AUS
116	**Zoutori (AUS)**	7	AUS
116	**Audarya (FR)**	6	GB

Rating		Age	Trained
116	**Emaraaty Ana (GB)**	6	GB
116	**Got The Greenlight (SAF)**	6	SAF
116	**Grand Glory (GB)**	6	FR
116	**Lieutenant Dan (USA)**	6	USA
116	**Lost And Running (NZ)**	6	AUS
116	**Marche Lorraine (JPN)**	6	JPN
116	**Nonconformist (AUS)**	6	AUS
116	**Panfield (CHI) (ex Look Pen)**	6	HK
116	**Riodini (NZ)**	6	AUS
116	**Rio Querari (SAF)**	6	SAF
116	**Sky Field (AUS)**	6	HK
116	**Wellington (AUS)**	6	HK
116	**Aristoteles (JPN)**	5	JPN
116	**Catch Twentytwo (SAF)**	5	SAF
116	**Express Train (USA)**	5	USA
116	**Happy Saver (USA)**	5	USA
116	**Helvic Dream (IRE)**	5	IRE
116	**Hukum (IRE)**	5	GB
116	**Linebacker (SAF)**	5	SAF
116	**Mischevious Alex (USA)**	5	USA
116	**Sonnyboyliston (IRE)**	5	IRE
116	**Tagaloa (AUS)**	5	AUS
116	**Western Empire (NZ)**	5	AUS
115	**Secret Ambition (GB)**	9	UAE
115	**Whitmore (USA)**	9	USA
115	**Benbatl (GB)**	8	GB
115	**C Z Rocket (USA)**	8	USA
115	**Glen Shiel (GB)**	8	GB
115	**Homesman (USA)**	8	AUS
115	**Persian Knight (JPN)**	8	JPN
115	**Streets of Avalon (AUS)**	8	AUS
115	**Trekking (AUS)**	8	AUS
115	**Walton Street (GB)**	8	UAE
115	**Arctos (JPN)**	7	JPN
115	**Belgarion (SAF)**	7	SAF
115	**Classique Legend (AUS)**	7	AUS
115	**Columbus County (NZ) (ex Sword In Stone)**	7	HK
115	**Firenze Fire (USA)**	7	USA
115	**Glorious Dragon (IRE) (ex Stephensons Rocket)**	7	HK
115	**Omega Perfume (JPN)**	7	JPN
115	**Raging Bull (FR)**	7	USA
115	**Regal Power (AUS)**	7	AUS
115	**United (USA)**	7	USA
115	**Atletico El Culano (URU)**	6	URU

Rating		Age	Trained
115	**By My Standards (USA)**	6	USA
115	**Casino Fountain (JPN)**	6	JPN
115	**Ce Ce (USA)**	6	USA
115	**Colette (AUS)**	6	AUS
115	**Duhail (IRE)**	6	FR
115	**Dunbar Road (USA)**	6	USA
115	**Gustavus Weston (IRE)**	6	IRE
115	**Ivar (BRZ)**	6	USA
115	**Japan (GB)**	6	IRE
115	**Lucky Patch (NZ) (ex Paleontologist)**	6	HK
115	**Motakhayyel (GB)**	6	GB
115	**Mozu Bello (JPN)**	6	JPN
115	**Mutually (JPN)**	6	JPN
115	**Nahaarr (IRE)**	6	GB
115	**Oxted (GB)**	6	GB
115	**Royal Flag (USA)**	6	USA
115	**Royal Ship (BRZ)**	6	USA
115	**Search For A Song (IRE)**	6	IRE
115	**Sir Busker (IRE)**	6	GB
115	**Superstorm (AUS)**	6	AUS
115	**Two Emmys (USA)**	6	USA
115	**Vin de Garde (JPN)**	6	JPN
115	**Aegon (NZ)**	5	NZ
115	**Al Suhail (GB)**	5	GB
115	**Althiqa (GB)**	5	GB
115	**Beau Rossa (AUS)**	5	AUS
115	**Cafe Pharoah (USA)**	5	JPN
115	**Cezanne (USA)**	5	USA
115	**Country Grammer (USA)**	5	USA
115	**Daring Tact (JPN)**	5	JPN
115	**Explosive Jack (NZ)**	5	AUS
115	**Gold Trip (FR)**	5	FR
115	**I'm Thunderstruck (NZ)**	5	AUS
115	**Independence Hall (USA)**	5	USA
115	**Jackson Pollock (BRZ)**	5	BRZ
115	**Lauda Sion (JPN)**	5	JPN
115	**Lion's Roar (NZ)**	5	AUS
115	**Luthier Blues (ARG)**	5	ARG
115	**Nerium (IRE)**	5	GER
115	**Prague (AUS)**	5	AUS
115	**Russian Emperor (IRE)**	5	HK
115	**Shedaresthedevil (USA)**	5	USA
115	**Silver State (USA)**	5	USA
115	**Tizamagician (USA)**	5	USA

THE DERBY STAKES (GROUP 1)
EPSOM DOWNS ON SATURDAY 3 JUNE 2023

SECOND ENTRIES BY NOON 4 APRIL; SUPPLEMENTARY ENTRIES BY NOON 29 MAY.

HORSE	TRAINER
ACADEMIAN	Joseph Patrick O'Brien
ADARE MANOR (IRE)	Aidan O'Brien
ADELAIDE RIVER (IRE)	Aidan O'Brien
A DUBLIN LAD	John & Thady Gosden
AGATHON (IRE)	Joseph Patrick O'Brien
AGE OF KINGS (IRE)	Aidan O'Brien
ALBERT PARK (IRE)	Joseph Patrick O'Brien
ALDER (IRE)	Donnacha Aidan O'Brien
ALEXANDRA GARDENS (IRE)	Joseph Patrick O'Brien
ALEXANDROUPOLIS (IRE)	Aidan O'Brien
ALFRED MUNNINGS (IRE)	Aidan O'Brien
AL KHAWANEEJ STORM (IRE)	Owen Burrows
AL RIFFA (FR)	Joseph Patrick O'Brien
AMLETO (IRE)	William Haggas
AN BRADAN FEASA (IRE)	Joseph Patrick O'Brien
ANNADER (IRE)	William Haggas
ASTRODOME	John & Thady Gosden
AUGUST (IRE)	John & Thady Gosden
AUGUSTE RODIN (IRE)	Aidan O'Brien
BALLSBRIDGE (USA)	Aidan O'Brien
BALNARRING BEACH (IRE)	Joseph Patrick O'Brien
BATEMANS BAY (FR)	Ralph Beckett
BERKSHIRE SUNDANCE (IRE)	Andrew Balding
BERTINELLI (USA)	Aidan O'Brien
BORN RULER	Sir Mark Prescott Bt
BOY SCOUT	Aidan O'Brien
BRAVE KNIGHT	
BURGLAR	John & Thady Gosden
CANBERRA LEGEND (IRE)	James Ferguson
CAPE BRIDGEWATER (IRE)	Aidan O'Brien
CAPITANO	Hugo Palmer
CATANI GARDENS (IRE)	Joseph Patrick O'Brien
CHARLES BIANCONI (IRE)	Aidan O'Brien
CHARMING STAR (IRE)	
CHINDWIN	Sylvester Kirk
CIRCLE OF FIRE	Sir Michael Stoute
CITY OF CHICAGO (IRE)	Aidan O'Brien
CLAN CHIEFTAIN	Ralph Beckett
CLASSIC	Richard Hannon
CLEVER RELATION	Hughie Morrison
CLOCKWORK (IRE)	Aidan O'Brien
CONGO RIVER (USA)	Aidan O'Brien
COVENT GARDEN (IRE)	Aidan O'Brien
CRISIUM (IRE)	France
CRYSTAL MARINER (IRE)	Sir Michael Stoute
DARK SIDE (IRE)	
DAVIDEO	Ralph Beckett
DEAKIN (FR)	Joseph Patrick O'Brien
DELTA LEGEND (IRE)	William Haggas
DENMARK	Aidan O'Brien
DESERT HERO	William Haggas
DESFONDADO (IRE)	Simon Dow
DRUMROLL (IRE)	Aidan O'Brien
DUKE CADOR (IRE)	Aidan O'Brien
DUKE OF VIENNA (USA)	Aidan O'Brien
ENFJAAR (IRE)	
EPICTETUS (IRE)	John & Thady Gosden
ERUPTIVE (USA)	

HORSE	TRAINER
ESPIONAGE (IRE)	Aidan O'Brien
EXOPLANET (FR)	Roger Varian
FARNBOROUGH (IRE)	Aidan O'Brien
FISHERMAN'S BEACH (IRE)	Joseph Patrick O'Brien
FLAGSTAFF GARDENS	Joseph Patrick O'Brien
FORCEFUL SPEED (IRE)	George Boughey
FOX VISION	Roger Varian
GALIXO (FR)	Joseph Patrick O'Brien
GARDEN ROUTE (IRE)	William Haggas
GILLINGHAM	
GIMMIE SHELTER (USA)	Joseph Patrick O'Brien
GLORIOUS LION	James Ferguson
GODWINSON	William Haggas
GOOLOOGONG (IRE)	Aidan O'Brien
GRAN CABALLO (USA)	Joseph Patrick O'Brien
GREENLAND (IRE)	Aidan O'Brien
GREEN MACHINE (IRE)	Andrew Balding
GUARD	John & Thady Gosden
GULF OF MEXICO (IRE)	Aidan O'Brien
HANS ANDERSEN	Aidan O'Brien
HIAWATHA (IRE)	Aidan O'Brien
HIPPODROME (IRE)	Aidan O'Brien
HUMANITY (IRE)	John & Thady Gosden
HURST PARK (IRE)	Aidan O'Brien
HUTTON (IRE)	Joseph Patrick O'Brien
IKIGAI STAR (IRE)	Joseph Patrick O'Brien
INDEMNITY (IRE)	Roger Varian
INSPIRITUS (IRE)	Roger Varian
INTELLOTTO (IRE)	Joseph Patrick O'Brien
ITHACA'S ARROW	Dominic Ffrench Davis
JACOPO PERI (IRE)	Aidan O'Brien
JEFF KOONS (IRE)	John & Thady Gosden
JOAQUIN SOROLLA (IRE)	Aidan O'Brien
KALYMNOS (IRE)	A. Fabre France
KING LEODEGRANCE (IRE)	Aidan O'Brien
KING OF STEEL (USA)	David Loughnane
KING OF THE PLAINS (IRE)	Charlie Johnston
KLONDIKE	William Haggas
KNIGHT TO KING (IRE)	D. K. Weld
LAND LEGEND (FR)	James Ferguson
LAND OF DRAGONS (FR)	P. Bary France
LEADING LION (IRE)	John & Thady Gosden
LEGACY POWER	Andrew Balding
LIEBER POWER	Andrew Balding
LIKE A TIGER	James Ferguson
LION KINGDOM	James Fanshawe
LION OF WAR	Charlie Johnston
LION TAMER	John & Thady Gosden
LISBOA (IRE)	
LONDONER (IRE)	Aidan O'Brien
LOSE YOUR WAD (IRE)	Charles Hills
LOVING FEELING	John & Thady Gosden
LUNATICK	Hughie Morrison
MAHBOOB (IRE)	John & Thady Gosden
MAPOGO	James Ferguson
MAXIDENT	
MEDIEVAL GOLD	William Haggas
MIDDLE EARTH	John & Thady Gosden

HORSE	TRAINER
MILWAUKEE (USA)	Aidan O'Brien
MISTER MISTER (GER)	Joseph Patrick O'Brien
MOAB (IRE)	Joseph Patrick O'Brien
MODESTY (IRE)	Freddie & Martyn Meade
MOHATU	William Haggas
MOHAWK CHIEF (USA)	Aidan O'Brien
MORDOR (FR)	David Simcock
MOTRIFF (IRE)	William Haggas
MR BUSTER (IRE)	Ralph Beckett
MR MISTOFFELEES (IRE)	Hughie Morrison
NAQEEB (IRE)	William Haggas
NATION'S CALL (IRE)	D. K. Weld
NAZYMBEK (FR)	Roger Varian
NDAAWI	Andrew Balding
NEWPORT	Donnacha Aidan O'Brien
NOPOLI	
NURBURGRING (IRE)	Joseph Patrick O'Brien
OVIEDO (IRE)	
OYAMAL	Owen Burrows
PADDINGTON	Aidan O'Brien
PEKING OPERA (IRE)	Aidan O'Brien
PICCADILLY CIRCUS (IRE)	William Haggas
PJANOO	Richard Spencer
PLEDGEOFALLEGIANCE (IRE)	Sir Mark Prescott Bt
POWER AND GLORY (IRE)	Aidan O'Brien
PRAGUE (IRE)	Aidan O'Brien
PRIDE AND GLORY (USA)	John & Thady Gosden
PRINCE MAXI (IRE)	Richard Hannon
PROSPER LEGEND (IRE)	William Haggas
PROUD AND REGAL (IRE)	Donnacha Aidan O'Brien
QUEENSTOWN (IRE)	Aidan O'Brien
RAPPAREE CHAMP (IRE)	Joseph Patrick O'Brien
REBEL RED	
RELENTLESS VOYAGER	Andrew Balding
REPETITION (IRE)	Aidan O'Brien
ROARING LEGEND (FR)	James Ferguson
ROGUE LION	Tom Clover
SAFEGUARD (IRE)	Aidan O'Brien
SAINT GEORGE	Andrew Balding
SALT BAY (GER)	Ralph Beckett
SALT LAKE CITY (IRE)	Aidan O'Brien
SAN ANTONIO (IRE)	Aidan O'Brien
SATURN (IRE)	Mrs J. Harrington
SAVANNA KING	John & Thady Gosden
SCINTILLANTE	Andrew Balding
SEA LEGEND (FR)	J. A. Stack
SERENGETI SUNSET	John & Thady Gosden
SHADOW OF WAR	John & Thady Gosden
SIR CILIA	Eve Johnson Houghton
SIR LAURENCE GRAFF (IRE)	John & Thady Gosden
SLIPOFTHEPEN	John & Thady Gosden
SQUARE MILE (IRE)	Aidan O'Brien
ST VINCENTS GARDEN (IRE)	Joseph Patrick O'Brien
SUBZERO (IRE)	Aidan O'Brien
SULEIMAN ARTIST (IRE)	Joseph Patrick O'Brien
SULLIVAN BAY (IRE)	Joseph Patrick O'Brien
SUPERBOLT (IRE)	Joseph Patrick O'Brien
SWORDOFHONOR (IRE)	Andrew Balding
SYLLABUS (IRE)	William Haggas
TAKEED	
TALISMAN	Richard Hannon
THE BLACK TIGER (USA)	Aidan O'Brien
THE FOXES (IRE)	Andrew Balding
THEORYOFEVERYTHING	John & Thady Gosden
THE PRAIRIE (IRE)	Aidan O'Brien
THUNDER CAT	

HORSE	TRAINER
TIME TELLS ALL (IRE)	D. K. Weld
TONY MONTANA	John & Thady Gosden
TORITO	John & Thady Gosden
TORRE DEL ORO (IRE)	Andrew Balding
TOWER OF LONDON (IRE)	Aidan O'Brien
TRUE LEGEND (IRE)	
TUJJAAR	Richard Hannon
TWIN EARTH (IRE)	Andrew Balding
UNIFICATION (IRE)	J. S. Bolger
VICTORIA ROAD (IRE)	Aidan O'Brien
VILLAGE LEGEND (IRE)	James Ferguson
WAIPIRO (IRE)	Ed Walker
WARRIOR LION	Joseph Patrick O'Brien
WITCHING HOUR	
YOSEMITE VALLEY	Donnacha Aidan O'Brien
YOUNG (IRE)	J. S. Bolger
YOUTH'S VOICE	Owen Burrows
ZARAZA (GER)	William Haggas
ZIVANIYA	Hugo Palmer
EX BEAUTY BRIGHT (IRE)	Joseph Patrick O'Brien
EX CROWN QUEEN (USA)	Roger Varian
EX DREAM CHILD (IRE)	Ismail Mohammed
EX HYDRANGEA (IRE)	Aidan O'Brien
EX LOVE AND BUBBLES (USA)	William Haggas
EX MOLLY MALONE (FR)	
EX PERFECT NOTE	
OPERA KING	Andrew Balding
BOLDLY (IRE)	John & Thady Gosden
BECCARA ROSE (IRE)	Charlie Fellowes

RACING POST CHAMPIONS 2022

ONLY HORSES WHICH HAVE RUN IN EUROPE ARE INCLUDED

FOUR-YEAR-OLDS AND UP

BAAEED 136
NATURE STRIP 129
KYPRIOS 128
TORQUATOR TASSO 126
BAY BRIDGE 125
MINZAAL 125
PYLDEDRIVER 125
REAL WORLD 125

THREE-YEAR-OLD COLT

VADENI 126
DESERT CROWN 125
LUXEMBOURG 124
MY PROSPERO 124
ALFLAILA 123
AL HAKEEM 123
COROEBUS 123

THREE-YEAR-OLD FILLY

INSPIRAL 123
EREVANN 122
HOMELESS SONGS 122
PLACE DU CARROUSEL 120
NASHWA 119
TUESDAY 119

SPRINTER

NATURE STRIP 129
MINZAAL 125
HIGHFIELD PRINCESS 124
ALCOHOL FREE 123
ART POWER 123
KINROSS 122
NAVAL CROWN 121

STAYER

KYPRIOS 128
TRUESHAN 126
HAMISH 121
QUICKTHORN 120
STRADIVARIUS 120
MOJO STAR 119

TWO-YEAR-OLD COLT

LITTLE BIG BEAR 123
AUGUSTE RODIN 120
NOBLE STYLE 119
CHALDEAN 118
ROYAL SCOTSMAN 117
BLACKBEARD 116

TWO-YEAR-OLD FILLY

TAHIYRA 116
COMMISSIONING 112
LEZOO 112
BLUE ROSE CEN 111
MEDITATE 110
NOVAKAI 109
TRILLIUM 109

MEDIAN TIMES 2022

The following Raceform median times are used in the calculation of the Split Second speed figures. They represent a true average time for the distance, which has been arrived at after looking at the winning times for all races over each distance within the past five years, except for those restricted to two or three-year-olds.

Some current race distances have been omitted as they have not yet had a sufficient number of races run over them to produce a reliable average time.

ASCOT

Distance	Time
5f	1m 1.50
6f	1m 14.90
7f	1m 30.34
7f 213y Round	1m 41.60
1m Straight	1m 41.40
1m 1f 212y	2m 10.75
1m 3f 211y	2m 35.37
1m 6f 34y	3m 10.39
1m 7f 209y	3m 34.49
2m 3f 210y	4m 25.11
2m 5f 143y	4m 52.56

AYR

Distance	Time
5f	1m 0.42
5f 110y	1m 7.20
6f	1m 14.73
7f 50y	1m 32.76
1m	1m 44.06
1m 2f	2m 13.83
1m 5f 26y	2m 59.10
1m 7f	3m 33.80

BATH

Distance	Time
5f 10y	1m 0.60
5f 160y	1m 10.40
1m	1m 42.66
1m 2f 37y	2m 12.60
1m 3f 137y	2m 31.41
1m 5f 11y	2m 53.77
1m 6f	3m 4.10
2m 1f 24y	3m 51.40

BEVERLEY

Distance	Time
5f	1m 4.30
7f 96y	1m 35.50
1m 100y	1m 48.45
1m 1f 207y	2m 6.00
1m 4f 23y	2m 45.84
2m 32y	3m 37.30

BRIGHTON

Distance	Time
5f 60y	1m 3.32
5f 215y	1m 11.30
6f 210y	1m 23.10
7f 216y	1m 35.50
1m 1f 207y	2m 6.40
1m 3f 198y	2m 36.56

CARLISLE

Distance	Time
5f	1m 2.10
5f 182y	1m 12.70
6f 195y	1m 28.00
7f 173y	1m 41.90
1m 1f	2m 1.00
1m 3f 39y	2m 29.70
1m 6f 32y	3m 13.00
2m 1f 47y	3m 55.00

CATTERICK

Distance	Time
5f	1m 0.00
5f 212y	1m 14.20
7f 6y	1m 26.60
1m 4f 13y	2m 40.00
1m 5f 192y	3m 0.00
1m 7f 189y	3m 34.70

CHELMSFORD (A.W)

Distance	Time
5f	59.40
6f	1m 12.20
7f	1m 25.80
1m	1m 38.50
1m 2f	2m 6.10
1m 5f 66y	2m 53.60
1m 6f	3m 0.20
2m	3m 29.00

CHEPSTOW

Distance	Time
5f 16y	1m 0.30
6f 16y	1m 12.30
7f 16y	1m 24.40
1m 14y	1m 35.80]
1m 2f	2m 10.00
1m 4f	2m 37.30
2m	3m 39.10

CHESTER

Distance	Time
5f 15y	1m 3.50
5f 110y	1m 7.00
6f 17y	1m 16.40
7f 1y	1m 28.00
7f 127y	1m 35.70
1m 2f 70y	2m 14.30
1m 3f 75y	2m 30.40
1m 4f 63y	2m 44.00
1m 5f 84y	3m 0.60
1m 6f 87y	3m 10.00
1m 7f 196y	3m 34.00
2m 2f 140y	4m 4.60

DONCASTER

Distance	Time
5f 3y	1m 0.30
5f 143y	1m 8.10
6f 2y	1m 13.10
6f 111y	1m 19.60
7f 6y	1m 26.40
7f 213y Round	1m 38.00
1m Straight	1m 37.70
1m 2f 43y	2m 12.30
1m 3f 197y	2m 33.20
1m 6f 115y	3m 9.00
2m 109y	3m 40.40
2m 1f 197y	3m 55.00

EPSOM

Distance	Time
5f	55.23
6f 3y	1m 9.10
7f 3y	1m 24.40
1m 113y	1m 46.90
1m 2f 17y	2m 11.18
1m 4f 6y	2m 40.19

FFOS LAS

Distance	Time
5f	59.30
6f	1m 10.90
7f 80y	1m 34.10
1m	1m 42.90
1m 2f	2m 11.30
1m 3f 209y	2m 38.20
1m 6f	3m 9.60
2m	3m 33.70

GOODWOOD

Distance	Time
5f	59.80
6f	1m 13.42
7f	1m 29.09
1m	1m 42.50
1m 1f 11y	2m 0.57
1m 1f 197y	2m 11.14
1m 3f 44y	2m 30.58
1m 3f 218y	2m 40.40
1m 6f	3m 7.44
2m	3m 40.26

HAMILTON

Distance	Time
5f 7y	1m 0.40
6f 6y	1m 13.20
1m 68y	1m 48.40
1m 1f 35y	1m 59.10
1m 3f 15y	2m 24.60
1m 4f 15y	2m 39.60
1m 5f 16y	2m 52.60

HAYDOCK

Distance	Time
5f	1m 0.60
5fl	1m 0.60
6f	1m 15.40
6fl	1m 15.40
6f 212yl	1m 28.80
7f 37y	1m 32.20
7f 212yl	1m 42.70
1m 37y	1m 45.60
1m 2f 42yl	2m 13.80
1m 2f 100y	2m 16.60
1m 3f 140yl	2m 32.60
1m 3f 175y	2m 37.50
1m 6fl	3m 9.40
1m 6f	3m 9.40
1m 6f 1y	3m 9.00
2m 45yl	3m 36.70
2m 45y	3m 36.70

KEMPTON (A.W)

Distance	Time
5f	1m 0.50
6f	1m 12.80
7f	1m 26.20
1m	1m 39.40
1m 1f 219y	2m 8.00
1m 2f 219y	2m 21.00
1m 3f 219y	2m 34.50
1m 7f 218y	3m 30.10

LEICESTER

Distance	Time
5f	1m 0.50
6f	1m 11.90
7f	1m 24.70
1m 53y	1m 46.80
1m 2f	2m 8.70
1m 3f 179y	2m 40.40

LINGFIELD

Distance	Time
4f 217y	58.70
6f	1m 11.50
7f	1m 24.30
7f 135y	1m 31.70
1m 1f	1m 56.90
1m 2f	2m 12.20
1m 3f 133y	2m 34.00
1m 5f	2m 45.40
1m 6f	3m 6.20

LINGFIELD (A.W)

Distance	Time
5f 6y	58.30
6f 1y	1m 11.90
7f 1y	1m 24.80
1m 1y	1m 37.30
1m 2f	2m 5.30
1m 4f	2m 32.10
1m 5f	2m 46.00
1m 7f 169y	3m 25.70

MUSSELBURGH

Distance	Time
5f 1y	1m 0.10
7f 33y	1m 29.00
1m 2y	1m 40.00
1m 208y	1m 53.10
1m 4f 104y	2m 44.50
1m 5f	2m 51.70
1m 5f 216y	3m 3.90
1m 7f 217y	3m 31.50

NEWBURY

5f 34y.......... 1m 2.40
6f.......... 1m 13.20
6f 110y.......... 1m 22.10
7f Straight.......... 1m 26.90
1m Straight.......... 1m 40.90
1m 2f.......... 2m 9.50
1m 3f.......... 2m 24.20
1m 4f.......... 2m 36.90
1m 5f 61y.......... 2m 54.40
2m.......... 3m 39.40
2m 110y.......... 3m 46.30

NEWCASTLE (A.W)

5f.......... 1m 0.90
6f.......... 1m 13.59
7f 14y.......... 1m 27.60
1m 5y.......... 1m 41.95
1m 2f 42y.......... 2m 13.98
1m 4f 98y.......... 2m 44.69
2m 56y.......... 3m 41.22

NEWMARKET

5f Rowly.......... 1m 0.90
6f Rowly.......... 1m 12.50
7f Rowly.......... 1m 27.40
1m Rowly.......... 1m 40.00
1m 1f Rowly.......... 1m 53.10
1m 2f Rowly.......... 2m 6.60
1m 4f Rowly.......... 2m 34.50
1m 6f Rowly.......... 3m 2.00
2m Rowly.......... 3m 27.30
2m 2f Rowly.......... 3m 53.00

NEWMARKET (JULY)

5f July.......... 58.80
6f July.......... 1m 12.50
7f July.......... 1m 27.39
1m July.......... 1m 39.90
1m 2f July.......... 2m 6.30
1m 4f July.......... 2m 36.25
1m 5f July.......... 2m 45.52
1m 6f July.......... 3m 0.81
2m July.......... 3m 26.33

NOTTINGHAM

5f 8yl.......... 1m 1.50
5f 8y.......... 1m 1.50
6f 18y.......... 1m 15.00
1m 75y.......... 1m 47.80
1m 75yl.......... 1m 47.80
1m 2f 50y.......... 2m 12.80
1m 2f 50yl.......... 2m 18.50
1m 6fl.......... 3m 9.40
1m 6f.......... 3m 9.40
2m.......... 3m 40.00
2ml.......... 3m 40.00

PONTEFRACT

5f 3y.......... 1m 4.10
6f.......... 1m 17.10
1m 6y.......... 1m 45.90
1m 2f 5y.......... 2m 15.00
1m 4f 5y.......... 2m 41.10
2m 1f 27y.......... 3m 52.30
2m 2f 2y.......... 4m 9.80
2m 5f 139y.......... 4m 58.00

REDCAR

5f.......... 58.50
5f 217y.......... 1m 11.80
7f.......... 1m 25.00
7f 219y.......... 1m 38.10
1m 1f.......... 1m 54.50
1m 2f 1y.......... 2m 7.90
1m 5f 218y.......... 3m 5.00
1m 7f 217y.......... 3m 33.70

RIPON

5f.......... 1m 1.00
6f.......... 1m 13.50
1m.......... 1m 42.50
1m 1f 170y.......... 2m 5.60
1m 2f 190y.......... 2m 22.00
1m 4f 10y.......... 2m 39.30
1m 6f.......... 3m 4.40
2m.......... 3m 30.40

SALISBURY

5f.......... 1m 2.50
6f.......... 1m 16.50
6f 213y.......... 1m 30.50
1m.......... 1m 43.50
1m 1f 201y.......... 2m 9.30
1m 4f 5y.......... 2m 43.60
1m 6f 44y.......... 3m 8.00

SANDOWN PARK

5f 10y.......... 1m 0.30
7f.......... 1m 30.70
1m.......... 1m 44.89
1m 1f.......... 1m 59.30
1m 1f 209y.......... 2m 12.34
1m 6f.......... 3m 12.70
2m 50y.......... 3m 39.87

SOUTHWELL (A.W)

4f 214y.......... 59.50
6f 16y.......... 1m 16.20
7f 14y.......... 1m 29.60
1m 13y.......... 1m 43.60
1m 3f 23y.......... 2m 29.30
1m 4f 14y.......... 2m 42.40
1m 6f 21y.......... 3m 8.50
2m 102y.......... 3m 46.00
2m 2f 98y.......... 4m 15.50

THIRSK

5f............ 59.40
6f............ 1m 12.10
7f............ 1m 28.50
7f 218y............ 1m 42.50
1m 4f 8y............ 2m 41.90
1m 6f............ 3m 3.00
2m 13y............ 3m 32.00

WETHERBY

5f 110y............ 1m 6.00
7f............ 1m 28.20
1m............ 1m 43.60
1m 2f............ 2m 11.50
1m 6f............ 3m 8.00
2m............ 3m 30.70

WINDSOR

5f 21y............ 1m 1.10
6f 12y............ 1m 13.20
1m 31y............ 1m 46.10
1m 2f............ 2m 11.50
1m 3f 99y............ 2m 32.40

WOLVERHAMPTON (A.W)

5f 21y............ 1m 1.90
6f 20y............ 1m 14.50
7f 36y............ 1m 28.80
1m 142y............ 1m 50.10
1m 1f 104y............ 2m 0.80
1m 4f 51y............ 2m 40.80
1m 5f 219y............ 3m 1.00
2m 120y............ 3m 39.30

YARMOUTH

5f 42y............ 1m 2.00
6f 3y............ 1m 13.50
7f 3y............ 1m 27.10
1m 3y............ 1m 38.20
1m 1f 21y............ 1m 54.00
1m 2f 23y............ 2m 8.80
1m 3f 104y............ 2m 29.90
1m 6f 17y............ 3m 4.70

YORK

5f............ 58.88
5f 89y............ 1m 4.82
6f............ 1m 12.60
7f............ 1m 25.50
7f 192y............ 1m 39.00
1m 177y............ 1m 50.40
1m 2f 56y............ 2m 12.30
1m 3f 188y............ 2m 32.20
1m 5f 188y............ 3m 0.20
2m 56y............ 3m 36.50

RACING POST RECORD TIMES (FLAT)

ASCOT

DISTANCE	TIME	AGE	WEIGHT	GOING	HORSE	DATE
5f	58.80	2	9-1	Good To Firm	**NO NAY NEVER**	Jun 20 2013
5f	57.44	6	9-1	Good To Firm	**MISS ANDRETTI**	Jun 19 2007
6f (Str)	1m 12.39	2	9-1	Good To Firm	**RAJASINGHE**	Jun 20 2017
6f	1m 11.05	3	9-1	Good To Firm	**BLUE POINT**	May 3 2017
6f 110y	1m 21.15	2	8-6	Good	**PENNY'S GIFT**	Sep 26 2008
6f 110y	1m 20.21	3	9-2	Good To Firm	**KHABFAIR**	Sep 24 2004
7f	1m 25.73	2	9-3	Good	**PINATUBO**	Jun 22 2019
7f	1m 24.28	4	8-11	Good To Firm	**GALICIAN**	Jul 27 2013
7f 213y (Rnd)	1m 39.55	2	8-12	Good	**JOSHUA TREE**	Sep 26 2009
7f 213y (Rnd)	1m 35.89	3	9-0	Good To Firm	**ALPHA CENTAURI**	Jun 22 2018
1m (Str)	1m 36.60	4	9-0	Good To Firm	**RIBCHESTER**	Jun 20 2017
1m 1f 212y	2m 1.90	5	8-11	Good To Firm	**THE FUGUE**	Jun 18 2014
1m 3f 211y	2m 24.60	4	9-7	Good To Firm	**NOVELLIST**	Jul 27 2013
1m 5f 211y	2m 59.36	3	9-4	Good	**BIG ORANGE**	Oct 3 2014
1m 7f 209y	3m 24.12	4	8-12	Good To Firm	**MIZZOU**	Apr 29 2015
2m 3f 210y	4m 16.92	6	9-2	Good To Firm	**RITE OF PASSAGE**	Jun 17 2010
2m 5f 143y	4m 45.24	9	9-2	Good To Firm	**PALLASATOR**	Jun 23 2018

AYR

DISTANCE	TIME	AGE	WEIGHT	GOING	HORSE	DATE
5f	56.89	2	8-12	Good To Firm	**VERTIGINOUS (IRE)**	Sep 17 2021
5f	55.68	3	8-11	Good To Firm	**LOOK BUSY**	Jun 21 2008
6f	1m 9.73	2	7-10	Firm	**SIR BERT**	Sep 17 1969
6f	1m 8.37	5	8-6	Good To Firm	**MAISON DIEU**	Jun 21 2008
7f 50y	1m 28.99	2	9-0	Good	**TAFAAHUM**	Sep 19 2003
7f 50y	1m 26.43	4	9-4	Good To Firm	**HAJJAM**	May 22 2018
1m	1m 39.18	2	9-7	Good	**MOONLIGHTNAVIGATOR**	Sep 18 2014
1m	1m 36.00	4	7-13	Firm	**SUFI**	Sep 16 1959
1m 1f 20y	1m 50.30	4	9-3	Good	**RETIREMENT**	Sep 19 2003
1m 2f	2m 4.02	4	9-9	Good To Firm	**ENDLESS HALL**	Jul 17 2000
1m 5f 26y	2m 45.81	4	9-7	Good To Firm	**EDEN'S CLOSE**	Sep 18 1993
1m 7f	3m 13.16	3	9-4	Good	**ROMANY RYE**	Sep 19 1991
2m 1f 105y	3m 45.20	4	6-13	Firm	**CURRY**	Sep 16 1955

BATH

DISTANCE	TIME	AGE	WEIGHT	GOING	HORSE	DATE
5f 10y	59.50	2	9-2	Firm	**AMOUR PROPRE**	Jul 24 2008
5f 10y	58.75	3	8-12	Firm	**ENTICING**	May 1 2007
5f 160y	1m 8.70	2	8-12	Firm	**QALAHARI**	Jul 24 2008
5f 160y	1m 7.40	4	9-10	Firm	**MOTAGALLY**	Sep 14 2020
1m 5y	1m 39.51	2	9-2	Firm	**NATURAL CHARM**	Sep 14 2014
1m 5y	1m 37.20	5	8-12	Good To Firm	**ADOBE**	Jun 17 2000
1m 5y	1m 37.24	3	9-4	Good To Firm	**EMERGING (IRE)**	Jun 30 2021
1m 2f 37y	2m 5.80	3	9-0	Good To Firm	**CONNOISSEUR BAY**	May 29 1998
1m 3f 137y	2m 25.74	3	9-0	Hard	**TOP THE CHARTS**	Sep 8 2005
1m 5f 11y	2m 46.11	4	10-1	Firm	**CARAMELISED**	Jun 22 2022
1m 6f	2m 58.97	4	9-10	Firm	**CHARLIE D**	Sep 15 2019
2m 1f 24y	3m 43.41	6	7-9	Firm	**YAHESKA**	Jun 14 2003

BEVERLEY

DISTANCE	TIME	AGE	WEIGHT	GOING	HORSE	DATE
5f	1m 0.85	2	9-5	Good To Firm	**BILLIAN**	Aug 12 2020
5f	59.51	7	9-2	Good To Firm	**TIS MARVELLOUS**	Aug 28 2021
7f 96y	1m 31.10	2	9-7	Good To Firm	**CHAMPAGNE PRINCE**	Aug 10 1995
7f 96y	1m 31.10	2	9-0	Firm	**MAJAL**	Jul 30 1991
7f 96y	1m 29.50	3	7-8	Firm	**WHO'S TEF**	Jul 30 1991
1m 100y	1m 43.30	2	9-0	Firm	**ARDEN**	Sep 24 1986
1m 100y	1m 42.20	3	8-4	Firm	**LEGAL CASE**	Jun 14 1989
1m 1f 207y	2m 1.00	3	9-7	Good To Firm	**EASTERN ARIA**	Aug 29 2009
1m 4f 23y	2m 33.35	5	9-2	Good To Firm	**TWO JABS**	Apr 23 2015
2m 32y	3m 28.62	4	9-11	Good To Firm	**CORPUS CHORISTER**	Jul 18 2017

BRIGHTON

DISTANCE	TIME	AGE	WEIGHT	GOING	HORSE	DATE
5f 60y	1m 0.10	2	9-0	Firm	**BID FOR BLUE**	May 6 1993
5f 60y	59.30	3	8-9	Firm	**PLAY HEVER GOLF**	May 26 1993
5f 215y	1m 8.10	2	8-9	Firm	**SONG MIST**	Jul 16 1996
5f 215y	1m 7.01	6	9-8	Good To Firm	**KENDERGARTEN KOP &**	Jun 1 2021
		4	9-7		**BATCHELOR BOY**	
6f 210y	1m 19.90	2	8-11	Hard	**RAIN BURST**	Sep 15 1988
6f 210y	1m 19.53	4	9-2	Good To Firm	**ARABIC CHARM**	Jun 1 2021
7f 211y	1m 32.80	2	9-7	Firm	**ASIAN PETE**	Oct 3 1989
7f 211y	1m 30.50	5	8-11	Firm	**MYSTIC RIDGE**	May 27 1999
1m 1f 207y	2m 4.70	2	9-0	Good To Soft	**ESTEEMED MASTER**	Nov 2 2001
1m 1f 207y	1m 57.20	3	9-0	Firm	**GET THE MESSAGE**	Apr 30 1984
1m 3f 198y	2m 25.80	4	8-2	Firm	**NEW ZEALAND**	Jul 4 1985

CARLISLE

DISTANCE	TIME	AGE	WEIGHT	GOING	HORSE	DATE
5f	1m 0.10	2	8-5	Firm	**LA TORTUGA**	Aug 2 1999
5f	58.80	3	9-8	Good To Firm	**ESATTO**	Aug 21 2002
5f 193y	1m 12.30	2	9-2	Good To Firm	**BURRISHOOLE ABBEY**	Jun 22 2016
5f 193y	1m 10.83	4	9-0	Good To Firm	**BO MCGINTY**	Sep 11 2005
6f 195y	1m 26.34	2	8-12	Good	**MAKALU**	Aug 26 2021
6f 195y	1m 24.30	3	8-9	Good To Firm	**MARJURITA**	Aug 21 2002
7f 173y	1m 40.04	2	9-4	Good To Firm	**PERFECT PLAY**	Aug 30 2022
1m 1f	1m 53.84	3	9-0	Firm	**LITTLE JIMBOB**	Jun 14 2004
1m 3f 39y	2m 20.46	5	10-0	Good To Firm	**AASHEQ**	Jun 27 2018
1m 3f 206y	2m 29.13	5	9-8	Good To Firm	**TEMPSFORD**	Sep 19 2005
1m 6f 32y	3m 2.20	6	8-10	Firm	**EXPLOSIVE SPEED**	May 26 1994

CATTERICK

DISTANCE	TIME	AGE	WEIGHT	GOING	HORSE	DATE
5f	57.60	2	9-0	Firm	**H HARRISON**	Oct 8 2002
5f	57.10	4	8-7	Firm	**KABCAST**	Jul 6 1989
5f 212y	1m 11.40	2	9-4	Firm	**CAPTAIN NICK**	Jul 11 1978
5f 212y	1m 9.86	9	8-13	Good To Firm	**SHARP HAT**	May 30 2003
7f 6y	1m 24.10	2	8-11	Firm	**LINDA'S FANTASY**	Sep 18 1982
7f 6y	1m 22.56	6	8-7	Firm	**DIFFERENTIAL**	May 31 2003
1m 5f 192y	2m 54.80	3	8-5	Firm	**GERYON**	May 31 1984
1m 7f 189y	3m 20.80	4	7-11	Firm	**BEAN BOY**	Jul 8 1982

CHELMSFORD (AW)

DISTANCE	TIME	AGE	WEIGHT	GOING	HORSE	DATE
5f	58.19	2	9-2	Standard	**SHALAA ASKER**	Sep 13 2020
5f	57.30	7	8-13	Standard	**BROTHER TIGER**	Feb 7 2016
6f	1m 10.62	2	9-4	Standard	**KOEPP**	Oct 8 2020
6f	1m 9.74	5	9-13	Standard	**CITY WALK**	Sep 15 2022
7f	1m 22.53	4	9-2	Standard	**JUMAIRA BAY**	Jun 16 2021
1m	1m 37.15	2	9-3	Standard	**DRAGON MALL**	Sep 26 2015
1m	1m 34.73	3	9-2	Standard	**CROUPIER**	Oct 13 2022
1m 2f	2m 1.81	5	9-7	Standard	**BIN BATTUTA**	Sep 28 2019
1m 5f 66y	2m 47.00	4	8-7	Standard	**COORG**	Jan 6 2016
1m 6f	2m 55.61	3	9-0	Standard	**BRASCA**	Sep 5 2019
2m	3m 21.93	3	9-3	Standard	**MOUNTAIN ROAD**	Sep 24 2022

CHEPSTOW

DISTANCE	TIME	AGE	WEIGHT	GOING	HORSE	DATE
5f 16y	57.60	2	8-11	Firm	**MICRO LOVE**	Jul 8 1986
5f 16y	56.80	3	8-4	Firm	**TORBAY EXPRESS**	Sep 15 1979
6f 16y	1m 8.50	2	9-2	Firm	**NINJAGO**	Jul 27 2012
6f 16y	1m 8.10	3	9-7	Firm	**AMERICA CALLING**	Sep 18 2001
7f 16y	1m 20.48	2	9-0	Good	**FESTIVAL DAY**	Sep 17 2019
7f 16y	1m 19.30	3	9-0	Firm	**TARANAKI**	Sep 18 2001
1m 14y	1m 33.10	2	8-11	Good To Firm	**SKI ACADEMY**	Aug 28 1995
1m 14y	1m 31.60	3	8-13	Firm	**STOLI**	Sep 18 2001
1m 2f	2m 3.37	3	9-2	Good	**BALEARIC**	Jul 15 2021
1m 2f 36y	2m 4.10	3	8-5	Good To Firm	**ELA ATHENA**	Jul 23 1999
1m 2f 36y	2m 4.10	5	8-9	Hard	**LEONIDAS**	Jul 5 1983
1m 2f 36y	2m 4.10	5	7-8	Good To Firm	**IT'S VARADAN**	Sep 9 1989
1m 4f 23y	2m 31.00	5	8-11	Hard	**THE FRIEND**	Aug 29 1983
1m 4f 23y	2m 31.00	3	8-9	Good To Firm	**SPRITSAIL**	Jul 13 1989
2m 49y	3m 27.70	4	9-0	Good To Firm	**WIZZARD ARTIST**	Jul 1 1989
2m 2f	3m 56.40	5	8-7	Good To Firm	**LAFFAH**	Jul 8 2000

CHESTER

DISTANCE	TIME	AGE	WEIGHT	GOING	HORSE	DATE
5f 15y	59.85	2	9-7	Good	**CHANGEOFMIND**	Jun 25 2022
5f 15y	58.88	3	8-7	Good To Firm	**PETERKIN**	Jul 11 2014
5f 110y	1m 6.39	2	8-7	Good To Soft	**KINEMATIC**	Sep 27 2014
5f 110y	1m 4.32	6	8-11	Good	**KING OF TONGA**	Aug 20 2022
6f 17y	1m 12.34	2	9-2	Good	**ALL THE TIME**	Aug 20 2022
6f 17y	1m 12.02	5	9-5	Good To Firm	**DEAUVILLE PRINCE**	Jun 13 2015
7f 1y	1m 25.16	2	9-5	Good	**FRANKNESS**	Aug 20 2022
7f 1y	1m 23.75	5	8-13	Good To Firm	**THREE GRACES**	Jul 9 2005
7f 127y	1m 32.29	2	9-0	Good To Firm	**BIG BAD BOB**	Sep 25 2002
7f 127y	1m 30.37	4	9-8	Good	**PERCY'S LAD**	Aug 20 2022
1m 2f 70y	2m 7.15	3	8-8	Good To Firm	**STOTSFOLD**	Sep 23 2006
1m 3f 75y	2m 22.17	3	8-12	Good To Firm	**PERFECT TRUTH**	May 6 2009
1m 5f 84y	2m 45.43	5	8-11	Firm	**RAKAPOSHI KING**	May 7 1987
1m 7f 196y	3m 20.33	4	9-0	Good To Firm	**GRAND FROMAGE**	Jul 13 2002
2m 2f 140y	3m 58.89	7	9-2	Good To Firm	**GREENWICH MEANTIME**	May 9 2007

DONCASTER

DISTANCE	TIME	AGE	WEIGHT	GOING	HORSE	DATE
5f 3y	58.04	2	9-1	Good	**GUTAIFAN**	Sep 11 2015
5f 3y	57.30	5	9-11	Good To Firm	**KHAADEM**	Sep 8 2021
5f 143y	1m 5.38	4	9-7	Good	**MUTHMIR**	Sep 13 2014
6f 2y	1m 10.33	2	9-4	Good To Firm	**COMEDY**	Jun 29 2018
6f 2y	1m 9.36	3	9-9	Good To Firm	**STARMAN**	Aug 15 2020
6f 111y	1m 17.19	2	8-9	Good	**MR LUPTON**	Sep 10 2015
6f 111y	1m 16.62	4	8-10	Good	**BADR AL BADOOR**	Sep 12 2014
7f 6y	1m 22.78	2	9-5	Good	**BASATEEN**	Jul 24 2014
7f 6y	1m 21.81	6	8-7	Good To Firm	**SIGNOR PELTRO**	May 30 2009
7f 213y (Rnd)	1m 38.37	2	8-6	Good To Soft	**ANTONIOLA**	Oct 23 2009
7f 213y (Rnd)	1m 34.46	4	8-12	Good To Firm	**STAYING ON**	Apr 18 2009
1m (Str)	1m 36.45	2	9-0	Good To Firm	**LILAC ROAD**	Aug 15 2020
1m (Str)	1m 34.95	6	8-9	Firm	**QUICK WIT**	Jul 18 2013
1m 2f 43y	2m 4.81	4	8-13	Good To Firm	**RED GALA**	Sep 12 2007
1m 3f 197y	2m 27.48	3	8-4	Good To Firm	**SWIFT ALHAARTH**	Sep 10 2011
1m 6f 115y	3m 0.27	3	9-1	Good To Firm	**LOGICIAN**	Sep 14 2019
2m 109y	3m 34.52	7	9-0	Good To Firm	**INCHNADAMPH**	Nov 10 2007
2m 1f 197y	3m 48.41	4	9-4	Good To Firm	**SEPTIMUS**	Sep 14 2007

EPSOM

DISTANCE	TIME	AGE	WEIGHT	GOING	HORSE	DATE
5f	55.02	2	8-9	Good To Firm	**PRINCE ASLIA**	Jun 9 1995
5f	54.00	6	8-13	Good To Firm	**ORNATE**	Jun 1 2019
6f 3y	1m 7.85	2	8-11	Good To Firm	**SHOWBROOK**	Jun 5 1991
6f 3y	1m 6.20	9	8-11	Good To Firm	**WATCHABLE**	Jun 1 2019
7f 3y	1m 21.30	2	8-9	Good To Firm	**RED PEONY**	Jul 29 2004
7f 3y	1m 19.88	7	9-5	Good	**SAFE VOYAGE**	Jul 4 2020
1m 113y	1m 42.80	2	8-5	Good To Firm	**NIGHTSTALKER**	Aug 30 1988
1m 113y	1m 40.46	4	9-6	Good To Firm	**ZAAKI**	Jun 1 2019
1m 2f 17y	2m 3.50	5	7-11	Firm	**CROSSBOW**	Jun 7 1967
1m 4f 6y	2m 31.33	3	9-0	Good To Firm	**WORKFORCE**	Jun 5 2010

FFOS LAS

DISTANCE	TIME	AGE	WEIGHT	GOING	HORSE	DATE
5f	56.03	2	8-6	Good To Firm	**FOX DEGREE**	Jul 11 2022
5f	56.35	5	8-8	Good	**HAAJES**	Sep 12 2009
6f	1m 9.00	2	9-5	Good To Firm	**WONDER OF QATAR**	Sep 14 2014
6f	1m 7.46	6	10-2	Good To Firm	**HANDYTALK**	Jul 29 2019
7f 80y	1m 30.15	2	9-2	Good To Firm	**FOX TAL**	Jul 24 2018
7f 80y	1m 28.26	6	8-12	Good To Firm	**MABO**	Aug 3 2021
1m	1m 39.36	2	9-2	Good To Firm	**HALA HALA**	Sep 2 2013
1m	1m 37.12	5	9-0	Good To Firm	**ZEBRANO**	May 5 2011
1m 2f	2m 4.85	8	8-12	Good To Firm	**PELHAM CRESCENT**	May 5 2011
1m 3f 209y	2m 31.18	3	9-9	Good	**TRUESHAN**	Aug 29 2019
1m 6f	2m 58.61	4	9-7	Good To Firm	**LADY ECLAIR**	Jul 12 2010
2m	3m 25.42	4	9-3	Good To Firm	**LONG JOHN SILVER**	Jul 24 2018

GOODWOOD

DISTANCE	TIME	AGE	WEIGHT	GOING	HORSE	DATE
5f	56.50	2	9-2	Good To Firm	**THE PLATINUM QUEEN (IRE)**	Jul 27 2022
5f	55.62	6	9-7	Good To Firm	**BATTAASH**	Jul 31 2020
6f	1m 9.66	2	9-2	Good To Firm	**ROYAL SCOTSMAN**	Jul 28 2022
6f	1m 9.10	6	9-0	Good To Firm	**TAMAGIN**	Sep 12 2009
7f	1m 24.99	2	8-11	Good To Firm	**EKRAAR**	Jul 29 1999
7f	1m 23.62	4	9-3	Good To Firm	**TORO STRIKE**	Aug 29 2021
1m	1m 37.21	2	9-0	Good	**CALDRA**	Sep 9 2006
1m	1m 35.28	3	8-13	Good To Firm	**BEAT LE BON**	Aug 2 2019
1m 1f 11y	1m 56.27	2	9-3	Good To Firm	**DORDOGNE**	Sep 22 2010
1m 1f 11y	1m 52.42	7	9-12	Good To Firm	**AJERO (IRE)**	Jul 30 2022
1m 1f 197y	2m 2.81	3	9-3	Good To Firm	**ROAD TO LOVE**	Aug 3 2006
1m 3f 44y	2m 22.77	3	9-3	Good	**KHALIDI**	May 26 2017
1m 3f 218y	2m 31.39	3	9-1	Good To Firm	**CROSS COUNTER**	Aug 4 2018
1m 6f	2m 57.61	4	9-6	Good To Firm	**MEEZNAH**	Jul 28 2011
2m	3m 21.55	5	9-10	Good To Firm	**YEATS**	Aug 3 2006
2m 4f	4m 11.75	3	7-10	Firm	**LUCKY MOON**	Aug 2 1990

HAMILTON

DISTANCE	TIME	AGE	WEIGHT	GOING	HORSE	DATE
5f 7y	57.95	2	8-8	Good To Firm	**ROSE BLOSSOM**	May 29 2009
5f 7y	57.20	5	9-4	Good To Firm	**DAPPER MAN**	Jun 27 2019
6f 6y	1m 10.00	2	8-12	Good To Firm	**BREAK THE CODE**	Aug 24 1999
6f 6y	1m 8.70	6	9-9	Good To Firm	**JORDAN ELECTRICS**	Jun 28 2022
1m 68y	1m 45.46	2	9-5	Good To Firm	**LAAFIRAAQ**	Sep 20 2015
1m 68y	1m 42.70	6	7-7	Firm	**CRANLEY**	Sep 25 1972
1m 1f 35y	1m 53.60	5	9-6	Good To Firm	**REGENT'S SECRET**	Aug 10 2005
1m 3f 15y	2m 17.60	3	9-7	Good To Firm	**WEST WIND BLOWS (IRE)**	Jul 15 2022
1m 4f 15y	2m 30.52	5	9-10	Good To Firm	**RECORD BREAKER**	Jun 10 2009
1m 5f 16y	2m 45.10	6	9-6	Firm	**MENTALASANYTHIN**	Jun 14 1995

HAYDOCK

DISTANCE	TIME	AGE	WEIGHT	GOING	HORSE	DATE
5f	58.56	2	8-2	Good To Firm	**BARRACUDA BOY**	Aug 11 2012
5f	56.39	5	9-4	Firm	**BATED BREATH**	May 26 2012
5f (Inner)	58.51	2	9-1	Good	**FOUR DRAGONS**	Oct 14 2016
5f (Inner)	57.30	6	9-2	Good To Firm	**LOOK OUT LOUIS**	Sep 3 2022
6f	1m 10.98	4	9-9	Good To Firm	**WOLFHOUND**	Sep 4 1993
6f	1m 8.56	3	9-0	Firm	**HARRY ANGEL**	May 27 2017
6f (Inner)	1m 10.58	2	9-2	Good To Firm	**PRESTBURY PARK**	Jul 21 2017
6f (Inner)	1m 8.75	4	9-5	Good To Firm	**MINZAAL**	Sep 3 2022
6f 212y (Inner)	1m 26.15	2	9-9	Good To Firm	**ALBAHR**	Jul 17 2021
6f 212y (Inner)	1m 23.52	4	9-1	Good To Firm	**AL SUHAIL**	Sep 2 2021
7f 37y	1m 27.57	2	9-2	Good To Firm	**CONTRAST**	Aug 5 2016
7f 37y	1m 25.50	3	8-11	Good	**FORGE**	Sep 1 2016
7f 212y (Inner)	1m 38.83	2	9-6	Good To Firm	**LEITZEL**	Sep 2 2022
7f 212y (Inner)	1m 37.80	3	9-4	Good To Firm	**SIDEWINDER**	May 26 2017
1m 37y	1m 41.21	2	9-2	Good To Firm	**TRIPLE TIME**	Sep 4 2021
1m 37y	1m 38.50	4	8-11	Good To Firm	**EXPRESS HIMSELF**	Jun 10 2015
1m 2f 42y (Inner)	2m 7.25	3	8-9	Good To Firm	**LARAAIB**	May 26 2017
1m 2f 100y	2m 7.53	4	9-5	Good To Firm	**TEODORO**	Aug 11 2018
1m 3f 140y (Inner)	2m 25.52	5	9-9	Good To Firm	**DECEMBER SECOND**	Aug 8 2019
1m 3f 175y	2m 25.53	4	8-12	Good To Firm	**NUMBER THEORY**	May 24 2012
1m 6f	2m 55.20	5	9-9	Good To Firm	**HUFF AND PUFF**	Sep 7 2012
2m 45y	3m 26.98	5	8-13	Good To Firm	**DE RIGUEUR**	Jun 8 2013

KEMPTON (AW)

DISTANCE	TIME	AGE	WEIGHT	GOING	HORSE	DATE
5f	58.96	2	8-6	Standard	**GLAMOROUS SPIRIT**	Nov 28 2008
5f	58.07	5	8-12	Standard	**A MOMENTOFMADNESS**	Apr 7 2018
6f	1m 11.02	2	9-1	Standard To Slow	**INVINCIBLE ARMY**	Sep 9 2017
6f	1m 9.79	4	8-11	Standard	**TRINITYELITEDOTCOM**	Mar 29 2014
7f	1m 23.79	2	8-0	Standard	**ELSAAKB**	Nov 8 2017
7f	1m 23.10	6	9-9	Standard	**SIRIUS PROSPECT**	Nov 20 2014
1m	1m 37.26	2	9-0	Standard	**CECCHINI**	Nov 8 2017
1m	1m 35.73	3	8-9	Standard	**WESTERN ARISTOCRAT**	Sep 15 2011
1m 1f 219y	2m 2.93	3	8-11	Standard To Slow	**PLY**	Sep 25 2017
1m 2f 219y	2m 15.65	4	8-8	Standard To Slow	**FORBIDDEN PLANET**	Mar 30 2019
1m 3f 219y	2m 28.99	6	9-3	Standard	**SPRING OF FAME**	Nov 7 2012
1m 7f 218y	3m 21.50	4	8-12	Standard	**COLOUR VISION**	May 2 2012

LEICESTER

DISTANCE	TIME	AGE	WEIGHT	GOING	HORSE	DATE
5f 2y	58.40	2	9-0	Firm	**CUTTING BLADE**	Jun 9 1986
5f 2y	57.85	5	9-5	Good To Firm	**THE JOBBER**	Sep 18 2006
5f 218y	1m 9.99	2	9-0	Good	**EL MANATI**	Aug 1 2012
5f 218y	1m 9.12	6	8-12	Good To Firm	**PETER ISLAND**	Apr 25 2009
7f	1m 22.83	2	9-5	Good To Firm	**CLOUDBRIDGE**	Aug 2 2020
7f	1m 22.02	4	9-4	Good To Firm	**OUTRUN THE STORM**	Jun 11 2022
1m 53y	1m 44.05	2	8-11	Good To Firm	**CONGRESSIONAL**	Sep 6 2005
1m 53y	1m 41.89	5	9-7	Good To Firm	**VAINGLORY**	Jun 18 2009
1m 1f 216y	2m 5.30	2	9-1	Good To Firm	**WINDSOR CASTLE**	Oct 14 1996
1m 1f 216y	2m 2.40	4	9-6	Good To Firm	**LADY ANGHARAD**	Jun 18 2000
1m 1f 216y	2m 2.40	3	8-11	Firm	**EFFIGY**	Nov 4 1985
1m 3f 179y	2m 27.10	5	8-12	Good To Firm	**MURGHEM**	Jun 18 2000

LINGFIELD (TURF)

DISTANCE	TIME	AGE	WEIGHT	GOING	HORSE	DATE
4f 217y	56.76	2	9-2	Good	**GLORY FIGHTER**	May 11 2018
4f 217y	56.09	3	9-4	Good To Firm	**WHITECREST**	Sep 16 2011
6f	1m 9.41	2	9-0	Good To Firm	**COMPANY MINX**	Jul 10 2019
6f	1m 8.48	4	9-6	Good To Firm	**REWAAYAT**	Jul 17 2019
7f	1m 20.55	2	8-11	Good To Firm	**HIKING**	Aug 17 2013
7f	1m 20.44	3	9-5	Good	**ADDITIONAL**	Jun 26 2020
7f 135y	1m 29.32	2	9-3	Good To Firm	**DUNDONNELL**	Aug 4 2012
7f 135y	1m 26.73	3	8-6	Good To Firm	**HIAAM**	Jul 11 1987
1m 1f	1m 50.45	4	9-3	Good To Firm	**ENZEMBLE**	May 30 2019
1m 2f	2m 4.83	5	9-8	Good To Firm	**HAIRDRYER**	Jul 21 2018
1m 3f 133y	2m 23.95	3	8-5	Firm	**NIGHT-SHIRT**	Jul 14 1990
1m 6f	2m 58.88	3	8-13	Good To Firm	**TIMOSHENKO**	Jul 21 2018
2m 68y	3m 23.71	3	9-5	Good To Firm	**LAURIES CRUSADOR**	Aug 13 1988

LINGFIELD (AW)

DISTANCE	TIME	AGE	WEIGHT	GOING	HORSE	DATE
5f 6y	56.94	2	10-3	Standard	**BEDFORD FLYER**	Nov 25 2020
5f 6y	56.65	5	8-2	Standard	**STRONG POWER**	Jan 7 2022
6f 1y	1m 9.76	2	9-4	Standard	**RED IMPRESSION**	Nov 24 2018
6f 1y	1m 8.32	6	9-0	Standard	**KACHY**	Feb 2 2019
7f 1y	1m 22.67	2	9-3	Standard	**COMPLICIT**	Nov 23 2013
7f 1y	1m 21.41	4	8-12	Standard	**TADREEB**	Feb 19 2022
1m 1y	1m 35.70	2	8-13	Standard	**QAADDIM**	Oct 3 2019
1m 1y	1m 33.90	6	9-5	Standard	**LUCKY TEAM**	Mar 30 2018
1m 2f	2m 0.29	3	9-1	Standard	**MISSED THE CUT**	Nov 12 2022
1m 4f	2m 26.99	6	9-11	Standard	**PINZOLO**	Jan 21 2017
1m 5f	2m 39.70	3	8-10	Standard	**HIDDEN GOLD**	Oct 30 2014
1m 7f 169y	3m 15.18	4	9-1	Standard	**WINNING STORY**	Apr 14 2017

MUSSELBURGH

DISTANCE	TIME	AGE	WEIGHT	GOING	HORSE	DATE
5f 1y	57.66	2	9-2	Good To Firm	**IT DONT COME EASY**	Jun 3 2017
5f 1y	56.77	9	9-10	Good To Firm	**CASPIAN PRINCE**	Jun 9 2018
7f 33y	1m 27.46	2	8-8	Good	**DURHAM REFLECTION**	Sep 14 2009
7f 33y	1m 25.00	9	8-8	Good To Firm	**KALK BAY**	Jun 4 2016
1m 2y	1m 40.34	2	8-12	Good To Firm	**SUCCESSION**	Sep 26 2004
1m 2y	1m 36.83	3	9-5	Good To Firm	**GINGER JACK**	Jul 13 2010
1m 208y	1m 50.42	8	8-11	Good To Firm	**DHAULAR DHAR**	Sep 3 2010
1m 4f 104y	2m 36.80	3	8-3	Good To Firm	**HARRIS TWEED**	Jun 5 2010
1m 5f	2m 46.41	3	9-5	Good To Firm	**ALCAEUS**	Sep 29 2013
1m 5f 216y	2m 57.98	7	8-5	Good To Firm	**JONNY DELTA**	Apr 18 2014
1m 7f 217y	3m 25.62	4	8-3	Good To Firm	**ALDRETH**	Jun 13 2015

NEWBURY

DISTANCE	TIME	AGE	WEIGHT	GOING	HORSE	DATE
5f 34y	1m 0.24	2	9-2	Good To Firm	**CUBAN MISTRESS**	Aug 12 2022
5f 34y	58.40	3	9-0	Good	**LAZULI**	Sep 19 2020
6f	1m 9.70	2	9-1	Good	**ALKUMAIT**	Sep 19 2020
6f 8y	1m 9.42	3	8-11	Good To Firm	**NOTA BENE**	May 13 2005
6f 110y	1m 18.06	2	9-5	Good To Firm	**TWIN SAILS**	Jun 11 2015
7f (Str)	1m 23.04	2	8-11	Good To Firm	**HAAFHD**	Aug 15 2003
7f (Str)	1m 20.80	3	9-0	Good To Firm	**MUHAARAR**	Apr 18 2015
1m (Str)	1m 37.66	2	8-12	Good	**YIBIR**	Sep 18 2020
1m (Rnd)	1m 36.98	3	9-1	Good To Firm	**HE'S OUR STAR**	Jun 26 2018
1m (Str)	1m 35.07	4	8-11	Good To Firm	**RHODODENDRON**	May 19 2018
1m 1f	1m 49.65	3	8-0	Good To Firm	**HOLTYE**	May 21 1995
1m 2f	2m 1.29	3	8-7	Good To Firm	**WALL STREET**	Jul 20 1996
1m 3f	2m 17.71	3	8-10	Good	**STAY ALERT**	Sep 17 2022
1m 4f 5y	2m 28.26	4	9-7	Good To Firm	**AZAMOUR**	Jul 23 2005
1m 5f 61y	2m 46.99	3	8-11	Good To Firm	**ZECHARIAH**	Aug 13 2022

NEWCASTLE (AW)

Distance	Time	Age	Weight	Going	HORSE	Date
5f	58.05	2	8-6	Standard	**SPIN DOCTOR**	Oct 25 2016
5f	57.73	5	9-2	Standard To Slow	**FINE WINE (FR)**	Dec 2 2022
6f	1m 9.95	2	9-2	Standard	**MAZYOUN**	Oct 25 2016
6f	1m 9.86	3	9-2	Standard	**UNABATED**	Mar 22 2017
7f 14y	1m 25.50	2	9-5	Standard	**COMMANDER COLE**	Oct 18 2016
7f 14y	1m 24.10	3	9-0	Standard	**NORTHERNPOWERHOUSE**	Dec 18 2019
1m 5y	1m 36.26	2	9-1	Standard	**KAMEKO**	Nov 1 2019
1m 5y	1m 36.10	4	9-8	Standard	**ALFRED RICHARDSON**	Nov 9 2018
1m 2f 42y	2m 4.88	3	8-6	Standard	**PALISADE**	Oct 16 2016
1m 4f 98y	2m 36.76	3	8-7	Standard	**AJMAN PRINCE**	Oct 14 2016
2m 56y	3m 29.87	4	9-8	Standard	**DANNYDAY**	Jun 25 2016

NEWMARKET (ROWLEY MILE)

DISTANCE	TIME	AGE	WEIGHT	GOING	HORSE	DATE
5f	58.04	2	9-5	Good To Firm	**EYE OF HEAVEN**	Jun 4 2020
5f	56.81	6	9-2	Good To Firm	**LOCHSONG**	Apr 30 1994
6f	1m 9.31	2	9-0	Good	**EARTHLIGHT**	Sep 28 2019
6f	1m 9.55	3	9-1	Good To Firm	**CAPTAIN COLBY**	May 16 2015
7f	1m 22.37	2	9-1	Good	**U S NAVY FLAG**	Oct 14 2017
7f	1m 21.98	3	9-0	Good To Firm	**TUPI**	May 16 2015
1m	1m 35.13	2	9-0	Good	**ROYAL DORNOCH**	Sep 28 2019
1m	1m 34.07	4	9-0	Good To Firm	**EAGLE MOUNTAIN**	Oct 3 2008
1m 1f	1m 46.94	4	8-8	Good	**MAJESTIC DAWN**	Sep 26 2020
1m 2f	2m 2.53	2	9-4	Good	**FLYING HONOURS**	Oct 8 2022
1m 2f	2m 0.13	3	8-12	Good	**NEW APPROACH**	Oct 18 2008
1m 4f	2m 25.89	5	9-0	Good To Firm	**GHAIYYATH**	Jun 5 2020
1m 6f	2m 55.69	6	9-1	Good	**NATE THE GREAT**	May 13 2022
2m	3m 18.64	5	9-6	Good To Firm	**TIMES UP**	Sep 22 2011
2m 2f	3m 45.59	4	8-8	Good	**WITHHOLD**	Oct 14 2017

NEWMARKET (JULY COURSE)

Following remeasurement of the track by the BHA and RCA in 2017, some starts were moved to retain traditional race distances.

DISTANCE	TIME	AGE	WEIGHT	GOING	HORSE	DATE
5f	57.31	4	9-2	Good To Firm	**MOUNTAIN PEAK**	Jul 12 2019
6f	1m 9.09	2	9-3	Good To Firm	**RAFFLE PRIZE**	Jul 12 2019
6f	1m 9.31	3	9-0	Good To Firm	**TEN SOVEREIGNS**	Jul 13 2019
7f	1m 23.33	2	9-1	Good To Firm	**BIRCHWOOD**	Jul 11 2015
7f	1m 21.78	3	8-13	Good To Firm	**LIGHT AND DARK**	Jul 12 2019
1m	1m 37.47	2	8-13	Good	**WHIPPERS LOVE**	Aug 28 2009
1m	1m 35.89	4	9-7	Good To Firm	**VERACIOUS**	Jul 12 2019
1m 2f	2m 0.61	3	9-7	Good To Firm	**WALKINTHESAND**	Jul 12 2019
1m 4f	2m 27.26	3	8-9	Good To Firm	**KATARA**	Aug 1 2020
1m 5f	2m 39.96	3	9-1	Good To Firm	**SPANISH MISSION**	Jul 11 2019
1m 6f	2m 53.40	7	9-3	Good To Firm	**WITHHOLD**	Aug 1 2020

NOTTINGHAM

DISTANCE	TIME	AGE	WEIGHT	GOING	HORSE	DATE
5f 8y (Inner)	58.43	2	9-0	Good To Firm	**LOST ANGEL**	Apr 26 2022
5f 8y (Inner)	57.01	3	8-12	Good To Firm	**GARRUS**	Apr 10 2019
5f 8y	57.90	2	8-9	Firm	**HOH MAGIC**	May 13 1994
5f 8y	57.58	5	7-11	Good To Firm	**PENNY DREADFUL**	Jun 19 2017
6f 18y	1m 11.40	2	8-11	Firm	**JAMEELAPI**	Aug 8 1983
6f 18y	1m 10.00	4	9-2	Firm	**AJANAC**	Aug 8 1988
1m 72y (Inner)	1m 45.14	2	9-6	Good	**RASHFORD'S DOUBLE**	Nov 2 2016
1m 72y (Inner)	1m 41.25	4	9-6	Good	**FAST MEDICINE**	Apr 16 2022
1m 75y	1m 43.50	2	9-7	Good	**FABILIS**	Sep 27 2020
1m 75y	1m 41.75	3	9-1	Good To Firm	**SIAM FOX**	Jun 2 2021
1m 2f 50y	2m 7.13	5	9-8	Good To Firm	**VASILY**	Jul 19 2013
1m 2f 52y (Inner)	2m 16.66	2	9-3	Soft	**LETHAL GLAZE**	Oct 1 2008
1m 2f 52y (Inner)	2m 8.36	3	9-5	Good	**SAVVY KNIGHT**	Apr 16 2022
1m 6f	2m 57.80	3	8-10	Firm	**BUSTER JO**	Oct 1 1985
1m 7f 219y (Inner)	3m 34.39	3	8-0	Good	**BENOZZO GOZZOLI**	Oct 28 2009
2m	3m 25.25	3	9-5	Good	**BULWARK**	Sep 27 2005

PONTEFRACT

DISTANCE	TIME	AGE	WEIGHT	GOING	HORSE	DATE
5f 3y	1m 1.10	2	9-0	Firm	**GOLDEN BOUNTY**	Sep 20 2001
5f 3y	1m 0.49	5	9-5	Good To Firm	**JUDICIAL**	Apr 24 2017
6f	1m 14.00	2	9-3	Firm	**FAWZI**	Sep 6 1983
6f	1m 12.60	3	7-13	Firm	**MERRY ONE**	Aug 29 1970
1m 6y	1m 42.80	2	9-13	Firm	**STAR SPRAY**	Sep 6 1983
1m 6y	1m 42.80	2	9-0	Firm	**ALASIL**	Sep 26 2002
1m 6y	1m 40.60	4	9-10	Good To Firm	**ISLAND LIGHT**	Apr 13 2002
1m 2f 5y	2m 10.10	2	9-0	Firm	**SHANTY STAR**	Oct 7 2002
1m 2f 5y	2m 8.20	4	7-8	Hard	**HAPPY HECTOR**	Jul 9 1979
1m 2f 5y	2m 8.20	3	7-13	Hard	**TOM NODDY**	Aug 21 1972
1m 4f 5y	2m 33.72	3	8-7	Firm	**AJAAN**	Aug 8 2007
2m 1f 27y	3m 40.67	4	8-7	Good To Firm	**PARADISE FLIGHT**	Jun 6 2005
2m 2f 2y	3m 51.10	3	8-8	Good To Firm	**KUDZ**	Sep 9 1986
2m 5f 139y	4m 47.80	4	8-4	Firm	**PHYSICAL**	May 14 1984

REDCAR

DISTANCE	TIME	AGE	WEIGHT	GOING	HORSE	DATE
5f	56.88	2	9-7	Good To Soft	**WOLFOFWALLSTREET**	Oct 27 2014
5f	56.01	10	9-3	Firm	**HENRY HALL**	Sep 20 2006
5f 217y	1m 8.84	2	8-3	Good To Firm	**OBE GOLD**	Oct 2 2004
5f 217y	1m 8.60	3	9-2	Good To Firm	**SIZZLING SAGA**	Jun 21 1991
7f	1m 21.28	2	9-3	Firm	**KAROO BLUE**	Sep 20 2006
7f	1m 20.67	3	9-0	Good To Firm	**DREAMLOPER**	Jul 27 2020
7f 219y	1m 34.37	2	9-0	Firm	**MASTERSHIP**	Sep 20 2006
7f 219y	1m 32.42	4	10-0	Firm	**NANTON**	Sep 20 2006
1m 1f	1m 52.44	2	9-0	Firm	**SPEAR**	Sep 13 2004
1m 1f	1m 48.50	5	8-12	Firm	**MELLOTTIE**	Jul 25 1990
1m 2f 1y	2m 10.10	2	8-11	Good	**ADDING**	Nov 10 1989
1m 2f 1y	2m 1.40	5	9-2	Firm	**ERADICATE**	May 28 1990
1m 5f 218y	2m 59.54	6	8-5	Good To Firm	**LEODIS**	Jun 23 2018
1m 7f 217y	3m 24.90	3	9-3	Good To Firm	**SUBSONIC**	Oct 8 1991

RIPON

DISTANCE	TIME	AGE	WEIGHT	GOING	HORSE	DATE
5f	57.80	2	8-8	Firm	**SUPER ROCKY**	Aug 5 1991
5f	57.80	2	9-5	Good	**ORNATE**	Jul 18 2015
5f	57.28	5	8-12	Good	**DESERT ACE**	Sep 24 2016
6f	1m 10.40	2	9-2	Good	**CUMBRIAN VENTURE**	Aug 17 2002
6f	1m 9.04	8	9-9	Good	**JUSTANOTHERBOTTLE**	Jun 16 2022
1m	1m 38.77	2	9-4	Good	**GREED IS GOOD**	Sep 28 2013
1m	1m 36.62	4	8-11	Good To Firm	**GRANSTON**	Aug 29 2005
1m 1f	1m 49.97	6	9-3	Good To Firm	**GINGER JACK**	Jun 20 2013
1m 2f	2m 2.60	3	9-4	Firm	**SWIFT SWORD**	Jul 20 1991
1m 4f 10y	2m 31.04	3	9-7	Good To Firm	**JUST HUBERT**	Jul 8 2019
2m	3m 23.90	4	9-10	Firm	**PANAMA JACK**	Jun 23 1988

SALISBURY

DISTANCE	TIME	AGE	WEIGHT	GOING	HORSE	DATE
5f	59.30	2	9-0	Good To Firm	**AJIGOLO**	May 12 2005
5f	58.85	4	9-9	Good To Firm	**GLAMOROUS BREEZE**	Aug 10 2022
6f	1m 12.10	2	8-0	Good To Firm	**PARISIAN LADY**	Jun 10 1997
6f	1m 11.09	3	9-0	Firm	**L'AMI LOUIS**	May 1 2011
6f 213y	1m 25.97	2	9-0	Firm	**MORE ROYAL**	Jun 29 1995
6f 213y	1m 24.91	3	9-4	Firm	**CHILWORTH LAD**	May 1 2011
1m	1m 40.48	2	8-13	Firm	**CHOIR MASTER**	Sep 17 2002
1m	1m 38.29	3	8-7	Good To Firm	**LAYMAN**	Aug 11 2005
1m 1f 201y	2m 4.70	3	8-8	Firm	**ALPINISTA**	Aug 13 2020
1m 4f 5y	2m 31.69	3	9-5	Good To Firm	**ARRIVE**	Jun 27 2001
1m 6f 44y	3m 0.48	7	9-2	Good To Firm	**HIGHLAND CASTLE**	May 23 2015

SANDOWN PARK

DISTANCE	TIME	AGE	WEIGHT	GOING	HORSE	DATE
5f 10y	59.48	2	9-3	Firm	**TIMES TIME**	Jul 22 1982
5f 10y	58.57	3	8-12	Good To Firm	**BATTAASH**	Jul 8 2017
7f	1m 26.56	2	9-0	Good To Firm	**RAVEN'S PASS**	Sep 1 2007
7f	1m 26.36	3	9-0	Firm	**MAWSUFF**	Jun 14 1986
1m	1m 43.90	2	9-5	Good	**VIA DE VEGA**	Sep 18 2019
1m	1m 39.21	4	8-12	Good To Firm	**EL HAYEM**	Jul 8 2017
1m 1f	1m 55.76	3	8-7	Good To Firm	**VEE SIGHT**	Jun 11 2022
1m 1f 209y	2m 2.14	4	8-11	Good	**KALAGLOW**	May 31 1982
1m 6f	3m 1.08	3	8-9	Good	**JUST HUBERT**	Jul 25 2019
2m 50y	3m 29.38	6	9-0	Good To Firm	**CAUCUS**	Jul 6 2013

SOUTHWELL (AW)

DISTANCE	TIME	AGE	WEIGHT	GOING	HORSE	DATE
4f 214y	57.18	2	8-13	Standard To Slow	**BROWNLEE**	Dec 15 2022
4f 214y	56.92	4	8-13	Standard To Slow	**DIGITAL**	Feb 22 2022
6f 16y	1m 13.26	2	9-3	Standard To Slow	**ROCKING ENDS**	Dec 15 2022
6f 16y	1m 12.49	4	9-1	Standard To Slow	**BLIND BEGGAR**	Dec 15 2022
7f 14y	1m 27.74	2	9-2	Standard	**PASTICHE**	Oct 9 2022
7f 14y	1m 24.95	8	8-13	Standard	**ANIF**	Nov 16 2022
1m 13y	1m 41.14	2	9-3	Standard	**DREAMING PRINCESS**	Dec 6 2022
1m 13y	1m 38.14	4	9-0	Standard	**GEORGE MORLAND**	Nov 16 2022
1m 3f 23y	2m 20.19	3	9-2	Standard	**DAME ETHEL SMYTH**	Nov 1 2022
1m 4f 14y	2m 33.67	6	8-12	Standard	**HAMMY END**	Nov 16 2022
1m 6f 21y	3m 2.02	3	9-8	Standard	**VAYNOR**	Oct 20 2022
2m 2f 98y	4m 6.17	4	9-10	Standard To Slow	**BLAZEON FIVE**	Dec 16 2022

THIRSK

DISTANCE	TIME	AGE	WEIGHT	GOING	HORSE	DATE
5f	57.20	2	9-7	Good To Firm	**PROUD BOAST**	Aug 5 2000
5f	56.92	5	9-6	Firm	**CHARLIE PARKES**	Apr 11 2003
6f	1m 9.20	2	9-6	Good To Firm	**WESTCOURT MAGIC**	Aug 25 1995
6f	1m 8.80	6	9-4	Firm	**JOHAYRO**	Jul 23 1999
7f	1m 23.70	2	8-9	Firm	**COURTING**	Jul 23 1999
7f	1m 22.80	4	8-5	Firm	**SILVER HAZE**	May 21 1988
7f 218y	1m 37.97	2	9-0	Firm	**SUNDAY SYMPHONY**	Sep 4 2004
7f 218y	1m 34.80	4	8-13	Firm	**YEARSLEY**	May 5 1990
1m 4f 8y	2m 29.90	5	9-12	Firm	**GALLERY GOD**	Jun 4 2001
1m 6f	2m 57.95	4	9-6	Good To Firm	**WOR WILLIE**	Apr 30 2022
2m 13y	3m 22.30	3	9-0	Firm	**TOMASCHEK**	Jul 17 1981

WETHERBY

DISTANCE	TIME	AGE	WEIGHT	GOING	HORSE	DATE
5f 110y	1m 5.01	2	9-3	Good To Firm	**FEARBY**	Jun 8 2021
5f 110y	1m 4.25	3	9-1	Good To Firm	**DAPPER MAN**	Jun 19 2017
7f	1m 26.23	2	8-9	Good	**RAYAA**	Jul 21 2015
7f	1m 24.72	4	9-2	Good	**SLEMY**	Jul 21 2015
1m	1m 37.75	7	9-2	Good To Firm	**SIX STRINGS**	Jun 8 2021
1m 2f	2m 5.13	5	9-5	Good	**FIRST SARGEANT**	Jul 21 2015
1m 6f	3m 0.31	4	9-9	Good	**DANNI CALIFORNIA (IRE)**	Jun 7 2022

WINDSOR

DISTANCE	TIME	AGE	WEIGHT	GOING	HORSE	DATE
5f 21y	58.69	2	9-7	Good To Firm	**AL DASIM**	Jul 25 2022
5f 21y	58.03	5	10-1	Good To Firm	**SPRING BLOOM**	Jul 11 2022
6f 12y	1m 10.50	2	9-5	Good To Firm	**CUBISM**	Aug 17 1998
6f 12y	1m 9.54	5	9-5	Good	**ALJADY**	Jul 13 2020
1m 31y	1m 41.73	2	9-5	Good To Firm	**SALOUEN**	Aug 7 2016
1m 31y	1m 39.47	4	9-6	Good To Firm	**MATTERHORN**	Jun 29 2019
1m 1f 194y	2m 1.62	6	9-1	Good	**AL KAZEEM**	Aug 23 2014
1m 2f	2m 3.01	7	9-7	Good To Soft	**REGAL REALITY**	Aug 27 2022
1m 3f 99y	2m 21.50	3	9-2	Firm	**DOUBLE FLORIN**	May 19 1980

WOLVERHAMPTON (AW)

DISTANCE	TIME	AGE	WEIGHT	GOING	HORSE	DATE
5f 21y	59.75	2	9-6	Standard	**QUATRIEME AMI**	Nov 13 2015
5f 21y	59.33	5	9-6	Standard	**LOMU**	Dec 3 2019
6f 20y	1m 12.16	2	9-2	Standard	**MUBAKKER**	Nov 1 2018
6f 20y	1m 11.44	5	9-6	Standard	**KACHY**	Dec 26 2018
7f 36y	1m 26.77	2	8-11	Standard	**RICHARD R H B**	Nov 23 2019
7f 36y	1m 25.35	4	9-3	Standard	**MISTER UNIVERSE**	Mar 12 2016
1m 142y	1m 47.38	2	9-5	Standard	**JACK HOBBS**	Dec 27 2014
1m 142y	1m 45.43	4	9-4	Standard	**KEYSTROKE**	Nov 26 2016
1m 1f 104y	1m 57.99	2	9-2	Standard	**EMISSARY**	Oct 12 2019
1m 1f 104y	1m 55.91	6	8-8	Standard	**STORM AHEAD**	Nov 18 2019
1m 4f 51y	2m 33.44	4	9-5	Standard	**PATHS OF GLORY**	Oct 19 2019
1m 5f 219y	2m 57.16	4	9-11	Standard	**TRIBAL ART**	Apr 19 2022
2m 120y	3m 31.18	4	9-0	Standard	**AIRCRAFT CARRIER**	Jan 14 2019

YARMOUTH

DISTANCE	TIME	AGE	WEIGHT	GOING	HORSE	DATE
5f 42y	59.00	2	9-2	Good To Firm	**THE LIR JET**	Jun 3 2020
5f 42y	58.57	11	9-10	Good To Firm	**CASPIAN PRINCE**	Sep 16 2020
6f 3y	1m 10.40	2	9-0	Firm	**LANCHESTER**	Sep 15 1988
6f 3y	1m 8.85	3	9-1	Good To Firm	**DESERT GULF**	Jul 14 2021
7f 3y	1m 22.20	2	9-0	Good To Firm	**WARRSHAN**	Sep 14 1988
7f 3y	1m 21.32	3	9-7	Firm	**MISTER SNOWDON**	Jun 3 2020
1m 3y	1m 35.40	2	9-2	Good To Firm	**FOREST FALCON**	Sep 17 2020
1m 3y	1m 33.00	4	9-5	Firm	**MAYDANNY**	Jun 3 2020
1m 1f 21y	1m 52.00	3	9-5	Good To Firm	**TOUCH GOLD**	Jul 5 2012
1m 2f 23y	2m 2.83	3	8-8	Firm	**REUNITE**	Jul 18 2006
1m 3f 104y	2m 23.10	3	8-9	Firm	**RAHIL**	Jul 1 1993
1m 6f 17y	2m 57.80	3	8-2	Good To Firm	**BARAKAT**	Jul 24 1990
2m	3m 26.70	4	8-2	Good To Firm	**ALHESN**	Jul 26 1999

YORK

DISTANCE	TIME	AGE	WEIGHT	GOING	HORSE	DATE
5f	57.11	2	9-0	Good	**BIG TIME BABY**	Aug 20 2016
5f	55.90	5	9-11	Good To Firm	**BATTAASH**	Aug 23 2019
5f 89y	1m 3.20	2	9-3	Good To Firm	**THE ART OF RACING**	Sep 9 2012
5f 89y	1m 1.72	4	9-7	Good To Firm	**BOGART**	Aug 21 2013
6f	1m 8.90	2	9-0	Good	**TIGGY WIGGY**	Aug 21 2014
6f	1m 8.23	3	8-11	Good To Firm	**MINCE**	Sep 9 2012
7f	1m 22.32	2	9-1	Good To Firm	**DUTCH CONNECTION**	Aug 20 2014
7f	1m 21.00	3	9-1	Good To Firm	**SHINE SO BRIGHT**	Aug 24 2019
7f 192y	1m 36.92	2	9-5	Good	**AWESOMETANK**	Oct 14 2017
7f 192y	1m 34.59	4	9-2	Good	**BLUE FOR YOU**	Aug 18 2022
1m 177y	1m 46.76	5	9-8	Good To Firm	**ECHO OF LIGHT**	Sep 5 2007
1m 2f 56y	2m 5.29	3	8-11	Good To Firm	**SEA THE STARS**	Aug 18 2009
1m 3f 188y	2m 25.40	4	8-8	Good To Firm	**TAMREER**	Aug 23 2019
1m 5f 188y	2m 52.97	6	9-5	Good To Firm	**MUSTAJEER**	Aug 24 2019
2m 56y	3m 27.06	5	9-6	Good To Firm	**STRADIVARIUS**	Aug 23 2019

TOP FLAT JOCKEYS IN BRITAIN 2022

(1 JANUARY - 31 DECEMBER)

WINS-RUNS	%	JOCKEY	2ND	3RD	TOTAL PRIZE	WIN PRIZE
201-750	27%	**WILLIAM BUICK**	127	105	3,719,116	6,757,469
151-1006	15%	**HOLLIE DOYLE**	142	135	1,970,863	3,299,511
144-1147	13%	**DAVID PROBERT**	141	135	1,240,115	2,774,824
128-853	15%	**DANIEL MUSCUTT**	124	109	863,056	1,643,035
127-889	14%	**TOM MARQUAND**	93	118	2,647,607	4,406,353
116-758	15%	**KEVIN STOTT**	96	107	750,270	1,448,909
116-770	15%	**ROSSA RYAN**	110	81	925,969	1,840,086
112-632	18%	**JACK MITCHELL**	88	82	771,384	1,441,699
111-673	16%	**DANIEL TUDHOPE**	87	76	1,616,448	2,721,362
108-714	15%	**PAUL MULRENNAN**	91	85	594,268	1,169,668
103-860	12%	**JASON HART**	109	95	1,060,112	1,815,524
103-1118	9%	**LUKE MORRIS**	135	123	860,377	1,484,359
98-681	14%	**RICHARD KINGSCOTE**	88	93	2,483,487	3,235,297
96-515	19%	**BEN CURTIS**	70	56	857,690	1,458,186
93-666	14%	**DAVID EGAN**	88	78	1,660,991	2,736,077
91-450	20%	**JAMES DOYLE**	74	67	1,900,447	3,534,043
90-415	22%	**JIM CROWLEY**	43	50	3,225,859	4,262,211
90-737	12%	**CONNOR BEASLEY**	93	111	843,204	1,413,323
82-541	15%	**CLIFFORD LEE**	74	59	949,353	1,639,254
81-676	12%	**JASON WATSON**	87	92	552,737	1,086,734
78-602	13%	**P J MCDONALD**	70	70	1,226,890	1,777,046
77-386	20%	**ANDREA ATZENI**	54	54	1,090,372	2,124,946
71-548	13%	**SEAN LEVEY**	63	64	748,605	1,452,037
71-667	11%	**DAVID ALLAN**	73	85	427,840	921,505
68-380	18%	**RYAN MOORE**	50	52	3,045,087	4,907,475
67-379	18%	**BENOIT DE LA SAYETTE**	57	48	439,732	789,458
67-456	15%	**HARRY DAVIES**	61	57	438,959	931,893
67-497	13%	**NEIL CALLAN**	63	61	657,836	1,226,411
67-504	13%	**ROBERT HAVLIN**	77	67	790,475	1,271,538
67-669	10%	**KIERAN O'NEILL**	64	63	318,341	627,056
66-560	12%	**CIEREN FALLON**	91	71	508,675	1,160,272
66-589	11%	**SAM JAMES**	60	80	445,797	813,017
66-679	10%	**ROB HORNBY**	78	78	1,011,975	2,171,737
64-457	14%	**RAY DAWSON**	51	50	626,994	1,089,828
64-462	14%	**MARCO GHIANI**	58	65	410,930	808,720
62-413	15%	**FRANNY NORTON**	61	59	493,480	934,641
56-410	14%	**ROSS COAKLEY**	62	48	323,619	621,136
55-568	10%	**GRAHAM LEE**	47	58	269,128	555,993
50-373	13%	**RYAN SEXTON**	52	46	254,456	504,836
49-362	14%	**HECTOR CROUCH**	45	41	235,568	474,750
49-387	13%	**CALLUM RODRIGUEZ**	45	39	274,013	522,960
47-410	11%	**RHYS CLUTTERBUCK**	45	36	237,472	425,932
46-360	13%	**PAT COSGRAVE**	51	47	325,465	629,884
46-418	11%	**SAFFIE OSBORNE**	43	44	362,663	688,221
46-487	9%	**JOANNA MASON**	45	53	261,496	492,355
45-379	12%	**KIERAN SHOEMARK**	38	49	587,211	1,055,959
45-512	9%	**CALLUM SHEPHERD**	66	54	303,031	702,262
45-561	8%	**ANDREW MULLEN**	43	62	194,797	509,184
41-292	14%	**JOE FANNING**	46	34	482,870	746,657
41-323	13%	**OISIN ORR**	41	43	254,688	650,516

TOP FLAT TRAINERS IN BRITAIN 2022

TRAINER	LEADING HORSE	W-R	2ND	3RD	4TH	WIN PRIZE	TOTAL PRIZE
CHARLIE APPLEBY	Naval Crown	152-488	100	61	41	3,562,463	6,251,358
WILLIAM HAGGAS	Baaeed	167-671	102	94	80	4,071,705	5,818,202
JOHN & THADY GOSDEN	Mishriff	128-591	118	75	52	2,948,066	5,133,204
ANDREW BALDING	Alcohol Free	133-927	138	128	136	2,220,707	4,597,646
ROGER VARIAN	Bayside Boy	140-639	91	84	79	2,527,686	3,606,167
K R BURKE	Cold Case	117-783	116	102	88	1,646,289	2,924,899
SIR MICHAEL STOUTE	Bay Bridge	36-247	40	36	37	2,254,474	2,921,355
CHARLIE & MARK JOHNSTON	Living Legend	176-1267	179	170	135	1,566,056	2,919,814
A P O'BRIEN	Kyprios	15-84	6	9	12	1,839,261	2,819,785
RALPH BECKETT	Kinross	88-565	76	73	71	1,708,498	2,772,335
RICHARD HANNON	Chindit	110-1058	124	126	137	1,144,880	2,698,222
DAVID O'MEARA	Get Shirty	110-904	91	115	107	1,230,679	2,137,981
GEORGE BOUGHEY	Cachet	136-787	122	83	82	1,255,735	1,994,760
RICHARD FAHEY	Perfect Power	103-878	91	88	94	1,147,929	1,953,379
TIM EASTERBY	Boardman	117-1453	133	169	150	759,583	1,722,078
CHARLES HILLS	Pogo	67-405	51	49	46	997,736	1,644,288
KEVIN RYAN	Fonteyn	65-609	75	70	77	732,751	1,554,397
MICHAEL APPLEBY	Raasel	107-882	119	93	106	614,455	1,438,497
SIMON & ED CRISFORD	Jadoomi	82-347	61	59	34	747,708	1,400,328
SAEED BIN SUROOR	Real World	49-234	30	37	27	669,244	1,206,192
WILLIAM MUIR & CHRIS GRASSICK	Pyledriver	28-241	30	30	35	896,914	1,186,007
ARCHIE WATSON	Eddie's Boy	79-591	76	66	63	663,635	1,183,595
MICHAEL DODS	Commanche Falls	57-499	61	66	50	623,684	1,079,794
CLIVE COX	Harry Three	61-473	53	60	50	601,625	1,074,118
JOHN QUINN	Highfield Princess	45-347	54	33	52	720,252	1,054,608
ED WALKER	Amichi	42-364	48	39	44	481,746	1,031,763
HUGO PALMER	Flaming Rib	43-419	55	53	42	399,535	997,976
OWEN BURROWS	Hukum	21-67	11	5	8	890,832	956,200
ALAN KING	Trueshan	30-289	44	28	34	596,367	947,402
IAN WILLIAMS	Alfred Boucher	35-392	33	41	38	451,705	901,282
DAVID EVANS	Rohaan	65-540	62	68	61	458,102	827,147
MARCO BOTTI	Giavellotto	51-396	44	55	43	395,994	825,782
HUGHIE MORRISON	Quickthorn	28-261	38	29	30	402,377	822,815
JIM GOLDIE	Call Me Ginger	60-539	43	64	59	403,348	801,348
MICK CHANNON	Majestic	46-426	49	52	51	482,594	792,354
KEITH DALGLEISH	Evaluation	49-553	68	60	69	327,424	765,685
TONY CARROLL	Night Bear	84-926	100	108	91	351,162	733,086
KEVIN PHILIPPART DE FOY	El Habeeb	60-381	61	51	42	390,461	729,856
HARRY & ROGER CHARLTON	Thesis	52-293	37	40	34	448,855	729,793
EVE JOHNSON HOUGHTON	Streets Of Gold	46-388	45	51	45	378,077	729,754
WILLIAM KNIGHT	Sir Busker	22-218	33	33	28	251,070	687,941
JOSEPH PATRICK O'BRIEN	State Of Rest	1-16	2	1	2	599,708	686,203
CHARLIE FELLOWES	Marbaan	34-289	34	33	37	343,268	680,987
RICHARD HUGHES	Merlin's Beard	57-384	57	48	53	323,783	660,385
ED DUNLOP	Haunted Dream	58-513	54	59	61	282,590	646,035
DAVID SIMCOCK	Bless Him	36-291	42	40	37	306,771	644,780
DAVID LOUGHNANE	Go Bears Go	39-381	47	39	51	302,747	642,893
JANE CHAPPLE-HYAM	Saffron Beach	22-227	33	30	23	289,753	639,518
MICHAEL BELL	Indian Dream	38-330	52	62	37	233,888	600,424
SIR MARK PRESCOTT BT	Alpinista	32-210	38	18	20	447,382	594,014

TOP FLAT OWNERS IN BRITAIN 2022

OWNER	LEADING HORSE	W-R	2ND	3RD	4TH	WIN PRIZE	TOTAL PRIZE
GODOLPHIN	Naval Crown	209-772	138	106	72	4,642,941	8,010,205
SHADWELL ESTATE COMPANY LTD	Baaeed	59-182	24	25	17	3,162,575	3,720,595
SHEIKH MOHAMMED OBAID AL MAKTOUM	Cold Case	47-220	36	33	30	896,632	1,678,665
JUDDMONTE	Chaldean	45-199	36	29	14	937,743	1,569,649
SAEED SUHAIL	Desert Crown	16-72	12	6	12	1,212,028	1,351,402
CHEVELEY PARK STUD	Inspiral	31-201	36	23	22	638,149	1,136,974
JAMES WIGAN & BALLYLINCH STUD	Bay Bridge	2-4	1	0	0	782,5980	1,031,228
SHEIKH AHMED AL MAKTOUM	Jadoomi	43-170	23	31	19	520,219	913,460
KING POWER RACING CO LTD	The Foxes	44-365	36	62	40	443,761	907,824
SUNDERLAND HOLDING INC	Sea La Rosa	21-58	11	13	1	518,734	861,986
AMO RACING LIMITED	Persian Force	39-236	35	25	32	322,979	849,043
LA PYLE PARTNERSHIP	Pyledriver	4-19	4	2	2	725,939	845,876
KHK RACING LTD	Eldar Eldarov	15-41	11	6	2	751,557	794,329
MARC CHAN	Kinross	9-50	6	5	12	631,745	752,246
TEME VALLEY & BALLYLINCH STUD	Bayside Boy	3-8	1	1	1	690,814	701,232
J C SMITH	Alcohol Free	15-95	13	14	9	446,205	699,892
MRS FITRI HAY	Khaadem	15-110	12	14	14	355,751	676,861
MISS K RAUSING	Alpinista	14-129	15	21	13	484,420	664,780
PRINCE A A FAISAL	Mishriff	3-27	8	4	3	39,101	659,826
MICK AND JANICE MARISCOTTI	Coltrane	8-52	14	5	11	210,606	656,356
MRS JOHN MAGNIER/MICHAEL TABOR/DERRICK SMITH/WESTERBERG	Tuesday	3-28	2	3	3	363,589	627,082
SHEIKH RASHID DALMOOK AL MAKTOUM	Perfect Power	20-79	15	10	10	414,782	619,716
STATE OF REST PARTNERSHIP	State Of Rest	1-1	0	0	0	599,708	599,708
MOYGLARE,MAGNIER,TABOR,SMITH,WESTERBERG	Kyprios	2-2	0	0	0	567,100	567,100
CLIPPER LOGISTICS	Fresh	23-175	18	17	20	346,611	517,542
TRAINERS HOUSE ENTERPRISES LTD	Highfield Princess	3-10	1	1	0	459,393	480,410
IMAD ALSAGAR	Nashwa	6-39	4	4	6	395,617	480,304
SINGULA PARTNERSHIP	Trueshan	3-5	1	1	0	395,740	477,490
SHEIKH JUMA DALMOOK AL MAKTOUM	Swingalong	15-135	30	23	17	266,526	460,945
H H AGA KHAN	Vadeni	1-2	0	1	0	448,363	460,737
AHMAD AL SHAIKH	Hoo Ya Mal	5-26	9	2	4	21,889	432,502
K K HO	Deauville Legend	13-64	15	8	9	280,770	428,386
JOHN AND JESS DANCE	Asjad	24-144	23	24	17	247,847	401,441
M TABOR & D SMITH & MRS J MAGNIER & WESTERBERG	Meditate	3-15	2	1	2	227,221	397,256
PAUL TURNER	Haunted Dream	43-306	26	40	39	220,027	395,037
JON AND JULIA AISBITT	Lilac Road	14-53	3	7	3	225,985	382,645
THE QUEEN	King's Lynn	20-110	20	17	12	185,338	374,767
BARBARA & ALICK RICHMOND	Living Legend	6-37	6	8	2	245,289	370,165
AKELA THOROUGHBREDS LIMITED	Get Shirty	10-49	2	3	9	304,992	369,322
ISA SALMAN & ABDULLA AL KHALIFA	Commissioning	2-2	0	0	0	364,503	364,503
HIGHCLERE T'BRED RACING - WILD FLOWER	Cachet	2-3	0	0	0	328,918	342,368
GEORGE STRAWBRIDGE	Mimikyu	15-60	11	5	7	232,198	339,891
D SMITH,MRS J MAGNIER,M TABOR,WESTERBERG	Blackbeard	2-16	1	2	2	215,152	336,237
MARC CHAN AND ANDREW ROSEN	Prosperous Voyage	4-7	2	0	0	204,600	333,600
JABER ABDULLAH	Queen Me	22-129	18	23	18	143,421	322,064
B E NIELSEN	Stradivarius	5-29	5	6	5	139,194	319,548
A E OPPENHEIMER	Megallan	14-74	16	9	8	185,888	316,672
SHEIKH HAMDAN BIN MOHAMMED AL MAKTOUM	Enfranchise	14-132	16	21	8	141,920	316,245
WESTERBERG,MRS J MAGNIER,M TABOR,D SMITH	Changingoftheguard	2-7	0	2	0	204,439	303,923
LLOYD WEBBER, TACTFUL FINANCE, S RODEN	Emily Upjohn	1-2	0	0	0	283,550	300,425

TOP FLAT HORSES IN BRITAIN 2022

HORSE (AGE)	WIN & PLACE £	W-R	TRAINER	OWNER	BREEDER
BAAEED (4)	1,742,625	4-5	William Haggas	Shadwell Estate Company Ltd	Shadwell Estate Company Ltd
BAY BRIDGE (4)	1,031,228	2-4	Sir Michael Stoute	James Wigan & Ballylinch Stud	London Thoroughbred Services Ltd
DESERT CROWN (3)	1,008,870	2-2	Sir Michael Stoute	Saeed Suhail	Strawberry Fields Stud
PYLEDRIVER (5)	804,550	1-2	William Muir & Chris Grassick	La Pyle Partnership	Knox & Wells Ltd & R Devlin
NAVAL CROWN (4)	702,227	1-4	Charlie Appleby	Godolphin	Godolphin
BAYSIDE BOY (3)	690,558	2-4	Roger Varian	Teme Valley & Ballylinch Stud	Ballylinch Stud
KINROSS (5)	625,750	3-6	Ralph Beckett	Marc Chan	Lawn Stud
ELDAR ELDAROV (3)	605,082	3-4	Roger Varian	KHK Racing Ltd	Miss K Rausing
STATE OF REST (4)	599,708	1-1	Joseph Patrick O'Brien	State Of Rest Partnership	Tinnakill Bloodstock Ltd
COROEBUS (3)	567,100	2-2	Charlie Appleby	Godolphin	Godolphin
KYPRIOS (4)	567,100	2-2	A P O'Brien	Moyglare,Magnier,Tabor,Smith,Westerberg	Moyglare Stud Farm Ltd
MISHRIFF (5)	519,484	0-3	John & Thady Gosden	Prince A A Faisal	Nawara Stud Limited
EMILY UPJOHN (3)	495,502	3-5	John & Thady Gosden	Lloyd Webber, Tactful Finance, S Roden	Lordship Stud & Sunderland Holding Inc
ALCOHOL FREE (4)	495,156	1-5	Andrew Balding	J C Smith	Churchtown House Stud
TUESDAY (3)	480,461	1-3	A P O'Brien	Mrs John Magnier/Michael Tabor/Derrick Smith/Westerberg	Coolmore
HIGHFIELD PRINCESS (5)	480,410	3-7	John Quinn	Trainers House Enterprises Ltd	Trainers House Enterprises Ltd
TRUESHAN (6)	477,490	3-5	Alan King	Singula Partnership	Didier Blot
CHALDEAN (2)	469,776	4-5	Andrew Balding	Juddmonte	Whitsbury Manor Stud
MODERN GAMES (3)	463,593	0-2	Charlie Appleby	Godolphin	Godolphin
VADENI (3)	448,363	1-1	J-C Rouget	H H Aga Khan	Haras De S A Aga Khan Scea
NASHWA (3)	444,105	3-4	John & Thady Gosden	Imad Alsagar	Blue Diamond Stud Farm (uk) Ltd
HOO YA MAL (3)	442,878	1-6	Gai Waterhouse & Adrian Bott	Go Bloodstock Australia, Sneesby Racing Et Al	Meon Valley Stud
TRAWLERMAN (4)	420,802	3-6	John & Thady Gosden	Godolphin	Godolphin
COLTRANE (5)	385,159	3-9	Andrew Balding	Mick and Janice Mariscotti	Rockfield Farm
COMMISSIONING (2)	368,823	3-3	John & Thady Gosden	Isa Salman & Abdulla Al Khalifa	Abdulla Al-Khalifa & Isa Salman
NEW LONDON (3)	363,000	3-5	Charlie Appleby	Godolphin	Godolphin
INSPIRAL (3)	352,909	1-3	John & Thady Gosden	Cheveley Park Stud	Cheveley Park Stud Limited
CACHET (3)	342,368	2-3	George Boughey	Highclere T'Bred Racing - Wild Flower	Hyde Park Stud
PERFECT POWER (3)	328,918	2-5	Richard Fahey	Sheikh Rashid Dalmook Al Maktoum	Tally-Ho Stud
ADAYAR (4)	305,270	1-2	Charlie Appleby	Godolphin	Godolphin
ALPINISTA (5)	302,689	1-1	Sir Mark Prescott Bt	Miss K Rausing	Miss K Rausing
CREATIVE FORCE (4)	302,487	0-3	Charlie Appleby	Godolphin	Owenstown Bloodstock Ltd
DEAUVILLE LEGEND (3)	297,952	3-5	James Ferguson	K K Ho	G B Partnership
NATURE STRIP (8)	283,550	1-1	Chris Waller	R A E Lyons, P D Harrison Et Al	Golden Grove Stud Farm
COLD CASE (2)	275,597	3-6	K R Burke	Sheikh Mohammed Obaid Al Maktoum	Whitsbury Manor Stud
TORQUATOR TASSO (5)	268,750	0-1	Marcel Weiss	Gestut Auenquelle	Paul H Vandeberg
POGO (6)	266,846	3-6	Charles Hills	Gary And Linnet Woodward	Thomas Foy
NATIVE TRAIL (3)	264,839	1-4	Charlie Appleby	Godolphin	Le Haras D'Haspel
PROSPEROUS VOYAGE (3)	263,579	1-4	Ralph Beckett	Andrew Rosen And Marc Chan	Lynch Bages & Camas Park Stud
STRADIVARIUS (8)	260,542	1-3	John & Thady Gosden	B E Nielsen	Bjorn Nielsen
HUKUM (5)	252,359	1-1	Owen Burrows	Shadwell Estate Company Ltd	Shadwell Estate Company Limited
WESTOVER (3)	251,583	1-3	Ralph Beckett	Juddmonte	Juddmonte Farms Ltd
LEZOO (2)	249,680	4-5	Ralph Beckett	Marc Chan & Andrew Rosen	Chasemore Farm
CHANGINGOFTHEGUARD (3)	247,587	2-3	A P O'Brien	Westerberg,Mrs J Magnier,M Tabor,D Smith	B V Sangster
MINZAAL (4)	247,575	2-4	Owen Burrows	Shadwell Estate Company Ltd	Ringfort Stud
KHAADEM (6)	244,107	2-4	Charles Hills	Mrs Fitri Hay	Yeomanstown Stud
SEA LA ROSA (4)	240,223	2-4	William Haggas	Sunderland Holding Inc	G B Partnership
LIVING LEGEND (6)	239,344	3-8	Charlie & Mark Johnston	Barbara & Alick Richmond	A Oliver
MY PROSPERO (3)	229,622	2-4	William Haggas	Sunderland Holding Inc	Sunderland Holding Inc
QUICKTHORN (5)	229,618	2-5	Hughie Morrison	Lady Blyth	Lemington Grange Stud

TOP NH JOCKEYS IN BRITAIN 2021/22

WINS-RUNS	%	JOCKEY	2ND	3RD	TOTAL PRIZE	WIN PRIZE
204-956	21%	**BRIAN HUGHES**	161	147	1,094,146	1,892,606
105-731	14%	**SAM TWISTON-DAVIES**	123	77	1,042,896	1,796,262
104-508	20%	**HARRY SKELTON**	83	76	883,595	1,691,199
99-427	23%	**HARRY COBDEN**	78	61	1,218,241	2,051,684
94-491	19%	**SEAN BOWEN**	63	71	687,062	1,090,041
87-408	21%	**PADDY BRENNAN**	77	63	576,349	1,025,713
80-417	19%	**JAMIE MOORE**	61	51	602,520	952,594
78-634	12%	**SEAN QUINLAN**	85	88	509,054	954,684
74-352	21%	**NICO DE BOINVILLE**	43	31	869,736	1,214,759
74-388	19%	**JAMES BOWEN**	64	52	588,785	953,158
74-431	17%	**TOM CANNON**	53	73	661,830	1,046,293
72-493	15%	**TOM O'BRIEN**	68	64	546,003	1,114,744
70-524	13%	**ADAM WEDGE**	46	59	642,380	981,073
68-338	20%	**AIDAN COLEMAN**	68	53	933,878	1,551,254
65-460	14%	**BRENDAN POWELL**	67	50	582,271	1,139,470
64-396	16%	**GAVIN SHEEHAN**	67	55	291,641	655,533
64-507	13%	**TOM SCUDAMORE**	75	57	385,769	846,089
63-455	14%	**JONATHAN BURKE**	62	55	440,243	771,218
59-360	16%	**JONJO O'NEILL JR**	43	52	401,066	796,873
53-452	12%	**NICK SCHOLFIELD**	45	40	283,548	633,266
51-414	12%	**TOM BELLAMY**	61	57	310,445	676,843
49-342	14%	**HARRY BANNISTER**	47	46	330,565	560,506
49-410	12%	**CONOR O'FARRELL**	42	48	276,030	529,808
48-317	15%	**CHARLIE DEUTSCH**	41	37	861,206	1,388,829
47-239	20%	**STAN SHEPPARD**	29	26	514,556	742,513
47-278	17%	**KEVIN BROGAN**	38	34	231,764	397,515
43-245	18%	**BRYONY FROST**	33	32	385,015	645,289
40-385	10%	**CRAIG NICHOL**	52	36	195,012	470,165
39-262	15%	**CHARLIE HAMMOND**	32	36	252,304	416,207
39-308	13%	**BEN JONES**	38	34	206,591	371,585
36-447	8%	**JAMES BEST**	53	45	142,077	357,239
34-266	13%	**DAVID BASS**	42	36	342,588	587,376
34-270	13%	**DEREK FOX**	27	42	365,462	603,132
33-236	14%	**THEO GILLARD**	29	35	173,401	324,308
33-323	10%	**KIELAN WOODS**	41	39	299,227	546,204
33-337	10%	**RYAN MANIA**	41	40	295,213	562,188
32-167	19%	**A P HESKIN**	28	29	370,265	594,284
32-184	17%	**LIAM HARRISON**	33	24	169,650	311,125
32-230	14%	**REX DINGLE**	33	30	157,636	376,300
31-211	15%	**RICHARD PATRICK**	32	22	232,866	419,103
31-226	14%	**DARYL JACOB**	27	40	289,329	585,913
31-285	11%	**DANNY MCMENAMIN**	38	27	222,343	435,861
29-253	11%	**JACK TUDOR**	34	27	239,400	482,640
29-308	9%	**CIARAN GETHINGS**	36	44	179,470	424,317
28-223	13%	**MITCHELL BASTYAN**	26	29	118,969	243,743
28-228	12%	**FERGUS GREGORY**	18	35	109,202	225,017
27-273	10%	**JAMIE HAMILTON**	28	37	140,513	283,637
27-331	8%	**HENRY BROOKE**	43	48	114,920	305,442
26-338	8%	**RICHIE MCLERNON**	24	47	128,726	306,606
24-204	12%	**CHARLIE TODD**	23	25	168,411	273,408

TOP NH TRAINERS IN BRITAIN 2021/22

TRAINER	LEADING HORSE	W-R	2ND	3RD	4TH	WIN PRIZE	TOTAL PRIZE
PAUL NICHOLLS	Greaneteen	143-629	113	85	57	1,727,306	2,964,486
NICKY HENDERSON	Epatante	119-557	80	68	44	1,610,497	2,408,791
DAN SKELTON	Protektorat	135-742	100	97	84	1,099,227	2,116,783
W P MULLINS	Energumene	15-89	7	11	7	1,216,900	1,730,527
VENETIA WILLIAMS	L'Homme Presse	60-292	36	35	35	996,914	1,567,452
NIGEL TWISTON-DAVIES	Guard Your Dreams	68-468	70	47	62	848,693	1,392,308
FERGAL O'BRIEN	Paint The Dream	128-735	131	110	90	693,384	1,378,280
ALAN KING	Edwardstone	63-435	69	72	49	722,291	1,319,630
DONALD MCCAIN	Minella Drama	155-663	102	98	77	817,455	1,301,327
GARY MOORE	Porticello	91-441	71	52	43	734,754	1,151,009
PHILIP HOBBS	Thyme Hill	70-506	77	64	55	545,834	1,150,362
COLIN TIZZARD	Eldorado Allen	62-450	54	56	50	582,332	1,143,452
OLLY MURPHY	Brewin'upastorm	92-526	98	82	64	603,662	1,124,937
HENRY DE BROMHEAD	A Plus Tard	5-45	3	6	2	840,319	1,123,360
GORDON ELLIOTT	Sire Du Berlais	16-123	20	12	8	428,452	1,033,367
EVAN WILLIAMS	Coole Cody	53-450	38	51	51	597,191	888,251
JONJO O'NEILL	An Tailliur	82-507	54	70	52	459,492	867,611
LUCINDA RUSSELL	Ahoy Senor	46-405	53	70	56	417,576	759,545
DR RICHARD NEWLAND	Captain Tom Cat	66-398	70	48	57	373,926	688,941
EMMA LAVELLE	Paisley Park	41-258	49	42	29	358,230	686,142
DAVID PIPE	Gericault Roque	47-427	57	41	51	283,490	675,401
HARRY FRY	Love Envoi	38-213	34	33	29	400,003	674,891
TOM LACEY	Glory And Fortune	50-275	43	22	31	394,371	669,657
CHRISTIAN WILLIAMS	Win My Wings	34-256	33	17	23	409,290	659,089
MILTON HARRIS	Knight Salute	56-254	41	42	23	396,220	595,489
NEIL MULHOLLAND	Kansas City Chief	62-448	63	50	62	309,293	588,759
KIM BAILEY	Two For Gold	35-269	42	34	25	338,374	574,965
EMMET MULLINS	Noble Yeats	1-12	1	1	2	500,000	529,133
CHARLIE LONGSDON	Snow Leopardess	47-282	44	40	28	325,138	520,784
BEN PAULING	Global Citizen	44-341	43	47	44	259,971	508,674
SAM THOMAS	Iwilldoit	20-102	18	13	14	335,968	490,707
JAMIE SNOWDEN	Kiltealy Briggs	49-258	47	40	32	255,856	480,394
CHRIS GORDON	Aucunrisque	43-253	24	42	32	271,104	466,870
PETER BOWEN	Mac Tottie	35-243	25	31	24	313,548	437,288
NICKY RICHARDS	Nells Son	37-289	48	39	42	208,857	430,527
HENRY DALY	Fortescue	30-154	27	22	12	264,824	417,730
ANTHONY HONEYBALL	Sam Brown	35-188	33	26	21	214,917	414,279
BRIAN ELLISON	Cormier	21-182	33	22	20	224,474	393,499
TOM GEORGE	Bun Doran	33-262	26	39	34	182,116	392,461
SANDY THOMSON	Hill Sixteen	20-187	31	20	20	143,625	383,188
SUE SMITH	Midnight Shadow	27-232	21	29	23	220,340	371,544
GAVIN CROMWELL	Flooring Porter	2-26	9	6	1	187,070	370,558
IAN WILLIAMS	Party Business	27-217	33	21	25	201,184	340,761
JOSEPH PATRICK O'BRIEN	Fakir D'oudairies	4-16	1	2	1	277,905	340,465
MICKY HAMMOND	Geryville	33-401	33	44	50	155,693	337,073
N W ALEXANDER	Wakool	35-226	26	31	35	190,751	335,613
JEREMY SCOTT	Dashel Drasher	19-172	30	22	18	138,942	327,504
OLIVER GREENALL	El Borracho	36-367	47	49	44	131,027	317,510
REBECCA MENZIES	Fonzerelli	31-228	31	38	32	157,933	312,831
STUART EDMUNDS	Gentleman At Arms	20-148	27	29	18	137,558	311,738

TOP NH OWNERS IN BRITAIN 2021/22

OWNER	LEADING HORSE	W-R	2ND	3RD	4TH	WIN PRIZE	TOTAL PRIZE
JOHN P MCMANUS	Epatante	97-545	58	68	72	1,638,811	2,689,969
CHEVELEY PARK STUD	A Plus Tard	4-12	0	2	2	754,007	822,140
SIMON MUNIR & ISAAC SOUEDE	Sceau Royal	28-164	24	27	21	420,480	797,891
ROBERT WALEY-COHEN	Noble Yeats	2-22	6	2	2	502,673	517,104
EXORS OF THE LATE TREVOR HEMMINGS	Cloudy Glen	30-130	20	17	12	326,542	477,402
GIGGINSTOWN HOUSE STUD	Delta Work	2-33	4	2	0	95,292	355,645
WALTERS PLANT HIRE & POTTER GROUP	Before Midnight	15-49	8	4	7	195,345	289,503
MRS S RICCI	Royale Pagaille	2-19	3	3	0	118,677	285,290
MRS J DONNELLY	Shishkin	5-24	3	3	1	211,987	276,540
TONY BLOOM	Energumene	1-7	2	0	1	226,672	262,201
KENNETH ALEXANDER	Honeysuckle	2-12	1	0	0	257,299	261,313
IAN HAMILTON	Tommy's Oscar	13-33	6	4	3	192,020	243,908
ROBERT ABREY, IAN THURTLE	Edwardstone	5-11	2	0	0	215,188	241,832
FLOORING PORTER SYNDICATE	Flooring Porter	1-2	1	0	0	182,877	235,652
SIR A FERGUSON G MASON J HALES & L HALES	Protektorat	1-12	2	2	3	44,775	227,533
KATE & ANDREW BROOKS	Saint Calvados	4-40	10	5	4	58,194	227,097
CHRIS GILES	Greaneteen	4-14	1	0	5	193,468	226,763
MCNEILL FAMILY	Threeunderthrufive	10-44	8	4	4	144,161	225,133
MRS JOHNNY DE LA HEY	Pic D'Orhy	9-49	6	3	3	157,736	220,152
DFA RACING (PINK & EDWARDS)	L'Homme Presse	5-6	0	1	0	205,392	218,124
WAYNE CLIFFORD	Coole Cody	4-23	1	3	4	189,593	214,732
TIM SYDER	Killer Clown	15-71	12	18	3	123,065	210,571
MR & MRS P K BARBER, G MASON & SIR A FERGUSON	Clan Des Obeaux	1-3	1	1	0	140,525	201,442
JAMES & JEAN POTTER LTD	Vienna Court	5-28	5	4	2	133,885	200,436
J HINDS	Glory And Fortune	4-23	5	0	3	125,214	193,305
MRS C WYMER & PJS RUSSELL	Ahoy Senor	4-15	2	4	1	124,512	190,196
COLM DONLON	Langer Dan	14-54	8	6	3	110,586	188,947
T G LESLIE	Minella Trump	21-76	11	8	10	124,937	183,494
R A BARTLETT	Stattler	5-12	1	1	1	141,646	183,399
MIKE AND EILEEN NEWBOULD	Third Time Lucki	4-24	2	3	3	123,231	181,131
MRS DIANA L WHATELEY	Thomas Darby	13-69	13	11	13	101,524	176,431
MR & MRS WILLIAM RUCKER	The Last Day	9-82	5	11	5	118,391	175,697
MY RACING MANAGER FRIENDS	Funambule Sivola	3-26	6	4	2	58,140	173,818
FOUR CANDLES PARTNERSHIP	Knight Salute	7-11	0	1	0	172,467	173,241
SUE HOWELL	Win My Wings	7-38	3	1	3	150,018	159,803
R J BEDFORD & ALL STARS SPORTS RACING	Kitty's Light	4-26	8	3	2	24,016	158,732
GALLOPING ON THE SOUTH DOWNS PARTNERSHIP	Larry	7-35	8	4	6	97,448	156,269
DAVID BRACE	Paint The Dream	10-61	9	7	8	77,774	153,803
BECTIVE STUD	Zanahiyr	3-39	6	7	3	12,253	146,723
THE MEGSONS	Global Citizen	5-34	5	6	5	87,974	144,941
J P ROMANS & TERRY WARNER	Eldorado Allen	2-12	1	3	0	74,983	143,533
T F P PARTNERSHIP	Tornado Flyer	1-2	0	0	0	143,045	143,045
O S HARRIS	Porticello	10-48	9	5	2	96,366	134,394
MICHAEL BUCKLEY	Constitution Hill	3-8	1	2	1	124,450	133,307
BARRY MALONEY	Minella Indo	0-3	1	0	0	0	132,500
ANNE-MARIE & JAMIE SHEPPERD	I Like To Move It	4-23	3	1	3	85,111	132,491
GRAHAM AND ALISON JELLEY	Guard Your Dreams	3-25	2	5	2	91,493	130,799
MRS AAFKE CLARKE	Midnight Shadow	2-17	0	4	1	99,780	129,731
ROBCOUR	Bob Olinger	2-15	0	0	1	120,551	129,472
STEVE & JACKIE FLEETHAM	Mac Tottie	2-8	0	1	1	125,347	128,887

TOP NH HORSES IN BRITAIN 2021/22

HORSE (AGE IN 2021)	WIN & PLACE £	W-R	TRAINER	OWNER	BREEDER
NOBLE YEATS (6)	509,616	1-3	Emmet Mullins	Robert Waley-Cohen	Mrs Kristene Hunter
A PLUS TARD (7)	466,552	2-2	Henry De Bromhead	Cheveley Park Stud	Mme Henri Devin
EPATANTE (7)	357,211	3-4	Nicky Henderson	John P McManus	Francois-Xavier & Anne Doulce Lefeuvre
ENERGUMENE (7)	258,727	1-2	W P Mullins	Tony Bloom	Christophe Dubourg
HONEYSUCKLE (7)	253,215	1-1	Henry De Bromhead	Kenneth Alexander	Dr G W Guy
EDWARDSTONE (7)	240,628	5-7	Alan King	Robert Abrey, Ian Thurtle	R Abrey & I Thurtle
FLOORING PORTER (6)	235,652	1-2	Gavin Cromwell	Flooring Porter Syndicate	Sean Murphy
FAKIR D'OUDAIRIES (6)	227,493	2-2	Joseph Patrick O'Brien	John P McManus	Comte Michel De Gigou
L'HOMME PRESSE (6)	218,124	5-6	Venetia Williams	DFA Racing (Pink & Edwards)	Bernard Camp
ALLAHO (7)	211,425	1-1	W P Mullins	Cheveley Park Stud	Eric Leffray
GREANETEEN (7)	202,774	2-4	Paul Nicholls	Chris Giles	Bertrand Compignie
CLAN DES OBEAUX (9)	201,442	1-3	Paul Nicholls	Mr & Mrs P K Barber, G Mason & Sir A Ferguson	Mme Marie Devilder
ANY SECOND NOW (9)	200,000	0-1	T M Walsh	John P McManus	Mrs Noreen McManus
GLORY AND FORTUNE (6)	183,167	3-9	Tom Lacey	J Hinds	P Connell
AHOY SENOR (6)	180,181	3-6	Lucinda Russell	Mrs C Wymer & Pjs Russell	D P Constable
KNIGHT SALUTE (3)	168,383	6-7	Milton Harris	Four Candles Partnership	Minster Stud And Mrs H Dalgety
PROTEKTORAT (6)	158,382	1-4	Dan Skelton	Sir A Ferguson G Mason J Hales & L Hales	Guy Cherel & Mme Isabelle Pacault
FUNAMBULE SIVOLA (6)	157,602	2-6	Venetia Williams	My Racing Manager Friends	Gilles Trapenard
COOLE CODY (10)	153,486	2-7	Evan Williams	Wayne Clifford	Timothy Considine
JONBON (5)	148,508	4-5	Nicky Henderson	John P McManus	Lotfi Kohli
SCEAU ROYAL (9)	145,724	2-7	Alan King	Simon Munir & Isaac Souede	Guy Vimont
TORNADO FLYER (8)	143,045	1-2	W P Mullins	T F P Partnership	Sweetmans Bloodstock
ELDORADO ALLEN (7)	142,405	2-6	Colin Tizzard	J P Romans & Terry Warner	Bruno Vagne
SHISHKIN (7)	142,375	2-3	Nicky Henderson	Mrs J Donnelly	C J & E B Bennett
CLOUDY GLEN (8)	142,375	1-3	Venetia Williams	Exors Of The Late Trevor Hemmings	Gleadhill House Stud Ltd
SIRE DU BERLAIS (9)	142,119	1-3	Gordon Elliott	John P McManus	Jean-Marc Lucas Et Al
DELTA WORK (8)	139,022	1-2	Gordon Elliott	Gigginstown House Stud	C Magnien & J Magnien
WIN MY WINGS (8)	138,060	3-6	Christian Williams	Sue Howell	Mrs Patricia A Byrne
MINELLA INDO (8)	132,500	0-2	Henry De Bromhead	Barry Maloney	Mrs R H Lalor
MAC TOTTIE (8)	128,887	2-7	Peter Bowen	Steve & Jackie Fleetham	Steve & Jackie Fleetham
FIDDLERONTHEROOF (7)	128,754	1-4	Colin Tizzard	Taylor, Burley & O'Dwyer	Treaty Pals Syndicate
TWO FOR GOLD (8)	124,994	2-4	Kim Bailey	May We Never Be Found Out Partnership 2	Neil R Tector
CONSTITUTION HILL (4)	124,450	3-3	Nicky Henderson	Michael Buckley	Mrs S A Noott
ROYALE PAGAILLE (7)	124,111	1-5	Venetia Williams	Mrs S Ricci	Philippe Mace
GUARD YOUR DREAMS (5)	119,864	2-7	Nigel Twiston-Davies	Graham And Alison Jelley	Little Lodge Farm & Mr & Mrs Twr Chugg
CHAMP (9)	118,237	1-4	Nicky Henderson	John P McManus	Philip And Mrs Jane Myerscough
KITTY'S LIGHT (5)	117,685	0-8	Christian Williams	R J Bedford & All Stars Sports Racing	The Daraiyna Syndicate
SNOW LEOPARDESS (9)	116,318	3-4	Charlie Longsdon	A Fox-Pitt	O And Mrs Fox-Pitt
MIDNIGHT SHADOW (8)	113,641	1-4	Sue Smith	Mrs Aafke Clarke	Capt A L Smith-Maxwell
BRAVEMANSGAME (6)	111,999	4-5	Paul Nicholls	John Dance And Bryan Drew	Dr Vet M Guiot & Dr Vet B Stoffel
LOVE ENVOI (5)	111,881	5-5	Harry Fry	Noel Fehily Racing Syndicates Love Envoi	Ciaran O'Toole
WAR LORD (6)	111,301	3-6	Colin Tizzard	The Wychwood Partnership	Gestut Etzean
HEWICK (6)	107,517	2-4	John Joseph Hanlon	T J McDonald	William Quinn
HITMAN (5)	106,654	0-4	Paul Nicholls	Mason, Hogarth, Ferguson & Done	Mme C Villaud Ameline & Mr Q Villaud
CAP DU NORD (8)	103,845	1-7	Christian Williams	The Can't Say No Partnership	S C E A Raymond Jean-Christian
BOB OLINGER (6)	101,564	1-1	Henry De Bromhead	Robcour	Kenneth Parkhill
TOMMY'S OSCAR (6)	99,235	4-7	Ann Hamilton	Ian Hamilton	Mrs E Kelly
THIRD TIME LUCKI (6)	99,031	3-6	Dan Skelton	Mike And Eileen Newbould	G Delaney
IWILLDOIT (8)	98,834	2-2	Sam Thomas	Diamond Racing Ltd	R L Brown
MARIE'S ROCK (6)	98,515	3-6	Nicky Henderson	Middleham Park Racing XLII	D Breen

LEADING SIRES OF 2022 IN GREAT BRITAIN AND IRELAND

STALLION	BREEDING	RNRS	WNRS	WINS	TOTAL	BEST HORSE
DUBAWI	by Dubai Millennium	193	99	152	£6,387,336	Naval Crown
SEA THE STARS	by Cape Cross	168	71	103	£5,054,148	Baaeed
FRANKEL	by Galileo	172	73	108	£5,053,284	Westover
GALILEO	by Sadler's Wells	160	66	88	£4,164,751	Kyprios
DARK ANGEL	by Acclamation	288	136	206	£3,807,546	Khaadem
NEW BAY	by Dubawi	86	43	69	£3,274,685	Bay Bridge
KINGMAN	by Invincible Spirit	178	76	108	£3,194,762	Kinross
KODIAC	by Danehill	308	125	191	£3,058,071	Ramazan
LOPE DE VEGA	by Shamardal	206	97	150	£2,811,633	Summerghand
NO NAY NEVER	by Scat Daddy	147	47	83	£2,639,528	Alcohol Free
INVINCIBLE SPIRIT	by Green Desert	158	72	112	£2,251,480	Pearls Galore
NATHANIEL	by Galileo	111	44	61	£2,191,967	Desert Crown
CAMELOT	by Montjeu	118	34	49	£2,144,946	Luxembourg
NIGHT OF THUNDER	by Dubawi	120	49	70	£2,134,289	Highfield Princess
STARSPANGLEDBANNER	by Choisir	152	55	76	£2,024,789	State of Rest
ZOFFANY	by Dansili	187	68	108	£1,998,637	Prosperous Voyage
DANDY MAN	by Mozart	226	85	132	£1,996,227	Hellsing
SHOWCASING	by Oasis Dream	188	62	91	£1,938,161	Cold Case
MEHMAS	by Acclamation	153	63	103	£1,876,677	Minzaal
EXCEED AND EXCEL	by Danehill	134	58	110	£1,693,260	Manaccan
MASTERCRAFTSMAN	by Danehill Dancer	134	43	64	£1,667,420	Coltrane
OASIS DREAM	by Green Desert	145	52	79	£1,631,827	Native Trail
CHURCHILL	by Galileo	120	50	70	£1,571,526	Vadeni
MUHAARAR	by Oasis Dream	150	61	98	£1,544,943	Run To Freedom
IFFRAAJ	by Zafonic	170	66	94	£1,454,004	My Prospero
TEOFILO	by Galileo	102	36	65	£1,409,915	Get Shirty
GOLDEN HORN	by Cape Cross	95	33	54	£1,370,925	Trawlerman
CAMACHO	by Danehill	148	43	60	£1,361,469	Galeron
MAYSON	by Invincible Spirit	123	63	111	£1,341,246	Rohaan
SIYOUNI	by Pivotal	102	43	68	£1,265,247	Tahiyra

LEADING TWO-YEAR-OLD SIRES OF 2022 IN GREAT BRITAIN AND IRELAND

STALLION	BREEDING	RNRS	WNRS	WINS	TOTAL	BEST HORSE
NO NAY NEVER	by Scat Daddy	60	25	43	£1,375,109	Meditate
HAVANA GREY	by Havana Gold	76	36	57	£1,070,064	Shouldvebeenaring
KINGMAN	by Invincible Spirit	59	19	24	£919,922	Commissioning
KODIAC	by Danehill	105	38	48	£917,713	Ramazan
CAMACHO	by Danehill	70	15	23	£917,563	Galeron
SHOWCASING	by Oasis Dream	62	21	27	£788,437	Cold Case
DANDY MAN	by Mozart	84	18	22	£705,125	Hellsing
SIOUX NATION	by Scat Daddy	65	29	40	£645,774	Matilda Picotte
FRANKEL	by Galileo	35	9	14	£611,900	Chaldean
DUBAWI	by Dubai Millennium	57	29	36	£568,656	Queen Me
COTAI GLORY	by Exceed And Excel	44	16	24	£527,051	The Platinum Queen
DARK ANGEL	by Acclamation	71	22	27	£502,624	The Antarctic
HAVANA GOLD	by Teofilo	29	12	20	£481,565	Streets of Gold
SIYOUNI	by Pivotal	26	11	15	£471,844	Tahiyra
LOPE DE VEGA	by Shamardal	56	21	24	£466,517	Novakai
HARRY ANGEL	by Dark Angel	45	21	33	£434,152	Marshman
ZOUSTAR	by Northern Meteor	53	14	19	£402,751	Lezoo
MEHMAS	by Acclamation	33	13	17	£387,832	Persian Force
INVINCIBLE SPIRIT	by Green Desert	45	19	23	£381,865	Shartash
EXCEED AND EXCEL	by Danehill	38	16	22	£377,971	Mawj
GLENEAGLES	by Galileo	37	11	13	£363,005	Royal Scotsman
KESSAAR	by Kodiac	42	20	24	£351,388	Tostado
GALILEO	by Sadler's Wells	42	17	18	£336,261	Proud And Regal
STARSPANGLEDBANNER	by Choisir	58	15	16	£318,485	Papilio
MUHAARAR	by Oasis Dream	48	15	21	£289,400	Polly Pott
EXPERT EYE	by Acclamation	54	18	22	£288,303	Misty Blues
OASIS DREAM	by Green Desert	59	14	19	£287,582	Marbaan
SAXON WARRIOR	by Deep Impact	42	13	15	£283,409	Killybegs Warrior
CHURCHILL	by Galileo	48	15	21	£249,220	The Foxes
TASLEET	by Showcasing	38	13	15	£245,106	Bradsell

LEADING FIRST CROP SIRES OF 2022 IN GREAT BRITAIN AND IRELAND

STALLION	BREEDING	RNRS	WNRS	WINS	TOTAL	BEST HORSE
HAVANA GREY	by Havana Gold	76	36	57	£1,070,064	Shouldvebeenaring
SIOUX NATION	by Scat Daddy	65	29	40	£645,774	Matilda Picotte
HARRY ANGEL	by Dark Angel	45	21	33	£434,152	Marshman
KESSAAR	by Kodiac	42	20	24	£351,388	Tostado
EXPERT EYE	by Acclamation	54	18	22	£288,303	Misty Blues
SAXON WARRIOR	by Deep Impact	42	13	15	£283,409	Killybegs Warrior
TASLEET	by Showcasing	38	13	15	£245,106	Bradsell
ROARING LION	by Kitten's Joy	49	8	12	£153,451	Dubai Mile
JUSTIFY	by Scat Daddy	11	5	6	£145,842	Statuette
U S NAVY FLAG	by War Front	35	8	10	£144,235	Catherine of Siena
CRACKSMAN	by Frankel	39	9	12	£138,246	Dance In The Grass
MASSAAT	by Teofilo	24	6	8	£122,905	Coco Jamboo
WASHINGTON DC	by Zoffany	21	6	6	£116,208	Washington Heights
JAMES GARFIELD	by Exceed And Excel	23	5	7	£108,478	Maria Branwell
UNFORTUNATELY	by Society Rock	17	7	11	£102,763	Looking For Lynda
RAJASINGHE	by Choisir	10	8	11	£101,864	Waiting All Night
JUNGLE CAT	by Iffraaj	7	2	3	£62,255	Miss Jungle Cat
POET'S WORD	by Poet's Voice	4	2	2	£46,074	Zabbie
LIGHTNING SPEAR	by Pivotal	8	4	6	£44,076	Destiny's Spirit
GUSTAV KLIMT	by Galileo	15	3	3	£22,341	Whispering Royal
MENDELSSOHN	by Scat Daddy	3	1	1	£22,204	Congo River
HAWKBILL	by Kitten's Joy	9	1	2	£14,251	Harry's Hero
BOLT D'ORO	by Medaglia d'Oro	1	1	1	£12,078	Bold Discovery
SMOOTH DADDY	by Scat Daddy	7	1	1	£10,112	Prince Nabeel
MASTER CARPENTER	by Mastercraftsman	4	1	2	£8,968	Princess Naomi
CLOTH OF STARS	by Sea The Stars	4	1	1	£6,426	Laafi
FRONTIERSMAN	by Dubawi	1	0	0	£6,033	Miss Dolly Rocker
SEAHENGE	by Scat Daddy	3	0	0	£3,220	Radetsky Marsch
MIDI	by Frankel	2	0	0	£2,450	Cherokee Run
GOOD MAGIC	by Curlin	1	0	0	£2,192	Miss New York

LEADING MATERNAL GRANDSIRES OF 2022 IN GREAT BRITAIN AND IRELAND

STALLION	BREEDING	RNRS	WNRS	WINS	TOTAL	BEST HORSE
GALILEO	by Sadler's Wells	473	192	284	£6,380,168	Galeron
PIVOTAL	by Polar Falcon	302	114	175	£4,119,716	Nashwa
DANSILI	by Danehill	302	116	186	£3,627,016	Naval Crown
OASIS DREAM	by Green Desert	340	126	204	£3,570,455	Quickthorn
DUBAWI	by Dubai Millennium	203	88	143	£3,285,014	Homeless Songs
DANEHILL DANCER	by Danehill	219	77	106	£2,701,260	Tuesday
SHAMARDAL	by Giant's Causeway	254	112	159	£2,636,033	Lilac Road
DANEHILL	by Danzig	86	35	53	£2,509,751	Kyprios
KINGMAMBO	by Mr. Prospector	48	16	22	£2,358,348	Baaeed
INVINCIBLE SPIRIT	by Green Desert	277	96	156	£2,304,323	Twilight Calls
SEA THE STARS	by Cape Cross	98	39	72	£2,275,174	Eldar Eldarov
TEOFILO	by Galileo	155	53	81	£2,192,226	Coroebus
CAPE CROSS	by Green Desert	189	69	103	£2,129,005	Fonteyn
MONTJEU	by Sadler's Wells	158	51	76	£2,021,577	Hoo Ya Mal
EXCEED AND EXCEL	by Danehill	222	91	141	£1,985,353	Current Option
ACCLAMATION	by Royal Applause	218	74	117	£1,974,596	Broome
DALAKHANI	by Darshaan	130	45	68	£1,839,943	Meditate
GREEN DESERT	by Danzig	101	35	63	£1,812,517	Desert Crown
NEW APPROACH	by Galileo	121	44	76	£1,751,202	Modern Games
SELKIRK	by Sharpen Up	101	39	50	£1,662,664	Kinross
MONSUN	by Konigsstuhl	39	17	31	£1,597,965	Vadeni
STREET CRY	by Machiavellian	120	52	87	£1,576,657	Royal Champion
RAVEN'S PASS	by Elusive Quality	75	26	36	£1,418,034	Mishriff
DUTCH ART	by Medicean	108	42	69	£1,346,299	Chaldean
HERNANDO	by Niniski	38	15	21	£1,330,110	Alpinista
HOLY ROMAN EMPEROR	by Danehill	137	51	87	£1,307,604	Eddie's Boy
LE HAVRE	by Noverre	23	12	19	£1,226,521	Pyledriver
ANABAA	by Danzig	47	18	27	£1,171,222	Bayside Boy
FASTNET ROCK	by Danehill	110	36	48	£1,135,844	High Definition
MULTIPLEX	by Danehill	11	3	8	£1,079,755	Bay Bridge

LEADING TRAINERS ON THE FLAT: 1906-2022

1906 Hon G Lambton
1907 A Taylor
1908 C Morton
1909 A Taylor
1910 A Taylor
1911 Hon G Lambton
1912 Hon G Lambton
1913 R Wootton
1914 A Taylor
1915 P P Gilpin
1916 R C Dawson
1917 A Taylor
1918 A Taylor
1919 A Taylor
1920 A Taylor
1921 A Taylor
1922 A Taylor
1923 A Taylor
1924 R C Dawson
1925 A Taylor
1926 F Darling
1927 Frank Butters
1928 Frank Butters
1929 R C Dawson
1930 H S Persse
1931 J Lawson
1932 Frank Butters
1933 F Darling
1934 Frank Butters
1935 Frank Butters
1936 J Lawson
1937 C Boyd-Rochfort
1938 C Boyd-Rochfort
1939 J L Jarvis
1940 F Darling
1941 F Darling
1942 F Darling
1943 W Nightingall
1944 Frank Butters
1945 W Earl
1946 Frank Butters
1947 F Darling
1948 C F N Murless
1949 Frank Butters
1950 C H Semblat
1951 J L Jarvis
1952 M Marsh
1953 J L Jarvis
1954 C Boyd-Rochfort
1955 C Boyd-Rochfort
1956 C F Elsey
1957 C F N Murless
1958 C Boyd-Rochfort
1959 C F N Murless
1960 C F N Murless
1961 C F N Murless
1962 W Hern
1963 P Prendergast
1964 P Prendergast
1965 P Prendergast
1966 M V O'Brien
1967 C F N Murless
1968 C F N Murless
1969 A M Budgett
1970 C F N Murless
1971 I Balding
1972 W Hern
1973 C F N Murless
1974 P Walwyn
1975 P Walwyn
1976 H Cecil
1977 M V O'Brien
1978 H Cecil
1979 H Cecil
1980 W Hern
1981 M Stoute
1982 H Cecil
1983 W Hern
1984 H Cecil
1985 H Cecil
1986 M Stoute
1987 H Cecil
1988 H Cecil
1989 M Stoute
1990 H Cecil
1991 P Cole
1992 R Hannon Snr
1993 H Cecil
1994 M Stoute
1995 J Dunlop
1996 Saeed bin Suroor
1997 M Stoute
1998 Saeed bin Suroor
1999 Saeed bin Suroor
2000 Sir M Stoute
2001 A O'Brien
2002 A O'Brien
2003 Sir M Stoute
2004 Saeed bin Suroor
2005 Sir M Stoute
2006 Sir M Stoute
2007 A O'Brien
2008 A O'Brien
2009 Sir M Stoute
2010 R Hannon Snr
2011 R Hannon Snr
2012 J Gosden
2013 R Hannon Snr
2014 R Hannon Jnr
2015 J Gosden
2016 A O'Brien
2017 A O'Brien
2018 J Gosden
2019 J Gosden
2020 J Gosden
2021 C Appleby
2022 C Appleby

CHAMPION JOCKEYS ON THE FLAT: 1905-2022

1905 E Wheatley … 124
1906 W Higgs … 149
1907 W Higgs … 146
1908 D Maher … 139
1909 F Wootton … 165
1910 F Wootton … 137
1911 F Wootton … 187
1912 F Wootton … 118
1913 D Maher … 115
1914 S Donoghue … 129
1915 S Donoghue … 62
1916 S Donoghue … 43
1917 S Donoghue … 42
1918 S Donoghue … 66
1919 S Donoghue … 129
1920 S Donoghue … 143
1921 S Donoghue … 141
1922 S Donoghue … 102
1923 S Donoghue … 89
1923 C Elliott … 89
1924 C Elliott … 106
1925 G Richards … 118
1926 T Weston … 95
1927 G Richards … 164
1928 G Richards … 148
1929 G Richards … 135
1930 F Fox … 129
1931 G Richards … 145
1932 G Richards … 190
1933 G Richards … 259
1934 G Richards … 212
1935 G Richards … 217
1936 G Richards … 174
1937 G Richards … 216
1938 G Richards … 206
1939 G Richards … 155
1940 G Richards … 68
1941 H Wragg … 71
1942 G Richards … 67
1943 G Richards … 65
1944 G Richards … 88
1945 G Richards … 104
1946 G Richards … 212
1947 G Richards … 269
1948 G Richards … 224
1949 G Richards … 261
1950 G Richards … 201
1951 G Richards … 227
1952 G Richards … 231
1953 Sir G Richards … 191
1954 D Smith … 129
1955 D Smith … 168
1956 D Smith … 155
1957 A Breasley … 173
1958 D Smith … 165
1959 D Smith … 157
1960 L Piggott … 170
1961 A Breasley … 171
1962 A Breasley … 179
1963 A Breasley … 176
1964 L Piggott … 140
1965 L Piggott … 160
1966 L Piggott … 191

1967 L Piggott 117
1968 L Piggott 139
1969 L Piggott 163
1970 L Piggott 162
1971 L Piggott 162
1972 W Carson 132
1973 W Carson 164
1974 Pat Eddery 148
1975 Pat Eddery 164
1976 Pat Eddery 162
1977 Pat Eddery 176
1978 W Carson 182
1979 J Mercer 164
1980 W Carson 166
1981 L Piggott 179
1982 L Piggott 188
1983 W Carson 159
1984 S Cauthen 130
1985 S Cauthen 195
1986 Pat Eddery 176
1987 S Cauthen 197
1988 Pat Eddery 183
1989 Pat Eddery 171
1990 Pat Eddery 209
1991 Pat Eddery 165
1992 M Roberts 206
1993 Pat Eddery 169
1994 L Dettori 233
1995 L Dettori 211
1996 Pat Eddery 186
1997 K Fallon 196
1998 K Fallon 185
1999 K Fallon 200
2000 K Darley 152
2001 K Fallon 166
2002 K Fallon 144
2003 K Fallon 208
2004 L Dettori 192
2005 J Spencer 163
2006 R Moore 180
2007 S Sanders 190
J Spencer 190
2008 R Moore 186
2009 R Moore 174
2010 P Hanagan 191
2011 P Hanagan 165
2012 R Hughes 172
2013 R Hughes 203
2014 R Hughes 161
2015 S De Sousa 132
2016 J Crowley 148
2017 S De Sousa 155
2018 S De Sousa 148
2019 O Murphy 168
2020 O Murphy 142
2021 O Murphy 153
2022 W Buick 157

CHAMPION APPRENTICES ON THE FLAT 1986-2022

1986 G Carter 34
1987 G Bardwell 27
1988 G Bardwell 39
1989 L Dettori 71
1990 J Fortune 46
1991 D Holland 79
1992 D Harrison 56
1993 J Weaver 60
1994 S Davies 45
1995 S Sanders 61
1996 D O'Neill 79
1997 R Ffrench 77
1998 C Lowther 72
1999 R Winston 49
2000 L Newman 87
2001 C Catlin 71
2002 P Hanagan 81
2003 R Moore 52
2004 T Queally 59
2005 S Golam 44
H Turner 44
2006 S Donohoe 44
2007 G Fairley 65
2008 W Buick 50
D Probert 50
2009 F Tylicki 60
2010 M Lane 41
2011 M Harley 57
2012 A Ryan 40
2013 J Hart 51
2014 O Murphy 74
2015 T Marquand 54
2016 J Gordon 50
2017 D Egan 61
2018 J Watson 77
2019 C Fallon 50
2020 C Fallon 48
2021 M Ghiani 51
2022 B D L Sayette 61

LEADING OWNERS ON THE FLAT: 1900-2022

1900 H.R.H. The Prince of Wales
1901 Sir G Blundell Maple
1902 Mr R S Sievier
1903 Sir James Miller
1904 Sir James Miller
1905 Col W Hall Walker
1906 Ld Derby (late)
1907 Col W Hall Walker
1908 Mr J B Joel
1909 Mr "Fairie"
1910 Mr "Fairie"
1911 Ld Derby
1912 Mr T Pilkington
1913 Mr J B Joel
1914 Mr J B Joel
1915 Mr L Neumann
1916 Mr E Hulton
1917 Mr "Fairie"
1918 Lady James Douglas
1919 Ld Glanely
1920 Sir Robert Jardine
1921 Mr S B Joel
1922 Ld Woolavington
1923 Ld Derby
1924 H.H. Aga Khan
1925 Ld Astor
1926 Ld Woolavington
1927 Ld Derby
1928 Ld Derby
1929 H.H. Aga Khan
1930 H.H. Aga Khan
1931 Mr J A Dewar
1932 H.H. Aga Khan
1933 Ld Derby
1934 H.H. Aga Khan
1935 H.H. Aga Khan
1936 Ld Astor
1937 H.H. Aga Khan
1938 Ld Derby
1939 Ld Rosebery
1940 Lord Rothermere
1941 Ld Glanely
1942 His Majesty
1943 Miss D Paget
1944 H.H. Aga Khan
1945 Ld Derby
1946 H.H. Aga Khan
1947 H.H. Aga Khan
1948 H.H. Aga Khan
1949 H.H. Aga Khan
1950 M M Boussac
1951 M M Boussac
1952 H.H. Aga Khan
1953 Sir Victor Sassoon
1954 Her Majesty
1955 Lady Zia Wernner
1956 Maj L B Holliday
1957 Her Majesty
1958 Mr J McShain
1959 Prince Aly Khan
1960 Sir Victor Sassoon
1961 Maj L B Holliday
1962 Maj L B Holliday
1963 Mr J R Mullion
1964 Mrs H E Jackson
1965 M J Ternynck
1966 Lady Zia Wernher
1967 Mr H J Joel
1968 Mr Raymond R Guest
1969 Mr D Robinson
1970 Mr C Engelhard
1971 Mr P Mellon
1972 Mrs J Hislop
1973 Mr N B Hunt
1974 Mr N B Hunt

1975 Dr C Vittadini
1976 Mr D Wildenstein
1977 Mr R Sangster
1978 Mr R Sangster
1979 Sir M Sobell
1980 S Weinstock
1981 H.H. Aga Khan
1982 Mr R Sangster
1983 Mr R Sangster
1984 Mr R Sangster
1985 Sheikh Mohammed
1986 Sheikh Mohammed
1987 Sheikh Mohammed
1988 Sheikh Mohammed
1989 Sheikh Mohammed
1990 Mr Hamdan Al-Maktoum
1991 Sheikh Mohammed
1992 Sheikh Mohammed
1993 Sheikh Mohammed
1994 Mr Hamdan Al-Maktoum
1995 Mr Hamdan Al-Maktoum
1996 Godolphin
1997 Sheikh Mohammed
1998 Godolphin
1999 Godolphin
2000 H.H. Aga Khan
2001 Godolphin
2002 Mr Hamdan Al-Maktoum
2003 K Abdullah
2004 Godolphin
2005 Mr Hamdan Al-Maktoum
2006 Godolphin
2007 Godolphin
2008 HRH Princess Haya of Jordan
2009 Mr Hamdan Al-Maktoum
2010 K Abdullah
2011 K Abdullah
2012 Godolphin
2013 Godolphin
2014 Mr Hamdan Al-Maktoum
2015 Godolphin
2016 Godolphin
2017 Godolphin
2018 Godolphin
2019 Mr Hamdan Al-Maktoum
2020 Mr Hamdan Al-Maktoum
2021 Godolphin
2022 Godolphin

LEADING SIRES ON THE FLAT: 1900-2022

1900 St Simon
1901 St Simon
1902 Persimmon
1903 St Frusquin
1904 Gallinule
1905 Gallinule
1906 Persimmon
1907 St Frusquin
1908 Persimmon
1909 Cyllene
1910 Cyllene
1911 Sundridge
1912 Persimmon
1913 Desmond
1914 Polymelus
1915 Polymelus
1916 Polymelus
1917 Bayardo
1918 Bayardo
1919 The Tetrarch
1920 Polymelus
1921 Polymelus
1922 Lemberg
1923 Swynford
1924 Son-in-Law
1925 Phalaris
1926 Hurry On
1927 Buchan
1928 Phalaris
1929 Tetratema
1930 Son-in-Law
1931 Pharos
1932 Gainsborough
1933 Gainsborough
1934 Blandford
1935 Blandford
1936 Fairway
1937 Solario
1938 Blandford
1939 Fairway
1940 Hyperion
1941 Hyperion
1942 Hyperion
1943 Fairway
1944 Fairway
1945 Hyperion
1946 Hyperion
1947 Nearco
1948 Big Game
1949 Nearco
1950 Fair Trial
1951 Nasrullah
1952 Tehran
1953 Chanteur II
1954 Hyperion
1955 Alycidon
1956 Court Martial
1957 Court Martial
1958 Mossborough
1959 Petition
1960 Aureole
1961 Aureole
1962 Never Say Die
1963 Ribot
1964 Chamossaire
1965 Court Harwell
1966 Charlottesville
1967 Ribot
1968 Ribot
1969 Crepello
1970 Northern Dancer
1971 Never Bend
1972 Queen's Hussar
1973 Vaguely Noble
1974 Vaguely Noble
1975 Great Nephew
1976 Wolver Hollow
1977 Northern Dancer
1978 Mill Reef (USA)
1979 Petingo
1980 Pitcairn
1981 Great Nephew
1982 Be My Guest (USA)
1983 Northern Dancer
1984 Northern Dancer
1985 Kris
1986 Nijinsky (CAN)
1987 Mill Reef (USA)
1988 Caerleon (USA)
1989 Blushing Groom (FR)
1990 Sadler's Wells (USA)
1991 Caerleon (USA)
1992 Sadler's Wells (USA)
1993 Sadler's Wells (USA)
1994 Sadler's Wells (USA)
1995 Sadler's Wells (USA)
1996 Sadler's Wells (USA)
1997 Sadler's Wells (USA)
1998 Sadler's Wells (USA)
1999 Sadler's Wells (USA)
2000 Sadler's Wells (USA)
2001 Sadler's Wells (USA)
2002 Sadler's Wells (USA)
2003 Sadler's Wells (USA)
2004 Sadler's Wells (USA)
2005 Danehill (USA)
2006 Danehill (USA)
2007 Danehill (USA)
2008 Galileo (IRE)
2009 Danehill Dancer (IRE)
2010 Galileo (IRE)
2011 Galileo (IRE)
2012 Galileo (IRE)
2013 Galileo (IRE)
2014 Galileo (IRE)
2015 Galileo (IRE)
2016 Galileo (IRE)
2017 Galileo (IRE)
2018 Galileo (IRE)
2019 Galileo (IRE)
2020 Galileo (IRE)
2021 Frankel
2022 Dark Angel (IRE)

LEADING BREEDERS ON THE FLAT: 1916-2022

1916 Mr E Hulton
1917 Mr "Fairie"
1918 Lady James Douglas
1919 Ld Derby
1920 Ld Derby
1921 Mr S B Joel
1922 Ld Derby
1923 Ld Derby
1924 Lady Sykes
1925 Ld Astor
1926 Ld Woolavington
1927 Ld Derby
1928 Ld Derby
1929 Ld Derby
1930 Ld Derby
1931 Ld Dewar
1932 H.H. Aga Khan
1933 Sir Alec Black
1934 H.H. Aga Khan
1935 H.H. Aga Khan
1936 Ld Astor
1937 H.H. Aga Khan
1938 Ld Derby
1939 Ld Rosebery
1940 Mr H E Morriss
1941 Ld Glanely
1942 National Stud
1943 Miss D Paget
1944 Ld Rosebery
1945 Ld Derby
1946 Lt- Col H Boyd-Rochfort
1947 H.H. Aga Khan
1948 H.H. Aga Khan
1949 H.H. Aga Khan
1950 M M Boussac
1951 M M Boussac
1952 H. H. Aga Khan
1953 Mr F Darling
1954 Maj L B Holliday
1955 Someries Stud
1956 Maj L B Holliday
1957 Eve Stud
1958 Mr R Ball
1959 Prince Aly Khan and the late
H.H. Aga Khan
1960 Eve Stud Ltd
1961 Eve Stud Ltd
1962 Maj L B Holliday
1963 Mr H F Guggenheim
1964 Bull Run Stud
1965 Mr J Ternynck
1966 Someries Stud
1967 Mr H J Joel
1968 Mill Ridge Farm
1969 Lord Rosebery
1970 Mr E P Taylor
1971 Mr P Mellon
1972 Mr J Hislop
1973 Claiborne Farm
1974 Mr N B Hunt
1975 Overbury Stud
1976 Dayton Ltd
1977 Mr E P Taylor
1978 Cragwood Estates Inc
1979 Ballymacoll Stud
1980 P Clarke
1981 H.H. Aga Khan
1982 Someries Stud
1983 White Lodge Stud
1984 Mr E P Taylor
1985 Dalham Stud Farms
1986 H.H. Aga Khan
1987 Cliveden Stud
1988 H. H. Aga Khan
1989 Mr Hamdan Al-Maktoum
1990 Capt. Macdonald- Buchanan
1991 Barronstown Stud
1992 Swettenham Stud
1993 Juddmonte Farms
1994 Shadwell Farm & Estate Ltd
1995 Shadwell Farm & Estate Ltd
1996 Sheikh Mohammed
1997 Sheikh Mohammed
1998 Sheikh Mohammed
1999 H. H. The Aga Khan's Studs
2000 H. H. The Aga Khan's Studs
2001 Shadwell Farm & Estate Ltd
2002 Gainsborough Stud
2003 Juddmonte
2004 Juddmonte
2005 Shadwell Farm & Estate Ltd
2006 Darley
2007 Darley
2008 Darley
2009 Darley
2010 Juddmonte
2011 Juddmonte
2012 Juddmonte
2013 Darley
2014 Darley
2015 Darley
2016 Darley
2017 Darley
2018 Godolphin
2019 Godolphin
2020 Godolphin
2021 Godolphin
2022 Godolphin

LEADING TRAINERS OVER JUMPS: 1951-2022

1951-52 N Crump
1952-53 M V O'Brien
1953-54 M V O'Brien
1954-55 H R Price
1955-56 W Hall
1956-57 N Crump
1957-58 F T T Walwyn
1958-59 H R Price
1959-60 P V F Cazalet
1960-61 T F Rimell
1961-62 H R Price
1962-63 K Piggott
1963-64 F T T Walwyn
1964-65 P V F Cazalet
1965-66 H R Price
1966-67 H R Price
1967-68 Denys Smith
1968-69 T F Rimell
1969-70 T F Rimell
1970-71 F T Winter
1971-72 F T Winter
1972-73 F T Winter
1973-74 F T Winter
1974-75 F T Winter
1975-76 T F Rimell
1976-77 F T Winter
1977-78 F T Winter
1978-79 M H Easterby
1979-80 M H Easterby
1980-81 M H Easterby
1981-82 M W Dickinson
1982-83 M W Dickinson
1983-84 M W Dickinson
1984-85 F T Winter
1985-86 N J Henderson
1986-87 N J Henderson
1987-88 D R C Elsworth
1988-89 M C Pipe
1989-90 M C Pipe
1990-91 M C Pipe
1991-92 M C Pipe
1992-93 M C Pipe
1993-94 D Nicholson
1994-95 D Nicholson
1995-96 M C Pipe
1996-97 M C Pipe
1997-98 M C Pipe
1998-99 M C Pipe
1999-00 M C Pipe
2000-01 M C Pipe
2001-02 M C Pipe
2002-03 M C Pipe
2003-04 M C Pipe
2004-05 M C Pipe
2005-06 P F Nicholls
2006-07 P F Nicholls
2007-08 P F Nicholls
2008-09 P F Nicholls
2009-10 P F Nicholls
2010-11 P F Nicholls
2010-11 P F Nicholls
2011-12 P F Nicholls
2012-13 N J Henderson
2013-14 P F Nicholls
2014-15 P F Nicholls
2015-16 P F Nicholls
2016-17 N J Henderson
2017-18 N J Henderson
2018-19 P F Nicholls
2019-20 N J Henderson
2020-21 P F Nicholls
2021-22 P F Nicholls

CHAMPION JOCKEYS OVER JUMPS: 1906-2022

Prior to the 1925-26 season the figure relates to racing between January and December

1906 F Mason 58
1907 F Mason 59
1908 P Cowley 65
1909 R Gordon 45
1910 E Piggott 67
1911 W Payne 76
1912 I Anthony 78
1913 E Piggott 60
1914 Mr J R Anthony 60
1915 E Piggott 44
1916 C Hawkins 17
1917 W Smith 15
1918 G Duller 17
1919 Mr H Brown 48
1920 F B Rees 64
1921 F B Rees 65
1922 J Anthony 78
1923 F B Rees 64
1924 F B Rees 108
1925 E Foster 76
1925-26 T Leader 61
1926-27 F B Rees 59
1927-28 W Stott 88
1928-29 W Stott 65
1929-30 W Stott 77
1930-31 W Stott 81
1931-32 W Stott 77
1932-33 G Wilson 61
1933-34 G Wilson 56
1934-35 G Wilson 73
1935-36 G Wilson 57
1936-37 G Wilson 45
1937-38 G Wilson 59
1938-39 T F Rimell 61
1939-40 T F Rimell 24
1940-41 G Wilson 22
1941-42 R Smyth 12
1942-43 No racing
1943-44 No racing
1944-45 H Nicholson 15
T F Rimell 15
1945-46 T F Rimell 54
1946-47 J Dowdeswell 58
1947-48 B Marshall 66
1948-49 T Moloney 60
1949-50 T Moloney 95
1950-51 T Moloney 83
1951-52 T Moloney 99
1952-53 F Winter 121
1953-54 R Francis 76
1954-55 T Moloney 67
1955-56 F Winter 74
1956-57 F Winter 80
1957-58 F Winter 82
1958-59 T Brookshaw 83
1959-60 S Mellor 68
1960-61 S Mellor 118
1961-62 S Mellor 80
1962-63 J Gifford 70
1963-64 J Gifford 94
1964-65 T Biddlecombe 114
1965-66 T Biddlecombe 102
1966-67 J Gifford 122
1967-68 J Gifford 82
1968-69 B R Davies 77
T Biddlecombe 77
1969-70 B R Davies 91
1970-71 G Thorner 74
1971-72 B R Davies 89
1972-73 R Barry 125
1973-74 R Barry 94
1974-75 T Stack 82
1975-76 J Francome 96
1976-77 T Stack 97
1977-78 J J O'Neill 149
1978-79 J Francome 95
1979-80 J J O'Neill 117
1980-81 J Francome 105
1981-82 J Francome 120
P Scudamore 120
1982-83 J Francome 106
1983-84 J Francome 131
1984-85 J Francome 101
1985-86 P Scudamore 91
1986-87 P Scudamore 123
1987-88 P Scudamore 132
1988-89 P Scudamore 221
1989-90 P Scudamore 170
1990-91 P Scudamore 141
1991-92 P Scudamore 175
1992-93 R Dunwoody 173
1993-94 R Dunwoody 197
1994-95 R Dunwoody 160
1995-96 A P McCoy 175
1996-97 A P McCoy 190
1997-98 A P McCoy 253
1998-99 A P McCoy 186
1999-00 A P McCoy 245
2000-01 A P McCoy 191
2001-02 A P McCoy 289
2002-03 A P McCoy 256
2003-04 A P McCoy 209
2004-05 A P McCoy 200
2005-06 A P McCoy 178
2006-07 A P McCoy 184
2007-08 A P McCoy 140
2008-09 A P McCoy 186
2009-10 A P McCoy 195
2010-11 A P McCoy 218
2011-12 A P McCoy 199
2012-13 A P McCoy 185
2013-14 A P McCoy 218
2014-15 A P McCoy 231
2015-16 R Johnson 235
2016-17 R Johnson 189
2017-18 R Johnson 176
2018-19 R Johnson 200
2019-20 B Hughes 141
2020-21 H Skelton 152
2021-22 B Hughes 204

LEADING OWNERS OVER JUMPS: 1951-2022

(Please note that prior to the 1994-95 season the leading owner was determined by win prize money only)

1951-52 Miss D Paget
1952-53 Mr J H Griffin
1953-54 Mr J H Griffin
1954-55 Mrs W H E Welman
1955-56 Mrs L Carver
1956-57 Mrs Geoffrey Kohn
1957-58 Mr D J Coughlan
1958-59 Mr J E Bigg
1959-60 Miss W H Wallace
1960-61 Mr C Vaughan
1961-62 Mr N Cohen
1962-63 Mr P B Raymond
1963-64 Mr J K Goodman
1964-65 Mrs M Stephenson
1965-66 Duchess of Westminster
1966-67 Mr C P T Watkins
1967-68 Mr H S Alper
1968-69 Mr B P Jenks
1969-70 Mr E R Courage
1970-71 Mr F Pontin
1971-72 Capt T A Forster
1972-73 Mr N H Le Mare
1973-74 Mr N H Le Mare
1974-75 Mr R Guest
1975-76 Mr P B Raymond
1976-77 Mr N H Le Mare
1977-78 Mrs O Jackson
1978-79 Snailwell Stud Co Ltd
1979-80 Mr H J Joel
1980-81 Mr R J Wilson
1981-82 Sheikh Ali Abu Khamsin
1982-83 Sheikh Ali Abu Khamsin
1983-84 Sheikh Ali Abu Khamsin
1984-85 T Kilroe and Son Ltd
1985-86 Sheikh Ali Abu Khamsin
1986-87 Mr H J Joel
1987-88 Miss Juliet E Reed
1988-89 Mr R Burridge
1989-90 Mrs Harry J Duffey
1990-91 Mr P Piller
1991-92 Whitcombe Manor Racing Stables Ltd
1992-93 Mrs J Mould
1993-94 Pell-Mell Partners
1994-95 Roach Foods Limited
1995-96 Mr A T A Wates
1996-97 Mr R Ogden
1997-98 Mr D A Johnson
1998-99 Mr J P McManus
1999-00 Mr R Ogden
2000-01 Sir R Ogden
2001-02 Mr D A Johnson
2002-03 Mr D A Johnson
2003-04 Mr D A Johnson
2004-05 Mr D A Johnson
2005-06 Mr J P McManus
2006-07 Mr J P McManus

2007-08 Mr D A Johnson
2008-09 Mr J P McManus
2009-10 Mr J P McManus
2010-11 Mr T Hemmings
2011-12 Mr J P McManus
2012-13 Mr J P McManus
2013-14 Mr J P McManus
2014-15 Mr J P McManus
2015-16 Gigginstown House Stud
2016-17 Mr J P McManus
2017-18 Mr J P McManus
2018-19 Mr J P McManus
2019-20 Mr J P McManus
2020-21 Mr J P McManus
2021-22 Mr J P McManus

LEADING AMATEUR RIDERS OVER JUMPS: 1955-2022

1955-56 Mr R McCreery 13
Mr A H Moralee 13
1956-57 Mr R McCreery 23
1957-58 Mr J Lawrence 18
1958-59 Mr J Sutcliffe 18
1959-60 Mr G Kindersley 22
1960-61 Sir W Pigott-Brown 28
1961-62 Mr A Biddlecombe 30
1962-63 Sir W Pigott-Brown 20
1963-64 Mr S Davenport 32
1964-65 Mr M Gifford 15
1965-66 Mr C Collins 24
1966-67 Mr C Collins 33
1967-68 Mr R Tate 30
1968-69 Mr R Tate 17
1969-70 Mr M Dickinson 23
1970-71 Mr J Lawrence 17
1971-72 Mr W Foulkes 26
1972-73 Mr R Smith 56
1973-74 Mr A Webber 21
1974-75 Mr R Lamb 22
1975-76 Mr P Greenall 25
Mr G Jones 25
1976-77 Mr P Greenall 27
1977-78 Mr G Sloan 23
1978-79 Mr T G Dun 26
1979-80 Mr O Sherwood 29
1980-81 Mr P Webber 32
1981-82 Mr D Browne 28
1982-83 Mr D Browne 33
1983-84 Mr S Sherwood 28
1984-85 Mr S Sherwood 30
1985-86 Mr T Thomson Jones 25
1986-87 Mr T Thomson Jones 19
1987-88 Mr T Thomson Jones 15
1988-89 Mr P Fenton 18
1989-90 Mr P McMahon 15
1990-91 Mr K Johnson 24
1991-92 Mr M P Hourigan 24
1992-93 Mr A Thornton 26
1993-94 Mr J Greenall 21
1994-95 Mr D Parker 16
1995-96 Mr J Culloty 40
1996-97 Mr R Thornton 30
1997-98 Mr S Durack 41
1998-99 Mr A Dempsey 47
1999-00 Mr P Flynn 41
2000-01 Mr T Scudamore 24
2001-02 Mr D Crosse 19
2002-03 Mr C Williams 23
2003-04 Mr O Nelmes 14
2004-05 Mr T Greenall 31
2005-06 Mr T O'Brien 32
2006-07 Mr T Greenall 31
2007-08 Mr T Greenall 23
2008-09 Mr O Greenall 23
2009-10 Mr O Greenall 41
2010-11 Mr R Mahon 19
2011-12 Miss E Sayer 11
2012-13 Mr N de Boinville 16
2013-14 Mr H Bannister 11
2014-15 Mr H Bannister 15
2015-16 Mr D Noonan 19
2016-17 Mr J King 15
2017-18 Miss P Fuller 16
2018-19 Mr D Maxwell 18
2019-20 Mr D Maxwell 18
*2020-21 Miss G Andrews 4
Mr J King 4
Miss B Smith 4
Miss L Turner 4
2021-22 Mr T Durrell 15

*Truncated season for amateurs owing to COVID

LEADING SIRES OVER JUMPS: 1989-2022

1989-90 Deep Run
1990-91 Deep Run
1991-92 Deep Run
1992-93 Deep Run
1993-94 Strong Gale
1994-95 Strong Gale
1995-96 Strong Gale
1996-97 Strong Gale
1997-98 Strong Gale
1998-99 Strong Gale
1999-00 Strong Gale
2000-01 Be My Native (USA)
2001-02 Be My Native (USA)
2002-03 Be My Native (USA)
2003-04 Be My Native (USA)
2004-05 Supreme Leader
2005-06 Supreme Leader
2006-07 Presenting
2007-08 Old Vic
2008-09 Presenting
2009-10 Presenting
2010-11 Presenting
2011-12 King's Theatre
2012-13 Beneficial
2013-14 King's Theatre
2014-15 King's Theatre
2015-16 King's Theatre
2016-17 King's Theatre
2017-18 King's Theatre
2018-19 Flemensfirth
2019-20 Milan
2020-21 Stowaway
2021-22 Yeats
Getaway

FLAT STALLIONS' EARNINGS FOR 2022

(Includes every stallion who sired a winner on the Flat in Great Britain and Ireland in 2022)

STALLIONS	RNRS	WNRS	WINS	PLACES	TOTAL (£)
ACCLAMATION (GB)	157	62	95	220	1190597
ACLAIM (IRE)	54	21	23	58	275468
ADAAY (IRE)	95	26	38	102	412691
ADLERFLUG (GER)	2	1	2	4	343251
AIR CHIEF MARSHAL (IRE)	3	1	1	2	9807
AIR FORCE BLUE (USA)	15	3	4	17	42713
AJAYA (GB)	13	4	5	13	106593
AL KAZEEM (GB)	28	8	19	32	165948
AL WUKAIR (IRE)	2	2	2	0	11140
ALBAASIL (IRE)	7	2	2	6	14469
ALHEBAYEB (IRE)	57	13	25	63	392746
ALMANZOR (FR)	16	5	6	9	53876
AMERICAN PHAROAH (USA)	24	7	7	19	231132
ANIMAL KINGDOM (USA)	6	2	3	8	32741
ANJAAL (GB)	41	15	23	34	188053
ANTONIUS PIUS (USA)	2	1	1	1	5945
APPROVE (IRE)	10	5	7	11	77900
AQLAAM (GB)	11	6	10	14	96552
ARABIAN GLEAM (GB)	5	2	2	2	10565
ARCADIO (GER)	5	1	1	1	38387
ARCANO (IRE)	36	9	16	38	147953
ARCHIPENKO (USA)	30	15	25	36	191873
ARDAD (IRE)	57	20	29	41	492082
ART CONNOISSEUR (IRE)	4	2	3	11	34119
ARTIE SCHILLER (USA)	1	1	1	2	5757
ASK (GB)	3	1	1	3	13819
ASSERTIVE (GB)	8	3	3	14	49669
ATRAF (GB)	1	1	1	1	5672
AUSSIE RULES (USA)	11	3	4	14	56187
AUSTRALIA (GB)	139	55	93	130	1959244
AUTHORIZED (IRE)	29	12	16	26	406881
AVONBRIDGE (GB)	4	2	2	4	12960
AWTAAD (IRE)	73	30	53	91	643688
BAHAMIAN BOUNTY (GB)	10	6	14	23	158152
BAHRI (USA)	4	2	5	3	26647
BALTIC KING (GB)	7	1	3	6	17346
BASHKIROV (GB)	4	1	2	4	17978
BATED BREATH (GB)	136	50	82	168	1002868
BATTLE OF MARENGO (IRE)	17	5	9	10	63213
BEAT HOLLOW (GB)	8	1	2	3	16007
BELARDO (IRE)	59	27	46	75	424327
BERNARDINI (USA)	3	1	1	2	8303
BIG BAD BOB (IRE)	21	5	5	27	63630
BLAME (USA)	4	1	1	6	14849
BOBBY'S KITTEN (USA)	56	16	24	69	357667
BORN TO SEA (IRE)	55	14	24	52	440077
BOW CREEK (IRE)	2	1	1	2	4661
BRAZEN BEAU (AUS)	82	31	52	91	517961
BRILLIANT SPEED (USA)	1	1	1	1	3934
BUNGLE INTHEJUNGLE (GB)	66	22	35	91	625568
BURATINO (IRE)	42	10	13	31	165580
BURWAAZ (GB)	3	3	6	7	52258
BUSHRANGER (IRE)	9	1	2	2	10643
CABLE BAY (IRE)	89	38	62	134	1127778
CACIQUE (IRE)	15	5	10	11	96698
CAMACHO (GB)	140	44	66	165	609133
CAMELOT (GB)	138	57	83	137	1522460

STALLIONS	RNRS	WNRS	WINS	PLACES	TOTAL (£)
CAMPANOLOGIST (USA)	1	1	3	3	80644
CANFORD CLIFFS (IRE)	66	17	22	64	262971
CANNOCK CHASE (USA)	10	1	1	4	13218
CAPE CROSS (IRE)	41	12	19	31	409096
CAPPELLA SANSEVERO (GB)	14	1	1	15	36427
CAPTAIN GERRARD (IRE)	15	6	8	11	58444
CARAVAGGIO (USA)	64	19	23	49	586775
CASAMENTO (IRE)	45	10	13	45	179163
CHAMPS ELYSEES (GB)	60	21	32	70	450989
CHARM SPIRIT (IRE)	46	22	31	83	259962
CHARMING THOUGHT (GB)	33	13	23	42	221834
CHOISIR (AUS)	12	6	15	21	161265
CHURCHILL (IRE)	64	18	22	49	328231
CITYSCAPE (GB)	53	17	28	62	243942
CLODOVIL (IRE)	41	14	19	55	225853
COACH HOUSE (IRE)	65	23	43	75	280428
COCKNEY REBEL (IRE)	2	1	2	2	8269
COMPTON PLACE (GB)	12	3	4	13	47519
CONDUIT (IRE)	1	1	1	2	5070
COTAI GLORY (GB)	71	26	36	54	501107
COULSTY (IRE)	25	8	13	15	92990
DABIRSIM (FR)	47	16	19	49	205884
DAIWA MAJOR (JPN)	1	1	1	3	61371
DALAKHANI (IRE)	8	3	5	8	67077
DANDY MAN (IRE)	190	76	132	321	1613541
DANSILI (GB)	59	27	45	60	521852
DARK ANGEL (IRE)	290	134	208	396	3115662
DAWN APPROACH (IRE)	93	33	51	99	1351539
DECLARATION OF WAR (USA)	30	9	14	37	212162
DECORATED KNIGHT (GB)	21	5	6	11	69634
DEEP IMPACT (JPN)	11	5	9	6	823806
DELEGATOR (GB)	22	11	15	46	186261
DENOUNCE (GB)	2	1	3	0	28389
DIALED IN (USA)	3	2	5	8	39384
DICK TURPIN (IRE)	10	7	8	12	61207
DISTORTED HUMOR (USA)	10	5	10	15	134444
DIVINE PROPHET (AUS)	12	1	1	5	16286
DRAGON PULSE (IRE)	85	31	48	88	406686
DREAM AHEAD (USA)	53	22	40	66	805380
DUBAWI (IRE)	186	101	163	185	3591530
DUE DILIGENCE (USA)	58	20	38	66	390351
DUNADEN (FR)	11	3	5	9	116369
DUNKERQUE (FR)	2	1	1	0	6554
DUTCH ART (GB)	66	28	43	79	862970
DYLAN THOMAS (IRE)	22	6	16	23	141929
ECTOT (GB)	2	1	1	3	9938
EL KABEIR (USA)	37	7	11	26	296792
ELM PARK (GB)	2	1	1	2	6109
ELNADIM (USA)	6	5	7	6	69460
ELUSIVE CITY (USA)	5	3	3	17	42096
ELUSIVE PIMPERNEL (USA)	22	4	6	17	121970
ELUSIVE QUALITY (USA)	8	4	10	6	52116
ELVSTROEM (AUS)	1	1	1	1	12555
ELZAAM (AUS)	99	37	57	93	603978
ENGLISH CHANNEL (USA)	3	2	2	7	37938
EPAULETTE (AUS)	65	26	42	81	364192
EQUIANO (FR)	124	44	65	149	752061
ES QUE LOVE (IRE)	13	5	13	19	111622
ESTIDHKAAR (IRE)	54	16	24	46	187579
EXCEED AND EXCEL (AUS)	146	66	102	181	1242077
EXCELEBRATION (IRE)	58	22	35	66	572611

STALLIONS	RNRS	WNRS	WINS	PLACES	TOTAL (£)
ACCLAMATION (GB)	144	49	79	189	1211293
ACLAIM (IRE)	66	31	48	78	843797
ADAAY (IRE)	91	28	49	106	712267
ADLERFLUG (GER)	3	1	2	2	559277
AIR CHIEF MARSHAL (IRE)	2	1	1	5	10662
AIR FORCE BLUE (USA)	12	2	2	11	39691
AJAYA (GB)	7	2	4	10	101474
AL KAZEEM (GB)	32	13	28	38	260827
AL RIFAI (IRE)	1	1	2	1	77511
ALBAASIL (IRE)	6	2	2	11	27440
ALHEBAYEB (IRE)	53	17	22	62	304823
ALMANZOR (FR)	31	11	17	38	219151
AMERICAN PHAROAH (USA)	18	6	9	10	190777
AMERICAN POST (GB)	2	1	3	1	33508
ANIMAL KINGDOM (USA)	5	3	5	8	41609
ANJAAL (GB)	32	6	10	26	145968
APPROVE (IRE)	6	3	5	11	63257
AQLAAM (GB)	5	2	3	6	105388
ARCANO (IRE)	16	4	11	12	76434
ARCHIPENKO (USA)	14	5	7	18	71047
ARDAD (IRE)	80	24	35	83	827106
AREION (GER)	2	1	1	0	4235
ART CONNOISSEUR (IRE)	2	1	1	2	14683
ARVICO (FR)	1	1	1	1	6592
ASSERTIVE (GB)	6	1	1	6	23298
ATRAF (GB)	1	1	4	1	12926
AUSSIE RULES (USA)	6	1	1	4	182222
AUSTRALIA (GB)	147	37	56	126	1126644
AUTHORIZED (IRE)	23	5	6	25	367176
AWTAAD (IRE)	87	36	55	102	810505
AXXOS (GER)	1	1	3	3	104879
AZAMOUR (IRE)	2	1	1	2	11418
BAHAMIAN BOUNTY (GB)	7	4	5	7	49326
BAHRI (USA)	3	2	2	4	17274
BAL A BALI (BRZ)	1	1	1	4	35042
BALTIC KING (GB)	2	1	1	0	7437
BASHKIROV (GB)	3	1	1	2	7971
BATED BREATH (GB)	121	43	72	144	1020825
BATTLE OF MARENGO (IRE)	12	3	5	10	45605
BELARDO (IRE)	78	30	58	112	721402
BERKSHIRE (IRE)	1	1	1	1	9487
BIG BAD BOB (IRE)	14	2	3	10	28400
BIRCHWOOD (IRE)	3	1	1	3	35243
BOBBY'S KITTEN (USA)	57	17	29	76	451942
BOLT D'ORO (USA)	1	1	1	1	11714
BORN TO SEA (IRE)	35	14	19	28	254977
BOW CREEK (IRE)	2	1	2	2	9569
BRAZEN BEAU (AUS)	83	31	49	109	594821
BRILLIANT SPEED (USA)	1	1	4	4	20496
BUNGLE INTHEJUNGLE (GB)	87	30	38	101	468438
BURATINO (IRE)	51	14	19	50	240651
BURWAAZ (GB)	5	3	6	4	37073
BUSHRANGER (IRE)	3	1	1	4	13022
CABLE BAY (IRE)	71	31	50	108	871965
CACIQUE (IRE)	8	5	6	3	88470
CAMACHO (GB)	148	43	60	186	1326659
CAMELOT (GB)	118	34	49	124	2103235
CANFORD CLIFFS (IRE)	35	15	23	42	195417
CANNOCK CHASE (USA)	7	1	1	2	8289
CAPE CROSS (IRE)	17	2	2	15	77651
CAPPELLA SANSEVERO (GB)	12	4	5	6	51433

STALLIONS	RNRS	WNRS	WINS	PLACES	TOTAL (£)
CAPTAIN GERRARD (IRE)	10	3	6	25	78077
CARAVAGGIO (USA)	101	35	48	100	852467
CARPE DIEM (USA)	2	1	1	5	14069
CASAMENTO (IRE)	27	5	6	28	112276
CHAMPS ELYSEES (GB)	38	12	15	30	150321
CHARM SPIRIT (IRE)	54	18	24	64	317695
CHARMING THOUGHT (GB)	35	13	21	47	267808
CHOISIR (AUS)	5	2	3	2	130095
CHURCHILL (IRE)	120	50	70	108	1565413
CITYSCAPE (GB)	71	22	38	78	431974
CLODOVIL (IRE)	30	12	17	36	226132
CLOTH OF STARS (IRE)	4	1	1	0	6426
COACH HOUSE (IRE)	51	15	20	62	212102
COMPTON PLACE (GB)	4	2	4	7	46040
CONDUIT (IRE)	2	1	2	4	127401
COTAI GLORY (GB)	106	45	61	110	909276
COULSTY (IRE)	15	4	8	15	60976
CRACKSMAN (GB)	39	9	12	18	138081
DABIRSIM (FR)	52	16	26	62	303460
DALAKHANI (IRE)	3	1	1	3	14269
DANDY MAN (IRE)	226	85	133	343	1980984
DANON BALLADE (JPN)	5	3	4	5	31095
DANSILI (GB)	34	16	25	29	321121
DARIYAN (FR)	5	1	1	3	33854
DARK ANGEL (IRE)	288	136	206	374	3797877
DARTMOUTH (GB)	2	1	1	2	9371
DAWN APPROACH (IRE)	78	15	19	58	303091
DECLARATION OF WAR (USA)	13	4	4	9	32493
DECORATED KNIGHT (GB)	27	13	18	33	178528
DEEP IMPACT (JPN)	14	7	9	16	351761
DELEGATOR (GB)	16	6	9	28	125138
DICK TURPIN (IRE)	5	2	3	9	36953
DISTORTED HUMOR (USA)	7	3	5	17	97674
DIVINE PROPHET (AUS)	15	8	10	27	97515
DRAGON PULSE (IRE)	88	24	42	91	449226
DREAM AHEAD (USA)	33	16	37	48	352785
DUBAWI (IRE)	193	99	152	189	6382897
DUE DILIGENCE (USA)	42	12	18	52	239899
DUKE OF MARMALADE (IRE)	4	1	1	3	9540
DUNADEN (FR)	11	1	1	10	25407
DUTCH ART (GB)	39	20	32	49	417986
DYLAN THOMAS (IRE)	14	6	7	9	66822
ECTOT (GB)	3	1	2	3	19226
EL KABEIR (USA)	61	12	18	61	485270
ELIOT (GER)	1	1	1	0	8429
ELM PARK (GB)	2	2	2	0	9564
ELUSIVE CITY (USA)	5	2	2	17	53865
ELUSIVE PIMPERNEL (USA)	14	2	3	7	31432
ELUSIVE QUALITY (USA)	2	1	1	2	8964
ELZAAM (AUS)	94	26	41	82	595285
EMPIRE MAKER (USA)	1	1	2	1	10722
ENGLISH CHANNEL (USA)	3	1	1	4	34342
EPAULETTE (AUS)	45	20	34	67	301373
EQUIANO (FR)	104	28	43	137	699587
ES QUE LOVE (IRE)	8	4	6	8	56665
ESTIDHKAAR (IRE)	44	7	8	39	139995
EXCEED AND EXCEL (AUS)	134	58	110	167	1689900
EXCELEBRATION (IRE)	40	10	17	50	316233
EXCHANGE RATE (USA)	3	2	2	5	22527
EXPERT EYE (GB)	54	18	22	40	286161
FAMOUS NAME (GB)	12	3	5	3	187781

STALLIONS	RNRS	WNRS	WINS	PLACES	TOTAL (£)
FARHH (GB)	55	28	32	61	617009
FASCINATING ROCK (IRE)	33	9	10	17	135863
FAST COMPANY (IRE)	150	48	69	132	1043731
FASTNET ROCK (AUS)	75	29	42	73	637612
FINJAAN (GB)	4	1	1	4	11521
FINSCEAL FIOR (IRE)	6	1	1	5	11184
FIREBREAK (GB)	2	1	1	3	10261
FLEMENSFIRTH (USA)	2	1	1	1	7651
FLINTSHIRE (GB)	7	2	5	12	36210
FOOTSTEPSINTHESAND (GB)	131	45	60	166	875628
FOUNTAIN OF YOUTH (IRE)	24	10	19	26	150200
FOXWEDGE (AUS)	11	6	10	22	105087
FRACAS (IRE)	11	1	1	9	39634
FRANKEL (GB)	172	73	108	151	5032177
FREE EAGLE (IRE)	63	24	41	73	438276
FRENCH FIFTEEN (FR)	5	2	2	4	95044
FRENCH NAVY (GB)	18	5	8	9	171681
FROZEN POWER (IRE)	8	1	2	12	26215
FULBRIGHT (GB)	23	4	6	10	50759
GALE FORCE TEN (GB)	15	4	11	10	194317
GALILEO (IRE)	158	66	88	158	4126353
GALILEO GOLD (GB)	70	22	30	61	504483
GALIWAY (GB)	1	1	2	2	16203
GARSWOOD (GB)	55	11	21	52	224817
GETAWAY (GER)	3	1	1	0	5340
GIANT'S CAUSEWAY (USA)	1	1	2	0	12129
GLENEAGLES (IRE)	119	43	60	128	1186738
GOLDEN HORN (GB)	95	33	54	115	1368532
GOLDENCENTS (USA)	1	1	2	1	9068
GREGORIAN (IRE)	37	16	24	34	287366
GUILIANI (IRE)	2	1	1	0	3984
GUSTAV KLIMT (IRE)	15	3	3	3	21993
GUTAIFAN (IRE)	96	32	58	108	821715
HAAFHD (GB)	7	3	4	17	46531
HAATEF (USA)	7	1	2	10	43797
HALLING (USA)	3	1	1	0	6440
HALLOWED CROWN (AUS)	13	7	10	12	177221
HARBOUR WATCH (IRE)	33	15	32	64	1243163
HARD SPUN (USA)	5	2	2	10	26979
HARRY ANGEL (IRE)	45	21	33	61	432860
HARZAND (IRE)	22	8	14	22	250072
HAVANA GOLD (IRE)	114	44	68	163	1253069
HAVANA GREY (GB)	76	36	57	108	1066567
HAWKBILL (USA)	9	1	2	3	14238
HEART'S CRY (JPN)	1	1	1	0	8181
HEERAAT (IRE)	63	21	34	79	357545
HELLVELYN (GB)	26	5	5	22	54958
HELMET (AUS)	70	27	47	88	522414
HENRYTHENAVIGATOR (USA)	6	2	2	4	21714
HIGH CHAPARRAL (IRE)	6	4	4	7	53870
HIGHLAND REEL (IRE)	55	9	11	43	226469
HIT IT A BOMB (USA)	2	1	2	2	11452
HOLY ROMAN EMPEROR (IRE)	106	36	57	120	939144
HOT STREAK (IRE)	50	15	22	59	265707
HUNTER'S LIGHT (IRE)	7	1	1	7	21655
HURRICANE RUN (IRE)	1	1	1	2	7796
I AM INVINCIBLE (AUS)	2	1	1	1	9394
IFFRAAJ (GB)	170	66	93	183	1425621
IMPERIAL MONARCH (IRE)	1	1	1	0	6197
INDIAN HAVEN (GB)	1	1	3	1	13785
INTELLO (GER)	52	16	25	43	336980

STALLIONS	RNRS	WNRS	WINS	PLACES	TOTAL (£)
INTENSE FOCUS (USA)	7	3	4	16	115128
INTIKHAB (USA)	5	2	2	8	36391
INTRINSIC (GB)	9	3	6	4	84925
INVINCIBLE SPIRIT (IRE)	158	72	111	217	2234119
IVAWOOD (IRE)	33	12	17	16	146847
JACK HOBBS (GB)	4	2	3	2	34932
JAMES GARFIELD (IRE)	23	5	7	13	108469
JEREMY (USA)	8	2	2	4	19963
JET AWAY (GB)	5	1	1	3	10367
JOHNNY BARNES (IRE)	5	1	1	4	25597
JUKEBOX JURY (IRE)	7	4	6	4	98224
JUNGLE CAT (IRE)	7	2	3	8	62256
JUSTIFY (USA)	11	5	6	9	142837
KALANISI (IRE)	6	2	3	1	25981
KAMSIN (GER)	2	1	1	2	6608
KANTHAROS (USA)	4	1	1	2	7656
KARAKONTIE (JPN)	7	2	3	8	194887
KARPINO (GER)	1	1	1	0	5454
KAYF TARA (GB)	1	1	1	1	6966
KENDARGENT (FR)	18	5	9	18	127655
KESSAAR (IRE)	42	20	24	47	348537
KHELEYF (USA)	7	2	2	10	32932
KINGMAN (GB)	178	76	108	183	3191415
KING'S BEST (USA)	1	1	1	0	5767
KINGSTON HILL (GB)	12	2	3	9	29767
KITTEN'S JOY (USA)	39	8	11	50	187826
KODI BEAR (IRE)	86	29	47	91	745141
KODIAC (GB)	308	125	191	410	3038158
KUROSHIO (AUS)	22	8	14	17	169972
KYLLACHY (GB)	19	10	12	28	121976
LAWMAN (FR)	67	22	33	71	439480
LE HAVRE (IRE)	55	17	23	49	493515
LEMON DROP KID (USA)	5	2	3	5	38882
LETHAL FORCE (IRE)	76	37	66	125	972744
LIGHTNING SPEAR (GB)	8	4	6	6	43498
LILBOURNE LAD (IRE)	11	1	1	22	75630
LITERATO (FR)	1	1	2	1	12326
LOPE DE VEGA (IRE)	206	97	150	256	2796619
LORD KANALOA (JPN)	5	3	3	1	27632
LORD OF ENGLAND (GER)	4	1	1	3	9610
LORD SHANAKILL (USA)	8	3	3	8	31758
MAGICIAN (IRE)	4	2	2	5	18337
MAJESTIC MISSILE (IRE)	1	1	1	2	6503
MAJOR CADEAUX (GB)	5	2	3	9	35233
MAKE BELIEVE (GB)	73	22	31	74	1127381
MAKFI (GB)	5	2	4	4	54393
MANDURO (GER)	5	3	4	5	38251
MARCEL (IRE)	6	1	1	5	13473
MARKAZ (IRE)	34	16	25	48	333220
MASSAAT (IRE)	24	6	8	19	122905
MASTER CARPENTER (IRE)	4	1	2	2	8968
MASTERCRAFTSMAN (IRE)	134	43	64	139	1662829
MASTEROFTHEHORSE (IRE)	2	1	1	1	7748
MATTMU (GB)	6	2	4	12	77271
MAXIOS (GB)	15	3	5	12	146211
MAYSON (GB)	123	63	110	159	1311413
MAZAMEER (IRE)	8	2	2	5	16607
MEDAGLIA D'ORO (USA)	4	1	1	1	9322
MEDICEAN (GB)	11	1	2	2	17967
MEHMAS (IRE)	153	63	103	220	1872557
MENDELSSOHN (USA)	3	1	1	4	21559

STALLIONS	RNRS	WNRS	WINS	PLACES	TOTAL (£)
MIDNIGHT LEGEND (GB)	2	1	1	2	42018
MILAN (GB)	5	1	1	4	11179
MISU BOND (IRE)	1	1	2	2	11346
MIZZEN MAST (USA)	5	4	7	14	61929
MONDIALISTE (IRE)	40	9	12	43	128768
MONSIEUR BOND (IRE)	24	6	11	22	90866
MONTMARTRE (FR)	1	1	1	0	5454
MOOHAAJIM (IRE)	4	1	2	4	15851
MORE THAN READY (USA)	13	3	3	9	53770
MORPHEUS (GB)	21	8	12	23	104233
MOST IMPROVED (IRE)	7	2	4	3	27224
MOTIVATOR (GB)	6	3	4	5	220634
MOUNT NELSON (GB)	18	5	8	19	118570
MR MEDICI (IRE)	1	1	1	4	7744
MUHAARAR (GB)	150	61	98	144	1538982
MUKHADRAM (GB)	53	17	34	57	325945
MULTIPLEX (GB)	9	5	10	13	70794
MUSIC MASTER (GB)	7	2	2	6	16134
MUSTAJEEB (GB)	3	2	4	5	31418
MYBOYCHARLIE (IRE)	5	2	4	10	36284
NATHANIEL (IRE)	111	44	61	113	2191332
NATIONAL DEFENSE (GB)	17	4	7	14	67554
NAYEF (USA)	14	4	9	17	86056
NEW APPROACH (IRE)	99	32	47	96	700056
NEW BAY (GB)	86	43	68	97	3258762
NICCONI (AUS)	1	1	1	0	283550
NIGHT OF THUNDER (IRE)	120	49	70	124	2123836
NO NAY NEVER (USA)	147	47	83	154	2625904
NOBLE MISSION (GB)	14	6	7	20	134613
NORSE DANCER (IRE)	2	1	1	2	5759
NOTNOWCATO (GB)	2	1	2	0	11529
OASIS DREAM (GB)	145	52	79	141	1629884
OLDEN TIMES (GB)	2	2	2	2	71665
OLYMPIC GLORY (IRE)	22	5	7	15	181989
ORATORIO (IRE)	2	1	1	0	3024
ORIENTOR (GB)	15	6	12	21	214637
OSCAR (IRE)	3	1	2	1	120571
OUTSTRIP (GB)	68	26	40	99	441666
PACO BOY (IRE)	21	12	16	34	139691
PAPAL BULL (GB)	4	1	1	3	11970
PARISH HALL (IRE)	7	1	1	3	14034
PASSING GLANCE (GB)	6	2	2	4	14923
PASTORAL PURSUITS (GB)	30	7	12	22	105658
PASTORIUS (GER)	4	3	3	4	29955
PEACE ENVOY (FR)	7	2	4	4	22418
PEARL SECRET (GB)	23	9	14	20	172139
PHOENIX REACH (IRE)	6	2	2	4	14354
PICCOLO (GB)	3	1	1	1	15465
PIVOTAL (GB)	49	23	45	63	556107
PLANTEUR (IRE)	4	3	5	8	494611
POET'S VOICE (GB)	44	21	37	74	314825
POET'S WORD (IRE)	4	2	2	12	46073
POSTPONED (IRE)	49	16	25	44	290559
POUR MOI (IRE)	10	3	4	4	69455
POWER (GB)	29	11	20	37	194119
PRESENTING (GB)	2	1	1	3	11671
PRIDE OF DUBAI (AUS)	45	20	36	51	499066
PRINCE OF LIR (IRE)	40	14	27	40	354048
PROCONSUL (GB)	7	1	2	7	17892
PROFITABLE (IRE)	123	38	58	126	721973
QUALITY ROAD (USA)	11	4	8	2	147057

RAJASINGHE (IRE)	10	8	11	19	101868
RAJJ (IRE)	5	1	2	3	16630
RAJSAMAN (FR)	6	2	2	6	22549
RAVEN'S PASS (USA)	37	12	20	55	377125
RECORDER (GB)	16	5	6	11	40767
RED JAZZ (USA)	36	10	14	39	196779
REDOUTE'S CHOICE (AUS)	3	1	1	1	7015
RELIABLE MAN (GB)	7	2	3	6	33613
REQUINTO (IRE)	28	11	18	30	232273
RIBCHESTER (IRE)	79	20	30	84	547401
RIO DE LA PLATA (USA)	5	2	3	5	31855
RIP VAN WINKLE (IRE)	10	3	8	21	82412
ROARING LION (USA)	49	8	12	27	152923
ROCK OF GIBRALTAR (IRE)	20	8	13	16	104968
RODERIC O'CONNOR (IRE)	20	9	13	22	125593
ROYAL APPLAUSE (GB)	12	4	5	21	63115
RULER OF THE WORLD (IRE)	23	2	3	11	255155
SAGEBURG (IRE)	4	1	1	3	9968
SAKHEE (USA)	2	2	2	1	8965
SAKHEE'S SECRET (GB)	7	3	3	9	44420
SAMUM (GER)	2	1	1	1	6413
SAXON WARRIOR (JPN)	42	13	15	28	278418
SAYIF (IRE)	10	2	5	7	44195
SCAT DADDY (USA)	6	2	3	4	35380
SCHIAPARELLI (GER)	2	1	3	2	12761
SCISSOR KICK (AUS)	1	1	1	1	14534
SEA MOON (GB)	2	1	2	1	12709
SEA THE MOON (GER)	76	23	32	69	384813
SEA THE STARS (IRE)	168	71	103	166	5050740
SEPOY (AUS)	31	17	29	37	331832
SHALAA (IRE)	38	18	30	56	361427
SHAMARDAL (USA)	84	39	59	95	1200930
SHANTOU (USA)	6	1	1	2	48693
SHIROCCO (GER)	5	1	1	2	6323
SHOLOKHOV (IRE)	3	1	1	4	9426
SHOWCASING (GB)	188	62	91	179	1936392
SIDESTEP (AUS)	4	1	1	4	22608
SILVER POND (FR)	1	1	1	2	6790
SIOUX NATION (USA)	65	29	40	67	642516
SIR PERCY (GB)	53	21	35	66	436222
SIR PRANCEALOT (IRE)	39	20	28	51	476481
SIXTIES ICON (GB)	57	17	30	64	311394
SIYOUNI (FR)	102	43	68	111	1252823
SLADE POWER (IRE)	64	28	48	87	515623
SLEEPING INDIAN (GB)	5	2	4	8	28192
SMOOTH DADDY (USA)	7	1	1	2	10102
SO YOU THINK (NZ)	5	1	1	6	30576
SOCIETY ROCK (IRE)	24	11	22	38	211724
SOLDIER HOLLOW (GB)	5	2	2	3	41362
SPEIGHTSTOWN (USA)	10	5	8	7	47652
SPILL THE BEANS (AUS)	7	1	2	11	38603
STARSPANGLEDBANNER (AUS)	152	56	77	182	2019463
STEELE TANGO (USA)	2	2	2	7	21681
STIMULATION (IRE)	12	2	2	16	38237
STOWAWAY (GB)	2	1	1	1	10109
STRATEGIC PRINCE (GB)	1	1	1	1	8555
STRATH BURN (GB)	4	1	2	0	21181
STREET CRY (IRE)	3	1	2	5	14283
STREET SENSE (USA)	4	1	2	3	13475
STRONG MANDATE (USA)	1	1	1	0	6206
STYLE VENDOME (FR)	4	2	3	5	20501
SUMMER FRONT (USA)	3	1	2	1	12856

STALLIONS	RNRS	WNRS	WINS	PLACES	TOTAL (£)
SUN CENTRAL (IRE)	2	1	2	2	11761
SWISS SPIRIT (GB)	56	26	52	85	597537
T H APPROVAL (USA)	1	1	2	1	21496
TAGULA (IRE)	18	6	8	15	73723
TAMAYUZ (GB)	63	23	32	79	433247
TASLEET (GB)	38	13	15	29	243937
TELESCOPE (IRE)	6	2	4	9	28178
TEMPLE CITY (USA)	1	1	2	3	15298
TEOFILO (IRE)	102	36	65	106	1402760
TERRITORIES (IRE)	75	25	32	63	917091
THE CARBON UNIT (USA)	6	2	6	7	92084
THE FACTOR (USA)	2	2	5	5	27079
THE GREY GATSBY (IRE)	2	1	4	3	16134
THE GURKHA (IRE)	62	24	41	76	470844
THE LAST LION (IRE)	30	8	12	40	132523
THE WOW SIGNAL (IRE)	1	1	1	1	4580
THEWAYYOUARE (USA)	5	2	3	7	27666
TIME TEST (GB)	69	17	25	42	409282
TOBOUGG (IRE)	3	1	1	2	10653
TORONADO (IRE)	42	13	21	52	282819
TOUGH AS NAILS (IRE)	10	3	5	11	40943
TWILIGHT SON (GB)	107	32	48	129	825851
TWIRLING CANDY (USA)	4	1	1	5	10510
U S NAVY FLAG (USA)	35	8	10	31	143402
ULTRA (IRE)	3	1	1	2	9653
ULYSSES (IRE)	75	31	44	97	827957
UNFORTUNATELY (IRE)	17	7	11	15	102740
UNIVERSAL (IRE)	6	2	4	7	71820
URGENT REQUEST (IRE)	1	1	1	2	6343
VADAMOS (FR)	46	13	20	34	279898
VALIRANN (FR)	3	2	3	2	68165
VERGLAS (IRE)	1	1	1	1	4454
VIRTUAL (GB)	1	1	2	3	12368
VOCALISED (USA)	27	6	8	21	123897
WAR COMMAND (USA)	52	16	25	55	352909
WAR FRONT (USA)	25	10	13	37	351764
WASHINGTON DC (IRE)	21	6	6	18	116212
WELL CHOSEN (GB)	1	1	1	0	5702
WILDCAT HEIR (USA)	1	1	1	3	6639
WINGS OF EAGLES (FR)	3	2	5	6	60588
WOOTTON BASSETT (GB)	35	15	22	30	765115
WORKFORCE (GB)	2	1	1	1	11487
WORTHADD (IRE)	5	1	1	6	19364
WROTE (IRE)	1	1	3	5	18576
XTENSION (IRE)	3	2	2	3	26311
YEATS (IRE)	10	1	1	4	12853
YORGUNNABELUCKY (USA)	6	1	1	8	23401
YOUMZAIN (IRE)	5	2	6	4	50523
ZAMINDAR (USA)	1	1	2	1	31358
ZANZIBARI (USA)	2	2	2	1	12298
ZARAK (FR)	10	4	7	12	95940
ZEBEDEE (GB)	43	19	29	36	570628
ZELZAL (FR)	8	2	2	11	46103
ZOFFANY (IRE)	186	67	107	202	1985266
ZOUSTAR (AUS)	53	14	19	41	402290

BY KIND PERMISSION OF WEATHERBYS

NH STALLIONS' EARNINGS FOR 2021/22

(Includes every stallion who sired a winner over jumps in Great Britain and Ireland in 2021/22)

STALLIONS	RNRS	WNRS	WINS	PLACES	TOTAL (£)
ADLERFLUG (GER)	2	1	2	0	5602
AGENT BLEU (FR)	1	1	1	1	8903
AIR CHIEF MARSHAL (IRE)	6	3	6	4	59732
AIZAVOSKI (IRE)	40	14	20	25	225834
AL KAZEEM (GB)	7	1	1	6	15051
AL NAMIX (FR)	37	8	11	27	171158
ALANADI (FR)	1	1	1	1	12723
ALBAASIL (IRE)	1	1	1	1	6202
ALBERTO GIACOMETTI (IRE)	4	1	2	4	22801
ALEXANDROS (GB)	1	1	1	1	4960
ALFLORA (IRE)	9	3	4	6	50817
ALHEBAYEB (IRE)	14	3	6	10	48020
ALKAADHEM (GB)	11	2	3	9	116223
ALKAASED (USA)	2	1	3	1	63084
AMERICAIN (USA)	3	1	2	3	16600
AND BEYOND (IRE)	8	1	1	3	23596
ANODIN (IRE)	3	2	2	3	25227
ANZILLERO (GER)	8	3	5	12	76339
AOLUS (GER)	2	1	1	3	11107
APPLE TREE (FR)	7	2	2	3	16085
APPROVE (IRE)	3	1	1	4	11509
APSIS (GB)	7	4	4	10	85650
AQLAAM (GB)	6	1	2	2	10448
ARAKAN (USA)	50	15	22	47	295824
ARCADIO (GER)	143	30	47	119	710072
ARCANO (IRE)	12	1	1	7	16530
ARCHIPENKO (USA)	12	4	5	21	58655
ARCTIC COSMOS (USA)	45	8	9	40	141583
ARVICO (FR)	19	3	5	10	74405
ASIAN HEIGHTS (GB)	5	3	5	3	31079
ASK (GB)	109	35	45	87	474192
ASTARABAD (USA)	3	1	1	0	6745
ASTRONOMER ROYAL (USA)	1	1	2	0	6667
AUSSIE RULES (USA)	5	1	1	7	12042
AUSTRALIA (GB)	29	3	3	16	53616
AUTHORIZED (IRE)	72	22	43	77	752329
AWTAAD (IRE)	5	1	1	7	14439
AXXOS (GER)	3	1	2	3	34253
AZAMOUR (IRE)	8	5	6	14	95143
BACH (IRE)	7	2	2	1	16188
BAHRI (USA)	5	2	5	5	48606
BALAKHERI (IRE)	1	1	1	4	6448
BALKO (FR)	40	9	14	44	195836
BALLINGARRY (IRE)	27	5	9	17	124455
BARASTRAIGHT (GB)	4	1	2	3	109861
BARATHEA (IRE)	1	1	1	2	5543
BARELY A MOMENT (AUS)	8	2	2	0	8535
BATED BREATH (GB)	7	2	2	5	18250
BATHYRHON (GER)	3	1	2	2	14622
BATTLE OF MARENGO (IRE)	19	4	5	14	54466
BEAT HOLLOW (GB)	62	14	18	46	518863
BENEFICIAL (GB)	96	27	33	100	675893
BERNARDINI (USA)	1	1	2	0	8846
BIENAMADO (USA)	3	2	2	2	10453
BIG BAD BOB (IRE)	20	7	11	19	111520
BLACK SAM BELLAMY (IRE)	109	31	46	113	707652
BLUE BRESIL (FR)	63	12	19	40	568412

STALLIONS	RNRS	WNRS	WINS	PLACES	TOTAL (£)
BOBBY'S KITTEN (USA)	4	1	1	5	13176
BOLLIN ERIC (GB)	10	1	1	1	7222
BONBON ROSE (FR)	6	2	2	5	19623
BORIS DE DEAUVILLE (IRE)	5	1	2	7	24766
BORN KING (JPN)	3	1	1	1	11710
BORN TO SEA (IRE)	42	17	25	51	448673
BRAVE MANSONNIEN (FR)	8	3	9	4	163780
BRIAN BORU (GB)	44	12	21	42	303008
BUCK'S BOUM (FR)	22	7	7	11	102722
BURATINO (IRE)	8	2	2	4	16388
CABLE BAY (IRE)	2	2	3	1	17218
CACIQUE (IRE)	9	2	5	12	68972
CALIFET (FR)	100	23	31	70	516532
CAMACHO (GB)	22	2	4	17	43542
CAMELOT (GB)	56	11	15	39	167420
CANFORD CLIFFS (IRE)	35	7	11	22	131155
CANNOCK CHASE (USA)	6	1	1	8	16559
CAPE CROSS (IRE)	22	4	4	20	72304
CAPTAIN RIO (GB)	3	1	2	1	8729
CARLOTAMIX (FR)	33	10	14	30	123122
CASAMENTO (IRE)	30	7	8	14	53507
CHAMPS ELYSEES (GB)	63	8	13	53	198527
CHARMING THOUGHT (GB)	5	2	2	2	19163
CHOISIR (AUS)	1	1	1	0	5446
CIMA DE TRIOMPHE (IRE)	4	1	1	5	49801
CLOUDINGS (IRE)	38	8	11	36	268624
CLOVIS DU BERLAIS (FR)	4	1	1	0	2964
COACH HOUSE (IRE)	2	1	1	4	8922
COASTAL PATH (GB)	48	19	25	46	454742
COKORIKO (FR)	37	11	19	16	206198
CONDUIT (IRE)	18	1	2	4	20926
CORRI PIANO (FR)	1	1	1	0	3594
COURT CAVE (IRE)	161	44	62	144	902840
CRAIGSTEEL (GB)	31	9	13	30	175438
CRILLON (FR)	17	5	6	11	63704
CROSSHARBOUR (GB)	4	3	4	3	35926
CROSSPEACE (IRE)	4	1	1	1	9296
CURTAIN TIME (IRE)	10	1	1	6	36494
DABIRSIM (FR)	3	1	1	1	5664
DAHJEE (USA)	3	1	1	4	11585
DAIWA MAJOR (JPN)	1	1	1	0	6893
DANDY MAN (IRE)	7	1	1	5	16143
DANEHILL DANCER (IRE)	1	1	1	2	7957
DANSANT (GB)	17	1	2	9	38258
DANSILI (GB)	20	5	8	9	63004
DAPPER (GB)	4	2	7	3	49730
DARK ANGEL (IRE)	26	11	15	25	186917
DARSI (FR)	12	5	7	12	90388
DAVIDOFF (GER)	6	1	2	9	106834
DAWN APPROACH (IRE)	29	4	5	16	49283
DAY FLIGHT (GB)	8	2	3	7	44496
DAYLAMI (IRE)	7	1	1	5	17717
DECLARATION OF WAR (USA)	11	3	4	11	46463
DEFINITE ARTICLE (GB)	15	6	7	13	116409
DELEGATOR (GB)	5	2	2	7	32780
DELLA FRANCESCA (USA)	9	3	4	4	28981
DENHAM RED (FR)	7	3	9	8	476258
DEPORTIVO (GB)	2	1	6	3	31663
DESIR D'UN SOIR (FR)	2	1	1	2	9365
DIAMOND BOY (FR)	43	17	31	50	530678
DIAMOND GREEN (FR)	3	1	1	3	13104

STALLIONS	RNRS	WNRS	WINS	PLACES	TOTAL (£)
DINK (FR)	1	1	1	1	68390
DISTANT PEAK (IRE)	1	1	1	0	5601
DOCTOR DINO (FR)	26	12	25	28	699173
DOUBLE ECLIPSE (IRE)	7	2	3	6	26932
DOYEN (IRE)	144	49	79	131	1063411
DR MASSINI (IRE)	30	9	14	39	168248
DRAGON DANCER (GB)	4	1	2	6	18736
DRAGON PULSE (IRE)	26	4	6	12	64944
DREAM AHEAD (USA)	10	1	3	4	31433
DREAM EATER (IRE)	5	1	2	4	13158
DREAM WELL (FR)	7	7	11	7	348683
DUBAI DESTINATION (USA)	48	19	28	52	566351
DUBAWI (IRE)	11	6	10	6	58155
DUKE OF MARMALADE (IRE)	10	2	2	10	30066
DUNADEN (FR)	16	4	6	7	38684
DURBAN THUNDER (GER)	3	1	2	1	15571
DUTCH ART (GB)	6	2	4	6	25175
DYLAN THOMAS (IRE)	129	33	59	111	896315
EAGLE TOP (GB)	4	1	1	1	3161
EARLY MARCH (GB)	4	2	2	3	24149
EASTERN ANTHEM (IRE)	6	1	1	3	7678
ECHO OF LIGHT (GB)	5	2	2	9	35757
EL SALVADOR (IRE)	8	2	3	4	23102
ELIOT (GER)	2	1	2	1	16799
ELUSIVE PIMPERNEL (USA)	59	8	9	37	196607
ELZAAM (AUS)	19	2	2	9	35436
ENGLISH CHANNEL (USA)	1	1	3	3	41318
ENRIQUE (GB)	7	2	2	8	113302
EPAULETTE (AUS)	18	3	4	16	52862
EQUERRY (USA)	1	1	1	2	8368
ESKENDEREYA (USA)	1	1	1	2	8064
EXCEED AND EXCEL (AUS)	5	2	4	2	27417
EXCELEBRATION (IRE)	21	4	6	23	92400
EXCELLENT ART (GB)	4	1	2	4	18904
EXCHANGE RATE (USA)	2	1	2	0	16767
EXIT TO NOWHERE (USA)	3	2	3	2	12780
FAIR MIX (IRE)	36	12	15	32	183396
FAIRLY RANSOM (USA)	8	2	8	11	84242
FALCO (USA)	14	7	9	9	183512
FAME AND GLORY (GB)	324	120	185	301	2538533
FAMOUS NAME (GB)	23	10	13	19	106436
FARHH (GB)	12	1	1	4	21023
FASCINATING ROCK (IRE)	7	1	1	6	16778
FAST COMPANY (IRE)	29	10	17	28	180067
FASTNET ROCK (AUS)	16	3	4	8	39740
FED BIZ (USA)	2	1	1	0	5796
FEEL LIKE DANCING (GB)	5	2	2	3	12606
FINE GRAIN (JPN)	1	1	1	2	25385
FIRST DEFENCE (USA)	1	1	2	2	10806
FLEMENSFIRTH (USA)	236	73	92	174	1529587
FLYING LEGEND (USA)	7	2	3	3	115169
FOOTSTEPSINTHESAND (GB)	23	1	1	7	21440
FORESTIER (FR)	3	1	1	1	6642
FOXWEDGE (AUS)	10	2	2	6	17744
FRACAS (IRE)	17	4	6	10	75117
FRAGRANT MIX (IRE)	7	3	3	10	74321
FRAMMASSONE (IRE)	12	6	8	11	116181
FRANKEL (GB)	16	2	2	13	46617
FREE EAGLE (IRE)	26	3	3	11	45204
FREE PORT LUX (GB)	2	1	2	0	11862
FRENCH FIFTEEN (FR)	4	2	4	4	29457

STALLIONS	RNRS	WNRS	WINS	PLACES	TOTAL (£)
FROZEN POWER (IRE)	9	3	7	8	44354
FRUITS OF LOVE (USA)	16	6	12	19	80115
FUISSE (FR)	13	6	12	15	92848
FULBRIGHT (GB)	4	2	2	1	13185
FULL OF GOLD (FR)	6	1	1	8	36861
GALE FORCE TEN (GB)	10	1	2	2	17407
GALILEO (IRE)	47	18	25	48	319783
GALIWAY (GB)	2	1	3	2	203329
GAMUT (IRE)	22	3	5	5	34821
GARSWOOD (GB)	8	1	2	7	35705
GARUDA (IRE)	1	1	1	1	5018
GENEROUS (IRE)	7	2	2	5	31639
GENTLEWAVE (IRE)	40	9	13	17	132055
GEORDIELAND (FR)	28	12	18	30	142790
GERMANY (USA)	5	2	2	7	33414
GETAWAY (GER)	352	108	163	363	2044113
GIANT'S CAUSEWAY (USA)	1	1	1	0	8402
GLENEAGLES (IRE)	19	3	3	18	73342
GOLAN (IRE)	19	3	3	13	41643
GOLD AWAY (IRE)	1	1	2	1	13203
GOLD WELL (GB)	131	50	71	116	1149757
GOLDEN HORN (GB)	16	9	16	19	173909
GOLDEN LARIAT (USA)	15	7	12	21	344417
GOLDEN TORNADO (IRE)	5	1	1	2	18767
GOLDMARK (USA)	3	1	1	1	7956
GRANDERA (IRE)	2	1	1	0	5357
GRAPE TREE ROAD (GB)	1	1	3	1	10102
GREAT PRETENDER (IRE)	63	21	30	46	541194
GREGORIAN (IRE)	9	2	4	4	40066
GRIS DE GRIS (IRE)	15	5	11	16	141474
GUTAIFAN (IRE)	11	1	1	4	13346
HAAFHD (GB)	13	1	2	6	26142
HALLING (USA)	4	2	4	5	26717
HALLOWED CROWN (AUS)	11	1	2	5	17392
HARBOUR WATCH (IRE)	11	2	5	11	54813
HARD SPUN (USA)	4	3	3	3	19881
HARZAND (IRE)	5	1	3	2	15133
HAVANA GOLD (IRE)	6	2	2	6	25020
HEERAAT (IRE)	12	1	3	6	27176
HELMET (AUS)	25	6	7	20	95326
HENRYTHENAVIGATOR (USA)	7	2	3	3	30325
HERNANDO (FR)	1	1	1	0	6188
HIGH CHAPARRAL (IRE)	18	5	6	16	67894
HIGH ROCK (IRE)	2	1	2	4	35788
HILLSTAR (GB)	8	3	4	7	30014
HOLY ROMAN EMPEROR (IRE)	21	10	14	25	128837
HUNTER'S LIGHT (IRE)	7	1	3	5	20718
HURRICANE CAT (USA)	4	2	2	6	23950
IFFRAAJ (GB)	23	5	6	12	50830
IMPERIAL MONARCH (IRE)	81	15	20	51	208982
INCLUDE (USA)	1	1	1	0	5080
INDIAN DANEHILL (IRE)	5	1	2	6	30638
INDIAN RIVER (FR)	11	4	5	10	82466
INSATIABLE (IRE)	2	2	2	0	7826
INTELLO (GER)	22	5	6	17	57302
INTENSE FOCUS (USA)	5	1	1	4	11015
INTIKHAB (USA)	9	1	1	6	14312
INVINCIBLE SPIRIT (IRE)	13	2	2	9	24954
IRISH WELLS (FR)	6	3	4	10	40508
IT'S GINO (GER)	6	4	5	7	68702
IVAWOOD (IRE)	10	1	1	0	5891

STALLIONS	RNRS	WNRS	WINS	PLACES	TOTAL (£)
JAMMAAL (GB)	2	1	2	1	9796
JEREMY (USA)	143	58	92	151	1452746
JET AWAY (GB)	59	22	30	52	302242
JIMBLE (FR)	3	1	1	1	5135
JOSHUA TREE (IRE)	9	2	3	8	27580
JUKEBOX JURY (IRE)	18	5	9	17	208091
KADASTROF (FR)	2	1	1	1	10999
KALANISI (IRE)	138	25	37	85	518969
KALLISTO (GER)	2	1	2	1	13053
KAMSIN (GER)	12	4	8	21	66521
KAP ROCK (FR)	9	4	5	15	76174
KAPGARDE (FR)	87	41	65	98	1758154
KAYF TARA (GB)	203	60	87	179	1345220
KELTOS (FR)	1	1	2	1	13457
KENDARGENT (FR)	8	3	4	9	65422
KENTUCKY DYNAMITE (USA)	5	3	6	8	81028
KHALKEVI (IRE)	9	3	6	8	249647
KILLER INSTINCT (GB)	1	1	1	1	5779
KING'S BEST (USA)	2	1	2	5	23188
KING'S THEATRE (IRE)	37	12	17	33	556061
KINGSALSA (USA)	5	3	3	6	28147
KINGSTON HILL (GB)	21	4	5	16	50812
KITKOU (FR)	3	2	2	0	10094
KITTEN'S JOY (USA)	6	1	1	1	9463
KODI BEAR (IRE)	8	1	1	6	20652
KODIAC (GB)	17	2	2	4	19244
KONIG SHUFFLE (GER)	2	2	3	1	29964
KONIG TURF (GER)	8	3	9	16	185457
KUTUB (IRE)	5	1	3	3	22574
KYLLACHY (GB)	5	1	1	2	10313
LAURO (GER)	4	1	1	1	5808
LAVEROCK (IRE)	10	2	2	3	16936
LAWMAN (FR)	28	9	16	23	132853
LE FOU (IRE)	36	12	17	41	249890
LE HAVRE (IRE)	22	4	6	18	160521
LE HOUSSAIS (FR)	1	1	2	5	16599
LE TRITON (USA)	1	1	2	2	11653
LEADING LIGHT (IRE)	115	26	32	70	420971
LEGOLAS (JPN)	6	1	1	6	21069
LETHAL FORCE (IRE)	9	1	1	2	7682
LIBERTARIAN (GB)	27	6	10	15	70576
LIBRETTIST (USA)	3	2	2	2	11759
LILBOURNE LAD (IRE)	6	2	2	9	26455
LINDA'S LAD (GB)	16	4	5	17	73151
LOPE DE VEGA (IRE)	21	5	8	12	168850
LORD DU SUD (FR)	20	5	6	25	147648
LORD OF ENGLAND (GER)	6	2	3	5	29418
LORD SHANAKILL (USA)	10	1	2	13	32525
LUCARNO (USA)	21	5	5	16	51355
MAHLER (GB)	254	81	129	221	1400875
MAKE BELIEVE (GB)	13	8	11	15	93572
MAKFI (GB)	10	3	5	9	109440
MALINAS (GER)	97	36	54	78	594023
MAMOOL (IRE)	7	2	6	9	81829
MANBOLIX (FR)	1	1	1	3	9351
MANDURO (GER)	17	4	8	19	165784
MARESCA SORRENTO (FR)	29	8	9	33	216495
MARIENBARD (IRE)	5	1	1	3	12803
MARTALINE (GB)	111	39	62	118	1170193
MASKED MARVEL (GB)	22	9	19	24	216973
MASTERCRAFTSMAN (IRE)	65	19	29	48	403751

STALLIONS	RNRS	WNRS	WINS	PLACES	TOTAL (£)
MASTEROFTHEHORSE (IRE)	17	4	4	8	44134
MASTERSTROKE (USA)	13	1	1	9	23502
MAWATHEEQ (USA)	3	1	1	8	12097
MAXIOS (GB)	35	14	20	52	293105
MAYSON (GB)	5	1	3	3	19522
MEDAALY (GB)	2	1	1	4	40889
MEDICEAN (GB)	14	5	11	12	151361
MESHAHEER (USA)	1	1	4	2	45995
MIDNIGHT LEGEND (GB)	117	54	84	155	1400001
MILAN (GB)	244	70	113	219	1639498
MILLENARY (GB)	19	5	7	17	71501
MISTER FOTIS (USA)	1	1	1	4	14888
MONITOR CLOSELY (IRE)	2	1	1	8	17484
MONSIEUR BOND (IRE)	3	1	1	2	9657
MONTMARTRE (FR)	49	16	23	54	403743
MOON BALLAD (IRE)	1	1	2	1	6462
MORES WELLS (GB)	9	3	6	8	42988
MOROZOV (USA)	53	21	38	44	310118
MORPHEUS (GB)	13	2	4	9	38504
MOST IMPROVED (IRE)	16	2	3	4	19940
MOTIVATOR (GB)	21	9	13	22	227577
MOUNT NELSON (GB)	44	12	14	17	121800
MOUNTAIN HIGH (IRE)	48	14	29	30	232575
MR DINOS (IRE)	12	3	3	11	37496
MUHAYMIN (USA)	5	1	1	3	11772
MUHTATHIR (GB)	25	8	16	29	319277
MUKHADRAM (GB)	16	4	4	7	32414
MULTIPLEX (GB)	39	9	13	11	92903
MUSTAJEEB (GB)	4	1	1	3	8024
MUSTAMEET (USA)	40	10	14	32	137545
MY RISK (FR)	5	3	6	9	40858
MYBOYCHARLIE (IRE)	5	1	1	2	15836
NAAQOOS (GB)	1	1	1	7	26422
NATHANIEL (IRE)	64	21	28	58	644345
NATIVE RULER (GB)	11	4	6	6	33569
NAYEF (USA)	21	1	1	14	30867
NETWORK (GER)	54	16	26	46	480865
NEW APPROACH (IRE)	27	4	5	14	129678
NEW BAY (GB)	3	1	1	3	11659
NICKNAME (FR)	7	3	4	7	176975
NIDOR (FR)	4	2	2	13	52084
NIGHT OF THUNDER (IRE)	2	1	1	2	5932
NIGHT WISH (GER)	1	1	1	2	9559
NO NAY NEVER (USA)	10	3	3	9	33888
NO RISK AT ALL (FR)	55	19	37	50	1182324
NOM DE D'LA (FR)	2	1	1	0	5509
NOROIT (GER)	16	8	11	21	265957
NORSE DANCER (IRE)	35	7	11	32	133778
NORTHERN LEGEND (GB)	1	1	1	1	9775
NOTNOWCATO (GB)	33	4	7	22	120136
NUTAN (IRE)	3	1	3	4	13861
OASIS DREAM (GB)	14	1	1	5	17869
OBSERVATORY (USA)	1	1	1	2	14705
OCOVANGO (GB)	96	20	28	56	270324
OLDEN TIMES (GB)	6	2	2	4	17996
OLYMPIC GLORY (IRE)	11	3	3	8	24708
ON EST BIEN (IRE)	3	1	3	3	21004
ORPEN (USA)	2	1	1	4	12550
OSCAR (IRE)	158	39	53	129	1127365
OUTSTRIP (GB)	7	1	1	5	16783

STALLIONS	RNRS	WNRS	WINS	PLACES	TOTAL (£)
PACO BOY (IRE)	5	1	1	1	3834
PALACE EPISODE (USA)	2	1	1	4	15841
PALAVICINI (USA)	5	1	2	1	16543
PAPAL BULL (GB)	21	1	2	11	47950
PASSING GLANCE (GB)	70	24	38	69	485328
PASTERNAK (GB)	4	1	1	5	14103
PASTORIUS (GER)	6	3	5	4	44472
PEDRO THE GREAT (USA)	2	1	1	1	9084
PEINTRE CELEBRE (USA)	1	1	3	4	29760
PETHER'S MOON (IRE)	18	3	3	6	15109
PHOENIX REACH (IRE)	20	6	8	17	71636
PIVOTAL (GB)	9	1	1	7	17171
PLANTEUR (IRE)	6	2	2	2	14089
POET'S VOICE (GB)	37	13	20	40	256003
POINT OF ENTRY (USA)	2	1	1	2	9500
POLICY MAKER (IRE)	17	3	3	13	146801
POLIGLOTE (GB)	22	8	11	23	419707
POUR MOI (IRE)	31	12	15	28	205267
POWER (GB)	17	4	6	12	102471
PRESENTING (GB)	231	61	92	227	1390205
PRIDE OF DUBAI (AUS)	6	2	2	3	13571
PRIMARY (USA)	8	3	3	7	138152
PRINCE FLORI (GER)	4	3	6	5	36671
PRINCE GIBRALTAR (FR)	3	1	1	2	9002
PRINCE OF LIR (IRE)	2	1	1	2	9649
PROTECTIONIST (GER)	2	1	1	3	8731
PROTEKTOR (GER)	4	1	1	3	5894
PUBLISHER (USA)	6	3	5	4	39091
PUIT D'OR (IRE)	3	3	4	6	19562
PUTRA PEKAN (GB)	2	1	2	1	15089
RACINGER (FR)	9	5	7	16	159958
RAIL LINK (GB)	20	6	10	26	102879
RAJSAMAN (FR)	10	5	6	21	68778
RAVEN'S PASS (USA)	14	3	5	10	58748
RECITAL (FR)	7	5	7	11	68163
RED DUBAWI (IRE)	1	1	3	1	23746
RED JAZZ (USA)	11	2	2	2	21604
RED ROCKS (IRE)	3	1	2	6	20865
RELIABLE MAN (GB)	4	2	3	4	53522
REVOQUE (IRE)	2	2	2	0	6982
RIP VAN WINKLE (IRE)	16	6	7	9	67809
ROBIN DES CHAMPS (FR)	64	19	33	46	318621
ROBIN DES PRES (FR)	33	10	13	35	157319
ROCAMADOUR (GB)	3	1	1	1	8656
ROCK OF GIBRALTAR (IRE)	19	3	5	12	59570
RODERIC O'CONNOR (IRE)	12	2	2	4	18398
ROYAL ANTHEM (USA)	18	5	8	11	64426
ROYAL APPLAUSE (GB)	3	1	1	4	9847
RUDIMENTARY (USA)	1	1	1	2	6177
RULE OF LAW (USA)	14	2	3	18	39287
RULER OF THE WORLD (IRE)	8	2	3	6	17589
SADDEX (GB)	12	5	6	11	100080
SADDLER MAKER (IRE)	62	29	44	64	523648
SADDLER'S ROCK (IRE)	2	1	1	0	3004
SAGAMIX (FR)	5	1	1	6	15688
SAGEBURG (IRE)	80	15	23	37	189256
SAINT DES SAINTS (FR)	72	27	45	79	1298491
SAKHEE (USA)	6	1	1	2	13334
SALUTINO (GER)	12	5	6	11	156516
SAMUM (GER)	12	6	10	23	122199

SANDMASON (GB)	8	1	1	6	33154
SANS FRONTIERES (IRE)	57	12	18	37	149692
SANTIAGO (GER)	2	1	4	3	27978
SATRI (IRE)	4	2	2	1	13011
SAYIF (IRE)	4	2	2	3	15639
SCHIAPARELLI (GER)	77	23	35	75	476987
SCISSOR KICK (AUS)	1	1	2	1	19311
SCORPION (IRE)	156	37	46	121	564324
SEA MOON (GB)	10	2	3	7	35869
SEA THE MOON (GER)	26	8	8	19	233780
SEA THE STARS (IRE)	39	9	13	30	151447
SECRET SINGER (FR)	8	4	4	14	61276
SELKIRK (USA)	2	1	1	2	5755
SEPOY (AUS)	9	2	4	3	24462
SEPTEMBER STORM (GER)	28	7	7	17	99021
SHAMARDAL (USA)	9	1	2	6	14671
SHANTARAM (GB)	9	2	2	4	15639
SHANTOU (USA)	180	59	99	152	1422732
SHIROCCO (GER)	267	85	122	212	1489374
SHOLOKHOV (IRE)	113	37	64	120	995368
SHOWCASING (GB)	8	2	3	3	21951
SILVANO (GER)	1	1	2	1	21178
SILVER FROST (IRE)	6	1	1	11	27111
SINNDAR (IRE)	23	9	15	22	147542
SINTARAJAN (IRE)	1	1	1	5	12531
SIR PERCY (GB)	34	11	21	29	314127
SIR PRANCEALOT (IRE)	11	1	2	4	40673
SIXTIES ICON (GB)	39	10	13	16	81870
SIYOUNI (FR)	8	1	1	2	12600
SKINS GAME (GB)	1	1	1	2	86635
SLADE POWER (IRE)	10	1	1	3	7628
SLICKLY ROYAL (FR)	1	1	1	0	6321
SMADOUN (FR)	4	2	3	3	17060
SNOW SKY (GB)	10	1	1	5	17597
SO YOU THINK (NZ)	17	4	7	12	78802
SOCIETY ROCK (IRE)	4	1	3	8	26887
SOLDIER HOLLOW (GB)	11	3	4	7	179042
SOLDIER OF FORTUNE (IRE)	80	25	30	52	267481
SOMMERABEND (GB)	1	1	1	4	12092
SPANISH MOON (USA)	30	14	22	36	309227
SPECIAL KALDOUN (IRE)	4	2	3	4	31508
SPIDER FLIGHT (FR)	9	3	5	10	33421
SPIRIT ONE (FR)	4	1	2	4	14327
SPRING AT LAST (USA)	2	1	1	0	3555
STARSPANGLEDBANNER (AUS)	7	1	1	4	10797
STOWAWAY (GB)	164	53	79	170	1486168
STRATEGIC PRINCE (GB)	1	1	1	1	3069
STREET CRY (IRE)	4	2	2	4	12926
SUBTLE POWER (IRE)	5	1	1	7	83869
SULAMANI (IRE)	74	34	51	101	994538
SUMITAS (GER)	1	1	1	1	6579
SUNDAY BREAK (JPN)	10	5	8	14	79710
TAGULA (IRE)	6	1	1	1	6098
TAJRAASI (USA)	3	1	2	4	18055
TAMARKUZ (USA)	1	1	1	0	6874
TAMAYUZ (GB)	13	4	7	11	90768
TELESCOPE (IRE)	43	4	4	23	53261
TEOFILO (IRE)	37	7	8	12	70190
TERRITORIES (IRE)	5	2	2	9	40083
THE GURKHA (IRE)	9	5	7	8	63300
THEWAYYOUARE (USA)	13	5	7	21	111022
TIGER GROOM (GB)	17	5	6	15	88219

TIGER HILL (IRE)	3	1	1	4	13582
TIKKANEN (USA)	18	3	3	14	47957
TIMOS (GER)	1	1	3	0	133168
TIRWANAKO (FR)	4	2	3	6	93703
TOBOUGG (IRE)	18	9	13	17	139988
TOUCH OF LAND (FR)	15	3	4	12	37742
TOUGH AS NAILS (IRE)	6	1	1	2	12198
TRANS ISLAND (GB)	38	13	19	36	274518
TRIPLE THREAT (FR)	1	1	1	0	49580
TURGEON (USA)	20	7	10	22	174239
TURTLE BOWL (IRE)	3	1	1	2	4985
TWILIGHT SON (GB)	4	2	2	2	19306
UNION RAGS (USA)	3	1	3	3	40891
UNIVERSAL (IRE)	29	9	11	26	102267
URBAN POET (USA)	10	2	3	3	20224
VADAMOS (FR)	20	2	3	12	52459
VALANOUR (IRE)	1	1	1	2	7488
VALE OF YORK (IRE)	8	1	1	7	17020
VALIRANN (FR)	49	16	23	25	246289
VERTICAL SPEED (FR)	6	1	2	1	27150
VERTIGINEUX (FR)	2	1	1	0	5268
VINNIE ROE (IRE)	31	8	10	25	145921
VIRTUAL (GB)	12	3	7	6	145383
VISION D'ETAT (FR)	9	6	8	11	91616
VITA VENTURI (IRE)	5	1	1	3	23939
VOCALISED (USA)	12	1	3	8	30956
VOILADENUO (FR)	5	2	2	0	8629
VOIX DU NORD (FR)	14	4	4	8	210419
WAKY NAO (GB)	1	1	1	1	4493
WALDPARK (GER)	7	5	6	4	75797
WALK IN THE PARK (IRE)	133	41	58	105	901390
WAR COMMAND (USA)	18	2	4	7	36319
WAR FRONT (USA)	3	1	1	2	6123
WATAR (IRE)	21	6	10	16	66388
WAY OF LIGHT (USA)	2	1	2	0	19854
WELL CHOSEN (GB)	47	17	25	26	248218
WELL MADE (GER)	2	1	1	1	3665
WESTERNER (GB)	193	61	99	191	1321221
WESTLAKE (GB)	1	1	1	0	5156
WHERE OR WHEN (IRE)	3	1	1	5	20736
WHIPPER (USA)	2	1	1	0	5618
WHITMORE'S CONN (USA)	12	5	6	9	46969
WILLYWELL (FR)	2	1	1	2	11687
WINDSOR KNOT (IRE)	15	5	7	12	61972
WINGED LOVE (IRE)	38	15	17	25	221421
WITH THE FLOW (USA)	4	1	1	1	4336
WITNESS BOX (USA)	10	3	4	5	47994
WOOTTON BASSETT (GB)	3	1	1	0	12507
WORKFORCE (GB)	4	1	2	1	20197
WORTHADD (IRE)	3	1	2	5	22245
YEATS (IRE)	281	109	169	311	2954363
YORGUNNABELUCKY (USA)	24	7	12	17	155910
ZAMBEZI SUN (GB)	8	3	7	13	137314
ZAMINDAR (USA)	3	1	1	1	29171
ZANZIBARI (USA)	7	2	4	6	30710
ZEBEDEE (GB)	9	2	4	10	34822
ZERPOUR (IRE)	2	1	3	3	22935
ZOFFANY (IRE)	45	7	8	30	111083

BY KIND PERMISSION OF WEATHERBYS

HIGH-PRICED YEARLINGS OF 2022 AT TATTERSALLS SALES

The following yearlings realised 120,000 guineas and over at Tattersalls Sales in 2022:

Name and Breeding	Purchaser	Guineas
B C FRANKEL (GB) - SO MI DAR (GB)	GODOLPHIN	2800000
B C FRANKEL (GB) - SWEEPSTAKE (IRE)	M MAGNIER/WHITE BIRCH	2400000
B C FRANKEL (GB) - BOLD LASS (IRE)	RICHARD KNIGHT BS AGENT	2000000
B C FRANKEL (GB) - BLUE WALTZ (GB)	M MAGNIER/WHITE BIRCH	1900000
B F LOPE DE VEGA (IRE) - ANNA LAW (IRE)	RICHARD KNIGHT BS AGENT	1800000
B C DUBAWI (IRE) - HOW (IRE)	GODOLPHIN	1600000
B C DUBAWI (IRE) - WILLOW VIEW (USA)	JS COMPANY	1600000
B C DUBAWI (IRE) - GOD GIVEN (GB)	GODOLPHIN	1500000
B C DUBAWI (IRE) - RING THE BELL (IRE)	GODOLPHIN	1500000
B F FRANKEL (GB) - SHAMBOLIC (IRE)	M MAGNIER/WHITE BIRCH	1500000
B C FRANKEL (GB) - WITHOUT YOU BABE (USA)	GODOLPHIN	1300000
B F DUBAWI (IRE) - JAZZI TOP (GB)	GODOLPHIN	1300000
B C DUBAWI (IRE) - URBAN FOX (GB)	GODOLPHIN	1100000
B F KINGMAN (GB) - TRAFFIC JAM (IRE)	SHADWELL ESTATE COMPANY	1050000
B C DUBAWI (IRE) - PERSUASIVE (IRE)	GODOLPHIN	1000000
B C DUBAWI (IRE) - FRANGIPANNI (IRE)	MANOR HOUSE FARM	1000000
B C DUBAWI (IRE) - BUFERA (IRE)	VENDOR	900000
B F SIYOUNI (FR) - LAH TI DAR (GB)	SHADWELL ESTATE COMPANY	880000
BR C DUBAWI (IRE) - HORSEPLAY (GB)	GODOLPHIN	800000
CH F NIGHT OF THUNDER (IRE) - BULRUSHES (GB)	BEN MCELROY	800000
B C SEA THE STARS (IRE) - KITCARINA (FR)	STROUD COLEMAN BS	800000
B C FRANKEL (GB) - AULD ALLIANCE (IRE)	M MAGNIER/WHITE BIRCH	800000
B C DUBAWI (IRE) - VIA CONDOTTI (IRE)	GODOLPHIN	800000
B F SEA THE STARS (IRE) - FARADAY LIGHT (IRE)	OLIVER ST LAWRENCE BS	800000
B F DUBAWI (IRE) - WISDOM MIND (IRE)	BBA IRELAND	800000
MULTIPLE CHOICE (IRE) B F NO NAY NEVER (USA) - MULTILINGUAL (GB)	TINA RAU BS/SCHLENDERHAN	780000
B C FRANKEL (GB) - EVITA PERON (GB)	GODOLPHIN	750000
B C DUBAWI (IRE) - ALINA (IRE)	GODOLPHIN	750000
B C KINGMAN (GB) - WALL OF SOUND (GB)	RICHARD KNIGHT BS AGENT	750000
B C GALILEO (IRE) - WALDLERCHE (GB)	JILL LAMB BS	725000
CLOVE HITCH (IRE) B F SIYOUNI (FR) - CONTEMPTUOUS (IRE)	JUDDMONTE FARMS	725000
CH C SEA THE STARS (IRE) - ALONG CAME CASEY (IRE)	ROGER VARIAN	700000
CH C FRANKEL (GB) - QAWS (GB)	BBA IRELAND	700000
B F SIYOUNI (FR) - TRUTH (IRE)	DE BURGH EQUINE	680000
B F GALILEO (IRE) - LAUGH OUT LOUD (GB)	BBA IRELAND	675000
B C DUBAWI (IRE) - DABYAH (IRE)	GODOLPHIN	650000
B F LOPE DE VEGA (IRE) - GALLITEA (IRE)	STROUD COLEMAN BS	650000
CH F GLENEAGLES (IRE) - PLYING (USA)	M V MAGNIER	650000
GR F NIGHT OF THUNDER (IRE) - SERENA'S STORM (IRE)	SOLIS/LITT & MONCEAUX	650000
B/BR C SEA THE STARS (IRE) - AMORELLA (IRE)	RICHARD KNIGHT BS AGENT	650000
B C NO NAY NEVER (USA) - BEAULY (GB)	M MAGNIER/WHITE BIRCH	650000
BR C DUBAWI (IRE) - I'M WONDERFUL (USA)	GODOLPHIN	625000
B F NO NAY NEVER (USA) - FOLLOW A STAR (IRE)	MV MAGNIER & PARTNERS	625000
B F SIYOUNI (FR) - WALDLIED (GB)	DAVID REDVERS	600000
LAUTREC (GB) B C KINGMAN (GB) - CABARET (IRE)	JUDDMONTE FARMS	600000
B G SEA THE STARS (IRE) - HUNAINA (IRE)	HONG KONG JOCKEY CLUB	600000
B G INVINCIBLE SPIRIT (IRE) - TEPPAL (FR)	HONG KONG JOCKEY CLUB	600000
B F SEA THE STARS (IRE) - PINKSTER (GB)	RICHARD KNIGHT BS AGENT	600000
B C TOO DARN HOT (GB) - TURRET ROCKS (IRE)	DAVID REDVERS	600000
B F BATED BREATH (GB) - ALWAYS A DREAM (GB)	GODOLPHIN	600000
B C MEDAGLIA D'ORO (USA) - BEATRIX POTTER (IRE)	BEN MCELROY AGENT	600000
B C GALILEO (IRE) - ALIVE ALIVE OH (GB)	M MAGNIER/WHITE BIRCH	600000
CH C STARSPANGLEDBANNER (AUS) - GREAT DAME (IRE)	RICHARD KNIGHT BS AGENT	600000
TEN DIMES (GB) BR F NO NAY NEVER (USA) - CUSHION (GB)	BOBBY FLAY	600000
CH C NIGHT OF THUNDER (IRE) - ASIDIOUS ALEXANDER (IRE)	JAMIE MCCALMONT	575000
CH C NIGHT OF THUNDER (IRE) - SARASOTA BAY (GB)	CHAUVIGNY GLOBAL EQUINE	575000
CAPTAIN STAR (FR) B C STARSPANGLEDBANNER (AUS) - MARECHALE (FR)	BADGERS BS	550000
B C DUBAWI (IRE) - PEACE IN MOTION (USA)	GODOLPHIN	550000
B C STARSPANGLEDBANNER (AUS) - WOWCHA (IRE)	HONG KONG JOCKEY CLUB	550000
B C NO NAY NEVER (USA) - DETAILED (IRE)	GODOLPHIN	550000
CH F NIGHT OF THUNDER (IRE) - SWEETY DREAM (FR)	GODOLPHIN	550000
B C SEA THE STARS (IRE) - SUNNY AGAIN (GB)	GODOLPHIN	550000
B C SEA THE STARS (IRE) - SAHRAWI (GER)	GODOLPHIN	550000
B C LOPE DE VEGA (IRE) - TESORO (IRE)	VOUTE SALES	525000
B C DUBAWI (IRE) - BRODERIE ANGLAISE (IRE)	GODOLPHIN	525000
B F NIGHT OF THUNDER (IRE) - PACIFICA HIGHWAY (USA)	CHAUVIGNY GLOBAL EQUINE	525000
B F LOPE DE VEGA (IRE) - GABRIELLE (FR)	JUSTIN CASSE FOR J OXLEY	525000
B C SIYOUNI (FR) - KLASSIQUE (GB)	GODOLPHIN	525000
FIAFA (IRE) B F GALILEO (IRE) - JACQUELINE QUEST (IRE)	VOUTE SALES	500000
B F SIYOUNI (FR) - VILLA D'AMORE (IRE)	STROUD COLEMAN BS	500000
B C KINGMAN (GB) - TIME SAVER (GB)	RICHARD KNIGHT BS AGENT	500000
CH C NO NAY NEVER (USA) - ADVENTURE SEEKER (FR)	GODOLPHIN	500000

Name and Breeding	Purchaser	Guineas
CATCH THE LIGHT (GB) CH F SIYOUNI (FR) - BAY LIGHT (IRE)	CHEVELEY PARK STUD	500000
B F WOOTTON BASSETT (GB) - CHRYSOCOLLA (FR)	JUSTIN CASSE	500000
B C DARK ANGEL (IRE) - CNOC AN OIR (IRE)	RICHARD KNIGHT BS AGENT	500000
B C KINGMAN (GB) - AME BLEUE (GB)	DAVID REDVERS	500000
B C ADVERTISE (GB) - SQUASH (GB)	RICHARD KNIGHT BS AGENT	500000
B C DUBAWI (IRE) - ASANTA SANA (IRE)	MIKE RYAN	500000
CH C DUBAWI (IRE) - BOUND (IRE)	VENDOR	500000
B C DUBAWI (IRE) - MAIN EDITION (IRE)	JOE FOLEY	500000
B C SEA THE STARS (IRE) - BAINO HOPE (FR)	BLANDFORD BS	500000
B C GALILEO (IRE) - MISSROCK (AUS)	HIGHCLERE AGENCY	500000
B F WOOTTON BASSETT (GB) - CHARM APPEAL (FR)	JOSEPH O'BRIEN	485000
B C WOOTTON BASSETT (GB) - TRANSCENDENCE (IRE)	M MAGNIER/WHITE BIRCH	480000
CH C NEW BAY (GB) - HAIRY ROCKET (GB)	RICHARD KNIGHT BS AGENT	475000
B C NIGHT OF THUNDER (IRE) - ELSHAADIN (GB)	PETER & ROSS DOYLE BS	475000
B F KODIAC (GB) - SHOBOBB (GB)	GODOLPHIN	475000
B F MEHMAS (IRE) - NO LIPPY (IRE)	RICHARD KNIGHT BS AGENT	450000
CH F NIGHT OF THUNDER (IRE) - ELLTHEA (IRE)	SOLIS/LITT	450000
BYE BYE SALAM (GB) CH C FRANKEL (GB) - SEPTEMBER STARS (IRE)	BLANDFORD BS	450000
B C KODIAC (GB) - FOLEGANDROS ISLAND (FR)	RICHARD KNIGHT BS AGENT	450000
CH F FRANKEL (GB) - ZINDAYA (USA)	GODOLPHIN	450000
B F SAXON WARRIOR (JPN) - WROOD (USA)	AL SHIRA'AA RACING	450000
GR C DARK ANGEL (IRE) - ISABEAU (IRE)	RICHARD KNIGHT BS AGENT	450000
B C CAMELOT (GB) - THE FAIRY (IRE)	M MAGNIER/WHITE BIRCH	450000
B C KINGMAN (GB) - BEST TERMS (GB)	RICHARD KNIGHT BS AGENT	450000
CH F FRANKEL (GB) - HOUSEHOLD NAME (GB)	AL SHIRA'AA RACING	425000
B F GALILEO (IRE) - PENCHANT (GB)	BBA IRELAND	425000
CH C NEW BAY (GB) - FACT OR FOLKLORE (IRE)	STROUD COLEMAN BS	425000
CH F FRANKEL (GB) - VIA LAZIO (GB)	BBA IRELAND	425000
ANCIENT MYTH (IRE) B C CAMELOT (GB) - QUEEN RABAB (IRE)	ANDREW BALDING	425000
ESTRANGE (IRE) GR F NIGHT OF THUNDER (IRE) - ALIENATE (GB)	CHEVELEY PARK STUD	425000
B F LOPE DE VEGA (IRE) - CHABLIS (IRE)	GODOLPHIN	425000
B C LOPE DE VEGA (IRE) - FOREST CROWN (GB)	BLANDFORD BS	420000
DEAD OF NIGHT (GB) B C SEA THE MOON (GER) - PEARLY SPIRIT (FR)	OCEANIC BS	410000
B C SIYOUNI (FR) - SECRET GAZE (GB)	DAVID REDVERS	400000
B F CHURCHILL (IRE) - WHERE'S SUE (IRE)	C GORDON WATSON BS	400000
B C FARHH (GB) - LAJATICO (GB)	KEVIN RYAN	400000
B C FRANKEL (GB) - DESIROUS (GB)	GODOLPHIN	400000
B F WOOTTON BASSETT (GB) - GLORYETTE (GB)	JEREMY BRUMMITT	400000
CH C DUBAWI (IRE) - PEPITA (IRE)	GODOLPHIN	400000
B C FRANKEL (GB) - CASH IN THE HAND (USA)	GODOLPHIN	400000
B F TOO DARN HOT (GB) - ZURIGHA (IRE)	MIKE RYAN	400000
B F CAMELOT (GB) - DANEHILL'S DREAM (IRE)	BLANDFORD BS	400000
SAOUDITE (GB) B F FRANKEL (GB) - DABAN (IRE)	THOROUGHBRED RACING CORP	400000
B F FRANKEL (GB) - SPECTRE (FR)	WHITE BIRCH FARM	380000
B C LOPE DE VEGA (IRE) - DARK CRUSADER (IRE)	JOSEPH O'BRIEN	380000
B C KINGMAN (GB) - DIAMOND FIELDS (IRE)	SUMBE	375000
GR C KINGMAN (GB) - SKY LANTERN (IRE)	VENDOR	375000
B C SEA THE STARS (IRE) - NATURAL BEAUTY (GB)	SACKVILLEDONALD	375000
B F NO NAY NEVER (USA) - SILENT THOUGHTS (IRE)	NEWTOWN ANNER STUD	375000
TANCREDI (GB) B C KINGMAN (GB) - INTRICATELY (IRE)	JUDDMONTE FARMS	375000
B F LOPE DE VEGA (IRE) - MOI MEME (GB)	PADDY TWOMEY	375000
B F NO NAY NEVER (USA) - PARK BLOOM (IRE)	MANOR HOUSE FARM	375000
B C SIYOUNI (FR) - HOSTESS (GB)	M MAGNIER/WHITE BIRCH	375000
B F GALILEO (IRE) - PRINCESS NOOR (IRE)	RABBAH BS	370000
B C NO NAY NEVER (USA) - BRIGHT SAPPHIRE (IRE)	M V MAGNIER	360000
B F GALILEO (IRE) - SONG OF MY HEART (IRE)	M V MAGNIER	360000
TWILIGHT VISION (IRE) B F SEA THE STARS (IRE) - FLYING FAIRIES (IRE)	RABBAH BS	360000
BR F LE HAVRE (IRE) - INNEVERA (FR)	DAVID REDVERS	350000
MEGASTAR (GB) CH C SIYOUNI (FR) - STARSCOPE (GB)	VENDOR	350000
CH C MASAR (IRE) - GREAT HOPE (IRE)	GODOLPHIN	350000
B F LOPE DE VEGA (IRE) - CERCLE D'OR (IRE)	MIKE RYAN AGENT	350000
CH C EXCEED AND EXCEL (AUS) - EJAAZAH (IRE)	CHAUVIGNY GLOBAL EQUINE	350000
B F SAXON WARRIOR (JPN) - PYREAN (IRE)	ROGER VARIAN	350000
B C SEA THE STARS (IRE) - WAITINGFORTHEDAY (IRE)	STROUD COLEMAN BS	350000
B F SEA THE STARS (IRE) - AMAZONE (GER)	HIGHCLERE AGENCY	350000
CH F SIYOUNI (FR) - DANCING BREEZE (IRE)	SHADWELL ESTATE COMPANY	350000
B F COTAI GLORY (GB) - POYLE SOPHIE (GB)	BLANDFORD BS	350000
B F FRANKEL (GB) - LEGERETE (USA)	HADDEN BS	350000
B F LE HAVRE (IRE) - NISREEN (IRE)	RICHARD KNIGHT BS AGENT	350000
B F LE HAVRE (IRE) - DARTING (GB)	A C ELLIOTT	350000
B C STARSPANGLEDBANNER (AUS) - MRS GALLAGHER (GB)	RICHARD KNIGHT BS AGENT	350000
B C INVINCIBLE SPIRIT (IRE) - TIANA (GB)	SACKVILLEDONALD	350000
CH F SIYOUNI (FR) - SEA OF GRACE (IRE)	ROGER VARIAN	350000
B C NIGHT OF THUNDER (IRE) - SYNDICATE (GB)	STROUD COLEMAN BS	340000
B F STARSPANGLEDBANNER (AUS) - A HUGE DREAM (IRE)	HUGO MERRY BS	340000

Name and Breeding	Purchaser	Guineas
B C SEA THE STARS (IRE) - AWESOMETANK (GB)	STROUD COLEMAN BS	335000
B C FRANKEL (GB) - MIDNIGHT CROSSING (IRE)	BBA IRELAND	330000
B F INVINCIBLE SPIRIT (IRE) - CHIQUITA PICOSA (USA)	WHITE BIRCH FARM	325000
B C HAVANA GREY (GB) - DOTTED SWISS (IRE)	KARL & KELLY BURKE	325000
CH C NEW BAY (GB) - PARABOLA (GB)	BLANDFORD BS	325000
B F LE HAVRE (IRE) - GLENMAYNE (IRE)	JAKE SCOTT CAMPBELL	325000
BR C NO NAY NEVER (USA) - BELLE ISLE (GB)	KEVIN RYAN	325000
B C NO NAY NEVER (USA) - CZABO (GB)	C GORDON WATSON BS	325000
NATURAL BLONDE (IRE) CH F LOPE DE VEGA (IRE) - INTENSE PINK (GB)	C GORDON WATSON BS	325000
B F ZOUSTAR (AUS) - DICE GAME (GB)	KARL & KELLY BURKE	325000
B F BLUE POINT (IRE) - REHN'S NEST (IRE)	BLANDFORD BS	320000
B F GALILEO (IRE) - ALPHABET (GB)	BBA IRELAND	320000
GR C DARK ANGEL (IRE) - THE MUMS (GB)	BEN MCELROY AGENT	320000
B F INVINCIBLE SPIRIT (IRE) - PLAYFUL SOUND (GB)	A C ELLIOTT	320000
SUMMIT (IRE) B F KODIAC (GB) - SHAREVA (IRE)	CHEVELEY PARK STUD	320000
B F TOO DARN HOT (GB) - SECRET SENSE (USA)	SHADWELL ESTATE COMPANY	320000
CH C SAXON WARRIOR (JPN) - ALICE LIDDEL (IRE)	HIGHCLERE AGENCY	320000
B F LOPE DE VEGA (IRE) - MOTEO (IRE)	STROUD COLEMAN BS	320000
HUTCHENCE (GB) CH C FRANKEL (GB) - BAISSE (GB)	A C ELLIOTT, AGENT	310000
BR C NO NAY NEVER (USA) - AURORA SPRING (IRE)	STEPHEN HILLEN BS	310000
B C SEA THE STARS (IRE) - COME APRIL (GB)	JAMIE MCCALMONT BS	310000
B C SIYOUNI (FR) - PELLIGRINA (IRE)	M MAGNIER/WHITE BIRCH	300000
B C TEOFILO (IRE) - ALNAAS (GB)	JOSEPH O'BRIEN	300000
QAZAQ (FR) B C KINGMAN (GB) - QABALA (USA)	SUMBE	300000
B C SEA THE STARS (IRE) - CAVA (IRE)	ANDREW BALDING	300000
B F KODIAC (GB) - AFRICAN MOONLIGHT (UAE)	MANOR HOUSE FARM	300000
EXPLORINGTHESTARS (GB) CH C GALILEO (IRE) - PATH OF PEACE (GB)	WALMAC FARM LLC	300000
B F ADVERTISE (GB) - ARDIENTE (GB)	BEN MCELROY AGENT	300000
B F LOPE DE VEGA (IRE) - YARROW (IRE)	A C ELLIOTT	300000
B C TOO DARN HOT (GB) - FRANKEL LIGHT (IRE)	STROUD COLEMAN BS	300000
B C SAXON WARRIOR (JPN) - POUR DEUX (IRE)	ROGER VARIAN	300000
B C SHOWCASING (GB) - GIVE AND TAKE (GB)	KARL & KELLY BURKE	300000
B C CAMELOT (GB) - CLIQUE (GB)	M MAGNIER/WHITE BIRCH	300000
B C SEA THE STARS (IRE) - GREENISLAND (IRE)	MV MAGNIER	300000
B F KINGMAN (GB) - WINNING WAYS (AUS)	C GORDON WATSON BS	300000
GR C FRANKEL (GB) - AMERICA NOVA (FR)	C GORDON WATSON BS	300000
B C MAGNA GRECIA (IRE) - MARIA LEE (IRE)	MANOR HOUSE FARM	300000
B C FRANKEL (GB) - SILENT MORNING (GB)	BBA IRELAND	300000
B F LE HAVRE (IRE) - MATAURI PEARL (IRE)	MIKE RYAN	290000
CH C SIYOUNI (FR) - FLORIA TOSCA (IRE)	AMO RACING	290000
B C LOPE DE VEGA (IRE) - DEUCE AGAIN (GB)	EBONOS	290000
B F GOLDEN HORN (GB) - LIVIA'S DREAM (IRE)	WILLIAM HAGGAS	290000
B C NIGHT OF THUNDER (IRE) - ZEB UN NISA (GB)	A C ELLIOTT, AGENT	280000
B G AUSTRALIA (GB) - ULTRA APPEAL (IRE)	HONG KONG JOCKEY CLUB	280000
B C WOOTTON BASSETT (GB) - BLOSSOM MILLS (GB)	MANOR HOUSE FARM	280000
B F ZOUSTAR (AUS) - STELLAR GLOW (IRE)	DAITHI HARVEY	280000
STEP TO SOMEWHERE (GB) B F SEA THE STARS (IRE) - FRESH TERMS (GB)	MOYGLARE STUD FARM	280000
BR C DARK ANGEL (IRE) - SAMAAH (IRE)	A C ELLIOTT, AGENT	280000
SHAHA (IRE) B F CRACKSMAN (GB) - BOARD MEETING (IRE)	THOROUGHBRED RACING CORP	280000
CH F SIYOUNI (FR) - VIVIANITE (IRE)	SACKVILLEDONALD	280000
B C EXCEED AND EXCEL (AUS) - SHORTMILE LADY (IRE)	OLIVER ST LAWRENCE BS	270000
B F NIGHT OF THUNDER (IRE) - PURPLEST (GB)	BLANDFORD BS	270000
B C BLUE POINT (IRE) - DANETIME OUT (IRE)	BLANDFORD BS	270000
B C KINGMAN (GB) - FLECHE D'OR (GB)	A C ELLIOTT	270000
BR C SEA THE STARS (IRE) - SOLTADA (IRE)	GODOLPHIN	270000
B C NIGHT OF THUNDER (IRE) - ANCESTRAL (GB)	JOE FOLEY	270000
B C BLUE POINT (IRE) - VINTAGE MOLLY (GB)	PETER & ROSS DOYLE BS	265000
B F NIGHT OF THUNDER (IRE) - VIOLET'S GIFT (IRE)	AVENUE BS FOR MV MAGNIER	265000
CH C TEOFILO (IRE) - EMPRESS CONSORT (GB)	GODOLPHIN	260000
B F FRANKEL (GB) - BIG BROTHERS PRIDE (FR)	BBA IRELAND	260000
BR C TEN SOVEREIGNS (IRE) - FASHION DARLING (IRE)	M MAGNIER/WHITE BIRCH	260000
B C KINGMAN (GB) - LOVING THINGS (GB)	MIKE RYAN	260000
B C MEHMAS (IRE) - MY BETTER HALF (GB)	ROGER VARIAN	260000
B C SHOWCASING (GB) - MEGAN LILY (IRE)	STROUD COLEMAN BS	260000
B C WOOTTON BASSETT (GB) - BEAUTY SALON (GB)	JOE FOLEY	260000
GR F NIGHT OF THUNDER (IRE) - NAMHROODAH (IRE)	H MACAULEY BS/J LOGAN BS	260000
CH F LOPE DE VEGA (IRE) - SCREEN STAR (IRE)	JOSEPH BURKE BS	260000
FRIGHTENING (GB) B F NIGHT OF THUNDER (IRE) - TWIST 'N' SHAKE (GB)	A C ELLIOTT, AGENT	260000
CH C NEW BAY (GB) - ISPANKA (GB)	C GORDON WATSON BS	260000
SEEK AND DESTROY (IRE) B F SEA THE STARS (IRE) - SWIZZLE STICK (IRE)	A C ELLIOTT, AGENT	260000
B C BLUE POINT (IRE) - OUR JOY (IRE)	ANDREW BALDING	250000
CH C SIOUX NATION (USA) - REFUSETOLISTEN (IRE)	KEVIN RYAN	250000
B F NO NAY NEVER (USA) - GEMS (GB)	SACKVILLEDONALD	250000
B C KINGMAN (GB) - BALTIC BEST (IRE)	MIKE RYAN	250000
B C SIYOUNI (FR) - DAME DU ROI (IRE)	ROGER VARIAN	250000

Name and Breeding	Purchaser	Guineas
B C LOPE DE VEGA (IRE) - YUMMY MUMMY (GB)	BALLYLINCH STUD	250000
CH C MASAR (IRE) - SWEET LADY ROSE (IRE)	SACKVILLEDONALD	240000
B F TOO DARN HOT (GB) - GALICUIX (GB)	RABBAH BS	240000
B F STARSPANGLEDBANNER (AUS) - PERMISSION (GB)	M V MAGNIER	240000
B F COTAI GLORY (GB) - DIAMINDA (IRE)	SACKVILLEDONALD	240000
B C NO NAY NEVER (USA) - CHICA WHOPA (IRE)	BLANDFORD BS	240000
B F SEA THE STARS (IRE) - ZAIN HANA (GB)	BLANDFORD BS/MV MAGNIER	240000
B F TOO DARN HOT (GB) - MINWAH (IRE)	STROUD COLEMAN BS	230000
B F BATED BREATH (GB) - ADORE (GB)	MANOR HOUSE FARM	230000
B C NO NAY NEVER (USA) - FLOWER FASHION (FR)	JAMIE MCCALMONT BS	230000
B F GALILEO (IRE) - NAPLES BAY (USA)	BBA IRELAND	230000
TOPANGA (GB) B F SIYOUNI (FR) - TIME TUNNEL (GB)	BLANDFORD BS	230000
B C DARK ANGEL (IRE) - DR SIMPSON (FR)	HUBERT GUY	230000
B F FRANKEL (GB) - POPULIST (IRE)	BEN MCELROY	230000
B F GALILEO (IRE) - CHINTZ (IRE)	BBA IRELAND	230000
RO/GR C LOPE DE VEGA (IRE) - MAID UP (GB)	STROUD COLEMAN BS	230000
VALVANO (IRE) CH C NIGHT OF THUNDER (IRE) - VUELA (GB)	A C ELLIOTT, AGENT	220000
SANAT (IRE) B C INVINCIBLE SPIRIT (IRE) - SANTE (IRE)	SUMBE	220000
B C NO NAY NEVER (USA) - CONNIPTION (IRE)	C GORDON WATSON BS	220000
B C FRANKEL (GB) - LIMONAR (IRE)	MIKE RYAN	220000
B F MAKE BELIEVE (GB) - WONDERFULLY (IRE)	KATSUMI YOSHIDA	220000
KILT (IRE) B C KINGMAN (GB) - DANK (GB)	VENDOR	220000
CH C HAVANA GREY (GB) - DUNDUNAH (USA)	STROUD COLEMAN BS	220000
B F INVINCIBLE SPIRIT (IRE) - SHE'S MINE (IRE)	VENDOR	220000
CH F MEHMAS (IRE) - SPEED FREAK (GB)	SHADWELL ESTATE COMPANY	220000
B C INVINCIBLE SPIRIT (IRE) - MONDELICE (GB)	BEN MCELROY	220000
B F ZOFFANY (IRE) - INNOCENT AIR (GB)	JS BS	220000
NOBLE PASSION (IRE) CH F SEA THE STARS (IRE) - NOUVELLE NOBLESSE (GER)	POWERSTOWN STUD	220000
B C STARSPANGLEDBANNER (AUS) - KEEP DANCING (IRE)	HONG KONG JOCKEY CLUB	220000
B C CHURCHILL (IRE) - MISS FRANGIPANE (IRE)	SUZANNE ROBERTS	210000
B F KINGMAN (GB) - SPARKLING SURF (GB)	BEN MCELROY AGENT	210000
CH C MEHMAS (IRE) - QUEENSGATE (GB)	JOE FOLEY	210000
B F ZOUSTAR (AUS) - CRIMSON ROSETTE (IRE)	BLANDFORD BS	210000
B/BR F KODI BEAR (IRE) - SCARLET PLUM (GB)	KEVIN RYAN	210000
CH F LOPE DE VEGA (IRE) - RUBILEO (GB)	MIKE RYAN	210000
BR C SHOWCASING (GB) - FALSAFA (GB)	EBONOS	210000
B F NIGHT OF THUNDER (IRE) - DREAMING TIME (GB)	MIKE RYAN	210000
YOU GOT TO ME (GB) B F NATHANIEL (IRE) - BRUSHING (GB)	A C ELLIOTT, AGENT	200000
B/BR F NO NAY NEVER (USA) - PRICELESS (GB)	VENDOR	200000
B C ARDAD (IRE) - FELICIANA (GB)	BLANDFORD BS	200000
B C LOPE DE VEGA (IRE) - BELLA ESTRELLA (IRE)	MCKEEVER BS/C HILLS	200000
STOP THE CAVALRY (GB) B F LOPE DE VEGA (IRE) - CARTIEM (FR)	A C ELLIOTT, AGENT	200000
B C NIGHT OF THUNDER (IRE) - AFDHAAD (GB)	VENDOR	200000
B C NATHANIEL (IRE) - ROBEMA (GB)	STROUD COLEMAN BS	200000
B C FARHH (GB) - SEA CHORUS (GB)	STROUD COLEMAN BS	200000
B C SIYOUNI (FR) - ILLAUNMORE (USA)	M MAGNIER/WHITE BIRCH	200000
B C SEA THE STARS (IRE) - MISS KATIE MAE (IRE)	JAMES FERGUSON RACING	200000
B F NIGHT OF THUNDER (IRE) - ISTORIA (IRE)	PURA VIDA	200000
CH F SHOWCASING (GB) - BIRI'S ANGEL (IRE)	SHADWELL ESTATE COMPANY	200000
B F KINGMAN (GB) - SANS EQUIVOQUE (GER)	MIKE RYAN	200000
B C AUSTRALIA (GB) - MERVILLE (FR)	BADGERS BS	200000
B C ZOUSTAR (AUS) - TALAMPAYA (USA)	BLANDFORD BS	200000
B F NIGHT OF THUNDER (IRE) - MALASPINA (IRE)	KATSUMI YOSHIDA	200000
B C BLUE POINT (IRE) - SIAMSAIOCHT (IRE)	GODOLPHIN	200000
ARMORIAL (IRE) B C CAMELOT (GB) - LADY MAGDALA (IRE)	RICHARD RYAN	200000
CH C NIGHT OF THUNDER (IRE) - PLAYFULL SPIRIT (GB)	GAINSBOROUGH TB	200000
B C ACLAIM (IRE) - DOUGH ON THE GO (USA)	ARMANDO DUARTE	200000
CH C NIGHT OF THUNDER (IRE) - ANTHEM ALEXANDER (IRE)	JOSEPH O'BRIEN	200000
B F SIYOUNI (FR) - FOREIGN LEGIONARY (IRE)	KARL & KELLY BURKE	200000
CH C LOPE DE VEGA (IRE) - GOLDEN SONG (GB)	STEPHEN HILLEN BS	200000
B C LOPE DE VEGA (IRE) - REGALLINE (IRE)	VENDOR	200000
B C NO NAY NEVER (USA) - MISS NOURIYA (GB)	GODOLPHIN	200000
B C CHURCHILL (IRE) - APTICANTI (USA)	BADGERS BS	200000
MISS ALPILLES (GB) B F SEA THE STARS (IRE) - ALMA LINDA (GB)	NORRIS/HUNTINGDON	200000
CH F NO NAY NEVER (USA) - EASTER (IRE)	NORTH HILLS CO	200000
B C GALILEO (IRE) - VANZARA (FR)	BADGERS BS	200000
GOLDEN MYRRH (IRE) B F FRANKEL (GB) - SHEPHERDIA (IRE)	BBA IRELAND	200000
RHETORICAL (GB) B C WOOTTON BASSETT (GB) - MOTIVATION (FR)	HIGHCLERE AGENCY	200000
B F ADVERTISE (GB) - SWING OUT SISTER (IRE)	KILBRIDE EQUINE	200000
B C KINGMAN (GB) - BEYOND THE SEA (USA)	VENDOR	200000
CH C NIGHT OF THUNDER (IRE) - PARTRIDGE (IRE)	JOE FOLEY	195000
B C NIGHT OF THUNDER (IRE) - LOOKS A MILLION (GB)	STROUD COLEMAN BS	190000
B F BLUE POINT (IRE) - MOOJHA (USA)	HIGHCLERE AGENCY	190000
B C CAMELOT (GB) - ALOUJA (IRE)	HIGHCLERE AGENCY	190000
B F TOO DARN HOT (GB) - AL MAHMEYAH (GB)	LONGWAYS STABLES	190000

Name and Breeding	Purchaser	Guineas
B C BLUE POINT (IRE) - WILD CHILD (IRE)	MIKE RYAN	190000
B C KINGMAN (GB) - ZONDAQ (USA)	JOE FOLEY	190000
B F DARK ANGEL (IRE) - LIDANSKI (IRE)	BBA IRELAND	190000
B F LE HAVRE (IRE) - ELLE MAXIMA (GER)	MANOR HOUSE FARM	190000
B F DUBAWI (IRE) - GEISHA GIRL (IRE)	JOE FOLEY	190000
B C INVINCIBLE SPIRIT (IRE) - WADAA (USA)	MIKE RYAN	190000
CH C FRANKEL (GB) - NOYELLES (IRE)	JOSEPH O'BRIEN	190000
CH C NIGHT OF THUNDER (IRE) - IL PALAZZO (USA)	FEDERICO BARBERINI	185000
B F DARK ANGEL (IRE) - PASTORAL GIRL (GB)	JOE FOLEY	180000
B C GALILEO (IRE) - AMAZING MARIA (IRE)	JOE FOLEY	180000
GODSEND (GB) CH C NATHANIEL (IRE) - FLORISS (GB)	OLIVER ST LAWRENCE BS	180000
B C NIGHT OF THUNDER (IRE) - IMPALA (GB)	VENDOR	180000
B C DARK ANGEL (IRE) - SILENT MOMENT (USA)	HONG KONG JOCKEY CLUB	180000
B F WOOTTON BASSETT (GB) - KAZEERA (GB)	CHERIE DEVAUX/D INGORDO	180000
B C WOOTTON BASSETT (GB) - LINCOLN TALE (IRE)	STROUD COLEMAN BS	180000
GR C DARK ANGEL (IRE) - BELDALE MEMORY (IRE)	CLIVE COX RACING	180000
B F INVINCIBLE SPIRIT (IRE) - ALWAYSANDFOREVER (IRE)	A C ELLIOTT, AGENT	180000
B C MEHMAS (IRE) - AJLA (IRE)	BBA IRELAND	180000
B C LAND FORCE (IRE) - SCARBOROUGH FAIR (GB)	RICHARD KNIGHT BS AGENT	180000
CH C NIGHT OF THUNDER (IRE) - STEP SEQUENCE (GB)	KEVIN RYAN	180000
B C WOOTTON BASSETT (GB) - QUARA (IRE)	JOE FOLEY	180000
B C TERRITORIES (IRE) - ACQUAINTED (GB)	JOHN FOOTE BS	180000
CH C DUBAWI (IRE) - FADHAYYIL (IRE)	YEOMANSTOWN STUD	180000
B F INNS OF COURT (IRE) - SOFT POWER (IRE)	JS BS	175000
B C NIGHT OF THUNDER (IRE) - ELSHAADIN (GB)	BALLYHIMIKIN STUD	175000
B C BLUE POINT (IRE) - SHEMIYLA (FR)	STROUD COLEMAN BS	170000
B F IFFRAAJ (GB) - GALMARLEY (GB)	FEDERICO BARBERINI	170000
GAMES PEOPLE PLAY (IRE) B F SEA THE STARS (IRE) - PRETTY DIAMOND (IRE)	A C ELLIOTT, AGENT	170000
B C SHOWCASING (GB) - BROGAN (GB)	BEN MCELROY AGENT	170000
B C TOO DARN HOT (GB) - COMPOSTELA (GB)	BLANDFORD BS	170000
B C NIGHT OF THUNDER (IRE) - FAIRY DANCER (IRE)	JOHN FOOTE BS	170000
CH C NIGHT OF THUNDER (IRE) - AL ANDALYYA (USA)	BBA IRELAND	170000
B C BLUE POINT (IRE) - AFFABILITY (IRE)	JOHN BUTLER RACING	170000
BR C CALYX (GB) - DAZZLING ROSE (GB)	M V MAGNIER	170000
B F NIGHT OF THUNDER (IRE) - SHEMDA (IRE)	MIKE RYAN	170000
FEIGNING MADNESS (GB) CH C ULYSSES (IRE) - DANCE THE DREAM (GB)	A C ELLIOTT, AGENT	170000
GR F DANDY MAN (IRE) - WRONG ANSWER (GB)	JAMIE MCCALMONT BS	170000
B C SIYOUNI (FR) - WALK IN BEAUTY (IRE)	VENDOR	170000
B F NIGHT OF THUNDER (IRE) - HAVRE DE PAIX (FR)	BLANDFORD BS	170000
B F SHOWCASING (GB) - MIDNIGHTLY (GB)	PADDY TWOMEY	160000
RECALL (GB) B C GOLDEN HORN (GB) - ALWAYS REMEMBERED (IRE)	OLIVER ST LAWRENCE BS	160000
CH C MASAR (IRE) - SHALANAYA (IRE)	QATAR RACING	160000
SUGAR ROAD (GB) CH C MASAR (IRE) - MUSCOVADO (USA)	ANDREW BALDING	160000
ECONOMICS (GB) CH C NIGHT OF THUNDER (IRE) - LA POMME D'AMOUR (GB)	HIGHCLERE AGENCY	160000
B C FARHH (GB) - THELADYINQUESTION (GB)	JAMES FERGUSON RACING	160000
B C CRACKSMAN (GB) - WONDERWORLD (GER)	DURCAN BS	160000
B C KODIAC (GB) - VIBE QUEEN (IRE)	C GORDON WATSON BS	160000
B F NO NAY NEVER (USA) - BALANKIYA (IRE)	VENDOR	160000
B F JUSTIFY (USA) - SOUTH SEA PEARL (IRE)	MONCEAUX	160000
B C CAMELOT (GB) - PARSNIP (IRE)	BLANDFORD BS	160000
CH F ZOUSTAR (AUS) - FAST LILY (IRE)	RICHARD HUGHES RACING	160000
B F SIYOUNI (FR) - MOONLIT GARDEN (IRE)	STROUD COLEMAN BS	160000
B F LOPE DE VEGA (IRE) - FINE TIME (GB)	BLANDFORD BS	160000
B F GALIWAY (GB) - KENDAM (FR)	MCKEEVER BS/C HILLS	160000
B C BLUE POINT (IRE) - SAR OICHE (IRE)	ABDULLAH ALMALEK ALSABAH	160000
APPROVAL (GB) CH C LE HAVRE (IRE) - ALNORAS (GB)	HIGHCLERE AGENCY	160000
B F TOO DARN HOT (GB) - ARCTIC OCEAN (IRE)	C GORDON WATSON BS	160000
CUBAN MELODY (GB) B F HAVANA GREY (GB) - JACQUOTTE DELAHAYE (GB)	HIGHCLERE AGENCY	155000
B F KESSAAR (IRE) - RAJMAHAL (UAE)	DURCAN BS	155000
BR C NO NAY NEVER (USA) - LADY CORSICA (IRE)	BBA IRELAND	155000
B C MEHMAS (IRE) - DUTCH MONARCH (GB)	BBA IRELAND	150000
CH C SEA THE STARS (IRE) - SWANSDOWN (GB)	MARTYN MEADE	150000
B C DUBAWI (IRE) - PREFER (IRE)	RABBAH BS	150000
B C KODIAC (GB) - INTAGLIA (GB)	JOHN FOOTE BS	150000
B C KODIAC (GB) - IRISH STEPS (USA)	JS BS	150000
DARING LEGEND (GB) B C DARK ANGEL (IRE) - SWISS AIR (GB)	AVENUE BS	150000
B C ULYSSES (IRE) - SACRE CAROLINE (USA)	EBONOS	150000
B C SEA THE STARS (IRE) - KISSABLE (IRE)	GODOLPHIN	150000
B F TOO DARN HOT (GB) - IONIC (GB)	VENDOR	150000
B F NIGHT OF THUNDER (IRE) - PENNY PEPPER (IRE)	JASON KELLY BS	150000
B C SEA THE STARS (IRE) - NEWTON'S ANGEL (IRE)	AVENUE BS	150000
B F KINGMAN (GB) - PREDAWN (IRE)	VENDOR	150000
CH C CHURCHILL (IRE) - FLAWLESS JEWEL (FR)	STROUD COLEMAN BS	150000
B C MAGNA GRECIA (IRE) - CHIBOLA (ARG)	VENDOR	150000
BR C PROFITABLE (IRE) - GRACE RAFAELA (IRE)	PETER & ROSS DOYLE BS	150000

Name and Breeding	Purchaser	Guineas
CH F NO NAY NEVER (USA) - POLDHU (GB)	RABBAH BS	150000
B C ACCLAMATION (GB) - PARTY FOR EVER (IRE)	MANOR HOUSE FARM	150000
B C INVINCIBLE SPIRIT (IRE) - EFFERVESCE (IRE)	JS BS/T CLOVER RACING	150000
KJELL HROAR (IRE) B C ZOFFANY (IRE) - ALPINE AIR (GB)	PAUL HARLEY BS	150000
B C GALILEO GOLD (GB) - SAGELY (IRE)	BLANDFORD BS	150000
B F NO NAY NEVER (USA) - SHERANDA (IRE)	PETER & ROSS DOYLE BS	150000
B C TEN SOVEREIGNS (IRE) - WESTERN SKY (GB)	ANDREW BALDING	150000
HAVANA CIGAR (GB) GR C HAVANA GREY (GB) - SPECULATING (IRE)	OCEANIC BS	150000
DILARA (IRE) CH F NIGHT OF THUNDER (IRE) - DIVISIMO (GB)	SUMBE	150000
B C FRANKEL (GB) - UMNIYAH (IRE)	GODOLPHIN	150000
AUTUMN DREAM (IRE) B F SIOUX NATION (USA) - YDILLIQUE (IRE)	TROY STEVE BS	150000
B C LOPE DE VEGA (IRE) - BURNING RULES (IRE)	WILLIAM HAGGAS	150000
B F KODIAC (GB) - ELKMAIT (GB)	C GORDON WATSON BS	150000
B F SIYOUNI (FR) - SO HI SOCIETY (IRE)	PETER & ROSS DOYLE BS	150000
HALVA (IRE) B F KODIAC (GB) - HOME CUMMINS (IRE)	SUMBE	150000
B C LOPE DE VEGA (IRE) - MODERNSTONE (GB)	VENDOR	150000
B C SEA THE STARS (IRE) - DUCHESS OF FRANCE (IRE)	EBONOS	150000
B C LOPE DE VEGA (IRE) - AZANARA (IRE)	AVENUE BS	150000
HEATER (IRE) BR C NO NAY NEVER (USA) - WEEKEND FLING (USA)	A C ELLIOTT, AGENT	145000
AL MUDHAFFAR (IRE) B C WOOTTON BASSETT (GB) - FAIRLY FAIR (FR)	JOSEPH O'BRIEN	145000
CH F CALYX (GB) - MIA DIVINA (GB)	ANDREW BALDING	145000
CH C CHURCHILL (IRE) - BARTER (GB)	ROGER CHARLTON	145000
CH C MASTERCRAFTSMAN (IRE) - PLAYWITHMYHEART (GB)	VENDOR	145000
BASIC INSTINCT (IRE) B F MEHMAS (IRE) - AHAALY (GB)	VENDOR	145000
B C SEA THE STARS (IRE) - SEQUILLA (FR)	PETER & ROSS DOYLE BS	145000
CH C STARSPANGLEDBANNER (AUS) - FEDERATION (GB)	DONNACHA O'BRIEN	140000
B C STUDY OF MAN (IRE) - ALMA MATER (GB)	AVENUE BS	140000
B F SEA THE STARS (IRE) - LUSTROUS (GB)	BBA IRELAND	140000
CH C LOPE DE VEGA (IRE) - HERTFORD DANCER (GB)	JAMES FERGUSON RACING	140000
B C MEHMAS (IRE) - FANCIFUL MISS (GB)	STROUD COLEMAN BS	140000
B C SIYOUNI (FR) - LAMORLAYE (IRE)	VENDOR	140000
THE BITTER MOOSE (IRE) B C KODIAC (GB) - BARONESS (IRE)	SACKVILLEDONALD	140000
B C KINGMAN (GB) - STELLAR PATH (FR)	POWERSTOWN STUD	140000
FLAG OF LOVE (IRE) GR F STARSPANGLEDBANNER (AUS) - APHRODITE'S ANGEL (IRE)	VENDOR	140000
B C SHOWCASING (GB) - NEW DAY DAWN (IRE)	SHADWELL ESTATE COMPANY	140000
B C CAMELOT (GB) - BLACK ENVY (GB)	VENDOR	140000
CH C SIYOUNI (FR) - WALDNAH (GB)	VENDOR	140000
CH C STARSPANGLEDBANNER (AUS) - CRISTAL FASHION (IRE)	BADGERS BS	140000
B C INVINCIBLE SPIRIT (IRE) - QUEEN OF PARIS (GB)	NOEL WILSON	140000
CH F ZOUSTAR (AUS) - CASTLE HILL CASSIE (IRE)	KARL BURKE	140000
B C INVINCIBLE ARMY (IRE) - FANCY FEATHERS (IRE)	SACKVILLEDONALD	140000
B C ZOUSTAR (AUS) - GOLDEN STUNNER (IRE)	JILL LAMB BS	140000
B C GLENEAGLES (IRE) - SHANNOW (IRE)	CORMAC MCCORMACK	140000
B F ZOUSTAR (AUS) - CAROLINAE (GB)	STROUD COLEMAN BS	140000
B C MEHMAS (IRE) - CLASSIC IMAGE (GB)	PETER & ROSS DOYLE	135000
CH C GALILEO (IRE) - AFTER (IRE)	D FARRINGTON	135000
BLUE COLLAR (IRE) B C STARSPANGLEDBANNER (AUS) - NAVIGATE BY STARS (IRE)	PETER & ROSS DOYLE BS	135000
B C NOBLE MISSION (GB) - QUEEN OF TIME (GB)	SACKVILLEDONALD	135000
B C CAMELOT (GB) - PATINEUSE (IRE)	JOSEPH O'BRIEN	135000
CH F WALDGEIST (GB) - CYNTHIANA (FR)	MIKE RYAN	135000
B F OASIS DREAM (GB) - BARROCHE (IRE)	CHERIE DEVAUX/D INGORDO	135000
B C LAND FORCE (IRE) - I HEARYOU KNOCKING (IRE)	FEDERICO BARBERINI	135000
B F IFFRAAJ (GB) - PERFECT BLESSINGS (IRE)	VENDOR	135000
WILD WAVES (IRE) CH C CRYSTAL OCEAN (GB) - GUENEA (GB)	ANDREW BALDING	135000
B C TOO DARN HOT (GB) - IMPRESSIONIST (IRE)	JOE FOLEY	130000
AMSTERDAM (GB) CH C DUTCH ART (GB) - WILDE AMBITION (IRE)	SACKVILLEDONALD	130000
WITHOUT ME (IRE) CH F FRANKEL (GB) - DULCIAN (IRE)	A C ELLIOTT, AGENT	130000
CH C NO NAY NEVER (USA) - LADY AQUITAINE (USA)	EIGHTEEN BS	130000
LET'S GET EM (GB) B C WOOTTON BASSETT (GB) - LOAVES AND FISHES (GB)	A C ELLIOTT, AGENT	130000
B F U S NAVY FLAG (USA) - STOR MO CHROI (IRE)	GALLOWAY STUD	130000
B C KODIAC (GB) - SEA OF DREAMS (IRE)	JILL LAMB BS	130000
GR C EXCEED AND EXCEL (AUS) - LADY ROSAMUNDE (GB)	VENDOR	130000
B C MAGNA GRECIA (IRE) - SHALOUSHKA (IRE)	STROUD COLEMAN BS	130000
B C ARDAD (IRE) - MARA GREY (IRE)	BLANDFORD BS	130000
MART (GB) B/GR C DARK ANGEL (IRE) - ADORN (GB)	A C ELLIOTT, AGENT	130000
B F TEN SOVEREIGNS (IRE) - FLAVIA TATIANA (IRE)	HUGO MERRY BS	130000
B C BLUE POINT (IRE) - SOLAR EVENT (GB)	PETER & ROSS DOYLE BS	130000
B C GALILEO (IRE) - PINK DOGWOOD (IRE)	MARTYN MEADE	130000
B C TIME TEST (GB) - STAY FOREVER (FR)	A C ELLIOTT, AGENT	130000
B C CABLE BAY (IRE) - RAINBOW VALE (FR)	KEN CONDON	130000
GENERAL ASSEMBLY (IRE) CH C STARSPANGLEDBANNER (AUS) - BLACK RODDED (GB)	RICHARD RYAN	130000
B C CRACKSMAN (GB) - PERFECT DELIGHT (GB)	SACKVILLEDONALD	130000
B C BLUE POINT (IRE) - ROMAN VENTURE (IRE)	ABDULLAH ALMALEK ALSABAH	130000
LIGHTNING LEO (GB) CH C NIGHT OF THUNDER (IRE) - SHADA (IRE)	A C ELLIOTT, AGENT	130000
B C FRANKEL (GB) - HOH MY DARLING (GB)	TALLY-HO STUD	130000

Name and Breeding	Purchaser	Guineas
B C MEHMAS (IRE) - HASSAAD (GB)	FEDERICO BARBERINI	125000
B F BLUE POINT (IRE) - VIA LATTEA (IRE)	BLANDFORD BS	125000
SALAH AL DEEN (IRE) B C MAGNA GRECIA (IRE) - FASNELA (IRE)	JOSEPH O'BRIEN	125000
B C CAPPELLA SANSEVERO (GB) - GOODNIGHT AND JOY (IRE)	SACKVILLEDONALD	125000
B F CRACKSMAN (GB) - CONSTANT DREAM (GB)	STROUD COLEMAN BS	125000
BERYL (GB) CH F LOPE DE VEGA (IRE) - CRYSTAL ZVEZDA (GB)	JUDDMONTE FARMS	125000
B F HAVANA GREY (GB) - SO BRAVE (GB)	JOE FOLEY	125000
CH C SAXON WARRIOR (JPN) - PURE SYMMETRY (USA)	ROGER CHARLTON	125000
B C GALILEO (IRE) - TIMBUKTU (IRE)	JEREMY BRUMMITT	125000
GR C CARAVAGGIO (USA) - SHIRLEY BLADE (IRE)	SUZANNE ROBERTS	125000
B C SAXON WARRIOR (JPN) - SHORT CALL (IRE)	D FARRINGTON	125000
PHOENIX PASSION (IRE) B C TOO DARN HOT (GB) - SOUVENIR DELONDRES (FR)	OPULENCE THOROUGHBREDS	125000
CH C EXCEED AND EXCEL (AUS) - ALCHEMILLA (GB)	SACKVILLEDONALD	125000
FLEURS DES BOIS (IRE) CH F WALDGEIST (GB) - FLEURISSIMO (GB)	STROUD COLEMAN BS	125000
B C BELARDO (IRE) - PETITS POTINS (IRE)	SACKVILLEDONALD	125000
B F LAND FORCE (IRE) - SEEING RED (IRE)	SHADWELL ESTATE COMPANY	120000
B F TOO DARN HOT (GB) - SMART CHANGE (USA)	VENDOR	120000
B C NO NAY NEVER (USA) - ELOQUENT (IRE)	RABBAH BS	120000
B C ACCLAMATION (GB) - PELLUCID (GB)	C GORDON WATSON BS	120000
B C FASTNET ROCK (AUS) - PURPLE MAGIC (GB)	JEBEL ALI STABLES	120000
B C DANDY MAN (IRE) - PERFECT BEAUTY (GB)	C GORDON WATSON BS	120000
RETRACEMENT (IRE) CH C AUSTRALIA (GB) - PICCADILLY FILLY (IRE)	HIGHFLYER BS	120000
B F CHURCHILL (IRE) - FEARN'S PIPPIN (GB)	EBONOS	120000
B F NATHANIEL (IRE) - ROYAL EMPRESS (IRE)	STROUD COLEMAN BS	120000
B F EXPERT EYE (GB) - MISS ATOMIC BOMB (GB)	PURA VIDA 2022	120000
B F ZOUSTAR (AUS) - CORAL SEA (GB)	CHRIS WALLER RACING	120000
B/BR F LAND FORCE (IRE) - BONHOMIE (GB)	A C ELLIOTT, AGENT	120000
B C CHURCHILL (IRE) - MISTIME (IRE)	GAELIC BS	120000
B F TOO DARN HOT (GB) - MIRROR CITY (GB)	JAMIE MCCALMONT BS	120000
GR C DARK ANGEL (IRE) - SHANG SHANG SHANG (USA)	EBONOS	120000
BR F LE HAVRE (IRE) - ALTHEA ROSE (IRE)	DONNACHA O'BRIEN	120000
B C SEA THE STARS (IRE) - COMPLEXION (GB)	VENDOR	120000
CH F LOPE DE VEGA (IRE) - COCONUT CREME (GB)	JONATHAN BARNETT	120000
TIME SIGNATURE (GB) B C DARK ANGEL (IRE) - BETTY F (GB)	BLANDFORD BS	120000
B C LOPE DE VEGA (IRE) - TERRE (FR)	VENDOR	120000
B C SHALAA (IRE) - DREAM DANA (IRE)	OLIVER ST LAWRENCE BS	120000
B C CAMELOT (GB) - EGYPTIAN SKY (IRE)	JOSEPH O'BRIEN	120000
CH C TERRITORIES (IRE) - WEARING WINGS (GB)	ANDREW BALDING	120000
GR F DARK ANGEL (IRE) - SHELBYSMILE (USA)	MIKE RYAN	120000
CH C SEA THE MOON (GER) - NIMIETY (GB)	RICHARD HUGHES RACING	120000
B F AWTAAD (IRE) - ZAAQYA (GB)	OLLIE SANGSTER	120000
B F ADVERTISE (GB) - SELF CENTRED (GB)	HUGO MERRY BS	120000
B F CHURCHILL (IRE) - QATAR PRINCESS (IRE)	VENDOR	120000
B F CALYX (GB) - PROMISE ME (IRE)	RABBAH BS	120000
B F TEN SOVEREIGNS (IRE) - MAID TO DREAM (GB)	BLANDFORD BS & PARTNERS	120000

HIGH-PRICED YEARLINGS OF 2022 AT GOFFS IRELAND

The following yearlings realised 76,000 euros and over at Goffs Ireland Sales in 2022:

Name and Breeding	Purchaser	Euros
B/BR F NO NAY NEVER (USA) - MUIRIN (IRE)	RICHARD KNIGHT BS AGENT	2600000
B F GALILEO (IRE) - SIGNORA CABELLO (IRE)	NEWTOWN ANNER STUD	750000
ODIN LEGACY (IRE) B C KODIAC (GB) - FIKRAH (GB)	PETER & ROSS DOYLE BS	575000
B F NIGHT OF THUNDER (IRE) - RAPACITY ALEXANDER (IRE)	BBA IRELAND	525000
B/BR C TEN SOVEREIGNS (IRE) - INDIGO BUTTERFLY (FR)	WEST BS	500000
CH F SEA THE STARS (IRE) - ZVARKHOVA (FR)	HUGO MERRY BS	460000
B C GALILEO (IRE) - BELESTA (GB)	JUSTIN CASSE, AGENT	450000
CH C NEW BAY (GB) - FALLING PETALS (IRE)	AMANDA SKIFFINGTON	450000
B F GALILEO (IRE) - NICKNAME (USA)	BBA IRELAND	430000
TOUCH THE MOON (IRE) B C SEA THE STARS (IRE) - HOLDA (IRE)	MANOR HOUSE FARM	425000
B F BLUE POINT (IRE) - BADR AL BADOOR (IRE)	MV MAGNIER	420000
B F NO NAY NEVER (USA) - CANADA WATER (GB)	MV MAGNIER	360000
B C FRANKEL (GB) - MISS KELLER (IRE)	PETER & ROSS DOYLE BS	360000
HEAT OF PASSION (GB) B F DUBAWI (IRE) - HERE TO ETERNITY (USA)	BBA IRELAND	350000
GR F NIGHT OF THUNDER (IRE) - PRINCESS DE LUNE (IRE)	AVENUE BLOOSTOCK	350000
CH F NIGHT OF THUNDER (IRE) - SKILL SET (IRE)	RABBAH BS	340000
CH F STARSPANGLEDBANNER (AUS) - BALAKERA (IRE)	OLIVIA PERKINS MACKEY	330000
B F STARSPANGLEDBANNER (AUS) - WILLOUGHBY (IRE)	BBA IRELAND	325000
B C KINGMAN (GB) - MAJESTIC SILVER (IRE)	ROGER VARIAN	320000
B C GALILEO (IRE) - TAKE ME WITH YOU (USA)	JOE FOLEY	310000
B F ZOUSTAR (AUS) - BABYLONIAN (GB)	NEWTOWN ANNER STUD	300000
B C PRINCE OF LIR (IRE) - BISOUS Y BESOS (IRE)	PETER & ROSS DOYLE BS	300000
B G SIYOUNI (FR) - HIBISCUS (IRE)	HKJC	300000
B F ADVERTISE (GB) - TREELINE (GB)	D HAYDEN	300000
B F TEN SOVEREIGNS (IRE) - SAUCY SPIRIT (GB)	RABBAH BS/KILFRUSH	300000
B F BLUE POINT (IRE) - COSMIC LOVE (GB)	B GRASSICK BS	300000
B F FRANKEL (GB) - IMPROVE (IRE)	VENDOR	290000
B/BR C NO NAY NEVER (USA) - QUEEN ISEULT (GB)	JASON TAYLOR EQUINE, USA	280000
B F INVINCIBLE SPIRIT (IRE) - SOPHIE GERMAIN (IRE)	DAVID REDVERS	280000
B C NIGHT OF THUNDER (IRE) - BUYING TROUBLE (USA)	BLANDFORD BS	270000
B C NO NAY NEVER (USA) - QUESTION TIMES (GB)	RICHARD KNIGHT BS AGENT	260000
B F MEHMAS (IRE) - CHAMPAGNE OR WATER (IRE)	PADDY TWOMEY	260000
B F KODIAC (GB) - BIONIC BUFFY (IRE)	MIKE FOWLER FOR TEAM D	260000
B C GALILEO (IRE) - WHERE (IRE)	DONNACHA O BRIEN	250000
CH C STARSPANGLEDBANNER (AUS) - FIUNTACH (IRE)	HAMISH MACAULEY BS	250000
KILDARE LEGEND (IRE) CH C SEA THE STARS (IRE) - MISS AIGLONNE (GB)	AVENUE BS	250000
B F CHURCHILL (IRE) - ISHVANA (IRE)	MYRACEHORSE/MV MAGNIER	250000
B F ZOUSTAR (AUS) - TIGER EYE (IRE)	JIM RYAN	250000
B F TEOFILO (IRE) - HYMN OF THE DAWN (USA)	BBA IRELAND	245000
JUNGLE DEMON (IRE) B C GALILEO (IRE) - TERROR (IRE)	MANOR HOUSE FARM	240000
B F KINGMAN (GB) - KNOCKNAGREE (IRE)	FORM BS	240000
B C NO NAY NEVER (USA) - HEIGHT OF ELEGANCE (IRE)	PHILIP ANTONACCI	235000
B C SIYOUNI (FR) - FLORA DANICA (IRE)	BBA IRELAND	235000
BR F TEN SOVEREIGNS (IRE) - SODASHY (IRE)	JONATHAN GREEN/DJ STABLE	235000
B F INVINCIBLE SPIRIT (IRE) - I AM BEAUTIFUL (IRE)	BBA IRELAND	235000
B C FRANKEL (GB) - SIVOLIERE (IRE)	BBA IRELAND	230000
B F FRANKEL (GB) - MONROE BAY (IRE)	BBA IRELAND	230000
TECHNICAL FAULT (IRE) CH C NO NAY NEVER (USA) - SHAHRALASAL (IRE)	MANOR HOUSE FARM	230000
B F CHURCHILL (IRE) - NAJMA (GB)	AMANDA SKIFFINGTON	230000
B F FRANKEL (GB) - LOVE MAGIC (GB)	J HARRINGTON RACING	230000
CH G NIGHT OF THUNDER (IRE) - BLANCHE NEIGE (GB)	HKJC	220000
NEVERSTOPDREAMING (IRE) GR/GR F NO NAY NEVER (USA) - SNOWFLAKES (IRE)	MANOR HOUSE FARM	220000
B C NIGHT OF THUNDER (IRE) - MYTHIE (FR)	AMANDA SKIFFINGTON	220000
B C TEN SOVEREIGNS (IRE) - FANCY VIVID (IRE)	MV MAGNIER	220000
B F KINGMAN (GB) - SOLAGE (GB)	VENDOR	220000
B F CHURCHILL (IRE) - YOU'LL BE MINE (USA)	BBA IRELAND	215000
B C INVINCIBLE SPIRIT (IRE) - WORLD OF GOOD (GB)	PETER & ROSS DOYLE BS	210000
B F BLUE POINT (IRE) - DUCHESS OF DANZIG (GER)	LINEHAN BS/J MURTAGH	210000
CH C SHOWCASING (GB) - SOLFILIA (GB)	BBA IRELAND	200000
B F CHURCHILL (IRE) - NAYARRA (IRE)	OLIVER ST LAWRENCE BS	200000
B F SEA THE STARS (IRE) - PURE ART (GB)	CREIGHTON SCHWARTZ BS	200000
CH F COTAI GLORY (GB) - FIDAAHA (IRE)	KEN CONDON	200000
B F WALDGEIST (GB) - EZALLI (IRE)	VENDOR	200000
GR F PHOENIX OF SPAIN (IRE) - THAMES PAGEANT (GB)	BEN MCELROY AGENT	200000
B F MAGNA GRECIA (IRE) - QUICK CHAT (USA)	JASON TAYLOR EQUINE, USA	200000
CELESTIAL REIGN (IRE) B C ZOFFANY (IRE) - SARAWATI (IRE)	RICHARD RYAN	200000
B C SIYOUNI (FR) - ISABEL DE URBINA (IRE)	GROVE STUD (P.S.)	200000

Name and Breeding	Purchaser	Euros
B F WALDGEIST (GB) - ALAVA (IRE)	LEASON BS	200000
NU DISCO (IRE) B C SIYOUNI (FR) - SEQUINED (USA)	MANOR HOUSE FARM	200000
CH C CHURCHILL (IRE) - LADY'S PURSE (GB)	SACKVILLEDONALD	200000
CUBAN TIGER (GB) B C HAVANA GREY (GB) - SHIRLEY'S KITTEN (USA)	ANDREW BALDING	200000
B C DANDY MAN (IRE) - MORE RESPECT (IRE)	BBA IRELAND	195000
B F ACCLAMATION (GB) - QUALITY TIME (IRE)	J DAVISON	195000
B C ACCLAMATION (GB) - RAMONE (IRE)	QATAR RACING	190000
B F VIOLENCE (USA) - DARING DIVA (GB)	NIALL BRENNAN	190000
STARSHINE LEGEND (IRE) B C SEA THE STARS (IRE) - BLISSFUL BEAT (GB)	AVENUE BS	190000
B C STUDY OF MAN (IRE) - STARLIT SANDS (GB)	QATAR RACING	185000
B C WOOTTON BASSETT (GB) - SANDRA'S SECRET (IRE)	JOE FOLEY	185000
B C DARK ANGEL (IRE) - AZWAH (GB)	JILL LAMB BS	185000
B C GALILEO (IRE) - MUSIC BOX (IRE)	HARAS D'ETREHAM (P.S.)	180000
B C SIYOUNI (FR) - RETICENT ANGEL (IRE)	VENDOR	180000
B C LOPE DE VEGA (IRE) - WAHEEBAH (IRE)	PHILIP ANTONACCI	180000
B F INVINCIBLE SPIRIT (IRE) - SEA MONA (USA)	D HAYDEN	180000
BR C KODIAC (GB) - KENDAL MINT (GB)	JOE FOLEY	180000
CH F DUTCH ART (GB) - SCHEME (GB)	M V MAGNIER	180000
B C GALILEO (IRE) - SNOW QUEEN (IRE)	BBA IRELAND	180000
B C TOO DARN HOT (GB) - OVER THE MOON (IRE)	DWAYNE WOODS	180000
CH F GLENEAGLES (IRE) - MISS MACNAMARA (IRE)	PADDY TWOMEY	175000
B F GLENEAGLES (IRE) - TASTE THE SALT (IRE)	SACKVILLEDONALD	175000
B C NO NAY NEVER (USA) - LIKE A STAR (IRE)	JOSEPH O'BRIEN (P.S.)	175000
B F TEN SOVEREIGNS (IRE) - BODAK (IRE)	KEN CONDON	170000
B F CHURCHILL (IRE) - MNEMONIC ALEXANDER (IRE)	MIKE FOWLER AND TEAM D	170000
B C INNS OF COURT (IRE) - VIDA AMOROSA (IRE)	AMO RACING/ROBSON AGUIAR	170000
B C MAKE BELIEVE (GB) - FLEUR DE CACTUS (IRE)	FEDERICO BARBERINI	170000
B F TEOFILO (IRE) - SULARINA (IRE)	JOE FOLEY	165000
BORN THIS WAY (IRE) B C LOPE DE VEGA (IRE) - WIZZ KID (IRE)	JAMES FERGUSON RACING	160000
B F KODIAC (GB) - MONTELLO (GB)	MIKE FOWLER AND TEAM D	160000
B F SIYOUNI (FR) - DREAM OF TARA (IRE)	JOHN MCCONNELL RACING	160000
B F DARK ANGEL (IRE) - HAY CHEWED (IRE)	RICHARD RYAN	160000
B F KODIAC (GB) - HUMBLE AND PROUD (IRE)	MIKE AKERS	160000
MADA MIA (IRE) GR F WOOTTON BASSETT (GB) - MIA CAPRI (IRE)	PETER & ROSS DOYLE BS	160000
B C NIGHT OF THUNDER (IRE) - LAUREN'S GIRL (IRE)	GROVE STUD	160000
B C U S NAVY FLAG (USA) - MANY HEARTS (USA)	SACKVILLEDONALD	160000
B F LOPE DE VEGA (IRE) - COTTONMOUTH (IRE)	GROVE STUD	160000
B C CAMELOT (GB) - QUEEN OF INDIA (IRE)	D FARRINGTON	160000
B C BLUE POINT (IRE) - FIREBIRD SONG (IRE)	ROBSON AGUIAR	155000
B/BR C MAGNA GRECIA (IRE) - RIO FESTIVAL (USA)	BLANDFORD BS	155000
STIPULATION (IRE) B C NEW BAY (GB) - DANAMIGHT (IRE)	MANOR HOUSE FARM	155000
B C MASTERCRAFTSMAN (IRE) - MONTE SOLARO (IRE)	H MACAULEY BS	150000
B C SIOUX NATION (USA) - KNOCK STARS (IRE)	D FARRINGTON	150000
CH C MEHMAS (IRE) - BROADWAY DUCHESS (IRE)	ROBSON AGUIAR	150000
B F CALYX (GB) - SHINE (GB)	CLAY SCHERER	150000
B F GLENEAGLES (IRE) - BURKE'S ROCK (GB)	JANE BUCHANAN, AGENT	150000
B F DARK ANGEL (IRE) - LAYLA JAMIL (IRE)	RABBAH BS	150000
B C NOT THIS TIME (USA) - MOREDIAMONDSPLEASE (USA)	JB BS	150000
B F NO NAY NEVER (USA) - INCA WOOD (UAE)	BBA IRELAND (P.S.)	150000
CH C SEA THE MOON (GER) - TRULY HONOURED (GB)	SACKVILLEDONALD	150000
B F CRACKSMAN (GB) - CARMENS FATE (GB)	FEDERICO BARBERINI	145000
B C MAGNA GRECIA (IRE) - CALLISTO STAR (IRE)	GETINTHEGAME.IE	145000
B/BR F CALYX (GB) - SURPRISINGLY (IRE)	AMO RACING/ROBSON AGUIAR	145000
B F EXPERT EYE (GB) - IT'S A WISH (GB)	PETER & ROSS DOYLE BS	145000
RIVIERA QUEEN (IRE) GR F CAMELOT (GB) - PAKORA (FR)	PETER & ROSS DOYLE BS	140000
B F GLENEAGLES (IRE) - SHENANIGANS (IRE)	BRIAN GRASSICK BS	140000
B C MAGNA GRECIA (IRE) - PRIMA LUCE (IRE)	MCKEEVER BS/C HILLS	140000
B/BR F NO NAY NEVER (USA) - BEST OF MY LOVE (IRE)	KEN CONDON	140000
B F NO NAY NEVER (USA) - LOVED (IRE)	JOSEPH O'BRIEN	140000
B F SEA THE STARS (IRE) - MAGNOLIA SPRINGS (IRE)	RABBAH BS	140000
UNIVERSAL STORY (IRE) B F SEA THE STARS (IRE) - NARRATIVE (IRE)	MANOR HOUSE FARM	140000
B F CHURCHILL (IRE) - SCHOOL RUN (IRE)	MERIDIAN INTERNATIONAL	135000
CH F GALILEO (IRE) - QUEEN BOUDICA (GB)	BBA IRELAND	135000
B F INNS OF COURT (IRE) - LADY LUCIA (IRE)	JASON KELLY BS	135000
B C EXCEED AND EXCEL (AUS) - INCHIKHAN (GB)	JIM TILTON	135000
BR F MAGNA GRECIA (IRE) - CHEETAH (GB)	GER LYONS RACING	130000
BLUE THUNDER (IRE) B F BLUE POINT (IRE) - PUSSYCAT LIPS (IRE)	RT RACING	130000
B F INVINCIBLE SPIRIT (IRE) - KERRY GAL (IRE)	VENDOR	130000
ANGEL PASS (IRE) B F DARK ANGEL (IRE) - AINTISARI (IRE)	SIR MARK PRESCOTT	130000
B F GREGORIAN (IRE) - ONOMATOMANIA (USA)	BEN MCELROY AGENT	130000

Name and Breeding	Purchaser	Euros
B F EXCEED AND EXCEL (AUS) - SA MOLA (GER)	JUSTIN CASSE (P.S.)	130000
B C SHOWCASING (GB) - CASCELLA (IRE)	LEGION BS/HOOLIE RACING	130000
ROCKING TREE (IRE) B C KODIAC (GB) - ROCKTIQUE (USA)	RICHARD RYAN	130000
HEARTFULLOFSTARS (IRE) B F STARSPANGLEDBANNER (AUS) - KENDAMARA (FR)	PETER & ROSS DOYLE BS	125000
B C CALYX (GB) - RHIANNON (IRE)	VENDOR	125000
B C CLOTH OF STARS (IRE) - NICOLE (FR)	DWAYNE WOODS	125000
CH F STARSPANGLEDBANNER (AUS) - KENDAR ROUGE (FR)	NICHOLAS CLEMENT/RGS	125000
B C NIGHT OF THUNDER (IRE) - AFDHAAD (GB)	ABBEYLANDS FARM	125000
SENNOCKIAN (IRE) CH C NO NAY NEVER (USA) - LADY GORGEOUS (GB)	JOHNSTON RACING	120000
FAMILY SILVER (IRE) GR F DARK ANGEL (IRE) - CHERISHED (IRE)	JAVIER MALDONADO	120000
PIANOFORTE (GB) B C LAND FORCE (IRE) - MUSICAL ART (IRE)	HIGHCLERE AGENCY	120000
B C TOO DARN HOT (GB) - KITTY LOVE (USA)	RICHARD KNIGHT BS AGENT	120000
B F SOLDIER'S CALL (GB) - SPANISH FLY (IRE)	JAMIE MCCALMONT	120000
B F ZOUSTAR (AUS) - CROSS PATTEE (IRE)	FORM BS	120000
B C NO NAY NEVER (USA) - LUCKY AT THE BAY (USA)	JASON TAYLOR EQUINE, USA	120000
CH C NO NAY NEVER (USA) - RAZZMATAZZ (GB)	MAGNOLIA II	120000
B F NO NAY NEVER (USA) - JUST IMAGINING (USA)	STRIPES STABLES LLC	120000
B F CAMELOT (GB) - KEYSTONE GULCH (USA)	VENDOR	119000
B C CAMELOT (GB) - WHAZZUP (GB)	VENDOR	119000
B F DARK ANGEL (IRE) - PLAGIARISM (USA)	R O RYAN/R FAHEY	115000
B F FASTNET ROCK (AUS) - CRUCK REALTA (GB)	VENDOR	115000
CHET'S FANCY (IRE) B C NIGHT OF THUNDER (IRE) - LETHAL PROMISE (IRE)	D K WELD	110000
CH F NIGHT OF THUNDER (IRE) - ABOVE THE MARK (USA)	SAM SANGSTER BS	110000
B F CHURCHILL (IRE) - MONA LISA'S SMILE (USA)	CLONMANON STUD	110000
B F CHURCHILL (IRE) - KISSEPAL (IRE)	BO BROMAGEN	110000
B C ZOFFANY (IRE) - TISSIAK (IRE)	WEST BS	110000
B F LOPE DE VEGA (IRE) - AGAINST RULES (FR)	VENDOR	110000
B F NO NAY NEVER (USA) - DEEP WINTER (GB)	ARTHUR HOYEAU, AGT	110000
CH C CALYX (GB) - FANCY (IRE)	CARFENTON UNLIMITED	110000
GR C DARK ANGEL (IRE) - ROYAL MAJESTIC (GB)	MANOR HOUSE FARM	110000
CH F NIGHT OF THUNDER (IRE) - EXPENSIVE DATE (GB)	WILLIE MCCREERY	110000
GR C TASLEET (GB) - RAWAAF (IRE)	JILL LAMB BS	110000
B C KODIAC (GB) - SHOW ME OFF (GB)	VENDOR	110000
CHESSALLA (IRE) B F KESSAAR (IRE) - CHELLALLA (GB)	JOHN MCCORMACK BS LLC	110000
B F NIGHT OF THUNDER (IRE) - OASIS SUNSET (IRE)	MIKE FOWLER AND TEAM D	110000
B F MAGNA GRECIA (IRE) - STATUESQUE (GB)	PHILIP ANTONACCI	105000
B C U S NAVY FLAG (USA) - LIFTING ME HIGHER (IRE)	ROBSON AGUIAR	105000
CH C CHURCHILL (IRE) - PASSION OVERFLOW (USA)	PRICE BS MANAGEMENT	105000
B C MEHMAS (IRE) - RAY OF LIGHT (IRE)	AIDAN O'RYAN	105000
CH C STARSPANGLEDBANNER (AUS) - HECUBA (GB)	CRAMPSCASTLE BS	105000
B C NIGHT OF THUNDER (IRE) - RAWAAQ (GB)	HAMISH MACAULEY BS	105000
HAVANAGREATTIME (IRE) B C HAVANA GREY (GB) - DAME SHIRLEY (GB)	RICHARD HUGHES	105000
B F TEN SOVEREIGNS (IRE) - HINT OF PINK (IRE)	MV MAGNIER	105000
B F U S NAVY FLAG (USA) - NEVER BUSY (USA)	STRIDE RACING	105000
CH C MASAR (IRE) - PAS DE SOUCIS (IRE)	FEDERICO BARBERINI	105000
CH C ULYSSES (IRE) - VEGA'S ANGEL (GB)	KEVIN ROSS BS	105000
BITESOF LUCK (IRE) B F U S NAVY FLAG (USA) - BUNOOD (IRE)	FILIP ZWICKY	100000
B C U S NAVY FLAG (USA) - RAW SILK (USA)	OCEAN REEF RACING	100000
B C NIGHT OF THUNDER (IRE) - KOZY (IRE)	JOHNNY MURTAGH	100000
B F U S NAVY FLAG (USA) - AWOHAAM (IRE)	LEGION BS	100000
B C NIGHT OF THUNDER (IRE) - DIANTHA (IRE)	CHURCH FARM	100000
B F TOO DARN HOT (GB) - TRANSHUMANCE (IRE)	BBA IRELAND	100000
B C TOO DARN HOT (GB) - LIBERATING (GB)	MCKEEVER BS/C HILLS	100000
BEAUTY THUNDER (IRE) B C NIGHT OF THUNDER (IRE) - TAWAYNA (IRE)	GAELIC BS	100000
PEGGY O'NEIL (IRE) B F ZOFFANY (IRE) - LIVIA GALILEI (IRE)	JOE MURPHY	100000
CH C ZOUSTAR (AUS) - MERCI LAYAN (IRE)	VENDOR	100000
B F KODIAC (GB) - VALLECUPA (ITY)	KEVIN RYAN	100000
VETIVER TONKA (IRE) GR C CARAVAGGIO (USA) - PEACE ROYALE (GER)	BBA IRELAND (P.S.)	100000
B C TEN SOVEREIGNS (IRE) - MISS UNDERSTOOD (IRE)	DE BURGH EQUINE	100000
B C COTAI GLORY (GB) - LA CUVEE (GB)	B MCELROY	100000
B C INVINCIBLE SPIRIT (IRE) - ULEAVEMEBREATHLESS (GB)	MYRACEHORSE	100000
B F U S NAVY FLAG (USA) - RUGGED UP (IRE)	BBA IRELAND	100000
WESTERN (IRE) B C MAGNA GRECIA (IRE) - MURHIBAANY (USA)	HIGHCLERE AGENCY	100000
B F CABLE BAY (IRE) - ART INSTITUTE (USA)	TOP LINE SALES	100000
B C DARK ANGEL (IRE) - CLEM FANDANGO (FR)	MCKEEVER BS/C HILLS	100000
B F ADVERTISE (GB) - FLIGHT TO FANCY (GB)	BBA IRELAND	100000
CH C PROFITABLE (IRE) - GROTTA DEL FAUNO (IRE)	MAGNOLIA II	98000
B C ACCLAMATION (GB) - SHADY SHAM (IRE)	VENDOR	98000
B C GOLDEN HORN (GB) - RUE RENAN (IRE)	PETER & ROSS DOYLE BS	95000
FOREVER NOAH (GB) B C DARK ANGEL (IRE) - POPPET'S PASSION (GB)	NICOSTEN	95000

Name and Breeding	Purchaser	Euros
B C CALYX (GB) - HONOURABLY (IRE)	CH THOROUGHBREDS	95000
WHERE I WANNA BE (IRE) B F CAMELOT (GB) - TRAVEL (USA)	BADGERS BS	95000
B F TOO DARN HOT (GB) - JASMINE BLUE (IRE)	MARQUEE BS/OGMA USA	95000
B C NO NAY NEVER (USA) - LASILIA (IRE)	SAM SANGSTER BS	95000
B F MEHMAS (IRE) - GRACIOUS LADY (GB)	D K WELD	95000
B F CHURCHILL (IRE) - SOLSTICE (GB)	CORMAC MCCORMACK/F STACK	95000
B F TEN SOVEREIGNS (IRE) - MISSISSIPPILANDING (IRE)	RICHIE GALWAY	95000
B/BR F NO NAY NEVER (USA) - SWEET CHARITY (FR)	VENDOR	95000
B F DARK ANGEL (IRE) - NIGELLA (GB)	BOBBY O RYAN	95000
B C AWTAAD (IRE) - QUIRITIS (GB)	RICHARD HUGHES	90000
B C INVINCIBLE ARMY (IRE) - MASAYA (GB)	GER LYONS RACING	90000
B F CALYX (GB) - IHTIRAAM (IRE)	CHURCH FARM & HORSE PARK	90000
B F NIGHT OF THUNDER (IRE) - GUANA (IRE)	GROVE STUD	90000
B/GR C DARK ANGEL (IRE) - REGENCY GIRL (IRE)	MAGNOLIA II	90000
B/BR F NO NAY NEVER (USA) - MY SISTER SANDY (USA)	SOUTHERN COMFORT (P.S.)	90000
B C NO NAY NEVER (USA) - LA NATUREL (IRE)	M & M BS	90000
B F SIOUX NATION (USA) - SKYLIGHT (IRE)	E CHILCOT/GET IN THE GAME	90000
B F TEOFILO (IRE) - LILY'S ANGEL (IRE)	VENDOR	90000
B F CAMELOT (GB) - UNIVERSAL BEAUTY (GB)	STRIPES STABLES/T RACING	90000
B F WOOTTON BASSETT (GB) - JUBLIANT GIRL (USA)	VENDOR	90000
B C NO NAY NEVER (USA) - CATCH THE EYE (IRE)	MAGS O TOOLE	87000
B F HOLY ROMAN EMPEROR (IRE) - BRIGHT BIRDIE (IRE)	RABBAH BS	85000
B C OASIS DREAM (GB) - GRANNY BEA (IRE)	MCKEEVER BS/C HILLS	85000
CH F CHURCHILL (IRE) - FRENCH FLIRT (GB)	VENDOR	85000
GR C DARK ANGEL (IRE) - ISAAN QUEEN (IRE)	VENDOR	85000
GR C PHOENIX OF SPAIN (IRE) - CLENAGHCASTLE LADY (IRE)	MIDDLEHAM PARK RACING	85000
B F CALYX (GB) - KAABARI (USA)	TOP LINE SALES	85000
CH F CALYX (GB) - RACHEVIE (IRE)	RABBAH BS	85000
MIDNIGHT DRIVE (FR) B F TEN SOVEREIGNS (IRE) - CRUISE CONTROL (IRE)	HIGHCLERE AGENCY	85000
B C STARSPANGLEDBANNER (AUS) - CALLISTAN (IRE)	MANOR HOUSE FARM	85000
CH C CHURCHILL (IRE) - JIRA (GB)	KEVIN CONNOLLY	85000
WODKA LEMON (IRE) B C WALDGEIST (GB) - MODEEROCH (IRE)	RONALD RAUSCHER, AGENT	85000
CH F PHOENIX OF SPAIN (IRE) - ZARIYNA (IRE)	BECTIVE STUD	82000
B C ZOUSTAR (AUS) - WHITE ROSA (IRE)	NICK BRADLEY RACING	82000
MARHABA MILLION (IRE) CH C GALILEO (IRE) - KHELEYF'S SILVER (IRE)	JOHNSTON RACING	82000
B C DARK ANGEL (IRE) - PLEASEMETOO (IRE)	P & R DOYLE BS/NAJD STUD	82000
B C SHOWCASING (GB) - ULTRASONIC (USA)	FOZZY STACK (P.S.)	80000
B C MAGNA GRECIA (IRE) - DIKTA DEL MAR (SPA)	JASON KELLY BS	80000
GR C DARK ANGEL (IRE) - STIRRING BALLAD (GB)	MANOR HOUSE FARM	80000
B F NEW BAY (GB) - KAPRIA (FR)	VENDOR	80000
CH C CRACKSMAN (GB) - NABARAAT (USA)	JS BS (P.S.)	80000
B C ZOFFANY (IRE) - MANY COLOURS (GB)	JOHNSTON RACING (P.S.)	80000
WASHEEK (IRE) B C SAXON WARRIOR (JPN) - DESERT VERSION (GB)	FEDERICO BARBERINI	80000
CH C NEW BAY (GB) - KAYAK (GB)	DURCAN BS/S LAVERY	80000
B C DAWN APPROACH (IRE) - STRAPLESS (IRE)	AC ELLIOTT, AGENT	80000
YOU BETTER MOVE ON (IRE) B C EXCEED AND EXCEL (AUS) - EYE WITNESS (GER)	MARIANNE HALBERG	80000
SIGHTER (GB) B F EXPERT EYE (GB) - TANOUMA (USA)	PETER & ROSS DOYLE BS	80000
B F BLUE POINT (IRE) - COPPLESTONE (IRE)	RABBAH BS	80000
CH F STARSPANGLEDBANNER (AUS) - OWASEYF (USA)	MIKE AKERS	80000
B F TERRITORIES (IRE) - ROSEISAROSE (IRE)	KEN CONDON	80000
GR C INVINCIBLE ARMY (IRE) - SILVER RAINBOW (IRE)	PETER NOLAN/NOEL MEADE	80000
B F INNS OF COURT (IRE) - YORK EXPRESS (GB)	JAMIE PIGGOTT/N TINKLER	80000
B C ZOUSTAR (AUS) - NATURAL (IRE)	FORM BS	80000
FOREST FAIRY (IRE) CH F WALDGEIST (GB) - BAHAMA GIRL (IRE)	A.C. ELLIOTT,AG	78000
B C DANDY MAN (IRE) - ARCHETYPAL (IRE)	JOE FOLEY	78000

HIGH-PRICED YEARLINGS OF 2022 AT GOFFS UK (DONCASTER)

The following yearlings realised £39,000 and over at Goffs UK Sales in 2022:

Name and Breeding	Purchaser	Pounds
PETRA MY LOVE (IRE) CH F NIGHT OF THUNDER (IRE) - THISWAYCADEAUX (IRE)	BLANDFORD BS	240000
BR C NIGHT OF THUNDER (IRE) - PIOUS ALEXANDER (IRE)	AVENUE BS	230000
SYMBOLOGY (GB) GR F HAVANA GREY (GB) - SHOWSTOPPA (GB)	HIGHCLERE AGENCY	230000
PERSICA (IRE) CH C NEW BAY (GB) - RUBIRA (AUS)	PETER & ROSS DOYLE BS	200000
GR C DARK ANGEL (IRE) - STAR APPROVAL (IRE)	PETER & ROSS DOYLE BS	200000
B C FRANKEL (GB) - TAI HANG DRAGON (IRE)	RICHARD HUGHES	200000
B C ACCLAMATION (GB) - ISOLE CANARIE (IRE)	HKJC	200000
FOOL'S GOLD (IRE) B C GALILEO GOLD (GB) - THRILLED (IRE)	RICHARD SPENCER	170000
SPACE NINJA (IRE) B C KODIAC (GB) - NIGHT QUEEN (IRE)	MANOR HOUSE FARM	160000
B C TOO DARN HOT (GB) - WHISPERING BELL (IRE)	R.S. & B.F.BROOKHOUSE	150000
TRIBAL RHYTHM (GB) CH C ULYSSES (IRE) - RUSSIAN PUNCH (GB)	MANOR HOUSE FARM	150000
B F TEN SOVEREIGNS (IRE) - RAINBOW MOONSTONE (IRE)	MANOR HOUSE FARM	150000
B C SHOWCASING (GB) - EMINENTLY (GB)	JB BS	140000
HACKMAN (IRE) CH C MEHMAS (IRE) - ISHIMAGIC (GB)	SACKVILLEDONALD	130000
B C INNS OF COURT (IRE) - KEY TO POWER (GB)	ROBSON AGUIAR/AMO RACING	125000
B C KUROSHIO (AUS) - PIVOTAL ERA (GB)	AVENUE BS	120000
CHUCHUWA (IRE) CH F BATED BREATH (GB) - BOUNCE (GB)	MANOR HOUSE FARM	120000
B F TEN SOVEREIGNS (IRE) - GRAND ZAFEEN (GB)	RICHARD HUGHES	110000
CH C SOLDIER'S CALL (GB) - RUSH (GB)	JOE FOLEY	105000
B C PHOENIX OF SPAIN (IRE) - CHICITA BANANA (GB)	BROOKHOUSE RACING	105000
CH C STARSPANGLEDBANNER (AUS) - EMERALD APPROACH (IRE)	DWAYNE WOODS	105000
CH C SHOWCASING (GB) - SARBACANE (GB)	VENDOR	100000
B C MAGNA GRECIA (IRE) - LOULWA (IRE)	DONNACHA O'BRIEN	100000
HAVANA BALL (GB) GR F HAVANA GREY (GB) - ENCHANTED LINDA (GB)	A.C.ELLIOTT , AGENT	100000
B C SIOUX NATION (USA) - DALAKANIA (IRE)	LONGWAYS STABLES	95000
B C INVINCIBLE ARMY (IRE) - SHES RANGER (IRE)	MANOR HOUSE FARM	95000
LOVE BILLY BOY (IRE) B C INVINCIBLE ARMY (IRE) - KATRINE (IRE)	PETER & ROSS DOYLE BS	90000
B C TASLEET (GB) - OLIVIA POPE (IRE)	OLIVER ST LAWRENCE BS	90000
B C CRACKSMAN (GB) - PAVILLON (GB)	DURCAN BS	90000
B F INVINCIBLE ARMY (IRE) - EDGE OF THE WORLD (IRE)	JS BS	88000
GR C HAVANA GREY (GB) - TWILIGHT THYME (GB)	CLIVE COX RACING LTD	85000
TWILIGHT ROMANCE (GB) B C TWILIGHT SON (GB) - RED BOX (GB)	RICHARD KNIGHT/S QUINN	85000
INSIGNIA (GB) B C LAND FORCE (IRE) - KASUMI (GB)	CLIVE COX RACING LTD	85000
B C EXCEED AND EXCEL (AUS) - SCARLET AND GOLD (IRE)	MIDDLEHAM PARK RACING	85000
BOUBOULE (IRE) B F KESSAAR (IRE) - TRUMP ALEXANDER (IRE)	JOSEPH O'BRIEN	85000
SHEILA'S PARADISE (GB) GR C HAVANA GREY (GB) - SHEILA'S ROCK (IRE)	VENDOR	85000
GR C DARK ANGEL (IRE) - ISAAN QUEEN (IRE)	AL MOHAMEDIYA RACING	82000
B F U S NAVY FLAG (USA) - RHYTHM QUEEN (IRE)	WESLEY WARD	82000
BR C WOOTTON BASSETT (GB) - MISS MINDING (IRE)	VENDOR	80000
DARK VIPER (GB) B/GR C DARK ANGEL (IRE) - GRANDE BLEUE (IRE)	PETER & ROSS DOYLE BS	80000
DOOLEY (IRE) B C MAGNA GRECIA (IRE) - GREATEST PLACE (IRE)	MCKEEVER BS/C.HILLS	80000
B C KINGMAN (GB) - QUEEN PHILIPPA (USA)	OLIVER ST LAWRENCE BS	80000
B F ARDAD (IRE) - ATHBAH (GB)	RICHARD HUGHES	80000
CH C SIOUX NATION (USA) - ANNIE FIOR (IRE)	CLIVE COX RACING LTD	80000
B C BLUE POINT (IRE) - MUSIC CHART (USA)	OLIVER ST LAWRENCE BS	80000
B C LAND FORCE (IRE) - BASQUE BEAUTY (GB)	OLIVER ST LAWRENCE BS	78000
RATING (IRE) CH F PROFITABLE (IRE) - SAVOY SHOWGIRL (IRE)	SAM SANGSTER BS	78000
B C ADVERTISE (GB) - VELVET REVOLVER (IRE)	JOE FOLEY	75000
B/BR C BLUE POINT (IRE) - RISKIT FORA BISKIT (IRE)	RABBAH BS LTD	75000
ZELOSA (IRE) B F ACCLAMATION (GB) - KANES PASS (IRE)	DURCAN BS/S. LAVERY	75000
B C ZOUSTAR (AUS) - GOLDEN SPELL (GB)	AVENUE BS	72000
B C EXCEED AND EXCEL (AUS) - KYLLARNEY (GB)	SAM SANGSTER BS	70000
B C COTAI GLORY (GB) - DELIZIOSA (IRE)	HILLEN/RYAN	70000
B C ZOFFANY (IRE) - SO DEVOTED (IRE)	MIDDLEHAM PARK RACING	70000
B C ZOUSTAR (AUS) - AINIPPE (IRE)	DAVID REDVERS/R.D.PEGUM	70000
B C PROFITABLE (IRE) - KASANKAYA (IRE)	JS BS	68000
B F SHOWCASING (GB) - IMAGE (GB)	COMPAS EQUINE/D.LOUGHNANE	68000
B C DANDY MAN (IRE) - OAKLEY STAR (GB)	JOE FOLEY	68000
CH F HAVANA GREY (GB) - LITTLE CLARINET (IRE)	MEGAN NICHOLLS	68000
CH C AUSTRALIA (GB) - YEAH BABY (IRE)	JOE FOLEY	67000
SUCCESSION (IRE) B C SHOWCASING (GB) - LADY ARIA (GB)	CLIVE COX RACING LTD	65000
CH C SOLDIER'S CALL (GB) - IN THE LURCH (GB)	MICHAEL EASTERBY	65000
PILGRIM (GB) GR C HAVANA GREY (GB) - HOT SECRET (GB)	HARROWGATE BS LTD	65000
GAIDEN (IRE) B F MEHMAS (IRE) - SILQUE (GB)	PETER & ROSS DOYLE BS	65000
GR F DARK ANGEL (IRE) - LADY KERMIT (IRE)	INGLEBY BS LTD	65000
QUANTUM FORCE (GB) B C LAND FORCE (IRE) - HIGH LUMINOSITY (USA)	HIGHCLERE AGENCY	65000

Name and Breeding	Purchaser	Euros
AIDAN ANDABETTIN (GB) B C BLUE POINT (IRE) - NADIA GLORY (GB)	BOBBY O'RYAN	65000
BR C HAVANA GREY (GB) - DOLLY COLMAN (IRE)	A O'RYAN	62000
B F INNS OF COURT (IRE) - AZAGBA (FR)	JC BS	62000
B F COTAI GLORY (GB) - SPRING GREEN (GB)	PETER & ROSS DOYLE BS	62000
B F CHURCHILL (IRE) - LAND GIRL (USA)	MCKEEVER BS/C.HILLS	62000
CH C SHOWCASING (GB) - MODIFY (GB)	SACKVILLEDONALD	60000
B C SOLDIER'S CALL (GB) - AHAZEEJ (IRE)	JS BS	60000
B F DANDY MAN (IRE) - ZIPPY ROCK (IRE)	BOBBY O'RYAN/R FAHEY	60000
B F SHOWCASING (GB) - MUST BE ME (GB)	OLIVER ST LAWRENCE BS	60000
PILOTO PARDO (IRE) B C BATED BREATH (GB) - IVORY CHARM (GB)	PETER & ROSS DOYLE BS	58000
B C KODIAC (GB) - GET UP AND DANCE (GB)	OLIVER ST LAWRENCE BS	58000
B C EXPERT EYE (GB) - KING'S MIRACLE (IRE)	SAM SANGSTER BS	58000
B F NO RISK AT ALL (FR) - ONLY FOR LOVE (GB)	COOLMARA STABLES	56000
B F SHOWCASING (GB) - HELLO GLORY (GB)	VENDOR	55000
B C TEN SOVEREIGNS (IRE) - LOST IN SILENCE (IRE)	LONGWAYS STABLES	55000
PANNONICA (IRE) B F ACCLAMATION (GB) - SPRING LEAF (FR)	PETER & ROSS DOYLE BS	55000
B C KINGMAN (GB) - TEARS OF THE SUN (GB)	JOHNSTON RACING	55000
B C INNS OF COURT (IRE) - MISFORTUNATE (IRE)	GARY HALPIN	55000
B F TEN SOVEREIGNS (IRE) - ERIA (IRE)	VENDOR	55000
B F KODIAC (GB) - TALIYNA (IRE)	RABBAH BS LTD	55000
B F AWTAAD (IRE) - MIN BANAT ALREEH (IRE)	NB BS	55000
BETTERBEGOODTOME (GB) B F TERRITORIES (IRE) - KARIJINI (GER)	A.C. ELLIOTT, AGENT	55000
BESTIE (GB) B C ADVERTISE (GB) - SIMMY'S TEMPLE (GB)	MARTYN MEADE	54000
B C CABLE BAY (IRE) - SHAMANDAR (FR)	KUBLER RACING	54000
B C INNS OF COURT (IRE) - MOON SISTER (IRE)	OLLIE PEARS/C.C.R.	52000
CHRISTIAN DAVID (IRE) B C PROFITABLE (IRE) - LIBERTY SKY (IRE)	PETER & ROSS DOYLE BS	52000
SACRED ANGEL (IRE) GR F DARK ANGEL (IRE) - SACRED ASPECT (IRE)	MANOR HOUSE FARM	52000
B C MEHMAS (IRE) - YIN (GB)	MAGS O'TOOLE	52000
BR C TWILIGHT SON (GB) - ZAWIYAH (GB)	JASON KELLY BS	52000
CH C STARSPANGLEDBANNER (AUS) - BUTTERFLY KISS (USA)	SAM SANGSTER BS	52000
STANLEY SPENCER (IRE) B C IFFRAAJ (GB) - MARSH HAWK (GB)	ANTHONY HOGARTH	50000
B F CARAVAGGIO (USA) - DARAJAAT (USA)	SACKVILLEDONALD	50000
B F SOLDIER'S CALL (GB) - RADIO GAGA (GB)	OLIVER ST LAWRENCE BS	50000
MY MARGIE (IRE) B F DANDY MAN (IRE) - AGAPANTHA (USA)	RICHARD HUGHES	50000
B C DANDY MAN (IRE) - DUCHESS OF FOXLAND (IRE)	PETER & ROSS DOYLE BS	50000
B F MAGNA GRECIA (IRE) - NEW TERMS (GB)	AMY LYNAM	50000
B C TEN SOVEREIGNS (IRE) - JOYCE COMPTON (IRE)	J.B.BS	50000
BR C DARK ANGEL (IRE) - PRADEN (USA)	DIEGO DIAS	50000
BARNABY (IRE) B C SOLDIER'S CALL (GB) - AEGEAN SUNSET (IRE)	HILLEN/RYAN	50000
CH C MASAR (IRE) - DULARAME (IRE)	AVENUE BS	50000
NOVATION (GB) B/BR C HAVANA GREY (GB) - CAPRELLA (GB)	HURWORTH BS	50000
DIMSONS (IRE) CH C FOOTSTEPSINTHESAND (GB) - HERRIDGE (IRE)	PETER & ROSS DOYLE BS	50000
B C LE BRIVIDO (FR) - RIOTICISM (FR)	MARTYN MEADE	50000
WARRENDALE WAGYU (GB) B C TASLEET (GB) - TUMBLEWIND (GB)	RICHARD KNIGHT/S QUINN	50000
B F JACK HOBBS (GB) - QUEEN OF THE STAGE (IRE)	ALNE PARK STUD	50000
CATENA (IRE) B F CABLE BAY (IRE) - KODURO (IRE)	NICK BRADLEY RACING	49000
B C IFFRAAJ (GB) - TWINKLE TWINKLE (GB)	OLIVER ST LAWRENCE BS	48000
B C KESSAAR (IRE) - KHIBRAH (GB)	OLIVER ST LAWRENCE BS	48000
BR C INNS OF COURT (IRE) - KINGDOMFORTHEBRIDE (IRE)	LONGWAYS STABLES	48000
B F OASIS DREAM (GB) - SASSY GAL (IRE)	VENDOR	48000
SHIMMERING MOON (IRE) B F KUROSHIO (AUS) - SUBTLE SHIMMER (GB)	MANOR HOUSE FARM	48000
CH C BUNGLE INTHEJUNGLE (GB) - SHAWHILL (GB)	MIDDLEHAM PARK RACING	48000
B G ADVERTISE (GB) - POWERFUL STAR (IRE)	NIGEL TINKLER	48000
B F PHOENIX OF SPAIN (IRE) - BEACH WEDDING (IRE)	SAM SANGSTER BS	48000
B F DARK ANGEL (IRE) - HIDDEN STEPS (GB)	HILLEN/RYAN	48000
GR F HAVANA GREY (GB) - PERFECT COVER (IRE)	RICHARD HUGHES	48000
B C U S NAVY FLAG (USA) - TEDSMORE DAME (GB)	CLIVE COX RACING LTD	47000
B F ZOFFANY (IRE) - ACCIPITER (GB)	J GLOVER/NIGEL TINKLER	46000
B G BATED BREATH (GB) - HALA HALA (IRE)	SAM SANGSTER BS	45000
B C KODIAC (GB) - SYANN (IRE)	VENDOR	45000
B F DANDY MAN (IRE) - FLOATING ALONG (IRE)	PETER & ROSS DOYLE BS	45000
GR C ACLAIM (IRE) - ANALYTICAL (GB)	OLIVER ST LAWRENCE BS	45000
CH C MEHMAS (IRE) - BACHELIERE (USA)	TALLY HO STUD	45000
VENI VIDI VINCI (IRE) B F INVINCIBLE ARMY (IRE) - LISA GHERARDINI (IRE)	PETER & ROSS DOYLE BS	45000
B C STARSPANGLEDBANNER (AUS) - TIME TO EXCEED (IRE)	KILRONAN	45000
B/GR F HAVANA GREY (GB) - INFAMOUS ANGEL (GB)	CARACCIOLO ANTONINO	45000
B C KODIAC (GB) - MARTINA FRANCA (GB)	SACKVILLEDONALD	45000
B C ZOUSTAR (AUS) - PEPPER LANE (GB)	JASON KELLY BS	45000
CH C EL KABEIR (USA) - SWEET DRAGON FLY (GB)	LILLINGSTON BS	45000

Name and Breeding	Purchaser	Euros
B F INVINCIBLE ARMY (IRE) - MANYATTA (IRE)	RABBAH BS LTD	45000
B C LAND FORCE (IRE) - AVESSIA (GB)	BLANDFORD BS	45000
VANTHEMAN (IRE) B C INVINCIBLE ARMY (IRE) - LAILA HONIWILLOW (GB)	HILLEN/RYAN	45000
CH C MAYSON (GB) - COLLEGIATE (IRE)	R.O'RYAN/RICHARD FAHEY	45000
B C SEA THE MOON (GER) - MARY ELISE (IRE)	OAK TREE FARM	43000
SOLDIER OF ROME (GB) B C CRACKSMAN (GB) - TYRANA (FR)	TOWNLEY HALL BS	43000
B F KODIAC (GB) - ELMALIYA (IRE)	PETER & ROSS DOYLE BS	43000
CH F GETAWAY (GER) - JELAN (IRE)	SWANBRIDGE BS	43000
B/GR F HAVANA GREY (GB) - INAGH RIVER (GB)	BOZZI/GUERRIERI	42000
EYE OF DUBAI (GB) B C HAVANA GREY (GB) - LILY CARSTAIRS (GB)	RICHARD KNIGHT/S QUINN	42000
B C INVINCIBLE ARMY (IRE) - MULUK (IRE)	RABBAH BS LTD	42000
B C TWILIGHT SON (GB) - PRODIGIOUS (GB)	KEVIN ROSS BS	42000
B F MASAR (IRE) - ITIQAD (GB)	FINBAR KENT	42000
STATES (GB) B C TERRITORIES (IRE) - STEREOPHONIC (IRE)	RICHARD HUGHES	42000
BR C KODIAC (GB) - DANCE CLUB (IRE)	OLLIE PEARS (P.S.)	42000
B F SOLDIER'S CALL (GB) - MOONLIGHT BAY (GB)	FEDERICO BARBERINI	42000
B C UNFORTUNATELY (IRE) - VULNICURA (IRE)	KARL BURKE	42000
B C TOO DARN HOT (GB) - KELLY NICOLE (IRE)	POWERSTOWN STUD	42000
B/BR C KODI BEAR (IRE) - PASSIONATTA (IRE)	MARTYN MEADE	41000
B C DUE DILIGENCE (USA) - TRUMPET LILY (GB)	JOE FOLEY	40000
B F IFFRAAJ (GB) - WORSHIP (IRE)	TRADEWINDS	40000
B F ZOFFANY (IRE) - INALA (GB)	JASON KELLY BS	40000
ARCTURIAN (IRE) CH C COTAI GLORY (GB) - STAR OF MALTA (GB)	RICHARD HUGHES	40000
B F EXPERT EYE (GB) - SUNCHISETAGIOO (GB)	TROY STEVE B/STOCK LTD	40000
B C CAMACHO (GB) - MANDORIA (GER)	MCKEEVER BS/C.HILLS	40000
B C IFFRAAJ (GB) - ISOLA VERDE (GB)	BYRON RODGERS/STAR BS	40000
B C LAND FORCE (IRE) - THREE SUGARS (AUS)	ADAM POTTS/DONOVAN BS	40000
B C KODIAC (GB) - CLAIOMH GEAL (GB)	VENDOR	40000
B F MAGNA GRECIA (IRE) - FOUR'S COMPANY (IRE)	MANOR HOUSE FARM (P.S.)	40000
B C SHOWCASING (GB) - FRABJOUS (GB)	JACK JONES RACING	40000
B F DANDY MAN (IRE) - SUMMARISE (GER)	RICHARD HUGHES	40000
B F HARRY ANGEL (IRE) - HILARY J (GB)	INGLEBY BS LTD	40000
B C TASLEET (GB) - POPPY PIVOT (IRE)	DWAYNE WOODS	40000
B C ADVERTISE (GB) - POET'S PRINCESS (GB)	FINBAR KENT (P.S.)	40000
B F U S NAVY FLAG (USA) - BY JUPITER (GB)	JASON KELLY BS	40000
ROGUE FIGHTER (IRE) B C DARK ANGEL (IRE) - REDMAVEN (IRE)	JS BS/T.CLOVER RACING	40000
B G SOLDIER'S CALL (GB) - SUEDEHEAD (GB)	JAMIE PIGGOTT	40000
B C LAND FORCE (IRE) - JAZZ WALK (GB)	GREENHILLS FARM	40000
B F MAGNA GRECIA (IRE) - VIOLA D'AMOUR (IRE)	KEVIN ROSS BS	40000
B C INVINCIBLE ARMY (IRE) - CAPE JOY (IRE)	ROBSON AGUIAR	39000
B F EXPERT EYE (GB) - BALAYAGE (IRE)	VENDOR	39000

HIGH-PRICED YEARLINGS OF 2022 AT TATTERSALLS IRELAND SALES

The following yearlings realised 34,000 euros and over at Tattersalls Ireland Sales in 2022:

Name and Breeding	Purchaser	Euros
B C NEW BAY (GB) - TOBAIR AN SHEEDA (IRE)	A C ELLIOTT	115000
B C INNS OF COURT (IRE) - SILK FAN (IRE)	MANOR HOUSE FARM	110000
KELBELLE (IRE) B F INNS OF COURT (IRE) - ZIGGY'S SECRET (GB)	HIGHFLYER BS	100000
WIND RIVER (IRE) CH C SIOUX NATION (USA) - DECORATIVE (IRE)	HIGHFLYER BS	100000
BR C FOOTSTEPSINTHESAND (GB) - SCIOLINA (IRE)	JOHN LAVERY	100000
BR C BATED BREATH (GB) - CAPED LADY (IRE)	JOE FOLEY	100000
B C STARSPANGLEDBANNER (AUS) - HIGH REGARDS (IRE)	MANOR HOUSE FARM	95000
CH C HAVANA GOLD (IRE) - MEANING OF TIME (GB)	KEVIN ROSS BS	95000
B C AWTAAD (IRE) - ORIENTAL STEP (IRE)	PETER & ROSS DOYLE & MPR	87000
B F INVINCIBLE SPIRIT (IRE) - WOOLSTONE (GB)	VENDOR	85000
B F MEHMAS (IRE) - LISFANNON (GB)	MANOR HOUSE FARM	80000
B C HOLY ROMAN EMPEROR (IRE) - MY TWINKLE (IRE)	K J CONDON/RPG BS	80000
B F CARAVAGGIO (USA) - SNEAKY SNOOZE (IRE)	JOE FOLEY	80000
BR F DUE DILIGENCE (USA) - RIOT OF COLOUR (GB)	JOE FOLEY	78000
TRYFAN (GB) B C NATHANIEL (IRE) - RHAGORI (GB)	THE ARTIS PARTNERSHIP	75000
SOUTH PARADE (IRE) B F INVINCIBLE ARMY (IRE) - RURAL CELEBRATION (GB)	R O'RYAN/H STEEL	75000
GR F MEHMAS (IRE) - DAY CREEK (GB)	STROUD COLEMAN BS	75000
NATIVE AMERICAN (IRE) B C SIOUX NATION (USA) - PENCARROW (GB)	R O'RYAN/R FAHEY	75000
NEW KINGS ROAD (IRE) B C SIOUX NATION (USA) - THISTLESTAR (USA)	BLANDFORD BS	72000
B F CALYX (GB) - CONDENSED (GB)	MICK FLANAGAN, AGENT	70000
CH C SHOWCASING (GB) - ROSE MARMARA (GB)	CHURCH FARM/HORSE PARK	70000
B F TOO DARN HOT (GB) - SUFFUSED (GB)	JOE FOLEY	70000
NOTTA NOTHER (GB) GR C HAVANA GREY (GB) - TULIP DRESS (GB)	PETER & ROSS DOYLE	70000
CH F NIGHT OF THUNDER (IRE) - MISS BUCKSHOT (IRE)	YEOMANSTOWN STUD	70000
B C SHOWCASING (GB) - SALSA BELLA (FR)	MARCO BOZZI BS	70000
GR F HAVANA GREY (GB) - GLACE (IRE)	HAMISH MACAULEY	68000
B C COTAI GLORY (GB) - ASRAFAIRY (IRE)	GARY HALPIN/SEAN DAVIS	65000
B C PROFITABLE (IRE) - PILATES (IRE)	VENDOR	65000
B C CARAVAGGIO (USA) - SWEET DREAMS BABY (IRE)	KILBRIDE EQUINE	65000
B C INVINCIBLE ARMY (IRE) - LITTLE AUDIO (IRE)	MANOR HOUSE FARM	65000
OLIGOPOLY (GB) B C HAVANA GREY (GB) - NOBLE CAUSE (GB)	HIGHFLYER BS	65000
B C KUROSHIO (AUS) - MYSTERIOUS BURG (FR)	ROBSON AGUIAR	65000
B C INNS OF COURT (IRE) - ZAKYAH (GB)	NICK BELL	65000
BR C HIGHLAND REEL (IRE) - FOUR ELEVEN (CAN)	LILLINGSTON BS	65000
HE'S GOT GAME (IRE) B C OASIS DREAM (GB) - THAFEERA (USA)	SACKVILLEDONALD	62000
B C INVINCIBLE SPIRIT (IRE) - MARTINI MAGIC (GB)	BARRY LYNCH/JOHN BOURKE	62000
B F INVINCIBLE ARMY (IRE) - TARAEFF (IRE)	VALFREDO VALIANI	62000
B C MEHMAS (IRE) - LOOKS GREAT (GB)	CHURCH FARM/HORSE PARK	62000
PERFECT BALL (FR) B C NO RISK AT ALL (FR) - PRINCESSE KAP (FR)	KIERAN SHIELDS	62000
B F DARK ANGEL (IRE) - HUSHING (GB)	HOWSON & HOULDSWORTH BS	60000
B F CHURCHILL (IRE) - DEVIOUS DIVA (IRE)	GERRY AHERNE	60000
REDNBLUE SOVEREIGN (IRE) B C TEN SOVEREIGNS (IRE) - MILLE TANK (GB)	SACKVILLEDONALD	60000
B C WALK IN THE PARK (IRE) - MYZTIQUE (IRE)	JASON HIGGINS	60000
HARVANNA (GB) B F HAVANA GREY (GB) - WEISSE SOCKEN (IRE)	KARL & KELLY BURKE	58000
B C FAST COMPANY (IRE) - THE SINGING HILLS (GB)	LILLINGSTON BS	58000
CH F NEW BAY (GB) - WHISPERED DREAMS (USA)	PETER & ROSS DOYLE	56000
B C ZOFFANY (IRE) - GUARDIA (GER)	CORMAC FARRELL BS	55000
B C INNS OF COURT (IRE) - TEELINE (IRE)	BLANDFORD BS	55000
B C MEHMAS (IRE) - PARTY ANIMAL (GB)	DERRYCONNOR STUD	54000
B C MILAN (GB) - BALLINCARD SAINT (IRE)	JAMES DOYLE	54000
B C SEA THE MOON (GER) - APURA (IRE)	KILRONAN	52000
B C MUHAARAR (GB) - MOQLA (GB)	BELIAR BS	52000
B C AWTAAD (IRE) - SCHOLARLY (GB)	SACKVILLEDONALD	52000
CH C CHURCHILL (IRE) - GLASS SLIPPER (IRE)	PETER NOLAN/NOEL MEADE	52000
MERCIAN WARRIOR (IRE) B C SAXON WARRIOR (JPN) - LOQUACITY (GB)	HIGHFLYER BS	52000
GR C HAVANA GREY (GB) - MUSICAL MIRAGE (USA)	MARCO BOZZI BS	52000
GR F DARK ANGEL (IRE) - PORTMANTEAU (GB)	JOE FOLEY	52000
B C PROFITABLE (IRE) - PEIG (IRE)	M DODS	52000
B F BLUE POINT (IRE) - HUMA BIRD (GB)	BROWN ISLAND STABLES	52000
B C HAVANA GREY (GB) - MADAME PACO (GB)	SACKVILLEDONALD	50000
VIENNOISE (IRE) B F ZOFFANY (IRE) - VOISCREVILLE (IRE)	BLANDFORD BS	50000
B F PHOENIX OF SPAIN (IRE) - MEETING IN PARIS (IRE)	KEVIN ROSS BS	50000
BR C SIOUX NATION (USA) - CAN DANCE (GB)	BBA IRELAND	50000
CH C ZOFFANY (IRE) - STRASBOURG PLACE (GB)	HAMISH MACAULEY BS	50000
CH C MEHMAS (IRE) - GLITTERDUST (GB)	MICHAEL CLEERE	50000
B F HAVANA GREY (GB) - CLIFFHANGER (GB)	VENDOR	50000
CH C SHOWCASING (GB) - IRISH MADAM (GB)	DONOVAN BS/CONOR MAHON	50000
B F SHOWCASING (GB) - MINORIA (GB)	PADDY TWOMEY	50000
B/BR C TWILIGHT SON (GB) - RYTHMIQUE (IRE)	CRAIG BRYSON	50000

Name and Breeding	Purchaser	Euros
CH C SEA THE STARS (IRE) - ENIGMATIQUE (GB)	VENDOR	50000
B C BLUE BRESIL (FR) - TELL IT TO ME (GB)	REDBRIDGE STABLES	50000
CH F NEW BAY (GB) - FINDHORN MAGIC (GB)	BBA IRELAND	50000
B C INVINCIBLE SPIRIT (IRE) - ANNE BONNEY (GB)	A OLIVER	50000
CH C FOOTSTEPSINTHESAND (GB) - VENUS DE MEDICI (IRE)	PETER & ROSS DOYLE	50000
B F TEN SOVEREIGNS (IRE) - BLUE SAPHIRE (GB)	LINDA SHANAHAN	50000
CH C FREE EAGLE (IRE) - PRINCESA DEL SOL (GB)	A C ELLIOTT	50000
B F NO NAY NEVER (USA) - FORCES OF DARKNESS (IRE)	ADAM POTTS/K J CONDON	50000
B C MEHMAS (IRE) - ON THE SAME PAGE (IRE)	CLIVE COX RACING	50000
B C KODI BEAR (IRE) - LETS TRY (IRE)	JOE FOLEY	50000
B C SHOLOKHOV (IRE) - CARRIGEEN LECHUGA (IRE)	GEAROID O'LOUGHLIN	50000
B F SOLDIER'S CALL (GB) - COCONUT KISSES (GB)	BLANDFORD BS	48000
B F AWTAAD (IRE) - AGHAANY (GB)	DE BURGH EQUINE	48000
GR F DARK ANGEL (IRE) - FAITHFUL DUCHESS (IRE)	M DODS	48000
B C BLUE BRESIL (FR) - AISANCE (FR)	RICHARD FRISBY	48000
INSPIRING SPEECHES (IRE) CH C CHURCHILL (IRE) - VALLAMBROSA (IRE)	M DODS	47000
SARAJEVO BOY (IRE) CH C DRAGON PULSE (IRE) - SARAJEVO ROSE (IRE)	MEGAN EVANS	47000
B F CHURCHILL (IRE) - WITHORWITHOUTYOU (IRE)	DE BURGH EQUINE	47000
B F BATED BREATH (GB) - SAJANJL (GB)	BBA IRELAND	46000
B C BLUE BRESIL (FR) - FIVE STAR PRESENT (IRE)	IAN FERGUSON	46000
B F DARK ANGEL (IRE) - KELSEY ROSE (GB)	VENDOR	45000
GR C TAMAYUZ (GB) - RAAQY (IRE)	A C ELLIOTT, AGENT	45000
BR F SOLDIER'S CALL (GB) - HARLEM DANCER (GB)	COMPAS EQUINE	45000
B F DANDY MAN (IRE) - CHASING THE RAIN (GB)	MEGAN EVANS	45000
B C KODIAC (GB) - GOLDCREST (GB)	GAVIN CROMWELL	45000
B C CRYSTAL OCEAN (GB) - BATTLE MELODY (IRE)	T HILLMAN	45000
B F DANDY MAN (IRE) - DREAM SLEEP (GB)	KARL & KELLY BURKE	44000
CH C STARSPANGLEDBANNER (AUS) - CELESTIAL BOW (IRE)	CORMAC FARRELL BS	44000
ABSOLUTE ADVANTAGE (GB) B C TASLEET (GB) - PERMAISURI (IRE)	HIGHFLYER BS	43000
GR C SOLDIER'S CALL (GB) - ALICIA DARCY (IRE)	KARL & KELLY BURKE	42000
CH F MEHMAS (IRE) - BIG VIOLETT (IRE)	JOHN MCCONNELL RACING	42000
B F EL KABEIR (USA) - PAPER DREAMS (IRE)	ROBSON AGUIAR	42000
B C SOLDIER'S CALL (GB) - QUEEN ELSA (IRE)	NICK BRADLEY RACING	42000
B C TEOFILO (IRE) - TAYARA (GB)	TODAY BS	42000
BR F STUDY OF MAN (IRE) - CHIAREZZA (AUS)	TOMMY MCGRATH	42000
B F SIOUX NATION (USA) - REAL MAGIC (IRE)	LINEHAN BS/J MURTAGH	42000
B F CAMACHO (GB) - HIDDEN GIRL (IRE)	MIDDLEHAM PARK RACING	42000
B F SIOUX NATION (USA) - ART NOUVELLE (IRE)	BBA IRELAND	42000
GR F DARK ANGEL (IRE) - LAVINIAD (IRE)	MEADOWVIEW STABLES	42000
B C MAGNA GRECIA (IRE) - LINA DE VEGA (IRE)	J S BS/T CLOVER RACING	42000
B C YEATS (IRE) - WOOD LILY (IRE)	JOHN LYNCH	41000
GR F DARK ANGEL (IRE) - VIA BALLYCROY (IRE)	JOANNE LAVERY	40000
B C HOLY ROMAN EMPEROR (IRE) - SMOKEN ROSA (USA)	P HARLEY/F REUTERSKIOLD	40000
B F SOLDIER'S CALL (GB) - DUSHLAN (IRE)	KARL & KELLY BURKE	40000
B C PROFITABLE (IRE) - COLD COLD WOMAN (GB)	ROBSON AGUIAR	40000
B F INVINCIBLE SPIRIT (IRE) - BOLDARRA (USA)	MEADOWVIEW STABLES	40000
B F ACCLAMATION (GB) - CARIBBEAN ACE (IRE)	MANOR HOUSE FARM	40000
B F MAGNA GRECIA (IRE) - DANIDH DUBAI (IRE)	DERRYCONNOR STUD	40000
B F HARRY ANGEL (IRE) - MEJALA (IRE)	AMANDA SKIFFINGTON	40000
B C SOLDIER OF FORTUNE (IRE) - BENEFIT BALL (IRE)	IAN FERGUSON	40000
BR F FOOTSTEPSINTHESAND (GB) - INSTINCTIVELY (IRE)	VENDOR	40000
B F WOOTTON BASSETT (GB) - PHILONIKIA (GB)	CRAIG BRYSON	40000
B F ZOFFANY (IRE) - BOUCHERON (GB)	O'BYRNE & GRASSICK	40000
B C MAGNA GRECIA (IRE) - PROSPER (GB)	BBA IRELAND	40000
WIT'S END (IRE) B F CHURCHILL (IRE) - SHAMANKIYNA (FR)	TOM DASCOMBE RACING	40000
B C GETAWAY (GER) - ITSALARK (IRE)	IAN FERGUSON	40000
B C TWILIGHT SON (GB) - FLORETT (IRE)	FOLISTOWN FARM	39000
B F MEHMAS (IRE) - FORCEFULL (IRE)	VENDOR	38000
CH F SAXON WARRIOR (JPN) - MALAKITE (IRE)	GUILLERMO ARIZKORRETA	38000
B F ACCLAMATION (GB) - UP AT LAST (GB)	C H THOROUGHBREDS	38000
B C INVINCIBLE ARMY (IRE) - SONNET (IRE)	BEACHLEA BS/MCCORMACK	38000
B C CALYX (GB) - ASAWER (IRE)	MARCO BOZZI BS	38000
B F NEW BAY (GB) - SPECIAL GAL (FR)	PADDY TWOMEY	38000
B C SHOLOKHOV (IRE) - BABIES PRESENT (IRE)	JAMESTOWN HOUSE STUD	38000
B C MEHMAS (IRE) - DUNIATTY (GB)	SHANAVILLE STABLES	37000
B C POET'S WORD (IRE) - TORNADO SKY (IRE)	T HILLMAN	37000
SEE ALL MATCH (IRE) B C ACCLAMATION (GB) - PEPPARD (GB)	BARAGIOLA SAGAM	37000
ANGLESEY LAD (IRE) B C KODI BEAR (IRE) - SIGN FROM HEAVEN (IRE)	COMPAS EQUINE	37000
B F ADVERTISE (GB) - DELICIOUS (GB)	ADAM POTTS	37000
B F CALYX (GB) - ALLEGRAMENTE (GB)	GUILLERMO ARIZKORRETA	37000
CH C EXCEED AND EXCEL (AUS) - KESKA (GB)	JOHN BUTLER RACING	37000
B C INNS OF COURT (IRE) - ELYSIUM DREAM (GB)	P D EVANS	37000

Name and Breeding	Purchaser	Euros
B C JAMES GARFIELD (IRE) - WIND IN HER SAILS (IRE)	CLIVE COX RACING LTD	37000
CH C GENTLEWAVE (IRE) - SANTA ADELIA (FR)	T HILLMAN	37000
B F KODIAC (GB) - MOON CLUB (IRE)	JASON KELLY BS	36000
B F FOOTSTEPSINTHESAND (GB) - CRYSTAL VALKYRIE (IRE)	JOHNSTON RACING	36000
B F KODIAC (GB) - RAYDA (IRE)	MARK FLANNERY	36000
B C BLUE BRESIL (FR) - ROAMING WILD (IRE)	RICHARD ROHAN	36000
B C ACCLAMATION (GB) - RUSSIAN DREAM (IRE)	THOMAS MCGRATH	36000
BR C SMOOTH DADDY (USA) - LIBYS DREAM (IRE)	DIEGO DIAS	36000
GR F PHOENIX OF SPAIN (IRE) - KRISTAL XENIA (IRE)	SACKVILLEDONALD	36000
B F CRYSTAL OCEAN (GB) - REINE ANGEVINE (FR)	VENDOR	36000
B F DANDY MAN (IRE) - END OF AN ERA (IRE)	LINEHAN BS/J MURTAGH	35000
B F WALK IN THE PARK (IRE) - GAMBLING GIRL (IRE)	VENDOR	35000
VIADEIPISPINI (IRE) B C PROFITABLE (IRE) - KIKONGA (GB)	ALESSANDRO BOTTI	35000
BATED BREEZE (IRE) B C BATED BREATH (GB) - OLGA DA POLGA (IRE)	GARY MOORE RACING	35000
B C CAMACHO (GB) - SATIN KISS (USA)	SAN ANTONE LODGE	35000
CH F SIOUX NATION (USA) - HYLAND HEATHER (IRE)	RODRIGO GONCALVES	35000
SEA THE BOSS (GB) CH F SEA THE MOON (GER) - SHAELLA (IRE)	BBA IRELAND	35000
B F SAXON WARRIOR (JPN) - TUPELO HONEY (IRE)	BBA IRELAND	35000
BELLA TASLINA (GB) CH F TASLEET (GB) - BELLA CATALINA (GB)	CLIVE COX RACING LTD	35000
B F TIRWANAKO (FR) - BENEFIT LODGE (IRE)	BALLYKERGHAN STABLES	35000
B C SOLDIER'S CALL (GB) - FOREVER MORE (IRE)	KARL & KELLY BURKE	34000
B C KUROSHIO (AUS) - NUALA TAGULA (IRE)	GAELIC BS	34000

2,000 GUINEAS STAKES (3y) Newmarket - 1 mile

Year	Owner	Winner and Price	Jockey	Trainer	Second	Third	Ran	Time
1985	Maktoum Al Maktoum's	**SHADEED** (4/5)	L Piggott	M Stoute	Bairn	Supreme Leader	14	1 37.41
1986	K Abdullah's	**DANCING BRAVE** (15/8)	G Starkey	G Harwood	Green Desert	Huntingdale	15	1 40.00
1987	J Horgan's	**DON'T FORGET ME** (9/1)	W Carson	R Hannon	Bellotto	Midyan	13	1 36.74
1988	H H Aga Khan's	**DOYOUN** (4/5)	W R Swinburn	M Stoute	Charmer	Bellefella	9	1 41.73
1989	Hamdan Al-Maktoum's	**NASHWAN** (3/1)	W Carson	R Hern	Exbourne	Danehill	14	1 36.44
1990	John Horgan's	**TIROL** (9/1)	M Kinane	R Hannon	Machiavellian	Anshan	14	1 35.84
1991	Lady Beaverbrook's	**MYSTIKO** (13/2)	M Roberts	C Brittain	Lycius	Ganges	14	1 37.83
1992	R Sangster's	**RODRIGO DE TRIANO** (6/1)	L Piggott	P Chapple-Hyam	Lucky Lindy	Pursuit of Love	16	1 38.37
1993	K Abdullah's	**ZAFONIC** (5/6)	P Eddery	A Fabre	Barathea	Bin Ajwaad	14	1 35.32
1994	G R Bailey Ltd's	**MISTER BAILEYS** (16/1)	J Weaver	M Johnston	Grand Lodge	Colonel Collins	23	1 35.08
1995	Sheikh Mohammed's	**PENNEKAMP** (9/2)	T Jarnet	A Fabre	Celtic Swing	Bahri	11	1 35.16
1996	Godolphin's	**MARK OF ESTEEM** (8/1)	L Dettori	S bin Suroor	Even Top	Bijou D'Inde	13	1 37.59
1997	M Tabor & Mrs J Magnier's	**ENTREPRENEUR** (11/2)	M Kinane	M Stoute	Revoque	Poteen	16	1 35.64
1998	M Tabor & Mrs J Magnier's	**KING OF KINGS** (7/2)	M Kinane	A O'Brien	Lend A Hand	Border Arrow	18	1 39.25
1999	Godolphin's (Run on July Course)	**ISLAND SANDS** (10/1)	L Dettori	S Bin Suroor	Enrique	Mujahid	16	1 37.14
2000	Saeed Suhail's	**KING'S BEST** (13/2)	K Fallon	Sir M Stoute	Giant's Causeway	Barathea Guest	27	1 37.77
2001	Lord Weinstock's	**GOLAN** (11/1)	K Fallon	Sir M Stoute	Tamburlaine	Frenchmans Bay	18	1 37.48
2002	Sir A Ferguson & Mrs J Magnier's	**ROCK OF GIBRALTAR** (9/1)	J Murtagh	A O'Brien	Hawk Wing	Redback	22	1 36.50
2003	Moyglare Stud Farm's	**REFUSE TO BEND** (9/2)	P J Smullen	D Weld	Zafeen	Norse Dancer	20	1 37.98
2004	Hamdan Al Maktoum's	**HAAFHD** (11/2)	R Hills	B Hills	Snow Ridge	Azamour	14	1 36.60
2005	Mr M Tabor & Mrs John Magnier's	**FOOTSTEPSINTHESAND** (13/2)	K Fallon	A O'Brien	Rebel Rebel	Kandidate	19	1 36.10
2006	Mrs J Magnier, Mr M Tabor & Mr D Smith's	**GEORGE WASHINGTON** (6/4)	K Fallon	A O'Brien	Sir Percy	Olympian Odyssey	14	1 36.80
2007	P Cunningham's	**COCKNEY REBEL** (25/1)	O Peslier	G Huffer	Vital Equine	Dutch Art	24	1 35.28
2008	Mrs J. Magnier's	**HENRYTHENAVIGATOR** (11/1)	J Murtagh	A O'Brien	New Approach	Stubbs Art	15	1 39.14
2009	C Tsui's	**SEA THE STARS** (8/1)	M Kinane	J Oxx	Delegator	Gan Amhras	15	1 35.88
2010	M Offenstadt's	**MAKFI** (33/1)	C Lemaire	M Delzangles	Dick Turpin	Canford Cliffs	19	1 36.35
2011	K Abdullah's	**FRANKEL** (1/2)	T Queally	H Cecil	Dubawi Gold	Native Khan	13	1 37.30
2012	D Smith, Mrs J Magnier & M Tabor's	**CAMELOT** (15/8)	J O'Brien	A O'Brien	French Fifteen	Hermival	18	1 42.46
2013	Godolphin's	**DAWN APPROACH** (11/8)	K Manning	J Bolger	Glory Awaits	Van Der Neer	13	1 35.84
2014	Saeed Manana's	**NIGHT OF THUNDER** (40/1)	K Fallon	R Hannon jnr	Kingman	Australia	14	1 36.61
2015	M Tabor, D Smith & Mrs J. Magnier's	**GLENEAGLES** (4/1)	R Moore	A O'Brien	Territories	Ivawood	18	1 37.55
2016	Al Shaqab Racing's	**GALILEO GOLD** (14/1)	L Dettori	H Palmer	Massaat	Ribchester	13	1 35.91
2017	M Tabor, D Smith & Mrs J Magnier's	**CHURCHILL** (6/4)	R Moore	A O'Brien	Barney Roy	Al Wukair	10	1 36.61
2018	D Smith, Mrs J Magnier & M Tabor's	**SAXON WARRIOR** (3/1)	D O'Brien	A O'Brien	Tip Two Win	Masar	14	1 36.55
2019	D Smith/Mrs J Magnier/M Tabor & Flaxman Stables's	**MAGNA GRECIA** (11/2)	D O'Brien	A O'Brien	King of Change	Skardu	19	1 36.84
2020	Qatar Racing Limited's	**KAMEKO** (10/1)	O Murphy	A Balding	Witchita	Pinatubo	15	1 34.72
2021	Mrs J Bolger's	**POETIC FLARE** (16/1)	K Manning	J S Bolger	Master Of The Seas	Lucky Vega	14	1 35.69
[illegible]	[illegible]	[illegible]	[illegible]	[illegible]	Native Trail	Luxembourg	15	1 36.27

1,000 GUINEAS STAKES (3y fillies) Newmarket - 1 mile

Year	Owner	Winner and Price	Jockey	Trainer	Second	Third	Ran	Time
1985	Sheikh Mohammed's	**OH SO SHARP** (2/1)	S Cauthen	H Cecil	Al Bahathri	Bella Colora	17	1 36.85
1986	H Ranier's	**MIDWAY LADY** (10/1)	R Cochrane	B Hanbury	Maysoon	Sonic Lady	15	1 41.54
1987	S Niarchos's	**MIESQUE** (15/8)	F Head	F Boutin	Milligram	Interval	14	1 38.48
1988	Ecurie Aland's	**RAVINELLA** (4/5)	G W Moore	Mme C Head	Dabaweyaa	Diminuendo	12	1 40.88
1989	Sheikh Mohammed's	**MUSICAL BLISS** (7/2)	W R Swinburn	M Stoute	Kerrera	Aldbourne	7	1 42.69
1990	Hamdan Al-Maktoum's	**SALSABIL** (6/4)	W Carson	J Dunlop	Heart of Joy	Negligent	10	1 38.06
1991	Hamdan Al-Maktoum's	**SHADAYID** (4/6)	W Carson	J Dunlop	Kooyonga	Crystal Gazing	14	1 38.18
1992	Maktoum Al-Maktoum's	**HATOOF** (5/1)	W R Swinburn	Mme C Head	Marling	Kenbu	14	1 39.45
1993	Mohamed Obaida's	**SAYYEDATI** (4/1)	W R Swinburn	C Brittain	Niche	Ajfan	12	1 37.34
1994	R Sangster's	**LAS MENINAS** (12/1)	J Reid	T Stack	Balanchine	Coup de Genie	15	1 36.71
1995	Hamdan Al-Maktoum's	**HARAYIR** (5/1)	R Hills	Major W R Hern	Aqaarid	Moonshell	14	1 36.72
1996	Wafic Said's	**BOSRA SHAM** (10/11)	Pat Eddery	H Cecil	Matiya	Bint Shadayid	13	1 37.75
1997	Greenbay Stables Ltd's	**SLEEPYTIME** (5/1)	K Fallon	H Cecil	Oh Nellie	Dazzle	15	1 37.66
1998	Godolphin's	**CAPE VERDI** (100/30)	L Dettori	S Bin Suroor	Shahtoush	Exclusive	16	1 37.86
1999	K Abdullah's (Run on July Course)	**WINCE** (4/1)	K Fallon	H Cecil	Wannabe Grand	Valentine Waltz	22	1 37.91
2000	Hamdan Al-Maktoum's	**LAHAN** (14/1)	R Hills	J Gosden	Princess Ellen	Petrushka	18	1 36.38
2001	Sheikh Ahmed Al Maktoum's	**AMEERAT** (11/1)	P Robinson	M Jarvis	Muwakleh	Toroca	15	1 38.36
2002	Godolphin's	**KAZZIA** (14/1)	L Dettori	S Bin Suroor	Snowfire	Alasha	17	1 37.85
2003	Cheveley Park Stud's	**RUSSIAN RHYTHM** (12/1)	K Fallon	Sir M Stoute	Six Perfections	Intercontinental	19	1 38.43
2004	Duke of Roxburghe's	**ATTRACTION** (11/2)	K Darley	M Johnston	Sundrop	Hathrah	16	1 36.70
2005	Mrs John Magnier & Mr M Tabor's	**VIRGINIA WATERS** (12/1)	K Fallon	A O'Brien	Maids Causeway	Vista Bella	20	1 36.50
2006	M Sly, Dr Davies & Mrs P Sly's	**SPECIOSA** (10/1)	M Fenton	Mrs P Sly	Confidential Lady	Nasheej	13	1 40.50
2007	M Ryan's	**FINSCEAL BEO** (5/4)	K Manning	J Bolger	Arch Swing	Simply Perfect	21	1 34.94
2008	S. Friborg's	**NATAGORA** (11/4)	C Lemaire	P Bary	Spacious	Saoirse Abu	15	1 38.99
2009	Hamdan Al-Maktoum's	**GHANAATI** (20/1)	R Hills	B Hills	Cuis Ghaire	Super Sleuth	14	1 34.22
2010	K Abdullah's (The first two placings were reversed by the Stewards)	**SPECIAL DUTY** (9/2)	S. Pasquier	Mme C Head-Maarek	Jacqueline Quest	Gile Na Greine	17	1 39.66
2011	Godolphin's	**BLUE BUNTING** (16/1)	L Dettori	M Al Zarooni	Together	Maqaasid	18	1 39.27
2012	Mrs John Magnier, M Tabor & D Smith's	**HOMECOMING QUEEN** (25/1)	R Moore	A O'Brien	Starscope	Maybe	17	1 40.45
2013	B Keswick's	**SKY LANTERN** (9/1)	R Hughes	R Hannon	Just The Judge	Moth	15	1 36.38
2015	Ballymore Thoroughbred Ltd's	**MISS FRANCE** (7/1)	M Guyon	A Fabre	Lightning Thunder	Ihtimal	17	1 37.40
2015	M Tabor, D Smith & Mrs J Magnier's	**LEGATISSIMO** (13/2)	R Moore	D Wachman	Lucida	Tiggy Wiggy	13	1 34.60
2016	D Smith, Mrs J Magnier & M Tabor's	**MINDING** (11/10)	R Moore	A O'Brien	Ballydoyle	Alice Springs	16	1 36.53
2017	Mrs John Magnier, M Tabor & D Smith's	**WINTER** (9/1)	W Lordan	A O'Brien	Rhododendron	Daban	14	1 35.66
2018	Pall Mall Partners & Partners'	**BILLESDON BROOK** (66/1)	S Levey	R Hannon	Laurens	Happily	15	1 36.62
2019	M Tabor, D Smith & Mrs John Magnier's	**HERMOSA** (14/1)	W Lordan	A O'Brien	Lady Kaya	Qabala	15	1 36.89
2020	M Tabor, D Smith & Mrs John Magnier's	**LOVE** (4/1)	R Moore	A O'Brien	Cloak Of Spirits	Quadrilateral	15	1 35.80
2021	D Smith, Mrs J Magnier & M Tabor's	**MOTHER EARTH** (10/1)	L Dettori	A O'Brien	Saffron Beach	Fev Rover	11	1 36.37
2022	Highclere T'Bred Racing - Wild Flower's	**CACHET** (16/1)	J Doyle	G Boughey	Prosperous Voyage	Tuesday	13	1 36.55

OAKS STAKES (3y fillies) Epsom - 1 mile 4 furlongs 6 yards

Year	Owner	Winner and Price	Jockey	Trainer	Second	Third	Ran	Time
1985	Sheikh Mohammed's	**OH SO SHARP** (6/4)	S Cauthen	H Cecil	Triptych	Dubian	12	2 41.37
1986	H Ranier's	**MIDWAY LADY** (15/8)	R Cochrane	B Hanbury	Untold	Maysoon	15	2 35.60
1987	Sheikh Mohammed's	**UNITE** (11/1)	W R Swinburn	M Stoute	Bourbon Girl	Three Tails	11	2 38.17
1988	Sheikh Mohammed's	**DIMINUENDO** (7/4)	S Cauthen	H Cecil	Sudden Love	Animatrice	11	2 35.02
1989	Saeed Maktoum Al Maktoum's	**SNOW BRIDE** (13/2)	S Cauthen	H Cecil	Roseate Tern	Mamaluna	9	2 34.22
	(Aliysa finished first but was subsequently disqualified)							
1990	Hamdan Al-Maktoum's	**SALSABIL** (2/1)	W Carson	J Dunlop	Game Plan	Knight's Baroness	8	2 38.70
1991	Maktoum Al-Maktoum's	**JET SKI LADY** (50/1)	C Roche	J Bolger	Shamshir	Shadayid	9	2 37.30
1992	W J Gredley's	**USER FRIENDLY** (5/1)	G Duffield	C Brittain	All At Sea	Pearl Angel	7	2 39.77
1993	Sheikh Mohammed's	**INTREPIDITY** (5/1)	M Roberts	A Fabre	Royal Ballerina	Oakmead	14	2 34.19
1994	Godolphin's	**BALANCHINE** (6/1)	L Dettori	H Ibrahim	Wind In Her Hair	Hawajiss	10	2 40.37
1995	Maktoum Al Maktoum/ Godolphin's	**MOONSHELL** (3/1)	L Dettori	S Bin Suroor	Dance A Dream	Pure Grain	10	2 35.44
1996	Wafic Said's	**LADY CARLA** (100/30)	P Eddery	H Cecil	Pricket	Mezzogiorno	11	2 35.55
1997	K Abdullah's	**REAMS OF VERSE** (5/6)	K Fallon	H Cecil	Gazelle Royale	Crown of Light	12	2 35.59
1998	Mrs D Nagle & Mrs J Magnier's	**SHAHTOUSH** (12/1)	M Kinane	A O'Brien	Bahr	Midnight Line	8	2 38.23
1999	F Salman's	**RAMRUMA** (3/1)	K Fallon	H Cecil	Noushkey	Zahrat Dubai	10	2 38.72
2000	Lordship Stud's	**LOVE DIVINE** (9/4)	T Quinn	H Cecil	Kalypso Katie	Melikah	16	2 43.11
2001	Mrs D. Nagle & Mrs J Magnier's	**IMAGINE** (3/1)	M Kinane	A O'Brien	Flight Of Fancy	Relish The Thought	14	2 36.70
2002	Godolphin's	**KAZZIA** (100/30)	L Dettori	S Bin Suroor	Quarter Moon	Shadow Dancing	14	2 44.52
2003	W S Farish III's	**CASUAL LOOK** (10/1)	M Dwyer	A Balding	Yesterday	Summitville	15	2 38.07
2004	Lord Derby's	**OUIJA BOARD** (7/2)	K Fallon	E Dunlop	All Too Beautiful	Punctilious	7	2 35.40
2005	Hamdan Al Maktoum's	**ESWARAH** (11/4)	R Hills	M Jarvis	Something Exciting	Pictavia	12	2 39.00
2006	Mrs J Magnier, Mr M Tabor & Mr D Smith's	**ALEXANDROVA** (9/4)	K Fallon	A O'Brien	Rising Cross	Short Skirt	10	2 37.70
2007	Niarchos Family's	**LIGHT SHIFT** (13/2)	T Durcan	H Cecil	Peeping Fawn	All My Loving	14	2 40.38
2008	J H Richmond-Watson's	**LOOK HERE** (33/1)	S Sanders	R Beckett	Moonstone	Katiyra	16	2 36.89
2009	Lady Bamford's	**SARISKA** (9/4)	J Spencer	M Bell	Midday	High Heeled	10	2 35.28
2010	Anamoine Ltd's	**SNOW FAIRY** (9/1)	R Moore	E Dunlop	Remember When	Rumoush	15	2 35.77
	(Meeznah finished second but was subsequently disqualified)							
2011	M J & L A Taylor's	**DANCING RAIN** (20/1)	J Murtagh	W Haggas	Wonder of Wonders	Izzi Top	13	2 41.73
2012	D Smith, Mrs J Magnier & M Tabor's	**WAS** (20/1)	S Hefferman	A O'Brien	Shirocco Star	The Fugue	12	2 38.68
2013	J L Rowsell & M H Dixon's	**TALENT** (20/1)	R Hughes	R Beckett	Secret Gesture	The Lark	11	2 42.00
2014	Hamdan Al Maktoum's	**TAGHROODA** (5/1)	P Hanagan	J Gosden	Tarfasha	Volume	17	2 34.89
2015	Mrs C C Regalado-Gonzalez's	**QUALIFY** (50/1)	C O'Donoghue	A O'Brien	Legatissimo	Lady of Dubai	11	2 37.41
2016	D Smith, Mrs J Magnier & M Tabor's	**MINDING** (10/11)	R Moore	A O'Brien	Architecture	Harlequeen	9	2 42.66
2017	K Abdullah's	**ENABLE** (6/1)	L Dettori	J Gosden	Rhododendron	Alluringly	9	2 34.13
2018	M Tabor, D Smith & Mrs J Magnier's	**FOREVER TOGETHER** (7/1)	D O'Brien	A O'Brien	Wild Illusion	Bye Bye Baby	9	2 40.39
2019	Helena Springfield Ltd's	**ANAPURNA** (8/1)	L Dettori	J Gosden	Pink Dogwood	Fleeting	14	2 36.09
2020	M Tabor, D Smith & Mrs J Magnier's	**LOVE** (11/10)	R Moore	A O'Brien	Ennistymon	Frankly Darling	8	2 34.06
2021	D Smith, Mrs J Magnier & M Tabor's	**SNOWFALL** (11/2)	L Dettori	A O'Brien	Mystery Angel	Divinely	14	2 42.67

DERBY STAKES (3y) Epsom - 1 mile 4 furlongs 6 yards

Year	Owner	Winner and Price	Jockey	Trainer	Second	Third	Ran	Time
1985	Lord H. de Walden's	**SLIP ANCHOR** (9/4)	S Cauthen	H Cecil	Law Society	Damister	14	2 36.23
1986	H H Aga Khan's	**SHAHRASTANI** (11/2)	W Swinburn	M Stoute	Dancing Brave	Mashkour	17	2 37.13
1987	L Freedman's	**REFERENCE POINT** (6/4)	S Cauthen	H Cecil	Most Welcome	Bellotto	19	2 33.90
1988	H H Aga Khan's	**KAHYASI** (11/1)	R Cochrane	L Cumani	Glacial Storm	Doyoun	14	2 33.84
1989	Hamdan Al-Maktoum's	**NASHWAN** (5/4)	W Carson	R Hern	Terimon	Cacoethes	12	2 34.90
1990	K Abdullah's	**QUEST FOR FAME** (7/1)	Pat Eddery	R Charlton	Blue Stag	Elmaamul	18	2 37.26
1991	F Salman's	**GENEROUS** (9/1)	A Munro	P Cole	Marju	Star of Gdansk	13	2 34.00
1992	Sidney H Craig's	**DR DEVIOUS** (8/1)	J Reid	P Chapple-Hyam	St Jovite	Silver Wisp	18	2 36.19
1993	K Abdullah's	**COMMANDER IN CHIEF** (15/2)	M Kinane	H Cecil	Blue Judge	Blues Traveller	16	2 34.51
1994	Hamdan Al-Maktoum's	**ERHAAB** (7/2)	W Carson	J Dunlop	King's Theatre	Colonel Collins	25	2 34.16
1995	Saeed Maktoum Al Maktoum's	**LAMMTARRA** (14/1)	W Swinburn	S Bin Suroor	Tamure	Presenting	15	2 32.31
1996	K Dasmal's	**SHAAMIT** (12/1)	M Hills	W Haggas	Dushyantor	Shantou	20	2 35.05
1997	L Knight's	**BENNY THE DIP** (11/1)	W Ryan	J Gosden	Silver Patriarch	Romanov	13	2 35.77
1998	Sheikh Mohammed Obaid Al Maktoum's	**HIGH-RISE** (20/1)	O Peslier	L Cumani	City Honours	Border Arrow	15	2 33.88
1999	The Thoroughbred Corporation's	**OATH** (13/2)	K Fallon	H Cecil	Daliapour	Beat All	16	2 37.43
2000	H H Aga Khan's	**SINNDAR** (7/1)	J Murtagh	J Oxx	Sakhee	Beat Hollow	15	2 36.75
2001	M Tabor & Mrs J Magnier's	**GALILEO** (11/4)	M Kinane	A O'Brien	Golan	Tobougg	12	2 33.27
2002	M Tabor & Mrs J Magnier's	**HIGH CHAPARRAL** (7/2)	J Murtagh	A O'Brien	Hawk Wing	Moon Ballad	12	2 39.45
2003	Saeed Suhail's	**KRIS KIN** (6/1)	K Fallon	Sir M Stoute	The Great Gatsby	Alamshar	20	2 33.35
2004	Ballymacoll Stud's	**NORTH LIGHT** (7/2)	K Fallon	Sir M Stoute	Rule Of Law	Let The Lion Roar	14	2 33.70
2005	The Royal Ascot Racing Club's	**MOTIVATOR** (3/1)	J Murtagh	M Bell	Walk In The Park	Dubawi	13	2 35.60
2006	A E Pakenham's	**SIR PERCY** (6/1)	M Dwyer	M Tregoning	Dragon Dancer	Dylan Thomas	18	2 35.20
2007	Saleh Al Homaizi & Imad Al Sagar's	**AUTHORIZED** (5/4)	L Dettori	P Chapple-Hyam	Eagle Mountain	Aqaleem	17	2 34.77
2008	HRH Princess Haya of Jordan's	**NEW APPROACH** (5/1)	K. Manning	J Bolger	Tartan Bearer	Casual Conquest	16	2 36.50
2009	C Tsui's	**SEA THE STARS** (11/4)	M Kinane	J Oxx	Fame And Glory	Mastereofthehorse	12	2 36.74
2010	K Abdullah's	**WORKFORCE** (6/1)	R Moore	Sir M Stoute	At First Sight	Rewilding	12	2 31.33
2011	Mrs John Magnier, M Tabor & D Smith's	**POUR MOI** (4/1)	M Barzalona	A Fabre	Treasure Beach	Carlton House	13	2 34.54
2012	D Smith, Mrs J Magnier & M Tabor's	**CAMELOT** (8/13)	J O'Brien	A O'Brien	Main Sequence	Astrology	9	2 33.90
2013	Mrs John Magnier, Michael Tabor & Derrick Smith's	**RULER OF THE WORLD** (7/1)	R Moore	A O'Brien	Libertarian	Galileo Rock	12	2 39.06
2014	D Smith, Mrs J Magnier, M Tabor & T Ah Khing's	**AUSTRALIA** (11/8)	J O'Brien	A O'Brien	Kingston Hill	Romsdal	16	2 33.63
2015	A E Oppenheimer's	**GOLDEN HORN** (13/8)	L Dettori	J Gosden	Jack Hobbs	Storm The Stars	12	2 32.32
2016	H H Aga Khan's	**HARZAND** (13/2)	P Smullen	D Weld	US Army Ranger	Idaho	16	2 40.09
2017	D Smith, Mrs J Magnier, M Tabor's	**WINGS OF EAGLES** (40/1)	P Beggy	A O'Brien	Cliffs of Moher	Cracksman	18	2 33.02
2018	Godolphin's	**MASAR** (16/1)	W Buick	C Appleby	Dee Ex Bee	Roaring Lion	12	2 34.93
2019	Mrs J Magnier, M Tabor & D Smith's	**ANTHONY VAN DYCK** (13/2)	S Heffernan	A O'Brien	Madhmoon	Japan	13	2 33.38
2020	Mrs J Magnier, M Tabor & D Smith's	**SERPENTINE** (25/1)	E McNamara	A O'Brien	Khalifa Sat	Amhran Na Bhfiann	16	2 34.43
2021	Godolphin's	**ADAYAR** (16/1)	A Kirby	C Appleby	Mojo Star	Hurricane Lane	11	2 36.85
2022	Saeed Suhail's	**DESERT CROWN** (5/2)	R Kingscote	Sir M Stoute	Hoo Ya Mal	Westover	17	2 36.38

ST LEGER STAKES (3y) Doncaster - 1 mile 6 furlongs 115 yards

Year	Owner	Winner and Price	Jockey	Trainer	Second	Third	Ran	Time
1985	Sheikh Mohammed's	**OH SO SHARP** (8/11)	S Cauthen	H Cecil	Phardante	Lanfranco	6	3 7.13
1986	Duchess of Norfolk's	**MOON MADNESS** (9/2)	Pat Eddery	J Dunlop	Celestial Storm	Untold	8	3 5.03
1987	L Freedman's	**REFERENCE POINT** (4/11)	S Cauthen	H Cecil	Mountain Kingdom	Dry Dock	7	3 5.91
1988	Lady Beaverbrook's	**MINSTER SON** (15/2)	W Carson	N A Graham	Diminuendo	Sheriff's Star	6	3 6.80
1989	C St George's (Run at Ayr)	**MICHELOZZO** (6/4)	S Cauthen	H Cecil	Sapience	Roseate Tern	8	3 20.72
1990	M Arbib's	**SNURGE** (7/2)	T Quinn	P Cole	Hellenic	River God	8	3 8.78
1991	K Abdullah's	**TOULON** (5/2)	Pat Eddery	A Fabre	Saddlers' Hall	Micheletti	10	3 3.12
1992	W J Gredley's	**USER FRIENDLY** (7/4)	G Duffield	C Brittain	Sonus	Bonny Scot	7	3 5.48
1993	Mrs G A E Smith's	**BOB'S RETURN** (3/1)	P Robinson	M Tompkins	Armiger	Edbaysaan	9	3 7.85
1994	Sheikh Mohammed's	**MOONAX** (40/1)	Pat Eddery	B Hills	Broadway Flyer	Double Trigger	8	3 4.19
1995	Godolphin's	**CLASSIC CLICHE** (100/30)	L Dettori	S Bin Suroor	Minds Music	Istidaad	10	3 9.74
1996	Sheikh Mohammed's	**SHANTOU** (8/1)	L Dettori	J Gosden	Dushyantor	Samraan	11	3 5.10
1997	P Winfield's	**SILVER PATRIARCH** (5/4)	Pat Eddery	J Dunlop	Vertical Speed	The Fly	10	3 6.92
1998	Godolphin's	**NEDAWI** (5/2)	J Reid	S Bin Suroor	High and Low	Sunshine Street	9	3 5.61
1999	Godolphin's	**MUTAFAWEQ** (11/2)	R Hills	S Bin Suroor	Ramruma	Adair	9	3 2.75
2000	N Jones'	**MILLENARY** (11/4)	T Quinn	J Dunlop	Air Marshall	Chimes At Midnight	11	3 2.58
2001	M Tabor & Mrs J Magnier's	**MILAN** (13/8)	M Kinane	A O'Brien	Demophilos	Mr Combustible	10	3 5.16
2002	Sir Neil Westbrook's	**BOLLIN ERIC** (7/1)	K Darley	T Easterby	Highest	Bandari	8	3 2.92
2003	Mrs J Magnier's	**BRIAN BORU** (5/4)	J P Spencer	A O'Brien	High Accolade	Phoenix Reach	12	3 4.64
2004	Godolphin's	**RULE OF LAW** (3/1)	K McEvoy	S Bin Suroor	Quiff	Tycoon	9	3 6.20
2005	Mrs J Magnier & M Tabor's	**SCORPION** (10/11)	L Dettori	A O'Brien	The Geezer	Tawqeet	6	3 19.00
2006	Mrs S Roy's (Run at York)	**SIXTIES ICON** (11/8)	L Dettori	J Noseda	The Last Drop	Red Rocks	11	2 57.20
2007	G Strawbridge's	**LUCARNO** (7/2)	J Fortune	J Gosden	Mahler	Honolulu	10	3 1.90
2008	Ballymacoll Stud's	**CONDUIT** (8/1)	L Dettori	Sir M Stoute	Unsung Heroine	Look Here	14	3 7.92
2009	Godolphin's	**MASTERY** (14/1)	T Durcan	S Bin Suroor	Kite Wood	Monitor Closely	8	3 4.81
2010	Ms R Hood & R Geffen's	**ARCTIC COSMOS** (12/1)	W Buick	J Gosden	Midas Touch	Corsica	10	3 3.12
2011	B Nielsen's	**MASKED MARVEL** (15/2)	W Buick	J Gosden	Brown Panther	Sea Moon	9	3 0.44
2012	Godolphin's	**ENCKE** (25/1)	M Barzalona	M Al Zarooni	Camelot	Michelangelo	9	3 3.81
2013	Derrick Smith & Mrs John Magnier & Michael Tabor's	**LEADING LIGHT** (7/2)	J O'Brien	A O'Brien	Talent	Galileo Rock	11	3 9.20
2014	Paul Smith's	**KINGSTON HILL** (9/4)	A Atzeni	R Varian	Romsdal	Snow Sky	12	3 5.42
2015	QRL, Sheikh Suhaim Al Thani & M Al Kubaisi's	**SIMPLE VERSE** (8/1)	A Atzeni	R Beckett	Bondi Beach	Fields of Athenry	7	3 7.12
2016	Mrs Jackie Cornwell's	**HARBOUR LAW** (22/1)	G Baker	Mrs L Mongan	Ventura Storm	Housesofparliament	9	3 5.48
2017	Derrick Smith & Mrs John Magnier & Michael Tabor's	**CAPRI** (3/1)	R Moore	A O'Brien	Crystal Ocean	Stradivarius	11	3 4.04
2018	Derrick Smith & Mrs John Magnier & Michael Tabor's	**KEW GARDENS** (3/1)	R Moore	A O'Brien	Lah Ti Dar	Southern France	12	3 3.34
2020	Galileo Chrome Partnership's	**GALILEO CHROME** (4/1)	T Marquand	J O'Brien	Berkshire Rocco	Pyledriver	11	3 1.94
2021	Godolphin's	**HURRICANE LANE** (8/11)	W Buick	C Appleby	Mojo Star	The Mediterranean	10	3 4.28
2022	KHK Racing Ltd's	**ELDAR ELDAROV** (9/2)	D Egan	R Varian	Haskoy	New London	9	3 8.39

KING G[illegible]ORGE [illegible]I AND QUEEN ELIZABETH STAKES Ascot - 1 mile 3 furlongs 211 yards

Year	Owner	Winner and Price	Jockey	Trainer	Second	Third	Ran	Time
1985	Lady Beaverbrook's	**PETOSKI** 3-8-8 (12/1)	W Carson	R Hern	Oh So Sharp	Rainbow Quest	12	2 27.61
1986	K Abdullah's	**DANCING BRAVE** 3-8-8 (6/4)	Pat Eddery	G Harwood	Shardari	Triptych	9	2 29.49
1987	L Freedman's	**REFERENCE POINT** 3-8-8 (11/10)	S Cauthen	H Cecil	Celestial Storm	Triptych	9	2 34.63
1988	Sheikh Ahmed Al Maktoum	**MTOTO** 5-9-7 (4/1)	M Roberts	A C Stewart	Unfuwain	Tony Bin	10	2 37.33
1989	Hamdan Al-Maktoum's	**NASHWAN** 3-8-8 (2/9)	W Carson	R Hern	Cacoethes	Top Class	7	2 32.27
1990	Sheikh Mohammed's	**BELMEZ** 3-8-9 (15/2)	M Kinane	H Cecil	Old Vic	Assatis	11	2 30.76
1991	F Salman's	**GENEROUS** 3-8-9 (4/6)	A Munro	P Cole	Sanglamore	Rock Hopper	9	2 28.99
1992	Mrs V K Payson's	**ST JOVITE** 3-8-9 (4/5)	S Craine	J Bolger	Saddlers' Hall	Opera House	8	2 30.85
1993	Sheikh Mohammed's	**OPERA HOUSE** 5-9-7 (8/1)	M Roberts	M Stoute	White Muzzle	Commander in Chief	10	2 33.94
1994	Sheikh Mohammed's	**KING'S THEATRE** 3-8-9 (12/1)	M Kinane	H Cecil	White Muzzle	Wagon Master	12	2 28.92
1995	Saeed Maktoum Al Maktoum's	**LAMMTARRA** 3-8-9 (9/4)	L Dettori	S Bin Suroor	Pentire	Strategic Choice	7	2 31.01
1996	Mollers Racing's	**PENTIRE** 4-9-7 (100/30)	M Hills	G Wragg	Classic Cliche	Shaamit	8	2 28.11
1997	Godolphin's	**SWAIN** 5-9-7 (16/1)	J Reid	S Bin Suroor	Pilsudski	Helissio	8	2 36.45
1998	Godolphin's	**SWAIN** 6-9-7 (11/2)	L Dettori	S Bin Suroor	High-Rise	Royal Anthem	8	2 29.06
1999	Godolphin's	**DAYLAMI** 5-9-7 (3/1)	L Dettori	S Bin Suroor	Nedawi	Fruits Of Love	8	2 29.35
2000	M Tabor's	**MONTJEU** 4-9-7 (1/3)	M Kinane	J Hammond	Fantastic Light	Daliapour	7	2 29.98
2001	Mrs J Magnier & M Tabor's	**GALILEO** 3-8-9 (1/2)	M Kinane	A O'Brien	Fantastic Light	Hightori	12	2 27.71
2002	Exors of the late Lord Weinstock's	**GOLAN** 4-9-7 (11/2)	K Fallon	Sir M Stoute	Nayef	Zindabad	9	2 29.70
2003	H H Aga Khan	**ALAMSHAR** 3-8-9 (13/2)	J Murtagh	J Oxx	Sulamani	Kris Kin	12	2 33.26
2004	Godolphin's	**DOYEN** 4-9-7 (11/10)	L Dettori	S Bin Suroor	Hard Buck	Sulamani	11	2 33.10
2005	H H Aga Khan's (Run at Newbury)	**AZAMOUR** 4-9-7 (5/2)	M Kinane	J Oxx	Norse Dancer	Bago	12	2 28.20
2006	M Tabor's	**HURRICANE RUN** 4-9-7 (5/6)	C Soumillon	A Fabre	Electrocutionist	Heart's Cry	6	2 30.20
2007	Mrs J Magnier & M Tabor's	**DYLAN THOMAS** 4-9-7 (5/4)	J Murtagh	A O'Brien	Youmzain	Maraahel	7	2 31.10
2008	Mrs J Magnier & M Tabor's	**DUKE OF MARMALADE** 4-9-7 (4/6)	J Murtagh	A O'Brien	Papal Bull	Youmzain	8	2 27.91
2009	Ballymacoll Stud's	**CONDUIT** 4-9-7 (13/8)	R Moore	Sir M Stoute	Tartan Bearer	Ask	9	2 28.73
2010	Highclere Thoroughbred Racing (Adm. Rous)'s	**HARBINGER** 4-9-7 (4/1)	O Peslier	Sir M Stoute	Cape Blanco	Youmzain	6	2 26.78
2011	Lady Rothschild's	**NATHANIEL** 3-8-9 (11/2)	W Buick	J Gosden	Workforce	St Nicholas Abbey	5	2 35.07
2012	Gestut Burg Eberstein & Teruya Yoshida's	**DANEDREAM** 4-9-4 (9/1)	A Starke	P Schiergen	Nathaniel	St Nicholas Abbey	10	2 31.62
2013	Dr Christophe Berglar's	**NOVELLIST** 4-9-7 (13/2)	J Murtagh	A Wohler	Trading Leather	Hillstar	8	2 24.60
2014	Hamdan Al Maktoum's	**TAGHROODA** 3-8-6 (7/2)	P Hanagan	J Gosden	Telescope	Mukhadram	8	2 28.13
2015	Sheikh Mohammed Obaid Al Maktoum's	**POSTPONED** 4-9-7 (6/1)	A Atzeni	L Cumani	Eagle Top	Romsdal	7	2 31.25
2016	D Smith, Mrs J Magnier & M Tabor's	**HIGHLAND REEL** 4-9-7 (13/8)	R Moore	A O'Brien	Wings of Desire	Dartmouth	7	2 28.97
2017	K Abdullah's	**ENABLE** 3-8-7 (5/4)	L Dettori	J Gosden	Ulysses	Idaho	10	2 36.22
2018	S Suhail's	**POET'S WORD** 5-9-7 (7/4)	J Doyle	Sir M Stoute	Crystal Ocean	Coronet	7	2 25.84
2019	K Abdullah's	**ENABLE** 5-9-4 (8/15)	L Dettori	J Gosden	Crystal Ocean	Waldgeist	11	2 32.42
2020	K Abdullah's	**ENABLE** 6-9-4 (4/9)	L Dettori	J Gosden	Sovereign	Japan	3	2 28.92
2021	Godolphin's	**ADAYAR** 3-8-10 (9/4)	W Buick	C Appleby	Mishriff	Love	5	2 26.54
2022	La Pyle Partnership's	**PYLEDRIVER** 5-9-9 (18/1)	P J McDonald	W Muir & C Grassick	Torquator Tasso	Mishriff	6	2 29.49

PRIX DE L'ARC DE TRIOMPHE ParisLongchamp - 1 mile 4 furlongs

Year	Owner	Winner and Price	Jockey	Trainer	Second	Third	Ran	Time
1985	K Abdullah's	**RAINBOW QUEST** 4-9-4 (71/10)	P Eddery	J Tree	Sagace	Kozana	15	2 29.50
	(The first two placings were reversed by the Stewards)							
1986	K Abdullah's	**DANCING BRAVE** 3-8-11 (11/10)	P Eddery	G Harwood	Bering	Triptych	15	2 27.70
1987	P de Moussac's	**TREMPOLINO** 3-8-11 (20/1)	P Eddery	A Fabre	Tony Bin	Triptych	11	2 26.30
1988	Mrs V Gaucci del Bono's	**TONY BIN** 5-9-4 (14/1)	J Reid	L Camici	Mtoto	Boyatino	24	2 27.30
1989	A Balzarini's	**CARROLL HOUSE** 4-9-4 (19/1)	M Kinane	M Jarvis	Behera	Saint Andrews	19	2 30.80
1990	B McNall's	**SAUMAREZ** 3-8-11 (15/1)	G Mosse	N Clement	Epervier Bleu	Snurge	21	2 29.80
1991	H Chalhoub's	**SUAVE DANCER** 3-8-11 (37/10)	C Asmussen	J Hammond	Magic Night	Pistolet Bleu	14	2 31.40
1992	O Lecerf's	**SUBOTICA** 4-9-4 (88/10)	T Jarnet	A Fabre	User Friendly	Vert Amande	18	2 39.00
1993	D Tsui's	**URBAN SEA** 4-9-1 (37/1)	E Saint Martin	J Lesbordes	White Muzzle	Opera House	23	2 37.90
1994	Sheikh Mohammed's	**CARNEGIE** 3-8-11 (3/1)	T Jarnet	A Fabre	Hernando	Apple Tree	20	2 31.10
1995	Saeed Maktoum Al Maktoum's	**LAMMTARRA** 3-8-11 (2/1)	L Dettori	S Bin Suroor	Freedom Cry	Swain	16	2 31.80
1996	E Sarasola's	**HELISSIO** 3-8-11 (18/10)	O Peslier	E Lellouche	Pilsudski	Oscar Schindler	16	2 29.90
1997	D Wildenstein's	**PEINTRE CELEBRE** 3-8-11 (22/10)	O Peslier	A Fabre	Pilsudski	Borgia	18	2 24.60
1998	J-L Lagardere's	**SAGAMIX** 3-8-11 (5/2)	O Peslier	A Fabre	Leggera	Tiger Hill	14	2 34.50
1999	M Tabor's	**MONTJEU** 3-8-11 (6/4)	M Kinane	J Hammond	El Condor Pasa	Croco Rouge	14	2 38.50
2000	H H Aga Khan's	**SINNDAR** 3-8-11 (6/4)	J Murtagh	J Oxx	Egyptband	Volvoreta	10	2 25.80
2001	Godolphin's	**SAKHEE** 4-9-5 (22/10)	L Dettori	S Bin Suroor	Aquarelliste	Sagacity	17	2 36.10
2002	Godolphin's	**MARIENBARD** 5-9-5 (158/10)	L Dettori	S Bin Suroor	Sulamani	High Chaparral	16	2 26.70
2003	H H Aga Khan's	**DALAKHANI** 3-8-11 (9/4)	C Soumillon	A De Royer-Dupre	Mubtaker	High Chaparral	13	2 32.30
2004	Niarchos Family's	**BAGO** 3-8-11 (10/1)	T Gillet	J E Pease	Cherry Mix	Ouija Board	13	2 25.00
2005	M Tabor's	**HURRICANE RUN** 3-8-11 (11/4)	K Fallon	A Fabre	Westerner	Bago	15	2 27.40
2006	K Abdullah's	**RAIL LINK** 3-8-11 (8/1)	S Pasquier	A Fabre	Pride	Hurrricane Run	8	2 26.30
	(Deep Impact disqualified from third place)							
2007	Mrs J Magnier & M Tabor's	**DYLAN THOMAS** 4-9-5 (11/2)	K Fallon	A O'Brien	Youmzain	Sagara	12	2 28.50
2008	H H Aga Khan's	**ZARKAVA** 3-8-8 (13/8)	C Soumillon	A De Royer-Dupre	Youmzain	Soldier of Fortune/It's Gino	16	2 28.80
2009	C Tsui's	**SEA THE STARS** 3-8-11 (4/6)	M Kinane	J Oxx	Youmzain	Cavalryman	19	2 26.30
2010	K Abdullah's	**WORKFORCE** 3-8-11 (6/1)	R Moore	Sir M Stoute	Nakayama Festa	Sarafina	18	2 35.30
2011	Gestut Burg Eberstein & T Yoshida's	**DANEDREAM** 3-8-8 (20/1)	A Starke	P Schiergen	Shareta	Snow Fairy	16	2 24.49
2012	Wertheimer & Frere's	**SOLEMIA** 4-9-2 (33/1)	O Peslier	C Laffon-Parias	Orfevre	Masterstroke	18	2 37.68
2013	H E Sheikh Joaan Bin Hamad Al Thani's	**TREVE** 3-8-8 (9/2)	T Jarnet	Mme C Head-Maarek	Orfevre	Intello	17	2 32.04
2014	Al Shaqab Racing's	**TREVE** 4-9-2 (11/1)	T Jarnet	Mme C Head-Maarek	Flintshire	Taghrooda	20	2 26.05
2015	A E Oppenheimer's	**GOLDEN HORN** 3-8-11 (9/2)	L Dettori	J Gosden	Flintshire	New Bay	17	2 27.23
2016	M Tabor, D Smith & Mrs J Magnier's	**FOUND** 4-9-2 (6/1)	R Moore	A O'Brien	Highland Reel	Order of St George	16	2 23.61
	(Run at Chantilly)							
2017	K Abdullah's	**ENABLE** 3-8-9 (10/11)	L Dettori	J Gosden	Cloth of Stars	Ulysses	18	2 28.69
	(Run at Chantilly)							
2018	K Abdullah's	**ENABLE** 4-9-2 (Evs)	L Dettori	J Gosden	Sea Of Class	Cloth Of Stars	19	2 29.24
2019	Gestut Ammerland & Newsells Parks's	**WALDGEIST** 5-9-5 (131/10)	P-C Boudot	A Fabre	Enable	Sottsass	12	2 31.97
2020	White Birch Farm's	**SOTTSASS** 4-9-5 (73/10)	C Demuro	J-C Rouget	In Swoop	Persian King	11	2 39.30
2021	Gestut Auenquelle's	**TORQUATOR TASSO** 4-9-5 (72/1)	R Piechulek	M Weiss	Tarnawa	Hurricane Lane	14	2 37.62
2022	Miss K Rausing's	**ALPINISTA** 5-9-2 (33/10)	L Morris	Sir M Prescott	Vadeni	Torquator Tasso	20	2 35.71

GRAND NATIONAL STEEPLECHASE Aintree - 4m 2f 74y (4m 4f before 2013)

Year	Winner and Price	Age & Weight	Jockey	Second	Third	Ran	Time
1977	**RED RUM** (9/1)	12 11 8	T Stack	Churchtown Boy	Eyecatcher	42	9 30.30
1978	**LUCIUS** (14/1)	9 10 9	B R Davies	Sebastian V	Drumroan	37	9 33.90
1979	**RUBSTIC** (25/1)	10 10 0	M Barnes	Zongalero	Rough and Tumble	34	9 52.90
1980	**BEN NEVIS** (40/1)	12 10 12	Mr C Fenwick	Rough and Tumble	The Pilgarlic	30	10 17.40
1981	**ALDANITI** (10/1)	11 10 13	R Champion	Spartan Missile	Royal Mail	39	9 47.20
1982	**GRITTAR** (7/1)	9 11 5	E Saunders	Hard Outlook	Loving Words	39	9 12.60
1983	**CORBIERE** (13/1)	8 11 4	B de Haan	Greasepaint	Yer Man	41	9 47.04
1984	**HALLO DANDY** (13/1)	10 10 2	N Doughty	Greasepaint	Corbiere	40	9 21.04
1985	**LAST SUSPECT** (50/1)	11 10 5	H Davies	Mr Snugfit	Corbiere	40	9 42.70
1986	**WEST TIP** (15/2)	9 10 11	R Dunwoody	Young Driver	Classified	40	9 33.00
1987	**MAORI VENTURE** (28/1)	11 10 13	S C Knight	The Tsarevich	Lean Ar Aghaidh	40	9 19.30
1988	**RHYME `N' REASON** (10/1)	9 11 0	B Powell	Durham Edition	Monanore	40	9 53.50
1989	**LITTLE POLVEIR** (28/1)	12 10 3	J Frost	West Tip	The Thinker	40	10 06.80
1990	**MR FRISK** (16/1)	11 10 6	Mr M Armytage	Durham Edition	Rinus	38	8 47.80
1991	**SEAGRAM** (12/1)	11 10 6	N Hawke	Garrison Savannah	Auntie Dot	40	9 29.90
1992	**PARTY POLITICS** (14/1)	8 10 7	C Llewellyn	Romany King	Laura's Beau	40	9 06.30
1993	RACE VOID - FALSE START						
1994	**MIINNEHOMA** (16/1)	11 10 8	R Dunwoody	Just So	Moorcroft Boy	36	10 18.80
1995	**ROYAL ATHLETE** (40/1)	12 10 6	J Titley	Party Politics	Over The Deel	35	9 04.00
1996	**ROUGH QUEST** (7/1)	10 10 7	M Fitzgerald	Encore Un Peu	Superior Finish	27	9 00.80
1997	**LORD GYLLENE** (14/1)	9 10 0	A Dobbin	Suny Bay	Camelot Knight	36	9 05.80
1998	**EARTH SUMMIT** (7/1)	10 10 5	C Llewellyn	Suny Bay	Samlee	37	10 51.40
1999	**BOBBYJO** (10/1)	9 10 0	P Carberry	Blue Charm	Call It A Day	32	9 14.00
2000	**PAPILLON** (10/1)	9 10 12	R Walsh	Mely Moss	Niki Dee	40	9 09.70
2001	**RED MARAUDER** (33/1)	11 10 11	R Guest	Smarty	Blowing Wind	40	11 00.10
2002	**BINDAREE** (20/1)	8 10 4	J Culloty	What's Up Boys	Blowing Wind	40	9 09.00
2003	**MONTY'S PASS** (16/1)	10 10 7	B J Geraghty	Supreme Glory	Amberleigh House	40	9 21.70
2004	**AMBERLEIGH HOUSE** (16/1)	12 10 10	G Lee	Clan Royal	Lord Atterbury	39	9 20.30
2005	**HEDGEHUNTER** (7/1)	9 11 1	R Walsh	Royal Auclair	Simply Gifted	40	9 20.80
2006	**NUMBERSIXVALVERDE** (11/1)	10 10 8	N Madden	Hedgehunter	Clan Royal	40	9 41.00
2007	**SILVER BIRCH** (33/1)	10 10 6	R M Power	McKelvey	Slim Pickings	40	9 13.60
2008	**COMPLY OR DIE** (7/1)	9 10 9	T Murphy	King Johns Castle	Snowy Morning	40	9 16.60
2009	**MON MOME** (100/1)	9 11 0	L Treadwell	Comply Or Die	My Will	40	9 32.90
2010	**DON'T PUSH IT** (10/1)	10 11 0	A P McCoy	Black Apalachi	State Of Play	40	9 04.60
2011	**BALLABRIGGS** (14/1)	10 11 0	J Maguire	Oscar Time	Don't Push It	40	9 01.20
2012	**NEPTUNE COLLONGES** (33/1)	11 11 6	D Jacob	Sunnyhillboy	Seabass	40	9 05.10
2013	**AURORAS ENCORE** (66/1)	11 10 3	R Mania	Cappa Bleu	Teaforthree	40	9 12.00
2014	**PINEAU DE RE** (25/1)	11 10 6	L Aspell	Balthazar King	Double Seven	40	9 09.90
2015	**MANY CLOUDS** (25/1)	8 11 9	L Aspell	Saint Are	Monbeg Dude	39	8 56.80
2016	**RULE THE WORLD** (33/1)	9 10 7	D Mullins	The Last Samuri	Vics Canvas	39	9 29.00
2017	**ONE FOR ARTHUR** (14/1)	8 10 11	D Fox	Cause of Causes	Saint Are	40	9 03.50
2018	**TIGER ROLL** (10/1)	8 10 13	D Russell	Pleasant Company	Bless The Wings	38	9 40.10
2019	**TIGER ROLL** (4/1)	9 11 5	D Russell	Magic of Light	Rathvinden	40	9 01.00
2020	RACE CANCELLED - CORONAVIRUS PANDEMIC						
2021	**MINELLA TIMES** (11/1)	8 10 3	R Blackmore	Balko Des Flos	Any Second Now	40	9 15.16
2022	**NOBLE YEATS** (50/1)	7 10 10	Mr S Waley-Cohen	Any Second Now	Delta Work	40	9 03.06

WINNERS OF GREAT RACES

LINCOLN HANDICAP
Doncaster-1m
2013 **LEVITATE** 5-8-4 22
2014 **OCEAN TEMPEST** 5-9-3 17
2015 **GABRIAL** 6-9-0 22
2016 **SECRET BRIEF** 4-9-4 22
2017 **BRAVERY** 4-9-1 22
2018 **ADDEYBB** 4-9-2 20
2019 **AUXERRE** 4-9-3 19
2020 RACE CANCELLED
2021 **HAQEEQY** 4-8-12 18
2022 **JOHAN** 5-9-4 22

GREENHAM STAKES (3y)
Newbury-7f
2013 **OLYMPIC GLORY** 9-0 5
2014 **KINGMAN** 9-0 10
2015 **MUHAARAR** 9-0 9
*2016 **TASLEET** 9-0 3
2017 **BARNEY ROY** 9-0 10
2018 **JAMES GARFIELD** 9-0 7
2019 **MOHAATHER** 9-0 8
2020 RACE CANCELLED
2021 **CHINDIT** 9-0 11
* Run at Chelmsford City on Polytrack
2022 **PERFECT POWER** 9-0 6

EUROPEAN FREE HANDICAP (3y)
Newmarket-7f
2013 **GARSWOOD** 9-0 10
2014 **SHIFTING POWER** 9-1 6
2015 **HOME OF THE BRAVE** 8-13 5
2016 **IBN MALIK** 9-6 6
2017 **WHITECLIFFSOFDOVER** 9-7 7
2018 **ANNA NERIUM** 8-11 10
2019 **SHINE SO BRIGHT** 9-3 7
2020 RACE CANCELLED
2021 **TACTICAL** 9-5 7
2022 **NEW SCIENCE** 9-7 5

CRAVEN STAKES (3y)
Newmarket-1m
2013 **TORONADO** 9-1 4
2014 **TOORMORE** 9-3 6
2015 **KOOL KOMPANY** 9-3 7
2016 **STORMY ANTARCTIC** 9-0 6
2017 **EMINENT** 9-0 7
2018 **MASAR** 9-0 6
2019 **SKARDU** 9-0 8
2020 RACE CANCELLED
2021 **MASTER OF THE SEAS** 9-0 10
2022 **NATIVE TRAIL** 9-0 6

JOCKEY CLUB STAKES
Newmarket-1m 4f
2013 **UNIVERSAL** 4-8-12 4
2014 **GOSPEL CHOIR** 5-9-0 8
2015 **SECOND STEP** 4-9-0 4
2016 **EXOSPHERE** 4-9-0 6
2017 **SEVENTH HEAVEN** 4-9-1 5
2018 **DEFOE** 4-9-1 5
2019 **COMMUNIQUE** 4-9-1 ....
2020 RACE CANCELLED
2021 **SIR RON PRIESTLEY** 5-9-1 ....
2022 **LIVING LEGEND** 6-9-1 ....

SANDOWN MILE
Sandown-1m
2013 **TRUMPET MAJOR** 4-9-0 ....
2014 **TULLIUS** 6-9-1 ....
2015 **CUSTOM CUT** 6-9-5 ....
2016 **TOORMORE** 5-9-4 ....
2017 **SOVEREIGN DEBT** 8-9-1 ....
2018 **ADDEYBB** 4-9-1 ....
2019 **BEAT THE BANK** 5-9-1 ....
2020 RACE CANCELLED
2021 **PALACE PIER** 4-9-1 ....
2022 **LIGHTS ON** 5-8-12 ....

CHESTER VASE (3y)
Chester-1m 4f 63yds
2013 **RULER OF THE WORLD** 8-12 ....
2014 **ORCHESTRA** 9-0 ....
2015 **HANS HOLBEIN** 9-0 ....
2016 **US ARMY RANGER** 9-0 ....
2017 **VENICE BEACH** 9-0 ....
2018 **YOUNG RASCAL** 9-0 ....
2019 **SIR DRAGONET** 9-0 ....
2020 RACE CANCELLED
2021 **YOUTH SPIRIT** 9-0 ....
2022 **CHANGINGOFTHEGUARD** 9-2 ....

CHESTER CUP
Chester-2m 2f 140yds
2013 **ADDRESS UNKNOWN** 6-9-0 ....
2014 **SUEGIOO** 5-9-4 ....
2015 **TRIP TO PARIS** 4-8-9 ....
2016 **NO HERETIC** 8-8-13 ....
2017 **MONTALY** 6-9-6 ....
2018 **MAGIC CIRCLE** 6-9-3 ....
2019 **MAKING MIRACLES** 4-9-0 ....
2020 RACE CANCELLED
2021 **FALCON EIGHT** 6-9-10 ....
2022 **CLEVELAND** 4-9-0 ....

OAKS TRIAL (3y fillies)
Lingfield-1m 3f 133yds
2013 **SECRET GESTURE** 8-12 ....
2014 **HONOR BOUND** 9-0 ....
2015 **TOUJOURS L'AMOUR** 9-0 ....
2016 **SEVENTH HEAVEN** 9-0 ....
2017 **HERTFORD DANCER** 9-0 ....
2018 **PERFECT CLARITY** 9-0 ....
2019 **ANAPURNA** 9-0 ....
2020 **MISS YODA** 9-0 ....
2021 **SHERBET LEMON** 9-0 ....
2022 **ROGUE MILLENNIUM** 9-2 ....

DERBY TRIAL (3y)

Lingfield-1m 3f 133yds

2013 **NEVIS** 8-12....4
2014 **SNOW SKY** 9-0....9
2015 **KILIMANJARO** 9-0....5
2016 **HUMPHREY BOGART** 9-0....5
2017 **BEST SOLUTION** 9-5....8
2018 **KNIGHT TO BEHOLD** 9-0....9
2019 **ANTHONY VAN DYCK** 9-0....10
2020 **ENGLISH KING** 9-0....8
2021 **THIRD REALM** 9-0....6
2022 **UNITED NATIONS** 9-2....4

MUSIDORA STAKES (3y fillies)

York-1m 2f 56yds

2013 **LIBER NAUTICUS** 8-12....6
2014 **MADAME CHIANG** 9-0....9
2015 **STAR OF SEVILLE** 9-0....5
2016 **SO MI DAR** 9-0....7
2017 **SHUTTER SPEED** 9-0....5
2018 **GIVE AND TAKE** 9-0....7
2019 **NAUSHA** 9-0....10
2020 **ROSE OF KILDARE** 9-0....6
2021 **SNOWFALL** 9-0....7
2022 **EMILY UPJOHN** 9-2....5

DANTE STAKES (3y)

York-1m 2f 56yds

2013 **LIBERTARIAN** 9-0....8
2014 **THE GREY GATSBY** 9-0....6
2015 **GOLDEN HORN** 9-0....7
2016 **WINGS OF DESIRE** 9-0....12
2017 **PERMIAN** 9-0....10
2018 **ROARING LION** 9-0....9
2019 **TELECASTER** 9-0....8
2020 **THUNDEROUS** 9-0....6
2021 **HURRICANE LANE** 9-0....10
2022 **DESERT CROWN** 9-2....8

MIDDLETON STAKES (fillies and mares)

York-1m 2f 56yds

2013 **DALKALA** 4-9-0....8
2014 **AMBIVALENT** 5-9-0....8
2015 **SECRET GESTURE** 5-9-0....8
2016 **BEAUTIFUL ROMANCE** 4-9-0....7
2017 **BLOND ME** 5-9-0....4
2018 **CORONET** 4-9-0....7
2019 **LAH TI DAR** 4-9-0....6
2020 RACE CANCELLED
2021 **QUEEN POWER** 5-9-0....5
2022 **LILAC ROAD** 4-9-2....6

YORKSHIRE CUP

York-1m 5f 188yds

2013 **GLEN'S DIAMOND** 5-9-0....8
2014 **GOSPEL CHOIR** 5-9-0....12
2015 **SNOW SKY** 4-9-0....6
2016 **CLEVER COOKIE** 8-9-1....5
2017 **DARTMOUTH** 5-9-1....8
2018 **STRADIVARIUS** 4-9-1....8
2019 **STRADIVARIUS** 5-9-4....8
2020 RACE CANCELLED
2021 **SPANISH MISSION** 5-9-4....5
2022 **STRADIVARIUS** 8-9-6....5

DUKE OF YORK STAKES

York-6f

2013 **SOCIETY ROCK** 6-9-13....17
2014 **MAAREK** 7-9-13....13
2015 **GLASS OFFICE** 5-9-8....15
2016 **MAGICAL MEMORY** 4-9-8....12
2017 **TASLEET** 4-9-8....12
2018 **HARRY ANGEL** 4-9-13....5
2019 **INVINCIBLE ARMY** 4-9-8....10
2020 RACE CANCELLED
2021 **STARMAN** 4-9-8....12
2022 **HIGHFIELD PRINCESS** 5-9-7....9

LOCKINGE STAKES

Newbury-1m

2013 **FARHH** 5-9-0....12
2014 **OLYMPIC GLORY** 4-9-0....8
2015 **NIGHT OF THUNDER** 4-9-0....16
2016 **BELARDO** 4-9-0....12
2017 **RIBCHESTER** 4-9-0....8
2018 **RHODODENDRON** 4-8-11....14
2019 **MUSTASHRY** 6-9-0....14
2020 RACE CANCELLED
2021 **PALACE PIER** 4-9-0....11
2022 **BAAEED** 4-9-0....9

HENRY II STAKES

Sandown-2m 50yds

2013 **GLOOMY SUNDAY** 4-8-11....10
2014 **BROWN PANTHER** 6-9-4....11
2015 **VENT DE FORCE** 4-9-0....7
2016 **PALLASATOR** 7-9-6....4
2017 **BIG ORANGE** 6-9-2....7
2018 **MAGIC CIRCLE** 6-9-2....8
2019 **DEE EX BEE** 4-9-4....5
2020 **DASHING WILLOUGHBY** 4-9-2....5
2021 **LISMORE** 4-8-12....5
2022 **QUICKTHORN** 5-9-4....8

TEMPLE STAKES

Haydock-5f

2013 **KINGSGATE NATIVE** 8-9-4....10
2014 **HOT STREAK** 3-8-10....9
2015 **PEARL SECRET** 6-9-4....11
2016 **PROFITABLE** 4-9-4....11
2017 **PRICELESS** 4-9-1....12
2018 **BATTAASH** 4-9-9....11
2019 **BATTAASH** 4-9-2....5
2020 RACE CANCELLED
2021 **LIBERTY BEACH** 4-9-1....6
2022 **KING'S LYNN** 5-9-6....10

BRIGADIER GERARD STAKES

Sandown-1m 1f 209yds

2013 **MUKHADRAM** 4-9-0....5
2014 **SHARESTAN** 6-9-0....3
2015 **WESTERN HYMN** 4-9-3....5
2016 **TIME TEST** 4-9-5....7
2017 **AUTOCRATIC** 4-9-0....7
2018 **POET'S WORD** 5-9-0....5
2019 **REGAL REALITY** 4-9-0....6
* 2020 **LORD NORTH** 4-9-0....5
2021 **EUCHEN GLEN** 8-9-3....4
2022 **BAY BRIDGE** 4-9-2....5

* Run at Haydock Park (1m 2f 42yds)

CORONATION CUP
Epsom-1m 4f 6yds

2013 **ST NICHOLAS ABBEY** 6-9-0 5
2014 **CIRRUS DES AIGLES** 8-9-0 7
2015 **PETHER'S MOON** 5-9-0 4
2016 **POSTPONED** 5-9-0 8
2017 **HIGHLAND REEL** 5-9-0 10
2018 **CRACKSMAN** 4-9-0 6
2019 **DEFOE** 5-9-0 9
*2020 **GHAIYYATH** 5-9-0 7
2021 **PYLEDRIVER** 4-9-0 6
2022 **HUKUM** 5-9-2 6

* Run at Newmarket

CHARITY SPRINT HANDICAP
York-6f

2013 **BODY AND SOUL** 8-11 19
2014 **SEE THE SUN** 8-7 20
2015 **TWILIGHT SON** 8-10 16
2016 **MR LUPTON** 9-7 17
2017 **GOLDEN APOLLO** 8-3 18
2018 **ENCRYPTED** 8-8 20
2019 **RECON MISSION** 9-2 22
2020 RACE CANCELLED
2021 **FIRST FOLIO** 9-3 17
2022 **HARRY THREE** 9-7 19

QUEEN ANNE STAKES
Ascot-1m (st)

2013 **DECLARATION OF WAR** 4-9-0 13
2014 **TORONADO** 4-9-0 10
2015 **SOLOW** 5-9-0 8
2016 **TEPIN** 5-8-11 13
2017 **RIBCHESTER** 4-9-0 16
2018 **ACCIDENTAL AGENT** 4-9-0 15
2019 **LORD GLITTERS** 6-9-0 16
2020 **CIRCUS MAXIMUS** 4-9-0 15
2021 **PALACE PIER** 4-9-0 11
2022 **BAAEED** 4-9-2 7

PRINCE OF WALES'S STAKES
Ascot-1m 2f

2013 **AL KAZEEM** 5-9-0 11
2014 **THE FUGUE** 5-8-11 8
2015 **FREE EAGLE** 4-9-0 9
2016 **MY DREAM BOAT** 4-9-0 6
2017 **HIGHLAND REEL** 5-9-0 8
2018 **POET'S WORD** 5-9-0 7
2019 **CRYSTAL OCEAN** 5-9-0 8
2020 **LORD NORTH** 4-9-0 7
2021 **LOVE** 4-8-11 6
2022 **STATE OF REST** 4-9-2 5

ST JAMES'S PALACE STAKES (3y)
Ascot-7f 213yds (rnd)

2013 **DAWN APPROACH** 9-0 9
2014 **KINGMAN** 9-0 7
2015 **GLENEAGLES** 9-0 5
2016 **GALILEO GOLD** 9-0 7
2017 **BARNEY ROY** 9-0 8
2018 **WITHOUT PAROLE** 9-0 10
2019 **CIRCUS MAXIMUS** 9-0 11
2020 **PALACE PIER** 9-0 7
2021 **POETIC FLARE** 9-0 13
2022 **COROEBUS** 9-2 11

COVENTRY STAKES (2y)
Ascot-6f

2013 **WAR COMMAND** 9-1 15
2014 **THE WOW SIGNAL** 9-1 15
2015 **BURATINO** 9-1 17
2016 **CARAVAGGIO** 9-1 18
2017 **RAJASINGHE** 9-1 18
2018 **CALYX** 9-1 23
2019 **ARIZONA** 9-1 17
2020 **NANDO PARRADO** 9-1 15
2021 **BERKSHIRE SHADOW** 9-1 17
2022 **BRADSELL** 9-3 17

KING EDWARD VII STAKES (3y)
Ascot-1m 4f

2013 **HILLSTAR** 8-12 8
2014 **EAGLE TOP** 9-0 9
2015 **BALIOS** 9-0 7
2016 **ACROSS THE STARS** 9-0 9
2017 **PERMIAN** 9-0 12
2018 **OLD PERSIAN** 9-0 9
2019 **JAPAN** 9-0 8
2020 **PYLEDRIVER** 9-0 6
2021 **ALENQUER** 9-0 6
2022 **CHANGINGOFTHEGUARD** 9-2 6

JERSEY STAKES (3y)
Ascot-7f

2013 **GALE FORCE TEN** 9-1 21
2014 **MUSTAJEEB** 9-4 23
2015 **DUTCH CONNECTION** 9-4 16
2016 **RIBCHESTER** 9-6 19
2017 **LE BRIVIDO** 9-1 20
2018 **EXPERT EYE** 9-1 21
2019 **SPACE TRAVELLER** 9-1 18
2020 **MOLATHAM** 9-1 13
2021 **CREATIVE FORCE** 9-1 18
2022 **NOBLE TRUTH** 9-3 15

DUKE OF CAMBRIDGE STAKES (fillies & mares)
Ascot-1m (st)

2013 **DUNTLE** 4-8-12 9
2014 **INTEGRAL** 4-9-0 14
2015 **AMAZING MARIA** 4-9-0 6
2016 **USHERETTE** 4-9-3 14
2017 **QEMAH** 4-9-0 14
2018 **ALJAZZI** 5-9-0 11
2019 **MOVE SWIFTLY** 4-9-0 17
2020 **NAZEEF** 4-9-0 10
2021 **INDIE ANGEL** 4-9-0 12
2022 **SAFFRON BEACH** 4-9-7 7

QUEEN MARY STAKES (2y fillies)
Ascot-5f

2013 **RIZEENA** 8-12 23
2014 **ANTHEM ALEXANDER** 9-0 21
2015 **ACAPULCO** 9-0 20
2016 **LADY AURELIA** 9-0 17
2017 **HEARTACHE** 9-0 23
2018 **SIGNORA CABELLO** 9-0 22
2019 **RAFFLE PRIZE** 9-0 25
2020 **CAMPANELLE** 9-0 18
2021 **QUICK SUZY** 9-0 21
2022 **DRAMATISED** 9-2 21

CORONATION STAKES (3y fillies)
Ascot-7f 213yds (rnd)
2013 **SKY LANTERN** 9-0 17
2014 **RIZEENA** 9-0 12
2015 **ERVEDYA** 9-0 9
2016 **QEMAH** 9-0 13
2017 **WINTER** 9-0 7
2018 **ALPHA CENTAURI** 9-0 12
2019 **WATCH ME** 9-0 9
2020 **ALPINE STAR** 9-0 7
2021 **ALCOHOL FREE** 9-0 11
2022 **INSPIRAL** 9-2 12

COMMONWEALTH CUP (3y)
Ascot-6f
2016 **QUIET REFLECTION** 9-0 10
2017 **CARAVAGGIO** 9-3 12
2018 **EQTIDAAR** 9-3 22
2019 **ADVERTISE** 9-3 9
2020 **GOLDEN HORDE** 9-0 16
2021 **CAMPANELLE** 8-11 15
2022 **PERFECT POWER** 9-2 20

ROYAL HUNT CUP
Ascot-1m (st)
2013 **BELGIAN BILL** 5-8-11 28
2014 **FIELD OF DREAM** 7-9-1 28
2015 **GM HOPKINS** 4-9-3 30
2016 **PORTAGE** 4-9-5 28
2017 **ZHUI FENG** 4-9-0 29
2018 **SETTLE FOR BAY** 4-9-1 30
2019 **AFAAK** 5-9-3 28
2020 **DARK VISION** 4-9-1 23
2021 **REAL WORLD** 4-8-6 30
2022 **DARK SHIFT** 4-9-1 29

QUEEN'S VASE (3y)
Ascot-1m 6f 34yds (2m before 2017)
2013 **LEADING LIGHT** 9-4 15
2014 **HARTNELL** 9-3 10
2015 **ALOFT** 9-3 13
2016 **SWORD FIGHTER** 9-3 18
2017 **STRADIVARIUS** 9-0 13
2018 **KEW GARDENS** 9-0 12
2019 **DASHING WILLOUGHBY** 9-0 13
2020 **SANTIAGO** 9-0 8
2021 **KEMARI** 9-0 13
2022 **ELDAR ELDAROV** 9-2 12

PLATINUM JUBILEE STAKES
Ascot-6f (Diamond Jubilee Stakes before 2022)
2013 **LETHAL FORCE** 4-9-4 18
2014 **SLADE POWER** 5-9-4 14
2015 **UNDRAFTED** 5-9-3 15
2016 **TWILIGHT SON** 4-9-3 9
2017 **THE TIN MAN** 5-9-3 19
2018 **MERCHANT NAVY** 3-9-3 12
2019 **BLUE POINT** 5-9-3 17
2020 **HELLO YOUMZAIN** 4-9-3 10
2021 **DREAM OF DREAMS** 7-9-3 12
2022 **NAVAL CROWN** 4-9-5 14

NORFOLK STAKES (2y)
Ascot-5f
2013 **NO NAY NEVER** 9-1 14
2014 **BAITHA ALGA** 9-1 9
2015 **WATERLOO BRIDGE** 9-1 10
2016 **PRINCE OF LIR** 9-1 11
2017 **SIOUX NATION** 9-1 17
2018 **SHANG SHANG SHANG** 8-12 10
2019 **A'ALI** 9-1 14
2020 **THE LIR JET** 9-1 12
2021 **PERFECT POWER** 9-1 15
2022 **THE RIDLER** 9-3 10

GOLD CUP
Ascot-2m 4f
2013 **ESTIMATE** 4-8-11 14
2014 **LEADING LIGHT** 4-9-0 12
2015 **TRIP TO PARIS** 4-9-0 12
2016 **ORDER OF ST GEORGE** 4-9-0 17
2017 **BIG ORANGE** 6-9-2 14
2018 **STRADIVARIUS** 4-9-1 9
2019 **STRADIVARIUS** 5-9-2 11
2020 **STRADIVARIUS** 6-9-2 8
2021 **SUBJECTIVIST** 4-9-1 12
2022 **KYPRIOS** 4-9-3 9

RIBBLESDALE STAKES (3y fillies)
Ascot-1m 4f
2013 **RIPOSTE** 8-12 9
2014 **BRACELET** 9-0 12
2015 **CURVY** 9-0 10
2016 **EVEN SONG** 9-0 14
2017 **CORONET** 9-0 12
2018 **MAGIC WAND** 9-0 10
2019 **STAR CATCHER** 9-0 11
2020 **FRANKLY DARLING** 9-0 11
2021 **LOVING DREAM** 9-0 13
2022 **MAGICAL LAGOON** 9-2 6

HARDWICKE STAKES
Ascot-1m 4f
2013 **THOMAS CHIPPENDALE** 4-9-0 8
2014 **TELESCOPE** 4-9-1 10
2015 **SNOW SKY** 4-9-1 7
2016 **DARTMOUTH** 4-9-1 9
2017 **IDAHO** 4-9-1 12
2018 **CRYSTAL OCEAN** 4-9-1 5
2019 **DEFOE** 5-9-1 8
2020 **FANNY LOGAN** 4-8-12 9
2021 **WONDERFUL TONIGHT** 4-8-12 10
2022 **BROOME** 6-9-3 7

WOKINGHAM STAKES
Ascot-6f
2013 **YORK GLORY** 5-9-2 26
2014 **BACCARAT** 5-9-2 28
2015 **INTERCEPTION** 5-9-3 25
2016 **OUTBACK TRAVELLER** 5-9-1 28
2017 **OUT DO** 8-8-13 27
2018 **BACCHUS** 4-9-6 28
2019 **CAPE BYRON** 5-9-5 26
2020 **HEY JONESY** 5-9-3 22
2021 **ROHAAN** 3-9-8 21
2022 **ROHAAN** 4-9-12 26

KING'S STAND STAKES
Ascot-5f
2013 **SOLE POWER** 6-9-4 19
2014 **SOLE POWER** 7-9-4 16
2015 **GOLDREAM** 6-9-4 18
2016 **PROFITABLE** 4-9-4 17
2017 **LADY AURELIA** 3-8-9 17
2018 **BLUE POINT** 4-9-4 14
2019 **BLUE POINT** 5-9-4 12
2020 **BATTAASH** 6-9-4 11
2021 **OXTED** 5-9-5 16
2022 **NATURE STRIP** 7-9-7 16

NORTHUMBERLAND PLATE
Newcastle-2m 56y Tapeta (2m 19y turf before 2016)
2013 **TOMINATOR** 6-9-10 18
2014 **ANGEL GABRIAL** 5-8-12 19
2015 **QUEST FOR MORE** 5-9-4 19
2016 **ANTIQUARIUM** 4-9-5 20
2017 **HIGHER POWER** 5-9-9 20
2018 **WITHHOLD** 5-9-1 20
2019 **WHO DARES WINS** 7-9-1 19
2020 **CARAVAN OF HOPE** 4-8-5 18
2021 **NICHOLAS T** 9-8-10 20
2022 **TRUESHAN** 6-10-8 20

ECLIPSE STAKES
Sandown-1m 1f 209yds
2013 **AL KAZEEM** 5-9-7 7
2014 **MUKHADRAM** 5-9-7 9
2015 **GOLDEN HORN** 3-8-10 5
2016 **HAWKBILL** 3-8-10 7
2017 **ULYSSES** 4-9-7 9
2018 **ROARING LION** 3-8-11 7
2019 **ENABLE** 5-9-4 8
2020 **GHAIYYATH** 5-9-3 7
2021 **ST MARK'S BASILICA** 3-8-11 4
2022 **VADENI** 3-8-13 6

LANCASHIRE OAKS (fillies and mares)
Haydock-1m 3f 175yds
2013 **EMIRATES QUEEN** 4-9-5 8
2014 **POMOLOGY** 4-9-5 9
2015 **LADY TIANA** 4-9-5 10
2016 **ENDLESS TIME** 4-9-5 6
2017 **THE BLACK PRINCESS** 4-9-5 7
2018 **HORSEPLAY** 4-9-5 7
2019 **ENBIHAAR** 4-9-5 6
2020 **MANUELA DE VEGA** 4-9-5 5
2021 **ALPINISTA** 4-9-5 9
2022 **FREE WIND** 4-9-7 7

DUCHESS OF CAMBRIDGE STAKES (2y fillies)
Newmarket-6f (Cherry Hinton Stakes before 2013)
2013 **LUCKY KRISTALE** 8-12 8
2014 **ARABIAN QUEEN** 9-0 5
2015 **ILLUMINATE** 9-0 9
2016 **ROLY POLY** 9-0 10
2017 **CLEMMIE** 9-0 8
2018 **PRETTY POLLYANNA** 9-0 9
2019 **RAFFLE PRIZE** 9-3 7
2020 **DANDALLA** 9-0 7
2021 **SANDRINE** 9-0 8
2022 **MAWJ** 9-2 6

BUNBURY CUP
Newmarket-7f
2013 **FIELD OF DREAM** 6-9-7 19
2014 **HEAVEN'S GUEST** 4-9-3 13
2015 **RENE MATHIS** 5-9-1 17
2016 **GOLDEN STEPS** 5-9-0 16
2017 **ABOVE THE REST** 6-8-10 18
2018 **BURNT SUGAR** 6-9-1 18
2019 **VALE OF KENT** 4-9-4 17
2020 **MOTAKHAYYEL** 4-9-7 17
2021 **MOTAKHAYYEL** 5-9-10 18
2022 **BLESS HIM** 8-9-3 18

PRINCESS OF WALES'S STAKES
Newmarket-1m 4f
2013 **AL KAZEEM** 4-9-5 6
2014 **CAVALRYMAN** 8-9-2 6
2015 **BIG ORANGE** 4-9-2 8
2016 **BIG ORANGE** 5-9-2 7
2017 **HAWKBILL** 4-9-2 6
2018 **BEST SOLUTION** 4-9-6 7
2019 **COMMUNIQUE** 4-9-9 6
2020 **DAME MALLIOT** 4-9-3 7
2021 **SIR RON PRIESTLEY** 5-9-9 5
2022 **YIBIR** 4-9-8 6

JULY STAKES (2y)
Newmarket-6f
2013 **ANJAAL** 8-12 11
2014 **IVAWOOD** 9-0 12
2015 **SHALAA** 9-0 9
2016 **MEHMAS** 9-0 9
2017 **CARDSHARP** 9-0 12
2018 **ADVERTISE** 9-0 8
2019 **ROYAL LYTHAM** 9-0 7
2020 **TACTICAL** 9-0 9
2021 **LUSAIL** 9-0 11
2022 **PERSIAN FORCE** 9-2 7

FALMOUTH STAKES (fillies & mares)
Newmarket-1m
2012 **GIOFRA** 4-9-5 10
2013 **ELUSIVE KATE** 4-9-5 4
2014 **INTEGRAL** 4-9-7 7
2015 **AMAZING MARIA** 4-9-7 7
2016 **ALICE SPRINGS** 3-8-12 7
2017 **ROLY POLY** 3-8-12 7
2018 **ALPHA CENTAURI** 3-8-12 7
2019 **VERACIOUS** 4-9-7 6
2020 **NAZEEF** 4-9-7 6
2021 **SNOW LANTERN** 3-8-12 13

SUPERLATIVE STAKES (2y)
Newmarket-7f
2013 **GOOD OLD BOY LUKEY** 9-0 8
2014 **ESTIDHKAAR** 9-1 8
2015 **BIRCHWOOD** 9-1 8
2016 **BOYNTON** 9-1 9
2017 **GUSTAV KLIMT** 9-1 10
2018 **QUORTO** 9-1 7
2019 **MYSTERY POWER** 9-1 8
2020 **MASTER OF THE SEAS** 9-1 10
2021 **NATIVE TRAIL** 9-1 9
2022 **PROSPEROUS VOYAGE** 9-0 5

JULY CUP
Newmarket-6f
2013 **LETHAL FORCE** 4-9-5....11
2014 **SLADE POWER** 5-9-6....13
2015 **MUHAARAR** 3-9-0....14
2016 **LIMATO** 4-9-6....18
2017 **HARRY ANGEL** 3-9-0....10
2018 **U S NAVY FLAG** 3-9-0....13
2019 **TEN SOVEREIGNS** 3-9-0....12
2020 **OXTED** 4-9-6....12
2021 **STARMAN** 4-9-6....19
2022 **ALCOHOL FREE** 4-9-5....13

WEATHERBYS SUPER SPRINT (2y)
Newbury-5f 34 yds
2013 **PENIAPHOBIA** 8-8....24
2014 **TIGGY WIGGY** 9-1....24
2015 **LATHOM** 9-0....22
2016 **MRS DANVERS** 8-0....23
2017 **BENGALI BOYS** 8-7....23
2018 **GINGER NUT** 8-5....25
2019 **BETTYS HOPE** 8-4....24
2020 **HAPPY ROMANCE** 8-5....25
2021 **GUBBASS** 8-10....22
2022 **EDDIE'S BOY** 9-2....20

SUMMER MILE
Ascot-7f 213yds (rnd)
2013 **ALJAMAAHEER** 4-9-1....11
2014 **GUEST OF HONOUR** 5-9-1....9
2015 **AROD** 4-9-1....6
2016 **MUTAKAYYEF** 5-9-1....10
2017 **MUTAKAYYEF** 6-9-1....7
2018 **BEAT THE BANK** 4-9-1....8
2019 **BEAT THE BANK** 5-9-4....8
2020 **MOHAATHER** 4-9-1....11
2021 **TILSIT** 4-9-1....9
2022 **CHINDIT** 4-9-3....6

PRINCESS MARGARET STAKES (2y fillies)
Ascot-6f
2013 **PRINCESS NOOR** 8-12....10
2014 **OSAILA** 9-0....8
2015 **BESHARAH** 9-0....6
2016 **FAIR EVA** 9-0....12
2017 **NYALETI** 9-0....7
2018 **ANGEL'S HIDEAWAY** 9-0....7
2019 **UNDER THE STARS** 9-0....9
2020 **SANTOSHA** 9-0....7
2021 **ZAIN CLAUDETTE** 9-0....10
2022 **LEZOO** 9-2....9

LENNOX STAKES
Goodwood-7f
2013 **GARSWOOD** 3-8-9....10
2014 **ES QUE LOVE** 5-9-3....7
2015 **TOORMORE** 4-9-3....7
2016 **DUTCH CONNECTION** 4-9-3....8
2017 **BRETON ROCK** 7-9-3....13
2018 **SIR DANCEALOT** 4-9-3....12
2019 **SIR DANCEALOT** 5-9-3....9
2020 **SPACE BLUES** 4-9-3....11
2021 **KINROSS** 4-9-3....8
2022 **SANDRINE** 3-8-9....11

STEWARDS' CUP
Goodwood-6f
2013 **REX IMPERATOR** 4-9-4....27
2014 **INTRINSIC** 4-8-11....24
2015 **MAGICAL MEMORY** 3-8-12....27
2016 **DANCING STAR** 3-8-12....27
2017 **LANCELOT DU LAC** 7-9-5....26
2018 **GIFTED MASTER** 5-9-6....26
2019 **KHAADEM** 3-9-6....27
2020 **SUMMERGHAND** 6-9-10....27
2021 **COMMANCHE FALLS** 4-9-1....27
2022 **COMMANCHE FALLS** 5-9-5....28

GORDON STAKES (3y)
Goodwood-1m 4f
2013 **CAP O'RUSHES** 9-0....7
2014 **SNOW SKY** 9-1....7
2015 **HIGHLAND REEL** 9-1....9
2016 **ULYSSES** 9-1....9
2017 **CRYSTAL OCEAN** 9-1....5
2018 **CROSS COUNTER** 9-1....4
2019 **NAYEF ROAD** 9-1....9
2020 **MOGUL** 9-1....6
2021 **OTTOMAN EMPEROR** 9-1....8
2022 **NEW LONDON** 9-3....10

VINTAGE STAKES (2y)
Goodwood-7f
2013 **TOORMORE** 9-0....12
2014 **HIGHLAND REEL** 9-1....8
2015 **GALILEO GOLD** 9-1....8
2016 **WAR DECREE** 9-1....9
2017 **EXPERT EYE** 9-1....10
2018 **DARK VISION** 9-1....12
2019 **PINATUBO** 9-1....7
2020 **BATTLEGROUND** 9-1....10
2021 **ANGEL BLEU** 9-1....6
2022 **MARBAAN** 9-2....9

SUSSEX STAKES
Goodwood-1m
2013 **TORONADO** 3-8-13....7
2014 **KINGMAN** 3-9-0....4
2015 **SOLOW** 5-9-8....8
2016 **THE GURKHA** 3-9-0....10
2017 **HERE COMES WHEN** 7-9-8....7
2018 **LIGHTNING SPEAR** 7-9-8....8
2019 **TOO DARN HOT** 3-9-0....7
2020 **MOHAATHER** 4-9-8....7
2021 **ALCOHOL FREE** 3-8-11....9
2022 **BAAEED** 4-9-10....7

RICHMOND STAKES (2y)
Goodwood-6f
2013 **SAAYERR** 9-0....10
2014 **IVAWOOD** 9-3....8
2015 **SHALAA** 9-3....8
2016 **MEHMAS** 9-3....4
2017 **BARRAQUERO** 9-0....7
2018 **LAND FORCE** 9-0....9
2019 **GOLDEN HORDE** 9-0....8
2020 **SUPREMACY** 9-0....7
2021 **ASYMMETRIC** 9-0....7
2022 **ROYAL SCOTSMAN** 9-2....8

KING GEORGE STAKES

Goodwood-5f

2013 **MOVIESTA** 3-8-12 17
2014 **TAKE COVER** 7-9-1 15
2015 **MUTHMIR** 5-9-6 15
2016 **TAKE COVER** 9-9-2 17
2017 **BATTAASH** 3-8-13 11
2018 **BATTAASH** 4-9-5 11
2019 **BATTAASH** 5-9-5 8
2020 **BATTAASH** 6-9-7 7
2021 **SUESA** 3-8-9 13
2022 **KHADEEM** 6-9-4 11

GOODWOOD CUP

Goodwood-2m

2013 **BROWN PANTHER** 5-9-7 14
2014 **CAVALRYMAN** 8-9-8 8
2015 **BIG ORANGE** 4-9-8 11
2016 **BIG ORANGE** 5-9-8 14
2017 **STRADIVARIUS** 3-8-8 14
2018 **STRADIVARIUS** 4-9-9 7
2019 **STRADIVARIUS** 5-9-9 9
2020 **STRADIVARIUS** 6-9-9 7
2021 **TRUESHAN** 5-9-9 8
2022 **KYPRIOS** 4-9-11 9

MOLECOMB STAKES (2y)

Goodwood-5f

2013 **BROWN SUGAR** 9-0 8
2014 **COTAI GLORY** 9-1 8
2015 **KACHY** 9-1 10
2016 **YALTA** 9-1 9
2017 **HAVANA GREY** 9-1 10
2018 **RUMBLE INTHEJUNGLE** 9-1 11
2019 **LIBERTY BEACH** 8-12 13
2020 **STEEL BULL** 9-1 10
2021 **ARMOR** 9-1 11
2022 **TRILLIUM** 9-0 8

NASSAU STAKES (fillies and mares)

Goodwood-1m 1f 197yds

2013 **WINSILI** 3-8-11 14
2014 **SULTANINA** 4-9-7 6
2015 **LEGATISSIMO** 3-8-12 9
2016 **MINDING** 3-8-11 5
2017 **WINTER** 3-8-13 6
2018 **WILD ILLUSION** 3-8-13 6
2019 **DEIRDRE** 5-9-7 9
2020 **FANCY BLUE** 3-8-12 7
2021 **LADY BOWTHORPE** 5-9-7 6
2022 **NASHWA** 3-9-0 8

HUNGERFORD STAKES

Newbury-7f

2013 **GREGORIAN** 4-9-3 5
2014 **BRETON ROCK** 4-9-5 6
2015 **ADAAY** 3-9-2 11
2016 **RICHARD PANKHURST** 4-9-6 6
2017 **MASSAAT** 4-9-6 8
2018 **SIR DANCEALOT** 4-9-9 8
2019 **GLORIOUS JOURNEY** 4-9-6 7
2020 **DREAM OF DREAMS** 6-9-6 9
2021 **SACRED** 3-8-11 10
2022 **JUMBY** 4-9-8 9

GEOFFREY FREER STAKES

Newbury-1m 5f 61yds

2013 **ROYAL EMPIRE** 4-9-4 10
2014 **SEISMOS** 6-9-4 11
2015 **AGENT MURPHY** 4-9-5 6
2016 **KINGS FETE** 5-9-7 5
2017 **DEFOE** 3-8-10 8
2018 **HAMADA** 4-9-5 6
2019 **TECHNICIAN** 3-8-10 5
2020 **HUKUM** 3-8-9 7
2021 **HUKUM** 4-9-8 10
2022 **ZECHARIAH** 3-8-11 5

INTERNATIONAL STAKES

York-1m 2f 56yds

2013 **DECLARATION OF WAR** 4-9-5 6
2014 **AUSTRALIA** 3-8-12 6
2015 **ARABIAN QUEEN** 3-8-9 7
2016 **POSTPONED** 5-9-6 12
2017 **ULYSSES** 4-9-6 7
2018 **ROARING LION** 3-8-13 8
2019 **JAPAN** 3-8-13 9
2020 **GHAIYYATH** 5-9-6 5
2021 **MISHRIFF** 4-9-6 5
2022 **BAAEED** 4-9-8 6

GREAT VOLTIGEUR STAKES (3y)

York-1m 3f 188yds

2013 **TELESCOPE** 8-12 7
2014 **POSTPONED** 9-0 9
2015 **STORM THE STARS** 9-0 7
2016 **IDAHO** 9-0 6
2017 **CRACKSMAN** 9-0 6
2018 **OLD PERSIAN** 9-3 9
2019 **LOGICIAN** 9-0 5
2020 **PYLEDRIVER** 9-3 8
2021 **YIBIR** 9-0 8
2022 **DEAUVILLE LEGEND** 9-2 6

LOWTHER STAKES (2y fillies)

York-6f

2013 **LUCKY KRISTALE** 9-1 9
2014 **TIGGY WIGGY** 9-0 9
2015 **BESHARAH** 9-0 9
2016 **QUEEN KINDLY** 9-0 8
2017 **THREADING** 9-0 9
2018 **FAIRYLAND** 9-0 9
2019 **LIVING IN THE PAST** 9-0 10
2020 **MISS AMULET** 9-0 14
2021 **ZAIN CLAUDETTE** 9-0 10
2022 **SWINGALONG** 9-2 13

YORKSHIRE OAKS (fillies and mares)

York-1m 3f 188yds

2013 **THE FUGUE** 4-9--7 7
2014 **TAPESTRY** 3-8-11 7
2015 **PLEASCACH** 3-8-11 11
2016 **SEVENTH HEAVEN** 3-8-11 12
2017 **ENABLE** 3-8-12 6
2018 **SEA OF CLASS** 3-8-12 8
2019 **ENABLE** 5-9-7 4
2020 **LOVE** 3-8-12 6
2021 **SNOWFALL** 3-8-12 7
2022 **ALPINISTA** 5-9-9 7

EBOR HANDICAP
York-1m 5f 188yds
2013 **TIGER CLIFF** 4-9-0 14
2014 **MUTUAL REGARD** 5-9-4 19
2015 **LITIGANT** 7-9-1 19
2016 **HEARTBREAK CITY** 6-9-1 20
2017 **NAKEETA** 6-9-0 19
2018 **MUNTAHAA** 5-9-9 20
2019 **MUSTAJEER** 6-9-5 22
2020 **FUJAIRA PRINCE** 6-9-8 21
2021 **SONNYBOYLISTON** 4-9-8 20
2022 **TRAWLERMAN** 4-9-3 20

GIMCRACK STAKES (2y)
York-6f
2013 **ASTAIRE** 8-12 7
2014 **MUHAARAR** 9-0 9
2015 **AJAYA** 9-0 8
2016 **BLUE POINT** 9-0 10
2017 **SANDS OF MALI** 9-0 10
2018 **EMARAATY ANA** 9-0 9
2019 **THREAT** 9-0 12
2020 **MINZAAL** 9-0 9
2021 **LUSAIL** 9-3 11
2022 **NOBLE STYLE** 9-2 12

NUNTHORPE STAKES
York-5f
2013 **JWALA** 4-9--8 17
2014 **SOLE POWER** 7-9-11 13
2015 **MECCA'S ANGEL** 4-9-10 19
2016 **MECCA'S ANGEL** 5-9-8 19
2017 **MARSHA** 4-9-8 11
2018 **ALPHA DELPHINI** 7-9-11 15
2019 **BATTAASH** 5-9-11 11
2020 **BATTAASH** 6-9-11 8
2021 **WINTER POWER** 3-9-6 14
2022 **HIGHFIELD PRINCESS** 5-9-12 13

LONSDALE CUP
York-2m 56yds
2013 **AHZEEMAH** 4 9-3 7
2014 **PALE MIMOSA** 5-9-0 7
2015 **MAX DYNAMITE** 5-9-3 8
2016 **QUEST FOR MORE** 6-9-3 7
2017 **MONTALY** 6-9-3 9
2018 **STRADIVARIUS** 4-9-6 9
2019 **STRADIVARIUS** 5-9-6 4
2020 **ENBIHAAR** 5 9-0 7
2021 **STRADIVARIUS** 7-9-3 4
2022 **QUICKTHORN** 5 9-5 6

PRESTIGE STAKES (2y fillies)
Goodwood-7f
2013 **AMAZING MARIA** 9-0 7
2014 **MALABAR** 9-0 8
2015 **HAWKSMOOR** 9-0 9
2016 **KILMAH** 9-0 7
2017 **BILLESDON BROOK** 9-0 10
2018 **ANTONIA DE VEGA** 9-0 8
2019 **BOOMER** 9-0 7
2020 **ISABELLA GILES** 9-0 5
2021 **MISE EN SCENE** 9-0 9
2022 **FAIRY CROSS** 9-2 8

CELEBRATION MILE
Goodwood-1m
2013 **AFSARE** 6-9-1 8
2014 **BOW CREEK** 3-8-12 8
2015 **KODI BEAR** 3-8-12 6
2016 **LIGHTNING SPEAR** 5-9-4 5
2017 **LIGHTNING SPEAR** 6-9-4 6
2018 **BEAT THE BANK** 4-9-7 8
2019 **DUKE OF HAZZARD** 3-8-12 6
2020 **CENTURY DREAM** 6-9-4 6
2021 **LAVENDER'S BLUE** 5-9-1 7
2022 **JADOOMI** 4-9-6 5

SOLARIO STAKES (2y)
Sandown-7f 16yds
2013 **KINGMAN** 9-0 4
2014 **AKTABANTAY** 9-1 5
2015 **FIRST SELECTION** 9-1 10
2016 **SOUTH SEAS** 9-1 10
2017 **MASAR** 9-1 7
2018 **TOO DARN HOT** 9-1 6
2019 **POSITIVE** 9-1 6
2020 **ETONIAN** 9-1 7
2021 **REACH FOR THE MOON** 9-1 6
2022 **SILVER KNOTT** 9-3 6

SPRINT CUP
Haydock-6f
2013 **GORDON LORD BYRON** 5-9-3 13
2014 **G FORCE** 3-9-1 17
2015 **TWILIGHT SON** 3-9-1 15
2016 **QUIET REFLECTION** 3-8-12 14
2017 **HARRY ANGEL** 3-9-1 11
2018 **THE TIN MAN** 6-9-3 12
2019 **HELLO YOUMZAIN** 3-9-1 11
2020 **DREAM OF DREAMS** 6-9-3 13
2021 **EMARAATY ANA** 5-9-3 16
2022 **MINZAAL** 4-9-5 12

SEPTEMBER STAKES
Kempton-1m 3f 219yds Polytrack
2013 **PRINCE BISHOP** 6-9-4 10
2014 **PRINCE BISHOP** 7-9-12 7
2015 **JACK HOBBS** 3-9-3 7
2016 **ARAB SPRING** 6-9-5 6
2017 **CHEMICAL CHARGE** 5-9-5 6
2018 **ENABLE** 4-9-2 4
2019 **ROYAL LINE** 5-9-5 12
2020 **ENABLE** 6-9-9 6
2021 **HAMISH** 5-9-5 5
2022 **MOSTAHDAF** 4-9-10 8

MAY HILL STAKES (2y fillies)

Doncaster-1m

2013 **IHTIMAL** 8-12 7
2014 **AGNES STEWART** 9-0 8
2015 **TURRET ROCKS** 9-0 8
2016 **RICH LEGACY** 9-0 9
2017 **LAURENS** 9-0 8
2018 **FLEETING** 9-0 11
2019 **POWERFUL BREEZE** 9-0 9
2020 **INDIGO GIRL** 9-0 9
2021 **INSPIRAL** 9-0 6
2022 **POLLY POT** 9-2 8

PORTLAND HANDICAP

Doncaster-5f 143yds

2013 **ANGELS WILL FALL** 4-9-2 21
2014 **MUTHMIR** 4-9-7 20
2015 **STEPS** 7-9-7 20
2016 **CAPTAIN COLBY** 4-9-0 20
2017 **SPRING LOADED** 5-8-9 22
2018 **A MOMENTOFMADNESS** 5-9-4 21
2019 **OXTED** 3-9-4 22
2020 **STONE OF DESTINY** 5-9-0 21
2021 **HURRICANE IVOR** 4-9-10 16
2022 **CHIPSTEAD** 4-8-10 19

PARK HILL STAKES (fillies and mares)

Doncaster-1m 6f 115yd

2013 **THE LARK** 3-8--6 9
2014 **SILK SARI** 4-9-5 13
2015 **GRETCHEN** 3-8-7 11
2016 **SIMPLE VERSE** 4-9-5 12
2017 **ALYSSA** 4-9-5 10
2018 **GOD GIVEN** 4-9-5 7
2019 **ENBIHAAR** 4-9-5 8
2020 **PISTA** 3-8-9 7
2021 **FREE WIND** 3-8-9 8
2022 **MIMIKYU** 3-8-11 8

DONCASTER CUP

Doncaster-2m 1f 197yds

2013 **TIMES UP** 7-9-3 7
2014 **ESTIMATE** 5-9-0 12
2015 **PALLASATOR** 6-9-3 11
2016 **SHEIKHZAYEDROAD** 7-9-3 8
2017 **DESERT SKYLINE** 3-8-5 9
2018 **THOMAS HOBSON** 8-9-5 8
2019 **STRADIVARIUS** 5-9-10 5
2020 **SPANISH MISSION** 4-9-5 7
2021 **STRADIVARIUS** 7-9-8 6
2022 **COLTRANE** 5-9-7 6

CHAMPAGNE STAKES (2y)

Doncaster-7f 6yds

2013 **OUTSTRIP** 8-12 4
2014 **ESTIDHKAAR** 9-3 6
2015 **EMOTIONLESS** 9-0 6
2016 **RIVET** 9-0 6
2017 **SEAHENGE** 9-0 7
2018 **TOO DARN HOT** 9-0 6
2019 **THREAT** 9-3 5
2020 **CHINDIT** 9-0 7
2021 **BAYSIDE BOY** 9-0 4
2022 **CHALDEAN** 9-2 3

PARK STAKES

Doncaster-7f 6yds

2013 **VIZTORIA** 3-8-11 9
2014 **ANSGAR** 6-9-4 7
2015 **LIMATO** 3-9-0 15
2016 **BRETON ROCK** 6-9-4 8
2017 **ACLAIM** 4-9-4 8
2018 **MUSTASHRY** 5-9-4 9
2019 **SIR DANCEALOT** 5-9-7 5
2020 **WICHITA** 3-9-0 8
2021 **GLORIOUS JOURNEY** 6-9-4 6
2022 **KINROSS** 5-9-9 6

FLYING CHILDERS STAKES (2y)

Doncaster-5f

2013 **GREEN DOOR** 9-0 7
2014 **BEACON** 9-1 14
2015 **GUTAIFAN** 9-1 9
2016 **ARDAD** 9-1 11
2017 **HEARTACHE** 8-12 9
2018 **SOLDIER'S CALL** 9-1 9
2019 **A'ALI** 9-1 7
2020 **UBETTABELIEVEIT** 9-1 10
2021 **CATURRA** 9-1 11
2022 **TRILLIUM** 9-0 8

AYR GOLD CUP

Ayr-6f

2013 **HIGHLAND COLORI** 5-8-13 26
2014 **LOUIS THE PIOUS** 6-9-4 27
2015 **DON'T TOUCH** 3-9-1 25
2016 **BRANDO** 4-9-10 23
*2017 **DONJUAN TRIUMPHANT** 4-9-10 17
2018 **SON OF REST** 4-9-3 dead heated with
BARON BOLT 5-8-12 25
2019 **ANGEL ALEXANDER** 3-8-13 24
2020 **NAHAARR** 4-9-5 24
2021 **BIELSA** 6-9-1 24
2022 **SUMMERGHAND** 8-9-5 24

*Run at Haydock Park

MILL REEF STAKES (2y)

Newbury-6f 8yds

2013 **SUPPLICANT** 9-1 7
2014 **TOOCOOLFORSCHOOL** 9-1 6
2015 **RIBCHESTER** 9-1 6
2016 **HARRY ANGEL** 9-1 7
2017 **JAMES GARFIELD** 9-1 9
2018 **KESSAAR** 9-1 7
2019 **PIERRE LAPIN** 9-1 8
2020 **ALKUMAIT** 9-1 8
2021 **WINGS OF WAR** 9-1 9
2022 **SAKHEER** 9-3 7

ROYAL LODGE STAKES (2y)

Newmarket-1m

2013 **BERKSHIRE** 8-12 5
2014 **ELM PARK** 9-0 6
2015 **FOUNDATION** 9-0 6
2016 **BEST OF DAYS** 9-0 8
2017 **ROARING LION** 9-0 5
2018 **MOHAWK** 9-0 7
2019 **ROYAL DORNOCH** 9-0 7
2020 **NEW MANDATE** 9-0 5
2021 **ROYAL PATRONAGE** 9-0 7
2022 **THE FOXES** 9-2 4

CHEVELEY PARK STAKES (2y fillies)

Newmarket-6f

2013 **VORDA** 8-12 7
2014 **TIGGY WIGGY** 9-0 9
2015 **LUMIERE** 9-0 8
2016 **BRAVE ANNA** 9-0 6
2017 **CLEMMIE** 9-0 11
2018 **FAIRYLAND** 9-0 11
2019 **MILLISLE** 9-0 11
2020 **ALCOHOL FREE** 9-0 8
2021 **TENEBRISM** 9-0 12
2022 **LEZOO** 9-2 10

SUN CHARIOT STAKES (fillies and mares)

Newmarket-1m

2013 **SKY LANTERN** 3-8-13 7
2014 **INTEGRAL** 4-9-3 7
2015 **ESOTERIQUE** 5-9-3 9
2016 **ALICE SPRINGS** 3-9-0 8
2017 **ROLY POLY** 3-9-0 13
2018 **LAURENS** 3-9-0 9
2019 **BILLESDON BROOK** 4-9-3 9
2020 **NAZEEF** 4-9-3 12
2021 **SAFFRON BEACH** 3-9-0 12
2022 **FONTEYN** 3-9-2 9

CAMBRIDGESHIRE

Newmarket-1m 1f

2013 **EDUCATE** 4-9-9 31
2014 **BRONZE ANGEL** 5-8-8 31
2015 **THIRD TIME LUCKY** 3-8-4 34
2016 **SPARK PLUG** 5-9-4 31
2017 **DOLPHIN VISTA** 4-8-7 34
2018 **WISSAHICKON** 3-9-5 33
2019 **LORD NORTH** 3-8-10 30
2020 **MAJESTIC DAWN** 4-8-8 27
2021 **BEDOUIN'S STORY** 6-9-5 26
2022 **MAJESTIC** 4-7-11 28

CUMBERLAND LODGE STAKES

Ascot-1m 4f

2013 **SECRET NUMBER** 3-8-7 7
2014 **PETHER'S MOON** 4-9-6 5
2015 **STAR STORM** 3-8-8 8
2016 **MOVE UP** 3-8-13 9
2017 **DANEHILL KODIAC** 4-9-2 9
2018 **LARAAIB** 4-9-2 5
2019 **MORANDO** 6-9-5 7
2020 **EUCHEN GLEN** 7-9-0 4
2021 **HUKUM** 4-9-5 7
2022 **HAMISH** 6-9-9 9

Run at York

FILLIES' MILE (2y fillies)

Newmarket-1m

2013 **CHRISELLIAM** 8-12 8
2014 **TOGETHER FOREVER** 9-0 7
2015 **MINDING** 9-0 10
2016 **RHODODENDRON** 9-0 8
2017 **LAURENS** 9-0 11
2018 **IRIDESSA** 9-0 8
2019 **QUADRILATERAL** 9-0 9
2020 **PRETTY GORGEOUS** 9-0 10
2021 **INSPIRAL** 9-0 8
2022 **COMMISSIONING** 9-2 8

MIDDLE PARK STAKES (2y)

Newmarket-6f

2013 **ASTAIRE** 9-0 10
2014 **CHARMING THOUGHT** 9-0 6
2015 **SHALAA** 9-0 7
2016 **THE LAST LION** 9-0 10
2017 **U S NAVY FLAG** 9-0 12
2018 **TEN SOVEREIGNS** 9-0 8
2019 **EARTHLIGHT** 9-0 8
2020 **SUPREMACY** 9-0 8
2021 **PERFECT POWER** 9-0 10
2022 **BLACKBEARD** 9-2 8

CHALLENGE STAKES

Newmarket-7f

2013 **FIESOLANA** 4-9-0 9
2014 **HERE COMES WHEN** 4-9-7 13
2015 **CABLE BAY** 4-9-3 10
2016 **ACLAIM** 3-9-1 12
2017 **LIMATO** 5-9-3 11
2018 **LIMATO** 6-9-3 8
2019 **MUSTASHRY** 6-9-8 5
2020 **HAPPY POWER** 4-9-3 9
2021 **AL SUHAIL** 4-9-3 9
2022 **AL SUHAIL** 6-9-5 8

DEWHURST STAKES (2y)

Newmarket-7f

2013 **WAR COMMAND** 9-1 6
2014 **BELARDO** 9-1 6
2015 **AIR FORCE BLUE** 9-1 7
2016 **CHURCHILL** 9-1 7
2017 **U S NAVY FLAG** 9-1 9
2018 **TOO DARN HOT** 9-1 7
2019 **PINATUBO** 9-1 9
2020 **ST MARK'S BASILICA** 9-1 14
2021 **NATIVE TRAIL** 9-1 8
2022 **CHALDEAN** 9-3 7

CESAREWITCH

Newmarket-2m 2f

2013 **SCATTER DICE** 4-8-8 33
2014 **BIG EASY** 7-8-7 33
2015 **GRUMETI** 7-8-2 34
2016 **SWEET SELECTION** 4-8-8 33
2017 **WITHHOLD** 4-8-8 34
2018 **LOW SUN** 5-9-2 33
2019 **STRATUM** 6-9-7 30
2020 **GREAT WHITE SHARK** 6-8-6 34
2021 **BUZZ** 7-8-13 32
2022 **RUN FOR OSCAR** 7-8-11 21

ROCKFEL STAKES (2y fillies)

Newmarket-7f

2013 **AL THAKHIRA** 8-12 8
2014 **LUCIDA** 9-0 9
2015 **PROMISING RUN** 9-0 7
2016 **SPAIN BURG** 9-0 8
2017 **JULIET CAPULET** 9-0 10
2018 **JUST WONDERFUL** 9-0 9
2019 **DAAHYEH** 9-0 8
2020 **ISABELLA GILES** 9-0 5
2021 **HELLO YOU** 9-0 9
2022 **COMMISSIONING** 9-2 14

QIPCO BRITISH CHAMPIONS SPRINT STAKES

Ascot-6f

2013 **SLADE POWER** 4-9-0 14
2014 **GORDON LORD BYRON** 6-9-2 15
2015 **MUHAARAR** 3-9-1 20
2016 **THE TIN MAN** 4-9-2 13
2017 **LIBRISA BREEZE** 5-9-2 12
2018 **SANDS OF MALI** 3-9-1 14
2019 **DONJUAN TRIUMPHANT** 6-9-2 17
2020 **GLEN SHIEL** 6-9-2 16
2021 **CREATIVE FORCE** 3-9-1 20
2022 **KINROSS** 5-9-4 18

QUEEN ELIZABETH II STAKES (BRITISH CHAMPIONS MILE)

Ascot-1m

2013 **OLYMPIC GLORY** 3-9-0 12
2014 **CHARM SPIRIT** 3-9-1 11
2015 **SOLOW** 5-9-4 9
2016 **MINDING** 3-8-12 13
2017 **PERSUASIVE** 4-9-1 15
2018 **ROARING LION** 3-9-1 13
2019 **KING OF CHANGE** 3-9-1 16
2020 **THE REVENANT** 5-9-4 14
2021 **BAAEED** 3-9-1 10
2022 **BAYSIDE BOY** 4-9-6 9

QIPCO BRITISH CHAMPIONS LONG DISTANCE CUP

Ascot-2m

2013 **ROYAL DIAMOND** 7-9-7 12
2014 **FORGOTTEN RULES** 4-9-7 9
2015 **FLYING OFFICER** 5-9-7 13
2016 **SHEIKHZAYEDROAD** 7-9-7 10
2017 **ORDER OF ST GEORGE** 5-9-7 13
2018 **STRADIVARIUS** 4-9-7 6
2019 **KEW GARDENS** 4-9-7 6
2020 **TRUESHAN** 4-9-7 13
2021 **TRUESHAN** 5-9-7 10
2022 **TRUESHAN** 6-9-9 8

QIPCO BRITISH CHAMPIONS FILLIES' AND MARES' STAKES

Ascot-1m 4f

2013 **SEAL OF APPROVAL** 4-9-3 8
2014 **MADAME CHIANG** 3-8-12 10
2015 **SIMPLE VERSE** 3-8-12 12
2016 **JOURNEY** 4-9-5 13
2017 **HYDRANGEA** 3-8-13 10
2018 **MAGICAL** 3-8-13 11
2019 **STAR CATCHER** 3-8-13 12
2020 **WONDERFUL TONIGHT** 3-8-13 12
2021 **ESHAADA** 3-8-13 8
2022 **EMILY UPJOHN** 3-9-1 14

QIPCO CHAMPION STAKES (BRITISH CHAMPIONS MIDDLE DISTANCE)

Ascot-1m 2f

2013 **FARHH** 5-9-3 10
2014 **NOBLE MISSION** 5-9-5 9
2015 **FASCINATING ROCK** 4-9-5 13
2016 **ALMANZOR** 3-9-0 10
2017 **CRACKSMAN** 3-9-1 10
2018 **CRACKSMAN** 4-9-5 8
2019 **MAGICAL** 4-9-2 12
2020 **ADDEYBB** 6-9-5 10
2021 **SEALIWAY** 3-9-1 9
2022 **BAY BRIDGE** 4-9-7 9

BALMORAL HANDICAP

Ascot-1m

2015 **MUSADDAS** 5-8-2 20
2016 **YUFTEN** 5-9-1 19
2017 **LORD GLITTERS** 6-9-3 20
2018 **SHARJA BRIDGE** 4-9-5 20
2019 **ESCOBAR** 5-9-6 20
2020 **NJORD** 4-9-5 18
2021 **ALDAARY** 3-9-6 20
2022 **SHELIR** 6-9-5 20

CORNWALLIS STAKES (2y)

Newmarket-5f (run at Ascot before 2014)

2013 **HOT STREAK** 9-0 12
2014 **ROYAL RAZALMA** 8-12 12
2015 **QUIET REFLECTION** 8-12 11
2016 **MRS DANVERS** 8-12 9
2017 **ABEL HANDY** 9-1 12
2018 **SERGEI PROKOFIEV** 9-1 14
2019 **GOOD VIBES** 8-12 12
2020 **WINTER POWER** 8-12 11
2021 **TWILIGHT JET** 9-1 12
2022 **RUMSTAR** 9-3 11

TWO-YEAR-OLD TROPHY (2y)

Redcar-6f

2013 **VENTURA MIST** 8-7 23
2014 **LIMATO** 8-12 23
2015 **LOG OUT ISLAND** 9-2 20
2016 **WICK POWELL** 8-3 20
2017 **DARKANNA** 8-11 23
2018 **SUMMER DAYDREAM** 8-9 21
2019 **SUMMER SANDS** 8-3 17
2020 **LULLABY MOON** 8-9 21
2021 **CHIPOTLE** 9-1 15
2022 **COLD CASE** 9-4 16

HORRIS HILL STAKES (2y)

Newbury-7f

2013 **PIPING ROCK** 8-12 11
2014 **SMAIH** 9-0 6
2015 **CRAZY HORSE** 9-0 9
2016 **PLEASELETMEWIN** 9-0 13
2017 **NEBO** 9-0 6
2018 **MOHAATHER** 9-0 8
2019 ABANDONED
2020 **MUJBAR** 9-0 12
2021 **LIGHT INFANTRY** 9-0 7
2022 **KNIGHT** 9-2 9

VERTEM FUTURITY TROPHY (2y)

(Racing Post Trophy before 2018)
Doncaster-1m (St)

2013 **KINGSTON HILL** 9-0 11
2014 **ELM PARK** 9-1 8
2015 **MARCEL** 9-1 7
2016 **RIVET** 9-1 10
2017 **SAXON WARRIOR** 9-1 12
2018 **MAGNA GRECIA** 9-1 11
2019 **KAMEKO** 9-1 11
2020 **MAC SWINEY** 9-1 8
2021 **LUXEMBOURG** 9-1 8
2022 **AUGUSTE RODIN** 9-3 8

Run at Newcastle 1m 5yds (Tapeta)

NOVEMBER HANDICAP

Doncaster-1m 3f 197yds

2013 **CONDUCT** 6-9-2 23
2014 **OPEN EAGLE** 5-8-12 23
2015 **LITIGANT** 7-9-10 22
2016 **PRIZE MONEY** 3-8-10 15
2017 **SAUNTER** 4-8-13 23
2018 **ROYAL LINE** 4-9-8 23
2019 ABANDONED
2020 **ON TO VICTORY** 6-9-0 23
2021 **FARHAN** 3-8-3 23
2022 **METIER** 6-8-10 21

WINNERS OF PRINCIPAL RACES IN IRELAND

IRISH 2,000 GUINEAS (3y)
The Curragh-1m
2013 **MAGICIAN** 9-0 10
2014 **KINGMAN** 9-0 11
2015 **GLENEAGLES** 9-0 11
2016 **AWTAAD** 9-0 8
2017 **CHURCHILL** 9-0 6
2018 **ROMANISED** 9-0 11
2019 **PHOENIX OF SPAIN** 9-0 14
2020 **SISKIN** 9-2 11
2021 **MAC SWINEY** 9-2 11
2022 **NATIVE TRAIL** 9-2 9

TATTERSALLS GOLD CUP
The Curragh-1m 2f 110yds
2013 **AL KAZEEM** 5-9-3 4
2014 **NOBLE MISSION** 5-9-3 5
2015 **AL KAZEEM** 7-9-3 6
2016 **FASCINATING ROCK** 5-9-3 6
2017 **DECORATED KNIGHT** 5-9-3 8
2018 **LANCASTER BOMBER** 4-9-3 5
2019 **MAGICAL** 4-9-0 5
2020 **MAGICAL** 5-9-9 6
2021 **HELVIC DREAM** 4-9-5 8
2022 **ALENQUER** 4-9-5 8

IRISH 1,000 GUINEAS (3y fillies)
The Curragh-1m
2013 **JUST THE JUDGE** 9-0 15
2014 **MARVELLOUS** 9-0 11
2015 **PLEASCACH** 9-0 18
2016 **JET SETTING** 9-0 10
2017 **WINTER** 9-0 8
2018 **ALPHA CENTAURI** 9-0 13
2019 **HERMOSA** 9-0 10
2020 **PEACEFUL** 9-2 11
2021 **EMPRESS JOSEPHINE** 9-2 14
2022 **HOMELESS SONG** 9-2 14

IRISH DERBY (3y)
The Curragh-1m 4f
2013 **TRADING LEATHER** 9-0 9
2014 **AUSTRALIA** 9-0 5
2015 **JACK HOBBS** 9-0 8
2016 **HARZAND** 9-0 9
2017 **CAPRI** 9-0 9
2018 **LATROBE** 9-0 12
2019 **SOVEREIGN** 9-0 8
2020 **SANTIAGO** 9-2 14
2021 **HURRICANE LANE** 9-2 11
2022 **WESTOVER** 9-2 8

PRETTY POLLY STAKES (fillies and mares)
The Curragh-1m 2f
2013 **AMBIVALENT** 4-9-10 9
2014 **THISTLE BIRD** 6-9-10 8
2015 **DIAMONDSANDRUBIES** 3-8-12 9
2016 **MINDING** 3-8-12 5
2017 **NEZWAAH** 4-9-8 11
2018 **URBAN FOX** 4-9-8 6
2019 **IRIDESSA** 3-8-12 5
2020 **MAGICAL** 5-9-12 5
2021 **THUNDERING NIGHTS** 4-9-12 8
2022 **LA PETITE COCO** 4-9-12 8

IRISH OAKS (3y fillies)
The Curragh-1m 4f
2013 **CHICQUITA** 9-0 7
2014 **BRACELET** 9--0 10
2015 **COVERT LOVE** 9-0 9
2016 **SEVENTH HEAVEN** 9-0 11
2017 **ENABLE** 9-0 10
2018 **SEA OF CLASS** 9-0 7
2019 **STAR CATCHER** 9-0 8
2020 **EVEN SO** 9-2 8
2021 **SNOWFALL** 9-2 8
2022 **MAGICAL LAGOON** 9-2 7

PHOENIX STAKES (2y)
The Curragh-6
2013 **SUDIRMAN** 9-3 5
2014 **DICK WHITTINGTON** 9-3 6
2015 **AIR FORCE BLUE** 9-3 7
2016 **CARAVAGGIO** 9-3 5
2017 **SIOUX NATION** 9-3 8
2018 **ADVERTISE** 9-3 5
2019 **SISKIN** 9-3 5
2020 **LUCKY VEGA** 9-5 10
2021 **EBRO RIVER** 9-5 8
2022 **LITTLE BIG BEAR** 9-5 5

MATRON STAKES (fillies and mares)
Leopardstown-1m
2013 **LA COLLINA** 4-9-5 12
2014 **FIESOLANA** 5-9-5 10
2015 **LEGATISSIMO** 3-9-0 9
2016 **ALICE SPRINGS** 3-9-0 8
2017 **HYDRANGEA** 3-9-0 10
2018 **LAURENS** 3-9-0 7
2019 **IRIDESSA** 3-9-0 7
2020 **CHAMPERS ELYSEES** 3-9-2 11
2021 **NO SPEAK ALEXANDER** 3-9-2 13
2022 **PEARLS GALORE** 5-9-7 9

IRISH CHAMPION STAKES
Leopardstown-1m 2f
2013 **THE FUGUE** 4-9-4 6
2014 **THE GREY GATSBY** 3-9-0 7
2015 **GOLDEN HORN** 3-9-0 7
2016 **ALMANZOR** 3-9-0 12
2017 **DECORATED KNIGHT** 5-9-7 10
2018 **ROARING LION** 3-9-1 7
2019 **MAGICAL** 4-9-4 8
2020 **MAGICAL** 5-9-6 6
2021 **ST MARK'S BASILICA** 3-9-3 4

2022 **LUXEMBOURG** 3-9-3 7

IRISH CAMBRIDGESHIRE

The Curragh-1m
2013 **MORAN GRA** 6-8-13 20
2014 **SRETAW** 5-8-8 21
2015 **HINT OF A TINT** 5-9-3 22
2016 **SEA WOLF** 4-9-5 24
2017 **ELUSIVE TIME** 9-8-9 27
2018 **KENYA** 3-9-2 21
2019 **JASSAAR** 4-8-8 25
2020 **LAUGHIFUWANT** 5-9-10 20
2021 **BOPEDRO** 5-9-3 27
2022 **FEDERAL** 4-8-11 25

MOYGLARE STUD STAKES (2y fillies)

The Curragh-7f
2013 **RIZEENA** 9-0 7
2014 **CURSORY GLANCE** 9-0 10
2015 **MINDING** 9-0 9
2016 **INTRICATELY** 9-0 7
2017 **HAPPILY** 9-0 8
2018 **SKITTER SKATTER** 9-0 10
2019 **LOVE** 9-0 9
2020 **SHALE** 9-2 13
2021 **DISCOVERIES** 9-2 8
2022 **TAHIYRA** 9-2 11

VINCENT O'BRIEN NATIONAL STAKES (2y)

The Curragh-7f
2013 **TOORMORE** 9-3 5
2014 **GLENEAGLES** 9-3 5
2015 **AIR FORCE BLUE** 9-3 5
2016 **CHURCHILL** 9-3 7
2017 **VERBAL DEXTERITY** 9-3 7
2018 **QUORTO** 9-3 7
2019 **PINATUBO** 9-3 8
2020 **THUNDER MOON** 9-5 10
2021 **NATIVE TRAIL** 9-5 7
2022 **AL RIFFA** 9-5 6

IRISH ST LEGER

The Curragh-1m 6f
2013 **VOLEUSE DE COEURS** 4-9-8 10
2014 **BROWN PANTHER** 6-9-11 11
2015 **ORDER OF ST GEORGE** 3-9-0 11
2016 **WICKLOW BRAVE** 7-9-11 4
2017 **ORDER OF ST GEORGE** 5-9-10 10
2018 **FLAG OF HONOUR** 3-9-1 6
2019 **SEARCH FOR A SONG** 3-8-11 10
2020 **SEARCH FOR A SONG** 4-9-8 8
2021 **SONNYBOYLISTON** 4-9-11 13
2022 **KYPRIOS** 4-9-11 11

IRISH CESAREWITCH

The Curragh-2m
2013 **MONTEFELTRO** 5-9-4 30
2014 **EL SALVADOR** 5-9-5 21
2015 **DIGEANTA** 8-9-10 20
2016 **LAWS OF SPIN** 3-8-6 20
2017 **LORD ERSKINE** 4-8-5 24
2018 **BRAZOS** 4-8-12 24
2019 **ROYAL ILLUSION** 7-8-5 18
2020 **CAPE GENTLEMAN** 4-9-0 21
2021 **LINE OUT** 9-8-9 30
2022 **WATERVILLE** 3-8-9 30
* Run at Navan

LADBROKES HURDLE (HANDICAP)

Leopardstown-2m
(Various sponsors)
2013 **ABBEY LANE** 8-10-8 28
2014 **GILGAMBOA** 6-10-9 24
2015 **KATIE T** 6-10-9 24
2016 **HENRY HIGGINS** 6-10-10 23
2017 **ICE COLD SOUL** 7-10-2 20
2018 **OFF YOU GO** 5-9-10 28
2019 **OFF YOU GO** 6-11-5 19
2020 **THOSEDAYSAREGONE** 7-9-12 22
2021 **DROP THE ANCHOR** 7 10-5 22
2022 **CALL ME LYREEN** 6-11-4 27

IRISH CHAMPION HURDLE

Leopardstown-2m
2013 **HURRICANE FLY** 9-11-10 5
2014 **HURRICANE FLY** 10-11-10 4
2015 **HURRICANE FLY** 11-11-10 6
2016 **FAUGHEEN** 8-11-10 5
2017 **PETIT MOUCHOIR** 6 11-10 4
2018 **SUPASUNDAE** 8-11-10 8
2019 **APPLE'S JADE** 7-11-3 6
2020 **HONEYSUCKLE** 6-11-3 9
2021 **HONEYSUCKLE** 7-11-5 6
2022 **HONEYSUCKLE** 8-11-5 5

IRISH GOLD CUP

Leopardstown-3m(Hennessy Gold Cup before 2016)
2013 **SIR DES CHAMPS** 7-11-10 4
2014 **LAST INSTALMENT** 9-11-10 7
2015 **CARLINGFORD LOUGH** 9-11-10 8
2016 **CARLINGFORD LOUGH** 10-11-10 10
2017 **SIZING JOHN** 7-11-10 7
2018 **EDWULF** 9-11-10 10
2019 **BELLSHILL** 9-11-10 4
2020 **DELTA WORK** 7-11-10 8
2021 **KEMBOY** 9-11-12 5
2022 **CONFLATED** 8-11-10 8

IRISH GRAND NATIONAL

Fairyhouse-3m 5f
2013 **LIBERTY COUNSEL** 10-9-5 28
2014 **SHUTTHEFRONTDOOR** 7-10-13 26
2015 **THUNDER AND ROSES** 7-10-6 28
2016 **ROGUE ANGEL** 8-10-6 27
2017 **OUR DUKE** 7-11-4 28
2018 **GENERAL PRINCIPLE** 9-10-0 30
2019 **BURROWS SAINT** 6-10-8 30
2020 RACE CANCELLED
2021 **FREEWHEELIN DYLAN** 9-10-8 28
2022 **LORD LARIAT** 7-9-12 27

WINNERS OF PRINCIPAL RACES IN FRANCE

PRIX GANAY
ParisLongchamp-1m 2f 110yds
2013 **PASTORIUS** 4-9-2 9
2014 **CIRRUS DES AIGLES** 8-9-2 8
2015 **CIRRUS DES AIGLES** 9-9-2 7
* 2016 **DARIYAN** 4-9-2 10
* 2017 **CLOTH OF STARS** 4-9-2 7
2018 **CRACKSMAN** 4-9-2 7
2019 **WALDGEIST** 5-9-2 5
** 2020 **SOTTSASS** 4-9-2 5
2021 **MARE AUSTRALIS** 4-9-2 7
2022 **STATE OF REST** 4-9-2 6
* Run at Saint-Cloud
** Run at Chantilly

POULE D'ESSAI DES POULAINS (3y)
ParisLongchamp-1m
2013 **STYLE VENDOME** 9-2 18
2014 **KARAKONTIE** 9-2 12
2015 **MAKE BELIEVE** 9-2 18
* 2016 **THE GURKHA** 9-2 13
* 2017 **BRAMETOT** 9-2 13
2018 **OLMEDO** 9-2 11
2019 **PERSIAN KING** 9-2 10
* 2020 **VICTOR LUDORUM** 9-2 9
2021 **ST MARK'S BASILICA** 9-2 12
2022 **MODERN GAMES** 9-3 15
* Run at Deauville

POULE D'ESSAI DES POULICHES (3y filllies)
ParisLongchamp-1m
2013 **FLOTILLA** 9-0 20
2014 **AVENIR CERTAIN** 9-0 16
2015 **ERVEDYA** 9-0 14
* 2016 **LA CRESSONNIERE** 9-0 14
* 2017 **PRECIEUSE** 9-0 18
2018 **TEPPAL** 9-0 14
2019 **CASTLE LADY** 9-0 10
* 2020 **DREAM AND DO** 9-0 12
2021 **COUERSAMBA** 9-0 13
2022 **MANGOUSTINE** 9-1 15
* Run at Deauville

PRIX SAINT-ALARY (3y fillies)
ParisLongchamp-1m 2f
2013 **SILASOL** 9-0 8
* 2014 **VAZIRA** 9-0 8
2015 **QUEEN'S JEWEL** 9-0 9
** 2016 **JEMAYEL** 9-0 9
** 2017 **SOBETSU** 9-0 11
2018 **LAURENS** 9-0 5
2019 **SIYARAFINA** 9-0 11
*** 2020 **TAWKEEL** 9-0 7
2021 **INCARVILLE** 9-0 11
2022 **ABOVE THE CURVE** 9-0 6
* We Are disqualified from first place
** Run at Deauville
*** Run at Chantilly

PRIX D'ISPAHAN
ParisLongchamp-1m 1f 55yds
2013 **MAXIOS** 5-9-2 7
2014 **CIRRUS DES AIGLES** 8-9-2 6
2015 **SOLOW** 5-9-2 4
* 2016 **A SHIN HIKARI** 5-9-2 9
* 2017 **MEKHTAAL** 4-9-2 5
2018 **RECOLETOS** 4-9-2 6
2019 **ZABEEL PRINCE** 6-9-2 9
* 2020 **PERSIAN KING** 4-9-6 8
2021 **SKALLETI** 6-9-2 6
2022 **DREAMLOPER** 5-8-13 8
* Run at Chantilly

PRIX DU JOCKEY CLUB (3y)
Chantilly-1m 2f 110yds
2013 **INTELLO** 9-2 19
2014 **THE GREY GATSBY** 9-2 16
2015 **NEW BAY** 9-2 14
2016 **ALMANZOR** 9-2 16
2017 **BRAMETOT** 9-2 12
2018 **STUDY OF MAN** 9-2 16
2019 **SOTTSASS** 9-3 15
2020 **MISHRIFF** 9-2 16
2021 **ST MARK'S BASILICA** 9-2 19
2022 **VADENI** 9-2 15

PRIX DE DIANE (3y fillies)
Chantilly-1m 2f 110yds
2013 **TREVE** 9-0 11
2014 **AVENIR CERTAIN** 9-0 12
2015 **STAR OF SEVILLE** 9-0 17
2016 **LA CRESSONNIERE** 9-0 16
2017 **SENGA** 9-1 16
2018 **LAURENS** 9-0 13
2019 **CHANNEL** 9-0 16
2020 **FANCY BLUE** 9-0 11
2021 **JOAN OF ARC** 9-0 17
2022 **NASHWA** 9-0 17

GRAND PRIX DE SAINT-CLOUD
Saint-Cloud-1m 4f
2013 **NOVELLIST** 4-9-2 11
* 2014 **NOBLE MISSION** 5-9-2 7
2015 **TREVE** 5-8-13 9
2016 **SILVERWAVE** 4-9-2 11
2017 **ZARAK** 4-9-2 10
2018 **WALDGEIST** 4-9-3 6
2019 **CORONET** 5-9-0 7
2020 **WAY TO PARIS** 7-9-2 5
2021 **BROOME** 5-9-2 8
2022 **ALPINISTA** 5-8-13 9
* Spiritjim disqualified from first place

PRIX JEAN PRAT (3y)
Chantilly-7f (1m before 2019)
2013 **HAVANA GOLD** 9-2 12
2014 **CHARM SPIRIT** 9-2 7
2015 **TERRITORIES** 9-2 8

2016 **ZELZAL** 9-2 9
2017 **THUNDER SNOW** 9-3 5
2018 **INTELLOGENT** 9-2 7
2019 **TOO DARN HOT** 9-2 12
2020 **PINATUBO** 9-2 11
2021 **LAWS OF INDICES** 9-2 13
2022 **TENEBRISM** 8-13 11

GRAND PRIX DE PARIS (3y)

ParisLongchamp-1m 4f
2013 **FLINTSHIRE** 9-2 8
2014 **GALLANTE** 9-2 11
2015 **ERUPT** 9-2 6
2016 **MONT ORMEL** 9-2 8
2017 **SHAKEEL** 9-2 9
2018 **KEW GARDENS** 9-3 6
2019 **JAPAN** 9-2 8
2020 **MOGUL** 9-3 10
2021 **HURRICANE LANE** 9-2 11
2022 **ONESTO** 9-3 6
Run at Saint-Cloud

PRIX ROTHSCHILD (fillies and mares)

Deauville-1m
2013 **ELUSIVE KATE** 4-9-2 12
2014 **ESOTERIQUE** 4-9-2 4
2015 **AMAZING MARIA** 4-9-2 8
2016 **QEMAH** 3-8-9 10
2017 **ROLY POLY** 3-8-9 10
2018 **WITH YOU** 3-8-9 10
2019 **LAURENS** 4-9-3 9
2020 **WATCH ME** 4-9-4 6
2021 **MOTHER EARTH** 3-8-11 14
2022 **SAFFRON BEACH** 4-9-4 7

PRIX MAURICE DE GHEEST

Deauville-6f 110yds
2013 **MOONLIGHT CLOUD** 5-8-13 14
2014 **GARSWOOD** 4-9-2 14
2015 **MUHAARAR** 3-8-11 12
2016 **SIGNS OF BLESSING** 5-9-2 15
2017 **BRANDO** 5-9-3 13
2018 **POLYDREAM** 3-8-10 20
2019 **ADVERTISE** 3-8-13 15
2020 **SPACE BLUES** 4-9-4 11
2021 **MARIANAFOOT** 6-9-4 12
2022 **HIGHFIELD PRINCESS** 5-9-1 14

PRIX JACQUES LE MAROIS

Deauville-1m
2013 **MOONLIGHT CLOUD** 5-9-1 13
2014 **KINGMAN** 3-8-13 5
2015 **ESOTERIQUE** 5-9-1 9
2016 **RIBCHESTER** 3-8-13 11
2017 **AL WUKAIR** 3-8-13 6
2018 **ALPHA CENTAURI** 3-8-9 11
2019 **ROMANISED** 4-9-5 8
2020 **PALACE PIER** 3-8-13 7
2021 **PALACE PIER** 4-9-5 8
2022 **INSPIRAL** 3-8-9 9

PRIX MORNY (2y)

Deauville-6f
2013 **NO NAY NEVER** 9-0 10
2014 **THE WOW SIGNAL** 9-0 9
2015 **SHALAA** 9-0 5
2016 **LADY AURELIA** 8-10 5
2017 **UNFORTUNATELY** 9-0 8
2018 **PRETTY POLLYANNA** 8-10 9
2019 **EARTHLIGHT** 9-0 8
2020 **CAMPANELLE** 8-10 9
2021 **PERFECT POWER** 9-0 14
2022 **BLACKBEARD** 9-0 5

PRIX JEAN ROMANET (fillies and mares)

Deauville-1m 2f
2013 **ROMANTICA** 4-9-0 6
2014 **RIBBONS** 4-9-0 11
2015 **ODELIZ** 5-9-0 11
2016 **SPEEDY BOARDING** 4-9-0 10
2017 **AJMAN PRINCESS** 4-9-0 10
2018 **NONZA** 4-9-0 9
2019 **CORONET** 5-9-0 8
2020 **AUDARYA** 4-9-0 11
2021 **GRAND GLORY** 5-9-0 8
2022 **ARISTIA** 4-9-0 7

PRIX DU MOULIN DE LONGCHAMP

ParisLongchamp-1m
2013 **MAXIOS** 5-9-2 7
2014 **CHARM SPIRIT** 3-8-11 10
2015 **ERVEDYA** 3-8-9 6
* 2016 **VADAMOS** 5-9-3 6
* 2017 **RIBCHESTER** 4-9-3 7
2018 **RECOLETOS** 4-9-4 11
2019 **CIRCUS MAXIMUS** 3-8-13 10
2020 **PERSIAN KING** 4-9-3 6
2021 **BAAEED** 3-9-0 6
2022 **DREAMLOPER** 5-9-1 9
* Run at Chantilly

PRIX VERMEILLE (fillies and mares)

ParisLongchamp-1m 4f
2013 **TREVE** 3-8-8 10
2014 **BALTIC BARONESS** 4-9-3 9
2015 **TREVE** 5-9-3 9
* 2016 **LEFT HAND** 3-8-8 6
* 2017 **BATEEL** 5-9-3 11
2018 **KITESURF** 4-9-3 8
2019 **STAR CATCHER** 3-8-9 9
2020 **TARNAWA** 4-9-5 10
2021 **TEONA** 3-8-10 7
2022 **SWEET LADY** 4-9-4 11
* Run at Chantilly

PRIX DE LA FORET

ParisLongchamp-7f
2013 **MOONLIGHT CLOUD** 5-8-13 11
2014 **OLYMPIC GLORY** 4-9-2 14
2015 **MAKE BELIEVE** 3-9-0 13
* 2016 **LIMATO** 4-9-2 11
* 2017 **ACLAIM** 4-9-2 10
2018 **ONE MASTER** 4-8-13 15
2019 **ONE MASTER** 5-8-13 12
2020 **ONE MASTER** 6-8-13 9

2021 **SPACE BLUES** 5-9-2 15
2022 **KINROSS** 5-9-2 10
* Run at Chantilly

PRIX DU CADRAN

ParisLongchamp-2m 4f
2013 **ALTANO** 7-9-2 10
2014 **HIGH JINX** 6-9-2 8
2015 **MILLE ET MILLE** 5-9-2 10
*2016 **QUEST FOR MORE** 6-9-2 12
*2017 **VAZIRABAD** 5-9-2 6
2018 **CALL THE WIND** 4-9-2 8
2019 **HOLDTHASIGREEN** 7-9-2 10
2020 **PRINCESS ZOE** 5-8-13 9
2021 **TRUESHAN** 5-9-2 13
2022 **KYPRIOS** 4-9-2 12
* Run at Chantilly

PRIX DE L'ABBAYE DE LONGCHAMP

ParisLongchamp-5f
2013 **MAAREK** 6-9-11 20
2014 **MOVE IN TIME** 6-9-11 18
2015 **GOLDREAM** 6-9-11 18
*2016 **MARSHA** 3-9-7 17
*2017 **BATTAASH** 3-9-11 13
2018 **MABS CROSS** 4-9-7 16
2019 **GLASS SLIPPERS** 3-9-7 16
2020 **WOODED** 3-9-11 11
2021 **A CASE OF YOU** 3-9-11 14
2022 **THE PLATINUM QUEEN** 2-8-4 18
* Run at Chantilly

PRIX JEAN-LUC LAGARDERE (2y)

ParisLongchamp-1m (7f before 2015)
2013 **KARAKONTIE** 9-0 8
*2014 **FULL MAST** 9-0 9
2015 **ULTRA** 9-0 11
2016 **NATIONAL DEFENSE 9-0 7
2017 **HAPPILY 8-10 6
2018 **ROYAL MARINE** 9-0 6
2019 **VICTOR LUDORUM** 9-0 7
2020 **SEALIWAY** 9-0 5
2021 **ANGEL BLEU** 9-0 9
2022 **BELBEK** 9-0 7
* Gleneagles disqualified from first place
** Run at Chantilly

PRIX MARCEL BOUSSAC (2y fillies)

ParisLongchamp-1m
2013 **INDONESIENNE** 8-11 12
2014 **FOUND** 8-11 12
2015 **BALLYDOYLE** 8-11 8
*2016 **WUHEIDA** 8-11 11
*2017 **WILD ILLUSION** 8-11 7
2018 **LILY'S CANDLE** 8-11 8
2019 **ALBIGNA** 8-11 9
2020 **TIGER TANAKA** 8-11 12
2021 **ZELLIE** 8-11 8
2022 **BLUE ROSE CEN** 8-11 12
* Run at Chantilly

PRIX DE L'OPERA (fillies and mares)

ParisLongchamp-1m 2f
2013 **DALKALA** 4-9-2 9
2014 **WE ARE** 3-8-11 11
2015 **COVERT LOVE** 3-8-11 13
*2016 **SPEEDY BOARDING** 4-9-2 7
*2017 **RHODODENDRON** 3-8-11 13
2018 **WILD ILLUSION** 3-8-11 15
2019 **VILLA MARINA** 3-8-11 12
2020 **TARNAWA** 4-9-2 12
2021 **ROUGIR** 3-8-11 14
2022 **PLACE DU CARROUSEL** 3-8-11 16
* Run at Chantilly

PRIX ROYAL-OAK

ParisLongchamp-1m 7f 110yds
2013 **TAC DE BOISTRON** 6-9-4 15
2014 **TAC DE BOISTRON** 7-9-4 13
2015 **VAZIRABAD** 3-8-10 13
*2016 **VAZIRABAD** 4-9-4 15
2017 **ICE BREEZE 3-8-10 9
2018 **HOLDTHASIGREEN** 6-9-4 8
2019 **TECHNICIAN** 3-8-10 6
2020 **SUBJECTIVIST** 3-8-10 8
2021 **SCOPE** 3-8-10 12
2022 **IRESINE** 5-9-4 10
* Run at Chantilly
** Run at Saint-Cloud

CRITERIUM INTERNATIONAL (2y)

Saint-Cloud-1m (7f 2015-2019)
2013 **ECTOT** 9-0 4
2014 **VERT DE GRECE** 9-0 9
2015 **JOHANNES VERMEER** 9-0 8
2016 **THUNDER SNOW** 9-0 9
2017 ABANDONED
*2018 **ROYAL MEETING** 9-0 6
2019 **ALSON 9-0 2
2020 **VAN GOGH** 9-0 6
2021 **ANGEL BLEU** 9-0 6
2022 **PROUD AND REGAL** 9-0 7
* Run at Chantilly
** Run at ParisLongchamp

CRITERIUM DE SAINT-CLOUD (2y)

Saint-Cloud-1m 2f
2013 **PRINCE GIBRALTAR** 9-0 12
2014 **EPICURIS** 9-0 6
2015 **ROBIN OF NAVAN** 9-0 10
2016 **WALDGEIST** 9-0 13
2017 ABANDONED
2018 **WONDERMENT** 8-10 9
2019 **MKFANCY** 9-0 8
2020 **GEAR UP** 9-0 7
2021 **EL BODEGON** 9-0 9
2022 **DUBAI MILE** 9-0 9

WINNERS OF OTHER OVERSEAS RACES

SAUDI CUP
Riyadh-1m 1f dirt
2020 **MAXIMUM SECURITY** 4-9-0 14
2021 **MISHRIFF** 4-9-0 14
2022 **EMBLEM ROAD** 4-9-0 14

PEGASUS WORLD CUP
Gulfstream Park-1m 1f dirt
2017 **ARROGATE** 4-8-12 12
2018 **GUN RUNNER** 5-8-12 12
2019 **CITY OF LIGHT** 5-8-12 12
2020 **MUCHO GUSTO** 4-8-12 10
2021 **KNICKS GO** 5-8-11 12
2022 **LIFE IS GOOD** 4-8-11 9

DUBAI WORLD CUP
Meydan-1m 2f Tapeta
2013 **ANIMAL KINGDOM** 5-9-0 13
2014 **AFRICAN STORY** 7-9-0 16
2015 **PRINCE BISHOP** 8-9-0 9
2016 **CALIFORNIA CHROME** 5-9-0 12
2017 **ARROGATE** 4-9-0 14
2018 **THUNDER SNOW** 4-9-0 10
2019 **THUNDER SNOW** 5-9-0 12
2020 RACE CANCELLED
2021 **MYSTIC GUIDE** 4-9-0 12
2022 **COUNTRY GRAMMER** 5-9-0 10

KENTUCKY DERBY
Churchill Downs-1m 2f dirt
2013 **ORB** 9-0 19
2014 **CALIFORNIA CHROME** 9-0 19
2015 **AMERICAN PHAROAH** 9-0 18
2016 **NYQUIST** 9-0 20
2017 **ALWAYS DREAMING** 9-0 20
2018 **JUSTIFY** 9-0 20
2019 **COUNTRY HOUSE** 9-0 19
2020 **AUTHENTIC** 9-0 15
2021 **MEDINA SPIRIT** 9-0 19
2022 **RICH STRIKE** 9-0 20
Maximum Security disqualified from first place

BREEDERS' CUP TURF
Various courses-1m 4f
2013 **MAGICIAN** 3-8-10 12
2014 **MAIN SEQUENCE** 5-9-0 12
2015 **FOUND** 3-8-7 12
2016 **HIGHLAND REEL** 4-9-0 12
2017 **TALISMANIC** 4-9-0 13
2018 **ENABLE** 4-8-11 13
2019 **BRICKS AND MORTAR** 5-9-0 12
2020 **TARNAWA** 4-8-11 10
2021 **YIBIR** 3-8-10 14
2022 **REBEL'S ROMANCE** 4-9-0 13

BREEDERS' CUP CLASSIC
Various courses-1m 2f dirt
2013 **MUCHO MACHO MAN** 5-9-0 11
2014 **BAYERN** 3-8-10 14
2015 **AMERICAN PHAROAH** 3-8-10 8
2016 **ARROGATE** 3-8-10 9
2017 **GUN RUNNER** 4-9-0 11
2018 **ACCELERATE** 5-9-0 14
2019 **VINO ROSSO** 4-9-0 11
2020 **AUTHENTIC** 3-8-10 10
2021 **KNICKS GO** 5-9-0 8
2022 **FLIGHTLINE** 4-9-0 8

MELBOURNE CUP
Flemington-2m
2013 **FIORENTE** 5-8-9 24
2014 **PROTECTIONIST** 4-8-13 22
2015 **PRINCE OF PENZANCE** 6-8-5 24
2016 **ALMANDIN** 6-8-3 24
2017 **REKINDLING** 3-8-2 23
2018 **CROSS COUNTER** 3-8-0 24
2019 **VOW AND DECLARE** 4-8-3 24
2020 **TWILIGHT PAYMENT** 7-8-10 23
2021 **VERRY ELLEEGANT** 6-9-0 23
2022 **GOLD TRIP** 5-9-1 22

JAPAN CUP
Tokyo-1m 4f
2013 **GENTILDONNA** 4-8-9 17
2014 **EPIPHANEIA** 4-9-0 18
2015 **SHONAN PANDORA** 4-8-9 18
2016 **KITASAN BLACK** 4-9-0 17
2017 **CHEVAL GRAND** 5-9-0 17
2018 **ALMOND EYE** 3-8-5 14
2019 **SUAVE RICHARD** 5-9-0 15
2020 **ALMOND EYE** 5-8-9 15
2021 **CONTRAIL** 4-9-0 18
2022 **VELA AZUL** 5-9-0 18

WINNERS OF PRINCIPAL NATIONAL HUNT RACES

PADDY POWER GOLD CUP (HANDICAP CHASE)
Cheltenham-2m 4f 78yds
(BetVictor Gold Cup before 2020)
2013 **JOHNS SPIRIT** 6-10-2 20
2014 **CAID DU BERLAIS** 5-10-13 18
2015 **ANNACOTTY** 7-11-0 20
2016 **TAQUIN DU SEUIL** 9-11-11 17
2017 **SPLASH OF GINGE** 9-10-6 17
2018 **BARON ALCO** 7-10-11 18
2019 **HAPPY DIVA** 8-11-0 17
2020 **COOLE CODY** 9-10-5 16
2021 **MIDNIGHT SHADOW** 8-11-5 19
2022 **GA LAW** 6-11-0 14

BETFAIR CHASE
Haydock-3m 1f 125yds (3m 24yds before 2017)
2013 **CUE CARD** 7-11-7 8
2014 **SILVINIACO CONTI** 8-11-7 9
2015 **CUE CARD** 9-11-7 5
2016 **CUE CARD** 10-11-7 6
2017 **BRISTOL DE MAI** 6-11-7 6
2018 **BRISTOL DE MAI** 7-11-7 5
2019 **LOSTINTRANSLATION** 7-11-7 4
2020 **BRISTOL DE MAI** 9-11-7 5
2021 **A PLUS TARD** 7-11-7 7
2022 **PROTEKTORAT** 7-11-0 5

LADBROKES TROPHY HANDICAP CHASE
Newbury-3m 1f 214yds
(Run as Hennessy Gold Cup before 2017)
2013 **TRIOLO D'ALENE** 6-11-1 21
2014 **MANY CLOUDS** 7-11-6 19
2015 **SMAD PLACE** 8-11-4 15
2016 **NATIVE RIVER** 6-11-1 19
2017 **TOTAL RECALL** 8-10-8 20
2018 **SIZING TENNESSEE** 10-11-3 12
2019 **DE RASHER COUNTER** 7-10-10 24
2020 **CLOTH CAP** 8-10-0 18
2021 **CLOUDY GLEN** 8-10-8 21
2022 **LE MILOS** 7-11-0 15

TINGLE CREEK CHASE
Sandown-2m
2013 **SIRE DE GRUGY** 7-11-7 9
2014 **DODGING BULLETS** 6-11-7 10
2015 **SIRE DE GRUGY** 9-11-7 7
2016 **UN DE SCEAUX** 8-11-7 6
2017 **POLITOLOGUE** 6-11-7 6
2018 **ALTIOR** 8-11-7 4
2019 **DEFI DU SEUIL** 6-11-7 8
2020 **POLITOLOGUE** 9-11-7 5
2021 **GREANETEEN** 7-11-7 5
2022 **EDWARDSTONE** 8-11-10 6

CHRISTMAS HURDLE
Kempton-2m
2013 **MY TENT OR YOURS** 6-11-7 6
2014 **FAUGHEEN** 6-11-7 6
2015 **FAUGHEEN** 7-11-7 5
2016 **YANWORTH** 6-11-7 5
2017 **BUVEUR D'AIR** 6-11-7 4
2018 **VERDANA BLUE** 6-11-0 5
2019 **EPATANTE** 5-11-0 10
2020 **SILVER STREAK** 7-11-7 5
2021 **EPATANTE** 7-11-0 5
2022 **CONSTITUTION HILL** 5-11-10 5

KING GEORGE VI CHASE
Kempton-3m
2013 **SILVINIACO CONTI** 7-11-10 9
2014 **SILVINIACO CONTI** 8-11-10 10
2015 **CUE CARD** 9-11-10 9
2016 **THISTLECRACK** 8-11-10 5
2017 **MIGHT BITE** 8-11-10 8
2018 **CLAN DES OBEAUX** 6-11-10 10
2019 **CLAN DES OBEAUX** 7-11-10 5
2020 **FRODON** 8-11-10 9
2021 **TORNADO FLYER** 8-11-10 9
2022 **BRAVEMANSGAME** 7-11-10 9

WELSH GRAND NATIONAL (HANDICAP CHASE)
Chepstow-3m 5f 110yds
2013 **MOUNTAINOUS** 8-10-0 20
2014 **EMPEROR'S CHOICE** 7-10-8 19
** 2015 **MOUNTAINOUS** 11-10-6 20
2016 **NATIVE RIVER** 6-11-12 20
*** 2017 **RAZ DE MAREE** 13-10-10 20
2018 **ELEGANT ESCAPE** 6-11-8 20
2019 **POTTERS CORNER** 9-10-4 17
**** 2020 **SECRET REPRIEVE** 7-10-1 18
2021 **IWILLDOIT** 8-10-0 20
2022 **THE TWO AMIGOS** 10-10-1 17
** Run in January 2016
*** Run in January 2018
**** Run in January 2021

CLARENCE HOUSE CHASE
(Victor Chandler Chase before 2014)
Ascot-2m 167yds
2013 **SPRINTER SACRE** 7-11-7 7
2014 **SIRE DE GRUGY** 8-11-7 7
2015 **DODGING BULLETS** 7-11-7 5
2016 **UN DE SCEAUX** 8-11-7 5
* 2017 **UN DE SCEAUX** 9-11-7 7
2018 **UN DE SCEAUX** 10-11-7 5
2019 **ALTIOR** 9-11-7 3
2020 **DEFI DU SEUIL** 7-11-7 5
2021 **FIRST FLOW** 9-11-7 8
2022 **SHISHKIN** 8-11-7 4
* Run at Cheltenham

BETFAIR HANDICAP HURDLE
Newbury-2m 69yds)

2013	**MY TENT OR YOURS** 6-11-2	21
2014	**SPLASH OF GINGE** 6-10-3	20
2015	**VIOLET DANCER** 5-10-9	23
2016	**AGRAPART** 5-10-5	22
2017	**BALLYANDY** 6-11-1	16
2018	**KALASHNIKOV** 5-11-5	24
*2019	**AL DANCER** 6-11-8	14
2020	**PIC D'ORHY** 5-11-5	24
2021	**SOARING GLORY** 6-10-7	23
2022	**GLORY AND FORTUNE** 7-11-8	14

* run at Ascot over 1m 7 ½f

SUPREME NOVICES' HURDLE
Cheltenham-2m 87yds

2013	**CHAMPAGNE FEVER** 6-11-7	12
2014	**VAUTOUR** 5-11-7	18
2015	**DOUVAN** 5-11-7	12
2016	**ALTIOR** 6-11-7	14
2017	**LABAIK** 6-11-7	14
2018	**SUMMERVILLE BOY** 6-11-7	19
2019	**KLASSICAL DREAM** 5-11-7	16
2020	**SHISHKIN** 6-11-7	15
2021	**APPRECIATE IT** 7-11-7	8
2022	**CONSTITUTION HILL** 5-11-7	9

ARKLE CHALLENGE TROPHY (NOVICES' CHASE)
Cheltenham-1m 7f 199yds

2013	**SIMONSIG** 7-11-7	7
2014	**WESTERN WARHORSE** 6-11-4	9
2015	**UN DE SCEAUX** 7-11-4	11
2016	**DOUVAN** 6-11-4	7
2017	**ALTIOR** 7-11-4	9
2018	**FOOTPAD** 6-11-4	5
2019	**DUC DES GENIEVRES** 6-11-4	12
2020	**PUT THE KETTLE ON** 6-10-11	11
2021	**SHISHKIN** 7-11-4	5
2022	**EDWARDSTONE** 8-11-4	11

CHAMPION HURDLE
Cheltenham-2m 87yds

2013	**HURRICANE FLY** 9-11-10	9
2014	**JEZKI** 6-11-10	9
2015	**FAUGHEEN** 7-11-10	8
2016	**ANNIE POWER** 8-11-3	12
2017	**BUVEUR D'AIR** 6-11-10	11
2018	**BUVEUR D'AIR** 7-11-10	11
2019	**ESPOIR D'ALLEN** 5-11-10	10
2020	**EPATANTE** 6-11-3	17
2021	**HONEYSUCKLE** 7-11-3	10
2022	**HONEYSUCKLE** 8-11-13	10

QUEEN MOTHER CHAMPION CHASE
Cheltenham-1m 7f 199yds

2013	**SPRINTER SACRE** 7-11-10	7
2014	**SIRE DE GRUGY** 8-11-10	11
2015	**DODGING BULLETS** 7-11-10	11
2016	**SPRINTER SACRE** 10-11-10	10
2017	**SPECIAL TIARA** 10-11-10	10
2018	**ALTIOR** 8-11-10	9
2019	**ALTIOR** 9-11-10	10
2020	**POLITOLOGUE** 9-11-10	5
2021	**PUT THE KETTLE ON** 7-11-3	9
2022	**ENERGUMENE** 8-11-10	7

BALLYMORE NOVICES' HURDLE
Cheltenham-2m 5f 26yds

2013	**THE NEW ONE** 5-11-7	8
2014	**FAUGHEEN** 6-11-7	15
2015	**WINDSOR PARK** 6-11-7	10
2016	**YORKHILL** 6-11-7	11
2017	**WILLOUGHBY COURT** 6-11-7	15
2018	**SAMCRO** 6-11-7	14
2019	**CITY ISLAND** 6-11-7	16
2020	**ENVOI ALLEN** 6-11-7	12
2021	**BOB OLINGER** 6-11-7	7
2022	**SIR GERHARD** 7-11-7	9

BROWN ADVISORY NOVICES' CHASE
(RSA Insurance Novices' Chase before 2021)
Cheltenham-3m 80yds

2013	**LORD WINDERMERE** 7-11-4	11
2014	**O'FAOLAINS BOY** 7-11-4	15
2015	**DON POLI** 6-11-4	8
2016	**BLAKLION** 7-11-4	8
2017	**MIGHT BITE** 8-11-4	12
2018	**PRESENTING PERCY** 7-11-4	10
2019	**TOPOFTHEGAME** 7-11-4	12
2020	**CHAMP** 8-11-4	10
2021	**MONKFISH** 7-11-4	6
2022	**L'HOMME PRESSE** 7-11-4	9

STAYERS' HURDLE
(World Hurdle before 2017)
Cheltenham-2m 7f 213 yds

2013	**SOLWHIT** 9-11-10	13
2014	**MORE OF THAT** 6-11-10	10
2015	**COLE HARDEN** 6-11-10	16
2016	**THISTLECRACK** 8-11-10	12
2017	**NICHOLS CANYON** 7-11-10	12
2018	**PENHILL** 7-11-10	15
2019	**PAISLEY PARK** 7-11-10	18
2020	**LISNAGAR OSCAR** 7-11-10	15
2021	**FLOORING PORTER** 6-11-10	15
2022	**FLOORING PORTER** 7-11-10	10

TRIUMPH HURDLE (4y)
Cheltenham-2m 179yds

2013	**OUR CONOR** 11-0	17
2014	**TIGER ROLL** 11-0	15
2015	**PEACE AND CO** 11-0	16
2016	**IVANOVICH GORBATOV** 11-0	15
2017	**DEFI DU SEUIL** 11-0	15
2018	**FARCLAS** 11-0	9
2019	**PENTLAND HILLS** 11-0	14
2020	**BURNING VICTORY** 10-7	13
2021	**QUILIXIOS** 11-0	8
2022	**VAUBAN** 11-0	12

CHELTENHAM GOLD CUP
Cheltenham-3m 2f 110yds

2013	**BOBS WORTH** 8-11-10	9
2014	**LORD WINDERMERE** 8-11-10	13
2015	**CONEYGREE** 8-11-10	16
2016	**DON COSSACK** 9-11-10	9
2017	**SIZING JOHN** 7-11-10	13
2018	**NATIVE RIVER** 8-11-10	15
2019	**AL BOUM PHOTO** 7-11-10	16
2020	**AL BOUM PHOTO** 8-11-10	12
2021	**MINELLA INDO** 8-11-10	12
2022	**A PLUS TARD** 8-11-10	11

RYANAIR CHASE (FESTIVAL TROPHY)
Cheltenham-2m 4f 166yds
2013 **CUE CARD** 7-11-10 8
2014 **DYNASTE** 8-11-10 11
2015 **UXIZANDRE** 7-11-10 14
2016 **VAUTOUR** 7-11-10 15
2017 **UN DE SCEAUX** 9-11-10 8
2018 **BALKO DES FLOS** 7-11-10 6
2019 **FRODON** 7-11-10 12
2020 **MIN** 9-11-10 8
2021 **ALLAHO** 7-11-10 11
2022 **ALLAHO** 8-11-10 7

BOWL CHASE
Aintree-3m 210yds
2013 **FIRST LIEUTENANT** 8-11-7 8
2014 **SILVINIACO CONTI** 8-11-7 6
2015 **SILVINIACO CONTI** 9-11-7 7
2016 **CUE CARD** 10-11-7 9
2017 **TEA FOR TWO** 8-11-7 7
2018 **MIGHT BITE** 9-11-7 8
2019 **KEMBOY** 7-11-7 6
2020 RACE CANCELLED
2021 **CLAN DES OBEAUX** 9-11-7 9
2022 **CLAN DES OBEAUX** 10-11-7 9

MELLING CHASE
Aintree-2m 3f 200yds
2013 **SPRINTER SACRE** 7-11-10 6
2014 **BOSTON BOB** 9-11-10 10
2015 **DON COSSACK** 8-11-10 10
2016 **GOD'S OWN** 8-11-10 6
2017 **FOX NORTON** 7-11-7 9
2018 **POLITOLOGUE** 7-11-7 6
2019 **MIN** 8-11-7 6
2020 RACE CANCELLED
2021 **FAKIR D'OUDAIRIES** 6-11-7 7
2022 **FAKIR D'OUDAIRIES** 7-11-7 10

AINTREE HURDLE
Aintree-2m 4f
2013 **ZARKANDAR** 6-11-7 9
2014 **THE NEW ONE** 6-11-7 7
2015 **JEZKI** 7-11-7 6
2016 **ANNIE POWER** 8-11-0 6
2017 **BUVEUR D'AIR** 6-11-7 6
2018 **L'AMI SERGE** 8-11-7 9
2019 **SUPASUNDAE** 9-11-7 7
2020 RACE CANCELLED
2021 **ABACADABRAS** 7-11-7 11
2022 **EPATANTE** 8-11-0 7

SCOTTISH GRAND NATIONAL (H'CAP CHASE)
Ayr-3m 7f 176 yds
2013 **GODSMEJUDGE** 7-11-3 24
2014 **AL CO** 9-10-0 29
2015 **WAYWARD PRINCE** 11-10-1 29
2016 **VICENTE** 7-11-3 28
2017 **VICENTE** 8-11-10 30
2018 **JOE FARRELL** 9-10-6 29
2019 **TAKINGRISKS** 10-10-1 23
2020 RACE CANCELLED
2021 **MIGHTY THUNDER** 8-11-1 22
2022 **WIN MY WINGS** 9-10-12 23

BET365 GOLD CUP (H'CAP CHASE)
Sandown-3m 4f 166yds
2013 **QUENTIN COLLONGES** 9-10-12 19
2014 **HADRIAN'S APPROACH** 7-11-0 19
2015 **JUST A PAR** 8-10-0 20
2016 **THE YOUNG MASTER** 7-10-12 20
2017 **HENLLAN HARRI** 9-10-0 13
2018 **STEP BACK** 8-10-0 20
2019 **TALKISCHEAP** 7-10-11 15
2020 RACE CANCELLED
2021 **POTTERMAN** 8-11-9 16
2022 **HEWICK** 7-11-4 15

DISTANCE CONVERSION

5f	1,000m	10f	2,000m	15f	3,000m	20f	4,000m
6f	1,200m	11f	2,200m	16f	3,200m	21f	4,200m
7f	1,400m	12f	2,400m	17f	3,400m	22f	4,400m
8f	1,600m	13f	2,600m	18f	3,600m		
9f	1,800m	14f	2,800m	19f	3,800m		

JOCKEYS' AGENTS

Jockeys' agents and their contact details

Agent	Telephone	Mobile/Email
NICKY ADAMS	01488 72004/72964	07796547659 nickadams2594@hotmail.com
NEIL ALLAN	01243 543870	07825549081 aneilallan@aol.com
ROSS BIRKETT	07855 065036	rbirkett1989@hotmail.co.uk
LINDSEY BRENNAN	07920407447	lindsey_hunting@hotmail.com
PAUL BRIERLEY		07824828750 bbjockeys@hotmail.co.uk
ADAM BROOK		07399390303 info@brooksportsmanagement.com
ALAIN CAWLEY		07951945573 apcawley@hotmail.com
GLORIA CHARNOCK	01653 695004	07951576912 gloriacharnock@hotmail.com
PAUL CLARKE	01638 660804	07885914306 paul.clarke79@btinternet.com
GORDON CLARKSON	01451 509496	07767296053 gordonclarkson@live.co.uk
STEVEN CROFT		07809205556 steven.croft6@googlemail.com
CHRIS DIXON	01604 248950	07557129536 chrisdixon2003@yahoo.com
SIMON DODDS	01509 734496	07974924735 simon.dodds@btinternet.com
SHELLEY DWYER	01638 493123	07949612256 shelleydwyer4031@outlook.com

Agent	Telephone	Mobile/Email
SHIPPY ELLIS	01638 668484	07860864864 shippysjockeys@jockeysagent.com
JAMES FOREST		07985333761 jfjockeyagent@gmail.com
MARK FURNASS		07474242332 jockeysagent@gmail.com
RICHARD HALE	01768 88699	07909520542 richardhale77@hotmail.co.uk
NIALL HANNITY	01677 423363	07710141084 niallhannity@yahoo.co.uk
ALAN HARRISON	01969 326248	07846187991 ahjockagent60@yahoo.co.uk
TONY HIND	01638 724997	07807908599 tonyhind@jockeysagent.com
GAVIN HORNE	01392 433610	07821 361215 renoodriver2@gmail.com
CHRIS HUMPLEBY		07712608969 chris.humpleby13@gmail.com
RUSS JAMES	01653 699466	07947414001 russjames2006@btconnect.com
HENRY JAMES	07527203330	henryg.james0405@gmail.com
GUY JEWELL	01672 861231	07765248859 guyjewell@btconnect.com
SARA-LOUISE METCALFE	01635 269647	07918525354 troopersjockeys@hotmail.co.uk
LUCIE MOORE	07867784945	lucie20@hotmail.co.uk
JOHN NEILSON	01388 730249	07813874970 john@jlnjockeys.co.uk
MEGAN NICHOLLS	07792440002	megannicholls2@googlemail.com
TARA OATLEY	07466751027	taraleeoatley@gmail.com
GARETH OWEN	01603 569390	07958335206 garethowenracing@gmail.com

Agent	Telephone	Mobile/Email
IAN POPHAM		07759 439286 ianpopham28@outlook.com
WILSON RENWICK		07860949577 wilsonrenwick@aol.com
SHASHI RIGHTON	01353 688594	07825381350 srighton.sr@googlemail.com
PHILIP SHEA	01638 667456	07585120297 psheajockeysagent@gmail.com
SAM STRONG	01488 72819	07775727778 samstrong@hotmail.com
ANNA WALLACE		07867923642 awallace51@yahoo.com
LAURA WAY	01704 834488	07775777494 laura.way@btconnect.com
NOEL WILSON	07506761481	andycookracing@gmail.com

FLAT JOCKEYS

Riding weights and contact details

An index of agents appears on page 700

Jockey	Weight	Agent
DAVID ALLAN	8 - 10	Mrs G. S. Charnock
ANDREA ATZENI	8 - 5	Mr S. Croft
CONNOR BEASLEY	8 - 6	Mr G. R. Owen
ALED BEECH	7 - 13	Mr L. R. James
CHARLIE BENNETT	8 - 6	Mr James Christopher Forrest
CHARLES BISHOP	8 - 10	Mr Neil Allan
SEAN BOWEN	8 - 12	A. P. Cawley
PADDY BRADLEY	8 - 12	Mr James Christopher Forrest
ANDREW BRESLIN	8 - 0	Mr N. Hannity
JOSHUA BRYAN	8 - 10	Mr G. D. Jewell
GEORGE BUCKELL	8 - 12	
WILLIAM BUICK	8 - 6	Mr Tony Hind
HARRY BURNS	8 - 4	Mr Christopher Humpleby
NEIL CALLAN	8 - 10	Mr S. Croft
WILLIAM CARSON	8 - 6	Mr Neil Allan
ROSS COAKLEY	8 - 12	Mr G. D. Jewell
PAT COSGRAVE	8 - 9	Mr Paul Clarke
DOUGIE COSTELLO	8 - 10	Mr A. T. Brook
LAURA COUGHLAN	7 - 13	Mr Paul Brierley
WILLIAM COX	8 - 4	Mr N. M. Adams
HECTOR CROUCH	8 - 11	Mr G. D. Jewell
JIM CROWLEY	8 - 7	Mr Tony Hind
NICOLA CURRIE	8 - 0	Mr G. J. Horne
BEN CURTIS	8 - 5	Mr S. T. Dodds
RAY DAWSON	8 - 4	Mr A. T. Brook
PHIL DENNIS	8 - 12	Mrs G. S. Charnock
FRANKIE DETTORI	8 - 9	07703 606162
PAT DOBBS	8 - 9	Mr Tony Hind
STEVIE DONOHOE	8 - 8	P. C. Shea
GEORGE DOWNING	8 - 9	Mr G. D. Jewell
HOLLIE DOYLE	8 - 0	Mr G. D. Jewell
JAMES DOYLE	8 - 10	Mr Christopher Humpleby
JACK DUERN	8 - 4	Miss A. Wallace
MARTIN DWYER	8 - 3	Mr S. T. Dodds
TOM EAVES	8 - 7	Mr R. A. Hale
LEWIS EDMUNDS	8 - 9	Mr S. T. Dodds
DAVID EGAN	8 - 4	Mr Tony Hind
JOHN EGAN	8 - 3	Mr Paul Brierley
ANDREW ELLIOTT	8 - 4	Mr Paul Brierley
JANE ELLIOTT	8 - 0	07731546370
JONATHAN ENGLAND	9 - 7	Mr R. A. Hale
JOHN FAHY	8 - 6	Mr Paul Brierley
CIEREN FALLON	8 - 5	Mr C. Dixon
JOE FANNING	8 - 2	Mr N. Hannity
DURAN FENTIMAN	8 - 0	Mr Alan Harrison
ROYSTON FFRENCH	8 - 3	Mr R. Birkett
JONATHAN FISHER	8 - 7	M. Furnass
ISOBEL FRANCIS	7 - 10	Mr James Christopher Forrest
BILLY GARRITTY	8 - 8	K. W. Renwick
JACK GARRITTY	9 - 0	K. W. Renwick
JOSEPHINE GORDON	8 - 4	Mr A. T. Brook
SHANE GRAY	8 - 4	Mr N. Hannity
THOMAS GREATREX	8 - 10	Mr G. D. Jewell
TONY HAMILTON	8 - 8	Mr N. Hannity
PAUL HANAGAN	8 - 6	Mr R. A. Hale
THORE HAMMER HANSEN	8 - 0	Mr C. Dixon
CAM HARDIE	8 - 0	Mr R. A. Hale
MARTIN HARLEY	8 - 11	
JASON HART	8 - 9	Mr Alan Harrison
ROBERT HAVLIN	8 - 7	Mr Neil Allan
JOEY HAYNES	8 - 5	Mr A. T. Brook
SAM HITCHCOTT	8 - 5	Mr N. M. Adams
DYLAN HOGAN	8 - 6	Mr Paul Brierley
ROB HORNBY	8 - 10	Mr N. M. Adams
RHIAIN INGRAM	8 - 0	
SAM JAMES	8 - 6	K. W. Renwick
CHARLOTTE JONES	9 - 0	Mr J. L. Neilson
DARRAGH KEENAN	8 - 7	Mr S. T. Dodds
SHANE KELLY	8 - 9	Mr N. M. Adams
LIAM KENIRY	8 - 8	Mr N. M. Adams
RICHARD KINGSCOTE	8 - 8	Mr G. D. Jewell
ADAM KIRBY	9 - 0	Mr N. M. Adams
THEODORE LADD	8 - 0	Mr G. D. Jewell
CLIFFORD LEE	8 - 10	Mr G. R. Owen
GRAHAM LEE	8 - 9	Mr R. A. Hale
SEAN LEVEY	8 - 10	Mr S. M. Righton
ELLIE MACKENZIE	8 - 6	
GINA MANGAN	8 - 0	Mr L. R. James
TOM MARQUAND	8 - 7	Mr S. M. Righton
FINLEY MARSH	8 - 12	Mr S. T. Dodds
JOANNA MASON	8 - 5	Mr N. Hannity
PADDY MATHERS	8 - 5	Mr James Christopher Forrest
P. J. MCDONALD	8 - 6	Mr S. T. Dodds
BARRY MCHUGH	8 - 6	K. W. Renwick
FAYE MCMANOMAN	7 - 13	Mr Paul Brierley
JACK MITCHELL	8 - 9	Mr S. Croft
SORIN MOLDOVEANU	8 - 10	
MARC MONAGHAN	8 - 10	
RYAN MOORE	8 - 9	Mr Tony Hind
LUKE MORRIS	8 - 0	Mr Neil Allan
PAULA MUIR	8 - 0	Mr Paul Brierley
ANDREW MULLEN	8 - 3	Mr R. A. Hale
PAUL MULRENNAN	8 - 10	Mr R. A. Hale
OISIN MURPHY	8 - 6	GJ Horne
CONNOR MURTAGH	8 - 9	K. W. Renwick
DANIEL MUSCUTT	8 - 10	Mr Paul Clarke
CAMERON NOBLE	8 - 9	Mr James Christopher Forrest
DAVID NOLAN	9 - 1	Mr R. A. Hale
FRANNY NORTON	8 - 0	Mr N. Hannity
DANE O'NEILL	8 - 7	Mr N. M. Adams
KIERAN O'NEILL	8 - 0	Mr N. M. Adams
RICHARD OLIVER	8 - 0	Mrs L. H. Way

OISIN ORR	8 - 10	Mr N. Hannity
ABBIE PIERCE	8 - 2	Miss A. Wallace
DAVID PROBERT	8 - 7	Mr Neil Allan
TOM QUEALLY	8 - 11	Mr S. T. Dodds
JIMMY QUINN	8 - 0	Miss A. Wallace
ALISTAIR RAWLINSON	8 - 11	Mr C. Dixon
BEN ROBINSON	8 - 9	Mr S. T. Dodds
CALLUM RODRIGUEZ	9 - 0	Mr G. R. Owen
GEORGE ROOKE	8 - 1	Mr N. M. Adams
ROSSA RYAN	8 - 7	Mr S. Croft
TYLER SAUNDERS	8 - 7	Miss A. Wallace
KIERAN SCHOFIELD	8 - 0	Mr James Christopher Forrest
ROWAN SCOTT	8 - 5	Mr N. Hannity
HARRISON SHAW	8 - 5	Mr R. A. Hale
CALLUM SHEPHERD	8 - 9	Mr N. M. Adams
KIERAN SHOEMARK	8 - 9	Mr G. D. Jewell
RAUL DA SILVA	8 - 0	M. Furnass
JEFFERSON SMITH	8 - 2	M. Furnass
SILVESTRE DE SOUSA	8 - 0	Mrs Shelley Dwyer
JAMIE SPENCER	8 - 7	Mr Christopher Humpleby
LOUIS STEWARD	8 - 11	Mr A. T. Brook
COLLEN STOREY	8 - 5	Ms T. L. Oatley
KEVIN STOTT	8 - 12	Miss M. Nicholls
JAMES SULLIVAN	8 - 0	Mr R. A. Hale
DALE SWIFT	8 - 9	Mr G. R. Owen
ROBERT TART	8 - 8	
HARRIET TUCKER	9 - 0	Mr L. R. James
DANIEL TUDHOPE	8 - 11	Mrs L. H. Way
HAYLEY TURNER	8 - 2	Mr G. D. Jewell
EOIN WALSH	8 - 10	Mrs G. S. Charnock
JASON WATSON	8 - 4	Mr C. Dixon
AMIE WAUGH	7 - 7	Mr J. L. Neilson
TREVOR WHELAN	8 - 7	P. C. Shea
JOE WILLIAMSON	9 - 7	Mr Paul Brierley
GEORGE WOOD	8 - 8	Mr S. T. Dodds

APPRENTICES

Riding weights and contact details

An index of agents appears on page 700

Apprentice	Weight	Contact
MUHAMMAD ADEEL (Sir Mark Prescott Bt)	8 - 8	c/o 01638 662 117 Use First
LOUISE AKEHURST (Kevin Ryan)	7 - 6	c/o 01845 597622
GEORGE BASS (Mick Channon)	8 - 5	Mrs Shelley Dwyer
LEVI BEDFORD (George Scott)	9 - 4	c/o 07833461294
ALICE BOND (Joseph Parr)	8 - 1	Miss S. L. Metcalfe
JOE BRADNAM (Michael Bell)	8 - 3	c/o 07802 264514
AIDEN BROOKES (Micky Hammond)	7 - 13	K. W. Renwick
SYDNEY CALE (Archie Watson)	7 - 12	c/o 01488 491247 (Also home)
TYRESE CAMERON (Richard Hannon)	8 - 2	c/o 01264 850254
WILLIAM CARVER (Andrew Balding)	8 - 3	P. C. Shea
LUKE CATTON (Stuart Williams)	8 - 9	Mr G. D. Jewell
STEFANO CHERCHI (Amy Murphy)	8 - 3	Mrs Shelley Dwyer
JACOB CLARK (Tom Clover)	8 - 4	c/o 01638660055
SOPHIE CLEMENTS (Nigel Tinkler)	7 - 8	Mr Alan Harrison
RHYS CLUTTERBUCK (Gary Moore)	8 - 10	Mr N. M. Adams
MARK CREHAN (Alice Haynes)	8 - 10	c/o 07585 558717 Preferred
ELLE-MAY CROOT (Ivan Furtado)	8 - 2	Miss A. Wallace
HARRY DAVIES (Andrew Balding)	8 - 0	P. C. Shea
ROSE DAWES (Mick Channon)	7 - 10	Mr R. Birkett
GEORGIA DOBIE (Eve Johnson Houghton)	8 - 3	c/o 01235 850480 CALL FIRST
ADAM FARRAGHER (William Haggas)	7 - 10	Mr S. M. Righton
SAM FEILDEN (K. R. Burke)	8 - 5	K. W. Renwick
ALEX FIELDING (Paul Midgley)	8 - 10	Mr R. A. Hale
TAYLOR FISHER (Archie Watson)	8 - 7	Mr Paul Clarke
KAIYA FRASER (Harry Eustace)	8 - 7	Mrs Shelley Dwyer
BRADLEY FURNISS (Marco Botti)	8 - 3	Mr Paul Brierley
ANNA GIBSON (Gary Moore)	7 - 7	c/o 01403 891 912
MOLLY GUNN (Tony Carroll)	8 - 2	M. Furnass
OLIVIA HAINES (David Simcock)	8 - 3	c/o 07808 954109
EMILIE HASSELBALCH-HOLM (J. S. Moore)	9 - 1	c/o 0148873887
PAIGE HOPPER (Michael Dods)	8 - 6	c/o 07860 411 590
CHRISTIAN HOWARTH (Henry Spiller)	8 - 3	Mr A. T. Brook
AMY HUNT (Micky Hammond)	8 - 4	c/o 07808 572777
CALLUM HUTCHINSON (Andrew Balding)	8 - 0	Mr N. M. Adams
EMILY IVORY (Dean Ivory)	7 - 11	c/o 01923 855337
TOMMIE JAKES (Jane Chapple-Hyam)	6 - 7	P. C. Shea
PIERRE-LOUIS JAMIN (K. R. Burke)	8 - 3	Mr G. D. Jewell
ALEX JARY (Nigel Tinkler)	8 - 3	Mr Paul Brierley
AIDAN KEELEY (Gary Moore)	8 - 2	Mr N. M. Adams
SEAN KIRRANE (Tim Easterby)	8 - 9	Mrs G. S. Charnock
FREDERICK LARSON (Michael Appleby)	8 - 2	Mr R. Birkett
JOE LEAVY (Richard Hannon)	8 - 6	P. C. Shea
OWEN LEWIS (Charles Hills)	8 - 0	Mr James Christopher Forrest
BILLY LOUGHNANE (Mark Loughnane)	8 - 7	Mr S. M. Righton
JAY MACKAY (Michael Bell)	7 - 7	c/o 07802 264514
CONNER MCCANN (Lucinda Russell)	8 - 7	K. W. Renwick
OISIN MCSWEENEY (Kevin Ryan)	8 - 3	Mr N. Hannity
SHARIQ MOHD (Alice Haynes)	8 - 0	Mrs L. H. Way
MIKKEL MORTENSEN (Charlie Fellowes)	8 - 4	c/o 01638666948
MIA NICHOLLS (Eve Johnson Houghton)	7 - 6	Mr N. M. Adams
SAFFIE OSBORNE (Jamie Osborne)	8 - 4	Mr N. Hannity

ERIKA PARKINSON (Michael Appleby) .... 8 - 0 c/o 01572 722772 Preferred
MADI PATZELT (Philip Kirby) .... 8 - 3 c/o 07984 403 558
LAURA PEARSON (Ralph Beckett) .... 8 - 4 Mr S. Croft
JONNY PEATE (Roger Fell) .... 8 - 0 Mr N. Hannity
MOLLIE PHILLIPS (Tony Carroll) .... 8 - 0 Miss S. L. Metcalfe
MOLLY PRESLAND (Phil McEntee) .... 7 - 8 Mrs G. S. Charnock
WILLIAM PYLE (Craig Lidster) .... 8 - 0 Mr N. Hannity
SOPHIE REED (Hughie Morrison) .... 8 - 0 c/o 07836 687 799
DEON LE ROUX (Richard Hughes) .... 8 - 10 P. C. Shea
HARRY RUSSELL (Brian Ellison) .... 8 - 7 K. W. Renwick
BEN SANDERSON (Ian Williams) .... 8 - 7 Mr S. T. Dodds
GIANLUCA SANNA (David & Nicola Barron) .... 8 - 7 Mr R. A. Hale
BENOIT DE LA SAYETTE (John & Thady Gosden) .... 8 - 10 Mr Paul Clarke
OLIVER SEARLE (Rod Millman) .... 7 - 12 Mr G. J. Horne
RYAN SEXTON (Adrian Keatley) .... 8 - 6 K. W. Renwick
OLIVER STAMMERS (Charlie Johnston) .... 8 - 10 Mr S. T. Dodds
MOHAMMED TABTI (Paul & Oliver Cole) .... 8 - 0 M. Furnass
EMMA TAFF (Ed Walker) .... 8 - 6 c/o 01488 674148 prefered
COURTNEY THOMAS (Roger Teal) .... 7 - 7 c/o 07710 325521 preferred
OLIVIA TUBB (Jonathan Portman) .... 8 - 3 c/o 01488 73894
ALEC VOIKHANSKY (Richard Hannon) .... 7 - 9 Mr G. D. Jewell
SHANNON WATTS (Jim Goldie) .... 8 - 0 c/o 04119 36989
ZAK WHEATLEY (Declan Carroll) .... 8 - 5 Mr R. A. Hale
ELISHA WHITTINGTON (Scott Dixon) .... 7 - 13 Miss A. Wallace
ISABEL WILLIAMS (Evan Williams) .... 8 - 12 c/o 01446 754069
JORDAN WILLIAMS (Bernard Llewellyn) .... 8 - 10 Mr L. R. James
LEVI WILLIAMS (T. J. Kent) .... 8 - 2
POPPY WILSON (Iain Jardine) .... 8 - 11 c/o 07944 722011 Val Renwick (Secretary)
CURTIS WILSON-RUDDOCK (Kevin Ryan) .... 8 - 5 Mr R. A. Hale
MARK WINN (David O'Meara) .... 8 - 0 Mr R. A. Hale
LIAM WRIGHT (Darryll Holland) .... 8 - 3 Miss A. Wallace
ARCHIE YOUNG (Charlie Johnston) .... 8 - 4 c/o 07848 642746

JUMP JOCKEYS

Riding weights and contact details

An index of agents appears on page 700

Jockey	Weight	Contact
AARON ANDERSON	9 - 7	Mr Paul Brierley
JOE ANDERSON	9 - 11	Mr Gordon Clarkson
BRIDGET ANDREWS	9 - 5	Mr I. P. Popham
EDWARD AUSTIN	10 - 0	Mr J. L. Neilson
HARRY BANNISTER	9 - 7	Mr Gordon Clarkson
DAVID BASS	10 - 5	Mr Gordon Clarkson
MITCHELL BASTYAN	10 - 0	Mr I. P. Popham
TOM BELLAMY	10 - 5	Mr Gordon Clarkson
JAMES BEST	10 - 2	Mr I. P. Popham
HARRISON BESWICK	10 - 0	Mr I. P. Popham
CALLUM BEWLEY	10 - 2	Mr R. A. Hale
JONATHON BEWLEY	10 - 0	01450860651
NICO DE BOINVILLE	10 - 0	Mr S. Stronge
JAMES BOWEN	10 - 0	A. P. Cawley
SEAN BOWEN	9 - 7	A. P. Cawley
CONNOR BRACE	10 - 0	A. P. Cawley
PADDY BRENNAN	9 - 12	07779302115
KEVIN BROGAN	10 - 0	A. P. Cawley
HENRY BROOKE	10 - 0	K. W. Renwick
JONATHAN BURKE	10 - 0	Mr Gordon Clarkson
DANNY BURTON	9 - 9	Mr L. R. James
TOM CANNON	10 - 5	Mr S. Stronge
BRYAN CARVER	10 - 2	Mr S. Stronge
ROSS CHAPMAN	9 - 8	Mr R. A. Hale
HARRY COBDEN	10 - 0	Mr S. Stronge
AIDAN COLEMAN	10 - 0	A. P. Cawley
SAM COLTHERD	9 - 12	Mr R. A. Hale
PATRICK COWLEY	10 - 0	Mr I. P. Popham
JAMES DAVIES	10 - 0	Mr L. R. James
BEN FFRENCH DAVIS	9 - 9	Mr L. R. James
CHARLIE DEUTSCH	10 - 0	Mr Gordon Clarkson
REX DINGLE	10 - 2	Mr S. Stronge
THOMAS DOWSON	10 - 0	Mr J. L. Neilson
ALAN DOYLE	9 - 10	Mr R. A. Hale
ROBERT DUNNE	10 - 7	Mr I. P. Popham
ALEX EDWARDS	10 - 0	Mr Gordon Clarkson\Mr I. P. Popham
LEE EDWARDS	10 - 0	Mr Gordon Clarkson
DAVID ENGLAND	10 - 0	Mr I. P. Popham
JONATHAN ENGLAND	9 - 10	Mr R. A. Hale
DEREK FOX	10 - 0	A. P. Cawley
BRYONY FROST	9 - 12	Mr S. Stronge
PAGE FULLER	9 - 6	Mr L. R. James
LUCY GARDNER	10 - 0	07814 979 699
THOMAS GARNER	10 - 2	07816496202 1st contact
BILLY GARRITTY	9 - 7	K. W. Renwick
JACK GARRITTY	9 - 0	K. W. Renwick
CIARAN GETHINGS	10 - 2	Mr Gordon Clarkson
MARC GOLDSTEIN	10 - 0	Mr S. Stronge
FERGUS GREGORY	10 - 7	Mr I. P. Popham
JAMIE HAMILTON	10 - 0	Mr R. A. Hale
CHARLIE HAMMOND	10 - 2	Mr S. Stronge
A. P. HESKIN	10 - 0	A. P. Cawley
DANIEL HISKETT	9 - 10	
SEAN HOULIHAN	9 - 11	Mr Gordon Clarkson
BRIAN HUGHES	10 - 0	Mr R. A. Hale
DARYL JACOB	10 - 3	Mr S. Stronge
ALAN JOHNS	10 - 0	Mr I. P. Popham
ALISON JOHNSON	9 - 7	07549142203
BEN JONES	10 - 0	Mr Gordon Clarkson
CHARLOTTE JONES	8 - 11	Mr J. L. Neilson
JONJO O'NEILL JR.	10 - 4	A. P. Cawley
MAX KENDRICK	9 - 9	Mr Gordon Clarkson
WILLIAM KENNEDY	10 - 0	Mr Gordon Clarkson
JOHN KINGTON	10 - 0	07525 818872
CILLIN LEONARD	9 - 11	Mr I. P. Popham
RYAN MANIA	10 - 5	Mr Gordon Clarkson
JAMES MARTIN	10 - 13	Mr I. P. Popham
RICHIE MCLERNON	10 - 2	A. P. Cawley
DANNY MCMENAMIN	9 - 7	Mr R. A. Hale
JAMIE MOORE	10 - 0	Mrs Lucie Moore
NATHAN MOSCROP	10 - 5	Mr R. A. Hale
STEPHEN MULQUEEN	10 - 0	K. W. Renwick
CRAIG NICHOL	10 - 0	K. W. Renwick
MICHEAL NOLAN	10 - 4	Mr Gordon Clarkson
DAVID NOONAN	10 - 0	K. W. Renwick
HUGH NUGENT	9 - 9	Mr Gordon Clarkson
PAUL O'BRIEN	10 - 3	Mr I. P. Popham
TOM O'BRIEN	10 - 2	Mr Gordon Clarkson
CONOR O'FARRELL	10 - 3	K. W. Renwick
RICHARD PATRICK	9 - 7	Mr Gordon Clarkson
BEN POSTE	9 - 12	Mr S. Stronge
BRENDAN POWELL	9 - 11	Mr S. Stronge
DAVID PRICHARD	10 - 0	Mr I. P. Popham
JACK QUINLAN	9 - 10	K. W. Renwick
SHANE QUINLAN	9 - 7	Mr I. P. Popham
SEAN QUINLAN	10 - 0	Mr R. A. Hale
HARRY REED	9 - 7	Mr I. P. Popham
CONOR RING	10 - 5	Mr I. P. Popham
BEN ROBINSON	8 - 9	Mr S. T. Dodds
DANIEL SANSOM	10 - 5	Mr L. R. James
JACK SAVAGE	10 - 5	07778 683721
NICK SCHOLFIELD	10 - 3	Mr S. Stronge
TOM SCUDAMORE	10 - 0	Mr C. Dixon
WILLIAM SHANAHAN	10 - 3	Mr L. R. James
GAVIN SHEEHAN	10 - 0	Mr Gordon Clarkson
STAN SHEPPARD	10 - 4	Mr Gordon Clarkson
HARRY SKELTON	10 - 0	Mr I. P. Popham
NICK SLATTER	9 - 7	
LEWIS STONES	9 - 11	Mr I. P. Popham
ALEXANDER THORNE	9 - 7	Mr S. Stronge
CHARLIE TODD	10 - 0	Mr I. P. Popham
HARRIET TUCKER	9 - 3	Mr L. R. James
JACK TUDOR	9 - 7	Mr S. Stronge
SAM TWISTON-DAVIES	10 - 0	Mr Gordon Clarkson
CHRIS WARD	9 - 12	Mr L. R. James
AMIE WAUGH	8 - 0	Mr J. L. Neilson
ADAM WEDGE	10 - 0	Mr Gordon Clarkson
LORCAN WILLIAMS	10 - 9	Mr I. P. Popham
ROBERT WILLIAMS	10 - 7	07538 462942
JOE WILLIAMSON	9 - 7	Mr Paul Brierley
KIELAN WOODS	10 - 3	Mr Gordon Clarkson
TABITHA WORSLEY	9 - 9	Mr L. R. James

CONDITIONALS

Riding weights and contact details

An index of agents appears on page 700

BENJAMIN ABBOTT (Sam Allwood) 10 - 0 c/o 07738 413579
PHILIP ARMSON (David Pipe) 9 - 7 Mr I. P. Popham
JAMIE BRACE (Jonjo O'Neill) 10 - 0 Mr I. P. Popham
NATHAN BRENNAN (Nicky Henderson) 9 - 12 Mr S. Stronge
BEN BROMLEY (Harry Fry) 9 - 9 Mr S. Stronge
TOM BUCKLEY (Paul Nicholls) 9 - 0 Mr S. Stronge
ANGUS CHELEDA (Paul Nicholls) 9 - 10 Mr S. Stronge
ELLIS COLLIER (Christian Williams) 9 - 10 Mr S. Stronge
DAIRE DAVIS (Olly Murphy) 9 - 3 Mr I. P. Popham
LEWIS DOBB (L J Morgan) 9 - 8 Mr Tommy Morgan
THOMAS DOGGRELL (Neil Mulholland) 10 - 4 Mr Gordon Clarkson
TRISTAN DURRELL (Dan Skelton) 9 - 7 Mr I. P. Popham
EDDIE EDGE (Lucy Wadham) 9 - 10 Mr Gordon Clarkson
THOMASINA EYSTON (Neil Mulholland) 9 - 7 Mr Gordon Clarkson
WILL FEATHERSTONE (Jamie Snowden) 9 - 5 c/o 01488 72800
NED FOX (Venetia Williams) 9 - 10 Mr Gordon Clarkson
ELIZABETH GALE (Philip Hobbs) 9 - 1 Mr Gordon Clarkson
FERGUS GILLARD (David Pipe) 9 - 7 Mr I. P. Popham
THEO GILLARD (Donald McCain) 10 - 7 Mr R. A. Hale
FREDDIE GINGELL (Paul Nicholls) 9 - 5 Mr S. Stronge
BEN GODFREY (Anthony Honeyball) 9 - 4 Mr S. Stronge
ROB HARGREAVES (Gary Moore) 10 - 3 c/o 01403 891 912
BRADLEY HARRIS (Milton Harris) 9 - 2 Mr I. P. Popham
LIAM HARRISON (Fergal O'Brien) 9 - 6 Mr S. Stronge
JACK HOGAN (Fergal O'Brien) 10 - 5 A. P. Cawley
NIALL HOULIHAN (Gary Moore) 9 - 7 Mr S. Stronge
DILLAN HURST (Susan Corbett) 9 - 7 Mr J. L. Neilson
CAMERON ILES (Tom Lacey) 9 - 0 c/o 07768 398604 Call first
DYLAN JOHNSTON (Rose Dobbin) 9 - 4 K. W. Renwick
PETER KAVANAGH (Donald McCain) 9 - 0 Mr R. A. Hale
HARRY KIMBER (Joe Tizzard) 9 - 7 Mr Gordon Clarkson
DYLAN KITTS (Warren Greatrex) 9 - 5 Mr S. Stronge
JAY KOZACZEK (Philip Kirby) 9 - 10 c/o 07984 403 558
FINN LAMBERT (Nigel Twiston-Davies) 10 - 3 Mr Gordon Clarkson
ROBERT LAW-EADIE (Tom George) 9 - 10 c/o 01452 814267
KAI LENIHAN (Kim Bailey) 9 - 8 Mr Gordon Clarkson
BRUCE LYNN (N. W. Alexander) 10 - 0 K. W. Renwick
AIDAN MACDONALD (Micky Hammond) 9 - 10 c/o 07808 572777
CHARLIE MAGGS (Donald McCain) 9 - 0 c/o 01829 720 352
WILLIAM MAGGS (Donald McCain) 9 - 4 c/o 01829 720 352
JACK MARTIN (Philip Hobbs) 10 - 4 Mr Gordon Clarkson
ABBIE MCCAIN (Donald McCain) 9 - 9 Mr R. A. Hale
CONNER MCCANN (Lucinda Russell) 8 - 10 K. W. Renwick
DAIRE MCCONVILLE (Ian Williams) 9 - 10 c/o 01564 822 392
TOM MIDGLEY (Sam England) 10 - 0 Mr R. A. Hale
BEAU MORGAN (Ben Pauling) 10 - 0 Mr Gordon Clarkson
LUCA MORGAN (Ben Pauling) 10 - 3 Mr S. Stronge
LORCAN MURTAGH (Harry Fry) 9 - 11 Mr Gordon Clarkson
JORDAN NAILOR (Nigel Twiston-Davies) 9 - 7 Mr Gordon Clarkson
SEAN O'BRIAIN (Nicky Henderson) 9 - 12 Mr S. Stronge
LILLY PINCHIN (Charlie Longsdon) 10 - 0 Mr Gordon Clarkson
CHARLIE PRICE (Tim Vaughan) 9 - 2 Mr I. P. Popham
CAOILIN QUINN (Gary Moore) 10 - 0 Mr S. Stronge
CONOR RABBITT (Nicky Richards) 9 - 12 Mr R. A. Hale
BRADLEY ROBERTS (Charlie Longsdon) 9 - 12 Mr Gordon Clarkson
LUKE SCOTT (Dr Richard Newland) 9 - 10 Mr I. P. Popham
EMMA SMITH-CHASTON (Micky Hammond) 9 - 7 K. W. Renwick

JOSHUA THOMPSON (Micky Hammond)	9 - 8	Mr J. L. Neilson
JAY TIDBALL (Alastair Ralph)	10 - 2	Mr Gordon Clarkson
PATRICK WADGE (Lucinda Russell)	9 - 0	K. W. Renwick
JACK WILDMAN (Emma Lavelle)	9 - 10	Mr Gordon Clarkson
CHESTER WILLIAMS (Mrs Jane Williams)	10 - 2	c/o 07977457350
ISABEL WILLIAMS (Evan Williams)	9 - 7	c/o 01446 754069
THOMAS WILLMOTT (Sue Smith)	9 - 7	Mr R. A. Hale
TOBY WYNNE (Oliver Greenall & Josh Guerriero)	10 - 0	Mr I. P. Popham

AMATEUR RIDERS

Riding weights and contact details

An index of agents appears on page 700

ADAMS, K. 9 - 2 07826328432
AGAR, J. 10 - 4 ....
ALEXANDER, C. 9 - 10 .... 07799 191093
ANDREWS, D. I. J. 10 - 10 .... 07817 322974
ANDREWS, G. 10 - 0 .... Mr Gordon Clarkson
ANDREWS, J. 10 - 7 .... Mr I. P. Popham
ATKINS, H. 8 - 8 ....
ATKINSON, P. L. 8 - 5 .... 01609 772691
BAILEY, H. G. 12 - 0 .... 07834 641078
BAIN, S. A. 8 - 8 ....
BAKER, C. 9 - 7 .... 07563 692386
BAKER, Z. C. N. 10 - 10 .... Mr Gordon Clarkson
BAMENT, C. L. 10 - 2 ....
BAMENT, J. J. 10 - 7 .... 07964 587682
BARFOOT-SAUNT, G. C. 10 - 12 .... 01684 833227
BARLOW, P. C. F. 9 - 0 .... Mr Tommy Morgan
BARRACLOUGH, J. A. 9 - 0 ....
BARTON, V. 9 - 0 .... Mr Tommy Morgan
BEDI, J. I. 8 - 10 .... 01642 780202
BELL, A. 9 - 4 .... 07971 675180
BENNETT, J. J. S. 10 - 7 ....
BETTS, R. D. 8 - 11 ....
BEVAN, M. J. 10 - 3 ....
BIDDICK, W. E. T. 11 - 0 .... 07976 556823
BIDDLE, C. 9 - 4 ....
BIRKETT, R. A. 10 - 0 .... 07855 065036 Preferred
BLAKEMORE, A. 9 - 0 ....
BODDY, C. 10 - 7 07944581502
BOSTOCK, K. L. 8 - 8 ....
BOWEN, S. L. 9 - 0 .... Mr S. M. Righton
BOYDEN, O. 10 - 0 ....
BRACKENBURY, B. E. 10 - 11 ....
BRADBURN, T. M. 8 - 4 ....
BRADSTOCK, L. A. N. 9 - 6 07972161732
BRIDGER, M. 9 - 4 07961349301
BROOKES, M. R. 8 - 3 ....
BROOKS, C. 9 - 0 ....
BROTHERTON, S. 8 - 12 ....
BROUGHTON, T. P. 10 - 0 .... 07853 012620
BROWN, L. 9 - 10 ....
BROWN, M. W. 9 - 12 07482639103
BROWN, P. J. 9 - 5 ....
BRYAN, P. J. 10 - 7 07538655128
BRYANT, M. P. 9 - 12 .... 07976 217542
BUCKLEY, F. 10 - 10 ....
BURNS-LEWIS, B. D. 9 - 7 ....
BUTLER, C. G. 10 - 5 ....
CAGNEY, E. 9 - 0 .... Mr Paul Brierley
CASE, C. 10 - 10 07807652305
CATER, J. J. 9 - 7 ....
CHADWICK, A. 10 - 0 ....
CHATFEILD-ROBERTS, T. 10 - 7 .... 07876 394421
CHATTERTON, B. A. 10 - 0 ....
CHESTER, C. 9 - 7 ....
CLARKE, S. 10 - 10 ....
CLEARY, P. 9 - 4 .... 00 353 858784431
CLOVER, C. 10 - 5 ....
COBBOLD, C. J. 10 - 2 ....
COLLIER, A. 9 - 0 .... Mrs G. S. Charnock
COLMER, B. 8 - 4 ....
COOKSON, N. P. 8 - 6 07711910653
COOPER, L. 10 - 0 ....
CORRADO, A. 9 - 6 ....
COWLEY, G. H. 10 - 6 ....
COX, A. 8 - 2 .... 07813 386642
CROW, H. 10 - 7 .... 07794 379295
DALY, G. 10 - 0 07469811361
DAWSON, J. A. 10 - 7 .... 07525984547 2022 Renewal
DICKINSON, K. 9 - 8 ....
DIXON, J. 9 - 7 ....
DIXON, J. 9 - 7 .... Mr James Christopher Forrest
DODD, M. 9 - 0 ....
DRING, H. E. 9 - 0 ....
DUN, C. 9 - 10 07766592287
DUNSDON, D. 10 - 6 .... Mr S. T. Dodds
DWAN, E. 8 - 0 ....
EASTERBY, E. A. 8 - 7 07854733689
EASTERBY, T. E. 10 - 7 ....
EASTERBY, W. H. 9 - 7 .... 07772 216 507
EDDERY, G. 9 - 4 ....
EDWARDS, D. M. 11 - 7 ....
EDWARDS, H. 10 - 4 ....
ELLIS, D. F. 9 - 2 ....
EMSLEY, C. J. R. 9 - 5 ....
ENNIS, M. C. 9 - 12 .... Mr C. Dixon
FEAKES, E. 9 - 4 .... 07771 902739
FENWICKE-CLENNELL, G. 9 - 5 ....
FERNANDES, J.F. 8 - 10 ....
FOX, A. S. G. E. J. 9 - 7 ....
FOX, M. 9 - 4 ....
FRANK, L. G. 9 - 0 07508285003
FURNESS, C. J. W. 10 - 6 .... 07871 449210
GAMBIN, J. 9 - 6 ....
GARTON, K. 8 - 12 ....
GARVEN, A. M. 8 - 9 .... Mr Paul Brierley
GERMANY, S. 9 - 0 ....
GIBBS, B. 10 - 10 .... 07818 407883
GIBSON, G. J. A. 9 - 0 ....
GLANVILLE, P. 10 - 0 ....
GORDON, F. 9 - 10 .... Mr S. Stronge
GORDON, L. 10 - 10 .... 01285 740445
GORMAN, G. 10 - 5 .... 01403 730596

GOUGH, W. 10 - 12
GREENWOOD, T. O. M. 10 - 12 07904889779
GUNN, P. 9 - 2
GUY, F. 7 - 10
HAMPSON, B. 9 - 12
HAMPTON, M. 11 - 0
HARBISON, J. E. A. 10 - 7 .... 01280 812057
HARDING, J. 9 - 10 .... Miss A. Wallace
HARDY, H. 10 - 5
HARNEY, G. 10 - 0 .... Mr I. P. Popham
HARPER, L. 9 - 1
HARRIS, C. 9 - 6
HAWKER, R. 10 - 12 .... 07891 960356
HENDERSON, F. 11 - 4 .... 07824 954461
HERBERT, I. 10 - 1
HERBERT, M. 11 - 0
HERBISON, E. 10 - 0 .... Mr Gordon Clarkson
HILLHOUSE, C. J. 9 - 0
HISCOCK, G. 10 - 7 .... 07815 475518
HISLOP, L. 10 - 0 07718607885
HODGINS, L. W. 10 - 5 .... Mr J. L. Neilson
HOLDER, E. 9 - 0
HOLLADAY, E. 8 - 10
HOLLIDAY, J. 9 - 10 07553773454
HOMER, A. 9 - 3 07581532460
HOPKINS, T. 8 - 0
HOWARTH, R. 9 - 2
HYSON, K. 9 - 2
IRVINE, N. 9 - 12
JACKSON-FENNELL, A. 10 - 7
JAKES, V. J. 10 - 2
JARDEBACK, S. S. 8 - 12
JEAVONS, J. 10 - 0
JEFFRIES, M. 10 - 0 .... 07985 327140
JOHNSON, M. S. 9 - 7
JOHNSTONE-BAKER, C. 9 - 7 07808093979
JONES, L. 9 - 0
JORDAN, M. 8 - 10 .... Miss A. Wallace
KATTENHORN, B. 10 - 0
KEEN-HAWKINS, L. 11 - 0
KEIGHLEY, A. M. 10 - 0
KELLARD, W. A. 11 - 0
KELLY, R. 9 - 2
KENT, L. 9 - 0
KING, G. 8 - 0 07741244698
KING, J. 10 - 7 .... Mr I. P. Popham
KYNE, D. B. 10 - 10
LANDAU, M. 9 - 4
LANDER, J. 8 - 13
LANGLEY, T. 8 - 5
LAWRENCE, P. 10 - 12
LEECH, R. 9 - 0 .... Mr I. P. Popham
LEGG, M. 8 - 7
LEVICK, I. 8 - 10
LEWIS, A. 8 - 7
LEWIS, Z. 8 - 5
LLEWELLYN, J. 9 - 0
MAIN, H. 9 - 7
MALZARD, V. A. 10 - 0 .... Mr Gordon Clarkson
MARGARSON, R. A. 9 - 0 07595888757
MARSHALL, C. 10 - 10 .... 07516 296716
MARSHALL, I. 9 - 0 .... Mr Gordon Clarkson
MASON, P. W. 11 - 4 07921707292
MATHIAS, I. 8 - 8
MAXWELL, D. 11 - 0 .... 0207 799 3429
MAYO, E. 8 - 13
MCBRIDE, A. 10 - 0
MCCLUNG, A. E. 9 - 7 07775740004
MCGARTY-JONES, E. 10 - 0
MCINTYRE, M. J. 10 - 4
MCLOUGHLIN, M. 8 - 7
MICKLEWRIGHT, M. 8 - 4 07525466455
MILLMAN, P. B. 9 - 7 .... Mr Ian Wood
MITCHELL, F. 10 - 0 .... Mr Philip Mitchell
MITCHELL, G P 10 - 0
MOONEY, D. 9 - 0 .... Mr J. L. Neilson
MORGAN, O. D. H. 10 - 3
MORRIS, C. 8 - 10
MORTON, E. C. 9 - 4 .... 07528 546596
MURPHY-KNIGHT, J. J. 9 - 3
MURRAY, T. H. 11 - 0 .... 07595 396806
MYDDELTON, H. D. 10 - 12 07713837857
NAUGHTON, A. 9 - 6
NEILD, J. D. 9 - 0 07577605914
NEWMAN, J. 9 - 10
NICHOLLS, O. 9 - 3 07850013672
NORECI, L. 9 - 5
O'BRIEN, D. J. 11 - 0 .... 07764 304906
O'BRIEN, F. 8 - 3
O'BRIEN, T. M. 10 - 7
O'KEEFFE, J. A. 9 - 7
O'NEILL, A. J. 10 - 0 07585400544
O'SHEA, A. 9 - 10 .... Mr J. L. Neilson
O'SHEA, C. 10 - 7 .... 07779 788748
O'SHEA, G. 10 - 0
OLIVER, N. H. 11 - 5
ORPWOOD, N. 11 - 0 .... 07831 836 626
ORTTEWELL, G. 9 - 4 07703351178
OSBORNE, M. 10 - 7
PADGETT, T. 8 - 9
PALIN, H. 9 - 9 07932322958
PALMER, O. 8 - 12 07444332547
PARKER, N. L. 9 - 5
PATERSON, E. 9 - 2
PERKINS, A. 7 - 11
PETERS, D. M. 11 - 3 .... 07789 997367
PHILIPSON-STOW, F. 10 - 4
PHIPPS, H. J. 10 - 6 .... 07715 207438
POWELL, K. C. 9 - 5
POWER, J. W. 10 - 0
PRITCHARD, C. 10 - 4
PROCTER, A. 9 - 7
PUFFETT, O. 10 - 10
QUEEN, L. D. M. 8 - 0

RADFORD, O. 10 - 8
RAHMAN, N. 9 - 7
RAMSAY, W. B. 11 - 12 .... 07764 960 054
RAYNER, K. P. 9 - 3
REDDINGTON, J. 10 - 2 07766767464
REES, E. M. 8 - 12
REES, J. 10 - 0
RILEY, D. L. 8 - 5 07904867045
RIPPON, S. 9 - 7
ROBINSON, I. P. B. 9 - 2 .... 07581 361986
ROBINSON, K. 9 - 3 .... 07400 134479
ROBINSON, M. 10 - 5
RUDDY, K. 8 - 1
RYDER, I. J. 9 - 2
SANDERS, L. 9 - 10
SAUNDERS, L. 9 - 4 .... Mr I. P. Popham
SCOTT, P. 8 - 10
SEERY, N. P. 9 - 9
SENSOY, H. 10 - 0 07595985025
SINCLAIR, K. S. 9 - 0 07554457681
SKELTON, K. 9 - 5
SLATER, M. L. 8 - 5
SMITH, J. M. 9 - 0
SMITH, R. 9 - 2 .... K. W. Renwick
SMITH, S. 7 - 10
SOLE, J. D. 10 - 1
SOLLITT, V. A. 10 - 6 .... 07540 229941
SPENCER, L. 9 - 0
SPRAKE, C. G. 10 - 3
STEARN, R. R. P. 11 - 0 .... 07879 412 414
STEPHENS, K. 8 - 10
STEVENS, A. L. 9 - 7 .... Mr I. P. Popham
STEVENS, H. M. 8 - 7 .... 07925 069749
STEVENSON, J. W. 10 - 0
STEWART, E. 9 - 0
STEWART, J. 9 - 6
SUMMERS, P. F. 10 - 0 07552219962
SUMMERSBY, C. 9 - 5
SUPPLE, J. M. 9 - 10
SUTTON, B. 10 - 11
TEAL, J. 10 - 4 .... 07984 649070
TEAL, L. 8 - 12
THOMAS, H. A. 9 - 0
THOMAS, P. J. 9 - 0
THORNTON, N. 8 - 7
TRAINOR, M. 9 - 7 .... 07554 992851
TROTT, L. 10 - 5 .... 01460 259139
TRY, M. E. 9 - 12
TUCKER, A. 8 - 7
TUER, A. L. 9 - 4
TURNER, J. 10 - 0 .... Mr Gordon Clarkson
TURNER, L. M. 10 - 0 .... 07984 531836
VOIKHANSKY, M. 9 - 9 01213772133
VOYCE, A. 8 - 10
WAGGOTT, J. J. 10 - 2
WALKER, S. A. 9 - 7 .... Mr S. T. Dodds
WALKINGSHAW, G. E. 10 - 6
WEAVER, A. 10 - 6
WEBSTER, V. 11 - 2 07960421013
WILLIAMS, E. 9 - 6
WILLIAMS, E. L. 9 - 4 07714170651
WILMOT, J. 10 - 6
WILSON, M. 10 - 4
WINGROVE, J. 9 - 4
WINGROVE, M. 9 - 9 07710562173
WRIGHT, A. 10 - 10 07515373070
WRIGHT, M. 7 - 13
YARHAM, F. R. 9 - 10
YORK, P. 10 - 7 .... 07774 962168
YOUNG, E. 8 - 13

NOTES

NOTES

CAVALOR
INHALE.
EXHALE.
REPEAT.
Cavalor Bronchix Pulmo opens airways and supports capillary elasticity and resilience during intensive training or competition. It promotes oxygen uptake during heavy efforts and protects the airway system.
CAVALOR
BRONCHIX
PULMO
1L